MILLION SELLING RECORDS

RECORDS

FROM THE 1900S
TO THE 1980S

AN ILLUSTRATED
DIRECTORY

The Beatles, *circa* **1964**

MILLION SELLING RECORDS

FROM THE 1900S TO THE 1980S

AN ILLUSTRATED DIRECTORY

Joseph Murrells

ARCO PUBLISHING, INC. New York

© Joseph Murrells 1984
First published 1984
Published 1985 by Arco Publishing Inc.
215 Park Avenue South
New York, NY 10003

Part of this book is based on *The Book
of Golden Discs*, 1978 edition

Library of Congress Cataloging in Publication Data

Murrells, Joseph, 1904–
    Million-selling records from the 1900s to the 1980s.
    Includes indexes.
    1. Music, Popular (Songs, etc.)—Discography.
2. Music, Popular (Songs, etc.)—Chronology. 3. Music,
Popular (Songs, etc.)—Bio-bibliography. I. Title.
ML156.4.P6M88   1985   789.9′12   84–24218
ISBN 0-668-06459-5

Typeset and printed in Great Britain

Front jacket shows:

Dolly Parton (photo © RCA)	ABBA (photo © A. Hanser/Polar Music Int. AB)
The Playmates	
Carly Simon (photo © WEA)	Ray Charles
The Police (photo © A&M)	McFadden and Whitehead (photo © Philadelphia International Records)

Spine shows:

Cliff Richard

Michael Jackson
(photo © CBS Inc.)

Back jacket shows:

The Impalas	Art Garfunkel (photo © CBS Inc.)	Jim Reeves
	Sophie Tucker	
The Hollies		Jean-Michel Jarre (photo © Polydor)
Cyril Stapleton (photo © Decca)		Ferrante and Teicher

Contents

85 436

Preface

The aim of this book is to set out in chronological order the details and story of every record disc which has been certified or reliably reported to have sold one million or more units globally.

The order within any given year is alphabetical except that musical-show albums and filmtrack albums are listed at the beginning of their year of issue. When both sides of a disc are known to have contributed to the sale, the full details are given for both recordings. When an artist has a string of such discs his or her personal details will normally be found under the first million seller.

The exact point in time when a golden disc was first given by a company to an artist has not been established with certainty. The germ of the idea, we think, started in 1905, when the Gramophone Company of Britain presented a bracelet to Marie Hall who was the first woman violinist to become a popular recording artist. The presentation charm bracelet was made of gold and pearls and displayed a minute violin, a tapered gramophone arm, and seven tiny *golden discs*, representing her seven bestselling records. The first gold disc ever awarded to an artist is believed to have been given to the Glenn Miller orchestra by RCA-Victor on 10 February 1942, over the Chesterfield Radio Broadcast. The presentation was for Miller's recording of 'Chattanooga Choo Choo' which sold over 1,200,000 copies on RCA's Bluebird label, and it was in the form of a gold-lacquered stamper. Brad McCuen, RCA-Victor artists and repertoire producer, found mention of this while preparing a new album by the orchestra under its leader, Buddy DeFranco, in 1968. The framed record was then found in the possession of Miller's daughter. Perfectionist Miller had every Chesterfield Radio Broadcast of the band's performance put on records for his private use, and these were left intact at the time of Miller's untimely death on 15 December 1944. It was from one of these that McCuen heard the presentation by RCA's Wally Earl taking place on the recording, dated 10 February 1942.

The first country gold record was awarded to Elton Britt for 'There's a Star Spangled Banner Waving Somewhere' in 1944. It was presented by him to the Country Music Hall of Fame on 23 May 1968.

Before 1958, gold discs were given to artists on an informal basis. Since 1958, the gold discs have been certified by the Recording Industry Association of America (R.I.A.A.) for 1,000,000 single sales and a gross of $1,000,000 for album sales.

The criteria for Gold Record Award certification by R.I.A.A. for a long-playing record and/or its counterparts on pre-recorded tape cassettes or cartridges was changed for all recordings released on or after 1 January 1975. The new standard became a minimum sale of 500,000 units regardless of the list price of the record album and/or its counterparts. Recordings released before that date continued to qualify at the prior standard of $1 million at the manufacturer's level. Platinum Record Award certifications commenced on 1 April 1976 for long-playing record albums and their counterparts on pre-recorded tapes achieving a minimum sale of one million units, and for single records selling a minimum of two million units for recordings released on or after 1 January 1976. (This book is based on the sale of discs.)

Gold discs are also awarded in smaller countries for sale of 10,000, 25,000, 50,000, 100,000, etc., or as the case may be, taking into consideration the total population of the country concerned, those being their equivalent of a 'million' sale.

Individual entries give the label under which the record was released in its country of origin. Discs may subsequently have been issued on different labels in other countries, but this information is not given in every case.

Sales Figures

The *million-selling discs* listed in the body of this work were either reported as having reached that figure by the manufacturers themselves to various musical magazines and newspapers or the information appeared in the general press. Since only some of the sales figures have been certified by actual audit the Compiler cannot verify the listings, but has passed on such information as many years of research have led him to believe is derived from acceptable reports.

Joseph Murrells

Acknowledgements

The compiler and publisher gratefully acknowledge the assistance of the following individuals and organizations, who in the latter case have either given permission to quote from their files or have supplied publicity photographs, which are copyright. In certain cases the publisher and compiler have not been able to trace the copyright holder; any omissions will be rectified in future editions.

ABC Television Ltd; A & M Records; American Society of Composers, Authors and Publishers; Apple Records; Arista Records; Asylum Records; Atco; Atlantic Records; Jacques Aubert-Philips; BBC Records; Tony Barrow International Ltd; *Billboard*; Broadcast Music Inc.; Brunswick; CBS Records; Capitol Records; *Cash Box*; Chess Records; Chrysalis Records; Columbia Pictures; Cotillion Records; Paul Cox; Syd Cullingham; *Current Biography*; Decca Record Co. Ltd; Deram Records; Deutsche Grammophon; *Down Beat*; N.V. Dureco; EMI Records; Roger Easterby; Electric and Musical Industries; Elektra Records; Epic Records; the late Brian Epstein; Leslie Gaylor; Philip Gotlop Photographic Ltd; H & L Records; Sue Harwood; Dezo Hoffman Ltd; Island Records; James J. Kriegsmann; Liberty Records; London Features International Ltd; Janet Lord; MCA; MGM; Major-Minor Records; J. Marcham; Mercury Records; Metromedia Records; Monitor Press; Monument Records; Motown Records; Brian Mulligan; Parlophone; Philips Records Ltd; Phonogram Ltd; Photo-Reportage Ltd; Pinnnacle Records; Barry Plummer; Polar Music Int. AB; Polydor Records; Patricia A. Pretty; Pye Records; RAK Records; RCA Records; Rann Productions Ltd; *Record Mirror*; *Record World*; G. Ricordi & Co. (London) Ltd; Bob Roberts; Rocket Records; Rockfield; Rogers & Cowan, Inc.; Roulette Records; Starshine Corporation; Stax Records; Tamla Motown Records; *Time;* United Artists; Universal Pictorial; *Variety;* Virgin Records; Vogue Records Ltd; WEA Records Ltd; Warner Brothers Ltd; Warner/Reprise; Clive Woods; P. F. Worger

Sales of U.S. records and tapes*

Year	Million dollars**
1920	100
1925	25
1930	75
1935	1
1940	50
1945	85
1950	200
1955	250
1960	650
1965	800
1970	1195
1975	2400
1980	3700

* Tapes started in 1966.
** To the nearest five million.

These figures are based on R.I.A.A. statistics. Figures for later years have not been given due to the increasing number of independent producers who are not members of R.I.A.A., as well as to changes in the way the figures are assessed, which could make direct comparisons misleading.

Definition of silver/gold/platinum record awards by country

Country	Silver Disc Albums	Silver Disc Singles	Gold Disc Albums	Gold Disc Singles	Platinum Disc Albums	Platinum Disc Singles	Comments
Australia	–	–	15,000	50,000	–	–	No Silver or Platinum Discs
Austria	–	–	25,000	100,000	–	–	No Silver or Platinum Discs
Belgium	10,000	50,000	25,000	100,000	50,000	200,000	
Canada	–	–	50,000	75,000	100,000	–	No Silver Discs
Czechoslovakia	–	–	250,000	–	500,000	–	Silver/Gold/Platinum Discs given to artists who sell the maximum number of discs in a year (all recordings counted together)
Denmark	25,000	25,000	50,000	50,000	–	–	Albums include records and cassettes
Finland	–	–	15,000	10,000	–	–	No Silver or Platinum Discs
France	–	–	100,000	500,000	–	–	No Silver or Platinum Discs
Hungary	–	–	50,000	100,000	–	–	No Silver or Platinum Discs
Ireland	–	50,000	–	100,000	–	–	No Silver or Platinum Discs for singles
Italy	500,000	–	1,000,000	1,000,000	–	–	No Silver or Platinum Discs for singles
Netherlands	10,000	50,000	25,000	100,000	50,000	250,000	
Norway	20,000	Kr.250,000	40,000	Kr.500,000	–	–	Singles based on unit sales, albums according to sales value
Poland	–	–	125,000	250,000	–	–	No Silver or Platinum Discs
Spain	–	–	100,000	100,000	–	–	No Silver or Platinum Discs
Sweden	–	50,000	25,000	100,000	50,000	–	No Silver Discs for LPs and no Platinum Discs for singles

| Country | Silver Disc | | Gold Disc | | Platinum Disc | | Comments |
	Albums	Singles	Albums	Singles	Albums	Singles	
United Kingdom	60,000	250,000	100,000	500,000	300,000	1,000,000	
U.S.A.	–	–	$1,000,000	1,000,000	–	–	(Up to 31 Dec. 1974)
	–	–	500,000	1,000,000	–	–	(From 1 Jan. 1975)
	–	–	500,000	1,000,000	1,000,000	2,000,000	(From 1 Apr. 1976)
West Germany	125,000	500,000	250,000	1,000,000	500,000	2,000,000	Gold Disc for sales of 200,000 musicassettes
Yugoslavia	–	50,000	25,000	100,000	–	–	No Platinum Discs, and no Silver Discs for albums

The charts

The first *song ratings* were based on the combined audiences of radio and television appearing in John G. Peatman's 'Weekly Survey' which started on 3 June 1942 in the U.S.A. The *Melody Maker* started publishing similar song lists in Britain in 1946.

The grand-daddy of Top 40 radio was born on 20 April 1935, was called 'Your Lucky Strike Hit Parade' and featured the fifteen most popular song hits of the week in the U.S.A. At that time sheet music sold much better than discs. Recent research has revealed that the first programme was introduced by Warren Hill, and the first No 1 song was 'Soon'. The series terminated on 29 April 1959, after being transferred to television on 10 July 1950.

Disc charts started in the U.S.A., the first appearing on 20 July 1940 in *Billboard*. Britain's first chart appeared in the *New Musical Express* on 14 November 1952, based on gramophone dealers' returns of sales.

The highest positions and the most weeks in the charts mentioned in this book were selected from the following musical publications:
  U.S.A.: *Billboard, Cash Box, Variety, Record World.*
  Britain: *New Musical Express, Melody Maker, Record Mirror, Disc.*

Awards

The National Academy of Recording Arts and Sciences (NARAS) was founded in 1957. The award known as the 'Grammy' began in 1958 for artistic achievement within the recording field, based on artistry in writing, performance, musicianship and engineering.

The Academy of Motion Picture Arts and Sciences was founded in 1927. The award known as the 'Oscar' began in 1934 for Musical Scoring and Best Film Song of the Year.

Country Music Hall of Fame (U.S.A.)

The Country Music Association of America was first organized in November 1958 and, since its inception, devoted to the promotion of country music and its exposure in all parts of the world.

In 1961, the first famous country artists and personalities in this field were elected to the Country Music Hall of Fame with a special plaque in their honour displayed in Nashville, Tennessee, the recognized centre of country music. In 1965, the com-

mittee nominated seventy people, the undermentioned being elected to the Hall of Fame. The foundation of a museum in Nashville became a reality when the building was officially opened on 31 March 1967, and since then has been a great attraction to thousands of visitors every year. (See also the album, 'Famous Country & Western Artists' Original Hits', 1965, in main section of this book and the note on country music under Jimmie Rodgers, 'Brakeman's Blues', 1928.)

Elected to the Hall of Fame:		Born	Died
1961	Jimmie Rodgers	8 September 1897	26 May 1933
	Fred Rose	24 August 1897	1 December 1954
	Hank Williams	17 September 1923	1 January 1953
1962	Roy Acuff	15 September 1903	
1964	Tex Ritter	12 January 1907	2 January 1974
1965	Ernest Tubb	9 February 1914	
1966	George D. Hay	9 November 1895	8 May 1968
	Uncle Dave Macon	7 October 1870	22 March 1952
	Eddy Arnold	15 May 1918	
	James R. Denny	28 February 1911	27 August 1963
1967	J. L. (Joe) Frank	15 April 1900	4 May 1952
	Red Foley	17 June 1910	19 September 1968
	Jim Reeves	20 August 1924	31 July 1964
	Stephen H. Sholes	12 February 1911	22 April 1968
1968	Bob Wills	6 March 1905	13 May 1975
1969	Gene Autry	29 September 1907	
1970	Original Carter Family:		
	Alvin Pleasant Carter	15 December 1891	7 November 1960
	Sarah Carter	21 July 1899	8 January 1979
	Maybelle Carter	10 May 1909	23 October 1978
	Bill Monroe	13 September 1911	
1971	Uncle Art Satherley	19 October 1889	
1972	Jimmie Davis	11 September 1904	
1973	Chet Atkins	20 June 1924	
	Patsy Cline	8 September 1932	5 March 1963
1974	Owen Bradley		
	Frank (Pee Wee) King	18 February 1914	
1975	Minnie Pearl	25 October 1912	
1976	Kitty Wells	30 August 1919	
	Paul Cohen		
1977	Merle Travis	29 November 1917	
1978	Grandpa Jones	20 October 1913	
1979	Hank Snow	9 May 1914	
	Hubert Long		
1980	Johnny Cash	26 February 1932	
	Connie B. Gay (founding President of C.M.A.)	22 August 1914	
	Original Sons of the Pioneers:		
	Hugh Farr	6 December 1903	17 March 1980
	Karl Farr	29 April 1909	20 September 1961
	Bob Nolan	1 April 1908	15 June 1980
	Lloyd Perryman	29 January 1917	31 May 1977
	Roy Rodgers	5 November 1911	
	Tim Spencer	13 July 1908	26 April 1974
1981	Vernon Dalhart	6 April 1883	14 September 1948
	Grant Turner	17 May 1912	
	Lefy Frizzell	31 March 1928	19 July 1975
	Roy Horton	5 November 1914	
1982	Marty Robbins	26 September 1925	8 December 1982
1983	Little Jimmy Dickens	19 December 1920	

1903-1939

ENRICO CARUSO

VESTI LA GIUBBA (On with the motley) *Victor* [*USA*] (from the opera *Pagliacci* by Ruggiero Leoncavallo). It is fitting that Caruso, the world's greatest operatic tenor, should be the first artist to achieve a million sale through subsequent years. Caruso was born in Naples on 25 February 1873 and died there on 2 August 1921. He was reared amid humble surroundings as a member of a large family, and began serious vocal training in 1891 under Guglielmo Vergine, studied for three years and finished under Vicenzo Lombardi. He made his debut in April 1895 in the role of Faust at Caserta (near Naples), but was scarcely known until his appearance in 1896 at the Fondo Theatre, Naples, in *La Traviata*, then *La Favorita* and *La Gioconda*. He became firmly established with his engagement at the Teatro Lirico in Milan, where he was chosen to create the role of Loris in Giordano's *Fedora* (1898). Thereafter he sang for two winter seasons at Petrograd, and during five summer seasons at Buenos Aires (1899-1903). In 1902 he made his London debut and in 1903 first appeared in the United States. His immense popularity in London dated from his summer season of 1903 at Covent Garden. He made his first recordings prior to 1903 for the Gramophone Co. of London in Milan (1901), The Zonophone Co., and the Anglo-Italian Commerce Co. of Genoa. From the autumn of 1903 he made his first recordings for Victor Records in the U.S.A. and was their exclusive artist until his death. Caruso was the leader in the parade of great artists who transformed the phonograph record from a toy into the greatest medium of home entertainment. For more than 30 years after his death he was still one of Victor's top bestselling artists. By 1952 the total royalties earned by his discs, both during his lifetime and since his death, was over $3,500,000 representing the largest single royalty figure accrued by any artist in RCA-Victor's history up to that time.

'Vesti la giubba' had further sales impetus when RCA-Victor, using the new electrical techniques, re-recorded Caruso's voice and those of other famous artists by making them clearer and truer than when first recorded. Sale of Caruso's discs came back strongly after the release of the film *The Great Caruso* (1951) with Mario Lanza in the star role. Caruso made his first version of 'Vesti la giubba' with piano accompaniment only on 12 November 1902 for the Gramophone Co. in Italy, using the new Victor Master Disc method, and with orchestral accompaniment in 1907 for Victor in U.S.A.

A further disc, also 10-inch with piano accompaniment, was made in 1903, both being released in America in 1903 and 1904-1905 respectively. Caruso's remaining recording career was basically in Camden, N. J. for Victor. He recorded 'Vesti la giubba' again between 1906 and 1908 on a 12-inch disc with orchestra under the single faced number 88061. In 1909-1911 he re-

'Non, Pagliaccio non son' on single faced 12-inch disc number 88279, and the two were subsequently backed on one 12-inch disc (6001). The collective sales of 'Vesti la giubba' easily surpassed the million, the bulk probably being the orchestral version. This was re-recorded after electrical recordings were introduced in 1925.

ARTHUR COLLINS

THE PREACHER AND THE BEAR *Victor* [*USA*]. This famous American song was written in 1904 by Joe Arzonia (pseudonym of the publisher, Arthur Longbrake). Collins re- corded the song for all the disc companies at that time. The disc was imported to Britain (on HMV - then The Gramophone Co.), and each record was accompanied by an explanatory leaflet so that the British public could understand the blackface dialect and know when to laugh at the humour in the story of the Negro preacher who was driven up a tree by a grizzly bear after going hunting on Sunday.

Over a period of 20 years, probably more copies of Arthur Collins' 'Preacher and the Bear' were sold than of any other record. Song was revived by Phil Harris in 1947 with fair success.

Previous page, top, left to right: Bing Crosby, Harry James; bottom: Nelson Eddy and Jeanette MacDonald, Paul Whiteman.

BURT SHEPARD
LAUGHING SONG *Gramophone Co. (Zonophone)* [*Britain*]. Written by George Washington Johnson, a burly Negro, born into slavery on a Virginian plantation, who went to Washington, D.C. to make a living by singing and whistling on the streets. He made thousands of records when Columbia and Berliner opened their studios there. Becoming prosperous and famous, he and his wife went on tour with a minstrel group, but his genial personality changed through drink. In a drunken rage he threw his wife out of a window and was hanged for murder. His records had all been cut out of the catalogues or remade by other artists around 1910. Oddly, an imitation of Johnson's version, made by Burt Shepard, an English comedian, became a big seller throughout the world. It was particularly popular in Oriental countries such as India, and is estimated to have sold over a million in that part of the world alone. Johnson's 'Laughing Song' remained a favourite with amateur minstrel shows for many years.

(Burt Shepard's name appears in the very early Victor (U.S.A.) catalogue of 1903 with the disc 'Limburger Cheese'.)

AL JOLSON
RAGGING THE BABY TO SLEEP *Victor* [*USA*]. Ragtime originally flourished in the U.S.A. during the latter part of the 19th century and was played considerably right up to 1928. It was around 1911 that a craze started, producing many new songwriters in this idiom and creating huge sheet music sales and many new dance steps. The most popular of the latter was the Turkey Trot. Irving Berlin came into prominence with his 'Alexander's Ragtime Band' in 1911 and recordings of ragtime tunes created rapidly increased sales, the first golden age of discs, in 1912.

Al Jolson was one of the earliest artists to be signed by Victor Records to record such songs. He recorded 'Ragging the Baby to Sleep' (written by L. Wolfe Gilbert with music by Lewis F. Muir) on 17 April 1912. One report said this disc (Victor 17081) sold 1,069,000 copies. The backing of the disc was 'Movin' Man Don't Take My Baby Grand', an appropriate title for the thousands of pianists who were thumping out ragtime at that time.

Jolson also recorded approximately 70 songs later for Columbia Records and subsequently went over to Brunswick label, then Decca. (See 1928 for Jolson biography.)

AL JOLSON
THE SPANIARD THAT BLIGHTED MY LIFE *Victor* [*USA*]. Jolson recorded this on 7 March 1913 (on Victor 17318) and sales were reported of 1,846,000. The song was written and originally sung by famous British artist Billy Merson in 1911 and Jolson revived it in a duet disc with Bing Crosby in 1946 (q.v.).

The backing of this disc was 'My Yellow Jacket Girl'. (See 1928 for Jolson biography.)

JOE HAYMAN (comedian)
COHEN ON THE TELEPHONE *Columbia* [*Britain*]. This is the first known million selling comedy dialogue disc. It was exported to the U.S.A. and released there in June 1914, coupled with a Fred Duprez monologue 'Happy tho' Married'. Hayman, an American by birth, was a popular British music hall attraction. This disc is said to have sold over two million in the U.S.A. It started a series of telephonic misadventures of Mr Cohen.

ALMA GLUCK (soprano) WITH MALE CHORUS AND ORCHESTRA
CARRY ME BACK TO OLD VIRGINNY backed with OLD BLACK JOE *Victor* [*USA*]. James A. Bland, writer of this immortal song 'Carry Me Back to Old Virginny', was born in Flushing, N.Y. on 22 October 1854. He came of a good Negro family and spent most of his boyhood in Washington, D.C. where his father was an examiner in the U.S. Patent Office, the first Negro to be appointed to such a position following the Civil War. James enrolled with his father at Howard University to study law, but his musical talents were ideal for the minstrel shows, and he decided to write and sing instead. At 21 he joined Callender's Original Georgia Minstrels, and for the next 25 years toured the U.S.A. and Europe with the Callender-Haverley combination, remaining in Britain for several years where he became a great favourite. He wrote approximately 700 songs of which only 37 are on file in the Library of Congress. James was improvident and careless with money and, despite his success abroad, returned to Washington a poor man. He finally drifted to Philadelphia where he died on 5 May 1911. 'Virginny' was written in 1878. In 1940 it was made the official State song of the Old Dominion by the Virginia Legislature.

During the 20 years when he was the idol of the English music halls, 'the prince of Negro songwriters' gave command performances for Queen Victoria and her son, Edward, Prince of Wales. In his homeland he was practically unknown, though his songs were sung by white singers. His unmarked grave on the outskirts of Merion, Pa., was located in 1939 through the efforts of ASCAP, and a headstone erected. Bland's other famous songs were 'Golden Slippers' and 'In the Evening by the Moonlight'.

'Old Black Joe' was written in 1860 by Stephen C. Foster who was born in Lawrenceville (Pittsburgh), Pa. on 4 July 1826. Foster married his childhood sweetheart Jane McDowell in 1850. The song was the result of a promise Foster made to the McDowell's coachman–butler that he would put the old Negro in a song some day. He became the most famous of American balladeers, unmatched by any other songwriter for consistent popularity over a period of almost 100 years. His enduring songs included 'Old Folks at Home', 'Mass's in de Cold, Cold Ground', 'Oh Susanna', 'My Old Kentucky Home', 'Camptown Races', 'Old Black Joe', 'Nelly Was a Lady', 'Old Dog Tray', 'Old Uncle Ned', 'Nelly Bly', 'Jeannie with the Light-Brown Hair' and 'Beautiful Dreamer'. Like James Bland, he too was improvident, for after living in Allegheny almost continuously until 1860 with his wife, he went to New York where his financial condition grew steadily worse, and his wife left him for the second time (1861). He then lived alone, almost destitute, and died in Bellevue Hospital, New York on 31 January 1864.

A new Stephen Foster Memorial was formally dedicated on the campus of the University of Pittsburgh on 2 June 1937. It houses the priceless collection of Fosteriana owned by Josiah Kirby Lilly.

Soprano Alma Gluck (real name Reba Fiersohn) was born in Bucharest, Rumania on 11 May 1884 and as a child of five her parents brought her to New York where she was educated. She studied singing there under Buzzi-Peccia from 1906–1909 and made her debut at the Metropolitan Opera House as Sophie in Massenet's *Werther* on 16 November 1909. The following morning she awoke to find herself famous, and numerous concert engagements followed. She continued as a member of the Metropolitan Opera until 1912 where she was heard in more than 20 operatic roles, then abandoned the operatic stage for concert work. She deservedly claims the major credit for the modern revival and permanently established popularity of 'Carry Me Back to Old Virginny'. Alma Gluck died on 27 October 1938 in New York.

The recording of 'Carry Me Back to Old Virginny' was made in the period before 1918, probably some time between 1911 and 1915, and first released on a 12-inch single-faced disc (No. 74420) and finally coupled with 'Old Black Joe' (No. 74442) on a double-faced disc (No. 6141) maybe around 1915. According to Marcia Davenport, a successful writer and critic, and the daughter of Alma Gluck by her first marriage, the newly issued disc sold over one million copies, the first popular ballad to do so, by 1918.

HENRY BURR (tenor vocalist)

JUST A BABY'S PRAYER AT TWILIGHT *Victor* [*USA*]. Henry Burr, born in St Stephen, N.B., Canada, on 15 January 1882, who later became known as 'The Dean of Ballad Singers', started recording in the days of cylindrical records and reached the height of his fame with this song, written by Sam M. Lewis and Joe Young (words) and M. K. Jerome (music). It is said to have sold over a million. His forte was in the singing of nostalgic ballads. He later (1925) recorded with Art Landry and his orchestra and (1926) with Roger Wolfe Kahn and his orchestra for Victor Records. From 1921 to 1925 he managed a show business troupe known as the Eight Popular (or Famous) Victor Artists, which proved an effective publicity idea for the label. They played everywhere in the U.S.A. and Canada, a complete sell-out wherever they appeared, and to relieve the tedium of travel organized The Order of Beards. They adorned their faces with

long red or black beards, equipped themselves with hatchets, waving and muttering as they stalked through the train causing uproar. The Eight consisted of Burr, Al Campbell, John Meyer and Frank Croxton (The Peerless Quartet), Billy Murray (comedian), Monroe Silver (The 'Cohen on the Telephone' monologue specialist and U.S.A. counterpart of Joe Hayman who first recorded these comedy dialogues), Rudy Wiedoeft (one of the world's greatest saxophone players), and Frank Banta (pianist who recorded with many famous jazz bands in the late 1920s). Murray and Burr were the top pop artists of horn recording, Murray having the highest individual sales and Burr making more titles than anyone else. Henry Burr died on 6 April 1941.

'Just a Baby's Prayer at Twilight' was also a million sheet music seller.

Billy Murray died on 17 August 1954.

HENRY BUSSE (trumpet)

WANG WANG BLUES *Victor* [*USA*]. Henry Busse, composer, trumpeter, conductor, radio and recording artist, was born 19 May 1894 in Magdeburg, Germany. He went to the U.S.A. in 1916 and after playing in a film house pit orchestra, led a five-piece band that eventually made its way to San Francisco. Busse joined Paul Whiteman's band after Paul had ended his service in the U.S. Navy in 1918 and stayed with him until 1928 when Busse formed his own band. Henry's band got its first break at Castle Farms, near Cincinnati and then moved to the Chez Paree in Chicago. He later made two films, *Rhapsody in Blue* (1945) and *Lady, Let's Dance* (1944) in addition to night-club, radio, recording and dance hall engagements. He also made

concert tours of Europe and the U.S.A.

Busse was a contemporary of such early jazz giants as Jack Teagarden, Bix Beiderbecke, Frankie Trumbauer and the Dorsey Brothers who all gained prominence under the Whiteman banner, and Henry's trumpet solo on 'When Day is Done' with the Whiteman Band (1927) started a vogue for 'sweet jazz'. He was also the first trumpeter to use the mute, and develop a shuffle rhythm for his background section.

'Wang Wang Blues' was Busse's first important composition, written in collaboration with Gus Mueller and 'Buster' Johnson, both Whiteman instrumentalists (clarinet and trombone respectively). It was first recorded with Whiteman in Camden, N.J. on 9 August 1920. The initial sale was 457,000, and together with his composition 'Hot Lips' (co-writers Henry Lange and Lou Davis), also recorded with Whiteman in New York on 27 June 1922 plus his own band's version later of the two tunes back to back, the sale through the years is estimated at over the million. The latter (1935) Decca coupling is still considered to be one of the U.S.A.'s perennial singles hits and is kept in constant supply.

Henry Busse died of a heart attack in Memphis, Tennessee on 23 April 1955 after his orchestra had completed a special engagement there.

BEN SELVIN AND HIS NOVELTY ORCHESTRA

DARDANELLA *Victor* [*USA*]. The first known 'pop' dance disc to sell a million. Ben Selvin (born 1898), violinist-bandleader-recording manager, started in the profession around 1905. He made more band discs than anybody in the world: 9,000 during his long career under thirty-nine different names for nine different companies from 1919 when he was 21. He was presented with a Gold Disc on 14 March 1963 by RCA-Victor Co., on his retirement at the age of 65. 'Dardanella' sold 6,500,000 discs on collective labels without the benefit of any radio or motion-picture plugs – one of the biggest selling songs on disc in the early years of recording. It was written by Felix Bernard and Johnny S. Black (music) and Fred Fisher (words) and was also a million seller in sheet music. Its popularity can be attributed to its continuous pattern in the bass, and may be the first example of 'boogie-woogie' in American music. No publisher would touch 'Dardanella' under its original title 'Turkish Tom Toms'. Fred Fisher renamed it, wrote the lyrics and published it in 1919. Selvin recorded it in February 1920 – Victor Record No 18633.

PAUL WHITEMAN AND HIS ORCHESTRA

WHISPERING backed with JAPANESE SANDMAN *Victor* [*USA*]. This disc sold nearly two million by 1921, and helped to establish Whiteman as the leading orchestra of that time. He was born in Denver, Colorado on 28 March 1890, the son of an artistic and affluent family. His father was Musical Supervisor to the schools in Denver and is reputed to have organized the first high school orchestra. His mother was equally prominent in local choir and oratorio circles. As a youngster, Paul was presented with a violin but later studied the viola, playing in one of his father's orchestras. At 17, he was first viola in the Denver Symphony Orchestra, then with the San Francisco People's Orchestra and the Minetti String Quartet. During the First World War he served in the Navy as bandmaster at Bear Island, California, with a 57-piece orchestra. Whiteman's training at the Navy's radio

school gave him a technical appreciation of the properties and performance of the microphone which stood him in good stead. In 1919 he led his own orchestra, after having first encountered jazz in a dance spot on the Barbary Coast and being fired from John Tait's Café Band after one day because he could not play jazz. He introduced his 'symphonic jazz' while playing at a hotel in Santa Barbara and later that year in Hotel Alexandria, Los Angeles, where film stars became his ardent admirers. When his nine-piece ensemble was asked to play at the Ambassador Hotel at Atlantic City, Paul introduced his new musical style – jazzing the classics. Ferde Grofe, the pianist he first met with the Tait Band, scored Whiteman's unique arrangements, and the orchestra attracted great attention, soon making discs for Victor Records. Whiteman had 'made a lady' out of jazz, and popular music would not have reached its present stage of development without his pioneering efforts in the field of symphonic orchestration. Paul's earnings soared – he organized 52 orchestras in the U.S.A., Europe and Mexico, appeared on Broadway and in vaudeville; appeared in London in 1923; and packed theatres everywhere he went. In 1924 he held his first concert at the Aeolian Hall, New York, entitled 'An experiment in Modern Music' which was outstanding for the first performance of George Gershwin's 'Rhapsody in Blue', orchestrated by Ferde Grofe. The orchestra then made appearances in most of the principal European cities and toured the U.S.A. In 1930 Paul Whiteman and his band starred in the Universal film *The King of Jazz* dedicated to him, a title he had won for himself. The film brought before the world the greatest and most popular light baritone of all time, Bing Crosby. Apart from his many concert appearances, Paul Whiteman was a popular radio personality from 1932. In 1943 he was appointed Musical Director to the Blue Network, and in 1945, ABC put on a special anniversary show, 'The First Twenty-Five Years', built around the band-leader's music. This disc was released in November 1920.

'Whispering' was written by Malvin Schonberger (words) and John Schonberger (music), and 'Japanese Sandman' by Raymond B. Egan (words) and Richard Whiting (music). Both were million sellers in sheet music as well as on disc.

Whiteman's first record was a 12-inch disc of 'Avalon', and 'Dance of the Hours' from *Gioconda*, also in 1920. It took almost a whole day to make, due to the nerves of the members of the band being on edge, who made interjections when anything went wrong, thus ruining the record. The band eventually got used to recording techniques thereafter and seldom took more than two hours for a session. Paul Whiteman died on 29 December 1967.

ISHAM JONES AND HIS ORCHESTRA
(featuring Louis Panico – trumpet)

WABASH BLUES *Brunswick* [*USA*]. Isham Jones, born on 31 January 1894 in Coalton, Ohio, had musical aspirations as a youngster, and studied the piano and saxophone while in grade and high school. At the age of 20, he organized his first orchestra, playing for dances in Bay City, Saginaw and other Michigan cities. After a year of advanced musical study in Chicago (1915) and working as a saxophonist with local bands, he organized his own professional orchestra in Chicago, playing to packed crowds at the Green Mill, opened the million-dollar Rainbow Gardens and then had a six-year engagement at the College Inn. His orchestra became the pride of Chicago and one of the most popular of the 1920s. The band made a triumphal tour of the U.S.A. in vaudeville, were a colossal success at New York's Rue de la Paix, toured Europe and captivated the clientele at London's famous Kit Kat Club. They later made tours of clubs, ballrooms, and hotels throughout America, and made many recordings. The songs he composed and made popular were closely

associated with the orchestra of violins, clarinets, saxophones and muted brass he directed, and several of some 200 he wrote have become standard dance band items, including 'On the Alamo', 'Swinging Down the Lane', 'It Had to Be You', 'I'll See You in my Dreams', 'Spain', 'The One I Love Belongs to Somebody Else', 'Ida, I Do' and 'You've Got Me Crying Again'.

A top bandleader of the 1920s and 1930s, Isham Jones retired around 1938, but continued writing songs at his California ranch. He was certainly one of the early radio and recording stars.

'Wabash Blues', written by Dave Ringle (words) and Fred Meinken (music) was probably the biggest hit of 1921–22, and Isham Jones' disc is said to have sold nearly two million. It also sold over 750,000 via the Benson Orchestra of Chicago's recording on the Victor label.

Isham Jones had the double distinction of making history with both conducting and composing. He died in Hollywood, Florida, on 19 October 1956.

1922

ART LANDRY AND HIS CALL OF THE NORTH ORCHESTRA

DREAMY MELODY *Gennett* [*USA*]. Art Landry, bandleader/violinist, estimated that his recording of this tremendously popular waltz song of 1922-1923 written by Ted Koehler, Frank Magine and C. Naset, sold around 1,500,000 in the U.S.A. - probably the biggest seller for the small Gennett Company. The Gennett label, long since defunct, was one of the earliest to record dance and jazz combinations in the early 1920s which included many now famous names such as Hoagy Carmichael,

Muggsy Spanier, Miff Mole, Adrian Rollini, Bix Beiderbecke, Phil Napoleon and Sam Lanin.

Landry is said to have made 2,000 records under countless names during his career. He first recorded for Gennett with his Syncopatin' Six, then his Call of the North Orchestra. In 1924 he went over to Victor Records recording as Art Landry and his Orchestra. He made few discs after 1932, and on retirement went to live in Ticonderoga, New York, where in 1953 he did a daily remote broadcast over a Rutland, Vermont station. He was born in 1900.

1923

'FIDDLIN' JOHN' CARSON

YOU WILL NEVER MISS YOUR MOTHER UNTIL SHE IS GONE *Okeh* [*USA*]. This song was written by Carson (words) with music by E. B Brockman. A former version (1885) was a great favourite with the Minstrels, written by Harry Birch.

OLD JOE CLARK *Okeh* [*USA*]. This American folk song and fiddle tune was written even earlier, certainly some time before 1850.

Recordings of hillbilly songs began around 1923 when Okeh Records sent a scouting expedition into rural America - the south-eastern section and the hills of Tennessee, Louisiana, Virginia, Kentucky and the Carolinas. They proved to be a most fruitful area. The recording men travelled by horse, mule, on foot and by Tin Lizzies, and discovered many potential back-country stars. Among them was the late 'Fiddlin' John' Carson, a Georgia fiddle player who made many records including these two discs. In these days, the recording as well as the singing and playing were bad from a recording standpoint, but were, nevertheless, sensationally successful in Southern redbrush bailiwicks. It has been estimated that the discs sold around a million copies before Okeh decided they must be re-recorded. Okeh also had another star in Henry Whitter (see Dalhart, 1924) whose disc of 'The Wreck of the Old 97' and 'The Lonesome Road Blues' swept the South.

Among the seven most noted of the field recording pioneers were Ralph Peer (see Rodgers, 1928) who was first with Okeh then with Victor; Art Satherley - a Britisher - and Don Satherley with Columbia; Dave Kapp and Paul Cohen with Decca; Frank Walker, first with Columbia then Victor and MGM; and Steve Sholes with Victor. Their discoveries created steady sales in the so-called 'country market', and their dedicated work laid the foundation and preserved for posterity the distinctive folk music of America. In the 1930s and 1940s, the great country catalogues - both songs and records - were firmly established, the process continuing into the 1950s. It was during the 1940s and early 1950s that the outstanding country artists and songs came to the fore, a golden epoch that produced the great stylists and what is now known as traditional country music.

'Fiddlin' John' Carson was born on 13 March 1868 on a farm in Fannin County in the heart of the Blue Ridge Mountains and began to play on his grandfather's instrument at the age of 10. He was still playing the fiddle while a young racehorse jockey in Cobb County. When he became too big to ride, he went to the annual Atlanta Interstate Fiddlers' Conventions, and earned a living by odd jobs as a textile hand and painter, and played his fiddle at political rallies and fiddlers' conventions. In March 1922, the *Atlanta Journal* opened WSB, the first commercial broadcasting station in the South, and Carson was probably the

first hillbilly performer to play on the then infant radio. He made his radio debut on 9 September 1922. It was the beginning of his career, for he was an instant success with requests pouring in for more of the old backwoods tunes. His first discs were 'The Little Old Log Cabin in the Lane' and 'The Old Hen Cackled and the Rooster's Going to Crow', recorded under Ralph Peer's direction in an improvised studio, and first issued without a label number for local Atlanta buyers. The session was on 14 June 1923, in Atlanta, and was Okeh's first out-of-town session and the first of any of the big companies to record traditional artists in the South. Carson thus sparked the hillbilly trend for Okeh, although Henry Whitter preceded him by four months as a record artist. In November 1923, Polk C. Brockman, a young Atlanta record dealer who discovered Carson and who had introduced him to Peer, sent the artist to New York to make more recordings for Okeh. Other disc companies soon followed Okeh into the South.

'Fiddlin' John' Carson died in Atlanta in 1949 on 11 December.

WENDELL HALL

IT AIN'T GONNA RAIN NO MO' *Victor* [*USA*]. Wendell Hall, composer, author, poet, singer, guitarist, radio, film and TV artist, was born 23 August 1896 in St George, Kansas, and was educated at University of Chicago preparatory school. He became a singing xylophonist in vaudeville and with orchestras. Wendell started as a staff artist for $25 a week on Chicago's KYW radio, and during the 1920s was a star in this medium, playing the ukulele (1922), a four-stringed instrument originating in Hawaii, resembling a small guitar. His performances on this helped to popularize the instrument all over the world. He was known as 'Red Headed Music Maker' and subsequently toured the world broadcasting, singing and playing his own compositions. He also wrote much material for the ukulele. This disc was issued on 16 November 1923 (Victor 19171).

Wendell was a friend of Carson Robinson with whom he went to New York, both working for Victor Talking Machine Co. He wrote 'It Ain't Gonna Rain No Mo' (based on an old country dance tune) and his recording, self accompanied on the ukulele, sold over two million. It has also sold over five million combined record and sheet music copies to date, and composer Hall was still active as a writer in 1966. Another of his popular compositions was 'Mellow Moon'. He died in Alabama on 2 April 1969.

BESSIE SMITH

DOWN HEARTED BLUES *Columbia* [*USA*]. Bessie Smith, who in her lifetime became known as The Empress of the Blues, and sold over 10 million records, was born into poverty in Chattanooga, Tennessee on 15 April 1895. She lost her father when she was an infant, her mother when she was nine. At the age of 11, she toured with the Rabbit Footing Minstrels, where Gertrude ('Ma') Rainey - the primogenitress of all female blues singers - began to school her greatest offspring. They toured the Southern states, and Bessie got her big break with them, the star of the group Ma Rainey becoming the first big-time blues singer to appear in theatres throughout the Midwest and, next to Bessie, probably the greatest blues singer who ever recorded. Bessie was discovered by Frank Walker, pioneer record man of Columbia Records, in Selma, Alabama, in the early 1920s, and Walker later sent the composer/pianist Clarence Williams to bring her North. Bessie recorded 180 songs for Columbia during her lifetime, the first being 'Down Hearted Blues', 15 February 1923, originally recorded by Alberta Hunter who wrote it with pianist Lovie Austin. Bessie's disc sold an incredible 800,000 (at 75 cents each) in 1923 and was Columbia's first pop hit, inspiring the company to start its 'race series'. Sales through the years plus the bootlegging of her discs must have made it a million seller.

Bessie was often accompanied by such great musicians as Louis Armstrong, Joe Smith, Tommy Ladnier, James P. Johnson and Fletcher Henderson. Her tours on the black concert circuit were a big success. In 1929 she made a short film entitled *St Louis Blues* and reached the height of her fame, earning from $1,500 to $2,500 a week. She was extraordinarily popular until 1930, the time of the Depression when her popularity waned and she stopped making records. She was convinced the blues were finished, and at the time (1932) she was right. Most of the coloured people were turning for a time to white-oriented musical values and Bessie found herself touring in the South for as little as $140 a week.

When Bessie's star and fortune had all but vanished, John Hammond, a great admirer of Bessie since he heard her sing at the Alhambra Theatre, Harlem, in October 1927 when he was 16, began working at Columbia Records and produced her final recording session on 24 November 1933. As the Depression had left Columbia virtually bankrupt, Hammond could only raise $150 for Bessie for the four sides she cut, plus another $150 for the sidemen such as Chew Berry, Benny Goodman, Jack Teagarden and others. Bessie then fell on hard times, singing in second-rate night clubs. She died tragically in an automobile accident on a highway outside Clarksdale, Mississippi on 26 September 1937.

Bessie was gifted with a deep voice of great beauty and a phenomenal sense of pitch, and could shade a vowel or vary her intonation according to the sense of the lyrics that few *lieder* singers could match, revealing the instincts of a genius. When Bessie sang the blues, she was the blues.

In the early 1960s, the blues began to have an international impact, helped by such acts as The Beatles, The Rolling Stones and others. Hammond has said: 'For years blues in America sold only in the Negro market; but during that era the British people generally dug the idiom.' Europe generally reissued a considerable amount of blues recordings. Blues dominated the pop scene in the 60s in much the same way that jazz did in the late 1930s and early 1940s.

In 1970, John Hammond started the reissue of every one of Bessie Smith's records (160 of which still exist) in a series of five two-LP albums, each containing 32 songs. The first album, containing Bessie's first acoustic recordings (1923) and her last electrics (1930-1933) released in June 1970, had big sales. The project was perfectly timed and the most ambitious reissue job ever attempted. The album transfers engineered by Hammond and his associates (notably blues expert Chris Albertson) have removed all surface noises from the shellac originals, and more

importantly gave the original sound new lustre without resort to artificial echo or phony stereo.

Bessie thus got the acclaim she deserved.

The greatest tribute to the legendary blues singer came in 1970 when artist Janis Joplin said, 'She showed me the air and taught me how to fill it'. This prompted a letter from a woman to the *Philadelphia Inquirer* asking where Bessie was buried. Janis Joplin, Juanita Green (a registered nurse from Philadelphia) and John Hammond, among others, shared the cost of a stone for the grave that had lain unmarked in Sharon Hill, Pa., since Bessie's death in 1937.

The inscription reads, 'The Greatest Blues Singer in the World Will Never Stop Singing - Bessie Smith - 1895-1937.'

Note: Although Bessie Smith is considered to be the greatest of all female blues singers, she was not the first to record. This distinction is held by Mamie Smith (born 16 September 1890, Cincinatti, Ohio; died New York, 30 October 1946) who made history when she recorded 'Crazy Blues' for the Okeh label in New York on 10 August 1920 under famed director Ralph Peer. Okeh had been unable to obtain white star Sophie Tucker for that date and Peer took the advice of Perry Bradford, composer of the song, to use Mamie Smith - the first recording of a vocal blues by a black artist. It is said to have sold 800,000 and started Okeh on its 'race series'. Soon other labels followed suit. Mamie's disc brought the blues to Northern cities in the U.S.A. and thus helped a segregated music out of its ghetto origins. Composer Perry Bradford died 20 April 1970. Mamie's first recording was 'That Thing Called Love', another Perry Bradford song, in mid February 1920 also for Okeh. It marked the historic beginning of the 'race record' era.

TED WEEMS AND HIS ORCHESTRA
SOMEBODY STOLE MY GAL *Victor* [*USA*]. Songwriter Leo Wood, composer of special material for vaudeville performers and U.S.A. productions, first wrote this highly successful popular song in 1918, but it was not until 1923 that it attained hit status through this recording by Ted Weems made in Camden, New Jersey on 20 November 1923. It was one of Weems' first recordings for the Victor label, an association that lasted for ten years until 1933. The disc is said to have sold a million.

The song became the signature tune for Britain's Billy Cotton and his Band. (See 1929 for Weems biography.)

PAUL WHITEMAN AND HIS ORCHESTRA
THREE O'CLOCK IN THE MORNING *Victor* [*USA*]. The second million seller for Paul Whiteman. The tune was first published in New Orleans (1919), composed by Julian Robledo, who paid for its publication himself, and according to one report it was originally a ribald drinking song. U.S. lyricist Dorothy Terriss (Dolly Morse) made it into a ballad, and she was also associated as a lyricist with Paul Whiteman and Ferde Grofe in 'Wonderful One'. A feature of 'Three O'Clock in the Morning' is its middle strain echoing the chime of London's 'Big Ben'. This song was also a million sheet music seller. The disc was reported to have sold 3½ million.

PAUL WHITEMAN AND HIS ORCHESTRA WITH MIKE PINGATORE – BANJO
LINGER AWHILE *Victor* [*USA*]. Third million seller for Paul Whiteman, the song written by Harry Owen (words) and Vincent Rose (music). It became one of Paul Whiteman's specialities, and featured the banjo playing of the diminutive Mike Pingatore who was with Whiteman for 25 years.

1924

VERNON DALHART
THE PRISONER'S SONG backed with THE WRECK OF

THE OLD 97 *Victor* [*USA*]. This was the biggest selling Victor record of the pre-electric epoch. Estimates of sales run between six and seven million with the electric re-recording still in circulation as late as 1952. Dalhart's real name was Marion Try Slaughter, but he took his stage name from two towns, Vernon and Dalhart, near his childhood home. He was born in Jefferson, Texas, 6 April 1883. Dalhart deserves the title of champion all-time hillbilly recording artist – although not born a hillbilly. His disc sales for several years made all the rest (including the legendary Jimmie Rodgers) seem small by comparison. After a thorough musical training he went to New York and became a member of the Century Opera Co. as tenor singer in light operas, and frequently appeared in Gilbert and Sullivan productions. He began making records in 1916, and was able to sing with a convincing Negro accent as well as in a voice free from imitation. A dramatic change in his career took place when he heard the Okeh recording of 'The Wreck of the 97' made by its reputed original writer, Henry Whitter, a Virginia mountain musician of Fries, Virginia, who played mouth harp, guitar, and sang through his nose. Being familiar with many southern and western folk tunes of his Texas boyhood, Dalhart, who also played mouth harp, was convinced there would be big money in hillbilly records. He copied Whitter's words of 'Wreck' and first recorded it for Edison Records. He then coupled it with 'Prisoner's Song' and recorded it for Victor Records (No. 19,427), with the most spectacular sales result for a disc at that time (1924). This was but the beginning of his hillbilly career. He sang, without exception, for every American disc company east of the Mississippi – some 30 or more – and recorded 'Prisoner's Song' for at least 28 labels under various names, with an estimated tally of 25 million. His discs could be bought under his own name and over 70 pseudonyms at various prices, e.g. as Jeff Calhoun (on Madison) and as Mack Allen (on Velvet Tone). His speciality was songs of wrecks and disasters, most of them being written by Carson J. Robison who later became so popular with his Hillbilly band in Britain in vaudeville and radio from 1932. Dalhart's disaster discs sold in staggering quantities from 1924 to 1930 during which period he made thousands of titles and colossal aggregate sales. Dalhart's decline as a hillbilly artist came about through a split with Robison, who had become his duet partner, over demands on royalties from songs written by Robison. Robison then teamed with Frank Luther, and Dalhart's disc sales began to drop. By 1931 he was on the way out, but by then the record industry had started a decline owing to the economic slump. Dalhart made a brief come-back on Bluebird label in 1939, but his discs did not sell. He died on 14 September 1948. 'The Prisoner's Song' is credited to Guy Massey, who is said to have actually spent some time in jail, and who Dalhart claimed on occasion to be his cousin. The disc was released on 3 October 1924.

Of the many names used by Dalhart as a recording artist 'Guy Massey' was a well-known one. It has also been claimed that Nathaniel Shilkret, then musical director for Victor, was mainly responsible for the finished product. 'The Wreck of the Old 97', based on a wreck which took place near Danville, Virginia in 1903, has no known composer. The tune was undoubtedly lifted from Henry C. Work's 'The Ship That Never Returned', a mournful song of the Civil War period. Victor Records advertised for information as to the writer of the song, intending to pay royalties, but after about 50 claims came in, all obviously spurious, the matter was dropped, though the song had probably caused more litigation than any other. Present day 'Wreck' sheet music lists the authors as Henry Whitter, Charles W. Noell and Fred J. Lewey, but the real lyricist still remains a mystery. This disc was a million seller by 1925. 'Prisoner's Song' was also a million sheet music seller.

ERNEST VAN (POP) STONEMAN
(country-and-western vocalist, guitar)

THE SINKING OF THE *TITANIC* Okeh [*USA*]. 'Pop Stoneman, born 25 May 1893 near the mining community of Iron Ridge, Carroll County, Virginia, was considered to be America's oldest recording artist, his career spanning the history of discs from Edison cylinders to the present day discs. In his early days he made over 250 records and Edison cylinders. It was on 1 September 1924 that he made this, his first disc, under the great field recording director Ralph S. Peer, the forerunner of many Stoneman releases that sold into the millions. 'Titanic', another of the wreck and disaster recordings so popular in America at that time, is said to have sold two million. It tells the story of the ill-fated $7½ million White Star liner which struck an iceberg off Cape Race, Newfoundland, 15 April 1912, on its maiden voyage from Southampton to New York with 2,223 persons aboard; 1,517 (including 103 women and children) were lost, 706 rescued.

Stoneman sang many religious songs and at one time recorded under 18 different names for 8 different labels. In 1927 he recorded some of the famous Powers Family's sacred songs for Victor. He also claimed he suggested the name 'Hillbillies' to Al Hopkins, a popular group of 1925–29, and thus the band named the music.

The 1929 Depression was a great blow to the Stoneman family who had spent the big money earned from many hit records on cars and furnishings. From then on they faced dire poverty, living in dilapidated shacks. 'Pop' who was a skilled carpenter eventually worked at the U.S. Naval Gun Factory near Washington, D.C., while his children were beginning to find an interest in music. His marriage resulted in 23 children, 13 of whom were still living in 1968.

The family's home life became filled with music and Pop and the children were soon playing for parties and dances in the Washington area. In 1956, Pop won a small fortune of $20,000 in a geography TV quiz programme 'The Big Surprise'.

In 1964, those of his children who had decided on a musical career – daughters Donna, Roni and sons Van Hayden, Calvin Scott and Jim – moved to California where they began to acquire valuable experience in the active folk music scene, and performed at the Monterey Folk Festival and on several national TV shows. A feature article in the *Washington Post* helped them to become exceedingly well known between 1964 and 1966. America thus took 40 years to discover their music.

The Stoneman Family appeared on the Jimmy Dean ABC-TV country music show (a series started in 1963) and in 1966 moved to Nashville with immediate success. Within two months they were signed to a contract for their own TV show, 'Those Stonemans', which premiered in May 1966, also a recording contract with MGM Records. By 1968, their TV show proved the most sought after item in national syndication. The Stoneman Family appealed to a much broader audience than the traditional 'Country' audience because of their exceptionally fine musicianship and delivery. In 1967 they won the Country Music Association's First Annual Award for Best Vocal Group which then consisted of Pop Stoneman (guitar/auto harp), Calvin Scott Stoneman (a fine fiddle player), Van Hayden Stoneman (bass), Donna Stoneman (guitar) and Roni Stoneman (banjo).

They featured 'bluegrass' music, better described as folk music handed down by tradition and embellished with new ideas. They have also recorded for the Starday, Folkways and World Pacific labels.

'The Sinking of the Titanic' is a traditional song, as is the backing of the disc 'The Face That Never Returned'. A recording by the group of 'Titanic' was released around 1963, arranged by William York.

Pop Stoneman's last recording session took place on 11 April 1968 soon after which he was hospitalized and died 14 June 1968 in Nashville.

MORAN AND MACK

TWO BLACK CROWS (comedy discs) *Okeh* [*USA*]. Moran and Mack's series of humorous duologues were an enormous success in the late 1920s and sold, it is said, in their millions. The first of these famous laughing discs by the duo who called themselves The Two Black Crows was 'The Early Bird Catches the Worm' in 1926, a fantastic success. This was followed by 'All about Lions' and 'Curiosities on the Farm' (both in 1927). 'No Matter How Hungry a Horse Is' (He Can't Eat a Bit), 'In Jail' and 'Two Black Crows in Hades' (all in 1928) and 'Foolishments' and 'Esau Buck and the Bucksaw' (both in 1929). All were issued on 10-inch discs by Okeh in U.S.A. and in Britain on Columbia.

There were no inhibitions in the yesteryear 'coon songs' and 'darky' brand of Moran and Mack humour, and their discs were still in the Columbia catalogue until the start of World War II.

George Moran died in 1949.

GEORGE OLSEN AND HIS BAND

WHO? *Victor* [*USA*]. George Olsen, born in 1893, was leader of a top popular orchestra from 1923 to 1934, immediately before the advent of the swing era. During that period, bands were featured in musical shows and in vaudeville. George Olsen's band played in numerous musicals on Broadway, including *Kid Boots*, *The Girl Friend*, *Whoopee*, *Good News* and *Sunny* and this song 'Who?' was the hit from *Sunny* produced at the New Amsterdam Theatre on 22 September 1925 where it ran for 517 performances, starring Marilyn Miller and Jack Donahue. Olsen's recording is said to have sold a million. *Sunny* was also a big success in Britain at the London Hippodrome with the stars Jack Buchanan and Binnie Hale.

The band played at the RKO Palace when that theatre was a twice-a-day mecca of vaudeville, and at the Capitol and Loew's State also on Broadway.

Olsen's was one of the bands featured at the NBC (New York) inaugural on 15 November 1926. He gave up his hotel stand for radio in 1927 for which he was paid $2,500 a week, and was also featured on network radio via the Canada Dry coast-to-coast show.

His first wife, Ethel Shutta, was the band's vocalist during the mid-1930s and became a top singer as a result of her band vocal assignments.

The band featured novelty instrumental effects which were used in Olsen's signature tune, 'Beyond the Blue Horizon', and his closing number 'Going Home Blues' with choo-choo train sounds by members of the band.

It was actress Fanny Brice who induced Flo Ziegfield, Jr. to hire the band for the Eddie Cantor show *Kid Boots* (1923) for which Olsen received $800 a week.

Olsen fronted his band for nearly 30 years, working in hotels across the U.S.A. and in theatres and shows, until his last hotel date at the Edgewater Beach Hotel, Chicago in 1950. He retired from music in 1951 and entered the restaurant business in Paramus, N.J.

Throughout his career, he recorded for RCA-Victor which reissued an album in its Vintage series in 1968 - 'George Olsen and His Music'. He died on 18 March 1971 in Paramus.

'Who?' was written by Otto Harbach and Oscar Hammerstein (words) with music by Jerome Kern. The vocal trio on this disc were Fran Frey, Bob Rice and Jack Fulton. An additional vocalist with the band was Bob Borger.

SOPHIE TUCKER (vocalist, cabaret artiste) WITH TED LEWIS AND HIS BAND

SOME OF THESE DAYS *Columbia* [*USA*]. Sophie Tucker was introduced to this in 1910, and it is one of the songs which started the ragtime fever in the U.S.A. Sophie's maid, a friend of composer/pianist/vaudeville entertainer Shelton Brooks, got Sophie to hear it, and it started her on the road to stardom. It became her most famous song, and she also used it for the title of her autobiography. Brooks (who also composed the famous 'Darktown Strutters' Ball' later in 1917) got the idea when he overheard two lovers arguing in a Cincinnati restaurant. 'You'd better not walk out on me, honey,' said the girl, 'for some of these days you're gonna miss me.' The song sold over a million in sheet music and Sophie's disc is estimated to have sold a million through the years. This original version was still in Columbia's catalogue for years afterwards, and Sophie also recorded it for Decca and Victor, with inclusion in her subsequent albums.

Ted Lewis, a jazz clarinettist and vocalist, was famous in vaudeville throughout the great jazz period of the 1920s on both sides of the Atlantic. He appeared on stage with his band, always immaculately dressed and wearing a top hat. Lewis made a great many records for Columbia between 1919 and 1933, and innumerable stage comebacks throughout his long career. He still worked periodically with Sophie until 3 months before she died.

Sophie Tucker was born on 13 January 1884 (some references give 1888) in Poland of Russian parents named Kalish. The family fled to America and changed their name to Abuza. She first appeared as a singer in her father's café in Hartford in 1905. In 1906, she was engaged at the German Village in New York for $15 a week, after an early marriage to Louis Tuck from which came her professional name. Then followed a 'black-face' act at New York's Music Hall (1906) and by 1909 she was performing in *Ziegfield Follies*. Here she was a big success. Appearances in various shows followed until 1912 when she returned to vaudeville. By 1914 she was earning $1,000 a week and from 1916 toured in various shows, then to Boston (1919) in *Shubert Gaieties* and *Earl Carroll Vanities* in New York (1924). Her first appearance in Britain was in 1922 in cabaret, with subsequent variety at London's Palladium and principal music halls. Other British appearances were in *Round in Fifty* (London Hippodrome, 1922) and a star part in *Follow a Star* (Winter Garden Theatre, 1930). Subsequent British appearances were in cabaret 1936, 1948, and in 1964 on TV. She also worked in films from as early as 1920 in *Honky Tonk*, followed by *Broadway Melody of 1937*, *Thoroughbreds Don't Cry* and *Atlantic City*. Sophie was a tremendous hit in Cole Porter's *Leave It to Me* musical on Broadway in 1938.

During her 60-year show business career, Sophie mastered every medium of entertainment - stage, film, cabaret, radio, TV, recording - and became affectionately known as 'The Last of the Red Hot Mamas', the title of one of the many spicy songs she introduced in cabaret. She sang all types of songs - jazz, blues, swing - in her brassy voice which became known throughout the world, and was among the last of a great breed of entertainers of an era that was one of the most colourful in show business. Her final engagement was in October 1965 at New York's Latin Quarter. She died on 9 February 1966 in New York. Sophie first recorded in 1910.

Ted Lewis, born in Circleville, Ohio, on 6 June 1890, died in New York on 25 August 1971. His real name was Theodore Leopold Friedman. 'Some of These Days' was recorded in Chicago on 23 November 1926.

GENE AUSTIN

MY BLUE HEAVEN *Victor [USA]*. Gene Austin became a singer in a vaudeville double act in the U.S.A. in 1923, then made many discs, sang on radio, stage and screen. This song, his first million seller disc, was written in 1927 by George Whiting (words) and Walter Donaldson (music) and was also a million sheet music seller then. This disc is reputed to have sold 5 million, and made Gene Austin rich and famous. He was born on 24 June 1900 in Gainsville, Texas, and served in the U.S. Army on a Mexican Punitive Expedition in 1916 and then in World War I. On his return, he attended Baltimore University. Austin was also known as the composer of several songs. This disc was recorded in December 1927. Austin's real name was Eugene Lucas. He died on 24 January 1972.

ERNEST LOUGH (boy soprano) WITH CHOIR OF TEMPLE CHURCH, LONDON, WITH ORGAN ACCOMPANIMENT BY G. THALBEN-BALL

HEAR MY PRAYER backed with OH, FOR THE WINGS OF A DOVE *His Master's Voice [Britain]*. This beautiful rendering of the famous Mendelssohn work, with Lough singing the solo parts, caused a sensation when the disc was issued, and it has been a favourite request item ever since. The million sale was reached in 1962, when Lough was presented with a Gold Disc, HMV's first presentation for a classical singles disc, 35 years after it was made. A similar award was made to the organist, Thalben-Ball.

RED NICHOLS (cornet) AND HIS FIVE PENNIES

IDA, SWEET AS APPLE CIDER *Okeh [USA]*. Red Nichols (real name Ernest Loring Nichols) born 8 May 1905 in Ogden, Utah, son of a local professor of music, played the cornet when he was 12 in the town band led by his father. A cornettist for several years, he was one of the few players who clung to this instrument before switching to the trumpet. He was certainly one of the 'greats' of Dixieland style.

After expulsion from Culver Military Academy for smoking when 17, he returned to Ogden and led a threepiece pit orchestra in the town's theatre. Having heard Isham Jones' band, he went east, playing with various bands and made his first discs for the since defunct Gennett Studios in October 1922 in Richmond, Indiana (one of the birthplaces of early jazz on discs) with a group called 'The Syncopatin' Five'. None of them were paid – in fact they each had to pay $25 for the privilege of recording – and got, it is said, 25 copies of the disc apiece. By 1923, Red formed in New York his first of many combinations, 'The Five Pennies', although the group usually exceeded six in number. They made discs for 14 different labels under various pseudonyms such as Nichols Stompers, Varsity Eight, The Redheads, Alabama Red Peppers, Six Hottentots, University Six, Arkansas Travellers, Louisiana Rhythm Kings, Wabash Dance Orchestra, Midnight Airedales, We Three, Miff's Stompers, Charleston Chasers, Miff Mole's Molers and, on occasion, Red Nichols and His Five Pennies. All of these discs became the prize possessions of collectors for years afterwards. Red was thus being featured on many 'hot' discs when he was 17 with other young jazz musicians, most of whom became famous players. These included Arthur Schutt (piano), Miff Mole (trombone), Adrian Rollini (bass sax), Jimmy Dorsey (clarinet), Eddie Lang (guitar), Vic Berton (drums) and Joe Venuti (violin). Other greats of jazz who worked for Red early in their careers include Glenn Miller, Tommy Dorsey, Benny Goodman, Gene Krupa and Jack Teagarden.

By 1924, Nichols led one of the liveliest of all recording jazz groups, as the disc business really came to the fore, and he probably made more jazz discs than any other bandleader during this period. 'Ida, Sweet as Apple Cider' was one of the first of those to sell a million, although doubtless other records by his band have done likewise. (The arrangement for this one was by Lennie Hayton, pianist and husband and accompanist of the famous singer, Lena Horne.) Red also appeared on the radio networks when they began, and organized and conducted pit bands for several musicals on Broadway between 1926 and 1932. When Dixieland style went out in the early 1930s, swing music came in, and he disbanded his own swing band, which was a disaster and cost him most of his savings. A further calamity was his daughter's polio illness. He spent eight years with his wife in nursing her, while he worked in a shipyard during World War II. His daughter recovered and she induced him to take up playing again. He made a sensational comeback in 1945 with his reformed Five Pennies and Dixie style. A film, *The Five Pennies*, was made in 1958 (with Danny Kaye as Red Nichols) and the recordings for it were made by Red. His 40th anniversary as a bandleader in February 1962 drew a show business galaxy to the celebrations. Red signed with Capitol Records after the war and continued working, mostly around the U.S.A. coast. In 1962 he went on a State Department tour of 11 countries and in autumn 1964 played commercial dates in Japan. He died in Las Vegas on 28 June 1965.

It is interesting to note that the great songwriter Harry Warren made his vocal debut with Nichols' band in 1924.

'Ida, Sweet as Apple Cider' is an old song of 1903, written by the well-known U.S. artist Eddie Leonard, and became identified with the late comedian/singer Eddie Cantor. The song was also a million sheet music seller years ago. Disc recorded in New York on 15 August 1927.

Red Nichols' scores of disc sessions virtually defined the New York 'Golden Age' jazz style.

JIMMIE RODGERS (country-and-western and blues vocalist with guitar)

THE SOLDIER'S SWEETHEART *Victor* [*USA*]. The first recording ever made by this artist whose name stands foremost in the country music field as 'the man who started it all'. Recorded in Bristol, Tennessee on 4 August 1927. It is said to have subsequently sold a million. (See 1928 for further data and biography of Jimmie Rodgers.)

This song was written by him and his initial royalty was a mere $27 for the recording.

1928

GENE AUSTIN

RAMONA *Victor* [*USA*]. This was written by L. Wolfe Gilbert (words) and Mabel Wayne (music) on the spur of the moment in 1927 for the exploitation of the silent film *Ramona*. It made Tin Pan Alley history as the first of the great film songs and sold fantastically on disc, piano-player rolls and sheet music all round the world. It was also the first of the songs that were bought not by one million but by several, so marking the beginning of a new era. Composer Mabel Wayne is America's First Lady of Song. This disc was Gene Austin's second million seller.

THE CARTER FAMILY (vocal and instrumental)

WILDWOOD FLOWER *Victor* [*USA*]. The famous Carter Family, consisting of Alvin Pleasant Carter (bass vocalist), his wife Sarah, born 21 July 1899, (lead vocalist and autoharp player) and Maybelle her first cousin (alto vocalist and lead guitar) made their first records in a makeshift studio using portable equipment in Bristol, Tennessee, on 1 August 1927. It was here that they were discovered, along with the great Jimmie Rodgers, by the late Ralph Peer, pioneer recording scout from Victor Records.

On 9 May 1928, in Victor's modern studios at Camden, New Jersey, the group recorded two songs, 'Meet Me by Moonlight Alone' and 'Little Darling, Pal of Mine' for which it is said people lined up to buy. Next day they made 10 songs among which was 'Wildwood Flower', a traditional song. This became the Carter Family's most popular love song and a favourite ever since. It is said to have sold over a million in 78 rpm discs alone. Maybelle's guitar playing in a clear-toned style made her unique among players of this instrument. The Carter Family's simple songs of breaking hearts and disappointed love affairs made a great contribution in modern music worldwide. Each of the 12 songs recorded became popular, a record in itself. During their recording years over three decades, they put on disc 250 of their songs, a great number of them written by A. P. Carter. One of his most popular in later years was 'I'm Thinking Tonight of My Blue Eyes' (written in 1930).

A. P. Carter, born 15 December 1891, left the Virginia hill country as a young carpenter to find work in Detroit, but after a very short stay returned to Scott County, where he began to sell fruit trees. He died on 7 November 1960. Some of his recordings were on the Acme and Bluebird labels.

Maybelle Carter was born in Michellsville, Virginia, 10 May 1909, and sang with the Carter Sisters. She had radio experience over the WNOX, Knoxville and WJHL-TV, Johnson, Tennessee, stations, also on WSM's 'Grand Ole Opry'. She has recorded for Victor, Decca, Columbia and other labels and wrote many country and sacred songs. She later recorded with her 3 daughters, June, Helen and Anita.

The Carter family were elected to the Country Music Hall of Fame in 1970.

Sarah Carter died in Lodi, California on 8 January 1979.

Maybelle Carter died 23 October 1978 in Nashville, Tennessee.

AL JOLSON

SONNY BOY backed with THERE'S A RAINBOW ROUND MY SHOULDER *Brunswick* [*USA*]. The first million seller of the talking-film era, both sung by Jolson in his second film *The Singing Fool*, the first musical film to gross over $4 million. 'Rainbow' was written by Al Jolson, Billy Rose and Dave Dreyer, and the tear-jerking 'Sonny Boy' by Al Jolson, B. G. de Sylva, Lew Brown and Ray Henderson. Both also sold a million in sheet music. 'Sonny Boy' swept the world and was revived in 1949 (*q.v.*) when it again sold a million discs, making over 3 million in aggregate. Al Jolson (born Asa Joelson on 26 March 1886 in Washington, D.C.) was the son of an orthodox rabbi. (It has also been stated that he was born on 28 May 1886 in St Petersburg, Russia, the family emigrating to the U.S.A. when he was a child.) He studied music with his father and deputized for him as a synagogue cantor in Washington at the age of 13. He made his first stage appearance in 1899 as one of the mob in *The Children of the Ghetto*. He abandoned the career of a Jewish cantor to become a popular singer, travelled with minstrel shows and circuses, then found his trademark in Brooklyn in 1909, when his hired dresser suggested the blackface routine. From there he joined Lew Dockstader's Minstrels for $75 a week as end man. In 1911, the famous Shuberts spotted him and he became the hit of their *La Belle Paree* in New York. For the next 10 years his rise to stardom continued with the Shuberts' shows and in 1924 his appearance in *Big Boy* brought a film offer of $10,000 a week. He made his screen debut in *The Jazz Singer* (1927), the first motion picture with dialogue, which grossed $5 million, and pioneered the new talkie field. It was a triumph in Europe as well as the U.S.A. Then followed more films, concerts, and his return to the stage full time in 1931 in *Wonder Bar*. More movies followed. In 1940 he temporarily quit the show *Hold on to Your Hats* through ill-health, rejoining it in 1941. Then came World War II and he devoted his time to the war effort, entertaining the troops in a long, exhausting tour from the Aleutians to India. Everybody thought Jolson was a spent force, a view shared by Warner Bros., whom he had helped to reach the heights in the film capital 20 years before. A Hollywood executive heard him at a Sunday-night benefit show at the Hillcrest Country Club in Beverly Hills, where Jolson had to follow top talent from screen and radio. He was a sensation, and the executive took a gamble. *The Jolson Story* was the result, with Larry Parks taking the title role and the soundtrack carrying the voice of Jolson. It was a colossal financial success, as was the follow-up film *Jolson Sings Again* (see 1945 and 1946). Then came Korea and more entertaining of the American Forces. A fortnight after his return he suddenly died of a heart attack while playing cards with his accompanist Harry Akst and arranger Martin Fried in a San Francisco hotel on 23 October 1950. He left $4 million of his $5 million estate to Jewish, Protestant and Catholic charities, and to hospitals in California and New York, and to New York City colleges.

JIMMIE RODGERS

BLUE YODEL *Victor* [*USA*]. Considered to be the greatest of all country artists, the legendary Jimmie Rodgers was installed as the first member of the Country Hall of Fame on 3 November 1961 by unanimous vote of a panel of qualified experts in the country music field. A huge plaque immortalizing 'Jimmie' now stands on display in the Tennessee State Museum in Nashville.

Jimmie Rodgers was born on 8 September 1897 in Meridian, Mississippi, son of a railroad man, Aaron Rodgers, a section foreman on the Mobile & Ohio Railroad. As a teenager, Jimmie was an assistant to his father, working on the railroad for 14 years as flagman, brakeman, and baggageman. During this time, he absorbed the railroad lore. He loved trains and railroad songs. He was not robust in health and sought another means of livelihood, as professional entertainer, whereby he could use his knowledge of railroad ballads and songs. His first group included three musicians and himself as vocalist and guitarist, called 'The Jimmie Rodgers Entertainers'. A local radio station in Asheville, North Carolina booked them. Jimmie wrote many songs, generally in the blues idiom or making use of well-known blues images. He was noted for his high-pitched yodel, which he used with great effect, as in his famous 'Blue Yodels', of which he wrote and also recorded 13. It was while his group was on tour that he auditioned for Ralph Peer, who, in the late 1920s, was in charge of RCA Victor's field recording activity. Peer (who died on 19 January 1960) was a pioneer in the 'race records' field (a term he established) - which ultimately became rhythm and blues. His recording experience stamped him as one of the finest recording directors of the music of the South in the late 1920s. Peer discovered and developed Jimmie Rodgers, the Carter Family and others. He also published their works in special song books in the joint publishing venture he organized with Victor, and which he later took over. Jimmie Rodgers' first test record 'The Soldier's Sweetheart', was made in a 'portable studio' in Bristol, Tennessee on 4 August 1927 under Ralph Peer's direction. On St Valentine's Day, 1928, he recorded 'The Sailor's Plea' in Victor's Camden, New Jersey studios with J. R. Ninde and E. T. Cozzens accompanying him. 'Yodelling Cowboy' was recorded by Jimmie in Dallas, Texas on 22 December 1929 with just his own guitar accompaniment. Peer said that Rodgers was best recorded as a vocalist with guitar, although he did cut a few records with orchestral backing.

Thus, Jimmie recorded in various Victor studios around the U.S.A. and particularly in New York. He was however suffering from tuberculosis, and in 1933, with his finances in a bad way, went to New York to record. He was critically ill, and made his last discs, 12 sides over a period of eight days at Victor's 24th Street Studios, whilst propped up on a cot. The final disc was made on 24 May 1933. He died two days later.

Jimmie Rodgers left a legacy of over 100 recordings, practically all his own compositions, and during his short recording career is said to have sold five million discs, and a great number since his death. Many artists copied his yodels, guitar runs, side comments and vocal style in general. Legend has it that, in his heyday, general-store customers would approach the counter and say 'Let me have a pound of butter, a dozen eggs and the latest Jimmie Rodgers record'. Like all the great country artists, he had a threefold ability - songwriter, recording artist, and live performer. 'The Singing Brakeman', also termed 'Father of the Country Field', was one of the great originals. He was never replaced, but his influence over the years cannot be doubted. In the history of the music business, he made a contribution of lasting value. Although small in stature, he was a giant among singers, and started a trend in the musical tastes of millions. It is no wonder he was the first for America's Country Hall of Fame. (See note below.)

This disc of 'Blue Yodel' is said to have sold a million over the years, and was first published in 1928. It was written by Jimmie Rodgers. It is one of RCA-Victor's all-time best country-and-western sellers.

BRAKEMAN'S BLUES *Victor* [*USA*]. Another Jimmie Rodgers' composition. First published in 1928.

Note - '**Country music**': Jimmie Rodgers' career had a profound effect on American music in this century, and parallels the start of the 'Grand Ole Opry' which, without his influence, might never have risen to its great popularity in the U.S.A. It all started as 'Barn Dance' on Nashville's radio station on 28 November 1925, when George D. Hay, a one-time newspaperman, presented himself as the 'solemn old judge' and introduced his lone artist, 80-year-old Uncle Jimmy Thompson, who boasted he could play a thousand tunes on his fiddle. It drew crowds to the small studio which had to be enlarged and moved several times to accommodate the growing audiences. In 1927, the 'Solemn Ole Judge' christened it 'Grand Ole Opry' from the stage of the Ryman Auditorium in Nashville. The auditorium was re-named 'Grand Ole Opry House' in 1963. With the Opry as its folk-music hub, Nashville quickly became the centre for top country talent. (See also Acuff, 1942.)

SOPHIE TUCKER WITH TED SHAPIRO AND HIS ORCHESTRA

MY YIDDISHE MOMME *Columbia* [*USA*]. This famous song was written in 1925 by Jack Yellen and Lew Pollack. Sophie's disc was recorded in English on one side and in Yiddish on the other. It has of course been tremendously popular with the Jewish fraternity for a great number of years and this original recording was still in the Columbia catalogue as late as 1957, thirty years after it was made, and eventually transferred to her albums. Sophie also recorded the song for Decca.

Ted Shapiro was Sophie's accompanist for 46 years, up to the time of her death, and wrote much special material for her. He was born 31 October 1899, in New York.

1929

TED WEEMS AND HIS ORCHESTRA
(vocal – Parker Gibbs)

PICCOLO PETE *Victor* [*USA*]. This was the first 'novelty' song to sell a disc million, written and composed by Phil Baxter, an early member of Paul Whiteman's band in World War I and later noted for his novelty of orchestration. Ted Weems was born in Pitcairn, Pennsylvania, on 26 September 1901 and formed his first band soon after leaving University of Pennsylvania. His band played the top ballroom and hotel locations before World War II, and was noted for its arrangements that frequently featured the use of whistlers. His orchestra was also a talent incubator for top vocalists including Perry Como. During the last war he served with the Merchant Marines. When name bands were slipping in the late 1940s, Weems came right back with a revival of 'Heartaches' (see 1933). He was composer, radio and recording artist for many years, and went into semi-retirement in 1958, returning with a new band in 1961. He died in Tulsa, Oklahoma on 6 May 1963. This disc recorded on 28 June 1929, in Camden, New Jersey.

THE MILLS BROTHERS

TIGER RAG backed with NOBODY'S SWEETHEART *Brunswick* [*USA*]. The first million seller by a vocal quartet through subsequent years. The Mills Brothers (John, Herbert, Harry and Donald) were born in Piqua, Ohio, and began their career singing over a Cincinnatti radio station. After a stage appearance at a Piqua opera house, the group was soon on its way to a long career and its reputation became established in 1934 when it was already well known on discs, and had appeared in films. After the death of John in 1935, the boys' father, John Sr, joined the group, which then went on to its biggest successes, notably in 1942 with 'Paper Doll' (see 1942). The group signed with Decca in 1934. 'Tiger Rag', written in 1917 by the Original Dixieland 'Jass' Band, was made famous by them at that time. This vocal disc of the Mills Brothers was a sensational hit. 'Nobody's Sweetheart' is another oldie of 1924, written by Gus Kahn, Ernie Erdman, Billy Meyers and Elmer Schoebel and is also a jazz standard. Birthdays: John, 11 February; Herbert, 2 April; Donald, 29 April; Harry, 19 August. John Mills Sr died 8 December 1967, aged 85.

DON AZPIAZU AND HIS HAVANA CASINO ORCHESTRA

THE PEANUT VENDOR (El Manisero) *Victor* [*USA*]. This song was discovered in 1930 by Herbert Marks, son of the famous American music publisher, who heard it while on honeymoon in Havana. Marks was informed by the hotel manager that it was written by his brother Moises Simons (1888–1945), a reputed local composer. Marks was introduced to the composer and brought the song back to New York, where Louis Rittenberg wrote an English lyric. This however proved unsuitable, and Marion Sunshine of the vaudeville act Tempest and Sunshine, married to the brother of Cuban conductor, Don Azpiazu, wrote a more practical lyric assisted by Wolfe Gilbert. Don Azpiazu featured it at Keith's Palace Theatre, then recorded it. It was a tremendous hit and is said to have sold over the million through subsequent years. With Latin American rumba rhythms just beginning to challenge established dance rhythms, this disc made history in that field. Azpiazu and his band came to London and played at the old Alhambra Theatre. The song was also featured in the film *Cuban Love Song* (1931) by Lawrence Tibbett.

CAB CALLOWAY AND HIS ORCHESTRA

MINNIE THE MOOCHER (The 'Ho De Ho' Song) *Brunswick* [*USA*]. Written by Cab Calloway and Irving Mills.

Recorded in New York on 9 March 1931, this was the theme song of Cab Calloway. It achieved tremendous popularity by reason of Cab's 'scat' singing, whereby audiences joined in repeating his 'Hi de hi's' and 'Ho de ho's' of the refrain, and brought him fame with the public.

Not until 1978 was it revealed that this recording had sold 2,500,000, thus making it the longest 'sleeper' million seller after 47 years, his second known million seller (see Calloway, 1939). The song was re-recorded and re-released by Hologram Records in 1978 (distributed by RCA).

TED WEEMS AND HIS ORCHESTRA WITH ELMO TANNER (whistling)

HEARTACHES *Bluebird – Victor* [*USA*]. This song written in 1931 by John Klenner (words) and Al Hoffman (music) took 14 years to provide Ted Weems with his second million seller. Here is the story: Weems' disc was not a success when issued in 1933. In 1947, a Charlotte, North Carolina disc jockey, Kurt Webster, found the disc by chance, and as he liked it, played it each day for a week on his programme. Record dealers in the South of the U.S.A. were swamped with orders. In just over two years it sold over the million and brought renewed popularity to Ted Weems. The bandleader showed his appreciation by flying his complete band to Charlotte to play at the birthday party for the disc jockey who made 'Heartaches' a million seller, 14 years after it had been recorded.

Disc was a No 1 chart seller in the U.S.A. (1947) for 12 weeks. Recorded in Chicago on 4 August 1933.

GID TANNER AND HIS SKILLET LICKERS (hillbilly quartet)

DOWN YONDER *Victor* [*USA*]. 'Down Yonder' was written in 1921, by veteran author/publisher L. Wolfe Gilbert (born Odessa, Russia in 1886), and was revived with considerable success in the late 1940s and early 1950s, apart from Gid Tanner's big hit with it in 1934.

James Gideon Tanner was born 6 June 1885 in Thomas Bridge, near Monroe, Georgia, and learned to play the fiddle at 14. In the 1920s he was a frequent competitor at the fiddling contests of 'Fiddlin' Joe' Carson (see 1923). In 1956 at the age of 71, he was named as Georgia's top old time fiddler.

It was Frank Walker, Columbia's talent scout who invited him to make some recordings in New York in early 1924, and with Riley Puckett on guitar, they made their first discs on 7 March 1924. They were the first Southern country artists to record for the label.

Earlier, in 1923, Gid helped to form 'The Lick Skillet Band' at Davula, Georgia, composed of himself (fiddle), Clayton McMichen (fiddle), Riley Puckett (guitar) and Fayte Norris (banjo). Tanner, who played what is known as 'hoe-down fiddling', later formed his own group under the name of 'Gid Tanner and the Skillet Lickers', and he recorded over 565 numbers for Columbia and Victor during his career, mostly the traditional tunes in hillbilly style. During the 1930s, Gid worked at radio stations in Covington, Kentucky, Cleveland, Chicago and Atlanta, and, in his active performing years, travelled to play engagements throughout the south-eastern states. His younger brother Arthur recorded with some of the group between 1926 and 1929, playing banjo and guitar, and Gordon, one of his five sons, played fiddle with the Skillet Lickers on their 1934 recordings.

All four members of the band contributed to the vocals, with Puckett taking the lead. 'Down Yonder', according to an interview with Gid, was said to have sold four million, and another big seller was 'Corn Liquor Still in Georgia'.

Gid Tanner returned to his chicken farming in the 1930s until his death on 16 May 1962 at Winder, Georgia.

He was undoubtedly one of the performing pioneers of early American country music.

Riley Puckett was born in Alpharetta, Georgia, 7 May 1890. He was blinded at the age of 3 through an accident and attended the Georgia School for the Blind at Macon. At the age of 12 he began to play the 5 string banjo, later learning the guitar. His radio debut was on Atlanta's WSB on 28 September 1922, and

later he played personal appearances throughout the States. After the Skillet Lickers disbanded in 1931 he worked in Convington and Cincinnatti with McMichen's Georgia Wildcats. Riley recorded on Columbia, Decca and Bluebird labels. At the time of his death on 13 July 1946 in East Point, Georgia, he was singing with the Stone Mountain Boys over Atlanta's WACA station.

Clayton McMichen was born on 26 January 1900 in Allatoona, Georgia, and learned the fiddle at age 11 from his father. The family moved to Atlanta in 1913. He began his career in the early 1920s playing over a small radio station belonging to the Georgia Railroad that broadcast privately to the train passengers. His radio debut was on WSB Atlanta on 18 September 1922. His band was called the Hometown Boys String Band and the Lick the Skillet Band (originally two violins, two guitars and a mandolin). Puckett joined them after his debut broadcast. McMichen formed the Georgia Wildcats after the Skillet Lickers disbanded and appeared over radio stations in Cincinnatti, Covington, and finally Louisville where he settled. He was a Columbia Records artist. McMichen was National Fiddling Champion from 1934 to 1949. He died on 3 January 1970 in Battletown, Kentucky.

1936

CLYDE McCOY (trumpet) AND HIS ORCHESTRA
SUGAR BLUES *Decca* [*USA*]. Featuring famous 'wa-wa' trumpet solist Clyde McCoy. Composed by early jazz writer Clarence Williams in 1923, words by Lucy Fletcher, it was Clyde McCoy's only million seller disc, achieving that figure in 1946. He was the first to take his whole band, intact, into the service – the U.S. Navy in 1942.

JEANETTE MACDONALD AND NELSON EDDY (soprano and baritone)
INDIAN LOVE CALL *Victor* [*USA*]. First musical show tune to top the million mark on disc. It also sold a million in sheet music. The song is the outstanding duet from the stage musical of 1924 in the U.S.A. – *Rose Marie*, written by Otto Harbach and Oscar Hammerstein II (words) and Rudolf Friml (music). This disc has the stars from the film version (1936).

Jeanette MacDonald was born in Philadelphia, Pennsylvania, on 18 June 1907, and made her first appearance, aged 12, in the chorus of a New York revue. She subsequently appeared in the road show of *Irene* and other productions, getting her first big role at Greenwich Village Theatre in *Fantastic Fricasse* followed by *The Magic Ring*. Other musicals followed until 1929 when she started her screen career, and made concert tours abroad in Paris and London. She became internationally known through the film *The Love Parade* (1929) co-starring with Maurice Chevalier. More star roles in film musicals followed with *Vagabond King*, *Love Me Tonight*, *Cat and the Fiddle*, *Merry Widow*, *Naughty Marietta*, *Rose Marie*, *Maytime*, *The Firefly*, *New Moon*, *Sweethearts* and *Bitter Sweet*. Then came successful concert appear-

ances until 1950 when Jeanette reappeared on the regular stage. She died 14 January 1965.

Nelson Eddy (born on 29 June 1901 in Providence, Rhode Island) was educated at University of Southern California and had a B.A. He was successively a telephone operator, shipping clerk and newspaper artist, reporter and copyreader in Philadelphia, also an advertising agency copywriter. He studied voice and entered the operatic and concert field; appeared in the Operatic Society and Civic Opera in Philadelphia, with his New York debut in *Wozzek*. Eddy's screen debut was in 1933, and he co-starred with Jeanette MacDonald in the film musicals *Naughty Marietta* (1934), *Rose Marie* (1936), *Maytime* (1937), *Bitter Sweet* (1940) and others. He died 6 March 1967.

PATSY MONTANA
I WANT TO BE A COWBOY'S SWEETHEART *Columbia* [*USA*]. Said to be the first million seller by a female country singer, this was written by her.

Patsy Montana was born on 30 October 1914 in Hot Springs, Arkansas, and educated at the University of West L.A. She became a singer in radio, was a member of the Montana Trio, and also appeared in films.

The backing of this disc was another country-and-western favourite, 'Ridin' Old Paint'.

Patsy always sang 'western' songs during her more than 40 years as a performer. Nashville was considered 'country', and it was not until 1971 that she made her first appearance there in Grand Ole Opry.

1937

THE ANDREWS SISTERS
BEI MIR BIST DU SCHON *Brunswick* [*USA*]. The first million seller by a female group. The sisters hail from Minneapolis (Patti, born 16 February 1920, Maxine, born 3 February 1918, and Laverne, born 6 July 1915) and started there by winning a children's contest at the Orpheum Theatre. The theatre bandleader was impressed and hired them to sing with his group. They caught on in vaudeville and with other bands. Then followed many dates in Chicago nightclubs, but it was not

until this recording that they became famous. Patti continued with the trio singing lead and most of the solo passages until 1953, when she became solo artist. The original version of this song was written by Sholem Secunda (music), a composer for the Jewish stage, and Jacob Jacobs (lyrics) in 1932, and was sold for $30. The English version, written by Sammy Cahn and Saul Chaplin, grossed $3 million by 1961, the original composer collecting only a meagre $4,325 since 1954. Collective labels are estimated to have sold 2½ million. This Andrews Sisters' disc sold around 100,000 on its initial release with a reputed million through subsequent years. Orders for the song poured into baffled dealers as 'the new French song', 'Buy a Beer Monsieur Shane', 'Mr Barney McShane' and 'My Mere Bits of Shame'. The Andrews Sisters' disc sales through the years have been estimated at 60 million. They appeared in 17 important films in addition to playing variety and cabaret in all the leading venues throughout America and in many countries abroad. It was Jack Kapp of Brunswick Records who first discovered them at the Hotel Edison, New York. 'Bei Mir Bist Du Schön' was the second record they made for the company. Recorded on 24 November 1937, in New York.

BING CROSBY WITH LANI McINTIRE AND HIS HAWAIIANS
SWEET LEILANI *Decca* [*USA*]. Recorded on 23 February 1937, in Los Angeles, this was the first of Bing's 22 million-selling discs. Seven figures were achieved by 1946. The song, written by Harry Owens, leader of the Royal Hawaiians orchestra, was included in Crosby's film *Waikiki Wedding* (1937) and won the Academy Award for the best film song of that year. Harry Lillis Crosby was born in Tacoma, Washington on 2 May 1904. Bing said he got his nickname of 'Bing' during his childhood in Spokane through his liking for a character called Bingo in his favourite comic book *The Bingville Bugle*. He attended Gonzaga University to study law, and teamed up there with Al Rinker and formed a seven-piece band. In 1924 they quit school and in a battered old car set out to see Rinker's sister, swing-style vocalist Mildred Bailey, who got them an engagement at the Tent Café in Los Angeles at $65 a week each. They appeared in Pacific coast nightclubs and vaudeville until 1927 when Paul Whiteman heard them and signed them up at $150. Whiteman took them to New York where Harry Barris joined and so was formed Paul Whiteman's Rhythm Boys who became a sensation in Broadway nightclubs thereafter. After being with Whiteman for three years, the trio was booked alone into the Los Angeles Coconut Grove, where Bing's reputation as a soloist was built. He began to make bestselling discs, and when his brother Everett sent one, 'I Surrender Dear', to both NBC and CBS in New York, both wanted an audition. CBS signed him up, and on the morning of this 1931 premiere over a nation-wide hookup he temporarily lost his voice. The doctor found nodules. These nodules, since insured for a large sum, produced the effect of a man 'singing into a rain barrel'. It made Bing famous. Before long he was broadcasting twice nightly over CBS and appearing at New York's Paramount theatre. Next came the start of a lengthy film career with an eventual Academy Award for his starring role in *Going My Way* (1944). His enormous popularity

in films, on recordings, and over the air continued unabated for over 20 years, and he was presented with a special Platinum Disc in June 1960 to commemorate his 200 millionth record sold. Bing made over 2,600 records, and had the biggest album release in 'Bing's Hollywood', 15 discs of his film songs from 1934 to 1956 comprising 189 songs, released by Decca in 1962. By 1975, his disc sales were estimated at 400 million. Since he made his first disc 'I've Got the Girl' on 18 October 1926, apart from his singles issue, around 120 albums and 60 EPs were also released by the First Citizen of the Recording Industry. He made a gift of a library to Gonzaga University, Spokane, and it also houses his musical and cinema awards in the Crosbyana Room – a special tourist attraction. He died in Madrid, Spain, on 14 October 1977.

Lani McIntire was born 15 December 1904, in Honolulu.

TOMMY DORSEY AND HIS ORCHESTRA
(Jack Leonard, vocal, with chorus)
MARIE *Victor* [*USA*]. The first million seller for the younger of the fabulous Dorsey brothers, Tommy and Jimmy. This was a superb swing arrangement of Irving Berlin's waltz song of 1928. The song was a million seller also in sheet music. This disc reached a million sales by 1946.

James Francis Dorsey (born 29 February 1904) and Thomas Francis Dorsey (born 19 November 1905) were reared in Mahoney Place, Pennsylvania. They played in a family quartet (saxophone) with their father, Thomas Sr, and a sister, Mary, then together formed their first orchestra 'Dorsey's Novelty Six – The Jazz Band of 'em All'. Two years later they became 'Dorsey's Wild Canaries', then disbanded and joined the 'Scranton Sirens'. They next played and recorded with Eddie Elkins and the Californian Ramblers, toured with Jean Goldkette's orchestra from Detroit, and joined Paul Whiteman in 1946, settling into radio and recording work in New York. They assembled various recording orchestras between 1929 and 1934, and in 1934 formed the Dorsey Brothers' orchestra. Tommy withdrew in 1935 to lead his own band and went on to parallel success with the Jimmy Dorsey orchestra throughout the 1930s and 1940s. In 1953 Jimmy disbanded and joined Tommy in the new Dorsey Brothers' orchestra. They also appeared in films and were the subject of a film made in 1947 – *The Fabulous Dorseys* in which they themselves starred. Tommy and Jimmy are each credited with five million seller discs (see 1937, 1938, 1941, 1942, 1943, 1944, 1957). The brothers died within a few months of each other, Tommy on 26 November 1956; Jimmy on 12 June 1957. The Tommy Dorsey orchestra was then taken over by Warren Covington (see 1958). This disc recorded 29 January 1937, in New York.

TOMMY DORSEY AND HIS ORCHESTRA
BOOGIE WOOGIE (Pinetop's Boogie Woogie) *Victor* [*USA*]. This, by 1941, was the second million seller for Tommy. The disc is an outstanding example of 'boogie woogie', composed by Clarence 'Pinetop' Smith, of the very old piano style based on eight beats to the bar that became exceedingly popular in the late 1930s and early 1940s.

The term 'boogie woogie' was first used by composer/singer/pianist Clarence Smith, one of the pioneers and probably the greatest exponent of this style. He was called 'Pinetop' because his conical head resembled a pine tree. He first recorded the work in 1928 under the title 'Pinetop's Boogie Woogie', and a few years later this became well known under the short title of 'Boogie Woogie'. Pinetop was accidentally shot during a quarrel between two people in a Chicago dance hall in 1929, a decade before boogie woogie became nationally famous with the help of Tommy Dorsey's orchestral version, arranged by Dean Kincaide. Re-

corded 16 September 1938, in New York.

ARTHUR FIEDLER AND BOSTON POPS ORCHESTRA
JALOUSIE (Jealousy) *Victor* [*USA*]. This magnificent recording of Danish composer Jacob Gade's famous 'Tango Tzigane', first written in 1926, was the first million seller of a light orchestral piece. Over 200 different recordings have been made to date. This disc sold a million by 1952. Fielder was born on 17 December 1894 in Boston. He studied at the Royal Academy of Music, Berlin. From 1915 he was violinist of the Boston Symphony Orchestra, and conductor of Boston Pops Orchestra from 1929 for over 30 years. Fiedler has sold around 5 million albums and 10 million singles discs to date. He recorded 'Jalousie' for Victor during his first session in 1935. It was released in 1938. He died on 10 July 1979 near Boston, U.S.A.

ELLA FITZGERALD WITH CHICK WEBB AND HIS ORCHESTRA

A-TISKET, A-TASKET *Decca* [*USA*]. 'The First Lady of Jazz' achieved by 1950 her first million seller with this disc. The song is an adaptation of the old nursery rhyme by Ella in collaboration with Al Feldman. Ella was born in Newport News, Virginia, on 25 April 1918, and ran away from home to compete in an amateur hour at Harlem Opera House in 1934. She won a $25 prize, and a contract to sing with Chick Webb's orchestra in 1935, with whom she remained until the leader's death. Later she led the band herself for a time. In 1940, she started out solo and since has headlined New York's Paramount Theatre, the Earle in Philadelphia, the Regal in Chicago, the Paradise in Detroit and most other big theatres in the U.S.A. Ella Fitzgerald has been a Decca artist since the day she made her theatrical debut in the late 1930s and has won every major popularity poll there is to be gained in the field of jazz singing in America. Her total disc sales are in excess of 25 million. Leading American jazzmen voted her the 'Greatest Ever Female Singer'. Ella has appeared in films, *Pete Kelly's Blues* (1955) and *St Louis Blues* (1958) and also made tours abroad, including Britain and the Continent. This disc was recorded 2 May 1938, in New York.

WILL GLAHE AND HIS ORCHESTRA

BEER BARREL POLKA *Victor* [*USA*]. This song was originally 'Skoda Lasky' (Lost Love) by two Czech writers, Vasek Zeman and Vladimir A. Timm (words) and music by Jaromir Vejvoda composed in 1934. English words were supplied by Lew Brown. The song proved to be one of the most popular of World War II, and this disc sold a million by 1943. It also includes a striking accordion solo by Will Glahe. Disc originally recorded in Germany.

HARRY JAMES AND HIS ORCHESTRA (trumpet)

ONE O'CLOCK JUMP *Brunswick* [*USA*]. Harry James found here his first million seller. The tune was composed by the great jazz pianist-bandleader Count Basie who had previously (1937) made it extremely popular with jazz enthusiasts. Recorded on 5 January 1938, in New York. (See 'Ciribiribin', 1939, for biography.)

ARTIE SHAW AND HIS ORCHESTRA

BEGIN THE BEGUINE backed with INDIAN LOVE CALL *Bluebird – Victor* [*USA*]. Shaw recorded both in New York on 24 July 1938, and it was the first recording of Cole Porter's famous song from the show *Jubilee* (1935). It sold a million by 1944. 'Indian Love Call' is the famous song from *Rose Marie* (1924) written by Otto Harbach and Oscar Hammerstein II (words), and Rudolf Friml (music). Both sides are outstanding 'swing' arrangements.

Artie Shaw (real name Arthur Arshawsky) was born on 23 May 1910 in New York, became a professional musician at the age of 15, playing saxophone in the pit band at New Haven's Olympic Theatre. He next took up the clarinet, an instrument on which he has become world famous. He learned arranging, and joined Irving Aaronson's Commanders. Later Shaw switched to Red Norvo's band. A period as a radio musician in New York followed, then in 1935 he took part in New York's first swing concert at the Imperial Theatre, performing an original jazz work. Artie then formed his first band which rose to great popularity with this disc of 'Begin the Beguine' by 1939. He disbanded briefly, then returned with another band which he kept until the Pearl Harbor raid that brought the United States into the war. During the war he led a Navy band, and returned to civilian life with a big band. After leading various groups, Shaw formed a new band in 1953, this being a version of his earlier recording group, the Gramercy Five. He appeared in the film *Second Chorus* (1940) with his orchestra in which he featured his 'Swing Concerto' for clarinet. One of the great musicians and bandleaders of the last war period, Shaw's discs sold the colossal total of 43 million for Victor Records. In commemoration of his 25 years with Victor, he was presented with eight gold records by them in November 1962 to mark the sale of eight of his recordings that each sold over one million.

'Indian Love Call' was the backing of 'Nightmare' on the English issue, with the vocal by Tony Pastor. Tony died 31 October 1969 in Old Lyme, Connecticut.

NIGHTMARE *Bluebird – Victor* [*USA*]. Artie Shaw's second disc with an eventual million sale. It reached a seven figure sale in 1943. Another outstanding 'swing' arrangement and Shaw's own composition. He wrote it around 1936.

The U.S.A. backing was 'Non-Stop Flight' (both recorded 27 September 1938, in New York) and the English release backed with 'Indian Love Call'.

BACK BAY SHUFFLE *Bluebird – Victor* [*USA*]. This number, composed by Artie Shaw and Teddy McRae, was Artie's third million seller through subsequent years. Recorded 24 July 1938, in New York.

1939

LALE ANDERSEN

LILI MARLENE *Electrola* [*Germany*]. This was the first German disc known to sell over one million copies. In fact the sales hit two million through subsequent years. The song was composed by Norbert Schultze in 1938. He took the lyrics from 'Der Junge Wachtposten' (The Young Sentinel) written by Hans Liep during the First World War. Danish singer, Lale Andersen, born 23 March 1910, in Bremerhaven, a young lass with a husky voice, made this disc. The song did not register until later, in 1940, when the German Soldier Network in Belgrade in occupied Yugoslavia chose it as its sign-off song. It made the voice of Lale Andersen internationally known. Her disc was one of the few the German Soldier Network in Belgrade had available when they started broadcasting. Lale was considered rather controversial by Goebbels, and he never allowed her to appear on the Belgrade Station in person as many other artists did at that time. The song became a favourite of the allied armies as well, and it has been said that both Sir Winston Churchill and John Steinbeck were among famous people who favoured the tune. 'Lili' has been translated into 42 different languages, the English words being by England's Tommie Connor (1941). Lili Marlene was the only classic song of World War II. Lale Andersen was a star for many years, but her career sagged and she went into semi-retirement. But in 1960, she recorded 'Never on Sunday' in German and sold over 800,000 records of the tune, and once again took up her status as a top star in Germany. She won the 'Song for Europe' contest in Germany (1961) and Hollywood made a film about her life. An LP of her top hits was issued in 1962. She died in Vienna on 29 August 1972.

Hans Liep's poem was written in April 1915, when he was in the German army on the way to the Russian front. 'Lili Marleen' (which became 'Lili Marlene' in World War II) was based on the names of two girls, his own and a friend's. It was published in 1937 in a Hans Liep collection *Die Hafenorgel*, and picked up in Munich by Lale Andersen, then a young cabaret actress. Her composer friend Rudy Zink did a setting in waltz tempo that her audiences liked. In 1938, composer Schultze, who was favoured by the Nazi Party, met Lale at a cabaret in Berlin and showed her his setting that a disc company wanted. She recorded this in a marching tempo in March 1939.

GENE AUTRY

THAT SILVER HAIRED DADDY OF MINE *Columbia* [*USA*]. The first million seller for Autry - 'Oklahoma Yodeling Cowboy' - was this song written by him and his father-in-law, Jimmy Long, in 1932. He was born on 29 September 1907, near Tioga, Texas, his folks being pioneer settlers in the hills of Grayson County. At the age of 10, he joined a travelling medicine show, covering a round of nearby Texas towns, and eight years later exchanged a job of herding steers to working as railroad telegrapher on the San Francisco railroad at Sapulpar, Oklahoma. Autry was encouraged by his boss, Jimmy Long, who heard him singing and playing his old guitar. Long worked with him for many years, co-writing his songs and later joining him on some of his early recording dates. Long persuaded Gene to spend his annual holiday by travelling to New York for a recording test. He used the experience to turn professional, working on radio in Tulsa, and began recording in 1930 with Victor Records, and later with Okeh, Columbia, Starr, Perfect and Conqueror. Apart from radio, and recording, he did rodeo work and made his screen debut in 1934 in a bit part in *In Old Santa Fe* starring Ken Maynard. Next followed many topgrade Western films. He was voted Top Western Star 1936 and 1946 to 1954. From 1942 to 1945 he served as Flight Officer in the U.S.A.A.F. Thereafter he resumed his radio career and was star of first Madison Square Garden Rodeo. Autry each year toured 100 cities in the U.S.A., and formed Gene Autry Productions Inc. Gene has also been responsible for several of the top-grade Western films shown on TV but today confines his public appearances to radio and the live theatre. He holds the unique distinctions of being the first cowboy to make recordings; the first to make singing Westerns; and first cowboy to head a rodeo in New York. His biggest disc achievement was in 1949 with 'Rudolph the Red-Nosed Reindeer' (*q.v.*). 'Silver Haired Daddy' sold five million by 1940 through one mail-order house alone. He toured Britain in 1939, and introduced 'South of the Border'. In 1969, Autry was made a member of the Country Music Hall of Fame.

CAB CALLOWAY AND HIS ORCHESTRA

JUMPIN' JIVE *Columbia* [*USA*]. This was Calloway's only million seller, recorded on 17 July 1939, in New York, written in conjunction with Jack Palmer and Frank Froeba. He was born on Christmas Day 1907 in Rochester, N.Y. and was attracted to show business by his sister, Blanche, then conducting a band, and became a drummer-singing bandleader. Calloway had originally studied law. In the mid 1930s he achieved phenomenal success as 'The King of Hi-de-ho', his name becoming inextricably linked with the song 'Minnie the Moocher', and his band toured Europe, furthering jazz abroad. In 1943 he received an award for his work in the film *Stormy Weather*. In the early 1950s Calloway was outstanding for his role of 'Sporting Life' in Gershwin's *Porgy and Bess*. 'Jive' was one of the most popular dances during the Second World War, hence the demand for Calloway's disc.

JUDY GARLAND (vocal) WITH VICTOR YOUNG AND HIS ORCHESTRA

OVER THE RAINBOW *Decca* [*USA*]. Judy Garland was only 16 when she starred in the film version of *The Wizard of Oz* in 1939, her greatest triumph. Of the many outstanding songs, all written by E. Y. Harburg (words) and Harold Arlen (music), 'Over the Rainbow' won Oscars for the writers, and for Herbert Stothart who did the musical score. The song, which was a big seller in sheet music, is now considered one of the world's greatest standards. Judy's disc is estimated to have sold a million or more over the years and is still in steady demand. The song has become associated with her name and was also her signature tune. (See 1954 for biography.)

The Wizard of Oz was chosen as one of the Ten Best Films of 1939 and was directed by Victor Fleming.

Judy was voted a special Oscar for her distinguished services to the screen by the Motion Picture Academy of Arts and Sciences in 1939.

She was one of the youngest-ever recording artists when she cut 'Swing Mr Charlie' and 'Stomping at the Savoy' with the Bob Crosby orchestra in 1936 while still only 13 years old.

COLEMAN HAWKINS (tenor saxophone) AND HIS ORCHESTRA

BODY AND SOUL *Bluebird - Victor* [*USA*]. Coleman Hawkins, one of America's greatest jazz players, was born on 24 November 1904 in St Joseph, Missouri, and began playing the piano at five, the cello at seven and fingering a saxophone at nine. He formally studied music theory at Washburn College, Topeka, Kansas, making his debut at the age of fifteen when he joined Mamie Smith's Jazz Hounds and playing professionally in the Kansas City area. The group went to New York in 1922 to record and Coleman then played with Wilbur Sweetman's band and in various Harlem nightclubs. That same year he joined the famous Fletcher Henderson orchestra and played the Club Alabam and the Roseland Ballroom between 1923 and 1927, making his first record with the band in 1923. He stayed with Henderson until 1933 and during his ten years with the band, raised the saxophone to the status of a major solo instrument, virtually single handed. In 1933, Hawkins formed his own combo, featuring Henry (Red) Allen on trumpet, Horace Henderson on piano and J. C. Higginbotham on bass, and in 1934 travelled to England and teamed up with bandleader Jack Hylton for a European tour, playing in England, France (including a concert in 1935 at the Salle Pleyel in Paris), Switzerland and Holland. Returning to the U.S.A. in 1939 while working with his own combo in New York City, he recorded this instrumental version of 'Body and Soul' on 11 October in the new style he had developed - intricate involved phrases and altered notes or improvized melody employed with great feeling on the hidden melodies within a commonplace tune. The disc became one of the masterpieces of jazz, selling over a million, and throughout the years his most requested item.

From 1943 to 1945 he played as soloist with many small bands in New York and Los Angeles nightclubs and with 'Jazz at the Philharmonic', reaching the peak of his popularity during this time. In 1948 he appeared in the Semaine du Jazz in Paris and returned to Europe again in 1949 for an extensive tour. From 1950 he played mostly in New York nightclubs, keeping abreast of later changes from 'swing' to 'bop'.

Coleman Hawkins' famous legato phrases and lush, warm style were his trademark and it is said that in a sense he created the tenor sax. Hawkins loved Bach and Beethoven as much as strong solo jazz. His friends called him 'Bean' (he loved every kind of bean - and popcorn). He was No 1 on all the Esquire Jazz Polls and generally No 1 tenor sax soloist on the Playboy, Downbeat and Metronome polls. He died on 19 May 1969 in New York.

'Body and Soul' was composed by John Green who is also a conductor, arranger, pianist and producer of stage and screen, and holder of four Academy Awards (see *American in Paris*, 1952). The song was introduced by Libby Holman in *Three's a Crowd* (revue) in 1930. It was also used as theme for the film *Body and Soul* (1947). Lyrics were written by Edward Heyman, Robert Sour and British author Frank Eyton.

Coleman Hawkins left a rich legacy of his talents on such labels as Apollo, Keynote, Victor, HMV, CMS, Savoy and Capitol.

WOODY HERMAN AND HIS ORCHESTRA

AT THE WOODCHOPPER'S BALL *Decca* [*USA*]. Woody Herman's first million seller was a joint work by him and 'blues' writer Joe Bishop. This title became a million seller by 1948. (See 1945 for Herman biography.) Recorded on 12 April 1939 in New York.

HARRY JAMES (trumpet) AND HIS ORCHESTRA

CIRIBIRIBIN *Columbia* [*USA*]. Harry 'The Horn' James wisely chose this song as his signature tune and it subsequently sold a million. It was originally written in Italy in 1898 by A. Pestalozza. This disc was an instant success and made Harry (the alternate sweet and torrid trumpet player) famous. He was born Harry Haag James on 15 March 1916 in Albany, Georgia, while his parents were working with the Mighty Haag Circus – hence his second name. His father led the band and his mother was a trapeze artist. At the age of six James learned how to play 'hot' drums in his father's band and in the following four years he mastered the trumpet and was soon conducting the second band for Christy Brothers Circus. The family finally settled down at Beaumont, Texas, and Harry attended school there, winning a state contest for trumpet playing. He then 'sat in' with dance orchestras around the south-west, gaining some notice. At 15 he travelled with Joe Gale's orchestra and in 1935 was hired by Ben Pollack. While with Pollack he composed 'Peckin' which started a dance craze among jazz-mad youngsters. A disc of this with Harry playing trumpet solo brought him to the attention of Benny Goodman, then 'King of Swing', and in 1937 Harry joined Goodman's band as featured trumpet player. In 1939 he decided to start his newly-organized band, with Goodman lending him $42,000. It was not a success as a 'hot band', so Harry developed a simple sweet style, cool trumpet with a mass of strings. He alternated from blues to boogie woogie to Viennese waltzes and technical specialities on his own trumpet. In 1941 he recorded 'You Made Me Love You' and at last found himself in the 'big time'. That summer he was the idol of the youngsters. He made his sensational appearance at New York's Paramount Theatre in April 1943, and 'The World's Number One Trumpeter' had arrived. Then RKO signed him for the film *Syncopation*, followed by Universal's *Private Buckeroo*, *Springtime in the Rockies* for 20th Century/Fox and *Two Girls and a Sailor* (M.G.M.). Eventually 20th Century/Fox signed him up on a long-term contract commencing with *Do You Love Me* (1946) followed by *If I'm Lucky* (1946). Other feature films were *Best Foot Forward* (1943) and *Bathing Beauty* (1944), both for M.G.M.

Harry James was married to the film star Betty Grable with whom he played an extensive one-nighter tour in a vaudeville act in 1953. They were divorced in October 1965. He was fond of classical music, and was also a fine performer in this field as his rendering of 'Flight of the Bumble Bee' shows. His band was still earning over £200,000 in 1963. This disc recorded on 20 February 1939, in New York. (James made a second recording also, in Los Angeles on 8 November 1939, with a Frank Sinatra vocal.)

Harry James died 5 July 1983 in Las Vegas.

KAY KYSER AND HIS ORCHESTRA
THREE LITTLE FISHES *Columbia* [*USA*]. This number written by 'Saxie' (Horace Kirby) Dowell, became Kay Kyser's first million seller by 1941. Kay was born in Rocky Mount, North Carolina on 18 June 1906, the 'Ol' Professor' being baptized James Kern Kyser. He attended university in his home state. At college, he organized his first band and carried on with it professionally later. In the U.S.A. he became a national institution with his 'Kollege of Musical Knowledge' on the radio, and he looked the part of a college professor. Apart from its comedy, the band alternated from sweet ballads to jive numbers with the greatest ease, and many other bandleaders adopted his methods, a flattering tribute to this maestro of jive and jump. Kay did an endless series of appearances at military camps during World War II and many broadcasts for Forces' radio. His unique group was soon appearing in films, such as *You'll Find Out* (1940), *Swing Fever* (1943), *Thousands Cheer* (1943) and *Carolina Blues* (1944). The latter film featured the antics of Kay's ace-trumpet playing stunt-man, Ish Kabibble (real name, Merwin Bogue), as well as actress Ann Miller and Victor Moore. Other films were *That's Right You're Wrong* (1939), *Playmates* (1941), *My Favourite Spy* and *Around the World* (1943).

'Three Little Fishes' was so catchy that in 1939 a Kansas State Penitentiary inmate killed another convict who persisted in singing it.

GLENN MILLER AND HIS ORCHESTRA
LITTLE BROWN JUG *Victor* [*USA*]. This Bill Finegan arrangement of the old song written by R. A. Eastburn (pseudonym of J. E. Winner) in 1869, provided Glenn Miller's estate with its first million seller by 1945. (See 1942 for Miller biography.) This disc recorded on 10 April 1939.

IN THE MOOD *Victor* [*USA*]. This second million seller for Glenn Miller (by 1945) was written by Andy Razaf (words) and Joe Garland (music). Recorded on 1 August 1939.

SUNRISE SERENADE backed with MOONLIGHT SERENADE *Victor* [*USA*]. These two sides were third and fourth million sellers for Glenn Miller. Sales of two million were reached by 1944. 'Sunrise Serenade' was written in 1938 by Jack Lawrence (words) and Frankie Carle (music). 'Moonlight Serenade' by Mitchell Parish (words) and Glenn Miller (music) was the band's signature tune, which three times a week for nearly three years thrilled listening millions. 'Moonlight Serenade' was recorded on 4 April 1939, and 'Sunrise Serenade' on 10 April 1939.

Glenn Miller did not write his famous 'Moonlight Serenade' for a theme song. The first part of the tune was an original warming-up exercise he used for getting his mouth in shape for trombone playing. This was while he was with Ray Noble's band. He later completed the melody and arranged it. By the time he had organized his own band, the tune became identified with his name. (See 1942 for Miller biography.)

ARTIE SHAW AND HIS ORCHESTRA
TRAFFIC JAM *Bluebird - Victor* [*USA*]. This number, written by Artie Shaw and Teddy McCrae, eventually became Artie Shaw's fourth million seller. Recorded on 12 June 1939, in Hollywood.

LEOPOLD STOKOWSKI AND PHILADELPHIA ORCHESTRA
TALES FROM THE VIENNA WOODS backed with THE BLUE DANUBE *Victor* [*USA*]. Both composed by Johann Strauss, 'Vienna Woods' was first performed in 1868 (9 June), in Vienna and 'Blue Danube' in 1867 (13 February), also in Vienna. This disc was a million seller by 1952. Stokowski was born of a Polish father and Irish mother on 18 April 1882 in London. He began to play the piano and violin in his childhood and while at Queen's College, Oxford he studied composition, and instrumentation at the Paris Conservatoire. He was organist at St James's, Piccadilly, London for a time and organist and choirmaster at St Bartholomew's, New York from 1905 to 1908 before becoming conductor of the Cincinnati Symphony Orchestra (1909-1912). In 1912 Stokowski became conductor of the Philadelphia Symphony Orchestra until 1936, continuing to conduct a part of each season. He brought this orchestra to a brilliant standard of execution. He thereafter made many appearances as guest conductor and his film debut in *The Big Broadcast of 1937*. Other major films were *One Hundred Men and a Girl* (1937), *Fantasia* (Disney film of 1940) as musical director in the experiment in multiple track sound, and *Carnegie Hall* (1947). He died on 12 September 1977 in Nether Wallop, Hampshire, England. Full name: Leopold Antonio Stanislaw Boleslawowicz Stokowski.

ORRIN TUCKER AND ORCHESTRA
(Bonnie Baker – vocal)
OH, JOHNNY, OH *Columbia* [*USA*]. This song was originally a big hit in World War I, when it sold a million in sheet music, repeating its popularity in World War II with a million on disc. Tucker and Bonnie Baker had millions singing this through 1940 and 1941. The song was written by Ed Rose (words) and Abe Olman (music) in 1917.

Orrin Tucker, who is also an author/composer, was born in St Louis, Missouri on 17 February 1911, educated at Northwestern University, and North Central College. He conducted his own orchestra in theatres, ballrooms throughout America. He also appeared on 'Hit Parade' for one year, was in the United States Navy in World War II, and had his own TV programme.

THE 1940s

1940

BING CROSBY WITH BOB CROSBY ORCHESTRA
SAN ANTONIO ROSE *Decca* [*USA*]. Again this song by Bob Wills reached a million; this time it provided his second million seller for Bing, accompanied by brother Bob's orchestra. This disc sold a million by 1946. Recorded on 16 December 1940 in Los Angeles. It reached No 7 in the U.S.A. charts.

JOHNNY LONG AND HIS ORCHESTRA WITH VOCAL ENSEMBLE
IN A SHANTY IN OLD SHANTY TOWN *Decca* [*USA*]. The outstanding feature of this million seller disc is the vocal ensemble. Song is an oldie hit of 1932, written by Joe Young (words) and Little Jack Little and John Siras (music). Johnny Long hails from Newall, North Carolina and, at the age of 10, this pop violinist and band leader was performing at concerts in his home town. At 16 he helped form a college band at Duke University. After graduation, the band took professional dates and soon became nationally known. They then played innumerable theatre and club dates. Johnny died on 31 October 1972 in Parkersburg, W.Va (aged 56).

GLENN MILLER AND HIS ORCHESTRA
PENNSYLVANIA SIX-FIVE THOUSAND *Victor* [*USA*]. This song, written by Carl Sigman (words), Jerry Gray (music), arranger of many of the band's numbers, provided Glenn Miller's estate with a fifth million by 1945. The title is the telephone number of the former Hotel Pennsylvania in New York. Recorded on 28 April 1940.

TUXEDO JUNCTION *Victor* [*USA*]. Written by Buddy Feyne (words) and Erskine Hawkins, William Johnson and Julian Dash (music), 'Tuxedo Junction' scored a million sales by 1945 and was Miller's sixth million seller. Tuxedo is a small place in Alabama. Recorded on 5 February 1940.

ARTIE SHAW AND HIS ORCHESTRA
FRENESI *Victor* [*USA*]. Artie Shaw's fifth million seller was the first song by any Mexican writer – Alberto Dominguez – to sell a million discs. English words were written by Ray Charles and S. K. Russell. Recorded on 3 March 1940, in Hollywood. It was No 1 for 13 weeks and remained 23 weeks in the U.S.A. bestsellers.

STARDUST *Victor* [*USA*]. This sixth million seller for Artie, by 1946, was written by Hoagy Carmichael in 1927. It sold over a million sheet music copies, and is one of the world's most recorded songs (another is 'St Louis Blues') with 1,000 different American disc versions and countless others around the world. The words were written by Mitchell Parish. Recorded 7 October 1940, in Hollywood. It reached No 6 in the U.S.A. charts.

ARTIE SHAW AND HIS GRAMERCY FIVE
SUMMIT RIDGE DRIVE *Victor* [*USA*]. This original composition by Artie Shaw, gained him his seventh million seller. The disc featured a harpsichord. Recorded 3 September 1940, in Hollywood, it was No 10 in the U.S.A. charts.

BOB WILLS AND HIS TEXAS PLAYBOYS
SAN ANTONIO ROSE *Okeh* [*USA*]. Bob Wills, born on 6 March 1905 in Groesbeck, Texas, a country and western artist, wrote this song. It is his only million seller of the many discs he made for Columbia.

Described as a key exponent of Western Swing, and sometimes referred to as its 'daddy', Wills has had extensive experience in radio since 1932 with the Light Crust Doughboys, Pappy O'Daniel and others. He played the fiddle and organized his Texas Playboys in 1932, appearing on many radio shows throughout Texas, Oklahoma, ABC-TV and in many Hollywood films. He was also on other labels including Decca, Harmony and Liberty, and was named to the Country and Western Music Hall of Fame in 1968.

He died on 13 May 1975 in Fort Worth, Texas.

1941

JIMMY DORSEY AND ORCHESTRA
(Bob Eberle and Helen O'Connell – vocal)
AMAPOLA *Decca* [*USA*]. This first million seller for Jimmy Dorsey, by 1946, was a revival of Joseph M. Lacalle's hit of 1924. New English words were written in 1940 by Albert Gamse. (See 'Marie', 1937, for Jimmy Dorsey's biography.) Recorded on 3 February 1941, in New York, it was No 1 for 10 weeks, and 14 weeks in the U.S.A. bestsellers.

GREEN EYES *Decca* [*USA*] (Bob Eberle and Helen O'Connell – vocal). Jimmy Dorsey enjoyed his second million selling success with this number by 1946. The song ('Aquellos ojos verdes') comes from Latin America, written in 1929 by Adolfo Utrera (1902–1931) (words) and Milo Menendez (music). The English version was by E. Rivera and E. Woods. Recorded 19 March 1941, in New York, it was No 1 for four weeks, and 21 weeks in the U.S.A. bestsellers.

MARIA ELENA *Decca* [*USA*] (Bob Eberle – vocal). Here was a third million seller for Jimmy Dorsey, by 1946. This Latin American song was written in 1933 by Lorenzo Barcelata. The English words were by S. K. Russell. The song was dedicated to the wife of Mexico's President Pontes Gill, whose name was Maria Elena. Recorded 19 March 1941, in New York, it was No 1 for two weeks, and 17 weeks in the U.S.A. bestsellers.

HORACE HEIDT AND HIS MUSICAL KNIGHTS
DEEP IN THE HEART OF TEXAS *Columbia* [*USA*]. This was the only million seller for Heidt. He ran many national amateur contests on radio and made personal appearances. This song, written by June Hershey (words) and Don Swander (music), became almost a plague on both sides of the Atlantic with its simple bugle melody and novel hand-clapping effect in the refrain. The disc achieved No 7 in the U.S.A. charts.

HARRY JAMES (trumpet) AND HIS ORCHESTRA
YOU MADE ME LOVE YOU *Columbia* [*USA*]. Harry James' third million seller disc was one which still further enhanced his reputation. James featured this in both his films of that year – *Syncopation* and *Private Buckeroo* – and the disc sold a million by 1946. Originally written in 1913 by Joe McCarthy (words)

Previous page, top, left to right: **Glen Miller, Nat King Cole, Dinah Shore**; bottom: **Ella Fitzgerald, Frank Sinatra.**

and James V. Monaco (music), it soon became a million sheet music seller. Recorded on 20 May 1941, in New York, it was No 5 in the U.S.A. charts.

FREDDY MARTIN AND HIS ORCHESTRA
(vocal – Clyde Rogers)

PIANO CONCERTO No 1 in B flat minor (Tchaikovsky) (Tonight We Love) *Victor* [*USA*]. This disc, a million seller by 1946, was an adaptation of the opening theme of Tchaikovsky's Concerto No 1 arranged as a song 'Tonight We Love' by Ray Austin with words by Bobby Worth. It sparked off 16 different versions of the tune, ending with one entitled 'Boogie de Concerto'. Freddy Martin was born on 9 December in Springfield, Ohio, and was orphaned at the age of four. He played drums in the orphanage band and sax at Ohio State University, where he formed his own student group which got its first booking as an off-night substitute for Guy Lombardo's orchestra. After a trip to Finland with a military band, Martin joined Eddy Hodges' Band of Pirates, then played tenor sax with Jack Albin's orchestra, forming his own orchestra in 1932. This disc brought him to prominence. He has recorded extensively for Victor Records. The disc was No 1 for eight weeks, and 24 weeks in the U.S.A. bestsellers.

GLENN MILLER AND HIS ORCHESTRA
(vocal – Tex Beneke, Marion Hutton and The Modernaires)

CHATTANOOGA CHOO CHOO *Victor* [*USA*]. This seventh million seller for Glenn hit seven figure sales as early as 1942. The number was a lively 'novelty' song by Mack Gordon (words) and Harry Warren (music), from the film *Sun Valley Serenade* in which the band appeared as co-stars with Norway's Sonja Henie, the Winter Olympic Games ice skating gold medallist. Recorded on 7 May 1941, it was No 1 for nine weeks, and 23 weeks in the U.S.A. bestsellers. (See also preface note.)

VAUGHN MONROE AND HIS BAND

RACING WITH THE MOON *Victor* [*USA*]. Monroe achieved his first million seller by 1952. This song was composed by him with P. Pope and J Watson. Monroe was born in Akron, Ohio, on 7 October 1911, and began his career with Gibby Lockhard's orchestra, as trumpeter. He then studied voice at the Carnegie Technical School of Music while working during the evenings with such bands as Austin Wylie's and Larry Funk's. From 1940 to 1953, he travelled with his own band as vocalist-leader. He thereafter became well established (1945) with a big hit disc 'There I've Said It Again' (*q.v.*) and made many more discs, appeared on the screen, TV, and radio. He became a solo artist in 1953. Monroe died on 21 May 1973 in Florida.

RAY NOBLE AND HIS ORCHESTRA
(vocalist – Roy Lanson)

BY THE LIGHT OF THE SILVERY MOON *Columbia* [*USA*]. Famous British composer-bandleader Ray Noble was born on 17 December 1903 in Brighton, Sussex, England, and was educated at Dulwich College in south-east London. He started writing songs in the late 1920s, his first success being 'Nobody's Fault But Your Own' with Alan Murray in 1928. He came to fame in 1929 when he won an arranging competition sponsored by *The Melody Maker* and became an arranger with Jack Payne's BBC Dance Orchestra. From July 1929 to August 1935 Ray was Musical Director to HMV Records for whom he made hundreds of recordings, those with the house band (The New Mayfair Orchestra) still regarded by dance band connoisseurs as some of the finest of their kind ever produced. This orchestra consisted of Britain's finest instrumentalists. He also wrote songs for the British films *Little Damozel* (1933), *The Camels are Coming* (1934), *Brewster's Millions* (1934) and *Princess Charming* (1934).

In September 1934 he took his vocalist Al Bowlly and drummer Bill Harty with him to the U.S.A. where he became arranger

and musical director for Radio City, New York. He engaged Glenn Miller to organize and arrange for his band which played in the famous Rainbow Room there. Glenn also played in the band as did many other famous U.S. instrumentalists such as Charlie Spivak (trumpet) and they recorded for the Victor label from 1935 to 1937 and then for Columbia (in California). The band was an outstanding financial success and a great favourite with the American people. Later Ray decided to remain in Hollywood and concentrated on radio work. A 13-year association with the famous ventriloquist Edgar Bergen (and his 'dummy' Charlie McCarthy) in Bergen's radio show was one of the longest in American show business history. His band also appeared in several films, notably *The Big Broadcast of 1936* (starring Bing Crosby) and *Damsel in Distress* (starring Fred Astaire) in 1937.

Many of Ray's compositions were big sellers. His 'Goodnight Sweetheart' (1931), 'Love Is the Sweetest Thing' (1932), 'The Very Thought of You' (1934), 'The Touch of Your Lips' (1936), 'I Hadn't Anyone Till You' (1938) and 'Cherokee' (1938) have all become standards in the dance band repertoire.

Vocalist Roy (Snooky) Lanson, born in Memphis, Tennessee, was a semi-pro boxer in his teens. He became vocalist in 1934 with WSM radio station and later joined Ray Noble's band. During World War II he signed with Ted Weems' band when it enlisted in the U.S. Navy as a unit. After discharge (1945) Lanson returned to WSM as a singer and disc jockey. His successful disc of 'The Old Master Painter' landed him the featured singing spot on 'Your Hit Parade' (1950) which he retained for eight years, followed by personal appearances in practically every big club in the American continent, plus his own TV shows in Atlanta and Shreveport. In 1968 he made his first discs for the Starday label.

This disc of 'By the Silvery Moon' was a big hit in the U.S.A. where it is said to have sold 1,500,000. The song was written in 1909 and revived for the Bing Crosby-Mary Martin film *The Birth of the Blues* in 1941. Edward Madden wrote the words and Gus Edwards the music. It was a million sheet music seller in its day.

Ray Noble toured both Britain and the U.S.A. in variety in 1938. He bears the distinction of being the first British bandleader to become successful in America. He died in London on 2 April 1978.

ARTIE SHAW AND HIS ORCHESTRA
DANCING IN THE DARK *Victor* [*USA*]. This became the eighth million seller for Artie Shaw through subsequent years. The tune was written in 1931 by Howard Dietz (words) and Arthur Schwartz (music) for the U.S. show *The Band Wagon*. Recorded 23 January 1941, in Hollywood, it achieved No 9 in the U.S.A. charts.

DINAH SHORE
BLUES IN THE NIGHT *Victor* [*USA*]. The mood and style of this outstanding song by Johnny Mercer (words) and Harold Arlen (music) suggests the true form of Negro folk music, and was Dinah's first million seller disc, through subsequent years. She was born Frances Rose Shore in Winchester, Tennessee, on 1 March 1917, and sang in local church choirs. While at Vanderbilt University she sang on Nashville radio, using 'Dinah' as her signature tune, later adopting the name legally. She went to New York in 1937 and started singing on a radio spot, then returned to college to get her degree in sociology, and so back to New York. In 1939 she signed to sing with Ben Bernie's orchestra on CBS, filling in on NBC's 'Chamber Music Society of Lower Basin Street' that made her nationally famous within only two years of leaving Nashville. By late 1940, her voice was known to millions via radio, juke-box, and disc. Her first hit was 'Yes My Darling Daughter', an adaptation by Jack Lawrence of an old Russian folk song, introduced by her on the Eddie Cantor show. Then came 'Blues in the Night'. By 1944, Dinah had her own show and from then grew even more famous in recording, radio, film, and TV. She made her film debut in *Thank Your Lucky Stars* (1943) followed by *Up In Arms* (1944), *Follow the Boys* (1944), *Belle of the Yukon* (1944), *Fun and Fancy Free* (1947) and *Aaron Slick from Pumpkin Crick* (1952). Dinah Shore won innumerable awards as Top Vocalist from 1941 to 1957 on radio, TV, and disc.

This song was first introduced by William Gillespie in *Blues in the Night* (film), 1941. The disc got to No 4 in the U.S.A. charts.

KATE SMITH
ROSE O'DAY *Columbia* [*USA*]. This fast waltz song with patter effects by Charles Tobias and Al Lewis was Kate Smith's first million seller. She was born Kathryn Elizabeth Smith on 1 May 1909 in Greenville, Virginia. She became a singer, commentator, and actress, making her stage debut in *Honeymoon Lane* in 1926; then followed *Flying High* (1930) and theatre and vaudeville dates across the U.S.A. She became internationally known through her star role in the film *Hello Everybody* in 1932. After some years of mainly radio work came the film *This is the Army* in 1943 and her own daytime weekly TV show in the late 1950s.

She launched the famous Irving Berlin song 'God Bless America' on her radio programme on 11 November 1939, and it virtually became the second national anthem in the States. All the royalties go the Boy Scouts and Girl Scouts of America. Kate made her first ever appearance in Britain in TV's 'Sunday Night at the Palladium' on 2 October 1966. The disc was No 8 in the U.S.A. charts.

ERNEST TUBB (country-and-western vocal)
WALKIN' THE FLOOR OVER YOU *Decca* [*USA*]. Ernest Tubb, 'The Texas Troubadour', wrote this in 1941 and it became his signature tune. Decca presented him with a Gold Disc for his recording in 1965 – 25 years after being with the company. Tubb was born on 9 February 1914 on a ranch in the heart of the cattle country near Crisp, Texas. He grew up in the country tradition and sang on a San Antonio radio station in 1933. Jimmie Rodgers was his childhood idol. Mrs Jimmie Rodgers wrote to Decca's recording manager, Dave Kapp, saying 'the lad could do just what Jimmie did'. When Kapp met him in San Antonio, Tubb entered the studio wearing Jimmie Rodgers' famous guitar around his neck, a present from Mrs Rodgers.

Ernest entered show business via radio in 1941 and, in 1942, he and his troupe joined 'Grand Ole Opry' in Nashville, Tennessee. His son Justin, then aged eight, first appeared with him in the show, and is now a disc, radio, TV and 'Grand Ole Opry' artist himself.

Ernest made three 'Western' films in Hollywood and was one of the first country artists to perform overseas.

Tubb was named to the Country Music Hall of Fame in October 1965 – the greatest honour that can be bestowed on a country artist.

WILEY WALKER AND GENE SULLIVAN (country-and-western duo)
WHEN MY BLUE MOON TURNS TO GOLD AGAIN *Columbia* [*USA*]. This duo was discovered by Columbia's talent scout Art Satherley, a Britisher, and one of the most noted field recording pioneers in the early 1920s. The song was written by Walker and Sullivan and their disc is said to have sold millions. It was also a big hit for Gene Autry on Okeh, and a success for Elvis Presley in 1957.

ROY ACUFF AND HIS SMOKY MOUNTAIN BOYS
WABASH CANNON BALL *Columbia* [*USA*]. Roy Acuff's popularity was in great part due to his authentic and sympathetic treatment of music from the Tennessee hills. A pioneer in American folk-style music, he learned to play the fiddle while recovering from a serious illness caused by sunstroke which ended his career as a baseball player shortly before receiving an offer to play with the New York Yankees. He formed a group called 'The Crazy Tennesseans'. He began his musical careeer on the radio at Knoxville, Tennessee, in 1938. By 1941 he was featured on 'Grand Ole Opry' over the Nashville radio, first as a compere. It was on this show that he sang his own song 'The Great Speckled Bird' which was an instant success. He made many personal appearances with his Smoky Mountain Boys around the South and also appeared in films such as *Hi Neighbour* (1942), *My* *Darling Clementine* (1943), *Sing, Neighbour, Sing* (1944), *Cowboy Canteen* (1944), and *Night Train to Memphis* (1946). In 1948 he ran for governor of Tennessee but was defeated.

With the late Fred Rose, he founded the now-famous Acuff-Rose firm upon which the present-day country-and-western market blossomed and thrived, making Nashville the accepted centre since its inception. Both Acuff (in 1962) and Rose (in 1961) were named to the Country Music Hall of Fame by the Country Music Association of America.

Roy was born in Maynardsville, Tennessee, 15 September 1903, the son of a judge. Most of the many songs he has written were recorded by him under Columbia's label. His discs have been estimated at over 25 million in sales. 'Wabash Cannon Ball' is a great traditional train song arranged by A. P. Carter, and is Roy's only known million seller so far.

Roy has been described as 'the undisputed king of country music'. He went to Britain in 1965 to launch his Hickory label.

ELTON BRITT

THERE'S A STAR SPANGLED BANNER WAVING SOMEWHERE *Bluebird-Victor* [*USA*]. Britt was born in Marshall, Arkansas, on 27 June 1913, and was discovered when he was 15 by talent scouts touring Arkansas and Oklahoma for an authentic cowboy-country boy who could sing and yodel. His radio experience included shows over KMPC, Hollywood, ABC-TV, NBC and CBS Radio, WSM - 'Grand Ole Opry', 'The Elton Britt Show', 'Camel Caravan' and many others. He recorded for over 22 years for Victor and also made discs for Decca, Ampar and ABC-Paramount. He also appeared in the films *Laramie*, *The Prodigal Son* and others. Britt also wrote many songs.

This song, written by Paul Roberts and Shelby Darnell (co-authored by Bob Miller, a prominent publisher of hillbilly songs), was probably the most timely song of 1942-43 in the U.S.A. in World War II, and possibly the biggest sheet music and disc seller of 1943. It sold over a million discs by 1944 with practically no exploitation, and (1944) received the first official Gold Disc for a country recording.

Elton died on 23 June 1972.

BING CROSBY WITH KEN DARBY SINGERS AND JOHN SCOTT TROTTER ORCHESTRA

WHITE CHRISTMAS (from the film *Holiday Inn*) *Decca* [*USA*]. This remarkable disc took four years to provide Bing Crosby with his third million seller. By 1968 it had established, at 30 million, a world selling record for any single. Collective sales on discs, by Christmas 1970, made the colossal total of 68 million and sheet music sales 5,500,000 for the U.S.A. and Canada alone. Foreign disc sales were 32 million to 1970. The copyright of 'White Christmas' is the most valuable song property in the world. Written by Irving Berlin for the film *Holiday Inn*, it has been translated into at least seven different languages (German, French, Spanish, Italian, Hawaiian, Polish and Dutch). Because of the song's unique calibre as a standard, it replenishes itself year after year with many new versions. There were over 400 to the end of 1968.

The song is virtually a publishing business all by itself. When Berlin demonstrated the song to Bing, the latter removed his pipe laconically and observed, 'This is one you don't have to worry about.' 'Otherwise,' said Berlin, 'Crosby never says anything.' Various arrangements for instrumentals, octavo, band, and orchestrations sold 927,738 copies in the U.S.A. and Canada, making a grand total of 5,587,259 in printed editions (including sheet music) to 31 December 1962.

This disc was recorded in Los Angeles on 29 May 1942, and was No 1 for 11 weeks, and 72 weeks in the U.S.A. bestsellers.

BING CROSBY WITH MAX TERR CHOIR AND JOHN SCOTT TROTTER ORCHESTRA

SILENT NIGHT backed with ADESTE FIDELES *Decca* [*USA*]. Only four months after 'White Christmas' came another colossal seasonal disc by Bing that quickly sold over seven million. Bing donated all royalties from the disc to a fund for American missions in China, and later to finance an entertainment unit for the Forces. This was his fourth million seller.

'Silent Night' (Stille Nacht, Heilige Nacht) was written on Christmas Eve 1818 in the tiny hamlet of Hallein in the Austrian Alps by Father Joseph Mohr, a priest. The village organist Franz Gruber set the words to music, and his 'Song from Heaven', as the author called it, was sung by the villagers on Christmas Day. It took some time for the song to become known and loved all over the mountain district. It was, however, the Strasser Sisters (Caroline, Andreas and Amalie) and their brother Joseph who made it world famous. Every year they helped their father to sell the gloves he made at the Leipzig Trade Fair where they also frequently sang some old Tyrolean airs. Invited to sing in the Guild House at Leipzig one day, they sang their favourite 'Song from Heaven' which was received with such acclamation that the King and Queen of Saxony, who were present, asked them to sing to their children. From then, the 'Song from Heaven' or 'Silent Night' as we all know it has been a message of peace for everyone at Christmas time.

'Adeste Fideles' (O Come All Ye Faithful) is a traditional song from the Latin with a mediaeval melody. The English translation was made by Frederick Oakeley (1802-1880).

By 1964, it was being said that this disc had equalled, if not passed, the 'White Christmas' success, but the claim could not be confirmed from the record sales statistics. Both titles were recorded in Los Angeles on 8 June 1942.

TOMMY DORSEY AND HIS ORCHESTRA (Frank Sinatra (vocalist) and the Pied Pipers)

THERE ARE SUCH THINGS *Victor* [*USA*]. This disc took only two years to become Tommy's third million seller. The song was written by three of America's best-known writers - Stanley Adams, Abel Baer and George W. Meyer. The notable feature was the quality of Sinatra's vocal, before he became solo singer and film star a year later. Recorded on 1 July 1942, in New York, it was No 1 for five weeks, and 24 weeks in the U.S.A. bestsellers.

HARRY JAMES (trumpet) AND HIS ORCHESTRA

EASTER PARADE *Columbia* [*USA*]. This was the fourth million seller for Harry James by 1943. The melody for this song from the stage show of 1933 *As Thousands Cheer* was used by the composer Irving Berlin for a song that flopped, 'Smile and Show Your Dimple'. 'Easter Parade' was also a million seller in sheet music. Recorded on 24 February 1942 in New York.

I HAD THE CRAZIEST DREAM (Vocal - Helen Forrest) *Columbia* [*USA*]. This song was a feature in the film *Springtime in the Rockies* (1942) which starred Harry James' orchestra and Betty Grable, whom he married the following year. It was another big song for writers Mack Gordon (words) and Harry Warren (music). The disc sold a million by 1943, and was Harry James' fifth to reach seven figures. Recorded on 22 July 1942 in Hollywood, it was No 1 for two weeks, and 18 weeks in the U.S.A. bestsellers.

I'VE HEARD THAT SONG BEFORE backed with MOON-LIGHT BECOMES YOU (Vocals - John McAfee and Helen Forrest) *Columbia* [*USA*]. Sales of this disc topped a million by 1943 and furnished Harry James with his sixth golden disc. 'I've Heard That Song Before' was written by Sammy Cahn (words) and Jule Styne (music) for the film *Youth on Parade* and is sung on the disc by Helen Forrest. She hails from Atlantic City, New Jersey, and first worked with Artie Shaw and Benny Goodman. 'Moonlight Becomes You' was written by Johnny Burke (words) and Jimmy van Heusen (music), the hit song of the Bing Crosby, Bob Hope, Dorothy Lamour film *The Road to Morocco*. The vocal here is by John McAfee, saxophonist of the James' orchestra. The recordings were made in Hollywood on 31 July 1942 and 15 July 1942 respectively. The disc was No 1 for 13 weeks, and 20 weeks in the U.S.A. bestsellers.

SPIKE JONES AND HIS CITY SLICKERS
DER FUEHRER'S FACE *Victor* [*USA*]. This was the first million seller for Spike Jones (see biographical data, 1944). His orchestra was the first to parody tunes which the band members had to play seriously over the air.

The song, by Oliver G. Wallace, a British composer who went to the U.S.A. in 1906 and became conductor-composer for Walt Disney from 1936, was originally written for a Donald Duck cartoon 'In Nutsy Land'. After Spike's disc was released, Disney changed the title to 'Der Fuehrer's Face'. The disc is said to have sold over one and a half million very quickly, and acted as a wartime morale booster with its zany musical portrait of Hitler, capped by Bronx cheers made by rubber razzers purchased for a few cents apiece from any candy store at that time. It was the start of a series of burlesque discs on 'pop' songs using wash-boards, gunshots, barking, car hooters, cowbells, hiccoughs, etc. Jones made a fortune with his general musical mayhem. He toured a show from 1947 for several years entitled 'Musical Depreciation Revue'. The disc reached No 3, and was in the U.S.A. bestsellers for 10 weeks.

KAY KYSER AND HIS ORCHESTRA
PRAISE THE LORD AND PASS THE AMMUNITION *Columbia* [*USA*]. The first war song of 1942 to get high in the bestsellers and sell a million discs. It was written by Frank Loesser who was destined to win a big reputation in a fairly short time. The text was supposedly built on a phrase uttered by a U.S. Navy chaplain during the Japanese attack on Pearl Harbor, 7 December 1941.

Its popularity was so great that radio stations were asked to limit its use to only once every four hours. The record was Kay Kyser's second million seller. It was No 2, and in the U.S.A. bestsellers for 13 weeks.

STRIP POLKA *Columbia* [*USA*]. Kyser's third million seller disc was written and composed by Johnny Mercer. It reached No 5 in the charts.

WHO WOULDN'T LOVE YOU *Columbia* [USA]. Kyser's fourth million seller disc was written by Bill Carey and Carl Fischer. It was No 2, and in the U.S.A. bestsellers for 22 weeks.

JINGLE JANGLE JINGLE *Columbia* [*USA*]. Kyser's fifth million seller disc, the hit of the film *Forest Rangers*, was written by Frank Loesser (words) and Joseph J. Lilley (music), one Sunday night in 1941. A simple catchy tune which made use of the round form on the second chorus, it was immensely popular with the Forces. The disc was No 1 for eight weeks, and 13 weeks in the U.S.A. bestsellers.

PEGGY LEE (vocal) WITH BENNY GOODMAN AND HIS ORCHESTRA
WHY DON'T YOU DO RIGHT? (Get me some money, too) *Columbia* [*USA*]. Written by Joe McCoy, this song was first introduced by Lil Green. Peggy Lee recorded it with Goodman in New York on 27 July 1942 and they also performed it in the

film *Stage Door Canteen* in 1943. The disc became a standard seller and has well passed the million sale through the years. It was No 4, and in the U.S.A. bestsellers for 12 weeks.

(See 1948 for Peggy Lee biography, and Benny Goodman biography.)

FREDDY MARTIN AND HIS ORCHESTRA
WHITE CHRISTMAS (from the film *Holiday Inn*) *Victor* [*USA*]. This version of Irving Berlin's famous song took six years to sell a million and provided Martin with his second million seller.

GLENN MILLER AND HIS ORCHESTRA
(vocal – Tex Beneke, Marion Hutton and The Modernaires)
KALAMAZOO (I've Got a Gal in) *Bluebird-Victor* [*USA*]. Written by Mack Gordon (words) and Harry Warren (music) for the film *Orchestra Wives*, this song provided an eighth million seller nine years after issue for the late Glenn Miller. Recorded on 20 May 1942, the disc was No 1 for 7 weeks, and 18 weeks in the U.S.A. bestsellers.

AMERICAN PATROL *Victor* [*USA*]. This fine Jerry Gray arrangement of the famous march written by F. W. Meacham in 1891 was just one of the big hits for Glenn Miller. Glenn was born in Clarinda, Iowa, on 1 March 1904. His family moved to North Platts, Nebraska, U.S.A., where Glenn received much of his schooling. At 13, he paid for a trombone by milking cows at $2 a week. During high school at Fort Morgan (1920-1924) and University of Colorado (1924-1926) he worked briefly with Boyd Senter's band in Denver. After college he headed for the West Coast working in small bands, then joined Ben Pollack, and did arrangements for other bands, notably for Paul Ash. Miller left Pollack in New York, working as a trombonist and arranger to Red Nichols, Victor Young, Freddy Rich and others, and in 1935 helped Britain's Ray Noble to organize his band when Ray arrived in the U.S.A. Glenn saved the money he was earning so that he could start his own band. In 1935 he organized a strings-and-swing combination for Columbia, which was an exclusive recording group. In 1937 Glenn started to rehearse his own band, suspended it in January 1938 through the illness of his wife and his dissatisfaction with the rhythm section, and then reorganized it in the spring of 1938. Then followed a series of one-night stands and within a short time Glenn and his orchestra were playing at a New York theatre to 'standing room only'. Then the band went into the Meadowbrook, and with 10 air shows a week, this Pompton Turnpike roadhouse which has helped to establish many big bands also helped the rise of Glenn. Just prior to this, they had worked for the summer (1939) at Glen Island Casino where the band broke records established by Casa Loma, Dorsey Brothers and Larry Clinton bands. By 1941, Glenn Miller was the toast of the U.S.A. His band had been carefully built up with the emphasis on smooth section work and skilled use of varied intonation in the reeds and brasses. His success was more in the popular than the 'hot' field, and his band was voted Best Sweet Band of 1940 and 1941. Undoubtedly the most popular danceband leader in the world earned an income of over $750,000 a year. In 1942 Glenn enlisted in the U.S. Forces at the peak of his career. The band's film appearances were a great success, notably *Sun Valley Serenade* (1941) and *Orchestra Wives* (1942). While in the U.S. Forces, with the rank of Captain and later Major, he entertained the Forces, and also went to Britain in 1944. The same year, in an aircraft en route to France from England, his plane disappeared over the English Channel on 15 December, a bitter blow to the world of popular music.

'American Patrol' was a million seller by 1944. A biographical film *The Glenn Miller Story* was a big hit in 1954. Sales of his discs were over 60 million by 1970. This disc was recorded on 2 April 1942 in Hollywood.

THE MILLS BROTHERS

PAPER DOLL *Decca* [*USA*]. The reincarnation of this 1915 song and its colossal success could not be explained even by its publisher. It was written by Johnny Black (real name Huber), also part-writer of 'Dardanella' (see 1919), who was killed in 1936 during a roadhouse brawl over 25 cents. He was an eccentric, and cornered the publisher, E. B. Marks, one afternoon, and pressed him into buying 'Paper Doll'. Black played it for hours on a violin with a trained canary perched on his shoulder chirping the rhythm. This disc sold a million by 1943. The Mills Brothers once claimed that it actually sold eleven million (by 1959). It was the Mills Brothers' second million seller. The song was a million seller in sheet music. The disc was No 1 for 12 weeks, and in the U.S.A. bestsellers for 30 weeks.

ELLA MAE MORSE (vocal) WITH FREDDIE SLACK AND HIS ORCHESTRA

COW-COW BOOGIE (Cum-ti-yi-yi-ay) *Capitol* [*USA*]. This was the newly formed (1942) Capitol Records' first big hit with a subsequent million sale, the song written by Don Raye, Gene de Paul and Benny Carter in 1941 for the film *Ride 'em Cowboy* in which it was sung by the great Ella Fitzgerald. Morse sang it also in the film *Reveille with Beverly* (1943). The tune is based on a boogie-woogie figure. (See 1952 for Morse biography.)

Frederic Charles Slack, composer, author, conductor, pianist, was born in La Crosse, Wisconsin, on 7 August 1910, and educated at the American Conservatoire, Chicago. A talented musician, he became pianist and arranger with various dance orchestras from around 1930, including the bands of Lennie Hayton, Ben Pollack, Jimmy Dorsey and Will Bradley until 1941 when he moved to Hollywood to work for Universal Pictures. It was here on the film studio's cutting floor that he picked up the tune 'Cow-cow Boogie' and the girl to sing it – Ella Mae Morse. Johnny Mercer, a founder of Capitol Records, agreed it would be a good novelty song for Ella and Freddie's first disc for the label. It gained considerable renown for them in the boogie-woogie era of the 1940s.

Slack also groomed Margaret Whiting as vocalist with his band, wrote some popular instrumental items including 'Riffette' and 'Cuban Sugar Mill' in addition to recording two bestseller boogie-woogie albums and had success in a dozen movie performances and personal appearances throughout the U.S.A. From 1950 until his death on 10 August 1965 in Hollywood, Freddie played in a duo-piano team and with his own trio in hotels and restaurants mainly on the Nevada circuit and various San Fernando Valley venues. He formed his first orchestra in Los Angeles in 1941.

This disc was one of Capitol's first releases – 1 July 1942. It reached No 9 in the U.S.A. charts.

FRED WARING AND HIS PENNSYLVANIANS (glee club and orchestra)

'TWAS THE NIGHT BEFORE CHRISTMAS *Decca* [*USA*]. The music for this is by Ken Darby (composer-arranger for Walt Disney). The words were written in 1822 by Clement Clarke Moore. It provided Waring's only million seller disc. He was born in Tyrone, Pennsylvania, on 9 June 1900, and learned to play the banjo in his childhood. At 16, with his brother Tom, on the piano, Fred Buck on banjo and Poley McClintock on drums, he formed a quartet – 'Waring's Banjazzatra' to play at local dances, and later used this as a nucleus for his first orchestra – 'Waring's Collegians'. Fred left Pennsylvania State College to play one-night stands in the eastern states and wielded a baton ever since. He expanded his original orchestra to include a glee club, and Waring and his Pennsylvanians began a long radio career in 1933, entering TV in 1949. The group has recorded widely on Decca. Waring was the first U.S. musician to record a rumba tune, with songs that Hoagy Carmichael brought from Cuba. He is also an inventor, manufacturer, and teacher, having instructed over 2,000 amateur directors for radio work. Waring also composed songs, of which more than 125 were college and service songs written 'to order'.

1943

ORIGINAL THEATRE CAST

OKLAHOMA (album) (78 rpm discs) *Decca* [*USA*]. This was the first time a complete score of a Broadway musical was put on wax. By 1945 sales were at half a million but rose to over two million and a half when released in the new 33 rpm Long Player form (see 1949).

BING CROSBY

I'LL BE HOME FOR CHRISTMAS *Decca* [*USA*]. Written by Kim Gannon, Walter Kent, and Buck Ram, this song provided Bing with his fifth million seller. Recorded in Los Angeles on 1 October 1943, it reached No. 3 in the U.S.A. charts.

BING CROSBY WITH KEN DARBY SINGERS

SUNDAY, MONDAY OR ALWAYS *Decca* [*USA*]. Bing's big hit from his film *Dixie* was another succes for writers Johnny Burke (words) and Jimmy van Heusen (music). It was Bing's sixth million seller. Recorded in Los Angeles on 2 July 1943, it was No. 1 for 7 weeks, and 18 weeks in the U.S.A. bestsellers.

BING CROSBY WITH THE ANDREWS SISTERS AND VIC SCHOEN'S ORCHESTRA

PISTOL PACKIN' MAMA *Decca* [*USA*]. This was the big novelty song of 1943, written by Al Dexter who also had a million disc in his own right (see below). It added a seventh golden disc to Crosby's soaring collection. Recorded in Los Angeles on 27 September 1943, it reached No. 2, and was 9 weeks in the U.S.A. bestsellers.

JINGLE BELLS *Decca* [*USA*]. The sale of this recording was estimated at over 6 million discs. Written in the 1850s by J. S. Pierpont, the original title was 'The One-Horse Open Sleigh'. The composer wrote it for a local Sunday School entertainment, but never imagined it was destined for immortality. Thus yet again Crosby scored a million seller – his eighth – with a seasonal theme. Recorded in Los Angeles on 27 September 1943.

TED DAFFAN AND HIS TEXANS

BORN TO LOSE backed with NO LETTER TODAY *Okeh* [*USA*]. Ted Daffan (Theron Eugene Daffan) was born in Beauregard Parish, Louisiana, on 21 September 1912, and became a professional musician in 1934 when he played steel guitar with the Blue Ridge Playboys along with his friend Floyd Tillman. He also worked later with the Bar X Cowboys, a well-known band in Houston, Texas, and after several years with them formed his own band. He became notable both as songwriter and artist. In 1939 he wrote his first hit song 'Truck Drivers' Blues', the first song ever to be written about truck drivers, and this was recorded for Decca by Cliff Bruner with Moon Mullican as vocalist (1939). It was such a big hit that Art Satherley of Columbia Records gave him a recording contract and Ted recorded his first song 'Worried Mind' (1940) for their Okeh label. It was also his own composition and sold over 350,000 copies in spite of being covered by 12 other prominent artists including Bob Wills, Roy Acuff and Wayne King. He continued to record for Columbia for the next 10 years and had many hits on the label. 'Born to Lose' and 'No Letter Today' were both written by him under the pseudonym of Frankie Brown (1943). Both sides of the disc were hits and won him one of the rare country gold discs for a million sale. From 1944 to 1946 he played with his western swing band in Los Angeles, then returned to Texas working in Dallas and Fort Worth for several years. He returned to Houston until 1958 and joined Hank Snow as partner in music publishing in Nashville. From 1961 he was general manager of a Houston music publishing house.

Practically every country artist has recorded one or more of his songs and many pop artists including Ray Charles, Les Paul and Mary Ford, Connie Francis, Dean Martin, Tennessee Ernie Ford, Kay Starr, Patti Page, Ray Anthony and Gene Pitney have also used his material.

Ted Daffan and his Texans were leading exponents of music on the range and a thoroughly versatile group. Daffan's original arrangements and unique styling played 'straight' or with instrumental tricks by his string band made delightful and entertaining music. Both Ted and the Texans had considerable experience as performers over KPRC station in Houston.

His contribution to country music is outstanding. Over 16 million records of his songs by various artists have been sold over the years, with 'Born to Lose' totalling 7 million of this figure.

AL DEXTER AND HIS TROOPERS
PISTOL PACKIN' MAMA *Okeh* [*USA*]. This very simple song, written by Al Dexter, consisting of several short stanzas set to a nondescript melody, made the U.S.A. 'Dexter-conscious'. It was the big novelty song of 1943 and soon sold a million and also a million for Bing Crosby (see above). The song was inspired by the oft-repeated story of a roadside café proprietress, Molly Jackson, in Texas, whose husband and brother in earlier days ran an illicit whisky still, deep in the Kentucky mountains. Armed with a pistol for protection she rode out at weekends to bring them home. On approaching the still she called her husband to come down and he would reply, 'Lay that pistol down, Ma, or we ain't comin'.' Dexter frequented Molly's place and she would often given him his meals when he had no money and say, 'Write a song about me some day.'

Dexter's song earned him $50,000 in royalties and a $3,500 personal appearance contract. He appeared on Broadway in a huge $30 white Stetson hat. Dexter came from East Texas and started playing music from the age of 15, singing while he worked and entertaining his fellow workers. He played every stringed instrument and wrote his own tunes, all with an unmistakable Texas flavour. A paper hanger by trade, he joined a hillbilly band in the days of the economic depression playing guitar and calling square dances in Texas cow towns. He enjoyed tremendous success throughout the south-west of the U.S.A. for a decade and made many discs for Columbia.

He was born in Jacksonville, Texas, on 14 May 1919, and his real name was Albert Poindexter. This disc was No 1 for one week, and was 17 weeks in the U.S.A. bestsellers.

JIMMY DORSEY AND HIS ORCHESTRA WITH KITTY KALLEN AND BOB EBERLE
BESAME MUCHO (Kiss Me) *Decca* [*USA*]. Originally written in 1941 by Mexican lady composer Consuelo Velazquez, with English lyrics by Sunny Skylar. The recording was a number that caught on immediately, and is considered one of the most representative of Mexican tunes. In August 1962, a series of celebrations in Guadalajara, where pianist-composer Velazquez lived, marked the song's 20th anniversary in which many recording artists participated, with a big climax at the Palace of Fine Arts, in Mexico City. This tune has been recorded in virtually every idiom. The disc eventually became Jimmy Dorsey's fourth million seller. It was No 1 for seven weeks, and was 16 weeks in the U.S.A. bestsellers.

DICK HAYMES AND THE SONG SPINNERS
YOU'LL NEVER KNOW *Decca* [*USA*]. This first million seller for Haymes was written by ace writers Mack Gordon (words) and Harry Warren (music) for the film *Hello 'Frisco Hello*, who won the Academy Award for the best film song of 1943. Haymes was born in Buenos Aires, Argentina, on 13 September 1916, reared in the U.S.A., and educated at Loyola University, Montreal. Trained in singing by his mother, a vocal teacher, he became a radio announcer, then singer with the Carl Hoff, Eddie Martin, and Orrin Tucker bands. His first big break was when he replaced Frank Sinatra as vocalist with Harry James' band in 1939, and he again followed Sinatra as singer with the Tommy Dorsey orchestra in 1943, then joined Benny Goodman briefly, breaking away to become a single artist. Haymes soon branched out in radio and films, with film debut in 1944 in *Irish Eyes Are Smiling*, followed by many others, including *Four Jills in a Jeep, Diamond Horseshoe, State Fair, Do You Love Me?, The Shocking Miss Pilgrim, Up in Central Park, Banjo on my Knee*, and *All Ashore*. He formed his own production company in 1955 and played in nightclubs and made also TV appearances. The disc was No 1 for four weeks, and 16 weeks in the U.S.A. bestsellers.

FRANK SINATRA WITH HARRY JAMES ORCHESTRA
ALL OR NOTHING AT ALL (Re-issue of 1939 recording) *Columbia* [*USA*]. This disc, when first issued, created no enthusiasm, selling, it is said, only about 8,000. In 1943, both Sinatra and bandleader James became national celebrities, and the re-issued disc subsequently sold the million. The song was written by Jack Lawrence and Arthur Altman. Sinatra was born Francis Albert Sinatra in Hoboken, New Jersey, on 12 December 1915, was educated at Demarest High School there and sang in its glee club. From 1933 to 1936 he worked as helper on a delivery truck for the *Jersey Observer*. Seeing a Bing Crosby film he decided to give up his job and become a singer, and in 1937, with three instrumentalists billed as 'The Hoboken Four', appeared on a Major Bowes amateur show, winning a contract as a touring unit. In 1939, after a brief period as a singing waiter and master of ceremonies at the Rustic Cabin, Teaneck, New Jersey, he was heard and signed by Harry James as vocalist for his newly organized orchestra. Sinatra's first recording was 'From the Bottom of My Heart', backed with 'Melancholy Mood' on 13 July 1939 with the Harry James orchestra. Six months later he joined Tommy Dorsey (see 1942). In 1943 he broke away on his own, and when he landed the star spot on radio's 'Hit Parade' series he became an overnight sensation. The same year Sinatra had his first star role in *Higher and Higher* and began a film career destined to reach the heights. (His film debut was with Tommy Dorsey in *Las Vegas Nights* in 1941.) Subsequent star roles were in *Step Lively, Anchors Aweigh, Till the Clouds Roll By, It Happened in Brooklyn, The Kissing Bandit, Miracle of the Bells, Everybody's Cheering*, and *On the Town*. For the next couple of years, Frank devoted his time mainly to appearances on U.S. television and night-club bookings (1950-1952). Then in 1953, the former idol of the early and late 1940s made a sensational 'comeback', not through singing, but by his Academy Award winning role as 'Maggio' in the film version of *From Here to Eternity* - an impressive portrayal of an aggressive GI. His disc sales, particularly his albums, achieved big figures globally, 'Songs for Swinging Lovers' being the first to gain a place in Britain's bestseller lists in 1956. Later he enjoyed the starring roles in the films *Young at Heart, The Tender Trap, Suddenly, Guys and Dolls, Man with the Golden Arm, High Society, Pal Joey, The Joker is Wild*, and *Can-Can*. Apart from singing and acting, Sinatra's knowledge of classical music is considerable. He has had long disc careers with Columbia and Capitol, then his own label, Reprise. The very talented Sinatra - known as 'The Voice' - is undoubtedly one of the most remarkable figures in the entertainment world. In 1963, he sold Reprise Records to Warner Bros., and the same year became Vice President and Consultant of Warner Brothers Picture Corp.

This disc was recorded on 17 September 1939 in New York, reached No 2, and was in the U.S.A. bestsellers for 18 weeks.

THE ANDREWS SISTERS WITH VIC SCHOEN AND HIS ORCHESTRA

RUM AND COCA-COLA *Decca* [*USA*]. This great hit provided a second million seller disc for the sisters (actually their fourth counting the two with Bing in 1943). The song is pure Calypso and the music traditional. It was brought back from Trinidad by Morey Amsterdam who wrote words for it with music arranged by Paul Baron, also known as a conductor, and Jeri Sullivan, the singer. This was the freak song of 1944–1945, which sparked off a Calypso trend. The revised title for Britain was 'Rum and Limonada'. Composer Amsterdam became well known in 1963 through his performance in the Dick Van Dyke comedy TV series.

The song was the subject of a well-known plagiarism suit in the U.S.A. The court found that the music to 'Rum and Coca-Cola' was taken from Lionel Belasco's work 'L'Annee Passee', written in Trinidad in 1906. The lyrics are an adaptation of a Calypso sung in Trinidad during World War II.

BING CROSBY WITH THE JOHN SCOTT TROTTER ORCHESTRA

SWINGING ON A STAR *Decca* [*USA*]. This record was from Bing's film *Going My Way*. It proved another big success for Johnny Burke (words) and Jimmy Van Heusen (music), and was the winner of the Academy Award for best film song for 1944. One of the best popular songs of modern times, this whimsical ditty was later honoured by being included in a standard U.S. school songbook. 'Swinging on a Star' was Bing's ninth million seller. Recorded in Los Angeles on 7 February 1944. Vocal backgrounds by the Williams Brothers, which included Andy Williams. The disc was No 1 for nine weeks, and in the U.S.A. bestsellers for 20 weeks.

BING CROSBY WITH THE VICTOR YOUNG ORCHESTRA

TOO-RA-LOO-RA-LOO-RAL (That's an Irish Lullaby) *Decca* [*USA*]. Also from Bing's film *Going My Way*, this revival of a popular song of 1914 written by J. R. Shannon became Bing's tenth million selling disc. Recorded in Los Angeles on 7 July 1944, and a new matrix made on 17 July 1945. It reached No 4, and was nine weeks in the U.S.A. bestsellers.

BING CROSBY WITH THE ANDREWS SISTERS AND THE VIC SCHOEN ORCHESTRA

DON'T FENCE ME IN *Decca* [*USA*]. Originally an interpolated number in the film *Hollywood Canteen*, this recording enjoyed great popularity throughout 1945. It was written by the famed composer/lyricist, Cole Porter, and became Bing's eleventh million seller, and the Andrews Sisters' fifth. The song was also a million sheet music seller. Recorded in Los Angeles on 25 July 1944.

George Eells, biographer of the late Cole Porter, states in his book, *The Life That Late He Led*, that Porter bought the rights to the poem, 'Don't Fence Me In', from the author, Robert H. Fletcher, for $150. In the *Variety* obituary of Fletcher, it was stated that Porter's song had no relationship to Fletcher's poem. Eells said that Fletcher's poem came to Porter's attention when he was working on a film for Twentieth-Century Fox.

After buying the rights from Fletcher, Porter used the title 'Don't Fence Me In' and some phrases from the original poem in his song. The song was originally intended as a theme for a film about Will Rogers, but was introduced by cowboy singer Roy Rogers and reprised in the 1944 Warner Bros. film, *Hollywood Canteen*, by the Andrews Sisters who had the bestselling disc on Decca Records.

It was No 1 for eight weeks, and in the U.S.A. bestsellers for 18 weeks.

TOMMY DORSEY AND ORCHESTRA

OPUS NO. 1 *Victor* [*USA*]. Composed by Sy Oliver, this record after 15 years of selling became Tommy Dorsey's fourth disc to reach seven figures. Recorded on 14 November 1944.

TOMMY DORSEY AND HIS ORCHESTRA WITH THE SENTIMENTALISTS (vocalists)

ON THE SUNNY SIDE OF THE STREET *Victor* [*USA*]. Written by Dorothy Fields (words) and Jimmy McHugh (music), two of America's greatest song writers, this was first sung by Harry Richman in Lew Leslie's *International Revue* in 1930 and subsequently became tremendously popular. Between 1939 and 1944, famous arranger, trumpeter, singer and bandleader 'Sy' Oliver became arranger for Tommy Dorsey, and this was one of his characteristically simple, power-packed swinging arrangements that made the big band era so memorable. The disc became equally popular in the U.S.A. and Britain and sold over a million. The recording was made on 14 November 1944.

ELLA FITZGERALD AND THE INK SPOTS

INTO EACH LIFE SOME RAIN MUST FALL *Decca* [*USA*]. Ella's second and the Ink Spots' first million seller disc was by Allan Roberts (words) and Doris Fisher (music). Doris is the daughter of the songwriter, Fred Fisher.

The Ink Spots: Orville 'Happy' Jones, bass and cello (died November 1944); Billy Kenny, tenor; Charlie Fuqua, bass and guitar; and Ivory 'Deek' Watson, tenor – were originally porters at New York's Paramount Theatre. They were heard by an artists' representative who arranged for them to record (*circa* 1937), came up with their first big hit 'If I Didn't Care' in 1939, and achieved top billing in U.S. variety by 1941. They made a great number of discs, and became renowned for their famous talking choruses. The Ink Spots appeared at the Palladium, London, in 1948. Recorded 30 August 1944.

EDDIE HEYWOOD (pianist) AND HIS ORCHESTRA

BEGIN THE BEGUINE *Decca* [*USA*]. This first million seller for Eddie Heywood was the second time this famous Cole Porter song, written in 1935 for the U.S. musical *Jubilee*, became a million seller.

Recorded on 15 December 1944. (See 'Canadian Sunset', 1956 for Heywood biography.)

SPIKE JONES AND HIS CITY SLICKERS

COCKTAILS FOR TWO *Victor* [*USA*]. A second million seller for Spike, the song by Sam Coslow (words) and Arthur Johnston (music) was originally written for the film *Murder at the Vanities* in 1934. Spike was born on 14 December 1911 in Long Beach, California, and, while in high school, organized a dance-band, 'Spike Jones and his Five Tacks', and played over local radio stations. He then played drums with Ray West, later substituting for Vic Barton in the Al Jolson show. Spike Jones remained in radio until 1941 when he organized a group of musicians to play novelty music. Their background for Walt Disney's cartoon 'Der Fuehrer's Face' (1942) established them, and the band became consistent disc sellers. They subsequently played concert and theatre dates, and also made various TV appearances. This disc became a million seller by 1946. Spike's real name was Lindley Armstrong Jones. He died on 1 May 1965. (See also 1942.) The disc reached No 4 in the U.S.A. charts.

LOUIS JORDAN AND HIS TYMPANY FIVE

IS YOU IS OR IS YOU AIN'T MY BABY? *Decca* [*USA*]. Jazz critic Leonard Feather has said that when one gets right down to the nub (a prehistoric term for fundamentals), teenage pop came from rock which came from rhythm and blues which came from Louis Jordan. Louis began to strike it rich in 1941 with 'Knock Me a Kiss' and 'I'm Gonna Move to the Outskirts of Town', just three years after leaving Chick Webb's band and forming his own. (See 1946 for Louis Jordan data.) Throughout the 1940s he became one of the greatest show business names ever to emerge from jazz, and the rhythmic character of his band had a tremendous influence on the course of popular music.

This disc was a big hit and is said to have sold over a million. The song, written by Louis Jordan and Billy Austin in 1943, was also a great dance hit in Europe. It was sung by Louis in the film *Follow the Boys* (1944) and by the Delta Rhythm Boys in the film *Easy to Look At* (1945). The disc reached No 5 in the U.S.A. charts.

THE MILLS BROTHERS

YOU ALWAYS HURT THE ONE YOU LOVE *Decca* [*USA*]. This record became the third million seller for the brothers, and a second major hit for the writers Allan Roberts (words) and Doris Fisher (music). It was No 1 for five weeks, and was 20 weeks in the U.S.A. bestsellers.

DAVID ROSE AND HIS ORCHESTRA

HOLIDAY FOR STRINGS *Victor* [*USA*]. This brilliant original composition and scoring made David famous, and gave him his first million seller. He was born in London on 15 June 1910 and went to the U.S.A. at the age of 4, eventually studying music at Chicago College of Music. He next became a professional pianist with Chicago orchestras, then staff arranger for Chicago radio station and held similar posts in Los Angeles, where his arranging talents brought him to Hollywood for extensive studio work. During the last war he was in the armed forces as composer and director of *Winged Victory*, an Army/Air Force production.

He formed his own orchestra and gravitated towards composing and conducting. He has recorded many selections since for MGM, including his own compositions, arranged and conducted for the Red Skelton TV show and for NBC TV spectaculars. David has been conductor of the Pasadena Pops Concerts for several years, and conducted the David Rose Concerts at Hollywood Bowl. This disc became a million seller by 1958. It reached No 2, and was 19 weeks in the U.S.A. bestsellers.

FRANK SINATRA WITH THE KEN LANE SINGERS AND ORCHESTRA DIRECTED BY AXEL STORDAHL

WHITE CHRISTMAS *Columbia* [*USA*]. Sinatra's second million seller (through subsequent years) was the third time composer Irving Berlin achieved a million seller with the title. It was recorded on 14 November 1944, two days after the 27 months' recording ban by the American Musicians Union was lifted, and reached No 7 in the U.S.A. charts.

MARGARET WHITING WITH THE BILLY BUTTERFIELD ORCHESTRA

MOONLIGHT IN VERMONT *Capitol* [*USA*]. This first million seller for Margaret was written by John Blackburn (words) and Karl Suessdorf (music). Margaret was born on 22 July 1924 in Detroit, daughter of the famous songwriter, Richard Whiting, and was reared in Hollywood. She used to sing for Johnny Mercer, who wrote songs with her father long before Mercer started Capitol Records in 1941, and her first radio spot was on a show starring Johnny Mercer. Then after a period with Freddie Slack's orchestra, Mercer gave her her big break with a Capitol contract. Margaret Whiting, thereafter, proved to be an important acquisition for Capitol and made many hit discs, appeared on TV and radio shows, and also visited Britain. Since her father's death in 1938, she successfully revived many of his songs and made an LP of Whiting singing Whiting. In 1947 she was the first female vocalist to enter music publishing and to exploit many famous songs written by her father, including about 150 he never managed to get published. Her 'sing-it-to-me' style put her in the $200,000-a-year income bracket between 1945 and 1950. Many songs reached the Hit Parade, and Margaret also brought back the vogue for duet singing by doubling with Jimmy Wakely, Jack Smith, Frank DeVol and Bob Hope.

William Charles (Billy) Butterfield was born 14 January 1917 in Middletown, Ohio, and educated at Transylvania College, Lexington, Kentucky. He studied medicine in his youth, but soon abandoned it for a musical career. He left school in 1936 and toured with a small college band, later taken over by Austin Wylie, and subsequently played trumpet with Bob Crosby, Artie Shaw and Benny Goodman before turning to radio work as CBS staff musician in New York in 1942. Other famous bandleaders who included his golden trumpet tone in their brass sections were Les Brown and Harry James. Butterfield had a further stint with ABC and a period in the Army, after which he formed his own orchestra at war's end and recorded for Capitol. From 1948, he again became a staff musician for ABC. His longest spell with a 'name' orchestra was a three-year period with Bob Crosby's Dixieland Band during the mid thirties.

His trumpet playing is noted for its expressive tone and technical command.

1945

LES BROWN AND HIS ORCHESTRA WITH DORIS DAY (vocal)

SENTIMENTAL JOURNEY *Columbia* [*USA*]. Written by Les Brown, with Bud Green and Ben Homer, this was a big hit in 1945, earning the band first place in a poll of that year. Les organized his first band at Duke University with, later, profes-

sional dates and recordings till 1937. After a period of arranging, he formed a new band in 1938, and conducted for Bob Hope. This disc (his first million seller) started Doris Day on the road to stardom. Les was born in Reinertown, Pennsylvania, on 14 March 1912. The disc was recorded 20 November 1944, was No 1 for nine weeks, and was in the U.S.A. bestsellers for 23 weeks.

CARMEN CAVALLARO AND HIS ORCHESTRA

POLONAISE IN A (Chopin) *Decca* [*USA*]. Cavallaro's only million seller disc arose from an interpretation of Chopin in the rhythmic idiom. He began his career as pianist with an orchestra, later joining Abe Lyman and Rudy Vallee. Cavallaro formed his own orchestra in 1939 which soon attracted nation-wide attention. He later became a recording artist and made piano recordings for the biographical film, *The Eddy Duchin Story* (1956). Carmen was born in New York City on 6 May 1913. The British sales of the record reached 300,000. It reached No 3 in the U.S.A., and was in their bestsellers for 19 weeks.

PERRY COMO WITH THE RUSS CASE ORCHESTRA

TILL THE END OF TIME (based on Chopin's Polonaise in A flat) *Victor* [*USA*]. Chopin's music was extremely popular in 1945, thanks both to the rhythmic version by the Cavallaro orchestra, and the piano solo of the original work by Iturbi (see below). It was inevitable a vocal version would be made, and it was this disc, a popular song version by Buddy Kaye and Ted Mossman, that helped to put Perry Como on the road to fame. The recording sold three million by 1951. Perry Como was born Pierino Como in Canonsburg, Pennsylvania, on 18 May 1913. Third Avenue, the street on which his family lived, has been re-named Perry Como Avenue. His mother and father had come from Italy. By the time Perry was 11, he worked after school in a barber's shop, and three years later was paying instalments on his own shop, but his father made him suspend the venture until he had completed high school in 1929. By 1934, Como was established in Canonsburg as a barber. He successfully auditioned for Freddie Carlone's Band and travelled with them as vocalist through the Midwest for three years. In 1937, Ted Weems heard him and signed him up with his orchestra until 1942 when Weems entered the armed forces. Como then signed with General Amusement Corporation and appeared at nightclubs and theatres. In 1943 he signed a contract with Victor. By 1945 his voice became widely known over juke-box and record-playing radio programmes. Also in 1943 he was signed to a seven-year film contract with 20th-Century/Fox, later released at his own request in 1947. In the interval, however, he featured in *Something for the Boys* and *Doll Face*, reaching full stardom in *If I'm Lucky* (1946). Como's discs sold very strongly, and he was the first popular singer to reach the two million sale on two releases at the same time – this disc and 'If I Loved You' – both in 1946 which hit the target within the same week. Perry was given the title of 'Maker of Songs' by *Variety* for his success with revivals. He was also starred on a thrice-weekly TV show, and later 'The Perry Como Show'. Between 1952 and 1957 he won many TV poll awards, and by 1969 sales of his discs were estimated at over 50 million. Perry's relaxed baritone voice has earned him the title of 'the world's most casual singer'. His supremacy as a TV performer was well matched by his dominance in the music world. This disc was No 1 for 10 weeks, and 17 weeks in the U.S.A. bestsellers.

IF I LOVED YOU backed with I'M GONNA LOVE THAT GIRL *Victor* [*USA*]. The title provided Perry's second million seller by 1946. The song 'If I Loved You' was the hit from the musical *Carousel* written by Oscar Hammerstein II (words) and Richard Rodgers (music). The reverse side is by Frances Ash, the pen-name for Britain's famous bandleader Ted Heath and his wife Moira, which was originally entitled 'I'm Gonna Love That Guy'. 'If I Loved You' was No 3, and 13 weeks in the U.S.A. bestsellers. 'I'm Gonna Love That Girl' was No 7.

PERRY COMO WITH THE SATISFIERS

A HUBBA-HUBBA-HUBBA (Dig You Later) *Victor* [*USA*]. This became a third million seller for Perry by 1951. The song is from Perry Como's own film *Doll Face*. It was written by Harold Adamson (words) and Jimmy McHugh (music). The disc was No 3, and 12 weeks in the U.S.A. bestsellers.

TEMPTATION *Victor* [*USA*]. By 1953 this title provided a fourth million seller for Perry Como. This revival of the great song, written in 1933 by Arthur Freed (words) and Nacio Herb Brown (music) for the film *Going Hollywood*, was originally sung by Bing Crosby.

BING CROSBY WITH CARMEN CAVALLARO (piano accompaniment)

I CAN'T BEGIN TO TELL YOU *Decca* [*USA*]. This twelfth million seller for the 'Old Groaner' Bing, was written for the film *The Dolly Sisters* by Mack Gordon (words) and James V. Monaco (music). Recorded in Los Angeles on 7 August 1945, it was No 1 for one week, and 17 weeks in the U.S.A. bestsellers.

BILLY ECKSTINE AND HIS ORCHESTRA

COTTAGE FOR SALE *National* [*USA*]. Billy Eckstine, born on 8 July 1913 in Pittsburgh, Pennsylvania, first sang at a church bazaar at the age of 11. Although he had taken piano lessons he had no tuition in singing. His family moved to Washington, D.C., where Billy attended Armstrong High School and had a preference for baseball and football rather than the glee club. At 17, he won his first amateur competition by imitating Cab Calloway. On one of the many subsequent amateur shows, he was heard by bandleader Tommy Miles who hired him to sing with his band for a summer season. Billy then accepted an athletic scholarship to play football for St Paul University, Lawrenceville, but after breaking his collar bone, he ended his football days, left college, and returned to Washington. He worked as a singer and master of ceremonies at numerous clubs in the East and Midwest, and in 1939 was heard by bandleader Earl Hines at the De Liso Club in Chicago, and became the band's regular vocalist for four years. During this period he learned to play the trumpet. Billy then discovered Sarah Vaughan (see 1959) at the Apollo Theatre in New York on amateur night and took her to Earl Hines who featured her with Billy. In 1943, Billy left the band to become a solo artist at New York's Onyx Club, but in June 1944, his agent suggested a Billy Eckstine Big Band. This included many now famous names in jazz such as Charlie Parker, Diz Gillespie, Fats Navarro, Miles Davis, Howard McGhee, Lucky Thompson, Gene Ammons, Dexter Gordon and Art Blakey. They played modern jazz in a declining swing era. In 1947, tired of one-night stands, the group disbanded and Billy went out as a 'single' artist again, and for the next five years broke records everywhere he appeared and became known as the 'Fabulous Mr B'. He toured Europe in 1954 and returned practically every year. He was one of the first jazz singers to become a world-wide star. Billy's rich baritone voice and jazz style have made him a top attraction in the world of entertainment. 'Cottage for Sale', written by Larry Conley (words) and Willard Robison (music) in 1930, was the first of two million seller discs for Billy on the National label, a company that specialized in coloured artists' recordings. Billy signed with National in 1945, MGM in 1947, and the new Tamla-Motown label in 1965.

Recorded on 2 May 1945.

PRISONER OF LOVE *National* [*USA*]. This was the second million seller for Billy Eckstine. The song was written in 1931 by Leo Robin, Clarence Gaskill and Russ Columbo. Recorded September 1945.

WOODY HERMAN AND HIS ORCHESTRA
LAURA *Columbia* [*USA*]. This was the theme of the film *Laura*, composed by David Raksin, with words provided later by Johnny Mercer. Woody Herman was born on 16 May 1913 in Milwaukee, Wisconsin, and was a vaudeville trouper at the age of only eight. At nine he was billed as 'The Boy Wonder of the Clarinet'. He studied music at the Marquette Music School in Milwaukee, and at 14 worked with local bands, joining Tom Gerum's orchestra in 1929, sharing the vocal work with Ginny Simms and Tony Martin. In 1933 Woody joined Harry Sosnick for a short period, then Isham Jones' orchestra whose band he conducted when Jones retired in 1938. The band formed a co-operative organization but changed status when the war-time draft caused personnel shifts, and Woody took over the control in 1941. He converted the Dixieland style to more modern music. In 1946, the band premiered Stravinsky's 'Ebony Concerto' at Carnegie Hall, New York, and then broke up, but not before it had been placed first in five popularity polls. In 1947, Woody reorganized his band which he retained until 1949. Woody then broke up his second team to go to Cuba and formed a small group, reorganizing yet again with a big band in 1950. He thereafter formed his own firm, Mars Records. 'Herman's Herd' was voted best band in 1949. This fine musician's real name is Woodrow Wilson Herman. Recorded 19 February 1945, the disc was No 7 in the U.S.A. charts.

JOSE ITURBI (piano)
POLONAISE IN A FLAT (Chopin) *Victor* [*USA*]. It was Iturbi's off-screen playing of Polonaise in the Chopin 'biopic', *A Song to Remember*, that started a Chopin year (see also Perry Como and Carmen Cavallaro). This disc sold a million by 1947. Iturbi, born in Valencia on 28 November 1895, toured Europe, South America, and the U.S.A. from 1923, and made his debut as a conductor in 1933. He portrayed himself in the film *Thousands Cheer* in 1943, and in 1943 signed a contract with MGM, and appeared thereafter in films with such stars as Frank Sinatra, Jeanette MacDonald, Mario Lanza, Jimmy Durante and Kathryn Grayson.

CLAIR DE LUNE (Debussy) *Victor* [*USA*]. This classical recording by Iturbi also sold a million but the magic figure was not reached until 1949.

AL JOLSON WITH ORCHESTRA DIRECTED BY CARMEN DRAGON
APRIL SHOWERS backed with SWANEE *Decca* [*USA*]. Jolson's fourth million seller disc carried songs he made extremely popular in earlier years: 'Swanee' (words by Irving Caesar, music by the great George Gershwin - his first hit) dating back to 1919 and 'April Showers' (words by B. G. de Sylva, music by Louis Silvers), first heard in 1921, then a million sheet music seller. Both songs were hits (together with other songs (see 1946)) in the film *The Jolson Story*. This film gave Jolson the chance to make a remarkable comeback after nearly 20 years of being out of the limelight. This disc was part of the process of introducing him to a new generation. (See also 1928 and 1946.)

LOUIS JORDAN AND HIS TYMPANY FIVE
CALDONIA (What makes your big head so hard?) *Decca* [*USA*]. Written by Fleecie Moore, this disc is said to have sold a million. The song was also a hit for Woody Herman and his orchestra in their disc version and the song a very popular one on both sides of the Atlantic. The disc reached No 6 in the U.S.A.

STAN KENTON AND HIS ORCHESTRA WITH JUNE CHRISTY (vocal)
TAMPICO *Capitol* [*USA*]. This number provided Kenton's first million seller disc. His band was top in the polls of 1947, 1950, 1951 and 1952. After leaving school he played the piano in clubs, then graduated to movie studio and radio work. Kenton formed his band in 1940 and from 1948 gave up ballroom work and launched his orchestra in concerts of progressive jazz and modern music. June Christy joined him in 1945, and was with him on tours, in between solo stints. This song was the third big success for writers Allan Roberts and Doris Fisher. Kenton was

born in Wichita, Kansas, on 19 February 1912. June Christy (real name Shirley Luster) was born in Decatur, Illinois, on 20 November 1925. Recorded July 1945, the disc was No 4, and 13 weeks in the U.S.A. bestsellers. Stan Kenton died 26 August 1979 in Los Angeles.

STAN KENTON (piano) AND HIS ORCHESTRA
ARTISTRY IN RHYTHM *Capitol* [*USA*]. Written by Stan Kenton in 1941, this was used as the theme for his orchestra. The disc is a production on the theme and one of the series of 'Artistry' discs he recorded in various rhythmic styles and played at his concerts of progressive jazz and modern music. This disc is believed to have been made around 1945.

ROY MILTON
R. M. BLUES *Specialty* [*USA*]. This original song by Roy proved to become his only million seller disc. He was born in 1915 in Tulsa, Oklahoma. Drummer and vocalist of his small band in California, Milton played mainly a repertoire of blues numbers.

VAUGHN MONROE AND HIS BAND
THERE I'VE SAID IT AGAIN *Victor* [*USA*]. By 1949 this number provided Monroe with a second disc to sell a million. The success of this disc consolidated Monroe's fame. Song written by Redd Evans and David Mann. Mann was personal pianist to President Truman in 1945-1946. This disc reached No 2, and was 20 weeks in the U.S.A. bestsellers.

THE PIED PIPERS WITH PAUL WESTON'S ORCHESTRA
DREAM *Capitol* [*USA*]. This was the first million seller disc by the Pied Pipers. They started in 1937 with seven boys and a girl, eventually becoming the quartet: John Huddlestone, Chuck Lowry, Clark Yokum and Jo Stafford. They got their big break when Tommy Dorsey heard them and put them on his radio show in 1939. Their unique and captivating style made them an immediate success and helped create a sudden, wide demand for vocal groups. Johnny Mercer brought them to his Capitol Records and they backed him on all the big hits he was making. The words and music of this song were written by Johnny Mercer. This disc was No 5, and 15 weeks in the U.S.A. bestsellers.

TINO ROSSI (tenor vocalist)
PETIT PAPA NOEL *Columbia* [*France*]. Tino Rossi was a popular singer in France in the 1940-1950 period. Many of his records were released in U.S.A. on Columbia, all sung in French, and included such hits as 'Le Chaland qui Passe', 'Reginella', 'Vieni Vieni' and 'Le Rêve'.

This disc 'Petit Papa Noel' is said to have sold around 20 million copies over the years. It received a Gold Disc award in 1945, the first such award ever presented in France, and was the real thing – 22-carat gold.

ARTHUR SMITH (country-and-western guitarist) AND HIS CRACKERJACKS
GUITAR BOOGIE *Super Disc/MGM* [*USA*]. Arthur earned himself the name of 'Guitar Boogie' Smith through this outstanding recording, his own composition.

Arthur Smith was born 1 April 1921 in Clinton, South Carolina, and became one of the most popular performers in the state. He has broadcast over WBT Radio in Charlotte, and on TV for over 20 years, the shows also being heard on more than 200 stations in the South and South-west of the USA. His discs were top sellers for MGM in 1948. Sales were also gigantic in other countries.

A great number of his discs are in the 'boogie' idiom and he was the first to establish and popularize this style on the guitar, composing much of his own material. He is also a brilliant exponent of mandolin and banjo.

1946

PERRY COMO
PRISONER OF LOVE *Victor* [*USA*]. Perry's fifth million seller was this song written in 1931 by Leo Robin, Russ Colombo and Clarence Gaskill. It was No 1 for three weeks, and 19 weeks in the U.S.A. bestsellers.

PERRY COMO WITH THE SATISFIERS AND RUSS CASE ORCHESTRA
I'M ALWAYS CHASING RAINBOWS *Victor* [*USA*]. Perry Como's sixth million seller was this song by Joe McCarthy with musical adaptation from Chopin's 'Fantasie Impromptu' in C sharp minor by Harry Carroll, written in 1918. The song was at that date a million sheet music seller. This disc reached No 7 in the U.S.A.

BING CROSBY WITH THE JESTERS AND BOB HAGGART AND HIS ORCHESTRA
McNAMARA'S BAND *Decca* [*USA*]. This delightful Irish song disc by Bing and the Jesters vocal group goes back to 1917. It was written by John H. Stamford (words) and Shamus O'Connor (music), and this version was arranged and adapted by Carlson, Bonham and Dwight Latham. Latham formed the Jesters Trio when at school and entered radio in 1925, thereafter was leader of the group for 20 years in radio, film and recording work.

'McNamara's Band' was lucky 13 in Bing's list of million sellers. Recorded in Los Angeles on 6 December 1945.

BING CROSBY AND THE ANDREWS SISTERS WITH VIC SCHOEN AND HIS ORCHESTRA
SOUTH AMERICA, TAKE IT AWAY *Decca* [*USA*]. This best song from the U.S.A. show *Call Me Mister* in 1946 was written and composed by Harold Rome, and became the fourth million seller disc for Bing in partnership with the Andrews Sisters. Individually it was Bing's fourteenth million seller disc, and the Andrews Sisters' sixth. Recorded in Los Angeles on 11 May 1946, the disc was No 2, and 17 weeks in the U.S.A. bestsellers.

EDDY HOWARD AND HIS ORCHESTRA
TO EACH HIS OWN *Majestic* [*USA*]. This was only one of three discs covering this song, written for but not used in the film *To Each His Own*, that sold a million. This version reached two million by 1957. It was written by Ray Evans (words) and Jay Livingston (music), a team who were to win further laurels for their songs. The song was also a million sheet music seller. Eddy began his career by singing on radio, then travelled with various bands including Ben Bernie's and Dick Jurgens'. In 1939 he formed his own band which he conducted until the early 1950s, thereafter confining himself to recordings. This was Howard's first million seller disc. Eddy was born on 12 September 1914 in Woodland, California, and died on 23 May 1963. This disc was No 1 for five weeks, and 19 weeks in the U.S.A. bestsellers.

THE INK SPOTS

TO EACH HIS OWN *Decca* [*USA*]. This million-selling disc of this extremely successful vocal group was the immediate big seller of those issued in 1946 on this song, discarded from the film *To Each His Own*. It was the group's first solo million seller, also their second million disc (see 1944). It was No 1 for one week, and 11 weeks in the U.S.A. bestsellers.

THE GYPSY *Decca* [*USA*]. The Ink Spots' third million seller, and second solo million seller, was provided by an English writer, Billy Reid, whose accordion band and partnership with vocalist Dorothy Squires, achieved considerable fame in Britain during the war. Reid had two other songs that were million sellers in the U.S.A. (see 1948 and 1953), and became the first British writer to achieve such distinction. This disc was No 1 for 10 weeks, and 18 weeks in the U.S.A. bestsellers.

AL JOLSON WITH MORRIS STOLOFF'S ORCHESTRA

ROCKABYE YOUR BABY backed with CALIFORNIA, HERE I COME *Decca* [*USA*]. 'Rockabye' was written by Sam Lewis and Joe Young (words) and Jean Schwartz (music) in 1918. 'California' was written by Al Jolson, B. G. de Sylva and Joseph Meyer in 1924.

YOU MADE ME LOVE YOU backed with MA BLUSHIN' ROSIE *Decca* [*USA*]. 'You Made Me Love You' - words by Joe McCarthy, music by James V. Monaco - was written in 1913 when it enjoyed a million sheet music sales. 'Ma Blushin' Rosie - words by Edgar Smith, music by John Stromberg - was written even earlier in 1900.

SONNY BOY backed with MY MAMMY *Decca* [*USA*]. 'Sonny Boy', written by B. G. de Sylva, Lew Brown, Ray Henderson and Al Jolson, was first heard in 1928. 'My Mammy' by Joe Young and Sam M. Lewis (words) and Walter Donaldson (music) dated back to 1920. Both songs were also million sheet music sellers in their day.

ANNIVERSARY SONG backed with AVALON *Decca* [*USA*]. 'Anniversary Song' by Al Jolson and Saul Chaplin (an adaptation of J. Ivanovici's 'Waves of the Danube' waltz of the 1880s) was written in 1946. 'Avalon', by Al Jolson and Vincent Rose, was written in 1920. 'Anniversary Song' was a bestseller in both the U.S.A. and Britain. This reached No 2, and was 14 weeks in the U.S.A. bestsellers.

NOTES ON JOLSON DISCS

All the foregoing titles, together with 'April Showers' and 'Swanee' (see 1945) were featured either in the film *The Jolson Story* released in 1947 which grossed $8 million, or *Jolson Sings Again* released in 1950 which grossed $5 million. Jolson's voice was recorded for these films and he was portrayed by Larry Parks. The 'Sonny Boy' disc became a million seller for the second time (see 1928), while the 'Anniversary Song' became an international hit. Morris Stoloff received an Academy Award for the best scoring of a musical picture with *The Jolson Story*.

AL JOLSON

THE JOLSON STORY *Decca* [*USA*]. Album of singles discs (issued October 1946). This Jolson souvenir album contained several of the above titles and is reputed to have sold well over a million, the first album to reach such a sale. It was later put out as an album entitled 'Rock-a-bye Your Baby (The Jolson Story)'.

'The Jolson Story' was one of the first 'soundtrack' albums, although it was not technically a soundtrack. All the tracks were specially recorded for the album to acquaint the musical public with Jolson's name before the film was shown. 'The Anniversary Song' was taken out of the album and was the first single ever to come out of a soundtrack.

SPIKE JONES AND HIS CITY SLICKERS

GLOW WORM *Victor* [*USA*]. A burlesque version of Paul Lincke's famous work provided a third million seller for Spike. (See Mills Brothers, 1952, for data concerning the tune.)

LOUIS JORDAN AND HIS TYMPANY FIVE

BEWARE, BROTHER, BEWARE *Decca* [*USA*]. Written in 1945 by Morry Lasco, Dick Adams and Fleecie Moore, Louis' disc was a bestseller of 1946 and is said to have sold a million.

CHOO CHOO CH'BOOGIE *Decca* [*USA*]. Louis Jordan's fourth million seller disc was written by Milton Gabler (words) with Vaughn Horton and Denver Darling (music). Louis played the alto saxophone for seven years with the famous Chick Webb band from 1932, then formed his own group. He is also the vocalist on this disc. Louis was born on 8 July 1908, in Brinkley, Arkansas. He began his musical studies in early childhood, and was educated at Arkansas Baptist College, Little Rock. He played with Ruby Williams in Hot Springs, then joined Charlie Gains in 1930 in Philadelphia, afterwards trekking to New York to work with Kaiser Marshall and Le Roy Smith before joining Chick Webb. Recorded 23 January 1946, the disc reached No 8 in the U.S.A. Louis died in Los Angeles in 1975 on 4 February.

VICTOR JORY (narrator)
TUBBY THE TUBA *Cosmopolitan* [*USA*]. Produced on two 10-inch records, 'Tubby the Tuba' was named by *Information Please Almanac* in the U.S.A. as the best children's record of 1946. 'Tubby' was the brain-child of Paul Tripp, author, born 20 February 1911 in New York. After education at the College of the City of New York and Brooklyn Law School, he began his career in the theatre as a singer, and later as actor and director. He taught dramatics to children in settlement houses and wrote three prize-winning anti-war plays and many children's plays. While in the U.S. Air Force (1942-45) part of his time in the Special Services was spent editing the post newspaper and as director of dramatics, also writing training films for the Signal Corps. He was in charge of a signal centre in China for one year. He later became writer, lyricist and star of weekly CBS-TV shows, notably 'Mr I. Magination' (1949-52) and 'On the Carousel' (1954-59). He narrated his own works with symphony orchestras and on discs, collaborating with composers George Kleinsinger and Ray Carter.

Tripp wrote several 'Tubby' adventures, 'Tubby the Tuba' being his biggest success. Actor Victor Jory's disc was the first, and is now considered a classic, sales said to be over the million. It was also a big hit on disc for Danny Kaye in the early 1950s.

Jory's disc proved to be the biggest seller for the Cosmopolitan Record Co. (formed in 1942 but since defunct). Victor Jory was born 23 November 1902 in Dawson City, Alaska, and after stage appearances, worked mainly in films in Hollywood (1932-43) with further stage and film work thereafter.

STAN KENTON AND HIS ORCHESTRA WITH JUNE CHRISTY (vocal)
SHOO-FLY PIE AND APPLE PAN DOWDY *Capitol* [*USA*]. Written by Sammy Gallop (words) and Guy Wood (music) this number furnished Kenton with his third disc to sell a million. Recorded 1 November 1945, it reached No 8 in the U.S.A.

GUY LOMBARDO AND HIS ROYAL CANADIANS
HUMORESQUE *Decca* [*USA*]. Lombardo's first million seller disc. This famous piano solo was written by Anton Dvorak back in 1894 and this dance version was a steady seller for a long time. Lombardo and his 'Sweetest Music This Side of Heaven' were one of the most durable and popular performers in the U.S.A. and resident band at New York's Hotel Roosevelt for 33 years until 1962. Over 6 million people have danced to his band and he sold more than 100 million records. He started in Ontario aged 12, with a three-piece band, himself and his brothers Carmen and Lebert, later expanding to nine. Lombardo then toured the Canadian provinces and finally went to New York in 1929. He

played his own type of music, a sweet tone with balance and stress on melody to which he has adhered, with enormous success, despite changing fads. He introduced over 275 tunes eventually classified as top songs of their day. As a hobby Lombardo was a speedboat enthusiast who won the sport's highest prize, the Gold Cup, in 1946 with his big speedboat 'Tempo VI'. Generally known as 'The King of Corn' for his style, Lombardo could always claim that his corn was quite definitely golden. Guy Lombardo was born in London, Ontario, on 19 June 1902, and died in Houston, Texas, on 5 November 1977.

GUY LOMBARDO AND HIS ROYAL CANADIANS WITH THE ANDREWS SISTERS
CHRISTMAS ISLAND backed with WINTER WONDERLAND *Decca* [*USA*]. This became by 1948 Lombardo's second and the Andrews Sisters' seventh million seller disc. Both are great seasonal songs, a new one 'Christmas Island' by Lyle Moraine, and an oldie 'Winter Wonderland' written in 1934 by Dick Smith (words) and Felix Bernard (music). It was Bernard who also collaborated on the big hit 'Dardanella' (see 1920). The collective sales of 'Winter Wonderland' are over 40 million.

TONY MARTIN
TO EACH HIS OWN *Mercury* [*USA*]. This was the third disc of this Ray Evans-Jay Livingston song discarded from the film *To Each His Own* to sell a million, and Tony's only disc to do so, a figure he reached by 1955. Tony was a saxophone player, then sang in a hotel band in San Francisco. After a radio broadcast he joined a band at the Chicago World's Fair in 1933. Finally he went to Hollywood where he acted and sang in many musical films, to become internationally known. Tony Martin (real name Al Morris) was born on Christmas Day 1914 in Oakland, California. His films include *Sing Baby Sing*, *You Can't Have Everything*, *Ali Baba Goes to Town*, *Music in My Heart*, *Ziegfeld Girl*, *Till the Clouds Roll By*, *Casbah*, *Two Tickets to Broadway*, *Here Come the Girls*, *Easy to Love*, *Deep in My Heart*, *Hit the Deck* and *Let's Be Happy*. The disc reached No 4, and was 12 weeks in the U.S.A. bestsellers.

FRED WARING AND HIS PENNSYLVANIANS (Glee Club) AND ORCHESTRA
'TWAS THE NIGHT BEFORE CHRISTMAS (Christmas Songs) (album) *Decca* [*USA*]. Originally released as an album of 78 rpm singles discs, this was later issued on a 10-inch 33 rpm album around 1954, and is said to have sold a million of the collective versions. The title for the album was taken from Fred Waring's first million selling singles disc (see 1942).

The album contained the following: ''Twas the night before Christmas', by Clement Clarke Moore (1822) and Ken Darby (1942); 'Silent Night, Holy Night', by Joseph Mohr and Franz Gruber (1818); 'Come unto Him' (from *The Messiah*), by Handel (1742); 'Oh, Gathering Clouds', arranged by Marjorie Bain; 'Adeste Fideles', traditional, from the Latin; 'O Holy Night', by Adams; 'O Little Town of Bethlehem', by Phillips Brooks and Lewis H. Redner; 'The First Noel', traditional carol; 'Carol of the Bells', by Leontovitch, arranged by Peter J. Wilhousky; 'Beautiful Saviour', anon., arranged by Arnaud.

EDDY ARNOLD AND HIS TENNESSEE PLOWBOYS
I'LL HOLD YOU IN MY HEART *Victor* [*USA*]. Written by Eddy himself in collaboration with Hal Horton and Tommy Dilbeck, this disc was a big success in both 1947 and 1948, selling an estimated million through the years.

Eddy Arnold, born on a farm near Henderson, West Tennes-

see, on 15 May 1918 (real name Richard Edward Arnold) is unquestionably one of America's greatest country and folk music artists, his tally of disc sales to 1969 said to be over 60 million for Victor Records over the past 25 years. He first received musical instruction from his mother, learned the guitar, and started playing for square dances in the Blue Ridge Mountain area as a youngster. Before becoming a professional (1943), he was a share

cropper and plough boy. After a long series of local personal and radio appearances, he went to St Louis and joined forces with a young fiddler named Howard McNatt, where they made their first professional appearance over KWK radio station. Eddy got his first big break as singer/guitarist with Pee Wee King's Golden West Cowboys, then appearing in Grand Ole Opry. He became very popular, formed his own band and eventually went solo with plenty of radio, TV and some film work. Over the years, Eddy has had a number of very big hits, making a wide impact on the American public. He began recording for RCA Victor in 1945. In 1948, four of his songs were No 1, in the country-and-western charts.

He made his first TV appearance in Britain in March 1966. His first successful disc was 'It's a Sin' in 1947. He was voted the most popular singer of 1966 and elected to the Country Music Association of America's Hall of Fame the same year.

GENE AUTRY
HERE COMES SANTA CLAUS *Columbia* [*USA*]. Gene Autry wrote this song with Oakley Haldeman. The disc became his second million seller by 1950. It was a No 1 in the U.S.A. charts.

PERRY COMO WITH THE SATISFIERS AND LLOYD SCHAFFER'S ORCHESTRA
WHEN YOU WERE SWEET SIXTEEN *Victor* [*USA*]. By 1952, this was Perry's seventh million seller disc. It is a great revival of a great song, written in 1898 by James Thornton. The song had been previously featured in *The Great John L*, the biographical film of John L. Sullivan, the former heavyweight boxing champion, produced in 1945 by Bing Crosby. The composer Thornton was Sullivan's favourite drinking companion in earlier days. This song was also a million sheet music seller. The disc was No 2, and 12 weeks in the U.S.A. bestsellers.

FRANCIS CRAIG (piano) AND HIS ORCHESTRA (vocalist: Bob Lamm)
NEAR YOU *Bullet* [*USA*]. The recording of this was made on 29 March 1947 in WSM's studio and piped by telephone line across the street to the Castle Recording Studio in Nashville's old Tulane Hotel. The success of the disc led to the establishment of the first record pressing plant in Nashville.

In 1947, there were no more than six or seven nationally

distributed labels in the U.S.A. and Bullet was probably the first independent label to sell nationally in a big way. There was some resistance to the Bullet version, many buyers refusing to buy it and preferring its availability through one of the major disc companies. It was subsequently re-released on Decca and re-cut for the Dot label.

Francis Craig was born on 10 September 1900 in Dickson, Tennessee, educated at preparatory school in Pulaski, and at Vanderbilt University, Nashville. He wrote the university's official football song 'Dynamite'. After World War I service in the U.S. Army, he organized his own orchestra and played for 21 consecutive years at Nashville's Hermitage Hotel. He was also a staff member of Nashville radio station for 25 years and was on NBC network for 12 years. During his career he introduced many now celebrated artists including Dinah Shore, Kay Armen, Phil Harris and Kitty Kallen.

Craig's recording of 'Near You' came about by pure chance. After he had retired, he approached Jim Bulleit, owner of Bullet, a small independent label, and arranged to record his own orchestral theme tune 'Red Rose'. Bulleit told him that another song would be required for the reverse side of the disc, this being a phase of the disc industry then in its early stages in Nashville. Craig selected his 'Near You' for which words had been written by Kermit Goell. With his hastily regrouped orchestra providing the accompaniment to his piano playing and with Bob Lamm providing the vocals, it became an instant hit. The disc was the top seller of 1947, No 1 for 12 weeks in the U.S.A., and 21 weeks in the bestsellers. It was also a big hit for other artists on disc in 1947 including The Andrews Sisters, Larry Green, Elliott Lawrence and Alvino Rey, with many recordings by other artists through the years. It is now considered to be a standard song, and is still Milton Berle's signature tune after many years.

This disc sold around 2½ million, putting both the composer and his band in the limelight, and enhancing the fortunes of the manufacturer. Craig's follow-up disc 'Beg Your Pardon', also composed by him, was another prodigious singles hit in 1948 and may well have also sold a million.

Francis Craig died on 19 November 1966 in Sewanee, Tennessee.

BING CROSBY
MERRY CHRISTMAS (album) *Decca* [*USA*]. Since Bing first immortalized Irving Berlin's 'White Christmas' in the film *Holiday Inn* (1942), this album (the only one to include his original recording) has been taken for granted by the record-buying public ever since it was put out in 1947, then on 78 rpms. With the introduction of the new speeds in 1948, it was inevitable that it would be transferred to the new albums, Decca doing so on a 10-inch disc in 1954 which sold half a million by 1956. This was later extended to a 12-inch album (1963) with some additional titles. The combined sales of the disc in its various forms make it not only the No 1 seller in the Decca catalogue, but, according to Sid Goldberg, a vice president, the number one seller in the record industry's history. It is still a big seller every Christmas. The original album contained the following:

'Silent Night' (a & d), by Joseph Mohr and Franz Gruber (1818); 'Adeste Fideles' (a & d), traditional, from the Latin; 'White Christmas' (b & d), by Irving Berlin (1942); 'God Rest Ye Merry, Gentlemen' (a & d), traditional (16th century); 'I'll Be Home for Christmas' (d), by Kim Gannon, Walter Kent and Buck Ram (1943); 'Faith of Our Fathers' (a & d), traditional; 'Jingle Bells' (c & e), by J. S. Pierpont (*circa* 1850); 'Santa Claus Is Comin' to Town' (c & e), by Haven Gillespie and J. Fred Coots (1934); Refrain, Bing Crosby (vocal) with (a) Max Terr's chorus, (b) The Ken Darby Singers, (c) The Andrews Sisters, (d) John Scott Trotter and his orchestra, (e) Vic Schoen and his orchestra.

This disc was Bing's seventeenth million seller.

A belated R.I.A.A. Gold Disc was awarded in 1970 for the 12-inch album of 1963 which had the additional titles of:

'Silver Bells', by Ray Livingston and Jay Evans (1950) (from film *Lemon Drop Kid*); 'It's Beginning to Look a Lot Like Christmas', by Meredith Willson (1951); 'Christmas in Killarney', by John Redmond, James Cavannaugh and Frank Weldon (1950); 'Mele Kalikamaka', by Anderson (Hawaiian song – 'Merry Christmas').

BING CROSBY WITH AL JOLSON WITH MORRIS STOLOFF ORCHESTRA

ALEXANDER'S RAGTIME BAND backed with THE SPANIARD THAT BLIGHTED MY LIFE *Decca* [*USA*]. This million seller disc is unique, being the only one made by these two world-famous artists together. 'Alexander's Ragtime Band', Irving Berlin's song, started off the ragtime craze when written in 1911, and when it was a million sheet music seller. 'The Spaniard that Blighted my Life', also written in 1911, is a British song by that great artist Billy Merson, who originally made it famous. Thus a fifteenth Golden Disc was chalked up for Bing.

Both titles recorded on 25 March 1947 in Los Angeles.

BING CROSBY WITH FRED WARING AND GLEE CLUB

WHIFFENPOOF SONG *Decca* [*USA*]. This was Bing's sixteenth million seller disc, by 1950. The song, 'revised' by Rudy Vallee in 1936, and originally credited to Meade Minnegerode and George S. Pomeroy (words) and Tod B. Galloway (music), was adopted by the Whiffenpoof Society of Yale University in 1909. The tune was probably composed by Guy Scull, a Harvard student in about 1893–94, using the words freely adapted from Rudyard Kipling's poem 'Gentlemen Rankers'. It was mainly a disc by Robert Merrill in 1947 that gave the University song renewed prominence, but Bing's rendering with the Glee Club eventually proved to be the big attraction and so sales rocketed. Recorded in Los Angeles on 5 June 1947, it reached No 7 in the U.S.A.

DORIS DAY WITH BUDDY CLARK

CONFESS backed with LOVE SOMEBODY *Columbia* [*USA*]. This is actually Doris Day's second disc in the million seller bracket; she was previously the vocalist on Les Brown's recording of 'Sentimental Journey' in 1945. Hailing from Cincinnati, she became a singer after a leg injury cancelled her career as a dancer. Doris first sang with Barney Rapp's band, then with Fred Waring, Bob Crosby and Les Brown, and it was her recording with Brown that led to subsequent stardom in films as actress-singer. Buddy Clark took up singing after leaving law school and went on radio in New York, and thereafter joined the staff of Columbia Broadcasting System, resuming recording after World War II. 'Confess' was written by Bennie Benjamin and George Weiss, 'Love Somebody' by Joan Whitney and Alex Kramer. Doris Day (real name Kappelhoff) was born in Cincinnati, Ohio, on 3 April 1924. It was Barney Rapp, a bandleader and owner of a nightclub in Cincinnati, who offered Doris a singing spot but told her something had to be done about her name Kappelhoff. Rapp christened her 'Doris Day' because of her singing 'Day After Day'. Doris, who was unknown except as a danceband singer before 1948, became one of the top female box-office attractions of motion pictures after an appearance at New York's Little Club, when she was summoned to Hollywood for a screen test. Stardom soon followed in *Romance on the High Seas* (British title *It's Magic*) in 1948. Other starring roles included the films *Young Man with a Horn*, *Tea for Two*, *On Moonlight Bay*, *I'll See You in My Dreams*, *Calamity Jane*, *Young at Heart*, *Love Me or Leave Me*, *By the Light of the Silvery Moon*, *The Man Who Knew Too Much*, *Pajama Game* and *Move Over Darling*. Buddy Clark was killed in an air crash in 1949.

'Love Somebody' was No 6, and 24 weeks in the U.S.A. bestsellers. 'Confess' was No 16, and 11 weeks in the U.S.A. bestsellers.

BILLY ECKSTINE

EVERYTHING I HAVE IS YOURS *MGM* [*USA*]. This was Billy's third million seller and his first on the MGM label. He was the second artist MGM signed when the label started in that year. The song was originally written for the 1933 MGM film, *Dancing Lady*, starring Joan Crawford, Clark Gable, Franchot Tone and Fred Astaire, with words by Harold Adamson and music by Burton Lane.

'DUSTY' FLETCHER

OPEN THE DOOR, RICHARD *National* [*USA*]. This absurd song by 'Dusty' Fletcher and John Mason (words), Jack McVea and Don Howell (music) stems from a well-known vaudeville routine performed mainly in Negro theatres in the U.S.A. in the 1930s and 1940s by Dusty Fletcher and John Mason. It became the nuisance song of the year and also had hit recordings by composer Jack McVea, Count Basie and his orchestra, Louis Jordan and his Tympany Five, and The Three Flames.

The song was discovered by Jerry Blaine (then with National Records and later head of Jubilee Records) in California, where McVea's original recording on the Black and White label was getting much public attention and where it was a big local hit. Blaine remembered artist Dusty Fletcher whom he had heard at New York's Paradise Restaurant. They got together and worked on the song for two days. Released in January 1947, the disc eventually sold over a million.

'Dusty' Fletcher was top male vocalist on Race Records on U.S. juke boxes in 1947.

ARTHUR GODFREY

TOO FAT POLKA backed with FOR ME AND MY GAL *Columbia* [*USA*]. This was Godfrey's only million seller disc. He was born on 31 August 1903 in New York; left home at the age of 14 and travelled the U.S.A. as a coalminer, office boy, cab driver and insurance salesman. He entered vaudeville in 1924 as banjoist after four years in the Navy, joined the Coast Guard and entered radio on his discharge in 1930. Godfrey then became a disc jockey, announcer and well-known personality through his 'Arthur Godfrey Talent Scouts' and 'Arthur Godfrey and His Friends' which were broadcast at the same time on radio and TV. 'Too Fat Polka' was written by Ross Maclean and Arthur Richardson. 'For Me and My Gal' by Edgar Leslie and E. Ray Goetz (words) and George W. Mayer (music) is an oldie of 1917, when it was a million sheet music seller. The disc was No 2, and was 16 weeks in the U.S.A. bestsellers.

THE HARMONICATS

PEG O' MY HEART *Mercury* [*USA*], *originally Vitacoustic* [*USA*]. This number, which sold a million by 1950, was the Harmonicats' only million seller. Jerry Murad was born in Turkey and went to the U.S.A. at the age of six. He took up the harmonica in high school. Later he went on tour with a Borrah Minnevitch unit and met Al Fiore. They left the unit in 1944 and with Bob Nes, an amateur harmonicist who was working in a department store in Chicago, formed their trio, and played in Helsing's Vodvil Lounge, Chicago. In 1945 they made a Vitacoustic disc which when exploited on the Mercury label rocketed them to fame. 'Peg O' My Heart' was written in 1913 by Alfred Bryan (words) and Fred Fisher (music), and was a million sheet music seller in that year. This disc was No 1 in the charts for four weeks, and 21 weeks in the U.S.A. bestsellers.

BETTY HUTTON WITH JOE LILLEY ORCHESTRA

I WISH I DIDN'T LOVE YOU SO *Capitol* [*USA*]. Betty Hutton became one of the biggest names in show business, and the 'Blonde Bombshell', born Betty June Thornberg in Battle Creek, Michigan, on 26 February 1921, began singing professionally in her teens. She soon became vocalist with the Vincent Lopez orchestra, Lopez changing her name to Hutton. As the result of a featured spot at Billy Rose's 'Casa Mañana' nightclub in New York and a subsequent vaudeville tour with Lopez, she was cast in the revue *Two for the Show* on Broadway and in 1940 Buddy De Sylva chose her for his smash musical *Panama Hattie*, playing second lead to Ethel Merman. This led to a motion picture contract and her screen debut in *The Fleet's In* for Paramount, where De Sylva was production chief (1942). She exploded into prominence with this film and her famous rendition of the song 'Arthur Murray Taught Me Dancing in a Hurry'. Subsequent films were *Incendiary Blonde, Star Spangled Rhythm, Happy Go Lucky, And the Angels Sing, Here Comes the Waves, Duffy's Tavern, The Stork Club, The Perils of Pauline, Annie Get Your Gun, Let's Dance, The Greatest Show on Earth, Somebody Loves Me*. Betty also appeared with great success as a vaudeville headliner at the London Palladium and the Palace in New York.

When Buddy De Sylva started Capitol Records he brought her there to record where she had a big hit with 'Doctor, Lawyer, Indian Chief' from the film *The Stork Club* (1945) followed by this disc of 'I Wish I Didn't Love You So' from the film *The Perils of Pauline* (1947). This sold a million around the world. The disc reached No 6 in the U.S.A.

The song was written by author/composer Frank Loesser. It was also a very big hit in the U.S.A. on disc for Dinah Shore.

MAHALIA JACKSON (gospel singer)

MOVE ON UP A LITTLE HIGHER *Apollo* [*USA*]. Mahalia Jackson, 'Queen of the Gospel Singers', was born in New Orleans, Louisiana, on 26 October 1911. She was a church singer by the time she was five years of age, singing in her father's church. Taken by her parents to Chicago when 16, she worked as a maid, nurse and laundress, and sang in the churches there. In Chicago she was offered a job with the Earl Hines band which she refused on religious grounds and joined instead the Greater Salem Baptist Church choir. The choirmaster immediately formed a gospel quintet featuring Mahalia and sent them on tours to various churches. She still worked, saved and opened a beauty salon, later a flower shop, and then branched into real estate. She recorded her first gospel songs in 1935 and by 1949 her fame in coloured religious circles spread with enormous success not only in the U.S.A. but throughout the world. Mahalia said she would never sing with jazz musicians but, after a meeting with Duke Ellington, Duke persuaded her to sing part of his 'Black and Beige' suite, and a moving version of the 23rd Psalm.

She also recorded with the Percy Faith orchestra, and toured Europe in 1952. An extended European tour in 1961, which also took in Israel, was enormously successful. Her singing was inspired by the great blues singer Bessie Smith. Mahalia had a deep voice with perfect control and astounding inflexions. This disc of 'Move On Up a Little Higher', a gospel song, was recorded for a small disc company in the U.S.A. in 1947 and subsequently sold two million.

Mahalia made a tremendous impact with her singing of 'The Lord's Prayer' at the close of the prize-winning film, *Jazz on a Summer's Day* (1960).

She died on 27 January 1972.

GORDON JENKINS AND HIS ORCHESTRA WITH CHARLES LA VERE (vocal) AND CHORUS

MAYBE YOU'LL BE THERE *Decca* [*USA*]. This was a first million seller for Jenkins. He was born in Webster Groves, Missouri, 12 May 1910. A multi-instrumentalist, he decided to turn arranger while playing on a St Louis radio station. He then conducted the band for *The Show Is On* on Broadway (1936) and was hired by the late Isham Jones as pianist and arranger. His work was used by Paul Whiteman, Vincent Lopez, and Andre Kostelanetz, and for a time in films. Jenkins signed with Decca in 1945 and was later made managing director. He has backed many artists including Patti Andrews and Louis Armstrong.

'Maybe You'll Be There' was written by Sammy Gallop (words) and Rube Bloom (music). This disc was No 3, and 30 weeks in the U.S.A. bestsellers.

FRANKIE LAINE

THAT'S MY DESIRE *Mercury* [*USA*]. This was the first of several million sellers for Frankie, who began singing with a four-piece band. In 1937 he replaced Perry Como as vocalist with Freddy Carlone's band, but left to become a solo artist, entering radio as a staff singer in New York. Laine built up his act with pianist Carl Fischer's aid after World War II and attracted attention in a Hollywood nightclub. Soon he became both a theatre and disc star. This recording brought both Mercury Records and Frankie Lane commercial success. The song was written in 1931 by Carroll Loveday (words) and Helmy Kresa (music). Frankie Laine was born on 30 March 1913. His real name is Frank Lo Vecchio. He sold nearly 100 million discs by 1969, and has 14 Gold Disc awards. This disc was No 7 in the U.S.A. charts.

GUY LOMBARDO AND HIS ROYAL CANADIANS WITH DON RODNEY (vocal)

EASTER PARADE *Decca* [*USA*]. This number was subsequently Guy's third million seller disc; thus he emulated Harry James' similar achievement of 1940. This Irving Berlin song - a hit of 1933 - was also a million seller in sheet music.

ART LUND

MAM'SELLE *MGM* [*USA*]. This number furnished Lund's only million seller. He was a teacher of mathematics at a high school in Kentucky, and sang with local bands as a sideline before giving up school teaching to tour with Jimmy Jay's orchestra. Lund was subsequently signed for Benny Goodman's pre-war band. He rejoined Goodman after a stint in the U.S. Navy in 1946 and then left to go solo, since then appearing on radio and TV. This song was written for the film *The Razor's Edge* by Mack Gordon (words) and Edmund Goulding (music). Goulding, a prominent movie director, born in Britain, wrote it on a sudden inspiration. He was one of the first to write songs in the early talkie days. The disc became a million seller by 1952. Lund was born in Salt Lake City, Utah. This disc was a No 1 chart seller for two weeks, and was 11 weeks in the U.S.A. bestsellers.

GORDON MACRAE WITH PAUL WESTON AND HIS ORCHESTRA

I STILL GET JEALOUS *Capitol* [*USA*]. Originally introduced by Nanette Fabray and Jack McCauley in the Broadway musical *High Button Shoes* in 1947, this song was written by Sammy Cahn (words) and Jule Styne (music).

Gordon MacRae's version was immensely popular in both the U.S.A. and Britain and sold an estimated global million.

VAUGHN MONROE AND HIS BAND

BALLERINA (Dance, Ballerina, Dance) *Victor* [*USA*]. By 1948 this title became Monroe's third disc to sell a million. Written by Bob Russell (words) and Carl Sigman (music), the disc was a No 1 seller for 10 weeks in U.S.A. in 1948, and 21 weeks in the bestsellers.

ART MOONEY AND HIS ORCHESTRA FEATURING MIKE PINGATORE (banjo)

I'M LOOKING OVER A FOUR LEAF CLOVER *MGM* [*USA*]. By 1955 this number provided a first million seller for Mooney. The song was an oldie of 1927 by Mort Dixon (words) and Harry Woods (music), one of the U.S.A.'s great song-writing teams. Mooney was born in Lowell, Massachusetts, and became well known through nightclub, radio, TV and personal appear-

ances. This disc features Mike Pingatore, noted banjoist who played with Paul Whiteman's orchestra where he first started in 1920, and stayed with him for over 25 years. This disc was No 1 seller for three weeks in the U.S.A. during 1948, and 16 weeks in the bestsellers.

MOON MULLICAN

NEW JOLE BLON (New pretty blonde) *King* [*USA*]. This country and western singer's million selling disc was his first and the first for the King label. Aubrey Mullican, born 29 March 1909, hails from Polk County, Texas. The disc, written by Sydney Nathan and Mullican, was a million seller by 1950. Mullican was also a pianist and was on Louisiana Governor Jimmy Davis' staff for four years (1960-63), returning to Nashville in 1964 for professional bookings. He was known as the 'King of Hillbilly Piano Playing'. He died on 1 January 1967.

JACK SMITH WITH THE CLARK SISTERS AND INSTRUMENTAL ACCOMPANIMENT

YOU CALL EVERYBODY DARLING *Capitol* [*USA*]. Written in 1946 by Sam Martin, Ben Trace and Clem Watts (pseudonym of bandleader Al Trace), this song was also a bestseller disc in the U.S.A. for Al Trace and his orchestra. It reached No 13, and was nine weeks in the U.S.A. bestsellers.

Singer Jack Smith made several discs with the Clark Sisters in the early days of Capitol Records and also recorded with Margaret Whiting for the label. This disc is said to have sold a global million.

Jack Smith appeared in the film *By the Light of the Silvery Moon* (1953) with Doris Day and Gordon MacRae.

JO STAFFORD WITH RED INGLE AND THE NATURAL SEVEN

TEMPTATION (Tim-tayshun) *Capitol* [*USA*]. This delightful 'hick' version of the Arthur Freed-Nacio Herb Brown song from the 1933 film *Going Hollywood* was Jo Stafford's first solo million seller, the disc label naming Jo as 'Cinderella G. Stump'. It is a really great hillbilly parody. Jo was born in Coainga, California, and studied voice from early childhood. She formed a trio with her sisters and began singing in a radio series in 1935. She joined the Pied Pipers group (see 1945) in 1937 until 1944 when she left to become solo artist. Since then she has done much radio and record work, and in 1953 began her own TV series. Jo Stafford was winner of a poll in 1943 and 1945 as best singer of those years. She had sold 25 million discs by 1955 for the Columbia label alone, and was presented with a special diamond-studded disc award. This disc reached No 2, and was 13 weeks in the U.S.A. bestsellers.

TED WEEMS AND HIS ORCHESTRA

MICKEY *Mercury* [*USA*]. By 1950 this record produced a fourth million seller for Ted Weems. The song was written in 1918 by Harry Williams (words) and Neil Moret (music) for the film *Mickey* starring Mabel Normand. Weems first recorded it for Decca around 1941-42. It reached No 10 in the U.S.A. charts.

TEX WILLIAMS AND THE WESTERN CARAVAN

SMOKE, SMOKE, SMOKE THAT CIGARETTE *Capitol* [*USA*]. This was the top country-and-western disc of the year and it put Tex well on the map. It was written by Tex Williams with another Capitol singer Merle Travis. Two weeks after its release, Tex was suddenly a nationally prominent entertainer, and it made him known internationally. He made his professional debut at 13 on radio in Decatur, Illinois, then toured the U.S., Canada and Mexico, singing and playing guitar with small hillbilly and western bands. Williams then formed his Western Caravan, a co-operative orchestra successful around southern California for one year before this song was heard. The disc sold over $2\frac{1}{2}$ million, was No 1 for six weeks, and 12 weeks in the U.S.A. bestsellers. Tex was born in Illinois, 23 August 1917.

1948

EDDY ARNOLD AND HIS TENNESSEE PLOWBOYS

BOUQUET OF ROSES backed with TEXARKANA BABY *Victor* [*USA*]. Both titles were No. 1 in the U.S.A. country-and-western charts in 1948. 'Bouquet of Roses' was written by Steve Nelson and Bob Hilliard, 'Texarkana Baby' by Cottonseed Clark and Fred Rose (famous country songwriter/publisher). This disc became a million seller within a year, and firmly established Eddy as one of America's greatest singers of gently flowing country ballads.

ANY TIME *Victor* [*USA*]. Originally written in 1921 by Herbert Happy Lawson, Eddy's revival in this year subsequently sold a million discs. It was a No 1 in the U.S.A. country-and-western charts, instituted by the American journal *Billboard* on 15 May 1948. (See note.) The song was also a million seller later for Eddie Fisher (see 1951).

Note: *Billboard*'s first column was 'Folk Songs and Blues' (January 1944).

JUST A LITTLE LOVIN' WILL GO A LONG, LONG WAY *Victor* [*USA*]. Another big hit for Eddy Arnold, written by him and Zeke Clements, with an estimated million sale through the years. This also was a No 1 in the U.S.A. country-and-western charts in 1948.

NAT 'KING' COLE WITH ORCHESTRA CONDUCTED BY FRANK DE VOL

NATURE BOY *Capitol* [*USA*]. The year 1948 saw Nat 'King' Cole stepping into the front rank of disc personalities. This record was the one that made him internationally famous. Nathaniel 'King' Cole, son of an ordained minister, was born on 17 March 1919 in Montgomery, Alabama, and was educated at public schools, and studied piano in Chicago privately. While in school he organized his own band for local engagements. Nat toured with a band in a revue *Shuffle Along* (1936). He then worked as a pianist in nightclubs. His singing career started by accident in a Hollywood nightclub when an enthusiast insisted that he sing 'Sweet Lorraine'. His free and easy relaxed style was so popular that he had to sing more than he wanted to, so much so that he became a singer accompanying himself on the piano in the mind of the American public. This was Cole's situation in 1937 when he formed his well-known Nat King Cole Trio. In 1940 he recorded 'Sweet Lorraine' for Decca. Nat inserted the extra name 'King' after being given a paper crown, but he did indeed become a king of the jazz and blues circles. The trio became a stage, radio and nightclub attraction, and were signed by Capitol Records in 1943 with subsequent soaring sales. Nat then became a solo artist on the nightclub circuits. In 1958 he was starred in the film *St Louis Blues*, the story of the blind and renowned blues composer, W. C. Handy. Nat's piano style was inspired by Earl Hines, and his singing owed much to Louis Armstrong.

'Nature Boy' was written by 'eden ahbez' (a Brooklyn Yogi who believed that only divinities deserved capital letters). As a youth, he hitchhiked across the U.S.A. eight times and walked across once. The song is said to have been left by him at the stage door of a California theatre where Nat was playing. The disc leapt into immediate and amazing popularity. It enjoyed the No 1 position for seven weeks, stayed 15 weeks in the bestsellers, and was voted an outstanding hit of the year in the U.S.A. and elsewhere. By 1968, Nat's estimated disc sales were 75 million. After a short illness he died on 15 February 1965.

Frank De Vol, composer, conductor, arranger, was born on 20 September 1911 in Moundsville, West Virginia, and was reared in Ohio. He took piano and violin lessons from his father and began studying arranging when only nine, turning out his first complete score at 16. After graduating at Miami University, Oxford, Ohio, in 1929 he led a motion picture theatre pit band, and joined his father's theatre orchestra as saxophonist, arranger and deputy conductor, subsequently joining, in succession, the Emerson Gill orchestra, the George Olsen-Ethel Shutta troupe, Horace Heidt and Alvino Rey. He also worked with Ben Bernie and Rudy Vallee. In 1940 he returned to Heidt as chief arranger and conductor, then left music for an aircraft job during the war. Thereafter came two years as managing director at KHJ, Los Angeles, and his own network show, 'Musical Depreciation', and eventually writing and conducting for Capitol Records. He provided accompaniments for Margaret Whiting, Jack Smith, Kay Starr and Nat 'King' Cole, one of his most outstanding being the distinctive orchestral background for this disc of 'Nature Boy'. De Vol has also written many background scores for films, notably *The Big Knife*, *Send Me No Flowers*, *Hush ... Hush, Sweet Charlotte*, *Flight of the Phoenix*, *Cat Ballou*, *The Glass Bottom Boat*, and *Guess Who's Coming to Dinner?*

NAT 'KING' COLE TRIO

LITTLE GIRL *Capitol* [*USA*]. 'Little Girl' was first written in 1931 by Madeline Hyde and Francis Henry and originally introduced and popularized by Guy Lombardo and his Royal Canadians. Nat is the vocalist on this disc, and it was a big success in Britain and elsewhere in Europe, selling a subsequent global million.

Composer Henry was guitarist with Lombardo for 21 years and also played with the Ray Miller and Isham Jones orchestras.

PERRY COMO WITH THE RUSS CASE ORCHESTRA

BECAUSE *Victor* [*USA*]. By 1951 'Because' became Perry's eighth million seller. The song is by the British writers Edward Teschemaker (words) and Guy d'Hardelot (music), being the respective pseudonyms of Edward Lockton and Mrs W. I. Rhodes. This world-famous ballad was written in 1902. The disc reached No 4, and was 18 weeks in the U.S.A. bestsellers.

COWBOY COPAS

TENNESSEE WALTZ *King* [*USA*]. Country-and-western artist Lloyd T. Copas was born 15 July 1913, and reared in and around Muskogee, Oklahoma, and spent his childhood on a small ranch. He learned to play his mother's guitar at an early age and was taught to sing by his father. At the age of 11, he won second prize in a radio amateur contest in Tulsa. His family moved to Ohio, and Copas began to play and sing at square dances and local affairs. At 14, he began to appear at country fairs, since when he has appeared in person at over 200 radio stations, and travelled across the U.S.A., Canada and Mexico doing personal appearances. In 1946, he joined the 'Grand Ole Opry', which proved to be the turning point of his career. Thereafter his personal appearances tripled. During the 1940s and 1950s he had a succession of hits on the King label, and switched in 1959 to the Starday label. He was killed in an air crash on 5 March 1963, with Patsy Cline and her manager and Hawkshaw Hawkins, another artist, when returning to Nashville from Kansas City after a benefit performance. 'Tennessee Waltz' was also a million seller in sheet music by 1950. It was made an official state song of Tennessee in 1965, and has sold over 10 million discs. It was written by Pee Wee King and Redd Stewart.

SIGNED, SEALED AND DELIVERED *King* [*USA*]. Cowboy Copas' second million seller was written in 1947 by Copas himself and Lois Mann. This number enjoyed a revival in 1962.

BING CROSBY WITH THE KEN DARBY CHOIR

NOW IS THE HOUR *Decca* [*USA*]. This is Bing's eighteenth million seller disc, either solo or with other artists. The song is unusual in that its range is only six notes, and its origin is Maori. Written in 1913 by Maewa Kaihau (words) and Clement Scott (music), it became a popular New Zealand song, adopted by the Maoris as a farewell song to visitors, under its original title 'Haere Ra'. Words for the English version were written by Dorothy Stewart of the U.S.A., who also gave it the title 'Now is the Hour'. First recorded in Britain by Gracie Fields, it became a big seller so 24,000 were shipped to the U.S.A., the biggest shipment of foreign discs ever imported. But it was finally the Crosby disc that predominated in the U.S.A. This song was also a million sheet music seller. Recorded in Los Angeles on 8 November 1947, it reached No 2, and was 23 weeks in the U.S.A. bestsellers.

BING CROSBY WITH ORCHESTRA DIRECTED BY VICTOR YOUNG

GALWAY BAY *Decca* [*USA*]. This song written in 1926 by Dr Arthur Colahan, a prominent British neurological specialist, became Bing's nineteenth million seller disc. Dr Colahan was shooting snipe in western Ireland that year when he saw people nearby digging 'praties'. Then he realized they did not understand one word of English, hence the line 'the strangers came and tried to teach us their ways'. The doctor was never impressed by his song's success. He was too busy with his medical work and regarded the composing of songs as only a hobby. Recorded in Los Angeles on 27 November 1947, it reached No 3, and was 17 weeks in the U.S.A. bestsellers.

DORIS DAY WITH ORCHESTRA DIRECTED BY GEORGE SIRAVO

IT'S MAGIC *Columbia* [*USA*]. This song is the hit from Doris Day's first film *Romance on the High Seas* and made her an internationally known singer-actress star. It provided her with her third million seller and a second million seller for writers Sammy Cahn (words) and Jule Styne (music). The disc was No 2, and 21 weeks in the U.S.A. bestsellers.

THE DINNING SISTERS (vocal trio) WITH ART VAN DAMME ORCHESTRA

BUTTONS AND BOWS *Capitol* [*USA*]. This popular trio consisted of three sisters - Lou Dinning, born in Kentucky, 29 September 1922, and twins Ginger Dinning and Jean Dinning, born in Braman, Oklahoma, on 29 March 1924. These three, of a family of nine, were discovered to have perfect pitch at the age of three and sang together from the age of five.

They started their career at a very early stage in their lives with bandleader Herbie Holmes in 1935, and toured the Middlewest singing at clubs and theatres. They arrived in Chicago completely unknown in 1939 and after a radio audition were a hit. For six years they were featured in regular coast-to-coast broadcasts.

This disc achieved Top 10 status in the U.S.A. and is said to have sold a million internationally.

The song was written by Jay Livingston and Ray Evans for the Bob Hope-Jane Russell film *The Paleface* and won an Oscar for the writers for Best Film Song of the year.

Art Van Damme was born on 9 April 1920 in Norway, Michigan, and was reared in Chicago. He studied piano and accordion with Pines Caviani in Iron Mountain, Michigan, and accordion with Andy Rizzo in Chicago, then joined Ben Bernie in 1941. After playing with local orchestras, etc. in Chicago he became an NBC staff musician there in 1944, and continued in this capacity for a long period and playing on star TV shows. The disc was No 7, and 16 weeks in the U.S.A. bestsellers.

FATS DOMINO (beat vocalist and pianist)

THE FAT MAN *Imperial* [*USA*]. Here was the first of New Orleans rhythm-and-blues pianist-singer Fats (Antoine) Dom-

ino's many million seller discs. The Fat Man in the number is Domino himself, who weighs 16 stone (224 lb). The song was jointly written by Dave Bartholomew of Imperial Records (who first spotted Domino) and Fats himself. He started playing the piano at the age of 10 and eventually performed at a local roadhouse. The news of his sensational act reached the president of Imperial Records. Domino's collaboration with Bartholomew on material for recordings proved to be one of the most formidable and consistently successful composing partnerships the 'beat era' has ever known. Estimates of Fats Domino's disc sales to date are over 60 million. Apart from recording, he appeared in nightclubs, films and at concerts. He climbed to nationwide fame in 1956–57 and earned the title of Rhythm-and-Blues personality of the year. Most of the numbers he recorded are his own composition. This disc sold a million by 1953. Fats was born on 26 February 1928 in New Orleans.

BILLY ECKSTINE

BLUE MOON *MGM* [*USA*]. This fourth million seller for Billy was written in 1934 by lyricist Lorenz Hart and composed by Richard Rodgers.

'Blue Moon' was originally written in 1934 with a different lyric under the title of 'Prayer' and sung in an unproduced film *Hollywood Revue of 1933* by Jean Harlow. A second lyric under the title 'The Bad in Every Man' was sung by Shirley Ross to the tune in the film *Manhattan Melodrama*. With the third and final lyric of 'Blue Moon' title, it became the only successful Rodgers and Hart song not associated with the stage, films or TV.

BENNY GOODMAN AND HIS ORCHESTRA (Al Hendrickson – vocalist)

ON A SLOW BOAT TO CHINA *Capitol* [*USA*]. Benny Goodman, the 'King of Swing', was born in Chicago on 30 May 1909, the twelfth child of Russian parents. His father was a hard-working tailor in a sweat shop on the West Side of the city and found it hard to provide for his large family. As a youngster, Benny showed unusual ability on the harmonica, and became attracted to the clarinet when he was six. When Benny was nine, his father learned of a synagogue that loaned instruments to youngsters and charged 25 cents for a lesson. Benny learned the rudiments of clarinet playing from Boguslawski, leader of the synagogue band. His father heard about a boys' band being started at Hull House and that they were handing out new instruments and uniforms to suitable applicants. Benny passed the audition and continued with his studies and at 13 played with local bands. His introduction to jazz came through chancing

commencing with Ben Pollack's band in 1926. He enjoyed great commercial success particularly between 1936 and 1942 with his Trio, Quartet, Sextet and Big Band. His Quartet included Teddy Wilson on piano, the extraordinary Lionel Hampton on vibraphone and Gene Krupa on drums, and his Sextet the great guitarist Charlie Christian, Cootie Williams on trumpet, and Count Basie on piano for a while when Basie gave up his own band. He also had wonderful coloured arrangers including Fletcher Henderson on 'When Buddha Smiles', 'Blue Skies' and 'Sometimes I'm Happy' (1935); also Jimmy Mundy, Mary Lou Williams and Edgar Sampson. Most of the great jazz instrumentalists have played with his band, and became famous bandleaders themselves.

Goodman played the London Palladium in the early 1950s, and a film *The Benny Goodman Story* (with Steve Allen as Benny) was released in 1956. In 1962 he played to an ecstatic audience in Leningrad.

There are few more astonishing episodes in the entire history of the popular art of our century than the career of Chicago clarinettist Benny Goodman, pioneer of the great dance orchestras of the Swing Age.

His recording of 'On a Slow Boat to China' (written by U.S. composer Frank Loesser) is said to have sold a global million by 1949. It reached the Top Ten in the U.S.A. charts in that year, and was 12 weeks in the bestsellers. It is, however, probable that some of his earlier jazz discs such as those mentioned above plus his sextet recordings of 'Star Dust' (1939), 'Royal Garden Blues' (1940) and 'I Found a New Baby' (1941) have also accumulated a million global sale each over the years.

Benny Goodman holds an all-time record of 27 awards in *Down Beat*'s annual readers poll – Top Swing Band: 1936, 1937, 1938, 1939, 1940, 1941 and 1943 – Top or Favourite Soloist: 1936, 1937, 1938, 1939, 1940, 1941, 1943, 1944, 1945, 1946, 1947 and 1949 – Top Clarinettist: 1937, 1938 and 1939 – Top Quartet: 1928 and Top Small Combo: 1939, 1940, 1941 and 1942; indeed 'The King of Swing'.

BUDDY GRECO (beat vocalist and pianist)

OOH LOOK-A THERE, AIN'T SHE PRETTY *Musicraft* [*USA*]. This title provides Buddy's only reputed million seller disc so far known. He says he got just $30 for making it. Soon after making this disc he received an invitation to join Benny Goodman's band (1949-51) as featured singer and pianist. He then launched out solo, making discs and appearing on TV. Greco, a brilliant pianist and stylish songster, became one of America's most sought-after night-club entertainers. The song was written in 1933 by Clarence Todd and Carmen Lombardo.

upon a record by Ted Lewis. He then heard that Central Park Theatre had started 'Jazz Nights' and decided to join in. A little later the manager sent for Benny to fill in when one of the acts folded and he received five precious dollars, the first money he ever earned.

Benny then studied for two years with Franz Schoepp, who once taught at the Chicago Musical College, and this laid the foundation for a legitimate technique. At 16, Benny was engaged by Ben Pollack with whom he stayed for three years, leaving in 1929 after a New York engagement. He next played with Arnold Johnson and Red Nichols, and later became a radio studio musician in New York. Mad about swing music, he decided in 1934 to form his own orchestra and their debut took place at Billy Rose's Music Hall on Broadway. He received the booking there because his band promised to be a musical phenomenon. Their swing music certainly astonished everybody but proved no sensational success at the beginning. The band then played at the Roosevelt Hotel where Guy Lombardo had been popular with his 'sweetest music this side of heaven'. Benny's intricate and bizarre hot choruses did not please the hotel's sedate clientele. This was disappointing to a band which had come to national attention through the radio's 'Let's Dance' show.

Following a coast-to-coast tour, Benny's band finally became a sensation at Los Angeles Palomar Ballroom where they opened on 21 August 1935, and again on 6 November at the Congress Hotel, Chicago, where their four weeks' booking kept being extended. They were now a national craze. Business increased, their records were selling well, and *Metronome* nominated them the best band of 1935. Their appearance at New York's Pennsylvania Hotel was yet another step up the ladder to fame, and thousands acclaimed Benny playing his clarinet. An appearance in the film *Big Broadcast of 1937* introduced the band to a wider public and when they opened at the Paramount Theatre, New York, in March 1937, practically everyone was Goodman-conscious. 21,000 people paid to hear them on the first day. Benny holds the distinction of having played the first jazz concert at Chicago's Congress Hall in 1935 and of playing the first ever jazz concert at New York's Carnegie Hall, on 16 January 1938.

He played everything – films, radio, one-night stands, hotels, theatres and his records sold millions, a conservative estimate being 50 million internationally. He recorded on many labels,

Buddy was born 14 August 1927 in Philadelphia, and made his first radio appearance at four years of age. He has had many years on radio as both actor and singer.

KEN GRIFFIN (organ) AND JERRY WAYNE (vocalist)

YOU CAN'T BE TRUE, DEAR *Rondo* [*USA*]. The circumstances of this recording are unique. Organist Ken Griffin made the disc for the Rondo label some time earlier than 1948, primarily as music to accompany iceskaters in the public rinks. It attracted considerable attention from the skaters and was brought to the notice of songwriter/publisher Dave Dreyer of New York. Dreyer was aware that the tune could not be successful for him without a vocal, so he got Jerry Wayne (a Hollywood film actor and later star of the London production of *Guys and Dolls*) to dub a lyric on to the Griffin disc. The words were literally written while the singer waited to do the recording. In the studio, Wayne was fitted with headphones into which was fed the organ solo, and he tried for some time to match the words with the tune. Although the original recording made no provision for a vocal and there was no break in the melody to allow a voice to slip in, in addition to which it was in the wrong key for Wayne, the dubbing was finalized to everyone's satisfaction. The resultant disc is probably the first big success for a recording made by the superimposition of voice on to an already existent recording. It is said to have sold around 3 million, and was one of the top sellers of 1948.

The song was originally written in 1935 in Germany – 'Du kannst nicht treu sein' – words by Gerhard Ebeler and music by Hans Otten. The English words were by Hal Cotton with the musical adaptation by Ken Griffin from Otten's original tune. The disc was No 2, and 22 weeks in the U.S.A. bestsellers.

The song was also a hit for Dick Haymes in the U.S.A. and for Vera Lynn in Britain.

DICK HAYMES WITH FOUR HITS AND A MISS, GORDON JENKINS AND ORCHESTRA

LITTLE WHITE LIES *Decca* [*USA*]. This song, written in 1930 by ace songwriter Walter Donaldson, gave Haymes his second million seller. After his first hit disc in 1943, Dick went into radio and films (1944). In 1955 he formed a production company with Rita Hayworth. This disc became a million seller within the year. It was No. 3, and 23 weeks in the U.S.A. bestsellers.

JOHN LEE HOOKER

I'M IN THE MOOD *Modern* [*USA*]. This disc sold nearly a million in the first rush after issue. It established the artist in the blues circles in the U.S.A. Hooker, who wrote the number with Jules Taub, was born in Clarksdale, Mississippi, on 22 August 1917 and learned to play the guitar under his grandfather's tuition. He decided that a settled life on the Mississippi farm was not for him and wandered around as a hobo for nearly 14 years on the road. He got his first chance to perform professionally at the Monte Carlo in Detroit where he was spotted by a talent scout who signed him up. 'I'm in the Mood' was one of his first discs. He made his debut on TV in Detroit in 1949, and his radio debut as a disc jockey in 1952. In that year he signed an exclusive contract with the newly formed Vee Jay Record Co. He has since made many discs of blues folklore material and several albums.

Hooker integrated many of his own songs into the stricter blues repertoire and became even better known when his discs were released in Britain from 1962. He made personal appearances in Britain in 1964. Both this disc and 'Boogie Chillun' (below) were originally 'taped' for the small Sensation Record Co. in Detroit in 1948. 'I'm in the Mood' was a hit in 1951.

BOOGIE CHILLUN *Modern* [*USA*]. This second million seller for John Lee Hooker was a disc which still further enhanced his reputation as a remarkable rhythm-and-blues artist. The song was written by Hooker himself.

PEE WEE HUNT AND HIS ORCHESTRA

TWELFTH STREET RAG *Capitol* [*USA*]. After being around for a long time, this massive hit provided Pee Wee with his first million seller. He began playing trombone in Jean Goldkette's great band of the middle twenties. In 1928, with other Goldkette men, Glen Gray included, Hunt formed the memorable Casa Loma aggregation, with himself in the triple role of trombonist, vocalist and vice-president for 16 years. He then served in the Merchant Marine during the war, after which he reorganized his combination with bookings in Los Angeles and a long period at the Hollywood Palladium (33 weeks), returning a month later for a further 23 weeks. It was here that his small Dixieland intermission orchestra in 1947 played their loose-limbed arrangement of '12th Street Rag' which got a big hand from the crowd. Hunt decided to wax it on one of his Capitol recording dates. What happened was phenomenal. This number became one of the biggest records Capitol had had. The tune was written by Euday L. Bowman in 1914, with lyrics by two or three different writers in later years. This disc sold its million by 1951, and was No. 1 seller for 8 weeks in the U.S.A. in 1948, and 32 weeks in the bestsellers. Pee Wee was born in Mount Healthy, Ohio, 1907 and died in Plymouth, Mass., on 22 June 1979.

RED INGLE (vocal) AND THE NATURAL SEVEN WITH THE MIGHT AND MAIN STREET CHORAL SOCIETY

CIGAREETS, WHUSKY AND WILD, WILD WOMEN *Capitol* [*USA*]. This unique comedy song was first introduced by the very popular Sons of the Pioneers in 1947 and was written by Tim Spencer, one of its members.

Red Ingle, born Ernest Jansen Ingle in Toledo, Ohio, in 1906, played the violin at the age of seven and in his teens joined Paul Whiteman's Kentucky Kernels. He subsequently played both violin and saxophone with the Jean Goldkette and Ted Weems orchestras.

His own band of musical jesters made adaptations and played burlesque versions of popular tunes with more effect than anyone else in show business. He put this one over with great gusto and it is in fact a riot. This disc, together with his previous hit 'Timtayshun' (1947), brought him great prominence and an eventual trip to Britain where he was a big success in the music halls.

The disc was popular on both sides of the Atlantic and sold a million internationally.

LONNIE JOHNSON (jazz guitar)

TOMORROW NIGHT *King* [*USA*]. Lonnie Johnson, blues singer and jazz guitarist, hit a million sales for this number by 1950 and three million through the years. Born in New Orleans on 8 February 1900, Johnson first learned to play violin, then guitar. With his brother James (pianist, violinist), he played in New Orleans from 1919 to 1921 and from 1925 to 1926 in Charlie Creath's band on the riverboats from St Louis. Here he won a blues contest and was given a contract by Okeh Records, making several discs which gave him prominence. From 1927 to 1930, Johnson went to New York and Chicago in the great jazz days and recorded with such famous bands as Louis Armstrong, The Chocolate Dandies, Duke Ellington, The Cotton Pickers and others. He gave up music after the 1929 financial crash and worked in a tyre factory and steel foundry, returning some years later to play with small bands such as Lil Armstrong's, Johnny Dodds', and Jimmie Noone's. He then worked mainly as a soloist in nightclubs from 1937 and made a large number of discs. Lonnie Johnson visited England in 1952 and again in 1963. His New Orleans style, beautiful tone, remarkable technique and brilliant phrasing stamp him as one of the great guitarists of jazz.

'Tomorrow Night' was written in 1939 by Sam Coslow (words) and Will Grosz (music). Lonnie died on 17 June 1970 in Toronto, Canada.

SPIKE JONES AND HIS CITY SLICKERS

ALL I WANT FOR CHRISTMAS (is my two front teeth) *Victor* [*USA*]. The comedy team achieved its fourth million seller with this title by 1949. The disc was a number one seller for one week in the U.S.A. in 1948. The song was written by Don Gardner.

EVELYN KNIGHT WITH THE STAR DUSTERS (vocalists)

A LITTLE BIRD TOLD ME *Decca* [*USA*]. This disc was Evelyn's only million seller, and was number one seller for seven weeks in the U.S.A., and 21 weeks in the U.S.A. bestsellers. She hails from Washington, D.C. and turned professional by singing on a local radio show. She made her first club appearance at the King Cole Room, Washington, and, since then, many nightclub appearances and recordings. The song is by Harvey O. Brooks, who was the first Negro to write a complete film score (for Mae West's *I'm No Angel*, 1933).

KAY KYSER AND HIS ORCHESTRA

WOODY WOODPECKER SONG *Columbia* [*USA*]. This sixth million seller for Kay Kyser was a number one seller for six weeks in the U.S.A., and was 15 weeks in the bestsellers. It became almost a disease with its infectious 'ha ha ha ha ha' phrase. The song was written by George Tibbles, author of much material for big stars, and Ramez Idriss, TV scriptwriter and instrumentalist. This disc sold a million by 1949.

(vocals – Harry Babbitt and Gloria Wood)

ON A SLOW BOAT TO CHINA *Columbia* [*USA*]. Kay Kyser's seventh million seller was an extremely original song by ace songwriter Frank Loesser. Its extreme popularity was reflected by a million sales within the year. The disc was No 2, and 19 weeks in the U.S.A. bestsellers.

FRANKIE LAINE WITH CARL FISCHER'S ORCHESTRA

SHINE *Mercury* [*USA*]. This revival of a great 'pop' song by Cecil Mack and Lew Brown (words) and Ford Dabney (music) written in 1924 furnished Frankie Laine with his second million seller. 'Shine' was also a million seller in sheet music in 1924. The disc was No 12 in the U.S.A. charts.

WHEN YOU'RE SMILING *Mercury* [*USA*]. Written in 1928 by Mark Fisher, Joe Goodwin and Larry Shay, this very popular song was first recorded in New York on 11 September 1929 by the great Louis Armstrong who made it famous.

Frankie Laine's recording made it a hit again in 1948, and it was sung by him in the film of the same title in 1950. Through the years it became a million seller, his 14th in this category.

Frankie kept smiling during the depression years by entering dance marathon contests - and holds the all-time world's record of 3501 hours, established in Atlantic City, New Jersey, in 1932. (See 1947 for Frankie Laine biography.)

PEGGY LEE WITH DAVE BARBOUR AND THE BRAZILIANS

MAÑANA *Capitol* [*USA*]. Peggy Lee broke into show business as vocalist in a Hollywood nightclub, eventually joining Will Osborne's band. 'Mañana' was her first seven-figure seller. Benny Goodman heard her in Chicago and signed her in 1941 and so brought her into prominence. She made her first disc with the band on 15 August 1941. She retired temporarily in 1943, but later resumed her career via records. Following the success of 'Mañana', she became a disc and nightclub star. Miss Lee made her screen debut in *Mr Music* with Bing Crosby and was a sensation in *Pete Kelly's Blues* (1955). She wrote 'Mañana' in collaboration with Dave Barbour (guitarist, arranger, conductor for the recording company) who accompanies her on this disc, one of Capitol's biggest hits. Peggy was born on 26 May 1920 in Jamestown, North Dakota. Her real name is Norma Engstrom. This disc was the No 1 seller for nine weeks in the U.S.A., and 21 weeks in the bestsellers.

NELLIE LUTCHER (vocalist and pianist)

HURRY ON DOWN backed with FINE BROWN FRAME *Capitol* [*USA*]. Nellie Lutcher, born 15 October 1915 in Lake Charles, Louisiana, is the eldest of ten children. She was musical at a very early age and learned the organ from her mother (a church organist) and musical theory from her father, one of the best-known bass players in the South. At school she took up the mandolin and guitar, as well as piano. A promising pianist at 14, she played in her father's dance band and later joined Clarence Hart's Imperial Orchestra as pianist, staying with them for six years. Then, with the Southern Rhythm Boys, she did her first professional singing. In 1935 she moved to Hollywood, playing in small clubs as a solo artiste and heading her own small groups, for around 12 years. It was not until 1947 that her big break came. In this year she volunteered to entertain in a March of Dimes Benefit in Los Angeles and it was this that brought her to the attention of Nat 'King' Cole who introduced her to Dave Dexter, prominent executive of Capitol Records. Dave arranged for her first recording session in which Nellie delivered these two songs. Her distinctive voice, 'hep' wording of her jazz idiom and punchy piano style got the disc into the U.S.A. Top 10, and within six months her records sold a million copies. Her unique singing style led to her first major engagement as the 'Real Gone Gal' (after her recording of 'He's a Real Gone Guy', a self-penned song) at Café Society Downtown in New York where she took the crowd by storm. A successful Broadway appearance followed, then a coast-to-coast theatre and nightclub tour, also a tour of Europe and Britain where she became an international favourite.

This disc was immensely popular in Britain where it was introduced over the radio by disc jockey Jack Jackson. It sold a global million.

'Hurry On Down', written by Nellie herself in 1947, catapulted the husky-voiced Negro jazz singer/pianist to fame. The backing 'Fine Brown Frame' was written by Guadalupe Cartiere and J. Mayo Williams in 1944.

THE MILLS BROTHERS

LAZY RIVER *Decca* [*USA*]. Originally written by Sidney Arodin (words) and the great Hoagy Carmichael (music) in 1931, this song had a revival in the 1946 film *The Best Years of Our Lives* in which the composer both acted and sang the song. The Mills Brothers' disc issued soon after also gave the song, now a standard, renewed prominence, and is said to have sold over a million, the group's fourth.

ART MOONEY AND HIS ORCHESTRA

BABY FACE *MGM* [*USA*]. This song is an oldie million seller sheet music hit of 1926, written by two of America's great writers, Benny Davis and Harry Akst. Its renewed popularity gave Art Mooney his second million seller seven years after issue. The disc was No 5, and 14 weeks in the U.S.A. bestsellers.

BLUEBIRD OF HAPPINESS *MGM* [*USA*]. This third million seller for Art Mooney was written in 1934 by Edward Heyman (words) and Sandor Harmati (music). It had already proved a hit in Britain in 1940 when both words and music were revised by Harry Parr Davies. This disc was No 9, and 22 weeks in the U.S.A. bestsellers.

EDWARD R. MURROW, K.B.E.(hon.) (radio news correspondent)

I CAN HEAR IT NOW (album of 78 rpm discs) *Columbia* [*USA*]. Goddard Lieberson, President of Columbia Records, claimed that this was the top-selling spoken-word album, and that it sold over a million as a *single-record* album. This comprised some of the famous Ed R. Murrow's pre-war broadcasts. Murrow was born in 1904 in Greensboro, North Carolina, and graduated from Washington State University in 1930, having majored in political science, speech and international relations. For two years he was a compassman and topographer for timber cruises in north-west Washington, British Columbia and Alaska. From 1930 to 1932 he visited over 300 American colleges and universities, and travelled extensively in Europe and arranged the first international debates between U.S. and European universities. In 1935 his talents as a public speaker earned him his first post with CBS as a director of Columbia's Department of Talks and Special Events. He was sent to England as Columbia's sole European representative in 1937, and in 1938 flew to Vienna, arriving there in time to describe the invasion of Austria by German troops. He was also on hand to tell of the end of democratic Czechoslovakia in 1939. It was, however, his graphic descriptions night after night on the roof of Britain's BBC building of the flaming air raids which he relayed to American listeners, in spite of the danger, that made him one of the greatest news reporters of our time, and one of the most famous broadcasters known to Britain, and in his own country. His own book *This is London* appeared in 1941 and showed, as one critic stated, 'almost poetic insight into the feeling of the war-stricken British'. He was made an Honorary Knight Commander of the Order of the British Empire in 1965. Murrow died on 27 April 1965.

THE PIED PIPERS
(with instrumental accompaniment)
MY HAPPINESS *Capitol* [*USA*]. The second big hit for the Pied Pipers, the disc getting into the U.S.A. Top Ten. It is said to have sold a million globally.

The song, written by Betty Peterson (words) and Borney Bergantine (music), was also a big hit for other artists on disc in 1948 including Ella Fitzgerald and John and Sandra Steele.

The backing of the disc, 'Highway to Love', written by Floyd H. Huddlestone (words) and Al Rinker (music) with the orchestral accompaniment by Paul Weston and his orchestra, was also very popular.

June Hutton replaced Jo Stafford (who went solo in 1945) on this disc which was No 4, and 25 weeks in the U.S.A. bestsellers.

DINAH SHORE
BUTTONS AND BOWS *Columbia* [*USA*]. Dinah's second million seller disc was the big hit from the Bob Hope-Jane Russell film *The Paleface* (1948), written by Jay Livingston and Ray Evans. It won the writers the Academy Award for the Best Film Song of the year. The disc was No 1 in the U.S.A. for 10 weeks, and 24 weeks in the bestsellers.

JO STAFFORD AND GORDON MACRAE WITH THE STARLIGHTERS
SAY SOMETHING SWEET TO YOUR SWEETHEART *Capitol* [*USA*]. The first recording of this song written by Sid Tepper and Roy Brodsky was made in Britain by Anne Shelton and Sam Browne. Jo and Gordon's disc was a hit in the U.S.A.

and also abroad, with an estimated million global sale. It reached No 20 in the U.S.A. charts.

JOHN AND SANDRA STEELE
MY HAPPINESS *Damon* [*USA*]. This song, written by Betty Peterson (words) and Borney Bergantine (music), became the Steeles' only million seller after three years, and sold between four and five million by 1969. It also enjoyed a big comeback in 1959 when Connie Francis made it a million seller again, at the very time when Betty Peterson and her family had all been seriously ill and her finances were in a bad way. One of the top songs of 1948, it stayed in the bestseller lists for 28 weeks, reaching No 3.

HANK THOMPSON (country-and-western vocal)
HUMPTY DUMPTY HEART (I've got a) *Capitol* [*USA*]. Hank Thompson wrote this song himself in 1947 and his disc was a bestseller in 1948. Through the years it is estimated to have sold a million. (For biography, see 1952.)

SONNY THOMPSON AND HIS BAND
LONG GONE (parts 1 and 2) *Miracle* [*USA*]. Considered a standard rhythm-and-blues disc, 'Long Gone' provided Sonny with his only million seller. He was born in Chicago, Illinois, on 22 August 1923.

The number was written by Chris Smith.

MARGARET WHITING
A TREE IN THE MEADOW *Capitol* [*USA*]. This was Margaret's second million seller disc, written by England's Billy Reid. Thus Reid achieved for the second time the magic figure in the U.S.A. (see 1946 and 1953). Margaret was born in Detroit, but was reared in Hollywood. Her first radio spot was on a show with Johnny Mercer. Then came a stint with Freddie Slack's orchestra and a contract with Capitol Records. This disc was No 1 seller for two weeks in the U.S.A., and 23 weeks in the bestsellers.

FRANK YANKOVIC AND BAND
BLUE SKIRT WALTZ *Columbia* [*USA*]. This number provided Yankovic with his only million seller. He was from Davis, West Virginia, where he was a self-taught accordionist at 15 years of age. He had a popular polka band and made many recordings in this idiom. Frank is also a TV, nightclub and personal-appearance artist. This successful song is by Mitchell Parish (words) and R. Dvorsky and Vaclav Blaha (music), and originally published as 'Red Skirt Waltz' in Czechoslovakia in 1944. The disc got to No 14, and was in the U.S.A. bestsellers for 23 weeks.

1949

The year 1949 was notable for the big battle between Victor and Columbia record companies over the merits of the new 45 and 33⅓ rpm speeds. When the talkies came in in 1927 at Hollywood, the old type disc material was too coarse for micro-grooves, the needles too blunt and the playing arms too heavy for film work. After World War II, vinylite, a tough almost grainless material, was developed, and fine-point styli and delicate pick-ups were devised. It was on 26 June 1948 that Columbia officially unveiled the 33⅓ rpm records to the press in the U.S.A., and on 18 September 1948 published a complete list of album releases. Victor favoured the 45 rpm disc at that time, and brought out a new 3-speed player (78, 45, and 33 rpm) in 1952. By 18 June 1949, Columbia figures showed album sales of 3,500,000 in the first year and it was evident that a new era in the disc world had begun. Capitol and Decca followed suit in 1949, going over to

the new speeds. In a few years, the 78 rpm discs had all but disappeared from the market.

ORIGINAL THEATRE CAST (ALFRED DRAKE, JOAN ROBERTS, HOWARD DA SILVA, CELESTE HOLM, LEE DIXON, WITH ORCHESTRA AND CHORUS DIRECTED BY JAY BLACKTON)
OKLAHOMA (album) *Decca* [*USA*]. This stage musical by Oscar Hammerstein II (book and lyrics) and Richard Rodgers (music) is based on the play *Green Grow the Lilacs* by Lynn Riggs. One of the most important productions in the theatre, *Oklahoma*, brought in almost a new art form - a literate, credible book, enhanced but not interrupted by the musical numbers and use of a ballet in the development of plot and character. It was the first of the Hammerstein-Rodgers long run of phenomenal

successes. Produced in 1943 (31 March) at St James's Theatre, New York, it ran for 2,212 performances, a record until *My Fair Lady* came along in 1956. This disc includes all the now famous songs – 'People Will Say We're in Love', 'Oh What a Beautiful Morning', 'Surrey with the Fringe on Top', 'Out of My Dreams', 'I Can't Say No', 'Oklahoma', 'Many a New Day', 'All or Nothin'', 'Pore Jud Is Dead', 'Kansas City'. It sold over 1,750,000 by 1956, and 2,500,000 by 1960. It was the first of the new 33⅓ rpm albums to strike such figures. By 1968, sales total was $15 million. (See also 1943.)

ORIGINAL THEATRE CAST (MARY MARTIN, EZIO PINZA, JUANITA HALL, WILLIAM TABBERT, BARBARA LUNA, WITH ORCHESTRA CONDUCTED BY SALVATORE DELL'ISOLA)

SOUTH PACIFIC (album) *Columbia* [*USA*]. This next colossal Hammerstein-Rodgers musical success was produced at the Majestic Theatre, New York, on 7 April 1949 with a subsequent 1,925 performances. Adapted from James A. Michener's Pulitzer Prize-winning novel *Tales of the South Pacific* by Hammerstein and Joshua Logan, it was a sensational success, featuring outstanding stars of the stage: the glamorous Mary Martin and the famous Metropolitan Opera bass-baritone Ezio Pinza. The disc includes 'Some Enchanted Evening', 'I'm Gonna Wash That Man Right Outa My Hair,' 'A Wonderful Guy', 'Bali Hai', 'This Nearly Was Mine', 'Cock-eyed Optimist', 'There Is Nothing Like a Dame', 'Younger than Springtime', 'Happy Talk', 'Honey Bun', 'Dites-moi', 'Carefully Taught', 'Bloody Mary' and 'Twin Soliloquies'. It sold a million by 1958 and 2,250,000 by 1960, almost 3,000,000 by 1963, and enjoyed a record stay of 427 weeks in the U.S.A. sellers charts up to 1962 plus the most weeks for any album at No 1 – 69 weeks. Gold Disc award R.I.A.A., 1966.

PATTI ANDREWS WITH CHORUS, AND GORDON JENKINS AND HIS ORCHESTRA

I CAN DREAM, CAN'T I? *Decca* [*USA*]. Patti is one of the famous Andrews Sisters who rose to fame in 1938. This disc was a million seller by 1950. The song was written by Irving Kahal (words) and Sammy Fain (music) in 1937. It was Sammy Fain's big year – he had another big hit with Crosby as well (see 'Dear Hearts and Gentle People'). This disc was No 1 seller for four weeks in the U.S.A., and 25 weeks in the bestsellers.

GENE AUTRY

PETER COTTONTAIL *Columbia* [*USA*]. Autry's third million seller disc, this was written by Steve Nelson and Jack Rollins. Steve is the son of songwriter Edward G. Nelson who wrote many successful songs, including 'Peggy O'Neil'.

RUDOLPH THE RED-NOSED REINDEER *Columbia* [*USA*]. Columbia's all-time bestseller. Gene Autry's fourth million seller proved to be his biggest success of all. Reaching 1,000,000 by 1950, this record went on to sell over 7,000,000. The U.S.A. total on collective discs rose to 60 million by 1970, thanks to over 450 versions. A further 31 million were sold overseas. This number is runner-up to 'White Christmas' as the top seasonal song. Sheet music sales ran to over 4,500,000. The song was written and published by Johnny Marks, the lyrics being based on Robert L. May's book of the same name. Autry introduced the song at Madison Square Garden. It was No 1 for a week in U.S.A. Over 115 different arrangements were published for a total sale of over 10 million copies. A belated Gold Disc was awarded by R.I.A.A. on 10 November 1969. It was in the U.S.A. bestsellers for 19 weeks.

BLUE BARRON AND HIS ORCHESTRA

CRUISING DOWN THE RIVER *MGM* [*USA*]. Barron's only million seller disc was an English song, written by two middle-aged women, Eily Beadell and Nell Tollerton, in 1945. It won the British nationwide song contest 'Write-a-tune for £1,000', run by the Hammersmith Palais de Danse in collabor-

ation with the BBC. Both writers played in a restaurant orchestra. The song shot to fame at the time of H.M.S. *Amethyst*'s defiant dash down the Yangtse – the crew singing it as they defied Chinese guns. It sold over 750,000 sheet music copies. A United States publisher had it for three years, then Blue Barron recorded it and it was an overnight hit in the U.S.A. Barron was born in Cleveland, Ohio, on 22 March 1911, and educated at Ohio State University. For a long time he had a ballroom 'sweet' band which broadcast in the U.S.A. and made recordings. (See also Russ Morgan orchestra 1949.) This disc was No 1 for two weeks in the U.S.A., and 19 weeks in the bestsellers.

SIDNEY BECHET (jazz clarinet and saxophone) WITH CLAUDE LUTER AND ORCHESTRA

LES OIGNONS (The Onions) *Vogue* [*France*]. This number was the first big success for the newly-formed (1947) Vogue Record Co., which had been started by a small group of Paris jazz fans. Sidney Bechet, composer of 'Les Oignons', veteran U.S.A. jazzman of clarinet and soprano sax, was the first exclusive recording artist for the label. He received an award for a million sale at the Bechet Golden Disc Concert in October 1955,

at the Salle Pleyel, Paris. (See 'Petite Fleur', 1959, for Bechet's biography.) Claude Luter (clarinet and bandleader) was born in Paris, France, on 23 July 1923. He formed a band in 1945, and played for several years in the Latin Quarter of Paris, and represented France in the first international Jazz Festival in Nice, 1948. From 1949 he often played with Bechet, whose influence became most marked. Luter is one of the white musicians who assimilated the Negro spirit and New Orleans style, playing very much in the King Oliver style of the great period 1922-24. Recorded 14 October 1949.

LES BROWN AND HIS ORCHESTRA

I'VE GOT MY LOVE TO KEEP ME WARM *Columbia* [*USA*]. Les Brown's second million seller disc was a revival of the great Irving Berlin song from the 1937 film *On the Avenue*, which starred Dick Powell. The disc was a belated issue. It was first recorded on 16 September 1946, reaching No 7, and was in the U.S.A. bestsellers for 16 weeks.

BING CROSBY WITH PERRY BOTKIN'S STRING BAND

DEAR HEARTS AND GENTLE PEOPLE *Decca* [*USA*]. Written by Bob Hilliard (words) and Sammy Fain (music), 'Dear Hearts' brought Bing Crosby his twentieth million seller. This number was Fain's second big hit of the year (see 'I Can Dream, Can't I?', 1949). Recorded in Los Angeles on 26 October 1949, it was No 2, and 16 weeks in the U.S.A. bestsellers.

VIC DAMONE

AGAIN *Mercury* [*USA*]. This first million seller disc for Damone was written by Dorcas Cochrane (words) and Lionel

Freddy Martin's disc is said to have sold a million in the U.S.A., and was his third to do so.

Vocalist Merv Griffin, born in San Mateo, California, eventually became a country, folk and bar-room ballad singer, then a popular TV personality on NBC. From 1964 he recorded for Cameo-Parkway and for Dot from 1968.

This disc was No 8, and 17 weeks in the U.S.A. bestsellers.

VAUGHN MONROE AND HIS ORCHESTRA

RIDERS IN THE SKY *Victor* [*USA*]. This fourth million seller disc for Monroe was written by Stan Jones. It was the top song of 1949. By utilizing a strain from 'When Johnny Comes Marching Home Again' with an original cowboy legend story and a pounding beat, Monroe produced a sound that was irresistible. This most original Western disc was No 1 for eleven weeks in the U.S.A., and 22 weeks in the bestsellers.

GEORGE MORGAN (country-and-western vocalist)

CANDY KISSES *Columbia* [*USA*]. George Morgan wrote this song himself in 1948, his first recording a big seller, and a No 1 country-and-western disc. The song was also immensely popular in Britain.

George was born 28 June 1924, in Waverly, Tennessee, and became a member of the Grand Ole Opry around the end of the 1950s. 'Candy Kisses' made him a 'super star' on Columbia.

In 1969 he signed a long-term contract with Stop Records. This disc subsequently passed the million mark.

George Morgan died in Nashville on 7 July 1975.

RUSS MORGAN AND HIS ORCHESTRA, WITH THE SKYLARKS (with organ)

CRUISING DOWN THE RIVER *Decca* [*USA*]. Russ Morgan's only million seller disc was the second recording of this song by Britain's Eily Beadell and Nell Tollerton to reach this figure. (See Blue Barron orchestra, 1949.) Russ Morgan, born on 29 April 1904, worked in the coal mines of his native Scranton, Pennsylvania, during his teens, then switched to playing the piano in a local theatre. Changing to trombone, he joined a local band, and at 18 trekked to New York, where he was an arranger for John Philip Sousa and Victor Herbert, later touring Europe with Paul Specht. On his return, Morgan led and arranged for Jean Goldkette's orchestra and finally became music director of a Detroit radio station before forming his own band. This disc was No 1 for seven weeks in the U.S.A., and 22 weeks in the bestsellers. At one time during the year, Russ Morgan had six discs in the U.S. Top 10, a record unequalled by any other dance band.

He died in Las Vegas on 7 August 1969.

PATTI PAGE

WITH MY EYES WIDE OPEN I'M DREAMING *Mercury* [*USA*]. Patti Page's first disc hit that started her on her succession of bestsellers. Through subsequent years, along with Patti's popularity, it amassed a million sale. The song was written in 1934 by Mack Gordon and Harry Revel for the film *Shoot the Works*. The disc was No 13, and 11 weeks in the U.S.A. bestsellers.

(See Patti Page, 1950, for biography.)

KEN ROBERTS (country-and-western vocalist)

I NEVER SEE MAGGIE ALONE *Coral* [*USA*]. Kenny's disc was probably the first British composition to make the Top Ten in the U.S.A. country charts. The song was first written in 1926 by Harry Tilsley (words) and Everett Lynton (music), both British songwriters, and published in Britain. 'Everett Lynton' is one of the many pseudonyms of composer/publisher Lawrence Wright of London, also well known as 'Horatio Nicholls' and 'Gene Williams'.

Kenny Roberts, 'The Jumping Cowboy', was born on 14 October 1926 in Lenoir City, Tennessee, and came into promi-

Newman (music) and originally sung by Ida Lupino in the film *Road House* in late 1948. Damone, who hails from Brooklyn, New York, got his first job as part-time usher at the Paramount Theatre, New York, during schooldays. He became a headliner there five years later, but in the interim did club dates and radio work that led to a small part in a club revue in New York. After one successful disc, Damone appeared on CBS 'Saturday Night Serenade', then in nightclubs, and made his film debut with a star part in *Rich, Young and Pretty* (1951). Vic resumed his career in 1953 after two years in the army. His name is Vito Farinola and he was born on 12 June 1928.

This disc was No 11, and 15 weeks in the U.S.A. bestsellers.

YOU'RE BREAKING MY HEART *Mercury* [*USA*]. Vic Damone's second million seller disc was this song by Pat Genaro and Sunny Skylar. It is based on 'Mattinata' ('Tis the day), written in 1904 by Ruggiero Leoncavallo (1858–1919), composer of the opera *Pagliacci*. This disc was No 1 seller for four weeks in the U.S.A., and sold over three million. It was 26 weeks in the bestsellers.

BILLY ECKSTINE

CARAVAN *MGM* [*USA*]. The fifth million seller for Billy was this song written in 1937 by Irving Mills (words), Duke Ellington and Juan Tizol (music).

LOUIS JORDAN AND HIS TYMPANY FIVE

SATURDAY NIGHT FISH FRY *Decca* [*USA*]. Louis Jordan's fifth million seller, written by him with Ellis Walsh, and his last big hit before his 15 years with Decca ended in 1953. It reached No 27 in the U.S.A.

FRANKIE LAINE

MULE TRAIN *Mercury* [*USA*]. Frankie's third million seller disc was written by Johnnie Lange, Hy Heath and Fred Glickman. It was a most original song with a pounding rhythm to a 'clippety-clop' refrain. The story of the mule train's cargo was put over by Frankie in distinctive and dramatic style. Sales hit the million mark by 1950. This disc was a No 1 seller for six weeks in the U.S.A., and 13 weeks in the bestsellers.

THAT LUCKY OLD SUN *Mercury* [*USA*]. Another great song for Frankie, his fourth million seller disc, also sold a million by the year following release. Written by Haven Gillespie (words) and Beasley Smith (music) the disc was No 1 in the charts for eight weeks in the U.S.A., and 22 weeks in the bestsellers.

FREDDY MARTIN AND HIS ORCHESTRA (Merv Griffin – vocalist)

I'VE GOT A LOVELY BUNCH OF COCONUTS *Victor* [*USA*]. This extremely popular comedy fairground song, first written by Fred Heatherton (pseudonym of British writers Elton Box and Desmond Cox with American Irwin Dash) in 1944, was first introduced by Billy Cotton and his band around 1948-49.

nence when he sang this song over the WLW station in 1949. The disc was subsequently estimated to have sold a million. He later recorded for Decca and Starday. After practical retirement from country music, he was host of the 'Kenny Roberts Show' on WNEM-TV in Saginaw, Michigan, for three years. From around 1964, he became active again in personal appearances at nightclubs, etc., and on WWVA's live 'Jamboree' show. He became popular in the New York area in 1967. Ken is probably America's leading exponent of yodelling. This disc was No 9, and 13 weeks in the U.S.A. bestsellers.

EDMUNDO ROS AND HIS RUMBA BAND
WEDDING SAMBA *Decca [Britain]*. In 1939, Edmundo Ros was a drummer at London's Old Florida. By the early 1940s he started recording with his own band and subsequently became Britain's biggest name in Latin-Americana, making a great number of discs in this idiom.

'Wedding Samba' was originally written in 1940 under the Yiddish title 'Der Nayer Sher' by Abraham Ellstein, Allan Small and Joseph Liebowitz. Ros recorded this with his Rumba Band at The Bagatelle Restaurant, London, in 1949 and it is said to have sold around three million globally. His disc was a big seller on both sides of the Atlantic, and was released on the London

label in U.S.A., where it reached No 16 in the charts. The Andrews Sisters also had a big success with the song in the U.S.A.

Edmundo Ros was born on 7 December 1910 in Venezuela. As a Latin name he was a formidable force on the world market – particularly in America and Japan, his discs selling strongly since the end of World War II. One of his albums, 'Rhythms of the South', was a particularly big seller since release in 1957.

He played 42 concerts in Japan during a seven-week tour and every venue was sold out. The Japanese sent him military marches and folk songs to be recorded in 'Western' style with a Latin-American beat.

GEORGE SHEARING (modern jazz pianist) QUINTET
SEPTEMBER IN THE RAIN *MGM [USA]*. George Shearing was born in Battersea, London, on 13 August 1920. He is blind, and began studying the piano at the age of five. After his student days at Linden Lodge School for the Blind, he toured Britain with an all-blind band under the direction of well-known British pianist Claude Bampton, then worked with the Bert Ambrose and Ted Heath orchestras. He began recording for British Decca in 1938 as solo pianist and with his sextet. After making his name as a swing pianist he played in various nightclubs throughout

World War II. He broadcast frequently with Arthur Young on two pianos. From 1939 to 1946 he won the *Melody Maker* poll as England's top swing pianist many times, and played in Harry Hayes' band and with a trio. In 1946, famous jazz music critic Leonard Feather brought Shearing to the U.S.A., where the pianist formed a combination playing nightclubs, theatres, recording for MGM and touring with jazz concert groups with enormous success. His quintet (himself on piano, Margie Hymans on vibraphones, Chuck Wayne on guitar, Denzil Best on drums and John Levy on bass) was formed in 1949. They suddenly stumbled on a sound that was not only an intriguing jazz development, but which also captured the imagination of the disc-buying public. George's playing with locked hands on piano, plus Denzil's wire brush effects on drums and the other members' individual rhythmic effects together produced a unique brand of music. The group actually came together more or less by accident. Their disc of 'September in the Rain', written by Al Dubin (words) and Harry Warren (music) – both famous film songwriters – was a tremendous hit, selling over 900,000 in the U.S.A. alone and with big sales in Britain and elsewhere. It was originally written for James Melton to sing in the film *Melody for Two* in 1937, one of the outstanding songs of that year. Shearing, a gifted musician, began playing jazz inspired by the great Art

Tatum, a pianist who is almost blind. George's greatest success as a composer is his famous 'Lullaby of Birdland' which he wrote in 1952 as the theme of New York's Birdland, a popular jazz club there. It was written in ten minutes. He was a Capitol artist from 1956.

JO STAFFORD AND GORDON MACRAE WITH PAUL WESTON AND HIS ORCHESTRA

WHISPERING HOPE *Capitol* [*USA*]. Although this famous duet for soprano and alto was written as long ago as 1868, it is still a great favourite today, particularly in America. The composer Alice Hawthorne was really a Philadelphia music publisher named Septimus Winner who had a number of tremendously popular songs to his credit including 'Listen to the Mocking Bird' (1854), 'Oh Where Oh Where Has My Little Dog Gone?' (words to a German folk tune (1864)), 'Ten Little Indians' (1868), and 'What Is Home Without a Mother?' (1854). Jo Stafford's delightful duetting disc with Gordon MacRae of 'Whispering Hope' took over 10 years to pass the million mark. The song's popularity was mainly due to the fact that the two voices could sing in very close harmony, sometimes just one tone apart.

This disc was No 6, and 23 weeks in the U.S.A. bestsellers.

Gordon MacRae, born 12 March 1921, in East Orange, New Jersey, was a child actor on radio. He won the prize in a magazine contest in 1940 - two weeks at New York's World's Fair singing with the Harry James and Les Brown bands. Then came a vocalist's berth with Horace Heidt, a Broadway stage role in *Junior Miss* and a CBS network show (replacing Frank Sinatra), which he interrupted for a tour of Air Force service. Afterwards came the singing lead in Ray Bolger's musical *Three to Make Ready* (1946). Back in radio, MacRae was MC for NBC's 'Teen Timer' show, appeared regularly on two other network summer programmes, being heard on some 580 stations per week. Capitol Records signed him quickly in August 1947, since when he has sold a great number of records for them. Stardom in films followed including *Look for the Silver Lining* (1949), *Tea for Two*, *West Point Story* (1950), *On Moonlight Bay*, *Starlift* (1951) - these latter four with Doris Day - *About Face* (1952), *By the Light of the Silvery Moon* with Doris Day, *Desert Song*, *Three Sailors and a Girl* (1953), *Oklahoma* (1955) and *Carousel* (1956) - both with Shirley Jones - *Best Things in Life Are Free* (1956).

Gordon's father 'Wee Willie' MacRae was an early radio star who encouraged his son's show business career.

(Jo Stafford biography: see 1947.)

MARGARET WHITING AND JIMMY WAKELY

SLIPPING AROUND *Capitol* [*USA*]. Margaret Whiting's third million seller disc was Jimmy Wakely's first. He hails from Mineola, Arkansas, and was schooled in Oklahoma, where he worked on ranches in his spare time. In 1937 Jimmy started singing over the radio there, then, after two years on Gene Autry's 'Melody Ranch' programme, he followed with film work. Wakely formed a band in 1943 - a trio called The Saddle Pals - for a series of Columbia pictures. This song is by Floyd Tillman. The disc sold 1,750,000 and made Margaret Whiting queen of the juke boxes for 1949. Wakely was born on 16 February 1914.

A top country-and-western disc. Nationally it achieved No 2, and was 22 weeks in the U.S.A. bestsellers.

ESTHER WILLIAMS AND RICARDO MONTALBAN

BABY, IT'S COLD OUTSIDE *MGM* [*USA*]. Composer Frank Loesser wrote this very clever duet in 1948 and frequently sang it with his wife at Hollywood parties. It was introduced in the film *Neptune's Daughter* (1949) by Esther Williams and Ricardo Montalban. Taken off the film soundtrack and issued as a single, it subsequently sold a million and started the vogue for a great number of boy-and-girl songs. The song received the Academy Award for Best Film Song of 1949.

Esther Williams, actress, born 8 August 1923 in Los Angeles,

California, was educated at the University of Southern California. She appeared at the San Francisco World's Fair Aquacade and was an accomplished swimmer, also a professional model. Esther first appeared on the screen in *Andy Hardy Steps Out* (1942). Her aquatic prowess and beauty were displayed in the highly popular film *Bathing Beauty* (1944) and she later appeared with Montalban in *Fiesta*, *On an Island With You* and *Neptune's Daughter*. Other films were *A Guy Named Joe*, *Ziegfeld Follies*, *Easy to Wed*, *Pagan Love Song*, *Dollar Mermaid* and *Dangerous When Wet*. She was voted one of the Top Ten Money-Making Stars in a 1950 poll.

Ricardo Montalban, actor, born in Mexico City, Mexico, first appeared in his native country in films from 1941 to 1945. He then went to the U.S.A. and appeared in films with Esther Williams (as above). Later films included *Two Weeks with Love*, *Across the Wide Missouri* and *Sombrero*.

HANK WILLIAMS WITH HIS DRIFTING COWBOYS

LOVESICK BLUES *MGM* [*USA*]. This top country-and-western disc of the year, was Hank's first million seller. The song was written way back in 1922 by Irving Mills (words) and Cliff Friend (music).

Hank was born on a farm at Mount Olive, near the Georgia and Alabama line, on 17 September 1923. While still a child, he learned without instruction to play the guitar given him by his parents. When he was twelve years old, the family moved to Montgomery, Alabama. Hank sang in the local church choir and sang his first composition, 'W.P.A. Blues', on amateur night at the Empire Theatre, winning $15 in prize money. At 13, he formed his own band, The Drifting Cowboys (Don Helms, steel guitar, Jerry Rivers, violin, Hillous Buttram, bass, and Bob McNett, guitar), and they performed over the local radio at Montgomery and at local dances until 1948. In 1946, Williams cut several records for the Stirling label. Hank's rise to fame was due to two factors - his talent, and a fortunate meeting with Fred Rose, a great songwriter who settled in Nashville to join Roy Acuff in the publishing firm of Acuff-Rose which laid the foundation stone of the present country-and-western market. Hank's wife Audrey asked Fred Rose to hear her husband's songs. They went to Nashville's radio studios and soon after (12 April 1948) Hank was signed to an exclusive Acuff-Rose writers' contract. At this time, Frank Walker was organizing MGM Records and wanted Fred Rose, a great lover of country music, to record material for him. Hank was then signed to the MGM label, his first release being 'Move It on Over'. From then on, both Rose and Walker made it possible for Hank to produce many great songs and records in a brief span. Hank's catalogue of songs and the discs, all owned by MGM, are often referred to as the chief jewel in the country music treasury. The wistful and nostalgic quality of Hank's songs, many of his own composition, led to many other artists modelling themselves on his style. Since his tragic death in a car accident on 1 January 1953, he has become a legend in country circles, his regular performances on 'Grand Ole Opry' from 1948 having made him one of the U.S.A.'s greatest artists. Both Hank Williams and Fred Rose (also deceased) were named to the Country Music Hall of Fame in 1961 by the Country Music Association of America.

In 1964, a biographical film based on Hank's life, called *Your Cheatin' Heart* was made by MGM, thus documenting his great contribution to American music. All the songs on the soundtrack were recorded by his son, Hank Williams Junior, who is also a recording star. The film included most of Hank's great songs such as 'Cold Cold Heart', 'Ramblin' Man', 'Long Gone Lonesome Blues', 'Your Cheatin' Heart', 'Jambalaya', 'Kaw Liga', 'Hey Good Looking' and 'Lovesick Blues'.

Sales of his discs to 1965 exceeded 20,000,000 singles and 2,500,000 albums. MGM awarded 11 gold records for singles sales.

Hank's original Stirling recordings were purchased by Wesley Rose and turned over to MGM.

'Lovesick Blues' was also a million seller disc for Frank Ifield in Britain (1962). Hank's disc was released in the U.S.A. in February 1949.

MY BUCKET'S GOT A HOLE IN IT *MGM* [*USA*]. Second million seller, through subsequent years, for Hank Williams. The song was written by C. Williams. A Gold Disc was awarded by MGM. It was a No 2 country-and-western disc.

YOGI YORGESSON WITH THE JOHN DUFFY TRIO

I YUST GO NUTS AT CHRISTMAS backed with YINGLE BELLS *Capitol* [*USA*]. This was the first Swedish seasonal disc to sell 1,000,000 and Yorgesson's only one. 'I Yust Go Nuts' was written by Harry Stewart, who also wrote 'Yingle Bells', an adaptation of Pierpont's famous 'Jingle Bells'. Yorgesson's real name is Harry Stewart.

THE 1950s

Decca Records were the first to launch the modern long-playing albums in Britain in this year.

AMES BROTHERS

RAG MOP backed with SENTIMENTAL ME *Coral* [*USA*]. The Ames Brothers (Joe, Gene, Vic and Ed in order of seniority) were born and reared in Malden, a suburb of Boston, Massachusetts. They sang together from grammar school days. Their first professional engagement was with a band at the 'Foxes and Hounds' in Boston, followed by a singing act of their own at the Roxy Theatre, New York. Thereafter, they starred at Ciro's in Hollywood, Chez Paree in Chicago, and the Riviera at Fort Lee, New Jersey. They made many TV appearances and became recording favourites. This disc, their first million seller, was popular for both sides. 'Rag Mop', a bouncy rhythmic number, simply spells out the title and utilizes a range of only six notes. It was written by Johnnie Lee Wills and Deacon Anderson. 'Sentimental Me' is a complete contrast, a slow melodic song written by Jim Morehead and Jimmy Cassin in 1949. 'Rag Mop' was a No 1 seller in the U.S.A. for one week, and 14 weeks in the bestsellers. 'Sentimental Me' was No 3, and 27 weeks in the bestsellers.

GENE AUTRY

FROSTY THE SNOW MAN *Columbia* [*USA*]. This was Autry's fifth million seller disc, and the second big hit for the 'Peter Cottontail' writers, Steve Nelson and J. Rollins. A great seasonal disc for the cowboy film star following on the sensational 'Rudolph' of the previous year. This disc was a million seller by 1951. It reached No 7 in the U.S.A. charts.

EILEEN BARTON

IF I KNEW YOU WERE COMING I'D HAVE BAKED A CAKE *National* [*USA*] and *Mercury* [*USA*]. The one and only million seller disc for Eileen, this song was written by Al Hoffman, Bob Merrill and Clem Watts. An obscure publisher of hymns in Chicago, Maurice Wells, bought the song for $300 and got friends to sing it on the Breakfast Club Radio Show at 7 o'clock one morning. By nightfall, seven top New York publishers were flying to Chicago to outbid one another for possession of the song. Wells sold out for a princely sum, and within a week the song was a rage in the U.S.A. and Europe. Eileen Barton was born in Brooklyn, New York. Her parents, Elsie and Ben Barton, were a song and dance team. Eileen made her debut in Kansas City at $2\frac{1}{2}$ and at 4 was a stooge for Ted Healey. Before her teens she had sung on 'Children's House' and the Eddie Cantor and Rudy Vallee programmes. She was also a regular stooge for Milton Berle on radio and stage. She has played nightclubs, had many radio and TV guest spots, and also appeared in Broadway plays. This disc was the No 1 seller for two weeks in the U.S.A., and issued on two different labels simultaneously. It was 15 weeks in the bestsellers.

TERESA BREWER

MUSIC, MUSIC, MUSIC *London* [*USA*]. Teresa Brewer's first million seller, and the one that made her known internationally, was written by Stephen Weiss and Bernie Baum. Teresa was born in Toledo, Ohio, on 7 May 1931, and first

appeared in a kiddie show over radio there. At five years of age she started a seven-year tour with 'Amateur Hour' and at 12 was permanent singer on the 'Pick and Pat' show. At 16 she was back in radio winning talent shows. Soon after came this disc hit. Miss Brewer made her movie debut in *Those Redheads from Seattle* (1953). This disc was No 1 seller for four weeks in the U.S.A., and 17 weeks in the bestsellers.

ROY BROWN

HARD LUCK BLUES *De Luxe* [*USA*]. Roy Brown, born in 1925, is one of the earliest rhythm-and-blues songwriter/vocalists, and this song written and recorded by him has become one of the standards in the rhythm-and-blues idiom. It is said to have sold a million through the years. Roy has recorded for several labels, starting out in the 1940s and early 1950s on De Luxe (and later King) Records. One of his first rhythm-and-blues hits was the 1947 'Good Rocking Tonight' which he wrote, and was later recorded by Wynonie Harris, Elvis Presley, Pat Boone, Ricky Nelson, Arthur Prysock and James Brown. His other hits, most of which he wrote as well as recorded, include ''Long About Midnight', 'Miss Fanny Brown', 'Rainy Weather Blues' and 'Don't Love Nobody'.

In 1970 he was a success at the Monterey Jazz Festival where he sang 'Love for Sale', a song written by him and his wife. This he recorded at his own expense on his own Friendship label, and it was released in 1970 on the Mercury label with whom Roy signed a recording contract.

NAT 'KING' COLE WITH
LES BAXTER ORCHESTRA AND CHORUS

MONA LISA *Capitol* [*USA*]. Nat's third million seller disc was this song by Ray Evans and Jay Livingston from the film *Captain Carey, U.S.A.* The writers won the Academy Award (their second) for the Best Film Song of the year. This disc was the No 1 seller in the U.S.A. for five weeks, and sold over two million. It was 27 weeks in the bestsellers.

DON CORNELL WITH
SAMMY KAYE ORCHESTRA

IT ISN'T FAIR *Victor* [*USA*]. This was Don's first million seller and reached 1,000,000 by 1952. Don hails from New York City. Soon after high school graduation he successfully auditioned for the orchestra at the Edison Hotel. More band singing followed until 1942 when he joined Sammy Kaye. He rejoined him in 1946, after wartime service in the Army, and became a singles artist in 1949. This song is an oldie of 1933 by Richard Himber (words) and Himber, Frank Warshauer and Sylvester Sprigato (music). Himber was a famous bandleader (for Sophie Tucker), recording artist, stage, screen and radio performer with his own orchestra in the 1920s and 1930s. This disc was No 3 in the charts, and 22 weeks in the bestsellers.

BING AND GARY CROSBY WITH
MATTY MATLOCK'S ALL STARS ORCHESTRA

SAM'S SONG backed with PLAY A SIMPLE MELODY *Decca* [*USA*]. Two hits for Bing and son Gary's first duet disc. This was Bing's 21st million seller. 'Sam's Song' was a new number by Jack Elliott (words) and Lew Quadling (music) and 'Simple Melody' an Irving Berlin oldie from his first Broadway revue *Watch Your Step* of 1914. Both were recorded in Los Angeles on 23 June 1950, and were No 3 in the U.S.A., and 19 weeks in the bestsellers.

Previous page, top, left to right: **Dean Martin, Brenda Lee, Johnny Ray**; bottom: **Buddy Holly, Elvis Presley, Sarah Vaughan.**

BILLY ECKSTINE

MY FOOLISH HEART *MGM* [*USA*]. This was Billy's sixth million seller disc, reaching 1,000,000 by 1951. The song was written in 1949 by Ned Washington (words) and Victor Young (music) for the film *My Foolish Heart*. The disc was No 6, and 19 weeks in the U.S.A. bestsellers.

RED (Clyde Julian) FOLEY

CHATANOOGIE SHOE-SHINE BOY *Decca* [*USA*]. One of the biggest country-and-western discs of the year, and No 1 for four weeks in the U.S.A. It was Foley's first million seller. The song was written by Harry Stone and Jack Stapp, Vice President/General Manager and Programme Director respectively of Nashville's WSM station. Foley started in the early 1930s to gain fame on a Chicago radio station where he was singing. His first discs appeared in 1941, after which he has made many very successful country-and-western and near-pop discs. Foley's home town was Blue Lick, Kentucky. He was born in Berea, Kentucky, on 17 June 1910, was educated at college, and was a star athlete in high school. At the age of 17 he won the Atwater-Kent singing contest. In 1960 he was the star of ABC-TV's 'Country Jubilee'. In addition to singing he played the guitar and harmonica. His daughter Shirley married disc star Pat Boone. Red Foley was elected to the Country Music Hall of Fame in 1967. He died 19 September 1968 in Fort Wayne, Indiana.

STEAL AWAY *Decca* [*USA*]. This second million seller for Foley is his own arrangement of the famous traditional Negro spiritual, first introduced in 1871 by the Fisk Jubilee Singers from Nashville's Fisk University.

(with the Jordanaires)

JUST A CLOSER WALK WITH THEE *Decca* [*USA*]. Foley's arrangement of another great American traditional sacred song became his third million seller.

TENNESSEE ERNIE FORD

THE SHOT GUN BOOGIE *Capitol* [*USA*]. Written by Tennessee Ernie himself, this was his first big hit disc and sold over 900,000 in 1950 and subsequently achieved a million. It was also a No 1 country-and-western hit. (See Ford, 1955, for biography.)

PHIL HARRIS

THE THING *Victor* [*USA*]. His only million seller disc, it reached 1,000,000 by 1951. Written by Charles Grean of the Victor pop records staff, it is the tune of an old Rabelasian ditty 'The Tailor's Boy' with new lyrics. The words never specify what 'The Thing' is; there is just a pause when singer Harris waits for three resounding booms of the bass drum. The 'boom boom boom' caught on fast, the disc selling 400,000 in ten days, then an all-time record for Victor, and spread like the measles. Harris was from Linton, Indiana, and all his discs had a comedy flavour. This disc was No 1 for four weeks in the U.S.A. and four weeks in the bestsellers.

IVORY JOE HUNTER

I ALMOST LOST MY MIND *MGM* [*USA*]. Ivory Joe Hunter, son of a preacher, was born in Kirbyville, Texas, in 1911. A rhythm-and-blues artist, singer, pianist and composer, he made his first disc 'Blues at Sunrise' in Oakland, California for his own Ivory label in 1943. He migrated to California from Texas in search of work during World War II. Instead, he found a secure niche in the pantheon of rhythm-and-blues pioneers. Ivory Joe made a big impression in the late 1940s for Syd Nathan's King Records of Cincinnati, and was backed by Duke Ellington's orchestra on all his King sessions. His biggest record during this period was 'Guess Who' which featured the sax playing of Johnny Hodges.

Joe then moved over to MGM and had his first big pop hit with this disc of 'I Almost Lost My Mind', a song written by himself. It passed the million mark by 1956. Pat Boone revived the number in 1956 and sold a million with his recording, and

Elvis Presley also recorded some of Joe's songs, including 'My Wish Came True', and 'Ain't That Loving You, Baby'. Hunter made a comeback as a recording artist in 1971 with an album entitled, appropriately 'The Return of Ivory Joe Hunter' on the Epic label.

Recording country material was not unusual for Joe. He was the first R & B artist to record Hank Williams' tunes commercially, for MGM in the early 1950s, a decade before Ray Charles' famous 'Modern Sounds in Country and Western Music' albums in 1962. Ivory Joe Hunter died on 8 November 1974 in Houston.

GORDON JENKINS AND ORCHESTRA, WITH THE WEAVERS (vocalists)

GOOD NIGHT, IRENE backed with TZENA, TZENA, TZENA *Decca* [USA]. This was Gordon Jenkins' second and the Weavers' first million seller disc. It actually sold more than 2,000,000, as both titles were extremely popular. 'Irene' is an adaptation by folklorist John Lomax of Huddie ('Lead Belly') Leadbetter's famous song (which Leadbetter thought he had learned from his uncle) recorded just before Huddie was sent to prison in Texas for murder in 1918. He added verses as they came to him and made the song a prison favourite. He was eventually pardoned, and died in 1949. 'Tzena, Tzena', also a folk song (Jewish), was composed in 1941 by Issachar Miron (Michrovsky) and re-written in 1947 by Julius Grossman. Spencer Ross arranged the melody and Gordon Jenkins wrote the English lyrics, the original version being voided by legal action. The Weavers were brought to Decca by Jenkins, and they sparked off a renaissance of folk music with these songs. The original Weavers were Lee Hayes (from Arkansas), Fred Hellerman (from Brooklyn, New York), Ronnie Gilbert (leader) and Pete Seeger (born on 3 May 1919 in New York City). Seeger left in 1958 to become solo and was replaced by Erik Darling, who formed the Rooftop Singers in 1962. This disc had the then longest tenure as No 1 seller in the U.S.A.'s Top 100 Charts – thirteen weeks, and in the bestsellers for 25 weeks. 'Tzena, Tzena, Tzena' was No 2, and 17 weeks in the bestsellers.

AL JOLSON

SONGS HE MADE FAMOUS (EP disc) *Decca* [*USA*]. This million seller 45 rpm disc contained four of Jolson's greatest songs – 'Swanee', 'California, Here I Come', 'April Showers' and 'Rock-a-bye Your Baby With a Dixie Melody', following the enormous success of the second of the Jolson story films *Jolson Sings Again*, released in February 1950.

ANTON KARAS (zither)

HARRY LIME ('THIRD MAN') THEME *Decca* [*Britain*]. This theme of the famous Orson Welles film *The Third Man* caused as much furore as Carol Reed's directing, and was said to have sold 4,000,000 discs. The film demanded music appropriate to post-World War II Vienna, and Reed did not want waltzes. One night he heard Karas in a wine-garden in Vienna, and was fascinated by the twangy jangling melancholy of his music. He later brought the 43-year-old Karas to London and kept him plucking away at his tunes for six weeks while he recorded a soundtrack. Then zither-playing tours and disc royalties earned him a small fortune. Karas was born in Vienna on 7 July 1906, and had made a living from zither-playing since the age of 18. 'The Harry Lime Theme' ('Lime' being the character played by Welles in the film) was composed in 1949 by cleverly rearranging an 8-measure melody he had remembered from a zither study book. Karas owned (up to September 1966) a winehouse de luxe in Grinzing, appropriately named 'The Third Man', where the lights were dimmed and waiters stopped serving for 10 minutes when he appeared to entertain the sophisticated audience. Collective disc sales were estimated to have reached 40 million by 1963. This disc was No 1 for 11 weeks in the U.S.A., and 27 weeks in the bestsellers.

FRANKIE LAINE

CRY OF THE WILD GOOSE *Mercury* [*USA*]. Frankie's fifth million seller disc was a song written in 1949 by Terry Gilkyson. It reached No 4, and was 11 weeks in the bestsellers.

MARIO LANZA

BE MY LOVE *Victor* [*USA*]. The famous tenor's first million seller disc reached seven figures by 1951. The song was written by Sammy Cahn (words) and Nicholas Brodszky (music) for the film *Toast of New Orleans*, in which Lanza starred with Kathryn Grayson. Lanza (real name Alfredo Arnold Cocozza) was born on 31 January 1921 in Philadelphia. He attended school in South Philadelphia where he became champion weight-lifter. Initially he studied voice in amateur fashion via his father's collection of Caruso's discs. At 19 Mario studied under Irene Williams and later with Enrico Rossati and Giacomo Spadoni, former tutors of Caruso and Gigli. After two years in the U.S. Air Force, during which he appeared in the chorus in an all-soldier show *Winged Victory*, he pursued further studies and in 1946 began giving concerts. Lanza made his screen debut in 1949 in *That Midnight Kiss*, subsequently starring in the title role for *The Great Caruso* followed by *Because You're Mine*, *Toast of New Orleans*, *Serenade*, *Seven Hills of Rome* and *For the First Time*. One of the finest tenors in the world, his death on 7 October 1959 in Rome, at the age of 38, was a great loss to music – a truly great artist. This disc was a No 1 seller in the U.S.A. for a week, and was 34 weeks in the bestsellers. By 1965 over four million Lanza albums had been sold. Philadelphia officially proclaimed 7 October as Mario Lanza day. His name was derived from his mother's maiden name Maria Lanza.

JOE LIGGINS

PINK CHAMPAGNE *Specialty* [*USA*]. This first million seller disc by rhythm-and-blues artist Liggins was written by the performer himself. It became top rhythm-and-blues disc of 1950. He was born in Guthrie, Oklahoma on 9 July 1916.

I GOTTA RIGHT TO CRY backed with HONEYDRIPPER *Specialty* [*USA*]. This number eventually became Joe Liggins' second million seller disc. Again Liggins himself was the writer.

GUY LOMBARDO AND HIS ROYAL CANADIANS, AND DON RODNEY (guitar)

THIRD MAN (HARRY LIME) THEME *Decca* [*USA*]. This

American version of Anton Karas' famous theme from the film *The Third Man* (see Karas) was, by 1954, Lombardo's fourth million seller disc. It reached No 2, and was in the U.S.A. bestsellers for 27 weeks.

GUY MITCHELL

MY HEART CRIES FOR YOU *Columbia* [*USA*]. This was the first million seller of several for Guy. This one reached the figure by 1951. It was written by Carl Sigman and Percy Faith who adapted the melody from 'Chanson de Marie Antoinette' supposedly written by France's queen of the 18th century. Mitchell comes from Detroit. As a child he was signed by Warner Bros. for grooming as a moppet actor-singer-dancer, and sang on their

radio station. After his family moved to San Francisco, he sang in his high school band and over radio. The Navy beckoned in 1946 and after discharge he joined Carmen Cavallaro's band as vocalist, until illness forced him out. In 1949 Mitchell won an Arthur Godfrey Talent Scouts competition and in 1950 a contract with Columbia Records. He was born on 21 February 1927 in Detroit. His real name is Al Cernik. This disc was No 2, and 21 weeks in the U.S.A. bestsellers.

MOON MULLICAN

I'LL SAIL MY SHIP ALONE *King* [*USA*]. Written by Lois Mann, Henry Bernard, Morry Burns and Henry Thurston, this number became a second million seller disc for this country-and-western singer. A top country-and-western disc.

PATTI PAGE

TENNESSEE WALTZ *Mercury* [*USA*]. This was a smash hit with a total sale by 1967 of over six million for Patti's disc, and over one million sheet music sales, the last to do so before disc sales displaced sheet sellers. Written by Redd Stewart and Pee Wee King in 1948, it had already been recorded by Cowboy Copas (see 1948) with a moderate sale, and originated from the country-and-western centre, Nashville. Patti's disc caught on without any publisher exploitation and sold its first million in 1951. Collective disc sales are estimated at well over ten million. Patti Page (Clara Ann Fowler, real name) was born in Tulsa, Oklahoma, and received her professional name as a hillbilly singer over radio. She was heard by the manager of Jimmy Joy's band and joined as vocalist. Then she broke away to become solo performer playing clubs in Milwaukee and Chicago, and had a spot on the 'Breakfast Club' radio show. Then started a chain of disc bestsellers and top billing in theatres and nightclubs, and Patti became the star of her own TV series. This disc, an historic multiple-voiced recording, was No 1 seller for nine weeks in the U.S.A., and top selling disc ever made by a girl singer. It sold over three million in its first year of release, and was 25 weeks in the U.S.A. bestsellers.

ALL MY LOVE *Mercury* [*USA*]. Originally introduced in France as 'Bolero' by Jacqueline François and written by Henri Contet (words) and Paul Durand (music) in 1948, Patti's disc with its English title 'All My Love' (words by Mitchell Parish, 1950) was a further big success for the singer, with a subsequent million sale. It reached No 2, with 22 weeks in the U.S.A. bestsellers.

EDITH PIAF

LA VIE EN ROSE *Pathe-Marconi* [*France*]. This song was written in 1946 by Edith Piaf (words) and Louiguy (music). An English lyric was written for Britain by Frank Eyton in 1947 and for the U.S.A. by Mack David in 1950. The British title was 'Take Me to Your Heart Again', while the U.S.A. title was 'You're Too Dangerous, Cherie'. Edith Piaf's disc is reputed to have sold, through the years, three million in global sales on the original label and on the Columbia label in both U.S.A. and Britain. It was originally recorded by Pathé on 1 April 1947 but 1950 was the year when the song attained great prominence.

Edith Piaf, was born Edith Giovanna Gassion on 19 December 1915, in Belleville, a working-class district of Paris. Her mother was an Italian café singer, and her father a Norman circus acrobat. Abandoned by her mother when she was two months old she was taken away by her grandmother to live in Bernay, Normandy, at the age of two. At the age of three the child suddenly became blind until she was seven. Edith attributed the restoration of her sight to her grandmother's taking her to the shrine of St Teresa of Lisieux.

She travelled with her father on his circus tours and noticing her musical talent, he encouraged her to sing in the circus, and this she developed in market places and cafés. At 15 she left for Paris, auditions proving fruitless, and sang in the streets for pennies. During this period she was discovered by Louis Leplée, proprietor of Gerny's, a smart cabaret where he presented her, changing her name to 'Piaf' (Parisian slang for 'Sparrow'), insisting she wear the sweater and skirt in which he had first seen

her, and selecting ten new songs more suited to her. Her first appearance was greeted with long applause from the audience, among whom were Maurice Chevalier and Mistinguett. The engagement lasted six months, ending when Leplée was found murdered in a robbery, the tragedy deeply affecting Edith Piaf. After further engagements she met Raymond Asse who wrote songs for her and gained her wider recognition. In 1935 she was acclaimed a 'hit' at a large vaudeville theatre in Paris, subsequently enlarging her repertoire with haunting and blues-type songs by famous writers, such as Michel Emer, Henri Contet and Marguerite Monnot. A play written for her by Jean Cocteau followed in 1940 and during World War II she sang several times to French prisoners held in Germany, and helped several to escape. She appeared in films from 1945 and travelled for two years with 'Les Compagnons de la Chanson', a group of nine Frenchmen. Her U.S. debut was in October 1947 with Les Compagnons in New York, with return dates in 1948, 1949, 1950. She sang 'La vie en rose' on U.S. television in late 1950 where it became a top hit. The disc reached No 3, with 23 weeks in the U.S.A. bestsellers. The French chanteuse fought ill health for five years, but the world famous husky voice kept returning to the stage until her death on 11 October 1963, when millions mourned her passing. She was indisputably one of the world's greatest cabaret and music-hall artists – 'a singer with dramatic power, a suggestion of greater inner fire, and a hint of unquenchable tragedy of heart' as one critic described her. In 1966, the French public subscribed for a memorial plaque at 72 Rue de Belleville, where she was born.

MERV SHINER (country-and-western vocalist)

PETER COTTONTAIL *Decca* [*USA*]. Written by Steve Nelson and Jack Rollins in 1949, Merv's disc is said to have sold nearly three million over the years, making the song for the second time a seven figure seller (see Autry, 1949). Merv, known as the old 'hoppin' down the bunny trail' boy, worked for a big music publishing company, but still performed and recorded, and was MC for occasional shows.

Real name: Mervin Shiner. He was born in Bethlehem, Pennsylvania, 20 February 1921.

HANK SNOW

I'M MOVIN' ON *Victor* [*USA*]. Written by Hank himself, this disc was a bestseller of 1950-1951 and a No 1 country-and-western disc of 1950. It stayed at No 1 in the country-and-western charts for a record 21 weeks. 'I'm Movin' On' is in the idiom of the train song, and established the artist in a big way on Victor's American catalogue. Hank made his first appearance on Grand Ole Opry on 7 January 1949, and his performance evoked little enthusiasm. He was thinking of returning to Texas, somewhat discouraged, when 'I'm Movin' On' caught on with the public and Opry audiences then began to take notice of everything he sang. He celebrated his 20 years with Grand Ole Opry on 11 January 1969. (See 1954 for Hank Snow biography.)

This disc subsequently sold a million.

BILL SNYDER (piano) AND HIS ORCHESTRA

BEWITCHED, BOTHERED AND BEWILDERED *Tower* [*USA*]. By 1957 this title provided Bill Snyder with his only million seller. It was written by Lorenz Hart (words) and Richard Rodgers (music) in 1940, being one of the songs from their stage musical *Pal Joey*. This disc features Snyder in a truly 'bewitching' piano arrangement of the now famous tune. It was No 3, and 19 weeks in the U.S.A. bestsellers. Snyder was born in Park Ridge, Illinois, on 11 July 1916 and studied the piano in his childhood, turning professional later by organizing a two-piano team and playing in radio until he entered the Services. Back in civilian life, he formed an orchestra shaped around his piano style and soon became an established nightclub attraction. This disc made him internationally known.

Snyder is the composer of 'The Chicago Concerto'.

THE THREE SUNS

TWILIGHT TIME *Victor* [*USA*]. This number was written by Buck Ram and the trio of Morty Nevins, Al Nevins and Artie Dunn in 1944 and had been recorded earlier on Majestic label (1946) by the Three Suns. It sold over four million. Al Nevins (guitarist) originally studied violin and viola and plays virtually any stringed instrument. Morty Nevins (accordionist) also plays piano. They both hail from Washington, D.C. Their cousin Artie Dunn (organist-vocalist) comes from Boston and was theatre organist in Dorchester, Massachusetts, then pianist for a New York music publisher before teaming with Morty and Al. This trio was the first guitar-organ-accordion combination. Al Nevins formed Aldon Music in the late 1950s with Don Kirschner (they put their Christian names together for this purpose) and the firm, just one part of the giant Nevins-Kirschner organization of top New York publishers, disc producers and managers, became one of the most profitable music concerns in America. It employed over thirty of America's top writers, notably the tremendously successful husband-and-wife teams Carole King and Gerry Goffin (since divorced), Cynthia Weill and Barry Mann, also Neil Sedaka, Howard Greenfield, Tony Orlando and Jack Keller. In April 1963, the organization was affiliated to Columbia Pictures–Screen Gems Music. The Three Suns' first big hit was 'Peg O' My Heart'.

HANK WILLIAMS WITH HIS DRIFTING COWBOYS

LONG GONE LONESOME BLUES *MGM* [*USA*]. Hank Williams wrote this number, his third million seller. A big seller in the U.S.A., it made the No 1 position in the country-and-western charts.

MOANIN' THE BLUES *MGM* [*USA*]. Hank Williams also wrote and performed this title, which eventually became his fourth million seller.

FLORIAN ZABACH (violin)

HOT CANARY *Decca* [*USA*]. Florian Zabach became a concert violinist at the age of 12 and toured Europe and the U.S.A. as a youth. He then switched to the popular idiom, breaking into radio in Chicago as a staff musician and soloist with Dr Roy Shield, Henry Weber and Percy Faith. He spent two years in the Army, then formed his own orchestra, appearing on the Arthur Godfrey Show and at New York's Strand Theatre. He subsequently appeared on radio and TV shows, and became a big attraction for supper club work.

In 1948, composer/conductor/violinist Paul Nero, of the Pittsburgh and CBS Symphony orchestras and soloist of the Chamber Music Society of Lower Basin Street, took a popular European piece entitled 'Le Canari' written by Paul Yakin ('F. Poliakin') and originally published in Belgium (date unknown). He made a jazz version of it – 'Hot Canary' – and also recorded it. It was, however, Zabach's disc that subsequently proved the bestseller with over a million sales through the years.

The disc is notable for Zabach's facile playing and expert use of harmonics – flute-like tones produced on the violin and such instruments by lightly placing the finger on the strings instead of pressing and resulting in vibrations to produce overtones of considerably strength. Zabach was thus able to produce a perfect imitation of a canary's chirping. It was No 13, and 10 weeks in the U.S.A. bestsellers.

Another of Zabach's hit discs was 'Jalousie'.

THE AMES BROTHERS WITH LES BROWN AND HIS ORCHESTRA

UNDECIDED *Coral* [*USA*]. This rhythmic number, written in 1939 by Sid Robin (words) and Charlie Shavers (music), became a second million seller for the Ames Brothers and a third for Les Brown. Robin specializes in writing lyrics for evergreen jazz favourites, as well as composing. He was formerly a member of Woody Herman's saxophone section. Charlie Shavers is a well-known jazz trumpeter. This disc was a million seller by 1956. Recorded 25 June 1951, it was 20 weeks in the U.S.A. bestsellers, and reached No 6.

LEROY ANDERSON AND HIS 'POPS' CONCERT ORCHESTRA

THE SYNCOPATED CLOCK *Decca* [*USA*]. Anderson was one of America's most celebrated composer-conductor-arrangers whose works have become famous by their outstanding acoustic effect. This was the first million seller of his many now famous descriptive pieces. He was born on 29 June 1908 in Cambridge, Massachusetts, and graduated with honours from Harvard in 1929. For the following five years he directed the Harvard band, then he acted as music tutor at Radcliffe College. In Boston, Anderson, with fine versatility, contributed to musical life as a choirmaster, church organist, double-bass player and conductor of orchestras. In 1935 he became an arranger and orchestrator for Arthur Fiedler and the Boston Pops orchestra, and it was Fiedler who introduced many of his works. 'The Syncopated Clock' has been described as a mesmeric work and became widely known through the U.S.A. television 'Late Show'. It was written in 1946. The disc was 14 weeks in the U.S.A. bestsellers, and reached No 12.

Anderson died on 18 May 1975, in Woodbury, Connecticut.

BLUE TANGO *Decca* [*USA*]. This second million seller for

Leroy Anderson, its composer, became the most popular for five weeks in the U.S.A. in 1952, and was 38 weeks in the U.S.A. bestsellers.

EDDY ARNOLD (country-and-western vocalist)

I WANNA PLAY HOUSE WITH YOU *Victor* [*USA*]. Eddy's fifth million seller disc, the song was written by Cy Coben. A seven-figure sale was achieved through subsequent years. The disc was a No 1 in the U.S.A. country-and-western charts in 1951.

FRED ASTAIRE AND JANE POWELL

HOW COULD YOU BELIEVE ME WHEN I SAID I LOVED YOU WHEN YOU KNOW I'VE BEEN A LIAR ALL MY LIFE? (The Liar Song) *MGM* [*USA*]. This song, with its extraordinary long title was written by Alan Jay Lerner (words) and Burton Lane (music) in 1950 and sung by Fred Astaire and Jane Powell in the film *Royal Wedding* (1951). In Britain the film was re-titled *Wedding Bells*.

Jane Powell, actress (real name Suzanne Burce), was born on 1 April in Portland, Oregon, where she subsequently had her own radio programme over station KOIN. She then became a singer on the national networks of the U.S.A. and made her screen debut in *Song of the Open Road* (1944). Later films included *Holiday in Mexico*, *Three Daring Daughters*, *Luxury Liner*, *A Date with Judy*, *Nancy Goes to Rio*, *Two Weeks With Love*, *Royal Wedding*, *Rich Young and Pretty*, *Seven Brides for Seven Brothers*, *Athena*, *Hit the Deck* and *The Girl Most Likely*.

Fred Astaire, dancer, actor (real name Frederick Austerlitz), was born 10 May 1899, in Omaha, Nebraska. He made his professional debut as a dancer at 11 in Paterson, New Jersey. He first appeared in New York in vaudeville in 1911, but being under age was forced to abandon his performance and was not seen again until 1916 when he toured with his actress-dancer sister Adele in vaudeville in the U.S.A. and Canada. From 1917, the duo appeared in 10 musicals together until 1931 including the famous *Stop Flirting*, *Lady, Be Good* and *Funny Face* (London and New York productions). Adele retired in 1931 and Fred then appeared in *The Gay Divorcee* (London and New York). In 1933, he entered the film world with his debut in *Dancing Lady*, followed by a further 29 musical films to 1957. These included (co-starring Ginger Rogers) - *Flying Down to Rio*, *The Gay Divorcee*, *Top Hat*, *Swing Time*, *Story of Irene and Vernon Castle*, *Follow the Fleet*, *Shall We Dance?*, *Roberta*, *Carefree* and *The Barkleys of Broadway*. The Rogers-Astaire scintillating song and dance routines captivated the world. Other great film successes were *Damsel in Distress*, then *Holiday Inn* and *You Were Never Lovelier* (both with Rita Hayworth), *Blue Skies*, *Easter Parade* (with Judy Garland) and *Band Wagon* and *Silk Stockings* (both with Cyd Charisse). Fred Astaire made his first dramatic role in *On the Beach* (1960) returning to a musical *Finian's Rainbow* (co-starring Petula Clark) in 1968. Acclaimed as one of the world's greatest dancers, he started a chain of dance studios throughout the U.S.A. Astaire was voted Money-Making Star in Motion Pictures for 1935, 1936 and 1937 in polls and was also given a special Academy Award for 'raising the standards of all musicals' in 1949.

He has been featured on TV specials and also TV series. Songwriting is another of his talents.

This disc of 'The Liar Song' was reported in 1968 to have sold a million, and was taken from the original film soundtrack.

TONY BENNETT

BECAUSE OF YOU *Columbia* [*USA*]. Tony's real name is Anthony Dominick Benedetto, and he was born on 3 August 1926 on Long Island, New York. Raised by a widowed mother, he literally sang for his supper while still a youngster, earning $15 for a weekend's work, then attending school. He made his first public appearance at seven years of age in a church minstrel show. The war broke his musical career and he served three years as a front-line infantry soldier in Europe. He had a tough time after the war until Ray Muscarelle got him on an Arthur Godfrey 'Talent Scouts' show which led to a television contract. Bob Hope also invited Bennett to sing in his Paramount Theatre Show. The writers of the song in 1940 were Arthur Hammerstein

(uncle of lyricist Oscar Hammerstein II) and Dudley Wilkinson and it was introduced in the film *I Was an American Spy*. The disc sold a million by 1952, and was No 1 seller for eight weeks in U.S.A., and 31 weeks in the bestsellers.

TONY BENNETT WITH THE PERCY FAITH ORCHESTRA

COLD, COLD HEART *Columbia* [*USA*]. This second million seller for Tony, by 1952, was a chart topper for six weeks in the U.S.A. The song was written by famous country-and-western artist Hank Williams in 1951 whose own disc also sold a million. This disc was 27 weeks in the bestsellers.

ROSEMARY CLOONEY

COME-ON-A MY HOUSE *Columbia* [*USA*]. This song made a big reputation for Rosemary, the little girl from Maysville, Kentucky, where she was born on 23 May 1928. Dramatist William Saroyan, and his cousin, Ross Bagdasarian, both of Armenian extraction, wrote it to the tune of an Armenian folk song of their childhood while driving through New Mexico in 1939. Saroyan used the song in his play *The Son* in 1950. Bagdasarian was later responsible for the famous 'Chipmunk' disc (see 1958). Rosemary Clooney began her career as half of the Clooney Sisters singing team. She sang with her sister Betty with Tony Pastor's Band from 1946 after being heard over the Cincinnati radio. In 1949, Mitch Miller of Columbia set her on her record, film, cabaret and TV career, after a vocal spot on TV's 'Songs for Sale'. 'Come-on-a My House' rocketed her to fame in 1951, and she became an international film star through such films as *Here Come the Girls* (with Bob Hope) and *White Christmas* (with Bing Crosby). This disc, her first million seller, was also the first pop song with an Armenian folk song flavour to hit the market, and was No 1 seller for six weeks in the U.S.A., and 17 weeks in the bestsellers.

NAT 'KING' COLE WITH ORCHESTRA CONDUCTED BY LES BAXTER

TOO YOUNG *Capitol* [*USA*]. Nat's fourth million seller disc was written by Sylvia Dee (words) and Sid Lippman (music). The song was top of the 1951 Hit Parade for five weeks in the U.S.A., and 29 weeks in the bestsellers.

PERRY COMO

IF *Victor* [*USA*]. This ninth million seller for Perry Como was written by the all-British team of Robert Hargreaves and Stanley J. Damerell (words) with music by Tolchard Evans in 1934, when it was a considerable success in England. This revival was No 1 for six weeks in the U.S.A. and a world hit. It was 22 weeks in the bestsellers.

DORIS DAY WITH THE PAUL WESTON ORCHESTRA

A GUY IS A GUY *Columbia* [*USA*]. This title provided Doris Day with her fourth million seller. Words and music of the song are by Oscar Brand. It was adapted by Brand from a parody song of ancient origin. A World War II version was 'A Gob is a Snob'. Disc was No 4 for four weeks in the U.S.A. (1952), and 19 weeks in the bestsellers.

BILLY ECKSTINE

I APOLOGIZE *MGM* [*USA*]. This seventh million seller for Billy is an oldie of 1931, written by Al Hoffman, Al Goodhard and Ed Nelson. This disc was 19 weeks in the U.S.A. bestsellers, and reached No. 8.

EDDIE FISHER

ANYTIME *Victor* [*USA*]. Within two years 'Anytime' provided Eddie with his first million seller. Fisher was born on 10 August 1928 in Philadelphia and sang over local radio stations in his teens. Next he went to New York as band vocalist and production singer at the Copacabana nightclub. In 1949 at an engagement in the Catskills, Fisher was spotted by Eddie Cantor who signed him for a cross-country tour. The song was originally written in 1921 by Herbert 'Happy' Lawson. This disc was No 3 for two weeks in the U.S.A. charts (1952), and 28 weeks in the bestsellers.

RED FOLEY

PEACE IN THE VALLEY *Decca* [*USA*]. This fourth million seller for Foley is an inspirational or gospel composition by Thomas A. Dorsey, written in 1939.

THE FOUR ACES WITH ORCHESTRA FEATURING AL ALBERTS

TELL ME WHY *Decca* [*USA*]. This first million seller for this outstanding group was written by Al Alberts (words) and Marty Gold (music), the arranger for the group. The vocal group was organized in 1949 by Al Alberts, their leader. After part-time work, Al with Dave Mahoney, Lou Silvestri and Sol Vocarro, worked full-time in Ye Olde Mill near Philadelphia, where they introduced their version of 'Sin'. They were asked to record it and it brought them fame. It was followed by 'Tell Me Why', which incidentally was backed by the English song 'Garden in the Rain' written by James Dyrenforth (words) and the late band leader Carroll Gibbons (music). The Four Aces had sold over 22 million discs by 1970. This disc was No 2 for six weeks in the U.S.A. charts (1952), and 24 weeks in the bestsellers.

THE FOUR ACES

SIN (It's no sin) *Victoria* [*USA*]. The Four Aces recorded this for the small independent company Victoria Records before signing with Decca, and paid for the recording out of their own funds. It went to a million sale just after 'Tell Me Why' reached that target. (See 'Tell Me Why' above for further data.) 'Sin' was written by Chester R. Shull (words) and George Hoven (music). The disc was No 4 in the U.S.A. charts (1952), and 22 weeks in the bestsellers.

EDDY HOWARD

SIN (It's no sin) *Mercury* [*USA*]. Eddy's second million seller, and chart topper for two weeks in the U.S.A., sold one million by 1956. The song was written by Chester R. Shull (words) and George Hoven (music). The disc was 23 weeks in the bestsellers.

PEE WEE KING AND HIS GOLDEN WEST COWBOYS

SLOW POKE *Victor* [*USA*]. The only million seller by this group reached the million by 1953. This song was written by Frank (Pee Wee) King, Redd Stewart and Chilton Price, and the disc appeared in Britain under the revised title of 'Slow-Coach'. King was born in Abrams, Wisconsin, and educated in Milwaukee where he won an amateur contest with his harmonica. By switching to accordion and organizing a four-piece combo, he landed a spot on a Racine, Wisconsin, radio station. He then toured with Gene Autry's western band, and joined the Log Cabin Boys in Louisville, Kentucky. Soon after King formed his own group - the Golden West Cowboys who appeared for ten years on the 'Grand Ole Opry' show over radio in Nashville. Pee Wee made movies and wrote such tunes as 'Bonaparte's Retreat'. This disc was No 3 in the U.S.A. charts (1952), and a top country-and-western disc, and was 22 weeks in the bestsellers. Pee Wee King was born on 18 February 1914.

FRANKIE LAINE

JEZEBEL *Columbia* [*USA*]. Frankie's sixth million seller disc was written by Wayne Shanklin in 1950. It reached No 2, and was 21 weeks in the U.S.A. bestsellers.

JALOUSIE (Jealousy) *Columbia* [*USA*]. A hit vocal version (words by Vera Bloom in 1931) of Jacob Gade's famous instrumental composition originally written by the Danish composer in 1926. Frankie Laine's disc is said to have sold a million. It reached No 3 in the U.S.A., and was 14 weeks in the bestsellers.

FRANKIE LAINE WITH THE NORMAN LUBOFF CHOIR

ROSE, ROSE I LOVE YOU (Make Way oh Make Way) *Columbia* [*USA*]. This traditional Chinese melody 'Mei Kuei' first came to light through a recording by Chinese artist Hue Lee. Its tune greatly attracted disc jockey Wilfred Thomas who discovered the disc, and while he was in Britain compering BBC radio programmes, he wrote English lyrics for it and give it its title. His adaptation of the music was then arranged by Chris Langdon of music publishers Chappell & Co. Frankie Laine's subsequent recording in the U.S.A. with the Luboff Choir was a very big hit, and the first Chinese melody to achieve Top Ten status there and sell a reported million. The song was also a big success in Britain and elsewhere.

Norman Luboff, composer/conductor/arranger/singer, was born in Chicago, Illinois on 14 May 1917 and educated there. He became a teacher, then singer, arranger and coach for radio shows in Chicago. He later (1948) went to Hollywood for 'Railroad Hour' then with Warner Brothers. He led his own choral group in concerts and made many fine discs for Columbia and R.C.A. with his choir. His biggest hit as a composer is probably 'Yellow Bird' which he adapted from a West Indian folk song, in 1957.

This disc was 16 weeks in the U.S.A. bestsellers and reached No 3.

MARIO LANZA

THE LOVELIEST NIGHT OF THE YEAR *Victor* [*USA*]. Lanza's second million seller was written by Paul Francis Webster (words) and Irving Aaronson (music), who adapted Juvenito Rosas's 'Sobre las Olas' waltz composed in the latter part of the 19th century. It was the hit song of the film *The Great Caruso* in which Lanza took the star role in the story of the world's greatest operatic tenor (see 1903). The song was introduced in the film by Ann Blyth.

The disc was No 3 and 34 weeks in the U.S.A. bestsellers.

MANTOVANI AND HIS ORCHESTRA

CHARMAINE *Decca* [*Britain*]. In 1951, Mantovani was asked to record some favourite tunes especially for the American market. This was taken off the album and issued as a single in Britain and America because of its intriguingly different arrangement of 'cascading strings' perfected by Mantovani, aided by composer-arranger Ronald Binge. It soon sold a million and 'Monty' became an international attraction. Born Annunzio Paolo Mantovani in Venice, Italy, on 15 November 1905, he was without question one of the most popular orchestra leaders in the world. His father was first violinist at the famed La Scala, Milan, then under Arturo Toscanini, and he thus inherited his artistic tastes. The family moved to England and at 16, 'Monty' was a professional violinist and four years later had installed an orchestra at the Hotel Metropole, London (1925), and began broadcasting. In the early 1930s he formed the Tipica Orchestra and began a series of lunchtime broadcasts from the Monseigneur Restaurant, Piccadilly, also recording for Regal Zonophone. Thereafter, Mantovani conducted for many stars, including Noel Coward, Leslie Henson and Pat Kirkwood. He also had his own TV show. Mantovani, who started recording for Decca in 1940, is in a class of his own for album sales, 15 selling over 250,000 each. 'Monty' was the first musician in the world to sell a million stereo albums. His figures in this department alone reached four million by 1965. He visited the U.S.A. often for long concert tours, playing to vast audiences and capturing the imagination of the American public. 'Charmaine' used as a theme for the silent film *What Price Glory?* in 1926 by Erno Rapee was given its title and lyric by Lew Pollack who did not think much of the song at the time, but it became a million sheet music seller. The backing was another famous Rapee-Pollack composition of 1927 – 'Diane'. 'Charmaine' was first composed in Hungary in 1913. The disc reached No 10, and was 19 weeks in the U.S.A. bestsellers.

Mantovani died 30 March 1980, Tunbridge Wells, Kent.

WYOMING *Decca* [*Britain*]. Another Mantovani disc that eventually sold a million in the U.S.A. on the London label.

It was written in 1919 by Gene Williams, the pseudonym of British composer-publisher Lawrence Wright.

PERCY MAYFIELD

PLEASE SEND ME SOMEONE TO LOVE *Specialty* [*USA*]. The only million seller by this rhythm-and-blues artist, was written by him in 1950. Percy was born on 12 August 1920 in Shreveport, Louisiana. Released in 1950, it was a top rhythm-and-blues disc.

GUY MITCHELL WITH THE MITCH MILLER ORCHESTRA

THE ROVING KIND *Columbia* [*USA*]. This song was written in 1950 by Jessie Cavanaugh and Arnold Stanton and provided Guy Mitchell with his second million seller. Publisher Howie Richmond came across the lyrics while reading Sinclair Lewis' novel *Arrowsmith*, ultimately discovering from the British Museum that it as an old British sea shanty, 'The Pirate Ship'. It was the famous Weavers folk outfit who retitled the tune, and although theirs was the first disc cut, Guy Mitchell's version became the bestseller. It was No 4, and 17 weeks in the U.S.A. bestsellers.

MY TRULY, TRULY FAIR *Columbia* [*USA*]. This third million seller for Guy Mitchell was written by Bob Merrill, one of the most consistent hit writers of the early 1950s, who wrote many successes for Mitchell and other artists in the disc field. It was No 5, and 19 weeks in the U.S.A. bestsellers.

PATTI PAGE

MOCKIN' BIRD HILL *Mercury* [*USA*]. Patti's fourth million seller was originally written in 1949 by Vaughn Horton. It reached No 3, and was 22 weeks in the U.S.A. bestsellers.

WOULD I LOVE YOU (LOVE YOU, LOVE YOU)? *Mercury* [*USA*]. The fifth big hit for Patti with an estimated subsequent million sale. It was written by Bob Russell (words) and Harold

Spina (music). This disc was No 7, and 17 weeks in the U.S.A. bestsellers.

DETOUR *Mercury* [*USA*]. Sixth million seller for Patti Page, a revival of a popular country-and-western song written by Paul Westmoreland in 1945. It reached No 12, and was 14 weeks in the U.S.A. bestsellers.

MISTER AND MISSISSIPPI *Mercury* [*USA*]. Seventh million seller for Patti Page, written by Irving Gordon, noted for his unique use of American states in his songs (see 'Delaware', 1960). It was No 9, and 13 weeks in the U.S.A. bestsellers.

LES PAUL (guitar) MARY FORD (vocal)

MOCKIN' BIRD HILL *Capitol* [*USA*]. This other million seller disc of the Vaughn Horton song was the first for the unique multitrack electric-guitar star Les Paul and his then wife Mary Ford (vocalist and guitar). Les Paul was born in Waukesha, Wisconsin on 9 June 1916, and played guitar on radio jobs in Racine and Milwaukee as a teenager. After a period on the staff of NBS in Chicago and a spot on the Ben Bernie Show, he joined NBC in Hollywood before entering the Army in 1944. It was, however, in the winter of 1941, after a bad car accident that he worked out the details of his multi-track guitar records idea while in hospital. He had been a radio amateur and keen dabbler in electronics for years. In 1942, Paul assembled a Western show for radio work to help pay for his recording experiments and engaged Mary Ford, a native of Pasadena, California, who had been playing guitar and singing on hillbilly radio shows from childhood. They married in 1948 (since divorced). After his discharge from the army the Pauls worked out a joint act in 1951. Paul had made records for Decca and Columbia with bands, with his trio, and as 'Rhubarb Red', a hillbilly, and had worked with big and small bands including Fred Waring's, Ben Bernie's and his own. He had also played the Eastern theatre circuit with his trio. His 'new sound' multiple recordings catapulted him to stardom when he joined Capitol in 1948, the first disc 'Lover' backed with 'Brazil' taking the disc world by storm. This disc of 'Mockin' Bird Hill' (and the following two titles) were in all probability recorded prior to 1951, but this was undoubtedly the big year for Les and Mary. Paul's real name is Leslie Polfuss. This disc was No 3, and 24 weeks in the U.S.A. bestsellers. Mary Ford's real name was Colleen Summers. She was born 7 July 1928 and died 30 September 1977 in the U.S.A..

HOW HIGH THE MOON *Capitol* [*USA*]. This second million seller for Les Paul and Mary Ford was originally written for a musical *Two for the Show* in 1940 by Nancy Hamilton (words) and Morgan Lewis (music). The disc was probably recorded about 1948. It was a No 1 seller for nine weeks in the U.S.A., and 25 weeks in the bestsellers.

THE WORLD IS WAITING FOR THE SUNRISE *Capitol* [*USA*]. This third million seller for Les Paul and Mary Ford is a rhythmic version of the outstanding ballad written in 1919 by Eugene Lockhart (words), the famous stage and screen actor, and Ernest Seitz (music), both being of Canadian extraction. It reached No 3, and was 16 weeks in the U.S.A. bestsellers.

JOHNNY RAY WITH THE FOUR LADS

CRY backed with LITTLE WHITE CLOUD THAT CRIED *Okeh-Columbia* [*USA*]. Johnny's first big hit sold over two million as he cried himself into a fabulous fortune in 1952, creating excitement and fervour not seen since the height of the Sinatra craze. He was born on 10 January 1927 in Dallas, Oregon. Ray left home at 17 after trying to crash Hollywood and wound up playing piano and singing in small bistros around Los Angeles and later in the Middlewest, writing his own material. Meanwhile, Bernie Lang, a freelance song plugger, was attracted by his songs and became his personal manager. During a nightclub tour, Johnny was spotted (in April 1951) at The Flame, Detroit, by disc jockey Robin Seymour who persuaded Danny Kessler of Columbia to hear Ray. Kessler signed Johnny in June, and he soon scored with this disc. 'Little White Cloud' was written by him. 'Cry' was written by Churchill Kohlman, a watchman at a dry-cleaning establishment at Werners, Pittsburgh. He entered it for an amateur songwriting contest conducted by the Copa Night Club in Pittsburgh. It was weeded out in the first round, and another of Kohlman's tunes 'Appreciation' got into the finals. 'Cry' never got anywhere until Johnny Ray recorded it for the Okeh label. It was No 1 for eleven weeks in the U.S.A. from the end of December 1951 into 1952, and 27 weeks in the bestsellers. 'Little White Cloud' was No 2 in the U.S.A. charts (1952), and 22 weeks in the bestsellers.

HERE AM I BROKEN-HEARTED *Columbia* [*USA*]. This second million seller for Johnny Ray was a most appropriate song title follow-up to his big hit 'Cry'. This song is an oldie of 1927, written by famous songwriting team of B.G. de Sylva, Lew Brown and Ray Henderson. The disc was No 9, and 14 weeks in the U.S.A. bestsellers.

DEBBIE REYNOLDS AND CARLETON CARPENTER WITH THE MGM STUDIO ORCHESTRA AND CHORUS CONDUCTED BY GEORGE STOLL

ABA DABA HONEYMOON *MGM* [*USA*]. This was the only million seller disc for this duo, although Debbie had a solo million disc later. The song is an oldie, written in 1914 by Arthur Fields and Walter Donovan, revived for the film *Two Weeks with Love* made in 1950 in which the singers starred. The disc, probably the first million seller taken directly from a soundtrack, sold three million. Debbie Reynolds (Mary Frances Reynolds) was born in El Paso, Texas, on 1 April 1932. Her high school talents were comedy and music, principally impersonations, in school theatricals, and she also played French horn with the Burbank Youth Symphony in school. She won the 'Miss Burbank' beauty contest in 1948, was spotted by talent scouts and given a screen contract. Debbie continued her education specializing in dramatics, voice and dancing, thereafter becoming a star with MGM. Carleton Carpenter, actor, pianist, songwriter, dramatic coach and soft-shoe virtuoso, was born in Bennington, Vermont. He began his career with a magic act as 'Professor Upham', performing at various clubs, camps and hospitals. After four years, at 14 years of age he toured with a carnival, ran away from school and landed a job in the chorus of *The Chocolate Soldier* in New York, but returned to complete his education. In 1944 he was signed for second comedy lead in *Bright Boy* in New

York. Carpenter served for 18 months in the Seabees, and then went back to New York in radio, TV and on Broadway. Eventually he signed to MGM and it was his role with Debbie in *Two Weeks with Love* that made them stars. This disc was No 3, and 15 weeks in the U.S.A. bestsellers.

JO STAFFORD

SHRIMP BOATS *Columbia* [*USA*]. Jo Stafford's delightful rendering of the charming 'Shrimp Boats A-Comin', There's Dancin' Tonight' sold an estimated million by 1952. The words and music were by Paul Mason Howard and composer-conductor-arranger Paul Weston. Paul Weston, born in Springfield, Massachusetts, 12 March 1912, was musical director and arranger for Capitol Records for seven years (1943-1950) then with Columbia, and from 1958 had an exclusive recording contract with Capitol. He provided the accompaniments on the hit discs of many stars including Doris Day, Johnny Ray, Frankie Laine, Rosemary Clooney and Jo Stafford. Paul married Jo Stafford. He devoted a lot of his time to music of a more serious nature. This disc was No 2 in the U.S.A. charts (1952), and 17 weeks in the bestsellers.

JOE TURNER

CHAINS OF LOVE *Atlantic* [*USA*]. This was a first million seller by this rhythm-and-blues artist. Turner was born in Kansas City on 18 May 1911, and has made nightclub and theatrical personal appearances. This song was written by 'Nugetre' (words) - Ahmet Ertegun, Van Walls (music), and the disc reached the million by 1954. Turner was a famous blues singer before World War II.

THE WEAVERS AND TERRY GILKYSON WITH CHORUS AND ORCHESTRA CONDUCTED BY VIC SCHOEN

ON TOP OF OLD SMOKEY *Decca* [*USA*]. This title provided a second million seller for the famous folk group, The Weavers. The words of the song are anonymous, and the tune is an old folk song of the hills. This arrangement was made by Pete Seeger, one of the original group who became a soloist in 1958. Gilkyson was born in Phoenixville, Pennsylvania on 17 June 1916. He studied music composition and harmony at the University of Pennsylvania from 1938 to 1940. From 1941 to 1946 Gilkyson was a singer of American folk songs on the Armed Forces Radio. He went on to become a hit songwriter. Pete Seeger was born 3 May 1919 in New York.

This disc was No 2, and 22 weeks in the bestsellers.

SLIM WHITMAN (country-and-western vocalist with guitar)

INDIAN LOVE CALL *Imperial* [*USA*]. This first million seller for Slim was written by Otto Harbach and Oscar Hammerstein II (words) and Rudolf Friml (music) for the famous musical *Rose Marie* in 1924. It brought great prominence to Slim. He was born on 20 January 1924, in Tampa, Florida and was educated there, where he also became a promising baseball player. After leaving school, he worked in a Tampa shipyard and enlisted in the U.S. Navy in 1943. He found an old guitar aboard his first ship, and although he strummed it left-handed, he enjoyed accompanying his own singing and was asked to appear on the ship's shows. On discharge in 1945, he returned to his shipfitting job until friends convinced him of a singing future. He decided to go for show business in 1948 and was eventually signed to a disc contract. 'Indian Love Call' gave him world-wide renown. Although he is considered mainly a country-and-western singer, his rich, melodic voice is equally at home with ballads and semi-classics as well as cowboy laments. His yodelling versions of songs were great favourites.

Slim was the first western artist to tour England on his own and was also the first western vocalist to perform at the London Palladium. His real name is Otis Dewey Whitman, Junior.

This disc was No 10, and 14 weeks in the U.S.A. bestsellers.

HANK WILLIAMS

COLD, COLD HEART *MGM* [*USA*]. This was a seventh million seller for this famous country-and-western disc star. The song was written by him and also became a million seller for Tony Bennett (see 1952). This was the top country-and-western disc of 1951, staying 46 weeks in the country-and-western charts, reaching No 2.

HANK WILLIAMS WITH HIS DRIFTING COWBOYS

HEY, GOOD LOOKIN' *MGM* [*USA*]. This number provided million seller number five for Hank. The song written by Hank himself was a hit in 1951 in the country-and-western charts, reaching No 2, and stayed 20 weeks in the country-and-western bestsellers.

RAMBLIN' MAN *MGM* [*USA*]. This number was also written by Hank Williams. The disc achieved the million sale through subsequent years.

DEL WOOD (piano)

DOWN YONDER *Tennessee* [*USA*]. Miss Del Wood, born 22 February 1920 in Nashville, Tennessee, was probably the first female country solo instrumentalist to register in a big way. She became known as the 'Down Yonder Girl' through the success of this disc which is said to have sold a million throughout the mid-1950s. 'Down Yonder', written by veteran author/publisher L. Wolfe Gilbert in 1921, has been revived several times since its publication (see Gid Tanner, 1934) and has become a standard ragtime work.

Del had some difficulty with Tennessee Records of Nashville over this disc, and a settlement was made out of court with Del obtaining a complete release from the label (since defunct) and a settlement of $5,000 in back royalties, in 1953.

She became a member of 'Grand Ole Opry' in 1951.

Subsequent recording came with the Victor, Class and Mercury labels and further hit discs with 'Piano Roll Blues', 'Muskat Ramble' and 'Johnson Rag', all played in her distinctive country ragtime and honky-tonk style.

In 1968, she went on a personal tour of the Far East including Viet Nam, South Korea and the Philippines, and also appeared in the Japanese version of 'Grand Ole Opry' in Tokyo.

'Down Yonder' achieved Top Ten status in the U.S.A. country-and-western charts, and was in the Hit Parade for 18 consecutive weeks. Nationally it was No 6, and 25 weeks in the bestsellers.

1952

FILM SOUNDTRACK OF FILM WITH GENE KELLY, GEORGES GUETARY, LESLIE CARON, OSCAR LEVANT (PIANIST) AND MGM STUDIO ORCHESTRA CONDUCTED BY JOHNNY GREEN

'AN AMERICAN IN PARIS' (album) *MGM* [*USA*]. The late U.S. composer George Gershwin wrote his famous instrumental work 'An American in Paris' in various hotels he stayed at during a trip (his last) to Europe in the spring of 1928. The entire 'blues' section was written at the Hotel Majestic in Paris. Damrosch sponsored its first performance and it has been popular with symphony organizations ever since. MGM based their film of the same title on this work and used all Gershwin songs of the past for its musical score which was arranged by Saul Chaplin and Johnny Green, both of whom received the Academy Award for the Best Musical Film Score of 1951. Green also conducted the orchestra for the film. It was a tremendous success for actor-dancer Gene Kelly, who also co-directed and arranged the choreography. He received a special Academy Award for advancing dance films (1951). The film also introduced the talented singer/actor Georges Guetary of France and French actress/dancer Leslie Caron (see biography 1953). An Oscar was also awarded to MGM for Best Feature Film of 1951.

Oscar Levant, the concert pianist who appeared as soloist in many Gershwin programmes at the Lewisohn Stadium (New York) and Hollywood Bowl, was also in the film and played Gershwin's 'Concerto in F' composed in 1925.

MGM Records issued a 10-inch album of the film soundtrack in 1952 which over the years was periodically repackaged and reissued; the collective sales were reported in 1970 as over the million mark.

The various musical items on these included the following from the film:

'An American in Paris' Ballet (The Orchestra) - George Gershwin (1928); 'I'll Build a Stairway to Paradise' (Georges Guetary) (from *George White's Scandals*, 1922) - B.G. De Sylva, Arthur Frances/George Gershwin; 'I Got Rhythm' (Gene Kelly) (from *Girl Crazy*, 1930) - Ira Gershwin/George Gershwin; 'Embraceable You' (Leslie Caron) (from *Girl Crazy*, 1930) - Ira Gershwin/George Gershwin; ''Swonderful' (Gene Kelly & Georges Guetary) (from *Funny Face*, 1927) - Ira Gershwin/George Gershwin; 'Love Is Here to Stay' (Gene Kelly) (from *Goldwyn Follies*, 1938) - Ira Gershwin/George Gershwin; 'By Strauss' (Kelly, Guetary & Caron) (from *The Show Is On*, 1936) - Ira Gershwin/George Gershwin; 'Liza' (from *Show Girl*, 1929) - Gus Kahn, Ira Gershwin/George Gershwin.

Musical director Johnny Green had four Oscar awards - *Easter Parade* (1948), *An American in Paris* (1951), *West Side Story* (1961) and *Oliver* (1968).

WINIFRED ATWELL (piano)

BLACK AND WHITE RAG *Decca* [*Britain*]. Winnie's first disc to sell a million. She was born in Tunapuna, Trinidad, West Indies, began playing the piano at the age of four and gave classical recitals when six. Miss Atwell studied for a degree in chemistry, and when she had qualified, worked in her father's chemist store, only playing the piano for friends and charity in her spare time. She also gave concerts in the Services Club, Trinidad. Winnie later went to New York to study piano under Alexander Borovsky, and then to Britain's Royal Academy of

Music under Harold Craxton. Finding the going difficult to become a concert pianist, she developed her earlier talents by playing boogie and managed to obtain a few engagements. Winifred Atwell's big chance came at a charity concert at the London Casino, where she was an instant success and which decided her future in becoming a top-liner. She made her first broadcast in 1947 and her first records for Decca in 1951. Decca then hit on the idea of a worn-out piano. Winnie found one that had the 'tinny' sound for which she was looking in a junk shop in Battersea for 50 shillings. Her disc on this old upright was the 'corny' 'Black and White Rag' which, played on the BBC's Jack Jackson Record Show, zoomed into the top sellers overnight. Winnie's 'other piano' became part of her stage act and she was acclaimed as a wonderful new star. Then came the star billing at the London Palladium, her own Radio Luxembourg programme (1952) and radio, cabaret, TV and tours abroad, with spectacular success in Australia. 'Black and White Rag' was written way back in 1908 by George Botsford who died just three days before Winnie made this disc. She died in Australia, 28 February 1983 (aged 69).

EARL BOSTIC (alto saxophone) AND HIS ORCHESTRA

FLAMINGO *King* [*USA*]. This was Bostic's only million seller. He was born in Tulsa, Oklahoma, on 25 April 1913, and played clarinet and sax in the school band. After attending Creighton University, Omaha, and Xavier University, New Orleans, he was taught harmony, theory and several new instruments by a nun, Sister Letitia. Bostic became director of the college symphony orchestra and sideman with dance bands after graduating. Then he went to New York with Don Redman, Cab Calloway and others. From 1945 he spent two years with the Lionel Hampton orchestra writing arrangements for the band and for other bands including Paul Whiteman's. Earl had his own band in 1938 for three years in Harlem. In 1946 with a new nine-piece combo, Bostic joined a small rhythm-and-blues company, Gotham Records, and began to achieve identification by his biting saxophone tone, backed by heavy rhythm and swing style. After the war Bostic switched to the King label. This disc made only a mild impression at first, but, after some broadcasts, sales rocketed sensationally. The composition is by Ted Grouya, originally piano instructor at Bucharest Conservatoire, Rumania, with words by Ed Anderson. 'Flamingo' was written and recorded in 1951. Bostic died in New York on 28 November 1965.

JIMMY BOYD

I SAW MOMMY KISSING SANTA CLAUS *Columbia* [*USA*]. Jimmy's only million seller was recorded when he was not quite 13 years of age. He was born in McComb, Missouri, 9 January 1940. At seven he started singing Western tunes for local affairs, accompanied by his father on guitar and harmonica. He then toured for a year with Texas Jim Lewis's troupe, and won a talent contest. After a guest appearance on the Frank Sinatra TV show he was contracted to Columbia. He has also had his own radio programme in Los Angeles, and attended the Hollywood Professional School for Children. This disc broke all records at Columbia who sold 248,000 in one day, 700,000 in ten days from 1 to 10 December, and over one million just before Christmas 1952. Total sales to date exceed 2,500,000. The song was written by famous British songwriter Tommie Connor (of 'Lili Marlene' - see 1939) who went to the U.S.A. in 1952 for a period. He had been unable to place the song in England, and the trip certainly made it worth while. It became No. 1 in the U.S.A. Hit Parade in three weeks, and stayed top for two weeks. Collective disc sales of the song by 1966 were 11 million. No 3 in Britain, and six weeks in the bestsellers.

TERESA BREWER

TILL I WALTZ AGAIN WITH YOU *Coral* [*USA*]. This number provided Miss Brewer with her second million seller. The song was written by Sidney Prosen. This disc was No 1 seller for five weeks in the U.S.A., and 22 weeks in the bestsellers.

RUTH BROWN

FIVE, TEN, FIFTEEN HOURS *Atlantic* [*USA*]. Within three years this number provided Ruth Brown, who was born in Portsmouth, Virginia, with her first million seller. In her native town she sang spirituals and hymns under her father's direction at church. Turning professional, she sang with the Lucky Millinder band until 1948. En route to New York for her debut at the Apollo Theatre, Harlem, she sustained multiple injuries in a car accident, but after a year in hospital she started recording with considerable success. This song was written by Rudolph Toombs.

KAREN CHANDLER

HOLD ME, THRILL ME, KISS ME *Coral* [*USA*]. This song, written by Harry Noble, was Miss Chandler's only seven-figure disc. Karen, a native of Rexburg, Ohio, was band vocalist at Brigham Young University. After graduation, she tried to crash New York City, without success. Then with husband, conductor/arranger Jack Pleis, she went to Hollywood where Jerry Lewis heard her auditioning for a local NBC show. This led to a spot on the Martin-Lanza TV series. She then made a demonstration disc of this song for Fred Amsel, who signed her to a personal management contract and arranged a regular recording session with a subsequent long-term contract with Coral.

This disc was 18 weeks in the U.S.A. bestsellers, and reached No 7.

ROSEMARY CLOONEY

TENDERLY *Columbia* [*USA*]. The song, written by Jack Lawrence (words) and Walter Gross (music) in 1946, has become one of the standard waltz successes of all time. It became Rosemary's second million seller, and reached No 30 in the U.S.A. charts.

BOTCH-A-ME *Columbia* [*USA*]. This third million seller for Rosemary was originally Italian - 'Ba-Ba-Baciami Piccina' - written by R. Morbelli and L. Astore, in 1941, with English words and music adaptation by Eddie Y. Stanley in 1952. Stanley made the 'Baciami' into 'Botch-a-me' for this half English, half Italian version. The disc was 26 weeks in the U.S.A. bestsellers, and reached No 2.

HALF AS MUCH *Columbia* [*USA*]. This song, written by Curley Williams in 1951, provided a fourth million seller for Rosemary, making it a big year for her. It was 26 weeks in the U.S.A. bestsellers, reaching No 2. No 3 in Britain, and nine weeks in the bestsellers.

PERRY COMO
DON'T LET THE STARS GET IN YOUR EYES *Victor* [*USA*]. Here, by 1953, was Perry's tenth million seller. Both the words and music are by Slim Willet (real name: Winston Moore), Cactus Pryor and Barbara Trammel. This disc was No 1 seller for five weeks in the U.S.A., and chart topper in Britain in 1953 for five weeks. It was 21 weeks in the U.S.A. bestsellers, and 15 in Britain.

DON CORNELL
I'M YOURS *Coral* [*USA*]. This second million seller for Don was written by Robert Mellin. It reached No 5, and was 16 weeks in the U.S.A. bestsellers.

FATS DOMINO
GOIN' HOME *Imperial* [*USA*]. This second million seller for Fats was written by him and Alvin E. Young. A top rhythm-and-blues disc.

EDDIE FISHER WITH HUGO WINTERHALTER ORCHESTRA AND CHORUS
TELL ME WHY *Victor* [*USA*]. This second million seller for Eddie was written by Al Alberts (words) and Marty Gold (music) (see Four Aces, 1951). It reached No 7, and was 19 weeks in the U.S.A. bestsellers.

EDDIE FISHER
LADY OF SPAIN backed with OUTSIDE OF HEAVEN *Victor* [*USA*]. Eddie's third million seller 'Lady of Spain' was written in 1931 by Errol Reaves and S.J. Damerell (words) with music by Tolchard Evans. This British song was put back in the popularity market by this disc and became world famous. 'Outside of Heaven', by American writers Sammy Gallop (words) and Chester Conn (music), was a No 1 seller in Britain in 1953, reached No 10 in the U.S.A., and was 12 weeks in the bestsellers. 'Lady of Spain' reached No 9 in the U.S.A., and was 17 weeks in the bestsellers.

WISH YOU WERE HERE *Victor* [*USA*]. This was the hit song of the American musical of 1952 *Wish You Were Here* and sung therein by Jack Cassidy. The complete score was by famous composer-author-librettist-pianist Harold J. Rome.

Eddie Fisher's disc sold an estimated global million, his fourth to do so. Much of the show's success was attributed to Eddie's disc, which was No 3 in the U.S.A. charts, and 21 weeks in the bestsellers. No 8 and nine weeks in the bestsellers in Britain.

GEORGIA GIBBS
KISS OF FIRE *Mercury* [*USA*]. This first million seller and No. 2 in the U.S.A. charts for Georgia was written by Lester Allen and Robert Hill (music adapted from A.G. Villoldo's famous 'El Choclo', an Argentine tango of 1913). Georgia Gibbs (nicknamed 'Her Nibs' by Garry Moore) hails from Worcester, Massachusetts, where she got her first show experience over a local radio station. She commuted on weekends to sing at the Plymouth theatre by day and the Theatrical Club by night. She then joined the Will Hudson-Eddie de Lange band, was next on the Herb Shriner radio show, and later the Jimmy Durante-Garry Moore programme. She got her first disc break in 1944 with 'Shoo Shoo Baby', with continued success thereafter. Her real name is Freda Gibson.

This disc was 20 weeks in the U.S.A. bestsellers.

DON HOWARD (vocal with guitar)
OH HAPPY DAY *Essex - Triple A* [*USA*]. This song, with a folk-like origin, was one of the bestselling records of 1952–53. Don Howard (Donald Howard Koplow) a 17-year-old Cleveland, Ohio, high school junior first heard it sung by an Ohio State girl friend, who had picked it up on the campus. Don changed it a little after working it out on his guitar, wrote some lyrics, sang it at parties and copyrighted it. In September 1952,

Phil McClean, a Cleveland disc jockey, played a home recording of it on the air and about 20 requests came in for it to station WERE each week. A new disc company, Triple A, pressed it for quick release and sold 21,000 around Cleveland before leasing it to the Essex label for national distribution. By February 1953, it had sold over 500,000, and had become a rare type of hit, without planning or plugging. Nobody ever understood why such a rudimentary composition, a happy tune rendered by Don Howard with the croaking lilt of a fogbound ferry whistle, ever became a hit. It went on to sell an estimated million. It reached No 4, and was 15 weeks in the U.S.A. bestsellers.

The interesting sequel came when Nancy Binns Reed, an amateur Washington, D.C., songwriter, claimed authorship. She had apparently written the song some years before while a counsellor at a girl's camp, but did not put it on paper. It was sung by the camp girls as Miss Reed's tune, and Howard had heard it from one of these girls. He agreed to sharing the royalties with Miss Reed and crediting her as co-writer. Don was born in Cleveland, Ohio, on 11 May 1935.

JONI JAMES
WHY DON'T YOU BELIEVE ME? *MGM* [*USA*]. This was Joni's third recording and it put her in the bestseller charts – her first million seller. Born Joan Carmella Babbo in Chicago in 1930 on 22 September, she studied dancing as a child, and on graduation from high school in 1948 joined a troupe for a summer tour of Canadian exhibitions and fairs. After a stint in the chorus at Edgewater Beach Hotel, Chicago, she switched to singing and touring nightclubs in the Midwest. In 1951, after a booking at the Vince Gardens, Chicago, and a TV performance, she was signed with MGM. This song is by Lew Douglas, King Laney and Roy Rodde. Joni actually paid for and staged the recording session herself. The disc was No 1 seller for four weeks in the U.S.A., and sold two million, with 22 weeks in the bestsellers. It reached No 11 in Britain.

FRANKIE LAINE
HIGH NOON (Do Not Forsake Me, Oh My Darling) *Columbia* [*USA*]. This ninth million seller for Frankie was the theme of the famous Western film *High Noon*, written by Ned Washington (words) and Dmitri Tiomkin (music). It received the Academy Award for the Best Film Song of 1952. It was 19 weeks in the U.S.A. bestsellers, reaching No 5. No 7, and seven weeks in the bestsellers in Britain.

FRANKIE LAINE AND DORIS DAY
SUGARBUSH *Columbia* [*USA*]. The original version of this song was first published in 1942 in the collection 'Songs from the Veld' by South African composer Josef Marais. Marais, born on 17 November 1905 in Sir Lowry Pass, South Africa, was brought up on the veld, or 'prairie', of Africa. His original compositions are based on melodies and Dutch-Afrikaans ditties he heard as a child. He made his first album of veld songs for Decca in 1940 and from that year steadily built up a reputation as a specialist in folk and children's songs. He and his Dutch wife Miranda accompanied themselves – playing a guitar, tom-toms and an occasional native instrument – he singing in English and Afrikaans, his wife piping a shy descant. Marais became an American citizen in 1945. In 1952, he turned popular songsmith by converting his songs from folk to pop. His veld songs such as 'Sugarbush', 'Ay-round the Corner', etc., had recordings by many star artists including Jo Stafford and Doris Day. The vogue of hillbilly and country tunes may have had something to do with Marais' popularity with the juke-box trade. His songs have an engaging Calypso-style rhythm of their own and original turns of phrase in the lyrics.

This buoyant, happy recording by Frankie and Doris reached the Top Ten in the U.S.A. and was also a similar success in Britain and elsewhere. It soon achieved the million sale, reaching No 10, with 12 weeks in the U.S.A. bestsellers. No 8, and eight weeks in Britain's bestsellers.

MARIO LANZA WITH CHOIR

BECAUSE YOU'RE MINE *Victor* [*USA*]. Lanza's million seller was from the film of the same title in which he starred. It was written by Sammy Cahn (words) and Nicholas Brodszky (music) in 1951. The disc was No 7, and 19 weeks in the U.S.A. bestsellers, No 3 and 24 weeks in the British bestsellers.

PEGGY LEE

LOVER *Decca* [*USA*]. This song written by the great Lorenz Hart (words) and Richard Rodgers (music) in 1932 for the Maurice Chevalier/Jeanette MacDonald film *Love Me Tonight* had long been a great favourite with Peggy. She recorded it as a triple-gaited mambo with a 37-piece accompaniment, giving the old waltz tune a new sound. A quarter of a million were sold in its first two weeks, and it soon passed the million mark, her second disc to do so. It reached No 10, and was 12 weeks in the U.S.A. bestsellers.

VERA LYNN WITH ORCHESTRA DIRECTED BY ROLAND SHAW AND CHORUS OF SOLDIERS, SAILORS AND AIRMEN OF HIS MAJESTY'S FORCES

AUF WIEDERSEH'N SWEETHEART *Decca* [*Britain*]. This was the first disc to top the Hit Parade on both sides of the Atlantic, an unprecedented achievement for a British artist. Total sales were over the two million mark. The tune was written by Eberhard Storch (and originally published in Germany in 1949) with words (1952) by John Sexton (Geoffrey Parsons) and John Turner (Jimmy Phillips). Vera Lynn (née Vera Margaret Welsh) was born on 20 March 1919 at East Ham, London, and started singing at the age of seven, joining a children's troupe at eleven. She had her own dancing school when 15. After a year or two she went out as a cabaret act at local affairs, and her voice, once described as 'a freak mezzo-soprano with an irresistible sob', attracted local bandleader Howard Baker who booked her to sing with his band. She then gave an audition to Joe Loss which led to a broadcast. She was next signed by pianist-leader Charles Kunz and joined his band at Casani's Club in London, broadcasting regularly for 18 months before joining Ambrose and his orchestra for three years. In 1941 Vera began a solo career and joined the revue *Apple Sauce* at the Palladium, and she launched her 'Sincerely Yours' idea, which became a radio series of immense popularity with servicemen all over the world. She en-

deared herself so much to the troops that she became known as 'The Sweetheart of the Forces'. Variety star-billing and films followed and much touring abroad singing for the troops. After a short retirement in 1946, she returned to show business and back into the limelight in 1951. Then came the 'Auf Wiederseh'n' disc to start a new Vera Lynn boom with stardom in the *London Laughs* revue, personal appearances in the U.S.A. and more disc hits. She recorded for Decca from 1938 until the early 1960s. This disc was issued on the London label in the U.S.A., and was No 1 seller there for nine weeks, with 21 weeks in the bestsellers. It was No 10 in Britain.

In 1969, Vera Lynn received the royal accolade – the award of the O.B.E. and in 1975 she was made a Dame of the British Empire.

VERA LYNN

YOURS *Decca* [*Britain*]. This second million seller for Vera, which she first sang in the *Apple Sauce* revue in 1941, became her signature tune. This revival of the original 1941 recording in 1952 became a million seller thanks to American sales. The song was originally Latin-American by Augustin Rodriguez (1886–1957) (Spanish words) and Gonzalo Roig (music). English words are by Jack Sherr. It was first published in 1931, entitled 'Quiereme Mucho'. The disc was issued on Decca's London label in the U.S.A. and reached No 8.

MANTOVANI AND HIS ORCHESTRA

GREENSLEEVES *Decca* [*Britain*]. This was Mantovani's third singles disc to sell a million in the U.S.A. on the London label. The tune has been a favourite from the time of Queen Elizabeth I (died 1603) to the present day, and was first mentioned in the Registers of the Stationers' Company in September 1580. It had evidently attained some popularity before that time and was probably a tune of Henry VIII's reign (1509–47), then styled 'a new Northern Dittye of the Lady Greene Sleeves'.

RALPH MARTERIE AND HIS ORCHESTRA

CARAVAN *Mercury* [*USA*]. Ralph Marterie, trumpeter, began his career with Danny Russo's Oriole orchestra. At 17 he joined the Chicago theatre band, and then spent seven years playing NBC shows in Chicago. He entered the Navy in 1942 and organized a service band. On discharge, Marterie returned to radio with his own show on ABC and in 1949 he was signed by Mercury. In 1951 Ralph left the studios to tour with his own band.

This song is the famous oldie of 1937 composed by Duke Ellington and Juan Tizol, with words by Irving Mills. Marterie was born in Accerra, Italy. 'Caravan' was his first million seller. It was No 11, and 10 weeks in the U.S.A. bestsellers.

AL MARTINO

HERE IN MY HEART *Capitol* [*USA*]. This was Martino's first million seller. Born Alfred Cini, on 7 October 1927, he hails from South Philadelphia, and is a first generation Italian-American. Martino grew up in an atmosphere which favoured the traditional Italian opera and song, as was the case with his boyhood friend, Mario Lanza, whose success encouraged Al. He was a bricklayer by day, in his father's construction business, but sang in local clubs at night which led to his big break in 1952 when he recorded this song, his first hit. Other successes followed. He became more successful in Europe than in his native America, and played at leading theatres, clubs and concerts there for five years. For a few years he had been developing as a performer in the hope of a revival of the big legitimate voice, and made a great comeback in the summer of 1963 with 'I Love You Because', which stood high in the sellers' charts. 'Here in My Heart' was written by Pat Genaro, Lou Levinson and Bill Borelli. The disc was No 1 for three weeks in the U.S.A., and chart topper in Britain for nine weeks. It was 19 weeks in the U.S.A. bestsellers, and 18 weeks in Britain.

THE MILLS BROTHERS WITH HAL McINTYRE AND HIS ORCHESTRA

GLOW WORM *Decca* [*USA*]. This fifth million seller for the Mills Brothers has an interesting song history. It was originally published in Germany in 1902 and written by composer, Paul Lincke. By 1907 it had become the rage of Europe and the U.S.A., with sheet music sales in various arrangements going well over the four million mark. English lyrics were written in 1907 by Lilla Cayley Robinson. In the 1940s Spike Jones and his City Slickers' comedy version on Victor records is said to have topped the million mark. To keep ahead of the market, Edward N. Marks, the American publisher of the tune, got the famous lyricist Johnny Mercer to write new lyrics for this rhythmic version which soon got the Mills Brothers' disc into the bestseller lists, where it remained for 21 weeks in the U.S.A. and reached No 2; No 10 in Britain.

GUY MITCHELL WITH THE MITCH MILLER ORCHESTRA

PITTSBURGH, PENNSYLVANIA (There's a pawnshop round the corner in) *Columbia* [*USA*]. This fourth million seller for Guy, was also another big success for songwriter, Bob Merrill. It was No 6 for two weeks in the U.S.A. charts, and 17 weeks in the bestsellers.

GEORGE MORGAN

ALMOST *Columbia* [*USA*]. The second million seller for country-and-western artist George Morgan, written in 1951 by Vic McAlpin and Jack Toombs.

ELLA MAE MORSE WITH ORCHESTRA CONDUCTED BY NELSON RIDDLE

BLACKSMITH BLUES *Capitol* [*USA*]. Ella was born in Dallas, Texas, and began her music with a small dance band run by her parents. At 12, she was singing over Dallas radio, and at 15 was auditioned and hired by Jimmy Dorsey, who was disappointed with the appeal of her voice to New York audiences. So Ella went home, and after several small jobs was heard by Freddie Slack in a San Diego club. Slack signed her for his first Capitol session and 'Cow Cow Boogie' (1942) brought her instant fame. 'Blacksmith Blues' was written originally in 1950 by Jack Holmes, under the title 'Happy Payoff Day'. It was No 3 for three weeks in the U.S.A. charts, and 20 weeks in the bestsellers.

PATTI PAGE

I WENT TO YOUR WEDDING *Mercury* [*USA*]. This eighth million seller for Patti was written by Jessie Mae Robinson. The disc was a No 1 seller for six weeks in the U.S.A., and 21 weeks in the bestsellers.

LLOYD PRICE

LAWDY, MISS CLAWDY *Specialty* [*USA*]. The first million seller by this rhythm-and-blues artist was written by Price himself. He was born on 9 March 1933 in New Orleans, of a musical family. He began studying trumpet at high school and formed a five-piece band which was signed to a local radio station. He wrote numbers for the station break commercials. This song caught on in a big way and he was put under contract to Specialty Records. A succession of hits followed. Lloyd Price then entered the U.S. Forces, was assigned to special services in the Far East and formed a swinging band out of service colleagues. They visited Korea and Japan, Lloyd being the featured vocalist and heading the band. On discharge he formed a nine-piece band, composing and arranging for it, and recording for ABC-Paramount. This was a top rhythm-and-blues disc.

JO STAFFORD

YOU BELONG TO ME *Columbia* [*USA*]. This fifth million seller for Jo was written by Western band leader Pee Wee King, Redd Stewart and Chilton Price, writers of 'Slow Poke' (see 1951). The disc was a No 1 seller for five weeks in the U.S.A., and was a chart topper in Britain in 1953. It was 24 weeks in the U.S.A. bestsellers, and 19 weeks in the British.

EARLY AUTUMN backed with JAMBALAYA (on the Bayou) *Columbia* [*USA*]. 'Early Autumn', a sixth million seller for Jo, was written by Johnny Mercer (words) and Ralph Burns and Woody Herman the famous bandleader (music) in 1948. 'Jambalaya' was written by the country-and-western star, Hank Williams, who also sold a million with his own version. The disc was No 3, and 20 weeks in the U.S.A. bestsellers, and reached No 11 in Britain.

JOHNNY STANDLEY (vocal) WITH HORACE HEIDT AND HIS MUSICAL KNIGHTS

IT'S IN THE BOOK *Capitol* [*USA*]. Standley's only million seller was written in conjunction with Art Thorsen. This comedy disc – a parody of religious fervour – mocks fundamentalist preachers. This disc was a No 1 seller for two weeks in the U.S.A., and 19 weeks in the bestsellers.

KAY STARR WITH ORCHESTRA CONDUCTED BY HAROLD MOONEY

WHEEL OF FORTUNE *Capitol* [*USA*]. This first million seller for Kay established her as a top name in pop music. Born Katherine Starks on an Indian reservation, 21 July 1922, in Dougherty, Oklahoma, she sang over the local radio at 13, and when the family moved to Memphis, she sang with famous jazz violinist Joe Venuti and his band at 15. On leaving high school, Venuti hired her, then Bob Crosby brought her to New York on his Camel Caravan. Here she made some records with Glenn Miller, later rejoining Venuti. Then Kay transferred to Charlie Barnet's band for two years, before becoming a popular soloist, playing famous clubs and, from 1945, recording with Capitol. Her discs clocked up strong sales. In 1955 she signed with Victor Records for a period, then returned to Capitol. She starred at the London Palladium for two weeks in 1953 and has also appeared in films with Charlie Barnet, Frankie Laine and Billy Daniels. Kay made her major radio debut with Bing Crosby. This song was written by Bennie Benjamin and George Weiss. The disc was a No 1 seller for nine weeks in the U.S.A., and 22 weeks in the bestsellers.

HANK THOMPSON WITH HIS BRAZOS VALLEY BOYS

THE WILD SIDE OF LIFE *Capitol* [*USA*]. Hank's second million seller was the top country-and-western disc of 1952. The song was written by A. Carter and W. Warren. Hank was born in Waco, Texas. He steadily climbed to success for about 10 years, striking the most fruitful years in 1952-1954. After serving in the Navy, Thompson made his first disc for a small record firm. A few months later he made another for them, then Capitol took over his contract. In 1949, after several years of working alone, Hank built his first Western swing band to back his personal appearances. His full name is Henry William Thompson, born 3 September 1925.

KITTY WELLS (country-and-western vocalist)

IT WASN'T GOD WHO MADE HONKY TONK ANGELS *Decca* [*USA*]. Known as the 'Queen of Country Music', Kitty Wells was born Muriel Deason in Nashville, Tennessee, on 30 August 1919. Her husband, singer Johnnie Wright, gave her the name Kitty Wells when he married her, inspired by a song sung on the 'Grand Ole Opry' in the early 1930s titled 'I Could Marry Kitty Wells'.

Kitty learned her art as a child from her guitar-playing railroader father, big Charlie Carey Deason. She got her start in radio on WSIX in Nashville in 1937 and since then has appeared on Knoxville, Shreveport, Raleigh and many other radio stations. She was also a featured soloist for many years on the 'Louisiana Hayride' and 'Grand Ole Opry'.

Kitty came out of an early retirement in 1952 to record 'It Wasn't God Who Made Honky Tonk Angels' for Decca. This was an 'answer song' to Hank Thompson's version of 'Wild Side of Life', and she recorded her song, written by J.D. Miller, at the Castle Studio, located in Nashville's old Tulane Hotel. The disc sold over 500,000 copies in its first six months from release, and remained the number one selling record for over one year. 'Honky Tonk Angel' was produced by Owen Bradley, an assistant A & R man for Decca at that time, and featured only four musicians - Paul Warren, Shot Jackson, Jack Anglin and Johnnie Wright. Since then, Bradley produced every Kitty Wells record made. In June 1972, she was honoured on the occasion of her 20th anniversary with Decca at a surprise luncheon when she was presented with a gold record for selling over one million copies of 'Honky Tonk Angels'. Over her 20 years with Decca her record sales averaged over one million a year.

Kitty Wells ranks as one of the all-time great performers. This is an achievement, particularly in a field dominated by men as far as longevity of fame is concerned. In 1953, Frank G. Clement, Governor of Tennessee, presented her with a plaque that read, in part, 'Kitty Wells, in addition to her artistry, demonstrated that she is an outstanding wife and mother in keeping with the finest traditions of Southern womanhood'. Her two daughters, Ruby and Sue, recorded for Cadence and her son, Bobby, for Decca. Kitty had a lifetime recording contract with Decca, and has been voted the top female country singer in America many times. She was elected to the Country Music Hall of Fame in 1976.

HANK WILLIAMS WITH HIS DRIFTING COWBOYS

JAMBALAYA (on the Bayou) *MGM* [*USA*]. Hank Williams wrote his own eighth million seller. The million mark was achieved by 1958. A top country-and-western disc, it reached No 23 in the charts.

YOUR CHEATIN' HEART backed with KAW-LIGA *MGM* [*USA*]. This ninth million seller for Hank Williams, the 'Kaw-Liga' song, was written by him with Fred Rose, his Nashville publisher. The disc tells the story of the wooden Indian and the Indian maiden in the antique store. 'Your Cheatin' Heart', also written by Hank Williams, was recorded in late 1952, and issued in January 1953, just after Hank's tragic death. (See Hank Williams, 1949.) It was the top country-and-western disc of 1953.

HONKY TONK BLUES *MGM* [*USA*]. This tenth million seller for Hank Williams was his own composition of 1948. This disc, released in the U.S.A. in February 1952, took several years to reach the million mark.

I'LL NEVER GET OUT OF THIS WORLD ALIVE *MGM* [*USA*]. Hank Williams' eleventh million seller, a No 1 in the country-and-western charts and a bestseller in 1952-1953. It was written by Hank with his Nashville publisher, Fred Rose.

1953

FAYE ADAMS

SHAKE A HAND *Herald* [*USA*]. A first record for the Herald label started by Al Silver in 1953. He started business in 1947 with his own pressing plant. This song was written by Joe Morris and the disc reported in 1968 to have sold a million. It was also a hit for Red Foley in 1953.

REX ALLEN (country-and-western vocalist)

CRYING IN THE CHAPEL *Decca* [*USA*]. Artie Glenn's song, first introduced by his son Darrell who had a hit with it, proved to be a real money spinner in 1953 with this Rex Allen recording and by The Orioles. It was also a success for Elvis Presley (see 1965).

Rex Allen, born 31 December 1922, in Wilcox, Arizona, achieved national prominence with this disc which sold 928,000 before the end of 1953, and went on to reach the million sale. Rex made his professional debut over a Phoenix radio station at 13. On graduation from high school, he started on the rodeo circuit, then augmented his income from a low-paying radio job while working at a rubber mill in Trenton, N.J. where he had settled. He was a vaudeville and radio actor for WLS, Chicago for five years and for WTTM, Trenton for two years. In March 1945 he landed on 'The National Barn Dance' and commenced a tour of the Middlewest and East. From around 1950 came stardom in Republic Pictures, makers of Western films, followed by a recording contract with Mercury, then Decca. He became a particularly hot rodeo attraction, earning anywhere from $4,500 to $10,000 a week for playing the big rings at Illinois State Fair, Chicago World's Championship Rodeo, etc., plus personal appearances. He was voted one of the ten best Money-Making Western Stars in the *Motion Picture Herald-Fame* polls of 1951, 1952, 1953 and 1954. Rex has also written over 300 songs. This disc was No 10 and 11 weeks in the U.S.A. bestsellers.

THE AMES BROTHERS

YOU, YOU, YOU *Victor* [*USA*]. This third million seller for the Ames Brothers was written by Robert Mellin (words) and the German composer Lotar Olias (music) in 1952. Olias wrote most of the Freddy (Quinn) million seller songs on disc. This disc sold two million. The original German words were by Walter Rothenberg. It was No 2, and 31 weeks in the U.S.A. bestsellers.

WINIFRED ATWELL WITH HER 'OTHER PIANO' AND RHYTHM ACCOMPANIMENT

LET'S HAVE A PARTY *Philips* [*Britain*]. (Medley comprising: 'If You Knew Susie'; 'The More We Are Together'; 'That's My Weakness Now'; 'Knees Up Mother Brown'; 'Daisy Bell'; 'Boomps-a-Daisy'; 'She Was One of the Early Birds'; 'Three

O'clock in the Morning'.) It was No 14 and 6 weeks in Britain's bestsellers.

By 1956 this disc was a second million seller for Winnie. Played by her on her 'tinny' piano, this disc of eight popular party songs and dance tunes of the past was an immense seasonal success over Christmas 1953. (See also 1954.)

TONY BENNETT WITH THE PERCY FAITH ORCHESTRA

RAGS TO RICHES *Columbia* [*USA*]. This third million seller for Tony was written by Richard Adler and the late Jerry Ross, the composers of the U.S. musicals, *Pajama Game* and *Damn Yankees*. The disc was a No 1 seller for six weeks in the U.S.A., and 24 weeks in the bestsellers.

STRANGER IN PARADISE *Columbia* [*USA*]. Tony's fourth million seller was the outstanding song from the musical show *Kismet*, written and composed by Robert Wright and George Forrest, who together have long been active in Hollywood scoring pictures (including *Firefly*, *Maytime* and *Sweethearts*), and then musical plays (*Song of Norway* and *Kismet*). *Kismet* is based on themes from the Russian classical composer, Alexander Borodin (1833–1887), and was produced in 1953. This number was a top disc in Britain for two weeks in 1955. It was No 3 in the U.S.A., and 19 weeks in the bestsellers; 16 weeks in Britain's bestsellers.

TERESA BREWER

RICOCHET *Coral* [*USA*]. With words and music by Larry Coleman, Joe Darion and Norman Gimbel, 'Ricochet' was, by 1954, a third million seller for Teresa, reaching No 4, and was 19 weeks in the U.S.A. bestsellers.

RUTH BROWN AND HER RHYTHM-MAKERS

MAMA, HE TREATS YOUR DAUGHTER MEAN *Atlantic* [*USA*]. This second million seller for Ruth Brown, rhythm-and-blues singer, was written by Johnny Wallace and Herbert J. Lance. A top rhythm-and-blues disc.

EDDIE CALVERT (trumpet) WITH NORRIE PARAMOR AND HIS ORCHESTRA

O MEIN PAPA *Columbia* [*Britain*]. Eddie's one and only million seller was a really fantastic hit. It not only topped the British bestseller charts for nine weeks in 1954, but climbed high in the U.S. lists, selling nearly three million in all, the first million by early 1954. It was the first British instrumental record to achieve

this figure. Eddie was born in Preston, Lancashire, England, on 15 March 1922, and got his first cornet lessons from his father, a boot repairer and noted brass-band musician, when he was eight. He played principal cornet with the Preston Town Silver Band at 11, and on leaving school was an apprentice electrician. Called up in the Forces at $17\frac{1}{2}$, Calvert became a despatch rider and was discharged after crashing in 1942. After a stint with Jimmy McMurray's band at Birmingham Casino, he was offered an engagement with Billy Ternent's band at the BBC's war-time base at Bangor, North Wales, and in 1945 joined Geraldo's band for two years for an ENSA tour of Europe. Calvert then led bands of his own for West End nightclub engagements, and while at Selby's Restaurant began to make solo appearances on radio and started recording in 1951 with Melo-disc. In 1952 came his first variety dates. By then he was recording with Columbia and in 1953 made 'O Mein Papa', a number he had heard one night on his car radio. His popularity climbed and the disc made him a star attraction thereafter. 'O Mein Papa' (original German words and music were written by Paul Burkhard in 1948) was published in Switzerland and first used in a musical *Schwarze Hecht* in Zurich. The show was reproduced in Hamburg, Germany, in 1953 as *Feuerwerke* (Fireworks) when the song started to gain great popularity. The English lyric is by Britain's John Turner (Jimmy Phillips) and Geoffrey Parsons and is almost a literal translation of the German (Swiss) original. (See also Eddie Fisher—'O Mein Papa', 1953.) In the U.S.A. this disc was No 9, and nine weeks in the bestsellers, 21 weeks in the British bestsellers. Calvert died 7 August 1978 in Johannesburg, South Africa.

LESLIE CARON AND MEL FERRER

HI-LILI, HI-LO *MGM* [*USA*]. This delightful lilting waltz song from the film *Lili* starring Leslie Caron and Mel Ferrer was written in 1952 by Helen Deutsch (words) and Bronislau Kaper (music). Composer Kaper, a veteran of film music, won an Academy Award for his musical score of the film *Lili* in 1953. He had previously written songs and film music in Warsaw, Berlin, Vienna and London prior to going to Hollywood.

Leslie Caron, dancer, actress, was born 1 July 1931 in Paris, France, and educated there at the Convent of Assumption and the Conservatory of France. After small solo parts, she became a star of the Ballet des Champs Elysées. In 1950, Leslie was signed for the lead role in *An American in Paris* by MGM. *Man in a Cloak*, *Glory Alley* and *Story of Three Loves* followed, then *Lili*, *Glass Slipper*, *Daddy Long Legs*, and *Gaby*. Her greatest success was in *Gigi* (1958) – this film winning 10 Academy Awards. Later films were *Fanny*, *Promise Her Anything* and *Is Paris Burning?* (1966).

Mel Ferrer, actor, producer and director, was born 25 August 1917 in Elberon, New Jersey. He was educated at Princeton University. During his college and early career he spent his summers at Cape Cod Playhouse, Dennis, Massachusetts, then became an author in Mexico, and wrote a children's book *Tito's Hats*. He later became editor of the Stephen Day Press in Vermont. On reaching leading-man status at Dennis, he left publishing and made his first two Broadway appearances in dancing roles. He then entered radio in small towns and became producer-director for NBC, his shows including 'The Hit Parade' and the Hildegarde programme. In 1945, Mel entered motion pictures as dialogue director for Columbia, then returned to Broadway in the leading role in *Strange Fruit*. He helped produce *The Fugitive* and *Vendetta* films and acted in *Lost Boundaries*, *Born to Be Bad* and *Ondine on Broadway* (1954). Further films included *Scaramouche*, *Lili*, *Knights of the Round Table*, *War and Peace* and *Sex and the Single Girl* (1964).

This disc of 'Hi-Lili, Hi-Lo' was reported in 1968 to have sold a million. It was taken from the original film soundtrack.

FRANK CHACKSFIELD AND HIS ORCHESTRA

'LIMELIGHT' THEME (Terry's Theme) *Decca* [*Britain*]. After eight years 'Limelight' became a first million seller for

Frank. He was born on 9 May 1914 in Battle, Sussex, England, and was a church organist in his teens, worked in a solicitor's office, then switched to music in the mid-1930s, forming a band shortly before World War II. While in the Army, Frank began broadcasting over the BBC, later becoming a staff arranger for the Services entertainment, 'Stars in Battle Dress'. After the war, he recorded for several labels, and it was this disc, his first for Decca, that brought him to the attention of the U.S.A., making him a noted arranger on both sides of the Atlantic. The theme was written by Charlie Chaplin for his film *Limelight* with Claire Bloom as co-star. A vocal version 'Eternally' was also published with lyrics by John Turner (Jimmy Phillips) and Geoffrey Parsons. The disc was issued on the London label in the U.S.A. where it was No 6, and 13 weeks in the bestsellers. In Britain it was No 2 for eight weeks and 24 weeks in the bestsellers.

EBB TIDE *Decca* [*Britain*]. This disc became a second million seller for Chacksfield, by 1961. It was a great follow-up to his 'Limelight Theme', and a hit on both sides of the Atlantic. Written by Robert Maxwell (music) and Carl Sigman (words) the disc was issued on the London label in the U.S.A., reaching No 2, and was 23 weeks in the bestsellers, No 9 and two weeks in the British bestsellers.

FATS DOMINO
GOING TO THE RIVER *Imperial* [*USA*]. This third million seller for Fats was written by Fats himself and Dave Bartholomew.

YOU SAID YOU LOVED ME *Imperial* [*USA*]. Likewise the fourth million seller for Fats was written by Fats himself and Dave Bartholomew.

PLEASE DON'T LEAVE ME *Imperial* [*USA*]. By 1957 the remarkable Fats achieved a fifth million seller with his own composition.

I LIVED MY LIFE *Imperial* [*USA*]. Dave Bartholomew collaborated with Fats for his sixth million seller.

RUSTY DRAPER
GAMBLER'S GUITAR *Mercury* [*USA*]. This first million seller for Rusty was written by Jim Lowe. Rusty entered show business at 12, singing and playing guitar over the radio in Tulsa, Oklahoma. After five years of radio work in Tulsa, Des Moines and Quincy, Illinois, he became the singing Master of Ceremonies at the Mel Hertz Club in San Francisco. Then followed a seven-year long spell at Hermie King's Rumpus Room in the same city. This disc was No 10, and 13 weeks in the U.S.A. bestsellers.

THE DRIFTERS
MONEY, HONEY *Atlantic* [*USA*]. Written by Jesse Stone, this first single by The Drifters formed in this year by Clyde McPhatter (see 1958) was a massive hit and became a standard rhythm-and-blues disc. Sales of two million through the years were reported in 1968, and made five million sellers by then for the group. (See Drifters, 1959, for biographical data.)

PERCY FAITH AND HIS ORCHESTRA (vocal by Felicia Sanders)
THE SONG FROM 'MOULIN ROUGE' (Where is your heart?) *Columbia* [*USA*]. Faith's first million seller became the top disc of 1953. The tune is by the classical composer, Georges Auric of France (words by William Engvick), and was composed for the film *Moulin Rouge* that starred José Ferrer as the painter, Toulouse Lautrec. Percy Faith was born on 7 April 1908 in Toronto, Canada, and played with the Canadian orchestra, later turning to arranging and conducting, and then becoming staff arranger for the Canadian Broadcasting Co. in the mid-1930s. In 1940, Faith went to the U.S.A. as conductor of 'The Contented Hour'. He specialized in 'middle-brow' arrangements of pop tunes. Percy Faith held the post of musical director at Columbia

and recorded with his studio orchestra, also conducting on radio and TV. This disc sold two million, and was No 1 for ten weeks in the U.S.A. with 24 weeks in the U.S. bestsellers. The original title was 'Le Long de la Seine' with the French words by Jacques Larue. Percy Faith died in Los Angeles on 9 February 1976.

EDDIE FISHER WITH THE HUGO WINTERHALTER ORCHESTRA
I'M WALKING BEHIND YOU *Victor* [*USA*]. Eddie's fifth million seller was also the third big hit for British songwriter, Billy Reid. This disc was No 1 for two weeks in the U.S.A., and a chart topper in Britain. It was in the U.S.A. bestsellers for 22 weeks, and 18 weeks in the British bestsellers.

OH MEIN PAPA (with chorus) *Victor* [*USA*]. This sixth million seller for Eddie Fisher was the inevitable vocal version following the Eddie Calvert instrumental disc. (See Eddie Calvert, 1953, for details of song.) Eddie Fisher's disc was No 1 for eight weeks in the U.S.A. in 1954, and 19 weeks in the bestsellers; it reached No 9 in Britain.

STAN FREBERG (vocal) WITH DAWS BUTLER AND JUNE FORAY (talking)
ST GEORGE AND THE DRAGONET backed with LITTLE BLUE RIDING HOOD *Capitol* [*USA*]. Freberg's only million seller was an outstanding comedy disc by a brilliant satirist. Freberg hails from Pasadena and entered show business at 11 as

a stooge for his magician uncle. In his late teens, he landed a two-year radio contract with Cliffie Stone, on whose show he did vocal impersonations. After two years in the Army (1945-1947) his trick voices were used in animated cartoons at Warner Brothers, Disney, Lantz, Paramount and Columbia studios. Freberg then gained national attention by entertaining children with comedian, Daws Butler, in a TV series, 'Time for Beany'. Stan started his comedy-disc career in 1950 with 'John and Marsha', followed by a succession of more comedy discs. This 1953 disc with two saucy satires was a big hit, both being written by Stan Freberg, Daws Butler and Walter Schumann (music).

This disc lampoons the legend of 'St George and the Dragon', with a slick parodied satire of the monotoned 'Dragnet' theme, composed by Walter Schumann for the radio-TV series. 'Riding Hood' is parodied in the same way. Capitol sold 400,000 in the first week of release. The take-off of the radio-TV show's technique via these favourite children's fables was one of the funniest records for many years. The demand caused a jam-up in front of several New York record shops where the disc was relayed into the streets. This disc was No 1 for four weeks in the U.S.A. Freberg was born on 7 August 1926.

THE GAYLORDS

TELL ME YOU'RE MINE *Mercury* [*USA*]. This sole million seller for the Gaylords reached seven figures by 1958. Ronnie Gaylord was a solo artist on Mercury in the mid-1950s, then a trio was formed, which finally became a duo – Burt Bonaldi and

Ronnie –both hailing from Detroit. They have performed in theatres, nightclubs and TV with Bonaldi playing guitar. The song comes from Italy (originally 1939), written by U. Bertini (Ronald Fredianelli) and D. Vasin (Nino Ravasini) and entitled 'Per un bacio d'amour'. English words by Ronnie Vincent. This disc was No 3, and 22 weeks in the U.S.A. bestsellers.

JACKIE GLEASON AND HIS ORCHESTRA

MELANCHOLY SERENADE *Capitol* [*USA*]. Jackie's only million seller was his own composition. He hails from Brooklyn, New York and was born on 26 February 1916. Gleason's childhood was very melancholy. His brother died when he was three, his father disappeared when he was eight and his mother died when he was 16. He won an amateur contest at 15, then turned professional comedian/Master of Ceremonies in theatres and nightclubs.

After spells as a carnival barker, dare-devil driver in auto

circuses, exhibition diver in water follies and radio disc jockey, Gleason began a stage career in the late 1930s with appearances in the musicals *Follow the Girls* and *Along 5th Avenue*. In 1940, Jackie played variety and nightclubs and signed a Warner Brothers' contract, appearing in five films. Then came Broadway in the title role of 'The Life of Riley', and in 1952, his own TV shows on CBS which brought him much fame. Gleason's albums of mood music were the biggest sellers in this field until Mantovani superseded him. Gleason later starred in films for Paramount and made albums with either his Society Dance orchestra or piano solo, plus bass and drums. Gleason also recorded his comic characterizations for Capitol.

'Melancholy Serenade' became the theme song of the Jackie Gleason show on American TV.

THE HILLTOPPERS

P.S. I LOVE YOU *Dot* [*USA*]. The only million seller for this group is an oldie of 1934 written by the famous writers, Johnny Mercer (words) and Gordon Jenkins (music). The Hilltoppers were founded as a serenading quartet at Western Centre College, Bowling Green, Kentucky, in 1952. They only appeared spasmodically then, because some of the members were still attending school, and one of the group was in the Army. Their first disc, 'Trying', established the quartet which consisted of Jimmy Sacca, Don McGuire, Seymour Spiegelman and Billy Vaughn (musical director, writer of 'Trying'). Vaughn subsequently became musical director for Dot Records. Sacca and McGuire were born in Hazard, Kentucky; Jimmy was born in Lockport, New York; Spiegelman was born in Seneca Falls, New York; and Vaughn was born in Bowling Green, Kentucky. This disc was No 4, and 18 weeks in the U.S.A. bestsellers.

PEE WEE HUNT AND HIS ORCHESTRA

OH *Capitol* [*USA*]. This second million seller for Pee Wee Hunt was a wonderful revival of a 1919 song written by Byron Gay (words) and Byron Gay and Arnold Johnson (music).

This disc sold two million, was 23 weeks in the U.S.A. bestsellers, reaching No 3.

JONI JAMES

YOUR CHEATIN' HEART *MGM* [*USA*]. This big success for Joni (her second million seller) was written in 1952 by Hank Williams. It reached No 7, and was 15 weeks in the U.S.A. bestsellers.

HAVE YOU HEARD? *MGM* [*USA*]. Written in 1952 by Lew Douglas, Frank Lavere and Roy Rodde, 'Have You Heard?' provided a third million seller for Joni James, reaching No 5, with 14 weeks in the U.S.A. bestsellers.

FRANKIE LAINE

I BELIEVE *Columbia* [*USA*]. This semi-religious song by Ervin Drake, Irvin Graham, Jimmy Shirl and Al Stillman was Frankie's eighth million seller. It was written in 1952. It was also extremely popular in Britain where it set a record by remaining in the No 1 position in the sellers' lists for 18 weeks. The disc sold three million. This song was again an outstanding success in 1964. (See The Bachelors, 1964.) In the U.S.A. the disc was No 2, and 23 weeks in the bestsellers, 36 weeks in the British bestsellers.

FRANKIE LAINE AND JIMMY BOYD

TELL ME A STORY *Columbia* [*USA*]. This song was written by Terry Gilkyson, and proved a successful follow-up hit for young Jimmy Boyd (see 1952). The disc achieved Top Ten status in the U.S.A. and was also popular in Britain. It is said to have subsequently passed the million sale. It was No 4, and 12 weeks in the U.S.A. bestsellers. It was No 5 and 16 weeks in the British bestsellers.

JULIUS LA ROSA

EH, CAMPARI *Cadence* [*USA*]. The song is traditional Italian, transcribed by Julius La Rosa and Archie Bleyer. La Rosa had his only million seller with this number. He was discovered by Arthur Godfrey while still in the U.S. Navy. He doffed his uniform to make his first professional appearance on the Godfrey TV show in November 1951. In two years he became well known through TV and his Cadence discs. Thereafter, La Rosa remained established by playing at theatres and night-clubs, making frequent appearances on the Ed Sullivan TV Show and through his own radio programme. This disc was 20 weeks in the U.S.A. bestsellers, reaching No 2.

SYLVANA MANGANO

ANNA (El Negro Zumbon) *MGM* [*USA*]. This tune was written in 1952 by R. Vatro, with words by a fellow Italian, F. Giordano, for Sylvana's film *Anna*, and is recorded from the soundtrack. English words were written for it by William Engvick who was lyricist for 'Song from Moulin Rouge'. Sylvana, whose only million seller this was, was born in Rome and studied dancing at the Academy of Jia Ruskaja. She was a model until 1949, then an actress in several major Italian films in which she starred. This disc was No 6, and 17 weeks in the U.S.A. bestsellers.

MANTOVANI AND HIS ORCHESTRA

SONG FROM 'MOULIN ROUGE' *Decca* [*Britain*]. This was a chart topper in Britain, and eventually sold a million. It was specially written for the film *Moulin Rouge*, the music for which was by Georges Auric, with words by William Engvick. (See also Percy Faith, 1953.) This disc was No 13 in the U.S.A. and 23 weeks in the British bestsellers.

SWEDISH RHAPSODY *Decca* [*Britain*]. This delightful instrumental work by the Swedish composer Hugo Alfven, with adaptation by Percy Faith, became a million seller in Britain. The tune, also known as 'Midsummer Vigil', is based on folk music themes by Alfven. The disc was No 2 for two weeks in Britain, and 18 weeks in the bestsellers.

CHRISTMAS CAROLS (album) *Decca* [*Britain*]/*London*. This was a 10-inch album issued in 1953 both on the London label in the U.S.A. and, titled 'An Album of Christmas Music', on the Decca label in Britain. It sold half a million in the U.S.A. in 1953, and, with the release of the 12-inch album on stereo in 1958, totalled a collective million by 1965. The contents of the 10-inch disc were: 'The First Noel' (traditional); 'Hark the Herald Angels Sing' (Mendelssohn); 'God Rest Ye Merry, Gentlemen' (traditional); 'Good King Wenceslas' (traditional); 'O Holy Night' (traditional); 'Joy to the World' (Watts/Handel); 'Silent Night, Holy Night' (J. Mohr/Franz Gruber) (1818); 'Nazareth' (traditional: arr. Miller); 'O Little Town of Bethlehem' (P. Brooks/Lewis H. Redner); 'Adeste Fideles' (traditional). Additional titles on stereo album (1958) were: 'White Christmas' (Irving Berlin) (1942); 'O Tannenbaum' (traditional); 'Midnight Waltz' (Lambrecht); 'Skaters Waltz' (Emil Waldteutel) (1882). Gold Disc award, R.I.A.A., 1961.

STRAUSS WALTZES (album) *Decca* [*Britain*]/*London*. Here was a second million-selling album for Mantovani. First issued in 1953 as a 10-inch album, there were additional titles on a 12-inch stereo album issued in 1958.

Contents: 'The Blue Danube' (op. 314), by Johann Strauss, Jr. (1825-1899); 'Voices of Spring' (op. 410), by Johann Strauss, Jr.; 'Thousand and One Nights' (op. 346), by Johann Strauss, Jr.; 'Treasure Waltz' (op. 418), by Johann Strauss, Jr.; 'Emperor Waltz', (op. 437), by Johann Strauss, Jr.; 'Wine, Women and Song' (op. 333), by Johann Strauss, Jr.; 'Tales from the Vienna Woods' (op. 325), by Johann Strauss, Jr.; 'Du und du' (from *Die Fledermaus*) (op. 367), by Johann Strauss, Jr. Additional titles on the 12-inch stereo album (1958) were: 'Village Swallows' (op. 234), by Johann Strauss, Jr.; 'Morning Papers' (op. 279), by Johann Strauss, Jr.; 'Roses from the South' (op. 388), by Johann Strauss, Jr.; 'Accelerations' (op. 164), by Johann Strauss (1827-1870).

This disc had a half million sale in the U.S.A. in 1953, and, with the release of the stereo album in 1958, totalled a collective million by 1965. This record was issued on the London label in the U.S.A. Gold Disc award R.I.A.A., 1961.

RALPH MARTERIE AND HIS ORCHESTRA

PRETEND *Mercury* [*USA*]. Marterie's second million seller was written by Lew Douglas, Frank Lavere and Cliff Parman in 1952. It reached No 16 in the U.S.A. charts.

DEAN MARTIN WITH DICK STABILE AND HIS ORCHESTRA

THAT'S AMORE - THAT'S LOVE *Capitol* [*USA*]. This first million seller for Dean was written by Jack Brooks (words) and Harry Warren (music), and sung by Martin in the film *The Caddy* in which he starred with Jerry Lewis. Dean was born Dino Crocetti in Steubenville, Ohio, on 17 June 1917, and occupied himself variously as gas station attendant, steel worker, prize fighter and card dealer before entering show business as vocalist with Sam Watkins' band in Cleveland. Changing his name to Dino Martini, he played the Tiobamba nightclub, New York as a single, then changed his name again to Dean Martin, playing other nightclubs and theatres alone until 1946. He then teamed up with Jerry Lewis, a phonograph-record pantomimist he had met by chance in 1942 in New York during an engagement at the 500 Club, Atlantic City. Their act was a flop until they indulged in a riotous slap-stick routine, putting them in the $15,000-per-week bracket and on CBS-TV. Their first film was *My Friend Irma* in 1949, followed by ten successful years together on stage, screen, radio and TV. Dean began a career as solo singer in 1956 and later as a dramatic actor. This disc sold over four million by 1964, was 22 weeks in the U.S.A. bestsellers and reached No 2. It was No 2 and 11 weeks in the British bestsellers.

THE ORIOLES FEATURING SONNY TIL

CRYING IN THE CHAPEL *Jubilee* [*USA*]. The only million seller by this rhythm-and-blues group, was written by Artie Glenn of Knoxville, Tennessee in 1953. The Orioles worked around Baltimore until they got their first break on the Arthur Godfrey 'Talent Scouts' show which led to a guest shot on his day-time programme, then appearances on the rhythm-and-blues circuit, which included recording. A top rhythm-and-blues disc, it reached No 11 in the U.S.A. charts.

PATTI PAGE

THAT DOGGIE IN THE WINDOW *Mercury* [*USA*]. Patti's ninth million seller was a charming song, written in 1952, by that 'boy wonder of Tin Pan Alley' Bob Merrill. The disc was a No 1 seller for eight weeks in the U.S.A., and sold three million by 1967, and was in the bestsellers for 21 weeks. It was No 9 and five weeks on the British bestsellers.

CHANGING PARTNERS *Mercury* [*USA*]. By 1954 this title provided a tenth million seller for Patti Page. It was written by Joe Darion (words) and Larry Coleman (music). The disc was No 4, and 19 weeks in the U.S.A. bestsellers.

LES PAUL (electric guitar) MARY FORD (vocal)

VAYA CON DIOS (May God be with you) *Capitol* [*USA*]. This very big hit for Les and Mary became their fourth million seller. The number was written by Larry Russell, Inez James and Buddy Pepper. The disc was a No 1 seller for 11 weeks in the U.S.A. and 31 weeks in the bestsellers. No 7 and four weeks in the British bestsellers.

JIM REEVES

MEXICAN JOE *Abbott* [*USA*]. Jim Reeves' first million seller was written by Mitchell Torok, also a country-and-western disc artist, for the Abbott label. Jim Reeves hailed from Panola County, Texas. He was born on 20 August 1924. College educated, he was forced to quit as a professional baseball pitcher for Houston Buffaloes through a leg injury, and he was also a full-time radio announcer at one stage of his career. He started recording in 1945. Jim owned and operated two music companies and two radio stations. He also wrote songs and played guitar. In 1961, the citizens of Henderson, Texas, saluted him with a 'Jim Reeves Day'. He was killed in an air crash in his private plane on 31 July 1964. Reeves made only one film *Kimberley Jim* (filmed in South Africa) during his career. It was released in 1965. He was elected to the Country and Western Music Hall of Fame in 1967. A top country-and western disc.

BIMBO *Fairway–Abbott* [*USA*]. This second million seller for Jim Reeves was written by Rod Morris.

KERMIT SCHAFER (humorist)
RADIO BLOOPERS (album disc) *Jubilee* [*USA*]. Jubilee Records started in 1947 and Schafer's was the first album for the label. It became one of the all-time bestsellers and sold almost five million through the years. This and the subsequent 'Blooper' series, together with Rusty Warren's risqué comedy albums from 1958, established Jubilee as one of the first and foremost disc companies in humorous recordings. 'Radio Bloopers' was certainly the first comedy album to sell a million.

Kermit Schafer, a radio and TV producer of long standing, coined the word 'blooper' when a radio announcer Harry Von Zell announced: 'Ladies and gentlemen, the President of the United States, Hoobert Heever'. From then on, Schafer monitored certain types of shows most likely to result in bloopers such as children's programmes or audience participation. It was through his Jubilee recordings that Schafer's bloopers first attained national prominence, and started the highly successful 'Pardon My Blooper' series of albums. He formed Bloopers Inc. and, in addition to his comedy recordings, had a daily syndicated newspaper column, blooper books, a series of radio and TV commercials based on bloopers, blooper toys, napkins containing bloopers, calendars, a song 'Pardon My Blooper' and other selling side-lines.

FRANK SINATRA WITH ORCHESTRA CONDUCTED BY NELSON RIDDLE
YOUNG AT HEART *Capitol* [*USA*]. This third million seller for Frank Sinatra was one of his biggest successes. The song is by Carolyn Leigh (words) and Johnny Richards (music). The melody was taken from a song titled 'Moonbeam' written by the composer in 1939. This disc sold 750,000 in the U.S.A. alone, sales elsewhere making a global million. It was No 2, and 22 weeks in the U.S. bestsellers; No 12 in Britain.

JOE TURNER
HONEY HUSH *Atlantic* [*USA*]. Joe Turner's second million seller was written by Lou Willie Turner and achieved the sale through the years. The disc, a bestseller 1953-1954, became a standard rhythm-and-blues pop song.

1954

WINIFRED ATWELL WITH HER 'OTHER PIANO' AND RHYTHM ACCOMPANIMENT
LET'S HAVE ANOTHER PARTY *Philips* [*Britain*]. (Medley comprising: 'Somebody Stole My Gal'; 'I Wonder Where My Baby Is Tonight'; 'Bye-bye Blackbird'; 'When the Red Red Robin'; 'Sheik of Araby'; 'Another Little Drink'; 'Lily of Laguna'; 'Honeysuckle and the Bee'; 'Broken Doll'; and 'Nellie Dean'.) This third million seller for Winnie, played on her famous 'tinny' piano, was her second big Christmas disc of party tunes. Its success made her the first British artist with three million sellers. This medley was a chart topper in Britain for four weeks, and was eight weeks in the bestsellers.

THE AMES BROTHERS WITH THE HUGO WINTERHALTER ORCHESTRA
NAUGHTY LADY OF SHADY LANE *Victor* [*USA*]. The fourth million seller for this group had an original lyrical twist (the naughty lady being a baby). It was written by Sid Tepper and Roy C. Bennett. It was No 3 for four weeks (1955), and 15 weeks in the U.S. bestsellers; No 6, and six weeks in the British bestsellers.

HANK BALLARD AND THE MIDNIGHTERS
WORK WITH ME, ANNIE *Federal* (*King*) [*USA*]. The Midnighters, featuring Hank Ballard whose home town is Detroit, rank as one of the most consistent, long-running hit makers on the music scene. Beginning as favourites in the rhythm-and-blues field, they became equally important in the pop category with a string of chart winners including the discs below. They were responsible for the first version of the dance sensation 'The Twist' (see 1960). They also turned out many money-making albums. Ballard, who wrote this winner, is prolific as a songwriter and arranger. The group was originally called 'The Royals'. A top rhythm-and-blues disc.

SEXY WAYS *Federal* (*King*) [*USA*]. This second million seller for Hank Ballard and the Midnighters was written by Hank.

ANNIE HAD A BABY *Federal* (*King*) [*USA*]. This third million seller for Hank Ballard and the Midnighters was written by Henry Glover and Lois Mann. A top rhythm-and-blues disc.

PROFESSOR ALEX BRADFORD AND HIS SINGERS
TOO CLOSE TO HEAVEN backed with I DON'T CARE WHAT THE WORLD MAY DO *Specialty* [*USA*]. The only million seller by this artist, who is a prominent gospel singer and professor. The Professor and his choir became internationally known through their performances with the gospel show, *Black Nativity*, which went to Britain in 1962.

THE CHORDETTES
MISTER SANDMAN *Cadence* [*USA*]. The Chordettes, who were a prototype of many later groups, scored their first million with the title. The group consisted of Jimmy Lochard, Carol Bushman, Nancy Overton and Lynn Evans, all of whom were college educated. They were originally organized for impromptu folk festivals, then they won an Arthur Godfrey 'Talent Scout Show' and were with him for four years, appearing in nightclubs and on TV. This song was written by Pat (Francis Drake) Ballard, who was for several years music editor of *College Humor*, and author of numerous articles on popular songs and songwriting. 'Mister Sandman' was No 1 for seven weeks in the U.S.A. and 20 weeks in the bestsellers; No 11 and eight weeks in the British bestsellers.

ROSEMARY CLOONEY WITH BUDDY COLE AND HIS ORCHESTRA
HEY THERE! *Columbia* [*USA*]. Rosemary's fifth million seller was written by Richard Adler and Jerry Ross. It was the hit song of their musical *The Pajama Game*. The disc was No 1 for six weeks in the U.S.A. and 27 weeks in the bestsellers; No 4, and 11 weeks in the British bestsellers.

THIS OLE HOUSE *Columbia* [*USA*]. This sixth million seller for Rosemary Clooney was written by Stuart Hamblen. The song was inspired when Hamblen, who was out hunting mountain lions with a friend, discovered a dilapidated hunter's hut about 20 miles from the nearest road. In the hut lay a dead man. Inside this weird Texas cabin all was in a shocking state. Much moved, Hamblen wrote his song on the back of an old sandwich bag. Unable to get a reasonable advance on the song, Hamblen published it himself. Rosemary's disc sold over two million in the U.S.A. alone, and his own disc on Victor sold half a million. The Clooney-version disc was a chart topper for one week both in the U.S.A. and in Britain. Coupled with 'Hey There!', this disc was 27 weeks in the U.S.A. bestsellers.

MAMBO ITALIANO *Columbia* [*USA*]. Rosemary Clooney's seventh million seller was written by ace songwriter Bob Merrill. This title was a chart-topper disc in Britain in 1955 for three weeks. It was No 10, and 12 weeks in the U.S. bestsellers; 16 weeks in the British bestsellers.

NAT KING COLE WITH CHORUS AND ORCHESTRA DIRECTED BY NELSON RIDDLE
ANSWER ME, MY LOVE *Capitol* [*USA*]. Originally written in 1952, German words and music by Gerhard Winkler and Fred Rauch, the English words were written in 1953 by U.S. songsmith Carl Sigman.

The song was also a big seller on disc in Britain for Frankie Laine (No 1 for six weeks) and David Whitfield (No. 1 for one week) in 1953.

Nat King Cole's disc was the big seller in U.S.A., reaching No 6 with 19 weeks in the bestsellers, and the million sale was reported in the press in 1971. The backing of his disc was an English hit by Michael Carr - 'Dinner For One Please James'.

PERRY COMO WITH CHORUS
PAPA LOVES MAMBO *Victor* [*USA*]. As an eleventh million seller for Perry, this song was the second mambo-type song of 1954 to reach seven figures. It was written by Al Hoffman, Dick Manning and Bix Reichner, reaching No 4, and was 18 weeks in the U.S. bestsellers; No 16 in Britain.

PERRY COMO WITH THE HUGO WINTERHALTER ORCHESTRA
WANTED *Victor* [*USA*]. Perry Como's twelfth million seller was written by Jack Fulton and Lois Steele. This disc was No 1 for eight weeks in the U.S.A. with 22 weeks in the bestsellers, reaching the million mark in 1955. No 4 and 15 weeks in the British bestsellers.

DON CORNELL
HOLD MY HAND *Coral* [*USA*]. This third million seller for Don was written by Jack Lawrence and Richard Myers and featured in the film (1954), *Susan Slept Here*, starring Dick Powell and Debbie Reynolds. The disc was a chart topper in Britain for five weeks, and reached No 5 with 18 weeks in the U.S. bestsellers; 21 weeks in the British bestsellers.

THE CREW CUTS
SH-BOOM (Life could be a dream) *Mercury* [*USA*]. The only million seller for this quartet of singers, Rudi Maugeri, Pat Barrett, Roy Perkins and Johnnie Perkins - all from the Toronto Cathedral Choir School in Canada.

The song was first recorded and written by James Keyes, Claude and Carl Feaster, Floyd F. McRae and James Edwards, a coloured group called The Chords. It was a 'head song' composed in the studio as it was recorded. Atlantic Records weren't quite sure what do to with this so they released it on a new label, Cat, which does not seem to have had any other releases. This became a No 1 bestseller in Los Angeles and no doubt accounted for the Crew Cuts cover version on the Mercury label.

The Crew Cuts version is now considered to be the first rock and roll hit, starting a transition period whereby white artists made hit disc versions of coloured artists' rhythm-and-blues songs. It was 20 weeks in the U.S. bestsellers; No 12, and nine weeks in the British bestsellers.

DORIS DAY
SECRET LOVE *Columbia* [*USA*]. The sixth million seller for Doris, this was written by ace songwriters, Paul Francis Webster (words) and Sammy Fain (music) for the film *Calamity Jane*, starring Doris Day and Howard Keel. The film was first shown in late 1953 and considerably enhanced Doris Day's career. Webster and Fain wrote the complete score and received the Academy Award for 'Secret Love' as the Best Film Song of 1953. This disc was No 1 for three weeks in the U.S.A. with 22 weeks in the bestsellers, and a chart topper in Britain for nine weeks, with 29 weeks in the bestsellers.

FATS DOMINO
LOVE ME *Imperial* [*USA*]. This seventh million seller for Fats was written by Dave Bartholomew and Fats.

DON'T LEAVE ME THIS WAY *Imperial* [*USA*]. Likewise, this eighth million seller for Fats Domino was jointly written by Dave Bartholomew and Domino himself.

EDDIE FISHER
I NEED YOU NOW *Victor* [*USA*]. This seventh million seller for Eddie was written by Jimmie Crane and Al Jacobs in 1953. The disc was No 1 for three weeks in the U.S.A. and 23 weeks in the bestsellers; No 13 and eight weeks in the British bestsellers.

THE FONTANE SISTERS WITH BILLY VAUGHN'S ORCHESTRA
HEARTS OF STONE *Dot* [*USA*]. The only million seller by this trio was written by Eddy Ray and Rudy Jackson. The sisters, Bea, Geri and Marge, whose family name is Rosse, hail from New Milford, New Jersey. After high school they joined an all-girls' unit for an eight-month cross-country tour. They then teamed with their brother Frank (guitar) for a family act, playing theatres and radio until World War II in which Frank lost his life. The girls reorganized in 1944 and in 1948 sang for several seasons on the Perry Como radio shows, which led to their similar berth on his T V programmes. They first recorded for Victor from 1949. This disc was No 1 seller in the U.S.A. in 1955 for one week, and 18 weeks in the bestsellers.

THE FOUR ACES
THREE COINS IN THE FOUNTAIN *Decca* [*USA*]. This third million seller for the Four Aces was written by Sammy Cahn (words) and Jule Styne (music) for the film of the same title. The song received the Academy Award for the Best Film Song of 1954. The disc was No 2, and 18 weeks in the U.S. bestsellers, No 5 and six weeks in the British bestsellers.

STRANGER IN PARADISE *Decca* [*USA*]. The Four Aces achieved their fourth million seller with this song from the musical *Kismet* of 1953, written by Robert Wright and George Forrest -based on the themes of Borodin. It reached No. 5 and was 16 weeks in the U.S. bestsellers; No 6 and six weeks in the British bestsellers.

THE FOUR KNIGHTS (vocal quartet with orchestral accompaniment)
OH BABY MINE (I get so lonely) *Capitol* [*USA*]. The opening phrase of this song is said to be adapted from an old non-copyright melody, probably 'Gently Down the Stream' by Nelson Kneas, a leader in the minstrel days of the latter part of the 19th century. Kneas was adept at taking old German tunes and arranging them and helped to popularize them with the minstrels. This song 'Oh Baby Mine' was written by Pat (Francis Drake) Ballard, a native of the small town of Troy, Pennsylvania (pop.

1,200), in 1953, originally as a sad ballad. It turned out to be a rhythm tune and made Pat a local celebrity, with demands for personal appearances at country dances with the jigged-up hill-billy version of his song. It was first called 'When I Dream About You', then 'I Get So Lonely When I Dream About You', but public demand was for a song and record called 'Oh Baby Mine'. The Four Knights disc was high on all the U.S.A. charts, and is estimated to have sold a global million. It reached No 3, and was 23 weeks in the U.S. bestsellers; No 5 and 11 weeks in the British bestsellers.

The group featured a fine bass singer named Oscar Broadway, and made many discs for Capitol in the 1950s.

THE FOUR TUNES

I UNDERSTAND (Just how you feel) *Jubilee* [*USA*]. The first million seller by this new group, was written by Pat Best. It enjoyed a big revival in 1964. (See Freddie and the Dreamers.) This group are rhythm-and-blues singers, comprising William H. Best of Wilmington, North Carolina, James E. Nabbie of Tampa, Florida, James B. Gordon of Dover, Oklahoma, and Danny Owens of Newark, New Jersey. The disc was No. 8 and 15 weeks in the U.S.A. bestsellers.

MARIE. This second million seller for The Four Tunes was an oldie of 1928 by the famous composer, Irving Berlin. Recorded in 1953, it reached No 18 in the U.S.A. charts.

JUDY GARLAND
(film actress, vocalist)

THE MAN THAT GOT AWAY *Columbia* [*USA*]. This was the hit song from the film *A Star is Born* as sung by Judy. Her film co-star was James Mason. It was written by Ira Gershwin (words) and Harold Arlen (music).

Judy, one of the world's greatest singing and film stars, could rightly claim to have brought the popular song to the concert halls. This she amply demonstrated when she gave a recital in early 1961 at New York's Carnegie Hall. A million selling double-album (see Judy Garland, 1961) was released that year.

Judy was born on 10 June 1922 in Grand Rapids, South Dakota (her real name was Frances Gumm), the third of three daughters of vaudeville artists Frank and Ethel Gumm. From the age of three she toured with her sisters in vaudeville. At the age of 12 she was signed to MGM Pictures. She made her first film, a 'short' called 'One Sunday Afternoon', with Deanna Durbin in 1935, and it was the great George Jessel who suggested her name change to Judy Garland. Judy grew up with the screen. Her first big film was *Pigskin Parade* (1936), followed by *Broadway Melody of 1938*, *Listen Darling*, *Everybody Sing* and *Thoroughbreds Don't Cry* –all in 1937-1938, and then a series of Andy Hardy films with Mickey Rooney. In 1939 came her greatest triumph, *The Wizard of Oz*, which won her an Academy Award and introduced the Harold Arlen-E. Y. Harburg never-to-be-forgotten song 'Over the Rainbow'. During the war years she starred in several big musical films, notably *Strike Up the Band*, *Babes on Broadway*, *For Me and My Girl*, *Girl Crazy* and *Meet Me in St Louis*. From 1946, she was the star of *The Harvey Girls*, *Easter Parade* and *In the Good Old Summertime*. Her last film for MGM was *If You Feel Like Singing* (1950).

In 1950 Judy had to withdraw from *Annie Get Your Gun* through a nervous collapse and her brilliant career seemed finished. She gradually recovered and in the summer of 1951 made her historic London Palladium bow. She was a sensational success, and on return to the U.S.A. repeated her victory on Broadway. Hollywood became interested again and Warner Brothers engaged her for the star part in *A Star is Born* (1954), a remake of a 1937 drama. As a musical it was a tremendous hit, Judy's song, 'The Man That Got Away', being in a way autobiographical. Judy was the gal that got away. But she came back. She then did several tours and TV shows. She was a very powerful singer with clarity, drive and rhythm. She recorded first for Decca then

MGM, and Columbia. She died in London, England on 22 June 1969.

SLIM GUITAR (Guitar Slim)

THE THINGS THAT I USED TO DO *Specialty* [*USA*]. Eddie 'Guitar Slim' Jones himself wrote his only million seller disc, in 1953. A top rhythm-and-blues disc. Slim was born 9 December 1926. He died on 7 February 1959.

BILL HALEY AND HIS COMETS

SHAKE, RATTLE AND ROLL *Decca* [*USA*]. This first million seller by Haley's Comets was written by Charles Calhoun. Bill Haley was the artist who started the 'rock-'n'-roll' craze, which was destined to usher in almost a new way of life for millions. William John Clifton Haley was born at Highland Park, a suburb of Detroit, Michigan, on 6 July 1925. His parents were musical, his father a banjoist/mandolinist, and his mother a pianist/organist. At 13, Bill became a professional vocalist/guitar player with a country-and-western troupe. He organized his own group at 15 (1940), for local events. In 1951, Haley made his first record for a small American label, with his 'Rocket 88' and 'Rock the Joint'. He switched from western music to the rhythm-and-blues idiom in 1952, his Comets achieving some success with a disc of 'Crazy Man, Crazy'. Then came this disc with Decca, and later the sensational 'Rock Around the Clock' (see below), and nationwide and other tours with his Comets, including Britain. This most fantastic group of music makers the world had yet known started a frenzied new era of their own creation. Haley's discs sold like wildfire in almost every country of the world. Haley and his Comets were starred in the films, *Rock Around the Clock* and *Don't Knock the Rock*. The undisputed 'Kings of Rock-'n'-Roll', sold over 60 million discs up to 1970. This disc was recorded on 12 April 1954, reaching No 7, with 27 weeks in the U.S. bestsellers. No 4 and 14 weeks in the British bestsellers. Bill Haley died Haelingen, Texas, 9 February 1981.

ROCK AROUND THE CLOCK *Decca* [*USA*]. This second million seller for Bill Haley was written in 1953 by Max C. Freedman and Jimmy De Knight (real name James Myers). The disc was also first recorded on 12 April 1954, and launched the rock 'n' roll era. It sold the million by 1955 and proved to be one of the most fantastic hits of all time. The tune was given added impetus when extensively featured in the film *Blackboard Jungle* (1955), and world sales of Bill's disc were estimated at 16 million up to 1970. Apart from its huge sales in the U.S.A., it was the first disc to sell over one million in Britain alone. 'Rock Around the Clock' has been featured in 14 different films, and recorded in 35 different languages with over 140 versions globally. It was No 1 chart topper for seven weeks in the U.S.A. in 1955, and also a No 1 in Britain for five weeks. The collective sales of 'Rock

Around the Clock' have been estimated at over 100 million. It was 29 weeks in the U.S. bestsellers, with a further 14 weeks when it was revived in 1974, and 19 weeks in the British bestsellers in 1955.

LEROY HOLMES AND HIS ORCHESTRA WITH FRED LOWRY (whistling)

THE HIGH AND THE MIGHTY *MGM* [*USA*]. Composed by Dmitri Tiomkin (with words by Ned Washington) this was the theme of the film of the same title. Leroy was born in Pittsburgh on 22 September 1913, and studied music at Northwestern University, at Juilliard and privately with composer, Ernest Toch. After six years as a staff arranger for Vincent Lopez, he became chief arranger to Harry James, then transferred from band work to studio arranging in Hollywood. After a routine job arranging four tunes for Alf Lund's debut session

on MGM, his work brought him to the attention of the film-sponsored disc company, which he joined later as an arranger-conductor. Holmes then started recording material with his own band, and also composed and conducted scores for children's discs. Composer Tiomkin was born in Russia and over a period of 30 or more years has probably written more motion picture themes than anybody. He holds four Academy Awards for film music, one of which is for his scoring of the film *The High and the Mighty*, and is the outstanding Western-style music composer in this field. The disc was No 9, and 14 weeks in the U.S.A. bestsellers.

KITTY KALLEN

LITTLE THINGS MEAN A LOT *Decca* [*USA*]. This was the top disc of 1954 and it made Kitty a star nightclub attraction. She hails from South Philadelphia, born on 25 May 1926, and became a professional singer as a child. She was rooming with Dinah Shore in the early 1940s when she got an offer from Jimmy Dorsey to sing with his band. It was with him that she recorded 'Besame Mucho' with Bob Eberly – her first big disc. 'Little Things Mean a Lot' was her first solo million seller. Kitty has also sung with Jack Teagarden and Harry James and was featured singer on the Danny Kaye, David Rose and Alec Templeton shows on radio. 'Little Things' was written by Carl Stutz, a Richmond (Virginia) disc jockey, and Edith Lindeman, amusement editor on the Richmond *Times-Despatch*. This disc was No 1 for nine weeks in the U.S.A., with 26 weeks in the bestsellers, and a chart topper in Britain for one week, with 23 weeks in the bestsellers.

IN THE CHAPEL IN THE MOONLIGHT *Decca* [*USA*]. Kitty Kallen's second (solo) million seller was written in 1936 by

Billy (William J.) Hill, the famous 'hillbilly' songsmith of 'Last Round-Up', 'Wagon Wheels' and 'Empty Saddles', who as a youth travelled extensively in the Far West, rode the range, played violin and piano, and who is said to have had the first jazz band of the Far West in Salt Lake City. This disc is reputed to have sold a million through the years. It reached No 5, and was 14 weeks in the U.S.A. bestsellers.

MARIO LANZA

Songs from 'THE STUDENT PRINCE' and Other Great Musical Comedies (album) *Victor* [*USA*]. Side 1 contained the following songs from the original *stage* show of 1924, words by Dorothy Donnelly, music by Sigmund Romberg:
Orchestral introduction; 'Serenade'; 'Drink, Drink, Drink'; *'Deep in My Heart Dear'; 'Gaudeamus Igitur' (traditional); and the following from the *film* version (1954), words by Paul Francis Webster, music by Nicholas Brodszky: 'Beloved'; 'I'll Walk with God'; *'Summertime in Heidelberg'; *duet with Elizabeth Doubleday.

Side 2 contained: 'Yours Is My Heart Alone' (*Land of Smiles*, 1929), English words by Harry Bache Smith, music Franz Lehar; 'Romance', Edgar Leslie/Walter Donaldson (1929); 'I'll See You Again' (*Bitter Sweet*, 1929) Noel Coward; 'If I Loved You' (*Carousel*, 1945) Oscar Hammerstein II/Richard Rodgers; 'I'll Be Seeing You', Irving Kahal/Sammy Fain (1938); 'One Night of Love' (film *One Night of Love*) Gus Kahn/Victor Schertzinger (1934).

Lanza's untimely death in 1959 (see Lanza, 1950) together with his great popularity made this disc a wonderful memorial souvenir of this great artist. It sold a million by 1961 and received a Gold Disc award from R.I.A.A., and was a No 1 album in the U.S.A. for 36 weeks.

MANTOVANI AND HIS ORCHESTRA

LONELY BALLERINA *Decca* [*Britain*]. This sixth million seller single for Mantovani was written by Lambrecht and Britain's Michael Carr. No 16 and four weeks in the British bestsellers.

MANTOVANI PLAYS THE IMMORTAL CLASSICS *Decca* [*Britain*]. Issued on both 10-inch and 12-inch albums, this album had collective sales of a million up to 1965.

The 10-inch disc contained: 'Prelude in C Sharp Minor', by Rachmaninoff; 'Minuet in D Major', K334, by Mozart; 'Simple Aveu', by Francis Thome; 'On Wings of Song', by Mendelssohn; 'Barcarolle' (*Tales of Hoffmann*), by Offenbach; 'Cradle Song' (Wiegenlied), by Brahms; 'Etude No 3 in E Major', by Chopin; 'Waltz from Serenade for Strings', by Tchaikovsky.

For the 12-inch album additional titles were: 'Romance', by Rubinstein; 'Largo', by Handel; 'Ave Maria', by Schubert; 'Air on the G String', by Bach.

GLENN MILLER AND HIS ORCHESTRA

THE GLENN MILLER STORY (album) *Victor* [*USA*]. Victor Records issued a 10-inch album of Glenn Miller's original hit recordings of 1939 and the early 1940s in 1954, when the biopic of the famous bandleader was premiered that year.

In 1956, other original recordings were added to make a 12-inch album which was awarded a Gold Disc in 1961 by R.I.A.A. for a million dollar sale. This was later re-titled 'Glenn Miller Plays Selections from *The Glenn Miller Story* and Other Hits', with a further R.I.A.A. Gold Disc award in 1968, making a total of a million units sold.

The 10-inch album consisted of: †*Moonlight Serenade (F), Mitchell Parish/Glenn Miller (1939); †*American Patrol (F), F. W. Meacham (1891) arranged by Jerry Gray; †*Pennsylvania 6-5000 (F), Carl Sigman/Jerry Gray (1940); †*In the Mood (F), Andy Razaf/Joe Garland (1939); †*Tuxedo Junction (F), Buddy Feyne/Wm. Johnson, Julian Dash and Erskine Hawkins (1940); †*Little Brown Jug (F), R.A. Eastburn (1869) arranged by Bill Finegan; *String of Pearls (F), Eddie de Lange/Jerry Gray

(1942); I Know Why (F), (from film *Sun Valley Serenade*), Mack Gordon/Harry Warren (1941); At Last (F), (from film *Sun Valley Serenade*, 1941, and featured in film *Orchestra Wives*, 1942), Mack Gordon/Harry Warren (1941); †Chattanooga Choo-Choo (F), (from film *Sun Valley Serenade*), Mack Gordon/Harry Warren (1941).

The 12-inch album consisted of the titles marked by asterisk (*) plus: †Kalamazoo ('I've got a gal in') (from film *Orchestra Wives*, 1942), Mack Gordon/Harry Warren (1942); Boulder Buff, Fred Norman/Eugene Novello; Farewell Blues, Leon Rappolo, Paul J. Mares and Elmer Schoebel (1923); King Porter Stomp (originally written in 1906), Ferdinand Joseph (Jelly Roll) Morton (1924); St Louis Blues (F), W. C. Handy (1914).

The eleven titles marked (F) were all included in the Universal International film *The Glenn Miller Story* (1954) in which Glenn was portrayed by James Stewart. These were arranged and modernized in Miller's style by Henry Mancini (see Mancini, 1959). The original soundtrack of the film was released by Decca in 1954 and also sold over half a million.

† Indicates sold a million as a single.

PATTI PAGE
CROSS OVER THE BRIDGE *Mercury* [*USA*]. This eleventh million seller for Patti was written by Bennie Benjamin and George Weiss. It was No 3 and 19 weeks in the U.S.A. bestsellers.

THE PENGUINS
EARTH ANGEL (Will you be mine?) *Dooto* [*USA*]. The only million seller for this rhythm-and-blues group, figure achieved by 1957. By 1966 the disc had sold almost four million. The song was written in 1954 by Curtis Williams (Jesse Belvin) and is considered to be one of the great rhythm-and-blues songs of the 1950s. It reached No 8, and was 15 weeks in the U.S.A. bestsellers. The Penguins were discovered by Buck Ram (see Platters, 1955).

Curtis Williams was lead singer of the quartet. Other members were Cleveland Duncan, Dexter Tisby and Bruce Tate.

WEBB PIERCE (country-and-western vocalist)
MORE AND MORE *Decca* [*USA*]. This was a bestseller of 1954/55 and a No 1 country-and-western disc, the song written by Webb Pierce and Merle Kilgore. It is said to have sold a million.

Pierce was born in West Monroe, Louisiana, on 8 August 1926 and has been one of Decca's most consistent country hit makers, starting with 'Wondering' in 1951, and nine No 1 country-and-western hits up to 1969. His particular brand of magic started at 16 when he became an entertainer on radio in his hometown, West Monroe, on station KMLB. Webb served three years in the Army, then settled in Shreveport, playing for various bands throughout Louisiana. After an audition for the famous 'Louisiana Hayride' radio show, he subsequently got star billing after a flood of mail and made his first Decca hit release and became one of America's foremost country singers. He has sold millions of discs and popularized hundreds of folk songs, a great number of which he wrote himself. His big hits include 'Back Street Affair' (1952), 'It's Been So Long', 'There Stands the Glass' (1953), 'Slowly' (1954), 'I Don't Care', 'In the Jailhouse Now', 'Love, Love, Love' (1955), 'Crazy Arms', 'Why, Baby, Why?' (1956) with a string of successes since.

HANK SNOW
I DON'T HURT ANY MORE *Victor* [*USA*]. This second million seller for Hank Snow ('The Singing Ranger') was a record 52 weeks (1954–55) in the country-and-western charts. Hank (real name Clarence E. Snow) was born in Liverpool, Nova Scotia, of a poor family. He left home at 12 and took a job as cabin boy on a freighter for four years. He became devoted to the music of the American West and the Canadian plains. With six dollars he earned unloading a freighter of salt cargo, he bought

his first guitar and taught himself to play, guided by his prized collection of Jimmie Rodgers' records. Rodgers' influence was so great that he christened his first son Jimmy Rodgers Snow, also a country performer and, since, a travelling evangelist. Hank landed his first radio job in his native Canada on the local station in Halifax and later was featured on 'The Canadian Farm Hour'. In 1934 he appeared on CBS as a regular daily performer with his own early morning show. In 1935 he opened his own studio for guitar tuition. In 1936, the country-and-western singer first began recording for Victor Records and they gave him a special reception in 1961 to celebrate his 25 years with the label. He made his first personal appearance in the U.S.A. in 1944, broadcasting over the Philadelphia network, making an instantaneous hit. His discs, hitherto recorded at Victor's studios in Canada, had only been released there, but his successful American tour in 1948 brought him nationwide publicity and a place in Victor's American catalogues, in 1950. In 1950, he signed with Nashville radio and later made a tour of Japan and Europe. By 1958, he came to be regarded by most country enthusiasts as one of the great performers, equal in some respects to the legendary Jimmie Rodgers himself, who died in 1933. 'I Don't Hurt Any More' was written by Don Robertson (music) and Jack Rollins (words). A top country-and-western disc.

JO STAFFORD
MAKE LOVE TO ME *Columbia* [*USA*]. The tune of this seventh million seller for Jo Stafford goes back to 1923. It was originally a jazz instrumental number 'Tin Roof Blues', with music by five members of the famed 'New Orleans Rhythm Kings' (Leon Rappolo, Paul Mares, Benny Pollack, George Brunies and Mel Stitzel) and Walter Melrose, the composer-author-publisher of most of the early jazz numbers in the early 1920s. The New Orleans Rhythm Kings were probably the finest white jazz group of all time. Walter Melrose wrote the original lyrics for 'Tin Roof Blues'. The new lyrics for this version of 'Make Love to Me' were written by Bill Norvas and Allan Copeland in 1953. The disc was No 1 for three weeks in the U.S.A. and 21 weeks in the bestsellers, going to No 8 in Britain.

JOAN WEBER WITH ORCHESTRA DIRECTED BY JIMMIE CARROLL
LET ME GO, LOVER *Columbia* [*USA*]. Joan's only million seller was originally written in 1953 by Jenny Lou Carson under the title 'Let Me Go, Devil', with an Alcoholics Anonymous pitch against demon rum. Mitch Miller, artists chief at Columbia,

suggested a revision of the lyrics which were written by Al Hill (1954). Miller recorded the tune with his new discovery, 18-year-old Miss Weber, who had been trying to get into recording for a couple of years, and got the producers of TV's 'Studio One' to plug it in their play about a disc jockey involved in a murder. Snatches of the disc were played six times during the show and public reaction was immediate. Within a fortnight orders for 500,000 hit Columbia, and the million sale soon followed. Joan Weber sang with her husband's dance band around her home town of Paulsboro, New Jersey. Then she got a chance to audition for a New York manager and almost immediately found herself facing a microphone, taking directions from Mitch Miller. Her disc was the first to catapult a pop tune into the hit parade overnight by means of concentrated TV plugging. The disc was No 1 for two weeks in the U.S.A. in 1955 and 15 weeks in the bestsellers; it was No 16 in Britain.

DAVID WHITFIELD WITH CHORUS AND MANTOVANI AND HIS ORCHESTRA

CARA MIA *Decca* [*Britain*]. David Whitfield was the first British male singer to have a million seller pop disc in the U.S.A. This disc was a hit on both sides of the Atlantic, and achieved the magic figure by 1956. The song was written by Lee Lange and Tulio Trapani – pseudonyms for Bunny Lewis and Mantovani – both English writers. David Whitfield came from Hull, Yorkshire, England. Born 2 February 1926, he was possessed of a fine tenor voice, and sang to his mess-mates while in the Royal Navy and in the late 1940s. After discharge in 1950, he was given three broadcasts in the Hughie Green programme on Radio Luxembourg, travelling to London for the recordings, but still working in Hull in a pre-cast stonemaker's yard. He became popular around Hull through club dates. Then Hughie Green asked him to appear at a charity concert at the Criterion Theatre, London, where he was introduced to impresario, Cecil Landeau, who put him in a show at the Washington Hotel for three months. Here (1953), he met Bunny Lewis, Decca's exploitation chief and started recording. Then followed variety and a hit disc 'Answer Me' with further successes, more variety, pantomime and then this disc of 'Cara Mia' to make him internationally known, when released on London label in the U.S.A. In 1963 David started an operatic career. This disc was a chart topper in Britain for 10 weeks. In the U.S.A. it was No 10 and 18 weeks in the bestsellers; 25 weeks in the British bestsellers. David Whitfield died on 16 January 1980 in Sydney, Australia.

SLIM WHITMAN

SECRET LOVE *Imperial* [*USA*]. Slim's second million seller is a song from the film *Calamity Jane* (see Doris Day, 1953), written by Paul F. Webster (words) and Sammy Fain (music).

ROSE MARIE *Imperial* [*USA*]. Slim Whitman's third million seller was his second song from the 1924 musical *Rose Marie* to reach this figure (see 1951). The words are by Otto Harbach and Oscar Hammerstein II, with music by Rudolf Friml. This disc was a chart topper in Britain in 1955 for 11 consecutive weeks, and 19 weeks in the bestsellers.

LINK WRAY AND HIS RAY MEN (instrumental group)

RUMBLE *Cadence* [*USA*]. Link Wray was born in 1930 in Fort Bragg, North Carolina and learned to play guitar on an old four-dollar instrument. His immediate influences were country music styles, but later a black blues singer named Hambone showed him how to play blues, using open chords tuned with fingers and a knife. He probably developed his musical insight from his mother who was a singer.

Link began living in commune fashion long before it became the style. Link and his brothers, their parents, their women and 16 children always worked and lived together – a closely united family.

He formed his first band in 1942, playing songs like 'Stardust' and 'Deep Purple'. Service in the Army followed, including a tour of duty in the Korean War where he contracted tuberculosis and spent a year in hospital after the war.

'Rumble', written by Milt Grant and Link Wray, said to have been recorded in 1954, sold a reported million by 1958, reaching No 16 with 14 weeks in the U.S.A. bestsellers, and during those four years Link vanished for a while until January 1959 when he reappeared briefly to make another monster hit 'Rawhide' (see 1959) for the Epic label. Again he vanished, determined to record and produce the way he wanted to do. This took him nearly 12 years, and was accomplished in an old chicken shack adjoining his farm at Accokeek in Maryland on a beat-up three-track machine. His method was somewhat primitive. When his guitar was too loud, the amplifier was put in the yard outside and the microphones placed through the window. For some time his backing musicians were without drums, so they improvised by stamping on the floor and rattling a tin of nails.

By 1971 he completed his first album – 'Link Wray' – a production of amazingly high quality, in his 'studio' dubbed 'Wray's Shack Three-Track'. The album happily reflects Wray's country roots and contained five tunes by him, five by friend Verroca and one by Willie Dixon - mostly rock-blues (Polydor label). The album was produced by Steve Verroca (drummer/percussionist) and Ray Vernon in association with Bob Feldman. Recording engineer was Vernon Wray.

The Family includes: Link Wray (lead vocals, dobro, guitar, bass); Billy Hedges (piano, organ); Bobby Howard (mandolin, piano); Doug Wray and Steve Verroca (drums, percussion); Mordicaw Jones (guitar, vocals).

ORIGINAL SOUNDTRACK FROM THE FILM WITH GORDON MACRAE, GLORIA GRAHAME, GENE NELSON, CHARLOTTE GREENWOOD, JAMES WHITMORE, SHIRLEY JONES, ROD STEIGER, JAY C. FLIPPEN AND CHORUS AND ORCHESTRA CONDUCTED BY JAY BLACKTON

OKLAHOMA (album) *Capitol* [*USA*]. For the second time this famous musical provided a million-selling album. This film-track version contains all the famous Oscar Hammerstein II and Richard Rodgers wonderful songs: Overture; Oh What a Beautiful Morning; Surrey with the Fringe on Top; Kansas City; I Can't Say No; Many a New Day; People Will Say We're in Love; Poor Jud is Daid; Out of My Dreams; Farmer and the Cowman; All or Nothin'; and Oklahoma. The film received the Academy Award for Best Musical Picture Score (by Robert Russell Ben-

nett, Adolph Deutsch and Jay Blackton) of 1955. The film was the first Todd-AO giant screen production. Gold Disc award R.I.A.A., 1958. This disc was in the U.S.A. bestseller charts for 255 weeks and hit the million in 1959.

EDDY ARNOLD WITH HUGO WINTERHALTER AND HIS ORCHESTRA

CATTLE CALL *Victor* [*USA*]. The sixth million seller through subsequent years for Eddy, an old song of 1934, written by Tex Owens. The disc was a No 1 in the U.S.A.'s country-and-western charts of 1955.

(See 1956 for Winterhalter biography.)

LA VERN BAKER

TWEEDLE DEE *Atlantic* [*USA*]. La Vern's first million seller was written by Winfield Scott in 1954. Rhythm-and-blues singer, LaVern Baker, was born in Chicago on 11 November 1928, and nicknamed 'Little Miss Sharecropper'. While still in her teens she sang at the Chicago Club DeLisa. She was heard by Fletcher Henderson who got her a date to record on the Okeh label. After more club work she toured with Todd Rhodes and his band and then signed with King Records. This disc was No 22, and 11 weeks in the U.S.A. bestsellers.

LES BAXTER AND HIS ORCHESTRA WITH CHORUS

UNCHAINED MELODY *Capitol* [*USA*]. The first million seller for Les Baxter was written by Hy Zaret (words) and Alex North (music) for the film *Unchained* in which it was sung by Todd Duncan, the famous baritone of *Porgy and Bess* by George Gershwin. Les Baxter was born in Mexia, Texas, on 14 March 1922. He studied piano at Detroit Conservatory and Pepperdine College, Los Angeles. Since the late 1930s he lived in Hollywood where he conducted orchestras and choruses for radio shows – including Bob Hope's, Abbot and Costello's – and at the Los Angeles Coconut Grove. Les was a one-time member of Mel Torme's singing group, the Meltones. A skilled arranger, he was signed to a long-term contract in 1950 with Capitol, and has arranged for Frank DeVol, Margaret Whiting and Nat King Cole. His first big disc was 'April in Portugal' (1953). This disc was No 2 for five weeks in the U.S. charts and 21 weeks in the bestsellers; No 10, and nine weeks in the British bestsellers.

CHUCK BERRY

MAYBELLENE *Chess* [*USA*]. This first big hit for Charles (Chuck) Edward Berry was written with the assistance of Alan Freed and Russ Fratto. Rock'n'roll singer Chuck, who also plays guitar, sax and piano, was born in San José, California on 15 January 1931, but spent most of his youth in St Louis where he started singing when the 'big beat' began to get under way. He became as popular as Bill Haley and Little Richard, sharing the bill with them on tours after signing with Chess and making this hit disc. He appeared on TV coast-to-coast shows and in rock'n'roll films, including *Rock Rock Rock*, *Mr Rock and Roll*, *Go Johnny Go* and *Jazz on a Summer's Day*. He later toured West Germany and appeared in Britain in 1964. Chuck was educated

at high school in St Louis and actually entered show business at the age of 16. He plays a swinging guitar and writes most of his songs. He worked as a hairdresser before he wrote and recorded 'Maybellene'. Co-writer Alan Freed, a disc jockey, is credited with having created the term 'rock'n'roll'. This disc was No 5 for four weeks in the U.S.A. charts and 14 weeks in the bestsellers, and a top rhythm-and-blues disc. It is also known as 'Mabelline'.

PAT BOONE

AIN'T THAT A SHAME *Dot* [*USA*]. This first of many million sellers for Pat Boone was written by Dave Bartholomew and Fats Domino (whose own disc also sold a million in this year). Pat (real names Charles Eugene Boone) was born on 1 June 1934 in Jacksonville, Florida, and is the great-great-great-great grandson of the legendary American pioneer Daniel Boone.

He was educated at Lipscombe College and North Texas State College, and graduated from Columbia University (1958) with a B.S. degree in speech and English. He won a prize in the Ted Mack Amateur Hour Show (1954), and then signed with Dot Records after winning on the Arthur Godfrey Talent Scout programme as a professional. A steady flow of rock'n'roll and ballad hits established his reputation among young and old, and led to several network TV shows of his own, and in 1956 a million-dollar film contract with 20th Century Fox for one picture a year for seven years. He became the hottest property next only to Elvis Presley on discs. Pat married Shirley Foley, daughter of famous country-and-western singer, Red Foley. Pat's talents now cover a wide range of show-business endeavours. His film debut was in *Bernadine*; then followed star roles in *April Love*, *Mardi Gras*, *State Fair*, *The Main Attraction*. This disc was No 2 for four weeks in the U.S. charts and 26 weeks in the bestsellers; No 7, and nine weeks in the British bestsellers.

TERESA BREWER

I GOTTA GO GET MY BABY *Coral* [*USA*]. This fourth million seller for Teresa Brewer was written by Marvin Rainwater.

LET ME GO LOVER *Coral* [*USA*]. This fifth million seller for Teresa was written by Jenny Lou Carson (in 1953), with revised lyrics by Al Hill (1954). (See Joan Weber, 1954, for song data.) It reached No 8, and was 11 weeks in the U.S. bestsellers; No 9 and 10 weeks in the British bestsellers.

DON CHERRY

BAND OF GOLD *Columbia* [*USA*]. American balladeer Don Cherry was born on 11 January in Dallas, Texas. A keen golf player, he quit a tournament in his home town to fly to New York in the early 1950s to make recordings in New York. From then on, he became a nightclub and theatre artist, with only occasional time to play golf. He subsequently was featured on both television and radio shows. His first recordings were with Decca, then Columbia, and in 1966 he was recording for the Monument label.

The song was first introduced by Kit Carson, formerly known as Liza Morrow (on the Mars and Capitol label), and was written by Bob Musel (words) and Jack Taylor (music). Don's disc was a bestseller from 1955 to 1956 and eventually sold an estimated million. It was also a hit in Britain, reaching No 6 in the charts in 1956. Disc was No 5 in the U.S.A. for two weeks in 1956, and notable for having the first arrangement by Ray Conniff for Columbia (see Conniff, 1966). It was 22 weeks in the bestsellers; 11 weeks in the British bestsellers.

NAT KING COLE

A BLOSSOM FELL *Capitol* [*USA*]. This song, by three British writers - Howard Barnes, Harold Cornelius (Harold Fields) and Dominic John (Joe Roncoroni) - was a big hit for Nat King Cole on both sides of the Atlantic. It was No 2 in the U.S.A. and in the Top Ten for 14 weeks, also No 3 in Britain and in the Top Ten for five weeks, with a combined sale of a million. The song was written in 1954, and was 20 weeks in the U.S. bestsellers; 10 weeks in the British bestsellers.

FATS DOMINO

THINKING OF YOU *Imperial* [*USA*]. The ninth million seller for Fats was written by R. Hall.

AIN'T THAT A SHAME *Imperial* [*USA*]. The tenth million seller for Fats Domino was written by Dave Bartholomew and Fats himself. A top rhythm-and-blues disc, it reached No 16 with nine weeks in the U.S. bestsellers; No 23 in Britain.

ALL BY MYSELF *Imperial* [*USA*]. The eleventh million seller for Fats Domino was written by Dave Bartholomew and Fats.

I CAN'T GO ON *Imperial* [*USA*]. The twelfth million seller for Fats Domino was written by Dave Bartholomew and Fats.

POOR ME *Imperial* [*USA*]. Yet another million seller for Fats Domino, again written by him and Dave Bartholomew.

LONNIE DONEGAN AND HIS SKIFFLE GROUP

ROCK ISLAND LINE *Decca* [*Britain*]. This was Lonnie Donegan's first big success and one which earned him a Gold Disc award in 1961 for its million sale (700,000 in the U.S.A. and 350,000 in Europe). It was first recorded in 1953 as part of an album 'New Orleans Joys' (Chris Barber's Jazz Band and The Lonnie Donegan Skiffle Group) at a Royal Festival Hall concert in London, and first came to the attention of U.S. music fans in 1954. In 1955, 'Rock Island Line' was issued as a single and quickly became a hit on both sides of the Atlantic, by 1956. The song is by Huddy Ledbetter. Donegan was born in Glasgow, Scotland, on 29 April 1931. Since youth he had been influenced by music, his father being an accomplished violinist. Lonnie showed an ardent interest in folklore and folk music, becoming quite an authority on these subjects. At 17 he bought his first guitar, and soon became interested in jazz, making his first appearance with a group before being called up for National Service in 1949. He played drums with the Wolverines Jazz Band in the Army, and on discharge, played banjo with the Ken Colyer Band which is credited with sowing the seeds of Britain's skiffle

craze - the skiffle sound based on the 'home-made' instruments developed by American Negroes. In 1951, Lonnie formed his own group and later joined forces with Chris Barber, making his disc debut with Chris on the album 'New Orleans Joys' for which he received a recording-session fee of £2 10s. He changed his name from Anthony to Lonnie after he appeared with his own band on the same bill in the Royal Festival Hall as U.S. blues artist (and Donegan idol), Lonnie Johnson. In 1956 he left Barber to go solo, singing with Pye Records, and made his variety debut in America. In 1957 he used his comedy talents playing in pantomime in London, becoming a top performer in that field. He made his film debut with a guest appearance in 1958 and later appeared before the Queen in Scotland's first Royal Command Variety Performance. In 1959 he presented his TV series 'Putting on the Donegan', with three series in all. He had paid three visits

to the U.S.A. and visited the Continent, and was a great success in Australia and New Zealand. He held the unique distinction of making a hit out of every single released, and was the first Briton to earn three Gold Discs for million sellers (see 1959 and 1960). This disc is said to have sold two million globally by 1966. It reached No 8 in Great Britain, and No 10 in the U.S.A. with 17 weeks in the bestsellers, 22 weeks in the British bestsellers.

RUSTY DRAPER

SHIFTING, WHISPERING SANDS *Mercury* [*USA*]. Rusty Draper's second million seller was a song originally written in 1950 by V. C. Gilbert (words) and Mary M. Hadler (music). It was also a hit for Billy Vaughn on the Dot label recorded on both sides of a disc in two parts. This disc reached No 7, and was 14 weeks in the U.S. bestsellers.

THE DREAM WEAVERS

IT'S ALMOST TOMORROW *Decca* [*USA*]. The only million seller by this vocal group was written by Wade Buff (words) and Gene Adkinson (music) in 1953. This disc was a chart topper in Britain in 1956 for three weeks, 18 weeks in the British bestsellers and reached No 8 in the U.S.A. with 23 weeks in the bestsellers. The group was organized by Adkinson for recording.

EDDIE FISHER

DUNGAREE DOLL *Victor* [*USA*]. This disc was released in December 1955, the exploitation concentrated on the second title of the disc 'Everybody's Got a Home But Me' from the stage musical *Pipe Dream* written by Oscar Hammerstein (words) and

Richard Rodgers (music). It was however 'Dungaree Doll' written by Ben Raleigh and Edward Sherman that proved the bigger attraction and made the disc a million seller in 1956, the eighth for Eddie Fisher.

TENNESSEE ERNIE FORD

SIXTEEN TONS *Capitol* [*USA*]. This disc of Tennessee Ernie Ford's leapt to the top of the U.S.A. bestseller lists as fast as any record then made. The song was written by Merle Travis, a Kentucky coal-miner's son from Beech Creek (pop. 788) who, remembering the long, workless summers of his father, decided to record some coal-miners' songs in 1947. There were hardly any to be found, so he wrote some, including 'Sixteen Tons'. The chorus is from a saying Travis' father often used, a somewhat homey cynicism that struck a chord in Americans' hearts (particularly the line 'I owe my soul to the company store'), most of whom live on credit. Tennessee Ernie was born on a farm outside Bristol, Tennessee, on 13 February 1919, where he attended school, sang in the choir and played trombone in the school band. He worked as a radio announcer and singer, playing Western tunes as a disc jockey in Pasadena, before entering the Air Force in 1941. In 1949, as singer in a quartet, he joined the 'Hometown Jamboree' show over Pasadena radio. A Capitol representative heard him on a car radio and three days later signed him to an exclusive contract (1948). In 1950 he started to build his career with such discs as 'I'll Never Be Free' (with Kay Starr) and 'Shot Gun Boogie' - his own composition - that made him well known.

Then followed personal appearances, TV and more recordings, and subsequently this big disc, with a reputed four million global sale. It was No 1 for seven weeks in the U.S.A., and a chart topper in Britain in 1956 for six weeks. A top country-and-western disc. It was released in October 1955 and sold over 400,000 in its first 11 days on the market, and was 22 weeks in the U.S. bestsellers; 11 weeks in the British bestsellers.

THE FOUR ACES

LOVE IS A MANY-SPLENDORED THING *Decca* [*USA*]. This fifth million seller for the Four Aces is from the film of the same title, written by Paul Francis Webster (words) and Sammy Fain (music). It won the Academy Award for the Best Film Song of 1955—the second such award for its writers. The disc was No 1 for five weeks in the U.S.A. and 15 weeks in the bestsellers; No 2, and 13 weeks in the British bestsellers.

THE FOUR LADS

MOMENTS TO REMEMBER *Columbia* [*USA*]. The first million seller for this group was written by Al Stillman (words) and Robert Allen (music). The Four Lads (Frank Busseri, Bernard Toorish, James Arnold and Corrie Coderini) hail from Toronto where, like the 'Crew Cuts' (see 1954), they attended the Cathedral Choir School for general education and musical training. They formed their act while in school. When the Golden Gate Quartet played an engagement at the Casino Theatre there, the boys went backstage and got 'Dad' Wilson, the Quartet's lead bass, to hear them. Wilson wired his manager in New York and shortly after, the Four Lads were booked into Le Ruban Bleu, New York. They then played many clubs, theatres and TV as well as recording. They backed Johnny Ray on his disc of 'Cry' (see 1951), starting their own solo recording career in 1953, first becoming known through their recordings of 'Istanbul' and 'Down by the Riverside'. This disc was No 3 for one week in the U.S. charts, and 18 weeks in the bestsellers.

GEORGIA GIBBS

TWEEDLE DEE *Mercury* [*USA*]. This second million seller for Georgia was also the second one for this song written by Winfield Scott in 1954. It was No 3 for two weeks in the U.S.A. and 19 weeks in the bestsellers; No 20 in Britain.

DANCE WITH ME HENRY *Mercury* [*USA*]. This third million seller for Georgia Gibbs and No 2 in the U.S.A. charts, was written and composed by Etta James, Johnny Otis and Hank Ballard. The song was also known as 'The Wallflower', a revised version of Hank Ballard's 'Work with Me Annie'. This disc was 18 weeks in the U.S. bestsellers.

BARRY GORDON WITH THE ART MOONEY ORCHESTRA

NUTTIN' FOR CHRISTMAS *MGM* [*USA*]. Barry's only million seller was written by Sid Tepper and Roy C. Bennett. It reached No 7 in the U.S. charts.

GOGI GRANT

SUDDENLY THERE'S A VALLEY *Era* [*USA*]. This first million seller for Gogi, who was born in 1937 and hails from Los Angeles, was written by Chuck Meyer and Biff Jones. Gogi made personal appearances, worked at nightclubs and on TV, and in 1961 started her own disc company. She has also recorded for Victor and Liberty. Her real name is Audrey Brown. This disc reached No 14, and was 11 weeks in the U.S. bestsellers.

BILL HAYES

THE BALLAD OF DAVY CROCKETT *Cadence* [*USA*]. This was Bill Hayes' only million seller—in fact it sold close on two million altogether. The song was a routine job in 1954 by Tom Blackburn (words) and his collaborator George Bruns (music), a Dixieland trombone-playing member of the Walt Disney music staff, for Disney's 'Ballad of Davy Crockett' (Disneyland) series on ABC-TV in the U.S.A. The story concerns the exploits of the fearless frontiersman. It captured the imagination of the youngsters, and up to 1955 proved to be the fastest selling entity in the history of the disc industry. Collective 'Crockett' discs on more than 20 different labels sold an estimated seven million in under six months. It also created a fantastic sale of more than 100 varieties of merchandise, for example, coonskin caps, a quiz game, outfits, dolls, shirts and buckskins, eagerly snapped up by the youngsters in the 'Crockett' boom that hit the major department stores. Fess Parker, who starred as Davy Crockett in the series, waxed the song for Columbia which sold close to a million in just over a month. This disc was No 1 for five weeks in the U.S.A. and was 20 weeks in the bestsellers. No 2, and nine weeks in the British bestsellers. Bill Hayes was born in Harvey, Illinois.

AL HIBBLER (vocal) WITH THE JACK PLEIS ORCHESTRA

UNCHAINED MELODY *Decca* [*USA*]. Al Hibbler, who rose to fame and fortune as a pop singer, was born 16 August 1915 in Little Rock, Arkansas and has been blind since birth. As a youngster, he attended the School for the Blind in Little Rock and became interested in music, joining the school choir. He later entered an amateur talent show in Memphis and won first prize and joined a local band, subsequently forming his own band which appeared at the Famous Door and the El Rancho. On disbanding this, he became vocalist with Jay McShann and his band and recorded with them in the early 1940s. His first discs were not successful, and he had a difficult time until Duke Ellington took an interest in his recordings. Duke then featured him as a vocalist with his band for eight years, during which Al toured the globe with them. In 1950, Al did a stint with Universal Pictures and then became a solo artist. Then came his big hit with 'Unchained Melody', written by Hy Zaret (words) and Alex North (music) for the film *Unchained*, with an estimated million sale.

The disc was a perennial seller over a long period. Al also had another big hit with 'He' in 1955. 'Unchained Melody' was No 5 for four weeks in the U.S. charts and 18 weeks in the bestsellers; No 2, and 17 weeks in the British bestsellers.

JONI JAMES

HOW IMPORTANT CAN IT BE? *MGM* [*USA*]. By 1958 this disc became Joni's fourth million seller. The song was written by Bennie Benjamin and George Weiss. This disc was No 8 and 15 weeks in the U.S. bestsellers.

B. B. KING (rhythm-and-blues vocalist)

EVERY DAY (I have the blues) *RPM* [*USA*]. Riley B. King was born on 16 September 1925 in Itta Bona near Indianola, Mississippi, on a plantation, and raised in the heart of the cotton producing bottomlands of the Mississippi Delta where some of the greatest blues-men were nurtured. His early youth was spent working in the fields. He learned the guitar from an uncle who was a Baptist minister, sang in gospel groups, and at around 14 got his first guitar as part of his wages through his employer. He then began performing spirituals with three other youths from his area, learning the rudiments of the instrument at the same time. He became interested in the blues through hearing visiting blues performers who performed from time to time at plantation dance halls and gambling establishments in the Indianola area. In World War II, King performed on street corners in local towns. After the war he moved to Memphis, where harmonica player Sonny Boy Williamson launched him on a full-time career as a blues performer. In 1945 he joined WGRM-Greenwood, Mississippi and in Memphis was hired as a disc jockey by station WDIA in addition to performing himself. WDIA was the first Negro-manned radio station in Memphis and, during his years of daily broadcasting, King learned a great deal about the blues and the tastes of blues audiences. It was at this station that the manager, Don Kern, named him 'The Blues Boy' which became shortened to simply 'B.B.'. In 1949, King made his first hit record 'Three O'Clock Blues' for RPM Records for which he wrote the music and in 1952 this was in the top position on the rhythm-and-blues charts for over four months. A string of successes followed, many of them his own compositions.

He later recorded for ABC Records who have many of his discs in their catalogue and in 1967 when the label formed Blues Way discs King was the first to record an album in their highly successful series devoted exclusively to the blues. For much of his career he worked with bands.

There is little doubt that B.B. King is the undisputed King of the Blues of this generation. His unique vocal and guitar style have been imitated by almost every other bluesman. It took 20 years for white audiences to discover the most potent and polished blues they had ever heard. This came about through the wave of white, blues-oriented rock started through the playing of gifted musicians such as Mike Bloomfield, Eric Clapton (then of The Cream) and Larry Coryell. It was a group of British performers who awoke Americans to a thing they had overlooked for a hundred years, and brought the sudden burst of recognition for B.B. King who until early 1968 had been confined to a dreary circuit of one-night performances in back-country roadhouses and big-city ghetto clubs. In 1969 he performed for an audience of over 6,000 at London's Royal Albert Hall.

King made 500 singles and 20 albums up to 1969. 'Every Day' written by Peter Chatman was originally titled 'Nobody Loves Me' and introduced in 1950 by Lowell Fulson. There was also a bestseller disc by Joe Williams with the Count Basie Orchestra.

B.B. King's disc is said to have sold at least four million through the years.

LITTLE RICHARD (vocal) AND BAND

TUTTI FRUTTI *Specialty* [*USA*]. With a sale of over three million by 1968, this first million seller for Little Richard was written by D. La Bostrie, R. Penniman and Joe Lubin. This vocalist hails from Macon, Georgia, and was born on Christmas Day, 1935. He started as soloist in the choir of his local church at 14 and also played the organ. At 15 he was singing, dancing and selling herb tonic for a medicine show, and a year later won a talent contest at an Atlanta, Georgia, theatre. Little Richard's first disc contract (Victor Records) brought little reward, so he returned home and became a member of the Temple Toppers group. They made discs for another company (Peacock Records), as did the re-styled group The Upsetters. Still without success, Little Richard made a private tape and submitted it to Specialty Records (it contained 'Tutti Frutti'), which when recorded in the studio became a hit on both sides of the Atlantic. A five-year contract to Hollywood followed and more hits on discs, including 'Long Tall Sally' (see 1956), which established him. In 1958 he set aside show business to enter the Oakwood Adventurist College on a two-year intense study, concentrating on religious activities, returning to show business in 1960. He appeared with Bill Haley in the film *Don't Knock the Rock* (1956), and the rock'n'roll spectacular film *The Girl Can't Help It* (1956). He has, since 1961, made gospel records. His real name is Richard Penniman, and he is part writer of this song 'Tutti Frutti'. He signed with Okeh Records in 1966. His disc sales equalled 32 million to 1968. This disc reached No 21, and was 12 weeks in the U.S. bestsellers; No 29 in Britain.

JULIE LONDON
CRY ME A RIVER *Liberty* [*USA*]. Actress-singer Julie was born in Santa Rosa, California, worked as a lift attendant in a departmental store, was discovered there by Sue Carol, and subsequently appeared on TV with the Steve Allen and Perry Como shows, also in several films. This is her only million seller disc. The song was written by Arthur Hamilton in 1953. Her real name is June Webb. This disc was No 13, and 20 weeks in the U.S. bestsellers; No 22 in Britain.

JOHNNY MADDOX (piano)
WITH THE RHYTHMASTERS
CRAZY OTTO MEDLEY (Parts 1 and 2) *Dot* [*USA*]. (Comprising: Ivory Rag; In der nacht ist der mensch nicht gern alleine; Das machen nur die Beine von Dolores; Was macht der Alte Seeman; Play a simple melody; Humoresque; Do, do, do; When you wore a tulip.) Johnny Maddox hails from Gallatin, Tennessee. His hobby of collecting old records, sheet music and piano rolls was responsible for this popular disc. He was a Dot Record artist from the early 1950s.

'Crazy Otto' (real name Fritz Schulz-Reichel) is the German recording artist famous for his honky tonk piano playing, who has been with the Polydor label since 1951. He was awarded (1957) the 'Golden Gramophone' for sales of over a million of his albums of 'Bar Music and Honky Tonk' over the years, a trophy normally given only to classical musicians. He was the first pop artist to receive this award, in recognition of outstanding and unusual recordings and for 'indefatigable activity in the service of music over the entire world'.

This disc was No 2 for six weeks in the U.S. charts, and 20 weeks in the bestsellers.

THE MCGUIRE SISTERS
SINCERELY *Coral* [*USA*]. 'Sincerely' was a first million seller for the three sisters: Christine (born 1929), Dorothy (born 1930) and Phyllis (born 1931), all from Middleton, Ohio. They sang with local church choirs in their teens, then sang at a local radio station. They started their professional career touring the U.S.A., entertaining at Army camps and veterans' hospitals. On returning to Ohio, they joined the staff of a radio station in Cincinatti, then did local club dates before going to New York and playing eight weeks on the Kate Smith show. They then won an Arthur Godfrey 'Talent Scouts' contest, joining the cast of his regular shows. Heard by Milt Gabler of Decca, they were signed for its Coral label in 1953, and were the only female vocal group in the U.S.A. at that time. Then came a hit 'Goodnight Sweetheart, Goodnight' (1954), followed by this disc of 'Sincerely' in the rhythm-and-blues idiom that zoomed into the hit parade overnight, and brought them fame, more recordings, nightclubs, TV and personal appearances in the U.S.A. and abroad.

Christine is a fine pianist and Dorothy an accomplished saxophonist. The song was written in 1954 by Harvey Fuqua and disc jockey Alan Freed. The disc was No 1 for six weeks in the U.S.A. and 20 weeks in the bestsellers.

MANTOVANI AND HIS ORCHESTRA
SONG HITS FROM THEATRELAND (album) *London/ Decca* [*Britain*]. This fourth million selling album for Mantovani reached the half million in the U.S.A. in 1955 and a million by 1965 for combined sales of the monaural (1955) disc and stereo disc (1958).

The contents were: 'If I Loved You' (from *Carousel*), by Oscar Hammerstein and Richard Rodgers (1945); 'Wunderbar' (from *Kiss Me Kate*), by Cole Porter (1948); 'I've Never Been in Love Before' (from *Guys and Dolls*), by Frank Loesser (1950); 'Bewitched' (from *Pal Joey*), by Lorenz Hart and Richard Rodgers (1940); 'I Talk to the Trees' (from *Paint Your Wagon*), by A.J. Lerner and Fredk. Loewe (1951); 'Some Enchanted Evening' (from *South Pacific*), by O. Hammerstein and Richard Rodgers (1949); 'Out of my Dreams' (from *Oklahoma*), by O. Hammerstein and Richard Rodgers (1943); 'Stranger in Paradise' (from *Kismet*) by Robt. Wright and Geo. Forrest (1953); 'C'est Magnifique' (from *Can-Can*), by Cole Porter (1953); 'Almost Like Being in Love' (from *Brigadoon*), by A.J. Lerner and Fredk. Loewe (1947); 'Hello Young Lovers' (from *The King and I*), by O. Hammerstein and Richard Rodgers (1951); 'They Say It's Wonderful' (from *Annie Get Your Gun*), by Irving Berlin (1946).

This disc was issued on the London label in the U.S.A., and on Decca in Britain. Gold Disc award R.I.A.A., 1961.

DEAN MARTIN
MEMORIES ARE MADE OF THIS *Capitol* [*USA*]. This second million seller for Dean was written by Terry Gilkyson, Richard Dehr and Frank Miller. The disc was No 1 for five weeks (U.S.A.) in 1956 with 24 weeks in the bestsellers, and a chart topper in Britain, also in 1956, with 16 weeks in the bestsellers.

MITCH MILLER AND HIS ORCHESTRA AND CHORUS
YELLOW ROSE OF TEXAS *Columbia* [*USA*]. This was a U.S. Civil War campfire song, adapted to a marching beat by Don George, who was tipped off to its 'pop' potentiality by a Cleveland disc jockey, Bill Randle. This adaptation's success induced Don George, a fine composer, organist, conductor, violinist and producer to give up his job of selling juke boxes, and return to writing which he had done in 1934. Mitch Miller was born on 4 July 1911 at Rochester, New York. He began studying oboe in high school at 12 and is today considered one of the top classical players on that instrument. At 15, he was second oboist in the Eastman School of Music's symphony orchestra and also made his first professional appearance with the Rochester Philharmonic, then with the Syracuse Philharmonic and others. In 1936, he joined CBS radio, and for 11 years was soloist with the CBS Symphony, playing with such orchestras as Percy Faith, Andre Kostelanetz, The Roth String Quartet, Budapest Quartet and The Mannes Trio. He then became a director of Mercury Records' 'pop' division, and in 1950 held a similar post with Columbia. In recent years, he has had tremendous success with his albums – 'Singalong' issues – which not only sold in millions, but were the start of an idea for an entire series of popular TV shows (see 1958). His association with Columbia since 1950 has produced big successes for singers Tony Bennett, Johnny Mathis, the Percy Faith orchestra and many others. 'The Yellow Rose of Texas' – Mitch Miller's first million seller disc – was one of the great marching songs around 1864 during the War between the North and South, when it was known as 'The Gallant Hood of Texas', a favourite with the soldiers under General John. B Hood, the Texas soldier of the Confederacy. This disc was No 1 for six weeks in the U.S.A. and 10 weeks in the bestsellers; No 2 and 13 weeks in the British bestsellers.

ART MOONEY AND HIS ORCHESTRA
(with vocal refrain)
HONEY BABE *MGM* [*USA*]. This fourth million seller for Art Mooney was written for the film *Battle Cry* by Paul Francis Webster (words) and Max Steiner (music) and was based on a traditional air ('Will You Be Mine?'). It was No 6 in the U.S. charts for four weeks and 17 weeks in the bestsellers.

THE PLATTERS
ONLY YOU (AND YOU ALONE) *Mercury* [*USA*]. The first million seller for this group, which comprised a male quartet – Tony Williams of Roselle, New Jersey, David Lynch of St Louis, Paul Robi of New Orleans, Herbert Reed of Kansas City – plus one girl, Zola Taylor. The song was written by Buck Ram and Ande Rand. Buck Ram, an enterprising song writer, heard Tony Williams singing and invited him to join a group he was in the process of grooming – The Platters. All were working as parking lot attendants in Los Angeles. Zola Taylor then joined the group. Buck secured the group a contract with Mercury. This disc, No 5 for two weeks, put them right on top, and they became a major

personal appearance attraction in many parts of the world, under the management of Buck, also later appearing in four films. Zola Taylor did not record with the group until their next big hit 'The Great Pretender'. Tony Williams became solo in 1961 and was replaced by Sonny Turner. This disc is also reputed to have sold a million in France on the Barclay label, becoming the first to do so in that country. The Platters had achieved nine gold discs by 1965. The group originally recorded (1952) on the Federal label. A top rhythm-and-blues disc, it was 22 weeks in the U.S. bestsellers. No 18 in Britain.

PEREZ PRADO AND HIS ORCHESTRA
(trumpet: Billy Regis)

CHERRY PINK AND APPLE BLOSSOM WHITE *Victor* [*USA*]. This first million seller for Prado 'King of the Mambo' was originally published in Paris in 1950 under the title 'Cerisier Rose et Pommer Blanc', words by Jacques Larue, music by Louiguy. Mack David provided English words in 1951. It was featured by Prado and his orchestra in the film *Underwater* (1955) starring Jane Russell and became one of the top sellers of the year, and the biggest instrumental disc on the Victor label. Perez Prado was born on 23 November 1918 in Mantanzas, Cuba, where he received his musical education and played with the Orquesta Casino de la Playa. Mambo syncopations were in Prado's head as long ago as 1942, and he wrote them into arrangements for local bands. In 1948, he formed his own band in Mexico and the mambo beat began to catch on, but it took six years for it to work its way through half a dozen tropical and semi-tropical countries before it hit the U.S.A. in 1954, with Rosemary Clooney and Perry Como discs in that year. Prado soon appeared in films, nightclubs and theatres throughout Latin America, then in the U.S.A. in nightclubs and ballrooms, notably the Roseland State Ballroom in Boston in 1954. He had recorded 'Cherry Blossom' originally in 1951 but R K O films selected the tune as theme music for *Underwater*. This resulted in Prado being recalled to cut this new version for Victor Records. The disc was No 1 for 10 weeks in the U.S.A. with 26 weeks in the bestsellers, and a chart topper in Britain for two weeks, with 17 weeks in bestsellers.

FRANK SINATRA WITH ORCHESTRA DIRECTED BY NELSON RIDDLE

LOVE AND MARRIAGE *Capitol* [*USA*]. Written by the great U.S. song-writing team of Sammy Cahn (words) and James van Heusen (music) for the musical version of Thornton Wilder's *Our Town*, a TV production in which it was introduced by Frank Sinatra. The disc sold 900,000 in the U.S.A. with sales elsewhere bringing the total over the million. It was No 5 in the U.S. charts and 17 weeks in the bestsellers; No 3 and eight in the British bestsellers.

LEARNIN' THE BLUES *Capitol* [*USA*]. Another tremendous hit for Frank Sinatra was the song written by Dolores Vicki Silvers. This also had a sale in the U.S.A. of 900,000 and topped the million with sales elsewhere. The disc was No 2 in Britain's charts for six weeks, and No 2 in U.S.A. for two weeks, with 20 weeks in the bestsellers; 13 weeks in the British bestsellers.

THE SINGING DOGS

JINGLE BELLS *RCA* [*USA*]. This record was born in 1955 when a Dane named Don Charles (Carl Weismann) put together a tape of various toned dog barks set to the music of 'Jingle Bells'. The five-dog team recorded this in Copenhagen and completed the 45 rpm disc with three other tunes, 'Patty Cake', 'Three Blind Mice' and 'Oh Susanna', as a four-tune medley. The disc was released by RCA in U.S.A. and sold 500,000 copies. Release in Britain around the same time was on Pye-Nixa label, on a 78 rpm disc.

Howard Smith, host of a four-hour talk/music show over the WABC-New York FM outlet, WPLJ, who liked to play anything weird or new on his programme, first started playing the original 45 rpm disc at Christmas 1970. Smith played the disc for many weeks prior to Christmas 1971 and told some RCA executives at a record party about the public response to his playing their old record. RCA unearthed the original parts at their plant in Indianapolis and rushed the disc into release in early December 1971. In three weeks alone it sold 420,000 copies, the combined sales through the years making it a million seller. It was No 13 and four weeks in the British bestsellers.

Many of Smith's callers stated that their own dogs sang along with the record. *Life* magazine printed a story of this canine novelty in its 19 December 1955 issue. The disc has now become a standard Yule-time hit.

CYRIL STAPLETON AND HIS ORCHESTRA

BLUE STAR *Decca* [*Britain*]. This was the theme for 'Medic', a U.S.A. TV series, written by Edward Heyman (words) and Victor Young (music) in 1955. It was initially a bestseller for Les Baxter and his orchestra in America, but Stapleton's recording reached No 2 for two weeks in Britain, was 12 weeks in the charts, and is said to have sold a million globally.

Cyril Stapleton began playing the violin at age seven, and later served with various theatre pit bands in the silent picture era. He was leading his own band in the provinces at age 20. He became well known with the old Henry Hall dance band, and later with the Royal Air Force Orchestra, before joining the BBC. He was a big radio favourite in Britain in the early postwar years when he became known as 'Mr Music' as maestro of BBC's Showband which he created in 1952. In World War II he conducted the Royal Air Force Symphony at the Potsdam summit conference and, during the 5 years he was with the BBC Showband, played with artists like Frank Sinatra, Nat 'King' Cole and Irving Berlin, and gave radio and TV breaks to 'Born Free' singer Matt Munro and Tommy Steele. He joined Pye Records in January 1966 with his band and became A & R controller and independent producer later.

Stapleton was born on 31 December 1914 and died on 25 February 1974.

GALE STORM

I HEAR YOU KNOCKING *Dot* [*USA*]. Gale Storm's only million seller was written by Dave Bartholomew and Pearl King. Actress-singer Gale Storm was born on 5 April 1922 in Bloomington, Texas, and became interested in dramatics at high school, winning a prize for being the best female actress of her years in an inter-scholastic dramatic competition in Houston. From 1939 she appeared in many films, including musicals and westerns. She also appeared in her own U.S. television shows, 'My Little Margie' and 'The Gale Storm Show'. This disc was No 3 in the U.S. charts, and 18 weeks in the bestsellers.

JOE TURNER

FLIP FLOP AND FLY *Atlantic* [*USA*]. Another standard rhythm-and-blues disc for Joe Turner which has sold a million through the years. The song was written by Charles Calhoun and Lou Willie Turner. Joe Turner signed with Ronn Records in 1969.

CATERINA VALENTE

THE BREEZE AND I *Decca [USA] Polydor [Germany]*. This vocal version of the famous Cuban composer Ernesto Lecuona's 'Andalucia' (1928) was first published in 1940, the words by Al Stillman. Caterina Valente was born in Paris of Italian parents and was immersed in the art of entertainment from birth, her mother Maria acknowledged by many to be the most gifted clown in the world and billed as 'The Female Grock', her father known as Di Zazzo was a famed accordion virtuoso, and one of her brothers had mastery of 33 musical instruments. Her diverse background enabled her to interpret lyrics with equal facility in English, Spanish, French, Italian, German and Swedish. She took time off from her work as feed comedian in her mother's circus act to audition with the Kurt Edelhagen Band in 1953 and her singing outstripped most of her rivals ever since. Her first major disc was Lecuona's 'Malagueña' which established her reputation in the U.S.A. and Britain. Then came 'The Breeze and I', an even greater success. Her exciting version appeared in the bestseller lists for a long time, and indeed is still popular today. Caterina is also an accomplished dancer. She has toured the world with her husband-manager Eric Von Aro and made 90 recordings in many languages in one year. She celebrated her 25th year in show business in 1962. She is undoubtedly one of Europe's greatest stars, her discs selling all over the world. 'The Breeze and I' has sold a reputed million globally through the years. It reached No 13, and was 14 weeks in the U.S. bestsellers; No 5 and 14 weeks in the British bestsellers.

BILLY VAUGHN AND HIS ORCHESTRA

MELODY OF LOVE *Dot [USA]*. By 1958 this became a first million seller for Billy Vaughn. The tune is the famous 'Melodie d'amour' written by H. Engelmann in 1903 with lyrics written by Tom Glazer in 1954. Billy Vaughn hails from Bowling Green, Kentucky. He sang with a vocal quartet in 1952, then developed into one of the most consistent hit-producing studio orchestra leaders in the disc world. As a member of the Hilltoppers and also their musical director in 1952, he wrote and recorded 'Trying' with the group. This led to a Dot Records contract and a hit record, with a follow-up hit 'P.S. I Love You' (see 1953). Then, as musical director at Dot, Vaughn had an important arranging-conducting hand in producing many of their hits with Pat Boone, Gale Storm and others. His own singles, and especially albums, have been tremendously successful not only in the U.S.A. but in other parts of the world. He has a particularly large

following in Germany. This disc was No 2 in the U.S. charts, and 27 weeks in the bestsellers.

OTIS WILLIAMS AND THE CHARMS

HEARTS OF STONE *De Luxe [USA]*. This group's first million seller, was the second for the song (see Fontane Sisters, 1954). It was written by Eddy Ray (words), and Rudy Jackson (music) in 1954, and the disc was released then. A top rhythm-and-blues disc.

ROGER WILLIAMS (piano) WITH ORCHESTRA DIRECTED BY GLENN OSSER

AUTUMN LEAVES *Kapp [USA]*. This was both a first million seller for Roger Williams and for the Kapp label. The song is the well-known one by Joseph Kosma, originally published in France (French lyrics are written by the poet Jacques Prevert, English words by Johnny Mercer) and copyrighted there in 1947. Roger Williams learned to play the piano by ear before his third birthday and wrote his first original composition when he was four. At the age of eight he could also perform on 12 other instruments. He conducted the school orchestra and choir in his Iowa high school days in Des Moines. After service in the U.S. Navy he returned to Des Moines in late 1945 to continue his piano studies, was given his own radio show, and accepted professional concerts throughout the Midwest. He returned to Idaho State College in 1949 to get his B.Sc. degree and in 1950 his M.A. degree in Music at Drake University, Des Moines. He subsequently received a Doctorate of Music. In 1952, Roger decided to move to New York, enrolled at the famous Juilliard College where he met jazz pianist Teddy Wilson who encouraged him to continue in the jazz medium, and he later studied with another fine jazz musician, Lennie Tristano. As a result, he won an Arthur Godfrey 'Talent Scouts' show and a $1,000 prize on the 'Chance of a Lifetime' TV show in New York. Dave Kapp, head of Kapp Records, heard him playing in a cocktail lounge and asked him to record for his company, and he made an album titled 'The Boy Next Door'. Soon after, he recorded 'Autumn Leaves' which was a No 1 seller for four weeks in the U.S.A. and 15 weeks in the bestsellers. Then came radio, TV and concerts all over the U.S.A. and Canada. In 1960 in a disc jockey poll, Roger Williams was voted 'the most played' and 'favourite solo instrumentalist'. A consistent album seller, his sales were over eight million by 1965. 'Autumn Leaves' subsequently sold two million globally. Roger Williams (real name Louis Weertz) was born in 1925.

ORIGINAL SOUNDTRACK OF FILM WITH BING CROSBY, GRACE KELLY, FRANK SINATRA, CELESTE HOLM, LOUIS ARMSTRONG AND HIS BAND AND MGM STUDIO ORCHESTRA CONDUCTED BY JOHNNY GREEN

HIGH SOCIETY (album) *Capitol [USA]*. *High Society* is a screenplay based on Philip Barry's stage play *The Philadelphia Story*. Famous lyricist/composer Cole Porter wrote the complete score, which as usual contained big hits, and a cast of big stars. Grace Kelly and Bing Crosby's song 'True Love' eventually sold a million as a singles disc and several of the other songs were and are continually performed today, particularly 'Who Wants to Be a Millionaire?', 'I Love You, Samantha' and 'Now You Has Jazz', the latter being a most original song in the manner in which it introduces the instruments of the jazz orchestra to a build-up by Bing Crosby and Louis Armstrong. Frank Sinatra was also outstanding in both his solo songs and duet with Celeste Holm. This album was reported to have sold three million by 1970. Its contents were: 'Overture High Society'; 'High Society Calypso' (Louis Armstrong); 'Little One' (Bing Crosby); 'Who

Wants to be a Millionaire?' (Celeste Holm and Frank Sinatra); 'True Love' (Grace Kelly and Bing Crosby); 'You're Sensational' (Frank Sinatra); 'I Love You, Samantha' (Bing Crosby); 'Now You Has Jazz' (Bing Crosby and Louis Armstrong); 'Well, Did You Evah?', (originally from *Leave It to Me*, 1938) (Bing Crosby and Frank Sinatra); 'Mind If I Make Love to You' (Frank Sinatra).

FILM SOUNDTRACK WITH DEBORAH KERR, YUL BRYNNER, RITA MORENO, TERRY SAUNDERS, CARLOS RIVAS, REX THOMPSON. CHORUS AND ORCHESTRA CONDUCTED BY ALFRED NEWMAN

'THE KING AND I' (album) *Capitol [USA]*. The original musical play with book and lyrics by Oscar Hammerstein II and music by Richard Rodgers is based on the novel *Anna and the King of Siam* by Margaret Landon. It ran for 1,246 performances from 29 March 1951, at New York's St James Theatre, an impressive show, beautifully set, sumptuously costumed, and a triumphant successor to *South Pacific*.

It tells the story of Anna Leonowens, a Victorian lady, who in the 1860s became teacher to the royal princes and princesses at the court of the King of Siam, and encountered many crises both in the classroom and in the realm of the King's affairs. She became very influential and after the King's death stayed in Siam. The late Gertrude Lawrence played the part of Anna until 11 August 1952, when she became ill and died in New York on 7 September 1952. She was succeeded by several other actresses - Constance Carpenter, Annamary Dickey and Patricia Morison. Yul Brynner played the King, later being replaced by Alfred Drake. The English production at the Drury Lane Theatre from 8 October 1953 ran for 926 performances with Valerie Hobson as Anna and Herbert Lom as the King.

20th Century Fox's magnificent film of the musical was released in the U.S.A. on 28 June 1956 with Yul Brynner as the King and Deborah Kerr as Anna, the songs being sung for her by Marni Nixon.

Capitol's soundtrack album stayed in the bestsellers for 259 weeks and received a Gold Disc award from R.I.A.A. in 1964, with an eventual million sale. Contents of the album: Overture; 'I Whistle a Happy Tune' (Deborah Kerr and Rex Thompson); 'My Lord and Master' (Rita Moreno); 'Hello, Young Lovers' (Deborah Kerr); 'The March of the Siamese Children'; 'A Puzzlement' (Yul Brynner); 'Getting to Know You' (Deborah Kerr, children and King's wives); 'We Kiss in a Shadow' (Rita Moreno and Carlos Rivas); 'I Have a Dream' (Rita Moreno and Carlos Rivas); 'Shall I Tell You What I Think of You?' (Deborah Kerr); 'Something Wonderful' (Terry Saunders); 'Song of the King' (Yul Brynner); 'Shall We Dance?' (Deborah Kerr and Yul Brynner); Finale (The Company).

Conductor Alfred Newman received his 8th Academy Award (Oscar) for his musical score of the film. His 9th came in 1967 for the score of the film *Camelot*, 10th for *Hello Dolly* in 1970. He holds the most Academy Awards for musical scores of films.

Alfred Newman died on 17 February 1970.

ORIGINAL THEATRE CAST WITH JULIE ANDREWS, REX HARRISON, STANLEY HOLLOWAY, ROBERT COOTE, MICHAEL KING, GORDON DILWORTH, ROD MCLENNAN, PHILIPPA BEVANS

MY FAIR LADY (album) *Columbia* [*USA*]. The most fabulous musical show ever produced the greatest selling musical show album, with an estimated six million plus sold up to 1 January 1966. This disc is said to have cost Columbia $40,000 to produce, and it brought in over $15 million. 'MFL' is a musical version of Bernard Shaw's famous play *Pygmalion*. Early in 1952, Alan Jay Lerner (lyricist) and Frederick Loewe (composer) were approached by producer Gabriel Pascal to write this version. After working on it for three months, Lerner and Loewe abandoned it. In July 1954, they renewed their work on an adaptation after Pascal's death that year. CBS put up the necessary $360,000 for the show which was directed by Moss Hart, and presented by Herman Levin at the Mark Hellinger Theatre on Broadway, 15 March 1956. It turned out to be the greatest musical comedy hit in theatrical history, running for six and a half years (to 29 September 1962) with 2,717 performances (the longest ever for an American musical on either side of the Atlantic up to 1965), grossed $20,257,000 on Broadway and over $66,000,000 from all productions including the U.S.A. It made a star of English actress Julie Andrews who had been chosen for the part of Eliza while playing in *The Boy Friend* in New York, and an unknown to practically everybody in the U.S.A. It added lustre to the established reputations of Rex Harrison and Stanley Holloway. These three and Robert Coote of the original Broadway cast also had the roles in the London production which opened on 30 April 1958 at the Drury Lane Theatre. It ran until 19 October 1963 with 2,281 performances - a record for an American musical in Britain up to 1963. The film rights were sold to Warner Brothers in 1962 for an amazing $5,500,000, then the highest ever paid, and the film cost $17 million to produce. 'MFL' has

also had record-breaking runs in 17 different countries with LP albums in nine languages adding to the astronomical disc income. This disc contains all the now famous songs; 'On the Street Where You Live', 'I Could Have Danced All Night', 'Wouldn't It Be Loverly?', 'With a Little Bit of Luck', 'Get Me to the Church on Time', 'I've Grown Accustomed to Her Face', 'The Rain in Spain', 'Just You Wait', 'Why Can't the English?', 'I'm an Ordinary Man', 'A Hymn to Him', 'Without You', 'You Did It', 'Show Me', and the 'Ascot Gavotte' and 'Overture'. The disc was No 1 in the U.S.A. for 15 weeks and was still in bestseller album charts nine years after its release in 1956 - for 482 weeks. Gold Disc award, R.I.A.A., 1964.

LES BAXTER AND HIS ORCHESTRA AND CHORUS

POOR PEOPLE OF PARIS (Poor John) *Capitol* [*USA*]. This disc, Les Baxter's second million seller, got its title 'Poor People of Paris' because of a cabled freak. The original title of this French song by René Rouzaud (words) and the French composer Marguerite Monnot was 'La goulant du pauvre Jean' (The Ballad of Poor John) as first sung in Paris by Edith Piaf. It told the story of the Frenchman who winds up with the wrong sort of girls. The title was cabled by Capitol's Paris representative to the Hollywood head office (or it came out incorrectly in the transmission) as 'pauvre gens' - 'gens' meaning 'people'. Whereupon Capitol forgot about 'poor Jean', resulting in the title change. The English lyric was written by Jack Lawrence. Marguerite Monnot, the composer, wrote the music for *Irma La Douce*, a big success on both sides of the Atlantic and a most unusual satirical musical play. She also composed hit songs for France's Edith Piaf, Yves Montand and the choral group Compagnons de la Chanson. She died aged 58, in 1961. 'Poor People of Paris' was a big instrumental success. This disc was No 1 seller for six weeks in the U.S.A. and 24 weeks in the bestsellers.

HARRY BELAFONTE

CALYPSO (album) *Victor* [*USA*]. Comprising: 'Banana Boat Song', by Harry Belafonte, Burgess (Lord Burgie) and Bill Attaway, 'Jack-ass Song', 'Hosanna', 'Come Back Liza' all by Attaway and Burgess, 'I Do Adore Her' and 'Dolly Dawn' both by Burgess, 'Jamaica Farewell', traditional - arrangement Burgess, 'Will His Love Be Like His Rum?' by Attaway and Belafonte, 'Man Smart' by Seagel and Belafonte, 'Star O' by Attaway, Burgess and Belafonte, 'Brown Skin Girl', traditional.

Harold George Belafonte was born in Harlem, New York City, on 1 March 1927, where he spent his first eight years, then five years in Jamaica, returning to New York at 13 to attend George Washington High School. After three years in the U.S. Navy he enrolled at the American Negro Theatre Workshop and later developed his acting talents at the Dramatic Worshop. After a

try at Broadway, he gave up his dramatic career for an eight-hour-a-day job as messenger and package wrapper in the garment district. Monte Kaye, a product-manager, heard him sing one evening at Broadway's Royal Roost Jazz Club with the band 'just for laughs' which resulted in a 22-week engagement there. He made some recordings, and played the Five O'Clock Club in Miami. Dissatisfied with 'pop' singing he quit and opened a restaurant in New York's Greenwich Village, where during informal song festivals he discovered a love for folk songs, sought out his friend Millard Thomas (now his accompanist) and together they built a repertoire of folk songs and ballads. After eight months he closed the restaurant and entered the entertainment world, at New York's Village Vanguard with a 22-week engagement. Other engagements followed, the Blue Angel, the Black Orchid in Chicago, the Chase Hotel in St Louis, then signing with Victor Records and later star roles in the films *Bright Road, Carmen Jones, Island in the Sun* and *The World, the Flesh and the Devil*. This album of 'Calypso' was a great success. 'Banana Boat Song' eventually sold a million as a single disc (1957). His album 'Belafonte Sings of the Caribbean' (1957) transformed Belafonte from a nightclub headliner into an international show business celebrity, earning him the nickname of 'King of the Calypso'. His albums are continually programmed by disc jockeys around the world and he has set attendance records everywhere, with high ratings on TV. There are few recording artists who rate with him. This disc sold 500,000 by 1957, with a reputed million by 1959, so becoming the first 33 rpm album by a solo artist to achieve seven figures. Gold Disc award R.I.A.A., 1963. It was No 1 for 31 weeks in the U.S.A.

CHUCK BERRY

ROLL OVER BEETHOVEN *Chess* [*USA*]. Second million seller for Chuck through subsequent years. The song was written by him and the disc reached No 29 in the U.S.A. It was also a hit for The Beatles in 1964.

PAT BOONE

I'LL BE HOME *Dot* [*USA*]. Second million seller for Pat Boone was written by Ferdinand Washington and Stan Lewis. The disc was a chart topper in Britain for five weeks, and No 5 in the U.S.A. for two weeks with 22 weeks in the bestsellers, in both countries.

I ALMOST LOST MY MIND *Dot* [*USA*]. This third million seller for Pat Boone was also the second time million seller for the writer Ivory Joe Hunter who composed and recorded it in 1950 (see 1950). This disc was No 1 for two weeks in the U.S.A. and 24 weeks in the bestsellers.

FRIENDLY PERSUASION (Thee I Love) *Dot* [*USA*]. Pat Boone's fourth million seller was the theme of the film *Friendly Persuasion* (1956), and another big success for composer Dmitri Tiomkin. The lyrics were supplied by Paul Francis Webster. Pat Boone also recorded the song for the film. This disc was No 8 for four weeks in the U.S.A. and 24 weeks in the bestsellers; No 3 in Britain with 21 weeks in the bestsellers.

REMEMBER YOU'RE MINE *Dot* [*USA*]. This fifth million seller for Pat Boone made it a golden year for him, with four major hits altogether. This number was written by Kal Mann and Bernie Lowe. The disc reached No 20, and was 21 weeks in the U.S. bestsellers; No 5 and 18 weeks in the British bestsellers.

TERESA BREWER

A TEAR FELL *Coral* [*USA*]. This sixth million seller for Teresa Brewer was written by Dorian Burton and Eugene Randolph. It reached No 7, and was 24 weeks in the U.S. bestsellers; No 2 and 15 weeks in the British bestsellers.

JAMES BROWN AND THE FAMOUS FLAMES

PLEASE, PLEASE, PLEASE *Federal* [*USA*]. This was a first million seller for this rhythm-and-blues group. Screamer-singer, songwriter and showman James Brown was born 17 June 1928

at Pulaski, Tennessee. As a youngster, he augmented the family income by working as a shoeshine and newspaper boy in Augusta, Georgia, where he was brought up. He learned a lot from his father, and soon became proficient on the piano and organ. Later he mastered the drums and bass-guitar. After completing high school, he could have become a baseball player or a boxer, but went on the road to sing gospel-derived songs with a group which he named 'The Famous Flames'. After very rough progress, they began to be noticed. In 1956, James discovered his own talent for composing and with the aid of John Terry wrote 'Please, Please, Please' which was recorded by the group at a local radio station. They pooled their resources to pay for this and got a disc jockey friend to play the record on the air. The response was so great that, within a week, James Brown was signed to a recording contract with King Records and the disc became a national hit.

He got his big break when he appeared on a nationwide TV show. Many big-beat groups in Britain fashioned their music on rhythm-and-blues singers like James Brown, Joe Turner and John Lee Hooker, and Brown decided to promulgate 'the real thing' after the British groups (including the immortal Beatles) had invaded the American disc market around 1963 with their 'synthetic' versions of a purely American idiom. He organized the 'James Brown Show', consisting of 40 singers, dancers and musicians, and made 300 appearances in 300 different cities in the U.S.A. in 1964 and again in 1965, playing to over a million and a quarter fans each year. He grossed over $1 million in 1965 and played to audiences of up to 27,000. His show was presented on British TV on 11 March 1966. Brown produces the whole show - the songs, costumes, lighting, routines, arrangements and dancing - and his dynamic stage act on five nights per week the whole year round electrifies audiences and musicians alike. The frenzied atmosphere he creates has earned him the names of 'Mr Dynamite', 'Mr Showbusiness' and 'The Biggest Negro Cat', and an estimated $250,000 a year for his performances alone - a spectacular achievement for an artist whose first 25 years were spent in poverty.

'Please, Please, Please' is a wild, pleading, religious-style song, and a reflection of Brown's Baptist church days and when he was a member of various gospel quartets.

By 1968, James Brown was considered to be a new leader of the black people in America. After Martin Luther King's assassination in that year, he appeared on American TV telling the people to 'Cool it. Don't do anything you'll regret tomorrow.'

People cleared from the streets and some of the impending violence died away. He was invited to the White House three times.

His records became as powerful as any political movement in the U.S.A. as exemplified in his disc 'Say It Loud. I'm Black and Proud'. His message wasn't Black Power but simply Soul Power.

Collective sales of James Brown's discs are estimated at 50 million (to 1971) of which it has been said some 24 singles titles sold over a million each. Five of these were officially confirmed by 1971. He is also said to have two gold albums.

BUCHANAN AND GOODMAN
FLYING SAUCER *Luniverse* [*USA*]. The only million seller by this duo was written by Mae Boren Axton, who gave Elvis Presley his great hit 'Heartbreak Hotel'. It was No 4 in the U.S. charts.

JOHNNY CASH
I WALK THE LINE *Sun* [*USA*]. Johnny's first million seller was a song he wrote himself. He was born in Kingsland, Arkansas, on 26 February 1932. The family were mainly hymn singers, being Baptists, but his mother taught him how to strum on her old guitar. At 12, he was writing poems, songs and stories. At 22 he enlisted in the U.S.A.F. and, while in Germany for three years, found his talents greatly in demand, singing at the air base and in German clubs. On discharge Cash became a salesman for electrical appliances, singing after working hours. In 1954, he and two friends – billed as Johnny Cash and The Tennessee Two – got a tryout with Sun Records (who also discovered Elvis Presley) and their first song 'Cry, Cry, Cry' was a hit. After that everything Johnny turned out became a hit, and everything he composed came easily. He finally switched to Columbia Records. One of U.S.A.'s top country music artists, he held the unique distinction that each of his discs from 1956 to 1959 reached the top ten in the country-and-western charts. Nationally this disc was No 19, and 22 weeks in the bestsellers.

GEORGE CATES AND HIS ORCHESTRA
MOONGLOW and Theme from 'PICNIC' *Coral* [*USA*]. Second million selling disc of these titles from the film *Picnic*. 'Moonglow' by Will Hudson, Eddie De Lange and Irving Mills was written in 1934 and 'Theme from Picnic' by George W. Duning in 1955.

George Cates, composer, conductor, arranger and producer was born in New York, 19 October 1911, and educated at New York University. He became a producer for Coral and Dot Records and was music supervisor for the Lawrence Welk show.

This disc was No 4 for two weeks in the U.S.A. and 22 weeks in the bestsellers.

PERRY COMO WITH MITCHELL AYRES' ORCHESTRA AND THE RAY CHARLES SINGERS
HOT DIGGITY (Dog Ziggity Boom) *Victor* [*USA*]. This 13th million seller for Perry was written by Al Hoffman (words) and Dick Manning (music). The melody was adapted from the first theme of Chabrier's (1841–1894) 'España' Rhapsody for orchestra. The million sale was achieved by 1957, and the disc was No 2 for three weeks in the U.S.A. with 23 weeks in the bestsellers. No 4 and 13 weeks in the British bestsellers.

Mitchell Ayres died September 1969 in Las Vegas.

MORE backed with GLENDORA *Victor* [*USA*]. Perry Como's 14th million seller was written by Tom Glazer (words) and Alex Alstone (music). 'Glendora' was written by Ray Stanley, and was No 14, and 17 weeks in the bestsellers. 'More' was No 9, and 18 weeks in the bestsellers. In Britain 'Glendora' was No 18 and 6 weeks in the bestsellers and 'More' was No 10 and 12 weeks in the bestsellers.

BING CROSBY AND GRACE KELLY
TRUE LOVE *Capitol* [*USA*]. This was a first for Grace and the 22nd million seller for Bing. The song is one of the many outstanding hits from the film *High Society*, all written by the great Cole Porter. This wonderful film starred Bing, Grace, Frank Sinatra, Celeste Holm and Louis Armstrong and his orchestra. This disc sold a million by 1957 and was taken from the filmtrack. Grace Kelly was born in Philadelphia, her father being a successful and wealthy building contractor and, in his youth, single sculls champion in the Olympic Games of 1920 and 1924. She made her non-professional acting debut at the age of 11. Educated at Philadelphia's Raven Hill Academy and Stevens School, she persuaded her parents to let her enter the American Academy of Dramatic Arts in New York City in 1948, studying there for two years, and working as a commercial photographers' and artists' model, becoming highly successful in this and appearing on covers of numerous magazines. Then came a role on Broadway and TV appearances, with over 50 in dramatic TV shows. Next followed her film career and a notable start with *High Noon* (1952). Miss Kelly won an 'Oscar' for her work in the film *The Country Girl* (1954). She also starred in *Rear Window* (1953) and played roles in *The Bridges at Toko-Ri*, *Green Fire* and *To Catch a Thief* (1954). Finally came *The Swan* and *High Society* (1956). Soon after the latter, she married Prince Rainier of Monaco.

Recorded on 22 February 1956 in Hollywood, this disc was No 4 in the U.S.A. (1957), and 31 weeks in the bestsellers. No 4 and 27 weeks in the British bestsellers. Grace Kelly died on 14 September 1982 after a car crash.

ALAN DALE
SWEET AND GENTLE *Coral* [*USA*]. This was a first million seller for Alan Dale, whose real name is Aldo Sigismondi. The song was originally a mambo-cha-cha 'Me lo Dijo Adela', 1953 from Cuba, by Otilio Portal. The English words were by George Thorn, 1955.

CHERRY PINK AND APPLE BLOSSOM WHITE *Coral* [*USA*]. Alan Dale's second million seller was a vocal disc of the famous French tune written in 1950 by Louiguy, with English lyrics by Mark David. (See also Perez Prado, 1955.)

VIC DAMONE
ON THE STREET WHERE YOU LIVE *Columbia* [*USA*]. This third million seller disc for Vic Damone meant a major comeback for this singer (whose last million sellers had been in 1949) with one of the big hits from *My Fair Lady* by Alan Jay Lerner (words) and Frederick Loewe (music). The disc was a chart topper in Britain in 1958, and No 8 in the U.S.A. with 25 weeks in the bestsellers, and 17 weeks in the British bestsellers.

DORIS DAY
WHATEVER WILL BE, WILL BE (Que Sera, Sera) *Columbia* [*USA*]. This was the big hit from the Alfred Hitchcock re-make of his famous film of 1934 *The Man Who Knew Too Much*, starring James Stewart and Doris Day, in which Doris sang the song. Written by Ray Evans and Jay Livingston in 1955 the title won the Academy Award for Best Film Song of 1956, the third such award for these writers. The disc was Doris Day's sixth million seller, and was a chart topper in Britain for six weeks, and No 2 in the U.S.A. with 27 weeks in the bestsellers; 22 weeks in Britain.

THE DELLS (rhythm-and-blues quintet)
OH, WHAT A NIGHT *Vee Jay* [*USA*]. The Dells all come from Harvey, Illinois, and first met while at Thornton Township High School there around 1954. After long hours of study and rehearsal they signed with Chess Records, but their first disc was no success. They then signed with Vee Jay Records and among their hits for the label 'Oh, What a Night' proved the biggest. The disc became a rhythm-and-blues standard and subsequently

amassed a million estimated sale. The song was written by Marvin Junior and John Funches.

The group played many of the top supper clubs in the U.S.A. and also toured with Ray Charles and the late Dinah Washington. It consists of: Marvin Junior (lead guitar); Chuck Barksdale (bass); Michael McGill (baritone); Johnny Carter (tenor); Verne Allison (second tenor).

(See also Dells, 1969.)

BILL DOGGETT (swing organist)

HONKY TONK (Parts 1 and 2) *King* [*USA*]. This only million seller for Bill Doggett was composed by him, Billy Butler, Shep Sheppard and Clifford Scott with lyrics by Henry Glover. Doggett hails from Philadelphia and has arranged for the Ink Spots, Lionel Hampton, Louis Jordan and many other star disc artists. In 1960 he switched to the new Warner Brothers label. The disc was No 2 in the U.S. charts with 29 weeks in the bestsellers, and a top rhythm-and-blues disc.

FATS DOMINO

BO WEEVIL *Imperial* [*USA*]. The 14th million seller for Fats was based on the insect, the boll weevil, the ravenous little eater that can devastate the cotton crop. This song was written by Fats Domino and Dave Bartholomew around the American folk song of the same title. This disc reached No 35 in the U.S. charts.

I'M IN LOVE AGAIN *Imperial* [*USA*]. The 15th million seller for Fats Domino was written by Dave Bartholomew and Fats. It was No 5 in the U.S. charts, and a top rhythm-and-blues disc. No 12 and 14 weeks in the British bestsellers.

BLUEBERRY HILL *Imperial* [*USA*]. The 16th million seller for Fats Domino was an oldie of 1940, written by Al Lewis, Larry Stock and Vincent Rose. It was No 4 for five weeks in the U.S.A. and was 27 weeks in the bestsellers. No 6 and 15 weeks in the British bestsellers. A top rhythm-and-blues disc.

BLUE MONDAY *Imperial* [*USA*]. The 17th million seller for Fats Domino - again written in conjunction with Dave Bartholomew - was for the film *The Girl Can't Help It* which featured several disc stars. Fats sang it in this film. It was No 9 for five weeks and 18 weeks in the U.S. bestsellers, and a top rhythm-and-blues disc of 1957. It reached No 23 in Britain.

ANTAL DORATI CONDUCTING THE MINNEAPOLIS SYMPHONY ORCHESTRA

1812 OVERTURE (Tchaikovsky, Opus 49) *Mercury* [*USA*]. Of all the available recordings of this immortal overture, Antal Dorati's version unquestionably towers over all its rivals. It is probably the best classical seller in history. By 1963 it was awarded an R.I.A.A. Gold Disc for $1 million in sales, the equivalent of half a million discs, and has been selling at the rate of 50,000 every year since. By the end of 1965, U.S. sales amounted to over $2,500,000. In Europe, the album was released by Philips in 1961 and sold the equivalent of $500,000, thus bringing the total sales to over one million discs. The Ampex Corporation of U.S.A.'s tape recording of the Dorati recording (1965) was also a bestseller.

The recording is unique in that it includes the booming of the University of Minnesota Brass Band bronze cannon and the bells of Harkness Memorial Tower, Yale University, with a spoken commentary by Deems Taylor, famous U.S. composer, author, journalist, music critic, radio commentator and linguist - for the monaural recording. The stereo disc has the bells of the Laura Spelman Rockefeller Memorial carillon.

Antal Dorati was born 9 April 1906 in Budapest, Hungary, and studied music with Zoltan Kodaly, Leo Weiner and Bela Bartok. His career began at the age of 18 when he was conductor at Budapest's Royal Opera House. From 1929 to 1932 he conducted the Municipal Opera Orchestra at Munster and then led the Ballet Russe de Monte Carlo orchestra from 1934 to 1940. He then settled in the U.S.A. and was director of the Ballet

Theatre orchestra from 1945 to 1949, thereafter becoming permanent conductor of the Minneapolis Symphony Orchestra for several years. In recent years he was principal conductor for the BBC Symphony Orchestra, a post he relinquished in June 1966, and conductor of the Washington (DC) Symphony.

There is no doubt that this remarkable album will continue to sell for a long time to come.

FIVE SATINS

IN THE STILL OF THE NITE (I'll Remember) *Ember* [*USA*]. Now a standard, this disc was later re-issued on the Flashback label, and sales are a reputed million to date. This disc was 24 weeks in the U.S. bestsellers between 1956 and 1961. The Five Satins, one of the many groups formed at the start of the 'rock' era, included Willie Wright, a vocalist, who subsequently became a disc jockey for the WFIF (Milford, Conn.) radio station.

The song was written by Fred Parris, lead singer of the group.

TENNESSEE ERNIE FORD

HYMNS (Album) *Capitol* [*USA*]. Tennessee Ernie Ford (see also 1955) is probably one of the two great country music artists closest to the church—the other being Red Foley. Ford has become one of the world's most successful singers of religious music, the outcome of closing each of his TV shows with a hymn. Of the 26 albums he made for Capitol up to 1966, 16 were religious or inspirational, the biggest seller being 'Hymns'. This is, in fact, the largest selling album ever recorded by a Capitol artist, Ford receiving a Gold Disc award from R.I.A.A. in 1959. On 5 November 1963, he was awarded a platinum-plated master record of the 'Hymns' album with a solid gold plaque inscribed: 'HYMNS, The Largest Selling Album ever recorded by a Capitol Artist, presented to Tennessee Ernie Ford by Capitol Records'. It sold the half million by 1959 and has now passed two million. The disc was in the U.S.A. charts for 276 weeks to 31 December 1962. It comprised the following: 'Who at My Door is Standing?' (anon.); 'Rock of Ages' (A. M. Toplady and Thomas Hastings, 1832, adaptation and arrangement by Jack Fascinato and Ernest J. Ford); 'Softly and Tenderly' (adaptation and arrangement by J. Fascinato and E.J. Ford); 'Sweet Hour of Prayer' (adaptation and arrangement by J. Fascinato and E.J. Ford); 'My Task' (Maude Louise Ray and Emma L. Ashford, 1903); 'Let the Lower Lights Be Burning' (adaptation and arrangement by J. Fascinato and E.J. Ford); 'The Ninety and Nine' (E.C. Clephane and Ira D. Sankey, 1876, adaptation and arrangement by J. Fascinato and E.J. Ford); 'The Old Rugged Cross' (Rev. George Bennard, 1913); 'When They Ring the Golden Bells' (J. Fascinato and Tennessee Ernie Ford); 'In the Garden' (C. Austin Miles, 1912); 'Ivory Palaces' (anon.); 'Others' (C.D. Meigs and Arthur A. Penn, 1875–1941).

By 1962, Tennessee Ernie Ford had 5 religious albums in the half million sellers, with Gold Disc awards from R.I.A.A. for four of them.

This disc was released in the U.S.A. in October 1956, and still sells around 75,000 annually.

THE FOUR LADS

NO, NOT MUCH *Columbia* [*USA*]. The second million seller for this group was written by Al Stillman (words) and Robert Allen (music) who had given them their first million seller song in 1955. It was No 3 in the U.S. charts, and 24 weeks in the bestsellers.

FREDDY (Quinn)

HEIMWEH (Memories are made of this) *Polydor* [*Germany*]. Freddy (real name Manfred Petz) is a major European pop-record champion for million sellers. This was his first to sell a million by this year, and it went on to sell two million by 1958 for which he received two Golden Disc awards. The song, written by U.S. writers Terry Gilkyson, Richard Dehr and Frank Miller in 1955, was also a hit for Dean Martin (see 1955). Freddy was

13 when the Red Army advanced on Vienna in 1945. In the confusion he escaped to Belgium, earning a living shining combat boots for U.S. Army units. He later joined a small travelling circus for eighteen months, then came a 'wanderlust' to Naples, Tunis, Casablanca, Paris, Rotterdam, Hamburg, playing a guitar and singing the hillbilly songs he'd learned from U.S. Army buddies. Between 1951 and 1953 he sailed in a Finnish tanker from Odessa to Mexico to the Far East. When he returned to Germany (1953) he changed his name from Manfred Petz to Freddy Quinn and began to play in nightclubs and on TV and radio spots. Then he recorded this German version of 'Memories Are Made of This', and he says 'the people discovered me'. He went on to become Germany's bestselling disc artist and a top film star (11 films). Making only two discs a year, they all reached high positions in the sellers' charts between 1956 and 1962, and his album of 'Sailors' Ballads' was the first German album to sell over 100,000 in West Germany. He speaks fluent English and has recorded in Spanish, French, Italian and Finnish. By the end of 1969, Freddy had reportedly sold 20 million records in 13 years on the Polydor label.

GOGI GRANT
THE WAYWARD WIND *Era* [*USA*]. This second million seller for Gogi was written by Herb Newman (words) and Stan Lebowsky (music). The disc was No 1 for seven weeks in the U.S.A. and 28 weeks in the bestsellers; No 9, and 11 weeks in the British bestsellers.

BILL HALEY AND HIS COMETS
SEE YOU LATER, ALLIGATOR *Decca* [*USA*]. The third million seller for this famous 'rock 'n' roll' band was written by Robert Guidry in 1955. It was No 6 for three weeks in the U.S. charts, and 19 weeks in the bestsellers; No 7 and 13 weeks in the British bestsellers.

GEORGE HAMILTON IV
A ROSE AND A BABY RUTH *ABC-Paramount* [*USA*]. By 1957 this title provided Hamilton with his first million seller. It was also a first million seller disc for this label. Hamilton was born 19 July 1938 in Winston-Salem, North Carolina, and began his career in the country-and-western field. He became a regular listener to the 'Grand Ole Opry' Friday night 'clambakes' and used this influence to pattern his early style. He broadcast regularly over the Winston-Salem station while still in high school, and continued his radio work in the 'Town and Country Time' programmes in Washington, D.C. This led to many appearances on network TV shows and then to Arthur Godfrey's 'Talent Scouts'. Experience before TV cameras thus led to his own shows on TV with CBS and ABC after his signing with ABC-Paramount, and then this million seller. This song was written by John D. Loudermilk. This disc was No 6 in the U.S.A. and 20 weeks in the bestsellers.

DICK HYMAN (swing harpsichord, organ) TRIO
MORITAT (theme from *The Threepenny Opera*) *MGM* [*USA*]. This theme was first heard in Berlin in 1928 (the opera being vaguely based on John Gay's 18th-century original *The Beggar's Opera*), written by Kurt Weill (music) and Bertolt Brecht (German words). In 1956, Marc Blitzstein translated the Berlin slang effectively into American and it was Louis Armstrong who first popularized this revival, under the new title of 'Mack the Knife', a bitter satire of society and of schmalzy popular music. About 20 different versions were issued in 1956, Dick Hyman's Trio being the most successful instrumental version and his only million seller. Bobby Darin's vocal version achieved even bigger sales (see 'Mack the Knife', 1959).

Richard R. Hyman, composer, conductor, pianist, organist and arranger, was born 8 March 1927 in New York. He was educated at Columbia University where he wrote the Varsity show. He became pianist in jazz groups including Lester Young and Tony Scott, and made a tour of Europe in 1950 with Benny Goodman. From 1951 to 1952 he was staff pianist/organist on station WMCA and additionally conductor with WNBC from 1952 to 1957. His work as pianist and arranger with orchestras included those of Mitch Miller and Percy Faith, and his own trio. Dick was co-musical director of the series 'Encyclopedia of Jazz Concerts' and he also conducted and arranged for vocal groups. In 1958 he became musical director of the 'Arthur Godfrey Show' and in 1962 accompanist to Johnny Desmond. He has made many records.

This disc was No 9, and 20 weeks in the U.S. bestsellers; No 9 and 10 weeks in the British bestsellers.

DICK JACOBS AND HIS ORCHESTRA
MAN WITH THE GOLDEN ARM (main theme) *Coral* [*USA*]. This million seller for Dick Jacobs was written by Elmer Bernstein for the film of the same title which starred Frank Sinatra. Bernstein, a musical prodigy in the classical field at the age of 12, became a concert pianist. He decided to compose popular music after five years in the U.S.A.A.F., and Columbia Pictures invited him to go to Hollywood to write background music. His music for *The Man with the Golden Arm* was the first time modern jazz had been used to any great extent in the movie industry, and Bernstein thus acquired a trade mark. He has since recorded many of his soundtracks, and composed modern jazz-styled themes for TV programmes, notably for the 'Staccato' series. He was also responsible for the music of Cecil B. de Mille's gigantic film *The Ten Commandments*.

Dick Jacobs, composer, conductor and record executive, was born on 29 March 1918 in New York and educated at New York University. He became musical director for 'Hit Parade' on TV in the U.S.A., 1957–58.

This disc was No 26 and 14 weeks in the U.S. bestsellers.

JERRY LEWIS
ROCK-A-BYE YOUR BABY WITH A DIXIE MELODY *Decca* [*USA*]. Jerry's only million seller is an oldie of 1918 by Sam Lewis and Joe Young (words) and Jean Schwartz (music). It was one of Al Jolson's early hits which he revived in *The Jolson Story* film (see Jolson, 1946). Jerry Lewis (born Joseph Levitch in Newark, New Jersey, on 16 March 1926) began at the age of 14 serving as a bus boy in resort hotels where his parents entertained professionally. Jerry worked up a record-pantomime act at Brown's in Loch Sheldrake, New York. His first professional booking came at 15 in a Buffalo burlesque house. Then followed five years touring theatres and clubs with the act, until 1946 when he teamed up with Dean Martin (see 'That's Amore', 1953). Their comedy act became a headliner in nightclubs, films, TV and radio for ten years. Jerry has made occasional discs with Capitol, mainly comedy material, and also recorded with his wife, Patti. This disc was No 10 in the U.S. charts (1957) and 19 weeks in the bestsellers.

LITTLE RICHARD AND HIS BAND
LONG TALL SALLY *Specialty* [*USA*]. This second million seller for Little Richard was the disc which did more to establish him than any other. It was written and composed by Enotris Johnson, Robert Blackwell and Richard Penniman, the latter being the real name of 'Little Richard'. A top rhythm-and-blues disc, it was No 13, and 9 weeks in the U.S. bestsellers; No 3 and 16 weeks in the British bestsellers.

RIP IT UP *Specialty* [*USA*]. The third million seller for Little Richard was another big rock'n'roll number, this time written by John Marascalco and Robert Blackwell. A top rhythm-and-blues disc, it was No 27, and 18 weeks in the U.S. bestsellers; No 30 in Britain.

LITTLE WILLIE JOHN AND BAND
FEVER *King* [*USA*]. A first million seller for Little Willie John was written by John Davenport and Eddie Cooley. The song was later also a hit for Peggy Lee (see 1958). Little Willie John was

born in Camden, Arkansas, 15 November 1937. He started his professional career at 17, and was also a songwriter. Davenport is a pseudonym for Otis Blackwell. Little Willie died 26 May 1968 in Washington State Penitentiary. This disc was No 27, and 15 weeks in the U.S. bestsellers.

JIM LOWE WITH THE HIGH FIVES
THE GREEN DOOR *Dot* [*USA*]. This was a million seller by 1957. The song was written by Marvin Moore (words) and Bob Davie (music). The number was inspired by the yellow door of an artists' club in Dallas, and the young men who used to hang around outside because they didn't have a union card to get them in. Jim Lowe was born in Springfield, Missouri, on 7 May 1927 and became a disc jockey and songwriter in New York. He wrote 'Gambler's Guitar', the big hit for Rusty Draper (see 1953). This disc was No 1 for three weeks in the U.S. charts, and 26 weeks in the bestsellers; No 8 and nine weeks in the British bestsellers.

THE MCGUIRE SISTERS
MOONGLOW and Theme from 'PICNIC' *Coral* [*USA*]. This was the third million seller disc of the popular 'Picnic' Theme (written by George W. Duning in 1955 for the film) introducing 'Moonglow' (written by Will Hudson, Eddie De Lange and Irving Mills in 1934).

The success of the instrumental versions by Morris Stoloff and George Cates resulted in Steve Allen writing the lyrics for this vocal version, the third million seller for the McGuire Sisters. It was No 13, and 20 weeks in the U.S. bestsellers.

CLYDE MCPHATTER
TREASURE OF LOVE *Atlantic* [*USA*]. The first solo disc for Clyde McPhatter, formerly of The Drifters (see McPhatter, 1958), the song written by J. Shapiro and Lou Stallman. It was reported to have sold two million by 1968 in the U.S.A. alone, reaching No 22 with 17 weeks in the bestsellers. It was No 27 in Britain. McPhatter died 13 June 1972 (aged 41).

JOHNNY MATHIS WITH THE RAY CONNIFF ORCHESTRA
WONDERFUL, WONDERFUL *Columbia* [*USA*]. The first million seller for Johnny was written by Ben Raleigh (words) and Sherman Edwards (music). Johnny was born in San Francisco on 30 September 1935, the fourth of seven children. He became an outstanding all-round athlete at George Washington High School in San Francisco, and established a local high-jump record at San Francisco State College. His father, a former vaudeville artist, began teaching him songs from the age of 10, then a local musical teacher took him on for seven years without

fee. Mathis was heard by Helen Noga singing with a group at her Black Hawk club in San Francisco. She introduced him to George Avakian of Columbia Records and became his manager. Johnny remarkably made his debut on disc with a whole album. This promptly ended his plans to teach physical education. Columbia sent him on a nationwide tour. He cut more discs and appeared on major TV shows, concert halls, nightclubs and films. None of his discs was of the teen-beat variety, his success being thus the more outstanding in an era of rock'n'roll. Today he is in the top bracket of leading album sellers, several of which have passed the half million mark in sales. His album 'Johnny's Greatest Hits' was in the sellers' charts consistently from 1958. He is now one of the richest singers in the business and probably one of the few millionaires among black entertainers in the U.S.A. This disc was No 17, and 39 weeks in the U.S. bestsellers.

MELACHRINO ORCHESTRA CONDUCTED BY GEORGE MELACHRINO
IMMORTAL LADIES (album) *Victor* [*USA*]. This disc was recorded in late 1954 by EMI for the American market and included: 'Laura', by Johnny Mercer and David Raksin (1945); 'Rosalie', by Cole Porter (1937); 'Sweet Sue, Just You', by Will J. Harris and Victor Young (1928); 'Mona Lisa', by Jay Livingston and Ray Evans (1949); 'Chloe', by Gus Kahn and Neil Moret (1927); 'Dolores', by Frank Loesser and Louis Alter (1941); 'Irene', by Joseph McCarthy and Harry Tierney (1919); 'Louise', by Leo Robin and Richard A. Whiting (1929); 'Liza', by Gus Kahn, Ira Gershwin and George Gershwin (1929); 'Sally', by Harry Leon, Leo Towers and Bill Haines (1931); 'Marie', by Irving Berlin (1928); 'Dinah', by Sam M. Lewis, Joe Young and Harry Akst (1925).

A British release (10-inch album) titled 'My Fair Lady' included only the first eight songs as above.

George Melachrino was born in London on 1 May 1909 of Greek parentage. At 14 he won a scholarship to the Trinity College of Music, specializing in chamber music and stringed instruments, winning the highest praise from his tutors. At 18, he was already well known at the BBC studio in Savoy Hill, playing and singing over '2LO'. Every instrument became a challenge, and, in the following 12 years, he became an expert multi-instrumentalist, adding the viola, clarinet, saxophone and oboe to his prowess on the violin. Melachrino also had a highly-developed talent for composing and arranging. Forming his own band in 1939, he landed one of the best engagements in the profession — resident orchestra leader at London's Café de Paris, but this was terminated during the Battle of Britain. He joined the Army in 1940, working his way up from a private to Regimental Sergeant Major, and became musical director when the band of the A.E.F. was formed. It was during the war that Melachrino found the musical sound which made him famous. His senior at the War Office, Eric Maschwitz, said he wanted to hear 'Pennsylvania Polka' played by an orchestra of 80, thus George was the first to introduce sweet, sentimental mood music by the use of masses of strings, so paving the way for Mantovani and other exponents of the shimmering strings sound. The Melachrino Sound sold over three million albums, mainly in the American market, when the album era started in the early 1950s. These included his 'Music for ...' records, such as 'Music for Reading', 'Music for Relaxation', 'Music for Day-dreaming', 'Music to Help You Sleep' and so on.

George's theme tune 'First Rhapsody' became a regular feature in his broadcasts. Other of his compositions include 'Woodland Revel', 'Winter Sunshine', 'Vision d'Amour', 'Portrait of a Lady' and songs for the London Hippodrome show *Starlight Roof* (1947), all of which featured his orchestra. Probably his biggest selling singles disc is 'The Legend of the Glass Mountain'.

Progress from his early days as a member of Carroll Gibbons' Savoy Hotel Orchestra and a jazz musician to world acclaim with his Melachrino Strings was an outstanding achievement. George was the first British orchestra leader to receive a gold disc; this was presented to him by RCA chief George Marek for this outstanding album - 'Immortal Ladies'. George Melachrino died on 18 June 1965, but his music is timeless. He was a musician's musician.

MICKEY AND SYLVIA

LOVE IS STRANGE *Groove* [*USA*]. The sales of the original Groove recording of this song, written by Mickey (Baker) and Ethel Smith, were over 800,000. The duo later switched to RCA-Victor and the disc was issued on their Vik label with subsequent reputed aggregate sales of one million. The disc has become a standard rhythm-and-blues item, reaching No 13 with 18 weeks in the U.S. bestsellers.

Mickey Baker was born on 15 October 1925 and hails from Louisville, Kentucky. He has written many textbooks on music, one a bestseller, *Jazz Guitar*, dealing with an instrument that he plays. Sylvia Robinson was born on 6 March 1936 and hails from New York City. She also plays guitar. Both are songwriters. The duo gained fame at nightclubs, by making personal appearances, and on TV.

This song was the subject of an action for the infringement of 'Billy Blues'. The decision went in favour of the defendants in the U.S. Court of Appeals after four years, and provided one of the rare cases in which a copyright infringement was tried by a judge and jury rather than by a judge alone. The court held that the two tunes were not substantially or materially similar and that 'Love Is Strange' was not copied from 'Billy Blues' consciously or otherwise.

GUY MITCHELL WITH RAY CONNIFF ORCHESTRA

SINGING THE BLUES *Columbia* [*USA*]. This song was written in 1954 by Melvin Endsley, a polio victim since the age of three, who was confined to a wheel-chair. 'Singing the Blues' was Endsley's first accepted and successful song, bringing comfort and recognition to its Arkansas composer and a yield of over £15,000 in royalties, at the age of 22. The reputed sale is 2,500,000. The disc, which was Guy Mitchell's fifth million seller, was No 1 in the U.S.A. for eight weeks from December 1956 with 16 weeks in the bestsellers, and a chart topper in Britain in 1957, with 22 weeks in the bestsellers. Ray Conniff was born 6 November 1916 in Attleboro, Massachusetts.

PATTI PAGE

ALLEGHENY MOON *Mercury* [*USA*]. Patti's twelfth million seller was written by Al Hoffman and Dick Manning. It was No 2 in the U.S. charts, and 27 weeks in the bestsellers.

OLD CAPE COD *Mercury* [*USA*]. Patti's thirteenth million seller, through subsequent years. It sold two million by the end of 1966. The disc was a bestseller 1956-57, reaching No 7 with 23 weeks in the U.S. bestsellers. The song written by Claire Rothrock, Milt Yakus and Allan Jeffrey.

PATIENCE AND PRUDENCE

TONIGHT YOU BELONG TO ME *Liberty* [*USA*]. The only million seller for this duo is an oldie of 1926 (a million seller in sheet music then) written by famed Billy Rose (words) and Lee David (music). It was No 4 in the U.S. charts, with 25 weeks in the bestsellers; No 28 in Britain.

CARL PERKINS

BLUE SUEDE SHOES *Sun* [*USA*]. Carl Perkins' only million seller is the song he also composed in 1955. It was written on a potato sack on a Jackson housing project and sold two million altogether. Carl Lee Perkins, country-and-western artist, hails from Jackson, Tennessee, and this was the second disc to be recorded by him, attaining a high position in the sellers' charts in the U.S.A. Carl was born in Tipton County, Tennessee, in 1930, the son of a farmer. With his two brothers, J. B. and Clayton, he became interested in music at an early age, performing for small dances in western Tennessee. After spots on local radio he made his first disc in 1955. Later the trio made several national TV appearances, and Carl appeared in the film *Jamboree*. His brother J. B. plays rhythm guitar, while Clayton plays bass. W.S. Holland is their drummer. This disc was No 3 for three weeks in the U.S. charts, with 21 weeks in the bestsellers. No 10 and eight weeks in the British bestsellers. Disc released 1 January 1956 (recorded 26 December 1955). Perkins was born on 4 September 1930. Carl's career came to a halt due to a car accident but, in recent years, he has begun to make a comeback, appearing at the country-and-western festival in London in 1978.

THE PLATTERS

THE GREAT PRETENDER *Mercury* [*USA*]. The second million seller for this group was written and composed by their manager Buck Ram. It was No 1 for two weeks in the U.S. charts, with 24 weeks in the bestsellers. Released in 1955, it was a top rhythm-and-blues disc.

MY PRAYER *Mercury* [*USA*]. The third million seller for the Platters was No 1 for five weeks in the U.S.A., and 23 weeks in the bestsellers. This revival of a 1939 hit was originally composed as 'Avant de mourir' by Georges Boulanger. It was lyrically and musically adapted as a song by England's famous songwriter, Jimmy Kennedy, in 1939.

ELVIS PRESLEY

HEARTBREAK HOTEL backed with I WAS THE ONE [*RCA*] [*USA*]. The first of Elvis' over 50 discs to sell a million. This one sold over two million to earn him two Gold Disc awards, one for each title and was top disc of 1956 in the U.S.A. for eight weeks. 'Heartbreak Hotel' was written by Mae Boren Axton, Tommy Durden and Elvis Presley. Elvis Aaron Presley, born in Tupelo, Mississippi, on 8 January 1935, is peerless in this era. His fantastic acceptance and unbelievable sales success throughout the world were unmatched by any other disc artist popular for the same short period of time as Elvis. He was an artist in a class all to himself. By February 1961, he had sold $76 million worth of discs. He also achieved the greatest sales ever in one year (1956) (until The Beatles arrived in the 1960s) with 10 million discs and earnings of over one million dollars. His discs were at No 1 for 25 weeks in 1956 and 24 weeks in 1957. His family moved to Memphis in 1948, and Elvis graduated from Hume High School there, then worked as theatre usher and truck driver at 19. He then made a private recording for his mother's birthday, which attracted the attention of Sun Records who signed him up a year later. His first disc was 'That's All Right, Mamma' backed with 'Blue Moon of Kentucky' and the first night it was played over Memphis WHBQ radio, they received 14 telegrams and 47 phone calls in three hours, and disc jockey Dewy Phillips had to play the same disc seven times. During the following week, 7,000 of his first records were sold in Memphis alone. Then RCA-Victor A & R chief Steve Sholes heard about this sensational singer and bought Elvis' contract from Sun Records for $35,000 along with his original recordings and four additional discs. Then came his disc of 'Heartbreak Hotel' and 'I Was the One', recorded on 10 January 1956 in Nashville. Thereafter his records were the sensation of the music world with an endless list of top hits, 18 of them at No 1 between 1956 and 1962, even while he was in the U.S. Army. He made nationwide TV and personal appearances, accompanied by the screams of legions of teenage fans and in 1956 signed with producer Hal Wallis to make his film debut in the 20th Century-Fox film *Love Me Tender* (followed by the films *Loving You*, *Jailhouse Rock* and *King Creole*), the film company recouping the cost of 'Love Me Tender' in the first three days of release, an achievement probably unprecedented in film history. Elvis served from 1958 to 1960 in the Army without losing his leadership and popularity in the disc world, and on discharge resumed recording and made the films *Flaming Star*, *G.I. Blues*, *Wild in the Country*, *Blue*

Hawaii, Follow That Dream, Kid Galahad, Girls, Girls, Girls and *It Happened at the World's Fair*, up to the end of 1962, and many more thereafter. His gross income to December 1963 was estimated at $20 million, and in 12 years with Victor Records, his sales were over 85 million singles, over 18 million albums, and over 14 million EP discs. By December 1970 he had sold 160 million disc units globally, with gross returns to RCA-Victor of $280 million. His biggest-selling disc was 'It's Now or Never' (1960) with world sales reputed of over 20 million (five million of these in the U.S.A. alone) and he held more gold disc awards for million sales than any other artist in the world (his nearest rivals being The Beatles, Fats Domino and Bing Crosby). 'I Was the One' was written by Aaron Schroeder, Claude de Metruis, Hal Blair and Bill Peppers. A top country-and-western disc 'Heartbreak Hotel' was 27 weeks in the U.S. bestsellers, and 'I Was the One' reached No 23 with 16 weeks in the bestsellers. 'Heartbreak Hotel' was No 2 and 21 weeks in the British bestsellers.

Elvis Presley died in Memphis, Tennessee on 16 August 1977.

I WANT YOU, I NEED YOU, I LOVE YOU *Victor* [*USA*]. This third million seller for Elvis – 'I Want You, I Need You' was written by Maurice Mysels (words) and Ira Kosloff (music). The disc was No 1 for three weeks in the U.S.A. with 24 weeks in the bestsellers; No 25 in Britain. The Gold Disc was awarded on U.S. sales alone. Recorded 11 May 1956 in Nashville.

DON'T BE CRUEL backed with HOUND DOG *Victor* [*USA*]. This colossal hit for Elvis (recorded 2 July 1956 in New York), selling six million, furnished his fourth and fifth Gold Discs. It was No 1 in the U.S.A. charts for 11 weeks, with 28 weeks in the bestsellers. 'Hound Dog' was No 2 and 23 weeks in the British bestsellers. 'Don't Be Cruel' was written by Otis Blackwell and Elvis Presley, and 'Hound Dog' by Jerry Leiber and Mike Stoller in 1952. Leiber and Stoller wrote other hits for Elvis, and The Coasters, with total sales of 30 million discs by 1960. This was also a top rhythm-and-blues and country-and-western disc.

LOVE ME TENDER backed with ANY WAY YOU WANT ME *Victor* [*USA*]. This sixth and seventh million seller for Elvis was No 1 in the U.S.A. charts for five weeks, and is the first known disc to have had an advance sale of over one million. 'Love Me Tender' was written by Elvis Presley and Vera Matson and is based on an old song 'Aura Lee' of 1861, and was sung by Elvis in his first film *Love Me Tender* in this year. (*Note* – The original 'Aura Lee' was written by W. W. Fosdick and George R. Poulson and was a favourite Civil War song with the Union Army.)

'Any Way You Want Me' was written by Aaron Schroeder and Cliff Owens. This disc sold two million, and was awarded a Gold Disc for each title on U.S.A. sales alone. 'Love Me Tender' was 23 weeks in the U.S. bestsellers. 'Any Way You Want Me' reached No 2 and was 10 weeks in the bestsellers. 'Love me Tender' was No 11 and nine weeks in the British bestsellers.

RAY PRICE
CRAZY ARMS *Columbia* [*USA*]. This first million seller for Ray was rated the top country-and-western disc of the year. The song was written by Ralph Mooney and Chuck Seals. Ray began his career studying veterinary medicine, but decided he would rather sing about animals than mend them. He lives in Perryville, Texas. As a 'Grand Ole Opry' star, he has had more than 25 hits in the top record charts over ten years from 1951 and is one of the big sellers on the Columbia label. Price has also had many awards for his exceptional singing ability, and is a country artist in the grand manner with a wardrobe without compare in this field.

MARVIN RAINWATER (cowboy vocalist)
GONNA FIND ME A BLUEBIRD *MGM* [*USA*]. Marvin wrote this song himself and it provided his first million seller. He was born in Wichita, Kansas, on 2 June 1925, a full-blooded

Cherokee. He began composing songs at the age of eight. In 1946, Marvin left an Oregon logging camp to try his hand at show business and managed to guest-star on Red Foley's 'Ozark Jubilee'. The Springfield, Missouri, radio station received many requests for encores from 'that new singer with the Indian name' and Foley gave him a regular spot on his show, with Marvin receiving offers for personal appearances all over the U.S.A., including Washington, D.C., with radio, stage and other spots. Then came a tour of the Middle West with a 'Grand Ole Opry' troupe, and eventually success on an Arthur Godfrey 'Talent Scout' show in 1955. Godfrey held Rainwater over for four weeks on his TV show and this won him his first disc contract with Coral Records, for whom he recorded only two songs. In January 1956 Marvin moved to MGM Records and his debut was made with 'Gonna Find Me a Bluebird'. His real name is Marvin Percy but he used his mother's maiden name Rainwater for career purposes. In addition to singing and songwriting (he has written over 400) he plays piano and guitar, and arranges. This disc became a million seller by 1957. It reached No 22 with 22 weeks in the U.S. bestsellers.

JOHNNY RAY
JUST WALKIN' IN THE RAIN *Columbia* [*USA*]. Johnny's third million seller was written in 1953 by Johnny Bragg and Robert S. Riley. This disc was a chart topper in Britain for seven weeks. The song was first recorded by some inmates of Tennessee State Prison, named 'The Prisonaires'. This disc was No 2 in the U.S. charts and 28 weeks in the bestsellers, and 19 weeks in the British bestsellers.

NELSON RIDDLE AND HIS ORCHESTRA
LISBON ANTIGUA (In Old Lisbon) *Capitol* [*USA*]. Recorded in late 1955, this number was a million seller by 1956. It was originally published in Lisbon in 1937, under title 'Lisboa Antigua' with Portuguese words by Jose Galhardo and Amadeu do Vale and music by Raul Portela. The English words were written by Harry Dupree. Nelson Riddle was born on 1 June 1921, hails from Ordell, New Jersey, and began his musical training at the age of eight, abandoning the piano at 14 for his father's instrument, the trombone. Before long he was playing and arranging for Charlie Spivak, Jerry Wald and Tommy Dorsey. With Dorsey in 1945 he was drafted into the Army and played with an Army band. On discharge he got a job with Bob Crosby which took him to the West Coast, where he gave up the trombone in favour of becoming a staff arranger for NBC. In 1950 Nelson gave up his job there for freelance arranging and before long his work on Nat King Cole's 'Too Young' and 'Mona

Lisa' brought him to the attention of recording executives. His name became known widely through Ella Mae Morse's 'Blacksmith Blues' (see 1952) which brought him many new artists including Frank Sinatra, Margaret Whiting and Betty Hutton. Capitol brought Nelson and Sinatra together, with the result that disc sales and Sinatra's popularity once again rose to the heights, taking of course Nelson along with them. 'Lisbon Antigua' was his first million seller. He was the arranger of most of Nat Cole's hits and is exceedingly busy on his own recording sessions, arranging and conducting for artists, motion pictures, radio and TV shows. He scored for the film *Lolita* in 1962. In 1962 he came to England for a concert tour with Britain's Shirley Bassey. This disc was No 1 for four weeks in the U.S.A. and 29 weeks in the bestsellers.

DON ROBERTSON (vocalist)

THE HAPPY WHISTLER *Capitol* [*USA*]. Don Robertson, an accomplished pianist and songwriter, was born in Peking, China, on 5 December 1922, the son of a distinguished physician and Head of the Department of Medicine at Peking Union Medical College. When he was four, the family moved to Chicago and Don was educated at both the university and musical college there. In his childhood a strong friendship developed between the Robertson family and poet-folk historian Carl Sandburg whom they met during their summers at Birchwood Beach, Michigan, where Sandburg lived. Don was thus very early introduced to the folk music world, for Sandburg, who had just completed his collection of songs for the first edition of his now famous *Songbag*, loved to perform. Don became a student of the piano at four when his mother began to teach him. After studying at the Chicago Musical College, he got a job in radio and worked as musical arranger for a period at station WGN. At the age of 23, he migrated to Los Angeles and made demos for publishers and songwriters, eventually landing a job as rehearsal and demonstration pianist at Capitol Records. Don had been composing since he was seven, and in the early 1950s decided to make songwriting his career. Publisher Julian Aberbach of Hill and Range eventually offered Don and his partner Hal Blair an exclusive contract and in 1953 he came up with hit No 1 'I Really Don't Want to Know' and in 1954 with 'I Don't Hurt Anymore' – a million seller for Hank Snow. Many hits followed, more than 30 figuring in the careers of Eddy Arnold, Elvis Presley, Hank Locklin, Hank Snow, Les Paul/Mary Ford, Carl Smith, Faron Young, Kitty Wells, Jerry Wallace, Nancy Wilson, The Chordettes and others. He wrote 12 songs for Presley, five of which were included in Elvis' films.

Don experimented with guitar figuration and had previously employed a chord device with a harmony note, instead of melody, on top. His new idea in 1959 was the use of a whole tone as a grace note instead of the usual half-tone. Chet Atkins, the famous guitarist, was very intrigued by this when he heard it on Don's demo disc of 'Please Help Me I'm Falling', and so was pianist Floyd Cramer who used it for the first time on the recording of his own composition 'Last Date'. Don's demo disc thus launched the Nashville piano style.

'The Happy Whistler' was written by Don and his disc was in the U.S.A.'s Top Ten in 1956, world-wide sales topping the million subsequently. It was No 9 and 20 weeks in the U.S. bestsellers, and No 8 in Britain, with nine weeks in the bestsellers.

DON RONDO (vocalist)

TWO DIFFERENT WORLDS *Jubilee* [*USA*]. This first million seller for Don Rondo was written by Sid Wayne (words) and Al Frisch (music), the sale being a global one. Don became a singer of commercials and the voice behind many TV and radio spots in America, through subsequent years. He was signed to a long-term contract in 1967 by United Artists Records. This disc reached No 19 with 18 weeks in the U.S. bestsellers.

BOBBY SCOTT (vocalist)

CHAIN GANG *ABC-Paramount* [*USA*]. Talented composer, author, pianist, singer, arranger Bobby Scott was born 29 January 1937 in Mount Pleasant, New York. He studied music and became pianist in dance bands in his early teens. By the time he was 17 he was playing piano on the 'Jazz at the Philharmonic' circuit and toured with the famous Gene Krupa orchestra. He also arranged for many star artists including Bobby Darin, Harry Belafonte and Sarah Vaughn.

His career became highlighted through his incidental music for the Broadway play *A Taste of Honey* (1960). His now famous theme of this title which was introduced instrumentally as interlude music by Bobby (piano) and his combination during the play won the Grammy Award for Best Instrumental Theme in 1962. The tune was a very big hit for Herb Alpert and his Tijuana Brass and a bestseller 1965-66, for which Alpert received three Grammy Awards for 'Record of the Year' and 'Best Instrumental Performance – Non Jazz' and 'Best Instrumental Arrangement', 1965.

Bobby's disc of 'Chain Gang' was reported to have sold the million subsequently. The song was written by Sol Quasha and Herb Yakus. It reached No 15 and was 13 weeks in the U.S. bestsellers.

Bobby Scott has recorded both vocal and straight jazz albums for ABC-Paramount, MGM and Mercury labels, and for Columbia (1968).

SHIRLEY AND LEE

LET THE GOOD TIMES ROLL *Aladdin* [*USA*]. The only million seller for Shirley Pixley and Lee Leonard was written by Lee. Known as 'The Sweethearts of the Blues' they hail from New Orleans where they compose and arrange their own songs. This disc was also the first million seller for the Aladdin label. No 27 and 19 weeks in the U.S. bestsellers.

KAY STARR WITH THE HUGO WINTERHALTER ORCHESTRA

ROCK AND ROLL WALTZ *Victor* [*USA*]. This second million seller for Kay was recorded in late 1955, and reached a million sale by 1956. The song was written by Dick Ware (words) and Shorty Allen (music) in 1955. This outstanding hit for Kay and Victor Records had great appeal for old and young alike. The disc was No 1 in both the U.S.A. (four weeks) and in Britain (one week), and 25 weeks in the U.S. bestsellers, and 20 weeks in Britain.

MORRIS STOLOFF (piano) AND ORCHESTRA

MOONGLOW and Theme from 'PICNIC' *Decca* [*USA*]. Both titles are from the film *Picnic* (1956), starring William Holden, Rosalind Russell and Kim Novak, for which Morris Stoloff was musical director. 'Moonglow' is an oldie of 1934 by Will Hudson, Eddie De Lange and Irving Mills, revived for the film, and 'Theme from Picnic' by Steve Allen (words) and George W. Duning (music) was written in 1955. Stoloff was born on 1 August 1898 in Philadelphia, and studied the violin. W. A. Clark, Jr., backer of the Los Angeles Philharmonic Orchestra, financed his musical education. Morris was a pupil of Leopold Auer, and at 16 went on a U.S.A. concert tour, later joining the Los Angeles Philharmonic Orchestra as its youngest member, to become years later its guest conductor. From 1928 he became associated with Paramount Pictures as concert-master, and in 1936 was appointed musical director of Columbia Pictures. Stoloff was given the Academy Award for best scoring of the musical pictures *Cover Girl* in 1944, *The Jolson Story* in 1946 and *Song Without End* in 1960. The film *Picnic* received three Academy Awards. This disc was five weeks at No 2 in the U.S. charts, and 27 weeks in the bestsellers, and No 7 in Britain, with 11 weeks in the bestsellers.

SYLVIA SYMS

I COULD HAVE DANCED ALL NIGHT *Decca* [*USA*]. One of the songs from *My Fair Lady*, written by Alan Jay Lerner (words) and Frederick Loewe (music), provided Sylvia with a major hit in the U.S.A. which is reputed to have subsequently sold a million. She signed with Prestige Records in 1965. This disc was No 35, and 14 weeks in the U.S. bestsellers.

Sylvia hails from The Bronx, New York.

THE TEENAGERS WITH FRANKIE LYMAN

WHY DO FOOLS FALL IN LOVE? *Gee* [*USA*]. The only million seller for this group was written by Frankie Lyman and George Goldner. Frankie Lyman was born in New York in September 1942. At the age of 13, this teen star with a soprano-type voice and a group of four other teenagers were singing gospel songs on a street corner when Richard Barrett, who led a group called the Valentines, heard them. He took them all along to Gee Records who recorded them with this, their first song, which sold a million very quickly. Frankie, still at Quintano's Professional School in New York City, was hailed in the business as a 'natural', vocally speaking. He'd never had singing lessons in his life. In 1957 he changed over to Roulette Records, made more discs and visited Britain the same year. He eventually became a solo artist. Lyman made TV, nightclub and personal appearances and in 1960 went to South America. In addition to songwriting, he played drums and was a dancer. This disc was a chart topper in Britain for three weeks, and No 7 in the U.S.A. for one week, and a top rhythm-and-blues disc. Global sale over two million. Frankie Lyman died 27 February 1968 in New York. The Teenagers - Joe Negroni, Sherman Garnes, Frankie Lyman, Herman Santiago and Jimmy Merchant - was formed in 1954. Lyman was the youngest-ever star to top the bill at the London Palladium (in 1957 for two weeks). This disc was 21 weeks in the U.S. bestsellers, and 16 weeks in Britain.

JOE TURNER

CORRINE, CORRINA *Atlantic* [*USA*]. The fourth million seller for Joe Turner is a traditional blues number with adaptation by J.M. Williams, Mitchell Parish and Bo Chatman in 1932. This disc was No 41 and 10 weeks in the U.S. bestsellers.

LEROY VAN DYKE
(country-and-western vocalist)

THE AUCTIONEER *Dot* [*USA*]. Leroy Van Dyke was born on 4 October 1929 in Spring Fork, Sedalia, Missouri, and worked on his father's farm and in the family trucking business as a youth. He took a particular interest in cattle and, after graduating from high school, decided on agriculture and animal husbandry as a career. He gained a B.Sc. degree in agriculture from the University of Missouri, then served in the U.S. Forces in Korea, using his spare time practising on a guitar with a singing career as his objective. On discharge, he attended the Auctioneering School in Decatur, Illinois, and went into livestock auctioneering and promotion, also working as a field representative for the *Corn Belt Dailies*, a chain of Midwest livestock newspapers. This work inspired him to write songs, and he began to appear in talent contests on radio and TV, some of which he won. In one of these he sang his own song 'The Auctioneer', written in collaboration with Buddy Black, resulting in a recording contract with Dot Records and a subsequent $2\frac{1}{2}$ million selling disc. A regular spot in 'Jubilee, U.S.A.' followed and then a contract with Mercury Records, for whom he had a big hit with 'Walk On By' in 1961.

'The Auctioneer', his first release for the Dot label, developed into a two-market hit - in both the country-and-western and national charts. The song, of course, is based on the life of a livestock auctioneer. It gained him the reputation as a top country-and-western artist. Leroy signed with the Warner label in 1965. He made his film debut in *What Am I Bid?* in 1967. This disc was No 29, and 15 weeks in the U.S. bestsellers.

GENE VINCENT (vocalist) AND HIS BLUE CAPS

BE-BOP-A-LULA *Capitol* [*USA*]. This first million seller for Gene was written by Gene himself and Sheriff T. Davis. Gene Vincent Craddock was born on 11 February 1935 in Norfolk, Virginia. He made his first public appearances at local county fairs in and around Norfolk after leaving the U.S. Navy in 1956. Self-taught in music, he played guitar and piano in addition to singing. In 1956, he won a Capitol Records audition from 200 other applicants and then recorded this song. Next followed his radio debut in the U.S., Virginia's 'Country Showtime', and his first important public appearance at the Sands Hotel in Las Vegas. Other hits in the rock'n'roll idiom - many of his own composition - were recorded by Capitol. Gene made his TV debut in Britain in 'Boy Meets Girl' on 12 December 1959 while on tour. His radio debut in Britain was on BBC's 'Saturday Club' on 5 March 1960. This disc was No 8 in the U.S. charts, and 20 weeks in the bestsellers, and No 16 in Britain and seven weeks in the bestsellers. Gene Vincent died in California in 1971.

BLUEJEAN BOP *Capitol* [*USA*]. By 1957 this title proved a second million seller for Gene Vincent. It was written by Gene himself in conjunction with Levy. It was No 16 in Britain and five weeks in the bestsellers.

OTIS WILLIAMS AND THE CHARMS

IVORY TOWER *Deluxe* [*USA*]. The second million seller for this group was written by Jack Fulton and Lois Steele. It was No 12 and 21 weeks in the U.S. bestsellers.

HUGO WINTERHALTER AND HIS ORCHESTRA
WITH EDDIE HEYWOOD (piano)

CANADIAN SUNSET *Victor* [*USA*]. Winterhalter's first million seller was composed by the well-known pianist Eddie Heywood. Winterhalter hails from Wilkes-Barre, Pennsylvania, and was born on 15 August 1909. He is now a veteran arranger-conductor. As artists and repertoire manager at RCA-Victor, Winterhalter has produced and arranged hit records for many artists including Perry Como and Eddie Fisher. He is also arranger-writer-conductor for TV, films and Broadway musicals. In addition to these talents Hugo plays saxophone and violin. Winterhalter first played violin in a campus orchestra at St Mary's College in Emmitsburg, Maryland, later switching to reeds and playing in such bands as Larry Clinton's, Raymond Scott's and Jack Jenney's. After 12 years as a sideman, he began orchestrating in 1944 for Tommy Dorsey, and later arranging for Will Bradley, Vaughn Monroe, Jimmy Dorsey, Claude Thornhill, Kate Smith, Billy Eckstine, Count Basie. He was musical director at both MGM and Columbia before joining Victor as both director and recording artist. Hugo was presented with a Gold Disc award for a million sale of this disc in 1961.

Eddie Heywood, composer of 'Canadian Sunset', began his career in his teens, substituting for his father as piano soloist and bandleader in an Atlanta, Georgia, vaudeville house, later joining Clarence Love's band in Kansas City where he met in 1939 the well-known Benny Carter. Carter landed Heywood the job of arranging for blues singer Billie Holliday and accompanying her on several disc dates. He then formed his own trio, scoring success at New York's Café Society, a downtown nightclub. He later became a solo piano disc artist. Heywood was born on 4 December 1915 in Atlanta. Lyrics for 'Canadian Sunset' were later written by Norman Gimbel, the song version proving a success for Andy Williams. This disc was No 2 for two weeks in U.S. charts, and 31 weeks in the bestsellers.

ORIGINAL THEATRE CAST WITH LARRY KERT, CAROL LAWRENCE AND CHITA RIVERA

WEST SIDE STORY (album) *Columbia* [*USA*]. This disc sold a million by 1963, but over two million by 1964. Lyrics were by Stephen Sondheim, with music by Leonard Bernstein. The idea of making a modern musical out of *Romeo and Juliet* was conceived by Jerome Robbins who directed the production. The story of violence rule and rival gangs on New York's West Side, and the love of Tony and Maria, of 'The Jets' and 'The Sharks' respectively, furnished music and dancing to interpret *West Side Story* perfectly, and make this vivid representation of a modern tragedy one of the finest musicals of our time. It was first produced on 26 September 1957 at New York's Winter Garden Theatre and ran for 732 performances. When it came to England in 1958, it ran for 1,039 performances. Bernstein's music accomplished a very important landmark by bridging the gap between popular and classical, from blues to operatic, and the dancing was of the finest seen in any musical. Born in Lawrence, Massachusetts, on 25 August 1918, Bernstein, educated at Boston Latin School, studied music and piano there, and later was assistant conductor of the New York Philharmonic Symphony 1943–1944, eventually becoming its chief. He has composed classical music, film music, and scores for the musicals *On the Town, Wonderful Town* and *Candide*, and has a vast following on American TV as a lecturer of serious music. *West Side Story* was made into a film in 1961 with spectacular success (see 1961). This original theatre cast album contains the songs: 'Tonight' and 'I Feel Pretty', 'Prologue', 'Jet Song', 'Something's Coming', 'The Dance at the Gym', 'Maria', 'America', 'Somewhere' (ballet), 'Gee, Officer Kropke', 'A Boy Like That', 'I Have a Love' and 'Finale'. This disc was in the bestseller charts in the U.S.A. for 186 weeks. Gold Disc award R.I.A.A. 1962.

THE AMES BROTHERS

MELODIE D'AMOUR *Victor* [*USA*]. The fifth million seller for this successful group was written by Leo Johns (pseudonym for Jimmy Phillips) and Marcel Stellman (music) and Henri Salvador (words). The original French words were by M. Lanjean, and the title was 'Maladie d'Amour'. This disc was No 12 and 20 weeks in the U.S. bestsellers.

PAUL ANKA

DIANA *ABC Paramount* [*USA*]. Paul Anka wrote this number when he was just over 14 years of age and his disc was a sensation. An estimated nine million were sold globally, this figure including over three million in the U.S.A., and over a million in Britain. Over a period of six years there were 320 different recordings of 'Diana' in 22 countries. By 1970, Paul had sold over 40 million discs of his songs around the world. He has written over 225 and three or four film theme songs. Born on 30 July 1941, in Ottawa, Canada, his parents being restaurant proprietors, Paul showed a great interest in music and show business from an early age. At the age of 12, while at Fisher Park High School, Paul formed a vocal trio and appeared at local functions. The trio received offers for bookings in theatres and teenage clubs throughout Canada. He then decided to become a single act and persuaded his father to send him to Hollywood where he had an uncle with connections in the film world. He managed to sign with a small company in Los Angeles for whom he made two sides, with disappointing sales results. His first song 'Blau Wildebeeste Fontaine' sold a mere 3,000 copies. He then wrote 'Diana' and approached Don Costa, A & R chief of ABC-Paramount with this and three other songs he had written. He was signed to a long-term contract and his recorded version of 'Diana' rocketed him to international fame and made him the first Canadian singer soloist to sell over a million of one record. Then followed more hits and intensive touring all over the world. Today Paul runs a musical empire from Manhattan that includes two music companies and a production company. He has had a million dollar contract with Victor Records since 1962, when he bought up all his original ABC-Paramount recordings, and an estimated annual income of £500,000. In 1961, he wrote the theme song for the epic film of the last war *The Longest Day*, and also had a role in the film. 'Diana' was a No 1 seller in the U.S.A. for one week, 29 weeks in the bestsellers, and chart topper in Britain for nine weeks, with 25 weeks in the bestsellers. A top rhythm-and-blues disc.

LAVERN BAKER

JIM DANDY *Atlantic* [*USA*]. This second million seller for LaVern Baker, the rhythm-and-blues singer, was written by Lincoln Chase. It reached No 22, with 19 weeks in the U.S. bestsellers.

HARRY BELAFONTE

BELAFONTE SINGS OF THE CARIBBEAN (Album) *Victor* [*USA*]. This second million seller for Belafonte comprises: 'Lucy's Door!', 'Cordelia Brown!' and 'Don't Ever Leave Me' – all by Burgess (Lord Burgie), 'Angelique-O' by Burgess and Bill Attaway, 'Scratch Scratch', 'Haiti Cherie' and 'Lead Man Holler' – by Belafonte and Burgess.

BANANA BOAT SONG (Day-O) *Victor* [*USA*]. This third million seller for Belafonte was taken from his album 'Calypso' of 1956. It was written by Harry Belafonte, Bill Attaway and Burgess (Lord Burgie). Another version of this popular calypso song by Eric Darling, Bob Carey and Alan Arkin was also a hit in this year. This disc was No 5 for five weeks, and 20 weeks in the U.S. bestsellers, and No 2 with 18 weeks in Britain's bestsellers.

MAMA LOOKA BOO BOO *Victor* [*USA*]. The fourth million seller for Harry Belafonte was written by Lord Melody (Fitzroy Alexander.) It reached No 13, with 20 weeks in the U.S. bestsellers.

MARY'S BOY CHILD *Victor* [*USA*]. Belafonte's fifth million seller achieved this figure in Britain in only eight weeks. This calypso-type Christmas song has become a standard seasonal seller. The song was written by Jester Hairston in 1956, and was taken from Belafonte's album 'An Evening with Belafonte'. The disc was a chart topper in Britain for seven weeks with 12 weeks in the bestsellers. In the U.S.A. it reached No 15.

TONY BENNETT WITH THE RAY ELLIS ORCHESTRA

IN THE MIDDLE OF AN ISLAND *Columbia* [*USA*]. This fifth million seller for Tony was written by Nick Acquaviva and Ted Varnick. It reached No 9, and had 21 weeks in the U.S.A. bestsellers.

CHUCK BERRY

SCHOOL DAY *Chess* [*USA*]. The third million seller for this rhythm-and-blues artist was written by Chuck. A top rhythm-and-blues disc, it was No 5, and 26 weeks in the U.S. bestsellers. No 24 in Britain.

ROCK AND ROLL MUSIC *Chess* [*USA*]. The fourth million seller for Chuck was likewise written by him. It reached No 8, with 19 weeks in the U.S. bestsellers.

BILLIE AND LILLIE

LAH DEE DAH *Swan* [*USA*]. The only million seller for this duo was written by Frank C. Slay Jr. and Bob Crewe. Slay, a Texan, worked with the British Information Service in New York and teamed with Crewe (one of New York's top male models for magazines and a talented painter) in 1953. They wrote, arranged and recorded their numbers, then sold them to various recording companies. (See also 'Crewe Generation', 1966.) This disc was No 9 and 13 weeks in the U.S. bestsellers.

PAT BOONE WITH ORCHESTRA CONDUCTED BY BILLY VAUGHN

LOVE LETTERS IN THE SAND *Dot* [*USA*]. The sixth million seller for popular Pat Boone is an oldie of 1931, written by Nick and Charles Kenny (words) and J. Fred Coots (music). This disc sold over 3½ million, was No 1 for five weeks in the U.S.A., and 34 weeks in the bestsellers, and No 2 and 21 weeks in the British bestsellers. This record earned Pat a special Platinum Disc award.

DON'T FORBID ME *Dot* [*USA*]. The seventh million seller for Pat Boone was written in 1956 by Charles Singleton. It was No 1 in U.S.A. for one week, and 22 weeks in the bestsellers, and No 2 and 16 weeks in the British bestsellers.

WHY, BABY WHY? *Dot* [*USA*]. The eighth million seller for Pat Boone had words and music by Luther Dixon and Larry Harrison, reaching No 6 in the U.S. charts, with 21 weeks in the bestsellers. No 17 and seven weeks in the British bestsellers.

APRIL LOVE backed with WHEN THE SWALLOWS COME BACK TO CAPISTRANO *Dot* [*USA*]. By 1958 this became a ninth million seller for Pat Boone with both sides very popular. 'When the Swallows' is an oldie of 1940, written by Leon Rene, and 'April Love' by Paul Francis Webster (words) and Sammy Fain (music) comes from Pat's first musical film of the same title in which he sang it. This was No 1 for two weeks in the U.S.A., and 26 weeks in the bestsellers, and No 7 and 23 weeks in the British bestsellers.

JIMMY BOWEN (vocal) WITH THE RHYTHM ORCHIDS

I'M STICKIN' WITH YOU *Roulette* [*USA*]. Written by Jimmy Bowen and Buddy Knox, million seller by 1961. Jimmy Bowen, born 30 November 1937 in Dumas, Texas, became a star athlete; and that earned him a scholarship to West Texas State College. His co-authorship of 'Party Doll' (see Buddy Knox, 1957) hastened his departure from college into the world of singing. From 1957 he was an artiste and producer for Roulette Records, and his own disc of 'I'm Stickin' With You' got into the U.S.A. Top Ten. He later moved to Crest Records as producer, then into professional management, and in 1962 to Chancellor Records before joining Reprise Records in 1963. Since then he has directed the recording careers of some of the world's top stars including Dean Martin, Frank Sinatra, Nancy Sinatra and Keely Smith. In 1969, Bowen launched his own label – Amos Records.

His accompanying group, The Rhythm Orchids, on this disc includes Buddy Knox playing guitar. Jimmy was the bass player of the group. This disc reached No 14, and was 17 weeks in the U.S. bestsellers.

RUTH BROWN

LUCKY LIPS *Atlantic* [*USA*]. Ruth's third million seller was written by Jerry Leiber and Mike Stoller (composers for Elvis Presley and other prominent artists). The song had a successful revival in 1963 with Britain's Cliff Richard, whose disc also sold a million. This disc was No 26, and nine weeks in the U.S. bestsellers.

THE COASTERS

SEARCHIN' backed with YOUNG BLOOD *Atco* [*USA*]. This was a first million seller for this rhythm-and-blues group, comprising Carl Gardner (leader) from Texas, Billy Guy from Hollywood, Cornelius Gunter from Los Angeles, Dub Jones from Los Angeles and Adolph Jacobs from Oakland, California, guitarist. The group formed in 1955, calling themselves The Coasters because all were living in Los Angeles on the West Coast. They started off in 1956 with a disc 'Down in Mexico', a fair hit, and after more records came 'Searchin''. It was the flip side 'Young Blood' that first got exploitation by disc jockeys, and a few weeks later the other side. Before long it had sold a million and became one of the most successful rhythm-and-blues discs of 1957. Then followed appearances at the major U.S.A. theatres, an extensive nightclub circuit tour and TV, with more big disc hits in 1958 and 1959. 'Searchin'' was written by ace writers Jerry Leiber and Mike Stoller, 'Young Blood' by Jerry Leiber, Mike Stoller and Doc Pomus. This disc sold over two million, and was a No 1 rhythm-and-blues disc of the year. 'Searchin'' reached No 5, with 26 weeks in the U.S. bestsellers. 'Young Blood' was No 8, and 24 weeks in the bestsellers. 'Searchin'' reached No 30 in Britain.

EDDIE COCHRAN (vocal)

SITTIN' IN THE BALCONY *Liberty* [*USA*]. This song was written by famous country songwriter John D. Loudermilk who also recorded it himself on the Colonial label under the name of Johnny Dee.

Eddie Cochran was born 3 October 1938 in Oklahoma City, U.S.A. Self-taught in music, he learned to play the guitar, bass, drums, piano and saxophone, making his first public appearance at South Gate Town Hall, California. He entered show business during his mid-teens. 'Sittin' in the Balcony' was Eddie's first singles disc for Liberty, which sold a million, and he followed this with three other big hits: '20 Flight Rock' (1957), and 'C'mon Everybody' and 'Summertime Blues' (1958) – the first written in collaboration with Fairchild and the latter two with Jerry Capehart. It is quite probable that each of these also sold a million for they reached high positions in the charts in the U.S.A., England, Canada and European countries. Eddie wrote many other songs and, of the 64 known tracks released, 30 were written by him. This disc was No 18, and 13 weeks in the U.S. bestsellers.

He went to Britain in 1960 for a tour (and appeared on TV) and it was during this tour that he was killed in a car crash on 17 April at Chippenham, Wiltshire. With him at the time were his fiancée, songwriter Sharon Sheeley, the late Gene Vincent, and agent; a tragic end to a fine artist.

Eddie appeared in four films, *The Girl Can't Help It* (1956), *Untamed Youth*, *Go, Johnny, Go* and *Bop Girl*.

His last public appearance was at the Empire, Bristol.

PERRY COMO

ROUND AND ROUND backed with MI CASA SU CASA (My house is your house) *Victor* [*USA*]. This fifteenth million seller for Perry Como, 'Round and Round', was written by Joe Shapiro and Lou Stallman in 1956. 'Mi Casa Su Casa' is by Al Hoffman and Dick Manning. 'Round and Round' was No 1 for a week in the U.S.A., and 29 weeks in the bestsellers. 'Mi Casa Su Casa' reached No 50.

SAM COOKE

YOU SEND ME *Keen* [*USA*]. The first million seller (by 1958) for this rhythm-and-blues artist was the composition of his brother Charles L. Cooke, and it was Sam's very first attempt. It also was the first (2½) million seller for the Keen label, on their initial release. Disc was No 1 for two weeks in the U.S.A., and 26 weeks in the bestsellers. It was also a top rhythm-and-blues disc. No 29 in Great Britain.

I'LL COME RUNNING BACK TO YOU *Specialty* [*USA*]. This disc became Sam Cooke's second million seller by 1958. It was in fact recorded before his hit 'You Send Me' and released by Specialty on the success of that disc. It was also written by Charles Cooke. Sam hailed from Chicago, born in 1937, one of eight sons of the Rev. and Mrs S. Cooke, and educated at high school there. Brought up in a religious environment, he sang with a gospel group The Soul Stirrers, touring for several years, and the group was signed by Specialty Records for whom they recorded extensively. Specialty turned down 'You Send Me' and their A & R manager 'Bumps' Blackwell, convinced of Sam's potential as a pop singer, bought Sam's contract and the trial recording and took it to Keen Records. Specialty then dived into their archives and discovered they still retained one track; this was the disc of 'I'll Come Running Back to You'. Sam eventually played nightclubs, made TV appearances and toured the U.S.A. In 1960 he switched to the RCA-Victor label. Sam also played guitar. He sold over 15 million discs by 1964. He was tragically shot in a hotel incident in the U.S.A. on 11 December 1964. This disc was No 22, and 14 weeks in the U.S. bestsellers.

THE CRICKETS
THAT'LL BE THE DAY *Brunswick* [*USA*]. First million seller for this group, founded by the late Buddy Holly in 1955. The personnel on this disc is Buddy Holly, Jerry Allison (drums), born 31 August 1939, Niki Sullivan (guitar) and Joe Mauldin (bass). Song written by Buddy Holly, J. Allison and Norman Petty. (See also Buddy Holly, 1957.) Disc was a No 1 seller in both the U.S.A. (one week) and Britain (three weeks). In the U.S.A. it was 22 weeks in the bestsellers and 19 weeks in the British bestsellers. A belated Gold Disc was awarded by R.I.A.A. in 1969.

DANNY AND THE JUNIORS
AT THE HOP *ABC-Paramount* [*USA*]. The only million seller by this group was a rock'n'roll song written by A. Singer, J. Medora and D. White. The million sale was achieved by 1958. It was No 1 for seven weeks in the U.S.A., and 21 weeks in the bestsellers, and No 3 with 14 weeks in the British bestsellers. It was also a top rhythm-and-blues disc.

THE DEL-VIKINGS (vocal and instrumental)
COME GO WITH ME *Dot* [*USA*]. This group's only million seller was written by C.E. Quick, who formed the group, which had many personnel changes. The disc reached No 5 in the U.S. charts, with 31 weeks in the bestsellers.

THE DIAMONDS
LITTLE DARLIN' *Mercury* [*USA*]. The first million seller for The Diamonds was written by Maurice Williams. The group include Dave Somerville and Mike Douglas from Canada, and John Felton and Evan Fisher from California. The disc was No 2 for five weeks in the U.S. charts, and 26 weeks in the bestsellers, and No 3 with 17 weeks in Britain's bestsellers.

SILHOUETTES *Mercury* [*USA*]. Released in October 1957, this disc reached No 60, stayed on the U.S. bestsellers for 11 weeks, and the million sale was reported by Mercury Records in 1972.

The song was written by Frank C. Slay Jr and Bob Crewe, and this was the second time this title became a million seller on disc.

FATS DOMINO
I'M WALKIN' *Imperial* [*USA*]. Fats Domino's eighteenth million seller was written in conjunction with Dave Bartholomew. It reached No 5 and was 25 weeks in the U.S. bestsellers, and was a No 1 rhythm-and-blues disc in the U.S.A. No 19 and seven weeks in the British bestsellers.

IT'S YOU I LOVE *Imperial* [*USA*]. Fats Domino's nineteenth million seller was also written in conjunction with Dave Bartholomew. It was No 22, and 12 weeks in the U.S. bestsellers.

I STILL LOVE YOU *Imperial* [*USA*]. This twentieth million seller for Fats Domino was written by Fats, Dave Bartholomew, Watson and Palmer. It reached No 79 in the U.S. charts.

JIMMY DORSEY AND ORCHESTRA
SO RARE *Fraternity* [*USA*]. This fifth million seller for Jimmy Dorsey and his orchestra was a revival of an oldie of 1937 written by Jack Sharpe (words) and Jerry Herst (music), reaching No 2 in the U.S. charts, and was 38 weeks in the bestsellers.

THE EVERLY BROTHERS
BYE BYE LOVE *Cadence* [*USA*]. First of several million sellers for these famous brothers, Donald Isaac (born 1 February 1937) and Phil (born 19 January 1939) from Brownie, Kentucky. Their parents, Ike and Margaret Everly, were well-known country artists, and the boys worked with them as a family singing group on local radio shows from the time they were 6 and 8 years old respectively. After several years of touring as a family unit, with winters off for schooling Mr and Mrs Everly retired when their sons left high school. Soon after, Wesley Rose of the famous Nashville music publishing firm, Acuff-Rose, took them under his wing and had them signed to Cadence Records. He became their manager. This disc started off a fantastic string of hits. The

song was written by the husband and wife team, Felice and Boudleaux Bryant, who composed nearly all the Everlys' major hits, which resulted in over 11 million discs of their songs. The Everlys made personal and TV appearances, and a visit to Britain in 1960 before service in the U.S. Marine Corps together. The brothers have sold over 18 million discs globally, which puts them in the category reserved for only the biggest stars. In 1960 they signed with Warner Brothers Records. A top country-and-western disc, it reached No 2 with 27 weeks in the U.S. bestsellers, and was No 6 and 16 weeks in the British bestsellers.

WAKE UP LITTLE SUSIE *Cadence* [*USA*]. The second million seller for the Everly Brothers was also written by Felice and Boudleaux Bryant. It was No 1 seller for two weeks in the U.S.A. with 26 weeks in the bestsellers, and was a top country disc. In Britain it was No 2 and 16 weeks in the bestsellers.

THE FOUR PREPS
TWENTY SIX MILES (Santa Catalina) *Capitol* [*USA*]. This was a million seller by 1958 for this group which comprised Don Clarke, Bruce Belland, Glen Larson and Ed Cobb – all from Hollywood. They formed their group in high school and got their

first big break through being guests on the Tennessee Ernie Ford TV show. The song was written by Glenn Larson and Bruce Belland. The group's first hit was 'Dreamy Eyes' (1957) and a further success was 'Big Man' (1958). This disc was No 4, and 20 weeks in the U.S. bestsellers.

TERRY GILKYSON AND THE EASY RIDERS
MARIANNE *Columbia* [*USA*]. This was the first million seller for Terry Gilkyson, although he was concerned with another very popular disc in 1951 (see Weavers, 1951). He also wrote 'Cry of the Wild Goose' (see Frankie Laine, 1950). Gilkyson wrote 'Marianne' in 1955 with Frank Miller and Richard Dehr who are the 'Easy Riders' on this disc. 'Marianne' is an adaptation from a Bahaman folk song. The disc was No 5 in the U.S. charts and 19 weeks in the bestsellers.

CHARLIE GRACIE
BUTTERFLY *Cameo* [*USA*]. Charlie's only million seller was written by Bernie Lowe and Kal Mann under the pseudonym of Anthony September. Charlie Gracie was born 4 May 1936 in Philadelphia, U.S.A. He is an accomplished rock'n'roll guitarist, and also a songwriter. This disc was remarkably the first recording for Cameo, reaching No 5, with 17 weeks in the U.S. bestsellers, and was No 12 in Britain, with eight weeks in the bestsellers.

RUSS HAMILTON WITH JOHNNY GREGORY ORCHESTRA
WE WILL MAKE LOVE backed with RAINBOW *Oriole* [*Britain*]. Russ Hamilton (real name Ron Hulme) from Liverpool, England, was both singer and writer of these songs. An ex-Butlin holiday camp redcoat in Britain, Hamilton was the most successful newcomer on disc in Britain in 1957. It was a unique recording in that 'We Will Make Love' was the hit side in Britain (where

it was No 2 and 20 weeks in the bestsellers) and 'Rainbow' the hit side in the U.S.A., where it was issued on the Kapp label and reached No 7, with 23 weeks in the bestsellers.

THURSTON HARRIS (blues vocalist) WITH THE SHARPS
LITTLE BITTY PRETTY ONE *Aladdin* [*USA*]. This song was written by Robert Byrd, better known as disc artist Bobby Day. Thurston's version is said to have sold a million in the U.S.A. It reached No 6, with 17 weeks in the bestsellers.

BOBBY HELMS
MY SPECIAL ANGEL *Decca* [*USA*]. The first million seller for Bobby was written by Jimmy Duncan. Bobby hails from Bloomington, Indiana. A top country-and-western disc, it was No 7, and 23 weeks in the U.S. bestsellers; No 22 in Britain.

BUDDY HOLLY AND THE CRICKETS
PEGGY SUE backed with EVERY DAY *Coral* [*USA*]. This million seller for Buddy Holly was written by Jerry Allison and Norman Petty, the drummer and recording engineer respectively, associated with The Crickets, the well-known group founded by Buddy in 1955. Buddy (Charles Hardin Holley) was born in Lubbock, Texas, on 7 September 1936 and started his musical career at four with violin and piano. At seven he took up the guitar, and while in high school sang on local radio shows. From 1955 to 1958 he was with The Crickets and thereafter teamed up with two disc session men and also called this group The Crickets. Soon after, on 3 February 1959, Buddy and two other artists, Ritchie Valens and The Big Bopper, were killed in an air crash near Fargo, North Dakota. Since his death Buddy Holly has become somewhat of a legend and many of his discs have been released. A memorial album, 'The Buddy Holly Story', issued on Coral, containing all the hits by him and with The Crickets, has been a consistent seller, and one of the biggest ever for Coral. Buddy Holly himself said he had been greatly influenced by Elvis Presley, but his own beat and vocal style were based on different principles, a Texas-Mexican sound derived from the later country-and-western sounds and from old Negro gospel numbers. Paul McCartney (formerly of The Beatles) has recently purchased all the rights to Buddy Holly's songs. 'Peggy Sue' was No 3, and 22 weeks in the U.S. bestsellers. 'Every Day' was also a big hit, reaching No 6 in Britain with 17 weeks in the bestsellers.

IVORY JOE HUNTER
SINCE I MET YOU BABY *Atlantic* [*USA*]. The second million seller for Ivory Joe was written by the vocalist himself in 1956. Recorded in 1956, it was No 12 and 22 weeks in the U.S. bestsellers.

EMPTY ARMS *Atlantic* [*USA*]. This third million seller for Ivory Joe Hunter was also written by him. It reached No 43, and was 16 weeks in the U.S. bestsellers.

TAB HUNTER
YOUNG LOVE *Dot* [*USA*]. This million seller was written by Carole Joyner and Ric Cartey, in 1956. Tab Hunter was born on 11 July 1931 in New York. He was a champion ice skater in his teens, and later became a U.S. Coast Guard. He was discovered in 1948 and made his film debut in *The Lawless*. Hunter was an established movie star when he made this, his first record. His real name is Arthur Gelien. This disc was No 1 for six weeks in the U.S.A., with 21 weeks in the bestsellers, and a chart topper in Britain for seven weeks, with 18 weeks in the bestsellers.

FERLIN HUSKY (country-and-western vocalist)
GONE *Capitol* [*USA*]. Ferlin Husky was born on 3 December 1927 in Flat River, Missouri, and began his show business career after discharge from the Merchant Marines. He performed around California until Tennessee Ernie Ford's manager, Cliffie Stone, one day asked Ferlin to fill in for Ford who was on

vacation. Big things then began to happen for him with Stone giving him a featured spot on his 'Hometown Jamboree' show, and then a long-term contract with Capitol Records from 1953. Many country hits followed and his first really big hit in 1953 with 'A Dear John Letter' recorded with Jean Shepard. In 1957 he recorded 'Gone', a pop re-make of one of his earliest country sessions, the song originally written in 1952 by Smokey Rogers. This became a smash hit and a No 1 country-and-western disc that earned him a Gold Disc for a million sale. He later followed with another big hit in both the country and pop fields via his 'On the Wings of a Dove' stanza.

Ferlin appeared in a number of films and TV shows, and comedy routines under the name of Simon Crum in the Grand Ole Opry proved side-splitting to the audiences. This alter-ego also earned him further money and fame on discs.

This disc of 'Gone' was the first recording session where a vibraphone and modern vocal group were used in a country session. It was No 4, and 27 weeks in the U.S. bestsellers.

SONNY JAMES
YOUNG LOVE *Capitol* [*USA*]. This version was the second disc of this Carole Joyner-Ric Cartey song to sell a million. Sonny James was born in Hackelburg, Alabama, on 1 May 1929, the son of a musical family. At the age of four he was already a featured performer, and after his radio debut sang with his sisters on personal appearances. At seven he learned to play the violin. Later he signed his first full-time contract with a Birmingham, Alabama, radio station, defeating 52 contestants for the position. Three years later James was credited with three tri-State and two mid-South violin championships. He has since learned to play all the common instruments and was a featured vocalist from 1947 for 10 years with a Dallas, Texas, radio show. He spent 15 months in the Services in Korea, and entertained the troops with his violin and guitar. Sales of this disc eventually totalled two million. It was No 2 for three weeks in the U.S.A., and 21 weeks in the bestsellers, and No 11 in Britain with seven weeks in the bestsellers.

BILL JUSTIS AND HIS ORCHESTRA
RAUNCHY *Philips* [*USA*]. The only million dollar seller for Bill Justis was a tune he himself composed with Sidney Manker. Justis was born on 14 October 1926. He was musical director of the Tulane campus night shows in New Orleans, did choral arrangements for Arizona University; and then became musical director for Sun Records. This tune was originally called 'Backwoods'. This disc was No 3, and 20 weeks in the U.S. bestsellers, and No 11 in Britain and eight weeks in the bestsellers.

BUDDY KNOX
PARTY DOLL *Roulette* [*USA*]. Buddy wrote his first million seller with the help of Jimmy Bowen, D. Lanier and D. Alldred. He was born in Happy, Texas, and at college gained a degree in psychology and business administration. Preferring an outdoor life he took jobs at rodeo riding, stock theatre work and served a stint in the tank corps before deciding to become a singer. He then recorded with The Rhythm Orchids group for Roulette. This disc established him on TV, and personal appearances followed. In 1958 he switched to Liberty Records. This disc was No 1 for a week in the U.S.A., and 23 weeks in the bestsellers, and No 29 in Britain. In 1968 Buddy Knox signed with United Artists label.

FRANKIE LAINE
MOONLIGHT GAMBLER *Columbia* [*USA*]. The ninth million seller for Frankie was written in 1956 by Bob Hilliard (words) and Philip Springer (music). It was No 3 in the U.S. charts, and 22 weeks in the bestsellers, and No 13 with 12 weeks in the British bestsellers.

JERRY LEE LEWIS
WHOLE LOTTA SHAKIN' GOIN' ON *Sun* [*USA*]. The first million seller for Jerry was written by Dave Williams and

Sunny David in 1957. Jerry was born in Ferriday, Louisiana, on 29 September 1935. He was educated at the Bible Institute, Waxahatchie, Texas, and is self-taught in music. Apart from singing he plays piano, guitar, violin and accordion. He entered show business in 1947, making his first appearance in Natchez, Louisiana. He signed with Sun Records in 1955 and has had fantastic success with his booming rock'n'roll singing and frantic piano playing. He has made personal-appearance tours of the U.S.A. and in Europe. In movies, his first roles were in the MGM film *High School Confidential* (1958), *Disc Jockey* and *Jamboree* (1957). The reputed sale of this disc was three million. A top rhythm-and-blues and country disc. It was No 3 in the U.S. charts, and 29 weeks in the bestsellers, and No 8 with 10 weeks in the British bestsellers.

GREAT BALLS OF FIRE *Sun* [*USA*]. This second million seller for Jerry Lee Lewis was the song sung by him in the film *Jamboree* (1957). It was written by Jack Hammer and Otis Blackwell. The reputed sale of this disc was also three million. It was a chart topper in Britain in 1958 for two weeks. A top country-and-western disc, it was No 2 in the U.S. charts, and 21 weeks in the bestsellers, and 12 weeks in the British bestsellers.

LITTLE RICHARD AND HIS BAND
LUCILLE *Specialty* [*USA*]. The fourth million seller for Little Richard was written by Albert Collins with Richard Penniman who is in fact Little Richard. It was No 27, and 21 weeks in the U.S. bestsellers, and reached No 10 in Britain, with nine weeks in the bestsellers.

JENNY, JENNY *Specialty* [*USA*]. The fifth million seller for Little Richard was written by Enotris Johnson and again Penniman himself. It reached No 14, with 20 weeks in the U.S. bestsellers, and reached No 11 in Britain, with five weeks in the bestsellers.

KEEP A-KNOCKIN' *Specialty* [*USA*]. The sixth million seller for Little Richard was entirely his own work. It was No 8, and 18 weeks in the U.S. bestsellers, and reached No 21 in Britain and seven weeks in the bestsellers.

MANTOVANI AND HIS ORCHESTRA
FILM ENCORES (album) *London/Decca* [*Britain*]. This fifth million seller album for Mantovani reached the half million in the U.S.A. within the year of issue and a million up to 1965 for combined sales of both 12-inch monaural (1957) disc and stereo disc (1958).

Contents were: 'My Foolish Heart' (from *My Foolish Heart*), by Ned Washington and Victor Young (1950); 'Unchained Melody' (from *Unchained*), by Hy Zaret and Alex North (1955); *'Over the Rainbow' (from *Wizard of Oz*), by E. Y. Harburg and Harold Arlen (1939); 'Summertime in Venice' (from *Summertime*), by Carl Sigman and Icini (1955); 'Intermezzo' (from *Escape to Happiness*), by R. Henning and Heinz Provost (1936); *'Three Coins in the Fountain' (from *Three Coins in the Fountain*), by Sammy Cahn and Jule Styne (1954); *'Love is a Many Splendored Thing' (from *Love is a Many Splendored Thing*), by P.F. Webster and Sammy Fain (1955); 'Laura' (from *Laura*), by Johnny Mercer and David Raksin (1945); *'High Noon' (from *High Noon*), by Ned Washington and D. Tiomkin (1952); 'Hi-Lili, Hi-Lo' (from *Lili*), by Helen Deutsch and B. Kaper (1953); 'September Song' (from *Knickerbocker Holiday*), by Maxwell Anderson and Kurt Weill (1944); 'Theme from *Limelight*', by Charles Chaplin (1953).

The disc was issued on the London label in the U.S.A., and on the Decca label in Britain. This album was in the U.S.A. bestsellers list for 199 weeks. Gold Disc award R.I.A.A. 1961. *Academy Award winner as the Best Film Song of its year.

JOHNNY MATHIS WITH THE RAY CONNIFF ORCHESTRA

CHANCES ARE *Columbia* [*USA*]. This third million seller for Johnny Mathis was written by Al Stillman (words) and Robert Allen (music). It was No 5, and 28 weeks in the U.S. bestsellers.

IT'S NOT FOR ME TO SAY *Columbia* [*USA*]. This third million seller for Johnny Mathis was also written by Al Stillman (words) and Robert Allen (music). It was composed for the film *Lizzie* in which Johnny sang the title song. This disc was No 5, and 34 weeks in the U.S. bestsellers.

MITCH MILLER AND HIS ORCHESTRA

MARCH FROM 'BRIDGE ON THE RIVER KWAI' *Columbia* [*USA*]. This disc sold a million in the U.S.A. alone. The tune was written for the film starring William Holden and Sir Alec Guinness by the British composer Malcolm Arnold who received the Academy Award for the best dramatic film score of 1957. This disc was Mitch Miller's second million seller. It is also reputed to have sold four million in Germany. Arnold's arrangement included the 'Colonel Bogey March' by Kenneth J. Alford (composed in 1914) on the disc. The film received seven Academy Awards in all. The disc reached No 21 with 29 weeks in the U.S. bestsellers.

SAL MINEO

START MOVIN' (in my direction) *Epic* [*USA*]. The only million seller for 18-year-old Mineo reached seven figures within two months of its release. It was his very first disc. The song was written by David Hill (real name David Hess) and Bobby Stevenson. Actor Sal Mineo was born in New York on 10 January 1939 and educated there. He got his start at 11 in a Broadway play *The Rose Tattoo*, then a juvenile lead in *The Little Screwball* created attention from talent scouts, one of whom signed him for an upcoming musical *The King and I* in the role of Crown Prince for this great Rodgers and Hammerstein play. As he looked too young for the part, he was understudy for a year. He appeared in his first movie *Six Bridges to Cross* in 1955, then came more films (including *Rebel Without a Cause*), and a star role in *Rock Pretty Baby*, *The Young Don't Cry* and *Dino*. Mineo recorded 'Start Movin'' because his fans wanted him to. It was No 10 and nine weeks in the U.S. bestsellers, and was No 16 and 11 weeks in the British bestsellers.

Sal Mineo was murdered in Los Angeles, California, on 12 February 1976.

JANE MORGAN WITH THE TROUBADOURS

FASCINATION *Kapp* [*USA*]. This million seller for Jane by 1958 (three million by 1965) is an oldie, 'Valse Tzigane' of 1904 by F.D. Marchetti, with words (1954) by Dick Manning. It was featured in the film *Love in the Afternoon* (1957) starring Gary Cooper and Audrey Hepburn. Jane Morgan was born Jane Currier in Boston, Massachusetts, educated at college and the Juilliard School of Music (as lyric soprano) in New York. She sang at clubs to pay for her tuition. Offered a contract by French impresario Bernard Hilda, she became a hit in Paris in a few weeks. Her reputation spread throughout the Continent and Jane starred in Rome, Madrid, Brussels, Geneva and on the French Riviera, becoming a prolific linguist. Then America wanted her to star in the top clubs, and billed her as 'The American Girl from Paris'. She also appeared in many summer stock shows in the U.S.A. and in dramatic roles. She is one of the most sought-after nightclub entertainers. The French words of 'Fascination' were written by Maurice de Ferandy in 1942. This disc was No 11 and 29 weeks in the U.S.A. bestsellers.

RICKY NELSON

A TEENAGER'S ROMANCE backed by I'M WALKIN' *Verve* [*USA*]. A double-sided million seller emerged for Ricky from his first recording session. He was born Eric Hilliard Nelson on 8 May 1940 in Teaneck, New Jersey, son of show business parents – band leader Ozzie Nelson and singer Harriet Hilliard. Ricky made his first appearance on their long-running (18 years) series 'The Adventures of Ozzie and Harriet' on ABC-TV at the age of eight, and grew up in full sight of millions of TV viewers. Educated at Hollywood High School, Nelson was a fine athlete. At the age of 16 he branched out as a solo singer (1957) and turned out double-sided hit discs with unbelievable regularity. His fabulous career includes star parts in the films *Rio Bravo*, *The Wackiest Ship in the Army* and many others. Ricky also writes songs and apart from his singing, acting and dancing abilities, plays guitar, drums, clarinet and piano. 'I'm Walkin'' was written by Fats Domino and Dave Bartholomew. Ricky's disc made it a second time million seller for the song, 'Teenager's Romance' was written by David Gillan, the disc reaching No 8, with 19 weeks in the U.S. bestsellers. 'I'm Walkin'' was No 17 and 17 weeks in the bestsellers.

BE-BOP BABY *Imperial* [*USA*]. The second million seller (by 1960) for Ricky was written by Pearl Lendhurst. It reached No 5 with 20 weeks in the U.S. bestsellers.

STOOD UP backed with WAITIN' IN SCHOOL *Imperial* [*USA*]. This third million seller for Ricky Nelson enjoyed popularity on both sides. 'Stood Up' was written by Dub Dickerson and Erma Herrold; 'Waitin' in School' by Johnny and Dorsey Burnette. 'Stood Up' was No 5 and 18 weeks in the U.S. best-

sellers; 'Waitin' in School' was No 18 and 14 weeks in the bestsellers; 'Stood Up' reached No 27 in Britain.

ELVIS PRESLEY
TOO MUCH backed with PLAYIN' FOR KEEPS *Victor* [*USA*]. Here were eighth and ninth million sellers for Elvis. 'Too Much' was written by Lee Rosenberg and Bernard Weinman (in 1956); and 'Playin' for Keeps' by Stanley A. Kesler (in 1956). 'Too Much' was No 1 in the U.S. charts for three weeks, and sold two million, with 17 weeks in the bestsellers. 'Playin' for Keeps' was No 34 and nine weeks in the bestsellers; it reached No 6 in Britain, and eight weeks in the bestsellers.

ALL SHOOK UP backed with THAT'S WHEN YOUR HEARTACHES BEGIN *Victor* [*USA*]. Next came these tenth and eleventh million sellers for Elvis. 'All Shook Up' was written by Otis Blackwell and Elvis Presley; 'That's When Your Heartaches Begin' by William Raskin and Billy Hill (words), Fred Fisher (music), first written in 1940, revised in 1952. 'All Shook Up' was the top disc of 1957, and was No 1 in the U.S. charts for eight weeks with 30 weeks in the U.S. bestsellers, and also chart topper in Britain for seven weeks, where it stayed 20 weeks in the bestsellers. Sales were well over two million. A top rhythm-and-blues disc. 'That's When Your Heartaches Begin' reached No 58.

LOVING YOU backed with TEDDY BEAR (Let me be your) *Victor* [*USA*]. These 12th and 13th million sellers for Elvis both came from his film *Loving You*. The title song was written by Jerry Leiber and Mike Stoller; 'Teddy Bear' by Kal Mann and Bernie Lowe. This disc was No 1 in the U.S.A. for seven weeks and sold two million. A top rhythm-and-blues and country disc. 'Loving You' was No 28, and 22 weeks in the U.S. bestsellers. 'Teddy Bear' was 25 weeks in the bestsellers; it was No 3 and 19 weeks in the British bestsellers.

JAILHOUSE ROCK backed with TREAT ME NICE *Victor* [*USA*]. Both songs came from Presley's film *Jailhouse Rock* to provide his 14th and 15th million sellers. Both songs were written by Jerry Leiber and Mike Stoller. This disc sold well over two million and 'Jailhouse Rock' was No 1 in the U.S. charts for seven weeks with 27 weeks in the bestsellers, and No 1 for three weeks in Britain in 1958, with 19 weeks in the bestsellers. A top rhythm-and-blues and country disc. 'Treat Me Nice' was No 27 and 10 weeks in the bestsellers.

ELVIS (album) *Victor* [*USA*]. This first million seller album for Elvis was issued in Britain under the title 'Rock'n'Roll No 2'. Gold Disc award, R.I.A.A., 1960. It was No 1 for five weeks in the U.S.A.

Contents of the disc were: 'Rip It Up', by R. Blackwell and J. Marascalco (1956); 'Love Me,' by Jerry Leiber and Mike Stoller (1957); 'When My Blue Moon Turns to Gold Again', by Wiley Walker and Gene Sullivan (1941); 'Long Tall Sally', by Enotris Johnson, Richard Penniman and R. Blackwell (1956); 'First in Line', by Aaron Schroeder and Ben Weisman (1957); 'Paralysed', by Otis Blackwell and Elvis Presley (1957); 'So Glad You're Mine', by Arthur Crudup (1946); 'Old Shep', by Red Foley (1940); 'Ready Teddy', by R. Blackwell and J. Marascalco (1956); 'Any Place Is Paradise', by Joe Thomas; 'How's the World Treating You?', by Boudleaux Bryant and Chet Atkins (1952); 'How Do You Think I Feel?', by Wayne Walker and Webb Pierce (1954).

ELVIS' CHRISTMAS ALBUM (album) *Victor* [*USA*]. First released at Christmas 1957, this album received the R.I.A.A. Gold Record award for a million dollar sales in 1963. By December 1964 it had sold over 800,000 copies and a further 309,000 were sold in the three months before Christmas 1965, bringing the total to well over the million.

The disc contained the following: 'Santa Claus Is Back in Town', by Jerry Leiber and Mike Stoller (1957); 'White Christmas', by Irving Berlin (1942); 'Here Comes Santa Claus', by Gene Autry and Oakley Haldeman (1947); 'I'll Be Home for Christmas', by Walter Kent, Kim Gannon and Buck Ram (1943); 'Blue Christmas', by Billy Hayes and Jay Johnson (1948); 'Santa, Bring My Baby Back', by Aaron Schroeder and Claude de Metruis (1957), 'O Little Town of Bethlehem', by Bishop P. Brooks (1835–1893), melody traditional; 'Silent Night, Holy Night', by Joseph Mohr and Franz Gruber (1818); 'Peace in the Valley', by Thomas A. Dorsey (1939); 'I Believe', by Ervin Drake, Irvin Graham, Jimmy Shirl and Al Stillman (1952); 'Take My Hand, Precious Lord', by Thomas A. Dorsey; 'It Is No Secret What God Can Do', by Bernard Hamblen (1950).

This made global million seller No 51 for Elvis by the end of 1965, and his fifth million seller album.

MARVIN RAINWATER AND CONNIE FRANCIS
MAJESTY OF LOVE *MGM* [*USA*]. This second million seller for Marvin and first for Connie Francis (see 1958 for data) was written by Ben Raleigh and Don Wolf.

THE RAYS
SILHOUETTES *Cameo* [*USA*]. This male quartet comprises Hal Miller, Davy Jones and Harry James, all from Brooklyn, New York, and Walter Ford from Lexington, Kentucky. The song is by Bob Crewe and Frank Slay, Jr. The disc was No 3 and 20 weeks in the U.S. bestsellers.

JIM REEVES
FOUR WALLS *Victor* [*USA*]. The third million seller for Jim Reeves was written by George Campbell and Marvin Moore. This disc was No 12 and 22 weeks in the U.S. bestsellers, and was a top country-and-western song of the year.

DEBBIE REYNOLDS (with Universal International orchestra conducted by Joseph Gershenson)
TAMMY *Coral* [*USA*]. This is actually Debbie's second million seller, her first being a duet with Carleton Carpenter in 1951. The song is by Jay Livingston and Ray Evans from the film *Tammy and the Bachelor*, starring Debbie, in which she sang it. The disc is from the soundtrack of the film, and was No 1 for five weeks in the U.S.A. and 13 weeks in the bestsellers, and No 2 with 17 weeks in the British bestsellers.

MARTY ROBBINS WITH RAY CONNIFF ORCHESTRA
A WHITE SPORT COAT AND A PINK CARNATION *Columbia* [*USA*]. The first million seller for Marty was a song he wrote himself - one of hundreds of songs he composed. Country-and-western artist Marty was born on 26 September 1925 at Glendale, Arizona, and moved with his family to Phoenix when he was 12. At 19 he enlisted in the U.S. Navy and spent three years on a Pacific island where he taught himself to strum a guitar and began to compose songs. Then he sang several times as a guest in a friend's band at a Phoenix nightclub, and later was engaged as guitarist in the band, which was his first paid job. Later he had his own radio show and a TV programme called 'Western Caravan' in which he ranged from gospel songs and blues to Western ballads. With two radio programmes daily and a weekly TV show Marty made frequent guest appearances in 'Grand Ole Opry', becoming a regular member in 1953. He then began to make recordings, mostly of his own works. Marty also appeared in a number of movie Westerns. A top country-and-western disc, it was No 3 and 26 weeks in the U.S. bestsellers. Marty was the first Nashville artist to be booked into Las Vegas, and the first person to perform at the new Opry House.

He died on 9 December 1982.

JIMMY RODGERS WITH THE HUGO PERETTI ORCHESTRA
HONEYCOMB *Roulette* [*USA*]. This first million seller for Jimmy was remarkably his first recording. The song was written by Bob Merrill in 1954. Jimmy hails from Camus, Washington, where he was born on 18 September 1933, and was taught music

by his mother who had earlier played with bands. He later taught himself to play piano and guitar. During his four years with the U.S. Air Force he developed as a singer and entertained at camp shows and concerts, mostly with folk songs. On discharge he worked his way down the Pacific north-west coast to California working on logging camps and farms and finding new songs. While appearing in a small club in Nashville, Tennessee, Western star Chuck Miller loaned him enough money to go to New York. He entered, and won outright the Arthur Godfrey 'Talent Scout' TV show. He then sought an audition with Hugo Peretti and Luigi Creatori, founders of Roulette Records, but left without leaving an address. The company spent six months before locating him in his home town. More hit discs followed with TV, nightclub appearances and films. Rodgers' career as a folk singer flourished mainly through the simple sincerity of his style. He had a big hit in England in 1962 with 'English Country Garden' taken from one of his albums. 'Honeycomb' was No 1 for two weeks in the U.S.A. and 28 weeks in the bestsellers, No 30 in Britain, and a top rhythm-and-blues disc.

KISSES SWEETER THAN WINE *Roulette* [*USA*]. The second million seller for Jimmy Rodgers was written by Paul Campbell (words) and Joel Newman (music) in 1951. Campbell is a pseudonym for the famous Weavers (see 1950) and Newman for Huddie Ledbetter (see Jenkins, 1950). Song is an adaptation of an old Irish folk song 'Drimmers Cow'. The disc was No 7 and 21 weeks in the U.S. bestsellers, and No 7 in Britain, with 11 weeks in the bestsellers.

OH OH I'M FALLING IN LOVE AGAIN *Roulette* [*USA*]. The third million seller for Jimmy Rodgers was written by Al Hoffman, Dick Manning and Mark Markwell (pseudonym for Hugo Peretti and Luigi Creatore). It was No 22 and 15 weeks in the U.S. bestsellers; No 18 and six weeks in the British bestsellers.

DON RONDO (vocalist)
WHITE SILVER SANDS *Jubilee* [*USA*]. Second million seller for Don, written by Charles G. 'Red' Matthews. The song had a big revival in 1960 when it was again a million seller (see Bill Black, 1960). The disc was No 10 and 19 weeks in the U.S. bestsellers, and No 18 in Britain.

DAVID ROSE AND HIS ORCHESTRA
CALYPSO MELODY *MGM* [*USA*]. This well-deserved second million seller for this brilliant arranger-conductor-composer was composed by Larry Clinton, who himself is a notably versatile musician and composer. The disc reached No 42 and was 12 weeks in the U.S. bestsellers.

TOMMY SANDS
TEEN AGE CRUSH *Capitol* [*USA*]. This first million seller for Tommy was written in 1956 by Audrey and Joe Allison, sung by him in the TV show 'The Singin' Idol' in that year. Sands took the part over from Elvis Presley who was forced to withdraw because of pressure of work. Tommy was born on 27 August 1937 in Chicago, where his father was a pianist and his mother a former singer with Art Kassell's band. At the age of eight Tommy learned to play the guitar and at nine had broadcast twice over local radio. He became interested in dramatics at high school in Houston and at sixteen played an important role in a pre-Broadway production there. Later he guested on Tennessee Ernie Ford's TV series (1956) and then made a star appearance in 'The Singin' Idol', the turning point in his career. He has since appeared in films, notably *Mardi Gras* (1959) with Pat Boone and Gary Crosby, and recorded many more songs in his 'beat' style. This disc was No 2 in the U.S. charts, and 17 weeks in the bestsellers.

FRANK SINATRA WITH ORCHESTRA DIRECTED BY NELSON RIDDLE
ALL THE WAY backed with CHICAGO *Capitol* [*USA*]. Frank Sinatra's sixth million seller comes (both sides) from the film *The Joker is Wild* (1957). 'All the Way', written by Sammy Cahn (words) and James van Heusen (music) won the Academy Award for Best Film Song of 1957. 'Chicago' is the great oldie of 1922, written by Fred Fisher, and a million sheet music seller in that year. Sinatra's disc brought this latter song back in a big way in popularity, the disc reaching a million sale by 1958. 'All the Way' was No 15 and 30 weeks in the U.S. bestsellers; No 3 and 20 weeks in the British bestsellers. 'Chicago' reached No 84.

HUEY SMITH (rock'n'roll piano) WITH THE CLOWNS
ROCKIN' PNEUMONIA AND THE BOOGIE WOOGIE FLU *Ace* [*USA*]. Huey 'Piano' Smith was born in New Orleans on 26 January 1934. His piano playing incorporated the boogie styles of Pete Johnson, Meade Lux Lewis, Albert Ammons, the jazz style of Jelly Roll Morton and the piano playing of Fats Domino. Smith became interested in the technical aspects of recording and became a studio engineer after leaving school. He then wrote this song and recorded it himself. If turned out to be a tremendous hit in the offbeat rock style in the U.S.A. The lyrics were by John Vincent, and sung by Bobby Marchan. The disc reached No 52, and was 13 weeks in the U.S.A. bestsellers.

DON'T YOU JUST KNOW IT *Ace* [*USA*]. This second million seller for Huey Smith was also written by him, again with lyrics by John Vincent, sung by Bobby Marchan. It reached No 9 with 13 weeks in the U.S. bestsellers.

ART AND DOTTY TODD
CHANSON D'AMOUR *Era* [*USA*]. The only million seller by this duo was written by Wayne Shanklin. Arthur W. Todd was born on 11 March 1920 and Dotty Todd on 23 June 1923 – birthplace of both being Elizabeth, New Jersey. Art was educated at Syracuse University, studied the banjo and voice, and Dotty was educated at a business college, also studying piano and voice. The duo became a singing team in nightclubs, hotels, TV and on records. They had their own radio show on CBS for two years and on ABC for two years. They wrote many of their own songs. The disc was No 13 and 16 weeks in the U.S. bestsellers.

BILLY VAUGHN AND HIS ORCHESTRA
SAIL ALONG SILV'RY MOON *Dot* [*USA*]. Billy Vaughn's second million seller, this disc sold a reputed four and a half million globally, for which he received a special Platinum Disc award. Apart from selling over a million in the U.S.A., it also sold over a million in Germany where his discs have a big following and consistent sales (see 1955). The song is an oldie of 1937 by Harry Tobias (words) and Percy Wenrich (music). The disc was No 5 and 26 weeks in the U.S. bestsellers.

GENE VINCENT AND HIS BLUE CAPS
WEAR MY RING *Capitol* [*USA*]. This third million seller for Gene Vincent was written by Don Kirschner and disc artist Bobby Darin. Gene Vincent died 13 October 1971 in Newhall, California.

BILLY WARD AND THE DOMINOES (vocal) WITH THE JACK PLEIS ORCHESTRA AND CHORUS
STARDUST *Liberty* [*USA*]. 'Stardust' was the only million seller for this group of rhythm-and-blues singers. The song is the famous Mitchell Parish (words) and Hoagy Carmichael (music) standard of 1929.
Billy Ward, born in the U.S.A. on 19 September 1921, commercial artist, songwriter, arranger and singer, worked for a New York advertising agency after Army service. His employer, Rose Marks, sold her firm to devote all her time to managing Billy. Billy started as a vocal coach, but soon formed a quintet which landed a King Records contract as The Dominoes. Ward wrote their first disc hit, 1951, 'Sixty Minute Man', and recorded 'Have Mercy, Baby' and 'One Mint Julep', 1952, 'I'd Be Satisfied',

'Rags to Riches', 'These Foolish Things' in 1953, all sizeable hits, before going over to the Liberty label. This disc was No 13 and 24 weeks in the U.S. bestsellers, and No 13 with 11 weeks in the British bestsellers.

NANCY WHISKEY (vocal) WITH THE CHARLES MCDEVITT SKIFFLE GROUP

FREIGHT TRAIN *Oriole* [*Britain*]. This version was written by Paul James and Fred Williams in 1957. The original song version is attributed to Elizabeth Cotten (U.S.A.), who worked as a domestic for much of her life, and originated the unique guitar style known as 'Cotton Picking'. Song first introduced into Britain by Peggy Seeger. The disc reached No 40 in the U.S.A.; No 5 with 18 weeks in the British bestsellers.

ANDY WILLIAMS

BUTTERFLY *Cadence* [*USA*]. Andy's first million seller was a second time million seller for this song by Anthony September (Bernie Lowe and Kal Mann). Andy was born on 3 December 1928, Howard Andrew Williams, in Wall Lake, Iowa, and began his singing career when he and his three brothers along with their parents organized a church choir in their native Wall Lake. The four brothers later became very popular on their own radio shows from Chicago, Cincinnati and Des Moines.

The family moved to California where the brothers teamed up with comedienne Kay Thompson and formed a highly successful nightclub act. The group stayed together for six years until 1952 when Andy became a soloist. He achieved national prominence as a regular performer on Steve Allen's 'Tonight' show over the following two and a half years. Then came a recording contract with Cadence Records for whom he made many singles and albums. This disc of 'Butterfly' established him, and by 1959 he was star of his own CBS-TV show and named 'Personality of the Year' in 1959 by the Variety Clubs of America, an award given to other star performers such as Al Jolson, Steve Allen and Arthur Godfrey.

In 1961, Andy was signed by Columbia Records with a subsequent string of big selling albums including 'Moon River' and 'Days of Wine and Roses', both million sellers. He made his film debut in *I'd Rather Be Rich* (1964) and from then on recorded more million selling singles and by 1970 had received 13 gold disc awards from R.I.A.A. for albums.

It is interesting to note that Andy made his first recording with his brothers as backing group to Bing Crosby's 'Swinging on a Star' in 1944. Andy's relaxed facile singing style has certainly made him a star, for he is one of the biggest sellers in the world and a colossal attraction wherever he appears. His TV series was a great success when screened on Britain's TV.

'Butterfly', recorded on 23 January 1957, got to No 1 for 3 weeks in the U.S. charts with 20 weeks in the bestsellers, and was No 1 in Britain for two weeks, with 15 weeks in the bestsellers.

BILLY WILLIAMS (vocal) WITH THE JIMMY HASKELLE ORCHESTRA

I'M GONNA SIT RIGHT DOWN AND WRITE MYSELF A LETTER *Coral* [*USA*]. This song was a big hit for the late and inimitable Fats Waller when it first appeared in 1935. Written by Joe Young (words) and Fred E. Ahlert (music) it provided a first million seller for Billy Williams.

Born in 1910, blues singer Billy Williams was leader of the Charioteers and the Billy Williams Quartet. He was one of the first black artists to appear regularly on television.

The Rev. Clarence Cobbs found him 'down and out' in a hotel in 1965. Billy had lost his voice because of diabetes. He went to live with the minister and worked in the Model Cities Program helping alcoholics, after returning to school in 1971 to finish his degree at De Paul University. He died in a Chicago hospital on 12 October 1972. The disc was No 6 and 23 weeks in the U.S. bestsellers; No 22 and nine weeks in the British bestsellers.

LARRY WILLIAMS

SHORT FAT FANNY *Specialty* [*USA*]. Here was a first million seller for Larry, the rhythm-and-blues pianist-vocalist. Larry originally played a rattling 'beat' piano with Lloyd Price's band and it was while with Lloyd that he was spotted and signed by Specialty Records as a solo artist. The song is his own composition. Williams was born on 10 May 1935 in the U.S.A. The disc was No 6 and 21 weeks in the U.S. bestsellers, and reached No 21 in Britain and eight weeks in the bestsellers.

BONY MORONIE *Specialty* [*USA*]. This second million seller for Larry Williams was also written by him. It reached No 18 with 18 weeks in the U.S. bestsellers, and was No 11 in Britain and 20 weeks in the bestsellers.

ORIGINAL THEATRE CAST WITH ROBERT PRESTON, BARBARA COOK, EDDIE HODGES, PERT KELTON, IGGIE WOLFINGTON, PAUL REED AND THE BUFFALO BILLS

THE MUSIC MAN (album) *Capitol* [*USA*]. This disc contains the following songs, all written and composed by Meredith Willson: 'Seventy-Six Trombones', 'Marian the Librarian', 'The Sadder-but-Wiser Girl', 'Ya Got Trouble' (all sung by Robert Preston); 'Goodnight My Someone', 'My White Knight' (sung by Barbara Cook); 'Gary, Indiana', 'Wells Fargo Wagon' (sung by Eddie Hodges); 'It's You', 'Sincere' (sung by The Buffalo Bills); 'Shipoopi' (sung by Iggie Wolfington); 'Lida Rose', 'Will I Ever Tell You?' (sung by Barbara Cook and Buffalo Bills); 'Piano Lesson', 'Till There Was You' (sung by Barbara Cook and Pert Kelton); 'Rock Island' (sung by Paul Reed and Travelling Salesmen); 'Finale', 'Pick-a-Little, Talk-a-Little', 'Goodnight Ladies' (sung by The Company).

The Music Man was produced on 19 December 1957 at the Majestic Theatre, New York and ran for 1,377 performances. (The London production at Adelphi Theatre, 16 March 1961, ran for 395 performances.) Creatively a one-man show, with book, music and lyrics by Meredith Willson, it is a 1912 tale of an itinerant con man, who invades an Iowa town posing as a bandleader. Robert Preston, a longtime film actor, is the star of the show, bringing unrationed, old-fashioned high spirits. The show was composer Willson's first try for the theatre. He was born in Mason City, Iowa, in 1907, and played the flute in the local band, and at 14 in the famous 'March King' Sousa's band. At 21 he played the same instrument in the New York Philharmonic Symphony orchestra under Toscanini. From 1929 he was musical director for various radio networks, including 20 years with NBC. Willson's biggest song hits were 'You and I' (1941) and 'May the Good Lord Bless and Keep You' (1951), 'I See the Moon' (1953) and '76 Trombones' from *The Music Man* now in the repertoire of practically every brass band in the world. He says he did not have to make up anything for *The Music Man*. All he had to do was remember. He turned his recollections of Mason City into rhythm and song, starting on it in 1955. He rewrote the whole show at least 20 times before it was finalized to become one of Broadway's biggest hits. This album sold half a million by 1959, and a reputed million by 1963. It was in the bestseller charts in the U.S.A. for 244 weeks. Gold Disc award R.I.A.A. 1959. Grammy Award for Best Original Cast Show Album 1958. It was No 1 for 12 weeks in U.S.A.

FILM SOUNDTRACK WITH ROSSANO BRAZZI, MITZI GAYNOR, JOHN KERR, FRANCE NUYEN

SOUTH PACIFIC (album) *Victor* [*USA*]. (Containing: 'Overture', 'Dites-Moi', 'Cock-eyed Optimist', 'Some Enchanted Evening', 'Twin Soliloquies', 'Bloody Mary', 'My Girl Back Home', 'Bali Ha'i', 'I'm Gonna Wash That Man Right Outa My Hair', 'I'm in Love with a Wonderful Guy', 'Younger Than Springtime', 'Happy Talk', 'Honey Bun', 'Carefully Taught', 'This nearly was Mine', 'Finale'.)

This was the biggest-selling soundtrack album up to 1966 with five million sold. The film was the second Todd-AO giant screen production, an even bigger success than its predecessor *Oklahoma* in 1955, bringing the famous Oscar Hammerstein/Richard Rodgers stage musical of 1949 to a colossal world audience. The film by 1968 grossed over $17½ million in the U.S.A. and Canada alone, and shattered every record for a motion picture in Britain at London's Dominion Theatre with a 231 weeks' run from April 1958 to September 1962 and a total of 2,551 performances, grossing $5½ million. This disc was the first album to achieve a million (by November 1963) sale in Britain alone, one and a half million by 1966, and it had the then longest stay of any disc in Britain's bestseller charts (306 weeks) – over five years. Mitzi Gaynor, star of the film, is said to have received more in royalties from the disc than she was paid for making the film. This disc was in the Top 10 for nearly two years in the U.S.A., and in their bestseller charts for 259 weeks. Gold Disc award, R.I.A.A., 1959. The film received an Academy Award for best sound recording. This album was No 1 for 54 weeks in the U.S.A. By 1970 it had sold over eight million globally.

PAUL ANKA

YOU ARE MY DESTINY *ABC-Paramount* [*USA*]. The second million seller for Paul Anka was written by him in 1957. It was No 7 and seven weeks in the U.S. bestsellers. No 6 and 13 weeks in the British bestsellers.

TONI ARDEN

PADRE *Decca* [*USA*]. Originally a French song by Jacques Larue (words) and Alain Romans (music), written in 1957, with English lyrics by Paul Francis Webster in 1958. It was first introduced in the U.S.A. by Lola Dee (Mercury label).

Toni Arden, a talented lady vocalist and a true romantic singer, was invited by President Nixon to go to China on an art cultural exchange programme.

Her recording of 'Padre' reached No 18 in the U.S.A. and is said to have sold a million.

FRANKIE AVALON

DEDE DINAH *Chancellor* [*USA*]. The first million seller for Frankie Avalon was written by Bob Marcucci (words) and Peter de Angelis (music). Frankie (real name Frank Avallone) was born in Philadelphia on 18 September 1940. He learned trumpet as a youngster, played at local dances, and at 12 spent a summer season with a teenage band in Atlantic City. He had guest appearances as a child prodigy on Jack Gleason's, Paul Whiteman's and Ray Anthony's TV shows, and on radio. Frankie then developed his singing and was heard by Marcucci and De Angelis, music publishers, who became his managers and signed him as their first teenage artist for their Chancellor label. Avalon's film debut came in *Disc Jockey Jamboree* (1957) and was followed with roles in *Guns of the Timberland* (1960) and *The Carpetbaggers* (1962). The disc was No 7 and 15 weeks in the U.S.A. bestsellers.

FRED BERTELMANN WITH THE HANSEN QUARTET (vocalists)

DER LACHEND VAGABUND (Laughing Vagabond) *Electrola* [*Germany*]. This disc is one of Germany's all-time bestsellers. It sold over two million.

CHUCK BERRY

SWEET LITTLE SIXTEEN *Chess* [*USA*]. This fifth million seller for Chuck was written by him. A top rhythm-and-blues disc, it reached No 2 with 16 weeks in the U.S. bestsellers, and was No 16 in Britain, and five weeks in the bestsellers.

JOHNNY B. GOODE *Chess* [*USA*]. Likewise this sixth million seller for Chuck was written by him. It was No 8 and 15 weeks in the U.S. bestsellers.

BIG BOPPER

CHANTILLY LACE *Mercury* [*USA*]. Big Bopper's real name was J.P. Richardson, born on 24 October 1930 in Sabine Pass, Texas. He was educated at Lamar College in Beaumont, Texas, and 'J.P.' first became a disc jockey while in school. He also played in high school and college dance bands.

In 1954 he started writing songs, which was interrupted by service in the Army in 1955. After one year serving as radar instructor, he was discharged. Determined to reinstate his top position in local radio, he challenged the standing record for marathon broadcasting with a 'JAPE-A-THON' (presumably a title combining 'Jaypee' and 'Marathon') and was on the air for 122 hours 8 minutes of continuous broadcasting, breaking the existing world's record by eight minutes. Being heard by a local talent scout resulted in his being signed to a contract by Starrite Publishing Co. To his surprise, the audition tape of his tunes so impressed the company that he was asked to record his own material himself, and his first hit was 'Chantilly Lace', a self-penned song. Released in August 1958, it sold the million by the end of that year. The disc stayed on the U.S. bestsellers for 25 weeks and reached No 6, and was No 12 in Britain, and eight weeks in the bestsellers.

Big Bopper went on tour with Buddy Holly and Ritchie Valens and, on 3 February 1959, all were killed in an air crash near Fargo, North Dakota, a tragic end for three outstanding rock-and-roll artists.

PAT BOONE

A WONDERFUL TIME UP THERE backed with IT'S TOO SOON TO KNOW *Dot* [*USA*]. 'Wonderful Time', originally 'Gospel Boogie', written by Lee Roy Abernethy, and 'It's Too Soon to Know', written in 1947 by Deborah Chessler, provided Pat with his tenth million seller. The disc was No 10 and 19 weeks in the U.S. bestsellers, and No 2 with 17 weeks in the British bestsellers.

CHERIE, I LOVE YOU *Dot* [*USA*]. This eleventh million seller for Pat was an oldie of 1926 written by Lillian Rosedale Goodman, who was one of his vocal tutors. The disc reached No 63 in the U.S.A.

JAMES BROWN AND THE FAMOUS FLAMES

TRY ME (I NEED YOU) *Federal* [*USA*]. This second million seller for James Brown and his group was also written by Brown. A top rhythm-and-blues disc, it reached No 48 with 13 weeks in the U.S. bestsellers.

THE CHAMPS

TEQUILA *Challenge* [*USA*]. This group comprised Dave Burgess (leader) from Lancaster, California, Dale Norris, from Springfield, Massachusetts, Bobby Morris from Tulsa, Oklahoma, Jimmy Seals from Rankin, Texas, and Dash Grofts from Cisco, Texas. All were aged between 17 and 22 when they made this disc. Dave and Dale play guitars, Bobby bass, Jimmy sax and Dash plays the drums. This disc is instrumental, the composition of Chuck Rio, and was No 1 for five weeks in the U.S.A. with 19 weeks in the bestsellers, and a top rhythm-and-blues disc. It was No 5 in Britain and nine weeks in the bestsellers. Grammy Award for best rhythm-and-blues recording of 1958.

THE CHANTELS

MAYBE *End* [*USA*]. Written by George Goldner of End Records, this disc was a big rhythm-and-blues seller of 1958 and said to have sold a million through subsequent years, despite the disbanding of the group. This disc was released on the London label in Britain. It was No 15 and 18 weeks in the U.S. bestsellers.

THE CHORDETTS

LOLLIPOP *Cadence* [*USA*]. This second million seller for The Chordettes was written by Beverly Ross and Julius Dixon. It was No 2 and 15 weeks in the U.S. bestsellers, and reached No 6 in Britain, and eight weeks in the bestsellers.

JIMMY CLANTON

JUST A DREAM *Ace* [*USA*]. The first million seller for Jimmy came with a song written by him and Cosimo Matassa. Jimmy was born on 2 September 1940, at Baton Rouge, Louisiana, of an exceptionally musical family. Jimmy studied guitar and played

at local clubs while still attending school. He formed a four-piece band, 'The Rockets', and travelled to New Orleans, where Matassa, a studio owner, arranged an audition with Ace Records. Jimmy has also appeared in several 'beat' films including *Go, Jimmy, Go*. A top rhythm-and-blues disc, it was No 4 and 18 weeks in the U.S. bestsellers.

A LETTER TO AN ANGEL *Ace* [*USA*]. This second million seller for Jimmy was also written by him and Cosimo Matassa, who became his personal manager. The disc was No 25 and 12 weeks in the U.S. bestsellers.

THE COASTERS

YAKETY YAK *Atco* [*USA*]. This second million seller for The Coasters sold over two million. It was written by the very successful team of Jerry Leiber and Mike Stoller. A top rhythm-and-blues disc, it was No 1 for a week and 16 weeks in the U.S. bestsellers, and No 12 in Britain, with eight weeks in the bestsellers.

COZY COLE (jazz drummer)

TOPSY (Parts 1 and 2) *Love* [*USA*]. William 'Cozy' Cole was born on 17 October 1909 in Orange, New Jersey. He played with Blanche Calloway 1931-1932, Benny Carter 1933-1934, Willie Bryant 1935-1936, Stuff Smith 1936-1939 and Cab Calloway 1939-1942. He also acted in *Carmen Jones* on Broadway in 1943, founded a drums school, and has played with numerous small groups. From 1949-1953 he was in Louis Armstrong's band.

Cozy is universally considered to be one of the most perfect drummers jazz has produced, possessing an incomparable solid tempo with enormous power, extraordinary exactitude, cleanness of playing and unrivalled virtuosity.

He made a large number of records both with studio groups and regular bands.

This recording sold a million, the popular side being 'Topsy 2'. The music was written by Edgar Battle and Edward Durham, the words by Edgar Battle. Cozy's drum solo was based on 'Topsy' from Battle and Durham's 1939 composition 'Uncle Tom's Cabin'.

'Topsy 1' reached No 27, and 'Topsy 2' No 3 in the U.S. charts. The disc was 21 weeks in the bestsellers. It reached No 29 in Britain.

PERRY COMO

CATCH A FALLING STAR backed with MAGIC MOMENTS *Victor* [*USA*]. By 1959 this disc became a 16th million seller for Perry. Both these songs were very popular and the disc sold over two million. 'Catch a Falling Star' was written by Paul Vance and Lee Pockriss in 1957. 'Magic Moments' was written in 1957 by Hal David (words) and Burt F. Bacharach (music). This record was the top disc in Britain for eight weeks. Grammy Award for Best Solo (Male) Vocal Performance 1958. Gold Disc award, R.I.A.A., 1958. 'Catch a Falling Star' was No 9 and 23 weeks in the U.S. bestsellers. 'Magic Moments' was No 27 and 16 weeks in the bestsellers. 'Catch a Falling Star' was No 9 and ten weeks in the British charts and 'Magic Moments' 17 weeks.

KEWPIE DOLL *Victor* [*USA*]. This 17th million seller for Perry Como was written by Sid Tepper and Roy C. Bennett in 1957. It reached No 12 and 16 weeks in the U.S. bestsellers, and No 9 in Britain, and seven weeks in the bestsellers.

I MAY NEVER PASS THIS WAY AGAIN *Victor* [*USA*]. This fine philosophical song written by Murray Wizell and Irving Melsher in 1957 became an 18th million seller for Perry Como. It was No 15 and eight weeks in the British bestsellers.

WARREN COVINGTON AND THE TOMMY DORSEY ORCHESTRA

TEA FOR TWO CHA CHA *Decca* [*USA*]. Covington took over the Tommy Dorsey orchestra after Tommy's death in November 1956. This disc, a million seller by 1960, was a tremendous success. It was an arrangement of the famous Irving Caesar/Vincent Youmans very popular song 'Tea for Two' originally from the musical *No, No Nanette* (1924), in cha-cha tempo. The cha-cha dance was also a great favourite at this time, and this disc sparked off many other favourite dance tunes being played and recorded in this idiom. Covington was born 7 August 1921 in Philadelphia, Pennsylvania. The disc was No 7 and 20 weeks in the U.S. bestsellers, and No 3 with 19 weeks in the British bestsellers.

THE CRESCENDOS

OH, JULIE *Nasco* [*USA*]. The only million seller for this group was written by Kenneth R. Moffit and Noel Ball in 1957. This disc reached No 5 with 18 weeks in the U.S. bestsellers.

THE CRESTS

SIXTEEN CANDLES *Coed* [*USA*]. By 1959 'Sixteen Candles' became the Crests' only million seller. All in their late teens at the time of recording, the Crests comprised Johnny Mastro, Jay Carter, Harold Torres and Tommy Gough. This number was written by Luther Dixon and Allyson R. Khent. The disc was No 2 and 21 weeks in the U.S. bestsellers.

THE CRICKETS

MAYBE BABY *Brunswick* [*USA*]. This second million seller for The Crickets was written by Norman Petty and Buddy Holly. It reached No 18 and was 14 weeks in the U.S. bestsellers, and reached No 4 in Britain and was ten weeks in the bestsellers.

BOBBY DARIN

SPLISH SPLASH *Acto* [*USA*]. This first million seller for Bobby, written by him and Jean Murray, was the start of several hits which made him the pet of the teenagers. He was born on 14 May 1936 in New York's Bronx district. His father died a few months before he was born and he was raised by his mother, a former professional entertainer, and his older sister. At school he graduated with honours from Bronx High School where he studied science and won a scholarship to college. By the time he quit school he could play piano, drums, vibraphone, guitar and bass. He soon began playing in the small nightclubs in and around New York, and early in 1956 he wrote a song 'My First Love' with his close friend Don Kirschner (now a top music publisher) and took along a demonstration disc to artists manager George Scheck, who not only gave him a personal management contract, but secured Bobby a recording contract with Decca. Darin made his TV debut the same year on a show with the late Tommy Dorsey (March 1956). Nothing much happened for two years until he wrote 'Splish Splash'. Other big hits of his own writing followed, 'Queen of the Hop', and then his record 'Mack the Knife' which appealed to the adults as well as the rock'n'rollers. This brought his total disc sales to over seven million. Then came two contracts with Paramount films and NBC-TV. Darin's film appearances include *Pepe*, *Too Late Blues*, *Come September* (for which he wrote the music also), *Hell Is for Heroes* and *If a Man Answers*. Bobby was a versatile performer, he danced, wrote hit songs and played the vibraphone, drums and guitar between numbers. He had a remarkable sense of rhythm and in a short time made the transition from 'rock' singer to the more mature musical world, and infused a touch of artistry into the 'beat' music world. With films, TV and major nightclub bookings, Darin was in the $350,000 a year class by 1961. He also made a tour of Britain and Australia. In 1960 he married Sandra Dee, actress of the film *Come September* whom he met in Italy while making the film there. Bobby won the award for 'The Best New Singer' and for 'The Best Record of the Year' for 1959. His real name was Waldon Cassotto. This disc was No 3 and 14 weeks in the U.S. bestsellers; No 28 in Britain. Darin died on 20 December 1973.

QUEEN OF THE HOP *Atco* [*USA*]. This second million seller for Bobby Darin was written by Woody Harris in conjunction with Darin. It reached No 9 with 19 weeks in the U.S. bestsellers, and was No 24 in Britain.

BOBBY DAY

ROCKIN' ROBIN *Class* [*USA*]. This was the sole million seller for rock'n'roll singer Bobby (real name Robert Byrd) who hails from Los Angeles. The song was written by a lady composer, J. Thomas. The disc was a rhythm-and-blues chart topper for 1958, reaching No 2 nationally with 21 weeks in the U.S. bestsellers; No 29 in Britain.

THE DIAMONDS

THE STROLL *Mercury* [*USA*]. The third million seller for this group was written by Clyde Otis and Nancy Lee in 1957. It was No 5 and 21 weeks in the U.S. bestsellers.

FATS DOMINO

WHOLE LOTTA LOVIN' *Imperial* [*USA*]. This 21st million seller for Fats was, like so many of his successes, written by him with Dave Bartholomew. The million sale was achieved by 1960. The disc was No 6 and 15 weeks in the U.S. bestsellers.

DUANE EDDY (guitar) WITH THE REBELS

REBEL ROUSER *Jamie* [*USA*]. This was the first million seller for Duane Eddy, who discovered and started the now-famous 'twangy guitar' approach by playing the melody on the bottom instead of the top strings of his guitar. The composition is by Duane and Lee Hazlewood, his close friend and independent record producer, who had cut his discs before Eddy got his Jamie

Records contract. Several of Eddy's hits were written with Hazlewood. Eddy was born on 26 April 1938 in Corning, New York. When he was five he started playing the guitar, and at 13 the family moved to Phoenix, Arizona, where he was educated at Coolridge High School. After leaving at 16, he played for local dances and a year later (1955) met band leader Al Casey. Eddy sat in with Al's band, and began studying with well-known jazz guitarist Jimmy Wybele. It was at this point that he stumbled on the 'twangy' sound that has since made him one of the highest paid pop instrumentalists in the world, and started off a fantastic trend for this type of music, with groups everywhere. With his group, The Rebels (saxophone, fender bass and drums), it was not long before they were signed to Jamie Records with subsequent TV and personal appearances, first in the U.S.A. and later in England. Eddy sold five million discs in three years, and twelve million by 1963, a phenomenal score for a non-vocal performer. He made his TV debut in the U.S.A. in the series 'Have Gun – Will Travel' and his film debut in 1960 in *Because They're Young*, followed by *A Thunder of Drums* and *The Wild Westerner*. He also wrote the title tune for *Ring of Fire* (1961). His work might best be characterized as rock'n'roll copiously embellished with the blues. He later recorded for RCA-Victor. This disc was No 6 and 13 weeks in the U.S. bestsellers, and was No 19 in Britain, and 10 weeks in the bestsellers.

TOMMY EDWARDS

IT'S ALL IN THE GAME *MGM* [*USA*]. This tune was written in 1912 by Gen. Charles Gates Dawes, the Chicago banker, amateur musician (flute) and Vice President of the U.S.A. in the Coolidge Administration, 1925-1929. He entitled his simple melody 'Melody in A major'. In 1951, lyricist Carl Sigman wrote words for it under 'It's All in the Game' and several discs were released including those by Dinah Shore, Sammy Kaye, Carmen Cavallaro and Tommy Edwards. Tommy Edwards' disc of that time did not mean very much, but in 1957 he recorded it in a halfway rock'n'roll-ballad arrangement which by 1958 became a No 1 hit. Tommy hails from Richmond, Virginia. From the age of nine he had been in show business. He broke into the disc scene as a songwriter with 'All Over Again'. When MGM heard his demonstration tape of it they gave him a contract. After cutting several discs, this million seller made him well known. It was No 1 for six weeks in the U.S.A. and chart topper in Britain for seven weeks, reaching seven figures in 1961. A top rhythm-and-blues disc, it subsequently sold 3,500,000, and was 22 weeks in the U.S. bestsellers, and 17 weeks in the British ones.

Tommy was born on 17 February 1922. He died on 23 October 1969 in Henrico County, Virginia.

THE ELEGANTS
LITTLE STAR *Apt* [*USA*]. The only million seller for this group was written by Arnold Venosa and Vito Picone. The song is a modern rhythmic version of the old nursery rhyme, 'Twinkle, Twinkle, Little Star'. A top rhythm-and-blues disc, it was No 1 for a week and 19 weeks in the U.S. bestsellers, and was No 25 in Britain.

EVERLY BROTHERS
ALL I HAVE TO DO IS DREAM backed with CLAUDETTE *Cadence* [*USA*]. Here was a third million seller for the Everlys. The 'Dream' number was written by Boudleaux Bryant, while 'Claudette' was written by Roy Orbison who also had million sellers as a disc artist. 'All I Have to Do Is Dream' was No 1 for four weeks in the U.S.A. with 17 weeks in the bestsellers, and No 1 for nine weeks in Britain and 21 weeks in the bestsellers. 'Claudette' was No 30 and ten weeks in the bestsellers. A top rhythm-and-blues and country disc.

BIRD DOG backed with DEVOTED TO YOU *Cadence* [*USA*]. Both songs in this fourth million seller for the Everlys were written by Boudleaux Bryant. 'Bird Dog' was a No 1 seller for five weeks in the U.S.A.. and 18 weeks in the bestsellers, and a top seller in Britain with 16 weeks in their bestsellers. A top country-and-western disc.

PROBLEMS *Cadence* [*USA*]. The fifth million seller for the Everlys was jointly written by Felice and Boudleaux Bryant. 'Problems' was No 2 and 15 weeks in the U.S. bestsellers; No 6 and 12 weeks in Britain's bestsellers.

CONNIE FRANCIS ACCOMPANIED BY THE JOE LIPMAN ORCHESTRA
WHO'S SORRY NOW? *MGM* [*USA*]. This first (solo) disc for Connie was actually her second million seller (she had her first with Marvin Rainwater - see 1957). The song is a revival of the famous 1923 oldie by Bert Kalmar and Harry Ruby (words) and Ted Snyder (music), which was then a million sheet music seller. Connie's real name is Constance Franconero, and she was born in Newark, New Jersey, on 12 December 1938, and educated there at grammar school and Newark Arts High School (where she majored in music theory and orchestration) and Belleville High School, New Jersey. At Belleville she edited the school newspaper, wrote and produced a school musical show, and won the New Jersey State typing contest. From the age of four she played the accordion and appeared in local vaudeville and amateur radio shows. She first made her mark in show business when 11, as a singer/accordionist on the juvenile TV 'Startime', presented by George Scheck, her manager. A year later she won an Arthur Godfrey 'Talent Scout' show. Connie got a four-year engagement as the featured vocalist on the NBC-TV 'Startime' series, and was signed to MGM Records when she was 17 (1955). Then her father, who plays concertina as a hobby, suggested she record a triplet-backed version of the old song 'Who's Sorry Now?'. This became her first big hit. More followed. Connie is, without doubt, one of the most successful female singers on disc. By 1967 she had sold 35 million. The U.S.A. is only part of her domain in disc sales, for she has made a unique success in other countries including France, Germany, Spain, Italy and Japan with recordings in their native tongues. She has also made many varied-themed albums and major nightclub and TV appearances

all over the world. Her film debut was in *Where the Boys Are* for MGM in 1961, and she was the top female disc star in the polls conducted by *Cashbox*, *Billboard* and *New Musical Express* (1959) and winner of practically all the disc industry's most important awards. She was also the only artist in the industry with 10 solo discs which sold a million each in a space of only two years. 'Who's Sorry Now?' was first released in November 1957 and catapulted her into national fame. Connie also plays the piano, and writes songs, and has made an intensive study of psychology. This record was top disc in Britain for six weeks with 25 weeks in the bestsellers, and No 4 for two weeks in the U.S.A. with 22 weeks in the bestsellers.

FREDDY (Quinn)
HEIMATLOS (Homeless) *Polydor* [*Germany*]. This second million seller for Freddy, the German 'pop' champion, was written by Lotar Olias and Peter Mosser.

DON GIBSON (vocal and guitar)
OH LONESOME ME backed with I CAN'T STOP LOVING YOU *Victor* [*USA*]. Both songs were written by Don Gibson in 1957 for his first million seller. He was born on 3 April 1928 in Shelby, North Carolina, became a professional there at the age of 14, and eventually moved to the radio station in Knoxville, Tennessee, where he formed his own band. Then followed several years of dance dates, local radio and TV, with much lonely work in his specially-equipped recording trailer with resultant perfection of performance on guitar and singing for which he is noted today. Gibson signed with Victor Records in 1957; then came a chain of country pop hits. His song-writing prowess is reflected by the fact that he has written most of the tunes that have become his own hit discs, as well as many that other performers have made. 'I Can't Stop Loving You' was revived in 1962 by Ray Charles to become a top song again. This disc of his two songs was top country-and-western seller of 1958. Released in December 1957, 'Oh Lonesome Me' reached No 8 with 21 weeks in the U.S. bestsellers, and 'I Can't Stop Loving You,' reached No 81.

BILLY GRAMMER

GOTTA TRAVEL ON *Monument* [*USA*]. This only million seller for Billy Grammer was written by Paul Clayton, L. Ehrlich, D. Lazar and T. Six (The Weavers). Billy was born in Bento, Illinois, on 28 August 1925. He both sings and plays guitar and is a member of the Grand Ole Opry. The song is based on a traditional melody. This disc was No 4 with 20 weeks in the U.S. bestsellers.

Billy Grammer is founder of the Grammer guitar, one of the finest flat top guitars on the market, which by 1965 cost $18,000 in research and development. His 'very first and very expensive' guitar was installed into the Country Music Hall of Fame in Nashville on 1 March 1969 along with the first bass pickup for amplifying a bass electronically, designed by Everett Hull.

Billy later became a Mercury recording artist.

GEORGE HAMILTON IV

WHY DON'T THEY UNDERSTAND? *ABC-Paramount* [*USA*]. The combined sales of Britain and the U.S.A. gave a second (reputed) million seller to George Hamilton. This song is by British writers Jack Fishman (words) and Joe 'Piano' Henderson (music) and was written in 1957. This disc was No 17 and 19 weeks in the U.S. bestsellers. In Britain it was No 22 and nine weeks in the bestsellers.

BOBBY HELMS

JINGLE BELL ROCK *Decca* [*USA*]. It took five years for this number to become a second million seller for Bobby. This rock beat version of the famous Yuletide 'Jingle Bells', originally written by J.S. Pierpont in 1857, was by writers Joe Beal and Jim Boothe exactly a century later. The disc was No 6 and 21 weeks in the U.S. bestsellers.

BUDDY HOLLY

IT DOESN'T MATTER ANY MORE *Coral* [*USA*]. This second million dollar seller for Buddy was written by disc-star/songwriter Paul Anka. It was No 1 disc for three weeks in Britain (1959) and 21 weeks in the bestsellers. In the U.S.A. it was No 13 and 14 weeks in the U.S. bestsellers.

MAHALIA JACKSON

HE'S GOT THE WHOLE WORLD IN HIS HANDS backed with I BELIEVE *Columbia* [*USA*]. The great Mahalia Jackson sang 'He's Got the Whole World in His Hands' at the Newport Festival, Rhode Island, in 1958 and her recording was released around March. The song is a traditional gospel number adapted by Geoff Love, a British bandleader and well-known musician. The backing, 'I Believe', equally popular, was written in 1952 by Ervin Drake, Jimmy Shirl, Al Stillman and Irvin Graham.

Mahalia, originally with Apollo Records from 1946, signed with Columbia in 1954 who gave her a strong national publicity build-up and during this period she performed only in concert and annual gospel shows at the old Madison Square Garden, New York. In the 1960s, Miss Jackson became allied with the late Rev. Martin Luther King Jr. in the civil rights movement. One of the most poignant moments at King's funeral was her rendition of 'Precious Lord'. In the last few years of her life, she continued to perform despite a series of heart attacks and a considerable decline in the power of her voice, and appeared on several network TV shows and sang 'Just a Closer Walk With Thee' at the 1970 Newport Jazz Festival. She died on 27 January 1972 after a long illness, at Little Company of Mary Hospital, Evergreen Park, Illinois, near Chicago. Her estate was estimated at $1,000,000, an incredible sum for an artist who never sang pop tunes and refused to appear in nightclubs.

This double-sided hit disc sold well over the million in subsequent years. In the U.S.A. it reached No 69.

(Early biographical data on Mahalia Jackson, the Gospel Queen - see 1947.)

THE KALIN TWINS

WHEN *Decca* [*USA*]. The sole million seller for the Kalin Twins - Hal and Herbie - was written by Paul Evans and Jack Reardon. It was top disc for five weeks in Britain and 18 weeks in the bestsellers. In the U.S.A. it was No 5 with 15 weeks in the bestsellers.

THE KINGSTON TRIO

TOM DOOLEY *Capitol* [*USA*]. This million seller by the Trio was arranged by Dave Guard, and is a traditional American folk song that tells the story of Tom Dula who was arrested by Sheriff Jim Grayson and hanged for the murder of his girl (Laura Foster) about a century ago. The Kingston Trio is Nick Reynolds from Colorado, California, and Bob Shane and Dave Guard, both from Hawaii. All play guitar, Dave also banjo, and they were in their early twenties when this track was made for their first album 'The Kingston Trio'. It was constantly played by disc jockeys and had to be released as a single. They came together at San Francisco's Purple Onion in 1957, formed by Dave Guard, and all shared a common interest in native rhythms. They were soon signed to a long-term contract with Capitol, their albums becoming top sellers, receiving four awards in 1961 for sales totalling $4 million. By 1960 the Kingston Trio were earning $10,000 a week, doing TV, concerts and nightclubs, winning an award in 1961 for the 'Most played vocal group'. Dave Guard left the trio in 1961 and was replaced by John Stewart (from San Diego) who had written many of their arrangements and composed some of their tunes. The trio visited Britain in 1963. Their earnings have been estimated at $1 million a year. This disc sold 3,500,000 and was No 1 for one week in the U.S.A. with 21 weeks in the bestsellers. In Britain it was No 5 and 14 weeks in the bestsellers. By 1965 the Kingston Trio sold 18 million records of their 28 albums. Grammy Award for Best Country-and-Western Recording 1958. Gold Disc award, R.I.A.A., 1959.

THE KINGSTON TRIO (album) *Capitol* [*USA*]. The first of the many Kingston Trio albums, released in the U.S.A. on 2 June 1958. It received a Gold Disc award in 1960 from R.I.A.A. and was in the bestsellers for 195 weeks.

The disc is an outstanding collection of folk songs, most of which were arranged by the group's Dave Guard. It subsequently sold a million.

Contents: *Side 1* - 'Three Jolly Coachmen', *arr.* Dave Guard; 'Bay of Mexico', *arr.* Dave Guard; 'Banua', *arr.* Dave Guard; 'Tom Dooley', *arr.* Dave Guard; 'Fast Freight', Terry Gilkyson; 'Hard, Ain't It Hard', Woody Guthrie (born 1912, died 1967); *Side 2* - 'Saro Jane', *arr.* Louis Gotlieb, 'Wreck of the "John B"'', Lee Hays/Carl Sandburg (1951) (*see* 'Sloop John B' - Beach Boys, 1966, for history of song); 'Santy Anno', *arr.* Dave Guard; 'Scotch and Soda', *arr.* Dave Guard; 'Coplas', *arr.* Dave Guard; 'Little Maggie', *arr.* Dave Guard.

BRENDA LEE

ROCKIN' AROUND THE CHRISTMAS TREE *Decca* [*USA*]. Brenda recorded this in October 1958 for the seasonal market. It soon shot up the U.S.A. charts to give her her first million seller, subsequently. The disc has now become a perennial international hit. It reached No 14 in December 1960 in the U.S.A., and was No 6 in Britain. It was written by the Christmas-songwriter expert, Johnny Marks, who also wrote and published the now famous 'Rudolph the Red-Nosed Reindeer'. (See 1960 for Brenda Lee biography.)

PEGGY LEE

FEVER *Capitol* [*USA*]. This third million seller for Peggy was the second time this song by John Davenport and Eddie Cooley (who wrote it in 1956) reached a seven figure sale. A most original recording by Peggy with a mounting tension and drum effects to give it perfect atmosphere. Davenport is a pseudonym for Otis

Blackwell. This disc was No 8 and 15 weeks in the U.S. bestsellers, and No 5 and 13 weeks in the British bestsellers.

JERRY LEE LEWIS

BREATHLESS *Sun* [*USA*]. The third million seller for Jerry was written by Otis Blackwell. It was No 7 for one week in the U.S.A. and 15 weeks in the bestsellers, and was No 8 in Britain and seven weeks in the bestsellers.

HIGH SCHOOL CONFIDENTIAL *Sun* [*USA*]. This fourth million seller for Jerry Lee Lewis was written by Lewis himself in collaboration with Ron Hargrave. It came from the film of the same title in which Jerry sang it. It was No 21 in the U.S. charts and 11 weeks in the bestsellers, and was No 12 in Britain and six weeks in the bestsellers.

LITTLE ANTHONY AND THE IMPERIALS

TEARS ON MY PILLOW *End* [*USA*]. This was the sole million seller for this group consisting of Little Anthony (Anthony Gourdine), born 8 January 1941 in New York (lead singer); Sam Strain, born 9 December 1941 in Brooklyn, New York (first tenor); Ernest Wright, born 24 August 1941 in Brooklyn, New York (second tenor); and Clarence Collins, born 17 March 1941 in Brooklyn, New York (baritone-bass). The song was written by Sylvester Bradford and Al Lewis.

The Imperials grew up together in Brooklyn, and, although members of different groups, they often sang together at youth centres and on variety programmes. After graduating from high school, Anthony joined Ernest and Clarence in the Chesters group. In 1958 they were heard by Richard Barrett, who had also discovered The Isley Brothers and other groups. He changed their name to Little Anthony and The Imperials, with Sam Strain completing the quartet, and gave them a disc contract. 'Tears on My Pillow' was the result and a very big hit. The group then made appearances in major American cities, and toured Canada and Mexico. They later joined Don Costa's DCP Records and had further hits on that label in 1964.

The Imperials have also made an extensive world tour. This disc was No 4 in the U.S.A. and 19 weeks in the bestsellers.

LITTLE RICHARD

GOOD GOLLY, MISS MOLLY *Specialty* [*USA*]. This seventh million seller for Little Richard was written by Robert Blackwell and John Marascalco in 1957. It reached No 10 with 15 weeks in the U.S. bestsellers, and was No 8 in Britain, and nine weeks in the bestsellers.

LITTLE WILLIE JOHN AND HIS BAND

TALK TO ME, TALK TO ME *King* [*USA*]. This second million seller for Little Willie John was written by Joe Seneca. It was No 20 and 17 weeks in the U.S. bestsellers.

LAURIE LONDON WITH THE
GEOFF LOVE ORCHESTRA AND CHORUS

HE'S GOT THE WHOLE WORLD IN HIS HANDS *Parlophone* [*Britain*]. This disc was only a minor hit when issued in Britain, but when issued on Capitol in the U.S.A. it sold a million. Young Laurie London was 13 in 1957 when he made himself known by pushing his way through the crowd at London's Radio Show. In a few months this disc, his sole success, was the result. The song is an adaptation by Geoff Love of a gospel song. Laurie was born on 19 January 1944.

It was No 2 and 19 weeks in the U.S. bestsellers, and was No 12 in Britain with twelve weeks in the charts. Gold Disc award, R.I.A.A., 1958.

ROBIN LUKE

SUSIE DARLIN' *Dot* [*USA*]. This sole million seller for Robin was written by Luke himself. He was born in Los Angeles on 19 March 1942, and spent his childhood moving around the U.S.A. with his parents. He found a guitar easier to carry around than a piano. Since the age of eight he sang and composed, and at 16 wrote 'Susie Darlin'', inspired by his young sister, Susie. He started singing professionally in 1957, co-starring on a Honolulu TV show with Kimo McVay. This song was recorded in Hawaii and went to the top of the Honolulu hit parade 10 days after release. It was heard over their radio by Art and Dorothy Freeman, distributors for Dot Records in Cleveland, Ohio, while on honeymoon at Waikiki. They phoned Dot Records in Hollywood who bought the master disc. Robin travelled back to the U.S.A. to appear on TV shows after the success of the disc. It was No 5 and 17 weeks in the U.S.A. bestsellers, and was No 23 in Britain.

ARTHUR LYMAN AND HIS BAND
(The exotic sounds of)

TABOO (album) *Hi-Fi* [*USA*]. Disc contains: 'Taboo' by Baxter; 'Kalua', by Darby; 'Ring Oiwake', by Yoneyama and Ozawa; 'Sea Breeze', by Bush; 'Misirlou', by Roubanis, Fred Wise, Milton Leeds and Bob (S.K.) Russell (1943); 'China Clipper', by Paul Conrad; 'Sim Sim', by Baxter; 'Katsumi Love Theme', by Franz Waxman (1957); 'Caravan', by I. Mills, Duke Ellington and J. Tizol (1937); 'Akaka Falls', by Parker; 'Dahil Sayo' (traditional); 'Hilo March', by Pele. (Recorded in Henry J. Kaiser's Aluminium Dome outside the Hawaiian Village Hotel in Honolulu.)

By 1962, this album had sold close to two million. Arthur Lyman was born on the island of Kauai in 1934, the family moving to the island of Oahu after his father lost his eyesight in an accident, and settled in Makiki, a section of Honolulu. Arthur's introduction to music was a toy marimba on which he played along with Benny Goodman and Lionel Hampton records on the phonograph. He mastered every Hampton solo. By the time he was 14 (1947) he was good enough to play in a Honolulu jazz cellar, graduating from there to the Martin Denny Trio, which played music something like Lyman's but with more of a jazz feeling. While he was with Denny, Lyman discovered the value of bird calls by making some as he played. The audience answered back with all kinds of weird cries. It did in fact become Lyman's trademark when he started his own group. Lyman's group, himself and three members, played 'mistily exotic mood music' which drew the crowds to the Shell Bar in the Hawaiian Village Hotel where they played when not on tour. Their repertoire was varied and immense – over 300 songs ranging from Israeli folk to rock'n'roll. Lyman arranged them, building in parts for castanets, chimes, tambourines, cow bells and even the jawbone of an ass – so that they all took on the same exotic, oriental flavour. At intervals Lyman and his men made bird calls to give listeners the impression they were in the rain forests of Brazil. Lyman plays vibraphone, guitar, piano, drums, and also composes. The group has a delicate haunting sound that no imitators can match. Other members of band are John Kramer (bass ukelele, guitar, flute, clarinet, percussion), Alan Soares (piano, guitar, celeste) and Harold Chang (percussion, virtuoso and xylophone). Lyman became internationally known through his instrumental recording of 'Yellow Bird' in 1961.

MCGUIRE SISTERS

SUGARTIME *Coral* [*USA*]. This second million seller for the sisters was written by Charlie Phillips and Odis Echols in 1956. The disc reached No 5 with 23 weeks in the U.S. bestsellers. In Britain it was No 14, and had six weeks in the bestsellers.

CLYDE MCPHATTER

A LOVER'S QUESTION *Atlantic* [*USA*]. This second million seller for Clyde, who hails from Durham, North Carolina, was written by Brook Benton and Jimmy Williams. Clyde started his career as lead singer with Billy Ward and The Dominoes, leaving in 1953 to form his own group, The Drifters. He turned himself into a single act in 1956. This disc was No 6 in the U.S.A. A top rhythm-and-blues disc.

HENRY MANCINI AND HIS ORCHESTRA

'PETER GUNN' (album) *Victor* [*USA*]. This disc had the distinction of becoming the first million seller of a TV series soundtrack. The Hollywood-originated private eye TV series was a tremendous success and Mancini's suave and flippant score with its reed melodies and five-piece rhythm section backing was distinctive enough to be heard by itself. This album comprised 12 of the compositions by Mancini, taken from the actual soundtrack of the 39-week filmed series. Mancini was born 16 April 1924 in Cleveland and attended the music school of Carnegie Tech in Pittsburgh and the famous Juilliard School in New York where he studied with Mario Castelnuovo-Tedesco. His father was a steel worker and a flute player during his lunch hour. In 1951, Henry Mancini joined Universal Pictures as composer-arranger on the staff, and modernized, without taking away their originality, all the original Miller arrangements for the biographical film *The Glenn Miller Story* (1954), adding a few more numbers which included 'Love Theme'. He was nominated for an Oscar award. Then followed work for *The Benny Goodman Story*, *High Time* (Bing Crosby) and *Rock Pretty Baby*. During his career he also composed material for the club acts of Dinah Shore, Polly Bergen, Billy Eckstine and Betty Hutton. He spent six years as a staff arranger until 1958 when producer Blake Edwards of Spartan Productions for NBC-TV engaged him as composer-arranger-conductor for the 'Peter Gunn' series which had famous musicians playing original jazz music during the action of the filmed show. Mancini thus became the first jazz music script writer on TV, 'Peter Gunn' creating a precedent for the popularity of TV themes. It brought him a double award from the National Association of Recording Arts and Sciences for the Best Arrangement and Best Album of the Year (1958). He soon switched to films and in 1961 wrote the music for the film *Breakfast at Tiffany's* with the song 'Moon River' (words by Johnny Mercer) and received the Academy Award for this score and for the Best Film Song of that year. Mancini followed up in 1962 with another Best Film Song of the year Academy Award for *Days of Wine and Roses* (words also by Johnny Mercer). The 'Peter Gunn' album contains the following: Peter Gunn theme; Sorta Blue; The Brothers Go to Mother's; Dreamsville; Session at Pete's Pad; Soft Sounds; Fallout; The Floaters; Slow and Easy; A Profound Gass; Brief and Breezy; Not from Dixie – all composed by Mancini. By 1964 Mancini was selling a million soundtrack albums per year for Victor. This disc was in the U.S. bestseller charts for 107 weeks and sold one and a quarter million by 1965. Gold Disc award, R.I.A.A., 1959. It was No 1 for 11 weeks.

MANTOVANI AND HIS ORCHESTRA

GEMS FOREVER (album) *London/Decca* [*Britain*]. This sixth million seller album for Mantovani, sold half a million in the U.S.A. in 1958, and a million by 1965 for combined sales of both the 12-inch monaural (1958) disc originally titled 'Mantovani and Music by — —', and the stereo disc (1959).

Contents were: 'All the Things You Are' (from *Very Warm for May*), by O. Hammerstein and Jerome Kern (1944); 'True Love' (from *High Society*), by Cole Porter (1956); 'I Could Have Danced All Night' (from *My Fair Lady*), by A.J. Lerner and Fredk. Loewe (1956); 'You Keep Coming Back Like a Song' (from *Blue Skies*), by Irving Berlin (1946); 'A Woman in Love' (from *Guys and Dolls*), by Frank Loesser (1950); 'This Nearly Was Mine' (from *South Pacific*), by O. Hammerstein and Richard Rodgers (1959); 'Summertime' (from *Porgy and Bess*), by Du Bose Heyward and Geo. Gershwin (1935); 'Something to Remember You By' (from *Three's a Crowd*), by Howard Dietz and Arthur Schwartz (1930); 'Love Letters' (from *Love Letters*), by Edward Heyman and Victor Young (1945); 'The Nearness of You' (from *Romance in the Dark*), by Ned Washington and Hoagy Carmichael (1938); 'An Affair to Remember' (from *An Affair to Remember*), by H. Adamson, Leo McCarey and Harry Warren (1957); 'Hey There' (from *The Pajama Game*), by Richard Adler and Jerry Ross (1953).

Issued in the U.S.A. on the London label, and on Decca in Britain. Gold Disc award, R.I.A.A., 1961.

DEAN MARTIN

RETURN TO ME (Ritorna a me) *Capitol* [*USA*]. This third million seller for Dean, was written by Danny Di Minno (words) and Carmen Lombardo (music) in 1957. Martin sings the song in both Italian and English. The disc was No 4 and 21 weeks in the U.S. bestsellers, and No 2 with 22 weeks in Britain's bestsellers.

VOLARE (Nel blu, dipinto di blu) *Capitol* [*USA*]. The fourth million seller for Dean Martin was written by Domenico Modugno and F. Migliacci (words) and Domenico Modugno (music). The English words are by Mitchell Parish. (See Modugno, 1958, for data on this song.) The disc reached No 15 with 13 weeks in the U.S. bestsellers, and No 2 with 14 weeks in Britain's bestsellers.

JOHNNY MATHIS

JOHNNY'S GREATEST HITS (album) *Columbia* [*USA*]. This album sold half a million by 1959 and well over two million after ten years of consistent sales. The disc was in the U.S.A. charts for a record 490 weeks to 1968. It comprised the following songs: 'Chances Are', by Al Stillman and Robert Allen (1957); 'Teacher, Teacher', by Al Stillman and Robert Allen (1957); 'The Twelfth of Never', by P.F. Webster and Jerry Livingston (1957); 'When I Am with You', by Al Stillman and Ben Weisman (1957); 'Wonderful, Wonderful', by Ben Raleigh and Sherman Edwards (1956); 'It's Not for Me to Say', by Al Stillman and Robert Allen (1956); 'Come to Me', by Peter Lind Hayes and Robert Allen (1957); 'Wild Is the Wind' (from the film *Wild Is the Wind*), by Ned Washington and Dmitri Tiomkin (1958); 'Warm and Tender', by Hal David and Burt Bacharach (1957); 'No Love But Your Love', by Billy Myles (1957); 'I Look at You', by Robinson and Johnny Mathis (1958).

R.I.A.A. Gold Disc award 1959.

MITCH MILLER AND THE GANG

SING ALONG WITH MITCH (album) *Columbia* [*USA*]. This disc contains the following popular songs: *'That Old Gang of Mine', by Billy Rose, Morton Dixon, Ray Henderson (1923); *'Down by the Old Mill Stream', by Tell Taylor (1910); *'By the Light of the Silvery Moon', by Edward Madden and Gus Edwards (1909); 'You Are My Sunshine', by Jimmie Davis and Chas. Mitchell (1940); *'Till We Meet Again', by Raymond B. Egan and Richard Whiting (1918); *'Let the Rest of the World

Go By', by J. Keirn Brennan and Ernest R. Ball (1919); 'Sweet Violets', by Cy Coben and Charles Green (1951); 'I've Got Sixpence', by Box, Cox and Hall (1941); 'I've Been Working on the Railroad' (traditional); 'That's Where the Money Goes', by Walter Daniels and R.P. Lilly; 'She Wore a Yellow Ribbon', by M. Ottner (1949); 'Don't Fence Me In', by Cole Porter (1944); 'There Is a Tavern in the Town', anon. (1883); 'Show Me the Way to Go Home', by Irving King (1925); 'Bell Bottom Trousers', by Moe Jaffe (1944). Items marked (*) were originally million sheet music sellers.

This was the first 'Singalong' album to sell a million by 1962. The idea sparked off a long series of TV shows, also many more albums, Mitch having made 17 by 1963 which enjoyed very big sales. This disc was his third million seller. This disc was in the U.S. bestseller charts for 201 weeks. Gold Disc award, R.I.A.A., 1959. It was No 1 for eight weeks in the U.S.A.

MITCH MILLER AND SINGERS
CHRISTMAS SING ALONG WITH MITCH (album) *Columbia* [*USA*]. The fourth million seller for Mitch Miller was, by 1962, his second album million seller. The contents are:

'Joy to the World' (trad.); 'Hark The Herald Angels Sing' (Mendelssohn); 'What Child Is This?' (trad.); 'We Three Kings of Orient Are' (trad.); 'It Came Upon the Midnight Clear' (trad.); 'Silent Night, Holy Night' (J. Mohr and Franz Gruber); 'Deck the Halls with Boughs of Holly' (trad.); 'God Rest Ye Merry, Gentlemen' (trad.); 'O Come, All Ye Faithful' (trad.); 'The First Noel' (trad.); 'The Coventry Carol' (trad.); 'Away in a Manger' (W.J. Kirkpatrick); 'O Little Town of Bethlehem' (trad.).

Gold Disc award, R.I.A.A., 1960.

MORE SING ALONG WITH MITCH (album) *Columbia* [*USA*]. This fifth million seller for Mitch Miller had contents as follows: 'Pretty Baby', by Gus Kahn, Tony Jackson and E. van Alstyne (1916); 'Be My Little Baby Bumble Bee', by Stanley Murphy and Henry I. Marshall (1912); *'Sweet Adeline', by Richard H. Gerard and Harry Armstrong (1903); *'Let Me Call You Sweetheart', by Beth Slater Whitson and Leo Friedman (1910); *'Shine on Harvest Moon', by Nora Bayes and Jack Norworth (1908); *'For Me and My Gal', by Edgar Leslie, E. Ray Goetz and George W. Meyer (1917); *'Moonlight and Roses', by Edwin H. Lemare, Ben Black and Neil Moret (1925) (song adaptation of Lemare's famous 'Andantino' written in 1892); 'If You Were the Only Girl in the World', by Clifford Grey and Nat D. Ayer (1916); *'My Buddy', by Gus Kahn and Walter Donaldson (1922); 'Whiffenpoof Song', by Meade Minnigerode, George S. Pomeroy and Tod B. Galloway (revised by Rudy Vallee, 1936); *'Carolina in the Morning', by Gus Kahn and Walter Donaldson (1922); *'When Irish Eyes Are Smiling', by Chauncey Olcott, George Graff, Jr. and Ernest R. Ball (1912); *'My Wild Irish Rose', by Chauncey Olcott (1899); 'You Can Tell Me Your Dream, I'll Tell You Mine', by Seymour A. Rice, Al H. Brown and Chas. N. Daniels (1908); *'There's a Long, Long Trail', by Stoddard King and Zo Elliott (1913); 'In the Evening by the Moonlight', by James A. Bland (1879). (*) indicates song originally a million sheet music seller.

The disc was in the U.S. bestseller charts for 160 weeks R.I.A.A. Gold Disc award, 1960.

DOMENICO MODUGNO
NEL BLU, DIPINTO DI BLU (Volare) *Fonit* [*Italy*]. This was a big hit in Italy when first released, selling nearly a million but when issued on Decca in the U.S.A. it sold over two and a half million, and eight million collective discs. 'Volare' was the top seller of 1958. The song, written by Modugno (music) with words by Modugno and Franco Migliacci (who supplied the idea for it, an inspiration from the back of a cigarette packet). When entered for the San Remo Festival of Music, the song won and rocketed Modugno to fame. He was born in Polignano a Mare, Italy, 9 January 1928. His father, a District Head in Sicily, wanted him to be well educated in a high-class school, but after his elementary studies, Domenico took his belongings, 2,000 lire (£2) and his guitar, to seek fame in Rome. He wanted to be a film star. He sat for an entrance examination for a college for screen actors, but conscription intervened. Back in civvies again he got into a college, studying with Sophia Loren as a fellow pupil. After two years Modugno was given small parts. Cast as a balladeer in *Il Mantello Rosso* (The Red Cloak), fame came to him as a singer, then followed a contract on Italian radio. Modugno sang his own songs 'Lu piscispada' and 'La Donna Riccia' in Sicilian dialect on Walter Chiari's programme. The latter song became so popular it was recorded by many vocalists in Italy. In 1957 his entry 'Lazzarella' for the Neapolitan Song Festival won second prize, then came this great win at San Remo with 'Nel blu, dipinto di blu' in 1958. With subsequent U.S.A. and European nightclub and TV appearances, Modugno could command £2,500 a week to sing in New York. His song is better known as 'Volare' (To Fly) with English words written by Mitchel Parish. Modugno won the San Remo Festival again in 1959 with 'Piove' (It's Raining), the English words were also by Parish and the song generally known as 'Ciao, Ciao, Bambina' and for third and fourth times with 'Addio, Addio' in 1962, and 'Dio Come Ti Amo' in 1966. Modugno has been hailed as 'the music genius of Italy', and no one can compete with him as composer, singer and actor at the same time. Some of his songs now belong to Italy's folklore, and many claim that he wrote his best songs when he was unknown. He also plays piano and accordion. He wrote his first song when he was 15, a lullaby entitled 'Ninna Nanna'. His disc sales exceeded 20 million by 1965. 'Volare' was No 1 for five weeks in the U.S.A. and 16 weeks in the bestsellers, and No 10 and 12 weeks in the British bestsellers. Grammy Awards for 'Song of the Year' 1958, and Record of the Year 1958.

THE MONOTONES
BOOK OF LOVE *Argo-London* [*USA*]. The sole million seller for this vocal group was written by W. Davis, G. Malone and C. Patrick, in 1957. The disc was No 5 and 18 weeks in the U.S. bestsellers.

RICKY NELSON
BELIEVE WHAT YOU SAY *Imperial* [*USA*]. Ricky's fourth million seller was written by Johnny and Dorsey Burnette. It was No 8 and 12 weeks in the U.S. bestsellers.

POOR LITTLE FOOL *Imperial* [*USA*]. Ricky Nelson's fifth million seller was written by Shari (Sharon) Sheeley. This disc was a No 1 seller for two weeks in the U.S.A. and 15 weeks in the bestsellers, and No 4 and 13 weeks in Britain's bestsellers.

LONESOME TOWN *Imperial* [*USA*]. The sixth million seller for Ricky Nelson was this song written by Baker Knight. It reached No 7 with 18 weeks in the U.S. bestsellers.

PATTI PAGE
LEFT RIGHT OUT OF YOUR HEART (Hi-lee, hi-lo, hi-lup-up-up) *Mercury* [*USA*]. The 14th million seller for Patti, the girl with the most discs in this category. It was written by Earl Shuman (words) and Mort Garson (music), reaching No 13 with 12 weeks in the U.S. bestsellers.

THE PLATTERS
TWILIGHT TIME *Mercury* [*USA*]. This fourth million seller for The Platters was the second time the song hit seven figures (see 1950). Buck Ram, Al and Morty Nevins and Artie Dunn wrote the song in 1944. The disc was a top of charts seller in the U.S.A. for one week with 17 weeks in the bestsellers, and a top rhythm-and-blues disc. It was No 3 in Britain with 18 weeks in the bestsellers.

SMOKE GETS IN YOUR EYES *Mercury* [*USA*]. The fifth million seller for The Platters is the famous song from the 1933 stage musical *Roberta*, written by Otto Harbach (words) and composer Jerome Kern. The disc was a No 1 seller for three weeks in the U.S.A. (with 19 weeks in the bestsellers) and likewise for three weeks in Britain (1959), with 20 weeks in their bestsellers.

THE PLAYMATES

BEEP, BEEP *Roulette* [*USA*]. The sole million seller for this vocal group was written by C. Cicchetti and D. Claps. The group were Donny Conn, born 29 March 1930; Morey Carr, born 31 July 1932; and Chick Hetti, born 26 February 1930. All hail from Waterbury, Connecticut. The disc was No 4 and 15 weeks in the U.S. bestsellers.

PEREZ PRADO AND HIS ORCHESTRA

PATRICIA *Victor* [*USA*]. Prado's second million seller was an instrumental composition by him – a swing cha-cha of great rhythmic originality. The words were written by Bob Marcus. A top rhythm-and-blues disc, it was No 1 for a week and 21 weeks in the U.S. bestsellers. No 8 and 16 weeks in the British bestsellers. Gold Disc award, R.I.A.A., 1958.

ELVIS PRESLEY

DON'T backed with I BEG OF YOU *Victor* [*USA*]. The 17th and 18th million sellers for Elvis came as usual in a pair. 'Don't' was written by Jerry Leiber and Mike Stoller in 1957; 'I Beg of You' by Rose McCoy and Kelly Owens was written in 1957. The disc sold two million and 'Don't' was No 1 for five weeks in the U.S. charts, with 20 weeks in the bestsellers, and was No 2 in Britain with 11 weeks in the bestsellers.

WEAR MY RING AROUND YOUR NECK *Victor* [*USA*]. Elvis's 19th million seller – 'Wear My Ring' – was written by Bert Carroll, Russell Moody and M. Schack. It reached No 3 and 15 weeks in the U.S. bestsellers, and was No 3 in Britain, 10 weeks in the bestsellers.

ELVIS' GOLDEN RECORDS (album) *Victor* [*USA*]. This second big selling album for Elvis sold a half million by 1961, and a reputed million subsequently. It comprises most of Presley's earlier singles million sellers of 1956 and 1957. Contents: 'Hound Dog', by Jerry Leiber and Mike Stoller (1956); 'I Love You Because', by Leon Payne (1949); 'All Shook Up', by Otis Blackwell and Elvis Presley (1957); 'Heartbreak Hotel', by Mae Boren Axton, Tommy Durden and Elvis Presley (1956); 'You're a Heartbreaker', by Sallee; 'Love Me', by Jerry Leiber and Mike Stoller (1954); 'Too Much', by Lee Rosenberg and Bernard Weinman (1956); 'Don't Be Cruel', by Otis Blackwell and Elvis Presley (1956); 'That's When Your Heartaches Begin', by Fred Fisher and Billy Hill (1940); 'I'll Never Let You Go', by Jimmy Wakeley; 'Love Me Tender', by Vera Matson and Elvis Presley (1956); 'I Forget to Remember to Forget', by S.A. Kesler and Chas. Feathers (1955); 'Any Way You Want Me', by Aaron Schroeder and Cliff Owens (1956); 'I Want You, I Need You, I Love You', by Maurice Mysels and Ira Kosloff (1956).

Here was million seller No 20 for the fabulous Elvis. R.I.A.A. Gold Disc award, 1961.

'KING CREOLE' Vol. 1 (EP disc) *Victor* [*USA*]. The million sale for this disc was reported 10 years later in 1968, making a belated 58th Gold Disc for Elvis. It comprised four songs from his film *King Creole*: 'King Creole', by Jerry Leiber and Mike Stoller; 'New Orleans', by Sid Tepper and Roy C. Bennett; 'As Long as I Have You', by Fred Wise and Ben Weisman; 'Lover Doll', by Sid Wayne and Abner Silver.

HARD HEADED WOMAN *Victor* [*USA*]. This 21st million seller for Elvis came from his film *King Creole*. 'Hard Headed Woman' was written by Claude de Metrius. The disc was No 1 for two weeks in the U.S.A. with 13 weeks in the bestsellers, and was No 2 in Britain with 11 weeks in the bestsellers. Gold Disc award, R.I.A.A., 1958.

I GOT STUNG *Victor* [*USA*]. The 22nd million seller for Elvis

Presley was 'I Got Stung', by Aaron Schroeder and David Hill. This disc was No 1 for three weeks in Britain (1959). Gold Disc award for U.S. sales, where it was No 8 and 16 weeks in the bestsellers; 12 weeks in the British bestsellers.

RAY PRICE

CITY LIGHTS *Columbia* [*USA*]. The second million seller for Ray was written by Bill Anderson. A top country-and-western disc, it reached No 71 in the U.S.A. charts.

LOUIS PRIMA (jazz trumpet and vocalist) WITH HIS BAND AND KEELY SMITH (vocal)

THAT OLD BLACK MAGIC *Capitol* [*USA*]. This famous song was written by Johnny Mercer (words) and Harold Arlen (music) in 1942 for the Bing Crosby-Bob Hope film *Star Spangled Rhythm*. Louis Prima was born in New Orleans on 7 December 1911. He studied the violin for seven years as a child, and then the trumpet for three years. At 17, he got his first job as trumpeter and singer in a New Orleans theatre, then from 1930 to 1933 he shuttled from New Orleans to New York, playing with Red Nichols' band. In 1933 Prima formed his own Dixieland group which attracted attention at New York's 'Famous Door' nightclub in 1935. He then appeared in motion pictures in Hollywood, and from 1940 was leader of his own large band, which has been active ever since, appearing on stage, screen, radio and TV. He has written many songs including 'It's the Rhythm in Me' and 'Sunday Kind of Love'. He married vocalist Keely Smith (since divorced), and they set up a talent management firm to record their own masters. In 1960 they switched to the Dot label.

Keely Smith was born in Norfolk, Virginia, on 9 March 1932 and entered show business in 1950. She made her first appearance with Prima in 1953, and came to fame as a jazz-influenced vocalist

with his band. In 1964 she made an album of 12 of The Beatles' songs, and came to Britain in 1965 for TV, radio and recording work, with a hit disc of 'You're Breaking My Heart' in Britain's charts. She later recorded for the Reprise label. The disc received Grammy Award for Best Vocal (Group) Performance of 1958. The disc reached No 18 with 13 weeks in the U.S. bestsellers.

JIMMY RODGERS

SECRETLY *Roulette* [*USA*]. This fourth million seller for Jimmy Rodgers was written by Al Hoffman, Dick Manning and Mark Markwell (Hugo Peretti and Luigi Creatore). It was No 4 with 16 weeks in the U.S.A. bestsellers.

JACK SCOTT

MY TRUE LOVE backed with LEROY *Carlton* [*USA*]. The first million seller for Jack Scott was with songs both written by him. He was born on 24 January 1938 and hails from Windsor, Ontario, Canada. He also plays guitar, an instrument his father bought him when he was eight. Scott (real name Scafone) moved with his family to Detroit where he was educated. His friend Leroy Johnson was jailed for fighting, and Jack wrote 'Leroy' and played it to him in the jail. He then taped 'My True Love' and played them both to Joe Carlton of Carlton Records, who signed him to the label. The disc sold a million in a few weeks. Amateur talent contents put him on the road to fame, and he made his bandleading debut at 18, with the Southern Drifters, with an impressive following at weekly barn dances in Detroit. He was invited to appear in Detroit disc jockey Jack Eirie's programme, and his popularity spread with this and subsequent discs. 'My True Love' was No 3 and 17 weeks in the U.S. bestsellers. No 9 and 10 weeks in the British best sellers. 'Leroy' reached No 25 with 13 weeks in the bestsellers.

DAVID SEVILLE AND HIS ORCHESTRA

WITCH DOCTOR *Liberty* [*USA*]. Here was the first million seller for David Seville whose real name Ross Bagdasarian indicates his Armenian extraction. He was born in Fresno, California, on 27 January 1919, his father being a grape grower. At 19, David went to New York and became an actor in his cousin, William Saroyan's, play *The Time of Your Life* for nearly two years. Then he became assistant stage manager of another show. During this period he wrote with Saroyan the song 'Come on-a My House' (see 1951), only his second attempt at songwriting. Then Seville spent four years in the Air Force, including one year in Britain and one year in France, and so back to grape farming. He later moved with his wife and family to Los Angeles where Rosemary Clooney subsequently recorded 'Come on-a My House'. In 1956, he decided to record some of his own works and concocted the name David Seville. In January 1958 he decided to write an unusual novelty song, inspired by the title of a book *Duel with the Witch Doctor*, recorded an orchestral track at half speed, played it back at normal speed and did likewise with the words of 'Witch Doctor'. Put together on tape, the finished product was put out by Liberty Records in 24 hours, the sinister 'Witch Doctor' selling one and a half million. In September 1958, David decided to try for a Christmas novelty. He wrote a song, and made the singers animals. When he finished the recording of his voice at varying distorted speeds they sounded like chipmunks and after three months, and four separate versions, the disc was finalized. It became the 'Chipmunk Song', the then fastest selling record of all time. It sold three and a half million in five weeks, with over five million eventually, bringing both David and his Chipmunks fame and fortune. David appeared in several movies including *Rear Window*, *The Proud and the Profane*, *The Deep Six* and *The Devil's Hairpin*. He said he loved witch doctors, chipmunks, and most of all – tape machines. The Chipmunks' names were taken from three of Liberty Records' chiefs: Theodore (from Theodore Keep, chief recording engineer), Simon (from Si Waronker, president and general manager) and Alvin (from Al Bonnett, vice chairman and general manager). They were thus immortalized on disc and, because of the enormous popularity of the Chipmunks, felt it something of an honour. Total sales of Chipmunk discs to 1970 were over 30 million. This disc was No 1 for three weeks in the U.S.A. and 16 weeks in the bestsellers, and was No 11 in Britain with six weeks in the bestsellers.

Bagdasarian died on 16 January 1972.

THE CHIPMUNK SONG (Christmas Don't Be Late) *Liberty* [*USA*]. This second million seller for David Seville was due to his electronic friends 'The Chipmunks' (see David Seville – 'Witch Doctor', above, for data). It was No 1 for four weeks in the U.S.A., and sold seven million. It was 13 weeks in the U.S. bestsellers (1958) and 28 weeks up to 1962. Three Grammy

Awards, for Best Comedy Performance, Best Engineering Contribution (Novelty Recording), and Best Recording for Children in 1958.

THE SILHOUETTES

GET A JOB *Ember* [*USA*]. This sole million seller for this vocal group was the song written by them – E. T. Beal, R. W. Edwards, W. F. Horton and R. A. Lewis – in 1957. A top rhythm-and-blues disc, it was nationally No 1 for two weeks in the U.S.A. with 15 weeks in the bestsellers.

HARRY SIMEONE CHORALE

SING WE NOW OF CHRISTMAS (Re-titled THE LITTLE DRUMMER BOY in 1963) (album) *20th Century Fox* [*USA*]. This has become a standard Christmas album in the U.S.A., and has appeared on their charts every year since its debut. Through the tremendous popularity of one of the songs thereon, 'The Little Drummer Boy', the original album was given this title in 1963. Performances of the song add impetus to the album sales at Christmas time.

20th Century Fox reported on 23 October 1965 that the album had sold the incredible number of 11,267,341 copies up to that date – the bestselling Christmas album *ever*. The contents are: *Side 1* – 'Sing We Now of Christmas' (traditional); 'Angels We Have Heard on High' (traditional French carol); 'Away in a Manger' (W.J. Kirkpatrick, 1838-1921); 'What Child Is This?' (traditional carol); 'Joy to the World' (Isaac Watts, 1674-1748, G.F. Handel, 1685-1759); 'Go Tell It on the Mountain' (traditional); 'It Came Upon the Midnight Clear' (E.H. Sears, 1850); 'Good King Wenceslas' (Dr J.M. Neale, 1818-1866, 16th-century Swedish melody); 'We Three Kings of Orient Are' (Rev. J. Hopkins, 1820-1891); 'Hark the Herald Angels Sing' (Charles Wesley, 1707-1788, Mendelssohn 1809-1847); 'Bring a Torch, Isabella' (traditional French carol); 'Lo How a Rose E'er Bloomed' (traditional); 'Deck the Halls' (traditional Welsh carol); 'Christian Men Rejoice' (from the Latin, 14th-century German tune); 'Masters in this Hall' (William Morris, traditional English tune); 'O Tannenbaum' (traditional German carol); *Side 2* – 'O Holy Night' (traditional); 'The Little Drummer Boy' (Henry Onorati, Katherine Daws and Harry Simeone – written in 1958); 'Coventry Carol' (traditional English carol, 1591); 'Rise Up Shepherd' (traditional American spiritual); 'God Rest Ye Merry, Gentlemen' (traditional 16th-century carol); 'O Little Town of Bethlehem' (Bishop P. Brooks, 1835-1893, traditional melody); 'O Come Little Children' (German carol by C. von Schmid and P. Schultz); 'Ding Dong Merrily on High' (G.R. Woodward and Thoinot Arbeau, 1588); 'While Shepherds Watched' (Nahum Tate, 1696, 16th-century melody); 'The First Noel' (traditional English carol); 'The Friendly Beasts' (English Carol by Robert Davis); 'Silent Night, Holy Night' (Joseph Mohr and Franz Gruber, 1818); 'Adeste Fideles' (traditional, from the Latin); 'A Christmas Greeting' (traditional).

The album was also issued in Britain in 1959 on the Top Rank label under the title 'Salute to Christmas'. R.I.A.A. Gold Disc 1969.

DODIE STEVENS

PINK SHOELACES *Crystalette* [*USA*]. This million seller (by 1959) for Dodie was recorded when she was only 11 years old. The song was written by Mickie Grant. Dodie was born 17 February 1947 in Temple City, California. Her real name is Geraldine Ann Pasquale. The disc was No 3 and 19 weeks in the U.S. bestsellers.

THE TEDDY BEARS

TO KNOW HIM IS TO LOVE HIM *Dore* [*USA*]. This sole million seller for this vocal trio was written by Phil Spector. He is a member of and the group's arranger. Phil was born on 26 December 1940 in the Bronx, and raised in Los Angeles. He met the other two members, Annette Bard (real name Kleinbard) and

Marshall Lieb, at Fairfax High School, Los Angeles, their respective ages at this time being 18, 16 and 19. The group started out with the idea simply to enjoy a pastime. Given a recording test with the small disc company, Dore Records, they sang this song for their audition and were signed up on the spot. Their TV debut followed on the coast-to-coast Dick Clark Show with guest appearances in other important productions; then came a contract for Imperial Records. This song was inspired by a photo of the engraving 'To Know Him Was to Love Him' on Phil Spector's father's tombstone in New York's Beth David Cemetery. Phil was only nine when his father died. The family moved to California in 1953. The song came quite naturally one night in 1958 when Phil started humming the words, and realized he had changed the past to the present tense - to know him *is* to love him. After a short rehearsal with his group, they made a pilot disc with the eventual release by Dore Records and a sale of 1,200,000 in the U.S.A. Phil Spector, a talented writer, later started his own company - Philles Records - and in 1962 discovered the outstanding group 'The Crystals' and wrote songs for their sessions. He also discovered Bob B. Soxx and the Blue Jeans, and The Ronettes. This disc was No 1 for three weeks in the U.S.A. with 23 weeks in the bestsellers; No 2 and 16 weeks in the British bestsellers. Global sales are a reputed two and a half million.

CONWAY TWITTY

IT'S ONLY MAKE BELIEVE *MGM* [*USA*]. Twitty, whose real name is Harold Jenkins, had his professional name chosen by his agent; the 'Conway' part came from a road map. This song was written by Twitty and Jack Nance. Twitty's father piloted a Mississippi River ferry out of Helena, Arkansas, and taught him to play the guitar at a very early age. At 10, Twitty sang his first solo on the radio. At 12 he formed his own band - the Phillips Country Ramblers. Later, in the Services, Twitty formed The Cimmarons and had a programme over Tokyo radio. On discharge he formed his own band for one-night stands over the U.S.A. He met his manager, Don Seat, during Army service. Twitty sent Seat some tapes which led to his MGM contract. Rock'n'roll singer Twitty wrote 'It's Only Make Believe', his first million seller, in seven minutes during an intermission at the Flamingo Lounge in Hamilton, and it is said to have netted him $400,000, plus big money for TV appearances, and film roles.

Twitty's movie debut was in *Sexpot Goes to College* followed by *Platinum High School* (*Rich, Young and Deadly* was the British title) and *College Confidential*. Twitty was born in 1935 in Mariana, Arkansas. This disc was No 1 for two weeks in the U.S.A. with 21 weeks in the bestsellers, and for five weeks in Britain (1959), with 15 weeks in their bestsellers. Global sales four million.

VAN CLIBURN (piano) WITH KIRIL KONDRASHIN AND SYMPHONY ORCHESTRA

PIANO CONCERTO NO. 1 - TCHAIKOVSKY (album) *Victor* [*USA*]. This was the first classical album to sell a million. It sold half a million in its first year of release. Cliburn was born on 12 July 1934 in Kilgore, Texas, and could read music and play the piano before he was three years old. Taught by his mother (a former concert pianist) as a youngster, he went to New York in 1951 to study with Mme Rosina Lhevinna. He won the Texas State Prize in a piano competition in 1947 at the age of 13, and the National Musical Festival in 1946. In 1952 Cliburn won two awards, the G.B. Dealey award in Dallas and the Kosciuszko Foundation Chopin award. In 1953, while a student at Juilliard, he won the concerto competition there, and in 1954 won the important U.S. piano competition, the Edgar M. Leventritt Foundation award, which earned him his debut with the New York Philharmonic. Van Cliburn's greatest triumph was winning the Tchaikovsky Piano Competition in the U.S.S.R. in April 1958, with the subsequent album breathlessly awaited by music lovers. As concert artist, his appearances are sell-outs, and as a personality he attracts attention wherever he performs. Van Cliburn is a perfectionist, and records a whole work rather than a section at a time as some artists do. His full name is Harvey Lavan (Van) Cliburn. This disc had sold two million globally by 1965. Gold Disc award R.I.A.A. 1961. It was 97 weeks in the U.S. bestseller charts to 1961, and a further 200 weeks to end of 1970. Grammy Award for Best Classical (Instrumental Solo with Orchestra) of 1958.

RITCHIE VALENS

DONNA backed with LA BAMBA *Del-Fi* [*USA*]. 'Donna' was written by Ritchie Valens and 'La Bamba' (traditional Spanish song) sung by Valens in Spanish was written by William Clauson. Ritchie was born on 13 May 1941, and raised in Pacoima, a suburb of Los Angeles. At an early age he sang and played the guitar at school assemblies. Del-Fi Records signed him up in 1958 at the age of 17, his rock'n'roll style being in tune with the teenagers. Valens' first disc was 'Come On, Let's Go', written by Ritchie himself, which sold 750,000, then followed this disc, which was his sole million seller. His career came to a tragic end when he was killed in an air crash with Buddy Holly and Big Bopper on 3 February 1959. His real name was Richard Valenzuela. 'Donna' was No 2 and 28 weeks in the U.S. bestsellers. 'La Bamba' was No 22 and 15 weeks in the bestsellers; No 29 in Britain.

BILLY VAUGHN AND HIS ORCHESTRA

LA PALOMA *Dot* [*USA*] *Teldec* [*Germany*]. Vaughn's third million seller sold a million in Germany alone, where his recordings are very popular. The tune is the famous tango written by Sebastian Yradier in 1877. The million sale was achieved by 1963. The disc was No 26 and 10 weeks in the U.S. bestsellers.

RUSTY WARREN (comedienne)

SONGS FOR SINNERS (album) *Jubilee* [*USA*]. This disc of risqué comedy material was the first million seller for Rusty. Billed as 'The Knockers Up Girl' (the title of her second album), she was born Ilene Goldman in 1931 in New York, and raised in Milton, Massachusetts. She studied at New England Conservatory of Music to be a concert pianist, starting to learn piano at the age of six. After her first year at the Conservatory, Rusty switched to popular music, playing at local clubs and hotels, adding a song here and there in her act. She then added jokes and funny lines, and began writing her own routines, and soon successfully toured the U.S.A. The turning point in her career came when Stanford Zucker, the agent, saw her perform, became her agent, and brought her to California to perform. Her first big success came at the Pomp Room in Phoenix, where she cut this, her first album. Her albums have sold well over eight million and made her a $5,000-a-week nightclub star. She holds a degree from the New England Conservatory of Music, and once played the piano under the direction of the famous Arthur Fiedler.

ROGER WILLIAMS (piano)

TILL *Kapp* [*USA*]. This second million seller for Roger was written in 1956 by Carl Sigman (words) and Charles Danvers (music). The disc was No 27 and 17 weeks in the U.S. bestsellers.

CHUCK WILLIS

WHAT AM I LIVING FOR? *Atlantic* [*USA*]. This was a sole million seller for Chuck, the rhythm-and-blues singer. It was the top rhythm-and-blues disc of 1958. The song was written by Fred Jay and Art Harris. Chuck died in 1958, soon after the release of this disc. He was born in Atlanta, Georgia, on 31 January 1928, and died on 10 April 1958. The disc was No 15 and nine weeks in the U.S.A. bestsellers.

SHEB WOOLEY

THE PURPLE PEOPLE EATER *MGM* [*USA*]. This sole million seller for Sheb (by 1960) was written by him, a most original 'rock' number about 'the thing a'comin' out of the sky'. Sheb was born on 10 April 1921, and raised on his father's farm in Erick, Oklahoma. His early years centred around rodeo riding and country music. When his interest in country music developed, he began entertaining in clubs and rodeos throughout Oklahoma. He formed his own western band in 1946 and toured the south-west with a resultant three-year booking on a radio network. MGM signed him to a recording contract in 1948. A screen test in 1951 got him a role in Errol Flynn's film *Rocky Mountain*. He has since appeared in nearly 50 pictures. His role as Pete Nolan in the popular TV 'Rawhide' series of 105 episodes earned him wide acclaim. Sheb also recorded under the name of Ben Colder. He has written several songs and is one of show business's most versatile personalities. 'Purple People Eater' was No 1 for six weeks in the U.S.A. and 13 weeks in the bestsellers, and No 12 in Britain with eight weeks in the bestsellers.

1959

VARIOUS ARTISTS (on two albums)

60 YEARS OF MUSIC AMERICA LOVES BEST (Volumes I and II) *Victor* [*USA*]

Side	Title	Artist	Author/Composer
1	Vesti la giubba (*Pagliacci*)	Caruso (vocal)	Leoncavallo (1892)
	Whispering	Paul Whiteman orchestra	Schonberger (1920)(*)
	Variations on themes from *Carmen*	Horowitz (piano)	Bizet-Horowitz (1875)
	Ramona	Gene Austin (vocal)	Gilbert/Wayne (1927) (*)
	Prelude in C sharp minor	Rachmaninoff (piano)	Rachmaninoff (1898)
	Indian Love Call (Rose Marie)	N. Eddy/J. Macdonald (vocal)	Harbach, Hammerstein/Friml (1924) (*)
	Ave Maria	Marian Anderson (vocal)	Schubert
2	Minuet in G	Paderewski (piano)	Paderewski (1888)
	Begin the Beguine	Artie Shaw orchestra	Cole Porter (1935)
	Hora Staccato	Heifetz (violin)	Dinicu-Heifetz (1930)
	Jalousie	Fiedler and Boston Pops orchestra	J. Gade (1926)
	Liebesfreud	Kreisler (violin)	Kreisler (1910)
	Sunrise Serenade	Glenn Miller orchestra	Lawrence/Carle (1938)
	Blue Danube Waltz	Stokowski and Philadelphia Symphony orchestra	J. Strauss (1867 (*)
3	And the Angels Sing	Benny Goodman orchestra	Mercer/Elman (1939)
	Take the 'A' Train	Duke Ellington orchestra	Strayhorn (1941)
	Piano Concerto No 1	Freddy Martin orchestra	Tchaikovsky
	There Are Such Things	T. Dorsey orchestra with Frank Sinatra (vocal)	Adams, Bear and Mayer (1942)
	Polonaise in A flat	Jose Iturbi (piano)	Chopin
	Bluebird of Happiness	Jan Peerce (vocal)	Heyman, Davies, Harmatti (1940)
4	Peg o' My Heart	Three Suns (vocal)	Bryan/Fisher (1913) (*)
	Ritual Fire Dance	Arthur Rubenstein (piano)	de Falla (1924)
	Bouquet of Roses	Eddy Arnold (vocal)	Nelson and Hilliard (1948)
	Be My Love	Mario Lanza (vocal)	Cahn/Brodszky (1950)
	Prelude (Act 3) (*Lohengrin*)	Toscanini and NBC Symphony orchestra	Wagner (1848)
	Cherry Pink and Apple Bossom White	Perez Prado orchestra	Larue-Louiguy (1950)
	Naughty Lady of Shady Lane	Ames Bros (vocal)	Tepper and Bennett (1954)
	Canadian Sunset	Hugo Winterhalter orchestra	Gimble/Heywood (1956)
	Day-O (Banana Boat)	Harry Belafonte (vocal)	Attaway and Burgess (1956)

Several of the titles on these two discs of '60 Years of Music' sold a million as singles discs. Those marked (*) are known to have sold a million in sheet music through the years. The dates given are those when the work was first written or published. Sale of half a million of the collective discs was reached in 1960 and the million sale reputed since. Vol. 1 was in the U.S.A. bestseller list for 78 weeks and Vol. 2 for 40 weeks. R.I.A.A. Gold Disc award, 1960.

ORIGINAL THEATRE CAST WITH PAT SUZUKI, MIYOSHI UMEKI, ROSE QUONG, LARRY BLYDEN, KEYE LUKE, JUANITA HALL, CONRAD YAMA, ANITA ELLIS, P. ADIARTE, ARABELLA HONG, ED KENNY, JACK SOO AND SALVATORE DELL'ISOLA ORCHESTRA

'FLOWER DRUM SONG' (album) *Columbia* [*USA*]. This disc contains the following all written by Oscar Hammerstein II (words) and Richard Rodgers (music): Overture; You are Beautiful; A Hundred Million Miracles; I Enjoy Being a Girl (sung by Pat Suzuki); I Am Going to Like It Here (sung by Miyoshi Umeki); Entr'acte; Grant Avenue (sung by Pat Suzuki and Ensemble); Love Look Away; At the Celestial Bar; Gliding Through My Memoree; The Other Generation; Sunday (sung by Larry Blyden and Pat Suzuki); Wedding Parade and Finale.

'Flower Drum Song', set in San Francisco's Chinatown, is another great Hammerstein and Rodgers musical, oriental in flavour. Produced on 1 December 1958, it ran for 600 performances at the St James Theatre, New York, the book being by Hammerstein and Joseph Fields. It also came to Britain with a different cast in 1960 (Palace Theatre, London, 24 March). While not such a big success as the writer and composer's previous musicals, the songs were very popular, and this album stayed in the bestseller charts in the U.S.A. for 137 weeks (two and a half years), selling half a million by 1962 and a reputed million globally subsequently.

Gold Disc award, R.I.A.A., 1962. It was No 1 for three weeks in the U.S.A.

PAUL ANKA

LONELY BOY *ABC-Paramount* [*USA*]. This third million seller for Paul Anka was written by Paul in 1958. It was No 1 for four weeks in the U.S.A. and 15 weeks in the bestsellers, and No 3 and 17 weeks in the British bestsellers.

PUT YOUR HEAD ON MY SHOULDER *ABC-Paramount* [*USA*]. This fourth million seller for Paul Anka was also written by Paul in 1958. It reached No 2 with 18 weeks in the U.S. bestsellers, and No 7 with 12 weeks in the British bestsellers.

FRANKIE AVALON

VENUS *Chancellor* [*USA*]. Frankie's second million seller was written by Ed Marshall. It was No 1 for five weeks in the U.S.A. and 17 weeks in the bestsellers. No 16 in the British charts and six weeks in bestsellers.

JUST ASK YOUR HEART *Chancellor* [*USA*]. A third million seller for Frankie Avalon was written by Diane De Nota, Peter Damato and Joe Ricci. It reached No 7 and was 16 weeks in the U.S. bestsellers.

WHY *Chancellor* [*USA*]. The fourth million seller for Frankie was written by Bob Marcucci (words) and Peter de Angelis (music). The tune was later the subject of much litigation on both sides of the Atlantic, it being claimed to be similar to the oldie 'In a Little Spanish Town' of 1926. The English High Court ruling was that though there was a definite degree of similarity between the two tunes, similarity itself was not sufficient to constitute an infringement. The plaintiffs had to prove that there was a conscious or subconscious act of copying. The court ruled that there was no infringement of copyright. 'Why' was a No 1 disc seller in the U.S.A. for one week with 16 weeks in the bestsellers, and also a big hit for Britain's Anthony Newley; in Britain this disc reached No 20.

LAVERN BAKER

I CRIED A TEAR *Atlantic* [*USA*]. This third million seller for LaVern was written by Al Julia and Fred Jacobson (Fred Jay) in 1958. It reached No 6 with 21 weeks in the U.S. bestsellers.

CHRIS BARBER AND HIS JAZZ BAND
(Monty Sunshine, clarinet)

PETITE FLEUR (Little Flower) *Pye-Nixa* [*Britain*]. This was a sole million seller for Britain's jazz trombonist, Chris Barber, and his band, which also brought his clarinet player Monty Sunshine to the fore. The disc achieved the million in the U.S.A. by 1960 when released there on the Laurie label. The tune was written by Sidney Bechet in Paris in 1952, who, besides being a great exponent of the soprano saxophone, was also a clarinettist of the highest order. Bechet was born in New Orleans in the latter part of the last century – some say on 14 May 1897. He was one of the greatest jazz players. He played in Russia; was one of the first jazzmen to leave America; made discs with Louis Armstrong and Clarence Williams; and in the 1930s he made an historic series of discs under the title 'Sidney Bechet and his New Orleans Footwarmers'. After the last war he settled permanently in Paris – his popularity being enormous in France. Bechet died in 1959.

Chris Barber was born on 17 April 1930 in Welwyn Garden City, Hertfordshire, and after the war played trombone around London clubs. He left Cy Laurie's band in 1949, formed his own band in 1950 but had to disband it, and joined Ken Colyer's band which he took over when Ken left in 1954. Barber set up small groups within the band, one of which was a skiffle group which included Lonnie Donegan. Barber's band soon developed into Britain's top traditional jazz band and his success both on discs and in person on the Continent resulted in 'Petite Fleur' being released as a single, taken from his album, 'Chris Barber Plays, Vol. 3', recorded in 1956. The disc single was put out in Germany, where it was a big seller. The Americans decided it might have a good sale in the States. When released there it stormed the bestseller lists. Chris in fact did not play on this number; it was a solo clarinet feature for Monty Sunshine. Barber's earliest discs were on Esquire in 1953. His band was the first British combo to be televised live in the U.S.A. on the Ed Sullivan Show (March 1959).

The disc was No 5 and 15 weeks in the U.S. bestsellers, and No 3 with 24 weeks in Britain's bestsellers.

HARRY BELAFONTE

BELAFONTE AT CARNEGIE HALL (2 albums) *Victor* [*USA*]. *Side 1* – Introduction; 'Darlin' Cora', by Fred Brooks; 'Sylvie', by Huddie Ledbetter and Paul Campbell (The Weavers); 'Cotton Fields', by C.C. Carter; 'John Henry', by Paul Campbell (The Weavers); 'Take My Mother Home', by Paul Johnson; *Side 2* – 'The Marching Saints', by C.C. Carter; 'Day-O', by Belafonte, Burgess and Attaway (1955); 'Jamaica Farewell', traditional, arranged by Lord Burgess (1955); 'Man Piaba', by Belafonte and Jack K. Rollins; 'All My Trials', by Rita Green and C.C. Carter; *Side 3* – 'Mama Look a Boo Boo', by Lord Melody (1957); 'Come Back Liza', by Lord Burgess and Bill Attaway; 'Man Smart (Woman Smarter)', by Belafonte and Jack Seagal; 'Hava Nageela', Israeli folk song, arranged by Belafonte and Lorin; 'Danny Boy', traditional, arranged F.E. Weatherly (1913); 'Merci bon Dieu', by Frantz Casseus; *Side 4* – 'Cu-cu-ru-cu-cu-paloma', by Tomas Mendez; 'Shenandoah', traditional; 'Matilda, Matilda,' by Harry Thomas (1953).

This is Belafonte's sixth million seller (third album). It sold half a million by 1960 and a million subsequently of the collective discs. It was recorded in New York's famous Carnegie Hall. The disc stayed in the U.S. bestsellers for 168 weeks, with five weeks at No 1.

Gold Disc award R.I.A.A. 1961. Grammy Award for Best Engineering Contribution (Popular Recording) 1959.

BROOK BENTON

IT'S JUST A MATTER OF TIME backed with SO MANY WAYS *Mercury* [*USA*]. This was a first million seller for Benton (real name Benjamin Franklin Peay). 'It's Just a Matter of Time' was written by Benton with Clyde Otis and B. Hendricks in 1958. 'So Many Ways' was written by Bobby Stevenson in 1958.

Benton was born in Camden, South Carolina, on 19 September 1931 and educated there at Jackson High School. He learned to sing with a local gospel group. At 12 he was delivering milk for a local dairy, then later in New York he worked for a garment centre pushing a hand-truck, and later as truck driver. During this time he wrote songs, and appeared in minor nightclubs and made some discs for Epic and Vik labels. He wrote about 300 songs and some were recorded by such famous stars as Nat King Cole, Clyde McPhatter and Roy Hamilton. It was Clyde Otis, artists' manager of Mercury Records, who gave Benton his biggest break by recording this double-sided hit disc. After this came personal appearances and more recording, his albums becoming big sellers. Songs either recorded or written by 'velvet-toned' Benton or written by him for other stars sold over 15 million by 1962. This disc was one of the top rhythm-and-blues sellers of 1959. Benton appeared on British TV in 1963. 'It's Just a Matter of Time' was No 3 and 18 weeks in the U.S. bestsellers. 'So Many Ways' reached No 6 and was in the bestsellers for 16 weeks.

BILL BLACK AND HIS COMBO

SMOKIE (Part 2) *Hi* [*USA*]. This first million seller for Bill Black's Combo was composed by Black himself. Bill, who lived in Memphis, where he was born 17 September 1926, was a bass player, and with guitarist Scott Moore played on most of Elvis Presley's discs until Elvis entered the U.S. Army. He then formed a group of his own, with Carl McVoy (piano), Martin Wills (sax), Reggie Young (guitar) and Jerry Arnold (drums). This combo evolved a distinctive rock-a-boogie style resulting in a hit with this disc (Parts 1 and 2, Part 2 being the popular side). Bill later added an organ to the group. In 1960 he won a poll as 'Most Played Instrumental Group'.

This was a No 1 rhythm-and-blues seller of 1960. It reached No 17 and was 12 weeks in the U.S. bestsellers.

Bill Black died on 21 October 1965.

THE BROWNS

THE THREE BELLS *Victor* [*USA*]. This was a first million seller for this trio of Jim, Maxine and Bonnie Brown, then aged 25, 27, and 22 respectively, in 1959. The two sisters and brother hail from Pine Bluff, Arkansas, and have sung together since childhood. Jim and Maxine won an amateur radio contest in Little Rock in 1952 which led to a booking on the country radio series 'Louisiana Hayride'. A long concert tour followed and then Bonnie made the group a trio, when they became featured artists on the 'Ozark Jubilee' TV show (1955). This song was composed in 1945 by the French writer Jean Villard (Gilles) as 'Les Trois Cloches'; it was also a big hit for the famous French artiste Edith

Piaf, and also for Les Compagnons de la Chanson. In 1948, Bert Reisfield wrote this disc's English lyric, and later, in 1948, Dick Manning wrote a lyric entitled 'While the Angelus Was Ringing'. Les Compagnons visited Britain in 1951 with their English version, 'The Jimmy Brown Song'. The Browns' disc however proved to be the biggest hit of all, and was No 1 for four weeks in the U.S.A. with 17 weeks in the bestsellers, and No 6 with 13 weeks in Britain's bestsellers. A top country disc.

EDD BYRNES AND CONNIE STEVENS

KOOKIE, KOOKIE, LEND ME YOUR COMB *Warner* [*USA*]. The sole million seller for this duo was written by Irving Taylor, from the TV series '77 Sunset Strip' in which Edd Byrnes played the role of Kookie. He was born on 30 July 1933 in New York. Before becoming an actor he was an ambulance driver, machine shop hand and delivery truck driver. His first professional engagement was in a play at New York's Ziegfeld Theatre. His first TV appearance was as a gunman in 'Cheyenne' and his first Hollywood engagement came in 1956. Edd had both TV and disc contracts with Warner, also an outside business interest in a U.S. comb manufacturing firm. His nickname is of course 'Kookie' but his real name Eddie Breitenberger. Connie Stevens was born on 8 August 1938 and hails from Brooklyn, where she was educated at high school and later at the Hollywood Professional School. Her real name is Concetta Ann Ingolia. She first entered show business at 16, making her film debut in *18 and Anxious* in 1957. She got her big break in 1959 when Jerry Lewis signed her as his leading lady in his film *Rock-a-bye Baby*. Then TV played a big part in her career with a guest appearance in the 'Tenderfoot' TV series and other TV shows, including some appearances with Edd Byrnes in '77 Sunset Strip'. Connie then appeared regularly in the 'Hawaiian Eye' TV series and in more films as well as recording for the Warner label. This disc was No 4 and 13 weeks in the U.S. bestsellers, and No 27 in Britain and eight weeks in the bestsellers.

FREDDY CANNON

TALLAHASSIE LASSIE *Swan* [*USA*]. The first million seller for Freddie Cannon was this song written by Frank C. Slay, Jr., Bob Crewe and Frederick A. Picariello. Freddy (real name Freddy Picariello) was born on 4 December 1940 in Lynn, Massachusetts, educated there in high school and started to think about a musical career in his middle teens. He learned to play the guitar, then formed his own band to play at school functions. He was spotted by Boston disc jockey Jack McDermott who groomed him and arranged a recording test with Swan Records who signed him up. 'Tallahassie Lassie' which he wrote with Slay and Crew was his first waxing. Then came a big break at a concert at the famous Hollywood Bowl. From this followed TV dates and engagements abroad in Britain, Holland, South Africa, Japan, Scandinavia and Australia. Known to his friends as 'Boom Boom Cannon' he was billed in the U.S.A. as 'the last of the rock stars'. He appeared in the film *Just for Fun* made in Britain in 1962. This disc was No 6 and 15 weeks in the U.S. bestsellers, and No 17 in Britain and eight weeks in the bestsellers.

WAY DOWN YONDER IN NEW ORLEANS *Swan* [*USA*]. The second million seller for Freddy was a revival of the famous song of 1922 written by Henry Creamer and J. Turner Layton (of the famous Layton and Johnstone team who were such a big vaudeville attraction in Britain in the 1920s). The song was a million sheet music seller years ago. The disc got to No 3 in the U.S. charts and was 15 weeks in the bestsellers, and No 3 with 16 weeks in Britain's bestsellers.

RAY CHARLES

WHAT'D I SAY (Parts 1 and 2) *Atlantic* [*USA*]. The first million seller for Ray Charles was written by Ray himself. Ray Charles Robinson was born in Albany, Georgia, on 23 September 1932 and was blinded by illness at six and orphaned at 15. He went to school just long enough to learn Braille, and at 17 formed his own trio (playing piano) which toured the U.S.A. He settled for a while in Seattle playing a Nat King Cole-ish style until well into his 20s. He had his own sponsored TV show in Seattle. Then in a flash of insight, he decided to be himself. He began singing and playing his mixture of rhythm and blues, jazz and shouting gospel music, or 'soul music'. His big disc break came when he was signed to Atlantic Records for which he made several hit singles and albums. Ray is one of the best blues singers around, and although he still sings the same 'race music', there is no modern singer who has not learned something from him. He also plays alto sax, clarinet and organ and has earned the name of 'The Genius'. In a nationwide concert tour in 1963 he had capacity attendances. Ray has also played concerts in Paris and London and he had his own supporting artists, a 16-piece band, The Raelets (led by Margie Hendrix) and singer Jean King. In 1960 he switched to the ABC-Paramount label with further outstanding disc successes. By 1963, Ray was a leading record-album seller and concert performer in jazz, blues and popular music, and he is also one of the few blacks ever to make a big hit in country-and-western music. His disc sales in 1962 were $8 million. (This disc was recorded on 19 February 1959 and was released in June of that year.) A top rhythm-and-blues disc, it reached No 6 with 15 weeks in the U.S. bestsellers.

JIMMY CLANTON

SHIP ON A STORMY SEA *Ace* [*USA*]. This third million seller for Jimmy was written by him in conjunction with Cosimo Matassa, Seth David and Malcolm Rebennack.

THE COASTERS

CHARLIE BROWN *Atco* [*USA*]. The third million seller for The Coasters was written by the very successful team of Jerry Leiber and Mike Stoller. It reached No 2 with 15 weeks in the U.S.A. bestsellers, and No 6 and 12 weeks in Britain's bestsellers.

POISON IVY *Atco* [*USA*]. The fourth million seller for The Coasters was also written by Jerry Leiber and Mike Stoller and proved yet another big hit for these songwriters. A top rhythm-and-blues disc, it was No 7 and 16 weeks in the U.S. bestsellers, and No 15 in Britain, with seven weeks in the bestsellers.

RUSS CONWAY, D.S.M. (swing piano)

SIDE SADDLE *Columbia* [*Britain*]. The year 1959 was a vintage one for British recording artists, and a particular triumph for Russ Conway who had no fewer than seven big hits. This disc of 'Side Saddle' was No 1 in Britain for three weeks, and 30 weeks in the bestsellers, and his follow-up, 'Roulette', also for three weeks. Both were Conway's own compositions. His third hit was 'China Tea'. All three topped the sheet music bestsellers. 'Side Saddle' is said to have sold a million discs globally.

Russ (real name Trevor H. Stanford) was born on 2 September 1927 in Bristol, and actually entered show business at the age of 10. He was educated at Merrywood Primary School, Bristol, and then took advanced studies at a local commercial college. Before entering show biz professionally, he was a plumber's mate, shop salesman, civil servant, barman, travelling salesman and solicitor's junior clerk. At 15 (1942) he joined the Merchant Navy as galley boy for two years, then became a signalman in the Royal Navy for three years. He lost the first joint of the third finger on his right hand in the first month in the Navy, when he was operating a bread slicer. He re-signed for a further two years and won the Distinguished Service Medal. In 1951 he rejoined the Merchant Navy until discharge in 1955. While at Naval Training School at 14, he played the bugle, cornet, French horn, euphonium and E flat bass. He also plays the organ, but the piano is definitely his forte. Russ is entirely self-taught in music. He sang with a church choir in his home town, and at 10 made his first public appearance with an accordion band at Bristol's Ideal Home Exhibition. Noted dancer Irving Davies heard Russ playing in a club around 1957 and introduced him to a recording manager at EMI. He made his first discs in April of that year,

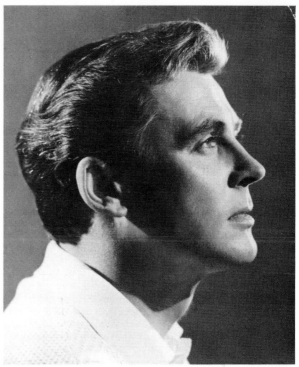

and had a seasonal bestseller with 'Party Pops' (1957). Russ accompanied many British variety stars including Lita Roza, Dennis Lotis, Dorothy Squires, Joan Regan and Shani Wallis. He also flew to Malta to accompany Gracie Fields in 1956. His first solo variety appearance was at the Metropolitan Theatre, London, in October 1957, followed by TV in November on the 'Jack Jackson Show' on ATV, and radio in 'Midday Music Hall' in 1958. He had his own TV series with Granada, which ran for nine months, and has made many major TV appearances, notably with BBC's 'Billy Cotton Band Show'. Russ recorded a number of popular albums and EPs, and was first to receive a Silver Disc award for sale of 250,000 albums (in 1961) in Britain.

With Norman Newell, his recording manager, he wrote the music for the West End production *Mr Venus* (1958) and the score for 'Beauty and the Beast', a TV pantomime, in 1956.

He has a most pleasant personality and smile and is still a favourite with people of all ages, playing popular rhythmic numbers and semi-classical and theme tunes.

BOBBY DARIN

DREAM LOVER *Atco* [*USA*]. This third million seller for Darin was written by Bobby himself. This disc was a chart topper in Britain for four weeks. In the U.S.A. it was No 2 and 17 weeks in the bestsellers, and 19 weeks in Britain's bestsellers.

MACK THE KNIFE *Atco* [*USA*]. The fourth million seller for Bobby Darin was a fabulous success with over two million sales in all. It was one of the top discs of 1959. Bobby first recorded this driving version of the famous song from Bertolt Brecht and Kurt Weill's *Threepenny Opera* for an album entitled 'That's All' and it was released as a single later in the year to become a million seller in 1960. It became Bobby's trademark. (See Hyman, 'Moritat'; 1956, for details of the song.) This disc was No 1 for nine weeks in the U.S.A. with 26 weeks in the bestsellers and a chart topper in Britain for two weeks with 17 weeks in the bestsellers. Grammy Award for Record of the Year (1959).

TOMMY DEE AND CAROL KAY

THREE STARS *Crest* [*USA*]. This song was written by Tommy Dee, who is a country-and-western disc jockey in the Nashville, Tennessee, area, as a tribute to the three disc stars

Buddy Holly, Ritchie Valens and the Big Bopper (J.P. Richardson) who were all killed in an air crash on 3 February 1959. It is sung by Carol Kay with a narration by Tommy Dee. The disc is estimated to have sold a million by 1966, reaching No 11 with 12 weeks in the U.S. bestsellers.

MARTIN DENNY AND HIS ORCHESTRA
QUIET VILLAGE *Liberty* [*USA*]. This sole million seller for Martin Denny was an instrumental work by Les Baxter, the conductor-arranger-composer, who is also a million seller on discs with his own orchestra. Martin Denny was born on 10 April 1911 and hails from New York City. He is a composer-arranger, and was an executive for Liberty Records in Honolulu, Hawaii. The tune, originally written in 1951, was part of Les Baxter's album 'Le Sacre du Sauvage'. Combination of band: Denny (piano), August Colon (bongos), John Kramer (bass) and Arthur Lyman (vibes). They played at the famous Hawaiian Village in Hawaii, their oriental music providing a great attraction for tourists. Kramer also played for Arthur Lyman (see 1958). This disc was No 4 and 16 weeks in the U.S. bestsellers.

DION AND THE BELMONTS
A TEENAGER IN LOVE *Laurie* [*USA*]. The first million seller for Dion and his group The Belmonts was written by Jerome 'Doc' Pomus and Mort Shuman. Dion Di Mucci was born on 18 July 1939 in The Bronx, New York, and educated there. He started singing at the age of five, his musical interest undoubtedly arising from the fact that his father was a singer and his mother in a stage act. He made his first public appearance on the Paul Whiteman TV show in 1954. Originally a single act, he was teamed with a group, The Timberlanes, on the Mohawk label. Laurie Records then signed him and brought him in as lead singer with The Belmonts - Fred Milano, second tenor; Carlo Mastangelo, baritone; Angel d'Aleo, first tenor. They sang together from 1957 until 1960 when Dion became a solo performer and disc artist with further big hits in 1961. He made his film debut in *Teenage Millionaire* and appeared in *Twist Around the Clock*. He has also toured Australia and appeared on TV, radio and stage in Britain (1961). Dion also plays guitar. In 1963 he took up a stage career. This disc was No 5 and 15 weeks in the U.S. bestsellers, and was No 28 in Britain.

CARL DOBKINS, JR
MY HEART IS AN OPEN BOOK *Decca* [*USA*]. Carl's only million seller was written by Hal David (words) and Lee Pockriss (music) in 1957. Carl was born in January 1941 and comes from Cincinnati. He sings and also plays banjo, and is interested in dancing and songwriting. The disc was No 3 and 24 weeks in the U.S. bestsellers.

FATS DOMINO
BE MY GUEST *Imperial* [*USA*]. The 22nd million seller for Fats Domino was written by him in collaboration with John Marascalco and Tommy Boyce. It was No 8 and 14 weeks in the U.S. bestsellers, and No 11 with 12 weeks in the British bestsellers.

LONNIE DONEGAN
DOES YOUR CHEWING GUM LOSE ITS FLAVOUR? (on the bed-post over night) *Pye* [*Britain*]. This title became a second million seller for Britain's Lonnie Donegan by 1961. It reached the million after being put out on the Dot label in the U.S.A. in 1961. The song is an oldie, originally 1924, entitled 'Does the Spearmint Lose Its Flavour on the Bed Post Over Night?', written by Billy Rose and Marty Bloom (words) and Ernest Breuer (music). 'Chewing gum' was substituted for 'spearmint' as in Britain there might have been some proprietary difficulties. Lonnie found the song in an old Boy Scouts' song book, it being a number that he used to sing as a boy. It reached No 5 in the U.S. charts (1961), and was 11 weeks in the bestsellers, and was No 3 with 12 weeks in the British bestsellers.

DICKEY DOO AND THE DONT'S
TEAR DROPS WILL FALL *Swan* [*USA*]. The sole million seller for this group was written by Dickey Doo and Marion Smith. The disc reached No 61.

THE DRIFTERS
THERE GOES MY BABY *Atlantic* [*USA*]. This was a second million seller for this group which originally sang with Clyde McPhatter in 1953. The group comprised Ben E. King (lead), Elsberry Hobbs (bass), Doc Green, Jr. (baritone), Charlie Thomas (tenor) and Reggie Kimber (guitar). The Drifters were formed in late 1953, with Clyde McPhatter as lead singer. Their first disc 'Money, Honey' for Atlantic was a big success. After McPhatter went into the U.S. Forces (1955), the remaining Drifters continued recording and playing at theatres, becoming big favourites on tour, through appearances in 'The Biggest Stars of 1957-1958' and with the Dick Clark Caravan in the U.S.A. Then came this big seller disc. As each member of the group had drifted from one vocal group to another before they became a team, they chose 'The Drifters' as their group name. This song was written by B. Nelson (Ben E. King), L. Patterson and G. Treadwell. The disc reached No 2 and was 19 weeks in the U.S. bestsellers.

Ben E. King left the group in 1960 to become a successful solo artist on the Atco label. Real name Benjamin Earl Solomon.

PAUL EVANS AND THE CURLS
SEVEN LITTLE GIRLS (Sitting in the back seat) *Guaranteed* [*USA*]. This sole million seller for Paul Evans was written by Bob Hilliard (words) and Lee Pockriss (music). It is a most original automobile comedy ditty. Paul Evans' home town is Queens, New York. He is a songwriter, radio and TV commercial writer and producer, folk and nightclub performer. The disc was No 9 and 18 weeks in the U.S. bestsellers, and was No 25 in Britain.

EVERLY BROTHERS
TAKE A MESSAGE TO MARY *Cadence* [*USA*]. The sixth million seller for Everly Brothers was written by Felice and Boudleaux Bryant. It reached No 16 with 13 weeks in the U.S. bestsellers, and was No 20 in Britain, and nine weeks in bestsellers.

('TIL) I KISSED YOU *Cadence* [*USA*]. The seventh million seller for the Everlys was written by Don Everly. It was No 4 and 16 weeks in the U.S. bestsellers, and No 2 and 15 weeks in the British bestsellers.

FABIAN

TIGER *Chancellor* [*USA*]. This was the sole million seller for Fabian, whose real name is Fabiano Forte. The song was written by Ollie Jones. Fabian was born in Philadelphia on 6 February 1943 and educated there. A chance meeting with Bob Marcucci and Peter De Angelis of Chancellor Records resulted in their having his voice trained and then signing him up. After one or two disc flops they sent him on a road tour (1957) with a big publicity campaign, and rock'n'roll singer Fabian's discs, 'I'm a Man' and 'Turn Me Loose', shot into the hit parade. Then came 'Tiger' and the adulation of the teenagers. He was then signed to a film contract, making his debut in *Hound Dog Man* (1959) followed by *High Time* with Bing Crosby, *North to Alaska* with John Wayne (both 1960) and *Love in a Goldfish Bowl* (1961). This disc was No 3 and 13 weeks in the U.S. bestsellers.

THE FALCONS (rhythm-and-blues vocal group)

YOU'RE SO FINE *Unart* [*USA*]. The Falcons, a now-defunct group, were one of the top groups in the Detroit area in this year. It included Eddie Floyd, Mack Rice, Joe Stubbs (brother of Levi Stubbs of Four Tops fame), Lance Finney and Willie Schofield. This song was written by Schofield with Lance Finney and Bob West, and the disc subsequently sold a million and became a standard rhythm-and-blues number.

The group later included Wilson Pickett (discovered by Schofield), who wrote many hits for the group and later became a solo artist of international fame.

The Falcons started in 1956 in Montgomery, Alabama, as a gospel group, singing, travelling and making records for seven years. They moved gradually into rhythm-and-blues. This disc was No 17 and 20 weeks in the U.S. bestsellers.

ERNIE FIELDS AND HIS ORCHESTRA

IN THE MOOD *Rendezvous* [*USA*]. This was a sole million seller for Fields and his rock'n'roll group. The song is a revival of the 1939 Glenn Miller hit, written by Andy Razaf (words) and Joe Garland (music). Ernie hails from Tulsa, Oklahoma. Fields' personal instrument is the trombone. The disc was No 4 and 19 weeks in the U.S. bestsellers, and was No 13 in Britain and six weeks in the bestsellers.

THE FLEETWOODS

COME SOFTLY TO ME *Dolton* [*USA*]. This was a first million seller for this trio, which comprised Gretchen Diane Christopher, born 29 February 1940, and Barbara Laine Ellis, born 20 February 1940, both from Olympia, Washington, and Gary Robert Troxel, born 28 November 1939 from Centralia, Washington, all aged 19 when this disc was recorded. The song was written by them. The trio got together first at high school where they discovered an almost perfect form of popular harmonization. Soon came a disc contract with full-time recording and further big hits. The disc was No 1 for four weeks in the U.S.A. and 16 weeks in the bestsellers, and was No 6 in Britain, and eight weeks in the bestsellers.

MISTER BLUE *Dolton* [*USA*]. The second million seller for The Fleetwoods was this song written by Dewayne Blackwell. It was a No 1 disc in the U.S.A. for one week, and 20 weeks in the bestsellers.

EMILE FORD WITH THE CHECKMATES
(Emile's three brothers on sax, bass and guitar, with John Cuffly drums)

WHAT DO YOU WANT TO MAKE THOSE EYES AT ME FOR? *Pye-Nixa* [*Britain*]. The sole million seller for Emile Ford was a revival of the 1916 song written by Joe McCarthy, Howard Johnson and James V. Monaco. Emile was born on 16 October 1937 in Nassau, in the Bahamas. His family sailed to Britain where Emile was educated at Paddington Technical College, London. He learned to play the guitar while at school, then made regular appearances in London coffee bars, developing as a singer. After winning a talent contest at Soho Fair with his group he was signed by Pye Records with radio and TV dates. He also plays the piano, violin and electric bass. This disc was a chart topper in Britain for six weeks, and 26 weeks in the bestsellers.

FRANKIE FORD

SEA CRUISE *Ace* [*USA*]. This was a sole million seller for Frankie Ford, the vocalist. He was born on 4 August 1940 and hails from Fretna, Louisiana. He won a scholarship to nearby South-eastern College, Hammond, and formed a band with a group of other students. This song was written by Smith and Frankie Ford. The disc reached No 14 with 17 weeks in the U.S. bestsellers.

CONNIE FRANCIS

MY HAPPINESS *MGM* [*USA*]. The third million seller (second solo) for Connie was originally composed by Betty Peterson (words) and Borney Bergantine (music) in 1933. It was also a million seller disc in 1948 (see John and Sandra Steele). The accompaniment is by the David Rose orchestra. It reached No 2 with 18 weeks in the U.S. bestsellers, and No 4 and 15 weeks in the British bestsellers.

LIPSTICK ON YOUR COLLAR backed with FRANKIE *MGM* [*USA*]. The song 'Lipstick' was written by Edna Lewis (words) and George Goehring (music). 'Frankie' was written by Howard Greenfield (words) and Neil Sedaka (music). This disc gave Connie her fourth million sale. 'Lipstick' reached No 5 with 17 weeks in the U.S. bestsellers, and No 3 and 16 weeks in Britain's bestsellers. 'Frankie' was No 9 and 15 weeks in the U.S. bestsellers.

AMONG MY SOUVENIRS *MGM* [*USA*]. This fifth million seller (fourth solo) for Connie Francis is a revival of 1927, written by Edgar Leslie (words) and Britain's Horatio Nicholls (music). It was a million sheet music seller when first published. The disc was No 7 and 15 weeks in the U.S. bestsellers, and No 11 and 10 weeks in Britain's bestsellers.

FREDDY (Quinn)

DIE GITARRE UND DAS MEER (The guitar and the sea) *Polydor* [*Germany*]. The third million seller for Freddy was written by Aldo Pinelli (words) and Lotar Olias (music) for the film of the same title, starring Freddy.

WILBERT HARRISON

KANSAS CITY *Fury* [*USA*]. The sole million seller for Wilbert was written by Mike Stoller (words) and Jerry Leiber (music). This song was No 1 for two weeks in the U.S.A. and 16 weeks in the bestsellers, and was originally written in 1952 under the title 'K.C. Loving'. Harrison was born 21 January 1929 in the U.S.A.

BUDDY HOLLY

THE BUDDY HOLLY STORY (album) *Coral* [*USA*]. Released in April 1959, two months after Buddy Holly's tragic death on 3 February 1959, this consistent selling memorial album sold the million by August 1970 when a Gold Disc was presented to his parents in his home town of Lubbock, Texas. The disc was in the bestseller charts for 166 weeks to March 1964 and contains most of Buddy's big hits.

Contents: 'Raining in My Heart', by Boudleaux and Felice Bryant (1958); 'Early in the Morning', by Woody Harris and Bobby Darin (1958); *'Peggy Sue', by Jerry Allison and Norman Petty (1957); *'Maybe Baby', by Norman Petty and Buddy Holly (1958); 'Every Day', by Charles Hardin (Buddy Holly) and Norman Petty (1957); 'Rave On', by Sunny West, Bill Tilghman and Norman Petty (1958); *'That'll Be the Day', by Jerry Allison,

Buddy Holly and Norman Petty (1957); 'Heartbeat', by Norman Petty and Montgomery (1958); 'Think It Over', by J. Allison, Buddy Holly and Norman Petty (1958); 'Oh, Boy', by Sunny West, Bill Tilghman and Norman Petty (1957); 'It's So Easy', by Buddy Holly and Norman Petty (1958); *'It Doesn't Matter Any More' (Buddy Holly with The Crickets), by Paul Anka (1958). (*) denotes was million seller singles disc.

A second album, 'The Buddy Holly Story Vol. 2', was released in 1960. (See Buddy Holly, 1957, for biography.)

JOHNNY HORTON
BATTLE OF NEW ORLEANS *Columbia* [*USA*]. This top country-and-western disc of 1959 (and first million seller for Johnny Horton) reached seven figures within seven weeks of its release. The song, written by Jimmy Driftwood in 1957, tells of the battle of 1814 and the decisive victory of the Americans against the British at New Orleans. It made Johnny the most talked about singer in the U.S.A. (The original melody is said to be an 1815 fiddle tune, entitled 'The Eighteenth of January'; which was composed in celebration of the victory.) He was born in Tyler, Texas, on 30 April 1927 of a farming family. He was educated at Gallatin, Texas, and later Seattle University, where he majored in petroleum engineering. Horton began writing songs as a hobby at university; won a talent contest; then worked on radio in Pasadena. Johnny then became the star of 'Louisiana Hayride', the top-rate country-and-western show in Shreveport, Louisiana, every Saturday, touring on week-days with his varied repertoire of folk and pop songs at nightclubs, dances and concerts. He wrote much of his own material and was an accomplished guitarist. He was killed in an auto crash on 5 November 1960. This disc started a craze for semi-historical country-and-western ballads or 'saga' songs in the U.S.A. This disc was No 1 there for six weeks and 21 weeks in the U.S. bestsellers. No 16 and four weeks in the British bestsellers.

Grammy Awards to Composer – Song of the Year (1959), and Best Country-and-Western Recording (1959). Gold Disc award R.I.A.A. 1966.

THE IMPALAS
SORRY (I ran all the way home) *Cub* [*USA*]. The sole million seller for this rock'n'roll group was written by Harry Giosasi and Artie Zwirn in 1958. The group was discovered by Giosasi. The disc reached No 2 with 18 weeks in the U.S. bestsellers, and No 28 in Britain.

THE ISLEY BROTHERS
SHOUT *Victor* [*USA*]. This song, written by the Isley Brothers, was the direct outcome of a performance by them of 'Lonely Teardrops' which they were singing at the Howard Theatre,

Washington, D.C., in the summer of 1959. In one line of the song, the leader, in a stroke of inspiration yelled 'You know, you want to make me SHOUT'. It electrified the crowd and produced pandemonium. RCA promotion man Howard Argie Bloom who was present told them to report at the studios, and backed by guitarist Joe Richardson, Professor Herman Stephens, organist of the boys' family church, plus six studio musicians, they recorded 'Shout'. It went on to sell a million, and became second only to 'The Twist'. (See Isley Brothers, 1962, for further data.) It reached No 47 and was nine weeks in the U.S. bestsellers.

STONEWALL JACKSON
WATERLOO *Columbia* [*USA*]. This sole million seller for Jackson was written by John Loudermilk and Marijohm Wilkin. Jackson was born in 1932 and hails from a backwoods district of North Carolina. Songwriting became his hobby as a youth while plucking away on an improvised guitar. He joined the U.S. Navy in 1949 as a cabin boy, aged 17, and made himself proficient on a guitar he borrowed from an officer. After discharge, he made nightclub and personal appearances and was in Grand Ole Opry. Stonewall's home town is Nashville, Tennessee. A top country-and-western disc, it reached No 4 with 16 weeks in the U.S. bestsellers, and No 24 in Britain. Jackson was born on 6 November 1932 in Moultrie, Georgia.

JOHNNY AND THE HURRICANES
RED RIVER ROCK *Warwick* [*USA*]. The sole million seller for this rock'n'roll instrumental group is a 'beat' version of the well-known cowboy song 'Red River Valley' (traditional), arranged by Tom King, Ira Mack and Fred Mendelsohn. The group's use of an organ (Hammond chord model) set the trend for that instrument with other groups. The personnel of the group are Johnny Paris (sax), Paul Tesluk (organ), Lionel 'Butch' Mattice (bass) and David York (guitar), all from Toledo, and Lynn Bruce (drums) from Detroit. They were all in their late teens when this disc was made. The group came together to entertain at local high school dances, and during the summer were very popular with rock'n'roll fans in Toledo's Pearson Park. Then came club dates and local TV, plus a contract with Warwick Records and their first hit 'Crossfire', soon followed by 'Red River Rock' and other successes. They made tours in the U.S.A. and visited Britain in 1963. This disc was No 5 and 17 weeks in the U.S. bestsellers, and No 3 and 16 weeks in the British bestsellers.

MARV JOHNSON
YOU GOT WHAT IT TAKES *United Artists* [*USA*]. Marv Johnson made his first recording 'Come to Me' in Detroit in 1959 where he was discovered by Berry Gordy, Jr. and this was the start of the now famous Tamla-Motown organization built up by Gordy. Marv's disc was the first Tamla release, although at the time it was not actually a label. Gordy got United Artists to release it nationally, as was also the case with 'You Got What It Takes'. The disc became a big hit in 1960 with a million sale. It also registered in Britain where it was No 5 in the charts in 1960. In the U.S.A. it reached No 10 with 22 weeks in the bestsellers, and was 16 weeks in Britain's bestsellers.

The song was written by Berry Gordy, Jr., Gwen Gordy and Tyran Carlo (Raquel Davis) and the disc is now considered a standard rhythm-and-blues seller.
(See Johnson, 1960, for biography.)

JERRY KELLER
HERE COMES SUMMER *Kapp* [*USA*]. Jerry's only million seller was this song which he wrote. He was born in Arkansas on 20 June 1938, the family moving to Tulsa when he was six. He formed 'The Lads of Note' quartet in his teens, joined the Tulsa Boy Singers and toured the Midwest. He then won a talent contest organized by bandleader Horace Heidt which led to a resident vocalist job with Jack Dalton's orchestra. After nine months as a disc jockey in Tulsa, Keller quit and went to New

York (1956), taking a job as clerk with an oil company, studying singing and trying to crash the disc world by cutting demo discs. Pat Boone, who attended the same church as Jerry, gave him a list of people to see, one being Marty Mills who became his manager, with the resultant Kapp recording. This disc was a chart topper in Britain for one week. In the U.S.A. it was No 14 and 13 weeks in the bestsellers; 14 weeks in the British bestsellers.

WINK MARTINDALE WITH
MILT ROGERS ORCHESTRA

DECK OF CARDS *Dot* [*USA*]. This sole million seller for Winston ('Wink') Martindale is an ingenious monologue - the story of a soldier bringing out a pack of cards in church. When brought before the marshal, the soldier explains the religious significance of each card, and that a deck of cards acts as his Bible, prayer book, and almanac. The music was composed and words written and adapted by T. Texas Tyler in 1948, who had recorded it at the time. Wink was born in 1933, and hails from Jackson, Tennessee. He began his career as a disc jockey in Jackson at 17. At that time he sang in the church choir. He sent a tape of his voice to a Memphis radio station and was soon working there as a music librarian, then as a disc jockey, at 4 a.m. each day, attending Memphis State in between to get his B.A. degree in speech and drama. After meeting Randy Wood, the Dot Records chief, he cut this disc and recited his way to fame. As a regular church-goer he was able to make the disc with real feeling. He moved to Hollywood where he had his own TV show - 'Teenage Dance Party'. This disc also had considerable success in Britain in 1963. In the U.S.A. it was No 7 and 17 weeks in the bestsellers, and was No 18 in Britain with eight weeks in the bestsellers. It was No 5 and 21 weeks in the British bestsellers in 1963.

JOHNNY MATHIS

MISTY *Columbia* [*USA*]. This fifth million seller for Johnny was written in 1955 by Johnny Burke (words) and the famous pianist Erroll Garner (music). The tune was first introduced as an instrumental in 1954 by The Erroll Garner Trio. It reached No 12 with 17 weeks in the U.S. bestsellers, and No 12 and 13 weeks in Britain's bestsellers.

MERRY CHRISTMAS (album) *Columbia* [*USA*]. The sixth million seller (second album) for Johnny Mathis contained the following songs and carols: 'Winter Wonderland', by Dick Smith and Felix Bernard (1934); 'Christmas Song', by Robt. Wells and Mel Torme (1946); 'Sleigh Ride', by M. Parrish and Leroy Anderson (1950); 'Blue Christmas', by B. Hayes and J. Johnson (1948); 'I'll Be Home for Christmas', by Kim Gannon, Walter Kent and Buck Ram (1943); 'White Christmas', by Irving Berlin (1942); 'O Holy Night', traditional; 'What Child Is This?', traditional; 'The First Noel', traditional; 'Silver Bells', by Jay Livingston and Ray Evans (1950); 'It Came Upon the Midnight Clear', by Rev. E. H. Seers and R. S. Willis (*c*. 1850); 'Silent Night, Holy Night', by Joseph Mohr and Franz Gruber (1818).
Gold Disc award R.I.A.A. 1960.

HEAVENLY (album) *Columbia* [*USA*]. The seventh million seller for Johnny, another fine collection of great songs. The disc stayed in the bestsellers for 235 weeks and comprised the following songs: *Side 1* - 'Heavenly', by Sidney Shaw and Burt F. Bacharach (1959); 'Hello, Young Lovers' (from *The King and I*), by O. Hammerstein II and Richard Rodgers (1951); 'A Lovely Way to Spend an Evening' (from film *Higher and Higher*), by Harold Adamson and Jimmy McHugh (1943); 'A Ride on a Rainbow' (from *Ruggles of Red Gap* TV musical), by Leo Robin and Jule Styne (1957); 'More Than You Know' (from *Great Day*), by William Rose, Edward Eliscu and Vincent Youmans (1929); 'Something I Dreamed Last Night' (from *George White's Scandals of 1939*), by Herb Magidson, Jack Yellen and Sammy Fain (1939); *Side 2* - 'Misty', by Johnny Burke and Erroll Garner (1955); 'Stranger in Paradise' (from *Kismet*), by Robert Wright

and George Forrest (1953), based on a theme by Borodin; 'Moonlight Becomes You' (from film *Road to Morocco*), by Johnny Burke and Jimmy Van Heusen (1942); 'They Say It's Wonderful' (from *Annie Get Your Gun*), by Irving Berlin (1946); 'I'll Be Easy to Find', by Bart Howard (1959); 'That's All', by Alan and Bob Haymes (1952) (originally 'C'est tout', an instrumental number).
Gold Disc award R.I.A.A. 1960.

MITCH MILLER AND THE GANG

STILL MORE SING ALONG WITH MITCH (album) *Columbia* [*USA*]. The sixth million seller for Mitch Miller (and fourth album million seller) included the following numbers: 'In a Shanty in Old Shanty Town', by Joe Young, Little Jack Little and John Siras (1932); 'Smiles', by J. Will Callahan and Lee Roberts (1917) (*); 'I'll Be with You in Apple Blossom Time', by Neville Fleeson and A. von Tilzer (1920) (*); 'Memories,' by Gus Kahn and Egbert van Alstyne (1915) (*); 'When Day is Done', by Bud G. De Sylva and Robt. Katscher (1926) (*); 'Good Night, Sweetheart', by J. Campbell, R. Connelly and Ray Noble (1931); 'Tip-toe Thru' The Tulips With Me', by Al Dubin and Joe Burke (1929); 'Daisy (a bicycle built for two)', by Harry Dacre (1892); 'Put on Your Old Grey Bonnet', by Stanley Murphy and Percy Wenrich (1902) (*); 'I'm Just Wild about Harry', by Eubie Blake and Noble Sissle (1921); 'The Band Played On', by John E. Palmer and Chas. B. Ward (1895); 'Oh You Beautiful Doll', by A. Seymour Brown and Nat D. Ayer (1911); 'Hinky Dinky Parlay Voo', by Al Dubin, Irving Mills, Jimmy McHugh and Irwin Dash (1924); 'She'll Be Comin' Round the Mountain', traditional hillbilly song; 'Beer Barrel Polka', by Lew Brown, V. Timm and J. Vejvoda (1934); 'When You Were Sweet Sixteen', by James M. Thornton (1898) (*); 'Silver Threads Among the Gold', by E.E. Rexford and H.P. Danks (1873) (*).
(*) indicates that the number was also a million sheet music seller in its day.
This disc was in the U.S. bestseller charts for 122 weeks. Gold Disc award R.I.A.A. 1960.

PARTY SING ALONG WITH MITCH (Album) *Columbia* [*USA*]. The seventh million seller for Mitch Miller (and fifth album million seller) was in the U.S. bestseller charts for 92 weeks. A Gold Disc award from R.I.A.A. in 1962. The disc is a collection of very popular vintage songs of the 19th and early 20th centuries.
Contents: 'I Love You Truly', by Carrie Jacobs Bond (1906) (*); 'In the Shade of the Old Apple Tree', by Harry H. Williams and E. van Alstyne (1905) (*); 'In the Good Old Summer Time', by Ren Shields and George Evans (1902), arr. Jimmy Carroll (*); 'The Sweetest Story Ever Told', by R.M. Stultz (1892), arr. Jimmy Carroll; 'Meet Me Tonight in Dreamland', by Beth Slater Whitson and Leo Friedman (1909) (*); 'I Wonder Who's Kissing Her Now', by Frank R. Adams, Will M. Hough, Harold Orlob and Joseph E. Howard (1900) (*); 'Good Night, Ladies', traditional song (circa 1859), arr. Jimmy Carroll; 'Home, Sweet Home', by John Howard Payne and Sir Henry Bishop (1823), arr. Jimmy Carroll (*); 'My Gal Sal', by Paul Dresser (1905) (*); 'Cuddle Up a Little Closer', by Otto Harbach and Karl Hoschna (1908); 'Ramblin' Wreck from Georgia Tech.', traditional college song, arr. Jimmy Carroll; 'A Bird in a Gilded Cage', by Arthur J. Lamb and Harry von Tilzer (1900) (*); 'Wait Till the Sun Shines, Nellie', by Andrew B. Sterling and Harry von Tilzer (1905) (*); 'Oh What a Pal was Mary', by Edgar Leslie, Bert Kalmar and Pete Wendling (1919) (*); 'Harrigan', by George N. Cohan (1907); 'School Days', by Will D. Cobb and Gus Edwards (1907) (*); 'Sweet Rosie O'Grady', by Maud Nugent (1896), arr. Jimmy Carroll (*); 'The Sidewalks of New York', by Charles B. Lawlor and James W. Blake (1894), arr. Jimmy Carroll (*); 'I'll Take You Home Again, Kathleen', by Thomas P. Westendorf (1876), arr. Jimmy Carroll.
(*) denotes song was a million sheet music seller.

GUY MITCHELL

HEARTACHES BY THE NUMBER *Columbia* [*USA*]. The sixth million seller for Guy was written by Harland Howard. This disc was No 1 for two weeks in the U.S.A. and 20 weeks in the bestsellers, and No 5 and 15 weeks in Britain's bestsellers.

RICKY NELSON

NEVER BE ANYONE ELSE BUT YOU backed with IT'S LATE *Imperial* [*USA*]. This seventh million seller for Ricky, 'Never Be Anyone' was written by Baker Knight while 'It's Late' was written in 1958 by Dorsey Burnette. 'Never Be Anyone' was No 6 and 16 weeks in the U.S. bestsellers, and No 14 and 10 weeks in the British bestsellers. 'It's Late' was No 9 and 13 weeks in the U.S. bestsellers, and No 3 with 20 weeks in the British bestsellers.

JUST A LITTLE TOO MUCH *Imperial* [*USA*]. The eighth million seller for Ricky Nelson was written by Johnny Burnette. It reached No 9 with 13 weeks in the U.S. bestsellers, and No 11 in Britain and eight weeks in the bestsellers.

SANDY NELSON (drums)

TEEN BEAT *Original Sound* [*USA*]. 'Teen Beat' provided a first million seller for Sandy (real name Sander L. Nelson) who was born on 1 December 1938 in Santa Monica, California. He made his first appearances with local rock'n'roll shows as drummer with the Kip Tyler Band. He found work in nearby Hollywood playing on sessions as a studio musician. While on a session with Original Sound he asked if he could record a little drum epic called 'Teen Beat'. He made the disc, literally packed with 'beat', which was a big success. His TV debut was on the 'Dick Clark Show', and he made a tour of the Midwest and visited Britain in late 1959. He also plays piano, bass and guitar. This number was written by Sandy Nelson and A. Egnoian. It reached No 4 with 16 weeks in the U.S. bestsellers, and No 9 and 12 weeks in the British bestsellers.

PHIL PHILLIPS

SEA OF LOVE *Mercury* [*USA*]. This sole million seller for Phil Phillips was written by George Khoury and Phil Battiste. Phil was born on 14 March 1931 and hails from Lake Charles, Louisiana. He was a bellhop, then served in the U.S. Navy. Phillips started in local radio and TV as a member of the Gateways Quartet. His real name is Phillip John Baptiste, and he wrote this song with the assistance of his personal manager George Khoury.

A top rhythm-and-blues disc, it was No 2 and 18 weeks in the U.S. bestsellers.

FRANCK POURCEL AND HIS ROCKIN' STRINGS

ONLY YOU *Pathe-Marconi* [*France*]. 'Only You' is a very original version of the 1955 song written by Buck Ram and Ande Rand, by the French string orchestra leader whose discs were popular from around 1956. This song was also a million seller for The Platters (see 1955). Pourcel sold 15 million discs by 1970. 'Only You' was released by Capitol in the U.S.A. and sold over two million. Pourcel studied music at the Paris Conservatoire, his instrument being the violin. He was a great admirer of Stephane Grappelli and Eddie South, and tried to play like Grappelli for a time. His first successful disc was 'Blue Tango' in 1952. Since then, he has won many musical awards, conducted in New York, Los Angeles, Denver, Hollywood and San Francisco. This disc was No 9 and 16 weeks in the U.S. bestsellers.

ELVIS PRESLEY

A FOOL SUCH AS I backed with I NEED YOUR LOVE TONIGHT *Victor* [*USA*]. This 23rd million seller for Elvis in fact sold two million. The song was written by Bill Trader in 1952. 'I Need Your Love Tonight' was written by Sid Wayne and Bix Reichner. 'A Fool Such As I' was No 1 in Britain for five weeks; No 2 in the U.S.A. with 15 weeks in the bestsellers.

'I Need Your Love Tonight' was No 4 and 13 weeks in the U.S. bestsellers. The disc was 15 weeks in Britain's bestsellers.

A BIG HUNK O' LOVE backed with MY WISH CAME TRUE *Victor* [*USA*]. This 24th million seller for Presley sold two million copies and was No 1 in the U.S.A. for two weeks. 'Big Hunk o' Love' was written by Aaron Schroeder and Sid Wyche; 'My Wish Came True' by Ivory Joe Hunter (in 1957). 'A Big Hunk o' Love' was 14 weeks in the U.S. bestsellers, and No 4 with 9 weeks in Britain's bestsellers. 'My Wish Came True' reached No 12 with 11 weeks in the bestsellers in the U.S.A.

LLOYD PRICE

STAGGERLEE *ABC-Paramount* [*USA*]. Price wrote his second million seller in conjunction with Harold Logan in 1958. This was a top rhythm-and-blues disc of 1959, and No 1 seller for four weeks in the U.S.A. Lloyd heard an old American folk song called 'The Ballad of Stack-O-Lee' while in the services in the Far East, and rewrote it in modern style. Reaction with the servicemen was so great that he decided to record it on his discharge from the Forces. The song is the story of two gamblers who meet with a tragic end. Released in 1958, it was 21 weeks in the U.S. bestsellers, and No 7 and 14 weeks in the British bestsellers.

I'M GONNA GET MARRIED *ABC-Paramount* [*USA*]. This third million seller for Lloyd Price was also written in conjunction with Harold Logan. A top rhythm-and-blues disc, it reached No 3 with 14 weeks in the U.S. bestsellers, and was No 23 in Britain.

PERSONALITY (You've got) *ABC-Paramount* [*USA*]. Price's four million seller was written by the same team of Logan and Price. A top rhythm-and-blues disc, it was No 2 and 19 weeks in the U.S. bestsellers, and No 9 and 10 weeks in the British bestsellers.

MARVIN RAINWATER

MY LOVE IS REAL *MGM* [*USA*]. This was the third million seller for Marvin, the cowboy vocalist.

MY BRAND OF BLUES *MGM* [*USA*]. Rainwater's fourth million seller was his own composition.

HALF BREED *MGM* [*USA*]. The fifth million seller for Marvin Rainwater was written by John D. Loudermilk.

DELLA REESE

DON'T YOU KNOW *Victor* [*USA*]. Della was born Dellareese Taliaferro in Detroit on 6 July 1932, and sang in a choir at six years of age and with a group headed by the great gospeller

Mahalia Jackson at 13. At Wayne University she formed her own gospel group before going out as a solo cabaret artist and on radio and TV. This prominent gospel singer visited Britain in 1959 and 1962. This song, Della's only million seller, was based on 'Musetta's Waltz' by G. Puccini (1896). The lyrical and musical adaptation was by Bobby Worth. A top rhythm-and-blues disc, it was No 2 and 18 weeks in the U.S. bestsellers.

JIM REEVES

HE'LL HAVE TO GO *Victor* [*USA*]. Sales of this subsequently topped three million. This fourth million seller for Jim was one of the top country discs of 1960. The song was written by Joe and Audrey Allison. The disc reached No 2 in the U.S. charts (1960) with 23 weeks in the bestsellers, and No 12 and 30 weeks in the British bestsellers.

CLIFF RICHARD (with The Drifters)

LIVING DOLL *Columbia* [*Britain*]. Here was the first million seller for Britain's top solo artist. The song was written by Britain's top songwriter Lionel Bart (composer of the tremendously successful stage musical *Oliver*). Cliff (real name Harry Roger Webb) was born on 14 October 1940 in Lucknow, India, and educated at Stanley Park Road Secondary School, Carshalton, Surrey, and Cheshunt Secondary School, Hertfordshire. He became an office clerk after leaving school and learned to play the guitar. Cliff made his first public appearance with a vocal group, The Drifters – himself (vocal), Terry Smart (drums), and Ian Samwell (guitar) – during a Youth Fellowship dance in Cheshunt in 1954; the group became very popular locally. They later appeared at the '2 I's' coffee bar in Soho where Cliff found Jet Harris (bass), Hank Marvin (guitar) and Bruce Welch (guitar) and replaced his original drummer by Tony Meehan. These four became 'The Shadows', later to be a sensational instrumental group with their own disc hits. Various engagements at London cinemas followed and in 1958, agent George Canjou saw Cliff appearing at the Shepherd's Bush Gaumont and fixed a recording test. Cliff's first disc was 'Move It' backed with 'Schoolboy Crush' which soon put Cliff and his Drifters into the British hit parade. Cliff made his TV debut in September 1958 and started his first major one-night tour in October 1958 with America's Kalin Twins. His variety debut at the Metropolitan, London, followed in November. The group changed its name to The Shadows to avoid confusion with the U.S. group 'The Drifters'. Ian Samwell left to concentrate on songwriting, before The Shadows were formed (1958). In 1959, Cliff appeared in the film *Serious Charge* and sang *Living Doll* which, when released as a single, topped the hit parade and sold a million. Since then, he and The Shadows have topped the bill in every major theatre in Britain, made overseas tours to America, South Africa, Scandinavia, Australasia and on the Continent of Europe. Cliff was top of the poll as Best British Male Singer from 1959 to 1966 and for 1970. He appeared in the film *Espresso Bongo* (1960) and starred in *The Young Ones* (1961), and *Summer Holiday* – to win a similar honour in 1963. He has had his own TV series and starred in every major TV variety show, also appeared at three Royal Variety Performances. His discs are automatic hit paraders. This disc was a chart topper in Britain for six weeks. In the U.S.A. it was No 30 and 13 weeks in the bestsellers, and 23 weeks in the British bestsellers. Recorded 25 May 1959. Cliff received an O.B.E. in January 1980.

IVO ROBIC

MORGEN (Morning) *Polydor* [*Germany*]. This first million seller for Ivo Robic was the first German sung tune to break into the top position of the American Hit Parade when released there on the Laurie label. The song was written and composed by Peter Mosser. Later an English version entitled 'One More Sunrise' was written by Noel Sherman. Ivo was born in 1927 and hails from Zagreb, Yugoslavia, completing his education at the Music Conservatory. He had a 15-piece band and was a star before going to Germany to record 'Morgen' for his first Polydor

disc. He had made about 50 records for the Jugoton label in Yugoslavia previously. Robic sings in German, French, Italian, Spanish and English and his native tongue; he plays the piano, clarinet, sax, flute and double bass. Robic has made personal appearances in the U.S.A. and all over the world. The disc reached No 13 with 17 weeks in the U.S. bestsellers, and was No 23 in Britain.

MARTY ROBBINS

EL PASO *Columbia* [*USA*]. Grammy Award for 'Best Country-and Western Performance' 1960. This second million seller for Marty was written by him. The disc was No 1 for two weeks in the U.S.A. in 1960, and originally on Marty's album 'Gunfighter Ballads and Trail Songs'. A top country disc, it was 22 weeks in the U.S. bestsellers, and was No 19 in Britain, and eight weeks in the bestsellers.

BOBBY RYDELL

WE GOT LOVE *Cameo* [*USA*]. The first million seller for Bobby was written by Kal Mann (words) and Bernie Lowe (music). Rydell's real name is Robert Louis Ridarelli; he was born in Philadelphia on 26 April 1940. His friends, Fabian and Frankie Avalon, went to the same boys' club and all three had the same ambition – to become singers. At 12, Bobby did a double act with Avalon, and he also appeared on a teenage TV show for Paul Whiteman whose suggestion it was that he change his name to Rydell. Later Bobby joined a rock'n'roll group – Rocko and his Saints – on drums, with Frankie Avalon on trombone in Atlantic City (1957). Then when the group were playing at a nightclub in New Jersey, Bobby met Frankie Day – a bass player with another group. Day got Bobby signed to a Cameo disc contract which included personal grooming in music, voice and dancing. Much rehearsing paid big dividends when his discs began to hit with regularity. Bobby also plays bass and composes, in addition to singing and drumming, and is an excellent impressionist. He was enthusiastically acclaimed at New York's Copa in 1961 and had a star role in the film version of the

stage musical *Bye Bye Birdie* in 1963. The disc was No 6 and 17 weeks in the U.S. bestsellers.

WILD ONE backed with LITTLE BITTY GIRL *Cameo* [*USA*]. This second million seller for Bobby Rydell comprised 'Wild One' written by Bernie Lowe, Kal Mann and Dave Appell and 'Little Bitty Girl' written by Fred Tobias and Clint Ballard, Jr. 'Wild One' was No 2 in the U.S. charts (1960) with 16 weeks in the bestsellers, and No 7 in Britain, with 14 weeks in the bestsellers. 'Little Bitty Girl' was No 19 and 15 weeks in the U.S. bestsellers.

SANTO AND JOHNNY
SLEEP WALK *Canadian-American* [*USA*]. This sole million seller for this duo, the brothers Santo and Johnny Farina who were aged 21 and 18 respectively, was written with the help of Ann Farina. 'Sleep Walk' turned out to be one of the few purely instrumental discs to top the U.S. lists up to that time. It owes its appeal to the pulsating slow background beat of Johnny's rhythm guitar and a melancholy somewhat exotic melody of Santo's steel guitar. The brothers were born in Brooklyn; Johnny on 30 April 1941, Santo on 24 October 1937. Santo began studying steel guitar at nine and Johnny the ordinary rhythm guitar at 12. They played together regularly while at high school and were established local favourites by 1955. After this disc came a major personal tour of the U.S.A., with their distinctive brand of Hawaiian-flavoured rhythm-and-blues delighting audiences everywhere. This disc was No 1 for two weeks in the U.S.A. and 18 weeks in the bestsellers; it was No 22 and 4 weeks in the British bestsellers.

NEIL SEDAKA
I GO APE *Victor* [*USA*]. 'I Go Ape' was 1950s slang for 'I go wild, crazy, idiotic' – but it meant the first million seller for talented Neil Sedaka. The song was written by Howard Greenfield (words) and Neil Sedaka (music). Neil was born on 13 March 1939, in Brooklyn, New York, the son of a taxi driver, and educated there at Lincoln High School. He is of Turkish descent. His father was determined his son should be permitted to develop his obvious talent for music. Neil intended to become a concert pianist and studied both piano and composition. At high school he developed a flair for writing pop music, writing several tunes for school productions, with awards for his activities. He was originator, arranger and member of a quartet known as The Tokens. He taught piano locally, sang and played with dance bands and acted as musical director at summer camps during school holidays. He won a scholarship to the famous Juilliard School of Music and was chosen by Arthur Rubinstein to play on a radio programme featuring school-age musical talent (1956). With Howard Greenfield, a neighbour in Brooklyn, Neil built up a repertoire of pop songs, and had discs of some by famous recording stars including Connie Francis, LaVern Baker, Jimmy Clanton, Roy Hamilton and Clyde McPhatter. Then in 1958 he made a private recording singing one of his own compositions. Publishers Al Nevis and Don Kirschner heard it and were more excited about the singer than the song. The demo disc was taken to RCA-Victor's Steve Sholes, head of artists and repertoire and discoverer of Elvis Presley, who immediately signed Neil to an exclusive disc contract. His first release for Victor was 'The Diary' (1958) which was a sizeable hit. Then came 'I Go Ape'. By 1960 Neil had composed around 400 songs, mostly with Howard Greenfield. Today, Neil is in great demand for TV guest appearances and tours. His discs are extremely popular in Japan, where he became No 1 in the sellers with all his releases being hits there. He has great talent as a classical pianist and is one of the most consistent hit-makers in the disc industry. In 1960, Neil Sedaka and Greenfield wrote the entire score for the MGM film *Where the Boys Are*, released in 1961, in which Connie Francis made her film debut. This disc was No 42 in the U.S. charts, and No 9 and 13 weeks in the British bestsellers.

OH CAROL *Victor* [*USA*]. The second million seller for Neil Sedaka was written by him (music) and Howard Greenfield (words). It reached No 9 with 18 weeks in the U.S. bestsellers, and No 3 in Britain's bestsellers.

DAVID SEVILLE AND THE CHIPMUNKS
ALVIN'S HARMONICA *Liberty* [*USA*]. This third million seller for David Seville was the second for his famous 'Chipmunks'. The number was written by Seville (Ross Bagdasarian). The disc was No 3 and 12 weeks in the U.S. bestsellers.

RAGTIME COWBOY JOE *Liberty* [*USA*]. Then came the fourth million seller for David Seville and a third for the 'Chipmunks'. The original song was written in 1912 by Grant Clarke (words) and Lewis F. Muir and Maurice Abrahams (music). The disc was No 16 and 9 weeks in the U.S. bestsellers.

HARRY SIMEONE CHORALE
LITTLE DRUMMER BOY *20th Century Fox* [*USA*]. This most beautiful recording of a religious song was written by Harry Simeone, Henry Onorati and Katherine Davis in 1958 who took the tune from the Spanish song 'Tabolilleros'. It tells the story of the poor boy who has no great gift to bring to the Nativity, but only his playing on the drum. Harry Simeone was born on 9 May 1911, and hails from Newark, New Jersey. After graduating from the famous Juilliard School of Music, he immediately joined CBS, staying there until bandleader Fred Waring recognized his arranging ability in 1939 by taking Harry on his permanent staff. He later moved to Paramount Pictures, working in conjunction with the late Victor Young, the famous composer/conductor, on such pictures as *Here Come the Waves*, *The Affairs of Susan* and the Bing Crosby–Bob Hope 'Road' series. From 1952 to 1959 he was arranger/conductor for the popular weekly U.S. TV show 'The Firestone Hour'. This disc had a 'different' sound – a strangely haunting and captivating charm. At least for a while it even shook the United States out of its overwhelming 'rock' mentality. It has now become a perennial Christmas seller with 150 different versions totalling 25 million sales up to the end of 1970. It first appeared on the Harry Simeone Chorale album, 'Sing We Now of Christmas' (see 1958). It reached No 13 with 28 weeks in the U.S. bestsellers (1958–1962), and was No 13 in Britain, with seven weeks in the bestsellers.

NINA SIMONE
I LOVES YOU PORGY *Bethlehem* [*USA*]. This was a sole million seller for Nina (real name Eunice Waymon) who comes from Tryon, North Carolina. The song is by Ira Gershwin (words) and George Gershwin (music) from his great Negro opera *Porgy and Bess* (1935). Nina was educated at college and the Juilliard School of Music and appeared at nightclubs, concerts, on TV and made personal appearances. She later recorded for Victor. Her style is modern jazz vocal and piano, and she also plays the organ. Nina was born on 21 February 1933 in Tryon, North Carolina. She made appearances in Britain in 1965. The disc was No 18 with 15 weeks in the U.S.A. bestsellers.

TERRY SNYDER AND HIS ALL STARS ORCHESTRA
PERSUASIVE PERCUSSION Vol. 1 (stereo album) *Command* [*USA*]. Stereophonic discs were first introduced in 1958, sales being very slow at the start, due, it is said, to lack of recordings with effective interest on a musical level. This album, Command's initial release in early 1959, was probably the first to put stereo discs on the map. It brought to light the startling *musical* aspects of stereo sound on records. It sold half a million by 1961, thereafter averaging 150,000 sales per year, passing the million mark and $5 million worth in sales by 1965.

Terry Snyder, born in New York, was educated at high school where he started playing the drums. He won a gold medal on graduation and a music scholarship. Starting work at 16, he played with big bands such as Paul Whiteman, Jimmy Dorsey, Jan Savitt and Benny Goodman, and became a featured vibraphone and drum player for WNEW in New York, from 1940. He then became instrumentalist in 1943 on the Perry Como show, an association of long duration. Terry did freelance work for practically every label in the U.S.A. on sessions conducted by most of the big names including Percy Faith, Hugo Winterhalter, Leonard Bernstein and Ralph Flanagan. He was one of the first exponents of 'ping-pong' music, but his fame undoubtedly rests with his extremely successful 'Persuasive Percussion' albums, made under the skilled direction of Command's 'Mister Stereo', Enoch Light. In 1961 Snyder was with United Artists and in 1962 with Ultra Audio Records. He died in 1963.

Contents of this album were: 'I'm in the Mood for Love', by Dorothy Fields and Jimmy McHugh (1935); 'Whatever Lola Wants', by Richard Adler and Jerry Ross (1955); 'Misirlou', by Leeds, Wise and Russell and R.N. Roubanis (1941); 'I Surrender Dear', by Gordon Clifford and Harry Barris (1931); 'Orchids in the Moonlight', by Gus Kahn, E. Eliscu and V. Youmans (1933); 'I Love Paris', by Cole Porter (1953), 'My Heart Belongs to Daddy', by Cole Porter (1938); 'Taboo', by Margarita Lecuona (1934); 'The Breeze and I', by Al Stillman (1940) and Ernesto Lecuona (1928), adapted T. Camarata (1940); 'Aloha Oe', by Queen Liliuokalani (1878); 'Japanese Sandman', by Raymond Egan and Richard Whiting (1920); 'Love is a Many Splendored Thing', by P.F. Webster and Sammy Fain (1955).

CYRIL STAPLETON AND HIS ORCHESTRA

CHILDREN'S MARCHING SONG (also known as THIS OLD MAN and NICK NACK PADDY WHACK) *Decca* [*Britain*]. The original words and music of this children's song were written by the famous folk song collector, Cecil J. Sharp, and S. Baring Gould. Malcolm Arnold adapted both the words and music and arranged the song for the film *Inn of the Sixth Happiness*, the story of an English missionary, Gladys Aylward (portrayed by Ingrid Bergman), who marched a band of orphans to safety over the rugged mountains during the Japanese invasion of China before World War II, singing this song together to keep up morale.

Stapleton's disc was a hit on both sides of the Atlantic, reaching No 13 in the U.S.A. on the London label and selling a reputed global million. The tune was also a hit in the U.S.A. for Mitch Miller where it was No 14 on the Columbia label. This disc was 14 weeks in the U.S. bestsellers.

BARRETT STRONG

MONEY (That's what I Want) *Tamla* [*USA*]. Songwriter Barrett Strong joined the famous Berry Gordy disc company soon after it came into existence in 1959, and this recording of a song written by Berry Gordy and Janie Bradford became the first million seller for Gordy's Motown Records and its affiliated labels. The disc was a bestseller in 1960.

Barrett Strong (born 5 February 1941) and Norman Whitfield (born 1940) came into prominence when they wrote 'I Wish It Would Rain' in 1967, following up with 'Cloud Nine', 'I Heard It Through the Grapevine', 'War' and 'Ball of Confusion'. They began collaborating as a team in the production area and are highly creative and in-demand producers.

Strong eventually recorded 'Let's Rock' as the first release on the Tamla label, the foundation of the Tamla-Motown operation. (See Berry Gordy data under Jackie Wilson, 'Lonely Teardrops' disc, 1959.)

Though Strong played a significant role in the Detroit story since the early days, he found the ideal partner in Whitfield for the continuation of his creativity.

The disc reached No 23 in the U.S. charts and 17 weeks in the bestsellers.

SARAH VAUGHAN

BROKEN HEARTED MELODY *Mercury* [*USA*]. The first million seller for Sarah was written by Hal David (words) and Sherman Edwards (music) in 1958. Sarah, born 27 March 1924, made her first public appearance in her native Newark, New Jersey, as a child choir singer. She later won an amateur contest at New York's Apollo Theatre, and a week's engagement with Earl Hines' band, which led to a permanent job with them, where she was co-featured with Billy Eckstine. When Eckstine formed his own orchestra, Sarah joined him as vocalist. She later became a member of the John Kirby orchestra. Miss Vaughan appeared in nightclubs, theatres and concerts and toured Europe in 1953. Sarah is also a pianist and organist. She visited Britain in 1963 with Count Basie and his band. This disc was No 7 and 19 weeks in the U.S. bestsellers, and No 7 and 13 weeks in the British bestsellers.

JERRY WALLACE

PRIMROSE LANE *Challenge* [*USA*]. This was a sole million seller for Jerry Wallace, who hails from Kansas City. He was born on 15 December 1933, and is both a songwriter and guitarist. This song was written by George Callender (words) and Wayne Shanklin (music). The disc reached No 8 with 21 weeks in the U.S. bestsellers.

RUSTY WARREN (comedienne)

KNOCKERS UP (album) *Jubilee* [*USA*]. The second album success for Rusty Warren was comprised of her particular brand of comedy songs. This disc sold a half million in 1959 and earned her the name of 'The Knockers Up Girl'. It sold a reputed million by 1963, and stayed in the bestsellers in the U.S.A. for 181 weeks. Sales by 1968 were $3\frac{1}{2}$ million.

THOMAS WAYNE

TRAGEDY *Fernwood* [*USA*]. Written in 1958 by Gerald H. Nelson and Fred B. Burch, Wayne's disc is said to have sold a million. It was No 5 in the U.S.A. with 19 weeks in the bestsellers.

Wayne (real name Thomas Wayne Perkins) was the brother of Luther Perkins, long-time guitar player for Johnny Cash, who died in a fire in 1968. Born in 1940, singer Wayne was a recording engineer up to the time of his death in a car collision in Memphis on 15 August 1971.

'Tragedy' was revived in 1961 by The Fleetwoods.

ANDY WILLIAMS

HAWAIIAN WEDDING SONG backed with HOUSE OF BAMBOO *Cadence* [*USA*]. 'Hawaiian Wedding Song' ('Ke Kali nei ou') was written in 1926 by Charles E. King. English words were provided in 1958 by Al Hoffman and Dick Manning. 'House of Bamboo' is a British song, with a 'rock' cha-cha rhythm, written in 1958 by Norman Murrells, who is a well-known accompanist and son of the compiler of *Million-Selling Records*. This disc was Andy's second million seller. Recorded on 3 November 1958, it was No 11 with 20 weeks in the U.S. bestsellers.

JACKIE WILSON

LONELY TEARDROPS *Brunswick* [*USA*]. The first million seller for Jackie was written by Gwen Gordy, Berry Gordy, Jr. and Tyran Carlo in 1958. Wilson hails from Detroit and began his singing career in 1953. One year after graduation from Highland Park High School he signed with Billy Ward's Dominoes as their lead voice. In late 1957 he decided to leave the Dominoes and try singing on his own. Nat Tarnpol, a Detroit publisher, recognized Jackie's talents and gave him a personal management contract which led to an exclusive pact with Brunswick Records and subsequent hit discs. Jackie then made top nightclub, theatre and TV appearances. Jackie sings rock'n'roll and ballads with equal facility. His success is in large part due to his mother's insistence on Jackie giving up a promising career as a boxer in 1948. (He entered and won a Golden Gloves welter-weight crown at the age of 16, by claiming to be 18.)

A top rhythm-and-blues disc, 'Lonely Teardrops' was released in 1958, reaching No 7 with 21 weeks in the U.S. bestsellers.

(*Note*. Songwriter Berry Gordy, Jr., a one-time auto assembly-line worker, started Gordy Records in 1959 with a loan of $800, developing it into the U.S.A.'s biggest independent producer of 45 rpm discs by 1965. As Motown Records (short for 'motor town') of Detroit and including the Tamla label, their stable of artists includes Mary Wells, The Supremes and Martha and the Vandellas. They introduced the 'Motown Sound' and with 42 bestselling songs and 12 million sales, dominated the rock'n'roll market in the U.S.A. in 1964.)

LINK WRAY AND HIS RAY MEN

RAWHIDE *Epic* [*USA*]. The second million-selling instrumental disc for this group, written by Milt Grant and Link Wray, released in January 1959. It was No 23 and 13 weeks in the U.S. bestsellers.

THE 1960s

ORIGINAL THEATRE CAST WITH MARY MARTIN, THEODORE BIKEL, PATRICIA NEWAY, LAURI PETERS, BRIAN DAVIES, KURT KASZNER, MARION MARLOWE, KAREN SHEPARD, ELIZABETH HOWELLS, MURIEL O'MALLEY, CHILDREN, NUNS AND FRANK DVONCH ORCHESTRA

THE SOUND OF MUSIC (album) *Columbia* [*USA*]. Here was another monumental stage musical success for Oscar Hammerstein (words), his last work, and Richard Rodgers (music).

The contents of the disc: 'The Sound of Music', (Mary Martin); 'Do-Re-Mi' (Mary Martin and children); 'The Lonely Goatherd' (Mary Martin and children); 'Edelweiss' (Theodore Bikel); 'So Long, Farewell' (The children); 'Climb Ev'ry Mountain' (Patricia Neway); 'Processional' (The Nuns); 'No Ordinary Couple' (Mary Martin and Theodore Bikel; 'The Sound of Music' (Martin, Bikel and children); 'My Favourite Things' (Mary Martin and Pat Neway); 'Sixteen Going Seventeen' (Mary Martin and Lauri Peters); 'Sixteen Going on Seventeen' (Brian Davies and Lauri Peters); 'How Can Love Survive?' (Kurt Kaszner and Marion Marlowe); 'No Way to Stop It' (Bikel, Kaszner and Marlowe); 'Maria' (Eliz. Howells, Muriel O'Malley, Pat Neway and Karen Shepard); 'Climb Ev'ry Mountain' (The Company); 'Laendler' (Frank Dvonch orchestra); 'Praedludium' (Frank Dvonch orchestra).

The Sound of Music was first produced at the Lunt-Fontanne Theatre in New York on 16 November 1959 and ran for 1,443 performances to 15 June 1963. The London production at the Palace Theatre opened on 18 May 1961 with 2,385 performances (the most ever for an American musical in Britain) until its closing on 14 January 1967. The play was adapted from *The Trapp Family Singers*, originally written by Maria Augusta Trapp, which tells the story of the famous Austrian vocalists. This album sold half a million by 1960, reached the million towards the end of 1961, and two million by 1963. It was lyricist Oscar Hammerstein II's last musical - he died in 1960. His fabulous partnership with Richard Rodgers resulted in over 30 million albums of their various musicals (stage and film) being sold by 1970, a seemingly unbeatable record. This disc was No 1 for 12 weeks in the U.S.A., and in the bestseller list for 277 weeks. Gold Disc award R.I.A.A. 1960. Grammy Award for Best Original Cast Album (1960).

PAUL ANKA

PUPPY LOVE *ABC-Paramount* [*USA*]. Paul wrote his fifth million seller in 1959, and the disc was No 2 for two weeks in the U.S.A. and 14 weeks in the bestsellers, and No 33 in Britain.

MY HOME TOWN *ABC-Paramount* [*USA*]. This sixth million seller for Paul was also written by the vocalist himself. It was No 8 for two weeks in the U.S.A. and 13 weeks in the bestsellers.

HANK BALLARD AND THE MIDNIGHTERS

THE TWIST *King* [*USA*]. This fourth million seller for Hank was written by him in 1958. This song created a dance craze in 1961 when popularized by Chubby Checker (*q.v.*) and set the

entire world 'Twisting'. 'The Twist' became a million selling disc by 1962, reaching No 28 with 16 weeks in the U.S. bestsellers.

FINGER POPPIN' TIME *King* [*USA*]. This fifth million seller for Hank Ballard and the Midnighters was also written by Hank. It was No 7 in the U.S.A. charts, and 26 weeks in the bestsellers.

LET'S GO, LET'S GO, LET'S GO *King* [*USA*]. Sixth million seller for Hank Ballard and the Midnighters, composed by Hank. This was No 8 in the U.S. charts with 16 weeks in the bestsellers, and a No 1 rhythm-and-blues disc.

BELLE BARTH (comedienne and singer)

IF I EMBARRASS YOU, TELL YOUR FRIENDS (album) Annabelle (Belle) Barth (née Salzman) was the youngest of nine children of a Manhattan merchant, and was born in 1912. She started in show business at an early age, working the Borsch Circuit as a singer, piano player and teller of bawdy stories. After 30 years she rose to the top of her field, then appeared in spots ranging from New York's Carnegie Hall to Las Vegas' Caesar's Palace, and beach hotels such as the Eden Roc and Saxony, and the now defunct Copa City in Miami. She became an institution in Miami Beach during two decades (1950-1970), her greatest success locally coming from the Saxony, where the Red Room was named after her and was her base of operations from which she travelled to dates in Las Vegas, New York, Chicago and Atlantic City. She first arrived in the Miami Beach area in 1945, where she established a reputation as an entertainer who used words no one else dared on stage. Her stories and songs were slightly bolder than Sophie Tucker's essays in the same style. Belle was one of the better-known names on 'party discs' which were sold *sub rosa* by less reputable disc stores of that time. She was the forerunner of other artists such as Pearl Williams, Rusty Warren and Red Foxx who also became 'party disc' and café personalities with their sex-angled comedy songs.

This album was her first, recorded in 1960, which is said to have sold two million without any radio exploitation or much publicity.

Belle was taken ill during a Las Vegas engagement in May 1970 and did not work again. She died at her Miami home on 14 February 1971.

The name of the 'offbeat' label that produced the disc is unknown.

BILL BLACK AND HIS COMBO

WHITE SILVER SANDS *Hi* [*USA*]. This second million seller (by 1963) for Bill Black and his Combo was written by Chuck 'Red' Matthews and G. Reinhardt, 1957. (Matthews's original version of 1949 was entitled 'If I knew'.) It reached No 9 in the U.S. charts with 13 weeks in the bestsellers, and was a No 1 rhythm-and-blues disc; in Britain it was No 50.

JOSEPHINE *Hi* [*USA*]. This third million seller for Bill Black and his Combo was written by Gus Kahn, B. Rivens and Wayne King way back in 1937. It reached No 18 with 10 weeks in the U.S. bestsellers, and No 32 in Britain.

DON'T BE CRUEL *Hi* [*USA*]. Bill Black's instrumental version of this song written in 1956 by Otis Blackwell and Elvis Presley was the fourth million seller for the combo. It was one of the top instrumental discs of 1960 and became a standard in the rhythm-and-blues field. It was No 11 with 13 weeks in the U.S. bestsellers.

JEANNE BLACK

HE'LL HAVE TO STAY *Capitol* [*USA*]. The sole million seller for rock'n'roll singer Jeanne was written by J. and A. Alison

Previous page, top, left to right: Stevie Wonder, Petula Clark, Paul Simon and Art Garfunkel; bottom: The Cream, Dusty Springfield.

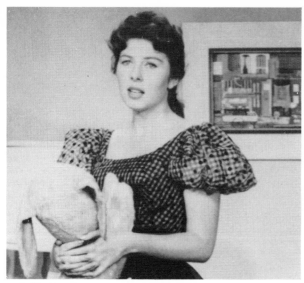

and Charles Green. Jeanne was born on 25 October 1937 and hails from Mount Baldy, California. She started singing duos with her sister Janie in the back seat of the family car. Cliff Stone discovered her, then she made many appearances on his local TV show, 'Hometown Jamboree'. The disc was No 4 for two weeks in the U.S.A. and 11 weeks in the bestsellers, and No 41 in Britain.

THE BLUE DIAMONDS
RAMONA *Fontana* [*Holland*] 'Ramona' was the first million seller for this duo – the brothers Rudi (age 21) and Riem (age 19) de Wolff – who went to Holland from Indonesia in 1949. They started with a Hawaiian band. Both brothers play guitar and are rhythm-and-blues vocalists. Inspired by the Everly Brothers, the de Wolffs made their first disc in 1959 which was an immediate success. This disc of 'Ramona' was the first ever to sell over 250,000 in Holland, and over one million in Germany when released on the Decca label, and it was also a hit in the U.S.A. The brothers have made guest appearances in all parts of the world. This disc sold the million by 1961. The song was written in 1928 by L. Wolfe Gilbert (words) and Mabel Wayne (music). The disc reached No 72 in the U.S.A.

BROTHERS FOUR
GREEN FIELDS *Columbia* [*USA*]. The sole million seller for this quartet was written by Terry Gilkyson, Richard Dehr and Frank Miller in 1956. The 'brothers', all from Washington state, and then aged 20-22, are Bob Glick, Mike Kirkland, John Paine and Richard Foley. As fraternity brothers they met at the University of Washington, and made nightclub and personal appearances. The disc was No 2 for four weeks in the U.S.A. and 20 weeks in the bestsellers, and was No 40 in Britain.

CHARLES BROWN (vocalist)
PLEASE COME HOME FOR CHRISTMAS *King* [*USA*]. Recorded on 21 September 1960 at King Records' studio in Cincinnati, this disc sold a million by February 1968 and is now considered a standard. A Gold Disc was presented to Gene Redd, artists and repertoire chief for King Records in early 1968, who both wrote the song and was responsible for its recording. It reached No 76 in the U.S.A.

Charles Brown made a number of Christmas recordings including the popular 'Merry Christmas Baby'.

HEIDI BRUHL
WIR WOLLEN NEIMALS AUSEINANDERGEH'N (We will never part) (Ring of gold) *Philips* [*Germany*]. Here was the first million seller for the German actress-singer Heidi Bruhl who was born 30 January in Munich in 1942. She started as a dancer and has been a versatile entertainer since she was six years of age. Heidi became a skilled ballerina by 1956 and then started singing. In 1955 she had her first leading role in Germany, becoming very popular there. She appeared in a number of films, became a popular magazine cover girl and received a major award in 1961 as the top TV personality of the year. In 1960, she sang 'Wir wollen neimals' in the 'Song for Europe' TV contest and gained second place, and her subsequent disc of the song sold over a million in Germany. Heidi started her disc career in 1959, and then perfected a one-woman show which took Germany by storm. She has visited the U.S.A. and in 1962 was signed for a leading role in MGM's film *Captain Sinbad*. This song was written by Bruno Balz and Gloria De Voss (words) and Michael Jary (music). The English lyric was written by Al Stillman.

ANITA BRYANT
PAPER ROSES *Carlton* [*USA*]. Ballad and beat vocalist Anita achieved her first million seller with a song written by Fred Spielman (music) and Janice Torre (words). Anita was born on 25 March 1940 in Barnsdale, Oklahoma, and started singing as a child, becoming popular at local functions. At nine she won a talent contest and became known as 'Oklahoma's Red Feather Girl' which led to appearances on the local TV station at Oklahoma City, then at the Tulsa station. Talent scout Arthur Godfrey heard her and booked her for his New York talent contest which she won. She then became in demand for guest spots on TV throughout the States and did tours. Anita had previously been 'Miss Oklahoma' in the Miss America Pageant and was second runner-up to 'Miss America' in 1958. This disc reached No 5 in the U.S. charts and 17 weeks in the bestsellers, and was No 24 in Britain.

IN MY LITTLE CORNER OF THE WORLD *Carlton* [*USA*]. The second million seller for the beauty queen Anita Bryant was written by Bob Hilliard (words) and Lee Pockriss (music). It was No 10 in the U.S. charts and 14 weeks in the bestsellers, and was No 48 in Britain.

TILL THERE WAS YOU *Carlton* [*USA*]. This third million seller for Anita is one of the major numbers from *The Music Man*, the stage musical of 1957, which was written by Meredith Willson. It was No 30 and 13 weeks in the U.S. bestsellers.

PAPA BUE AND VIKING JAZZ BAND
SCHLAFE MEIN PRINZCHEN *Storyville* [*Denmark*]. Papa Bue (real name Arne Bue Jensen) was born in 1931. He started an amateur band in the Copenhagen harbour district of Nyhavn, where his sextet was soon discovered by the Storyville-Sonet firm. This disc was his sole million seller by 1962. Papa Bue plays the trombone, and his combo is one of the Continent's most travelled bands with frequent tours of Europe, including Britain. The tune on this disc is 'Wiegenlied', often attributed to Mozart, but actually written by one of his contemporaries, Bernard Flies. Bue's version is, of course, in the traditional jazz style.

JOHNNY BURNETTE
DREAMIN' *Liberty* [*USA*]. First million seller for Johnny Burnette, written by Ted Ellis and Barry De Vorzon. Rock'n'roll singer John Joseph Burnette was born in Memphis, Tennessee, on 25 March 1934, started playing the guitar at a very early age, and made appearances at local functions. He was also a Golden Gloves city champion for boxing in Memphis in his teens. In 1955 he formed his own rock'n'roll trio, himself as lead singer, his older brother Dorsey on bass vocals and Paul Burlison on electric guitar. They first played at a local fairground, then moved to California, won first place three times on Ted Mack's 'Original Amateur Hour' on TV, and went on a three-week tour with the show in South America. On return they found several contracts for recording awaiting them, and Johnny signed for Coral Records. Their first disc 'Tear It Up' was not a success, but their second 'The Train Kept A'rollin'' in 1957 was a hit only in

Boston. In June 1958, Johnny disbanded the trio and started writing songs with his brother, and they were asked to write for Rick Nelson. They came up with three million-selling discs songs for Rick and subsequently Johnny signed for Liberty Records. Brother Dorsey became a hit disc artist on the Era label. Johnny's first discs for Liberty were not successful until July 1960 when, with 18 violins instead of his guitar backing him, he recorded 'Dreamin''. It reached No 11 with 15 weeks in the U.S. bestsellers, was No 5 and 16 weeks in the British bestsellers, and has become a standard seller through the years. Other hits followed and in early 1964 he formed his own record label which had just one release before Johnny's death in a boating accident at Clear Lake, California, on 15 August 1964.

Before becoming a professional singer, Johnny was a deckhand on Mississippi tugboats. He entered show business at the age of 22 – his TV debut being on the Steve Allen Show.

YOU'RE SIXTEEN *Liberty* [*USA*]. Johnny Burnette's second million selling disc, the song written by Bob and Dick Sherman who later achieved fame with their Oscar-winning score of *Mary Poppins* (1964). 'You're Sixteen' got to No 8 in the U.S. charts and 15 weeks in the bestsellers, and No 3 and 12 weeks in Britain's bestsellers.

RAY CHARLES
GEORGIA ON MY MIND *ABC-Paramount* [*USA*]. The second million seller for Ray Charles is an oldie of 1930, written by Stuart Gorrell (words) and ace composer Hoagy Carmichael. This disc was a No 1 seller in the U.S.A. for one week and 13 weeks in the bestsellers, and was No 24 in Britain with eight weeks in the bestsellers. Grammy Awards for Best Male Vocal Recording 1960 and Best Pop Single Performance 1960. Disc released 19 August 1960.

CHUBBY CHECKER
THE TWIST *Cameo-Parkway* [*USA*]. Chubby (real name Ernest Evans) was born on 3 October 1941 in Philadelphia. After school hours he worked in a chicken market, and the owner, Henry Colt, was so impressed with his singing as he worked that

he contacted Kal Mann (songwriter of Chubby's first disc, 'The Class') and Chubby was signed to a long-term contract with Cameo-Parkway. Chubby's second disc was 'The Twist', a commercialized cover version of the Hank Ballard disc. His rocking version of this was so popular (it sold over three million) that it started a dance craze all over the world. According to King Records, the song was first conceived by Hank Ballard early in 1958 to fit a dance step for his group in their act, then he composed the music and lyric to fit the new step which he called the 'Twist'. Chubby got his name from Mrs Dick Clark, the famous American disc jockey's wife, when visiting the studio as Chubby was cutting his first record. She remarked that he looked like a young Fats Domino – thus she derived 'Chubby Checker' from Fats' name. Chubby also plays piano and drums. This disc was a No 1 in 1960 for one week and again in 1962 for two weeks in the U.S. It was 18 weeks in the U.S. bestsellers list between 1960 and 1961, and a further 18 weeks, 1961-1962, making a record stay of 36 weeks in all; it was No 44 in Britain.

By 1965, Chubby had sold over 15 million discs.

PERRY COMO
DELAWARE *Victor* [*USA*]. The 19th million seller (globally) for Perry Como was written by Irving Gordon in 1959. This most original ditty, utilizing the names of the states of the U.S.A. in the lyrics as puns, e.g. 'Why did Cali phone ya' (for California), 'Where has Orry gone (Oregon), 'He's gone to pay his Taxes' (Texas) and of course 'What did Della wear' (Delaware). The disc was No 22 and 11 weeks in the U.S. charts, and No 3 and 13 weeks in Britain's bestsellers.

SAM COOKE
WONDERFUL WORLD *Keen* [*USA*]. The third million seller for Sam was written by Barbara Campbell, with Lou Adler and Herb Alpert in 1959. It was No 12 and 15 weeks in the U.S. bestsellers, and No 27 in Britain and eight weeks in the bestsellers.

CHAIN GANG *Victor* [*USA*]. The fourth million seller for Sam Cooke was written by Sol Quasha and Herb Yakus in 1956. It was No 2 for two weeks in the U.S. charts and 16 weeks in the bestsellers, and No 9 and 11 weeks in the British bestsellers.

DON COSTA (mandolin) ORCHESTRA
NEVER ON SUNDAY *United Artists* [*USA*]. The sole million seller for Don Costa was written in 1960 for the film *Jamais le Dimanche* (Never on Sunday) starring Melina Mercouri and Jules Dassin and composed by Manos Hadjidakis. Lyrics in English were written by Billy Towne. 'Never on Sunday' won the Academy Award for Best Film Song of 1960, and was the first European song to do so. In 12 months, global sales of collective discs exceeded ten million, with the major part in Europe on the large number of versions issued there. Don Costa was born on 10 June 1925 in Boston. He began his professional career at 15 with a staff orchestra of a local radio station. He arranged for Vaughn Monroe, Vic Damone, Sarah Vaughan, Rusty Draper, Georgia Gibbs, the Ames Brothers and many more. He also appeared as arranger/singer on local TV shows. He became the artists and repertoire director of ABC-Paramount Records, then he filled a similar role for United Artists Records. Original Greek title of the song was 'Tu Pedea Tou Pirea' (The Children of Pireaus). The disc was No 19 and 26 weeks in the U.S. bestsellers, and No 27 and 10 weeks in Britain's bestsellers.

FLOYD CRAMER (piano)
LAST DATE *Victor* [*USA*]. The first million seller for the rhythm pianist Floyd Cramer was his own composition. He was born in Shreveport, Louisiana, on 27 October 1933 and showed interest in music from the age of five. His family bought him a piano, and he actually began playing by ear before taking music lessons. After leaving school, he joined the 'Louisiana Hayride' and accompanied many leading artists. In 1955 he joined the

Grand Ole Opry. His piano was featured on Elvis Presley's disc 'Heartbreak Hotel' (1956). He won a disc jockey poll in 1960 as 'The Most Promising Solo Instrumentalist', and in 1961 as 'Favourite and Most Played Solo Instrumentalist'. The disc was No 2 for four weeks in the U.S. charts and 20 weeks in the bestsellers.

BOBBY DARIN

BEYOND THE SEA (La Mer) *Atco* [*USA*]. This fifth million seller for Bobby was originally written and sung by the great French entertainer Charles Trenet in 1945. English words were written in 1947 by Jack Lawrence for the U.S. market. This record provides a particularly fine 'beat' version of a great song. It reached No 6 in the U.S. charts and 14 weeks in the bestsellers, and No 8 and 10 weeks in the British bestsellers.

MARK DINNING

TEEN ANGEL *MGM* [*USA*]. The sole million seller for rock'n'roll beat vocalist Mark Dinning was written by Jean and Red Surrey in 1959. Mark was born in 1933 in Grant County, Oklahoma. He played guitar as well as singing, and is a brother of the well-known Dinning Sisters Trio. This disc was No 1 for two weeks in the U.S.A. and 18 weeks in the bestsellers, and No 37 in Britain.

FATS DOMINO

WALKIN' TO NEW ORLEANS backed with DON'T COME KNOCKIN' *Imperial* [*USA*]. This was the 23rd million seller for the consistent Fats. 'Walkin' to New Orleans' was written by Dave Bartholomew, R. Guidry and Fats himself. 'Don't Come Knockin'' was all Fats' own work. 'Walkin' to New Orleans' reached No 6 in the U.S. charts with 14 weeks in the bestsellers. 'Don't Come Knockin'' was No 21 and 11 weeks in the bestsellers. The disc was No 19 and 10 weeks in the British bestsellers.

LONNIE DONEGAN

MY OLD MAN'S A DUSTMAN *Pye* [*Britain*]. Lonnie became the first British vocalist to achieve the distinction of a third million seller. This disc was No 1 for four weeks with 13 weeks in the bestsellers and sold a million in Britain alone. Its comedy lines and cockneyish flavour had a great appeal for the British public. The words were written by Lonnie Donegan, Peter Buchanan and Beverley Thorn, the tune being based on a traditional air, and sung by the troops in World War I when on the march – 'My old man was a farmer, Now what do you think of that?

He's wearing khaki trousers and a little gawdblimey hat.' (The hat being the soft, floppy type of Service cap which some officers wore.) Lonnie and his co-writers of course made a modern version about the dustman who 'lives in a Council flat'.

THE DRIFTERS

TRUE LOVE, TRUE LOVE backed with DANCE WITH ME *Atlantic* [*USA*]. This third million seller for the Drifters comprised 'True Love' written by Doc Pomus and Mort Shuman and 'Dance with Me' written by L. Lebish, G. Treadwell, I. Nahan and Glick (Jerry Leiber and Mike Stoller). Lead singer on this disc was Ben E. King. Disc released in 1959. 'True Love' was No 33 and 11 weeks in the U.S. bestsellers. 'Dance with Me' was No 15 and 15 weeks in the bestsellers.

SAVE THE LAST DANCE FOR ME *Atlantic* [*USA*]. This even more popular 4th million seller for the Drifters was written by Jerome (Doc) Pomus and Mort Shuman. The disc was No 1 for three weeks in the U.S.A. Lead singer also Ben E. King. Released in 1959 and a top rhythm-and-blues disc, it was 18 weeks in the U.S. bestsellers, and No 2 and 18 weeks in the British bestsellers.

DUANE EDDY

BECAUSE THEY'RE YOUNG *Jamie* [*USA*]. This second million seller for Duane was written by Aaron Schroeder and Walley Gold (words) and Don Costa (music) for the film *Because They're Young*. In it Duane made his film debut and played the title number. Disc was No 4 for two weeks in the U.S.A. and 15 weeks in the bestsellers, and No 2 and 18 weeks in Britain's bestsellers.

EVERLY BROTHERS

CATHY'S CLOWN *Warner* [*USA*]. The eighth million seller for the Everlys was their own composition. It was No 1 for five weeks in the U.S.A. with 17 weeks in the bestsellers, and a chart-topper in Britain for nine weeks with 18 weeks in the bestsellers. A top rhythm-and-blues disc.

PERCY FAITH AND HIS ORCHESTRA

THEME FROM 'A SUMMER PLACE' *Columbia* [*USA*]. The second million seller for Faith became the undisputed top disc of 1960. This tune was written for the film *A Summer Place* by Max Steiner in 1959. This disc sold over two million and was No 1 for nine weeks in the U.S.A. and 21 weeks in the bestsellers, and No 2 and 30 weeks in the British bestsellers. Grammy Award for 'Record of the Year' 1960. Gold Disc award, R.I.A.A., 1962.

FERRANTE AND TEICHER (piano duettists) WITH ORCHESTRA

THEME FROM 'THE APARTMENT' *United Artists* [*USA*]. Here was the first million seller for this brilliant and most popular piano duo ever. The number was written in 1949 by the British composer Charles Williams, an instrumental work originally titled 'Jealous Lover', and used as the theme for the Jack Lemmon-Shirley MacLaine film *The Apartment* in 1960. Arthur Ferrante was born in New York (7 September 1921), and Louis Teicher in Wilkes-Barre, Pennsylvania (24 August 1924). They met at the age of six while students at Manhattan's Juilliard School of Music. Both graduated as piano majors and following schooling did a brief period of concert work, then returned to Juilliard as faculty members, combining teaching and a limited concert schedule. Their increasing popularity made them give up teaching in 1947 for full-time concert work, and they became professional duo-pianists. In 1948, they loaded their Steinway pianos on to an old delivery truck they had bought, and played in cafeterias, churches, gymnasia, ballparks and even a boxing ring, as well as with the leading orchestras throughout the U.S.A. and Canada. In the first 12 years they used up three trucks and twelve motors. Gradually drifting into popular music, their unique recitals combining classics with their own arrangements of tunes by Gershwin, Kern, Cole Porter, Rodgers and others, they devised a series of 'original gadgets' to extend the tonal range of their pianos. They used strips of sandpaper, cardboard wedges, etc., in their pianos applied to the strings for weird effect to resemble drums, xylophone, castanets, gongs and harpsichord, reaching into the pianos to pluck, strum and pound on the strings in novelty numbers. They appeared on TV and for two years on ABC's 'Piano Playhouse'. From around 1954 they started recording for Columbia, Westminster, ABC and MGM labels until 1960 when they were signed to United Artists with whom they began a string of film-theme hits. 'The Apartment' theme was the first, and also the first with orchestral accompaniment. They were so successful that they decided to drop their classical repertory, added some comedy routines and changed their billing from piano duettists to 'a two-man show'. From 1960 to 1970 they sold over 20 million records. Their biggest selling album was 'West Side Story'. *The Apartment* film received 5 Academy Awards. This disc reached No 10 in the U.S. charts with 20 weeks in the bestsellers, and was No 44 in Britain.

EXODUS - MAIN THEME *United Artists* [*USA*]. The second million seller for this duo was the tune from the film *Exodus*, composed by Ernest Gold, who received an Academy Award for his musical score and Grammy Award for 'Song of the Year' 1960. The disc was released in late 1960, reaching the million soon after in 1961. It was a top chart seller of 1961, and 120 different discs of the tune were made up to 1965. This disc reached No 2 in the U.S.A. with 21 weeks in the bestsellers, and No 6 and 17 weeks in Britain's bestsellers.

CONNIE FRANCIS
MAMA backed with TEDDY *MGM* [*Britain/USA*]. The sixth million seller (fifth solo) for Connie Francis was 'Mama' from Italy, originally written in 1941 by B. Cherubini (words) and C. A. Bixio (music) with English lyrics by Harold Barlow and Phil Brito (1955), and 'Teddy' was written by Paul Anka (1959). 'Mama' was accompanied by Tony Osborne and orchestra and recorded in Britain; 'Teddy' by Gus Levene and orchestra was made in the U.S. 'Mama' was No 8 in the U.S.A. and 13 weeks in the bestsellers. 'Teddy' was No 17 and 11 weeks in the U.S. bestsellers, and No 2 and 19 weeks in Britain's bestsellers.

EVERYBODY'S SOMEBODY'S FOOL backed with JEALOUS OF YOU *MGM* [*USA*]. The seventh million seller (sixth solo) for Connie comprised 'Fool' by Jack Keller and Howard Greenfield and 'Jealous of You', originally 'Tango della gelosia' from Italy (1930) by Peppino Mendes (words) and Vittorio Mascheroni (music). English words were by Marjorie Harper (1960). The latter was sung in part Italian, part English by Connie Francis. The accompaniments were by Joe Sherman's and Stan Applebaum's orchestras respectively for the two titles. 'Fool' was No 1 in the U.S.A. for two weeks and 13 weeks in the bestsellers, and No 5 with 19 weeks in Britain's bestsellers. 'Jealous of You' was No 19 and 11 weeks in the U.S. bestsellers.

MY HEART HAS A MIND OF ITS OWN *MGM* [*USA*]. The eighth million seller for Connie Francis (seventh solo) was written by Howard Greenfield and Jack Keller, with accompaniment by the Joe Sherman orchestra. This disc was top seller for two weeks in the U.S.A. and 17 weeks in the bestsellers, and No 3 with 15 weeks in Britain's bestsellers.

MANY TEARS AGO *MGM* [*USA*]. The ninth million seller for Connie Francis (eighth solo) was written by Winfield Scott. The accompaniment was by the Stan Applebaum orchestra. The disc reached No 7 in the U.S. charts with 13 weeks in the bestsellers, and No 12 with 9 weeks in Britain's bestsellers.

FREDDY (Quinn)
UNTER FREEMDEN STERNEN (Under foreign stars) *Polydor* [*Germany*]. The fourth million seller for champion German pop singer Freddy was written by Aldo Pinelli (words) and Lotar Olias (music).

ROCCO GRANATA
MARINA *Electrola* [*Germany*]. 'Marina' was a big success on the Continent of Europe, and was written in 1959 by Italian pop ballad and rock vocalist Granata himself. The English words are by Ray Maxwell. The song was originally published in Belgium. Rocco, born in 1939, lived at Waterschei, Belgium. He plays the accordion and guitar in addition to writing songs. This disc sold a million in Germany alone. It was No 31 and 11 weeks in the U.S. bestsellers.

ROLF HARRIS (vocal) WITH HIS WOBBLE BOARD AND THE RHYTHM SPINNERS
TIE ME KANGAROO DOWN, SPORT *Columbia* [*Britain*]. Rolf Harris certainly started a new craze when he invented his now famous wobble board. Rolf, a cabaret and TV artist who also aspired to be a painter, was born in Australia, the son of Welsh parents who emigrated there from Cardiff. In 1958, Rolf had placed an oil painting on Masonite board on an oil heater to dry. The board got very hot, so he held it by the edges and wobbled it back and forth to cool it. This produced a resounding twang like the sound of a tight-skinned bongo drum, and Rolf decided the sound was just the background he required for his kangaroo song. He recorded the number and it soon rocketed to the top of Australia's bestsellers. Rolf's wobbling of his oil painting on a TV show resulted in the Masonite firm turning out 200 boards as giveaways in a promotion plan with Rolf's help. The demand was so big that the company were obliged to engage extra hands to produce them. They sold over 55,000 in Australia alone. The craze spread to England and the U.S.A. Rolf's disc was a big hit in Australia and Britain, and reached No 4 in the U.S.A. with 11 weeks in the bestsellers when released there on the Epic label, making an estimated million combined global sale. Rolf Harris was born 30 March 1930 in Perth, Australia. Apart from being a very talented entertainer, he is an artist, cartoonist, sculptor, pianist and composer. He first studied the piano at the age of nine, and later taught it to children every week in his riverside home in Perth, Australia. Seeking a show business career, he eventually got a spot on the major Australian talent show 'The Amateur Hour' and as a result was given many engagements. He saved enough to give up teaching and sailed for England. After two years in London, his savings dwindled and things became rather difficult. He then got his break through an audition for Josephine Douglas, a TV producer, who signed him for an appearance on one of her shows. Thereafter, his TV appearances increased, and he became widely known in Britain for his cartoon characters on children's TV shows.

Then came recording for Columbia with further successes on disc including his 'Sun Arise' (based on an aboriginal chant) in 1962. This was also a hit on both sides of the Atlantic. In 1966, Rolf had his own BBC-TV series 'Hey Presto, It's Rolf', and a much talked-about Anglia-TV wildlife series, 'Survival', on which he was both singer and narrator.

He was also a big success (1966) at London's 'Talk of the Town' with 'Jake the Peg', a humorous act about a character with *three* legs.

Rolf received the Royal accolade in 1968 when he was made a Member of the Order of the British Empire (M.B.E.), and again in 1977 when he was awarded the O.B.E.

His 'Rolf Harris' BBC-TV shows have achieved colossal success and brought the 'Young Generation' group of singers and dancers into prominence.

This disc was No 9 and 13 weeks in the British bestsellers.

THE HOLLYWOOD ARGYLES
ALLEY-OOP *Lute* [*USA*]. This was the sole million seller for this septet which comprised: Gary Paxton, Bobby Rey (also a songwriter), Ted Marsh (bass player), Gary Webb (drums), Deary Webb (songwriter/guitarist), Deary Weaver and Ted Winters. They all hail from California. The song for this rock'n'roll vocal group was written by Dallas Frazier. This disc

was a No 1 seller in the U.S.A. for one week and 15 weeks in the bestsellers. No 24 and 10 weeks in the British bestsellers.

JOHNNY HORTON

NORTH TO ALASKA Columbia [USA]. This second million seller for Johnny was written by Mike Phillips and sung by Johnny in the film North to Alaska. It was No 4 in the U.S. charts with 23 weeks in the bestsellers, and a top country disc. No 23 and 11 weeks in British bestsellers.

BRIAN HYLAND

ITSY, BITSY, TEENIE, WEENIE, YELLOW POLKA DOT BIKINI Kapp [USA] (originally recorded on Leader label). The first million seller for Brian was written by Paul J. Vance and Lee Pockriss. It was the biggest novelty hit of the year. Brian was born on 12 November 1943 in Woodhaven, New York, and began singing at the age of nine in his church choir. When 12, he organized a vocal group – The Delphis – to perform at local functions. The group made a demonstration disc which Brian took around New York disc companies. Dave Kapp of Kapp Records was impressed with Brian and signed him up. His first disc release was 'Rosemary', then came this 'Bikini' disc which brought Brian international recognition. In 1961, he signed with ABC-Paramount Records. In addition to singing, Brian plays the guitar, flute and clarinet. This disc was a No 1 in the U.S.A. for one week with 15 weeks in the bestsellers, and sold over two million. No 8 and 13 weeks in the British bestsellers.

JAN AND KJELD

BANJO BOY Ariola [Germany]. This was the sole million seller (by 1961) for this duo who were labelled 'The Kids from Copenhagen'. The song was written in 1959 for the film Kein Mann Zum Heiraten by Charlie Niessen. English words were written by the U.S. lyricist Buddy Kaye in 1960. In the U.S.A. the disc was No 58, and No 36 in the British bestsellers.

MARV JOHNSON

(YOU'VE GOT TO) MOVE TWO MOUNTAINS United Artist [USA]. Rock'n'roll singer Marv was born on 15 October 1938 and hails from Detroit. At 13 he formed a vocal group, The Serenaders, performing at local functions and later at semi-professional dates throughout Michigan. Johnson also directed and acted in amateur theatricals. Marv was spotted by Berry Gordy, a Tamla Records representative, while his group sang on a lorry during a Detroit Carnival Parade and signed him for his first recording, the disc released on the United Artists label. This song, Marv's second million seller, was written by Berry Gordy, Jr., who subsequently signed Marv to his Tamla label. This disc was No 20 and 11 weeks in the U.S. bestsellers.

JIMMY JONES

HANDY MAN Cub [USA]. This first million seller for rock'n'roll singer Jimmy Jones was written by him and Otis Blackwell, in 1959. Jimmy was born on 2 June 1937 and hails from Birmingham, Alabama. It reached No 2 in the U.S. charts with 18 weeks in the bestsellers, and No 3 and 21 weeks in the British bestsellers.

GOOD TIMIN' Cub [USA]. The second million seller for Jimmy Jones was written by Clint Ballard, Jr. and Fred Tobias. This disc was a No 1 chart topper in Britain for three weeks, and No 3 for three weeks in the U.S.A. with 15 weeks in the bestsellers and 15 weeks in the British bestsellers.

BERT KAEMPFERT AND HIS ORCHESTRA

WONDERLAND BY NIGHT (Wunderland bei nacht) Polydor [Germany]. This first million seller for Kaempfert was written by Lincoln Chase (words) and Klauss-Gunter Neuman (music) in 1959. Kaempfert was born on 16 October 1923 in Hamburg, Germany, and showed musical gifts at an early age, later becoming a graduate at Hamburg School of Music. He played four instruments – piano, clarinet, sax and accordion – was also composer, arranger, producer and conductor for Polydor Records, Germany. He made his debut on radio with Hans Busch's orchestra in Danzig and after the last war formed his own band. As producer/arranger, he was responsible for 'Die Gittare und das Meer' for Freddy, and 'Morgen' for Ivo Robic. Both were million sellers. His unique orchestral sound captured the popularity of the world, and after this disc of 'Wonderland by Night' (a salute to Manhattan) he was the first European to be honoured as the 'Up-and-Coming Orchestra of the Year' in a U.S. disc jockey poll. Bert then made more hit singles and albums, and background music for the film 90 Minutes to Midnight which he wrote and conducted. He spent part of his time in New York and Miami Beach, his permanent home being in Hamburg. This disc was No 1 seller for three weeks in the U.S.A. in 1961 and 17 weeks in the bestsellers. It also sold another million copies outside the U.S.A. Kaempfert was the first man to record The Beatles when he hired them to back Tony Sheridan in Hamburg. (See Sheridan, 1961.) He died whilst on holiday in Spain on 22 June 1980.

BRENDA LEE

SWEET NOTHIN'S Decca [USA]. Here was the second million seller for Brenda Lee ('Little Miss Dynamite') reaching No 4 in the U.S. charts with 24 weeks in the bestsellers. The song was written by Ronnie Self in 1959. Brenda was born at Lithonia, near Atlanta, Georgia, on 11 December 1944, and educated at Maplewood School, Nashville. She won a talent contest at the age of six in Atlanta. She was later (1956), at the age of 11, heard by the country-and-western star Red Foley, singing in an amateur talent contest in Augusta, Georgia. Foley was so impressed with her singing that he arranged for her to make her TV debut at the famous country-and-western 'Ozark Jubilee' show (31 March 1956). Her success led to further major TV appearances and a recording contract with Decca from 21 May 1956. Her first disc release was 'Jambalaya' (1956), and after a string of bestsellers, she attained star-disc status with 'Sweet Nothin's', followed by 'I'm Sorry' backed with 'That's All You Gotta Do'. Brenda's voice has been described as 'part whisky, part negroid and all woman', and this 'explosive bundle of charm' can 'transform herself from a comics-reading teenager into a tortured woman', with a clap of her hands. From 1956, Brenda appeared on many major shows including those of Perry Como, Steve Allen and Dick Clarke and toured not only the U.S.A. but South America. She appeared on TV in Britain and elsewhere in Europe. Paris hailed her as the 'most dynamic American artist since Judy Garland'. She started her acting career with a role in The Two Little Bears. Her discs enjoy big sales, and her first two albums – 'This is Brenda' and 'Brenda Lee' – were particularly successful. Her real name is Brenda Lee Tarpley. She was voted the world's top female singer for 1962, 1963 and 1964. No 4 and 19 weeks in the British bestsellers.

I'M SORRY backed with THAT'S ALL YOU GOTTA DO Decca [USA]. 'I'm Sorry' was written by Ronnie Self and Dub Albritton (Brenda's legal guardian and personal manager). 'That's All You Gotta Do' was written in 1958 by J. Reed. 'I'm Sorry', Brenda's third million seller, was No 1 seller in the U.S.A. for three weeks and 23 weeks in the bestsellers. 'That's All You Gotta Do' was No 6 and 14 weeks in the bestsellers. 'I'm sorry' reached No 12 and 16 weeks in the British bestsellers.

HANK LOCKLIN (country-and-western vocalist/guitar)

PLEASE HELP ME I'M FALLIN' Victor [USA]. Written by Don Robertson and Hal Blair, Hank's disc of the song was No 1 for 14 weeks in the U.S. country-and-western charts and top song in this category for 1960. It reached No 8 with 22 weeks in the U.S. bestsellers. It was also the first of the contemporary country-and-western discs to break through the barrier of strictly purist country-and-western and direct 'pop' in Britain where it achieved Top 20 status (1960) and paved the way for others. No 9 and 19 weeks in the British bestsellers.

Lawrence Hankins Locklin was born in McLellean, Florida, on 15 February 1918, and was inspired by his musically gifted parents from an early age. He played guitar for amateur contests in Milton, Florida, at the age of 10 and soon became featured at Pensacola's WCOA station, also playing and singing for school parties and plays. He then did mostly shipyard work and farming in his home state. At the age of 20 he made his first professional appearance at the Community Centre in Whistler, Alabama, followed by many tours, broadcasts and personal appearances in the southern states before moving to Texas. In 1953 he started recording for 4-Star Records, his initial disc 'Let Me Be the One' becoming quite a success. Two years later he signed with Victor Records and recorded under famed guitarist Chet Atkins' direction in Nashville. His biggest seller (collectively) is 'Send Me the Pillow You Dream On' recorded for both 4-Star and Victor and written by him. 'Please Help Me I'm Fallin'' is estimated to have sold a million by 1967 and was also a hit for Skeeter Davis.

From 1960, Hank became a member of the famous Grand Ole Opry just 10 years after deciding on a professional career in 1950. He has made several visits to Britain, Germany and other countries in Europe.

LOLITA

SEEMANN (Sailor) *Polydor* [*Germany*]. This sole million seller for Lolita (real name Ditta) was written by Werner Scharfenberger (of Vienna) with the German words by Fini Busch. An English lyric was written by David West – the pseudonym of Norman Newell, well-known artists' and repertoire manager of EMI in Britain. Lolita hails from Vienna, and is the daughter of a civil servant. She worked as a children's nurse and as a secretary, and sang in the local church choir. After a radio spot on Radio Linz, her debut was such a success that she began working full time in cabaret. Then came recording for Polydor, films, TV appearances and stage shows. 'Seemann' was the first German song sung by a female artist to reach a high position in the U.S. hit parade, reaching No 5 with 18 weeks in the bestsellers, when

released there on the Kapp label. The song was also a big hit for Petula Clark on the Pye label and Ann Shelton on the Philips label in Britain. Lolita's hobby is cooking, and after giving her favourite recipe for a cake on TV, it appeared in the national press. In Denmark where she is very popular, the Danish bakers named a cake after her, 'Gâteau à la Lolita'. Lolita was born in St Poelten, about 40 miles from Vienna.

MANTOVANI AND HIS ORCHESTRA

'EXODUS' AND OTHER GREAT THEMES (album) *London/Decca* [*Britain*]. The seventh million seller for maestro Mantovani started with half a million sale in the U.S.A. in 1961 on the London label, and built up to a global million by 1965. The contents of this disc are: 'Main theme from *Exodus*', by Ernest Gold (1960); 'Karen' (from *Exodus*), by Ernest Gold (1960); 'Theme from *A Summer Place*', by Max Steiner (1960); 'The Green Leaves of Summer' (from *The Alamo*), by P. F. Webster and Dimitri Tiomkin (1960); 'Theme from *The Sundowners*', by Dmitri Tiomkin (1960); '76 Trombones' (from *The Music Man*), by Meredith Willson (1957); 'I Love Paris' (from *Can-Can*), by Cole Porter (1953); 'Song Without End' (from *Song Without End*), by Ned Washington, Morris Stoloff and George Duning (1960); 'Irma la Douce' (from *Irma la Douce*), by Marguerite Monnot (1958); 'Carousel Waltz' (from *Carousel*), by O. Hammerstein and Richard Rodgers (1945); 'The Sound of Music' (from *The Sound of Music*), by O. Hammerstein and Richard Rodgers (1959); 'Mister Wonderful' (from *Mr Wonderful*), by Jerry Bock, Larry Holofcener and George Weiss (1956).

This disc was in the U.S. bestsellers' lists for 65 weeks. Gold Disc award R.I.A.A., 1963.

MITCH MILLER AND THE GANG

SENTIMENTAL SING ALONG WITH MITCH (album) *Columbia* [*USA*]. The eight million seller for Mitch Miller (his sixth album million seller) with 103 weeks in the U.S. bestseller charts, and Gold Disc award from R.I.A.A. in 1962.

The contents were: 'Singin' in the Rain' (from film *Hollywood Revue of 1929*), by Arthur Freed and Nacio Herb Brown (1929); 'All I Do is Dream of You' (from film *Sadie McKee*), by Arthur Freed and Nacio Herb Brown (1934); *'Toot, Toot, Tootsie, Good-bye' (from show *Bombo*), by Gus Kahn, Ernie Erdman and Dan Russo (1922); 'The Gang That Sang "Heart of my heart"', by Ben Ryan (1926); 'Little Annie Rooney', by Michael Nolan (1889); *'Hello, Ma Baby', by Joseph E. Howard and Ida Emerson (1899); 'Our Boys Will Shine Tonight', (traditional war song); 'Give My Regards to Broadway' (from show *Little Johnny Jones*), by George M. Cohan (1904); 'While Strolling Through the Park One Day', by Ed Haley (1880); *'Ida, Sweet as Apple Cider', by Eddie Leonard (1903); 'When the Saints Go Marching In', (traditional); 'Jeannine, I Dream of Lilac Time' (from film *Lilac Time*), by L. Wolfe Gilbert and Nathaniel Shilkret (1928); 'Just A-wearyin' for You', by Frank Stanton and Carrie Jacobs-Bond (1901); *'I'll See You in My Dream', by Gus Kahn and Isham Jones (1924); 'When I Grow Too Old to Dream' (from film *The Night Is Young*), by O. Hammerstein and Sigmund Romberg (1935); 'Jeannie with the Light Brown Hair', by Stephen C. Foster (1854); *'Three O'clock in the Morning', by Dorothy Terris and Julian Robledo (1922).

(*) denotes song was a million sheet music seller.

MEMORIES SING ALONG WITH MITCH (album) *Columbia* [*USA*]. Mitch Miller's ninth million seller (his seventh album million seller) with 75 weeks in the U.S. bestsellers. A Gold Disc was awarded by R.I.A.A. in 1962.

Contents of the disc: *'My Blue Heaven', by George Whiting and Walter Donaldson (1927); 'I'm Nobody's Baby', by Benny Davis, Lester Santly and Milton Ager (1921); 'You Were Meant for Me' (from film *Broadway Melody*), by Arthur Freed and Nacio Herb Brown (1929); 'At Sundown', by Walter Donaldson (1927); 'Five Foot Two, Eyes of Blue', by Sam M. Lewis, Joe Young and Ray Henderson (1925); 'Meet Me in St Louis, Louis', by Andrew B. Sterling and Kerry Mills (1904), arranged by Jimmy Carroll; 'Bill Bailey, Won't You Please Come Home', by Hughie Cannon (1902), arranged by Jimmy Carroll; 'The Bowery' (from *A Trip to Chinatown*), by Charles H. Hoyt and Percy Gaunt (1892), arranged by Jimmy Carroll; 'The Yankee Doodle Boy', (from *Little Johnny Jones*), by George M. Cohan (1904), arranged by Jimmy Carroll; 'I'm Going Back to Dixie' ('Dixie'), by Dan D. Emmett (1860), arranged by L. L. Riker 'Honey', by Seymour Simons, Haven Gillespie and Richard Whiting (1928); *'Sleepy Time Gal', by J. R. Alden, Raymond B. Egan, A. Lorenzo and Richard A. Whiting (1925); *'Ramona' (from film *Ramona*), by L. Wolfe Gilbert and Mabel Wayne (1927); *'Peg O' My Heart', by Alfred Bryan and Fred Fisher (1913); *'Peggy O'Neil', by Harry Pease, Ed G. Nelson and Gilbert Dodge (1921); 'I Love You' (from *Little Jessie James*), by Harlan Thompson and Harry Archer (1923); *'Home on the Range', (traditional, *circa* 1873), arranged by Jimmy Carroll; 'Battle Hymn of the Republic', by Julia Ward Howe (1861), tune 'Glory, Glory, Hallelujah' ascribed to William Steffe (*circa* 1856), arranged by Jimmy Carroll.

(*) denotes million sheet music seller.

ROY ORBISON

ONLY THE LONELY *Monument* [*USA*]. Roy wrote his first million seller with the help of Joe Melson. Roy Kelton Orbison was born in Vernon, Texas, on 23 April 1936 and was educated at Wink Texas High School and North Texas State College. His father, an oil-rig driller, taught Roy to play the guitar when he was six. He became extremely proficient with an instrument on which he might well have gained fame alone, if his vocal ability

had not also been discovered. In his early teens, Roy was leading the 'Wink Westerners' and conducting a talent show over the local radio station. At 16, he represented the Lone Star State at the International Lions Conclave in Chicago. While a student (and disc artist at the time) at college, Pat Boone advised him to look for disc hits instead of oil. In 1956 he was signed to Sun Records and in 1958 agreed to a writer/management pact with Wesley Rose then over to Victor Records and subsequently to the Monument label and further big successes. Roy's radio debut was in Vernon in 1944, and first important stage appearance in Richmond, Virginia, in 1956 and TV debut in Dick Clark's 'American Bandstand' in 1960. Roy is a songwriter and also plays the harmonica. The disc was No 2 in the U.S.A. with 21 weeks in the bestsellers, and a chart topper in Britain for three weeks with 24 weeks in the bestsellers. He later recorded for MGM and sold 27 million records by 1972.

BLUE ANGEL *Monument* [*USA*]. The second million seller (globally) for Roy Orbison, also written by him with Joe Melson. It reached No 9 in the U.S. charts with 14 weeks in the best-sellers, and No 11 and 16 weeks in the British bestsellers.

ELVIS PRESLEY

STUCK ON YOU backed with FAME AND FORTUNE *Victor* [*USA*]. Here was the 25th million seller for Elvis. 'Stuck on You' was written by Aaron Schroeder and J. Leslie McFarland. 'Fame and Fortune' was written by Fred Wise and Ben Weisman. Reputed sale was two million, and the disc was top seller for four weeks in the U.S.A. with an amazing advance order of 1,275,077 copies - a record at that time. The Gold Disc award was for 'Stuck on You' which had 16 weeks in the bestsellers. 'Fame and Fortune' was No 17 and 10 weeks in the bestsellers, 'Stuck on You' No 3 and 14 weeks in the British bestsellers.

IT'S NOW OR NEVER backed with A MESS OF BLUES *Victor* [*USA*]. 'It's Now or Never' was originally written in 1901 under the title 'O sole mio' in Italy by G. Capurro (words) and Eduardo Di Capua (music). It was the U.S. writers Aaron Schroeder and W. Gold who wrote the new lyric for Elvis' recording. It turned out to be the biggest hit of his already phenomenal career; global sales were reported at 20 million (five million in the U.S.A., one million in Britain, one million in Germany and the remainder from other countries, including Sweden and Japan). The disc was No 1 in the U.S.A. for five weeks and a chart topper in Britain where it was No 1 in its first week and for nine weeks in all and 19 weeks in the bestsellers. Elvis received Gold Disc awards for both titles in the U.S.A. (his 26th and 27th) and Gold Discs for 'It's Now or Never' from both Britain and Germany. 'A Mess of Blues' was written by Doc Pomus and Mort Shuman. Backing for the British release was 'Make Me Know It' written by Otis Blackwell. On 1 October 1960, Elvis said, 'I've recorded 26 singles releases, and in fact I have 33 gold records because some of them went over two million'. 'It's Now or Never' was 20 weeks in the U.S. bestsellers. 'A Mess of Blues' was No 32 and 11 weeks in the bestsellers. No 2 and 18 weeks in the British bestsellers.

ARE YOU LONESOME TONIGHT? backed with I GOTTA KNOW *Victor* [*USA*]. Two more Gold Disc awards (the 28th and 29th) for Elvis's U.S.A. sales of both titles. 'Are You Lonesome Tonight?' was written in 1926 by Roy Turk and Lou Handman; 'I Gotta Know' was the work of Paul Evans and Matt Williams. The global sale was four million. 'Are You Lonesome Tonight?' was No 1 for six weeks in the U.S.A. with 16 weeks in the bestsellers, and for five weeks in Britain in 1961, with 15 weeks in the bestsellers. 'I Gotta Know' was No 20 and 11 weeks in the U.S. bestsellers.

G.I. BLUES (album) *Victor* [*USA*]. This 30th million seller for Elvis Presley (his third album million seller) consisted of songs from the original soundtrack recording of his film *G.I. Blues*. The contents were: 'Tonight Is So Right For Love', by Sid Wayne and Abner Silver (1960) (adaptation of Offenbach's 'Bacarolle'); 'What's She Really Like?', by Sid Wayne and Abner Silver (1960); 'Frankfurt Special', by Sid Wayne and Sherman Edwards (1960); 'Wooden Heart', by Fred Wise, Ben Weisman, Kay Twomey and Bert Kaempfert (1960); 'G.I. Blues', by Sid Tepper, Roy C. Bennett and Aaron Schroeder (1960); 'Pocketful of Rainbows', by Fred Wise and Ben Weisman (1960); 'Shoppin' Around', by Sid Tepper, Roy C. Bennett and Aaron Schroeder (1960); 'Big Boots', by Sid Wayne and Sherman Edwards (1960); 'Didja' Ever', by Sid Wayne and Sherman Edwards (1960); 'Blue Suede Shoes', by Carl Lee Perkins (1955); 'Doin' the Best I Can', by Doc Pomus and Mort Shuman (1960).

This album sold half a million in 1961 and two million subsequently. It was No 1 for eleven weeks in the U.S.A., 1960-1961. A Gold Disc was awarded by R.I.A.A. in 1963. This disc was in the U.S. bestsellers' lists for two years (111 weeks).

WOODEN HEART *Victor* (*Teldec*) [*Germany*]. Elvis's 31st million seller achieved a seven-figure sale in Europe alone on the Teldec label, the representatives for Victor (RCA) in Germany. The song is from Presley's film *G.I. Blues* based on the adventures of the same military outfit with which he served in Germany in 1959-1960 during his spell in the U.S. 3rd Armoured (Spear-head) Division. (See also the album 'G.I. Blues', 1960.) This song was written by Fred Wise, Ben Weisman, Kay Twomey and Berthold Kaempfert (famous German composer-arranger-orchestra leader-recording artist) and is an adaptation of an old German folk song 'Muss I denn zum Stadtele naus'. Elvis sings it partly in German and partly in English. The disc was No 1 seller in Britain for three weeks in 1961 and 27 weeks in the bestsellers.

JOHNNY PRESTON

RUNNING BEAR *Mercury* [*USA*]. This first million seller for rock'n'roll vocalist Johnny Preston is the story of an Indian brave and his love for a maiden of an enemy tribe. It was written in 1959 by J. P. Richardson, better known as 'The Big Bopper', who was killed in an air crash with Buddy Holly in early 1959. Johnny hails from Port Arthur, Texas, was born on 18 August 1939, and started singing with the school choir, later forming a combo called 'The Shades' for local dances. He won a Certificate of Achievement and Richardson encouraged him to make his first recording. He signed a contract with Mercury, toured the U.S.A. and appeared on TV and on radio. This disc made him internationally known, and was No 1 in the U.S.A. for three weeks with 27 weeks in the bestsellers, and a chart topper in Britain for one week with 14 weeks in the bestsellers.

CHARLIE RICH (vocalist)

LONELY WEEK-ENDS *Philips International* [*USA*]. Pianist-vocalist Charlie Rich wrote this himself and his recording was reported to have sold the million. He was raised in Arkansas and has been involved with music for most of his life. He studied piano and saxophone as a youth and later played with various bands while in high school. He studied music for two years at Arkansas University and, while in the U.S. Air Force during his tour of duty, formed a swing group called The Velvetones which had a weekly TV show. On discharge, he started playing piano in a small club, The Sharecropper, in Memphis, Tennessee, where he developed his now famous style, his sound encompassing the country, jazz and popular fields of music. This disc was No 22 and 21 weeks in the U.S. bestsellers.

BOBBY RYDELL

DING-A-LING backed with SWINGIN' SCHOOL *Cameo* [*USA*]. Both tunes were very popular in this third million seller for Bobby. They were written by Kal Mann (words), Bernie Lowe and Dave Appell (music). 'Swingin' School' was No 5 in the U.S.A. charts and 12 weeks in the bestsellers. 'Ding-a-Ling' was No 18 and 11 weeks in the bestsellers.

VOLARE *Cameo* [*USA*]. The fourth million seller for Bobby Rydell was the third time the famous 'Nel blu dipinto di blu' song of 1958, written by Domenico Modugno (music) with English words by Mitchell Parish, provided a million seller. The disc reached No 4 in the U.S. charts and 15 weeks in the bestsellers, and was No 22 in Britain.

JACK SCOTT

WHAT IN THE WORLD'S COME OVER YOU? *Top Rank* [*USA*]. The second million seller for Scott was a song written by Scott himself in 1959. It reached No 5 in the U.S. charts and 16 weeks in the bestsellers, and No 11 and 15 weeks in Britain's bestsellers.

THE SHADOWS (instrumental group)

APACHE *Columbia* [*Britain*]. The first million seller for Britain's famous instrumental quartet was written by Britain's Jerry Lordan. The group, comprising Hank Marvin (lead guitar),

Bruce Welch (rhythm guitar), Jet Harris (guitar) and Tony Meehan (drums), were the regular backing unit for Cliff Richard, Britain's famous vocalist. (See Cliff Richard, 1959.) This disc, The Shadows' fourth release in their own right, established them as the then premier British group, and with Cliff Richard they became internationally known. Hank was born on 28 October 1941 in Newcastle; Bruce on 2 November 1941 in Bognor Regis; Jet (Terence) on 7 July 1939 in Kingsbury, London; and Tony on 2 March 1942 in London. This disc was a chart topping disc for six weeks and a million seller by 1963 in Britain, with 21 weeks in the bestsellers. Jet was eventually replaced by John Rostill and Tony by Brian Bennett. (Photo does not show original line-up.)

THE SHIRELLES

DEDICATED TO THE ONE I LOVE *Scepter* [*USA*]. This female group comprises Addie Harris, Shirley Owens, Doris Kenner and Beverley Lee. They began their musical activities at their high school in Passaic, New Jersey, and were discovered while performing there in a talent show in late 1957, which brought them a Decca contract. Their first disc for Decca 'I Met Him on Sunday' established them as a show-business attraction.

They then began to record with Scepter Records, a label formed by their manager Florence Greenberg, with great success. This disc was recorded in late 1959 and eventually passed the million sale. The Shirelles' first million seller was written in 1957 by L. Pauling and R. Bass. The disc was No 3 for two weeks in the U.S.A. in 1961 and 20 weeks in the bestsellers (including four weeks in 1959).

TONIGHT'S THE NIGHT *Scepter* [*USA*]. This second million seller for The Shirelles was written by Owens, and Luther Dixon (artists' and repertoire manager and arranger for Scepter). This disc was recorded in late 1960, reaching No 39 with 12 weeks in the U.S. bestsellers.

WILL YOU LOVE ME TOMORROW? *Scepter* [*USA*]. The third million seller for The Shirelles was written in 1960 by husband-and-wife Gerry Goffin and Carole King, one of U.S.A.'s most successful songwriting teams in recent years. The disc was recorded in late 1960, and was a top seller for two weeks in the U.S.A. in 1961 with 19 weeks in the bestsellers. No 4 and 15 weeks in the British bestsellers.

RAY SMITH (rhythm-and-blues vocalist)
ROCKIN' LITTLE ANGEL *Judd* [*USA*]. This sole million-seller for both Ray Smith and the Judd label was just another addition to the great number of 'rock' discs of the period.

Ray Smith was born on 31 October 1938 in Paducah, Kentucky, and educated at high school. He had his own local TV show and made personal appearances at clubs. He played guitar and piano in addition to singing. In 1969 he signed with the Celebrity label. The disc was No 22 and 16 weeks in the U.S. bestsellers.

CONNIE STEVENS
SIXTEEN REASONS *Warner Bros.* [*USA*]. The second million seller (but first solo) for Connie was written by Bill and Doree Post in 1959. (See Edd Byrnes and Connie Stevens, 1959, for Connie's biographical data.) It reached No 3 in the U.S. charts with 24 weeks in the bestsellers; No 9 and 12 weeks in the British bestsellers.

ROLAND STONE
SOMETHING SPECIAL *Ace* [*USA*]. The first million seller for Roland Stone was written by Mac Rebennack.

JOHNNY TILLOTSON
POETRY IN MOTION *Cadence* [*USA*]. The first million seller for Tillotson was written by Paul Kaufman and Mike Anthony. Johnny was born on 20 April 1939 in Jacksonville, Florida, and at the age of eight moved to Palatka, in the same state, and there developed his early musical interest – country music. He had earned a local reputation as a fine performer before he entered high school. Then came a three-year contract as a regular on a TV variety show, 'The Tom Dowdy Show'. Heard by Lee Rosenburg, who arranged an audition with Cadence, Johnny was immediately signed to the label, in 1958. He plays ukulele and guitar as well as singing, and holds two degrees as a graduate of the University of Florida. This disc was top seller in Britain for three weeks in 1961, and reached No 2 in the U.S. charts with 15 weeks in the bestsellers and 15 weeks in Britain.

IKE AND TINA TURNER
A FOOL IN LOVE *Sue* [*USA*]. Ike Turner, born on 4 November 1938 in Clarksdale, Mississippi, became interested in music at the age of six. He played piano in the house of a lady from the church. After high school he formed a group called the Kings of Rhythm which went to Nashville following local success. They recorded 'Rocket 88', Ike's first rhythm-and-blues hit. Dates around St Louis followed with Howling' Wolf and B. B. King. In 1956, Ike met Annie Bullock (born 26 November 1939 in Brownsville, Tennessee) who became Tina Turner. Tina started singing in gospel choirs and talent shows in Knoxville. She went to nightclubs with her sister and often asked Ike if she could sing. He'd say 'O.K.' but never called her to the stage. One night he was playing organ and the drummer put a microphone in front of Tina's sister for her to sing. She refused, so Tina took over, ending up by singing several numbers and later joining the group and becoming Ike's wife.

In 1959, Ike wrote 'A Fool in Love', but the singer never turned up for the session. Tina filled in, the result being a hit record that sold over a million.

From 1960 they took their own 15-piece 'Ike and Tina Turner Revue' around America. Tina's sensuous singing, wild and frantic vocal backed by the four Ikettes and the Kings of Rhythm orchestra, evoked great audience enthusiasm, and they followed up their disc success with a string of big hits. In 1964 they signed with the Warner label, then Philles label, and subsequently with United Artists and Liberty.

They gained ready acceptance in England, due to the fantastic success of their 1966 single 'River Deep, Mountain High' (produced by Phil Spector) on Philles label. Some critics described this as the most passionate performance ever put on record until Aretha Franklin. Tina Turner sings more gutsily than ever in the 1980s.

'A Fool in Love' reached No 2 in the U.S. rhythm-and-blues charts. It was No 27 and 13 weeks in the national bestsellers.

CONWAY TWITTY
LONELY BLUE BOY *MGM* [*USA*]. The second million seller for Twitty was originally called 'Danny' (from Presley's film *King Creole*) written in 1958 by Fred Wise (words) and Ben Weisman (music). It reached No 6 in the U.S. charts and 15 weeks in the bestsellers.

BOBBY VEE AND THE SHADOWS
DEVIL OR ANGEL *Liberty* [*USA*]. The first million seller for rock'n'roll vocalist Bobby Vee was written by Blanche Carter in 1955. Bobby (real name Bobby Velline) was born on 30 April 1943 in Fargo, North Dakota. Several members of his family circle made music their hobby, his father being an accomplished violinist and pianist; his uncle played sax and his two elder brothers the guitar. Bobby learned to play the guitar while at high school. His brothers let him sit in with their 15-piece band on practice sessions. In 1959, the group was asked to fill in on a date for Buddy Holly who had been killed in an air crash. The boys bought identical sweaters, called themselves The Shadows and put Bobby on as vocalist because he knew all the lyrics to the six numbers in their limited repertoire. The audience loved the band, especially young Bobby. It aroused enough professional interest to have the group signed to a Liberty contract and Bobby cut his first disc 'Susie, Baby'. Since then he and the (American) Shadows have had a string of hits, with TV dates and personal appearances in the States and a tour of Britain. The Shadows (American group) were led by Bobby's elder brother Bill (lead guitar, rhythm guitar and composer) with Jim Stillman (electric bass guitar) and Bob Korum (drums). This disc was No 6 for two weeks in the U.S. charts and 19 weeks in the bestsellers.

RUBBER BALL *Liberty* [*USA*]. The second million seller for Bobby Vee was written by Annie Orlowski and Aaron Schroeder. It reached No 6 in the U.S. charts and 14 weeks in the bestsellers, and was No 4 and 11 weeks in the British bestsellers.

THE VENTURES (instrumental rock'n'roll group)
WALK, DON'T RUN *Dolton* [*USA*]. The first million seller for this group was written by Johnny Smith. The group comprises Don Wilson, Bob Bogle, Nokie Edwards (guitars) and Howie Johnson (drums); all were between 23 and 25 years of age when they made this disc. Don and Bob met while working as tuckpointers (removing mortar from brick buildings for new to be inserted) and later teamed up with Nokie and Howie, sending a tape recording to several disc companies without success. They then recorded 'Walk, Don't Run' on the Blue Horizon label (a company they had formed) and circularized the disc jockeys. It was an overnight success for the quartet who had named themselves The Ventures, simply because they were venturing into a new field. Then came an award as 'The most promising instrumental group of 1960', also several successful tours of the U.S.A. and further hit discs. This disc was the best instrumental single of the year. The Blue Horizon venture was affiliated to Dolton Records, a company which had encouraged the boys not to give up. This disc was No 2 in the U.S. charts and 18 weeks in the bestsellers, and No 8 and 13 weeks in the British bestsellers. Don Wilson born 10 February 1937 in Tacoma, Washington. Bob Bogle born 16 January 1937 in Portland, Oregon.

LARRY VERNE

MISTER CUSTER *Era* [*USA*]. This was a sole million seller for Larry who hails from Minneapolis. He was born on 8 February 1936. Larry, a country-and-western beat vocalist, plays the guitar. This is a song with a historical flavour, written by Fred Darian, Al de Lory and Joe Van Winkle. The disc was a No 1 seller in the U.S.A. for one week and 13 weeks in the bestsellers.

DINAH WASHINGTON WITH BROOK BENTON

BABY (You got what it takes) *Mercury* [*USA*]. This first million seller for Dinah was the second for Brook. The song was written in 1959 by Murray Stein and Clyde Otis. This disc is a conversational duet. Dinah (real name Ruth Jones), known as 'Queen of the Blues', was born 29 August 1924 in Tuscaloose, Alabama. She sang and directed the church choir in Chicago, and at the age of 19 became band vocalist with Lionel Hampton. She appeared in nightclubs and theatres, then as a solo artist - one of the best of the coloured jazz singers. She visited Britain in 1959 and appeared on TV and in the film *Jazz on a Summer's Day*. She died on 14 December 1963. (See 1959 for Brook Benton data.) This disc was No 5 in the U.S. charts with 15 weeks in the bestsellers, and a No 1 rhythm-and-blues disc.

MAURICE WILLIAMS AND THE ZODIACS

STAY *Herald* [*USA*]. The first million seller for this group was written by Maurice Williams himself. The disc was No 1 in the U.S.A. for one week and 18 weeks in the bestsellers; No 14 and nine weeks in the British bestsellers.

The group comprised Maurice Williams (born 26 April 1938), Henry Gasten, Willie Bennet and Charles Thomas, all from Lancaster, South Carolina. The group won first prize in a talent show in 1955 at Barr High School in Lancaster. They were then known as The Charms. They travelled the South and came to Nashville where they hoped to be recorded. Williams, the leader-piano player and songwriter, had written 'Little Darlin' which he recorded for Excello label. It was, however, The Diamonds' disc of this that made it a hit (see 1957). The group at this time was called The Gladiolas. They also played under the names of The Royal Charms and The Excellos, and finally The Zodiacs. A contract with Herald Records was signed and then came this big hit 'Stay'.

JACKIE WILSON

NIGHT backed with DOGGIN' AROUND *Brunswick* [*USA*]. This second million seller for Jackie ('Night') was by Johnny Lehman and Herb Millier written in 1959. 'Doggin' Around' was written by Lena Agree. 'Night' is based on a classical theme. 'Night' was No 4 for 2 weeks in the U.S.A. with 17 weeks in the bestsellers, and a No 1 rhythm-and-blues single. 'Doggin' Around' was No 15 and 16 weeks in the U.S. bestsellers.

ORIGINAL THEATRE CAST WITH JULIE ANDREWS, RICHARD BURTON, ROBERT GOULET, ROBERT COOKE, RODDY McDOWALL, NEL DOWD

CAMELOT (album) *Columbia* [*USA*]. Another fine musical show by Alan Jay Lerner (lyrics) and Frederick Loewe (music) following their *My Fair Lady*. Further big laurels came the way of English actress/singer Julie Andrews. *Camelot* was produced on 3 December 1960 at the Majestic Theatre, New York, and ran into 1962, probably the most complex, biggest and most beautiful set musical play yet attempted, compressing into one evening the essence of the legend of King Arthur and his Knights of the Round Table. There were 200 people in the show including 46 stage hands, 41 musicians and 56 actors. This album sold half a million by 1962 with a million by 1963. The contents of disc are as follows: 'Overture'; 'I Wonder What the King is Doing Tonight'; 'The Simple Joys of Maidenhood'; 'Camelot'; 'Follow Me'; 'The Lusty Month of May'; 'C'est moi'; 'Then You May Take Me to the Fair'; 'How to Handle a Woman'; 'If Ever I Would Leave You'; 'Parade'; 'Before I Gaze at You Again'; 'The Seven Deadly Virtues'; 'What Do the Simple Folks Do'; 'Fie on Goodness'; 'I Loved You Once in Silence'; 'Guinevere'; 'Camelot'.

Camelot cost $480,000 to produce, the money being put up by CBS. It was directed by Moss Hart. The disc was No 1 in the U.S.A. for six weeks, and in the bestsellers list for 265 weeks. Gold Disc award R.I.A.A. 1962.

ORIGINAL SOUNDTRACK WITH NATALIE WOOD, RICHARD BEYMER, RUSS TAMBLYN, RITA MORENO, GEORGE CHAKIRIS AND TUCKER SMITH

WEST SIDE STORY (album) *Columbia* [*USA*]. For a second time this famous musical show of 1957 by Stephen Sondheim (lyrics) and Leonard Bernstein (music) sold a million discs. This filmtrack album sold five million by 1970 in the U.S.A., plus three million elsewhere. *West Side Story* won 10 Academy Awards including the Best Motion Picture of 1961. The disc contains the following: 'Prologue'; 'Jet Song' (Russ Tamblyn and the Jets); 'Something's Coming' (Richard Beymer); 'Dance at the Gym' (orchestra); 'Maria' (Richard Beymer); 'America' (Rita Moreno, George Chakiris, Sharks and Girls); 'Tonight' (Richard Beymer and Natalie Wood); 'Quintet' (Richard Beymer, Natalie Wood, Rita Moreno, Jets); 'I Feel Pretty' (Natalie Wood and Girls); 'One Hand, One Heart' (Beymer and Wood); 'The Rumble' (orchestra); 'Cool' (Tucker Smith and Jets); 'A Boy Like That' (Wood and Moreno); 'I Have a Love' (Wood and Moreno); 'Somewhere' (Beymer and Wood).

The stereo disc was No 1 for 54 weeks (May 1962-63); in the Top 10 for nearly two years in the U.S.A.; and in the bestsellers charts for 198 weeks. Gold Disc award R.I.A.A. 1963. Grammy Award, 'Best Original Cast Album Recording' (1961).

Note: Natalie Wood's voice in these songs is not her own. The dubbing was by Marni Nixon, and some of Beymer's songs were also dubbed. Betty Wand dubbed for some of Rita Moreno's songs.

THE ALLISONS

ARE YOU SURE? *Fontana* [*Britain*]. This was the sole million seller for the 'Brothers' John and Bob - real names John Brian Alford born on 31 December 1939, London, and Bob Colin Day, born in Trowbridge 21 February 1942. Both were educated in London and first sang together in a church choir. They had a mutual passion for composing and singing, and, after perfecting their style by playing in coffee bars and local concerts, they won a talent contest in 1960 and an audition for Fontana Records. Fame came overnight when they took second place for Great Britain in the Eurovision Song Contest in March 1961 with their own composition 'Are You Sure?' Prior to entering show business Johnny was an engineering draughtsman, and Bob a clerk. They made many guest appearances after the success of this song. This disc was No 1 in Britain for two weeks with 16 weeks in the bestsellers.

KENNY BALL (traditional jazz trumpet) AND HIS BAND

MIDNIGHT IN MOSCOW *Pye* [*Britain*]. This first million seller for Kenny Ball. 'Midnight in Moscow' is based on a song by the Russian writers, Vassili Soloviev-Sedoi and M. Matusovsky, arranged by Kenny Ball. Kenneth Daniel Ball was born on 22 May 1931 in Ilford, Essex and started his career as a semi-professional with Charlie Galbraith's All Star Jazz Band in 1951, his former occupations being a salesman and working in an advertising agency. He entered show business when 23. He first joined Sid Phillips' Band, then Eric Delaney's Band and Terry Lightfoot's New Orleans Jazzmen, making his first important public appearance with Lightfoot at the Festival of Jazz in London's Royal Albert Hall in 1959 as a soloist, and his TV debut around the same time. In December 1958 he formed his own band of trumpet (himself), trombone, clarinet, piano, drums, bass and banjo, making a successful debut at a British resort after intensive rehearsals. After their TV debut in 'New Faces' (March 1959) and BBC radio dates, the band toured the Continent, playing at jazz clubs with seasons in 1959 and 1960 at Storyville Club, Frankfurt, Germany. Lonnie Donegan heard them at a TV audition and was so impressed that he brought them to the attention of Pye Records who signed them up. Their first disc hit was 'Samantha' (1961), then came the 'Moscow' disc, which enjoyed tremendous sales all over the world, reaching No 2 position in the U.S. hit parade in March 1962 with 14 weeks in the U.S. bestsellers, when released there on the Kapp label. It was No 2, and 21 weeks in the British bestsellers. One of the best traditional jazz bands, they have visited the U.S.A., toured Australia and New Zealand, the Far East and returned to make more European appearances. Kenny also sings and plays the mouth-organ. In 1963 Kenny was the first British jazzman to become an honorary citizen of New Orleans. Original Russian title of song was 'Padmeskoveeye Vietchera'.

JOE BARRY (pop ballad vocalist)

I'M A FOOL TO CARE Smash [USA]. Joe Barry (real name Joe Barious) was born on 13 July and hails from Cut Off, Louisiana. He was educated at high school and started singing with gospel groups. He also studied music with famed Al Hirt and Pete Fountain.

Joe appeared at record hops and also on TV. He plays guitar, drums and piano and writes his own arrangements.

The song was written in 1948 by country-and-western artist/ songwriter Ted Daffan. Barry's disc reached No 24 in the U.S. charts with 12 weeks in the bestsellers, and No 49 in Britain, the million sale being reported in 1968.

He was signed to Nugget records in 1968.

RALF BENDIX

BABYSITTIN' BOOGIE Electrola [Germany]. This first million seller for Ralf Bendix was an American song with German words written by Joachim Relin. Bendix was both a disc star and a director of TWA airlines in Dusseldorf, Germany. His first disc success was 'Kriminal Tango' which sold over 750,000 in 1960, followed by 'Babysittin' Boogie'. In 1955 he appeared on a regular show for Pittsburgh TV in the U.S.A. He is a seasoned performer, speaks several languages and does a top stage show. He appeared in Las Vegas in 1961 and did another U.S. tour in 1962. This disc sold its million on the Continent. This number was written by the U.S.A. composer J. Parker in 1960.

BROOK BENTON

BOLL WEEVIL SONG Mercury [USA]. The third million seller for Brook Benton was written in 1960 by Clyde Otis and Brook Benton himself. It is a new version of an old American song, telling the story of the farmer and the boll weevil bugs – the little eaters that devastate the cotton crops. The disc was No 2 for three weeks in the U.S. charts and 16 weeks in the bestsellers, and No 30 in Britain and nine weeks in the bestsellers.

MR ACKER BILK (traditional jazz clarinet) WITH LEON YOUNG STRING CHORALE

STRANGER ON THE SHORE Columbia [USA]. Here is the first million seller for Britain's top jazz clarinettist. Its global sales were around four million by 1967, with the first million being sold by April 1962. The disc is said to have grossed £36,000

for Acker Bilk. The disc had the longest reign up to 1966 in the British bestsellers – 55 weeks, being No 1 for one week in 1962; and was a No 1 chart hit in the U.S.A. also (for one week in 1962) with 21 weeks in their bestsellers. The tune was composed by Acker Bilk and issued by Atlantic Records in the U.S.A. as part of an album 'Sentimental Journey'. Bilk named it 'Jenny' after one of his children. About this time the BBC was planning to feature Bilk playing the signature tune for a children's TV series called 'Stranger on the Shore', so 'Jenny' was retitled and issued in Britain as a single to tie in with the series. It immediately shot into the sellers' charts. Bernard Stanley Bilk was born on 28 January, in Somerset in 1929. His father was a Methodist lay preacher, his mother a church organist. He took up the clarinet to pass the time while in an Army jail in Egypt for three months through falling asleep on guard (1947). After Army discharge, he gave up his job as a blacksmith, and again took up the clarinet forming his own group, 'The Paramount Jazz Band', in 1958. After a period of semi-professional playing around the Bristol area, the band went to Dusseldorf, playing jazz in beer cellars. They made their first recordings for the independent producer Denis Preston of Record Supervision in London. Acker's first hit was a quiet blues 'Summer Set' (1960), written by his former pianist Dave Collett. Then came 'Stranger on the Shore' to give Acker international fame and fortune, and to make him the 'Best Instrumentalist' of 1962 here and in the U.S.A. In his familiar bowler hat and coloured waistcoat, Acker (rural name for 'mate') and his band were in great demand. He appeared in the Royal Variety show in 1961. The disc was issued on the Atco label in the U.S.A. Gold Disc award, R.I.A.A., 1 June 1967.

GARY 'U.S.' BONDS

QUARTER TO THREE Le Grand [USA]. The first million seller for Gary, whose real name is Gary Anderson, was written by J. Royster, G. Barge, G. Anderson and F. Guida. Rock'n'roll singer Gary was born on 6 June 1939, in Jacksonville, Florida and began singing at the age of nine in his church choir, and from 13 performing in different churches and choir groups. In 1952 he formed his own group The Turks, and became a solo artist after it disbanded. For some 12 years he was a resident of Norfolk, Virginia, singing in various local nightclubs. He then met Frank J. Guida, head of the Norfolk Recording Studio who felt he had great promise. His first disc 'New Orleans' was a big hit, then came 'Quarter to Three' followed by other hit singles in 'rock' style. This disc was No 1 in the U.S.A. for two weeks and 15 weeks in the bestsellers, and No 7 and 13 weeks in Britain's bestsellers.

PAT BOONE

MOODY RIVER *Dot* [*USA*]. This 12th million seller for Pat Boone was written by Gary D. Bruce. The disc was a No 1 in the U.S.A. for one week and 15 weeks in the bestsellers, and No 18 and 10 weeks in Britain's bestsellers.

DAVE BRUBECK QUARTET (instrumental jazz group)

TAKE FIVE *Columbia* [*USA*]. Dave (David Warren) Brubeck was born 6 December 1920 in Concord, California, and originally wanted to be a veterinarian in order to continue his father's cattle business. From local grammar schools, he went on to study at the College of the Pacific at Stockton, California, in 1938, and from 1942 studied under Darius Milhaud (one of the avant garde composers) at Mills College, Oakland, California, and later at the University of California. He also studied music under Arnold Schoenberg. He naturally found the lure of music very strong, and the talented pianist formed an octet at college in 1948. After serving in the Army during World War II, he joined a band headed by the outstanding alto saxophonist Paul Desmond for a short while, and continued his studies under Milhaud, then formed various groups and became a great favourite of college campuses all over the U.S.A. as a result of his definitive jazz stylings and arrangements. Around 1950 his quartet, which then included Paul Desmond, made frequent appearances on radio, TV, nightclubs and a series of concert tours which made him one of the most sought-after musicians in the country. He started recording for the Fantasy label of Oakland, California, and from 1954 was signed by Columbia, for whom he recorded many singles and albums. One of these albums 'Time Out', recorded in 1959, included 'Take Five', a composition by Paul Desmond, the first famous jazz tune in 5/4 tempo.

Both this album and another 'Time Further Out' had very big sales during 1962 and appeared in the Top Ten of the album charts. The uniqueness of 'Take Five' resulted in its release as a singles disc in 1961 and it reached No 25 in the U.S. charts with 12 weeks in the bestsellers, a high position for a jazz disc at a time when rock'n'roll still predominated. The disc was also a great favourite in Britain where it was No 5 for one week in 1961 and 15 weeks in the bestsellers. Sales around the world are said to be several millions.

The Dave Brubeck Quartet were voted the Top Instrumental Group of 1961, and consisted of Dave Brubeck (piano), Paul Desmond (alto sax), Joe Morello (drums) and Eugene Wright (bass).

JERRY BUTLER

MOON RIVER *Vee Jay* [*USA*]. This faboulously successful song, introduced by Audrey Hepburn in the film *Breakfast at Tiffany's*, received three Grammy Awards and had countless recordings. The biggest seller on disc was this version by Jerry Butler, which according to artist Andy Williams (who also had a big hit with it) sold over the million. Jerry's disc was released around October 1961, reached No 8 for two weeks and stayed in the U.S. bestsellers for 17 weeks.

The song was written by Johnny Mercer (words) and Henry Mancini (music). Mancini, who scored the music for the film also had a hit with his version that reached No 11 and stayed in the U.S. charts for 20 weeks. (See also Mancini, 1961, for additional data, and 1969 for Butler biography.)

RAY CHARLES

HIT THE ROAD, JACK *ABC-Paramount* [*USA*]. The third million seller for Ray was written by disc artist Percy Mayfield. The disc was No 1 in the U.S.A. for two weeks and 13 weeks in the bestsellers, and was No 6 in Britain with 12 weeks in the charts. Winner of N.A.R.A.S. Award for 'Best Rhythm-and-Blues Recording' 1961. A top rhythm-and-blues disc. Released 21 August 1961.

ONE MINT JULEP *ABC-Paramount* [*USA*]. Released in March 1961, this disc soon reached No 8 for two weeks on the U.S. charts with 13 weeks in the bestsellers, subsequently selling a million, his fourth to do so. The song was a revival of a 1953 hit written by Rudolph Toombs who had a big success then with recordings by The Clovers and Louis Prima.

CHUBBY CHECKER

PONY TIME *Cameo-Parkway* [*USA*]. Chubby's second million seller was written in 1960 by Don Covay and John Berry. This disc was No 1 in the U.S.A. for three weeks with 16 weeks in the bestsellers; No 27 and six weeks in the British charts. A top rhythm-and-blues disc, this is a rewrite of Pinetop Smith's famous 'Boogie Woogie' (see Dorsey, 1938).

LET'S TWIST AGAIN *Cameo-Parkway* [*USA*]. The third million seller for Chubby was written by Kal Mann and Dave Appell, both of Cameo's Artists and Repertoire Department. This disc was a top seller in Britain for two weeks in 1962, and got to No 8 in the U.S. charts with 12 weeks in the bestsellers. Winner of N.A.R.A.S. Award for 'Best Rock and Roll Recording' 1961. With revivals up to 1975 it was 44 weeks in the British bestsellers.

THE FLY *Cameo-Parkway* [*USA*]. Chubby's fourth million seller was written by J. Madara and D. White. It got to No 7 in the U.S. charts with 13 weeks in the bestsellers.

DEE CLARK

RAINDROPS *Vee Jay* [*USA*]. Dee wrote his own million seller 'Raindrops'. He was born in Blythsville, Arkansas, on 7 November 1938, and is one of six children, having two brothers and three sisters. His family moved in 1940 to Chicago where he attended Farren Grammar School and, after moving again, graduated from Calhoun Grammar School. His musical interest stems from his mother, Delecta, a spiritual singer. In 1952, Dee joined a group, the Hambone Kids, and made a disc 'Hambone' for Okeh Records. In 1955 he was with a group called The Goldentones, and they won first prize at Roberts Show Lounge in Chicago, a talent contest. This brought them to the attention of Herb Kent, a Chicago disc jockey who changed their name to The Kool Gents and took them to Vee Jay's studios. Their disc of 'The Convention' had Dee in the lead and Vee Jay's artists and repertoire executive Calvin Carter saw tremendous potential in him as a singles artist. After a few discs, Dee's 'Nobody But You', a song he wrote, put him on the road to success, followed eventually by this hit 'Raindrops', which achieved No 2 in the U.S. charts with 16 weeks in the bestsellers.

PETULA CLARK

ROMEO *Pye* [*Britain*]. 'Romeo' was reputedly the first million seller for Petula Clark, with its sale achieved in Europe in 1962. This song was originally published in Germany in 1920 under the title 'Salome', written by Robert Stolz, famous in Europe for his operettas. The English lyric for the new title 'Romeo' is by Britain's Jimmy Kennedy (1961). (See 'Monsieur', 1962, for biographical data on Petula Clark.) The disc was No 3 for two weeks in Britain and 15 weeks in the bestsellers.

THE COUSINS (instrumental group)

KILI WATCH *Palette* [*Belgium*]. 'Kili Watch' was both the first record for the Palette label and the first million seller (on the Continent) by this quartet of students: Adrien Ransy (drums), Gus Devon (lead guitar), Andre Vandemeerschoot (rhythm guitar) and Jacky (rhythm guitar). They were discovered at the club 'Les Cousins' in Brussels, Belgium, from which they took their name. The disc got into the bestsellers' lists immediately and made the group one of the hottest combinations on the Continent. They appeared on TV and radio in Belgium, Holland, France, Sweden, Germany and Italy. This traditional tune was adapted and written by Gus Derse.

FLOYD CRAMER (piano)

ON THE REBOUND *Victor* [*USA*]. This second million seller for Floyd was his own composition. Written in 1960, it reached No 4 with 13 weeks in the U.S. bestsellers, and No 1 and 14 weeks in the British bestsellers.

JAMES DARREN

GOODBYE CRUEL WORLD *Colpix* [*USA*]. This first million seller for Darren was written by Gloria Shayne. Darren (real name James Ercolani) was born in Philadelphia on 8 June 1936, and studied at the Epiphany and Southern High Schools there. While at school he took lessons on the trumpet and became very proficient, and formed his own jazz band for local functions. As far as he could remember, he always wanted to be a singer and an actor. On leaving school he took lessons with the drama coach Stella Adler and shortly afterwards was spotted by a talent scout for Columbia Pictures, with whom he has a long-term contract. His film debut was in *Rumble on the Docks* (1959), and later he starred in such films as *The Gene Krupa Story*, *The Guns of Navarone*, *Gidget* and many others. Columbia signed him to their record subsidiary Colpix, and Jimmy made discs in between making films, this disc being his biggest success. It was No 3 for two weeks in the U.S. charts and 17 weeks in the bestsellers, and was No 28 in Britain, with nine weeks in the bestsellers.

JIMMY DEAN

BIG BAD JOHN *Columbia* [*USA*]. This was a first million seller for country-and-western singer Dean. He wrote the song. He was born on 10 August 1928 on a farm outside Plainview, Texas, and began his musical career at the age 10, first learning to play the piano, then mastering the accordion and guitar. Dean's musical and Air Corps careers developed simultaneously. He filled in as a replacement with the Tennessee Haymakers, a country-music quartet made of Air Force buddies who played during off-duty hours in their Washington Base bars for $5 a night. In 1952, Dean caught the eye of Connie B. Guy who hired him to perform for the U.S. troops in the Caribbean. After this tour Dean worked on radio and TV in Washington, and in 1957 began his CBS-TV network show, winning many fans. In April 1957 he was signed to Columbia Records. 'Big Bad John' was his first big pop hit, and was a top seller in the U.S.A. for five weeks and in the bestsellers for a total of 16 weeks. It was No 2 and 13 weeks in the British charts. Winner of N.A.R.A.S. Award for 'Best Country-and-Western Recording' 1961. A top country seller. It tells the story of the heroism of a big and immensely strong bad man of repute who saves others in a mine disaster but sacrifices his own life. Disc received Gold Disc award from R.I.A.A., 1961.

JOEY DEE AND THE STARLITERS

PEPPERMINT TWIST *Roulette* [*USA*]. Joey Dee and his Starliters comprise Carlton Latimor (organist); Willie Davis (drums); Larry Vernieri and David Brigati (song and dance). 'Peppermint Twist' was written by Joey Dee and Henry Glover. Dee was born on 11 June 1940 in Passaic, New Jersey. The group started in 1958, and played for over 12 months from 1960 at New York's famous Peppermint Lounge, without doubt the home of twist music, a nightclub that developed into a gold mine. From late 1961 they went on a nationwide tour with audiences going wild for their music. They also appeared in films including *Hey Let's Twist* and *Vive le Twist*. They were a versatile group, each member a competent instrumentalist (they all play saxophone and at least one other instrument) and vocal soloist. The Starliters were 'twisting' at every opportunity. Roulette Records rapidly signed the group to record this their first million seller and their biggest hit. They also had a hit with their album 'Doing the Twist at the Peppermint Lounge'. 'Peppermint Twist' was No 1 for three weeks in the U.S.A. in 1962 and 18 weeks in the bestsellers, and was No 33 in Britain, with eight weeks in the bestsellers.

DICK AND DEEDEE

THE MOUNTAIN'S HIGH (*Lama*) *Liberty* [*USA*]. This first million seller for Dick and Deedee was written by Dick (real name Dick St John Gosting). Dick was 21 when he recorded the disc with an 18-year-old girl – Deedee. Dick had been recording for some time without success when he met the Wilder Brothers and Don Ralke who became managers and arrangers for them. They took Dick to a small California studio called Lama Records, to cut a song 'I Want Someone' that Dick and Deedee (real name Sperling) had written. A female voice was needed for the flip side of the disc, so Dick called on Deedee whom he had known since junior high school for his song 'The Mountain's High'. It was this side of the disc that broke first in San Francisco, spreading rapidly throughout the U.S.A., when later released by Liberty Records. The duo did a tour of Texas with other disc stars, both returning to college and cutting more discs between studies, Dick at Los Angeles Art Center and Deedee at Santa Monica City College. This disc was No 2 for two weeks in the U.S. charts and 15 weeks in the bestsellers. It reached No 37 in Britain.

DION WITH ORCHESTRA CONDUCTED BY GLEN STUART

RUNAROUND SUE *Laurie* [*USA*]. This second million seller for Dion (originally of the team Dion and The Belmonts) (see 1959) was his first solo hit. The song was written by Ernie Maresca and Dion himself. This disc was No 1 in the U.S.A. for two weeks and 14 weeks in the bestsellers, reaching No 11 with nine weeks in the British bestsellers.

THE WANDERER *Laurie* [*USA*]. The third million seller for Dion was entirely the work of Ernie Maresca. Written in 1960, the disc reached No 2 with 18 weeks in the U.S. bestsellers, and No 10 with 21 weeks in the British bestsellers (1962 and 1976).

LEE DORSEY

YA YA *Fury* [*USA*]. This million seller for beat vocalist Lee Dorsey was written by C. Lewis, M. Robinson and Dorsey himself ('Ya Ya' means a boy or girl friend.) The song was also a success for Britain's Petula Clark.

Lee Dorsey was born on 4 December 1926 in Portland, Oregon, where he developed into a top contender for the World Lightweight Boxing Championship. His career was interrupted for four years when he joined the U.S. Navy. He returned to boxing and gave up when he was discovered singing in New Orleans while underneath a car repairing it at his automobile shop, resulting in his recording of 'Ya Ya'. Another hit 'Do-Re-Mi' followed, both becoming collectors' classics. After a while he stopped recording and returned to his car businesses plus a grocer's shop, then re-commenced recording later with a big hit in 'Ride Your Pony' for the Amy label in 1965.

He went to London in 1966 for a club tour. Lee was known in America as 'Mr T.N.T.'

This disc achieved the No 7 position in the U.S. charts with 13 weeks in the bestsellers, and was a top rhythm-and-blues disc.

THE DOVELLS

BRISTOL STOMP *Cameo-Parkway* [*USA*]. This vocal group comprised Len Barry, lead singer; Arnie Satin, baritone; Jerry Summers, first tenor; Danny Brooks, bass; and Mike Dennis, second tenor. They all hailed from Philadelphia, singing together from 1957 mostly for local and school functions. After their first disc, which was not a success, they went their separate ways, but got together again in December 1960. In the spring of 1961 they gave an audition for Dave Appell, a director of Parkway Records, and were signed to a contract. The Dovells then made this disc which quickly put them in the U.S.A. limelight, following up with a string of hits. This song, the Dovells' first million seller, was written by Kal Mann and Dave Appell of Cameo Records. It was No 2 for two weeks in the U.S. charts and 16 weeks in the bestsellers.

JOE DOWELL

WOODEN HEART *Smash* [*USA*]. The U.S.A. release of this version of the song also recorded by Elvis Presley in Europe, also sold a million. Joe Dowell's disc reached No 1 for a week and stayed in the U.S. bestsellers for 16 weeks. Release was in June 1961.

Joe Dowell was born in 1943 in Bloomington, Illinois. He had a college education, and later made personal appearances. He is also a songwriter and plays guitar.

'Wooden Heart' is based on the German folk song 'Muss I denn zum Stadtele naus' with words and adaptation by Ben Weisman, Kay Twomey and Bert Kaempfert (famous arranger/conductor) and written in 1960.

JIMMY ELLEDGE (vocalist)

FUNNY (How time slips away) *Victor* [*USA*]. Written by Willie Nelson, this disc is said to have sold a million through the years.

Born on 8 January 1943 in Nashville, Tennessee, Jimmy decided to become a recording artist, wrote a song, put it on tape and submitted it to Chet Atkins at RCA Victor. Chet signed him to a contract and 'Funny How Time Slips Away', his first record, became a bestseller. He later signed with the Hickory label. This disc reached No 22 with 14 weeks in the U.S. bestsellers.

THE EVERLY BROTHERS

WALK RIGHT BACK backed with EBONY EYES *Warner Bros.* [*USA*]. 'Walk Right Back' was written by Sonny Curtis in 1960, while 'Ebony Eyes' was written by John D. Loudermilk. This top disc seller in Britain for three weeks (with 16 weeks in the bestsellers) was the Everly Brothers' ninth million seller. 'Walk Right Back' reached No 7 in the U.S. charts and 13 weeks in the bestsellers. 'Ebony Eyes' was No 8 and 12 weeks in the bestsellers.

FERRANTE AND TEICHER

TONIGHT *United Artists* [*USA*]. This superb piano duet rendering of the hit song from the *West Side Story* musical of 1957 by Leonard Bernstein (music) and Stephen Sondheim (words) gave the wonderful team of Ferrante and Teicher their third million seller. It reached No 8 with 13 weeks in the bestsellers.

CONNIE FRANCIS

WHERE THE BOYS ARE *MGM* [*USA*]. This 10th million seller for Connie (her ninth solo) came from the film of the same title in which she made her debut. The song was written by Howard Greenfield (words) and Neil Sedaka (music) in 1960. It was No 4 for two weeks in the U.S.A. and 15 weeks in the bestsellers, No 5 and 14 weeks in the British bestsellers.

TOGETHER *MGM* [*USA*]. 'Together' is a revival of the hit of 1928 written by the great songwriting team of B. G. de Sylva, Lew Brown and Ray Henderson. The accompaniment is by the Cliff Parman orchestra. This was Connie's 11th million seller. It reached No 6 in the U.S. charts with 11 weeks in the bestsellers, and similarly in Britain.

FREDDY (Quinn)

LA PALOMA *Polydor* [*Germany*]. The melody of 'La Paloma' was written by Sebastian Yradier sometime before 1877. It is one of the world's best-known tango tunes. Freddy's vocal version was extremely popular on the Continent and produced a fifth million seller for him by 1962.

JUDY GARLAND (vocal) WITH ORCHESTRA CONDUCTED BY MORT LINDSEY

JUDY AT CARNEGIE HALL (double album) *Capitol* [*USA*]. This is a wonderful two-disc album of Judy's sensational per-

formance in New York's famous concert hall in May 1961. The album was No 1 in the U.S.A. for 13 consecutive weeks, and in the U.S. bestsellers' lists for 85 weeks. It sold half a million by 1962 and the million subsequently. Gold Disc award R.I.A.A. 1962, and Grammy Awards for Best Engineering Contribution (popular recording) and Best Album Cover, 1961. The contents of the discs are: *Overture* 'The Trolley Song', by Hugh Martin and Ralph Blane (1944); 'Over the Rainbow', by E. Y. Harburg and Harold Arlen (1939); 'Man That Got Away', by Ira Gershwin and Harold Arlen (1954); 'When You're Smiling', by Mark Fisher, Joe Goodwin and Larry Shay (1928); *Medley* 'Almost Like Being in Love', by Alan J. Lerner and Frederick Loewe (1947); 'This Can't Be Love', by Lorenz Hart and Richard Rodgers (1938); 'Do It Again', by B. G. De Sylva and George Gershwin (1922); 'You Go to My Head', by Haven Gillespie and J. Fred Coots (1938); 'Alone Together', by Howard Dietz and Arthur Schwartz (1932); 'Who Cares?' by Ira Gershwin and George Gershwin (1931); 'Puttin' on the Ritz', by Irving Berlin (1929); 'How Long Has This Been Going On?' by Ira Gershwin and George Gershwin (1927); 'Just You, Just Me', by Raymond Klages and Jesse Greer (1929); 'The Man That Got Away', by Ira Gershwin and Harold Arlen (1954); 'San Francisco', by Gus Kahn, W. Jurmann and B. Kaper (1936); 'I Can't Give You Anything but Love', by Dorothy Fields and Jimmy McHugh (1928); 'That's Entertainment', by Howard Dietz and Arthur Schwartz (1953); 'Come Rain or Come Shine', by Johnny Mercer and Harold Arlen (1946); 'You're Nearer', by Lorenz Hart and Richard Rodgers (1940); 'A Foggy Day', by Ira Gershwin and George Gershwin (1937); 'If Love Were All', by Noel Coward (1929); 'Zing, Went the Strings of My Heart', by James F. Hanley (1935); 'Stormy Weather', by Ted Koehler and Harold Arlen (1933); *Medley* 'You Made Me Love You', by Joe McCarthy and Jas. V. Monaco (1913); 'For Me and My Gal', by Edgar Leslie, E. Ray Goetz and George W. Meyer (1917); 'The Trolley Song', by Hugh Martin and Ralph Blane (1944); 'Rock-a-bye Your Baby with a Dixie Melody', by Sam M. Lewis, Joe Young and Jean Schwartz (1918); 'Over the Rainbow', by E. Y. Harburg and Harold Arlen (1939); 'After You've Gone', by Henry Creamer and Turner Layton (1918); 'Chicago', by Fred Fisher (1922).

EARL GRANT (organist/vocalist)

EBB TIDE *Decca* [*USA*]. Earl Grant, Negro singer-organist, was born in 1931, and started playing the organ at the age of four, performing at the services presided over by his father, a Baptist minister. He became a music teacher. It was while serving as a soldier at Fort Bliss, Texas, in the 1950s that he made his mark as a singing organist and subsequently appeared at nightclubs, in TV, films and personal appearances in the U.S.A. and abroad. He started to record for Decca in 1957 and had a long string of hits on the label including 50 albums, the biggest being 'Ebb Tide, Beyond the Reef' and other instrumental favourites released after the success of the singles disc 'Ebb Tide' in 1961. The album sold half a million and the singles disc went over the million. Earl Grant played frequently at the Pigalle Club in Los Angeles and he also appeared in such films as *Tender Is the Night* (1962), *Imitation of Life* and *Tokyo Night*.

His numerous successful singles include 'House of Bamboo' (written by British composer Norman Murrells), 'The End' and 'Ol' Man River'. 'Ebb Tide' was written by Carl Sigman (words) and Robert Maxwell (music) in 1953.

After an appearance at the La Fiesta Club in Juarez, Mexico, on 10 June 1970, he was killed in an automobile crash in the New Mexico desert near Lordsburg, New Mexico, when his Rolls Royce swerved off a road.

Earl also played piano, drums and trumpet. His home town was Oklahoma City.

BUDDY GRECO WITH ORCHESTRA

THE LADY IS A TRAMP *Epic* [*USA*]. Buddy Greco considers that his biggest break was when he had this hit record that sold over a million. His swinging singing and piano style is aptly suited to this standard written by the late Lorenz Hart (words) and Richard Rodgers (music) for their musical *Babes in Arms* in 1937. Buddy says his biggest influence was Art Tatum, the jazz pianist with whom he studied for two years. (See 1948 for further biography.)

This disc was released in Britain on the Fontana label, and was No 26 and eight weeks in the bestsellers.

JOHNNY HALLYDAY

LET'S TWIST AGAIN (Viens danser le Twist) *Philips* [*France*]. Johnny Hallyday, the French 'Elvis', is reputed to have sold a million of his combined English and French versions of this American twist song written by Kal Mann and Dave Appell in 1961. French words by Gosset. Teenbeat vocalist/guitarist Johnny (real name Jean Philippe Smet) was born in Paris in spring 1943 of a French mother and Belgian father. After his parents parted he was reared from the age of six by his aunt, wife of an American dancer in vaudeville named Lee Hallyday. With them he travelled the world from Cairo to Mexico City, eventually joining their song and dance act. He became France's first and most authentic rock'n'roller, the idol of the teenagers, the highest paid pop singer by 1961 on the Continent ($1,000 a night) and sold two-and-a-half million discs in 1961, a phenomenon in France. In his act, he sang about half the time in English and has acquired a unique hillbilly accent. In 1961 he made a feature movie *Les Parisiennes*. By 1969 his disc sales totalled 12 million.

THE HIGHWAYMEN

MICHAEL (Row the boat ashore) *United Artists* [*USA*]. The first million seller for this vocal quintet, is a traditional song which originated among the slaves in Georgia, Alabama, who travelled by boat each day between the mainland and their quarters on the islands dotted along the coast. This version was arranged by Dave Fisher. The group, all senior honour students at Wesleyan University, Middletown, Connecticut, came into existence by mere coincidence. They got together to prepare an act for a party. It went over so well that they decided to continue with it, performing for their fellow students at college. In late 1960, they went to New York where they met Ken Greengrass, later their manager, who got the group signed to United Artists. They made an album which included 'Michael' which, when released as a single, zoomed to the top of the U.S.A. hit parade to become one of the top sellers of 1961. The personnel are Steve Butts, guitar and bass singer from New York City; Chan Daniels, guitar, charango and baritone singer; Bob Burnett, guitar, bongos, maracas and tenor singer, from Mystic, Connecticut; Steven Trott, guitar and tenor singer from Mexico City; and Dave Fisher, guitar, banjo, recorder, bongos, lead tenor, arranger and organizer from New Haven, Connecticut. The Highwaymen sang in English, French, Hebrew and Spanish, doing a spread of folk songs both American and foreign. They turned down countless offers of tours and personal appearances after this disc hit in order to concentrate on their studies. This disc was No 1 for two weeks in the U.S.A. with 17 weeks in the bestsellers, and top seller in Britain for one week with 14 weeks in the bestsellers.

CHRIS KENNER

I LIKE IT LIKE THAT *Instant* [*USA*]. Allen Toussaint and Chris Kenner jointly wrote this number, which reputedly became the first million seller for the teenbeat singer Chris. It was No 2 for three weeks in the U.S. charts and 17 weeks in the bestsellers.

GLADYS KNIGHT AND THE PIPS

EVERY BEAT OF MY HEART *Vee Jay* [*USA*]. Gladys Knight began her singing career at the age of four, and classical training at seven when she appeared on the Ted Mack Amateur Hour and won first prize in the finals. Prior to this she sang in church choirs and at recitals in her native town of Atlanta, Georgia. Until 1955 she made many public appearances as a solo artist and then became part of a group. In 1958, Gladys Knight and The Pips was formed, a family group consisting of her brother Merald 'Bubber' Knight, and her two cousins William Guest and Edward Patten. All started singing from an early age in high school together, the boys writing their own material as well. When they were ready to work, they proved to be a great success on their tours and were contracted to Vee Jay Records for whom they recorded this song, originally written by Johnny Otis in 1952. It is said to have sold a million in 1967, and was a No 1 in the rhythm-and-blues charts of 1961. It reached No 45 in the U.S. national charts.

The group have appeared throughout America at theatres and on TV with their soul singing. In 1967 they joined the famed Tamla-Motown recording company of Detroit.

'Every Beat of My Heart' is a slow, delicate soul ballad with a spine-tingling vocal by Gladys.

Merald Knight and William Guest are expert bongo-drummers as well as singers.

BOBBY LEWIS

TOSSIN' AND TURNIN' *Beltone* [*USA*]. The top hit of 1961 and was the first million seller for Bobby Lewis. It was written by Ritchie Adams and Malou Rene. Bobby was born on 17 February 1933 in Indianapolis and spent most of his early life in an orphanage. At the age of five, the orphanage board of directors sponsored him for piano lessons when he showed a remarkable talent for music. He proved an apt student. He was adopted at the age of 12, and taken to live in Detroit. Bobby began his career with an early morning radio show on a local station, then he travelled the usual round of local clubs and theatres. Teenbeat-singer Bobby took a long time to become a success, his disc career taking him through several labels, when he was finally spotted

by Joe Rene of Beltone Records who put his abilities as a vocalist to good use in his initial Beltone release of 'Tossin' and Turnin'' of which Rene was part writer. This disc was No 1 for seven weeks in the U.S.A. with 23 weeks in the bestsellers, and a top rhythm-and-blues disc.

GENE McDANIELS
ONE HUNDRED POUNDS OF CLAY *Liberty* [*USA*]. This song was written by B. Elgin, L. Dixon and K. Rogers. Gene was born on 12 February 1935 in Kansas City, Kansas. His strongest early influence was his father, a minister of religion. At 13, Gene joined and toured with a gospel group playing the sax. During high school in Omaha, he was a fine basketball player. After high school, Gene formed his own quartet, including everything from gospel to jazz in its repertoire. While touring with them he found time to attend Omaha University, Nebraska University and Omaha Conservatory of Music. He then signed with Liberty Records and gained attention with some discs, including 'In Times Like These' and 'The Green Door', finally breaking through with his first million seller 'One Hundred Pounds of Clay' (No 3 in the U.S. charts and 15 weeks in the bestsellers), followed by other successes such as 'Tower of Strength'.

HENRY MANCINI AND HIS ORCHESTRA
'BREAKFAST AT TIFFANY'S' (album - soundtrack) *Victor* [*USA*]. The second album to sell a million (by 1966) for composer/conductor Mancini. The stereo disc was No 1 for 12 weeks in early 1962 and the monaural disc was No 2 for two weeks. Both stayed high in the U.S.A. charts for many weeks and discs enjoyed a run of almost 18 months from the time of release in August 1961. They included 'Breakfast at Tiffany's' (theme), 'Holly', 'Something for the Cat', 'Moon River', 'Sally's Tomato', 'Mr Yunioshi', 'The Big Blow Out', 'Hubcap and Tail Lights', 'Latin Golightly', 'Loose Caboose', 'The Big Heist', from the tremendously successful film that starred Audrey Hepburn and George Peppard, all composed by Mancini.

The song 'Moon River' (with lyrics written by Johnny Mercer) won the Academy Award for Best Film Song of 1961, and a second award went to Mancini for the best scoring of a dramatic

or comedy picture. He also had two Grammy Awards for 'Moon River' - 'Best Song of the Year' 1961, and 'Best Arrangement' 1961. By 1968, there were around 500 different recordings of 'Moon River' and almost one million sheet music sales, the song earning Mancini $230,000 and Mercer over $100,000 by the end of the March 1966.

Mancini says he wrote the song in half an hour, once he had figured out the character of Holly Golightly (played by Audrey Hepburn). The tune is sobbed by a plaintive harmonica, repeated by strings, hummed and sung by a chorus, and finally resolved with harmonica. Its haunting appeal made it the most successful melody from a film score for several years, and Mancini the most sought after musician in Hollywood.

This album received Gold Disc award from R.I.A.A. in 1962, and Grammy Award for Best Film Soundtrack Album (1961).

MANTOVANI AND HIS ORCHESTRA
ITALIA MIA (album) *London/Decca* [*Britain*]. This eighth million seller album for Mantovani had the by now expected big sales in the U.S.A. and elsewhere. 'Italia Mia' achieved this figure by 1965. The disc contained the best of the famous Italian melodies and songs played in Mantovani's inimitable style. They were: 'Catari, Catari', by S. Cardillo (1911); 'Capriccio Italien' theme, by Tchaikovsky, arr: Milner; 'Italia Mia', by Mantovani (1961); 'Vissi d'arte' (from *La Tosca*), by G. Puccini (1901); 'Carnival of Venice' variations by Frosini; 'Mattinata' ('Tis the day), by R. Leoncavallo (1904); 'Bersaglieri March' by Eduardo di Capua; 'Come Back to Sorrento', by G.D. de Curtis and E. de Curtis (1911); 'Return to Me', by Danny Di Minno and Carmen Lombardo (1957); 'Nessun Dorma' (from *Turandot*), by G. Puccini (1926); *Italian fantasia medley* - 'Tarantella' (anon.); 'O Sole Mio', by G. Capurro and E. di Capua (1901); 'A frangesa', by Costa; 'Santa Lucia', by T. Cottrau (1849); 'Maria, Mari', by Russo and E. di Capua; 'Funiculi, Funicula', by Luigi Denza (1895).

The disc was issued on the London label in the U.S.A., and on the Decca label in Britain. This album was in the U.S.A. bestsellers' lists for 50 weeks.

THE MARCELS
BLUE MOON *Colpix* [*USA*]. This quintet, a teenbeat vocal group, comprised: Cornelius Hart; Fred and Allen Johnson (bro-

thers); Ronald Mundy; and Walter Maddox, all from Pittsburgh and then aged between 18 and 20. Their version of this famous song writen by Lorenz Hart (words) and Richard Rogers (music) in 1934 was barely recognizable from the original, but the disc had a fantastic entertainment value, selling nearly two million. The quintet had formed and disbanded several times before their manager, Julius Kruspir, thought them ready for Colpix Records. The Marcels appeared in the film *Twist Around the Clock* in 1961. 'Blue Moon' their first disc, was a No 1 in the U.S.A. for three weeks (with 14 weeks in the bestsellers) and in Britain for two weeks (with 13 weeks in the bestsellers). A top rhythm-and-blues disc.

THE MAR-KEYS
LAST NIGHT *Satellite* [*USA*]. This novelty instrumental rhythm-and-blues group was made up by Jerry Johnson (drums); Steve Cropper (guitar); Don 'Duck' Dunn (bass); Charles Axton (tenor sax); Don Nix (baritone); Wayne Jackson (trumpet); and Jerry Lee 'Smoochie' Smith (piano or organ). After being organized for three years, the group, which first consisted of four musicians, was in 1961 augmented by a brass section and an organist. These seven staff musicians for Satellite Records (now called Stax Records) of Memphis, decided to try a disc of their own, and helped by artists' and repertoire manager, 'Chips' Moman, they wrote and arranged 'Last Night'. Teenagers took to their original sounding group and the disc zoomed into the hit parade, selling a million by 1962. It was No 3 in the U.S. charts for two weeks and 14 weeks in the bestsellers.

THE MARVELETTES
PLEASE MISTER POSTMAN *Tamla* [*USA*]. This female vocal beat group, comprising Gladys Horton (lead singer), Katherine Anderson, Georgeanna Tillman, Juanita Cowart and Wanda Young, were all in their senior year at Inkster High School in Detroit, when they recorded this their first million seller. The Marvelettes were discovered by songwriter and Tamla Records' chief, Berry Gordy, Jr., at their school talent show early in 1961. He signed them to a disc contract. This, their first disc, soon got into the hit parade; the group then did a tour of theatre dates on the strength of its success in the U.S.A. Further disc hits followed. The song was written by B. Holland, R. Bateman and F. Gorman. The disc was a No 1 seller in the U.S.A. for one week with 23 weeks in the bestsellers, and a top rhythm-and-blues disc. Released 16 September 1961.

THE MIRACLES
SHOP AROUND *Tamla* [*USA*]. This teenbeat vocal quintet, comprising Warren Moore, Robert Rogers, Ronald White, Bill Robinson and Claudette Rogers (Mrs Robinson), all come from Detroit and were then around 21 years of age. This song was written by Bill Robinson and Berry Gordy, Jr (their manager and president of Tamla/Motown Records). The disc, released 3 October 1960, sold a million by 1962. The group was formed in 1958. The disc was No 2 in the U.S.A. charts and 16 weeks in the bestsellers, and No 1 in rhythm-and-blues.

BOB MOORE AND HIS ORCHESTRA (novelty vocal and instrumental group)
MEXICO *Monument* [*USA*]. Bob Moore (born Nashville, Tennessee, on 30 November 1932), living in the centre of the country music field, took up bass playing and after a few years of study obtained many studio dates. He made numerous cross-country tours of the U.S.A. accompanying the established artists including Connie Francis, Brenda Lee, Elvis Presley and Red Foley. Fred Foster, head of Monument Records, recognized his ability as a musical director and engaged him for heading the orchestra on Roy Orbison's sessions. His band was so successful that it led to instrumental dates of his own. His first disc was 'My Three Sons', a fair hit, then came 'Mexico' written by the famous songwriters Felice and Boudleaux Bryant. It is reputed to have

sold a million to date. The disc reached No 7 in the U.S. charts with 15 weeks in the bestsellers.

NANA MOUSKOURI WITH ORCHESTRA DIRECTED BY MANOS HADJIDAKIS
WEISSE ROSEN AUS ATHEN (The White Rose of Athens) *Fontanna-Philips* [*Germany*]. This disc reached the half million sale by January 1962 and the million later in the year. The song comes from the film *Traumland der Sehnsucht* (Dreamland of Desire), the tune being an adaptation of an old Greek song also known as 'The Water and the Wine'. It was written and arranged for the film by Manos Hadjidakis. English words were written later by Norman Newell and Archie Bleyer. The voice of longing is the keynote of Nana Mouskouri's success. She was born 10 October 1936 in Athens, Greece, and was already a success there before going to Germany. She got her biggest break when she met Manos Hadjidakis (composer of the sensational hit 'Never on Sunday') in 1958. He heard her sing and promised her material. In 1959 she made her first record in Greece and within one year was established as a top-disc artist. After winning several song contests, she went to Germany to record, her first disc there being this one of 'Weisse Rosen aus Athen', which earned her a gold award. Greek words were by Nikos Gatsas.

RICKY NELSON
HELLO MARY LOU backed with TRAVELLIN' MAN *Imperial* [*USA*]. The ninth million seller for Ricky was 'Hello Mary Lou' written by Gene Pitney and 'Travellin' Man' written in 1960 by Jerry Fuller. 'Travellin' Man' was No 1 for two weeks in the U.S.A. with 16 weeks in the bestsellers. 'Hello Mary Lou' was No 9 with 15 weeks in the bestsellers. Composer Pitney is also a successful disc artist (see 1961) and is said to have made over £15,000 from 'Hello Mary Lou' broadcast fees alone. The disc was No 2 in Britain with 18 weeks in the bestsellers. A belated Gold Disc was awarded by R.I.A.A. on 10 August 1977.

SANDY NELSON (drums)
LET THERE BE DRUMS *Imperial* [*USA*]. This second million seller for Sandy established him as one of the most consistent money-making percussionists. The number was written by Richard Podolor and Nelson. It reached No 7 with 16 weeks in the U.S. bestsellers, and No 3 and 16 weeks in the British bestsellers.

ROY ORBISON
RUNNIN' SCARED *Monument* [*USA*]. This third million seller for Roy was written by Joe Melson and Orbison. The disc was the top seller in the U.S.A. for one week with 17 weeks in the bestsellers, and No 9 and 15 weeks in Britain's bestsellers. Song written in 1952.

CRYIN' backed with CANDY MAN *Monument* [*USA*]. The fourth million seller for Roy Orbison, No 2 in the U.S. charts and 16 weeks in the bestsellers and No 25 in Britain, was also written by Joe Melson and Orbison. 'Candy Man' was written by Beverly Ross and Fred Neil, and reached No 25 with 14 weeks in the U.S. bestsellers, and nine weeks in the British bestsellers.

I'M HURTIN' *Monument* [*USA*]. Still another million seller (globally) for Roy, again written in collaboration with Joe Melson, their fifth. It reached No 27 in the U.S. charts.

EMILIO PERICOLI (pop ballad vocalist)
AL DI LA *Ricordi* [*Italy*]. 'Al Di La' was the winner of the San Remo Song Festival in 1961 in which it was sung by Betty Curtis. The song, written by 'Mogol' (Guilio Rapetti) (words), and Carlo Donida (music), eventually amassed around 50 different recordings. An English lyric was written by Ervin Drake.

Pericoli's disc sold over 400,000 in the U.S.A. on the Warner label (1961) and by 1965 is said to have sold 1,300,000 globally, with particularly heavy sales in Latin American countries, despite only moderate sales in Italy itself. Emilio sang the song in the film *Rome Adventure* and this proved to be his international stepping stone to success. It was also used as the theme for Warner's film *Lovers Must Learn*, with shots of Emilio singing the song sparking off a rush for the disc, which achieved a position of No 6 in the U.S. charts (1962) and 14 weeks in the bestsellers. It reached No 30 with 14 weeks in the British bestsellers.

Pericoli was born in 1928 at Cesenatico, Italy, the son of a sailor, the family living near Milan. He trained as an accountant, but developed his acting and singing abilities while at school, becoming popular in local plays. This convinced him that his future was in acting and after some time in repertory he won acclaim as a TV actor. He first sang professionally in 1960 after bringing the house down with a spontaneous act in a nightclub in Italy.

In 1962, Pericoli won a U.S.A. poll as Favourite International Artist, and in 1965 made his American debut at the Three Rivers Inn, Syracuse, New York.

GENE PITNEY

TOWN WITHOUT PITY *Musicor* [*USA*]. This was the theme song for the film of the same title sung by Pitney. The song was written by Ned Washington (words) and Dmitri Tiomkin (music). Gene was born on 17 February 1941 in Hartford, Connecticut and was educated at Rockville High School, the University of Connecticut and Ward's Electronic School. He took guitar tuition for one year. Pitney began his career as a songwriter, supplying other performers with disc material, then with a disc rendition of his own song 'I Wanna Love My Life Away' in which he produced all seven voices heard on the disc by means of electronics. This versatile singer, composer, arranger also plays the piano and drums in addition to guitar. His songs have been recorded by such artists as June Valli, Tommy Edwards, Steve Lawrence, Roy Orbison and Ricky Nelson. Gene has a voice that can reach such high notes that he does chorus bits of his own discs, aided by multi-tracking. He has made tours of Australia, New Zealand, Canada, Hawaii, England, Italy, Germany and France, and was particularly popular in England in 1963 when he came over to help promote his very popular disc of '24 Hours from Tulsa'. 'Town Without Pity' is said to have sold a million by 1962. It was No 13 for two weeks in the U.S. charts (1962) and 19 weeks in the bestsellers, reaching No 32 with six weeks in the British bestsellers.

ELVIS PRESLEY

SURRENDER *Victor* [*USA*]. The 32nd million seller for Elvis had a reputed global sale of five million. The song is a new version of the 1911 Italian ballad 'Torna a Sorrento' ('Come back to Sorrento'), originally written by G.D. de Curtis (words) and E. de Curtis (music). The new English words and adaptation were by Doc Pomus and Mort Shuman in 1960. 'Surrender' was No 1 in its first week in Britain and stayed there for four weeks. It was No 1 in the U.S.A. for two weeks and 12 weeks in the bestsellers; 15 weeks in the British bestsellers.

I FEEL SO BAD backed with WILD IN THE COUNTRY *Victor* [*USA*]. The 33rd million seller for Elvis Presley, 'I Feel So Bad' was written by Chuck Willis; 'Wild in the Country' was written by Hugo Peretti, Luigi Creatore and George Weiss and sung by Elvis in his film of the same title. This disc was a top seller in Britain (with 12 weeks in the bestsellers) and a global million seller. 'I Feel So Bad' was No 5 in the U.S. charts with nine weeks in the bestsellers. 'Wild in the Country' reached No 26.

LITTLE SISTER backed with HIS LATEST FLAME *Victor* [*USA*]. These titles provided Elvis with his 34th million seller. Both songs were written by Doc Pomus and Mort Shuman. The disc was No 1 for three weeks in Britain and 13 weeks in the bestsellers, and a global million seller. It reached No 5 in the U.S. charts with 13 weeks in the bestsellers.

CAN'T HELP FALLING IN LOVE backed with ROCK-A-HULA BABY *Victor* [*USA*]. Both Elvis's 35th and 36th million selling titles were from his film *Blue Hawaii*. 'Can't Help Falling in Love', adapted from 'Plaisir d'Amour' by Giovanni Martini (1714-1816), was written by George Weiss, Hugo Peretti and Luigi Creatore (Gold Disc award on U.S. sales). 'Rock-a-Hula Baby', written by Fred Wise, Ben Wiseman and Dolores Fuller, achieved a global million sale. Both were taken from the filmtrack album 'Blue Hawaii' and issued as a singles disc. 'Can't Help Falling in Love' got to No 2 in the U.S. charts with 14 weeks in the bestsellers. 'Rock-a-Hula Baby' was No 23. The disc was No 1 and 20 weeks in the British bestsellers. Gold Disc award, R.I.A.A., 1962.

'BLUE HAWAII' (film soundtrack) (album) *Victor* [*USA*]. The 37th million seller for Elvis was his fourth album million seller. Released in October 1961, this album sold 600,000 in three months in the U.S.A. alone and an eventual three million globally. All the songs on the disc were sung by Elvis in his film *Blue Hawaii*. The contents of the disc are: 'Blue Hawaii', by Leo Robin and Ralph Rainger (1937); 'Can't Help Falling in Love' and 'Ku-u-i-po', by George Weiss, Hugo Peretti and Luigi Creatore; 'Rock-a-Hula Baby', by Fred Wise, Ben Weisman and Dolores Fuller; 'Hawaiian Wedding Song', by Chas E. King (1926), English words: A. Hoffman and Dick Manning (1958); 'Aloha Oe', by Queen Liliuokalani (1878), arranged and adapted by Presley; 'Almost Always True', by Fred Wise and Ben Weisman; 'No More', by Don Robertson and Hal Blair; 'Moonlight Swim,' by Sylvia Dee and Ben Weisman; 'Ito Eats', 'Slicin' Sand', 'Hawaiian Sunset', 'Beach Boy Blues', 'Island of Love' (Kaui), by Sid Tepper and Roy C. Bennett.

This album was No 1 seller for 20 weeks in the U.S.A. and Presley's biggest success for Victor Records. It was in the bestsellers' lists for nearly 18 months. Gold Disc award R.I.A.A., 1961.

LINDA SCOTT

I'VE TOLD EVERY LITTLE STAR *Canadian-American* [*USA*]. The first million seller for teenage singer Linda Scott was a revival of the song written in 1932 for the stage musical in the U.S.A. *Music in the Air* by Oscar Hammerstein II (words) and Jerome Kern (music). Linda (real name Linda Joy Sampson) was born on 11 June 1945 in Queens, New York and has been performing as a singer since she was four. She moved to Teaneck, New Jersey when 11 and enrolled at the high school there. In 1960-1961 she divided her time between appearances at local functions and preparing for a disc career, which materialized with this recording. It got to No 3 in the U.S.A. charts with 14 weeks in the bestsellers, and No 7 and 13 weeks in the British bestsellers.

DEL SHANNON

RUNAWAY *Big Top* [*USA*]. The first million seller for Shan-

non was a song written by him with the help of Max Crook. Del was born in Grand Rapids, Michigan on 30 December 1939. At 14, he began playing the guitar and singing. In 1957 he entered the Army, and was stationed in Germany as a radioman. On discharge Del was spotted by a disc jockey who was instrumental in getting him a disc session. This disc was No 1 for five weeks in the U.S.A. (with 17 weeks in the bestsellers) and four weeks in Britain (with 22 weeks in the bestsellers). Shannon's real name is Charles Westover.

HATS OFF TO LARRY *Big Top* [*USA*]. The second million seller for Del Shannon was entirely his own work. It reached No 5 in the U.S. charts and was 13 weeks in the bestsellers, No 6 and 12 weeks in the British Bestsellers.

HELEN SHAPIRO (pop ballad vocalist) WITH ACCOMPANIMENT DIRECTED BY MARTIN SLAVIN

YOU DON'T KNOW *Columbia* [*Britain*]. Helen Shapiro was the most sensational British discovery of 1961. She was born in London's East End on 28 September 1946, and started singing lessons in 1961, at the Maurice Berman School of Singing. John Schroeder of EMI called at the Berman School to find out whether there was any worthwhile talent, and heard Helen in the middle of her lesson. He was so impressed that he arranged for her to make some trial recordings. These were so good that the

artists' and repertoire boss signed her up. John Schroeder specially wrote 'Don't Treat Me Like a Child' for Helen which became a hit. Then came 'You Don't Know' which topped Britain's charts for three weeks with well over the quarter million sale, and a subsequent reputed million globally. By the end of the year her discs had sold over a million in Britain alone, at a time when she was still 14 and attending Clapton Girls' School. She became the only girl to make over a dozen radio and TV appearances before her 15th birthday. She was also featured in a documentary film *Look at Life*. After leaving school she made many tours and personal appearances round the globe. For a young singer she had dynamic drive and an inherent rhythmic sense, with confidence, assurance and personality quite outstanding for her age. She was voted No 1 Female British Singer for 1961 and 1962. The disc was 23 weeks in Britain's bestsellers.

HELEN SHAPIRO WITH ACCOMPANIMENT DIRECTED BY NORRIE PARAMOR

WALKING BACK TO HAPPINESS *Columbia* [*Britain*]. This second big success for Helen Shapiro was No 1 for four weeks in Britain (with 19 weeks in the bestsellers) with almost half a

million sale, with global sales making it over the million. The song was written by Mike Hawker (words) and John Schroeder (music).

TONY SHERIDAN AND THE BEATLES

MY BONNIE backed with WHEN THE SAINTS GO MARCHING IN *Polydor* [*Germany*]. This rhythmic version was recorded in Germany when Tony Sheridan sang with the Beatles, a group only really well known to their local Liverpudlians at that time. The disc had a small sale when first released in Britain (1962), although it sold 100,000 in Germany, but by 1964 it is reputed to have sold the million globally because The Beatles had by then become the most sensational group in disc history (see 1963 for full biography). This disc was released in the U.S.A. by MGM in 1964, selling well over 300,000 there alone. Sheridan's real name is Anthony Esmond Sheridan McGinnity, an ex-art school student from Norwich, where he was born in 1941. He was in Germany in 1961 joining in with all the groups who arrived in Hamburg. He met The Beatles at the Top Ten Club there, when they were a quintet comprising Stuart Sutcliffe, John Lennon, Paul McCartney, Pete Best (the drummer who was later replaced by Ringo Starr) and George Harrison. Both songs were designated as 'traditional', although 'My Bonnie' is believed to have been written by Charles T. Pratt under the pseudonyms of J.T. Wood and H.J. Fulmer around 1881. By 1964, Tony Sheridan had became a big seller on discs in Germany. This disc reached No 26 in the U.S.A. and No 48 in Britain.

TROY SHONDELL

THIS TIME (we're really breaking up) *Liberty* [*USA*]. Troy Shondell was born and raised in Indiana and was educated at Valparaiso University and Indiana University. He wrote his first song at the age of 14 which was recorded by Little Anthony and the Imperials, and also learned to play five instruments. His recording career began with 'This Time' in 1961, which is said to have sold a million. It was written by Chips Moman in 1958. The disc reached No 6 for a week with 13 weeks in the U.S. bestsellers and was released in September 1961. It was No 22 and 11 weeks in the British bestsellers.

From 1961, Troy toured the U.S.A. with many other top recording artists. In 1968 he became a songwriter for Acuff-Rose in Nashville and made the first recording for TRX Records, a branch of Hickory for whom he made some popular discs until 1969 when he went into the music publishing field. In October 1969, Troy was appointed as Assistant Regional Director of ASCAP's Southern Regional Office in Nashville.

THE STRING-A-LONGS (country and western instrumental group)

WHEELS *Warwick* [*USA*]. This group comprised Jimmy Torres, lead guitar; Don Allen on drums; Aubrey Lee de Cordova on bass and guitar; Richard Stephens on guitar; and Keith McCormack on rhythm guitar, also vocalist. They started playing together in high school at local dances and parties. In late 1960, they auditioned and recorded for Norman Petty in Clovis, New Mexico. Petty liked the group and took their disc of 'Wheels' to Warwick Records who signed them up. This tune was written by Jimmy Torres and Richard Stephens in 1960 in collaboration with Norman Petty. The disc was No 3 in the U.S. charts for two weeks and 16 weeks in the bestsellers, and No 8 and 16 weeks in Britain's bestsellers.

SUE THOMPSON

SAD MOVIES (make me cry) *Hickory* [*USA*]. The first reputed million seller for Sue was written by John D. Loudermilk. Her real name is Eva Sue McKee. She was born on a farm near Nevada, Missouri. From the age of seven she began singing and playing the guitar and entertaining at school and church functions. After the family moved to Sheridan, California, Sue kept singing while at high school and working at summer jobs. She

entered a contest at the vaudeville theatre in San José, winning a fortnight's engagement there and a movie role. Local radio soon booked her, also TV, and then came recording for Mercury Records under Murray Nash. She also recorded for Columbia and Decca, eventually signing with the Hickory label and producing her first chart topping disc 'Sad Movies'. Many successful club and TV appearances followed, mostly in Las Vegas, where she lives with her artist husband Hank Perry. This disc reached No 5 in the U.S. charts and was 14 weeks in the bestsellers, and was No 46 in Britain.

NORMAN *Hickory* [*USA*]. The second million seller for Sue Thompson was an even bigger success than 'Sad Movies'. It was also written by John D. Loudermilk. This disc achieved No 3 in the U.S. charts and 16 weeks in the bestsellers.

THE TOKENS
THE LION SLEEPS TONIGHT *Victor* [*USA*]. The Tokens, a folk, country-and-western teenbeat vocal quintet, comprise Mitchel Margo, Phillip Margo, Hank Medress, Jay Siegel and Joseph Venneri, all from Brooklyn, New York. They were originally a quartet formed by disc-star Neil Sedaka around 1958. 'The Lion Sleeps Tonight' is a new version by Hugo Peretti, Luigi Creatore, George Weiss and Albert Stanton who revised the music and added new lyrics to the original song 'Wimoweh', a South African (Zulu) folk song 'Mbube', adapted and arranged by Paul Campbell, with English words by Roy Ilene, in 1951. This disc was No 1 for three weeks in the U.S.A. and 15 weeks in the bestsellers, and No 11 and 12 weeks in the British bestsellers. Gold Disc award, R.I.A.A., 1962.

TONIGHT I FELL IN LOVE *Warwick* [*USA*]. This disc was released in March 1961, reaching No 15 in the U.S. charts. The Tokens first soared to pop-rock fame with this which subsequently sold a million. It was released on the Parlophone label in Britain. The group signed later in the year with RCA Victor. In 1969 they signed a long-term contract with Buddah Records.

The song was written by M. Margo and Hank Medress of the group. The disc was 14 weeks in the U.S. bestsellers.

PHILIP UPCHURCH COMBO (rock'n'roll instrumental group)
YOU CAN'T SIT DOWN (Part 2) *Boyd* [*USA*]. Phil Upchurch recorded this disc (Parts 1 and 2) in Oklahoma City, and it was Part 2 that caught the fancy of the fans. It is said to have sold a million in the U.S.A. subsequently, and became a standard rave record. The disc was released five years later in Britain (1966) by

Sue Records. It was written by Dee Clark, Cornell Muldrow and Kal Mann in 1960, and reached No 29 in the U.S.A. charts, and No 39 in Britain.

LEROY VAN DYKE
WALK ON BY *Mercury* [*USA*]. The second big success for Leroy with an estimated $1\frac{1}{2}$ million sale. The song was written by Kendall Hayes and the disc a No 1 in the U.S. country-and-western charts. It was No 5 for three weeks in the U.S. national charts and 16 weeks in the bestsellers; No 5 and 17 weeks in the British bestsellers.

BILLY VAUGHN AND ORCHESTRA
WHEELS *Dot* [*USA*]. The fourth million seller for Billy Vaughn was the second time a million seller for the tune by Jimmy Torres and Richard Stephens (of 'The String-a-Longs') in collaboration with Norman Petty. Billy's disc was a million seller by 1962, reached No 28 in the U.S.A., and also sold a million in Germany on its Teldec label release there.

BOBBY VEE
TAKE GOOD CARE OF MY BABY *Liberty* [*USA*]. This third million seller for Bobby Vee was another big song success for writers (husband and wife) Gerry Goffin and Carole King. The disc was No 1 for three weeks in the U.S.A. and 15 weeks in the bestsellers, and a chart topper in Britain for one week with 16 weeks in bestsellers.

RUN TO HIM *Liberty* [*USA*]. Million seller No 4 for Bobby Vee, written by Gerry Goffin and Jack Keller. Issued in November 1961, it was No 2 in the U.S. charts by the end of the year, stayed 15 weeks on the bestsellers and sold the million by 1962. The disc was also popular in Britain, reaching No 6 in the charts (1962) with 15 weeks in bestsellers.

THE VENTURES (instrumental rock'n'roll group)
PERFIDIA *Dolton* [*USA*]. The tune of this second million seller for The Ventures is a Latin American oldie of 1939 written by Alberto Dominguez. The disc was No 15 and 13 weeks in the U.S.A. bestsellers, and No 4 and 13 weeks in Britain's bestsellers.

LAWRENCE WELK AND HIS ORCHESTRA
CALCUTTA *Dot* [*USA*]. The first million seller for the now famous Lawrence Welk orchestra was written by German composer Heino Gaze in 1958 with the title 'Tivoli Melody'. The tune then appeared as 'Take Me Dreaming'; next came the piano version called 'Nicolette'; fourth it appeared as a song in 1960 in Germany titled 'Kalkutta liegt am Ganges'; and finally as 'Calcutta' in the U.S.A., before it finally caught on with this great Welk orchestra version. English words by Lee Pockriss and Paul J. Vance.

Lawrence Welk was born 11 March 1903 in Strasbourg, North Dakota. His parents and their family of four sons and four daughters left Alsace-Lorraine in 1878 fleeing Bismarck's invasion of their country. Theer sole possession was a three-generation, handed-down accordion when they settled in Strasbourg. The second son, Lawrence, took an interest in the instrument on which his father played the polka and folk dance music. At 13, he was playing it for local dances and church socials. At 21 he left the family, joined travelling bands and eventually formed his own group, 'the biggest little band in America', which began to broadcast over the Yankton, South Dakota station in 1925. Ballroom and hotel dates followed and from 1928 he became one of the most popular orchestra leaders in the U.S.A., with TV and recording in addition to his ballroom work. In 1951, Welk was engaged for six weeks at the Aragon Ballroom in Pacific Ocean Park, California; the engagement was extended to nine years! He had a successful run with Coral Records, then moved over to Dot to get his first million seller with 'Calcutta', and further successes followed in the singles and album field. 'Calcutta' was No 1 for two weeks in the U.S.A. with 17 weeks in the bestsellers, and No 1 in Germany. Gold Disc award, R.I.A.A., 1961.

MAURICE WILLIAMS AND THE ZODIACS

MAY I *Herald* [*USA*]. Second big hit, through subsequent years, for this group, with an estimated million sale. The song was written by Clyde Otis, De Jesus and famous disc artist Brook Benton.

FARON YOUNG (country-and-western vocalist)

HELLO WALLS *Capitol* [*USA*]. Faron Young was born on 25 February 1932 in Shreveport, Louisiana. His father bought a small dairy farm and moved away from the city, and it was here that Faron got his first guitar, and sang mostly to the cattle.

Later came an opportunity to sing on the 'Louisiana Hayride' on Shreveport's radio station KWKH. He did so well that they kept him for two years. In 1951 a talent scout for a small record label heard him on the show, and soon after he recorded 'Tattle Tale Tears' for the Gotham label – his first hit.

His professional career began with this, and after a second Gotham release, Ken Nelson, Capitol Records' brilliant country producer who had heard Faron on this 15-minute morning radio show for KWKH, signed him to the label. Jack Stapp, programme manager for WSM's Grand Ole Opry, booked Faron for two guest appearances. Faron came for two weeks and stayed on the show for 11 years as a feature performer.

Hubert Long, a former record distributor, became Faron's manager, got bookings and helped get Faron in the movies. One of the movies Faron made in the early 1950s was *The Young Sheriff*, a label that stuck. Faron later called himself 'The Singing Sheriff'.

He made some bad business investments and nearly went broke, so he started working for low fees and gradually lifted them up to a minimum of between $1,800 and $2,500 a night. Faron's career was interrupted when he was drafted in the Army in the early 1950s and on release he literally had to start all over. He subsequently became much in demand for TV. Throughout his career he had scores of hits for Capitol, the biggest being this disc of 'Hello Walls' written by RCA artist Willie Nelson, one of the many people Faron befriended when in need. These also included Roger Miller, Johnny Cash and songwriter Kris Kristopherson. Faron later switched to Mercury Records, with most of his releases making the Top Ten.

He is also a successful business man, becoming president of *Music City News*, a Nashville newspaper concerned solely with country music, distributed throughout the world.

By 1971, Faron Young had recorded over 35 albums and nearly 500 songs, 57 of his songs making the Top Ten charts of the national trade publications.

'Hello Walls' was released in February 1961 and eventually sold over two million. It reached No 12 for two weeks in the U.S. charts and was 15 weeks in the bestsellers.

Faron's other films were *Daniel Boone*, *Country Music Holiday* and *Hidden Guns*. He has appeared on network and syndicated TV programmes and also visited Europe, Canada and Mexico.

HERB ALPERT (trumpet) AND HIS TIJUANA BRASS

THE LONELY BULL *A & M* [*USA*]. Herb Alpert, born 31 March 1937 of Jewish descent, hails from Los Angeles, California, and was educated at the University of Southern California. An ex-Army trumpeter, he started experimenting with a tape recorder in his garage and found that by overdubbing one trumpet solo on top of another it produced the effect of a 'Spanish flair'. He achieved the most successful results from a song, 'Twinkle Star', written by his friend Sol Lake. A little later, while in Tijuana witnessing his first bullfight, he decided to add the roaring 'olés' of the crowd and the sounds of the mariachi band on to the beginning and end of 'Twinkle Star', recording the sounds by a microphone suspended by a wire in the arena. With $200 he produced his disc, calling it 'The Lonely Bull' which eventually, 1962–1963, went high in the U.S. charts (No 6) with 14 weeks in the bestsellers, selling over a million, and was No 22 in Britain with nine weeks in the bestsellers. Alpert's new quasi-Mexican music, part jazz, 'hot' mariachi and a touch of rock'n'roll soon became known as Ameriachi – a combination of American and Mariachi. He plays both parts of the trumpet duet, the recording achieving a two-dimensional effect by a slight alteration of synchronization and one trumpet playing a trifle sharp or flat by a secret process. Alpert also composes, arranges and conducts his band which consists of trumpets, trombone, piano drums, mandolin (sometimes two electric guitars) and his voice. The simple slick arrangements including maracas, tambourines, and other percussion instruments produce the most infectious music. By the end of 1965, Alpert had three albums in the bestsellers: 'Going Places', 'South of the Border' and 'Whipped Cream and Other Delights', and scheduled appearances on practically every major TV show. In fact, Herb Alpert and the Tijuana Brass was 1965's outstanding new instrumental group.

Herb is also artists and repertoire producer, partner and vice-president with Jerry Moss of A & M Records. One release, 'Up Cherry Street', became the signature theme tune for the popular BBC radio series 'Newly Pressed', and Alpert gets a bigger following with his 'olé' shouting fans in every record released. Alpert's six sidemen (The Brass) are Lou Pagani (piano), Tonni Kalash (trumpet), John Pisano (guitar), Nick Ceroli (drums), Pat Senatore (guitar), and Bob Edmondson (trombone and band comic).

THE LONELY BULL (album) *A & M* [*USA*]. With the success of the singles disc of the same title the newly-formed A & M Records followed up with the release of this their first album in December 1962. It had a fair sale in early 1963 and came back with increasing sales in 1965 and 1966 through the big success of Herb Alpert and his 'Whipped Cream and Other Delights' album, reaching No 10 in the U.S. charts and Gold Disc award from R.I.A.A. in 1966. By March 1966 it had sold 758,000 and passed the million sale by the end of 1967. It was in the bestsellers for 157 weeks.

Contents: 'The Lonely Bull', (El solo toro), by Sol Lake (1962); 'El lobo' (The wolf), by Green and Sol Lake (1962); 'Tijuana Sauerkraut', by Jerry Moss and Herb Alpert (1962); 'Desafinado', by Newton Mendonca and Antonio Carlos Jobim (1959); 'Mexico', by Felice and Boudleaux Bryant (1961); 'Never on Sunday' (film title number), by Billy Towne and Manos Hadjidakis (1960); 'Struttin' with Maria', by Herb Alpert (1962); 'Let It Be Me', by Pierre Delanoe and Gilbert Becaud (1955) (English words by Mann Curtis); 'Acapulco 1922', by Eldon Allan (1962); 'Limbo Rock', by Jon Sheldon and William E. Strange (1962); 'Crawfish', by Elsa Doran and Sol Lake (1962); 'A Quiet Tear' (Lagrima quieta), by Herb Alpert (1962).

RICHARD ANTHONY WITH ORCHESTRA CONDUCTED BY CHRISTIAN CHEVALIER

J'ENTENDS SIFFLER LE TRAIN (500 miles away from home) *Columbia* [*France*]. This French version of the American song '500 Miles Away from Home' was written by Hedy West, Bobby Bare and Charles Williams (originally recorded by Peter, Paul and Mary) and sold over one million. It is said that Richard was the first French singer to attain this figure. He was born on 13 January 1938 in Egypt and was one of the first French singers with a rock'n'roll release – 'Peggy Sue' in 1959. He had to wait, however, for three years before the twist rage reached France, and after 1962 was Johnny Hallyday's main rival. Real name Richard Anthony Btesh.

THE BEATLES

LOVE ME DO backed with P.S. I LOVE YOU *Parlophone* [*Britain*]. This was the first disc by The Beatles, and their first British recording to prove a major hit. Both songs were written by John Lennon and Paul McCartney of the group which also included George Harrison and Ringo Starr. (See 1963 for full biographies.) A global million sale was attained in 1964 after the group had made their first sensational appearances in the U.S.A. and when the disc was released on the Tollie label there, making the No 1 spot for one week, in May 1964. Disc released in Britain on 4 October 1962. 'Love Me Do' was 14 weeks in the U.S. bestsellers. 'P.S. I Love You' reached No 10 with 8 weeks in the bestsellers; 'Love Me Do' was No 17 and 18 weeks in the British bestsellers.

TONY BENNETT

I LEFT MY HEART IN SAN FRANCISCO *Columbia* [*USA*]. One of his biggest successes, Tony's sixth million seller sold almost two million by 1964, with Grammy Awards 'Best Male Vocal Performance' and 'Record of the Year' 1962. The song was written by Douglas Cross and George Cory in 1954. Disc released in July 1962. It was in the U.S. bestsellers for 21 weeks reaching No 19. It was No 25 and 14 weeks in the British bestsellers.

Tony's gold record of this song was presented by him on 27 August 1970 to the people of San Francisco. Presentation was made to Mayor Joseph Alioto in his offices at the City Hall.

MARCIE BLAINE (vocalist)

BOBBY'S GIRL *Seville* [*USA*]. Marcie's father, a high school teacher specializing in band instruments, was a professional musician which undoubtedly accounts for his daughter's talents. Marcie Blaine was born on 21 May 1944, in Brooklyn, New York, and educated at college. She was discovered by Seville's artists and repertoire man Marv Holtzman who got her to record this song, written by Henry Hoffman and Gary Klein. It got to No 2 in the U.S. charts with 16 weeks in the bestsellers and sold an estimated million by 1963. The song also put Britain's Susan Maughan on the recording map, Susan's disc reaching No 4 in Britain and selling over a quarter million.

Marcie's hobbies are dancing and folk singing. She is also an instrumentalist and plays violin, piano, flute and guitar.

PAT BOONE

SPEEDY GONZALES *Dot* [*USA*]. Far from unlucky, the 13th million seller for consistent Pat Boone enjoyed a reputed global sale of two million. This song was written by Buddy Kaye, David Hill and Ethel Lee in 1961. The disc was No 6 for three weeks in the U.S. charts and 13 weeks in the bestsellers, and No 2 and 19 weeks in the British bestsellers.

BOOKER T AND THE MGs

GREEN ONIONS *Stax* [*USA*]. This novelty pop instrumental group takes its title from the initials of 'Memphis Group'. Booker (real name Booker T. Jones) also hails from Memphis. He was born 12 November 1944. Booker's instruments include string bass and organ. The number was written by the group, Booker T. Jones, Steve Cropper (guitar), Lewis Steinberg (bass) and Al Jackson (drums). The disc got to No 3 in the U.S. charts with 16 weeks in the bestsellers, and was a top rhythm-and-blues seller.

FREDDY CANNON

PALISADES PARK *Swan* [*USA*]. This song was written to commemorate the opening of a huge American fun fair. The writer was Chuck Barris, manager of ABC-TV's day-time programmes, and it provided Freddy with his third million seller. It was No 3 for two weeks in the U.S. charts and 15 weeks in the bestsellers, and No 20 in Britain, with eight weeks in the bestsellers.

GENE CHANDLER ('Duke of Earl')

DUKE OF EARL *Vee Jay* [*USA*]. The first million seller for Gene (now known as Duke of Earl) was written in 1961 by Earl Edwards, Eugene Dixon and Bernice Williams. Gene Chandler (formerly Eugene Dixon) hails from Chicago and was born on 6 July 1937. He began singing at the age of eight and soon organized a number of groups to sing at parties and clubs. He became a professional performer in 1960 when Mrs Bruce Williams, a young woman business manager, heard him, signed him to a contract and took him to the Chicago agent Bill Sheppard who negotiated a disc contract with Vee Jay Records after an audition. The disc was released 10 days afterwards, and quickly reached the top of the hit parade charts. The disc was No 1 for three weeks in the U.S.A. with 15 weeks in the bestsellers, and a top rhythm-and-blues disc.

BRUCE CHANNEL WITH ACCOMPANIMENT DIRECTED BY MARVIN MONTGOMERY

HEY BABY *Smash* [*USA*]. This first million seller for Bruce was written by him and Margaret Cobb in 1961. Teenbeat singer Bruce was born 28 November 1940, in Jacksonville, Texas, of a musical family. He was singing and playing the guitar from the age of five. After his family moved to Dallas, and while in high school Bruce entertained at youth centres and local shows. His father took him to Shreveport, Louisiana, to seek an audition with Tillman Franks, producer of the famous 'Louisiana Hayride' show. Franks signed him for an appearance on the show and he became a regular on it for six months. In 1961 Smash Records signed him to an exclusive disc contract. 'Hey Baby' reached the top of the hit parade charts. The disc was No 1 for three weeks in the U.S.A. with 15 weeks in the bestsellers and No 2 for three weeks in Britain with 12 weeks in the bestsellers. It features the harmonica of Delbert McLinton.

RAY CHARLES

I CAN'T STOP LOVING YOU *ABC-Paramount* [*USA*]. The fourth million seller for Ray was one of the top discs of 1962 with a sale of over two million. The song for this singles disc, taken from Ray's big selling album 'Modern Sounds in Country-and-Western Music', was written by Don Gibson in 1957, who also had a million seller with it in 1958 (q.v.). This was the top disc in the U.S.A. for five weeks with 18 weeks in the bestsellers, and for one week in Britain with 17 weeks in the British bestsellers. A top rhythm-and-blues disc. The backing of this disc was 'Born to Lose' (written by Ted Daffan in 1943). Grammy Award for 'Best Rhythm-and-Blues Recording' 1962. Gold Disc award, R.I.A.A., 1962. Released 23 April 1962.

MODERN SOUNDS IN COUNTRY-AND-WESTERN MUSIC (album) *ABC-Paramount* [*USA*]. The fifth million seller for Ray Charles was his first album million seller. It sold half a million by September 1962. The contents of the album are: 'Bye Bye, Love', by Felice and Boudleaux Bryant (1957); 'You Don't Know Me', by Cindy Walker and Eddy Arnold (1955); 'Half as Much', by Curley Williams (1951); 'I Love You So Much It Hurts', by Floyd Tillman (1948); 'Just a Little Lovin', by Eddy Arnold and Zeke Clements (1948); 'Born to Lose', by Frankie Brown (Ted Daffan) (1943); 'Worried Man' (traditional); 'It Makes No Difference Now', by Floyd Tillman (1939); 'You Win Again', by Hank Williams (1952); 'Careless Love', traditional, arrangement by Ray Charles; 'I Can't Stop Lovin' You', by Don Gibson (1957); 'Hey Good Lookin'', by Hank Williams (1951).

This disc was No 1 for 14 weeks in the U.S.A., and in their bestseller charts for 100 weeks. Gold Disc award R.I.A.A., 1962. Released January 1962.

YOU DON'T KNOW ME *ABC-Paramount* [*USA*]. The sixth million seller for Ray Charles, written in 1955 by Cindy Walker and Eddy Arnold, was also culled from Charles' big seller album of 'Modern Sounds in Country-and-Western Music'. It got to

No 2 in the U.S. charts with 11 weeks in the bestsellers; No 9 and 13 weeks in the British bestsellers. It was a top rhythm-and-blues seller. Released 10 July 1962.

CHUBBY CHECKER

SLOW TWISTIN' *Cameo-Parkway* [*USA*]. The fifth million seller for Chubby was written by Jon Sheldon. It was No 3 in the U.S. charts an 14 weeks in the bestsellers, and No 23 in Britain with eight weeks in the charts.

LIMBO ROCK backed with POPEYE *Cameo-Parkway* [*USA*]. The sixth million seller and No 2 for two weeks for Chubby Checker comprised 'Limbo Rock', written by W.E. Strange and Jon Sheldon, and 'Popeye', the work of Kal Mann and Dave Appell, both on the staff of Cameo Records. 'Limbo Rock' was 23 weeks in the U.S. bestsellers; No 32 with 10 weeks in the British bestsellers. 'Popeye' reached No 10 with 13 weeks in the bestsellers.

LOU CHRISTIE (vocalist)

THE GYPSY CRIED *Roulette* [*USA*]. First (reputed) million seller for Lou Christie, the song written by him and Twyla Herbert. It achieved the No 18 chart position in the U.S.A. in early 1963 with 13 weeks in the U.S. bestsellers.

Lou Christie (real name Geno Sacco) was born in Glen Willard near Pittsburgh, Pennsylvania. He won a state scholarship at Moon Township High School and studied classical music and singing. In 1963, Lou moved to New York and sang in backgrounds on other artists' discs after persistently asking record companies for a test. He eventually got a contract,with this disc as his first release. Lou collaborated with Twyla Herbert, a mystic 20 years older than himself, who he says predicted his hits and often had visions of his future. After two years' Army service in the U.S.A., Lou and Twyla came up with a big hit in the late 1965 – 'Lightnin' Strikes' – and Lou also signed with MGM for films. He has since toured all over the States and appeared on all the major TV shows.

JIMMY CLANTON

VENUS IN BLUE JEANS *Ace* [*USA*]. Jimmy Clanton's fourth million seller disc, the song written in 1961 by Howard Greenfield and Jack Keller. The song was also a hit in Britain with Mark Wynter's disc. Clanton's disc was No 7 and 13 weeks in the U.S. bestsellers.

PETULA CLARK

MONSIEUR *Vogue* [*Germany*]. This disc by Britain's actress-singer Petula Clark sold 250,000 in Germany alone by December 1962, and totalled two million on the Continent. Petula Sally Olwen Clark was born on 15 November 1932 in West Ewell, Surrey, England, and studied music from her earliest childhood. She first performed with a music chorus in Cardiff, later on local radio, from the age of nine. During her teens, her career went into high gear, and between 11 and 18 she made more than 20 films and won an award in 1950 for the most outstanding TV artist. An experienced performer of stage, screen and radio, she signed a recording contract with Pye (Britain) in 1955, her first major hits being 'Sailor' (1960) and 'Romeo' (see 1961), then 'My Friend the Sea', followed by 'Ya Ya Twist', a Continental smash hit. Petula married Claud Wolff, publicity director for Vogue Records in France. Petula has become one of the biggest disc stars and performers on the Continent, recording in English, French and German. 'Monsieur' was her disc in the latter language. Petula's first film was *A Medal for the General* (1944) followed by *Strawberry Road, I Know Where I'm Going, London Town, Here Come the Huggetts, The Card, The Gay Dog, Track the Man Down, Easy Money, Vote for Huggett, Goodbye Mr Chips* and many others. She has appeared in TV plays in Britain and France, with her own series in Britain. She has also performed in South Africa. Her first recordings were for Columbia and Polygon. Petula's double professional ambition to reach full status as

an actress and carry on her career as a singer has been fully achieved. This song was written by Kurt Hertha (words) and Karl Goetz (music) in Germany. Petula had sold over 25 million discs in Europe and the U.S.A. by 1970. She was awarded the Grand Prix du Disque by the French Disc Academy for this record in 1963.

CHARIOT *Vogue* [*France*]. This reputed million seller for Petula Clark (sung in French) achieved its sale on the Continent. It was written by Jacques Plant (words) and J.W. Stole and Del Roma (pseudonyms of famous French Orchestra conductors Frank Pourcell and Paul Mauriat) (music). 'Chariot' was also a million seller for Little Peggy March under the U.S. title 'I Will Follow Him' in 1963 (see 1963). This disc was No 39 in Britain and seven weeks in the bestsellers.

NAT 'KING' COLE WITH ORCHESTRA AND CHORUS DIRECTED BY BELFORD HENDRICKS

RAMBLIN' ROSE *Capitol* [*USA*]. The sixth million seller for Nat came after an interval of 11 years. This song was written by Joe and Noel Sherman. The disc also sold over 250,000 in Britain, reaching No 5 with 14 weeks in the bestsellers. It was 16 weeks in the U.S. bestsellers, reaching No 2.

RAMBLIN' ROSE (album) *Capitol* [*USA*]. Capitol issued this disc in August 1963, following the great success of his singles disc of the same title. The album sold the half million by 1964, receiving a Gold Disc award from the R.I.A.A. Since Nat's death on 15 February 1965, Capitol have had very big sales of his various albums, with this 'Ramblin' Rose' album reaching the two million sale by 1968. The contents are: 'Ramblin' Rose', by Joe and Noel Sherman (1962); 'Wolverton Mountain', by Claude King and Merle Kilgore (1962); 'Twilight on the Trail', by Sydney Mitchell and Louis Alter (1936); 'I Don't Want It That Way', by Joe and Noel Sherman (1962); 'He'll Have to Go', by Joe and Audrey Allison (1959); 'When You're Smiling', by Mark Fisher, Joe Goodwin and Larry Shay (1928); 'Goodnight Irene', by Huddie Ledbetter and John Lomax (1950); 'Your Cheatin' Heart', by Hank Williams (1952); 'One Has My Heart, the Other My Name', by Eddie Dean, Dearest Dean and Hal Blair (1948); 'Skip to My Lou', by Hugh Martin and Ralph Blane (1944); 'The Good Times', by Ron Miller and Lee Porter (1962); 'Sing Another Song (and We'll All Go Home)', by Burke and Romoff (1962).

This album was in the U.S. bestsellers for 162 weeks.

THE CONTOURS

DO YOU LOVE ME? *Gordy* [*USA*]. This vocal rhythm-and-blues sextet consisted of Bill Gordon, Billy Hoggs, Joe Billingslea, Sylvester Potts, Hubert Johnson and Huey Davis – all were in their 20s. Around 1958, when The Contours were a quartet, Johnson joined and was instrumental in getting his distant cousin, disc star Jackie Wilson, to hear the group which led to an audition for Berry Gordy of Gordy Records for whom they made their first disc 'Whole Lotta Woman'. In early 1962, guitar player Huey Davies was added to their act, then came this hit disc. This first million seller for The Contours was written by Berry Gordy, Jr. A top rhythm-and-blues disc. Released 18 August 1962, it reached No 3 with 18 weeks in the U.S. bestsellers.

SAM COOKE

TWISTIN' THE NIGHT AWAY *Victor* [*USA*]. Sam wrote his own fifth seven figure seller, which enjoyed a reputed global sale of over 1,500,000. It got to No 9 in the U.S. charts with 15 weeks in the bestsellers and No 6 and 14 weeks in the British bestsellers. A top rhythm-and-blues disc.

THE CRYSTALS (vocal quartet)

HE'S A REBEL *Philles* [*USA*]. This was the first million seller for the Philles label, a disc company started by singer-songwriter Phil Spector in 1960 (see Teddy Bears, 1958). The song was written by disc artist-songwriter Gene Pitney, and the disc was No 1 for two weeks in the U.S.A. with 18 weeks in the bestsellers and No 19 and 13 weeks in the British bestsellers. (See Crystals, 1963 for biography.)

BOBBY DARIN

THINGS *Atco* [*USA*]. This six million seller for Darin was written by Bobby himself in 1961. It got to No 3 in the U.S. charts with 12 weeks in the bestsellers, and No 2 and 17 weeks in the British bestsellers.

SAMMY DAVIS JR. (jazz vocalist, instrumentalist, dancer and impressionist)

WHAT KIND OF FOOL AM I? *Reprise* [*USA*]. Sammy Davis Jr. is one of the world's outstanding entertainers. He has been appearing before the public since the age of two, when he made his professional debut. He was born on 8 December 1925 in New York City, into a family already well known to vaudeville audiences. His father, Sammy Davis Sr, and his uncle Will Mastin were a popular act before he was born. From 1933 the trio played nightclubs and theatres across the U.S.A. In 1943, Sammy Jr. went into the Army. In 1946, he rejoined his father and uncle at 'Slapsie Maxie's' in Hollywood and they broke every previous record there. In 1954 he lost an eye and had his nose smashed in a car accident in Las Vegas. In 1956, Sammy added Broadway to his career with *Mr Wonderful*, in which he starred. Then came recording for Decca, TV and radio star spots, also films, including *Anna Lucasta*, *Porgy and Bess* (1959), *Pepe* (1961), *The Three-Penny Opera* (1963), *Robin and the Seven Hoods* with Sinatra, Crosby and Dean Martin (1964).

Sammy's versatility is astounding. Apart from his terrific jazz vocalizing, dancing and impressions, he plays the piano, bass, drums, vibraphone, trumpet and is also a songwriter. His incredible 'one-man' show took Britain by storm when he came over in 1963 to make some special appearances on BBC-TV. He made a considerable number of singles, EPs and albums for Decca in the U.S.A. before switching to the Reprise label which was started by Frank Sinatra (sold to Warner Brothers in 1963). 'What Kind of Fool Am I?' from the stage show *Stop the World – I Want to Get Off*, written by Leslie Bricusse (words) and Anthony Newley (music) and first produced in Britain in 1961, was his first hit disc by British writers. It is said to have sold a global million, reaching No 7 with 15 weeks in the U.S. bestsellers and No 26 and eight weeks in the British bestsellers. Sammy's follow-up was another British song 'As Long as He Needs Me' from Lionel Bart's *Oliver*.

Sammy Davis is indisputably one of the world's greatest coloured entertainers, his performance in the film of Gershwin's great Negro opera *Porgy and Bess* being outstanding. His disc sales by the end of 1969 were over eight million. Grammy Award to the writers for 'Song of the Year, 1962'.

'SKEETER' DAVIS (country-and-western popular ballad vocalist)

THE END OF THE WORLD *Victor* [*USA*]. Skeeter Davis (real name Mary Frances Penick) was born on 30 December 1931 in Sparta, Kentucky, the eldest of six children. Her parents encouraged their talented daughters Skeeter and Bee Jay. After attending high school in Dixie Heights from 1945 to 1949, Skeeter sang with pop bands. Country music however was her real love. She appeared on Nashville's 'Grand Ole Opry' and the Ernest Tubb show. Skeeter became known for her disc of 'I Forget More than You'll Ever Know' which she recorded with her sister, Bee Jay, in 1953. This was a very big hit for the Davis Sisters, as they were then known, as record artists. They received the 'Cash Box' annual award that year for 'The Most Programmed Record of 1953'. This brief joint success ended when Bee Jay was killed in a car crash. Steve Sholes, Victor's artists and repertoire chief, persuaded Skeeter to do a solo session in 1957 – an important turning point in her career – and she received

the 1958 *Cash Box* award as 'The Most Promising Female Country Vocalist'. She recorded 'The End of the World' in late 1962, the disc staying at No 2 for three weeks in the U.S. charts in 1963 with an eventual million sale by 1964. She was voted 'Favourite Female Country Artist' in the *Billboard* Disc Jockey Poll of 1964. 'The End of the World' was written in 1962 by Sylvia Dee and Arthur Kent, Skeeter's disc becoming a hit also in Britain, reaching No 18 with 13 weeks in the bestsellers. It was 17 weeks in the U.S. bestsellers.

JOEY DEE AND THE STARLITERS

SHOUT *Roulette* [*USA*]. This song, written in 1959 by the Isley Brothers, was the seond million seller for Joey Dee, and the second time the song produced a million selling version. The disc got to No 6 in the U.S. charts with 12 weeks in the bestsellers.

DUANE EDDY

(DANCE WITH) THE GUITAR MAN *Victor* [*USA*]. The third million seller for Duane Eddy was written by him in conjunction with Lee Hazlewood. It achieved No 12 in the U.S. charts with 16 weeks in the bestsellers, and No 4 and 16 weeks in Britain's bestsellers.

SHELLEY FABARES

JOHNNY ANGEL *Colpix* [*USA*]. This song was written by Lee Pockriss (music) and Lyn Duddy (words). Shelly (real name Michele Fabares) hails from Santa Monica, California. Niece of Nanette Fabray, she started as a dancer, her first break coming in 1953 with an appearance on a Frank Sinatra TV show. She started her own showbiz career as an actress and moved into dramatic parts on several top rating TV shows. Her film break came in 1955 with *Never Say Goodbye*, then featured parts in *Rock Pretty Baby* and *Summer Love*. Shelley subsequently played the role of Donna Reed's daughter on the U.S. TV series 'The Donna Reed Show'. In 1962 she started her singing career with her first tune for Colpix Records, this disc of 'Johnny Angel'. This first million seller for 19-year-old Shelley almost overnight reached top place in the sellers charts (for two weeks in the U.S.A. with 15 weeks in the bestsellers, and reaching No 41 in Britain), so adding another laurel to her varied talents.

BENT FABRIC (piano)

ALLEY CAT *Metronome* [*Denmark*]. Bent Fabric (real name Bent Fabricus Bjerre) was born on 7 December 1924 in Copenhagen. A multi-talented artist, Bent had a jazz band in his teens and made some early Danish jazz discs. He then went into the pop field in which he has remained ever since. In 1950 he took over Metronome Records in Denmark. In addition he is also a successful artists and repertoire man, composer, pianist and TV personality. As host and star of a popular Saturday night Danish TV show called 'Around a Piano' he presented guest stars and played piano. The tune of 'Alley Cat' was written by Frank Bjorn (pseudonym of Fabric). This disc sold a million when released on the Atco label in the U.S.A., and was at No 12 in the charts with 18 weeks in the bestsellers. Lyrics by Jack Harlem were written later for a song version. The disc was Denmark's first entry into the American bestseller charts to reach a high position. Winner of N.A.R.A.S. Award for 'Best Rock and Roll Recording' 1962.

LARRY FINNEGAN (pop ballad vocalist)

DEAR ONE *Old Town* [*USA*]. Written in 1961 by Larry and Vincent Finnegan, this disc reached No 11 in the U.S. charts with 14 weeks in the bestsellers, and is said to have sold a global million by 1966. It was his first recording.

John Lawrence Finnegan was born in New York in 1939, and was educated at Notre Dame. His musical interests were playing the guitar, piano, drums and songwriting. He is also an apt dancer and made radio, TV and personal appearances. In 1966 Larry who was living in Stockholm, Sweden, set up his own independent record company, Svensk-American.

He sings in the country style and is a successful songwriter in Denmark, Sweden, Norway and Germany.

THE FOUR SEASONS

SHERRY *Vee Jay* [*USA*]. This teenbeat vocal quartet comprised: Bob Gaudio (tenor singer, piano and organ, and composer of the song) born 17 November 1942; Franki Valli (leader and tenor) born 3 May 1937; Nick Massi (bass and vocal arrangements) born 19 September 1935; and Tommy de Vito (baritone and guitarist) born 19 June 1935. All four hail from New Jersey. Except for Bob Gaudio, who joined the group after leaving the Royal Teens, the others had been working together for about six years under the name Four Lovers. After enjoying only mild success they met record producer Bob Crewe in Gotham who changed their name to The Four Seasons and gave them fresh material. 'Sherry' reached the top of the bestseller charts as did their second disc 'Big Girls Don't Cry' (see below) to make the

boys a household name throughout the U.S.A. and achieve fame elsewhere. 'Sherry' was top disc for five weeks in the U.S.A. with 14 weeks in the bestsellers, and No 8 and 16 weeks in the British bestsellers. The group previously recorded for the Gone label. A top rhythm-and-blues seller.

BIG GIRLS DON'T CRY *Vee Jay* [*USA*]. Likewise this second million seller for The Four Seasons reached the top of the U.S. charts, and was a bestseller for 16 weeks reaching No 13 with 10 weeks in the British bestsellers. The number was written by Bob Crewe, and Robert Gaudio (of the group). A top rhythm-and-blues disc.

FREDDY (Quinn)

JUNGE KOMM BALD WIEDER (Son, come home soon) *Polydor* [*Germany*]. This sixth million seller for Freddy was written by Walter Rothenburg (words) and Lotar Olias (music). The English version was released in late 1963 in the U.S.A., with words by Charles Singleton and Quinn. The song is the hit number from the German musical *Homesick for St Pauli*, that starred Freddy Quinn. Disc sold 2 million by end of 1967.

CONNY FROBOESS

ZWEI KLEINER ITALIENER (Two little Italians) *Electrola* [*Germany*]. The first million seller for Conny was written by Christian Bruhn and George Buschor. Conny was born in Berlin on 28 October 1943 and made her first appearance there in 1950 when she was seven and her first record the same year. After a top career as a child star on discs and in films she eventually established herself as Germany's top teenage songstress. Already a veteran of several years in show business she continued her career as a top star of stage, screen and TV. Her recording of this disc sold half a million by December 1962 in Germany and subsequently over the million with Continental sales (1,225,000 by June 1965). She won the 'Song for Europe' contest in Germany in 1962 and visited the U.S.A. in 1963. She also made her first English-speaking record in 1962 for EMI in England.

STAN GETZ (modern tenor sax) AND CHARLIE BYRD (modern jazz guitar)

DESAFINADO (Slightly out of tune) *Verve* [*USA*]. The music for this million seller was written in 1959 by Antonio Carlos Jobim, with the original text by Newton Mendonca, and was published in Brazil. English lyrics were written by Jon Hendricks and Jessie Cavanaugh in 1962. Charlie Byrd, the talented jazz and classical guitarist, was born on 16 September 1925 in Chuckatuck, Virginia. He began on the guitar at the age of nine, learning from his father. He played with local groups during high school and college, later in a U.S. Army Band show. He then met famed jazz guitar Django Reinhardt and was greatly impressed by his technique. After discharge from the Army, from 1946 to 1950, Byrd was building his name on the American jazz scene, and studied with Sophocles Papas, the classical teacher, and worked on composition with Thomas Simmons. This led to a stay in Italy with the world's greatest classical guitarist Andres Segovia, with whom he became a private student. An avid student of Latin-American music, Byrd was chosen for a tour of South America by the U.S. State Department in 1961, during which he picked up the Bossa Nova sound and became a leading exponent by featuring much of it in his repertoire and on discs when he returned to the States in 1962. Together with Stan Getz, Byrd was thus responsible for introducing the Bossa Nova craze, 'Desafinado' being the first big hit in this idiom. Byrd has also made several albums of classical music including some from the 16th and 17th centuries. He spent a lot of time on tour with Woody Herman's swing-band, and likes to take his trio on concert tours of serious music. His album 'Jazz Samba' with Getz, made in 1962, was a big seller being in the charts for well over 12 months. Stan Getz was born on 2 February 1927, the son of Russian-Jewish immigrants (real name: Gayetzsky), and hails from Philadelphia. A veteran tenor sax player, and a mainstay of modern jazz, Getz has played with many top bands including Stan Kenton, Benny Goodman and Jimmy Dorsey. He tours with his quartet on college, club and TV dates. 'Desafinado' was taken from the 'Jazz Samba' album and issued as a single. It became a million seller in 1963, being the first Bossa Nova to climb the seller charts. Byrd played for several years in the Showboat Lounge and at his own club, The Byrd Cage, in Washington DC, working over classic, jazz and folk material. Grammy Award for 'Best Jazz Performance (Small Group)' 1962. Sales were over 1,600,000 by 1967. The disc reached No 15 and was 16 weeks in the U.S. bestsellers, and No 11 and 11 weeks in the British bestsellers.

JAZZ SAMBA (album) *Verve* [*USA*]. This album is reputed to have sold a million by 1964; it was one of 1962's biggest sellers in the U.S.A. It contained the famous 'Desafinado' (see above). Titles on the album are: 'Desafinado', by Antonio Carlos Jobim (1959): 'Samba Deese Days', by Charlie Byrd; 'O Pata', by J. Silva and N. Teixeira (1962); 'Samba triste', by Baden Powell and Blanco; 'Samba de una nota so', by Antonio Carlos Jobim and Newton Mendonca (1959); 'E Luxo so', by Peixota and Ary Barroso; 'Baia', by Ary Barroso (1939).

This disc was in the U.S. bestsellers lists for 70 weeks.

FRANÇOISE HARDY (pop vocalist)
TOUS LES GARÇONS ET LES FILLES (All the boys and girls) *Vogue* [*France*]. Françoise Hardy is considered to be one of France's prettitest stars and certainly one of its biggest sellers on disc. She was born in Paris on 17 January 1944 and studied at Le Bruyère College. Given a guitar when she graduated, she taught herself to play and began writing songs. In April 1960 she began auditioning at various record companies and was immediately signed to Vogue. She continued however to study and obtained a degree in German. In addition she speaks English, Spanish and Italian as well as her native French.

In June 1962 her disc of 'Tous les garçons et les filles' was released. Written by her, it became an international hit and was particularly big in France and in Italian for their market. It stayed in the Continental charts for several weeks and subsequently amassed the million sale. By 1966 she was selling more discs than any other French singer. Apart from her singing, Françoise was in great demand as a model and acquired a name for being a trendsetter of fashion. She was one of the first stars to wear her hair very long and straight. *Time* (30 December 1966) described her face as one of 'intricate refinement' and saw her as 'a symbol of the mystery of youth'. Her photogenic qualities resulted in a great number of French magazines putting her on their covers with much press publicity in France and abroad. She appeared in several of Vadim's films, making her debut in Sagan's *A Castle in Sweden*. Her first major U.S. film was *Grand Prix* (1966) co-starring with Yves Montand, James Garner and Genevieve Page.

Françoise is a very talented composer and writes many of her own songs.

Demands for her appearances became extensive and in addition to major TV and cabaret in France and Britain, she regularly commuted between almost every European country. She has also visited the U.S.A.

Italian version of the song was 'Quelli della mia eta'. The disc was No 36 in Britain and seven weeks in the bestsellers.

BRIAN HYLAND
SEALED WITH A KISS *ABC-Paramount* [*USA*]. This second million seller for Brian was written in 1960 by Peter Udell (words) and Gary Geld (music). The disc was No 3 for two weeks in the U.S. charts and 14 weeks in the bestsellers, and No 3 with 15 weeks in the British bestsellers.

FRANK IFIELD
I REMEMBER YOU *Columbia* [*Britain*]. Frank Ifield's sensational country-and-western style recording of this song sold two

million. It sold 102,000 in one day, and 367,000 in five days after its release in June 1962. The song was written in 1942 by famed Johnny Mercer (words) and the late Victor Schertzinger (music) for the Dorothy Lamour, Bob Eberly, Helen O'Connell, Jimmy Dorsey and orchestra film *The Fleet's In*. Frank was born on 30 November 1937 in Coventry, England. He actually began his career at the age of 15 in Australia where he spent two-thirds of his life. He was the first artist to appear on TV in Sydney when it was officially opened, and had several of his own TV and radio series 'down under'. To further his career he travelled to England in 1959 and within a few months signed a disc contract with Columbia Records. Frank furthered his fame by winning second place with Britain's entry in the Eurovision TV contest. He eventually became the first singer ever to get his three hits to No 1 in Britain's bestseller charts. Ifield also plays guitar, ukulele, piano, and bass as well as singing. This disc was No 1 for eight weeks in Britain with 28 weeks in the bestsellers, and a success in the U.S.A. where it reached No 5 with 11 weeks in the bestsellers.

LOVESICK BLUES *Columbia* [*Britain*]. The second million seller for Frank Ifield was an oldie of 1922 written by Irving Mills (words) and Cliff Friend (music). It was No 1 disc for five weeks in Britain, and reached No 44 in the U.S.A. with seven weeks in the bestsellers, and 17 weeks in the British bestsellers.

THE ISLEY BROTHERS
TWIST AND SHOUT *Wand* [*USA*]. The second million seller for the Isley Brothers was written by Bert Russell (Berns) and Phil Medley in 1960. The Isley Brothers, Ronald, Rudolph and O'Kelly, hail from Cincinatti. They previously recorded for RCA Victor. This song also a big hit for Brian Poole and the Tremeloes, and The Beatles in Britain. The Brothers' disc got to No 17 in the U.S. charts with 16 weeks in the bestsellers and reached No 42 in Britain.

CLAUDE KING
WOLVERTON MOUNTAIN *Columbia* [*USA*]. A top country-and-western disc, this first million seller for Claude King was written by Merle Kilgore and King himself. Claude, country-and-western vocalist, was born in Shreveport, Louis-

iana. He bought his first guitar when he was 12 for 50 cents from a farmer, and began songwriting at an early age. He attended the University of Idaho and a business college at Shreveport. This disc got to No 7 in the U.S. charts with 16 weeks in the bestsellers. This song is an adaptation of a traditional American mountain song.

STEVE LAWRENCE (accompaniment arranged and conducted by Marion Evans)

GO AWAY LITTLE GIRL *Columbia* [*USA*]. The first million seller for Steve was another big success for husband and wife songwriting team Gerry Goffin and Carole King. Steve Lawrence (real name Sam Leibowitz) was born in New York on 8 July 1933. He received early encouragement from his father who was a cantor. In early days he tried his hand at the piano and sax, composing and arranging. In 1952, he caught the public eye when he won an Arthur Godfrey 'Talent Scout' show, then appeared with it for a week on TV and radio, and later as a regular on the Steve Allen TV show. Through this latter association, he met Eydie Gorme, also a regular on the show. They married in 1957 and eventually became one of the most successful nightclub acts in the U.S.A. Steve was heard by King Records who signed him up and he had his first hit with 'Poinciana' (1953). In 1954, he signed with Coral Records and enjoyed a hit with 'Party Doll'. In 1959 he switched to ABC-Paramount and hits 'Pretty Blue Eyes' and 'Footsteps' followed. In 1961 came 'Portrait of My Love' on the United Artists label, then this million seller on Columbia. Steve and Eydie, a husband-wife team of rare talent, have starred in their own TV shows and have been acclaimed wherever they appeared. Eydie Gorme is also a disc star with hits 'Yes My Darling Daughter' and 'Blame It on the Bossa Nova'. This disc was No 1 for two weeks in the U.S.A. in 1963 and 17 weeks in the bestsellers.

BRENDA LEE

ALL ALONE AM I *Decca* [*USA*]. This fourth million seller for Brenda was written by Arthur Altman (words) and Manos Hadjidakis (music). Original Greek words by Jean Ioannidis. It reached No 3 with 15 weeks in the U.S. bestsellers, and was No 7 and 17 weeks in the British bestsellers.

DICKEY LEE (country vocalist)

PATCHES *Smash* [*USA*]. Dickey Lee, talented singer-guitarist-composer, was born and raised in Memphis. He became a graduate of Memphis State University where he participated in sports and majored in physical education. He is a former Golden Gloves champion.

Producer Jack Clement, who aided him in every phase of his career - writing, singing, confidence - was one of the major influences of his success.

'Patches' was written in 1960 by Barry Mann and Larry Kolber. Dickey's recording for Smash got to No 6 and was on the U.S. bestsellers for 14 weeks. It was reported that the disc subsequently sold over a million.

In 1965, Dickey had a hit with 'Laurie' on the 20th Century-Fox-distributed TCF-Hall label, and later joined RCA Records as an exclusive artist.

KETTY LESTER

LOVE LETTERS *Era* [*USA*]. The first million seller for Ketty was written in 1945 for the film *Love Letters* by Edward Heyman (words) and the late Victor Young (music). Ketty was born in Hope, Arkansas, and after college enrolled for training as a nurse at the City College, San Francisco. She joined the college choir which made her realize that it was music, not nursing, for which she was destined. She took singing and acting lessons and a music course at San Francisco State College. Passing an audition she sang at the Purple Onion, a top 'Frisco' night spot, and toured France, Germany, Italy, and Switzerland. Ketty then met Cab Calloway, the famous bandleader and musical star, who took her on tour to South America. Then came a spot with Ziegfeld

Follies in New York and on the road. Miss Lester's disc chance came through two artists and repertoire men from Era Records hearing her nightclub act. They offered her 'Love Letters' which racked up big sales through her rendering and the unique new treatment particularly in the original accompaniment. Era then signed her to a five year pact. The disc was No 5 and 14 weeks in the U.S. bestsellers, and No 4 and 12 weeks in the British bestsellers.

LITTLE EVA

THE LOCO-MOTION *Dimension* [*USA*]. The first million seller for teenbeat vocalist Little Eva was yet another big hit for husband-wife songwriters Goffin and Carole King. Little Eva (Eva Narcissus Boyd) was born on 29 June 1945 in Belhaven, North Carolina, one of a family of fourteen. She moved to New York at 15 to stay with relatives and attend high school. Songwriters Goffin and King hired her in the evenings as their baby-sitter while they worked on new compositions. Eva sang as she went about the house. Her pleasant voice and easy style struck the trained ear of the Goffins as she sang a Dee Dee Sharp song, so they suggested she cut some demonstration discs. Dimension Records were impressed and let her record the Goffins' latest song 'The Loco-motion'. The disc went to the top of the hit parade charts for one week. Little Eva demonstrated the dance on TV which for a while superseded the Twist, from which it was a development. She later appeared in Britain. A top rhythm-and-blues disc, it was 16 weeks in the U.S. bestsellers, and No 2 and 17 weeks in the British bestsellers.

VAUGHN MEADER WITH NAOMI BROSSART

THE FIRST FAMILY (album) *Cadence* [*USA*]. This comedy disc by Vaughn Meader, assisted by Naomi Brossart, a series of skits on the U.S. President John F. Kennedy and his family, was up to 1962 the disc industry's fastest and all-time bestseller comedy album with an estimated five-and-a-half million sale in as many months. Released in mid-November 1962, this disc sold 1,600,000 in two weeks, and 3,250,000 in a month, continuing at the rate of 100,000 per day for some time thereafter. 'The First Family' was at No 1 for nine weeks. Vaughn Meader was born on 20 March 1936 in Boston. He worked for a radio station in Boston prior to his four-year Army service. He started in show business as a pianist in the country field and switched to comedy while playing in clubs around New England. Eventually he came to New York and secured an engagement at the Phase 2 in Greenwich Village, and got his first big break on a 'Talent Scouts' TV show in 1962. From then he made numerous appearances on TV and played many of the top supper clubs throughout the U.S.A. One of his assets was a resemblance to President Kennedy, and he even had the same kind of haircut. In his take off of the President in the album, he perfectly captured the voice of the chief executive. Naomi Brossart impersonated the President's wife, Jacqueline, on part of the disc. After the President's assassination on 22 November 1963, all copies of the disc were withdrawn from the record stores. Gold Disc award, R.I.A.A., 1962. Grammy Awards for 'Album of the Year' 1962 and 'Best Comedy Performance' 1962.

NED MILLER
FROM A JACK TO A KING (re-issue of 1957 recording) *Fabor* [*USA*]. This disc was released in December 1962 and by July 1963 had sold an estimated two million. The song, written by Ned Miller in 1957 was waxed by him then on Fabor Records who leased it to Dot Records, but it failed to register. Then Fabor Robinson decided to try again and orders started to come in with spectacular results. Ned Miller comes from Salt Lake City, Utah, where he was raised (he was born in Rains, Utah, 12 April 1925). He bought his first guitar at the age of nine, his mother teaching him to play. At 16, he was writing songs. He served three years in the Marine Corps in the South Pacific, and after service studied for two years under the G.I. Bill and became a pipefitter. Miller then wrote 'Dark Moon', a hit for Gale Storm (1957), and, in all, 100 other songs. This disc reached No 6 with 13 weeks in the U.S. bestsellers, and No 2 and 21 weeks in the British bestsellers.

MINA
HEISSER SAND (Hot Sand) *Italdisc* [*Italy*] *Polydor* [*Germany*]. This disc was a million seller, mainly in Europe, by 1965. The song was written by Kurt Feltz (a producer of operettas for Polydor since 1945) with music by Werner Scharfenberger. The song was specially recorded in Italy for release in Germany by Polydor, Mina's first disc in German.

Mina was born in Busto Arsizio, Italy in 1940, and has become a very popular singing personality. She was discovered at a talent show. In addition to her disc success, she has starred in films and on TV, toured Europe, Japan and South America. Her first disc hit was 'Il cielo in una stanza' (1961) which sold almost a million to win her nationwide acclaim. Then followed 'Renato', 'Strigimi forte I polsi' and 'Chihuahua' in 1962. In 1963 her disc of 'Stessa piaggia stesso mare' was a big hit in Italy. Then came 'Heisser Sand' and recording in several languages. Mina became contracted to RI.FI Records.

THE MIRACLES
YOU'VE REALLY GOT A HOLD ON ME *Tamla* [*USA*]. Second million seller for The Miracles, written by group leader William 'Smokey' Robinson. The disc was a big hit in early 1963 and also a top rhythm-and-blues number. Released on 8 December 1962, it reached No 8 with 16 weeks in the U.S. bestsellers.

LOU MONTE
PEPINO THE ITALIAN MOUSE *Reprise* [*USA*]. The first million seller for Lou Monte was issued in late 1962 and reached a million sale by 1963. Comedy vocalist Lou was born on 2 April 1917 and hails from Oakland, New Jersey. For many years he has made singing and playing the guitar his career. He started before the war as a solo act, then enlisted in the U.S. Army. After the war, he got his first break with his own radio show over a Newark Station, and did local club dates. His manager, George Brown, brought Lou and the song 'Dark-Town Strutters Ball' – Italian arrangement – to Victor Records, for whom he recorded it – a hit disc – followed by a string of others including 'Italian

Hucklebuck', 'Lazy Mary' and 'Sheik of Araby'. 'Pepino' was written by Ray Allen and Wanda Merrell. The disc was No 5 and 10 weeks in the U.S. bestsellers.

CHRIS MONTEZ
LET'S DANCE *Monogram* [*USA*]. The first million seller for teenbeat vocalist Chris was written by Jim Lee (chief of Monogram Records). It got to No 6 in the U.S. charts and was 14 weeks in the bestsellers. It reached No 2 and was 18 weeks in the British charts. Chris was born on 17 January 1943 in Los Angeles. His brothers taught him to play guitar, and at 15 he began to sing and write songs. After high school in 1961, he met Jim Lee, a young impresario, who was looking for talent to start his Monogram Records. Chris first recorded one of his own songs 'All You Had to Do Was Tell Me' which got some attention, then came this million seller. His real name is Christoper Montanez.

SOME KINDA FUN *Monogram* [*USA*]. The second million seller for Chris Montez was written by Jim Lee (of Monogram Records) and Montez himself. It reached No 43 and was nine weeks in the U.S. bestsellers.

ROY ORBISON
DREAM BABY *Monument* [*USA*]. Roy's sixth million seller reached No 3 in the U.S.A. (with 12 weeks in the bestsellers), and No 2 and 14 weeks in the British charts. This song was written by Cindy Walker.

WORKIN' FOR THE MAN *Monument* [*USA*]. This was the seventh estimated (global) million seller subsequently for Roy, his own composition. It reached No 33 with 11 weeks in the U.S. bestsellers, and was No 50 in Britain.

THE ORLONS
THE WAH-WATUSI *Cameo* [*USA*]. The first million seller for the Orlons was written by Kal Mann and Dave Appell (of Cameo Records). This vocal group comprises Shirley Brickley (born 9 December 1944); Rosetta Hightower (born 23 June 1944); Marlena Davis (born 4 October 1944); and Steve Caldwell (born 22 November 1942). Originally the Orlons were a quintet who met in junior high school in Philadelphia and sang together for about five years at school assemblies and local functions. They disbanded and then Stephen Caldwell got the group together after locating two of the original members to form this quartet. After about a year, they were signed up by Cameo and came up with this big hit which got to No 2 in the U.S. charts and 14 weeks in the bestsellers.

DON'T HANG UP *Cameo* [*USA*]. The second million seller for the Orlons was also written by Kal Mann and Dave Appell (of Cameo Records). It reached chart position No 4 in the U.S.A. with 15 weeks in the bestsellers, and was No 39 in Britain.

PAUL AND PAULA
HEY, PAULA *Philips* [*USA*]. Issued in late 1962, this disc sold over one million in the U.S.A. and globally two million by 1963. The duo's real names are Ray Hildebrand, writer of the song, from Harlingen, Texas, and Jill Jackson, from Brownwood, Texas. Paul, an accomplished songwriter and guitarist, sang it at college with Paula. As students at Howard Payne College in Brownwood, Texas, they teamed up after singing for a Cancer Fund drive radio programme. They travelled to Fort Worth in November 1962 for an audition with Major Bill Smith, well-known star maker, only to learn he was scheduled to record an artist and could not hear them. Determined to get a hearing they waited. The scheduled artist did not turn up. As Smith walked out, the duo began singing 'Hey, Paula' and within minutes Smith realized their talent and cut a demonstration disc the same day on the Lecam label, Philips Records acquiring global rights. It soon zoomed to No 1 in the charts and stayed top for three weeks in the U.S.A. in 1963, as well as being 15 weeks in the

bestsellers. It was No 8 and 17 weeks in the British bestsellers. Ray was born 21 November 1940 in Joshua, Texas. A top rhythm-and-blues disc.

Gold Disc award, R.I.A.A., 1963.

PETER, PAUL AND MARY

PETER, PAUL AND MARY (album) *Warner* [*USA*]. Issued in March 1962, this album sold over a million in the U.S.A. by mid-1963, and two million by mid-1965. The trio's full names are Peter Yarrow (born in New York on 31 May 1938), Paul Stookey (born 30 November 1937 in Baltimore, Maryland) and Mary Allin Travers (born on 7 November 1937 in Louisville, Kentucky). Peter holds a psychology degree from Cornell University where he was also an instructor in a folk ballad course. He was discovered at the Newport Folk Festival in 1960 after appearing as a single artist in his own very successful tour of various nightclub spots catering for folk music fans. He plays the guitar. Paul played an electric guitar for a high school rock'n'roll group on local TV and worked his way through Michigan State University, also doing stand-up comic routines in Greenwich Village, and helping Mary make a comeback as a singer after she had worked in a Broadway flop, *The Next President*, with Mort Sahl. Mary appeared with several teenage folk groups, and then twice at Carnegie Hall. Life-long interest in folk music led the three to Greenwich Village where they formed a trio, touring the country from The Blue Angel to the Hungry I, after seven months working up their initial repertoire of 18 numbers with the assistance of Milton Okun (formerly with Harry Belafonte) to polish their arrangements. They developed their style and acquired a big following. Their fortunes began to rise with this album, one of the songs 'Lemon Tree' taken from for it and issued as a single bringing the trio into the national limelight. 'If I Had a Hammer' further enhanced their reputation. Their success was a phenomenal one with fantastic strides both as recording artists and personal appearance attractions. The trio visited Britain in September 1963 and then appeared in other European countries. This album was in the U.S. bestsellers lists for 185 weeks. Gold Disc award R.I.A.A. 1962.

The disc contained the following songs: 'Early in the Morning', by Paul Stookey; 'Five Hundred Miles', by Hedy West, Bobby Bare and Charlie Williams (1962); 'Sorrow', by Paul and Peter Yarrow; 'This Train', by Peter Yarrow; 'Bamboo', by Van Ronk and Weisman;'It's Raining', by Paul Stookey; 'If I Had My Way', by Davis; 'Cruel War', by Peter Yarrow; 'Lemon Tree', by Will Holt (1960); 'If I Had a Hammer', by Lee Hays and Pete Seeger (1958); 'Autumn to May', by Peter Yarrow and Paul Stookey; 'Where Have All the Flowers Gone?' by Peter Seger (1961) (additional verses by Joe Hickerson).

ESTHER PHILLIPS (rhythm-and-blues vocalist)

RELEASE ME *Lenox* [*USA*]. Esther Phillips was born on 23 December 1935 in Houston. At the age of 13, she was discovered by bandleader Johnny Otis in Los Angeles where she won an amateur contest, and was signed by Otis to sing with his orchestra soon after. She was billed as 'Little' Esther Phillips at the famous Barrelhouse Club in that West Coast R & B centre in the 1940s and 1950s. Her first disc appeared on the Modern label in late 1948, with Otis backing her up, but this met with little success. In 1949, Johnny and Esther moved over to the Savoy label and had a big hit with 'Double-Crossin' Blues', followed by 'Cupid's Boogie' in 1950. In 1952, Otis folded things up for a while and Esther went out as a solo act but with little success. She recorded for a variety of Southern labels including Federal and Warwick, then ill health and personal problems forced her home to Houston in the mid-1950s for a couple of years' recuperation. She then took to the road again. Lenox Records executives Bob Gans and Lilan Rogers found her performing at a local night spot in Houston and signed her to the label, and in 1962 she recorded the country/western tune 'Release Me' for the New York-based Lenox label. This sold a million, and led to a whole, much-disputed album of C & W tunes and landed her a reputation in the supper-club easy-listening circles that contrasted solidly with her tough, little-girl role in the forties and fifties. Atlantic Records bought up her contract in 1965, at first continuing with the C & W style songs, but soon allowing her to cover The Beatles' 'And I Love Her' that turned out to be her last big hit. Atlantic followed with some albums of 'standards' by her.

Esther Phillips returned in 1971 with a marvellous album – 'Esther Phillips/Burnin'' – which was recorded live at Freddie Jett's Pied Piper Club in Los Angeles. This was another stepping stone in her up-and-down career. It proved Esther to be an extraordinary blues singer, coupled with a jazz ballad sense of timing à la Dinah Washington or Nina Simone. This album included a live version of her come-back tune, 'Release Me'.

'Release Me' was written by Eddie Miller and W.S. Stevenson in 1954, and is one of he biggest selling country songs on discs, and one of the world's most performed songs.

Release of this disc was in October 1962. It was No 8 for two weeks in the U.S.A. and 14 weeks in the bestsellers.

BOBBY (Boris) PICKETT AND THE CRYPT KICKERS

MONSTER MASH *Garpax* [*USA*]. Bobby Pickett himself and Leonard Capizzi wrote 'Monster Mash' which became a million seller by 1963, and No 1 in the U.S.A. for two weeks with 14 weeks in the bestsellers, and No 3 and 13 weeks in the British bestsellers.

GENE PITNEY

THE MAN WHO SHOT LIBERTY VALANCE *Musicor* [*USA*]. The second reputed million seller for Gene Pitney took a title inspired by the film of the same name, and was written by Hal David (words) and Burt Bacharach (music). It was No 4 in the U.S. charts and 13 weeks in the bestsellers.

IF I DIDN'T HAVE A DIME backed with ONLY LOVE CAN BREAK A HEART *Musicor* [*USA*]. This third million seller for Gene consisted of the 'Dime' song written by Bert Russell (Berns) and Phil Medley with arrangement and conducting by Chuck Sagle. The 'Heart' song was written by Hal David (words) and Burt Bacharach (music) with arrangement and conducting by the composer Bacharach. 'Only Love Can Break a Heart' was No 2 and 14 weeks in the U.S. bestsellers. 'If I Didn't Have a Dime' was No 31 and eight weeks in the bestsellers.

ELVIS PRESLEY

GOOD LUCK CHARM backed with ANYTHING THAT'S PART OF YOU *Victor* [*USA*]. The 38th and 39th million sellers for Elvis were 'Good Luck Charm' written by Aaron Schroeder and Wally Gold and 'Anything That's Part of You' by Don Robertson. A Gold Disc was awarded for the former title for its U.S. sales. This disc also sold another million globally and was No 1 disc for two weeks in the U.S.A. (with 13 weeks in the bestsellers) and for five weeks in Britain. 'Anything That's Part of You' was No 31 and eight weeks in the bestsellers. 'Good Luck Charm' was 17 weeks in the British bestsellers.

SHE'S NOT YOU Victor [USA]. The 40th million seller for Elvis Presley was written by Jerry Leiber, Mike Stoller and Doc Pomus. It was a No 1 disc for three weeks in Britain and was a global million seller. The disc was No 5 in the U.S. charts and 10 weeks in the bestsellers. 17 weeks in the British bestsellers.

RETURN TO SENDER backed with WHERE DO YOU COME FROM? Victor [USA]. The 41st and 42nd million sellers for Elvis were both songs taken from Elvis' film Girls, Girls, Girls. 'Return to Sender' was written by Otis Blackwell and Winfield Scott and 'Where Do You Come From?' was the work of Ruth Batchelor and Bob Roberts. The first title was awarded a Gold Disc for its U.S.A. million sale alone. In fact the disc sold another million globally and was No 1 disc for two weeks in Britain and 14 weeks in the bestsellers and No 2 for three weeks in the U.S.A. with 16 weeks in the bestsellers. 'Where Do You Come From?' reached No 99 in the U.S.A.

CLIFF RICHARD AND THE SHADOWS

THE YOUNG ONES Columbia [Britain]. This second million seller for Cliff Richard provided the second occasion on which a British artist entered the seller charts in Britain at No 1 in the week of release. The disc had at that time an all-time peak advance sale for Britain of 524,000 copies by day of release. The song is the title number from Cliff Richard's first big film starring role, The Young Ones, written by Sid Tepper and Roy C. Bennett in 1961. It was the outstanding British musical film of 1962. This disc was No 1 for six weeks in Britain with 21 weeks in the bestsellers.

BACHELOR BOY backed with THE NEXT TIME Columbia [Britain]. The third million seller for Cliff Richard. Both songs came from his second starring film role in Summer Holiday. The disc was released in December 1962, and the film in 1963. 'Bachelor Boy' was written by Cliff Richard and Bruce Welch (of The Shadows) and it featured Cliff accompanied by The Shadows. 'The Next Time' was written by Buddy Kaye and Philip Springer of U.S.A.; in it Cliff was accompanied by The Shadows and by the Norrie Paramor Strings. The film was one of the outstanding musical pictures of 1963, while the disc was No 1 in Britain and 17 weeks in the bestsellers.

TOMMY ROE

SHEILA ABC-Paramount [USA]. The first million seller for teenbeat vocalist Tommy was his own composition. Thomas David Roe was born in Atlanta, Georgia, on 9 May 1942 and educated there, at Brown High School. At 16 he formed his own group - The Satins - for school and local dates. The group actually recorded 'Sheila' on the Judd label in 1960 but it did not register then. Tommy then signed with ABC-Paramount. He has written over 125 songs. His singing style is based on Buddy Holly's. This disc was No 1 for two weeks in the U.S.A. with 14 weeks in the bestsellers, and No 3 and 14 weeks in the British bestsellers. Tommy was first recognized as a performer in Britain where he spent a great deal of his time. A Gold Disc was awarded by R.I.A.A. in 1969.

DAVID ROSE AND HIS ORCHESTRA

THE STRIPPER MGM [USA]. This third million seller for David Rose was his own composition. 'The Stripper' was top seller in the U.S. charts for two weeks, and 17 weeks in the bestsellers.

KYU SAKAMOTO

SUKIYAKI (Ueo Muite Aruko) Toshiba [Japan]. 'Sukiyaki' was the first million selling Japanese disc in the U.S.A. It was written in 1962 by pianist Hachidai Nakamura with lyrics by Rokusuke Ei entitled 'Ueo Muite Aruko' (Walk with Your Chin Up) for an album. The disc was heard in December 1962 by Louis Benjamin, head of Pye Records (Britain) while on a business trip to Japan. He brought it back to England for Kenny Ball and his band to record it, dubbing it 'Sukiyaki' for simplicity's sake. Kenny Ball's instrumental version was a hit in Britain. Capitol Records, therefore, released the original vocal version by Sakamoto under the title of 'Sukiyaki' and it became the No 1 bestseller in the U.S.A. in 1963 for four weeks with 14 weeks in the bestsellers, selling a million there; it was No 6 and 13 weeks in the British bestsellers. Kyu Sakamoto was a big star in Japan for some years, with eight bestselling albums and 15 hit singles in that time, as well as acting in films and making TV appearances. His career started in the teahouses of Tokyo until, in 1960, the Toshiba label heard him and signed him up. His very first disc was a big hit. 'Sukiyaki' is a lilting, melancholy song of nocturnal loneliness. It sold half a million copies in Japan when first released there. Kyu is a native of the industrial city of Kawasaki, and he first sang with a group, the Paradise Kings. It was disc jockey Rich Osborne of radio station KORD in Pasco, Washington, who introduced the original Japanese version from the Toshiba album to his night time U.S.A. audience. He was immediately swamped with requests to repeat both the music and the announcement of the song's title and artist. Osborne repeated the song on his day time programme with the same results, and it soon became immensely popular in Washington State, and eventually all over America. Kyu (pronounced 'Q') also registered with his follow-up disc 'China Nights' in 1963.

NEIL SEDAKA

BREAKING UP IS HARD TO DO Victor [USA]. This third million seller for Neil was a top of the charts seller. The song was written by Howard Greenfield and Sedaka himself. The disc was No 1 for two weeks in the U.S.A. with 14 weeks in the bestsellers and No 7 and 16 weeks in the British bestsellers.

THE SHADOWS
WONDERFUL LAND *Columbia [Britain]*. This disc had a big sale in Britain, the Commonwealth and on the Continent with combined sales reputed at a million. The tune was written by Jerry Lordan, British composer of their first hit 'Apache'. This disc was top seller in Britain for eight weeks with 19 weeks in the bestsellers.

DEE DEE SHARP
MASHED POTATO TIME *Cameo [USA]*. The first million seller for teenage vocalist Dee Dee was written by Jon Sheldon and Harry Land. Dee Dee (real name Dione LaRue) was born on 9 September 1945 and hails from Philadelphia. She started her rise to stardom after answering a newspaper advertisement for a girl singer when 15, and soon was doing backgrounds on recordings at various Philadelphia sessions. She eventually auditioned for Cameo and recorded as part of a group for a disc that was not released. Dee Dee then impressed the company's artists and repertoire director Dave Appell who asked her to sing for him alone but the department was too busy at the time to record her. Several months later, Chubby Checker recorded 'Slow Twistin'' which seemed to lack the punch of his previous efforts. Head man Bernie Lowe of Cameo suggested using a female vocalist to give the record added sound. Dee Dee was called in for the sessions, and Lowe was so overcome with her talent that he decided to record her first solo that same night. This disc 'Mashed Potato Time' was the result. Dee Dee then went on to make more hit discs while still at Overbrook High School, and made radio, TV and personal apperances. This disc was No 2 for two weeks in the U.S.A. charts with 18 weeks in the bestsellers and a top R & B disc.

RIDE (I'm gonna get on my pony and ride) *Cameo [USA]*. This second million seller for Dee Dee Sharp was written by Jon Sheldon and Dave Leon. It achieved No 5 in the U.S.A. charts and 13 weeks in the bestsellers.

ALLAN SHERMAN
MY SON, THE FOLK SINGER (album) *Warner [USA]*. This exceedingly funny album sold a million in 10 weeks in the U.S.A. Comedian Allan Sherman was born on 30 November 1924 in Chicago, raised by his mother, his father and three successive stepfathers in Los Angeles, Miami, Chicago and New York. He went to 21 public schools and the University of Illinois. His writing activities began at the university where he studied journalism as well as writing lyrics and starring in and directing three consecutive Varsity shows. Then World War II erupted and, after it, Sherman set out on his show business career. He created special material for many nightclub performers; worked in TV for some years; and devised and produced the panel game 'I've Got a Secret'. He then made this album to become a world famous comedian. Allan was one of the few professional comedy writers who performed in front of the audiences just as wittily as he wrote for others. This disc was the outcome of his penchant for entertaining friends by singing familiar songs with lyrics marinated in Jewish humour, and he thus emerged from anonymity to convulse audiences on his own. His follow-up disc (1963) was 'My Son, the Celebrity'. The 'My Son' series of albums totalled three million sales. Gold Disc award R.I.A.A. 1962.

THE SHIRELLES
SOLDIER BOY *Scepter [USA]*. The fourth million seller for The Shirelles was No 1 seller in the U.S. charts for three weeks, and 14 weeks in the bestsellers. It was No 23 and nine weeks in the British charts. The song was written in 1961 by Florence Green and Luther Dixon, the latter being the Shirelles' artists and repertoire manager and arranger at Scepter Records.

RAY STEVENS WITH THE MERRY MELODY SINGERS
AHAB THE ARAB *Mercury [USA]*. The first million seller for Ray Stevens was his own composition. Ray, born 24 January 1941, hails from Clarkdale, Georgia. He became a disc jockey at the age of 15, and had his own TV show at 16. He plays the piano, trumpet, sax, clarinet, bass drums, tube mellophone and violin in addition to being a songwriter, and teenbeat vocalist. The disc got to No 5 in the U.S. charts and 11 weeks in the bestsellers.

THE TORNADOS (novelty instrumental group)
TELSTAR *Decca [Britain]*. This disc was No 1 seller for five weeks in Britain and for three weeks in the U.S.A., and global sales are estimated at five million. The tune was composed by Joe Meek, then aged 29, an ex-junior studio engineer who started a hit-making factory in a small lounge in Holloway Road, North London. In early 1962, he advertised for a group and picked five applicants, groomed them and sent them out on tour with John Leyton and Don Charles, vocalists. He then took them to Decca and got them a disc contract, and a season backing Billy Fury at Great Yarmouth. Thrilled by the brilliant achievement of the first Telstar trans-Atlantic transmission (23 July 1962), Meek felt the strong urge to write a tune in his studio. He phoned the Tornados immediately he had finished it to tell them to come to London the following weekend. They arrived and within an hour had worked out an arrangement and in a further half hour had recorded it. The disc was released on Decca (Britain) and on London (USA) with reputed earnings for Joe Meek of £30,000. The personnel of the Tornados is: Clem Cattini (drums) born 28 August 1939 in London; Alan Caddy (violin and guitar) born 2 February 1940 in Chelsea, London; George Bellamy (guitar) born 8 October 1941 in Sunderland; Roger Jackson (piano and organ) born 11 November 1938 in Kidderminster; and Heinz Burt (bass) born 25 July 1942 in Hargin, Germany. This was the biggest disc seller in Britain up to 1962. It was 16 weeks in the U.S.A. bestsellers, and 25 weeks in the British bestsellers. Composer Meek died tragically on 3 February 1967.

BOBBY VEE
THE NIGHT HAS A THOUSAND EYES *Liberty [USA]*. This fifth million seller for Bobby Vee was written by Ben Weisman, Dottie Wayne and Marilyn Garrett in 1962 for the film *Just for Fun* in which Bobby featured it. It reached No 3 with 14 weeks in the U.S. bestsellers, and No 3 and 12 weeks in Britain's bestsellers.

BOBBY VINTON
ROSES ARE RED (my love) *Epic [USA]*. The first big hit for Vinton produced a sale of nearly two million. The song was written in 1961 by Al Byron and Paul Evans (see 1959). This disc was top seller for four weeks in the U.S. charts and was 15 weeks in the bestsellers, and No 15 in Britain with eight weeks in the charts. Stanley Robert Vinton hails from Canonsburg, Pennsylvania, born 16 April 1935. He organized his first band in high school and later began to sing with the band. Epic Records signed him to a contract after hearing some of his recorded tapes. After the success of this disc he won a poll as the Most Promising Male Vocalist of 1962. Vinton appeared in London in 1962 on a promotional trip for filming in *Just for Fun*.
Gold Disc award R.I.A.A., 1962.

GERHARD WENDLAND
TANZE MIT MIR IN DEN MORGEN (Dance with me in the morning) *Philips [Germany]*. Wendland was born in Berlin in 1932. He started his career as a singer in 1952. It was interrupted by the war but he came back afterwards to make records. He is a top stage star and also does much film work and TV work. This song was written by Karl Goetz (words) and Kurt Hertha (music).

ANDY WILLIAMS WITH ORCHESTRA CONDUCTED BY ROBERT MERSEY

'MOON RIVER' AND OTHER GREAT MOVIE THEMES (album) *Columbia* [*USA*]. This third million seller for Andy Williams was his first album in this category. Robert Mersey both arranged and conducted the songs. The disc includes five songs (marked *) that were winners of the Academy Award for best film songs of their year. The contents of the disc are: *Side 1* – 'Love is a Many-Splendored Thing' (film of same title)*, by P.F. Webster and Sammy Fain (1955); 'A Summer Place' (film, same title), by Mack Discant and Max Steiner (1959); 'Maria' (film *West Side Story* 1962) by S. Sondheim and L. Bernstein (1957); 'Never on Sunday' (film, same title)*, by B. Towne and M. Hadjidakis (1960); 'As Time Goes By' (film *Casablanca* 1943), by Herman Hupfeld (orig. 1931); 'Exodus' (film *Exodus*), by Pat Boone (1961) and Ernest Gold (1960); *Side 2* – 'Moon River' (film *Breakfast at Tiffany's*)*, by J. Mercer and Henry Mancini (1961); 'Tonight' (film *West Side Story* 1962), by S. Sondheim and L. Bernstein (1957); 'The Second Time Around' (film *High Time*) by S. Cahn and J. Van Heusen (1960); 'Tender is the Night' (film, same title), by P.F. Webster and Sammy Fain (1962); 'It Might as Well Be Spring'* (film *State Fair*) (1945), by O. Hammerstein and R. Rodgers (1945); 'Three Coins in the Fountain'* (film, same title), by Sammy Cain and Julie Styne (1954).

This disc a two million seller by 1967, was in the U.S. best-sellers list for 176 weeks. Gold Disc award R.I.A.A., 1963.

1963

JOHN FITZGERALD KENNEDY – A MEMORIAL ALBUM (album) *Premier* [*USA*]. This disc – a recapitulation of a memorial tribute produced and broadcast by radio station WMCA-New York on 22 November 1963, the day of his assassination, with special recorded material from the files of Radio Press International – sold four million copies in six days (7-12 December 1963). Both Premier Records and WMCA Radio Station turned over all royalties to the Joseph Kennedy Jr. Foundation for Mental Retardation. The disc was the fastest seller of all time, and beat the previous record set by the satirical album 'The First Family' made by Vaughn Meader for Cadence Records in 1962. The disc is narrated by Ed Brown. It was sold at 99 cents, and included the inaugural address in its entirety as well as a collection of the late President's speeches. Gold Disc award, R.I.A.A., 1964.

THE PRESIDENTIAL YEARS (of John F. Kennedy) (album) *Pickwick* [*USA*]. Close to one million copies of this album were sent out in the first six days of its release. Sales passed the million soon after. This disc was also sold at 99 cents.

VARIOUS ARTISTS

ALL-STAR FESTIVAL (album) *United Nations*. This uniquely promoted album was produced by the United Nations High Commissioner for Refugees, and released in February 1963 on a worldwide basis for their benefit. The million sale was reached by June 1963. Presentations of the disc were made to numerous heads of state in Europe, to U Thant and President Kennedy in America, and to numerous dignitaries throughout the world. Contents of the disc: 'Lazy River' (Bing Crosby and Louis Armstrong) by Sidney Arodin and Hoagy Carmichael (1931); 'The Everlasting Arms' (Doris Day) by Paul F. Webster and Martin Broones; 'Ximeroni' (Nana Mouskouri) by Manos Hadjidakis; 'La vie est une belle fille' (Maurice Chevalier) by Albert Willemitz and Joseph Kosma; 'First Star I See Tonight' (Patti Page) by Corso, Otis and Hendricks; 'All of Me' (Ella Fitzgerald) by Seymour Simons and Gerald Marks (1931); 'Je m'imagine' (Edith Piaf) by Raya and Marguerite Monnot; 'When You Belong to Me' (Nat 'King' Cole) by Merrick and Cochran; 'Greensleeves' (Anne Shelton) traditional, arranged by Wally Stott; 'Adonde Vas, Nino?' (Luis Alberto de Parano of Los Paraguayos) by Don Rafirio Camar; 'Nobody but You Lord' (Mahalia Jackson) by M. Jackson; 'La Golondrina' (Caterina Valente) by Narciso Serradell arranged: Flor.

All the artists, music publishers, disc companies and many others associated with the production of this disc contributed their services and waived royalties so that the maximum profits might be obtained for the refugees.

THE ANGELS

MY BOYFRIEND'S BACK *Smash* [*USA*]. This was the first million seller for this (female) trio, consisting of two sisters, Barbara and Jiggs, and another girl, Peggy. The song was written by Robert Fieldman, Gerald Goldstein and Richard Gottehrer. The disc was No 1 in U.S. charts for three weeks and 14 weeks in the bestsellers, and was No 50 in Britain. The trio got together in 1961 and had two hits with 'Til' and 'Cry Baby Cry' on the Caprice label. They travelled across the U.S.A. with a nightclub act and have sung on coast-to-coast TV. Jiggs went to college, but left to sing with the group when they recorded 'Til'. She planned to become a teacher before she started her show business career. Barbara studied at the Juilliard School of Music and intended to be an arranger and producer. She arranged the trio's early hits. Peggy wrote and sang on commercials for WINS-New York before joining the sisters. She also appeared in *Do Re Mi* on Broadway. Barbara and Jiggs hail from Orange, New Jersey, Peggy from Bellville, New Jersey.

CHARLES AZNAVOUR

LA MAMA *Barclay* [*France*]. This first million seller for Aznavour achieved its sale in France alone. The song was written by Robert Gall (words) and Aznavour (music) and first recorded by the famous Les Compagnons de la Chanson in 1963. Aznavour's own version made it a big hit and France's No 1 by early January 1964, following his performances of it on a TV show 'Discorama'. The day after, it became the talk of France. Aznavour was born on 22 May 1924 in Paris of Armenian parentage. His father, an ex-baritone, was then running a restaurant on the Rue de la Huchette frequented by central European refugees where young Charles heard many songs from his homeland. After leaving school he obtained various small parts in Shakespearean and other plays, and then a big part in the film *La guerre des gosses*. From 1940 and throughout the war he was able to continue his theatrical studies and went on several tours around France. Around 1942, he wrote his first songs 'Il y a deux hiboux dans le beffroi' and 'Pere Noel est swing'; joined 'L'école du music -hall'; and finally teamed up with Pierre Roche and wrote several hit songs with him. They were encouraged by Maurice Chevalier, Mistinguette and Raul Breton and began to make a reputation in the music hall world, becoming protégés of Edith Piaf. They went on to the Latin Quarter and Café Society in New York and triumphed at the Maison Doré in Montreal, Canada. On returning to France in 1950 from Montreal, Charles had a lean time until 1956 when his singing became the feature of the Olympic Theatre in Paris, making him a star. Then followed the lead in films, radio and TV and recording. His first songwriting success was 'Sur ma vie', 1955, and subsequent hits included 'If faut savoir', 'J'm voyais déjà', 'Alleluia' and 'Je t'attends' which from 1961 helped to make him an international favourite. An English version of 'La Mama' entitled 'For Mama', was written in 1964, with words by Don Black. Aznavour made his first U.S.A. discs in English in 1965, and is said to have written around 500 songs.

He was the highest paid French entertainer of 1965 and was presented with 12 Gold Discs on 17 July 1966, one for each of the big hits he had recorded for Barclay label.

BOBBY BARE (vocalist)

DETROIT CITY *Victor* [*USA*]. Written in 1962 by Danny Dill and Mel Tillis, Bobby's disc is said to have sold a million by 1964. He was born on 7 April 1935 in Ironton, Ohio, and was left motherless at the age of 5. He became a farm worker by the time he was 15 and later started writing rock'n'roll songs. In 1958 he recorded 'All-American Boy' which was released on the Fraternity label to become a hit. Earlier home town TV experience proved valuable and while in the U.S. Army he appeared in an 'Ed Sullivan Show'. In 1961 he wrote three rock'n'roll songs for Chubby Checker's film *Teenage Millionaire* and the same year appeared in a movie *A Distant Trumpet*. Bobby had many successes after 'Detroit City' and was also made a regular member of WSM's 'Grand Ole Opry' radio programme.

This disc reached No 13 in the U.S. charts with 12 weeks in the bestsellers, and was winner of N.A.R.A.S. Award for 'Best Country-and-Western Recording' 1963.

500 MILES AWAY FROM HOME *Victor* [*USA*]. Bobby wrote this song with Hedy West and Charles Williams in 1962. It was a big hit for Peter, Paul and Mary and also for French singer Richard Anthony. Bobby recorded it himself in 1963 when it reached No 10 in the U.S. charts with 11 weeks in the bestsellers, and was later coupled with his recording of 'Detroit City', this becoming a standard seller, and both titles estimated million sellers.

THE BEACH BOYS

SURFIN' USA *Capitol* [*USA*]. Surfing, or riding on high rolling waves, became a craze with youngsters on the west coast of the U.S.A. in 1963. In November 1962, surfer Dennis Wilson, then aged 17, decided it was time somebody wrote a song about it, so he took an idea to his musically-talented family. His cousin, Mike Love, wrote 'Surfin''. Then his brother Brian got together a vocal group consisting of Mike, Dennis, and a third brother Carl. Their father Murray Wilson, a long-time songwriter, got a recording session and the song was a success. This was heard by a young Capitol producer Nick Venet who signed them to an exclusive contract. Their first disc for Capitol was 'Surfin' Safari' in late 1962 which became a nationwide hit (No 3 in 1963). Then came 'Surfin' USA', written by Brian Wilson in 1963 to an old Chuck Berry tune 'Sweet Little Sixteen' of 1958. Brian also collaborated on 'Surf City' (see Jan and Dean, 1963). The group also included David Marks, and all the quintet came from Hawthorne, California. Brian Wilson, who wrote most of their numbers, died in 1983. At the time of recording 'Surfin' USA' the quintet was Mike Love, lead vocal and bass guitar; Brian Wilson, bass guitar; Carl Wilson on lead guitar; Dennis Wilson, guitar; and David Marks, vocalist of high falsetto parts. Later Al Jardine, rhythm guitar, replaced Marks. The group have sold over sixteen million discs, and were awarded the most Gold Discs for million dollar albums in 1965 - five in all. This disc was 17 weeks in the U.S. bestsellers, and reached No 34 in Britain with seven weeks in the bestsellers.

SURFER GIRL *Capitol* [*USA*]. The second reputed million seller for the Beach Boys was written in 1962 by Brian Wilson. It was No 5 for three weeks in the U.S. charts and 14 weeks in the bestsellers.

BE TRUE TO YOUR SCHOOL *Capitol* [*USA*]. The third reputed million seller for the Beach Boys was also written by Brian Wilson. This was No 6 in the U.S. charts and 12 weeks in the bestsellers.

THE BEATLES

SHE LOVES YOU *Parlophone* [*Britain*]. The success story of The Beatles is one of the most remarkable in disc history.

In 1955, John Lennon, Eric Griffiths, Pete Shotton and Colin Hanson formed The Quarrymen - named after John Lennon's school, Liverpool's Quarrybank School.

On 15 June 1956 Paul McCartney was introduced to John by a mutual friend, and Paul subsequently joined The Quarrymen. George Harrison had his own group, The Rebels, at this time. On 29 August 1958 George joined The Quarrymen and by 1959 The Quarrymen were down to a trio. John, Paul and George entered a talent contest as Johnny and The Moondogs, and later that year played variously as The Rainbows and The Silver Beatles. In 1960, Stu Sutcliffe joined as bass guitarist and the group, now the Silver Beatles, was chosen by Larry Parnes to back singer Johnny Gentle on a Scottish tour.

Later in the year they went on their first German tour with Pete Best on drums. From 24 February 1961, the group played regular lunchtime dates at The Cavern in Liverpool for £8 per show, playing some 292 times at the club and making frequent trips back to Hamburg. At the Top Ten Club there, they met Tony Sheridan (see 1961) and the group was then a quintet which included Sutcliffe (who died in Hamburg on 10 April 1962) and Best. With Tony they made some recordings for Polydor. The Silver Beatles first met Richard Starkey (Ringo

Starr) in the Kaiserkeller, Hamburg, in 1960, and this friendship later resulted in Ringo joining the original trio to form the famous quartet, The Beatles, for their first British recordings in 1962. Their version of 'My Bonnie' (see 1961) for Polydor in Germany resulted in Liverpool fans enquiring for the disc from local businessman Brian Epstein. Epstein discovered The Beatles in a cellar club in the city. He decided to go to Germany to find out if he could import the disc to Britain. The group had previously played in Hamburg's rowdy and raucous Indra (Star) Club. Brian Epstein was so impressed that, in spite of knowing little about show business, he became their manager. The disc was released by Polydor in Britain, and through Epstein's efforts The Beatles, turned down by Decca, began to record for the Parlophone label, under recording manager George Martin. By this time Pete Best had been replaced by Ringo Starr on drums. Their first British recording was 'Love Me Do' backed with 'P.S. I Love You' in 1962, both written by Paul McCartney and John Lennon of the group, and this was the start of a string of hits for these two writers. The Beatles were virtually 'born' on Granada TV on 17 October 1962 when first introduced to British TV audiences, and were brought back eleven times on TV between April and December 1963. Their second disc 'Please Please Me' (January 1963) was a sizeable hit within forty-eight hours of release and a No 1 chart seller in Britain by the end of February 1963. 'From Me to You (No 1 for seven weeks) followed, as did 'She Loves You', their first million seller (No 1 for six weeks with 14 weeks in the U.S. bestsellers, and 33 weeks in the British bestsellers) and 'I Want to Hold Your Hand' (No 1 for six weeks). During 1963, under Epstein's guidance, a landslide of publicity and top bookings in Britain and TV shows, their popularity became unprecedented. There were riots at personal performances, swooning and screaming fans, and fabulous incomes from their disc sales of £6,000,000 in six months. 'Beatlemania' swept Britain, then the U.S.A. and subsequently all around the world, and opened up the gates for a floodtide of other British talent in the U.S.A. From obscurity, The Beatles became a legend in less than twelve months, selling millions of discs (seven million in Britain alone in 1963). They made pop music history by topping Britain's bestselling disc charts with singles and albums for four weeks in December 1963. In mid-December, their singles discs were Nos 1 and 2; EP discs Nos 1, 2 and 3; albums 1 and 2 - all at the same time, an unprecedented achievement in disc history. Their 'Twist and Shout' had a tally of well over 650,000. The group's John Lennon and Paul McCartney wrote practically all The Beatles' songs (around 180 published by the end of 1969). Some of their material topped the sellers' charts for nineteen weeks during the year, the copyrights earning Lennon and McCartney and their publisher Dick James of Northern Music over £1,000,000 ($4 million) in 1964, in royalties from disc and music sales. In February 1964, following the colossal success of 'I Want to Hold Your Hand' on both sides of the Atlantic, they appeared in New York, with the most enthusiastic scenes ever known in America. They took America by storm, and their discs swamped the U.S. bestseller charts for weeks. On 4 April 1964, the five top positions were held by Beatles discs - 'Can't Buy Me Love', 'Twist and Shout', 'She Loves You', 'I Want to Hold Your Hand', 'Please Please Me', and two albums 'Meet the Beatles' and 'Introducing the Beatles' at Nos 1 and 2 - all at the same time. They had fifteen discs in the top hundred sellers at one time and 60 per cent of all discs in the U.S. air waves were by The Beatles - the most amazing avalanche in disc history. They went on to break practically every record in the business, including the biggest fee (to 1964) ever paid for a performance, $150,000 (£53,571) in Kansas City on 17 September 1964 during their second tour of the U.S.A. from August to September, which earned them $1 million. Lennon and McCartney were the top songwriters of 1964, gaining ten awards out of the best 100 songs in the U.S.A. Their first film *A Hard Day's Night* (see 1964) was a sensation. Apart from the inescapable so-termed 'Liverpool sound', merchandized goods including wigs of their distinctive 'mushroom' haircuts - their

collective trademark - sold in huge quantities in Britain and abroad. Their discs topped the charts in practically every country, a staggering global impact. By January 1970 it was estimated that Beatles disc sales were over 330 million singles discs (counting an album as six singles), the biggest sales for any artists in a period of seven years. The quartet, all born and educated in Liverpool, were Paul McCartney (born 19 June 1942); John Lennon (born 9 October 1940); George Harrison (born 25 February 1943); Richard Starkey ('Ringo Starr') (born 7 July 1940). The latter is so named through wearing four rings on his fingers. The disc of 'She Loves You' written by Lennon and McCartney became almost a plague with its 'yeah, yeah' in the refrain. It sold over one and a half million in Britain alone by January 1964 and a further three million by March 1964 on the Swan label in the U.S.A., where it was No 1 for two weeks. The reverse side of the disc was 'I'll get You' for both Britain and the U.S.A., written by Lennon and McCartney. The global sales of this disc are estimated at well over five million. In June 1965, The Beatles were made Members of the British Empire (M.B.E.) in the Birthday Honours, the first beat group to be so recognized in an honours list, and probably the youngest-ever to receive awards of this kind in peacetime.

By 1965 there were 1,920 cover versions of Beatles songs - all written by Lennon and McCartney - and hundreds more since. John Lennon was murdered in New York on 8 December 1980.

I WANT TO HOLD YOUR HAND *Parlophone [Britain]*. This disc held the British record for an advance sale of 950,000 (November 1963) up to that time. It sold over 1.5 million in Britain by mid-January 1964 (finally 1,509,000), was a No 1 chart entry in its first week, remaining in that position for six weeks. Issued on Capitol label in the U.S.A. on 30 December 1963, this disc sold one million in less than three weeks, and topped their charts for eight weeks with 15 weeks in the bestsellers. It had 21 weeks in the British bestsellers. It was Capitol's fastest-selling disc up to that time, also their biggest seller, with a 4,900,000 U.S. sale. The disc was Britain's biggest-ever world single with around 11 million sold globally. The backing of the British disc was 'This Boy', and the U.S. disc 'I Saw Her Standing There'. All three were written by the group's John Lennon and Paul McCartney. Gold Disc award, R.I.A.A., 1964.

PLEASE PLEASE ME *Parlophone [Britain]*. This was The Beatles' first British big seller, in early 1963. It sold over a million in the U.S.A. when released there in early 1964 on the Vee Jay label, reaching No 3 with 13 weeks in the bestsellers. The song was written by John Lennon and Paul McCartney of The Beatles in 1962. It was the No 1 chart seller in Britain for one week and 18 weeks in the bestsellers. The coupling in Britain was 'Ask Me Why', and 'From Me To You' in the U.S.A. Both written by Lennon and McCartney.

TWIST AND SHOUT (single and EP disc) *Parlophone [Britain]*. For the second time this song, written by Bert Russell (Berns) and Phil Medley in 1960, became a million seller. The Beatles 'Twist and Shout' EP disc sold over 650,000 in Britain alone, the biggest EP sale for Britain up to 1963. The song sold over a million within three weeks in the U.S.A. when released there as a singles disc by Tollie label in 1964. It was Tollie's first issue - a new label put out by Vee Jay Records - and was chart topper for one week in the U.S.A. and 11 weeks in the bestsellers. The tune for 'Twist and Shout' is an adaptation of a traditional Spanish air 'La Bamba' (see Valens, 1958). The backing was 'There's a Place', written by John Lennon and Paul McCartney in 1963. Over 13½ million copies overall of 'Twist and Shout' have been sold in Britain and the U.S.A. alone.

The Beatles' 'Twist and Shout' EP contained the following: 'Twist and Shout', by Bert Russell and Phil Medley (1961); 'A Taste of Honey', by Rick Marlow and Bobby Scott (1960); 'Do You Want to Know a Secret?' by John Lennon and Paul McCartney (1963); 'There's a Place', by John Lennon and Paul McCartney (1963).

It was No 1 for 21 weeks in Britain and 52 weeks in the charts.

DO YOU WANT TO KNOW A SECRET? *Parlophone [Britain]*. Although written by The Beatles' John Lennon and Paul McCartney, this song was originally a No 1 chart topper for two weeks in Britain for Billy J. Kramer and The Dakotas. It sold a million in the U.S.A. when The Beatles' disc was released there in 1964 on the Vee Jay label. The reverse side in the U.S.A. was 'Thank You Girl' by Lennon and McCartney. In the U.S.A. the disc reached No 2 with 11 weeks in the bestsellers.

FROM ME TO YOU *Parlophone [Britain]*. 'From Me to You' was a strong seller in Britain and No 1 for seven weeks with 21 weeks in the bestsellers. It was released in the U.S.A. in 1964 where it was No 41 and 6 weeks in the bestsellers. Global sales subsequently reached over a million. The number was written by Lennon and McCartney. The U.S.A. release on Vee Jay label was coupled with their 'Please Please Me', and in Britain with their 'Thank You Girl'.

ASK ME WHY (EP disc) *Parlophone [Britain]*. Again written by Lennon and McCartney this song was released by Vee Jay in the U.S.A. in 1964 on an EP disc with 'Anna', 'Misery' and 'A Taste of Honey' and priced as a single. It sold a reputed million in the U.S.A.

WITH THE BEATLES *Parlophone [Britain]* MEET THE BEATLES *Capitol [USA]* (album). All the songs on both discs were recorded in Britain by Parlophone in 1963. Both discs included nine titles in common with differing additional numbers as noted below. 'With the Beatles' reached 270,000 in advance sales one week before release on 22 November and sold 530,000 by 29 November 1963. By the end of 1964 the tally was 980,000, with the million reached in 1965. This was an all-time high for a British album. This disc was No 1 in Britain for twenty-one weeks to 25 April 1964. Capitol's release in the U.S.A. was even more astonishing. This sold 750,000 in its first week of release, soon passing the million mark. By mid-February 1964, it had sold 1,600,000, by early March 2,800,000 and 3,650,000 by mid-March with an estimated five million by December 1966. It was No 1 in the U.S.A. charts for 11 weeks to 25 April and is the biggest selling pop album to 1966.

The nine songs common to both albums were as follows: 'It Won't Be Long', by John Lennon and Paul McCartney (1963); 'All I've Got to Do', by John Lennon and Paul McCartney (1963); 'All My Loving', by John Lennon and Paul McCartney (1963); 'Little Child', by John Lennon and Paul McCartney (1963); 'Hold Me Tight', by John Lennon and Paul McCartney (1963); 'I Wanna Be Your Man', by John Lennon and Paul McCartney (1963); 'Not a Second Time', by John Lennon and Paul McCartney (1963); 'Don't Bother Me', by George Harrison (1963); 'Till There Was You' (from *The Music Man*), by Meredith Wilson (1960); *'With the Beatles' additional titles:* 'Please Mister Postman', by B. Holland, F. Gorman and R. Bateman (1961); 'Roll Over Beethoven', by Chuck Berry (1956); 'You've Really Got a Hold on Me', by William Robinson (1963); 'Devil in Her Heart', by Richard Drapkin (1963); 'Money', by Berry Gordy, Jr. and J. Bradford (1960); *'Meet the Beatles' additional titles:* 'I Want to Hold Your Hand', by John Lennon and Paul McCartney (1963); 'This Boy', by John Lennon and Paul McCartney (1963); 'I Saw Her Standing There', by John Lennon and Paul McCartney (1963).

Gold Disc award R.I.A.A. 1964. Disc was in the U.S. bestsellers for 71 weeks.

PLEASE PLEASE ME *Parlophone [Britain]*. INTRODUCING THE BEATLES *Vee Jay [USA]* (albums). The 'Please Please Me' disc was issued in Britain in early 1963 and sold well over 500,000 staying in Britain's charts at No 1 for 30 weeks. Its counterpart titled 'Introducing the Beatles' was issued in the U.S.A. in February 1964 and was runner-up there for several weeks to 'Meet the Beatles' album, selling well over a million, making a combined world sale of over 1,500,000. Both discs included the following 12 songs: 'I Saw Her Standing There', by John Lennon and Paul McCartney (1963); 'Please Please Me',

by John Lennon and Paul McCartney (1963); 'Do You Want to Know a Secret?' by John Lennon and Paul McCartney (1963); 'There's a Place', by John Lennon and Paul McCartney (1963); 'Ask Me Why', by John Lennon and Paul McCartney (1963); 'Anna' (Go to him), by Arthur Alexander (1963); 'Boys', by Wesley Farrell and Luther Dixon (1960); 'Chains', by Gerry Goffin and Carole King (1962); 'Twist and Shout', by Bert Russell and Phil Medley (1961); 'A Taste of Honey', by Rick Marlow and Bobby Scott (1960); 'Baby It's You', by Mack David, Burt Bacharach and Barney Williams (1962); 'Misery', by John Lennon and Paul McCartney (1963).

There were two additional songs on the British album of 'Please Please Me' which were: 'Love Me Do', by John Lennon and Paul McCartney (1962); and 'P.S. I Love You', by John Lennon and Paul McCartney (1962).

'Introducing the Beatles' was in the U.S. bestsellers for 49 weeks.

BOBBY (Blue) BLAND (rhythm-and-blues vocalist)

CALL ON ME backed with THAT'S THE WAY LOVE IS *Duke [USA]*. Bobby Bland was born on 27 January 1930 in Rosemark, Tennessee. He formed his own group at high school and joined the Duke label at the height of the rock'n'roll craze. His first big seller was 'Turn on Your Lovelight'. In 1960 he was voted 'Best Rhythm-and-Blues Male Singer'. Both songs were written by D. Malone in 1962. A top rhythm-and-blues disc, 'Call on Me' was No 22 and 12 weeks in the U.S. bestsellers. 'That's the Way Love Is' was No 33 and 10 weeks in the bestsellers.

THE CASCADES (vocal instrumental group)

RHYTHM OF THE RAIN *Valiant [USA]*. This male quintet comprises John Gummoe, Eddie Snyder, Dave Stevens, Dave Wilson and Dave Zabo, who all hail from San Diego, California. Before making this, their first million-selling disc, they had built up a reputation at teenage and school dances in and around San Diego, then throughout the southern California area, chiefly at the Peppermint Stick nightclub. The Cascades play a variety of instruments in addition to their fine ultra-smooth singing style. This song was written by John Gummoe in 1962. The disc was No 3 and 16 weeks in the U.S. bestsellers and No 5 and 16 weeks in the British bestsellers.

JOHNNY CASH

RING OF FIRE *Columbia [USA]*. On 1 August 1958, Johnny Cash, previously with Sun Records, with whom he had had a string of hits, signed with Columbia. With his group known as The Tennessee Three (i.e. the original Tennessee Two – Marshal Grant and guitarist Luther Perkins, plus W.S. Holland on drums) he produced a number of hit discs for their new label. Suddenly a decline in Cash's popularity set in and a series of mediocre recordings followed. Then in 1963, he burst back on to the scene with 'Ring of Fire', a song written by Merle Kilgore and June Carter (who subsequently became his wife).

This recording enabled Johnny to 'experiment' with sounds while still retaining the rhythmic simplicity of Luther Perkins' lead-guitar, and defying all country music principles, Johnny dared to incorporate a Tijuana Brass sound on 'Ring of Fire' and it provided him with his biggest hit since 'I Walk the Line' in 1956, and established him in the U.S. pop charts where it was No 14 for a week and in the bestsellers for 13 weeks. The million sale was reported in 1971.

This disc was the true beginning of the Cash legend. The disc was a No 1 in the country-and-western charts also in 1963.

Luther Perkins (born 8 January 1928 in Memphis) together with Marshal Grant were in the main responsible for Cash's earlier successes by virtue of the unique sound they produced – a sound that stripped a song to its soul and replaced it with a hard-driving, rockabilly sound.

Perkins died on 5 August 1968 as a result of burns received on 2 August. His place was subsequently taken by guitarist Bob Wooton.

RAY CHARLES

TAKE THESE CHAINS FROM MY HEART *ABC-Paramount* [*USA*]. This seventh million seller for Ray was written in 1952 by Fred Rose and Hy Heath. Released on 27 March 1963, it was No 8 and 11 weeks in the U.S. bestsellers; No 5 and 20 weeks in the British bestsellers.

BUSTED *ABC-Paramount* [*USA*]. Written in 1962 by Harlan Howard, this song was first introduced by Johnny Cash. Ray Charles' disc was released on 23 August 1963 and got to No 2 for a week in the U.S. charts with 12 weeks in the bestsellers, and No 21 and 10 weeks in the British bestsellers, selling a reported million, his eighth.

The disc won a Grammy Award for the Best Rhythm-and-Blues record of 1963.

THE CHIFFONS (vocal group)

HE'S SO FINE *Laurie* [*USA*]. This song was a No 1 seller in the U.S.A. for four weeks and 15 weeks in the bestsellers, and No 16 and 12 weeks in the British bestsellers. The Chiffons are a female quartet consisting of Barbara Lee, Patricia Bennet, Sylvia Peterson and Judy Craig (lead singer and comedienne), all then in their late teens and from the Bronx and Upper

Manhattan districts of New York. This song was written by Ronald Mack (in 1962) who, with William Rigler, brought the girls together; Mack became their manager. Sylvia and Patricia had been singing for six or seven years whilst high school graduates. Barbara formerly worked in a telephone exchange. A top rhythm-and-blues disc.

LOU CHRISTIE

TWO FACES HAVE I *Roulette* [*USA*]. Second million seller for Lou, also written by him and Twyla Herbert. It achieved No 3 position on the U.S. charts and 15 weeks in the bestsellers.

DAVE CLARK FIVE

GLAD ALL OVER *Columbia* [*Britain*]. Here was the first British group to topple the Beatles from the No 1 chart position in England, causing quite a sensation in the Press. This song was written by Dave Clark (born 15 December 1942 in Tottenham, London), who is the group's drummer; and Mike Smith (born 12 December 1943 in Edmonton, London), the pianist, organist and vibraphonist. The other members are Denis West Payton (born 8 August 1943 in Walthamstow, London) - sax, guitar, clarinet and harmonica player; Leonard Davidson (born 30 May 1944 in Enfield, London) - guitarist; and Richard Huxley (born 5 August 1942 in Dartford, Kent) - bass guitarist and harmonica. Prior to Dave's twenty-first birthday, the group's musical activities were playing three nights a week in a Tottenham ballroom, and making an occasional recording for the Piccadilly label. All had regular jobs: Dave, a film stunt man; Mike, a finance correspondent; Denis, an electronic engineer; Leonard, a progress clerk; and Richard, a lighting engineer. For a year they were a

big success in Tottenham and received a major award - the Mecca Gold Cup for the best band of 1963. They later received an invitation to play at the annual Buckingham Palace Staff Ball, the beginning of a popularity that increased immensely. Then came this disc which sold over 800,000 in Britain, to top Britain's charts for two weeks in January 1964. Their success resulted in a contract from impresario Harold Davison, guaranteeing them £50,000 a year from March 1964. In early 1964 they followed The Beatles to the U.S.A. and were a terrific success, and 'Glad All Over' sailed up the U.S. charts to sell a million over there for the Epic label, reaching No 6 with 14 weeks in the bestsellers, and in Britain was 19 weeks in the bestsellers. Mike Smith did most of the vocals and the group wrote much of their own material. Dave's pounding drum work and the total musical effect soon became known as the 'Tottenham Sound'. Their second hit 'Bits and Pieces' soon followed to become another big chart success on both sides of the Atlantic and elsewhere. 'Glad All Over' sold two-and-a-half million globally, and up to December 1970 the group had sold over 35 million discs.

THE CRYSTALS (vocal quartet)

DA DOO RON RON *Philles* [*USA*]. This song was written by Phil Spector (owner of Philles Records), Ellie Greenwich and Jeff Barry. This female quartet was made up of Barbara Alston Deedee Wright, and Pat Thomas - all then aged 18 - and Lala Brooks, 17. All are Brooklyn-born. They began singing together in high school. Originally a quintet - with another girl named Mary - Phil Spector discovered them when they had been singing together for about four months in 1962. They recorded 'There Is No Other (like my baby)' and 'Uptown' and registered late in that year with a No 1 chart seller 'He's a Rebel', followed in 1963 by 'Da Doo Ron Ron'. Each of the quartet plays the piano. Phil Spector is their personal manager. The disc was No 3 and 13 weeks in the U.S. bestsellers No 5 and 24 weeks in the British bestsellers (1963 and 1974).

THEN HE KISSED ME *Philles* [*USA*]. Written by ace American writers, Jeff Barry, Ellie Greenwich and Phil Spector, the disc was released in July. The British release was on the London label. It was the third million seller for the group before their

popularity waned as Beatlemania set in. The disc reached No 6 in the U.S.A. with 12 weeks in the bestsellers, and No 2 for 2 weeks in Britain with 14 weeks in the bestsellers.

This was another classic example of the 'Spector Sound', formulated by Phil Spector, owner of Philles Records.

DALE AND GRACE

I'M LEAVING IT UP TO YOU *Montel-Michele* [*USA*]. Written by Don Harris and Dewey Terry in 1957, this number was first recorded by the composers in that year. Dale (Houston) and Grace (Broussard) made this up-dated version which sold a million globally, when released by the Jaimie-Guyden disc company in 1963, and it was the No 1 seller for two weeks in the U.S.A. with 15 weeks in the bestsellers. It reached No 42 in Britain. Dale and Grace had sung in local Baton Rouge, Louisiana, bistros for several years before teaming up. Grace first sang with brother Van, while Dale worked as a soloist. It was at producer Sam Montel's studio that they met and did an impromptu session. Montel was greatly impressed with their version of 'I'm Leaving It Up to You'. The disc was an immediate success in the Southern States and a hit when Jaimie-Guyden released it for national distribution. It gave the new team a national hit with their first disc. Grace hails from Prairieville, Louisiana, and Dale from Baton Rouge. Both were 19 when this disc was made.

THE DRIFTERS

UP ON THE ROOF *Atlantic* [*USA*]. The fifth million seller for The Drifters was written by the ace husband and wife team of Gerry Goffin and Carole King in 1962. It reached No 5 with 20 weeks in the U.S. bestsellers.

DAVE DUDLEY (country vocalist)

SIX DAYS ON THE ROAD *Golden Wing* [*USA*]. Written by two Alabama truck drivers, Earl Green and Carl Montgomery, the success of this disc made truck drivers so keen on Dave's music that the Teamsters Union presented him with a gold, permanent membership card.

Dave Dudley was born on 3 May 1928 in Stevens Point, Wisconsin, and played big league baseball before becoming a singer. In 1950 he was obliged to give up his professional baseball career through a serious arm injury. His next-door neighbour Vern Shepherd was a local disc jockey, and one morning in the studios Dave picked up Shepherd's guitar and started to play and sing along with the country records. The next day, Shepherd asked him to rush down to the studio and do some songs. The locals liked his singing and Dave became a professional musician/disc jockey/singer for a year in Stevens Point.

In 1953, he formed the Dudley Trio, working nightclubs and lounges, and he and his wife Jean stayed on the road for almost nine years. He then joined the local country music radio station in Minneapolis until December 1960 when a car accident hospitalized him for 6 months. With very little money left, he set up a session for himself at the local Kaybank studios, Minneapolis. His long time friend Jimmy Key, a Nashville music publisher, sent a song called 'Six Days on the Road'. A dubbing of the recording found its way to Soma Records, Minneapolis. Two months later the Golden Wing release was definitely established as an all-time country bestseller. The disc reached No 32 but stayed in the U.S. bestsellers for 11 weeks. Through the years it has sold over the million.

Dave later signed with Mercury Records and made many albums and hit singles. He was featured in 3 movies up to 1971, and appeared all over North America and parts of Europe. He has a four-piece country-and-western combination, The Road Runners, which he organized in 1963. Dudley is a regular visitor to Nashville's Grand Ole Opry.

THE ESSEX

EASIER SAID THAN DONE *Roulette* [*USA*]. This quintet (four men and one girl) comprises Walter Vickers from New Brunswick, New Jersey; Rodney Taylor from Gary, Indiana; Billie Hill from Princeton, New Jersey; Rudolph Johnson from New York; and Anita Humes from Harrisburg, Pennsylvania. All the boys were members of the United States Marine Corps and the group was started by Vickers and Taylor who met while stationed on Okinawa in the Pacific. On return to Camp Lejeune, North Carolina, they added Hill and Johnson to the partnership. They worked at perfecting their sound, but not until they heard Anita Humes singing at an NCO club and asked her to join them, were they satisfied with their group. They decided to make the rounds of record companies while on short leave from Camp Lejeune, and their first and only stop was Roulette Records, who recorded their first two sides, including 'Easier Said Than Done'. Their first release was an immediate hit. The song was written by William Linton and Larry Huff, and the disc was top of the charts sellers for two weeks in the U.S.A. with 13 weeks in the bestsellers; No 41 and 5 weeks in the British bestsellers.

THE FOUR SEASONS (accompaniment arranged and conducted by Chas. Calello)

WALK LIKE A MAN *Vee Jay* [*USA*]. The third million seller for this group was top of the sellers' charts for three weeks in the U.S.A. and 13 weeks in the bestsellers. No 12 and 12 weeks in the British bestsellers. This song was written in 1962 by Bob Crewe and Bob Gaudio.

INEZ FOXX

MOCKINGBIRD *Symbol* [*USA*]. The first million seller for Inez Foxx was written by her brother Charlie, who is also her manager, and by Inez herself. This disc sold around 800,000 in th U.S.A. and over a million globally. Inez was born in Greensboro, North Carolina, on 9 September 1942. She started singing in a church choir, her first public recital being with the Gospel Tide Chorus in Greensboro. She was discovered by Clarence Fuller who booked her at Greensboro's ABC Club. Inez appeared at other clubs in the district over following months. In 1959 she decided to try her luck on her own and went to New York. After three to four years of bad breaks, she caught the attention of Sue Records who signed her to their Symbol label. 'Mockingbird' was her first release. It was No 7 in the U.S. charts and 18 weeks in the bestsellers; No 34 and five weeks in the British bestsellers.

FREDDIE AND THE DREAMERS

I'M TELLING YOU NOW *Columbia* [*Britain*]. Freddie and the Dreamers first recorded this in 1963; it was only their second recording for Columbia. Freddie Garrity, vocalist and guitarist, was born in Manchester on 14 November 1940. A self-taught musician, he made his first public appearance in the Red Sox skiffle group. He became an engineer and then a milk roundsman. The Dreamers comprised Derek Quinn (lead guitar, harmonica – born 24 May 1942); Roy Crewdson (rhythm guitar, piano, drums – born 29 May 1941); Pete Birrell (bass guitar, bass, accordion – born 9 May 1941) and Bernie Dwyer (drummer, piano – born 11 September 1940), all from Manchester. They were extremely popular in the north of England. Individually and collectively they were natural comedians and their clowning brought a fresh approach to the music scene. They made their debut on BBC TV in 'Let's Go' in October 1961, and their radio debut in 'Beat Show' from Manchester in 1961. The group moved south to dates at Margate's Dreamland, Stevenage Locarno and Leyton Baths, etc. They turned professional early in 1963, and achieved instant success with their first disc 'If You Gotta Make a Fool of Somebody', quickly followed by 'I'm Telling You Now' and 'You Were Made for Me'. Their zany antics brought them a contract to appear in the film *What a Crazy World* (1963). In 1963 they appeared at the Top Ten Club in Hamburg and thereafter came much work in ballrooms, clubs, stage, radio and TV, so building up the enviable following. In 1965, they appeared on American TV in the 'Shindig' and 'Hullabaloo' shows, in which Freddie introduced a new dance 'The

'Freddie'. This sensational performance made them a major attraction in the States, and they were hailed as the biggest thing since The Beatles came on the scene. Their discs started to zoom up the charts and 'I'm Telling You Now' became No 1 there for two weeks (released on the Tower label) in early April 1965 with 11 weeks in the bestsellers, passing the half million sale to make it a global million seller. They also had another tremendous hit with 'I Understand' (see 1964), at the same time, and their album 'Freddie and the Dreamers' had advance orders for close on 200,000, then the biggest for any album in Mercury Records' history. Freddie is a talented songwriter. He wrote 'I'm Telling You Now' with ace British songwriter Mitch Murray. The group made a world tour in early 1965, including Australia and New Zealand and a further appearance in the U.S.A.

This disc was No 2 in Britain and 11 weeks in the bestsellers.

YOU WERE MADE FOR ME *Columbia* [*Britain*]. This next big hit for Freddie and the Dreamers was written by Mitch Murray. It sold over 250,000 in Britain in this year, and topped the million with continued sales when released in the U.S.A. in 1965 on the Tower label. It was No 17 for two weeks in the U.S.A. and seven weeks in the bestsellers and No 3 for one week in Britain and 15 weeks in the bestsellers.

JIMMY GILMER AND THE FIREBALLS (vocal and instrumental trio)

SUGAR SHACK *Dot* [*USA*]. The first million seller for Gilmer was written in 1962 by Keith McCormack and Faye Voss. Gilmer, then aged 23, came from Amarillo, Texas, and began singing as a youngster in La Grange, Illinois. In 1951 he moved with his family to Amarillo where he studied the piano for four years at the Musical Arts Conservatory. In 1957, he organized his own rock'n'roll band, playing for schools and other teenage functions. While attending Amarillo College (for an engineering degree), he continued to perform. He met the Fireballs (Stan Lark, Eric Budd and George Pomsco) at Norman Petty's recording studios in Clovis, New Mexico. The Fireballs had already had some success on disc, and Jimmy teamed up with them as singer and rhythm guitarist. Their first hit was 'Quite a Party'. Then came 'Sugar Shack', and subsequent tours of Canada and Europe. Jimmy was born in Chicago in 1939. This disc was No 1 for five weeks in the U.S.A. with 15 weeks in the bestsellers; No 45 in Britain and eight weeks in the bestsellers, and a top rhythm-and-blues seller.

Gold Disc award, R.I.A.A., 1963.

GITTE (vocalist)

ICH WILL EINEN COWBOY ALS MANN (I want to marry a cowboy) *Electrola-Columbia* [*Germany*]. This song, written by Rudy von den Dovenmuhle and Nils Nobach, was winner of the 1963 German Song Festival in which it was sung by Gitte. The disc was No 1 for seven weeks in Germany, and sold over half a million there by year's end and 1,050,000 by mid-1965.

Gitte Haenning was born 29 July 1946 in Copenhagen, Denmark. She made her first record at the age of eight with her father Otto Haenning, a singer, teacher and composer, and her first solo disc in 1960. She became a top German and Scandinavian attraction on disc and TV, and was teamed with Rex Gildo, another teenage idol.

LESLEY GORE (arranged and conducted by Claus Ogerman)

IT'S MY PARTY *Mercury* [*USA*]. This was the first million seller for Lesley Gore. She hails from Tenafly, New Jersey, born on 2 May 1946, the daughter of a wealthy American swimwear manufacturer, and was educated at an exclusive girls' school near her home. This song was written by Herb Wiener, Wally Gold and John Gluck Jr. Lesley first sang it at a friend's birthday party. A guest suggested a private recording which was sent to Mercury Records who quickly realized her hit-making potential and signed her to an exclusive disc contract. The disc was a No 1 seller in the U.S. charts for two weeks, with 13 weeks in the bestsellers. It was No 9 and 12 weeks in the British bestsellers. The final record was cut on the first take, Lesley with her unusual abilities performing like a seasoned professional. She was completely unknown before cutting 'It's My Party'. A top rhythm-and-blues disc.

YOU DON'T OWN ME *Mercury* [*USA*]. The second million seller for Lesley, the disc released in December 1963 and reaching No 2 for two weeks in the U.S. charts by February 1964 and 13 weeks in the bestsellers.

The song was written by John Madara and David White.

EYDIE GORME (accompaniment, arrangement and conducting by Al Kasha)

BLAME IT ON THE BOSSA NOVA *Columbia* [*USA*]. This song was written in 1962 by the husband and wife team Barry Mann and Cynthia Weill. Eydie was born on 16 August 1933 and hails from the Bronx, New York. After high school graduation she worked as a Spanish interpreter, attending City College at night and singing occasionally with a band formed by Ken Greengrass, a schoolday friend. She became a regular vocalist for him and later joined Tommy Tucker and Tex Beneke, before breaking away as a solo singer in 1952. She came into prominence in the U.S.A. when she was a regular performer on the Steve Allen 'Tonight' show where she met her husband-to-be, singer Steve Lawrence. Together they became one of the most popular nightclub circuit acts in the States, and on TV. Eydie also had a sizeable hit in 1962 with 'Yes, My Darling Daughter'. 'Blame it on the Bossa Nova' was No 7 and 15 weeks in the U.S. bestsellers and was No 32 in Britain and six weeks in the bestsellers.

AL HIRT (jazz trumpet) AND HIS BAND

JAVA *Victor* [*USA*]. This first million seller for Al ('The Monster') Hirt was written in 1958 by Allen Toussaint, Alvin O. Tyler and Freddy Friday (Murray Sporn). Al was born in 1923, the son of a New Orleans policeman, who gave him a trumpet when he was six. Hirt studied classical music at high school and then entered Cincinnati Conservatory on a scholarship. Here he noticed less gifted students earning a few dollars per night with dance bands. This decided Al that money lay outside the classics, so by listening to Harry James and Roy Eldridge discs he turned himself into a jazz musician while still earning a living as a salesman for an exterminating company and playing his trumpet for some 15 years in comparative anonymity. New Orleans musicians gradually recognized him as a great player and, after forming his own small band in 1955, he began to acquire a local following. He has also toured with the bands of Tommy and Jimmy Dorsey, Ray McKinley and Horace Heidt, and did four years in the U.S. Army. He first recorded for the Southland label in New Orleans then with Audio-Fidelity. His manager, Joe Glaser, and RCA-Victor executives finally got him to leave Louisiana and he recorded albums 'He's the King' (1961), 'Al

Hirt - Greatest Horn in the World', 'Horn A-Plenty', 'Al Hirt at the Mardi Gras' and in 1963 his first million seller album 'Honey in the Horn'. By 1964 he gained an award for the best performance by an instrumentalist through his million selling singles disc of 'Java'. Hirt now has his own nightclub on New Orleans' Bourbon Street called simply 'Al Hirt', in the same locality where his success began in June 1961 at the Pier 600 Club. His nickname 'The Monster' derives from his huge stature and weight (6 ft. 2 in., 300 lb.). He is bush-bearded and when on the bandstand, his trumpet looks like a toy in his big hands. He plays everything from Dixieland to modern jazz in an explosive and dynamic style. One associate described it as 'blowing down the throat of a hurricane'. 'Java' was released in late 1963 and became a million seller in 1964, reaching No 4 with 16 weeks in the U.S. bestsellers. It was originally included on Al Hirt's album 'Honey in the Horn'.

HONEY IN THE HORN (album) *Victor* [*USA*]. This album made its debut in August 1963 and sold half a million by April 1964 and the million by February 1965. It included 'Java' which was released as a single in late 1963 and sold a million in 1964. The contents of the album: 'I Can't Get Started (with you)', by Ira Gershwin and Vernon Duke (1936); 'Java' by Allen Toussaint, Alvin O. Tyler and Murray Sporn (1958); 'Man with a Horn', by Eddie De Lange, Lake and Jenney (1948); 'Tansy', by Norrie Paramor (1961); 'Night Theme', by Peterson and Cogswell; 'Talkin' 'bout that River', by Ray Charles; 'Fly Me to the Moon (In other words)', by Bart Howard (1954); 'To Be in Love', by Smith and Best; 'Al Di La', by Carl Donida and Mogol (Guilio Rapetti) (1962); 'Malibu', by Weiss and Attwood; 'Theme from a Dream', by Boudleaux Bryant; 'I'm Movin' On', by Hank Snow (1950).

Gold Disc award R.I.A.A. 1964. It was in the U.S. bestsellers for 104 weeks.

JOHN LEE HOOKER

DIMPLES *Vee Jay* [*USA*]. Hooker wrote his own third reputed million seller. It was originally included in a rhythm-and-blues album of various artists entitled 'The Blues' in 1962. This disc was No 23 and 10 weeks in the British bestsellers.

JAN AND DEAN

SURF CITY *Liberty* [*USA*]. 'Surfing' music became a rage in the U.S.A. in 1963 and this is one of the million sellers in that idiom, and the first for Jan Berry and Dean Torrence. This song was written by Jan Berry and Brian Wilson (of the Beach Boys). Jan and Dean hail from Southern California. They went through high school together, Jan going to the University of Southern California, specializing in advertising art and design, and Dean to the University of California, Los Angeles on a pre-medical course. They collaborated in song-writing, Dean the writer, pianist and guitarist, Jan also writing, playing and working on the arrangements. They cut their first record 'Jennie Lee' in Jan's garage in 1958; it was a small hit. Then Dean was conscripted for six months' army service, rejoining his partner on demob with successful discs, including 'Baby Talk, 'There's a Girl' and 'Clementine' on the Arwin label and 'Heart and Soul' on the Challenge label. In 1961, they switched over to the Liberty label and came up with a success in 'Linda'. Then surf music became a craze in the U.S.A. and the boys came in with the tide with 'Surf City'. Their recording studio was a converted garage underneath their apartment in Bel Air, Hollywood. 'Surf City' was No 1 seller for two weeks in the U.S.A. and 13 weeks in the bestsellers, and was No 26 and 10 weeks in the British bestsellers.

THE KINGSMEN (vocal and instrumental quintet)

LOUIE LOUIE *Wand* [*USA*]. This song, written by Richard Berry, provided a first million seller (by April 1964) for this quintet and for the Wand label. The Kingsmen are Lynn Easton (vocalist and saxophone); Garry Abbot (drums); Don Gallucci (organ); Mike Mitchell (lead guitar); and Norman Sundholm (guitar and bass). They were first organized by Lynn Easton in 1957 when he was a freshman in Portland's David Douglas High School, the group at that time consisting of three members - Lynn, Gary and Mike. They began to develop a distinctive hard-driving bluesy instrumental style and over six years worked in a wide variety of media such as fairs, fashion shows, TV commercials, dances and one-night tours, developing an impressive reputation in north-west U.S.A. The Kingsmen also had their own float in the annual Portland Rose Festival parade. Throughout 1963, they were the house band at Portland's popular teenage nightspot, The Chase, and their first album was recorded there by producer Jerry Dennon. In addition to their performing, Gary was a barber and Mike a clothing salesman. 'Louie Louie' was a chart topper for two weeks in early 1964 in the U.S.A. with 16 weeks in the bestsellers plus 2 weeks in 1966; No 26 in Britain and seven weeks in the bestsellers, and a top rhythm-and-blues seller.

BILLY J. KRAMER WITH THE DAKOTAS

BAD TO ME *Parlophone* [*Britain*]. This song was written by The Beatles' famous songsmiths Paul McCartney and John Lennon. The disc was No 1 for two weeks in Britain. When released in the U.S.A. in 1964 on the Imperial label the combined U.S.A./British sales topped the million - 340,000 in Britain, 540,000 in the U.S.A., plus sales in other countries. Billy was born in Bootle, Liverpool on 19 August 1943, and educated there at St George of England Secondary Modern School. His real name is William Ashton, the youngest member of a family of seven. On leaving school he took up an engineering apprenticeship with British Railways in Liverpool. He started out as a spare time rhythm guitar player with his own local self-formed group, switching to vocal work in 1962. As a former leading singer in school music festivals, this was a natural thing to do. He was then backed by a new group, the Coasters, changing his name to Kramer, and began playing the more important clubs while still holding his British Railways job. He was discovered in Liverpool by The Beatles' manager, Brian Epstein, who signed him to an exclusive management contract in 1963, at which time he left British Railways to become professional. In February 1963, Epstein teamed him up with the leading Manchester group The Dakotas (Tony Mansfield, drums, born Salford, 28 May 1943; Mike

Maxfield, lead guitar, born Manchester, 23 February 1944; Robin Macdonald, rhythm guitar, born Nairn, Scotland, 18 July 1943; and Raymond Jones, bass guitar, born Oldham, 20 October 1939). In March 1963 they had a month's session in Germany at Hamburg's Star Club, and with the backing of the group Billy returned to England to make his first disc 'Do You Want to Know a Secret?' which became a chart topper. Then followed 'Bad to Me' and other big hits, with the inevitable TV, radio and tours. The U.S. backing was 'Little Children' (see 1964) which reached No 7 with 15 weeks in the bestsellers. 'Bad to Me' was No 9 and 10 weeks in the U.S. bestsellers and 14 weeks in the British bestsellers.

BRENDA LEE

LOSING YOU *Decca* [*USA*]. Brenda's fifth million seller was originally written by Pierre Havet and Jean Renard in France, in 1961. The U.S. lyricist Carl Sigman wrote English words for it in 1963. Disc got to No 6 in the U.S. charts with 13 weeks in the bestsellers; No 10 and six weeks in the British bestsellers. Original French title was 'Un ange est venu'.

LITTLE PEGGY MARCH

I WILL FOLLOW HIM *Victor* [*USA*]. This song, originally 'Chariot' from France, was written in 1962 by Jacques Plant (words) and J.W. Stole and Del Roma (noms de plume of Frederick Pourcell and Paul Mauriat) (music), and was a big hit there for Britain's Petula Clark (see 1962). This version has English lyrics by Arthur Altman and Norman Gimbel, and the disc was No 1 for three weeks in the U.S.A. with 14 weeks in the

bestsellers. Peggy March was born in Lansdale, Pennsylvania in March 1948, and began singing at the age of two, winning a talent contest at five against fifteen other children. At six, she auditioned for Rex Trailer's TV show and became a regular member of his cast. She travelled with local shows and a Western band for four years, appearing and working with such names as Salley Starr and the Three Stooges. Her career really started in a big way when she won a Children's House (a Sunday morning children's TV show) new faces contest a few years later. It was a relative who heard her singing 'Lazy River' at her cousin's wedding who became her manager and arranged an audition with RCA Victor Records. Little Peggy March has appeared at Atlantic City's Steel Pier, in Tony Grant's Stars of Tomorrow and other contests. In 1963 she made a tour of Europe and did radio and TV work in Britain. The disc was her first million seller. Her real name is Battavio.

LITTLE STEVIE WONDER

FINGERTIPS - Part 2 *Tamla* [*USA*]. This first million seller for Little Stevie was a No 1 seller in the U.S.A. for three weeks and 15 weeks in the bestsellers. It was written by Clarence Paul and Henry Cosby. Stevie (real name Steve Hardaway) was born in Saginaw, Michigan on 13 May 1950. Though blind from birth, he developed his talents and began playing piano and harmonica at the age of five. At his premier performance at Detroit's Latin Quarter he sang, played the piano, harmonica, bongos, organ and drums. On a visit to the home of Ronnie White, a member of the Miracles, where he played with Ronnie's young brother, Little Stevie's singing and harmonica playing so impressed Ronnie that he introduced him to Brian Holland, artists and repertoire director of Tamla Records. His first release for them was 'I Call It Pretty Music' which was a moderate success. Then came 'Fingertips' a rousing harmonica solo, which was 15 weeks in the U.S. bestsellers when Stevie was only 12. Stevie lived with his mother, three brothers and sister in Detroit. He has the distinction of being the first artist to have a single, this one of 'Fingertips', and an album 'That 12-year-old Genius' both at No 1 in the U.S. charts. Stevie visited Britain in 1965 and appeared on TV.

A top rhythm-and-blues disc. Released 22 June 1963.

TRINI LOPEZ

IF I HAD A HAMMER *Reprise* [*USA*]. This song was originally written in 1958 by Lee Hayes and Pete Seeger, members of the famous Weavers (see 1950) - a new version of a Negro folk song. This disc is Trini's first million seller. He was born in Dallas, Texas on 15 May 1937. At 15, he began playing the guitar and singing Latin-American songs in Dallas nightclubs, with excellent audience response. Lopez then formed his own five piece combo and toured the south-west, spending four years in the U.S.A. playing clubs, after finishing high school. With his group he took a professional engagement in Hollywood, his first two weeks' engagement at Ye Little Club developing into a year's stay. He then played other clubs including the world-famous Ciro's and made his TV debut on the Steve Allen show. While the group was performing at P.J.'s they were heard by recording manager Don Costa who was so impressed that he signed Trini to an exclusive disc contract with Reprise. The recording was made during a session at P.J.'s in Hollywood where Trini performed for 18 months. Trini visited Britain in 1963. This disc also sold half a million on the Ariola label in Germany, over a million in the U.S.A., and globally four-and-a-half million. It was No 3 for three weeks in the U.S.A. charts and 14 weeks in the bestsellers, and No 4 and 17 weeks in the British bestsellers.

LOS INDIOS TABAJARAS (instrumental guitar duo)

MARIA ELENA *Victor* [*USA*]. The presence of this disc in the hit parade (No 6 in the U.S.A. with 14 weeks in the bestsellers, and No 5 in Britain with 17 weeks in the bestsellers) of two Brazilian Indians playing the simplest ever version of a 30-year-old Mexican tune on guitars without any electrical aid, and without even a change of key throughout the whole performance, astounded everyone in the disc business. Its success was also 1963's strangest hit parade story.

The two brothers, Musiperi and Herundy, sons of a Tabajaras Indian chieftain, were born in Ceara, in the isolated jungles of northeastern Brazil. It is said that years ago they found a guitar in the jungle left there by white men who had been exploring the vicinity. When they touched the strings and found it made a sound, they became guitar addicts, and taught themselves to play. After becoming proficient instrumentalists, they travelled 1,200 miles to Rio de Janeiro and made their debut playing the guitar as an accompaniment to their tribal folk songs. They were discovered by a theatrical agent who arranged instruction and bookings in Mexico, and the brothers eventually became completely schooled in folklore, literature and the classics, experts on Chopin, Bach and Beethoven as well as the contemporary Latin American music. They also speak six languages - Italian, German, Greek, Portuguese, Spanish and their native 'Tupi'. Their names were changed to Natalicio and Antenor Lima as their original Indian names were too difficult to pronounce. Following concerts in South America, they then toured Europe.

They made several albums for Victor Records, starting in 1943, mainly for the South American market, but 'Maria Elena' was their first single to be released in the U.S.A., where it had a big sale. It also sold over 250,000 in Britain by 1964 and according to RCA Italiana, 536,350 by March 1966 in Italy alone, thus making it an indisputable global million seller. The disc's quietness, simplicity and attractive melody came as a refreshing change in an era of Beatlemania and rock and roll.

'Maria Elena' was written in 1933 by Mexican composer Lorenzo Barcelata. (See also Jimmy Dorsey, 1941.)

LONNIE MACK (guitarist)

MEMPHIS *Fraternity* [*USA*]. Lonnie Mack (real name Lonnie McIntosh) was born in 1941 in Harrison, Indiana and had his first guitar, a $10 Lone Ranger model, at the age of four. By the time he was six, Lonnie was playing country music and singing with his brother and sisters. At the age of 12 he was receiving fees for performing at a local hotel. As a teenager, he got his first electric guitar and worked clubs with his brother, Alvin. Then at 14 he had his own rock'n'roll band.

He continued to make his living as a guitarist, and in 1963, caught the attention of Harry Carlson of Fraternity Records who was so impressed with the young instrumentalist that he recorded him immediately.

This first disc for the artist was a big success and reached No 5 for one week in the U.S.A. charts and 13 weeks in the bestsellers. The composition is by famous composer/artist Chuck Berry who wrote it in 1959.

A fine instrumental disc, it was released in May 1963, with subsequent million sale.

THE MARKETTS (instrumental group)

OUT OF LIMITS *Warner* [*USA*]. The Marketts were a group of five Hollywood high school graduates under the direction of Dick Glasser, all aged between 18 and 21 when they made their first records, 'Start' and 'Surfer's Stomp', in 1962. The surfing craze was then a popular sport with the youngsters in America. After recording 'Balboa Blue' and 'Stompede' in 1963, the group followed with 'Out of Limits', written by Michael Z. Gordon, an intriguing up-beat disc with a galloping rhythm. It reached No 3 in the U.S.A. charts by early 1964 with 14 weeks in the bestsellers, and subsequently sold a million globally. It brought the group national prominence, and many radio, nightclub and personal appearances. They became professional musicians after graduating. The combination is three guitars, saxophone and drums.

MARTHA AND THE VANDELLAS

HEATWAVE *Gordy* [*USA*]. The first million seller for this trio, consisting of Martha Reeves, born 18 July 1941; Betty Kelly; and

Rosalind Ashford, born 2 September 1943. Martha became a secretary at the Tamla/Motown/Gordy Record Corporation. Part of her job was to sing lyrics of a tune on tape for artists to learn. She never thought she would ever be likely to get a singing career, but one day an artist became ill and she was asked if she would like to sing on the session which had been previously arranged. The studio was pleased with the result and she then did some backing work with two other girls, Betty and Rosalind. Their first disc backing was for artist Marvin Gaye's 'Stubborn Kind of Fellow', and they were used on several of his subsequent discs. Tamla then gave the girls a disc contract of their own, and their second disc 'Come and Get These Memories' got into the U.S.A. charts. They then changed their style and 'Heatwave' resulted, a vibrant rock number written by Eddie Holland, Lamont Dozier and Brian Holland (artists and repertoire director of Tamla Records). This disc was No 4 for two weeks in the U.S.A. charts and 14 weeks in the bestsellers and a top rhythm-and-blues seller. Released 27 July 1963.

GARNET MIMMS AND THE ENCHANTERS (vocal quartet)

CRY BABY *United Artists* [*USA*]. The first million seller for this quartet was written by Bert Russell (Berns) and Norman Meade. Garnet Mimms and The Enchanters each sang individually and collectively for a number of years. Garnet came from West Virginia, and sang in church choirs and small groups whenever it was possible to do so. Zola Pearnell, from Philadelphia, had much experience in her musical background. She travelled in Europe with a vocal group, sang with the Paul Roberts Choir and did solo work with Philadelphia orchestras. Samuel Bell, from Philadelphia, appeared with gospel groups all over the east of America before joining the group. He is also a successful songwriter. Charles Boyer, born in North Carolina, had extensive background experience with vocal groups including five years with a group called The Ambassadors. This disc was No 4 in the U.S.A. charts with 14 weeks in the bestsellers, and a top rhythm-and-blues disc.

THE MIRACLES

MICKEY'S MONKEY *Tamla* [*USA*]. Third million seller for The Miracles, written by the outstanding songwriting team of Eddie Holland, Brian Holland and Lamont Dozier. The disc got to No 8 for two weeks in the U.S.A. charts with 12 weeks in the bestsellers. Released 17 August 1963.

THE NEW CHRISTY MINSTRELS

GREEN, GREEN *Columbia* [*USA*]. Randy Sparks (born 29 July 1933 in Leavenworth, Kansas) conceived both the name and idea for his vocalist-instrumentalists from Edwin P. Christy who formed the famous Christy Minstrels way back in 1842, and who were America's foremost interpreters of the great Stephen Foster songs.

Randy actually commenced in show business while in college. He sought a part time job and made his first appearance at the Purple Onion in San Francisco. Subsequently he appeared at New York's Blue Angel, followed by the entire Playboy circuit, and often worked on TV. He planned the Christys as a recording group in 1961, but Columbia Records insisted they stayed together full-time to build an 'in-person vitality' and an audience. The Group started with a week's engagement in July 1962 at Hollywood's Troubadour Café and were so successful there that they stayed for three months, with crowds queuing up to hear them. Their eventual national exposure on the Andy Williams TV show gave them great prominence, introducing their folk choral sound, humour and ultra-modern minstrel sound to millions. Their first album 'The New Christy Minstrels in Person' was a big seller, and their 'Ramblin'' album sold over the half million. They all sing and play folk instruments, two on banjo, six on guitar, one on double bass and one on tambourine - also a variety of assorted instruments such as harmonica and even the fife.

'Green, Green' was written by Randy Sparks and Barry McGuire and is said to have sold a million to date. McGuire, who also wrote 'Green Back Dollar' for the Kingston Trio, became a solo artist in 1964 when he left the group, and had a tremendous hit with 'Eve of Destruction' in 1965.

The New Christy Minstrels have sung everywhere - for President Johnson; at the Hollywood Bowl; Carnegie Hall, New York; in London; and at the 1965 San Remo Song Festival in Italy.

Randy Sparks sold out his interest in the New Christy Minstrels in 1964 to a management company on the coast for $2,500,000 and went on to organize groups in the folk field, owning several music publishing concerns, and his own disc label - American Gramophone. This song is based on fragments of traditional material. This disc was No 14 in the U.S.A. charts and 12 weeks in the bestsellers.

ROY ORBISON
IN DREAMS *Monument* [*USA*]. The eighth (global) million seller for Roy was his own composition. This disc was a sizeable seller in the U.S.A. (No 10 in their charts and 13 weeks in the bestsellers) and sold over a quarter million in Britain (No 5 in the charts and 23 weeks in the bestsellers).

MEAN WOMAN BLUES backed with BLUE BAYOU *Monument* [*USA*]. 'Mean Woman Blues' was No 5 in both the U.S.A. (with 13 weeks in the bestsellers) and Britain (with 19 weeks in the bestsellers). The song was written by Jerry West and Whispering Smith. 'Blue Bayou', written by Roy Orbison and Joe Melson, was also high in the charts in both countries (No 29 for two weeks in the U.S.A. and 10 weeks in the bestsellers; No 3 in Britain).

The disc had big sales in the U.S.A. and sold over a quarter million with global sales being estimated at over the million. It was thus Roy's ninth disc to achieve a seven figure sale.

FALLING *Monument* [*USA*]. Written by Roy himself, this disc was a hit in both the U.S.A. and Britain and sold an estimated (global) million. It was Roy's 10th million seller, reaching No 22 with 8 weeks in the U.S. bestsellers; No 9 and 11 weeks in the British bestsellers.

THE ORLONS
SOUTH STREET *Cameo* [*USA*]. This third million seller for the Orlons was written by Kal Mann and Dave Appell, both of Cameo Records. It was No 3 in the U.S.A. charts and 13 weeks in the bestsellers.

RITA PAVONE (pop vocalist)
LA PARTITA DI PALLONE (The Football Match) *RCA* [*Italy*]. Rita Pavone is probably the world's smallest singer (height 5 feet, weight 80 pounds) but nevertheless she is certainly one of Italy's most powerful and successful vocalists and has become known as the 'Little Queen of Italian Song'.

She was born on 23 August 1945 in Turin, Italy, the daughter of a body worker at the Fiat plant. Her father entered her for a competition organized by RCA in 1962, called by him 'The Unknowns Festival'. Rita was the winner and was automatically signed by the label. 'La Partita di Pallone' was her first recording and it immediately entered the charts, soon selling over a quarter million, and subsequently an estimated million globally. Promotion to a spot on 'Studio 1', Italy's most popular TV show, made her immediately popular. Her second disc 'Come to non c'e' nessumo' sold half a million, and was top Italian disc of 1963. This was followed by 'Cuore' backed with 'Il ballo del Mattone', another tremendous hit (see below).

Practically all Rita's discs have become chart toppers, and her collective disc sales to the end of 1970 were estimated at over ten million. Her extraordinary talent resulted in big success in many countries. She became a sensation in Spain, Germany, Brazil, Japan, Argentina and Holland as well as in her native land. Her first British appearance was in October 1966 on TV. She also made several appearances on the famous Ed Sullivan show in the U.S.A.

Rita records in English, French, German and Spanish and is also a talented performer on screen and stage. Her 1966 Italian film *Rita the Mosquito* became a top box office success. This song was written by Rossi and Vianello.

RITA PAVONE (with accompaniment directed by Luis Enriquez)
CUORE (Heart) backed with IL BALLO DEL MATTONE *RCA* [*Italy*]. 'Cuore' (Italian version by Rossi of the American song 'Heart' written in 1962 by the U.S.A. husband-wife team of Barry Mann and Cynthia Weill) together with the backing 'Il ballo del Mattone' by Verde and Canfora was the second million seller globally for Rita Pavone. It was No 1 for nine weeks in Italy; No 27 and 12 weeks in the British bestsellers.

PETER, PAUL AND MARY
PUFF (THE MAGIC DRAGON) *Warner* [*USA*]. Written by Leonard Lipton and Peter Yarrow (member of the trio) the disc was released in March 1963, reaching No 2 for a week and staying in the U.S.A. bestsellers for 14 weeks. The song tells of a little boy's friendship with a dragon and of his sadness when it does not appear any more. The disc had a great appeal for children and sales of over a million were reported through subsequent years.

BLOWIN' IN THE WIND *Warner* [*USA*]. Peter, Paul and Mary first sang this famous Bob Dylan song at the Newport Festival in 1963. It became one of the most powerful protest songs of America. The disc was released in June 1963, reaching No 2 for two weeks and staying in the U.S. bestsellers for 15 weeks. It reached No 13 and 16 weeks in the British bestsellers. It also received two Grammy awards - 'Best Folk Recording' and 'Best Performance by a Vocal Group' of 1963. The tremendous popularity of the song soon made it a million selling disc.

MOVING (album) *Warner* [*USA*]. This album by the famous folk trio was released in February 1963. It remained in the Top 10 in the U.S.A. for 40 weeks and reached No 2. The million sale plus platinum award was reported in December 1973. R.I.A.A. awarded a Gold Disc for $1 million sales on 27 August 1963. Contents of the album: 'Settle Down' (Goin' Down the Highway), by Mike Settle; 'Gone the Rainbow', by Stookey, Yarrow, Travers and Okun; 'Flora', by Stookey, Travers and Mizetti; 'Pretty Mary', traditional, arranged by Stookey, Mizetti and Okun; 'Puff, the Magic Dragon', by Leonard Lipton and Peter Yarrow (1963); 'This Land is Your Land', by Woody Guthrie (1956); 'Man Come into Egypt', by Hellerman and Minkoff; 'Old Coat', traditional, arranged by Stookey, Travers and Mizetti; 'Tiny Sparrow', traditional, arranged by Stookey, Mizetti and Okun; 'Big Boat', by Willie Dixon; 'Morning Train', traditional, arranged by Mizetti; 'A-soulin'', by Stookey, Batteaste and Mizetti.

IN THE WIND (album) *Warner* [*USA*]. Released towards the end of 1963, this album reached No 1 in 1963 and was a bestseller for a long time. A Gold Disc was awarded for $1 million sales by R.I.A.A. on 13 November 1973, and a Platinum Disc was awarded for million units sale in December 1973. Contents of the album: 'Very Last Day', by Yarrow and Stookey; 'Hush-a-bye', traditional, arranged by Yarrow and Stookey; 'Long Chain On', by Jimmy Driftwood; 'Rocky Road', by Yarrow, Stookey and Grossman; 'Tell It on the Mountain', traditional, arranged by Yarrow, Stookey and Travers; 'Polly Von', arranged by Yarrow, Stookey and Travers; 'Stewball', traditional, arranged by Mizetti, Okun, Stookey and Travers; 'All My Trials', traditional, arranged by Yarrow, Stookey and Okun; 'Don't Think Twice, It's All Right', by Bob Dylan; 'Freight Train', by Elizabeth Cotton, arranged by Mizetti, Travers, Yarrow and Stookey; 'Quit Your Low Down Ways', by Bob Dylan; 'Blowin' in the Wind', by Bob Dylan.

GENE PITNEY (arrangement conducted by Burt Bacharach)

24 HOURS FROM TULSA *Musicor* [*USA*]. The fourth million seller for Gene Pitney was written by Hal David (words) and Burt Bacharach (music). The disc had a strong sale in the U.S.A. and sold over a quarter of a million in Britain (1964). It was No 17 in the U.S.A. and 11 weeks in the bestsellers; No 5 and 19 weeks in the British bestsellers.

ELVIS PRESLEY

(YOU'RE THE) DEVIL IN DISGUISE *Victor* [*USA*]. The 43rd million seller for Elvis was written by Bill Grant, Bernie Baum and Florence Kaye. The million sale was achieved globally. It was No 3 for two weeks in the U.S. charts and 11 weeks in the bestsellers; No 1 and 12 weeks in the British bestsellers.

BOSSA NOVA BABY *Victor* [*USA*]. Elvis' song from his film *Fun in Acapulco* was written by Jerry Leiber and Mike Stoller. The disc was a million seller globally and Elvis' 44th. It was No 8 for two weeks in the U.S. charts and 10 weeks in the bestsellers. No 13 and eight weeks in the British bestsellers.

ONE BROKEN HEART FOR SALE *Victor* [*USA*]. This number was sung by Elvis in his film *It Happened at the World's Fair*. It was written by Otis Blackwell and Winfield Scott. The 45th million seller for Elvis in aggregate world sales, it reached No 11 with nine weeks in the U.S. bestsellers, and was No 12 in Britain and nine weeks in the British bestsellers.

CLIFF RICHARD WITH THE SHADOWS

LUCKY LIPS *Columbia* [*Britain*]. The fourth million seller for Cliff Richard achieved half the million in Germany where it was No 1 for 10 weeks. This song was written in 1957 by the successful songwriters Jerry Leiber and Mike Stoller. 'Lucky Lips' was also a million seller for Ruth Brown in the U.S.A. In the U.S.A. Cliff's disc was No 62 and eight weeks in the bestsellers; No 4 and 15 weeks in the British bestsellers.

THE RONETTES (instrumental and vocal group)

BE MY BABY *Philles* [*USA*]. The Ronette trio consists of

Veronica Bennett, born 10 August 1945; Nedra Talley, born 27 January 1946; and Estelle Bennett, born 22 July 1944. All were raised in New York. Veronica and Estelle are sisters, and Nedra their first cousin. They began singing together from 1956 and performed at many famous twist houses throughout the U.S.A. including the Peppermint Lounges in New York and Miami Beach. In 1963 they were heard by Phil Spector, head of Philles Records, who was so impressed with the group that he signed them to an exclusive disc contract and put this, their first record, into production. It soon zoomed into the charts. The song was written by Phil Spector, Ellie Greenwich and Jeff Barry. Disc was No 1 for one week in the U.S. charts and 13 weeks in the bestsellers; No 4 and 13 weeks in the British.

THE ROOFTOP SINGERS (folk and pop ballad, vocal and instrumental group)

WALK RIGHT IN *Vanguard* [*USA*]. This trio comprised Erik Darling, born 1933 (formerly of the Weavers), balladeer, guitarist and vocalist; Lynne Taylor, vocalist in leading Miami Beach and New York nightclubs and originally with the Benny Goodman Band for one year; and Bill Svanoe, graduate of Oberlin College and University of Minnesota, guitarist of seven years' standing. 'Walk Right In' was written in 1930 by Gus Cannon and Hosie Woods. When recorded by the Rooftop Singers, it was thought to be a traditional song until it was discovered to be an original composition by Gus Cannon (then 79), a yard man of Memphis, living in a little house near the railroad tracks. For years he had strummed the banjo, singing songs he wrote himself. Fifty years before he toured the South of the U.S.A. with a medicine show. He worked along the Mississippi levees and tramped around Beale Street, where honest blues were invented. In winter 1962, he had no work and no money and almost froze. He even had to 'hock' his banjo for $20 worth of coal. Then this disc was made and it walked right in among the U.S.A.'s top hits. Gus was sought out and taken to Atlantic Records' studio to make an album for the Stax label. The Voice of America radio station broadcast its 'Gus Cannon Story' to Europe, Africa and the Near East in April 1963. This disc was No 1 for two weeks in the U.S.A. and 13 weeks in the bestsellers, and No 10 and 12 weeks in Britain's bestsellers. Gus Cannon's Jug Stompers first introduced the song on Victor Records around 1930.

BOBBY RYDELL

FORGET HIM *Cameo-Parkway* [*USA*]. The fifth million seller for Bobby was written by Mark Anthony (real name Tony Hatch, the well-known musical director and songwriter of Pye Records, Britain). The disc reached No 4 for a week in the U.S. charts in early January 1964 and 16 weeks in the bestsellers; No 13 and 14 weeks in the British bestsellers.

SHEILA (vocalist)

L'ECOLE EST FINIE (School is over) *Philips* [*France*]. Two independent artists and repertoire men, Carrere and Plait, discovered teenage singer Sheila in France, selected her songs, made recordings and gave Philips Records the exploitation rights. Carrere wrote this song with André Salvet and it was a very big success, the disc holding the No 1 chart position in France for eight weeks, with a subsequent million sale. It was the first time a disc was put on the French market by independent producers.

Sheila, born in 1946, is considered the most surprising phenomenon that the French disc world has ever known. She made 10 records for Disques Philips/Productions Carrere, from 1963 to 1966, and all of them reached No 1. She became an idol of the French teenagers. Her real name is Anny Chancel.

ALLAN SHERMAN

HELLO MUDDAH, HELLO FADDAH *Warner* [*USA*]. The second million seller for Allan is a comedy disc about a boy's first day at a summer camp and his letter to the folks back home. Set to the music of Poncielli's 'Dance of the Hours' it was written and adapted by Allan Sherman and Lou Busch (who is the artist

Joe 'Fingers' Carr, and recording producer for Sherman). Disc was No 1 for one week in U.S.A. with 10 weeks in the bestsellers; No 14 and 10 weeks in the British bestsellers. Grammy Award for 'Best Comedy Performance' 1963.

THE SINGING NUN (Soeur Sourire) WITH CHORUS OF FOUR NUNS

DOMINIQUE *Philips* [*Belgium*]. The extraordinary story of a Belgian nun singing in French having a hit in both America and Britain began in 1961, when Sister Luc-Gabrielle of the convent at Fichermont, near Brussels, began to entertain the young girls studying there. They asked the sister to make some recordings of her songs – private recordings just for them. With the Mother Superior's permission, Sister Luc-Gabrielle and a companion travelled to Philips Records' offices in Brussels to seek their aid. The Company were busy and the nuns were politely turned down. Three months later (1962), Sister Luc-Gabrielle and four other nuns went again to the recording studios and this time were permitted to record some songs. When executives of Philips heard them, they liked them and instead of pressing just 200, pressed thousands and released them commercially. The discs were sent out as the songs of Soeur Sourire – 'Sister Smile' – and were an almost instant success throughout Europe. An album of the songs was released in the U.S.A., but it meant nothing until publisher Paul Kapp took the song 'Dominique' (which lauds the virtues of the Dominican Order) out of the album and transferred it to a single. This disc was sent to 360 radio stations and from the first broadcasts was an immediate success. Between October and December 1963 it sold over 750,000 in the U.S.A., with a million by early 1964, and 250,000 in Britain by December 1963. There were also big sales on the Continent of Europe and elsewhere. The disc was No 1 for four weeks in the U.S.A. with 13 weeks in the bestsellers, and No 7 and 13 weeks in the British bestsellers, and both this and her album were No 1 sellers simultaneously in the U.S.A., the first time such a double had been achieved. Grammy Award for 'Best Gospel or Religious Recording' 1963. Soeur Sourire was so named by Philips Records after a poll was taken in France and Belgium. She plays the guitar and most of the songs, all written by her, are in a religious vein. She was born in 1928. All the money earned from 'Dominique' and her album (estimated at over £30,000) was spent on foreign missions. Soeur Sourire is also a very talented artist and designed and drew the cover for the sleeve of the album. She left the convent in October 1966. Her real name is Jeanine Dekers.

THE SINGING NUN (album) *Philips* [*Belgium*]. All the songs on the disc were written by Sister Luc-Gabrielle (Soeur Sourire) and recorded by her, with a chorus of nuns, in Belgium in 1962. (See 'Dominique' for data.) The disc sold over 750,000 by December 1963, with an eventual million by 1964, and was No 1 seller for 10 weeks in the U.S.A. Contents are: 'Plume de radis'; 'Mets ton joli jupon' (Put on your pretty skirt); 'Resurrection'; 'Alleluia'; 'J'ai trouvé le Seigneur' (I have found the Lord); 'Entre les étoiles' (Among the stars); 'Dominique' (Dominic); 'Soeur Adele' (Sister Adele); 'Fleur de cactus' (Cactus flower); 'Complainte pour Marie-Jacques' (Lament for Marie-Jacques); 'Je voudrais' (I would like); 'Tous les chemins' (All the paths). Gold Disc award R.I.A.A. 1963.

JIMMY SOUL

IF YOU WANNA BE HAPPY *S.P.Q.R.* [*USA*]. Jimmy Soul, born in Harlem in 1942, was a boy preacher at the age of seven and got his name from the church elders who whispered 'He's got soul' whenever Jimmy preached.

His parents returned to their farm in North Carolina when he was young and Jimmy listened to the circuit-riding ministers in his rural area and soon became a circuit minister himself. Later his parents moved to Portsmouth, Virginia and Jimmy both preached and became a member of various local gospel singing groups. For one year, he travelled with the famed gospellers The Nightingales all over the U.S.A. He then discovered his forte in singing pop tunes and rock'n'roll. He auditioned with a rock'n'roll combination for an engagement at the Azalea Gardens Club in Norfolk, Virginia, and the group had its week's engagement extended into several months. Jimmy then formed his own organization, adopting the name 'Wonder Boy', recalling the days when he was so-called on the North Carolina preaching circuit. He and his manager approached Frank Guida, head of S.P.Q.R. Records, who had done so much for Norfolk area performers, and Jimmy made his first disc 'Twisting Matilda' in 1962. Then came his 'If You Wanna Be Happy' recording in 1963. The disc was No 1 in the U.S.A. for two weeks and 14 weeks in the bestsellers, and was No 39 in Britain. In addition to his singing ability, Jimmy is also an excellent dancer and plays the piano, drums and guitar.

The song was written by Frank Guida, Carmela Guida and Joseph Royster. A top rhythm-and-blues disc.

DUSTY SPRINGFIELD WITH ORCHESTRA DIRECTED BY IVOR RAYMONDE

I ONLY WANT TO BE WITH YOU *Philips* [*Britain*]. Dusty Springfield (real name Mary O'Brien) was born on 16 April 1939 in Hampstead, London, and educated at convents in High Wycombe and Ealing, England. At 16 she started work in a record store. The family held musical evenings in a room with a built-in amplifier and microphone. Dusty shared her brother Tom's interest in Latin American music. She took up the guitar and gave up her job to accompany Tom, who was becoming a successful entertainer. She continued with day work, in a departmental store, eventually joining Tom and his partner at that time – Tim Feild – forming The Springfields in 1960. By 1961 they were Britain's top vocal group and were voted No 1 in 1961 and 1962 in their class. They had a big hit in the U.S.A. with 'Silver Threads and Golden Needles' in 1963. Later in that year the group split up (after Feild had been replaced by Mike Longhurst-Pickworth), each member going solo. This disc, Dusty's first solo recording, was a big hit in Britain, and in the U.S.A. in 1964 where it reached No 12 and 10 weeks in the bestsellers, with global sales over a million. It reached No 4 in Britain with 18 weeks in the bestsellers. The song was written by Mike Hawker and her musical director Ivor Raymonde.

Dusty was voted World Female Singer No 1 in 1965, 1966 and 1967 polls in Britain.

THE SPRINGFIELDS

SILVER THREADS AND GOLDEN NEEDLES *Philips* [*Britain*]. The Springfields ascended to fame via this country-and-western classic written in 1956 by Dick Reynolds and Jack Rhodes, recorded in Britain. It was, however, in the U.S.A. that the disc was a hit, reaching No 10 with an estimated million sale. Tom Springfield was born 2 July 1934 in Hampstead, London. (For data on The Springfields see Dusty Springfield, 1963.)

APRIL STEVENS AND NINO TEMPO

DEEP PURPLE *Atco* [*USA*]. A big hit for brother and sister Nino and April, and chart topper for two weeks in the U.S.A. with 15 weeks in the bestsellers. It reached No 17 and 11 weeks in the British bestsellers. The song is the famous oldie of 1939 by Mitchell Parish (words) and Peter de Rose (music), originally composed by de Rose in 1934 for piano solo, and a great favourite for over 30 years with orchestras.

The duo hail from Niagara Falls, New York. Nino has been a performer since the age of three. By the time he was seven, he sang with the famous Benny Goodman orchestra and later with Glenn Miller's band. He is a skilled musician, and plays clarinet, saxophone, piano and guitar in addition to singing. He has also arranged and composed many songs for big name artists including Rosemary Clooney and Steve Lawrence. It was not until he teamed with April that he became a big name himself, although he had recorded one success 'Sweet and Lovely'. April had a hit with her first single disc 'I'm in Love Again', followed by two or three other successes included 'Gimme a Little Kiss' and 'And

So to Sleep Again'. She was a regular performer in the top paying nightclubs and first recorded for a small label – 'Society Recordings' – in 1950. Their teaming together on 'Deep Purple' produced a big success in the States and in several places around the world, the disc becoming a million seller by 1965. Grammy Award for 'Best Rock and Roll Recording' 1963.

THE SURFARIS (instrumental and vocal quintet)

WIPE OUT *Dot* [*USA*]. 'Wipe Out' is a surfing term, meaning that one has been knocked off the board while 'surfing' or riding the waves. This disc was yet another million seller of the surfing craze that achieved such wide prominence amongst teenagers in the U.S.A. in 1963. 'Wipe Out' was written by the Surfaris, all five of whom hail from Glendora, California. The group comprises Jim Pash, saxophonist; Ron Wilson, drummer; Pat Connolly, leader and bass guitar; Jim Fuller, lead guitar; and Bob Berryhill, rhythm guitar. Because of their schooling, their personal appearances were restricted to local dances in and around Glendora. They later switched to the Decca label. This disc was No 2 for one week in the U.S.A. with 16 weeks in the bestsellers, and had a big revival in 1966 when it reached No 16 with 14 weeks in the bestsellers, and No 5 and 14 weeks in the British bestsellers.

THE TYMES (vocal quintet)

SO MUCH IN LOVE *Parkway* [*USA*]. This male quintet consists of Donald Banks, Al Berry, Norman Burnett, George Hilliard and George Williams, Jr, then all in their early twenties. Banks and Hilliard hail from Franklin, Virginia, and Berry, Burnett and Williams from Philadelphia. This song was written by George Williams (of the group), William Jackson and Roy Straigie. The group came into being when Burnett and Hilliard met at a summer camp in 1956 and started singing together for their own amusement. In the autumn, they teamed with Banks, Berry and Williams, singing and working together on the group's sound with the idea of a show business future. They sang for amateur shows and at local record dances. In April 1963 they appeared at a Philadelphia theatre on the WADS talent show, were spotted and asked to record for Parkway. 'So Much in Love' was their first disc, and No 1 for one week in the U.S. charts with 15 weeks in the bestsellers; No 21 and eight weeks in the British bestsellers.

BOBBY VINTON (with arrangement and orchestra conducted by Burt Bacharach)

BLUE VELVET *Epic* [*USA*]. This second million seller for Bobby was No 1 in the U.S.A. for three weeks and 15 weeks in the bestsellers. The song was written in 1951 by Bernie Wayne and Lee Morriss.

BOBBY VINTON (with arrangement and orchestra conducted by Stan Applebaum)

THERE I'VE SAID IT AGAIN *Epic* [*USA*]. For a second time this song produced a million seller on disc (see also Monroe, 1945). It was written by Redd Evans and Dave Mann in 1941. This version was the third million seller for Bobby Vinton. The disc was No 1 in the U.S.A. for four weeks in 1964 and 13 weeks in the bestsellers, with big sales there, and was No 34 and 10 weeks in the British bestsellers, additional sales elsewhere making it a global million.

DALE WARD

A LETTER FROM SHERRY *Dot* [*USA*]. 'Pop' vocalist Dale Ward made this disc in 1963 when it was released in late December. By February 1964 it reached No 25 in the U.S.A. charts, was 11 weeks in the bestsellers and subsequently sold the million.

The song was written by Kenneth R. Moffit, and the disc backed with another of his songs 'Oh Julie' which he wrote in 1957 with Noel Ball – a million seller in 1958 for The Crescendos.

Dale joined the trend of pop stars gone country in 1971.

DIONNE WARWICK (arrangement and orchestra conducted by Burt Bacharach)

ANYONE WHO HAD A HEART *Scepter* [*USA*]. Dionne was born in East Orange, New Jersey, 12 December 1941, her family being gospel singers. She studied music from the age of six. After schooling in her native town, she studied at the Hartt College of Music in Hartford, becoming an accomplished singer and pianist, and still playing and singing in church every Sunday. She then sang in the background chorus in New York on several recording

sessions. Her unique style of singing greatly attracted the songwriter-producers Hal David (author) and Burt Bacharach (composer) who wrote this song. They introduced her to Scepter Records and a hit 'Don't Make Me Over' followed. Then came 'Anyone Who Had a Heart' which with big sales in the U.S.A. and abroad topped the million. It reached No 8 with 14 weeks in the U.S. bestsellers; No 42 and three weeks in the British bestsellers. Dionne toured all over Europe and thus established a big international reputation with her audiences and on disc. 'Anyone Who Had a Heart' was also a big hit for Britain's Cilla Black in 1964.

MARY WELLS

TWO LOVERS *Motown* [*USA*]. The first million seller for Mary was written in 1962 by William 'Smokey' Robinson, vice president of Motown. Mary was born in Detroit, 13 May 1943, and started singing at the age of 10. She was discovered by Motown during the firm's regular audition sessions and signed to a contract. Her first disc and own song 'Bye Bye Baby' became a hit. Since then Mary has done many TV and club dates, and visited Britain in 1964. The full name of this very talented coloured artist is Mary Esther Wells. Released December 1962 it was a top rhythm-and-blues disc, reaching No 7 with 13 weeks in the U.S.A. bestsellers.

ANDY WILLIAMS (accompaniment arranged and conducted by Robert Mersey)

CAN'T GET USED TO LOSING YOU *Columbia* [*USA*]. This fourth million seller for Andy (No 2 in the U.S. charts with 15 weeks in the bestsellers, and No 2 and 18 weeks in the British bestsellers) was written by ace writers Doc Pomus and Mort Shuman in 1962.

DAYS OF WINE AND ROSES (album) *Columbia* [*USA*]. The second million seller album for Andy Williams, with Robert Mersey's arrangements and conducting. It sold around 2,000,000 by end of 1967. The release in Britain was changed to 'Can't Get Used to Losing You', the title of his million selling single (see above) that is included on the disc.

A Gold Disc was awarded by R.I.A.A. in 1963. This album was No 1 in the U.S.A. for 16 weeks in 1963 and stayed in the bestsellers lists for 107 weeks. It includes the Academy Award winning film song of 1962 'Days of Wine and Roses' from the movie of the same title, which also gained a Grammy Award for Henry Mancini for 'Record of the Year' 1963.

Contents of the disc are: *Side 1* - 'Falling in Love with Love' (from *The Boys from Syracuse*), by Lorenz Hart/Richard Rodgers (1938); 'I Left My Heart in San Francisco', by Douglas Cross/ George Corey (1954); 'You Are My Sunshine', by Jimmie Davis and Chas. Mitchell (1940); 'What Kind of Fool Am I?' (from *Stop the World - I Want to Get Off*), by Leslie Bricusse/Anthony Newley (1961); 'When You're Smiling', by Mark Fisher, Joe Goodwin and Larry Shaw (1928); 'Days of Wine and Roses' (from the film), by Johnny Mercer/Henry Mancini (1962); *Side 2* - 'It's a Most Unusual Day' (from the film *A Date with Judy*), by Harold Adamson/Jimmy McHugh (1948); 'My Colouring Book', by Fred Ebb/John Kander (1962); 'Can't Get Used to Losing You', by Doc Pomus and Mort Shuman (1962); 'I Really Don't Want to Know', by Howard Barnes/Don Robertson (1953); 'Exactly Like You', by Dorothy Fields/Jimmy McHugh (1930); 'May Each Day' (Andy Williams' theme song), by Morton J. Green/George Wyle (1963).

1964

ORIGINAL THEATRE CAST WITH ZERO MOSTEL, MARIA KARNILOVA, BEATRICE ARTHUR, JULIA MIGENES, MICHAEL GRANGER, SUE BABEL, CAROL SAWYER, BERT CONVY, AUSTIN PENDLETON, LEONARD FREY, PAUL LIPSON, JOANNA MERLIN, TANYA EVERETT, ORCHESTRA CONDUCTED BY MILTON GREENE

FIDDLER ON THE ROOF (album) *Victor* [*USA*]. 1964 saw a new musical which has now become something of a theatrical legend. *Fiddler on the Roof*, with book by Joseph Stein, is based on stories by Sholom Aleichem, and combines the elements of Jewish folklore with those of a musical play. The lyrics are by Jerry Bock and music by Sheldon Harnick. Opening on 22 September 1964 at New York's Imperial Theatre (later transferred to Majestic Theatre) it proved to be one of America's greatest musicals, playing to capacity audiences at every performance. This saga from folk tales of a Jewish village in Russia in 1905 was brilliantly directed by Jerome Robbins, and Zero Mostel's performance as Teyve the milkman added his name to the small circle of really great stars. Filled with laughter, emotion, tenderness, popular song, dance and comedy, the play is most moving in its demonstration of the cruelty of bigotry in the form of anti-Semitism. Although the ending is emotional as the long persecuted Jews are driven from their miserable village, it is essentially a humorous show. Mostel's rendering of the outstanding comedy song 'If I Were a Rich Man' and the very moving 'Sabbath Prayer' are superlative, and also the beautiful 'Sunrise, Sunset' with Maria Karnilova as his wife. The show naturally had a special appeal for Jewish audiences. RCA-Victor's album of the show became one of their hottest sellers as early as 10 days after release and was awarded a Gold Disc in 1965 by R.I.A.A. It stayed in the bestsellers for 187 weeks. The show ran until 3 July 1972, with 3,242 performances, a record for a musical in the U.S.A. The album subsequently sold over a million.

In Britain the show opened on 16 February 1967 at Her Majesty's Theatre and Topol in the star part gave a superb performance and thus introduced this outstanding Israeli actor to England. His part was later taken over by English actor Alfie Bass with great success. This production was still running at the end of 1970 in London, closing in 1971 with 2,030 performances. Other productions were seen in Israel, Holland, Finland and Denmark.

The album contents: *Side 1* - 'Tradition' (Zero Mostel and Chorus); 'Matchmaker, Matchmaker' (Julia Migenes, Joanna Merlin and Tanya Everett); 'If I Were a Rich Man' (Zero

Mostel); 'Sabbath Prayer' (Zero Mostel, Maria Karnilova and Chorus); 'To Life' (Zero Mostel, Michael Granger and men); 'Miracle of Miracles' (Austin Pendleton); *Side 2* - 'Teyve's Dream' (Zero Mostel, Maria Karnilova, Sue Babel, Carol Sawyer and Chorus); 'Sunrise, Sunset' (Zero Mostel, Maria Karnilova and Chorus); 'Now I Have Everything' (Bert Convy and Julia Migenes); 'Do You Love Me?' (Zero Mostel and Maria Karnilova); 'Far from the Home I Love' (Julia Migenes and Zero Mostel); 'Anatevka' (Zero Mostel, Maria Karnilova, Michael Granger, Beatrice Arthur, Leonard Frey and Paul Lipson).

ORIGINAL SOUNDTRACK OF FILM MUSIC

GOLDFINGER (album) *United Artists* [*USA*]. One of America's biggest selling discs from time of release in November 1964 and throughout 1965. It sold over 400,000 in its first three months and over $2 million worth in six months, was No 1 for three weeks and stayed high in the charts for 70 weeks in the U.S.A.

Composer John Barry (surname Prendergast) was born 3 November 1933 in York, England, and grew up in Fulford, three miles outside the city. His father, owner of theatres, presented both classical and jazz concerts at his Rialto theatre in York and young John was thus able to meet many artists at the Prendergast home. He thus matured in both musical idioms - classical and jazz. He was educated at St Peter's, a northern uppercrust school, and took initial musical training under Dr Francis Jackson, Master of Music at the cathedral of York Minster, followed by Shillinger and Bill Russo courses. When he did his Army service, he signed for an extra 12 months, using this period as a musician, mostly with the 1st Division of the Green Howards in Egypt and Cyprus, playing trumpet and studying the Bill Russo (Stan Kenton's arranger) correspondence course in composition. Back in civilian life, he spent six months arranging for top jazz orchestras such as Ted Heath, Johnny Dankworth and Jack Parnell. Jack Parnell suggested Barry should form a band, and so the John Barry Seven was formed in 1957 playing for concerts and starring on TV. It became a top instrumental group in polls, backed stars on discs and was the swinging nucleus of a big recording combination. He decided in September 1961 to devote his time to writing, but kept his band on the road - and remained as their agent, manager, arranger and composer without going on tour with them. He had just previously written his first film score for rock'n'roll singer Adam Faith's debut in *Beat Girl*. This led to an invitation to doctor the score for *Dr No*, the first of the James Bond thrillers written by the late Ian Fleming, which included Monty Norman's '007' (1962), the now famous 'Bond Theme' used in subsequent Bond films - *From Russia with Love* (1963), *Goldfinger* (1964), *Thunderball* (1965) and others. Lionel Bart wrote the title song for *From Russia with Love*, but Barry arranged it and composed the rest of the score. In *Goldfinger* he wrote the entire musical content, apart from the lyrics of the title song, and similarly for *Thunderball*. For the latter two films he composed the principal parts in only two days. His scoring was a colossal world-wide triumph, particularly as the film music domain had been virtually exclusive to American writers until a few years before. During 1965 his scores for first-rate films included *Séance on a Wet Afternoon*, *King Rat*, *The Knack*, *The Ipcress File*, following *Zulu* and *The Winstone Affair*, and many others. In 1966 he became the first composer to be presented to Queen Elizabeth at a Royal Film Performance of *Born Free* for which he also wrote the music, a thoroughly merited accolade for Barry personally, and recognition of the British composer's expanding role in film music.

The *Goldfinger* film (starring Sean Connery in the role of James Bond - agent 007) had grossed over $22 million in the U.S.A. and Canada alone by January 1968, and with receipts from other countries totalled £16 million in one year. The title song from the film also sold a million as a singles disc (see Bassey, 1964), while the 'Goldfinger' album was only outsold very narrowly by The Beatles' 'Hard Day's Night' album in 1965.

Barry composed 15 film scores from 1961 to 1965, seven of them in 1965 alone. He has the unique ability of being able to project the mood of a film, his music setting the scene or creating tension, yet always remaining unobtrusive.

The 'Goldfinger' album comprises the following, all the music composed by John Barry: Goldfinger (title song) (sung by Shirley Bassey) lyrics by Leslie Bricusse and Anthony Newley; *Themes from the film:* Miama, Golden Girl, Alpine Drive, Auric's Fancy, Death of Tilley, Odd Job's Pressing Engagement, The Laser Beam, Bond Back in Action Again, Pussy Galore's Flying Circus, Teasing the Korean, Gassing the Gangsters, Dawn Raid on Fort Knox, Arrival of the Bomb, Count Down, Death of Goldfinger.

ORIGINAL SOUNDTRACK OF FILM WITH JULIE ANDREWS, DICK VAN DYKE, DAVID TOMLINSON, GLYNIS JOHNS, KAREN DOTRICE, MATTHEW GARBER, ED WYNN (ARRANGED AND CONDUCTED BY IRWIN KOSTAL)

MARY POPPINS (album) *Buena Vista* [*USA*]. This disc, released in the U.S.A. on 6 July 1964, sold over 4 million in the U.S.A. alone and over six million globally by 1 January 1968 with sales still mounting. 'Mary Poppins' was No 1 for 16 weeks in the U.S.A.

The film (biggest gross of 1965 in the U.S.A. - $31 million), based on the *Mary Poppins* books by Miss P.L. Travers, premiered in the U.S.A. in August 1964, is undoubtedly Walt Disney's greatest. (Disney accumulated 34 Oscars and won over 900 other awards and five honorary doctorates - unequalled in the history of the motion picture industry.) A musical fantasy, mingling live action and animation as only Disney can produce, it appealed to people of all ages. The dream-world story of the English nanny (Julie Andrews) arriving on the East Wind to take over the household of a London banker (David Tomlinson), his wife (Glynis Johns) and their two young children, and changing their lives, is sheer entertainment. It made Julie Andrews a scintillating new film star and was also a triumph for Dick Van Dyke as a Jack-of-all-trades, permitting him to display his wide range of talents. The film won five Academy Awards for 1964: for Best Actress (Julie Andrews), Best Song ('Chim Chim Cher-ee'), Best Music Score, Best Visual Effects and Best Editing. It also sparked off a tremendous sale for the songs, 'Poppins' comics, colouring books, dolls, toys, apparel and other merchandise in the U.S.A. and elsewhere. An additional ten-song album sold over 750,000 and a storyteller album over 300,000 by the end of 1965. The songs were written by Richard M. Sherman and Robert B. Sherman, sons of famed U.S. songwriter Al

Sherman. Both were staff writers for Disney, and they also wrote the songs for two previous Disney films *The Parent Trap* and *Summer Magic*, both of which starred Hayley Mills.

Songs in the soundtrack: 'Overture' (orchestra and chorus); 'Sister Suffragette' (Glynis Johns); 'The Life I Lead' (David Tomlinson); 'Perfect Nanny' (Karen Dotrice and Matthew Garber); 'Pavement Artist' (Chim Chim Cher-ee) (Dick Van Dyke); 'A Spoonful of Sugar' (Julie Andrews); 'Jolly Holiday' (Julie Andrews and Dick Van Dyke); 'Supercalifragilisticexpialidocious' (Julie Andrews, Dick Van Dyke and Pearlies); 'Stay Awake' (Julie Andrews); 'I Love to Laugh' (Ed Wynn, Julie Andrews and Dick Van Dyke); 'A British Bank' (Julie Andrews and David Tomlinson); 'Feed the Birds' (Tuppence a Bag) (Julie Andrews and chorus); 'Fidelity, Fiduciary Bank' (Dick Van Dyke, David Tomlinson and Bankers); 'Chim Chim Cher-ee' (Dick Van Dyke, Karen Dotrice, Julie Andrews and Matthew Garber); 'Step in Time' (Chimney Sweeps' Dance) (Dick Van Dyke and Chimney Sweeps; 'A Man has Dreams', 'Life I Lead', and 'Spoonful of Sugar' (David Tomlinson and Dick Van Dyke); 'Let's Go Fly a Kite' (Tomlinson, Van Dyke and Londoners).

Gold Disc award R.I.A.A., 1964 and Grammy Awards for 'Best Original Film Song' 1964, 'Best Recording for Children' 1964. Disc was in the U.S. bestsellers for 114 weeks. By end of 1969 the film had grossed over $60 million (£25,000,000).

ORIGINAL FILM SOUNDTRACK WITH AUDREY HEPBURN, REX HARRISON, STANLEY HOLLOWAY AND JEREMY BRETT

MY FAIR LADY (album) *Columbia* [*USA*]. This film of the greatest ever stage musical, based on Bernard Shaw's play *Pygmalion*, with lyrics by Alan Jay Lerner and music by Frederick Loewe, can only be described as a box office gold mine, and superlative entertainment. In its first year it grossed £16,300,000 at the box office, £10 million of it in the U.S.A. and Canada. Warner Brothers paid the world record figure of $5,500,000 for the film rights. Audrey Hepburn, who has the star role of Eliza, originally played by Julie Andrews in the stage show, does not sing the songs in the film or on the disc. These were dubbed by Marni Nixon (soprano and wife of composer Ernest Gold of 'Exodus' fame) who can sing in the accents of any unmusical star. Lerner and Loewe wrote some new material for the film, and it was then the most expensive musical and studio film in the industry's history, costing in all $17,000,000. *My Fair Lady* won eight Academy Awards (1964).

This album was issued in the U.S.A. in October 1964 and sold 500,000 before the film opened with a 1½ million sale by early 1966. The disc contained all the familiar songs: 'Wouldn't It Be Loverly?'; 'I Could Have Danced All Night'; 'Just You Wait'; 'Without You'; 'Show Me'; 'The Rain in Spain'; 'On the Street Where You Live'; 'Get Me to the Church on Time'; 'With a Little Bit of Luck'; 'I've Grown Accustomed to Her Face'; 'I'm Just an Ordinary Man'; 'You Did It'; 'The Ascot Gavotte'; 'Why Can't the English?'; 'A Hymn to Him'.

Gold Disc award R.I.A.A. 1964. This album was in the U.S. bestsellers for 111 weeks.

THE ANIMALS (rhythm-and-blues vocal and instrumental group)

HOUSE OF THE RISING SUN *Columbia* [*Britain*]. The first million seller (combined sales Britain and U.S.A.) for this group was written by Alan Price of the Animals, based on a Negro folk song. The disc was No 1 for two weeks in Britain with 12 weeks in the bestsellers and No 1 for three weeks in the U.S.A. (on the MGM label). The group consisted of Alan Price (electric organ), born 19 April 1942, in Fatfield, Co. Durham; Bryan Chandler (bass guitar), born 18 December 1938 in Heaton, Newcastle-on-Tyne; Hilton Stuart Patterson Valentine (lead guitar), born 2 May 1943 in North Shields, Northumberland; Eric Victor Burdon (vocalist), born 19 May 1941 in Newcastle-on-Tyne; and John Steel (drums), born 4 February 1941 in Gateshead, Co. Durham. All are self-taught in music. Alan started as an income tax officer, Bryan a ship's instrument maker, Hilton a machinist,

singles disc made by the group. The song was originally a success for veteran folk singer Josh White. The Animals toned down the original rather bawdy lyrics for their version. Dave Rowberry (born 4 July 1940) replaced Alan Price in 1965. Their recording manager was Mickie Most. Subsequent sales globally were estimated at five million.

PAUL ANKA (with Ennio Morricone orchestra and the Cantori Moderni)

OGNI VOLTA *RCA [Italy]*. This was a first million seller for Paul in the Italian market, and it was sung by him in Italian. 'Ogni Volta' was introduced by Paul at the San Remo Song Festival in February 1964, taking second place in the contest. The disc passed the million sale in Europe by mid-May. It actually sold a million in Italy alone, becoming the second disc to achieve such a figure in the country – the first being by Bobby Solo (*q.v.*). The U.S. title for the song was 'Every Time'. The writers are Rossi and Robifer. This disc was Paul Anka's seventh million seller. He sold five million records in Italy alone by mid-1966.

LOUIS ARMSTRONG (vocal and jazz trumpet)

HELLO, DOLLY *Kapp [USA]*. This song, one of the biggest hits to come from the U.S.A., was originally written as a production number to get actress/singer Carol Channing on stage in the second act of the Broadway musical *Hello Dolly*, produced at St James Theatre, New York, on 16 January 1964, with the music and lyrics by Jerry Herman. It became so fantastically popular that it was played and sung everywhere, by the big disc artists, dance bands, orchestras, Dixieland groups and modern jazz groups. *Hello Dolly*'s producer gave the tune exclusively to Lyndon B. Johnson for the Democratic campaign in the Presidential election of 1964 when it was sung everywhere as 'Hello Lyndon'. It was Louis Armstrong's recording in his inimitable rasping rhythmic style that gave the song qualities it never had in the original show version, and it became the first disc to knock the Beatles from their long period at the top of the U.S.A.'s hit parade in May 1964. After a long and successful career in the jazz world, it was Louis' first million seller, and that at the age of 64, and was No 1 for one week in the U.S.A. and 22 weeks in the bestsellers. Total sales were over 2 million. It reached No 4 and 14 weeks in the British bestsellers.

Louis Armstrong was born 4 July 1900 in New Orleans, and was destined to become one of the true immortals of jazz. He learned to play the cornet in a reform school where he had been

Eric a designer, postman and draughtsman, John a technical illustrator and salesman. The group started under the name of the Alan Price Combo, playing rhythm-and-blues items in Newcastle where they became fantastically popular with their fans, with a following there almost as fervent as that acquired by The Beatles in Liverpool. The audience were heard talking about 'the animals' and the group eventually realized it was a reference to themselves. They therefore adopted the name. They took over a resident berth at the Club à Gogo in Newcastle, basing much of their work on Ray Charles and Bo Diddley. They made a demonstration disc and their fans found out about it and bought up 500 copies. This disc was brought to London by their manager who played it to agents and secured them sufficient work in the South. They arrived in London in January 1964, becoming full-time London residents, with packed houses wherever they played. They made their radio debut on BBC 'Saturday Club' on 27 December 1963, and appeared in their first TV on Tyne-Tees' 'Roundabout' and Granada's 'Scene at 6.30'. They made a tour with Chuck Berry in 1964 in Britain and also toured in the U.S.A. in this year. A Gold Disc was presented to the group by MGM Records of the U.S.A. in September 1964, before they returned to Britain. 'House of the Rising Sun' was the second

sent in 1913 for discharging a pistol, which he found in his home, in the streets on New Year's Day. On release in 1917, he met famed King Oliver who became his teacher, and the following year he replaced Oliver as trumpeter with Kid Ory's band, then joined Fate Marable's band on the Mississippi steamboats for two years. In 1922, he was with Oliver's band in Chicago, and in 1924 played with Fletcher Henderson in New York, later with Ollie Powers, Erskine Tate, Caroll Dickerson and Clarence Jones until 1927 when he formed his own band. In 1929, he was featured in the 'Hot Chocolate' revue in New York, which helped to increase his fame. In 1931 he returned to Chicago and got together a band, and in 1932 visited England, enjoying enormous success at the London Palladium. He made a second tour of England and went on the Continent (1933-1935), appeared in several motion pictures including *Pennies from Heaven* (1936), *Artists and Models* (1937), *Every Day's a Holiday* (1937). In subsequent years Armstrong appeared in many big films including *Going Places, Cabin in the Sky, Jam Session, Glenn Miller Story* and the tremendously successful *High Society* in 1956 with Crosby, Sinatra and Grace Kelly. In 1949 he again toured Europe, also in 1952, 1956, 1962 and 1965. Louis' recording career must be the longest in the world. He made his first disc on 31 March 1923 in Richmond, Indiana, as a member of King Oliver's Creole Jazz Band. The first time his distinctive gravel-voice was heard on disc was 1925 when he did 'vocal breaks' for 'Everybody Loves My Baby' with Fletcher Henderson's orchestra and it was around this time he was billed as 'The World's Greatest Jazz Cornetist.' He played his instrument as no one had ever done before and for him it talked and sang like a human voice. His gifts of creation and inventiveness, rhythm and tone are unsurpassed, and his singing evolved the same style as his trumpet playing. Armstrong's influence in jazz history has been greater than that of anyone else. In 1928 he made a series of records for Okeh with his 'Hot Five' and 'Hot Seven' which were some of the finest jazz discs ever recorded. From 1935, he recorded for Decca and through the years has made hundreds of discs. Louis has two nicknames – 'Pops' and 'Satchmo' (or Satchel-mouth). He was undoubtedly a genius. Around 200 different versions of 'Hello Dolly' were made up to January 1966. It received a Grammy Award in the U.S.A. for 'Song of the Year' 1964, and an award to Louis for Best Vocal Performance. Louis died on 6 July 1971 in New York.

An interesting sequel to the song was its similarity (first four bars) to 'Sunflower' written by Mack David in 1948. David sued for infringement but the case was settled out of court. Herman paid $250,000 to retain exclusive rights to 'Hello Dolly'.

THE BACHELORS (vocal trio and instrumentalists)

DIANE *Decca* [*USA*]. The first million seller for this extremely popular trio came from the combined sales from Britain, the U.S.A. and other countries. The song was originally written in 1927 by Lew Pollack (words) and Erno Rapee (music). Rapee's tune was first entitled 'Valse Dramatique' for the Janet Gaynor/Charles Farrell silent film *Seventh Heaven* for which it was used as the theme. The Bachelors were all born in Dublin: Con Cluskey, 18 November 1941; his brother Declan Cluskey, 12 December 1942; and John James Stokes, 13 August 1940. Con and Declan both studied piano, and John music theory. They were all educated in Dublin colleges, Declan becoming a design draughtsman, Con a heating engineer and John a builder. The trio came together in 1953 and formed a harmonica group, calling themselves the Harmonichords. They performed semi-professionally at dances and on radio and TV in Dublin. They became such a success that they were eventually asked to appear on the Ed Sullivan TV show in America, and also performed on a number of radio shows, playing mostly classical music. On their return to Dublin they did a six-month period on a top-rate radio show. In 1959, they toured England with Patrick O'Hagan who encouraged them to sing folk songs in their act. Soon after, they laid aside their instruments and devoted all their time to singing,

and changed their name to The Bachelors, on the suggestion of Decca's artists and repertoire producer Dick Rowe who auditioned them in late 1962. They then cut their first disc 'Charmaine' which soared to the top of the charts in 1963. Then followed this international hit, 'Diane', sung also in a charming melodic rhythmic style. It reached No 10 with 13 weeks in the U.S. bestsellers, and No 1 and 19 weeks in Britain's bestsellers. The trio play several instruments: Con – piano, guitar, banjo and tin whistle; Declan – piano, guitar, banjo and harmonica; and John – guitar, double bass and harmonica. The Bachelors' disc sales by end of 1965 were estimated at 10 million.

I BELIEVE *Decca* [*Britain*]. The second big seller for the Bachelors hit a 600,000 sale in Britain and 300,000 in the U.S.A. Sales from other countries helped to make it a million. The song was written in 1952 by Ervin Drake, Irvin Graham, Jimmy Shirl and Al Stillman, and was previously a tremendous hit for Frankie Laine (see Laine, 1953). The disc was No 33 and 8 weeks in the U.S. bestsellers. It was No 2 and 17 weeks in the British bestsellers.

BOBBY BARE

FOUR STRONG WINDS *Victor* [*USA*]. Another big hit through subsequent years for Bobby Bare, with an estimated million sale. Written by Ian Tyson in 1963 the disc entered the top 10 in the country-and-western charts in the U.S.A. Nationally it was No 60 with 7 weeks in the bestsellers.

SHIRLEY BASSEY (jazz vocalist)

GOLDFINGER *Columbia* [*Britain*]. Shirley recorded this, the title song for the sensationally successful *Goldfinger* film (the third of the famous 'James Bond' thrillers from Ian Fleming's novels). It had a good sale in Britain but when released on the

United Artists label in the U.S.A. in November 1964 it sold (by May 1965) a fast million. The music is by Britain's ace film composer John Barry, who became internationally famous for his scores of the James Bond films *Dr No, From Russia with Love, Goldfinger* and *Thunderball*. The soundtrack album of 'Goldfinger' also sold over a million in the U.S.A. The words of the song are by the famous British stage musical songwriting team of Anthony Newley and Leslie Bricusse. Barry's royalties from 'Goldfinger' are estimated to be in excess of £60,000.

Shirley Veronica Bassey was born on 8 January 1937 in the tough Tiger Bay area of Cardiff, the youngest of seven children.

Her father died when she was two. She first worked in an enamel factory. Self-taught in music, she made her first appearance at Luton, Bedfordshire, in the chorus of a touring revue *Memories of Al Jolson* at the age of 16. In 1955, she was heard by the late impresario Jack Hylton at London's Astor Club, and this led to her first big break in the West End in the *Such is Life* review. Her first successful disc was 'Banana Boat Song' (1956), then 'As I Love You' (1958) and 'Kiss Me Honey, Honey Kiss Me' (1959) for the Philips label. She then joined Columbia Records and became a consistent chart entrant with big hits including 'If You Love Me' (1959), 'As Long as He Needs Me' (1960), 'Climb Every Mountain' (1961), 'You'll Never Know' (1961), 'Far Away' (1962), 'What Now My Love' (1962), 'I' (who have nothing) (1963).

Shirley now has a big international reputation for her cabaret appearances in London, Las Vegas, Monte Carlo, Hollywood and other extensive visits to Australia, Sweden and Belgium. She has made many major appearances on TV, and in 1961 a fantastically successful appearance at New York's Persian Room undoubtedly set the seal on her career, making her one of the world's most sought after artists. This disc was No 7 in the U.S. charts and 13 weeks in the bestsellers, and No 21 in Britain, with nine weeks in the bestsellers.

THE BEACH BOYS

I GET AROUND *Capitol* [*USA*]. This fourth million seller for this group was written by their own member Brian Wilson. The disc was No 1 for two weeks in the U.S.A. and 15 weeks in the bestsellers. No 7 and 13 weeks in the British bestsellers. Belated R.I.A.A. Gold Disc award 1982.

FUN, FUN, FUN *Capitol* [*USA*]. This fifth reputed million seller for The Beach Boys was written by Brian Wilson but this time with the help of Mike Love. It reached No 5 with 11 weeks in the U.S. bestsellers.

THE BEATLES

CAN'T BUY ME LOVE *Parlophone* [*Britain*]. This disc holds the record to date for the biggest advance sale of any single – 2,100,000 in the U.S.A., on the Capitol label, and over one million in Britain. By the first week of release in Britain it sold 1,226,000 and 1,500,000 during its first week in the U.S.A., both all-time highs. It was No 1 (in its first week) and for four weeks in Britain and five weeks in the U.S.A. with 10 weeks in the U.S. bestsellers, and 14 weeks in the British. It topped the charts all over the globe. World sales have been estimated at between five and six million. Backing was 'You Can't Do That', again written by Lennon and McCartney.

MEET THE BEATLES (album) *Capitol* [*USA*]. (See 'With the Beatles', 1963, for data.)

INTRODUCING THE BEATLES (album) *Vee Jay* [*USA*]. (See 'Please Please Me', 1963, for data.)

THE BEATLES' SECOND ALBUM (album) (original recordings by *Parlophone, Britain*) *Capitol* [*USA*]. This album of recordings made in Britain in 1963 (with the exception of 'You Can't Do That' recorded in 1964) was also released in the U.S.A. in April 1964 and was No 1 seller in a week, selling 250,000 on the first day. It was the fastest selling album in Capitol's history up to that time. It was No 1 for five weeks in the U.S.A. All the songs were originally issued by Parlophone either on single, EP, or albums. Contents of the album were: 'Roll over Beethoven', by Chuck Berry (1956); 'You've Really Got a Hold on Me', by William Robinson (1963); 'Devil in Her Heart', by Richard Drapkin (1963); 'Money', by Berry Gordy, Jr. and J. Bradford (1959); 'Please Mister Postman', by B. Holland, F. Gorman and R. Bateman (1961); 'Long Tall Sally', by E. Johnson, R. Blackwell and R. Penniman (1956); 'She Loves You', by John Lennon

and Paul McCartney (1963); 'I'll Get You', by John Lennon and Paul McCartney (1963); 'You Can't Do That', by John Lennon and Paul McCartney (1964); 'Thank You Girl', by John Lennon and Paul McCartney (1963); 'I Call Your Name', by John Lennon and Paul McCartney (1963).

Gold Disc award R.I.A.A., 1964. This disc was in the U.S. bestsellers for 55 weeks.

A HARD DAY'S NIGHT *Parlophone* [*Britain*]. This number comes from the Beatles' film of the same title; it was written by John Lennon and Paul McCartney. The disc was No 1 (in its first week) and for four weeks in Britain (with 13 weeks in the bestsellers), and three weeks in the U.S.A. (with 13 weeks in the bestsellers) on Capitol label, entering the U.S. charts at No 21 in its first week, the highest ever (up to 1964) for a new disc. The backing for Britain was 'Things We Said Today' and 'I Should Have Known Better' for the U.S.A. Both backing numbers were also written by Lennon and McCartney. This disc was a million seller in both the U.S.A. and Britain, and also a world chart topper. Grammy Award for 'Best Vocal Group Performance' 1964. Gold Disc award, R.I.A.A., 1964.

'A HARD DAY'S NIGHT' (album) *Parlophone* [*Britain*] *United Artists* [*USA*]
'SOMETHING NEW' (album) *Capitol* [*USA*]. 'A Hard Day's Night' was issued in July 1964, and this soundtrack album of the Beatles' first film had advance orders of 250,000 in Britain and one million in the U.S.A., making it one of the fastest selling albums in the history of the disc industry. It was No 1 seller in a week and by October it had passed the two million mark in the U.S.A. and by December over 600,000 in Britain. The United Artists film reaped $5,800,000 in U.S. rentals in six weeks, around £4,000,000 world gross, and achieved the unprecedented world print order of between 1,500 and 1,800 – a global saturation which even included a showing behind the Iron Curtain. Over 800 prints were booked solid in the U.S.A. and 170 in Britain. The film was released just prior to The Beatles' second U.S. tour in August, and was a sensational global success. The group's 24 nights of appearances in the U.S.A. earned around $1 million, and at Kansas City's Municipal Stadium on 17 September they received a then world record fee of $150,000 for the one performance. They proved to be the most astonishing act in the history of show business. One estimate of their earnings abroad was as high as $56 million in one year. The 'Hard Day's Night' album was released by United Artists in the U.S.A. (producers of the film in Britain) with seven songs from the film on Side 1, and six other songs, mostly new, on Side 2. The disc was No 1 for 21 weeks in Britain and for 14 in the U.S.A., and in their bestsellers for 51 weeks.

'Something New' album had an advance order in the U.S.A. of half a million, with subsequent sales of a million. This was issued by Capitol in July, with six songs from 'A Hard Day's Night' and six other numbers. United Artists had the exclusive rights to the film soundtrack. The two albums had nine titles common to both as follows: 'A Hard Day's Night', by John Lennon and Paul McCartney (1964); 'I Should Have Known Better', by John Lennon and Paul McCartney (1964); 'If I Fell', by John Lennon and Paul McCartney (1964); 'I'm Happy Just to Dance with You', by John Lennon and Paul McCartney (1964); 'And I Love Her', by John Lennon and Paul McCartney (1964); 'Tell Me Why', by John Lennon and Paul McCartney (1964); (all the above from the film); 'Any Time at All', by John Lennon and Paul McCartney (1964); 'The Things We Said Today', by John Lennon and Paul McCartney (1964); 'I'll Cry Instead' (written for but cut from the film), by John Lennon and Paul McCartney (1964).

'A Hard Day's Night' album also included: 'Can't Buy Me Love' (in film), by John Lennon and Paul McCartney (1964); 'When I Get Home', by John Lennon and Paul McCartney (1964); 'You Can't Do That', by John Lennon and Paul McCartney (1964); 'I'll Be Back', by John Lennon and Paul McCartney (1964).

'Something New' album also included: 'Matchbox', by Carl Lee Perkins (1957); 'Slow Down', by Larry Williams (1958); 'Komm gib mir deine Hand' (German version of 'I Want to Hold Your Hand'), by John Lennon and Paul McCartney (1963).

Gold Disc award R.I.A.A., 1964 to Capitol. It stayed in the U.S. bestsellers for 41 weeks.

I FEEL FINE backed with SHE'S A WOMAN *Parlophone* [*Britain*]. Both songs were written by John Lennon and Paul McCartney. This disc had an advance order of 750,000 in Britain, and sold one million within 12 days of release. It also sold a million in its first week of release (27 November) in the U.S.A. on Capitol label. It was No 1 in Britain immediately, and stayed top for six weeks, with 14 weeks in the bestsellers. 'I Feel Fine' was also No 1 for four weeks in the U.S.A. and 11 weeks in the bestsellers. 'She's a Woman' was No 4 and 9 weeks in the bestsellers. Gold Disc award R.I.A.A., 1964.

BEATLES FOR SALE (album) *Parlophone* [*Britain*]
BEATLES '65 (album) *Capitol* [*USA*]. 'Beatles for Sale' released on 4 December 1964 started with the biggest advance sale ever in Britain for an album of 750,000. The disc was No 1 immediately, and for eleven weeks. Its counterpart 'Beatles '65', released in the U.S.A. on 14 December 1964, also had an advance order of 750,000 and was No 1 in a week, staying at the top for nine weeks. Capitol sold over one million during the first week, 2,124,000 in four weeks and over three million in six weeks, making it the fastest-selling pop album up to 1964.

Both discs contained the following songs: 'No Reply', by John Lennon and Paul McCartney (1964); 'I'm a Loser', by John Lennon and Paul McCartney (1964); 'Baby's in Black', by John Lennon and Paul McCartney (1964); 'I'll Follow the Sun', by John Lennon and Paul McCartney (1964); 'Honey Don't', by Carl Lee Perkins (1956); 'Everybody's Trying to Be My Baby', by Carl Lee Perkins (1958); 'Rock'n'roll Music', by Chuck Berry (1957); 'Mister Moonlight', by Roy Lee Johnson (1962, published 1964). 'Beatles for Sale' additional songs were: 'Kansas City', by Mike Stoller and Jerry Leiber (1959); 'Words of Love', by Buddy Holly (1958); 'Eight Days a Week', by John Lennon and Paul McCartney (1964); 'Every Little Thing', by John Lennon and Paul McCartney (1964); 'What You're Doing', by John Lennon and Paul McCartney (1964); 'I Don't Want to Spoil the Party', by John Lennon and Paul McCartney (1964). 'Beatles '65' additional songs were: 'I'll Be Back', by John Lennon and Paul McCartney (1964); 'I Feel Fine', by John Lennon and Paul McCartney (1964); 'She's a Woman', by John Lennon and Paul McCartney (1964).

Gold Disc award R.I.A.A., 1964 to Capitol. This album stayed in the U.S. bestsellers for 70 weeks.

THE BEATLES' STORY (Double album) *Capitol* [*USA*]. This double album was put out in the U.S.A. in mid-November 1964 to commemorate The Beatles' first anniversary there when their first Capitol single 'I Want to Hold Your Hand' started a disc industry revolution (December 1963). The discs are a narrative and musical biography of Beatlemania, a documentary with all the Beatles songs in chronological order, interviews with each Beatle and an excerpt from their Hollywood Bowl Concert. It hit the million-dollars sales mark within the first week, and went on to sell a million copies subsequently. Gold Disc award R.I.A.A., 1964. The disc was in the U.S. bestsellers for 17 weeks.

LONG TALL SALLY (EP disc) *Parlophone* [*Britain*]. This global million seller for The Beatles was their third EP to hit seven figures. This disc was No 1 for seven weeks in Britain, with over a quarter million sales by early 1965; the remainder of the million sales came from around Europe and elsewhere. The disc contained the following: 'Long Tall Sally', by E. Johnson, R. Blackwell and R. Penniman (1956); 'Matchbox', by Carl Lee Perkins (1957); 'Slow Down', by Larry Williams (1958); 'I Call Your Name', by John Lennon and Paul McCartney (1963).

CILLA BLACK WITH ACCOMPANIMENT DIRECTED BY JOHNNY PEARSON

ANYONE WHO HAD A HEART *Parlophone* [*Britain*]. Cilla Black (real name Priscilla Maria Veronica White) was born in Liverpool 27 May 1943. After schooling at St Anthony's Junior and Secondary Schools and Anfield Commercial College, Liverpool, she became a typist and secretary with a local firm when aged 15. In 1960 at 'The Iron Door', a well-known rock'n'roll club in Liverpool, she was singing along with the music of the group there, and the bass player noted her enthusiasm. He took a microphone over and asked her to sing a song. The audience and the group were very impressed and she sang with them for the remainder of the evening. She was then invited to join another well-known local group as vocalist, singing with them and keeping her office job. She often sang at Liverpool's famous 'The Cavern' with then unknowns like The Beatles and Gerry and The Pacemakers. In September 1963 she deputized for the Fourmost group on The Beatles' show at Southport's

Odeon and during this month was spotted by Brian Epstein (manager of The Beatles, Billy J. Kramer and others) who signed her up and persuaded her to become a full-time professional. She made her radio debuts on 'Friday Spectacular' 13 September 1963 on Radio Luxembourg, and on 'Easy Beat' December 1963 on BBC. Her TV debut was in 'Ready, Steady, Go' 27 September 1963. It was Epstein who changed her name, as so many people had said her voice sounded black rather than white. Cilla's first recording was 'Love of the Loved', a John Lennon/Paul McCartney song. Then Billy J. Kramer brought back 'Anyone Who Had a Heart' from the U.S.A. which he was certain was the right song for Cilla. He could not have chosen more suitable material, for Cilla's disc became No 1 in Britain for four weeks (with 17 weeks in the bestsellers), selling over 800,000 in just over a month. This earned her a summer season at the London Palladium in 1964, where she was a great success. This song was written in 1963 by Hal David (words) and Burt Bacharach (music).

YOU'RE MY WORLD *Parlophone* [*Britain*]. Cilla Black's second million seller, was No 1 for three weeks in Britain (and 17 weeks in the bestsellers) and also a success in the U.S.A. (reaching No 26 with 7 weeks in the bestsellers), and elsewhere. Combined British-U.S. sales are estimated at 1,500,000. The disc was issued on the Capitol label in the U.S.A. The song was written in 1963 in Italy, originally titled 'Il mio mondo', by Gino Paoli (words) and Umberto Bindi (music). The English lyrics were written by Carl Sigman in 1964.

GIGLIOLA CINQUETTI (accompaniment and direction by F. Monaldi)

NON HO L'ETA PER AMARTI (I'm not old enough to love you) *C.G.D.* [*Italy*]. This song, written by Nicola Salerno and Mario Panzeri, won the San Remo Festival and the Eurovision Song Contest in 1964, and was sung by Gigliola in both.

She was born in Verona on 20 December 1947 and started singing at the age of five, starring in the local Christmas show. She won a local TV competition at 11 and was first in another contest among 4,200 entrants. She graduated from local concerts to the bigger Italian shows, with schooling and singing lessons in between. Then at 17 came her triumphs in the San Remo and Eurovision festivals.

This disc topped the charts all over Europe. It was No 1 for four weeks in Italy, four weeks in France, six weeks in Denmark, two weeks in Belgium, and one week in both Holland and Spain. It was No 17 and 17 weeks in Britain's bestsellers. Cinquetti was presented with a special Platinum Disc in mid-August 1964 for global sales of two million, the final tally being three million. An English version of the song was a minor hit for Vera Lynn under the title 'This is My Prayer'.

Gigliola's real ambition was to win a degree as an architect/designer.

DAVE CLARK FIVE

BITS AND PIECES *Columbia* [*Britain*]. Here was another pounding beat rhythmic number for this group, written by Dave Clark and group member Mike Smith. This disc (it was No 4 in the U.S.A. with 11 weeks in the bestsellers, and No 2 in Britain with 11 weeks in the bestsellers) was their second million seller. It sold 590,000 in Britain and over half a million in the U.S.A. on the Epic label.

DO YOU LOVE ME? *Columbia* [*Britain*]. Another big success, the 3rd million seller, for this group, the song originally written by Berry Gordy Jr in 1962 when it was a million seller for The Contours (see 1962). Dave Clark's disc achieved the No 8 chart position in the U.S.A. with 10 weeks in the bestsellers when released there on the Epic label, with the bulk of its sale there, and was also No 30 in Britain, making a subsequent million global sale.

CAN'T YOU SEE THAT'S SHE MINE *Columbia* [*Britain*]. The fourth million seller for Dave Clark Five with its combined sale in the U.S.A. and other countries. This song, written by Dave Clark and Mike Smith, was released on the Epic label in the U.S.A. It was No 4 in the U.S.A. with 10 weeks in the bestsellers, and No 10 in Britain with 11 weeks in the bestsellers.

BECAUSE *Columbia* [*Britain*] *Epic* [*USA*]. The fifth million seller for this group sold well in the U.S.A. while at the height of popularity there. This attractive rock-a-cha-cha beat number, recorded in an ear-arresting manner, was written by Dave Clark, and got to No 3 in the U.S. charts and 10 weeks in the bestsellers.

ANY WAY YOU WANT IT *Columbia* [*Britain*] *Epic* [*USA*]. Another pounding 'pull out all the stops' number by the Dave Clark Five, their sixth million seller, globally. But the bulk of the sales made were in the U.S.A. on the Epic label. It got to No 8 in the U.S. charts in early 1965 and 12 weeks in he bestsellers. It was No 25 in Britain. Written by Dave Clark.

PETULA CLARK

DOWNTOWN *Pye* [*Britain*]. Petula's fourth million seller is her biggest hit to date. This song was written by Pye's musical director Tony Hatch. The disc was No 2 for two weeks in Britain (with 15 weeks in the bestsellers) with well over the quarter million sale, but when released on the Warner label in the U.S.A. in December 1964 it soon shot to the top of the charts in January 1965, and was No 1 for two weeks with 15 weeks in the bestsellers, selling over a million there. Only one other female British artist had ever attained No 1 in America - Vera Lynn in 1952 - so this

was a wonderful achievement for Petula with global sales over three million. She received the Gramophone Academy Award of the U.S.A. for this disc as the best rock'n'roll single of 1964. Gold Disc award, R.I.A.A., 1965.

BILL COSBY (comedian)

BILL COSBY IS A VERY FUNNY FELLOW, RIGHT? (album) *Warner* [*USA*]. The first album of his inimitable comedy material recorded by Bill Cosby. It received a Gold Disc award from R.I.A.A. in 1966 and sold one and a half million units by 1968.

The album includes: 'A Nut in Every Car'; 'Superman'; 'Hoof and Mouth'; 'Karate'; 'Planes'; 'Wives'; 'Baby'. (See Cosby, 1966 for biography.) It was in the U.S. bestsellers for 128 weeks.

I STARTED OUT AS A CHILD (album) *Warner* [*USA*]. Bill Cosby's second album with Gold Disc award from R.I.A.A. in 1966 and million units sale by July 1967. It was produced by his fellow comedian Allen Sherman and recorded 'live' at Mr Kelly's in Chicago.

Contents of the album: 'Sneakers'; 'Street Football'; 'The Water Bottle'; 'Christmas Time'; 'The Giant'; 'Opps'; 'The Lone Ranger'; 'Ralph Jameson'; 'Medic'; 'My Pet Rhinoceros'; 'Half Man'; 'Rigor Mortis'; 'The Neanderthal Man'; 'T.V. Football'; 'Seattle'. (See Cosby, 1966, for biography.) It was in the U.S. bestsellers for 140 weeks and sold 1,200,000 up to then.

Grammy Award for Best Comedy Performance, 1964.

THE DIXIE CUPS

CHAPEL OF LOVE *Red Bird* [*USA*]. Here was a first million seller for this coloured female trio: Barbara Anne Hawkins; her sister Rose Lee Hawkins (both educated at Southern University in New Orleans); and Joan Marie Johnson (educated at high school in New Orleans). The trio started their musical career singing in the school chorus in elementary school. In 1963 they organized as a group with a show business career in mind, and in just over a year were discovered by Joe ('You talk too much') Jones at a talent show in New Orleans. He became their manager, rehearsed them for four months and brought them to New York to see songwriters Jerry Leiber and Mike Stoller who signed them immediately for their comparatively new Red Bird label, calling them The Dixie Cups. This, their first disc, soon became a top seller, and was No 1 for three weeks in the U.S.A. with 13 weeks in the bestsellers, and was No 22 in Britain. The group visited Britain at the end of 1964 and appeared on TV and broadcast on radio. This song was written by Phil Spector, Jeff Barry and Ellie Greenwich.

PETE DRAKE (country-and-western vocalist/guitarist)

FOREVER *Smash* [*USA*]. Pete Drake, the 'talking steel guitar man', achieved national limelight in the U.S.A. with this disc which although only reaching No 22 with 11 weeks in the bestsellers was a steady seller and through the years is said to have sold a million. The composition is by Buddy Killen (1959). It was on this disc that Pete first featured the 'Talking Steel'.

He was born 8 October 1932 in Augusta, Georgia, and saved the money from his first job as a clerk in a grocery store to buy his first guitar, a cheaply-made mail-order instrument. He saved for a further two years to buy a good steel guitar. He was encouraged by his two musician brothers and won his first professional job as a musician on WLMA-Atlanta while still a teenager.

In 1959, his prowess became recognized throughout the South and he moved to Nashville, working with artists who came to record there. He soon played dates on the Grand Ole Opry where his popularity grew and earned him regular Saturday night dates with the show.

He became one of the busiest musicians in Nashville. In 1968 he became President of his own Stop Records. Pete has recorded with big names such as Elvis Presley, Perry Como and The Monkees in addition to all the top country stars.

GEORGIE FAME (rhythm-and-blues vocalist, organist) WITH THE BLUE FLAMES

YEH YEH *Columbia* [*Britain*]. Georgie Fame's disc of this song written in 1963 by Rodgers Grant, Pat Patrick and Jon Hendricks achieved No 1 position in Britain's charts for one week in January 1965 with 12 weeks in the bestsellers, and sold over 250,000. It was also a success in the U.S.A. (reaching No 21 with eight weeks in the bestsellers) and elsewhere, making an estimated million global sale.

Georgie Fame (real name Clive Powell) was born 26 June 1943 at Leigh, near Manchester, and took piano lessons when he was seven. At 15 he left Leigh Central County Secondary School and worked in a cotton-weaving factory, playing the piano at nights with a group called The Dominoes. In 1959 he sang in a Butlin's holiday camp contest at Pwllelhi, Wales, and was offered a job

by the bandleader Rory Blackwell. After Butlin's he went to London and was playing in Islington, North London, when composer Lionel Bart called to see Blackwell. Georgie was singing and he was asked to audition for Larry Parnes. Parnes changed his name to Georgie Fame and employed him as pianist in a group to accompany visiting American artists. One of the singers was missing one night, so Georgie took over and was given a solo spot in the show. The group eventually became The Blue Flames, and worked solely with artist Billy Fury. Later, the group decided to stay together and played weekend all-night dances at London's Flamingo Club, becoming the resident group. In 1962, Georgie switched to the electric organ and the club business trebled, attracting 1,000 people at the Saturday all-night sessions with his jazz-based rock'n'roll music and blues. His driving self-termed 'rockhouse' music became a cult among visiting West Indians and Americans, Georgie's singing to his organ accompaniment sounding like the singers of America's deep South. 'Live' recordings were made at the Flamingo, then came 'Yeh Yeh'. The inevitable TV, radio and personal appearances followed.

The Blue Flames consists of Colin Green (guitar), Peter Coe (alto/tenor saxes and flute), Tony Makins (bass guitar), Bill Eyden (drums) and Speedy Acquaye (congo drums). Georgie Fame is generally considered to be the best rhythm-and-blues artist in Britain.

THE FOUR SEASONS

RAG DOLL *Philips* [*USA*]. The fourth million seller for this group was written by Bob Crewe and Bob Gaudio (of the group) and the disc was No 1 for two weeks in the U.S.A. and 12 weeks in the bestsellers, and No 2 and 13 weeks in the British bestsellers.

Gold Disc award, R.I.A.A., 1964.

THE FOUR TOPS (rhythm-and-blues vocal quartet)

BABY, I NEED YOUR LOVING *Motown* [*USA*]. Signed by the Tamla-Motown organization in 1964, this disc was the first release for the group, the song written by the famous team Eddie Holland, Lamont Dozier and Brian Holland. It reached No 11 in the U.S.A. with 12 weeks in the bestsellers, and was also a hit in Britain (No 15). Subsequent global sale estimated at one million. (See 1965 for Four Tops biography.) Released 15 August 1964.

FREDDIE AND THE DREAMERS

I UNDERSTAND (just how you feel) *Columbia* [*Britain*]. This third global million seller for Freddie was written by Pat Best in 1953. This disc sold around 500,000 in Britain and a further half million in the U.S.A. on the Mercury label when released there in 1965, following the group's sensational TV appearance in New York. This number was a previous million seller (see 'Four Tunes', 1954). In the U.S.A. the disc was No 36 and 9 weeks in the bestsellers, and in Britain it was No 5 and 15 weeks in the bestsellers.

FREDDY (Quinn)

VERGANGEN, VERGESSEN, VORUEBER *Polydor* [*Germany*]. The seventh million seller for Freddie was composed by Lotar Olias. It is said to have sold 1,800,000 by July 1965, mainly in Germany and other Continental countries. The literal translation of the title is 'Gone, Forgotten, All Over'.

GALE GARNETT (vocalist)

WE'LL SING IN THE SUNSHINE *Victor* [*USA*]. Gale Garnett was born in Auckland, New Zealand, on 17 July 1942, the eldest daughter of an English carnival pitchman, musical hall entertainer and a Russian émigré. The family left the South Pacific for America when she was nine and travelled throughout the U.S.A. before going to New York. She began her career at 12 as a stage actress, left home at 14 after her father died and got her first apartment in New York's Lower East Side. She made her professional debut as an actress at 15, after having worked as a waitress and as a janitress in an off-Broadway theatre. Circumstances forced her to buy her clothes at the Salvation Army. Three years after her high school career ended, she got a role in the touring company of *The Drunkard* (a famous play first produced in 1843 and credited with the longest run of any show at one theatre in the world). Thereafter she was featured in no fewer than 60 TV shows with acting leads in 'Hawaiian Eye', '77 Sunset Strip', 'Adventures in Paradise', 'Bonanza' and many others. She has also appeared in the stage productions of *Threepenny Opera*, *Guys and Dolls*, *Showboat*, *World of Suzie Wong* and others.

In 1960, she went to Europe for a part in a French film *La Fille Liza* but was unable to work through having no working papers. She stayed in Paris for a while to absorb Gallic culture. On return to the U.S.A. she made her singing debut at Los Angeles' Garrett Club, then club dates across the country in key spots.

Gale wrote songs as a hobby and took 25 of them to RCA-Victor. Although primarily an actress up to that time, Victor signed her to a contract after hearing her sing. She had only been singing professionally for three months before 'We'll Sing in the Sunshine', her own composition (1963), got to No 1 for one week in the U.S. charts and stayed in the Top Ten for two months and 17 weeks in the bestsellers, with an eventual estimated million sale.

This disc won the 1964 Grammy Award as 'The Best Folk Recording of the Year'. Gale has been singing in the sunshine ever since. The song was her first recording. She became a full-time singer.

GERRY AND THE PACEMAKERS

DON'T LET THE SUN CATCH YOU CRYING *Columbia* [*Britain*]. The first million seller for this British group was written by Gerry (Marsden) himself. It sold 206,000 in Britain, over 650,000 in the U.S.A. on the Laurie label, topping the million with sales in other countries. Personnel: Gerry (Gerry Marsden) born 24 September 1942 in Liverpool, educated at a convent school; and The Pacemakers: Leslie Maguire, born 27 December 1941 in Wallasey, Cheshire; John Chadwick, born 11 May 1943 in Liverpool; and Freddy Marsden (Gerry's brother) born 23 October 1940 in Liverpool. After school they became: British Railways employee (Gerry); joiner and music assistant (Leslie); bank clerk (John); and clerk (Freddy). Gerry first played guitar with a skiffle group, then formed his own group, 'The Mars Bars', singing and playing clubs in the Liverpool area for six months before breaking up. Gerry then formed the original Pacemakers (1959) and soon after got an offer to appear in Hamburg. They turned professional and had a major success for two months at the famous Top Ten Club there, returning to Britain and again working round Liverpool and the north-west, often on dates with The Beatles. Artists' and repertoire man George Martin was persuaded to watch them in action in a Birkenhead ballroom while in Liverpool on business. He signed them on the spot for their first sessions, recording 'How Do You Do It', which became an eventual chart topper. The group had been signed six months earlier (June 1962) to an exclusive management contract by Beatles manager Brian Epstein. Gerry and his brother Freddy worked together for six years in various 'rock' groups before forming the Pacemakers in 1959 with Chadwick. They remained a trio until 1961 when Maguire joined as pianist. They play the following instruments – Gerry (guitar, piano, drums), Freddy (drums), Chadwick (guitar, bass, piano), Maguire (piano, sax, flute, clarinet). Gerry is a talented songwriter. The group became one of the most popular in Britain, and had their first three discs all at No 1 in Britain. This disc was No 4 and 12 weeks in the U.S. bestsellers, and No 6 and 11 weeks in the British bestsellers.

ASTRUD GILBERTO (vocal) AND
STAN GETZ (tenor saxophone)

THE GIRL FROM IPANEMA *Verve* [*USA*]. The success of this disc was largely the result of an afterthought. Verve had planned an album to be built around the two bossa nova giants – Stan Getz, the American adaptor, and Joao Gilberto, designated 'father' of bossa nova in Brazil. It was decided to have the Portuguese lyrics to one of the tracks for the song 'Girl from Ipanema' and to also have them sung in English. Astrud, wife of Joao, was invited to sing the English lyrics (written by Norman Gimbel) for the disc. When the disc was issued as a single, Astrud came into her own. The album version had to be shortened, and the shortened single version contained only the inspired tenor sax of Stan Getz and plaintive haunting voice of Astrud. The disc reached No 5 for two weeks in the U.S.A. with 12 weeks in the bestsellers, and became a global hit with an estimated over one million sale.

Astrud Gilberto hails from an area around Rio de Janeiro and somewhere near the beach of Ipanema, of which she sings. She has had practically no musical training which would seem to account for her appeal. Her rendering of the song, backed by Getz' outstanding obligatos, is unique in its simplicity and lack of affectation.

Astrud was born in 1941. The original song was written by Vincius de Moraes (Portuguese words) and Antonio Carlos Jobim (music). It was composer Jobim, working in company with singer Joao Gilberto who launched the Bossa Nova movement in pop music in Brazil. (See also Getz/Byrd, 1962.) Grammy Award for 'Record of the Year' 1964.

BOBBY GOLDSBORO

SEE THE FUNNY LITTLE CLOWN *United Artists* [*USA*]. Bobby comes from Maryanna, Florida, where he was born on 15 January 1941. His family moved to Dotham, Alabama, and after Bobby's graduation from high school there, he studied at Auburn University for two years. He learned to play the guitar and after a brief period of freelance work, joined Roy Orbison as a guitarist in January 1962, also deciding to write his own songs. Orbison encouraged him to go solo for a while.

In 1964, a friend took a recording of Bobby's voice to Jack Gold, an A & R director at United Artists Records in New York. Gold immediately took a plane to Dotham and signed Bobby to an exclusive contract, the first release being this disc which got to No 9 in the U.S. charts with 13 weeks in the bestsellers, with an eventual million sale (by 1967).

Bobby has played various dates around the U.S.A. and Canada. He also toured Britain with Roy Orbison.

This song was written by Bobby in 1963, the arrangement and conducting for the disc by Garry Sherman.

LORNE GREENE (TV actor, pop ballad vocalist)

RINGO *Victor* [*USA*]. At a time when pop groups and teenage music saturated the musical scene, Lorne Greene's disc created a big surprise. Lorne, born 1914, is best known as one of the stars of the TV series 'Bonanza', in which he played the role of Pa Cartwright of the Ponderosa Ranch for over four years. His interest in drama dates back to his Linger Collegiate Institute days in Ottawa. He received a fellowship to study at New York's Neighbourhood Playhouse after being noticed in Canada's annual drama festival. Lorne did a few years of radio jobs in Canada and some acting in TV in Gotham, then he was featured in the Hollywood films *The Silver Chalice* and *Tight Spot*. These were followed by acting assignments on Broadway and at the Shakespearian Festival at Stratford and then the immensely successful 'Bonanza' TV series.

In 1964, Lorne recorded some numbers for Victor although he had had no experience in this field. An album 'Welcome to the Ponderosa' was the outcome that included 'Ringo', sung in monologue style and dramatically portraying the story of how he saved the life of notorious gunman Johnny Ringo. Nothing happened to the album until a Texas disc jockey played it. The result was sensational, and was repeated when another disc jockey played it. RCA-Victor were obliged to release it as a single and it sold well over the half million very quickly and got to No 1 for one week in the U.S. charts and 12 weeks in the bestsellers. It was also popular in Britain (where it was No 22) and in many other countries, selling over a million globally. Requests poured in for Lorne to make personal appearances at rodeos and fairs and he opened in Reno in April 1965. He received a stupendous mail, prepared a five-times-a-week radio show and some TV productions, commanding a big salary. Lorne is also the inventor of a stopwatch which runs backwards, made for the benefit of radio personnel.

'Ringo' was written by Don Robertson and Hal Blair in 1963.

HERMAN'S HERMITS

I'M INTO SOMETHING GOOD *Columbia* [*Britain*]. The first million seller for this Manchester group was No 1 in Britain for three weeks and 15 weeks in their bestsellers. This song was written by famous husband-and-wife team Gerry Goffin and Carole King. It sold over 470,000 in Britain and 250,000 in its first ten days in the U.S.A. on the MGM label, passing the million globally soon after. Herman (real name Peter Noone) was born in Manchester on 5 November 1947, and was educated at St Bedde's College and Stretford Grammar School. He sang a little at school, combining his first drama lessons with singing when he had a part in the TV series 'Knight Errant' which required him to sing. He then attended Manchester School of Music for both drama and singing classes at 14. He appeared in 'Coronation Street', 'Saki', two children's plays and in several other TV shows. While visiting his local youth club one night, the group there, The Heartbeats, were short of a singer. Peter joined them, and gave up his acting career. The personnel of the group changed several times after its formation. Karl Anthony Green (bass guitar and harmonica) remained the only member of the original group. He was born in Salford on 31 July 1947,

and was a process engraver. Others were Jan Berry Whitham (drums), born 21 July 1946 in Manchester and a hairdresser; Keith Hopwood (guitar), born 26 October 1946 in Manchester, and a telephone engineer; Derek Leckenby (guitar), born 14 May 1946 in Leeds, who was a student. Peter (or Herman) played the piano.

The name Herman came from a cartoon character in a TV show 'The Bullwinkle Show'. The group were amused at the similarity of one character called Sherman to that of their lead singer Peter, so they christened him Herman, adding The Hermits as it fitted the first name so well. The group were brought to the attention of independent record producer Mickie Most, who had been responsible for the hits of The Animals and The Nashville Teens. He travelled to Bolton to see them at a concert, was impressed by their stage show and signed them to a recording contract. Mickie Most chose this song for their disc debut which was released in three weeks. The group had more big hits in the U.S.A. in 1965, and were a fantastic success there on tour. This group had sold 17 million records by the end of 1967. They also made two films for MGM in 1965. In the U.S.A. this disc was No 13 and 13 weeks in the bestsellers.

JOE HINTON (rhythm-and-blues vocalist)

FUNNY (how time slips away) *Backbeat* [*USA*]. Originally a hit for Jimmy Elledge in 1961, this country song written by Willie Nelson was recorded by Joe Hinton in a gospel soul-flavoured style for the new Backbeat label, a subsidiary of Duke/Peacock Records in the U.S.A.

The disc reached No 12 with 12 weeks in the U.S. bestsellers, and is said to have subsequently sold a million.

Joe Hinton was born in 1929, and died in Boston on 13 August 1968.

AL HIRT (jazz trumpet) AND HIS BAND

SUGAR LIPS *Victor* [*USA*]. Another big success for 'The Monster' Al Hirt, written by William D. (Buddy) Killen (executive vice president and co-owner of Tree Publishing Co., Inc and Dial Records) with Billy Sherrill. This disc was estimated to have sold a million by 1965 and the composition both included in and used as the title for Hirt's million-dollar-selling album. Released July 1964, the disc was No 20 in the U.S. charts and 7 weeks in the bestsellers.

COTTON CANDY *Victor* [*USA*]. The third singles million seller for Al Hirt, written by Russ Damon, the disc was released

in April 1964. It was No 15 for two weeks in the U.S. charts and 12 weeks in the bestsellers, and the title was used for another of Hirt's albums which became a million-dollar seller.

Al Hirt signed with GWP Records, a new label, in 1969.

THE HONEYCOMBS

HAVE I THE RIGHT? *Pye* [*Britain*]. This new British group had a million seller with their disc debut. This song was written by their two managers Alan Blaikley and Ken Howard. It was No 1 for two weeks in Britain and 15 weeks in the bestsellers. The million sale came from the combined British (over 250,000), U.S.A. and other countries' totals. Personnel: Martin Murray (guitar), born 7 October 1941 in the East End of London; Alan Ward (guitar, piano, organ), born 12 December 1945, Nottingham; Denis Dalziel (piano, guitar, harmonica, jews harp), born 10 October 1943, Whitechapel, London; John Lantree (bass), born 20 August 1940 in Newbury, Berkshire; Ann ('Honey') Lantree (drums), born 28 August 1943, Hayes, Middlesex.

The group was formed in 1963 by Martin Murray. He started playing guitar in the skiffle era with various groups, but wanted a new 'sound' different from other groups. He finally advertised in a musical paper and met Ward, the group's lead guitar. Martin had known Honey Lantree for some time as they were both in the hairdressing business. She had an unusual hobby for a girl – drumming. He finally persuaded her to join the group. She became one of the few female drummers in Britain. Her brother John joined the group when Martin's previous bass player had to leave. Martin then met Denis through a friend's suggestion that he would fit in as a good vocalist. The group played dates in the West End and all around London including the famous pub, The Mildmay Tavern, in North London. They submitted some of their original numbers to independent producer Joe ('Telstar') Meek. He chose 'Have I the Right?', recorded it and then took the disc to Pye. It soon put The Honeycombs' up-beat number into the hit parade, with subsequent radio, TV and personal appearances in Britain, France, Australia and New Zealand. This number was released on the Interphon label in the U.S.A. where it reached No 4 in their charts and 13 weeks in the bestsellers.

THE KINKS

YOU REALLY GOT ME *Pye* [*Britain*]. The Kinks are four art students with a flair for rhythm-and-blues, but also a great musical appreciation ranging from Chuck Berry to Bach. Their distinctive dress of hunting pink jackets, white frilled shirts, and black silk stockings, plus long hair, makes them look like characters from Dickens. They came together in 1961 playing and singing in the Muswell Hill, London, area, with the idea of making money to help with their studies, mainly in art. They

soon became extremely well known through their music and 'kinky' clothes - hence the group's name. Two young businessmen, Grenville Collins, a stockbroker, and Robert Wace, became interested in them and invited the group to play at a few debutante and society parties. Their success and obvious great potential as professionals were apparent and they were brought to the attention of Larry Page who signed them up immediately. A Pye contract soon followed and their first disc was 'Long Tall Sally'. Their third was 'You Really Got Me', which became No 1 in Britain for two weeks and was 12 weeks in the bestsellers. It sold over a quarter million in Britain and when released in the U.S.A. on the Reprise label, the combined sales topped the million, reaching No 7 with 15 weeks in the bestsellers. The song was written by group member Raymond Davies.

The Kinks are two brothers, Raymond Davies (born 21 June 1944, London), who plays guitar, harmonica and piano; and David Davies (born 3 February 1947, Muswell Hill), who plays guitar, piano and banjo; with Michael Avory (born 15 February 1944, Hampton Court), drums; and Peter Quaife (born 31 December 1943, Tavistock, Devon), bass, guitar and bongo. Raymond, David and Peter all sing. The group toured Britain in 1964 with Gerry and The Pacemakers, and Gene Pitney, and toured Australia and New Zealand in 1964.

BILLY J. KRAMER (vocal) AND THE DAKOTAS
LITTLE CHILDREN *Parlophone* [*Britain*]. This was a second million seller for Billy and the group. Sales in Britain were 600,000 with the U.S.A. and other countries making the million. The song is a most attractive one by American writers Mort Shuman and John Leslie McFarland. The disc was No 1 in Britain for one week, with 13 weeks in the bestsellers. In the U.S.A. it was released on the Imperial label, backed by 'Bad to Me' (see 1963), reaching No 7 with 15 weeks in the bestsellers.

GARY LEWIS AND THE PLAYBOYS
THIS DIAMOND RING *Liberty* [*USA*]. This disc was released in late December 1964, and by April 1965 had sold a million in the U.S.A. It was No 1 for two weeks there and 12 weeks in the bestsellers. The song was written by Bobby Brass, Irwin Levine and Al Kooper.

Gary Lewis, born 1946, is the son of the famous comedian and film star Jerry Lewis, and made up his mind on a show business career early in life. In 1964, after many months of drum practice, he formed a small band just for parties and personal enjoyment. Gary took the group to Disneyland and auditioned for a summer job, unknown to his parents. They were engaged and played most of the summer for teenage dancers at the famous amusement park. The park officials did not know until several weeks later that Gary was the son of a famous star. The group completed their summer engagement by appearing in a Universal picture *Swinging Summer*.

With his parents' and friends' encouragement, Gary asked Liberty Records for an audition, the result being this big hit on which he is the vocalist. The Playboys are Dave Costell, Dave Walker and Al Ramsey.

MAHINA STARS AND KAZUKO MATSUO
OZASHIKI KOUTA *Victor* [*Japan*]. Here was the first local Japanese hit to sell well over one-and-a-half million. A Gold Disc was awarded to Hiroshi Wada's Mahina Stars on 22 January 1965 in Tokyo. The disc was No 1 for 21 weeks in Japan from September 1964 into 1965.

The composer is unknown. Royalties are paid to the Japanese Bureau of Justice until the writer is established.

SIV MALMQUIST (ballad vocalist)
LIEBESKUMMER LOHNT SICH NICHT (Love problems aren't worthwhile) *Metronome* [*Germany*]. Siv Malmquist's disc was No 1 in the German charts for 11 weeks in 1964, after running away with first prize in the German Pop Music Festival

in Baden Baden (13 July 1964). It sold 100,000 in a fortnight, and 880,000 in a year with an estimated million in Germany by the end of 1965. The song was written by Christian Bruhn and Georg Buschor, who also wrote the winning Festival song in 1962.

Siv Malmquist (Siw Malmkvist) was born in Landskrona, Sweden, on 31 December 1936 and made her debut on records for Metronome of Sweden in 1955 with 'Tweedle Dee'. She is also an actress and made films in Denmark. At the end of 1961, she was on the stage in Turku, Finland, in *Irma la Douce* and appeared later in other musicals. She made many tours in European countries and has been seen on TV all over Europe. Siv has recorded in Swedish, Danish, Norwegian, German, English, French and Dutch and in 1961 was introduced on records in the U.S.A. as 'the girl from Sweden'.

MANFRED MANN AND THE MANFREDS
DO WAH DIDDY DIDDY *H.M.V.* [*Britain*]. This number was written in 1963 by the Americans Jeff Barry and Ellie Greenwich. Manfred's disc sold 650,000 in Britain and over 750,000 in the U.S.A. on the Ascot label. It was also said to have sold one million on the Continent, mainly in Germany on the Electrola label. This disc was No 1 in Britain for two weeks with 14 weeks in the bestsellers, and in the U.S.A. for two weeks with 13 weeks in the bestsellers. Manfred Mann, real name Manfred Lubowitz, was born on 21 October 1940 in Johannesburg, and played in a coffee bar there for a while. He was educated in his native town, and musically at the famed Juilliard School of Music, New York, and Vienna State Academy. He plays the piano and organ. Mike Hugg (drums, vibes and piano) met Manfred at Butlin's holiday camp. They teamed as The Blues Brothers, progressing from jazz to rhythm-and-blues with the group they formed together. Mike Hugg was born 11 August 1942 in Andover, Hampshire. Tom McGuiness was born 2 December 1941 in Wimbledon, London. He joined the group in May 1964, and played the guitar, and bass guitar. He played with many groups before joining Manfred and had been interested in music for several years. Paul Jones (born 24 February 1942 in Portsmouth) was educated at Oxford University, and played the harmonica. Michael Vickers (born 18 April 1941 in Southampton) played the alto sax, guitar, flute, clarinet and piano. The group first became popular with their (1964) recording of '5-4-3-2-1', and 'Hubble Bubble (Toil and Trouble)'. Then came this sensational disc 'Do Wah Diddy Diddy' to make them well known on both sides of the Atlantic. They toured Australia, New Zealand and the Far East.

SHA LA LA *H.M.V.* [*Britain*]. The second million seller globally for Manfred Mann is a version of the song that was successful earlier for the Shirelles, written by Robert Mosley and Robert Taylor. It was No 3 in Britain and 12 weeks in the bestsellers, and No 12 in the U.S.A. with 12 weeks in their bestsellers, on the Ascot label, with big sales in both countries and elsewhere.

MARTHA AND THE VANDELLAS (pop, ballad and rhythm-and-blues vocal trio)
DANCING IN THE STREET *Gordy* [*USA*]. The second estimated million seller for this trio, the song written by disc artist Marvin Gaye and William Stevenson. It achieved the No 2 position in the U.S. charts for two weeks and 14 weeks in the bestsellers.

Betty Kelly, born 16 September 1944, replaced Annette Beard on this disc. Released 22 August 1964.

DEAN MARTIN, WITH ACCOMPANIMENT DIRECTED BY ERNIE FREEMAN
EVERYBODY LOVES SOMEBODY *Reprise* [*USA*]. This song was written in 1948 by Irving Taylor (words) and Ken Lane (music), and first recorded by Sinatra. This version sold a million

in the U.S.A. and was No 1 for one week and 15 weeks in the bestsellers. This was Dean's fifth million seller, and constituted a major comeback for him. It was No 11 for two weeks in Britain and 13 weeks in the bestsellers. Gold Disc award, R.I.A.A., 1964.

Subsequent research revealed music actually written by Sam Coslow, though attributed to Ken Lane.

ROGER MILLER
DANG ME *Smash* [*USA*]. The first million seller for country-and-western singer Roger Miller was his own composition and his first recording for the Smash label.

Roger Dean Miller was born on 2 January 1936 in Fort Worth, Texas. After his father died, he was raised in Erick, Oklahoma, by an uncle on a farm. At school, he was influenced by Hank Williams' singing and determined to go into show business. He saved to buy a guitar, started writing songs and earned prize money to get a violin. He spent three years in the U.S. Army in Korea as a driver, then on discharge was a page-boy at the Andrew Jackson Hotel in Nashville. One night a disc executive heard him singing one of his own compositions and Roger got a disc contract. His first three records didn't sell. Columbia's Ray Price wanted a comedian-singer for his travelling show and hired Roger, also recording Roger's song, 'Invitation to the Blues', which was quite a big hit. He then joined country-and-western star Faron Young as a drummer in 1962 and started singing again. That year, Tennessee Ernie Ford booked him as a guest on his TV show, and Roger built a big following with his fast-paced wit, great ad-libbing capabilities and singing. Then in 1964 came 'Dang Me', with an earthy, humorous lyric, infectious melody and compelling rhythm. Smash recorded 25 songs on two albums, all but one of them his own, which included this song and another 'goofy' number 'Chug-A-Lug', both of which were released as singles. Roger, whose parents were very poor, has not allowed life's misfortunes to get the better of him. They have in fact given him a most valuable sense of humour which spills out in his conversation as well as his songs. He also plays bass and mandolin in addition to violin and guitar. 'Dang Me' won three Grammy Awards for the best Country-and-Western performance, single disc and song of 1964 in the U.S.A. It got to No 7 in the U.S. charts with 11 weeks in the bestsellers, and was a top country-and-western disc.

CHUG-A-LUG *Smash* [*USA*]. The second million seller for Roger Miller was also his own composition reaching No 6 in the U.S. charts and 13 weeks in the bestsellers.

MILLIE (with accompaniment directed by Harry Robinson)
MY BOY LOLLIPOP *Fontana* [*Britain*]. This song was written in 1956 by Robert Spencer and Johnny Roberts. It sold over 600,000 in Britain (where it reached No 2 with 18 weeks in the bestsellers) and nearly a million on the Smash label in the U.S.A. where it reached No 2 with 12 weeks in the bestsellers. Millicent 'Dolly May' Small was born on 6 October 1948 in the parish of Clarendon, Jamaica. She started to take an interest in music at nine, and at 12 won a talent contest in Kingston, with a recording test as a prize. Her first disc 'We'll Meet' (Island label) was No 1 there in six weeks and she became a big attraction in Jamaica. Further discs followed, with stage producers and cabaret managers vying for her services. Chris Blackwell who ran the disc firm which released West Indian music on Island discs in England went to Jamaica to find out about Millie. He signed her up and brought her back and introduced her work to artists and repertoire manager Jack Baverstock of Fontana Records. This completely changed little Millie's life. They got her to make her first disc 'Don't You Know' (1963), then came 'My Boy Lollipop' which Millie gave out with her native 'Ska' style, or 'Bluebeat' as it became known. Millie is in fact called 'Queen of the Bluebeat'. Millie was enrolled at the Italia Conti Stage School to study dancing and diction soon after her arrival in Britain. In 1964 she became a great favourite with her bubbling explosive personality

and powerful voice, appearing on radio, TV and at concerts around Britain.

Global sale of the disc – 3¾ million by 1969.

HARUO MINAMI
TOKYO GORIN ONDO (Tokyo Olympic Song) *Teichiku* [*Japan*]. This was written for the Olympic Games in Tokyo, 1964, by Takashi Miyata (words) and Masao Koga (music). The disc sold over 1,300,000, and was No 1 in Japan for 16 weeks.

THE MOODY BLUES
GO NOW *Decca* [*Britain*]. This group had great success in a short space of time. They are five young men: Denny Laine (real name Brian Hines), born 29 October 1944 in a boat off the Jersey coast; Mike Pinder, born 27 December 1942, Birmingham; Graham Edge, born 30 March 1942, Rochester, Staffordshire; Ray Thomas, born 29 December 1942, Stourport-on-Severn; and Clint Warwick (real name Clinton Eccles), born 25 June 1949, Birmingham.

Denny Laine, lead singer and lead guitarist, originally fronted a top Birmingham group, The Diplomats. He also plays the ukulele, piano, organ, guitar and bass player, originally played with The Crew Cats in Hamburg and Hanover. Graham Edge, the drummer played with three different groups in Birmingham. Ray Thomas plays the harmonica. He also played with several groups, notably El Riot and The Rebels who worked with The Beatles on TV. Clint Warwick, bass guitarist, played with The Rainbows at Ayr.

With rhythm-and-blues so popular on the music scene, Denny Laine formed The Moody Blues who achieved fantastic success

in Birmingham within a few months. They then came to London's Marquee Club and their initial performance established them as one of Britain's best groups, with subsequent radio, TV and personal appearances. Their first disc was 'Lose Your Money', then came 'Go Now' which was No 1 in Britain for two weeks with 14 weeks in the bestsellers and sold over 250,000. The disc was No 10 in the U.S.A. and 14 weeks in the bestsellers on the London label, a big success there, bringing the global sale to an estimated million. The song was written in 1963 by Larry Banks and Milton Bennett, a romantic heartbreak song performed by The Moody Blues in a fascinating rock'n'roll-waltz-like manner. Denny Laine subsequently joined Paul McCartney's group Wings.

GIANNI MORANDI
IN GINOCCHIO DA TE (On My Knees to You) *RCA* [*Italy*]. Gianni Morandi, a singer of extraordinary talent, revealed himself as one of the top artists of 1964. Singing this song, with which he won the Cantagiro Summer Song Contest, he topped the Italian charts for 14 weeks, the longest stay at No 1. By March 1966 the disc had sold almost 750,000 and the million was reported in 1968. Song written by Franco Migliacci and Bruno Zambrini.

NON SON DEGNA DI TE (Not Good Enough for You) *RCA* [*Italy*]. Gianni Morandi's follow-up song was as big a success as his former hit. This was introduced in and won the Festival Delle Rose, a televised show in Rome, in October 1964 and sung by him. It was a chart topper for many weeks, the disc selling over 825,000 by March 1966, with the million reported by 1968. Song written by Franco Migliacci and Bruno Zambrini.

THE NEWBEATS
BREAD AND BUTTER *Hickory* [*USA*]. This trio consists of Dean (Louis Al) Mathis, born 17 March 1939; his brother Mark (Marcus F.) Mathis, born 9 February 1942 – birthplace of both was Hahira, Georgia – and Larry Henley, born 30 June 1941 in Arp, Texas.

Their mother taught Dean and Mark the guitar as children, but they soon mastered other instruments – the piano, bass and drums. They both played in the band at Bremen High School, Georgia, where they were educated. They decided on a show business career on leaving school. Dean joined Paul Howard's 'Western Swing Band' in 1956 as pianist, then joined Dale Hopkins' band where his brother Mark joined on bass. They stayed with this band for two years and then recorded 'Tell Him No' as a duo for the Chess label. They then started their own eight-piece band and played in their home town of Shreveport, Louisiana. It was here that Larry first met Dean and Mark when he came up from the audience and asked to sing with the band, his first public appearance. The audience were so enthusiastic that he was asked to join the band. After a time they went separate ways, Larry as solo artist, Mark and David as a duo, all recording independently for Wesley Rose. After about 18 months, they met again and made a demonstration disc of 'Bread and Butter' together, sent it to Wesley Rose (Hickory Records) who asked them to record it for the label. The trio did so under the name of The Newbeats. When issued it soon shot up the U.S. charts, reaching No 2 for two weeks and 12 weeks in the bestsellers, and was also a hit later in Britain where they appeared in 1964, reaching No 15. The song was written by Larry Parks and Jay Turnbow.

ROY ORBISON
OH PRETTY WOMAN *Monument* [*USA*]. Roy's eleventh million seller was written by him with the help of Bill Dees. It sold a million in the U.S.A. and 680,000 in Britain, 350,000 in Germany and 180,000 in Canada. This disc was the first for many months to gain No 1 chart position for three weeks simultaneously in Britain (where it was 18 weeks in the bestsellers) and America, where it was 15 weeks in the bestsellers. Global sale estimated at 4 million. Gold Disc award R.I.A.A. 1964.

IT'S OVER *Monument* [*USA*]. Another global estimated million seller (Roy's twelfth) was written again by him and Bill Dees. The disc got to No 9 in the U.S. charts with 11 weeks in the bestsellers and was No 1 in Britain for two weeks (and 18 weeks in the bestsellers) where it sold well over quarter of a million. Roy appeared on TV in Britain in 1964 and proved highly popular.

JOHNNY PEARSON (piano) AND SOUNDS ORCHESTRAL (pop concert orchestra)
CAST YOUR FATE TO THE WIND *Piccadilly* [*Britain*]. Written in 1960 this tune composed by Vince Guaraldi and Frank Werber (words) was a big success in the U.S.A. for modern jazz pianist Guaraldi and his Trio at that time. It was brought to the attention of Piccadilly Records who had been looking for material to create something orchestral, but at the same time totally different from most orchestral pieces and still within commercial boundaries. The disc, a quiet off-beat arrangement, features the brilliant piano playing of Britain's Johnny Pearson.

Sales started quietly at first but the disc eventually got to No 5 in Britain's charts in 1965 with 16 weeks in the bestsellers and sold well over 250,000. Issued on the Parkway label in the U.S.A. it got to No 9 in their charts and sold a million globally. It firmly established a new concept in orchestral sound.

Johnny Pearson (born 18 June 1925 in Plaistow, London) started to learn the piano at the age of seven, and when he was nine won a scholarship to the London Academy of Music, where he studied for four years with the great classical concert pianist Solomon. This enabled him to develop a formidable piano technique, and he was giving recitals and concerts at London's Westminster Central Hall before he was 12. As a teenager he started on a new career from the classics to jazz, was a semi-professional musician at 16, and later formed his own group, The Rhythm Makers. Then came Army service, in which he became pianist and drummer in the Royal Artillery Band. After demobilization, Johnny worked at TV audition studios, and in 1948 became founder member of the well-known Malcolm Mitchell Trio that toured the Continent and later played West End clubs. He began broadcasting and made some TV appearances with subsequent provincial tours and music hall engagements all over Britain. The trio disbanded in 1954, and Johnny then worked with many stars including Lena Horne, Vanessa Lee, Shirley Bassey, Connie Francis and subsequently Cilla Black (1964) in recordings, on stage and in cabaret. BBC producer Johnnie Stewart was greatly impressed by his piano technique and Johnny became soloist every week with the famed Peter Yorke Concert Orchestra on radio. He took an intense interest in arranging and proved himself in all spheres of music as solo pianist, conductor, arranger and composer. Pearson became musical director for the long-running BBC radio series 'Music for Sweethearts'; then 'Swingalong' as pianist and arranger, the star spot in radio's 'Younger than Springtime'; and 'The Johnny Pearson Show'. He started recording in his own right. He has written signature tunes and incidental music for several TV series and conducted orchestras for many top TV shows.

PETER AND GORDON
WORLD WITHOUT LOVE *Columbia* [*Britain*]. The first million seller for this duo sold 550,000 in Britain and over 400,000 in the U.S.A., as well as sales from other countries. The disc was No 1 in Britain for two weeks (with 14 weeks in the bestsellers) and for one week in the U.S.A. with 12 weeks in the bestsellers. It was released on the Capitol label in the States. Peter Asher (born 22 June 1944 in London) and Gordon Trueman Riviere Waller (born 4 June 1945, Braemar, Scotland) first met at boarding school in 1959. They both had piano tuition, and Peter also plays the guitar and double bass and Gordon the guitar. They began playing the guitar and singing together, performing at school concerts and eventually at local coffee bars. During a two-month booking at London's Pickwick Club, they were brought to the attention of EMI Records who sent an artists and repertoire man to hear them. Next day they were summoned to EMI to record one of their own songs 'If I Were You'. But a strong number was needed for the reverse side of the disc. The duo then remembered that Beatles John Lennon and Paul McCartney had written a song for them which was not completed, 'World Without Love'. When finished it turned out to be a big hit for all concerned. The duo then did radio, TV and personal appearances in Britain; Peter also appearing in such TV productions as 'Robin Hood' and 'Sword of Freedom'. They also went to the U.S.A. in 1964 and did a long tour, becoming extremely popular there. Asher later became a prominent producer in the U.S.A.

NOBODY I KNOW *Columbia* [*Britain*]. The second million seller for Peter and Gordon was also written by The Beatles' John Lennon and Paul McCartney. It was No 12 and nine weeks in the U.S. bestsellers, and No 10 and 11 weeks in Britain's bestsellers.

PETER, PAUL AND MARY

IN CONCERT (album) *Warner* [*USA*]. Another big success for the famous folk trio, with a Gold Disc award from R.I.A.A. on 21 January 1965. A million unit sale gave them a Platinum Disc award in December 1973, making this their fourth million-seller album. Contents of the album: 'The Times They Are A-Changin'', by Bob Dylan (1963); 'A-soulin'', by Paul Stookey; '500 Miles', by Hedy West, Bobby Bare and Charlie Williams (1962); 'Blue', by Peter Yarrow, Paul Stookey and Mary Travers; 'Three Ravens', by Yarrow, Stookey, Travers and Okun; 'One Kind Favor', by Yarrow, Stookey and Travers; 'Blowin' in the Wind', by Bob Dylan (1962); 'Car, Car', by Woody Guthrie; 'Puff, the Magic Dragon', by Leonard Lipton and Peter Yarrow (1963); 'Jesus Met the Woman', traditional, arranged by Yarrow, Travers and Okun.

ELVIS PRESLEY

VIVA LAS VEGAS *Victor* [*USA*]. From Elvis' film of the same title and written by Doc Pomus and Mort Shuman this disc rapidly became a million seller globally. It was the 46th Golden Disc for Presley, and got to No 16 in the U.S.A. with 7 weeks in the bestsellers. It reached No 16 in Britain with 12 weeks in the bestsellers.

KISSIN' COUSINS *Victor* [*USA*]. From Elvis' film of the same title and written by Fred Wise and Randy Starr the disc likewise became a million seller globally, and the 47th such success for Elvis. It was No 10 in the U.S.A. and 9 weeks in the bestsellers. It reached No 9 in Britain with 11 weeks in the bestsellers.

AIN'T THAT LOVIN' YOU BABY *Victor* [*USA*]. This song, written by Clyde Otis and Ivory Joe Hunter in 1958, was originally recorded that year in Nashville, Tennessee. With the Midas touch of Presley, it became his 48th million seller, the disc getting to No 13 for two weeks in the U.S.A. and 10 weeks in the bestsellers. It was No 14 in Britain with 8 weeks in the bestsellers.

JIM REEVES

I LOVE YOU BECAUSE *Victor* [*USA*]. This song by blind composer Leon Payne (1949) had originally been a big hit for Al Martino in 1963 in the U.S.A. It was Jim Reeves' version that was the big hit in Britain when released by RCA-Victor in 1964 making over 860,000 sales. This disc was Reeves' fifth million seller globally. It was No 5 in Britain with 39 weeks in the bestsellers.

I WON'T FORGET YOU *Victor* [USA]. This sixth million seller for Jim Reeves was written by Harlan Howard in 1962 in which year it was first recorded on the album 'The Country Side of Jim Reeves'. The single was issued in Britain just after Jim's tragic death in a plane accident and sold 750,000 in Britain alone, reaching No 3 with 26 weeks in the bestsellers.

THE RIGHTEOUS BROTHERS

YOU'VE LOST THAT LOVIN' FEELIN' *Philles* [*USA*]. This disc was No 1 in both the U.S.A. (with 16 weeks in the bestsellers) and Britain (with 10 weeks in the bestsellers) for two weeks simultaneously in February 1965. It was released in the U.S.A. in late 1964, and was written by Phil Spector (of Philles Records) and the husband-and-wife team Barry Mann and Cynthia Weill. The disc was released on the London label in Britain and the combined sales from both countries took it well over the million by early 1965.

The Righteous Brothers are not brothers at all. The duo consists of Bill Medley, born 19 September 1940 in Los Angeles, and Bobby Hatfield, born 10 April 1940 at Beaver Dam, Wisconsin. Bill, who also plays the piano and bass guitar, is a fine songwriter. Before they teamed up in 1963, they both had follow-ings as solo performers in Southern California. Their first hit was 'Little Latin Lupe Lu' (written by Bill).

JOHNNY RIVERS

MEMPHIS *Imperial* [*USA*]. This song was written in 1959 by famous Chuck Berry and Johnny's disc rocketed him to fame in the U.S.A., reaching No 2 in their charts for two weeks with 12 weeks in the bestsellers. His swift rise to stardom, however, cannot be called an overnight success. He was born in New York City on 7 November 1943, the family moving to Baton Rouge, Louisiana, when Johnny was three. His father was a housepainter and the family were exceedingly poor. Johnny picked up guitar playing and singing when quite young, obviously influenced by his father who played guitar and mandolin. The summers of his teenage years were spent in New York and Nashville pursuing a musical career. His first musical inspiration can be attributed to Fats Domino, B. B. King, Ray Charles and other great classical blues singers. He soon became popular locally with a large following, and became a fine songwriter. His innumerable hits included 'I'll Make Believe' for Ricky Nelson in 1958.

After completing school he settled in Nashville briefly, then moved to New York and Los Angeles where, in 1960, he decided to give up performing and produce records for other vocalists, singing and writing occasionally to earn money to produce another disc. In 1963 he was enticed from his studios to fill in at Hollywood's Whiskey à Go-Go as a favour to a friend. This was a great triumph and resulted in his album, 'Johnny Rivers at the Whiskey à Go-Go', being in the bestsellers charts for 45 weeks from June 1964.

During 1964, Johnny had offers from every top club in the U.S.A., including The Sands and Flamingo in Las Vegas and Mr Kelly's in Chicago, as well as offers from all the major TV shows such as Ed Sullivan, Jimmy Dean and Jack Paar, etc.

In addition to being a fine songwriter and performer, Johnny formed his own label – Soul City. He also arranges, and is, in fact, the complete musician.

Johnny also has his own music publishing company dealing with the works of outstanding new songwriters such as Jim Webb ('Up, Up and Away', 'By the Time I Get to Phoenix'). His greatest interest is producing records, working with and creating new sounds.

JULIE ROGERS WITH THE JOHNNY ARTHEY ORCHESTRA AND CHORUS

THE WEDDING (La Novia) *Mercury* [*Britain*]. This song, originally published in 1960 in Argentina as 'La Novia', was written by Joaquin Prieto. The English lyrics were written by Fred Jay. It had previously been a success in 1961 for both Anita Bryant and Malcolm Vaughan, but this was the disc which proved the top seller. Julie Rogers' version sold well over the quarter million in Britain and many more in the U.S.A. on Mercury label. By 1972 it was reported to have sold 7 million.

Julie (real name Julie Rolls) was born in Bermondsey, London, on 6 April 1943. She took piano lessons as a child and started her career after schooling at the age of 16. While on holiday in Spain, she and a girl friend applied for jobs as dancers and to their surprise were hired. Nine months later they were back in England. Julie then became a secretary and did one trip as a stewardess on a ship to Africa. She then auditioned for bandleader Teddy Foster who booked her to sing with his band. Then came cabaret dates in London with Foster as a duo. It was during these that she was heard by artists and repertoire director Johnny Franz and she recorded 'It's Magic' after he had signed her to a disc contract. Then came the disc of 'The Wedding', a song Julie had remembered in its original Spanish version of four years previously. Julie's disc also sparked off the sale of the sheet music which was the bestseller of 1964. Her TV debut was on Southern TV's 'Day by Day', and her radio debut in 1962 on 'Music with a Beat'. This disc was No 10 in the U.S.A. for two weeks with 11 weeks in the bestsellers, and No 3 in Britain for two weeks with 23 weeks in the bestsellers.

THE ROLLING STONES

IT'S ALL OVER NOW *Decca* [*Britain*] *London* [*USA*]. Written by B. and S. Womach, this song was a success firstly (1964) for the U.S. group, The Valentinos. The Rolling Stones' cover version is described as 'an infectious thumper' and got to No 1 in the British charts for one week and 15 weeks in the bestsellers. It was also a success in the U.S.A. in 1964 when the group appeared there, reaching No 25 with 10 weeks in the bestsellers. Sales reached a global million by the end of 1966. (See 1965 for Rolling Stones biography.)

TIME IS ON MY SIDE *Decca* [*Britain*] *London* [*USA*]. This was originally included in the Rolling Stones' album 'The Rolling Stones – No 2' on Decca in Britain, but when released as a single in the U.S.A., proved to be a big hit there, reaching No 6 in their charts for three weeks and 13 weeks in the bestsellers. Global sale of a million by 1966. The song is a pulsating blues number, written by Norman Meade (pseudonym of Jerry Ragovoy) in 1963.

RONNY AND THE DAYTONAS

G.T.O. *Mala* [*USA*]. In addition to the surfing craze in the U.S.A., the younger generation had a craze for 'hot rods' or 'stock cars' with souped-up engines for racing. 'G.T.O.' was the first big hit in hot-rod music, and it established this group's reputation.

Ronny Dayton, leader of the group, was born in Tulsa, Oklahoma, on 26 April 1946. The Daytonas consist of his close musical friends Lynn Williams (drums); Johnny Johnson (guitar); and Van Evans (bass).

When Ronny was 11 and living in Nashville, he had already had three years' guitar tuition. In his early teens he entered local talent shows and this decided him to pursue a musical career. He then formed his group and called them The Daytonas.

'G.T.O.' is the composition of John Wilkin. The disc got to No 4 in the U.S. charts with 13 weeks in the bestsellers, and is estimated to have sold an eventual million.

THE SEARCHERS

NEEDLES AND PINS *Pye* [*Britain*]. This disc was No 1 for three weeks in Britain (with 15 weeks in the bestsellers) and such a hit in the U.S.A. that global million sales were reached by April 1964. There it reached No 12 with 10 weeks in the U.S.A. bestsellers. 'Needles and Pins' was issued on the Kapp label in the U.S.A. The song was written by Americans Jack Nitzsche and Sonny Bono (later of Sonny and Cher; see 1965) in 1963.

Personnel of the group are: Chris Curtis (born 16 August 1941, Oldham, Lancashire); Mike Pender (born 3 March 1942, Liverpool); John McNally (born 30 August 1941, Liverpool); and Tony Jackson (born 16 July 1940, Liverpool). Instruments played are: Chris (piano, guitar, drums); Mike (violin, piano, drums, guitar); John (guitar, harmonica); Tony (bass guitar). Chris, Mike and John all met while at school. The group was founded by John in Liverpool in 1960 and became the backing group for the Liverpool singer Johnny Sandon, but left him to branch out as The Searchers, taking their name from the John Wayne film. They made appearances in Liverpool and the north-west, and appeared at Hamburg's Star Club. In 1963, Pye recording manager Tony Hatch was told about the group, visited Liverpool and signed them to a disc contract. Their first disc 'Sweets for My Sweet' was a big hit. 'Sugar and Spice' another hit followed, then came 'Needles and Pins'. In one year they achieved recognition as one of the top beat groups in Britain, and later appeared on tour with Roy Orbison, Tommy Roe, Bobby Rydell and other disc stars. During 1964 they visited America, New Zealand, Australia, Hong Kong, toured Britain and appeared on radio and TV numerous times. The Searchers became one of the best-known names on the beat scene in Britain and America, and with a big following globally. Tony Jackson left in 1964 to form his own group, and was replaced by an old friend of The Searchers, Frank Allen (born 14 December 1943 in Hayes, Middlesex), who also plays bass guitar and sings. The Searchers' earnings in 1964 were estimated at around £150,000.

THE SHANGRI-LAS

REMEMBER (Walkin' in the sand) *Red Bird* [*USA*]. The Shangri-Las – Mary Ann and Margie Ganser (twins) and Betty and Mary Weiss (sisters) – started singing together while at Andrew Jackson High School in Queens, New York, around the beginning of 1964. The idea (and the song itself for the disc) came from George (Shadow) Morton, who discovered the group. He got them to make a demonstration disc for presentation to Artie Ripp, of Kama Sutra Productions. Ripp played this to writers Jeff Barry and Ellie Greenwich, and the trio decided to produce the final master. This they took to George Goldner, head of Red Bird Records, with the Shangri-Las being immediately signed to a long-term contract. George Morton, a producer for Red Bird, included the cries of seagulls to the disc to add atmosphere to the seashore locale of the song, which is a haunting plaintive love song with an off-beat rapidly changing hard-shuffling measure. The disc was No 5 for five weeks in the U.S.A. and 11 weeks in the bestsellers, and also a hit in Britain where it reached No 14 (with 13 weeks in the bestsellers), when the group visited in early 1965 and also toured Europe. Their very first disc is estimated to have sold well over a global million. They were still attending school when the disc was made, and later appeared on many top TV shows.

LEADER OF THE PACK *Red Bird* [*USA*]. The second global million seller for the Shangri-Las was also written by George (Shadow) Morton, Ellie Greenwich and Jeff Barry. The song is a heartbreaking number about a girl in love with the leader of a motorcycle gang, of her parents' disapproval, and how he loses his life in a crash. Sounds of motorcycle engines and screaming tyres gave the disc an extremely realistic backing. The disc was No 1 in all the U.S. charts for one week with 14 weeks in the bestsellers, and it was also a big seller in Britain where it got to No 11 for 2 weeks. It was reissued in Britain in 1972 and reached No 3. Subsequent reissues 1974 and 1976 gave it a total of 44 weeks in the British charts.

DEL SHANNON

KEEP SEARCHIN' *Amy* [*USA*]. The third million seller, globally, for Del was his own composition. It was a hit in the U.S.A. (No 9 in the charts with 14 weeks in the bestsellers) and in Britain (No 3 in the charts with 11 weeks in the bestsellers).

BOBBY SOLO WITH THE GIANNIN MARCHETTI ORCHESTRA

UNA LACRIMA SUL VISO (A Tear on Your Face) *Ricordi* [*Italy*]. Bobby Solo's disc of this song, written by 'Mogol' (Giulio Rappetti) (words) and Lunero (music), was the first disc to sell

one million in Italy. Six hundred thousand of these were sold within 10 days of its release, and the total sale was 3 million. This was the top sale in the history of the Italian record market for a singles disc. Bobby was born in 1946. In June 1963, he entered the 'Ribalta per San Remo' – a competition to find new talent – which he won, and was immediately signed to a recording contract to wax the contest song 'Ora che sei gia una donna', following up with 'Blue e blue'/'Marrone'. As winner of that talent competition he automatically qualified to appear at the San Remo Song Festival in February 1964, and it was there that he first sang 'Una lacrima sul viso' (A tear on your face). The song did not win the contest but can be considered the real winner in so far as overall popularity is concerned. It can also be termed the greatest song to come from any San Remo event. After the success of his disc, he made a film of the same title. This disc was No 1 in Italy for nine weeks.

TERRY STAFFORD

SUSPICION *Crusader* [*USA*]. Terry Stafford was born and educated in Amarillo, Texas, and started singing the songs of his two idols, Elvis Presley and Buddy Holly, at school dances. With the help of his mother, he went to Hollywood and, after two years of playing nightclubs and record hops, was heard by John Fisher and Les Worden, executives of the newly-formed Crusader Record Company. They rushed him to a studio where he recorded 'Suspicion', a song previously recorded by Elvis Presley. It reached No 3 for 2 weeks in the U.S. charts, the runner-up position to The Beatles who were at Nos 1 and 2 at that time and had nine weeks in the British bestsellers. Terry's disc stayed in the charts for 15 weeks and the million sale was reported in 1970. It was No 31 in Britain. The disc was released in February 1964 and the song written by Doc Pomus and Mort Shuman in 1962.

Terry, a sports enthusiast, earned letters in basketball, baseball and football, in addition to awards for water skiing and horseback riding. A tall Texan, he stands at 6 feet 3 inches. In 1970 he signed with MGM Records.

LUCILLE STARR

THE FRENCH SONG *Almo* [*USA*] *Barry* [*Canada*]. Lucille Starr, otherwise known as Fern Regan, and her husband Rob Regan (Robert Frederickson) are called the 'Canadian Sweethearts' in their act. The song was written by Lucille a few years ago and she first recorded it for a small Canadian label – Rodeo Records. In 1964 she recorded it for Almo (a label of A & M Records, Hollywood, and owned by the famous bandleader Herb Alpert with partner Jerry Moss) and this was released on the Barry label in Canada, a subsidiary of Quality Records. Lucille's disc, sung in both English and French, soon topped the Canadian charts, and together with the U.S. sales sold a million. It made her the first Canadian artiste to do so. In the U.S.A. it reached No 54 with 8 weeks in the bestsellers. In 1965, the disc was also very popular in Europe.

Lucille was born and raised in St Boniface, Manitoba.

THE SUPREMES

WHERE DID OUR LOVE GO? *Motown* [*USA*]. The first million seller for this coloured female trio was written by Brian Holland, Eddie Holland and Lamont Dozier. The disc was No 1 for two weeks in the U.S.A. with 14 weeks in the bestsellers. The trio was Diana Ross, born 26 March 1944 in Detroit; Mary Wilson, born 6 March 1944 in Mississippi; and Florence Ballard, born 30 June 1943 in Detroit. All were close friends from childhood days in Detroit. In their last year at school they won a talent contest which brought them to the notice of Motown Records. They were signed to the label and made their first disc 'I Want a Guy'. Then came this big hit and subsequent personal appearances in New York, Washington and elsewhere. They appeared on British radio and TV in late 1964 with great success. They

are the only girl group to have eleven discs at No 1 in the U.S.A. (by 1968). It was No 3 in Britain with 14 weeks in the bestsellers.

BABY LOVE *Motown* [*USA*]. The second million seller for The Supremes was also written by Brian Holland, Eddie Holland and Lamont Dozier. It was No 1 for three weeks in the U.S.A. with 13 weeks in the bestsellers, and for two weeks in Britain (on Stateside label) with 15 weeks in the bestsellers. The sales in Britain were over a quarter of a million. A top rhythm-and-blues disc.

COME SEE ABOUT ME *Motown* [*USA*]. The third million seller for The Supremes was yet another song by the team of Brian Holland, Eddie Holland and Lamont Dozier. It was No 1 for one week in the U.S.A. with 14 weeks in the bestsellers, and reached the million sale in early 1965. It was No 27 in Britain.

JOE TEX (rhythm-and-blues vocalist)

HOLD WHAT YOU'VE GOT *Dial* [*USA*]. Joe Tex (Joseph Arrington, Jr.) was born on 8 August 1936 in Baytown, Texas, and received musical training throughout his high school days there. His first step toward fame came in 1954 when he won an amateur talent contest in Baytown, the prize being a two-week expenses-paid trip to New York. Here he entered an amateur show at the Apollo, and took another first prize. He soon returned to that theatre on a fee basis and stayed there for four weeks. Apart from his vocal talents, Joe is a prolific songwriter and has penned several hundred songs, including 'Hold What You've Got'. Many have been recorded by famous disc stars including James Brown, Ernie K-Doe and Jerry Butler.

This disc was a hit in early 1965, achieving the No 5 chart position in the U.S.A. with 11 weeks in the bestsellers, and sold the million by 1966. A top rhythm-and-blues seller.

Joe appeared on TV, radio and club dates in Britain in December 1965, after successful personal appearances in the U.S.A.

His early church training is evident in his emotional 'soul' performances of a semi-'preaching' style.

THE VENTURES

WALK – DON'T RUN '64 *Dolton* [*USA*]. This up-dated version of The Ventures' 1960 hit 'Walk - Don't Run', written by John H. Smith, Jr. and performed with a far more subtle relaxed feeling, reached No 8 for 2 weeks in the U.S.A. and earned the group and song a second Gold Disc for a million sale, and brought their total of million sellers to three. This disc was recorded in July 1964.

The Ventures sold 20 million records in the U.S.A. and a further 10 million in Japan where they became immensely popular. By 1970 they had made 38 albums, and Don Wilson and Bob Bogle were still with the group. The original drummer Howie Johnson retired from music after an auto accident, and was replaced by Mel Taylor from New York some time after this disc was made. Nokie Edwards, the original guitarist, left in 1967 and was replaced by Jerry McGee, a noted guitarist, and an organist, Johnny Durrill from Houston (formerly with The Five Americans), was added in 1967. The group travelled more than a million miles in successful tours of Australia, Hawaii, Mexico and the Orient.

DIONNE WARWICK (arrangement and orchestra conducted by Burt Bacharach)

WALK ON BY *Scepter* [*USA*]. This second million seller globally for Dionne was another big hit for songwriters Hal David (words) and Burt Bacharach (music). The disc besides being high in the U.S. charts was also a great favourite in Britain and Europe. In the U.S.A. it was No 6 for 2 weeks with 13 weeks in the bestsellers. In Britain it was No 9 for 2 weeks and 14 weeks in the bestsellers. The song was written in 1963. A top rhythm-and-blues disc.

MARY WELLS

MY GUY *Motown* [*USA*]. The second million seller for Mary Wells was written for her by Motown's vice-president William 'Smokey' Robinson. The disc was No 1 for two weeks in the U.S.A. and 15 weeks in the bestsellers, and a top rhythm-and-blues seller. In Britain it reached No 3 with 14 weeks in the bestsellers. The disc was released in the U.S.A. on 4 April 1964.

J. FRANK WILSON AND THE CAVALIERS

LAST KISS *Josie* [*USA*]. This song, written in 1961 by Wayne Cochran, deals with a young man and his girl friend who become involved in an auto accident in which the girl is killed. It was somewhat prophetic for in October when the disc was at its highest (No 2) in the U.S. charts, the group's manager was killed in a road crash, and members of the group injured. J. Frank Wilson was born in 1941 in Lufkin, Texas, a lumber town. After graduation from high school there he joined the U.S. Air Force, and was stationed at San Angelo, Texas, where he became lead vocalist with the group called The Cavaliers. With them, he became No 1 attraction in that area at teenage dances. On discharge from the Forces, he decided to stay in show business but had a tough time for 18 months. Then in the spring of 1964 the independent producer Sonley Rush recorded some tunes with them. Major Bill Smith, an associate of their manager, took J. Frank Wilson's demonstration disc of 'Last Kiss' to Josie Records and it soon got into the charts. The disc was 15 weeks in the U.S. bestsellers, and sold a million by early 1965. The Cavaliers are Phil Trunzo from Geneva, New York; Jerry Graham from Flint, Michigan; Bobby Woods from Memphis and Gene Croyle from San Antonio.

THE ZOMBIES

SHE'S NOT THERE *Decca* [*Britain*]. The Zombies consists of Colin Blunstone (vocalist-guitarist) born 24 June 1945, Hatfield, Hertfordshire; Paul Atkinson (lead guitarist) born 19 March 1946, Cuffley, Hertfordshire; Rodney Argent (piano, organ, harmonica, clarinet and violin) born St Albans, Hertfordshire, 14

June 1945; Hugh Grundy (drums) born 6 March 1945, Winchester, Hampshire; and Chris Taylor White (bass, guitar and double bass) born Barnet, Hertfordshire, 7 March 1943.

The quintet were all classmates at St Alban's School, the group being founded by Rod, Hugh and Paul. They began by playing for local clubs and school dances, and were joined later by Chris and Colin. Rod and Paul were set for university, Chris for a teacher-training college. Hugh worked in a bank and Colin as an insurance broker. The group was in danger of breaking up, but after winning the *Evening News* Hearts Beat Competition their fortunes changed. Rod Argent then wrote 'She's Not There' and submitted a demonstration disc to Decca. On release it became a hit in Britain reaching No 12 for 2 weeks, with 11 weeks in the bestsellers. When released on the Parrott label in the U.S.A. it got to No 1 in their charts for one week with 15 weeks in the bestsellers. Many TV, nightclub, ballroom and stage appearances followed in Britain, with the disc estimated to have sold a global million.

The group was actually started in 1963, and with the success of this disc they decided to become professionals.

1965

VARIOUS COUNTRY-AND-WESTERN ARTISTS

FAMOUS ORIGINAL HITS (album) *CMA* (*Country Music Association*) [*USA*]. This unique disc bears the distinction of being the first album to sell over a million through mail orders only and without ever hitting the U.S. charts. The sale was achieved without the benefit of retail sales or newspaper and magazine advertisements. Advertising, in order to obviate high promotional costs on this $2 disc, was restricted to mail-order, radio and TV spots, amounting to one million of these from the time of release (27 September) for about a month, at a weekly rate of 7,000 on 300 TV and 35,000 on 500 radio stations, making it the largest radio-TV coverage ever known for a single record. Final sales of four million were anticipated in 18 months.

The disc, which features 25 of the top artists in country music, was sponsored by Martin Gilbert, a local Hollywood disc executive, for the foundation of a museum in the country music centre of Nashville. With the help of CMA director Roy Horton, the co-operation of Capitol, Columbia, Victor, Decca, Mercury, MGM, Hickory and Starday labels was solicited in borrowing material of their famous country artists - the labels, publishers and artists waiving their royalties to make the album possible. Martin Gilbert donated $25,000, and a guaranteed royalty of $85,000. In appreciation, CMA named a room in the Nashville museum after him. The building was officially opened on 31 March 1967.

The album contained the following: Roy Acuff, 'Wabash Cannonball'*, trad. arr. A. P. Carter (1942); Bill Anderson, 'Still', by Bill Anderson (1963); Eddy Arnold, 'Bouquet of Roses'*, by Steve Nelson and Bob Hilliard (1948); Bobby Bare, 'Detroit City'*, by Danny Dill and Mel Tillis (1963); Johnny Bond, 'Cimarron' (Roll on), by Johnny Bond (1942); Johnny Cash, 'I Walk the Line'*, by Johnny Cash (1956); Patsy Cline, 'I Fall to Pieces', by Harlan Howard and Hank Cochran (1961); Dave Dudley, 'Six Days on the Road', by Earl Green and Carl Montgomery (1963); Red Foley, 'Chattanooga Shoe Shine Boy'*, by Jack Stapp and Harry Stone (1950); Lefty Frizzell, 'If You've Got the Money', by Lefty Frizzell and Jim Beck (1950); Don Gibson, 'I Can't Stop Loving You'*, by Don Gibson (1958); Pee Wee King, 'Tennessee Waltz', by Pee Wee King and Red Stewart (1947); Roger Miller, 'You Don't Want My Love', by Roger Miller (1964); George Morton, 'Candy Kisses'*, by George Morgan (1948); Buck Owens, 'Act Naturally', by J. Russell and V. Morrison (1963); Ray Price, 'Heartaches by the Number', by Harlan Howard (1959); Jim Reeves, 'He'll Have to Go'*, by J. and A. Allison (1959); Tex Ritter, 'Rye Whiskey', trad. arr. J. Bond; Marty Robbins, 'Singing the Blues', by Melvin Endsley (1954); Hank Snow, 'I'm Movin' On'*, by Hank Snow (1950); Hank Thompson, 'Humpty Dumpty Heart'*, by Hank Thompson (1948); Merle Travis, 'So Round, So Firm, So Fully Packed', by Merle Travis, Cliffie Stone and Eddie Kirk (1947); Ernest Tubb, 'Walkin' the Floor Over You'*, by Ernest Tubb (1941); Kitty Wells, 'It Wasn't God Who Made Honky Tonk Angels'*, by J. D. Miller (1952); Hank Williams, 'Your Cheatin' Heart'*, by Hank Williams (1952).

Titles marked * were originally million seller discs for the artists concerned.

A second album was released in October 1966.

FILM SOUNDTRACK WITH JULIE ANDREWS, CHRISTOPHER PLUMMER, PEGGY WOOD, MARNI NIXON, DANIEL TRUHITTE AND THE SEVEN CHILDREN: CHARMIAN CARR, HEATHER MENZIES, NICHOLAS HAMMOND, DUANE CHASE, ANGELA CARTWRIGHT, DEBBIE TURNER, KYM KARATH; ORCHESTRA CONDUCTED BY IRWIN KOSTAL

'SOUND OF MUSIC' (album) *Victor* [*USA*]. This album, released in the U.S.A. on 2 March 1965, achieved Gold-Disc status faster than any other soundtrack in record history, selling the half million in the first two weeks of release. The initial pressing of a quarter million was quickly exhausted and re-orders poured in. According to *Time* magazine (23 December 1966) it had sold seven million, a sales record for all show or soundtrack albums with sales continuing globally. Britain alone sold two million (by October 1968) and there were big sales in Canada, Australia and Japan. It holds the record for the longest stay in Britain's charts at No 1 - 69 weeks. The album was No 1 in the U.S.A. for only two weeks in 1965 but stayed in the Top Ten there from May 1965 with the exception of a week or two right up to the end of May 1967. The film became one of the all-time moneymakers in film history, easily beating *Gone with the Wind* which grossed $41 million in U.S.-Canada rentals over a period of 27 years (1938-65). *The Sound of Music* achieved this figure in only 22 months on a reserved-seat basis in 53 cities.

The film, a superb adaptation of the stage musical of 1959 by the late Oscar Hammerstein II and Richard Rodgers, starred Julie Andrews and Christopher Plummer in the famous story of the Von Trapp family singers. This was another tremendous triumph for Julie Andrews immediately following her *Mary Poppins* film. Marni Nixon, whose voice was used for Audrey Hepburn's in *My Fair Lady*, Natalie Wood's in *West Side Story* and Deborah Kerr's in *The King and I*, made her first film appearance.

Sound of Music received five Academy Awards (1965) for Best Picture, Best Director, Best Film Editing, Best Sound and Best Scoring of Music.

This album was in the U.S. bestsellers chart for 198 weeks and in Britain for 362 weeks up to the end of 1973. Sales were then reported at around 14 million globally, and record world rentals for any film - around $150 million by 1 January 1969.

'Sound of Music' was the first stereo 8 tape cartridge to become a million-seller in the entire industry.

The contents of the disc: 'Prelude' (orchestra); 'Overture' (orchestra); 'Morning Hymn and Alleluia' (Nuns' chorus); 'Maria' (Marni Nixon, Peggy Wood and Nuns' quartet); *'I Have Confidence in Me' (Julie Andrews); *'Something Good' (Julie Andrews and Christopher Plummer); 'Sixteen Going on Seventeen' (Charmian Carr and Daniel Truhite); 'My Favourite Things' (Julie Andrews and Children); 'Climb Every Mountain' (Peggy Wood); 'Lonely Goatherd' (Julie Andrews); 'The Sound of Music' (Julie Andrews and Christopher Plummer); 'Do-Re-Mi' (Julie Andrews and Children); 'Processional' (orchestra); 'Edelweiss' (Christopher Plummer and Julie Andrews); 'So Long, Farewell' (The Children); 'Climb Every Mountain' (The Company).

Items marked * were specially written for the film version by Richard Rodgers, Hammerstein having died in 1960.

Gold Disc award, R.I.A.A., 1965.

JEWEL AKENS

THE BIRDS AND THE BEES *Era* [*USA*]. Jewel Akens, born in Texas in 1940, had a million seller with this his first recording, the song written by Herb Newman (of Era Records).

His unusual name came about because his mother wanted a daughter and liked the name so much that she retained it even when she had a son. Jewel is one of ten children, and began singing in the church when he was only 11 years old, and this early training undoubtedly accounts for his success. He can sing in a variety of styles - folk, gospel, rhythm-and-blues, rock'n'roll and ballad.

'Birds and the Bees' is a multi-voiced shuffle rock'n'roll recording. It got to No 2 in the U.S.A. for two weeks with 14 weeks in the bestsellers, and was No 29 in Britain.

HERB ALPERT (trumpet) AND THE TIJUANA BRASS

SOUTH OF THE BORDER (album) *A & M* [*USA*]. Another big success for Alpert, the disc issued in January 1965. It got to No 6 in the U.S. charts in 1966 and was awarded a Gold Disc by R.I.A.A., staying in the charts for 163 weeks. Sales by March 1966 were 770,000. It topped the million by the end of 1967.

Contents: 'South of the Border', by Jimmy Kennedy and Michael Carr (1939); 'The Girl from Ipanema', by Vincius de Moraes/Antonio Carlos Jobim (1963) (Eng. words by Norman Gimbel); 'Hello Dolly' (from stage musical), by Jerry Herman (1963); 'I've Grown Accustomed to Her Face' (from *My Fair Lady*), by A. J. Lerner/Frederic Loewe (1956); 'Up Cherry Street', by Julius Wechter (1964); 'Mexican Shuffle', by Sol Lake (1964); 'El Presidente', by Sol Lake (1964); 'All my Loving', by John Lennon and Paul McCartney (1963); 'Angelito', by Rene Herrera and Rene Ornellos (1964); 'Salud amor y dinero', by Sol Lake (1964); 'Numero cinco', by Ervan Coleman (1964); 'Adios, mi corazon', by Sol Lake (1964).

WHIPPED CREAM AND OTHER DELIGHTS (album) *A & M* [*USA*]. Issued in the U.S.A. in April 1965, this album sold 1,100,000 by the end of the year. It was No 1 for eight weeks in the U.S.A., with 2,283,000 sold by March 1966 and over 4,500,000 by end of 1966.

Herb Alpert's new 'Ameriarchi' sound (see Alpert, 1962) made him world famous by the end of 1965, with all his other discs enjoying very big sales, and numerous demands for personal appearances. This album contained the following: 'A Taste of Honey' (film title number), by Ric Marlow and Bobby Scott (1960); 'Green Peppers' by Sol Lake; 'Tangerine', by J. Mercer and V. Schertzinger (1942); 'Bittersweet Samba', by Sol Lake; 'Lemon Tree', by Will Holt (1960); 'Whipped Cream', by Naomi Neville (1964); 'Love Potion No 9', by Jerry Leiber and Mike Stoller (1959); 'El Garbanzo', by Sol Lake; 'Ladyfingers', by Toots Thielmans; 'Butterballs', by Mike Henderson; 'Peanuts', by Luis Guerrero (1965); 'Lollipops and Roses', by Tony Velona (1959).

Gold Disc award, R.I.A.A., 1965; also their second Gold Cartridge award (see Alpert 1966) from I.T.C.C. (International Tape Cartridge Company). The disc was in the U.S. bestsellers for 185 weeks.

GOING PLACES (album) *A & M* [*USA*]. This album sold 1,561,000 by 1 March 1966, just six months after release in the U.S.A., when it also became No 1 in their charts and for six weeks. It stayed in the charts for many months, nine of these in the Top 10, and was in the bestsellers for 164 weeks.

It contained: 'Tijuana Taxi', by Ervan Coleman (1965); 'I'm Getting Sentimental Over You', by Ned Washington/George Bassman (1933); 'More and More Amor', by Sol Lake (1965); 'Spanish Flea', by Julius Wechter (1965); 'Mae' (from film *Yellow Rolls Royce*), by Riz Ortolani (1965); 'Third Man' theme, by Anton Karas (1950); 'Walk, Don't Run', by Johnny Smith (1960); 'Felicia', by John Pisano (1965); 'And the Angels Sing', by Johnny Mercer/Ziggie Elman (1939); 'Cinco de mayo', by Chris Montez (1965); 'A Walk in the Black Forest', by Horst Jankowski (1965); 'Zorba the Greek' title number, by Mikis Theodorakis (1964).

Gold Disc award, R.I.A.A., December 1965.

SPANISH FLEA *A & M* [*USA*]. Originally on Alpert's album 'Going Places', this novelty number played in the band's inimitable style was a big hit when issued as a singles disc, particularly in Britain where it sold over 250,000 and was No 3 for three weeks and 20 weeks in the bestsellers. Sales in Europe were also big. The disc was No 19 in the U.S.A. with seven weeks in the bestsellers. The combined sale was over the million.

Tune written by Julius Wechter.

CHRIS ANDREWS (vocalist)
YESTERDAY MAN *Decca* [*Britain*]. Chris Andrews has been described as the young man with the golden touch for, apart from being one of England's most successful young songwriters, his disc of this song, his own composition, made him a hit disc star. Christopher Frederick Andrews was born on 15 October 1942 in Romford, Essex, and started playing guitar and singing when he was eleven. He also had six years' tuition on the piano, started composing when he was eleven, and made his first amateur public appearance then in a public house locally. Four years later (1957) came his first professional appearance at the Ilford Palais de Dance, and later his first big break on his TV debut in 'Oh Boy'. Chris formed his own group called Chris Ravell and The Ravers in late 1963, and started writing for the group rather than perform the current popular songs. After his return from Hamburg, Germany, he was introduced to Evelyn Taylor, manager for Britain's pop stars Adam Faith and Sandie Shaw. She asked to hear some of his songs. From then on his career as a professional songwriter started. Adam recorded his song 'The First Time' and so one of the most successful composer/singer partnerships was formed. Chris then heard Sandie Shaw, who had been discovered by Adam and was asked to write songs for her. He came up with 'Long Live Love', 'Girl Don't Come' and 'Message Understood', all of which were big hits. He then recorded his song 'Yesterday Man' himself, an immediate hit with a No 2 achievement in the British charts for three weeks, 15 weeks in the bestsellers, and over 250,000 sale. Life then changed rapidly, for he was engaged up and down Britain for stage, radio and TV appearances. His disc was released in Germany on the Vogue label in 1966 and was No 1 for two weeks, No 1 Austria and Switzerland, and No 94 in the U.S.A. It sold half a million in Germany in two months and a million in four months, staying in their charts for 20 weeks. He received a Gold Disc award in May 1966.

Chris returned to Germany for a TV appearance in March 1966 and played Hamburg's famous Star Club. He also starred in a big TV spectacular in Wiesbaden in May 1966. The tremendous success of 'Yesterday Man' established him as one of the most in-demand stars in Germany, with his tours there becoming sell-outs. Quite a success story for singer/songwriter Chris who a few years before was an unknown, and playing on the same bill with another group unknown at that time – The Beatles.

LEN BARRY (vocalist)
1, 2, 3 *Decca* [*USA*]. Falling in love, Len Barry explains, is as elementary as 1-2-3, or A-B-C. Len (real name Leonard Borisoff) wrote the song with John Madara and David White. The disc got to No 2 in the U.S.A. with 15 weeks in the bestsellers, and was No 1 for one week in Britain and 14 weeks in the bestsellers. The British sales were over 250,000 and the American sales 1,500,000.

Len was born in West Philadelphia on 6 December 1942. He studied at Temple University there where he and four friends formed a group, playing for over two years at local gatherings, and school functions. Calling themselves The Dovells, they auditioned for Cameo-Parkway Records in 1961 and had a million seller hit with 'Bristol Stomp' (see 1961). Later, Len left to become a solo artist. His first disc 'Lip Sync' didn't become a hit but '1-2-3' finally gave him prominence.

He is the typical personification of the 'All-American Boy' – six feet one tall, blond hair and blue eyes – with a high tenor voice.

FONTELLA BASS (pop, rhythm-and-blues vocalist)
RESCUE ME *Checker* [*USA*]. Coloured-artist Fontella Bass (born 24 August 1942 in St Louis, Missouri) was educated at Golden High School, St Louis, and Lincoln University. Her mother sang with the Clara Ward Singers and started coaching Fontella at the age of four. At five she was playing the piano and singing in a church choir in her native town. She eventually became the choir's director and an accomplished pianist and organist. Fontella made her first public appearance playing the piano and organ in the St Louis 'Gospel Blues Show'. Chess Records' star Little Milton heard her singing in church in 1960 and was so impressed that he immediately engaged her to play the piano and sing in his band – a post she held for four years. In

June 1964, Little Milton took her to Chess Records and introduced her to artists and repertoire manager, Billy Davis, who in turn introduced her to a young singer Bobby McClure. Davis arranged for them to make their first disc together – 'Don't Mess Up a Good Thing'. It was not, however, until August 1965 that she got her big chance for stardom. Sitting in the rehearsal studio with two of the Chess writers, Carl Smith and Raynard Miner, arranger Phil Wright called in. The outcome was the birth of 'Rescue Me' – 'a sure-fire hit', said Marshall Chess. It certainly was. Fontella's rollicking rhythmic version about a love-sick girl begging her boy friend for another chance in romance got to No 4 in the U.S. charts with 13 weeks in the bestsellers, and No 7 in Britain with 10 weeks in the bestsellers, selling a global million.

Fontella visited Britain in December 1965 and again in January 1966. She has appeared on several important American shows including 'Hollywood à Gogo', 'Shindig', 'Shabang' and 'The Dick Clark Show'. Her TV debut was in 'St Louis Hop' in 1961.

A top rhythm-and-blues disc in both the U.S.A. and Britain.

THE BEACH BOYS
HELP ME RHONDA *Capitol* [*USA*]. This sixth million seller for the Beach Boys was written by the group's Brian Wilson. It was No 1 for two weeks in the U.S.A. and 14 weeks in the bestsellers, and sold an eventual million globally. It was No 27 and 10 weeks in Britain's bestsellers.

BARBARA ANN *Capitol* [*USA*]. The seventh million seller (globally) for America's top male group, the song written by Fred Fassert in 1961. It was No 1 for two weeks in the U.S.A. with 11 weeks in the bestsellers, and reached No 3 in Britain in 1966 with 10 weeks in the bestsellers. The disc was also exceedingly popular on the Continent of Europe in 1966 and sold over 200,000 in Germany alone. Issued mid-December 1965.

THE BEATLES

TICKET TO RIDE backed with YES IT IS *Parlophone [Britain]*. The disc sold 700,000 in Britain and had an advance sale of 750,000 in the U.S.A. on the Capitol label. 'Ticket to Ride' was No 1 immediately, and for five weeks in Britain (with 12 weeks in the bestsellers) and one week in the U.S.A. with 11 weeks in the bestsellers. 'Yes It Is' was No 46 and 4 weeks in the U.S. bestsellers. Both songs were written by The Beatles' John Lennon and Paul McCartney.

EIGHT DAYS A WEEK backed with I DON'T WANT TO SPOIL THE PARTY *Capitol [USA] (original Parlophone recording in Britain)*. Both songs were included in The Beatles' album 'Beatles for Sale' (Britain) and 'Beatles '65' (U.S.A.) issued in December 1964. They were issued as a singles disc in February 1965 on the Capitol label in the U.S.A. This recording soon sold a million, and 'Eight Days a Week' was No 1 for three weeks in the States with 10 weeks in the bestsellers. The backing was No 39 and 6 weeks in the bestsellers. The songs were written by John Lennon and Paul McCartney. Gold Disc award, R.I.A.A., 1965.

HELP backed with I'M DOWN *Parlophone [Britain]*. This record consists of the title song from The Beatles' second film *Help* (see album data) and the backing also written by John Lennon and Paul McCartney. This disc sold 500,000 in one week and 800,000 in three weeks in Britain where it was No 1 immediately and for four weeks, with 14 weeks in the bestsellers. It also sold a million in the U.S.A. in one week and was No 1 there for three weeks with 13 weeks in the bestsellers, issued on Capitol label. Gold Disc award, R.I.A.A., 1965.

BEATLES VI (album) *Capitol [USA]*. All songs on this album were originally recorded for Parlophone, Britain. This disc sold 500,000 in five days in the U.S.A. and eventually a million - the Beatles' eighth album to do so in America. The album comprised the following songs: 'You Like Me Too Much', by George Harrison (1965); 'Tell Me What You See', by John Lennon and Paul McCartney (1965); 'Every Little Thing', by John Lennon and Paul McCartney (1964); 'What You're Doing', by John Lennon and Paul McCartney (1964); 'Eight Days a Week', by John Lennon and Paul McCartney (1964); 'Yes It Is', by John Lennon and Paul McCartney (1965); 'I Don't Want to Spoil the Party', by John Lennon and Paul McCartney (1964); 'Bad Boy', by Larry Williams (1958); 'Dizzy Miss Lizzie', by Larry Williams (1958); 'Words of Love', by Buddy Holly (1958); 'Kansas City', by Jerry Leiber and Mike Stoller 1959).

The disc was No 1 in the U.S.A. for six weeks. Gold Disc award, R.I.A.A., 1965. It stayed in the U.S. bestsellers for 41 weeks.

HELP (album) *Parlophone [Britain] Capitol [USA]*. For the first time in the history of the record industry, a definite order of more than one million albums was received in the States for a disc. Thus 'Help' qualified for an instant Gold Disc to Capitol from R.I.A.A. The Beatles chalked up their ninth million seller album in the U.S.A. The Capitol disc included the seven songs from the film, and the soundtrack music composed by Ken Thorne. It was in the U.S. bestsellers for 44 weeks. Contents: 'Help', by John Lennon and Paul McCartney (1965); 'Another Girl', by John Lennon and Paul McCartney (1965); 'The Night Before', by John Lennon and Paul McCartney (1965); 'You're Going to Lose That Girl', by John Lennon and Paul McCartney (1965); 'You've Got to Hide Your Love Away', by John Lennon and Paul McCartney (1965); 'Ticket to Ride', by John Lennon and Paul McCartney (1965); 'I Need You', by George Harrison (1965).

The British issue by Parlophone included the above seven songs on Side 1 and the following (not from the film) on Side 2: 'Act Naturally', by Van Morrison and John Russell (1963); 'Dizzy Miss Lizzie', by Larry Williams (1958); 'You Like Me Too Much', by George Harrison (1965); 'It's Only Love', by John Lennon and Paul McCartney (1965); 'Tell Me What You See', by John Lennon and Paul McCartney (1965); 'I've Just Seen a Face', by John Lennon and Paul McCartney (1965); 'Yesterday', by John Lennon and Paul McCartney (1965).

The advance order in Britain was 250,000, but the disc actually sold 270,000 in one week.

The film (in colour) broke all box-office records previously set up by their first film *A Hard Day's Night*, both in Britain and the U.S.A.

The Beatles paid their third visit to the U.S.A. in August 1965 for a tour and broke their previous record fee for a single performance when they appeared at New York's Shea Stadium on 16 August before an audience of 56,000 fans, and received $160,000 (£57,000). Gross takings for the tour were over $1 million for the second time.

'Help' album was No 1 for 11 weeks in Britain and for 10 weeks in the U.S.A. R.I.A.A. certified Gold Disc awards for both album and singles disc for the first time simultaneously.

YESTERDAY backed with ACT NATURALLY *Capitol [USA]*. These two songs were taken from the British Parlophone disc 'Help' album and issued as a singles disc in the U.S.A. by Capitol. 'Yesterday', a solo by Paul McCartney accompanying himself on guitar with the addition of a string quartet, is said to be the best Lennon-McCartney composition of all their many songs. This plaintive romantic song proved to be a colossal hit in the U.S.A., selling over one million in 10 days plus R.I.A.A. Gold Disc award and staying at No 1 there for four weeks with 11 weeks in the bestsellers, with final total of 1,800,000 sold. The backing is a solo by Beatles drummer, Ringo Starr, with Paul harmonizing and a guitar interlude from George Harrison of the group. 'Act Naturally' is an American song about show business success, sung in country style. It was No 47 and seven weeks in the U.S. bestsellers. It was written by Van Morrison and John Russell in 1963 when it was a No 1 country-and-western hit for Buck Owens. 'Yesterday' was also No 1 in Hong Kong, Finland, Spain, Norway and Belgium. Total sales estimated at well over two and a half million. Over 1,186 recordings of the tune were current by December 1972.

RUBBER SOUL (album) *Parlophone [Britain] Capitol [USA]*. With this disc, The Beatles topped themselves. Issued on the Capitol label in the U.S.A. on 6 December 1965 it sold 1,200,000 in its first nine days on the market, breaking every sales record held by the group. Sales thereafter continued at a tremendous rate in 1966. The disc qualified for an immediate Gold Disc award to Capitol by R.I.A.A. and soon passed the two million mark. It was No 1 in the U.S.A. for 7 weeks.

In Britain, the disc was released on 10 December 1965 with advance orders of over 500,000, so becoming an immediate No 1 seller and staying for 13 weeks in the charts. The album is particularly notable for the first use in 'pop' discs of the sitar, an Indian instrument, by George Harrison in 'Norwegian Wood', and the song 'Michelle', sung by Paul McCartney, telling Michelle, in the only words he knows in French with added English, how much he needs her, and recorded in a bluesy French manner. 'Michelle' (Grammy Award to writers for 'Song of the Year', 1966) was immediately taken up by a great number of other artists with 629 different versions recorded in all parts of the world by the end of 1972. The British disc includes the first composing credit to drummer Ringo Starr for the country-and-western style song 'What Goes On?', thus making all members of the group songwriters. Both discs include the following: 'Think for Yourself', by George Harrison (1965); 'Norwegian Wood', by John Lennon and Paul McCartney (1965); 'The Word', by John Lennon and Paul McCartney (1965); 'Michelle', by John Lennon and Paul McCartney (1965); 'Girl', by John Lennon and Paul McCartney (1965); 'I'm Looking Through You', by John Lennon and Paul McCartney (1965); 'In My Life', by John Lennon and Paul McCartney (1965); 'Wait', by John Lennon and Paul McCartney 1965); 'You Won't See Me', by John Lennon and Paul McCartney (1965); 'Run for Your Life', by John Lennon and Paul McCartney (1965).

Additional titles on the Capitol disc: 'It's Only Love', by John Lennon and Paul McCartney (1965); 'I've Just Seen a Face', by John Lennon and Paul McCartney (1965).

Additional titles on Parlophone disc: 'If I Needed Someone', by George Harrison (1965); 'Nowhere Man', by John Lennon and Paul McCartney (1965); 'Drive My Car', by John Lennon and Paul McCartney (1965); 'What Goes On?' by John Lennon, Paul McCartney and Ringo Starr (1965).

'Rubber Soul' was the tenth album million seller for the Beatles in the U.S.A., making a total of 11 (including one in Britain). It was in the U.S. bestsellers for 51 weeks.

DAY TRIPPER backed with WE CAN WORK IT OUT *Parlophone* [*Britain*] *Capitol* [*USA*]. Another tremendous double-sided hit for the fabulous Beatles, both again were written by the prolific John Lennon and Paul McCartney. Issued in Britain on 3 December 1965, it sold a million by 20 December, was an immediate No 1 and stayed there for six weeks with 12 weeks in the bestsellers. Issued on the Capitol label in the U.S.A. in early December the disc also reached No 1 (within three weeks) and sold over a million. The world sales are estimated at three million. The disc was No 1 for four weeks in the U.S.A., and received Gold Disc award from R.I.A.A. in 1966.

By the end of 1970, The Beatles' tally of million sellers was:

25	Singles	(U.S.A.)
1	EP	(U.S.A.)
19	Albums	(U.S.A.)
7	Singles	(Britain)
1	Album	(Britain)
2	Singles	(Combined U.S.A./Britain)
2	EPs	(Global)
2	Singles	(Global)

Total 59

JAMES BROWN AND THE FAMOUS FLAMES
PAPA'S GOT A BRAND NEW BAG *King* [*USA*]. Written by James Brown himself, this disc was a big hit in the U.S.A. (No 6 in their charts with 13 weeks in the bestsellers) and also a success in Britain, with global sales estimated at two million. A top rhythm-and-blues disc. It was No 21 in Britain, with seven weeks in the bestsellers.

The song received the Grammy Award for the best rhythm-and-blues recording of 1965.

I GOT YOU (I feel good) *King* [*USA*]. Another self-penned song by James Brown and a big seller, with a million sale and Gold Disc presentation in January 1966. It achieved one week at the No 1 position in the U.S. charts with 12 weeks in the bestsellers, was No 29 in Britain, and was a top rhythm-and-blues disc.

THE BYRDS
MR TAMBOURINE MAN *Columbia* [*USA*]. This disc, the group's first recording for Columbia, was No 1 for one week in the U.S.A. (with 13 weeks in the bestsellers), and for two weeks in Britain (with 14 weeks in the bestsellers). It achieved big sales in the U.S.A. and over 250,000 in Britain, with global sales estimated at over the million. This song was written in 1964 by Bob Dylan, king of the folk-rock protest songs so popular in 1965.

Personnel of the group: Chris Hillman, born 4 December 1942 in Los Angeles, who was formerly a cowboy, played bass guitar and mandolin. Gene Clark, born 17 November 1941 at Tipton, Missouri, played the guitar, harmonica, tambourine and sang; he was originally with the New Christy Minstrels. Jim McGuinn, born 15 July 1942 in Chicago, contributed lead guitar, banjo and bass voice; he formerly played with the Chad Mitchell Trio for two years and for one year with Bobby Darin. Mike Clarke, born 3 June 1944 in New York City, played the drums and the harmonica. David Crosby, born 14 August 1941 in Los Angeles,

played the guitar and sang; he formerly was a folk singer-guitarist for five years in folk clubs all over the U.S.A.

Chris Hillman originally had his own group, The Hillmen, active in country music.

The group were formed in Los Angeles in August 1964. Their management, realizing the group's collective experience, trained and prepared them for the highly competitive folk music field, with successful results both in recording and personal appearances.

Actually, this disc was not due for release in Britain, but had to be rush released because the disc was being played on the 'pirate' station Radio Caroline. It eventually became a success in other European countries.

TURN, TURN, TURN *Columbia* [*USA*]. This is the first instance of a million selling disc being inspired by the Bible. The song (written in 1962) is a fine emotional rendering of folk singer and writer Pete Seeger's adaptation of 'Turn, Turn, Turn' from the Book of Ecclesiastes. It became the No 1 disc for three weeks in America with 14 weeks in the bestsellers, also a success in Britain where it was No 26 with eight weeks in the bestsellers and was the second million seller for the Byrds.

FREDDY CANNON
ACTION *Warner* [*USA*]. The fourth million seller for Freddy, and his first on the Warner label. An action-packed beat number with a tremendous vocal sound, written by Tommy Boyce and Steve Venet. The disc reached the No 13 position in both the U.S.A. (with nine weeks in the bestsellers) and Britain with subsequent global million sale.

MEL CARTER
HOLD ME, THRILL ME, KISS ME *Imperial* [*USA*]. Mel Carter's recording of this 1952 song written by Harry Noble made it a million seller for the second time. His disc reached No 8 in the U.S. charts and stayed in the bestsellers for 15 weeks. It was released in June 1965.

Mel Carter was born on 22 April 1943 in Cincinnati, and made his first disc at the age of four, a Negro spiritual sung in a 25-cent recording booth in a penny arcade while held up to the microphone by his grandmother. At nine, he entered and won an amateur contest at Cincinnati's Regal Theatre that resulted in a regular spot with Lionel Hampton, following his experience entertaining at church functions and on local radio. From then on he performed with other well-known bands including Jimmy Scott, Paul Gayton and the Raymond Rasberry Male Gospel Group until he was 16 when he joined the Air Force. In the Service, he joined the Robert Anderson Singers and also won a scholarship to Cincinnati Conservatory of Music, later becoming leading soloist and assistant director of the Greater Cincinnati Youth and Young Adult Choral Union. In 1957, Mel won an award as America's top tenor in the gospel field. In 1959 he formed his own gospel group The Carvetts.

Moving to Los Angeles in 1960 after leaving the Air Force, he appeared at large and small clubs including Ciro's and the Crescendo. By January 1962 he had been a guest on the Ed Sullivan Show.

Mel first recorded in 1963 for Sam Cooke's Derby Records and came up with a successful disc 'When a Boy Falls in Love'. Then came a contract with the Imperial label, this big hit, and other successes such as 'Band of Gold' and 'My Heart Sings'.

Soon after this he played the famous Coconut Grove and became one of the busiest people in show business.

Coloured singer Mel Carter enjoyed writing songs and teaching young people to sing. In 1968 he recorded for the Bell label.

LOU CHRISTIE

LIGHTNIN' STRIKES *MGM* [*USA*]. Third million seller for Lou, the song again written by him with Twyla Herbert. The disc was issued in late 1965 and was No 1 for two weeks in the U.S.A. in 1966 with 15 weeks in the bestsellers, and No 11 in Britain with eight weeks in the bestsellers. Gold Disc award from R.I.A.A. in March 1966. Sales were two million.

DAVE CLARK FIVE

I LIKE IT LIKE THAT *Epic* [*USA*]. The song was originally written in 1961 by Chris Kenner (whose disc is said to have sold a million then) and Allen Toussaint. It also sold a million for Dave Clark in 1965 in the U.S.A., reaching No 6 on their charts, and 11 weeks in the bestsellers. This disc was Dave's seventh million seller.

CATCH US IF YOU CAN *Columbia* [*Britain*]. From the film of the same title, starring the Dave Clark Five, this song was written by group members, Dave Clark and Leonard Davidson. The disc sold a global million (their eighth) by October 1965 and was a big hit on the Epic label in the U.S.A., reaching No 4 in their charts with 11 weeks in the bestsellers. It was also No 4 in Britain with 11 weeks in the bestsellers.

OVER AND OVER *Epic* [*USA*]. The ninth million seller for Dave Clark, based on U.S. sales, was written in 1958 by Robert Byrd and the disc was No 1 for one week in the States and 12 weeks in the bestsellers. It was No 45 in Britain.

Byrd was a disc star under the name of Bobby Day (see 1958).

PETULA CLARK

MY LOVE *Warner* [*USA*]. Petula's first recording in America, and issued in December 1965. It sold a global million by March 1966, and was No 1 in the U.S. charts for two weeks with 13 weeks in the bestsellers, and No 4 in Britain with nine weeks in the bestsellers. Song was written by Petula's recording manager Tony Hatch (of Pye Records, Britain) and the disc made history, it being the first time that a British female artist topped the U.S. charts twice - Petula's first being 'Downtown'.

Tony Hatch completed 'My Love', one of three songs he wrote for Petula, on a transatlantic flight in November 1965, for her to launch on the Ed Sullivan show. He started on it somewhere over the North Pole and finished it by the time the plane touched down in Los Angeles. Pet recorded it in Los Angeles with an American studio orchestra.

BILL COSBY

WHY IS THERE AIR? (album) *Warner* [*USA*]. Bill Cosby's third album, which deals mainly with the problems of an expectant father, sold 951,000 by July 1967 with the million sale by the end of the year. It received a Gold Disc award from R.I.A.A. in 1966.

The album included 'The Toothache', 'Kindergarten', 'Driving in San Francisco'. It stayed in the U.S. bestsellers for 152 weeks.

It was recorded at the Flamingo Hotel, Las Vegas, and produced by Roy Silver and fellow comedian Allan Sherman. Sales by end of 1967 were 1,400,000.

(See Cosby, 1966, for biography.)

Grammy Award for Best Comedy Performance, 1965.

DRAFI DEUTSCHER (vocalist)

MARMOR, STEIN UND EISEN BRICHT (Marble, stone and iron break) *Decca* [*Germany*]. Written by Drafi himself in collaboration with Christian Bruhn, this disc sold 800,000 in Germany alone up to April 1966 and was No 1 there for 12 weeks from December 1965. It was issued in the U.S.A. in 1966 under the title 'Marble Breaks and Iron Bends' on the London label with English lyrics by Marcel Stellman, and subsequently reached a million global (combined) sale. The song is a teen-type number with a hard driving chorus and strongly worded recitation breaks.

Drafi Deutscher was born in Berlin on 9 May 1946, his father being Hungarian. At the age of 11, he won a talent contest on the accordion and two years later formed his first band 'Charlie and his Timebombs'. They couldn't appear in public as they were all minors. A year later, Drafi formed another group called 'The Magics' which won first prize in 1961 at a twist festival in Berlin. They became firmly established in German 'beat' circles over the following two years. In 1963, Drafi won another competition, this time for his vocal talents, resulting in an opportunity to record. His first disc was an overnight hit, and all his succeeding records followed the same pattern. In 1966, he was voted Germany's 'No 1 male vocalist'.

KEN DODD

TEARS *Columbia* [*Britain*]. With beat groups predominating in Britain, Ken Dodd's recording of this old sentimental song was the biggest surprise of 1965, and the year's greatest hit. By the end of November it passed the million mark to become Britain's biggest disc of 1965. Sales by August 1966 were 1,600,000.

The song, written by Frank Capano (words) and Billy Uhr (music), both Americans, was originally recorded by Rudy Vallee in 1929.

Ken Dodd was born in Liverpool, England, on 8 November 1932, son of a coal merchant. He became interested in entertaining when he was seven by giving backyard concerts to school friends. He later gave a show as a ventriloquist to pupils of local Knotty Ash School, and at 13 an audition at a Liverpool theatre who advertised for dancers. He got the only vacant male role - leading Cinderella's coach. On leaving school, he worked with his father, then started selling pots and pans on the city's housing estates. In the evenings, he entertained at clubs and by 1954 was so busy with engagements he became a full-time professional comedian. He studied the theories on laughter by philosophers such as Freud, Kant and Schopenhauer, and carefully noted audience reaction to his gags, thereby making his hilarious performances suited to everybody. Ken's trademark - his teeth - are insured for £10,000. On stage, he presents the appearance of a village idiot, with his hair reminiscent of having seen a ghost. Apart from his unique comedy, he is a fine singer of romantic ballads, and this opened up a new career for him on discs. His first recording and first success was 'Love Is Like a Violin' issued in June 1960 on Decca label, and in 1964 came a hit with 'Happiness' on Columbia.

He appeared in the Royal Variety Show in 1965 at the London Palladium in which he also sang 'Tears', the song that stayed No 1 for six weeks in Britain's charts with 24 weeks in the bestsellers.

EARLE DOUD AND ALEN ROBIN

WELCOME TO THE LBJ RANCH (album) *Capitol* [*USA*]. Earle Doud, who was producer of the famous 'First Family' album in 1962, teamed up with Alen Robin - head of the U.S.A.'s 'Tonight' show - to produce this brilliant comedy disc. By matching interview questions with authentic but unrelated statements made by well known political officials including President

Lyndon B. Johnson, Dwight Eisenhower, Governor Nelson Rockefeller, Senator Barry Goldwater, their unique comedy idea resulted in an uproarious album with colossal sales in the U.S.A. The clever tape editing involved some 40 lawyers employed by Capitol Records to clear the legal side before it was released on 2 November 1965. The disc sold half a million by 1 December and gained an R.I.A.A. Gold Disc award. It went on to sell an estimated million (1966), was No 3 for two weeks and stayed high on the U.S. charts for most of its 25-week run.

The actual voices of prominent men in politics are used for this political spoof together with the voices of noted U.S. commentator John Cameron Swayze, Westbrook Van Voorhis, John St Leger and Doud and Robin themselves. The producers combed through 480,000 feet of tape to obtain the right answers to their questions. Additional voices on the disc - Senator Robert Kennedy, Lady Bird Johnson, Senator Everett Dirksen and Vice-President Richard Nixon.

BOB DYLAN

LIKE A ROLLING STONE *Columbia* [*USA*]. Bob Dylan (born Bob Zimmerman in Duluth, Minnesota, on 24 May 1941) was the undisputed king of the new folk rock wave that swept the U.S.A., Britain and elsewhere during 1965. His songs, combining the big beat with folk themes of unsentimental love and protest, were sensationally successful. This one, written by him, tells the story of a girl's decline from boarding school to street walker. It was No 1 for a week in the U.S.A. with 12 weeks in the bestsellers, and No 2 in Britain, with 12 weeks in the bestsellers, easily selling a global million.

Bob started to sing and play guitar when he was ten and wrote his first song at 15. He attended high school in Hibbing, Minnesota, and then the University of Minnesota for six months. Like so many of his restless generation he could not settle to college life. He did in fact run away from Hibbing seven times between the ages of 12 and 18. By the age of 15 he had taught himself the piano, autoharp and harmonica. His wanderings took him to several States where he assimilated the songs of all kinds of folk singers from cowboy ballads to Negro-blues artists, thus absorbing all the techniques of the folk-song tradition. In 1961, he went East, where he visited Woody Guthrie, the father figure of white folk music who had been ill in Greystone Park Hospital,

New Jersey, with Huntington's chorea since 1954. Here he talked folk music for hours on end with Guthrie, sang Guthrie songs and played in the Guthrie manner. His life-long idol thus became a marked influence on his career. It was John Hammond, a talent director for CBS, who discovered Dylan when Bob attended a rehearsal for another folk singer whom Hammond wanted to record. Up to this time, Bob found it hard going to work steadily at singing and even at times was forced to sleep in doorways. He soon started playing at folk clubs and festivals, attracting more and more fans. The real turning point in his career came at the Newport Folk Festival in 1963 where he captivated audiences and critics alike. It was here that the great folk singing trio Peter, Paul and Mary sang Bob's now famous 'Blowin' in the Wind', a powerful protest song, Peter describing it to the audience as 'written by the most important folk artist in America'. Dylan then appeared as part of Joan Baez's concerts, Joan having become the 'Queen of Folk' with a tremendous following everywhere and on discs. Other great Dylan songs include 'The Times They Are A-changin'', 'Mr Tambourine Man', 'Subterranean Homesick Blues', 'All I Really Want to Do' and 'Positively 4th Street'. He is entirely sincere in his role as a folk writer and singer. He is also a forthright spokesman for civil rights. The significance of Dylan goes far beyond Dylan the artist. He has established a brand of seemingly uncommercial music into a commodity the public really wants, borne out by the big demand for his albums such as 'The Freewheelin' Bob Dylan', 'Bringing It All Back Home', 'The Times They Are A-changing'' and 'Highway 61 Revisited', all big sellers in 1965. His songs have also been recorded by dozens of other artists, a great tribute to 'The King of Folk'. He took the name of Dylan in tribute to Dylan Thomas, the Welsh poet.

POSITIVELY 4TH STREET *Columbia* [*USA*]. The second million seller for Bob Dylan was also written by him. In it he criticizes those who would not accept him when he was unknown. The disc was No 7 in the U.S.A. with 9 weeks in the bestsellers, and No 8 in Britain's charts with 12 weeks in the bestsellers, the combined sales making the million.

SHIRLEY ELLIS

THE CLAPPING SONG *Congress* [*USA*]. This first million seller globally for Shirley was written by her manager Lincoln Chase, Mrs James McCarthy and Mrs Larry Kent.

Shirley, who lives in Gotham, started in show business by winning an amateur contest at the Apollo Theatre, New York, her native city. She used her natural talents by gaining valuable experience performing whenever possible in clubs, charity affairs and dances, and then joined a group, The Metronomes, which played every type of music from rock'n'roll to calypso. In 1958 she met Lincoln Chase for whom she had made some demonstration discs for Decca some years previously. Chase felt that Shirley had a natural talent after hearing her sing and signed her up to a management contract and became her professional tutor. After five years of intensive preparation, he wrote 'The Nitty Gritty' for her (1963) and 'The Name Game' (1964), both sizeable hits that got into the U.S.A.'s Top 10. Then came 'The Clapping Song', which took Shirley's disc up to No 8 in the U.S.A. with nine weeks in the bestsellers, and No 4 in Britain (London label) and 13 weeks in the bestsellers, with an estimated global million sale.

Shirley did TV musical work, made personal appearances in addition to recording, and Broadway shows. Lincoln Chase was himself a performer years ago but gave up his career to concentrate on building Shirley's career.

WAYNE FONTANA AND THE MINDBENDERS

GAME OF LOVE *Fontana* [*Britain*]. The first million seller (by the end of May 1965) for this group was compiled by 900,000 from combined U.S.-British sales and the remainder from other countries. The disc was No 1 for one week in the U.S.A. with 11 weeks in the bestsellers, and No 2 in Britain with 11 weeks in the

bestsellers. The song was written by Clint Ballard, Jr. in 1964.

Wayne Fontana (real name Glyn Geoffrey Ellis), vocalist, was born in Manchester, 28 October 1945. The Mindbenders are Eric Stewart (lead guitar), born 20 January 1945; Bob Lang (bass guitar), born 10 January 1946; and Ric Rothwell (drums), born 11 March 1944.

Wayne formed a group, himself and the Jets in 1963, singing semi-professionally in local Manchester clubs, and got an audition at the Oasis Club in the city - to be heard by artists' manager Jack Baverstock of Fontana Records. Only Wayne and Bob Lang arrived for the audition. Wayne asked two other boys who were in the club that night to help him out. They were Eric Stewart and Ric Rothwell. Baverstock was impressed and offered them a recording contract. When he enquired their names, Wayne borrowed the Mindbenders from a horror film he had recently seen. They made the British charts with their fifth disc - a revival of 'Um, Um, Um, Um, Um, Um' (1964). Then came 'Game of Love' with the resultant TV, radio and personal appearances, including a visit to the U.S.A. Wayne was a trainee telephone engineer after leaving school, and has been interested in music since he was five.

THE FOUR SEASONS
LET'S HANG ON *Philips* [*USA*]. The fifth million seller for this outstanding group, the song written by Denny Randell, Sandy Linzer and Bob Crewe. The disc was released in September 1965 and remained in the bestseller charts for 17 weeks, reaching No 1 for one week. It was also popular in Britain where it reached No 4 for one week with 16 weeks in the bestsellers.

THE FOUR TOPS (rhythm-and-blues vocal quartet)
I CAN'T HELP MYSELF *Motown* [*USA*]. This disc was released on 15 May 1965. The Four Tops, consisting of Abdul Fakir, Levi Stubbs, Renaldo Benson and Lawrence Payton, first came together in 1954 in their native Detroit. Since then, the group have formed a closely-knit association, despite many disappointments, for the pleasure of making music. Berry Gordy of Motown considered them one of his most talented acts, and their artistic teamwork and repertoire of widely different styles - pop songs, rhythm-and-blues, country-and-western, rock'n'roll and modern jazz - has paid off handsomely for the singers.

For many years they have appeared at many top nightclubs in the U.S.A. including Los Angeles' Moulin Rouge, Las Vegas, Thunderbird and the famous Playboy circuit. Billy Eckstine is one of their greatest admirers and they enhanced their reputations through appearances on Eckstine's road show. The Four Tops also appeared on radio and TV in Britain in May 1965.

'I Can't Help Myself', written by the tremendously successful team of Brian Holland, Eddie Holland and Lamont Dozier, gave them a big hit. The disc was No 1 for two weeks in the U.S.A. with 14 weeks in the bestsellers, a top rhythm-and-blues seller, and also was a hit in Britain (No 22) with nine weeks in the bestsellers. It sold well over the million. The song is a rollicking hand-clapping number.

THE GENTRYS (rock and roll instrumental and vocal septet)
KEEP ON DANCING *MGM* [*USA*]. The Gentrys were first organized in Memphis, Tennessee, in May 1963 as a rock'n'roll group for local dances, and were very successful playing for high school dates. In September 1964 they won third place in the Mid-South Fair Talent Competition and auditioned for the Ted Mack Amateur Hour. They soon became the most popular teenage band in the mid-South and in 1964 won the Memphis Battle of the Bands. In December of 1964 the group were given a contract by a local record label and made their first disc of 'Sometimes' which was very popular locally in early 1965. Then came 'Keep on Dancing', which was leased for national distribution by MGM Records. It achieved No 3 for two weeks in the national charts with 14 weeks in the bestsellers, and subsequently sold a million.

The Gentrys proved adroit with their fine vocals, instrumental backgrounds of varied guitar, organ, piano or horn rhythms, and on instrumentals with a variety of popular sounds through the use of trumpet and tenor saxophone harmony.

The members of the group are: Larry Raspberry (leader, guitar, vocalist); Larry Wall (drums); Jimmy Johnson (trumpet, organ); Bobby Fisher (tenor sax, electric piano); Pat Neal (bass guitar); Bruce Bowles (vocalist); Jimmy Hart (vocalist).

'Keep on Dancing' was written by Allen A. Jones and Willie David Young. The group started recording for Bell Records in 1968.

BOBBY GOLDSBORO
LITTLE THINGS *United Artists* [*USA*]. Second million seller (reported by 1967) for Bobby, the song was written by him in 1964. It reached No 12 in the U.S. charts with 12 weeks in the bestsellers.

HERMAN'S HERMITS
CAN'T YOU HEAR MY HEARTBEATS? *Columbia* [*Britain*]. The second million seller for this English quintet was written by John Carter and Ken Lewis (pseudonyms for John Shakespeare and Kenneth Hawker). The million sale was achieved on the MGM label in the U.S.A. by May, just prior to the group's immensely successful tour there. This disc reached No 2 in the U.S. charts and was 15 weeks in the bestsellers.

SILHOUETTES *Columbia* [*Britain*]. The third million seller for Herman's Hermits was also issued on the MGM label in the U.S.A. prior to the group's American tour. It sold well over the half million there, over a quarter million in Britain with the global sale totalling over one million. It had a 400,000 advance sale in the U.S.A.

This song was written by Bob Crewe and Frank Slay, Jr in 1957, and was also a million seller for The Rays in the U.S.A. 1957-58. The 'Silhouettes' disc was No 4 in the U.S.A. with 13 weeks in the bestsellers, and No 2 in Britain with 13 weeks in the bestsellers.

MRS BROWN YOU'VE GOT A LOVELY DAUGHTER *Columbia* [*Britain*]. This song was originally written in 1963 and sung by actor Tom Courtenay in a British TV play. The author-composer is Trevor Peacock. Herman's Hermits were popular on their first album 'Introducing Herman's Hermits' which sold well over half a million. This song from it became so popular with disc jockeys playing over the air, that MGM were obliged to issue 'Mrs Brown' as a singles disc. It had a 600,000 advance sale in April, and sold over the million by mid-May in the U.S.A., while the group were there on tour. This disc was No 1 for four weeks in their charts, entering at No 12 the first week, the highest any new disc had ever achieved before in the U.S.A., and it stayed for 11 weeks in the bestsellers.

With a Gold Disc award for the album and the single disc (both in U.S.A.) by R.I.A.A. the group thus received five Gold Disc awards in three months, including one for 1964's disc of 'I'm Into Something Good'. Herman's Hermits became the hottest selling act in the U.S.A. in 1965.

I'M HENERY THE EIGHTH, I AM *MGM* [*USA*]. This song, written by Fred Murray and R. P. Weston, was made famous in 1911 by Harry Champion, the great Cockney comedian. It was recorded by Herman's Hermits for Columbia (Britain), and included on their second album 'Herman's Hermits on Tour' for the U.S. market. It became so popular with U.S. disc jockeys that MGM released it as a single disc, with orders of 600,000 in two days, in June 1965. It became No 1 (for 1 week) in the U.S.A. within six weeks, with 10 weeks in the bestsellers, eventually passing the million sale, their fifth singles disc to do so. Gold Disc award, R.I.A.A., 1965.

WONDERFUL WORLD *Columbia* [*Britain*]. A rhythmic and blues-tinged styling by the group of this 1959 song written by Barbara Campbell (joint pseudonym of Sam Cooke, Lou Adler and Herb Alpert) gave Herman's Hermits their sixth million seller, global sale. Issued on the MGM label in the U.S.A. it reached No 4 in their charts with 10 weeks in the bestsellers, and was No 7 in Britain and nine weeks in the bestsellers.

JUST A LITTLE BIT BETTER *Columbia* [*Britain*] *MGM* [*USA*]. The seventh million seller for Herman's Hermits, a major success on both sides of the Atlantic. It was No 10 in Britain and nine weeks in the bestsellers and No 7 in America with 10 weeks in their bestsellers. The song was written in 1964 by Kenny Young. The disc sold an estimated million globally, but the bulk of the sales were in the U.S.A.

THE BEST OF HERMAN'S HERMITS (album) *MGM* [*USA*]. An impressive collection of the group's biggest hits, this album was issued in the U.S.A. in November 1965 after their fantastic successes both on tour and on disc.

In twelve months this album sold 900,000 in America and reached the million in 1967. A Gold Disc was awarded by R.I.A.A. on 11 January 1966, for sales of $1 million. The original recordings were made on the Columbia label in Britain.

Contents of the disc: *'Just a Little Bit Better', by Kenny Young (1964); *'I'm Henery the Eighth, I Am', by R. P. Weston and Fred Murray (1911); *'Mrs Brown You've Got a Lovely Daughter', by Trevor Peacock (1963); *'Silhouettes', by Bob Crewe and Frank Slay, Jr. (1957); *'I'm Into Something Good', by Gerry Goffin and Carole King (1964); *'Can't You Hear My Heartbeats?', by John Carter and Ken Lewis (1965); *'Wonderful World', by Barbara Campbell (1959); 'Mother in Law', by Allen Toussaint (1961); 'The End of the World', by Sylvia Dee and Arthur Kent (1962); 'Sea Cruise', by Frankie Ford and Huey Smith (1959); 'I Gotta Dream On', by Gordon (1965). Items marked * were million seller singles for the group.

This album was No 5 for three weeks and stayed in the Top Ten for 17 weeks. It was in the bestseller charts for 105 weeks.

HORST JANKOWSKI (piano)
WITH HIS ORCHESTRA

A WALK IN THE BLACK FOREST *Philips* [*Germany*]. Horst was voted top jazz pianist for the previous nine years in German polls, but it was this disc, taken from an album 'Eine Schwarzwaldfahrt' issued by Philips originally and put out as a single by Mercury label in the U.S.A., that gave him prominence globally.

Pianist Horst Jankowski was born in Berlin on 30 January

1936. His family moved from Berlin when the heavy bombing began. His father died when he was eight. In 1947, he and his mother moved back to Berlin where he attended the Berlin Conservatory of Music through the efforts of his mother working and sacrificing to pay for his tuition. Here he studied tenor saxophone, contra-bass and trumpet in addition to the piano. His instructors found jobs for him playing popular and jazz music. When he was 16, he met Caterina Valente who asked him to work with her for two years on a tour of Africa, Spain and France. He then joined a big band and started doing arrangements and composing. In 1960, he started a choir, made up of entirely amateur singers from all walks of life. He used this choir of 18 with his orchestra in a similar style to America's famous Ray Conniff. He certainly created something of a 'new sound' in instrumentals, and his fame spread rapidly throughout Germany, with much recording and TV work. His albums sell in a big way; one of them 'The Genius of Jankowski' is especially popular in the U.S.A. (see below).

Jankowski has toured Europe with his orchestra which he also leads.

'A Walk in the Black Forest', his own composition written in 1962, sold over 250,000 in Britain and more in the U.S.A., with big European sales, making a total of over the million.

He still plays a lot of jazz music apart from his choir and has worked with many famous musicians including Oscar Peterson, Ella Fitzgerald, Gerry Mulligan and Miles Davis. He also played in Benny Goodman's band in Brussels for four months. This disc was No 3 in Britain with 18 weeks in the bestsellers, and No 9 in the U.S.A. where it was 13 weeks in the bestsellers.

THE GENIUS OF JANKOWSKI (album) *Philips* [*Germany*]. This album sold a global million by March 1966. It included the now famous Jankowski composition 'A Walk in the Black Forest' which sold a million as a singles disc. Mercury label released the album in the U.S.A. where it had very big sales, reaching No 11 in their charts, and a run of 31 weeks in the bestsellers.

Jankowski received the Philips International Gold Record award in early 1966.

Contents of the disc: 'My Yiddishe Momme', by Jack Yellen and Lew Pollack (1925); 'Clair de lune', by Debussy (1905), arr. Jankowski; 'Eine Schwarzwaldfahrt' (A Walk in the Black Forest), by Horst Jankowski; 'When the Girls Go Marching In', by Jankowski and Rabe; *'Donkey Serenade' (from *The Firefly*), by H. Sothart and Rudolf Friml (1937); 'Sing-song', by Lehn; 'Serenata No 1', by Enrico Toselli (1900), arr. Jankowski; 'Simpel gimpel', by Horst Jankowski; 'Parles-moi d'amour', by Bruce Sievier/Jean Lenoir (1930); 'Caroline-Denise', by Horst Jankowski; 'Bald klopft das gluck auch mel an deine Tur' (Soon good luck will knock at your door), by Forell; 'Nola', by Felix Arndt (1915).

*Originally 'Chanson - In Love', by Rudolf Friml, a piano solo (1923).

TOM JONES

IT'S NOT UNUSUAL *Decca* [*Britain*]. Tom Jones (full name Thomas Jones Woodward) was born on 7 June 1942 in Trefforrest, Glamorgan, Wales, a miner's son. He began his singing career in his chapel choir, influenced by his father and uncle, both singers. Tom had several jobs and a short spell in the building trade, and began playing drums around South Wales men's clubs with various groups. He then formed his own group, The Playboys, started singing with them and working in ballrooms. In 1962 he was booked for the BBC-TV show 'Donald Peers Presents', and was so successful that he was given a return date. A Decca recording contract quickly followed and he made his first disc 'Chills and Fever'. His manager, Gordon Mills, wrote 'It's Not Unusual' with songwriter-musical director Les Reed, and Tom's disc of it topped Britain's charts for one week with 14 weeks in the bestsellers, and sold over half a million. It was also high in the U.S. charts (Parrot label) and the combined sales globally are estimated to have passed the million.

Tom was then booked for a great number of top TV and radio shows in England. He went to America with the release of his recording of 'What's New, Pussycat?', a song he sang for the film of the same title, which was another big hit for him.

Both Jerry Lee Lewis and Solomon Burke, U.S.A. artists, had considerable influence on Tom's career. His voice is very powerful, and his vitality on stage is an important part of his act. He also plays the guitar.

Tom's spectacular success with 'It's Not Unusual' is a classic example of what one hit can do. It virtually quadrupled his earning power overnight.

The disc was No 8 for two weeks in the U.S.A. and 12 weeks in the bestsellers.

WHAT'S NEW, PUSSYCAT? *Decca* [*Britain*]. The second big hit for Tom Jones was written by Hal David (words) and Burt Bacharach (music) for the film starring Peter Sellers, Peter O'Toole and Romy Schneider. On Parrot label it had big sales in the U.S.A. (No 3 in their charts and 12 weeks in the bestsellers) and sold nearly a million by the end of August with an estimated global million by the end of the year. It was No 10 in Britain and 10 weeks in the bestsellers.

BERT KAEMPFERT AND HIS ORCHESTRA

RED ROSES FOR A BLUE LADY *Decca* [*USA*]. An outstanding revival of the 1948 song written by Sid Tepper and Roy Brodsky. Kaempfert's instrumental version was released in January 1965 and reached No 10 for two weeks in U.S.A., subsequently selling a million. It was on the bestseller charts there for 14 weeks. It was also included in one of Kaempfert's bestselling albums 'Blue Midnight'.

YUZO KAYAMA (vocalist)
WITH THE LAUNCHERS

KIMI TO ITSUMADEMO (Forever with you) (Love forever) *Toshiba* [*Japan*]. Yuzo Kayama, who is one of Japan's most brilliant film stars, is also well known as a composer under the name of Kosaku Dan. He made this record, his own composition (with lyrics by Tokiko Iwatani), with his band The Launchers in December 1965. It was No 1 in the Japanese charts for 16 weeks into 1966 and stayed in their charts for 24 weeks, and was reported to have sold over two million, the biggest selling disc up to that time in the history of the Japanese recording industry.

It was released in the U.S.A. on Capitol under the title 'Love Forever', in July 1966.

Kayama and his group became Japan's top pop group as a result of this disc.

JONATHAN KING

EVERYONE'S GONE TO THE MOON *Decca* [*Britain*]. Jonathan King (real name Kenneth King) was born on 6 December 1944 in London. After education at London's Charterhouse School, he became a student at Trinity College, Cambridge, to study English. In between he went on a round-the-world trip. He became a pop fan after hearing Buddy Holly's disc 'It Doesn't Matter Any More'. He later produced a record 'Gotta Tell' sung by Terry Ward that sold a meagre 3,000 copies, and then met Ken Jones, a skilled arranger who became his recording manager after hearing Jonathan's song 'Everyone's Gone to the Moon'. Ken produced the disc which was sold to Decca.

Jonathan was his own personal manager and road manager, and, at the time, had the smallest recording organization in existence. He became one of the most consistently successful independent producers in England, forming U.K. Records in July 1972.

Jonathan also wrote a very successful pop column and a novel. His first professional appearance was on Britain's 'Juke Box Jury' in July 1965.

'Everyone's Gone to the Moon', a haunting, dreamy, and somewhat poetic number, reached No 3 in Britain with 11 weeks in the bestsellers, and, with a re-release in 1969 at the time of

America's first moon landing, was No 17 in the U.S.A. (Parrot label). It subsequently sold a global million.

THE KINKS

TIRED OF WAITING FOR YOU *Pye* [*Britain*]. Written in 1964 by Raymond Douglas Davies of the group, this Kinks' disc was No 1 in Britain for one week with 10 weeks in the bestsellers, selling over a quarter of a million, and No 6 for two weeks in the U.S.A. on the Reprise label with 11 weeks in the bestsellers, the combined sales and those from other countries making a global million. The song is a shuffle-beat lament of the boy who is upset about waiting for his girl getting ready for their date.

This was the second million seller for the Kinks.

BARBARA LEWIS

BABY, I'M YOURS *Atlantic* [*USA*]. Barbara Lewis was born on 9 February 1945 in Detroit, where she grew up and was educated in high school. At the age of nine, she wrote her first song, due no doubt to the fact that she came from a family of musicians. She later took some of her songs to Ollie McLaughlin who saw great possibilities in both her voice and her songs, and decided to record her.

She scored firstly with her own song 'Hello Stranger', a hit of 1964, and followed with her 'Puppy Love'.

'Baby, I'm Yours' was written by Van McCoy in 1964 and Barbara's disc got to No 10 in the U.S. charts with 14 weeks in the bestsellers, and an eventual million sale.

RAMSEY LEWIS TRIO (modern jazz pianist with drum and bass)

THE 'IN' CROWD *Argo-Cadet* [*USA*]. Ramsey Lewis, born 27 May 1935 in Chicago, caught the fancy of the American record-buying public in a very big way with this disc. It got to No 5 in their charts with 16 weeks in the bestsellers, and sold over a million by the end of 1965.

'The "In" Crowd', written by Bill Page in 1964, was originally a success in early 1965 for singer Dobie Grey.

Ramsey Lewis began studying the piano at six, his father being the major influence musically during his childhood. He graduated from school in 1948 after winning the American Legion Award as an outstanding scholar, and a special award for services as pianist at the Edward Jenner Elementary School plus a $150 scholarship. He then began his musical career as piano accompanist for the choir at Chicago Zion Hill Missionary Baptist Church, then to Chicago Musical College, aspiring to become a concert pianist. He married at 18 and left college, became a clerk in a record shop, and joined a seven-piece dance band, The Clefs.

The rhythm section were bass player El Dee Young and drummer Isaac Holt with whom Ramsey formed a trio. They switched to jazz and played for around 10 years together in some of the best-known jazz clubs in the U.S.A.

In July, Ramsey heard a rock'n'roll version of 'The "In" Crowd' on a juke box and decided to put his version on the market. He insisted this should be recorded in a nightclub where he would have the infectious handclapping and enthusiastic 'Yeah Yeah' cries from the audience. As a result his fees trebled almost overnight from $2,500 to $6,500 for one-week club dates. Coloured pianist Ramsay, with his 'join-the-party' type performances, made jazz into something people both enjoyed and understood and made them really feel part of the 'in' crowd. This disc was originally released by Argo, the label being changed later to Cadet. Grammy Award for Best Instrumental Jazz Performances (Small Group).

HANG ON SLOOPY *Cadet* [*USA*]. Ramsey Lewis' version of the McCoys' big hit of this year was also a success, selling a reported million. The disc reached No 11 in the U.S. charts with eight weeks in the bestsellers, and still further enhanced their popularity. Composition by Bert Russell (Berns) and Wes Farrell in 1964.

THE McCOYS (vocal and instrumental quartet)

HANG ON SLOOPY *Bang* [*USA*]. This song, written in 1964 by Bert Russell (Berns) and Wes Farrell, was also a hit in Canada with Little Caesar and The Consuls. The McCoys performed the romantic blues pounding song in a soulful manner. It was No 1 in the U.S.A. for two weeks with 14 weeks in the bestsellers, and got to No 4 on the Immediate label (a new disc company, and their first hit) in Britain with 13 weeks in the bestsellers. American sales alone were a million.

The McCoys first started as a duo, Rick Zehringer (then aged 17) and his brother Randy (aged 16), when they lived in Ohio. Later in Indiana, Dennis Kelly, a neighbour, made it a trio as bass guitarist. The brothers then met Ronnie Brandon (aged 18), a pianist who learned the organ and joined the group. After Dennis left for college, Randy Hobbs (aged 17) joined them, the group playing for dances in their vicinity where they became well known as one of the pop bands in the Midwest. On an engagement in Dayton, Ohio, they met The Strangeloves band who were greatly impressed with their performance, and brought The McCoys to New York to meet their producers and Bang Records. Within two days of their arrival they were signed to the label and cut their first disc 'Hang on Sloopy', a tremendous hit. It made them internationally celebrated, only two years after their formation.

Ricky is lead vocalist and lead guitarist; his brother Randy is the drummer; Hobbs is bass guitarist and vocalist. Ronnie is also the comedian of the group in addition to his organ playing. Randy's other instruments are bass, piano and harmonica. Ricky and Randy Zehringer's home town is now Union City, Indiana.

Recorded versions of 'Hang on Sloopy' have sold an estimated 10 million copies globally. It was first recorded in 1964 by The Vibrations on Atlantic label.

BARRY MCGUIRE

EVE OF DESTRUCTION *Dunhill* [*USA*]. The year 1965 was notable for the popularity of protest songs among the younger generation, and this, written by 19-year-old P. F. Sloan and Steve Barri as an anti-war song, was a tremendous hit in the U.S.A. where it sold over the million (nearly two million globally).

Barry McGuire, born 15 October 1935 in Oklahoma City, made his first public appearance as an amateur at the Frankenstein Coffee House, Laguna Beach, in 1960; his first professional appearance at Ye Little Club, Beverly Hills, 1961; his TV debut in a 'Route 66' episode. He worked with another singer Barry Kane for a while as Barry and Barry and was then hired by Randy Sparks when Randy formed The New Christy Minstrels (1962). He became a lead singer with them and made a tour of Europe with the group, including Britain. Leaving the group in 1964 to become a solo singer, he met Lou Adler of Dunhill Records in June 1964 and told him about Sloan's song, and it was then recorded. Although the disc was banned by some U.S. stations and for broadcasting by the BBC, it was aired by pirate radio stations. In the U.S.A. it was a chart-topper for one week with 14 weeks in the bestsellers, and reached No 3 in Britain with 12 weeks in the bestsellers.

Barry has had no musical education, but plays guitar, banjo and harmonica in addition to singing. He is also a talented songwriter, and wrote 'Green Back Dollar', a hit for the Kingston Trio, and 'Green Green' for The New Christy Minstrels (see 1963).

THE MAMAS AND THE PAPAS (vocal quartet)

CALIFORNIA DREAMIN' *Dunhill* [*USA*]. This song was a tremendous hit in the U.S.A., a consistent seller with 17 weeks in their charts and reaching No 4 in 1966. The group had a somewhat chequered history in the folk field before achieving success. John Phillips, from New York, born 30 August 1941, leader of the group in the vocals, also did their arrangements and wrote most of their songs, including this one. He played in many spots in and around Greenwich Village and with a group called The Journeymen. Michelle Gilliam, from Long Beach, California, was a New York model and married John whom she met in New York (now divorced). They formed a friendship with Cass Elliott from Baltimore, then aged 23 – she having formerly travelled across America in satirical revues – and Denny Doherty from Halifax, Nova Scotia, aged 24, who were in a group called The Mugwumps. Other groups with whom the four performed included The Big Three and The Halifax Three. John, Michelle and Denny decided on a holiday in the Virgin Islands. Cass followed to take a job as a waitress. They then decided to form a group. They stayed for eight months, living in tents near the beach and strumming their guitars and singing. The governor of the islands suggested they moved on. American pop culture for the natives did not contribute much to the Islands.

They arrived in Los Angeles where they met 'Eve of Destruction' singer Barry McGuire. Tanned but very hungry, they were taken by Barry to his record producer Lou Adler who heard them sing and signed them to the Dunhill label. John also played guitar, Denny was lead guitar, and all four were singers.

These singers had a unique vocal style. John and Denny called the girls 'Mamas' as a joke. When they signed with Dunhill, and were asked the name of the group they said they had been calling each other Mamas and Papas, and so thus they became known. Disc released December 1965, it became a million seller in early 1966 with R.I.A.A. Gold Disc award. In Britain it reached No 23, with nine weeks in the bestsellers.

AL MARTINO
SPANISH EYES *Capitol* [*USA*]. Musical director/composer Bert Kaempfert originally wrote this as an instrumental item 'Moon Over Naples' for his Polydor (Germany) album 'Magic Music of Faraway Places'. Issued as a singles disc it was a world-wide bestseller.

Charles Singleton and Eddy Snyder wrote lyrics for the tune giving it a new title 'Spanish Eyes', and Al Martino's disc was a big success. It got to No 11 for two weeks in the U.S.A. with 12 weeks in the bestsellers, and was a big seller. It also sold 800,000 in Germany. Sales of 1,500,000 were reported at the end of 1967. In 1973 it was No 5 and 21 weeks in the British bestsellers.

Al Martino's success with the song resulted in an album for Capitol of the same title, including the song. This gained an R.I.A.A. Gold Disc award for million dollar sales in December 1966.

'Spanish Eyes' was Martino's second million seller, 13 years after his first with 'Here in My Heart' (1952).

ROGER MILLER
KING OF THE ROAD *Smash* [*USA*]. A top country-and-western disc. The popular country-and-western folk singer Roger Miller wrote this song himself in 1964. The disc climbed high in the charts on both sides of the Atlantic, No 3 with 13 weeks in the U.S. bestsellers, and No 1 in Britain with 15 weeks in the bestsellers.

It sold 550,000 within 18 days of release in the U.S.A., soon passing the million, and subsequently reached two million. This was Miller's third Golden Disc. Gold Disc award, R.I.A.A., 1965 and winner of five Grammy Awards for best Rock and Roll recording, Best Rock and Roll (Male) Performance, best Country-and-Western Recording, Best Country-and-Western Song and Best Country-and-Western Performance 1965.

THE MIRACLES
TRACKS OF MY TEARS *Tamla* [*USA*]. This fourth million seller for The Miracles was written by three members of the group – William 'Smokey' Robinson, Warren Moore and Marvin Taplin. The disc achieved No 16 in the U.S. charts with 12 weeks in the bestsellers. Release was on 10 July 1965.

Claudette ('Smokey's' wife), who took Warren Moore's place when he was called up for 21 months' service with the U.S. Forces, left the group in December 1964 to devote her time to youth clubs and the church. The group then consisted of 'Smokey' Robinson, Bobby Rogers, Ronnie White and Warren Moore. Lead guitarist Marv Taplin and drummer Donald White completed the personnel. (See also 'Shop Around', 1961, for further data.)

The Miracles paid their first visit to Britain in November 1964. In 1969 it was No 9 and 13 weeks in the British bestsellers.

GOING TO A GO GO *Tamla* [*USA*]. Issued on 25 December 1965, this disc provided The Miracles with their fifth million seller by 1966. It got to No 9 in the U.S. charts with 12 weeks in the bestsellers. It reached No 44 with five weeks in the British bestsellers. Song written by group members William 'Smokey' Robinson, Warren Moore, Robert Rogers and Marv Taplin.

YUKIKO NINOMIYA
MATSUNOKI KOUTA *King* [*Japan*]. This disc was issued in Japan in January 1965 and sold a million by April. The song is a type of Ozashiki melody. The disc was No 1 for ten weeks in Japan from 3 April to 5 June 1965. The composer is unknown,

so under Japanese law a certain sum in royalties has to be paid into the Bureau of Justice until the composer is established.

PETER AND GORDON
TRUE LOVE WAYS *Columbia* [*Britain*]. Another big hit for this very popular duo made it their third million seller from combined British and American sales. The disc was No 2 in Britain with 15 weeks in the bestsellers and No 14 in the U.S.A. with 11 weeks in the bestsellers. The song is an oldie of 1958 written by Norman Petty and the late Buddy Holly.

The disc was issued on the Capitol label in the U.S.A.

WILSON PICKETT (rhythm-and-blues vocalist)
IN THE MIDNIGHT HOUR *Atlantic* [*USA*]. Wilson Pickett was born in Prattville, Alabama, on 18 March 1941, his family moving to Detroit when Wilson was in his teens. For four years he was a spiritual singer and performed with groups and as a soloist in and around Detroit. In 1959 he became a singer with The Falcons (see 1959), a top group in the area, where he became aware for the first time of the rhythm-and-blues music world that was to have a profound effect on his future. After a time with the group he found he had a talent for songwriting and composed many songs for the group including their first hit 'I Found a Love'. His solo career was sparked off by an audition in 1963 for artist Lloyd Price's label Double L and his first self-written solo 'If You Need Me' became a hit and eventually a rhythm-and-blues standard. His second self-written song 'It's Too Late' was also a hit for Double L.

In 1964, Pickett signed with Atlantic Records and continued his string of hits on his new label, including his own compositions 'For Better or Worse', 'I'm Gonna Cry', 'In the Midnight Hour' and 'Mustang Sally'. He then became one of the most sought-after artists for concerts and one-nighter tours, and appeared on most of TV's top rock and roll shows in both New York and Hollywood. In 1968 he had several discs in the charts in the U.S.A.

Wilson Pickett appeared in Britain for the first time in November 1965 to promote 'In the Midnight Hour' and other songs.

This disc was No 19 for two weeks in the U.S.A. with 21 weeks in the bestsellers, and reached No 12 for a week in Britain with 11 weeks in the bestsellers, and he became very popular there. The song was written by Wilson Pickett and Steve Cropper and first released in the U.S.A. in July 1965. The disc sold over the million globally.

The artist has one of the largest collections of spiritual albums of any performer.

GENE PITNEY
LOOKING THROUGH THE EYES OF LOVE *Musicor* [*USA*] *Stateside* [*Britain*]. This big success for Gene was shared with the writers husband/wife Barry Mann and Cynthia Weill. The disc was such a success in Britain (No 3 in the charts and 12 weeks in the bestsellers) and in the U.S.A. that global sales made it Pitney's fifth million seller. Chart position in the U.S.A. was No 23 and the disc was eight weeks in the bestsellers.

ELVIS PRESLEY
CRYING IN THE CHAPEL *Victor* [*USA*]. This song was originally written in 1953 by Artie Glenn and was then a million dollar seller for The Orioles. Elvis Presley originally recorded the song, a particular favourite of his, for an album in 1960 but it was omitted from the disc. This belated issue got to No 3 in the U.S. charts with 14 weeks in the bestsellers and was No 1 in Britain for two weeks in June 1965 with 15 weeks in the bestsellers. The combined sales of over a quarter million in Britain added to a million in the U.S.A. and sales elsewhere, made it Elvis' 49th (global) million seller. The final tally was said to be 1¾ million.

I'M YOURS backed with (It's a) LONG LONG LONELY HIGHWAY *Victor* [*USA*]. The two songs are from Elvis' film

Tickle Me. 'I'm Yours' was written by Don Robertson and Hal Blair in 1961. 'Lonely Highway' was written by Doc Pomus and Mort Shuman, making the 50th million seller globally for the champion winner of Gold Disc awards.

This disc was No 11 for two weeks in the U.S.A. and 11 weeks in the bestsellers.

(*Note:* See 1957 for Presley's 51st million seller by 1965.)

TELL ME WHY *Victor* [*USA*]. Written by Titus Turner in 1956, Elvis' disc, issued in late December 1965, sold over half a million in the U.S.A. and a global million by early 1966. Disc achieved No 20 in U.S. charts with 7 weeks in the bestsellers, and No 14 in Britain with 10 weeks in the bestsellers.

Elvis' 52nd million seller.

THE ROLLING STONES

THE LAST TIME *Decca* [*Britain*]. This million seller, globally, for the controversial Rolling Stones was written by Mick Jagger and Keith Richard of the group. The disc was No 1 for four weeks in Britain with 13 weeks in the bestsellers, and No 9 for two weeks in the U.S. charts where it stayed 10 weeks in the bestsellers.

Personnel for this recording: Mick (Michael Philip) Jagger (vocalist, harmonica) born 26 July 1943 Dartford, Kent, educated at the London School of Economics; Brian Jones (guitar, harmonica) born 28 February 1944, Cheltenham (died July 1969); Keith Richard (guitar) born 18 December 1943, Dartford, Kent; Bill Wyman (bass), born 24 October 1941, Lewisham, London; Charles Robert Watts (drums), born 2 June 1941 in London.

The group's music is quite different from that of any other English group – a basic rhythm-and-blues approach. Their music attracted big crowds. They first met in London's Marquee Club where they listened to music and then formed the group, originally a sextet including pianist and maraccas player Ian Stewart who dropped out to become their manager on the road. The starting point of the Rolling Stones' career was the Station Hotel, Richmond, Surrey, in late 1962 and into 1963 where their reputation was built. Film producer Giorgio Gomelsky informed the *Record Mirror* he was filming a session by the group. The paper's writers praised them so highly that all the disc companies wanted them. Decca won the bid for what turned out to be one of the hottest groups in the country. Their first discs were 'Come On' (1963), 'I Wanna Be Your Man' (1964) by Lennon and McCart-

ney of The Beatles; 'Not Fade Away' (1964) their first quarter million plus seller in Britain; an EP disc 'Five by Five' which was No 1 for 23 weeks; and two singles 'It's All Over Now' and 'Little Red Rooster' (No 1 for two weeks). All were quarter million sellers (1964). Their first album 'The Rolling Stones' sold over 200,000 (1964) and was No 1 for 12 weeks. 'Rolling Stones Vol. 2' album sold over 400,000 in 1965 and was No 1 for 13 weeks. They visited the U.S.A. in 1964 and 1965 and were a great success there both with personal appearances and disc sales. All their records have been hits. 'The Rolling Stones' is the title of an old Muddy Waters blues song.

(I can't get no) SATISFACTION *London* [*USA*]. This song, recorded in Hollywood, written by Mick Jagger and Keith Richard of the group, sold a million on the London label in the U.S.A. by the end of June 1965. It was the group's biggest hit to date. It was No 1 in the States for four weeks (with 14 weeks in the bestsellers) and for three weeks in Britain (with 12 weeks in the bestsellers) achieving a global sale of 4½ million by mid-1966. Gold Disc award, R.I.A.A., 1965.

GET OFF MY CLOUD *London* [*USA*]. Another million seller for the controversial Rolling Stones, written by group members Mick Jagger and Keith Richard. It was recorded in Hollywood during their U.S. tour in 1965.

The disc was No 1 for two weeks simultaneously in Britain and the U.S.A. (and 12 weeks in both bestsellers). It topped Britain's charts for three weeks in all, selling over 250,000 alone on the Decca label and enjoyed very big sales in the U.S.A. and elsewhere. Released on 22 October 1965 in Britain.

AS TEARS GO BY *London* [*USA*]. Written by Mick Jagger and Keith Richard of the group with their recording chief Andrew Loog Oldham, this was first recorded in 1964 by Britain's Marianne Faithfull for whom it became a big hit in Britain and America. The Rolling Stones' own recording was released in the U.S.A. in late December 1965 and got to No 3 in their charts in early 1966 and in the bestsellers for 9 weeks, with million sale globally by the beginning of 1967.

OUT OF OUR HEADS (album) *Decca* [*Britain*] *London* [*USA*]. America issued the album with this title in July 1965 which contained the following (Nanker and Phelge are pseudonyms for Jagger and Richard): *'Mercy, Mercy', by Don Covay and Ronnie Miller (1964); *'Hitch Hike', by Marvin Gaye, William

Stevenson and Paul (1965); 'The Last Time', by Mick Jagger and Keith Richard (1965); *'That's How Strong My Love Is', by Jamison (1965); *'Good Times', by Sam Cooke (1964); 'I'm All Right', by Nanker and Phelge (1965); 'Satisfaction', by Mick Jagger and Keith Richard (1965); *'Cry to Me', by Bert Russell (1961); *'The Under Assistant West Coast Promotion Man', by Nanker and Phelge (1965); 'Play with Fire', by Nanker and Phelge (1965); 'The Spider and the Fly', by Nanker and Phelge (1965); 'One More Try', by Mick Jagger and Keith Richard (1965).

The British issue (24 September 1965) contained the following and the six titles marked * as above: 'She Said "Yeah"', by Jackson and Christy (1965); 'Gotta Get Away', by Mick Jagger and Keith Richard (1965); 'Talkin' 'Bout You', by Chuck Berry (1961); 'Oh Baby' (we got a good thing tonight), by Ozen (1965); 'Heart of Stone', by Mick Jagger and Keith Richard (1965); 'I'm Free', by Mick Jagger and Keith Richard (1965).

Three other musicians, Jack Nitzsche (the group's road manager in the U.S.A.), Ian Stewart and J. W. Alexander, assisted in organ, piano and percussion work. The album was produced by Andrew Oldham in Chicago and Hollywood.

Combined sales went well over the million globally. Sales in the U.S.A. were big, the disc staying in the charts for 65 weeks and reaching No 1 for three weeks. In Britain its run was 26 weeks in the charts with two weeks at No 2.

R.I.A.A. Gold Disc award 12 October 1965.

DECEMBER'S CHILDREN (album) *London* [*USA*]. Second million seller album for the group, U.S.A. sales, with R.I.A.A. Gold Disc award on 15 January 1966. It was No 2 for three weeks and stayed in the bestsellers for 33 weeks.

Contents: 'She Said "Yeah"', by Jackson and Christy (1965); 'Talkin' 'Bout You', by Chuck Berry (1961); 'You Better Move On', by Arthur Alexander; 'Look What You've Done', by Margonfield (1965); 'Get Off My Cloud', by Mick Jagger and Keith Richard (1965); 'The Singer not the Song', by Green (1965); 'Route 66', by Bob Troup (1965); 'As Tears Go By', by Mick Jagger, Keith Richard and Andrew Oldham (1964); 'I'm Free', by Mick Jagger and Keith Richard (1965); 'Gotta Get Away', by Mick Jagger and Keith Richard (1965); 'Blue Turns to Grey', by Mick Jagger and Keith Richard (1965); 'I'm Movin' On', by Hank Snow (1950).

Released in the U.S.A. in December 1965.

NINI ROSSO (trumpet)

IL SILENZIO (The Silence) *Durium* [*Italy*]. This disc became a big hit all over Europe, No 1 in Italy (for six weeks), West Germany (five weeks), Austria, Holland, Belgium and Switzerland. It sold over 750,000 in Italy and two million in Germany. Global sales have been estimated at five million by end of 1967. Nini was presented with the first European Common Market Gold Disc in Hamburg in September 1965. The tune, written by Nini Rosso and Guglielmo Brezza, is a trumpet solo - a variation of 'The Last Post'.

Nini (real name Celeste Rosso) was born in Turin on 19 September 1926 and ran away from home at the age of 19 to follow a musical career instead of an academic one - against his parents' wishes. He was found playing a trumpet in a Nice nightclub by the police and sent back to his family. They allowed him to continue playing, and he formed a small orchestra, toured all over Italy, the rest of Europe and India. On return he was engaged by Radio Turin, later going to Rome where he soon became known as one of Italy's best jazz players. His first disc was 'La ballata della tromba', an instant hit. Then came 'Concerto disperato', another of his compositions (1963) that became the theme of Stewart Granger's film *The Legion's Last Patrol*, a hit in Italy and other countries including Japan.

'Il silenzio' was also a success in Britain, reaching No 8 with 14 weeks in the bestsellers, where it was additionally recorded by Eddie Calvert, and in the U.S.A. by Al Hirt.

MITCH RYDER AND THE DETROIT WHEELS (vocal and instrumental quintet)

JENNY TAKE A RIDE *New Voices* [*USA*]. The first recording for this group took their disc to No 10 in the U.S.A. charts within as many weeks from date of release in December 1965 with 12 weeks in the bestsellers, and was reported to have sold the million. It was No 33 in Britain, and five weeks in the bestsellers.

The group was first called Billy Lee and The (Detroit) Rivieras, the name being changed to Mitch Ryder and The Detroit Wheels by their manager Alan Stroh. Mitch Ryder formerly sang with rhythm-and-blues groups in the Detroit area, and, when the Dave Clark Five from England appeared in Detroit in 1965, the group appeared on the same bill under their original name. They were scheduled to sing only two numbers, but were on stage for almost an hour and a half. Famous producer Bob Crewe, notified by WXYZ-Detroit's disc jockey Dave Prince, was in the audience and immediately signed them. Under his guidance, this disc resulted plus five consecutive top records, and personal appearances through the U.S.A.

Besides Mitch Ryder, the group consisted of 'Little' John Badenjek (drums), Jimmy McCartney (lead guitarist), Earl Eliot (bass guitarist) and Joe Cubert (rhythm guitarist).

The composition is by E. Johnson and R. Penniman (real name of 'Little Richard').

SAM THE SHAM AND THE PHARAOHS

WOOLY BULLY *Penn* (*released*) *MGM* [*USA*]. Sam the Sham (real name Domingo Samudio) was born and raised in Dallas, Texas. After graduation he joined the U.S. Navy for four years, and decided to devote himself to music upon his discharge. He then worked on building sites and saved enough money for the entrance fee to Arlington State College in Texas, and began singing with various groups. Seeking a distinctive sound for a group, he taught himself to play the organ and saved enough to buy one. Organists being scarce, he found no difficulty in getting work. Moving to Louisiana, he joined a friend's band which became popular in many clubs in and around Memphis until its leader returned home. Sam and the bass player David Martin stayed on, added guitarist Ray Stinnet and drummer Jerry Paterson, and later saxophonist Butch Gibson, adopting the name Sam the Sham and The Pharaohs. Stan Kessler, a producer for Penn Records, invited them to the studios for an audition. They arrived in their black hearse which they used for transportation. Their first disc was (May 1964) 'Haunted House'. Then came 'Wooly Bully', written by Sam in 1964 - a thudding beat number with a tongue-twisting chorus and nonsense lyrics, which when released on MGM label became a big hit, reaching No 2 in the U.S. charts in June 1965 with 18 weeks in the bestsellers, and an eventual two million sale with another million abroad. It was No 11 in Britain with 15 weeks in the bestsellers.

Sam explains the term 'sham' as rhythm-and-blues jargon for shuffling, twisting or jiving around to music. Before he started playing the organ, Sam 'shammed' while he sang. The group wore wild clothing, Sam a jewelled jacket and feathered turban, the Pharaohs special costumes including Arab dress. All were aged 23 or 25 when this disc was made.

Gold Disc award, R.I.A.A., 1965.

THE SEEKERS (instrumental and vocal quartet)

I'LL NEVER FIND ANOTHER YOU *Columbia* [*Britain*]. This first big hit for an Australian group was a million seller for The Seekers in their very first recording in Britain. Over 700,000 copies in Britain plus big sales from the U.S.A. and elsewhere totalled 1,750,000.

The quartet was one girl and three boys: Judith Durham, born in Melbourne on 3 July 1943, who also plays the piano, guitar, the harmonica, castanets and tambourine; Bruce Woodley, born Melbourne, 25 July 1942, plays Spanish guitar and five-string banjo; Keith Potger, born Columbo, Ceylon, 2 March 1941, plays guitar, banjo and recorder; and Athol Guy, born Victoria, Australia, 5 January 1940, double bass and zimbuka. Keith's family moved to Australia when he was six. The quartet met (1964) in Australia and was started purely as a hobby after their day jobs (Bruce and Athol worked for an advertising agency in Melbourne, Judith was a pathologist's secretary, and Keith a radio producer). They appeared on local TV shows around Melbourne, and becoming very popular decided to give up their jobs and try their luck in Britain. After some work on board ships, one of the trips finished in Britain. Within three weeks of arriving in London they made their first TV appearance on 'Sunday Night at the Palladium'. They then made their first disc in Britain, 'I'll Never Find Another You' which was No 1 for two weeks and 23 weeks in the bestsellers. In the U.S.A. the disc was No 4 and 13 weeks in the bestsellers. This song was written in 1964 by Tom Springfield (of the Springfields' group).

The Seekers were unusual in that their style was more folk song than electronic, and they were the first Australian group to become successful abroad. They held the Australian record for crowds with 200,000 – drawn at Melbourne's Myer Music Bowl in 1967.

A WORLD OF OUR OWN *Columbia* [*Britain*]. The second million seller for The Seekers, the song also the work of Tom Springfield. The disc was No 2 in Britain with 18 weeks in the bestsellers and duplicated the success of their first disc, with big sales in Britain (half a million or more), in the U.S.A., and elsewhere around the world, making well over the magic seven figures. The song, of a pop-folk message type, delineates the future in a more pleasant world. The disc was issued on the Capitol label in the U.S.A. where it was No 19 for two weeks and 10 weeks in the bestsellers.

THE CARNIVAL IS OVER *Columbia* [*Britain*]. The Seekers firmly established themselves with this number as a top group of 1965. Issued in October 1965, this disc soon achieved the No 1 spot in Britain for three weeks with 17 weeks in the bestsellers, and sold a million by the year's end. An 'end of a romance' song, it was Tom Springfield's third consecutive big hit for the group. The composer adapted the melody from an old Russian folk song 'Stenjka Razin', but half the tune is his own composition and the lyric entirely his own work. A million sale was achieved in Britain alone.

SIMON AND GARFUNKEL
(vocal and instrumental duo)
THE SOUNDS OF SILENCE *Columbia* [*USA*]. Paul Simon, the writer of this song (in 1964), and Art Garfunkel first met in grade school and started singing together from the age of 13. At the time of making this disc, Art was working for his degree in mathematics at New York University, then became a graduate student at Columbia University. Paul graduated from N.Y. University, then majored in English literature at Queen's College and started songwriting, joining Art when college work wasn't too involved. From school functions and private gatherings, they gained full professional status at Gerde's Folk City, New York, and performed in the Greenwich Village coffee houses, and later at the Edinburgh Folk Festival, etc. Engagements also took them to London and Paris in concerts and folk nightclubs. Both were in their twenties when they recorded this beautiful song with its profound lyrics of the inability of people to communicate with one another. Paul says it took him six months to write the song – a line a day. The duo's songs are in the traditional folk idiom with 'rock' overtones. Most of Paul's songs are extremely intellectual and deeply poetic. 'The Sounds of Silence' brought them international fame. It was in the U.S. bestseller charts for 14 weeks, two of these at No 1 in January 1966, and was awarded a Gold Disc by R.I.A.A. for a million sale in February 1966.

Paul wrote the songs and Art did the vocal arrangements and played guitar. Both their material and performances were of the highest order. They first performed under the name of Tom and Jerry, recording for Big Records (1962).

Paul Simon was born on 13 October 1941, Newark, New Jersey. Art Garfunkel was born on 5 November 1941, New York City. They have since broken up and now have very successful solo careers, Art adding acting to his, having appeared in films such as *Carnal Knowledge*.

SONNY AND CHER (vocal duo)
I GOT YOU BABE *Atco* [*USA*]. 'I Got You Babe' was a major success for this duo on both sides of the Atlantic, selling half a million in Britain (on the Atlantic label) and over a million in the U.S.A., totalling three million globally. This disc was No 1 for three weeks in the U.S.A. (with 14 weeks in the bestsellers) and one week in Britain (with 12 weeks in the bestsellers). Gold Disc award, R.I.A.A., 1965.

Cher (Cherilyn La Pierre Sakisian) was born on 20 May 1946 in El Centro, California, and has Cherokee blood in her. Her mother, who had been acting in Hollywood for a number of years, started Cher on an acting career some years ago, when she was tutored by Jeff Corey, prominent acting teacher in Hollywood. She met Sonny Bono in 1963 at a recording session for Phil Spector where they were engaged to sing background music for The Ronettes. They teamed up and married (since divorced). Sonny (Salvatore Bono) was born 16 February 1935 in Detroit, and has been in show business all his life. He spent most of his time in Los Angeles and has had a long friendship with Phil Spector (of Philles Records), playing and singing with The Ronettes, The Crystals, Darlene Love and The Righteous Brothers. In 1964 he wrote the big hit 'Needles and Pins' (see Searchers, 1964). Other successes were 'Baby Don't Go', 'The Boy Next Door' and 'Dream Baby'. He is also the composer of 'I Got You Babe'. Cher cut some solo discs for Imperial. The couple signed a long-term contract with Atlantic Records.

Sonny and Cher were part of the leading exponents of the rock-folk-message type of song, a hybrid combining the instrumentation of rock music with folk lyric and often lyrics of protest.

They wore completely unconventional clothes, the visual impact being tremendous and their discs have a very weird and original sound.

'Look at Us' their first album issued in August in the U.S.A. was a big success.

They made appearances in Britain in 1965 on TV and created a sensation. Their 'Sonny and Cher' TV show in the U.S.A. was an enormous success.

LOOK AT US (album) *Atco* [*USA*]. This tremendous hit for Sonny and Cher's first album passed the 750,000 sale in just over two months after release in the U.S.A. With sales from all over Europe and the Far East, the global tally was over two million.

The contents of the disc: 'I Got You Babe', by Sonny Bono (1965); 'Unchained Melody' (from the film *Unchained* 1955), by Hy Zaret/Alex North (1955); 'Then He Kissed Me', by Jeff Barry, Ellie Greenwich and Phil Spector (1963); 'Sing C'est La Vie', by Bono, Greene and Stone (1965); 'It's Gonna Rain', by Sonny Bono (1965); '500 Miles Away From Home', by Bobby Bare, Hedy West and Charles Williams (1962); 'Just You', by Sonny Bono (1965); 'The Letter', by Don Harris and Dewey Terry; 'Let It Be Me' (orig. 'Je t'appartiens' in France, 1955), by Pierre Delanoe and Gilbert Becaud (English words: Mann Curtis, 1960); 'You Don't Love Me', by Raye; 'You Really Got a Hold on Me', by William 'Smokey' Robinson (1962); 'Why Don't They Let Us Fall in Love?', by Jeff Barry, Ellie Greenwich and Phil Spector (1965).

This disc helped to put the husband-and-wife team into the big money class – around $3,000,000 gross for 1965. In 1964 their income was $3,000. Gold Disc award, R.I.A.A., 1965.

THE SUPREMES
STOP, IN THE NAME OF LOVE *Motown* [*USA*]. The fourth million seller for The Supremes was written by Brian Holland, Eddie Holland and Lamont Dozier. This disc was No 1 for two weeks in the U.S.A. with 12 weeks in the bestsellers, their fourth consecutive disc to hit the top position. In Britain it reached No

7 with 12 weeks in the bestsellers. Disc released in the U.S.A. on 20 February 1965.

BACK IN MY ARMS AGAIN *Motown* [*USA*]. This was the fifth consecutive disc by The Supremes to sell a million and to top the U.S. charts (for one week) with 11 weeks in the bestsellers. It was No 40 in Britain with five weeks in the bestsellers. The song was written again by Brian Holland, Eddie Holland and Lamont Dozier. Released on 1 May 1965; a top rhythm-and-blues disc.

NOTHING BUT HEARTACHES *Motown* [*USA*]. Had it not been for The Beatles and Sonny and Cher who monopolized the U.S. charts during August and September 1965, there is no doubt the disc would have got to No 1. It did, however, get a high position (No 8) with 9 weeks in the bestsellers, and sold a million just the same. The song was again by the same team of Brian Holland, Eddie Holland and Lamont Dozier. Disc released on 31 July 1965.

I HEAR A SYMPHONY *Motown* [*USA*]. This disc was released on 23 October 1965. The seventh million seller for the fantastically popular Supremes was also the seventh consecutive hit written for them by their successful songwriting team. 'I Hear a Symphony' was the trio's sixth disc to get to No 1 in the U.S. charts, this time for two weeks, and was 10 weeks in the bestsellers. It was No 39 in Britain with five weeks in the bestsellers. Global sales over two million.

THE TEMPTATIONS (rhythm-and-blues vocal quintet)

MY GIRL *Gordy* [*USA*]. The Temptations got together around 1961 and soon after found an opening for their talent in a local theatre's rock and roll show. Choosing the name they are now known by, they got the job.

They were subsequently signed to the Gordy label, run by Berry Gordy, Jr. who founded the now famous Motown Record company and the Motown sound by putting groups of talented performers together who had a background in gospel music.

The group became nationally famous via their Gordy recordings, notably 'The Girl's All Right with Me', 'My Baby' and this disc of 'My Girl'. They also developed an extensive choreographed club routine, their rendition of 'Ole Man River' in *a capella* style (after the manner of church music) proved to be

outstanding. Over the years they have sold several million discs.

'My Girl' was written by Ronald White and William 'Smokey' Robinson, both members of the famous Miracles group who were also successful Motown artists for Gordy. The disc was No 1 for one week in the national charts with 10 weeks in the bestsellers, and No 1 in the rhythm-and-blues charts in the U.S.A. It was No 43 in Britain. Release was on 9 January 1965.

Members of the Temptations are: Melvin Franklin, born 12 October 1942 in Montgomery, Alabama; Paul Williams, born 2 July 1939 in Birmingham, Alabama; David Ruffin, born 18 January 1941 in Meridian, Mississippi; Otis Miles, born 30 October 1941 in Texarkana, Texas; Eddie Kendricks, born 17 December 1939 in Birmingham, Alabama. All are lead singers, who take over the role from number to number. The immediate lead separates from the others; the other four group in a mixture of intricate choreography and subtle vocal harmonies.

The disc became a standard rhythm-and-blues item and subsequently sold over a million.

THE TOYS

A LOVER'S CONCERTO *Dyno Voice* [*USA*]. This million seller was the very first recording by The Toys, a coloured female trio consisting of Barbara Harris (lead singer), born on 18 August 1945 in Elizabeth City, North Carolina; June Montiero, born 1 July 1946 in Queens, New York; and Barbara Parritt, born 10 January 1944 in Wilmington, North Carolina.

They all went to the Woodrow Wilson High School in Jamaica, New York, where they discovered that they all liked to sing. They teamed up and rehearsed for a few weeks, then contracted a U.S. disc company Genius Inc., making an appointment with Vince Marc. Greatly impressed, Marc called in his songwriting producers Sandy Linzer and Denny Rendell who went to work on a Bach five-finger exercise and wrote 'A Lover's Concerto' for their first session. Within three months, their disc got to No 2 in the U.S.A. for one week and stayed in No 2 position for three weeks, with 15 weeks in the bestsellers, passing the million sale soon after. In Britain it was No 5 and 13 weeks in the bestsellers.

The Toys made their TV debut in 'Shindig' and their first tour with Gene Pitney, followed by many other TV appearances in the U.S.A., and TV in Britain in 1965. Vince Marc is their personal manager. They were also featured in a film *The Girl in Daddy's Bikini*.

Global sales of this disc – two million. Gold Disc award, R.I.A.A., 1965.

THE WALKER BROTHERS

MAKE IT EASY ON YOURSELF *Philips* [*Britain*] *Smash* [*USA*]. The remarkable fact about this American trio is that it was not until they came to Britain in this year that they became a big success, due to this disc that got them to No 1 in the British charts for one week with 14 weeks in the bestsellers. It was also a hit (No 16) in the U.S.A. later on the Smash label and was 10 weeks in the bestsellers.

The Walkers are not actually brothers, but Gary Walker (real name Gary Leeds), born 3 September 1944, Glendale, California (drummer); John Walker (real name John Maus), born 12 November 1943, New York City (guitarist); and Scott Walker (real name Scott Engel), born 9 January 1944, Hamilton, Ohio (bass guitarist). Gary had been to England on a tour with the U.S. artist P. J. Proby, and on his return to the States found John and Scott playing in Gazzarri's in Hollywood. They let their hair grow long for eight months and were ahead of most artists in their musical approach. They teamed up and appeared on a major local TV show which became a nationwide success ('Hollywood à Gogo'). They had decided to leave for England at this time and try for their big break there, rightly assuming that three Americans with long hair would be something entirely new. They were firstly a success at novelties, but English audiences began to take notice that they had good voices when they sang 'Make It Easy on Yourself'. Their disc soon sold over 250,000 in Britain where it was 14 weeks in the bestsellers, and U.S. sales and elsewhere eventually made a global million. The song was written by ace American songsmiths Hal David (words) and Burt Bacharach (music) in 1962.

The Walker Brothers were all Californian college students before becoming professionals, Scott being educated at California Institute of Arts, John at El Camingo College and Gary at Glendale College. Gary says his biggest break was playing with Elvis Presley when Elvis' drummer was ill. He had also played for other U.S. stars while still at college. Scott is also a bass player. John is also a violinist, clarinettist and saxophonist. At the age of 12 he took part in a TV series 'Hello Mom' with Betty Hutton.

The trio chose the name of The Walker Brothers simply because they liked it. Scott was helped by Eddie Fisher who took him on several major TV shows after hearing him sing at a Palm Springs luncheon, and has also had working experience with Sonny (Bono) and Phil Spector of the Philles label.

WE FIVE (vocal and instrumental quintet)

YOU WERE ON MY MIND *A & M* [*USA*]. This song, a folk-influenced ballad written in 1964 by Sylvia Fricker, was the debut disc for the group and achieved the No 2 spot in the U.S. charts for two weeks. It sold a million by the end of 1965.

The 'We Five' story began in 1962 when Mike Stewart, brother of John (a member of the famous Kingston Trio), formed The Ridge Runners, a mainly folksinging group. John brought his brother's group to the attention of Frank Werber, The Kingston Trio's manager, as he was convinced of Mike's great ability. Werber thought the group good but urged them to abandon the folk idiom and search for their own unique sound. For the following two years they perfected their sound and Werber became convinced of their potentiality after auditioning them at his newly-formed Trident Productions. Werber groomed them for eight months, rehearsing, developing new ideas and polishing tunes, etc., and finally on 20 April 1965 took the group to a recording studio and produced 'You Were on My Mind'. A deal was made for A. & M. Records (owned by Herb Alpert and Jerry Moss) to release the singles disc. It stayed in the U.S. bestsellers for 15 weeks.

The group consisted of: Mike Stewart, leader and arranger, writer of several songs for The Kingston Trio, who hails from Riverside, California, and was educated at San Francisco University and Mt San Antonio College; Beverly Bivens, the only female member and lead singer, born in Orange, California, educated at Santa Anna High School where she was a member of the school's glee club; Bob Jones, a keen jazz guitarist from Honolulu, educated at St Louis High School, Hawaii, then attended the same university and college as Mike Stewart in San Francisco; Jerry Burgan, born in Kansas City and raised in San Diego, California, who also attended the same colleges as Mike and Bob, a versatile guitarist who highlighted the group's driving, rhythmic beat; Pete Fullerton, a native of Pomona, California, star football athlete at Clarmont High School, then a graduate of Mt San Antonio College, the drummer of the group.

(Little) STEVIE WONDER

UP TIGHT *Tamla* [*USA*]. The second big hit for (erstwhile 'Little') Stevie, the song written by Henry Cosby, Sylvia Moy and Stevie Judkins (Stevie Wonder). Released on 11 December 1965, it achieved the No 3 position in 1966 in the U.S. charts, and a run of 14 weeks in the bestsellers. The disc was also a success in Britain where it was No 13 in 1966 with 10 weeks in the bestsellers. It is estimated to have sold a million globally.

A top rhythm-and-blues disc in U.S.A. and Britain.

THE YARDBIRDS (rhythm-and-blues vocal and instrumental quintet)

FOR YOUR LOVE *Columbia* [*Britain*]. Personnel of this group are Keith Relf (harmonica and vocalist) born Richmond, Surrey, 22 March 1943; Eric Clapton (guitar); Chris Dreja (rhythm guitar) born Surbiton, Surrey, 11 November 1945; Paul Samwell-Smith (bass guitar) born south-west London, 8 May 1945; and Jim McCarty (drums) born Liverpool, 25 July 1943. They had all played with various groups before joining up and becoming The Yardbirds. The group were offered the residency of the Crawdaddy Club, Richmond, replacing The Rolling Stones in 1963. With The Rolling Stones so popular, it took The Yardbirds a few months to win back the fans to the club, but this they did, beating the crowds The Stones had brought in. Further appearances at London's Marquee Club and Liverpool were also big successes.

'For Your Love' was their third disc and in a few weeks got to No 1 in Britain's charts for one week with 12 weeks in the bestsellers, and brought The Yardbirds national recognition. On release in the U.S.A. on the Epic label it achieved No 6 position with 12 weeks in the bestsellers, and sold a global million. Eric Clapton left the group just after this disc was released and was replaced by Jeff Beck (lead guitar) who was born 24 June 1944.

'For Your Love' was written by Graham Gouldman.

ORIGINAL FILM SOUNDTRACK: MGM STUDIO ORCHESTRA (conducted by Maurice Jarre)

'DOCTOR ZHIVAGO' (album) *MGM* [*USA*]. The music for this outstanding film was written by Maurice Jarre, one of France's leading modern composers, who also wrote the score for the film *Lawrence of Arabia* (1962) that won him an Oscar.

Jarre began work on the *Zhivago* score - one of the most monumental ever undertaken for a motion picture - while the film was being shot in Spain. The film is a multi-million production of the Nobel Prize-winning novel by the Russian author Boris Pasternak. The novel was banned in Russia and political

pressure made it impossible for the author-poet to accept the Nobel Prize for Literature. The film was directed by David Lean who also directed *Lawrence of Arabia* that earned him an Oscar. *Doctor Zhivago* was awarded five Oscars, and the film was made in 22 foreign language versions, the greatest number for a single film in the studio's history. Filming took nine months and a total of three years to complete. The Moscow street set, dominated by an amazingly realistic background of the Kremlin, was constructed over a ten-acre area in the Madrid suburb of Canillas and took five and a half months to complete. Other scenes were shot in Finland.

The dramatic story of Doctor Zhivago evokes the whole experience of Russia, and its Revolution, over the past 50 years. The film had an international cast, with Omar Sharif as Zhivago, Julie Christie as Lara, Alec Guinness, Geraldine Chaplin, Tom Courtenay, Siobhan McKenna, Ralph Richardson, Rod Steiger and Rita Tushingham.

Maurice Jarre's music, lending vivid insight into the story and its characters, soars with grace and beauty.

The album was released in January 1966, sold 300,000 in six months, a further 300,000 the first fortnight in August and easily passed the million by year's end – the biggest all-time soundtrack seller for the MGM label – with R.I.A.A. Gold Disc award. It occupied a high position in the U.S. charts for many months, and was No 1 for five weeks.

Contents of the album: 'Overture' from *Doctor Zhivago*; 'Main title' from *Doctor Zhivago*; 'Lara Leaves Yuri'; 'At the Student Café'; 'Komarovsky and Lara's Rendezvous'; 'Revolution'; 'Lara's theme' from *Doctor Zhivago*; 'The Funeral'; 'Sventytski's Waltz'; 'Yuri Escapes'; 'Yonya Arrives at Varykino'; 'Yuri Writes a Poem for Lara'.

Song version of 'Lara's theme', 'Somewhere My Love' (words by Paul Francis Webster), subsequently published.

Sales by 1967 were two million. The album was 157 weeks in the U.S. bestsellers. Grammy Award for Best Film Soundtrack, 1966.

ORIGINAL FILM SOUNDTRACK WITH PIERRE BAROUCH AND NICOLE CROISELLE (vocals)

UN HOMME ET UNE FEMME (A Man and a Woman) (album) *United Artists* [*USA*]. The first French film soundtrack (put out in the U.S.A. by United Artists) to sell a million, with Gold Disc award from R.I.A.A. in 1967. The film, starring Anouk Aimée and Jean Trintignant and featuring Pierre Barouch, Valerie Legrange and Simone Paris, was directed and filmed by the do-it-yourself French film-maker Claude Lelouch, and is the story of a racing car driver and his love affair with a widow. The film won the Grand Prize at the Cannes Film Festival in 1966 and then became a great international success.

This album included the very popular 5/4 tempo semi-bossa nova theme of the same title. It had very many different recordings by other artists.

The music was composed by Francis Lai, and the author was Pierre Barouch who sings on the disc and appeared in the film. He and Nicole Croiselle sing the following (in French): 'A Man and a Woman'; 'Samba Saravah'; 'Today It's You'; 'Stronger Than Us'; 'In Our Shadow'; '124 Miles an Hour'.

The million sale was reported in September 1967 and the disc was in the bestsellers for 73 weeks.

ORIGINAL THEATRE CAST WITH RICHARD KILEY, IRVING JACOBSON, RAY MIDDLETON, ROBERT ROUNSEVILLE, JEAN DIENER, ELEANOR KNAPP, MIMI TURQUE, GINO CONFORTI, HARRY THEYARD; ORCHESTRA CONDUCTED BY NEIL WARNER

MAN OF LA MANCHA (album) *Kapp* [*USA*]. This musical adaptation of Miguel de Cervantes-Saavedra's world-famous novel, *Don Quixote*, written in 1605 (part 1) and 1615 (part 2) – with book by Dale Wasserman, lyrics by Joe Darion and music by Mitch Leigh – had its first try out in the summer of 1965 at the Goodspeed Opera House, and was then produced at the ANTA Washington Square Theatre, New York, on 22 November 1965. It was composer Mitch Leigh's first Broadway musical and earned both the composer and Richard Kiley (cast as 'Don Quixote') the top awards in the New York Drama Critics Poll of 1965-1966. Another top award went to Howard Bay for the Best Scenic Design. When the ANTA Theatre was demolished, the show moved to New York's Beck Theatre (spring 1968) and played a total of 2,329 performances, making it one of the top 20 long-runners on Broadway. The London production opened on 24 April 1968 at the Piccadilly Theatre with 253 performances

and Keith Michell as Don Quixote, and a revival there from 10 June 1969 with Richard Kiley in his original role. By the end of 1968, the show had made a profit of around $3 million. Cervantes' *Don Quixote*, however, brought him fame but little profit. The show was produced in several countries abroad. Rounseville was in all productions – a record of 2,412 performances.

This album was released in January 1966 and stayed on the charts in U.S.A. for 167 weeks, receiving a Gold Disc award from R.I.A.A. in 1967. It sold the million units by 1969.

The show's principal song 'The Impossible Dream' became immensely popular, with over 150 different recordings by January 1968. Contents of the album are: 'Overture'; 'Man of La Mancha' (I, Don Quixote) (Richard Kiley, Irving Jacobson); 'It's All the Same' (Jean Diener); 'Dulcinea' (Richard Kiley); 'I'm Only Thinking of Him' (Mimi Turque, Robert Rounseville, Eleanor Knapp); 'I Really Like Him' (Irving Jacobson and Jean Diener); 'What Do You Want of Me' (Jean Diener); 'Barber's Song'/'Golden Helmet' (Gino Conforti, Kiley and Jacobson); 'To Each His Own Dulcinea' (Robert Rounseville); 'The Impossible Dream' (Richard Kiley); 'Little Bird, Little Bird' (Harry Theyard); 'Dubbing' (Ray Middleton, Kiley, Diener and Jacobson); 'Abduction' (Harry Theyard); 'Aldonza' (Jean Diener, Richard Kiley); 'Little Gossip' (Irving Jacobson); 'Dulcinea'/'Impossible Dream' (Jean Diener, Kiley, Jacobson, Rounseville and entire company); 'Man of La Mancha'/'Psalm'/'Finale'.

HERB ALPERT AND THE TIJUANA BRASS

WHAT NOW MY LOVE (album) *A. & M.* [*USA*]. Another tremendous success for Alpert and his disc firm A. & M. It had initial orders of close to one million and was released in early May, reached No 2 in its second week and then No 1 for 12 weeks in the U.S. charts. By the end of May it had sold 1,600,000 and subsequently passed the two million mark. The disc received an immediate Gold Disc award from R.I.A.A. and the first 'Gold Cartridge' Award (from I.T.C.C.) for record-breaking retail sales of their stereo tape cartridge release of the same song selection. In its first three weeks, the cartridge sales exceeded $250,000. (*Note*: The new tape cartridges for cars became big business in the U.S.A. in 1966, opening up a new medium for the entertainment industry.) By June 1968, Alpert had sold over 20 million albums. A. & M.'s gross sales in 1964 were $600,000 for its third year of operation. In 1965 the gross dramatically soared to $7,-600,000, with each of Alpert's nine album releases gaining R.I.A.A. Gold Discs by 1967. A. & M.'s sales grossed over $25 million for 1966, and over $50 million in 1967.

The album contains the following: *Side 1* – 'What Now My Love' (originally 'Et maintenant' 1962 in France), by P. Delanoe/Gilbert Becaud (English words Carl Sigman, 1962); 'Freckles', by Ervan Coleman; 'Memories of Madrid', by Sol Lake; ***'It Was a Very Good Year', by Ervin Drake (1961); 'So What's New?', by John Pisano; 'Plucky', by Herb Alpert and John Pisano; *Side 2* – 'Magic Trumpet', by Bert Kaempfert; 'Cantina Blue', by Sol Lake; 'Brasilia', by Julius Wechter; 'If I Were a Rich Man' (from show *Fiddler on the Roof*), by Sheldon Harnick/Jerry Bock (1964); 'Five Minutes More', by Sammy Cahn/Jule Styne (1946); 'The Shadow of Your Smile' (from film *The Sandpiper* – song was Oscar winner of 1965), by P. F. Webster/Johnny Mandel (1965).

* From Frank Sinatra's CBS-TV special show, introduced therein by him.

This disc was in the bestsellers for 128 weeks and received Grammy Awards for Best Performance by an Orchestra, and Best Arrangement, 1966.

S.R.O. (album) *A & M* [*USA*]. An extremely appropriate title for this album, 'S.R.O.' (short for 'Standing Room Only'). It had the incredible advance order of 1,700,000, a record up to the end of 1967. Alpert was voted 'The Record Man of the Year' for 1966, his seven albums dominating the album charts in 1966 as no other artist had ever done in history. The Brass sold more than twice the number of albums as The Beatles and more than all the soundtracks combined in the first ten months of the year.

This album was No 1 for three weeks and stayed in the Top Ten in the U.S.A. for six months from time of release in late 1966 through 1967.

Its contents were: *Side 1* - 'Our Day Will Come', by Mort Garson/Bob Hilliard (1962); 'Mexican Road Race', by Sol Lake; 'I Will Wait for You' (from film *Umbrellas of Cherbourg*), by Jacques Demy/Michel Legrand (1964) (English words N. Gimbel); 'Bean Bag', by John Pisano, Julius Wechter and Herb Alpert; 'The Wall Street Rag', by Ervan Coleman; 'Work Song', by Oscar Brown Jr./Nat Adderley (1960); *Side 2* - 'Mame' (from show *Mame*), by Jerry Herman (1966); 'Blue Sunday', by Julius Wechter; 'Don't Go Breaking My Heart', by Hal David/Burt Bacharach; 'For Carlos', by John Pisano, Nick Ceroli and Herb Alpert; 'Freight Train Joe', by John Pisano; 'Flamingo', by Ed Anderson/Ted Grouya (1951).

By the end of 1967 sales of this album were well over the 2,500,000 figure. The disc was in the bestsellers for 85 weeks. R.I.A.A. Gold Disc award February 1967.

THE ANIMALS

THE BEST OF THE ANIMALS (album) *MGM* [*USA*]. This album of the group's big hits recorded by them up to the end of 1965 was issued in the U.S.A. in early 1966 and sold over 800,000 by the end of the year, with sales continuing into 1967. It was also issued in Britain on the Columbia label as 'The Most of the Animals' in April 1966, the combined global sales being over the million mark. A Gold Disc was awarded by R.I.A.A. on 28 July 1966.

The contents were: 'We've Gotta Get Out of This Place', by Barry Mann and Cynthia Weill (1965); 'Don't Let Me Be Misunderstood', by Bernie Benjamin, Sol Marcus and Gloria Caldwell (1965); 'Boom, Boom', by John Lee Hooker; 'Baby, Let Me Take You Home', by Bert Russell and Wes Farrell (1963); 'Bright Lights, Big City', by J. Reed (1961); 'I'm Crying', by Alan Price and Eric Burdon (1964); 'House of the Rising Sun', traditional, arranged Alan Price (1964); 'It's My Life', by Roger Atkins/Carl Derrilo (1965); 'Mess Around', by 'Nugetre' (Ahmet Ertegun) (1954); 'Dimples', by John Lee Hooker; 'Bring It on Home to Me', by Sam Cooke (1962); 'Gonna Send You Back to Walker', by J. Matthews and Jake Hammonds, Jr. (1963); 'I'm Mad Again' by John Lee Hooker; 'Talkin' 'Bout You', by Ray Charles (1959).

Recordings originally made on Columbia in Britain. The disc was in the bestsellers for 113 weeks.

THE ASSOCIATION
(vocal and instrumental sextet)

CHERISH *Valiant* [*USA*]. The Association's success with this disc helped to put the small Valiant label on its financial feet. The disc was No 1 for three weeks in the U.S.A. with 14 weeks in the bestsellers, and sold a million in two months. The song was written by group member Terry Kirkman.

The group was formed in February 1965 and made their debut in July the same year. They first played in Los Angeles nightclubs and folk clubs, then Disneyland and the college and university circuit. Bob Dylan's 'One Too Many Mornings' was their first record, followed by 'Along Comes Mary', a hit that reached No 7 in the U.S. charts. 'Cherish' became the first major hit for the Valiant label, with Gold Disc award, R.I.A.A. The Association quickly became a top attraction in America with their unique vocal blending.

The group comprised Gary Alexander (first lead guitar, composer-arranger); Ted Bluechel (drummer, third rhythm guitar); Brian Cole (bass); Russ Giguere (lead singer, second rhythm guitar); Terry Kirkman (lead singer, composer); and Jim Yester (first rhythm guitar, lead singer).

THE BEACH BOYS

SLOOP JOHN B. *Capitol* [*USA*]. Yet another outstanding disc of an old folksong, arranged by the group's Brian Wilson, sung and played in a fine rhythmic and rousing style. It sold 500,000 within two weeks of release, reaching No 3 in the U.S. charts for one week with 11 weeks in the bestsellers, and No 2 in Britain for one week with 15 weeks in the bestsellers. It was also No 1 in Holland and Norway and popular generally in Europe, with an estimated global million sale.

The song was originally published in a collection by famous American folksong specialist Carl Sandburg, and apparently originates from the West Indies. The historic 'John B.' lies embedded in the sand at Governor's Harbour, Nassau. An expedition sent in 1926 salvaged two items from the craft, a knee of horseflesh and a ring-bolt, which are preserved in the Watch Tower on the southern coast. The song became exceedingly popular around Nassau.

Lee Hays (of the famous Weavers) made an adaptation of this – 'The John B. Sails' – in 1951, re-titling it 'I Wanna Go Home' (Wreck of the John B.). Britain's Lonnie Donegan revived it with much success in 1960.

This disc by The Beach Boys was reported to have sold faster than any of their previous singles.

GOOD VIBRATIONS *Capitol* [*USA*]. The basic plan for this disc came to Brian Wilson in a Hollywood recording studio in April 1966. An instrumental track was completed after two sessions but the vocals weren't coming out right. The song was shelved, but later, after six more recording sessions, it still wasn't right. Then, in order to get the proper sound for each phase of the recording, Brian used four different studios, Western Recorders, Gold Star, Columbia and Sunset Sound and also re-introduced the 'therimin', an electronic instrument first used in the movie *Spellbound*. Track after track of Beach Boys singing was overlaid, the content changing week by week. Finally, after six months it was ready for the vocal lead, taken over by Carl Wilson, and within six weeks of release was No 1 in the U.S. charts (for one week) and 14 weeks in the bestsellers, with a million sale and R.I.A.A. Gold Disc award. The catchy easy-driving song with its new sounds was also No 1 in Britain for two weeks and 13 weeks in the bestsellers with sales of over 300,000 and big sales elsewhere. This disc also included the assistance of Bruce Johnson, an accomplished performer on bass, guitar and organ and regarded as a substitute for Brian Wilson on stage, singing all the difficult falsetto harmonies. He also performed this function on some of the group's discs. Bruce was born on 24 June 1944 in Chicago.

Song was written by Brian Wilson and Mike Love. Disc released in the U.S.A. 24 October 1966.

THE BEATLES

NOWHERE MAN backed with WHAT GOES ON? *Capitol* [*USA*]. Issued 15 February 1966 in the U.S.A., this disc sold a million in three weeks. Both were written by the group's John Lennon and Paul McCartney and were originally on the British release of their album 'Rubber Soul' issued in Britain by Parlophone in 1965, but not included in the U.S. release of the album. 'Nowhere Man' got to No 1 for two weeks in their charts with 9 weeks in the bestsellers. 'What Goes On?' was No 81 in the U.S.A.

Gold Disc award, R.I.A.A., in April 1966.

PAPERBACK WRITER backed with RAIN *Parlophone* [*Britain*]. Another Gold Disc award for the Beatles from R.I.A.A. in July 1966. This disc was No 1 in both the U.S.A. and Britain simultaneously for two weeks, selling over the million in the U.S.A., and over 500,000 in Britain. 'Paperback Writer' has some of the most startling harmony singing, while Ringo Starr emphasizes the drive with terrific cymbal effects. Both were written by Paul McCartney and John Lennon. Disc released in the U.S.A. on 4 June and in Britain on 10 June. It was also a big hit in Europe and was No 1 in Holland, Norway, Denmark, Germany, Austria and Ireland, and as far away as New Zealand, Australia, Hong Kong, Malaysia and Singapore. Estimates of total sales are well over two million. Side one features the double-tracked voice of Paul, and 'Rain' the double-tracked voice of John. 'Paperback Writer' was 10 weeks in the U.S. bestsellers and 11 weeks in the British bestsellers. 'Rain' achieved No 23 with 7 weeks in the U.S. bestsellers.

YESTERDAY ... AND TODAY (album) *Capitol* [*USA*]. In June 1966, Capitol shipped 750,000 of this album to their various branches. It was awarded an R.I.A.A. Gold Disc two weeks after release on 15 June and subsequently sold over a million, staying at No 1 in the U.S. charts for five weeks and in the bestsellers for 31.

The disc demonstrates the considerable change of the group's sound from their earlier discs.

The contents were: 'Yesterday' (sung by Paul McCartney), by John Lennon and Paul McCartney (1965); 'Doctor Robert', by John Lennon and Paul McCartney (1966); 'I'm Only Sleeping', by John Lennon and Paul McCartney (1966); 'And Your Bird Can Sing', by John Lennon and Paul McCartney (1966); 'We Can Work It Out', by John Lennon and Paul McCartney (1965); 'Day Tripper', by John Lennon and Paul McCartney (1965); 'Nowhere Man', by John Lennon and Paul McCartney (1965); 'What Goes On?', by John Lennon, Paul McCartney and Ringo Starr (1965); 'Drive My Car', by John Lennon and Paul McCartney (1965); 'If I Needed Someone', by George Harrison (1965); 'Act Naturally' (sung by Ringo Starr), by Van Morrison and John Russell (1963).

REVOLVER (album) *Parlophone* [*Britain*] *Capitol* [*USA*]. This Beatles' album again demonstrates the incredible ingenuity of the group with its new sounds and new ideas. A wide range of musical influences were absorbed in the album including French horn, sitar, trumpet, clavichord, violin, viola and piano in addition to the group's usual three guitars and drums. This remarkable album set a new direction for the pop music field. It was released in Britain on 5 August and in the U.S.A. on 8 August. Advance orders in Britain were 300,000 and with U.S. sales it soon sold a million, plus their 20th Gold Disc award from R.I.A.A. after three weeks.

The album became the most 'covered' ever to emerge on the British disc scene with more than half a dozen other artists recording the songs before the album was on sale, followed by many more versions – all anxious to make or enhance their disc careers with a Beatles song.

The album included the following on both British and U.S. releases: 'Taxman', by George Harrison (1966); 'Eleanor Rigby', by John Lennon and Paul McCartney (1966); 'Love You Too', by George Harrison (1966); 'Here, There and Everywhere', by John Lennon and Paul McCartney (1966); 'Yellow Submarine', by John Lennon and Paul McCartney (1966); 'She Said, She Said', by John Lennon and Paul McCartney (1966); 'Good Day Sunshine', by John Lennon and Paul McCartney (1966); 'For No One', by John Lennon and Paul McCartney (1966); 'I Want to Tell You', by George Harrison (1966); 'Got to Get You into My Life', by John Lennon and Paul McCartney (1966); 'Tomorrow Never Knows', by John Lennon and Paul McCartney (1966).

The British release also included: 'Doctor Robert', by John Lennon and Paul McCartney (1966); 'And Your Bird Can Sing', by John Lennon and Paul McCartney (1966); 'I'm Only Sleeping', by John Lennon and Paul McCartney (1966).

Features of the disc are George Harrison joining with Anil Bhagwat in 'Love You Too' to play some sitar jangles, and 'Yellow Submarine' and 'Eleanor Rigby' (see singles disc data).

It was an immediate No 1 in Britain, staying seven weeks at the top, and in the U.S.A. No 1 for eight weeks, also chart topper in many other countries. Global sales are estimated at well over two million.

The disc was in the U.S. bestsellers for 79 weeks.

YELLOW SUBMARINE backed with **ELEANOR RIGBY** *Parlophone* [*Britain*] *Capitol* [*USA*]. Released in Britain on 5 August and in the U.S.A. on 8 August during the group's fourth tour (global this time) which commenced on 24 June, culminating in yet again breaking their previous record fees of 1964 and 1965 with their performance at New York's Shea Stadium on 23 August 1966. This time it was $189,000 (£67,785).

Both songs on this singles disc were written by The Beatles' John Lennon and Paul McCartney and advance orders were over 250,000 in Britain. It was No 1 in Britain for four weeks with 13 weeks in the bestsellers, and No 1 in the U.S.A. for one week. The songs were composed for the group's new album 'Revolver' and it was the first time that EMI of Britain released a Beatles singles disc simultaneously from and with the album.

'Yellow Submarine', with 9 weeks in the U.S. bestsellers, with the solo vocal by Ringo Starr, is a simple children's song with all kinds of sound effects such as swirling water, and including a massed chorus and a brass band. 'Eleanor Rigby', which reached No 11 with 8 weeks in the U.S. bestsellers, sung by Paul McCartney is a folksy ballad with a classical sound provided by a string octet, and tells the wistful tale of the lonely Miss Rigby.

This disc sold 1,200,000 in its first four weeks in the U.S.A. and received a Gold Disc award from R.I.A.A. (their 21st) making the most ever earned by any act in R.I.A.A. history.

It was No 1 also in Germany, Norway, Sweden, Holland, Canada, Switzerland, Australia and New Zealand. Global sale estimated at over two million.

A Grammy award was made to Paul McCartney for 'Eleanor Rigby' for Best Contemporary Rock and Roll Solo Male Performance, 1966.

'Yellow Submarine' was later included in a colour cartoon film of the same title for which The Beatles wrote new songs and sang. The film, described as a swirling splurge of phantasmagoria, was a tremendous success, and particularly a smash hit in the U.S.A. It gave new magic to animation, and was chosen as one of the ten Best Movies of 1968.

ROY BLACK

GANZ IN WEISS (All in white) *Polydor* [*Germany*]. Roy Black, a teenage singer from Augsburg, Germany, first appeared with a beat band but gave up these activities to become one of Germany's most popular ballad singers of the teenage set. He entered the German Pop Music Festival and this resulted in a two-sided hit disc with both sides high on the German charts. His first big hit was 'Du bist nicht allein' (You Are Not Alone) in 1965 which sold half a million, to establish him in his native country. He then became a firm favourite on tours and TV. Each of his disc releases racked up big sales and made top positions in the German charts.

'Ganz in Weiss' written by Arland and Hertha, sold half a million by mid-1966 and achieved the million sale by the end of 1967. The disc was No 1 for six weeks.

His first album was a bestseller at Christmas 1966 and his 'Roy Black II' album (November 1967) had advance orders of 50,000.

GRAHAM BONNEY

SUPER GIRL *Columbia* [*Britain*]. Graham Bonney was born on 2 June 1945 in Stratford, East London, and at the age of four attended a dancing school. A few years later he was appearing in pantomime, on TV and in films, both acting and dancing. Around 1961 he became interested in popular music and played semi-professionally with various groups including the well-known Riot Squad. He also did session work for prominent artists including The Ivy League, Julie Rogers and Jet Harris. After a trip to Paris in 1965, playing with Michael Chaplin, Graham switched to solo singing, songwriting and record production. He wrote both the songs for his first solo disc released in November 1965 and collaborated with Barry Mason on 'Super Girl', his second disc, released in February 1966. This was only a minor success in Britain, but when released in Germany later it went to the top of their charts for six weeks with an estimated million sale. Bonney built up an enormous following in Germany where he appeared on many TV and radio shows.

'Super Girl' was one of Germany's 'Top 10 Hits of 1966'. It was No 19 and eight weeks in the British bestsellers.

THE BUCKINGHAMS

KIND OF A DRAG U.S.A. [USA]. A million seller for their first recording by this new American teenage group of five vocalists, and their 'Chicago' sound. Written by J. Holvay, it sold the million by 1967 and was No 1 in the U.S.A. for two weeks with 13 weeks in the bestsellers. In early 1967, the group signed an exclusive contract with Columbia Records and went on a 30-city concert tour of America.

CATERINA CASELLI (vocalist)

NESSUNO MI PUO GIUDICARE (No one can judge me) C.G.D. [Italy]. Caterina Caselli, young Italian songstress born 1948, was quite unknown until she sang this song in the San Remo Song Festival in February 1966. Although placed second in the contest, it proved to be the biggest seller of the entries. Caterina was discovered and introduced on the disc market by C.G.D. (Compagna Generale del Discs) in 1965. This disc became one of the biggest sellers in Italy during the winter of 1966 and reached a 650,000 figure in early 1967, with subsequent million sale and a Gold Disc award on 26 April 1967 by C.G.D. It was No 1 for nine consecutive weeks in Italy and was also a success in Argentina. American disc star Gene Pitney also had a big success with his disc on the same label of around half a million sale. He also sang it in the same Festival.

In 1966, Caterina won the Juke Box 'Festival Bar' with 'L'uomo d'oro' which sold half a million. By 1967 she was performing at concerts all over Italy and partnered Giorgio Gaber in a weekly TV series 'Diamoci del Tu' - one of the most popular Italian TV musical shows.

'Nessumo mi puo giudicare' was written by M. Panzeri, D. Pace, Beretta and Prete, and is a pulsating up-tempo romantic ballad with a contagious repeating riff.

RAY CONNIFF WITH HIS ORCHESTRA AND THE CONNIFF SINGERS

SOMEWHERE MY LOVE (album) Columbia [USA]. Ray Conniff, born on 6 November 1916 in Attleboro, Massachusetts, received his first musical training from his father who doubled as leader and trombonist for the Attleboro Jewelry City Band, and

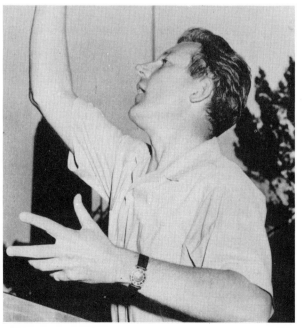

additional inspiration from his mother who played piano. While at high school, Ray joined a local band as trombonist and, with the aid of a mail-order course, taught himself arranging. He made his first arrangements for the band that pleased the outfit and the audience. After graduation in 1934, Ray went to Boston and got his first engagement as a professional with Dan Murphy's society orchestra, the 'Musical Skippers'. He stayed with them for two years, improving his playing and arranging technique. In 1936, he headed south to New York and got his first job in the city as trombonist-arranger with Bunny Berigan, making quite a name for himself with the band in this capacity. In 1938, he was hired by Bob Crosby as trombonist-arranger for The Bobcats. The following year he was offered a job with the famous Artie Shaw, and it was while with the band that he really emerged as an arranger of distinction. During his four years with Shaw he became known for his trombone solos, and also appeared on many radio shows and studied at the famous Juilliard School of Music. He next worked with Glen Gray's orchestra until 1944 when he became arranger for various groups on the Armed Forces Radio Services, and working with Meredith Willson and Walter Schumann. After Army release, he became arranger for the Harry James band. In the late 1940s, Ray turned to freelancing and also took on some non-musical jobs to keep his wife, three children and himself. For three years he made a private and intense study of hit records and felt assured he had discovered the key to certain success for recording. In late 1953 he was introduced to Columbia's Mitch Miller and in 1954 invited by the label to prove his 'success theory' by making an arrangement for their artist Don Cherry. The lucky disc was 'Band of Gold', an eventual million seller (see 1955) followed by a string of Conniff-arranged sessions and chart toppers for Johnnie Ray, Guy Mitchell, Frankie Laine, and later Marty Robbins and Johnny Mathis. Columbia then decided to give Ray a session of his own, the result being his first album with his special sound. This was 'S'wonderful' (1956) which sold half a million. Many more big selling albums followed and he became a top seller and artist on the Columbia label.

Ray's successful formula is the use of mixed choruses as instruments of an orchestra, skilfully blended. His orchestra consists of 18 musicians, with chorus of four girls and four boys. The Conniff Singers are a group of 25 (12 girls and 13 boys) usually backed by eight musicians. By 1970 he had been awarded nine Gold Discs by R.I.A.A. for million dollar selling albums, including this album of 'Somewhere My Love' which sold a million units by February 1967. Gold Disc award for this was on 20 September 1966. It was issued in July 1966, the title taken from the vocal version of 'Lara's Theme' from the film Doctor Zhivago. This particular theme became one of the biggest and most durable successes in the history of film background music and a colossal success in Europe. There is no doubt that Ray Conniff's version of this album played a big part in the tune's popularity.

Contents of the album: Side 1 - 'Red Roses for a Blue Lady', by Sid Tepper and Roy C. Bennett (1948); 'Downtown', by Tony Hatch (1964); 'Charade' (from film Charade), by Johnny Mercer/Henry Mancini (1963); 'King of the Road', by Roger Miller (1964); 'Edelweiss' (from Sound of Music), by O. Hammerstein II/Richard Rodgers (1960); 'Young and Foolish' (from Plain and Fancy), by Arnold B. Horwitt/Albert Hague (1954); Side 2 - 'Somewhere My Love' ('Lara's theme' from film Doctor Zhivago), by Paul Francis Webster/Maurice Jarre (1965); 'Days of Wine and Roses' (from film Days of Wine and Roses), by Johnny Mercer/Henry Mancini (1962); 'Tie Me Kangaroo Down Sport', by Rolf Harris (1960); 'Wouldn't It Be Lovely?' (from My Fair Lady), by Alan J. Lerner/Frederick Loewe (1956); 'So Long, Farewell' (from Sound of Music), by O. Hammerstein/Richard Rodgers (1960).

This album was 18 weeks in the Top Ten, and reached No 2 in the U.S.A. It was in the bestsellers for 90 weeks.

The 'Ray Conniff in Moscow' album, cut by him with a Russian chorus in December 1974 in Moscow, was released in

Moscow in 1975. Conniff was the first American pop performer to record in the U.S.S.R.

BILL COSBY

WONDERFULNESS (album) *Warner Brothers* [*USA*]. Bill Cosby has the distinction of hitting the gold album jackpot (1966) with four R.I.A.A. awards at the same time, including this album which went over the million mark on 4 April 1967, just under one year since release in May 1966, selling 1,400,000 by year's end.

Cosby is one of America's funniest comedians and could have become a big name in the athletic field. After service in the U.S. Navy medical corps, he attended Temple University on a football scholarship, but somewhere along the line decided on show business as a career. He gave up both football and college after two years and took a part-time job as a bartender, the customers being highly amused with his unusual brand of comedy. He soon had a big following and was eventually booked into the Gaslight Café in Greenwich Village, New York, where he was 'discovered' by one of the city's journalists with subsequent tremendous publicity. In New York he met fellow comedian Allan Sherman who speedily introduced him to the Warner Brothers label for whom he made his first album 'Bill Cosby Is a Very Funny Fellow' (1964). The same year he co-starred with Robert Culp in the popular 'I Spy' TV series and in 1965 came to fame through his many TV appearances on the Jack Paar, Jimmy Dean and Andy Williams shows. His second album 'I Started Out as a Child' (1964) was followed by 'Why Is There Air?' (1965) with 'Wonderfulness' amassing the largest initial order ever garnered on a comedy album in a single day - 200,000. It got to No 7 in the U.S. charts.

Bill Cosby is a native of Philadelphia and was in his mid-twenties when he made this disc. His witty and hilarious monologues are based on his great talent for discovering humour in everyday happenings of life and his amusing and penetrating observations of human behaviour are far reaching in their scope. 'Wonderfulness' contains some of his funniest material including 'Tonsils', 'Go Carts', 'Chicken Heart' and 'The Playground'. All four albums were in the Top Sellers lists for most of 1966 continuing into 1967, earning him a Grammy Award as Best Comedy Artist of 1966.

Bill Cosby has also appeared before the President of the United States. He was born on 12 July 1937.

This album was in the U.S. bestsellers for 106 weeks.

THE BOB CREWE GENERATION (instrumental)

MUSIC TO WATCH GIRLS GO BY *DynoVoice* [*USA*]. Written by Tony Velona and Sid Ramin, this was the campaign theme of Diet Pepsi (Pepsi-Cola Company). Bob Crewe's disc got to No 9 in the U.S. charts with 12 weeks in the bestsellers, and sold an estimated million by mid-1967. The disc is a 'brass filled thumper' played by the Generation - an aggregation of 17 instrumentalists (seven brass, three saxophones, three guitars, piano, drums, tympani and xylophone) headed by Bob Crewe, the famous songwriter. It also proved to be a big hit for Andy Williams as a song.

Bob Crewe, born 12 November 1937, became one of New York's top male models. He also became a noted artist, some of his canvases selling for as much as $1,200. For Vik Records he wrote 'Charm Bracelet' with Frank Slay, Jr and made a disc for them on which he was the vocalist. Bob met Frank in 1953 for songwriting and recording sessions while still in other full-time jobs. They were among the first independent record producers who wrote, arranged and then sold the masters of their recorded tunes to various record companies. Crewe's hit 'Silhouettes' which he produced with The Rays (see 1957) opened the gates for the deluge of independent disc producers. With his brother, Dan, they started a publishing and recording business and in ten years had 62 hits and over 100 million records sold bearing Bob's name on the label. He is head of his own operation, the Crewe Group of Companies, which includes three music publishing companies, two record labels (DynoVoice and New Voice Records), a record production company, Genius, Inc., Crewe Group Films and a TV production unit, Crewe Video Productions. He sparked a new generation of creative talent in show business. *Record World* (9 December 1967) said, 'Crewe has been called a communicator to the today generation and "generation" seems to be a key word emerging in any attempt to describe him, applying as much to a description of his process as it does to the appeal of his product.' Quite naturally he called his own group of young musicians the Bob Crewe Generation. Bob has produced such great artists as The Four Seasons, The Highwaymen, Lesley Gore and Mitch Ryder.

THE CYRKLE (vocal and instrumental pop quartet)

RED RUBBER BALL *Columbia* [*USA*]. The Cyrkle, originally The Rondells, was renamed by Brian Epstein, manager of The Beatles, and John Lennon contributed the unique spelling of the name. It was Epstein's sole American group. The song was written by Paul Simon (of Simon and Garfunkel) and Bruce Woodley (of The Seekers), a hard-driving rhythmic ode about a boy who has just got over an unhappy romance and finally sees the light of day. The Cyrkle's disc was released in the U.S.A. in April 1966 and in Britain on 12 August 1966. It was, however, not a success in Britain, but in the U.S.A. reached No 2 with 13 weeks in the bestsellers, and went on to sell a million.

The group originally began as a three-man unit at Lafayette College, later becoming a quartet. Each of the Cyrkles is a college graduate, their music sometimes having a folk-like campus flavour. They became exceedingly popular on the Gotham discotheque scene, and in addition to their own sound had an amazing talent for imitating sounds of other groups such as The Four Seasons and The Beach Boys, and performing favourite older tunes.

They appeared on 14 of the dates in the U.S. Beatles tour in 1966.

The members are: Tom Dawes, born 25 July 1944 in Albany, New York, who plays 12-string guitar, five-string banjo, bass guitar and sitar; Don Danneman, born 9 May 1944 in Brooklyn, New York, who plays piano and guitar; Marty Fried, born 1944 in Wayside, New Jersey, who plays drums; Earl Pickens, who plays organ.

'Red Rubber Ball' was their first Columbia release.

THE SPENCER DAVIS GROUP (instrumental and vocal rhythm-and-blues quartet)

GIMME SOME LOVIN' *Fontana* [*Britain*]. This group which became one of Britain's fastest rising outfits was formed by Spencer Davis, a Birmingham University student who became interested in rhythm-and-blues while with the University Jazz Band as guitarist. While with the band he heard the Muff-Woody quartet who at that time had 13-year-old Stephen Winwood playing piano. A few months later Spencer got them to join him, the group consisting of himself, Stephen Winwood, his brother Mervyn (Muff) Winwood and Peter York. They played in the Birmingham area for a considerable time gaining experience and building up engagements. Their first professional appearance was at The Golden Eagle in Birmingham in 1964. Chris Blackwell of Fontana records signed them to the label and also became their recording and personal manager. They made their film debut in *Pop Gear* in 1964 which show-cased most of Britain's pop artists including The Beatles, The Animals, Herman's Hermits, Billy J. Kramer, Peter and Gordon, The Honeycombs, Susan Maughan and other rising artists in the pop world.

They finally broke through with their disc 'Keep On Running' recorded in 1965, a No 1 disc for three weeks in 1966 which sold over 400,000, followed by another No 1 'Somebody Help Me'. 'Gimme Some Lovin' ', written by Steve, Mervyn Winwood and Spencer Davis, was their third big hit in a row, selling over

250,000 in Britain (No 2 for two weeks with 12 weeks in the bestsellers) and big sales in the U.S.A. (No 5 for two weeks, 1967 with 13 weeks in the bestsellers). The combined global sales were well over the million.

Their success resulted in an exclusive contract to United Artists Records in the U.S. The disc has a primitive sound about it – an absolute tour-de-force from the group – with Steve pulling out all the stops on both organ and vocally.

The group made a big name for themselves all over Europe on tours apart from becoming the most saluted group in Britain. Steve and Mervyn Winwood quit the group in April 1967.

Personnel: Spencer Davis, born 17 July 1941, Swansea, Wales (guitar, harmonica, piano accordion, vocal); Peter York, born 15 August 1942, Redcar, Yorkshire (drums, vibraphone, vocal); Mervyn (Muff) Winwood, born 15 June 1943, Birmingham (bass guitar, vocal); Stephen Winwood, born 12 May 1948, Birmingham (piano, organ, guitar, vocal lead).

This disc released on 28 November 1966.

DAVE DEE, DOZY, BEAKY, MICK AND TICH (pop vocal and instrumental quintet)

BEND IT *Fontana* [*Britain*]. Written by Howard Blaikley (joint pseudonym of Ken Howard and Alan Blaikley who managed the group) this disc was No 2 in Britain, 12 weeks in the bestsellers and with over 250,000 sale and a particularly big hit on the Continent of Europe. It was No 1 in Germany and high up other European charts. In order to obtain the bouzouki sound (a bouzouki being a Greek stringed instrument), an electrified mandola was used. With deliberate tempo accelerations the disc caught the flavour of Greek music. The combined British and European sales were over a million.

The group came from Salisbury, England, and first gained recognition through their disc 'You Make It Move' and then their quarter-million seller 'Hold Tight' (1966) also written by Howard Blaikley. This also was a hit in Germany where the group performed. They became musical globe-trotters and visited Greece, Africa and Australia in addition to native performances. The name of the group was partly taken from nicknames of three of them. They became noted for their dazzling colour combinations in stage clothing.

Personnel of the group: Dave Dee (David Harman), born 17 December 1943, Salisbury, Wiltshire (jews harp); Dozy (Trevor Leonard Ward Davies), born 27 November 1944, Enford, Wiltshire (bass guitar, drums, bongos); Beaky (John Dymond), born 10 July 1944, Salisbury, Wiltshire (guitar, drums, bass accordion); Mick (Michael Wilson), born 4 March 1944, Amesbury, Wiltshire (drums); Tich (Ian Frederick Stephen Amey), born 15 May 1944, Salisbury, Wiltshire (lead guitar).

NEIL DIAMOND

CHERRY, CHERRY *Bang* [*USA*]. Neil's first million selling disc, the song written by him. It was released in August 1966

and reached No 5 in the U.S. charts for one week with 12 weeks in the bestsellers. Neil switched to the Uni label in 1969 after having written big hits for The Monkees, and became a major artist for that label. (See 1969 for biographical data.)

DONOVAN (folk vocalist, guitar and harmonica)

SUNSHINE SUPERMAN *Epic* [*USA*]. Donovan (Donovan Phillips Leitch) is one of the few British artists to appear on TV before making his first record, and achieved national recognition through his appearance on the 'Ready, Steady, Go' programme. His new and refreshing approach to folk music singing brought him prominence.

He was born 10 May 1946 in Maryhill, Glasgow, and was educated at St Audrey's Secondary School, Hatfield, and attended The Campus, Welwyn Garden City, for a year. He left college to roam, and travelled throughout Britain, often in the company of a kazoo player named Gypsy Dave, and sang and wrote on the beaches of St Ives, Cornwall, for a while. He had purchased a guitar and taught himself to play. He worked in hotels occasionally and did a few jobs at art clubs. Other com-

panions of Donovan were Julian, a harmonica player, and some young and talented classical guitarists. Donovan met his manager, Peter Eden, at Southend, Essex, who liked his songs and for whom he later recorded some tapes in London. This resulted in a meeting with Bob Bickford of 'Ready, Steady, Go' TV programmes and his first appearance thereon, also an eventual Pye Records contract (1965). His first recording, 'Catch the Wind', his own composition, sold over 200,000 (No 4 in the British charts), followed by another self-penned hit 'Colours' and then his biggest success, a U.S. song 'Universal Soldier' (on an EP of the same title) which was No 1 for eight weeks. Donovan made his first American appearance on their 'Shindig' TV shows in the summer of 1965, after a tour in Britain with pop groups. He again appeared in the U.S.A. in November 1965 for several concerts and TV shows, and has since become an international name with appearances in France, Norway, Sweden, Finland, Denmark and Belgium.

'Sunshine Superman' was written by him and recorded especially for the American market. It sold 800,000 in six weeks and soon passed the million mark, achieving the No 1 chart position for one week in U.S.A. with 13 weeks in the bestsellers. His album of the same title had an advance order of a quarter million and quickly sold half a million.

The song is described as a 'blues-soaked romance' about a boy determined to snare the girl of his dreams, and was completely different from his former folk songs. The disc is strongly Indian flavoured, incorporating the sitar, tambura and electric guitar.

Donovan is a writer, singer and poet of considerable talent and one of Britain's top folksinging personalities.

This disc also sold over 250,000 when released in Britain (Pye label) where it was No 3 and 11 weeks in the bestsellers.

MELLOW YELLOW *Epic* [*USA*]. Second million seller for Donovan, an off-beat rock number also written by him for the American market. It was No 1 for three weeks in the U.S. charts and 12 weeks in the bestsellers, and No 8 in Britain. R.I.A.A. Gold Disc award, February 1967.

THE EASYBEATS (quintet)

FRIDAY ON MY MIND *United Artists* [*Britain*]. Although designated as an Australian group, all its members are sons of European parents who emigrated to Australia. The young immigrants met in a hostel in Sydney and played at various clubs in the vicinity. After a year or so they made their first disc, 'For My Woman', which had only small success. The second disc 'She's So Fine' got them the No 1 position in the Australian charts and established them. By July 1966, four of their six discs reached the top chart position, making them the most popular group 'down under', with riots wherever they appeared, and several awards - Best Group, Most Original Group and Best Vocal Group in Australia. The Easybeats made their first big impact on the pop music scene in April 1965 when they appeared at The Village, Sydney, receiving plaudits that started to gain them recognition in the U.S.A.

'Friday on My Mind' was the group's first English-produced disc by United Artists. It was issued on Parlophone in Australia and stayed No 1 there for eight weeks. It got to No 6 in Britain with 15 weeks in the bestsellers, and No 16 in the U.S.A. (staying 14 weeks in the charts). Sales in Britain were over 250,000 and a Gold Disc for a global million was presented to them in May 1967 in Australia.

They made a short tour of America and toured Germany in 1967 in addition to British appearances.

Personnel: George Young, born 6 November 1947 in Glasgow, Scotland; Gordon 'Snowy' Fleet, born 16 August 1945 in Bootle, Lancashire; Dick Diamonde, born 28 December 1947 in Hilversum, Holland; Harry Vanda, born 22 March 1947 in The Hague, Holland; Little Stevie Wright, born 20 December 1948 in Leeds, Yorkshire.

Vanda and Young play guitar, Wright plays drums and guitar, Diamonde plays bass and Fleet plays drums - in addition to their singing.

'Friday on My Mind' was written by Young and Vanda who wrote most of the group's songs.

THE FOUR TOPS

REACH OUT I'LL BE THERE *Motown* [*USA*]. Yet another triumph for songwriter team Eddie Holland, Brian Holland and Lamont Dozier, and the third million seller for the highly-professional Four Tops. A pulsating rhythm-and-blues romantic song, the disc was No 1 for two weeks in the U.S.A., with 15 weeks in the bestsellers, and for four weeks in Britain with 16 weeks in the bestsellers (with over 250,000 sales).

A top rhythm-and-blues disc in both the U.S.A. and Britain. Release in the U.S.A. was 3 September 1966.

STANDING IN THE SHADOWS OF LOVE *Motown* [*USA*]. Fourth million seller for The Four Tops, also written by Eddie Holland, Brian Holland and Lamont Dozier. A driving romantic

number in the group's powerful style. It was No 6 for two weeks in the U.S.A. and 10 weeks in the bestsellers, and No 5 for one week in Britain, with eight weeks in the bestsellers.

Release in the U.S.A. was 17 December 1966.

BOBBY GOLDSBORO

IT'S TOO LATE *United Artists* [*USA*]. Third million seller for Bobby also written by him, sale reported by 1967. The disc achieved No 22 position in the U.S. charts and 8 weeks in the bestsellers.

THE HAPPENINGS (vocal quartet)

SEE YOU IN SEPTEMBER *B. T. Puppy* [*USA*]. The members of this group, Dave Libert (lead baritone and arranger), Tom Juliano (tenor and second lead), Bob Miranda (lead singer) and Ralph Divito (baritone, high falsetto and comedian), all hail from Paterson, New Jersey. They spent the three years from 1964 in planning, training and practising. After the usual rounds of one record company to another, they had a recording session produced by the successful recording group The Tokens. Their second session was much more successful and included 'See You in September' (written in 1959 by Sid Wayne, author, and Sherman Edwards, composer). The recording on the B. T. Puppy label (owned by Jubilee Records) was finally a big success in Boston, Massachusetts, and quickly spread throughout the U.S.A., becoming No 1 for a week and occupying a high position in most of the charts for several weeks and 14 weeks in the bestsellers, with an eventual million sale, and Gold Disc award by Jubilee Records.

GO AWAY LITTLE GIRL *B. T. Puppy* [*USA*]. This revival of the 1962 hit song by Gerry Goffin and Carole King made it the second time it was a million seller for the husband and wife songwriter team. The disc was produced by The Tokens, and The Happenings' version reached No 9 in the U.S. charts with 9 weeks in the bestsellers, a successful follow-up to their 'See You in September', with a seven-figure sale subsequently.

BOBBY HEBB

SUNNY *Philips* [*USA*]. Bobby is known in the U.S.A. as the 'song-a-day man'. He started writing in 1958 and his output to date is over 3,000 songs, with around 1,000 of them published. 'Sunny' is a fine example of his work, soulful singing with a gently swinging accompaniment. He wrote it in the dawn of the day following President Kennedy's assassination (1963), his sleep having been disturbed by the event, and this no doubt accounts for the rather poignant lyrics. It took over two years to get the song on disc, but, when released, opened up a promising career for Bobby. The disc got to No 1 in the U.S.A. for one week with 15 weeks in the U.S. bestsellers, also reaching No 11 in Britain, with nine weeks in the bestsellers.

Bobby Hebb was born 26 July 1941 in Nashville and started performing at the age of four. When he was 12, Roy Acuff invited him to be the first negro to appear on the Grand Ole Opry show. On leaving high school in Nashville he learned to play the trumpet, graduated from a dental technician's course in Chicago, resuming his music studies and on occasion played spoons at Bo Diddley's recordings. He played trumpet with a jazz combo during his U.S. Navy service and on discharge moved on to other brass instruments, then guitar studies with famous Chet Atkins whom he credits with launching him into a recording career. He also plays four-string banjo and drums, and is virtually a 'one-man band'. Bobby then joined the Mickey and Sylvia team in New York which finally became just Bobby and Sylvia for a while (1961), working together for two years. Bobby then sang in New York and local clubs on his own. Two of his early recordings were 'Night Train to Memphis' and 'You Broke My Heart and I Broke Your Jaw'. The success of 'Sunny' earned Bobby a booking as a supporting attraction with The Beatles' 1966 U.S. tour and several coast-to-coast TV appearances.

Bobby is one of seven children. Both his parents are blind.

Many famous artists have recorded Bobby's material including Percy Sledge, Mary Wells, Marvin Gaye, Billy Preston and Herb Alpert. 'Sunny' was also recorded by many other artists including Cher, Georgie Fame and Gloria Lynne.

HERMAN'S HERMITS

LISTEN, PEOPLE *MGM* [*USA*]. The big hit from the film *When the Boys Meet the Girls*, a re-make of a George Gershwin musical *Girl Crazy* of 1930, in which the group were starred. The song was written by Britain's Graham Gouldman for the film, the disc taken from the soundtrack. It had advance orders of 600,000.

The disc sold a million in the U.S.A. by early March 1966 and was No 3 in their charts and 9 weeks in the bestsellers.

THE HOLLIES (vocal and instrumental pop quintet)

BUS STOP *Parlophone* [*Britain*] *Imperial* [*USA*]. The Hollies, one of Britain's top swinging combinations, was first formed in Manchester in 1963. They created a big impression when their former manager Tommy Sanderson brought them to London for a recording test with Parlophone. Their first disc 'Ain't That Just Like Me' caused quite a stir when the producer of a film starring Frankie Vaughan heard it. He booked The Hollies for a screen test. Again in 1963, their next two discs 'Searching' and 'Stay' reached No 10 and No 8 respectively in the charts, and in early 1964 'Just One Look' sold over 250,000. The group topped the bill in several shows (1964), and in 1965 toured with The Rolling Stones, had their first No 1 with 'I'm Alive', made a tour of the U.S.A., Sweden and Denmark. In 1966, their tenth hit 'I Can't Let Go' was a speedy No 1, followed by a six-week tour of the U.S.A. Soon after this their original bass guitarist Eric Haydock was taken ill and he left the group, being replaced by Bernie Calvert. Then came the release of 'Bus Stop' on 24 June 1966, written by Graham Gouldman, which reached No 3 in both Britain and the U.S.A. with nine weeks in the British bestsellers and with 14 weeks in the U.S. bestsellers, selling a million in the U.S.A. alone by the end of 1967.

The personnel for this recording was: Graham Nash, born 2 February 1942 in Blackpool, England (guitar); Allan Clarke, born 5 April 1942 in Salford (guitar, harmonica); Tony Hicks, born 16 December 1943 in Nelson (guitar, drums); Bobby Elliot, born 8 December 1942 in Burnley, Lancashire (drums); Bernie Calvert, born 16 September 1944 (bass guitar).

By December 1967, The Hollies had four million-seller singles in U.S.A. plus a million dollar selling album 'The Hollies' Greatest Hits', and were presented with five Gold Discs following their 1967 tremendously successful tour of the U.S.A.

STOP, STOP, STOP *Parlophone* [*Britain*] *Imperial* [*USA*]. Second million seller in the U.S.A. for The Hollies, released in Britain on 7 October 1966, and written by three members of the group, Graham Nash, Tony Hicks and Allan Clarke. The million sale was achieved by the end of 1967. The disc was No 2 in Britain for two weeks with 12 weeks in the bestsellers and reached No 5 in the U.S.A. with 10 weeks in the bestsellers.

TOMMY JAMES AND THE SHONDELLS (vocal and instrumental group)

HANKY PANKY *Snap* [*USA*] re-released on *Roulette* [*USA*]. Written by the famous U.S. husband/wife songwriters Jeff Barry and Ellie Greenwich, 'Hanky Panky' did not sell when first issued in 1963 on Snap label. A job lot of the discs was bought up in 1966 and some action was obtained on Pittsburgh radio when it was aired by a disc jockey. It sold 28,000 in ten days with other broadcasts in Cleveland and Memphis. A scramble to obtain the master disc ended with the rights going to Roulette Records for $10,000. When subsequently nationally promoted by them, it shot to No 1 position on the charts for two weeks with 12 weeks in the U.S. bestsellers, and sold a million. The disc was No 38 in

Britain. The group were presented with a Gold Disc in August 1966 by R.I.A.A.

Lead singer Tommy James, born 29 April 1947 in Dayton, Ohio, originally started a group in Niles, Michigan, called Tommy and The Tornados when he was 13. All the Shondells come from Greensboro, a small town in the Pittsburgh suburbs; three of them, Joe, Ronnie and George, went to the same college – St Vincent's in Latrobe, Pennsylvania. Tommy James met The Shondells (six members) one night in Pittsburgh and decided to join them.

They are managed by Bob Mack of Pittsburth, who negotiated the deal with Roulette Records, and who operates 11 teen-type nightclubs in the city.

The Shondells are Joe Kessler, guitarist; George Magura, saxophonist, bass and organist; Vinnie Pietropaoli, drummer; Ronnie Rosman, piano and organ; and Mike Vale, bass, piano and vocalist.

TOM JONES

GREEN, GREEN GRASS OF HOME *Decca* [*Britain*]. Tom Jones first sang this country-flavoured song, composed by Curly Putman of the U.S.A., in 1965 – on a TV show in Britain. The great number of requests for Tom to record the song led directly to its release on 28 October 1966, and by the end of the year it sold a million, giving Tom his first Gold Disc for a British sale alone. It topped the British charts for seven weeks (1966–1967) and was 22 weeks in the bestsellers. The song, rendered by Tom with great depth and feeling, was previously recorded by U.S. artists including country-and-western stars Ferlin Husky and Porter Wagoner, but it was Tom Jones' disc that was the biggest success and a personal triumph for him. It was No 11 and 12 weeks in the U.S. bestsellers.

UDO JURGENS

MERCI CHERIE *Vogue* [*Germany*]. This song, a dreamy romantic ballad with an 'Ave Maria'-like lilt, won for Udo Jurgens and Austria the Grand Prix of the 1966 Eurovision Song Contest at the Villa Louvigny, Luxembourg, on 5 March. The words are by Thomas Hoerbiger with music by Udo Jurgens. It was the third time Udo had entered for the contest and the first time he won. He featured it accompanying himself at the piano, and it was heard and seen by 200 million throughout Europe and North Africa.

Udo Jurgen Beckelman was born on 30 September 1934 in Klagenfurt, Austria, and spent his childhood days in his parents' 800-year-old home, Ottmanach Castle, once Napoleon's Austrian residence. He learned to play the harmonica at five and, soon after, the accordion. He studied music in 1948 at the music college in Klagenfurt – and took a five-year course in composition, music theory and singing. During this course, his composition 'Je t'aime' won a national competition and this award resulted in his directing the big band of Radio Klagenfurt, in 1951. At the age of 20 Udo made his first record which was unsuccessful. In 1960 at the Knokke (Belgium) Song Festival he gained a prize for the best solo singer, and immediately afterwards had a hit in Belgium with his own song 'Jenny'. During 1961 and 1962, he became well known through a series of films he made, and in 1963 achieved big acclaim when his song 'Warum nur warum' got fifth place in the 1964 Eurovision Contest. This became a big hit all over Europe and was a success for Britain's Matt Munro under its English title of 'Walk Away'. Udo then became a top export item in Germany, and an established European star both as artist and composer all over Europe.

'Merci Cherie' sold over 350,000 in France and over 250,000 in Germany plus big sales in his native Austria (No 2 in the charts) and in Holland. It sold over the million globally and Deutsche Vogue presented him with a Gold Disc.

LOS BRAVOS (Spanish vocal and instrumental group)

BLACK IS BLACK *Decca* [*Britain*]. This recording generated tremendous vocal and musical excitement. Los Bravos were the first Spanish group to reach a high position in Britain's charts, this disc achieving No 2 for a week with 13 weeks in the bestsellers, and later No 4 for a week and 12 weeks in the bestsellers when released in the U.S.A. on the Press label put out by London/Decca. The combined sales globally easily passed the million.

The group, made up of four Spanish boys and one German, was formed in 1965, an amalgamation of two pop groups Los Sonor and The Runaways. Los Bravos made their radio debut in Madrid and quickly became very popular throughout Spain where they were subsequently voted the No 1 group.

A copy of one of their discs sung in Spanish was sent by Decca's Spanish branch to Britain. Musical director Ivor Raymonde was very impressed and went to Madrid to hear them play a number of British songs he took with him, including 'Black Is Black'. He then invited the group to come to London for their first British recording sessions in April 1966, when they made 'Black Is Black' plus several Spanish songs for release in Spain. This disc was released in Britain on 17 June and in a very short time rocketed the group to fame in Britain, all over Europe, and subsequently in the U.S.A. They appeared on top TV and radio shows in Britain and elsewhere in Europe.

The song was written by Tony Hayes and Steve Wadey from the village of Hoo near Rochester, Kent, where the duo had their own recording studio for cutting demo discs. It was their very first song, but nobody wanted it for a British group.

Los Bravos consists of: Antonio Martinez (guitar), born 3 October 1945 in Madrid; Manuel Fernandez (electric organ) born 29 September 1943 in Seville; Miguel Vicens Danus (bass guitar) born 21 June 1944 in Mallona, Palma; Pablo Gomez (drums) born 5 November 1943 in Barcelona; Mike Kogel (lead singer/guitar) born 25 April 1945 in Berlin.

KEITH

98.6 *Mercury* [*USA*]. Written by Tony Powers (words) and George Fischoff (music) this disc was produced by Jerry Ross, responsible for or associated with a string of bestselling hit records.

The disc reached No 7 and was 14 weeks in the bestsellers in the U.S.A., with a reported million sale by 1967. It reached No 24 with seven weeks in the British bestsellers.

RAMSEY LEWIS TRIO

WADE IN THE WATER *Cadet* [*USA*]. Continuation of the Ramsey Lewis success story, this disc was No 19 in the U.S. charts and had a 13-weeks' spell in the bestsellers. It was No 31 in Britain with eight weeks in the British bestsellers. The music was arranged by Ramsey Lewis and is based on a pre-Civil War slave song. A million sale was subsequently reported.

THE LOVIN' SPOONFUL

DAYDREAM *Kama Sutra* [*USA*]. This group with its extraordinary name first met in New York's famed Greenwich Village where they became friends through a mutual love of music and were teamed by their manager Bob Cavallo and producer Erik Jacobson. After their formation, they obtained a booking at

Greenwich Village's Night Owl Café, but the manager wasn't too impressed and said they needed more practice. The group took his advice and literally went underground, to the basement of a nearby hotel and emerged two months later professionally polished. The Night Owl Café owner then engaged them for an indefinite period and many famous personalities in the entertainment world came to hear them. They made their first disc 'Do You Believe in Magic?' which hit the U.S. charts in August 1965. It achieved the No 4 position for two weeks in October and was the start of a quick rise to fame. 'You Didn't Have to Be So Nice' followed with a high chart position, and in early 1966 their 'Daydream' got to No 1 for a week with 12 weeks in the bestsellers, and to No 2 for two weeks in Britain with 13 weeks in the bestsellers (over 250,000 sale). With big U.S. sales, the disc is estimated to have sold a global million. The song is an easy-going blues-tinged happy-go-lucky item, somewhat reminiscent of the idiom of the 1930s.

The group's style continually changes and they have a modern approach to current trends. The members are Zal Yanovsky (lead guitarist), born 19 December 1944; John Sebastien (guitar, harmonica and autoharp), born 17 March 1943; Steve Boone (electric bass), born 23 September 1943; and Joe Butler (drums), born 16 September 1943. 'Daydream' was written by John Sebastien. Most of their songs are penned by members of the group.

The Lovin' Spoonful visited Britain in April 1966 for TV and club appearances, then Sweden and Ireland.

SUMMER IN THE CITY *Kama Sutra* [*USA*]. Second million seller for the The Lovin' Spoonful, with Gold Disc award from R.I.A.A. for a million sale in the U.S.A. alone. This infectious hard-driving blues beat number rocketed to No 1 for three weeks in America with 11 weeks in the bestsellers, and was also a hit in Britain (No 7 with 11 weeks in the bestsellers) and in Germany. It was written by Steve Boone, John Sebastien and M. Sebastien.

THE MAMAS AND THE PAPAS

IF YOU CAN BELIEVE YOUR EYES AND EARS (album) *Dunhill* [*USA*]. This first album by the group, following their tremendous success with their first singles disc, proved to be a gold mine. It contained 'Monday, Monday', issued as a singles disc, and is said to have sold three million by early 1967, just twelve months after release in February 1966. It achieved the No 1 position for one week and was in the top ten for 20 weeks, staying in the bestsellers for 105 weeks.

More than half the songs on the album were written by the group's John Phillips. Gold Disc award, R.I.A.A., 10 June 1966.

Contents of the disc: Side 1 - 'Monday, Monday', by John Phillips (1966); 'Straight Shooter', by John Phillips (1966); 'Got a Feelin'', by Denny Doherty and John Phillips (1966); 'I Call Your Name', by John Lennon and Paul McCartney (1963); 'Do You Wanna Dance?', by Freeman; 'Go Where You Wanna Go, by John Phillips (1966); Side 2 - 'California Dreamin'', by John Phillips (1965); 'Spanish Harlem', by Jerry Leiber and Phil Spector (1961); 'Somebody Groovy', by John Phillips (1966); 'Hey Girl', by John and Michelle Phillips (1966); 'You Baby', by P. F. Sloan and Steve Barri (1966); 'The "In" Crowd', by Billy Page (1965).

The British release was titled 'The Mamas and the Papas' album.

MONDAY, MONDAY *Dunhill* [*USA*]. The second big hit for this group, an even bigger success than their first. Written by the group's lead singer John Phillips, the disc was No 1 for three weeks in the U.S. charts and 12 weeks in the bestsellers, and was No 3 for three weeks in Britain with 13 weeks in the bestsellers, and also a success in Europe and abroad.

With a Gold Disc for million dollar sales of their first and second albums, this made four Gold Discs from R.I.A.A. for the group.

This disc released on 24 March 1966. Grammy Award for Best Contemporary Rock'n'Roll Group Performance, 1966.

THE MAMAS AND THE PAPAS (album) *Dunhill* [*USA*]. Second album by America's most successful group of 1966 with an estimated two million sale by early 1967. Again most of the songs were written by the group's John Phillips. It was No 4 for seven weeks, in the Top Ten for 11 weeks and in the bestsellers for 76 weeks. The disc was released in September 1966. Gold Disc award, R.I.A.A., 1 December 1966.

The group were reported to have sold six million singles and five million albums in just over a year, making a gigantic success for themselves and the Dunhill label which was bought up by ABC-Paramount in May 1966.

Contents of disc: Side 1 - 'No Salt on Her Tail', by John Phillips (1966); 'Trip, Stumble and Fall', by John Phillips and Michelle Gilliam (1966); 'Dancing Bear', by John Phillips (1966); 'Words of Love', by John Phillips (1966); 'My Heart Stood Still', by Lorenz Hart/Richard Rodgers (1927); 'Dancing in the Street', by William Stevenson and Marvin Gaye (1964); Side 2 - 'I Saw Her Again', by Denny Doherty and John Phillips (1966); 'Strange Young Girl', by John Phillips (1966); 'I Can't Wait', by John Phillips (1966); 'Even if I Could', by John Phillips (1966); 'That Kind of Girl', by John Phillips (1966); 'Once Was a Time I Thought', by John Phillips (1966).

The British album was titled 'Cass, John, Michelle, Denny'.

THE MINDBENDERS (vocal and instrument trio)

A GROOVY KIND OF LOVE *Fontana* [*Britain*]. The first big hit for The Mindbenders who, after being with Wayne Fontana (see 1965), went out on their own. The song was written by American teenager Toni Wine with Carole Bayer in 1965 and the disc was No 1 for one week in Britain with 14 weeks in the bestsellers, and sold over 250,000. With the release on the Fontana label in the U.S.A. where it was also No 1 for a week and 13 weeks in the bestsellers with big sales, the disc reached an estimated million. (See 'Game of Love' 1965 for biographies of The Mindbenders.)

Eric Stewart, the group's lead guitarist, doubles as lead vocalist on the disc. The Mindbenders made a long personal appearance tour throughout the U.S.A. in 1965.

THE MONKEES (vocal and instrumental rock and roll quartet)

LAST TRAIN TO CLARKSVILLE *Colgems* [*USA*]. The Monkees were hailed as a unique experiment in popular music. The idea for the group came from two TV producers - Robert Rafelson and Bert Schneider of Raybert Productions. They advertised in the *Hollywood Reporter* on 8 September 1965 for 'four insane boys, aged 17 to 21' to form a group for a TV show, the show to reflect the 'adventures' of an unknown, young, long-haired, modern-dressed group and its dreams on the way to fame and fortune. These 'dreams' actually came true. Out of the 437 applicants, it brought together Mickey (George Michael) Dolenz, born 8 March 1945 in Los Angeles - son of famous actor George Dolenz - formerly TV's 'Circus Boy' for three years and other acting appearances in 'Peyton Place', 'Route 66' and 'Mr Novak'. He became drummer of the group. Peter Halsten Tork (real name Thorkelson), born 13 February 1942 in Washington, D.C. - son of H. J. Thorkelson, an Associate Professor of Economics at the University of Connecticut - formerly training for a career as a teacher but decided on singing instead. He became vocalist/guitarist of the group, and was also a pianist, and French horn player. Robert Michael Nesmith, born 30 December 1942 in Dallas, Texas, first appeared in San Antonio folk clubs, becoming performer/composer in California cafes and known as 'Wool Hat' Nesmith. He became second vocalist/guitarist. David Thomas Jones, born 30 December 1946 in Manchester, England - formerly a TV actor with parts in 'Coronation Street', 'Z Cars', 'Ben Casey' and 'Farmer's Daughter', on stage in the U.S.A. as the Artful Dodger in *Oliver* and Sam Weller in *Pickwick*. He was third guitarist of the group.

Don Kirschner, president of Colgems (see 'Twilight Time' 1950), then spent two months in grooming them in singing and supervised their disc sessions as well as their TV series.

'Last Train to Clarksville' was written and produced by Tommy Boyce and Bobby Hart, exclusive writers for Screen Gems, the Columbia Music Publishing Company. The song, a hard-driving, pulsating number with a catchy repeating 'riff', was the group's first disc for the newly formed Colgems label. It was released on 16 August 1966 with extensive promotion, and just prior to the filmed Screen Gems TV show 'The Monkees', a comedy-fantasy series especially created for them, with the debut on 12 September. Their first album 'The Monkees' was also released on this date to coincide with the series. The single reached No 1 in the U.S. charts in nine weeks with 15 weeks in the bestsellers, and sold nearly two million, with R.I.A.A. Gold Disc award (31 October). It stayed at the top for two weeks. It was No 23 in Britain with seven weeks in the bestsellers. The album also received a Gold Disc award from R.I.A.A. at the

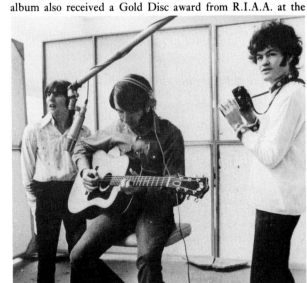

same time (setting a precedent) – after only five weeks in the charts, and was No 1 for 15 weeks. The success of the TV series and the disc made the group the rage of the U.S.A., emulating The Beatles' success. The TV series also became a tremendous hit in Britain from January 1967. Monkee merchandise from guitars to comic books and Monkee pants grossed $20 million by the end of 1966 in America. The group's quick rise to fame is an outstanding example of American show business co-ordination and planned promotion.

The backing of this disc was 'Take a Giant Step' by husband and wife team Gerry Goffin and Carole King. Due to pressure of work, the group actually do only the singing on the disc.

THE MONKEES (album) *Colgems* [*USA*]. This first album by the group, issued on 12 September (the first showing of their TV series), sold over 3,200,000 in just over three months on the U.S. market – faster than The Beatles did at their launching there in 1964. It was No 1 in the U.S.A. for 15 weeks, and in Britain for eight weeks (on the RCA label) in 1967. R.I.A.A. Gold Disc award in December 1966.

By 1 January 1968, it had sold around five million with sales still continuing, and was in the U.S. bestsellers for 78 weeks.

The album contained two songs written by group member Mike Nesmith and six by their writer/producers Tommy Boyce and Bobby Hart.

Contents were: *Side 1* – Theme from 'The Monkees', by Tommy Boyce and Bobby Hart; 'I Wanna Be Free', by Tommy Boyce and Bobby Hart; 'Tomorrow's Gonna Be Another Day', by Tommy Boyce and Steve Venet Gates; 'Saturday's Child', by Gates; 'Papa Jean's Blues', by Mike Nesmith; 'Take a Giant Step', by Gerry Goffin and Carole King; *Side 2* – 'Last Train to Clarksville', by Tommy Boyce and Bobby Hart; 'This Just Doesn't Seem to Be My Day', by Tommy Boyce and Bobby Hart; 'Let's Dance On', by Tommy Boyce and Bobby Hart; 'I'll Be True to You', by Gerry Goffin and Russ Titelman; 'Sweet Young Thing', by Mike Nesmith, Gerry Goffin and Carole King; 'Gonna Buy Me a Dog', by Tommy Boyce and Bobby Hart.

I'M A BELIEVER *Colgems* [*USA*]. This second single by the Monkees had an advance order of 1,051,280 before release on 26 November and was awarded an immediate Gold Disc by R.I.A.A. It was the first time that RCA Victor (manufacturers and distributors of the Colgems label) had advance orders in excess of one million on a single record release, with the exception of Elvis Presley.

The song, written by Neil Diamond, is a medium-paced rock number performed by the group with outstanding harmonies and infectious sounds. It was produced by Jeff Barry.

The disc was No 1 in the U.S.A. for seven weeks (with 15 weeks in the bestsellers) and in Britain for four weeks – four weeks simultaneously with U.S.A. – and was 17 weeks in the bestsellers. It sold over three million in America in its first two months on the market, and over 750,000 in Britain on the RCA label in two weeks to March 1967. Global sales are estimated at around ten million. It was No 1 in Australia, Eire, Finland, New Zealand, Norway and South Africa in early 1967.

The backing of this disc was '(I'm not your) Steppin' Stone', written by Tommy Boyce and Bobby Hart.

Here again, only the singing is by the group on this disc.

NAPOLEON XIV (comedy vocalist)

THEY'RE COMING TO TAKE ME AWAY, HA-HAAA *Warner* [*USA*]. Napoleon XIV is in reality a New York recording engineer and composer named Jerry Samuels, who wrote and recorded this number himself. He hired a studio for $15 and made the record in 1½ hours, then took the tape to George Lee, a top executive of Warner/Reprise, who immediately signed him to the company. When the disc was released, it sold over half a million in five days, the bestselling single in the history of the company, and proved to be the novelty single of the past decade. In one month it had sold 775,000, was No 1 in the U.S. charts for one week and 6 weeks in the bestsellers, and sold an eventual

million plus. Jerry Samuels was a 28-year-old composer, and lead singer of a rock-and-roll group in which he performed in a mask as Napoleon XIV, in addition to being a record producer. He decided to write a comedy song that would be entirely different. The completed song is about a man going mad because his dog leaves him, but this is not apparent at the beginning. Most of the American radio stations banned it on the grounds of bad taste, believing it to refer to a man who has lost his girl. This however did not stop the disc selling in huge quantities. It also turned out to be quite a big seller in Britain and reached No 4 in the charts with 10 weeks in the bestsellers.

The song is recited, more than sung, with a catchy martial backing consisting of drum, tambourine and hand clapping plus Napoleon's voice getting higher and higher, finally like the Chipmunks.

An additional novelty is the reverse side of the disc – 'Aaah-Ah Yawa Em Ekat Ot Gnimoc Er-Yeht' – the complete song played backwards.

AARON NEVILLE

TELL IT LIKE IT IS *Par-lo* [*USA*]. This disc sold a million after being in the U.S. charts for five weeks to the end of 1966 and was the No 1 rhythm-and-blues number for five weeks in early 1967. It reached No 2 for one week in the U.S. national charts and was 14 weeks in the bestsellers.

Aaron Neville hails from New Orleans where he was educated, and studied vocal and instrumental music and manuscript writing. His compositions include 'Every Day' and 'Humdinger'. Aaron literally grew up in show business, having made his debut at the age of five. His first public appearance was at the Y.M.C.A. in New Orleans as an amateur and his first professional appearance at the Roosevelt Hotel there when he was 13.

This song was written by Lee Diamond (words) and George Davis (music).

THE NEW VAUDEVILLE BAND
(Geoff Stevens, vocalist)

WINCHESTER CATHEDRAL *Fontana* [*Britain*]. The New Vaudeville Band came into being through the keen interest of composer Geoff Stevens in old recordings of the 1920s and the sounds of vaudeville. After working as a schoolteacher in Southend, Essex, teaching English, French, games and religious instruction, he became a training executive in an advertising agency. He then helped to write a fairly successful amateur revue and started writing short sketches for the B.B.C. An advertisement by a London music publisher landed him a job with them for two years, resulting in big successes with 'Tell Me When' for The Applejacks and 'The Crying Game' for Dave Berry in 1964. He also discovered Donovan whose first three records he produced.

Geoff decided to write a simple tuneful song as he was con-

vinced other writers were trying to make popular music too complicated. He organized a group of musicians for a recording session of 'Winchester Cathedral', a song about a boy who is deserted by his girl at or near that edifice. He named the group 'The New Vaudeville Band' and decided to sing on the record himself in order to obtain the interpretation he wanted. To the old style accompaniment of the band singing through the old fashioned megaphones of the 1930s, the strangled adenoidal tones of that era were thus produced. It was so different from modern group styles that the disc soon got into Britain's charts (No 4 with 19 weeks in the bestsellers) with a sale of over 200,000. The release by Fontana in the U.S.A. was even more astonishing. This sold over 1½ million in six weeks and became No 1 there for three weeks, America's biggest British hit of 1966, and an unprecedented feat for a group playing ordinary band instruments in a style devoid of modern rock and roll. A promotional trip to the U.S.A. with appearances on the Ed Sullivan TV show and elsewhere were a sensational success, bringing back the sound of the Rudy Vallee era, and sparking off a search for old megaphones by others to get the pre-electronic sound of the late 1920s. Many other U.S. artists including Frank Sinatra recorded the song, making Geoff Stevens the most covered British composer since The Beatles' Lennon and McCartney. By 1970 it was reported there were 400 cover versions.

Geoff Stevens, born in New Southgate, London, on 1 October 1934, sang only on the disc and did not tour with the band, his function being performed by Alan Klein who adopted the title of 'Tristram, seventh Earl of Cricklewood'. The group projected the nostalgic image of the late 1920s by dressing in old-time clothes and lolling around stage like good-for-nothing aristocrats. None of them played on the original recording which was made by session musicians. The rest of the group are Mick Wilsher (lead guitar) born 21 December 1945 in Sutton, Surrey; Bobby 'Pops' Kerr (trumpet, saxophone and French horn) born 14 February 1943 in Kensington, London; Hugh Watts (trombone) born 25 July 1941 in Watford, Hertfordshire; Neil Korner (bass) born 6 October 1942 in Ashford, Middlesex; Henry Harrison (drums) born 6 June 1943 in Watford, Hertfordshire; Stan Heywood (piano, organ, accordion) born 23 August 1947 in Dagenham, Essex; Alan Klein born 29 June 1942 in Clerkenwell, London.

Global sales of this disc were over three million and over seven million on collective discs. Grammy Award for 'Best Contemporary Rock'n'Roll Recording'. Gold Disc award by R.I.A.A.

CHIYO OKUMURA
HOKKAIDO SKIES *Toshiba* [*Japan*]. Written by the U.S. group The Ventures, who became extremely popular in Japan during the mid and late 1960s via their personal tours and disc sales. They wrote many songs about Japan, with recordings by popular Japanese singers.

This song was a million seller for female singer Chiyo Okumura who followed up with another hit 'Ginza Lights'.

THE OUTSIDERS
(vocal and instrumental quintet)
TIME WON'T LET ME *Capitol* [*USA*]. The Outsiders' first single was virtually an immediate hit for them. The song was written by the group's leader-guitarist-composer-arranger Tom King. Tom became interested in music when he transposed the zither part of the 'Third Man Theme' to guitar, and started a career with the formation of The Outsiders. He played in various night spots in Cleveland where he met Sonny Geraci, a young singer. The duo then invited Bill Bruno, a Pittsburgh university student to join them as a lead guitarist, then Rick Baker (real name Biagiola) from Cleveland on drums, and Mert Madsen a native of Denmark on bass. The group played in and around Cleveland. Tom King wrote this song, and after a four-hour recording session they took it to a Capitol executive who immediately signed them to a contract. The disc was released in

February in the U.S.A. and reached No 5 for two weeks in the national charts with 15 weeks in the bestsellers, and a subsequent million sale.

The group personnel data: Tom King (guitar-composer-arranger-leader) born Cleveland 1944; Bill Bruno (lead guitar) born Pittsburgh 1946; Sonny Geraci (lead vocalist) born Cleveland 1948; Rick Biagola (drums) born Cleveland 1949; Mert Madsen (bass, accordion, harmonica and guitar) born Denmark. Later, Madsen was replaced by Ritchie D'Amato, born Cleveland 1949.

ROBERT PARKER
BAREFOOTIN' *Nola* [*USA*]. Robert Parker's disc reached No 7 for two weeks in the U.S.A. and is a consistent seller for 14 weeks in their charts, selling, it is claimed by the small Nola company, over one million there.

Robert was born in New Orleans in 1942 and the recording was his first. The song, a raunchy blues novelty, was written by him. It was released on the Island label in Britain where it was No 24, with eight weeks in the bestsellers.

Parker started his musical career as a tenor sax player and gained experience playing with Sonny Stitt, Miles Davis and Gene Ammons in jam sessions in New York. On his return to New Orleans, he started playing on backing sessions for other artists. He then wrote his first song 'All Night Long' followed by 'Across the Tracks', the discs of these becoming local New Orleans hits. Nola Records then signed him up and 'Barefootin'' became a big success very quickly, with resultant bookings and a tour of the U.S.A.

PETER AND GORDON
LADY GODIVA *Columbia* [*Britain*]. The fourth million seller for this popular British duo, the song written by Mike Leander and Charles Mills. The disc reached No 16 for two weeks in Britain with 16 weeks in the bestsellers, and was released in September 1966. It was an even bigger success in the U.S.A. on the Capitol label, achieving No 5 for two weeks with 14 weeks in the bestsellers, the combined sales totalling the million by 1967.

WILSON PICKETT
LAND OF A THOUSAND DANCES *Atlantic* [*USA*]. Originally a bestseller in 1963 for the writers Kris (Chris) Kenner and Fats Domino on the Instant label. Wilson Pickett's recording was released in July 1966 and was No 6 in the U.S.A. charts for two weeks and 11 weeks in the bestsellers, and achieved No 22 in Britain with nine weeks in the bestsellers to make a million global sale. Is now a standard rhythm-and-blues disc.

MUSTANG SALLY *Atlantic* [*USA*]. Written by Wilson Pickett, his disc was released in the U.S.A. in November 1966 and was No 16 for one week with 9 weeks in the bestsellers. In Britain it reached No 22 for a week with seven weeks in the bestsellers and global sale estimated at one million. It is now considered a standard rhythm-and-blues item.

SANDY POSEY (country vocalist)
BORN A WOMAN *MGM* [*USA*]. Sandy Posey was born in 1945 in Jasper, Alabama, and began singing when she was five years old, harmonizing to the music of the radio. In her late teens she moved to West Memphis, Arkansas, just across the Mississippi River from Memphis, a top recording centre in the South. While working as a receptionist at the American Studios, she filled in as a background singer for many famous artists including Tommy Roe, Bobby Goldsboro, Bobby Bare, Joe Tex, Percy Sledge and Skeeter Davis.

In mid-1965 she signed a recording contract with Chips Moman, an independent hit record producer. He found a great piece of material for her first recording in 'Born a Woman' written by Martha Sharp. The demo disc when released by MGM got to No 9 for 2 weeks and stayed in the bestsellers for 14 weeks, and subsequently sold the million. Release was in July

1966 in the U.S.A. and 19 August 1966 in Britain, where it was No 22, with 11 weeks in the bestsellers.

Sandy later recorded for Columbia. She received every major award and is recognized as one of the most outstanding female singers.

SINGLE GIRL *MGM* [*USA*]. Second big hit for Sandy Posey, also written by Martha Sharp and released in the U.S.A. in November 1966. It reached No 10 in 1967 and stayed in the bestsellers for 12 weeks.

In Britain it reached No 15 and was 13 weeks in the bestsellers, in 1967.

ELVIS PRESLEY

LOVE LETTERS *Victor* [*USA*]. Elvis recorded this fine melodic song written in 1945 for the film *Love Letters* by Edward Heyman (words) and Victor Young (music), in a slow shuffling lyrical style. It was released in June 1966 and achieved No 15 in the U.S. charts with 7 weeks in the bestsellers, subsequently selling a million globally. Elvis thus chalked up his 53rd million seller.

The disc was a hit in Britain, reaching No 5 in the charts, with 10 weeks in the bestsellers.

FRANKIE AND JOHNNY *Victor* [*USA*]. The title song from the film of the same name starring Elvis Presley. This version of the classical American gutter song – the story of Frankie and her man – was written by Gottlieb, Fred Karger and Ben Weisman. The song was originally known as the Frankie and Albert song and well known along the Mississippi river and among railroad men of the Middle West as early as 1888. There have been a great number of different versions since then, the Frankie and Johnny song being of later development.

Elvis' disc was released in March 1966 and was No 17 for two weeks in the U.S. charts and 8 weeks in their bestsellers, and No 20 for one week in Britain with nine weeks in the bestsellers. It sold the global million by 1968, making Gold Disc No 55.

ELVIS PRESLEY WITH THE JORDANAIRES

ALL THAT I AM *Victor* [*USA*]. Another belated global million seller for Elvis Presley released in October 1966 and reaching the seven-figure sale by 1968, his 56th. The song comes from Elvis' film *Spinout* (British title *California Holiday*) and was written by Sid Tepper and Roy C. Bennett. The disc reached No 39 in the U.S. charts with 8 weeks in the bestsellers, and No 18 in Britain, and it was the first Presley disc to feature an orchestral accompaniment.

ELVIS PRESLEY WITH THE JORDANAIRES AND THE IMPERIALS QUARTET

IF EVERY DAY WAS LIKE CHRISTMAS *Victor* [*USA*]. Presley's friend Bob West wrote this for him and the disc achieved substantial sales at Christmas 1966 and 1967, with the million by 1968. It was released in December 1966 and was quite a success in Britain where it was No 9 in the charts with seven weeks in the bestsellers. This made million seller No 57 for Elvis (by 1968) globally.

JAMES AND BOBBY PURIFY

I'M YOUR PUPPET *Bell* [*USA*]. James Lee Purify and Robert Lee Dickey are the real names of this duo who are cousins. James was born in Pensacola, and Bobby in Tallahassee, Florida. James left Pensacola and was raised in Chicago, and Bobby on a farm outside Tallahassee.

From 1963 until 1966 they played the school and nightclub road circuit throughout Florida, Georgia and Alabama. They first started out in the music field by forming a group called the Dothan Sextet.

This disc by the talented duo was No 5 for two weeks in the U.S.A. and 14 weeks in the bestsellers. It reached No 12 with 10 weeks in the British bestsellers and sold an estimated million. It was released in September 1966.

The song was written by Lindon Oldham and Dan Penn.

? (QUESTION MARK) AND THE MYSTERIANS
(vocal and instrumental quintet)

96 TEARS *Cameo* [*USA*]. This quintet was a Mexican/American group out of Detroit via Acapulco. The Mysterians were discovered by Bob Dell, a programme director of WTAC-Flint, Michigan, who launched the group in the record business. Lead singer Question Mark joined the group one night when they were playing at Michigan's Mount Holly Ski Lodge. Not even the group were said to know his real name or anything about his past. He lived alone and never removed his sun glasses. The Mysterians were Bobby Balderamma (lead guitar), Frank Lugo (bass guitar), Eddie Serrato (drummer) and Frank Rodriquez (organist).

'96 Tears', a beat-blues number with a powerful organ backing, was written by Rudy Martinez. The disc, their first, reached the No 1 spot in the U.S. charts for two weeks with 15 weeks in the bestsellers, and was also a top seller in Canada. It reached No 37 with four weeks in the British bestsellers.

Cameo-Parkway Records presented the group with a gold record for a million sale in November 1966, just 12 weeks after its release. R.I.A.A. Gold Disc award also.

THE RIGHTEOUS BROTHERS

(You're my) SOUL AND INSPIRATION *Verve* [*USA*]. The second million seller for this duo, the song again written by the husband/wife team Barry Mann and Cynthia Weill. The disc sold 750,000 in the U.S.A. in two weeks, and the million in six weeks, with Gold Disc award from R.I.A.A. in May 1966, just 12 weeks after its release.

The disc was No 1 in the U.S. charts for three weeks and 13 weeks in the bestsellers. It reached No 15 and was 10 weeks in the British bestsellers.

JOHNNY RIVERS

SECRET AGENT MAN *Imperial* [*USA*]. This song was written by P. J. Sloan and Steve Barri who also had a tremendous hit with 'Eve of Destruction'. Johnny Rivers' recording reached No 2 in the U.S. charts with 11 weeks in the bestsellers, and he was presented with a Gold Disc in May 1966 on his return visit to Hollywood's Whiskey à Go Go, the scene of his initial triumph in 1964.

The song is described as 'bluesy' and was sung in an infectious soulful manner by Johnny over the credits on the popular CBS-TV series of the same title. The disc was issued in March 1966.

TOMMY ROE

SWEET PEA *ABC-Paramount* [*USA*]. Another self-penned success for singer Tommy Roe with consistent sales over 16 weeks in the U.S. charts and reaching the No 5 position. Subsequent sales made this the second million seller for him, with a belated Gold Disc award by R.I.A.A. in March 1969.

THE ROLLING STONES

19th NERVOUS BREAKDOWN *Decca* [*Britain*] *London* [*USA*]. This sold a global million in a few weeks (by March 1966) and was No 1 in Britain for three weeks with eight weeks in the bestsellers and No 1 in the U.S.A. for one week with 10 weeks in the bestsellers. British sales were over 250,000, the rest from the U.S.A. and elsewhere. Song, written by the group's Keith Richard and Mick Jagger, typifies their unique humorous song-writing style. The disc was released in Britain on 4 February. Originally recorded in Hollywood.

PAINT IT BLACK *Decca* [*Britain*] *London* [*USA*]. Another Keith Richard-Mick Jagger composition. The disc had advance orders in Britain of over 300,000 before release on 13 May and was No 1 in the charts for one week with 10 weeks in the bestsellers. Sales were much bigger in the U.S.A. where the disc was No 1 for two weeks with 11 weeks in the bestsellers, making a global sale of over a million.

The disc has a strong Eastern flavour and highlights the use of the sitar, an Indian stringed instrument.

The song was written during The Rolling Stones' Australian tour earlier in the year and was recorded by them in Hollywood afterwards.

HAVE YOU SEEN YOUR MOTHER, BABY, STANDING IN THE SHADOW? *Decca [Britain] London [USA]*. Although difficult to catch much of the lyrics, this disc with its wild rhythms and startling sounds proved another big hit for The Rolling Stones. It sold a combined U.S.A./Britain million in just over a fortnight. It was recorded by them in Hollywood and written by Mick Jagger and Keith Richard during their U.S. tour in 1966. The disc was No 4 in the U.S.A. for one week with 7 weeks in the bestsellers, and No 5 in Britain for two weeks, with 8 weeks in the bestsellers.

MOTHER'S LITTLE HELPER backed with LADY JANE *London [USA]*. Both titles were recorded by the group in Hollywood as part of their album 'Aftermath'. This singles release subsequently sold a million. 'Mother's Little Helper' reached No 4 (with 9 weeks in the bestsellers) and 'Lady Jane' No 24 (with 6 weeks in the bestsellers) in the U.S. charts. Both were written by Mick Jagger and Keith Richard of the group, the first title being an amusing song with catchy words and the latter a pretty medieval number.

AFTERMATH (album) *Decca [Britain] London [USA]*. Third million seller for The Rolling Stones, with heavy sales in the U.S.A. where it was No 1 for two weeks and stayed in the charts for 50 weeks. Sales in Britain were also big, the disc achieving No 1 for nine weeks and staying in the charts for 27 weeks. Combined sale well over the million globally. Gold Disc award from R.I.A.A. on 9 August 1966.

The album is a collection of songs all written by the group's prolific writer/members Mick Jagger and Keith Richard and makes use of the sitar, an Indian stringed instrument, by group member Brian Jones in the song 'Mother's Little Helper'. Jack Nitzsche (road manager) and Ian Stewart helped with piano and organ spots. Contents: 'Mother's Little Helper'; 'Stupid Girl'; 'Lady Jane'; 'Under My Thumb'; 'Doncha Bother Me'; 'Goin' Home'; 'Flight 505'; 'High and Dry'; 'Out of Time'; 'It's Not Easy'; 'I Am Waiting'; 'Take It or Leave It'; 'Think'; 'What to Do'.

The disc was recorded under the supervision of their manager Andrew Oldham at RCA-Victor Studios in Hollywood, on three separate visits to the U.S.A.

Released 15 April 1966 in Britain and in July 1966 in the U.S.A.

BIG HITS (High Tide and Green Grass) (album) *Decca [Britain] London [USA]*. Fourth million seller album for the group, with big sales in the U.S.A., Britain and globally. It was No 3 for three weeks in America and stayed in the bestsellers for 98 weeks. In Britain it was No 3 for one week and 14 weeks in the charts.

The album contains most of the momentous highlights from the group's recording career. Sales were over two million by end of 1967.

Contents (British release); *'Have You Seen Your Mother, Baby, Standing in the Shadow?' by Mick Jagger and Keith Richard (1966); *'Paint It Black', by Mick Jagger and Keith Richard (1966); *'It's All Over Now', by B. and S. Womack (1964); *'The Last Time', by Mick Jagger and Keith Richard (1965); 'Heart of Stone', by Mick Jagger and Keith Richard (1965); 'Not Fade Away', by Charles Hardin and Norman Petty (1957); *'Satisfaction (I can't get no)', by Mick Jagger and Keith Richard (1965); *'Get Off My Cloud', by Mick Jagger and Keith Richard (1965); *'As Tears Go By', by Mick Jagger, Keith Richard and Andrew Loog Oldham (1964); *'19th Nervous Breakdown', by Mick Jagger and Keith Richard (1966); *'Lady Jane', by Mick Jagger and Keith Richard (1966); *'Time Is On

My Side', by Norman Meade (1963); 'Come On', by Chuck Berry (1961); 'Little Red Rooster', by Willie Dixon (1961).

Items marked * were million seller singles.

This album was released in the U.S.A. in April 1966 and in Britain in November 1966. Gold Disc award from R.I.A.A. on 27 April 1966, soon after release of disc.

The American release contained most of the above songs with substitution of three titles for: 'Tell Me', by Mick Jagger and Keith Richard (1964); 'Good Times, Bad Times', by Mick Jagger and Keith Richard (1964); 'Play with Fire', by Nanker and Phelge (pseudonyms of Jagger and Richard) (1965).

THE ROYAL GUARDSMEN

SNOOPY VERSUS THE RED BARON *Laurie [USA]*. Evolved from the popular U.S. comic strip 'Peanuts' by Charles Schulz in which the hero's dog Snoopy imagines himself to be a World War I pilot hunting the skies for the Red Baron from Germany, this gimmick song proved to be a big hit. The Royal Guardsmen, six American cowboy-booted singers and instrumentalists, give a highly individual telling of the story, written by Phil Gernhard and Dick Holler. The Red Baron was actually the famous World War I aviator Baron Maurice von Richthofen (born 1888) who between 1917 and 1918 brought down over 80 Allied machines and then met his match in April 1918 when he was shot down behind the British lines by Captain Roy Brown of the Royal Flying Corps. Richthofen's exploits were told in a film entitled *The Blue Max* (1966). In his honour, Richthofen squadrons were formed in the regenerated post-war German Air Force.

This disc was first broadcast in early December 1966 over the Tampa, Florida, and Abilene, Texas, airwaves, spread to Pittsburgh, Albany, Providence and then right across the U.S.A., selling over 360,000 in a few days. It soon reached No 2 in the charts, remaining in that position for five weeks with 12 weeks in the bestsellers, with an eventual million sale in early 1967 and a Gold Disc award from R.I.A.A. (February 1967). Global sale over three million.

The catchy tune is in the style of an Army march with a big brass sound, and was one of the novelties of the year. It also had quite a success in Britain in 1967 when released on the Stateside label, reaching No 6 position in the charts with 13 weeks in the bestsellers.

The Royal Guardsmen all hail from Florida's town of Ocala and were all at high school or university when they made this disc. The group comprises John Burdett (drums), Bill Balogh (bass), Barry Winslow (rhythm guitarist/vocalist), Tom Richards (lead guitarist), Billy Taylor (organist) and Chris Nunley (vocalist/percussionist). They performed around Oklawaha, their reputation coming to the attention of Phil Gernhard, a producer, who groomed them until he decided they were ready to make their first record 'Baby Let's Wait' for the Laurie label. This was not a success, but the label decided to give the group a second try at the end of 1966 with 'Snoopy', with sensational results.

STAFF SERGEANT BARRY SADLER

THE BALLAD OF THE GREEN BERETS *Victor [USA]*. Barry's disc was released on 11 January 1966 and proved to be the fastest seller for Victor Records, selling the million in a fortnight, with an R.I.A.A. Gold Disc award. The song was inspired by Robin Moore's bestseller book *The Green Berets*, and was written by Robin Moore with music by Barry Sadler. The disc was No 1 in the U.S.A. for five weeks and 13 weeks in the bestsellers and sold over five million. A German version by Freddy (Quinn) on Polydor titled '100 Mann und ein befehl' was No 1 for nine weeks there and sold over 600,000. It was No 24 in Britain, with eight weeks in the bestsellers.

Handsome Staff Sergeant Barry Sadler was born in New Mexico in 1941, his father being a plumber who died when Barry was seven. His mother was a barmaid. After leaving school at 15, Barry tramped around for three years before joining the U.S. Air Force at 18 for four years. On discharge in 1962 a friend taught him the drums and guitar, and they formed a group which was unsuccessful. Barry then joined the U.S. Army and after about a year's rigorous training, qualified for his green beret as a combat medic. Along the way, at Fort Sam Houston, he started writing songs. A few months later, while on patrol in Vietnam, he fell into a man-trap and a pungi stake (a poisoned spear made of sharpened bamboo) plunged into his leg. He operated on himself between fainting spells and was ultimately found and carried to safety. This ended his combat career and left him with one leg scarred and partially numb. He had written a number of songs during his Army career and during off-duty hours in Vietnam, mostly about men at war, and once back in America, he contacted the publisher to whom he had given his first song 'The Ballad of the Green Berets'. The publisher was a friend of the author of the book *The Green Berets* who required a model to pose for the cover illustration of a paperback edition. As a result, Barry's face appeared on the cover. The songwriter was then brought to the attention of RCA-Victor who put him under contract immediately, and he recorded the song, being possessed of a raw tenor voice. With America deeply involved in the Vietnam conflict, his disc made a tremendous impact and rocketed him to fame and fortune, with demands for his personal appearances so great that the Army specially assigned a lieutenant colonel to handle his bookings. Barry's earnings as writer and performer from the song and the album brought him well over $500,000 for himself alone. About another dozen versions of the song in the U.S.A. and many foreign were recorded, totalling 75 by the end of 1966 (see also 'Ballads of the Green Berets' album).

This disc was America's biggest hit of 1966.

BALLADS OF THE GREEN BERETS (album) *Victor* [*USA*]. All the arrangements for this album of songs written and sung by Barry Sadler were by Sid Bass. It was released on 19 January 1966, No 1 for seven weeks (four of these simultaneously with the single) and sold well over two million. Both this album and the single were certified simultaneously for Gold Disc awards, the second time in the history of R.I.A.A. - the first being 'Help' by The Beatles. The album is also one of the fastest selling in RCA-Victor's history. It stayed in the bestseller charts for 32 weeks and sold the first million in five weeks.

Contents of disc: 'Ballad of the Green Berets', by Robin Moore/Barry Sadler; 'Letter from Vietnam', by Barry Sadler; 'Saigon', by Barry Sadler; 'The Soldier Has Come Home', by Barry Sadler; 'I'm Watching the Raindrops Fall', by Barry Sadler; 'Trooper's Lament', by Barry Sadler; 'Bamiba', by Barry Sadler; 'Badge of Courage', by Barry Sadler; 'Salute to the Nurses', by Barry Sadler; 'I'm a Lucky One', by Barry Sadler; 'Garet Trooper', by Barry Sadler; 'Lullaby', by Barry Sadler.

SAM AND DAVE (rhythm-and-blues duo)
HOLD ON, I'M COMING *Stax* [*USA*]. Written by Isaac Hayes and David Porter, composers of several hits for this out-

standing duo and the first million seller for them. The disc was released in the U.S.A. in April 1966 and became a No 1 on the rhythm-and-blues charts in addition to reaching No 15 on the national charts with 13 weeks in the bestsellers. It is now considered to be a standard rhythm-and-blues disc.

(See 1967 for data on Sam and Dave.)

SAM THE SHAM AND THE PHARAOHS
LI'L RED RIDING HOOD *MGM* [*USA*]. Second million seller for Sam the Sham, with R.I.A.A. Gold Disc award in August 1966 after two months on the market. It was No 1 in the U.S.A. for one week and stayed high in their charts for three months with 14 weeks in the bestsellers. It reached No 46 with three weeks in the British bestsellers. It was written by Ronald Blackwell, and is a low-key blues type romantic number borrowed freely from the children's fairy tale of the same name.

THE SEEKERS
GEORGY GIRL *Capitol* [*USA*] *Columbia* [*Britain*]. The fourth million seller for The Seekers and composer Tom Springfield, the words by Jim Dale. It was written for the film *Georgy Girl* (starring James Mason, Alan Bates and Lynn Redgrave as 'Georgy') as a replacement for another song, and sung for the film by The Seekers. The disc is a compilation of the two sets of lyrics written for the opening and closing of the film which was a tremendous success. The disc was first released in the U.S.A. and became No 1 there for one week with 16 weeks in the bestsellers. It was issued in Britain early 1967 on the Columbia label and reached No 3 in the charts with 11 weeks in the bestsellers. It was also a big hit in the group's native land Australia (No 1 for two weeks) where they received a Gold Disc in March 1967 for a million global sale, and also appeared before an audience of 200,000 at the Myer Music Bowl in Melbourne. Total sales of this disc were subsequently three million.

The song was nominated for an Academy Award, 1966. Gold Disc award, R.I.A.A., 1967.

THE SHADOWS OF KNIGHT
(vocal and instrumental quintet)
GLORIA *Dunwich* [*USA*]. First big hit for the Dunwich label (distributed in U.S.A. by Atlantic) and first million seller for this group.

The quintet, all high school graduates, began their swift rise to the top in the summer of 1965 at The Cellar in Arlington Heights, a suburb of Chicago, their fame spreading further afield very rapidly. They played teenage clubs and dances in and around Chicago for a year. Then came this disc which reached No 6 in the U.S. charts with 12 weeks in the bestsellers, with eventual sales of a million.

The song was written by Van Morrison in 1965. The group consists of: Jim Sohns (lead singer) born 23 August 1949, Prospect Heights, Illinois; Warren Rogers (lead guitar); Jerry McGeorge (rhythm guitar); Tom Schiffour (drums); Joe Kelly (bass). In 1968 the group was assigned to Team Records.

FRANK SINATRA
STRANGERS IN THE NIGHT *Reprise* [*USA*]. A great triumph for Sinatra. This disc was No 1 for one week in the U.S.A. and No 1 for three weeks in Britain (one week of these simultaneously with the U.S.A.). Sinatra had only topped Britain's charts once before - in 1954 with 'Three Coins in the Fountain' - but this time it was to the tune of over half a million sale. The disc was made on 11 April 1966 and stayed in the U.S. charts for 15 weeks and in Britain for 20 weeks. Combined U.S./British sales were over a million.

The tune was written by famous German conductor/composer Bert Kaempfert as part of the score of the Universal picture *A Man Could Get Killed* - Kaempfert's first musical assignment for an American film. The publisher realized its potentialities as a hit song for Sinatra and lyrics were written by Charles Singleton and Eddy Snyder. No fewer than 85 other performers also recorded it, making it the biggest success the composer has ever had.

Frank Sinatra's big hit with this disc immediately followed his daughter Nancy's success with 'These Boots Are Made for Walkin' ' – making a 1966 'double' No 1 for the Sinatras.

'Strangers in the Night' was also No 1 in Argentina, Italy, Switzerland, Austria, Belgium, France (over 600,000 sold), Australia and Eire and thus created a worldwide resurgence for the Sinatra 'magic'. His album of the same title also won a Gold Disc award. There were (1966) four Grammy Awards for 'Strangers in the Night' – 'Record of the Year', 'Best Vocal (Male) Performance', 'Best Engineering Contribution (Popular Recording)' and 'Best Arrangement'.

NANCY SINATRA
THESE BOOTS ARE MADE FOR WALKIN' *Reprise* [*USA*]. Written by Lee Hazlewood (composer of many hits for guitarist Duane Eddy), Nancy's disc sold a million in the U.S.A. in eight weeks and received an R.I.A.A. Gold Disc award in March 1966. It was No 1 there for one week (with 14 weeks in the bestsellers) and for four weeks in Britain (one week of these simultaneously with the U.S.A. and 14 weeks in the bestsellers). British sales were well over 250,000, Germany over 400,000, and this disc was No 1 also in Australia, New Zealand, Germany, Holland, South Africa, Eire and Singapore with global sales estimated at four million.

Nancy, daughter of Frank Sinatra, was born in Jersey City, New Jersey, in 1941. When she moved to Los Angeles, Nancy attended University High and studied economics for 1½ years at the University of Southern California. She decided to develop her own talents rather than bask in her father's fame, and spent many years studying the arts – 11 years of piano, five years' voice and singing lessons, eight years of dance and five years of dramatics. She first attracted attention when she sang on a TV show with her father and Elvis Presley in 1959. Since then she has appeared on many TV shows as singer and dramatic actress. In 1961, she signed exclusively with Reprise Records and began to build an international reputation. Her first disc 'Cuff Links and a Tie Clip' was quite a success, and by 1963 such discs as 'Tonight You Belong to Me', and 'Like I Do' were hits in Japan, Italy, South Africa, Holland and Belgium. She appeared in four movies, including *Marriage on the Rocks* which starred Frank Sinatra and Dean Martin and, in 1966, *The Last of the Secret Agents*.

With 'These Boots Are Made for Walkin' ', Nancy was the first U.S. girl singer since Connie Francis (in 1958) to top the British charts, and followed her father in the golden disc route. With his 'Strangers in the Night' success it was a memorable year for the Sinatras and the Reprise label.

SUGAR TOWN *Reprise* [*USA*]. Another big success for Nancy and the composer Lee Hazlewood, the disc achieving the No 4 position in early 1967 in the U.S. charts and a run of 13 weeks. It also had a good sale in Britain where it was No 8 in 1967, with 10 weeks in the bestsellers.

U.S. sales were over a million. Gold Disc, R.I.A.A., in 1967.

PERCY SLEDGE (rhythm-and-blues vocalist)
WHEN A MAN LOVES A WOMAN *Atlantic* [*USA*]. The very first disc for Percy Sledge. It became No 1 after seven weeks in the U.S. charts and stayed there for two weeks in all, in early June 1966, was 13 weeks in the bestsellers, and sold a million by mid-August, with Gold Disc award from R.I.A.A. The disc also got to No 4 in Britain with 17 weeks in the bestsellers.

Percy Sledge, born 1941, hails from Muscle Shoals in the deep south of Alabama. He began singing at the age of 15. After leaving school, he became a male nurse at Colbert County Hospital near his home town, and also devoted some of his time by singing in the choirs of Galilee Baptist Church and other churches near his home. He also managed to eke a living as member of a group called The Esquires Combo. Finally, Percy decided to call in on Quin Ivy at his 'Ivy's Tune Town Record Shop' in Sheffield, Alabama. Quin, a former disc jockey, asked him to sing, then said he would record him as soon as he could. Quin and a man named Greene, guitarist and A & R man, supervised the session at a small studio in Sheffield. Manager-agent Phil Walden – closely associated with Otis Redding's successes – flew to Sheffield to hear the result of the session. He decided that Sledge was a potential hit; so did the Atlantic executives. With very little promotion and even less publicity, the virtually unknown singer was a success in a very short time, with the resultant countless shows, radio and TV appearances and more recording.

The song, written by C. Lewis and A. Wright, is an easy going, moving blues-based chant.

A top rhythm-and-blues disc in both the U.S.A. and Britain.

THE SPIDERS (septet)
YUHI GA NAITEIRU (Sad Sunset) *Philips* [*Japan*]. The Spiders, one of Japan's top recording groups, had an advance order of 150,000 for this disc which sold half a million in six months and the million by eight months (July 1967). Composition is by Kuranosuke Hamaguchi.

The group was formed by drummer Sochi Tanabe in 1962, and made its debut at a jazz tea-house in Kinshico, Tokyo. Their reception was mild, but they kept pace with American pop styles such as the twist and surfing music, adapting them to their own fashion. Their popularity gradually increased by playing in tea-houses and at American military camps. They finally became national favourites in 1964 when the group's arrangements of Beatle-type sounds began to make an impact with their fans. They were then invited to appear with visiting artists such as The Animals, Beach Boys, Peter and Gordon, etc., and made their film debut in *Seishun-a-Go-Go*.

They made their first promotional tour of Europe in 1966, and a personal appearance tour in Hawaii and America in 1967.

Their beat music, known in Japan as 'eleki', remains recognisably oriental in flavour. This disc was No 1 for 14 weeks from November 1966 to February 1967 and stayed in the charts in Japan for 20 weeks.

Personnel: Sochi Tanabe (drummer) born 1942; Katsuo Ohno (steel guitar and organ) born 1943; Takayuki Inoue (lead guitarist and vocalist) born 1944; Hirochi Kamayatsu (rhythm guitarist and vocalist) born 1942; Masaaki Sakai (tambourine and vocalist) born 1947; Mitsuru Kato (bass) born 1939; Jun Inoue (vocalist) born 1948.

DUSTY SPRINGFIELD WITH ORCHESTRA DIRECTED BY IVOR RAYMONDE

YOU DON'T HAVE TO SAY YOU LOVE ME *Philips* [*Britain*]. This song came from an Italian San Remo Song Contest in 1965. The original title – 'Io che non vivo (senzate)' by V. Pallavicini (words) and P. Donaggio (music). The English lyrics are by Vicki Wickham and Simon Napier-Bell.

Dusty's disc sold over 250,000 in Britain where it was No 1 for two weeks. It had a big sale in the U.S.A. where it reached No 3 in their charts and stayed high up for six weeks with 13 weeks in the bestsellers. It had 18 weeks in the British bestsellers. Global sale a million by 1967.

THE SUPREMES

MY WORLD IS EMPTY WITHOUT YOU *Motown* [*USA*]. The eighth million seller for The Supremes, and for the writers Eddie Holland, Brian Holland and Lamont Dozier. Release was on 15 January 1966, the disc reaching No 4 for a week in the U.S. charts with 11 weeks in the bestsellers.

YOU CAN'T HURRY LOVE *Motown* [*USA*]. The ninth million seller for the U.S.A.'s greatest female group and for their writers Brian Holland, Eddie Holland and Lamont Dozier. The disc attained a high position in the U.S. charts very quickly and was No 1 for two weeks with 13 weeks in the bestsellers. The song is a throbbing pop rhythm-and-blues number about romance, performed in their inimitable style and 'Motown' sound. The disc also reached No 3 in Britain's charts with 12 weeks in the bestsellers. It was The Supremes' seventh disc to top the U.S.A. charts, a feat matched only by The Beatles. Released 13 August 1966.

A top rhythm-and-blues disc in both the U.S.A. and Britain.

YOU KEEP ME HANGIN' ON *Motown* [*USA*]. Tenth million seller for The Supremes with big sales in the U.S.A. where it was No 1 for two weeks and 12 weeks in the bestsellers, and also a hit in Britain (No 5 with 10 weeks in the bestsellers).

It was their eighth disc to top the U.S. charts, again very quickly. The song was also written for them by the talented team of Brian Holland, Lamont Dozier and Eddie Holland, a pulsating rock number with a driving guitar figure throughout. Released 29 October 1966.

A top rhythm-and-blues disc in both the U.S.A. and Britain.

B. J. THOMAS WITH THE TRIUMPHS

I'M SO LONELY I COULD CRY *Scepter* [*USA*]. The first big hit for B. J. Thomas and the one that brought him national prominence. It was recorded in late 1965 and by 1966 after release in February, reached No 5 for two weeks on the U.S. charts and was 13 weeks in the bestsellers. The song was written in 1949 by country-and-western singer Hank Williams, one of his own personal favourite numbers. Release in Britain was 25 March 1966. The million sale was reported in 1970.

The Triumphs, a seven-piece band from Rosenberg, Texas, made 15 recordings with B. J. Thomas before he became a solo artist in 1966. (See 1968 for B. J. Thomas biography.)

THE TROGGS (vocal and instrumental quartet)

WILD THING *Fontana* [*Britain*]. The most promising new group in Britain in 1966, the year of their formation. 'Wild Thing' was written by Chips Taylor who has also had hit songs recorded by The Hollies and Peggy Lee. An outstanding feature of this disc is Reg Presley's ocarina playing.

The group comprised – Reg Presley, born Andover, Hampshire, 12 June 1943, formerly a bricklayer. He was bass guitarist with his previous group but became lead vocalist with The Troggs. Chris Britton, born Watford, Hertfordshire, 21 June 1945. He studied classical guitar for four years, joined a local group at 16 and was an apprentice lithographic camera operator. Peter Staples, born Andover, Hampshire, 3 May 1944, an electrician. Learned to play guitar at 14, and played in various local groups from 15, and was with Chris prior to The Troggs' for-

mation. Ronnie Bond, born Andover, Hampshire, 4 May 1943. All were educated at Andover schools.

The group got its biggest break when they met Larry Page who became both their personal and recording manager. They made their radio debut on 'Saturday Club' and TV debut in 'Thank Your Lucky Stars'. Ronnie plays drums, Chris the guitar, Reg the bass and ocarina, Peter bass and rhythm guitar.

'Wild Thing' became a very fast-moving hit, and two American labels Atco and Fontana claimed the U.S. distribution rights. It was released there on both*, the Fontana label backed with 'From Home' and the Atco with 'With a Girl Like You' (see below). The song was No 1 in the U.S.A. for two weeks with 11 weeks in the bestsellers, and No 1 for one week in Britain with 12 weeks in the bestsellers. A Gold Disc for global million sale was presented by Page One Records, the independent company which produced their discs. 'Wild Thing' was released on 22 April 1966.

*Dual label releases occurred only once before in the U.S.A. – in 1950 (see Eileen Barton).

WITH A GIRL LIKE YOU *Fontana* [*Britain*]. Written by The Troggs' member Reg Presley. This was also released by both Atco and Fontana in the U.S.A., reached No 29 with 8 weeks in the U.S. bestsellers, and sold a global million. It was No 1 for two weeks in Britain and 12 weeks in the bestsellers, with over 250,000 sales. Disc was backed by 'I Want You' on the Fontana label in the U.S.A.

The group adopted their name from the shortened form of the word 'troglodyte' (cave-dweller) because they liked it.

MAO TSE-TUNG

SING ALONG WITH MAO (*Chinese Disc*) Red China's Chairman Mao Tse-Tung made this disc in late November 1966. It contains excerpts from his quotations which he chants, 'live' recordings of his three meetings with the Red Guards, and recordings of speeches by Defence Minister Lin Piao and Premier Chou En-lai at Red Guard rallies in Peking.

According to the Chinese newspaper the *People's Daily*, the Shanghai record factory that produced the disc was taken over by the Red Chinese government because it had been making many records that were 'decadent influences of the bourgeois and feudal classes', and because the former management had been under 'powerholders within the party who took the capitalist road'. 'In the great cultural revolution, all capitalist powerholders have been overthrown and swept clear, and the record factory has become a school of Mao Tse-Tung's thought,' said the paper.

The disc is said to have easily gone over the million mark and replaced the former No 1 favourite disc in Red China, 'The East is Red', a collection of revolutionary opera music.

JACKY YOSHIKAWA AND HIS BLUE COMETS

AOI HITOMI (Blue eyes) *CBS* [*Japan*]. Jacky Yoshikawa and his Blue Comets formed in May 1965, became extremely popular in their native Japan in 1966, and made their debut with this disc released on 20 March. It sold half a million by July and the million sale was reported in May 1967. The disc stayed in the Japanese bestseller charts for six months, was No 2 for eight weeks and No 1 for one week.

The song, a Japanese folk-rock original, was written by Jun Hashimoto (words) and Tadao Inoue (music). Disc was also released on the Epic label in the U.S.A.

THE YOUNG RASCALS (instrumental and vocal quartet)

GOOD LOVIN' *Atlantic* [*USA*]. The Young Rascals were first formed in January 1965, and their first engagement was the Choo Choo Club, Garfield, New Jersey. Then came an engagement on The Barge, a real barge lying in the waters off Southampton, Long Island, where they performed for 2½ months. Here they were tremendously popular and were discovered by Sid Bernstein, a New York promoter who signed them to Atlantic Records against bids from practically every other major U.S. recording company. Their first release was 'I Ain't Gonna Eat My Heart Out Any More' (1965) which got into the national charts. Then came 'Good Lovin'' written by Rudy Clark and Arthur Resnick, that put them at No 1 for two weeks in the charts with 14 weeks in the U.S. bestsellers, with a Gold Disc award from Atlantic for the million sale of this hard-pounding rhythmic number.

Their tours throughout America in clubs, arenas, concert halls and 'rock' shows made them a major attraction by the group's showmanship and the excitement they created. They were also a success on an English tour and became much in demand in other countries.

The group did their own arrangements for recording.

Personnel of the group: Eddie Brigati (lead vocalist) of Garfield, New Jersey; Felix Cavaliere (organ) of Pelham, New York; Gene Cornish (guitar) of Rochester, New York; Dino Danelli (drums) of Jersey City.

1967

THE AMERICAN BREED (vocal and instrumental quartet)

BEND ME, SHAPE ME *Acta* [*USA*]. The American Breed's disc proved to be the all-time bestselling locally-produced single in Chicago, selling well over 150,000 there alone. It also became No 1 for one week in the U.S. national charts in early 1968 with 14 weeks in the bestsellers, and went over the million mark. Song was written by Scott English and Laurence Weiss, and the disc released in late 1967. It was also a good seller in Britain in early 1968 when released there on the Stateside label. It reached No 24, and stayed six weeks in the charts. R.I.A.A. Gold Disc award February 1968.

The group became especially popular in the Chicago area at dance dates and were originally called Gary and The Nite Lights. Their discovery was a 'fortunate accident'. Kenny Myers, Acta's general manager, was caught in a blizzard in the winter of 1966 and forced to stay in Chicago. He wandered down to one of the recording studios and ran into Bill Traut of Dunwich Productions who played him some tapes of a new group he was producing called The Mauds. Sandwiched between their takes was a foursome from Cicero who had previously recorded for MGM – a number titled 'I Don't Think You Know Me' by Gary and The Nite Lights. Myers signed them immediately for the new Acta label (a division of Dot Records) and the song was the label's first release, under the group's new name of The American Breed. This got into the U.S. charts and their second disc got to No 10. A successful album followed and the group were booked at top venues all over the Southern states. 'Bend Me, Shape Me' set the seal of fame on the group with performances all over the U.S.A.

The personnel of the group: Gary Loizzo (lead singer, lead guitarist) born 16 August 1945; Charles 'Chuck' Colbert (bass guitarist) born 29 August 1944; Alan Ciner (12-string guitarist) born 14 May 1947; Lee Anthony Graziano (drummer, trumpet) born 9 November 1943.

LOUIS ARMSTRONG (vocal)

WHAT A WONDERFUL WORLD *ABC* [*USA*]. Louis' debut disc on the ABC label projected a new image of this famous artist in a beautiful slow ballad with flower-child lyrics about the beautiful things. This lovely song was written by George David Weiss and George Douglas (Robert Thiele) and produced by composer Robert Thiele. The disc, issued in September in the U.S.A., did not make much headway there, but when released in Britain (27 October) it was by 1968 a big success, selling over half a million. Internationally the disc was a million seller. Release in Britain was on the Stateside label, and the disc was No 1 for four weeks there, with 29 weeks in the bestsellers.

Louis sang this song when he visited Britain in 1968 to appear for two weeks at the Variety Club, Batley. He received a reported record fee of £20,000 and was a tremendous attraction.

THE ASSOCIATION

WINDY *Warner* [*USA*]. Second million seller for this group and another R.I.A.A. Gold Disc award. The disc was No 1 in the U.S.A. for four weeks and 14 weeks in the bestsellers. The song was written by 19-year-old Ruthann Friedman.

NEVER MY LOVE *Warner* [*USA*]. This beautiful slow-paced ballad featuring The Association's brilliant harmony was written by Don and Dick Addrisi and released in August 1967. By November it sold a million and was awarded a Gold Disc by R.I.A.A. It was No 1 for one week in the U.S. charts and 14 weeks in the bestsellers.

AL BANO

NEL SOLE (In the sun) *EMI* [*Italy*]. Al Bano was awarded La Maschera d'Argent in Rome (October 1967) as the most popular young singer of that year. He also won the fourth International Roses Festival with the song 'L'oro del mondo'.

'Nel Sole' was written by Vito Pallavicini and Pino Massara (Bano's producer). The disc sold over 600,000 in its first three months on the Italian market, with the million reported in July 1968 plus Gold Disc award. It stayed in a high position in the Italian charts for 22 weeks after release in July 1967, and was No 1 for 11 of those weeks.

The song was first introduced on the TV-radio contest 'A Disc for the Summer' in Italy.

Al Bano was born in Southern Italy in 1943. His real name is Albano Carrisi.

THE BEATLES

PENNY LANE backed with STRAWBERRY FIELDS FOR-EVER *Parlophone* [*Britain*] *Capitol* [*USA*]. The 22nd Gold Disc award from R.I.A.A. for the group (March 1967), both songs written by the prolific John Lennon and Paul McCartney. 'Penny Lane' was No 1 for two weeks in the U.S.A. with 10 weeks in the bestsellers, and No 2 for three weeks in Britain with 11 weeks in the bestsellers. Issued on 13 February on Capitol in the States, over 1,100,000 were ordered, the highest quantity of any one single ever pressed and shipped in a three-day period by the label. It also sold 350,000 in its first three days in Britain where it was released on 17 February, and easily passed the half million mark later. U.S.A. sales were over 1,500,000 and the global total well in excess of two million.

'Strawberry Fields Forever', which reached No 8 with 9 weeks in the U.S. bestsellers, has a complex backing of flutes, cellos, harpsichord and weird sounds and dissonances, achieved partly through space-age electronic effects and tapes played backwards at various speeds. Through the use of this electronic medium, The Beatles bridged the hitherto impassable gap between 'rock' and classical music. The tempos are mixed – four-four, six-eight and three-four, the song building to a bustling crescendo with crisp brass. 'Penny Lane' is more commercial sounding, with flutes and brass prominent to a jaunty rhythm and catchy tune with a colourful lyric.

The titles for both were taken from two places in the group's native Liverpool.

SERGEANT PEPPER'S LONELY HEARTS CLUB BAND

(album) *Parlophone* [*Britain*] *Capitol* [*USA*]. This album dramatised musically and lyrically the genius of the 'new' Beatles, still the same group, yet far removed from their style of the early 1960s when they first attained world acclaim. Even the cover of the album, with its photo montage of a crowd around a grave, seemingly proclaimed by self-mockery the demise of the old Beatles to make way for the new.

The disc took 700 hours of night-time sessions four times to six times a week over a period of three months to record under the direction of George Martin, Britain's top pop producer who guided the group and produced all their discs. Martin scored all the arrangements, and played on several tracks in addition to acting as electronics expert. The result of the disc, with its contrived, original and distorted music with mysterious, and sometimes meaningless lyrics, was a major step forward in the development that has been described as the 'total' album – an important first.

The album contained 13 tracks with virtually no bands of 'silence' between the tracks, as follows: *Side 1* – 'Sergeant Pepper's Lonely Hearts Club Band' (lead singer: Paul McCartney), by John Lennon and Paul McCartney; 'With a Little Help from my Friends' (lead singer: Ringo Starr), by John Lennon and Paul McCartney; 'Lucy in the Sky with Diamonds' (John Lennon), by John Lennon and Paul McCartney; 'Getting Better' (Paul McCartney), by John Lennon and Paul McCartney; 'Fixing a Hole' (Paul McCartney, including guitar solo by George Harrison), by John Lennon and Paul McCartney; 'She's leaving Home' (John Lennon and Paul McCartney, accompanied by string quartet and harp obligato), by John Lennon and Paul McCartney; 'Being for the Benefit of Mr Kite' (John Lennon, with George Martin on Hammond organ and other organ sounds plus electronic echoes), by John Lennon and Paul McCartney; *Side 2* – 'Within You Without You' (George Harrison, solo vocal with sitars, tamboura and swormandel plus percussion and strings), by George Harrison; 'When I'm 64' (Paul McCartney), by John Lennon and Paul McCartney; 'Lovely Rita' (Paul McCartney), by John Lennon and Paul McCartney; 'Good Morning, Good Morning' (John Lennon), by John Lennon and Paul McCartney; 'Sergeant Pepper's Lonely Hearts Club Band (reprise: Paul McCartney), by John Lennon and Paul McCartney; 'A Day in the Life' (John Lennon and Paul McCartney including a 41-piece orchestra), by John Lennon and Paul McCartney.

The disc was released in Britain and the U.S.A. on 1 June 1967. It sold 250,000 in Britain in its first week and over 500,000 in a month. In the U.S.A., advance orders were over one million and over 2½ million sales in three months. In Germany it sold 100,000 in its first week, a new sales record for that territory, and topped the charts all over the world. In Britain it was No 1 for 27 weeks and in the U.S.A. No 1 for 19 weeks. An R.I.A.A. Gold Disc was awarded immediately - their 23rd.

One estimate of global sales was a probable seven million for the disc by the group - the forerunners of 'psychedelic sound'.

This album stayed in the U.S. charts for 113 weeks. It also took four Grammy Awards for Best Contemporary Album, Best Performance, Best Album Cover, and Best Engineered Recording of 1967.

ALL YOU NEED IS LOVE *Parlophone* [*Britain*] *Capitol* [*USA*]. Gold Disc award No 24 from R.I.A.A. for the world's greatest group. The disc also sold over half a million in Britain. Global sales were over three million. It was No 1 for two weeks in the U.S.A. (with 11 weeks in the bestsellers) and for four weeks in Britain (with 13 weeks in the bestsellers), and topped the charts in countries all over the globe. Written by John Lennon and Paul McCartney, who also wrote the backing 'Baby You're a Rich Man'. Disc released in Britain on 7 July.

'All You Need Is Love' had world-wide exposure to make it an immediate No 1 through its first performance by the group on the BBC-TV show 'Our World' on 25 June. This was a world-wide hook-up with an estimated 400 million viewers and was the first electronic trip around the world, live by satellite (excluding the Soviet states which dropped out at the last minute). The show was seen and heard by 26 nations on five continents and involved the TV systems of 14 countries.

HELLO, GOODBYE backed with I AM THE WALRUS *Parlophone* [*Britain*] *Capitol* [*USA*]. Released simultaneously in Britain and the U.S.A. on 24 November 1967, this disc sold its first half million in Britain and a million in the U.S.A. within three weeks of release. Both were written by the group's John Lennon and Paul McCartney.

'Hello, Goodbye', with Paul as lead singer, is simple in construction with a repetitive lyric and an urgent strumming beat, and extremely commercial. 'I Am the Walrus' with John as lead singer, is more complex in its scoring, with nonsense lyrics that require longer to absorb. It reached No 56 in the U.S.A. This latter title comes from *Magical Mystery Tour*, a TV film in colour screened over the Christmas period 1967 in Britain.

'Hello, Goodbye' was No 1 in Britain for seven weeks with 12 weeks in the bestsellers and No 1 in the U.S.A. for four weeks with 11 weeks in the bestsellers.

An R.I.A.A. Gold Disc was awarded for million sale on 15 December 1967. Global sales well over two million.

'MAGICAL MYSTERY TOUR' (album) *Capitol* [*USA*] (*orig. Parlophone recordings, Britain*). Released in the U.S.A. early December 1967, the title came from the London-produced TV colour film special featuring the famous group and screened by the BBC on 26 December 1967. The album contains the six songs from the film plus five other songs previously unavailable on album. It included, for the first time in five years of recording, an instrumental item 'Flying' composed by the quartet jointly. Contents: 'Magical Mystery Tour' (lead singer: Paul McCartney), by John Lennon and Paul McCartney; 'Your Mother Should Know' (lead singer: Paul McCartney), by John Lennon and Paul McCartney; 'I Am the Walrus' (lead singer: John Lennon), by John Lennon and Paul McCartney; 'The Fool on the Hill' (lead singer: Paul McCartney), by John Lennon and Paul McCartney; 'Flying' (instrumental number), by John Lennon, Paul McCartney, George Harrison and Ringo Starr; 'Blue Jay Way' (lead singer: George Harrison), written by George Harrison while on holiday in Los Angeles, and near a highway called 'Blue Jay Way'. All the above were from TV film *Magical Mystery Tour* and issued as a two-disc EP on Parlophone in Britain on 8 December. The album also included: 'Hello, Goodbye' (lead singer: Paul McCartney), by John Lennon and Paul McCartney; 'Penny Lane', by John Lennon and Paul McCartney; 'Strawberry Fields Forever', by John Lennon and Paul McCartney; 'All You Need Is Love', by John Lennon and Paul McCartney; 'Baby You're a Rich Man', by John Lennon and Paul McCartney.

The Parlophone two-EP issue in Britain of the six songs from *Magical Mystery Tour* had advance orders of 400,000, over 600,000 sold by mid-January 1968. The disc was No 2 for three weeks.

In the U.S.A. the album issue proved to be the biggest sales bonanza in the history of Capitol, passing eight million dollars in sales in its first three weeks on the market and 1¼ million sold by mid-January 1968. Global sales in both forms totalled well over three million. R.I.A.A. Gold Disc awarded on 15 December, the group's 26th.

This was the first time that The Beatles produced and directed their own film, made on a coach trip around the West Country of Britain, improvising dialogue and filming whatever struck their fancy. The result was a somewhat disjointed series of nightmares, daydreams, reveries and slapstick. The film was not very favourably reviewed by the press and caused considerable controversial discussion. Nevertheless, the 50-minute film which cost The Beatles over £30,000 ($90,000) brought in an estimated £1,000,000 (over $3 million) from overseas sales in addition to the disc royalties - an astonishing tribute to the popularity of the group.

The album was No 1 for eight weeks in the U.S.A. in 1968 and in the bestsellers for 59 weeks.

THE BEE GEES

NEW YORK MINING DISASTER (Have you seen my wife, Mr Jones?) *Polydor* [*Britain*]. The Bee Gees were originally a trio - twins Robin and Maurice Gibb plus their brother Barry. They began as amateurs (1956) in Manchester, England, when very young and in 1958 the family emigrated to Australia. By 1960, when the average age of the group was just ten years, they were starring in their own weekly half-hour TV series from Brisbane and during the following eight years became one of Australia's top pop acts. They made their first disc there in

January 1963, and their own song 'Coal Man' got to No 1. They returned to Britain in February 1967 and established a big reputation for themselves with their song 'New York Mining Disaster' which entered the charts on both sides of the Atlantic. This sold over 350,000 in America alone in three weeks, reaching No 14 for two weeks. It was actually written on the stairs in the dark at Polydor's studios before going into a recording session. They had sent a couple of their records to Brian Epstein on the off-chance when they returned to Britain and were signed by his agency prior to the recording, and had also added Colin Petersen to the group. A fifth member Vince Melouney then joined. 'New York Mining Disaster' was the Bee Gees' first British release (April 1967), the song by Maurice, Barry and Robin Gibb of the group. A global million sale was reported for this shuffling, soulful soft-rock recording by the end of the year. It was released in the U.S.A. in May 1967 on the Atco label, and achieved No 14 chart status for two weeks there with 7 weeks in the bestsellers, with over half a million sale. In Britain, the disc was No 12 for a week with 10 weeks in the bestsellers, and it was also a big seller in six other countries including Australia, New Zealand and Holland.

MASSACHUSETTS (The lights went out in) *Polydor* [*Britain*]. 'Massachusetts' was released in Britain on 1 September 1967 and

soon raced up the charts, becoming No 1 for four weeks with 17 weeks in the bestsellers, selling over 250,000, was No 11 for two weeks in the U.S.A. with 8 weeks in the bestsellers and big sales, and a No 1 in many other countries including Germany (three weeks), Japan (six weeks) with over 500,000 sold, Malaysia, South Africa, New Zealand, Singapore, Australia. The million sale was reported in mid-January 1968. The song was written by Barry, Robin and Maurice Gibb, a fine melodious ballad.

The precociousness of The Bee Gees was quite astounding. The three brothers had written around 300 songs (up to 1968). The group went to the U.S.A. in June 1967 for a promotional visit, and a million dollar tour there in 1968.

Personnel: Barry Gibb (guitar, piano, harpsichord) born 1 September 1947; Robin Gibb (guitar, piano, melodia and autoharp) born 22 December 1949; Maurice Gibb (bass guitar) born 22 December 1949 (birthplace of all three Douglas, Isle of Man); Colin Petersen (drums) born 24 March 1946 in Kinearoy, Queensland, Australia; Vince Melouney (lead guitarist) born 18 August 1945 in Sydney, Australia.

Sales of this disc were over five million.

WORLD *Polydor* [*Britain*]. Released in Britain on 17 November 1967. 'World' proved another outstanding song for the group, again written by the three group member brothers Barry, Robin and Maurice Gibb. It achieved No 7 in Britain with 16 weeks in the bestsellers, selling over 250,000 and then became a No 1 hit in Holland, Germany and Switzerland with big sales elsewhere in Europe and abroad. The final sales tally was two million.

The group's promotional tour of the U.S.A. in this year was a tremendous success. In the U.S.A. they were voted the World's Most Promising Group by one magazine and had other 'Top Musical Group' awards from Britain, Germany and Australia. In just over 12 months (to May 1968) their discs were No 1 for 27 times in 15 countries, with collective sales of over ten million.

THE BOX TOPS (vocal and instrumental quintet)

THE LETTER *Mala* [*USA*]. The first record for this group sold almost three million (of its four million global sales) in the U.S.A. where it was No 1 for four weeks with 16 weeks in the bestsellers, and received a gold disc award from R.I.A.A. It reached No 5 and was 12 weeks in the British bestsellers. The song was written by Wayne Carson Thompson.

The Box Tops are five young men from Memphis: Alex Chilton (lead guitar); Danny Smythe (drums); Bill Cunningham (bass guitar); Gary Talley (lead guitar); John Evans (organ).

They met while at college and formed the group in 1965. Their particular interest was in 'soul' music. The disc is power-packed with a good tune and lyric.

TOMMY BOYCE AND BOBBY HART

I WONDER WHAT SHE'S DOING TONIGHT? *A&M* [*USA*]. The talented American songwriting team, Tommy Boyce and Bobby Hart, wrote, sang and produced this disc which was released in early December 1967. The million sale was reported in February 1968, the disc having reached No 6 for two weeks in the U.S.A. charts with 14 weeks in the bestsellers. The song is a powerful beat number.

Tommy Boyce, born in Charlottesville, Virginia in 1944, went to Los Angeles with his parents when he was 12. His parents were both singers, and his father once had his own country-and-western band. His father began teaching Tommy guitar. While at school he wrote his first song, and later Fats Domino recorded 'Be My Guest' (1959) which he wrote with Fats and John Marascalco. This became a No 1 in the U.S.A. and Tommy's career was on the way as singer and songwriter.

Bobby Hart, born in Phoenix, Arizona in 1944, is the son of a preacher, and became influenced by music of the church. He served in the U.S. Army for six months, then went to Hollywood and worked at a job printing record labels after trying to break into show business. He then met Tommy and they began working together at weekends. After a car accident in which they were both injured, Tommy went to New York for treatment where he was joined by Bobby. Their song 'Come a Little Bit Closer' (1964) was a hit for Jay and The Americans. They then returned to Hollywood and a prior exclusive writers contract with Screen Gems landed them the music assignment for The Monkees project for whom they wrote and produced 80 per cent of the music and lyrics (1966).

In May 1967 they decided to form a duo and record their own material, released by A&M Records. 'I Wonder What She's Doing Tonight?' proved to be a big personal hit. They then worked on the one-nighter personal appearance circuit singing their own songs, backed by their own trio on stage.

Boyce and Hart contributed equally to music and lyrics. By mid-1968 they had written over 300 songs, and estimated that their compositions had sold 42 million records since June 1964.

JAMES BROWN AND THE FAMOUS FLAMES
COLD SWEAT (Parts 1 and 2) *King* [*USA*]. Written by the dynamic James Brown himself and A. Ellis, this throbbing, pounding disc proved another million seller for screamer-shouter James Brown. It was a No 1 'soul' record of the year and got to No 4 for two weeks in the national charts with 12 weeks in the bestsellers, and No 1 for four weeks in the rhythm-and-blues charts, in the U.S.A.

BUFFALO SPRINGFIELD (quintet)
FOR WHAT IT'S WORTH *Atco* [*USA*]. This top group from Los Angeles emerged from the 'underground'. They were born in the West Coast rock revolution of 1966/7 and survived for two years, during which stormy time they produced some of the most distinctive and enjoyable sounds to come out of that whole scene. They took their name from an American tractor company. Their soft country rock, tight playing and more relaxed approach never received the acclaim given to the heavier and flashier groups such as The Doors and Iron Butterfly, despite the fact that they cut three albums with moderate success. The group's greatest strength – and the eventual cause of its dissolution in 1968 – was the strongly contrasting musical personalities of its three writers, Steven Stills (writer of this recording), Richard Furay and Neil Young.

Stills wrote up-tempo songs in the main, Furay quiet romantic numbers, Neil Young songs of love, despair and regret.

The other members of the group were Dewey Martin (drums) and Jim Fielder (bass) plus occasional vocals by the group's engineer Jim Messina.

Their break-up makes interesting pop history. Fielder, once with The Mothers of Invention, left to join Blood, Sweat and Tears. Messina formed the country group Poco, Stills joined Al Kooper and Mike Bloomfield on the legendary 'Supersession' and then formed an alliance with Crosby and Nash. Young teamed with a trio called Crazy Horse and eventually with Crosby, Stills and Nash.

'For What It's Worth' reached No 7 in the U.S. charts for two weeks with 15 weeks in the bestsellers. The million sale was reported in 1970.

VIKKI CARR
IT MUST BE HIM *Liberty* [*USA*]. Vikki Carr (real name Florencia Bisenta de Casillas Martinez Cardona) was born on 19 July 1942 in El Paso, Texas, the eldest of seven children. Apart from many sports activities with her three brothers, she liked entertaining family and friends, and made her public debut at the age of four, singing 'Adeste Fideles' and 'Silent Night' in Latin at a Christmas programme. She moved to Los Angeles where she attended the San Gabriel Parochial and Rosemead High Schools, taking music courses and the leading roles in the school musical productions. After graduation she became a book-keeper in a local bank and soon after was chosen out of 30 girls who auditioned for an engagement in Palm Springs' Chi Chi Club with the Pepe Callahan Orchestra, a Mexican-Irish band,

travelling to Reno, Las Vegas, Lake Tahoe and Hawaii, over a period of three years. During her appearances in Reno with the Chuck Leonard Quartette at the Holiday Hotel, she staged a solo act and worked for nine months in Elko, Nevada. After a considerable time in club work, she made a demo disc, and after Liberty Records heard it was signed by them to a long-term contract. Her first disc was so successful in Australia that she toured that continent. Then came a 26 weeks' run as featured vocalist on Ray Anthony's TV show, appearances on the Jimmy Dean and Hollywood Palace TV shows and a dramatic debut on the Bing Crosby Show.

'It Must Be Him', written by Maurice Vidalin (words) and Gilbert Becaud (music) and originally published in France as 'L'étoile', had English words supplied by Mack David. Vikki's disc was No 3 for two weeks in the U.S.A. with 15 weeks in the bestsellers, and No 2 for one week in Britain with 30 weeks in the bestsellers, subsequently selling a global million.

JOHNNY CASH
GREATEST HITS (album) *Columbia* [*USA*]. Johnny Cash's great success in 1968 subsequently gave renewed interest in this album with a resurgence in sales in 1969 along with his other albums. 'Greatest Hits', a collection of his former disc successes, became a consistent seller and by February 1970 sold over one million in albums and tapes. It received a Gold Disc award from R.I.A.A. in 1969 and was in the bestsellers for 71 weeks.

The album contained: 'Jackson' (sung by Johnny Cash and June Carter), by G. Rodgers and B. Wheeler (1967); 'I Walk the Line', by Johnny Cash (1956); 'Understand Your Man', by Johnny Cash (1964); 'Orange Blossom Special', by E. T. Rouse (1965); 'The One on the Right Is on the Left', by Jack Clement (1966); 'Ring of Fire', by Merle Kilgore and June Carter (1962); 'It Ain't Me Babe', by Bob Dylan (1964); 'Ballad of Ira Hayes', by Peter La Farge (1962); 'Johnny Yuma' (Theme from 'The Rebel'); 'Five Feet High and Rising', by Johnny Cash (1959); 'Don't Take Your Guns to Town', by Johnny Cash (1958).

ADRIANO CELENTANO (vocalist)
LA COPPIA PIU' BELLA DEL MONDO (The most beautiful couple in the world) *Clan* [*Italy*]. Adriano is unquestionably one of Italy's most popular male singers. He was discovered by Guertler, and made his disc debut on Guertler's label, SAAR, in 1959, adopting Elvis Presley's style at the time of rock 'n' roll. His debut appearance was at Milan's Ice Palace where he sang 'Rock Around the Clock' at the 'Rock and Roll Festival'. Other appearances elsewhere followed with regular six-monthly disc releases by Guertler, all appearing high on Italy's charts. His biggest seller for SAAR was 'Nata per me' (Born for Me) which sold over 450,000 in 1962.

He then formed his own disc company, Clan Celentano, with an astonishing debut on the new label with the Italian version of 'Tower of Strength' that sold over 600,000, followed by 'Preghero' (Stand by Me) with over 700,000 between 1962 and 1963. Adriano was top-selling artist of 1961, 1962, 1963 and 1964, and he is also very popular in Argentina, France, Spain and Germany, where his discs over the subsequent years have also been consistent sellers.

This disc was released in July 1967 and after only five weeks on the Italian market sold 500,000 with the million by the beginning of 1968. It was No 1 for four weeks and stayed in the Italian charts for 18 weeks.

Adriano has starred in a number of films. He was born in Milan in 1938.

PETULA CLARK
THIS IS MY SONG (C'est ma chanson) *Pye* [*Britain*]. A great tribute to the composing talents of the celebrated Charles Chaplin, who at the age of 77 was probably the oldest writer of a new hit song. Chaplin wrote it for his film *A Countess from Hong Kong* (starring Sophia Loren and Marlon Brando). Petula Clark first recorded the song in French ('C'est ma chanson' with French

lyrics by Pierre Delanoe), and in Italian and German for the European market while in Hollywood. Claude Wolf, Petula's husband and manager, recorded the original English version (adding a second voice track) at the end of the session, there being some time to spare. The tape was sent to England and although Petula was not impressed with the song when she first heard it, her disc made an explosive impact in Britain and gave her her first-ever No 1 there (for two weeks with 14 weeks in the bestsellers), selling over 500,000. Her Continental versions sold over 700,000 in five months and topped the charts in France, Belgium, Holland and Eire, as well as being a big hit in Germany, Italy and Scandinavia. There were also big sales in the U.S.A., the disc reaching No 3 in their charts with 12 weeks in the bestsellers. The arrangement for the recording was by Ernie Freeman, the U.S. release on the Warner label and on Vogue for the Continent of Europe. The song proved to be one of the most lucrative copyrights of 1967.

England's Harry Secombe also recorded the song prior to Petula Clark, and his version reached No 1 for one week in Britain and sold over 250,000. World sales of Petula's versions are estimated at well over two million, and sparked off a whole series of recordings by many other countries.

Petula's disc was released in Britain on 16 January 1967.

CLASSICS IV (rhythm-and-blues quartet)

SPOOKY *Imperial* [*USA*]. Classics IV, a group of four young men, were discovered by Bill Lowery of Lowery Productions in Atlanta who produced this disc for Imperial Records. It was the group's first disc, released in November 1967, and in 1968 it got to No 2 for one week in the U.S.A. charts with 15 weeks in the bestsellers, and subsequently sold a million. It was No 46 in Britain. The disc was started off in Louisville over the radio to break into national popularity. It was written by Sharpe and Middlebrook.

The group (expanded to five members) consisted of: James Cobb (lead guitar); Dennis Yost (lead vocals); Wally Eaton (rhythm guitar); Kim Venable (drums); Joe Wilson (bass guitar and vocals).

Cobb, who arranged 'Spooky' was born in Birmingham, Alabama. He was a studio musician before joining the group. Yost hails from Jacksonville, Florida and was formerly an usher in a movie theatre. Eaton also comes from Jacksonville. Venable, from Alabama, first played at teenage dances and was a musician from age 14. Wilson wrote many tunes for the group.

ARTHUR CONLEY (blues vocalist)

SWEET SOUL MUSIC *Atco* [*USA*]. Arthur Conley got his start through a demo record called 'I'm a Lonely Stranger' played to Otis Redding, a prominent blues singer, in Baltimore in 1965. Redding, who became Conley's record producer, was

instrumental in getting him to record it on the Jotis label. Subsequent recordings under Redding were made for Jotis and Fame labels, then Redding produced Conley's 'Sweet Soul Music' on his own on the Atco label and Arthur Conley was on his way. The disc sold over the million, with R.I.A.A. Gold Disc award. It got to No 2 in the U.S.A. charts for two weeks with 15 weeks in the bestsellers, and to No 7 in Britain (with 14 weeks in the bestsellers), where it was also a top rhythm-and-blues seller for six weeks.

The song was jointly written by Otis Redding, Sam Cooke and Arthur Conley. Arthur Conley was born on 14 January 1946 in Atlanta, Ga.

BILL COSBY

REVENGE (album) *Warner* [*USA*]. A further hilarious disc from Bill Cosby, issued in the U.S.A. in April 1967. In the title track, the humorist grimly tracks down Junior Barnes, a childhood associate who committed the unpardonable sin of hitting him in the face with a slushball. This epic quest for retribution and other reminiscences of his boyhood experiences earned him a Gold Disc from R.I.A.A. with a million units sold by year's end. It got to No 1 for one week in the U.S. charts.

Cosby's five comedy albums over the past four years grossed $30 million for Warner's, a record sales figure for spoken-word discs. Grammy Award for Best Comedy Performance, 1967 – the fourth in a row.

LITTLE OLE MAN (Uptight-everything's all right) *Warner* [*USA*]. Bill Cosby's first singles disc for the Warner label and his first as a singer. The recording is a volatile version of the Stevie Wonder hit of 1965 written by Henry Cosby, Sylvia Moy and Stevie Wonder – 'Uptight'.

It reached No 4 in the U.S.A. charts with 11 weeks in the bestsellers, and sold a million.

THE COWSILLS (pop vocal and instrumental quintet)

THE RAIN, THE PARK AND OTHER THINGS *MGM* [*USA*]. The Cowsills' story is an extraordinary one of talent, determination and fortitude. 'America's First Family of Music', as they were known, was a complete family unit consisting of father, mother, daughter and six sons. Chief Petty Officer Bud Cowsill retired from the U.S. Navy after 20 years' service in 1963, and decided that his four singing, drumming, guitar-playing youngest sons were destined for better things than just local and family concerts. He teamed them with their 'mini-mom', Barbara, and took on his other sons Dick and Paul as road managers and sound engineers. With their then four-year-old sister Susan, they set out into the world of professional music. Father Bud enforced a firm Navy discipline and made the children keep up with their studies, and practise two hours every day to build up their repertoire of some 500 folk, country, pop and rock 'n' roll songs. Nothing however happened for them and the cost of musical instruments, transport and promotion put Bud in debt to the tune of around $100,000. During the winter their old 23-room house on top of one of the few Newport, Rhode Island hills became neglected, with the drive unattended to ward off debt collectors. They even had to chop up furniture for fires when they couldn't get any oil on credit.

Just as they were about to lose their home and not knowing which way to turn, Artie Kornfeld, a producer and writer, brought them to Leonard Stogel's personal management firm, who introduced the group to MGM. An album resulted which included 'The Rain, the Park and Other Things' (written by S. Duboff and Artie Kornfeld who also produced the disc). When released as a single in September 1967 this soon climbed the U.S. charts and reached No 1 for one week with 16 weeks in the bestsellers, was a consistent seller for over three months and awarded a Gold Disc on 19 December by R.I.A.A. for the million sale. MGM sent them on a 22-city personal-appearance tour of the West Coast for one month, spending $250,000 on an unprecedented promotional campaign. Their concert at New York's Town Hall on 28 December was reported as one of the year's best pop concerts. Susan Cowsill (then eight years of age) was also presented and proved to be the cutest eight-year-old in the business, and probably the most talented. 'Mom' Barbara also shone with her folk song number. The group's natural talent rocketed to the forefront, particularly in their blues and rock items.

The personnel of the group: Bill Cowsill (vocal), born 9 January 1948, also writer of own lyrics; Bob Cowsill (vocals), born 26 August 1949; Barry Cowsill (vocals and bass guitarist), born 14 September 1954; John Cowsill (drums), born 2 March 1956; Susan Cowsill born 1959; Barbara Cowsill born 1928, who lends her voice to the quartet's close-harmony whenever it is needed.

The Cowsills were signed to an exclusive TV contract, with subsequent films and tours.

THE CREAM (rhythm-and-blues instrumental and vocal trio)

DISRAELI GEARS (album) *Atco* [*USA*]. It was London agent Robert Stigwood who got together in 1966 three of Britain's top musicians - Eric Clapton (lead guitar), Jack Bruce (bass) and Peter 'Ginger' Baker (drums) - and called them The Cream. Stigwood produced the new outfit's first hit disc 'Wrapping Paper'. All three had previously played with some of Britain's top bands - Clapton with The Yardbirds, Bruce with Manfred Mann, and Baker with the Graham Bond organisation.

The Cream spent most of their time in the U.S.A. where their blues and psyche-orchestral flavour became exceedingly popular with teenagers, young adults and a mass of 'underground' listeners. (See Folk Crusaders 1967 for underground data.) They became one of the rock world's biggest names through their sheer, outstanding musical talent. Their first album 'Fresh Cream' in 1967 achieved a Gold Disc for million-dollar sales from R.I.A.A. in 1968. Their second album 'Disraeli Gears' for Atco was their biggest success and received a similar award, plus platinum disc award for sales of $2 million of their third (double) album 'Wheels of Fire'. This also received a Gold Disc award from R.I.A.A.

'Disraeli Gears' was produced by Felix Pappalardi in Atlantic City, and the group's discs were released in Britain on Polydor's Reaction label. In the U.S.A., it stayed in the Top Ten for eight months during 1968.

In 1968, The Cream, who had created a sensation in their short career together, decided to go their individual musical ways and gave their final U.S.A. performances at Madison Square Garden, New York on 2 November 1968 before a capacity audience of 21,000 young patrons and in Baltimore (3 November) and Providence (4 November). A farewell performance took place in Britain on 26 November 1968 in London's Royal Albert Hall before a rapturous audience of 5,000.

Each of the trio developed into individual virtuosos on their respective instruments. Bruce, in addition, is a vocalist and harmonica player of equally high status.

The group wrote most of their own material. 'Disraeli Gears' comprised the following: 'Strange Brew', by Collins, Pappalardi and Clapton; 'Sunshine of Your Love', by Bruce, Brown and Clapton; 'World of Pain', by Collins and Pappalardi; 'Dance the Night', by Bruce and Brown; 'Blue Condition', by Baker; 'Tales of Brave Ulysses', by Clapton and Sharp; 'Swlabu', by Bruce and Brown; 'We're Going Wrong', by Bruce; 'Outside Woman Blues', by Reynolds; 'Take It Back', by Bruce and Brown; 'Mother's Lament', traditional, arr. The Cream.

A notable first million selling 'underground' album. It was in the U.S.A. bestsellers for 69 weeks.

SUNSHINE OF YOUR LOVE *Atco* [*USA*]. Written by Eric Clapton, Jack Bruce and Peter Brown, this was originally included on The Cream's 'Disraeli Gears' album, and released in the U.S.A. in December 1967 as a single through popular demand. It stayed on the U.S.A. bestseller charts for 26 weeks in

1968, achieving No 4 for one week. Release in Britain was on 27 September 1968 on Polydor label but only reaching No 25.

The composition is described as a low-keyed, funk-flavoured blues. The disc sold a million in U.S.A. and was awarded a Gold Disc by R.I.A.A. in September 1968.

THE SPENCER DAVIS GROUP

I'M A MAN *Fontana* [*Britain*]. Second million seller for this group, the song written by Jimmie Miller and the group's Stevie Winwood. The disc was released in Britain on 20 January 1967, and reached No 2 for two weeks with seven weeks in the bestsellers, then No 6 for one week in the U.S.A. with 10 weeks in the bestsellers, with a subsequent estimated million combined sale. The record came from a promotional film the group made for America and was produced by Jimmie Miller, the American who also produced their first million seller 'Gimme Some Lovin''. The disc had a lengthy introductory riff, building to an intense swinging atmosphere with the crashing chords of Stevie Winwood's organ, plus banshee-like wailing by the group.

THE DOORS (instrumental and vocal quartet)

LIGHT MY FIRE *Elektra* [*USA*]. The Doors collectively wrote this. All became influenced by jazz, blues and rock music, welding these influences into their own style. Jim Morrison's vocals ring out over the striking electric sound that the group made their own. They performed to packed audiences in Los Angeles clubs, Hollywood, the Fillmore Auditorium in San Francisco and at Ondine's in New York, etc. This disc was No 1 for three weeks in the U.S.A. and 17 weeks in the bestsellers, and was awarded a Gold Disc by R.I.A.A. It was No 49 in Britain. Their first album (also a No 1) 'The Doors' received an R.I.A.A. Gold Disc for million-dollar sales at the same time. 'Light My Fire' was Elektra's first-ever top ten entry after 18 years of successful record production. The group comprised: Jim Morrison (vocal) born 8 December 1943, in Melbourne, Florida; Ray Manzarek (organ and piano) born 2 December 1942, in Chicago; Bobby Krieger (guitar) born 1 August 1946 in Los Angeles; John Densmore (drums) born 1 December 1944 in Santa Monica, California. Morrison died in Paris, France, on 3 July 1971.

THE DOORS (album) *Elektra* [*USA*]. By 1972, The Doors had reportedly sold over 4 million albums and almost 8 million singles. This album was their biggest with a sale of 1,234,919 by that year. After release in March 1967, it stayed in the U.S.A. bestsellers for 104 weeks and during that time was No 1 for 3 weeks and in the Top 10 for 23 weeks, and certified gold by R.I.A.A. in November 1967. Release in Britain was on Polydor label in September 1967.

The album contained their great hit 'Light My Fire', an eventual million seller as a single for the group and later for Jose Feliciano.

Contents of the album: *Side 1* - 'Break On Through (to the other side)', by The Doors; 'Soul Kitchen', by The Doors; 'The Crystal Ship', by The Doors; 'Twentieth Century Fox', by The Doors; (*)'Alabama Song', by Bertolt Brecht and Kurt Weill (1928); Light My Fire', by The Doors; *Side 2* - 'Back Door Man', by Dixon and Burnett; 'I Looked at You', by The Doors; 'End of the Night', by The Doors; 'Take It as It Comes', by The Doors; 'The End', by The Doors. (*) Also known as 'Moon of Alabama'. Originally published in Germany and introduced by Lotte Lenya in Leipzig, Germany in *The Rise and Fall of the City of Mahogany* (opera, 1930).

GEORGIE FAME
THE BALLAD OF BONNIE AND CLYDE *CBS* [*Britain*]. Written by two of Britain's leading songwriters of the day, Peter Callander and Mitch Murray. The song was inspired by the immensely successful film *Bonnie and Clyde* which was based on the real-life story of Bonnie Parker and Clyde Barrow, two Texas desperadoes who roamed the Southwest and Midwest in the early 1930s, robbing and killing.

The song was the first to be published by the writers themselves, but they were unable to think who might be best suited to record it. Then CBS phoned them for a new song for Georgie Fame and this proved ideal for him. His disc was released on 1 November and by mid-January 1968 reached No 1 in the British charts, selling over 300,000 with 13 weeks in the bestsellers. Sales in the U.S.A. were even more spectacular with a million on the Epic label and No 6 for two weeks in their charts and 14 weeks in the bestsellers. Global sales were subsequently estimated at well over five million, providing Georgie with his second million seller.

The song had over 100 disc versions by six months after release.

THE FIFTH DIMENSION (vocal quintet)
UP, UP AND AWAY *Soul City* [*USA*]. Written by America's outstanding young writer Jim Webb, the son of a Baptist minister. Webb started to play piano and organ at 11 and to compose at 13. Raised in Oklahoma and Texas, he started music studies at California's San Bernardino Valley College in 1966 at the age of 18, then went to Hollywood to become a songwriter. After disappointments he wrote a wistful ballad 'By the Time I Get to Phoenix' which when recorded by Glen Campbell won a Grammy Award for the singer for the best male vocal performance of 1967. In the meantime, Webb and a friend planned a movie about a balloon trip, but the only thing that soared was the title song which when recorded by the Fifth Dimension got to No 4 in the U.S.A. charts with 12 weeks in the bestsellers, sold 875,000 and by 1968 topped the million, and put the group on the map (see Fifth Dimension 1968 for further data). Jim Webb was also up, up and away. Trans World Air Lines bought the rights to use the song in its TV and radio commercials, to make it a universal standard song.

The song is described as a bright, bouncy, mid-tempo romp. The disc was issued in May 1967.

THE FOLK CRUSADERS
KAETTE KITA YOPPARAI (I only live twice) *Toshiba* [*Japan*]. 'I Only Live Twice' was the first 'underground' record to be released in Japan by the Toshiba Record Co. in December 1967. It proved to be so popular with college students that it sold 1,200,000 by mid-February 1968, and was No 1 for five weeks in Japan.

Alternative radio, known as underground radio, a new radio form working on new stations or time periods with an avant-garde approach, provided an escape for a vast minority from radio's normally restricted format. One of the first of these free music experiments started around 1966 in Los Angeles, with sporadic broadcasts from midnight. The idea gradually spread to other American stations, becoming immensely popular particularly on college stations, and with students. The formats varied - from rock 'n' roll, to stations broadcasting blues, country-and-western, raga, modern electronic music, avant garde jazz and Japanese Koto.

Rock 'n' roll which had developed as an art form was no longer just music for teenagers, but appealed to a large section of society. The new rock thus created the new radio outlets.

The Folk Crusaders, an unknown student group, recorded this song at their own expense, created a sensation in the Kansai area and started an 'underground music' trend in Japan. Toshiba Records then obtained the recording rights.

THE FOUNDATIONS (rhythm-and-blues octet)
BABY, NOW THAT I'VE FOUND YOU *Pye* [*Britain*]. The unusual feature of this group was the difference in their ages ranging from 19 to 38. They were discovered by Barry Class, a London record dealer who had been listening to the group playing in a basement club, The Butterfly, underneath his office in Westbourne Grove, London. Intrigued by their sound, he contacted Tony Macauley, one of Pye's young recording managers, who agreed to record the group. With his partner John MacLeod, Tony wrote this song for their first recording which was released on 25 August 1967. It eventually got to No 1 for three weeks with 16 weeks in the bestsellers and sold between a quarter and a half million. It was released in the U.S.A. on the Uni label and got to No 9 in their charts in February 1968 with 13 weeks in the bestsellers. Sale of a combined million was reached in January 1968. Global sale - 3½ million.

Three of the group were born in London - Tim Harris (drums) on 14 January 1948 at St John's Wood, a musician since leaving school; Peter Macbeth (bass guitarist) born 2 February 1943 in Marylebone, formerly a teacher and in book publishing; Alan Warner (lead guitarist) born 21 April 1947 in Paddington, formerly a printer then with various groups. Five members were from the Commonwealth - Eric Allan Dale (trombonist) born 4 March 1936 in Dominica, West Indies, formerly with the Hammersmith Brass Band, then his own band and member of the Terry Lightfoot and Alex Walsh bands; Clem Curtis (lead singer) born 28 November 1940 in Trinidad, formerly a metal worker and professional boxer who came to England in 1956; Tony Gomez (organist) born 13 December 1948 in Colombo, Ceylon, formerly a clerical officer at London's County Hall; Pat Burke (tenor sax and flute) born 9 October 1937 in Jamaica, a musician with various groups since arrival in Britain in 1952; Mike Elliot (tenor sax) born 6 August 1929 in Jamaica, formerly with Colin Hicks group. He came to Britain in 1955.

The group was formed in January 1967.

ARETHA FRANKLIN (blues vocalist)
I NEVER LOVED A MAN (the way I love you) *Atlantic* [*USA*]. 1967 was the year that established the extremely talented Aretha Franklin as one of America's greatest blues singers. One of the five children of the Rev. C. L. Franklin of Detroit, she started singing with her brothers and sisters in the choir of The New Bethel Baptist Church, her father's pastorate. Her training in the gospel field was a great influence on her musical style, its roots retained in her singing. At the age of 14 she joined her father's evangelistic tours and sang in America's churches for four years. She then began to give serious thought to blues singing and was encouraged to do so by Major 'Mule' Holly, the bassist for pianist Teddy Wilson. Holly suggested an audition for John Hammond, A & R executive of Columbia Records, who was so impressed that he signed her to a contract. In 1966, Aretha joined Atlantic Records and her first release for the label was this disc which got to No 8 in the U.S.A. charts with 11 weeks in the bestsellers, and subsequently sold a million with R.I.A.A. Gold Disc award. The song was written by Ronny Shannon. Top rhythm-and-blues disc for seven weeks in U.S.A.

Aretha is a fine pianist as well as a gifted singer. She also developed an exciting nightclub act.

Her first eight releases for Atlantic were all million sellers - a precedent for a solo girl singer, and her album of the same title as this singles disc was also awarded a Gold Disc by R.I.A.A. for million dollar sales.

Aretha was born on 25 March 1942, and was named by *Billboard* as the top female vocalist of 1967.

RESPECT *Atlantic* [*USA*]. An even bigger success for Aretha Franklin, this disc was No 1 for three weeks in the U.S.A. with 12 weeks in the bestsellers, with Gold Disc award from R.I.A.A. for million sale, and also a good seller in Britain where it reached No 10 with 14 weeks in the bestsellers. The song was written by disc artist Otis Redding in 1965 and was originally on her album 'I Never Loved a Man'. It is a driving, wailing, up-beat number.

Top rhythm-and-blues disc in Britain for six weeks and eight weeks in the U.S.A. Grammy awards for Best Rhythm-and-Blues Recording, and Best Rhythm-and-Blues Solo (Female) Performance of 1967.

BABY I LOVE YOU *Atlantic* [*USA*]. Aretha's third million seller single in a row, a slow shuffling blues, gospel-flavoured with plenty of soul, written by Ronny Shannon. Gold Disc award by R.I.A.A. It achieved No 3 in the U.S. charts for three weeks with 11 weeks in the bestsellers, and was a top rhythm-and-blues disc for two weeks. It was No 39 in Britain.

CHAIN OF FOOLS *Atlantic* [*USA*]. Aretha's fourth consecutive million seller, written by Don Covay. Released in early December 1967, it sold a million in five weeks with R.I.A.A. Gold Disc award in mid-January 1968 and subsequent two million total sale.

It was No 1 for one week (in June 1968), 12 weeks in the bestsellers, and No 1 for four weeks in the U.S. charts. It was No 43 in Britain. Aretha was awarded a Grammy for this disc – Best Rhythm-and Blues Vocal Performance (Female) of 1968.

JOHN FRED AND HIS PLAYBOY BAND
JUDY IN DISGUISE (with glasses) *Paula* [*USA*]. This group of eight instrumentalists was formed for the purpose of playing weekend functions while in high school. After starting college at Louisiana State University, they concentrated more on recording. John Fred who is 6 ft. 5 in. tall made his first record in 1962. He is lead vocalist and harmonica player, the rest of the group consisting of Charlie Spinoza and Ronnie Goodson (trumpets), Andrew Bernard (baritone sax), Jimmy O'Rourke (guitar), Harold Cowart (bass), Joe Micelli (drums), and Tommy Dee (organ). The ensemble did its own writing, recording, arranging and producing and had a big sound.

Their first hit was 'Agnes English', and 'Judy in Disguise' (a play on The Beatles' 'Lucy in the Sky with Diamonds') was first included on their album of 'Agnes English'. When released as a single in November 1967, it soon rocketed to the top of the U.S.A. charts and stayed No 1 for two weeks with 16 weeks in the bestsellers. By mid-January 1968 it sold a million with R.I.A.A. Gold Disc award. It was written by John Fred and Andrew Bernard of the group, and has a hard rock beat with much humour and solid dance appeal.

The disc was also a success in Britain where it reached No 3 in the charts for one week with 12 weeks in the bestsellers.

Personnel data: Ron Goodson, born 2 February 1945 in Miami, Florida; Tommy Dee, born 3 November 1946 in Baton Rouge, Louisiana; Andrew Bernard, born 1945 in New Orleans, Louisiana; Harold Cowart, born 12 June 1944, in Baton Rouge, Louisiana; Joe Micelli, born 9 July 1946 in Baton Rouge, Louisiana; Charlie Spinoza, born 29 December 1948 in Baton Rouge, Louisiana; Jimmy O'Rourke, born 14 March 1947 in Fall River, Massachusetts; John Fred, born 8 May 1945 in Baton Rouge, Louisiana.

GENE AND DEBBE (vocal duo)
PLAYBOY *TRX* [*USA*]. Gene Thomas and Debbe Nevills had only been together for eight weeks when they made their first disc 'Go with Me' in Nashville, Tenn., which was an instant hit around October 1967. The boy-girl duo then became a much-sought-after act in the U.S.A., appearing on top TV shows and nightclubs.

'Playboy', their next disc (released on 17 November 1967), was first broadcast on 15 November from WMAK Nashville, a 'grass roots' station, and sold 18,000 immediately. WMAK kept playing the disc for around three months and it sold 250,000 before being taken up by the major markets, starting with 6,500 from Cleveland in January 1968. It then became a national success and got to No 11 for two weeks in the charts, with 16 weeks in the bestsellers, with an eventual million sale in 1968. Gene and Debbe received a Gold Disc in June 1968.

'Playboy' was written by Gene, and is a shuffling, easy-listening ballad. The duo hail from Nashville.

BOBBIE GENTRY
ODE TO BILLIE JOE *Capitol* [*USA*]. Bobbie Gentry, of Portuguese descent, was born on 27 July 1944 on a farm in Chicasaw County, Mississippi. She first appeared as a performer at the age of 11 on stage, strumming the guitar while accompanying a singer from Chicasaw County. Since then she has become proficient on piano, banjo, vibraphones and electric bass.

She studied philosophy at U.C.L.A. and counterpoint and composition at Los Angeles Conservatory of Music. She worked in various San Diego and Las Vegas night spots dancing as well as singing, and at the age of 13 acted in 'little theatre' locally and in the South.

In mid-1967, she recorded this song, her own composition, backed with 'Mississippi Delta' in Capitol's Studio C in less than half an hour, accompanied by half-a-dozen violins, two cellos and her own guitar, under the supervision of recording manager Kelly Gordon. After only two weeks, the disc shot into the top thirty, sold 750,000 in three weeks and was No 1 in the charts for four weeks and 14 weeks in the bestsellers. Soon after, this her very first recording was awarded a Gold Disc by R.I.A.A. and went on to sell two million (three million globally).

Bobbie proved to be America's brightest new singing discovery. This song in typical folk style tells of a certain Billie Joe Macallister who jumped off the Tallahatchie Bridge and whose suicide was scarcely noticed by his neighbours who were more interested in their supper. Bobbie wrote it to point out indifference.

She writes all her own material, the first one when she was only seven called 'My Dog Sergeant Is a Good Dog'. Her first album containing ten of her own compositions was also issued in 1967 and soon went to No 1 in the album charts gaining a fast R.I.A.A. Gold Disc award, completing a double for her very first recordings.

Bobbie appeared in Britain on TV in October 1967 and made her first extensive personal tour in this year. The disc reached No 13 in Britain with 11 weeks in the bestsellers.

1967 Grammy Awards for Best Solo (Female) Performance, Best Arrangement, Best Contemporary (Rock 'n' Roll) Vocal Performance, Best New Artist.

Disc released in U.S.A. on 10 July 1967. Bobbie's real name is Roberta Streeter. She changed it to Gentry after seeing the movie *Ruby Gentry*.

THE GRASS ROOTS (vocal and instrumental quartet)
LET'S LIVE FOR TODAY *Dunhill* [*USA*]. The Grass Roots are: Warren Entner (lead singer, guitar and piano); Rob Grill (joint lead singer, bass guitar); Rickey Coonce (drums); Creed Bratton (guitar, sitar and banjo).

Entner and Bratton met by accident while travelling through Israel in 1966 and both were originally folk artists. They teamed with Coonce and Grill in Los Angeles on return to America and formed the group. Entner, born in Boston, grew up in Los Angeles and holds a B.A. in theatre arts from U.C.L.A. where he specialised in film-making. He is self-taught on guitar and has been a singer and musician from the age of 12. Bratton, a native of California, played guitar during an extensive trip through virtually the whole of Europe, and while in Israel worked on the film *Cast a Giant Shadow* with Kirk Douglas. Grill was born in Hollywood and studied at Los Angeles City College and has been a professional musician and singer since his college days. Coonce, the group's drummer, has played in every sort of musical group from symphony orchestras to Dixieland bands. A native of Los Angeles, he was educated at Ventura College.

'Let's Live for Today', the English version of the Italian hit 'Piangi con me' written by Shel Shapiro, Mike Shepstone (both members of The Rokes) Mogol (Guilio Rapetti) and Julien, was their first recording. It reached No 3 in the U.S.A. charts with 12 weeks in the bestsellers, and is said to have sold a million. The disc was released in May 1967.

The group combined an exciting sound with a driving beat, expert musicianship and professionalism. British release of the disc (Pye Records) was on 2 June 1967.

THE HAPPENINGS
I GOT RHYTHM *B. T. Puppy* [USA]. A fine up-dated version of the famous song by Ira Gershwin (words) and George Gershwin (music) written in 1930 for the musical *Girl Crazy* in the U.S.A. It reached No 1 for one week with 13 weeks in the U.S. bestsellers, and got to No 28 in Britain with nine weeks in the bestsellers. It was released in April 1967.

MY MAMMY *B. T. Puppy* [USA]. Yet another fine up-dated version by this group of the famous song written by Joe Young and Sam Lewis (words) and Walter Donaldson (music) in 1920 and featured in the first talkie *The Jazz Singer* by the great Al Jolson in 1927.

The disc was released in the U.S.A. in July 1967 and reached No 12 in the national charts with 8 weeks in the bestsellers. It was No 34 in Britain with five weeks in the bestsellers. The million sale was reported in 1969.

ANITA HARRIS (pop vocalist)
JUST LOVING YOU *CBS* [Britain]. Anita Madeleine Harris was born 3 June 1944 in the small village of Midsomer Norton, Somerset, Britain. When quite young she started to sing and dance, and when aged eight took up ice-skating, continuing lessons in skating for eight years. Just before her 16th birthday while at a London ice rink, the manager there was impressed with Anita's skating ability and having heard of her interest in show business offered her her first professional job in Naples, Italy followed by six weeks in Las Vegas. On return to Britain she lived in Bournemouth, Hants., and worked locally. She then joined the Grenadiers and sang with the Cliff Adams Singers in 'Song Parade' on TV. In 1961 she decided to go solo and for four years worked on TV, radio, stage, cabaret and in recording. She represented Britain as vocalist in three European song festivals – at Montreux, Knokke-le-Zoute and San Remo. In late 1964 she met Mike Margolis and John Lane who ran an advertising consultancy, photographic and jingle work and a restaurant in Kensington. Anita decided they should jointly manage her.

Anita has recorded for the Parlophone, Vocalion and Pye labels in the past and in 1966 made her first important public appearance at the London Palladium - an eight-and-a-half months' run.

In June 1967, C.B.S. released 'Just Loving You' which got to No 6 in the British charts, was 30 weeks in the bestsellers and was a consistent seller for over six months with 625,000 sales in Britain and 200,000 in South Africa (where it was No 1). Sales from other European countries and Australia took the total over the million.

The song was another great success for British writer Tom Springfield whose compositions helped The Seekers to fame. It was inspired by a theme from Chopin's 'Fantaisie Impromptu'.

HEINTJE (pop boy vocalist)
MAMA *CNR* [Holland] *Ariola* [Germany]. 'Mama' was a big hit in Holland in 1967 and reached the Top Ten there very quickly. When released on the Ariola label in February 1968 in Germany, it sold over a million and was No 1 there for twelve weeks, only equalled by Drafi Deutscher. It was also in Germany's Top Ten for six months and, with another Heintje disc 'Du sollst nicht weinen', the two discs held the No 1 and No 2 positions for a week. At the same time, Heintje's Dutch release of 'Ich bau dir ein Schloss' was also No 1 in Holland.

It is not surprising therefore that he became known as Holland's 'Wonder Boy'. His disc sales were over two million in a few months. He was also a phenomenal seller in Switzerland.

Heintje was discovered by Addy Klyngeld, C.N.R.'s A & R representative, in 1967. Born in Bleijerheide, South Holland, on 12 August 1956, Heintje was only 11 years of age when he recorded 'Mama', one of the youngest hit makers in the industry.

The song was originally published in 1941 in Italy under the title 'Mamma', words by B. Cherubini and music by C. A. Bixio, and was a big hit for Connie Francis in 1960. It has been sung and recorded by most of the world's famous operatic tenors including Gigli, Tino Rossi, Sergio Franchi, and a great number of pop tenor vocalists.

Heintje recorded in German and his recordings were made in Germany. His singing was not in contemporary style, but straightforward and often unabashedly sentimental.

By mid-1970 he had sold over six and a half million singles and over four million albums.

HERMAN'S HERMITS
THERE'S A KIND OF HUSH *Columbia* [Britain] *MGM* [USA]. Released in Britain on 3 February, this disc was a good seller reaching No 4 with 11 weeks in the bestsellers. In the U.S.A. it had a big advance order and reached No 3 there with 12 weeks in the bestsellers, selling over a million with gold disc award from R.I.A.A. The album of the same title also achieved an R.I.A.A. Gold Disc for million dollar sales.

The backing of this singles disc was 'No Milk Today' in the U.S.A., previously a big hit in Europe, an English song by Graham Gouldman (1966).

'There's a Kind of Hush' was written by English song writers Geoff Stevens and Les Reed, and the 15th big hit for the group.

THE HOLLIES
ON A CAROUSEL *Parlophone* [Britain] *Imperial* [USA]. Third million seller for The Hollies issued in Britain on 11 February 1967 and second million seller for the writers, Allan Clarke, Tony Hicks and Graham Nash, members of the group. The disc sold its million in the U.S.A. by the end of the year, and was No 7 for two weeks with 14 weeks in the bestsellers. It got to No 4 in Britain, with 11 weeks in the bestsellers.

CARRIE ANNE *Parlophone* [Britain] *Epic* [USA]. Fourth million seller for The Hollies, the song again by group members Clarke, Hicks and Nash (their third). The disc was issued on 27 May 1967, in Britain, and was No 3 for two weeks with 11 weeks in the bestsellers. In the U.S.A. it climbed to No 5, staying in the bestsellers for 13 weeks, and sold a million there by year's end.

ENGELBERT HUMPERDINCK
RELEASE ME *Decca* [Britain]. Englebert Humperdinck (real name Arnold George Dorsey) was born 2 May 1936 in Madras, India where his father was a leading engineer. He had two brothers and seven sisters. In 1947 the family came to England, his father having retired and taken a house in Leicester, where 'Gerry' was educated at secondary school, and learned to play piano and saxophone by night. On leaving school he started out as an apprentice engineer for a short time, but the urge to make music proved too strong. He started to sing in local clubs and then did his National Service in the Army Corps of Signals. On discharge in 1956 he resumed his semi-professional singing in working-men's clubs and won a contest in the Isle of Man while

on holiday. This resulted in a London agent getting him a recording contract in London, and Decca released his first disc 'Mister Music Man' in 1958. After a solo spot on the TV 'Song Parade' he went out with top pop package tours, and by 1960, with no recordings and only occasional work, found himself engaged in a struggle both to eat and gain recognition. It was hard for him to find the rent for his flat in Paddington. Then came a six months' sojourn in hospital with a chest complaint and six months to recuperate. 1963 and 1964, he says, were the starvation years of his life, and he had also married which made matters even more difficult. In 1965 he met up again with a former flatmate, Gordon Mills who had become Tom Jones' manager. Mills decided to manage Gerry and suggested he change his name to Engelbert Humperdinck, borrowed from the famous German composer. He got a new chance with Decca and recorded 'Stay', and was sent with the Decca team to the Knokke-le-Zoute Song Festival in Belgium (1966). He was a big success and his disc of 'Dommage, Dommage' sold over 100,000 on the Continent. On 13 January 1967 his disc of 'Release Me' was issued. Soon after, he was asked to deputise for Dicky Valentine who was ill with a sore throat. It happened to be for TV's 'Sunday Night at the Palladium' on which he included 'Release Me' in his programme. Record shops were inundated the next day with orders for his disc which rocketed to No 1 and stayed there for six weeks, with a run of 56 weeks in the bestseller charts. In the U.S.A. this disc was No 4 and 14 weeks in the bestsellers. Sales in Britain alone went over the million, and globally it sold over five million. Engelbert had definitely arrived, and went on to record more million sellers before the year's end, with many TV, radio and personal appearances plus film offers. He started his own TV series 'The Engelbert Humperdinck Show' in November 1967.

'Release Me' was written in 1954 by U.S.A. songsmiths Eddie Miller and Dub Williams (W. S. Stevenson) when it was a success for country-and-western artists including Ray Price. It was acclaimed by the Music Operators of America as 'the most popular record of the year in coin-operated phonographs'. The song is also the world's most performed country music composition with collective disc sales of 12 million.

THERE GOES MY EVERYTHING Decca [Britain]. Engelbert's second big success of the year, a country-and-western number written by U.S.A. composer Dallas Frazier in 1965. The disc has a choir and string backing with a gentle beat. It soon sold over 250,000 in Britain where it was No 2 for four weeks with 29 weeks in the bestsellers, and then topped the 750,000 sales mark. In the U.S. it reached No 20 with 6 weeks in the bestsellers. The combined sales well exceeded a global million. Disc released 19 May.

The song was also a great hit in 1966 for U.S. country artist Jack Greene.

THE LAST WALTZ Decca [Britain]. A continuation of the Humperdinck success story, and his third million seller in a row. This is a British song written by Barry Mason and Les Reed; the latter also provided the arrangement. Released on 18 August it sold a million in Britain alone in two months and was No 1 for six weeks with 27 weeks in the bestsellers. In the U.S.A. it was No 21 for two weeks and 9 weeks in the bestsellers.

The song was also recorded by several prominent disc artists including Petula Clark and Mireille Mathieu for the French market under the title 'La dernière valse' with French lyrics by Hubert Ithier.

Global sales over three million, two million in Europe alone. Collective disc sales were over eight million.

RELEASE ME (album) Decca [Britain] Parrot [USA]. Engelbert Humperdinck's tremendous success with his single 'Release Me' was followed by this album of the same title released in Britain on 12 May 1967 and soon after on the Parrot label in the U.S.A. It became a big seller on both sides of the Atlantic and the forerunner of several other successful albums. This album

stayed in Britain's bestsellers for 57 weeks, reaching No 6 for one week, and in the U.S.A. for 116 weeks, reaching No 7 for three weeks. By the end of 1969 it had sold well over a million, by which time Engelbert was established as a world star and, along with Tom Jones, a big money earner for Britain with sell-out performances in the U.S.A. A Gold Disc was awarded by R.I.A.A. in December 1967.

Contents of the album: *Side 1* - 'Release Me', by Eddie Miller and Dub Williams (1954); 'Quiet Night', by Jobim, Kaye and Lees; 'Yours Until Tomorrow', by Gerry Goffin and Carole King (1967); 'There's a Kind of Hush', by Les Reed and Geoff Stephens (1967); 'This is My Song', by Charles Chaplin (1967) (from film *Countess from Hong Kong*); 'Misty Blue', by Bob Montgomery (1967); *Side 2* - 'Take My Heart', by Gordon Mills (1967); 'How Near Is Love', by Ivor Raymonde, Marcel Stellman and Dix (1967); 'Walk Through This World', by Seamons and Savage; 'If I Was You', by Crewe and Rambeau; 'Talking Love', by Werner Scharfenberger and Kurt Feltz (Eng. words: Marcel Stellman); 'El mondo' (My World), by Pes, Fontana, Meccia and Mellin; 'Ten Guitars', by Gordon Mills (1967).

TOMMY JAMES AND THE SHONDELLS

I THINK WE'RE ALONE NOW Roulette [USA]. Second million seller for this group in the U.S.A., where the disc got to No 3 with 17 weeks in the bestsellers. The song, an easy paced 'rocker', was written by Ritchie Cordell.

MIRAGE Roulette [USA]. A fast driving rock number, written by Ritchie Cordell who also produced the disc. It registered No 7 for two weeks in the U.S.A. charts with 10 weeks in the bestsellers, and was No 10 for a week in Britain. Global sales estimated at over a million.

The arrangement was by Jimmy Wisner, and the disc was released in the U.S.A. in April 1967.

JAY AND THE TECHNIQUES

APPLES, PEACHES, PUMPKIN PIE (Ready or not) Smash [USA]. Written by Maurice Irby, Jr., the group's recording reached No 6 and was in the U.S.A. bestsellers for 17 weeks, with a million reported sale.

Jay Proctor, a Philadelphia-born vocalist, has been in close touch with music almost all his life. Proctor sang occasionally on WAEB-Allentown, Pennsylvania, with a group he formed with several friends in the late 1950s. He then played in other groups in the Pennsylvania area until helping form The Techniques with fellow member Karl Landis. Besides Proctor, the other members of the group are Landis, Chuck Crowl, George Lloyd, Ronnie Goosly, Dante Dancho and John Walsh. All of them lived in Allentown and its environs. They all got together one night with guitars, drums, trumpets and saxophones and tried to form a symphony orchestra, but ended up starting a rock group instead. 'Apples, Peaches, Pumpkin Pie', their first single for Smash records, was a hit, as was 'Keep the Ball Rollin''.

KEEP THE BALL ROLLIN' Smash [USA]. This second reported million seller for Jay and The Techniques was written by Denny Randell and Sandy Linzer. It reached No 14 and stayed 12 weeks in the U.S.A. bestsellers.

JEFFERSON AIRPLANE (rock septet)

SURREALISTIC PILLOW (album) RCA [USA]. Jefferson Airplane was formed in 1966 by Martin Balin, with Signe Anderson (vocals), Skip Spence (drums), Paul Kantner (vocals and guitar), Jorma Kaukonen (guitar) and Jack Casady (bass). When Signe Anderson left she was replaced by Grace Slick. Spence also left the group and was replaced by Spencer Dryden. The band subsequently included Papa John Creach (violin) and Johnny Barbata as a replacement to Dryden on drums. They first appeared at the Matrix Club in San Francisco where the group became one of the premier bands. Their first albums were quite extraordinary, with Balin, Slick and Kantner's vocal use of unorthodox musical intervals and Kaukonen's unusual and unpredictable guitar lines.

Their first album, 'Jefferson Airplane Takes Off', was released in 1966, followed by 'Surrealistic Pillow' which, by 1975, was reported as having sold 1,500,000. R.I.A.A. awarded a Gold Disc in 1967. It is notable for two of Grace Slick's songs, 'White Rabbit' and 'Somebody to Love', which were also released as a single, giving the group their first U.S.A. success.

Balin was replaced by David Freiberg in 1972, and Kaukonen and Casady formed their own group, Hot Tuna, while Slick and Kantner began recording solo albums. In 1974, the group changed their name to Jefferson Starship with the release of their 'Dragonfly' album, and in 1975 their 'Red Octopus' album reached No 1 in the charts. (See 1975 for personnel of Jefferson Starship.)

GLADYS KNIGHT AND THE PIPS

I HEARD IT THROUGH THE GRAPEVINE *Soul* [*USA*]. Written by N. Whitfield and B. Strong, this disc sold 1,500,000 by the end of 1967, the first million seller for the Soul label, put out by the Tamla-Motown Recording company. The recording

was one of the biggest hits in the history of the company and a great triumph for Gladys Knight and The Pips since their first million seller of 1961. The disc was No 1 for one week in the U.S. national charts with 17 weeks in the bestsellers, and No 1 for six weeks on the rhythm-and-blues charts. In Britain it reached No 47. Release was on 21 October 1967. A sale of two million was reported by 1969.

FAUSTO LEALI (pop vocalist)

A CHI *RiFi* [*Italy*]. This is an Italian version of an American hit 'Hurt', originally written in 1953 by Jimmy Crane and Al Jacobs, and previously (1963) a big success for singer Timi Yuro.

Fausto Leali's disc, released in April 1967, was No 1 for three weeks and stayed in the top 15 for 26 weeks in Italy. By mid-April 1968 it had sold over 800,000 and went on to pass the million mark.

THE LEMON PIPERS (vocal and instrumental quintet)

GREEN TAMBOURINE *Buddah* [*USA*]. The Lemon Pipers were five young men based in New York: Bill Albaugh (drummer); Reg Nave (organist, tambourine); Bill Bartlett (lead guitar),

born in South Harrow, Middlesex, England; Steve Walmsley (bass guitar), born in New Zealand; Ivan Browne (lead singer, rhythm guitar).

Issued in late 1967, this disc reached No 1 in the U.S.A. charts in February 1968 for two weeks with 13 weeks in the bestsellers, and subsequently sold two million. The number was written by S. Pinz and Paul Leka (producer of the disc). The disc achieved popularity also in Britain where it got to No 7 in 1968 and was 11 weeks in the bestsellers.

R.I.A.A. Gold Disc award February 1968.

LITTLE TONY (pop vocalist)

CUORE MATTO (Crazy Heart) *Durium* [*Italy*]. Little Tony (real name Antonio Ciacci) was born in 1940 in San Marino, Italy. He formed a trio with his two brothers, and in 1959 they were discovered by Jack Good, the British producer of the TV series 'Boy Meets Girl'. Good brought Tony to Britain in spite of the fact that he could not speak English, and Tony appeared on British TV and toured the country with Cliff Richard, staying in Britain for a year. His disc of 'Too Good' got into Britain's top ten. In 1961, Little Tony won second prize in the 1961 San Remo Festival with the song '24,000 Kisses', and again appeared in the Festival in 1964. In 1967 he sang 'Cuore matto' in the contest, which although not the winner, proved to be the bestselling song of the entries, reaching the million sale in three months. It was No 1 for ten weeks in Italy.

The song was written by Ambrosino and Toto Savio and the English version by Jackie Trent and Tony Hatch titled 'Long is the Lonely Night'. The English version was issued by Pye on 24 March 1967.

Little Tony received a Gold Disc award in Italy in May 1967 for the million sale.

LULU (pop vocalist)

TO SIR, WITH LOVE *Epic* [*USA*] (*orig. Columbia, Britain*). Little Marie McDonald McLaughlin Lawrie, professionally known as Lulu, was born 3 November 1948 at Lennox Castle, Lennoxtown, north of Glasgow, Scotland and began to sing at a very early age. She won a competition on holiday in Blackpool at the age of five and by the time she was nine appeared regularly with a local accordion band. In 1963 she was singing with a group (originally called the Gleneagles) and which was re-named Lulu and The Luvers (a six-piece band). Her impact on the audience at Glasgow's Le Phonographe Club inspired the owner Tony

Gordon to invite his sister Marian Massey in London, a show-business woman, to hear Lulu. Marian was greatly impressed by this young dynamic singer and became her manager. Lulu's first disc was 'Shout', recorded while she was still at school in 1964 and this entered the British charts. Then came another success with 'Satisfied'. She subsequently appeared on TV, radio and in pantomime and made British and Continental tours. She was in fact the first British girl artist to perform behind the Iron Curtain in Poland (March 1966). In 1967 Lulu had a hit with 'The Boat that I Row' and was chosen for a top acting role in the film *To Sir, With Love* starring Sidney Poitier. She was a tremendous success in this, the film breaking many box office records in the U.S.A. Her song of the same title written by Don Black (words) and Mark London (music) was released as a single in the U.S.A. and soon reached No 1 there, staying top for five weeks and selling over two million, the first time in recording history a British disc topped the U.S.A. charts without entering the British charts. Gold Disc award R.I.A.A. in November 1967.

This diminutive (5 feet 2 inches) redhead thus became universally acclaimed. She possesses a very powerful voice and projects her songs with infinite clarity.

She first recorded for Decca, switching to Columbia in 1967. This disc was first recorded for Columbia (Britain) and released on 23 June 1967.

VICTOR E. LUNDBERG (narrator)

AN OPEN LETTER TO MY TEENAGE SON *Liberty* [*USA*]. This controversial record, projecting Lundberg's opinions and advice concerning the world situation and the youth of the day became one of the fastest-selling discs in the U.S.A. It received orders for over 70,000 from Chicago and Los Angeles within three days in early November 1967 and sold over the million, within a month.

Victor E. Lundberg, born in 1923 in Grand Rapids, Michigan, where he is the owner of an advertising firm, served for five years during World War II in the Infantry and Psychological Warfare Department under General Omar Bradley. After the war, he started a broadcasting career and was an announcer and newsman at stations in Grand Rapids, Tulsa and Phoenix. He then moved into sales and management with the Imperial Broadcasting System of Hollywood and later started his own company, specialising in radio and TV advertising and production. He also became president of Admen, Inc., an advertising agency serving regional and national clients.

Lundberg recorded 'An Open Letter to My Teenage Son' because, as he wanted to give American youth food for thought, the best way to reach them was through the recording medium. He followed up with a narrative album on related social trends for the Liberty label.

This disc achieved No 6 for two weeks in the U.S. charts and was 6 weeks in the bestsellers.

SCOTT McKENZIE (pop vocalist)

SAN FRANCISCO (Be Sure to Wear Some Flowers in Your Hair) *Ode* [*USA*]. The 'hippies' emerged on the American scene in a big way by 1967, their aim being the change of Western society through 'flower power' and force of example. They preached 'altruism, mysticism, honesty, joy and non-violence, finding an almost childlike fascination in beads, blossoms and bells, ear-shattering music, exotic clothing and erotic slogans' (*Time*, 7 July 1967). They also popularised a new word, 'psychedelic'. San Francisco became the major musical centre as a result, spawning dozens of new groups.

Scott McKenzie, born in Alexandria, Virginia, recorded this song with charm and simplicity, believing it to be a reflection of the changing pattern on the West Coast of which he was part.

It was written by John Phillips, leader of The Mamas and the Papas, who also produced the disc, playing guitar himself and Mama Michelle playing bells.

Scott originally sang with John Phillips in The Journeymen

group some years before, when his range stretched from jazz to folk to blues.

The disc was No 3 for three weeks in the U.S.A. with 12 weeks in the bestsellers, and a big success in Britain where it was No 1 for four weeks and 17 weeks in the bestsellers with over 250,000 sales on the C.B.S. label. The disc was also No 1 in Germany, Belgium, Denmark and Norway and a big seller elsewhere abroad. It was re-released in 1977 with great success.

Global sales over seven million.

THE MAMAS AND THE PAPAS

DEDICATED TO THE ONE I LOVE *Dunhill* [*USA*]. A great revival of the Shirelles hit of 1960, written by L. Pauling and R. Bass in 1957. Performed by The Mamas and Papas in a harmonic soft rock style it soon reached the No 2 position for three weeks in the U.S.A. with 10 weeks in the bestsellers, and was also No 2 for two weeks in Britain and 17 weeks in the bestsellers, with a subsequent million global sale.

PAUL MAURIAT AND HIS ORCHESTRA

LOVE IS BLUE (L'amour est bleu) *Philips* [*France*] Philips [*USA*]. The background of this instrumental hit is one of the most surprising stories to come out of France. The song, by André Popp (music) and Pierre Cour (words), was written in early 1967 and chosen to represent Luxembourg in the 1967 Eurovision Song Contest. Polydor artist Vicky (real name Vicky Leandros) sang it and it got fourth place. Her recording was not, however, a sales success, although she recorded it for 19 different countries in various languages.

Paul Mauriat's instrumental version, released in late 1967 in the U.S.A., raced to the top of their charts in early 1968 and stayed No 1 for seven weeks with 18 weeks in the bestsellers, sparking off other instrumental versions and many vocal versions (with lyrics by Bryan Blackburn). This singles disc reached No 12 in Britain with 14 weeks in the bestsellers. Sheet music copies went over the million mark, and Paul's disc (featuring the harpsichord) well over four million in the U.S.A. Vicky's disc then became a hit in Canada.

Paul Mauriat, born in 1925, conductor-arranger, studied music from the age of four, while he lived in the provinces of France. His father, a musician descended from generations of classical musicians, took the family to Paris when Paul was ten. Paul completed his studies at the Conservatoire when 14, and first aspired to become a classical pianist. He became attracted to lighter music and the world of jazz. By the time he was 17, Paul had formed his own orchestra, touring the cabarets and concert halls of France and Europe. After several years' touring he went to Paris when a producer arranged a recording session. He was

then on his way, arranging and conducting for artists such as Charles Aznavour, and joining the select group of famous French band-leader arrangers which includes Caravelli, Raymond Lefevre and Franck Pourcell. These four regularly produced albums of orchestrated arrangements of international hits, Mauriat being the first to achieve disc success of considerable magnitude, and sparking off a swing towards instrumentals in France with similar success for his bandleader colleagues.

He made his first appearance on U.S.A. TV in February 1968. An album titled 'Blooming Hits' containing the tune was a very big seller in the U.S.A. in early 1968, and also reached No 1 for seven weeks.

Gold Disc award from R.I.A.A., March 1968.

Over 300 cover versions of the tune were recorded by August 1969. Collective versions sold over ten million globally. Paul later made regular appearances in Japan, Mexico and Latin America in addition to tours of the U.S.A. He is part writer of 'I Will Follow Him' (under a pseudonym) with Franck Pourcell.

BLOOMING HITS (album) *Philips [France] Philips [USA]*. Originally recorded in France, this album was released in December 1967 in the U.S.A. and sold 750,000 in three months with the million passed during 1968, and two million by mid-1968.

The disc, with its distinctive Mauriat sounds and arrangements played by his orchestra of soaring lush strings and horns with rocking rhythms, includes the million selling 'Love Is Blue' and other great international hits.

Contents of the album: *'Puppet on a String', by Bill Martin and Phil Goulter (1967) (winner of Eurovision Song Contest, 1967); *'This Is My Song', by Charles Chaplin (1967) (from film *Countess from Hong Kong*); *'Penny Lane', by John Lennon and Paul McCartney (1967); *'L'amour est bleu' (Love Is Blue), by Pierre Cour/André Popp (1967); 'Adieu à la nuit' (Adieu to the night), by M. Vidalin/Maurice Jarre (1967); 'Mama' (When My Dollies Have Babies), by J. Monty and Sonny Bono (1967); *'Somethin' Stupid', by C. Carson Parks (1966); 'Inch Allah', by Adamo (1967); *'There's a Kind of Hush', by Geoff Stevens and Les Reed (1967); 'Seul au monde' (Alone in the World), by A. Pascal and Paul Mauriat (1967).

Additional titles on British release: 'Ta, Ta, Ta-Ta', by Michel Polnareff and Gerald (1967); 'L'important c'est la rose', by Louis Amade/Gilbert Becaud (1967).

Titles marked * were million seller discs for various artists.

A Gold Disc was awarded by R.I.A.A. in March 1968 and the record was No 1 for seven weeks in the U.S.A., staying in the charts for 50 weeks.

'SMOKEY' ROBINSON AND THE MIRACLES

I SECOND THAT EMOTION *Tamla [USA]*. The famous Miracles added William 'Smokey' Robinson to the name of the group, and this song, written by 'Smokey' with the producer of the disc A. Cleveland, was a big hit in the U.S.A. where it reached No 3 for two weeks in their charts and 15 weeks in the bestsellers. It was also a hit in Britain where it achieved No 27 and was 11 weeks in the bestsellers.

THE MONKEES

MORE OF THE MONKEES (album) *Colgems [USA]*. The second tremendous seller for this group with an advance sale of 1,500,000, the biggest ever for a vocal album. The disc was No 1 for 18 weeks in the U.S.A. and two weeks in Britain. U.S. sales were reported at around five million. It was awarded an instant Gold Disc by R.I.A.A.

Released in the U.S.A. on 1 February and in Britain on 31 March. Disc includes two songs written by Mike Nesmith of the group. Contents: *Side 1* – 'She', by Tommy Boyce and Bobby Hart; 'When Love Comes Knockin' (at your door)', by Neil Sedaka and Carole Bayer; 'Mary, Mary', by Mike Nesmith; 'Hold on Girl', by Jack Keller, Raleigh and Carr; 'Your Auntie Grizelda', by Jack Keller and Diana Hilderbrand; '(I'm not your) Steppin' Stone', by Tommy Boyce and Bobby Hart (1966); *Side 2* – 'Look Out (here comes tomorrow)', by Neil Diamond; 'The Kind of Girl I Could Love', by Mike Nesmith and Roger Atkins; 'The Day We Fall in Love', by Sandy Linzer and Denny Randell; 'Sometime in the Morning', by Gerry Goffin and Carole King; 'Laugh', by Medress, Seigel, P. and M. Margo; 'I'm a Believer', by Neil Diamond (1966).

The disc was in the U.S.A. bestsellers for 70 weeks.

A LITTLE BIT ME, A LITTLE BIT YOU *Colgems [USA]*. Third million seller single for The Monkees and second for writer Neil Diamond. Advance orders were over 1½ million at the time of release in mid-March with a simultaneous Gold Disc award by R.I.A.A. Sales in Britain (R.C.A. label) were over 250,000 and the global well over two million.

The disc was No 1 for two weeks in the U.S.A. and 10 weeks in the bestsellers, and No 3 for three weeks in Britain with 12 weeks in the bestsellers.

HEADQUARTERS (album) *Colgems [USA]*. Issued on 16 May, advance orders were well over the million copies, their third consecutive album to achieve the seven-figure sale, plus a Gold Disc award from R.I.A.A. (23 May). The disc was recorded in Hollywood, and was No 1 for one week and No 2 for 11 weeks in the U.S.A. In Britain (R.C.A. label) it was No 2 for five weeks. Half of the songs on the album were written by members of the group – Mike Nesmith, Peter Tork, Mickey Dolenz and Davy Jones. Contents: *Side 1* – 'You Told Me', by Mike Nesmith; 'Forget that Girl', by Chip Douglas (Douglas Farthing Hatlelid); 'Band 6', by Mike Nesmith, Peter Tork, Davy Jones and Mickey Dolenz; 'I'll Spend My Life with You', by Tommy Boyce and Bobby Hart; 'You Just May Be the One', by Mike Nesmith; 'Shades of Grey', by Barry Mann and Cynthia Weill; 'I Can't Get Her Off My Mind', by Tommy Boyce and Bobby Hart. *Side 2* – 'For Pete's Sake', by Peter Tork and Joe Richards; 'Mr Webster', by Tommy Boyce and Bobby Hart; 'Sunny Girlfriend', by Mike Nesmith; 'Zilch', by Mike Nesmith, Peter Tork, Davy Jones and Mickey Dolenz; 'No Time', by Hank Cicalo; 'Early Morning Blues and Greens', by Diane Hilderbrand and Jack Keller; 'Alternate Title' (Randy S.), by Mickey Dolenz.

Sales by 31 December 1967 were estimated at over two million and continued into 1968. The disc was in the bestsellers for 50 weeks.

PLEASANT VALLEY SUNDAY *Colgems [USA]*. The fourth singles million for the popular Monkees, the song was written by ace American husband/wife team Gerry Goffin and Carole King. A fast-paced number with much instrumental punch and Monkee harmonising.

The disc was No 2 for a week in the U.S.A. and 10 weeks in the bestsellers, selling a million with R.I.A.A. Gold Disc award. It also sold well in Britain reaching No 10 in the charts.

Release in Britain was on 11 August (R.C.A. label). By October 1967, The Monkees' TV series was being screened in 39 different countries.

DAYDREAM BELIEVER *Colgems* [*USA*]. This fifth singles million seller for the Monkees, written by John Stewart, was awarded a Gold Disc from R.I.A.A. for the achievement a fortnight after the disc was released in November 1967. Davy Jones takes the vocal honours in this beautifully-constructed ballad with strings and brass lending atmosphere to the group's harmonisation.

It was No 1 in the U.S.A. charts for five weeks with 12 weeks in the bestsellers, and No 2 in Britain for one week with 17 weeks in the bestsellers where it was released on 10 November. The disc sold over two million by end of 1967.

PISCES AQUARIUS CAPRICORN AND JONES LTD (album) *Colgems* [*USA*]. The Monkees' fourth album, another huge success with an R.I.A.A. Gold Disc award for advance sales presented on 2 November. The disc was recorded in Hollywood in the summer of 1967 following the group's highly successful tour of the U.S.A. and Britain, and released on 25 October. The title of the album incorporates the names of the various Zodiac signs of the members of the group as well as that of Davy Jones, also in the group. Jones is also a Capricorn hence the addition of his name to the title. The album got to No 1 in its second week on the market and stayed top for five weeks, soon passing the million units sale, and continuing sales into 1968.

Group members Davy Jones, Mike Nesmith and Peter Tork contributed their own songs to the collection, full contents being: *Side 1* - 'Salesman', by Smith; 'She Hangs On', by Jeff Barry; 'Door into Summer', by Douglas and Martin; 'Love Is Only Sleeping', by Barry Mann and Cynthia Weill; 'Cuddly Toy', by Nilsson; 'Words', by Tommy Boyce and Bobby Hart; *Side 2* - 'Hard to Believe', by Davy Jones, Capli and Brick; 'What Am I Doing Hangin' Round?' by Travis Lewis and Boomer Clarke; 'Peter Percival Patterson's Pet Pig Porky', by Peter Tork; 'Pleasant Valley Sunday', by Gerry Goffin and Carole King; 'Daily Nightly', by Mike Nesmith; 'Don't Call on Me', by Mark London and Mike Nesmith; 'Star Collector', by Gerry Goffin and Carole King.

It stayed in the U.S.A. bestsellers for 47 weeks. Disc released in Britain on R.C.A. label 5 January 1968.

THE MOODY BLUES

NIGHTS IN WHITE SATIN *Deram* [*Britain*]. A catchy, unusual composition with a haunting quality written by Justin Hayward of the group was their second million seller (globally). It was taken from their album 'Days of Future Passed' and released as a single on 10 November 1967. It had a good sale in Britain, reaching No 19 with 11 weeks in the bestsellers. In France it was No 1 and achieved prominent chart status in Holland, Germany, and the U.S.A.

The personnel of the group for this disc was three original members - Graeme Edge, Mike Pinder and Ray Thomas - plus two others: John Lodge (bass guitar/cello) born 20 July 1945 in Birmingham, and Justin Hayward (guitar, piano, sitar) born 14 October 1946 in Swindon, Wiltshire, who joined the group in 1965. They replaced Denny Laine and Clint Warwick. This disc had a revival in 1972, selling a million in the U.S.A., was No 1 for a week and 18 weeks in their bestsellers.

THE MOODY BLUES (with The London Festival Orchestra)

DAYS OF FUTURE PASSED (album) *Deram* [*Britain*]. The Moody Blues experienced a lean period after their 1965 success with 'Go Now', but in 1968 enjoyed a resurgence of popularity with their Deram albums, 'Days of Future Passed' released in Britain in 1967 (No 24 in their charts) and 'In Search of the Lost Chord'. Both were successful in the U.S.A., the former staying

in their bestseller charts for 50 weeks over 1968-69. The group, with its swirling head sound and magnificent mating of instruments surrounded by words, appeared at New York's Carnegie Hall in December 1970, by which time they had still further enhanced their reputation with two more albums 'On the Threshold of a Dream' and their first release on their own Threshold label 'To Our Children's Children'.

Their original sound has virtually never been copied. They made two tours of the U.S.A. in 1972 and the 'Days of Future Passed' album experienced its own 'second coming' on the U.S.A. national charts, reaching No 1 for a week in the autumn and staying in the bestsellers into 1973, and almost unbelievably had the No 1 single with 'Nights in White Satin', a cut from the 'Days of Future Passed' album, at the same time. All The Moody Blues albums were certified gold million dollar sellers by R.I.A.A. while 'Days of Future Passed' sold over 1 million units by 1972.

Contents of the album: Days of Future passed - Symphonic Portrait of a Day, For Voices and Concert Orchestra - 'Day Begins'; 'Dawn'; 'Morning'; 'Lunch Break'; 'Afternoon'; 'Night'; 'Day Begins'.

Written and composed by The Moody Blues.

Their 1972 U.S.A. tours grossed between one and two million dollars.

VAN MORRISON (blues vocalist)

BROWN-EYED GIRL *Bang* [*USA*]. Van Morrison is acknowledged as one of Britain's foremost 'blueswailers', due to the influence of his father's big collection of blues records. He was born on 31 August in Belfast, Northern Ireland in 1945. At the age of 11 he sang with a skiffle group at the local palais de danse and in 1960 went to Germany, playing at U.S. bases for four months. On return to Belfast he formed a group called Them (1964) which was signed to Decca, their first disc being released in September 1964. The group's second disc got into the charts and their third 'Here Comes the Night' was a global hit followed by TV, national tours and much acclaim. Trouble over music policy caused the group to break up and Van returned to Belfast from London and formed a new Them group. One of the group's discs 'Gloria' was a hit in the U.S.A. in 1965, and was written by Van.

Van was subsequently signed to an exclusive contract by Bang Records in New York and 'Brown-Eyed Girl' was his first release (March 1967), a song he wrote himself. It got to No 7 in the U.S.A. charts and was 16 weeks in the bestsellers, with an eventual million sale.

The song has a big beat and a great vocal by Van with a chorus backing.

The artist writes much of his own material and made a tour of the U.S.A. following the success of this disc.

It was released on the London label in Britain on 28 July.

THE MUSIC EXPLOSION (beat quintet)

A LITTLE BIT O'SOUL *Laurie* [*USA*]. Another success for the Laurie label and their new group. The Music Explosion were five youngsters: James Lyons (lead singer, ocarina) from Galion, Ohio; Don (Tudor) Atkins (lead guitar) from Mansfield, Ohio; Richard Nesta (rhythm guitar) from Mansfield, Ohio; Burton Stahl (bass guitar, organ) from Mansfield, Ohio; Bob Avery (drums, harmonica) from Cohoes, New York.

This disc was No 1 for one week in the U.S.A. with 16 weeks in the bestsellers, and received an R.I.A.A. Gold Disc award for a million sales.

The song was written in the early 1960s by Britain's John Carter and Ken Lewis (members of The Ivy League vocal trio) who also wrote 'Can't You Hear my Heartbeats?' for Herman's Hermits.

PETER, PAUL AND MARY

ALBUM 1700 (album) *Warner* [*USA*]. The fifth million seller album for Peter, Paul and Mary, with a Gold Disc award for a million dollar sale on 27 January 1969. The million units sale was reported in December 1973. Contents of the album: 'I Did Rock and Roll Music', by Stookey, Mason and Dixon; 'Bob Dylan's Dream', by Bob Dylan; 'Great Mandella', by Peter Yarrow; 'The House Song', by Stookey and Bannard; 'If I Had Wings', by Yarrow and Yardley; 'I'm in Love with a Blue Frog', by Bernstein; 'No Other Name', by Paul Stookey; 'The Song Is Love', by Dixon, Kniss, Stookey, Yarrow and Travers; 'Weep for Jamie', by Peter Yarrow; 'Whatsername', by Stookey, Dixon and Kniss; 'Rolling Home', by Andersen; *'Leaving on a Jet Plane', by John Denver (1966).

* This was released as a singles disc in 1969 and sold a million. John Denver wrote it 1966 when he was a member of the Mitchell Trio.

WILSON PICKETT

FUNKY BROADWAY *Atlantic* [*USA*]. This was first recorded by Dyke and The Blazers in early 1967. Pickett's recording was released in July 1967 and reached No 6 for one week with 12 weeks in the U.S.A. bestsellers. It reached No 43 in Britain and had a total estimated million sale.

The song was written by Lester Christian.

ELVIS PRESLEY

INDESCRIBABLY BLUE *Victor* [*USA*]. R.C.A.-Victor released this on Elvis' 32nd birthday (8 January 1967). The song was written by Darrell Glenn, son of Artie Glenn the composer of 'Crying in the Chapel'.

The disc was No 26 for one week in the U.S.A. with 8 weeks in the bestsellers, and sold a global million by 1968. It was released in Britain on 3 February 1967 reached No 20 in the charts and had five weeks in the bestsellers.

The song is a beautiful lilting ballad, recorded with mandolin opening and a superb vocal backing by The Jordanaires, plus the Imperial Quartet.

This made million seller No 54 for Elvis.

THE PROCOL HARUM

A WHITER SHADE OF PALE *Deram* [*Britain*]. The Procol Harum story started around September 1966, when vocalist-pianist Gary Brooker found himself out of a job after a German tour with The Paramounts, a group from Southend, Essex.

Gary met Keith Reid through a mutual friend and they decided to write songs together, although Keith had nothing to do with the pop business except the desire to write. Keith had shown his poem 'A Whiter Shade of Pale' to publisher David Platz of Essex Music who was greatly impressed and told Reid to

get it set to music, which was done by Gary. The writers then decided to form a group and began advertising for players, resulting in the discovery of Matthew Fisher, a classical organist at the Royal Guildhall School, guitarist Ray Royer, bassist Dave Knights and drummer Bobby Harrison. Platz assisted with a loan of £100 ($280). Denny Cordell, an old friend of Gary's, produced the disc just prior to the group's first appearance at London's Speakeasy Club. The release of the disc on Decca's newly-formed (September 1966) label Deram on 12 May 1967 had dynamic reactions. It proved to be the fastest-selling single in the history of the company. Within days it was No 1 in the national charts and became a sensational success all over Europe. There were also huge sales in the U.S.A. In Britain the disc was No 1 for six weeks with 15 weeks in the bestsellers, selling 380,000 in 16 days and soon easily passing the half million. In France it was No 1 for 11 weeks and went on to sell over half a million – a rarity for that country. In the U.S.A. it got to No 3 with 12 weeks in their bestsellers. Global sales were reported at six million.

The lyrics of the song have been described as 'Dylanesque', and are set against a baroque organ riff or rock organ version based on one of the movements of Bach's Suite No 3 in D Major (Air on the G String). The group's style is described as 'Surrealyric Soul' and 'Bach Rock'. The disc is excitingly original in concept with an almost Gothic feel. Garry Brooker provides the soulful vocal, Matthew Fisher dominating with his celestial organ playing and Bach-inspired chords. Keith Reid became manager of the group.

Procol Harum took their name from a rare breed of Burmese cat, and is also Latin-derived, meaning 'beyond these things'.

The disc was also the fastest selling in Swiss disc history. Drummer Harrison did not play on the disc 'take' that was used owing to illness. Session drummer Bill Eyden deputised.

Personnel data: Gary Brooker (vocal, piano, organ), born 29 May 1945, Hackney, London; Matthew Charles Fisher (organ, piano, bass, guitar) born 7 March 1946, Croydon, Surrey; Ray Royer (lead guitar, violin) born 8 October 1945, The Pinewoods; Dave Knights (guitar, bass) born 28 June 1945, Islington, London; Bobby Harrison (drums, vibraphones) born 28 June 1943, East Ham, London.

Royer and Harrison left the group in July 1967 and were replaced by Robin Trower and Barrie J. Wilson.

Offers of engagements for the group poured in from all over Britain and Europe. They were a particularly resounding success at the Paris Olympia.

'A Whiter Shade of Pale' is estimated to have earned the group £50,000.

HOMBURG *Regal-Zonophone* [*Britain*]. Second million seller (globally) for Procol Harum, again written by Gary Brooker and Keith Reid, and released on 29 September, on the revived Regal-Zonophone label. Personnel of the group: Gary Brooker, Matthew Charles Fisher, Dave Knights – original members – and newcomers Robin Trower and Barrie J. Wilson. The disc, another powerful recording, features the piano and was No 5 in Britain, with 10 weeks in the bestsellers, but only achieved No 34 in the U.S.A. with 5 weeks in the bestsellers. It did well in other countries to eventually reach the seven-figure sale.

ROCKY ROBERTS AND THE AIREDALES (vocal and instrumental group)

STASERA MI BUTTO (Tonight I'll jump) *Durium* [*Italy*]. Rocky Roberts was born in the U.S.A. and is the first American artist to have started a career in Italy. He arrived in Europe as a Marine on board the ship *Enterprise* and was a member of its jazz band. In Europe he got his first contract to record on the Barclay label. He returned to the U.S.A. after his military service, then in 1965 came back to Europe and began to perform with his group The Airedales (six members) in Rome's popular 'beat' club The Piper. He then signed a long-term contract with Durium.

Early in 1967 he was given a 12 week series as leading group in the Italian TV top show 'Sabato Sera' (Saturday Night) and used as the theme of the show this tune 'Stasera mi butto'. Through these shows he became one of Italy's most popular personalities of the 'beat' scene and his disc of the theme tune became a No 1 in the charts, selling 100,000 in three weeks. In three months it had sold 600,000 and went on to sell a million for which he received a Gold Disc award at the Whiskey à Go Go in Cannes (October 1967). The disc was a runaway winner of the Festvalbar, a summer contest among a series of records in 30,000 Italian jukeboxes. It is said to have sold around 4 million by 1970.

The American version was made by dubbing English lyrics on to the original Continental recording, and was released by United Artists in the U.S.A.

The composition is by Amurri, B. Canfora and Doug Fowlkes (manager).

THE ROKES (vocal and instrumental quartet)

PIANGI CON ME (Cry with me) *RCA* [*Italy*]. The Rokes (I Rokes) became the best beat group in the Italian pop world, their story somewhat similar to that of The Beatles. The group are all English - Shel Shapiro, born 16 August 1944 in London; Johny, born 3 April 1944 in Walthamstow, London; Bobby Posner, born 6 May 1945 in Harrow, Middlesex; and Mike Shepstone, born 29 March 1944 in Weymouth, Dorset. Shel and Johny play guitar, Bobby the bass, and Mike on drums.

Shel, Bobby and Mike all went to Harrow County School and after leaving joined with a boy called Malcolm. At the end of 1961 they left for Hamburg and were invited to make a four-week tour of Italy. Malcolm returned to England, his place being taken by Johny (originally with a group The Londines in Paris). They made their first appearance at the Alcyone Theatre in Milan. Teddy Reno, a noted Italian talent scout, liked them and invited them to appear with Rita Pavone on two big package tours after they had won a national contest for unknown pop singers in 1963, the same Rita Pavone had won in 1962. In August 1963 they recorded 'Un' anima pura', an old melodic Italian song, Shel's fine beat arrangement catching the imagination of the youngsters. It was however in February 1965 that the group had their first lucky break and very big success when they appeared at Rome's first-ever beat club, The Piper, which had just opened. They played there for the first two months and became the symbols for Italy's teenagers. Most of their subsequent disc releases hit the top of the Italian charts, the group becoming Italy's top-selling disc makers on the beat scene for three years with four million sales.

'Piangi con me', written by Shel and Mike with Mogol and Julien, sold over 800,000 - an enormous figure for the Italian market - and with sales elsewhere totalled the million. The English version was entitled 'Let's Live for Today' and was released on 21 April 1967 in Britain. The song also achieved No 3 in the U.S.A. with The Grass Roots' recording.

Shel and Mike wrote nearly all the songs for the group. The Rokes also co-starred with Rita Pavone in the film *La Figlia Americana*, and had their own TV show in Italy.

THE ROLLING STONES

RUBY TUESDAY backed with LET'S SPEND THE NIGHT TOGETHER *Decca* [*Britain*] *London* [*USA*]. Both songs written by Mick Jagger and Keith Richard of the group. The disc was released in Britain on 13 January, selling over 250,000. Released in the U.S.A. around the same date, and the sales there topped the million with Gold Disc award by R.I.A.A. 'Ruby Tuesday' was No 1 for two weeks in the U.S.A. (with 12 weeks in the bestsellers) and No 2 for one week in Britain (with 10 weeks in the bestsellers). 'Let's Spend the Night Together' was No 55 and 8 weeks in the U.S.A. bestsellers.

WE LOVE YOU backed with DANDELION *Decca* [*Britain*] *London* [*USA*]. Again both songs by Mick Jagger and Keith Richard, the disc was released on 18 August. 'Dandelion' reached No 4 in Britain and No 6 in the U.S.A. and had 8 weeks in the bestsellers in both countries, and subsequently sold a global million. 'We Love You' was No 50 and 6 weeks in the U.S.A. bestsellers. By the end of 1967, The Rolling Stones were said to have earned almost £43,000,000 from sales abroad.

THEIR SATANIC MAJESTIES REQUEST (album) *Decca* [*Britain*] *London* [*USA*]. Issued simultaneously in Britain and the U.S.A. on 8 December 1967, this album was the fastest selling in London Records' history. It passed the $2 million mark after only ten days on the U.S.A. market, and was awarded an R.I.A.A. Gold Disc for advance sales on 6 December. It reached No 2 (for six weeks) by 1968 and in Britain No 3 for 1 week.

The album set a major landmark in the career of one of the record industry's most successful groups, and displays them in a new creative light - in the role of producers. The disc is entirely conceived, written and produced by the group and described as 'an integrated and ethereal experience with a cosmic quality'. All the items were written by Mick Jagger and Keith Richard except 'In Another Land', which is the composition of group member Bill Wyman, who performs his song as a solo vocalist. Each track of the four-track recording was carefully prepared for stereo effect. The album took many months to finalise and was cut in the Olympic Sound Studios in London and Bell Sound Studios in New York. The sleeve featured a 3-D colour picture of the group in which the figures move. The production and design of this cover cost over £10,000 ($30,000).

Contents: *Side 1* - 'Sing This All Together'; 'Citadel'; 'In Another Land'; '2,000 Man'; 'Sing This All Together' (See what happens); *Side 2* - 'She's a Rainbow'; 'The Lantern'; 'Gomper'; '2,000 Light Years from Home'; 'On with the Show'.

The fine piano playing, featured on nearly every track, is by Nicky Hopkins. The idea for the album title was Mick Jagger's, taken as a corruption from page 2 of a British passport which reads, 'Her Britannic Majesty . . . requests and requires', etc.

The million sale was reached in 1968, after being in the U.S. charts for 30 weeks.

SAM AND DAVE (rhythm-and-blues duo)

SOUL MAN *Stax* [*USA*]. Sam (Samuel David Moore) born 12 October 1935 and Dave (Dave Prater) born 9 May 1937 are two black artists from Miami Beach. Dave, son of a Baptist deacon in Miami, got much of his early training in the choir at his father's church. After graduating from high school he had to make the decision whether to be a gospel singer or go into pop music. He consulted his grandfather, a Baptist minister, who quoted the 100th Psalm ('Make a joyful noise unto the Lord'), and also said 'Whatever noise you're going to make, just be sure you make the best of it.'

Years later, while Sam was singing at Miami's King of Hearts club, he met Dave, a labourer's son from Ocilla, Ga., who had also sung in church, but on moving to Miami had supported himself as a cook and baker's assistant. One night at the club, dressed in his white baker's outfit, he joined Sam on stage for some clowning. They have made joyful noises ever since.

They broke through to prominence with their first Stax release of 'You Don't Know Like I Know' in 1965 which became a bestseller the following year. Of their subsequent releases for the label, 'Hold On' was also a big U.S. hit. Sam and Dave eventually made tours and personal appearances in addition to a stint at New York's famous Apollo Theatre. They also appeared on tour in Britain.

'Soul Man' was released in September 1967 and sold a million in the U.S.A. by November with a Gold Disc award by R.I.A.A. In addition to being No 1 in the U.S.A. national charts for a week and 15 weeks in the bestsellers, it was also No 1 in the U.S.A. rhythm-and-blues charts for seven weeks, and in Britain's rhythm-and-blues charts for nine weeks to the end of 1967. It also reached No 24 in the British national charts and had 14 weeks in the bestsellers.

The song was written by Isaac Hayes and David Porter (producer of the disc). This solid slamming song is performed by the duo with outstanding vigour and ability. On stage, their galvanic dancing and musicianship invoke great fervour with their audiences.

In 1968, their college tour with a 35-member troupe grossed around $1,500,000.

They received the Grammy Award for the Best Rhythm-and-Blues (Group) Performance of 1967.

SANDIE SHAW (pop vocalist) WITH ORCHESTRA, ACCOMPANIED BY KEN WOODMAN

PUPPET ON A STRING *Pye* [*Britain*]. After winning the British section, this song won the Eurovision Song Contest in 1967, the first ever for Britain, putting both the writers, Bill Martin and Phil Coulter, and Sandie Shaw, the singer, in the spotlight. Sandie's disc was No 1 for four weeks in Britain with 18 weeks in the bestsellers, and No 1 in practically every country in Europe. She received a Gold Disc for million plus combined British and European sales on 9 May. Global sales are estimated at four million plus and over 450 different recordings by the end of 1969. The disc was released on 10 March 1967.

Sandie Shaw (real name Sandra Goodrich) was born on 26 February 1947 in Dagenham, Essex, England and educated at the Robert Clack Technical School there. She decided to become a singer and at the age of 17 (1964) went backstage at a theatre where pop singer Adam Faith was appearing and sang for him. Adam was so impressed, as was his agent Eva Taylor, that, within a few weeks, the young singer who always sings with her shoes off was auditioned and signed to a contract by Pye Records. Her first release was 'As Long as You're Happy, Baby' followed by 'There's Always Something There to Remind Me' (No 1 for three weeks) and 'Girl Don't Come', both 250,000-plus sellers in 1964, and 'Long Live Love' likewise in 1965 (also No 1 for three weeks). She was then chosen by the BBC to represent Britain in the Eurovision contest which, in the finals on 8 April in Vienna, proved to be her greatest success. 'Puppet on a String' was voted the winner by a big majority by the various panels of judges in Europe, and brought her international acclaim, with fantastic demands for her services everywhere.

The outstanding arrangement for the disc was by Kenny Woodman whose orchestra accompanies her. With three No 1 chart toppers, she became one of Britain's outstanding female singers.

This disc sold over 500,000 in Britain and 750,000 in Germany.

NANCY SINATRA AND FRANK SINATRA

SOMETHIN' STUPID *Reprise* [*USA*]. A unique recording by a famous father and famous daughter, their first duet disc, the song was written by C. Carson Parks in 1966.

This beautiful ballad with its captivating arrangement by Billy Strange sold over the million in the U.S.A. and received a Gold Disc award from R.I.A.A. It was No 1 there for five weeks with 13 weeks in the bestsellers. It also sold over 250,000 in Britain where it was No 1 for two weeks simultaneously with the U.S.A. and had 18 weeks in the bestsellers.

The recording was made 'off the cuff' a few days before Nancy left the States to entertain troops in Vietnam and took only 35 minutes, one of the easiest recordings ever for Nancy's disc producer Lee Hazlewood, in collaboration with Jimmy Bowen (Frank's producer).

THE SMALL FACES (vocal and instrumental quartet)

ITCHYCOO PARK *Immediate* [*Britain*]. This group was formed in early 1965 by Ronnie 'Plonk' Lane. After leaving school he started working in a fairground and took up playing

guitar in his spare time. He decided to form a group, and his brother suggested Kenny Jones – a drummer he had heard playing in a local pub. Soon after, they recruited Steve Marriott who had appeared in the show *Oliver* for 18 months from the age of 12, and he brought in the fourth member Jimmy Winston, a guitarist-organist. Their first week together was at a club in Sheffield, then to Manchester, and then London, working in an East Ham London pub. A 'one-night stand' at the Cavern in Leicester Square resulted in a five-week booking there, and their popularity induced Don Arden, a top agent, to sign them up. Their first disc 'Watcha Gonna Do About It' on Decca was released on 6 August 1965 only a few weeks after the group's formation, and they were also signed for parts in a film. This included a song 'Sha-La-La-La-Lee' which got to No 2 in the charts. On 5 November, Winston left the group and was replaced by Ian McLagan. They made two highly successful nationwide tours in 1966 and had their first No 1 hit with 'All or Nothing'. Thereafter came a Scandinavian tour, and a tour with Roy Orbison (1967), a radio and TV promotion tour of Europe, and appearance in Germany's first ever TV colour transmission.

In May 1967 the group switched to the new Immediate label and were later managed by Andrew Loog Oldham.

'Itchycoo Park', released on 4 August 1967, reached No 3 in Britain with 14 weeks in the bestsellers, and got to No 12 in the U.S.A. (February 1968) with 17 weeks in the bestsellers, the global sales totalling over a million. The song was written by group members Steve Marriott and Ronnie Lane who together write most of the band's hits, the lyrics reflecting their freshness and modern approach in an ever-changing world of pop music.

The group personnel: Steve Marriott (guitar, drums, organ, harmonica) born 30 January 1947 in Bow, East London; Ronnie 'Plonk' Lane (bass and guitar) born 1 April 1946 in Plaistow, East London; Kenny Jones (drums) born 16 September 1948 in Stepney, London; Ian McLagan (organ) born 12 May 1946 in Hounslow, Middlesex.

The disc was re-released in 1977 with great success.

WHISTLING JACK SMITH

I WAS KAISER BILL'S BATMAN *Deram* [*Britain*]. The name of Whistling Jack Smith for this disc is somewhat misleading. The recording was said to have been made as a 'laugh' originally by The Mike Sammes Singers, a popular TV singing group, and Smith didn't exist at the time. When the disc hit the British charts, a singer named Billy Moeller who had previously recorded for the Decca organisation under his professional name of Coby Wells was given the name of Whistling Jack Smith to promote the disc on tour throughout Britain.

The recording got to No 5 in Britain with 12 weeks in the bestsellers, and No 14 in the U.S.A. with 7 weeks in the bestsellers, where the tune also had several other recordings and became an international hit, the first in this idiom to do so for many years. This catchy tune, whistled so professionally, subsequently sold a global million of the so-called Whistling Jack Smith version.

Billy Moeller was born on 2 February 1946 in Liverpool. The tune was written by Roger Greenaway and Roger Cooke, a talented pair of songwriters and recording artists known as David and Jonathan.

SONNY AND CHER

THE BEAT GOES ON *Atco* [*USA*]. Released in January 1967 this disc is said to have sold four million globally for the husband and wife team. It reached No 3 for a week in the U.S. charts with 11 weeks in the bestsellers. It reached No 29 with eight weeks in the bestsellers in Britain. The song was written by Sonny Bono.

THE SOUL SURVIVORS

EXPRESSWAY TO YOUR HEART *Crimson* [*USA*]. Written by K. Gamble and L. Huff who also produced the disc. It first broke big in Philadelphia, then New York, and three months after appearing in the U.S. charts, sold a million, after climbing to No 4 with 15 weeks in the bestsellers.

The Soul Survivors were a group of six youngsters.

SPANKY AND OUR GANG

SUNDAY WILL NEVER BE THE SAME *Mercury* [*USA*]. Written in 1966 by Gene Pistilli and Terry Cashman, Spanky and Our Gang's recording in 1967 reached No 9 and was 8 weeks in the U.S. bestsellers, with a reported million sale. Spanky McFarlane had been known for some years in folksinging circles. She had sung with the New Wine Singers and had gained an excellent musical reputation, particularly in the Chicago area. In early 1966 she left the group and moved to Florida. One night a hurricane struck the Miami area in which Spanky was living in a one-room converted chicken coop. Two young men named Nigel Pickering and Oz Bach took shelter in Spanky's quarters. While they waited for the winds to subside, the three passed the time by singing. Thus was born the idea for Spanky and Our Gang. They finally got together in Chicago and worked as a trio. Then they recruited a fourth member, Malcolm Hale, a folk singer who had also worked with the New Wine Singers. Pickering, before joining Spanky, had done a lot of singing, particularly country-and-western. Bach was at one time a well-known performer in Miami coffeehouses. Hale participated in a U.S. State Department tour of Vietnam while playing with the New Wine Singers. The quartet played what Spanky called 'good-time music . . . we want everyone around us to have fun'. Spanky and Our Gang first broke into the charts with 'Sunday Will Never Be the Same'. Bob Dorough and Stu Scharf took over production reins of the group in late 1967. Several personnel changes took place in the group when Oz Bach left to form his own unit. Malcolm Hale died of pneumonia late in 1968 and was not replaced.

LAZY DAY *Mercury* [*USA*]. Second reported million seller for Spanky and Our Gang, the song was written by Tony Powers (words) and George Fischoff (music). The disc reached No 14 and was in the U.S.A. bestsellers for 11 weeks.

THE STRAWBERRY ALARM CLOCK (jazz-rock sextet)

INCENSE AND PEPPERMINTS *Uni* [*USA*]. This sextet, exponents of jazz-rock, was composed of Mark Weitz (leader), organist; Randy Seol, vocalist, drums and vibraphones; Lee Freeman, rhythm guitar and lead vocalist; Ed King, lead guitar; Gary Lovetro, bass guitar (lead); and George Bunnell, special effects bass guitarist.

The group is a combination of two successful Southern Californian bands and had been together for less than a year when this disc hit the U.S.A. charts. It reached No 1 within two months and stayed on top for two weeks with 16 weeks in the bestsellers. A Gold Disc for million sale was awarded by R.I.A.A.

on 19 December. The group not only developed an unusual sound, but built themselves a top visual act. Randy Seol, drummer, developed a technique whereby he performed on bongos with his hands on fire during shows.

They appeared all over the West Coast of America at clubs, civic centres and many prominent TV shows. 'Incense and Peppermints' shows the influence of jazz and Oriental music. It was written by J. Carter and T. Gilbert.

THE SUPREMES

LOVE IS HERE AND NOW YOU'RE GONE *Motown* [*USA*]. A bright rhythmic, pulsating Motown-sound disc by the ever-popular Supremes, making their eleventh million seller. Another big hit for the songsmiths Eddie Holland, Lamont Dozier and Brian Holland. Release was on 28 January 1967.

It was No 1 for two weeks in the U.S.A. with 11 weeks in the bestsellers, and reached No 17 in Britain with 10 weeks in the bestsellers.

THE HAPPENING *Motown* [*USA*]. The twelfth million seller for the world's greatest female group, and their tenth disc to top the U.S.A. charts (for one week) with 11 weeks in the bestsellers. It also achieved the No 5 position in Britain for one week and had 12 weeks in the bestsellers.

A light, bouncy up-tempo number written by the great songwriting team of Eddie Holland, Brian Holland and Lamont Dozier (words) in collaboration with Frank de Vol (music), for the Columbia film of the same title.

The disc was also No 2 in Britain's rhythm-and-blues charts. U.S.A. release was on 8 April 1967.

DIANA ROSS AND THE SUPREMES

REFLECTIONS *Motown* [*USA*]. A throbbing blues lament for the group under its new billing of Diana Ross (lead singer) and

The Supremes. The recording utilises considerable electronic effects.

Yet another triumph for the Eddie Holland, Brian Holland and Lamont Dozier song-team, and the thirteenth million seller for the group. The disc was No 2 for two weeks in the U.S.A. and 11 weeks in the bestsellers, and a big success in Britain where it was No 4 for two weeks with 14 weeks in the bestsellers, and No 1 in the rhythm-and-blues charts for seven weeks. U.S.A. release was 5 August 1967.

Cindy Birdsong (formerly with Patty La Belle and The Bluebells) took over from Florence Ballard (an original member of the group), hence their new name. Mary Wilson remained as the third member of the trio.

GREATEST HITS (album) *Motown [USA]*. A superlative album containing all the million sellers to date by the world's greatest female group, and a remarkable tribute to their songwriters Eddie Holland, Brian Holland and Lamont Dozier who wrote every song (the music for 'The Happening' was written by Frank de Vol). The album was issued as a two-disc set in the U.S.A. in September 1967. It soon climbed to No 1 and was top for five weeks. The British issue as a single album was released in January 1968, and was No 1 for six weeks.

Contents: *'Stop, in the Name of Love' (1965); *'Nothing but Heartaches' (1965); 'When the Lovelight Starts Shining thru his Eyes' (1963); *'My World Is Empty Without You' (1966); *'Where Did our Love Go?' (1964); 'Love Is Like an Itching in my Heart' (1966); *'Come See about Me' (1964); *'I Hear a Symphony' (1965); *'Reflections' (1967); *'Back in my Arms Again' (1965); *'You Keep Me Hangin' On' (1966); 'Whisper You Love Me, Boy' (1965); *'The Happening' (1967); *'Love Is Here and now You're Gone' (1967); *'You Can't Hurry Love' (1966); *'Baby Love' (1964).

* Indicates million seller single in year given.

This album soon sold half a million and went to to the million mark in 1968. It was in the U.S.A. bestsellers for 89 weeks.

JOE TEX
SKINNY LEGS AND ALL *Dial [USA]*. Second million seller for Joe Tex, the song written by him. Issued in October, it reached No 7 for one week in the U.S. charts with 15 weeks in the bestsellers, and sold the million with R.I.A.A. Gold Disc award in January 1968.

THE TREMELOES (vocal and instrumental quartet)
HERE COMES MY BABY *CBS [Britain]*. The Tremeloes were originally a backing group for Brian Poole, the three original Tremeloes (Alan Blakely, Rick West and Dave Munden) breaking away in 1964 to go out on their own, spending most of their time on the road throughout England and Scotland. Chip Hawkes was added to make the foursome.

Brian Poole and The Tremeloes first came into prominence in 1963 through their recording of 'Twist and Shout', and their quarter million seller 'Do You Love Me?'. They toured with Roy Orbison and appeared at the Paris Olympia. In 1964 they made tours of South Africa and Australia, and also recorded their second quarter million seller 'Someone', followed by a film musical in Ireland *A Touch of Blarney*, and a concert tour in Sweden. 1965 saw them on a British tour, and Irish and Scandinavian tours. Up to 1966 The Tremeloes recorded for British Decca, afterwards going over to C.B.S.

'Here Comes My Baby' was their first hit on their new label, reaching No 4 for two weeks in Britain with 11 weeks in the bestsellers, and No 11 in the U.S.A. with 12 weeks in the bestsellers. The song was written by recording artist Cat Stevens and the disc achieved a million global sale by the end of the year.

Group personnel: Rick (Richard Charles Westwood) West (lead guitar, banjo) born 7 May 1943, Dagenham, Essex; Dave (Dave Charles) Munden (drums) born 2 December 1943, Dagenham, Essex; Chip (Leonard Donald) Hawkes (bass guitar)

born 11 November 1946, Shepherd's Bush, London; Alan Blakely (rhythm, organ, piano, drums) born 1 April 1942, Bromley, Kent.

Rick, Dave and Alan were all educated in Dagenham, Chip in Slough, Buckinghamshire.

SILENCE IS GOLDEN *CBS [Britain]*. The Tremeloes' revival of the song by American writers Bob Crewe and Bob Gaudio (1963) with its beautiful recording and falsetto singing proved to be the group's biggest hit. It sold well over 250,000 in Britain where it was No 1 for three weeks with 15 weeks in the bestsellers, and also reached No 9 in the U.S.A. with big sales there (14 weeks in the bestsellers) and around the globe. Released on 22 April 1967, it soon racked up a million-plus sale. The Tremeloes made an American tour during the summer 1967 following this disc's success.

EVEN THE BAD TIMES ARE GOOD *CBS [Britain]*. Third global million seller for The Tremeloes, one of England's top pop groups. This disc was released on 28 July 1967, and the song was written by two of Britain's top pop songsmiths Peter Callender (words) and Mitch Murray (music). It got to No 4 for a week in Britain and 13 weeks in the bestsellers, and had good sales in the U.S.A. (No 28 and 7 weeks in the bestsellers) plus additional sales from other countries.

THE TROGGS
LOVE IS ALL AROUND *Page One [Britain]*. Written by the group's Reg Presley, this disc reached No 4 in Britain with 14 weeks in the bestsellers, and No 7 in the U.S.A. where it was a hit on the Fontana label with 16 weeks in the bestsellers. The million sale globally was reached by May 1968, and the disc first released in Britain in October 1967.

The group made successful tours of the U.S.A.

THE TURTLES (pop vocal and instrumental sextet)
HAPPY TOGETHER *White Whale [USA]*. Formed in early 1965, the group commenced their career at Reb Foster's Rebelaire Club in Redondo Beach, California, although still at high school. An audition resulted in their being immediately signed as the Club's regular band, and adopting the name 'The Turtles' soon afterwards.

Foster then invited them to headline his celebrity night at Hollywood's Red Velvet Club. They were so successful that a new label, White Whale, signed them to a contract. Their first release 'It Ain't Me Babe' - a Bob Dylan composition - was a big hit for the label's initial issue. Three subsequent discs by the group also achieved prominent chart status, and were a major factor in putting the new label on the map. Then came 'Happy Together', a number performed against a background of subtle harmonies and counter harmonies, coupled with intriguing lyrics and a brilliantly imaginative orchestration and chorus. It got to No 1 in the U.S.A. for three weeks with 15 weeks in the bestsellers, and sold over a million with R.I.A.A. Gold Disc award. It reached No 12 in Britain with 12 weeks in the bestsellers.

The song was written by Garry Bonner and Alan Gordon. The group actually changed bass players and drummers a couple of times after its formation. The personnel on this recording was: Howard Kaylan (sax, clarinet, harmonica, lead singer) born 22 June 1947, New York; Mark Volman (clarinet, sax, vocals) born 19 April 1947, Los Angeles; Al Nichol (guitar, piano, organ, bass, trumpet, harpsichord, vocals); Jim Pons (bass, vocals) born 14 March 1943, Santa Monica, California; John Barbata (drums) born 1 April 1946, New Jersey; Jim Tucker (guitar, harmonica).

The group was featured in nationally-broadcast TV programmes, at the U.S.A.'s best known nightclubs and on tour with the Dick Clark Caravan and Herman's Hermits. They acquired the song from Bonner and Gordon while playing at the Phone Booth, a New York club.

SHE'D RATHER BE WITH ME *White Whale* [*USA*]. A pulsating rock number, again written by Garry Bonner and Alan Gordon for The Turtles, and their second million seller (globally). The disc was No 1 for one week in the U.S.A. and 11 weeks in the bestsellers, and got to No 4 in Britain with 15 weeks in the bestsellers.

THE UNION GAP (vocal and instrumental quintet)

WOMAN, WOMAN *Columbia* [*USA*]. Dressed in Civil War uniforms and named after the historic town of Union Gap, Washington, this group attracted a very large following in the U.S.A., playing at clubs and colleges.

Their leader, vocalist and guitarist 'General' Gary Puckett, is an accomplished songwriter, who was born in Minnesota in 1942. 'Sergeant' Dwight Bement (tenor sax) was a former music major at San Diego State. Canadian-born 'Corporal' Kerry Chater is bass-guitarist. 'Private' Gary ('Mutha') Withem plays woodwind and piano, and 'Private' Paul Whitbread is drummer.

The group was organised in January 1967 in San Diego, California. 'Woman, Woman', written by J. Grosen and J. Payne, got to No 2 in the U.S.A. charts with 17 weeks in the bestsellers, and sold the million by mid-February 1968, with R.I.A.A. Gold Disc award for their very first Columbia recording. It was No 48 in Britain. Personnel: Bement, born in San Diego, California, 1944; Withem, born in San Diego, California, 1945; Whitbread, born in San Diego, California, 1945; Chater, born in Vancouver, British Columbia, 1944.

FRANKIE VALLI

CAN'T TAKE MY EYES OFF YOU *Philips* [*USA*]. Frankie Valli, as lead singer to the famous group The Four Seasons, always wanted to make solo discs and the success of this one, his first, certainly justified the effort. It was No 1 for two weeks in the U.S.A. and 16 weeks in the bestsellers, and sold a million with R.I.A.A. Gold Disc award. The song was written by record producer Bob Crewe and The Four Seasons' Bob Gaudio.

Frank Valli was born on 3 May 1937 in Newark, New Jersey and started singing while still at high school. He was also a skilled though self-taught drummer. It was his fine tenor voice that gave The Four Seasons their characteristic and easily distinguishable sound.

BOBBY VEE AND THE STRANGERS

COME BACK WHEN YOU GROW UP *Liberty* [*USA*]. Bobby's first big seller since 1962 with R.I.A.A. Gold Disc award for the million sale in the U.S.A. The disc got to No 2 for a week there with 16 weeks in the bestsellers. The song was written by Martha Sharp.

DIONNE WARWICK

I SAY A LITTLE PRAYER backed with Theme from 'THE VALLEY OF THE DOLLS' *Scepter* [*USA*]. 'I Say a Little Prayer' was written by Hal David (words) and Burt Bacharach (music) who also produced both sides of the disc. In late 1967, this side reached No 4 for two weeks in the U.S.A. charts, the disc selling over 700,000. With the release of the film *Valley of the Dolls*, the reverse side became a big hit in early 1968 and took the sales to well over the million mark. Both sides were 13 weeks in the U.S.A. bestsellers. This was written by Dory Previn (words) and her composer/musical director then husband André Previn who scored the music for the film. It reached No 2 for two weeks in March 1968 in the U.S.A., and was No 28 in Britain with eight weeks in the bestsellers. R.I.A.A. Gold Disc award February 1968.

STEVIE WONDER

I WAS MADE TO LOVE HER *Tamla* [*USA*]. Third million seller for Stevie, written by him with Lula Hardaway, Henry Cosby and Sylvia Moy, and No 2 for two weeks in the U.S.A. with 15 weeks in the bestsellers, plus No 5 for one week in Britain with 15 weeks in the bestsellers. A driving, wailing, pulsating rhythm-and-blues number, it was also a top rhythm-and-blues chart number in the U.S.A., and in Britain (two weeks). Release in the U.S.A. was 3 June 1967.

BRENTON WOOD

GIMME LITTLE SIGN *Double Shot* [*USA*]. Brenton Wood (real name Alfred Smith) born 26 July 1941 in Shreveport, Louisiana, took his stage name from a district in Beverly Hills called Brent Wood. He went to California at the age of two and attended high school and college there. In Compton College he became lead singer of The Quotations group, but left later to become solo singer in nightclubs throughout the U.S.A. and Canada. In early 1967 he was signed to Double Shot Records and scored immediately with his own song 'The Oogum Boogum Song' which was a hit. Then came 'Gimme Little Sign', another self-written song which reached No 6 in the U.S.A. charts with 15 weeks in the bestsellers, and also got to No 8 in Britain when released there in 1968 with 14 weeks in the bestsellers.

Brenton derived much inspiration from listening to his favourites like Jesse Belvin, Sam Cooke, Diana Ross, Frank Sinatra and The Temptations.

'Gimme Little Sign' was the first million seller for the small Double Shot Record company in the U.S.A. It was also in the top ten in Australia, Canada, Mexico, Italy and Germany.

JACKY YOSHIKAWA AND HIS BLUE COMETS

BLUE CHATEAU *CBS* [*Japan*]. Released in Japan on 15 March 1967, this disc sold 500,000 in a month. By year's end the sales were over 1,300,000. It was awarded the Disc Grand Prize of Japan for 1967.

The group became one of the most popular in Japan and, in just over 2½ years after its formation, sold 8,180,000 discs by 31 December 1967.

The song was a second million-selling success for the writers Jun Hashimoto (words) and Tadao Inoue (music) who also wrote the group's 'Aoi hitomi' (Blue eyes) in 1966.

This disc was No 1 for four weeks in Japan and stayed in their charts for six months.

THE YOUNG RASCALS

GROOVIN' *Atlantic* [*USA*]. Second million seller for this group, with R.I.A.A. Gold Disc award. This disc was No 1 for four weeks in the U.S. charts with 13 weeks in the bestsellers, and was also a success in Britain where for two weeks it reached No 8 with 13 weeks in the bestsellers. It was written by Eddie Brigati and Felix Cavaliere of the group.

ORIGINAL THEATRE CAST WITH GEROME RAGNI, JAMES RADO, SHELLEY PLIMPTON, RONALD DYSON, LYNN KELLOGG, LAMONT WASHINGTON, MELBA MOORE AND COMPANY; ORCHESTRA CONDUCTED BY GALT MacDERMOT

HAIR (album) *RCA Victor* [*USA*]. *Hair*, billed as America's first 'tribal love-rock musical', became a Broadway landmark overnight and made producers realise that rock music could be successful on the legitimate stage. The story concerns the activities of a number of freaky contemporary youths, the music a pot-pourri of modern pop sounds linked together in composer Galt MacDermot's individual style. The book and lyrics were written by two actors, Gerome Ragni and James Rado, who, between 1965 and 1967, had spent two years listening to rock sounds among the devotees of 'underground' music. In 1967 they showed their first draft of the script of *Hair* to well-known author Nat Shapiro who suggested the wild and weirdly creative Galt MacDermot, a Canadian and son of a diplomat, musically educated in South Africa, to write the music. MacDermot had composed 'African Waltz' in 1961, a modern jazz work which was a sizeable hit (two Grammy Awards 1961), and was well equipped to undertake the score of *Hair* being one of the few musicians who understood the roots and dynamics of the new popular music. *Hair* was then chosen by Joseph Papp for the launching of his part-subsidised New York Shakespeare Public Theatre (October 1967). The eight-week run was a sell-out and RCA recorded an original cast album. The show was then moved to the Cheetah, a Broadway palais de danse, but this proved unsatisfactory. Eventually, Michael Butler brought the show to Broadway and presented it at the Biltmore Theatre on 29 April 1968 after substantial revision of the book, music and lyrics. It became an important contribution to the Broadway picture, a revolution both in theatre and in music. The London production opened on 27 September 1968 at the Shaftesbury Theatre, with productions following in Copenhagen, Stockholm, Acapulco, Munich, Los Angeles, Paris, Milan, Sydney, Tokyo, Belgrade, Amsterdam and every major city in the U.S.A. and Canada. By April 1969, *Hair* caught the pop music fancy and three of its tunes – the title song, 'Aquarius', 'Let the Sunshine In' – were Nos 1 and 2 on the U.S. singles charts and the album of the Broadway version No 1 on the album charts. There was also a flood of other recordings of the show's various songs in the U.S.A., Britain, Germany, Italy and Holland and elsewhere. The album of the Broadway theatre cast was issued in June 1968 and received a Gold Disc award in early 1969 from R.I.A.A. It subsequently went on to sell over five million copies by mid-1971 and received a Grammy Award for the Best Score from an Original Cast Show Album of 1968.

The Broadway cast album comprised: *Side 1* – 'Aquarius' (Ronald Dyson and the Company); 'Donna' (Gerome Ragni and the Company); 'Hashish' (The Company); 'Sodomy' (Steve Curry and the Company); 'Coloured Spade' (Lamont Washington and the Company); 'Manchester, England' (James Rado and the Company); 'I'm Black' (Washington, Curry, Ragni and Rado); 'Ain't Got No' (Curry, Washington, Melba Moore and the Company); 'Air' (Sally Eaton, Shelley Plimpton, Moore and the Company); 'Initials' (The Company); 'I Got Life' (Rado and the Company); 'Hair' (Rado, Ragni and the Company); 'My Conviction' (Jonathan Kramer); 'Don't Put It Down' (Ragni and the Company); 'Frank Mills' (Shelley Plimpton); 'Be-in' (The Company); *Side 2* – 'Where Do I Go' (Rado and the Company); 'Black Boys' (Diane Keaton, Suzannah Nostrand, Natalie Mosco); 'White Boys' (Moore, Lorri Davis, Emmaretta Marks); 'Easy to Be Hard' (Lynn Kellogg); 'Walking in Space' (The Company); 'Abie Baby' (Washington, Dyson, Donnie Burks and

Davis); 'Three-Five-Zero-Zero' (The Company); 'What a Piece of Work Is Man' (Dyson and Walter Harris); 'Good Morning Starshine' (Kellogg, Moore, Rado and Ragni); 'The Flesh Failures' – 'Let the Sunshine In' (Rado, Kellogg, Moore and the Company).

This album was No 1 in the U.S.A. for 20 weeks and in the bestseller charts for 151 weeks (into 1971).

Disc sales of 'Hair' recordings grossed $20 million by October 1969 alone, and by mid-1970 productions of the show in the U.S.A. and abroad were bringing in a take of almost $1 million every ten days. The close to 300 different recordings of the score (at 31 June 1970) made it the most successful score in history as well as the most performed score ever written for Broadway. *Hair* became really big business all around the world including further productions in Toronto, Boston, Helsinki and Sao Paulo. The rights were also sold to Israel, Italy, Belgium and Japan.

Norman Racusin, General Manager of RCA-Victor, said, 'I think the charm and the greatness in *Hair* is that it's one of a kind. There can never be another *Hair*!'

FILM SOUNDTRACK (THE BEATLES, GEORGE MARTIN – MUSICAL DIRECTOR)

YELLOW SUBMARINE (album) *Parlophone* [*Britain*] *Apple* [*USA*]. *Yellow Submarine* is probably the first film to be based on a song – the single recorded by The Beatles in 1966. This fantasy extravaganza animated cartoon was obviously inspired by the song and the 'Sergeant Pepper's Lonely Hearts Club Band' album, although apart from singing for the film The Beatles had little to do with it. It tells the story of The Beatles travelling in a yellow submarine to defend 'Pepperland' against an attack of anti-music missiles and various other monsters, combining every trick and treatment of film animation and take-offs on schools and art styles. After voyaging through fantasy lands of Outer Space or Sea Bottom inhabited by demons and all kinds of terrors, they finally return to 'Pepperland' and vanquish the monstrous Blue Meanies with Beatlemusic and love.

This surrealistic mixture of pictures, words, songs and images was the result of two years' work by an international collection of diverse talents. No one had tried anything new with cartoons since Walt Disney's masterpiece *Fantasia* (1940) which was a landmark in the development of animation. It was Al Brodax, head of the TV and Motion Pictures Division of King Features Syndicate, producer of over 500 animated shorts for TV, who started thinking about The Beatles in conjunction with Disney's masterpiece – a feature-length animated film on a Beatles theme. With the go-ahead from The Beatles, Brodax started to work with Heinz Edelmann, a Czech-born commercial artist, whose work he had seen in a German magazine. Edelmann drew all the characters and most of the backgrounds, then his sketches were turned over to 40 animators and 140 technical artists who made some half a million drawings. The result was a technically brilliant film, with the most astonishing colours ever seen in a cartoon.

It was first previewed on 16 July 1968 at the Pavilion, London, and, when generally released in the U.S.A. in November, was a tremendous success. The musical score was written by The Beatles' record producer George Martin and the album released in Britain on 6 December 1968 and in the U.S.A. in January 1969. In the U.S.A. it was No 2 for three weeks and in Britain No 3 for three weeks. In just over three months it sold over 800,000 and went on to the million mark later in 1969. A Gold Disc award was presented by R.I.A.A. after two weeks on the market, for million dollar sale.

The album featured The Beatles' songs on one side and the

George Martin musical score on the reverse. Contents: *Side 1* - 'Yellow Submarine', by John Lennon and Paul McCartney (1966); 'Only a Northern Song', by George Harrison (1968); 'All Together Now', by John Lennon and Paul McCartney (1968); 'Hey, Bulldog', by John Lennon and Paul McCartney (1968); 'It's All Too Much', by George Harrison (1968); 'All You Need Is Love', by John Lennon and Paul McCartney (1967); *Side 2* (Instrumental) - 'Pepperland', by George Martin (1968); 'Sea of Time', by George Martin (1968); 'Sea of Holes', by George Martin (1968); 'Sea of Monsters', by George Martin (1968); 'March of the Meanies', by George Martin (1968); 'Pepperland Laid Waste', by George Martin (1968); 'Yellow Submarine in Pepperland', by John Lennon and Paul McCartney (1968) (arranged by George Martin).

This album was in the U.S.A. bestsellers for 24 weeks.

The film also included the John Lennon/Paul McCartney songs 'Sergeant Pepper's Lonely Hearts Club Band', 'Eleanor Rigby', 'Lucy in the Sky with Diamonds', 'Nowhere Man', 'When I'm 64', and 'A Day in the Life'.

HERB ALPERT AND THE TIJUANA BRASS

THIS GUY'S IN LOVE WITH YOU *A & M* [*USA*]. This song, with its unusual range of an octave and a fifth, was written by ace songwriters Hal David (words) and Burt Bacharach (music) for trumpeter Herb Alpert to sing on a CBS-TV special (22 April 1968) – a programme supported by over $100,000 in merchandising and promotion for more than one million advance order pressings of the artists' tenth album 'The Beat of the Brass'.

Alpert wanted something different for the programme and he sang the number on the programme to his wife Sharon. He had no intention of releasing the record as a single, but after the TV show was flooded with calls the following morning, he put it out right away. It shot to No 1 within six weeks and stayed in that chart position for four weeks with 14 weeks in the U.S.A. bestsellers with Gold Disc award for million sale (August) from R.I.A.A. within three months of release. In Britain, the disc was released on 14 June and reached No 1 for one week, selling over 250,000 with 16 weeks in the bestsellers.

The disc was the first No 1 ever for the David-Bacharach team in the U.S.A.

Although this was the first big hit for Alpert as a singer, he had actually made two vocal records in 1960 while under contract for a year to RCA with the name of Dore Alpert, and in 1962 made his first vocal disc 'Tell It to the Birds' for A & M, one of the label's first records.

Alpert's six fellow performers were said to be the highest-paid sidemen of all time, earning between £50,000 and $100,000 each per year.

THE BEAT OF THE BRASS (album) *A & M* [*USA*]. Still another colossal success for Herb Alpert, his tenth album containing numbers from his CBS-TV special (22 April 1968). It was No 1 for four weeks in the U.S.A. and stayed in the charts for 54 weeks. Advance order pressings were over a million and R.I.A.A. Gold Disc award was made at the beginning of August.

Contents: 'Monday, Monday', by John Phillips (1966); 'A Beautiful Friend', by Sol Lake (1968); 'Cabaret' (from the show *Cabaret*), by Fred Ebb and John Kander (1966); 'Panama', by Julius Wechter (1968); 'Belz mein shtetele belz' (My home town), by Jacob Jacobs and Alexander Olshanetsky; 'Talk to the Animals' (from film *Dr Doolittle*), by Leslie Bricusse (1967); 'Slick', by Herb Alpert and John Pisano (1968); 'She Touches Me', by Sol Lake (1968); 'Thanks for the Memory' (from film *Big Broadcast of 1938*), by Leo Robin and Ralph Rainger (1938); 'The Robin', by John Pisano (1968); 'This Guy's in Love with You', by Hal David and Burt Bacharach (1968).

The TV show, produced by the Singer Company, was planned to demonstrate visually as well as musically the universal application and appeal of The Brass in the U.S.A.

ANTOINE (pop folk vocalist)

LA TRAMONTANA (The Bearings) *Vogue-Saar* [*Italy*]. Another big success for Italian songwriters D. Pace (words) and Mario Panzeri (music). Antoine's disc was No 1 for ten weeks in Italy and also a big hit in France. Italian sales reached a million.

The song was first sung by Antoine in the 1968 San Remo Song Festival, with French and German versions being recorded later. It is an amusing song expressly made in Antoine's 'Italian' style of direct folk inspiration with a catchy melody and samba rhythm.

Antoine (real name Pierre Antoine Muraccioli), born in 1945 in Tamatave, one of Madagascar's main ports, was the son of a Corsican public works engineer who took his family to Canada, America, and Africa before settling in Paris when Antoine was 16. Antoine quickly became one of France's leading pop-folk singers and he was awarded the Prix d'Honneur for his performance of this song. His shoulder-length coiffure, pastel flowered shirts and silk slacks helped to make him one of the biggest attractions in France and his discs were said to out-sell those by Charles Aznavour, Johnny Hallyday and Yves Montand combined. He first achieved success in early 1966 with his particular brand of protest songs such as 'La guerre' and modern-style love reflections as in his ballad of an impoverished wife who kills her nine children. 'Antoine's Lucubrations' in a lighter vein was a big seller in France. Maurice Chevalier observed, 'Never in French show business has an artist reached the top so fast.' It took Antoine four months to do so in 1966, after fantastic scenes at the Paris Olympic Music Hall. Up to 1968 (July) he appeared on TV in Italy, France and Germany.

Released in Britain 5 April 1968 on Vogue label.

APHRODITE'S CHILD (vocal and instrumental trio)

RAIN AND TEARS *Philips* [*France*]. 'Rain and Tears' is an old tune originally written by the seventeenth-century German organist-composer Johann Pachelbel of Nuremberg (1653–1706), arranged by Vangelis Papathanassiou of the group with B. Bergman.

The group started working and recording in Greece around 1963 and played English and American songs. They found it difficult to get real success with this type of music and decided to try their luck in England. Being held up by a transport strike in Paris during the student demonstrations proved to be lucky for them. They were heard by Philips Records producer Pierre Sberre who was greatly impressed and signed them to the label immediately. Their success with this song, sung in English, was almost instantaneous in France. It got into the charts there within three days and soon after was No 1, staying top for a record 14 weeks, and was also a huge hit right across the Continent and Scandinavia. It also achieved No 27 in Britain with seven weeks in the bestsellers.

Each of the trio are accomplished musicians. Vangelis Papathanassiou, born in Valos, Greece on 29 March 1943, plays organ, drums, vibraphone, flute and several typically Greek instruments, and inherits his talents from his parents. His father is a painter, his mother a singer. Vangelis studied art and classical music at college. He speaks fluent English and French. Demis Roussos was born in Alexandria (Egypt) of Greek parents on 15 June 1947, his parents also being artistic, father a classical guitarist and engineer, mother a singer. He first studied music in Egypt at the age of eight, then in music college in Athens. He plays trumpet, double bass and organ, and is a competent bouzouki player. Speaks English, French, Arabic and Greek. He has since gone solo and is now an international bestselling artist. Lucas Sideras was born in Athens on 5 December 1944. His mother is a classical pianist and music teacher. Lucas plays drums, and is also a linguist, speaking English, French and his native Greek.

Combined sales of 'Rain and Tears' estimated at well over the million.

THE BEATLES

LADY MADONNA backed with THE INNER LIGHT *Parlophone* [*Britain*] *Capitol* [*USA*]. 'Lady Madonna' was written by John Lennon and Paul McCartney, 'The Inner Light' by George Harrison.

The 'Madonna' song is a terrific rock-and-roll number in a blues style combining humour with pungent social comment on a hard-pressed mother. 'Inner Light' is an East Indian-oriented ballad sung by George Harrison, the first time he had both written and sung on a Beatles single. Paul McCartney sings lead on the former.

With 'Madonna', the the Beatles sparked a new interest in the 'old fashioned' rock 'n' roll in Britain with revivals of many former favourites in this idiom, and the disc sold a million in the U.S.A. during its first week of issue and over the quarter million in Britain. It was released simultaneously in the U.S.A. and Britain on 15 March, was No 2 in the U.S.A. for three weeks and No 1 in Britain for two weeks with eight weeks in the British bestsellers. The disc was also No 1 in Germany, Poland, Denmark, Sweden, France and Australia, the combined global sales totalling two million. 'Lady Madonna' was 11 weeks in the U.S.A. bestsellers. 'The Inner Light' was No 96 in the U.S.A.

Gold Disc award from R.I.A.A. April 1968, the group's 27th.

HEY JUDE backed with REVOLUTION *Apple* [*Britain*] *Apple* [*USA*]. The Beatles' first release (30 August) by their new company Apple Corps Ltd, organised in 1968 to co-ordinate their many business enterprises – films, TV, electronics, music publishing, recording – and to promote new talent. They also released three other discs at the same time by new artists.

'Hey Jude' entered the British charts at No 3 and was No 1 the following week, staying in top position for four weeks with 16 weeks in the bestsellers. In the U.S.A. it entered the charts at No 10, the highest for any new disc (beating Herman's Hermits who were No 12 in 1965 with a first entry in the U.S. charts of 'Mrs Brown You've Got a Lovely Daughter'). It reached No 1 the second week staying in that position for 9 weeks, with 19 weeks in the bestsellers, and sold over a million there in eight days with a final total of over four million. British sales were over a quarter million for the same period, and global sales totalled over two million in a fortnight, and well over six million by year's end.

'Hey Jude', featuring Paul McCartney in the main vocal role and also a 40-piece orchestra, is a beautiful, compelling song – one of the most haunting and poignant Lennon and McCartney ever wrote – Paul's lilting and soulful vocal exhorting a friend to overcome his fears and commit himself to love. It is the longest single the Beatles ever recorded – 7 minutes 11 seconds. A strain of the melody is repeated by orchestra and chorus for almost four minutes at the end with the Beatles shouting over it to a fadeout.

'Revolution', also by Lennon and McCartney, features mainly the group's John Lennon, with a highly topical lyric addressed to radicals all over the world. It is a message saying that though we all want to change the world, it is unwise to do so by destruction or hate. The song is performed in unashamed rock 'n' roll with a bouncing beat and excitement. It was No 12 and 11 weeks in the U.S. bestsellers.

The two contrasting titles once again proved that The Beatles were still a long way ahead of their nearest rivals in 1968.

It received a Gold Disc award from R.I.A.A. It was also No 1 in Germany, Holland, Ireland, Belgium, Malaysia, Sweden, Singapore, Norway, Denmark and New Zealand.

British sales at year's end were around 800,000, Europe and Japan combined over 1,500,000, Canada over 300,000.

THE BEATLES (The 'White' Album) (double album) *Apple* [*Britain*] *Capitol* [*USA*]. With this double album, the Beatles pulled back from their electronic style of 'Sergeant Pepper' to a more relaxed, modest, pure and simple Beatles. It proved to be their biggest ever album success. Released by their new Apple Records in Britain and via Capitol for the U.S.A. on 21 November, advance orders in Britain were over 300,000 and an incredible 1,900,000 in the U.S.A. It was an immediate No 1 in both countries, and subsequently a huge hit around the world. By the end of 1968 global sales were well over four million – in just over five weeks on the market – and continuing strongly into 1969. All songs written by The Beatles.

Contents of the double album: *Side 1* – 'Back in the U.S.S.R.' (Paul McCartney), by John Lennon and Paul McCartney; 'Dear Prudence' (John Lennon), by John Lennon and Paul McCartney; 'Glass Onion' (John Lennon), by John Lennon and Paul McCartney; 'Ob-La-Di, Ob-La-Da' (Paul McCartney), by John Lennon and Paul McCartney; 'Honey Pie (Part One)', by John Lennon and Paul McCartney; 'The Continuing Story of Bungalow Bill' (John Lennon), by John Lennon and Paul McCartney; 'While My Guitar Gently Weeps' (Paul McCartney), by George Harrison; 'Happiness Is a Warm Gun' (John Lennon), by John Lennon and Paul McCartney; *Side 2* – 'Martha My Dear' (Paul McCartney), by John Lennon and Paul McCartney; 'I'm So Tired' (John Lennon), by John Lennon and Paul McCartney; 'Blackbird' (Paul McCartney), by John Lennon and Paul McCartney; 'Piggies' (George Harrison), by George Harrison; 'Rocky Racoon' (Paul McCartney), by John Lennon and Paul McCartney; 'Don't Pass Me By' (Ringo Starr), by Richard Starkey (Ringo Starr); 'Why Don't We Do It in the Road?' (Paul McCartney), by John Lennon and Paul McCartney; 'I Will' (Paul McCartney), by John Lennon and Paul McCartney; 'Julia' (John Lennon), by John Lennon and Paul McCartney; *Side 3* – 'Birthday' (John, Paul, George and Ringo), by John Lennon and Paul McCartney; 'Yer Blues' (John Lennon), by John Lennon and Paul McCartney; 'Mother Nature's Son' (Paul McCartney), by John Lennon and Paul McCartney; 'Everybody's Got Something to Hide Except Me and My Monkey' (John, Paul, George and Ringo), by John Lennon and Paul McCartney; 'Sexy Sadie' (John Lennon), by John Lennon and Paul McCartney; 'Helter Skelter' (Paul McCartney), by John Lennon and Paul McCartney; 'Long, Long, Long' (John, Paul and George), by George Harrison; *Side 4* – 'Revolution 1' (John Lennon) by John Lennon and Paul McCartney; 'Honey Pie' (Paul McCartney), by John Lennon and Paul McCartney; 'Savoy Truffle' (George Harrison), by George Harrison; 'Cry Baby, Cry' (John and Paul), by John Lennon and Paul McCartney; 'Revolution 9' (non-vocal), by John Lennon and Paul McCartney; 'Goodnight' (Paul McCartney), by John Lennon and Paul McCartney.

The most popular of these numbers was 'Ob-La-Di, Ob-La-Da', a kind of West Indian number with a 'blue beat' sound, handclapping, Jamaican band backing, and a merry Caribbean flavour. It was immediately taken up by many other artists for recording, and was a big hit for a British group The Marmalade (No 1 in the charts) and for Arthur Conley in the U.S.A.

Final estimate of probable sales of this first colossal double album were put at around $6\frac{1}{2}$ million, with the U.S.A. accounting for over half this figure. It was awarded an immediate Gold Disc award from R.I.A.A. and was the fastest-selling disc ever for Capitol Records who released the Apple label in the U.S.A., staying in their bestsellers for 64 weeks.

It was No 1 for 14 weeks in the U.S.A., and eight weeks in Britain.

THE BEE GEES

WORDS *Polydor* [*Britain*]. A tense love song with a semi-soft, somewhat-rock sound obtained by use of near-classical piano, soaring strings and pop percussion rhythm with a brilliant vocal lead, the song written by the three brothers Barry, Robin and Maurice Gibb of the group. The disc was released in mid-January in the U.S.A. (Atco label) and in Britain on 26 January. It achieved No 8 in Britain for one week with 10 weeks in the bestsellers and No 15 in the U.S.A. for one week with 11 weeks in the bestsellers, but was even more successful in Europe where it was No 1 in Germany, Holland and Switzerland with big sales. It sold two million globally.

On 27 January 1968, The Bee Gees made a record-breaking concert debut in Anaheim's Convention Centre, California, singing their simple but subtle songs, all self-written, backed by the uncomplicated sound of a 30-piece orchestra (23 strings, six horns and harp). It proved the most exciting British export in the field since The Beatles.

I'VE GOTTA GET A MESSAGE TO YOU *Polydor* [*Britain*]. Another big hit for The Bee Gees, written by the three brothers Barry, Robin and Maurice Gibb, and one of their most powerful discs with a phenomenal arrangement. The song tells the story of a country-and-western condemned man, desperately trying to prepare a message for a loved one. The disc was released in Britain on 2 August 1968 and in the U.S.A. a week later. Sales in Britain were over 250,000 where it was No 1 for a week and 15 weeks in the bestsellers. In the U.S.A. it was No 3 for one week with 13 weeks in the bestsellers. The record was a global million seller by the end of September 1968.

ARCHIE BELL AND THE DRELLS (rhythm-and-blues quartet)

TIGHTEN UP *Atlantic* [*USA*]. Archie Bell and The Drells made this disc in Texas where it gained the approval of Don Sundeen, programme director for station KCOH-Houston and the station's disc jockey. Atlantic picked up the master through the station's enthusiasm in broadcasting it. The disc was released at the end of March 1968 and sold the million by May with R.I.A.A. Gold Disc award. It was No 1 for two weeks in the U.S.A. and 15 weeks in the bestsellers.

Song was written by Archie Bell and Billy Buttier.

BIG BROTHER AND THE HOLDING COMPANY WITH JANIS JOPLIN

CHEAP THRILLS (album) *Columbia* [*USA*]. This group comprised Sam Andrew (guitars), James Gurley (guitars), Pete Albin (bass) and David Getz (drums). They played regularly at the Avalon Ballroom, San Francisco, and went out on the road in January 1966. Pete Albin was vocalist at the time, but they needed another singer. Their manager decided on Janis Joplin. A small Chicago company, Mainstream, offered Big Brother a chance to record, and their first album was not released until the group got rave reviews and audience reaction at the Monterey Pop Festival in the summer of 1967. The album was not very good, but Clive Davis of Columbia Records was impressed with Janis' performance at the Festival. The group were then signed with Albert Grossman as manager in 1968 and in the spring, they recorded the album 'Cheap Thrills'. This was a colossal success after release in September, and received a Gold Disc award from R.I.A.A. for a million dollar sale on 15 October with a subsequent million units sale. It was No 1 for 8 weeks in the U.S.A. charts.

By the end of 1968, Janis Joplin's star status far outweighed the rest of the group, and she went solo.

Janis Joplin was born on 19 January 1943 in Port Arthur, Texas. She listened to Bessie Smith and Leadbelly records, and in the early 1960s began singing country and blues music with a bluegrass band. She worked in Austin, Texas, in 1961, and San Francisco in 1962. She also attended the University of Texas for a while and was in and out of colleges from 1962–66. On return to San Francisco in 1966, she joined Big Brother and the Holding Company in June, and in August 1967 won acclaim at the Monterey Festival, with the resultant 'Cheap Thrills' album success. Her performance on stage was very powerful, frantic and passionate. She made three other albums – 'I Got Dem Ol' Kozmic Blues Again Mamma' (1969), 'Pearl' (1971) (a very big hit), and 'In Concert' (1972), the last two released after her death from drug overdose in a hotel room in Hollywood on 4 October 1970. The tragedy of her early demise was probably due to her elevation to superstar status too quickly, as she seemed to overdo everything to sustain her reputation. An album of her greatest hits was released in 1973.

The contents of 'Cheap Thrills': 'Combination of the Two', by Sam Andrew; 'I Need a Man', by Janis Joplin and Sam Andrew; 'Summertime' (from *Porgy and Bess*), by DuBose Heyward and George Gershwin (1935); 'Piece of My Heart', by J. Ragovoy and B. Berns; 'Turtle Blues', by Janis Joplin; 'Oh, Sweet Mary', by Janis Joplin; 'Ball and Chain', by Mama Willie Mae Thornton.

THE BOX TOPS

CRY LIKE A BABY *Mala* [*USA*]. Second million seller (R.I.A.A. Gold Disc award) for The Box Tops, the song written by Dan Penn (producer of the disc for Bell Records) and Spooner Oldham. The disc was released in the U.S.A. in mid-February and sold the million by mid-May. It was No 2 for two weeks in the U.S.A. with 15 weeks in the bestsellers, and No 14 for one week in Britain with 12 weeks in the bestsellers. British release on 1 March 1968 (Bell label). It features a new hybrid instrument, the electric sitar. The composition is a mid-speed rock-blues.

In this year, Rick Allan took over the bass guitar duties in the group.

THE BROOKLYN BRIDGE (vocal and instrumental group)

THE WORST THAT COULD HAPPEN *Buddah* [*USA*]. The Brooklyn Bridge, a complete, self-contained show band, was formed in 1968 of four singers, each from different groups, with the idea of creating a totally unique musical organisation. The four singers were present at the first audition of a newly-formed seven-piece band which they liked, and they joined forces to build The Brooklyn Bridge group to play 'blue-eyed soul', hard rock, progressive contemporary sounds and everything in between.

The personnel of the group – ten men and one woman: Johnny Maestro (solo vocals), Fred Ferrara, Les Cauchi, and Mike Gregorie (solo vocals and harmonic backing), Tom Sullivan (band-leader/arranger/saxophonist), Carolyn Wood (organ), Jimmy Rosica (bass), Richie Macioce (guitar), Artie Catanzarita (drums), Shelly Davis (trumpet and piano), and Joe Ruvio (saxophone).

The group's recording of this brilliant song by famous song-smith Jim Webb – a power-packed ballad with excellent vocal and instrumental work – was released in November 1968 in the U.S.A. and, by mid-March 1969, sold over 1,250,000 with Gold Disc award from R.I.A.A. The disc was produced by Wes Farrell and reached No 3 for two weeks in the U.S.A. charts and 12 weeks in the bestsellers.

ARTHUR BROWN (The Crazy World of)

FIRE *Track* [*Britain*]. Arthur Brown's stage routine was one of the most dynamic. He appeared in flowing multi-coloured robes, his face streaked with colourful make-up, a helmet on his head, and his hair on fire. With a band backing him in a mixture of rock, rhythm-and-blues, jazz and pop, he electrified his audiences with shrieks, jumps, growling and singing.

Arthur Brown was born in Whitby, Yorks. on 24 June 1944. Arthur studied law at London University but failed his exams after one year. He then studied philosophy at Reading University, where he formed a college group in the area. Before entering show business he had various occupations such as teacher, dishwasher, road-digger, etc. His fire stage act stems from his preoccupation with fire in his youth, and his hobby of going to fun fairs.

'Fire' was written by him with Vincent Crane. It achieved No 1 for one week in Britain and 14 weeks in the bestsellers, and was No 2 for two weeks in the U.S.A. (Atlantic label) with 13 weeks in the bestsellers. The disc was awarded a Gold Disc from R.I.A.A. for the million sale in the U.S.A. alone and also had big sales elsewhere. It was released in Britain on 7 June.

GLEN CAMPBELL (country-and-western vocalist)

WICHITA LINEMAN *Capitol* [*USA*]. Glen Campbell, the seventh son of a seventh son in a family of 12 children, was born on 22 April 1936 on a farm near Delight, Arkansas, and since his entire family played musical instruments he was surrounded with music from birth. By the age of six he was singing and strumming the guitar on his local radio and at barn dances. He joined a western band in his teens, led by his uncle Dick Bills, in Albuquerque, New Mexico, and appeared with the band on radio and TV for five years. Glen then had his own band for several years before heading for the West Coast. He arrived in Hollywood in 1960 and started to record for the Crest label there, and worked with a vocal and instrumental group, The Champs. He then cut 'Turn Around, Look at Me' for Crest records and the disc brought him national popularity (1961). This success resulted in an exclusive contract with Capitol Records (1962). A proficient artist on drums, bass, violin, mandolin and harmonica, this helped Glen to find work as a studio musician, and he played on sessions for many star artists including Nat 'King' Cole and Frank Sinatra in addition to making some recordings himself.

It wasn't until he recorded 'Gentle on my Mind' (1967) that his name was noted seriously in America. This disc was a hit and the subsequent 'By the Time I Get to Phoenix' achieved No 1 in the U.S. charts plus three Grammy Awards. By 1968, Glen was the toast of the American music scene with three million-dollar albums simultaneously certified by R.I.A.A. in November 1968.

'Witchita Lineman', a melancholy love ballad with an eerie production atmosphere, was released in October 1968 and sold over 700,000 in two months, reaching the million by March 1969 plus a Gold Disc award by R.I.A.A. and a Grammy Award for the Best Engineered (Popular) Recording of 1968. The song was written by America's Jim Webb, and the disc was No 2 for one week and in the U.S. bestsellers for 15 weeks. It was also a success in Britain where it reached No 5 for one week with 13 weeks in the bestsellers. Glen's album of the same title had a 450,000 advance sale, the largest ever for the artist. He started his own CBS-TV weekly show in January 1969.

WALTER CARLOS AND BENJAMIN FOLKMAN

SWITCHED ON BACH (album) *Columbia* [*USA*]. Released in late 1968, this album was in the bestseller U.S.A. national charts for 58 weeks and on their best classical sellers chart for the whole of 1969, 1970 and 1971 and was No 1 classical seller for 94 weeks. The disc received three Grammy Awards for 1969 - Best Engineered Recording Classical (Engineer's award to Walter Carlos), Best Performance by Instrumental Soloist (to Walter Carlos on the Moog synthesizer), and Best Classical Album of the Year (performed on the Moog synthesizer by Walter Carlos). It was in the U.S. classical charts for 310 weeks to end of 1974.

The boom in electronic music and much of the credit for the Moog synthesizer's popularity is undoubtedly due to the sales of this Carlos/Folkman album on both the popular and classical bestseller lists. By May 1972 it sold the million, the second-bestselling classical album ever put out (after Van Cliburn's recording of Tchaikovsky's First Piano Concerto).

It was responsible for both the major Moog sales interest and for a tremendous amount of aesthetic controversy over the validity of transcribing Bach to synthesizer, the album catching the attention of purists because of the part played in it by Folkman who had already established his reputation as a musicologist. He advised Carlos, who moved from physics into music via composing commercials, and it was Carlos (born 1941) who in fact is credited with being the friend who persuaded Robert Moog to tag his name on to the electric keyboard synthesizers which he invented.

Dr Robert A. Moog of New York (born 1934) began work on the synthesizer in 1964 and after a few months the first, now primitive, model was made. His invention subsequently became the biggest thing to hit the music world since the electronic organ. This piece of electronic wizardry was used in commercials, films and on record to produce a seemingly endless variety of sound effects and music and is certainly the most successful and versatile instrument yet developed. The Moog synthesizer allows the player to predetermine and reconstitute not only any known

sound but also, of much greater importance, entirely new sounds, never before heard.

Dr Moog took his Ph.D. in engineering before he became interested in setting up the synthesizer in 1964 during his last year at college, and had a team of 20 people working with him, including composers.

The album contained: *Side 1* - 'Sinfonia to Cantata No 29'; 'Air on the G string'; 'Two-part Invention in F major'; 'Two-part Invention in B flat major'; 'Two-part Invention in D minor'; 'Jesu Joy of Man's Desiring'; 'Prelude and Fugue No 7 in E flat major' (from Book 1, *Well-Tempered Klavier*); *Side 2* - 'Prelude and Fuge No 2 in C minor' (from Book 1, *Well-Tempered Klavier*); 'Chorale Prelude - Wachet auf'; 'Brandenburg Concerto No 3 in G major' (1st, 2nd and 3rd movements).

A Gold Disc was awarded by R.I.A.A. in August 1969.

Released in Britain 21 February 1969 on the CBS label.

This album ranks as Columbia's all-time best classical seller, with a million sale by April 1980 (U.S.A.).

CLARENCE CARTER

SLIP AWAY *Atlantic* [*USA*]. Written by W. Armstrong, W. Terrell and M. Daniel, this song was recorded by Carter in Muscle Shoals, Alabama and produced by Rick Hall in his Fame Recording Studios.

The disc was released in the U.S.A. in May 1968 but did not begin to attract attention until July and thereafter climbed the charts steadily, reaching No 6 for one week in October with 16 weeks in the bestsellers, with Gold Disc award from R.I.A.A.

Clarence Carter was originally a gospel singer and made his first recordings with his partner Calvin Thomas for Rick Hall. Clarence, who has a degree in music from an Alabama college, is blind. He is a talented arranger, writer and musician, and plays guitar, piano and organ. He writes his arrangements in Braille which are then transposed for the studio musicians.

TOO WEAK TO FIGHT *Atlantic* [*USA*]. A similar type of love song to Clarence Carter's previous big seller 'Slip Away', this disc released in October 1968 sold over a million by mid-March and received a Gold Disc award from R.I.A.A. It was No 7 for 2 weeks in the U.S. charts and 13 weeks in the bestsellers. The song was written by Clarence Carter, G. Jackson and J. Keyes and arranged by Rick Hall (producer of the disc).

JOHNNY CASH

AT FOLSOM PRISON (album) *Columbia* [*USA*]. Because of Johnny Cash's great compassion for outcasts, he insisted that this album be recorded 'live' at a concert he gave at California's Folsom Prison. It is probably the first recording cut in a prison by any major artist. The collection of old and new Cash songs was released in May 1968 in the U.S.A. and in Britain on 28 May 1968 (No 7 for one week). It was a colossal success, reaching No 1 on the U.S.A. country charts for ten weeks and staying in the top ten for eight months. In the U.S. national charts it reached No 11. An R.I.A.A. Gold Disc for the million dollar sale was awarded in 1968 and the disc sold over the million units by June 1969. Johnny Cash, a solid country-and-western success since 1955, was finally discovered by the U.S.A. TV networks in 1969 and was given his own one-hour series on ABC-TV 'The Johnny Cash Show' from June 1969. In 1968 he is said to have made around $2 million. By then he had produced 400 original songs, made 19 record albums and was giving nearly 200 concerts a year. He became one of Columbia's top five in record sales - along with such favourites as Simon and Garfunkel, Barbra Streisand, Bob Dylan and Andy Williams.

Contents of the album: 'Folsom Prison Blues', by Johnny Cash (1956); 'Dark as the Dungeon', by Merle Travers (1968); 'I Still Miss Someone', by R. Cash and Johnny Cash (1958); 'Cocaine Blues', by T. J. Arnall (1968); '25 Minutes to Go', by Shel Silverstein (1962); 'Orange Blossom Special', by E. T. Rouse (1965); 'Long Black Veil', by Danny Dill and Marijohn Wilkin (1959); 'Send a Picture of Mother', by Johnny Cash

(1968); 'Wall', by Harlan Howard (1968); 'Dirty Old Egg-sucking Dog', by J. H. Clement (1966); 'Flushed from the Bathroom of Your Heart', by J. H. Clement (1968); 'Jackson', by G. Rodgers and B. Wheeler (1967); 'Give My Love to Rose', by Johnny Cash (1957); 'I Got Stripes', by Charlie Williams and Johnny Cash (1959); 'Green, Green Grass of Home', by Claude (Curly) Putman, Jr. (1965); 'Greystone Chapel', by G. Shirley (1968).

This album stayed in the bestseller charts in the U.S.A. for 122 weeks. It sold over two million in records and tapes.

CLASSICS IV

STORMY *Imperial* [*USA*]. Written by B. Buie and J. Cobb, 'Stormy' was No 2 for one week in the U.S.A. and 15 weeks in the bestsellers. The disc, issued in mid-September, was taken from the Imperial album 'Mammas and Papas'/'Soul Train'. The song is described as a fully loaded low-key rock number, and the disc sold a million, the second to do so for the group. R.I.A.A. Gold Disc award.

THE CREAM

WHITE ROOM *Atco* [*USA*]. Written by Jack Bruce and Ginger Baker of the trio, it was first included in their album 'Wheels of Fire' which was itself a very big seller. When this track was issued as a single by popular demand, it got to No 6 for three weeks in the U.S. charts with 11 weeks in the bestsellers, was No 28 in Britain with eight weeks in the bestsellers, and sold an estimated million globally.

CREEDENCE CLEARWATER REVIVAL

CREEDENCE CLEARWATER REVIVAL (album) *Fantasy* [*USA*]. The first album by this outstanding group was released in the spring 1968. It was awarded a Gold Disc by R.I.A.A. on 16 December 1970 for a million dollar sale and subsequently sold a million units. The album contained one of their big hits, 'Susie Q', which had a duration of $8\frac{1}{2}$ minutes. (See 1969 for Creedence Clearwater Revival biographical data.)

The contents of the album: 'I Put a Spell on You', by Screaming Jay Hawkins; '99$\frac{1}{2}$ Won't Do', by Wilson Pickett and S. Cooper; 'Susie Q', by Dale Hawkins, Stanley Lewis and Eleanor Broadwater (1957); 'Walk on the Water', by John Fogerty; 'Get Down Woman', by John Fogerty; 'Working Man', by John Fogerty; 'Porterville', by John Fogerty; 'Gloomy', by John Fogerty.

TYRONE DAVIS (blues vocalist)

CAN I CHANGE MY MIND *Dakar* [*USA*]. Blues singer Davis hails from Chicago and once served as a chauffeur for soul-singer Freddie King who also recorded for Cotillion Records, a new subsidiary label started by Atlantic Records in 1968. Cotillion distributed Dakar products, and this disc was its first million seller (by February 1969) which was released in November 1968. It reached No 5 for two weeks in the U.S.A. charts with 13 weeks in the bestsellers, and was awarded a Gold Disc by R.I.A.A. in February 1969. It was also No 1 for three weeks in the rhythm-and-blues charts.

The song was written by Barry Despenza and Carl Wolfolk and is described as a solid rhythm rouser.

DAVE DEE, DOZY, BEAKY, MICK AND TICH

LEGEND OF XANADU *Fontana* [*Britain*]. Another success for British writers Ken Howard and Alan Blaikley, and second million seller for the group. The disc was released on 9 February 1968 in Britain and in March in the U.S.A. It sold over 250,000 in Britain and sales from Europe and the Commonwealth and elsewhere made it a global million, although American sales were small, reaching only No 52 with 6 weeks in the bestsellers. The disc was No 1 for a week in Britain and 12 weeks in the bestsellers. The performance is in Mariachi-rock style with heavy rhythm, fine vocal and instrumental lines, and arresting cracking-whip effect.

DEEP PURPLE (rock quintet)

HUSH *Parlaphone* [*Britain*] *Tetragrammaton* [*USA*]. Deep Purple made their recording debut with this for the Parlophone label on 21 June 1968 in Britain but it was in the U.S.A. where the disc became a million seller in 1968, reaching No 4 there for two weeks via the Tetragrammaton label, with 10 weeks in the bestsellers.

One of Britain's top progressive rock bands, they were a big attraction all over Europe, making a name for themselves with their powerful, exhibitionist and musicianly rock. Though 'Hush' was a hit in the U.S.A. plus two high-placed albums there, it wasn't until the autumn of 1969 that the group made any impact in Britain. This occurred when they performed organist Jon Lord's 'Concerto for Group and Orchestra' at London's Royal Albert Hall with the London Philharmonic Orchestra, after which they returned to America for a third tour, climaxing in a 'Concerto' date at the Hollywood Bowl with the Los Angeles Philharmonic.

Personnel: Rod Evans (lead singer) born in Edinburgh and a professional since the age of 15. Lyric writer for the group's originals together with Jon Lord. Nicky Simper (bass guitar and vocal harmony) from Norwood Green, Southall, London. Jon Lord (organ and vocal harmony) from Leicester, born 9 June 1941. Studied piano at nine and was accomplished organist at 11. Switched from classics to jazz and pop music in his late teens. Ian Paice (drummer) from Nottingham, born 29 June 1948. Ritchie Blackmore (lead guitar) from Weston-super-Mare, born 14 April 1945.

These constituted the group for the 'Hush' recording, but Evans and Simper were later replaced by Roger Glover and Ian Gillan.

'Hush' was written by U.S.A. composer Joe South, a well known studio guitarist for several years in Atlanta, Ga. He received the Grammy Award for his 'Games People Play' - the Song of the Year (1969).

THE DELFONICS

LA LA (means I love you) *Philly Groove* [*USA*]. Written by William Hart (words) and the group's producer, Thom Bell, this was the first disc for The Delfonics. It reached No 4 and was 15 weeks in the U.S.A. charts. It reached No 19 and was 10 weeks in the British bestsellers. The million sale was reported in 1974. (See 1970 for The Delfonics biographical data.)

DION

ABRAHAM, MARTIN AND JOHN *Laurie* [*USA*]. This disc sparked a new career for Dion (Dion Di Mucci) the former teen-bopper rock star, who had recorded for the Laurie label from 1958 to 1962. Producer Phil Gernhard who achieved early success with 'Stay' (Maurice Williams and The Zodiacs) and later with the 'Snoopy' discs (The Royal Guardsmen) was anxious to be involved in more contemporary projects, and when Dick Holler, the songwriter signed to him, showed Gernhard his song 'Abraham, Martin and John' he got his wish.

Holler wrote the song the day after the assassination of Senator Robert F. Kennedy in Los Angeles (June 1968), expressing the tragedy personally in his own medium, a message ballad equating Abraham Lincoln, Dr Martin Luther King and John F. Kennedy.

Gernhard's search for a sensitive artist to sing the song ran into several months, until Gene Schwartz, Laurie's A & R chief, contacted Gernhard to ask him to arrange a meeting with Dion as Schwartz was interested in resuming what had once been a highly successful relationship between the artist and Laurie. Gernhard expected to find the old Dion, a rock and roll singer, but, after hearing Dion work, discovered that the artist was tuned to the style of the day and was amazed that he was not recording. He had found the right artist for Dick Holler's song. Dion's disc was released in September 1968, got to No 2 for one week in the U.S. charts with 14 weeks in the bestsellers, and by February 1969 sold the million with Gold Disc award by R.I.A.A.

The disc was released in Britain on 8 November 1968.

THE DOORS

HELLO I LOVE YOU *Elektra* [*USA*]. Written collectively by The Doors, this disc was released in U.S.A. in late June and became No 1 after five weeks, staying at the top for three weeks and 12 weeks in the bestsellers. R.I.A.A. awarded a Gold Disc in September 1968. In Britain, the disc was released on Elektra on 23 August and reached No 15 in the charts there for one week, with 12 weeks in the bestsellers.

The disc is a great rock number with a solid dance beat.

TOUCH ME *Elektra* [*USA*]. Another big hit written by The Doors themselves, a throbbing, driving disc with a beat in the group's hard-hitting style. It was released in December 1968, was No 1 for one week and 13 weeks in the bestsellers, and sold the million by February 1969 with Gold Disc award from R.I.A.A. (March 1969).

The disc was issued in Britain on 24 January 1969.

THE EQUALS (vocal and instrumental quintet)

BABY COME BACK *President* [*Britain*]. The Equals' disc of this song was originally released in Britain in late 1966 as the secondary number and did not register there until the summer of 1968.

Pat Lloyd, John Hall and Eddie Grant all went to school together at Acland Burghley School, North London, and decided to form a group. When Derve Gordon's twin brother Lincoln heard of this, he and Derve asked if they could join. Eddie, the only one who could play an instrument, began to teach them. They first started rehearsing on a council estate at Hornsey Rise, North London around 1965, Eddie writing most of their material. They later spent six months of each year on the Continent, building their popularity, and appeared in TV shows. A friend wanted to make a demo disc of this song and took the group to President Records. The label liked the song so much they suggested the group record it themselves. The disc - issued on Ariola in Germany - was a big hit there in 1967 and became a No 1 in Belgium and Holland in early 1968. Then quite quickly it began to climb the British charts and within eight weeks was No 1 for three weeks plus over 250,000 sale.

A Gold Disc was presented to the group in June 1968 for a combined million sale. In the U.S.A. it reached No 26 for one week with 9 weeks in the bestsellers.

Eddie Grant, who wrote the song, has also written material for other groups including the bluebeat spoof 'Train Trip to Rainbow City' and 'Wedding in Peyton Place'.

The group personnel: Derve Gordon (lead singer) born 29 June 1948 in Jamaica; Eddie Grant (lead guitarist) born 5 March 1948 in Guyana; Lincoln Gordon (rhythm guitar) born 29 June 1948 in Jamaica; John Hall (drummer) born 25 October 1947 in Holloway, London; Patrick Lloyd (rhythm guitarist) born 17 March 1948 in Holloway, London.

DON FARDON

INDIAN RESERVATION (Lament of the Cherokee Reservation Indian) *Pye-Youngblood* [*Britain*] *GNP Crescendo* [*USA*]. Famous U.S.A. songwriter John D. Loudermilk originally copyrighted this song in 1963. It is a lament concerning the plight of the Cherokee Indians, who, in 1791, were moved from their home in Georgia, when gold was found on the land, to Oklahoma. It was never recorded as a protest song, but when the record became a hit in the U.S.A., the Indians in Salt Lake City used it as a publicity song in their struggle for civil rights.

The disc was released in August 1968 in the U.S.A. and reached No 20 in the charts. It was issued in Britain by Pye in October 1968, but did not become popular until re-issue on the Youngblood label in 1970 in Britain, reaching No 2 with 17 weeks in the bestsellers. The disc was also a No 1 on the Continent. It can probably be classed as the longest 'sleeper' disc, taking two years to become a hit. The global sale is estimated at over the million.

Micki Dallon, Don Fardon's producer, made a deal with Crescendo Records in Hollywood for a number of masters including 'Indian Reservation', resulting in its U.S.A. release.

Don Fardon hails from Coventry, England, managed by Micki Dallon from 1965 when Don was a member of The Sorrows group. He promoted Don as a solo artist after the group broke up. Don spent much of his time working in cabaret both on the Continent and in Britain with his backing band A Touch of Raspberry - a 6-piece Scottish group with two vocalists. His discs were also successful in Canada, Australia, Germany, Italy, France and Brazil.

JOSE FELICIANO (vocalist, guitar)

LIGHT MY FIRE *Victor* [*USA*]. José Monserrate Feliciano was born in Puerto Rico in 1945 and has been blind since birth. One of a family of nine children, they moved to New York when José was very young and he displayed a talent for music at a very early age. His first performance in public was at the Teatro Puerto Rico in The Bronx as an accordionist when he was nine. José then discovered the guitar, an instrument on which he has become a virtuoso. He made his professional debut in Detroit's Retort Coffee House, and received wider exposure when he appeared in Gerde's Folk City in New York's Greenwich Village. He was discovered there quite accidentally when an RCA-Victor A & R man called in to see another act. He was so impressed by José that he forgot about the other artist, and signed Jose to a recording contract (1963). His first single was released in the autumn of 1964 - his own composition 'Everybody Do the Click' - and he also cut two albums for Victor. From then on he enjoyed great popularity with his Latin American records and successful radio, TV and nightclub appearances. After hearing The Doors' recording of their own composition 'Light My Fire', José decided to record it in a slower tempo as a 'soul' number. This was done with José singing and playing guitar plus bass and conga drums, special string arrangements and a jazz flautist improvising. The result was a disc that reached No 3 for three weeks in the U.S.A. with 12 weeks in the bestsellers, and No 6 for one week in Britain with combined sales of over the million, and 16 weeks in the bestsellers.

His album 'Feliciano' was a No 1 seller later in the year, and earned a Gold Disc award from R.I.A.A.

Jose is a rare artist. Apart from his virtuosity on the guitar, he plays many other instruments including banjo, organ, mandolin, harmonica and piano. His range of songs covers rock 'n' roll, folk, blues, pop and Latin-American music. He also sings in seven different languages. A multi-talented singer/entertainer who has embraced music with a fervor that is reflected in his performances.

The disc was issued in the U.S.A. in July 1968. Feliciano received two Grammy Awards for Best New Artist and Best Contemporary Pop Vocal (Male) Performance of 1968.

THE FIFTH DIMENSION (vocal quintet)
STONED SOUL PICNIC *Soul City* [*USA*]. The Fifth Dimension quintet was formed in 1965, and at that time was called The Versatiles, later The Vocals when on tour for six months with Ray Charles. During this tour they received high praise for their performances. Their first successful disc was 'Go Where You Wanna Go' and then, after meeting songwriter Jim Webb, they recorded in 1967 his 'Up, Up and Away' which achieved No 4 in the U.S. charts. This proved an immensely popular item with disc jockeys everywhere and resulted in the group becoming internationally known, gaining them five Grammy Awards for Record of the Year, Song of the Year, Best Vocal Performance, Best Contemporary Single and Best Contemporary Group Performance. By 1968 they had reached the top of their profession. The group's sound is best described as a sort of Hi-Los (a famous group who perfected a modern vocal technique) with a touch of added soul, but they can make the transition from their modernistic approach in singing to the earlier rhythm-and-blues idiom with a smoothness delightful both to watch and hear.

The group consisted of: Marilyn McCoo (born 1944), a graduate from U.C.L.A. with a B.A. degree in business administration after switching from theatre arts. She made her TV debut at 15. Also plays piano. Florence LaRue (born 1943), a B.A. in elementary education at Cal State in Los Angeles, and a schoolteacher for a short time before joining the group in 1966. Also plays violin and viola. Ron Townson (born 1933), a singer with choirs and spiritual groups from the age of six. Toured with Nat 'King' Cole and Dorothy Dandridge as a teenager, later joined the Wings Over Jordan Gospel Singers, and also played a small part in the film version of *Porgy and Bess*. LaMonte McLemore (born 1939), a former member of the U.S. Army Drum and Bugle Corps. Billy Davis, Jr., owner of a cocktail lounge in his hometown, St Louis. He used the lounge as an entertainment workshop.

'Stoned Soul Picnic' was written by Laura Nyro, then a promising new artist. The disc was released in mid-May 1968 and in Britain on 5 July (Liberty label). It was No 3 for three weeks in the U.S.A. and 16 weeks in the bestsellers, and sold a million by October with Gold Disc award from R.I.A.A.

The song is a warm description of a down-home picnic.

FLEETWOOD MAC
ALBATROSS *Blue Horizon* [*Britain*]. Fleetwood Mac are credited with having started the breakthrough to a blues boom in Britain in 1968, and were the first to be successful commercially with their great chart success in 'Albatross', an instrumental number of simplicity and great appeal written by the group's Peter Green. It was No 1 for three weeks in Britain soon after release in December 1968 and, by February 1969, had sold a global million, with 20 weeks in the bestsellers.

They were formed in August 1967, and their following started from their first stage appearance. Their second date was at London's Marquee Club where they broke all previous box office records. They were discovered by manager Clifford Davis when performing as a quartet. Davis added a fifth member, Danny Kirwan, whom he had under management. The group evoked the nearest thing in enthusiasm and excitement to the early Rolling Stones audiences. They gained a wider audience through their album 'Fleetwood Mac' in 1968, released by a small label, Blue Horizon, which was started in 1966 by Mike Vernon, a

producer for Decca for six years. This album was one of the top sellers in Britain in 1968 and Blue Horizon, who started with the small capital of £250 ($600), made a turnover of around £250,000 ($600,000) in its first year after completing a pressing and distribution deal with CBS Records who release their output.

The group consists of: Mick Fleetwood (drums) born 24 June 1947 in London; John McVie (bass guitar) born 25 November 1944 in London; Peter Green (vocal, guitar, harmonica) born 29 October 1946 in London (all the above originally with John Mayall's Bluesbreakers); Jeremy Spencer (guitar, piano) born 4 July 1948 in London; Danny Kirwan (guitar) born 13 May 1950 in London.

Fleetwood Mac made tours in America in 1968 and 1969.

THE FOUNDATIONS
BUILD ME UP, BUTTERCUP *Pye* [*Britain*]. Written by Tony Macauley (of Pye Records) and Mike D'Abo (of Manfred Mann group), an infectious rhythmic number which reached No 2 for a week in Britain with 15 weeks in the bestsellers and sold over 250,000 by early January 1969, just two months after release on 8 November 1968. The disc was released in the U.S.A. in late December on the Uni label and got to No 1 for two weeks in 1969 with 15 weeks in the bestsellers. Global sales totalled $4\frac{1}{2}$ million by April 1969, over one million of this total in the U.S.A. alone.

The lead singer for this recording was Colin Young, born 12 September 1944 in Barbados, West Indies, who replaced Clem Curtis. Mike Elliot had left the group, making it a septet.

R.I.A.A. Gold Disc award March 1969.

ARETHA FRANKLIN
SINCE YOU'VE BEEN GONE *Atlantic* [*USA*]. This song was written by Aretha Franklin and Ted White, the disc being released in February 1968 with a million sale by the end of March plus a Gold Disc award from R.I.A.A. It was Aretha's fifth successive million seller single. It was No 4 in the charts for four weeks and 12 weeks in the U.S.A. bestsellers. It was also the No 1 rhythm-and-blues disc for three weeks in the U.S.A. In Britain it achieved No 4 for three weeks.

The song, highly emotional, is rendered in a most powerful manner, with a tingling orchestral backing. Aretha, who had earned the name of 'Lady Soul', was named by *Billboard* as the Top Female Vocalist of 1967 and *Time* magazine devoted its feature article to her in June 1968. Disc released in Britain 1 March 1968 on Atlantic label.

THINK *Atlantic* [*USA*]. The sixth consecutive million seller for Aretha Franklin, the song again written by her with Ted White. The disc was released in May 1968, was No 7 for two weeks in the U.S.A. charts with 10 weeks in the bestsellers, and sold the million by July with R.I.A.A. Gold Disc award. In Britain it reached No 26 and was nine weeks in the bestsellers.

The song is yet another pressure-packed rhythm-and-blues number with wailing lyrics of a hard-luck love affair, recorded with tremendous rhythmic drive.

It was the No 1 rhythm-and-blues disc for three weeks in the U.S.A. and No 1 for five weeks in Britain's rhythm-and-blues charts. Disc released in Britain on 10 May 1968 on Atlantic label.

I SAY A LITTLE PRAYER backed with THE HOUSE THAT JACK BUILT *Atlantic* [*USA*]. Million seller single No 7 for Aretha and another Gold Disc R.I.A.A. award. 'I Say a Little Prayer' (written in 1967 by Burt Bacharach and Hal David) was previously (1967) a million seller for Dionne Warwick. This version was taken from Aretha's album 'Aretha Now' and released in August. It was No 10 for one week in the U.S.A. with 11 weeks in the bestsellers, and No 4 for two weeks in Britain and 14 weeks in the bestsellers. The backing 'House That Jack Built' (written by Bob Lance and Fran Robins) got to No 6 for two weeks in the U.S.A. with 9 weeks in the bestsellers. 'Prayer' was released in Britain on 2 August with a different backing. Both songs had tremendous vocals by Aretha with a hard orchestral accompaniment.

SEE SAW backed with MY SONG *Atlantic* [*USA*]. Released in mid-November, this double hit disc sold a million by early January 1969 with R.I.A.A. Gold Disc award. Both songs are revivals. 'See Saw' written by Steve Cropper and Don Covay was originally a hit for Don Covay in 1965. 'My Song' was written by Arthur Alexander in 1952 and was then a hit for Johnny Ace. The disc was produced by Atlantic's Jerry Wexler and made the eighth consecutive million seller for Aretha. She was voted Top Female Vocalist of 1968 by all the major polls, making it two years running for 'Lady Soul'.

'See Saw' was No 11 for one week, and 'My Song' No 31 for one week in the U.S.A. The titles were respectively, 14 and 7 weeks in the U.S.A. bestsellers.

MARVIN GAYE
I HEARD IT THROUGH THE GRAPEVINE *Tamla* [*USA*]. A million seller for the second time for this song, written in 1967 by Norman Whitfield and B. Strong and a hit then for Gladys Knight and The Pips. This version was No 1 in the U.S.A. for seven weeks and 15 weeks in the bestsellers, and sold over three million, by early 1969. The disc was released on 9 November, and Marvin's recording has striking vocals and percussion – a brilliant production job. It was also one of the top rhythm-and-blues numbers of the year (No 1 for seven weeks) and Tamla Motown's biggest hit.

This disc was also No 1 in Britain in 1969 for three weeks where it was released on 7 February, and 15 weeks in the bestsellers.

Marvin Gaye, born in 1939 in Washington, DC, was the son of a church minister. He grew up in the Capital, made his debut as a solo vocalist at the age of three and later both sang and played organ in church every Sunday. He continued singing religious music until his early teens, and in high school used his talents in popular music as vocalist-pianist-guitarist-drummer with the school orchestra.

His first break came when he was with a group of singers on tour called The Moonglows. He was playing at a party in Detroit where he was heard by Tamla-Motown president Berry Gordy, Jr. who persuaded Marvin to become a solo performer and signed him to a long-term contract. His first disc hit was 'Stubborn Kind of Fella' (1962) followed by 'Pride and Joy', 'Hitch Hike' and 'Can I Get a Witness'. These successes led to personal appearances in Brooklyn, San Francisco, Harlem and Chicago. In 1964 he made his first visit to Britain to promote his disc 'How Sweet It Is'. He later teamed up with Kim Weston. Marvin

became better known to the British public from 1965 onwards when the Tamla-Motown label was launched there.

Marvin Gaye was one of the pioneers of the Motown sound. He was a gifted composer and a versatile artist who could sing any type of song from ballad to rock 'n' roll, and also an accomplished musician.

He died after being shot by his father on his 45th birthday, 1 April 1984, in Los Angeles.

BOBBY GOLDSBORO
HONEY *United Artists* [*USA*]. 'Honey' written by Bobby Russell and issued in March 1968, proved to be Bobby Goldsboro's biggest hit so far. It sold its first million in just over three weeks and subsequently went over the three million mark. It sold over 250,000 in Britain where it was No 2 for three weeks and 15 weeks in the bestsellers. In the U.S.A. it achieved No 1 for five weeks and 15 weeks in the bestsellers, and was United Artists' fastest-selling singles disc. A Gold Disc was awarded by R.I.A.A. in April.

The song, a ballad of lovers' remembrances, has poignant lyrics and tune which accounted for the disc's tremendous popularity, aided by an outstanding arrangement by Don Tweety, plus Bobby Goldsboro's sensitive performance.

THE GRASSROOTS (vocal and instrumental quartet)
MIDNIGHT CONFESSIONS *Dunhill* [*USA*]. This disc was No 3 for a week and stayed in the U.S.A. charts for 18 weeks, subsequently amassing a million sale by early December plus R.I.A.A. Gold Disc award. It was released in August. The song was written by Lou Josie, arranged by Jimmy Haskell.

The group's first hit was 'Let's Live for Today' (No 3 in the U.S.A.), a former hit for the Italian group The Rokes (see 1967).

RICHARD HARRIS
MacARTHUR PARK *Dunhill* [*USA*]. Richard Harris was born on 1 October 1933 in Limerick, Ireland and attended the Royal Academy of Dramatic Art, London. He first became known to the public for his great performance in *This Sporting Life* which earned him an Academy Award nomination, and appeared in other films – *The Red Desert*, *Hawaii*, *Mutiny on the Bounty*, *The Guns of Navarone* and the star role as King Arthur in the film version of *Camelot* (1967).

At 23, he won a role in the play *The Quare Fellow* and then appeared in Arthur Miller's *A View from the Bridge*. A tour in Russia and Eastern Europe with *The Iron Harp* led to his contract with Associated British Pictures and his career in the movies was under way.

In January 1968, American songwriter Jim Webb came to Britain to record an entire album of his songs all sung by Harris entitled 'A Tramp Shining' which included 'MacArthur Park', a complex extravaganza and remembrance of springs past. When issued as a single, the disc, now considered a classic, swept up the U.S.A. charts and was No 2 for four weeks with 13 weeks in the bestsellers, selling over a million. In Britain it reached No 4 for two weeks and 12 weeks in the bestsellers. The record achieved a dramatic breakthrough in that it extends for over seven minutes as against the normal three for most singles. MacArthur Park does exist – at the end of Wilshire Boulevard in Los Angeles. Harris first met composer Jim Webb (then aged 21) in California in early 1967, where he was presenting a charity show. Johnny Rivers introduced Webb to Harris who asked the young composer to write some songs for him. Webb's first big hit was the multi-award-winning 'Up, Up and Away' (six Grammy Awards 1967), then 'By the Time I Get to Phoenix' (three Grammy Awards 1967). His lyrical presentation, complicated music scoring and mastery of the 'big orchestra' sound brought him acclaim as the greatest young pop composer in the world. The album 'A Tramp Shining' was also a bit hit, selling over 600,000 in its first three months on the U.S.A. market.

'MacArthur Park' was awarded a Grammy for Best Arrangement Accompanying Vocalist(s) of 1968.

HEINTJE (boy vocalist)

HEINTJE (album) *Ariola* [*Germany*]. Heintje's first album, which included his big first hit 'Mama', 'Ich bau dir ein Schloss' and 12 other songs, was a fantastic success for the singing youngster from Holland. It sold 1,250,000 in its first year on the market, probably a record for Germany. 68,000 were sold in Switzerland, a phenomenal figure for that country where sales of 6,000 are considered excellent. Total sales were over two million by 1970 when Heintje was presented with a platinum disc award. His disc sales 1968–1969 totalled over 10 million.

DU SOLLST NICHT WEINEN (You shouldn't cry) *Ariola* [*Germany*]. Boy-wonder Heintje's second million seller was released in Germany in May 1968 and was No 1 there for 11 weeks, staying in the top ten for over eight months (36 weeks). The disc also sold over 90,000 in Switzerland, a figure seldom if ever reached for a single there. It was additionally a big seller in Denmark in 1969.

The song is based on the famous Mexican air 'La Golondrina' (The Swallow) composed many years ago by Narciso Serradell, with new German lyrics. Backing of the disc: 'Ich bau dir ein Schloss'.

HEIDSCHI BUMBEIDSCHI *Ariola* [*Germany*] *CNR* [*Holland*]. Third million seller in a row for Heintje, released in Germany in October 1968. By mid-January 1969 it had sold over 800,000 and soon easily achieved the million. The disc was an immediate No 1 in Germany and for 16 weeks, the most for any in that country, staying in their top ten for over six months. It was also No 1 for four weeks in Holland and a hit in Denmark (1969).

'Heidschi Bumbeidschi' is based on an old German folk song, the title of which is untranslatable into English. This new version had new German lyrics.

By the end of 1968, Heintje was the most successful artist ever to have hit Germany, and his discs accounted for around 20 per cent of the country's total record sales at that time. By 1969 he had been awarded 12 Gold Discs in Germany, and a total of 27 by mid-1970 from various countries. Backing of the disc 'Ich sing ein lied fur dich'.

WEIHNACHTEN MIT HEINTJE (Christmas with Heintje) (album) *Ariola* [*Germany*]. Another colossal seller for Holland's boy wonder. This album of songs for Christmas had an initial pressing of one million in Germany and was soon completely sold out. Swiss advance orders were 20,000, a large amount for that country. Heintje sold around two million of his already released albums, the biggest Christmas sales ever for Ariola label.

MARY HOPKIN

THOSE WERE THE DAYS *Apple* [*Britain*]. The melody for this song is based on a Russian folk song 'Darogoi Dlimmoyo' (Dear for me), the first known recording of the original made in the 1920s by Alexander Wertinsky.

Another known recording was made in 1958 in Finland by Mrs Annikki Tahtiand, and the song was also recorded in 1966 by Finnish singer Martti Caram in tango rhythm. It was American composer and nightclub performer Gene Raskin who wrote the popular version in 1962 and it was first recorded by The Limeliters folk group in 1963.

Mary Hopkin was born in Pontardawe, Wales on 3 May 1950, daughter of the housing officer there. Mary began singing at the age of four and later took singing lessons every Saturday. She got engagements at working men's clubs and elsewhere from a local agent for around £6 ($15) per show and in 1968 appeared in the TV show 'Opportunity Knocks'. It was model Twiggy who told Beatle Paul MacCartney in Liverpool about Mary's performance and, when Paul returned to London, several others mentioned her. At this time Apple Records were looking for singers, and

Paul phoned her and asked her to come to London. Paul remembered Gene Raskin and his wife Francesca singing 'Those Were the Days' in the Blue Angel in London around 1966. A demo of the song was obtained from America by the English publishers and Mary recorded the song. The disc was released on 30 August along with three other discs (including The Beatles' 'Hey Jude') and gave the new Apple Records a second huge hit. In four weeks it sold 360,000 and around 750,000 in three months. In the U.S.A. the disc was issued in September and sold a million in two months with R.I.A.A. Gold Disc award. The disc became a No 1 all round the world and by year's end had sold over five million. It was No 1 for six weeks in Britain with 21 weeks in the bestsellers, and No 1 for four weeks in U.S.A. with 14 weeks in the bestsellers. Mary Hopkin gave the haunting, Mediterranean-style café song a gentle, swaying, lyrical performance. She sings in a high, clear soprano reminiscent of Joan Baez.

'Those Were the Days' is regarded as Mary's first single, but this is not correct. She made her first recording for a small independent label in Wales - Cambrian - but in her own language, Welsh. She also sang folk songs on Welsh TV programmes before her big disc success.

The tremendous success of Mary's disc was a unique feat for a British girl only 18 years of age.

By February 1969 the cumulative sales of this song in Mary Hopkin's recordings in English, French, German, Italian, Spanish and Hebrew topped the eight million mark. Of this figure U.S.A. sales were over 1,500,000.

THE INTRUDERS (rhythm-and-blues quartet)

COWBOYS TO GIRLS *Gamble* [*USA*]. First million seller for this group and for the Gamble label. The disc was issued in March 1968 and was awarded an R.I.A.A. Gold Disc for million sale in mid-May. It reached No 5 for one week with 14 weeks in the U.S.A. bestsellers. Release in Britain was on the Ember label.

The group consists of: Sam (Little Sonny) Brown (lead singer); Eugene Daughtry; Robert Edwards; Phillip Terry. All come from Philadelphia.

Song was written by K. Gamble and L. Huff (producer of the disc).

IRON BUTTERFLY (vocal and instrumental quartet)

IN-A-GADDA-DA-VIDA (album) *Atco* [*USA*]. Released in July 1968 in the U.S.A., this became the biggest selling album in the history of Atlantic-Atco Records, selling over three million by the end of 1970, and staying in the Top Ten for twelve months. It achieved No 4 for two weeks in November 1968. It was in the charts for 140 weeks. A Gold Disc was awarded by R.I.A.A. in December 1968.

The Iron Butterfly consists of: Doug Ingle (group leader and lead vocalist), composer of most of the group's numbers, born 1947; Ron Bushby (drums) born 1946; Lee Dorman (bass guitar) born 1946; Erik Keith Brann (lead guitar) born 1951.

Ingle, who spent most of his spare time composing, had played the organ for two years. Bushby had been drumming since school days and travelled considerably throughout the U.S.A. with his Army-career father. Dorman, who also played drums and piano, was the group's comedian. Brann was also a versatile performer, and also played violin and drums. He studied voice before he was a teenager. The group, noted for their incredible blending of light, airy sounds with a 'heavy' blues blend, broke into the charts with their first album 'Heavy', but it was 'In-A-Gadda-Da-Vida' that established them as a leading act in the U.S.A. The album includes the tune of the same title, which is a 17-minute composition that became a show-case for the group on its personal appearances. This, together with a contracted version of the work that was a hit single in 1968, greatly increased their following. They performed with The Cream and others in the film *Savage Seven* and Ingle wrote The Iron Butterfly's first Atco single 'Possession' backed with 'Unconscious Power' for this movie.

Contents of the album: 'Most Anything You Want', by Doug Ingle; 'Flowers and Beads', by Doug Ingle; 'My Mirage', by Doug Ingle; 'Termination', by Eric Brann and Lee Dorman; 'Are You Happy?' by Doug Ingle; 'In-A-Gadda-Da-Vida', by Doug Ingle.

A top disc of 1969 in the U.S.A. Release in Britain was in 1968 on the Atlantic label.

TOMMY JAMES AND THE SHONDELLS

MONY MONY *Roulette* [*USA*]. A throbbing rock recording with tremendous percussion accenting and group chanting, written by B. Bloom, Tommy James (of the group), Ritchie Cordell and Bo Gentry (producers of the disc). Released in March 1968, the disc was No 3 for two weeks in the U.S.A. and 17 weeks in the bestsellers, and a big hit in Britain where it was No 1 for five weeks (on Major Minor label) and 18 weeks in the bestsellers, with over 250,0000 sale.

Tommy James and Ritchie Cordell got the title for the song when they were writing one night. Outside the apartment was a sign that said 'Mutual of New York' which when lit up spelled MONY.

The personnel for this disc was Ronnie Rosman, Mike Vale, Tommy James, Peter Lucia and Eddie Gray.

Global sale was over 1,500,000.

CRIMSON AND CLOVER *Roulette* [*USA*]. This teen-type ballad with a strong finish, written by P. Lucia and Tommy James (of the group) was issued in early December 1968. It sold 700,000 in its first four weeks and over $2\frac{1}{2}$ million by mid-June 1969, Roulette's biggest seller. The disc was No 1 for two weeks in the U.S.A. charts with 16 weeks in the bestsellers, and another triumph for Tommy James and The Shondells, their fifth million seller. Global sale totalled 4 million.

JAY AND THE AMERICANS

THIS MAGIC MOMENT *United Artists* [*USA*]. This group was formed in the autumn of 1961 and made its first recording in 1962 with 'She Cried' which achieved No 5 in the charts, followed by other charts hits 'Only in America', 'Let's Lock the Door and Throw Away the Key' and 'Think of the Good Times'. In 1965 their disc of the British song 'Cara Mia' got to No 4 and was also instrumental in making a name for the group with this updated version in Britain.

The group worked steadily in and around New York for some time before discovering a new and different sound, then got an audition and a recording contract with United Artists. Eventually

they played at college concerts and rapidly developed a flair for comedy. Their interests became extended with music publishing, management, commercials and record production. Up to 1969 they had made two concert tours of Europe and travelled throughout America for engagements in every entertainment medium. They all come from Brooklyn.

Jay and The Americans were a quintet in 1965, comprising: Jay Black (lead singer) born 2 November 1941, originally a show salesman; Kenny Vance born 9 December 1943; Sandy Deane (real name Sandy Yaguda) born 30 January 1943; Marty Sanders born 28 February 1941; Howie Kane born 6 June 1942, a licensed mortician.

'This Magic Moment' was originally a hit for The Drifters in 1960, written by Doc Pomus and Mort Shuman. Jay and the The Americans' disc was released in November 1968 and reached No 4 for two weeks in the U.S.A. with 14 weeks in the bestsellers, and the certified million sale in early 1969 with R.I.A.A. Gold Disc award (16 May). The group for this disc was a quartet and excluded Howie Kane.

TOM JONES

DELILAH *Decca* [*Britain*]. This song, written by the enormously successful British composers Les Reed and Barry Mason, is probably Tom Jones' biggest disc success to date. Released on 23 February 1968, it sold well over half a million in Britain, and was No 2 for three weeks with 17 weeks in the bestsellers. It was a fantastic success abroad – No 1 in France, Israel, Switzerland, Germany (14 weeks), South Africa, Belgium, Eire, Spain and Finland, with big sales in the U.S.A. (Parrot label) where it achieved No 15 chart position with 14 weeks in the bestsellers. Global sales totalled five million.

The song has a catchy melody with a good story lyrically, a sparkling big-sounding backing devised by Les Reed, plus Tom Jones' fiery vocal packed with excitement and emotion.

Tom Jones was signed to a contract in June guaranteeing him a minimum of £9 million over the following three years, thus making him Britain's highest paid entertainer and the first British artist to have his own American TV series – 17 hour-long British-made shows screened in the States, in Britain and throughout the world.

By the end of the year there were 380 cover versions of the song.

FEVER ZONE (album) *Decca* [*Britain*] *Parrot* [*USA*]. Released in the U.S.A. in May 1968, this album sold the million by the end of 1970. A Gold Disc was awarded by R.I.A.A. in May 1969.

The album contained: 'Don't Fight It', by Wilson Pickett and Stephen Cropper (1965); 'You Keep Me Hanging On', by B. Holland, E. Holland and Lamont Dozier (1966); 'Hold on, I'm Coming', by David Porter and Isaac Hayes (1966); 'I Was Made to Love Her', by H. Crosby, S. Moy, L. Hardaway and Stevie Wonder (1967); 'Keep on Running', by Jackie Edwards (1965); 'Get Ready', by Smokey Robinson (1966); 'Delilah', by Les Reed and Barry Mason (1968); 'I Know', by Barbara George (1961); 'I Wake Up Crying', by Hal David and Burt Bacharach (1964); 'Funny How Time Slips Away', by Willie Nelson (1961); 'Danny Boy', by F.E. Weatherly (1913), arr. Blackwell (tune 'Londonderry Air'); 'It's a Man's Man's World', by James Brown (1966).

The British release was titled '13 Smash Hits' and included 'I'll Never Fall in Love Again', by Lonnie Donegan and Jim Currie (1967); 'Yesterday', by John Lennon and Paul McCartney (1965); plus all the songs on 'Fever Zone' except 'Delilah'.

Date of British release was December 1967 where the disc was No 4 for two weeks and in the bestsellers for 42 weeks. In the U.S.A. it was No 14 in 1969 for one week, but was a consistent seller for 82 weeks into 1970 by which time Tom Jones had became an international star, with several albums and singles becoming big hits in the U.S.A. after his 1969 tour there where he broke box office records wherever he performed. He was named Entertainer of the Year (1970) and voted World's No 1 Male Vocalist (1970) by a *Playboy* international poll.

GLADYS KNIGHT AND THE PIPS

THE END OF OUR ROAD *Soul* [*USA*]. The third million seller for this group, the song written by N. Whitfield, B. Strong and Roger Penzabene. The disc reached No 11 in the U.S.A. with 10 weeks in the bestsellers. The song is performed with a torrid vocal and pressure-packed instrumental lines. Released 10 February 1968.

LEAPY LEE (pop vocalist)

LITTLE ARROWS *MCA* [*Britain*]. Leapy Lee (real name Lee Graham) was born 2 July 1942 in Eastbourne, Sussex, England and educated there. He became active in school amateur dramatics and later formed his own rock group. At 15 he left school, and after working for a year in a factory, the group became professional. Leapy's career became highly diversified. He acted, was an entertainment manager, antique dealer, songwriter and singer. He made his TV debut in 'State Your Case', was one year at the London Palladium in *Large as Life* (1958), a few days in *Johnnie the Priest* at the Prince's Theatre and five weeks in Joan Littlewood's *Sparrows Can't Sing*. He also started a bingo hall in Shepherd's Bush, London.

In 1968 he found the song 'Little Arrows' written by Albert Hammond and Mike Hazlewood and recorded it for the new MCA label. It reached No 2 in Britain's charts for two weeks with 21 weeks in the bestsellers and was No 12 in the U.S.A. for two weeks with 14 weeks in the bestsellers (Decca label), with a combined global sale of three million.

The origin of the stage name: 'I was always a leaper.' Leapy also plays guitar and banjo.

The success of this disc resulted in American, Australian, South Africa and Continental tours.

The disc was released in August 1968 in Britain.

MANFRED MANN AND THE MANFREDS

MIGHTY QUINN (Quinn the Eskimo) *Fontana* [*Britain*]. Released on 19 April 1968, this disc was No 1 for two weeks in Britain and 11 weeks in the bestsellers with an over 250,000 sale and also a hit in the U.S.A. (Mercury label) where it reached No 4 with 11 weeks in the bestsellers. A fine rhythmic version of a Bob Dylan composition, a writer much favoured by the group who recorded many of his songs. It was also a huge hit in Germany, a No 1 there, and global sales totalled two million.

The group included singer Mike D'Abo (born 1 March 1944 in Bletchworth, Surrey) who replaced Paul Jones in 1969 when Paul became a solo artist, and Klaus Voormann who replaced Mike Vickers. (Picture shows original line-up.)

Other countries in which the disc was No 1 were Singapore, Sweden and Denmark.

THE MARMALADE (pop vocal and instrumental quintet)

OB-LA-DI, OB-LA-DA *CBS* [*Britain*]. Written by John Lennon and Paul McCartney, this West Indian-type number with an infectious melody and rhythm was first recorded by them on their double album 'The Beatles'. This outstanding recording by The Marmalade sold around half a million or more in Britain and the million globally by April 1969. It was released in Britain in November 1968.

The group were originally called The Gaylords and were exceedingly popular in Scotland where they were voted No 1

group from 1964 to 1966. They then decided to cross the border to England and appeared at the Windsor Jazz Festival in 1967 and all but stole the show on their night. This resulted in a regular Thursday night residency at London's Marquee Club, where other British groups such as Manfred Mann, The Yardbirds, The Traffic, Spencer Davis, The Herd, The Rolling Stones and The Animals acquired fame. Important engagements abroad included Holland. Their first disc success was 'Lovin' Things', No 6 in Britain in 1968, followed by 'Ob-la di, Ob-la-da' (No 1 for three weeks and 20 weeks in the bestsellers).

The personnel of the Marmalade: Alan Whitehead (drums) born 24 July 1946, originally a work-study trainee; Graham Knight (bass guitar) born 8 December 1946; Junior Wullie Campbell (guitar, piano, drums) born 31 May 1947, originally a plasterer; Patrick Fairley (six-string bass and rhythm guitar) born 14 April 1946, originally an industrial chemist; Dean Ford (real name Thomas McAleese) (lead vocalist, guitar, harmonica) born 5 September 1946, originally an office worker and apprentice plater.

HUGH MASEKELA (trumpet)

GRAZING IN THE GRASS *Uni* [*USA*]. Hugh Masekela is the son of a famous sculptor and was born in Witbank, Johannesburg, South Africa in 1939. He was raised by his grandmother until he was old enough to attend school. At the age of 13 he saw the film *Young Man with a Horn* which gave direction to his future. The school headmaster got him a trumpet and after a few months he began playing in the clubs and streets of Johannesburg, later travelled the country with a band, and eventually fled from the South African apartheid repressions. He won a scholarship to study at London's Royal Academy of Music and Guild Hall School, then went to the U.S.A. to study at the Manhattan School of Music. It was there he met Harry Belafonte who was impressed with his talent and sponsored him in America. Hugh worked in various New York clubs during his four years of study and in 1966 formed Chisa Records, his product later being released on the Uni label.

Hugh is described as an extremely exciting performer, his style a combination of traditional South African and contemporary pop, while his vocal numbers are mostly South African. He is usually assisted in his playing by a tenor/soprano sax, pianist, drummer and bass.

'Grazing in the Grass' was written by Philemon Hou and achieved No 1 in the U.S.A. charts for three weeks with 12 weeks in the bestsellers, with R.I.A.A. Gold Disc award for a million sale in July 1968 within three months of release.

Masekela was a sensational success on 15 June 1968 at New York's Carnegie Hall where he played to a packed house.

JUN MAYUZUMI (vocalist)

TENSHI NO YUWAKU *Toshiba* [*Japan*]. Written by Rei Nakanishi (words) and Kunihiko Suzuki (music) this disc was released through Toshiba Records (Japan) in May 1968. It was No 2 for two weeks in Japan and by year's end sold 1,700,000, with a 16 weeks' stay in their charts. The recording was awarded the Japan Gold Disc Prize of 1968.

Jun Mayuzumi was one of Japan's top female disc stars of the year.

THE MONKEES

VALLERI backed with TAPIOCA TUNDRA *Colgems* [*USA*]. The sixth million selling single for The Monkees, reaching the sale within three days of release in early March plus an immediate Gold Disc award from R.I.A.A. The song was written by ace American writers Tommy Boyce and Bobby Hart. The backing, also a sizeable hit, was the composition of the group's Mike Nesmith.

'Valleri' is a snappy up-tempo number in rock style with considerable teenage appeal, while 'Tapioca Tundra' is a fantasy number. The disc was No 1 for two weeks in the U.S.A. with 10 weeks in the bestsellers, and achieved No 12 for two weeks and was in the bestsellers for eight weeks in Britain where it was released on 22 March.

This disc marked the tenth Gold Disc for the Monkees in 18 months including the four for albums.

HUGO MONTENEGRO AND HIS ORCHESTRA AND CHORUS

THE GOOD, THE BAD AND THE UGLY *Victor* [*USA*]. Hugo Montenegro's disc of the fine theme from the Italian-made Western film of the same title ('Il buono, Il brutto, Il cattio') was an outstanding instrumental recording, reaching No 2 for one week in the U.S.A. and a consistent seller chartwise for 22 weeks. It sold a million there and over 250,000 in Britain where it was No 1 for four weeks and 24 weeks in the bestsellers. The tune was composed by Ennio Morricone. The disc was released in the U.S.A. in March and later in the year in Britain (RCA label). It was the first time in many years that an instrumental disc had topped Britain's charts.

Hugo Montenegro was born in 1925 and raised in New York City where he attended city schools. After two years in the U.S. Navy he graduated from Manhattan College. His arranging for Service bands was but a stepping stone to later success. He moved to California with his family and wrote and conducted the scores for Otto Preminger's *Hurry Sundown*, and *The Ambushers* (1967). From 1955, Hugo spent 13 years in the record industry making good music albums without ever having a hit. He had also been staff manager to André Kostalanetz and arranger conductor for Harry Belafonte. His first album for Victor was 'Music from The Man From U.N.C.L.E.'.

It was on what was to be his last RCA project that he decided to develop a different sound and use different colours. He got ten records his children had bought and listened for how to utilize

electric guitars and what the contemporary drum patterns were. Hitherto he had used sweeping strings and a sweet sound. It was the introduction that made 'The Good, the Bad and the Ugly' a hit, the use of an ocarina. Together with underlying Indian and Western sounds plus chorus, the disc caused a big stir, and Hugo Montenegro was greatly in demand for films.

This disc is a striking example of his writing, arranging and orchestral sound. He did in fact bring so-called background music very much to the foreground. Montenegro's disc made use of unusual instruments including an electric violin developed by Elliot Fisher and the only one then in existence, the piccolo trumpet (played by Manny Klein), and an electronic harmonica (played by Tommy Morgan). The ocarina, also known as the 'sweet potato', was played by Arthur Smith, a vocal group was led by and featured Ron Hicklin, and Muzzy Marcellino (whose whistling helped make 'The High and the Mighty' a hit) also performed on the record. 'Italian grunts' were added to the effect, these being just nonsense Italian syllables chanted out by Montenegro.

THE 1910 FRUITGUM COMPANY

SIMON SAYS *Buddah* [*USA*]. An old children's play song 'Simon Says' was the inspiration for this disc debut by this group with its extraordinary name.

The group consists of: Floyd Marcus (drums) born 1949; Pat Karwan (lead guitar) born 1949; Mark Gutkowski (organ) born 1950; Steve Mortkowitz (bass guitar) born 1949; Frank Jeckell (rhythm guitar) born 1947.

The quintet, all from Lynden, New Jersey, went to the same high school and formed the group in January 1967 and played under number of names including Jeckell and Hyde, The Odyssey, and The Lower Road. It was Frank Jeckell who coined the name 1910 Fruitgum Company after discovering an old bubble gum wrapper while going through a trunk in an attic.

'Simon Says', written by Elliot Chiprut, is a teenage 'bop' type of number, the arrangement being a collaboration between the group and their disc producers. It was issued in early January 1968 and sold a million by March with R.I.A.A. Gold Disc award. In the U.S.A. the disc was No 1 for one week with 14 weeks in the bestsellers, and in Britain No 2 for two weeks and 16 weeks in the bestsellers with over the 250,000 sale. It also sold a million in Canada, the global sales totalling around 3½ million. Released in Britain on Pye International, 3 May 1968.

Each member of the group shares the lead vocal spot on

different numbers. In April 1968, Bruce Shaw and Dave Peck replaced Marcus and Mortkowitz.

This disc sparked a trend for what became known as 'bubble-gum music' in the U.S.A., created for the sub-teenagers, the formula being set by actor and rock 'n' roll singer Neil Bogart, general manager of the newly-formed Buddah label in 1967. The label's sales were almost $6 million in its first year.

1. 2. 3. RED LIGHT *Buddah* [*USA*]. Second million seller for The 1910 Fruitgum Company, the song written by S. Trimachi and Bobbi Trimachi. The disc was released in the U.S.A. in July 1968 and achieved No 3 chart position for three weeks with 13 weeks in the bestsellers, with Gold Disc award from R.I.A.A. in October. The song, like the group's first hit, has a carefree children's-game motif, with lover's lyrics and hefty dance rhythm.

CLIFF NOBLES & CO

THE HORSE *Phil-LA of Soul* [*USA*]. A unique instrumental disc, due to a combination of funky rhythms, emanating a feeling of wanting to move with it. It was written by Jesse James who also produced the disc, and arranged by Bobby Martin. The song is unusual in the way it was put together, although no unusual instruments are used, the instruments being two bass guitars, drums, piano, baritone sax, tenor sax, three trumpets and trombone.

A new dance was fashioned around 'The Horse', and the disc was played on all types of stations.

The disc was No 2 for three weeks in the U.S.A. with 14 weeks in the bestsellers, and sold the million within three months of release plus Gold Disc award from R.I.A.A. in August 1968. Nobles was born in Mobile, Alabama in 1944.

ESTHER AND ABI OFARIM (vocal duo)

CINDERELLA ROCKEFELLA *Philips* [*Britain*]. Esther and Abi Ofarim first met when Esther was a student in Abi's dance studio in Haifa, Israel. Esther served four months in the Israeli Army and was released on her marriage to Abi. They started singing at home for fun and then decided to try to make it as a duo in Israel. Their first album (1961) went to No 1 and the same year, Frank Sinatra, who was touring the Orient doing shows for youth relief, chose Esther to perform in his Israeli concerts. She then did other dates with Sinatra in Europe. The Ofarims settled in Geneva. Esther won a prize in a festival in Poland (1961) and she represented Switzerland in the 1963 Eurovision Contest in London, was announced the winner but was deposed when a

judging mistake was discovered. The recorded version of her contest song, however, attained international popularity. In 1964, Esther won the Dutch prize at the Grand Gala du Disque and a top award came for the duo in Rome (1967). By this time, the duo had received Gold Disc awards for their albums 'Songs of the World', 'New Songs of the World' and 'Noch einen Tanz'. The same year they had completed a new album titled '2 in 3', produced by them in London, Paris and Munich which consisted of 13 songs in eight languages. The initial pressing was 100,000, then a record for Germany, with an eventual Gold Disc award. This album included 'Cinderella Rockefella', a nonsense song written in a somewhat 1920s style by Mason Williams and Nancy Ames of the U.S.A. in 1966. Williams, writer for The Smothers Brothers TV show in the U.S.A., was a personal friend of the singers. In December 1967, the duo appeared on the Eamonn Andrews Show on TV in Britain when they introduced the song. It was the start of their success in Britain and Philips Records were inundated with inquiries for the song and decided to issue it as a single (9 February 1968). In six weeks it sold a million and was No 1 for four weeks with 13 weeks in the bestsellers, and No 1 in Holland and Sweden. In the U.S.A. the disc was No 68 and 6 weeks in the bestsellers.

The Ofarims appeared on 170 TV shows around the world in three years. Apart from their native Hebrew they spoke fluent English, French and German. They had been singing together since 1960.

Esther Ofarim (real name Esther Zaled) was born 13 June 1943 in Safed, Israel and educated in Haifa. Abi Ofarim (real name Abraham Reichstadt) born 5 October 1939 in Tel Aviv, Israel and educated there, studied dancing and music.

Their music mainly revolves around updating folk music to make it more commercial. Many countries have claimed Esther as their own top singing star, but she is really international.

THE OHIO EXPRESS (vocal and instrumental quintet)

YUMMY, YUMMY, YUMMY *Buddah* [*USA*]. The Ohio Express consists of: Douglas Grassel (rhythm guitar) born 1949; Dale Powers (lead guitar) born 1948; Jim Pfahler (organ) born 1948; Tim Corwin (drums) born 1949; Dean Kastran (bass guitar) born 1949.

The group was formed in 1965 in Mansfield, Ohio, and was brought to the attention of Super K Productions' Jerry Kasenetz and Jeff Katz by Jamie Lyons, lead singer of the Music Explosion who also lives in Mansfield. Katz and Kasenetz gave the group a recording session during which they cut 'Beg, Borrow and Steal' (1967) which was a sizeable hit. They then made their first big public appearance opposite The Beach Boys in Cleveland and were a huge success with an audience of over 10,000 teenagers. 'Yummy, Yummy, Yummy', written by K. Resnick and J. Levine, was first played over WMCA-New York station. After two months it sold a million and was awarded a Gold Disc by R.I.A.A. in June.

It was No 4 for three weeks in the U.S.A. with 14 weeks in the bestsellers, and No 4 for two weeks in Britain with 15 weeks in the bestsellers.

Dean, Jim and Dale wrote most of the group's material, Jim doing the quintet's arrangement. Dale performed most of the singing with Jim occasionally joining in. Tim, Dean and Jim added the background harmony.

Released in Britain 17 May 1968 on Pye International label.

The disc was another big success for the new Buddah label and the subteen 'bubble-gum music' market. (See '1910 Fruitgum Company'.)

CHEWY CHEWY *Buddah* [*USA*]. Second million seller for The Ohio Express, again written by J. Levine and K. Resnick. Released in October, it sold 875,000 in two months and finally went on to seven-figure sale. The disc was another big hit on the 'bubble-gum music' market, and reached No 8 for one week in the U.S.A. charts and 13 weeks in the bestsellers.

R.I.A.A. Gold Disc award March 1969.

THE O'KAYSIONS (vocal and instrumental sextet)

GIRL WATCHER *ABC* [*USA*]. This group comprised: Donnie Weaver (lead vocals and organ); Wayne Pittman (lead guitar); Jim Hinnant (bass); Bruce Joyner (drums); Ronnie Turner (trumpet); Jim Speidel (saxophone).

The song was written by Pittman with B. Traill. Weaver and Hinnant started playing together in 1963, and although they knew all the other members of the group they only got together in the latter part of 1967. They wrote their own music in order to be part of the permanent rock scene.

'Girl Watcher' was No 4 for two weeks in the U.S.A. It was released in mid-August and received Gold Disc award for a million sale from R.I.A.A. in December. The disc stayed in the charts for 15 weeks.

PEPPERMINT RAINBOW

WILL YOU BE STAYING AFTER SUNDAY? *Decca* [*USA*]. Written by A. Kasha and J. Hirschhorn and arranged by Paul Leka who also produced the disc, which was released in December 1968 with reported million sale in 1969. The disc was No 20 for two weeks in the U.S.A. and stayed in the bestseller charts for 20 weeks.

PINKY AND THE KILLERS

KOI NO KISETSU *King* [*Japan*]. This group received an award as The Most Promising New Group in Japan of 1968. Their disc first entered the Japanese charts in September 1968 and stayed there right up to March 1969, holding the No 1 position for 17 weeks. It is estimated to have sold well over the million.

PATTY PRAVO

LA BAMBOLA *RCA* [*Italy*]. Released in May, Patty's disc was No 1 for nine weeks of its 20 weeks' stay in the Italian charts. It sold well over the half-million in four months and achieved the million by the end of the year.

Patty Pravo, born in 1948, made her debut in 1965 when she was 17 at Rome's Piper Club as vocalist with a band. She was discovered there by an RCA Italiana talent scout and signed to a long-term agreement in 1967. Her first disc 'Ragazzo Triste' (Sad Boy) brought her much popularity and appearances in song contests. Patty is a native of Venice.

ELVIS PRESLEY

IF I CAN DREAM *RCA* [*USA*]. Released in November 1968, this disc reached the million sale by the end of 1969. The song, written by W. Earl Brown, is a ballad with a message lyric – a plea for 'peace and understanding'. In the U.S.A. it was No 9 for a week with 13 weeks in the bestsellers, and in Britain No 11 for two weeks with 10 weeks in the bestsellers. This made million seller No 62 for Elvis.

THE RASCALS (originally The Young Rascals)

A BEAUTIFUL MORNING *Atlantic* [*USA*]. Written by Felix Cavaliere and Eddie Brigati of the group, this disc was released in the beginning of April 1968 and sold a million by July with gold disc award from R.I.A.A. achieving the No 2 chart position in the U.S.A. for three weeks with 13 weeks in the U.S.A. bestsellers.

The group perform the number in a gentle soul, easy rock, chanting and dreamy manner.

PEOPLE GOT TO BE FREE *Atlantic* [*USA*]. Also written by Felix Cavaliere and Eddie Brigati of The Rascals, this disc achieved No 1 in the U.S.A. in a month from date of release in mid-July and stayed top for five weeks with 14 weeks in the bestsellers. By mid-September it had sold over 1,500,000 and was awarded a Gold Disc by R.I.A.A. in August 1968. The disc was released on Atlantic label in Britain on 16 August.

This is a freedom song with a fine message lyric and the disc is packed with Memphis orchestral sound and oustanding rhythm work. The group became a big box office attraction in this year.

OTIS REDDING (rhythm-and-blues vocalist)

(Sittin' on) THE DOCK OF THE BAY *Volt* [*USA*]. Otis Redding, born 9 September 1941 in Dawson, Georgina, was one of the best exponents of soul music – the American blend of blues, gospel and pop which began in the late 1940s via the dedicated pioneers of rhythm-and-blues discs, put out by Atlantic, Savoy, Chess, King, Specialty, Imperial and Modern labels with a flock of new labels in the early 1950s and over 40 by the mid-1960s. The pioneer labels filled a long-felt need due to the larger labels having practically abandoned the rhythm-and-blues field during World War Two. By 1967, the rhythm-and-blues field became one of the most exciting and lucrative in the disc industry.

Otis' family moved to Macon, Georgia while he was still young and he attended the high school there. The enormous success of Little Richard (also from Macon) decided Otis to embark on a singing career. He entered local talent contests and won most of them. Then Otis joined forces with Phil Walden, another high school student who had been booking a local band in his spare time. Walden recognized Redding's talent and became his manager, and Otis cut several discs for various labels including 'Shout Bamalama' for Sue label and 'Fat Girl' for Bethlehem (a subsidiary of the King label). He then became vocalist with Johnny Jenkins and The Pinetoppers, their disc 'Love Twist' becoming a regional success on the Atlantic label. The group became established favourites in Southern colleges and universities. More discs were cut and then the group were scheduled for a session in Memphis, Tennessee for the Volt label. After the session, Otis asked if he could cut a demo disc and in less than an hour recorded 'These Arms of Mine', a self-written song. When issued by Volt and distributed by Atlantic, it sold around 750,000 and Redding's career was on its way. His next disc 'Pain in My Heart' (1963) was later recorded by Britain's The Rolling Stones. Otis reciprocated with a hit recording of their song 'Satisfaction'. His best beat number was 'Respect' which he recorded in 1965 and was written by him. It earned a Gold Disc for Aretha

Franklin in 1967 and his 'Sweet Soul Music' (1967) a similar award for Arthur Conley.

Otis formed his own disc company Jotis Records and his own Redwal Music Publishing Co.

In 1967 he came to Britain with the famous 'Hit the Road Stax' tour (Stax-Volt artists) and was recognized in France as an historic figure in rhythm-and-blues. In Britain he was voted Top Music Singer of 1967. Otis also played several instruments including bass, drums, organ, piano and guitar, in addition to arranging, song writing and producing.

'The Dock of the Bay' was recorded on 7 December 1967. Three days later (10 December) his plane crashed into icy Lake Monona, Madison, Wisconsin, killing Otis, four members of his musical revue, his valet and the pilot. The sole survivor was Ben Cauley, also with The Redding Show.

The lyrics of 'Dock of the Bay' had a strangely ironic air of premonition and in a burst of discovery, the U.S.A. record-buying public made it up to Redding with an almost two-million sale of the disc which was No 1 for four weeks with 16 weeks in the bestsellers, and awarded a Gold Disc by R.I.A.A. in March 1968.

Atlantic Records Vice President, Jerry Wexler said, 'All this acclamation for Otis is new. It's his epitaph and proves that a singer can do his own thing and still be commercially successful. Otis is tremendously responsible for the fact that so much of the young white audience now digs soul the way the black does.' A great tribute to a great blues exponent.

The song was written by Steve Cropper (producer of the disc) and Otis Redding. The disc was No 3 in Britain for one week with 15 weeks in the bestsellers, and top rhythm-and-blues disc in the U.S.A. for three weeks, and Britain for eight weeks.

Released in Britain 9 February 1968 on the Stax label.

This disc also sold over 400,000 in Japan. It received two Grammy Awards for Best Rhythm-and-Blues Vocal Performance (Male) and Best Rhythm-and-Blues Song of 1968.

CLIFF RICHARD

CONGRATULATIONS *Columbia* [*Britain*]. The Eurovision Song Contest of 1968 in London was won by a Spanish song 'La La La' (sung by Massiel) by just one point over Britain's entry 'Congratulations' sung by Cliff Richard. It was, however, the latter which emerged as the biggest hit from the record-buying public's point of view, and Cliff's disc eventually sold a global million with a Gold Disc award, his fifth, on 22 June 1968. The disc was released on 13 March, and after the contest at the Royal Albert Hall (6 April) quickly became an international success. It was No 1 for two weeks in Britain with 13 weeks in the bestsellers, and No 1 also in Belgium, Denmark, Norway, Spain, Malaysia, Holland, Sweden and Singapore. In the U.S.A. the disc reached No 99. It was Cliff's first big hit since 1963.

The song was written by Bill Martin and Phil Coulter who won the 1967 Eurovision Contest with 'Puppet on a String' (see Sandie Shaw, 1967).

JEANNIE C. RILEY (country-and-western vocalist)

HARPER VALLEY P.T.A. *Plantation* [*USA*]. 'Judge not lest ye be judged' is the story line of this unique song. It tells of a widowed wife criticised by the Harper Valley Parent Teacher Association for her high skirts and low life in a note brought home by her teenage daughter. The mother attends a meeting of the P.T.A. and exposes the hypocritical behaviour of her accusers.

Jeannie C. Riley recorded the song on 26 July 1968 and it launched the new Plantation label for Shelby S. Singleton, Jr, who also produced the disc, in Nashville. It was the fastest starting single he'd ever had dealings with and sold 1,750,000 in two weeks after hitting the turntables when it became No 1, and stayed top for three weeks with a total of 13 weeks in the U.S.A. bestsellers. The song was written by her friend Tom T. Hall, son of a Kentucky minister. A former disc jockey, he progressed

into a top songwriter and entertainer.

Jeannie C. Riley, a 22-year-old girl from Anson, Texas (born there 19 October 1945), made this multi-market monster after having been in Nashville only a few months. Her only previous show business experience had been routine song-demo sessions for various Nashville firms. Her superb performance of the song resulted in the inevitable nation-wide round of TV shows and meeting disc jockeys, netting her $15,000 per night personal appearances and record royalties of around $150,000.

Sales in the U.S.A. were four million, a further million in Canada and big sales elsewhere, making an estimated tally of $5\frac{1}{2}$ million globally. A Gold Disc award was made by R.I.A.A. in August, four weeks after the disc's release. Release in Britain (Polydor label) was on 20 August, the disc reaching No 10 for one week with 15 weeks in the bestsellers.

The first artist to record this song was Alice Joy who toured with the Marty Robbins Show. Her disc was never released, but it was after hearing her version that Jeannie Riley decided to record the song. It earned Jeannie a Grammy Award for Best Country Vocal Performance (Female) of 1968.

HARPER VALLEY P.T.A. (album) *Plantation* [*USA*]. Jeannie C. Riley's phenomenal success with her single disc of this title sparked the inevitable follow-up of an album. This was released in the U.S.A. in September 1968 and reached No 6 for two weeks, with Gold Disc award from R.I.A.A. in December. It stayed in the bestsellers for 27 weeks but consistent sales throughout 1969 made it a million copy seller by the end of that year. In Britain, the album was released in 1968 on the Polydor label.

Contents of the album: 'Harper Valley P.T.A.', by Tom T. Hall; 'Widow Jones', by Tom T. Hall; 'No Brass Band', by Groah, Groah and Steve Singleton; 'Mr Harper', by Tom T. Hall; 'Run, Jeannie, Run', by Bentley and Clark; 'Shed Me No Tears', by Steve Singleton; 'Cotton Patch', by Smith and Lewis; 'Sippin' Shirley Thompson', by Tom T. Hall; 'Little Town Square', by Ben Peters; 'Ballad of Louise', by Naomi Martin; 'Satan Place', by Ben Peters and Bentley.

TOMMY ROE

DIZZY *ABC* [*USA*]. Described as an easy riding, medium-paced pop dance disc with soft sound and violins, Tommy's disc, released in December 1968, was No 1 for four weeks (1969) with 15 weeks in the bestsellers, and sold two million by mid-April 1969 with Gold Disc award from R.I.A.A.

1968

The song was written by Tommy Roe and F. Weller. 'Dizzy' was also a big hit in Britain where it was No 1 for two weeks, 19 weeks in the bestsellers.

THE ROLLING STONES

JUMPIN' JACK FLASH *Decca* [*Britain*]. Yet another big hit for The Rolling Stones, written by their prolific Mick Jagger and Keith Richard. It was released in Britain on 24 May and in the U.S.A. a week later (London label). The disc was No 1 for two weeks in Britain (with 11 weeks in the bestsellers) and one week in the U.S.A. (with 12 weeks in the bestsellers) and was a return to the group's famous blues-beat style, with terrific drive and great vocal work. A really exciting disc. Combined British-U.S.A. sales were over the million.

MERRILEE RUSH (vocal)

ANGEL OF THE MORNING *AGP* [*USA*] *distributed by Bell* [*USA*]. This disc was released in April 1968, reached No 3 for three weeks on the U.S.A. charts and was in the bestsellers for 16 weeks. The million sale was reported in 1970.

Merrilee Rush studied classical piano for ten years, and also played organ with her backing group The Turnabouts, a quartet of saxophone, drums, bass and guitar. They made numerous TV appearances together. All were managed by Paul Revere and The Raiders.

This disc was Merrilee's first single. The song was written by C. Taylor.

BARRY RYAN (pop vocalist)

ELOISE *MGM* [*Britain*]. Barry Ryan's recording of a song written by his twin brother Paul achieved No 1 in Britain for one week with 12 weeks in the bestsellers and was also No 1 in Holland, Italy, Austria, Belgium, Switzerland and Germany, with prominent chart positions in most other European countries and abroad. In the U.S.A. it reached No 50 for one week. The disc was released in Britain in October and by January 1969 had sold a global million, with over three million by April 1969.

Paul and Barry Ryan (real name Sapherson) are the twin sons of well-known British singer Marion Ryan and were born on 24 October 1948 in Leeds. It took the twins three years to persuade their mother to let them make a record. Their first was 'Don't Bring Me Your Heartaches' (October 1965) which was a success. They then made a nationwide tour, TV and radio appearances plus Continental TV and radio performances. They continued recording for Decca until 1968 when they were signed to MGM who also signed them to a £100,000 film contract. 'Eloise' was the first disc for MGM with Barry who had turned solo performer, brother Paul having decided to concentrate on writing.

SAM AND DAVE

I THANK YOU *Stax* [*USA*]. The third million seller disc for this duo and for the writer-producers of the disc, Isaac Hayes and David Porter. It was released in the U.S.A. in January 1968 and reached No 8 on the national charts with 13 weeks in the bestsellers. In Britain it reached No 34 and was nine weeks in the bestsellers. Sam and Dave's rendering gives out pure fire and the disc has fascinating drum, guitar and sax work to put the finishing touches to this song from the Hayes-Porter catalogue.

THE SCAFFOLD (pop vocal trio)

LILY THE PINK *Parlophone* [*Britain*]. The Scaffold were first formed in the summer of 1962. John Gorman, a post office engineer, was invited to assist in organizing the Merseyside Arts Festival and was introduced to Roger McGough, a teacher and part-time poet. They organised poetry readings for the festival which were later supplemented by duologues and comedy sketches which called for the addition of Mike McGear, then an apprentice hairdresser. The Scaffold thus came into being. In December 1963 while appearing at Liverpool's Everyman

Theatre, an ABC-TV talent scout spotted them and signed them to a six-months' contract to supply humorous content to the late night TV show 'Gazette'. Their success in this and other shows encouraged them to turn professional in 1964. They became popular at beat clubs, cocktail parties, political meetings and universities and did a three-week residency at The Establishment in London. In September 1964 they introduced their revue 'Birds, Marriages and Deaths' as part of the Edinburgh Festival and later at London's Little Theatre for a month's run. In 1965 they returned to the Festival with new sketches and poems, and then appeared in 'The Marquee Show' for a tour of 16 English cities. Returning to the Traverse Theatre in 1966, they established themselves as firm favourites with Scottish audiences.

They first started using musical items at a show at the Everyman Theatre, which they closed with a number called 'Today's Monday'. In 1967, Mike McGear wrote 'Thank U Very Much' which when recorded by the trio was a big hit. It was only then that it was revealed that Mike McGear was actually Michael McCartney, brother of The Beatles' famous Paul. Mike had wanted to work without using The Beatles, and that was why he changed his name.

'Lily the Pink' was released on 18 October 1968 and was written by The Scaffold, based on an old traditional rugby song, telling the story of Lily who invented a medicinal compound 'most efficacious in every case'. It was an enormous success and sold 825,000 in three months and was No 1 for five weeks, staying in the British charts for 24 weeks. It was also popular in Norway, New Zealand and Malaysia in 1969 and subsequently went over the million mark. Despite the popularity of their songs, The Scaffold were basically a highly original humour group. Details of the trio: John Gorman, born 4 January 1937 in Birkenhead, educated at St Anselm's College, Liverpool; Mike McGear (Michael McCartney), born 7 January 1944 in Walton; Roger McGough, born 9 November 1937 in Liverpool, educated St Mary's College, Crosby and Hull University (where he obtained a B.A. degree in French and geography), wrote much of the group's material.

A French version of the song 'Le Sirop Typhon' recorded by Richard Anthony also sold around 800,000. The original traditional version was known as 'Lydia Pinkham'.

SIMON AND GARFUNKEL

MRS ROBINSON *Columbia* [*USA*]. An abbreviated version of this song appeared at the climax of the film *The Graduate* (1967) for which Paul Simon wrote the songs and Simon and Garfunkel sang them for the movie. An extended version with extra verses in the duo's album of the soundtrack music was issued as a single. It got to No 1 in the U.S.A. charts for four weeks with 13 weeks in the bestsellers. Issued in April 1968, it sold over the million by June and was awarded a Gold Disc by R.I.A.A. In Britain the disc was No 4 for one week and 12 weeks in the bestsellers.

The song is a booming beat satire on the problematic mother of the film, with glittering vocals and the unique lyrics of Paul Simon. The film had a world net rental of over $85,000,000 by January 1971.

Simon and Garfunkel had the distinction of five albums in the bestsellers at this time including 'The Graduate Soundtrack' and 'Bookends' at Nos 1 and 2.

'Mrs Robinson' gained Simon and Garfunkel a Grammy Award for the Best Contemporary Pop Performance by Vocal Duo or Group of 1968.

SIR DOUGLAS QUINTET PLUS TWO

MENDOCINO *Smash* [*USA*]. The Sir Douglas Quintet was formed in the early 1960s by Doug Sahm, born in Texas in 1943. Sahm himself started in music at the age of six, playing steel guitar, and at nine was a featured performer on the 'Louisiana Hayride' country show. He was a graduate of San Antonio's Sam Houston High School and leader of the group which also included four boys from the Lone Star State: August Meyers, Jackson Barber, John Perez and Franklin Morin. They had their first hit with 'She's About a Mover' (Tribe label) in 1965. The group moved to San Francisco and became caught up in the musical scene there.

They signed with Smash Records, calling the group Sir Douglas Quintet Plus Two as by that time the personnel had changed and increased. It actually became a front for the talents of writer-singer-producer Doug Sahm who also produced other acts for Smash Records.

Sahm wrote 'Mendocino', the group's disc being released in December 1968. It reached No 14 by early 1969 in the U.S.A. charts with 15 weeks in the bestsellers, but was much more successful in Europe selling over three million there and making the group one of the relatively few American bands to attain international acclaim. It was particularly successful in Germany and Belgium.

The personnel of the group for this recording: Doug Sahm (vocalist/guitarist); Franklin Morin (tenor); Wayne Talbert (piano); Martin Fierro (alto sax); Bill Atwood (trumpet); Mel Barton (baritone sax); Terry Henry (trumpet); Whitney Freeman (bass); George Rains (drums). All came from Texas except Freeman who is a Californian.

SLY AND THE FAMILY STONE (rhythm-and-blues vocal and instrumental septet)

EVERYDAY PEOPLE *Epic* [*USA*]. This group was formed in 1966 by Sly Stone who was a rhythm-and-blues disc jockey at KSOL-San Francisco and at KDIA-Oakland. It comprises: Sly Stone (leader, composer, organ) born 15 March 1944; Freddie 'Pyhotee' Stone (guitar, vocals); Rosemary Davis (Stone) (electric piano); Cynthia 'Ecco' Robinson (trumpet); Larry Graham (bass guitar, vocals); Jerry Martini (saxophone); Greg 'Handfeet' Errico (drums). Freddie and Rosemary are Sly's brother and sister. Sly wrote for and produced The Beau Brummels, The Mojo Men and Bobby Freeman for the Autumn label in Los Angeles at the age of 20.

The group rehearsed in Sly's basement before appearing on the local club circuit, then appeared at the Fillmore Auditorium, and spread to New York, Los Angeles, Chicago and Las Vegas. Their first disc 'Dance to the Music', issued in February 1968, was a big hit in the U.S.A. (No 5 for one week) and also in Britain (No 7). 'Everyday People' was released in the U.S.A. in November 1968 and was No 1 for four weeks in early 1969 with 19 weeks in the bestsellers, passing the million sale by February 1969 plus R.I.A.A. Gold Disc award. The disc was additionally a No 1 for a week in the U.S.A. rhythm-and-blues charts. In Britain it reached No 36 and was five weeks in the bestsellers. The song was written by Sylvester Stewart, real name of Sly, who writes much of the group's material. He made his first recording at the age of four, and in his senior year at high school was a member of The Viscanes group. He studied music theory and composition in college and led several groups, playing guitar and bass around the San Francisco nightclub circuit. He then

became producer for Autumn Records, and a radio disc jockey.

Sly described the group as 'a dance and concert combination', and their sound as 'the first fusion of psychedelia and rhythm-and-blues'. All its members were competent on many instruments, and could sing and dance.

O.C. SMITH

LITTLE GREEN APPLES *Columbia* [*USA*]. This tender ballad delivered a love message in a completely new and philosophical form, and was first recorded in February by country artist Roger Miller, then by Patti Page. It was written by Bobby Russell who also had a huge hit with 'Honey' in this year.

O.C. Smith's version was completely different in that he gave the song a bluesy approach rather than country-and-western. It proved to be a tremendous hit and two months after release (August) got to No 2 for a week in the U.S.A. charts with 17 weeks in the bestsellers, with Gold Disc award from R.I.A.A. for million sale.

Smith was raised in Los Angeles, and instructed in music by his mother. He attended high school and college there and performed whenever possible. He gained his first full-time semi-professional experience during his four years in the U.S. Air Force. His popularity during that time decided Smith to become professional after discharge. He obtained a singing job in New York's Club Baby Grand and was later hired by Count Basie with whom he worked for three years, making five trips to Europe. His recording of 'Son of Hickory Holler's Tramp' earlier in the year brought him prominence in both Britain and America. 'Little Green Apples' gave him global recognition. The song received two Grammy Awards for Song of the Year and Best Country Song of 1968.

STATUS QUO (vocal and instrumental quintet)

PICTURES OF MATCHSTICK MEN *Pye* [*Britain*]. The first million seller for this group, being the combined sale Britain, U.S.A. and elsewhere. The disc was released in Britain on 5 January 1968 and reached No 6 in the British charts with 12 weeks in the bestsellers. In the U.S.A. it achieved No 11 with 17 weeks in the bestsellers, the debut disc of the new Cadet Concept label.

Status Quo: Francis Rossi (lead guitar/vocalist) born 29 May 1949 in Forest Hill, London; Roy Lynes (organist/vocalist) born 25 November 1943 in Redhill, Surrey; Alan Lancaster (bass guitar) born 7 February 1949 in Peckham, London; John Coghlan (drummer) born 19 September 1946 in West Norwood, London; Rick Parfitt (rhythm guitar/vocalist) born 12 October 1948 in Woking, Surrey.

With the exception of Rick Parfitt, who joined the group in 1967, the others had played together professionally for $2\frac{1}{2}$ years and were previously known as The Traffic Jam which toured all over Britain and appeared in France. Status Quo appeared in TV, radio and concerts in Sweden, Holland, Germany and Switzerland.

The song was written by group member Francis Rossi, and the disc created an inventive electronic-blues experience. As a result of its success, the group made its first U.S.A. tour in September 1968.

STEPPENWOLF (vocal and instrument quintet)

BORN TO BE WILD *Dunhill* [*USA*]. Steppenwolf were formerly a Canadian group called Sparrow who migrated to Los Angeles and San Francisco during the West Coast rock rush. Steppenwolf emerged as a major force in rock. Their name was taken from Herman Hesse's novel, an immensely popular work with college students.

The group comprised John Kay (lead singer), Michael Monarch (lead guitar), Jerry Edminton (drummer), Nick St Nicholas (bass and harmony), Galdy McJohn (organ). Rushton Moore was originally bassist in early 1967 and John Russell Morgan in late 1968.

The group were discovered at midnight in a coffeehouse at Venice Beach in California. Their performances consist of hard blues, sinister psychedelics and rip-roaring rock numbers.

'Born to Be Wild', written by Mars Bonfield, is played in the rock style. The disc was released in July 1968 and was No 2 for three weeks in the U.S.A. charts and 13 weeks in the bestsellers, selling over a million with Gold Disc award from R.I.A.A. It was No 30 in Britain and nine weeks in the bestsellers.

John Kay is also second guitarist, harmonica player and a composer. The group had no commercial success until mid-1967 when they were called Steppenwolf.

MAGIC CARPET RIDE *Dunhill* [*USA*]. Released in the U.S.A. in October 1968, this disc reached No 2 in the charts and was a steady seller for 16 weeks into 1969 with subsequent reported million sale. The song was written by John Kaye (of the group) and Rushton Moore (formerly bassist of the group), and the disc was described as 'a super charged sampling of pure power and rhythm work with a vocal that tears into the teen psyche'.

DIANA ROSS AND THE SUPREMES

LOVE CHILD *Motown* [*USA*]. Another tremendous disc for The Supremes, the song written by Pam Sawyer, Dean Taylor, Frank Wilson and Deke Richards. It was released on 19 October and marked a new turn in Supreme sound plus a lyric which discusses a mother's concern for a slum child and her hopes of a better future. It sold 500,000 in its first week, and by year's end had reached two million. The disc was No 1 for four weeks in the U.S.A. with 16 weeks in the bestsellers, and reached No 11 in Britain for one week with 14 weeks in the bestsellers.

DIANA ROSS & THE SUPREMES AND THE TEMPTATIONS

I'M GONNA MAKE YOU LOVE ME *Motown* [*USA*]. Diana Ross and The Supremes first joined forces with The Temptations on the Ed Sullivan Show. The result was as though they had been together for years. Motown issued an album of the two groups together (November 1968) and one of the scintillating tracks was 'I'm Gonna Make You Love Me' written by K. Gamble, J. Ross and Jerry A. Williams. On 7 December this was issued as a single and sold an astonishing 900,000 in its first two weeks on the market, thereafter quickly passing the million mark. It became No 1 at the beginning of 1969 and stayed top for three weeks with a total of 13 weeks in the bestsellers. R.I.A.A. Gold Disc award March 1969. The disc was also No 3 for two weeks (1969) in Britain with 11 weeks in the bestsellers, where it was released on 24 January.

On 9 December 1968, the two groups presented their first joint TV special in colour 'Takin' Care of Business' (TCB) and the original soundtrack was released by Motown resulting in very big sales.

T.C.B. (Taking Care of Business) (album) *Motown* [*USA*]. The advance orders for this original soundtrack of the combined groups' first television special in colour on NBC-TV 9 December 1968 poured in at the fastest rate in Motown's history. The album was released immediately after the show and by April 1969 had easily passed the million sale, reaching No 1 in the U.S. charts for one week.

The complete programme was: 'Somewhere' (from *West Side Story*) (Diana Ross) by Stephen Sondheim and Leonard Bernstein (1957); 'Stop in the Name of Love' (Diana Ross and The Supremes) by E. Holland, L. Dozier and B. Holland (1965); 'You Keep Me Hangin' On' (Diana Ross and The Supremes) by E. Holland, L. Dozier and B. Holland (1966); 'Mrs Robinson' (from film *The Graduate*) (Diana Ross and The Supremes) by Paul Simon (1967); 'I Hear a Symphony' (Diana Ross and The Supremes) by E. Holland, L. Dozier and B. Holland (1965); 'With a Song in My Heart' (from *Spring is Here*) by Lorenz Hart and Richard Rodgers (1929) and 'Without a Song' (from *Great Day*) (medley – Diana Ross and The Supremes) by W. Rose, E. Eliscu and V. Youmans (1929); 'Come See About Me' (medley – Diana Ross and The Supremes) by E. Holland, L. Dozier and B. Holland (1964); 'My World Is Empty Without You' (medley – Diana Ross and The Supremes) by E. Holland, L. Dozier and B. Holland (1966); 'Baby Love' (medley – Diana Ross and The Supremes) by E. Holland, L. Dozier and B. Holland (1964); 'Eleanor Rigby' (Diana Ross) by John Lennon and Paul McCartney (1966); 'Reflections' (excerpt) (Diana Ross) by E. Holland, L. Dozier and B. Holland (1967); 'Do You Know the Way to San Jose?' (Diana Ross) by Hal David and Burt Bacharach (1968); 'Pata Pata' (The Temptations) by Ragavoy and Mackeba; 'Get Ready' (The Temptations) by William 'Smokey' Robinson (1966); 'A Taste of Honey' (The Temptations) by Ric Marlow and Bobby Scott (1960); 'Ain't Too Proud to Beg' (The Temptations) by E. Holland and N. Whitfield (1966); 'Hello Young Lovers' (from *The King and I*) (The Temptations) by O. Hammerstein II and Richard Rodgers (1951); 'For Once in My Life' (The Temptations) by Orlando Murdon and Ron S. Miller (1965); 'I'm Losing You' (The Temptations) by Grant, N. Whitfield and E. Holland (1967); 'My Girl' (excerpt) (The Temptations) by William 'Smokey' Robinson and Ronald White (1964); 'The Way You Do the Things You Do' (Diana Ross and The Temptations) by William 'Smokey' Robinson and Bobby Rodgers (1964); 'Respect' (The Supremes and The Temptations) by Otis Redding (1965); 'The Impossible Dream' (from *Man of La Mancha*) (The Supremes and The Temptations) by Joe Darion and Mitch Leigh (1966).

Personnel of The Temptations: Paul Williams, Eddie Kendricks, Otis Williams (Miles), Melvin Franklin, Dennis Edward (who replaced David Ruffin), The Supremes: Mary Wilson, Cindy Birdsong, Diana Ross (lead singer).

The album was in the U.S.A. bestsellers for 34 weeks.

JOHNNY TAYLOR

WHO'S MAKING LOVE? *Stax* [*USA*]. Johnny Taylor was born in 1940 in Memphis, Tennessee, and, like so many other popular singers, became interested in music in his local church where he sang in the choir. Although a deeply religious man, a show business career prompted him to take up more commercial material than gospel songs.

He became professional at the age of 16 (1956) and had quite a success with his first single for the Galaxy label – 'You'll Need Another Favor'. In 1963, he had another hit on Galaxy with 'Part Time Love'.

'Who's Making Love?' was written by Homer Banks, Betty Crutcher, Don Davis and Raymond Jackson and the disc got to No 4 for two weeks in the U.S.A. with 14 weeks in the bestsellers, and had a Gold Disc award from R.I.A.A. for a million sale.

The disc was released in October 1968.

Johnny became a solo artist after joining The Soul Stirrers in 1960 as a replacement for Sam Cooke, the group's leader.

THE TEMPTATIONS

I WISH IT WOULD RAIN *Gordy* [*USA*]. Written by B. Strong, Roger Penzabene and Norman Whitfield (producer of the disc) this disc achieved No 2 for one week in the U.S.A. and 14 weeks in the bestsellers. It was No 45 in Britain. Released in early January 1968, the million sale was reported in February. A fine bluesy ballad with hard percussion and coasting strings, giving solidity and gentleness to the soul vocalising.

CLOUD NINE *Gordy* [*USA*]. This disc was issued at the beginning of November and in four weeks sold 800,000, passing the million mark by early January 1969. It achieved No 4 for two weeks in the U.S.A. charts and was 12 weeks in the bestsellers. It was No 15 and 10 weeks in the British bestsellers. The song, written by B. Strong and Norman Whitfield (producer of the disc), is a dual-level narrative that has been interpreted as either dealing with narcotic addiction or a dream world without discrimination. The listener is left to decide which. This disc was considered to be the first intellectual soul recording, bringing the 'underground' to soul fans and the Motown sound to progressive rock fans.

The Temptations received a Grammy Award with this disc for Best Rhythm-and-Blues Performance by a Duo or Group of 1968.

THE TEMPTERS (rock and roll quintet)

EMERALD - NO DENSETSU (Legend of the emerald) *Philips* [*Japan*]. The Tempters were one of Japan's top selling rock'n'roll groups of 1968 and consisted of: She-Kan (real name Ken-ichi Hagiwara) (leader) born 1948, Y. Matsuzaki (guitar), Kireshi Oguchi (drums), Toshio Tanaka (guitar and organ), Noboru Takaku (bass).

The group sold several million of their disc releases (three albums and seven singles up to 1968). They had a near million seller with 'Kamisama enegai' released in April 1968 which was No 1 for four weeks and in the Top 10 for 14 weeks. Their following release in July 1968 of 'Emerald - no densetsu' was No 1 for two weeks and in the Top Ten for 13 weeks, selling over the million.

In October 1969, She-kan went to the U.S.A. as he wanted to be the first from Japan to try and get the Memphis Sound. She-Kan recorded ten songs brought from Japan and two written by Memphis songwriter Bob McDill. He sang the album in both Japanese and English.

B.J. THOMAS

HOOKED ON A FEELING *Scepter* [*USA*]. Billy Joe Thomas was born in Houston, Texas, in 1946 and joined the church choir and subsequently the high school choral group. His admiration for Roy Head led him to make a career in singing. While in high school, he became lead singer with a group called The Triumphs, a seven-piece outfit that subsequently provided the instrumental backing to many of his records. Thomas began performing with The Triumphs at teenage functions in and around Houston at weekends. His vocal ability and popularity began to soar after a performance at a state park in Texas, where Thomas sang his own song 'The Lazy Man', a single he had recorded months previously and which became a local hit. Here he was 'discovered' by independent producer Charlie Booth who became his manager and started his rise to national prominence. His first record 'I'm So Lonesome I Could Cry', a Hank Williams song, brought him to the attention of Scepter Records who bought the master and signed Thomas to a contract. The disc became a national hit and Thomas was on his way. Other hit tunes followed: 'Mama', 'Billy and Sue' and 'Tomorrow Never Comes'. The artist then became in great demand for appearances in nightclubs, colleges and all forms of live performances.

'Hooked on a Feeling' was written by Mark James and the disc

with 'a bit of Memphis and some beat spicing' released in the U.S.A. in October 1968, was No 5 for two weeks and stayed in the charts for 16 weeks. A Gold Disc for a million sale was awarded by R.I.A.A. in February 1969. Release of the disc in Britain was 3 December 1968.

THE THREE MECKYS

GEN ALTE SCHAU MI NET SO TEPPART AN *WM Produktion* [*Austria*]. This record was the first single to be issued on the WM Produktion label founded in 1968, and owned by the Austrian music publisher Wien Melodie. By 1971, there were 68 versions of this Viennese song in existence - 18 from the Netherlands. An instrumental version by famous orchestra leader James Last was very successful, the 'Non Stop Dancing '70' album containing it selling 422,000.

The Three Meckys, an Austrian folk trio who made this first Austrian million seller, were awarded a Gold Disc in October 1971.

It was by then the most successful Viennese song ever recorded. The group's disc was released on the Elite Special label in Germany and reached the Top Ten there (1969).

The song was written by Szälot and Ull.

THE UNION GAP (featuring Gary Puckett)

YOUNG GIRL *Columbia* [*USA*]. Second million seller for this group, the composition is by Jerry Fuller, arranged by Al Capps. Issued at the end of February 1968 it reached the magic figure by 13 April with Gold Disc award from R.I.A.A. The disc was No 1 for one week in the U.S.A. and 15 weeks in the bestsellers, and No 1 for five weeks in Britain with 17 weeks in the bestsellers, and features the group's leader Gary Puckett. A fine rhythmic and vocal performance of teenage material.

'Young Girl' also sold over 250,000 in Britain (CBS label).

LADY WILLPOWER *Columbia* [*USA*]. Third million seller and R.I.A.A. Gold Disc award (July 1968) in a row for Gary Puckett and The Union Gap, the song again written by Jerry Fuller and arranged by Al Capps. The recording is on the same lines as their previous million sellers with a fine orchestral showing and a spectacular lead vocal performance by Gary Puckett.

The disc was No 1 for one week in the U.S.A. charts with 13 weeks in the bestsellers, and No 5 for two weeks in Britain (CBS label) with 16 weeks in the bestsellers.

Released at end of May 1968 in the U.S.A.

OVER YOU *Columbia* [*USA*]. Fourth million seller and R.I.A.A. Gold Disc award (December 1968) for Gary Puckett and The Union Gap, and another triumph for writer Jerry Fuller. The disc was released in September 1968 and reached No

5 for two weeks with 11 weeks in the bestsellers. An exceptional ballad with the arrangement and power of their previous great successes.

BOBBY VINTON

I LOVE HOW YOU LOVE ME *Epic* [*USA*]. A tremendous comeback for Bobby, with a stunning oldie written by Barry Mann and Larry Kolber in 1961. Bobby's sparkling performance and interpretation of the lyrics made the number a very big hit for both teenage and middle-of-the-road markets. The disc was released in mid-October 1968 and got to No 4 for one week in the U.S. charts with 14 weeks in the bestsellers. A consistent seller for over three months, it sold a million by the end of the year and was awarded a Gold Disc by R.I.A.A.

THE VOGUES (vocal quartet)

TURN AROUND, LOOK AT ME *Reprise* [*USA*]. This song was written in 1961 by Jerry Capehart and provided The Vogues with their first million seller and Gold Disc award from R.I.A.A. The disc was released in June 1968 and attained No 4 chart position in the U.S.A. for one week with 15 weeks in the bestsellers.

The group, all then in their early twenties, comprised Bill Burkette (lead baritone); Don Miller (baritone); Hugh Geyer (first tenor); and Chuck Blasko (second tenor).

They all grew up together in Turtle Creek, near Pittsburgh, and formed a working partnership in 1960. They were originally called the Val-Aires, but changed the name to The Vogues, an apt choice since they all dressed very stylishly. They had several chart hits including 'Five o'clock World', 'Magic Town', 'You're the One' and 'Please Mr Sun' before this hit with 'Turn Around, Look at Me'. They were known almost as much for their club act as for their recordings. Their in-person performances appealed to all age groups, mainly because they had two different shows - one for teenage audiences and the other for adults. Their range therefore included everything from 'rock' to standards.

MASON WILLIAMS (guitar) WITH ORCHESTRA

CLASSICAL GAS *Warner-7 Arts* [*USA*]. Mason Williams was born in Abilene, Texas, on 24 August 1938 and learned to play guitar while studying mathematics at Oklahoma City University. He played at night after classes and toured with his folk music group The Wayfarers Trio. After service in the U.S. Navy during which he wrote songs commemorating every event, he began singing in folk clubs around Los Angeles where he met Glenn Yarborough of The Limeliters. Glenn introduced him to The Smothers Brothers who were appearing at Glenn's club. They used Mason's material on a new album they were recording and he has written for them ever since, also appearing on stage with them playing guitar. Many of his songs have been recorded by The Smothers Brothers, The Kingston Trio, Gale Garnett, Johnny Desmond, Claudine Longet and Glenn Yarborough in addition to his own versions on Warner-7 Arts label. He also wrote for a Petula Clark TV spectacular. Mason is a dramatic example of creative versatility. Apart from over 100 songs, he has written seven books, the biggest entitled *The Bus Book*, a life-sized photograph of a Greyhound bus which folds up into a small package. This was exhibited at the Pasadena Art Museum, on the Joey Bishop Show, in *Life* magazine and now hangs permanently in the New York Museum of Modern Art. His name became widely known when his song 'Cinderella Rockefella' became an international hit for the young Israeli duo Esther and Abi Ofarim. He wrote 'Classical Gas', a dreamy orchestral instrumental that includes a dose of everything from classical rock and bluegrass, for his first major album 'The Mason Williams Phonograph Record'. 'Classical Gas' was issued on 19

April 1968 as a single in Britain and reached No 9 for one week. In the U.S.A. it got to No 1 for a week with 14 weeks in the bestsellers, and sold a million. In Britain it was 13 weeks in the bestsellers.

The essence of the disc is the integration of various instruments. Mike Post, who produced the disc, used cellos to create a Fender bass sound, the string section to get a guitar sound and achieved a drum feeling from horns. The actual instruments used were ten violins, four cellos, one baritone sax, two tubin horns (Wagnerian tubin horn - a very rare instrument), two trombones, two pianos, one percussion, three guitars and a bass.

Although the disc took some time to make the charts, it was certainly one of the most unusual instrumental hits.

Apart from being an expert guitarist/folk singer, Mason Williams is author, poet, publisher, comedy writer and photographer, TV and nightclub performer.

The disc achieved three Grammy Awards for Best Instrumental Arrangement, Best Contemporary-Pop Performance and Best Instrumental theme of 1968. It was re-released in 1978.

STEVIE WONDER

FOR ONCE IN MY LIFE *Tamla* [*USA*]. The fourth million seller for Stevie, the song written by Orlando Murdon and Ron S. Miller (composer of special material for nightclubs) in 1965. The recording of this ballad in up-tempo and rhythm was No 1 for one week and 14 weeks in the bestsellers in the U.S.A. where it was released 2 November 1968. The million sale was reached in March 1969. It was also a hit in Britain (released 29 November 1968) where it was No 3 for four weeks and 13 weeks in the bestsellers.

TAMMY WYNETTE (country singer)

STAND BY YOUR MAN *Epic* [*USA*]. Tammy Wynette's first big hit was written by her and Epic's producer, Billy Sherrill. It reached No 19 and was 16 weeks in the U.S.A. bestsellers. It was reported in 1975 that the disc had sold over 2 million.

Tammy was awarded the Grammy for this song, the Best Country-and-Western Solo Vocal Performance (Female) for 1969. By the end of 1974, she had had more discs at No 1 than any other female country singer in the country charts - sixteen in all. (See 1969 for Tammy Wynette biography.)

'Stand by Your Man' had a tremendous success in 1975 when Tammy performed in Britain, her disc selling over 500,000 there. It reached No 1 and was 12 weeks in the bestsellers.

YOUNG-HOLT UNLIMITED (instrumental jazz rhythm trio)

SOULFUL STRUT *Brunswick* [*USA*]. This trio consists of Eldee Young (bass) and Isaac 'Red' Holt (drums), formerly two-thirds of the Ramsey Lewis Trio, plus Ken Chaney (piano).

Young studied at the American Conservatory of Music in Chicago, and started his professional career as a guitarist, later switching to bass. He recorded an album on which he made his debut as a cellist, and was the first to introduce the cello to soul sounds effectively. Holt also studied music at the same Conservatory as Young, and played professionally with the late Lester Young, Wardell Gray and James Moody. He is said to have introduced the tambourine to jazz. Chaney is a self-taught artist who began his career as a vocalist and then went over to piano. Before going to Chicago where he teamed with Young and Holt, Chaney resided in Detroit and played with such famous jazz artists as Donald Byrd and Kenny Burrell.

'Soulful Strut', written by E. Record and Sonny Sanders, is a jazz-rock flavour disc. It was No 1 for one week with 13 weeks in the U.S.A. bestsellers, and sold a million with R.I.A.A. Gold Disc award by the end of January 1969, just 2½ months after release in November 1968.

ORIGINAL FILM SOUNDTRACK

EASY RIDER (album) *Dunhill* [*USA*]. Released July 1969 (U.S.A.) and 28 November 1969 (Britain – Stateside label). The Columbia Films release of *Easy Rider*, a Pando Co.-Raybert Production, was the winner at Cannes Film Festival, May 1969. It was a directional debut for Dennis Hopper who teamed with Peter Fonda and Terry Southern to write the script. The story concerns two motorcyclists looking for freedom, who pull off a dope-selling deal in Mexico to get funds for the purpose. Their motorbike jaunt takes them across America from California to Louisiana (New Orleans' Mardi Gras) during which the two dropouts' search for freedom is thwarted by the bigoted violence in modern America. Their aborted trip ends in tragedy. The film employed recorded music tracks with rare aptitude, brilliantly edited to the film. Peter Fonda (as Captain America) and Dennis Hopper (as Billy) were the two motorbike stars of the film. This soundtrack was a big seller on both sides of the Atlantic and the U.S.A. reported a million sale by July 1970. The disc got to No 6 in the U.S.A. and stayed in their Top Twenty for 33 weeks. It was in the bestsellers for 72 weeks. In Britain it was No 2 for two weeks in 1970, in the Top Twenty for 42 weeks and the bestsellers for 71 weeks.

Contents of the album: *Side 1* - 'The Pusher' (Steppenwolf), by Hoyt Axton; 'Born to Be Wild' (Steppenwolf), by Mars Bonfield (1968); 'The Weight' (Smith), by Robertson; 'Wasn't Born to Follow' (The Byrds), by Gerry Goffin and Carole King; 'If You Want to Be a Bird' (Holy Modal Rounders), by Antonia; *Side 2* - 'Don't Bogart Me' (Fraternity of Man), by Elliott Ingber and Larry Wagner; 'If 6 Were 9' (Jimi Hendrix Experience), by Jimi Hendrix; *'Kyrie Eleison – Mardi Gras' (The Electric Prunes), by David Axelrod (1967); 'It's Alright, Ma' (Roger McGuinn), by Bob Dylan; 'Ballad of Easy Rider' (Roger McGuinn), by Roger McGuinn.

Note * From 'Mass in F Minor' (a 'rock' work) using extended classical forms by rock musicians, composed by Los Angeles record producer David Axelrod and recorded by The Electric Prunes in 1967.

A Gold Disc award presented by R.I.A.A. on 19 January 1970.

ORIGINAL FILM SOUNDTRACK (conducted by the composer Nino Rota)

ROMEO AND JULIET (album) *Capitol* [*USA*]. This beautiful film of Shakespeare's play was first released in 1968 and had its U.S.A. premiere in October at the Paris Theatre in New York. The film was directed by Franco Zefferelli and starred Leonard Whiting (then aged 17) and Olivia Hussey (aged 16), allegedly the youngest performers ever to play Shakespeare's 'star crossed lovers' professionally. An album was released in January 1969, strictly dialogue. It was enormously successful, stayed in the Top Ten from May to September for 16 weeks and achieved the No 1 position for one week. By 3 July it received a Gold Disc award for million dollar sale from R.I.A.A. and by year's end had passed the million units sale. The film's beautiful Love Theme became a million seller as a singles disc for Henry Mancini and his orchestra.

Contents of the album: Prologue, Romeo's foreboding, and feast at the house of Capulet. Song 'What Is Youth?'. Balcony scene. Romeo and Juliet are wed. Death of Mercutio and Tybalt. Farewell love scene. Likeness of death. In Capulet's tomb. All are punished.

A vocal version of the love theme - 'A Time for Us' with lyrics by Eddie Snyder and Larry Kusik was also published.

The above album stayed in the U.S.A. bestseller charts for 74 weeks.

Capitol issued a second album which was a combination of Nino Rota's lovely musical score and dialogue, on four discs. A third version of the entire Nino Rota score without dialogue was issued in January 1970, making the first time the label had issued three albums from the same film.

VARIOUS ARTISTS

STUNDE DER STARS (Hour of the Stars) (album) [*Germany*]. An album marketed specifically for raising funds for the 'Altershilfe' (old age relief) and the 'Muttergenesungswerk' (maternity homes). It sold over two million and produced a net profit of $540,000 (two million Deutschmarks) by February 1970.

VARIOUS ARTISTS

WORLD STAR FESTIVAL (album) *United Nations* Sixteen top disc artists and 12 British and U.S.A. record companies waived all fees and copyright royalties on the sales of this magnificent album, released in March 1969, in aid of the United Nations fund for refugees, the second of its kind (see also 'All-Star Festival' 1963). It was marketed through Philips Records and sold over 1,250,000 in over 130 different countries in four months, and was launched through the United Nations via the U.N. High Commissioner for Refugees, Prince Sadruddin Aga Khan.

Contents: *Side 1* - 'The Happening' (Diana Ross and The Supremes), by E. Holland, L. Dozier and B. Holland (1967); 'What the World Needs Now Is Love' (Dionne Warwick), by Hal David and Burt Bacharach (1966); 'Georgia on My Mind' (Ray Charles), by S. Gorrell and Hoagy Carmichael (1930); 'Cowboys and Indians' (Herb Alpert and The Tijuana Brass), by Sol Lake (1967); 'Homeward Bound' (Simon and Garfunkel), by Paul Simon (1966); 'For the First Time in My Life' (Tom Jones), by E. Greines (1969); 'The Beat Goes On' (Sonny and Cher), by Sonny Bono (1966); 'The Singer Sang His Song' (The Bee Gees), by Maurice, Barry and Robin Gibb (1968); *Side 2* - 'I've Got a Song for You' (Shirley Bassey), by L. Holmes and Al Stillman (1968); 'May Each Day' (Andy Williams), by Morton J. Green and George Wyle (1963); 'Thoroughly Modern Millie' (from the film) (Julie Andrews), by Sammy Cahn and James van Heusen (1967); 'I'll Go On Loving Her' (Je l'aimerai toujours) (Paul Mauriat and his Orchestra), by Charles Aznavour (1968); 'Talk to the Animals' (from film *Doctor Doolittle*) (Sammy Davis, Jr), by Leslie Bricusse (1967); 'I Think It's Going to Rain Today' (Dusty Springfield), by Randy Newman (1968); 'September of My Years' (Frank Sinatra), by Sammy Cahn and James van Heusen (1965); 'He Touched Me' (Barbra Streisand), by M. Schafer and I. Levin (1965).

Note Another album 'International Piano Festival' was also issued for the United Nations funds in October 1964.

ADAMO

PETIT BONHEUR *Pathe-HMV* [*France*]. Belgian singer Salvatore Adamo was born in 1944 and is of Sicilian origin, living in Belgium since boyhood. Before joining Pathe, he had cut a number of discs for Philips and Polydor which went unnoticed. In 1963 he had a meteoric rise with 'Sans toi Mamie' and was the Belgian 'discovery of the year'. All his songs from then on reached the top, and by 1964 he also became the rage of Holland, and later a top favourite in France. His self-written song 'Inch Allah' was a big hit in 1968. 'Petit Bonheur' also written by him got to No 7 in Belgium and No 5 in France in December 1969, and world sales totalled a million by April 1970. Adamo, who played guitar and wrote his own songs, sang in French, Spanish and Italian, and was a great favourite on the Continent of Europe.

APOLLO 11 ASTRONAUTS (narrated by Hugh Downs)

FIRST MAN ON THE MOON *MGM* [*USA*]. The successful

lunar landing on 20 July 1969 by the Apollo 11 astronauts in the lunar module 'Eagle' was one of the greatest events in human history.

Apollo 11 with astronauts Neil Armstrong, Edwin Aldrin and Michael Collins blasted off from Cape Kennedy on 16 July 1969 at 9.32 E.D.T. (13.32 G.M.T.) for the over 250,000-mile journey to the moon. At 13.47 E.D.T. (17.47 G.M.T.) on 20 July, the lunar module 'Eagle' separated from the command ship 'Columbus' for the descent to the moon's surface with Armstrong and Aldrin, while Collins orbited the moon in 'Columbus' to await their re-docking.

'Eagle' touched down on the moon's surface in the Sea of Tranquility at 16.17 and 42 secs. E.D.T. (20.17 and 42 secs. G.M.T.) on 20 July. Just over 6½ hours later at 22.56 and 20 secs. E.D.T. (02.56 and 20 secs. G.M.T. 21 July) Neil Armstrong became the first man ever to set foot on the moon, saying, as he planted his white left boot in the moon's grey dust, 'That's one small step for a man – a giant leap for mankind.' He was followed about 25 minutes later by Aldrin, the two astronauts walking on the moon for 2½ hours, collecting lunar rocks and soil and setting up various scientific instruments including a laser-beam reflector, a seismometer, solar wind instrument, solar panels and a camera to televise lunar activities to the world. They also made photographs of rock samples, and, before departing, left a U.S.A. flag and a silicon disc bearing goodwill messages for posterity from world leaders including Queen Elizabeth II, The Pope and President Tito; also a metal plaque bearing the names of the three astronauts and President Richard M. Nixon. The moon walk was seen by millions of people on television around the world and the voices of the astronauts were clearly heard, as was the message from President Nixon. 'Eagle' blasted off from the moon at 13.54 E.D.T. (17.54 G.M.T.) and re-docked with 'Columbus' at 17.35 E.D.T. (21.35 G.M.T.) on 21 July. After Armstrong and Aldrin had transferred to 'Columbus' the lunar module was jettisoned in lunar orbit and the command ship made its return to Earth, splashing down in the Pacific at 12.51 E.D.T. (16.51 G.M.T.) on 24 July.

The lunar module actually spent 21 hours 36 mins. 18 secs. on the moon, and the entire journey of over half a million miles took 195 hours 18 mins. 21 secs. - a masterpiece of scientific planning by N.A.S.A. and Mission Control at Houston, Texas, which employed, at its peak, 376,600 people.

Each of the three astronauts was born in 1930: Neil Alden Armstrong in Wapakoneta, Ohio on 5 August, Col. Edwin Eugene Aldrin in Montclair, New Jersey on 20 January and Lt.-Col. Michael Collins in Rome, Italy on 31 October.

This successful lunar landing launched a great outpouring of documentary discs, and the first to hit the U.S.A. market was this 45 rpm disc aimed at the chain stores and supermarkets. It traces the history of the U.S.A. space programme and features the actual voices of the astronauts. M.G.M. released the disc on 22 July and it quickly passed the million and a half mark with sales thereafter rapidly accelerating. Prices of the various discs and albums ranged from 39c to as high as $19.95 and aggregate sales ran into many millions.

In Britain, Philips manufactured a special disc for 12s. ($1.45) sold exclusively to readers of *The News of the World*, Britain's largest selling Sunday newspaper.

THE ARCHIES

SUGAR, SUGAR *Calendar* [USA]. Written by Jeff Barry (producer of the disc) and Andy Kim, this disc was released in the U.S.A. in July 1969 and by 30 August had sold the million with R.I.A.A. Gold Disc award. It got to No 1 for four weeks with 22 weeks in the bestsellers, and by October passed the three million sale in the U.S.A. The Archies were cartoon characters – Archie Andrews, Mr Weatherbee, Betty Cooper, Veronica Lodge, Reggie Mantle and Jughead Jones – who topped the TV ratings all over the U.S.A. with their Saturday morning CBS series. The series was based on a newspaper strip, originated in 1942 by the American cartoonist John L. Goldwater, which first

appeared in the late 1940s. Don Kirschner, who made The Monkees famous, was responsible for the music in the series.

This single was cut by studio singers who remained anonymous with the exception of Ron Dante (born 1948) who was later named as the lead singer.

In Britain the disc (RCA label) was No 1 for eight weeks and sold over a million there. It was also No 1 in many other countries including Spain, Denmark, Norway, Belgium, Germany, and Mexico, and sales brought the global tally up to six million, making it the top disc of 1969. Don Kirschner received the Carl-Alan Award in Britain for 'Sugar, Sugar' - the most popular disc of the year.

JINGLE JANGLE *Kirschner* [USA]. Second million seller for The Archies, again written by Jeff Barry and Andy Kim, a delightful, bubbly follow-up to 'Sugar, Sugar'. It was released in November and taken from the 'Jingle Jangle' album. The disc reached No 4 for a week with 13 weeks in the bestsellers, and received a Gold Disc award from R.I.A.A. in February 1970.

THE BEATLES (with Billy Preston)

GET BACK *Apple* [Britain] *Apple* [USA]. Another John Lennon and Paul McCartney song, and another giant seller for The Beatles. This disc was released in Britain on 15 April 1969 and was an immediate No 1, staying in that chart position for six weeks with 17 weeks in the bestsellers and selling over 530,000. In the U.S.A. release was in May, the disc at No 1 for five weeks, entering the charts at No 10 the first week with 12 weeks in the bestsellers, equalling, with the group's 'Hey Jude', the highest any new disc had ever achieved in the U.S.A. American sales were around two million and a Gold Disc awarded on 19 May by R.I.A.A. after only two weeks on the market. 'Get Back' was also No 1 in many other countries including Canada, Germany, France, Spain, Norway, Denmark, Holland, Australia, Belgium, Malaysia, Singapore and New Zealand, global sales totalling an estimated 4,500,000.

The disc features Billy Preston (who played Nat 'King' Cole as a child in a movie) on the organ. Preston, also a vocalist, was signed by Apple Records to record as a solo artist. He was born in 1947 in Houston, Texas, and was greatly influenced by Ray Charles whom he studied intensely. He subsequently spent two years with Charles on a world tour and recorded extensively with the band. It was George Harrison of The Beatles who first heard him play in Hamburg.

'Get Back' is a 'rock' disc, a return to the simple appeal that marked The Beatles' early efforts. The reverse side is 'Don't Let Me Down', also by Lennon and McCartney, with the lead vocal by John Lennon. Paul McCartney is lead singer on 'Get Back'.

A Gold Disc was awarded in 1970 to Billy Preston by R.I.A.A. for his organ back-up of the disc.

THE BEATLES

THE BALLAD OF JOHN AND YOKO *Apple* [Britain] *Apple* [USA]. This song by John Lennon and Paul McCartney tells of John Lennon and Yoko Ono's marriage, their trip to Paris and Amsterdam and their life in general. John takes the vocal lead for this 'rocker' in which he complains of people's attitude to the events which immediately preceded and followed the marriage in Gibraltar, the tension relieved by the driving rock backing of guitar, bass and drums. Paul McCartney joins in the last few choruses. The disc can be described as a 'stormer' and a great one to dance to. It was released in Britain on 30 May 1969, was No 1 for three weeks with 14 weeks in the bestsellers and sold around 300,000. Release in the U.S.A. was in June 1969, the disc achieving No 7 for two weeks with 9 weeks in the bestsellers, with Gold Disc award from R.I.A.A. on the 16 July. U.S.A. sales were around 1,250,000. Global sales estimated at 2,500,000.

The disc was also No 1 in Germany, Austria, Holland, Norway, Spain, Belgium, Denmark and Malaysia.

Reverse side of disc 'Old Brown Shoe' written by George Harrison.

The Beatles' Apple record company – one year old in August 1969 – had sold over 12 million singles in Britain and the U.S.A. alone since it was launched.

SOMETHING backed with COME TOGETHER *Apple* [*Britain*] *Apple* [*USA*]. Both tracks come from The Beatles' album 'Abbey Road', and this single was released in the U.S.A. on 15 October and in Britain on 31 October. 'Something' written by George Harrison, a beautiful love song with a floating, aching melody, is sung by George to his own simple but effective guitar style and a crying blend of piano and strings. The song is considered something of a milestone for him and the best he had written to date.

'Come Together' by John Lennon and Paul McCartney is a bass-orientated song with a rasping John Lennon vocal and thumping drum from Ringo Starr, probably the funkiest thing ever done by the group.

The disc entered the U.S. charts at No 20 and was No 1 after four weeks, staying in that position for five weeks with a total of 16 weeks in the bestsellers. It sold its first million in the U.S.A. within the first month on the market, with R.I.A.A. Gold Disc award 27 October 1969.

In Britain it reached No 4 for one week.

U.S.A. sales went to around 1,750,000. The global tally around 2,500,000.

ABBEY ROAD (album) *Apple* [*Britain*] *Apple* [*USA*]. Another monster selling album for The Beatles. It was named 'Abbey Road' in honour of the group's favourite recording studios in London. The album is a return to the modest style of 'Rubber Soul' and 'Revolver', combining a variety of music – old-line rock 'n' roll, low blues, high camp, and folk-melodic, inventive honest pop music, and is crammed with musical delights. Side 2 of the album is most intriguing, described as a 'long, interlocked medley – a kind of odyssey from innocence to experience'. (*Time*, 3 October 1969.)

The disc was released in Britain on 26 September 1969, and on 1 October in the U.S.A. It was No 1 immediately in Britain and No 1 in the U.S.A. within three weeks. R.I.A.A. Gold Disc award for million dollar sale in four weeks. This position was maintained in Britain for 18 weeks and in the U.S.A. for 14 weeks. The global impact was immense, and an estimated four million were sold in the first six weeks, with sales globally well over five million by end of 1969.

The mood of each song fits comfortably with every other, and, although most of them are written by John Lennon and Paul McCartney, one is by drummer Ringo Starr and two by George Harrison, the latter's 'Something' (see above) being considered by his three colleagues as the best song in the album.

The contents of the disc: *Side 1* – 'Come Together' (John Lennon), by John Lennon and Paul McCartney; 'Something' (George Harrison), by George Harrison; 'Maxwell's Silver Hammer' (Paul McCartney), by John Lennon and Paul McCartney; 'Oh Darling' (Paul McCartney), by John Lennon and Paul McCartney; 'Octopus's Garden' (Ringo Starr), by Ringo Starr; 'I Want You – She's So Heavy' (John Lennon), by John Lennon and Paul McCartney; *Side 2* – 'Here Comes the Sun' (George Harrison), by George Harrison; 'Because' (John Lennon), by John Lennon and Paul McCartney; 'You Never Give Me Your Money' (Paul McCartney), by John Lennon and Paul McCartney; 'Sun King' (John Lennon), by John Lennon and Paul McCartney; 'Mean Mr Mustard' (John Lennon), by John Lennon and Paul McCartney; 'Polythene Pam' (John Lennon), by John Lennon and Paul McCartney; 'She Came in Through the Bathroom Window' (Paul McCartney), by John Lennon and Paul McCartney; 'Golden Slumbers' (Paul McCartney), by John Lennon and Paul McCartney; 'Carry that Weight' (ensemble), by John Lennon and Paul McCartney; 'Ending – Her Majesty' (Paul McCartney), by Paul McCartney.

The album was produced by George Martin. It stayed in the U.S. bestsellers charts for 83 weeks. In Britain it was in the charts for 59 weeks.

Grammy Award (1969) for Best Engineered Recording (other than classical).

BROOK BENTON

RAINY NIGHT IN GEORGIA *Cotillion* [*USA*]. Recorded on the Cotillion label (youngest of the three Atlantic labels) and released in late December 1969, this disc achieved No 2 in the U.S. charts for a week in March 1970, by which time it had sold a million with R.I.A.A. Gold Disc award. The song, written by disc artist Tony Joe White, proved powerful material for Benton who sings it with charm and blues impact. It was recorded at the Criteria Studio in Miami, Benton being backed by the promising new Florida Rhythm Section 'Cold Grits' (a quartet) plus Cornell Dupree on guitar and Dave Crawford on piano.

JANE BIRKIN AND SERGE GAINSBOURG

JE T'AIME … MOI NON PLUS *Fontana* [*Britain*]. Jane Birkin (born 1947) and Serge Gainsbourg (born 1929) are two of France's most popular stars – both on disc and on the screen. Jane met Serge when she went to France in 1967 during rehearsals for the film *Slogan* and they became constant companions. Serge, a singer, actor, film music and pop composer, originally wrote 'Je t'aime' for famous actress Brigitte Bardot but, after recording it, Brigitte decided the song was too erotic and would not allow it to be released. In early 1969, Serge came to Britain and recorded an album 'Jane Birkin and Serge Gainsbourg' and included the song in it. The singles disc was released two weeks later (27 June) and by October was No 1 for a week in Britain. Although the song was sung in French, it proved to be the most controversial record of the decade and was banned by most of the radio networks. In France, the original Fontana (Philips) recording was handed over to an independent label DISC A2, as being too sensational, after selling around 750,000 in the French-speaking world. Global sales were estimated at two million. The disc was a big seller in France, Britain, Germany, Italy, Belgium, Norway, Switzerland, Denmark, Holland and Sweden and subsequently in the U.S.A. where it was released in early 1970, reaching No 58 with 10 weeks in the bestsellers. In Britain, the disc was eventually handed over to the Major Minor label. Sales went over 250,000 there.

Jane Birkin, who made seven films during 1969 and hails from Chelsea, London, rose from obscurity to stardom in 12 months through this disc and became the new sex symbol of France. She and Serge were voted France's Most Exciting Couple of 1969.

In Britain, the song became known under the title 'Love at First Sight'. The disc was No 1 also in Belgium, Denmark, Norway, Switzerland and Sweden.

ROY BLACK

DEINE SCHONSTES GESCHENK *Polydor* [*Germany*]. Another big success for Roy Black, the disc released in November 1969. By mid-January 1970 it sold over half a million, with the million sale plus Gold Disc by May 1970. It stayed at No 1 for nine weeks in Germany between January and March.

BLOOD, SWEAT AND TEARS (rock group)

BLOOD, SWEAT AND TEARS (album) *Columbia* [*USA*]. Blood, Sweat and Tears proved to be one of the most mature groups to emerge for a long time. Their different musical backgrounds made them successful in combining jazz-flavoured brass and reeds with rock guitar and rhythm, their musical prowess in complex arrangements being second to none in the rock world.

The nucleus of the group was born in New York in the summer of 1967, the brainchild of Al Kooper, an organist and singer previously a member of The Blues Project. He also gave the group its name. Kooper recruited guitarist Steve Katz from his old band, Katz brought in drummer Bobby Colomby, and Colomby discovered sax-pianist-arranger Fred Lipsius. Classical trained trombone-organist-arranger Dick Halligan and rock bass player Jim Fielder completed the band. They made a debut album 'Child Is Father to the Man' for Columbia (an early 1968 chart success) by which time trumpeters Randy Brecker and Jerry Weiss had made the group an octet. They were a big success in New York, attracting much attention at leading venues. After about a year, Kooper left to become a soloist and record producer, followed by Weiss and Becker. The group found new blood in vocalist David Clayton-Thomas and three seasoned brass men: trumpeters Lew Soloff and Chuck Winfield and trombonist Jerry Hyman making a nine-piece band.

In late December 1968 the new group's album entitled 'Blood, Sweat and Tears' was released and sold 600,000 in four months, and received a Gold Disc award from R.I.A.A. within three months. It was No 1 in the charts for seven weeks and stayed in the Top Ten for several months, selling two million by year's end.

This powerfully appealing 'rock' package introduced more music into rock at a time when more and more rock was being introduced into music. The group's individual musical backgrounds made this so, as the following personnel data shows:

David Clayton-Thomas, born 1944 in London, was raised in Toronto and previously led his own band in Canada; Steve Katz, born 1945 in Brooklyn on 16 May. Originally with the Blues Project; Fred Lipsius born 1944 in New York. Graduate of High School of Music and Art, also studied at Berklee Music School, Boston; Jim Fielder, born 1948 in Texas. Taught music by his father. Worked with The Mothers of Invention and Buffalo Springfield; Dick Halligan, born 1944 in New York. Studied at Manhattan School of Music where he received an M.A. in music. Originally led his own trio; Bobby Colomby, born 1945 in New York City. Has a B.A. in psychology; Chuck Winfield, born 1943 in Pennsylvania. Gained B.A. and Master's degrees in music at the Juilliard School of Music, New York; Jerry Hyman, born 1947 in Brooklyn. Studied at New York School of Music. Is also a pianist and flugel horn player; Lew Soloff, born Brooklyn, 1944. Studied at Juilliard School of Music, New York for six years, then at Eastman School of Music, Rochester, N.Y. where he obtained a Bachelor's degree, and later returned to Juilliard.

The contents of this exciting, progressive album were: Side 1 - *'Trois Tymopedies' - 1st and 2nd Movements, by Erik Satie (1866-1925); 'Smiling Phases', by Steve Winwood, Jim Capaldi and Chris Wood (all members of The Traffic); 'Sometimes in Winter' (sung by Steve Katz), by Steve Katz; 'More and More', by P. Vee and D. Juan; 'And When I Die', by Laura Nyro; 'God Bless the Child', by Arthur Herzog, Jr., and Billie Holiday (1941); Side 2 - 'Spinning Wheel', by David Clayton-Thomas; 'You've Made Me So Very Happy', by Berry Gordy, Jr., B. Holloway, P. Holloway and F. Wilson; 'Blues Part 2', by David Clayton-Thomas, Steve Katz, Fred Lipsius and Bobby Colomby; 'Trois Tymopedies' (reprise) by Erik Satie.

David Clayton-Thomas is the lead singer on this disc. The versatility of the group's musicianship ranges from hard blues-rock sound (as in 'Smiling Phases') to modern jazz (as in 'Blues Part 2'), chamber ensemble with flutes and Bartokian brass plus electronic sound effects (in 'Trois Tymopedies') and spiritual (in 'And When I Die').

This disc received the Grammy Award for Album of the Year (1969) and the Erik Satie variations (*) a Grammy Award for Best Contemporary Instrumental Performance (1969).

It was in the U.S. bestsellers for 109 weeks.

YOU'VE MADE ME SO VERY HAPPY Columbia [USA]. Taken from the group's album 'Blood, Sweat and Tears' by popular demand, this track was issued as a single in the U.S.A. in March 1969. It was No 2 for three weeks with 13 weeks in the U.S. bestsellers, and sold a million by 12 June with R.I.A.A. Gold Disc award. It was No 35 in Britain. Song written by Berry Gordy, Jr., B. Holloway, P. Holloway and F. Wilson.

SPINNING WHEEL Columbia [USA]. This powerhouse disc by Blood, Sweat and Tears was also taken from their album by popular demand and released as a single in May 1969, and sold a million by 23 July 1969 with R.I.A.A. Gold Disc award. The disc was No 2 for three weeks in the U.S. charts with 13 weeks in the bestsellers. The song written by David Clayton-Thomas, lead singer of the group. Grammy Award (1969) for Best Arrangement Accompanying Vocalist(s).

AND WHEN I DIE Columbia [USA]. An easy going arrangement of the tune by Laura Nyro, it was the third single taken from the album 'Blood, Sweat and Tears' to sell a million, the first time this had ever happened. It was released in October 1969 and was No 2 in the U.S.A. charts for two weeks with 13 weeks in the bestsellers. A Gold Disc was awarded by R.I.A.A. in January 1970.

JERRY BUTLER

ONLY THE STRONG SURVIVE Mercury [USA]. Jerry Butler's recording of this power-packed song lyric with hollow-string tension and rhythmic power was released in the U.S.A. in February 1969, and in Britain on 11 April 1969. It reached No 4 in America with 13 weeks in the bestsellers, and by 24 April sold the million with R.I.A.A. Gold Disc award. The song was written by Jerry with the producers of the disc - K. Gamble and L. Huff.

Jerry Butler was born on 8 December 1939 in Sunflower, Missouri, his family moving to Chicago in 1942 where his father was a railroad fireman for the Northwestern railroad. Jerry sang spirituals as a child on a Chicago radio station, and was active in choir singing from 12. He then joined the Northern Jubilee Gospel Singers. After graduation from Washburn School in Chicago he found singing was his main interest and sang with his own group, The Impressions, which included two members of his church choir, Curtis Mayfield and Sam Gooden. Eventually, the group came to the attention of Vee Jay Records' Ewart Abner, Jr., when they performed a tune for an ambitious songwriter. Abner didn't like the song, but signed The Impressions. Their first hit was 'For Your Precious Love' written by Jerry with Arthur and Richard Brooks in 1958, now a standard evergreen. Soon after, Jerry decided to become a soloist and made several hits including 'Aware of Love', 'He Will Break Your Heart', 'Love Me', 'Let It Be Me' and in 1961 an exceptionally fine recording of 'Moon River' which, although he did not create it, nevertheless had much to do with publicizing the tune.

Jerry has written or part written many of his successes.

GLEN CAMPBELL

GALVESTON Capitol [USA]. The second million seller singles disc for Glen, the song again written for him by Jim Webb. A pretty ballad with outstanding production touches. The disc was released in February 1969 and was awarded a Gold Disc by R.I.A.A. on 14 October. It was No 3 in the charts for two weeks in the U.S.A. with 12 weeks in the bestsellers. The title was also used for a million dollar selling album by Glen.

Release of this single in Britain was in May 1969 where it reached No 11 for one week and 10 weeks in the bestsellers.

GLEN CAMPBELL (musical director Al deLory)

LIVE (GLEN CAMPBELL - LIVE) (double album) Capitol [USA]. This two-record release on 29 August 1969 was Glen Campbell's first 'live' album of his sell-out concert at the Garden State Art Center, New Jersey on 24 July 1969. It contained 18 'on stage' recordings - nine of his previous hits and nine songs he had never before recorded - and was produced by Al deLory. It sold over 600,000 in one month and was awarded a Gold Disc by R.I.A.A. on 19 September for million dollars sale and easily sold a million units before year's end.

This U.S. release contained: 'More' (from film Mondo Cane), by M. Cioricolini, Riz Ortolani and N. Oliviero (1963) (English words by Norman Newell); 'Somewhere' (from West Side Story), by Stephen Sondheim and Leonard Bernstein (1957); 'Didn't We', by Jim Webb (1969); 'Dreams of the Everyday Housewife', by Chris Gantry (1969); 'By the Time I Get to

Phoenix', by Jim Webb (1968); 'For Once in My Life', by Orlando Murdon and Ron S. Miller (1965); 'Gentle on My Mind', by John Hartford (1968); 'Where's the Playground, Susie?' by Jim Webb (1968); 'Dock of the Bay (Sittin' on)', by Steve Cropper and Otis Redding (1967); 'If You Go Away' (Ne me quitte pas), by Rod McKuen and Jacques Brel (1969); 'Walk Right In', by Gus Cannon and Hosie Woods (1930); 'The Impossible Dream' (from *Man of La Mancha*), by Joe Darion and Mitch Leigh (1966); 'The Lord's Prayer' (biblical), music by Albert Hay Malotte (1935); 'Mountain Dew'; and four other titles.

It reached No 7 in the U.S. charts for two weeks, and was in the bestsellers for 29 weeks. The British release was a single disc album and contained the first 12 titles as above.

Glen Campbell made his first film in 1969, co-starring with John Wayne in *True Grit*, for which he received $100,000. Glen's earnings for 1967/1968 were $800,000. For 1968/1969 they were over $2 million from discs, concerts, TV and films.

JOHNNY CASH

A BOY NAMED SUE *Columbia* [*USA*]. A very amusing ditty about the disadvantages of a boy being saddled with a girl's name. Johnny Cash drawls this in his dark-brown tones accompanied by a peppy, finger-clicking beat. The song is one of the tracks from his album recorded at San Quentin, performed against a background of cheers and laughter from the prisoners, a clever piece of humorous material.

The song was written by Shel Silverstein and the disc released in July 1969. It was No 1 in the U.S.A. for one week with 12 weeks in the bestsellers, and sold a million with R.I.A.A. Gold Disc award on 14 August. It was also a No 1 country disc for five weeks.

In Britain it reached No 3 for one week.

Grammy Awards (1969) for Best Country Vocal Performance and Best Country Song.

AT SAN QUENTIN (Johnny Cash at San Quentin) (album) *Columbia* [*USA*]. A tremendous selling album for Johnny Cash. It was released in June 1969 in the U.S.A. and was awarded a Gold Disc for million dollar sales on 12 August. By year's end it had sold over two million in records and tapes. In the U.S.A. it achieved No 1 for four weeks and was in the Top Ten for 20 weeks with sales continuing strongly into 1970. In Britain it was No 1 for two weeks and in the Top Ten for 25 weeks into 1970. British release was in August 1969 on the C.B.S. label. The album contained the song 'A Boy Named Sue', a million seller as a single (see above).

It was the second album recorded by Johnny at a U.S. prison. Johnny was awarded five of the ten awards at the Country Music Association Festival in October 1969 - Entertainer of the Year, Male Vocalist of the Year, Singles Disc of the Year, Vocal Group (with wife June Carter) of the Year, and Album of the Year ('At San Quentin').

Contents of the album: 'Wanted Man', by Bob Dylan; 'Wreck of the Old '97', traditional: arr. Cash, Johnson and Blake; 'I Walk the Line', by Johnny Cash (1956); 'Darling Companion', by John Sebastien; 'Starkville City Jail', by Johnny Cash; 'San Quentin', by Johnny Cash; 'A Boy Named Sue', by Shel Silverstein (1969); 'Peace in the Valley', by Thomas A. Dorsey (1939); 'Folsom Prison Blues', by Johnny Cash (1956).

This album was in the bestsellers in the U.S.A. for seventy weeks.

CHAIRMEN OF THE BOARD

GIVE ME JUST A LITTLE MORE TIME *Invictus* [*USA*]. Produced by the great songwriting team of Holland, Dozier and Holland for their new label Invictus, the song written by R. Dunbar and E. Wayne. The disc was released in late December 1969, reached No 3 for a week in the U.S.A. with million sale plus R.I.A.A. Gold Disc award by May 1970. This was the first million seller for the Invictus label. The group are General

Johnson (formerly with The Showmen) - lead singer, Harrison Kennedy, Danny Woods and Eddie Curtis.

CHICAGO TRANSIT AUTHORITY

CHICAGO TRANSIT AUTHORITY (double album) *Columbia* [*USA*]. Chicago Transit Authority came into being as a club band around 1968, performing in local clubs in the Chicago area under the name of The Big Thing, probably to describe their booming sound. Jim Guercio, a producer for Columbia, met the group while attending De Paul University just outside Chicago. Having been associated with Chad and Jeremy and The Buckinghams, he was so impressed with The Big Thing that it made him devote most of his time and energy towards making the group a success. The name of Chicago Transit Authority came later, when the group signed with Columbia. Their first outing for the label was this now classic two-record set which initially was not a success but, after the release of their second double album in 1970, began to sell until it subsequently received a Gold Disc R.I.A.A. award and went on to platinum status for a million units sale. It reached No 25 for 2 weeks in the U.S. charts.

The group had its first singles success with 'I'm a Man' written by Stevie Winwood of Britain's Spencer Davis Group. Chicago Transit Authority had its first successful concert in Britain at London's Royal Albert Hall in 1970. In the U.S.A. their live performances engendered frenzy with their audiences. Each of the group's sequbsequent releases sold a million units (eight by 1975) and they became one of the most successful bands of the seventies.

The personnel of Chicago Transit Authority: Dan Seraphine (drums); Robert Lamm (organ, electric piano, vocals); Terry Kath (guitar, vocals); James Pankow (trombone); Peter Cetera (bass, vocals); Walter Parazaider (woodwinds); Lee Loughnane (trumpet, flugel horn).

Seraphine studied with Chuck Flores, ex-member of the Maynard Ferguson and Woody Herman bands; Parazaider studied with woodwind players in the Chicago Symphony; Loughnane studied for two years at Chicago Conservatory College and played in several Chicago rock groups and big bands; Cetera started playing accordion at 12 and worked with several local groups; and Pankow has played with the Bobby Christian and Ted Weems orchestra as well as his own jazz quintet and does much of Chicago Transit Authority's composition and brass arrangement. Lamm is one of the band's prolific writers and Kath is also a busy writer for the group.

This first album contained 12 tracks, the most outstanding being: 'Beginnings', 'Does Anybody Really Know What Time It Is?' and 'Questions 67 & 68'. Others on the album are: 'Introduction', 'Listen', 'Poem 58', 'South California Purples', 'I'm a Man', 'Someday' and 'Liberation'. It was 148 weeks in the U.S. bestsellers. Released in April 1969. Released in Britain on the CBS label.

CLASSICS IV

TRACES *Imperial* [*USA*]. A beautiful romantic ballad featuring

Dennis Yost, lead vocalist of the group, and written by James Cobb (of the group) with B. Buie and E. Gordy.

The disc was released in January 1969 and was No 2 chartwise for a week in the U.S.A. with 12 weeks in the bestsellers. It is estimated to have sold a million by April 1969, the third for the group.

Originally a quartet, they became an octet (see 1967) and the personnel for this recording had two changes, Auburn Burrell (lead guitar) and Dean Daughtry (organ) in place of James Cobb and Joe Wilson. Cobb left to remain in Atlanta as a writer.

THE COWSILLS

HAIR (from *Hair*) MGM [*USA*]. The phenomenal success of the Broadway musical *Hair* caught the pop music fancy, and after being around for over a year, its numerous songs were recorded by dozens of artists in the U.S.A., England, Germany and other countries.

The Cowsills' version of 'Hair' was rearranged and recorded by Bill and Bob Cowsill of the famous family group and released in March 1969. By the following month it had passed the million mark (24 April) and was awarded a Gold Disc by R.I.A.A. The disc was No 1 for three weeks with 15 weeks in the U.S. bestsellers. Bill Cowsill, the oldest member of the group, left in May 1969 to pursue a career in composing.

The disc was the second million seller for The Cowsills. The song was written by Gerome Ragni and James Rado (words) and Galt MacDermot (music).

CREEDENCE CLEARWATER REVIVAL (vocal and instrumental quartet)

PROUD MARY *Fantasy* [*USA*]. This group was formed around 1959 in San Francisco when the members were 13 and schoolboys in suburban E. Cerrito, California. Lead singer John Fogerty who wrote most of their material was a keen student of Chuck Berry and Bo Diddley records. Doug Clifford began to learn drums, and along with Stu Cook on piano and John's brother Tom on bass guitar, they called themselves The Blue Velvets, later changing this to The Golliwogs. They performed at teenage clubs and various military bases. After John was out of the Army in 1967, they practised together for six months and pooled their resources. In early 1968 they were ready for a new career and decided on a new name: Creedence (a mixture of creed and credence indicating belief in themselves) Clearwater (deep, pure and true) and Revival (symbolizing their new direction). They developed a blend of psychedelic electronic sounds with a firm blues base, performing songs about where they came from and about people's problems in a simple, rhythmic-blues straight sound. In 1968 they earned only $30 a night from occasional dates. By 1969 it was $30,000 a night.

In October 1968, their recording of 'Susie Q' rose to No 11 in the U.S. charts and subsequently sold a million. 'Proud Mary', a steady moving mid-speed rhythmic number written by John Fogerty was released in January 1969 and rose to No 1 for one week with 14 weeks in the bestsellers, selling the million by April,

the first for the Fantasy label. It was also a success in Britain, reaching No 8 (Liberty label) with 13 weeks in the bestsellers.

Creedence Clearwater Revival became the major factor in Fantasy's success, this outstanding rock group packing in big crowds with its astonishingly powerful music, impeccable instrumental style and fast delivery. Their first three albums passed the million dollar sales mark.

Leader John Fogerty also plays guitar and mouth harp, and sings with obvious blues inspirations. He was born on 28 May in Berkeley, California. Brother Tom born 9 November 1941, Berkeley, California. Doug Clifford born 24 April 1945 in Palo Alto, California. Stuart Cook born 25 April 1945 in Berkeley, California.

BAD MOON RISING *Fantasy* [*USA*]. Also written by the group's John Fogerty, the disc released in April 1969. Described as 'a powerhouse disc, and a blazing bayou rock outing' it sold the million by July, the second for now internationally famous Creedence Clearwater Revival. It was No 1 for a week in the U.S.A. with 14 weeks in the bestsellers, and was a very big success in Britain where it was No 1 for three weeks (Liberty label) and sold over 250,000. R.I.A.A. Gold Disc award 16 December 1970.

GREEN RIVER *Fantasy* [*USA*]. The third million seller in a row for this outstanding group, the song again written by their leader John Fogerty. A powerhouse disc, it developed the bayou-rock style of the group and was released in July 1969 with million sale in two months. Chartwise it was No 2 for one week in the U.S.A. and 13 weeks in the bestsellers.

The title was also used for an album by the group (see below).

BAYOU COUNTRY (album) *Fantasy* [*USA*]. Released in the U.S.A. in January 1969, this album by the Creedence Clearwater Revival reached No 8 for one week and was a consistent seller throughout 1969. By November 1969 it sold over a million. Most of the numbers were written by the group's John Fogerty. The album contained: 'Born on the Bayou', by John Fogerty; 'Bootleg', by John Fogerty; 'Graveyard Train', by John Fogerty; 'Good Golly, Miss Molly', by Robert Blackwell and John Marascalco (1957); 'Penthouse Pauper', by John Fogerty; 'Proud Mary', by John Fogerty; 'Keep on Chooglin', by John Fogerty.

It was in the U.S. bestsellers for 87 weeks. R.I.A.A. Gold Disc award, 1970 (December).

Release in Britain was on the Liberty label on 4 July 1969.

GREEN RIVER (album) *Fantasy* [*USA*]. Second million seller album by the end of 1969 for Creedence Clearwater Revival. The tremendous popularity of the group took this disc to No 1 for four weeks with sales continuing strongly into 1970. It was released in the U.S.A. in August 1969 and had advance orders of over $1,000,000. The group's leader, John Fogerty, was again responsible for nearly all the numbers thereon. The album contained: 'Green River', by John Fogerty; 'Commotion', by John Fogerty; 'Tombstone Shadow', by John Fogerty; 'Wrote a Song for Everyone', by John Fogerty; 'Bad Moon Rising', by John Fogerty; 'Lodi', by John Fogerty; 'Cross Tie Walker', by John Fogerty; 'Sinister Purpose', by John Fogerty; 'The Night Time Is the Right Time', by Herman.

It was in the U.S. bestsellers for 88 weeks. R.I.A.A. Gold Disc award, 1970 (December).

DOWN ON THE CORNER backed with FORTUNATE SON *Fantasy* [*USA*]. The fourth singles million for Creedence Clearwater Revival, both songs written by the group's John Fogerty. The disc was released in the U.S.A. in October 1969 and sold the million by early 1970 after reaching No 3 for a week with 15 weeks in the bestsellers. In Britain (Liberty label) it was No 26 for two weeks in early 1970, where it was released in February. 'Down on the Corner' is a slower bayou blues. 'Fortunate Son' is a stunning effort with early rock feeling. R.I.A.A. Gold Disc award December 1970.

WILLY AND THE POOR BOYS (album) *Fantasy* [*USA*]. This fourth album by the group was released in December 1969 and reached No 3 on the U.S. charts for five weeks staying in the Top Ten for 15 weeks in 1970 with a run of 60 weeks in the charts. It received a Gold Disc award from R.I.A.A. in December 1970 and by then had sold over the million.

The sleeve of the disc just about tells the group's whole story. Perhaps more than any other group, they were directly concerned with the simple lives of simple people, and this music reflected their sensibilities with honest, intense passion.

The contents of this outstanding disc were: 'Down on the Corner', by John Fogerty; 'Fortunate Son', by John Fogerty; 'Cotton Fields', by Huddie Ledbetter; 'The Midnight Special', traditional, arr.: J. Fogerty; 'It Came Out of the Sky', by John Fogerty; 'Poor Boy Shuffle', by John Fogerty; 'Feelin' Blue', by John Fogerty; 'Don't Look Now', by John Fogerty; 'Side of the Road', by John Fogerty; 'Effigy', by John Fogerty.

In Britain release was on the Liberty label in March 1970 where it reached No 10 for two weeks.

CROSBY, STILLS AND NASH

CROSBY, STILLS & NASH (album) *Atlantic* [*USA*]. Crosby, Stills and Nash, three formidable members of the royalty of rock, were formed as a group in the spring of 1969. Each had separated from the groups in which they had become famous – David Crosby, formerly of The Byrds; Stephen Stills, formerly of The Buffalo Springfield; and Graham Nash, formerly of The Hollies. All three are writers, singers and guitarists. They signed as a group with Atlantic Records and together produced this album, a magnificent debut and showcase for their combined talents. It was completed after many weeks of intensive work and released in the U.S.A. in June 1969. It was one of the most eagerly awaited albums of the year and got to No 5 for three weeks, and stayed in the Top Ten for 31 weeks into 1970 with sales of two million reported by March 1970. Its outstanding feature is the vocal harmony with haunting instrumental sound. A Gold Disc was awarded by R.I.A.A. and the group received the Grammy Award for 'Best New Artists of 1969'. The drummer with the group is Dallas Taylor. 'Marrakesh Express' written by Nash was a hit as a singles issue in the U.S.A. (No 17 for a week).

The album contents: 'Sweet Judy Blue Eyes', by Stephen Stills; 'Marrakesh Express', by Graham Nash; 'Guinevere', by David Crosby; 'You Don't Have to Cry', by Stephen Stills; 'Pre-Road Downs', by Graham Nash; 'Wooden Ships', by David Crosby and Stephen Stills; 'Lady of the Island', by Graham Nash; 'Helplessly Hoping', by Stephen Stills; 'Long Time Gone', by David Crosby; 'Bye-Byes', by Stephen Stills.

The album was released in Britain in August 1969, and was No 19 for two weeks. In the U.S.A. it stayed in the bestsellers for 100 weeks.

Stephen Stills was born on 3 January 1945.

THE CUFF LINKS (pop septet)

TRACY *Decca* [*USA*]. A melodic, pop-rock song rendered in light hearted fashion, 'Tracy' provided this new group with a smash hit. It was written by Paul Vance and Lee Pockriss. The group were in Vance's office (so the story went) and suddenly they started to sing. Vance was so impressed he suggested they record something straight away. The results were so good that a few days later, and after a rapid series of phone calls, the seven singers decided to quit the groups they had been with and form The Cuff Links. 'Tracy' was released in the U.S.A. in July 1969, shot up the charts to No 4 for two weeks with 12 weeks in the bestsellers, and subsequently sold a million. In Britain it was released on the MCA label in November 1969 and reached No 2 for two weeks with 16 weeks in the bestsellers, with over 250,000 sale by early 1970.

The personnel was: Pat Rizzo (sax, flute) ex-member and former child star with Joey Dee and The Starlighters, and The Riverboat Soul Band; Danny Valentine (drums); Rich Dimino (organist); Bob Gill (trumpet, flugel horn and flute); Dave Lavender (guitar); Andrew 'Junior' Denno (bassist); Joe Cord (vocalist).

Ron Dante (of The Archies group) was later named as the vocalist on this disc, and revealed The Cuff Links weren't actually on the disc at all. The recording was Dante's voice nine times over. The Cuff Links became an individual group, backing him on occasion.

DESMOND DEKKER AND THE ACES

ISRAELITES *Pyramid* [*Britain*]. Desmond Dekker (real name Desmond Dacres) was born 16 July 1941 in Kingston, Jamaica. He made his first appearance as an amateur in a church choir there, and his first professional appearance in 1962. He subsequently went to Britain for a tour, made his TV debut in 'Top of the Pops' and then made his own TV series 'Action' in Jamaica. Most of his recording was done in Jamaica. 'Israelites' written by him with Leslie Kong was arranged there, and is a novelty reggae number. The disc was issued in Britain in March 1969 and was No 1 for two weeks, selling over 250,000. It rose to No 6 in the U.S.A. on the Uni label with 10 weeks in the bestsellers and a global million sale was reported by June.

In addition to singing, Dekker plays piano, guitar and drums. Singer James Brown was the biggest influence on his career.

DESMOND DEKKER

IT MEK *Pyramid* [*Britain*]. This disc with its strange title, was recorded and released before Dekker's big hit 'Israelites' and withdrawn when the latter was a success. It was released again (June 1969) and achieved No 7 for two weeks in the British charts with 11 weeks in the bestsellers. The disc subsequently (by September 1970) sold over a million overseas, with Gold Disc award by Ember Records, the distributors of Dekker's recordings.

The song was written by L. Kong and D. Dacres (Dekker's real name) and recorded in Dekker's native land, Jamaica, with the brass accompaniment added in Britain. Dekker is an exponent of Jamaica's popular music which finally became known as 'reggae' – a mixture of ska, rock-steady and semi-calypso.

'It mek' is a West Indian phrase meaning 'that's why'.

THE DELLS

OH, WHAT A NIGHT *Cadet* [*USA*]. Written by Marion Junior (of the group) with John Funches, The Dells first released this in 1956 (q.v.). This recording, released in August 1969, thus made the song a million seller for the second time for them. It reached No 10 for two weeks in the U.S.A.'s national charts with 11 weeks in the bestsellers, and was also a No 1 rhythm-and-blues disc.

The personnel of The Dells was still the same after 15 years (see 1956).

JACKIE DE SHANNON

PUT A LITTLE LOVE IN YOUR HEART *Imperial* [*USA*]. Jackie De Shannon's (real name Sharon Myers) career has embraced acting, singing and song writing. She was born on 21 August 1945 in Hazel, Kentucky. At the age of six she showed remarkable precociousness and had her own radio show. She toured with The Platters, and with a group called The Cookies, early in her career. When Imperial Records heard she was both performing and producing her own radio show at the age of 12, they signed her to a contract. Jackie subsequently sang in clubs, in concert, and on TV and appeared as an actress in various TV shows including 'My Three Sons', 'Wild, Wild West' and 'Name of the Game'. In 1964 she went to Britain for a lengthy promotional visit and made recordings there for the Liberty label.

She is a prolific song writer, over 600 to date, and her recordings brought her four nominations from N.A.R.A.S. Artists who have recorded her songs include The Byrds, Brenda Lee, Rick Nelson, Bobby Vee, The Searchers and Helen Shapiro.

'Put a Little Love in Your Heart', written by Jackie with Jimmy Holiday and Randy Myers, is a beautiful song with a message. It was released in June 1969, reached No 3 in the U.S. charts with 14 weeks in the bestsellers, and was a certified

R.I.A.A. million seller by 29 September when it began to find its way on to new albums at a fantastic rate.

NEIL DIAMOND

SWEET CAROLINE *Uni* [*USA*]. Neil Diamond was born in Coney Island, New York, on 24 January 1945. At the age of seven, he moved to Memphis and at ten played with The Memphis Backstreet Boys who earned a living by singing in the streets and picking up the small money thrown from windows as they passed by. At 13, Neil ran away from home and landed in Kansas City, Mo., where he got together a folk group called The Roadrunners. They travelled the Midwest for a few years, during which time Neil absorbed various styles of folk music and also met the legendary Woody Guthrie. Neil subsequently left the Midwestern nightclub circuit for New York, and in 1964 was discovered by the songwriting team of Jeff Barry and Ellie Greenwich who put him on the road to fame as a songwriter. He wrote for Sonny and Cher, The Ronettes, Jay and The Americans and The Monkees, with two million sellers for the latter – 'I'm a Believer' and 'A Little Bit Me, a Little Bit You'.

Barry and Greenwich induced him to record, and he made his first vocal disc 'Solitary Man' in 1966, for the Bang label. Several of his discs on this label were chart items. In 1968, Neil signed with the Uni label and made an album 'Brother Love's Travelling Salvation Show' for them, released in 1969. This included 'Sweet Caroline' released in June 1969 as a single. It rose to No 3 in the U.S. charts for two weeks with 14 weeks in the bestsellers, and by 18 August sold a million with R.I.A.A. Gold Disc award. The song, a fine love ballad, was written by Neil.

Neil Diamond became one of the most sought-after songwriters. His compositions performed by himself and others accounted for 14 hits and sales of 12 million singles between 1966 and 1968 alone. He became the most highly paid performer in the world.

HOLLY HOLY *Uni* [*USA*]. A great follow-up disc for Neil Diamond, again written by him. This was released in October 1969 and got to No 4 for two weeks in the U.S. charts with 14 weeks in the bestsellers, with million sale and Gold Disc award from R.I.A.A. in January 1970.

DIMITRI DOURAKINE AND HIS ORCHESTRA

CASATSCHOK *Philips* [*France*]. Released in early 1969, 'Casatschok' a new dance craze created by François Patrice Saint-Hilaire sold over a million via Dourakine's disc throughout Europe. It was No 1 for ten weeks in France, and a big seller in Denmark (No 1), Italy (No 5), Holland (No 3), Spain, Germany, Belgium (sold 150,000) and Mexico (No 1). A near million by Philips artist Rika Zarai was also sold, this disc reaching No 2 in France. Dourakine was born in Russia. 'Casatschok' was written by Boris Rubashkin.

FERRANTE AND TEICHER

MIDNIGHT COWBOY *United Artists* [*USA*]. Theme of the film of the same title, written by British composer John Barry (a 3-time Academy Award winner) this disc was released in the U.S.A. in October, reaching No 10 and staying in the bestsellers for 15 weeks. It is said to have sold the million, making the fourth for the famous piano duo.

The film received the Academy Awards for Best Picture, Best Director of 1969, and Best Instrumental Theme.

THE FIFTH DIMENSION

THE AGE OF AQUARIUS (album) *Soul City* [*USA*]. A superlative album, released in the U.S.A. in May 1969, this was in the Top Ten for ten weeks and reached No 2 for two weeks, with Gold Disc award by R.I.A.A. on 14 July. By early January 1970 it had sold over a million units. It contained two titles that sold a million as singles by the group.

Contents were: 'Aquarius' (from *Hair*), by Gerome Ragni, James Rado and Galt MacDermot (1968); 'Blowing Away', by Laura Nyro; 'Skinny Man', by Kollander and Kollander; 'Wed-

ding Bell Blues', by Laura Nyro; 'Don'tcha Hear Me Callin' to Ya', by Stevenson; 'The Hideaway', by Jim Webb; 'Workin' On a Groovy Thing', by Roger Atkins and Neil Sedaka; 'Let It Be Me' (Je t'appartiens) by Pierre Delanoe and Gilbert Becaud (1955) (English words: Mann Curtis); 'Sunshine of Your Love', by Eric Clapton, Jack Bruce and Peter Brown (1967); 'The Winds of Heaven', by Dorough and Landesman; 'Those Were the Days', by Gene Haskin (1963); 'Let the Sunshine In' (from *Hair*) by Gerome Ragni, James Rado and Galt MacDermot (1968).

This album was in the U.S.A. bestsellers for 72 weeks.

In Britain, the disc was released on the Liberty label.

AQUARIUS/LET THE SUNSHINE IN (medley from the musical *Hair*) *Soul City* [*USA*]. The Fifth Dimension first saw the show *Hair* in the summer of 1968 and decided that the song 'Aquarius' would be a great one for them to record. Their vocal arranger Bob Alcivar and the group's producer Bones Howe worked out the rhythm arrangement and cut the basic track in Los Angeles in October 1968. The group's vocals for this were overdubbed in a studio at Las Vegas in December. The disc was released at the end of February 1969 and soon zoomed to No 1 where it stayed for six weeks with 17 weeks in the bestsellers, with R.I.A.A. Gold Disc award for a million sale by 30 April. By mid-May it had sold over two million. The disc rose to No 11 for a week in Britain (Liberty label) where it was released on 3 April 1969 with 11 weeks in the bestsellers. It had continued sales and became a standard item, with global tally of an estimated three million plus by the end of 1969.

This was the first big seller of the show's 26 songs written by Gerome Ragni and James Rado (words) and Galt MacDermot (music). By June 1969, 16 of the show's songs had been released as singles, with million sellers for The Cowsills and Oliver among them in the U.S.A. alone.

Grammy award (1969) for Best Contemporary Vocal Performance by a group.

WEDDING BELL BLUES *Soul City* [*USA*]. Released in September 1969 and taken from the Fifth Dimension's enormously successful album 'Age of Aquarius', this lovely soft song by Laura Nyro became No 1 in the U.S. charts for three weeks with 15 weeks in the bestsellers, and sold the million by 5 December 1969 with Gold Disc award from R.I.A.A. It was No 16 in Britain.

FLEETWOOD MAC

OH WELL *Reprise* [*Britain*]. Written by the group's Peter Green and released in September 1969, it helped to make Fleetwood Mac one of the top groups of the year. The disc was No 1 for a week in the U.S.A. and sold a global million by February 1970.

FLYING MACHINE (pop quintet)

SMILE A LITTLE SMILE FOR ME *Pye* [*Britain*] *Congress* [*USA*]. This disc, by five talented musicians with several years of combined experience, was released in Britain on the Pye label on 11 April 1969 but did not register as a hit. When released in the U.S.A. by Congress in June, it rose to No 4 for two weeks with 14 weeks in the bestsellers, and by 12 December had sold a million with R.I.A.A. Gold Disc award. Described as a 'stunning teenage romance-tune with a bittersweet touch', the song is the work of British writers Tony Macauley and Geoff Stevens.

Tony Newman (born 1947 in Rugby) vocalist, and Sam Kempe (born 1946 in Rugby) first played together in local groups, then with The Pinkertons for nearly five years, and later became friends with Stuart Colman (born 1945 in Rugby) who is a bass guitarist and electric piano player. When The Pinkertons split, they formed their own group. They met Steve Jones (born 1946 in Coventry) who is a guitarist and Paul Wilkinson (born 1948 in Coventry) when they were sharing a bill in Coventry, and then formed The Flying Machine. They developed a soft and provocative style. 'Smile a Little Smile' was their debut on the Pye label.

FRIENDS OF DISTINCTION (vocal quartet)

GRAZIN' IN THE GRASS *Victor* [*USA*]. The personnel of this group, two women and two men, is: Harry Elson, Floyd Butler, Jessica Cleaves and Barbara Jean Love. Elson was previously a professional baseball player for a time with the Los Angeles Angels, and then decided on a singing career when he joined a rock group in the early 1960s. When this group was a touring troupe with soul singer Ray Charles, Elson met Butler and formed the nucleus of the Friends of Distinction. Butler brought Jessica Cleaves into the group when they met in the Los Angeles Urban League, Butler being its assistant project director for two years. Barbara Jean Love, daughter of a West Coast disc jockey Reuben Brown, joined the group about six months before the act made its debut at the Daisy, a top Hollywood discotheque, in the summer of 1968.

The group was brought to the attention of RCA-Victor by actor Jim Brown who signed them to his firm after hearing them sing in their first professional engagement.

'Grazin' in the Grass', originally a million seller for trumpeter Hugh Masekela who composed it, was an instrumental number. Harry Elston, writer for The Friends, wrote lyrics for the tune and the result was the group's initial RCA recording. This was released in March 1969, rose to No 3 for one week on the U.S. charts with 16 weeks in the bestsellers, and sold the million by 10 June, with R.I.A.A. Gold Disc award.

GOING IN CIRCLES *Victor* [*USA*]. This disc was a consistent seller, staying in the U.S. charts for 20 weeks after release in July 1969 and reaching No 14 for two weeks, giving The Friends of Distinction their second Gold Disc award for million sale by R.I.A.A. in December 1969. It was written by Anita Poree and Jerry Peters in 1968.

BOBBY GENTRY

FANCY *Capitol* [*USA*]. Released in the U.S.A. in October 1969, the million sale reported in October 1970. It was written by Bobbie herself. The disc was a steady seller and stayed in the U.S. charts for 14 weeks, achieving No 31 for two weeks.

ROBIN GIBB

SAVED BY THE BELL *Polydor* [*Britain*]. The famous Bee Gees group broke up in 1969 and Robin Gibb, one of its original members, became a solo artist. This recording of a song he wrote himself was released in Britain on 4 July 1969 and was No 2 there for four weeks, selling a global million by mid-September. It was popular in Europe, particularly in Denmark (No 1), Holland, Germany and Belgium. The group has since re-formed.

GIORGIO

LOOKY LOOKY *Ariola* [*Germany*]. Giorgio (real name Giorgio Moroder) was both singer and producer of this disc which sold a million in Europe, mainly in West Germany, Austria and Switzerland. A Gold Disc was awarded by Ariola in October 1970. Song written by Giorgio and Rainford.

R. B. GREAVES

TAKE A LETTER, MARIA *Atco* [*USA*]. R. B. Greaves was born at a U.S. Air Force Base in South America, the son of a Captain in the Air Force. He moved to a Seminole reservation in Samona, California where, being half Indian, he was raised by his stepmother from the age of four. As a youngster, he spent most of his time developing the traits of a Westerner, and learned to play guitar in his spare time. He also acquired cowboy techniques, rode Indian style, and learned how to track in the wilderness. He became an accomplished songwriter and wrote this song himself, which tells of a man who is leaving his wife for his secretary. The vocal impact of this disc rocketed him to instant stardom and it was No 2 chartwise in the U.S.A. for a week with 15 weeks in the bestsellers, selling the million with Gold Disc award from R.I.A.A. on 11 December, just three months after its September release.

Greaves' singing is said to be 'an uncanny echo of his uncle, the late Sam Cooke'. In January 1970, he appeared as co-star with Stevie Wonder at New York's Apollo Theatre.

By 1970 sales of this disc totalled 2,500,000. Greaves won a Hank Williams show singing contest at the age of eight while visiting relatives in Memphis. In 1960 he went to Europe with a 14-piece band and joined up with other black performers. He performed with The Beatles at the Star Club in Hamburg.

The biggest date of his career was 6 August 1970 when he appeared for two weeks at New York's Copacabana.

GARLAND GREENE

JEALOUS KIND OF FELLA *Uni* [*USA*]. Written by singer Garland Greene, R. Browner, M. Dollison and Joe Armstead (producer of the disc), this was released in the U.S.A. in August 1969 and reached No 19 for a week with 10 weeks in the bestsellers. It was reported to have sold the million by March 1971. Garland Greene had previous hits on the Uni label with 'Ain't That Good Enough' and 'Don't Think I'm a Violent Guy'. He signed with the Cotillion label in March 1971.

THE GUESS WHO (vocal and instrumental quartet)

THESE EYES *Victor* [*Canada*]. The Guess Who, all of whom are from Winnipeg, Manitoba, consists of: Randy Bachman (leader and lead guitarist); Burton Cummings (lead singer, piano, organ, rhythm guitar, flute and harmonica); Garry Peterson (drummer); Jim Kale (bassist).

Garry made his debut at four in a show with Gisele Mackenzie and has also appeared on CBS radio and TV, and in concert with the Winnipeg Symphony. Jim gave voice recitals as a youngster at Shinn Conservatory of Music. Randy was composer of all the group's material with Burton, the duo having written this song.

The group had been in and around the Canadian scene since 1960 and won a silver record for their first single 'Shakin' All Over'. 'These Eyes' was turned down for several weeks by a leading pop radio station in Canada as being not suitable commercially. One station only broadcast the disc after an opposition station had given it successful exposure in the same city. The Guess Who then became the first group in Canadian history to top the charts from Newfoundland to British Columbia. Through this success, the disc got wide exposure in the U.S.A. where it rose to No 3 for two weeks after release in March 1969 with a subsequent 14 weeks in the bestsellers. By 25 June it sold over the million and was awarded a Gold Disc by R.I.A.A.

The Guess Who starred on a weekly show 'Where It's At' on CBC-TV in 1969. They undoubtedly opened up the U.S.A. market to local Canadian producers. The disc was produced by Jack Richardson and arranged by Ben McPeek for Nimbus 9 Productions, cut at the A & R Studios in New York and released through RCA-Victor. Randy Bachman later formed Bachman-Turner Overdrive.

LAUGHING *Victor* [*USA*]. Described as a 'finely wrought melancholy rock ballad', this disc was the second million seller for The Guess Who, again written by the group's Randy Bachman and Burton Cummings. It was released in July 1969 and sold the million by October, reaching No 5 for a week in the U.S.A. with 11 weeks in the bestsellers. R.I.A.A. Gold Disc award 28 October 1969.

NO TIME *RCA* [*USA*]. Third million seller in a row for this Canadian group, written by its two members Randy Bachman and Burton Cummings. It was released in December 1969 and sold the million by early 1970, reaching No 3 in the U.S. charts for one week with 14 weeks in the bestsellers.

MERLE HAGGARD (country-and-western vocalist)

OKIE FROM MUSKOGEE (also known as 'The Only Hippie in Muskogee') *Capitol* [*USA*]. Merle Haggard was born on 6

April 1937 and raised in Bakersfield, California. At the age of 14 he ran away from his Bakersfield home and embarked on a riot of vagrancy and wild living, and by 1960 had spent seven years of his life in reform school or jails, including a three-year term in San Quentin. He then decided to change his directions. While in San Quentin, he began to write and pick guitar for himself, and he was there when Johnny Cash came to record his 'Live at San Quentin' album. On release, his music showed no compromise. 'Mama Tried' tells of his rift with home, and 'Hungry Eyes' is from life. He entered the recording business when he signed with Tally Records, where he gained his first recognition among country music fans with a country hit called 'Strangers'. He then came to the attention of Capitol Records, and in 1965 was signed by them.

In February 1966 his talent was recognized by the Academy of Country-and-Western Music, which named him, at its first Annual Awards Show, 'The Most Promising Male Vocalist' of that year. In addition, he and his wife Bonnie Owens received the Academy's award for 'Best Vocal Group'. These awards were only the beginning for Merle. He has since become one of the biggest country disc sellers, with hit after hit in both singles and album form. His biggest singles were: (1966) 'Swinging Doors', 'The Bottle Let Me Down'; (1967) 'Sing Me Back Home', 'I'm a Lonesome Fugitive'; (1968) 'Mama Tried', 'I Take a Lot of Pride in What I Am'; (1969) 'Hungry Eyes', 'Workin' Man Blues' and his first million seller, this disc of 'Okie from Muskogee'.

'Okie' was written by Merle Haggard and Roy Edward Burris, and the disc reached No 41 in the national charts and was a Top 10 country-and-western hit. Merle got the idea for the song while driving into a small western town with his band The Strangers when someone looked out of the window and commented, 'I bet they don't smoke marijuana in Muskogee.' One line led to another and very quickly the whole song was put together. The song was adopted by the 'silent majority' and became the redneck's battle song. It virtually transformed Merle's career, and is now folklore.

Further hits followed, 'The Fightin' Side of Me' (1970), 'Someday We'll Look Back' and 'Soldier's Last Letter' (1971), 'Carolyn', 'Grandma Harp' (1972), 'Everybody's Had the Blues', 'I Wonder if They Ever Think of Me' (1973), 'If We Make It through December', 'Things Aren't Funny Anymore', 'Ole Man from the Mountain' (1974).

One of the biggest sellers of his many albums was 'The Best of Merle Haggard' (1968) which received a Gold Disc award in 1974 from R.I.A.A. for million dollars sale. With the continued global interest in country-and-western singers, Merle became one of the 'greats' by 1974 and was selected as a special feature in *Time* magazine in that year.

An album 'The Very Best of Merle Haggard' containing 16 of his most famous recordings was released in 1974.

ROLF HARRIS

TWO LITTLE BOYS *Columbia [Britain]*. 'Two Little Boys' is probably the oldest pop song to date to have topped the record charts. It was written way back in 1903 by the U.S. songwriters Edward Madden (words) and Theodore Morse (music) who penned many hits such as 'Blue Bell' and 'Down in Jungle Town' in the early part of this century.

Rolf Harris was on a four-months' working holiday around Northern Australia and during a party at the Eldo Tracking Station, met Ted Egan, a member of the Aborigine Welfare Department. At a sing-song after the meal, Ted mentioned a song his father had taught him, suggesting it would be ideal for Rolf to feature on his TV show. Rolf didn't think, after hearing it, that such a weepy song of boyhood friendship about an incident in the American Civil War would really suit him, but after singing it a few times it began to attract him. Egan put the song on tape and Rolf brought it back to England. Stewart Morris, producer of his British TV show, was keen, but Rolf found the tape had been over-recorded and phoned Egan in Australia and taped it across 13,000 miles as Egan sang it. Rolf featured it on his TV show, was inundated with requests, and made a commercial recording which shot up the British charts and stayed at No 1 for six weeks with 24 weeks in the bestsellers. The disc was released in Britain on 7 November 1969 and by 31 February 1970 sold over 900,000 in Britain, sales elsewhere easily making it a global million seller. It was the bestselling British-made record of 1969.

THE EDWIN HAWKINS SINGERS FEATURING DOROTHY COOMBS MORRISON

OH HAPPY DAY *Pavilion [USA]*. The Edwin Hawkins Singers were originally the Northern California State Youth Choir, founded in April 1967 by soprano Betty Watson and Edwin Hawkins, the members' ages ranging from 17 to 25. It was formed by drawing upon leading singers from Pentecostal choirs throughout the San Francisco area. Twenty-five-year-old choir director of the Ephesian Church of God in Christ, Edwin Hawkins of Oakland, California, who is also a pianist and music arranger, sent the 46-strong ensemble into the church with eight traditional gospel songs (1967) arranged by himself to make an album to raise funds for the choir. This was done on an ordinary two-track tape recorder. At a cost of $750 (£250) the choir decided to make 1,000 records from the tape, and the album titled 'Let Us Go into the House of the Lord' was recorded by an Oakland, California company that specialized in church sales. It sold about 600 in the limited gospel market at the Annual Youth Congress in Cleveland (June 1968) where the choir was placed first in the singing competition. The disc was then forgotten, but, in February 1969, a copy was unearthed by John Lingel, rock promotion director at Chatton Distributors in Oakland, and given to a local radio station KSAN-FM where disc jockey Abe Keshishian played the record heavily, especially the track of 'Oh Happy Day'. Record companies started bidding for the album but New York's Buddah Records got the distribution rights by paying a $55,000 advance plus a $25,000 bonus and changed the name of the choir to The Edwin Hawkins Singers. 'Oh Happy Day' was released as a single on Pavilion label in April, and its infectious, compelling exhilarating sound was broadcast on rhythm-and-blues stations, easy-listening stations and even rock stations 10 to 20 times a day from Los Angeles to Boston. In two weeks the disc sold over a million and rose to No 2 on the U.S. charts with 10 weeks in the bestsellers. Release in Britain was on the Buddah label on 18 May 1969, the disc being

No 2 for two weeks with 12 weeks in the bestsellers. R.I.A.A. awarded a Gold Disc on 3 June.

'Oh Happy Day' was the first black gospel record to catch on, and it became the biggest gospel seller of our time. Estimates of global sales have been put at over three million. In an era of rock and roll, the disc was an education in an authentic religious experience to thousands of young people. It accelerated the rush to make gospel records by the labels who were first responsbile for the removal of gospel and religious music from the black stations.

'Oh Happy Day' dates back to 1755, when it was written by Phillip Doddige. E. F. Rimbault revised it in 1855 and it is included in the Baptist Standard Hymnal. Edwin Hawkins' arrangement became one of the most recorded of 1969. The album, also released on the new Pyramid label owned by Edwin Hawkins and producer/engineer Lamont Beech, soon passed the million dollar sale. U.S.A. sales of 'Oh Happy Day' were over two million.

Grammy award (1969) for Best Soul Gospel.

THE HOLLIES

HE AIN'T HEAVY – HE'S MY BROTHER *Parlophone* [*Britain*]. Written by U.S.A. songwriters Bob Russell and Bobby Scott. Tony Hicks of The Hollies heard the song in a British publisher's office and was charmed by its beauty. The song came about through Father Flanagan, of Boys' Town, who saw one of his little boys carrying a much-bigger but crippled boy in his arms. Father Flanagan asked the little boy if that wasn't a heavy load, to which he replied 'He ain't heavy, he's my brother'. A Jesuit priest who knew the Boys' Town story, heard the song on the radio and contacted the disc jockey to tell him about it. The D.J. then related the story every time he played the disc and it soon became a hit, spreading to all the big cities in the U.S.A. where it was released on the Epic label in December 1969. It sold a million there by March 1970 and reached No 7 in the U.S. charts for two weeks with 19 weeks in the bestsellers. In Britain, the disc was released earlier – on 19 September 1969 – reaching No 2 for two weeks.

The lead vocal is by Allan Clarke, with the large orchestral accompaniment arranged and conducted by Johnny Scott. On this disc, Terry Sylvester replaced Graham Nash who had left to join the new supergroup of Crosby, Stills and Nash.

Global sales of over 2½ million were reported in March 1970.

MICHAEL HOLM

MENDOCINO *Ariola* [*Germany*]. A big success for Michael Holm who wrote the German lyrics. The disc was released in September 1969, reached No 3 for five weeks in 1970 in Germany and stayed in the Top Ten for over three months, selling over a million. Ariola presented a Gold Disc award in October 1970. Doug Sahm (of Sir Douglas Quintet) composed the tune.

EDDIE HOLMAN

HEY THERE, LONELY GIRL *ABC* [*USA*]. Originally 'Hey There, Lonely Boy' written by Earl Shuman (words) and Leon Carr (music) in 1963, when it was a hit for Ruby and The Romantics. Eddie Holman's version is described as a 'sweet soul-scorcher' and the disc was released in early November 1969. By February 1970, the disc was No 2 for three weeks with 14 weeks in the U.S. bestsellers, and received a Gold Disc award from R.I.A.A. for million sale in March 1970.

THE ISLEY BROTHERS

IT'S YOUR THING *T. Neck* [*USA*]. Released in February 1969, this disc sold half a million in its first three weeks on the market, and two million by June, the first big hit for the three Isleys (Rudolph, Ronald and Kelly) since 1962. It was the first release on their own T. Neck label, which they had planned for a year and a half after several years of hit records, extended tours and fame since their rock hit of 1959 – 'Shout'. 'It's Your Thing'

was thus written, produced and performed by the brothers with the help of their band which included two other Isley brothers, Ernest (who arranged and played a variety of instruments) and Marvin (who played bass and contributed arrangement ideas). The disc was No 2 for two weeks in the U.S. charts and 14 weeks in the bestsellers, and No 25 for two weeks in Britain. An R.I.A.A. Gold Disc for million sale was awarded 9 April 1969.

Grammy Award (1969) for Best Rhythm-and-Blues Vocal Performance by a duo or group.

THE JACKSON 5

I WANT YOU BACK *Motown* [*USA*]. Diana Ross of The Supremes discovered this talented quintet in Gary, Indiana at a talent show to which she had been invited by the city's black mayor. She was so impressed that she immediately took them back to Detroit where Motown chief Berry Gordy, Jr rushed them into the recording studio. 'I Want You Back' became one of the label's biggest hits, selling two million in its first six weeks after release in October. It achieved No 1 for a week and stayed in the U.S. charts for 19 weeks. In Britain it was No 1 for one week where it was released on 16 January 1970 and sold over 250,000.

Described as a dynamic group of child prodigies, the personnel was lead singer Michael (then aged 10), Marlon (aged 12), Jermaine (aged 14), Toriano (aged 15) and Sigmund Jackson (aged 18), all brothers. These new 'soul-kings' had the old Supremes/Four Tops flair with a bit of Sly Stone added. Their performance of the song, written by 'The Corporation' is certainly dynamic. 'The Corporation' is the team of Freddie Perren, Fonso Mizell, Deke Richards and Berry Gordy, Jr.

DIANA ROSS PRESENTS THE JACKSON 5 (also known as I WANT YOU BACK) (album) *Motown* [*USA*]. This was The Jackson 5's first album, released in the U.S.A. on 18 December 1969. It was No 5 for a week and stayed in the bestsellers for 32 weeks, amassing a reported million sale by the end of December 1970. The British release was on 6 March 1970. Contents of the album: 'Zip-A-Dee Doo Dah' (from the film *Song of the South*, 1946), by Ray Gilbert and Allie Wrubel (1945); 'Nobody', by The Corporation (1969); 'I Want You Back', by The Corporation (1969); 'Can You Remember?', by Thom Bell and William Hart; 'Standing in the Shadows of Love', by El Holland, B. Holland and L. Dozier (1966); 'You've Changed', by Reese; 'My Cherie Amour', by S. Wonder, H. Cosby and S. Moy (1968); 'Who's Lovin' You?', by Smokey Robinson; 'Chained', by Frank Wilson (1967); '(I Know) I'm Losing You', by Whitfield, Holland and

Grant; 'Stand', by Sly Stewart; 'Born to Love You', by Hunter and Stevenson.

JAGGERZ (rock sextet)

THE RAPPER *Kama Sutra* [*USA*]. Released in late December 1969 this disc got to No 1 for two weeks in the U.S.A. in March 1970 and sold over the million with R.I.A.A. Gold Disc award by then. It was written by D. Ierace, and performed with a belting bass line for rhythmic drive by the group with their hard rock sound. The song fuses bayou and 'bubble-gum' idioms.

The group played local dates around Pittsburgh for five years before making this, their first disc.

TOMMY JAMES AND THE SHONDELLS

SWEET CHERRY WINE *Roulette* [*USA*]. Described as a 'pulsing weighty-bass effort' this disc was released in mid-March 1969 and was No 5 for two weeks in the U.S.A. with 10 weeks in the bestsellers. The million sale was reported in June. The disc also sold another half million abroad. The song was written by Tommy James with Richie Grasso.

CRYSTAL BLUE PERSUASION *Roulette* [*USA*]. The fifth million seller for Tommy James and The Shondells, written by Tommy James and M. Vale (both of the group) with Ed Gray. It was released in May 1969 and was No 1 for one week in the U.S.A. and 15 weeks in the bestsellers, with the million sale reported in July. The song is a soft ballad. With this hit, the group had achieved seven Top Ten chart hits, plus an aggregate of 19 hits in a row.

TOM JONES

I'LL NEVER FALL IN LOVE AGAIN *Decca* [*Britain*] *Parrot* [*USA*]. Written by British writers Jim Currie and Lonnie Donegan, this disc was originally a big hit in Britain in 1967 where it was No 2 for four weeks and 25 weeks in the bestsellers with over 250,000 sale, released there in July. In 1969, Tom Jones made a tour of the U.S.A. and was a great success particularly in Las Vegas where a 'live' album was recorded, including this song and his other hits (see below). 'I'll Never Fall in Love Again' was released as a single in July 1969 by overwhelming demand, reached No 5 for two weeks in the U.S.A. on the Parrot label and sold over the million with Gold Disc award from R.I.A.A. on 3 October 1969. It stayed in the bestsellers there for 16 weeks.

Tom Jones became a TV, nightclub and disc phenomenon in this year in the U.S.A., and broke all existing records at New York's Copacabana, Las Vegas' Flamingo and all over the States. By the end of 1969 he had amassed five Gold Disc awards from R.I.A.A. for million-dollar selling albums.

WITHOUT LOVE (There is nothing) *Decca* [*Britain*] *Parrot* [*USA*]. This song is a classy updating of an inspirational ballad from the country and oldie archives written in 1957 by Danny Small of the U.S.A. It was originally a hit for The Platters. Tom Jones performs the song as a middle of the road rock-blues. The disc was first released in Britain on 28 November 1969 and reached No 9 in the charts. U.S. release was in December 1969, and Tom's great popularity in 1970 over there resulted in the disc reaching No 3 for a week in February 1970 and 11 weeks in the bestsellers, with Gold Disc award from R.I.A.A. for million sale in March.

LIVE IN LAS VEGAS (album) *Decca* [*Britain*] *Parrot* [*USA*]. Tom Jones' first engagement was at The Copacabana in New York for two weeks in May 1969. In July 1969 he was booked for the Flamingo Hotel in Las Vegas. Both proved to be attendance records, and the four weeks' Flamingo engagement was the biggest advance in the hotel's history. Tom was paid $280,000 for this Las Vegas appearance and his performance was recorded, the resultant album becoming his biggest seller, notching up almost two million by early 1971. This was released in the U.S.A. in late October 1969 and had a million dollar sales advance ten days before release, with Gold Disc award from R.I.A.A. on 27 October.

The disc quickly got to No 2 for a week and stayed in the Top Ten for 18 weeks and the Top Twenty for 23 weeks. It was also in the U.S. bestsellers for 51 weeks.

British release was around the same time, the disc reaching No 2 for a week and staying in the bestsellers for 23 weeks.

By the end of 1970 Tom Jones had sold over 30 million discs of all categories (100 million equivalent singles) around the world and his tremendous success in the U.S.A. on discs, his TV show 'This is Tom Jones' on ABC and personal appearances earned him a fantastic string of bookings in the U.S.A. throughout 1970.

The album contained: 'Turn on Your Love Light', by Deadric Malone and Joseph Scott (1961); 'The Bright Lights and You Girl', by Shepard; 'I Can't Stop Loving You', by Don Gibson (1958); 'Hard to Handle', by Isbell, Jones and Redding; 'Delilah', by Les Reed and Barry Mason (1968); 'Danny Boy', by F. E. Weatherly (tune 'Londonderry Air') (1913) arranged: Blackwell; 'I'll Never Fall in Love Again', by Lonnie Donegan and Jim Currie (1967); 'Help Yourself' (orig. 'Gli occhi miei' in Italy), by Mogul and C. Donida (1968) (English words by Jack Fishman); 'Yesterday', by John Lennon and Paul McCartney (1965); 'Hey Jude', by John Lennon and Paul McCartney (1968); 'Love Me Tonight' (orig. 'Alla fine della, strada' in Italy), by D. Pace/Pilat and M. Panzer (1969) (English words by Barry Mason); 'It's Not Unusual', by Gordon Mills and Les Reed (1965); 'Twist and Shout', by Bert Russell (Berns) and Phil Medley (1961).

THIS IS TOM JONES (album) *Decca* [*Britain*] *Parrot* [*USA*]. Released in both Britain and the U.S.A. in June 1969. It reached No 4 for four weeks and was in the bestsellers for forty-two weeks in the U.S.A., selling the million there by end of 1970. A Gold Disc was awarded by R.I.A.A. almost immediately on release. In Britain the disc was No 1 for four weeks and in the bestsellers for 16 weeks..

Contents of the album: 'Fly Me to the Moon' (In other words), by Bart Howard (1954); 'Little Green Apples', by Bobby Russell (1968); 'Wichita Lineman', by Jim Webb (1969), 'Dock of the Bay (Sittin' on the)', by Steve Cropper and Otis Redding (1968); 'Dance of Love', by Charles Rich (1969); 'Hey Jude', by John Lennon and Paul McCartney (1968); 'Without You' (orig. 'Non ce' che lei' in Italy), by Rossi and Tersi (English words: Barry Mason); 'That's All Any Man Can Say', by Tony Macauley and John Macleod (1969); 'That Wonderful Sound', by Les Reed and Geoff Stephens (1969); 'Only Once', by Clive Weslake (1969); 'I'm a Fool to Want You', by Jack Wolf, Joel Herron and Frank Sinatra (1951); 'Let It Be Me' (orig. 'Je t'appartiens' in France), by Pierre Delance and Gilbert Becaud (1955) (English words by Mann Curtis).

Sales were around two million by January 1971.

ANDY KIM

BABY, I LOVE YOU *Steed* [*USA*]. The first million seller (by September 1969) for Andy Kim, and for the Steed label, the disc released in May 1969. It rose to No 5 in the U.S. charts for two weeks with 16 weeks in the bestsellers. The song written by American songwriters Jeff Barry, Ellie Greenwich and Phil Spector.

Andy Kim was born in Montreal on 5 December 1946, the third of four sons in a Lebanese family. He left high school and hitch-hiked to New York, where he continually made the rounds of record companies. He learned to play the guitar in order to accompany himself on his self-written songs. His older brother became his manager.

The disc was also produced by writer Jeff Barry.

R.I.A.A. Gold Disc award 14 October 1969.

B. B. KING

THE THRILL IS GONE *Blues Way* [*USA*]. Written by Arthur H. Benson and Dale Pettite, this disc was released in the U.S.A. in December 1969 and reached No 13 for two weeks in early 1970 with 14 weeks in the bestsellers, selling a million by April 1970.

1969 was the year in which 'King of the Blues' B. B. King was recognized as one of the world's great artists, after some 20 years in comparative anonymity to white audiences. (See B. B. King, 1955.) This disc has a little of the Memphis touch with emotional charge, and is a powerful rhythm-and-blues performance. B. B. King received a Grammy Award for this disc – Best Rhythm-and-Blues Vocal Performance (Male) 1970.

LED ZEPPELIN (vocal and instrumental quartet)

LED ZEPPELIN (album) *Atlantic* [*USA*]. Led Zeppelin, a British rock group, consists of Jimmy Page (lead guitar, pedal steel guitar, acoustic guitar) born Heston, Middlesex, 9 January 1944; John Paul Jones, real name John Baldwin, (bass, organ, piano) born Sidcup, Kent, 3 January 1946; John Bonham (drums) born Redditch, Worcs., 31 May 1948; died Windsor, Berks., 25 September 1980; and Robert Plant (lead vocals, harmonica, occasional bass) born Bromwich, Staffs, 20 August 1939. Their success story stems mainly from Jimmy Page's drive and initiative. Jimmy, a brilliant young session player who had backed up such artists as The Rolling Stones, Donovan, and Jeff Beck on sessions, became lead guitarist of The Yardbirds in 1966 until the group dissolved in 1968. In October 1968, Led Zeppelin was born. At that time The Cream, who had pioneered the heavy instrumental rock band, were breaking up, and although Led Zeppelin was not created to take over their role, this did in fact happen with incredible swiftness. Britain was the last to hear about it. America made them the hottest act to come from Britain in some time. Their hard rock and blues sound established them as one of the supergroups, and their Carnegie Hall debut in New York in the autumn of 1969 was hailed as the biggest happening since The Beatles. They had become well known through this, their first album released in February 1969 by Atlantic who had signed them to a contract. Within two months it was No 8 in the charts, and stayed in the Top 20 for six months with sales continuing into 1970. It received a Gold Disc award from R.I.A.A. for million dollar sales on 22 July 1969 and sold over a million units by year's end. In Britain the disc reached No 5.

Robert Plant's voice is so powerful that screens were put around him while recording. Jimmy Page proved to be one of the great guitarists in modern music, a master of rock-blues and a super-fast instrumentalist. Drummer Bonham and bassist Jones were also masters of their instruments, stunning audiences with the driving sound they created together backing up Page and Plant. The group wrote most of their own numbers.

The album contained: 'Good Times, Bad Times', by J. Page, John P. Jones and John Bonham; 'Babe I'm Gonna Leave You', traditional: arr. Jimmy Page; 'You Shook Me', by Willie Dixon; 'Dazed and Confused', by Jimmy Page; 'Your Time Is Gonna Come', by Jimmy Page and John Paul Jones; 'Black Mountain Side', by Jimmy Page; 'Communication Breakdown', by J. Page, John P. Jones and John Bonham; 'I Can't Quit You Baby', by Willie Dixon; 'How Many More Times?', by J. Page, John P. Jones and John Bonham.

By April 1970, sales were around the two million mark in the U.S.A. alone.

It was in the U.S. bestsellers for 73 weeks.

LED ZEPPELIN II (album) *Atlantic* [*USA*]. Second big seller for this flashy, bluesy exciting group, with the same driving instrumental and vocal power. Disc released in the U.S.A. in October 1969. It received a Gold Disc award for million dollar sales from R.I.A.A. on 10 November within three weeks of release and the disc was No 1 at year's end, and for a further six weeks in 1970 (seven weeks in all). It was also No 1 in Britain for four weeks in 1970. The numbers on the album were all composed by the group's members.

U.S. sales swiftly reached the million, and both the group's albums gained gold and platinum awards for collective sales of over six million by mid-February 1970. By this time, they commanded a high fee of $25,000 per performance.

The album contained 'Whole Lotta Love' which was a big seller as a single when released in November 1969.

Album contents: 'Whole Lotta Love', by Jimmy Page and Robert Plant; 'What Is and What Should Never Be', by Jimmy Page and Robert Plant; 'The Lemon Song', by J. Page, R. Plant, John Bonham and John Paul Jones; 'Thank You', by Jimmy Page and Robert Plant; 'Heartbreaker', by J. Page, R. Plant, John Bonham and John Paul Jones; 'Livin' Lovin' Maid' (She's a woman), by Jimmy Page and Robert Plant; 'Ramble On', by Jimmy Page and Robert Plant; 'Moby Dick', by J. Bonham, J. Page and John Paul Jones; 'Bring It on Home', by Jimmy Page and Robert Plant.

This album was the fastest selling in Atlantic's history. It sold at the rate of 100,000 per week and was in the Top Ten in the U.S.A. for many weeks with sales by April 1970 approaching

three million there alone. It was in the bestsellers for 75 weeks. A million sale was also achieved in Europe.

Led Zeppelin made their first date at The Middle Earth in London. They started their fifth tour of the U.S.A. in March 1970.

WHOLE LOTTA LOVE *Atlantic* [*USA*]. Released in November 1969 as a single from the group's album 'Led Zeppelin II', the disc reached No 2 for two weeks in the U.S.A. in January 1970 with 15 weeks in the bestsellers, and sold the million by April 1970 with R.I.A.A. Gold Disc award. It was also a big hit in Germany (No 1) and in Belgium (No 1). Written by Jimmy Page and Robert Plant, both of the group.

MARK LINDSAY

ARIZONA *Columbia* [*USA*]. Written by Kenny Young and released in November 1969, the disc was No 9 for two weeks in the U.S.A. in early 1970 and sold a million, with R.I.A.A. Gold Disc award by April 1970, after 16 weeks in the bestsellers. It has a powerful brass arrangement to the teen-slanted lyrics. Mark Lindsay was born in Idaho. He was originally a bread delivery boy until he asked to be allowed to sing for Paul Revere, a drive-in hotel proprietor who played electric piano on local dates. Mark became lead singer and doubled on sax for Paul Revere and The Raiders (around 1963). The group became one of the top three in the U.S.A. by 1966, and Mark voted 'Super Star of the Year'. This disc was his second solo single.

KARUMEN MAKI

TOKINIWA HAHA NO NAIKO NO YOHNI (Sometimes I feel like a lonely baby) *CBS/Sony* [*Japan*]. The first million selling disc for the CBS/Sony label. Singer Karumen (Carmen) Maki's disc, her first recording, was No 2 in the Japanese charts for six weeks and in the bestsellers for three months. It was released in Japan in April 1969 and sold the million by July. CBS/Sony awarded her a Gold Disc in July.

HENRY MANCINI AND HIS ORCHESTRA

LOVE THEME FROM 'ROMEO AND JULIET' *Victor* [*USA*]. Mancini's beautiful arrangement of the love theme from the Franco Zeffirelli production of the film *Romeo and Juliet* became a top instrumental single recording in the U.S.A. The disc was released on 4 April 1969, was No 1 for two weeks in the U.S. charts with 14 weeks in the bestsellers, and sold the million by 25 June with R.I.A.A. Gold Disc award. The theme is based on Nino Rota's score for the film which starred Leonard Whiting, then aged 17, and Olivia Hussey, 16, said to be the youngest performers ever to play the ill-fated lovers professionally.

A vocal version of the theme titled 'A Time for Us' was written by Eddie Snyder and Larry Kuisk.

Mancini's instrumental version sold over 200,000 in one week alone.

Grammy Award (1969) for Best Instrumental Arrangement.

MARMALADE

REFLECTIONS OF MY LIFE *Decca* [*Britain*]. The Marmalade's first recording for Decca, written by W. Campbell and T. McAleese (both members of the group), this disc reached No 1 for a week in Britain in early 1970 with 12 weeks in the bestsellers. Release was on 14 November 1969. In the U.S.A. it was No 7 for a week and stayed on their bestseller charts for 15 weeks (London label).

Sales were quite big in both countries, and the million was reported in November 1971 when the group was presented with a Gold Disc for global sale.

A highly professional production, with subtleties of tone building to a powerful climax.

MEL AND TIM

BACKFIELD IN MOTION *Bamboo* [*USA*]. This song is described as one of 'football imagery with a strange and novel twist' that made it a teenagers' disc with blues. The disc was released in September 1969 and reached No 10 for a week in the U.S. charts with 14 weeks in the bestsellers, selling a million with R.I.A.A. Gold Disc award by the end of the year. This overnight success for Mel and Tim (real names Melvin Harden and Tim McPherson) who wrote the song was their debut disc for the Bamboo label. A soul-singing duo, they were originally employed as bus drivers in St Louis until the demo disc of their song was played to producer Gene Chandler who was so impressed that he cut it for his Scepter-distributed Bamboo label.

MERCY

LOVE (Can make you happy) *Sundi* [*USA*]. First hit for this new group and the small Sundi label. The song was written by J. Sigler, Jr., and the disc released through Jamie Records in April 1969, with million sale and R.I.A.A. Gold Disc award on 15 July. The disc was No 2 for three weeks in the U.S.A. and 13 weeks in the bestsellers. The group subsequently signed with Warner Brothers-Seven Arts label.

Mercy was the brainchild of Jack Sigler, Jr. who at the age of nine started learning guitar and then came into contact with members of what became the 'Love Can Make You Happy' group. In Brandon High School he formed his own group, all graduates at the school, and they gained experience by appearing at schools around Florida. Mercy underwent changes of personnel that eventually brought them to the attention of producer George Roberts. Roberts introduced the group to its future hit as part of his film *Fireball Jungle*, and their performance resulted in recording for Sundi Records in Florida.

OSAMU MINAGAWA

KURO NEKO NO TANGO (Black Cat Tango) *Victor* [*Japan*]. Osamu Minagawa is the youngest artist to achieve million sale of a recording. A native of Tokyo, Japan, he made this disc at the age of six in 1969. It was released there in November and swiftly leapt to No 1 in the Japanese charts, staying in that position for 15 weeks. By February 1970 it had sold two million, and achieved success mostly on the basis of Osamu's imitation of a mewing cat.

The song is a Japanese version of 'Volveo un gatto nero' (I wanted a black cat) from Italy where it was featured in the Golden Sequin Festival of Bologna. The disc sold 840,000 in its first 18 days on the Japanese market where Italian children's songs were becoming important on their disc scene. Total sales were around 3 million.

Osamu Minagawa was born in Tokyo on 22 January 1963, and started singing at the age of three. After activity in TV commercials, he performed in a TV series 'Songs for Mamma and Me' on TBS-TV from May 1968 for a year. He then appeared in a TBS-TV drama series 'Is It So? No It's Not'.

Reiko Okiai assisted Osamu on the recording. She was born in Tokyo on 28 October 1964.

GIANNI MORANDI

SCENDE LA POGGIA (It's raining) *RCA* [*Italy*]. This is the Italian version of the 1968 American hit 'Elenore' written by The Turtles (H. Kaylan, M. Volman, J. Pons, A. Nichel and J. Barbata). It was the winner of the top popular contest called 'Canzonissima' (The Best Song) organized by the Italian State Television by postcards sent to the TV company. Of the 20 million sent in, Morandi won with six million votes. The disc was issued in early January 1969 and sold 800,000 in a month, was No 1 for five weeks in the Italian charts and subsequently sold the million, making Morandi the most popular singer in Italy.

RYOKO MORIYAMA

KINIJIRARETA KOI (Unpermitted Love) *Philips* [*Japan*]. Ryoko Moriyama describes herself as a pop folk singer. By this year she had eight albums released in Japan, also her own radio and TV programmes. This disc was released in April 1969 and stayed at No 1 in the Japanese charts for 12 weeks with over a million subsequent sale (by October 1969).

In October 1969 she visited Nashville to record with local musicians to get the authentic Nashville sound.

1910 FRUITGUM CO.

INDIAN RIVER *Buddah* [*USA*]. The third million seller for this 'bubble-gum' band, released in January 1969. The disc received a Gold Disc award from R.I.A.A. on 31 March. The song, written by B. Gentry, R. Cordell and B. Bloom, features heavy drumming. It rose to No 3 for one week on the U.S. charts with 13 weeks in the bestsellers.

OLIVER

GOOD MORNING STARSHINE *Jubilee* [*USA*]. William Oliver Swofford was born on 22 February 1945 in North Wilkesboro, North Carolina, and started playing guitar at the age of 15. While at the University of North Carolina he sang with a group called The Virginians, and they moved to New York subsequently touring with the Mitch Ryder Show for a year in Canada. They had a regional hit 'Long Walk Back to Paradise' on the Epic label. Bill Cash, the group's manager, took them to Bob Crewe who signed them to a disc contract, and he changed the act's name to The Good Earth Trio, releasing an album by them. The group soon disbanded and Oliver joined Jim Dawson to form a duo called Good Earth. A song written by Oliver 'I Can See the Light' was a success for them. Dawson then left to form a new group and Oliver decided to be a soloist. He chose 'Good Morning Starshine', one of the hit songs from the fantastically successful musical *Hair* written by Gerome Ragni and James Rado (words) and Galt MacDermot (music), and the disc was produced and directed by Bob Crewe with a powerful rock-semi-folk base and a standout vocal. This version was released in May 1969 and achieved No 3 for two weeks on the U.S. charts with 13 weeks in the bestsellers. In Britain it was No 6 with 16 weeks in the bestsellers. By August it had sold the million with R.I.A.A. Gold Disc award, and put Oliver well and truly on

the road to fame. It was the third song from *Hair* in this year to sell a million or more on disc.

JEAN *Crewe* [*USA*]. With the success of 'Good Morning Starshine', an album of the same title by Oliver was released at the end of July 1969 on Bob Crewe's label. This included the song 'Jean' from the film *The Prime of Miss Jean Brodie* written by Rod McKuen which was released as a single in August by overwhelming demand. It sold the million by October with R.I.A.A. Gold Disc award 10 October. The disc was No 1 for one week in the U.S. charts and 14 weeks in the bestsellers.

PETER, PAUL AND MARY

LEAVING ON A JET PLANE *Warner-7 Arts* [*USA*]. A beautiful ballad written by John Denver with an especially fine arrangement. The disc, released in October 1969, highlights Mary as lead singer, and brought the trio even greater national prominence. It reached No 1 for two weeks with 17 weeks in the bestsellers, and sold the million by December 1969 with R.I.A.A. Gold Disc award.

British release was in January 1970, the disc reaching No 2 for one week with 16 weeks in the bestsellers.

THE PLASTIC ONO BAND

GIVE PEACE A CHANCE *Apple* [*Britain*] *Apple* [*USA*]. Written by The Beatles' John Lennon and Paul McCartney, this song with its very clever lyrics is described as a hypnotic chant. It was dreamed up by Lennon and his wife Yoko Ono during a week's 'bed-in' in their hotel in Montreal. The recording was made in Room 1472 of the Hotel La Reine Elizabeth, Montreal, on 2 June 1969, by John and Yoko with Tommy Smothers on one guitar, LSD advocate Dr Timothy Leary, Derek Taylor (Beatles' press officer), a Toronto rabbi and at least 35 others – journalists, TV cameramen, photographers and friends. John called them The Plastic Ono Band. An eight-track portable recording machine was hired, which with its crew cost £3,300 (around $8,000) for five hours. The hotel costs were more than £400 per day ($1,000). The disc was released in Britain on 4 July 1969 and about a week later in the U.S.A. In Britain it reached No 2 for two weeks with 13 weeks in the bestsellers, selling over 250,000. In the U.S.A. it was No 10 for two weeks with 9 weeks in the bestsellers, and sold 800,000. A further 900,000 were sold in the rest of the world, making a global total of around two million.

The number was cemented into fame when Pete Seeger sang it in 1969 at the Washington Monument during a Peace March by over 250,000 people.

THE POPPY FAMILY (vocal quartet)

WHICH WAY YOU GOIN' BILLY? *London* [*Canada*]. Released initially on the London label (Canada) in the summer of 1969, and in the U.S.A. on 30 September 1969. It reached No 2 for two weeks in the U.S.A. in June 1970, stayed on the bestsellers for 16 weeks and sold a million by July with R.I.A.A. Gold Disc award. Release in Britain was 31 October 1969 (Decca label) where it reached No 5 for one week in 1970 with 14 weeks in the bestsellers.

The song was written by Terry Jacks (of the group), and is sung on the disc by his wife Susan. The group is Canadian, comprising: Susan Jacks (vocals); Terry Jacks (rhythm guitar, composer, arranger); Craig MacCaw (guitar, sitar and harp); Satwan Singh (tabla, percussion, violin, organ).

The Poppy Family made their first appearance in the small town of Blubber Bay to an audience of 150 people, and subsequently played in Western Canada for four years. They were then chosen to represent Canada at Expo '70 in Osaka, Japan, a highlight of their career.

ELVIS PRESLEY

IN THE GHETTO *Victor* [*USA*]. Elvis made an album 'Elvis in Memphis' in this year, his first session there for 14 years. The album included 'In the Ghetto' written by Scott Davis (pseudonym for Mac Davis and Billy Strange) and this was released as a single in April 1969. It was No 1 for a week in the U.S.A. with 13 weeks in the bestsellers, and sold a million by 25 June with R.I.A.A. Gold Disc award. The disc was also a success in Britain, No 1 for a week with 17 weeks in the bestsellers, where it sold over 250,000.

The song was a new departure for Elvis - a protest song - with a vital lyric line of social consciousness delivered with great impact.

Soon after the success of this disc it was reported that Elvis had sold the equivalent of 250 million singles over the past 14 years. This disc made the 59th million seller for Elvis.

SUSPICIOUS MINDS *Victor* [*USA*]. This ballad, written by Mark James and released in September 1969, proved a big hit for Elvis Presley. His disc was No 1 for two weeks in the U.S. charts with 15 weeks in the bestsellers, and sold a million, his 60th. R.I.A.A. Gold Disc award 28 October 1969.

In Britain it sold over 250,000 and reached No 2 in the charts for one week with 14 weeks in the bestsellers.

DON'T CRY DADDY backed with RUBBERKNECKIN' *Victor* [*USA*]. A tremendous double-sided hit disc for Elvis Presley, released in November 1969 and reaching No 5 for three weeks in the U.S. charts with 13 weeks in the bestsellers. By mid-January 1970 it had sold the million with R.I.A.A. Gold Disc award, making the 61st million seller for Elvis.

'Don't Cry Daddy' was written by Scott Davis (pseudonym of Mac Davis and Billy Strange), and is a slow-moving bitter-sweet ballad. 'Rubberkneckin'' was written by Dory Jones and Bunny Warren. The disc reached No 7 in Britain.

CHARLEY PRIDE

THE BEST OF CHARLEY PRIDE (album) *RCA* [*USA*]. Charley Pride, believed to be the only black artist to work in a strict country-and-western style without any trace of the Negro blues sound, hails from Mississippi. From an early age, he spent several years working towards a baseball career. He played with the Los Angeles Angels, but after several seasons decided to try his luck as a singer in Nashville, the home of country-and-western music. Here he met famous guitarist and RCA artist/executive Chet Atkins who signed him to a contract.

Charley made several albums for RCA and in 1967 had two singles 'I Know One' and 'Just Between You and Me' in the Top Ten U.S. country charts. In 1968 he had three more singles and two albums in the charts, with more successes in 1969 and 1970 by which time he won the *Billboard* award for Best Male Country Vocalist and for the Best Album - 'The Best of Charley Pride',

originally released in the U.S.A. in October 1969. By March 1971 it had sold over the million (seven million dollars at retail) and a Gold Disc was awarded by R.I.A.A. in 1970. Charlie had a further three Gold Disc awards from R.I.A.A. for albums in March 1971.

'The Best of Charley Pride' album was produced by Chet Atkins who also produced all the singer's other discs. It contained the following: 'Just Between You and Me', by Jack Clement (1967); 'Does My Ring Hurt Your Finger?', by Robertson, Crutchfield and Clement; 'Kaw-Liga', by Fred Rose and Hank Williams (1952); 'The Snakes Crawl at Night', by Mel Tillis and Fred Burch; 'All I Have to Offer You (is me)', by A. L. Owens and Dallas Frazier (1969); 'The Easy Part's Over', by Jerry Foster and Bill Rice (1968); 'The Day the World Stood Still', by Jerry Foster and Bill Rice (1968); 'I Know One', by Jack Clement (1967); 'Gone, on the Other Hand', by Jack Clement; 'Before I Met You', by Seitz, Lewis and Rader (1957); 'Too Hard to Say I'm Sorry', by Clement and Johnson; 'Let the Chips Fall', by Jack Clement.

Release of the album in Britain was on 7 August 1970. In the U.S.A. it reached No 25 for two weeks and was in the bestsellers for 65 weeks.

Pride was born on 18 March 1938 at Sledge, Mississippi. He was the first black artist ever to appear at Nashville's Grand Ole Opry (1967).

LOU RAWLS (rhythm-and-blues vocalist)

YOUR GOOD THING (is about to end) *Capitol* [*USA*]. Lou Rawls was born 1 December 1937, a native of Chicago, and began singing in the choir of Greater Mount Olive Baptist Church there at seven. He graduated from Dunbar High School and later joined The Pilgrim Travelers, a gospel group, leaving the gospel field in 1958 following a car accident. After two years in the U.S. Army he played service clubs, and then on the backwater Midwestern nightclub circuit from around 1959, earning about ten dollars a night. He moved on to Los Angeles where he began singing blues. This pushed him into the jazz field, and he did a series of recordings that at various times labelled him as a jazz pop, gospel and even folk singer. He appeared with Dick Clark on a 'Hollywood Bowl' show, also the 'Steve Allen', 'Johnny Carson', 'Mike Douglas' and 'Jack Benny' TV shows. In 1964 he was a success at the Monterey Jazz Festival. Lou developed a style all his own, drawing from a mixed bag of songs and effortlessly improvising within a three-octave range - a sharp gospel wail down to a gritty, resonant bottom. In between he interspersed rhythmic rapid-fire monologues on anything that came to his mind, a device he used in the small Negro nightclubs to make himself heard above the noise. This Rawls speciality became known as 'soulin''. In early 1966, Lou decided to make a recording of his old 'chitlin' circuit' style, singing and soliloquizing, and invited a number of friends to the studio for the finger-clicking, hand-clapping accompaniment. The resultant album 'Lou Rawls LIVE' was a big hit and sold around 500,000, followed by 'Soulin'' album, another big seller. Both received Gold Disc awards from R.I.A.A. for million dollar sales. In a few months he was commanding $5,000 for a one-night stand. In his performance in January 1967 at Carnegie Hall, the first of a series of tours into virtually every major nightclub and concert hall, his blend of talk and song was an outstanding success.

'Your Good Thing', a powerful ballad, was written by Isaac Hayes and David Porter, who had provided big hits for Sam and Dave. The disc was released in July 1969 and by November sold over 900,000 subsequently reaching the million. It was No 15 chartwise for one week in the U.S.A. and in the bestsellers for 14 weeks.

MIGUEL RIOS (with orchestra and chorus conducted by Waldo De Los Rios)

HIMNO A LA ALEGRIA (Song of Joy) *Hispavox* [*Spain*] *A & M* [*USA*]. This disc, suitably commemorating the bicentennial of Beethoven (born 1770), was firstly a big hit in Spain where it achieved No 3. The song is based on the last movement of Beethoven's 9th ('The Choral') Symphony, the words by Orbe and musical adaptation by Waldo De Los Rios. It was released in the U.S.A. in May 1970 (A. & M. label) where it got to No 9 for a week and by July sold a million combined U.S./Canada sales and was awarded a Gold Disc by R.I.A.A. The English words were written by Ross Parker. 'Song of Joy' was a hit in Canada before the U.S.A., and then got into the charts in Portugal, Holland, France, Belgium and South America (No 1), Germany (No 1). Release in Britain was on 13 February 1970 (Hispavox label) but it was not a hit there until its U.S. success, when the disc was re-released and reached No 16 with 16 weeks in the bestsellers.

Miguel Rios was born in 1944 in Granada and started singing at six. At eight he was soloist in his school choir. After school he formed a rock group in Granada, playing local clubs. He then met a record man who invited him to make a disc, and 'Song of Joy' resulted in December 1969. The enormous choir and symphony orchestra that made the disc in Madrid gave a tasteful modern pop treatment and a fresh meaning to Beethoven's immortal melody, 200 years after his birth.

Conductor Waldo De Los Rios is well known as the composer of 'South American Suite'.

TOMMY ROE

JAM UP JELLY TIGHT *ABC* [*USA*]. Written by Tommy Roe with F. Waller, the disc was released in November 1969, reaching No 4 for a week in the U.S. charts with 14 weeks in the bestsellers. It was a big hit for the 'bubble-gum' devotees and sold a million by January 1970 with R.I.A.A. Gold Disc award.

KENNY ROGERS AND THE FIRST EDITION
(vocal and instrumental quintet)

RUBY, DON'T TAKE YOUR LOVE TO TOWN *Reprise* [*USA*]. Kenny Rogers, leader and lead singer of the group, was born on 21 August 1938 in Houston, Texas, and was formerly a bass man with The Bobby Doyle Trio, a jazz group which toured the U.S.A. and recorded for Columbia. They performed in nightclubs and concerts frequently with The Kirby Stone Four. On leaving the trio, Rogers joined The New Christy Minstrels for a year (1966) and then left to form The First Edition. Thelma Camacho, who had four years of classical voice training, had played roles in San Diego opera and light opera. She was with The New Christy Minstrels when she met Mike Settle (rhythm guitar), Kenny Rogers, and Terry Williams (guitar) and formed The First Edition. Terry, whose father played first trombone for Tommy Dorsey, and whose mother was vocalist with the band, took up the guitar at 14. Settle, while a member of The Cumberland Three, worked with John Stewart, later of The Kingston Trio. He wrote much of The First Edition's music. Mickey Jones (drummer) had played with Trini Lopez, Johnny Rivers and Bob Dylan.

'Ruby, Don't Take Your Love to Town' was written in 1966 by Mel Tillis and is now considered to be a country classic. It tells the story of a war cripple and has a deeply moving tune. The First Edition's disc was released in the U.S.A. in June 1969 and achieved No 6 for two weeks chartwise with 13 weeks in the bestsellers. In Britain, release was in October and it went to No 1 there for a week with 23 weeks in the bestsellers, selling over 250,000. Together with the U.S. sales and other countries it sold over a million.

Mike Settle was born in Muskogee, Oklahoma. Kenny Rogers has since gone solo.

THE ROLLING STONES

HONKY TONK WOMEN *Decca* [*Britain*] *London* [*USA*]. The first Rolling Stones single for over a year, the song written by the group's Mick Jagger and Keith Richard. The recording possessed an earthy gutsy sound and marked the debut of Mick Taylor, the 20-year-old guitarist who replaced Brian Jones (died 2 July 1969).

The disc was released in Britain on 4 July 1969 and sold well over 250,000 after being at No 1 for five weeks. It was released around the same time in the U.S.A. and was No 1 for four weeks with 15 weeks in the bestsellers, selling the million by 26 August with R.I.A.A. Gold Disc award. Global sales were well over two million.

The disc was a further extension of the group's rock and country fusion as in their 'Beggar's Banquet' album, and performed with astonishing vocals, pulsing rhythm and powerful impact.

THROUGH THE PAST, DARKLY (BIG HITS Vol. 2) (album) *Decca* [*Britain*] *London* [*USA*]. This second 'greatest hits' album by The Rolling Stones was specifically dedicated by the group to the late Brian Jones, one of its original members who died in 1969. It covers a further period of the group's history and was released in both Britain and the U.S.A. in August 1969.

Contents (British release): *'Honky Tonk Women', by Mick Jagger and Keith Richard (1969); *'Ruby Tuesday', by Mick Jagger and Keith Richard (1967); *'Jumpin' Jack Flash', by Mick Jagger and Keith Richard (1968); 'Street Fighting Man', by Mick Jagger and Keith Richard (1968); *'Let's Spend the Night Together', by Mick Jagger and Keith Richard (1967); '2,000 Light Years from Now', by Mick Jagger and Keith Richard (1967); *'Mother's Little Helper', by Mick Jagger and Keith Richard (1966); 'She's a Rainbow', by Mick Jagger and Keith Richard (1967); *'Dandelion', by Mick Jagger and Keith Richard (1967); 'You Better Move On', by Arthur Alexander (1964); *'We Love You', by Mick Jagger and Keith Richard (1967); 'Sitting on the Fence', by Mick Jagger and Keith Richard (1967).

The American release contained the first nine titles plus: *'Paint It Black', by Mick Jagger and Keith Richard (1966); *'Have You Seen Your Mother, Baby, Standing in the Shadow?' by Mick Jagger and Keith Richard (1966).

Items marked * were million seller singles.

In the U.S.A. the disc sold $1 million worth within two weeks on the market plus R.I.A.A. Gold Disc award (September 1969) and was No 2 for two weeks. It was in the U.S. bestsellers for 32 weeks.

In Britain the disc was No 1 for one week.

Well over an estimated million units were sold globally by the end of 1969, a year in which The Rolling Stones were at the height of their popularity and in which they made a tour of America from November, which grossed $238,612 (£99,420) on their opening night (8 November) at Los Angeles Forum in two performances before 35,286 people, thus establishing the largest all-time attendance record for any night event anywhere.

LET IT BLEED (album) *Decca* [*Britain*] *London* [*USA*]. Released in the U.S.A. during the group's first appearance there in three years, this album has the old power plus ominous tension. Its lyrics are mainly preoccupied with sex, drugs and violence, and the album includes two previously recorded Stones' songs 'Country Honk' - a country-and-western version of their million seller 'Honky Tonk Women' and 'You Can't Always Get What You Want'. It also features the first recorded vocal by Keith Richard. Release for the U.S.A. was 10 November, and the disc received an immediate Gold Disc award from R.I.A.A. for million dollar sale. It was No 3 for six weeks and stayed in the Top Ten for ten weeks. In Britain release was on 5 December 1969 and the disc was No 2 for one week and in the Top Ten for 11 weeks. By 1970, it had passed the million units sale.

Contents: 'Let It Bleed', by Mick Jagger and Keith Richard; 'Love in Vain', by Payne; 'Midnight Rambler', by Mick Jagger and Keith Richard; 'Gimme Shelter', by Mick Jagger and Keith Richard; 'You Got the Silver' (Keith Richard - vocal), by Mick Jagger and Keith Richard; 'You Can't Always Get What You Want', by Mick Jagger and Keith Richard; 'Live with Me', by Mick Jagger and Keith Richard; 'Monkey Man', by Mick Jagger and Keith Richard; 'Country Honk', by Mick Jagger and Keith Richard.

The album includes many artists on the various songs such as

Mary Clayton (vocalist), Ray Cooper (mandolin), Byron Berline (bluegrass violin), Ian Stewart (piano), Jimmy Miller (tambourine), Nick Hopkins (piano), Jack Nitzche (arrangements for London Bach Choir), Madeline Bell (vocalist), Doris Troy vocalist) and Nanette Newman (vocalist).

This album was 39 weeks in the U.S. bestsellers charts.

DIANA ROSS AND THE SUPREMES
SOMEDAY WE'LL BE TOGETHER *Motown* [*USA*]. Written by Jackey Beavers, Johnny Bristol and Harvey Fuqua in 1961, this disc of their soft ballad was released on 8 November 1969. It was No 1 for two weeks in the U.S.A. and sold the million by January 1970 with R.I.A.A. Gold Disc award. World sales by February 1970 were estimated at three million, another huge success for this famous female trio, the disc staying in U.S. bestsellers for 16 weeks.

The disc was popular in Britain where it reached No 10 for a week with 13 weeks in the bestsellers.

BARRY RYAN
LOVE IS LOVE *MGM* [*Britain*]. Written by Barry himself, and released in Britain during February 1969, his disc was not a success in his own country. Although Barry had never performed any live dates outside Britain, his discs were extremely popular on the Continent, particularly in Germany, Austria and Holland, and did in fact win a poll by several European papers as the most popular in that territory. 'Love Is Love' sold a million globally by August 1969, the second for Barry. It was No 25 in Britain.

SANTANA (rock sextet)
SANTANA (album) *Columbia* [*USA*]. The music of Santana is considered unique, using a fusion of rhythms - African, Cuban, Mexican, blues - as well as subtle Latin ingredients, producing an exotic sound that has rarely been heard in rock. Their raw, basic music caused the police to stop performances at times because the audience got too carried away. This album, with its Latin rhythms, created a unique sound, a kind of Mexicali soul excursion, and was the group's first album, released in September 1969. In 12 months it sold two million and earned the group $300,000 in royalties. It reached No 2 for a week in 1970 in the U.S.A.

The group started in San Francisco around 1966 and then included Gregg Rolie (pianist-organist), Carlos Santana (guitarist), Dave Brown (bass guitarist) and two others since departed.

They first called themselves The Santana Blues Band and were immensely popular in San Francisco's Spanish Mission District. In early 1969 they were joined by Jose Areas (conga drums, trumpet, timbales), Mike Carrabello (conga drums) and Mike Shrieve (drums), the group being managed from the beginning by Stan Marcum, a music-struck local barber. Marcum even sold his clothes for the group's benefit and went out to cut hair while the group stayed home and played music. In 1968, they were the star attraction at the famous Fillmore West without ever having made a record, and in the summer of 1969 were one of the longest and most arresting acts at the phenomenal Woodstock Festival. The group rarely uses lyrics though it offers an occasional vocal solo. It features principally solos on electric guitar, organ or electric piano. Carlos Santana the lead singer/guitarist was born in Autlan, Mexico.

The contents of the album: *Side 1* - 'Waiting', by The Santana Band; 'Evil Ways', by J. Zach; 'Shades of Time' by The Santana Band; 'Savor', by The Santana Band; 'Jin-go-lo-ba', by Michael Olatunje; *Side 2* - 'Persuasion', by The Santana Band; 'Treat', by The Santana Band; 'You Just Don't Care', by The Santana Band; 'Soul Sacrifice', by The Santana Band.

The album was in the Top Ten for 28 weeks, and in the bestsellers for 108 weeks in the U.S.A.

A Gold Disc award by R.I.A.A. in December 1969.

Release in Britain was on 14 November 1969 (CBS label).

BOBBY SHERMAN
LITTLE WOMAN *Metromedia* [*USA*]. Bobby Sherman became one of Metromedia's first successful artists. This disc released in August 1969 was No 1 for a week and 13 weeks in the U.S. bestsellers, and sold the million by October with R.I.A.A. Gold Disc award on 7 October. The song was written by D. Janssen.

In 1965, Bobby Sherman was a high school football star and engineering student, but in his spare time was a songwriter, record producer, and singer - mainly at parties. He was discovered at one of these by Natalie Wood and Sal Mineo, resulting in an audition and then an appearance on the ABC-TV network 'Shindig' show. When the series ended he became a featured character in the TV series 'Here Come the Brides'. 'Little Woman' was his first recording on the Metromedia label.

LA, LA, LA (If I had you) *Metromedia* [*USA*]. Follow-up hit for Bobby Sherman, again written by D. Janssen, released in November 1969. It was No 8 for one week in the U.S.A. and 11 weeks in the bestsellers, and sold the million by January 1970 with Gold Disc award from R.I.A.A. The disc is pretty material and has a fine vocal.

THE SHOCKING BLUE
(vocal/instrumental quartet)
VENUS *Pink Elephant* [*Holland*] *Colossus* [*USA*]. The success of The Shocking Blue, a quartet from The Hague, Holland, brought new optimism and enthusiasm to the Dutch music scene. Their leader, Robert van Leeuwen (born 1944) who is also lead guitar, was well known in Holland where he originally led The Motions for three years. He then went into record production for a year and soon after decided he wanted another group. The Shocking Blue was the result, and he produced this disc as well

as writing the song with P. & V. Stock. The disc was a big hit in Holland where it reached No 3 in the summer of 1969. Thereafter, it became No 1 in Belgium, France, Sweden, Austria and Switzerland, No 2 in Germany, where it sold 350,000 copies, and also entered the charts in Italy, Scandinavia, Australia and Canada. Its big Continental success resulted in the U.S. release on the Colossus label in November 1969 and it shot up their charts to No 1 and stayed there for three weeks in January 1970 with 14 weeks in the bestsellers, Holland's first American chart topper. It sold the million by the end of January 1970 and was awarded a Gold Disc by R.I.A.A. Global sales were over five million. In Britain, release was on the Penny Farthing label in January 1970 and the disc reached No 7 for one week.

The Shocking Blue's style is a mixture of rock and country with a simple rock beat and driving guitar riff. Their sudden success was attributed to the simplicity of their music at a time when the supergroups' music was getting more and more complicated.

The other three members of the group are: Mariska Veres (lead singer) born 1949, began singing and playing piano at a very early age, comes from musical family, her father a gipsy violinist and orchestra leader; she was discovered in an Amsterdam club; Klasse van der Wal (bass guitar); Cornelius van der Beek (drums).

The worldwide success of this disc not only put The Shocking Blue on the map, but also Robert van Leeuwen as producer and writer. He had written consistent hits in Holland and had an international hit song with 'My Love Is Growing' recorded by The Walker Brothers. The Shocking Blue sold 13½ million discs by 1973.

JOE SIMON (rhythm-and-blues vocalist)
THE CHOKIN' KIND *Sound Stage 7* [*USA*]. Soul singer Joe Smith's disc is a song about selfish love, performed against a

funky, percussive background which includes bongos and brass. It was written by Harland Howard. The disc was released in March 1969 and rose to No 11 in the U.S. charts for a week with 12 weeks in the bestsellers. By 16 June it sold the million and was awarded a Gold Disc by R.I.A.A.

Joe Simon was born in Simmesport, Louisiana, on 2 September 1943. He naturally absorbed the various musical influences of the deep South - jazz, rhythm-and-blues and gospel, and frequently sang in the public schools he attended as well as in churches throughout the area. At the age of 15 he moved to California, and later gained an introduction to Sound Stage 7 Records, a subsidiary of Monument Records, who signed him to a contract in 1966. His first release 'Teenager's Prayer' got into the charts and he followed up with a string of hits. Joe made a successful European tour in 1968 which took in Britain, France, Italy and Germany.

Grammy Award (1969) for Best Rhythm-and-Blues Vocal Performance (Male).

FRANK SINATRA
MY WAY *Reprise* [*USA*]. Written in 1967 by the French songsmiths Gilles Thibaut (words) and Claude François and Jacques Revaux (music) with the title 'Comme d'habitude'. The wonderful English lyrics telling of a man who has fought his way up through the pressures of life to do things 'my way' were written by famous disc artist Paul Anka in 1969. The disc only reached No 27 in the U.S.A. (with 8 weeks in the bestsellers) but got to No 4 in Britain. The million sale in Britain was reported in early 1970. It was released in the U.S.A. in March 1969 and Britain on 21 March 1970. The song was the No 1 sheet music seller in Britain 1969. Now an indisputable 'standard'.

The disc holds the then record for the longest stay in Britain's bestseller charts - 122 weeks into 1971.

By 1971 there were over 100 versions of 'My Way' which had earned lyricist Paul Anka $200,000.

SLY AND THE FAMILY STONE
THANK YOU (Falettin me be mice elf again) backed with EVERYBODY IS A STAR *Epic* [*USA*]. A big double-sided hit for this group, both songs written by their leader Sly (Sylvester Stewart). It was released in late December 1969 and was No 1 for two weeks in the U.S.A. The million sale Gold Disc was awarded in mid-February 1970, by R.I.A.A.

SMITH (pop quintet)
BABY IT'S YOU *Dunhill* [*USA*]. Smith quintet comprised one girl and four men: Gayle McCormick (lead singer) born in St Louis, Mo., Larry Moss (organ and kazoo); Jerry Carter (bass); Robert Evans (drums); Rich Cliburn (lead guitar).

'Baby It's You', a song written in 1961 by Mack David, Burt Bacharach and Barney Williams, was originally a hit for The Shirelles in 1962. Smith's disc was released in July 1969 and by October sold a million with R.I.A.A. Gold Disc award. It reached No 3 for two weeks and stayed in the U.S. bestsellers for 15 weeks.

Smith was managed by disc artist Del Shannon who selected the song from their repertoire for recording.

THE SPIRAL STAIRCASE
(vocal and instrumental quintet)
MORE TODAY THAN YESTERDAY *Columbia* [*USA*]. This group began in January 1964 at a nightclub in Sacramento, California. After a few years of name and personnel changes they were signed to Columbia Records. This was their second disc for the label and it rose to No 7 for a week in the U.S. charts with 15 weeks in the bestsellers after release in March 1969. By the end of August it had sold almost a million and reached the magic figure subsequently.

The Spiral Staircase consists of: Pat Upton (lead singer, guitar), writer of the group's material; Richard Lopes (organizer, leader of the act, saxophone and vocals); Bob Raymond (bass); Harvey Kaye (keyboards); Vinnie Panariello (drums).

All were in their early twenties and they have appeared in many clubs since 1962. The song for this disc was written by Pat Upton.

STEAM (sextet)
NA NA HEY HEY KISS HIM GOODBYE *Fontana* [*USA*]. Steam, a group of six men in their early twenties, came into prominence in late 1969 with this disc which was released in September. The recording has a 'Cher'-like vocal. The song was written by G. de Carlo, D. Frashuer and Paul Leka (discoverer of the group, also their manager and producer). It was No 1 in the U.S.A. for two weeks and 16 weeks in the bestsellers, and received Gold Disc award for million sale from R.I.A.A. on 8 December 1969.

Five of the group had been together since their early teens, and all lived together in Connecticut, practising in each other's houses. The group at that time consisted of: Hank Schorz (guitar, organ, piano, drums); Mike Daniels (bass); Bill Steer (vocalist); Tom Zuke (rhythm guitar); Jay Babins (lead guitar).

In 1969, Ray Corries (drums, bass and vocalist) was added to the group. Schorz then became lead vocalist. The recording was made at Mercury Sound Studios in New York.

STEPPENWOLF
ROCK ME *Dunhill* [*UDA*]. Written by John Kay of the group, this song comes from the film *Candy* for which the group sang the songs. The film included many stars – Charles Aznavour, Marlon Brando, John Huston, Richard Burton, 'Beatle' Ringo Starr and many others.

The disc was released in February 1969 and was No 7 for two weeks in the U.S. charts with 10 weeks in the bestsellers. A million sale was reported in May. 'Rock Me' is described as a 'supercharged disc with pulverizing vocal performance and intense rhythmic underpinnings'.

RAY STEVENS
GITARZAN *Monument* [*USA*]. Multi-instrumentalist and songwriter Ray Stevens, specialist in novelty songs, had a big hit with this humorous tongue-twister, a great story-line with a rock beat built around the vocal attributes of Tarzan, Jane and their pet chimpanzee. It was written by him and Bill Everett. The disc was released at the end of March 1969 and reached No 7 for two weeks in the U.S. charts with 13 weeks in the bestsellers, with million sale by 16 June and a Gold Disc award from R.I.A.A. Ray's first million seller was 'Ahab the Arab' (see 1962).

TEE-SET (quintet)
MA BELLE AMIE *TSR-Negram* [*Holland*] *Colossus* [*USA*]. It was Jerry Ross of Colossus Records who put The Tee-Set, a Dutch group, on the road to success. He heard their recording of 'Ma Belle Amie' when a friend in Zurich invited him to a discotheque and he moved quickly to get license to distribute the recording on his Colossus label in North and South America. The disc reached No 4 for a week in the U.S.A. in March 1970, was a hit in Belgium (Discostar label) and in Holland where it sold over 100,000 (the equivalent of a million seller there). Global sales went over the million. Release in the U.S.A. was December 1969.

The song was written by Hans Van Eyk and Petter Tetteroo (lead singer) of the group, the other members being Perry Lever, Franklin Madjid and Herman van Boeyen.

THE TEMPTATIONS
I CAN'T GET NEXT TO YOU *Gordy* [*USA*]. Another big hit for writers Norman Whitfield and Barrett Strong and for The Temptations. This song, with its new blues-rock love lyrics and powerful vocal performance by the group, sold a million after being No 1 for two weeks in the U.S. charts with 17 weeks in the bestsellers. It was No 13 in Britain. It was released 16 August 1969.

B.J. THOMAS
RAINDROPS KEEP FALLING ON MY HEAD *Scepter* [*USA*]. A sparkling ballad written by famous songsmiths Hal David (words) and Burt Bacharach (music), sung by B.J. Thomas for the film *Butch Cassidy and The Sundance Kid*. The disc was released in October 1969 and by the end of the year became No 1 for three weeks, with Gold Disc award from R.I.A.A. for million sale (December). By the end of January 1970, sales were estimated at two million in the U.S.A. alone. It stayed in the U.S. bestsellers for 22 weeks.

Release in Britain was on the Wand label on 5 December 1969 and it reached No 38. The song received the 'Oscar' for Best Film Song of the year, and the disc sold over a global three million.

THREE DOG NIGHT
(vocal trio with instrumental quartet)
ONE *Dunhill* [*USA*]. 'One' was written by artist-songwriter Harry Nilsson who first recorded it. Three Dog Night's disc was released in May 1969 and went to No 1 for a week in the U.S. charts with 16 weeks in the bestsellers, and sold the million by 23 July plus R.I.A.A. Gold Disc award, the first for the group.

This West Coast band performed with clean vocals and classy showmanship and comprised: vocalists: Danny Hutton, born in Buncrana, Donegal, Ireland; Cory Wells from New York; Chuck Negron from New York; backed by four exceptional musicians: Joe Sherman (bass); Jimmy Greenspoon (organ); Mike Alsup (lead guitar); Floyd Sneed (drums).

In addition to their U.S. appearances, the group performed in Britain at various clubs in 1969. 'Three Dog Night' is an Australian term meaning 'extreme cold'.

EASY TO BE HARD *Dunhill* [*USA*]. Yet another song from the musical *Hair* by Gerome Ragni and James Rado (words) with Galt MacDermot (music) to sell a million on disc. Three Dog Night's recording was released in August 1969 and reached No 1 for two weeks in the U.S.A. and stayed in the bestsellers for 13 weeks.

ELI'S COMING *Dunhill* [*USA*]. Third million seller in a row for Three Dog Night. This was taken from their album 'Suitable for Framing' and released in October 1969, achieving No 7 for two weeks in the U.S. charts with 14 weeks in the bestsellers. The recording is a version of the familiar song written by Laura Nyro, performed with powerful drive. By 1970, the group, whose roots reached into every branch of music, were considered to be one of America's greatest, their carefully planned performances receiving standing ovations all over the U.S.A.

VANITY FAIR (pop quintet)
EARLY IN THE MORNING *Page One* [*Britain*]. Vanity Fair, a group of lads all in their early twenties, had their first chart hit in 1968 with 'I Live for the Sun', and they also appeared in the BBC's 'Saturday Club' on radio and 'Dee Time' on TV in that year. They had made previous appearances on TV and radio in 1965. Their first important public appearances were a Scottish tour and at the London Palladium. They also had important engagements on German and Dutch TV shows. Their group name was taken from Thackeray's book of that title.

'Early in the Morning' was released on 20 June and reached No 7 for two weeks in Britain with 12 weeks in the bestsellers. Release in the U.S.A. was in November 1969 and here it achieved No 9 for two weeks in early 1970 with 13 weeks in the bestsellers, by which time the disc had sold a million globally.

The song is a very tuneful one, written by Mike Leander and Eddie Seago.

Vanity Fair consists of: Dick Allix, born 3 June 1945 in Gravesend, Kent, plays drums; Trevor Brice, born 12 February 1945 in Strood, Kent, lead vocalist, pianist; Tony Goulden, born 21 November 1944 in Rochester, Kent, lead and 12-string guitar also vocals; Tony Jarrett, born 4 September 1944 in Rochester,

Kent, bass guitar and vocals; Barry Landemann, born 25 October 1947 in Woodbridge, Suffolk, piano.

THE VENTURES

HAWAII FIVE-O *Liberty* [*USA*]. This theme from the successful TV series of the same title, was written by Mort Stevens. It achieved No 4 and stayed in the U.S. bestseller charts for 14 weeks.

It was around this year that The Ventures became exceedingly popular in Japan, resulting from a number of tours the group did there commencing in the early 1960s when they were completely unknown to the Japanese. Their discs were put out by Toshiba Records and became big sellers. By 1971 they had made 9 tours, and many of their compositions of a Japanese flavour were recorded by native artists, including 'Kyoto Doll', 'Kyoto Boy' (both by Yuko Nagisa), 'Hokkaido Skies' (Chiyo Okumura), and 'Stranger in Midosuji' (Fifi Ouyang), each selling over a million. By 1973, The Ventures had made 50 albums, their disc sales totalling over 30 million, with a large proportion of the sales in Japan.

THE WHO

TOMMY (Double album) *Decca* [*USA*] *Track* [*Britain*]. The Who were formed in London in 1964, consisting of: Peter Townshend (lead guitar) born 19 May 1945, Chiswick, London; Keith Moon (drums) born 23 August 1947, Wembley, London, died 7 September 1978; John Entwhistle (bass guitar, trumpet, French horn, piano) born 9 October 1945, Chiswick, London; Roger Daltrey (lead singer, guitar, harp) born 1 March 1945, Hammersmith, London.

Townshend, son of a dance-band saxophonist, met the other three in Acton County Grammar School, and their early local success came from imitations of U.S. blues and rock'n'roll performers. Later, they were the pioneers of pop-art costumes, e.g. jackets made from Union Jacks, etc., and in their act they began literally breaking things up, smashing instruments during the performance of their wild anti-parental hymn of hate 'My Generation'. Their fans went berserk at this most violent stage act in the business. They made a successful tour with The Beatles, then came much TV and radio. In the summer of 1967 they built up a big reputation with their smashed-instrument-ending performance in the U.S.A. at the Monterey Pop Festival, and also toured the States, winning frenzied admirers. Their singles successes were – in Britain 'My Generation' (No 3 for three weeks, 1965) on Brunswick label, 'I'm a Boy' (No 2 for two weeks 1966) Reaction label, 'Pictures of Lily' (No 4 for two weeks, 1967) Track label, 'Happy Jack' (No 3 for a week, 1967) Track label, 'Pinball Wizard' (No 4 for a week, 1969) Track label.

In April 1969, the group's double album of 'Tommy' was released. Composed by Peter Townshend with contributions by Who members John Entwhistle and Keith Moon, this 'rock' opera about a deaf, dumb and blind boy proved to be one of the most ambitious rock ventures ever undertaken. The *New York* *Times* said 'This might be the first pop masterpiece'. The Who included excerpts from it on their 1969 U.S. tour, and the album (released there May 1969) became a big seller, and received a Gold Disc award for million dollar sales from R.I.A.A. by December 1969. It reached No 1 for three weeks.

By mid-1970, after a final-performance-of-the-opera tour that opened at the Metropolitan Opera House, New York City, grossing $55,000 for the two shows, they were one of the most popular groups in the U.S.A., with both 'Tommy' and a new album 'Live at Leeds' both in the Top Ten. Renewed sales of 'Tommy' were more than 150,000 in July alone, the million sale reached in August. The album was 110 weeks in the U.S. bestsellers. In Britain it reached No 2 for two weeks in June 1969.

The double album contents were: Overture; It's a Boy: 1921; Amazing Journey; Sparks; Eyesight for the Blind (written by Sonny Boy Williamson); Miracle Cure; Sally Simpson; I'm Free; Welcome; Tommy's Holiday Camp; We're not Gonna Take It; Christmas, Cousin Kevin; Acid Queen; Underture; Do You Think It's All Right; Fiddle About; Pinball Wizard; There's a Doctor; Go to the Mirror; Tommy Can You Hear Me; Smash the Mirror; Sensation.

The Who's highly-distinctive sound incorporated violent drumming, smashing against amplifiers, elements of rhythm-and-blues and jazz – decidedly different from the traditional 'Mersey Beat' format.

The tape recording sold $1,500,000 worth by end of 1970. In 1971 'Tommy' was produced in the U.S.A. as a ballet. The album sold over 3 million by 1972. It was later made into a film.

Keith Moon died in London.

THE WINSTONS (vocal and instrumental sextet)

COLOR HIM FATHER *Metromedia* [*USA*]. A highly polished performing unit, The Winstons got their big break when they were heard by The Impressions in their home, Washington, D.C. They toured America as a back-up band for The Impressions and were soon touring on their own as a name act. They were signed with Metromedia Records in Atlanta, Georgia, and 'Color Him Father' was their debut disc for the label. It became an overnight hit and rose to No 6 for two weeks in the U.S. charts with 13 weeks in the bestsellers, after release in May, and by 24 July received a Gold Disc award from R.I.A.A. for million sale. The song, written by lead singer Richard Spencer, is a soft soul ballad – a family tale with smooth emotional magnetism and rhythm-and-blues slant.

Personnel of the group: Richard Spencer (lead singer, tenor sax) formerly worked with the Otis Redding band; Phil Tolotta (organist and second lead singer); Quincy Mattison (lead guitar and vocalist) also worked with Otis Redding and with Arthur Conley, backed Conley on his 'Sweet Soul Music' hit; Ray Maritano (alto sax and vocalist) a graduate of Berklee School of Music and played sax in the U.S. Air Force Band; Sonny Peckrol (bass guitar and vocalist) first began performing in teen clubs while at high school; G.C. Coleman (drummer and vocalist) also worked with Otis Redding and was drummer for two years for Tamla Motown label, principally with The Marvelettes.

Grammy Award (1969) for Best Rhythm-and-Blues Song.

DAVID ALEXANDER WINTER

OH LADY MARY *Riviera-CED* [*France*]. Dutch born singer Winter was triumphant at the 1969 Antibes Song Festival and was discovered by Riviera Records (an affiliate of the Barclay group). This disc was released in April 1969 and by September sold 750,000 and the million by November in France, where it was No 1 for five weeks and in the Top Ten for around six months. It was also a hit in Italy (No 4). The song was written by Carli and Bukey, and also became a hit in 1970 for Germany's Peter Alexander (No 1 for four weeks).

STEVIE WONDER

MY CHERIE AMOUR *Tamla* [*USA*]. Stevie Wonder became one of Tamla/Motown's greatest acquisitions and 1969 was a big year for this artist. This disc was released on 24 May 1969 and

reached No 3 for two weeks in the U.S. charts with 14 weeks in the bestsellers. The song was written by Stevie Wonder, Henry Cosby and Sylvia Moy in 1968. The disc was also a good seller in Britain where it was No 3 for two weeks, and released in July 1969.

YESTER ME, YESTER YOU, YESTERDAY *Tamla* [*USA*]. Written in 1966 by Ronald Miller and Bryan Wells, this was a second million seller in 1969 for Stevie Wonder after release in the U.S.A. on 18 October. It reached No 7 for two weeks in the U.S. charts and was 14 weeks in the bestsellers.

In Britain, release was July 1970, the disc selling over 250,000 there and achieving No 1 for one week.

TAMMY WYNETTE

GREATEST HITS (album) *Epic* [*USA*]. Tammy Wynette was born on 5 May 1942 in Red Bay, Alabama, the daughter of a talented musical family, and began to take music seriously in high school, singing and playing the piano. She later worked with Country Boy Eddie on a Birmingham TV show, wrote a number of songs, and made a successful appearance on Porter Wagoner's TV show which led to singing engagements in the South. She made a visit to Nashville to try to get Epic Records interested in some songs written by a friend but ended up with Epic's producer Billy Sherrill signing her to a disc contract. Within a few weeks, her first single 'Apartment No 9' was a hit with country music fans (1967) and instantly a favourite on country, pop and top 40 stations.

She then became top of the charts constantly with singles and albums, and winner of the Country Music Association of America's top female vocalist award for 1967, 1968, 1969, and 1970. 'I Don't Wanna Play House' won her a Grammy award, 1967, for Best Country-and-Western Solo Vocal Performance (Female), and likewise 'Stand by Your Man' for 1969. Tammy's heavy schedule of personal appearances with her then famous husband George Jones, included Kraft Music Hall, Johnny Cash Show, Mike Douglas Show and Joey Bishop Show.

She became the first female singer with a solely country repertoire to sell an album in excess of one million dollars, with R.I.A.A. Gold Disc award April 1970. By October 1971 it was also the first for a female country singer to sell a million units, for which she received a platinum disc award. Her producer is Glenn Sutton, the songwriter husband of Lynn Anderson, a top country-and-western singer.

The contents of the album were: 'Stand by Your Man', by Tammy Wynette and Billy Sherrill (1968); 'Lonely Street', by K. Fowder, C. Below and W.S. Stevenson; 'D-I-V-O-R-C-E', by B. Braddock and C. Putman (1968); 'Gentle on My Mind', by John Hartford (1967); 'Take Me to Your World', by Glenn Sutton and Billy Sherrill (1968); 'Almost Persuaded', by Glenn Sutton and Billy Sherrill (1966); 'Your Good Girl's Gonna Go Bad', by Glenn Sutton and Billy Sherrill (1967); 'Apartment No 9', by J. Payeheck and B. Austin (1967); 'Hey, Good Lookin' ', by Hank Williams (1951); 'I Don't Wanna Play House', by Glenn Sutton and Billy Sherrill (1967); 'My Arms Stay Open Late', by J. Lomas and C. Putnam; 'There Goes My Everything', by Dallas Frazier (1965).

This album stayed in the U.S. bestseller national charts for 61 weeks and reached No 37. It was released in Britain under the title 'The Best of Tammy Wynette' (CBS label).

THE YOUNGBLOODS

GET TOGETHER *Victor* [*USA*]. The Youngbloods were four completely 'different' young men: Jesse Colin Young (leader); Jerry Corbitt (harmonica, guitar); 'Banana' Lovell Levinger (comedian); Joe Bauer (drums) born Memphis, Tenn.

'Get Together', written by Chet Powers, was originally a track from the group's first album issued in 1967, and released then in September as a single when it had a fair sale, reaching a minor

position in the U.S. charts. Victor re-issued the disc in July 1969 when it achieved No 4 for two weeks, and sold the million with R.I.A.A. Gold Disc award (7 October). Although the group had made many recordings from 1967, this re-issue was their first big hit. It stayed in the U.S. bestsellers for 17 weeks and brought the group to national prominence. With a prior 8 weeks in the bestsellers in 1967, the final tally reached 25 weeks.

SAORI YUKI

YOAKE-NO SKAT (Scat in the dark) *Express* [*Japan*]. Released in Japan in April 1969, this disc was a tremendous hit and sold two million in two months. It was No 1 for 10 weeks and stayed in the Top Ten for four months.

The Express label is a subsidiary of Toshiba Records.

ZAGER AND EVANS (vocal duo)

IN THE YEAR 2525 (Exordium and Terminus) *Victor* [*USA*]. 'In the Year 2525' is one of the most unusual and remarkable success stories to emerge from the U.S.A. Denny Zager and Rick Evans, two country guitarists from Lincoln, Nebraska, were once part of a group called The Eccentrics, but after a while, they decided to become a duo and spent much time on songs and rehearsing an act. They had performed on-and-off together since 1960. Rick Evans wrote this song around 1964.

In November 1968 the duo were singing in a Lincoln motel lounge, and at this time, borrowed $500 and set off for Odessa, Texas, to record the song. They formed their own record company, Truth Records, had an initial pressing of 1,000 recordings, and sold copies to record shops from the back of their car whenever they could get it played by the local radio stations. The disc soon received constant airplay, and a further 10,000 copies were pressed and sold. Buoyed by this regional success, the duo sent copies to all the major disc companies in New York. The copy sent to RCA came to the attention of their executive producer, Ernie Altschuler, who immediately traced them to Zeplin, Missouri, where they were then playing. He signed them to an exclusive contract. RCA then put considerable promotional weight behind the disc which they released in June 1969, and after four weeks it was No 1, remaining in that position for six weeks and selling over a million in less than two months, with R.I.A.A. Gold Disc award on 8 July.

Zager and Evans' meteoric rise to fame from obscurity was entirely due to this remarkable song of futuristic nostalgia, which sounds, (*Time* 18 July 1969), 'as though it were composed by a computer at the Rand Corporation'. Starting in the year 2525, the lyrics tell of what might be happening to mankind then and in each 1,000 years hence, such as pills, machines and artificial insemination taking over and maybe God thinking it time for Judgement Day by 6565. Set to a simple tune with a nostalgic instrumental backing typical of the early 1950s, this most original song had 'hit' written all over it. It was also described as 'a compelling song of the future'. The disc was released in Britain (July 1969) on RCA label where it was No 1 for three weeks with 13 weeks in the bestsellers, sold over 250,000 and had further big sales abroad. Soon after the single's release in the U.S.A., RCA issued an album combining 'In the Year 2525' with nine of Rick Evans' other songs titled '2525 (Exordium and Terminus)' and the duo moved on from small nightclubs to concerts in front of 25,000 people.

The single sold 4 million (two million in the U.S.A. and two abroad).

THE ZOMBIES

TIME OF THE SEASON *Date* [*USA*]. Written by Rod Argent (of the group) this was taken from their album of the same title and issued as a single in January 1969. It reached No 1 for a week in the U.S.A. with 13 weeks in the bestsellers, and sold the million by 11 April with Gold Disc award by R.I.A.A. The group had its first million seller in 1964 (*q.v.*).

THE 1970s

VARIOUS ARTISTS

JESUS CHRIST, SUPERSTAR (double album) *MCA [Britain] Decca [USA]*. Described as far and away the most ambitious pop venture into the Scriptures, this English rock opera was released on 1 October 1970 in Britain and 27 October 1970 in the U.S.A. on an 87-minute double album. This musical retelling of the last seven days of Christ added an interesting new dimension to the gutsy honesty and directness of rock opera and unfolds in a different way from the story learned in Sunday School. It was suggested that the work would bridge the musical - and scriptural - generation gap.

The recording has an all-star cast, an 85-piece symphony orchestra, three choirs, a rock group, a jazz band, a pianist who won the 1970 Tchaikovsky Award in Moscow and a Moog synthesizer. The principal singers were:

Ian Gillan (of Deep Purple group): Jesus Christ; Murray Head (actor-tenor): Judas Iscariot; Yvonne Elliman: Mary Magdalene; Mike D'Abo (former lead singer with Manfred Mann group): King Herod; Victor Brox: Caiaphus the High Priest; John Gustafson: Simon Zealots; plus Paul Raven, Brian Keith, Barry Dennen, Paul Davis, Annette Brox and others. The basic backing band consisted of three of The Grease Band group - Bruce Rowland (drums), Alan Spenner (bass guitar), Henry McCullough (guitar) - plus Peter Robinson from Quatermass (keyboards), Chris Curtis (tenor), Neil Hubbard (guitar) and other musicians. The principal conductor was Alan Doggett with the strings of the City of London Ensemble (Principal - Malcolm Henderson).

The album had one of the most all-inclusive promotion, advertising and publicity campaigns in the history of Decca Records, and received the endorsement of England's and America's leading clergymen. It was produced in Britain, where it reached No 6 in the charts.

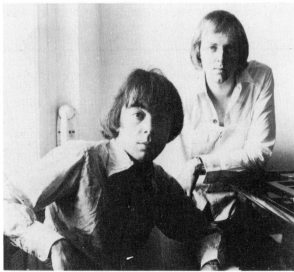

The work was written by Tim Rice (words) and Andrew Lloyd Webber (music) and took 18 months to complete. A single, 'Superstar', sung by Murray Head, was released first in December 1969 in the U.S.A. This sold over 500,000 globally by October 1970 and aroused considerable controversy, but received praise from many churchmen. The album got to No 1 in the

Previous page, top, left to right: Dolly Parton, Rod Stewart, David Bowie; bottom: David Essex, Elton John, Dionne Warwick.

U.S.A. by February 1971 for eight weeks and stayed in the Top 10 for 41 weeks, and 101 weeks in the bestsellers charts.

Lloyd Webber (son of a composer) was born on 22 March 1948. He studied music at the Guildhall School and the Royal College, and also went to Oxford. Rice, born on 10 November 1944, attended Lancing College and spent two years working towards a law career. He worked for EMI under Norrie Paramour, who produced hit discs for Cliff Richard and The Scaffold. The duo had met when both had left school and decided to write musicals, which didn't work out. While Rice was at EMI, they were asked to write a children's show. This was a version of the Old Testament's Joseph story, which they called *Joseph and the Amazing Technicolor Dream Coat*. This had a modest success. Manager David Lands asked them if he could underwrite their work. They agreed, and started on *Superstar*. Although Lloyd Webber grew up on Bill Haley and rock, his sound classical musical training fused *Superstar's* scoring with Rice's words into a convincing narrative style. The orchestral scoring was undoubtedly influenced by such composers as Hindemith, Penderecki and Ligeti.

A Broadway stage production had its preview in October 1971, and on 27 October its premiere. In Britain production opened on 9 August 1972 at the Palace Theatre, London, with 3,357 performances to 9 August 1980 - a record for a British musical. With productions in nearly every country in the world, it grossed more money than any other stage attraction. By August 1972 it had earned over $62 million in the U.S.A. alone. A screen version directed by Norman Jewison was produced in 1973.

Copies of the album are said to have sold in huge quantities on the Russian black market, and a report in early 1975 estimated earnings from various productions around the world, a film and recordings at £50,000,000 (approximately $125 million).

What this album will eventually sell is anyone's guess - probably millions. It could even be the greatest-selling album of all time. By 1974, sales of the double album were reported at $5\frac{1}{2}$ million with estimated earnings of £25,000,000. R.I.A.A. awarded a Gold Disc on 21 December 1970.

Contents: 'Heaven on their Minds': Murray Head; 'Everything's Alright': Yvonne Elliman, Murray Head, Ian Gillan; 'Hosanna': Victor Brox, Ian Gillan and the crowd; 'Pilate's Dream'; 'I Don't Know How to Love Him': Yvonne Elliman; 'The Last Supper': The Apostles; 'I Only Want to Say' (Gethsemane): Ian Gillan; 'King Herod's Song': Mike D'Abo; 'Superstar': Murray Head. The most popular song was 'I Don't Know How to Love Him', which had a great number of recordings and was sung by countless prominent vocalists all over the world.

FILM SOUNDTRACK

LOVE STORY *Paramount [USA]*. The film of Erich Segal's book *Love Story*, starring John Marley, Ray Milland, and Ali McGraw and Ryan O'Neal as the lovers, had its world premiere at Loew's State 1 and Loew's Tower East in New York on 17 December 1970. It became one of the biggest hits of all time. It made history and an enormous change in the entire motion picture industry. The audiences for *Love Story* bridged all gaps - generation, social, financial. It produced a return to romanticism, a revival of the story film, and brought people back into the theatres.

The music was scored by Francis Lai, who set the basic feel of the film with his haunting Chopinesque main love theme heard in four varying moods, and the use of Mozart and Bach selections as a pleasant addition. Carl Sigman wrote lyrics for the main love theme and the resultant song - 'Where do I begin?' - sold over 2 million sheet music copies. The song was widely recorded, and one disc - by Andy Williams - sold over a million.

The film took over $35 million in 282 collective theatres by mid–March 1971, and grossed over $50 million in the U.S.A. and Canada alone by the end of 1971. Segal's book sold over 1 million hardback and around 5 million paperback copies.

The album was released in the U.S.A. in November 1970 and sold 750,000 in the first 4 weeks, subsequently amassing a two million sale. It was No 1 for two weeks, No 2 for nine weeks, and in the Top 20 for five months, staying in the bestsellers for 39 weeks. In Britain, it reached No 8. It won an R.I.A.A. Gold Disc award in February 1971. Francis Lai won the Academy Award (the Oscar) for Best Original Score (1970). *Love Story* bears the unique position of simultaneously being the No 1 book, film and record in the U.S.A.

Contents: '*Love Story* Theme'; 'Snow Frolic' 'Sonata No 12 in F Major' – Allegro (Mozart); 'I Love You, Phil'; 'Christmas Trees'; 'Search for Jenny'; 'Bozo Barrett'; 'Skating in Central Park'; 'Long Walk Home'; 'Concerto No 3 in D Major' – Allegro (Bach); '*Love Story* Theme' – Finale. Piano solo by Georges Pludermacher.

ORIGINAL CAST TV SOUNDTRACK
THE SESAME STREET BOOK & RECORD *Columbia* [*USA*]. This is probably the best children's show in TV history, and one of the best parents' shows as well.

'Sesame Street' began in February 1966 at a dinner party given by Mrs Cooney, a producer for public TV in Manhattan. She was complaining about poor children's programming. One of her guests, Lloyd N. Morrisett, vice-president of the Carnegie Corporation, became very interested, and after Mrs Cooney submitted her report with the recommendation: 'Spend a lot of money on this', her Children's Television Workshop was granted $6 million by the Carnegie Corporation, the Ford Foundation, the U.S. Office of Education and related government agencies.

Mrs Cooney then consulted such diverse experts as psychologists and children's book illustrators, and, after 18 months studying children's interests across the country, an associate research professor from Oregon, Dr Edward L. Palmer, learned what children really wanted and what bored them. Joan Ganz Cooney created a McLuhanesque environment for the show, which commenced in November 1969. Monsters run the show (Cookie Monster, Big Bird, Oscar the Grouch and other creatures) plus human 'hosts' (a black couple, an Irish tenor, and a crusty old man). Between them, they demonstrate that problems can be solved only by cooperation in a series of instructional songs and 'selling' the alphabet and numbers with rhythmic breaks in the action, to sharpen children's cognitive skills. The 'switched-on' classroom education was a fantastic success. The first series reached almost 7 million pre-school children everyday, and won many awards and prizes for excellence. By 1971, 'Sesame Street' was being shown in over 50 countries.

The 'Sesame Street' album with illustrated book released in 1970 (July) held a position on the pop charts for 47 weeks, reaching No 23 for two weeks. By January 1972 it had sold over a million.

One of the songs, 'Rubber Duckie Song', was in the charts for nine weeks and the disc sold over 800,000 by January 1972 as a singles commercial release. The vocalist is Jim Henson, who sings for and animates 'Ernie'.

The cast included Matt Robinson (as Schoolteacher); Will Lee (as Grocer 'Gordon'); Carroll Spinney (as Puppeteer); Bob McGrath (vocalist); Jim Henson (as Ernie); Loretta Long (as Susan); and Jaime Sanchez.

FILM SOUNDTRACK
WOODSTOCK (triple album) *Cotillion* [*USA*] *Atlantic* [*Britain*]. The Woodstock Music and Arts Fair, held at Woodstock, an obscure town in New York State, for three days, August 16, 17 and 18, in 1969, was probably one of the greatest mass assemblies in history. Around 450,000 people attended this festival of love, peace and music in which many famous folk singers and rock groups performed. The whole event was filmed, and a virtually perfect record of the festival was brilliantly made by Michael Wadleigh, and reviewed in Hollywood on 25 March 1970, cut from 315,000 feet of film.

This triple album set was then the biggest pop package released (May 1970) with the highest list price ($14.98) and one of the most successful ever put out by Atlantic Records on their new Cotillion label, with expectations of becoming one of the biggest selling pop albums ever. The set sold 1,100,000 by September 1970 and two million by the end of the year, with sales still continuing long after. A Gold Disc was awarded by the R.I.A.A. before its release. It was No 1 for four weeks in the U.S. charts, stayed in the Top 10 for 24 weeks, and in the bestsellers for 68 weeks. In Britain it was released on 3 July 1970 where it reached No 17.

The set of three albums included 21 long tracks: *Side 1* - 'I Had a Dream' (John B. Sebastien), by John B. Sebastien; 'Going Up the Country' (Canned Heat) by Alan Wilson; 'Freedom' (Ritchie Havens), by Ritchie Havens; 'Rock and Roll Music' (Country Joe & The Fish), by McDonald, Melton, Hirsch, Barthol and Cohen; 'Coming into Los Angeles' (Arlo Guthrie), by Arlo Guthrie; 'At the Top' (Sha-Na-Na), by Singer, Medora and White; *Side 2* - 'The "Fish" Cheer/I-feel-like-I'm-fixin'-to-die-Rag' (Country Joe), by Joe McDonald; 'Drug Store Truck Drivin' Man' (Joan Baez, featuring Jeffrey Shurtloff), by McGuinn and Parsons; 'Joe Hill' (Joan Baez), by Robinson and Hayes; 'Suite: Judy Blue Eyes' (Crosby, Stills, Nash & Young), by Stephen Stills (1964); 'Sea of Madness' (Crosby, Stills, Nash & Young), by Neil Young; *Side 3* - 'Wooden Ships' (Crosby, Stills, Nash & Young), by David Crosby and Stephen Stills (1964); 'We're Not Gonna Take It' (The Who, from *Tommy*), by Peter Townshend (1969); 'With a Little Help From My Friends' (Joe Cocker), by John Lennon and Paul McCartney (1967); *Side 4* - 'Soul Sacrifice' (Santana), by Santana; 'I'm Going Home' (Ten Years After), by Alvin Lee; *Side 5* - 'Volunteers' (Jefferson Airplane), by Marty Balin and Paul Kantner; medley: 'Dance to the Music'/'Music Lover'/ 'I Want to Take You Higher' (Max Yasgur, Sly & The Family Stone), by Sylvester Stewart; 'Rainbows All Over Your Blues' (John B. Sebastien), by John B. Sebastien; *Side 6* - 'Love March' (Butterfly Blues Band), by Dinwiddie and Wilson; 'Star Spangled Banner'/'Purple Haze' and instrumental solo (Jimi Hendrix), by Jimi Hendrix.

Other artists who appeared at the Festival were: Melanie, Mountain, The Band, Creedence Clearwater Revival, Blood, Sweat & Tears, The Grateful Dead, Tim Harding, Keef Hartley, The Incredible String Band, Johnny Winter, Sweetwater, Quill, and Ravi Shankar.

ALIVE 'N KICKIN' (sextet)
TIGHTER, TIGHTER *Roulette* [*USA*]. A new sextet, five men and one girl, with their first million seller, the composition by T. James, B. King and arrangement by J. Wisner. It was released in May 1970 and stayed in the U.S. charts for 16 weeks, reaching No 3 for two weeks.

LYNN ANDERSON
(country-and-western vocalist)
ROSE GARDEN (I Never Promised You a) *Columbia* [*USA*] *CBS* [*Britain*]. Lynn Anderson was born on 26 September 1947 in Grand Forks, North Dakota, and graduated from Bella Vista High School in California. She started singing at the age of six at the San Jose, California, Civic Auditorium, before her family moved to Nashville. She became expert in guitar playing and horse-womanship, her quarter horses winning over 700 trophies and awards in seven years of showing. One of her horses, Top Mark, was the inspiration for the single 'Ride, Ride, Ride'. Top Mark and Lynn won 123 trophies and over 600 ribbons in horse shows, rodeos and parades all over California. She was 'Princess' of the 1965 State Fair Horse Show and 'California State Horse Shoe Queen' in 1966. Since 1967, she was a Top 5 Nashville female vocalist. Her mother, Liz Anderson, was a former RCA-

Victor recording artist. Lynn is married to songwriter Glenn Sutton, who produces all her recordings. 'Rose Garden', written by Joe South, is a light, bouncy, fingerclicking number with a catchy melody and brilliant lyrics. The name of the song comes from the title of a novel by Hannah Green, but there is no further connection between the song and the novel. It was taken from one of Lynn's albums and released in October 1970. It proved to be the biggest record of her career, and achieved the rare feat of a female country-and-western vocalist reaching No 1 in the U.S. charts for a week in February 1971, by which time it had sold a million, with R.I.A.A. Gold Disc award. It was also the No 1 country-and-western disc for five weeks, and on national best-seller charts for 17 weeks.

British release was in February 1971, and the disc reached No 2 for one week with 20 weeks in the bestsellers, selling over 250,000. It gained the Grammy Award for Best Country Vocal Performance (Female) 1970. Sales by August 1971 were 2,000,000.

BADFINGER

COME AND GET IT *Apple* [*Britain*] *Apple* [*USA*]. Written by Paul McCartney, this was recorded by Badfinger for the film *The Magic Christian* when they were still known as The Iveys. The Beatles persuaded them to change their name to Badfinger.

The group was signed to the Apple organization and was launched with a massive campaign, but nothing happened until Paul McCartney wrote 'Come and Get It' and produced the disc. This was released in January 1970, reaching No 3 for one week on both British (with 11 weeks in the bestsellers) and U.S. charts. It had the bigger sale in the U.S.A., where it sold a million. This group had a vocal sound that set them apart.

Personnel: Pete Ham (guitar, piano, organ) born 27 April 1947 in Swansea, Wales; Mike Gibbins (drums, guitars) born 12 March 1949 in Swansea, Wales; Tom Evans (guitar, piano, bass) born 21 June 1947 in Liverpool; Joe Molland (guitar, piano, bass) born 21 June 1947 in Liverpool (joined the group after this disc). They had their first big date at The Cavern, Liverpool. Pete Ham died on 24 April 1975 in Woking, Surrey.

NO MATTER WHAT *Apple* [*Britain*] *Apple* [*USA*]. Written by Pete Ham (of the group), this disc was released in the U.S.A. in October 1970 where it was No 4 for a week. British release was in January 1971, where it was No 5 for two weeks with 12 weeks in the bestsellers. Combined sales from the U.S.A. and Britain plus elsewhere made an estimated million sales for Badfinger.

GEORGE BAKER SELECTION (quintet)

LITTLE GREEN BAG *Negram* [*Holland*] *Colossus* [*USA*]. An infectious, softly rocking disc by a new Dutch group, and their initial release, which was a big seller in Europe and a success in the U.S.A. The combined sales exceeded a million. The disc was released in the U.S.A. in March 1970 and got to No 16 in the charts for two weeks.

The song was written by Jan Visser and Bouens (George Baker), both members of the group, Baker being vocalist. Other members were Jacques Greuter, George The and Jon Hop.

THE BEATLES

HEY JUDE (album) *Apple* [*USA*]. An album of old Beatles material, produced by George Martin especially for the American market. It was released on 26 February with a massive advertisement campaign and drew over 2 million in advance record orders and nearly one million for tape. A Gold Disc award from the R.I.A.A. was instantaneous. Sales after three months were reported at over 3,300,000 and 3,750,000 by the end of its 33 weeks' run in the bestseller charts. It reached No 1 for four weeks.

Contents: Hey Jude (1968); Revolution (1968); Paperback Writer (1966); I Should Have Known Better (1964); Lady Madonna (1968); Can't Buy Me Love (1964); Don't Let Me Down (1969); Ballad of John and Yoko (1969); Rain (1966); Old Brown Shoe (George Harrison, 1969). All songs by Lennon and McCartney unless otherwise indicated.

LET IT BE *Apple* [*Britain*]. An inspirational, soulful, gospel-style number with a profoundly philosophic lyric, expressed with great feeling by Paul McCartney plus his thudding piano, supported throughout by 'heavenly choir'. This beautiful soul ballad with its references to 'Mother Mary' is said to be dedicated to Paul's mother Mary, who died when he was young. Release on both sides of the Atlantic was 6 March 1970, and it was No 1 for four weeks in the U.S.A. with the R.I.A.A. Gold Disc award inside a month, and well over 1½ million sales. In Britain it was No 2 for a week with well over a quarter of a million sales. The disc was also No 1 in Canada, Switzerland, Malaysia, Poland, New Zealand, Norway, Holland, Italy, Germany and Australia, with global sales estimated at well over 3 million. The song was written by John Lennon and Paul McCartney some 12 months earlier for their film, and originally recorded at Twickenham Studios. The backing of the disc is 'You Know My Name', written by Lennon and McCartney, originally recorded in 1967, and has Billy Preston playing organ.

THE LONG AND WINDING ROAD backed with FOR YOU BLUE *Apple* [*USA*]. Both these songs were taken from the 'Let It Be' album and released in May 1970 as a single for the U.S. market only. It sold 1,200,000 in two days and was No 1 for two weeks, with an immediate Gold Disc award. 'The Long and Winding Road', written by Lennon and McCartney, features Paul McCartney as soloist with a large choir and orchestra. 'For You Blue' was written by Beatle George Harrison, and is a romantic ballad sung by Paul partly in falsetto.

'LET IT BE' (album) *Apple* [*Britain*] *Apple* [*USA*]. *Let It Be*, a semi-documentary colour movie lasting one hour and 20 minutes, was premiered in the U.S.A. on 13 May and in Britain (London and Liverpool) on 20 May 1970, its basic theme being 'a day in the recording life' of The Beatles. The record was planned as a 'soundtrack album' complete with false starts and in-between chatter. Most of the takes were recorded in early 1969 during the shooting of a Beatles film 'happening'. Former rock tycoon Phil Spector was brought in to give the album commercialism. It set a new record for the American disc industry by achieving a sale of 3,700,000 in just over two weeks, representing $25 million with an immediate Gold Disc award by the R.I.A.A. Its release was simultaneous in Britain and the U.S.A. on 13 May, and achieved No 1 for five weeks in the U.S.A. and six weeks in Britain.

The album was in the U.S. bestsellers for 54 weeks, and global sales are estimated at well over four million. It won a Grammy Award for Best Original Score written for a Motion Picture (Composer's Award) 1970.

1970 was also the year that saw the break-up of The Beatles as a group, each member starting to record individually. (See McCartney album and John Lennon album, and George Harrison. Ringo Starr also made a solo album 'Sentimental Journey' that sold half a million.) 'Let It Be' won the Academy Award (the Oscar) for Best Original Song Score for a Film (1970).

It was revealed in February 1971 that The Beatles' income from record royalties, tours, films and other sources from June 1962 to December 1968 was £7,864,126. From May 1969 to December 1970 it was £9,142,533, of which more than £8,000,000 came from record royalties, £700,000 from films and £300,000 from other sources, making a grand total of £17,006,659.

The album is notable for the first song written by all four Beatles, 'Dig It', which was improvised as they recorded it. Contents: 'Two of Us on Our Way Home'; 'Dig a Pony'; 'Across the Universe' (originally released on a charity album); 'Let It Be'; 'I've Got a Feeling'; 'One after 909' (originally written in the mid 1950s); 'Get Back'; 'I, Me, Mine' (George Harrison); 'For You Blue' (George Harrison); 'Dig It' (Lennon, McCartney, Harrison and Starr); 'Maggie May' (Liverpool folk song); 'The Long and Winding Road'. All songs written by Lennon and McCartney unless otherwise indicated.

THE BEE GEES

LONELY DAYS *Polydor [Britain] Atco [USA]*. Written by Barry, Robin and Maurice Gibb – the three brothers who are The Bee Gees recording as a trio in this year, the original group having split up. The disc was first released in Britain on 6 November 1970, but reached only No 26. In the U.S.A. it was a big hit, reaching No 1 there for a week in February 1971 after release in October 1970, and selling a million with R.I.A.A. Gold Disc award in April 1971.

It was in the bestseller U.S. charts for 14 weeks.

VINCENT BELL (guitarist)

'AIRPORT' THEME *Decca [USA]*. Written by Alfred Newman for the successful film *Airport*, for which he wrote the entire score, the last before his death on 17 February 1970. This exciting version of the theme with its bubbly underwater guitar sound sold a million globally. It achieved No 27 for a week in the U.S.A.

Vincent Bell, a veteran studio musician and recording artist in his own right, was the man responsible for the guitar sound on Ferrante and Teicher's version of the theme from the film *Midnight Cowboy*. The 'Airport' disc was made under the direction of Tom Morgan, A & R head of Decca and established Bell as a major recording artist. Release was in March 1970. The arrangement was by Nick Perito. The disc won a Grammy Award for Best Instrumental Composition (Composer's Award) 1970.

BLACK SABBATH

BLACK SABBATH (album) *Vertigo [Britain] Warner [USA]*. Black Sabbath group, comprising Tony Iommi (guitar), Geezer Butler (bass guitar), Bill Ward (drums) and John 'Ozzie' Osbourne (vocals and harmonica) emerged from Birmingham, England, around late 1966, where they established a fine local reputation and changed their name from Earth to Black Sabbath. They became deeply interested in black magic which is strongly reflected in their music, backed up by a huge barrage of sound. They became an 'underground' success with their highly individual conception of progressive sounds.

The group rapidly built up fanatical followings in small areas of Britain from 1969 and by 1970 were a hit group. They played the Star Club in Hamburg and were re-booked five times during 1969.

The 'Black Sabbath' album, their first, was released on 13 February 1970 in Britain, reaching No 8 for two weeks and staying in the top 20 for 12 weeks. In the U.S.A. it reached No 23 and was many weeks in the bestsellers, with R.I.A.A. Gold Disc award in 1971, and platinum award for million sale in August 1974.

Contents: 'Black Sabbath'; 'The Wizard'; 'Behind the Wall of Sleep'; 'N.I.B.'; 'Sleeping Village'; 'Warning' (Dunbar); 'Evil Woman' (Wiegand and Waggoner). All songs written by Iommi, Butler, Ward and Osbourne unless otherwise indicated.

PARANOID (album) *Vertigo [Britain] Warner [USA]*. The second album and second big hit for Black Sabbath. This was released in Britain in September 1970 following the success of their single 'Paranoid', released on 24 July. The album reached No 1 for two weeks and was in Britain's top 20 for 16 weeks. In the U.S.A. it was No 8 for a week and stayed 65 weeks in the bestsellers, with Gold Disc award from R.I.A.A. in 1971 and platinum award from Warner Bros. for million sale subsequently. The group's world-wide success stems from this album.

Contents: 'War Pigs'; 'Paranoid'; 'Planet Caravan'; 'Iron Man'; 'Electric Funeral'; 'Hand of Doom'; 'Rat Salad'; 'Fairies Wear Boots'.

All songs written by the group.

BLOOD, SWEAT AND TEARS

BLOOD SWEAT AND TEARS 3 (album) *Columbia [USA] CBS [Britain]*. Released in July 1970 in the U.S.A., this third album by the group with its dynamic fusing of rock and classics. Blood, Sweat and Tears produce a pulsating, exciting sound, matched by the raw vocals of David Clayton-Thomas. The album shipped more than a million units in the first week, and subsequently sold a million by the end of 1970. A Gold Disc was awarded by R.I.A.A. for $1 million sale almost immediately after release. The album was 41 weeks in the U.S. bestsellers. It was No 1 for three weeks and stayed in the Top 10 for three months. British release was in August and the disc reached No 13 for a week.

Contents: 'Hi-de Ho' (Carole King); 'The Battle' (Steve Katz and Dick Halligan); 'Lucretia McEvil' (David Clayton-Thomas); 'Lucretia's Reprise' (David Clayton-Thomas); 'Fire and Rain' (James Taylor); 'Lonesome Susie' (Richard Manuel); 'Symphony for the Devil' (Mick Jagger and Keith Richard; an overwhelming track which uses The Rolling Stones' words of their 'Sympathy for the Devil' but with different music. It took four months to complete); 'He's a Runner' (Laura Nyro); 'Something's Comin' On' (Joe Cocker); '40,000 Headsmen' (a unique track, using three different themes by three different composers, incorporating them into the Stevie Winwood song).

BLUES IMAGE (sextet)

RIDE CAPTAIN, RIDE *Atco [USA]*. Released in April 1970, this was taken from the group's album 'Open' (released January 1970). It was written by the group and is a well-constructed, clean instrumental and a good song. The disc got to No 4 for one week and was 16 weeks in the U.S. charts, selling the million by August, with R.I.A.A. Gold Disc award.

Most of the group members are from Florida and lived in Los Angeles, the notable exception being bass guitarist Malcolm Jones who emigrated from Wales in 1967. Blues Image were pioneers in the Latin-Rock wave and attained a growing underground reputation. They played the clubs and large arenas.

The personnel: Dennis Correll (vocals); Joe Lala (congas and vocals); Manuel Bertematti (drums); Skip Konte (keyboards); Kent Henry (lead guitar); Malcolm Jones (bass guitar).

BREAD (vocal and instrumental quartet)

MAKE IT WITH YOU *Elektra [USA]*. Bread are a Californian group originally formed by David Gates, James Griffin and Robb Royer, all respected Los Angeles session men until early 1969. Gates got them together for a Screen Gems TV show and found that they worked well. Mike Botts (drums) was added later.

Gates and Royer were songwriting together in 1968, when Gates used them on a session. The trio recorded an album and two singles were taken from it. A second album, 'On the Waters', was then made when Botts joined, and 'Make It With You' was taken from this. It was written by David Gates and is an attractively garnished ballad with a fine vocal and instrumental performance of soft, bittersweet teen material. The recording was made in Los Angeles and released in May 1970. British release was in July 1970. The disc was No 1 for a week in the U.S.A. and sold a million by August, with a Gold Disc award by R.I.A.A. In Britain it was No 5 for a week with 14 weeks in the bestsellers.

All three original members are multi-instrumentalists: David Gates (born Tulsa, Oklahoma) plays guitar, bass, keyboards, violin, viola, percussion and Moog synthesizer; James Griffin (born Memphis, Tennessee) plays guitar and percussion; Robb Royer plays flute, recorder, keyboards and guitar. Royer left the group around 1972, and was replaced by Larry Knechtel (born in Bell, California) who plays piano, organ, bass, guitar and harmonica.

ERIC BURDON AND WAR
SPILL THE WINE *MGM* [*USA*] *Polydor* [*Britain*]. Singer Eric Burdon first became prominent with The Animals, who were disbanded in early 1969. He then lived for many months in the hills of Laurel Canyon in Hollywood, striving for a career in motion pictures without success. He then got together a new group, himself and seven others, to produce their first album 'Eric Burdon Declares War' which was released in March 1970. 'Spill the Wine' was taken from this and released as a single in May. It got to No 1 for a week and sold the million by August with R.I.A.A. Gold Disc award. The disc was released in Britain 17 July 1970.

War comprised six sidemen and a Danish harmonica player. Their music proved to be dynamic, producing some of the most amazing rhythms ever heard, and a stage act of pure musical excitement.

The personnel: Dee Allen (congas); B.B. Dickerson (bass, vocal); Harold Brown (drums); Howard Scott (guitar, vocal); Charles Miller (tenor sax, flute); Lonnie Jordan (organ, piano) (all originally in a Los Angeles band called The Nightshift); Lee Oskar (harmonica); Eric Burdon (lead vocalist). The song was written by the group. (See also War, 1971.)

CANNED HEAT (instrumental and vocal quintet)
LET'S WORK TOGETHER *Liberty* [*USA*]. Written by Wilbert Harrison in 1969, Canned Heat's disc was taken from their album 'Future Blues' and was a big hit in Britain where it sold over 250,000 after release in January 1970, reaching No 2 for one week with 15 weeks in the bestsellers. The disc was also a big seller in Europe, the combined sales being over the million. In U.S.A. release was several months later and it reached No 17 for two weeks there.

The personnel: Bob Hite (known as 'The Bear'), lead singer, born 26 February 1943 in Torrance, California: also plays trumpet, harp and guitar; Alan Wilson (known as 'Blind Owl'), born 4 July 1943 in Boston, Mass., guitar, harmonica and vocals; Henry Vestine (known as 'Preacher'), born 25 December 1944 in Washington, guitar; Larry Taylor, born Brooklyn, N.Y., 26 June 1942, bass guitar; Adolpho De La Parra, born 8 February 1946 in Mexico City, drums, organ and guitar.

Hite began to sing while working as a box boy in a supermarket, then joined a jug band, started playing professional dates and ended up as lead singer to Canned Heat. Wilson majored in music at Boston University, and began playing New Orleans-style trombone at local clubs when he was 14. He joined the group after moving to Los Angeles in 1965. Vestine played every type of engagement from parties to blues sessions in the deep South. Taylor's first job professionally was backing Jerry Lee Lewis at the age of 14. De La Parra, a master of percussion, replaced the original drummer Frank Cook. It was during jam sessions and playing small clubs around Los Angeles that Canned Heat was formed.

THE CARPENTERS
CLOSE TO YOU (They long to be) *A & M* [*USA*]. The Carpenters' success story is one of waiting for their sound to develop, the right recording contract and the right song. The Carpenter family moved to Los Angeles in 1963 from New Haven, Connecticut. Richard Carpenter and his sister Karen began singing professionally in 1967 and were in groups for a while. One of these, Spectrum, became quite well known in the Los Angeles area. The duo decided to go out alone and took two members of Spectrum as part of their back-up group. One of their tapes got through to Herb Alpert, boss of A. & M. who signed them up. Their first disc was 'Ticket to Ride' (1969) a minor hit for them. Songwriter Burt Bacharach liked this disc and, after hearing the group sing one of his songs at a benefit party, took them with him on other shows in New York, St Louis and Hollywood. Alpert then gave The Carpenters 'Close to You', a Hal David/Burt Bacharach song written around 1963 which had been recorded on albums by Dionne Warwick and Dusty Springfield. This was the right song which after release in May 1970 achieved No 1 for four weeks in the U.S. charts, was awarded a Gold Disc by R.I.A.A. in August and sold over two million. Release in Britain was September 1970 where it reached No 3 for a week with 18 weeks in the bestsellers. Over three million were sold globally.

Richard Carpenter, born 1946 (piano and vocals), and Karen Carpenter, born 1950 (drums and vocals), are joined by Dan Woodhams (bass guitarist, vocalist), Gary Sims (guitarist, bassist, vocalist) and Douglas Strawn (reed player, vocalist) but Richard and Karen do all the voices on the recordings, and Richard does the arrangements. This disc brought them international prominence. They received Grammy Awards for Best New Artist of 1970 and for Best Contemporary Vocal Performance by a group (1970).

WE'VE ONLY JUST BEGUN *A. & M.* [*USA*]. This song was taken from The Carpenters' album 'Close to You' and released in September 1970. It got to No 1 for a week in the U.S.A. and by November had sold a million with Gold Disc award from R.I.A.A.

The song, written by Paul Williams and Roger Nichols, is a beautiful, tenderly haunting ballad, and offsets the voice of Karen Carpenter to perfect advantage. The strings, deft piano touches interwoven behind her voice, plus the tambourine stressing the rhythm and staccato brass chords punctuating the scoring in the chorus, make the recording outstanding.

Release in Britain was January 1971 where it was No 28.

Karen died on 4 February 1983 in California.

CLARENCE CARTER

PATCHES *Atlantic* [*USA*]. A powerful blues disc, and the story of a poor boy growing up, was written by Donald Dunbar and N. Johnson (General Johnson of The Chairmen of the Board group). This 'rags to riches' theme earned Clarence Carter a Gold Disc award by R.I.A.A. for the million sale by September 1970, just two months after its release in the U.S.A. (July).

The disc was No 1 there for a week and also a hit in Britain, where it reached No 2 for three weeks. It was Carter's third million seller. The disc was produced by Rick Hall and won a Grammy Award for Best Rhythm-and-Blues Song (Songwriter's Award) 1970.

GENE CHANDLER

GROOVY SITUATION *Mercury* [*USA*]. This disc, a sweet soul item, brought Gene ('Duke of Earl') Chandler back into the spotlight after eight years, giving him his second million seller. It was released in June in the U.S.A. and received a Gold Disc award from R.I.A.A. in November 1970, after being 15 weeks in the charts, and reaching No 10 for a week. The song was written by Russell Lewis and Herman Davis.

CHICAGO (Transit Authority)

CHICAGO II (Double album) *Columbia* [*USA*]. Chicago's second album release proved to be a big success and it was this that finally launched the group. It was No 4 in the U.S.A. for four weeks, and remained in the Top 10 for 31 weeks, with R.I.A.A. Gold Disc award and subsequent million units sale. In Britain it reached No 6, and was seven weeks in the Top 10.

It contained 23 tracks, the outstanding ones being: 'Wake Up Sunshine', 'Fancy Colours', '25 or 6 to 4', 'In the Country', 'Movin' In', 'Low Down' (Seraphine and Cetera), 'West Virginia Fantasies', 'Better End Soon', 'Poem for the People' and 'Ballet for a Girl from Buchanan'. A single, 'Make Me Smile', taken from the latter title, became a big hit standard. Other titles were 'The Road', 'So Much to Say, So Much to Give', 'Anxiety's Moment', 'Colour My World', 'To Be Free', 'Now More Than Ever', 'Prelude', 'A.M. Mourning', 'P.M. Mourning', 'Memories of Love' and 'Where Do We Go From Here?'.

This disc was 111 weeks in the U.S. bestsellers. It was released January 1970.

CHRISTIE (vocal and instrumental trio)

YELLOW RIVER *CBS* [*Britain*] *Epic* [*USA*]. Jeff Christie wrote 'Yellow River' in 1968 with The Tremeloes in mind for recording. They turned it down, so Christie formed his group initially for the purpose of recording it. The disc's very commercial sound proved to be a worldwide hit and is said to have been No 1 in 26 countries with global sales of over 3 million. Release was in Britain in April 1970 and it reached No 1 for a week with over 250,000 sale. In the U.S.A. release was in July and although it reached only No 16 there, it had a run of 23 weeks in their bestsellers and sold over the million. It was also awarded a Gold Disc in Japan where it was chosen as the most outstanding single of 1970. Yet another Gold Disc was collected by the group during its South American tour (autumn 1970) for 100,000 sale in Brazil – a rare event in that country. The success of the disc resulted in bookings in many countries including the U.S.A., Germany, Italy, Ireland, Sweden, Japan, Australia, New Zealand and Israel.

Christie are: Jeff Christie (born 12 July 1946 in Leeds, Yorkshire) guitar, organ, piano, bass; Vic Elmes (born 10 May 1947 in Dagenham, Essex) guitar; Michael Blakley (born 12 January 1947 in Bromley, Kent) drums, piano.

JOE COCKER

CRY ME A RIVER *A & M* [*USA*]. John Robert Cocker was born on 30 May 1944 in Sheffield, England, and educated at Central Technical School there, and later became a gas fitter with East Midlands Gas Board.

Ray Charles became an important influence, and at 15 he joined The Cavaliers, a local group, playing drums and harmonica. Two years later he was lead vocalist of the group when renamed Vance Arnold and The Avengers. In 1964, he was offered a contract by Decca and given six months' leave of absence from his job, which he resumed after his first disc was unsuccessful.

Cocker then formed a funk outfit, The Grease Band, which included Chris Stainton (keyboards) who became his guiding influence in later years. After playing mostly soul music in the north of England, he moved south and made another disc 'Marjorine'; an appearance at the Windsor Jazz and Blues Festival brought him prominence, with his next single 'With a Little Help From My Friends' reaching No 1 in Britain, and entering the U.S. Top 40, subsequently achieving Top 10 status.

In 1969, he made the album of the same title, using well-known session musicians such as Stevie Winwood, Jimmy Page and Albert Lee. The Grease Band's U.S. tour in 1969 gained him many friends, among whom was Leon Russell, an Oklahoma pianist who helped supervise his recordings in Los Angeles.

When Cocker arrived in the U.S. in 1970 wishing to cancel a Grease Band tour, Russell arranged instead a massive group of 40 or more musicians, old ladies and dogs, collectively called Mad Dogs and Englishmen, the result being a 114 minute carnival of high spirits and rock'n'roll. They performed 65 times in 57 days.

Cocker was virtually adopted by the Americans, particularly after his performance at the Woodstock Festival (1969) and its subsequent film showing.

'Cry Me a River', a former hit for Julie London, was a big hit for Joe Cocker in his Mad Dogs and Englishmen show, which he performed as a shouting, cathartic revival hymn with his friends. The song was written by Arthur Hamilton in 1953. The disc reached No 7 in the U.S. charts and a million sale was reported in early 1971.

In 1972, Cocker re-teamed with Stainton and a 12-piece band for a brief British tour and then went to Australia, subsequently returning to England after drugs trouble.

He was easily the most convincing blues/soul singer to come out of Britain.

JUDY COLLINS

AMAZING GRACE *Elektra* [*USA*]. Folksinger Judy Collins was born on 1 May 1939. Her father, Chuck Collins, was blind and a well-known figure in radio in Denver and on the West Coast. Judy, raised in Denver, studied piano and guitar for 10 years. She attended school in Jacksonville, Illinois, and at the University of Colorado, and developed an interest in folk music during summer vacations at Rocky Mountain National Park, when she decided a career as a concert pianist was not for her. She began singing regularly at folk clubs in Denver and Chicago. When the folk boom reached Denver she landed a TV pilot show with The Clancy Brothers and Tommy Makem, and signed with Elektra Records, making her first album in 1962 and many successful gold albums since. She developed her interest in contemporary folk music and performed with others on platforms at protest marches, singing the material of angry young folksingers such as Tom Paxton, Bob Dylan and Phil Ochs.

From the early 1960s her musical vision consistently outstripped everyone in the folk field, and her thorough musical training and ability at song arranging were recognized as outstanding. She has become one of the foremost singer/songwriters of our time, and has played every major booking including the Hollywood Bowl, Newport and Philadelphia Festivals, and Carnegie Hall, New York.

She recorded 'Amazing Grace' – a song The Weavers made big some time ago – simply because it was one of her favourites. It is an old shapenote hymn attributed by hymnals to the Rev. John Newton (1779), a famous Church of England preacher and hymn writer (1725-1807). Years ago in the Appalachian Mountains in the U.S.A., people couldn't read or write, so they

couldn't read music – but they could associate a certain shape with a certain note, and it became a sort of local code. The recording was made at St Paul's Chapel, Columbia University, on account of its aesthetic and acoustic qualities. Judy's disc of this very old hymn, arranged by her, was taken off her 'Whales and Nightingales' album, and issued as a single. It reached No 12 and was 15 weeks in the U.S. bestsellers charts. In Britain it reached No 4 for a week in 1971, and was 67 weeks in the charts, selling well over 250,000. With big sales in the U.S. and elsewhere, it is estimated to have well passed the million mark.

PERRY COMO

IT'S IMPOSSIBLE *RCA* [*USA*]. Perry Como, pop singer idol from the mid-1940s to the end of the 1950s, proved, with this song, that nothing is impossible. After an absence of 11 years, at the age of 57 he bounced right back into the charts on both sides of the Atlantic. The song was written by Sid Wayne and A. Manzanero, a catchy, commercial composition with a beautiful melody and outstanding lyrics that appealed to both old and young.

The disc was released in the U.S.A. in October 1970, and reached No 7 for a week. It stayed in their bestsellers for 15 weeks and sold a million by February 1971. In Britain release was on 8 January 1971 and it sold over 250,000 and reached No 2 for one week with 23 weeks in the bestsellers. It made million seller No 20 for Perry.

Composer Armando Manzanero, singer-songwriter, was the first Mexican RCA artist by 1968 to receive an award for exceeding one million dollars sales of his discs. Original Spanish title of 'It's Impossible' – 'Somos Novios'.

CREEDENCE CLEARWATER REVIVAL

TRAVELIN' BAND backed with WHO'LL STOP THE RAIN *Fantasy* [*USA*] *Liberty* [*Britain*]. Both songs written by the group's John Fogerty, side one featuring the group's updating of the 'Long Tall Sally' rock sound, and side two featuring their originated river-rock style. The disc was released in January 1970 and was No 2 for two weeks in the U.S.A. with Gold Disc awarded by R.I.A.A. in December for a million sale. In Britain the disc reached No 4 for a week (issued in March 1970). This was the group's fifth consecutive million seller.

UP AROUND THE BEND backed with RUN THROUGH THE JUNGLE *Fantasy* [*USA*] *Liberty* [*Britain*]. A powerfully sung double-sided disc, rather away from their usual 'bayou' styled music, and the sixth consecutive million seller for Creedence Clearwater Revival, with Gold Disc award from R.I.A.A. in December 1970. Both songs again written by the group's John Fogerty. Release in the U.S.A. was in April, the disc reaching No 2 for two weeks. In Britain release was in June 1970 and it reached No 3 for a week.

LOOKIN' OUT MY BACK DOOR backed with LONG AS I CAN SEE THE LIGHT *Fantasy* [*USA*] *Liberty* [*Britain*]. Seventh consecutive million seller for Creedence Clearwater Revival, with R.I.A.A. Gold Disc award in December 1970. Released in July, it sold a million in the U.S.A. after only five weeks on the market, and reached No 1 for a week. Both numbers again by the group's John Fogerty. Side one emphasises the group's early rock appeal, with side two being a more subtle recording of a slower-paced ballad from the blues school. Release in Britain was in August, and the disc reached No 19 for a week. Both songs were taken from their 'Cosmo's Factory' album and released as singles.

COSMO'S FACTORY (album) *Fantasy* [*USA*] *Liberty* [*Britain*]. Released in July 1970, this was the biggest seller of Creedence Clearwater Revival's albums, selling over two million in the U.S.A. by the end of October, where it was No 1 for nine weeks. A Gold Disc was awarded by R.I.A.A. in December. In Britain, release was in August 1970, and the disc reached No 1 for a week and had a big sale.

The album was dedicated to the group's Doug (Cosmo) Clifford, and the title taken from Cosmo's Factory, an old warehouse in Berkeley, California the group used as a poolroom, basketball court, clubhouse and rehearsal hall.

Contents: 'Ramble Tamble'; 'Before You Accuse Me' (Bo Diddley, 1958); 'Travelin' Band'; 'Ooby Dooby' (More/Penner, 1958); 'Lookin' Out My Back Door'; 'Run Through the Jungle'; 'Up Around the Bend'; 'My Baby Left Me' (Arthur Crudup, 1956); 'Who'll Stop the Rain'; 'I Heard It Through the Grapevine' (Whitfield and Strong, 1967); 'Long as I Can See the Light'. All songs by John Fogerty unless otherwise indicated.

'Cosmo's Factory' was in the U.S. bestsellers for 69 weeks. Sales of the album were reported at over three million by 1973.

The group was one of the biggest successes of 1970: sales of their discs (five albums and seven singles) all certified million sellers by R.I.A.A., grossing over $50 million by the end of the year.

PENDULUM (album) *Fantasy* [*USA*] *Liberty* [*Britain*]. The sixth album for this fantastically successful group. It had advance orders for over a million copies together with a $250,000 ad-promotion campaign, the label's biggest campaign up to that time. Release in the U.S.A. was in early December 1970, the album reaching No 2 for four weeks, in the Top 10 for 11 weeks, and in the U.S. bestsellers for 42 weeks. It was awarded an immediate Gold Disc by R.I.A.A. U.S. sales in the first six weeks were 1,200,000. Release in Britain was in January 1971, and the disc reached No 8 for one week.

The album was the group's best, most ambitious, polished and exciting one to date, with more subtle highlights and more variety of style. Heavy organ, sax, piano, vibes and other instruments were added to their familiar backing.

Contents: 'Chameleon'; 'Molina'; 'It's Just a Thought'; '(Wish I could) Hideaway'; 'Pagan Baby'; 'Sailor's Lament'; 'Born to Move'; 'Have You Ever Seen the Rain'; 'Rude Awakening No 2'; 'Hey Tonight'. All songs by John Fogerty.

Global sales are estimated at well over two million.

CROSBY, STILLS, NASH & YOUNG

DEJA VU (album) *Atlantic* [*USA*]. Crosby, Stills and Nash added Neil Young (originally with Buffalo Springfield) to produce one of the most distinctive blends in the disc business. The supergroup also included the trio's original drummer Dallas Taylor, plus bassist Greg Reeves.

The group made their only performance in Britain at the Royal Albert Hall, London, on 13 January 1970, and toured the U.S.A. in early 1970 for five weeks, commanding $150,000 a night. They then split up to pursue solo careers.

This recording of their album is notable for the splendid songs, marking each composer's individual style, and was produced by them at Wally Heider's small Hollywood studio, immaculately engineered by Bill Halverson, over a period of two months. Advance orders for the disc were $2 million, an unprecedented feat at Atlantic Records. The disc was released in mid-March 1970 with an immediate R.I.A.A. Gold Disc award, and sold over two million in the two weeks, and 2½ million by May in the U.S.A. alone. Chartwise it was No 1 there for four weeks, and in the bestsellers for 65 weeks. In Britain release was in April 1970, and it was No 5 for three weeks, and 22 weeks in their bestsellers. Global sales are estimated at around 3,500,000.

Contents: 'Carry on and Questions' (Stills); 'Teach Your Children' (Nash); 'Almost Cut My Hair' (Crosby); 'Helpless' (Young); 'Woodstock' (Joni Mitchell); 'Déjà Vu' (Crosby); 'Our House' (Nash); '4+20' (Stills); 'Country Girl' (Young) (three part song 'Whiskey Boot Hill', 'Down, Down, Down' and 'Country Girl'); 'Everybody I Love You' (Stills and Young).

(See also Crosby, Stills & Nash 1969).

DANA

ALL KINDS OF EVERYTHING *Rex* [*Britain*]. Dana (real name Rosemary Brown) born in London on 30 August 1951, moved to Ireland with her parents when she was two, and spent three years at a Romford, Essex, school to complete ballet training and general education. The family were all musical, her hairdresser father playing trumpet in local brass bands, and her three brothers and two sisters also local singers. In addition to her singing, Dana also played piano, organ and guitar. She began singing professionally at the age of 16 (1968), doing concert and cabaret work and many TV appearances in Ireland. She then won the Irish National Song Contest with this song to represent Ireland in the Eurovision Contest. This first win for Ireland is said to have made £20,000 each for the songwriters and artist.

The disc sold over 250,000 in Britain where it was No 1 for two weeks, and 100,000 in Ireland, the first time for such a sale there plus a special Gold Disc award. It was also No 1 in several countries including Ireland, South Africa, Australia and Singapore, the global sales estimated at 2 million by October 1970.

This song was written by two Dubliners, Derry Lindsay and Jackie Smith, both printers aged 28. It was the winner by six points over Britain's entry 'Knock, Knock, Who's There?' sung by Mary Hopkin in the Eurovision contest held in Amsterdam on 20 March 1970.

Rex Records are a subsidiary of British Decca.

TYRONE DAVIS

TURN BACK THE HANDS OF TIME *Dakar* [*USA*]. Written by Jack Daniels and Bonnie Thompson, Tyrone's recording of this 'softly stated ballad' with its superb orchestral backing was released in February 1970. It achieved the No 1 chart position for two weeks in the U.S.A. and sold the million, with R.I.A.A. Gold Disc award by May.

DAWN (vocal trio with instrumental accompaniment)

CANDIDA *Bell* [*USA*]. Dawn consists of Tony Orlando, Joyce Vincent and Telma Hopkins. The trio was founded by Tony, who had personal hits in the early 60s with 'Bless You' and 'Chills'. His teaming with two black girls proved an irresistible hit formula. All had been in the music business for a few years before forming Dawn, Tony as general manager of a music publisher, and Joyce and Telma doing sessions for Motown. An old friend, Hank Medress (of The Tokens), brought the song 'Candida' to Tony's office. Tony suggested Bell Records, but

they weren't impressed with the lead singer on the finished master. Tony was persuaded to record it, Medress decided on the name Dawn, and produced the disc with Dave Apell. It was released in July and sold a million by October 1970, plus R.I.A.A. Gold Disc award. In the U.S.A. it was No 1 for a week. British release was on 24 July 1970, but the disc was not successful until July 1971 when it reached No 6 with 11 weeks in the bestsellers. It is a story-song with a happy-go-lucky sound, written by Toni Wine and Irwin Levine, arranged by Norman Bergen. U.S. sales totalled one and a half million, global 2 million.

Instrumental accompaniment was by Norman Bergen (guitar), Ronnie Amodea (bass), Shenny Brown (horns), Lois Griffiths (percussion) and Carmine Celendo (drums). Tony Orlando was born in 1945 of Greek and Spanish parentage, and first started his singing career at the age of 12.

After their second hit (see below) they became the second biggest singles sellers of the U.S.A. without ever making appearances either live or on TV, and the group went on to further big hits in 1973 after touring America, England, Germany, France, Italy, Australia, South America and Japan between 1971 and 1973.

KNOCK THREE TIMES *Bell* [*USA*]. Second million seller (by December 1970) for Dawn, plus R.I.A.A. Gold Disc award. The song has a hint of Mexican styling, with percussion, brass and guitar featured strongly. It was produced by Hank Medress and Dave Apell, arranged by Norman Bergen, and written by L. Russell Brown and Irwin Levine. Release was in November 1970, the disc reaching No 1 for four weeks in January 1971, with 18 weeks in the bestsellers. British release was on 26 March 1971 where it was No 1 for five weeks and 27 weeks in their bestsellers with over 250,000 sale.

It was a tremendous seller for Dawn, with estimated total global sales of over six and a half million, three million of these in the U.S.A. alone.

THE DELFONICS (vocal trio)

DIDN'T I BLOW YOUR MIND THIS TIME *Philly Groove* [*USA*] *Bell* [*Britain*]. A trio, all from Washington, Pennsylvania. Brothers Wilbert and William Hart with Randy Cain began singing together in 1961. Wilbert and Randy both attended Overbrook High, and William went to Carr Heights in Washington. Their first hit single was 'La La Means I Love You' in 1968, which led to many bookings for the group, including New York, Washington, Chicago and Philadelphia.

'Didn't I Blow Your Mind' reached No 9 for two weeks in the U.S.A. after release in January, and by March was awarded a Gold Disc by R.I.A.A. for the million sale. This slow, harmonic song was written by Thomas R. Bell (producer of the disc) and William Hart (of the group). Philly Groove is a subsidiary of Bell Records. Release in Britain was on 13 March 1970. Grammy Award for Best Rhythm-and-Blues Vocal Performance by a duo or group, 1970.

MICHEL DELPECH

WIGHT IS WIGHT *Barclay* [*France*]. The third Isle of Wight Festival of Pop Music (26 August-1 September 1970) was probably the biggest mass attendance in Britain, and attracted well over 250,000. It was also probably the last occasion for such a big audience in Britain. Among those who performed were Kris Kristofferson, Arrival, Taste, Chicago, Family, Procol Harum, Voices of East Harlem, John Sebastien, Joni Mitchell, Tiny Tim, Miles Davis, Ten Years After, Emerson, Lake and Palmer, The Doors, The Who, Sly and The Family Stone, Free, Donovan, Pentangle, Moody Blues, Jethro Tull, Jimi Hendrix, Ritchie Havens and Joan Baez.

'Wight is Wight' is a story in song about the Festival. Sandie Shaw heard the disc in a discotheque in Rome and persuaded the disc jockey to part with it. She brought it back to Britain and wrote English lyrics to the French melody. Michel Delpech's original version is also about the island festival but the lyrics are in French hippy language. This very young singer's disc is said to have sold over the million on the Continent of Europe, mainly in France.

NEIL DIAMOND

CRACKLIN' ROSIE *Uni* [*USA*]. Another colossal hit for Neil Diamond. Neil wrote the song as the result of a trip to Canada in the winter of 1969. A medical missionary told him the beautiful story about a tribe of Red Indians which had more men than women. As there were not enough women to go around, the men bought bottles of sparkling rosé wine and that became their women for the weekend. The disc was released in August in the U.S.A. where it became No 1 for a week with R.I.A.A. Gold Disc award for million sale in November. In Britain, release was in November, the disc reaching No 2 for a week with 17 weeks in the bestsellers, selling over 250,000. Internationally it was a huge success and estimated to have sold six million, one of the bestselling singles in this market. It was No 1 in many countries including Australia, Belgium, Brazil, Canada, Malaysia, Mexico, New Zealand, South Africa and Sweden.

EDISON LIGHTHOUSE (instrumental and vocal quartet) (with Tony Burrows)

LOVE GROWS (where my Rosemary goes) *Bell* [*Britain and USA*]. Edison Lighthouse were originally a group called Greenfield Hammer. Songwriter-producer Tony Macauley put them together with singer Tony Burrows (originally with The Flower Pot Men, The Ivy League and The Kestrels) and gave them their name after he left Pye Records to join Bell Records. This song, written by Barry Mason and Tony Macauley, was Macauley's first record under his million-dollar deal with Bell and was released on 9 January 1970. An easy beat rocker, it was No 1 in Britain for five weeks with 12 weeks in the bestsellers where it sold over 250,000. The U.S. release was in February and it was No 4 there for four weeks, selling the million by April with R.I.A.A. Gold Disc award.

Personnel: David Taylor (born High Wycombe, 7 October 1950), guitar, bass guitar, Ray Dorey (born Windsor, Berkshire, 22 February 1949), guitar, bass guitar; Stuart Edwards (born Maidenhead, Berkshire, 9 June 1946), lead guitar; George Weyman (born Herne Bay, Kent, 18 May 1949), drums. Macauley chose the group after auditioning 30 groups in November 1969. Tony Burrows (born Exeter, 14 April 1942), lead vocalist, was a former sales clerk. He toured for seven years with various groups and then became a top session singer and featured vocalist with The Brotherhood of Man, White Plains and Pipkins. His four recordings with these three groups and Edison Lighthouse sold around 8 million.

DAVE EDMUNDS

I HEAR YOU KNOCKING *MAM* [*Britain*]. Dave Edmunds first achieved prominence in 1967 as guitarist on Love Sculp-

ture's rock version of Khachaturian's 'Sabre Dance' that reached No 1 in Britain. The band made a six week tour of the U.S.A. then split up, Dave returning to his home town Cardiff, determined to make it on his own. He spent the next two and a half years working at his own Rockfield Studios in Monmouthshire, mastering recording techniques.

'I Hear You Knocking', his first solo single, a remake of the 1955 number originally made popular by Smiley Lewis and Gale Storm in the U.S.A. and written by Pearl King and Dave Bartholomew, was released November 1970 with spectacular results. It reached No 1 for three weeks and stayed 12 weeks in Britain's bestsellers, selling well over 250,000 copies. It was later reported that the disc had sold three million globally. In the U.S.A. this disc reached No 4. Since then he has released occasional singles on his Rockfield label, put out by RCA, mostly re-creations with full and solid echo-laden vocals of the early 1960s Phil Spector-type sound, playing most of the instruments himself and produced at his own studios.

EMERSON, LAKE & PALMER

EMERSON, LAKE & PALMER (album) *Island* [*Britain*] *Cotillion* [*USA*]. From their formation in 1969, ELP, as they became known, established themselves as a trio of unique technical ability.

Keith Emerson had built up an outstanding reputation as an organist supreme, employing acrobatics such as organ-vaulting, flinging daggers and other musical sadism towards his equipment. In 1968 he was still a bank clerk in Worthing, Sussex, playing in pubs at weekends for small fees. He also played with a group called T-Bones, and The Nice. He then met Greg Lake (bass and vocals for King Crimson) and later added Atomic Rooster drummer Carl Palmer, the trio making their debut at the Isle of Wight Festival, 1970. They became entirely dedicated to improving the standards of contemporary music. Their music gradually gained recognition, despite the fact that they never issued a 'single' record – normally essential for commercial success – or appeared on TV shows of a pop nature.

With their line-up of Moog synthesizer, electric drums and bass guitar, plus Emerson's dazzling dexterity in classical passages on a grand piano, the trio's influence gave a new direction to pop music, evoking profound respect among intellectual musicians.

This first album by ELP, released around November, reached No 4 for a week and was 23 weeks in Britain's Top 30 bestsellers. U.S. release was in early 1971, where it reached No 18 for two weeks and was 23 weeks in the U.S.A.'s Top 50 bestsellers.

Emerson's music has been used by the Royal Swedish Ballet Company for an *avant garde* ballet, and his scores have been featured in films. The band's tours of America, Europe and Japan were complete sell-outs and earned them enormous sums. Their 1973 U.S. tour alone generated £1,000,000 worth of business and attracted 750,000 people to concerts in 40 cities. Emerson has said, 'You see, we don't write for the charts. I write what I hope is classical pop. Music that in, say, 50 years' time, musicians will still want to play.'

Contents: 'The Barbarian' (Emerson, Lake and Palmer); 'Take a Pebble' (Lake); 'Knife-edge' (Emerson, Lake and Fraser); 'The Three Fates: (a) Clotho (b) Lachesis (c) Atropos' (Emerson); 'Tank' (Emerson and Palmer); 'Lucky Man' (Lake).

All their albums – 'Emerson, Lake & Palmer', 'Tarkus' (1971), 'Pictures at an Exhibition' (1971), 'Trilogy' (1972), 'Brain Salad Surgery' (1973) and 'Welcome Back My Friends, to the Show That Never Ends' (1974) – have sold over a million each. By 1974, their album sales were estimated at 10 million plus.

FIFTH DIMENSION

ONE LESS BELL TO ANSWER *Bell* [*USA*]. A gently lilting ballad with melancholy reminders in the crafted Hal David and Burt Bacharach lyrics and music, and a sparkling disc with dramatic production. It was released in October 1970 in the U.S.A. and was No 2 there for two weeks with a million sale plus

R.I.A.A. Gold Disc award by December. It sold over 1,750,000 by January 1971 in the U.S.A. In Britain, release was on 15 January 1971 and the disc got to No 2 for two weeks.

THE FIVE STAIRSTEPS

OOH-OOH-CHILD *Buddah* [*USA*]. This quintet comprises the children of Clarence Burke - Clarence Jr, James, Aloha, Kenny and Dennis. Prior to making this disc they had appeared at New York's famous Apollo Theatre. The disc was released in March 1970 and reached No 4 for a week. Its consistent sales (22 weeks in the bestseller charts) resulted in the million sale by August with R.I.A.A. Gold Disc award. The song was written by S. Vincent.

KING FLOYD

GROOVE ME *Chimneyville* [*USA*]. Written by Floyd himself, this was the first single released on the new label distributed by Cotillion. The disc has a reggae beat with the full soul treatment. The million sale was reached by late December with Gold Disc award by R.I.A.A. Release in the U.S.A. was November and the disc reached No 4 for four weeks, staying in the bestsellers for 20 weeks.

King Floyd's hometown is New Orleans. He has been involved in music since the age of 12.

ARETHA FRANKLIN

DON'T PLAY THAT SONG *Atlantic* [*USA*]. Originally written by B. Nelson (i.e. Ben E. King, whose real name is Benjamin Earl Solomon, former lead singer with The Drifters) and A. Ertegun (of Atlantic Records) in 1962 when it was a hit then for Ben E. King. Release was in July in the U.S.A., the disc reaching No 7 for a week and selling a million by October with R.I.A.A. Gold Disc award, making the ninth million seller for Aretha. Release in Britain was in August, and the disc got to No 12 for two weeks with 11 weeks in the bestsellers. It won a Grammy Award for Best Rhythm-and-Blues Vocal Performance (Female) 1970.

FREE (vocal and instrumental quartet)

ALRIGHT NOW *Island* [*Britain*] *A & M* [*USA*]. Free was: Simon Kirke (born Chelsea, London, 28 July 1949) drums. Educated in Shrewsbury; played with The Maniacs and Heatwave, then Black Cat Bones; Paul Kossoff (born London, 14 September 1950) guitar, son of actor David Kossoff; Andy Fraser (born 3 July 1952) bass guitar, keyboards; played with John Mayall; Paul Rodgers (born 17 December 1949 in Middlesbrough) vocalist, guitar.

Kirke met Kossoff and joined Paul's blues band, Black Cat Bones. Kirke and Kossoff joined Rodgers, and Fraser was put in touch with Kossoff in early 1968 when Fraser was starting to form his own group. Free was thus started. The group made tours constantly and this disc was the result of a very bad date in Manchester. They came off stage and couldn't even look at each other, when Fraser started to play a lead line on acoustic guitar. The others joined in and chanted 'all right now' on the chorus part in memory of the date they had just done. It all happened in about three minutes. The recording was released in Britain in June and was No 1 for three weeks and 16 weeks in the bestsellers with over the 500,000 sale. In the U.S.A. release was in August where it reached No 3 for a week and was in their bestsellers for 22 weeks, making well over the million global sale. It was popular in many countries. The song was written by Andy Fraser and Paul Rodgers, who wrote most of the songs. An EP of this song was released in 1977.

Paul Kossoff died on 19 March 1976, during a flight to the U.S.A.

FRIJID PINK (vocal and instrumental quartet)

HOUSE OF THE RISING SUN *Parrot* [*USA*] *Deram* [*Britain*]. This traditional song of the U.S.A. was adapted and arranged by Alan Price in 1964 and was a million seller then for The Animals. Frijid Pink's disc, released in January 1970 in the U.S.A., has incredible instrumental punch and earthy rawness. It was No 5 for a week there and sold the million by May with R.I.A.A. Gold Disc award. In Britain it was No 3 for a week with 16 weeks in the bestsellers.

The group are all from Detroit and made their first New York appearance at Ungano's. Its members: Kelly Green, a first-rate blues vocalist and skilled harmonica player who also played drums; Gary Thompson, an exceptional blues guitarist; Thomas (Satch) Harris, an intense performer, bass guitarist; Rick Stevens, drums and vocal harmonies, also guitar. His drum effects are overpowering.

BOBBY GOLDSBORO

WATCHING SCOTTY GROW *United Artists* [*USA*]. Fifth million seller for Bobby Goldsboro (written by Mac Davis) in 1971. Disc released in December 1970. Chartwise it was No 6 for a week in the U.S.A., and stayed in the bestsellers for 13 weeks.

GRAND FUNK RAILROAD (instrumental and vocal rock trio)

LIVE ALBUM (double album) *Capitol* [*USA*]. The success of Grand Funk Railroad had its genesis with their appearance at the first Atlanta International Pop Festival on 4 July 1969. They performed free, before 180,000 people in 110°F heat, and acclaim was instantaneous. This album is a recording of their performance at 1970's Atlanta Pop Festival. It had the largest initial Capitol advance order since The Beatles. Capitol shipped 750,000 albums and 250,000 tapes, and release was on 16 November. By the end of the year it had soared past the two million mark. It reached No 4 for two weeks, was in the Top 10 for 10 weeks, and 62 weeks in the bestsellers. In Britain release was on 15 January 1971.

In early 1969 the trio were in separate and competitive bands playing the Flint and Detroit, Michigan, areas. They are: Mark Farner (lead guitarist/vocalist), Mel Schacher (bassist) and Don Brewer (drummer and occasional vocalist). All come from Flint, Michigan. It was DJ and rock performer Terry Knight who brought the three together and Grand Funk Railroad was born. Knight masterminded the promotion, production and timing of the group's rise. In two months of touring in the autumn of 1970, the group netted over $350,000. Visitors to New York in the summer of 1970 saw 60-foot portraits of the trio dominating Times Square from the largest billboard in the world, running along the west side of Broadway engulfing two full city blocks. It cost Knight $100,000, but no tourist from anywhere left New York without knowing of Grand Funk Railroad. This huge billboard carried a message about the group and its music: 'Three faces among the countless who belong to the New Culture, setting forth on its final voyage through a dying world . . . searching to find a way to bring us all closer to home.'

Their first three albums, 'On Time' (1969), 'Closer to Home' (1970) and 'Grand Funk' (1970) were all certified million-dollar sellers by R.I.A.A. and this 'Live Album' got a similar award immediately. The trio became one of Capitol's most outstanding financial ventures, with over five million sales by early 1971. Their concerts were an immediate sell-out and they became a national phenomenon. Their first appearance in Britain was on 15 January 1971 at London's Royal Albert Hall.

The double album is long by normal standards, with one hour and 20 minutes of music. Contents: 'Inside Looking Out' (Lomax, Burdon and Chandler); 'Into the Sun'; 'Mean Mistreater'; 'Paranoid'; 'Are You Ready?'; 'In Need'; 'Heartbreaker'; 'Words of Wisdom' (spoken); 'Mark Says Alright' (Farner, Brewer and Schacher); 'T.N.U.C.'. All songs by Mark Farner unless otherwise indicated.

NORMAN GREENBAUM

SPIRIT IN THE SKY *Reprise* [*USA*]. Norman Greenbaum together with Erik Jacobson (producer of the disc) wrote this enormously successful song described as a 'quasi-spiritual'. Release was in February 1970 in the U.S.A., where it was No 1 for two weeks, selling the million by May with R.I.A.A. Gold Disc award. It was immensely successful also in Britain where it sold well over the 250,000 and was No 1 for four weeks after release in May with 20 weeks in the bestsellers. The disc was a chart-topper simultaneously in both countries.

Greenbaum is a Bostonian. His musical interest began while in high school where he organized fraternity hops in the 1950s. He wanted to be a disc jockey and fraternized with them and promotion men. At 17 he got his first guitar and started playing in college. His first record centred around 'jug band' music. In 1965 he formed a group called Eggplant.

'Spirit in the Sky' earned Norman national recognition and sold over two million globally.

THE GUESS WHO
AMERICAN WOMAN backed with NO SUGAR TONIGHT *RCA* [*USA*]. Fourth consecutive million seller for this Canadian group, 'American Woman' written by all four members - Randy Bachman, Burton Cummings, Garry Peterson and Jim Kale - and 'No Sugar Tonight' by Randy Bachman. The tracks were taken from the group's R.I.A.A. certified million-dollar album 'American Woman'. This singles issue was released in March 1970 and reached No 1 for three weeks in the U.S.A. with Gold Disc from R.I.A.A. for million sale by May. In Britain the disc was No 19 for a week.

The disc was produced in Toronto, Canada, by Nimbus 9's Jack Richardson and distributed internationally by RCA.

SHARE THE LAND *RCA* [*USA*]. Fifth consecutive million seller for The Guess Who, the song written by Burton Cummings of the group. It was taken from their album of the same title which was a big seller also. The single was No 5 for a week in the U.S.A. and sold a million by early 1971.

MARK HAMILTON
COMME J'AI TOUJOURS ENVIE D'AIMER *Carrere* [*France*]. Another big hit for France's first full-time independent producer Claude Carrere, and a million seller for Canadian artist Mark Hamilton. The song, written by Carrere, is one of the many big hits he has written for his artists, including those for his star singer Sheila in 1962. Since then, he can legitimately claim to be one of the biggest hit makers.

GEORGE HARRISON
ALL THINGS MUST PASS (Triple album) *Apple* [*Britain*] *Apple* [*USA*]. This was Beatle George Harrison's first major statement as a writer. It follows his crowning writing achievement with the success of 'Something' which had 120 different recordings by the end of 1970, and emphasizes his writing versatility. This album took four months to produce, and comprises 16 of his own compositions, one co-written with Bob Dylan and one by Dylan, plus a jam session called 'Apple Jam', with performances by some of the world's leading musicians - Eric Clapton, Ginger Baker, Dave Mason, Pete Drake, Jim Gordon, Klaus Voormann, Ringo Starr, Billy Preston, Alan White, Gary Brooker and others - plus George Harrison himself. Religion, God and hope are prominent in Harrison's material. An outstanding track is 'My Sweet Lord' with its guitar opening and singing by George. A beautiful choir backing is produced through multiple tracking, all made up of his own voice plus the Hare Krishna chant. It is one of the most outstanding rock albums in years, musically and philosophically, and was co-produced with the U.S.A.'s Phil Spector. Release in the U.S.A. was on 25 November 1970, and over 1,500,000 albums and 250,000 tapes were shipped by Capitol Records within a week, and quickly sold. By mid-February 1971 it had passed the 2,500,000 sale there and was still selling strongly. It reached No 1 for eight weeks. In Britain release was also on 5 December, the disc

reaching No 1 for seven weeks. Global sales are estimated at well over 3 million.

Contents: 'I'd Have You Any Time' (Bob Dylan and George Harrison); 'My Sweet Lord'; 'Wah Wah'; 'Isn't It a Pity'; 'What Is Life?'; 'If Not For You' (Bob Dylan); 'Behind That Locked Door'; 'Let It Down'; 'Run of the Mill'; 'Beware of the Darkness'; 'Apple Scruffs'; 'Ballad of Sir Frankie Crisp'; 'Awaiting On You All'; 'All Things Must Pass'; 'I Dig Love'; 'Art of Dying'; 'Isn't It a Pity' (second version); 'Hear Me Lord'; jam session – 'Apple Jam': 'Out of the Blue' – 'It's Johnny's Birthday' (tune 'Congratulations' by Coulter & Martin) – 'Plug Me In' – 'I Remember Jeep' – 'Thanks for the Pepperoni'.

All songs by George Harrison unless otherwise indicated.

The album was 38 weeks in the U.S. bestsellers, and 23 weeks in Britain's bestsellers.

MY SWEET LORD backed with ISN'T IT A PITY *Apple* [*Britain*] *Apple* [*USA*]. Both written by Beatle George Harrison and taken from his tremendously successful album 'All Things Must Pass'. Issued as a single in late November 1970 in the U.S.A. and on 15 January 1971 in Britain. 'My Sweet Lord' is an outstanding track sung by George Harrison in a low moaning spiritual voice. 'Isn't It a Pity' is a seven-minute-long recording of a touching ballad with beautiful shaded notes and a big finish instrumental ending of the 'Hey Jude' type.

The disc sold over the million in the U.S.A. in two weeks with R.I.A.A. Gold Disc award on 14 December. It passed the two million mark by the end of the year. In Britain it sold over 700,000 in six weeks. It was No 1 for four weeks in the U.S.A. and No 1 for six weeks in Britain. The disc was 15 weeks in the U.S. bestsellers and 17 weeks in the British bestsellers. Other countries where it was No 1 were Switzerland, Singapore, Mexico, Spain, Sweden, Germany, Norway, France, Brazil, Australia, Malaysia, Austria. Global sales estimated at five million.

In 1981 judgement was awarded against Harrison for having subconsciously copied John Mack's melody 'He's So Fine', a hit for The Chiffons in 1963, for 'My Sweet Lord.'

HOTLEGS (vocal and instrumental trio)
NEANDERTHAL MAN *Fontana* [*Britain*] *Capitol* [*USA*]. The personnel of this trio is: Eric Stewart (born Manchester, 1 January 1945) guitars, tone generator engineer, vocals; Kevin Godley (born Manchester, 7 October 1945) drums, percussion, vibes, vocals; Lol Creme (born Manchester, 17 September 1947) acoustic guitars, recorders, piano, bass, vocals.

Kevin and Lol were graphic designers and long-standing friends of Eric, who is part owner of Strawberry Studios, Stockport, where 'Neanderthal Man' first matured. It was written by all three. They each made their first appearances in the Manchester area. Eric made his TV debut with 'Scene at 6.30' on Granada TV, and film debut in *To Sir, With Love*. He also had chart successes with The Mindbenders group. Kevin and Lol made their TV debut in 'Top of the Pops'.

'Neanderthal Man' was released in Britain on 19 June 1970, the disc reaching No 2 for two weeks and 14 weeks in the bestsellers, with a good sale. In the U.S.A. release was in August 1970 where it was No 11 for a week and sold a half million or more. The disc sold well in Europe and was No 1 in Italy and No 3 in both France and Germany. Other big sales came from Australia, Canada, Japan and other territories. Global sales estimated at two million by February 1971.

100 PROOF AGED IN SOUL (vocal trio)
SOMEBODY'S BEEN SLEEPING *Hot Wax* [*USA*]. A powerful disc with the Detroit sound, plus lyrics giving a new slant to *Goldilocks* and *Jack and the Beanstalk*. It was written by G. Perry, A. Bond and General Johnson (of Chairmen of the Board) and released in the U.S.A. in August 1970. The disc was No 6 for three weeks and sold a million by November with R.I.A.A. Gold Disc award. The disc stayed on the bestseller charts for 15

weeks. Release in Britain was on 30 October 1970.

This new trio comprised: Joe Stubbs (brother of Levi of Four Tops fame) who originally sang with The Contours and The Falcons; Eddie Anderson and Steve Mancha.

BRIAN HYLAND

GYPSY WOMAN *Uni* [*USA*]. A welcome return to the hit scene by Brian Hyland since his last million seller of 1962. This disc was released in August 1970 and was No 3 for two weeks, with 21 weeks in the U.S. bestseller charts. R.I.A.A. Gold Disc for million sale was awarded in January 1971. It was No 42 in Britain.

The song was written by celebrated black composer Curtis Mayfield, who was lead singer for ten years from 1960 with The Impressions, and composer for the successful film *Superfly* in 1972.

IDES OF MARCH

VEHICLE *Warner-7 Arts* [*USA*]. The million sale for this so far unidentified group was reported in November 1972. The song was written by Peterik, and the disc released in March 1970. It reached No 2 for one week in the U.S. charts, and No 31 in Britain.

THE JACKSON 5

A.B.C. *Motown* [*USA*]. Second consecutive million seller for this extremely talented young quintet. The song was written again by 'The Corporation' who are revealed as Freddie Perren, Fonso Mizell, Deke Richards and Berry Gordy, Jr, who also produced the disc. It was released in the U.S.A. on 24 February 1970, and was No 1 for two weeks, selling over two million in less than three weeks. In Britain release was on 8 May 1970 and it was No 8 for a week.

THE LOVE YOU SAVE *Motown* [*USA*]. Again written by The Corporation (see above) and produced by them, making the third consecutive million seller for The Jackson 5. Release in the U.S.A. was on 13 May 1970, the disc achieving No 1 for two weeks and selling over two million. British release was on 24 July 1970, and it reached No 7 for a week with 9 weeks in the bestsellers.

I'LL BE THERE *Motown* [*USA*]. This was taken from The Jackson 5's third album and was an ever bigger success than their previous 1970 releases, selling over 3,500,000 in the U.S.A. by November, after being at No 1 for five weeks. Release was on 28 August 1970. In Britain release was on 13 November 1970, and it got to No 4 for a week and sold over 250,000 by early 1971. Global sales estimated at over five million. This fourth consecutive million seller for The Jackson 5 was written by Berry Gordy, Jr, B. West, W. Hutch and H. Davies, the disc being produced by Hal Davis and arranged by Bob West. A slower disc than usual, the change of pace showcased the group's versatility. In the incredibly short space of nine months, the quintet sold over ten million singles, claimed to be in excess of sales figures by The Beatles within any given nine-month period. With these and other successes by Motown's artists, the label dominated the singles charts in America for 1970.

A.B.C. (album) *Motown* [*USA*]. Second million-selling album for this group, the sale reported in December 1970. The disc was released in the U.S.A. on 8 May 1970 and was No 4 for two weeks. British release 8 May 1970.

Contents: 'A.B.C.' (The Corporation); 'The Love You Save' (The Corporation); 'I Found That Girl' (The Corporation); 'One More Chance' (The Corporation); 'La La Means I Love You' (T. Bell and W. Hart); 'Never Had a Dream Come True' (H. Cosby, S. Wonder and S. Moy); 'I'm the One You Need' (E. Holland, L. Dozier and B. Holland); 'Don't You Know Why I Love You?' (D. Hunter, S. Wonder, L. Hardaway and P. Riser); 'True Love Can Be Beautiful' (B. Taylor and J. Jackson); 'I'll Bet You' (T. Clinton, S. Barnes and P. Lindsay); 'The Young

Folks' (H. Gordy and A. Story).

This album was 50 weeks in the U.S. bestsellers.

THIRD ALBUM (album) *Motown* [*USA*]. A third million-selling album for The Jackson 5, the sale also reported in December 1970. Release in the U.S.A. was on 8 October, the album being No 1 for two weeks. Release in Britain was in February 1971.

Contents: 'Reachin'' (Verdi); 'I'll Be There' (Gordy Jr, B. West, W. Hutch and H. Davies); 'Bridge Over Troubled Water' (Paul Simon); 'Oh How Happy' (Edwin Starr); 'The Love I Saw in You Was Just a Mirage' (M. Tarplin and Smokey Robinson); 'How Funky is Your Chicken?' (Carr, R. Hutch and W. Hutch); 'Can I See You in the Morning?' (Richards); 'Darling Dear' (H. and R. Gordy and A. Story); 'Mama's Pearl' (The Corporation); 'Ready or Not' (T. Bell and W. Hart); 'Going Back to Indiana' (The Corporation).

This album was 50 weeks in the U.S. bestsellers.

ELTON JOHN (rock vocalist/pianist)

ELTON JOHN (album) *DJM* [*Britain*] *Uni* [*USA*]. Elton John (real name Reginald Dwight) was born in Pinner, Middlesex, England, on 25 March 1947. He was educated at Pinner County Grammar School, and attended part-time at the Royal Academy of Music, studying the piano, starting at the age of 12. He played in his first band, The Corvettes, at small halls for six months when he was 13. Two years later with Stuart Brown, a former member of the group, he formed a new band, Bluesology, in which Elton played and sang occasionally. Up to that time he played weekends at a local pub, singing Jim Reeves-type songs, and spent his earnings on his first electric piano.

Bluesology worked as a back-up band for touring U.S. singers such as Doris Troy, The Drifters and Major Lance, and worked awhile on the Continent. Back in London, Elton was approached by Long John Baldry at London's Cromwellian club, and was invited to join the soul band Baldry was forming. During this period he auditioned as a singer for Liberty Records and was turned down. He saw no future in staying with Baldry and Bluesology, and left the group, deciding he would write. Through a music paper advert he met lyricist Bernie Taupin, and the duo began writing and recording their own demos. About this time he changed his name to Elton John, taking Elton from Elton Dean (a member of Bluesology) and John from Long John Baldry.

Dick James, head of DJM Music and Records, signed Elton and Bernie Taupin to a writers' contract. Elton made his first album 'Empty Sky' in 1969, but it didn't sell many copies. Despite this, Dick James started Elton's second album, 'Elton John', in early 1970. This took over 55 hours' recording time and cost over £6,500. It was released on 17 April 1970 and reached No 4 in Britain's charts (in 1971) for one week, with 17 weeks in the Top 30 bestsellers. James then sponsored an American promotional trip (August 1970) and Elton captivated the audience every night at Los Angeles' Troubadour Club. The album was released in the U.S.A. on MCA's Uni label (September) and reached No 5 for a week, staying 23 weeks in the Top 30. R.I.A.A. awarded a Gold Disc for million dollar sales in February 1971. By the end of 1972 it had sold a million copies with Platinum Disc award. Elton signed with MCA Records in 1970 and, from then on, practically all his albums became million sellers. His success in America was sudden and massive, and by 1974 he had made a spectacular rise to the top of the disc and music industries. He made extensive tours - America, Hawaii, Nassau, Canada - earning enormous sums with sell-out performances everywhere. In 1973, he launched Rocket Records, his own record company, and in 1974 made his first starring role in a motion picture, playing 'Pinball Wizard' in Ken Russell's version of The Who's rock opera *Tommy*.

Elton's regular accompanists at the time were Dee Murray (bass guitar) and Nigel Olsson (drums), both former members of The Spencer Davis Group, and Davey Johnstone (lead guitar, mandolin, sitar, banjo, lute) was recruited in 1972. This album marked the beginning of a long association with arranger Paul Buckmaster and producer Gus Dudgeon, and firmly established Elton John and the songwriting team. It finally sold over two million.

Contents: 'Your Song'; 'I Need You to Turn To'; 'Take Me to the Pilot'; 'No Shoe Strings on Louise'; 'First Episode at Heinton'; 'Sixty Years On'; 'The Border Song'; 'The Greatest Discovery'; 'The Cage'; 'The King Must Die'.

All songs written by Elton John and Bernie Taupin.

Elton's first recording is said to be 'From Denver to L.A.' for producer Michael Winner's film *The Games* in 1969, in which Elton was featured, and for which he is reputed to have been paid £25.

TUMBLEWEED CONNECTION (album) *Uni* [*USA*] *DJM* [*Britain*]. Second big success for Elton John, the album released in Britain on 20 November 1970 reaching No 2 for three weeks and staying in the Top 30 for 16 weeks. U.S.A. release was in January 1971 and it was No 5 for two weeks and 14 weeks in the Top 30.

R.I.A.A. awarded a Gold Disc for million dollars sale in March 1971, and a platinum award by MCA-Uni for million copies sale by December 1972.

Contents: 'Ballad of a Well-known Gun'; 'Come Down in Time'; 'Country Comfort'; 'Son of Your Father'; 'My Father's Gun'; 'Where to Now, St Peter?'; 'Love Song' (Lesley Duncan); 'Amoreena'; 'Talking Old Soldiers'; 'Burn Down the Mission'.

All songs by Elton John and Bernie Taupin unless otherwise indicated.

The album displayed lyricist Taupin's fondness for Old West mythology and the increasing personal style of Elton's singing.

FRANCIS LAI AND ORCHESTRA

LE PASSAGER DE LA PLUIE (Passenger of the rain) *Somethin' Else* [*France*]. Famous French composer Francis Lai wrote this for the film *Le Passager de la Pluie*, a sleek thriller directed by René Clement starring Charles Bronson and Marlene Jobert, previewed in Paris on 9 January 1970. The disc was released in 40 countries and was particularly successful in Japan (on the Nippon/Columbia label) where the composer received a Gold Disc award for million sales in September 1971.

A vocal version of this film title track was made by Severine, winner of the 1970 Eurovision Song Contest in Dublin.

LED ZEPPELIN

LED ZEPPELIN III (album) *Atlantic* [*USA*]. Released on 5 October 1970, this third album by Led Zeppelin had advance orders of over 700,000 and 250,000 tapes (Ampex's biggest initial order). The album was put together during the first six months of the year, and is a far cry from their first hectic session. It is more acoustic and subtle, lacking the funky, exciting live feeling of their previous albums, but nevertheless a turning point in the group's career. Vocalist Robert Plant is in fine voice throughout, plus the delicate artistry of Jimmy Page's acoustic work, John Paul Jones's organ playing and bass guitar work, and John Bonham's percussion.

The disc was No 1 for four weeks in the U.S.A., stayed in the Top 10 for 14 weeks, and in the bestsellers for 31 weeks. R.I.A.A. Gold Disc award was immediate. In Britain release was also in October 1970, and the disc reached No 1 for seven weeks and sales over the half million mark. It was in the Top 10 for 23 weeks and the bestsellers for 40 weeks.

Global sales estimated at over two million.

Contents: 'Immigrant Song'; 'Friends'; 'Celebration Day'; 'Since I've Been Loving You'; 'Out on the Tiles'; 'Gallows Pole' (trad. arr. Page and Plant); 'Tangerine'; 'That's the Way'; (*) 'Bron-y-aur Stomp'; 'Hats Off to (Roy) Harper' (Trad. arr. Charles Obscure).

All songs by the group unless otherwise indicated.

(*) This song is the title of a small derelict cottage in South Snowdonia, Wales, which helped provide much of the album's musical inspiration. 'Bron-y-aur' is Welsh for 'Golden Breast'.

JOHN LENNON

JOHN LENNON PLASTIC ONO BAND (album) *Apple* [*Britain*] *Apple* [*USA*]. Released in both the U.S.A. and Britain 11 December 1970, this album in the U.S.A. had an advance order of 2,500,000. This was Beatle John Lennon's biggest solo album following his 'Two Virgins' and 'Live Peace in Toronto' albums.

This long-awaited first solo effort by John Lennon has been described as 'self analysis in poetry and music' and in it he gets to grips with social problems. The album is often tragic and occasionally beautiful. It is certainly unique, and it is the lyrics which take priority over the melodies. Lennon wrote all the numbers and is vocalist. He also plays guitar and piano on the album. The Plastic Ono Band comprises Ringo Starr (drums), Klaus Voormann (bass), John Lennon (guitar/piano) with Billy Preston (keyboards) on occasion and similarly Phil Spector. Two songs – beginning and ending the album – are about mothers, Lennon's own mother having died early in his life. Lennon exposes his innermost feelings on this brilliant album, including his love for Yoko Ono and his concept of God.

The album was No 2 for two weeks in the U.S.A., in the Top 10 for eight weeks, and the bestsellers for 40 weeks. In Britain the album was No 11 for one week, and 10 weeks in the bestsellers.

Contents: 'Mother'; 'Hold On'; 'I Found Out'; 'Working Class Hero'; 'Isolation'; 'Remember'; 'Love'; 'Well Well Well'; 'Look at Me'; 'God'; 'My Mummy's Dead'. All songs by John Lennon.

The disc was produced by John and Yoko and Phil Speector and recorded in England.

INSTANT KARMA (We All Shine On) *Apple* [*Britain*] *Apple* [*USA*]. With words and music by John Lennon, this single, released on 6 February in both Britain and the U.S.A., was No 3 for four weeks in America and sold the million with R.I.A.A. Gold Disc award by December 1970. In Britain it was No 5 for two weeks with 9 weeks in the bestsellers. John Lennon pours it out in a most exciting involved manner. The song has a 1950s shuffle style. John is accompanied by The Plastic Ono Band.

GORDON LIGHTFOOT

IF YOU COULD READ MY MIND *Reprise* [*USA*]. Gordon Lightfoot, born in Orillia, Canada, spent his musically formative years, after emigrating to Los Angeles in 1958, studying piano and orchestration at Westlake College, and in England. On return

to Canada he built his own musical identity. He left Westlake to work as studio vocalist, arranger, writer and producer of commercial jingles.

He became interested in folk music after listening to Pete Seeger and others, and took up the guitar in 1960. He rose to popularity along with artists like Bob Dylan, Tom Paxton and Phil Ochs. His first album was released in the U.S.A. in 1966. A fine songwriter, his material was used by established artists Judy Collins, Harry Belafonte, Johnny Cash, Peter, Paul and Mary and others, and he is said to write an average of three songs each day. He actually wrote 15 in 1967 when he visited England for a week. Gordon played around 70 concerts each year and visited Britain annually, accompanied by Red Shea (guitar) and Richard Haynes (bass). He was voted Top Male Vocalist of 1971 in Canada.

'If You Could Read My Mind' was written by him, and the disc was No 3 for a week in the U.S.A., staying 15 weeks in the bestsellers. Released in December 1970 it sold the million by early 1971 globally, while the album of the same title received R.I.A.A. Gold Disc award. It was No 30 and 9 weeks in the British bestsellers. He was originally a United Artists recording star before joining Reprise Records.

For several years, Gordon was known as 'the guy who wrote "Early Mornin' Rain"', but the success of 'If You Could Read My Mind', his first U.S. charts hit, brought sudden recognition, generating interest in his earlier United Artists issues.

PAUL McCARTNEY

McCARTNEY *Apple* [*Britain*] *Apple* [*USA*]. Beatle Paul McCartney's first solo effort. The album was recorded at his home, at EMI (No 2 studio) and at Morgan Studios in London over a period of four months from Christmas 1969 to April 1970. Release was on 17 April 1970 and advance orders in the U.S.A. were over $2 million. It sold the million units in the first month and received an immediate R.I.A.A. Gold Disc award. In the U.S.A. it was No 1 for four weeks, 15 weeks in the Top 10, 47 weeks in the bestsellers. In Britain the disc was No 2 for three weeks, 16 weeks in the Top 10, and 22 weeks in the bestsellers.

All the songs were written by Paul McCartney himself and he sings all the lead parts and plays all the instruments - bass, drums, acoustic guitar, lead guitar, piano and organ-mellotron, toy xylophone. The disc marks the return to simple pleasures, expressed in a simple, countrified manner, somewhat characteristic of Bob Dylan's works at the time. Some of the songs were written in 1968 in India - 'Teddy Boy' and 'Junk' - and 'Hot as Sun' in the same year. His wife Linda also helps out with harmonies on some of the tracks, and she took all the photos and designed the package with Paul.

'Kreen-Akrorer' was inspired by the film about that tribe from the Brazilian jungle and how the white man is trying to change their way of life. Paul also pays tribute to his wife on the opening track - 'The Lovely Linda'. The album is varied, clever and full of humour.

Total sales were estimated at two million.

Contents: 'The Lovely Linda'; 'That Would be Something'; 'Valentine Day'; 'Every Night'; 'Hot as Sun'; 'Glasses'; 'Junk'; 'Man We Was Lonely'; 'Oo You'; 'Momma Miss America'; 'Teddy Boy'; 'Singalong Junk'; 'Maybe I'm Amazed'; 'Kreen-Akrorer'.

All songs were written by Paul McCartney.

PETER MAFFEY

DU (You) *Telefunken* [*Germany*]. This German singer's disc is said to have sold a million by the end of 1970. Peter Maffey, born in 1950, speaks five languages. He made one TV appearance, and his disc did not become a hit until a year after release. It reached No 1 in Holland (1971).

LEE MARVIN

WAND'RIN' STAR *Paramount* [*USA*]. Actor Lee Marvin was born in New York on 19 February 1924. He played in summer stock companies and made his Broadway debut in *Billy Budd*. He appeared in many motion pictures, including *Gun Fury*, *Wild One*, *Caine Mutiny*, *Bad Day at Black Rock*, *Not as a Stranger* and *Pete Kelly's Blues*. In 1969 he got a star role in the film version of the 1951 stage musical *Paint Your Wagon* for which the original score was written by Alan Jay Lerner and Frederick Loewe (of *My Fair Lady* fame). This film was premiered at Loewe's State 2, New York City, on 15 October 1969 and proved a very big attraction. Lee Marvin received a fee of $1 million.

Songwriter Alan Lerner persuaded ex-Marine Lee Marvin to sing the lyrics, though Marvin objected that he was not a singer, and that the song should be dubbed. Lerner finally got him to talk - or rather grate - his way through the number accompanied by full orchestra. Halfway through, Marvin dismissed the musicians because he said it sounded awful and absurd. He then continued talking the song without musical accompaniment which was added later. Marvin's gravelly-hoarse voice was 'a new sound', something that the record industry is always seeking. The song itself meant nothing when it was first written in 1951, but it reflected the mood and emotions in 1970 of a new restless generation. Lee Marvin portrays an ancient gold-miner in the film, a prototype of the 'hippy'.

The disc first started to register in Britain after release on 16 January 1970. It got to No 1 there for four weeks with 23 weeks in the bestsellers and sold over 500,000. The release of the film internationally made the disc a big seller, passing the two million mark. It was also very popular in Australia, where the film soundtrack was awarded a Gold Disc. U.S.A.'s R.I.A.A. awarded a Gold Disc for the soundtrack.

MASHMAKHAN

AS THE YEARS GO BY *Epic* [*Canada*]. It was reported in August 1971 that this disc had sold a global million, made up of 400,000 sales in the U.S.A., 400,000 in Japan, over 100,000 in Canada, plus sales elsewhere. Data on the artist is not so far available, neither the writer of the song.

JEAN FRANÇOIS MICHAEL

ADIEU JOLIE CANDY *Vogue* [*France*]. This disc, a 'sleeper' in the industry, started off very slowly. It was continually played in discotheques around France for several months until November 1970, when it started off in several other countries in Europe. It proved to be the surprise hit of the year in France. A million sale was reported in March 1971. Disc co-produced by Franck Pourcel.

THE MOMENTS

LOVE ON A TWO-WAY STREET *Stang* [*USA*]. Written by Sylvia Robinson and B. Keyes, this disc was released in March 1970, and by May had sold 1,250,000 in the U.S.A., with Gold Disc award by the R.I.A.A. in June. Total sales were 1,600,000. The disc was No 3 in the U.S.A. for two weeks. It sold two million globally.

The Moments are a black trio, comprising Al, Billy and John. It was the first million seller for the Stang label.

JACKIE MOORE

PRECIOUS, PRECIOUS *Atlantic* [*USA*]. Jackie wrote this with Dave Crawford who produced the disc. It was released in November 1970 and stayed in the U.S.A. bestsellers for 17 weeks, reaching No 11 for a week and selling a million by March 1971 with R.I.A.A. Gold Disc award. Jackie hails from Jacksonville, Florida, and the disc was the first recording she made for Atlantic and her first gold record.

MUNGO JERRY (vocal and instrumental quartet)

IN THE SUMMERTIME *Dawn* [*Britain*] *Janus* [*USA*]. Mungo Jerry comprised: Ray Dorset (born 21 March 1946 at Ashford, Middlesex), vocals and composer, also plays electric guitar, six-string acoustic, cabassa and stomp; Paul King (born

ANNE MURRAY

SNOWBIRD *Capitol* [*USA*]. Anne Murray was born in the mining town of Springhill, Novia Scotia, in 1945, the only girl in a family of six. She led an active, athletic life and subsequently graduated from New Brunswick University with a degree in physical training. She started working as an instructor in a Prince Edward Island school, a post she held for a year. Her piano and voice training gained her first prize in a number of local festivals in her home town. On her 21st birthday, she made her first major appearance on the popular 'Singalong Jubilee' show which was networked from Halifax. She became so popular that a regular featured soloist spot resulted, where she performed her own special brand of contemporary folk and country/rock. She then began a series of solo concerts ('An Evening with Anne Murray')

9 January 1948 at Dagenham, Essex), banjo, guitar and jug; Colin Earl (born 6 May 1942 at Hampton Court), piano; Mike Cole, string bass.

The group, which had always been based in London, started in early 1969 when Dorset and Earl formed a trio with Jo Rush. After Rush left, the band reached its present line-up when King sat in with them and Cole joined after answering an advertisement. They played together semi-professionally under several names, their repertoire taking in hard rock, progressive rock, skiffle, blues, Leadbelly numbers and country blues. They seemed to be able to play almost any date and never fail to have something for that particular performance. Barry Murray, producer of 'In the Summertime', was the first to hear and help them, initially when Dorset and two others replied to an ad for a progressive rock band. Barry could do nothing when the other two left to join other bands. A year later, when Ray was working with the present members, Barry noticed his name on an ad they'd put in to try and get work. A recording contract with Dawn (a Pye Records label) and a managerial contract with the Red Bus Company, Hollywood promoters, were the results. They decided on the name Mungo Jerry only two weeks before the disc was released on 12 May. Their recording debut also launched the new series of Dawn 'Maxi-Singles'. It proved to be a colossal runaway success, due to the new craze for the group's jug-blues-rock-folk-country music, as opposed to the so-called progressive pop music. The disc features Paul King who actually blows over the jug – an empty cider jar – the Mungo Jerry style being rather more contemporary than that used by the jug bands which originated in Chicago in the 1920s.

The disc was No 1 for seven weeks in Britain and stayed in their bestsellers for 20 weeks. In the U.S.A. it was No 1 for a week and sold over a million there, with Gold Disc award from R.I.A.A. by August, just two months after release. British sales were around 800,000. The disc was No 1 in 26 countries including Canada, Denmark, New Zealand, Holland, Norway, Finland, West Germany, Sweden, Switzerland, Singapore, Italy, Malaysia and France, selling 400,000 in France in the first month, just about the fastest seller ever known there, and subsequently a million. The group were presented with a Gold Disc on 23 November 1971 at the Olympia, Paris, by Vogue International label for the French million sale. Global sales totalled over six million by the end of the year.

Mungomania was possibly the most startling and unexpected pop phenomenon to hit Britain since the Beatles. Mungo Jerry made their first trip to the U.S.A. in September 1970.

and finally CBC recognised her talents and signed her for her own regular series. Capitol offered her a contract, and she made her first album, 'This Was My Way'. She was produced by Brian Ahearn and recorded at Bay Studios in Toronto.

'Snowbird', a delightful, melodious song, was written by Gene MacLellan. It became the first ever disc by a female Canadian artist to exceed a million sales in the U.S.A., and a Gold Disc award from the R.I.A.A. was presented on the Merv Griffin show on 10 November. Release in the U.S.A. was in July 1970, and the disc reached No 4 for two weeks and stayed in the bestsellers for 18 weeks. British release was on 28 August 1970, and it reached No 23.

YUKO NAGISA

KYOTO NO KOI (Kyoto Doll) *Liberty-Toshiba* [*Japan*]. Written by the American group The Ventures who were so popular in Japan, it is one of the many songs they wrote for Japanese artists during their several tours. Yuko Nagisa appeared with The Ventures on their ninth Japanese tour, and her disc was a tremendous success, selling a million by August 1971 after being No 1 in Japan for 11 weeks.

THE ORIGINALS (vocal quartet)

THE BELLS *Soul* [*USA*]. The Originals comprised: Walter Gaines (baritone) from Augusta, Georgia, who formed the group in 1965, C.P. Spencer (tenor), Henry Dixon (2nd tenor) and Freddie Gorman (bass), all from Detroit.

Their first hit single was 'Green Grow the Lilacs', and later 'Baby I'm for Real' in 1969 which was a big success. 'The Bells' followed and was released in the U.S.A. on 31 January 1970. By April it had sold a million with R.I.A.A. Gold Disc award. It achieved No 12 for two weeks. The disc is a soft soul recording with a polished vocal performance, written by Gaye, Gaye, Stover and Bristol. The disc was produced by Marvin Gaye.

THE PARTRIDGE FAMILY

I THINK I LOVE YOU *Bell* [*USA*]. The Partridge Family was created for a popular TV show in the U.S.A., as were The Monkees. The show depicts the humorous adventures of a widow and her five children. It proved to be a top-rating TV series, networked weekly by ABC-TV.

The Partridge Family was: David Cassidy, son of Jack Cassidy and Shirley Jones' real-life stepson. He was lead singer; Shirley Jones, actress and former star of films (*Oklahoma, Carousel*) and stage (*Call Me Madam, South Pacific*); Susan Dey; Jeremy Gelbwaks; Danny Bonaduce; Suzanne Crough.

Bell Records mounted a huge promotion campaign around the TV series, single, album and music from the show. 'I Think I Love You' was the first single released in August 1970 which was No 1 for four weeks with R.I.A.A. Gold Disc award in December for million sale. This very sweet and catchy song was written by Tony Romeo, and the disc produced by Wes Farrell. The tracks for The Family are done by studio musicians, as are the vocal backings.

Release in Britain was on 13 November 1970 and it reached No 17 with 9 weeks in the bestsellers. U.S. sales of the disc were three and a half million by January 1971, global sales, five million.

THE PARTRIDGE FAMILY ALBUM (album) (original TV cast) *Bell* [*USA*]. This album of numbers from The Partridge Family TV shows was released in October 1970 in the U.S.A. It was a huge success and sold a million by January 1971. A Gold Disc was awarded by the R.I.A.A. in December 1970. Chartwise it was No 4 for two weeks, 16 weeks in the Top 10, and 68 weeks on the U.S.A. chart bestsellers.

Contents: 'Brand New Me' (Wes Farrel and C. Singleton); 'Point Me in the Direction of Albuquerque' (Tony Romeo); 'Bandala' (Wes Farrell); 'I Really Want to Know You' (Barry Mann and Cynthia Weill); 'Only a Moment Ago' (Tashman and West); 'I Can Feel Your Heartbeat' (Farrell, Creptecos and Appel); 'I'm on the Road' (Barry Mann and Cynthia Weill); 'To Be Lovers' (Mark Sharon); 'Somebody Wants to Love You' (Farrell, Creptecos and Appel); 'I Think I Love You' (Tony Romeo); 'Singing My Song' (Farrell and Hilderbrand).

FREDA PAYNE

BAND OF GOLD *Invictus* [*USA*]. Freda Payne was born in Detroit, Michigan. She studied piano as a child and after six years was encouraged by her tutor to sing as well. She sang at talent shows, in church and at school events, winning every contest she entered. At the age of 18 she moved to New York to start serious musical study. Here she also took dancing and vocal tuition. She then met Quincy Jones and worked with his band. This led to a major European tour in 1965. She also sang with the Duke Ellington orchestra for six months in Las Vegas, and with Lionel Hampton and Count Basie - her career angled towards jazz.

Although at the age of 15 she had become a protegé of Berry Gordy, a contract with Tamla-Motown did not materialize. She started her recording career in 1965 cutting tracks for both MGM and Impulse and several times deputized in that year as understudy for Lesley Uggams in *Hallelujah Baby*. In 1969, Eddie Holland, owner of Invictus Records, convinced her that she would have a great future if she changed her singing style to more pop-influenced music, and she made her first single for the label, 'The Unhooked Generation', which established her with the rhythm-and-blues fans. Then came 'Band of Gold', written by Ron Dunbar (an ex-factory-worker and ex-Motown writer who worked for Invictus) and Edith Wayne. This was released in April 1970 and got to No 1 in the U.S. charts for a week, selling the million with R.I.A.A. Gold Disc award by August, and staying in their bestsellers for 20 weeks. In Britain release was 28 August 1970 where it was a No 1 disc for six weeks with 19 weeks in the bestsellers and selling well over 250,000. Global sales were estimated at around two million.

The song is a simple one, with interesting lyrics.

ELVIS PRESLEY

KENTUCKY RAIN *RCA* [*USA*]. A pounding teenage disc, the song written by E. Rabbitt and D. Heard. Release in the U.S.A. was in February 1970, and the disc reached No 10 for a week there. In Britain it was No 21 for a week with 11 weeks in the bestsellers. Global sales are estimated at over a million. This was Elvis' 63rd million seller.

THE WONDER OF YOU *RCA* [*USA*]. Originally written in 1958 by Baker Knight, Elvis Presley's recording was taken from his album 'On Stage' and released in May 1970. It was No 4 for two weeks there and sold a million by August, with R.I.A.A. Gold Disc award. It was also a big hit in Britain, where it was released on 3 July 1970, selling well over 250,000 and No 1 in the charts for six weeks and 20 weeks in the bestsellers. Global sales are estimated at two million. This was his 64th million seller.

YOU DON'T HAVE TO SAY YOU LOVE ME *RCA* [*USA*]. Second time round as a million seller for this song of Italian origin written by V. Pallavicini and P. Donaggio, with English lyrics by Vicki Wickham and Simon Napier-Bell. It was a big hit for Dusty Springfield in 1966 (*q.v.*).

Elvis' version was released in October 1970 and reached No 7 for a week. British release was on 18 December 1970, and it was No 9 there for a week with 10 weeks in the bestsellers. It was also a top single in Japan, where it sold a near million in 1971. Global estimate of sale is around two million.

RAY PRICE

FOR THE GOOD TIMES (album) *Columbia* [*USA*] *Philips* [*Britain*]. Released in September 1970, this album built up a steady sale over a lengthy period. R.I.A.A. awarded a Gold Disc for million dollar sales in March 1971. By 1973 it had sold a million copies with platinum award to popular country-and-western vocalist Ray Price by Columbia Records. The album was produced by Don Law.

Contents: 'For the Good Times' (Kris Kristofferson); 'Gonna Burn Some Bridges' (Mel Tillis); 'Crazy Arms' (Chuck Seals and Ralph Mooney, 1956); 'I'll Go to a Stranger' (R. Pennington and D. Kirby); 'Black and White Lies' (J. Fowler); 'Grazin' in Greener Pastures' (R. Pennington); 'Help Me Make It Through the Night' (Kris Kristofferson, 1970); 'Lonely World' (E. West); 'You Can't Take It With You' (H. Bynum and J. Kandy); 'Cold Day in July' (D. Kirby and G. Martin); 'Heartaches by the Number' (Harlan Howard, 1959).

RARE BIRD

SYMPATHY *Philips* [*Italy*] *Chrysalis* [*Britain*]. Rare Bird comprises: Stephen Gould (lead vocalist and guitar), Mark Ashton (drums), Dave Kaffinetti (electric piano) and Graham Field (organ).

The composition is by the group, who are utterly professional with outstanding musicianship. They were extremely popular in Europe, particularly in Italy, where 'Sympathy' got to No 1. The disc also sold 500,000 in France and is estimated to have sold a million globally. Rare Bird were formed shortly before the release of their first album in December 1969.

RARE EARTH (rock quintet)

GET READY *Rare Earth* [*USA*]. Rare Earth are one of the Tamla-Motown company's key acts that become a household word among rock fans. The label's namesake were five Detroit artists: Gil Bridges (sax, tambourine, vocals), John Parrish (bass, trombone, vocals), Rod Richards (guitar, vocals), Kenny James (organ, electric piano) and Pete Rivers (drums, vocals). They were formerly known as The Sunliners and had played together since 1961.

This disc was released on 14 March 1970 in the U.S.A. and got to No 2 for a week there, staying in the bestsellers for 20 weeks. The song was written by 'Smokey' Robinson in 1966. The disc had sold a million by the end of 1970.

THE RATTLES (vocal and instrumental group)

THE WITCH *Philips [Britain] Phonograph Ton [Germany]*. The Rattles, a German group, was formed in 1962, and consisted of Hans Joachim Kreutzfeldt (then 18) on guitar, Rewhard Tarrach (18) on drums, Achim Reishel (18) lead guitar and vocal, and Herbert Hilderbrandt (19) bass guitar and vocal. All came from Hamburg.

They met The Beatles in their Hamburg days (1962) and played with them on three occasions in Germany, once at Munich, once at Essen and once in Hamburg. They also did three weeks with them at the Hamburg Star Club. The Rattles' reputation spread by word-of-mouth appraisal from returning British bands, and they subsequently appeared at Liverpool's Cavern for two weeks with great success, and also appeared on British TV.

In 1968, they recorded 'The Witch', written by Hilderbrandt, a hit for them in Germany. The group were then forced to split up owing to army service and other reasons and a new group formed with Frank Mille (guitar), Herbert Bornhold (drums), Satto Lumgen (bass) and an Israeli singer simply known as Edna. This combination started in Italy, with Hilderbrandt staying on as composer and producer.

They recorded a new version of 'The Witch' in 1970 and this was a success in Britain where it reached No 5 for one week with 15 weeks in the bestsellers. Another version with strings and more voice was also made for the German market.

By April 1971 it was reported that 'The Witch' had sold a million. This very intriguing and original number certainly cast a spell. The disc was popular in the U.S.A., The Rattles being the first German group ever to appear in their charts.

JERRY REED (country vocalist and guitarist)

AMOS MOSES *RCA [USA]*. Jerry Reed (real name Jerry R. Hubbard) was born on 20 March 1937 in Nashville, Tennessee. He began to strum on his first guitar when he was eight and later played at local dances with his father who played mandolin, guitar and banjo. When the family lived in Atlanta, he worked days in cotton mills and performed nights in gin mills. He also had a spell on the road with Ernest Tubb and The Texas Troubadours. At 16, he was introduced to an Atlanta promoter/publisher Bill Lowery who got him a contract with Capitol Records as singer/writer, and made his first record. He stayed with Capitol for three years, then did his military service, when 22. Jerry then signed with Columbia but this was not very fruitful as he only played at recording sessions. He moved on to Nashville and did seven years there playing guitar on recording sessions, and met Chet Atkins who recorded a number of his intrumental compositions. Chet invited Jerry to make some records at RCA and an album was recorded and issued from which a single was taken called 'Guitar Man'. This got into the country charts and all his subsequent discs did likewise. He became known as the 'Guitar Man' after Elvis Presley had a hit with it.

Chet Atkins produced several albums by Jerry for RCA, and Jerry received the CMA award for 1970 and 1971 as Instrumentalist of the Year. He also won the 1970 Grammy award for his duet album with Chet Atkins - 'Me and Jerry' - Best Country Instrumental Performance, and a Grammy nomination for Best Country Male Vocal Performance 1970 with his disc 'Amos Moses', which he wrote.

'Amos Moses' is described as a 'gritty down-home song about Louisiana swamp folk' and was coupled with the old standard 'Preacher and the Bear', a frantic guitar 'pickin'' song written in 1904 (see Collins 1905 for song data). Both are up-tempo performances. 'Amos Moses' was released in September 1970 and reached No 5 in the U.S. charts for a week, staying in the bestsellers for 24 weeks. Release in Britain was 2 April 1971. The disc sold a million by April 1971 with R.I.A.A. Gold Disc award.

SMOKEY ROBINSON AND THE MIRACLES

TEARS OF A CLOWN *Tamla [USA]*. This song was originally written in 1967 by H. Cosby, Smokey Robinson and Stevie

Wonder. The disc was initially released in Britain on 17 July 1970 and proved a big success, selling well over 250,000 there and achieving No 1 for four weeks with 14 weeks in the bestsellers. Release in the U.S.A. was on 10 October 1970 and it got to No 1 for two weeks and sold a million. The song is a bright blues rock number.

DIANA ROSS

AIN'T NO MOUNTAIN HIGH ENOUGH *Motown [USA]*. A tremendous success for Diana Ross, who in 1970 became a star solo attraction. The song was written in 1968 by Nickolas Ashford and Valerie Simpson (both of whom produced the disc). Release was on 8 August 1970 in the U.S.A. and the disc was No 1 there for three weeks, selling well over two million. British release was on 2 October 1970, and it got to No 6 there for a week with 12 weeks in the bestsellers.

BOBBY SHERMAN

EASY COME, EASY GO *Metromedia* [*USA*]. A fine swinging number with overpowering instrumental touches, written by J. Keller and D. Hildebrand. It was released in the U.S.A. in January 1970 and was No 5 for one week. The million sale, Bobby's third disc to achieve this, was reached in April when it was awarded a Gold Disc by the R.I.A.A.

JULIE DO YA LOVE ME *Metromedia* [*USA*]. Fourth million seller in a row for Bobby Sherman. Released in the U.S.A. in July 1970, it was No 1 for a week and passed the million sale by mid-September with R.I.A.A. Gold Disc award. It did in fact sell 152,000 copies in one day (1 September), and total sales by November were over two million. The song, written by T. Bahles and arranged by Al Capps, is very tuneful and bouncy. The popular version in Britain was recorded by the group White Plains. The Sherman disc was No 28 in Britain.

SHOCKING BLUE

NEVER MARRY A RAILROAD MAN *Pink Elephant* [*Holland*] *Colossus* [*USA*]. A third million seller for this quartet, written by group member Robby van Leeuwen, released in late 1970.

It was a big success in Europe, reaching the Top 10 in Holland, Italy, Spain, France and Belgium. When released in Japan on the Nippon/Polydor label it was a tremendous hit, reaching No 2 with a reported million sale by September 1971, during the group's concert tour there.

MIGHTY JOE *Colossus* [*USA*]. Second million seller (globally) for this Dutch group written by R. van Leeuwen. This driving rock disc was released in the U.S.A. in February 1970 and reached No 27 for a week. It had a good sale there, with European sales making the million total. It was No 43 in Britain.

SIMON AND GARFUNKEL

BRIDGE OVER TROUBLED WATER *Columbia* [*USA*] *CBS* [*Britain*]. Written by Paul Simon, this was released in late January 1970 just before their album of the same title. The song, set in parable, is a love ballad – magnificent vocal performance and material. It was considered to be the top disc of 1970, and reached No 1 for six weeks in the U.S.A. A Gold Disc was awarded by the R.I.A.A. in March, and sales by April were over two million. In Britain it was also a great success, and it achieved No 1 for four weeks with 20 weeks in the bestsellers and sold well over 250,000.

The song had wide coverage by other artists, and Paul Simon was said to have made $7 million from the song by the end of 1970. Global sales are estimated to be in the five million bracket. Grammy Awards for Record of the Year (1970), Song of the Year (1970) and Best Contemporary Song (1970).

BRIDGE OVER TROUBLED WATER (album) *Columbia* [*USA*]. This magnificent album by Simon & Garfunkel was released in early February 1970. It showcases the duo on a variety of tunes ranging from gentle ballads to bouncy country-rock numbers, the music and words attaining new heights yet retaining their relative simplicity. Garfunkel's sensitive voice and the duo's intricate harmonies, all performed with ease, made this a brilliant achievement. The album was undoubtedly the top album of 1970. It was No 1 for 10 weeks in the U.S.A. and stayed in the bestsellers for 85 weeks. In Britain it was No 1 for 35 weeks (a million sale) and stayed in their bestsellers for 285 weeks.

U.S. sales were 2,500,000 by the end of the year, and it was still selling strongly into 1971. Global sales reported by Columbia were over 10 million by 1975.

Contents: 'Bridge Over Troubled Water' (1969); 'El Condor Pasa' (this song originates from the 18th century, the original story telling of Tupac Amaru's revolution against the Spanish. Paul Simon's lyrics are completely different); 'Cecilia' (1969); 'Keep the Customer Satisfied' (1970); 'So Long, Frank Lloyd Wright' (1969); 'The Boxer' (1969); 'Baby Driver' (1969); 'The Only Living Boy in New York' (1969); 'Why Don't You Write Me?' (1969); 'Bye, Bye, Love' (Felice & Boudleaux Bryant, 1957); 'Song for the Asking' (1970). All songs written by Paul Simon unless otherwise indicated.

Simon and Garfunkel achieved the rare feat of having this album and the single of the same title at No 1 for five weeks simultaneously, both selling two million in two months on the U.S. market. A Gold Disc for the album was awarded by the R.I.A.A. in March as well as Grammy awards for Album of the Year (1970), Best Arrangement Accompanying Vocalists (1970) and Best Engineered Recording (1970).

CECILIA *Columbia* [*USA*]. Taken from the above album and released as a single in April, this Paul Simon song, a mixture of rhythm-chant and Caribbean rock, was another huge seller. It was No 1 for a week, and sold a million by June, with R.I.A.A. Gold Disc award.

SLY & THE FAMILY STONE

GREATEST HITS (album) *Epic* [*USA*]. Released in the U.S.A. in November 1970, this album sold a million in less than two months. An R.I.A.A. Gold Disc was awarded two weeks after release. Release in Britain was in February 1971.

The songs were all written by Sly (real name Sylvester Stewart), and the album can be said to represent the original blueprint which helped change the stereotyped format of popular black music.

This album was No 1 for a week in the U.S.A. and in the Top 10 for 15 weeks.

Contents: 'Dance to the Music' (1968); 'I Want to Take You Higher' (1969); (*)'Thank You (falletin me be mice elf again)'; 'Life'; 'Stand'; (*)'Everyday People'; 'Everybody Is a Star'; 'Fun'; 'You Can Make It If You Try'; 'Hot Fun in the Summertime'; 'M'Lady'; 'Sing a Simple Song'. (*) denotes million sold as single.

EDWIN STARR

WAR *Gordy* [*USA*] *Tamla-Motown* [*Britain*]. Edwin Starr was born in Nashville, Tennessee in 1942 and educated at Cleveland, Ohio. He began his career by singing in school shows at East Technical High School, which resulted in his first professional engagement with the Futuretones on the Gene Carroll talent show at Cleveland's Circle Theater. The rhythm-and-blues singer became a solo performer and joined Golden World Recording Company, where he wrote and recorded his first hit 'Agent 00 Soul'. Berry Gordy, Jr, president of Motown, heard him and signed him with the firm's Gordy label. Starr had a hit, in 1966, 'S.O.S. Stop Her on Sight', which became bigger when revived in 1969, particularly in Britain, where the artist had by that year made his ninth tour.

He has played many top venues, including New York's Apollo Theater, Cleveland's Circle Ballroom, Detroit's Twenty Grand, Regal Theater in Chicago, The Blue Note in Toronto and Esquire Club in Montreal, and annually performed at many colleges and universities.

This song, written by Barrett Strong and Norman Whitfield (producer of the disc) is a condemnation of war. Release was on 11 July 1970 in the U.S.A., the disc making the No 1 spot chartwise for three weeks and selling a million. In Britain release was on 9 October 1970, and it was No 2 for a week.

Total sales of the disc are estimated at three million.

CAT STEVENS

LADY D'ARBANVILLE *Island* [*Britain*] *A & M* [*USA*]. Written by Cat Stevens (real name Stephen Georgiou), the disc was released in Britain in July 1970 and reached No 5 in the charts with 13 weeks in the bestsellers, after first being a big hit in France. With further sales in the U.S.A., a million sale was reported globally in 1971. The song is a track from the album 'Mona Bone Jakon'.

Stevens made his debut in 1966 with a hit, 'I Love My Dog', and followed up with a bigger success in 1967 with 'Matthew & Son', both on the new Deram label (Decca). Born in London on 21 July 1948, son of a Greek restaurant owner in London's Shaftesbury Avenue, he was educated in Sweden and became a serious student of classical music. By the age of 17 he had written many songs with a startlingly different approach. His musical ideas were brilliant, and his lyrics poetic. He was discovered by ex-Springfield member Mike Hurst. After a period of serious illness and a hospital stay of a year and a half, his new self knowledge led him to A & M Records who produced his album, 'Mona Bone Jakon'. After two U.S. tours came a successful album, 'Tea for the Tillerman' (1971), which went high in the U.S. charts, and in 1972 the album 'Catch Bull at Four', then 'Teaser and the Firecat' (1972) in which was the big hit 'Morning Has Broken', a big seller when released as a single. This really established him as an international artist, and one of the foremost singer/composers on both sides of the Atlantic.

RAY STEVENS
EVERYTHING IS BEAUTIFUL *Barnaby* [*USA*]. The third million seller for Ray, eight years after his 'Ahab the Arab' of 1962. Ray wrote the song, which has a gospel approach accented by a church choir-like chorus. It was the first single for the Barnaby label distributed by Columbia, and was released in late March 1970, achieving No 1 in the U.S.A. for two weeks and selling a million by July with R.I.A.A. Gold Disc award. Release in Britain was on the CBS label and the disc was No 6 for a week and 16 weeks in the bestsellers.

Ray became even more popular in 1970 through his many appearances on the Andy Williams TV show, and won a Grammy Award for Best Contemporary Performance (Male) of 1970).

KIYOKO SUIZENJI
DAISHOBU *Crown* [*Japan*]. This disc reached No 1 in the Japanese charts, and a reported million sale by April 1971.

THE SUPREMES
UP THE LADDER TO THE ROOF *Motown* [*USA*]. The first single from the new Supremes line-up – Jean Terrell, who joined in January 1970, Mary Wilson and Cindy Birdsong. It was released in the U.S.A. on 7 March 1970, and achieved No 7 for a week, subsequently selling a million. In Britain the disc was released on 24 April 1970 and was No 6 for a week with 15 weeks in the bestsellers. Jean Terrell takes the lead vocal in this recording of a happy uptempo song written by Vincent Dimirco and Frank Wilson. It was the 17th million seller single for The Supremes' various groupings, exclusive of former member Diana Ross's solo discs.

STONED LOVE *Motown* [*USA*]. The 18th million seller for The Supremes, written by Frank E. Wilson (producer of the disc) and Kenneth Thomas. It was released in the U.S.A. on 31 October 1970, and was No 5 for four weeks, staying on the bestsellers for 15 weeks. In Britain, release was on 8 January 1971, and it got to No 2 for two weeks. The million global sale was reported in March 1971.

JAMES TAYLOR
SWEET BABY JAMES (album) *Warner* [*USA*]. James Taylor was born in Boston, Massachusetts, on 12 March 1948, the son of a very distinguished North Carolina family. His father was Dean of the Medical School of the University of North Carolina and his mother had been a lyric soprano at New England Conservatory of Music.

James was educated at Milton Academy near Boston. He went into depression in his final year, and then into a mental hospital. After discharging himself, he proceeded to New York, and in 1966 formed a group, The Flying Machine, with three friends, but it broke up after a year. He then went to London, where after auditioning with various disc companies, was discovered in 1968 by producer Peter Asher, who signed him to The Beatles' Apple Records, and released his first solo album 'James Taylor'. James returned to the U.S.A. in December 1968 and re-entered hospital, but Asher, a former performer (Peter & Gordon) had great faith in him, becoming his friend, manager and guide in business matters. In December 1969 they went to California to record the album 'Sweet Baby James' which, when released in March 1970, sold 1,600,000 in a year. It was No 1 for a week, in the Top 10 for 15 weeks and in the bestsellers for 102 weeks. In Britain it was No 4 for a week, in the Top 10 for nine weeks, and in the bestsellers for 47 weeks. Sales of tapes and albums had soared way over the two million mark by the end of 1971.

His beautifully melodic songs and brilliant unique acoustic guitar playing earned him the title of 'The Dylan of the 70s'. His two brothers (Alex and Livingston) and sister (Kate) all made names for themselves as singers and songwriters in much the same style.

'Fire and Rain' on the album was issued as a single after the album had been released, and had big sales. It was this that started the amazing success of the album and sell-out national concert tours.

In February 1971, *Time*'s music critic William Bender attended a brilliant performance by James Taylor at New York's Philharmonic Hall, resulting in an honour rarely accorded pop stars - being featured on the front cover of *Time* magazine, plus an in-depth article about the artist.

R.I.A.A. awarded a Gold Disc on 16 October 1970.

James Taylor happened at the right time - just as pop, folk, country, rock and jazz all came together to form the new rock.

Contents: 'Sweet Baby James'; 'Lo and Behold'; 'Sunny Skies'; 'Steamroller'; 'Country Road'; 'O Susannah' (Stephen C. Foster, 1848); 'Fire and Rain'; 'Blossom'; 'Anywhere Like Heaven'; 'Oh Baby, Don't You Loose Your Lip On Me'; 'Suite for 20 G'. All songs written by James Taylor unless otherwise indicated.

THE TEMPTATIONS
BALL OF CONFUSION (That's what the world is today) *Gordy* [*USA*] *Tamla Motown* [*Britain*]. Another big success for writers Norman Whitfield and Barrett Strong and The Temptations. The disc was released in the U.S.A. on 23 May 1970, was No 1 for a week and sold a million by August. British release was on 4 September 1970 and it was No 7 for two weeks with 15 weeks in the bestsellers. The disc was produced by Norman Whitfield, and has a strong dance-beat plus a high powered performance by the quintet.

THREE DOG NIGHT
MAMA TOLD ME (not to come) *Dunhill* [*USA*] *Stateside* [*Britain*]. Written by Randy Newman, this disc has a powerful surcharge both musically and commercially. It was released in the U.S.A. in May 1970 and was No 1 for three weeks, selling a million by July with R.I.A.A. Gold Disc award. British release was on 24 July, the disc reaching No 3 for three weeks with 14 weeks in the bestsellers. It made million seller No 4 for the group.

VANITY FAIR
HITCHIN' A RIDE *Page One* [*Britain*]. The second million seller for this group. The disc was first released in Britain in January 1970, and was No 16 for a week and 13 weeks in the bestsellers, with quite a good sale. It was much more successful in the U.S.A.. where it was released in March and got to No 3 for a week, selling a million there by July with R.I.A.A. Gold Disc award. The song was written by Peter Callender and Mitch Murray, two of Britain's most successful composers.

STEVIE WONDER

SIGNED, SEALED, DELIVERED (I'm yours) *Tamla* [*USA*]. A big up-tempo arrangement by Paul Riser of this song written by Stevie Wonder, L. Garrett, S. Wright and Lil Hardaway, in which Stevie is joined by a vocal group, proved a big seller. It is said to have sold three million. Release in the U.S.A. was on 20 July 1970, and the disc reached No 1 for a week. In Britain it was released on 26 June and got to No 10 for a week with 10 weeks in the bestsellers.

ORIGINAL FILM SOUNDTRACK

FIDDLER ON THE ROOF (double album) (starring Topol, with Norma Crane) *United Artists* [*USA*]. This superb film of the then longest running American stage musical written by Jerry Bock and Shelton Harnick, was directed by Norman Jewison and premiered in the U.S.A. on 3 November 1971. It was a tremendous success. Topol, who starred in the London production of the stage show, was also the star of the film, which accounted for the highest ever advance sale for any house in the Rank circuit of $187,000, prior to its premiere on 9 December 1971 at London's Dominion Theatre.

The double album soundtrack achieved a million dollars in disc and tape sales after just one day of sales in the U.S.A. and quickly became the fastest-moving motion picture disc and tape in United Artists' history. Although only reaching No 30 for two weeks, it was a consistent seller in the U.S.A. for 90 weeks, and soon passed the million sale, with U.S. sales executives' prediction that it would become the firm's all-time top grosser. The R.I.A.A. Gold Disc award was awarded on 18 October 1971.

Topel excels in the songs 'If I were A Rich Man' and 'Sabbath Prayer', and also in 'Sunrise, Sunset', with leading lady Norma Crane as his wife. (See *Fiddler on the Roof* Stage Theatre Cast for details of the various songs – 1964). The sound of the 'fiddler' in the film is from virtuoso violinist Isaac Stern.

ORIGINAL FILM SOUNDTRACK

SHAFT (Double album) (Isaac Hayes) *Enterprise* [*USA*] *Stax* [*Britain*]. *Shaft* was the first film to be made by black people featuring blacks as heroes. It starred Richard Roundtree and co-starred Moses Gunn, and was a thriller in the ever-popular cops-and-robbers genre with the theme of the hard-hitting private eye. It appealed to the vast audiences which had followed the James Bond films, and captured the imagination of Americans of many different backgrounds and tastes. Isaac Hayes' score fused the purest kind of rhythm-and-blues with some of the most soulful string arrangements ever. Isaac plays many of the instrumental tracks himself – piano, electric piano, vibes, and organ – as well as adding vocals to three tracks. In a matter of days the album became the fastest selling in Stax Records' history. Released in August 1971 in the U.S.A., it went to No 1 for two weeks, staying in the bestsellers for 60 weeks. It was No 1 in the rhythm-and-blues and jazz charts, both for albums and tape cartridges and won a Grammy Award for Best Original Score written for a Motion Picture or TV Special (a composer's award). It qualified for a gold record for million dollar sales three weeks after release, and platinum record for over $2 million by the end of October. By mid-November the double-sleeve album racked up over one million units sale while the single release 'Theme from *Shaft*' went over 1,350,000 at the same time. It was released November 1971 in Britain and reached No 7 for a week.

Isaac Hayes was born in 1943 in Covington, Tennessee, and was raised by share-cropping grandparents, moving to Memphis in his teens. He joined the school band and learned to play several instruments. By about 1962 he had cut a few unsuccessful sides for a local label and had started playing piano. He gravitated to Stax Records after its president Jim Stewart heard him playing with The MarKeys, and he was asked to play sax on an Otis Redding session. At Stax, he became reunited with a former acquaintance David Porter, and the duo began songwriting with eventually a Stax contract. They produced hit after hit for Stax artists, including Johnnie Taylor, Carla Thomas and Sam and Dave. A Stax Christmas party led to the recording of his first album – 'Presenting Isaac Hayes' (1967) (Atlantic re-release as 'Blue Hayes'). Then came 'Hot Buttered Soul' (Stax 1969), 'Movement' (Stax 1970), 'To Be Continued' (Stax 1971). Hayes' involvement with *Shaft* was the outcome of a meeting between Stax and MGM, who had just bought the screen rights to Ernest Tidyman's novel. He was invited to do the music for the film which took him seven weeks while in the middle of a tour. He had never done a movie before and had to learn all the technicalities. The tremendous success of *Shaft* brought more offers of filmscore work.

Music aside, Hayes' concern is the Isaac Hayes Foundation, through which he helps poor and needy old people of all races. More than half his estimated earnings (at around $1,500,000 a year by 1971) were poured into community projects all over the world. He became known as 'Black Moses'. With clean-shaven head, heavy beard, dark shades, draped in robes and gold chains, for his stage image, he has earned great respect as a gifted artist and social benefactor.

'Shaft' album contained the following Isaac Hayes compositions: 'Theme from *Shaft*'; 'Bumby's Lament'; 'Walk from Regio's'; 'Ellie's Love Theme'; 'Shaft's Cab Ride'; 'Cafe Regio'; 'Early Sunday Morning'; 'Be Yourself'; 'A Friend's Place'; 'Soulville'; 'No Name Bar'; 'Bumby's Blues'; 'Shaft Strikes Again'; 'Do Your Thing'; 'The End Theme'.

LYNN ANDERSON

ROSE GARDEN (album) *Columbia* [*USA*]. Following the huge success of her singles recording, Lynn Anderson used the title for her album which sold a million units by October 1971 with Platinum Disc award. Released January 1971 in the U.S.A. it reached No 11 for 1 week and stayed in the bestsellers for 33 weeks. The R.I.A.A. Gold Disc award came on 25 March 1971.

Contents: 'Rose Garden' (Joe South, 1970); 'For the Good Times' (Kris Kristofferson, 1970); 'Snowbird' (Gene MacLellan, 1970); 'It's Only Make Believe' (Jack Nance and Conway Twitty, 1958); 'I Don't Wanna Play House' (Billy Sherrill and Glenn Sutton, 1967); 'Sunday Mornin' Comin' Down' (Kris Kristofferson, 1969); 'Another Lonely Night'; 'Your Sweet Love Lifted Me' (Billy Sherrill); 'I Still Belong to You'; 'I Wish I Was a Little Boy Again'; 'Nothing Between Us'.

BADFINGER

DAY AFTER DAY *Apple* [*Britain*] *Apple* [*USA*]. This was the second million seller for Badfinger. Written by the group's Peter Ham, it is a soothing love-song. It was released in November 1971 in the U.S.A. and gained No 1 for two weeks. British release was January 1972, and it reached No 9 for one week with 11 weeks in the bestsellers. It was certified as an R.I.A.A. million seller on 4 March 1972.

JOAN BAEZ

THE NIGHT THEY DROVE OLD DIXIE DOWN *Vanguard* [*USA*]. Joan Baez, born on Staten Island, New York, 9 January 1941, became the most important and most controversial female folksinger of the 1960s. Her mother was Anglo-Scottish and her father Mexican, a physics professor whose appointments took him to Paris, Rome, Switzerland and Baghdad, where young Joan revealed an amazing ability at memory and mimicry. She went to school in Palo Alto, California, studying music and biology. She also sang in the school choir, and bought a guitar. After high school, the family moved to Boston, Massachusetts, and Joan became interested in folk music early in 1958. Her father took Joan and her sisters one night to Tulla's Coffee Grinder in Boston where amateur folksingers could bring their guitars and sing. Joan was soon singing there and in similar venues around Boston. After a short period at Boston University studying theatre, she met several semi-pro folk singers who taught her songs and guitar techniques. She never studied voice, or folklore, but just soaked up the songs from those around her. With her exceptionally pure voice, she began appearing regularly at Club 47, Cambridge, Massachusetts, specializing in folk fare.

In 1959, she went along to the first Newport Folk Festival, Rhode Island, appearing before an audience of 13,000 where she received a great deal of favourable mention which brought her widespread national acclaim. At the Festival she was asked if she would like to meet Columbia Records' representative Mitch Miller. Joan had never heard of him, and not wanting to be exploited by a big company, signed with a small outfit called Vanguard who issued her first album 'Joan Baez Vol. 1' in 1960. This was an album of traditional folk material including many Scottish ballads. The reaction was immediate, and sales pushed it into the Top 50 of *BMW*'s Top Mono album chart. This was exceptional for an authentic folk-singer in the recording field. Joan then moved to the Californian coast, and lived in a squalid cabin for eight months along with five cats and five dogs, eventually moving to more comfortable quarters in nearby Carmel.

With regular concert performances and annual album releases by Vanguard, her popularity became enormous. Her third album (1962) included a song that became identified with her – 'We Shall Overcome' – which became the all-purpose protest song throughout the Western hemisphere. This clearly denoted a developing political awareness, and Joan sang it at a series of publicized protest meetings all over the U.S.A., culminating in the 1963 Freedom March on Washington. During this period she met the young Bob Dylan, and introduced him at her many concerts, also using much of Dylan's material and that by other contemporary writers. Politics became a major concern of her life, and in 1965 she founded the Institute for the Study of Non-Violence. Her refusal to pay taxes to help towards the war effort in Vietnam made her a national symbol of protest. In some quarters this turned her popularity into hatred and contempt, but despite this she remained true to her principles and a spokeswoman for civil rights and peace movements. By 1974, Vanguard had released 20 albums of Joan Baez. In 1971 Vanguard released her 'Blessed Are. . . .' album which contained 'The Night They Drove Old Dixie Down' (written by J. Robbie Robertson), a song of the American Civil War, and one quite different from her protest songs, with a very catchy chorus. This was released as a single in July 1971 in the U.S.A. and reached No 1 for a week, staying in the Top 50 of the bestsellers for 13 weeks. By 22 October it had sold over a million with R.I.A.A. Gold Disc award. In Britain the disc reached No 6 with 12 weeks in the bestsellers, released in September 1971.

Several of Joan Baez's albums were certified gold by the R.I.A.A., and her more recent ones contained much original material, composed either by herself or by her sister, Mimi Fariña.

THE BEE GEES

HOW CAN YOU MEND A BROKEN HEART? *Atco* [*USA*]. Another big success for The Bee Gees, composed by brothers Barry and Robin Gibb of the group. It was released in June 1971 in the U.S.A. and went to No 1 for four weeks, staying in the bestsellers for 14 weeks. The R.I.A.A. Gold Disc award came 26 August 1971.

THE BELLS (vocal and instrumental sextet)

STAY AWHILE *Polydor* [*USA*]. The Bells, a Canadian group from Montreal, consisted of: Jacki Ralph (vocals); Cliff Edwards (vocals); Doug Gravelle (drummer); Charlie Clarke (guitar);

Mike Wayne (bass); Denny Will (piano). The group was formed in 1965 after Jacki Ralph met Cliff Edwards at a ski resort outside Montreal. He was playing rock and roll at the time, while she was singing folksongs. They decided to team their talents, and thus The Bells were born. From around 1968 their recordings enjoyed considerable popularity in their native Canada where they made the transition from a tavern act to concert and supper club stature. 'Stay Awhile' passed the million copy sales mark even before the major U.S. radio stations had played it. Written by K. Tobias, it was released in the U.S.A. February 1971, staying at No 4 for 3 weeks, and 11 weeks in the Top 50. The R.I.A.A. awarded a Gold Disc 27 May 1971, and British release was in June 1971.

The Bells sound is intimate and controlled, a perfect counterpoint to the frenzied rock that was the rule for so long. They appeared in New York on the 'Tonight' TV programme in June 1971.

BLACK SABBATH

MASTER OF REALITY (album) *Vertigo* [*Britain*] *Warner* [*USA*]. Third big seller for Black Sabbath, with R.I.A.A. Gold Disc award 27 September 1971 and subsequent platinum award for million units sale. Released August 1971 in Britain it reached No 23 and stayed for 13 weeks in the Top 30. In the U.S.A. it went to No 8 for 2 weeks and stayed in the bestsellers for 43 weeks.

Contents: 'Sweet Leaf'; 'After Forever'; 'Embryo'; 'Children of the Grave'; 'Orchid'; 'Lord of This World'; 'Solitude'; 'Into the Void'.

All songs written by group (Tony Iommi, Geezer Butler, Bill Ward and Ozzie Osbourne).

BLOOD, SWEAT AND TEARS

BLOOD SWEAT & TEARS 4 (album) *Columbia* [*USA*]. This was one of the fastest-moving albums in Columbia's history. It was completely sold out within 24 hours of release and the stock had to be increased immediately. It was released July 1971, reached No 10 in the U.S. for 2 weeks, and stayed in the Top 50 for 11 weeks. R.I.A.A. Gold Disc award came swiftly, on 5 August 1971, and the million sale reported eventually.

Material for the album was supplied mainly by the group's outstanding vocalist David Clayton-Thomas, who in 1972 left to pursue a solo career, but returned in late 1974.

Contents: 'Go Down Gambling'; 'Cowboys and Indians' (Terry Kirkman and Dick Halligan); 'John the Baptist' (Phyllis Major and Al Kooper); 'Redemption'; 'Lisa Listen to Me'; 'Look to My Heart'; 'High on a Mountain' (Steve Katz, Dick Halligan and David Clayton-Thomas); 'Valentine Day' (Steve Katz); 'Rock Me for a Little While'; 'Take Me in Your Arms' (Isley Brothers); 'Mama Gets High' (Dave Bargeron and Steve Katz); 'For My Lady'. All songs by David Clayton-Thomas unless otherwise indicated.

BREAD

IF *Elektra* [*USA*]. Written by David Gates (of the group), 'If' was released March 1971 in the U.S.A. where it reached No 4 and stayed for 10 weeks in the Top 30. 'If' is a beautiful song in which David Gates recites some of the lyrics. It has been called 'a love poem that has touched the lives of millions of people'. It was revived in 1975 through a recording by Telly Savalas, the star of the TV series 'Kojak'. The original Bread recording sold a million globally, and was taken from their album 'Manna.'

BABY, I'M A WANT YOU *Elektra* [*USA*]. Written by David Gates (of the group), and released in the U.S.A., October 1971, this reached No 3 for two weeks and stayed in the bestseller charts for 12 weeks. In Britain it reached No 9 with 10 weeks in the bestsellers. It sold a million with R.I.A.A. Gold Disc award, 7 January 1972. The song was also the title of an album by Bread (1972).

JAMES BROWN
HOT PANTS (Part 1) (She got to use what she got to get what she wants) *People* (*Starday-King*) [*USA*]. This was the first big hit for the dynamic James Brown on his new label. Written by him, it was released in the U.S.A., June 1971 and reached No 10. It stayed 10 weeks in the Top 50 and had sold a million by August 1971.

JERRY BUTLER AND BRENDA LEE EAGER
AIN'T MISUNDERSTANDING MELLOW *Mercury* [*USA*]. Although this recording did not make No 1 it was a consistent seller for four months and sold the million by 1972,with Gold Disc award from R.I.A.A. on 6 April 1972. It was written by Polk and Talbert, released in the U.S.A. December 1971, and reached No 21 for 3 weeks, staying in the bestsellers chart 18 weeks.

Brenda Lee Eager was born in 1948. She made her singing debut in church at the age of four in Mobile, Alabama. After graduating from Blount High School in Mobile in 1965, she worked in a hospital in Mobile. She then went to New York and got a job at a piece work factory on 34th Street. She worked a few club dates in Brooklyn and then returned to Mobile and married.

In 1968, Brenda became a member of the 'Pipperettes', a female quartet, and went on the 'breadbasket' and 'campaign' trail for two years, working with Reverend Jesse Jackson, appearing all over the U.S.A. In 1970, the Reverend's brother, Chick Jackson, took a tape of a song she cut, 'It Was Real What I Feel', to Jerry Butler. Also in 1970, Brenda joined two other girls, Caroline Johnson and Deidra Teig, and Jerry Butler's sister Mattie, and formed the group Peaches. When Pattie La Belle & The Bluebells left Jerry Butler in late 1969 Jerry was not ready to work with another vocal group, but finally sister Mattie convinced him that Peaches were ready to do his vocal backgrounds. The need soon came, and Peaches joined Jerry in a performance at Chicago Auditorium. Peaches was on its way, and Brenda Lee Eager made this great disc with Jerry.

(See 1969 for Jerry Butler data.)

GLEN CAMPBELL
GLEN CAMPBELL'S GREATEST HITS (album) *Capitol* [*USA*]. This fine compilation of Glen Campbell's big hits was a consistent seller for several months in the U.S.A. and was awarded a Gold Disc by the R.I.A.A. on 15 May 1972. In Britain it was a huge success, and by 1975 had sold over 500,000, after having reached No 8 and stayed in their charts for 26 weeks.

Contents: 'Honey Come Back' (Jim Webb, 1970); 'Gentle on My Mind' (John Hartford, 1968); 'Everything a Man Could Ever Need' (Mac Davis, 1970); 'Galveston' (Jim Webb, 1968); 'Try a Little Kindness' (Bobby Allen Austin and Thos. Curt Sapaugh, 1969); 'Dreams of the Everyday Housewife' (Chris Gantry, 1969); 'By the Time I Get to Phoenix' (Jim Webb, 1968); 'Dream Baby' (Cindy Walker, 1971); 'Where's the Playground, Susie?' (Jim Webb, 1968); 'It's Only Make Believe' (Jack Nance and Conway Twitty, 1958); 'Wichita Lineman' (Jim Webb, 1968); 'All I have to Do Is Dream' (Boudleaux Bryant, 1958).

THE CARPENTERS
FOR ALL WE KNOW *A & M* [*USA*]. With lyrics by Robb Wilson and Arthur James, and music by Fred Karlin, this disc was released in the U.S.A. in January 1971, reaching No 3 for two weeks and lingering for 14 weeks in the Top 30. In Britain, it reached No 18 with 13 weeks in the bestsellers. By 12 April 1971, this disc had sold over 1,100,000 in the U.S.A. and received the Gold Disc award from the R.I.A.A. The song was the theme of the film *Lovers and Other Strangers* and was included on the soundtrack, sung by The Carpenters. Arthur James and Robb Wilson (the lyricists) are pseudonyms for Arthur Griffin and Robb Royer, two of the members of the Elektra recording group Bread. They changed their names so that their reputation as rock-'n'-roll artists wouldn't conflict with their image as song-writers for films.

The song received the Academy Award (the Oscar) for Best Film Song of 1970.

RAINY DAYS AND MONDAYS *A & M* [*USA*]. Another song by the talented brother and sister Richard and Karen Carpenter, this time with a wistful quality. Written by Roger Nichols and Paul Williams, it was released in the U.S.A. May 1971, reaching No 2 for two weeks, and staying in the bestsellers for 12 weeks. It sold a million and was awarded a Gold Disc by the R.I.A.A. on 21 July 1971.

SUPERSTAR *A & M* [*USA*]. This million seller was written by Leon Russell and Bonnie Bramlett. Released in the U.S.A. August 1971, it stayed at No 1 for a week, and in the Top 50 for 13 weeks. In Britain it reached No 18 with 13 weeks in the bestsellers. The Gold Disc award from the R.I.A.A. came on 18 October 1971. The Carpenters also received a Grammy Award for Best Vocal Performance by a duo, group or chorus with their 'Carpenters' album, 1971.

DAVID CASSIDY (pop vocalist)
CHERISH backed with COULD IT BE FOREVER *Bell* [*USA*]. David Cassidy, son of actor Jack Cassidy and actress/dancer Evelyn Ward, was born in New York, 12 April 1950. He entered show business at the age of 16 when he went to Los Angeles with the LA Theatre Group. At the age of 18, David decided to go to Florida to play in a band, but never made it as his mother had been offered a part in a play *And So To Bed* and David auditioned for the show and got a small bit part. After a Broadway production, *Fig Leaves Are Falling*, in which he had a part, flopped, he went to Hollywood and landed some TV parts, appearing in 'Bonanza', 'Ironside' and 'The FBI'. Songwriter/producer Wes Farrell auditioned him for a singing part in 'The Partridge Family' TV series. The show was a tremendous success and David become one of the biggest teen idols. He attracted thousands of screaming fans and was also a pop phenomenon in Britain when the TV series was screened there, and when he went to Britain in 1972.

'Cherish' (written by T. Kirkman) and 'Could It Be Forever?' (written by Wes Farrell and F. Janssen) was his first single. This was released in the U.S.A. in October 1971 and on 21 March 1972 in Britain. The disc was No 3 for two weeks in the U.S.A. and stayed in the bestsellers for 12 weeks, selling a million with R.I.A.A. Gold Disc award, 16 December 1971. In Britain, the disc was No 2 and stayed 10 weeks in the Top 10 with 17 weeks in the bestsellers.

David started doing live solo performances, and drew sell-out crowds wherever he appeared. (See Partridge Family, 1970.)

CHAKACHAS (rock septet)
JUNGLE FEVER *Polydor* [*USA*]. Written by B. Ador (William Albimoor) and released in December 1971, this reached No 5 for one week in the U.S.A. and stayed in the bestsellers for 15 weeks.

The record originated in Europe, where – according to Polydor – the group were established for several years. In 1958, they had their first hit with 'Eso Es El Amor', and subsequently were in demand throughout Europe, playing in France, Holland, Spain, Italy, Belgium and Germany. They also starred in a film in Rome, and became a big name on the Continent. They had the distinction of introducing the Twist in the early 1960s to Continental audiences, and kept up a heavy schedule until 1967. Their leader, Gaston Boogaerts, split from the group in the late 1960s to take up his former interest in painting. In 1970, he called the group to record an album, and 'Jungle Fever' resulted from the recording session. Besides Gaston, the group comprises: Kary, female lead singer; Victor Ingeveld, saxophone; and four other musicians on trumpet, sax, conga drums and bongos.

By 22 March 1972, 'Jungle Fever' had sold the million and gained an R.I.A.A. Gold Disc award.

CHEECH & CHONG (rock comedians)

CHEECH AND CHONG (album) *Ode* [*USA*]. Released in the U.S.A. September 1971, this album reached No 17 where it stayed for three weeks. It remained firmly lodged in the best-sellers for 64 weeks.

Richard 'Cheech' Marin and Thomas Chong are among the most successful comedians in the history of the record industry. Chong was born in Edmonton, Alberta, Canada, and began his career on stage as a guitar player in rhythm-and-blues bands around Western Canada. 'Cheech' was born in Watts, California, son of a Los Angeles policeman. As soon as he left San Fernando Valley College, he went to Canada where he met Chong. They were both in a group known as City Lights which consisted of three freaks, four topless dancers, a mime artiste and a roaring audience. When the group broke up, Cheech and Chong stayed together as a duo. They went south to the 'Hoot' night at the Troubadour, where Lou Adler, president of Ode Records, signed them up. Their first three albums 'Cheech and Chong', 'Big Bambu' and 'Los Cochinos' were all million sellers. The 'Cheech and Chong' album was awarded a Gold Disc by R.I.A.A. on 28 July 1972.

The duo became well known for their satiric portrayal of various roles in contemporary society, and were exceptionally popular among a drug-orientated generation, while poking fun at drug users, pushers, and outdated morality and laws. They became a symbol of freedom to the current generation, and set box office records everywhere – on stage, concert halls, college campuses, etc. Their comedy albums rank alongside other consistent 'rock-era' superstar supersellers, zooming sales to unheard-of heights and restoring viability to comedy albums.

This first album – all material by Cheech and Chong – contains: 'Blind Melon Chitlin''; 'Wink Dinkerson'; 'Acapulco Gold Filters'; 'Vietnam'; 'Trippin' in Court'; 'Dave'; 'Emergency Ward'; 'Welcome to Mexico'; 'The Pope'; 'Live at the Vatican'; 'Cruisin' with Pedro de Pacas'; 'Waiting for Dave'.

CHER

GYPSIES, TRAMPS AND THIEVES *Kapp* [*USA*] *MCA* [*Britain*]. Written by Bob Stone, released in the U.S.A. September 1971, this song stayed at No 1 for two weeks and in the bestsellers for 16 weeks. British release was November 1971, and it reached No 3 for one week, staying for 12 weeks in the bestsellers. It was the first big hit as a solo artist for Cher, with a million sale in the U.S.A. plus R.I.A.A. Gold Disc award, 19 November 1971. It also sold over 250,000 in Britain.

After Sonny & Cher's initial success in the mid-1960s, the duo became somewhat quiet in the acid rock period, making an anti-dope film (1968) for children. From 1969 to 1970 there was a lull in their fortunes, but in 1970 they went into nightclubs and the cabaret circuit. In 1971, they got a TV series with CBS and were back in popularity, with the success of the one-hour TV shows. Cher was subsequently divorced from Sonny Bono (1974), started a solo career with Kapp Records, and became a model working for *Vogue*, etc. In 1975 she embarked on a stormy, on-off marriage to Greg Allman (formerly of The Allman Bros.) and has subsequently recorded with him (Allman and Woman, 1977).

CHICAGO

CHICAGO 3 (Double album) *Columbia* [*USA*]. Released in the U.S.A. January 1971, this album reached No 2 for two weeks, staying in the bestsellers for 44 weeks (9 weeks in the Top 10). In Britain it reached No 14. The album was another big success for this group, with R.I.A.A. Gold Disc award on 4 February 1971. It went on to a subsequent million sale.

The double album contained 23 titles, including: 'Sing a Mean Tune Kid'; 'I Don't Want Your Money'; 'Free'; 'Motorboat to Mars'; 'When All the Laughter Dies in Sorrow'; 'Loneliness is Just a Word'; 'What Else Can I Say?'; 'Flight 602'; 'Free Country'; 'At the Sunrise'; 'Happy 'cause I'm Going Home'; 'Mother'; 'Lowdown'; 'An Hour in the Shower'; 'Off to Work'; 'Fallin'

Out'; 'Hard Rising Morning Without Breakfast'; 'Dreaming Home'; 'Canon'; 'Morning Blues Again' (all written by members of the group).

CHICAGO 'LIVE' AT CARNEGIE HALL (quadruple album) *Columbia* [*USA*]. Released October 1971 in the U.S.A. this package reached No 3 and stayed in the bestsellers for 33 weeks (12 weeks in the Top 10).

This was the first four-record set ever released by a rock group. Columbia anticipated the success of the set by manufacturing a large amount of sets before the usual industry gauge – retail recorders – were available. The package went over the million mark during the first 30-day period, and continued to accelerate. R.I.A.A. awarded the Gold Disc on 9 November 1971. It sold 250,000 immediately it was released. The package contained 37 titles, replete with rousing horns and vocal harmonies and included: 'Fancy Colours'; 'In the Country'; South California Purple'; 'Questions 67 and 68'; 'Does Anybody Really Know What Time It is?'; 'Sing a Mean Tune'; 'Beginnings'; 'It Better End Soon' (5 movements); 'Mother'; 'Lowdown'; 'Flight 602'; 'Motorboat to Mars'; 'Free'; '25 or 6 to 4'; 'Where Do We Go from Here?'; 'Colour My World'; 'I'm a Man'; 'West Virginia Fantasies'; 'A Song for Richard and His Friends'; 'I Don't Want Your Money'; 'Happy 'cause I'm Going Home'; 'Make Me Smile'. (All written by the group, except 'I'm a Man' by Stevie Winwood.)

THE CHI-LITES (rhythm-and-blues quartet)

HAVE YOU SEEN HER? *Brunswick* [*USA*]. Written by Barbara Acklin and Eugene Record, this was released in the U.S.A. on 23 October 1971 and stayed at No 1 for 2 weeks, and in the bestsellers for 14 weeks. It was released in Britain 17 December 1971, where it reached No 3, remaining in the bestsellers for 9 weeks.

The Chi-Lites, a black group, got together in 1961, and were originally known as the Hi-lites. They added the 'C' to identify more closely with the city (Chicago) of their origins. They are mainly a soul group, but also sing up-tempo numbers. They were actually formed from the split of two other groups. The major factor in the group's success story is Eugene Record, lead singer, main writer and producer of the Chi-Lites' chart-topping discs. By 1975 he was vice-president of Brunswick Records in charge of Artistes and Repertoire, but was a Chicago taxi cab driver when he auditioned for the group, which consisted of: Marshall Thompson (baritone), Robert 'Squirrel' Lester (tenor lead) and Creadel 'Red' Jones (bass). Record (also tenor lead) made up the quartet and the group broke into popularity with the advent of the Dakar product (issued through Atlantic) who signed them to

Revue, a subsidiary of MCA. Their first album was 'Give It Away' on MCA (1968) followed by 'Give More Power to the People' (1971). By then, MCA had switched the group to their main Brunswick label. 'Have You Seen Her?', a cut from 'Power to the People' album, was not intended to be a single until public demand and rhythm-and-blues airplay made it a hit before release. The album sold a near million, but the single sold around three million. Thereafter, every Brunswick single by the group sold a minimum of 250,000. Another major factor of the group's popularity is the long-term faith that rhythm-and-blues radio personnel had in their earlier years.

TONY CHRISTIE (vocalist)

IS THIS THE WAY TO AMARILLO? *MCA [Britain]*. Written by Howard Greenfield and Neil Sedaka, the single was released in Britain 8 October 1971, reached No 17 and stayed in the bestsellers for 13 weeks.

Tony Christie, born 25 April 1944 in Conisborough, near Doncaster, Yorkshire, made his first public appearance when 17, becoming a professional at 20. His first British radio date was in 1967, and TV in 1970. British writers Mitch Murray and Peter Callender both wrote and produced his first hit 'Las Vegas'(1970) and followed up with another hit 'I Did What I Did for Maria' in early 1971. They then chose 'Amarillo', a driving, up-tempo number, with a chorus that registered immediately, by the famous U.S. writers Greenfield and Sedaka, and, aside from its British success, it was No 1 in Germany, Spain, Austria, Belgium, Switzerland and Sweden, and into the Top 20 in six other countries. It subsequently amassed a million sales, with Gold Disc by September 1972. Tony's success brought him tours of Australia, New Zealand and South Africa. His real name is Anthony Fitzgerald. He plays the guitar.

TOM CLAY

WHAT THE WORLD NEEDS NOW IS LOVE backed with ABRAHAM MARTIN & JOHN *MoWest (Motown) [USA]*. Released in the U.S.A. July 1971, this double-sided hit reached No 7 for two weeks and stayed for eight weeks in the Top 30.

Tom Clay, American disc jockey, felt that such a powerful medium as radio should cover subjects in an interesting way, particularly serious subjects, and personally paid for the making of a disc to present on his programme. Berry Gordy (Motown's president) heard this disc on his car radio and put it out on his label. Both songs had been hits previously, but Clay's 'message' disc was eminently suitable for the U.S. market at the time. It ultimately sold a million (September 1971). There was also enormous reaction in other countries – Australia, New Zealand and Canada – where it became a Top 5 hit. The disc had over 10 minutes' playing time, and was produced by Clay, with arrangements by Gene Paige. 'What the World Needs Now' was written by the Bacharach/David team (1965) and 'Abraham, Martin and John' by Dick Holler (1968).

CLIMAX (vocal and instrumental quintet)

PRECIOUS AND FEW *Carousel [USA]*. Written by Walt Nims and released in the U.S.A., December 1971, this got to No 1 for one week, and stayed for 19 weeks in the bestsellers.

Climax was originally Tom King & The Starfires from Cleveland, Ohio. In order to get airplay, they changed their name to The Outsiders, and Sonny Geraci, lead singer, had a Top 10 single with 'Time Won't Let Me' (Capitol, 1966). Four albums and three more Top 40 singles later, the group went through some changes and stopped recording for a time. Geraci, who had been with The Outsiders from 1966 to 1968, left the group to form Climax with four of the most talented musicians he could find. These were Bob Neilson (drums), Rick Lip (jazzaccordion), Steve York (bass), and writer of a number of Climax songs, Walt Nims (guitar). Their contract was picked up by Carousel Records in California where the group had moved to. They had chosen

Climax as a name that seemed to register, and also as a name for the launching of an act that would be freer in approach.

'Precious and Few' was a big hit for them (distributed by Bell Records) and sold over the million with R.I.A.A. Gold Disc award on 21 February 1972. In order to avoid confusion with an Italian label, Carosello, they chose Rocky Road Records, as a new name for their label. Sonny Geraci kept the group free in a musical sense, utilizing jazz and classical influences when appropriate. (See also The Outsiders, 1966.)

DENNIS COFFEY & DETROIT GUITAR BAND

SCORPIO *Sussex [USA]*. Written by Dennis Coffey, released October 1971 in the U.S.A. this reached No 4 for one week and stayed in the bestsellers for 17 weeks.

Dennis Coffey, born in 1940, began playing in rock and roll bands, then spent five years studying music theory at Wayne State University in Detroit. He became a prominent session guitarist, his first being for The Temptations' recording of 'Cloud 9' (Motown). His 'wah wah' guitar and innovative guitar work resulted in his being on most of The Temptations' records, and his working on records by The Jackson 5, Gladys Knight, Wilson Pickett, Paul Anka and others. His riffs led to a contract with Sussex Records as a soloist, and 'Scorpio', a smash hit with R.I.A.A. gold record award on 9 December 1971. At the same time, his 'Evolution' album (1970) started to climb the charts.

CORNELIUS BROTHERS & SISTER ROSE

TREAT HER LIKE A LADY *United Artists [USA]*. A very talented family trio, Eddie, Carter and Rose Cornelius became a new asset to United Artists, their discs selling in a big way. 'Treat Her Like a Lady', a most consistent seller, reached the million sale by 2 August 1971 and was awarded a Gold Disc by R.I.A.A. It was written by Eddie Cornelius, released in the U.S.A. March 1971, reaching No 2 for one week and staying in the bestsellers for 21 weeks.

LES CRANE

DESIDERATA *Warner Bros [USA] Kinney [Britain]*. Released in the U.S.A. September 1971, 'Desiderata' reached No 8 for one week, and stayed in the bestsellers for 12 weeks. In Britain it was released February 1972, going to No 7 for one week and staying in the bestsellers for 14 weeks.

'Desiderata', a most beautiful piece of prose rich in advice for living a contented life, encapsulating man's hopes and desires, peace, freedom of thought and expression, etc., was written in 1906 by Max Ehrmann, an American author and lawyer, and appeared in a volume of his poems. It was first copyrighted under the title 'Go Placidly Amid the Noise and Haste' (the first stanza of the poem) in 1927, and with its present title 'Desiderata' in *The Poems of Max Ehrmann* edited by Mrs Ehrmann in 1948, three years after her husband's death. The rights were subsequently sold (1968) to Crescendo Publications of Boston.

The first recording of the poem, entitled 'Child of the Universe' featuring the 'Desiderata' words and set to a tune by singer Graham Bell, seems to be that by the British group Every Which Way in September 1970 formed by ex-Nice drummer Brian Davison, on their first and only album. In December 1970, the prose that made up Les Crane's recording was printed in full on a page advertisement for King Crimson's album 'Lizard', and King Crimson, who thought 'Desiderata' was an authentic ancient document, the words having appeared on a poster as 'found in Old Saint Paul's Church, Baltimore, dated 1692', was later obliged to make a settlement for infringement of copyright.

Producer/composer Fred Werner found the poster in a Los Angeles shop, and made his musical setting for Les Crane. Werner cleared his music copyright through a contract with Crescendo Publications. The disc was an undoubted bestseller and made the Top 10 in 12 different countries, with a million plus global sale. It also received the Grammy Award for Best Spoken Word Recording of 1971.

Kinney Records spent time and money tracing the right St

Paul's Church, eventually talking to the Rev. George P. Donnally who told them Old Saint Paul's Church was *founded in 1692* – the date on the poster, but the original link with 'Desiderata' and the church didn't occur until 1956 when the then rector Rev. Frederick Ward Kates used Ehrmann's poem as a sermon for his congregation. It was duplicated and passed around the pews for the parishioners to take home, to study, and put into practice. The Rev. Kates was thus directly responsible for 'Desiderata' becoming known throughout the world.

CREEDENCE CLEARWATER REVIVAL

HAVE YOU EVER SEEN THE RAIN? backed with HEY TONIGHT *Fantasy [USA] Liberty [Britain]*. Both songs were written by John Fogerty, and this disc was released January 1971 in the U.S.A. reaching No 3 for two weeks, and remaining for eight weeks in the Top 30. British release was in February 1971.

Taken from the group's big seller album 'Pendulum', it became their eighth million-selling single with R.I.A.A. Gold Disc award on 17 March 1971.

JOHN DENVER

POEMS, PRAYERS AND PROMISES (album) *RCA [USA]*. John Denver (real name Henry John Deutschendorf, Jr), born in Roswell, New Mexico on 31 December 1943, grew up in an Air Force family and was educated in various schools all over the U.S.A. His father was a pilot with three world records in military aviation. John had similar ambitions but was rejected by the U.S. Air Force for shortsightedness. As a youngster, his grandmother gave him an old 1910 Gibson guitar. Later, while at Texas Tech, where he was majoring in architecture, he decided to try his luck in show business on the West Coast. He changed his name to John Denver, which had a distinct country-and-western ring about it, and played a number of small spots, then auditioned successfully for Randy Sparks, well-known folk impresario in Los Angeles (1964).

Chad Mitchell had left the trio bearing his name, and Denver was chosen from over 250 applicants for the top job with that trio, working with them for nearly four years. The Mitchell Trio gave its last performance in November 1968, and John struck out on his own. The band, however, had debts of $40,000, and John was faced with a debt of $11,000. As he had not performed solo for over three years, nobody seemed interested in booking him, and a very worried Denver flew to Aspen, Colorado to find a job. He finally landed a week's engagement at The Leather Jug in nearby Snowmass, and this looked like the turning point in his career. A series of concerts at colleges followed, then his signing with RCA and his solo debut on the album 'Rhymes and Reasons' (1969). Also in 1969, his composition 'Leaving on a Jet Plane', which had been included in a Peter, Paul & Mary album in 1967, was released as a single by that trio, and was a smash-hit million seller. John Denver was designated as one of the most important

discoveries of the year, and recognized as an extremely talented songwriter.

His second album 'Take Me Tomorrow' featured six of Denver's own songs. The third album 'Whose Garden Was This?' (1970) had enthusiastic reviews while the fourth 'Poems Prayers & Promises' contained his first million-selling single 'Take Me Home Country Roads'. This fourth album released in March 1971 was awarded a Gold Disc by R.I.A.A. on 15 September. It reached No 15 for five weeks and stayed on the charts for 38 weeks. By March 1974 it had sold around two million.

All John Denver's recording is directed by Milton Okun. With many awards to his credit, John became a national institution by 1974. 'Poems, Prayers and Promises' was also released in Britain 1 October 1972. It contains: 'Poems, Prayers and Promises' (John Denver); (*) 'Take Me Home Country Roads' (Bill Danoff, Taffy Nivert and John Denver); (*) 'Sunshine on My Shoulders' (John Denver, Kniss and Taylor); 'Let It Be' (John Lennon and Paul McCartney, 1970); 'My Sweet Lady'; 'Wooden Indian'; 'Junk' (Paul McCartney, 1970); 'Gospel Changes'; 'I Guess He'd Rather Be In Colorado' (Bill Danoff and Taffy Nivert); 'Around and Around'; 'Fire and Rain' (James Taylor, 1969); 'The Box'. (*) denotes sold a million as a single.

TAKE ME HOME COUNTRY ROADS *RCA [USA]*. Written by John Denver, Bill Danoff and Taffy Nivert, this was released in the U.S.A. May 1971, climbing to No. 1 for two weeks, and lingering in the bestsellers for 24 weeks. It was John Denver's first great personal success, taken from his album 'Poems, Prayers and Promises'. It sold a million by 18 August with R.I.A.A. Gold Disc award.

Denver is one of the few writers able to give country-folk a solid significance over and above the hitherto simple sing-along. 'Take Me Home Country Roads' characterized the best in contemporary folk-rock.

THE DRAMATICS (vocal quintet)

WHATCHA SEE IS WHATCHA GET *Volt [USA]*. Written by Tony Hester this was released in the U.S.A. May 1971, reaching No 9 for one week and staying 12 weeks in the Top 50.

The Dramatics were five black artists from Detroit, Willie Lee Ford, Jr, William Franklin Howard, Elbert Vernell Wilkins, Larry Demps and Ronald Banks. They began singing together from the early 1960s and were originally founded by Banks and Demps who teamed up with Ford and Lenny Mayes (who later left the group) in a Detroit high school talent show. They spent days and nights rehearsing and played every club, hall and auditorium in the Detroit area. In 1969, they signed with Stax Records, and 'Whatcha See Is Whatcha Get' was their first album from which this single was taken. The group developed into a potent touring attraction and perfected a polished performance choreography, as well as a definitive Motor City sound of their own. They subsequently played to 'standing room only' audiences across Europe and the U.S.A.

Their success was part of a boom in soul music in the U.S.A., plus the songs provided and written by their producer Tony Hester who originally approached them at the Music Hall in Detroit and asked if he could work for them.

Their first album also produced another million seller 'In the Rain' when issued as a single in 1972.

'Whatcha See Is Whatcha Get' sold a million by December 1971.

JONATHAN EDWARDS

SUNSHINE *Capricorn [USA]*. Written by Jonathan Edwards, this was released in November 1971 in the U.S.A., reaching No 3 for two weeks, and stayed in the bestsellers for 17 weeks.

Jonathan Edwards made three albums before he got his big hit.

'Sunshine' was taken from his third album, 'Jonathan Edwards' and by 17 January 1972 had sold a fast million with R.I.A.A. Gold Disc award.

EIGHTH DAY

SHE'S NOT JUST ANOTHER WOMAN *Invictus* [*USA*]. Written by C. Wilson and R. Dunbar, and released in the U.S.A. May 1971. It reached No 8 for two weeks, and stayed for 12 weeks in the Top 50.

A big success for this new group and label. The disc sold a million by 15 September 1971, with R.I.A.A. Gold Disc award. The personnel of the group is unidentified.

EMERSON, LAKE & PALMER

TARKUS (album) *Island* [*Britain*] *Cotillion* [*USA*]. Released in June 1971 in Britain, the album reached No 1, staying 10 weeks in the Top 10 and 20 in the Top 30. In the U.S.A. it reached No 9 for two weeks, and remained for 15 weeks in the Top 50.

The second tremendous album by this unique and dynamic trio, it was a bigger success both in the U.S.A. and in Britain than their first.

Contents of the album (all written by members of the group): 'Eruption'; 'Stones of Years'; 'Iconoclast'; 'Mass'; 'Manticore'; 'Battlefield'; 'Aquatarkus'; 'Jeremy Bender'; 'Bitches Crystal'; 'The Only Way'; 'Infinite Space: (Conclusion)'; 'A Time and a Place'; 'Are You Ready, Eddy?' The R.I.A.A. Gold Disc award came on 26 August 1971, with a subsequent million sale.

PICTURES AT AN EXHIBITION (album) *Island* [*Britain*] *Cotillion* [*USA*]. Released November 1971 in Britain, the album reached No 2, staying 14 weeks in the Top 30, 4 in the Top 10. Release in the U.S.A. was December 1971, going to No 10 for one week, staying in the bestsellers for 23 weeks.

This was Emerson, Lake & Palmer's version of the work by Russian composer Mussorgsky (1839–81), a live album based on the long-standing stage act. It established the group as one of the principal architects of techno-rock.

Contents of the album: 'Promenade'; 'Gnome'; 'Sage'; 'Old Castle'; 'Blues Variation'; 'Hut of Baba Yaga'; 'Promenade'; 'Curse of Baba Yaga'; 'Hut of Baba Yaga'; 'Great Gates of Kiev'; 'End'; 'Nutrocker'. R.I.A.A. Gold Disc award 17 April 1972, with a subsequent million sale.

JEREMY FAITH

JESUS *Decca* [*France*]. This religious song, originally published in France, had many recordings in Europe by various artists in Italy, Germany, Holland, Belgium, Spain, France and Britain. Its biggest success was in France, where Jeremy Faith's disc was No 2 for six weeks. Decca of France awarded a Gold Disc for million sales in April 1972.

FIVE MAN ELECTRICAL BAND

SIGNS *Lionel-MGM* [*USA*]. Written by L. Emerson, this disc was released in the U.S.A. in May 1971, reaching No 3 for one week and staying 12 weeks in the Top 50. It was yet another success for one of the smaller labels and the many independent record producers in the U.S.A. 'Signs' sold a million by 30 August 1971, with R.I.A.A. Gold Disc award.

The Five Man Electrical Band personnel is unidentified.

ARETHA FRANKLIN

BRIDGE OVER TROUBLED WATER *Atlantic* [*USA*]. Written by Paul Simon (1970), Aretha's version of this song was released in the U.S.A. in April 1971, reaching No 2 for two weeks and staying 11 weeks in the Top 50. It is a most beautiful recording of this outstanding song by 'Lady Soul'. It sold a million by 13 May 1971, with Gold Disc award by R.I.A.A. It was her tenth million seller single. The disc also received the Grammy Award for Best Rhythm-and-Blues Vocal Performance (Female) of 1971.

SPANISH HARLEM *Atlantic* [*USA*]. Written by Jerry Leiber and Phil Spector (1960), released in the U.S.A. in July 1971, this reached No 1 for a week and stayed 11 weeks in the Top 30. The British release was in September 1971, reaching No 11 for two

weeks, and lasting eight weeks in the Top 30. Originally a hit for Ben E. King (1961) this was the eleventh million-seller single for Aretha Franklin. It was awarded the R.I.A.A. Gold Disc on 26 August 1971.

ROCK STEADY *Atlantic* [*USA*]. Released in the U.S.A. 11 October 1971, this went to No 6 for two weeks and stayed in the Top 30 for 9 weeks. This 'throbbing rocker', written by Aretha, was her twelfth million-seller single, making another highly successful year for her. R.I.A.A. Gold Disc awarded 13 December 1971.

MARVIN GAYE

WHAT'S GOING ON? *Tamla* [*USA*]. Written by Marvin Gaye, Al Cleveland and Renaldo Benson, released in the U.S.A. in February 1971, this got to No 1 for 1 week, stopping for 15 weeks in the Top 50. It was released in Britain on 28 May 1971.

Taken from Marvin's song-cycle album of the same name on social issues, and issued as a single, this disc with a surging message for everyone sold a million by June 1971.

MERCY, MERCY, ME (The Ecology) *Tamla* [*USA*]. Written by Marvin Gaye, and released in the U.S.A. June 1971, this reached No 2 for 2 weeks and stayed for 11 weeks in the Top 50.

Marvin Gaye's disc describes how man is destroying his environment. It sold a reported million by August 1971. Taken from his album 'What's Going On?'

INNER CITY BLUES *Tamla* [*USA*]. This was Marvin's third big seller on social issues, a frustrating look at life and the government from the ghetto. Taken from his album 'What's Going On?' Million sale reported September 1971. This was his third million seller in a row from the same album.

Written by Marvin Gaye and James Nyx, it was released in the U.S.A. in September 1971, reaching No 6 for a week and remaining in the Top 40 for eight weeks.

DANYEL GERARD

BUTTERFLY *CBS* [*France*]. Released in March 1971, 'Butterfly', a German beer-drinking song, was a colossal success in Europe. It sold over two million in West Germany where it was No 1 for 12 weeks, and was a hit in Holland (No 1 for two weeks), Switzerland (No 1 for five weeks), Austria (No 1 for five weeks) and No 1 in France and Sweden. Other countries where it was a hit were Canada (No 1), Denmark and Spain (in the Top 10 of both countries), and Japan. The disc sold over five million collectively by November 1971 as recorded by Gerard in German, French, Dutch and Japanese, and around seven million globally by May 1972. It actually achieved Top 10 status in 30 countries with nine Gold Disc awards, and was No 1 in 15 countries.

The song is of the hand-clapping, sing-along variety, written by Danyel Gerard, with English lyrics by Howard Barnes. Danyel Gerard, born in France in 1941, is the son of an Armenian father and Italian mother. He sang in church choirs, spent much of his early life in South America, and only took up music when a musician in a Paris club taught him to play guitar. After doing National Service in the French army he began writing songs for French stars like Johnny Hallyday, Sylvie Vartan and Richard Anthony, and then decided he might as well sing his own songs himself. He became a leading French 'rock' singer/writer, then switched to non-rock numbers and wrote a big hit 'Fais la rire' for Hervé Villard. His singing with the children's choir as a youngster at Notre Dame Cathedral in Paris stood him in good stead, and he was quite successful with compositions like 'Je', 'Il pleut dans ma maison' and 'Memphis Tennessee'. 'Butterfly' is indisputedly his greatest success. Danyel has a unique studio at St-Quen-L'Aumone, 25 miles from Paris. It is a castle where he records in Japanese, German, French and English. He owns a Mystère 70 jet, a music publishing company, record company and television studio. 'Butterfly' was made at the château studio. In Britain it was No 12 and eight weeks in the bestsellers.

GRAND FUNK RAILROAD

E PLURIBUS FUNK (album) *Grand Funk Railroad* (*distributed by Capitol*) [*USA*]. Released in the U.S.A., 29 November 1971, this went to No 3 for three weeks, staying in the bestsellers for 30 weeks. It was Grand Funk's first album on their own 'honorary' label from Capitol Records. Pre-release orders for the pressing topped the $6 million mark. It was certified gold by the R.I.A.A. soon after release and went on to pass the 1,250,000 unit mark in a month finally selling over 1,500,000.

Contents: 'Footstompin' Music'; 'People Let's Stop the War'; 'Save the Land'; 'Loneliness' (duration: 8 minutes 38 secs); 'Upsetter'; 'I Come Tumblin''; 'No Lies'. All titles composed by members of the group.

AL GREEN (rhythm-and-blues vocalist)

TIRED OF BEING ALONE *Hi* [*USA*] *London* [*Britain*]. Written by Al Green, this gutsy soul number was released in July 1971 in the U.S.A., going to No 6 for one week, staying in the bestsellers for 19 weeks. In Britain it reached No 3, lasting for seven weeks in the bestsellers.

Al Green, born 13 April 1946 in Forrest City, Alabama, was brought up in Grand Rapids, Michigan, and began singing from age nine in a family gospel group, The Green Brothers - a quartet with elder brothers, Robert, William and Walter. They sang in churches throughout Michigan, Illinois, Wisconsin, Indiana and Ohio. Al became interested in popular music, and in 1964 joined The Creations, a local group, and was signed as solo artist to the Hot Line Music Journal label formed by two of its members. His first hit was 'Back Up Train' (1968) distributed by Bell Records for Hot Line. Moving on to Memphis, Al met Willie Mitchell, legendary producer for Hi Records, and after a few nondescript efforts, scored with 'I Can't Get Next to You' from his album 'Get Next To You' (1970). This album stamped him as a soul singer with strong blues influences.

Al's first major success as a writer came with 'Tired of Being Alone' which sold the million with R.I.A.A. Gold Disc award, 26 October 1971. He gradually veered towards soft, gentle ballads, and developed a style similar to Otis Redding. Under Mitchell's recording prowess, he went on to record several more million seller singles and Gold Disc albums in the ensuing years, and became a dynamic stage performer, and successful songwriter.

LET'S STAY TOGETHER *Hi* [*USA*] *London* [*Britain*]. Written by Al Green, Willie Mitchell and Al Jackson, and released in the U.S.A., November 1971, this got to No 1 for 2 weeks, staying in the bestsellers for 17 weeks. It reached No 6 for one week in Britain, staying in the bestsellers for 9 weeks.

This was a second million seller for Al Green with R.I.A.A.

Gold Disc award on 6 January 1972. Producer Mitchell, whose band provides Al's backing and MG's drummer Al Jackson who collaborated on the song, also wrote many of Al's best numbers with him.

THE GUESS WHO

BEST OF THE GUESS WHO (album) *RCA* [*USA*]. Released in the U.S.A. March 1971, this compilation reached No 11 for two weeks, staying in the bestsellers for an impressive 45 weeks.

All the hits of The Guess Who. The album was awarded a Gold Disc by the R.I.A.A. on 15 June 1971, and the million units reported by March 1973 with platinum award.

Contents of the album: (*) 'These Eyes' (Randy Bachman and Burton Cummings, 1969): (*) 'Laughing' (Randy Bachman and Burton Cummings, 1969); (*) 'No Time' (Randy Bachman and Burton Cummings, 1969); (*) 'Share the Land' (Burton Cummings, 1970); (*) 'No Sugar Tonight' (Randy Bachman, 1970); 'Hand Me Down World' (Kurt Winter, 1970); 'Undun' (Randy Bachman); 'New Mother Nature'; 'Bus Rider'; 'Do You Miss Me Darlin'?'; 'Hang on to Your Life'. Titles marked (*) were million seller singles.

HAMILTON, JOE FRANK & REYNOLDS

DON'T PULL YOUR LOVE *ABC/Dunhill* [*USA*] *Probe* [*Britain*]. Written by Dennis Lambert and Brian Potter, this was released in the U.S.A. May 1971, going to No 1 for one week and staying 12 weeks in the Top 50. It was released in Britain on 2 July 1971.

The trio was formed in 1970 when Dan Robert Hamilton, Joe Frank Carollo and Thomas Clark Reynolds left the T-Bones group. Hamilton, born in Spokane, Washington, learned to play guitar when he was 13, and at 15 played with The Ventures, Jerry Lee Lewis, Ronny and The Daytonas and many other popular bands when he had moved to Los Angeles. He formed a group, The T-Bones, with his brother, and met Joe Frank while playing a date in Birmingham, Alabama. Joe joined the group. Joe Frank, born in Leland, Mississippi, started playing drums at 13, later moving on to bass. He attended Delta State College in Mississippi, where he majored in music and history. Moving to Los Angeles around 1967 where he attended Los Angeles City College, he became involved in rock and roll. In a trip back to Birmingham he met Danny Hamilton and joined T-Bones. Reynolds, born in New York, lived in Bermuda and the Virgin Islands. He was educated at Windsor, Connecticut and New Jersey. He started a group in the U.S.A. and was probably the only rock and roll musician who knew how to play steel drums, a talent left over from his Caribbean days.

The trio left T-Bones in the hopes of broadening their musical horizons. Their wide-ranging background of musical influences produced exciting music, and resulted in 'Don't Pull Your Love' topping the charts and selling a million with R.I.A.A. Gold Disc award on 11 August 1971.

Tommy Reynolds left the group in 1972 and was replaced by Alan Dennison (born in Marion, Ohio). He plays every kind of keyboard instrument, as well as flute, congas, trumpet, baritone horn, etc. - practically a one-man band. He met Hamilton in London in February 1972 and became part of the band, working and writing together. (See Hamilton, Joe Frank & Reynolds, 1975.)

GEORGE HARRISON & FRIENDS

CONCERT FOR BANGLADESH (triple album) *Apple* [*USA*]. Released in the U.S.A. December 1971, this huge enterprise went to No 1 for 5 weeks, staying in the bestsellers for 41 weeks. In Britain it was released 10 January 1972, going to No 1 for one week and staying in the bestsellers for 13 weeks.

The benefit concert on 1 August 1971 at New York's Madison Square Garden for the United Nations Children's Fund for the refugee children of the newly established Bangladesh was probably the biggest pop musical event since the Woodstock festival. The concert was both organized and mainly dominated by former

'Beatle' George Harrison, despite the high standing of the many other artists who took part. Within a matter of days, up to 31 December 1971, the impressively packaged triple album sold globally on disc and tape, 900,000 units, and by the end of 1972 an estimated three million. The album went directly into the U.S. charts at No 5, an incredible feat, and was eagerly purchased at $12.98 (£5.50 in Britain). Capitol Records presented a certified cheque for $3,750,000 to Apple Records as an advance payment on the album's sales, and the charity received a full $5 royalty fee for each unit sold. A further sum of $243,418 came from the concert gross.

The package was accompanied by a handsome 64-page brochure, giving full details of the artists, running order, pictures, etc.

Full details of the set: Side One: This side is subtitled 'Bangla Dhun.' George Harrison introduces Ravi Shankar, who then plays a sitar and sarod duet with Ali Abkar Khan. Then comes 'Dadra Tal' featuring Alla Rakah on tabla. Finally a piece called 'Teental' featuring Kamala Chakravarty. Side Two: Three songs written and sung by George Harrison – 'Wah-Wah', 'My Sweet Lord' and 'Awaiting On You All' – are followed by Billy Preston performing 'That's The Way God Planned It'. Side Three: Ringo Starr sings 'It Don't Come Easy'. Then George Harrison and Leon Russell duet in 'Beware of Darkness'. And George handles the solo vocal in 'While My Guitar Gently Weeps' and features in a guitar duet with Eric Clapton. Side Four: The Leon Russell solo 'Jumpin' Jack Flash' is followed by 'Youngblood', in which Leon is joined by Don Preston. Then follows 'Here Comes The Sun' by George Harrison. Side Five: Five tracks by Bob Dylan, in which he is accompanied by Leon Russell, George Harrison and Ringo Starr. They are 'A Hard Rain's Gonna Fall', 'It Takes a Lot to Laugh – It Takes a Train to Cry', 'Blowin' in the Wind', 'Mr Tambourine Man' and 'Just Like a Woman'. Side Six: This consists solely of two extended George Harrison tracks. They are 'Something' and 'Bangladesh'.

R.I.A.A. awarded a Gold Disc on 4 January 1972, and Grammy Award followed for 'Album of the Year' 1972.

FREDDIE HART (country-and-western vocalist)
EASY LOVING *Capitol* [*USA*]. Written by Freddie Hart, this reached No 12 for one week in the U.S.A., staying in the bestsellers for 17 weeks. It was released in the U.S.A. in August 1971.

Freddie Hart was born in Alabama, right in the middle of country music. His career began at the age of 17 when he met and was helped by famous country artist Lefty Frizzel. Freddie worked at logging, pipelining, farming, in the steel mills, the oil fields, and as a dishwasher in New York. He worked with Lefty until 1953 when he landed a Capitol recording contract, but moved to several other labels in subsequent years, returning to Capitol in 1969.

In the 1950s, as in the 1960s, and then in the 1970s Freddie wrote music for himself and for almost every country vocalist. His song 'Loose Talk' was picked up by 50 other artists, and he had several No 1 country hits such as 'My Hangup Is You', 'Got the Allovers for You', 'Super Kind of Woman,' 'Hang in There Girl', 'If You Can Feel It It Ain't There', 'Trip to Heaven' and 'Easy Loving' which was chosen as the Country Music Association's 'Song of the Year' in both 1971 and 1972.

Freddie reached a new peak in his career through the success of 'Easy Loving' which sold the million with a Gold Disc award from R.I.A.A. on 29 November 1971. He formed his own backup band, 'Heartbeats', and apart from much touring, appeared on many national television shows as well.

Freddie owns a trucking line, raises fruit and cattle, and holds a black belt in judo. He also spends a lot of time helping underprivileged children.

ISAAC HAYES
THEME FROM 'SHAFT' *Enterprise* [*USA*] *Stax* [*Britain*]. Released U.S.A. 29 September 1971, this was written by Isaac Hayes, arranged by Isaac Hayes and Johnny Allen and produced by Isaac Hayes. It reached No 1 for two weeks in the U.S.A., staying in the bestsellers for 13 weeks. In Britain it was released in November 1971, reaching No 2 for one week and staying in the bestsellers for 12 weeks.

The outstanding and unique 'Shaft' theme from the film, taken from the soundtrack, easily passed the million and a half in the U.S.A. In Britain it sold over 250,000. It won the Oscar for Best Film Song of 1971, and Grammy Award for Best Instrumental Arrangement (Arranger's Award) 1971, also Grammy Award for Best Engineered Recording (Engineer's Award) 1971.

Personnel on the disc: Isaac Hayes (vocal/organ); Lester Snell (electric piano); James Alexander (bass guitar); Michael Toles (lead/rhythm guitar); Charles Pitts (lead/rhythm guitar); Willie Hall (drums/tambourine); Gary Jones (bongos/congos); The Memphis Strings & Horns (arranged by Isaac Hayes & Johnny Allen). (See also *Shaft* soundtrack data, 1971.)

HEDVA & DAVID
I DREAM OF NAOMI (Ari Holem Al Naomi) *RCA* [*Japan*]. Written by David Krivoshei, this was No 1 in Japan for five weeks.

It was the winner of the Grand Prix at the 1970 International Song Festival of Tokyo. Composer/singer David Krivoshei's disc with partner Hedva (both Israeli) sold close to a million by mid-October 1971, and went on to amass 1,900,000 sales in the combined English and Japanese versions. 'Ari Holem Al Naomi' is the Japanese title.

THE HILLSIDE SINGERS
I'D LIKE TO TEACH THE WORLD TO SING *Metromedia* [*USA*]. Written by Roger Cook, Roger Greenaway, B. Backer and B. Davis, this singalong anthem was released in the U.S.A. in November 1971, reaching No 10 for two weeks and staying 12 weeks in the bestsellers.

The Hillside Singers' version of this extremely popular song was released just prior to The New Seekers' version, and made exciting rivalry between the two versions. Despite a slight tracking problem, subsequently corrected, The Hillside Singers' disc sold a reported million, but it was The New Seekers' version that sold on a much bigger scale. (See New Seekers, 1971, for data on the song's origin, etc.)

HONEY CONE (female rhythm-and-blues trio)
WANT ADS *Hot Wax* [*USA*]. Written by General Johnson, G. Perry and B. Parkins, this was released in the U.S.A. in April 1971 going to No 1 for two weeks and staying in the bestsellers for 16 weeks. British release was 14 May 1971.

Honey Cone consisted of Shelly Clark, Carolyn Willis and Edna Wright from the West Coast. All had built up individual reputations as backing singers for Motown before becoming a group. 'Want Ads' was a first big hit from them, selling a million with R.I.A.A. Gold Disc award on 14 May 1971.

The trio was formed when Andy Williams and Burt Bacharach needed a back-up group for a TV special. The backing singers sang a medley of Bacharach hits, and found they got on well together. Eddie Holland of the famous Holland-Dozier-Holland team, owners of Hot Wax Records, watched the show and signed them to the new Invictus/Hot Wax company (1969). The 'Want Ads' lyrics lament the end of an affair, and describe a unique way of starting the next by an ad for a young man with 'experience in love preferred'.

STICK-UP *Hot Wax* [*USA*]. Written by General Johnson, A. Bond and G. Perry, and released in the U.S.A. in July 1971, this got to No 7 for one week, and stayed 11 weeks in the Top 50.

It was a quick follow-up success for Honey Cone, with million sale and R.I.A.A. Gold Disc award on 23 September 1971.

THE JACKSON 5
MAMA'S PEARL *Motown* [*USA*]. Written by The Corporation (1970), this outtake from the group's third album of the same

name was an almost immediate hit. Released in the U.S.A. on 7 January 1971, it went to No 1 for a week and stayed 10 weeks in the Top 50. British release was 2 April 1971 where it was No 25 The million sale was reported by mid-March 1971.

NEVER CAN SAY GOODBYE *Motown* [*USA*]. Written by Clifton Davis and released in the U.S.A. on 16 March 1971, this got to No 1 for 1 week, remaining 11 weeks in the Top 50. It was released in Britain on 2 July 1971 and got to No 33.

This melodic song registered fantastic U.S. sales in its five days of release – 1,213,000 copies – unparalleled since the heyday of The Beatles. Final estimate of sales: 2 million plus. It was the group's sixth single, sixth consecutive No 1 and sixth million seller, these discs having racked up collective sales totalling over 16 million.

MICHAEL JACKSON

GOT TO BE THERE *Motown* [*USA*]. First single and solo disc for Michael Jackson of the talented Jackson 5. The million sale was reported for the U.S.A. in early 1972, a fantastic achievement for a 12-year-old, the youngest member of the group.

Written by E. Willensky, it was released in the U.S.A. on 7 October 1971, going to No 1 for a week and staying in the bestsellers for 14 weeks. Release in Britain came on 7 January 1972, the disc rising to No 4 for three weeks, staying in the bestsellers for 11 weeks.

JETHRO TULL (vocal and instrumental rock and roll, blues and jazz quintet)

AQUALUNG (album) *Chrysalis* [*Britain*] *Reprise* [*USA*]. Jethro Tull took its name from an 18th-century agriculturist. The group comprised: Ian Anderson (born 10 August 1947) flute, guitar, keyboards, vocals; Martin Barre (born 17 November 1946) guitar, flute; John Evan (born 28 March 1948) keyboards; Jeffrey Hammond-Hammond (born 30 July 1946) bass; Clive Bunker (born 30 December 1946) drums.

The group, some of whom played in the Blackpool area, travelled to London in 1967, where Anderson met Mick Abrahams and Clive Bunker, and, with original bass player Glenn Cornick, formed Jethro Tull as a quartet in 1968. They made their first discs for Island Records (Britain) and their album 'This Was' (1968) was a surprise success. Abrahams then left the group to form Blodwyn Pig, and Martin Barre took over his place. In 1969, Jethro Tull produced the hit single 'Living in the Past' and the album 'Stand Up'. A series of sell-out concerts followed, with singles chart successes, and U.S.A. success coming quickly. Their third album 'Benefit' was not such a success, but Jethro Tull's popularity increased in the U.S.A. By the time 'Aqualung' was made, John Evan had joined the group, and Hammond-Hammond replaced Cornick who left to form Wild Turkey. 'Aqualung' was Jethro Tull's first concept album. It devoted one side entirely to Anderson's views on organized religion.

The album included: 'Aqualung'; 'Cheap Day Return'; 'Up to Me'; 'Cross-eyed Mary'; 'Wond'ring Aloud'; 'Slip Stream'; 'Mother Goose'; 'My God'; 'Hymn 43'; 'Locomotive Breath'; 'Wind-up'. It received R.I.A.A. Gold Disc award on 1 July 1971 and by April 1972 sold 1,100,000. Released in Britain in March 1971, it went to No 4 for a week, staying in the bestsellers for 15 weeks. U.S. release was in May 1971. It went to No 7 for seven weeks. It was an immediate and successful seller, staying in the U.S. Top 20 for five months.

Through 1971–72, Jethro Tull made extensive tours abroad, and by 1975 had amassed six Gold Disc awards from R.I.A.A., the other albums being 'Stand Up', 'Thick as a Brick' (1972), 'Living in the Past' (1972), 'A Passion Play' (1973) and 'Minstrel in the Gallery' (1975).

Clive Bunker left the band in 1971 and was replaced by Barrie Barlow. The band announced 'retirement' from performance in 1973, citing hostile press reaction, but made comeback tours of

Britain and U.S.A. in late 1974 – early 1975, when Jeffrey Hammond-Hammond left to be replaced by John Glascock.

ELTON JOHN

MADMAN ACROSS THE WATER (album) *DJM* [*Britain*] *Uni* [*USA*]. Released simultaneously in Britain and the U.S.A. on 5 November 1971, it reached No 8 for two weeks in the U.S.A., staying in the bestsellers for 51 weeks.

Even up to end of 1975, this album was still one of Elton John's most consistent sellers. It was awarded a Gold Disc by the R.I.A.A. on 19 February 1972, and by the end of that year received a platinum award for million sales. The album also marked the end of what Elton called his 'strings period', and by the close of 1971 he embarked on a new phase of his career and subsequently became a superstar. Davey Johnstone (guitar) played at the recording sessions on this album, which contained: 'Tiny Dancer'; 'Levon'; 'Razor Face'; 'Madman Across the Water'; 'Indian Sunset'; 'Holiday Inn'; 'Rotten Peaches'; 'All the Nasties'; 'Goodbye'. All material written and composed by Bernie Taupin and Elton John.

Global sales estimated at two million.

ROBERT JOHN

THE LION SLEEPS TONIGHT *Atlantic* [*USA*]. An adaptation of the South African (Zulu) song 'Mbube' by Hugo Peretti, Luigi Creatore, George Weiss and Albert Stanton in 1961, this version was released in the U.S.A. in December 1971. It reached No 2 for two weeks in the U.S., staying in the bestsellers for 17 weeks.

The first recorded version of this song was made in South Africa in the 1930s by Solomon Linda. The first adaptation, titled 'Wimoweh', was by Paul Campbell (collective pseudonym for The Weavers who had a bestseller with it in 1951).

Robert John, born 1946, a graduate of Erasmus High School, Brooklyn, N.Y., started writing songs as a youngster. He first appeared on 'American Bandstand' in 1958, and has made numerous TV and radio appearances. First single 'If You Don't Want My Love' (Columbia, 1968) was quite a success. 'The Lion Sleeps Tonight' gave him prominence, the disc selling the million with R.I.A.A. Gold Disc award on 15 March 1972. (See also The Tokens, 1961).

TOM JONES

SHE'S A LADY *Parrot* [*USA*]. A striking ballad by famous disc artist Paul Anka, gave Tom Jones another million seller with R.I.A.A. Gold Disc award on 25 March 1971. It was released in the U.S.A. in January 1971, going to No 1 for a week and staying in the bestsellers for 13 weeks. In Britain it rose to No 10 and loitered in the bestsellers for eight weeks.

CAROLE KING (vocalist/pianist)

TAPESTRY (album) *Ode* [*USA*] *A & M* [*Britain*]. Released in March 1971 in the U.S.A. 'Tapestry' went to No 1 for 15 weeks staying in the bestsellers for an amazing 292 weeks. In Britain it was released in May 1971, going to No 1 for a week but staying in the charts for 87 weeks.

Carole King (née Klein), born 9 February 1942 in New York City, epitomizes 'The Great American Dream' from a musical standpoint. Her prowess as a popular songwriter is indisputable, and the hits she has composed since the early 1960s for a great many famous singers are legion. Carole first displayed her musical talents at the age of four when in her Brooklyn home she began singing and taking piano lessons from her mother. At 14, she formed a high school vocal quartet called The Co-sines and wrote music for them. Later (1958), at Queen's College, New York she met Gerry Goffin whom she later married. Gerry also proved to be the ideal partner for her in songwriting. In the late 1950s Carole was cutting demo discs with Paul Simon and, through this, the duo were later contracted to New York's top publisher, managers and record producers Al Nevins and Don

Kirschner who had put their first names together to form Aldon Music, eventually affiliated to Columbia Pictures-Screen Gems Music. Gerry at this time was working as a chemist.

Goffin and King's first big hit was 'Will You Love Me Tomorrow?' (1960) for the Shirelles. Thereafter they wrote hit after hit, their success being unparalleled. Their amazing list of rock'n'roll hits included 'Up on the Roof', 'The Loco-Motion', 'Chains', 'When My Little Girl Is Smiling', 'Take Good Care of My Baby', 'Go Away Little Girl', 'I'm into Something Good', 'Pleasant Valley Sunday', 'Run to Him', 'It Might as Well Rain until September' (Carole's first solo hit, 1962), also 'A Natural Woman'.

During the mid-1960s when British artists predominated in the international charts, the duo did not write much, but (1966) formed the Tomorrow label which was not a success. By 1968, Carole found it hard to maintain a marriage writing together and moved to Los Angeles 'to get together a new identity'. She separated from Goffin, and Lou Adler of Ode Records persuaded her to take up a solo career. She formed a group, The City, which included Charles Larkey (bass) whom she later married. Their one and only 'The City' (1968) became a collector's item.

Carole's next solo venture came in 1970 with the album 'Writer' which brought impressive acclaim and renewed interest in her. Lou Adler's Ode Records thus built up Carole to a peak with her third album 'Tapestry' which became one of the record industry's biggest sellers, and biggest selling record by a female artist. By the end of 1973 it sold 12 million globally, with over half this amount in the U.S.A. while sales still continued into the mid-1970s. 'Tapestry' was awarded the first gold tape cartridge (1971), the Grammy Award for Album of the Year (1971) and Grammy Award for Best Pop Vocal Performance (Female) 1971. Carole also received two other Grammy Awards of 1971 (see 'It's Too Late', 1971). R.I.A.A. Gold Disc award came on 7 June 1971.

Contents: 'I Feel the Earth Move'; 'So Far Away'; 'Home Again'; 'Beautiful'; 'Way Over Yonder'; 'You've Got a Friend'; 'Where You Lead'; 'Tapestry'; 'Will You Love Me Tomorrow?' (Gerry Goffin and Carole King, 1960); 'Smackwater Jack' (Gerry Goffin and Carole King); 'It's Too Late' (Toni Stern and Carole King); 'A Natural Woman (You make me feel like)' (Gerry Goffin, Jerry Wexler and Carole King). All songs by Carole King unless otherwise indicated.

IT'S TOO LATE *Ode* [*USA*]. Written by Toni Stern and Carole King, this single was released in the U.S.A. in May 1971, hitting No 1 for five weeks, and staying in the charts 17 weeks. In Britain it went to No 5 for two weeks, staying in the bestsellers for 9 weeks.

A sensitive ballad with a strong rock under-beat, taken from her sensationally successful album 'Tapestry', issued as a single with quick million sale and R.I.A.A. Gold Disc award on 21 July 1971. It also received the Grammy Award for Record of the Year, 1971. Carole also received a Grammy Award for Song of the Year, 1971 – 'You've Got a Friend' – from 'Tapestry' album, a big hit for her friend James Taylor (*q.v.*).

CAROLE KING MUSIC (album) *Ode* [*USA*] *A & M* [*Britain*]. Released early in December 1971 in the U.S.A. this album went to No 1 for three weeks, staying in the charts for 44 weeks. Released in Britain on 20 December 1971 it reached No 12 for one week, staying in the charts for 11 weeks.

The follow-up album to Carole King's gigantic 'Tapestry' seemed rather an anti-climax. Nevertheless it sold 1,300,000 on the day of release with instant Gold Disc award by R.I.A.A. 9 December 1971 and qualifying for a platinum award for million units sale. Final estimate was over two million. Featured musicians on the album include James Taylor and Danny Kortchmar, both of whom play guitar. Contents, all of which Carole again had a hand in writing, were: 'Brother Brother'; 'It's Going to Take Some Time' (Toni Stern and Carole King); 'Sweet Season' (Toni Stern and Carole King); 'Some Kind-a Wonderful' (Gerry

Goffin and Carole King, 1961); 'Surely'; 'Carry Your Load'; 'Song of Long Ago'; 'Brighter'; 'Growing Away from Me'; 'Too Much Rain' (Toni Stern and Carole King); 'Back to California'. All songs by Carole King unless otherwise indicated.

Carole visited Britain in 1972 for two weeks of concerts.

JEAN KNIGHT

MR BIG STUFF *Stax* [*USA*]. Written by Joe Broussard, Ralph Williams and Carroll Washington, this was released in the U.S.A. in May 1971, going to No 1 for one week and staying in the charts for 16 weeks.

This disc was made by Malaco Productions in their studios at Jackson, Mississippi. The musicians accompanying Jean Knight were Wardell Quezerque (piano/organ), James Carey Stroud (drums/percussion), Jerry Puckett (guitar) and William Laverne Robbins (bass). Wardell Quezerque produced and arranged.

The disc was a big seller, two million sold by the end of August 1971. It was Jean's first record. She was born 26 June 1943 in New Orleans.

DENIS LA-SALLE

TRAPPED BY A THING CALLED LOVE *Westbound* [*USA*]. Written by Denis La-Salle, released in the U.S.A. in August 1971, this went to No 9 for two weeks, remaining in the charts for 10 weeks. Westbound were another small label with a big hit by newcomer Denis La-Salle. R.I.A.A. Gold Disc award on 30 November 1971 for million sale.

LED ZEPPELIN

LED ZEPPELIN IV (Runes) (album) *Atlantic* [*USA*]. Released simultaneously on 8 November 1971 in Britain and the U.S.A., this album reached No 1 in both Britain and the U.S.A. for two weeks, staying 151 weeks in the U.S.A. charts but only 23 weeks in Britain's bestsellers.

Another stupendous album for Led Zeppelin, and a guaranteed million seller before its release. With its unusual title of four rune-like symbols, advance orders for the album and tapes totalled over $1 million. R.I.A.A. Gold Disc award was almost immediate, certification made on 16 November 1971. With an almost three-year run in the U.S.A. bestsellers plus sales elsewhere, it is estimated the album sold over three million by 1974.

This album consolidated the group's expanding maturity. Although it followed their familiar style of rock songs such as 'Rock and Roll' and 'Black Dog', it also contained subtle material like 'Stairway to Heaven', one of their finest and most popular numbers.

1971 was the year in which Led Zeppelin fever gripped Britain, resulting in huge demands for tickets for their concerts at the Empire Pool, Wembley, London and around the country. They returned to the U.S.A. in 1972.

'Led Zeppelin IV' was recorded nine months before it was released, the album tapes having been taken to the U.S.A. for the final mixing.

Contents of the album: 'Black Dog' (Jimmy Page, Robert Plant and John Paul Jones); 'Rock and Roll' (Robert Plant, Jimmy Page, John Paul Jones and John Bonham); 'The Battle of Evermore'; 'Stairway to Heaven'; 'Misty Mountain Hop' (Jimmy Page, Robert Plant and John Paul Jones); 'Four Sticks'; 'Going to California'; 'When the Levee Breaks' (Jimmy Page, Robert Plant, John Paul Jones and John Bonham). Songs showing no author are by Jimmy Page and Robert Plant.

JOHN LENNON & THE PLASTIC ONO BAND

IMAGINE (album) *Apple* [*USA & Britain*]. Released in the U.S.A. in September 1971 and Britain in October 1971, this went to No 1 for three weeks in both countries. It stayed in the U.S. charts for 30 weeks and in the British charts for 57 weeks (18 weeks in the Top 10).

This was John Lennon's fifth solo album and probably his best. It took less than a month to receive certification by the

R.I.A.A. Gold Disc was awarded on 1 October 1971, and the album had a million plus sale subsequently. This is a superb and beautiful album. The title track is outstanding and considered to be Lennon's most distinctive composition since the dissolution of The Beatles. All the songs have melody, class and sensitivity, and are beautifully structured.

Contents of the album: 'Imagine'; 'Crippled Inside'; 'Jealous Guy'; 'It's so Hard'; 'I Don't Want To Be a Soldier'; 'Give Me Some Truth'; 'Oh My Love'; 'How Do You Sleep?' (duration 5 mins 35 secs.); 'How?'; 'Oh Yoko'. All songs by John Lennon.

POWER TO THE PEOPLE *Apple* [*USA & Britain*]. Written by John Lennon, this record was released simultaneously in Britain and the U.S.A. in March 1971. It went to No 11 in the U.S.A. for two weeks, staying nine weeks in the Top 40, and to No 6 for one week in Britain, staying 6 weeks in the charts.

The disc's lyric line is basically a hand-clapping incantation of the title repeated over and over by a mass of voices, with a honky-tonk sax of the 1950s' rock style in the background. Like Lennon's 'Give Peace a Chance', it is a 'street' song, with atmospheric rock and roll rawness, recreated by Phil Spector who assisted production.

The million sale is an estimated global one.

LOBO

ME AND YOU AND A DOG NAMED BOO *Big Tree* [*USA*] *Philips* [*Britain*]. Written by Kent Lavoie, this was released in the U.S.A. in March 1971, and in Britain in May 1971. It went to No 5 for two weeks in the U.S.A., staying 11 weeks in the Top 50, and to No 4 for one week in Britain, also staying 11 weeks in the charts.

Lobo (real name Kent Lavoie) was born in Tallahasee, Florida, in 1944 of French/Indian parentage. He plays guitar, organ and piano. His early training on guitar, given to him during his early teens, came into use while he was at college. He became a professional singer-guitarist with beer-bar bands when he was working his way through Florida colleges. After marriage, he settled in the Tampa/St Petersburg/Clearwater Beach area, and continued to earn a living from long-term engagements at local nightclubs. In one of these clubs in Tampa, he met Phil Gernhard (producer of 'Stay' by Maurice Williams & The Zodiaks, 'Snoopy and the Red Baron' by The Royal Guardsmen and Dion's 'Abraham, Martin and John') who signed him up. Lobo spent three years writing songs in between working, some of which were local releases cut in an Atlanta, Georgia, studio before showing Gernhard 'A Dog Named Boo'. A master was cut and a contract made with Big Tree Records in New York, a label which was eventually distributed by Bell Records.

The success of this disc firmly established Lobo as both artist and songwriter, resulting in TV, concert appearances and touring with his group in the U.S.A. and abroad. The million sale of the disc was reported in September 1971.

Lobo chose the name for his billing so that if the record had flopped he could start afresh without detriment to his real name. The name Lobo means 'wolf' in Spanish, and symbolized the image of being a loner, a lone wolf. He became a successful writer of radio/TV jingles, preparing audition tapes on his home-based four-track studio.

LOS POP TOPS (vocal septet)

MAMMY BLUE *Explosion* [*Spain*]. This song was a great achievement for French songwriter Hubert Giraud (born 1927) whose musical career included playing harmonica with Django Reinhardt, and writing several hit songs. Giraud had sent a demo record of the tune to French publisher Claude Pascal. It stayed on the shelf for four months. An Italian impresario then used it as the debut recording for 16-year-old singer Ivana Spagna. This recording, in Italian on the Ricordi label, is the first commercial version of the song.

At the end of May 1971, Alain Milhaud, a French producer based in Spain, picked up the song for his group, Los Pop Tops,

and Pascal began to realise the international potential of the song. Los Pop Tops recorded it in London, with an English lyric by their lead singer, West Indian Phil Tris. Giraud was invited over for the recording, and when Pascal heard the version he restricted use of the song so as to arrange versions by other big name artists in various countries, agreeing however to give Milhaud a few days priority in each country before local versions were released. Barclay Records in France picked up the song for Joel Dayde (in English), Ricoletta (in French) and Milhaud licensed the Los Pop Tops version to Claude Carrere. France became 'Mammy Blue' crazy with all three versions at one time tying for first place. Orchestral versions by Paul Mauriat, Franck Pourcel, Raymond LeFevre, Georges Jouvin and Caravelli followed in rapid succession. With versions of the song all over Europe (more than 270 by January 1972), it became a valuable copyright. The Los Pop Tops recording (released June 1971 in Spain) was a hit in Belgium, Eire, Greece, Holland, Italy, Norway, Portugal (where Los Pop Tops recorded the song in Italian and Spanish) and Switzerland. It made the Top 50 in England, and was a success in West Germany (No 1). In the U.S.A. it got into the Top 100, but there were too many cover versions of the song for it to be a big hit there. A version by Ricky Shayne sold over 100,000 in Japan, and was also No 1 in Brazil. The exact sales figure of Los Pop Tops' version is not known, but its success all over Europe made an estimated million-plus.

'Mammy Blue' is based on a simple four-bar theme - a theme with a 'hook' which proved irresistible to everyone. The song was conceived amid the clamour and chaos of a Paris traffic jam.

PAUL McCARTNEY

ANOTHER DAY *Apple* [*Britain*]. Written by Paul and Linda McCartney, 'Another Day' went to No 1 for 1 week in Britain after its release in February 1971 in both Britain and the U.S.A. In the U.S.A. it hit No 5 for two weeks, staying 11 weeks in the Top 50. In Britain it stayed 10 weeks in the Top 30.

First hit single disc by Paul McCartney after he left The Beatles. It was co-written with his wife Linda, and is the story of a lonely girl waiting in her room for her lover to arrive (presumably because he's a married man). A wistful song with a bouncy beat, it typifies so many of Paul's songs. The disc is largely dual-tracked by Paul with a pungent acoustic guitar sound giving depth to the backing.

Sales in Britain, the U.S.A. and elsewhere made it an estimated million sale, reached on 21 September 1971 with Gold Disc.

PAUL & LINDA McCARTNEY

UNCLE ALBERT/ADMIRAL HALSEY *Apple* [*USA*]. Culled from the McCartneys' album 'Ram', this is a busy disc with everything happening and numerous key changes. It commences with a thunderstorm, then telephone warbles and a furious trumpet finale, and is a 'Noel Coward impression'. Written by Paul and Linda McCartney, it went to No 1 in the U.S.A. for a week, staying 12 weeks in the Top 30. It was released there in August 1971. The million sale was reached on 21 September 1971 with Gold Disc R.I.A.A. award. Paul McCartney also received a Grammy Award for Best Arrangement Accompanying Vocalist(s) – an Arranger's Award – for 1971.

RAM (album) *Apple* [*USA & Britain*]. Simultaneously released in the U.S.A. and Britain on 21 May 1971, the album hit No 2 in the U.S.A. for two weeks and No 1 in Britain for three weeks, staying for 37 weeks in the U.S. bestsellers and 24 in the British charts.

It was Paul McCartney's second album after leaving The Beatles, co-written and co-produced by Paul and his wife Linda, and for the most part was recorded in the winter of 1970 in New York and Los Angeles. Linda is featured vocally on all the tracks with Paul, and she also took all the photographs for the sleeve, designed by Paul. A section of the New York Philharmonic Orchestra is featured on 'Uncle Albert/Admiral Halsey', 'Long Haired Lady' and 'The Back Seat of My Car'. Other musicians used on the sessions were Denny Seiwell (drums), Dave Spinoza (guitar) and Hugh McCracken (guitar). 'Ram' is basically a 'country' Paul, obviously influenced by his Scottish hideaway and domestic happiness. It showcases his many talents – the rocking Paul, the country Paul, the ballad Paul, the blues Paul and the humorous Paul. On release, the reaction was somewhat critical – 'a mixed bag of psychedelic liquorice allsorts', was the way one critic described it. Nevertheless it was a big seller and received R.I.A.A. Gold Disc award on 9 June 1971 and subsequently passed the million sale.

Contents: 'Too Many People'; '3 Legs'; 'Ram On'; 'Dear Boy'; 'Uncle Albert/Admiral Halsey'; 'Smile Away'; 'Heart of the Country'; 'Monkberry Moon Delight'; 'Eat at Home'; 'Long Haired Lady'; 'Ram On': (reprise); 'The Back Seat of My Car'. All songs by Paul McCartney, Linda assisting on 'Dear Boy', 'Uncle Albert', 'Heart of the Country', 'Monkberry Moon Delight' and 'Eat at Home'.

DON McLEAN

AMERICAN PIE *United Artists* [*USA*]. Written by Don McLean, released in the U.S.A. in November 1971 and January 1972 in Britain, this went to No 1 in both countries, staying for five weeks in the U.S.A. and one week in Britain. It stayed in the U.S.A. bestsellers for 19 weeks and 16 weeks in the British charts.

Don McLean, born 12 October 1947, drifted in to the coffeehouse circuit when he left high school in 1964, his first engagement being at the Bitter End. In 1968 he signed on with the New York State Government to tour the Hudson River valley communities. He played in river communities, three a day for a month or more, the state paying him $200 per week. At the time, folk singer Pete Seeger was planning a project to save the Hudson River by sailing a boat down the river, carrying ecological messages to the towns McLean had been visiting. McLean joined the crew, which included Ramblin' Jack Elliott and Lou Killen, so he was in musical company. He started writing songs. His first album 'Tapestry', put out by Media Arts, was released in October 1970 (now United Artists). Then came the album 'American Pie' (1971). An edited version of his eight-and-a-half minute epic of the same title was taken from this, and the 'potted history of rock' became a fantastic success. 'American Pie' was Don's attempt to use all the metaphors he could to describe a certain loss that he felt in American music, Buddy Holly's death in 1959 being symbolic to him. He jammed 10 years of experience into 'American Pie'. The single sold over the million and was awarded a Gold Disc by R.I.A.A. on 3 January 1972. It was also a big hit in England where it sold over 250,000. The success of the disc and the album completely changed Don's life. He had formerly travelled over most of Canada and the U.S.A. and built up a select number of fans. 'American Pie' brought him large audiences at big venues where he topped the bill.

AMERICAN PIE (album) *United Artists* [*USA*]. Released in the U.S.A. in November 1971 and Britain in February 1972, the album hit No 1 in both countries for nine weeks in the U.S.A. and three weeks in Britain. It stayed for 48 weeks in the U.S. bestsellers and 38 weeks in Britain's charts. Both the album and the single were released in the U.S.A. at the same time, and both were at one time, in early 1972, simultaneously at the No 1 chart position for 3 weeks. The album's chart duration of almost a year plus its extraordinary popularity in both Britain and the U.S.A. made it a certain million seller. R.I.A.A. Gold Disc award came on 3 January 1972. All the songs were written by Don, and a second song from the album, 'Vincent', also sold over 250,000 in Britain as a single (three weeks at No 1). The album included: 'American Pie'; 'Vincent'; 'Winterwood'; 'Till Tomorrow'; 'Crossroads'; 'Empty Chairs'; 'Sister Fatima'; 'Babylon'; 'Everybody Loves Me Baby'.

Don McLean's 'American Pie' had the rock world completely baffled, and caused endless discussion. He consistently refused to give any interpretation of the songs.

MELANIE

BRAND NEW KEY *Neighborhood* [*USA*] *Buddah* [*Britain*]. Written by Melanie Safka. Released in the U.S.A. in October 1971, and Britain in December 1971, this went to No 1 for three weeks in the U.S.A. and No 3 for one week in Britain. It stayed for 18 weeks in the U.S. charts and 10 weeks in Britain.

Melanie Safka, born 3 February 1947 in New York City, is of Ukrainian/Italian parentage. Her mother was a jazz singer, and her father ran a chain of discount stores. Melanie played guitar when quite young. The family moved to New Jersey where Melanie attended high school, but she ran away to Los Angeles for a while until her father took her home. She returned to school and left at the age of 19, with a degree from the American Academy of Dramatic Art which she attended for two years, deciding to sing for a living. Arriving in New York she sang and played guitar in city bars for six months. Offered an audition for a small part in a play, she walked into the wrong office - to find herself facing record producer Peter Scherkeryk. He asked her to play and eventually encouraged her to move on to Buddah Records after Columbia would not let her record an album. With Buddah she had all her success.

Scherkeryk became her manager and her husband. From 1969 Melanie recorded several albums for Buddah - 'Born to Be' (1969); 'Affectionately Melanie' (1969); 'Candles in the Rain' (1970); 'Leftover Wine' (1970); 'All the Right Noises' (soundtrack) (1971); 'Good Book' (1971); 'Four Sides of Melanie' (1971); 'Garden in the City' (1972). She had singles hits with 'Ruby Tuesday' and 'What Have They Done to My Song, Ma?'. In 1972 she formed her own record label, Neighborhood Records, and her 'Gather Me' album was released in October; also the single from it, 'Brand New Key'. Both were big successes, both the album and the single receiving R.I.A.A. Gold Disc award for million sale on 16 December 1971. It sold over 250,000 in Britain and 2,500,000 globally by July 1972.

Melanie's other albums for Neighborhood were 'Stoneground Words' (1972), 'At Carnegie Hall' (1973) and 'Madrugada' (1974). Buddah released 'Please Love Me' in 1973. All her albums had good sales on both sides of the Atlantic.

'Brand New Key' is described as 'a highly refreshing and innocently delivered tune with much lyrical meaning, and an engaging ode to the joys of skating and generally riding around'. Melanie actually started writing songs at school when she was 15. Many of her songs are simple, covering a wide range of emotions and situations. They have a constantly recurring theme

- that cities stifle people and create sadness - and that people should return to the countryside to a simple uncomplicated way of life.

She gave annual birthday concerts in New York for her devoted fans.

MIDDLE OF THE ROAD (pop quartet)

CHIRPY, CHIRPY, CHEEP CHEEP *RCA* [*Italy*]. Written by Lally Stott. Released in Britain on 15 January 1971, where it went to No 1 for 5 weeks, and stayed in the bestseller charts for 34 weeks.

The group consists of Glaswegian brothers Eric and Ian Campbell Lewis (born 17 June 1949 and 15 July 1947 respectively), Ken (Ballantyne) Andrew (born 28 August 1946) and Sally (Sarah) Carr (born 28 March 1949). Eric played bass and piano, Ian guitars, flute, and bagpipes, Ken was on drums, piano, organ and vibes and Sally on percussion and vocals.

They were originally an amateur group in Glasgow called Part Four. They changed their name to Los Caracos to feature Latin American music as their speciality, always playing in Scotland near their jobs during the day. On 1 April 1970 they turned professional, and again changed their name, this time to Middle of the Road as it typified the music they played. The group arrived in Italy via a stint on the boats, and roughed it for a while as they were virtually penniless. They subsequently worked in Italian clubs and while in Rome were heard by RCA producer Giacomo Tosti. He got them to cut a demo disc of 'Chirpy, Chirpy, Cheep Cheep' which Liverpool composer Lally Stott had first recorded himself for the Italian market. Tosti decided this was the right song for Middle of the Road. It was actually released in Italy in October 1970, and was first a hit in Belgium, sweeping up all the European charts. In Britain it was a slow starter, but by June began to swiftly rise in the charts. By mid-August British sales were over 500,000, German over a million, Belgian 175,000 and other European sales made a total of over four million. The song became a hit in no fewer than 20 countries, the final tally being an estimated 10 million sales. Lally Stott is said to have netted over £100,000 from the song. Middle of the Road rose from virtual obscurity to international stars in less than a year through the song's success. Apart from its fantastic success in Belgium, Holland, Spain, Italy, Germany, Ireland and Sweden, it was a hit in Australia, Mexico and Argentina. Strangely, however, it did not register in the U.S.A.

'Chirpy, Chirpy' is an infectious and catchy little tune, its carefree appeal making it an obvious winner.

TWEEDLE DEE TWEEDLE DUM *RCA* [*Italy*]. Written by Lally Stott and 'Cassio' (Giosy and Maria Capuano), this was released in Britain on 27 August 1971, reaching No 2 for one week and staying in the charts for 12 weeks.

'Tweedle Dee' is an Italian melody with lyrics by Lally Stott, who wrote the group's big hit 'Chirpy, Chirpy'. Its story is about a clan feud between the McDougalls and the McGregors, an apt choice of material for the Scottish quartet. The recording was made in Rome under the same producer, Giacomo Tosti.

The disc was a hit in Denmark, Italy and Sweden before its

release in Britain. This follow-up hit was also a success and sold an estimated two million or more by the end of 1971.

SOLEY SOLEY *RCA* [*Italy*]. Written by Fernando Arbex, this was released in Britain on 26 November 1971 going to No 2 for a week, and staying in the charts for 12 weeks.

This happy simple pop song has a 'summer sound' and was the third big hit for Middle of the Road. Production again by Giacomo Tosti, and arrangers Giosy and Maria Capuano. Composer Arbex is Spanish.

The disc sold over 250,000 in Britain, and with sales in other countries it soon passed the million sale. It was particularly successful in South Africa, where it was No 1.

By early 1972, Middle of the Road with sales of over five million discs emerged as one of the bestselling aggregates in he world. Their discs were also big hits in several Latin-American countries.

YUKO NAGISA

KYOTO BOJYO (Kyoto Boy) *Toshiba* [*Japan*]. Second million seller for Yuko, a follow-up disc that was bigger than her previous hit 'Kyoto Doll'. It was composed by the American group The Ventures, who wrote her first hit.

TERRY NELSON

BATTLE HYMN OF LIEUTENANT CALLEY *Plantation* [*USA*]. Written by Julian Wilson, James M. Smith and Terry Nelson, this was released in the U.S.A. in March 1971, going to No 11 for one week and staying in the bestsellers for six weeks.

The recording of this was lying around the racks - mostly in the southern areas of America - from the time Lt William L. Calley Jr's court martial started in December 1970. It suddenly emerged as one of the hottest selling discs in recent years, following his conviction at the end of March 1971 for premeditated murder of at least 22 South Vietnamese civilians at Mylai in 1968. It was released 10 days prior to the Calley verdict (30 March) although it had been written several months before its release. It would have been a failure saleswise had Calley been acquitted. It sold 250,000 immediately and passed the million sale in just four days with R.I.A.A. Gold Disc award on 15 April 1971.

The impact of the disc was startling, with tremendous reaction to the lyrics, which stated in part: 'even though they made me out a villain, my truth was marching on ... when the smoke had cleared away 100 souls were dead ... but I tried to do my duty ... my truth was marching on'. American protestation of the verdict was immense.

The song, with music from the famous 'Battle Hymn of the Republic', was written by three people who never had anything to do with the music business before. They were engineer Julian Wilson and attorney James M. Smith, from Sheffield, Alabama, and the singer and disc jockey Terry Nelson from Russellville, Alabama. The disc was recorded in Muscle Shoals, Alabama. Some disc companies would not market their versions owing to the violent pros and cons, and some were not willing to glorify or vilify Calley in any form.

Twenty-seven-year-old Terry Nelson's hit - nearly two million sold - indicated that the public had accepted the 'Battle Hymn of Lt Calley' as a folksong of the 1970s.

THE NEW SEEKERS
(instrumental and vocal quintet)

I'D LIKE TO TEACH THE WORLD TO SING *Polydor* [*Britain*] *Elektra* [*USA*]. Written by Roger Cook, Roger Greenaway, B. Backer and B. Davis, this was released in the U.S.A. in November 1971 and Britain on 3 December 1971, going to No 7 for two weeks in the U.S.A. and No 1 for four weeks in Britain. It stayed for 12 weeks in the U.S. charts and 20 weeks in the British bestsellers.

This song originally started out under the title 'True Love and Apple Pie' by Cook and Greenaway. New words and musical

Song'. Success in Britain followed. In May 1971 they topped the bill at the London Palladium with their highly polished act that included singing, comedy, acting and dancing. Their performance resulted in unanimous raves from the critics and 'Seeker Fever' everywhere. A major concert tour of Britain featuring their own two-hour show was a complete sell-out. They were soon after chosen to sing before Queen Elizabeth II at the 1971 Royal Command Performance at the London Palladium.

Then came 'I'd Like to Teach the World to Sing' and their selection to represent Britain in the 1972 Eurovision Song Contest. They became one of the top sources of entertainment, earning an international reputation, appearing on television everywhere including the Andy Williams and Ed Sullivan shows in the U.S.A. and every major variety programme in Britain.

The New Seekers gave a farewell concert tour of Britain, completed by May 1974, and then split up. Up to that time they had sold an estimated 25 million records around the world.

NILSSON
WITHOUT YOU *RCA* [*USA*]. Written by Tom Evans and Peter Ham, this was released in the U.S.A. in December 1971 and in Britain on 14 January 1972. It went to No 1 in both countries, for four weeks in the U.S.A. and six weeks in Britain. It stayed for 28 weeks in the bestsellers in the U.S.A. and Britain.

Harry Edward Nilsson was born in the tough Brooklyn district of New York. When he was 12, the family moved to California where Harry began to take interest in rock music. He worked for the Security First National Bank there as a supervisor in the computer centre for seven years. During this time he wrote songs, taught himself the piano, and peddled demos round the music publishers of Los Angeles. He got his first break in music from producer Phil Spector who liked some of his songs and used two for The Ronettes and one for The Modern Folk Quartet. Nilsson left his bank job (1967) after hearing one of his songs, 'Cuddly Toy' sung by The Monkees, over the radio. He signed a contract with RCA (1967) – as an artist – and recorded his first album 'Pandemonium Shadow Show' (1968), then 'Aerial Ballet' (1968) – a title he took from the name of his grandparents' circus act, and 'Harry' (1969). His first album featured six of his own songs and one track fusing 11 Beatles' songs. The second featured Fred Neil's song 'Everybody's Talkin'' which was used in the soundtrack of the film *Midnight Cowboy*. Both albums were acknowledged, with high regard, by The Beatles. Subsequent albums were 'Nilsson sings Newman' (1970), 'The Point' (music for cartoon film, 1971), and 'Nilsson Schmilsson' (1971) which included his big hit 'Without You'. This album was recorded in London, and 'Without You' was written by two members of Badfinger, the English group signed to The Beatles' Apple organization. Further albums were 'Son of Schmilsson' (1972) 'Aerial Pandemonium Ballet' (1973), 'A Little Touch of Schmilsson in the Night' (1973) and the John Lennon-produced 'Pussy Cats' (1974).

Nilsson's song 'One' was a million seller for Three Dog Night in 1969. He also composed the score for the film *Skidoo*, and theme songs for U.S. TV. Many of his songs were recorded by prominent artists. He made a two-month promotional tour in Europe in 1968, and spent much of his time later in England where he recorded at the Trident Studios in London's Soho with some of the best session musicians under producer Richard Perry.

'Without You' sold over 400,000 in Britain (with Silver Disc award) and over the million in the U.S.A. where he received Gold Disc award from R.I.A.A. on 3 March 1972. Nilsson also received a Grammy Award for Best Male Pop, Rock & Vocal Performance (1972) with the song.

OCEAN (vocal quintet)
PUT YOUR HAND IN THE HAND OF THE MAN FROM GALILEE *Kama Sutra* [*USA*]. Written by Gene McLellan, this was released in the U.S.A. in March 1971, going to No 2 for three weeks and staying 13 weeks in the Top 50.

score were adapted from it for a Coca-Cola commercial with the collaboration of American writers Backer and Davis. It was popular on both sides of the Atlantic and was released as a single by public demand with slight alteration of the words. The original Coca-Cola version was recorded almost 12 months previously, and the modestly-converted commercial became a chart-topping spectacular in every part of the globe. It became Britain's greatest hit of 1972 and was the only disc there to sell over a million copies for three years, with a Gold Disc award. Despite strong competition in the U.S.A. at the same time as The Hillside Singers' version was released (see Hillside Singers, 1971) it sold over 1,500,000 with Gold Disc award by R.I.A.A. on 27 January 1972. World sales by July 1972 were four million and said to be six million by 1974.

The New Seekers are Eve Graham (vocalist), born 19 April 1943 in Perth, Scotland. Formerly a hairdresser, then solo singer with groups for 10 years and featured singer with the Cyril Stapleton Band; Lyn Paul (vocalist) born 16 February 1949 in Manchester. Also a dancer and comedienne and with own vocal trio; Peter Doyle (vocals and guitar) born 28 July 1949 in Melbourne, Australia. Formerly a child star in Australia, became member of a top Australian group, and also a talented songwriter. Paul Layton (vocals and bass guitar) born 4 August 1947 in Beaconsfield, Buckinghamshire. Originally a successful child actor in films, TV and stage, decided on music as a career when he was 18; Marty Kristian (vocals, guitar, banjo, harmonica) born 27 May 1947 in Leipzig, Germany. Son of Latvian parents who went to Australia when he was two. Studied as an architect, and at 18 started playing rock and roll. A trip to Europe resulted in an immediate audition for the musical *Hair*. The group was formed in 1969 by Keith Potger, a member of the original Seekers, 'to take up where the other group left off'. They gradually changed the folksy image of the original Seekers and developed a more contemporary sound that brought them world acclaim. This commenced in the U.S.A. right from the start where they had three big hits in quick succession – 'Look What They've Done to My Song, Ma', 'Beautiful People', and 'Nickel

An exceedingly attractive, melodic song in the 'pop gospel' vein, written by the composer of the equally popular 'Snowbird'. It sold the million by 3 May 1971 with Gold Disc award from R.I.A.A.

Ocean are a Canadian group (personnel so far unidentified). The song won a Grammy Award for black artist Shirley Caesar for Best Soul Gospel Performance of 1971.

THE OSMONDS (vocal and instrumental group)
ONE BAD APPLE *MGM* [*USA*]. Written by George Jackson, this was released in the U.S.A. in January 1971, went to No 1 for five weeks, and stayed 15 weeks in the bestsellers.

The Osmonds hail from Salt Lake City, Utah, and are strict Mormons. They first began singing in close harmony style for family gatherings at an early age, being taught by their mother who used to play the saxophone. Their father had sung in a choir and taught them to harmonize. The four eldest boys, Alan, Wayne, Merrill and Jay, formed a group and sang at parish functions, where they made such an impression that they became

regulars on the unpaid church circuit. On one trip they went to California, and the boys visited Disneyland where they were invited on stage. They then made their first professional engagement (1963) at Disneyland where they became resident for a long time.

Andy Williams' father heard their act and recommended them to Andy - with the result that they worked with him on his TV shows for five years. They then appeared in weekly shows with Jerry Lewis, and Donny Osmond became a member of the group. Their success in the U.S.A. was formidable and the group's appearances in Britain, when the youngest brother Little Jimmy Osmond was featured, brought fan hysteria wherever they appeared. This was in 1972.

Although their TV exposure made them America's most in-demand teenage attraction after the Jackson 5 furore, it wasn't until after they left the show (January 1971) that 'Osmondmania' accelerated, starting with this recording of 'One Bad Apple', which sold nearly three million and received R.I.A.A. Gold Disc award on 4 February 1971. By 1975 they had sold around 20 million discs (singles plus albums) and collected 10 Gold Discs for singles and 10 for albums from the R.I.A.A. either as a group, solo or duet.

Sister Marie Osmond made her first record in 1973 (*q.v.*). The Osmonds made TV specials, numerous guest-starring appearances on network variety shows in the U.S.A. and Japan, sell-out concerts, plus appearances in Germany and Britain, etc. They signed with MGM Records in June 1970.

The performing Osmonds are: Alan Osmond (lead guitar, vocals), born 22 June 1949; Wayne Osmond (guitar/saxophone, vocals), born 28 August 1951; Merrill Osmond (lead vocals, bass), born 1 May 1953; Jay Osmond (drums), born 1955; Little Jimmy Osmond (vocals), born 1964; Marie Osmond (vocals), born 13 October 1959; Donny Osmond (vocals/keyboards), born 12 September 1957. There are two elder brothers, Virl and Tom, who do not sing. The Osmonds were one of the biggest successes of 1971.

YO YO *MGM* [*USA*]. Written by Joe South, this was released in the U.S.A. in September 1971, hitting No 1 for two weeks and staying in the bestsellers for 12 weeks.

This was the second million seller for the Osmonds with R.I.A.A. Gold Disc award on 17 November 1971.

DONNY OSMOND
SWEET AND INNOCENT *MGM* [*USA*]. The first solo disc for Donny of the famous Osmonds group. It passed the million sale by 30 August and was awarded a Gold Disc by R.I.A.A.

Written by R. Hill and Billy Sherrill, it was released in the U.S.A. in March 1971, reaching No 5 for one week and staying 16 weeks in the charts.

GO AWAY LITTLE GIRL *MGM* [*USA*]. Written by Gerry Goffin and Carole King (1962), Donny's version was released in the U.S.A. in July 1971, going to No 1 for three weeks and staying 15 weeks in the bestseller charts.

The second solo disc for Donny Osmond, it received R.I.A.A. Gold Disc award on 13 October 1971. The song was a former million seller in 1962 for Steve Lawrence.

HEY GIRL *MGM* [*USA*]. Written by Gerry Goffin and Carole King (1963), released in the U.S.A. in November 1971, this went to No 9 for two weeks, staying 11 weeks in the charts.

The third million seller in a row for Donny, an oldie of 1963 again by Goffin and King. R.I.A.A. Gold Disc award for million sale on 28 July 1971, making 1971 a successful year for Donny and the group.

FUIFUI (FIFI) OUYANG
AME NO MIDOSUJI (Stranger in Midosuji) *Toshiba* [*Japan*]. A Japanese version of the American group The Ventures' song. Fuifui is probably the first Chinese singer to have a million seller in Japan.

THE PARTRIDGE FAMILY
(featuring David Cassidy)
DOESN'T SOMEBODY WANT TO BE WANTED? *Bell* [*USA*]. Written by Mike Appel, Jim Cretecos and Wes Farrell, this was released in the U.S.A. in February 1971 and in Britain on 16 April 1971. It went to No 1 for one week in the U.S.A., staying in the bestsellers for 12 weeks.

An easy beat rhythm item, it is a simple song about loneliness. It sold a million by 11 March 1971, with R.I.A.A. Gold Disc award.

UP TO DATE (album) *Bell* [*USA*]. Released in the U.S.A. on 25 March 1971 and in Britain on 1 September 1971, this album was No 3 for four weeks in the U.S.A. and stayed for 53 weeks in the bestsellers.

Second million seller album for the U.S. TV Partridge Family, it was a consistent seller for over a year. It received the R.I.A.A. Gold Disc award the same month as its release.

Contents: 'I'll Meet You Halfway'; 'You Are Always on My Mind;' 'Doesn't Somebody Want to Be Wanted?'; 'I'm Here, You're Here'; 'Umbrella Man' (J. Cavanaugh, Vincent Rose and Larry Stock, 1938); 'Lay It on the Line'; 'Morning Rider on the Road'; 'That'll Be the Day' (Jerry Allison, Buddy Holly and Norman Petty, 1957); 'There's No Doubt In My Mind'; 'She'd Rather Have the Rain'; 'I'll Leave Myself a Little Time'.

THE PARTRIDGE FAMILY CHRISTMAS CARD (album) *Bell* [*USA*]. Released in the U.S.A. in October 1971 and in Britain on 1 November 1972, this album qualified for a Gold Disc on the basis of pre-release orders. The award from R.I.A.A. was on 2 November 1971. It sold over a million in a few weeks. The album, containing Christmas material, was issued with an actual Christmas card featuring a photo of the TV family and signatures of the individual members slipped on to the front cover.

The Partridge Family albums were among the biggest gift selections of the holiday season, and sold in big quantities all over the U.S.A. in this year. It was reported that sales of their four albums totalled over 6 million by the end of 1971.

THE PARTRIDGE FAMILY SOUND MAGAZINE (album) *Bell* [*USA*]. Released in the U.S.A. in August 1971 and in Britain on 7 April 1972, this went to No 8 for two weeks in the U.S.A., staying in the charts for 35 weeks, and went to No 14 in Britain.

Sales of this album at one time moved at an incredible pace - 60,000 per week. R.I.A.A. awarded the Gold Disc on 27 September 1971, and it soon went over the million (see also David Cassidy, 1971). Contents: 'I Woke Up in Love This Morning' (Irwin Levine and L. R. Brown); 'Echo Valley 2-6809'; 'One Night Stand'; 'I Would Have Loved You Anyway'; '24 Hours a Day'; 'Love Is All That I Ever Needed'; 'You Don't Have to Tell Me'; 'Rainmaker'; 'I'm on My Way Back Home'; 'Summer Days'; 'Brown Eyes'.

FREDA PAYNE
BRING THE BOYS HOME *Invictus* [*USA*]. Written by G. Perry, A. Bond and G. Johnson, this was released in the U.S.A. in May 1971, reaching No 5 for two weeks and staying in the bestsellers for 15 weeks.

At a time when the U.S.A. was heavily involved in the Vietnam war, the disc was timely and extremely popular. It sold 1,008,000 by August 1971 and received Gold Disc award from R.I.A.A. on 27 August 1971.

THE PERSUADERS (vocal quintet)
THIN LINE, BETWEEN LOVE AND HATE *Atco* [*USA*]. Written by R. and R. Poindexter and Jockey Members, this went to No 9 for one week in the U.S.A., staying 9 weeks in the Top 50. It was released in the U.S.A. in August 1971.

This disc by The Persuaders, an unidentified soul *a capella* group, was produced by the Poindexter Brothers, and gave them their first Gold Disc from R.I.A.A. on 29 October 1971. It was also the group's first recording for the Atco label.

WILSON PICKETT
DON'T LET THE GREEN GRASS FOOL YOU *Atlantic* [*USA*]. Written by Akines, Bellman, Drayton and Turner, this was released in January 1971 in the U.S.A., rising to No 10 for three weeks and staying eight weeks in the Top 50.

Described as a 'soulful rocker and a high tensioned offering for blues and teen audiences', this was originally included on Pickett's album 'Wilson Pickett in Philadelphia'. It was produced by the famous Gamble and Huff team, and was the first certified R.I.A.A. single for the artist, with Gold Disc award on 22 March 1971.

DON'T KNOCK MY LOVE (Part 1) *Atlantic* [*USA*]. Written by B. Shapiro and Wilson Pickett, and released in April 1971 in the U.S.A., this hit No 7 for a week, staying ten weeks in the Top 50.

It is a wild, wailing recording of Pickett's own composition, his second R.I.A.A. certified million seller, with Gold Disc award on 22 June 1971.

CHARLEY PRIDE
KISS AN ANGEL GOOD MORNIN' *RCA* [*USA*]. Written by Ben Peters, this was released in the U.S.A. in November 1971 and in Britain on 26 May 1972. It rose to No 19 for one week in the U.S.A. and stayed 16 weeks in the top sellers.

Charley Pride's first single million seller with R.I.A.A. Gold Disc award on 8 March 1972. The disc was also a hit in the U.S. country charts and composer Ben Peters won a Grammy Award for the song - Best Country Song (Songwriter's Award) 1972. Charley made his first European tour in 1972, and at this time was RCA's biggest seller.

THE RAIDERS (PAUL REVERE AND THE RAIDERS)
(pop quintet)
INDIAN RESERVATION *Columbia* [*USA*]. Written by John D. Loudermilk in 1970, this version was released in the U.S.A., February 1971, going to No 1 for three weeks and staying 22 weeks in the bestsellers.

This song was originally a hit for Don Fardon in Britain in 1970. The Raiders' (originally Paul Revere & The Raiders) disc was Columbia's biggest selling single for a long time. It received R.I.A.A. Gold Disc award for million sale on 30 June 1971, and was also the group's first No 1 record.

Paul Revere & The Raiders were formed in Portland, Oregon, by Paul (an ex-barber turned restaurateur and apartment house owner by the time he was 21). The group specialized in playing teen dances and were exceedingly popular in their own area from their formation in 1962. Lead singer Mark Lindsay (see 1969) and Paul Revere were joined by Freddy Weller (lead guitar), Charlie Coe (bass) and Joe Correro (drums). Later (1969), Coe was replaced by Keith Allison, and Correro by Mike Smith.

They became a big box office draw on the West Coast and extremely popular in Honolulu. In 1965, Dick Clark's TV show 'Where the Action Is' featured the group and made them national stars, and lead singer Mark an instant teenage idol. By 1966 they were voted top group in America and their records shot into the Top 10 with several gold album awards. In 1967 they had their own series called 'Happening '68' which ran into 1969. The personnel changed several times, and those who played on 'Indian Reservation' were: Paul Revere (electric organ), Mark Lindsay (lead vocalist), Freddy Weller (lead guitar), Keith Allison (bass guitar) and Mike Smith (drums).

JERRY REED
WHEN YOU'RE HOT, YOU'RE HOT *RCA* [*USA*]. Written by Jerry Reed and released in the U.S.A. in May 1971, this got to No 8 for one week, staying 11 weeks in the Top 50. The million sale of this disc was reported in early June 1971. Jerry received the Grammy Award for Best Country Vocal Performance (Male) of 1971.

NEIL REID (juvenile vocalist)
MOTHER OF MINE *Decca* [*Britain*]. Written by Bill Parkinson and released in Britain on 3 December 1971, this achieved No 2 for three weeks, staying in the bestsellers for 21 weeks.

It was not until 1968 that his talents were recognized at a Christmas party given for old age pensioners. He then worked in clubs, sang at private functions and, during his summer holidays, appeared at King's Theatre, Glasgow, on the Calum Kennedy Show.

Appearance on British TV in 'Opportunity Knocks' in 1971 in which he was three-times winner, brought big success, and 'Mother of Mine' was an outstanding hit with over 250,000 sale in Britain, and over 2,500,000 globally. The disc, directed by Ivor Raymonde and produced by Dick Rowe for British Decca, also sold over 400,000 in Japan.

Neil Reid was the youngest-ever artist signed by Decca. His first album 'Neil Reid' (1972) reached No 1 and was in the British charts for four months. Composer Parkinson is lead guitarist of the group P.A.T.C.H. Neil was born in Scotland, 1960.

T. REX (rock quintet)
HOT LOVE *Fly* [*Britain*]. Written by Marc Bolan, this was released in Britain in February 1971, hitting No 1 for six weeks and staying 13 weeks in the bestsellers.

T. Rex comprised Marc Bolan (born Hackney, London, 1947, real name Mark Feld), vocals and guitar; Micky Finn, percussion; Steve Currie, bass; Bill Legend, drums; Jack Green, guitar.

Bolan drifted round Britain for a while after leaving school, doing some acting, then went to France where he lived with a magician for six months and became interested in folklore and mythology. On returning to Britain he met an American, Jim Economedes, sometime producer of The Beach Boys, who got

him his first recording 'The Wizard' on Decca (1965). The disc was sent to Radio London disc jockey John Peel, as was 'Hippy Gumbo' on Columbia, to play on his 'Perfumed Garden' programme. In 1968 Bolan teamed with percussionist Steve Peregrine Took and formed Tyrannosaurus Rex, and they were the only two surviving members of the attempt to form an electric band quintet. John Peel gave them considerable aid by putting them on his 'Top Gear' show and helped them with engagements at his own personal appearances. Practically all Bolan's songs were self-written.

The group graduated to London's 'Middle Earth' and gradually drew bigger audiences. Record companies wanted them, and they signed with Regal Zonophone (1968) making albums and singles. Steve Took then left after they did their first U.S. tour, and was replaced by Micky Finn (1970). They made the album 'Beard of Stars' (1970) in which Bolan played electric guitar, thus returning to the electric rock he played in the John's Children group (1967) before the formation of Tyrannosaurus Rex.

In late 1970, Bolan and Finn operated under the shortened name of T. Rex and had a hit with 'Ride a White Swan' on their debut with the Fly label. Currie and Legend were added to the band and they became a rage with the teenyboppers with 'Hot Love' which sold over 250,000 in Britain and an estimated million globally. A further hit 'Get It On' followed soon after, and more hit albums, including the highly successful No 1 album 'Electric Warrior' (1971).

Bolan was at the peak of his popularity with sell-out performances and mass teenage hysteria in the first half of 1972. 'Bolan Boogie' and 'The Slider' albums (1972) were big commercial successes. T. Rex album sales during 1971 and 1972 were a massive 14 million, and one tally of their sales over four years to 1973 was an estimated 37 million. By 1974, T. Rex fever had largely abated.

As a poet, Bolan was gifted and very successful. He became one of Britain's best selling poets with his book *Warlock of Love*. He was killed in an automobile crash in Barnes, London, on 16 September 1977, aged 30.

GET IT ON (Bang-a-Gong) *Fly* [*Britain*] *Reprise* [*USA*]. Written by Marc Bolan and released in Britain in July 1971, this went to No 1 for three weeks. In the U.S.A. it stopped at No 10 for two weeks. It stayed 12 weeks in the British bestseller charts and 15 weeks in the U.S. lists.

The disc sold over 250,000 in Britain and had further big sales in the U.S.A., making well over the million collectively.

'Bang-a-Gong' was the title used for the U.S. release.

THE ROLLING STONES

BROWN SUGAR *Rolling Stones* [*Britain & USA*]. Simultaneously released in the U.S.A. and Britain on 16 April 1971, it went to No 1 in both countries, staying for three weeks in the U.S.A. and one week in Britain. It spent 12 weeks in the Top 50 in the U.S.A. and 11 weeks in Britain's topsellers.

It was the first big hit on The Rolling Stones' own label, released just prior to their album 'Sticky Fingers' in which it was included. A solid rock disc with lusty lyrics about slave days in New Orleans. Jagger's vocals are reinforced by Keith Richard's biting guitar, Bobby Keys on saxophone, and Ian Stewart on piano. The disc was made over a long period; first at Muscle Shoals, Florida, in December 1969, then completed a long time after in London at Olympic and The Stones' Mighty Mobile Studios. Sales in Britain went over 250,000 and big sales in the U.S.A. and elsewhere made it an easy global million seller.

STICKY FINGERS (album) *Rolling Stones* [*Britain & USA*]. Released in the U.S.A. and Britain on 30 April 1971, this easily scooped No 1 in both places, staying there for four weeks in the U.S.A. and eight weeks in Britain. It remained in the bestsellers for 41 weeks in the U.S.A., 26 in Britain.

A remarkably varied album, produced by Jimmy Miller, it was made in three different places during a period of over a year, at Muscle Shoals, The Stones' Mighty Mobile Studios, and London's Olympic studio. The album, according to Britain's *New Musical Express*, was 'a grand celebration of Stones jet-set debauchery and chic demonic postures', whilst *Time* described its sleeve as 'a record-store attraction, and positively too dreadful to ignore'.

'Sticky Fingers' was the first album on their own label. With Mick Jagger's vocals, wild at times, and controlled elsewhere, plus the exceptional musicianship, it was certain to be a big success. It sold 500,000 in its first two weeks, the fastest seller ever in the U.S.A. for The Rolling Stones, was awarded a Gold Disc by R.I.A.A. on 11 May 1971, and soon passed the million units sale.

All the tracks were written by Mick Jagger and Keith Richard. Contents: 'Brown Sugar'; 'Sway'; 'Wild Horses'; 'Can't You Hear Me Knocking?'; 'You've Gotta Move'; 'Bitch'; 'I Got the Blues'; 'Sister Morphine'; 'Dead Flowers'; 'Moonlight Mile'. 'Sister Morphine', with its powerful lyric about drug withdrawal, was co-written with Marianne Faithfull. 'Moonlight Mile' includes the playing of the Buckmaster Strings and the piano of Jim Price. Billy Preston played organ on 'Can't You Hear Me Knocking?' and 'I Got the Blues'. Bobby Keys (saxophone) also plays on some of the tracks.

After a fairly quiet 18 months, the album marked the return of The Rolling Stones.

HOT ROCKS 1964-1971 (Double Album) *London* [*USA*]. Released in the U.S.A. in December 1971, this compilation went to No 4 for three weeks, and stayed in the bestsellers charts for an amazing 167 weeks.

Following the success of The Rolling Stones' album 'Sticky Fingers', London Records released this anthology of the group's former recordings on Decca (Britain) for the U.S. market only. It was the biggest ever seller for the group, and was awarded R.I.A.A. Gold Disc on 20 January 1972, one month after its release. Its long run in the U.S. bestsellers for over three years resulted in an estimated two million-plus units sale.

'Hot Rocks' was the first Stones two-record set ever to be released in the U.S.A. and was their 13th gold album in a row on London Records. It brought about a surge of new interest in their recordings at a time when rock had changed drastically to a musically softer and more lyrically inquisitive style, and when the age of the big group was at a historical turning point, such as the break up of The Beatles and the permanent closing of the great American rock houses Fillmores West and East.

Contents: (*) 'Time Is on My Side' (Norman Meade [Jerry Magovay], 1963); (*) 'As Tears Go By' (Mick Jagger, Keith Richard and Andrew Loog Oldham, 1964); 'Heart of Stone' (1965); (*) 'Get Off My Cloud' (1965); 'Play with Fire' (1965); (*) 'Satisfaction (I Can't Get No)' (1965); (*) 'Paint it Black' (1966); (*) 'Mother's Little Helper' (1966); (*) '19th Nervous

Breakdown' (1966); 'Under My Thumb' (1966); (*) 'Let's Spend the Night Together' (1967); (*) 'Ruby Tuesday' (1967); 'Sympathy for the Devil' (1968); (*) 'Jumping Jack Flash' (1968); 'You Can't Always Get What You Want' (1969); 'Gimme Shelter' (1969); (*) 'Honky Tonk Woman' (1969); 'Midnight Rambler' (live) (1969); 'Street Fighting Man' (1971): 'Wild Horses' (1971); (*) 'Brown Sugar' (1971). ((*) denotes million seller single originally.) All songs by Mick Jagger and Keith Richard unless otherwise indicated.

SANTANA
SANTANA (THIRD ALBUM) (Album) *Columbia* [*USA*]. Released in October 1971 in the U.S.A. and Britain, this went to No 1 for five weeks in the U.S.A., staying 39 weeks in the bestsellers. In Britain it went to No 5, staying in the bestsellers for ten weeks.

Santana's third album was an instant gold record on release, with more than $2,000,000 in advance orders. R.I.A.A. award on 5 October 1971. By the end of November it passed the million units sale. The group had Coke Escovedo in place of the ailing timbales player Areas, and added guitarist Neal Schon, and brought the band to its logical conclusion. The album was issued in Britain under the title 'Santana – The Third Album'.

It included the hit 'No One to Depend on Me'.

JOE SIMON
DROWNING IN THE SEA OF LOVE *Spring* [*USA*]. Released in the U.S.A. in November 1971, this went to No 6 for three weeks, stopping among the bestsellers for 15 weeks. A second million seller for Joe Simon written by Kenny Gamble and Leon Huff. It sold over 1,500,000 and received R.I.A.A. Gold Disc award on 6 January 1972.

This was a further big success for the talented writers/producers Gamble and Huff who had emerged as the dominant force in Philadelphia from the late 1960s via the Sigma Sound Studio. It was one of the discs that proved to be the spark for the tremendous impact and excitement that followed with the formation of Philadelphia International Records. Artists began to flock to Philadelphia to work with the two writers and their associate Thom Bell, these three helping to musically define the 1970s with the Phil-Internat sound.

SLY & THE FAMILY STONE
(IT'S A) FAMILY AFFAIR *Epic* [*USA*]. Written by Sly (Sylvester) Stone, this was released in the U.S.A. in November 1971, going to No 1 for four weeks and staying 14 weeks in the bestsellers. In Britain it went to No 14 for three weeks, staying nine weeks in the topsellers.

This disc achieved a million sale within a month of its release, and was awarded the R.I.A.A. Gold Disc on 30 November 1971. It went on to amass sales of over 2,500,000, and further established Sly as a writer.

SAMMI SMITH (country vocalist)
HELP ME MAKE IT THROUGH THE NIGHT *Mega* [*USA*]. This version of Kris Kristofferson's song was released in the U.S.A. in January 1971, going to No 7 for one week, and staying 16 weeks in the bestsellers.

Sammi Smith was born in Orange, California, in 1943, and moved to Oklahoma when she was three. She began her vocal career at the age of 12, singing each night at a club in Oklahoma City. Under the guidance of Gene Sullivan, a writer and studio executive, and owner of a local recording studio to whom she was introduced at 18, she cultivated her vocal and writing styles, penning many songs which were sung by established country artists.

After making some records for Columbia, Sammi signed with a new label – Mega Records – in Nashville (1970). She met an old friend, Kris Kristofferson, who had written 'Help Me Make It Through the Night', which was just right for her. Sammi was Mega's first artist when the company started in September 1970, and her disc sold 1,200,000 by mid-May 1971, with Gold Disc

award from R.I.A.A. on 26 April 1971. It went on to around a two million sale globally. Sammi received a Grammy Award for her recording – Best Country Vocal (Female) Performance of 1971, and composer Kristofferson a Grammy Award for Best Country Song (Songwriter's Award) of 1971. The artist also received many awards from *Cashbox*, *Billboard*, *Record World*, The Country Music Association, etc. and performed on U.S. TV on 'The Mike Douglas Show', 'The Johnny Cash Show' and 'American Bandstand', also making many guest appearances. She made her concert debut in Britain at London's Royal Albert Hall on 26 October 1972.

'Help Me Make It Through the Night' was undoubtedly the turning point in Sammi's career, and helped to make her one of America's leading female country singers.

SONNY & CHER
ALL I EVER NEED IS YOU *Kapp* [*USA*]. Released in the U.S.A. in October 1971, this song written by E. Reeves and J. Holiday, went to No 6 for one week, and stayed in the bestsellers for 16 weeks. In Britain it rose to No 8 for one week, staying in the top sellers for seven weeks.

This disc made a welcome return to the charts for the duo. It was also used as the title for their album which received an R.I.A.A. Gold Disc in 1972.

Sales of this single disc of a million globally were reported in early 1972. The duo were divorced in 1975. (See Cher, 1971.)

THE STAMPEDERS (vocal trio)
SWEET CITY WOMAN *Bell* [*USA*] *Stateside* [*Britain*]. Written by Rich Dodson, this was released in the U.S.A. in August 1971 and in Britain on 9 October 1971. It got to No 7 for two weeks, and stayed for 16 weeks in the U.S. topsellers.

The Stampeders originally started out as a sextet in 1963, when the founders were in their earliest teens in Calgary, Canada. They became a trio in 1965, comprising: Rich Dodson (guitar), Ronnie King and Kim Berkley. They were consistent hitmakers on the Canadian charts.

This disc sold a reported million by September 1971. It features an attractive banjo introduction.

THE STAPLE SINGERS (vocal quartet)
HEAVY MAKES YOU HAPPY *Stax* [*USA*]. Written by J. Barry and B. Bloom, this was released in the U.S.A. in January 1971, getting to No 24 for two weeks, staying 13 weeks in the bestsellers.

The Staple Singers were Roebuck 'Pop' Staples, born 28 December 1914 in Winona, Mississippi, and his daughters Mavis (lead vocals), Cleo and Yvonne. 'Pop' Staples was inspired to take up the guitar by players such as Robert Johnson and Blind Blake. He started to play harmonica after hearing Howlin' Wolf play. As a youngster, he taught himself the guitar, an instrument he saved up to buy for $5.

The Staples began to sing in Chicago churches, and would have been launched in 1948 had they not been forced to wait a few years before daughter Mavis' voice was developed. By 1953 they were well known through their church singing, and began performing their renditions of gospel classics on radio. They signed with United Records, a local label, and were then picked up by the larger black independent, Vee Jay Records, in 1956. Their first hit was 'Uncloudy Day' which had a rock and roll flavour mixed with gospel. In the 1960s, the group joined the Epic label without scoring a major hit. Their greatest successes came in the 1970s, first with Stax Records. 'Heavy Makes You Happy (Sha Na Boom Boom)' was a big pop and rhythm-and-blues hit with over a million sale. It firmly established The Staple Singers, and was the first of a run of big sellers.

Their songs were not gospel, but their message was of love and brotherhood, proving that inspirational music had a place on both black religious radio and white and black pop programmes as well.

In 1975, they joined the Curtom label.

RESPECT YOURSELF *Stax* [*USA*]. Written by Mack Rice and Luther Ingram and released in the U.S.A. in October 1971, this reached No 9 for two weeks, staying 14 weeks in the best-sellers.

The second million seller for The Staple Singers, reaching this figure while they were on a German tour during December 1971. The title was used for a successful album by the group – 'Beatitude: Respect Yourself' – in 1972.

RINGO STARR

IT DON'T COME EASY *Apple* [*Britain*]. Released in Britain and in the U.S.A. on 2 April 1971 and written by Richard Starkey (Ringo Starr), this went to No 1 for a week in the U.S.A. and No 4 for three weeks in Britain. It stayed 12 weeks in the Top 50 in the U.S.A. and nine weeks in the British Top 30.

The breakup of The Beatles in 1970 resulted in each of its members branching out on their own in the recording world. Drummer Ringo Starr started a career in films and gave a convincing performance in *That'll Be the Day* in 1973. It was in this year (1970) that he made his first solo album, 'A Sentimental Journey', then 'Beaucoups of Blues', followed by 'Ringo' (1973) and 'Goodnight Vienna' (1974).

This single, 'It Don't Come Easy', was his first big hit, a self-written song that sold a million in the U.S.A. with Gold Disc award from the R.I.A.A. on 3 August 1971. Further million sellers followed in 1973 to establish him as a solo artist.

ROD STEWART

EVERY PICTURE TELLS A STORY (Album) *Mercury* [*Britain*]. Released simultaneously in the U.S.A. and Britain in June 1971, this shot to No 1 for nine weeks in Britain and four weeks in the U.S.A. It stayed in the U.S. bestsellers for 52 weeks, and in the British top charts for 43 weeks.

Rod Stewart was born on 10 January 1945 in North London. His parents owned a newsagent's shop in Archway Road, Holloway, London. When Rod left school, he took various jobs such as grave digging and fence erecting, and later became an apprentice with Brentford Football Club which he left due to low wages. He decided to tour around Europe, mainly in Italy and Spain, with an English folk artist Wizz Jones from whom he learned to play banjo. He also learned to play guitar, and on returning to Britain began singing and playing harmonica with Jimmy Powell's Dimensions around Birmingham on semi-pro gigs. He made a record for Decca in 1964, and in 1965 joined The Hoochie Coochie Men with Long John Baldry in the vocal front line. He then joined Baldry's new Steam Packet rhythm-and-blues 'revue' with Brian Auger and Julie Driscoll, but left, after personal disagreements, to join Shotgun Express. This group was a failure, and Rod made occasional solo discs, etc. before joining the Jeff Beck group, along with Ronnie Wood (1968). Beck's outfit was well known in the U.S.A. and it was there that singer Stewart began to get wide recognition. He recorded two albums with them and then he and Ronnie Wood left. In 1969, Rod signed a solo contract with Mercury, and with Wood, joined Faces.

Although the group was billed occasionally as Rod Stewart and Faces, he was still almost unknown to British pop fans. His first album 'An Old Raincoat Will Never Let You Down' (Vertigo 1969) showed him to be a fine folk singer, rock singer and composer. His second 'Gasoline Alley' (Vertigo 1970) proved him to be a top writer and established him as a top solo singer in the U.S.A. Rod continued his recording career with The Faces and as solo singer. In 1971, 'Every Picture Tells a Story' was released and this plus the single from it, 'Maggie May', gave him prominence on both sides of the Atlantic. At one period, both album and single were No 1 in the charts in Britain and in the U.S.A. R.I.A.A. awarded a Gold Disc on 2 August 1971 and the album went on to sell over 2,500,000 copies.

Contents: 'Every Picture Tells a Story' (Rod Stewart); 'Seems Like a Long Time' (Rod Stewart); 'That's All Right' (Arthur Crudup, 1947); 'Tomorrow Is a Long Time' (Bob Dylan); 'Maggie May' (Rod Stewart and M. Quittenton); 'Mandolin Wind'

(Rod Stewart); '(I Know) I'm Losing You' (Cornelius Grant, Norman Whitfield and Eddie Holland, 1966); 'Reason to Believe' (Tim Hardin); 'Amazing Grace' (arranged Stewart).

MAGGIE MAY backed with REASON TO BELIEVE *Mercury* [*Britain*]. 'Maggie May', written by Rod Stewart and M. Quittenton, and 'Reason to Believe', written by Tim Hardin, was released as a double-sider in July 1971. It went to No 1 for five weeks in the U.S.A. and for six weeks in Britain. It stayed in the U.S. bestsellers for 21 weeks and 22 weeks in the British top sellers.

A tremendous hit for Rod Stewart, taken from his album 'Every Picture Tells a Story'. Both sides of the disc were popular, and were simultaneously hits in Britain and the U.S.A. Sales in Britain went over 250,000 and well over a million in the U.S.A. R.I.A.A. Gold Disc award on 1 October 1971.

THE STYLISTICS (vocal quintet)

YOU'RE A BIG GIRL NOW *Avco Embassy* [*USA*]. Written by Bryant and Douglas (1969), this was the first disc made by The Stylistics. It set them on the road to fame. They were heard by producer Bill Perry in 1969, who spent $400 to record the number at the Virtue Studios in Philadelphia. It was released on the Seabring label (1969) and did well in Philadelphia, New York, Washington and Baltimore. Avco Records took it over in late 1970 and released it on their Embassy label in January 1971 for national exposure. It subsequently sold a million (uncertified) and was the forerunner of a string of million sellers for the group.

(See also 'You Are Everything' 1971, for Stylistics data.)

YOU ARE EVERYTHING *Avco* [*USA*]. Written by Linda Creed and Thom Bell, this was released in the U.S.A. in October 1971 and went to No 9 for two weeks and stayed 16 weeks in the bestsellers.

The Stylistics, all from the Philadelphia area, are: Russell Thompkins, Jr (lead singer); Airrion Love (tenor); Herb Murrell (baritone); James Dunn (baritone) and James Smith (bass). The group was the outcome of personnel changes in the two groups, The Monarchs and The Percussions, that The Stylistics were working with. They formerly sang in the Philadelphia area while at school, and made jaunts to Atlantic City to work the clubs. They made a disc, 'You're a Big Girl Now', for a small label, Seabring of Philadelphia, which began to break in late 1969. This was picked up by Avco Records who decided the group should move into the pop field. Hugo Peretti and Luigi Creatore (better known as Hugo and Luigi) of Avco got Thom Bell as their producer, and 'You Are Everything' became a rhythm-and-blues hit via national distribution. It sold the million with R.I.A.A. Gold Disc award on 3 January 1972.

By the end of 1972, the distinctive sound of the five youthful soul singers sold over six million records. Their first album contained no fewer than four hits, when released as singles, and made the album probably the most productive nine-track disc ever made.

Their success took them right away from their black audiences and into immense popularity with the white. Producer Thom Bell created a high form of pure pop music for the group - rhythm-and-blues distilled down to pure emotion and embellished with romantic orchestration.

The Stylistics made tours of Europe, and were extremely popular in Britain as well as in the U.S.A.

THE SUPREMES

NATHAN JONES *Motown* [*USA*]. Released in the U.S.A. in May 1971 and in Britain on 13 August 1971, this song was written by L. Gaston and F. Wakefield. It got to No 8 for one week in the U.S.A. and No 4 for one week in Britain. It stayed in the U.S. bestsellers for eight weeks and in the British charts for ten weeks.

Taken from the album 'Touch', this single sold a reported million by early 1973. Produced by Frank Wilson, it was the third million seller for the Supremes new line-up of Jean Terrell, Mary Wilson and Cindy Birdsong.

SWEET (pop quartet)

FUNNY FUNNY *RCA* [*Britain*]. Released in Britain in March 1971 and written by Nicky Chinn and Mike Chapman, this went to No 13 for two weeks and stayed 14 weeks in the Top 30.

Sweet is: Brian Connolly (vocals) born Hamilton, Scotland, 5 October 1949; Andy Scott (guitar) born Wrexham, Wales, 30 June 1951; Steve Priest (bass) born Hayes, Middlesex, 23 February 1950; Mick Tucker (drums) born Harlesden, London, 17 July 1949.

Sweet was first formed in 1968 by Tucker and Connolly who

were previously members of Wainwright's Gentlemen, a group that included future Deep Purple members Ian Gillan and Roger Glover. Priest and guitarist Frank Torpky completed the original group which recorded 'Slow Motion' for the Fontana label and then three singles, 'Lollipop', 'Get on the Line' and 'All You'll Ever Get from Me', for EMI. All failed to make any impression. In 1969, Torpky was replaced by Mick Stewart who was himself replaced in 1970 by Scott, and the group made a management/ production deal with the new songwriting team of Nicky Chinn and Mike Chapman, plus producer Phil Wainman.

The Chinn-Chapman team were turning out top ten chart hits for Suzi Quatro and Mud. Sweet benefited from the partnership with a number of hit singles in Britain and throughout Europe, starting off with 'Funny Funny' which gave Sweet their first million global seller.

The group were, from the outset, regarded as a 'bubblegum' band but their lyrics and vocals gradually improved as did their instrumental work. By 1973 they became successful in the U.S.A. through the release of 'Little Willy' and by 1975 broke big in America with a 40-city headlining tour. They had by then broken away from Chinn and Chapman and were writing their own hits. By 1976, Sweet's singles sales totalled a staggering 13 million worldwide, and this while they were still considered a relatively new entity in the U.S.A.

CO-CO *RCA* [*Britain*]. Released June 1971 in Britain, and written by the 'pop-machine' Nicky Chinn and Mike Chapman, this went to No 2 for two weeks, staying for 12 weeks in the Top 30.

This disc sold over 250,000 in Britain and amassed a two million plus sale globally for the 'bubblegum' sound of Sweet, and a further triumph for the Chinn-Chapman songwriting team.

JAMES TAYLOR

YOU'VE GOT A FRIEND *Warner* [*USA*]. Released in the U.S.A. in May 1971 and in Britain in August 1971, this song was written by Carole King, and went to No 1 for one week in the U.S.A. and No 4 for two weeks in Britain. It stayed 15 weeks in the bestseller charts in U.S.A., 12 weeks in the British Top 30.

This first million selling single for James Taylor was taken from his album 'Mud Slide Slim and the Blue Horizon'. It was first recorded by composer Carole King on her 'Tapestry' album (*q.v.*).

R.I.A.A. awarded a Gold Disc on 13 September, and James Taylor received the 1971 Grammy Award for Best Pop Vocal Performance (Male). Carole King got the Grammy Award (Songwriter's Award) for Song of the Year, 1971.

THE TEMPTATIONS

JUST MY IMAGINATION (Runnin' away with me) *Gordy* [*USA*]. Released in the U.S.A. in February 1971 and in Britain in May 1971, the song was written by Norman Whitfield and Barrett Strong. It went to No 1 for two weeks in the U.S.A. and No 6 for one week in Britain. It stayed for 15 weeks in the U.S. bestsellers and 13 weeks in the British charts.

The personnel for this recording were: Eddie Kendricks, Melvin Franklin, Dennis Edwards, Paul Williams and Otis Williams. The disc was a big hit for The Temptations, and sold over two million.

THREE DOG NIGHT

LIAR *ABC/Dunhill* [*USA*]. Released in the U.S.A. in July 1971, this went to No 6 for a week, staying 13 weeks in the bestsellers.

The million sale of this disc was reported in August 1972. Composer Russ Ballard was guitarist with the English group Argent from its formation in 1970, but left in mid-1974.

JOY TO THE WORLD *ABC/Dunhill* [*USA*]. Released in the U.S.A. in March 1971 and in Britain on 8 April 1971, this went to No 1 for six weeks and stayed 17 weeks in the bestsellers.

This potent rock ballad written by Hoyt Axton was taken from the group's album 'Naturally' and sold over 1,250,000 in just over five weeks. It received R.I.A.A. Gold Disc award on 9 April 1971. By June the sales topped 2,750,000 in the U.S.A. alone and, by July, 4 million globally. The disc is the biggest seller in Dunhill's history.

AN OLD FASHIONED LOVE SONG *ABC/Dunhill* [*USA*]. Released in the U.S.A. in November 1971 and in Britain on 10 December 1971, this made No 4 for three weeks in the U.S.A. and stayed 11 weeks in the bestseller list.

Written by Paul Williams, this was the seventh million seller for Three Dog Night, taken from their album 'Harmony'. Gold Disc award from R.I.A.A. on 29 December 1971.

Three Dog Night's success in 1971 was fabulous. In 10 months of touring they grossed $5,012,345 from less than 100 dates, appearing before audiences aggregating 943,309.

TRAFFIC (rock quartet)
LOW SPARK OF HIGH HEELED BOYS (Album) *Island* [*Britain*]. Released in the U.S.A. in November 1971, this went to No 7 for two weeks and stayed 30 weeks in the bestsellers.

Traffic was formed in 1967, with Stevie Winwood (formerly with The Spencer Davis Group) on vocals, guitar and keyboards; Chris Wood, an outstanding jazz player, on saxophone and flute; Jim Capaldi, a fine lyricist, on vocals, drums and percussion; Dave Mason, composer, on guitar. Most of the group hailed from the Birmingham area in Britain. The quartet moved out to a Berkshire cottage to make music and produced some fine rock music in their peaceful retreat. They were immediately successful with their compositions 'Paper Sun' and 'Hole in My Shoe' (both in 1967). Their first album was 'Mr Fantasy' (1967). In 1968 they made the album 'Traffic', and the group split up in December of that year, but had release of their third album 'Last Exit' in early 1969. 'Best of Traffic' was released in 1969.

Winwood, Wood and Capaldi re-formed as a trio in 1970 and made the hit album 'John Barleycorn Must Die'. Bassist Rick Grech joined the group in November 1970.

In 1971, Reebop Kwaaku Baah (percussion) came in and, on the group's British tour, Jim Gordon replaced Capaldi. Mason rejoined the band for the tour, and the album 'Welcome to the Canteen' was released (1971), followed by 'Low Spark of High Heeled Boys' which was a big success in America. It was awarded an R.I.A.A. Gold Disc for half million sales in 1972.

Traffic broke up at the end of 1971, but the basic nucleus of Winwood, Capaldi, Wood and Reebop returned to America in 1972, when David Hood (bass) and Roger Hawkins (drums) – session men from Muscle Shoals – joined them for a U.S.A. tour. 'Shoot Out at the Fantasy Factory' album was released in 1973, another big success, and Traffic made a world tour, adding Barry Beckett from Muscle Shoals. Their next big hit was the album 'When the Eagle Flies' (1974).

'Low Spark of High Heeled Boys' subsequently sold a million units, reported in March 1976, when they received a platinum award.

The album included: 'Low Spark of High Heeled Boys'; 'Rock and Roll Stew'; 'Hidden Treasure'; 'Rainmaker'; 'Light Up or Leave Me Alone'; 'Many a Mile to Freedom'.

IKE AND TINA TURNER
PROUD MARY *Liberty* [*USA*]. Released in the U.S.A. in January 1971, this went to No 4 for a week, and stayed 11 weeks in the Top 50.

Ike and Tina received the 1971 Grammy Award with this disc, written by John Fogerty (1969), for the best Rhythm-and-Blues Vocal Performance by a duo or group, Vocal or Instrumental. R.I.A.A. awarded a Gold Disc for million sale on 6 May 1971. The song was originally a million seller for Creedence Clearwater Revival, of which composer John Fogerty is a member.

WAR (rock/soul septet)
SLIPPIN' INTO DARKNESS *United Artists* [*USA*]. Released in the U.S.A. in November 1971, this reached No 12 for a week and stayed 24 weeks in the bestsellers.

A composition by the group, the disc was a consistent seller over a long period. The million sale achieved by 26 June 1972 with R.I.A.A. Gold Disc award.

War was first formed around 1960 by Miller, Brown, Dickerson and Scott during high school in California. They were known as The Creators. Service in the U.S. forces split the band but, around 1968, they got together again in a group called The Nite Shift, formed to back Deacon Jones, a football player turned singer. English singer Eric Burdon saw them in a Los Angeles club in 1969 and Eric's friend Lee Oskar, a white harmonica player from Copenhagen, deputized with the group when Deacon Jones failed to appear. Next day, Burdon and his producer-friend Jerry Goldstein talked to the group, and asked them to change their name to War, and be the back-up band for Burdon. Burdon agreed to stay with them until War were successful and could go on alone. They made 'Spill the Wine', which became a million seller, and two albums, after which Burdon left the group. War then became one of the most successful American bands in the rock-soul field.

(See also Burdon and War, 1970.)

ANDY WILLIAMS
THEME FROM 'LOVE STORY' (Where do I begin?) *Columbia* [*USA*]. Released in the U.S.A. in February 1971 and in Britain in March 1971, this reached No 5 for two weeks in the U.S.A. and No 3 for one week in Britain. It stayed 17 weeks in the U.S. bestsellers and 18 weeks in the British charts.

Of the many recorded versions of this beautiful song by Francis Lai and Carl Sigman, Andy Williams' was the biggest seller, surpassing the million sale globally. (See 'Love Story' film soundtrack, 1970.)

BILL WITHERS
AIN'T NO SUNSHINE (when she's gone) *Sussex* [*USA*]. Released in the U.S.A. in July 1971, this went to No 3 for two weeks and stayed 16 weeks in the bestsellers.

Bill Withers was born on 4 July 1938 in the small mining town of Slab Fork, West Virginia, the youngest of a family of six children. After grade school and college he earned a living in bricklaying. His big problem was acute shyness and stuttering. His enlistment in the U.S. Navy was a big boon to him. Special speech therapy helped to overcome the stuttering. On leaving the Navy, at the age of 26, he started singing and playing guitar. With his savings, Bill went to a small California studio and cut some songs he had written. After another two years he met up with Booker T. Jones who got him a contract with Sussex Records (1971). His first album 'Just as I Am' included 'Ain't No Sunshine' which when released as a single became a big hit. It received R.I.A.A. Gold Disc award for million sale on 2 September 1971 and the 1971 Grammy Award for best Rhythm-and-Blues Song (Songwriter's Award).

At the time he made his first discs Bill was working at an aircraft factory. Although primarily a writer, his lyrics and haunting melodies established him as a major soul performer/composer. 'Ain't No Sunshine' subsequently became a soul standard.

By 1973 he was appearing on stage, backed by the Watts 103rd Street Rhythm Band, and writing many more hits.

BETTY WRIGHT
CLEAN UP WOMAN *Alston* [*USA*]. Released in the U.S.A. in November 1971 and written by Steve Alaimo (of Marlin Productions), this got to No 4 for two weeks, staying for 14 weeks in the bestsellers.

Betty Wright was born on 21 December 1953 in Miami, Florida. She began singing in her family spiritual group, Echoes of Joy, when she was only three. At the age of 11, she won a 'Guess the Tune' phone-in competition and, when she went along to pick up the prize, a copy of the disc, Clarence Reid and Willie Smith of the record store asked her to sing. A year later they recorded her, and put out the disc on their own Deep City label. Her next disc was leased to TK set-up and was a big success. Betty had her own two-hour TV show when she was 17. Then came 'Clean Up Woman' which sold a million, with R.I.A.A. Gold Disc award on 30 December 1971. She gained the title of Best New Female Singer of the year, and the *Cashbox* award for best single of the year.

Betty has an amazing voice, and is highly intelligent with an IQ calculated at 191.

1972

FILM SOUNDTRACK (DIANA ROSS)

LADY SINGS THE BLUES (Double album) *Motown* [*USA*]. Released in the U.S.A. in October 1972, this double soundtrack went to No 1 for two weeks, staying up in the charts for 54 weeks.

Lady Sings the Blues is a somewhat romanticized version of the life of Billie Holiday (born 7 April 1915 in Baltimore, Maryland), the jazz singer who made scores of records from 1933 until 1959, when she died in a New York hospital on 17 June. Billie's childhood and adolescence were spent in abject poverty, and her last 15 years under the shadow of drug addiction. Her sad story, which also included racial prejudice and a life of prostitution, was written by her with William Duffy in 1956, and the autobiography *Lady Sings the Blues* (from her nickname, Lady Day) was the basis and title of the film, which is set from 1939 to 1959. It is a deeply moving and entertaining movie with elements of truth in it, but parts of Billie's life were glossed over.

Despite the omission of various sordid events in the real story, the film was a tremendous success, and sparked off a big demand for Billie's old recordings.

The idea for the film came from producer Jay Weston who, after hearing Billie at Carnegie Hall, later read her autobiography, and it then took 11 months to clear legal entanglements to start on the film. After a further 21 months' negotiations with the CBS film section, it was finally agreed. In 1970 (October) Weston saw Diana Ross and realized that here was the star for the film. CBS were informed of his decision to use Diana Ross, but were unable to make a final decision. Weston then phoned Berry Gordy of Motown Records, and with film director Sidney J. Furie, formed Motown-Weston-Furie Productions, with Motown advancing the money. Diana Ross then immersed herself in Billie Holiday's recordings and, with great skill, captured the feeling of Billie's voice, and proved to be a marvellous actress. The film was previewed in Los Angeles on 12 October 1972.

The soundtrack double album was reported to have sold over a million globally. The film included many of Billie Holiday's songs, among which were: 'God Bless the Child' (Al Hertzog, Jr and Billie Holiday, 1941); 'Strange Fruit' (Lewis Allan, 1940); 'Billie's Blues' (Billie Holiday); 'Fine and Mellow' (Billie Holiday, 1940); 'Good Morning, Heartbreak' (Irene Higginbotham, Ervin Drake and Dan Fisher, 1946); 'Lover Man' (Jimmy Davis,

Roger Ramirez and Jimmy Sherman, 1943); 'Don't Explain' (A. Hertzog, Jr and Billie Holiday, 1946); 'Them There Eyes' (M. Pinkard, W. Tracey and Doris Tauber, 1930); 'The Man I Love' (Ira Gershwin and George Gershwin, 1924); 'Gimme a Pigfoot' (Kid Wesley and Sox Wilson, 1933); 'My Man (Mon Homme)' (A. Willemetz, Jacques Charles and Maurice Yvain, 1920, English words by Channing Pollock); "Taint Nobody's Business If I Do' (P. Grainger, G. Prince and C. Williams, 1922); 'Mean to Me' (Roy Turk and Fred E. Ahlert, 1929); 'All of Me' (Seymour Simons and Gerald Marks, 1931); 'I Cried for You' (A. Freed, Gus Arnheim and Abe Lyman, 1923); 'What a Little Moonlight Can Do' (Harry Woods, 1934); 'You've Changed' (Bill Carey and Carl Fischer, 1942).

All were sung by Diana Ross. Music for the film was written by Michel Legrand, and his theme became a song, 'Happy', with words by Smokey Robinson. Diana Ross was nominated for an Academy Award.

The album was reported to be the fastest selling in the history of Motown Record Corporation. The film was released by Paramount Pictures.

ORIGINAL SOUNDTRACK (CURTIS MAYFIELD AND BAND)

SUPERFLY (Album) *Curtom* [*USA*]. With a score by Curtis Mayfield, this was released in the U.S.A. in July 1972, going to No 1 for five weeks and staying in the charts for 46 weeks. It won the R.I.A.A. Gold Disc award on 7 September 1972.

Superfly is described as a 'fast, flashy and funky' adventure film, and concerns the big city drug traffic and how it relates to the black community. It proved to be one of the biggest action/adventure films of 1972. Apart from the outstanding score by Curtis Mayfield, its other two strengths are Ron O'Neal's performance in the lead, and the really ingenious ending that brings the film out of the ordinary and into greatness, as far as sheer enjoyment is concerned. It was Curtis Mayfield's first effort in the film musical scoring field, and he also acted and played with his band.

Curtis Mayfield was born in Chicago on 3 June 1942. His grandmother was a minister in the Travelling Souls Spiritualists' Church, and this is where he met Jerry Butler who was singing with the church. The duo then met a group called The Roosters, and combined to form The Impressions. In 1958, The Impressions had their first big hit with the Jerry Butler rendition of 'For Your Precious Love'. Jerry subsequently went solo, and Curtis, who is a fine and distinctive guitarist, fronted the band. Curtis had been writing songs since he was ten, and during the years with the band, gained a wealth of experience of life and its vicissitudes. It was also the period when his lyric power began to flower.

Curtis went solo in 1970, but still maintained his links with The Impressions as producer and owner of their recording label. Curtis Mayfield's songs reflected his gospel origins, and emphasized his attachment to themes of social and spiritual matters. The powerful gospel flavour of The Impressions' successes sprang from those spiritual roots. The gospel style immediately links Mayfield with his black audience. He built his own complex of music publishing companies and a recording company, Curtom, which became internationally prominent. Curtis' first major concert appearance was in December 1971 at the Philharmonic in New York, an immense success. It was at the reception after the performance that he was offered the first draft of the *Superfly* script. He accepted the challenge and wrote the complete score and the lyrics. For the film, he used his own band consisting of Craig McMullen (guitarist), Lucky Scott (bass), Henry Gison (percussion), Scotty Harris (a new drummer) and himself on guitar.

By November the album had sold 1,400,000 and over 2,000,000 by June 1973. It was also the first to receive a gold tape award for a million units from Ampex Music Corp in June 1973. Two releases as singles from the album, 'Freddie's Dead' and 'Superfly' theme sold a million each. The film grossed over $10 million by November 1972.

VARIOUS ARTISTS

22 EXPLOSIVE HITS (Volume 2) (Album) K-Tel [USA]. One of the first compilations of 'Original Hits by Original Stars' to go over the million sale, achieved in North America, by early 1973. It contained recordings of the early 1970s by arrangement with nine different disc companies, and included artists from the U.S.A., Britain, Spain, Germany and France.

Contents: (*) 'Nice to Be with You': Gallery (J. Gold, 1972); 'A Simple Man': Lobo (K. Lavoie); (*) 'Mammy Blue': Los Pop Tops (Phil Trim and Hubert Girard, 1971); (*) 'Popcorn': Hot Butter (Gershon Kingsley, 1972); (*) 'One Bad Apple': The Osmonds (George Jackson, 1971); 'Son of My Father': Georgio (P. Bellotte, Michael Holm and G. Moroder, 1971); (*) 'Candy Man': Sammy Davis, Jr (Anthony Newley and Leslie Bricusse, 1972); (*) 'Butterfly': Danyel Gerard (Bernet, Baines and Gerard, 1971); (*) 'Don't Pull Your Love': Hamilton, Joe Frank & Reynolds (Dennis Lambert and Brian Potter, 1971); 'If Not For You': Olivia Newton-John (Bob Dylan, 1971); (*) 'The Power of Love': Joe Simon (Gamble, Huff and Simon, 1972); 'Honky Tonk - Part 1': James Brown (James Brown); 'Power to the People': Chi-Lites (John Lennon, 1971); 'Layla': Derek & The Dominos (Eric Clapton and Jim Gordon, 1972); 'Rainy Day Feeling': The Fortunes (Greenaway, Cook and Macauley, 1971); 'You Could Have Been a Lady': April Wine; 'My Man a Sweet Man': Millie Jackson; 'Small Beginnin's': Flash; 'Wedding Song': James Last; 'Chicaboom': Daddy Dewdrops; 'You Are the One': Sugar Bears; 'Don't Let Me Take You': Detroit Emeralds.

((*) indicates was a million seller as a single originally.)

VARIOUS ARTISTS

TOP STAR FESTIVAL (Album) *United Nations* [Phonogram]. Released March 1972, this was a 'committee' album. A panel consisting of Burt Bacharach, Dave Brubeck and David Frost selected the recordings for this special U.N. album in aid of the United Nations International Children's Emergency Fund.

It consisted of a galaxy of international stars, the record manufactured and distributed throughout the world by Phonogram. Sales exceeded a million by August 1972 and included around 500,000 in the U.S.A., 100,000 in both Holland and Germany, 90,000 in Belgium, 50,000 in Australia, and over 30,000 in Britain. Japan sold well over 50,000 and final figures for the world are estimated at 2,000,000.

Contents: 'Quando, Quando': Engelbert Humperdinck (Boone, Tests and Renis, 1962); 'Where Do I Begin?' (*Love Story* theme): Mireille Mathieu (Carl Sigman and Francis Lai, 1970); 'Until It's Time for You to Go': Neil Diamond (Buffy Sainte-Marie, 1965); 'One Bad Apple': The Osmonds (George Jackson, 1971); 'Celia of the Seals': Donovan (Donovan Leitch, 1971); 'Home Lovin' Man': Andy Williams (Greenaway, Cook and Macauley, 1970); 'Rain': José Feliciano (José and Hilda Feliciano, 1971); 'My Way': Aretha Franklin (Paul Anka, G. Thibaut, C. François and Jacques Revaux, 1969); 'Fire and Rain': James Taylor (James Taylor 1969); 'Knock Three Times': James Last & Orchestra (I. Levine and L.R. Brown, 1971); 'A Boy Named Sue': Johnny Cash (Shel Silverstein, 1969); 'Oh Had I a Golden Thread': Nana Mouskouri; 'Innocent': Val Doonican; 'Vivace': Ekseption; 'My Lover My Friend': Anita Kerr; 'Mandrill': Mandrill.

THE ALLMAN BROTHERS BAND (instrumental and rock sextet)

EAT A PEACH (Album) *Capricorn* [USA]. Released in the U.S.A. in February 1972, this rose to No 3 for one week and lingered in the charts for 43 weeks, winning the R.I.A.A. Gold Disc award on 13 April 1972.

The Allman Brothers Band was formed in 1969 by Duane Allman who was born in 1946, raised in Nashville and later in Daytona Beach, Florida. Duane subsequently became acknowledged as the world's leading exponent of the bottleneck slide guitar. He first attracted notice through his guitar work on recording sessions for many prominent artists including Wilson Pickett, Aretha Franklin, Clarence Carter, King Curtis and other Atlantic stars. He led a band, Hourglass, with brother Greg Allman, and was later encouraged to form his own band. The two brothers joined up with a group called The Second Coming, led by Dickie Betts and Berry Oakley. Other members were Butch Trucks and Jai Johnany Johanson (drums, percussion). The band was an immediate success (1969) with the outstanding twin guitars of Duane Allman and Dickie Betts performing superb blues workouts and inventive music. They worked coast to coast and made several big-selling albums. By March 1971 they made their fourth appearance at the Fillmore East in New York.

During a vacation, on 29 October 1971, Duane Allman was killed in a motorcycle accident in Macon, Georgia. The five members of the band decided to carry on, and in December completed their fourth album 'Eat a Peach' which featured three tracks with Duane. The album met with great critical acclaim and became The Brothers' first platinum (million seller) disc. In mid-October 1972, pianist Chuck Leavell from Tuscaloosa, Alabama, joined the band. On 11 November 1972, bassist Berry Oakley was killed in a motorcycle accident very similar to Duane's. Lamar Williams was selected to take his place. Greg Allman later married Cher (of Sonny and Cher).

The new combination went on to further great success and in July 1973, headlined the largest outdoor rock concert ever, at Watkins Glenn, New York.

Contents of the album: 'Ain't Wastin' Time No More'; 'Les Brers in A Minor'; 'Melissa'; 'Mountain Jam'; 'One Way Out'; 'Trouble No More'; 'Stand Back'; 'Blue Sky'; 'Little Martha'.

Personnel for the disc: Duane Allman (guitar); Greg Allman (rhythm guitar, organ, vocals); Dickie Betts (slide guitar, lead guitar, vocals); Berry Oakley (bass guitar); Butch Trucks (drums, percussion); Johnany Johanson (drums, congas).

AMERICA (vocal and instrumental trio)

A HORSE WITH NO NAME *Warner Bros* [Britain & USA]. Written by Dewey Bunnell (of the group) this was released in Britain in January 1972 and in the U.S.A. in February 1972. It hit No 1 for one week in Britain and three weeks in the U.S.A., staying ten weeks in the British charts and 14 weeks in the U.S. bestsellers.

This disc sold a quick million in the U.S.A. and was awarded a Gold Disc by R.I.A.A. on 24 March. It also received the Grammy Award for Best New Artist(s) (1972).

America, a U.K.-based trio of young expatriate Americans, emerged in a very short time as one of the major contemporary acts of the 1970s. They were Gerry Beckley (vocals/guitar), Dewey Bunnell (vocals/guitar) and Dan Peek (vocals/guitar). Their average age was 20. They achieved the extremely uncommon feat of having a No 1 hit in both album and singles charts with first releases.

The trio met at an American school in Bushey, Hertfordshire, England, the sons of American officers stationed there. They all graduated from London Central High School in 1968, and played in various bands separately, occasionally joining one another after class for jam sessions. It wasn't until Dan Peek left for college in the U.S.A. then returned to England in 1969, that America became a serious proposition. They chose the name America while listening to an Americana jukebox. Some demo tracks were recorded in a studio built into an old farmhouse in Devon. The group then contacted Warner Brothers' English office which led to their debut album 'America' and their hit single 'A Horse with No Name'. The single took off immediately in Britain, so they embarked on a six-week North American tour where they were completely unknown. Their first concert was in the lunch room of a college in Ontario. Three weeks later the disc was No 1 in the U.S. charts, and they were topping the bill in Los Angeles. The single sent the 'America' album scurrying up the charts. The group's middle-of-the-road audiences both at home and abroad, plus their creative output, made them a major musical force. Theirs is the sort of success story that normally doesn't happen any more. The music industry usually takes many months or even years to build up an act to this status.

AMERICA (album) *Warner Bros* [*Britain & USA*]. Released in Britain in January 1972 and in the U.S.A. in February 1972, this got to No 11 for one week in Britain and No 1 for five weeks in the U.S.A. It stayed in the British bestsellers for seven weeks, and the U.S. charts for 40 weeks.

This London-produced album of original songs by the trio was a tremendous success in the U.S.A. at the same time as their single 'A Horse with No Name' (*q.v.*). It was awarded a Gold Disc by the R.I.A.A. on 10 March 1972, and went on to sell a million.

Contents: 'A Horse with No Name'; 'Children'; 'Clarice'; 'Donkey Jaw'; 'Everyone I Meet Is from California'; 'Here'; 'I Need You'; 'Never Found the Time'; 'Pigeon Song'; 'Rainy Day'; 'River Side'; 'Sandman'; 'Three Roses'.

All songs written by the group.

HOMECOMING (album) *Warner Bros* [*USA*]. Released in the U.S.A. in November 1972, this album went to No 5 for two weeks, staying in the charts for 32 weeks.

This album was recorded after America left Britain to take up residency in California. It was awarded a Gold Disc by the R.I.A.A. on 18 December 1972, and the million sale was reported in 1975.

Contents: 'California Revisited'; 'Don't Cross the River'; 'Head and Heart'; 'Saturn Nights'; 'Ventura Highway'; 'Till the Sun Comes Up Again'; 'Cornwall Blank'; 'Moon Song'; 'Only in Your Heart'; 'To Each His Own'.

All songs written by the group.

ARGENT (rock quartet)

HOLD YOUR HEAD UP *Epic* [*Britain*]. Released in Britain in March 1972 and in the U.S.A. in June 1972, this reached No 4 for two weeks in Britain and one week in the U.S.A. and stayed in the British charts for ten weeks and the U.S. bestsellers for 16 weeks. It was a global million-seller by November 1972.

Argent consisted of Rod Argent (keyboards/vocals), Russ Ballard (lead vocals/guitar), Jim Rodford (bass) and Robert Henrit

(drums). Rod Argent was originally a member of The Zombies (*q.v.*) which split up in 1968. Argent formed his band in 1970 with his cousin Jim Rodford and Ballard and Henrit from the group Unit Four Plus Two. They chose the name Argent, and thus became the second group to borrow a name directly from one member – the first being Manfred Mann.

The song has a strange history. It was originally to have been part of an album, but was put out as a single, six-and-a-half-minute version, written by Argent and Chris White (both ex-Zombie members) in 1971. This turned out to be a 'sleeper' over the following six months, and a shorter version was released in place of the original maxi-single. Sales then rocketed to 12,000 a day. The group subsequently made tours in Britain and the U.S.A. where they played to enthusiastic audiences. They had toured the U.S.A. in 1970 playing both Fillmores. The American concerts were, in fact, their very first dates as Argent, the initial interest in the States coming as a result of Rod's association with The Zombies.

EDWARD BEAR (vocal trio)

LAST SONG *Capitol* [*USA*]. Written by Larry Evoy, this was released in the U.S.A. in December 1972, going to No 2 for one week and staying in the charts for 18 weeks. It sold a million by 15 March 1973, and was awarded a Gold Disc by the R.I.A.A.

Edward Bear (the original name of Winnie the Pooh) was formed in the late 1960s, and it took six years before this big success came to them in the U.S.A. They had always been among the top performers in Canada, steadily working and recording. The organist on the disc is Paul Weldon (owner of a thriving jacket and graphic design firm) and it was his only disc with the group. He was later replaced by Bob Kendall.

The group appeared on 'Midnight Special' and 'American Bandstand'.

CHUCK BERRY

MY DING-A-LING *Chess* [*USA*]. Released in the U.S.A. in July 1972 and in Britain in October 1972, this slightly naughty ditty went to No 1 for two weeks in the U.S.A. and four weeks in Britain, staying in the British charts for 16 weeks and the U.S. bestsellers for 17 weeks.

Chuck Berry wrote 'My Ding-a-Ling' in the early 1950s. Mercury Records turned it down. It was however recorded by Dave Bartholomew in 1954 and by Chuck (under the new title of 'My Tambourine') in 1958. Chuck included the song under its original title on his album 'London Chuck Berry Session' (1972) and the single issue rocketed to No 1 with R.I.A.A. Gold Disc award by September 1972. It took Britain by storm and was their Christmas hit of 1972. The disc was cut at the Lanchester Arts Festival. This risqué novelty song was a surprise Anglo-American hit, and in Britain aroused attack by Mrs Mary Whitehouse, a 'clean-up TV' campaigner. The publicity undoubtedly enhanced his career, putting Chuck in the superstar category of rock hierarchy with repeats of his 1950s hits in his stage act.

'My Ding-a-Ling' was Chuck's first officially certified million seller, though some of his earlier discs had also reportedly sold likewise. It sold around two million globally.

Chuck's output up to 1972 was around 30 singles and 20 albums. To many people he was, and is, the king of rock'n'roll.

DANIEL BOONE

BEAUTIFUL SUNDAY *Penny Farthing* [*Britain*] *Discomate* [*Japan*]. Written by R. McQueen and Daniel Boone and released April 1972, this went to No 21 in Britain and No 15 for two weeks in the U.S.A., staying in the U.S. charts for 20 weeks.

Singer Daniel Boone's first success was in 1971 with the British song 'Daddy Don't You Walk So Fast' for the Penny Farthing Record Co., run by Larry Page. 'Beautiful Sunday' had a modest success in Britain but was high in the charts in the U.S.A. when released there on the Mercury label. A Gold Disc was awarded for a million global sales in July 1972. The disc was re-released in 1974 on a different label in Britain, again with modest sales. Larry Page then took it to a new publishing company (1976) in Japan – Shinko Publishing – who in turn took it to a new record company called Discomate in Tokyo. The song was adopted as the theme tune for a very popular Japanese TV programme, broadcast at the mind-sapping hour of 7 a.m., called Good Morning 720. The disc started to sell in a very big way, 540,000 copies the first week and a total of 900,000 in two weeks, and subsequently amassed a 2,000,000 plus sale, staying at No 1 in the Japanese charts for 16 weeks during 1976, and becoming one of the biggest records ever in Japan. Soon there were 18 cover versions of the song, two of them sung in Japanese with English chorus which reached the Japanese Top 10.

Boone then made a two-week promotional visit to Japan, and made more than 20 TV appearances in ten days, and established himself as a performer. His real name is Peter Green, born in Birmingham, England. He first worked in the jewellery trade, then formed The Beachcombers with three friends, and worked in the Midlands for five years with the group.

BREAD

EVERYTHING I OWN *Elektra* [*USA*]. Written by David Gates (of the group), this was released in the U.S.A. in January 1972, rising to No 5 for three weeks and staying in the charts for 16 weeks.

Another great disc by the instrumentally oriented rock quartet, whose speciality was close harmonic singing and precision playing. The million sale of this disc was reported at the end of March 1972. David Gates became a solo performer in 1972.

THE BRIGHTER SIDE OF DARKNESS

LOVE JONES *20th Century* [*USA*]. Written by Randolph Murph, Ralph Eskridge and Clarence Johnson, this was released in the U.S.A. in November 1972, going to No 8 for two weeks and staying 13 weeks in the charts.

This is said to be the very first record by a group of Chicago teenagers. Ralph Eskridge, Randolph Murph, and Larry Washington met at Windy City's Calumet High School. They had played at local dances, etc. for several months, when they were discovered by Mrs Anna Preston, mother of a musically-gifted family, who had been an entertainer herself for several years. Acting as manager/music director for the group, she added Darryl Lamont (then 12), whom she had been grooming, in order to round out her new discovery's vocal sound. She chose the group's name as it expressed her belief in their bright future. The quartet ran away with a local talent contest and came to the attention of General Entertainment Company producer/hit maker, Clarence Johnson, who recorded them with 'Love Jones', a song on which he, Ralph and Randolph collaborated.

The disc was taken to 20th Century Records' president Russ Regan, resulting in a long-term contract with the label. By 9 February 1973 it sold the million with R.I.A.A. Gold Disc award.

JAMES BROWN

(GET ON THE) GOOD FOOT – Part 1 *Polydor* [*USA*]. Written by James Brown, Fred Wesley and Joe Mims, this was released in the U.S.A. in July 1972, going to No 9 for two weeks and staying in the charts for 15 weeks.

The clean, crisp sound of this disc gave James Brown another million seller, with Gold Disc award from R.I.A.A. on 19 September 1972.

THE CARPENTERS

HURTING EACH OTHER *A & M* [*USA*]. Written by G. Geld and Peter Udell and arranged by Richard Carpenter, this was released in the U.S.A. in January 1972, zooming to No 1 for one week and staying in the bestsellers for 13 weeks.

A very quick million seller for Karen and Richard Carpenter, with R.I.A.A. Gold Disc award on 29 February 1972.

THE JIMMY CASTOR BUNCH
(vocal/instrumental quintet)

TROGLODYTE (Cave Man) *RCA* [*USA*]. Written by The Bunch, this novelty number was released in the U.S.A. in May 1972, going to No 2 for one week and sticking in the charts for 14 weeks. It was a million seller by 30 June 1972, and received a Gold Disc award from the R.I.A.A.

Jimmy Castor was born in The Bronx, New York City, in 1943. His early love of music subsequently won him admittance to New York's High School of Music and Art, where he got a fine background in musical theory and practice. He also plays saxophone and piano, and is vocalist, dancer, actor and songwriter.

As a teenager, he wrote a hit song 'I Promise to Remember' in 1956 for Frankie Lymon & The Teenagers. After graduation, he formed his own band playing New York nightspots, and came up with another success 'Hey Leroy' in 1966, when he left City College where he had been studying accountancy, and went into music full-time. 'Troglodyte' was a breakout in Washington, DC, from his album 'It's Just Begun'. Phone requests to station WOL forced its release as a single. The group's music is a cross between James Brown and Isaac Hayes – a sort of powerful, driving, soul music.

Jimmy's encompassing talents also include producing, arranging, and publishing, his skills earning him the name of 'Everything Man'.

Personnel of The Jimmy Castor Bunch: Jimmy Castor (vocals, sax and timbales), Gerry Thomas (trumpet and piano), Doug Gibson (bass), Harry Jensen (guitar) and Lenny Fridie, Jr (congas).

CHEECH & CHONG

BIG BAMBU (Album) *Ode* [*USA*]. Released in the U.S.A. in June 1972, this went to No 1 for one week, but took up residence in the charts for 100 weeks.

The second million seller for this outstanding comedy duo, with sales of 2,100,000 plus. A Gold Disc was awarded on 21 August 1972 by the R.I.A.A. This album of their inimitable satirical portrayals of their roles in contemporary society contained: 'Sister Mary Elephant'; 'Ralph and Herbie'; 'Bust'; 'Streets of New York or Los Angeles or San Francisco or . . .'; 'Rebuttal – Speaker Ashley Roachclip'; 'Continuing Adventures of Pedro de Pacas and Man'; 'Television Medley – Tortured Old Man/Empire Hancock/Let's Make It a Dope Deal/Unamerican Bandstand'.

All material by Cheech and Chong.

NAOMI CHIAKI

KASSAI (Applause) *Nippon Columbia* [*Japan*]. Released in Japan 10 September 1972, this went to No 1 for one week, and stayed 17 weeks in the Japanese Top 10.

Naomi Chiaki, an ex-office-girl, achieved a million sale in Japan with this disc by February 1973.

CHICAGO

CHICAGO V (Album) *Columbia* [*USA*]. Released in the U.S.A. in July 1972, this stayed at No 1 for nine weeks and in the charts for 39 weeks.

Another great album from Chicago, with a massive sale for this consistently successful jazz-rock band. It received the Gold Disc award from R.I.A.A. on 31 July, within days of release, and sold well over a million, their fifth consecutive album to do so. It contained the hit single 'Saturday in the Park', and some sensitive piano work by Robert Lamm in 'Alma Mater'.

Contents: 'All is Well'; 'Alma Mater'; 'Dialogue'; 'Goodbye'; 'A Hit by Varese'; 'Now That You've Gone'; 'Saturday in the Park'; 'State of the Union'; 'While the City Sleeps'.

All material by the group.

SATURDAY IN THE PARK *Columbia* [*USA*]. Written by Robert Lamm (of the group), this was released in the U.S.A. in July 1972, going to No 3 for two weeks and staying in the charts for 13 weeks.

The prime cut from the Chicago V album (backed with 'Dialogue'), produced by James William Guercio. The song paints a scene of inner city greenery. The million sale was reported on 9 November 1972, when R.I.A.A. awarded a Gold Disc.

CHICORY TIP (vocal/instrumental quartet)

SON OF MY FATHER *CBS* [*Britain*]. Written by P. Bellotte, Michael Holm and Giorgio Moroder (originally published in Germany under the title 'Nachts scheint die sonne'), the English words and adaptation are by Chicory Tip. It was released in Britain in January 1972, going to No 1 for two weeks and staying 10 weeks in the charts.

Chicory Tip personnel: Peter Hewson (lead singer) born 1 September 1950, Gillingham, Kent; Rick Foster (lead guitarist/synthesizer/keyboards); Barry Mayger (bass guitar) born 1 June 1950, Maidstone, Kent; Brian Shearer (drums) born 4 May 1951, Lewisham, London. The first three were together since school days, and the quartet was discovered in Maidstone in 1970 by Roger Easterby. Hewson chose the group's name from a coffee bottle which reminded him of chicory. They made their first public appearance at Tudor House, Maidstone, in 1968, and first broadcast in 'The Jimmy Young Show' in September 1970.

'Son of My Father' (by an Italian and two German writers) started off on the Continent, where it was a hit for composer-singer Giorgio Moroder. Chicory Tip's English version sold over 250,000 in Britain, and amassed the million with sales from other countries, by July 1972.

The prominent characteristic of the disc is the use made of a Moog synthesizer which was played by record producer Chris Thomas on the session. Foster was replaced by Rod Cloutt (lead guitar/synthesizer/organ/vocals) in October 1972.

THE CHI-LITES

OH GIRL *Brunswick* [*USA*]. Released in the U.S.A. in March 1972, this went to No 1 for two weeks and stayed in the charts for 15 weeks. In Britain it made No 12 for one week.

Writer Eugene Record also produced the disc which sold a million by May 1972, with Gold Disc award.

(See 1971 for Chi-Lites data.)

CORNELIUS BROTHERS & SISTER ROSE

TOO LATE TO TURN BACK NOW *United Artists* [*USA*]. Written by Eddie Cornelius, this was released in the U.S.A. in May 1972, making No 1 for one week, and staying in the charts for 15 weeks.

It was the second million seller for the talented trio. A Gold Disc was awarded by R.I.A.A. in August 1972.

CREEDENCE CLEARWATER REVIVAL

MARDI GRAS (Album) *Fantasy* [*USA*]. Released in the U.S.A. in April 1972, this went to No 12 for two weeks, and remained in the charts 24 weeks.

It was the final album by the group before it disbanded, and their only one as a trio, Tom Fogerty having left through a clash of personality. Although not one of the group's best albums, it did receive a Gold Disc award from R.I.A.A. on 12 June 1972, and is subsequently said to have sold a million units.

Contents of the album: 'Lookin' for a Reason'; 'Take It Like a Friend'; 'Someday Never Comes'; 'Sweet Hitch-Hiker'; 'Need Someone to Hold'; 'Tearin Up the Country'; 'What Are You Gonna Do?'; 'Sail Away'; 'Door to Door'; 'Up Around the Bend'.

All songs by John Fogerty.

CREEDENCE GOLD (Album) *Fantasy* [*USA*]. Released in the U.S.A. in November 1972, this classic compilation reached No 15 for one week and stayed in the charts 37 weeks. It was an album of original Creedence Clearwater Revival's classic series of hit performances taken from their bestselling albums. It received a Gold Disc award from R.I.A.A. on 26 January 1973, and subsequently sold a million units.

Contents: (*)'Proud Mary' (1969); (*)'Down on the Corner' (1969); (*)'Bad Moon Rising' (1969); 'I Heard It Through the Grapevine' (Norman Whitfield and Barrett Strong, 1967); 'The Midnight Special' (traditional, arranged John Fogerty, 1969); (*) 'Have You Ever Seen the Rain?' (1970); 'Born on the Bayou' (1969); 'Susie Q' (Dale Hawkins, Stanley Lewis and Eleanor Broadwater, 1957).

((*) denotes sold a million as a single.)

All songs by John Fogerty unless otherwise indicated.

MAC DAVIS (country-and-western vocalist)

BABY, DON'T GET HOOKED ON ME *Columbia* [*USA*]. Written by Mac Davis and released in the U.S.A. in July 1972 this hit No 1 for three weeks, staying up in the charts for 19 weeks. It was No 29 in Britain.

Mac Davis was born in Lubbock, Texas, on 21 January 1942. As singer and writer, his style can be traced back to childhood. His father made him sing in the church choir, and he soon started making up songs. At 15, he became fascinated with rock'n'roll, and his works reflect his origins with the dynamics of Southern rock'n'roll tempered with a country feel. At this time, he was playing in a band and writing rock songs like 'Mau Mau Mary' and 'I Got a Flea on Me'. After two years at college, Mac worked as a record promotion executive for Lowery Music in Atlanta, then as district manager for Liberty Records and, after five years, with the company's publishing outlet, Metric Music. He continued writing songs under two pseudonyms, Scott Davis and Mac Scott Davis, so as not to be confused with the lyricist Mack David. This made matters more confusing and he then decided to write under his own name. Mac had long hoped he would write for Elvis Presley. This ambition was achieved when Presley taped several of his songs, notably 'In the Ghetto'. Many other

artists wanted his material, including Bobby Goldsboro, Andy Williams, O.C. Smith, Kenny Rogers & The First Edition, Lou Rawls and Glen Campbell. His songs were heard in *Norwood*, the film starring Glen Campbell. He also wrote original material for Presley's first TV special and for two of his films.

As an artist he was repeatedly asked back for TV shows, and made personal appearances in Las Vegas and college concerts. His first record was 'The Song Painter' for Columbia. Then came 'Baby Don't Get Hooked on Me' (produced by Rick Hall) which he composed initially as a joke. This became a national hit, and received a Gold Disc award from R.I.A.A. on 20 September 1972 for million plus sale.

Mac Davis started publishing company of his own, Song Painter Music (Screen Gems).

SAMMY DAVIS, JR

CANDY MAN *MGM* [*USA*]. Written by Anthony Newley and Leslie Bricusse, this was released in the U.S.A. in January 1972, going to No 1 for three weeks and staying in the charts 21 weeks.

'Candy Man' was Sammy Davis' first big hit since 1962 and his first top single. It sold the million by 21 August 1972 and was awarded a Gold Disc by R.I.A.A. The song, from the Paramount film *Willy Wonka and the Chocolate Factory*, is a sort of children's novelty. Its popularity was completely unpredictable as the disc was not the type of record that normally made the playlists. It was, however, the aggressive promotion by the label that finally made a breakthrough on middle-of-the road stations, rarely a source of No 1 hits.

DEEP PURPLE

MACHINE HEAD (Album) *Purple* [*Britain*] *Warner* [*USA*]. Released in Britain in March 1972 and in the U.S.A. in May 1972, this went to No 6 for two weeks in the U.S.A. staying in the charts for 118 weeks. In Britain it made No 1, and stayed in the Top 10 for eight weeks. With over two years' run in the U.S. charts, this album firmly established the group in America, and was awarded a Gold Disc by R.I.A.A. on 6 November 1972. By April 1974 it had sold a million units, with Platinum Disc award.

Contents: 'Highway Star'; 'Maybe I'm a Leo'; 'Pictures of Home'; 'Never Before'; 'Smoke on the Water'; 'Lazy'; 'Space Truckin''.

In 1976, the personnel of the group was Glenn Hughes, Ian Paice, Jon Lord, David Coverdale and Tommy Bolin. Bolin died in Miami on 4 December 1976.

MADE IN JAPAN (double album) *Purple* [*Britain*] *Warner* [*USA*]. Released in Britain in December 1972 and in the U.S.A. in March 1973, this went to No 16 in Britain, but No 6 for two weeks in the U.S.A., staying in the charts for 52 weeks. It received the Gold Disc award from R.I.A.A. 31 May 1973.

This double album topped off the group's breakthrough around the world, and by April 1974 a million units sale was reported, with Platinum Disc award. Deep Purple is the first English group to record a complete package in Japan. The album comprises seven compositions including 'Smoke on the Water', 'Highway Star', 'Strange Kind of Woman' and 'Space Truckin''.

MICHEL DELPECH

POUR UN FLIRT (For a Flirt) *Barclay* [*France*]. A million sale for this popular French artist's disc was reported in July 1972.

JOHN DENVER

ROCKY MOUNTAIN HIGH (Album) *RCA* [*USA*]. Released in the U.S.A. in September 1972 and in Britain in January 1973, this reached No 1 for one week in the U.S.A. and No 11 in Britain. It stayed 53 weeks in the U.S. bestsellers. A Gold Disc was awarded by R.I.A.A. on 30 December 1972 for this big success for John Denver. By April 1974, the sale was almost two

million. An album of powerful material and performances, it contained: 'Rocky Mountain High' (John Denver and Mike Taylor); 'Mother Nature's Son' (John Lennon and Paul McCartney); 'Paradise' (John Prine); 'For Baby (For Bobbie)'; 'Darcy Farrow'; 'Prisoners'; 'Goodbye Again'; 'Season Suite: Summer, Fall, Winter, Late Winter, Early Spring (When Everybody Goes to Mexico) and Spring'. All material by John Denver unless otherwise indicated.

ROCKY MOUNTAIN HIGH *RCA* [*USA*]. Written by John Denver and Mike Taylor, this was released in the U.S.A. in November 1972, going to No 7 for one week and staying in the charts for 20 weeks.

This song was described as 'sparkling with sincerity and beautiful lyrical images', and the disc sold a global million. It was taken from Denver's album of the same title, and helped to take him further towards recognition as a talented singer/songwriter.

THE DETROIT SPINNERS (vocal quintet)

I'LL BE AROUND *Atlantic* [*USA*]. Written by Thom Bell and Phil Hurtt and released in the U.S.A. in July 1972, this reached No 1 for one week, staying 20 weeks in the charts. R.I.A.A. Gold Disc award on 30 October 1972.

The Detroit Spinners called themselves The Dominicos when they first began singing at Ferndale High in 1955. The original group, Pervis Jackson (bass lead singer), Henry Fambrough (baritone lead singer), Billy Henderson (tenor lead singer), Bobby Smith (tenor lead singer) and Crathman Spencer, all lived and grew up in the same area, Royal Oak Township, Ferndale, Michigan. They did the route of local talent contests and radio shows in the late 1950s, and U.S.O. shows that really gave them the chance to get together. In 1959-60, Harvey Fuqua, brother-in-law of Berry Gordy, took them in hand and helped to get them their first record on the Tri-Phi label, 'That's What Girls Are Made For' (1961). By this time, the group were known as The Spinners, and when Fuqua joined with Motown in 1965, taking his labels there, he took the group with him. They then became The Motown Spinners. Later they became The Detroit Spinners to avoid confusion with the British Spinners folk group. At Motown they were coached by Charlie Atkins and had some of the early Motown successes. They travelled on and off with The Supremes for two years and also worked with other Motown greats such as Gladys Knight and The Pips. In 1968, Crathman Spencer left and was replaced by Edgar Edwards, who was later replaced by George 'G.C.' Cameron. In 1970, Stevie Wonder produced their big hit 'It's a Shame'. In May 1971, Cameron was replaced by Phillipe Wynne. The Spinners joined Atlantic Records in 1972, teaming up with Thom Bell, the man mainly responsible for the smooth 'Philadelphia Sound'. He co-wrote their first Atlantic hit 'I'll be Around', The Spinners' first million-selling single on that label, and also produced, arranged and conducted the recording.

A dynamic quintet, with a wide repertoire, lively dance routine, comedy, impersonations, plus an ingenious blend of soulful, smooth songs, The Detroit Spinners have performed with most of the great names of soul, and played clubs and theatres from coast to coast, including New York's Philharmonic and Lincoln Center. The reverse side of this disc 'How Could I Let You Get Away' (by Yvette Davis) was also a hit.

COULD IT BE I'M FALLING IN LOVE? *Atlantic* [*USA*]. Released in the U.S.A. in December 1972 and in Britain in 1973, this hit No 1 for one week in the U.S.A. and No 11 in Britain. It stayed 15 weeks in the U.S. bestsellers and 11 weeks in the British lists. R.I.A.A. Gold Disc award on 13 February 1973.

A beautiful rhythm-and-blues ballad (written by Mystro and Lyric), and an outstanding production by Thom Bell. The disc sold a very quick million.

NEIL DIAMOND

SONG SUNG BLUE *Uni* [*USA*]. Released in the U.S.A. in April 1972 and in Britain in May 1972, this went to No 1 for two weeks in the U.S.A. and No 11 in Britain. It stayed in the U.S. charts 14 weeks, and 13 weeks in Britain.

A fine melodic song by singer/writer Neil Diamond. It received a Gold Disc award from R.I.A.A. for million sale on 27 July 1972.

MOODS (Album) *Uni* [*USA*]. Released in the U.S.A. and Britain in July 1972, the album went to No 4 for one week in the U.S.A. and No 7 in Britain. It stayed for 41 weeks in the U.S. bestsellers and 5 weeks in the British Top 10. R.I.A.A. awarded a Gold Disc on 31 August 1972. By December it had sold a reported million, and was given a Grammy Award for Best Engineered Recording of 1972.

Contents: 'Song Sung Blue'; 'Porcupine Pie'; 'High Rolling Man'; 'Canta Libre'; 'Captain Sunshine'; 'Play Me'; 'Gitchy Goomy'; 'Walk on Water'; 'Theme'; 'Prelude in E Major'; 'Morningside'.

All songs written by Neil Diamond.

HOT AUGUST NIGHT (Double album) *MCA* [*USA*]. Released in the U.S.A. in December 1972 this hit No 1 for one week, staying 71 weeks in the charts.

This album was recorded 'live' in the summer of 1972 during Diamond's record-breaking ten-day stand at the Greek Theatre in Los Angeles. It was the first on the new MCA Records label. R.I.A.A. awarded a Gold Disc on release on 23 December 1972. By early 1974 it had passed the million sale with platinum award, and later approached the two million mark. The album contained much of Neil's best-known material, including: 'Cracklin' Rosie'; 'Song Sung Blue'; 'Play Me'; 'Sweet Caroline'; 'Cherry Cherry'; 'Shilo'; 'Porcupine Pie'; 'Holly Holy'; 'I Am – I Said'; 'Soggy Pretzels'. Neil is supported by a 36-piece string section plus his own seven-member band. The album contained 17 songs in all.

DR HOOK & THE MEDICINE SHOW
SYLVIA'S MOTHER *Columbia* [*USA*]. Written by Shel Silverstein, this poignant tune was released in the U.S.A. in March 1972 and in Britain in June 1972. It went to No 1 for one week in the U.S.A., and No 2 for two weeks in Britain, staying 16 weeks in the U.S. bestsellers and 13 weeks on the British charts. R.I.A.A. Gold Disc award 2 August 1972.

Personnel of the group: Ray Sawyer (vocals); Dennis LaCorriere (vocals/guitar); George Cummings (guitar/steel guitar); Bill Francis (keyboards) and Jay David (drums).

The group got together playing the small bars and clubs in New Jersey, based around vocalists Ray Sawyer, a one-eyed ex-soul singer from Alabama, and LaCorriere from New Jersey. Songwriter Shel Silverstein saw them, and arranged for them to appear in and perform the music for the film *Who is Harry Kellerman and Why Is He Saying These Terrible Things About Me?* for which he had written the score. This resulted in the group being signed to CBS Records, for whom they recorded their first album 'Doctor Hook'. 'Sylvia's Mother' was a cut from this, and when issued as a single sold over a million, their very first.

Ray Sawyer is the strutting eye-patched Dr Hook of the group.

THE COVER OF ROLLING STONE *Columbia* [*USA*]. Released in the U.S.A. in November 1972, this went to No 4 for one week, staying in the bestsellers 21 weeks and receiving a R.I.A.A. Gold Disc award 4 April 1973.

Rolling Stone is a U.S. magazine that features musical and other articles on the current scene in America and elsewhere. This song is the story of what it's like to be on the cover of a magazine. It was the second huge success for the group and writer Shel Silverstein, with an over a million sale.

Rik Elswit (guitar) and Jans Garfat (bass) were added to the original quintet for this and subsequent recordings.

DOOBIE BROTHERS
TOULOUSE STREET (Album) *Warner* [*USA*]. Released in the U.S.A. in August 1972, this went to No 16 for one week, but rode the charts for 103 weeks, getting R.I.A.A. Gold Disc award 21 August 1973.

The Doobie Brothers (a 'doobie' is American slang for a joint) began in the student ghetto of San Jose, California, in 1971, playing in bars, and was formed as Pud by Tom Johnston (guitar, harp, keyboards), John Hartman (drums) and since departed Greg Murphy. Pat Simmons (guitar, vocals) was added, and the quartet made its first album 'The Doobie Brothers' (1972). A second drummer, Mick Hossack, and Tiran Porter (bass) were added in 1972 and the quintet recorded the album 'Toulouse Street'. This album, including the single 'Listen to the Music', brought them national attention, and was a consistent seller for two years. By August 1974 it had sold over a million and was awarded a Platinum Disc. The disc, however, was not a success in Britain, though the Doobies had sell-out performances at London's Rainbow theatre on their U.K. visit in early 1974.

Contents of the album: 'Listen to the Music'; 'Jesus is Just Alright'; 'Got-to-get-back-to Jamaica'; 'Disciple'; 'Rockin' Down the Highway'; 'Cotton Mouth' (Seals and Crofts); 'Don't Start Talkin' to Me' (Sonny Boy Williamson); 'Snake Man'.

THE DRAMATICS
IN THE RAIN *Stax-Volt* [*USA*]. Written by Tony Hester and released in the U.S.A. in February 1972, this went to No 3 for one week, staying in the charts 14 weeks.

It was the second million seller from the group's first album, 'Whatcha See Is Whatcha Get' (see Dramatics, 1971).

EMERSON, LAKE & PALMER
TRILOGY (Album) *Island* [*Britain*] *Cotillion* [*USA*]. Released in Britain in June 1972 and a month later in the U.S.A., this went to No 2 for one week in Britain and No 4 for two weeks in the U.S.A. It stayed for 26 weeks in the British charts and 37 weeks in the U.S. bestsellers. R.I.A.A. Gold Disc award 5 September 1972 made this the fourth subsequent million units seller for the trio.

Contents: 'Endless Enigma Part 1'; 'Fugue'; 'Endless Enigma Part 2'; 'From the Beginning'; 'Sheriff'; 'Hoedown'; 'Trilogy'; 'Living Sin'; 'Abaddon's Bolero'.

DONNA FARGO (country-and-western vocalist)
THE HAPPIEST GIRL IN THE WHOLE U.S.A. *Dot* [*USA*]. Written by Donna Fargo, this was released in the U.S.A. in 1972 going to No 7 for two weeks, staying in the charts 17 weeks. It received R.I.A.A. Gold Disc award on 23 August 1972 and a Grammy Award, Best Country Female Vocal Performance, 1972.

Donna Fargo (real name Yvonne Vaughn) was born in Mount Airy, North Carolina, raised in that state and educated at High Point (NC) College and University of Southern California. As a youngster, she always wanted to sing professionally, and after moving to California, her desire became even stronger. She became a schoolteacher, and started playing guitar and composing. At nights, she performed in small clubs in and around Los Angeles. During this period she met Stan Silver, who guided her career and became her husband. 'The Happiest Girl' was her first release for the Dot Label. It became a national hit and No 1 on the country-and-western charts with a million sale after three months on the market. The song was written in August 1971, and recorded the following November in Nashville. She continued teaching after the song became a hit, and then sang professionally all over the U.S.A. 'The Happiest Girl' was the most performed country song of 1972 and both song and singer received many awards. Donna stormed the music industry with her self-created sound.

THE HAPPIEST GIRL IN THE WHOLE U.S.A. (Album) *Dot* [*USA*]. Released in the U.S.A. in July 1972, this went to No 39 for week and stayed in the charts for 43 weeks. R.I.A.A. awarded a Gold Disc on 29 January 1973.

It had sold a million copies by June 1974 and received plati-

num status. The album, based on the title of her singles hit, included: 'The Happiest Girl in the Whole U.S.A.' (Donna Fargo); 'Funny Face' (Donna Fargo); 'Manhattan' (Richard Rodgers and Lorenz Hart, 1925); and 'Kansas'.

FUNNY FACE *Dot* [*USA*]. Released in the U.S.A. in August 1972, this reached No 5 for two weeks, staying 20 weeks in the charts, and winning a R.I.A.A. Gold Disc award 4 January 1973.

Taken from Donna's album 'The Happiest Girl in the Whole U.S.A.', this sold over a million, her second single to do so. The disc was her second No 1 in the U.S.A. country-and-western charts. 'Funny Face' was inspired by her husband, who always called her by that name, and is an emotional love ballad.

THE FIFTH DIMENSION
LAST NIGHT I DIDN'T GET TO SLEEP AT ALL *Bell* [*USA*]. Released in the U.S.A. in March 1972, this got to No 6 for three weeks and stayed in the charts 17 weeks. It won R.I.A.A. Gold Disc award on 12 July 1972. It made a personal triumph for British writer Tony Macauley, with a million sale for the famous American vocal quintet.

ROBERTA FLACK
THE FIRST TIME EVER I SAW YOUR FACE *Atlantic* [*USA*]. Written by Ewan MacColl, this was released in the U.S.A. in March 1972 and in Britain in May 1972. It went to No 1 for six weeks in the U.S.A. and No 14 for one week in Britain. It stayed in the U.S. bestsellers for 18 weeks and 15 weeks in the British charts. R.I.A.A. Gold Disc award came on 19 April 1972, and the disc won a Grammy Award for Record of the Year (1972). The Grammy Award for Song of the Year (Songwriter's Award) went to Ewan McColl.

Roberta Flack was born in Asheville, North Carolina, and raised in Virginia by her musically-inclined parents. Roberta was herself an accomplished pianist at the age of four. When 15, she graduated from Howard University with a BA in music. She then worked as a teacher in Washington, DC, and took a part-time job accompanying opera singers at the Tivoli Restaurant, directed an amateur production of *Aida* and then left teaching for a full-time musical career. Her residency (1967) in Washington at Mr Henry's pub brought her to the attention of many famous people, including Les McCann, a well-known jazz pianist, who took her to Atlantic Records where she cut her first album 'First Take' (1971). This included 'The First Time Ever I Saw Your Face' written by British folk singer/songwriter Ewan

MacColl. The producers of the film *Play Misty For Me* asked if they could use the song in the soundtrack, and when the film became a success, record dealers were inundated with requests for the song. Atlantic then issued it as a single, and after only one month, Roberta's rendering of the song sold over the million. It was the top song in the U.S.A. of 1972.

From then on, all Roberta's albums and singles were big sellers, and she became the potential contender to the 'Queen of Soul', Aretha Franklin's throne, though they are very different performers.

Songwriter Ewan MacColl was born in 1916 in Auchterarder, Perthshire, Scotland. In the 1950s he was a significant figure in British folk music, and subsequently a star of TV, radio, films and discs. He married Peggy Seeger, a well-known folksinger herself and sister of Pete Seeger.

ROBERTA FLACK WITH DONNY HATHAWAY
WHERE IS THE LOVE? *Atlantic* [*USA*]. Written by Ralph MacDonald and William Salter, this was released in the U.S.A. in May 1972, going to No 5 for two weeks, and staying in the charts for 14 weeks. In Britain it reached No 29. R.I.A.A. Gold Disc award came on 5 September 1972, and the duo won the Grammy Award for Best Pop Folk and Rock Vocal Performance by a duo, group or chorus, 1972.

Second million seller for Roberta, and first for brilliant arranger-singer-pianist Donny Hathaway. The song is a cut from the 'Roberta Flack and Donny Hathaway Album' (1972). Donny was born in Chicago in 1945 and at the age of three was billed as 'The Nation's Youngest Gospel Singer'. He attended Howard University, Washington, DC, in 1964 on a fine arts scholarship. Then he joined the Ric Powell Trio as pianist, and entered the recording industry as arranger, songwriter, producer, session keyboard and percussionist for Curtis Mayfield and The Impressions, then working with Roberta Flack, The Staple Singers, Woody Herman, Jerry Butler and many other stars. He recorded principally in New York with the top black session men to back his talents. Donny died in February 1979.

THE FOUR TOPS
KEEPER OF THE CASTLE *ABC/Dunhill* [*USA*]. Released in the U.S.A. in October 1972 and written by Dennis Lambert and Brian Potter, this rose to No 9 for one week in the U.S.A. and No 17 in Britain. It stayed in the U.S. charts 13 weeks.

The million sale of this disc was reported in early 1973. It is a cut from The Four Tops album of the same title. The group, still with the same personnel as in 1954 when first formed, scored many rhythm-and-blues hits since 1963 and have been one of the most consistent entertainers in the music industry in both recording and personal appearances. This was their first big hit on their new label, produced by writers Lambert and Potter with Steve Barri.

ARETHA FRANKLIN

DAY DREAMING *Atlantic* [*USA*]. Released in the U.S.A. in March 1972, this went to No 5 for one week, staying in the charts 16 weeks and winning R.I.A.A. Gold Disc award on 19 April 1972.

Yet another triumph and fast million seller for 'Lady Soul' Aretha, her 13th, and written by herself.

GALLERY

NICE TO BE WITH YOU *Sussex* [*USA*]. Released in the U.S.A. in February 1972, and written by J. Gold, this hit No 1 for one week and stayed in the charts 22 weeks; it achieved R.I.A.A. Gold Disc award on 20 June 1972.

Dennis Coffey, of 'Scorpio' hit (1971), produced Gallery. The members of the group are so far unidentified.

GARY GLITTER (rock vocalist)

ROCK & ROLL, Parts 1 & 2 *Bell* [*Britain*]. Released in Britain in March 1972 and in the U.S.A. in July 1972 and written by Gary Glitter and Mike Leander, this stayed at No 2 for three weeks in Britain and No 3 for one week in the U.S.A. It stayed in the British charts for 15 weeks, and the U.S. bestsellers 13 weeks.

Gary Glitter (real name Paul Gadd) was born 8 May 1944 in Banbury, Oxfordshire. He entered show business at the age of 14, appearing with two friends as guitar trio at the Safari Club, London, under the name of Paul Raven. He then toured with Tommy Steele, Engelbert Humperdinck and Cliff Richard, recording his first disc 'Alone in the Night' for Decca (1960). In

1961, he had a hit with 'Walk on By' and 'Tower of Strength' (both for Parlophone), played in German clubs, and made a total of 9 singles. In 1965, he met Mike Leander who became his co-writer and manager. A contract with MCA in 1967 resulted in his being featured on the album 'Jesus Christ Superstar'. He also recorded 'Here Comes the Sun' under the name of Paul Monday. It was, however, in 1971, when he signed with Bell Records and changed his name to Gary Glitter, that he really became famous with the disc of 'Rock & Roll' that sold three million plus globally, a million of these in America alone. The disc took four months to get in the British charts through the discotheques and night-clubs, and was the forerunner of a string of hits for him. By the end of 1975, he had sold 18 million records, and had made worldwide tours to enthusiastic teenagers.

AL GREEN

LET'S STAY TOGETHER (Album) *Hi* [*USA*]. Released in the U.S.A. in January 1972, this went to No 8 for two weeks, staying in the topsellers for 56 weeks and netting R.I.A.A. Gold Disc award on 28 April 1972.

The album was based on the million-seller single of the same title. The million sale, platinum status, was reported in May 1975.

Contents of the album: 'Let's Stay Together'; 'I've Never Found a Girl'; 'So You're Leaving'; 'It Ain't No Fun to Me'; 'Talk to Me'; 'Old Time Lovin' '; 'Judy'; 'What Is This Feeling?'; 'Tomorrow's Dreams'; 'How Can You Mend a Broken Heart?'; 'La-La for You'.

LOOK WHAT YOU DONE FOR ME *Hi* [*USA*]. Released in the U.S.A. in March 1972, this went to No 3 for three weeks, staying in the charts 14 weeks and getting R.I.A.A. Gold Disc award on 28 April 1972. It was No 44 in Britain.

A fast million-seller for Al Green, and his successful collaborators Willie Mitchell and Al Jackson.

I'M STILL IN LOVE WITH YOU *Hi* [*USA*]. Released in the U.S.A. in June 1972, this achieved No 1 for one week, staying in the charts for 14 weeks. R.I.A.A. Gold Disc award came on 29 August 1972. It was No 35 in Britain.

Yet another quick million-seller for Al Green and his writers Willie Mitchell and Al Jackson.

YOU OUGHT TO BE WITH ME *Hi* [*USA*]. Released in the U.S.A. in October 1972, this also went to No 1 for one week, staying in the charts for 15 weeks and claiming the R.I.A.A. Gold Disc award on 15 December 1972.

Third million-seller single in this year for Al, his co-writers, and the legendary producer Willie Mitchell.

I'M STILL IN LOVE WITH YOU (album) *Hi* [*USA*]. Released in the U.S.A. in October 1972, this went to No 3 for two weeks, and stayed for 67 weeks in the bestsellers. R.I.A.A. Gold Disc award was announced on 29 November 1972.

The second million-seller album in 1972 for Al Green, based on the title of his hit single disc. The million platinum-status figure was reported in May 1975.

The album included his two big hits, 'I'm Still in Love with You' and 'Look What You Done for Me', plus other material by Al Green, Al Jackson and producer Willie Mitchell.

ALBERT HAMMOND

IT NEVER RAINS IN SOUTHERN CALIFORNIA *Mums* [*USA*]. Written by Albert Hammond and M. Hazelwood this was released in the U.S.A. in October 1972, going to No 2 for one week, and staying in the charts 16 weeks. It got R.I.A.A. Gold Disc award on 9 January 1973.

Albert Hammond was born in England and spent most of his early years in Gibraltar. He began entertaining professionally at 13. Albert travelled with his brother in a group, The Diamond Boys, at 16, and two years later left the group and went to England. In his early 20s he played with a group called Los

Cuico Ricardos and was introduced to Mike Hazelwood at Radio Luxembourg, later collaborating with him on songs (1966). Their 'Little Arrows' (1968) was a million seller for Leapy Lee, and 'Gimme dat Ding' was another hit. Both were written for a children's TV show 'Oliver and the Overlord' in Britain for which they won awards. They had eight hits in Britain, and became involved singing in two groups, Family Dogg and Magic Lantern. Albert and Mike then decided to go to the U.S.A. It took 15 months during their sojourn in Southern California before their songs were taken up by Bobby Roberts who was forming his own label, Mums. Hammond was signed up and was the first Mums artist. His second record, 'It Never Rains in Southern California', soon zoomed up the charts and established him as a major artist.

THE HOLLIES
LONG COOL WOMAN (in a black dress) *Epic* [*USA*]. Written by Allan Clarke, Roger Cook and Roger Greenaway, this was released in the U.S.A. in June 1972, hitting No 1 for one week and staying in the charts for 16 weeks, and was No 32 in Britain. It won R.I.A.A. Gold Disc award on 11 September 1972.

This marked the return of The Hollies to the million sellers. It sold two million globally (one and a half million in the U.S.A.). Aside from lead singer Allan Clarke, only one original member remained in the group, Tony Hicks (lead, bass guitar, vocals). The other members for this recording were: Bobby Elliot (drums), Bernard Calvert (bass guitar, piano, organ) and Terry Sylvester (rhythm guitar, vocals).

CLINT HOLMES
PLAYGROUND IN MY MIND *Epic* [*USA*]. Written by Paul Vance and Lee Pockriss, this was released in the U.S.A. in June 1972, going to No 2 for three weeks and staying in the charts for 23 weeks. It won R.I.A.A. Gold Disc award on 3 July 1973.

Clint Holmes' very first single release amassed the million after five months in the bestsellers. Clint hails from Buffalo, NY. He made concert and TV appearances around the U.S.A., and taped an appearance for 'The Mike Douglas Show'. Writers Vance and Pockriss produced the disc. The song has a childhood theme.

HOT BUTTER
POPCORN *Musicor* [*USA*]. Written by Gershon Kingsley and released in the U.S.A. in June 1972, this went to No 7 for two weeks and stayed in the charts for 21 weeks. It went to No 3 in Britain, staying 12 weeks in the bestsellers.

Hot Butter is an instrumental group consisting of Stan Free's Moog synthesizer playing with a rhythm line-up. Stan Free, one of the best known and most experienced Moog players, made extensive recordings with the Moog on compositions ranging from classical to rock, including recordings with the Boston Pops Orchestra. 'Popcorn' was arranged and co-produced by Dave Mullaney and John Abbott along with Richard Talmadge, Steve and Bill Jerome and Danny Jordan. It became an international hit, and sold a million in France alone, one of that country's fastest million sellers. Sales in Britain went over 250,000. With big sales in the U.S.A., the disc amassed over two million globally.

LUTHER INGRAM
IF LOVING YOU IS WRONG (I dont want to be right) *Koko/Stax* [*USA*]. Written by Homer Banks, Raymond Jackson and Carl Hampton, this ballad was released in the U.S.A. in May 1972, achieving No 3 for two weeks, and hanging on in the charts for 18 weeks.

Luther Ingram was born in Jackson, Tennessee, in 1950, and raised in a small town outside St Louis. He moved to the Midwest with his parents when quite young and with his brothers sang at local parties, in church and at school, before starting a professional singing career. He subsequently moved to New York and worked as a session singer before meeting the white rock'n'soul producers Jerry Leiber and Mike Stoller, who got him a recording deal with Smash Records. He then recorded for Decca (1965) but got his big break when he met Johnny Baylor who was starting Koko Records, and made several successful singles and an album. Luther's first film appearance was in *Wattstax* in which he sang 'If Loving You Is Wrong', a soul-searing ballad. The impact was dynamic, the disc selling a reported four million. A second album for Koko was made, which like the first contained some of his own songs. Luther is a prolific writer, and contributed to Isaac Hayes' 'Black Moses' album and co-wrote The Staple Singers' million seller 'Respect Yourself' (1971).

JERMAINE JACKSON
DADDY'S HOME *Motown* [*USA*]. Written by J. Shepherd and W. Miller (1961), this was released in the U.S.A. in December 1972, reaching No 6 for two weeks, and staying 18 weeks in the charts.

The million sale for this disc, taken from Jermaine's album 'Jermaine', was reported in March 1973. It is a remake of the Shep and Limelites' classic of 1961. A great triumph for Jermaine, one of the Jackson 5.

MICHAEL JACKSON
ROCKIN' ROBIN *Motown* [*USA*]. Released in the U.S.A. in February 1972 and Britain May 1972, this hit No 1 for one week in the U.S.A. and No 3 for two weeks in Britain. In both countries it stayed 14 weeks in the bestsellers.

This oldie song of 1958, written by J. Thomas, was a hit in that year for Bobby Day. Michael Jackson, of the famous Jackson 5, made this a great comeback for the song and sold well over two million.

BEN *Motown* [*USA*]. Released in the U.S.A. in July 1972 and in Britain in November 1972, this went to No 1 for one week in the U.S.A. and No 5 for one week in Britain. It stayed 16 weeks in the U.S. bestsellers and 13 weeks in the British charts.

'Ben', written by Dee Black and Walter Scharf, is from the film of the same name. Michael Jackson, of the Jackson 5, sold over a million in the U.S.A. and the disc also sold 250,000 in Britain.

ELTON JOHN
HONKY CHATEAU (album) *DJM* [*Britain*] *Uni* [*USA*]. Released in Britain and the U.S.A. in May 1972, the album went to No 1 for five weeks in the U.S.A. and No 2 for two weeks in Britain. It spent 58 weeks in the U.S. bestsellers and 22 weeks in the British charts, going R.I.A.A. gold on 24 July 1972.

This was Elton John's first studio album as an Elton John group, and forerunner of his return to tremendous popularity. The million units, platinum status, was reported in December 1972. It was No 2 immediately in Britain. It was recorded at the Chateau d'Herouville in France. All the songs were written by Bernie Taupin (words) and Elton John (music).

Contents: (*)'Honky Cat'; 'Mellow'; 'I Think I'm Going to Kill Myself'; 'Susie (Dramas)'; (*)'Rocket Man'; 'Salvation'; 'Slave'; 'Amy'; 'Mona Lisas and Mad Hatters'; 'Hercules'.

(*) denotes million sellers when released as singles.

ROCKET MAN *DJM* [*Britain*] *Uni* [*USA*]. Written by Bernie Taupin and Elton John and released in the U.S.A. and in Britain in April 1972, this went to No 6 for one week in the U.S.A. and No 2 for two weeks in Britain. It stayed 15 weeks in the U.S. bestsellers and 13 weeks in the British charts. 'Rocket Man' was included on Elton's album 'Honky Chateau'. It easily surpassed the million sale globally by September 1972.

HONKY CAT *DJM* [*Britain*] *Uni* [*USA*]. Written by Bernie Taupin and Elton John and released in the U.S.A. and in Britain in August 1972, this reached No 7 for two weeks in the U.S.A. and No 24 in Britain. It stayed ten weeks in the U.S. bestsellers and six weeks in British charts.

The second cut from the 'Honky Chateau' album to sell, by September 1972, a global million. The song is described as 'a good old-fashioned "how you gonna keep me down on the farm" frolic'.

CROCODILE ROCK *DJM* [*Britain*] *MCA* [*USA*]. Released in Britain in October 1972 and in the U.S.A. in December 1972, this made No 1 for three weeks in the U.S.A. and No 4 for one week in Britain. It stayed 17 weeks in the U.S. bestsellers and 13 weeks in the British charts, going R.I.A.A. gold on 5 February 1973.

His first single release on the MCA label, and Elton's biggest single success up to this year; also his first U.S. certified million seller. The disc is Elton's (and Bernie's) own rendition of rock'n'roll history – the British answer to Don McLean's 'American Pie'.

CAROLE KING
RHYMES AND REASONS (Album) *Ode* [*USA*]. Released in the U.S.A. in October 1972, this went to No 1 for two weeks and stuck in the charts for 31 weeks. It was awarded R.I.A.A. Gold Disc on 1 November 1972.

Another fine album of Carole King singing her own compositions. It sold the million units by the end of 1973.

Contents: 'Come Down Easy'; 'My My, She Cries'; 'Peace in the Valley'; 'Feeling Sad Tonight'; 'The First Day in August'; 'Bitter with the Sweet'; 'Goodbye Don't Mean I'm Gone'; 'Stand Behind Me'; 'Gotta Get Through Another Day'; 'I Think I Can Hear You'; 'Ferguson Road'; 'Been to Canaan'.

VICKI LAWRENCE
THE NIGHT THE LIGHTS WENT OUT IN GEORGIA *Bell* [*USA*]. Released in the U.S.A. in November 1972, this went to No 1 for two weeks, staying in the U.S. charts 20 weeks. It received R.I.A.A. Gold Disc award on 2 April 1973.

Songwriter Bob Russell, composer of 'Honey', 'Little Green Apples' and many other hits, based 'The Night the Lights Went Out in Georgia' loosely on an actual murder-of-passion he had heard about, changing the names and locales of the story completely. During a visit to Nashville with his wife, singer Vicki Lawrence, he started working on some demos of his songs, and Vicki was pressed into service to sing a revised version he had written. When Snuff Garrett Music Enterprises heard the tape, Snuff was instantly impressed, stating that this was Russell's best song in years. He signed Vicki as a Snuff Garrett artist for Bell Records release. The entire instrumental background was taped in one session 24 October 1972 at United Records' Studio B with 21 musicians. Vicki went to the same studio two days later, vocalizing her lead and harmony overdubs in one or two takes for each part. The disc was Vicki's debut single. Within two weeks of release, it was the hottest record in the secondary AM markets of the South, making its first major breakout before Christmas in New Orleans, then Houston and Dallas. When sales momentum dropped, Bell had to convince radio in the rest of the U.S.A. that this was more than just a regional hit. They subsequently achieved big sales nationally through consistent enthusiasm and the disc finally amassed sales of two million plus.

VICKY LEANDROS
APRÈS TOI (Come what may) *Philips* [*France & Germany*]. Written by Yves Dessca and Mario Panas with English version by Norman Newell and German version by Klaus Munro, this was released in Britain in April 1972, going to No 2 for two weeks and staying in the charts 16 weeks.

Vicky Leandros was born in Greece in 1950, and was taught singing, classical guitar and ballet. She was raised in Hamburg, and apart from the vocal tuition by her father Leo Leandros (songwriter, manager and agent), Vicky's main hobby is languages of which she speaks seven. She made her first record in Germany when she was 15 – an immediate success. In 1967, she was invited to sing Luxembourg's entry 'Love is Blue' in the Eurovision Song Contest. The song was placed fourth, but proved to be the big seller globally. (See Mauriat, 1967.) Vicky then became a big success in Canada, and bigger still in Japan (1968) where she received the Japanese Prix du Disque. In 1972, she was again chosen to represent Luxembourg in the Eurovision Contest, and was the winner with 'Après Toi'. This was a hit all over Europe, selling in excess of a million with Gold Disc award.

JOHN LENNON, YOKO ONO & HARLEM COMMUNITY CHOIR WITH THE PLASTIC ONO BAND
HAPPY CHRISTMAS (War is over) *Apple* [*Britain*]. Released in Britain in November 1972, this went to No 2 for one week and stayed in the charts 7 weeks.

This successful Christmas song by the husband/wife team of former Beatles member John Lennon and Yoko Ono was reported by mid-January 1973 to have sold in excess of two million. It is a song expressing hope for peace between all nationalities.

LOBO
I'D LOVE YOU TO WANT ME *Big Tree/Bell* [*USA*]. Written by Lobo (Kent Lavoie), this was released in the U.S.A. in September 1972, going to No 1 for one week in the U.S.A., and somewhat later (1974) No 5 for one week in Britain with 11 weeks in the bestsellers. It stayed 15 weeks in the U.S. bestsellers and won R.I.A.A. Gold Disc award on 29 November 1972.

The second million seller for Lobo, it was re-issued in Britain in 1974 with reasonable success.

LOGGINS & MESSINA
YOUR MAMA DON'T DANCE *Columbia* [*USA*]. Released in the U.S.A. in October 1972 this went to No 4 for one week, staying in the charts 17 weeks and going R.I.A.A. gold on 7 March 1973.

Jim Messina hails from California and Ken Loggins from Seattle, Washington. Messina was with Buffalo Springfield in their late stages, and then with Poco, formed by Richie Furay, for a couple of years. The Loggins and Messina partnership was formed in 1971. Loggins was signed to do his first Columbia album, and Messina was called in to lend his musical talent and production skills. The result was a most fortuitous case of musical serendipity, the album 'Sittin' In' selling over 250,000. With their fine aggregation of ten musicians, the ensuing years saw seven albums (up to 1975) and numerous concert tours. Loggins and Messina write all their own material, and are polished performers. Their music is light and clean in the tradition of the West Coast school. Both play guitar, bass and do the vocals. Their performances generate enormous electricity, provoking dancing in the aisles through such numbers as 'Your Mama Don't Dance'. This number soon passed the million sale.

THE LONDON SYMPHONY ORCHESTRA & CHAMBER CHOIR, WITH GUEST SOLOISTS

TOMMY (rock opera) (Double album) *Ode* [*USA*]. Released in the U.S.A. in December 1972, this ambitious project went to No 2 for one week, stopping in the charts for 24 weeks and winning R.I.A.A. Gold Disc award on 13 December 1972.

A monumental production of Pete Townshend's classic rock opera (1969), with an all-star cast of everyone's favourite rock artists. The idea for this most ambitious of all rock albums was Lou Reizner's, the producer. He began the task of getting the album together in September 1971. The sessions began in March 1972. Intensive work went into all parts of the album, especially the mix, all done in London, over a nine-month period.

The line-up was: David Measham: Conductor of the London Symphony Orchestra; Peter Townshend: Narrator; Sandy Denny: The Nurse; Graham Bell: Tommy's Mother's Lover; Steve Winwood: Father; Maggie Bell: Tommy's Mother; Richie Havens: The 'Hawker'; Merry Clayton: 'The Acid Queen'; Roger Daltrey: Tommy; John Entwhistle: Cousin Kevin; Ringo Starr: Uncle Ernie; Rod Stewart: Pinball Wizard; Richard Harris: Doctor.

The album was shipped 'gold', and sold over a million globally by mid-March 1973. 'Tommy' received the 1973 Grammy Award for Best Album package. (See The Who, 1969, for further data on 'Tommy'.)

LOOKING GLASS (quartet)

BRANDY (You're a fine girl) *Epic* [*USA*]. Written by E. Lurie and released in the U.S.A. in June 1972 this made No 1 for one week, staying 16 weeks in the bestsellers.

Looking Glass consists of Elliot Lurie (guitar), Pieter Sweval (bass), Larry Gonsky (keyboards), Jeff Grob (drums). This disc was their first million seller, achieving a Gold Disc award from R.I.A.A. on 9 August 1972.

LOVE UNLIMITED (female vocal trio)

WALKIN' IN THE RAIN WITH THE ONE I LOVE *Uni* [*USA*]. Released in the U.S.A. in March 1972, this climbed to No 7 for two weeks in the U.S.A. and No 10 in Britain. It stayed 16 weeks in the U.S. charts. R.I.A.A. Gold Disc award came on 24 July 1972.

Love Unlimited comprises Diana Taylor, Linda James and Glodean James. Barry White, a producer of international scope who is also an artist and songwriter, met the trio when they were back-up singers in 1968. He soon became their adviser and mentor. After more than three years' grooming, White brought them to Russ Regan's Uni Records, and for them produced his own composition that was to change the course of his career as well as theirs, viz. the quickly certified million seller 'Walkin' in the Rain with the One I Love'. The disc had a 'sensual soul' sound, made by weaving monologue with tightly knit yet supple harmony. The arrangement was highlighted by electric piano and lush strings. 'Walkin' in the Rain' featured only 13 words from White, coming in a monologue form at the climax of the record. This was the first time that millions of people were exposed to his distinctive bass tones. Both Love Unlimited and Barry White became linked up with Russ Regan at 20th Century Records, with fantastic success and many Gold Discs in the ensuing years. (See also Barry White, 1973.)

MAIN INGREDIENT (vocal trio)

EVERYBODY PLAYS THE FOOL *RCA* [*USA*]. Written by Rudy Clark, Dede Dabney, J.R. Bailey and Ken Williams and released in the U.S.A. in July 1972, this made No 1 for one week and stayed in the charts 20 weeks, winning R.I.A.A. Gold Disc award on 20 September 1972.

Main Ingredient are a soul act comprising Luther Simmons, Tony Silvester and Cuba Gooding. They grew up together in Harlem, and found music their prime interest. They got their first contract in 1965 under the name The Poets, on Red Bird Records, with a hit called 'Merry Christmas Baby', later changing

the song to 'Chapel Bells Are Calling'. They then left the firm and called themselves The Insiders. After some three years rehearsing and writing, they met Tom Wilson of MGM, a black man dealing with white music. Wilson and another great influence, Clarence Avant, paid for their next session, which was sold to RCA. They didn't do too well the first time at RCA, due to the fact that RCA weren't really geared in 1967 to make and merchandise black product. The group went back to rehearsing. Simmons thought of 'main' and Silvester got 'ingredient' from a coke bottle, to form their new name. They went back to RCA where Buzzy Willis, head of the new rhythm-and-blues division, worked with them. Around 1970, the trio had consistent hits, finally coming up with their first million seller 'Everybody Plays the Fool'.

CURTIS MAYFIELD

FREDDIE'S DEAD (from the film *Superfly*) *Curtom* [*USA*]. Written by Curtis Mayfield and released in the U.S.A. in July 1972 this reached No 4 for two weeks and stayed 17 weeks in the bestsellers. It won R.I.A.A. Gold Disc award on 31 October 1972.

'Freddie's Dead' from the anti-drug film *Superfly* sold over 1,179,000 when released as a single.

(See 'Superfly' album for data on Mayfield and his band.)

SUPERFLY (from the film *Superfly*) *Curtom* [*USA*]. Released in the U.S.A. in November 1972, this went to No 6 for three weeks and stayed 15 weeks in the charts, winning R.I.A.A. Gold Disc award on 18 January 1973.

The second single release from the immensely successful album soundtrack to sell over a million.

(See 'Superfly' album for data on Mayfield and his band.)

MEL & TIM

STARTING ALL OVER AGAIN *Stax* [*USA*]. Written by Phillip Mitchell and released in the U.S.A. in June 1972, this climbed to No 16 and stayed 22 weeks in the charts.

The second million seller (reported in 1973) for Mel (Harden) and Tim (McPherson). The sale was amassed over a period of five months on the market.

HAROLD MELVIN & THE BLUE NOTES (rhythm-and-blues quintet)

IF YOU DON'T KNOW ME BY NOW *Philadelphia-International* [*USA*]. Written by Kenny Gamble and Leon Huff, this was released in the U.S.A. in September 1972, going to No 2 for one week, and staying in the charts for 17 weeks. It was awarded R.I.A.A. Gold Disc on 21 November 1972.

The group consists of Harold Melvin, Theodore Pendergrass, Lawrence Brown, Bernard Wilson and Lloyd Parks. The group were just 15-year old youngsters in Philadelphia when they made their first record 'If You Love Me' for the Josie label in 1956. This was a big success, but all they got was $500 each from the disc company. In 1960 they had a rhythm-and-blues hit with 'My Hero' on a long-forgotten label called Valve. In the early

1960s they had various soul hits on little labels, but never received much payment for them. Throughout the 1960s, as black music gradually fought its way to full acceptance in the white market, Melvin stayed out of the recording scene, and The Blue Notes went into the Silver Circuit showroom act, highly respected by the industry, but little-known to the public. They worked in Las Vegas, Lake Tahoe, Reno, Puerto Rico, Miami and the resort circuit, all making a comfortable living. The Blue Notes were one of the first black acts booked in predominantly white rooms by the William Morris Agency, to whom they were introduced by Martha Reeves of The Vandellas (1960).

It wasn't until Gamble and Huff put the Philadelphia Sound back on the map with their production, songs and groundbreaking arrangements by Thom Bell, that Melvin was ready to make another assault on making hit discs. Melvin signed The Blue Notes to Gamble-Huff's Philadelphia International label in 1971. Gamble, Huff and Melvin had known each other as schoolmates, South Philadelphia neighbours and would-be musicians in the late 1950s. It was natural that Gamble and Huff should write their first really big hit. 'If You Don't Know Me by Now' soon sold over the million.

SHIRO MIYA & THE PINKARA TRIO
ONNA NO MICHI (A woman's way) *Nippon-Columbia* [*Japan*]. Released in Japan in May 1972, this hit No 1 for 17 weeks in Japan. Written by Shiro Miya, the sales of this disc were believed to be a new record in Japan. It sold over 3,500,000 by the end of 1973. A tape of the same title by the group also established a new record in Japan with sales of over 500,000.

THE MOODY BLUES
NIGHTS IN WHITE SATIN *Deram* [*USA & Britain*]. Written by Justin Hayward (1967), this re-issue was released in the U.S.A. in August 1972 and re-released in Britain in October 1972. It went to No 1 for one week in the U.S.A. and No 9 in Britain. It stayed 18 weeks in the U.S. bestsellers and ten weeks in the British charts. R.I.A.A. Gold Disc was awarded on 18 December 1972.

'Nights in White Satin' first appeared as a single from the group's album 'Days of Future Passed' in 1967. It was re-issued when The Moody Blues made two successful tours of the U.S.A. in 1972, and became their biggest-selling single. Sales exceeded a million by December.

(See also The Moody Blues, 1967.)

MOUTH & MacNEAL
HOW DO YOU DO *Philips* [*USA*]. Written by Hans van Hemert and Van Hoff, this was released in the U.S.A. in April 1972, going to No 5 for one week, and staying 19 weeks in the charts. It won R.I.A.A. Gold Disc award on 2 August 1972.

Mouth (real name Willem Duyn) and his female partner Mac-Neal (real name Sjoukje Van't Spijker) teamed up after Mouth heard a tape of MacNeal at the Phonogram Studios in Amsterdam (1971). Mouth chose his name because he talks and shouts a lot. He was formerly a construction worker, then sang with several Dutch groups. MacNeal had trained as a classical singer, but preferred singing pop music. Their first record was 'Hey Love You', then came 'How Do You Do', originally re-leased in Europe in February 1972. The disc spent some time building in small markets, then broke big internationally, selling a million in the U.S.A. alone. Global sales were over two million. The duo also received awards from Belgium and Austria. They made innumerable tours around Europe, and represented Holland in the 1974 Eurovision Song Contest. They sing in English, German, French and Dutch.

JOHNNY NASH
I CAN SEE CLEARLY NOW *Epic* [*USA*]. Released in the U.S.A. in August 1972 and in Britain in June 1972, this hit No 1 for one week in the U.S.A. and No 4 in Britain. It stayed 21 weeks in the U.S. charts and 15 weeks in the British bestsellers,

winning R.I.A.A. Gold Disc award on 17 November 1972.

This disc, written by Johnny Nash, is cut from the album of the same title. Johnny Nash was born on 19 August 1940 in Houston, Texas, and educated at Jack Yates High School there. He sang in the Progressive New Hope Baptist Church choir, of which he was lead singer. He made his first appearance as an amateur in 'Matinee', a TV show on KPRC station, Houston, and then as a regular on this afternoon variety show for three years. At 16, he became the youngest member of The Arthur Godfrey Radio/TV Show. He also attended the School for Young Professionals in New York. Film star Burt Lancaster noted Johnny's vocal style and took him to Hollywood for a screen test which led to a starring role in *Take a Giant Step*, and then *Key Witness*. In addition to singing, he is a record producer, a prolific songwriter, and an expert guitarist. Johnny has also lived in London, New York, California, Scandinavia and the West Indies. From the latter, he developed a style that made him master of the Jamaican rock and reggae beat. He is extremely popular in Britain where all his disc releases were hits. Johnny appeared on most of the major TV shows in the U.S.A., and did in fact break the colour bar for many other black artists when Houston TV opened up for him in 1953.

'I Can See Clearly Now' established Johnny as a talent of magnetic proportions, possessing the wizardry, finesse and art of a major star. The song itself, said Johnny, 'is a reflection of my life in many ways'.

Since his first recording 'A Teenager Sings the Blues', he has made several albums for ABC Paramount, and later recorded for MGM before going over to the Epic label.

RICK NELSON
GARDEN PARTY *Decca* [*USA*]. Written by Rick Nelson and released in the U.S.A. in July 1972, this hit No 3 for one week and stayed for 19 weeks in the bestseller charts. It won R.I.A.A. Gold Disc award on 24 November 1972.

Rick (formerly Ricky) Nelson was one of the most successful rock artists of the late 1950s and early 1960s. In the mid 1960s he started singing ballads instead of rock and his popularity waned. In late 1971, Richard Nader, a super-promoter of rock nostalgia, engaged Rick for one of his 'Rock'n'Roll Revivals' at Madison Square Garden, New York, along with other artists. The audience were not impressed. Rick was not an ancient freak suitable for a 1971 musical sideshow. He went to Britain on tour, and met somebody who was at Madison Square Garden on that night. The memories of that unfortunate night all came back, and when he returned to the U.S.A., wrote 'Garden Party' in which he set down his feelings about rock revival shows. The song, a personal account of the unhappy moments at Madison Square Garden, was a smash hit, and Rick's disc went over the million and re-established his name, also reimbursing Decca label somewhat for the $1,000,000 they paid to lure him away from Imperial Records in 1963.

WAYNE NEWTON

DADDY DON'T YOU WALK SO FAST *Chelsea* [*USA*]. Written by Peter Callender and Geoff Stephens, and released in the U.S.A. in April 1972, this got to No 1 for two weeks and stayed 22 weeks in the bestsellers. It was awarded R.I.A.A. Gold Disc on 19 July 1972.

Wayne Newton was born in Norfolk, Virginia, in 1943, and began singing at church and school functions when just an infant. He got his first $5 payment for a performance when he was six. Several years later, after moving to Phoenix, Arizona, he had his own daily TV appearance on KOOL-TV while still a high school student. In 1959, he started a long-term engagement at the Fremont Hotel in Las Vegas with his brother Jerry. The duo played the southwest circuit concurrently, and got their biggest break with their first national exposure in 1962 on the opening 'Jackie Gleason Show'. Bobby Darin saw Wayne and signed him up, producing his first disc, 'Heart', which was placed with Capitol in 1963. This was followed by 'Danke Schoen' which raced to a high chart position. In 1972 he became the first artist signed by Wes Farrell's Chelsea label (distributed by RCA) and 'Daddy Don't You Walk So Fast', written by two of Britain's top composers, gave both Wayne and the Chelsea label their first Gold Disc for a million sale. The song had originally been a hit in Britain in 1971 for Daniel Boone.

Wayne has a distinctive voice encompassing three octaves, and he also plays virtually every musical instrument, and dances in his nightclub act. He made a well-received dramatic debut in the TV series 'Bonanza' and off-stage is deeply concerned with charity work including the American Indian problems. In May 1972, Wayne was the winner of the Nevada Governor's Trophy as Entertainer of the Year. He is one of the world's highest paid performers, and appeared at London's Talk of the Town, and in a Royal Variety show.

He resides on a 48-acre ranch in Las Vegas, where he breeds pure Arabian horses in his spare time.

THE O'JAYS (vocal trio)

BACK STABBERS *Philadelphia-International* [*USA*]. Written by Leon Huff, G. McFadden and J. Whitehead, this was released in the U.S.A. in June 1972 and in Britain in August 1972, going to No 1 for one week in the U.S.A. and No 14 for one week in Britain with 9 weeks in the bestsellers. It stayed for 18 weeks in the U.S. bestsellers, getting R.I.A.A. Gold Disc on 1 September 1972.

The O'Jays are Eddie Levert, Walter Williams and Bill Powell. They were originally a quintet known as The Mascots with Bobby Massey and Bill Isles in their home town of Canton, Ohio, in 1958. The group was renamed when they signed with local disc jockey Eddie O'Jay as their manager. In 1961, they recorded 'Miracles' in Detroit for the Wayco and Apollo labels, and after more recordings, went to the Imperial label in 1963. In 1966, Isles left the group when Imperial was bought by Liberty Records, and the group had a difficult period. Around 1967, they signed with Bell Records and had a chart hit with 'I'll Be Sweeter Tomorrow' in 1968. After a number of unsuccessful discs, they signed with Kenny Gamble and Leon Huff's Neptune label in 1969, cutting some classic discs, all recorded in Philadelphia with the arrangements by Thom Bell and Bobby Martin. Neptune Records finished owing to financial difficulties, and in 1971, the group made one disc for the small local Saru company. Bobby Massey then quit, leaving the group as a trio.

In 1972, the O'Jays re-contracted to the new Gamble/Huff Philadelphia International label, and had an immediate million seller with 'Back Stabbers', and long-awaited commercial success. Bill Powell retired in 1976 and was replaced by Sammy Strain, who had been singing with Little Anthony and The Imperials for 12 years. Powell (born 20 January 1942) died on 26 May 1977 in Canton, Ohio.

DANNY O'KEEFE

GOOD TIME CHARLEY'S GOT THE BLUES *Signpost* [*USA*]. Written by Danny O'Keefe, this was released in the U.S.A. in August 1972, getting to No 8 for two weeks, and staying in the charts for 14 weeks.

This disc was distributed via Atlantic Records and took several months to reach the million, in June 1973. It was Danny O'Keefe's sole success.

GILBERT O'SULLIVAN

ALONE AGAIN (Naturally) *MAM* [*Britain*]. Written by Gilbert O'Sullivan, this was released in Britain in February 1972 and in the U.S.A. in June 1972. It reached No 3 for six weeks in Britain and No 1 for six weeks in the U.S.A., spending 12 weeks in the British bestsellers and 18 weeks in the U.S. charts. It won R.I.A.A. Gold Disc award on 9 August 1972.

Gilbert O'Sullivan (real name Raymond O'Sullivan) was born on 1 December 1946 in Waterford, Southern Ireland. His family moved to Swindon, England, in 1960, and Gilbert enrolled at the local art college. He first played with semi-pro bands The Doodles and The Prefects, then Rick's Blues, while at college. His mother bought him a piano, but his thumping style relegated Gilbert and piano to the garden shed. He began to write songs, his major influences being The Beatles, Dylan and Rodgers & Hart. In 1965 he entered show business, first with CBS, then Major Minor, but left both through dissatisfaction with artistic direction. Some of the tapes he had been sending out reached Gordon Mills (of Tom Jones/Humperdinck fame) and he became fascinated by the catchy tunes and lyrics with a difference. They got together and worked on songs, and a year later (1970) 'Nothin' Rhymed' was recorded and Gilbert was launched. He chose a Chaplinesque mode of dress for his debut – flannel suit far too small, flat cap and short cropped hair which shocked Mills and the press, but people laughed at him and listened, and he won them over. Success followed success via his singles 'No Matter How I Try', 'Alone Again' and many others. All proved to be instant hits. In 1972, Gilbert O'Sullivan changed his image and a new long-haired trendy Gilbert emerged. The Continent of Europe and America fell under the O'Sullivan spell and he became a truly international star.

'Alone Again' soon sold the million in the U.S.A. and exceeded 250,000 in Britain, with big sales elsewhere round the globe. His albums 'Himself' (1971), 'Back to Front' (1972) and subsequent releases were also big sellers.

CLAIRE *MAM* [*Britain*]. Written by Gilbert O'Sullivan and released in Britain and the U.S.A. in October 1972, this hit No 1 for two weeks in Britain and No 2 for two weeks in the U.S.A. It stayed in the British charts for 13 weeks and the U.S. charts for 16 weeks, winning R.I.A.A. Gold Disc award on 22 March 1973.

A second tremendous success for Gilbert O'Sullivan. In addition to the million U.S. sale, it also sold over 250,000 in Britain and had huge sales elsewhere. His disc sales exceeded ten million in 1972, and made him the top star of the year.

THE OSMONDS

DOWN BY THE LAZY RIVER *MGM* [*USA*]. Released in the U.S.A. in January 1972, this reached No 3 for three weeks, staying in the charts for 14 weeks and winning R.I.A.A. Gold Disc award on 24 March 1972. It was No 40 in Britain.

The third million-seller for this fabulous and talented group, written by two of its members, Alan and Merrill.

DONNY OSMOND
PUPPY LOVE *MGM* [*USA*]. Released in the U.S.A. in February 1972 and in Britain in June 1972, this zoomed to No 2 for two weeks in the U.S.A. and No 1 for five weeks in Britain, spending 12 weeks in the U.S. bestsellers and 19 weeks in the British charts. R.I.A.A. Gold Disc award 24 March 1972.

This revival of a Paul Anka song was a fantastic hit for Donny of The Osmonds, and was reported to have sold over three million in the U.S.A. alone plus a further two million in Britain. It was the fourth million seller for Donny, the British sales due to the group's visit to Britain, and the teenage fever generated on both sides of the Atlantic. The song had also been a million seller for writer Paul Anka in 1960.

KIYOHIKO OZAKI
MATA AU HI MADE (Lovers and fools) *Philips Nippon Phonogram* [*Japan*]. Ozaki made his debut in Japan in September 1970, and by 1972 became the most popular singer there, topping both singles and album charts. His first disc was 'Wakare No Yoake' in 1970. 'Mata Au Hi Made' sold a reported million by July 1972. Ozaki's dynamic vocal technique is reminiscent of Tom Jones and Engelbert Humperdinck.

BILLY PAUL (rhythm-and-blues vocalist)
ME AND MRS JONES *Philadelphia-International* [*USA*]. Written by Gilbert, Leon Huff and Kenny Gamble and released in the U.S.A. in October 1972, this hit No 1 for three weeks in the U.S.A. and No 12 in Britain (with 9 weeks in the bestsellers). It stayed 17 weeks in the U.S. charts. It won R.I.A.A. Gold Disc award on 4 December 1972, and Grammy Award for Best Rhythm-and-Blues Male Vocal Performance, 1972.

This is one of the strongest rhythm-and-blues efforts of 1972, an outstanding vocal performance, also another great triumph for the Gamble/Huff label Philadelphia International. The disc soon sold the million, and subsequent sales were estimated at over four million.

Billy Paul, a black singer from North Philadelphia, began singing at the age of 12 and appeared on several local radio shows. He has been involved in singing jazz ever since, influenced by Nat King Cole, Tony Bennett, Nina Simone, Wayne Newton and others. He learned more about music at Temple University, West Philadelphia Music School, and the Granoff Music School. By the age of 16 he was good enough to appear at the Harlem Club in Philadelphia on the same bill as Charlie Parker in 1955. With his trio, they featured at the Harlem Club, and the group made their first recording 'Why Am I?' for the Jubilee label. They had all grown up together, and went to church together. After service in the army, he resumed his career (1959) recording for the New Dawn label, and around 1961 was one of Harold Melvin's Blue Notes. In 1965, he became involved with Gamble and Huff, an association which continued, ripening into success with 'Me and Mrs Jones'. He had made several records in the interval for the Gamble and Neptune labels. The influence of The Beatles made itself felt around 1965, and it was after hearing them that Billy moved away from jazz and standard ballad singing. The Beatles convinced him that rock'n'roll and rhythm-and-blues lyrics were important.

'Me and Mrs Jones' is a soul ballad, with arresting lyrics about an adulterous love affair. The impeccable production and Billy's unique voice were mainly responsible for its success, but probably the biggest selling point was the lyrics. It received a Grammy Award.

ELVIS PRESLEY
BURNING LOVE *RCA* [*USA*]. Released in the U.S.A. in August 1972 and in Britain in September 1972, this went to No 1 for one week in the U.S.A. and No 5 in Britain. It stayed for 16 weeks in the U.S. bestsellers and nine weeks in the British charts.

R.I.A.A. Gold Disc award on 27 October 1972.

Another successful disc for Elvis, a rock number, making his total 66 million sellers since 1956. Composer Dennis Linde, a native of Abilene, Texas, is a staff writer for Combine Music Company. The song was originally recorded by Arthur Alexander but didn't catch on, in his rhythm-and-blues version. Elvis gave it a 'rock' treatment after producer Felton Jarvis gave the song to him.

BILLY PRESTON
OUTA SPACE *A & M* [*USA*]. Written by Billy Preston and J. Greene, this was released in the U.S.A. in April 1972, hitting No 1 for one week and sticking in the charts for 17 weeks. It won R.I.A.A. Gold Disc award on 21 June 1972, and the Grammy award for Best Pop, Rock & Folk Instrumental Performance (1972).

Billy Preston became internationally famous in 1969, through his organ playing on The Beatles' 'Get Back' (*q.v.*) Billy learned piano at three, moved to Los Angeles and when he was ten appeared with a local symphony orchestra, conducted church choir and appeared on the 'Mahalia Jackson Show'. He was also cast as the young W. C. Handy ('Father of the Blues') in the film *St Louis Blues*. He joined the Little Richard and Sam Cooke show in 1962 at the age of 16, visited Britain winning considerable acclaim, and returned to the U.S.A. to record for Sam Cooke's Sar label. In 1965, Billy became resident keyboard player on the rock show 'Shindig'. He recorded rhythm-and-blues and gospel instrumentals, 'The Most Exciting Organ Ever (1965) and 'Gospel in My Soul' (1962) with the patronage of Ray Charles, and toured Europe with him 1967-8. His friendship with Beatle George Harrison resulted in The Beatles buying out his recording contract, and he cut 'That's the Way God Planned It' and 'Encouraging Words' for their Apple organization, with Harrison co-producing. After spending considerable time in Britain, Billy signed with A & M which produced 'I Wrote a Simple Song' (1971) with Harrison and David T. Walker on guitars and the arrangements by Quincy Jones. 'Outa Space' was the only instrumental item from this, his first album. It very soon sold a million, with two major awards.

Billy Preston became greatly interested in the electronic keyboard, and formed his own band, The God Squad, with three keyboard players sharing 16 instruments including electric piano, clarinet, organ and Moog, as well as being a vocalist and composer.

RASPBERRIES (vocal and instrumental rock quartet)
GO ALL THE WAY *Capitol* [*USA*]. Written by Eric Carmen, this was released in the U.S.A. in June 1972, going to No 3 for one week, and staying in the charts 18 weeks. R.I.A.A. Gold Disc award on 6 November 1972.

Raspberries consists of Eric Carmen (lead singer, piano, bass guitar), Wally Bryson (lead guitarist), David Smalley (rhythm guitar) and Jim Bonifanti (drums). All were born in 1949. Each had played in a band, and after going through high school, decided to form a band of their own. Eric Carmen is credited with most of the arrangements, but each member writes independently, Eric, with his creative touch, adding the necessary spice to the compositions. The group originated in Cleveland, playing local dances and clubs before coming to the attention of Capitol Records who signed them to a recording contract. 'Go All the Way' is a cut from their first album 'Raspberries' and became their first national hit. They appeared at Carnegie Hall on 26 September 1973, and were extremely popular on an extensive tour. Carmen later went solo.

HELEN REDDY
I AM WOMAN *Capitol* [*USA*]. Written by Helen Reddy and Ray Burton, this was released in the U.S.A. in May 1972, shooting to No 1 for two weeks and staying 22 weeks in the charts. It won R.I.A.A. Gold Disc award on 18 December 1972 and the

Grammy Award for Best Female Pop, Rock & Folk Vocal Performance, 1972.

Helen Reddy was born in Australia, daughter of Max Reddy and his wife Stella Lamond, a show business family. She first went on stage at the age of five at the old Tivoli Theatre in Perth. The family played 'the circuit' doing sketch comedy. At the age of 18, Helen was on her own. From band-singing at the Chevton Hotel in Melbourne, she moved into Australian TV, and was soon a regular on a show called 'In Melbourne Tonite' (1958) and a series 'Sunnyside Up'. She eventually had her own show 'Helen Reddy Sings'. She entered a song contest in 1966 along with 1,358 others, and won the first prize - a trip to New York, and after a lot of trouble collecting the money, took an air ticket for herself and bought one for her three-year-old child. At this time she was divorced. In New York, she discovered that the record companies were looking for male singers or groups, and that female vocalists were a drug on the market. She had a difficult time for several months doing odd jobs. On her birthday, some friends in New York gave her a party, and it was here that she met Jeff Wald, from the staff of the William Morris Agency. They married, and made some progress in 1968 when Helen cut a record called 'Go' which didn't. In 1969, Helen filled in her time taking UCLA extension courses, after moving to California. She heard (1970) the song 'I Don't Know How to Love Him' from *Jesus Christ Superstar* and Capitol Records decided to record her with this. Her husband spent $4,000 in eight months trying to get disc jockeys to play it. A boost from Flip Wilson came when he agreed to put her on TV when nobody else would, and it made the song a hit. Thereafter everybody wanted Helen. In May 1971, she made her first album based on the title of her hit, and this included her own song 'I Am Woman' which was released (1972) as a single. It was a long time contender for chart status, but finally got to No 1 and sold over the million. Other million-selling singles and albums followed. Helen was voted the Best Female Pop Vocalist of 1973-1974, and became an international star. Her second album 'Helen Reddy' was released in 1971.

I AM WOMAN (Album) *Capitol* [*USA*]. Released in the U.S.A. on 13 November 1972, this went to No 12 for one week, staying in the charts for 62 weeks. R.I.A.A. Gold Disc award on 7 March 1973.

Helen Reddy's third album. After more than a year in the charts it was reported platinum (one million unit sale) by August 1974. Based on the title of her successful single disc title, it contained: 'I Am Woman'; 'Peaceful' (Kenny Rankin); 'This Masquerade' (Leon Russell); 'I Didn't Mean to Love You' (A. Butler and K. Philipp); 'Where Is My Friend?' (B. Scott and D. Meehan); 'And I Love You So' (Don McLean); 'What Would They Say?' (Paul Williams); 'Where Is the Love?' (R. MacDonald and W. Walter); 'Hit the Road, Jack' (P. Mayfield); 'The Last Blues Song' (B. Mann and C. Weill).

RINGO WILLIE CAT
HELP, GET ME SOME HELP *Sonopresse* [*France*]. A big success for Ringo in France with reported million sale. He married Sheila (of 'L' école est finie' fame). Claude Carriere who produced and wrote that song also produced Ringo's disc.

JOHNNY RIVERS
ROCKIN' PNEUMONIA AND THE BOOGIE WOOGIE FLU *United Artists* [*USA*]. Released in the U.S.A. in September 1972, this went to No 4 for one week, staying 19 weeks in the charts. R.I.A.A. Gold Disc award on 29 January 1973.

Third million-seller for Johnny Rivers, vocal version of the old Huey Smith and John Vincent rock piano number made famous in 1957 by Huey Smith.

THE ROLLING STONES
EXILE ON MAIN STREET (Double album) *Rolling Stones* [*USA & Britain*]. Simultaneously released in Britain and the U.S.A. in May 1972, this hit No 1 for two weeks in Britain and 8 weeks in the U.S.A., staying in the British charts for 16 weeks and the U.S. bestsellers for 43 weeks. R.I.A.A. Gold Disc award on 30 May 1972.

This album was released to coincide with The Rolling Stones' third U.S. tour which began on 3 June and finished 26 July at Madison Square Garden in New York. The tour included 53 performances in 32 cities and grossed over $4,000,000, playing to over 750,000 fans, making them the most popular group in the world.

'Exile on Main Street' entered the U.S. charts immediately at No 10 and received a Gold Disc award simultaneously. It soon sold over the million units. Featured on the album are Billy Preston, Tammi Lynn, Jimmy Miller, Nicky Hopkins, Ian Stewart. The main line-up for the album was Mick Jagger (vocals), Keith Richard (guitar), Bill Wyman (bass), Charlie Watts (drums), plus Bobby Keyes (sax), Jim Price (trumpet/trombone) and Nicky Hopkins (piano). Other participants were Bill Plumber (bass), Clydie King & Vanetta (backing vocals), Al Perkins (steel guitar), Amyl Nitrate (marimbas), Jerry Kirkland (vocals), Shirley Goodman, Mac Rebennack and Joe Green (vocals).

Contents of album: 'Rocks Off'; 'Rip This Joint'; 'Hip Shake'; 'Casino Boogie'; 'Tumbling Dice'; 'Sweet Virginia'; 'Torn and Frayed'; 'Black Angel'; 'Loving Cup'; 'Happy'; 'Turd on the Run'; 'Ventilation Blues'; 'Just Wanna See His Face'; 'Let It Loose'; 'All Down the Line'; 'Stop Breaking Down'; 'Shine a Light'; 'Soul Survival'.

All songs by Mick Jagger and Keith Richard.

MORE HOT ROCKS (Double album) (Big Hits & Fazed Cookies) *London* [*USA*]. Released in the U.S.A. in December 1972, this collection made No 9 for three weeks, staying 29 weeks in the charts.

The second anthology of the group's former Decca recordings (Britain) compiled for the U.S. market only. It sold half a million in a month and received the Gold Disc award from R.I.A.A. on 17 January 1973, subsequently reaching a million units sale. All tracks in the album set include performances by the late Brian Jones. It was packaged by Andrew Loog Oldham, and contained 25 titles, eight of which had never before been released in the U.S.A. - denoted by (†). Oldham originally produced all the tracks.

Contents: 'Good Times, Bad Times' (1966); (*) 'The Last Time' (1965); 'Sittin' on a Fence' (1969); (*) 'Dandelion' (1967);

'She's a Rainbow' (1967); 'Child of the Moon' (1968); '2000 Light Years from Home' (1967); (*) 'Have You Seen Your Mother, Baby, Standing in the Shadow?' (1966); 'I'm Free' (1965); 'Out of Time' (1966); 'No Expectations' (1968); (*) 'Lady Jane' (1966); (*) 'We Love You' (1967); 'Let It Bleed' (1969); 'Tell Me' (1964); 'Not Fade Away' (Charles Hardin and Norman Petty, 1957); (*) 'It's All Over Now' (B. and S. Womack, 1964); (*) 'Fortune Teller' (B. Hurdon and Dyer Hurdon, 1961); (†) 'Bye Bye Johnnie' (Chuck Berry, 1960); (†) 'Come On' (Chuck Berry, 1961); (†) 'Poison Ivy' (Jerry Lieber and Mike Stoller, 1959); (†) 'What to Do' (1966); (†) 'I Can't Be Satisfied' (1964); (†) 'Long Long While' (1966). ((*) denotes sold a million as a single.)

All songs by Mick Jagger and Keith Richard unless otherwise indicated.

ROYAL SCOTS DRAGOON GUARDS
(pipes & drums & military band)
AMAZING GRACE *RCA* [*Britain*]. Originally written by John Newton (1779), and arranged by Judy Collins, this version was released in Britain on 24 March 1972, and in the U.S.A. in April 1972. It went to No 1 for six weeks in Britain and No 10 for two weeks in the U.S.A. It stayed 24 weeks in the British charts and 11 weeks in the U.S. bestsellers.

In July 1971, The Royal Scots Greys Band split up after 300 years and members of it got together with the 3rd Carabineers (Prince of Wales Dragoon Guards) to form The Royal Scots Dragoon Guards. Under that name, the band went into Redford Barracks in Edinburgh and cut 31 tracks – one of them being 'Amazing Grace'. This track from the album 'Farewell to the Greys' (only their third since their inception in 1678) was played on a late night BBC radio show. The result was remarkable. Listeners asked for more. It was issued as a single and within three weeks reached No 1 in Britain, selling over 300,000. By the end of May, sales were over 600,000. The disc then became a smash hit in Australia, Canada and Europe. It was rushed into the U.S. market, and ten days after release orders came in for an excess of 200,000. By July 1972, sales globally of over two million were reported. Dragoon mania hit an all-time high in Germany during April, the band also set to play several of the year's big festivals in Scotland and elsewhere. By mid-1977 this disc had sold seven million.

The bagpipes solo is played by Pipe Major Tony Crease, and the disc is the first million seller ever on bagpipes. This instrumental recording broke all the rules of the music business. RCA had eight record pressing plants all over Britain working at full pressure to keep up the phenomenal demand. The recording used 20 pipes and drums and a 30-piece military band. 'Amazing Grace' is only a 16-bar melody, and there are only six notes used throughout the melody.

(See Judy Collins, 1970 for further data on the melody and words.)

SEALS & CROFTS
SUMMER BREEZE (Album) *Warner* [*USA*]. Released in the U.S.A. in August 1972, this went to No 5 for two weeks and took up residence in the charts for 100 weeks. R.I.A.A. Gold Disc award on 14 December 1972.

Jim Seals (born 1943) and Dash Crofts (born 1942) began playing together in various bands from 1954. In 1958 they were with The Champs who had a tremendous instrumental hit with 'Tequila'. The group dissolved in 1964, and Jim and Dash continued playing in different units before trying their luck as a duo around 1969. They made many tours in the U.S.A. including outdoor summer festivals, and gradually established themselves. The release of 'Summer Breeze' was the big breakthrough for the duo. It was so popular that it stayed in the bestsellers for almost two years and received platinum award for a million units sale in January 1974.

They wrote all their own material, their songs relating to their thoughts and feelings of brotherhood and peace, and the realities of life. They attribute their creative talents and success to Abdul Baha to whom they made a pilgrimage at Haifa, Israel, the most sacred place in the Baha'i religion. At the shrine of Baha'u'llah they vowed to dedicate their lives, 'talents and material wealth to the unification of this planet through the teaching of Baha'u'llah'.

Seals & Crofts' success put them on many TV shows including 'The Midnight Special' and 'The Dinah Shore Show'. They also made a short tour of Europe in 1975. Other assignments included scoring for films.

The duo played four concerts at New York's Carnegie Hall, complete with backing 37-piece orchestra, to four sold-out houses.

Contents of the album: 'Humming Bird'; 'Funny Little Man'; 'Say'; 'Summer Breeze'; 'East of Ginger Trees'; 'Fiddle in the Sky'; 'Boy Down the Road'; 'Euphrates'; 'Advance Guards'; 'Yellow Dirt'.

CARLY SIMON
YOU'RE SO VAIN *Elektra* [*USA*]. Written by Carly Simon, released in the U.S.A. in November 1972 and in Britain in December 1972, this went to No 1 for three weeks in the U.S.A. and No 2 for one week in Britain. It stayed 17 weeks in the U.S. bestsellers and 14 weeks in the British charts. R.I.A.A. Gold Disc award on 8 January 1973.

Carly Simon was born in New York City in 1945, and grew up in a well-to-do home surrounded by music. Her father, a pianist, founded the famous book publishing firm of Simon & Schuster. All her uncles were in music; her sister Joanna became an opera singer. Sister Lucy and Carly became a singing duo known as The Simon Sisters in the heyday of urban folk. They worked regularly at New York's Bitter End and had one or two hits on Kapp Records. Carly spent a year in France not singing before she met Albert Crossman who wanted to turn her into a female Bob Dylan, which did not succeed. She later signed with the Elektra label.

She had her first big hit with 'That's the Way I've Always Heard It Should Be'. This became known as 'the first explicitly upper middle class blues ballad' (1971). Her first album 'Carly Simon' (1971) was followed by 'Anticipation' (1972) which gained an R.I.A.A. Gold Disc award. She also won a Grammy Award as Best New Artist of 1971. On 4 November 1972, Carly married disc star James Taylor, and the same month recorded

her third album 'No Secrets' which contained 'You're So Vain'. Issued as a single disc, this was an instant success and quickly sold over a million in the U.S.A. alone. Sales in Britain were over 250,000. This 'psychological rocker' caused tremendous interest regarding the identity of the subject of the song. Carly writes practically all her own material. She played The Troubadour in Los Angeles on 6 April 1971, and soon after in New York's Carnegie Hall, followed by her first album success. From being a singer's singer, Carly became a commercial proposition.

NO SECRETS (album) *Elektra* [*USA*]. Released in the U.S.A. in November 1972 and in Britain in December 1972, this reached No 1 for six weeks in the U.S.A. and one week in Britain. It stayed 71 weeks in the U.S. bestseller charts and 26 weeks in the British lists. R.I.A.A. Gold Disc award on 8 December 1972.

This album was recorded at the Air Studio in London in November 1972, and produced by Richard Perry. The disc is sprinkled with musician credits – artists known to Carly Simon – who joined in the recordings here and there. These included husband James Taylor, Mick Jagger, Warren Beatty, Cat Stevens, Kris Kristofferson, Nicky Hopkins, Klaus Voormann, Jimmy Ryan, and Paul and Linda McCartney.

Carly gained enormous commercial success with this album, which stayed in the bestsellers for almost 18 months. Her incredibly powerful voice really pours out from this magnificent album, which contained: 'You're So Vain'; 'It Was So Easy'; 'The Carter Family'; 'Her Friends Are More than Fond of Robin'; 'Embrace Me You Child'; 'Right Thing to Do'; 'Waited So Long'; 'We Have No Secrets'; 'Night Owl'; 'When You Close Your Eyes' (Carly Simon and Billy Merritt). All songs by Carly Simon. Sales of over two million have been estimated.

JOE SIMON
POWER OF LOVE *Spring* [*USA*]. Written by Kenny Gamble, Leon Huff and Joe Simon, this was released in the U.S.A. in June 1972, reaching No 6 for two weeks and staying in the charts 16 weeks. R.I.A.A. Gold Disc award on 29 August 1972.

Third certified million-seller for Joe Simon, and yet another hit for the prolific writers Gamble and Huff.

SIMON & GARFUNKEL
GREATEST HITS (album) *Columbia* [*USA*]. Released in the U.S.A. in June 1972 and in Britain in July 1972, this album went to No 1 for one week in the U.S.A. and ten weeks in Britain. It took up seemingly permanent residence in the charts, staying 131 weeks in the U.S. charts and 179 weeks in the British list. R.I.A.A. Gold Disc award 6 July 1972.

One of the many greatest hits albums by prominent artists, this album holds the record for duration in the British charts – three-and-a-half years. It was also a big seller in the U.S.A. for over two-and-a-half years, and the initial order there was in excess of 600,000 units, which qualified it for an instant Gold Disc award. What the actual sales of the disc were must be well over the two million mark globally, in view of the album's consistent sales.

It contained: (*) 'Bridge Over Troubled Water' (1969); (*) 'The Sounds of Silence' (1964); (*) 'Mrs Robinson' (1968); 'Scarborough Fair/Canticle' (Paul Simon and Art Garfunkel, 1966); 'I Am a Rock' (1965); 'For Emily, Whenever I May Find Her' (1966); 'Kathy's Song' (1966); 'Bookends' (1968); 'America' (1968); (*) 'Cecilia' (1969); 'El Condor Pasa (If I Could)' (Paul Simon, 1970, music arranged by Jorge Milchberg, 1963); 'The Boxer' (1968); 'Homeward Bound' (1966); 'The 59th Street Bridge Song (Feelin' Groovy)' (1966). ((*) denotes sold a million as a singles disc.)

All songs by Paul Simon unless otherwise indicated.

A definitive album of greatest hits from the American duo that has sold more albums than any other in history.

THE STAPLE SINGERS (vocal quartet)
I'LL TAKE YOU THERE *Stax* [*USA*]. Written by Alvertis Isbell and released in the U.S.A. in March 1972, this went to No 1 for two weeks staying 15 weeks in the charts. It was No 30 in Britain.

The third million-seller for The Staple Singers, achieved after one month on the U.S. market. Pervis Staples (guitar, vocals), one of the quartet's original members, went into record production, his place being taken by his youngest sister, in 1969. The disc has a West Indian sound. It subsequently sold two million.

CAT STEVENS
CAN'T KEEP IT IN *Island* [*Britain*]. Written by Cat Stevens and released in Britain in December 1972, this achieved No 9 in the charts with 13 weeks in the bestsellers.

This second big hit for Cat Stevens sold a reported million globally by mid-1973.

STONE & CHARDEN
L'AVENTURA *Disc AZ* [*France*]. Songwriter-singer Eric Charden and his wife, Stone, two young French artists, chalked up a bestseller with this disc in France. It was reported to have sold 1,500,000.

THE STYLISTICS
BETCHA BY GOLLY WOW *Avco* [*USA*]. Written by Thom Bell and Linda Creed, this was released in the U.S.A. in February 1972, going to No 3 for one week in the U.S.A. and No 13 in Britain, staying in the bestsellers for 16 weeks in the U.S.A. and 12 weeks in Britain. R.I.A.A. Gold Disc award on 17 April 1972.

This quick million-seller for The Stylistics featured Russell Thompson, Jr, and was yet another success for producer/writer Thom Bell.

I'M STONE IN LOVE WITH YOU *Avco* [*USA*]. Written by Thom Bell, Linda Creed and Anthony Bell, released in the U.S.A. in October 1972, this climbed to No 9 for one week in the U.S.A. and No 10 in Britain, and stayed 15 weeks in the U.S.A. bestsellers and 10 weeks in Britain. R.I.A.A. Gold Disc award on 13 December 1972.

The fast-selling Stylistics added yet another million-seller to their list of successes, and still further enhanced the outstanding reputation of producer/writer Thom Bell. A message song – 'Love conquers all'.

THE SUPREMES
FLOY JOY *Motown* [*USA*]. Released in the U.S.A. in January 1972 and in Britain in February 1972, this went to No 16 for one week in the U.S.A. and No 8 in Britain, staying in the U.S.A. bestsellers for 13 weeks and 10 weeks in Britain.

Famous writer Smokey Robinson wrote and produced this disc. The million sale was reported in March 1973. The disc was the fourth million-seller for The Supremes with the new line-up of Jean Terrell, Mary Wilson and Cindy Birdsong.

THE SWEET
POPPA JOE *RCA* [*Britain*]. Released in Britain in January 1972, this Chinnichap (Nicky Chinn and Mike Chapman) opus went to No 10 for one week and stayed in the charts for 11 weeks.

The million sale for this (their third) was for global sales, by 1973. The disc has a West Indian flavour, plus a liberal spattering of bongos and oil drum percussion. A catchy and easily memorable tune. (See The Sweet, 1971, for data.)

LITTLE WILLY *RCA* [*Britain*] *Bell* [*USA*]. Released in Britain in May 1972 and in the U.S.A. in January 1973, this went to No 3 for one week in Britain and three weeks in the U.S.A., staying in the topsellers 14 weeks in Britain and 23 weeks in the U.S. charts. R.I.A.A. Gold Disc award on 25 April 1973.

Another big hit for The Sweet and writers Chinn and Chapman, with simple lyrics and a catchy melody. It had good sales in Britain, but when released in the U.S.A. in 1973, sold over 1,500,000 there, making the group with the raunchy vocals and driving rhythm a big success in the States.

WIG-WAM BAM *RCA* [*Britain*]. Released in Britain in September 1972, going to No 4 for one week and staying 13 weeks in the charts.

Yet another success for The Sweet and writers Chinn and Chapman, a light-hearted tale of Red Indian love. It sold a million globally by February 1973. British sales alone were over 250,000.

THE TEMPTATIONS
PAPA WAS A ROLLING STONE *Gordy* [*USA*]. Written by Norman Whitfield and Barrett Strong, this was released in the U.S.A. in September 1972, going to No 1 for one week in the U.S.A. and No 14 in Britain. It stayed 16 weeks in the U.S. charts and nine weeks in the British charts. It won Grammy awards for Best Rhythm-and-Blues Performance by a Duo, Group or Chorus (1972); Best Rhythm-and-Blues Instrumental Performance (1972); and Best Rhythm-and-Blues Song (Songwriter's Award) to N. Whitfield and B. Strong (1972).

The famous Temptations climbed to the top again with this sensational piece of music. The million sale was reported in January 1973.

JOE TEX
I GOTCHA *Dial* [*USA*]. Written by Joe Tex and released in the U.S.A. in January 1972, this went to No 2 for two weeks, and stayed 20 weeks in the charts. R.I.A.A. Gold Disc award on 22 March 1972.

Joe Tex's third million-seller, his first big hit since 1967. The million sale was reached by March, and two million reported in August. From 1972 he became known as Joseph X.

TIMMY THOMAS
WHY CAN'T WE LIVE TOGETHER? *Glades* [*USA*]. Written by Timmy Thomas and released in the U.S.A. in November 1972, this went to No 2 for two weeks in the U.S.A. and No 10 in Britain. It stayed 16 weeks in the U.S. charts and 11 weeks in the British bestsellers.

This disc is said to have stirred emotions globally, and sold a reported two million. Timmy Thomas was born in Evansville, Indiana, in 1944. His father was a minister. Timmy's rapid musical development during his school days resulted in a 'Musician of the Year' award at high school, and also won him a stint at the Stan Kenton Jazz Clinic in 1962, where he studied under such great talents as Cannonball Adderley, Donald Byrd, Bobby Baker and Woody Herman, with performances at the Indiana Jazz Festival directed by Stan Kenton. He gained a scholarship to Lane College in Jackson, Tennessee, and mastered the keyboards. His first recording 'Have Some Boogaloo' was made in Memphis with good local sales. After 'Why Can't We Live Together?', his career was well on the way. His talent was acknowledged in *Billboard*'s 1972 national awards issue. Timmy appeared on 'Midnight Special' (ABC-TV) 'Soul Train' and '90 Minutes'. He also played on sessions with Betty Wright, K.C. and The Sunshine Band and others.

Glades Records were distributed by T.K. Productions of Hialeah, Florida. British release on Mojo label.

THREE DOG NIGHT
BLACK AND WHITE *Dunhill* [*USA*]. Written by D. Arkin and E. Robinson, and released in the U.S.A. in July 1972, this went to No 1 for two weeks, staying in the charts 14 weeks. R.I.A.A. Gold Disc award on 2 October 1972.

Another big hit for this extremely successful group. The disc is 'a song of brotherhood' from their album 'Seven Separate Fools'.

WAR
THE WORLD IS A GHETTO (album) *United Artists* [*USA*]. Released in the U.S.A. in October 1972, this went to No 1 for two weeks, staying in the charts for 68 weeks. R.I.A.A. Gold Disc award on 13 December 1972.

This album is the third by the group for United Artists. It proved to be their biggest, selling well over 1,500,000 units plus tapes sales exceeding 300,000. The group, who gave the term 'Afro-Rock' its original meaning, wrote all the numbers. The album included: (*) 'The World is a Ghetto'; (*) 'Cisco Kid'; 'Where Was You At?'; 'The 13-08'; 'City Country City'. (* denotes sold a million as a single.)

THE WORLD IS A GHETTO *United Artists* [*USA*]. Released in the U.S.A. in October 1972, this climbed to No 7 for one week, staying in the charts for 16 weeks. R.I.A.A. Gold Disc award on 2 March 1973.

Single release from the album of the same title. It subsequently went platinum status, with over two million sales.

THE EDGAR WINTER GROUP
THEY ONLY COME OUT AT NIGHT (album) *Epic* [*USA*]. Released in the U.S.A. in November 1972, this hit No 1 for one week, staying in the charts 80 weeks. R.I.A.A. Gold Disc award on 30 April 1973.

This group consists of Edgar Winter (born 28 December 1947 in Leland, Mississippi) on keyboards and alto sax, Ronnie Montrose (lead guitar), Chuck Ruff (drums), and Dan Hartman (bass).

Edgar, the younger brother of Johnny Winter the white blues tornado, played around the southern U.S. circuit with various bands. After Johnny became famous, Edgar joined his band where his solo keyboards and alto sax work attracted attention.

Edgar decided to experiment with Texas tap roots of early jump band jazz as opposed to Johnny's rock approach. In 1971, Edgar formed White Trash, and built his act on standard soul material. After his 'White Trash' album (1971) and 'Road Work' album (1972) he built a big following in the U.S.A. He finally split with White Trash and, teaming up with ex-McCoys guitarist Rick Derringer, formed the Edgar Winter Group, with Derringer producing the album 'They Only Come out at Night'. This sold 1,200,000 in a year, and with the hit single from it - 'Frankenstein', made the quartet a huge attraction in concerts in the U.S.A. The album became a landmark in Edgar Winter's career. It included: (*) 'Frankenstein'; 'Autumn'; 'When It Comes'; 'Round and Round'; 'Hangin' Around'; 'Free Ride'; 'Undercover Man'; 'We All Had a Real Good Time'; 'Rock 'n' Roll Boogie Woogie Blues'. (* denotes sold a million as a single.)

All material by Edgar Winter. Edgar Winter possesses a dynamic vocal style, in addition to his instrumental skill.

BILL WITHERS
LEAN ON ME *Sussex* [*USA*]. Written by Bill Withers and released in the U.S.A. in April 1972, this went to No 1 for three weeks in the U.S.A. and No 14 in Britain. It stayed 19 weeks in the U.S.A charts and 9 weeks in Britain. R.I.A.A. Gold Disc award on 20 June 1972.

A second million-seller for Bill. Sales subsequently topped three million.

USE ME *Sussex* [*USA*]. Written by Bill Withers and released in the U.S.A. in August 1972, this got to No 2 for two weeks, staying 19 weeks in the charts. R.I.A.A. Gold Disc award on 12 October 1972.

Third self-written million-seller in a row for Bill Withers, a 'basic funk' disc.

BOBBY WOMACK & PEACE

HARRY HIPPIE *United Artists* [*USA*]. Written by J. Ford and released in the U.S.A. in November 1972, this went to No 25 for one week, staying 12 weeks in the charts. R.I.A.A. Gold Disc award on 14 February 1973.

Bobby Womack was born in Cleveland, Ohio. He attended elementary and high school, also a technical high school. He began singing at four, and with his four brothers sang in church until his teens. His first claim to fame was as a member of Valentinos (who were his brothers) who cut the original of The Rolling Stones' hit 'It's All Over Now'. The song, written by Bobby, has become a rock classic. Bobby went on to compose songs for Wilson Pickett, Aretha Franklin, Joe Tex, Percy Sledge and Jerry Butler. He toured with the James Brown troupe, and later extensively with the Sam Cooke group. It was Cooke who took Womack and his brothers out of gospel music and into rhythm-and-blues, signing them to his Sar label. After 'It's All Over Now', the group disbanded, Bobby continuing with Cooke as guitarist right up to Cooke's death. He then became guitarist on most of Wilson Pickett's hits in the 1960s, recorded in his own right for Minit label and later the parent company United Artists. By the early 1970s he emerged as one of the new black superstars with his United Artists albums. Bobby inherited his love of the guitar from his father, who also gave him his first music lessons.

'Harry Hippie' was his first million seller, almost a decade since writing 'It's All Over Now' (1964).

STEVIE WONDER

TALKING BOOK (album) *Tamla* [*USA*]. Released in the U.S.A. in October 1972 and in Britain in January 1973, this went to No 3 for four weeks, staying in the charts for 109 weeks.

Stevie Wonder broke away from the Motown formula sound by his 21st birthday, in 1971, because the company had changed the course of pop music with its terrific roster of black talent. He received about $1 million which had been held in trust for him till he was 21 – a trust personally supervised by Motown's founder, Berry Gordy. Up to that time, Stevie had sold 30 million records. Stevie wanted to use his creative ability in his own way, and put $250,000 of his own money into studio time. He learned to play the Moog synthesizer, and recorded an album 'Music of My Mind'. In 1972 he toured nationally with The Rolling Stones, and thus exposed his music to a big new, mainly white audience. After finishing 'Music of My Mind' he went back to Motown with a much more favourable contract. Then came the album 'Talking Book' which stayed in the charts for over two years and easily sold over the million units. It contained: (*) 'You Are the Sunshine of My Life'; 'Maybe Your Baby'; 'You and I'; 'Tuesday Heartbreak'; 'You've Got It Bad'; (*) 'Superstition'; 'Big Brother'; 'Blame It on the Sun'; 'Lookin' for Another Pure Love'; 'I Believe (when I fall in love it will be forever)'. (* denotes sold a million as a single.)

All material by Stevie Wonder.

SUPERSTITION *Tamla* [*USA*]. Written by Stevie Wonder and released in the U.S.A. in November 1972, this went to No 1 for two weeks in the U.S.A. and No 11 in Britain (9 weeks in the bestsellers). It stayed 17 weeks in the U.S. charts and won Grammy Awards for Best Rhythm-and-Blues Male Vocal Performance (1973) and Best Rhythm-and-Blues Song (1973).

This tremendously successful award-winning song from Stevie's album 'Talking Book' sold well over two million. The disc has a voodoo beat, and expresses directly one of his extraordinary variety of musical moods.

TAKURO YOSHIDA (folk singer)

TABI NO YADO *Odyssey* [*Japan*]. Released in Japan in July 1972, this disc was No 1 for six weeks there, and in the Top 20 for 18 weeks. It sold a reported million by September 1972.

FARON YOUNG

(IT'S) FOUR IN THE MORNING *Mercury* [*USA*]. Written by J. Chestnut (1971) and released in Britain in July 1972, this went to No 3 and stayed in the charts for 23 weeks.

Faron Young's biggest hit since his 'Hello Walls' in 1961, it was first a big hit in Britain, where it sold over 500,000. It sold another 750,000 in North America by early 1973.

NEIL YOUNG

HEART OF GOLD *Reprise* [*USA*]. Released in the U.S.A. in January 1972, this went to No 1 for one week in the U.S.A. and No 7 in Britain, staying 15 weeks in the U.S. charts and 10 weeks in the British lists. R.I.A.A. Gold Disc award on 21 April 1972.

Neil Young was born 1945 in Toronto, son of a well-known journalist. He later moved to Winnipeg, and travelled around Canada and the border as a solo folksinger. He subsequently arrived in Los Angeles and formed Buffalo Springfield in 1966 with Steve Stills (see Buffalo Springfield). When they dissolved in 1968, Neil resumed as singer/guitarist at small U.S. clubs. By 1969, Neil formed Crazy Horse, but they were overshadowed by Crosby, Stills and Nash (1969). Neil was invited to join the trio, and his contribution to their second album 'Déjà Vu' resulted in a tremendous success for the quartet. It was one of the major albums of 1970. Neil continued his solo career, and in 1972 recorded his album 'Harvest', which took 18 months to complete. One of its songs 'Heart of Gold' proved to be a big hit and easily sold over the million.

HARVEST (Album) *Reprise* [*USA*]. Released in the U.S.A. in January 1972, this hit No 1 for four weeks in the U.S.A. and three weeks in Britain. It stayed 41 weeks in the U.S. charts and 32 weeks in British bestsellers. R.I.A.A. Gold Disc award on 18 February 1972.

This album went straight into the U.S. charts at No 12, and was No 1 in the second week. It stayed in the top area of their charts for the greater part of its 41 weeks' run and was undoubtedly the top album there of 1972. In Britain it also had a considerable success and was in the Top 10 for 12 weeks. U.S. sales quickly reached the million sale. Global sales are estimated at around two million.

Contents of the album: 'Out on the Week-end'; 'Harvest'; 'Man Needs a Maid'; 'Heart of Gold'; 'Are You Ready for the Country?'; 'Old Man'; 'There's a World'; 'Needle and the Damage Done'; 'Words (between the lines of age)'.

All songs by Neil Young.

ORIGINAL SOUNDTRACK

AMERICAN GRAFFITI (Double album) *MCA* [*USA*]. Released in the U.S.A. in August 1973, this went to No 9 for two weeks, staying 60 weeks in the charts. R.I.A.A. Gold Disc award on 21 December 1973.

One of the best youth-themed nostalgia films, set in 1962, but reflecting the culmination of the 1950s. The film recalls teenage attitudes and moods, and the cast included some extremely talented new players. It tells the story of a long summer night in the lives of four school chums: Curt (Richard Dreyfuss), Steve (Ronny Howard), John (Paul Le Mat) and Terry (Charlie Martin Smith). There is also a gang of toughs led by Bo Hopkins, and three girls: Laurie (Cindy Williams), Debbie (Candy Clark), and Carol (Mackenzie Phillips, 12-year-old daughter of composer John Phillips), disc jockey Wolfman Jack, plus a rock band, Flash Cadillac & The Continental Kids. The film was directed by George Lucas, who later made *Star Wars*. The soundtrack uses 41 disc hits, opening with Bill Haley's 'Rock Around the Clock'. By August 1974 the double album had achieved platinum status with 1,500,000 sold.

Contents: 'Rock Around the Clock': Bill Haley and The Comets (M. C. Freedman and J. De Knight, 1953); 'Do You Wanna Dance?': Bobby Freeman (Bobby Freeman, 1958); 'Sixteen Candles': The Crests (Luther Dixon and Allyson R. Khent, 1959); 'Fanny Mae': Buster Brown (Wayman Glasco, 1960); 'Runaway': Del Shannon (Del Shannon and Max Crook, 1961); 'Smoke Gets in Your Eyes': The Platters (Otto Harback and Jerome Kern, 1933); 'At the Hop': Flash Cadillac (A. Singer, J. Medora and D. White, 1957); 'She's So Fine': Flash Cadillac (Ronnie Mack, 1962); 'He's the Great Impostor': The Fleetwoods (The Fleetwoods, 1962); 'See You in September': The Tempos (Sid Wayne and Sherman Edwards, 1959); 'Since I Don't Have You': The Skyliners (Beaumont, Vogel, Verscharen, Lester, Taylor, Rock and Martin, 1959); 'The Stroll': The Diamonds (Clyde Otis and Nancy Lee, 1957); 'Surfin' Safari': The Beach Boys (Mike Love and Brian Wilson, 1962); 'All Summer Long': The Beach Boys (Brian Wilson, 1964); 'Almost Grown': Chuck Berry (Chuck Berry, 1959); 'Book of Love': The Monotones (W. Davis, G. Malone and C. Patrick, 1957); 'Love Potion No 9': The Clovers (Jerry Leiber and Mike Stoller, 1959); 'Ya Ya': Lee Dorsey (Lee Dorsey, C. Lewis and M. Robinson, 1961); 'Chantilly Lace': The Big Bopper (J. P. Richardson, 1958); 'The Great Pretender': The Platters (Buck Ram, 1955); 'To the Aisle': The Five Satins (Billy Dawn Smith and Stuart Wiener, 1957); 'You're Sixteen': Johnny Burnette (Dick and Bob Sherman, 1960); 'Little Darlin': The Diamonds (Maurice Williams, 1957); 'Barbara Anne': The Regents (Fred Fassert, 1961); 'Get a Job': The Silhouettes (The Silhouettes, 1958); 'Maybe Baby': Buddy Holly (Norman Petty and Buddy Holly, 1958); 'Ain't That a Shame': Pat Boone (Fats Domino and Dave Bartholomew, 1955); 'That'll be the Day': Buddy Holly (J. Allison, Buddy Holly, and Norman Petty, 1957); 'Teen Angel': Mark Dinning (Jean and Red Surrey, 1959); 'Only You': The Platters (Buck Ram and Ande Rand, 1955); 'Heart and Soul': The Cleftones (Frank Loesser and Hoagy Carmichael, 1938); 'Party Doll': Buddy Knox (Jimmy Bowen and Buddy Knox, 1957); 'Johnny B. Goode': Chuck Berry (Chuck Berry, 1958) 'A Thousand Miles Away': The Heartbeats (James Sheppard and W. H. Miller, 1956); 'Come Go with Me': The Del-Vikings (C. E. Quick, 1957); 'Green Onions': Booker T. & The MGs (S. Cropper, A. Jackson, L. Steinberg and Booker T. Jones, 1962); 'Goodnight, Well It's Time To Go': The Spaniels (Calvin Carter and James Hudson, 1954); 'Peppermint Twist': Joey Dee & The Starlighters (Joey Dee and Henry Glover, 1961); 'I Only Have Eyes For You': The Flamingoes (Al Dubin and Harry Warren, 1934); 'Crying in the Chapel': Sonny Till & The Orioles (Artie Glenn, 1953); 'Why Do Fools Fall in Love?': Frankie Lymon (Frank Lymon and George Goldner, 1956).

The film was first reviewed at the Directors Guild of America in Los Angeles on 15 June 1973. It was filmed in small towns north of San Francisco.

ORIGINAL FILM SOUNDTRACK

JESUS CHRIST SUPERSTAR (Double album) *MCA* [*USA*]. Released in the U.S.A. in June 1973 this went to No 21 for one week, staying in the charts 39 weeks. R.I.A.A. Gold Disc award on 5 September 1973.

Produced by Norman Jewison and Robert Stigwood and directed by Jewison, this film of the phenomenally successful rock opera was filmed on location in Israel, using natural settings. It featured the vocals of Ted Neeley (as Jesus), Carl Anderson (as Judas), Yvonne Elliman (as Mary Magdalene) and Barry Dennen (as Pontius Pilate). The score was orchestrated by its composer Andrew Lloyd Webber and conducted by André Previn. Lyrics by Tim Rice. It was the third time round for the opera on disc, having previously been released in 1970 and as a Broadway cast album in 1971. The film (MCA/Universal) was released in major U.S.A. cities on 27 June 1973 and globally by early 1974. By then, over 700,000 of the album had been sold in the U.S.A., 60,000 in Canada, over 45,000 in Britain and 30,000 in Holland. With sales from other countries around the world it easily passed one and a half million sales, and a million of these were in the U.S.A. alone. The film was reviewed at Universal Studios, Los Angeles on 29 May 1973.
(See 'Jesus Christ Superstar', 1970.)

ORIGINAL FILM SOUNDTRACK (NEIL DIAMOND)

JONATHAN LIVINGSTON SEAGULL (Album) *Columbia* [*USA*]. Released in the U.S.A. in October 1973, this avian opera hit No 1 for two weeks, staying in the charts 30 weeks. R.I.A.A. Gold Disc award on 30 October 1973.

The film version of Richard Bach's famous book *Jonathan Livingston Seagull* was produced and directed by Hall Bartlett, who also collaborated with Bach on the screenplay. It is a pastoral allegory, filmed with live birds and locations, with some well-known players speaking the dialogue. The nature photography is superb. The story is of Jonathan, a non-conformist bird who wants to dive for fish instead of foraging in garbage like gulls always do. He cruises the world after being banished from the flock, and passes to another level of existence before returning to his flock to instill his new ideas in younger birds. The music for this modern fable was composed by Neil Diamond, who spent more than a year in creating the soundtrack. He both wrote and sang his melodies, and shared the credit for the score and orchestration with Lee Holdridge. Jonathan's voice is dubbed by James Franciscus, his girl friend's by Juliet Mills, Elder's voice by Hal Holbrook, Chang's voice by Philip Ahn, Fletcher's voice by David Ladd, Kimmy's voice by Kelly Harmon and parents' voices by Dorothy McGuire and Richard Crenna. Paramount budgeted $1,500,000 for the production, which was a big success. The world premiere was in New York on 24 October 1973. One of Neil Diamond's numbers, 'Be', was released as a single.

By 1978, the album had sold more than 2,000,000 in the U.S.A. plus an additional million sales units from overseas markets. It was declared platinum by February 1975. Other hits on the album were 'Skybird' and 'Dear Father'.

Neil Diamond received the Grammy Award for Best Soundtrack Performance 1973.

VARIOUS ARTISTS

STARS FOR US (Album) (*German disc*). Many international disc stars participated in making this album for the campaign to combat world hunger. It sold over one million in the German-speaking countries of West Germany, Austria and Switzerland at 10 German marks ($4.20) of which 2 marks (80 cents) went to the campaign fund. The Dalai Lama of Tibet was the recipient of an unusual citation - The Golden Record Award - presented to him by pop singer Katja Ebstein when he appeared in West Germany during his tour for world peace before returning to his exile in India. A little Tibetan orphan Taschi was featured as 'cover boy' for the album.

AEROSMITH (rock quintet)

AEROSMITH (Album) *Columbia* [*USA*]. Released in the U.S.A. in September 1973, this made No 20 for two weeks (in 1976), and 50 weeks in the charts altogether. R.I.A.A. Gold Disc award on 11 September 1975.

Aerosmith consists of Joe Perry (guitar), Brad Whitford (guitar), Tom Hamilton (bass) and Joey Kramer (drums), all from Boston, and Steve Tyler (vocals) from Yonkers, NY. Tyler started in rock'n'roll playing drums in the band at his parents' small hotel in Sunapee, New Hampshire. In the early 1970s he met Hamilton and Perry and decided to be a vocalist, bringing in Kramer and Whitford to form the quintet. Their high-voltage, high-decibel rock music gradually made them one of the pre-eminent attractions in the U.S.A. via their incessant touring throughout the heartlands and East Coast. They were subsequently signed by Clive Davis to CBS and, by 1975, their catalogue of albums all began moving up the charts including this album 'Aerosmith'. Sell-out concerts resulted, with the final affirmation of the group's coming of age at Madison Square Garden on 10 May 1976.

They wrote their own material. This album included 'Dream On' (which reached No 6 as a single disc issue), 'Make it', 'One Way Street', 'Somebody' and 'Mama Kin'. It sold the million units by 1976.

THE ALLMAN BROTHERS BAND

BROTHERS AND SISTERS (Album) *Capricorn* [*USA*]. Released in the U.S.A. in August 1973, this album stayed No 1 for five weeks, remaining in the charts for 55 weeks. R.I.A.A. Gold Disc award on 21 August 1973.

This album was an instant success, reaching No 1 within two weeks of release and selling 760,000 in the first three weeks. It finally sold two million in the U.S.A. with total global sales between three and four million. It features lead vocals from Greg Allman and Dicky Betts, combined with their outstanding instrumental fusion. Betts' slide and lead guitar work are impressive, as is Allman's organ playing and the tight rhythm section. One of the strongest blues rock albums for quite some time.

Contents: 'Ramblin' Man'; 'Southbound'; 'Wasted Words'; 'Pony Boy'; 'Jelly Jelly'; 'Jessica'; 'Early Morning Blues'; 'Come and Go Blues'.

RAMBLIN' MAN *Capricorn* [*USA*]. Written by Richard Betts and released in the U.S.A. in August 1973, this went to No 1 for one week, staying in the charts 16 weeks.

A big success for Dicky Betts of the group, from the album 'Brothers and Sisters'. This single sold a reported million by March 1974.

THE BEATLES

THE BEATLES 1962-1966 (Double album) THE BEATLES 1967-1970 (Double album) *Apple* [*Britain & USA*]. Released in the U.S.A. and Britain on 2 April 1973, both albums went to No 1 for two weeks in the U.S.A.; the 1962-1966 album went to No 1 for one week in Britain and the 1967-1970 album to No 1 for two weeks. Both albums stayed in the U.S.A. charts for 77 weeks and in the British charts for 52 weeks R.I.A.A. Gold Disc awards on 13 April 1973, both albums.

These two albums of The Beatles' biggest hits were certified gold by the R.I.A.A. two days before their official release in the U.S.A. They show the maturation of the group, to the time they split up in 1970. They reveal the amazing career of the famous quartet and the way they revolutionized the world's approach to pop music, with the powerful songwriting team of John Lennon and Paul McCartney. Each album sold well over a million, one estimate being one-and-a-half million for the 1962-1966 album and almost two million for the 1967-1970 album.

1962-1966 album (all songs by John Lennon and Paul McCartney). (*)'Love Me Do' (1962); (*)'Please Please Me' (1963); (*)'From Me to You' (1963); (*)'She Loves You' (1963); (*)'I Want to Hold Your Hand' (1963); 'All My Loving' (1963); (*)'Can't Buy Me Love' (1964); (*)'A Hard Day's Night' (1964) 'And I Love Her' (1964); (*)'Eight Days a Week' (1964); (*)'I Feel Fine' (1964); (*)'Ticket to Ride' (1965); (*)'Yesterday' (1965); (*)'Help' (1965); 'You've Got to Hide Your Love Away' (1965); (*)'We Can Work It Out' (1965); 'Day Tripper' (1965); 'Drive My Car' (1965); 'Norwegian Wood' (1965); (*)'Nowhere Man' (1965); 'Michelle' (1965); 'In My Life' (1965); 'Girl' (1965); (*)'Paperback Writer' (1966); 'Eleanor Rigby' (1966); (*)'Yellow Submarine' (1966).

1967-1970 album (all songs by John Lennon and Paul McCartney unless otherwise indicated). 'Strawberry Fields Forever' (1967); (*)'Penny Lane' (1967); 'Sergeant Pepper's Lonely Hearts Club Band' (1967); 'With a Little Help from My Friends' (1967); 'Lucy in the Sky with Diamonds' (1967); 'A Day in the Life' (1967); (*)'All You Need Is Love' (1967); 'I Am the Walrus' (1967); (*)'Hello Goodbye' (1967); 'The Fool on the Hill' (1967); 'Magical Mystery Tour' (1967); (*)'Lady Madonna' (1968); (*)'Hey Jude' (1968); 'Revolution' (1968); 'Back in the U.S.S.R.' (1968); 'While my Guitar Gently Weeps' (George Harrison, 1968); 'Ob-La-Di, Ob-La-Da' (1968); (*)'Get Back' (1968); 'Don't Let Me Down' (1968); (*)'The Ballad of John & Yoko' (1968); 'Old Brown Shoe' (George Harrison, 1968); 'Here Comes the Sun' (George Harrison, 1969); (*)'Come Together' (1969); (*)'Something' (George Harrison, 1969); 'Octopus's Garden' (Ringo Starr, 1969); (*)'Let It Be' (1969); 'Across the Universe' (1970); (*)'The Long and Winding Road' (1970).

(* denotes sold a million as a single.)

BEGINNING OF THE END (male vocal instrumental group)

FUNKY NASSAU *TK-Drive* [*USA*] *Atlantic* [*Britain*]. Written by Raphael Munnings and Tyrone Fitzgerald, released in the U.S.A. in 1973 and in Britain in early 1974, it was No 31 and 6 weeks in the charts.

This disc was a big hit for the group (so far unidentified) in the Caribbean area, where it is reputed to have sold a million.

BLOODSTONE (rhythm and soul sextet)

NATURAL HIGH *London* [*USA*]. Written by Charles McCormick and released in the U.S.A. in April 1973, this went to No 5 for two weeks and stayed 20 weeks in the charts. It was No 40 in Britain. R.I.A.A. Gold Disc award on 19 July 1973.

The members of Bloodstone: Charles Love (guitar/vocals), Willis Draffen (rhythm guitar/vocals), Harry Williams (percussion/vocals), Charles McCormick (bass guitar/vocals), Roger Durham (percussion/vocals) and Melvin Webb (drums/vocals). The group were all together at Central High School in Kansas City, Missouri, around 1962, and fitted rehearsals in with their studies. They split up for a stint in the Services. They were originally known as The Sinceres, a strictly vocal group, but when they tried for success in Hollywood (1968) they were rewarded with starvation and the advice 'play your own instruments'. By 1971, they had changed over to an instrumental group. At this time, their manager George Bronstein suggested that Britain would be the best place to make it, so (1972) they made England their home for almost a year. The breakthrough came when they played the Rainbow Theatre in London with Al Green, and made their first album in Britain. The 'Natural High' album (including the single) was written in Britain, and it was Mike Vernon who produced their discs, travelling to Los Angeles to cut the album at The Village Recorder there. The group admitted they owed a lot to Britain and their British producer Mike Vernon.

Their Hollywood aspirations were realised in 1974 when they were signed to make the movie *Night Train*.

The single 'Natural High' has been described as 'beautifully ethereal'. Bloodstone wrote all their own songs, and the group's sound was diverse and versatile, built on traditional rhythm-and-blues harmonics embellished with progressive melodic instruments.

BLUE SWEDE

HOOKED ON A FEELING *EMI* [*Sweden*] *Capitol* [*USA*]. Written by Mark James, 1968 (real name Francis Rodney Zambon), and released in Sweden in May 1973 and in the U.S.A. in February 1974, this reached No 1 for two weeks in the U.S.A., staying in the charts 18 weeks. R.I.A.A. Gold Disc award on 28 March 1974.

Blue Swede was first formed in 1973, when Bjorn Skifs, a top male vocalist in Sweden, was looking for a band to accompany him during his live performances. Bengst Palmers, head of A & R for EMI in Sweden who worked with the group on its stage presentation, suggested they do 'Hooked on a Feeling', the 1968 hit for B.J. Thomas, because he thought it would be an effective number to encourage audience participation. It was so successful that when recorded it became an immediate hit in Sweden, due mainly to the rhythmic, chanting, distinctive background vocals. The disc was also a number one single in Canada, Australia and Holland. It sold a fast million in the U.S.A.

BROWNSVILLE STATION

SMOKIN' IN THE BOYS ROOM *Bell* [*USA*]. Written by Lutz and Koda, this was released in the U.S.A. in September 1973, going to No 2 for one week, staying in the charts 22 weeks. It was No 27 in Britain. R.I.A.A. Gold Disc award on 15 January 1974.

Taken from the group's album 'Yeah', this disc took five months to sell the million. Personnel of this group so far unidentified.

THE CARPENTERS

SING *A & M* [*USA*]. Released in the U.S.A. in February 1973, this rose to No 3 for two weeks, staying in the charts 15 weeks. R.I.A.A. Gold Disc award on 17 May 1973.

'Sing' comes originally from the successful TV show 'Sesame Street', with composer Joe Raposo as musical director. Kermit the Frog did the original on the gold, Grammy-winning first 'Sesame Street' album. The famous Carpenters - Karen and Richard - decided to include it in their album 'Now and Then', but the single was released prior to that album appearing on the market. The song became very popular in Britain later through the album.

YESTERDAY ONCE MORE *A & M* [*USA*]. Written by Richard Carpenter and John Bettis and released in the U.S.A. in May 1973 and in Britain in July 1973, this went to No 1 for one week in the U.S.A. and three weeks in Britain. It stayed 17 weeks in both the U.S.A. and British bestsellers. R.I.A.A. Gold Disc award on 13 August 1973.

Yet another hit for The Carpenters. The song is based on the inspiration Carpenter and Bettis got from the infectious lyrics and rhythms of the early 1960s. This single is a cut from the duo's 'Now and Then' album. In addition to the U.S.A. million-plus sale, it sold well over 250,000 in Britain, and over 600,000 in Japan by mid-1974.

TOP OF THE WORLD *A & M* [*USA*]. Again written by Richard Carpenter and John Bettis, this was released in the U.S.A. in September 1973 and in Britain in October 1973. It went to No 1 for two weeks in the U.S.A. and No 4 for two weeks in Britain, staying 20 weeks in the U.S.A. charts and 17 weeks in the British bestsellers. R.I.A.A. Gold Disc award on 11 December 1973.

A 1973 'hat-trick' of million sellers for The Carpenters. This single is a cut from their album 'A Song for You'. The disc also sold over 250,000 in Britain.

THE SINGLES 1969-1973 (Album) *A & M* [*USA*]. Released in the U.S.A. in November 1973 and in Britain in January 1974, this raced to No 1 for two weeks in the U.S.A. and 20 weeks in Britain. It lodged 49 weeks in the U.S. bestsellers and 102 weeks in the British charts. R.I.A.A. Gold Disc award on 11 December 1973.

A superlative album compilation of The Carpenters' biggest hits, to round off their most successful year since they came on the disc scene. In the U.S.A. it was No 1 by its fifth week, and No 1 by the third week on the market in Britain. Estimated sales were around three million globally, over a million of these in the U.S.A. alone.

Contents: (*)'We've Only Just Begun' (Paul Williams and Roger Nichols, 1970); (*)'Top of the World' (Richard Carpenter and John Bettis, 1973); 'Ticket to Ride' (John Lennon and Paul McCartney, 1969); (*)'Superstar' (L. Russell and B. Bramlett, 1971); (*) 'Rainy Days and Mondays' (Paul Williams and Roger Nichols, 1971); 'Goodbye to Love' (Richard Carpenter and John Bettis, 1972); (*)'Yesterday Once More' (Richard Carpenter and John Bettis, 1973); 'It's Going to Take Some Time' (Richard Carpenter and John Bettis, 1973); (*)'Sing' (Joe Raposo, 1973); (*)'For All We Know' (Robb Wilson, Arthur James and Fred Karlin, 1971); (*)'Hurting Each Other' (G. Geld and Peter Udell, 1972); (*)'Close to You' (Hal David and Burt Bacharach, 1970).

(* denotes sold a million as a single.)

By the end of 1975, The Carpenters had sold over 30 million records.

DAVID CASSIDY

DAYDREAMER backed with PUPPY SONG *Bell* [*USA*]. With 'Daydreamer' written by Tony Dempsey and 'Puppy Song' written by Harry Nilsson, this double sider was released in Britain October 1973, going to No 1 for three weeks and staying 11 weeks in the charts.

David Cassidy's popularity with the teenagers was still in evidence in Britain, and this disc released there sold a reported million subsequently around the world, with over 250,000 in Britain alone.

CHEECH & CHONG

LOS COCHINOS (Album) *Ode* [*USA*]. Released in the U.S.A. in August 1973, this went to No 1 for 1 week and stayed in the charts for 69 weeks. It received the R.I.A.A. Gold Disc award on 2 October 1973, and the Grammy Award for the Best Comedy Recording, 1973.

The album covers a range of subjects from dope to basketball. It includes the outrageous 'Basket Ball Jones (featuring Tyrone Shoelaces)' which features George Harrison, Carole King, Billy Preston and others on musical back-up. Other comic gems are 'Pedro and Man at the Drive-Inn' and 'Sargent Stadanko'. Its popularity with Americans earned it a Grammy Award. Platinum status (one million units sold) was reported in December 1973.

CHER

HALF BREED *MCA* [*USA*]. Written by Mary Dean and Al Capps, this ethnic lament was released in the U.S.A. in July 1973, going to No 1 for two weeks and lasting in the charts for 19 weeks. R.I.A.A. Gold Disc award on 12 October 1973.

First million-seller for Cher on her new (MCA) label, and

because of its title and Cher's interpretation, particularly popular with U.S.A. fans.

CHICAGO

CHICAGO VI (Album) *Columbia* [*USA*]. Released in the U.S.A. in July 1973 this shot to No 1 for five weeks, and stopped in the charts 70 weeks. R.I.A.A. Gold Disc award on 18 July 1973.

The sixth million units seller for this super group. The disc was No 1 in its third week of release. All the songs were written by the group.

Contents: 'Just You'n Me'; 'Critic's Choice'; 'Darlin' Dear'; 'Jenny'; 'What's This World Comin' To?'; 'Something in This City Changes People'; 'Hollywood'; 'In Terms of Two'; 'Rediscovery'; 'Feelin' Stronger Every Day'.

JUST YOU'N ME *Columbia* [*USA*]. Released in the U.S.A. in September 1973, this went to No 1 for one week and stayed in the charts 20 weeks. R.I.A.A. Gold Disc award on 2 January 1974.

The prime cut from the 'Chicago VI' album, written by group member James Pankow. It reached the million sale four months after release.

JIM CROCE

BAD, BAD LEROY BROWN *ABC Dunhill* [*USA*]. Released in the U.S.A. in April 1973, this rose to No 1 for two weeks and stayed there 22 weeks. R.I.A.A. Gold Disc award on 24 July 1973.

Singer/songwriter Jim Croce was born 1942 and grew up in the Philadelphia area. His involvement in music began while he was attending Villanova University where he ran a campus radio station (1961–1965) featuring folk music. He achieved modest success playing the fraternity party circuit, and during his junior year, his musical talents gained him a goodwill tour as a troubadour to the Baltic states, the Middle East and African nations for the U.S. Government. He then became a salesman at a soul radio station, a camp counselor and a teacher, finally going to New York to work the coffeehouse circuit. This led to a college tour, session work, and a recording contract with Capitol that produced his first album 'Approaching'. The record failed to catch on, and Jim found work, first with an excavating contractor, then as a truck driver. He moved to the wilds of Pennsylvania and once again hit the music trail, getting a recording contract and a hit record 'You Don't Mess Around with Jim' taken from his ABC/Dunhill album of the same title. His next album 'Life and Times' contained 'Bad Bad Leroy Brown' which sold a million as a singles release. He was a success also in Britain when he appeared (1973) at the Cambridge Folk Festival. Most of his best songs were from situations which capture people and the human condition.

On 20 September 1973, after an engagement at Northwestern Louisiana State University and on his way to a date in Sherman, Texas, the private plane in which he was a passenger failed to gain altitude and crashed at Natchitoches, Louisiana, killing Jim Croce, his guitar player Maury Muelheisen and his road manager. A tragic end for an outstanding folksinger who had just reached the top in his profession.

TIME IN A BOTTLE *ABC Dunhill* [*USA*]. Written by Jim Croce and released in the U.S.A. in November 1973, this gained No 1 for two weeks and stayed 17 weeks in the charts. R.I.A.A. Gold Disc award on 3 January 1974.

Jim Croce's tragic death in September 1973 sparked a greater interest in his richly humorous songs, and 'Time in a Bottle' was released posthumously with a quick million sale.

DAWN (featuring Tony Orlando)

TIE A YELLOW RIBBON (round the old oak tree) *Bell* [*USA*]. Written by Irwin Levine and L. Russell Brown, this insidious tune was released in the U.S.A. in January 1973 and in Britain in February 1973. It made No 1 for four weeks in the U.S.A. and

in Britain for five weeks. It stayed for a tenacious 23 weeks in the U.S.A. bestsellers and 40 weeks in the British charts. R.I.A.A. Gold Disc award on 2 April 1973.

The biggest hit of 1973. It sold well over two million in the U.S.A., 927,000 in Britain, and total global sales estimated at over six million. The song is based on a Civil War story about the homecoming of a soldier from Andersonville prison, written by journalist Pete Hamill as part of a PBS-TV series 'The Great American Dream Machine', a few months before the song itself was written. Tony Orlando and the writers estimated the song generated over 1,000 world-wide cover versions. It was the most performed song of 1973. By the end of 1975, Dawn had sold 25 million records.

SAY HAS ANYBODY SEEN MY SWEET GYPSY ROSE? *Bell* [*USA*]. Written by Irwin Levine and L. Russell Brown and released in the U.S.A. in June 1973 and in Britain in July 1973, this achieved No 3 for two weeks in the U.S.A. and No 11 for one week in Britain. It stayed 17 weeks in the U.S.A. bestsellers and 15 weeks in Britain. R.I.A.A. Gold Disc award on 9 October 1973.

Dawn officially changed their name to Tony Orlando & Dawn, as they found there were 14 other Dawns playing around the world, who were wrecking their reputation. This disc and the trio's Bell album 'Ragtime Follies' almost singlehandedly revived the ragtime style. Although the trio had hitherto made few live performances, when their 'Dawn's New Ragtime Follies' made its debut at the Riviera Hotel in Las Vegas on 9 November 1973, the novel stage act resulted in TV specials, summer replacement series and a show for the BBC. They became a top-rated musical-variety show on TV, via a regular season run on CBS starting in December 1974. Tony Orlando, Joyce Vincent Wilson and Telma Hopkins appealed to the widest possible cross-section of the public.

In 1975, the trio went over to Elektra/Asylum Records.

DEEP PURPLE

SMOKE ON THE WATER *Warner* [*USA*] *Purple Records* [*Britain*]. Written by Richie Blackmore, Ian Gillan and Roger Glover, this was released in the U.S.A. in May 1973, going to No 2 for one week and staying 16 weeks in the charts. R.I.A.A. Gold Disc award on 28 August 1973.

The most popular number from the group's 1972 album 'Machine Head' was a million seller for Deep Purple quite some time after the album release. The writers are members of the group.

THE DE FRANCO FAMILY (vocal/instrumental quintet)

HEARTBEAT (It's a love beat) *20th Century* [*USA*]. Written by Williams and Kennedy, this was released in the U.S.A. in June 1973, reaching No 1 for one week, staying 21 weeks in the charts. R.I.A.A. Gold Disc award on 6 November 1973.

The De Franco Family are Benny (born 11 July 1954), Nino (born 19 October 1956), Marisa (born 23 July 1955), Tony (born 31 August 1959) and Merlina (born 1958). All were raised in Welland, Ontario. They became popular in their local region of the Niagara Peninsula, Canada, and their faces became features in various newspapers around the country. One of these came to the attention of Charles Laufer, a publisher of teenage magazines in Hollywood. Laufer did a series of interviews and photographs of the quintet which were published in his magazines. The response to the articles convinced Laufer that The De Francos were something special. He signed the group to his entertainment concern, and hired Mike Post and Walt Meskill to produce them and record three sides for his LEG records. Russ Regan of 20th Century Records liked their sound, and made a deal to distribute the LEG-De Franco recordings. 'Heartbeat' was a big hit, and sold almost two million. Appearances on the Dick Clark show 'American Bandstand' (July 1973) and a national TV show with Jack Benny (January 1974) set the seal on The De Francos' future.

THE DELLS

GIVE YOUR BABY A STANDING OVATION *Cadet* [*USA*]. Written by Marv Johnson and Henry Williams and released in the U.S.A. in April 1973, this got to No 20 for two weeks and stayed 16 weeks in the charts. R.I.A.A. Gold Disc award on 30 July 1973.

First big hit for The Dells since 1969. They are one of the longest-serving American rhythm-and-blues groups, with only one change in their line-up since 1954 – Jerry Funches replacing Johnny Carter in 1968.

JOHN DENVER

GREATEST HITS (Album) BEST OF JOHN DENVER (title for Britain) *RCA* [*USA*]. Released in the U.S.A. in November 1973 and in Britain in March 1974, this compilation went to No 1 for four weeks in the U.S.A. and No 15 for one week in Britain. It persisted for 127 weeks (to mid-1976) in the U.S.A. charts and nine weeks in the British top sellers. R.I.A.A. Gold Disc award on 11 December 1973.

This lush and beautifully arranged album, produced by Milton Okun, is a collection of Denver's most esteemed hits. Its success in the U.S.A. was outstanding. The million units sale (platinum status) was reached by March 1974, two million by May 1974, three million by October 1974 and an incredible five-and-a-half million by December 1975. The final tally was over six million.

Contents: 'Leaving on a Jet Plane' (1967); (*)'Take Me Home Country Roads' (John Denver, B. Danoff and Taffy Nivert, 1971); 'Poems, Prayers and Promises' (1971); (*)'Rocky Mountain High' (John Denver and Mike Taylor, 1972); 'For Baby (For Bobbie)' (1972); 'Starwood in Aspen' (1971); 'Rhymes and Reasons' (1969); 'Follow Me' (1969); 'Goodbye Again' (1972); 'The Eagle and the Hawk' (1971); (*)'Sunshine on My Shoulders' (Denver, Kniss and Taylor, 1971).

(* denotes sold a million as a single.)

All songs by John Denver unless otherwise indicated.

THE DETROIT SPINNERS

ONE OF A KIND (LOVE AFFAIR) *Atlantic* [*USA*]. Written by Joseph B. Jefferson, this was released in the U.S.A. April 1973, going to No 8 for two weeks and staying for 15 weeks in the charts. R.I.A.A. Gold Disc award 13 July 1973.

The third million-seller for The Detroit Spinners, a continuation of their success story.

THE DOOBIE BROTHERS

THE CAPTAIN AND ME (Album) *Warner* [*USA*]. Released in the U.S.A. in March 1973, this went to No 7 for two weeks, staying in the charts 78 weeks. R.I.A.A. Gold Disc award on 3 July 1973.

The second million-seller album for this rock quintet, produced by Ted Templeman. It marks one of the high points in synthesizer rock. There are several strong tracks on the album including: 'Natural Thing'; 'Ukiah'; 'China Grove'; 'Dark-eyed Cajun Woman'; 'Long Train Runnin'' and 'Clear as the Driven Snow'.

EMERSON, LAKE & PALMER

BRAIN SALAD SURGERY (Album) *Manticore* [*Britain*]. Released in Britain in November 1973 and in the U.S.A. in December 1973, this went to No 1 for two weeks in Britain and No 7 for one week in the U.S.A. It stayed 14 weeks in the British charts and 47 weeks in the U.S.A. bestsellers. R.I.A.A. Gold Disc award on 12 December 1973.

The fifth million-seller album in a row for the trio.

DAVID ESSEX (rock vocalist)

ROCK ON *CBS* [*Britain*]. Written by David Essex, this was released in Britain in August 1973 and in the U.S.A. in October 1973. It went to No 1 for one week in both countries, staying 11 weeks in the British charts and 25 weeks in the U.S.A. topsellers. R.I.A.A. Gold Disc award on 26 March 1974.

David Essex (real name David Cook) was born in Plaistow, London, Britain on 23 July 1947 and grew up in the dockland area. At the age of 12 he became interested in pop music. He learned to play drums, and joined a local band when 14 and subsequently became a singer. The band was heard by Derek Bowman, a journalist on the *Daily Express*, and he became David's manager, persuading him to embark on a solo career and change his name from Cook to Essex. In 1963, David made his first record 'And The Tears Came Tumblin' Down' for Decca. He then toured for two years with a soul band calling themselves David Essex and the Mood Indigo. He made no real progress until 1970 when he made his debut film appearance in *Assault* and then *All Coppers Are . . .* His big break came when he auditioned successfully and gained the star part in a play *The Fantastics* and then the star part in *Godspell* to play Jesus (November 1971). This was followed by the lead part of Jim McLain, the central character in the immensely popular film *That'll Be The Day*. 'Rock On' was a big hit on both sides of the Atlantic.

David's career was now established, with a further hit 'Lamplight' and a second film *Stardust* in which he again played the McLain role. He also made a strong impression on U.S. audiences in 1974 with appearances on 'In Concert', 'In Session' and 'Touch of Gold'.

His co-star in the film *That'll Be The Day* was Beatle Ringo Starr.

ROBERTA FLACK

KILLING ME SOFTLY WITH HIS SONG *Atlantic* [*USA*]. Written by Norman Gimbel and Charles Fox, this had simultaneous release in the U.S.A. and Britain in January 1973. It rose to No 1 for three weeks in the U.S.A. and No 5 for one week in Britain. It remained 16 weeks in the U.S.A. charts and 14 weeks in the British topsellers. R.I.A.A. Gold Disc award on 22 February 1973 and three Grammy Awards: Best Record of 1973; Best Female Pop Vocal; Song of the Year 1973 to writers Gimbel and Fox.

Roberta Flack was not the first to record this beautiful song. She first heard Lori Lieberman's version on a plane flight from Los Angeles to New York. Roberta's million-plus sales and three Grammy Awards have made the song a world standard.

THE FOUR TOPS

AIN'T NO WOMAN (Like the one I've got) *ABC/Dunhill* [*USA*]. Written by Dennis Lambert and Brian Potter and released in the U.S.A. in January 1973, this went to No 1 for one week, notching up 15 weeks in the charts. R.I.A.A. Gold Disc award on 2 April 1973.

The second single from The Four Tops' album 'The Keeper of the Castle' to sell a million.

ARETHA FRANKLIN

UNTIL YOU COME BACK TO ME *Atlantic* [*USA*]. Written by Stevie Wonder, C. Paul and M. Bradnax, this was released in the U.S.A. in November 1973, hitting No 3 for one week and staying in the charts 21 weeks. R.I.A.A. Gold Disc award on 20 February 1973.

The 14th million-seller for Aretha.

MARVIN GAYE

LET'S GET IT ON *Tamla* [*USA*]. Written by Ed Townsend and released in the U.S.A. in July 1973, this enormous hit went to No 1 for two weeks, staying in the bestsellers for 21 weeks.

One of the largest-selling singles in Motown history, this disc sold two million within six weeks of release, finally amassing over three million. Writer Townsend was co-producer with Marvin Gaye. The disc was also No 1 for nine straight weeks on the rhythm-and-blues charts, and believed to be the highest number of record sales for a single recording in a comparable period since the early Beatles era.

LET'S GET IT ON (Album) *Tamla* [*USA*]. Released in the U.S.A. in September 1973, this album went to No 1 for two weeks and stayed in the charts for 54 weeks.

It was shipped and certified gold on 29 August, and sold a million by mid-October. It included: 'Let's Get It On'; 'Distant Lover'; 'Please Don't Stay'; 'Come Get to This'; 'Just to Keep You Satisfied'; 'What's Going On?'; 'If I Should Die Tonight'; 'Keep Gettin' It On'.

The album was produced by Ed Townsend and Marvin Gaye.

GARY GLITTER

I'M THE LEADER OF THE GANG *Bell* [*Britain*]. Written by Gary Glitter and Mike Leander, and released in Britain in July 1973, this thumping number went to No 1 for four weeks, staying in the charts for 12 weeks.

It sold over 500,000 in Britain and went on to the million sale globally, further establishing Gary's fame in the rock world.

I LOVE YOU LOVE ME LOVE *Bell* [*Britain*]. Written by Gary Glitter and Mike Leander, this was released in Britain in November 1973, climbing to No 1 for four weeks and staying in the charts for 13 weeks.

The third million-seller for Gary Glitter and his co-writer Mike Leander, the sale was in Britain alone, and Gary was the first British artist to be awarded a platinum record by the British Phonograph Society (1974). 1973 was a great year for Gary, who had many other hits in Britain, and was awarded four silver discs for 250,000 or more for each.

GRAND FUNK RAILROAD

WE'RE AN AMERICAN BAND *Capitol* [*USA*]. Written by Don Brewer and released in the U.S.A. in July 1973, this went to No 1 for one week, staying in the bestsellers 17 weeks. R.I.A.A. Gold Disc award on 9 October 1973.

First million-seller single for Grand Funk Railroad.

DOBIE GRAY

DRIFT AWAY *Decca* [*USA*]. Written by Mentor Williams and released in the U.S.A. in February 1973, this drifted to No 4 for two weeks, lingering in the charts for 21 weeks. R.I.A.A. Gold Disc award on 5 July 1973.

Dobie Gray (real name Leonard Victor Ainsworth) was born in Brookshire, Texas in 1942. As a teenager, he responded to a radio advertisement for new singers and went to Hollywood. Sonny Bono of Specialty Records heard him sing but could find no opening for him with the label. Sonny introduced him to Cor-Dak records and he made 'Look at Me!' which was a success (1963). He then recorded 'The "In" Crowd' for the Charger label which was a big hit in 1965. This brought him work on several tours. He based himself in Los Angeles to study law in college and concentrated on acting. He also joined a group called Pollution. His big break came when he met Mentor Williams who produced his album 'Drift Away' and the single of the same title for Decca. Both were big successes, the single selling over a million, and Dobie was back with the 'in crowd', a long-awaited comeback in his musical career.

AL GREEN

CALL ME (Come back home) *Hi* [*USA*]. Written by the established team of Al Green, Willie Mitchell and Al Jackson, this was released in the U.S.A. in February 1973, going to No 8 for two weeks and staying 12 weeks in the charts. R.I.A.A. Gold Disc award on 23 April 1973.

The sixth million-seller single in a row for Al Green.

HERE I AM (Come and take me) *Hi* [*USA*]. Written by Al Green and M. Hodges, this was released in the U.S.A. in June 1973, reaching No 10 for two weeks, and staying in the charts 16 weeks. R.I.A.A. Gold Disc award on 28 August 1973.

The incredible Al Green's seventh consecutive million-seller.

GEORGE HARRISON

LIVING IN THE MATERIAL WORLD (Album) *Apple* [*Britain*] *Capitol* [*USA*]. Released in the U.S.A. and Britain in June 1973, this went to No 1 for five weeks in the U.S.A. and No 2 for one week in Britain, staying 26 weeks in the U.S.A. bestsellers and 11 weeks in the British charts. R.I.A.A. Gold Disc award on 1 June 1973.

An immediate gold award for this collection of ballads, rock and rollers and heart-felt sentiments. The album was made in London, and Beatle George Harrison is joined in the studio by friends Nicky Hopkins, Gary Wright, Klaus Voormann, Jim Keltner, Ringo Starr, Jim Gordon, John Barham and Zakir Hussein. The album contents: 'Give Me Love'; 'Sue Me, Sue You Blues'; 'The Light That Has Lighted the World'; 'Don't Let Me Wait Too Long'; 'Who Can See it?'; 'Living in the Material World'; 'The Lord Loves the One that Loves the Lord'; 'Be Here Now'; 'Try Some Buy Some'; 'The Day the World Gets 'round'; 'That Is All'.

All material written by George Harrison.

The album was estimated to have sold more than two million in the U.S.A. and over three million globally.

THE INDEPENDENTS (vocal quintet)

LEAVING ME *Wand* [*USA*]. Written by M. Barge and J. Jiles and released in the U.S.A. in March 1973, this went to No 18 for one week, staying 14 weeks in the charts. R.I.A.A. Gold Disc award on 23 May 1973.

This group comprises Chuck Jackson (lead singer) born 22 March 1945 in Greenville, South Carolina, Maurice Jackson, born 12 June 1944 in Chicago, Eric Thomas, born in Chicago, Marvin Jerome Yancy, born 31 May 1950 in Chicago and Helen Curry, born Clarksdale, Mississippi. All had attended university and got together in Chicago. They all had prior experience in the world of music before emerging as a group. 'Leaving Me' was included on their album 'The First Time We Met' and was a big hit for them as a single release.

THE ISLEY BROTHERS

THAT LADY *T.Neck*/*Columbia* [*USA*]. Written by Ronald, O'Kelly and Rudolph Isley, this was released in the U.S.A. in July 1973 and in Britain in September 1973. It reached No 6 for three weeks in the U.S.A. and No 13 for one week in Britain. It stayed 20 weeks in the U.S.A. charts and eight weeks in the British bestsellers. R.I.A.A. Gold Disc award on 2 October 1973.

This song, written by the three Isley Brothers, was their first hit for CBS to whom they signed on their T.Neck label. It was a cut from their album '3 plus 3' and introduced younger brothers Ernie Isley (guitar), Marvin (bass) and brother-in-law Chris Jasper (keyboards), as back-up musicians. Ernie's rock-styled guitar playing took the group into a new sound. The disc sold over two million.

ELTON JOHN

DANIEL *DJM* [*Britain*] *MCA* [*USA*]. Written by Bernie Taupin and Elton John, this was released in Britain in January 1973 and in the U.S.A. in April 1973. It went to No 4 for one week in the U.S.A. and No 2 for two weeks in Britain, staying 15 weeks in the British charts and 11 weeks in the U.S.A. bestsellers.

'Daniel' is a cut from Elton's album 'Don't Shoot Me, I'm Only the Piano Player', and sold a global million by July 1973.

DON'T SHOOT ME, I'M ONLY THE PIANO PLAYER (Album) *DJM* [*Britain*] *MCA* [*USA*]. Released in the U.S.A. and Britain in February 1973, this album went to No 1 for three weeks in the U.S.A. and eight weeks in Britain. It stayed a staggering 89 weeks in the U.S.A. charts and 21 weeks in the British bestsellers. R.I.A.A. Gold Disc award on 12 February 1973.

A colossal success for Elton John and Bernie Taupin with an estimated global four million sale, over half of this in the U.S.A. alone. The multi-tracking and strings on the album provide a broad, rich, well-executed sound, and Elton's smooth voice and gentle piano on 'Blues for a Baby and Me' contrast starkly with the new rhythmic sound on 'Elderberry Wine'. The album included two items, 'Crocodile Rock' and 'Daniel', that each sold a million or more as single releases. The album was recorded at the Château d'Herouville in France, and contained: 'Daniel'; 'Teacher I Need You'; 'Elderberry Wine'; 'Blues for Baby and Me'; 'Midnight Creeper'; 'Have Mercy on the Criminal'; 'I'm Going to be a Teenage Idol'; 'Texan Love Song'; 'Crocodile Rock'; 'High Flying Bird'.

All written by Bernie Taupin and Elton John.

SATURDAY NIGHT'S ALRIGHT FOR FIGHTIN' *DJM* [*Britain*] *MCA* [*USA*]. Written by Bernie Taupin and Elton John and simultaneously released in Britain and the U.S.A. in July 1973, this went to No 8 for two weeks in the U.S.A. and No 4 for one week in Britain. It stayed 13 weeks in the U.S.A. charts and nine weeks in the British bestsellers.

This single was quite a success in both Britain and the U.S.A. and subsequently sold a global million. It was included on Elton's album 'Goodbye Yellow Brick Road'.

GOODBYE YELLOW BRICK ROAD *DJM* [*Britain*] *MCA* [*USA*]. Written by Bernie Taupin and Elton John, this was released in the U.S.A. and Britain in September 1973, going to No 1 for one week in the U.S.A. and No 4 for one week in Britain. It stayed 17 weeks in the U.S.A. bestsellers and 12 weeks in the British charts. R.I.A.A. Gold Disc award on 4 January 1974.

The second single from the album 'Goodbye Yellow Brick Road' to sell a million plus.

GOODBYE YELLOW BRICK ROAD (Double album) *DJM* [*Britain*] *MCA* [*USA*]. Released in the U.S.A. and Britain in October 1973, this shot to No 1 for eight weeks in the U.S.A. and two weeks in Britain. It lodged in the U.S.A. charts for 91 weeks and 72 weeks in the British bestsellers. R.I.A.A. Gold Disc award on 12 October 1973.

Elton's third album recorded at the Château d'Herouville in France. This double album highlights the hit single 'Saturday Night's Alright for Fightin' ' and the title track. The combination of soft, haunting ballads and rock'n'roll display the undoubted genius of Elton and lyricist Taupin. It also included a third title 'Benny and the Jets' which also sold a million in 1974 as a single release. The album was Elton's biggest hit up to 1973, selling an estimated seven million globally, at least half of these in the U.S.A. alone, after staying eight weeks at the top there, and remaining in the bestsellers in both U.S.A. and Britain for several months. The album contained: 'Funeral for a Friend'; 'Love Lies Bleeding'; 'Candle in the Wind'; 'Benny and the Jets'; 'Goodbye Yellow Brick Road'; 'This Song Has No Title'; 'Grey Seal'; 'Jamaica Jerk Off'; 'I've Seen that Movie Too'; 'Sweet Painted Lady'; 'The Ballad of Danny Bailey (1909–1934)'; 'Dirty Little Girl'; 'All the Girls Love Alice'; 'Your Sister Can't Twist (But She Can Rock'n'Roll)'; 'Saturday Night's Alright For Fightin' '; 'Roy Rogers'; 'Social Disease'; 'Harmony'.

All songs by Elton John and Bernie Taupin.

EDDIE KENDRICKS

KEEP ON TRUCKIN' *Tamla* [*USA*]. Written by Anita Poree, Frank Wilson and Leonard Caston, this was released in the U.S.A. in August 1973, going to No 1 for two weeks in the U.S.A. and No 18 for one week in the Britain with 14 weeks in the charts. It stayed 19 weeks in the U.S.A. charts.

The million sale for this disc was reported in November 1973. Caston and Wilson who co-wrote the song also produced the disc at Tamla-Motown.

Eddie Kendricks was born on 17 December 1939 in Birmingham, Alabama. He started singing at the age of eight. His first group was the local Cavaliers who moved to Cleveland, then Detroit where Eddie met Otis Williams who he joined in a group called The Distants, which in turn became The Elgins. Williams knew Berry Gordy and that is how the group joined Tamla who changed their name to The Temptations (1960). They went on during the ensuing years to become tremendously successful, their style influencing the whole development of soul. In 1971, Eddie decided to pursue a solo career, and with this first No 1 hit 'Keep on Truckin' ' he was catapulted into national prominence. The song is a cut from his album 'Eddie Kendricks'.

BOOGIE DOWN *Tamla* [*USA*]. Written by Anita Poree, Leonard Caston and Frank Wilson and released in the U.S.A. in December 1973, this went to No 1 for one week, staying in the U.S.A. charts for 19 weeks. It was No 39 in Britain.

This super follow-up to Eddie's 'Keep on Truckin' ' sold the million by February 1974. Again written by Poree and his disc producers at Motown.

CAROLE KING

FANTASY (Album) *Ode* [*USA*]. Released in the U.S.A. in June 1973, this went to No 1 for one week and stayed in the charts for 37 weeks. R.I.A.A. Gold Disc award on 26 June 1973.

Another fine album by composer/singer Carole King. Its contents analyse the frailties and banalities of human relationships. Produced by Lou Adler, the album highlights Carole's gently cooing voice, plus lush strings soaring above the brass and reeds, keeping pace with the pulse beat of the bass and conga. Carole's singing and the melodic sweep of the music made the album a million seller by December 1973.

Contents: 'Being at War with Each Other'; 'That's How Things Go Down'; 'Haywood'; 'A Quiet Place to Live'; 'Corazon'; 'You Light Up My Life'; 'Weekdays'; 'Fantasy Beginning'; 'Fantasy End'; 'Believe in Humanity'; 'You've Been Around Too Long'; 'Directions'.

All written by Carole King.

GLADYS KNIGHT & THE PIPS

NEITHER ONE OF US (wants to say goodbye) *Soul* [*USA*]. Released in the U.S.A. in January 1973, this made No 1 for one week, staying 16 weeks in the U.S.A. charts. It was No 31 in Britain. Grammy Award for Best Pop Vocal Performance by a Duo, Group or Chorus, 1973.

Composer Weatherly, born in Ponotoc, Mississippi, began playing guitar and writing songs from the age of 12. He graduated from the University of Mississippi, and is one of the many American composers of popular country-western-rock-soul music able to portray the musical version of the people of the Deep South.

The disc sold two million.

MIDNIGHT TRAIN TO GEORGIA *Buddah* [*USA*]. Released in the U.S.A. in August 1973, this made No 1 for two weeks, staying in the U.S.A. charts for 19 weeks. It was No 10 and 9 weeks in the British charts. R.I.A.A. Gold Disc award on 18 October 1973 and Grammy Award for Best Rhythm-and-Blues Vocal Performance by a Duo, Group or Chorus, 1973.

Second big hit for composer Jim Weatherly, and second Grammy Award for the group in 1973. The disc is said to have sold over two million, and is the first for Gladys Knight & The Pips on their new label, Buddah.

IMAGINATION (Album) *Buddah* [*USA*]. Released in the U.S.A. in October 1973, this album went to No 9 for one week, staying 53 weeks in the U.S.A. charts. R.I.A.A. Gold Disc award on 5 November 1973 and Grammy Award for Best Selling Album by a Female Soul Artist, 1974.

The million sale for this fine album was reported in April 1974. It included: 'Best Thing That Ever Happened to Me'; (*)'Midnight Train to Georgia'; (*)'I've Got to Use My Imagination'; 'I Can See Clearly Now'; 'Once in a Lifetime'; 'Perfect Love'; 'Storms of Troubled Times'; 'Where Peaceful Waters Flow'; 'Window Raisin' Granny'. (* denotes million-selling singles.)

I'VE GOT TO USE MY IMAGINATION *Buddah* [*USA*]. Written by Gerry Goffin and Goldberg and released in the U.S.A. in November 1973, this reached No 4 for two weeks and stayed 16 weeks in the charts. R.I.A.A. Gold Disc award on 30 January 1974.

This upbeat number with powerful vocals and strong horn breaks is a cut from the group's album 'Imagination', and made it a very successful year for them and their new label Buddah.

KOOL & THE GANG (rhythm and blues septet)

JUNGLE BOOGIE *De-Lite* [*USA*]. Written by Ronald Bell and Kool & The Gang, and released in the U.S.A. in December 1973, this rose to No 4 for one week, staying in the charts for 22 weeks. R.I.A.A. Gold Disc award on 21 February 1974.

Personnel of the group: Robert 'Kool' Bell (lead vocals/bass), born on 8 October 1950, Youngstown, Ohio, Ronald Bell (tenor sax), Claude Smith (lead guitar), Robert Mickens (trumpet), Rickey West (keyboards), George Brown (drums) and Reedman Thomas. The group started out as The Jazziacs in the mid-1960s in Jersey City, New Jersey, playing local clubs and occasional excursions to New York, opening by playing its jazz set and then as back-up to featured acts. They also provided the music for the Miss Black America Pageant - their 'Wild and Peaceful' serving as the contest's theme. Their adopted role was one of bridging the gap between funk and jazz. The group wrote, arranged and produced their own records, and toured clubs, theatres and colleges extensively.

'Jungle Boogie' was a tremendous success for them and De-Lite records.

KRIS KRISTOFFERSON

WHY ME, LORD? *Monument* [*USA*]. Written by Kris Kristofferson and released in the U.S.A. in March 1973, this went to No 16 for one week and stayed 38 weeks in the charts. R.I.A.A. Gold Disc award on 8 November 1973.

Kris Kristofferson was born in Brownsville, Texas on 22 June 1936. He moved to California while at high school. From Pomona College, he won a Rhodes Scholarship and went to England in 1958 to Oxford University. Here he began writing songs under the name Kris Carson. After obtaining an English degree, he joined the army and became a pilot, settling in Germany flying helicopters. He stayed in the forces for five years, and rose to the rank of captain. While in Germany he played NCO clubs and resumed songwriting, sending material to a publisher relative in Nashville. On return to the U.S.A. he spent a time in Nashville before taking a post as English teacher in West Point. Here he met Johnny Cash and decided on a singer/songwriter career. He moved to Nashville (1965) and his first professional job for Columbia records was cleaning Nashville Studios. He then became a janitor in a bar, another stint as helicopter pilot, and then continued songwriting in Nashville, where he was short of money and living in a tenement. As he was on the point of taking a construction job, artist Roger Miller asked him to go to California. Miller had decided to record one of his songs 'Me and Bobby McGhee' but finally recorded three. On return to Nashville he received a recording contract with Monument Records and cut the albums 'Silver Tongued Devil and I' (1971), 'Me and Bobby McGhee' (1972), 'Border Lord' (1972) and 'Jesus Was a Capricorn' (1973) from which 'Why Me?' was a singles release. This stayed in the bestsellers for 38 weeks, an incredibly long time for a gospel-type song.

Kris made tours and starred in the movies *The Last Movie* and *Cisco Pike*. His records sold in a big way, more than Bob Dylan's, it was reported in 1973. He married artist Rita Coolidge in 1973 and starred with her in the movie *Pat Garrett and Billy The Kid* which also featured Dylan. Kris quickly became a movie star because of his natural flair for acting. His seventh film was *A Star Is Born* (1967) in which he co-starred with Barbra Streisand and also wrote the songs. Many of his songs are now standards such as 'For the Good Times' and 'Help Me Make it Through the Night'.

LED ZEPPELIN

HOUSES OF THE HOLY (Album) *Atlantic [USA]*. Released in the U.S.A. and in Britain in March 1973, this hit No 1 for two weeks in both countries, staying for 76 weeks in the U.S.A. charts and 12 weeks in the British bestsellers. R.I.A.A. Gold Disc award on 10 April 1973.

Advance orders for this album were colossal. It went 'gold' in Germany before release and in the U.S.A. soon after release. Sales during the first month were 1,200,000, and over two million eventually globally. Led Zeppelin toured Europe from March to April and the U.S.A. where they played to larger crowds than any other band at that time. There were two sell-out concerts at Madison Square Garden, and at Tampa, Florida they broke the all-time American concert attendance record with 56,800 people plus 6,000 'gatecrashers' on 5 May 1973, at the stadium there. The previous record was held by The Beatles, who drew 55,000 people to the Shea Stadium. The Tampa event grossed $309,000, a new high one-day gross record.

Contents of the album: 'The Song Remains the Same'; 'The Rain Song'; 'Over the Hills and Far Away'; 'The Crunge'; 'Dancing Days'; 'D'Yer Mak' er'; 'No Quarter'; 'The Ocean'.

All songs written by the group.

LOVE UNLIMITED ORCHESTRA

LOVE'S THEME *20th Century [USA]*. Written by Barry White and released in the U.S.A. in November 1973, this went to No 1 for one week in the U.S.A. and No 10 in Britain. It stayed 19 weeks in the U.S.A. bestsellers and ten weeks in the British charts. R.I.A.A. Gold Disc award on 7 February 1974.

Barry White wrote, produced and conducted this smooth instrumental with a 41-piece orchestra, after changing his record label to 20th Century. This number was a cut from the album 'Stone Gon''.

LYNYRD SKYNYRD (rock septet)

PRONOUNCED LEH-NERD SKIN-NERD (Album) *Sounds of the South-MCA [USA]*. Released in the U.S.A. in August 1973, this went to No 56 for two weeks, staying in the charts for 58 weeks. R.I.A.A. Gold Disc award on 18 December 1974.

Lynyrd Skynyrd consisted of Ronnie Van Zant (lead singer), Ed King, Allen Collins, Gary Rossington (lead guitarists), Bobby Keys (reeds), and had Merry Clayton and Clydie King on vocal harmony. The band was formed in their hometown of Jacksonville, Florida. In 1972 they left Jacksonville, in search of jobs, bars and the joys of rock'n'roll life in Atlanta, Georgia, subsequently playing at a little rock club, Funocchio's – now defunct.

Here they were heard by Al Kooper who was recording in Atlanta for a while. The group gave him the idea of forming Sounds of the South Records, and with Al's help, this album was recorded. It sold 100,000 in six weeks, but it was not until their second album 'Second Helping' (1974) became a very big hit, that the first also became a similar success, receiving a Gold Disc 18 months after its release. By October 1976 it achieved platinum status with a million sale. The band were constantly on the road with a staggering 300 dates per year, and in 1974 they toured with The Who as an opening act, which gave them invaluable exposure and contributed to their success as disc sellers. By the end of 1976, their record sales reached an all-time peak. In January 1977, they started a tour of Hawaii, Japan, and then to England and Europe. Tragically, three members of the band were killed in an aircrash in October that year.

Lynyrd Skynyrd lyrics are written by Van Zant, with music by members of the group, principally Rossington, Ed King and Allen Collins. After personnel changes, the group at the end of 1976 was Van Zant, Collins, Rossington, Billy Powell, Leon Wilkeson, Artimus Pyle, (who replaced Bob Burns in 1975) and Steve Gaines (who replaced Ed King in 1976).

This first album included: 'I Ain't the One'; 'Tuesday Gone'; 'Things Goin' On'; 'Mississippi Kid'; 'Free Bird'.

PAUL McCARTNEY & WINGS

MY LOVE *Apple [USA and Britain]*. Written by Paul McCartney and released in Britain in March 1973 and the U.S.A. in April 1973, this went to No 7 for one week in Britain and No 1 for five weeks in the U.S.A., remaining 11 weeks in the British charts and 18 weeks in the U.S.A. bestsellers. R.I.A.A. Gold Disc award on 6 July 1973.

Wings was formed in the summer of 1971. At first, the band had no name, but featured Denny Laine, Denny Seiwell and Paul and Linda McCartney. Their first album 'Wild Life' (1971) was not a success. Henry McCullough (guitar) joined the band but he and Seiwell subsequently quit. Wings' second album 'Red Rose Speedway' (1973) included the song 'My Love' which was a big success, particularly in the U.S.A. The band toured Britain, playing at colleges, then Europe. It took the band some time to really get together and come up with good material, but 'Red Rose Speedway' dispelled all doubts, and Wings were then flying high.

Global sale of 'My Love' is estimated at two million.

BAND ON THE RUN (Album) *Apple [Britain] Capitol [USA]*. Released in the U.S.A. and Britain in November 1973 this shot to No 1 for eight weeks in Britain and five weeks in the U.S.A., settling for 101 weeks in the British charts and 74 weeks in the U.S.A. bestsellers. R.I.A.A. Gold Disc award on 4 June 1974.

This album gave Paul McCartney and Wings widespread acclaim and was the most commercially successful of all Beatles 'solo' projects. It included the classic rockers 'Jet' and 'Helen Wheels' and a beautiful love ballad 'No Words'. The band's harmonies and musicianship are superb. Linda McCartney and Denny Laine (guitar/vocals) are also featured. By August 1974, the album sold over two million in the U.S.A. and with British and other sales, well over two-and-a-half million globally. The million units sale in the U.S.A. was reported in April 1974. The album reached No 1 in the U.S.A. in March 1974, to return to the coveted position later. This repetition of No 1 status, after an absence, was an industry first. It was the best selling album in Britain in 1974, and the first ever McCartney record to be released in the Soviet Union (1976).

Contents of the album: 'Jet'; 'Band on the Run'; 'Bluebird'; 'Mrs Vandebilt'; 'Let Me Roll It'; 'Mamunia'; 'No Words'; 'Picasso's Last Words (Drink to Me)'; '1985'; 'Helen Wheels'.

All songs written and produced by Paul McCartney.

The album also gained two Grammy Awards in 1974 for Best Engineering Recording (Non-Classical), and Best Pop Vocal Performance by a Duo, Group or Chorus.

LIVE AND LET DIE *Apple* [*Britain*] *Capitol* [*USA*]. Written by Paul McCartney and Linda McCartney this was released in Britain and the U.S.A. in June 1973, going to No 1 for one week in the U.S.A. and No 7 for one week in Britain. It stayed 12 weeks in the British charts and 16 weeks in the U.S.A. bestsellers. R.I.A.A. Gold Disc award on 31 August 1973. Grammy Award to George Martin for Best Arrangement Accompanying Vocalists (1973).

In addition to the million-plus sale in the U.S.A., this disc also sold over 250,000 in Britain. The song was written for the James Bond film of the same name, in which it was sung by B.J. Arnau.

MAUREEN McGOVERN

THE MORNING AFTER *20th Century* [*USA*] *Pye* [*Britain*]. Written by Al Kasha and Joel Hirschhorn this was released in the U.S.A. in June 1973, reaching No 1 for two weeks and staying 18 weeks in the U.S.A. charts. R.I.A.A. Gold Disc award on 14 August 1973. 'Oscar' Award for Best Film Song of 1973 (Academy Award).

Maureen McGovern, born 1949, hails from Youngstown, Ohio. In 1972 she was working as a doctor's secretary in her home town. She also performed as a folksinger accompanied by guitar in small clubs and hotel chains around the Youngstown area. On one of her engagements, she was heard by Pat Padula of Destiny Inc., a theatrical agency in nearby Warren, Ohio. They made a demo disc and sent it to some record companies. Russ Regan, of 20th Century Records, heard it and signed her up. Her first single 'The Morning After' was cut in December 1972, produced by Carl Maduri. The song was featured in the film *The Poseidon Adventure*. Her disc had no initial success, but that all changed when the song won the Academy Award, and soon after, Maureen's disc finally reached the top of the U.S.A. charts, selling over a million. Release in Britain was February 1973.

BYRON MacGREGOR (narrator)

THE AMERICANS *Westbound – Chess/Janus* [*USA*]. Written by Gordon Sinclair and released in the U.S.A. in December 1973, this hit No 1 for one week, and stayed 13 weeks in the charts. R.I.A.A. Gold Disc award on 8 January 1974.

This most unlikely candidate for a hit record, a spoken word disc, began as an editorial by 72-year-old Gordon Sinclair, acknowledged dean of Canadian broadcast journalists, and was first broadcast on radio's CFRB-AM (Toronto) on 5 June 1973. Proclaiming Americans as one of the world's most unappreciated and unjustly maligned peoples, the editorial was reprinted in many newspapers. It came to the attention of CKLW's 25-year-old news chief, Byron MacGregor, who, like Sinclair, is a Canadian. MacGregor's tape of that editorial was first aired on the Detroit station on 2 December 1973, during a newscast. The station received a record 3,500 phone calls, which prompted Armen Boladian, head of Westbound Records in Detroit, to record 'The Americans' with an instrumental backing of 'America the Beautiful'. It was an instantaneous smash hit, selling 1,200,000 in just five days, and continuing at the rate of 250,000 a day. It went on to sell well over three million, despite hit recordings by Gordon Sinclair and country star Tex Ritter. 'The Americans' is unique in that never in the history of the singles charts has any spoken word disc had three charted versions. MacGregor and Peter Scheurmier, producer of the record, donated their royalties to the American Red Cross. One of the points raised in 'The Americans' is that the U.S.A. always provides assistance in major world disasters but foreign countries didn't reciprocate. As a result, the Red Cross was bankrupt halfway through its fiscal year.

HAROLD MELVIN & THE BLUE NOTES

THE LOVE I LOST (Part 1) *Philadelphia-International* [*USA*]. Written by Kenny Gamble and Leon Huff, this was released in the U.S.A. in September 1973, going to No 6 for one week and staying 18 weeks in the charts. In Britain it was No 21 and 8

weeks in the charts R.I.A.A. Gold Disc award on 28 December 1973.

Produced by famous writer/producers Gamble and Huff, who definitely put the Philadelphia Sound on the musical map. The composition is from the group's album 'Black and Blue', and is the second million-seller for them.

M.F.S.B. (Mother, Father, Sister, Brother)

T.S.O.P. (The Sound of Philadelphia) *Philadelphia-International* [*USA*]. Written by Kenny Gamble and Leon Huff, this was released in the U.S.A. in December 1973, going to No 1 for two weeks and staying 18 weeks in the charts. R.I.A.A. Gold Disc award on 1 April 1974. Grammy Award, Best Rhythm-and-Blues Instrumental Performance, 1974.

Used as the theme for the popular 'Soul Train' TV show, a major showcase for black talent, 'T.S.O.P.' was a big hit in the U.S.A. The disc was masterminded by Philadelphia International's Kenny Gamble, Leon Huff, and chief arranger/musical director Bobby Martin. Some 28 musicians are involved, most of whom had been together for over a decade at Philly's regular studio band. They were the musicians on Cliff Noble's million-selling 'The Horse' in 1968, and as Family on 'Family Affair' in 1971. M.F.S.B. comprises the regular session musicians of the Sigma Sound Studios, home of Gamble/Huff and Thom Bell's 'Philadelphia Sound', which began to emerge predominantly from the late 1960s as a force in popular music. Sigma Sound was the first proper four-track studio in the city. Philadelphia Sound with its lilting melodies and immediately recognisable style was definitely put on the map by Gamble, Huff and Bell, replacing, in a sense, the popularity of Detroit's Motown Sound. Their success was phenomenal. This outstanding disc created by the 'Family of Philadelphia' included Kenny Gamble (keyboards), Norman Harris (guitar), Lenny Pakula (organ), Zach Zachery (sax), Ronnie Baker (bass), Vince Montana (vibes), Larry Washington (percussion), Earl Young (drums), Roland Chambers (guitar), Ron Kersey (guitar), Bobby Eli (bass), plus strings, reeds and horns provided by contractor Don Renaldo.

STEVE MILLER BAND

THE JOKER *Capitol* [*USA*]. Written by Steve Miller, this was released in the U.S.A. in September 1973, hitting No 1 for one week, and sticking in the charts for 21 weeks. R.I.A.A. Gold Disc award, on 11 January 1974.

Steve Miller was born in Wisconsin and raised there and in Texas. While at the University of Wisconsin, he had a group called The Ardells, formed with boyhood friend Boz Scaggs. After college came a move to Chicago, where Steve became encouraged by such blues masters as Muddy Waters and Howlin' Wolf. He then moved to San Francisco, and The Miller Blues

Band (1966) became The Steve Miller Band (1967). Miller and his band became prominent figures in San Francisco and, in May 1968, made their first album 'Children of the Future'. Up to early 1972, they recorded seven quite popular albums and toured extensively. There were several changes in personnel. A fractured vertebra put Miller out of action for eight months following the release of his seventh album 'Recalling the Beginning . . . Journey from Eden' in March 1972. He then realigned his band, the personnel being Steve Miller (guitar), Dicky Thompson (keyboards), John King (drums), Gerald Johnson (bass), and composed material with which he returned with a flourish, as The Joker. The ninth album, 'The Joker', included the single of the same title, with resultant million sale. The album was also certified gold by R.I.A.A. The band then undertook a 40-city tour, an immensely successful one, highlighted by a New York performance the proceeds from which Steve donated to UNICEF's education fund.

Steve Miller and the band made their British debut in February 1972 at London's Rainbow Theatre.

OLIVIA NEWTON-JOHN

LET ME BE THERE *MCA* [*Britain & USA*]. Written by John Rostill and released in Britain in August 1973 and in the U.S.A. in November 1973, this reached No 4 for one week in the U.S.A., staying 20 weeks in the charts. R.I.A.A. Gold Disc award on 8 February 1974. Grammy Award, Best Female Country Vocal, 1973.

Olivia Newton-John was born in Cambridge, England on 26 September 1949, daughter of a Welsh-born father who had an academic background, and a German-born mother who was the daughter of a Nobel Prizewinning physicist. By the time Olivia was five, her family moved from Wales to Australia, and it was

there in Ormond College, where her father became Master of the College, that Olivia spent her time in making up tunes, although she had no musical training. She entertained friends with self-written musicals, and at 12 years of age, entered a local cinema contest to find 'the girl who most looked like Hayley Mills'. Two years later, Olivia formed a singing act with three other girls, called The Sol Four, but this was disbanded in 1969 as it interfered with school work, and Olivia continued singing on her own in a coffee lounge. A customer suggested she enter a local contest, held by Australian musical personality and TV star Johnny O'Keefe, which she won. As she was still at school, she had to wait a year before she could enjoy her prize - a trip to London. On arrival in London she formed a double act with another

Australian girl, a successful combination until her partner's visa ran out and she was forced to return to Australia. Olivia stayed, made one or two solo records, and became part of the group Tomorrow (1971).

Her first single 'If Not for You', recorded for Festival Records Inc. in 1971, was a hit in many countries including the U.S.A., Britain, Canada, Australia, South Africa, Norway and Belgium, and is a Bob Dylan tune. Also in 1971, her disc of 'Banks of the Ohio' sold over 250,000. The same year, Olivia made a tour of Europe with the Cliff Richard Show, and recorded a vocal duet with Cliff (the first time he had recorded with a girl). A three-week season followed at the London Palladium, and a subsequent tour of major British cities. In 1972, Olivia was a regular guest in the BBC-TV series 'It's Cliff Richard'. She was voted Best British Girl Singer by readers of *Record Mirror* for two years running. Her second album 'Olivia' was a success in 1972.

In 1973, Olivia took part in the Tokyo Song Festival, and a prestigious appearance on the 'Dean Martin' TV Show in the U.S.A. She also found herself with this big hit 'Let Me Be There' in the U.S. charts, winning her a coveted Grammy Award. The song was written by an ex-member of Cliff Richard's group The Shadows - John Rostill. Olivia also played the Sydney Opera House and toured again with Cliff Richard.

She is produced by Australian John Farrar and Bruce Welch (of The Shadows), is particularly fond of contemporary country songs, and became one of the most popular female vocalists in America, winning many awards and accolades, with virtually all her discs achieving million-seller status. She was awarded an O.B.E. in January 1979.

THE OHIO PLAYERS (septet)

FUNKY WORM *Westbound - Chess/Janus* [*USA*]. Written by The Ohio Players and released in the U.S.A. in January 1973 this got to No 13 for one week and stayed 19 weeks in the charts. R.I.A.A. Gold Disc award on 14 May 1973.

Although not reaching the No 1 position in the U.S.A. this cut from the group's album 'Pleasure' sold a million after three months in the bestsellers.
(See 1974 for biographical data.)

THE O'JAYS

LOVE TRAIN *Philadelphia-International* [*USA*]. Written by Kenny Gamble and Leon Huff and released in the U.S.A. in January 1973, this went to No 1 for one week and stayed 15 weeks in the charts. R.I.A.A. Gold Disc award on 9 February 1973.

Another big hit for the O'Jays, a cut from their 'Back Stabbers' album, with sales of over two million. It was written by writers/producers Kenny Gamble and Leon Huff. 'Love Train' is a universal song with an up-to-date message, the lyrics mentioning all areas around the world where there was conflict.

SHIP AHOY (album) *Philadelphia-International* [*USA*]. Released in the U.S.A. in November 1973 this made No 8 for two weeks, staying for 48 weeks in the charts. R.I.A.A. Gold Disc award on 21 January 1974.

A powerful session by The O'Jays, with the usual musical messages from the trio and Phil-Internat producer/writers Gamble and Huff.

By 1977, after 20 years of performing, The O'Jays were internationally recognized as world spokesmen for family traditions and the importance of family above monetary aspects of the theatrical profession. They reflected this philosophic message through their music as well as their professional and personal lives. This was proclaimed by both Ralph J. Perk, mayor of their hometown, Cleveland, and James A. Rhodes, Governor of Ohio, in special citations on the occasions of their 20th anniversary in 1977.

The album included: 'Put Your Hands Together'; 'For the Love of Money'; 'Just Call Me Brother'; 'You Got Your Hooks in Me'; 'Now That We Found Love'.

The million units (platinum status) sale was reported by mid-1974.

MIKE OLDFIELD (multi-instrumentalist)

TUBULAR BELLS (album) *Virgin* [*Britain*]. Released in Britain in July 1973 and in the U.S.A. in October 1973, this went to No 1 for 12 weeks in Britain and for one week in the U.S.A. It took up residence for 123 weeks in the British charts and 44 weeks in the U.S.A. bestsellers. R.I.A.A. Gold Disc award on 26 March 1974. Grammy Award, Best-Selling Pop Instrumental Album, 1974.

Mike Oldfield was born on 15 May 1953 in England. The son of a doctor from Reading, he began his career at the age of 14 with his elder sister Sally as a folk duo, and made their first record 'Sallyangie' for the Transatlantic label in 1968. Mike then formed a group, Barefeet, which only lasted a short time, and then joined Kevin Ayres & The Whole World as featured guitar/bass until it disbanded in mid-1971. Unable to get a full-time job in the orchestra for the musical *Hair* for which he was a stand-in musician, he had a lean time, and stayed in a tawdry bedsitter in Tottenham, London. He borrowed a friend's tape recorder and made a demo disc. He tried to place this for several months, but was turned down by five different record companies (all of which are now kicking themselves). The demo disc was eventually lost. Mike then met a friend, Richard Branson, who was starting a new label (Virgin), and signed him, making 'Tubular Bells' the first release. A year was spent by Mike at the Manor Studios, Oxfordshire, where, working entirely single-handed, he taped around 80 separate recordings, playing a combined total of 28 instruments ranging from tympani to mandolins. From the resultant dubbing and over-dubbing, the 'Tubular Bells' album was completed – a recording of $48\frac{1}{2}$ minutes. This debut album, an incredible fusion of rock and classic into a symphonic structure, was a sensation. It sold over 350,000 in Britain alone, and enjoyed fantastic success when much of it was used as background music for the film *The Exorcist*. The album had no lyrics – just a list of the many instruments Mike played and explored. It was regarded by many as one of the great musical works of the decade, and Mike was acclaimed a genius while still a teenager. British and American sales of the album each went over a million, and the global sales well over 6 million. The single release 'Tubular Bells (Theme from *The Exorcist*)' was also a million-seller (see 1974).

Mike Oldfield was then able to move to the peaceful area of Herefordshire, where he produced his second successful album, 'Hergest Ridge' named after the hill that faced his home. The over-dubs for the album were done by engineer Tom Newman.

Mike Oldfield was awarded the Freedom of the City, 1983 for his outstanding achievement with 'Tubular Bells'.

GILBERT O'SULLIVAN

GET DOWN *MAM* [*Britain*]. Written by Gilbert O'Sullivan, this was released in Britain in March 1973 and in the U.S.A. in June 1973, going to No 1 for two weeks in Britain and No 4 for two weeks in the U.S.A. It stayed 13 weeks in the British charts and 15 weeks in the U.S.A. bestsellers. R.I.A.A. Gold Disc award on 18 September 1973.

Another big hit for Gilbert on both sides of the Atlantic. Sales over a million in the U.S.A. and 250,000 in Britain.

DONNY OSMOND

THE TWELFTH OF NEVER *Kolob-MGM* [*USA*]. Written by Paul Francis Webster and Jerry Livingston (1956), this was released in the U.S.A. and Britain in February 1973. It went to No 1 for two weeks in Britain and No 5 for one week in the U.S.A. It stayed 13 weeks in the U.S.A. charts and 14 weeks in the British bestsellers. R.I.A.A. Gold Disc award on 14 September 1973.

A fine revival of the song originally made famous by Johnny Mathis in 1956. The melody is adapted from 'The Riddle Song', a folksong from Kentucky but probably of earlier English origin. This disc brought the Osmond family's ninth Gold Disc single for over a million sale. Global sales are estimated at two million.

MARIE OSMOND

PAPER ROSES *Kolob-MGM* [*USA*]. Written by Janice Toree and Fred Spielman (1960), this was released in the U.S.A. and Britain in September 1973. It went to No 4 for two weeks in the U.S.A. and No 2 for one week in Britain, and stayed 16 weeks in the U.S.A. charts and 15 weeks in the British bestsellers. R.I.A.A. Gold Disc award on 7 December 1973.

A recording debut for the Osmond family's 14-year-old daughter, Marie (born 13 October 1959). Originally a hit for Anita Bryant in 1960, it was produced in Nashville by country master Sonny James, and quickly made the crossover on to the national charts in the U.S.A. and abroad. Marie Osmond made her entry into the professional world in mid-1973, and started singing with her brothers at their concerts. Because of her feeling for country music, MGM Records suggested she join her brothers on the recording scene, and chose 'Paper Roses', which soon sold a million. The Osmonds made a major tour of Britain in late 1973, and Marie's disc was very popular there also. Global sales estimated at two million.

By 1976, Marie and Donny Osmond had their own TV show in America.

Kolob is the Osmond's label, marketed by MGM. 'Paper Roses' was the Osmond family's tenth Gold Disc single.

SIMON PARK ORCHESTRA

EYE LEVEL *Columbia* [*Britain*]. Written by Jack Trombey and released in Britain in September 1973, this reached No 1 for four weeks and stayed 22 weeks in the charts.

'Eye Level' was written for Britain's Thames TV series 'Van Der Valk' by Dutch composer Jack Trombey (real name Jules Staffaro) who also arranged it for the Simon Park Orchestra. It was recorded in France when Simon Park flew over to conduct and supervise the recording arrangement. A most attractive melody, the TV series sparked off a big demand by the British public and it soon sold over 500,000, and subsequently over a million globally.

Simon Park was born in Market Harborough, England in 1946 and gained a B.A. in music at Oxford. He plays piano and organ, and worked for the De Wolfe company which deals in consultations for film music and TV jingles.

BOBBY PICKETT & THE CRYPT KICKERS

MONSTER MASH *Parrot* [*USA*]. Written by Bobby Pickett and Lenny Capizzi (1962), this was re-released in the U.S.A. in April 1973 and in Britain in September 1973. It ascended to No 10 for one week in the U.S.A. and No 2 for one week in Britain.

It stayed 23 weeks in the U.S.A. charts and 13 weeks in the British bestsellers. R.I.A.A. Gold Disc award on 28 August 1973.

'Monster Mash' was previously a hit for Bobby Pickett in 1962 when it also sold a million. This re-issue on the Parrot label made it the third time it appeared on the U.S.A. national charts, and it again sold a million.

Bobby 'Boris' Pickett tried to get into acting in 1960 in California, and in between jobs formed a vocal quintet, The Cordials. Two years later, having left The Cordials, and still leading the life of a struggling actor, he wrote 'Monster Mash' with his friend Lenny Capizzi. It then reached No 1 on the now defunct Garpax label. For several years, Pickett wrote and harmonized in song and performance with his wife Joan Payne. They appeared in clubs and ski resorts around the U.S.A. until October 1973 and then settled in New York where he formed MP11 Ventures with lyricist Mike Meskill, merging with Alta Loma Music. Pickett's nickname 'Boris' came about through his impression of Boris Karloff, the actor of horror films, which he includes in his stage act. The revival of the old novelty disc 'Monster Mash' started when WOKY station in Milwaukee started to play the disc, and introduced the entertainment value of the recording to another generation of teenagers.

PINK FLOYD (rock quartet)

DARK SIDE OF THE MOON (album) *Harvest* [*Britain*]. Released in Britain in March 1973 and in the U.S.A. in March 1973, this went to No 1 for one week in both countries and stayed 180 weeks in the British charts and 132 weeks in the U.S.A. bestsellers. R.I.A.A. Gold Disc award on 17 April 1973.

Pink Floyd consists of David Gilmour (guitar/vocals), born 6 March 1946, Nick Mason (drums/percussion) born Birmingham 27 January 1945, Roger Waters (bass/vocals) born Cambridgeshire 6 September 1944, Richard Wright (keyboards/vocals), born London 28 July 1945.

Pink Floyd were formed towards the end of 1965, and originally contained six members, all students at London's Regent Street Polytechnic Architectural School: Mason, Waters, Wright, and bassist Clive Metcalf plus singers Keith Noble and Juliette Gale (later Mrs Richard Wright). They were then known as Sigma 6, changing to The Tea Set before finally becoming The Architectural Abdabs. When some of the original members left, Roger 'Syd' Barrett from Beckenham Art College, an old friend from Cambridge, was enlisted on guitar. Barrett suggested a name change from The Abdabs to The Pink Floyd Sound. (The name was inspired by the Georgia bluesmen Pink Anderson and Floyd Council.) Now a quartet, they became known as, simply, Pink Floyd. They gradually changed style from rhythm-and-blues towards original material and mixed-media experiments, and eventually became known as a prototype psychedelic group of 1966-1967. They signed with Columbia and in 1967 recorded two single hits, 'Arnold Layne' and 'See Emily Play', followed by their first album 'Piper at the Gate of

Dawn' (1967) and their second 'A Saucerful of Secrets' (1968). At this time Syd Barrett's songwriting dominated the group. He left in 1968 and was replaced by David Gilmour. One more album for Columbia, the soundtrack for *More* (1969), was followed by 'Ummagumma' (1969), 'Atom Heart Mother' (1970), 'Meddle' (1971), 'Obscured by Clouds' soundtrack (1972), all on the Harvest label, and 'Relics' (1971, Starline label). Their greatest success, 'Dark Side of the Moon', took nine months to record, and was premiered at the London Planetarium. It was a consistent seller in Britain, the U.S.A. and Europe, over three years in Britain and two and a half years in the U.S.A.

The contents of the album were: 'Speak to Me'; 'Breathe'; 'On the Run'; 'Time'; 'The Great Gig in the Sky'; 'Money'; 'Us and Them'; 'Any Colour You Like'; 'Brain Damage'; 'Eclipse'. All written by Pink Floyd.

Pink Floyd's gradual development towards the concept of 'concert' appearances required better quality and more elaborate equipment, and they became undisputed masters of quadraphonic sound. They use a vast assortment of special effects, around six-and-a-half tons of equipment, and were pioneers of stage presentation. Their tours of the U.S.A., Britain and France were fantastic successes.

'Dark Side of the Moon' sold an estimated two-and-a-half million, globally, at least 500,000 in both Britain and France, and million in the U.S.A. By 1981, global sales were 14 million.

Founder member Syd Barrett (real name Roger Keith Barrett) was born in Cambridge, England, on 6 January 1946.

ELVIS PRESLEY

ALOHA FROM HAWAII VIA SATELLITE (double album) *RCA* [*USA*]. Released in the U.S.A. and Britain in February 1973, this reached No 1 for two weeks in the U.S.A. and No 16 in Britain. It stayed 52 weeks in the U.S.A. charts and 5 weeks in the British bestsellers. R.I.A.A. Gold Disc award on 13 February 1973.

This was the first Elvis Presley album to be released simultaneously on a global basis. It had advance orders of over 500,000 even before release date and definite sale of one million immediately on release. Global sales are estimated at over two million. The album is the soundtrack of Elvis' one-hour concert from the Honolulu International Center Arena on 14 January 1973. The historic satellite-live television concert was beamed to viewers throughout the Far East, picking up some of the highest viewer ratings for any show, and the master tapes of the tele-recording were sent immediately to London. It was also screened in Europe, Africa, Latin America, Canada, and of course in America. The TV audience was estimated at one billion. Elvis was also the first artist in the industry to have a gold award for this, a four-channel (quadradisc) recording. The proceeds of the concert went towards the Kui Lee Cancer Fund. Kui Lee, Hawaii's best-known contemporary composer – a victim of cancer – had one of his songs 'I'll Remember You' included in the show.

The vocal backing on the show was provided by J.D. Sumner and The Stamps, Kathy Westmoreland and The Sweet Inspirations.

Contents of the album: 'See See Rider' (Ma Rainey, 1943); 'Burning Love' (Dennis Linde, 1972); (*)'Something' (George Harrison, 1969); (*)'You Gave Me a Mountain' (Marty Robbins, 1968); (*)'Steam Roller Blues' (James Taylor, 1970); (*) 'My Way' (Thibault, François and Revaux, 1967, English words by Paul Anka, 1969); 'Love Me' (Jerry Leiber and Mike Stoller, 1954); 'Johnny B. Goode' (Chuck Berry, 1958); (*)'It's Over' (Jimmie Rodgers, 1966); 'Blue Sude Shoes' (Carl Perkins, 1955); (*)'I'm So Lonesome I Could Cry' (Hank Williams, 1949); 'I Can't Stop Loving You' (Don Gibson, 1958); 'Hound Dog' (Jerry Leiber and Mike Stoller, 1956); (*)'What Now My Love?' (Delanoe and Becaud, English words by Carl Sigman, 1962); 'Fever' (John Davenport and Eddie Cooley, 1956); (*)'Welcome to My World' (Ray Winkler and John Hathcock, 1961); 'Suspicious Minds' (Fred Zambon, 1968); 'I'll Remember You' (Kui Lee); 'Long Tall Sally' (E. Johnson, R. Penniman and R.A.

Blackwell, 1956); 'Whole Lotta Shakin' Goin' On' (Dave Williams and Sunny David, 1957); 'American Trilogy' ('Marching Through Georgia', Henry Clay Work, 1865; 'John Brown's Body', words anon., music by Wm Steffe, 1861; 'All My Trials', traditional); 'Big Hunk of Love' (A. Schroeder and Sid Wyche, 1959); 'Can't Help Falling in Love' (G. Weiss, H. Peretti and L. Creatore, 1961). (* denotes songs never before recorded by Elvis Presley.)

BILLY PRESTON

WILL IT GO ROUND IN CIRCLES *A & M* [*USA*]. Written by Billy Preston and Bruce Fisher, this was released in the U.S.A. in February 1973, going to No 1 for two weeks, and staying 25 weeks in the charts. R.I.A.A. Gold Disc award on 26 June 1973.

The second gold record for Billy Preston during his two-year association with A & M Records. This million-seller was culled from his album 'Music Is My Life'.

SPACE RACE *A & M* [*USA*]. Written by Billy Preston and released in the U.S.A. in September 1973, this reached No 4 for two weeks, staying 18 weeks in the charts.

Another million seller for talented musician Billy Preston. This disc was released in the U.S.A. at the time Billy was appearing before 10,000 rock fans at the Empire Pool, Wembley, London.

Billy always carries a Bible with him, and finds inspiration for his songs in the Psalms. He has never forgotten it was in the church in 1962 that he was ironically launched on a showbiz career through his meeting at the Grace Memorial Church of God in Christ, Los Angeles, with disc star Little Richard. Preston donates 5% of his annual earnings to the Church.

SUZI QUATRO (rock vocalist)

CAN THE CAN *RAK* [*Britain*]. Written by Nicky Chinn and Mike Chapman, this was released in Britain in May 1973, hitting No 1 for three weeks and staying 14 weeks in the charts.

Suzi Quatro was born in Detroit, Michigan on 3 June 1950. She first played bongos at the Art Quatro band, run by her father, when she was seven. By the time she was 14, she formed Suzi Soul and The Pleasure Seekers with her three sisters, and toured for four years. She then had a band called Cradle for two years and played in Vietnam. In 1971, Mickie Most, the English producer of The Animals and Herman's Hermits fame, was in Detroit to record Jeff Beck, when he discovered Suzi at the East Town theatre. Realising her potential, he brought her to Britain (October 1971) and formed a band. Her first public performance was at Loughborough University in 1972. Writers Chapman and Chinn were brought in and wrote 'Can the Can' especially for her. It was No 1 in Britain, Spain, Switzerland, Australia, France, Germany and Japan, selling over two million globally. Chinn

and Chapman produced the disc. She also became successful in the U.S.A. and an instant superstar. She was described as a female Marc Bolan, with her gut-level rock'n'roll voice. Suzi also plays bass guitar, and is a pianist and drummer.

She is accompanied by Dave Neal (drums), Lennie Tuckey (lead guitar) and Alastair McKenzie (keyboards) on her engagements.

48 CRASH *RAK* [*Britain*]. Written by Nicky Chinn and Mike Chapman, and released in Britain in July 1973, this went to No 2 for two weeks, staying 10 weeks in the charts.

A successful follow-up disc for Suzi, with a reported million global sale.

HELEN REDDY

DELTA DAWN *Capitol* [*USA*]. Written by Alex Harvey and L. Collins, this was released in the U.S.A. in June 1973, going to No 1 for two weeks and staying 22 weeks in the charts. R.I.A.A. Gold Disc award on 30 August 1973.

Second million-seller single for Helen Reddy. It was also included in her album 'Long Hard Climb'.

LONG HARD CLIMB (album) *Capitol* [*USA*]. Released in the U.S.A. in July 1973, this rose to No 6 for two weeks, staying 43 weeks in the charts. R.I.A.A. Gold Disc award on 19 September 1973.

This album sold the million units, achieved platinum status by August 1974, and contained: 'Long Hard Climb' (Ron Davies); (*)'Leave Me Alone (Ruby Red Dress)' (Linda Laurie); (*)'Delta Dawn' (Alex Harvey and L. Collins); 'The Old Fashioned Way' (Garvarentz, Kasha and Hirschhorn); 'Until It's Time for You to Go' (Buffy Sainte-Marie); 'Lovin' You' (John Sebastien); 'Don't Mess with a Woman' (P. Moan, R. Curtis and M. Curtis); 'The West Wind Circus' (Adam Miller); 'A Bit O.K.' (C. Sager and P. Allen); 'If We Could Still Be Friends' (Paul Williams). (* denotes sold a million as a single release.)

LEAVE ME ALONE (RUBY RED DRESS) *Capitol* [*USA*]. Written by Linda Laurie and released in the U.S.A. in October 1973, this went to No 1 for one week, staying 16 weeks in the charts. R.I.A.A. Gold Disc award on 8 January 1974.

The third million-seller single for Helen, a cut from her hit album 'Long Hard Climb'.

CHARLIE RICH

BEHIND CLOSED DOORS *Epic* [*USA*]. Written by Kenny O'Dell and released in the U.S.A. in January 1973 and in Britain in April 1973, this went to No 13 for one week and to No 16 in Britain. It stayed 19 weeks in the U.S.A. charts and ten weeks in the British bestsellers. R.I.A.A. Gold Disc award on 4 September 1973. Grammy Awards: Best Country Vocal Performance (Male) 1973; Best Country Song (Composer's Award) 1973.

After Charlie Rich's big hit 'Lonely Weekends' in 1960, the country singer from Colt, Arkansas, had several years of comparative obscurity, during which time he played small clubs and had occasional hits such as 'Big Boss Man' and 'Mohair Sam'. He joined Epic Records in 1968 and soon became a successful country hitmaker, with country chart winners like 'Nice'n'easy'. Then in 1972, he had a really big success with 'I Take It On Home' and followed this with 'Behind Closed Doors' which turned out to be a monster hit. It was first a country hit, but after the cross-over to the national charts, soon sold well over a million. By the end of 1974 it had sold three million globally, and was the best Country Song of 1973.

BEHIND CLOSED DOORS (album) *Epic* [*USA*]. Released in the U.S.A. in May 1973, this went to No 5 for two weeks, staying 105 weeks in the charts. R.I.A.A. Gold Disc award on 27 November 1973.

Based on the title of his single hit, this album was a tremendous success for Charlie Rich, selling 3,500,000 by mid-June 1975, after two years in the bestsellers. It was also No 1 in the country charts for 14 weeks.

It contained: 'Behind Closed Doors'; 'I Take It On Home'; 'The Most Beautiful Girl'; 'A Sunday Kind of Woman'; ''Til I Can't Take It Anymore'; 'If You Wouldn't be My Lady'; 'I'm Not Going Hungry Anymore'; 'Peace on You'; 'Nothing in the World (to do with me)'; 'We Love Each Other'; 'You Never Really Wanted Me.' Grammy Award, Best Selling Album by a Male Country Artist, 1974.

THE MOST BEAUTIFUL GIRL *Epic* [*USA*]. Written by Norro Wilson, Billy Sherrill and Rory Bourke, this was released in the U.S.A. in September 1973 and in Britain in February 1974. It rose to No 1 for two weeks in the U.S.A. and No 2 for two weeks in Britain, staying 23 weeks in the U.S.A. charts and 14 weeks in the British bestsellers. R.I.A.A. Gold Disc award on 10 December 1973.

This cut from Charlie Rich's album 'Behind Closed Doors' provided the second single million seller, making it the most successful year ever for this popular artist. It was also the first disc by him to appear in the British charts.

SMOKEY ROBINSON
BABY COME CLOSE *Tamla* [*USA*]. Written by W. Robinson, P. Moffett and M. Tarplin, this was released in the U.S.A. in November 1973, rising to No 27 for one week, and staying 21 weeks in the charts.

This disc was reported to have sold 800,000 by February 1974 and went on to the million mark subsequently. Bill 'Smokey' Robinson, a founder of the famous group The Miracles, became a solo artist after leaving them in May 1972.

THE ROLLING STONES
ANGIE *Rolling Stones* [*Britain & USA*]. Written by Keith Richard and Mick Jagger, this ballad was released in the U.S.A. and Britain in August 1973. It went to No 1 for two weeks in the U.S.A. and No 2 for two weeks in Britain, staying 16 weeks in the U.S.A. charts and ten weeks in the British topsellers. R.I.A.A. Gold Disc award on 1 November 1973.

The prime cut from The Rolling Stones' album 'Goat's Head Soup', with over a million in U.S.A. sales. The album, also certified 'gold', was the fastest-selling album for the group in the U.S.A. and likewise reached No 1.

DIANA ROSS
TOUCH ME IN THE MORNING *Motown* [*USA*]. Written by Michael Masser and Ron Miller, this was released in the U.S.A. in May 1973 and in Britain in June 1973, going to No 1 for one week in U.S.A. and No 8 for one week in Britain. It stayed 22 weeks in the U.S.A. bestsellers and 12 weeks in the British charts.

Diana Ross's 'Touch Me in the Morning' album, and this million-selling single, followed her enormous success with the *Lady Sings the Blues* film and album.

SEALS & CROFTS
DIAMOND GIRL (album) *Warner* [*USA*]. Released in the U.S.A. in April 1973, this rose to No 4 for one week and stayed 77 weeks in the charts. R.I.A.A. Gold Disc award on 25 June 1973.

A brilliant album by this duo. It eventually achieved platinum status with the million units sale. The contents included a rock number, 'Standin' on a Mountain Top', they had written in 1964, and a contemplative ballad, 'We May Never Pass This Way (again)'. Dynamic material and strong musicianship throughout, and written entirely by Seals & Crofts.

PAUL SIMON
LOVES ME LIKE A ROCK *Columbia* [*USA*]. Written by Paul Simon and released in the U.S.A. in July 1973, this hit No 1 for one week, staying in the charts for 17 weeks. It was No 39 in Britain. R.I.A.A. Gold Disc award on 9 October 1973.

A fine solo performance by Paul (of the former Simon & Garfunkel partnership) released as a single from his album 'There Goes Rhymin' Simon', and his first solo million-seller since the duo parted in 1971.

SLADE (rock quartet)
MERRY XMAS EVERYBODY *Polydor* [*Britain*]. Written by Noddy Holder and Jim Lea, this raucous jubilation was released in Britain in December 1973, going to No 1 for four weeks and staying seven weeks in the charts.

Slade are Noddy Holder (guitar/vocals), born Walsall, 15 June 1950; Jim Lea (bass/piano/violin/vocals), born Wolverhampton, 14 June 1952; Dave Hill (guitar/vocals), born Fleetcastle, Devon, 4 April 1952; and Don Powell (drums), born Bilston, Staffordshire, 10 September 1950.

The group originated from the Midlands in Britain around 1969, and were first known as The 'N'Betweens, then Ambrose Slade. They were promoted as the first 'skinhead' group, an idea that was rejected by band bookers fearing audience reaction.

Slade made their first hit disc, Little Richard's number 'Get Down and Get With It', a popular number for them, evoking stomping and hand-clapping at their club appearances, and becoming their trademark. Thereafter, Holder and Lea wrote all the group's numbers in an aggressive pop style, with powerful vocals by Holder. Known as a 'working-class group', they stressed this by misspelling each song title: 'Coz I Luv You' (1971), 'Look Wot You Dun' (1972), 'Mama Weer All Crazee Now' (1972), 'Gudbuy T'Jane' (1972), 'Cum on Feel the Noize' (1973), 'Skweeze Me, Pleeze Me' (1973). Their continual success and rock performances made them one of Britain's important acts. Their albums 'Slade Alive' (1972) and 'Slayed' (1972) both reached No 1 and they had seven singles, including 'Merry Xmas Everybody', at No 1. This sold over 950,000 in Britain alone, and easily passed the million mark globally. They made a tour of Europe in 1973 and the U.S.A. in 1974.

SLY & THE FAMILY STONE
IF YOU WANT ME TO STAY *Epic* [*USA*]. Written by Sylvester Stewart, this was released in the U.S.A. in June 1973, going to No 12 for two weeks and staying 17 weeks in the charts. R.I.A.A. Gold Disc award on 12 September 1973.

JIM STAFFORD
SPIDERS AND SNAKES *MGM* [*USA*]. Written by David Bellamy and Jim Stafford, this was released in the U.S.A. in September 1973, going to No 3 for two weeks, and No 14 in Britain (with 8 weeks in the charts). It stayed 25 weeks in the U.S.A. charts. R.I.A.A. Gold Disc award on 6 March 1974.

Jim Stafford was born in Eloise, close to Winter Haven in Florida in 1944. He started playing rock'n'roll on guitar, and played at local dances. On leaving high school, he made his way to Nashville, and worked a little at the Opry and in local clubs. He wanted to be a performer rather than just a musician, and went to Atlanta, working there in clubs and eventually wended his way back to Florida. He then began writing for the first time. His first recording was 'Swamp Witch' which was produced by his friend Kent Lavoie, better known as Lobo. He signed with MGM after the session, and moved to Los Angeles to work there. Jim then came up with 'Spiders and Snakes', an offbeat, cute love tale. His record was a big hit and sold two million.

Jim's songs tend to deal with the supernatural at least in a figurative sense, and he has the ability to give a natural occurrence a decided twist, and turn a platitude into a new surprise by approaching it in a completely different form.

He evokes great enthusiasm with his performance on stage, integrating fast-paced comedy with country simplicity. A one-man band, he plays guitar, sings, and simulates a bass drum and bass line with two electronic foot pedals. He has been described as 'the O'Henry of lyrics and the Hitchcock of rock'.

THE STAPLE SINGERS

IF YOU'RE READY (Come go with me) *Stax* [*USA*]. Written by H. Banks, R. Jackson and C. Hampton, this was released in the U.S.A. in October 1973, going to No 8 for one week and staying 17 weeks in the charts. It was No 34 in Britain. R.I.A.A. Gold Disc award on 19 December 1973.

Another big success for this popular quartet, their fourth million seller.

RINGO STARR

RINGO (album) *Apple* [*Britain*] *Capitol* [*USA*]. Released in October 1973, this zoomed to No 1 for three weeks in the U.S.A. and No 6 in Britain. It stayed 37 weeks in the U.S.A. bestsellers and 18 weeks in the British charts. R.I.A.A. Gold Disc award on 8 November 1973.

Ringo Starr (former drummer of The Beatles) stopped recording in 1969. He then began a career in films, and made a fine convincing performance in *That'll Be The Day* (1973) with David Essex. On the break-up of The Beatles, Ringo, like the rest of that group, wanted to prove himself on record. His first album 'A Sentimental Journey' (1970) was compiled of old 1940s standards. His second 'Beaucoups of Blues' (1970) was made in Nashville with top sessioners. This third album, 'Ringo', produced by Richard Perry, featured songs by his three former colleagues plus guest appearances by artists including John Lennon, George Harrison, Billy Preston, Marc Bolan, Klaus Voorman, Jack Nitzche, Bobby Keyes, Nicky Hopkins, Harry Nilsson, Paul McCartney, Martha Reeves, Tom Scott, Steve Cropper, Linda McCartney, Jim Keltner, and Milt Holland.

Contents: 'I'm the Greatest' (John Lennon); 'Have You Seen My Baby?' (Randy Newman); (*)'Photograph' (John Lennon and George Harrison); 'Sunshine Life for Me' (George Harrison); (*)'You're 16' (Richard and Robert Sherman, 1960); 'Oh My My' (Vini Poncia and Ringo Starr); 'Step Lightly' (Ringo Starr); 'Six O'Clock' (Linda and Paul McCartney); 'Devil Woman' (Vini Poncia and Ringo Starr); 'You and Me (Babe)' (Mal Evans and George Harrison). (* denotes sold a million as single.)

The million units (platinum status) sale was reported in August 1974, with platinum disc awarded by Capitol Records. The album reached No 2 within two weeks in the U.S.A. then went on to No 1.

PHOTOGRAPH *Apple* [*USA & Britain*]. Written by Ringo Starr and George Harrison and released in the U.S.A. in September 1973 and in Britain in November 1973, this went to No 1 for one week in the U.S.A. and No 4 in Britain. It stayed 18 weeks in the U.S.A. bestsellers and 13 weeks in the British charts. R.I.A.A. Gold Disc award on 28 December 1973.

Single release from the album 'Ringo'. It sold over one-and-a-half million globally.

YOU'RE SIXTEEN *Apple* [*Britain & USA*]. Written by Richard and Robert Sherman (1960), this was released in the U.S.A. in December 1973 and in Britain in February 1974. It climbed to No 1 for one week in the U.S.A. and No 3 for one week in Britain, staying 16 weeks in the U.S. charts and ten weeks in the British bestsellers. R.I.A.A. Gold Disc award on 31 January 1974.

The second singles release from 'Ringo' album to sell over a million. It was originally a million-seller for Johnny Burnette in 1960.

STEALERS WHEEL

STUCK IN THE MIDDLE WITH YOU *A & M* [*USA & Britain*]. Written by Joe Egan and Gerry Rafferty, this was released in the U.S.A. in February 1973 and in Britain in May 1973. It reached No 3 for one week in the U.S.A. and No 6 for two weeks in Britain, staying 18 weeks in the U.S. bestsellers and nine weeks in the British charts.

Joe Egan and Gerry Rafferty went to the same school in Paisley, Scotland, but did not know each other until Egan, who played with a local band The Mavericks, met Rafferty when he joined as vocalist/guitarist. This was in 1964. They got themselves a contract with EMI and, in 1965 had a small local hit with 'Benjamin Day', written by Rafferty. After The Mavericks, Gerry went to London and joined The Humblebums. Joe stayed in Scotland studying languages at a local college, but the duo kept in touch. When The Humblebums split up, Gerry went on to make a superb album 'Can I Have My Money Back?' before meeting up with Joe again. They decided to form a band, and Stealers Wheel was chosen as the name. The band's tapes were distributed around and got into the hands of Jerry Leiber and Mike Stoller, writers of songs for Elvis Presley, The Coasters and The Drifters. They decided to produce the first Stealers Wheel album, the first British band they had ever worked with (1972). This rocketed up to No 29 in the U.S. charts, and the singles release from it, 'Stuck in the Middle With You', was a big hit with a reputed million plus global sale. An equal share of credit for the brilliant production goes to Leiber and Stoller along with the considerable talents of Egan and Rafferty.

The line-up behind Egan and Rafferty's vocals which are the crux of Stealers Wheel's sound was Luther Grosvenor (guitar/vocals), DeLisle Harper (bass), Rod Coombes (drums), and Paul Pilnick (guitar).

STORIES (vocal quintet)

BROTHER LOUIE *Kama Sutra* [*USA*]. Written by Errol Brown and Tony Wilson, this was released in the U.S.A. in June 1973, going to No 1 for two weeks, and staying 18 weeks in the charts. R.I.A.A. Gold Disc award on 22 August 1973.

A quick million-seller for this group, the personnel being Ian Lloyd (lead singer), Steve Love (lead guitar), Bryan Madey (drums), Kenny Aaronson (bass) and Kenny Bichel (keyboards).

BARBRA STREISAND

THE WAY WE WERE *Columbia* [*USA*]. Written by Marilyn and Alan Bergman and Marvin Hamlisch, this was released in the U.S.A. in November 1973, going to No 1 for two weeks and staying 22 weeks in the charts. It was No 31 in Britain. R.I.A.A. Gold Disc award on 6 February 1974. Grammy Award: Song of the Year (Songwriter's Award to Writers) 1974; Academy Award (The Oscar): Best Film Song of 1973.

Barbra Streisand, the Broadway star, was born 24 April 1942. She graduated at 16 from Erasmus High School in Brooklyn, near her birthplace, and attended acting classes while at school. She tried summer stock for a few weeks, then moved to Manhattan where she covered as many auditions as possible. She entered and won a Greenwich Village nightclub contest. She was soon singing in some of the best showcase clubs in New York. Producer David Merrick saw her act and signed her to play the star role in his production of *I Can Get It for You Wholesale* (1962). One of her numbers, 'Miss Marmelstein', stopped the show. The original cast recording of the show was followed by a recording of 'Pins and Needles' by the same composer, Harold Rome. Rome, who sings one of the leads on the latter album, chose Barbra as his co-star. Her successful recordings of these two show albums won Barbra a contract with CBS, who produced her first nationally released single 'My Colouring Book' coupled with 'Lover Come Back to Me'. Barbra's exclusive services with CBS for ten years included a special a year at the end of two seasons, and a series by mutual agreement. Her earnings for her first two seasons with the network were $1 million. With the release of her first album 'The Barbra Streisand Album' (1963) her national fame spread fast. The album received the NARAS award for best album of the year, and Barbra was named best female vocalist. Then came the leading role in the Broadway musical *Funny Girl* (1964), and with the release of the score's most powerful ballad 'People' following after three 'gold' Columbia albums, the hit firmly established Streisand as a recording artist and performer.

Although Barbra continued to record certified gold album after album in the following years, her singles were not really big

hits, with the exception of 'People' but two titles, 'Second Hand Rose' and 'He Touched Me', sold well and had many airings. Barbra played the star role in the film version of *Funny Girl* (1968) and in 1969 starred in the film version of the Broadway musical *Hello Dolly. Funny Lady* was another starring role in 1975. It was however, the film of *The Way We Were* in 1973 which produced her first certified gold single in the title song, with a million plus sale, and the Academy Award with an Oscar.

By the end of 1975, Barbra was credited with 16 certified R.I.A.A. gold albums, and her earnings ran into millions of dollars.

THE STYLISTICS

BREAK UP TO MAKE UP *Avco* [*USA*]. Written by Thom Bell, Linda Creed and Kenny Gamble, this was released in the U.S.A. in February 1973, and went to No 5 for one week, staying 14 weeks in the charts. It was No 34 in Britain. R.I.A.A. Gold Disc award on 6 April 1973.

Yet another million-seller for The Stylistics, and a continuation of the success story of the group and the producer/writers.

SWEET

BLOCKBUSTER *RCA* [*Britain*]. Written by Nicky Chinn and Mike Chapman, this was released in Britain in January 1973. It went to No 1 for five weeks, staying 15 weeks in the charts.

Sale of this disc in Britain was well over 250,000, and the global total over a million. The song showed that writers Chinn and Chapman were more than just 'bubble-gum' scribes. 'Blockbuster' brought hysteria back to pop audiences and indicated Sweet's transition from bubble-gum to rock music.

HELL RAISER *RCA* [*Britain*]. Written by Nicky Chinn and Mike Chapman and released in Britain in April 1973, this rose to No 2 for four weeks, staying 11 weeks in the charts.

A powerful hit by Sweet, proving their change of image and style. Advance orders were in excess of 100,000 and sale in Britain over 250,000. Another global million-seller for group and writers.

THE BALLROOM BLITZ *RCA* [*Britain*]. Written by Nicky Chinn and Mike Chapman and released in Britain in September 1973 and in the U.S.A. in June 1975, this went to No 1 for one week in Britain and No 5 for one week in the U.S.A. It stayed nine weeks in the British charts and 26 weeks in the U.S. bestsellers.

This disc was quite a success in Britain and also in the U.S.A. when released there in 1975. It is a hard rocker, following the trend of the group's other two hits in this year, and sold a global million. Chinn and Chapman became one of the most successful songwriting teams in pop music. This made million-seller number eight for Sweet.

SYLVIA

PILLOW TALK *Vibration* [*USA*]. Written by Sylvia Robinson and M. Burton, this was released in the U.S.A. in March 1973 and in Britain in June 1973. It went to No 2 for one week in the U.S.A. and No 10 for one week in Britain. It stayed 21 weeks in the U.S. charts and 11 weeks in the British topsellers. R.I.A.A. Gold Disc award on 21 May 1973.

Sylvia Robinson (of Mickey & Sylvia - see 1956) started her own labels Vibration and All Platinum in 1969 after the duo broke up and Mickey went to France, while Sylvia stayed in New Jersey. Here at Englewood, she was vice-president, writer, producer and engineer. Her recording set-up included a staff of studio musicians. Her first success was as writer and producer of several hits for The Moments, including their million-seller 'Love on a Two-Way Street'.

'Pillow Talk' was actually written in 1971 as a possible vehicle for Hi Records' star Al Green. Sylvia made the demo tape with full orchestration, and put in her own voice, including all the sexy breathing that caused so much interest in the song, for demonstration purposes. Green and Willie Mitchell in Memphis felt that the song was too sexy for Al and turned it down. Sylvia then tried the same instrumental tracks with several other All Platinum artists, but none could sing the song the way she wanted, so she decided to do it herself. It was Frankie Crocker, a disc jockey of WBLS-FM in New York who was the first to break the record. He put the song on the air and the phones went wild. Sylvia and her national manager of All Platinum records also credit Cecil Hale and E. Rodney Jones of WVON in Chicago for initiating national interest in the song.

'Pillow Talk' catapulted Sylvia back into the spotlight. The disc was a great success with over two million sale.

JOHNNY TAYLOR

I BELIEVE IN YOU (You believe in me) *Stax* [*USA*]. Written by Don Davis and released in the U.S.A. in June 1973, this went to No 5 for two weeks, staying 17 weeks in the charts. R.I.A.A. Gold Disc award on 23 October 1973.

Johnny Taylor's second million-seller single. His first was in 1968, but in the intervening period, he made several successful albums for Stax Records.

THREE DOG NIGHT

SHAMBALA *ABC/Dunhill* [*USA*]. Written by Daniel Moore and released in the U.S.A. in May 1973, this hit No 1 for one week, staying 22 weeks in the charts. R.I.A.A. Gold Disc award on 24 July 1973.

Composer Daniel Moore, a writer/artist with ABC/Dunhill from 1970 to 1972, had two recordings of this song on the U.S.A. market, due to a contretemps. RCA also had a tape sent to them which they retained and put out a disc by B. W. Stevenson. Both this and the Three Dog Night disc were successful, but it was the latter version that proved the biggest seller through the immense popularity of the group. It soon racked up a million sale.

IKE & TINA TURNER

NUTBUSH CITY LIMITS *United Artists* [*USA*]. Written by DuPree and Beldone, released in the U.S.A. in August 1973 and in Britain in September 1973, this rock number went to No 22 for one week in the U.S.A., but was properly appreciated in Britain where it reached No 2 for two weeks. It stayed 16 weeks in the U.S.A. bestsellers and 13 weeks in the British charts.

This disc had a big sale in Europe, and was given the Golden European Record Award, the first ever given for American artists who scored heavily in that area. It clocked up a combined million-plus sale, and was their third in this category.

WAR

THE CISCO KID *United Artists* [*USA*]. Written by War, this was released in the U.S.A. in March 1973, going to No 1 for one week, staying 15 weeks in the charts. R.I.A.A. Gold Disc award on 2 March 1973.

An immediate Gold Disc for this, a cut from their No 1 album 'The World Is a Ghetto' (1972). It was described as 'a Latino oriental musical experience' – a catchy rhythm item.

DELIVER THE WORLD (album) *United Artists* [*USA*]. Released in the U.S.A. in August 1973, this rose to No 6 for three weeks, staying 36 weeks in the charts. R.I.A.A. Gold Disc award on 11 September 1973.

The songs for this million-selling album were written by War.

ERIC WEISSBERG & STEVE MANDEL

DUELLING BANJOS *Warner* [*USA*]. Composed by Arthur Smith (1955) and released in the U.S.A. in January 1973 and in Britain in March 1973, this rose to No 1 for two weeks in the U.S.A. and No 17 for one week in Britain, staying 15 weeks in the U.S. bestsellers and seven weeks in the British charts. R.I.A.A. Gold Disc award on 7 March 1973. Grammy Award: Best Country Instrumental, 1973.

Used in the film *Deliverance*, where a banjo playing mountain kid (played by Hoyt J. Pollard) and a guitarist from the city (Ronnie Cox) meet. They gradually sound out each other's capabilities and then break out into a heated version of the old tune 'Duelling Banjos'. The music was recorded by Weissberg and Mandel, two well-known session men of New York. John Boorman, the film's director, decided to include it after James Dickey, author of *Deliverance*, heard it on the radio and thought it would be perfect for the film. Weissberg and Mandel then spent a few days on location in Georgia during the filming, teaching the actors how to mime the tune. The success of the disc with its million plus sale was phenomenal for Weissberg and Mandel. Weissberg was signed to a long-term contract by Warner's. The soundtrack is simply the one tune 'Duelling Banjos'.

There was a great deal of controversy over the tune. It was thought to be traditional, but composer/guitarist Arthur Smith (see 1945) said 'somebody heard the tune on and off since he wrote it in 1955 and figured it was non-copyright, and just put his name on an arrangement of it for the movie.' Smith's original title was 'Feuding Banjos'. It had been a success on MGM label in 1955. Weissberg, a veteran of recording, made an album 'Folk Blues' with banjoist Marshall Brickman in 1962 when they were in a group called The Tarriers, and he has known Mandel for around 15 years. Both worked on Judy Collins and John Denver albums. 'Duelling Banjos' was also recorded on an album 'Back Porch Bluegrass' (Elk label) in the mid-1960s by The Dillards. The tune sparked a resurgence of the country 'blue grass' sound, and Weissberg formed a group, naming them Deliverance, which included himself, Mandel, Charlie Brown (electric guitar), Tony Brown (bass) and Richard Crooks (drums). The group then made sell-out performances at Folk City and the Philharmonic Hall, both New York City, and elsewhere. Weissberg plays a total of ten instruments: bass (upright and Fender), guitar, fiddle, banjo, kazoo, mandolin, pedal steel, dobro and jews harp.

FRED WESLEY & THE JBs

DOIN' IT TO DEATH *People/Polydor* [*USA*]. Written by James Brown, this was released in the U.S.A. in May 1973, going to No 21 for one week, staying 11 weeks in the charts. R.I.A.A. Gold Disc award on 23 July 1973.

This million-seller single on James Brown's Polydor-distributed People label was also produced by him. Fred Wesley is the leader of the band that backs James Brown. The disc is a two-part extemporised call-and-answer session with the backing jazz musicians (The JBs). It repeats the patented 'party record' format so successful for The JBs over the years, but is dominated by the sound of Brown. Wesley has a fine trombone solo, and Maceo Parker a sax and flute solo.

BARRY WHITE

I'M GONNA LOVE YOU JUST A LITTLE MORE, BABY *20th Century* [*USA*]. Written by Barry White, this was released in the U.S.A. in March 1973 and in Britain in June 1973. It rose to No 3 for one week in the U.S.A. and No 17 in Britain. It stayed 18 weeks in the U.S. charts and five weeks in the British lists. R.I.A.A. Gold Disc award on 6 June 1973.

Barry White was born on 12 September 1944 in Galveston, Texas, his family moving to Los Angeles' East Side when he was six months old. His mother belonged to the church. Barry was a natural singer, and at age eight was singing with the church choir. He was playing the organ when he was ten and directed choirs. At 16, Barry joined a local rhythm-and-blues quintet, The Upfronts, spending two years with them singing and playing piano. His first entry into the charts came in 1963, when he wrote the music for the rhythm-and-blues hit 'The Harlem Shuffle' for a duo called Bob & Earl. Earl (Cosby) changed his name to Jackie Lee and Barry wrote the hit 'The Duck' for him (1965). As manager for Earl/Jackie he learned new facets of the industry. By 1967, Barry had become a producer of international scope. As part of his A & R directorship of Bronco Records, he was responsible for three hits with Felice Taylor and Viola Wills. Bronco Records folded, but Barry kept writing and a hit 'Under the Influence of Love' established three ladies: Linda & Glodean James and Diane Taylor, later known as Love Unlimited (see 1972). Four years after (1972) Barry's career as well as Love Unlimited's changed with the trio's powerful single 'Walkin' in the Rain With the One I Love'. The disc also laid very specific groundwork for White's development as a solo artist. His link-up with Russ Regan at 20th Century resulted in four gold singles and seven gold albums by the end of 1975. 'I'm Gonna Love You Just a Little More, Baby' soon passed the million sale.

Barry White is one of the record industry's most successful creator/businessmen. It was 1970 when his conceptions of the industry and his own role in it really began to take shape. He realised that many changes were going on when large numbers of employees were fired from the big disc companies, putting an end to the independent producers that caused the spending of too much money. Barry decided he was going to be *the* man on the west coast of the U.S.A., and spent 18 months talking to people and analysing what people were writing about – racial problems, the war, the ghetto, etc. He decided to write about whatever was fair between a man and a woman. His direct emotion, married to his sophisticated musical instinct, became the hallmark of the Barry White sound. He also set a new pace for the music industry and introduced one of the largest on-stage musical ensembles, the 41-piece strong Love Unlimited Orchestra.

Barry's early experiences of poverty and the terrible vices of Los Angeles inspired him, as a teenager, to change his life. He won many awards from boards of education for keeping problems down in school, and subsequently, the 'black maestro' spent much time and money to raise funds for various Los Angeles youth movements and underprivileged youth organisations.

NEVER, NEVER GONNA GIVE YA UP *20th Century* [*USA*]. Written by Barry White and released in the U.S.A. in October 1973 and in Britain in January 1974, this went to No 7 for one week in the U.S.A. and No 11 for one week in Britain. It stayed 18 weeks in the U.S. charts and 11 weeks in the British bestsellers. R.I.A.A. Gold Disc award on 7 February 1974.

Second million-seller single for Barry White, with a raw, sensuous vocal with much drive and power, plus a fine musical backing.

THE WHO

QUADROPHENIA (Double album) *Track* [*Britain*] *MCA* [*USA*]. Released in Britain and in the U.S.A. in October 1973, this went to No 2 for three weeks in Britain and in the U.S.A. for two weeks. It stayed 40 weeks in the U.S. charts and 12 weeks in the British lists. R.I.A.A. Gold Disc award on 29 October 1973.

'Quadrophenia', unlike The Who's famous *Tommy*, is the story of a lone Londoner of the 1960s, and tells of 'Jimmy's' aggression, sorrows and frustration, and his search for identity and fulfilment. The moods are brilliantly captured. Daltrey's vocals are superb, while Keith Moon and John Entwistle's rhythm section work and other specialities are *par excellence*, plus of course Pete Townshend's outstanding guitar. The album took a year to make, and is considered a masterpiece.

Contents: 'I Am the Sea'; 'The Real Me'; 'Quadrophenia'; 'Cut My Hair'; 'The Punk and the Godfather'; 'I'm One'; 'The Dirty Jobs'; 'Helpless Dancer'; 'Is It In My Head?'; 'I've Had Enough'; '5.15'; 'Sea and Sand'; 'Drowned'; 'Bell Boy'; 'Dr Jimmy'; 'The Rock'; 'Love Reign O'er Me'.

All songs by Pete Townshend.

The million units sale was reported by the end of 1973.

AL WILSON

SHOW AND TELL *Rocky Road* [*USA*]. Written by Jerry Fuller, this was released in the U.S.A. in October 1973, going to No 1 for one week and staying 22 weeks in the charts. R.I.A.A. Gold Disc award on 17 December 1973.

Al Wilson began his singing career in the U.S. Navy, where he was part of an enlisted man's combination. On discharge, he joined The Jewels. In 1960, he joined a new group The Rollers who had a substantial hit with 'Continental Walk'. He met Marc Gordon in 1966 who became his manager and introduced Al as a solo recording act to Johnny Rivers' Soul City label, on which he had a pop/soul hit 'The Snake' in 1968. A further hit was 'Lodi' in 1969. Al then moved to Carousel Records which eventually became Rocky Road. 'Show and Tell', written and produced by Jerry Fuller, first worked its way up the soul charts and then into the national charts. During his leaner times, Al took odd jobs including dishwasher and mechanic, and appeared at small clubs in order to perfect his talents. 'Show and Tell' was the big breakthrough, this million-seller making him a full-time professional singer.

THE EDGAR WINTER GROUP

FRANKENSTEIN *Epic* [*USA*]. Written by Edgar Winter and released in the U.S.A. in February 1973, this went to No 1 for two weeks in the U.S.A. and No 18 for one week in Britain. It stayed 20 weeks in the U.S. charts and nine weeks in the British lists. R.I.A.A. Gold Disc award on 19 June 1973.

This instrumental number, a singles release from the group's hit album 'They Only Come Out at Night' (1972) was indeed a 'monster', selling over two million in the first three months. 'Frankenstein' wasn't even intended to be recorded. It was merely a live work the group performed to showcase Edgar's new-found interest in the synthesizer. They called it 'Frankenstein' because of all the cutting. They had created something from a lot of different parts and instilled life into it.

WIZZARD (rock octet)

SEE MY BABY JIVE *Harvest* [*Britain*]. Written by Roy Wood and released in Britain in April 1973, this raced to No 1 for four weeks, staying 17 weeks in the charts.

Wizzard was formed in 1972, after Roy Wood left The Electric Light Orchestra, following his association with The Move, a group he had formed with Jeff Lynne. Wizzard consisted of Roy Wood (vocals, guitar, sax, cello, bassoon, tuba, clarinet, recorder, sitars, banjo, harmonica, string bass, drums); Rick Price (bass guitar, recorder, harmonica); Bill Hunt (piano, French horn, harpsichord, tuba); Mike Bernie (tenor sax); Nick Pentelow (tenor sax, flute, clarinet, piano); Charlie Grima (drums, bongos, percussion); Keith Smart (drums); and Hugh McDowell (electric cello, cello, piano).

The band stormed the U.K. single charts with its infectious rock'n'roll original works. This disc sold over 500,000 in Britain and amassed a million global sale.

STEVIE WONDER

YOU ARE THE SUNSHINE OF MY LIFE *Tamla* [*USA*]. Written by Stevie Wonder, this was released in the U.S.A. in March 1973 and in Britain in May 1973, shooting to No 1 for one week in the U.S.A. and No 5 for one week in Britain. It remained 17 weeks in the U.S. bestsellers and 11 weeks in the British charts.

This single release from Stevie's 1972 album success 'Talking Book' soon sold a million, and has since become a world standard. Stevie received the Grammy Award for this, the Best Male Pop Vocal of 1973, making five Grammy awards in all for 1973 for the 23-year-old artist.

INNER VISIONS (album) *Tamla* [*USA*]. Released in the U.S.A. in August 1973 and in Britain in October 1973, this went to No 1 for one week in the U.S.A. and No 8 for one week in Britain, staying 73 weeks in the U.S. bestsellers and 30 weeks in the British lists. Grammy Awards: Album of the Year (1973): Best Engineered Non-Classical Recording (1973).

A million-plus sale in the U.S.A. for this album and an estimated total sale of over two million. The album displays the different facets of Stevie's talents and personality.

Contents: 'Too High'; 'Visions'; 'Living for the City'; 'Golden Lady'; 'Higher Ground'; 'Jesus Children of America'; 'Don't You Worry 'Bout a Thing'; 'He's a Missta Know It All'.

All songs by Stevie Wonder.

ZZ TOP

TRES HOMBRES (album) *London* [*USA*]. Released in the U.S.A. in July 1973, this went to No 8 for one week, staying 71 weeks in the charts. R.I.A.A. Gold Disc award on 23 May 1974.

A super-tough rock trio, ZZ Top consists of Billy Gibbons (guitar/vocals), Dusty Hill (bass/vocals), and Frank Beard (drums/percussion). They became known as 'that little ol' band from Texas', formed in 1970, the culmination of the trio's years in the centre of the Texas blues/rock/psychedelic scene. Each had formerly played in either Houston or Dallas bands. The band was guided by manager/producer Bill Ham, and they cut their first album which was released in January 1971. This established them as a hard-driving, blues rock combination, and, with Ham's careful direction, they began making the public take notice. In bars, clubs in Texas and concerts, ZZ Top started paying their dues, and soon gained a firm place on the concert circuit generally. 'Rio Grande Mud' was their second album (March 1972). By the time this album 'Tres Hombres' was released, they were top of the bill, and thereafter set staggering attendance records. By 1975, they were hailed as a rock'n'roll phenomenon, and a Texas legend.

'Tres Hombres' achieved platinum (million units sale) status by December 1975, after 18 months on the bestseller charts.

ZZ Top write their own material.

1974

ORIGINAL FILM SOUNDTRACK

THE STING (Album). Released in the U.S.A. in January 1974, this went to No 1 for five weeks, staying in the charts 43 weeks. R.I.A.A. Gold Disc award on 19 April 1974. Grammy Award: Best Movie Soundtrack, 1974.

An outstanding film, the story of two confidence tricksters in Chicago of the 1930s, portrayed by Paul Newman and Robert Redford, out to fleece a bigtime racketeer played by Robert Shaw.

Adapter/conductor Marvin Hamlisch employed piano rags of the long forgotten composer Scott Joplin, known as 'King of the Ragtimers'. Hamlisch blended several of Joplin's tunes with some of his own original compositions so beautifully, that the music proved as big a success as the film, an unprecedented boom for Joplin's works and the ragtime idiom. The film was first reviewed at the Directors Guild of America, Los Angeles on 27 November 1973. The soundtrack album sold 1,825,000 units by the end of April 1974 and went on to double platinum status with over two million subsequently. The Scott Joplin tune from it, 'The Entertainer', that was originally written in 1902, was a smash hit when released as a single.

A great deal of credit for the musical success of *The Sting* must also be given to the film's director, George Roy Hill. A trained musician himself, he was introduced to the 'rags' of Scott Joplin through a new recording of the composer's work brought home by his son. Though Joplin's music preceded the period of the film, Hill decided it would fit perfectly, and built montages and sequences into the film where the rags could be featured. He abandoned the idea of scoring the music himself and brought in pianist Marvin Hamlisch whom he had known on Broadway and who had already scored several films, including the successful *The Way We Were*. Marvin liked the idea of using ragtime because Hill's Joplin favourites were also his, and the selection of material was easy. (See Marvin Hamlisch data, 1974.)

The album included: 'The Entertainer' (1902); 'Solace' (1909); 'Pineapple Rag'; 'Gladiolus Rag'; 'Rag Time Dance'; 'Easy Winners'; 'Hooker's Hooker' (Marvin Hamlisch); 'Luther' (Marvin Hamlisch); 'The Glove' (Marvin Hamlisch).

All tunes by Scott Joplin unless otherwise indicated. The album features Marvin Hamlisch at the piano.

The Sting won seven Academy Awards (Oscars) for: Best Picture; Best Director; Best Story and Screenplay; Best Art Direction; Best Film Editing; Best Original Song Score and Adaptation or Best Scoring; Best Costume Design, 1973.

ABBA (vocal quartet)

WATERLOO *Polar* [*Sweden*] *CBS* [*Britain*]. Written by Stig Anderson and Benny Andersson and Bjorn Ulvaeus, this was released in Sweden in 1974, and in Britain (English version) in April 1974, and in U.S.A. in May 1974. It went to No 1 in Sweden, No 1 in Britain for three weeks, and No 6 for one week in the U.S.A., staying nine weeks in the British charts and 17 weeks in the U.S. lists.

ABBA consists of two female singers – Agnetha Faltskog (born 5 April 1950 in Jonkoping, Sweden) and Anni-Frid Lyngstad

(born 15 November 1945 in Narvik, Norway) – and two male singers – Benny Andersson (born 16 December 1946 in Stockholm, Sweden) and Bjorn Ulvaeus (born 25 April 1945 in Gothenburg, Sweden).

The ABBA story begins in 1966, when Bjorn, a member of The Hootenanny Singers, met Benny, organist and writer for The Hep Stars, at a party in Vastervik. They decided to write songs together. Nothing much came of their first efforts although they were recorded. Bjorn was later invited to join The Hep Stars for a tour, and the duo began to collaborate more after The Hep Stars split up in 1969. Bjorn met Agnetha at about the same time as Benny met Anni and, by the autumn of 1970, they were billed as The Festfolk Quartet in a specially arranged floor show. The show had its premier at Tragarn in Gothenburg on 1 November 1970 – ABBA's first stage performance.

Bjorn and Benny then began to acquire a big reputation as trailblazers of the pop industry in Sweden, and wrote many songs for prominent Swedish artists and themes for two films. One of these, *Language of Love*, became their first international success (February 1971). Agnetha and Bjorn were married on 7 July 1971. On this very day, Bengt Bernhag, a co-founder and joint owner with Stig Anderson of the Polar Recording Co., died. Bjorn was invited to take Bengt's place as producer at Polar, but Bjorn wanted Benny with him which was agreed. They took up their permanent appointment at Polar in the autumn of 1971. The 'real' ABBA came in 1972 with Bjorn and Benny's recording of 'She's My Kind of Girl', with Agnetha and Anni singing in the background. The label only mentioned Bjorn and Benny. This was heard by a Japanese publisher visiting Paris, who asked for publishing rights. The disc was their first really big hit in Japan, selling 500,000. The duo were invited to the Tokyo Song Festival in November 1972, and put on a song 'Santa Rosa', helped out by the two girls. 'People Need Love' was their next hit. Thereafter, the label said 'Bjorn, Benny, Agnetha and Anni-Frid'. By taking the initials of the quartet's Christian names, they became a permanent group called ABBA, in 1974.

In 1973, 'Ring Ring' was written for the Swedish Song Contest, and as a probable contender for the Eurovision Contest. Although it did not win in Sweden, the disc was a firm international success, and was No 1 in several European countries and South Africa. ABBA's big breakthrough to subsequent world acclaim came in 1974 with the song 'Waterloo', a story of lovers meeting their defeat in the combat against passion. This was sung by them in the Eurovision Song Contest on 6 April at The Dome, Brighton, England, and voted the winner. From then on, they had a string of hits, amassing sales of 30 million singles and 12 million albums (i.e. over 100 singles equivalent) by 1976. They achieved international fame with their soft-rock style, reaching the top of the U.S. charts in 1977 with 'Dancing Queen'.

ABBA made a formidable impact on the world's pop market, a remarkable feat as they are essentially a non-touring group. Benny Andersson, Bjorn Ulvaeus and Stig Anderson (of Polar Records) write all the group's songs.

Anni-Frid first appeared on the stage at the age of ten. She eventually had an orchestra of her own and then had big success on TV programmes, and on disc as a solo singer before teaming with ABBA. Agnetha started singing with a dance band in 1965 and was a successful recording artist before she met Bjorn.

'Waterloo' sold 5,000,000 around the world. It was No 1 also in Sweden, Norway, Denmark, Holland and Belgium.

WATERLOO (album) *Polar* [*Sweden*] *CBS* [*Britain*]. Following their staggering success with the single of the same title, this album sold 400,000 in Sweden and amassed three million in European sales.

It contained: 'Waterloo'; 'Sitting in the Palm Tree'; 'King Kong Song'; 'Hasta Mañana'; 'My Mama Said'; 'Dance (While the Music Still Goes On)'; 'Honey, Honey'; 'Watch Out'; 'What About Livingstone?'; 'Gonna Sing You My Love Song'; 'Suzy-Hang-Around'; 'Ring Ring'.

All songs written by Bjorn Ulvaeus, Benny Andersson and Stig Anderson.

HONEY, HONEY *Polar* [*Sweden*]. Written by Benny Andersson, Stig Anderson and Bjorn Ulvaeus, this was released in Scandinavia (excluding Sweden).

From their 'Waterloo' album, this single sold a million in Europe.

SO LONG *Polar* [*Sweden*]. Written by Benny Andersson and Bjorn Ulvaeus, this was released in Sweden in November 1974.

ABBA's third million-seller single, the sale achieved in Europe.

AEROSMITH
GET YOUR WINGS (album) *Columbia* [*USA*]. Released in the U.S.A. in March 1974, this stayed 80 weeks in the U.S. charts. R.I.A.A. Gold Disc award on 18 April 1975.

This second million-seller album for Aerosmith was a consistent seller in the U.S. charts, although never reaching an upper position there. It gradually achieved popularity with the public when the group became nationally known around 1975. The million sale was reported in 1976.

The album included: 'Same Old Song and Dance'; 'Woman of the World'; 'S.O.S. (Too Bad)'; 'Seasons of Wither' and 'Train Kept a Rollin''.

All material written by Aerosmith.

PAUL ANKA
YOU'RE HAVING MY BABY *United Artists* [*USA*]. Written by Paul Anka, this tune was released in the U.S.A. in July 1974 and in Britain in October 1974. It went to No 1 for one week in the U.S.A. and No 4 for one week in Britain, staying 17 weeks in

the U.S. charts and seven weeks in the British charts. R.I.A.A. Gold Disc award on 14 August 1974.

Paul Anka's first product of his return to the studio since the mid-1960s. The disc crawled on to the charts and then grew up to become a million seller, his first since 1964. Throughout the intervening years, he became an unknown entity to the audience that initially made him a star - Top 40-oriented youth - but he maintained a strong international following as a club and concert personality. This disc is possibly Paul's best song since he wrote the lyrics for the great standard 'My Way'.

EDDIE ARNOLD (country-and-western vocalist)
THE GREATEST OF EDDIE ARNOLD (album) *Tele House* [*USA*]. This compilation of Eddie Arnold's hits became a top-selling album through direct sales television promotion. It sold well over 1,500,000 for a gross of over $8 million. All the songs by Eddie were originally cut for RCA Records, but Tele House licensed them for promotion via the TV medium. It sparked off renewed interest in Eddie's catalogue items at RCA where his sales had dropped off considerably in the preceding years.

AVERAGE WHITE BAND
PICK UP THE PIECES *Atlantic* [*USA*]. Written by Roger Ball and Hamish Stuart, this was released in the U.S.A. in December 1974 and in Britain in February 1975. It went to No 6 for one week in Britain and No 1 for one week in the U.S.A., remaining 21 weeks in the U.S. charts and nine weeks in the British lists. R.I.A.A. Gold Disc award on 6 March 1975.

Average White Band was formed in Scotland in early 1972 and consists of six Glaswegians: Allen Gorrie (bass/vocals); Hamish Stuart (lead guitar/vocals); Onnie McIntyre (vocals/rhythm guitar); Steve Ferrone (drums); Roger Ball (keyboards/tenor sax); Malcolm 'Molly' Duncan (tenor sax). Their music is the nearest a British band have come to authentic soul or black music. 'Pick Up the Pieces' gained the adulation of black youngsters and disc jockeys, and helped the band to achieve the distinction of topping the U.S. album and singles charts simultaneously. It also made them wealthy. They left Glasgow to become tax exiles in Los Angeles. The original drummer Robbie Macintosh died after a lethal dose of drugs was slipped into his drink at a Hollywood party in September 1974.

This disc features Roger Ball's saxophone work and the dual guitar efforts of McIntyre and Stuart, and sold well over the million. They made a number of successful albums and became a big attraction to U.S. audiences, playing rhythm-and-blues better than many so-called rhythm-and-blues acts. They are undeniably good exponents of black music. Bassist Alan Gorrie had backed many top U.S. soul acts before the band was formed.

AVERAGE WHITE BAND (Album) *Atlantic* [*USA*]. Material by Roger Ball and Hamish Stuart, released in the U.S.A. in October 1974, reaching No 2 for a week, and staying in the charts for 36 weeks. R.I.A.A. Gold Disc Award on 14 January 1975.

The group's first album for Atlantic Records. It stayed 15 weeks in the U.S. Top 20, and subsequently sold a million. The prime cut 'Pick Up the Pieces' sold a million as a single.

Contents of the album are: 'Got the Love'; 'I Just Can't Give You Up'; 'Just Want to Love You'; 'Keepin' It All to Myself'; 'Nothing You Can Do'; 'Person to Person'; 'Pick Up the Pieces'; 'There's Always Someone'; 'Work to Do'; 'You Got It'.

CHARLES AZNAVOUR

SHE *Barclay/RCA* [*Britain*]. Written by Herbert Kretzmer and Charles Aznavour, this was released in Britain in May 1974, going to No 1 for four weeks, and staying 14 weeks in the charts.

'She' was specially commissioned for the TV series 'The Seven Faces of Woman' in Britain, and was recorded in London with British musicians, arranged and co-produced by Del Newman. Aznavour collaborated with English journalist Herbert Kretzmer to write the song, a romantic number. The disc was a big hit in Britain, selling over 500,000. The million (global) sale was reported in July 1975.

BACHMAN-TURNER OVERDRIVE (rock quartet)

BACHMAN-TURNER OVERDRIVE II *Mercury* [*USA*]. Released in the U.S.A. in January 1974, this rose to No 4 for two weeks, staying 67 weeks in the charts. R.I.A.A. Gold Disc award on 9 May 1974. Grammy Awards: Best Selling Album 1974; Best Selling Album by a Group, 1974.

Randy Bachman (born 27 September 1943) was first with an early Canadian group, Chad Allen and the Expressions, who later became The Guess Who. Randy left The Guess Who in 1970 and formed Brave Belt with Chad Allen (vocals) and Robbie Bachman (drums). They made one album for Warner Brothers, then Allen was replaced by Fred Turner, and their second album, again unsuccessful, was recorded. The band then changed its name to Bachman-Turner Overdrive, 'Overdrive' taken from the name of a publication read by truck drivers all over the U.S.A. An additional guitarist Timmy Bachman was added and BTO made the album 'Bachman-Turner Overdrive' for the Mercury label (May 1973). 'Bachman-Turner Overdrive II' was a big hit, and sold over a million (albums plus tapes) by August 1974. It included a singles hit 'Takin' Care of Business'. BTO describe themselves as a 'heavy duty rock' band. Timmy Bachman left after this recording, and the band personnel became Randy Bachman (vocals/guitar); Fred Turner (bass/vocals); Robbie Bachman (drums) and Blair Thornton (guitar).

The album included: 'Takin' Care of Business'; 'Let It Ride';

'Tramp'; 'Give It Time'; 'Welcome Home'; 'Blown'; 'Stonegates'; 'I Don't Have to Hide'.

Most material by Randy Bachman and Fred Turner.

Bruce Allen, manager of BTO, is particularly responsible for the success of the band. His shrewd policy of getting them to perform in areas frequently ignored by most touring bands, paid off handsomely. These included really out-of-the-way places where rock fans came from a 500-mile radius.

NOT FRAGILE (Album) *Mercury* [*USA*]. Released in the U.S.A. in August 1974, this hit No 1 for one week and stayed 50 weeks in the U.S. bestsellers. R.I.A.A. Gold Disc award on 23 August 1974.

BTO was the first Canadian group to have two Top 100 albums (Nos 1 and 2) simultaneously in the charts. 'Not Fragile' sold a million by November 1974. It included: 'Not Fragile'; 'You Ain't Seen Nothin' Yet'; 'Sledgehammer'; 'Blue Moanin'; 'Free Wheelin'' (Blair Thornton); 'Givin' It All the Way'; 'Rock Is My Life'; 'Roll on Down the Highway' (Robbie Bachman and Fred Turner); 'Second Hand'.

Most material written by Randy Bachman and Fred Turner.

YOU AIN'T SEEN NOTHIN' YET *Mercury* [*USA*]. Written by Randy Bachman and released in the U.S.A. in September 1974 and in Britain in November 1974, this went to No 1 for one week in the U.S.A. and No 2 for three weeks in Britain. It stayed 18 weeks in the U.S. charts and 12 weeks in the British lists. R.I.A.A. Gold Disc award on 13 December 1974.

The prime track from BTO's hit album 'Not Fragile'. It sold well over the million. This is a rock number with Randy Bachman doing the vocals, combined with the best playing to date from the group. The reverse side of the disc is a number from the same album – 'Free Wheelin'', written by BTO's guitarist Blair Thornton.

BAD COMPANY (rock quartet)

BAD COMPANY *Swan Song* [*USA*]. Released in the U.S.A. in July 1974, this went to No 1 for one week, staying 49 weeks in the charts. R.I.A.A. Gold Disc award on 19 September 1974. Grammy Award: Best Selling Album by a New Artist, 1974.

Bad Company's debut album, also the first album for Led Zeppelin's new label Swan Song. Bad Company personnel: Paul Rodgers (vocals), Mick Ralphs (guitar), Boz Burrell (bass) and Simon Kirke (drums).

The group were formed quite casually in November 1973, the four musicians of notable yet diverse backgrounds. Rodgers and Kirke were formerly members of Free, Ralphs a founder member of Mott The Hoople and Burrell of King Crimson. They were the most popular new band in the U.K. and the most successful British band in the U.S.A. in 1974. Their first U.S.A. tour in 1974, managed by Led Zeppelin manager Peter Grant, aroused great enthusiasm, and they topped the charts there with this album and a single from it, 'Can't Get Enough'.

They fused a sound of powerful simplicity, and went on to further big success, with a sold-out coast-to-coast tour of America in early 1976, breaking attendance records in Jacksonville, Florida, Mobile, Alabama and Lubbock, Texas.

The album included: 'Seagull'; 'Can't Get Enough'; 'The Way I Choose'; 'Don't Let Me Down'; 'Ready for Love'; 'Bad Company'.

Material by Bad Company. The album sold over 1,300,000 by June 1975.

THE BEACH BOYS

ENDLESS SUMMER (Double album) *Capitol* [*USA*]. Released in the U.S.A. in July 1974, this went to No 1 for one week, staying for 71 weeks in the charts. R.I.A.A. Gold Disc award on 14 August 1974.

A compilation of previously released material by The Beach Boys, charting the 1962-1966 period when they captured the mood of the U.S.A.'s West Coast and eventually of teenagers throughout the country. The double album was the perfect summer record. It showcases the band's writing talents and almost perfect harmonizing, and every track is a reminder of summer. Brian Wilson thought of the title for the package, and also took part in the selection of material. He is either sole writer or co-writer of every number. It was Capitol Records' first TV advertising campaign on which they spent $250,000, plus another $75,000 for a combination of in-store merchandising, banner displays and radio giveaways.

By mid-September the album sold 620,000, and 290,000 tapes and cassettes. By year's end it had passed the million units sale and went on to sell an estimated two million.

Contents: (*) 'Surfin' U.S.A.' (revised version of Chuck Berry's 'Sweet Little 16' written in 1958, by Brian Wilson and Chuck Berry, 1963); (*) 'Surfer Girl' (1962); 'Catch a Wave' (1962); 'The Warmth of the Sun' (1964); (*) 'Be True to Your School' (1963); 'Surfin' Safari' (1962); 'Little Deuce Coupe' (1963); 'In my Room' (1964); 'Shut Down' (1963); (*) 'Fun, Fun, Fun' (1964); (*) I Get Around' (1964); 'The Girl on the Beach' (1964); 'Wendy' (1964); 'Let Him Run Wild' (1965); 'Don't Worry Baby' (1964); 'California Girls' (1965); 'Girl Don't Tell Me' (1965); (*) 'Help Me, Rhonda' (1965); 'You're So Good to Me' (1965); 'All Summer Long' (1964).

(* denotes originally a million-seller single.)

BIMBO JET (instrumental group)

EL BIMBO *Pathe-Marconi [France] EMI [Britain]*. Written by Claude Morgan and released in France in June 1974 and in Britain in August 1975, this went to No 1 in France and No 10 for one week in Britain. It stayed 20 weeks in the French charts and 11 weeks in the British lists.

French composer Claude Morgan took this tune to singer Laurent Rossi (son of Tino Rossi). Laurent saw the commercial potential of the number, and recorded it with a group (believed to be a sextet) of musicians. It was an instant hit in France, selling 1,300,000 there alone. Throughout the world it sold three million, and was No 1 in France, Spain, Italy, Denmark, Turkey and Lebanon. In Argentina it was No 2, and also a chart hit in Belgium, Switzerland, Mexico and the U.S.A. (where it got to the Top 30).

Its popularity in Britain came about through discotheque playing, and in the fact that it had its own dance, plus the demand from holiday makers returning from countries where it had been a hit and where they'd seen the dance.

BLUE MAGIC (vocal quintet)

SIDESHOW *Atco [USA]*. Written by Bobby Eli and Vinny Barrett, this was released in the U.S.A. in May 1974, going to No 5 for two weeks and staying 22 weeks in the charts. R.I.A.A. Gold Disc award on 16 August 1974.

The quintet - Vernon Sawyer (second tenor/baritone); Keith Beaton (second tenor); Wendell Sawyer (baritone); Richard Pratt (bass baritone); and Ted Mills (lead tenor/arranger), based in Philadelphia, combined the new 'Philadelphia Sound' with the singing style of the Philadelphia early 50s. All could sing lead. They did not make any appearances until they had signed their record contract and had a disc released. The first was 'Spell' in December 1973. After that, Blue Magic forged ahead very quickly and into national and international prominence. They were one of the best choreographed groups on stage, the dance routines being arranged by Keith Beaton. Vernon Sawyer designed the stage wardrobe.

'Sideshow' is a sparkling tune. It soon sold the million.

JEAN-CLAUDE BORELLI & HIS ORCHESTRA

DOLANNES MELODIE (Flute de Pan) *Delphine/Discodis [France] London [USA]*. Although first released in 1974, this disc did not take off until 1975, when after 'sleeping' for six months it sold 1,350,000 in France, 500,000 in Germany and 200,000 in Benelux. Many cover versions were made of this melody from a French movie soundtrack.

The disc incorporates an acoustic guitar line beneath a flighty flute solo played by Paul de Senneville and Oliver Toussaint.

'Dolannes Melodie' was No 1 for four weeks in France and Belgium. It also reached No 1 in Switzerland (Metronome label) and Germany (Telefunken label).

JAMES BROWN

THE PAYBACK (Part 1) *Polydor [USA]*. Written by James Brown, F. Wesley and J. Starks, this was released in the U.S.A. in March 1974, going to No 23 for two weeks and staying 13 weeks in the charts. R.I.A.A. Gold Disc award on 18 April 1974.

A quick million-seller for James Brown without ever getting into the top section of the U.S. charts. A great disco item. A U.S. report in this year stated that this disc, plus the album of the same title, were James Brown's 41st and 42nd Gold Discs of varying categories.

SHIRLEY BROWN

WOMAN TO WOMAN *Truth/Stax [USA]*. Written by James Banks, Eddie Marion and H. Thigpen, this was released in the U.S.A. in October 1974, reaching No 22 for one week, and staying 16 weeks in the charts.

Stax Records reported the million sale of this disc in December 1974. It was Shirley's first record, a poignant story about stealing another woman's man, taking the shape of a phone call. It was followed by other artists using a similar pattern.

B.T. EXPRESS (vocal & instrumental septet)

DO IT 'TIL YOU'RE SATISFIED *Scepter [USA]*. Written by B. Nichols and released in the U.S.A. in September 1974, this bounced to No 2 for two weeks, staying 20 weeks in the charts. R.I.A.A. Gold Disc award on 25 November 1974.

This group began as the King Davis House Rockers around 1970, then became Madison Street Express, and Brothers Trucking which begat B. T. Express. King Davis became their manager. Record producer Jeff Lane heard them and took them into the studios to record this disc for his Dock production company, the group's first record. This was taken up by Scepter Records' Roadshow label. Its infectious rhythm was perfect for disco stomping, and in due course it sold the million.

B. T. Express consists of Bill Risbrook (vocals/tenor sax/flute); his brother Louis Risbrook (bass); Richie Thompson (lead guitar/vocals); Carlos Ward (flute/alto sax/piccolo/clarinet); Terrell Woods (drums); Dennis Rowe (congas); and Barbara Joyce Lomas (vocals). All come from Brooklyn except Barbara who hails from Bessemer, Alabama, and had previously played with other groups. Carlos was born in Panama.

THE CARPENTERS

PLEASE, MISTER POSTMAN *A & M [USA]*. Written by B. Holland, F. Gorman and R. Bateman (1961), this was released in the U.S.A. in November 1974 and in Britain in January 1975. It went to No 1 for one week in the U.S.A. and Britain, staying 17 weeks in the U.S. charts and 12 weeks in the British lists. R.I.A.A. Gold Disc award on 11 February 1975.

This song was originally a hit for The Marvellettes in 1961 and then The Beatles in 1964. The Carpenters' version has their usual fine blending harmonies. A certain million seller from the day of release.

HARRY CHAPIN

CAT'S IN THE CRADLE *Elektra [USA]*. Written by Sandy and Harry Chapin, this was released in the U.S.A. in August 1974, going to No 1 for one week. It stayed 20 weeks in the charts. R.I.A.A. Gold Disc award on 31 December 1974.

Harry Chapin and his brothers Tom and Steve started playing together in the 1950s. After Harry left Cornell University, he reunited with his brothers in a Greenwich Village band. When the group disbanded, he joined forces with an old friend John Wallace, guitarist Ron Palmer and cellist Tim Scott. This was the foundation for his highly principled philosophy of composition – writing to communicate to others. He wrote poetry, studied philosophy and produced documentary films. His first hit single was 'Taxi' (1970) from his first Elektra album 'Heads and Tails'. In this and all his subsequent albums, he maintained the high ethical standards he set for himself and his music. He also made large donations to UNICEF.

Chapin's songs are story narratives. 'Cat's in the Cradle' is another of his fascinating lyrics, a story of a father and son and their changing roles in relationship over the years. The song is a collaboration between Harry and his wife Sandy.

He died on 16 July 1981.

CHER
DARK LADY *MCA* [*USA*]. Written by John Durrill and released in the U.S.A. in January 1974, this reached No 1 for one week and stayed 18 weeks in the charts. It was No 35 in Britain. R.I.A.A. Gold Disc award on 22 March 1974.

A powerful follow-up to her previous 'Half Breed' hit, this has a story line reminiscent of her great 'Gypsies, Tramps and Thieves'. A quick million-seller.

CHICAGO
CHICAGO VII (Double album) *Columbia* [*USA*]. Released in the U.S.A. in March 1974, this hit No 1 for one week, staying 69 weeks in the charts. R.I.A.A. Gold Disc award on 18 March 1974.

Seventh million units seller in a row for Chicago, with an almost immediate gold award. Again, all the material was written by the group.

Contents included: 'I've Been Searchin' So Long'; 'Call on Me'; 'Wishing You Were Here'; 'Hanky Panky'; 'Prelude to Aire'; 'Byblos'; 'Life Saver'; 'Italian from New York'; 'Air'; 'Devils Sweet'; 'Happy Man'; 'Mononucleosis'; 'Song of the Evergreens'; 'The Woman Don't Want to Love Me'; 'Skinny Boy'.

ERIC CLAPTON
I SHOT THE SHERIFF *RSO/Atlantic* [*USA*]. Written by Bob Marley, this was released in the U.S.A. in June 1974 and in Britain in July 1974. It got to No 1 for two weeks in the U.S.A. and No 7 for one week in Britain, staying 17 weeks in the U.S. charts and 8 weeks in the British topsellers. R.I.A.A. Gold Disc award on 19 September 1974.

Eric Clapton was born on 30 March 1945 in Ripley, Surrey, and studied stained-glass design. At 17, he took up the guitar and became a replacement in a local group The Yardbirds (see 1965). Eric left the group in 1965, and went on a world tour, and the same year joined John Mayall's Bluesbreakers. In 1966 he joined Cream (see 1967) and had his first real commercial success. He formed Blind Faith in 1969 after Cream split up, but they disbanded after a year. Then came a spell with Delaney & Bonnie, an American white-gospel duo. Eric toured with them (1970), also recorded an album with them and made his first solo album. In 1971, he formed Derek and The Dominoes with three ex-Delaney & Bonnie musicians, with whom he made a double album 'Layla'. It featured Eric as lead vocalist and Duane Allman as guest guitarist, and was one of his greatest achievements. After this group broke up, Eric's sole venture was a star-studded concert at the Rainbow Theatre, London (1973). He then re-appeared with a new band in mid-1974, and in Miami made his first studio recordings in almost four years. One of these was 'I Shot the Sheriff', recorded by Eric in the reggae style. It became a major hit globally, including singer/composer Bob Marley's native Jamaica. It sold well over a million in the U.S.A. alone, and brought Eric renewed prominence. His tally of albums with the many groups, etc. he played with was 20 up to 1975.

CHARLIE DANIELS BAND
FIRE ON THE MOUNTAIN (album) *Kama Sutra* [*USA*]. Released in the U.S.A. in December 1974, it reached No 30 for two weeks, staying 26 weeks in the charts.

Daniels was born in North Carolina, son of a lumber mill worker. He began playing music at an early age and continued throughout high school. He was 19 when Presley inspired in him a devotion to pop music. Before that it was only the bluegrass that was played on backwoods North Carolina radio. At 20 he played clubs around Washington. In the late 1960s, Charlie formed a band, the Jaguars, and toured the South and Mid-West. Early in 1970 he headed for Nashville, at the advice of record producer Bob Johnson. Johnson was preparing to produce a Bob Dylan album and let Daniels sit in at the sessions, taking over when the regular guitar player wasn't available. He became a studio musician and throughout the years has played scores of sessions. But he wanted his own career and teamed up with Joe Sullivan, a youthful livewire who had just formed a Nashville booking agency. Sullivan got Daniels a Buddah recording contract, and he soon established himself with songs like 'Uneasy Rider' and 'The South's Gonna Do It', with his newly formed Charlie Daniels Band challenging the other Southern rock bands like Marshall Tucker's, Lynyrd Skynyrd, and the Allman Brothers. He won all kinds of awards, played in the East Room of the White House, and grossed two million dollars on a mid-70s tour. His band consists of himself (violin) and five other musicians. His main hobby is songwriting.

This album sold 700,000 on the Buddha Records' Kama Sutra label in 1975. It was re-released when the band signed with CBS/Epic label in 1977, and sold a further 600,000. With other sales it reached the 1,500,000 mark. The band came into prominence in 1977. The million plus sale of 'Fire On The Mountain' was reported in August 1979.

JOHN DENVER
SUNSHINE ON MY SHOULDERS *RCA* [*USA*]. Written by Denver, Kniss and Taylor (1971), this was released in the U.S.A. in January 1974 and in Britain in March 1974. It went to No 1 for one week in the U.S.A., staying 18 weeks in the charts. R.I.A.A. Gold Disc award on 28 March 1974.

This soft, tender ballad originally appeared on Denver's album 'Poems, Prayers and Promises' (1971). It was re-cut for Denver's 'Greatest Hits' album (1973) and eventually released as a single due to popular demand with an eventual million-plus sale.

ANNIE'S SONG *RCA* [*USA*]. Written by John Denver and released in the U.S.A. in May 1974 and in Britain in July 1974. It reached No 1 for two weeks in the U.S.A. and for one week in Britain. It stayed 17 weeks in the U.S. charts and 12 weeks in the British lists. R.I.A.A. Gold Disc award on 26 July 1974.

John Denver's song about his wife, Annie, who he first met when he was singing with The Mitchell Trio at her college in Minnesota in 1965. They were married in June 1967 and set up house in Aspen, Colorado. This single is a track from Denver's album 'Back Home Again' which appeared on the U.S.A. market a month later. Over a million sale in the U.S.A. and an estimated two million globally.

BACK HOME AGAIN *RCA* [*USA*]. Written by John Denver and released in the U.S.A. in September 1974, this went to No 5 for two weeks, staying 19 weeks in the charts. R.I.A.A. Gold Disc award on 3 January 1975.

John Denver's third million-seller single in 1974 was arranged by Lee Holdridge.

BACK HOME AGAIN (album) *RCA* [*USA*]. Released in the U.S.A. in June 1974 and in Britain in August 1974, this stayed at No 1 for four weeks in the U.S.A. and No 3 for one week in Britain. The album loitered for 96 weeks in the U.S. charts and 26 weeks in the British bestsellers. R.I.A.A. Gold Disc award on 24 June 1974.

Another huge album success for Denver, with million (platinum) sale by July 1974, a month after release. Estimate of global sale well over three million.

Contents: 'Annie's Song'; 'Back Home Again'; 'Grandma's Feather Bed'; 'Matthew'; 'Thank God I'm a Country Boy'; 'The Music Is You'; 'It's Up to You'; 'Cool an' Green an' Shady'; 'Eclipse'; 'Sweet Surrender'; 'This Old Guitar'.

WILLIAM DE VAUGHN
BE THANKFUL FOR WHAT YOU'VE GOT *Roxbury* [*USA*]. Released in the U.S.A. in April 1974 and written by William De Vaughn, this went to No 1 for one week and stayed 20 weeks in the charts. R.I.A.A. Gold Disc award on 31 May 1974.

This disc was distributed by Chelsea/RCA. A very quick million-seller for De Vaughn, a new name on the recording scene.

NEIL DIAMOND
SERENADE (album) *Columbia* [*USA*]. Released in the U.S.A. in October 1974, this went to No 2 for three weeks, staying 27 weeks in the charts. R.I.A.A. Gold Disc award on 30 October 1974.

The album was described by Neil Diamond as 'a serenade, a hymn of sorts, at most a small portion for the soul'. It sold 1,200,000 by June, plus 700,000 overseas, and was declared platinum by January 1975.

Contents include: 'I've Been This Way Before'; 'Reggae Strut'; 'Longfellow Serenade'; 'The Gift of Song'; 'The Last Picasso'; 'Rosemary's Wine'; 'Yes I Will'; 'Lady Magdalene'. All songs written by Neil Diamond.

BO DONALDSON & THE HEYWOODS (vocal septet)
BILLY, DON'T BE A HERO *ABC* [*USA*]. Written by Peter Callender and Mitch Murray, this was released in the U.S.A. in March 1974, hitting No 1 for two weeks and staying 20 weeks in the charts. R.I.A.A. Gold Disc award on 5 June 1974.

Bo Donaldson and the group toured extensively in the U.S.A. with top name groups like The Raiders, The Rascals, and The Hermits. Following a stint with The Osmonds, they realized they didn't have to take second place to any group. All they needed was a hit record. Bea Donaldson, Bo's mother and manager of the group, decided to make a move. They made their first single for ABC Records - 'Deeper and Deeper' - which failed to register. Then two promotion men Chackler and Leseff who headed Chalice Productions, came up with the idea of 'Billy, Don't Be a Hero'. This English song was a No 1 in Britain for Paper Lace. Chackler and Leseff called in Steve Barri who decided that changes were needed to be made to the song before it could translate to the American market. Veteran Barri and the band did this in the studio. The result was a fantastic success, the disc selling 3,500,000. The song has an intriguing story line, concerning 'Billy' going off to war, and his attempt at survival, with his lady at home hoping for the best.

THE DOOBIE BROTHERS
WHAT WERE ONCE VICES ARE NOW HABITS (album) *Warner* [*USA*]. Released in the U.S.A. in March 1974, this reached No 9 for one week, staying 33 weeks in the charts. R.I.A.A. Gold Disc award on 2 April 1974.

Another big hit for The Doobies. Straight hard rock throughout the disc, with added percussive accents and the use of the Memphis horns - plus guest artists. The million units (platinum) sale was reported in February 1975.

Contents include: 'Black Water'; 'Down in the Track'; 'Tell Me What You Want To' and 'Pursuit on 53rd Street'.

BLACK WATER *Warner* [*USA*]. Released in the U.S.A. in December 1974, this was written by Pat Simmons of the group,

and went to No 1 for one week. It stayed 20 weeks in the charts. R.I.A.A. Gold Disc award on 14 April 1974.

An outstanding disc with bubbling guitars, flowing harmonies, drums and bass and fiddle, plus a big *a capella* finish. This cut was a highlight from the Doobies' album 'What Were Once Vices'.

CARL DOUGLAS
KUNG FU FIGHTING *Pye* [*Britain*] *20th Century* [*USA*]. Written by Carl Douglas and released in Britain in August 1974 and in the U.S.A. in September 1974, this reached No 1 for five weeks in Britain and two weeks in the U.S.A. R.I.A.A. Gold Disc award on 27 November 1974. Grammy Award: Best Selling Single, 1974.

Carl Douglas was born in Jamaica, and educated in America and Britain. He went to Britain to study engineering, then got into singing and worked as a semi-pro entertainer until 1964. Carl had some success as a writer when he penned the music for the Richard Roundtree film *Embassy*.

Kung Fu, the martial art of self defence in China, had been brought to the film world via the late actor Bruce Lee. At his funeral in the U.S.A., the Chinese gave him a hero's burial, with thousands lining the street. The Kung Fu craze moved to TV, and made a star out of David Carradine. The idea for the disc stemmed from Carl's evening out with his producer Biddu, when they saw a gang chopping and kicking and throwing each other about. Carl had an early interest in judo and started learning more about Kung Fu from 1973. Biddu's production of his hit was put to a reggae-style beat with lyrics about the universal fascination with the oriental art, believed to have started some 4,600 years ago by Huang Di, the Chinese Emperor who wanted a fast method of training his army.

'Kung Fu Fighting' was a big success on both sides of the Atlantic, over a million sale in the U.S.A., around half a million in Britain, and globally over four million. The disc started the Kung Fu step, a popular dance first in British discos, then in the U.S.A.

EMERSON, LAKE & PALMER
WELCOME BACK, MY FRIENDS, TO THE SHOW THAT NEVER ENDS - LADIES AND GENTLEMEN (triple album) *Manticore* [*USA*]. Written by Emerson, Lake & Palmer and released in the U.S.A. in August 1974, this bonanza package went to No 2 for two weeks. It stayed 24 weeks in the charts. R.I.A.A. Gold Disc award on 19 September 1974.

An almost immediate gold award for this triple album, which was reported to have been shipped platinum (one million copies). It was the sixth million-seller for the three musicians.

The album contains such epic pieces as 'Tarkus' (with its six subdivisions), 'Piano Improvisations', 'Take a Pebble', 'Karn Evil 9', 'Jerusalem', 'Toccata' and 'Hoedown'. The album is a live recording of their 1973-74 tour of the U.S.A.

ROBERTA FLACK
FEEL LIKE MAKIN' LOVE *Atlantic* [*USA*]. Written by E. McDaniels, this was released in the U.S.A. in June 1974, going to No 1 for one week and staying 18 weeks in the charts. It was No 34 in Britain. R.I.A.A. Gold Disc award on 8 August 1974.

Another soft rendering from Roberta, an infectious melody with percussion and keyboard. It soon sold a million.

GRAND FUNK RAILROAD
THE LOCO-MOTION *Capitol* [*USA*]. Written by Gerry Goffin and Carole King (1962), this revamped oldie was released in the U.S.A. in February 1974. It went to No 1 for two weeks and stayed 20 weeks in the charts. R.I.A.A. Gold Disc award on 24 April 1974.

Todd Rundgren's production of Grand Funk's cover version

of the Goffin/King classic. This million-seller with its fine guitar playing and inspired harmonization further enhanced both the song and the trio.

AL GREEN
SHA LA LA (makes me happy) *Hi* [*USA*] *London* [*USA*]. Written by Willie Mitchell and released in the U.S.A. in September 1974 and in Britain in November 1974, this made No 7 for one week in the U.S.A. and No 17 in Britain. It stayed 19 weeks in the U.S. charts and nine weeks in the British bestsellers. R.I.A.A. Gold Disc award on 22 January 1975.

A powerful composition with a soulful performance by Al Green, plus infectious Memphis horns and a super string section. Another million seller to continue the Al Green success story.

MARVIN HAMLISCH (pianist)
THE ENTERTAINER *MCA* [*USA*]. Written by Scott Joplin (1902) and released in the U.S.A. in March 1974 and in Britain in April 1974, this went to No 1 for one week in the U.S.A. and No 22 in Britain. It stayed 17 weeks in the U.S. charts and 12 weeks in the British lists. R.I.A.A. Gold Disc award on 7 June 1974. Grammy Award: Best Pop Instrumental Performance, 1974.

Marvin Hamlisch, pianist/composer/conductor was born on 2 June 1944 in New York. He was educated at a professional children's school, Juilliard and Queen's College. He became Musical Director for Equity Library Theatre Productions and later managing director and writer of musical scores for films. His first big success in the latter came with the Barbra Streisand film *The Way We Were* in 1973. He won the Oscar for the title song, and Grammy Awards for the song and Best Original Score for a Motion Picture.

'The Entertainer' is the prime cut from his score released as a single by popular demand from the album 'The Sting' (*q.v.*). The use of long-forgotten Scott Joplin, 'King of the Ragtimers', music in the film created a tremendous revival of Joplin's works. Joplin, born on 24 November 1868 in Texarkana, Texas, a fine pianist, played at the Maple Leaf Club in Sedalia, Missouri, a town revered by ragtimers. His famous 'Maple Leaf Rag' was published by a Sedalia house in 1899. He wrote dozens of ragtime tunes, and even two ragtime operas *A Guest of Honour* and *Treemonisha*, neither of which got much beyond a first performance. He also wrote a ballet *Rag Time Dance*. The success of 'Maple Leaf Rag' made him independent, and he left the honky tonk circuit and Sedalia and set himself up as a teacher in St Louis. Here he helped 'amateur players' learn how to keep a steady beat with the left hand while syncopating off the beat with the right. When jazz came in, ragtime was gradually forgotten. Scott virtually died with it, on 4 April 1919 in New York.

Joplin's opera *Treemonisha* composed in 1907 was mounted in a full production for the first time in 1972, and arrived at Broadway's Uris Theatre in 1974's Houston Grand Opera Production, and his ragtime tunes were once again played by thousands of pianists throughout the world.

'The Entertainer' became the most popular through this million-selling disc.

HERBIE HANCOCK (jazz rock instrumentalist)
HEADHUNTERS (Album) *Columbia* [*USA*]. Herbie Hancock, keyboard player, was born in 1940, and hails from Chicago. He started playing piano at the age of seven. By the age of 11 he was good enough to play the first movement of Mozart's Piano Concerto No 26 in D with the Chicago Symphony Orchestra. He became interested in jazz whilst at high school by listening to George Shearing and Oscar Peterson discs, and trying to duplicate their sounds. Herbie began arranging and composing at Iowa's Grinnell College, and gave a concert with a 17-piece band. After leaving college, he returned to Chicago, living with his parents, and played as many dates as he could. In 1960 he joined up with the visiting Donald Byrd and went to New York with him. His first success as composer came with 'Watermelon Man'

in 1963. Byrd took Hancock to Miles Davis to play some ballads which resulted in Herbie becoming a member of the Davis band. He was then on his way, staying with Miles Davis as composer and keyboard man from 1963-68, and making a big impression in the jazz community.

In 1968 Herbie formed his own group, a sextet, and made a series of innovative albums for Blue Note and Warner Bros, subsequently signing with Columbia, after disbanding his group for financial reasons in 1973. He decided to change his style from melodic lines and quick tempos to the more commercial funky music embracing the big beat, or jazz rock. The 'Headhunters' album attracted an entirely new audience of jazz lovers and rock fans. The album reached No 10 in the U.S. charts, and sold 700,000 in around four months, going on to pass the million, the biggest selling jazz album until George Benson came along in 1976. Herbie gave a concert of his jazz rock avant-garde electronics music at Carnegie Hall, New York, on 13 April 1974, a major event.

Herbie is a member of the Buddhist sect of Nisherin Shoshu.

'Headhunters' was released in the U.S.A. March 1974 and includes: 'Chameleon'; 'Watermelon Man'; 'Sky'; 'Vein Melter'; 'Rolling Stone'; and was in the U.S. bestsellers for 27 weeks.

Herbie Hancock was voted the Top Jazz Artist in several 1974 polls.

THE HOLLIES
THE AIR THAT I BREATHE *Polydor* [*Britain*] *Epic* [*USA*]. Written by Albert Hammond and Mike Hazelwood, this was released in Britain in January 1974 and in the U.S.A. in April 1974. It went to No 2 for two weeks in Britain and No 5 for one week in the U.S.A., staying 13 weeks in the British charts and 21 weeks in the U.S. bestsellers. R.I.A.A. Gold Disc award on 22 August 1974.

A great success in Britain, with over 250,000 sale, and the million following in the U.S.A. The Hollies' rendering of this tuneful ballad made it a hit in many markets. Allan Clarke, who had gone solo for a while, rejoined the group in late 1973.

HUES CORPORATION (soul trio)
ROCK THE BOAT *RCA* [*USA*]. Written by W. Holmes, this was released in the U.S.A. in February 1974 and in Britain in July 1974. It went to No 1 for one week in the U.S.A and No 5 for two weeks in Britain. It stayed 20 weeks in the U.S. bestsellers

and ten weeks in British lists. R.I.A.A. Gold Disc award on 24 June 1974.

Hues Corporation consisted of two males - St Clair Lee and Tommy Brown - and a girl, H. Ann Kelly. The newly formed trio made a rapid entry into both the disc scene and on the U.S. concert circuit. They perform this million-seller with driving rhythm and stylish vocal delivery. It was originally on their album 'Freedom for the Stallion'. 'Rock the Boat' sold well over two million.

TERRY JACKS

SEASONS IN THE SUN *Bell* [*USA*]. Written by Jacques Brel (English lyrics translated by Rod McKuen, 1964), this was released in the U.S.A. in January 1974 and in Britain in March 1974. It went to No 1 for three weeks in the U.S.A. and four weeks in Britain. It stayed 22 weeks in the U.S. charts and 12 weeks in the British bestsellers. R.I.A.A. Gold Disc award on 14 February 1974.

'Seasons in the Sun', by Belgian composer/singer Jacques Brel, was originally written in 1961 with the French title of 'Le Moribond', and is the story of a dying man. Terry Jacks, formerly of The Poppy Family (see 1969), first heard the song by the famous Kingston Trio in 1964, and in 1972 was involved in some Beach Boys' sessions when they cut the track but never released it. He decided to produce a re-make himself and re-wrote the last verse and re-arranged some of the chorus. His disc was released on his own Canadian label Goldfish Records, his first release for Goldfish and the third single on which he had been featured as solo artist as well as producer. Bell Records picked up the rights for the U.S.A. and it sold over three million there alone. World sales are well over six million.

Terry received only permission and not credit for changing some of the lyrics to 'lighten them up'. His main reason for recording it was the sudden death of a very close friend. British sales went over the 250,000 mark.

Composer Brel died in 1978.

THE JACKSON 5

DANCING MACHINE *Motown* [*USA*]. Written by H. Davis, D. Fletcher and W. D. Parks, this was released in the U.S.A. in March 1974, going to No 1 for one week. It stayed 22 weeks in the charts.

Taken from the group's album 'Get It Together', the million sale of this disc by the energetic quintet sold a reported million within a month of release. Its intricate rhythms, expansive harmonies and clear lyric line made it one of the group's best efforts.

JETHRO TULL

WAR CHILD (album) *Chrysalis* [*USA*]. Released in the U.S.A. in September 1974, this made No 2 for three weeks, staying 31 weeks in the charts. R.I.A.A. Gold Disc award on 8 November 1974.

A second million-selling album (by April 1975) for this super-group, containing a wealth of captivating material.

It included: 'War Child', 'Skating Away on the Thin Ice of the New Day' and 'Bungle in the Jungle', all by Ian Anderson.

ELTON JOHN

BENNIE AND THE JETS *MCA* [*USA*] *DJM* [*USA*]. Written by Bernie Taupin and Elton John, this was released in the U.S.A. in February 1974. It reached No 1 for one week, staying 18 weeks in the charts. R.I.A.A. Gold Disc award on 8 April 1974.

Culled from Elton's 'Goodbye Yellow Brick Road' album (1973), this single easily passed the million sale. A very strong number, and a rather long disc of 5 mins 10 secs' duration.

CARIBOU (album) *MCA* [*USA*] *DJM* [*Britain*]. Written by Bernie Taupin and Elton John and released in the U.S.A. and Britain in June 1974, this hit No 1 for five weeks in the U.S.A. and two weeks in Britain. It stayed 54 weeks in the U.S. charts

and 22 weeks in the British lists. R.I.A.A. Gold Disc award on 5 July 1974.

This big seller, estimated at four million, was recorded in the Caribou Ranch in Colorado.

Contents: 'The Bitch Is Back'; 'Pinky'; 'Grimsby'; 'Dixie Lily'; 'Solar Prestige a Gammon'; 'You're so Static'; 'I've Seen the Saucers'; 'Stinker'; 'Ticking'; 'Don't Let the Sun Go Down on Me'.

At this time, Elton signed his colossal contract, $8 million with MCA, making him one of the highest paid recording artists in history.

DON'T LET THE SUN GO DOWN ON ME *MCA* [*USA*] *DJM* [*Britain*]. Written by Bernie Taupin and Elton John, released in the U.S.A. and Britain in June 1974, this went to No 1 for one week in the U.S.A. and No 15 for one week in Britain. It stayed 17 weeks in the U.S. charts and eight weeks in the British bestsellers. R.I.A.A. Gold Disc award on 7 September 1974.

The single was a cut from his album 'Caribou'.

GREATEST HITS (album) *MCA* [*USA*] *DJM* [*Britain*]. All written by Bernie Taupin and Elton John, released in the U.S.A. and Britain in November 1974, this hit No 1 for eight weeks in the U.S.A. and 12 weeks in Britain. It lodged 117 weeks in the U.S. charts and 54 weeks in the British lists. R.I.A.A. Gold Disc award on 8 November 1974. Grammy Award: Best Selling Album by a Male Artist, 1974.

The album went platinum (one million sale) after only one month of release. By August 1976, it had sold over five million globally and went on to rack up an estimated tally of seven million.

It was compiled and produced by Gus Dudgeon, and the personnel are: Elton John (keyboards), Dee Murray (bass), Nigel Olsson (drums), Davey Johnstone (guitar). Additional players on some tracks.

Contents: 'Your Song'; 'Daniel'; 'Honky Cat'; 'Goodbye Yellow Brick Road'; 'Saturday Night's Alright for Fighting'; 'Rocket Man'; 'Candle in the Wind'; 'Don't Let the Sun Go Down on Me'; 'Border Song'; 'Crocodile Rock'. Most of these were million-seller singles.

The release of this album was the culmination of a successful year for Elton John: U.S. earnings over the year were reported at £3,500,000 (approximately $9 million). His 40-city tour of the U.S.A. sold out at every concert.

LUCY IN THE SKY WITH DIAMONDS *MCA* [*USA*] *DJM* [*Britain*]. Written by John Lennon and Paul McCartney (1967) and released in the U.S.A. and Britain in November 1974, this went to No 1 for two weeks in the U.S.A. and No 3 for two weeks in Britain. It stayed 14 weeks in the U.S. bestsellers and ten weeks in the British charts. R.I.A.A. Gold Disc award on 29 January 1975.

Only Elton could make a cover version of this Beatles classic and be certain it would reach No 1. He made considerable changes in time and dynamics at the end of this long recording. It was the first time Elton John and Bernie Taupin had had a hit with a song not written by themselves. The disc sold around two million globally.

ANDY KIM

ROCK ME GENTLY *Capitol* [*USA*]. Written by Andy Kim, this was released in the U.S.A. in June 1974, going to No 1 for one week in the U.S.A. and No 2 for one week in Britain. It stayed 20 weeks in the U.S. charts and 12 weeks in the British bestsellers. R.I.A.A. Gold Disc award on 3 October 1974.

Andy Kim's first big disc since 1969, on his new (Capitol) label. The Canadian-born singer had not appeared on the charts in the U.S.A. for over three years, but with this disc, which inched its way up the charts, he was back again to renewed popularity. Apart from writing the song, he put his own money into the project, and also produced the disc with a bunch of musicians unknown to him. The gamble succeeded, and 'Rock Me Gently' achieved the million plus sale, with an estimated two–three million globally.

GLADYS KNIGHT & THE PIPS

BEST THING THAT EVER HAPPENED TO ME *Buddah* [*USA*]. Written by Jim Weatherly and released in the U.S.A. in February 1974, this hit No 2 for one week, staying 18 weeks in the charts. R.I.A.A. Gold Disc award on 15 April 1974.

A powerful disc, one of the group's best, plus another million seller to add to their list.

ON AND ON *Buddah* [*USA*]. Written by Curtis Mayfield and released in the U.S.A. in May 1974, this reached No 5 for two weeks, staying 16 weeks in the charts. R.I.A.A. Gold Disc award on 15 July 1974.

This single disc was taken from the Gladys Knight & The Pips soundtrack album 'Claudine', and was the sixth consecutive gold record for them since signing with Buddah Records in early 1973. Curtis Mayfield wrote and produced the music for the film.

KOOL & THE GANG

HOLLYWOOD SWINGING *De-Lite* [*USA*]. Written by R. West and Kool & The Gang, this was released in the U.S.A. in April 1974, going to No 6 for one week and staying 19 weeks in the charts. R.I.A.A. Gold Disc award on 21 June 1974.

Another million seller to follow their incredibly successful 'Jungle Boogie'. A great dance disc by the group with the 'New York Sound'.

LABELLE (vocal trio)

LADY MARMALADE *Epic* [*USA*]. Written by Allen Toussaint, Bob Crewe and Kenny Nolan, this was released in the U.S.A. in November 1974 and in Britain in March 1975. It got to No 1 for one week in the U.S.A. and No 15 for one week in Britain, staying 20 weeks in the U.S. charts and nine weeks in the British bestsellers. R.I.A.A. Gold Disc award on 25 March 1975.

Labelle was originally a quartet of black ladies - Patti LaBelle, Nona Hendryx, Sarah Dash and Cindy Birdsong - known as Pattie LaBelle and The Bluebells. Their first fair-sized hits in the early 1960s were 'I Sold My Heart to the Junkman' and 'Down the Aisle'. Cindy Birdsong left in 1967 to join The Supremes. After going through a period of instability when they recorded for a number of different labels, they met British expatriate Vicki Wickham in 1970. She became their manager and they became simply Labelle, changing their act to a funkier style, with songs written by Nona Hendryx. Labelle made their first album 'Moonshadow' (Warner Bros, 1971), then 'LaBelle' (RCA, 1973), and 'Pressure Cookin'' (RCA, 1974) followed by 'Nightbirds' (1974) for the Epic label after Vicki and the trio decided on this change. This was recorded under New Orleans producer Allen Toussaint with The Meteors, his famed studio band. The album was a big success resulting in Labelle making musical history by becoming the first black popular act to perform at New York's Metropolitan Opera House. This was followed by an international tour with recognition by all the established stars.

'Lady Marmalade' was culled from the 'Nightbirds' album. This was an overnight sensation, due to the hook line in the song 'Voulez-vous coucher avec moi ce soir?'. The million sale was inevitable.

Labelle's act was exciting and thoroughly professional, and they appeared in futuristic silver outfits making the show a visual experience as well.

JOHN LENNON

WALLS AND BRIDGES (album) *Apple* [*USA & Britain*]. Written mostly by John Lennon, this was released in the U.S.A. and in Britain in October 1974. It went to No 1 for one week in both countries staying 27 weeks in the U.S. charts and 10 weeks in the British lists. R.I.A.A. Gold Disc award on 22 October 1974.

An almost instant gold award and platinum for million sales by November 1974. The album is loaded with powerful rock 'n' roll in the Lennon style with mood orchestrations in the right places, and is a skilful collaboration between him and a group of highly skilled creative musicians. The ensemble is Jim Keltner (drums), Klaus Voormann (bass), Jesse Ed Davis (guitar), Ken Ascher, Nicky Hopkins and Elton John (keyboards), Harry Nilsson (back-up vocals), Bobby Keys (tenor).

Contents: 'Steel and Glass'; 'Coming Down on Love'; 'Whatever Gets You Through the Night'; 'Old Dirt Road'; 'What You Got'; 'Bless You'; 'Scared'; 'Number 9 Dream'; 'Surprise Surprise'; 'Beef Jerky'; 'Nobody Loves You When You're Down and Out' (Cox); 'Ya Ya' (Lee Dorsey).

GORDON LIGHTFOOT

SUNDOWN *Reprise* [*USA*]. Written by Gordon Lightfoot and released in the U.S.A. in March 1974, this went to No 1 for one week, staying 19 weeks in the charts. It was No 33 in Britain. R.I.A.A. Gold Disc award on 18 June 1974.

A melodic pop rocker from the Canadian singer/composer, his best since 'If I Could Read Your Mind' in 1970. It sold a quick million.

SUNDOWN (album) *Reprise* [*USA*]. Released in the U.S.A. in January 1974, this went to No 1 for two weeks, staying for 45 weeks in the charts. R.I.A.A. Gold Disc award on 31 May 1974.

Gordon's album, based on the title of his successful single, sold the million by mid-September 1974. It made a big impact with its variety of songs in his troubadour style, and highlights his subtle vocals.

Contents included: 'Sundown'; 'High and Dry'; 'Circle of Steel'; 'The List'; 'Seven Island Suite' and 'Carefree Highway'. Songs written by Gordon Lightfoot.

LYNYRD SKYNYRD

SECOND HELPING (album) *MCA* [*USA*]. Released in the U.S.A. in April 1974, this went to No 12 for two weeks, staying 45 weeks in the charts. R.I.A.A. Gold Disc award on 20 September 1974.

The album that brought prominence to this group. It sold a million (platinum status) by June 1976.

Contents included: 'Sweet Home Alabama', 'I Need You' and 'Don't Ask Me No Questions'. All songs by the group. (See Lynyrd Skynyrd, 1973.)

PAUL McCARTNEY & WINGS

BAND ON THE RUN *Apple* [*Britain*] *Capitol* [*USA*]. Written by Paul McCartney (1973) and released in the U.S.A. in April 1974 and in Britain in June 1974, this hit No 1 for two weeks in the U.S.A. and No 2 for one week in Britain. It stayed 18 weeks in the U.S.A. charts and 11 weeks in the British lists. R.I.A.A. Gold Disc award on 4 June 1974. Grammy Award: Best Pop Vocal Performance by a Group.

Culled from the album of the same name (1973), this high-quality McCartney track was a quick million-seller in the U.S.A. Global sale is estimated at around two million.

GEORGE McCRAE

ROCK YOUR BABY *TK* [*USA*] *Jay Boy* [*Britain*]. Written by Richard Finch and H. W. Casey, this was released in the U.S.A. in May 1974 and in Britain in June 1974. It got to No 1 for two weeks in the U.S.A. and 3 weeks in Britain. It stayed 19 weeks in the U.S. bestsellers and 14 weeks in the British charts.

'Rock Your Baby', written by two resident writers/arrangers/producers at the small TK disc company in Florida, became one of 1974's biggest hits on both sides of the Atlantic. It sold over two million in the U.S.A., and another million or more in Europe. British sales were over 250,000 and the disc won RCA's first Gold Disc in Germany for 560,000 sales. Global sales were reported in excess of 15 million by 1977.

George McCrae was virtually unknown until he made this disc. His first group was The Fabulous Stepbrothers during school days. He then formed The Jets, went into the U.S.A. Navy where he ran the NAS Rockers, and on discharge worked the South Florida club circuit. He attracted attention while working with his wife at Fort Lauderdale and was signed by TK Records. A subsequent tour of Europe and elsewhere followed.

'Rock Your Baby' was distributed by RCA. It was No 1 in 53 countries.

MAIN INGREDIENT (vocal trio)

JUST DON'T WANT TO BE LONELY *RCA* [*USA*]. Written by Barrett, Freeman and Eli, this was released in the U.S.A. in February 1974, going to No 7 for one week. It stayed 20 weeks in the charts. It was No 27 in Britain. R.I.A.A. Gold Disc award on 10 May 1974.

Second million-seller for this trio.

BARRY MANILOW

MANDY *Bell* [*USA*]. Written by S. English and R. Kerr, this was released in the U.S.A. in October 1974 and in Britain in February 1975. It went to No 1 for one week in the U.S.A. and No 7 for one week in Britain, staying 21 weeks in the U.S. charts and nine weeks in the British lists. R.I.A.A. Gold Disc award on 31 January 1975.

Barry Manilow was born in Brooklyn, New York in 1947. He went to the Juilliard School of Music, and worked in the mail room at CBS. Here he started doing arranging, and wrote a musical *The Drunkard*. He did some arranging for the Ed Sullivan specials and, in due course, teamed up with singer Bette Midler and became her musical director, conductor and pianist.

Barry co-produced and created the arrangements for her best-selling 'Divine Miss M' album, and went on tour as a support act to Bette with some success. In 1973, he recorded his first album. His second album in 1974 included three hit numbers. 'Mandy' was taken from this, and was a big hit. It was also something of a shock to Barry, whose main claim to fame had previously been in writing some advertising jingles.

Barry got the song from a four-year-old demo tape. Its original title was 'Brandy'. As there was already a song of that title on the market, Barry changed the title to 'Mandy' and recorded it with a lush orchestration and doing some fine piano work himself. This classic love song sold the million by early 1975. Thereafter, Barry Manilow's disc output was in great demand, and his albums were big sellers.

SISTER JANET MEAD

THE LORD'S PRAYER *Festival* [*Australia*] *A & M* [*USA*]. With music by Arnold Strals, this was released in the U.S.A. in February 1974 and shot to No 4 for one week, staying 18 weeks in the charts. R.I.A.A. Gold Disc award on 8 April 1974.

1974's most unlikely hit, a rock version of the 2,000-year-old prayer. Sister Janet Mead, born 1938, became a member of the Sisters of Mercy Convent in Adelaide, Australia in 1955. The record is the result of Sister Janet's music via her weekly rock masses held in Adelaide Cathedral, and her weekly radio programme. Her tasteful and lilting 'Lord's Prayer' was recorded by Festival Records as the 'B' side of 'Brother Sun, Sister Moon'. Festival Records' manager saw its commercial potential, and A & M got the world rights. It sold over 1,500,000 in four months on the U.S. market, plus big sales elsewhere.

The disc was intended only for churches and schools, but when issued generally it became a hit. Sister Janet donated all the money from it to charity.

THE MIRACLES

DO IT BABY *Tamla* [*USA*]. Written by F. Perren and C. Yarien, this was released in the U.S.A. in July 1974, going to No 9 for one week and staying 16 weeks in the charts.

Another million-seller, by December 1974, for The Miracles.

MUD (pop vocal quartet)

TIGER FEET *RAK* [*Britain*]. Written by Nicky Chinn and Mike Chapman, this stomper was released in Britain in January 1974, going to No 1 for four weeks and staying 11 weeks in the charts.

Mud consists of Les Gray (lead singer) born 9 April 1946, Dave Mount (drums/vocals) born 3 March 1947, Rob Davis (lead guitar/vocals) born 1 October 1947, and Ray Stiles (bass guitar/vocals) born 20 November 1946. All were born in Carshalton, Surrey, England. They were formed in February 1966, became professionals in 1968 and played mainly at local gigs, etc. All had played in different groups before Mud's formation. They made their first disc for CBS in 1966 and another in 1968, followed by two for Philips in 1969 and 1970. In 1973 they recorded for RAK Records and came up with a success – 'Crazy' in 1973, by Britain's top songwriters Chinn and Chapman, who also wrote their next two successes 'Hypnosis' (1973) and 'Dyna-mite' (1973). Then came 'Tiger Feet' which sold over 500,000 in Britain and amassed a million sale globally. The group later signed with RCA Records.

OLIVIA NEWTON-JOHN

IF YOU LOVE ME LET ME KNOW *MCA* [*USA*]. Written by John Rostill, this was released in the U.S.A. in March 1974, rising to No 5 for two weeks and staying 20 weeks in the charts. R.I.A.A. Gold Disc award on 26 July 1974.

Olivia's natural follow-up to 'Let Me Be There' and with her career wide open on both the pop and country fronts, this new single was an inevitable million seller.

IF YOU LOVE ME LET ME KNOW (album) *MCA* [*USA*]. Released in the U.S.A. in May 1974, this went to No 1 for one week and stayed 61 weeks in the charts. R.I.A.A. Gold Disc award on 9 September 1974. Grammy Awards: Best Selling Album by a Female Artist, 1974; Best Selling Album by a Female Country Artist, 1974.

A superlative album by Olivia with the million (platinum) sale by November 1974, and the best album of 1974 for a female singer in the U.S.A.

It contained: (*) 'If You Love Me Let Me Know' (John Rostill); (*) 'I Honestly Love You' (P. Allen and John Barry); 'God Only Knows' (Tony Asher and Brian Wilson, 1966); 'You Ain't Got the Right'; 'Country Girl'; 'Free the People'; 'Mary Skeffington'; 'Home Ain't Home Any More'; 'River's Too Wide'; 'Changes'. (* denotes sold a million as a single disc.)

The album was produced by John Farrar.

I HONESTLY LOVE YOU *MCA* [*USA*]. Written by P. Allen and John Barry, this was released in the U.S.A. in August 1974, going to No 1 for two weeks and staying 15 weeks in the charts. R.I.A.A. Gold Disc award on 9 October 1974. Grammy Awards: Record of the Year, 1974; Best Pop Vocal Performance, Female, 1974.

Culled from Olivia's album 'If You Love Me Let Me Know', this million seller was a tender love song with a simple arrangement. Produced by John Farrar.

THE OHIO PLAYERS (septet)

SKIN TIGHT (album) *Mercury* [*USA*]. Released in the U.S.A. in April 1974, this climbed to No 8 for two weeks, staying 48 weeks in the charts. R.I.A.A. Gold Disc award on 28 June 1974.

This group, based in Dayton, Ohio (hence their name), consists of Clarence 'Satch' Satchell (tenor/soprano/baritone saxes, trumpet/flute/trombone), Marshall 'Rock' Jones (bass guitar), Ralph 'Pee Wee' Meadowbrook (trumpet/trombone/alto and tenor sax), Billy Beck (piano/organ/clarinet/synthesizer), Marvin 'Merv' Pierce (trumpet/valve trombone/flugelhorn), Leroy 'Sugar' Bonner (lead guitar) and Jimmy 'Diamond' Williams (drums/congas).

They are the residue of two local Dayton bands after being fired around 1968. In 1970 they made their first recordings, and then went back to college until 1971 and made an album at the small Westbound Studio, but it was not until 1973 that their second album 'Pleasure' gave them a hit with a single from it – 'Funky Worm'. In 1974, they signed with Mercury Records and their 'Skin Tight' album was a big hit, selling the million by January 1975. The Ohio Players then became a valuable property and with their brand of black rock 'n' roll achieved national prominence at year's end, with two gold singles and two platinum albums.

Their compositions are worked on in the studio sessions without any set ideas until sufficient tracks are approved to constitute an album. All members of the group share in the vocals.

Contents included: 'Streakin' Cheek to Cheek'; 'Heaven Must Be Like This'; 'Is Anybody Gonna be Saved?'; 'Jive Turkey'; 'It's Your Night/Words of Love' and 'Skin Tight'. All songs written by the group.

SKIN TIGHT *Mercury* [*USA*]. Written by The Ohio Players and released in the U.S.A. in July 1974, this reached No 11 for one week and stayed 16 weeks in the charts. R.I.A.A. Gold Disc award on 25 October 1974.

This funk-flavoured tune with powerful horn instrumentation and tight vocals was culled from their album of the same title, and sold a million within three months on the U.S.A. market.

FIRE (Album) *Mercury* [*USA*]. Released in the U.S.A. in November 1974, this achieved No 1 for one week, staying 29 weeks in the charts. R.I.A.A. Gold Disc award on 13 December 1974.

Another strong package from The Ohio Players. It sold a very quick million.

Contents included: 'Smoke'; 'Fire'; 'It's All Over'; 'I Want to be Free'; 'Runnin' From the Devil' and 'What the Hell'. All written by the group.

FIRE *Mercury* [*USA*]. Written by The Ohio Players and released in the U.S.A. in November 1974, this single hit No 1 for one week, staying ten weeks in the charts. R.I.A.A. Gold Disc award on 23 January 1975.

The title track from their album sold a million in less than three months.

THE O'JAYS

FOR THE LOVE OF MONEY *Philadelphia-International* [*USA*]. Written by Kenny Gamble and Leon Huff, this was released in the U.S.A. in April 1974. It got to No 7 for two weeks, staying 16 weeks in the charts. R.I.A.A. Gold Disc award on 12 June 1974.

Culled from the O'Jays' fine album 'Ship Ahoy'. Another huge success for the O'Jays and their producer/writers Gamble and Huff, with a million sale.

MIKE OLDFIELD

TUBULAR BELLS *Virgin* [*Britain*] *Atlantic* [*USA*]. Written by Mike Oldfield and released in the U.S.A. in February 1974, this went to No 5 for two weeks and stayed 16 weeks in the charts. It was No 31 in Britain. Grammy Award: Best Instrumental Composition, 1974.

Used as the theme for the film *The Exorcist*, it became known to thousands of people as a result of its inclusion in the soundtrack. The million sale of this cut from the album of the same title was reported in the U.S.A. in August 1974. It also sold a great number in other countries. (See also Mike Oldfield, 1973.)

DONNY AND MARIE OSMOND

I'M LEAVING IT ALL UP TO YOU *MGM* [*USA*]. Written by Don F. Harris and Dewey Terry, Jr (1957), this was released in the U.S.A. and Britain in June 1974. It went to No 1 for one week in the U.S.A. and No 2 for one week in Britain, remaining ten weeks in the U.S. charts and 16 weeks in the British best-sellers. R.I.A.A. Gold Disc award on 20 September 1974.

Originally a hit for Dale and Grace in 1963, this revival by Donny and Marie Osmond made it a million seller all over again.

PAPER LACE (pop quintet)

THE NIGHT CHICAGO DIED *Bus Stop* [*Britain*] *Mercury* [*USA*]. Written by Peter Callender and Mitch Murray, this was released in Britain in May 1974 and in the U.S.A. in June 1974. It went to No 3 for one week in Britain and No 1 for one week in the U.S.A., remaining 18 weeks in the U.S. charts and 11 weeks in the British lists. R.I.A.A. Gold Disc award on 9 August 1974.

Paper Lace are: Michael Vaughan (lead guitar/vocals) born Sheffield, Yorkshire, 27 July 1950; Cliff Fish (bass guitar/vocals) born Ripley, Derbyshire, 13 August 1949; Philip Wright (drums/lead vocals) born Nottingham, 9 April 1948; Chris Morris (guitar/vocals) born Nottingham, 1 November 1954; Carlo Santana (guitar/vocals) born near Rome, Italy, 29 June 1947.

They were formed in 1969, with a resident engagement at Tiffany's in Rochdale. The band's name came from Nottingham, the lace city. Their first broadcast was in the BBC's 'Terry Wogan Show' (1970) and first TV in 'Crackerjack' on the BBC (1970). In early 1974, they appeared in ITV's popular contest show 'Opportunity Knocks', which they won, this giving them national fame. In the show they sang 'Billy, Don't Be A Hero' (also written by Murray and Callender who had signed them to their record company Bus Stop). This song was a big hit in Britain and in the U.S.A. (see Bo Donaldson, 1974) and was thus a dual success for Paper Lace and the writer/producers. The follow-up, 'The Night Chicago Died', a strong novelty number taking the idea of the Roaring Twenties and the excitement of that era, was firstly a hit in Britain and a little later top of the charts in the U.S.A. This was an astonishing achievement, as Paper Lace triumphed in the U.S.A. at virtually the first attempt where so many other English groups of a similar mould had failed.

The disc sold over two million in the U.S.A. and globally around three million. The writers had written million sellers for other British artists from 1965 including 'Even the Bad Times are Good'.

Paper Lace subsequently made tours abroad, including the U.S.A. in 1975, and appeared in a Royal Variety Performance before Queen Elizabeth II.

ELVIS PRESLEY

ELVIS PRESLEY'S 40 GREATEST HITS *Arcade* [*Britain*]. Released in Britain in November 1974, this anthology went to No 1 for 11 weeks and stayed for 18 weeks in the charts.

This compilation of Elvis' Gold Discs was released in Britain only by Arcade label via an arrangement with RCA. It was a tremendous seller over the Christmas period, and sold over 1,500,000 in Britain.

BILLY PRESTON

NOTHING FROM NOTHING *A & M* [*USA*]. Released in the U.S.A. in June 1974, this hit No 1 for one week and stayed 20 weeks in the charts. R.I.A.A. Gold Disc award on 16 October 1974.

Billy sings this in virtually a jazz style, and includes some very fine piano inserts and a fine rhythm and orchestra section. A worthy million-seller for this experienced artist. The disc is a cut from his album 'The Kids and Me', and written by Billy Preston and B. Fisher.

SUZI QUATRO

DEVIL GATE DRIVE *RAK* [*Britain*]. Written by Nicky Chinn and Mike Chapman, this was released in Britain in February 1975 and in the U.S.A. in September 1974. It went to No 1 for three weeks in Britain, staying 11 weeks in the charts.

Third million-seller globally for Suzi Quatro and another hit for the English writers Chinn and Chapman.

It was very popular in Britain, but only mildly so in the U.S.A. As well as singing lead vocals, Suzi Quatro is a fine bass player.

ARIEL RAMIREZ (pianist)

MISA CRIOLLA (album) *Phonogram-Internat-Phillips* [*Holland*]. Argentinian pianist/composer Ariel Ramirez is a folk music expert. He visited many countries, and in 1962 was signed to the Philips label, subsequently producing the bestselling albums 'Coronacion del Folklore' and 'The Folk Mass'. He is also a theatre show producer. He recorded albums with Los Fronterizos, Eduardo Falu and Jaime Torores. In 1966 he produced 'Los Caudillos', another epic album.

'Misa Criolla' was first broadcast on Argentinian radio in 1966, when thousands of listeners demanded an immediate repeat. The radio station were forced to do this after their 'official' closedown - a unique occurrence in the history of sound broadcasting. Since then it was a huge success with listeners throughout the world. Ramirez' disc of the work sold a million and was presented with a platinum award in Holland, August 1974.

REDBONE (vocal & instrumental quartet)

COME AND GET YOUR LOVE *Epic* [*USA*]. Written by Lolly Vegas, this was released in the U.S.A. in January 1974, going to No 5 for two weeks and staying in the charts for 24 weeks. R.I.A.A. Gold Disc award on 22 April 1974.

Redbone are two brothers Lolly and Pat Vegas (guitar and bass), Tony Bellamy (guitar), Pete De Poe (drums). They claim to be the first genuine Red Indian band. De Poe was born on a reservation, the others are city Indians. They were formed in 1968 when they met in a West Coast club, and took their name from the cajun word for half-breed. The Vegas brothers' songs were sung by P. J. Proby, Bobbie Gentry, The Righteous Brothers and Aretha Franklin, and they backed visiting artists such as Odetta and John Lee Hooker on the West Coast. Their first album was 'Redbone' (1970), then 'Potlatch' (1970) and the third, 'Witch Queen of New Orleans', contained a single of the same title that was a hit in Britain in 1971, when they subsequently toured there. Following albums were 'Already Here' (1972), 'Wovoka' (1974) and 'Beaded Dreams Through Turquoise Eyes' (1974).

This million seller 'Come and Get Your Love' was their first in that category. The band introduced new rhythm to rock with a jerky cajun beat - a mixture of black and tribal influences. Lolly Vegas and Pete Welding co-produced their albums.

HELEN REDDY

ANGIE BABY *Capitol* [*USA*]. Written by A. O'Day and released in the U.S.A. in October 1974, this reached No 1 for one week, staying 17 weeks in the charts. It was No 5 and ten weeks in the British charts (1975). R.I.A.A. Gold Disc award on 13 January 1975.

Taken from her album 'Free and Easy', this haunting tune has an infectious lyric line. Helen's vocal is sparkling and the disc has a subtle instrumentation. In December 1974, Helen was sworn in as a United States citizen, eight years after she arrived in the U.S.A. with practically nothing, and wondering whether she had any future. This million seller and her previous big successes certainly proved that she had.

THE RUBETTES (vocal & instrumental quintet)

SUGAR BABY LOVE *Polydor* [*USA*]. Written by Wayne Bickerton and Tony Waddington, this was released in Britain in May 1974 and in the U.S.A. in June 1974. It reached No 1 for four weeks in Britain and No 24 for one week in the U.S.A. It also stayed ten weeks in the British charts and 15 weeks in the U.S.A. topsellers.

Rubettes are Alan Williams (guitar/flute/piano) born Welwyn Garden City, Hertfordshire, 22 December 1950; Tony Thorpe (guitar/piano/drums) born London, 20 July 1947; Mick Clarke (bass guitar) born Grimsby, 10 August 1946; Bill Hurd (keyboards) born East Ham, London, 11 August 1948; John Richardson (drums) born Dagenham, Essex, 3 May 1947.

They all knew each other for a number of years through playing on sessions and in different bands together. In early 1974 they were making a number of demo discs for Wayne Bickerton (of Polydor) and asked if they could possibly record one of the songs. This they were allowed to do a little later with Alan

Williams as lead vocalist. Wayne Bickerton (who wrote the song) also thought up the name Rubettes for the group. The disc was a very big success with over 500,000 in Britain sold and a reported global sale of three million. It is entertaining, dynamic and extremely commercial.

RUFUS (featuring Chaka Khan) (sextet)
TELL ME SOMETHING GOOD *ABC* [*USA*]. Written by Stevie Wonder and released in the U.S.A. in June 1974, this went to No 1 for one week, staying 19 weeks in the charts. R.I.A.A. Gold Disc award on 9 August 1974.

From 1967 to 1970, this group were known as American Breed before most of its members left. In its place, Ask Rufus emerged as the new band performing in clubs in Chicago. Some new members were added and it became Rufus. Their black girl lead singer, Chaka Khan, got involved with Rufus around 1972 when she was 18, and since then the rise of Chaka's and Rufus' popularity was phenomenal. Their first album 'Rufus' did not include Chaka, but just the five male members. The group went through some personnel changes and by 1974 became Rufus (featuring Chaka Khan) – its complement of musicians being founder member Kevin Murphy (organist); André Fischer (drums); Tony Maiden (guitar); Nate Morgan (electric piano); Bobby Watson (bass). It was Chaka who persuaded Stevie Wonder to write 'Tell Me Something Good' which gave them their first million seller single. This was also included on their second album 'Rags to Rufus'. They made personal appearances with such headliners as Stevie Wonder, Sly & The Family Stone, The O'Jays and Marvin Gaye, earning them tumultuous ovations and rave reviews. Their sound is a mixture of rhythm-and-blues, mixed with rock, mixed with jazz which they describe as 'Krudde', which really means funky in all terms – black, white or brown.

RAGS TO RUFUS (Album) *ABC* [*USA*]. Released in the U.S.A. in May 1974, this rose to No 4 for one week, staying 30 weeks in the charts. R.I.A.A. Gold Disc award on 5 September 1974.

This group's first million seller album, with the dynamic lead singer Chaka Khan. It sold a million in 40 days.

The album included: 'You Got Love'; 'I Got the Right Street'; 'Walkin' the Sun'; 'Rags to Rufus' (instrumental); 'Swing Down Chariot'; 'Sideways' (instrumental); 'Ain't Nothin' but a Maybe'; 'Tell Me Something Good' (Stevie Wonder); 'Look Through My Eyes'; 'In Love We Grow'; 'Smokin' Room'.

RUFUSIZED (album) *ABC* [*USA*]. Released in the U.S.A. in December 1974, this went to No 6 for two weeks, staying 24 weeks in the charts. R.I.A.A. Gold Disc on 27 December 1974.

Another very quick million-seller for Rufus/Chaka Khan. The album reflected the new rhythm-and-blues sound that took the U.S.A. by storm. With this, their third million seller of 1974, they proved to be one of the most outstanding groups of the time, and Chaka Khan emerged as one of the premiere female vocalists of the year.

Contents included: 'Once You Get Started'; 'Somebody's Watching'; 'Pack'd My Bags'; 'Your Smile'; 'Rufusized'; 'I'm a Woman'; 'Right Is Right'; 'Half Moon'; 'Please Pardon Me'; 'Stop on By'.

BOBBY SETTER & HIS CASH & CARRY
TCHIP TCHIP *Cannon* [*Belgium*] *Tara* [*USA*]. Written by Werner Thomas and T. Rendall, this was released in Belgium in early 1974 and in the U.S.A. in March 1974. It reached No 2 in Belgium.

An instrumental disc that sold a million in Europe. It was Louis van Rijmenant, President of Eurovox, who first heard the tune played by composer/accordionist Werner Thomas in a hotel bar in Davos, Switzerland in March 1973. The disc was released in the U.S.A. with fair success.

In 1981 it was revived in Britain by The Tweets and was a big success. Its infectious melody inspired the 'Birdie Dance', which became a positive disease all over Europe with recordings under the title 'Birdie Song'.

CARLY SIMON AND JAMES TAYLOR
MOCKINGBIRD *Elektra* [*USA*]. Written by Inez and Charlie Foxx (1963), this was released in the U.S.A. in January 1974. It went to No 3 for two weeks, staying for 16 weeks in the charts. It was No 34 in Britain. R.I.A.A. Gold Disc award on 14 May 1974.

A new version of the Inez Foxx hit of 1963 by Carly and her husband James, taken from her album 'Hotcakes'. Beautiful vocal interchange between the duo and a Dixieland horn arrangement gave the disc wide appeal, and subsequent million sale.

RAY STEVENS
THE STREAK *Barnaby* [*USA*] *Janus* [*Britain*]. Written by Ray Stevens and released in the U.S.A. in April 1974 and in Britain in May 1974, this hit No 1 for three weeks in the U.S.A. and two weeks in Britain. It stayed 17 weeks in the U.S. charts and 12

weeks in the British lists. R.I.A.A. Gold Disc award on 24 April 1974.

In the U.S.A., a new craze started with streakers dashing about in the nude. Ray Stevens, a master at mocking trends, captured the streaking craze with this humorous country disc. The disc 'streaked' into the charts and sold a million after only three weeks on the U.S. market. It also had a good sale in Britain. Global sale was four million.

BARBRA STREISAND

THE WAY WE WERE (Album) *Columbia* [*USA*]. Released in the U.S.A. in February 1974, this went to No 1 for two weeks, staying 30 weeks in the charts. R.I.A.A. Gold Disc award on 26 February 1974.

Barbra Streisand's film success *The Way We Were* resulted in her making this album of the same title. This was also a tremendous success for Barbra, and sold over a million by mid-June 1974. It is one of the 19 albums she had recorded for Columbia Records, all of them certified gold by R.I.A.A. up to the end of 1975. The album included: 'The Way We Were'; 'All in Love is Fair' (Stevie Wonder); 'What Are You Doing the Rest of Your Life?' (M. and A. Bergman and Michel Legrand); 'Summer Me, Winter Me' (M. and A. Bergman and Michel Legrand); 'The Best Thing You've Ever Done'; 'I've Never Been a Woman Before'; 'Pieces of Dreams'; 'Being at War with Each Other'.

THE STYLISTICS

YOU MAKE ME FEEL BRAND NEW *Avco* [*USA*]. Written by Thom Bell and Linda Creed, this plaintive song was released in the U.S.A. in March 1974 and in Britain in July 1974. It went to No 1 for one week in the U.S.A. and No 2 for two weeks in Britain. It stayed for 25 weeks in the U.S. charts and 14 weeks in the British bestsellers. R.I.A.A. Gold Disc award on 22 May 1974.

The sixth million-seller for The Stylistics. This is possibly their best track ever released as a single, taken from their album 'Let's Put It All Together'. Produced by Thom Bell.

BILLY SWAN

I CAN HELP *Monument* [*USA*]. Written by Billy Swan and released in the U.S.A. in September 1974 and in Britain in December 1974, this rose to No 1 for two weeks in the U.S.A. and No 6 for two weeks in Britain. It stayed 18 weeks in the U.S. charts and eight weeks in the British topsellers. R.I.A.A. Gold Disc award on 2 December 1974.

Billy Swan was born in Cape Girardeau, Missouri, on 12 May 1943. He became interested in music through listening to Hank Williams on radio, and by an uncle who played saxophone. Jerry Lee Lewis and Buddy Holly made him want to play rock'n'roll, so at 14 he took up drums and hitchhiked to local gigs. He later taught himself electric piano, organ and rhythm guitar. A trip to Memphis with some friends who were to record with Bill Black resulted in Billy getting Black to record 'Lover Please', one of his songs. This wasn't a hit till later when it was cut by Clyde McPhatter. After a stint of two years with Mirt Mirley & The Rhythm Steppers, Billy moved to Nashville, quit playing and toured as road manager for singer Mel Tillis. He also had a job sweeping floors and moving mikes around Columbia's studios.

His first break came from Fred Foster of Monument Records who allowed Billy to produce records. He also toured briefly with Kinky Friedman and Billy Joe Shaver, and worked closely with the then struggling Kris Kristofferson. Returning to Nashville, he went back to Monument Records to make his debut as artist. With over ten years extensive musical education in Nashville, his artistry was apparent, and 'I Can Help' became a big hit with over the million sale in the U.S.A. and over 250,000 in Britain.

Billy's genius influenced many other songwriters who held him in high esteem. This they showed by writing him into their songs. Kristofferson and Roger Miller were two of the stars who paid him this high tribute.

SWEET

TEENAGE RAMPAGE *RCA* [*Britain*]. Written by Nicky Chinn and Mike Chapman, this was released in Britain in January 1974 and in the U.S.A. in February 1974. It went to No 1 for one week in Britain, staying eight weeks in the charts.

Sweet's biggest seller so far, over 500,000 in Britain and a million plus globally. Over 200,000 were sold in Britain in its first week. Another triumph for writers Chinn and Chapman.

SYLVIA

Y VIVA ESPANA *Sonet* [*Sweden*]. Written by Leo Rozenstraten and Leo Caerts, this was released in Britain in August 1974. It went to No 4 for three weeks and stayed 28 weeks in the charts.

'Y Viva Espana' has a remarkable international history. It was written by two Belgians and first recorded there by Samantha – a big hit with 26 weeks in their charts and 130,000 sales. In Germany it was a big hit for Dutch girl Imca Marina, and there were 56 cover versions in that country including one by James Last. Total sales in Germany went over 1,500,000. In both Sweden and Spain it was a chart topper. It was, however, the Sonet version by Sylvia that really established its great popularity. Sylvia, real name Sylvia Vrethammar, one of Sweden's top female singers, got it into the British charts after it had been No 1 in her own country. She first sang it in 1972 while working in the Canary Islands. It soon became a kind of 'national anthem' in Spain where it had a big success through Samantha's version with Spanish lyrics.

A happy, holiday sing-along type of song, it rapidly became popular throughout Europe, mainly via holidaymakers who heard it played and sung everywhere. Sylvia's version was a huge success in Britain, selling well over 250,000, and globally it easily passed the million. The English lyrics were written by Eddie Seago.

THE THREE DEGREES (vocal trio)

WHEN WILL I SEE YOU AGAIN? *Philadelphia-International* [*USA*]. Written by Kenny Gamble and Leon Huff, this was released in Britain in July 1974 and in the U.S.A. in September 1974. It went to No 1 for four weeks in Britain and one week in the U.S.A. It stayed 16 weeks in the British charts and 18 weeks

in the U.S. bestsellers. R.I.A.A. Gold Disc award on 9 December 1974.

The Three Degrees – Fayette Pinkney, Valeria Holiday and Sheila Ferguson – were formed around 1968; Fay and Sheila are from Philadelphia, Valeria from Boston. They were compared to The Supremes, but it took them five years to be recognized as stars in their own right. Strangely it was the popularity of this disc in Britain that finally set the seal on their career where it reached the top of the charts and sold over 500,000 before its release in the U.S.A. where it repeated that success. It was another triumph also for the writers and the label. The Three Degrees regard themselves as being closely allied to the whole Philadelphia sound. The disc, culled from their album, released in England during the trio's tour there, has a great arrangement and strong vocal performance, with the usual excellent Gamble/Huff production.

Helen Scott subsequently replaced Sheila Ferguson.

THREE DOG NIGHT

THE SHOW MUST GO ON *ABC/Dunhill* [*USA*]. Written by D. Courtney and Leo Sayer, this was released in the U.S.A. in February 1974, going to No 1 for one week and staying 19 weeks in the charts. R.I.A.A. Gold Disc award on 14 May 1974.

This million seller for Three Dog Night is a great fun song with a circus atmosphere in the music. It had previously been a hit for British singer/writer Leo Sayer in England. Three Dog Night took it to further heights.

FRANKIE VALLI

MY EYES ADORED YOU *Private Stock* [*USA*]. Written by Bob Crewe and Kenny Nolan, this was released in the U.S.A. in November and in Britain in January 1975. It went to No 1 for one week in the U.S.A. and No 3 for one week in Britain. It stayed 26 weeks in the U.S. charts and 11 weeks in the British lists. R.I.A.A. Gold Disc award on 1 April 1975.

The first million-selling single for Private Stock Records in less than six months of active operation. A mellow ballad sung by Frankie Valli (of The Four Seasons) and written and produced by Bob Crewe, who used to do all The Four Seasons songs.

BOBBY VINTON

MY MELODY OF LOVE *ABC* [*USA*]. Written by H. Mayer and Bobby Vinton, this was released in the U.S.A. in August 1974, going to No 1 for one week and staying 20 weeks in the charts. R.I.A.A. Gold Disc award on 5 December 1974.

Bobby Vinton's most commercial disc for several years, his last big hit having been in 1968. 'My Melody of Love' has a strong international flavouring. Bobby went to a Polish school for eight years and learned how to speak Polish, which accounts for this bilingual disc.

WAR

WAR – LIVE (Album) *United Artists* [*USA*]. Written by War and released in the U.S.A. in March 1974, this went to No 10 for two weeks and stayed 35 weeks in the charts. R.I.A.A. Gold Disc award on 13 March 1974.

Another million-selling (platinum) disc for this talented group, including their hits. It sold two million by July 1974 and was gold almost on release. United Artists announced that up to this time War's sales were an unprecedented $33,640,000 for five albums and five singles. No large progressive black ensemble had ever achieved sales of a similar nature.

This album included: 'All Day Music'; (*) 'Cisco Kid'; 'Lonely Feelin''; (*) 'Slippin into Darkness'; 'Son Oh Son' (10½ minutes' duration); 'Get Down' (20½ minutes duration). (* denotes single million seller.)

DIONNE WARWICKE & THE DETROIT SPINNERS

THEN CAME YOU *Atlantic* [*USA*]. Written by S. Marshall and P. Hugh, and released in the U.S.A. in July 1974, this went

to No 1 for one week, staying 17 weeks in the charts. It was No 29 in Britain. R.I.A.A. Gold Disc award on 8 October 1974.

Great arrangement, both musically and vocally, matching the performance of these two hit-making entities. Dionne added the 'e' to her surname from this recording onwards. The disc sold a million in three months.

BARRY WHITE

CAN'T GET ENOUGH OF YOUR LOVE, BABE *20th Century* [*USA*] *Pye* [*Britain*]. Written by Barry White and released in the U.S.A. in July 1974 and in Britain in August 1974, this went to No 1 for one week in the U.S.A. and No 5 for one week in Britain. It stayed 15 weeks in the U.S. charts and 12 weeks in the British lists. R.I.A.A. Gold Disc award on 11 September 1974.

Another million seller for superstar Barry White, in the tradition he began in 1973. He is assisted by The Love Unlimited Orchestra.

YOU'RE THE FIRST, THE LAST, MY EVERYTHING *20th Century* [*USA*] *Pye* [*Britain*]. Written by Barry White, T. Sepe and P.S. Radcliffe, this was released in the U.S.A. and Britain in October 1974. It went to No 1 for one week in the U.S.A. and two weeks in Britain, staying 17 weeks in the U.S. charts and 14 weeks in the British lists. R.I.A.A. Gold Disc award on 18 December 1974.

Another million seller for Barry, culled from his 'Can't Get Enough' album, again accompanied by The Love Unlimited Orchestra, with lush orchestration.

CAN'T GET ENOUGH (Album) *20th Century* [*USA*]. Written by Barry White and released in the U.S.A. in August 1974. It reached No 1 for a week and was in the charts for 28 weeks. R.I.A.A. Gold Disc award on 19 September 1974.

A superlative album by Barry White, containing his usual self-penned songs of love and performed in his inimitable style. It included: (*) 'You're the First, the Last, My Everything'; 'I Can't Believe You Love Me'; (*) 'Can't Get Enough of Your Love, Babe'; 'Mellow Mood'; 'Oh Love, Well We Finally Made It'; 'I Love You More Than Anything'.

(* sold a million as a single.)

The million sale of this album was reported in January 1976.

BOBBY WOMACK

LOOKIN' FOR A LOVE *United Artists* [*USA*]. Written by J.W. Alexander and Z. Samuels (1972) this was released in the U.S.A. in January 1974, going to No 8 for one week and staying 19 weeks in the charts.

The song was successfully recorded in 1972 by The J. Geils Band. Bobby Womack's pop version with this funky number sold a million by 8 April 1974, when it was awarded an R.I.A.A. Gold Disc.

STEVIE WONDER

FULFILLINGNESS FIRST FINALE (Album) *Tamla* [*USA*]. Released in the U.S.A. in August 1974, this was at No 1 for four weeks, staying 50 weeks in the charts. Grammy Awards: Album of the Year, 1974; Best Pop Vocal Performance (Male), 1974.

This album is supposed to mark the end of the first phase of Stevie's musical career. Two of the songs from it were single million sellers, while the album itself easily exceeded the million.

Contents included: 'Boogie on Reggae Woman'; 'You Haven't Done Nothin''; 'Too Shy to Say'; 'Bird of Beauty'; 'High Fidelity'. All songs by Stevie Wonder.

YOU HAVEN'T DONE NOTHIN' *Tamla* [*USA*]. Written by Stevie Wonder and released in the U.S.A. in August 1974, this hit No 1 for one week and stayed 22 weeks in the charts.

Culled from Stevie's magnificent album 'Fulfillingness First

Finale', this is a track with memories of the earlier 'Superstition'. The first million seller from the album to sell a million, by December 1974.

BOOGIE ON REGGAE WOMAN *Tamla* [*USA*]. Written by Stevie Wonder and released in the U.S.A. in November 1974, this also hit No 1 for one week, staying 18 weeks in the charts.

Grammy Award: Best Rhythm-and-Blues Performance (Male), 1974.

The second cut from Stevie's album 'Fulfillingness First Finale' to sell over a million, by January 1975. The disc has a Jamaican motif, and Stevie brings his 'Fingertips' facile harmonica style back in the spotlight.

ORIGINAL FILM SOUNDTRACK

TOMMY (rock opera) (Double album) *Polydor* [*Britain & USA*]. Written by Pete Townshend with additional songs by John Entwhistle and Keith Moon (of The Who) this was released in the U.S.A. and Britain in March 1975. It went to No 2 for one week in the U.S.A. and No 10 for one week in Britain, staying 35 weeks in the U.S. charts and seven weeks in the British lists. R.I.A.A. Gold Disc award on 18 March 1975.

This double album is the third time round for the unique rock opera *Tommy*. The film, produced by the Robert Stigwood Organization, was directed by Ken Russell, with a star-studded cast, and had a twin premiere on 19 March 1975 in New York and Los Angeles, and on 26 March 1975 at London's Leicester Square Theatre. It features Roger Daltrey (of The Who) in the title role, Eric Clapton as the Preacher, Keith Moon as Uncle Ernie, Elton John as Pinball Wizard, Oliver Reed as Tommy's Stepfather, Robert Powell as Tommy's Father, Ann-Margret as Tommy's Mother, Tina Turner as the Acid Queen, Jack Nicholson as the Specialist, and The Who, the Rock Band.

The album contained all the familiar numbers as originally written and played by The Who (see 1969), and there are actually 32 tunes in all, for this film version. It was certified gold immediately and the million (platinum status) was achieved by November 1975.

The album included three new Pete Townshend songs which were not in the original *Tommy* score: 'Mother and Son', 'Champagne' and 'Bernie's Holiday Camp', and two other numbers by The Who.

The film is said to have cost over $3 million to produce, and Polydor Records were reported as paying $1 million for the soundtrack rights. The album of the soundtrack took several months to record, under the direct attention of Pete Townshend.

VARIOUS ARTISTS

CADEAU DE LA VIE (Album) (Gift of Life) *Pathe/Marconi/EMI* [*France*].

Produced and sold for the UNESCO campaign for the benefit of the Cancer Research Association, this album sold the million by 1979. The Association's President, Mr Crozemarie, received three gold records and a 200,000 franc cheque from EMI director Michel Bonnet on behalf of the authors, composers, publishers and artists of Pathe/Marconi/EMI, all of whom had waived royalties and fees.

ABBA

ABBA (Album) *Polar* [*Sweden*] *Epic* [*Britain*]. Released in Sweden in March 1975 and in Britain in February 1976, this went to No 10 for one week in Britain, lasting 10 weeks in the charts.

ABBA's first album was a colossal success throughout Europe in 1975, selling four million before release in Britain. There were four titles therein which sold a million each as single discs.

Contents of the album: (*) 'Mamma Mia'; 'Hey Hey Helen'; 'Tropical Loveland'; (*)'S.O.S.'; 'Man in the Middle'; 'Bang-a-Boomerang'; (*)'I Do, I Do, I Do'; 'Rock Me'; 'Intermezzo No 1'; 'I've Been Waiting for You'; (*)'So Long'.

(* sold a million as a single.)

All songs by Benny Andersson, Stig Anderson and Bjorn Ulvaeus.

I DO, I DO, I DO *Polar* [*Sweden*]. Written by B. Andersson, S. Anderson and B. Ulvaeus, this was released in Scandinavia (excluding Sweden). It was No 38 in Britain.

The fourth singles million seller for European group ABBA. Sales of this disc were 2,500,000, mainly in Europe.

S.O.S. *Polar* [*Sweden*] *Epic* [*Britain*]. Written by B. Andersson, S. Anderson and B. Ulvaeus, this was released in Britain in September 1975 and in the U.S.A. in August 1975. It went to No 4 for one week in Britain and No 10 for two weeks in the U.S.A. It stayed in the British charts for ten weeks and the U.S. bestsellers for 26 weeks.

The second of ABBA's discs to break into the U.S. and British charts. It was another triumph for the group, mainly in Europe where it sold four million.

MAMMA MIA *Polar* [*Sweden*] *Epic* [*Britain*]. Written by B. Andersson, S. Anderson and B. Ulvaeus, this was released in Scandinavia (excluding Sweden), and in Britain in December 1975. It went to No 1 for three weeks in Britain, staying 14 weeks in the charts.

European sales of this disc were 3,500,000, with over 500,000 in Britain alone, where ABBA's popularity was immense.

ABBA GREATEST HITS *Polar* [*Sweden*] *Epic* [*Britain*] *Atlantic* [*USA*]. Released in Sweden in 1975, in Britain in March 1976 and in the U.S.A. in September 1976. It reached No 1 for 13 weeks in Britain and No 56 in the U.S.A. It stayed in the British charts for 115 weeks (to June 1978) and for 28 weeks in the U.S. lists. R.I.A.A. Gold Disc award on 30 December 1976.

The fantastic success of this album brought international fame to ABBA. It sold over 1,500,000 in Britain alone, was at the top of the charts for three months, and kept on selling into 1978. In the U.S.A. it went gold and sold over 500,000 there. Global sales were well over 6,000,000. The album contained no fewer than seven titles each of which sold a million as single release.

Complete contents: (*)'S.O.S.'; 'He Is Your Brother'; 'Ring Ring'; 'Another Town, Another Train'; (*)'Honey Honey'; (*)'So Long'; (*)'Mamma Mia'; (*)'I Do, I Do, I Do'; 'People Need Love'; (*)'Waterloo'; 'Nina Pretty Ballerina'; 'Bang-a-Boomerang'; 'Dance (while the music still goes on)'; (*)'Fernando'.

(* denotes million-seller single 'Fernando' in 1976.)

Album produced by Benny Andersson and Bjorn Ulvaeus, and all songs written by Benny Andersson, Bjorn Ulvaeus and Stig Anderson. Australian sales of this album were over 900,000. It subsequently sold a million (by 1978) in U.S.A. with platinum R.I.A.A. award 20 July 1978.

AEROSMITH

TOYS IN THE ATTIC (Album) *Columbia* [*USA*]. Released in the U.S.A. in April 1975, this went to No 11 for one week, staying 60 weeks in the charts. R.I.A.A. Gold Disc award on 11 August 1975.

The third million seller (by December 1975) for this Boston-based 'heavy duty boogie band'. It included: 'Walk This Way'; 'Sweet Emotion'; 'You See Me Crying'; 'Uncle Salty'; 'Big 10-

Inch Record'; 'No More, No More'; 'Toys in the Attic'. All songs by Aerosmith.

MORRIS ALBERT

FEELINGS *Charger/RCA* [*USA*]. Written by Morris Albert and released in the U.S.A. in April 1975 and in Britain in September 1975, this achieved No 4 for one week in the U.S.A. and No 3 for two weeks in Britain. It stayed 32 weeks in the U.S. bestsellers and ten weeks in the British charts. R.I.A.A. Gold Disc award on 13 November 1975.

Singer/songwriter Morris Albert is a Brazilian, and his record of 'Feelings' had been No 1 in Brazil, Venezuela, Chile and Mexico before being rush-released on the American market by RCA. The success of this disc made Morris Albert an international star. The disc is a cut from his album of the same title, and was a bestseller in the U.S.A. for seven months.

AMERICA

HISTORY (America's Greatest Hits) (Album) *Warner* [*USA*]. Released in the U.S.A. in October 1975, this went to No 2 for four weeks, staying 49 weeks in the charts. R.I.A.A. Gold Disc award on 1 December 1975.

A fine album by this group who had many hits since breaking on to the disc scene in 1972. This album shows the progress of the trio from the pre-acoustic sound they started with to a much more varied musical approach. The million (platinum status) was achieved by January 1976.

Contents included: 'A Horse with No Name'; 'I Need You'; 'Ventura Highway'; 'Tin Man'; 'Sister Golden Hair'; 'Daisy Jane'; 'Sandman'; 'Lonely People'; 'Woman Tonight'.

Production was by George Martin (of Beatles fame) and all material written by the group.

BAD COMPANY

STRAIGHT SHOOTER (Album) *Swan Song* [*USA*]. Released in the U.S.A. in April 1975, this rose to No 3 for one week, staying 33 weeks in the charts. R.I.A.A. Gold Disc award on 8 May 1975.

The second million-selling album for Bad Company, the platinum status reported in 1976. The package shows off the exotic vocals and rock prowess of the quartet.

It included two outstanding tracks, 'Wild Fire Woman' and 'Good Lovin' Gone Bad', and other fine numbers. All material by Bad Company.

GEORGE BAKER SELECTION (quintet)

UNA PALOMA BLANCA (White Dove) *Negram* [*Holland*] *Warner* [*Germany*]. Written by Bouens (George Baker). This went to No 1 in Germany for 10 weeks, and topped the charts in Holland, Belgium, Switzerland, Austria, South Africa and New Zealand. It was released in Holland in April 1975.

This tune was a fantastic hit all over Europe and abroad. It sold over a million in Germany, and globally over four million. Vacationers in Europe were attracted by it immensely, and a successful cover version was put out in Britain, recorded by Jonathan King. It was George Baker Selection's biggest hit since his 'Little Green Bag' in 1970. It was also a sizeable hit in England, France and Italy. A most attractive melodic number.

JOAN BAEZ

DIAMONDS AND RUST (Album) *A & M* [*USA*]. Released in the U.S.A. in May 1975, this got to No 11 for one week, staying 46 weeks in the charts. R.I.A.A. Gold Disc award on 11 November 1975.

First big seller for Joan Baez of the many albums she has recorded, with sale of over a million on her new label.

It contained: 'Never Dreamed You'd Leave in Summer' (Stevie Wonder and Syreeta Wright); 'Blue Sky' (Richard Betts); 'Children and All That Jazz'; 'Diamonds and Rust'; 'Dida'; 'Fountain of Sorrow' (Jackson Browne); 'Hello in There' (John Prine); 'I Dream of Jeannie'/'Danny Boy' (Stephen C. Foster/

traditional); 'Jesse' (Janis Ian); 'Simple Twist of Fate' (Bob Dylan); 'Winds of the Old Days'.

Songs by Joan Baez unless otherwise indicated.

In this year, Joan Baez made a successful tour with Bob Dylan, and recorded another album, 'From Every Stage'.

BAY CITY ROLLERS (pop quintet)

BAY CITY ROLLERS (Album) *Arista* [*USA*]. Released in the U.S.A. in September 1975, this made its way to No 14 for one week, staying 33 weeks in the charts. R.I.A.A. Gold Disc award on 31 December 1975.

This album, released at the time The Bay City Rollers made their first tour of the U.S.A. (1975), contained all the hit songs that had made them the rulers of Britain's teenybopper kingdom. It sold half a million in the U.S.A. and global sales were reported in June 1977 at two million. All the recordings were originally made in Britain on the Bell label, and mostly produced by their writers Bill Martin and Phil Coulter.

Their hit numbers include: 'Keep on Dancing' (1971); 'We Can Make Music' (1972); 'Mañana' (1972); 'Saturday Night' (1973); 'Remember' (1973); 'Shang-a-Lang' (1974) 'Summer Love Sensation' (1974); 'All of Me Loves All of You' (1974); 'Bye Bye Baby' (1975); 'Give a Little Love' (1975); 'Money Honey' (1975).

BYE BYE BABY *Bell* [*Britain*]. Written by Bob Gaudio and Bob Crewe (1964) this was released in Britain in March 1975. It went to No 1 for six weeks, staying 15 weeks in the charts.

Bay City Rollers were formed in 1967 by brothers Derek and Alan Longmuir while at Tynecastle School in Edinburgh and were first called The Saxons. When they left school, they christened the group after an American place name. They stuck a pin in the map and it came down on Bay City; they added the word Rollers, unaware that Bay City was a popular surfing resort. Tam Paton, a resident band leader at Edinburgh Palais, got the Rollers their first booking at the city's Top Storey Club, and subsequently gave up his job to manage the group. The Rollers were heard by a Bell Records talent scout and they made their first disc 'Keep on Dancing' in 1971 which reached the Top 10. Changes in personnel had taken place between the band's formation and mid-1972. Eric Faulkner (guitar/violin) joined shortly after the first hit and toured with them through Europe and North Africa. In January 1973, founder-member Nobby Clarke and guitarist John Devine left The Rollers at the low ebb of their career and were replaced by Les McKeown (vocals/piano) and Stuart 'Woody' Wood (guitar). The band had released three singles in the meantime, and with the exception of 'Mañana' (their first success abroad, a No 1 in Israel and a chart hit in Germany, Belgium and France) it wasn't until The Rollers joined forces with the songwriting/producing team of Bill Martin and Phil Coulter (writers of the hit 'Puppet on a String') that hits in profusion came for the group. Their second collaboration 'Remember' (December 1973) heralded the start of The Year of the Rollers. In May 1974, 'Shang-a-Lang' was a hit followed by 'Summer Love Sensation' (August) and 'All of Me Loves All of You' (October) which sold almost 300,000 in Britain.

Their debut album 'Rollin'' hit the Top 20 in October 1974 at the time they embarked on their first headlining tour of Britain. This was an astounding tour with instant sell-outs to crowds of tartaned teenagers with scenes of wild enthusiasm unseen since the days of The Beatles and Rolling Stones. Their success was due to masses of emotion and energy that had been ignored since the days of teenybop hysteria. Thus was Rollermania born, the band greeted by screams, shouts and whistles – sheer hysteria. 'Bye Bye Baby', with its record-breaking six weeks as a chart topper, sold over a million – an incredible sale for Britain.

Their second album 'Once Upon a Star' (April 1975) shot up the charts to join 'Rollin'' and their second nationwide tour drew as many as 90,000 fans for one performance. The Bay City Rollers subsequently went to Australia and the U.S.A. where they repeated their fantastic success.

By the end of 1974 they had earned an estimated £750,000 in Britain alone, and were the top group of the year.

Personnel for this recording: Eric Faulkner (lead guitar/violin/mandolin), born Edinburgh, 21 October 1955; Stuart (Woody) Wood (guitar), born Edinburgh, 25 February 1957; Alan Longmuir (bass guitar/piano/accordion), born Edinburgh, 20 June 1950; Leslie McKeown (vocalist/guitar/piano), born Edinburgh, 12 November 1955; Derek Longmuir (drums), born Edinburgh, 19 March 1951.

SATURDAY NIGHT *Bell* [*Britain*] *Arista* [*USA*]. Written by Bill Martin and Phil Coulter (1973) and released in Britain in January 1973 and in the U.S.A. in October 1975, this reached No 1 for one week in the U.S.A., staying 20 weeks in the charts. R.I.A.A. Gold Disc award on 16 December 1975.

Originally recorded by The Bay City Rollers in 1973 in Britain, but not a success then. Their tour of the U.S.A. and the release of this disc with its two million plus sale brought the group world acclaim. This big sale was reported in January 1976.

THE BEACH BOYS

SPIRIT OF AMERICA (Double album) *Capitol* [*USA*]. Released in the U.S.A. in April 1975, this climbed to No 8 for two weeks, staying 30 weeks in the charts. R.I.A.A. Gold Disc award on 30 April 1975.

This package was both instant gold and instant platinum million seller. It included many Beach Boys gems such as: 'Dance, Dance, Dance'; 'The Little Girl I Once Knew'; 'Barbara Anne'; 'When I Grow Up' and '409'.

THE BEE GEES

MAIN COURSE (Album) *RSO/Atlantic* [*USA*]. Released in the U.S.A. in May 1975, this reached No 14 for one week, staying 47 weeks in the charts. R.I.A.A. Gold Disc award on 23 December 1975.

The Gibb brothers mix material embellished by disco-directed rhythm-and-blues with classic Bee Gees sounds. This album had sold a million by July 1976 and includes their big singles hit 'Jive Talkin'' and 'Come On Over', 'Nights on Broadway', 'Country Lanes'.

JIVE TALKIN' *RSO/Atlantic* [*USA*]. Written by Barry, Maurice and Robin Gibb, this was released in the U.S.A. in May 1975 and in Britain in June 1975. It went to No 1 for two weeks in the U.S.A. and No 3 for two weeks in Britain. It stayed 23 weeks in the U.S. charts and 10 weeks in the British bestsellers. R.I.A.A. Gold Disc award on 21 August 1975.

Another million seller for the Gibb brothers from their album 'Main Course'.

THE BLACKBYRDS (jazz/rock quintet)

WALKING IN RHYTHM *Fantasy* [*USA*]. Written by B. Perry, this was released in the U.S.A. in January 1975. It went to No 6 for two weeks, staying 17 weeks in the charts. It was No 23 in Britain.

The Blackbyrds were founded in 1973 by Donald Byrd, trumpet player, music instructor and director of jazz studies at Howard University, Washington, DC. The young black musicians, while remaining full-time students there, took the stage as a testing laboratory to develop Byrd's original theory of 'applied music' they had learned in the classroom. This resulted in three albums and two single records. The first album 'The Blackbyrds' on Fantasy label, broke into all the U.S. charts - jazz, soul and pop. 'Walking in Rhythm' is a cut from their second album 'Flying Start', described as 'a full-blown lyric and melodic concept, refreshing and catchy'. The group's skilful blending of jazz, rock and funk had great commercial appeal, and brought them national prominence.

With the aid of Donald Byrd, the group mastered the art of travelling while keeping their scholar status. The Blackbyrds are: Kevin Toney (band leader/keyboards) and Keith Killgo (lead singer/drums/percussion), both original members; Joe Hall (bass); Jay Jones (sax/flute). Orville Saunders (guitar) took over when three former members resigned to further their studies.

The million sale of this disc was reported in May 1975. Blackbyrds subsequently toured Europe and the U.S.A., stopping at various colleges and universities to give lecture/demonstrations.

DAVID BOWIE

FAME *RCA* [*Britain*]. Written by David Bowie, John Lennon and Carlos Alomar, this was released in Britain in July 1975 and in the U.S.A. in June 1975. It went to No 1 for two weeks in the U.S.A. and No 17 for one week in Britain. It stayed 26 weeks in the U.S. charts and eight weeks in the British bestsellers. R.I.A.A. Gold Disc award on 17 October 1975.

David Bowie (real name David Jones) was born in Brixton, London, on 8 January 1947. He attended Bromley Technical High School and, when 16, started playing tenor saxophone (an instrument he began studying at age 13). The same year, he formed a blues group under the name David Jones and The Lower Third, changing his name to Bowie because of another David Jones (Davy Jones of The Monkees). The group was then called David Bowie and The Buzz. They were soon disbanded, and David became interested in Buddhism, and then formed a mime group Feathers, also becoming a member of the Lindsay Kemp mime troupe. He returned to music after a while and made his first album for Deram, 'The World of David Bowie' (1967). His early discs did not meet with public approval but his association with Gus Dudgeon, a producer, brought about his first chart success, 'Space Oddity' (1969), followed by an album of the same title. He then retired to found and run Beckenham Arts Laboratory, but during this period made one of his best albums, the powerful, doom-laden 'The Man Who Sold The World' (1970).

In 1971, David signed a long-term multi-dollar contract with RCA in the U.S.A. plus completed a new album 'Hunky Dory', and thus began his first step towards national recognition. His taste for rock returned, and in order to achieve a stage identity he performed around Britain with Mick Ronson (guitar), Trevor Bolder (bass) and Woody Woodmansey (drums). In 1972 came the release of the album 'The Rise and Fall of Ziggy Stardust and The Spiders from Mars'. This became a huge seller as did the single 'Starman' taken from it. The creation of Ziggy Stardust enabled him to bring together many of his diverse ideas, the powerful imagery of his costume, and the choreography allied to his music, establishing a type of theatrical rock presentation never before experienced. His earlier passion for mime helped him in this.

After a 60-date British tour in mid-1973, David announced 'retirement' from stage work, but by then he had achieved considerable fame. He came out again in 1974 and toured the U.S.A. extensively, with enormous success.

His other albums were 'Aladdin Sane' (1973), 'Images 1966-1967' (1973) and 'Pin-Ups' (1973), the latter selling a near million. 'Diamond Dogs' and 'David Live' followed in 1974. 'Young Americans' album in 1975 was mainly recorded in Philadelphia's Sigma Sound studio with the help of local back-up musicians and singers, and reflected the influence of his year-long stay in the States. This included 'Fame', a number with an infectious guitar riff which Bowie gradually builds into a smooth and steady rhythm. It was composed in the studio, and co-writer ex-Beatle John Lennon joins with Bowie towards the end. Issued as a singles disc it stayed six months in the U.S. bestsellers and sold well over the million.

David Bowie writes virtually all the material for his recordings.

B.T. EXPRESS

EXPRESS *Scepter* [*USA*]. Written by Jeff Lane, this was released in the U.S.A. in January 1975, going to No 4 for three weeks and staying 16 weeks in the charts. It was No 34 in Britain. R.I.A.A. Gold Disc award on 4 August 1975.

Taken from the group's album 'Do It Till You're Satisfied', this million seller has the same compulsive beat as their hit of 1974.

GLEN CAMPBELL

RHINESTONE COWBOY *Capitol* [*USA*]. Written by Larry Weiss, this was released in the U.S.A. in May 1975 and in Britain in October 1975. It reached No 1 for two weeks in the U.S.A. and No 3 for one week in Britain. It lasted 25 weeks in the U.S. charts and nine weeks in the British topsellers. R.I.A.A. Gold Disc award on 5 September 1975.

A gigantic hit for Glen Campbell, with a sale of well over a million and a half. The disc was a continuous seller for six months in the U.S.A.

CAPTAIN & TENNILE

LOVE WILL KEEP US TOGETHER *A & M* [*USA*]. Written by Howard Greenfield and Neil Sedaka (1974) this was released in the U.S.A. in April 1975 and in Britain in August 1975. It went to No 1 for four weeks in the U.S.A. and No 29 for one week in Britain. It stayed 23 weeks in the U.S. charts and five weeks in the British lists. R.I.A.A. Gold Disc award on 1 July 1975. Grammy Award: Record of the Year, 1975.

Captain (real name Daryl Dragon) is the son of symphony conductor Carmen Dragon. He could have been a session musician, but joined The Beach Boys' live show from 1967 to 1972, concentrating primarily on arrangements for the group. Tennille (Toni Tennille) was raised for a theatrical career. Her father sang with Bob Crosby's band and her mother had a TV show in Montgomery, Alabama, her hometown. Tennille went to California around 1965 and worked in San Francisco with a musical she had written on ecology, *Mother Earth*. Daryl was recommended to her as keyboard player when the show played the Huntington Hartford Theatre. When the show closed (1971) Daryl called her for The Beach Boys' tour. They formed a nightclub act and worked clubs in between The Beach Boys' engagements. While on tour Toni wrote 'The Way I Want to Touch You'. The duo spent $250 on pressing 500 records to send to radio stations. Daryl played all the instruments and Toni sang all the vocal parts. The tape was cut in a tiny garage studio in 1973 in the San Fernando Valley. The song became a legend in Los Angeles. A & M purchased the record and immediately re-released it, and signed them to the label.

Toni wrote the song about the way she really felt about Daryl to whom she is married. She is the only 'Beach Girl' (she played piano) ever to tour with The Beach Boys, and among her other varied credits she worked as backing vocalist on Elton John's 'Caribou' album.

'Love Will Keep Us Together', their second disc, rose very quickly to the top of the charts, sold well over one-and-a-half million, and made the duo nationally famous. In addition to a Gold Disc, it was the best record of the year. Daryl hails from California.

THE WAY I WANT TO TOUCH YOU *A & M* [*USA*]. Written by Toni Tennille (1973). Re-released in the U.S.A. in September 1975, this went to No 3 for one week, staying 22 weeks in the charts. R.I.A.A. Gold Disc award on 17 December 1975.

Second million-seller single for this duo. Its re-release was inevitable following their success with 'Love Will Keep Us Together'.

LOVE WILL KEEP US TOGETHER (Album) *A & M* [*USA*]. Released in the U.S.A. in June 1975, this rose to No 2 for one week and stayed put in the charts for 106 weeks. R.I.A.A. Gold Disc award on 1 August 1975.

This album sold a million by October 1975, and stayed in the bestsellers for over two years with an estimated tally in 1977 of over two million. Fittingly, the album also contains renditions of two Beach Boys classics. Its success made it a wonderful year for the pair of brand new stars.

The album included: (*)'Love Will Keep Us Together'; (*)'The Way I Want To Touch You'; 'Cuddle Up'; 'The Good Songs'; 'Gentle Stranger'; 'I Write the Songs'; 'Honey Come Love Me'; 'Disney Girls' (Beach Boys number); 'God Only Knows' (Beach Boys number).

(* sold a million as a single.)

ERIC CARMEN

ALL BY MYSELF *Arista* [*USA*]. Written by Eric Carmen and released in the U.S.A. in December 1975 and in Britain in April 1976, this went to No 1 for one week in the U.S.A. and No 9 for one week in Britain. It stayed 25 weeks in the U.S. charts and seven weeks in the British lists. R.I.A.A. Gold Disc award on 21 April 1976.

Eric Carmen, born in 1949, hails from Cleveland, Ohio. At the age of two he started learning the piano and studied for the following 13 years. At five he started learning the violin. As a youngster, he became the mascot of the Cleveland Symphony Orchestra and sat next to the piano player or played in the cello

classes. After spending 15 years with classical music, he became impressed with The Who on a TV show, and taught himself to play drums and guitar, joining his first band The Fugitives in 1965, then Cyrus Erie and The Choir. By this time, rock became Eric's life. He dropped out of college in 1968, and formed The Raspberries in late 1970 (see Raspberries, 1972). The group disbanded in May 1975, and Eric found a band playing in a local club and went on tour with them as pianist and vocalist. He wrote 'All by Myself' around a three-year relationship with a girl and how it broke up. The tune is an adaptation of a theme from Rachmaninoff's Second Concerto.

The disc was in the U.S. charts for six months and sold the million by 1976, bringing Eric national and international prominence.

THE CARPENTERS

HORIZON (Album) *A & M* [*USA*]. Released in the U.S.A. and in Britain in June 1975, this, inevitably, went to No 10 for one week in the U.S.A. and No 1 for five weeks in Britain. It stayed 18 weeks in the U.S. charts and 24 weeks in British topsellers. R.I.A.A. Gold Disc award on 17 June 1975.

This album was actually more popular in Britain than in the U.S.A. and subsequently sold a global million. The album also features the melodic guitar sound of Tony Peluso, Joe Osborn on bass, Earl Dumier on oboe, and English horn additions. It contained: 'Solitaire' (Neil Sedaka); 'Happy' (Tony Peluso, Rubin and John Bettis); 'Love Me for What I Am' (Tony Peluso, Rubin and John Bettis); 'Please Mr Postman' (B. Holland, F. Gorman and R. Bateman, 1961); 'Only Yesterday' (Richard Carpenter and John Bettis); 'I Can Dream, Can't I?' (I. Kahal and Sammy Fain, 1937); 'Desperado' (Glen Frey and Don Henley); 'Aurora' (Richard Carpenter); 'Eventide' (Richard Carpenter); 'Goodbye and I Love You' (Richard Carpenter).

CHICAGO

CHICAGO VIII (Album) *Columbia* [*USA*]. Released in the U.S.A. in March 1975, this rose to No 1 for three weeks, staying 29 weeks in the charts. R.I.A.A. Gold Disc award on 31 March 1975.

Super-group Chicago's eighth million (platinum) seller in succession. It shipped over 500,000 on release, with instant gold award, and sold a million by mid-August 1975. A large part of the success of this album was due to a single disc, 'Harry Truman', so popular at the time, and this was included on the album. Contents included: 'Harry Truman'; 'Old Days'; 'Anyway You Want'; 'Brand New Love Affair, Parts 1 & 2'; 'Till We Meet Again'; 'Long Time No See'; 'Ain't It Blue?'; 'Hideaway'; 'Never Been in Love Before'.

All songs by Chicago.

CHICAGO'S GREATEST HITS (Album) *Columbia* [*USA*]. Released in the U.S.A. in November 1975, this collection hit No 1 for eight weeks, staying 69 weeks in the charts. R.I.A.A. Gold Disc award on 18 November 1975.

The best music from Chicago's eight platinum albums, showing the group's musical maturity through the years. It sold a million by February 1976.

Contents included: 'Beginnings'; 'Does Anybody Really Know What Time It Is?'; 'Make Me Smile'; (*)'Just You 'n' Me'; 'Wishing You Were Here'; (*)'Saturday in the Park'; 'Feelin' Stronger Every Day'; 'Colour My World'; '25 or 6 to 4'; 'I've Been Searchin' so Long'.

(* sold a million as a single disc.)

PERRY COMO

PERRY COMO'S 40 GREATEST HITS (Double album) *K-Tel* [*Britain*]. Released in Britain in October 1975, this was at No 1 for five weeks and slumbered 20 weeks in the charts. It also went to No 1 in Ireland.

This double album was a tremendous seller over the Christmas period in Britain and sold a million there by March 1976. A superb compilation of Perry Como's past successes marketed by K-Tel International by arrangement with RCA, it included several of his former million-seller singles.

The outstanding titles included were: 'It's Impossible'; 'And I Love You So'; 'I Think of You'; 'For the Good Times'; 'The Way We Were'; 'Walk Right Back'; 'Caterina'; 'Hot Diggity'; 'Round and Round'; 'Magic Moments'; 'Catch a Falling Star'; 'Delaware'.

JOHN DENVER

AN EVENING WITH JOHN DENVER (Double album) *RCA* [*USA*]. Released in the U.S.A. and Britain in February 1975, this went to No 2 for two weeks in the U.S.A., staying 50 weeks in their charts. R.I.A.A. Gold Disc award on 19 February 1975.

This was shipped gold (500,000 units, the new criterion for this award by the R.I.A.A. - the second under the new certification) and, as it was a double album, it qualified for over a million records shipped (platinum) at the same time. It was recorded at Denver's concerts in the summer of 1974 at the Universal Amphitheater, California, under the direction of Milton Okun.

Contents: 'The Music Is You'; 'Farewell Andromeda'; 'Mother Nature's Son'; 'Summer'; 'Today'; 'Saturday Night in Toledo, Ohio'; 'Matthew'; 'Rocky Mountain Suite (Cold Nights in Canada)'; 'Sweet Surrender'; 'Grandma's Feather Bed'; 'Annie's Song'; 'The Eagle and the Hawk'; 'My Sweet Lady'; 'Annie's Other Song'; 'Boy from the Country'; 'Rhymes and Reasons'; 'Forest Lawn'; 'Pickin' the Sun Down'; 'Thank God I'm a Country Boy'; 'Take Me Home, Country Roads'; 'Poems, Prayers and Promises'; 'Rocky Mountain High'; 'This Old Guitar'.

THANK GOD I'M A COUNTRY BOY *RCA* [*USA*]. Written by John Sommers (1974) and released in the U.S.A. in February 1975, this went to No 1 for one week, staying 22 weeks in the charts. R.I.A.A. Gold Disc award on 26 June 1975.

A cut from Denver's album 'An Evening with John Denver', this sincere song soon sold a million. It was written by John Sommers, the guitarist of his backing group, and was also included in 'Back Home Again' album (1974).

I'M SORRY backed with CALYPSO *RCA* [*USA*]. Both written by John Denver. Released in the U.S.A. and Britain in August 1975, this double-header went to No 1 for one week in the U.S.A., staying 21 weeks in the charts. R.I.A.A. Gold Disc award on 18 November 1975.

'I'm Sorry' is a song of lost love. 'Calypso' is dedicated to Captain Jacques-Yves Cousteau and the men who had served on the ship Calypso. Second million-seller single of the year for Denver.

WINDSONG (Album) *RCA* [*USA*]. Released in the U.S.A. and Britain in September 1975, this went to No 1 for five weeks in the U.S.A. and No 17 for one week in Britain. It stayed 35 weeks in the U.S. charts and seven weeks in the British topsellers. R.I.A.A. Gold Disc award on 19 September 1975.

Continuing the astounding success of John Denver, 'Windsong' sold an incredible 2,900,000 by the end of 1975 and well over 3,500,000 globally by early 1976. It comprised 12 new songs by him, and featured 'I'm Sorry', 'Calypso', 'Fly Away', and 'Looking for Space'.

It entered the U.S. charts at No 2 in its first week, and was certified gold almost immediately, passing the 1,250,000 unit mark in a little over two weeks of national release.

ROCKY MOUNTAIN CHRISTMAS (Album) *RCA* [*USA*]. Released in the U.S.A. in October 1975 and Britain in November 1975, this made No 7 for two weeks in the U.S.A., staying 11 weeks in the charts. R.I.A.A. Gold Disc award on 24 October 1975.

Denver's 'Rocky Mountain Christmas' was the first Christmas album in history to receive a gold award. By Christmas it had sold 1,200,000 in the U.S.A. and finally well over 1,500,000, making 1975 a phenomenal year for Denver and for RCA.

The album contained mainly traditional songs. An ABC-TV special, 'Rocky Mountain Christmas', seen by 65,000,000 viewers, added enormously to Denver's record sales. It was ABC's all-time high for a musical special.

Contents of the album: 'Silent Night'; 'Coventry Carol'; 'Away in a Manger'; 'Silver Bells'; 'Christmas Song'; 'What Child is This?'; 'Rudolph the Red-Nosed Reindeer'; 'Please Daddy Don't Get Drunk This Christmas' (Bill and Taffy Danoff); 'Aspenglow'; 'Christmas for Cowboys' (John Denver); 'A Baby Just Like You' (John Denver).

THE DETROIT SPINNERS
THEY JUST CAN'T STOP IT (Games people play) *Atlantic* [*USA*]. Written by J.B. Jefferson, B. Hawes and C. Simmons, this was released in the U.S.A. in August 1975, going to No 1 for one week and staying 23 weeks in the charts. R.I.A.A. Gold Disc award on 14 November 1975.

The fifth million seller for the popular Detroit Spinners.

BOB DYLAN
BLOOD ON THE TRACKS (Album) *Columbia* [*USA*]. Released in the U.S.A. and Britain in February 1975, this went to No 1 for three weeks in the U.S.A. and No 2 for two weeks in Britain. It stayed 24 weeks in the U.S. charts and 14 weeks in the British bestsellers. R.I.A.A. Gold Disc award on 12 February 1975.

The first album to go gold under the new R.I.A.A. standards (500,000 units) and Dylan's first album since returning to Columbia. It sold 400,000 album and tape units in the first week of its release, and subsequently amassed a million (platinum) sale.

It included: 'Tangled Up in Blue'; 'Idiot Wind'; 'Lily, Rosemary and the Jack of Hearts'; 'Meet Me in the Morning'; 'You're a Big Girl Now'; 'Simple Twist of Fate'. All songs by Bob Dylan.

EAGLES (country rock quintet)
ONE OF THESE NIGHTS (Album) *Asylum* [*USA*]. Released in the U.S.A. in June 1975 and in Britain in July 1975, this flew to No 1 for five weeks in the U.S.A. and No 4 for one week in Britain. It stayed 62 weeks in the U.S. charts and 36 weeks in the British bestsellers. R.I.A.A. Gold Disc award on 30 June 1975.

Eagles were formed in 1971 on the American West Coast, and originally were a quartet – Glenn Frey (guitar), Randy Meisner (bass), Don Henley (drums) and Bernie Leadon (guitar). All had played with other bands before teaming up – Glenn Frey with John David Souther; Leadon with Dillard and Clark, Linda Ronstadt, and The Burrito Brothers; Meisner an early member of Poco. Their first album for Asylum 'Eagles' (1972) featured 'Take It Easy', written by Jackson Browne and actually recorded in London's Olympic Studios. This was a hit in the U.S.A. and

brought the group national attention. The 'Desperado' album followed in 1973, then 'On the Border' in 1974. It was, however, their fourth album 'One of These Nights' in 1975 that gave them prominence in every sector of popular music. Three singles releases from it 'One of These Nights', 'Lyin' Eyes' and 'Take It To the Limit' were all chart hits. Don Felder (slide guitarist) had made the band a quintet when he joined in early 1974. After 'One of These Nights' album, Leadon left, and Joe Walsh, vocalist, guitarist, writer, and well-known solo performer, took Leadon's place (late 1975).

The first three albums were all certified gold in 1974, and Eagles paralleled their emergence as top recording stars with their impact as a live group. Steady touring in the U.S.A. and abroad drew vast international concert audiences. In 1975 around 850,000 fans paid over $5 million for 59 concert sites in the U.S.A. alone. Frey and Henley write most of the group's material, and the Eagles' 'Greatest Hits' album in early 1976 took them to the pinnacle of success with over five million sale. 'One of These Nights' album sold the million (platinum) by August 1975. It also included a fine track 'Too Many Hands' in addition to the titles mentioned above.

Contents of this album: 'One of These Nights' (Henley and Frey); 'Too Many Hands' (Meisner and Felder); 'Hollywood Waltz' (B. Leadon, T. Leadon, Henley and Frey); 'Journey of the Sorcerer' (B. Leadon); 'Lyin' Eyes' (Henley and Frey); 'Take It to the Limit' (Meisner, Henley and Frey); 'Visions' (Felder and Henley); 'After the Thrill Is Gone' (Henley and Frey); 'I Wish You Peace' (Davis and B. Leadon).

EARTH, WIND & FIRE (rock/soul band)
THAT'S THE WAY OF THE WORLD (Album) *Columbia* [*USA*]. Released in the U.S.A. in March 1975, this went to No 1 for four weeks and stayed 55 weeks in the charts. R.I.A.A. Gold Disc award on 9 April 1975.

A group of nine black artists – Maurice White (percussion/ vocalist/leader); Johnny Grahm (guitar); Ralph Johnson (drums); Al McKay (guitar/vocals); Phil Bailey (vocals/percussion); Lorenzo Dunhill (keyboards); Verdine White (bass); Freddy White (drums); Jessica Cleave (vocalist).

Maurice White, who formed the first Earth, Wind & Fire in 1970, was born and raised in Memphis, Tennessee, and sang in church when he was six. He later played drums in school bands, and spent three years at Chicago Music Conservatory, studying percussion, piano and composition. This led to his association with many famous black artists resulting in his playing in the studio on many hit records by John Coltrane, Sonny Stitt, Muddy Waters, The Impressions and others. His own big break came when he signed as drummer with The Ramsey Lewis Trio in 1966 and stayed with them until 1970. Moving to Los Angeles, he formed the first Earth, Wind & Fire which he disbanded after recording two albums for Warner Brothers label. A new band was formed and they made their first Columbia album 'Last Days in Time'. The next album 'Head to the Sky' was a big success (1973) followed by 'Open Our Eyes' (1974) and the group were by then one of the U.S.A.'s major successes.

The group's fourth album for Columbia 'That's the Way of the World' exploded on to the U.S. charts and sold a million by June 1975, at the same time as a single release from it, 'Shining Star'. The album was used as the original soundtrack of a film of the same name, in which the nine members of the group portray a rock'n' soul band.

The album included: 'Shining Star'; 'That's the Way of the World'; 'Happy Feelin''; 'All About Love'; 'Yearnin' Learnin''; 'See the Light'; 'Africano'. All songs by members of the group.

SHINING STAR *Columbia* [*USA*]. Written by M. White and P. Bailey, and released in the U.S.A. in March 1975, this hit No 1 for one week and stayed 24 weeks in the charts. R.I.A.A. Gold Disc award on 19 June 1975. Grammy Award: R & B vocal performed by a duo, group or chorus: Earth, Wind & Fire - 1975.

The prime cut from the group's album 'That's the Way of the World', written by two members of the band, selling a million at the same time as the album. It was a particular favourite with their audiences at the group's consistent sell-out concerts, in which they have an intriguing visual stage presence that adds immeasurably to their music.

SING A SONG *Columbia* [*USA*]. Written by M. White and A. McKay and released in the U.S.A. in November 1975, this achieved No 5 for two weeks, staying in the charts 21 weeks. R.I.A.A. Gold Disc award on 27 February 1976.

Second million-seller single for Earth, Wind & Fire, making 1975 a memorable year for them. Written by two members of the band.

FREDDY FENDER

BEFORE THE NEXT TEARDROP FALLS *ABC/Dot* [*USA*]. Written by V. Keith and B. Peters (1965), this was released in the U.S.A. in January 1975. It went to No 1 for one week, staying 21 weeks in the charts. R.I.A.A. Gold Disc award on 22 May 1975.

Freddy Fender (real name Baldemar G. Huerta) was born in 1937 in San Benito, Texas, his father being a Mexican. He began singing when he was ten and learned guitar when he was 11. At 16 he was playing local dances. He joined the U.S. Marines in 1954 and after service returned to Texas (1956), formed a small band, and made his first records for a small local company, Falcon Records. In 1960, he was arrested for marijuana possession in Baton Rouge, resulting in a five-year jail sentence. He served three years, where he played guitar to the other prisoners. On release, he returned to Texas and worked as engineer in a recording studio, then went to Louisiana for three years as resident singer in Poppa Joe's on Bourbon Street, New Orleans, returning again to Texas in 1969. In 1971 Freddy took a two-year college course in history at Corpus Christi, and worked as a mechanic. He then met legendary producer Huey Meaux and began working with him in Houston. He cut two albums on Meaux's Crazy Cajun label, and in 1974 recorded 'Before the Next Teardrop Falls', a song he had heard Charley Pride sing. The albums and this single were released to ABC/Dot. 'Teardrop', a mid-tempo mix of English and Spanish, country and rock, got to No 1 in both country and national charts, and Freddy

was America's new country star, on both records and live appearances.

Million seller 'Teardrop' was written some ten years before Fender recorded it.

WASTED DAYS AND WASTED NIGHTS *ABC/Dot* [*USA*]. Written by B. Huerta and W. Duncan (1959), this was released in the U.S.A. in June 1975, going to No 3 for one week and staying for 22 weeks in the charts. R.I.A.A. Gold Disc award on 18 September 1975.

Taken from Freddie's album of the same title, this million-seller single is a re-worked version of the song he wrote just before being jailed. Tex-Mex rockabilly music had really arrived.

FLEETWOOD MAC

FLEETWOOD MAC (Album) *Reprise* [*USA*]. Released in the U.S.A. in July 1975, this went to No 1 for one week and refused to budge from the charts for 122 weeks. R.I.A.A. Gold Disc award on 4 December 1975.

Fleetwood Mac made a number of albums for Blue Horizon label up to 1969, and switched to Reprise with continued success. Peter Green left the group in 1970, his place being taken by John McVie's wife Christine (Christine Perfect from Chicken Shack) and in February 1971, Jeremy Spencer left while the band were on tour in California, to join a religious sect. Bob Welch, a San Francisco guitarist/songwriter, replaced Spencer. Danny Kirwan also quit in 1972, Bob Weston taking over until 1974 when he left. A further change in 1974 came when Bob Welch left to embark on a solo career, and he was replaced by two Americans, Lindsey Buckingham and girl vocalist, Stevie Nicks. This duo influenced the style and direction of the group - now John McVie, Mick Fleetwood (the only two original members), Christine McVie, Nicks and Buckingham brought more possible harmonic combinations and songwriting depth with the group's tenth album 'Fleetwood Mac', produced with the help of Keith Olsen. This was an outstanding album and a gigantic success in the U.S.A., selling over 4,500,000 by July 1977. Final estimate of sales is well over 5 million.

It included two singles releases, 'Over My Head' and 'Rhiannon', both chart hits. Another fine track was 'Say You Love Me'.

Contents: 'Monday Morning' (Buckingham); 'Warm Ways' (McVie); 'Blue Letter' (Curtis); 'Rhiannon' (Nicks); 'Over My Head' (McVie); 'Crystal' (Nicks); 'Say You Love Me' (McVie); 'Landslide' (Nicks); 'World Turning' (McVie and Buckingham); 'Sugar Daddy' (McVie); 'I'm So Afraid' (Buckingham).

The band established itself through its nine-year history as one of the most consistently popular bands working in America, with sell-out concerts and ever-increasing audiences, although it was nearly wiped out when a former manager put another group on the road using the same name. Months of legal wrangling prohibited him from doing so after the real Fleetwood Mac won an injunction.

THE FOUR SEASONS

DECEMBER 1963 (Oh What a Night) *Warner/Curb* [*USA*]. Written by Bob Gaudio and J. Parker and released in the U.S.A.

in December 1975 and in Britain in January 1976, this went to No 1 for three weeks in the U.S.A. and two weeks in Britain. It remained 27 weeks in the U.S. charts and 10 weeks in the British bestsellers. R.I.A.A. Gold Disc award on 29 March 1976.

A great comeback for the re-formed Four Seasons (still headed by Frankie Valli), their first million seller since 1965. The disc was a big hit on both sides of the Atlantic and sold an estimated two million or more globally.

DICKIE GOODMAN
MR JAWS *Cash/Private Stock* [*USA*]. Written by B. Ramal and Dickie Goodman, this was released in the U.S.A. in August 1975, going to No 1 for one week. It stayed 19 weeks in the charts. R.I.A.A. Gold Disc award on 29 September 1975.

Inspired by the successful film *Jaws*, this million seller was Dickie Goodman's first success since he recorded 'Flying Saucer' in 1956.

AL GREEN
L.O.V.E. *Hi* [*USA*]. Written by Al Green, W. Mitchell and L. Hodge, this was released in the U.S.A. in February 1975 and in Britain in March 1975. It reached No 10 for one week in the U.S.A. and No 20 for one week in Britain. It lasted 14 weeks in the U.S. charts and nine weeks in the British bestsellers.

The continuing success story of Al Green. This was his ninth singles million seller in a row, subsequently achieving this with global sales.

HAMILTON, JOE FRANK & REYNOLDS
FALLIN' IN LOVE *Playboy* [*USA*]. Released in the U.S.A. in June 1975, this hit No 1 for one week, staying 19 weeks in the charts. It was No 33 in Britain. R.I.A.A. Gold Disc award on 13 September 1975.

A moving and sensitive sound for this second million seller for the trio. It was the first Playboy disc to reach gold status. Written by D. Hamilton and A. Hamilton.

STEVE HARLEY & COCKNEY REBEL
COME UP AND SEE ME (Make me smile) *EMI* [*Britain*]. Written by Steve Harley, this was released in Britain in February 1975. It notched No 1 for two weeks, staying nine weeks in the charts.

This group, consisting of Steve Harley (guitar/vocals); Jean-Paul Crocker (violin); Paul Avron Jeffrys (bass) and Milton Reame-James (keyboards), was formed in 1973 by ex-journalist Harley. He advertised for musicians, resulting in this line-up. With intelligent publicity and record production, the band were a big success with their second single 'Judy Teen' which incorporated fashionable styles into one original mode. This caused some provocation, as the social style kept Harley's name in the spotlight but brought about the break-up of the original Rebel through friction in the band. Harley came up with a new group in 1974 – including Jim Cregan (bass) and the band recorded the albums 'The Human Menagerie' (1974) and 'Psychomodo' (1974). The third album 'The Way We Used to Be' in 1975 contained 'Come Up and See Me', which was a big hit when released as a single, and sold a million globally.

HOT CHOCOLATE (vocal sextet)
YOU SEXY THING *RAK* [*Britain*] *Big Tree* [*USA*]. Written by Errol Brown and Tony Wilson this was released in the U.S.A. in October 1975 and in Britain in November 1975. It went to No 2 for one week in the U.S.A. and No 1 for one week in Britain. It stayed 26 weeks in the U.S. charts and 13 weeks in the British topsellers. R.I.A.A. Gold Disc award on 13 January 1976.

Hot Chocolate first came on the disc scene in Britain in 1970 when they had a hit with 'Love Is Life', followed by 'I Believe in Love' (1971) and 'Brother Louie' (1973). They have been a good acquisition for the English RAK label who signed them up. This disc of 'You Sexy Thing' was a big hit on both sides of the Atlantic, selling a quick million in the U.S.A. alone.

Errol Brown is the leader, and with member Tony Wilson writes the group's material.

JANIS IAN (folk singer)
BETWEEN THE LINES (Album) *Columbia* [*USA*]. Written by Janis Ian and released in the U.S.A. in May 1975. It reached No 10 for two weeks and stayed in the charts for 28 weeks. R.I.A.A. Gold Disc award on 11 November 1975. Grammy Award for the Best Engineered Recording (Non-Classical) in 1975.

Janis Ian grew up in New Jersey, her family moving to New York when she was 14. Her father was a music teacher. Janis had piano lessons at the age of three and started playing guitar at twelve. She attracted attention in the U.S.A. with her self-written single 'Society's Child' – a song about the hypocrisies of modern life. Her first album got into the charts when she was sixteen through disc-jockey Murray the K playing tracks from it each night. Janis still stayed with her family, and gave innumerable college concerts all over the U.S.A.

She made albums for Verve-Folkways: 'Janis Ian' (1967), 'For All the Seasons of the Mind' (1968) and 'The Secret Life of J. Eddy Fink' (1968). She then disappeared from the scene but continued writing and rehearsing a five-piece band, returning to the limelight with the band and a fine album 'Stars' for CBS in 1974. Then came 'Between the Lines' which put her back into national prominence. This album sold the million by 1976.

Janis writes all her material. Her band consists of Clair Bay (vocals/percussion); Barry Lazorowitz (drums); Stu Woods (bass); and Jeff Layton (guitar).

The contents of the album are: 'When the Party's Over'; 'At Seventeen'; 'From Me to You'; 'Bright Lights and Promises'; 'In the Winter'; 'Watercolours'; 'Between the Lines'; 'The Come On'; 'Light a Light'; 'Tea and Sympathy'; 'Lover's Lullaby'.

The song 'At Seventeen' made No 1 in the U.S. charts as a single release.

THE ISLEY BROTHERS

THE HEAT IS ON (Album) (featuring 'Fight the Power') *T-Neck* [*USA*]. Released in the U.S.A. in June 1975 this went to No 1 for three weeks, staying 40 weeks in the charts. R.I.A.A. Gold Disc award on 30 June 1975.

A quick Gold Disc for The Isleys with the million (platinum) sale by mid-November 1975. The album is another example of their remarkable consistency over two decades. It included: 'Fight the Power' (parts 1 & 2); 'The Heat is On'; 'Hope You Feel Better, Love' (parts 1 & 2); 'Sensuality' (parts 1 & 2); 'For the Love of You' (parts 1 & 2).

Material is written by the group.

FIGHT THE POWER (Part 1) *T-Neck* [*USA*]. Written by the group and released in the U.S.A. in June 1975, this rose to No 4 for one week, staying 18 weeks in the charts. R.I.A.A. Gold Disc award on 11 September 1975.

The prime cut from the group's hit album 'The Heat Is On' also sold a quick million.

JEFFERSON STARSHIP (rock octet)

RED OCTOPUS (Album) *Grunt* [*USA*]. Released in the U.S.A. in July 1975, this went to No 1 for four weeks, staying in the charts for 50 weeks. R.I.A.A. Gold Disc award on 22 August 1975.

Originally Jefferson Airplane (see 1967), the band became an octet and changed its name to Jefferson Starship. This consists of original members Grace Slick, Paul Kantner, Martin Balin (who returned to the group), Johnny Barbata, Papa John Creach, David Frieberg, Craig Chaquico and Peter Sears. The group won over millions of new fans, and this album sold a million (platinum status) very quickly. It included many fine tracks, notably 'Miracles', 'Play On Love', 'Tumblin'' and 'Love Theme'.

JIGSAW (quartet)

SKY HIGH *Chelsea* [*USA*] *Splash* [*Britain*]. Written by Des Dyer and Clive Scott and released in G.B. in November 1975 and in the U.S.A. in August 1975. It reached No 9 in Britain, staying in the charts for 11 weeks. In the U.S.A. it was at No 5 for one week, staying 26 weeks in the charts.

Jigsaw's line-up: Des Dyer (lead vocals/drums); Clive Scott (keyboards/vocals); Tony Campbell (lead guitar); and Barrie Bernard (bass guitar). They worked the tough 'live' circuit in the U.S.A., writing and performing songs of quality, and have a dozen albums to their credit. 'Sky High' was originally commissioned as the main theme for a Kung-Fu movie *The Man from Hong Kong*. The 3-minute track outshone and outlasted the film itself in reputation, and was a radio and disco DJ favourite for a long time, becoming a classic and a collector's item. It figured constantly for three years in the Japanese charts and is reputed to have sold 13 million, globally.

Jigsaw later recorded a new disco version, available as either a 12″ or 7″ single, released on 24 August 1979.

THE ELTON JOHN BAND

PHILADELPHIA FREEDOM *MCA* [*USA*] *DJM* [*Britain*]. Written by Bernie Taupin and Elton John, this was released in the U.S.A. in February 1975 and in Britain in March 1975. It made No 1 for three weeks in the U.S.A. and No 12 for one week in Britain, staying 21 weeks in the U.S. charts and nine weeks in the British topsellers. R.I.A.A. Gold Disc award on 23 April 1975.

This was one of Elton John's most elaborate creations, with performer credits listed as 'The Elton John Band' and the impressive arranger as Gene Page. Elton John's group in 1975 was Elton (piano); Davey Johnstone (guitar); Ray Cooper (percussion); Roger Pope (drums); Kenny Passarelli (bass); James Newton Howard (keyboards); Caleb Quaye (guitar).

'Philadelphia Freedom' sold over two million very quickly in the U.S.A.

ELTON JOHN

CAPTAIN FANTASTIC & THE BROWN DIRT COWBOY (Album) *MCA* [*USA*] *DJM* [*Britain*]. Released in the U.S.A. and Britain in May 1975, this was No 1 for 12 weeks in the U.S.A. and three weeks in Britain. It stayed 43 weeks in the U.S. charts and 22 weeks in the British lists. R.I.A.A. Gold Disc award on 21 May 1975.

Recorded at Caribou Ranch in Colorado, this album is a concept record, tracing the history of Elton John (Captain Fantastic) and Bernie Taupin (the Brown Dirt Cowboy) since they first met. It was issued in a double sleeve, containing two 16-page full colour booklets 'Lyrics' and 'Scraps'. The album was the first to enter the U.S. charts at No 1 in its first week of release, and was also the first time in the history of MCA Records that an album was declared gold and platinum upon its release. By the end of August 1975 it sold 2,600,000, and finally an estimated seven million plus globally. In the U.S.A. it sold an incredible 1,400,000 in the first four days on the market.

It contained: 'Captain Fantastic and the Brown Dirt Cowboy (Opening)'; 'Meal Ticket'; 'Someone Saved My Life Tonight'; 'We All Fall in Love Sometime'; 'Tower of Babel'; 'Saturday Night'; 'Bitter Fingers'; 'Tell Me When the Whistle Blows'; 'Writing'; 'Better Off Dead'; 'Curtains'. All songs by Elton John and Bernie Taupin.

Personnel also on the disc: Dee Murray, Davey Johnstone, Ray Cooper, Nigel Olsson.

In this year, Elton John received a platinum cassette and cartridge for 250,000 sales of his 'Greatest Hits' tape.

SOMEONE SAVED MY LIFE TONIGHT *MCA* [*USA*] *DJM* [*Britain*]. Written by Bernie Taupin and Elton John, this was released in the U.S.A. and Britain in June 1975. It made No 1 for one week in the U.S.A. and No 22 for one week in Britain. It stayed 14 weeks in the U.S. charts and five weeks in the British lists. R.I.A.A. Gold Disc award on 10 September 1975.

Culled from Elton's colossal album 'Captain Fantastic & The Brown Dirt Cowboy', this also sold a million.

ROCK OF THE WESTIES (Album) *MCA* [*USA*] *DJM* [*Britain*]. Released in the U.S.A. in October 1975 and in Britain in November 1975, this went to No 1 for five weeks in the U.S.A. and No 2 for two weeks in Britain. It lasted 26 weeks in the U.S. charts and nine weeks in the British topsellers. R.I.A.A. Gold Disc award on 21 October 1975.

This album was certified gold on day of release, and was his tenth million (platinum) album. It was recorded at Caribou Studios, Colorado, and sold an estimated four million globally.

Contents were: 'Grow Some Funk of Your Own'; 'Dan Dare (Pilot of the Future)'; 'Island Girl'; 'I Feel Like a Bullet (In the Gun of Robert Ford)'; 'Street Kids'; 'Street Fighting Man'; 'Feed Me'; 'Medley (Yell Help, Ugly and Wednesday Night)'; 'Hard Luck Story' (Anne Orson and Care Blanche); 'Billy Jones and the White Bird'.

Davey Johnstone collaborated on two of the songs with Elton John and Taupin. The backing vocals were by Labelle, Kiki Dee, Anne Orson and Clive Franks. Instrumentalists same as 'Philadelphia Freedom' listing.

The million sale was achieved by November 1975.

ISLAND GIRL *MCA* [*USA*] *DJM* [*Britain*]. Written by Bernie Taupin and Elton John and released in the U.S.A. and Britain in October 1975 this went to No 1 for three weeks in the U.S.A. and No 12 for one week in Britain. It stayed 20 weeks in the U.S. bestsellers and seven weeks in the British charts.

An outtake from Elton's album 'Rock of the Westies', yet another million seller single, making 1975 a highly successful year for Elton and Taupin, and MCA.

SAMMY JOHNS

CHEVY VAN *GRC* [*USA*]. Written by Sammy Johns and released in the U.S.A. in January 1975, this went to No 5 for two weeks, staying 20 weeks in the charts. R.I.A.A. Gold Disc award on 5 May 1975.

Described as 'a story of stationwagons and comfortable lovemakin', fueled with a difference', this disc was Sammy's first million seller, and the first for General Recording Corp. (GRC).

K.C. AND THE SUNSHINE BAND
(rhythm and blues group)

GET DOWN TONIGHT *TK* [*USA*]. Written by H.W. Casey and Rick Finch, this was released in the U.S.A. in May 1975, going to No 1 for two weeks and No 20 in Britain, staying 24 weeks in the U.S. charts and nine weeks in the British lists.

Writer Harry Wayne Casey had a brief career in record retailing before joining Tone Distributors, a large record wholesaler which housed TK studio in Miami, Florida, at the back of their warehouse. He met Rick Finch, former bass player for several Florida bands, who had been hired as part-time engineer by TK. They started writing together, and in 1973 wrote, arranged, produced and performed on the first Sunshine Band disc 'Blow Your Whistle', followed by 'Sound Your Funky Horn'. Both were chart hits. Casey was in great demand from then on as a studio performer and Rick as engineer for other producers at TK. In 1974 the big break happpened. A Casey/Finch song/production, George McCrae's 'Rock Your Baby' became a multi-million-selling, international No 1 record. Then came K.C.'s own album and single 'Queen of Clubs' which attained Top 10 status in England and prompted a six-week English tour. Audience response was overwhelming, and the breakthrough in the U.S. was about to begin for the band.

Casey and Finch got the idea for 'Get Down Tonight' while on the tour, and recorded it upon their return. This was a big hit in the U.S.A. after chart entry in Britain, which called for another tour in July 1975, and became an international hit with well over the million sale. K.C. and The Sunshine Band were thus recognized as the exponents of the 'Miami Sound'. Thenceforth, the careers of the band and Casey and Finch rocketed.

The band is nine-strong with Casey (keyboards); Rick Finch (bass); Jerome Smith (guitar); Robert Johnson (drums); Oliver Brown (congas); Ronnie Smith (trumpet); Denvil Liptrot (sax); James Weaver (trumpet); and Charles Williams (trombone).

THAT'S THE WAY I LIKE IT *TK* [*USA*]. Written by H.W. Casey and Rick Finch this was released in the U.S.A. in October 1975, going to No 1 for three weeks and staying 20 weeks in the charts. In Britain it was No 4 and ten weeks in the charts.

Second reported million seller for this group, again written by the two leading lights of the band – Casey and Finch.

K.C. AND THE SUNSHINE BAND (Album) *TK* [*USA*]. Released in the U.S.A. in July 1975, this reached No 8 for two weeks and stayed in the charts for 43 weeks.

The first million-selling album by this popular 'Miami Sound' group containing their previous hits. Platinum status was achieved in 1976.

It included: 'Who Do Ya (Love)?'; 'Do You Feel All Right?'; 'Queen of Clubs'; 'Sound Your Funky Horn'; 'Get Down Tonight'; 'That's the Way I Like It'; 'I'm So Crazy'.

KISS (rock quartet)

KISS ALIVE (Album) *Casablanca* [*USA*]. Released in the U.S.A. in October 1975, this went to No 9 for four weeks and stayed a staggering 104 weeks in the charts. R.I.A.A. Gold Disc award on 4 December 1975.

Kiss group was formed in 1972, consisting of Gene Simmons (bass); Paul Stanley (guitar); Peter Criss (drums); and Ace Frehley (lead guitar). All had grown up in New York. For a year, the group played clubs in Queens and on Long Island. On 23 May 1973 they gave their first Manhattan concert in a club called The Daisy at which only the group's girlfriends and a jukebox repair man were present. The quartet decided it had best change its image. They went beyond a mere make-up change. Simmons emerged as a vampire figure, Stanley transformed himself into a pouting-lipped sex symbol, Frehley a silver-eyed spaceman, and Criss a whiskered, sly, mysterious feline.

At a concert in the Crystal Ballroom of the Diplomat Hotel in Times Square on 4 July they were spotted by Bill Aucoin, a TV director who took on their management and signed them to Casablanca Records. Their first album was released in February 1974, the second, 'Hotter Than Hell' at the end of 1974, and their third, 'Dressed to Kill' in early 1975. It was, however, their fourth album 'Kiss Alive' that broke the barrier commercially. It sold a million by January 1976 and went over two million by January 1977. It contained the group's first hit single 'Rock and Roll All Night'.

Word of this bizarre quartet spread like wildfire, and Kissmania became a reality by the end of 1975. Their exciting stage presentation utilizing such effects as fire breathing, blood-spitting, a giant spark-making machine built for the movie *Frankenstein* in the late 1930s and other visual accoutrements, plus their outrageous make-up and elaborate costumes and blazing rock and roll, made them nationally popular.

The group made its first British tour in May 1976.

LED ZEPPELIN

PHYSICAL GRAFFITI (Double album) *Swan Song* [*USA*]. Released in the U.S.A. and Britain in March 1975, this zoomed to No 1 for six weeks in the U.S.A. and three weeks in Britain. It stayed 28 weeks in the U.S. charts and 25 weeks in the British bestsellers. R.I.A.A. Gold Disc award on 6 March 1975.

This album was considered to be Led Zeppelin's finest since their second album, and a milestone in their career. It was their first release on their own Swan Song label (distributed by Atlantic Records), the first certified gold on the Atlantic distributed label since the inauguration of the new R.I.A.A. standards of sales in excess of 500,000 units, and their sixth consecutive album to go gold and platinum. Advance shipments were actually in excess of 1,000,000 units, and an estimate of the U.S. sales were over 2,500,000, and globally around 4,500,000. It established Led Zeppelin as the most successful rock band in the world. A large part of 1974 was spent in working on the record.

Contents: 'Custard Pie'; 'The Rover'; 'In my Time of Dying'; 'Houses of the Holy'; 'Trampled under Foot'; 'Kashmir'; 'In the Light'; 'Bron-Y-Aur'; 'Down By the Seaside'; 'Ten Years Gone'; 'Night Flight'; 'The Wanton Song'; 'Boogie with Stu'; 'Black Country Woman'; 'Sick Again'.

All material by the band.

Led Zeppelin had an astute manager in Peter Grant, with his uncanny knack of making the right decisions at the right time. It was he who took the major step on the band's behalf by establishing Swan Song label in 1974, and took a large credit for the group's 18 million plus albums sold up to this point, and the colossal success of their concerts in the U.S.A. It has been estimated that Led Zeppelin's earnings at this period were around $30,000,000. 'Physical Graffiti' entered the U.S. charts at No 3, the highest entry within memory in the U.S.A. for an album up to that time. The group achieved great success without the help of a press agent or TV appearances.

C.W. McCALL

CONVOY *MGM* [*USA*]. Written by C.W. McCall and B. Fries, this was released in the U.S.A. in November 1975 and in Britain in February 1976. It went to No 1 for three weeks in the

U.S.A. and No 2 for one week in Britain, staying 24 weeks in the U.S. charts and 12 weeks in the British bestsellers. R.I.A.A. Gold Disc award on 19 December 1975.

C.W. McCall (real name Bill Fries) hails from Omaha, and was born in 1928. An ex-advertising executive, he put into song his fantasies of a thousand massive trucks speeding down the highway in strict convoy formation linked together by two-way radio (the C Bar – citizen's band wavelength), and the revolt of the truck drivers who abhorred speed limits against the 'smokey bears' (police) who enforce them. The song is spiced with Middle American slang and colourful truckers' expressions, and reveals a great deal about America.

McCall majored in Fine Arts at Iowa University, then joined the advertising world despite his love of country music and early classical training. He eventually became a $40,000-a-year advertising man, and in 1973 won a Cleo Award for a series of jingles he produced for a bread company, involving a character 'C.W. McCall'. Bob Sears, a local record studio owner, persuaded him to record a country-and-western song called 'Old Home' based on his soap opera about bread deliveries to the Old Home Filler-Up and Truckin' Café and the flirting with the manageress. The disc sold 35,000 and MGM signed him up, with a further sale of the disc to around 100,000 (1974). Then came 'Wolf Creek Pass' aimed at the trucking market, a hair-raising tale of brake failure that sold 250,000. Two more singles followed, then came 'Convoy' which took McCall out of the country charts and into the national charts. It sold over a million in the U.S.A. and over two million globally.

Fries (or C.W. McCall) rode with truckers as a youngster and grew up surrounded by the business, and researched the trucking jargon for a long time. Radio helped create the mystique and provided much publicity.

'Convoy' was a hit also in Britain, Canada, Australia and South Africa.

VAN McCOY & THE SOUL CITY ORCHESTRA

THE HUSTLE *Avco* [USA]. Written by Van McCoy and released in the U.S.A. in April 1975, and in Britain in May 1975, this instant tune got to No 1 for one week in the U.S.A. and No 2 for one week in Britain. It stayed 19 weeks in the U.S. charts and 12 weeks in the British bestsellers. R.I.A.A. Gold Disc award

on 26 June 1975, Grammy Award: Best Pop Instrumental Performance, 1975.

Van McCoy was born in Washington, D.C., in 1940. He started in the music business in 1955 in a high school group The Starlighters. He later joined The Heartbeats who were signed to Gone/End records for whom they made three singles. This group lasted until 1961 when McCoy went to Philadelphia, where he cut a record that cost $219 and sold to Rock Records for $4,000. The label was distributed by Scepter/Wand where A & R chief, Luther Dixon, suggested Van train under him for a year as record producer. He worked with The Shirelles for a time and then took a staff job with famous writers Leiber and Stoller in 1962. He wrote for Gladys Knight & The Pips, Bobby Vinton, Clyde Otis, then joined Blackwood Music as staff writer in 1964. He had hits with Aretha Franklin, Barbara Lewis and Peter & Gordon. In 1967 Van formed his own publishing company, writing hits for many artists.

Van McCoy, soul producer/writer/arranger turned hit recording artist, wrote this new U.S. dance craze 'The Hustle' which became the biggest 'dance' record of the 1970s, and the biggest disc of that genre in some nine years. It sold 1,500,000 in the U.S.A. alone by August 1975 and further big sales abroad, totalling over 10 million. McCoy died in New Jersey 13 July 1979.

GWEN McRAE

ROCKIN' CHAIR *TK-Cat* [USA]. Written by Clarence Reid and Willie Clark and released in the U.S.A. in April 1975. It climbed to No 10 for two weeks and stayed in the charts for 18 weeks.

Following her husband George McRae who had a tremendous hit with 'Rock Your Baby' in 1974, Gwen completed a double for the duo with this million seller.

MAJOR HARRIS

LOVE WON'T LET ME WAIT *Atlantic* [USA]. Written by B. Eli and V. Barrett this was released in the U.S.A. in March 1975, going to No 3 for two weeks and staying 19 weeks in the charts. It was No 37 in Britain. R.I.A.A. Gold Disc award on 25 June 1975.

A new Atlantic artist, his disc sold a million within three months.

BARRY MANILOW

I WRITE THE SONGS *Arista* [USA]. Written by Bruce Johnson, this was released in the U.S.A. in November 1975. It hit No 1 for one week, staying 24 weeks in the charts. R.I.A.A. Gold Disc award on 6 January 1976.

Second million seller for Barry, who steadily became one of America's bestselling artists. This number was also a hit in Britain for David Cassidy.

TRYIN' TO GET THE FEELING (Album) *Arista* [USA]. Released in the U.S.A. in October 1975, it reached No 8 for two weeks, staying 83 weeks in the charts. R.I.A.A. Gold Disc award on 30 December 1975.

This album is one of Barry Manilow's biggest successes. It was a consistent seller throughout 1976 and into 1977 with over two million records sold by June 1977.

BOB MARLEY & THE WAILERS

NO WOMAN, NO CRY *Island* [Jamaica]. Written by Bob Marley.

Bob Marley was born in the North Jamaican parish of St Ann, his father a retired British Army Captain and his mother a Jamaican, on 6 February 1945. He only saw his father once or twice before he died in the mid-seventies. His mother moved the family to Kingston when he was nine, residing in the city's ghetto areas, where he grew up listening to American rock and roll groups. Many transistor radios playing steel drum music and calypso from both black and white artists from the U.S.A. provided the background for Marley's early years. In 1963 two local musicians taught him the nuances of singing – Joe Higgs and percussionist Alvin 'Seeco' Patterson. He cut his first single 'One Cup of Coffee' in 1964, after Jimmy Cliff introduced him to producer Leslie Kong. In 1965 he formed a vocal group that featured Peter McIntosh (keyboard) (later called Peter Tosh), Bunny Livingston (congas, percussion) and three other singers. The group was originally called The Wailing Rudeboys, which after several name changes became The Wailers in 1966 with Marley, Tosh and Livingston as the only members. They had a succession of hits on the Coxsone label with mid-sixties Jamaican pop classics including: 'Simmer Down'; 'Ride Boy'; 'Put It On'; and Tosh's 'Steppin' Razor'. Marley acted as chief songwriter and arranger. In 1967, Bob started his own Wailin' Soul label which failed after a few releases. He then met and signed with Johnny Nash, made an unreleased album and a hit single 'Stir It Up'. For a while he lived with his mother in Wilmington, Delaware, working in a Chrysler plant at night and writing songs by day. On return to Jamaica he joined Tosh and Livingston and recorded 'Bend Down Low', 'Nice Time' and other singles for producer Clement Dodd. In 1968 drummer Carlton Barret and his brother, bassist Aston Barrett, were added to the group, providing a fuller instrumental gritty sound for the three-part harmonies and increasingly political lyrics of Marley and Tosh. In 1970 Marley formed the Tuff Gong label and had great local success with Wailers' releases such as 'Small Axe', 'Trenchtown Rock', 'Duppy Conquer' and others, many of them preaching the doctrine of Rastafarianism, which advocates the return of the Western hemisphere's black population to Africa.

In 1972 The Wailers signed with Chris Blackwell's Island Records which assured the band of international distribution and promotion. Their first hit album was 'Catch a Fire' (Island, 1973), then 'African Herbsman' (Trojan, 1973), 'Burnin' (Island, 1974) which included 'I Shot The Sheriff', a No 1 pop hit for Eric Clapton internationally, and 'Natty Dread' (1974). Tosh and Livingston then left The Wailers, leaving Marley as the principal Wailer and a real star. His prolific songwriting and charisma on stage made him the symbol of reggae music and a Third World political personality up to the time of his death on 1 May 1981 in Miami, U.S.A., from brain cancer. Marley, who supported in 1976 the then Jamaican Prime Minister Michael Manley in his re-election campaign, was to give a major outdoor concert, appearing with Manley. Marley was shot at, suffering chest and arm wounds, but despite this, he performed, and Manley won in a landslide.

'No Woman, No Cry' was a big hit for Marley and internationally sold well over the million. It was No 22 and seven weeks in Britain's bestsellers. Subsequent hits were 'Rastaman Vibration' (1976); 'Exodus' (1977); and 'Kaya' (1978), all major sellers in Europe, spawning hit singles such as 'Jamming' (1977). Marley was such an outstanding artist that Jamaican Prime Minister Edward Seaga and former P.M. Manley were present when Marley's body lay in state at the National Arena in Kingston for two days prior to the funeral. He was interred as a national hero in his birthplace, St Ann, Jamaica, and is universally acclaimed as Prince of Reggae. Jamaica issued a special postage stamp in his honour.

Origins of reggae go back to Africa, but it is also doubtless influenced by the rhythm and blues sound on the Jamaican scene from U.S. black R & B radio stations and discs taken home by West Indian workers. The new beat was named 'Ska' and 'Blue Beat', but subsequently became more complex and electric, and finally emerged into more up-tempo reggae. It gradually developed by mingling American rock with Caribbean calypso. (See also 'My Boy Lollipop', Millie, 1964.)

THE MIRACLES

LOVE MACHINE (Part 1) *Tamla* [*USA*]. Written by W. Moore and W. Griffith, this was released in the U.S.A. in October 1975 and in Britain in January 1976. It went to No 1 for one week in the U.S.A. and No 3 for three weeks in Britain, staying 28 weeks in the U.S. charts and nine weeks in the British lists.

Described as 'a relentless disco churner with chanting harmonies', this disc is a cut from the group's album 'City of Angels'. The million sale was reported by Tamla Records in March 1976.

MICHAEL MURPHEY

WILDFIRE *Epic* [*USA*]. Written by Michael Murphey and L. Cansler, and released in the U.S.A. in March 1975, this went to No 2 for two weeks, staying 22 weeks in the charts. R.I.A.A. Gold Disc award on 21 July 1975.

Culled from Murphey's album, 'Blue Sky, Night Thunder', this was the first million seller for 'cosmic cowboy' Michael.

NAZARETH (rock quartet)

LOVE HURTS *A & M* [*USA*]. Written by Boudleaux Bryant, this old standby was released in the U.S.A. in November 1975. It reached No 8 for two weeks and stayed 26 weeks in the charts. R.I.A.A. Gold Disc award on 8 April 1976.

Nazareth are Dan McCafferty (vocals); Manny Charlton (guitar); Pete Agnew (bass); Darryl Sweet (drums). Dan, Pete and Darryl played in The Shadettes in and around Dunfermline, Scotland, for eight years, changing their name to Nazareth when Manny Charlton joined in 1969. They became professionals after the release of their first album 'Nazareth' on the Pegasus label in 1971. Their second album was 'Exercises' (1972) then 'Razamanaz' (1973) for Mooncrest label. A successful single 'Broken Down Angel' from their third album got into the charts, and the follow-up 'Bad Boy', also from 'Razamanaz', was a success. They gradually became one of Britain's new attractions. Later, in the U.S.A., they were signed to A & M Records, and came up with 'Love Hurts', written by famous country songwriter Boudleaux Bryant. It was Nazareth's big break, selling the million and staying in the U.S. charts for six months. It is a cut from their album 'Hair of the Dog'.

WILLIE NELSON (country vocalist)

RED HEADED STRANGER (Album) *Columbia* [*USA*]. Songs written by Willie Nelson and released in the U.S.A. in June 1975. It reached No 4 in the country and western charts and was in the charts for over three years. R.I.A.A. Gold Disc award on 11 March 1976. Platinum award by Columbia in 1977.

Willie Nelson was born on 30 April 1933 in Fort Worth, Texas, and started his career as a guitar player, then became a disc jockey, vacuum cleaner salesman, and eventually a 'songwriter's songwriter'. He actually began writing songs at the age of six, and has since averaged one song a month over 40 years. His songs all have themes dear to the hearts of most country artistes – love, hard times, broken homes, despair, happiness – the lyrics subtle and carefully crafted like well-worked stories. Willie talks, speaks and recites them and many have been recorded by artists ranging from Perry Como to Little Anthony & The Imperials, Stevie Wonder to Harry James, Ray Price to Eydie Gorme and from Frank Sinatra to the late Patsy Cline. Willie's audiences packed every performance wherever the travelling Willie Nelson Show appeared, having an electrifying effect.

Nelson originals include many contemporary country standards such as 'Crazy', 'Hello Walls', 'My Own Peculiar Way', 'Funny How Time Slips Away' and 'Night Life'. A top attraction on the country club circuit, his appearances on the Glen Campbell Goodtime Hour, The Porter Wagoner Show, Hee-Haw, and with Bill Anderson brought him acclaim from national audiences. His bandwagon off the beaten country-music track in such places as Los Angeles' Troubadour Club, Las Vegas' Golden Nugget and Max's Kansas City in New York added further laurels from those rock-orientated venues.

Willie's determination to make music in his own style caused him to be seen as something of a renegade, even in the early years. He became known as the leader of a group called 'Nashville Outlaws', most of whom were Texans, but always seemed to include Waylon Jennings, Tompall Glaser, Billy Joe Shaver and Kris Kristofferson. He bridged the gap between country and rock, hippies and rednecks, young and old, creating a huge and appreciative audience in the process. Willie and the other 'Outlaws' convinced people that their music is the natural progression of country music.

He first recorded for the Liberty, Starday and Victor labels, making around 20 albums collectively, as well as a number of singles for Victor. 'Red Headed Stranger' was his first Columbia release, and also the label's first country platinum album. In 1976 he joined Waylon Jennings, Jessi Colter (Waylon's wife) and Tompall Glaser to record 'Wanted: The Outlaws' which resulted in the first country album on any label to ever go platinum. (See Jennings, etc., 1976.) 'Red Headed Stranger' was in the U.S. country charts for over three years, and achieved its million sale by 1977. It included: 'Blue Eyes Crying in the Rain'; 'Bandera'; 'Time of the Preacher'; 'Hands On the Wheel'; 'Red Headed Stranger'; 'Remember Me'; 'Down Yonder'. 'Blue Eyes Crying in the Rain' was a hit as a single, and won a Grammy Award for Best Country Vocal (Male) Performance in 1975. By 1976 Willie Nelson was firmly established as a superstar in the country and national fields.

OLIVIA NEWTON-JOHN

HAVE YOU NEVER BEEN MELLOW? (Album) *MCA* [*USA*]. Released in the U.S.A. in January 1975, this went to No 1 for two weeks, staying 33 weeks in the charts. R.I.A.A. Gold Disc award on 26 February 1975.

A fine mixture of country, soft rock and easy-listening cuts specially selected to appeal to Olivia's fans in all three areas. It had sold a million by April 1975.

Contents: 'Have You Never Been Mellow?' (John Farrar); 'Follow Me' (John Denver); 'Goodbye Again' (John Denver); 'Lifestream' (Rick Nelson); 'Please Mr Please' (Bruce Welch and John Rostill); 'The Air that I Breathe' (A. Hammond and M. Hazelwood); 'Loving Arms'; 'I Never Did Sing You a Love Song'; 'It's So Easy'; 'Water Under the Bridge'; 'And in the Morning'.

Produced by John Farrar.

HAVE YOU NEVER BEEN MELLOW? *MCA* [*USA*]. Released in the U.S.A. in January 1975, this hit No 1 for one week, staying 16 weeks in the charts. R.I.A.A. Gold Disc award on 5 March 1975.

Culled from Olivia's album of the same title. A quick million seller and a personal triumph for John Farrar who produces all her discs.

PLEASE MR PLEASE *MCA* [*USA*]. Released in the U.S.A. in May 1975, this again went to No 1 for one week. It stayed for 15 weeks in the charts. R.I.A.A. Gold Disc award on 16 September 1975.

Written by two members of Britain's famous Shadows (Welch and Rostill), this cut from Olivia's album 'Have You Never Been Mellow?' was the second million-seller single from that album, making another great year for Olivia.

TED NUGENT (rock guitarist)

TED NUGENT (Album) *Epic* [*USA*]. Released in the U.S.A. in December 1975, this reached No 43 for two weeks, staying in the charts for 50 weeks. R.I.A.A. Gold Disc award on 26 July 1976. Platinum award in October 1977.

Ted Nugent's passion for rock'n' roll came at an early age. At 14 he helped usher in the start of what soon became Detroit's heavy metal rock dynasty as a member of The Lourds. Two years later, he formed the original Amboy Dukes, his attack on rock's senses beginning in earnest. In the following ten years Ted and The Amboy Dukes became one of rock's most successful and publicized acts, with tours of more than 200 nights a year. His first Top 20 hit was 'Journey to the Center of Your Mind', one of his many regional successes, plus four albums by 1977. His dedication to rock'n' roll resulted in his signing with Epic in

1975. This album 'Ted Nugent' was his debut for Epic, and sales of his albums thereafter made him a 'platinum' artist in two years, and recognition not only in U.S.A. but throughout Europe where he toured extensively as one of the premier artists in the music industry.

The album includes: 'Stranglehold'; 'Hey Baby'; 'Just What the Doctor Ordered'.

THE OHIO PLAYERS

HONEY (Album) *Mercury* [*USA*]. Released in the U.S.A. in August 1975, this went to No 2 for one week, staying 36 weeks in the charts. R.I.A.A. Gold Disc award on 15 August 1975. Grammy Award: Best Album Package, 1975.

An almost immediate gold award for this album. It had sold a million by January 1976.

LOVE ROLLERCOASTER *Mercury* [*USA*]. Written by The Ohio Players, this was released in the U.S.A. in October 1975, going to No 1 for one week and staying 25 weeks in the charts. R.I.A.A. Gold Disc award on 5 January 1976.

Another big hit for this group, with million sale by the end of the year.

THE O'JAYS

I LOVE MUSIC (Part 1) *Philadelphia-International* [*USA*]. Written by Kenny Gamble and Leon Huff and released in the U.S.A. in October 1975 and in Britain in February 1976, this got to No 5 for two weeks in the U.S.A. and No 13 for one week in Britain. It stayed 19 weeks in the U.S. bestsellers and 10 weeks in the British charts.

A further triumph and million seller for The O'Jays and their writers Gamble and Huff.

FAMILY REUNION (Album) *Philadelphia-International* [*USA*]. Released in the U.S.A. in October 1975, this climbed to No 7 for one week, staying 32 weeks in the charts. R.I.A.A. Gold Disc award on 5 December 1975.

Second million seller album for The O'Jays by 1976.

TONY ORLANDO & DAWN

HE DON'T LOVE YOU (like I love you) *Elektra/Asylum* [*USA*]. Written by Jerry Butler, Clarence Carter and Curtis Mayfield, this was released in the U.S.A. in February 1975. It rose to No 1 for three weeks and stayed 17 weeks in the charts. R.I.A.A. Gold Disc award on 9 June 1975.

The first single to be released by Elektra/Asylum Records, written by three famous artist/writers, and another million seller for the international stars Orlando & Dawn.

PEOPLE'S CHOICE (vocal sextet)

DO IT ANYWAY YOU WANNA *Philadelphia-International* [*USA*]. Written by Leon Huff and released in the U.S.A. in August 1975, this went to No 11 for one week, staying 19 weeks in the charts. R.I.A.A. Gold Disc award on 17 November 1975.

Peoples Choice are Frankie Brunson (vocalist/piano/organ); David Thompson (drums); Roger Andrews (bass) - all originally members of The Fashions in 1970 - and Guy Friske (bass); Donald Ford (keyboards); and Darnell Jordan (guitar), who joined in 1973 to form the newly-named group. Producer/writer Kenny Gamble discovered them performing at the Apollo and signed them to his Phil-Int label. They are a completely self-contained group, and do their own arranging and writing, and never use any session men.

This disc sold the million in three months.

PILOT

MAGIC *Capitol* [*USA*] *EMI* [*Britain*]. Written by Dave Paton and Bill Lyall, this was released in Britain in November 1974 and in the U.S.A. in March 1975. It reached No 8 for one week in Britain and No 5 for two weeks in the U.S.A., staying 11 weeks in the British charts and 22 weeks in the U.S. charts. R.I.A.A. Gold Disc award on 13 August 1975.

This disc was first a moderate success in Britain in 1974, but when released in the U.S.A. in 1975 it was a big success there and sold a million. Pilot were an English group who were popular on British TV.

PINK FLOYD

WISH YOU WERE HERE (Album) *Columbia* [*USA*]. Released in the U.S.A. in September 1975, this hit No 1 for two weeks, staying 33 weeks in the charts. R.I.A.A. Gold Disc award on 17 September 1975.

This album was certified platinum for million sale by Columbia Records. It was the quartet's first album on that label.

Contents: 'Shine on You Crazy Diamond' (Wright, Waters and Gilmour); 'Welcome to the Machine' (Waters); 'Have a Cigar' (Waters); 'Wish You Were Here' (Waters and Gilmour).

QUEEN (rock quartet)

A NIGHT AT THE OPERA (Album) *EMI* [*Britain*] *Elektra* [*USA*]. Released in Britain in November 1975, and in the U.S.A. in December 1975, this went to No 4 for three weeks in the U.S.A. and No 1 for nine weeks in Britain. It stayed 50 weeks in the U.S. charts and 20 weeks in the British topsellers. R.I.A.A. Gold Disc award on 9 March 1976.

Queen are Freddie Mercury (vocals); Brian May (guitar); John Deacon (bass); and Roger Taylor (drums). The group was formed in 1972 when May and Taylor of the then recently disbanded Smile, joined singer Mercury. After six months' auditioning, John Deacon was chosen as bassist, and the new band spent a year and a half in rehearsing and practising. Mercury had many ideas for songs, and also came up with the name Queen, helping to develop the group's unique style and image. Queen were more than just an average rock group. Mercury was an art school graduate and graphic designer, May has a degree in physics and had worked toward a Ph.D. in infra-red astronomy, Taylor has been through dental college and Deacon has an honours degree in electronics from Chelsea College.

The group were signed to EMI in 1973, and Elektra in the U.S.A., after their first album 'Queen' (1973). This album had quick and strong acceptance, showing rare maturity for a debut disc. This became even more apparent after release of their single 'Seven Seas of Rhye' and during a brief U.S. tour with Mott The Hoople in 1974. 'Queen II' album followed in 1974 and also 'Sheer Heart Attack'. The latter contained the single hit 'Killer Queen' that definitely established the band on both sides of the Atlantic, and a world tour built their reputation in Europe, North

America and Japan. It revealed a new diversity – densely layered songs, contrasting with their earlier efforts.

'A Night at the Opera' album, superbly produced by Queen and former engineer Roy Thomas Baker, utilized studio methods to construct elaborate soundscape from the crescendos of operatic choruses during 'Bohemian Rhapsody'. The album soon sold a million.

It included: 'Bohemian Rhapsody'; 'You're My Best Friend'; ' '39'; 'Good Company'; 'The Prophet's Song'.

Mercury and May write the group's material.

BOHEMIAN RHAPSODY *EMI* [*Britain*]. Written by Freddie Mercury and released in the U.S.A. in December 1975 and in Britain in November 1975, this rococo number got to No 1 for nine weeks in Britain and No 4 for two weeks in the U.S.A. It stayed 18 weeks in the British charts and 27 weeks in the U.S. bestsellers. R.I.A.A. Gold Disc award on 3 June 1976.

The prime cut from Queen's successful album 'Night at the Opera'. It sold a million in Britain and over a million in the U.S.A., despite its length (six minutes). This disc, with operatic choruses, was the first single in this genre, and imprinted its sound on the minds of millions. Global sales estimated at well over three million.

HELEN REDDY

HELEN REDDY'S GREATEST HITS (Album) *Capitol* [*USA*]. Released in the U.S.A. in November 1975 and in Britain in January 1976, this went to No 5 for two weeks in both countries. It stayed 37 weeks in the U.S. charts and 15 weeks in the British bestsellers. R.I.A.A. Gold Disc award on 3 December 1975.

This fine compilation sold a million in the U.S.A. by July 1976, and over 150,000 in Britain. Global sales estimated at two million plus.

It contained: (*)'I Am Woman' (Helen Reddy and R. Burton); 'I Don't know How to Love Him' (Tim Rice and Andrew Lloyd Webber); (*)'Leave Me Alone (Ruby Red Dress)' (Linda Laurie); (*)'Delta Dawn' (A. Harvey and L. Collina); 'You and Me Against the World' (P. Williams and K. Ascher); (*)'Angie Baby' (Alan O'Day); 'Emotion' (V. Sanson and P. Dahlstrom); 'Keep On Singing' (Janssen, Hart and Davis); 'Peaceful' (Kenny Rankin); 'Ain't No Way to Treat a Lady' (Harriet Schock).

(* denotes sold a million as a single.)

The British release of the album was entitled 'The Best of Helen Reddy'.

RHYTHM HERITAGE

THEME FROM 'S.W.A.T.' *ABC* [*USA*]. Written by B. De Vorzan, this was released in the U.S.A. in November 1975, hitting No 1 for two weeks and staying 27 weeks in the charts. R.I.A.A. Gold Disc award on 11 February 1976.

First million seller for Rhythm Heritage (leader Michael Omartian). This theme from the U.S. TV series was a great disco favourite there.

MINNIE RIPERTON

LOVIN' YOU *Epic* [*USA*]. Written by Minnie Riperton and R. Rudolph, this was released in the U.S.A. in January 1975 and in Britain in April 1975. It rose to No 1 for one week in the U.S.A. and two weeks in Britain, staying 21 weeks in the U.S. charts and ten weeks in the British lists. R.I.A.A. Gold Disc award on 8 April 1975.

Minnie Riperton was born on the South Side of Chicago, and started singing with her large and musical family, and later in the church choir at the age of nine. Vocal tuition commenced shortly after, cultivating the now widely-renowed five-octave vocal range. At 14, she signed a recording contract with Chess/Janus. At school Minnie was tutored in operatic singing, but this was the hardest form to break into for a black girl. She formed a girl group, The Gems, staying with them for four years, and doing background vocals for radio commercials. In 1967 when she was 18, Minnie took a job as a secretary with Chess, and recorded as lead singer with The Rotary Connection, a new group the label formed, for two years. Six Rotary Connection sets were followed by her first and only solo album for Chess, 'Come to My Garden', which met with much critical acclaim.

In 1971, Minnie left Chess with her husband Richard Rudolph for some time, and settled in Gainesville, Florida. During this period, she gave up singing and concentrated on writing with her husband and raising her family. She was pursued by many disc companies, but held out for something she thought special. This came from Epic's A & R man, Don Ellis, who signed her to that label. An album followed, 'Perfect Angel', and 'Lovin' You', written by Minnie and her husband, was taken from it and released as a single. This sweet ballad was an excellent recording to show off her amazingly flexible five-octave range. The disc speedily sold over a million in the U.S.A. and had big sales in Britain and elsewhere.

Minnie died in Los Angeles, 12 July 1979.

DIANA ROSS

THEME FROM 'MAHOGANY' ('Do you know where you're going to?') *Motown* [*USA*]. Written by Gerry Goffin and M. Masser, this was released in the U.S.A. in October 1975, and in Britain in April 1976. It went to No 1 for one week in the U.S.A. and No 4 for one week in Britain. It stayed 21 weeks in the U.S. charts and eight weeks in the British lists.

Mahogany is a Berry Gordy film with Diana Ross in the name part. This fine theme song sold a quick million by January 1976, and together with the film further enhanced Diana Ross' career. The film was an enormous box office success.

DAVID RUFFIN

WALK AWAY FROM LOVE *Motown* [*USA*]. Written by C. Kipps, this was released in the U.S.A. in November 1975 and in Britain in January 1976. It went to No 8 for two weeks in the U.S.A. and No 10 for two weeks in Britain, staying 21 weeks in the U.S. charts and nine weeks in the British bestsellers.

First million seller for David since he left The Temptations and went solo in 1968. Taken from his album 'Who I Am', it sold a million by February 1976.

RUFUS (featuring Chaka Khan)

RUFUS, FEATURING CHAKA KHAN (Album) *ABC* [*USA*]. Released in the U.S.A. in November 1975, this went to No 7 for one week, staying 31 weeks in the charts. R.I.A.A. Gold Disc award on 14 January 1976.

Another million (platinum) for Rufus and outstanding girl singer Chaka Khan, the sale achieved by early 1976.

It contained: 'Fool's Paradise'; 'Have a Good Time'; 'Ooh I Love Your Lovin' '; 'Everybody Has an Aura'; 'Circle'; 'Sweet Thing'; 'Dance Wit' Me'; 'Little Boy Blue'; 'On Time'; 'Jive Talking'.

SEALS & CROFTS

SEALS & CROFTS' GREATEST HITS (Album) *Warner* [*USA*]. Released in the U.S.A. in October 1975, this went to No 6 for two weeks and stayed 32 weeks in the bestsellers. R.I.A.A. Gold Disc award on 5 December 1975.

Third million-selling album for Seals & Crofts by March 1976. A compilation of all their best numbers, it included: 'Diamond Girl'; 'Hummingbird'; 'Castles in the Sand'; 'We May Never Pass This Way (Again)'; 'I'll Play for You' and 'Summer Breeze'.

NEIL SEDAKA

BAD BLOOD *Rocket MCA* [*USA*]. Written by Neil Sedaka and P. Cody and released in the U.S.A. in September 1975, this went to No 1 for three weeks, staying 19 weeks in the charts. R.I.A.A. Gold Disc award on 25 November 1975.

Neil Sedaka, disc star of the late 1950s and early 1960s, retired from 1963 to 1970 when groups became predominant, and de-

voted himself to writing for other stars including Tom Jones, Fifth Dimension, Andy Williams, Peggy Lee, David Cassidy and Nancy Wilson. He commuted to England and discovered he was still popular. In 1971, a Royal Albert Hall concert in London proved successful. In 1972 came a successful revival of 'Oh Carole' (1972). After little success with his albums 'Emergence' (1971) and 'Solitaire' (1972) in the U.S.A., he recorded a third album 'Tra-La Days Are Over' (1973) using the same British session personnel (later known as 10 CC) as he had on 'Solitaire'. That album attracted Elton John's attention. They met at a party in London, and though Neil was then under contract to Polydor for world distribution (outside the U.S.A.) he asked Elton if he'd distribute his albums on Elton's new Rocket label. Elton readily agreed and they selected the best tracks from Sedaka's last few albums and issued the album 'Sedaka's Back' for release in the U.S.A. Within weeks of its release the first single from it 'Laughter in the Rain' was a hit (1974). Other single hits from the album were 'Solitaire' (a half-million seller for Andy Williams and hit for The Carpenters), 'Love Will Keep us Together' (multi-million seller for Captain & Tennille) and also hits for Bo Donaldson & The Heywoods, Maria Muldaur, and Helen Reddy.

Sedaka made his 'comeback' U.S. nightclub appearance at The Troubadour in Los Angeles, the same club that launched Elton John's career four years earlier. It was, however, the 'Tra-La Days Are Over' that started it all for Sedaka. This sold 100,000 in Britain and he began to play concerts all over Britain, The Talk of the Town in London for five weeks, and also a couple of BBC specials. Sedaka thus established himself as a contemporary star, and erased his old image.

Neil teamed up with Phil Cody and the album 'The Hungry Years' (1975) (titled 'Overnight Success' in Britain) was released. This contained the hit 'Bad Blood' that went over the million as a single.

Up to 1975, Neil Sedaka had written over 700 songs.

SILVER CONVENTION (female soul trio)

FLY, ROBIN, FLY *Midland International/RCA* [*USA*]. Written by S. Levay and S. Prager, this was released in the U.S.A. in October 1974, going to No 1 for three weeks and staying 20 weeks in the charts. R.I.A.A. Gold Disc award on 2 December 1975. Grammy Award: Best Rhythm-and-Blues Instrumental Performance, 1975.

Silver Convention line-up: Ramona Wulf (originally a solo artist); Linda G. Thompson (former member of Les Humphries Singers) both from Germany, and Penny McLean (former singer with several groups) born in Austria, but most of her life spent in Germany. They first appeared in the British charts with 'Save Me', followed by 'Fly, Robin, Fly' which got to No 28 only. Its release in the U.S.A. was immediate with a rapid million sale, an outstanding event for three ladies from Germany whose international success spread from there. They went on to bigger success in 1976.

PAUL SIMON

FIFTY WAYS TO LEAVE YOUR LOVER *Columbia* [*USA*]. Written by Paul Simon, this hit No 1 for three weeks in the U.S.A. and No 20 for one week in Britain. It stayed 20 weeks in the U.S. charts and seven weeks in the British bestsellers after release in the U.S.A. in December 1975 and in Britain in January 1976. R.I.A.A. Gold Disc award on 11 March 1976.

Second solo million seller for Paul Simon, particularly popular in the U.S.A.

THE STAPLE SINGERS

LET'S DO IT AGAIN *Curtom* [*USA*]. Written by Curtis Mayfield and released in the U.S.A. in October 1975, this went to No 1 for one week and stayed 20 weeks in the charts. R.I.A.A. Gold Disc award on 24 November 1975.

Continuing the success story of The Staple Singers, this disc was their fifth million seller.

CAT STEVENS

CAT STEVENS' GREATEST HITS *Island [Britain] A & M [USA]*. Released in the U.S.A. and Britain in July 1975, this achieved No 4 for one week in the U.S.A. and No 2 for one week in Britain. It stayed 35 weeks in the U.S. charts and 19 weeks in the British lists. R.I.A.A. Gold Disc award on 15 August 1975.

Cat Stevens had had an impressive string of hits from 1971. This mixture of ballads and easy rockers made an excellent package, and is a good history of the artist. It included 'Two Fine People'; 'Wild World'; 'Moonshadow'; 'Peace Train'; 'Morning Has Broken'; 'Another Saturday Night'; 'Lady D'Arbanville'.

THE STYLISTICS

BEST OF THE STYLISTICS (Album) *Avco [USA]*. Released in the U.S.A. in February 1975 and Britain in March 1975, this made No 41 for one week in the U.S.A. and No 1 for eight weeks in Britain. It stayed 30 weeks in the U.S. charts and 52 weeks in the British bestsellers.

This compilation of the group's big hits was the bestselling album of 1975 in Britain, where it sold over a million.

It contained: (*)'You Make Me Feel Brand New' (1974); (*)'Betcha By Golly Wow' (1972); 'Rockin' roll Baby' (1973); (*)'Break Up to Make Up' (1973); (*)'You're a Big Girl Now' (Bryant & Douglas, 1969); (*)'I'm Stone in Love with You' (1972); 'Stop, Look, Listen' (1972); 'Let's Put It All Together' (Hugo, Luigi and Geo. D. Weiss, 1974); (*)'You Are Everything' (1971); 'People Make the World Go Round' (1972).

All songs by Linda Creed and Thom Bell unless otherwise indicated.

(* denotes sold a million as a single.)

DONNA SUMMER

LOVE TO LOVE YOU BABY *Oasis/Casablanca [USA]*. Written by Giorgio Moroder, P. Bellotte and Donna Summer, this sexy ballad was released in the U.S.A. in November 1975 and in Britain in January 1976. It went to No 1 for one week in the U.S.A. and No 2 for four weeks in Britain, staying 22 weeks in the U.S. charts and ten weeks in the British bestsellers. R.I.A.A. Gold Disc award on 19 February 1976.

Donna Summer was born in September 1950 in a working-class Boston family. She wanted to be a singer from the age of ten. Mahalia Jackson was her first singing idol. She practised her singing throughout her school career, and landed her first professional job as a member of the Munich (Germany) cast of *Hair* for over a year, and stayed in Europe almost continuously afterwards, joining the Vienna Folk Opera's productions of *Porgy and Bess* and *Showboat*. She also took part in German stagings of *Godspell* and *The Me That Nobody Knows*. Additionally she worked as backing vocalist on several Munich recordings, and it was during one of these sessions she was spotted by Giorgio Moroder and Pete Bellotte, partners of a new label, Oasis Records. She made a number of singles that were hits in Northern Europe, the biggest being 'Hostage' and 'Lady of the Night', but nothing was released in the U.S.A. Inspired by the popular erotic 'Je t'aime' in France, she wrote and recorded 'Love to Love You Baby' which did not break big in Europe. This was one of three records that Moroder brought to Casablanca Records, and president Neil Bogart bought it. Bogart gave a party for his friends at his house, and on a whim, placed the disc on his turntable. The mood of the party changed immediately, and the disc was replayed several times. Bogart phoned Moroder in Germany requesting a re-cut of the song lengthening it from 4 minutes to a 20-minute version. Moroder complied with a 16 minute, 50 second version which became the rage of New York discos. Its lyric and sensual approach created a storm of controversy, and the irresistible drive and rhythm generated another furore in discos across the county.

Her subsequent albums 'Love to Love You Baby', 'Love Trilogy' and 'The Four Seasons of Love' all went gold, and her personal appearances in the U.S.A. established Donna as a major newcomer.

'Love to Love You Baby' sold a rapid million in the U.S.A. and big sales in Britain and elsewhere.

SWEET

FOX ON THE RUN *RCA [Britain]*. Written by the group Sweet (Connolly, Priest, Scott and Tucker) and released in Britain in March 1975 and in the U.S.A. in October 1975, this went to No 4 for three weeks in the U.S.A. and No 2 for two weeks in Britain. It stayed 22 weeks in the U.S. charts and ten weeks in the British lists. R.I.A.A. Gold Disc award on 23 February 1976.

The first number both written and produced by Sweet. It was an outstanding success on both sides of the Atlantic, and was also No 1 in Germany for nine weeks. U.S. sales went over the million, and global sale over two million.

ACTION *RCA [Britain]*. Written by the group Sweet (Connolly, Priest, Scott and Tucker) and released in the U.S.A. in February 1976 and Britain in July 1975, this hit No 10 for one week in the U.S.A. and No 14 for one week in Britain. It stayed for 14 weeks in the U.S. bestsellers and six weeks in the British charts.

Second single written solely by Sweet. A power-packed rocker, it sold a reported 1,500,000 globally.

THE SYLVERS (male and female sextet)

BOOGIE FEVER *Capitol [USA]*. Written by K. St Lewis and F. Perren and released in the U.S.A. in December 1975. It reached No 1 for one week and stayed 20 weeks in the charts. R.I.A.A. Gold Disc award on 20 April 1976.

The Sylvers consisted of two sisters and four brothers for the main group, but were originally a family act featuring nine members ranging in age (in 1976) from the mid-teens to the mid-twenties. They decided to get into the music business after they noted that the voices of Donny Osmond (The Osmonds) and Michael Jackson (Jackson Five) were breaking into a lower range. They re-grouped their act (named the Little Angels featuring the four elder Sylvers in the 1960s) around the clear falsetto voice of Foster, age 10. From the beginning they had hits like 'Fool's Paradise' and 'Misdemeanor' (a solo hit for Foster Sylvers). Then came 'Boogie Fever' which became one of the biggest crossover records from the rhythm-and-blues lists to the national charts. It sold over 2,500,000.

Their hit records were followed by concert, nightclub and TV appearances including The Donny & Marie Show, The Mac

Davis Show, The Cher Show and concerts at Caesar's Palace and Madison Square Garden.

The sextet are: James; Ricky; Edmond; Pat; Angie; and Foster. They shared the spotlight as one of America's top-selling groups for seven years. The soul/pop group had, for a time, a seventh member, Leon Sylvers, the oldest brother who left to handle the songwriting and production reins. They first recorded in 1973 for Pride Records.

B.J. THOMAS
ANOTHER SOMEBODY DONE SOMEBODY WRONG SONG *ABC* [*USA*]. Written by Chips Moman and L. Butler, this was released in the U.S.A. in January 1975, getting to No 1 for one week and staying 21 weeks in the charts. R.I.A.A. Gold Disc award on 23 May 1975. Grammy Award: Best Country Song, 1975.

First big hit for B.J. Thomas since 1968, when he dropped out of the music world for a complete rest and self re-evaluation. He came back in 1973 with an album, and at that time committed himself to Southern rock'n'roll. He then toured with his group Beverteeth, and subsequently made this million seller, produced by independent producer Chips Moman for ABC, with whom he co-wrote the song.

WAR
WHY CAN'T WE BE FRIENDS? *United Artists* [*USA*]. Written by the group War and released in the U.S.A. in April 1975, this got to No 5 for two weeks, staying 20 weeks in the charts. R.I.A.A. Gold Disc award on 23 July 1975.

This single sold a million in three months in the U.S.A.

WINGS (WITH PAUL McCARTNEY)
VENUS AND MARS ARE ALRIGHT TONIGHT (Album) *Apple* [*Britain*] *Capitol* [*USA*]. Released in the U.S.A. and Britain in June 1975, this shot to No 1 for one week in the U.S. and seven weeks in Britain. It stayed 36 weeks in the U.S.A. charts and 22 weeks in the British topsellers. R.I.A.A. Gold Disc award on 2 June 1975.

This album, mostly recorded in New Orleans in the Allen Toussaint-Marshall Schorn studios, had advance orders for 1,500,000, and was both gold and platinum almost on release. It hit the No 1 spot also in France and Japan.

The album is McCartney's most co-ordinated effort since leaving The Beatles, and is a set of fine rock, but he goes beyond his pop role to prove he can handle all kinds of music. His vocals range from smooth ballad style to raunchy rock sound. It also features Jimmy McCulloch (guitar) and Denny Laine switched to bass and vocal harmonies. Wife Linda McCartney is an improved singer. Guest musicians include Tom Scott, Allan Toussaint and Dave Mason. There are horn-filled tracks and some big brass arrangements. The album includes 'Listen to What the Man Said' issued as a single just prior to their album.

Contents: 'Venus and Mars'; 'Spirits of Ancient Egypt'; 'Rock Show'; 'Letting Go'; 'Listen to What the Man Said'; 'You Gave Me the Answer'; 'Magneto and Titanium Man'; 'Medicine Jar'; 'Call Me Back Again'; 'Treat Her Gently (Lonely Old People)'; 'Crossroads'; 'Love in Song'.

All songs by Paul McCartney.

Global sale estimated at well over two million.

LISTEN TO WHAT THE MAN SAID *Apple* [*Britain*] *Capitol* [*USA*]. Written by Paul McCartney and released in the U.S.A. in May 1975 and in Britain in June 1975, this went to No 1 for two weeks in the U.S.A. and No 6 for two weeks in Britain. It lasted 19 weeks in the U.S. charts and eight weeks in the British topsellers. R.I.A.A. Gold Disc award on 5 September 1975.

Released before the 'Venus and Mars' album, this single whetted the appetite for the album. It sold well over a million in the U.S.A. alone, and made big sales elsewhere.

GARY WRIGHT
THE DREAM WEAVER (Album) *Warner* [*USA*]. Released in the U.S.A. in August 1975, this rose to No 5 for two weeks, staying 50 weeks in the charts. R.I.A.A. Gold Disc award on 8 March 1976.

Gary Wright began his path to success in the 1960s, when he left his native New Jersey to study medicine in Europe. Around 1968 he joined the British underground rock scene playing in the group Spooky Tooth, a quintet which became the springboard for a number of prominent British musicians. Between 1968 and 1973, they made six albums for Island Records and one for Goodear label in 1974, also toured around. During this period, Gary made some solo experiments, production and session work with a variety of artists including George Harrison, Steve Gibbons and Tim Rose. Spooky Tooth finally broke up in 1974. On return to the U.S.A., Gary embarked on a solo career (1975) recording for Warner Brothers, and composed, produced and performed practically all the vocal and instrumental parts on his debut album 'Dream Weaver'. He toured for six months after the release of the album, and Warners kept pushing and promoting their artist. Their faith in him finally paid off, and Gary became an 'overnight sensation'. He leads an all-keyboard (plus drums) group, producing a sound with an appealing fusion of progressive rock and rhythm-and-blues. The former keyboards Spooky Tooth player thus confirmed, through his success on the charts and on the road, that he is one of the most professional artists in the contemporary field of music.

'Dream Weaver' album included two single hit releases, 'Dream Weaver' (a No 1 hit in 1976) and 'Love is Alive'.

Z.Z. TOP
FANDANGO (Album) *London* [*USA*]. Released in the U.S.A. in May 1975, this went to No 9 for two weeks, staying 41 weeks in the charts. R.I.A.A. Gold Disc award on 27 June 1975.

Second million-selling album for Z.Z. Top, the sale achieved by December 1975. It included: 'Tush'; 'Thunderbird'; 'Jailhouse Rock' (Jerry Leiber and Mike Stoller, 1957); 'Heard It on the X'; 'Nasty Dogs & Funky Kings'; 'Back Door Medley (Backdoor Love Affair, Mellow Down Easy, Backdoor Love Affair No 2, Long Distance Boogie)'.

Material written by Z.Z. Top.

1976

ORIGINAL FILM SOUNDTRACK (LED ZEPPELIN)
THE SONG REMAINS THE SAME (Double album) *Swan Song* [*USA*]. Released U.S.A. and Britain, October 1976. It climbed to No 2 in the U.S.A. and stayed there for three weeks, remaining in the charts for 20 weeks. In Britain it stayed in the charts for 13 weeks, reaching No 1 for one week. R.I.A.A. Gold Disc award on 3 November 1976. Platinum award on 15 December 1976.

Led Zeppelin's first full-length motion picture, the culmina-

tion of three years' work. It is part-documentary and part-fantasy, running for 136 minutes. The gala première was in New York on 20 October 1976. The four Lords Led are transported over ocean, hills and black mountainsides until they reach Led Zeppelin Land. Here they rule as benevolent despots, guided from behind by Grand Vizier Peter Grant. The drum solo 'Moby Dick' and guitar passages during the 26 minutes of 'Dazed and Confused' underlined what had been apparent for some years, that Jimmy Page and John Bonham were gifted musicians, and that Led Zeppelin was the world's most successful rock group.

Peter Grant was the group's manager. The album was produced by Jimmy Page.

The recurring themes of 'The Song Remains The Same' are the same as those which appeared in the group's seven albums – love, violence, aggression – portrayed in performance and dream sequences. Film directed by Peter Clifton and Joe Massot, sound synchronized by Jimmy Page.

Contents of album are: 'Rock'n'Roll'; 'Celebration Day'; 'The Song Remains The Same'; 'Dazed and Confused'; 'No Quarter'; 'Stairway to Heaven'; 'Moby Dick'; 'Whole Lotta Love'.

ORIGINAL FILM SOUNDTRACK (BARBRA STREISAND AND KRIS KRISTOFFERSON)

A STAR IS BORN (Album) *Columbia* [*USA*]. Released in U.S.A. in November 1976, and in Britain in February 1977. This was No 1 for seven weeks in the U.S.A., staying in the charts for 50 weeks. In Britain it stayed in the charts for 46 weeks. R.I.A.A. Gold Disc award on 23 December 1976. R.I.A.A. Platinum award on 21 January 1977.

The film is the love story of two rock stars, played by Barbra Streisand and Kris Kristofferson – both superstars in front of the camera and the microphone. The album features the music from their concerts in the film, including the now famous 'Love Theme' (Evergreen). The film captures the excitement and madness of the rock scene. Apart from the R.I.A.A. awards, it was five times winner of the Golden Globe awards (Best Musical Film; Best Actress in a Musical Film; Best Actor in a Musical Film; Best Song 'Evergreen', and Best Musical score).

'Evergreen' also won three Grammy Awards and the Academy Award (The Oscar) for Best Film Song of 1976. (See Barbra Streisand, 1976.) Other songs were 'Watch Closely Now', 'With One More Look at You', 'Everything', 'Woman in the Moon' and 'Hellacious Acres', all written by Kris Kristofferson. Sales of this album were 5 million by May 1978.

ABBA (vocal quartet)

FERNANDO *Polar* [*Sweden*], *Epic* [*Britain*], *Atlantic* [*USA*]. Written by B. Andersson and Stig Anderson and released in Sweden in 1975, in Britain in March 1976 and in the U.S.A. in August 1976. This was No 1 in Britain for six weeks, staying in the charts for 15 weeks. It reached No 14 in the U.S.A. and remained in the charts for 23 weeks.

'Fernando' was included in ABBA's 'Greatest Hits' album in 1975. Its release as a single in Britain and its place as No 1 seller in France made the group internationally famous. The disc sold over a million in Britain, and subsequently 6 million globally. It was ABBA's biggest international hit to date. Australian sales were over 250,000 in 10 weeks.

DANCING QUEEN *Polar* [*Sweden*], *Epic* [*Britain*], *Atlantic* [*USA*]. Written by B. Andersson, Bjorn Ulvaeus and Stig Anderson, released in Britain in August 1976, and in the U.S.A. in December 1976. R.I.A.A. Gold Disc award in April 1977. This was 15 weeks in the charts in Britain, with five weeks at No 1. In the U.S.A. it was No 1 for one week and 27 weeks in the charts.

A cut from ABBA's album 'Arrival', this was a sensational follow-up to 'Fernando' in Britain, where it sold a near million. The disc was No 1 all over Europe – Holland, Germany, Belgium, Sweden, Norway, Denmark, Switzerland and Austria – and No 1 in Australia. European sales were over 3 million before the disc was released in the U.S.A., where it sold another million plus. Total sales were over 4 million.

MONEY, MONEY, MONEY *Polar* [*Sweden*], *Epic* [*Britain*], *Atlantic* [*USA*]. Written by Benny Andersson and Bjorn Ulvaeus, this was released in Britain in November 1976, and in the U.S.A. in October 1977. This was No 2 for one week in Britain, with 11 weeks in the charts.

A second single from ABBA's album 'Arrival', with sales of over 500,000. The disc was high in the bestselling charts of most countries, and sold 3 million globally before release in the U.S.A.

ARRIVAL (Album) *Polar* [*Sweden*], *Epic* [*Britain*], *Atlantic* [*USA*]. Released in Scandinavia on 11 October 1976, in Britain in November 1976 and in the U.S.A. in January 1977. It was No 1 in Britain for 12 weeks and stayed in the charts for 61 weeks. In the U.S.A., this album was No 9 for one week and 7 weeks in their charts. R.I.A.A. Gold Disc award on 4 April 1977.

Advance sales for this album in Scandinavia were over 500,000, and subsequent total sales over a million. In Britain, advance sales were 300,0000, reported to make it the highest UK album advance order ever. By February 1977, it had sold 750,000 in Britain and went on to exceed the million there. It was a top seller all over the rest of Europe, No 1 in France for a long time, and No 1 in Australia and New Zealand, with many Gold Disc awards from around the world: a solid gold arrival for the group internationally. Global estimates of sales are well over 5 million. By August 1977, ABBA had sold over 50 million discs, including 20 million albums, and were considered to be the richest group in the world, with a reported fortune of £3 million and the likelihood of earning another £2-£3 million during 1977-1978. They made their first world tour in 1976, with particularly spectacular success in Australia on stage, TV and in disc sales.

Contents: 'When I Kissed the Teacher' (B. Andersson & B. Ulvaeus); (*) 'Dancing Queen' (B. Andersson & B. Ulvaeus and Stig Anderson); 'My Love, My Life' (B. Andersson & B. Ulvaeus and Stig Anderson); 'Dum Dum Diddle' (B. Andersson & B. Ulvaeus); (*) 'Knowing Me, Knowing You' (B. Andersson, B. Ulvaeus and Stig Anderson); (*) 'Money, Money, Money' (B. Andersson & B. Ulvaeus); 'That's Me' (B. Andersson, B. Ulvaeus and Stig Anderson); 'Why Did it Have to be Me?' (B. Andersson & B. Ulvaeus); 'Tiger' (B. Andersson & B. Ulvaeus), 'Arrival' (B. Andersson & B. Ulvaeus). (*) denotes sold a million as singles release. Instrumentalists who played on the album were: Rutger Gunnarsson (bass); Ola Brunkert (drums); Roger Palm; Malanda Gassama (rhythm instruments); Janne Schaffer (electric guitar); Anders Glenmark (electric guitar); Lasse Wellander (acoustic guitar); Bjorn Ulvaeus (acoustic and electric guitars); Benny Andersson (synthesizers, marimbas, chimes, accordion, piano); Anders Dahl (strings); Lasse Carlsson (saxophone). Arrangements by Sven Olof Walldoff and Rutger Gunnarsson. Recorded at Metronome Studio, Polar Recording Co., Sweden, 1976.

AEROSMITH

ROCKS (Album) *Columbia* [*USA*]. This was released in the U.S.A. in May 1976. It was No 3 there for four weeks and stayed in the charts for 45 weeks. R.I.A.A. Gold Disc award on 21 May 1976. R.I.A.A. Platinum Disc award on 9 July 1976.

A superlative album by Aerosmith of their own material, with an almost instant Gold Disc. It sold a million within 10 weeks of release. It included: 'Sick as a Dog': 'Home Tonight': 'Back in the Saddle': 'Rats in the Cellar: 'Last Child'.

AVERAGE WHITE BAND

SOUL SEARCHING (Album) *Atlantic* [*USA*]. This was released in the U.S.A. in July 1976 and was at No 9 for one week, staying in the charts for 17 weeks. R.I.A.A. Gold Disc award on 12 August 1976. R.I.A.A. Platinum Disc award on 30 December 1976.

A really big success for this British group so popular in the U.S.A. It achieved gold status within a month and consistent sales made it a million seller by the year's end. The album features vocalist Alan Gorrie, and sparkles with fine horns and rhythm throughout. Prime cuts on the album 'A Love of Your Own'; 'Queen of My Soul'; and 'Soul Searching'.

BAD COMPANY

RUN WITH THE PACK (Album) *Swan Song* [*USA*] *Island label* [*Britain*]. The material for this disc was written by Bad Company. It was released in the U.S.A. and Britain in February

1976. It climbed to No 3 in the U.S.A. and stayed there for four weeks, remaining in the charts for 24 weeks. In Britain it stayed in the charts for 11 weeks, reaching No 3. R.I.A.A. Gold Disc award on 10 February 1976. R.I.A.A. platinum award on 1 December 1976. The third album for this group to sell a million. It went gold immediately after release. Outstanding tracks were 'Run With the Pack'; 'Simple Man': 'Honey Child'; and 'Young Blood'.

THE BEACH BOYS

THE BEACH BOYS' 20 GOLDEN GREATS (Album) *Capitol-EMI* [*Britain*]. This was released in Britain on 25 June 1976 and was No 1 for 12 weeks, staying in the charts for 25 weeks.

EMI spent £175,000 on promoting this superb compilation with TV, radio and other advertising – the biggest backing they had ever given a record. It sold 750,000 in Britain in three months and went on to achieve the million sale. It had the longest stay at the top for any record in over two years, and contained all the Beach Boys' biggest hits from 1963-1970.

Contents: (*) 'Surfin' USA' (Chuck Berry & Brian Wilson 1963) (*) 'Fun, Fun, Fun' (Mike Love and Brian Wilson 1964) (*) 'I Get Around' (Brian Wilson 1964) 'Don't Worry Baby' (Roger Christian and Brian Wilson 1964) 'Little Deuce Coupé' (Roger Christian and Brian Wilson 1963) 'When I Grow Up (To be a Man)' (Brian Wilson 1964) (*) 'Help Me Rhonda' (Brian Wilson 1965) 'California Girls' (Brian Wilson 1965) (*) 'Barbara-Ann' (Fred Fassert 1961, 1965) (*) 'Sloop John B' (Traditional, arr. Brian Wilson 1966) 'You're So Good to Me' (Brian Wilson 1965) 'God Only Knows' (Tony Asher and Brian Wilson 1966) 'Wouldn't It Be Nice?' (Tony Asher and Brian Wilson 1966) (*) 'Good Vibrations' (Mike Love and Brian Wilson 1966) 'Then I Kissed Her' (Jeff Barry, Ellie Greenwich & Phil Spector – original 'Then He Kissed Me' 1963-1965) 'Heroes and Villains' (Van Dyke Parks and Brian Wilson 1967) 'Darlin'' (Mike Love and Brian Wilson 1968) 'Do It Again' (Mike Love and Brian Wilson 1968) 'I Can Hear Music' (Jeff Barry, Ellie Greenwich & Phil Spector – original 1966-1969) 'Break Away' (Mike Love & Brian Wilson 1969). (* denotes originally a million singles seller.)

THE BEATLES

ROCK'N'ROLL MUSIC (Double album) *Parlophone* [*Britain*], *Capitol* [*USA*]. This was released in Britain and the U.S.A. in June 1976. In Britain it was No 10 for one week, staying in the charts for 14 weeks. In the U.S.A. it reached No 2 for two weeks and remained in the charts for 18 weeks. R.I.A.A. Gold Disc award and platinum award on 14 June 1976.

This is a superb package in every way, the music tracing the band's roots right through to its most self-assured period. The publicity and promotion campaign in the U.S.A. was Capitol's most extensive ever. The album was simultaneously gold and platinum 3 days after release on June 11.

Contents: 'Long Tall Sally' (E. Johnson, R. Blackwell and R. Penniman 1956) 'Roll Over Beethoven' (Chuck Berry 1956) 'Rock'n'Roll Music' (Chuck Berry 1957) 'Matchbox' (Carl Lee Perkins 1957) 'Dizzy Miss Lizzy' (Larry Williams 1958) 'Bad Boy' (Larry Williams 1958) 'Slow Down' (Larry Williams 1958) 'Everybody's Trying to be My Baby' (Carl Lee Perkins 1958) 'Kansas City' (Mike Stoller and Jerry Leiber 1959) 'Money' (Berry Gordy Jnr and J. Bradford 1960) 'Boys' (Wesley Farrell and Luther Dixon 1960) 'Twist and Shout' (Bert Russell and Phil Medley 1961) 'I Call Your Name' (John Lennon and Paul McCartney 1963) 'I Saw Her Standing There' (John Lennon and Paul McCartney 1963) 'You Can't Do That' (John Lennon and Paul McCartney 1964) 'Any Time at All' (John Lennon and Paul McCartney 1964) 'I Wanna be Your Man' (John Lennon and Paul McCartney 1964) 'The Night Before' (John Lennon and Paul McCartney 1965) 'Drive My Car' (John Lennon and Paul McCartney 1965) 'I'm Down' (John Lennon and Paul McCartney 1965) 'Got To Get You Into My Life' (John Lennon

and Paul McCartney 1966) 'Taxman' (George Harrison 1966) 'Birthday' (John Lennon and Paul McCartney 1968) 'Hey Bulldog' (John Lennon and Paul McCartney 1968) 'Back in the U.S.S.R.' (John Lennon and Paul McCartney 1968) 'Helter Skelter' (John Lennon and Paul McCartney 1968) 'Revolution' (John Lennon and Paul McCartney 1968) 'Get Back' (John Lennon and Paul McCartney 1969). Estimated global sales were around 2 million.

THE BEE GEES

YOU SHOULD BE DANCING *RSO* [*USA*]. Written by Robin, Maurice and Barry Gibb and released in the U.S.A. and Britain in July 1976. It climbed to No 1 in the U.S.A. for one week and remained in the charts for 22 weeks. In Britain it was No 4 for one week, staying in the charts for 10 weeks. R.I.A.A. Gold Disc award on 15 September 1976.

Another hit by the Bee Gees, with a compulsive stomping beat. A million seller in the U.S.A. and fine sales elsewhere.

CHILDREN OF THE WORLD (Album) *RSO* [*USA*]. Written by Robin, Maurice and Barry Gibb, this was released in the U.S.A. in September 1976. It was No 8 there for three weeks and stayed in the charts for 29 weeks. R.I.A.A. Gold Disc award on 21 September 1976. R.I.A.A. Platinum Disc award on 23 December 1976.

A million seller for the Gibb brothers within three months. The album is superb disco material incorporating their distinctive sound. It includes their two million-seller singles 'You Should be Dancing' and 'Love So Right'. Other outstanding tracks: 'Children of the World'; 'Boogie Child' and 'You Can't Keep a Good Man Down'.

LOVE SO RIGHT *RSO* [*USA*]. This was written by Robin, Maurice and Barry Gibb and was released in the U.S.A. in September 1976. It was No 3 there for four weeks and stayed in the charts for 24 weeks. R.I.A.A. Gold Disc award on 29 December 1976.

Yet another million seller for the Bee Gees, a cut from their hit album 'Children of The World'.

GEORGE BENSON (jazz guitarist and vocalist)

BREEZIN' (Album) *Warner Brothers* [*USA*]. Released in the U.S.A. in March 1976, this rose to No 1 and stayed there for two weeks, remaining in the charts for 40 weeks. R.I.A.A. Gold Disc award on 4 June 1976. R.I.A.A. Platinum Disc award on 10 August 1976. Grammy Awards: Best Pop Instrumental Performance, 1976; Best Engineered Recording, 1976.

George Benson became involved in rhythm and blues and jazz in the early 1950s. He was 19 when Jack McDuff's band went to Benson's hometown of Pittsburgh one night in 1963. McDuff's guitar player was leaving the band, and Benson auditioned for the job. He stayed with Brother Jack McDuff's Quartet for over two years, and much of his guitar-playing growth happened during this period. The band made an album for Prestige in 1964. Benson left the band in 1965 to pursue a solo career, playing at clubs in the Bronx and Harlem. He made two albums with his band in 1965-66 for Columbia, and went on to record two 'big band' records on Verve (MGM) in 1967 and 1968. Following the death of guitarist Wes Montgomery, Creed Taylor of A & M Records, who had produced Montgomery's discs, cut three albums with Benson from 1968 to 1969. Creed Taylor then set up CTI Records and Benson made a single, 'The Gentle Rain' for the label in 1970, staying with CTI until 1976. During this period Benson made seven solo albums, five with other artists (Freddie Hubbard, Stanley Turrentine) and three singles. His single and album 'White Rabbit' (1972) made a name for him in the pop market. In 1976, George and CTI parted company, and George made the albums 'Benson Burner', 'Spirituals to Swing' (John Hammond's Anniversary Concert), and '50 Years of Jazz Guitar' for Columbia (1976). There was also a single 'Nadia's Theme' for A & M (1976) and an album 'Blue Benson' for Polydor (1976).

Benson was then signed by Warner Brothers and Tommy Li Puma, a staff producer for the company, made the Benson debut album for the label, 'Breezin'', which spearheaded the Warners' 'new music that stays new' campaign in 1976. The album included 'This Masquerade' (written by Leon Russell) - a hit as a single release - and other compositions from various traditions such as Upchurch's 'Six to Four' (Benson's disco contribution) - 'Affirmation' (by José Feliciano) and Bobby Womack's 'Breezin''. Ronnie Foster's 'Lady' and Benson's 'So This is Love' were also included in the album. Benson's interpretation of David Matthews' 'Theme from Good King Bad' was the winning entry in the Best R & B Instrumental Performance competition of the Grammy Awards, 1977. The accompanying band on the album were Phil Upchurch (guitar), Harvey Mason (drums), Ralph MacDonald (percussion) - the three members of Benson's regular touring band - plus Ronnie Foster (keyboards), Jorge Dalto (keyboards) and Stanley Banks (bassist).

By mid 1977 'Breezin'' had sold over 2 million.

Benson is now hailed as the most sparkling and inventive guitarist and definitive jazz guitarist/vocalist of our time. He is also an excellent impersonator and a natural comedian - an incredible performer. Benson's style has not changed much over the years. He still plays without the use of electronic gimmicks like fuzz and echo. It is interesting to note that he first secured a recording contract with RCA at the age of ten as a singer on sessions.

ELVIN BISHOP

FOOLED AROUND AND FELL IN LOVE *Capricorn* [*USA*]. This was written by Elvin Bishop and released in the U.S.A. in March 1976. It was No 3 in the U.S.A. for two weeks and stayed for 25 weeks in the charts. R.I.A.A. Gold Disc award on 23 June 1976.

Elvin Bishop was raised in Tulsa, Oklahoma, and was keen on music from an early age. He subsequently decided to learn the guitar, with blues music becoming the main influence. After graduation from high school, he headed for the University of Chicago under a National Merit Scholarship, and here he met Paul Butterfield. They played at clubs and parties around Chicago. Some years later, the Paul Butterfield Band was formed and established Paul, Elvin and Mike Bloomfield as bona fide rock stars.

Elvin left the band after they had made four albums. He formed a few bands, recorded several albums, none of which captured the true spirit of his music. During a New Year's Eve concert in San Francisco (1973-74), Richard Betts of The Allman Brothers Band introduced Elvin to Capricorn president Phil Walden. Walden signed Elvin to the label soon afterwards and work began on his first album. His album 'Let It Flow' was a good seller, and he gradually built up a steady following. The album included 'Travellin' Shoes', his first chart single. The second Capricorn album 'Juke Joint Jump' bettered his previous record and increased his list of fans. 'Sure Feels Good' taken from it saw considerable chart success. In 1976 came the 'Struttin' My Stuff' album which included the big hit single 'Fooled Around and Fell in Love' which resulted in a million sale. Elvin Bishop had arrived on the national musical scene.

BLUE OYSTER CULT

AGENTS OF FORTUNE (Album) *Columbia* [*USA*]. It was released in the U.S.A. in June 1976 and was No 32 for two weeks, staying in the charts for 35 weeks. R.I.A.A. Gold Disc award on 26 October 1976. R.I.A.A. platinum award on 17 July 1978.

The group's line-up is Allen Lanier (guitar/keyboards), Donald 'Buck Dharma' Roeser (lead guitar), Eric Bloom (vocalist/guitar), Joe Bouchard (bass), and Albert Bouchard (drums). They began in the late 60s as the Soft White Underbelly, later changed to the Stalk Forrest Group, and after landing a contract with Columbia, became Blue Oyster Cult. Their first album was 'Blue Oyster Cult' (1972), received with great acclaim by critics who appreciated their technical ability as well as their wit. By singing of motorcycle gang riots, outer space exploration, folk mythology and drug traffic murders, BOC proved from the outset to be a highly individual outfit, with both decibel and intellectual appeal. 'Tyranny Mutation', 'Secret Treaties (1974) and 'On Your Feet on Your Knees' were products of the first phase of their career, and they then developed material to expose each member's personality. 'Agents of Fortune' highlighted the musicians' individual contribution. In 1976 they developed the most sophisticated laser light show in rock by joining forces with one of America's most advanced physics laboratories, investing in more than 100,000 dollars of equipment.

'Agents of Fortune' contained their first hit single 'Don't Fear The Reaper', a melodic number with an intriguing (false) ending. By 1978, BOC had played 250 shows before half a million people in a year of engagements around the U.S.A. Eric Bloom sang almost the whole of their set in Japanese when they went to Japan.

BONEY M (male and female group)

DADDY COOL *Hansa* [*Germany*]. *Atlantic* [*Britain*]. Written by Farian & Reyman, this was released in Germany in summer 1976 and in Britain in November 1976. In Germany it climbed to No 1 and stayed there for nine weeks, staying in the charts for four months. It was No 6 in Britain and remained in the charts for 13 weeks.

A new German group achieving enormous success. This disc sold over 800,000 in Europe and, with sales elsewhere, easily topped the million. On 11 December 1976, Boney M were presented with a gold disc for German sales, one for sales in France (Disques Carrere), a platinum disc for sales in Benelux (Dureco and Fonior), and a silver disc for their album sales of 'Take the Heat Off Me' in Denmark (AEG Dansk). The album sold 200,000 copies in Germany alone. The single was rush-released in Sweden, Italy and Spain, and Atlantic Records acquired the rights for U.S.A., Britain, Japan and Australia.

The personnel of Boney M is three girls and one man: Marcia Barrett, born 1949 in Jamaica, and brought up in Surrey. Liz Mitchell, born 1953 in Jamaica, and brought up in Kensal Rise, London. Maisie Williams, born 1951 in Monsarrat, and brought up in Birmingham. Bobby Farrell, born 1950 in the Dutch West Indies, and brought up in Holland.

Frank Farian of Munich, a clever producer, recruited the group and sent them around endless 'discokellars' with a selection of backing tapes until Boney M became well-known. The group had four hits, 'Daddy Cool' being the biggest. The group's name was taken from the hero of a German TV series.

BOSTON (rock quintet)

BOSTON (Album) *Epic* [*USA*]. The material for this disc was written by Tom Scholtz. It was released in the U.S.A. in September 1976 and in Britain in December 1976. It was No 2 in the U.S.A. for four weeks, staying in the charts for 82 weeks. In Britain it was No 10 for one week and stayed for 14 weeks in the charts. R.I.A.A. Gold Disc award on 26 October 1976. Platinum award on 22 November 1976.

'Boston' was the brainchild of Tom Scholtz, electronics genius/guitarist/scientist, a highly paid employee of the Polaroid organization, and former graduate of the Massachusetts Institute of Technology. Whilst at Polaroid, he developed a passion for music, and started experimenting with his guitar, electronic machinery and tapes. It soon became more important than his job, and with his wife Cindy, a former horticulturist, he spent their savings buying demo tapes, recorders and amplifiers. Scholtz spent six years putting tapes together in his home-made studio, making one final demo on which he played most of the instruments. An old friend, Brad Delp, did the vocals. After approaching various record companies the recording was signed to the Epic label. Nobody expected the enormous success that was to follow. The album simply raced up the charts and stayed in the Top 10 in U.S.A. for nine months. By July 1978, it had sold over 6½ million, earning well over 40 million dollars for

Scholtz, the Epic label and the subsequently formed group. Boston had re-recorded the songs for the album in Los Angeles, and thus brought the group together in the studio for the first time. It included two additional songs to the demo originally made by Scholtz and Delp, one of which ('More Than a Feeling') became a singles chart hit. Another fine track is 'Smokin''. Other titles included were 'Television Politician', 'Hitch a Ride', 'Peace of Mind', 'Foreplay', 'Long Time', and 'Rock and Roll Band'.

Boston began touring almost immediately after the record was released, and the hard rocking quintet became a major attraction in Boston. Its fame soon spread across the U.S.A. with the added help of Charlie McKenzie (road manager) and Paul Ahern who had promoted the disc. All members of the group had previously made demos with Scholtz and had played in different combinations.

Personnel of Boston: Tom Scholtz (guitars, keyboards); Brad Delp (lead vocal, acoustic guitar and percussion); Barry Goudreau (lead and rhythm guitars); Fran Sheehan (bass); Sib Hasian (drums and percussion).

'Boston' was the most successful debut album of the decade.

DAVID BOWIE

CHANGESONEBOWIE (Album) *RCA [Britain]*. Written by David Bowie, this was released in the U.S.A. and Britain in May 1976. It was No 4 in Britain for two weeks, remaining 17 weeks in the charts. In the U.S.A. it was No 12 for one week and stayed in the charts (in the Top 30) for nine weeks. R.I.A.A. Gold Disc award on 2 August 1976. Platinum award on 15 September 1981.

Bowie's six sold-out concerts at the Empire Pool, Wembley, London, resulted in this Greatest Hits package called 'Changesonebowie', a selection of eleven songs from the repertoire of one of the most sensational singers of the 1970s. It opens with 'Space Oddity' - the song that gave him his first hit in 1969. This is followed by 'John, I'm Only Dancing' (1972) and 'Changes', 'Ziggy Stardust' (1972/1973), 'Suffragette City' and 'The Jean Genie'. Side two opens with 'Diamond Dogs' (1974), then 'Rebel Rebel' (from the 'Diamond Dogs' album), 'Young Americans' (from the album of the same title), the John Lennon/David Bowie composition 'Fame' (from the album 'Young Americans) and 'Golden Years' (from the album 'Station to Station').

The album demonstrates Bowie's musical and lyrical talents, his ability to express the feelings of his age, to mirror the times and move with them. It was a steady seller in the U.S.A. for 5 years, reaching the million sale mark in 1981.

BRASS CONSTRUCTION (nine-member group)

BRASS CONSTRUCTION (Album) *United Artists [USA]*. Released in the U.S.A. in January 1976, this was No 10 for one week, staying 25 weeks in the charts R.I.A.A. Gold Disc award on 31 March 1976. R.I.A.A. platinum award on 10 December 1976.

Brass Construction consists of: Randy Muller (vocalist); Wade Williamston (bass); Joseph Arthur Wong (guitar); Morris Price (trumpet and percussion); Wayne Parris (trumpet); Larry Payton (drums); Sandy Billups (percussion); Jesse Ward (tenor sax); Mickey Grudge (sax and clarinet). Brass Construction were one of the new wave of dance bands of the seventies. They were originally formed while members of the group attended junior high school in Brooklyn's notorious Brownsville, and introduced to music via high school bands. They began playing at parties, school dances and street festivals. Jeff Lane, producer of B.T. Express, spent three years preparing them for this, their first album, and nurturing the talents of group leader Randy Muller, a young musician with a flair for arranging. Lane eventually gave Muller the responsibility for arranging the B.T. Express albums.

The 'Brass Construction' album steadily moved up the U.S. charts and the group became a success on tour, with the album achieving the million sale by the year's end.

BROTHERHOOD OF MAN (vocal quartet)

SAVE YOUR KISSES FOR ME *Pye [Britain]*. Written by Lee Sheriden, Martin Lee and Tony Hiller, this was released in Britain in March 1976 and in the U.S.A. in May 1976. It was No 1 in Britain for six weeks, staying in the charts for 15 weeks. In the U.S.A. it was No 27 for one week and in the charts for 10 weeks.

Brotherhood of Man was founded in 1970 by Tony Hiller of Bethnal Green, London, whose great interest in music resulted in his gathering a group of session singers and musicians in the studio. Tony, also a well-known songwriter, selected four youngsters and worked on them. Their first hit disc was 'United we Stand' (1970) followed by several fair successes. Towards the end of 1974 and into 1975, the group worked successfully in Britain and throughout Europe, and had a hit on the Continent with a self-written song 'Lady'. This was No 1 in Holland and France, earning them major television and cabaret appearances in Austria, Portugal, Holland, France and Belgium. Then came 'Kiss Me, Kiss You Baby' which went 'gold' in France and Belgium, topping the charts in Scandinavia, Germany, Holland and France.

Tony Hiller then concentrated on a song for the Eurovision Song Contest, and with the group, spent a long time on choreography and the search for a suitable number. A thousand pounds was spent on stage clothes, and then the group made a promotion tour of five weeks in six different countries with 'Save Your Kisses For Me' as a run-in to the contest. The song won the British section of the contest, and Brotherhood of Man were then Britain's choice for the Eurovision Contest at The Hague on 3 April 1976. They were the winners, and the song and group rocketed to fame. The song sold a million in Britain by the end of April, and was also No 1 in Denmark, Holland, France, Eire, and Greece, No 2 in Finland, Austria and Norway, and a hit in Sweden. In Germany it sold 170,000 within 2 days of release. Estimates of collective sales are well over 5 million.

Brotherhood of Man consists of: Nicky Stevens. From Wales; she was only 15 when she first toured the Continent, and originally trained as a classical singer. Sandra Stevens (no relation to Nicky). Born in Leeds, she sang with the big bands of Ken Mackintosh and Joe Loss, and was resident singer at Wakefield Theatre Club. Lee Sheriden. Learned piano and later singing and guitar. Became resident musician on the Top Rank circuit, and broadcast with different bands, also making discs as a solo singer. Martin Lee. From Purley, Surrey, spent five years in Australia. Learned guitar and formed his own band on return to Britain, then worked with various bands. His writing brought him into contact with manager Tony Hiller.

'Save Your Kisses For Me' was the first time Britain had won the Eurovision Contest outright since Sandie Shaw with 'Puppet on a String' in 1967.

JACKSON BROWNE

THE PRETENDER (Album) *Elektra/Asylum [USA]*. Written by Jackson Browne and released in the U.S.A. in November 1976, this went to No 5 for two weeks, staying 27 weeks in the charts. R.I.A.A. Gold Disc award on 15 November 1976. R.I.A.A. platinum award on 12 April 1977.

Born in 1950, Jackson Browne left his native Los Angeles in 1967 and went to New York, where he performed in clubs throughout 1968. His songs began to gain attention, and on return to Los Angeles he concentrated on writing. His songs were taken up and recorded by other artists, including The Byrds, Linda Ronstadt, Tom Rush and Johnny Rivers. From 1975, his works were recorded by Greg Allman, Kiki Dee, The Eagles, Bonnie Raitt, Ian Matthews and Joe Cocker.

Browne was one of the first artists to be signed by Asylum Records and it was the Tom Rush disc of 'These Days' that brought his talents to prominence. His first album 'Jackson Browne' was released in October 1971, and the second 'For Everyman' in October 1973. His 'Saturate Before Using' (1972) featured David Crosby and Graham Nash on harmonies, and in that year he played British dates with Joni Mitchell. In the winter of 1973-74, he headlined a 40-city national tour with Linda

Ronstadt, and a 40-city tour with Bonnie Raitt in 1974. 'Late for the Sky' album, released in September 1974 was soon certified 'gold', and 'For Everyman' became 'gold' in 1975.

After a 45-city tour of the U.S.A., Jackson started his first major European tour on 1 December 1977, playing dates in Scotland, England, Holland, Sweden, Germany and Norway, followed by a tour of Australia and Japan. His songs have been described as constantly demanding, complex and mysterious. 'The Pretender' album was produced by Jon Landau, and contained the hit 'Here Come Those Tears Again' released as a single.

GLEN CAMPBELL

20 GOLDEN GREATS (Album) *EMI/Capitol* [*Britain*]. This was released in Britain in October 1976 and went to No 1 for six weeks, staying in the charts for 25 weeks.

This British release of Glen's big hits from the Capitol recordings by EMI came simultaneously with his four shows in the Royal Albert Hall, London, where he was awarded a platinum record for one million sales in Britain. The album is an extension of his former U.S. release 'Greatest Hits' (1971) and achieved the million by May 1977.

Contents: (*) 'Rhinestone Cowboy' (Weiss 1975) 'Both Sides Now' (Joni Mitchell 1970) 'By the Time I Get to Phoenix' (Jim Webb 1969) 'Gentle on My Mind' (John Hartford 1967) 'Too Many Mornings' (Place 1974) (*) 'Witchita Lineman' (Jim Webb 1968) 'One Last Time' (D. and D. Addris 1972) 'Don't Pull Your Love' (Lambert and Potter 1976) 'Then You Can Tell Me Goodbye' (John Loudermilk 1976) 'Reason to Believe' (Tim Hardin 1969) 'It's Only Make Believe' (Jack Nance and Conway Twitty 1958) 'Honey Come Back' (Jim Webb 1970) 'Give Me Back That Old Familiar Feeling' (Graham 1973) (*) 'Galveston' (Jim Webb 1968) 'Dreams of the Everyday Housewife' (Chris Gantry 1969) 'The Last Thing on My Mind' (Tom Paxton 1972) 'Where's the Playground, Susie?' (Jim Webb 1968) 'Try a Little Kindness' (Sapaugh and Austin 1970) 'Country Boy (You Got Your Feet in L.A.)' (Lambert and Potter 1975) 'All I Have to do is Dream' (with Bobbie Gentry) (Boudleaux Bryant 1958) 'Amazing Grace' (Newton arr. and adapted by Kelly). (*) denotes sold a million as singles release.

CAPTAIN & TENNILLE

LONELY NIGHTS (Angel Face) *A & M* [*USA*]. Written by Neil Sedaka and released in the U.S.A. in January 1976, this climbed to No 1 for one week and stayed 23 weeks in the charts. R.I.A.A. Gold Disc award on 8 April 1976.

A continuation of this duo's success - their third million-selling single. It is an up-tempo tune performed with vocal and instrumental dexterity.

SONG OF JOY (Album) *A & M* [*USA*]. This was released in the U.S.A. in March 1976 and went to No 5 for one week, remaining 59 weeks in the charts. R.I.A.A. Gold Disc award on 10 March 1976. R.I.A.A. platinum award on 23 September 1976.

An extremely popular album with over 12 months in the U.S. bestsellers - the duo's second million-selling album. It contained all their big hits including: 'Love Will Keep us Together, 'Lonely Nights', 'Shop Around', 'Muskrat Love', 'Song of Joy'.

SHOP AROUND *A & M* [*USA*]. Written by Berry Gordy and Smokey Robinson in 1961, this was released in the U.S.A. in April 1976. It went to No 4 for one week and stayed 26 weeks in the charts. R.I.A.A. Gold Disc award on 13 August 1976.

Captain's electronic keyboards and Tennille's dramatic gospel-flavoured vocals made this a fourth million seller single for them.

MUSKRAT LOVE *A & M* [*USA*]. Written by Willis Allan Ramsey and released in the U.S.A. in September 1976, this was No 2 for three weeks and stayed in the charts for 25 weeks. R.I.A.A. Gold Disc award on 8 December 1976.

A skilful interpretation of this fine ballad, the duo's fifth million seller single, making 1976 a memorable year for them.

CHICAGO

CHICAGO X (Album) *Columbia* [*USA*]. Written by Chicago, it was released in the U.S.A. in June 1976 and went to No 4 for two weeks, staying 40 weeks in the charts. R.I.A.A. Gold Disc award on 21 June 1976. R.I.A.A. platinum award on 14 September 1976. Grammy Award: Best Album Package, 1976.

Another superb album by Chicago with their distinctive horn-based sound, their tenth consecutive million seller package. It included: 'Another Rainy Day in New York City', 'If You Leave Me Now', 'Once or Twice', 'You Are On My Mind', 'Skin Tight', 'Mama Mama'.

IF YOU LEAVE ME NOW *Columbia* [*USA*]. Written by Peter Cetera (of Chicago), this was released in the U.S.A. in August 1976 and in Britain in October 1976. In the U.S.A it went to No 1 for two weeks, and stayed in the charts for 26 weeks. In Britain it was No 1 for six weeks, staying 16 weeks in the charts. R.I.A.A. Gold Disc award on 26 October 1976. Grammy Awards: Best Arrangement Accompanying Vocalists, 1976; Best Pop Vocal Performance by a Duo, Group or Chorus, 1976.

The outstanding cut from the group's tenth album, a ballad with a strong vocal line. It was also a big hit in Britain where it sold well over 500,000 in addition to the million plus in the U.S.A. One of 1976's best numbers.

ALICE COOPER (rock sextet)

I NEVER CRY *Warner Bros* [*USA*]. Written by Alice Cooper, this was released in the U.S.A. in September 1976 and went to No 8 for one week, staying 26 weeks in the charts. R.I.A.A. Gold Disc award on 5 April 1977.

Alice Cooper is the legal name of the lead singer and writer, and also the name of the band. Cooper (real name Vince Furnier) is the son of a minister in Phoenix where he was born on 4 February 1948. In 1964, his band (Glen Buxton - lead guitar; Michael Bruce - rhythm guitar; Dennis Dunaway - bass; Neal Smith - drums) were known as the Earwigs, the Spiders, and the Nazz, living and working out of Phoenix, Arizona, and changing the name to Alice Cooper before moving to Hollywood in 1968. In Hollywood they existed at starvation level, playing in poorly paid chicane clubs and bars. Then they met manager Shep Gordon and Frank Zappa, who signed them to his newly formed Straight label. Their first album 'Pretties For You' was released in November 1969, and their second 'Easy Action' in May 1970. At this time they were a rock group in bizarre costume and make-up. They were then signed by the Warner label, and the 'Love It To Death' album was released in 1971. This was the first real Cooper album, professionally produced by Bob Ezrin. The band were then based in Detroit.

Their stage show had new theatrical stunts to startle their audiences, such as the leader being guillotined or falling through a gallows trap-door, throwing live chickens into the audience, or bringing a boa constrictor on stage. Their make-up was designed to generate all kinds of sexual tensions in the audience. The band soon became a top box-office success in America. The 'Killer' album followed in 1971, and the sensational 'School's Out' in 1972. The latter contained the teenage anthem of the same title, a big hit as a single release in both U.S.A. and Britain. 'Billion Dollar Babies' (1973), 'Muscle of Love' (1974), 'Greatest Hits' (1974) and 'Welcome to my Nightmare' (1975) (Atlantic label) were all certified gold by R.I.A.A. - seven in total.

The band's 90-day, 56-city tour of America (1973) was seen by a million people who paid 4,500,000 dollars at the box offices. Ezrin's production established them as an international act, and they appeared also in 1973 in Britain. By 1974 their disc sales were around 10 million. They have been described as exponents of sado-masochistic rock, or the 'theatre of cruelty'. Alice Cooper certainly became rock's most outrageous superstar. This disc 'I Never Cry' was Alice Cooper's first certified million seller single.

Cooper's original musicians were replaced in 1974 by Dick Wagner and Steve Hunter (guitars), Prakash John (bass), Whitley Glen (drums), and Josef Chirowsky (keyboards), all of whom had played for Lou Reed. They are the personnel with Cooper on this single.

JULIE COVINGTON
DON'T CRY FOR ME ARGENTINA (from the musical 'Evita') *MCA [Britain]*. Written by Tim Rice and A. Lloyd Webber, this was released in Britain in December 1976. It was in the charts for 15 weeks and climbed to No 1 for one week.

In 1973, Tim Rice heard a programme on his car radio about Eva Peron, wife of the Argentine dictator, who died in 1952. Tim went off to Argentina in 1974 to do some research. In 1975, Tim's partner Lloyd Webber (with whom he wrote 'Jesus Christ Superstar') went to Majorca to see Hal Prince, the American king of musicals, and took the first demo tapes of 'Evita'. He was too busy to direct it so the writers decided to make a record first and await Hal's availability. The double album was released in Nov-

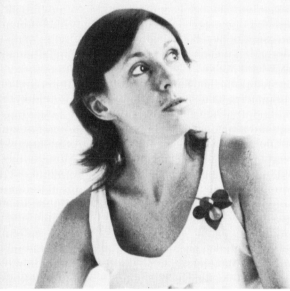

ember 1976. This sold 700,000 copies around the world before the show was finally produced at the Prince Edward Theatre, London, on 21 June 1978. The single of the big hit 'Don't Cry for Me Argentina' from the album, sung by Julie Covington, sold 1,700,000. Everyone assumed Julie would get the Evita role in the musical, but she declined it on political grounds, and disapproved of the issuing of the hit single 'out of context'. The role was given to 27-year-old Elaine Page, daughter of a Bognor Regis estate agent. The musical biography of Eva Peron was a tremendous success.

Julie Covington's background includes the Cambridge Footlights Club which produced many other TV, stage and recording successes. She became particularly well known to TV viewers through the series 'Rock Follies' in 1977. Recordings of the 'Evita' album and 'Don't Cry for Me, Argentina' were banned by the Argentine government.

BURTON CUMMINGS
STAND TALL *CBS/Portrait [USA]*. Written by Burton Cummings, it was released in the U.S.A. in September 1976. It went to No 5 for one week and stayed 25 weeks in the charts. R.I.A.A. Gold Disc award on 21 January 1977.

Burton Cummings started playing with a popular local band in Winnipeg, and was invited to join the Canadian group Guess Who on keyboards and lead vocals. With founder Randy Bachman, they wrote many hits including 'These Eyes', 'Undun', 'Laughing', 'American Woman' and 'No Time'.

In 1976 (July) he signed a solo contract with the new CBS/Portrait label, and his Richard Perry produced album, 'Burton Cummings', followed the single 'Stand Tall' up the U.S. charts. After a cross-country tour of his native Canada, with the able assistance of Richard Perry, Burton found that he could be successful on his own. He made his debut at the Roxy Theatre with a band composed of Jim Gordon (drums); Randy Strom and Danny Weis (guitars); Ian Gardiner (bass) and Mike Rheault (keyboards). He tested his act before big audiences as special guest star on several dates with the Bee Gees. By the end of 1976 he had indeed become successful, and returned to his Winnipeg home for celebrations with his friends and family. He then moved to Los Angeles where he continued to further his career, built on the standards achieved through hard work and attention to detail in his Guess Who days. 'Stand Tall' is a fine ballad, and was the first U.S. million seller for the new CBS label.

ENGLAND DAN & JOHN FORD COLEY
I'D REALLY LOVE TO SEE YOU TONIGHT *Big Tree [USA]*. Written by Parker McGee, this was released in the U.S.A. in May 1976, staying in the charts for 26 weeks and reaching No 2 for two weeks. R.I.A.A. Gold Disc award on 12 October 1976.

This duo had worked for over a decade in the musical profession before they were signed to Big Tree in 1976, and scored immediately with this song, produced by Kyle Lehning in Nashville. It brought them an extensive tour that included major TV appearances and successful album recording for Big Tree.

JIMMY DEAN
I.O.U. *Casino/GRT [USA]*. This was written by Jimmy Dean and released in the U.S.A. in April 1976. It went to No 46 and stayed in the charts for seven weeks. R.I.A.A. Gold Disc award on 20 May 1976.

A most unusual record in a number of ways. It was released several days after the label, Casino, had made a distribution arrangement with GRT. After plays on radio stations in Minneapolis, Chicago and Houston, the markets reported phenomenal requests. Dean wrote the song for his mother a long time ago, and it was originally planned as a release just for Mother's Day broadcasts. The extraordinary response revealed a widespread appeal far beyond the Mother's Day holiday. The disc is also unusual in that its duration is six minutes. It was a remarkable comeback for Dean, who had spent the past few years running a sausage business. In the 1960s he had had his own TV show and big hits such as 'Big Bad John' and 'P.T.109'. 'I.O.U.' was his first release on the Casino label. Jimmy's Mother's Day tribute was a hit on both Country and National charts and sold an exceedingly fast million. It has been described as 'the perfect ARB disc'.

RICK DEES AND HIS CAST OF IDIOTS
DISCO DUCK (Part 1) *RSO [USA]*. This composite disc by Rick Dees was released in the U.S.A. in August 1976 and in Britain in September 1976. In the U.S.A. it went to No 1 for three weeks, staying in the charts for 28 weeks. In Britain it went to No 6 and stayed nine weeks in the charts. R.I.A.A. Gold Disc award on 6 October 1976. R.I.A.A. platinum award on 13 December 1976.

This novelty hit exploded across the U.S.A., selling over 2 million. It was Rick Dees' first RSO single. Disco Duck is actually a disc jockey in Memphis, where he was a top DJ and programme director of the WMPS station. The 'Cast of Idiots' is a composite of tapes plus his own voice using various inflections. Dees, a graduate of North Carolina University, where he specialized in radio, TV and motion pictures, began his career in 1966 while still at high school, and went to WBGB station in Winston-Salem, North Carolina, as the Sunday morning DJ. He created the 'Cast of Idiots' in his early days in radio, taping voices of old recordings and contemporary politicians. With vocal tricks and numerous sound effects, his morning show incorporated 300 tape cartridges. 'Disco Duck' also had extensive broadcasting in the south of England on release, and then throughout the whole country.

JOHN DENVER

SPIRIT (Album) *RCA* [*USA*]. This was released in the U.S.A. and in Britain in August 1976. It went to No 2 for two weeks in the U.S.A. and stayed 28 weeks in the charts. In Britain it was No 7 for one week, staying in the charts for 9 weeks. R.I.A.A. Gold Disc award on 17 August 1976. R.I.A.A. Platinum award on 6 October 1976.

This album was ceremoniously unveiled at RCA's annual sales convention in San Francisco in August 1976 and coincided with RCA's 75th anniversary. Denver had become the label's biggest selling artist in the history of the company over the previous two years. 'Spirit' was produced once again by Milt Okun, assisted by Kris O'Connor, and includes a number of new Denver songs as well as an oldie, 'Polka Dots and Moonbeams' plus a new song by Bill Danoff (leader of the Starland Vocal Band). It was an immediate success with the American public and sold a million in less than two months.

THE DETROIT SPINNERS

RUBBERBAND MAN *Atlantic* [*USA*]. Written by Linda Creed and Thom Bell, this was released in the U.S.A. and in Britain in September 1976. It went to No 2 in the U.S.A. for three weeks, staying 27 weeks in the charts. In Britain it stayed in the charts for 11 weeks, reaching No 16. R.I.A.A. Gold Disc award on 8 December 1976.

This disc was produced by writer Thom Bell, and the song taken from the group's album 'Happiness is Being with The Spinners'. It was equally popular in both pop and R & B circles.

BARRY DE VORZON & PERRY BOTKIN JNR

NADIA'S THEME (from 'The Young and The Restless') *A & M* [*USA*]. Written by Perry Botkin Jnr and Barry De Vorzon, this was released in the U.S.A. in July 1976. It went to No 7 for two weeks and stayed 19 weeks in the charts. R.I.A.A. Gold Disc award on 18 January 1977.

The second big success for composer Barry De Vorzon (see 'S.W.A.T.' theme 1975) from a TV production. It had a long run in the U.S. charts, and its popularity earned it an award for a million sale.

NEIL DIAMOND

BEAUTIFUL NOISE (Album) *Columbia* [*USA*]. This was released in the U.S.A. in June 1976. It reached No 3 for one week and stayed in the charts for 29 weeks. R.I.A.A. Gold Disc award on 20 September 1976. R.I.A.A. Platinum award on 2 October 1976.

Neil 'retired' for 2 years in 1973 to write the musical score for 'Jonathan Livingston Seagull' and then came back on the concert circuit, after touring Australia, in 1976. His success there resulted in a Neil Diamond record in every fourth Australian home. In early July of 1976 he made musical history when he became the world's highest paid singer, earning £250,000 for a week's performances at Las Vegas' newest concert hall. This album of his own songs includes: 'If You Know What I Mean', 'Lady, Oh', 'Don't Think . . . Feel', 'Stargazer', 'Home is a Wounded Heart', 'Surviving Life', 'Beautiful Noise'.

DOCTOR HOOK & THE MEDICINE SHOW

ONLY SIXTEEN *Capitol* [*USA*]. Written by Barbara Campbell (pseudonym of Sam Cooke), L. Adler and Herb Alpert in 1958, this was released in the U.S.A. in January 1976. It went to No 5 for one week and stayed 25 weeks in the charts. R.I.A.A. Gold Disc award on 17 May 1976.

A successful revival of a song which was originally a hit for Sam Cooke in 1959.

DOOBIE BROTHERS

TAKIN' IT TO THE STREETS (Album) *Warner Bros* [*USA*]. Released in the U.S.A. in April 1976, it was No 9 for three weeks and stayed in the charts for 27 weeks. R.I.A.A. Gold Disc award on 11 May 1976. R.I.A.A. Platinum award on 27 July 1978.

Another great album by this exciting group. It finally made the million sale two years after release through consistent sales. It included 'Takin' It to the Streets' (McDonald).

BEST OF THE DOOBIES (Album) (title for Britain 'Greatest Hits') *Warner Bros* [*USA*]. Released in U.S.A. and in Britain in November 1976, it was 53 weeks in the U.S.A. charts, reaching No 5 for two weeks. R.I.A.A. Gold Disc award on 23 November 1976. R.I.A.A. Platinum award on 22 December 1976.

This album turned out to be one of the most successful packages to date. Contents: 'China Grove', 'Long Train Runnin'', 'Listen to the Music', 'Rockin' Down the Highway' (all written by Tom Johnston of the group), 'Takin' it to the Streets' (McDonald), 'Black Water' (Pat Simmons) 'Jesus is Just Alright' (Reynolds), 'It Keeps You Runnin' (McDonald), 'South City Midnight Lady' (Pat Simmons), 'Without You' (Doobie Bros), 'Take Me in Your Arms, Rock Me a Little While' (B. Holland, E. Holland and L. Dozier).

BOB DYLAN

DESIRE (Album) *Columbia* [*USA*]. This was released in the U.S.A. and in Britain in January 1976. In the U.S.A. it went to No 1 for five weeks and stayed 22 weeks in the charts. In Britain it climbed to No 1 for one week, staying in the charts for 32 weeks. R.I.A.A. Gold Disc award on 14 June 1976. R.I.A.A. Platinum award on 4 March 1977.

Dylan came back in this year with probably his greatest album to date. His writing was even better than before, his songs reflecting a new Dylan. Each of the narrative songs had tight instrumental work featuring Scarlett Rivera on violin, Rob Stoner on bass, Emmy Lou Harris on background vocals, Luther Rix on congas and Howie Wyeth on drums. They were also joined on some tracks by Ronee Blakley and Steve Soles on background vocals, with particular effect on the track 'Hurricane'. Dylan was responsible for harmonica, acoustic guitar, piano, and vocals. The album included: 'Sara', 'Isis', 'Romance in Durango', 'Mozambique', 'Hurricane', 'One More Cup of Coffee', 'Oh Sister', 'Joey'.

This album was also a big success in Britain where it made over £250,000 and gained a Gold Album Presentation.

EAGLES

THEIR GREATEST HITS, 1971-75 (Album) *Asylum* [*USA*]. Released in the U.S.A. in February 1976 and in Britain in March 1976, this went to No 1 in the U.S.A. for six weeks and stayed 104 weeks in the charts. In Britain it was No 1 for three weeks and stayed 79 weeks in the charts. R.I.A.A. Gold and Platinum Disc awards on 24 February 1976.

This was the first album to be shipped Platinum, under the new R.I.A.A. certification requirement. One of 1976's best-selling albums, it sold well over six million by May 1977. It was No 1 in the U.S.A. within two weeks of release. British sales were also spectacular – £250,000 plus a Gold Disc award. The appeal of this pre-eminent California country band was remarkable. It also stayed in the U.S.A. Top 20 for many months. Contents: 'Take it Easy' (Browne and Frey); 'Witchy Woman' (Henley and Leadon); 'Lyin' Eyes' (Henley and Frey); 'Already Gone' (Tempchin and Strandlund); 'Desperado' (Henley and Frey); 'One of These Nights' (Henley and Frey); 'Tequila Sunrise' (Henley and Frey); 'Take it To the Limit' (Meisner, Henley and Frey); 'Peaceful, Easy Feeling' (Tempchin); 'Best of My Love' (Henley, Frey and Souther).

HOTEL CALIFORNIA (Album) *Asylum [USA]*. This was released in the U.S.A. in December 1976 and in Britain in January 1978. It climbed to No 1 in the U.S.A. and stayed there for 11 weeks, staying in the charts for 73 weeks. In Britain it stayed in the charts for ten weeks, reaching No 2 for four weeks. R.I.A.A. Gold Disc award on 13 December 1976. R.I.A.A. platinum award on 15 December 1976.

This lush, smooth album contained only two rock tracks, 'Hotel California' and 'New Kid in Town', released as singles. Contents: 'Hotel California' (Frey, Henley and Felder); 'New Kid in Town' (Frey, Henley, and Souther); 'Life in the Fast Lane' (Walsh, Frey and Henley); 'Wasted Time' (Frey and Henley); 'Reprise' (Frey, Henley and Norman); 'Victim of Love' (Felder, Frey and Henley); 'Pretty Maids All in a Row' (Walsh and Vitale); 'Try and Love Again' (Randy Meisner); 'The Last Resort' (Henley and Frey).

This disc subsequently sold six million. Sales in Britain were over £300,000, resulting in a Gold Disc award. It entered the U.S.A. charts at No 4 and was No 2 in the second week.

NEW KID IN TOWN *Asylum [USA]*. Written by Glenn Frey, Don Henley and John David Souther, this was released in the U.S.A. and in Britain in December 1976. It went to No 3 in the U.S.A. for one week, staying 18 weeks in the charts. In Britain it went to No 20 for one week, staying 10 weeks in the charts. R.I.A.A. Gold Disc award on 21 March 1977.

One of the prime cuts from the 'Hotel California' album. Bernie Leadon left the band, and Joe Walsh (writer-vocals-guitar) joined, making his debut with the band on 1 May 1976 at Hughes Stadium, Sacramento.

EARTH, WIND & FIRE

SPIRIT (Album) *Columbia [USA]*. The material for this disc was written by the group and released in the U.S.A. in October 1976. It was No 2 there for three weeks and stayed 27 weeks in the charts. R.I.A.A. Gold Disc award on 7 October 1976. R.I.A.A. Platinum award on 13 October 1976. Another big success for the impressive rhythm and blues/pop style used by the group. Contents included: 'Getaway', 'Imagination', 'Saturday Nite', 'Earth Wind and Fire Theme Song', 'On Your Face', 'Burnin' Bush'.

'Getaway' sold a million as a single and prefaced the release of the album.

GETAWAY *Columbia [USA]*. Written by the group, this was released in the U.S.A. in July 1976 and went to No 10 for two weeks, staying 23 weeks in the charts. R.I.A.A. Gold Disc award on 29 October 1976.

This was the group's strongest single since 'Shining Hour'. The disc is a tapestry of electronics and syncopated vocals. It sold over 3 million.

ELECTRIC LIGHT ORCHESTRA (ELO)

A NEW WORLD RECORD (Double Album) *Jet [Britain] Jet/ United Artists [USA]*. Released in the U.S.A. and in Britain in October 1976, this went to No 5 in the U.S.A. for two weeks and to No 2 in Britain for one week. It stayed in the U.S.A. charts for 56 weeks and for 82 weeks in the British charts. R.I.A.A. Gold Disc award on 25 October 1976. Platinum award on 6 December 1976.

This outstanding British group that combined the rhythm of rock with classical instruments was originally formed by Roy Wood with two fellow members of their old band Move – Jeff Lynne and Bev Bevan – in 1969. They wanted to create a different sound from the old band. Wood left ELO to form Wizzard, and Lynne and Bevan recruited D'Albuquerque (bass/ vocals) and Colin Walker (cello) – the new band making their debut at Reading Festival with their first hit 'Roll Over Beethoven', a new arrangement of the Chuck Berry rock'n' roll classic. They made their first album 'No Answer', then 'Electric Light Orchestra (1971), 'ELO 2' (1973), 'Showdown' (1974), and 'Eldorado' (1975) for the Harvest label. ELO had included Wilf Gibson (violin), Mike Edwards (cello), and Richard Tandy (piano, moog, bass, guitar). 'Face the Music' followed and 'Olé ELO' which won a gold award in 1976 in U.S.A. – both of these on the Jet label. Then came 'A New World Record' (double album) recorded in Musicland Studios, Munich, after a year's work. The band became famous through its experimental attempts using strings and a certain amount of classical influence in the context of a rock'n' roll combination.

All the material for 'New World Record' was written by Jeff Lynne, and the orchestra conducted by Louis Clark. This album sold over 5 million worldwide. Contents: 'Do Ya'; 'Tight Rope'; 'Telephone Line'; 'Rockaria'; 'Mission'; 'So Fine'; 'Livin' Thing'; 'Above the Clouds'; 'Shangri-La'.

The 1976 line-up of the band was: Jeff Lynne (guitar/singer/ songwriter) born Birmingham, 30 December 1947; Bev Bevan (drums/percussion) born Birmingham 25 November 1945; Richard Tandy (keyboards) born Birmingham 26 March 1948; Kelly Groucutt (bass/backing vocals) born Coseley, 8 September 1945; Mik Kaminski (electric violin) born Harrogate, 2 September 1951; Hugh McDowell (cello) born Hampstead 31 July 1953; Melvyn Gale (cello) born London 15 January 1952. The members of the string section are all classically trained. ELO made phenomenally successful tours, particularly in the U.S.A.

FOGHAT

FOOL FOR THE CITY (album) *Bearsville [USA]*. This was released in the U.S.A. in January 1976 and went to No 22 for one week, staying 29 weeks in the charts. R.I.A.A. Gold Disc award on 12 March 1976.

The original members of Foghat were Rod Price (guitar); Dave Peverett (lead vocals/guitar); Nick Jameson (bass) – the latter replaced by bassist Craig MacGregor – and Roger Earl (drums). All were all born in Britain, except Jameson who was a native of Connecticut.

After the release of their debut album 'Foghat' in 1972, the quartet toured for eight or nine months a year with their brand of driving rock and roll which proved much more successful after five years of touring in the U.S.A. than in their native land.

'Fool for the City' was their second album, which was promoted on the U.S.A.'s FM rock stations, laying the groundwork for subsequent big successes. It had reached a reported million sale by November 1976. The album launched the hit single 'Slow Ride'. All members settled in the U.S.A., residing on Long Island's north shore.

PETER FRAMPTON

FRAMPTON COMES ALIVE (Double Album) *A & M [USA]*. This was released in the U.S.A. in January 1976 and in Britain in March 1976. In the U.S.A. it went to No 1 for 17 weeks and stayed 80 weeks in the charts. In Britain it went to No 4 for one week, staying in the charts for 37 weeks. R.I.A.A. Gold Disc award on 27 February 1976. R.I.A.A. platinum award on 8 April 1976.

Peter Frampton was born on 22 April 1950 in Beckenham, Kent. He first joined the Tru-Bears which became the teeny-bop group The Herd. In 1969 he co-founded Humble Pie, leaving in

1971 to record a solo album, 'Winds of Change', which included Ringo Starr, Klaus Voorman, Billy Preston, and Andy Brown among the session players. He then formed the group Frampton's Camel (1972) and made an album of that title in 1973. The personnel were Frampton (guitar/vocals/piano/drums/organ); Mick Gallagher (keyboards); Rick Wills (bass); and John Siomos (drums). Frampton's Camel was disbanded in late 1974. The albums 'Something's Happening' and 'Frampton' followed. America then offered him a greater opportunity, his agents Dee and Frank Barsalona putting him on the road for just as long as it took to establish him there. During a five-year period he performed up to 300 concerts a year before a total estimated audience of more than a million people. He also made important groundwork by visiting FM stations around the country. Then 'everything was primed for him!' said A & M promotion chief Harold Childs, 'Peter was just ready to happen.' They were blessed with an album – 'Frampton Comes Alive' – that was pre-sold to the artist's growing audience and the label started a merchandise campaign that literally exploded sales over 6 million in the U.S.A. alone. By the end of 1978 global sales were 12 million. Its 17 weeks at No 1 in the U.S.A. were a record up to this year, and it was the biggest selling live album. The first 40 minutes of the album is comprised of old material from the 'Winds of Change' album (notably 'Jumping Jack Flash' and 'Fig Tree Bay') and the 'Frampton's Camel' album (1972).

Peter Frampton is a great guitarist both technically and in rock terms, and was no doubt influenced by such players as Eric Clapton, Ken Burrell and Wes Montgomery. The Frampton sound is instantly recognizable, and he emerged as one of the major artists of the decade. The album was recorded in San Francisco, San Rafael and New York in the autumn of 1975. Peter (guitar/vocals) is accompanied by John Siomos (drums); Bob Mayo (guitar/vocals/keyboards); and Stanley Sheldon (bass/vocals). The album includes: 'Baby I Love Your Way'; 'Something Happening'; 'Show Me the Way'; 'I Wanna Go To The Sun'; 'It's a Plain Shame'; 'Jumping Jack Flash'; 'Lines on My Face'; 'Do You Feel Like We Do?'; 'Penny for Your Thoughts'; 'Shine On'; 'Fig Tree Bay'.

HENRY GROSS

SHANNON *Lifesong* [*USA*]. Written by Henry Gross, this was released in the U.S.A. in February 1976 and in Britain in August 1976. In the U.S.A. it was No 4 for one week and stayed in the charts for 26 weeks. In Britain it went to No 32 for one week and was four weeks in the charts. R.I.A.A. Gold Disc award on 18 June 1976.

Henry Gross hails from Brooklyn, New York and was formerly a lead guitarist in the group Sha Na Na. His first two albums (for A & M) were radio favourites. His band includes Jeremy Harris (drums); Andrew Pearson (rhythm guitar); and Warren Nichols (bass). He became a headliner in Memphis and Atlanta, and also toured with The Doobie Brothers, The Beach Boys and Aerosmith. Gross is basically a rocker. 'Shannon' – the tale of the death of a dog – illustrates his diverse talent. He is an outstanding guitarist, and became a star in his hometown with performances at New York's Bottom Line in this year. This million seller was the newly formed Lifesong Records' first major chart hit, and was taken from one of his albums.

DARYL HALL & JOHN OATES

SARA SMILE *RCA* [*USA*]. Written by Hall and Oates, this was released in the U.S.A. in February 1976 and in Britain in July 1976. It went to No 4 for two weeks in the U.S.A., staying in the charts for 31 weeks. R.I.A.A. Gold Disc award on 30 June 1976.

Hall and Oates both grew up in Philadelphia, where they met in 1967 while Oates was at college majoring in journalism and Hall was working for a production company and as a studio musician at Sigma Sound. They started writing songs together and joined a group called Gulliver which made an album in 1969 for Elektra. They left the group soon afterwards and decided to

work together in the various clubs around Philadelphia. In 1972 they went to California and signed up with Atlantic Records, then moved to New York and made their debut album 'Whole Oates'. Their second album 'Abandoned Luncheonette' was recorded in 1973 and contained a hit track 'She's Gone'. This was a hit for artist Lou Rawls and the song brought them national recognition as writers and performers. In 1974 they joined Todd Rundgren who produced, engineered and played lead guitar on their third album 'War Babies'. With these albums, their style and musical direction developed, and their fourth album 'Daryl Hall & Oates', made when they returned to Los Angeles in the spring of 1975 with their new label RCA, consolidated and refined their music, making them a formidable recording and writing team. Their blend of white soul, gospel, rhythm and blues, folk, and particularly rock 'n' roll has given them a most exciting sound on stage and disc, and one of the biggest rock 'n' roll acts of the decade.

They first visited Britain in 1975 at London's New Victoria Theatre and were given a standing ovation. In 1976 they returned for their first major tour. They also made TV dates in England, Germany, France and Sweden, and concerts in Amsterdam in 1975. 'Sara Smile' was taken from their debut RCA album 'Daryl Hall & John Oates'.

RICH GIRL *RCA* [*USA*]. Written by Hall & Oates, this was released in the U.S.A. in December 1976, going to No 1 for two weeks and staying 25 weeks in the charts. R.I.A.A. Gold Disc award on 1 April 1977.

This was the outstanding track from the duo's fifth album 'Bigger than Both Of Us'.

HEART

DREAMBOAT ANNIE (Album) *Mushroom* [*Canada*]. This was written by Ann and Nancy Wilson and was released in the U.S.A. in April 1976. It went to No 4 there for three weeks and stayed 65 weeks in the charts. R.I.A.A. Gold Disc award on 8 September 1976. R.I.A.A. platinum award on 5 November 1976.

Produced by Mike Flicker at Cab-Base Studios, Vancouver. Heart's manager Michael Fisher said the reason for the group was 'a love affair that got blown up out of all proportion and became mixed up in business and music'. The love affair involved himself and the group's lead singer, Ann Wilson, and then his brother Roger, the group's guitarist, fell for Ann's sister, Nancy. The two sisters, who front the band, come from a musical family. They gradually moved into rock after playing the Seattle folk circuit and their base was transferred to Vancouver. Heart was then formed with Steve Fossen (bass); Roger Fisher (lead guitar);

Mike Derosier (drums); and Howard Leese (keyboards), making them Vancouver's most important group since the Collectors in 1968. They were brought to the attention of producer Mike Flicker, who took them to Mushroom Records and recorded this album. Other players on the album were Kat Hendrikse and Duris Maxwell (both on drums); and Geoff Foubert (banjo).

Ann Wilson's fine voice is heard to better advantage on record than it was on stage, and Nancy's acoustic guitar playing is an enjoyable feature throughout the whole album, providing excitement and subtlety. The attraction of the disc stems from the wide range of material from frantic rock to soft and wistful melody. Two singles from it – 'Crazy on You' and 'Magic Man' were sizeable hits in the U.S.A. It was the first Canadian label to become established independently in the U.S.A. with such success. Contents: 'Dreamboat Annie'; 'Magic Man'; 'Crazy on You'; 'White Lightning and Wine'; 'Sing Child'; 'Heart'; 'I'll Be Your Song'; 'Soul of the Sea'.

HEATWAVE

TOO HOT TO HANDLE (Album) *GTO* [*Britain*] *CBS/Epic* [*USA*]. Written by Rod Temperton, this was released in Britain in October 1976 and in the U.S.A. in July 1977. In the U.S.A. it went to No 17 for two weeks and stayed in the charts for 33 weeks. R.I.A.A. Gold Disc award on 10 October 1977. Platinum award on 22 December 1977.

Heatwave were discovered playing to standing room only in Gullivers, a club in London's West End. They comprised Johnny Wilder (lead vocal); his brother Keith Wilder (vocals); Eric John (guitar); Mario Mantese (bass); Ernest Berger (drums); and Rod Temperton (songwriter/keyboards). They came from all over the world. Rod Temperton has been described as a wizard on the keyboards, and Johnny Wilder's ebullience is a real visual experience. This album was produced by Barry Blue, with the addition of brass and strings, and was the British Soul Album of the Year. The group established their name by working in all the small clubs in Britain and at various European venues. When the album was released in the U.S.A. in 1977, it was a very big hit, and their musical British/American amalgam resulted in visits to the States. The album subsequently (1977) spawned two million selling singles 'Boogie Nights' and 'Always and Forever' and more successes to follow. In 1978 they played in front of a 15,000-strong crowd for the Martin Luther King memorial concert in Atlanta, Georgia, and the CBS Convention in New Orleans. They were the forerunner of British soul. Heatwave is mainly based in West Germany and London. Contents of the album are: 'Too Hot to Handle'; 'Boogie Nights'; 'Ain't No Half Steppin'; 'Always and Forever'; 'Super Soul Sister'; 'All You Do is Dial'; 'Lay It On Me'; 'Sho' nuff Must be Love'; 'Beat Your Booty'; Sales in the U.S.A. were over 2 million.

THELMA HOUSTON

DON'T LEAVE ME THIS WAY *Tamla* [*USA*]. Written by Gamble, Huff and Davis, this was released in the U.S.A. in December 1976 and in Britain in February 1977. It went to No 1 for one week in the U.S.A. and to No 13 for one week in Britain. It stayed 25 weeks in the U.S.A. charts and eight weeks in the British charts. Grammy award: Best Rhythm and Blues Vocal Performance, Female, 1977.

Mississippi-born Thelma Houston has been described as a rare musical jewel. She started her professional career with ABC-Dunhill in 1969 and joined Tamla-Motown in 1972. Although she worked in clubs, she wanted to play in concert halls where her singing would have been more appreciated, but without a hit single it was hard to be a draw in this field. It was in 1975 that she appeared at the famous Carnegie Hall with Smokey Robinson, and was a sensation before a sell-out audience with her rendering of material from poignant ballads to gospel. This song was reported to have sold a million on disc by April 1977, a triumph for such a gifted artist who is a somewhat unknown quantity, seldom seen in person or heard on record.

She became a headline attraction, and a subsequent album, 'Any Way You Like It' went gold.

ENGELBERT HUMPERDINCK

AFTER THE LOVIN' *CBS/Epic* [*USA*]. Written by A. Bernstein and R. Adams and released in the U.S.A. in September 1976, this went to No 5 for two weeks and stayed 24 weeks in the charts. R.I.A.A. Gold Disc award on 15 February 1977.

Engelbert's first million seller for his new label Epic and his first major U.S. hit for several years.

AFTER THE LOVIN' (Album) *CBS/Epic* [*USA*]. This was released in the U.S.A. in December 1976, going to No 17 for two weeks and staying 20 weeks in the charts. R.I.A.A. Gold Disc award on 4 January 1977. Platinum award on 23 May 1977.

This album was recorded in New York and Philadelphia, and a fine debut album for Epic following his single success of the same title. It included: 'After the Lovin' '; 'Can't Smile Without You'; 'World Without Music'; 'Let Me Happen To You'; 'The Hungry Years' (Neil Sedaka).

ISLEY BROTHERS

HARVEST FOR THE WORLD *T-Neck* [*USA*]. Written by the Isley Brothers, this was released in the U.S.A. in May 1976. It went to No 9 for two weeks and stayed in the charts for 25 weeks. R.I.A.A. Gold Disc award on 3 June 1976.

A new phase in a brilliant career for this famous group. Up to this year they had sold over 35 million records. The album included: 'Who Loves You Better?'; 'People of Today'; 'Let Me Down Easy'; '(At Your Best) You are Love'; 'You Still Feel the Need'.

The million sale was reported later in the year.

THE JACKSONS

ENJOY YOURSELF *CBS/Epic* [*USA*]. Written by Kenny Gamble and Leon Huff, this was released in the U.S.A. in November 1976 and in Britain in March 1977. It reached No 7 for one week in the U.S.A. and stayed 27 weeks in the charts. In Britain it went to No 42 for one week and stayed in the charts for four weeks. R.I.A.A. Gold Disc award on 10 February 1977.

The Jacksons (originally The Jackson Five) changed the name when brother Jermaine left the group. This disc is the original four plus other members of the family who were too young to join when the group was first formed.

JEFFERSON STARSHIP

SPITFIRE (Album) *Grunt* [*USA*]. This was released in the U.S.A. in June 1976 and in Britain in July 1976. In the U.S.A. it climbed to No 1 and stayed there for one week, remaining in the charts for 27 weeks. R.I.A.A. Gold Disc award on 30 June 1976. Platinum award on 28 September 1976.

This is actually the group's 15th album since their first - 'Jefferson Airplane Takes off' (1966). The album is appropriately named after one of the most famous aircraft ever - 'Spitfire'. The group here is the same as for their previous 'Red Octopus' album except for Papa John Creach.

'Spitfire' again demonstrates the soaring harmonies and great songs of Marty Balin (like his single hit 'Miracles'). This album included: 'Cruisin''; 'Dance with the Dragon'; 'Ozymandias'; 'St Charles'; 'Don't Let it Rain'.

WAYLON JENNINGS, WILLIE NELSON, JESSI COLTER AND TOMPALL GLASER

WANTED: THE OUTLAWS (Album) *RCA* [*USA*]. Released in the U.S.A. in January 1976, this went to No 10 for two weeks and stayed 23 weeks in the charts. R.I.A.A. Gold Disc award on 30 March 1976. Platinum award on 24 November 1976.

The first country album on any label to go platinum. It also stayed in the U.S. country charts for over 2 years, and subsequently sold over 2 million.

Waylon Jennings was born on 15 June 1937 in Littlefield, Texas, where, at the age of 12, he became one of the youngest disc jockeys in radio. Through his teens he spun records and occasionally sang for home town audiences. At 21 he moved to Lubbock, Texas, as a DJ where he met Buddy Holly, and joined his group as an electric bass player. He travelled with the Holly troupe throughout 1958, singing as part of The Crickets. In 1959, Waylon fortunately missed the mid-Western plane flight which took Buddy's life. This served, in retrospect, to take Waylon off the pop/rock path The Crickets had been following. He returned to radio work before moving to Phoenix and formed his own group, The Waylors, playing the clubs where many audiences went wild over the band's hard-edged country rhythms. He was 'discovered' by Nashville A & R chief Chet Atkins who signed him with RCA-Victor. He subsequently appeared on virtually every country show in the nation and on TV. He sings primarily his own material on his many RCA albums.

Jessi Colter (née Miriam Johnson) was born in Phoenix, Arizona, daughter of a mechanical expert mining engineer/racing car builder/inventor father and evangelist mother. She got her nickname from Jesse James, but the spelling was given a feminine touch. Jessi became a church pianist when she was eleven, added the accordion, and started writing at fifteen. Switching from churches to clubs, she filled in her earlier years singing and playing until she met and married guitarist Duane Eddy, who encouraged her and recorded her as an artist. Jessi eventually moved to Nashville, where Waylon Jennings entered the scene, and their romance led to marriage. He was her producer for RCA, but she went over to Capitol in 1975. Tompall Glaser is a member of the 'Nashville Outlaws' headed by Willie Nelson (*see* 1975 for Willie Nelson data).

The idea for the 'Outlaws' album was conceived by Waylon Jennings. It was this group of four highly respected performers in contemporary country music appearing on one album that in the main created the upsurge of interest. They had expanded on the roots of country music without losing the Nashville feel.

Contents of album (singer in brackets): 'You Mean to Say' (Jessi Colter); 'My Heroes Have Always Been Cowboys' (Waylon Jennings); 'Honky Tonk Heroes' (Waylon Jennings); 'Good-Hearted Woman' (Jennings and Nelson); 'Heaven or Hell' (Jennings and Nelson); 'Suspicious Minds' (Jennings and Colter); 'I'm Looking for Blue Eyes' (Colter); 'Why You Been Gone So Long?' (Colter); 'Yesterday's Wine' (Nelson); 'Me and Paul' (Nelson); 'Put Another Log on the Fire' (Glaser); 'T for Texas' (Glaser).

JETHRO TULL

M.U. - THE BEST OF JETHRO TULL (Album) *Chrysalis* [*USA*]. This was released in the U.S.A. in January 1976. R.I.A.A. Gold Disc award on 25 February 1976. R.I.A.A. platinum award on 3 May 1978.

Everything worth while of the Jethro Tull group is on this album. It took just over two years to sell the million.

ELTON JOHN & KIKI DEE

DON'T GO BREAKING MY HEART *Rocket/MCA* [*Britain/USA*]. Written by Anna Orson and Carte Blanche, this was released in Britain and the U.S.A. in June 1976. In Britain it was No 1 for seven weeks and stayed 14 weeks in the charts. In the U.S.A. it was No 1 for five weeks, staying in the charts for 26 weeks. R.I.A.A. Gold Disc award on 17 August 1976.

A duet of rare charm and simplicity, enhanced by the strings provided by Newton-Howard. After a long career, it finally made Kiki Dee a big star.

Kiki Dee (née Pauline Matthews) was born in Bradford, England in 1947. She sang with a local dance band in northern England, then came to London in 1964 where she met well-known songwriter Mitch Murray. He provided both her new name and her first single 'Early Night'. She was five years with Philips Records and recorded one album 'I'm Kiki Dee', plus ten singles mainly after the Motown style. She was the only white English girl singer to be signed to the Motown label (1970) but recorded the wrong type of songs. Her career suffered as a result, so in 1972 she toured Australia and South Africa for seven months. On return, John Reid, Elton John's manager, made her an offer to join the newly formed Rocket label for which she made the 'Loving and Free' album (1973). This was favourably received, quite a boost after her disappointing album 'Great Expectations' for Tamla-Motown in 1971. Her first Top 20 hit 'Amoureuse' was followed by a flop, but the next single 'I've Got the Music in Me' entered both the British and the U.S. charts. Kiki made British and American tours as support act to Steely Dan and The Beach Boys. From then on her talent emerged, and with ace producer Gus Dudgeon, active vocal and financial support from Elton John and Rocket's staff plus a dynamic band comprising Phil Curtis (bass); Jo Partridge (guitar); Roger Pope (drums); Bias Boshell (keyboards); Mike Deacon and Peter Clarke, Kiki had arrived.

'Don't Go Breaking my Heart' sold well over 500,000 in Britain (with Gold Disc Award) and the writers received Britain's Ivor Novello Award for the Best Pop Record of 1976.

ELTON JOHN

BLUE MOVES (Double album) *Rocket* [*Britain*] *MCA* [*USA*]. The material for this was written by Bernie Taupin and Elton John and it was released in Britain and the U.S.A. in October 1976. In the U.S.A. it went to No 3 for three weeks, staying in the charts for 18 weeks. In Britain it was No 3 for one week and stayed 15 weeks in the charts. R.I.A.A. Gold Disc award on 29 October 1976. Platinum award on 9 December 1976.

An important release for Elton John and for Rocket, for which this is his debut (double) album. The record was produced by Gus Dudgeon. It was certified gold on release in the U.S.A. and sold over £300,000 worth in Britain with a Gold Disc award there. 'Sorry Seems to be the Hardest Word' sold a million when released as a single. Contents: (*)'Your Starter For'; 'Tonight'; 'One Horse Town'; 'Chameleon'; 'Boogie Pilgrim'; 'Cage the Songbird'; 'Crazy Water'; 'Shoulder Holster'; 'Sorry Seems to be the Hardest Word'; (*)'Out of the Blue'; 'Between Seventeen and Twenty'; 'The Wide-Eyed and Laughing'; 'Someone's Final Song'; 'Where's The Shoorah'; 'If There's A God In Heaven'; 'Idol'; (*)'Theme For A Non-Existent TV Series'; 'Bite Your Lip'. (*) Instrumental numbers featuring Caleb Quale (guitars) and Roger Pope (drums).

SORRY SEEMS TO BE THE HARDEST WORD *Rocket* [*Britain*] *MCA* [*USA*]. Written by Bernie Taupin and Elton

John, this was released in Britain and the U.S.A. in November 1976. It went to No 6 for three weeks in the U.S.A. and to No 11 for one week in Britain. It stayed 19 weeks in the U.S.A. charts and seven weeks in the British lists. R.I.A.A. Gold Disc award on 25 January 1977.

The prime cut from Elton's double album 'Blue Moves' with musicianship and vocals of the highest quality.

BROTHERS JOHNSON

LOOK OUT FOR NO. 1 (Album) *A & M [USA]*. This was released in the U.S.A. in February 1976, going to No 9 for two weeks and staying 36 weeks in the charts. R.I.A.A. Gold Disc award on 12 May 1976. R.I.A.A. platinum award on 13 September 1976.

Louis Johnson (bass guitar) born in 1956 and George Johnson (guitar) born in 1954 were discovered by Quincy Jones when they were playing with a back-up band on Quincy's session for his album 'Mellow Madness' which contained some of the Brothers' original material. Both had previously worked as sidemen on sessions with Billy Preston, Herbie Hancock, Bobby Womack and others. Quincy Jones took them with him on tour, and on their return signed them to his home label A & M. 'Look Out for Number One' was their debut album. Serious dedication and hard work had paid off. The addition of strong melodies and structure to the thumping beat that became their trademark brought them great success. The album included their compositions 'Dancin' and Prancin', and the big hit 'I'll Be Good To You'. Quincy Jones produced and co-arranged the album.

I'LL BE GOOD TO YOU *A & M [USA]*. Written by Brothers Johnson and released in the U.S.A. in April 1976, this was No 8 for one week and stayed in the charts for 23 weeks. R.I.A.A. Gold Disc Award on 18 January 1977.

The Brothers' first big singles hit, taken from their debut album 'Look Out For Number One', making a great year for this outstanding duo.

KANSAS

LEFTOVERTURE (Album) *Kirschner/CBS [USA]*. Written by Steve Walsh, Kerry Livgren and others in Kansas, this was released in the U.S.A. in October 1976, going to No 5 for four weeks and staying 42 weeks in the charts. R.I.A.A. Gold Disc award on 25 January 1977. Platinum award on 15 March 1977.

This Topeka-area rock band tried to break into the British music scene after a three-month stay there. Arriving back in the U.S.A. Phil Ehart called in Steve Walsh, a gifted writer and singer he had formerly played with. Then Robby Steinhardt, who had retired from music, was coaxed back. Rich Williams, another friend from West Topeka High, who had left a successful show band touring the midwest, asked if he could join, and together with Dave Hope, the quintet started as the group White Clover, building their sound in the bars and clubs of the area. They needed another writer and enlisted Kerry Livgren whose band had struck terrible luck. They went on the road in 1972, playing an average of 200 dates a year. A demo tape sent to Don Kirschner resulted in the band being signed to his own Kirschner Records. They produced the band's first album, released in 1974. As they were all natives of Kansas, they called themselves just that. They progressed from clubs to ballrooms as an opening band in the big West Coast venues. Two more albums followed: 'Song For America' and 'Masque'. Their fourth album of adventurous rock in 1976, 'Leftoverture', was a big hit, and the band then became permanent headliners. The album contained their biggest single hit up to this time, 'Carry on Wayward Son', and sold over 2 million.

KC & THE SUNSHINE BAND

(SHAKE, SHAKE, SHAKE) SHAKE YOUR BOOTY *TK [USA]*. Written by H.W. Casey and R. Finch, this was released in the U.S.A. in June 1976 and in Britain in July 1976. It was No 1 for one week in the U.S.A. staying 24 weeks in the charts. In Britain it was No 22 for one week staying 8 weeks in the charts.

Described as 'a hypnotic invitation to get on the floor and shake your booty', this disc was reported to have sold the million by September 1976. It was the group's first new recording for some time.

PART 3 (Album) *TK [USA]*. Written by H.W. Casey and R. Finch and released in the U.S.A. in October 1976, this went to No 13 for one week and stayed 45 weeks in the charts.

A million sale by August 1976 was reported, and 2 million by the end of the year. Around $2\frac{1}{2}$ million by 1977. This is a beautifully packaged set of songs of quality and danceability, containing all the band's previous hits. The band is said to have shaken Madison Square Gardens to its deepest foundations. The album includes: 'Shake your Booty'; 'Wrap Your Arms Around Me'; 'Baby I Love You'; 'I Like To Do It'; 'I'm Your Boogie Man'; 'Keep it Comin' Love'; 'Let's Go Party'; 'Come On In'.

KEEP IT COMIN' LOVE *TK [USA]*. Written by H.W. Casey and R. Finch, this was released in the U.S.A. in June 1977 and in Britain in 1976. It went to No 2 for three weeks in the U.S.A. and stayed 27 weeks in the charts. In Britain it was No 31 for one week and stayed in the charts for eight weeks.

Taken from the album 'Part 3', this sold a reported million in the U.S.A. in 1977.

KISS

DESTROYER (Album) *Casablanca [USA]*. Written by Kiss, this was released in the U.S.A. in March 1976 and in Britain in June 1976. It went to No 4 for two weeks in the U.S.A., staying 19 weeks in the charts. In Britain it went to No 18 for one week and stayed five weeks in the charts. R.I.A.A. Gold Disc award on 22 April 1976. Platinum award on 11 November 1976.

This album contained the group's big hit 'Beth'.

BETH *Casablanca [USA]*. Written by R. Ezrin, S. Penridge and Peter Criss and released in the U.S.A. in September 1976, this was No 7 for two weeks and stayed 22 weeks in the charts.

R.I.A.A. Gold Disc award on 5 January 1977.

This was the first million seller single for Kiss, being the prime track from their successful album 'Destroyer'.

ROCK AND ROLL OVER (Album) *Casablanca* [*USA*]. Written by Kiss and released in the U.S.A. in November 1976, this went to No 7 for one week, staying 41 weeks in the charts. R.I.A.A. Gold Disc award on 11 November 1976. R.I.A.A. platinum award on 5 January 1977.

A very good year for Kiss. This album sold over 1½ million before the end of 1977. It includes: 'See You in Your Dreams'; 'Hard Luck Woman'; 'Ladies Room'.

LED ZEPPELIN

PRESENCE (Album) *Swan Song* [*USA*]. This was released in the U.S.A. in March 1976 and in Britain in April 1976. In the U.S.A. it climbed to No 1, staying there for five weeks, and remained in the charts for 20 weeks. In Britain it was No 1 for one week and stayed 12 weeks in the charts. R.I.A.A. Gold Disc award on 1 April 1976. Platinum award on 12 April 1976.

Led Zeppelin added more than a touch of the bizarre to this latest disc, in their eighth year of existence: a crashing wall of sound music from perfectionists. The album was shipped gold and a million seller within two weeks. It was recorded at Musicland Studios, Munich, West Germany. All the material was written by the band's Jimmy Page and Robert Plant, except 'Royal Orleans' by John Bonham, John Paul Jones, Page and Plant. Global sales estimated at well over two million. The album includes: 'Achilles' Last Stand'; 'For Your Life'; 'Royal Orleans'; 'Nobody's Fault But Mine'; 'Candy Store Rock'; 'Hots on for Nowhere'; 'Tea for One'.

'Presence' was No 1 in the U.S.A. in its second week, and No 1 in Britain in its first week.

GORDON LIGHTFOOT

SUMMERTIME DREAM (Album) *Warner/Reprise* [*USA*]. Written by Gordon Lightfoot and released in the U.S.A. in June 1976, this went to No 16 for one week and stayed 38 weeks in the charts. R.I.A.A. Gold Disc award on 26 October 1976. Platinum award on 7 February 1980.

A delightful album by singer/songwriter Lightfoot. It gradually developed in popularity and sold the million after 3 years.

LYNYRD SKYNYRD

ONE MORE FROM THE ROAD (Double album) *MCA* [*USA*]. Written by the group and released in the U.S.A. in September 1976, it went to No 6 for one week and stayed 26 weeks in the charts. R.I.A.A. Gold Disc award on 26 October 1976. Platinum award on 30 December 1976.

An album recorded during three consecutive nights of 'sold out' performances at the Fox Theatre, Atlanta, Georgia. An exciting new Skynyrd release. The album includes: 'Free Bird' (their signature tune); 'Gimme Three Steps'; 'Sweet Home, Alabama' (from 'Second Helping' album of 1973); 'Saturday Night Special' (orig. 1974); 'T for Texas'; and nine other songs. It sold over 1½ million and the group started a British tour in January 1977.

MARILYN McCOO & BILLY DAVIS JR

YOU DON'T HAVE TO BE A STAR (To be in my Show) *ABC* [*USA*]. Written by Dean & Glover, this was released in the U.S.A. in September 1976 and in Britain in March 1977. In the U.S.A. it was No 1 for two weeks and stayed 30 weeks in the charts. In Britain it was No 7 for one week and stayed nine weeks in the charts. R.I.A.A. Gold Disc award on 30 November 1976. Grammy Award: Best Rhythm and Blues Vocal Performance by a Duo, Group or Chorus, 1976.

New Jersey-born Marilyn was brought up in Los Angeles where she gained a degree in business administration from U.C.L.A. and appeared on several talent shows, winning the Miss Bronze California Pageant. At the contest photographer Lamont McLemore invited her to join the Fifth Dimension. Billy was born in St Louis, sang in gospel groups before going solo, moved to Los Angeles, met McLemore and teamed up with Fifth Dimension. Bill married Marilyn in 1969. In 1975 they left Fifth Dimension to operate on their own. With the release of this, their first duet, and its great popularity, they appeared at the top supper clubs across the U.S.A. Their first album 'I Hope We Get To Love In Time' also zoomed up the U.S. Soul Charts, and Bill and Marilyn were back with a young audience all over again.

MARY MACGREGOR

TORN BETWEEN TWO LOVERS *Capitol/Ariola/America* [*USA*]. Written by Peter Yarrow and Phil Jarrell, this was released in the U.S.A. in November 1976 and in Britain in February 1977. In the U.S.A. it reached No 1, staying there for four weeks, and remained in the charts for 27 weeks. In Britain it went to No 4 for one week and stayed ten weeks in the charts. R.I.A.A. Gold Disc award on 10 January 1977.

A beautiful song by a newcomer to the pop scene. Ariola/America's first million seller. Co-writer Peter Yarrow was an original member of the famous trio Peter, Paul and Mary. The disc was also co-produced by him. Mary MacGregor hails from Steamboat Springs, Colorado.

THE MANHATTANS

KISS AND SAY GOODBYE *Columbia* [*USA*]. Written by W. Lovett, this was released in the U.S.A. in April 1976 and in Britain in June 1976. It went to No 1 for two weeks in the U.S.A. and to No 4 for two weeks in Britain. It stayed 29 weeks in the U.S.A. charts and 13 weeks in the British lists. R.I.A.A. Gold Disc award on 17 June 1976. Platinum award on 23 August 1976.

R.I.A.A. introduced a new award for singles in this year – a Platinum Award for 2 million sales. This was the second of such awards (Johnnie Taylor was the first). The Manhattans, a male quartet, were brought to Columbia by Mickey Eichner. Connoisseurs of soul harmonies had followed them through three or four record labels. This disc was taken from their album 'Manhattans' and burst out of the South to No 1 at station WQXI in Atlanta, Georgia, and then gained major airplay in New York and Los Angeles. It became one of the hottest sales items around the U.S.A. It had a devastating introduction, enhancing the lyrical concept and orchestration. With the current disco craze, and rock acts changing their sounds by putting black characteristics into their music, this black quartet helped to accelerate the momentum influenced mainly by the Philadelphia Sound. (See MFSB, 1973.)

BARRY MANILOW

THIS ONE'S FOR YOU (Album) *Arista* [*USA*]. Written by Barry Manilow and others and released in the U.S.A. in July 1976, this went to No 4 for two weeks and stayed 63 weeks in the charts. R.I.A.A. Gold Disc award on 17 August 1976. Platinum award on 6 January 1977.

Another big success for the versatile Barry. This album sold two million by April 1977 and went on to three million subsequently. It included: 'This One's For You'; 'Riders To the Stars'; 'Week End in New England'; 'Looks Like We Made It'.

MANFRED MANN EARTH BAND

BLINDED BY THE LIGHT *Warner Bros* [*USA*] *Bronze* [*Britain*]. Written by Bruce Springsteen, this was released in the U.S.A. in November 1976 and in Britain in September 1976. In the U.S.A. it was No 1 for one week, remaining in the charts for 29 weeks. In Britain it was No 6 for one week and stayed ten weeks in the charts. R.I.A.A. Gold Disc award on 1 March 1977.

Manfred Mann formed a new band, Manfred Mann Chapter Three, in 1969, having tired of recording hit singles with his former band in the mid-sixties. However, it was disbanded in

1971. Later in the year he formed the Earth Band, made albums for Philips Records and worked constantly on the road. He started using the synthesizer and the group developed a heavier and instrumentally more ambitious style. This song written by Bruce Springsteen enhanced their reputation and helped the composer back into the limelight and towards having eventual stardom himself two years later.

Manfred Mann's band comprised: Manfred Mann (organ/synthesizer); Mick Rogers (vocals/guitar); Chris Slade (drums); Colin Pattenden (bass).

JOHNNY MATHIS
WHEN A CHILD IS BORN *CBS* [*USA and Britain*]. Written by Zacar (Crio Dammico) with English words by Fred Jay, this was released in Britain in November 1976. It climbed to No 1 and stayed there for three weeks, staying in the charts for 11 weeks.

Crio Dammico, an obscure Italian composer, wrote this in 1973 as a love song. American lyricist Fred Jay found it in 1976 and it was an immediate hit in Britain, where it sold well over half a million. Sales of the disc over subsequent years made it a million seller there. Apart from its British success the song was recorded in 120 versions, recorded by 40 artists in Japan, 10 Italian singers, and translated into five South American languages in 1976. The total sales world wide to 1976 of the various versions were well over six million. Since then, it has appeared on discs every Christmas, and is now as popular as 'White Christmas'. It was the first No 1 hit in Britain for Johnny Mathis.

STEVE MILLER BAND
FLY LIKE AN EAGLE (Album) *Capitol* [*USA*] *Mercury* [*Britain*]. In the U.S.A. this was released in May 1976 and in Britain in June 1976. It went to No 3 for two weeks in the U.S.A., staying in the charts for 70 weeks. In Britain it was No 11 for one week and stayed seven weeks in the charts. R.I.A.A. Gold Disc award on 28 July 1976. Platinum award on 27 September 1976.

Miller's first album since 'The Joker' in 1973 is lyrical and gently flowing. Sales were three million by the end of 1977.

Contents include: 'Take the Money and Run' (Miller); 'Rock'n Me' (Miller); 'You Send Me' (C.L. Cooke - 1957); 'Blue Odyssey' (Miller); 'Sweet Maree' (Miller); 'The Window' (Miller and J. Cooper); 'Fly Like an Eagle' (Miller); 'Space Odyssey' (Miller); 'Mountain Honey' (S. McCarty); 'Serenade' (Miller and McCarty); 'Dance, Dance' (Miller and J. & B. Cooper); 'Mercury Blues' (K.C. Douglas).

FLY LIKE AN EAGLE *Capitol* [*USA*]. Written by Steve Miller and released in the U.S.A. in December 1976, this went to No 2 for three weeks and stayed 22 weeks in the charts. R.I.A.A. Gold Disc award on 18 April 1977.

Single taken from Miller's album of the same title. With two other singles from the album ('Take the Money and Run' and 'Rock'n Me') reaching high chart positions plus this million seller, Steve became one of the biggest success stories of 1976.

DOROTHY MOORE
MISTY BLUE *Malaco/TK* [*USA*]. Written by B. Montgomery, this was released in the U.S.A. in February 1976 and in Britain in May 1976. It went to No 3 for four weeks in the U.S.A., staying 26 weeks in the charts. In Britain it was No 5 and stayed 12 weeks in the charts.

A new singer with a stirring treatment of a rhythm and blues ballad, backed by a fine string accompaniment. She was named one of the most promising female R & B album vocalists of 1976. The million sale of 'Misty Blue' was reported in August 1977.

WALTER MURPHY & BIG APPLE BAND
A FIFTH OF BEETHOVEN *Private Stock* [*USA*]. Written by Walter Murphy, this was released in the U.S.A. and Britain in June 1976. In the U.S.A. it was No 1 for one week, staying 35 weeks in the charts. In Britain it was No 28 for one week, staying nine weeks in the charts. R.I.A.A. Gold Disc award on 8 September 1976.

Another new name on the 1976 scene, with a resounding million seller and a very original song title.

MAXINE NIGHTINGALE
RIGHT BACK WHERE WE STARTED *United Artists* [*USA and Britain*]. Written by Pierre Tubbs and Vince Edwards, this was released in Britain in October 1975 and in the U.S.A. in January 1976. It went to No 1 for one week in the U.S.A. and remained in the charts for 21 weeks. It went to No 8 for one week in Britain, staying eight weeks in the charts. R.I.A.A. Gold Disc award on 27 April 1976.

Maxine's father was one of the first black men in Wembley, London. Her singing career started around 1969 when she was 18, doing sessions in London and singing with various bands. She lived most of the time subsequently in Los Angeles, and it was in the U.S.A. that she very nearly lost her life when she collapsed during a tour. In her earlier years, apart from part-time singing, she went into fashion. She then joined the cast of 'Hair', and later 'Jesus Christ Superstar', followed by 'Savages', before doing session work. She recorded this song as a favour to producers/writers Tubbs and Edwards. When it was released in the U.S.A. it speedily climbed the charts, with a quick ascent to No 1 in Birmingham for two weeks. National coverage followed with airplay in every market. At 25, Maxine is an accomplished singer and actress and shared the 'Dinah' TV stage with Spiro Agnew in 1976.

KENNY NOLAN
I LIKE DREAMIN' *20th Century* [*USA*]. Written by Kenny Nolan and released in the U.S.A. in November 1976, this went to No 3 for one week and stayed 28 weeks in the charts. R.I.A.A. Gold Disc award on 21 March 1977.

Kenny Nolan's reputation as a hit songwriter began in 1969. His 'Back to Dreamin' Again' was recorded then by The Grassroots, and he became firmly established when Frankie Valli recorded his 'My Eyes Adored You', while Labelle recorded 'Lady Marmalade', and 'Get Dancin' was recorded by Disco Tex. 'I Like Dreamin' ' was turned down by the artist for whom it was originally intended, so Kenny decided to record it himself. It was responsible for giving Kenny a new career. His album, 'Kenny Nolan', which followed also helped to establish him as a major new recording artist.

TED NUGENT
FREE FOR ALL (Album) *Epic* [*USA*]. Released in the U.S.A. in September 1976, this went to No 16 for one week and stayed 25 weeks in the charts. R.I.A.A. Gold Disc award on 11 November 1976. R.I.A.A. platinum award on 27 September 1977.

Nugent's second album and second million seller.

PARLIAMENT
MOTHERSHIP CONNECTION (Album) *Casablanca* [*USA*]. Written by George Clinton, this was released in the U.S.A. in February 1976. It went to No 13 there for two weeks and stayed 33 weeks in the charts. R.I.A.A. Gold Disc award on 26 April 1976. Platinum award on 20 September 1976.

Originally called the Parliaments, when leader George Clinton wrote 'I Wanna Testify', which was a big hit for them in 1967. In 1969, due to legal problems, the group changed its name to Funkadelik and became a pioneering black group making the transition to rock. In the early 1970s they changed the name to Parliament and signed up with Casablanca. Clinton (born 1958) then developed a more vocal, danceable group, and this became a big success. 'Mothership Connection' was the foundation for the Earth Tour - a funk opera about extra-terrestrials returning to Earth in search of P-funk (Parliament Funkadelic) they had left here. Clinton (as Dr Funkenstein) prepared his audiences for the acceptance of P-funk. Clinton and his fans, affectionately called clones, raised the roof at their performances in 1977 on the Earth Tour with one of the most elaborate stage productions of the 70s. They engaged Jules Fischer, famous designer for stage and screen as well as for major rock acts like the Rolling Stones, Kiss and David Bowie. He designed the stage set involving a 275,000 dollar spaceship or Mothership with an 80-man crew. The Mothership ascends into the arena and onto the stage with laser beams and flashing lights. Good Dr Funkenstein has arrived, and the crowds are ecstatic. Clinton is a firm believer that 'fantasy is reality in the world today'.

Parliament's second album 'The Clones of Dr Funkenstein' continued the tale and also had big sales – around half a million. The 'Mothership Connection' album included two hit singles: 'Starchild' and 'Tear the Roof Off the Sucker'.

TEAR THE ROOF OFF THE SUCKER (Give up the Funk) *Casablanca* [*USA*]. Written by George Clinton and released in the U.S.A. in May 1976, this went to No 8 for one week, staying 23 weeks in the charts. R.I.A.A. Gold Disc award on 19 October 1976.

The prime track from the group's album 'Mothership Connection'. This huge rhythm and blues record achieved sensational success, first in Detroit and Memphis, and subsequently becoming a national hit.

LOU RAWLS
ALL THINGS IN TIME (Album) *Philadelphia International* [*USA*]. This was released in the U.S.A. in March 1976, going to No 16 for one week and staying in the charts for 23 weeks. R.I.A.A. Gold Disc award on 23 August 1976. Platinum award on 25 January 1977.

Lou Rawls' first big hit for seven years, and the first for his new label. It included the big hit 'You'll Never Find Another Love Like Mine'.

YOU'LL NEVER FIND ANOTHER LOVE LIKE MINE *Philadelphia International* [*USA*]. Written by Kenny Gamble and Leon Huff, this was released in the U.S.A. in April 1976 and in Britain in July 1976. It went to No 2 for two weeks in the U.S.A., staying 30 weeks in the charts. In Britain it went to No 10 for one week, staying 10 weeks in the charts. R.I.A.A. Gold Disc award on 19 August 1976.

This big hit was culled from Lou's album 'All Things In Time' and was his biggest singles hit to date.

CLIFF RICHARD
DEVIL WOMAN *MCA/Rocket* [*USA*] *EMI* [*Britain*]. Written by Christine Authors and Terry Britten, this was released in Britain in May 1976 and in the U.S.A. in June 1976. In the U.S.A. it was No 5 for three weeks and stayed 28 weeks in the charts. In Britain it was No 5 for one week and stayed in the charts for eight weeks. R.I.A.A. Gold Disc award on 20 October 1976.

Cliff Richard has been recognized as one of the world's top singers, but for the first 18 years of his career, for some inexplicable reason, he never had any success in the U.S.A., despite over 60 chart hits in Britain. In early 1976 he signed with Rocket Records who produced his album 'I'm Nearly Famous'. This title was somewhat prophetic, for soon afterwards the single 'Devil Woman' was a big hit in the U.S.A., and gave him the breakthrough. It also gave him his first U.S. Gold Disc. It was thus proved that with the right material and promotion Cliff could extend his success in that country. The recording is strong in the rhythm section and the disc was one of Cliff's best rock vocal performances in years. In September of this year, he received a tumultous reception in Leningrad and Moscow, playing to a total of 91,000 Russians.

THE ROLLING STONES
BLACK AND BLUE (Album) *Rolling Stones* [*Britain and*

USA]. This was released in the U.S.A. and Britain in April 1976. In the U.S.A. it was No 1 for two weeks and in Britain No 2 for two weeks. It stayed 16 weeks in the U.S.A. charts and 13 weeks in the British charts. R.I.A.A. Gold Disc award on 26 April 1976. Platinum award on 23 June 1976.

This album took three years to complete, with new friends and directions. All the tracks were recorded in Musicland, Munich, except for 'Melody' which was recorded with a mobile in Rotterdam. It was a huge success. The album is 'reggae' influenced with some straightforward blues and more traditional-sounding Stones items. Contents: 'Hot Stuff'; 'Memory Motel' (both with Harvey Mandel on guitar); 'Crazy Mama'; 'Hand of Fate'; 'Fool to Cry' (both with Wayne Perkins on electric guitar); 'Cherry Oh Baby'; 'Hey, Negrita' (both with Ronnie Wood on vocals and guitar); 'Melody' (horns arranged by Arif Mardin).

In addition to the players mentioned, Billy Preston played on piano, string synthesizer, vocals and organ; Nicky Hopkins on organ, piano and string synthesizer; Ollie E. Brown on percussion, plus of course the Rolling Stones (Charlie Watts, Bill Wyman, Keith Richard and Mick Jagger).

LINDA RONSTADT
HASTEN DOWN THE WIND (Album) *Asylum* [*USA*]. Released in the U.S.A. in August 1976, this went to No 2 for one week, staying 24 weeks in the charts. R.I.A.A. Gold Disc award on 30 August 1976. Platinum award on 28 October 1976. Grammy Award: Best Pop Vocal Performance, Female, 1976.

Country artist Linda Ronstadt was born in Tucson, Arizona, went to school there and then to the University of Arizona. Moving to South Carolina, together with two friends she formed the group Stone Poneys. They were successful and made some albums for Capitol, the best being 'Different Drum'. Linda left the group to go solo, formed her own band and started touring, with successful appearances at the Troubadour in Los Angeles, The Bitter End in New York, The Cellar Door in Washington DC, and many colleges throughout the U.S.A. There were also several important TV appearances as guest on a major network, including the Glen Campbell, Johnny Carson, Andy Williams, David Frost and Johnny Cash Shows. She had a hit with 'Long Long Time' from her album 'Silk Purse', followed by a top seller album 'Linda Ronstadt'. In 1974 a successful album 'Don't Cry Now' included 'Silver Threads and Golden Needles'. In 1976 she appeared at the Odeon in Birmingham, England, and triumphed there. 'Hasten Down the Wind' well and truly established her, with its inimitable style of country, rock and middle of the road items.

The album includes: 'Lo Siento Mi Vida' (Linda Ronstadt, Kenny Edwards and Gilbert Ronstadt); 'The Tattler' (Ry Cooder and Russ Titelman); 'Try Me Again' (Linda Ronstadt and Andrew Gold); 'Hasten Down The Wind' (Warren Zevon); 'Lose Again' (Karla Bonoff); 'Someone to Lay Down Beside Me' (Karla Bonoff); 'That'll Be the Day' (J. Allison, Buddy Holly and Norman Petty); 'Give One Heart' (John and Johanna Hall); 'Crazy' (Willie Nelson); 'If He's Ever Near' (Karla Bonoff).

GREATEST HITS (Album) *Asylum* [*USA*]. Released in the U.S.A. in December 1976, this went to No 6 for five weeks and stayed 28 weeks in the charts. R.I.A.A. Gold Disc award on 8 December 1976.

It was reported that by February 1977 this album had passed the million sale. It included: 'Desperado'; 'Heat Wave'; 'You're No Good'; 'That'll Be The Day'.

ROSE ROYCE (male and female vocal and instrumental group)
CAR WASH *MCA* [*USA*]. Written by Norman Whitfield, this was released in the U.S.A. in October 1976 and in Britain in January 1977. In the U.S.A. it went to No 1 for two weeks, staying in the charts for 24 weeks. In Britain it was No 5 for one week and stayed ten weeks in the charts. R.I.A.A. Gold Disc

award on 21 December 1976. Platinum award on 22 February 1977.

The members of Rose Royce are: Gwen Dickey (lead vocals); Lequient 'Duke' Jobe (bass and vocals); Kenji Chiba Brown (lead guitar and vocals); Freddie Dunn (trumpet); Kenny Copeland (trumpet and vocals); Michael Moore (saxophone and vocals); Henry Garner (drums and vocals); Mike Walsh (keyboards); Terral Santiel (percussion). Most of the members of this nine-piece group performed in the Los Angeles area for several years under the name 'Total Concept'. They backed artists including Edwin Starr, The Temptations and Yvonne Fair. They later toured with Starr in England and Japan. When Starr left on a career as a separate unit, the group met producer Norman Whitfield, then a prominent producer at Motown Records. He changed their name to Rose Royce and teamed them with his other successful group Undisputed Truth. They recorded and toured together. Gwen Dickey was the last to join Rose Royce. Undisputed Truth heard her in Miami in a group, and brought her to Whitfield's attention. Whitfield persuaded her to move to California where she soon became a member of Rose Royce. Whitfield, a talented composer, always wanted his own record label but it didn't actually happen until he left Motown (by then located in Los Angeles) to pursue a career of writing and producing. MCA was among the companies he first approached about financing and forming Whitfield, but it was with Warner Brothers that he finally reached agreement. MCA did however get 'Car Wash' for which Whitfield wrote the score. The group's first album 'Car Wash' rose with the great success of the film of the same name and reached platinum status according to some reports as yet unconfirmed or certified. The title track was a monster hit and achieved the coveted R.I.A.A. platinum award for the two million sale, the fifth single to do so. Norman Whitfield received a Grammy Award for Album of Best Original Score Writers for a Motion Picture or a TV Special: 'Car Wash' (1976).

RUFUS (featuring Chaka Khan)

SWEET THING *ABC* [*USA*]. Written by T. Maiden and Chaka Khan and released in the U.S.A. in January 1976, this went to No 5 for two weeks, staying 24 weeks in the charts. R.I.A.A. Gold Disc award on 2 March 1976.

Second million-seller single for Rufus, the prime track from the album 'Rufus, Featuring Chaka Khan' (1975).

RUSH

2112 (Album) *Mercury/Polygram* [*USA*]. The material for this disc was written by Rush. R.I.A.A. platinum award on 25 February 1981.

With the group's consistent success, this album sold the million after five years.

ALL THE WORLD'S A STAGE (Double album) *Mercury/Polygram* [*USA*]. Material by Rush. R.I.A.A. Gold Disc award on 16 November 1977. Platinum award on 4 March 1981.

This heavy metal power trio from Canada consists of Geddy Lee (lead vocalist/guitar); Neil Peart (drummer/lyricist); Alex Lifeson (guitar). As teenagers in Toronto, they were inspired by Led Zeppelin. The trio started in 1969, and were rejected by record companies and discouraging reviews. In 1974 their debut album 'Rush' was released by Mercury, then they spent eight months per year touring the U.S.A. and the remaining months on Canadian tours, and recording. They became concert headliners playing to audiences of 15,000 to 20,000. Subsequent albums were 'Fly by Night', 'Caress of Steel', '2112' and then 'All the World's a Stage', which became their biggest success to date.

LEO SAYER

ENDLESS FLIGHT (Album) *Warner Bros* [*USA*], *Chrysalis* [*Britain*]. This was released in the U.S.A. in October 1976 and in Britain in January 1977. It was No 15 for two weeks in the U.S.A., staying 43 weeks in the charts. In Britain it remained in the charts for 53 weeks. R.I.A.A. Gold Disc award on 26 April 1977. Platinum award on 17 September 1977.

Leo (real name Gerard) Sayer was born at Shoreham, Sussex, England, in 1948. He first worked periodically as a magazine illustrator, then became an itinerant poet and harmonica player. He briefly led a band named Patches. In 1971, Leo answered a newspaper advertisement which put him in touch with composer David Courtney as a songwriting partner. Courtney had played drums for artist Adam Faith, and Adam became Leo's manager. Soon afterwards, The Who's Roger Daltrey included some of their songs on his solo album. Leo recorded some hit singles for Chrysalis – 'The Show Must Go On' (1973); 'One Man Band' and 'Long Tall Glasses' (1974); 'Moonlighting' (1975). An album, 'Silverbird', was released by Chrysalis (1973). Adam Faith suggested a mask to put over Leo's dual character – confident extrovert and shy introvert. The idea was used for the 'Silverbird' cover, and Leo started wearing the clown make-up on stage. He abandoned the clown image on his first U.S.A. tour (1975). His appearances there were a big success as was this album that contained two songs released as singles, selling a million each. Contents of album are: 'Hold On To My Love' (Leo Sayer, Barry Mann and Cynthia Weill); (*)'You Make Me Feel Like Dancing' (Leo Sayer and Vini Poncia); 'Reflections' (B. Holland, L. Dozier and E. Holland); (*)'When I Need You' (Albert Hammond and Carole Sager); 'No Business Like Love Business' (B. Shapiro, C. Reid, S. Alaimo and Vini Poncia); 'I Hear Laughter' (Leo Sayer and Johnny Vastano); 'Magdalena' (Danny O'Keefe); 'How Much Love?' (Leo Sayer and Barry Mann); 'I Think We Fell In Love Too Fast' (Leo Sayer, Johnny Vastano and Vini Poncia); 'Endless Flight' (Andrew Gold). (* denotes sold a million as single.) This album was recorded in Los Angeles, 1976.

Sayer's appearance at Los Angeles' Universal Amphitheater in 1978 was an outstanding one. Here he gave an impersonal gathering of 5000 people the feeling of an intimate party. It proved to be an ideal showcase. Everyone in the audience realized that here was a singer/songwriter second to none. The magazine *Rolling Stone* labelled him 'the perfect star for the '70s'.

YOU MAKE ME FEEL LIKE DANCING *Warner Bros* [*USA*] *Chrysalis* [*Britain*]. Written by Leo Sayer and Vini Poncia, this was released in the U.S.A. and Britain in October 1976. In the U.S.A. it reached No 1 for one week and stayed 26 weeks in the charts. In Britain it went to No 2 for two weeks and stayed eight weeks in the charts. R.I.A.A. Gold Disc award on 28 December 1976. Grammy Award: Best Rhythm and Blues Song, 1977.

One of the tracks from Leo's album 'Endless Flight'.

BOZ SCAGGS

SILK DEGREES (Album) *Columbia* [*USA*]. Written by Boz (William Royce) Scaggs and released in the U.S.A. in April 1976, this was No 2 for five weeks, staying 78 weeks in the charts. R.I.A.A. Gold Disc award on 16 July 1976. Platinum award on 22 September 1976.

Scaggs was born in Ohio in June 1944, and raised in Oklahoma and Texas. He met Steve Miller when he was fifteen at school in Dallas and joined Miller's band, the Marksmen, as vocalist and tambourine player. Miller taught him rhythm guitar. Both went to the University of Madison, Wisconsin, where Boz joined Miller's Ardells group, playing rhythm and blues and rock'n'roll. He then formed Wigs R & B band on his return to Texas, and the group left university to go to England in 1964. They found there were a great number of R & B bands there, so the members returned to the U.S.A., whilst Scaggs became a folk singer on the continent, spending some time in Stockholm where he recorded the album 'Boz' (Polydor 1965). He also went as far as Bombay. He returned to the U.S.A. to join the Steve Miller Band in San Francisco in 1967 but musical clashes led Scaggs to split. His friend Jan Wenner, editor of *Rolling Stone* magazine, made an arrangement with Atlantic Records, and produced the album 'Boz Scaggs' in Muscle Shoals (1969).

Boz soon returned to the West Coast, formed a band, and signed with CBS (1970) recording three completely different albums – 'Moments' (1971); 'And Band' (1971) (this was cut in London) and 'My Time' (1972). 'Slow Dancer' followed, produced by ex-Motown producer Johnny Bristol for CBS. In 1976, he teamed up with producer Joe Wissart to create 'Silk Degrees'. This brought to fruition the growing partnership he has formed with David Paich, resulting in the fine song 'Lowdown' included on the album. Boz Scaggs' great success on both record and before audiences everywhere during 1976 certainly made it his year. The album includes: 'We're All Alone'; 'It's Over'; 'What Can I Say?'; 'Georgia Jump Street'; 'Lowdown'; 'Lido Shuffle'. The personnel for the band changed many times.

LOWDOWN *Columbia* [*USA*]. Written by Boz (William Royce) Scaggs and David Paich, this was released in the U.S.A. in June 1976. It went to No 1 for one week and stayed 27 weeks in the charts. R.I.A.A. Gold Disc award on 29 October 1976. Grammy Award: Best Rhythm and Blues Song, 1976.

The outstanding cut from the album 'Silk Degrees', with a feverishly soulful vocal and a fine rhythm.

JOHN SEBASTIAN
WELCOME BACK *Warner/Reprise* [*USA*]. Written by John Sebastian and released in the U.S.A. in March 1976, this climbed to No 1, staying there for two weeks, and remained 22 weeks in the charts. R.I.A.A. Gold Disc award on 19 May 1976.

The first million seller for newcomer John Sebastian.

BOB SEGER & THE SILVER BULLET BAND
'LIVE' BULLET (Album) *Capitol* [*USA*]. Written by Bob Seger and released in the U.S.A. in April 1976, this was No 49 for two weeks. R.I.A.A. Gold Disc award on 25 January 1977. Platinum award on 16 December 1977.

Bob Seger's musical career started in high school bands in 1960 in the area of Ann Arbor, Detroit. He became organist and singer with Doug Brown and The Omens, and then started his own band. His first recordings were made at the local Detroit label, Hideout, with the band named Last Heard. His product was picked up by Cameo label which unfortunately went out of business overnight. Seger was 16 when he turned professional, with much success in various parts of Detroit. The band had several name changes: Bob Seger & The Last Heard, Bob Seger System and, in 1975, Bob Seger and the Silver Bullet Band. The band signed with Capitol and had a sizeable hit with 'Ramblin' Gamblin' Man'. After a couple of albums for Capitol, he moved to Warner Brothers, a bad move on his part, then returned to Capitol which proved to be the turning point in the band's fortune.

The change in their success was dramatic. Whereas their previous albums (they made three for Warner) had been selling between 30,000 and 50,000, the first for their new deal with Capitol – 'Beautiful Loser' – sold 300,000. Then came ' 'Live' Bullet'. When 'Night Moves' was released later in the year, that became the big seller, and resulted in fans buying ' 'Live' Bullet' as well, which reached the platinum stage in late 1977. The band played their heavy rock all over the U.S.A. to capacity audiences, and in 1977 went to Britain, where they were an amazing success, as well as in Germany and France. Personnel of the band are: Bob Seger; Drew Abbott; Robyn Robbins (keyboards); Jack Teagarden (drums); Alto Reed (saxophone); Chris Campbell (bass).

NIGHT MOVES (Album) *Capitol* [*USA*]. Written by Bob Seger and released in the U.S.A. in November 1976, this went to No 7 for one week, staying 47 weeks in the charts. R.I.A.A. Gold Disc award on 25 January 1977. Platinum award on 25 March 1977.

This was the album that rocketed Bob Seger to stardom. It sold over two million in just over three months.

MASATO SHIMON
OYOGE TAIYAKIKUN *Canyon* [*Japan*]. This disc sold 3,700,000 – an all-time high figure for a tune that wasn't exposed on a music programme, but on a children's show. It was No 1 for nine weeks in Japan.

SHOWADDYWADDY (male vocal/instrumental group)
UNDER THE MOON OF LOVE *Bell* [*Britain*]. Written by Boyce and Lee and released in Britain in October 1976, this reached No 1 for three weeks and remained 15 weeks in the charts.

Showaddywaddy came into prominence in Britain in 1974 with their No 2 disc 'Hey Rock and Roll' and from then on were always well up the charts with subsequent releases. This British group had its first No 1 with 'Under the Moon of Love', written by the American songwriter Tommy Boyce, writer of several hits for The Monkees. He came to London in this year and placed several songs with prominent British artists including Petula Clark, David Essex and Demis Roussos, also producing the new band Darts. 'Under the Moon of Love' was a big seller in Britain and went on to top the million globally.

SILVER CONVENTION (female vocal group)
GET UP AND BOOGIE *RCA-Midland Internat* [*USA*] *Magnet* [*Britain*]. Written by Levay and Prager, this was released in the U.S.A. and Britain in March 1976. In the U.S.A. it was No 1 for one week and stayed 25 weeks in the charts. In Britain it was No 4 for one week and stayed 11 weeks in the charts. R.I.A.A. Gold Disc award on 7 June 1976.

Second million seller for this German female soul trio.

DAVID SOUL
DON'T GIVE UP ON US *Private Stock* [*USA and Britain*]. Written by Tony Macauley, this was released in Britain in December 1976 and in the U.S.A. in January 1977. It was No 1 for one week in the U.S.A., staying in the charts for 25 weeks. In Britain it was No 1 for four weeks, staying 13 weeks in the charts. R.I.A.A. Gold Disc award on 6 April 1977.

David Soul (real name Solberg) broke into show business in a musical review and later toured mid-Western U.S. college towns performing contemporary and folk material. He put together a production of 'Baal', a rarely staged work by German playwright Bertolt Brecht, and in addition to portraying Baal, composed special music for Brecht's ballads. David appeared in major roles on TV including 'Here come the Brides'; 'Cannon'; 'The Rookies'; 'Ironside'; 'Medical Center'; 'The Streets of San Francisco'; 'Star Trek'; 'McMillan and Wife'; 'Dan August'; and 'Owen Marshall, Counseller at Law'. He achieved super-star status on TV in the ABC series 'Starsky and Hutch', as the tough, soft-spoken, well-educated Ken Hutchinson. Although his acting career brought him success so early in life, he always wanted a place in the record industry. This came through Larry Uttal of the record business who believed in his talent. David Soul got that opportunity with Private Stock Records in England and the U.S.A. where his success was spectacular. 'Don't Give Up On Us' was written by English songwriter Tony Macauley and first released in Britain where it sold over 500,000. Another million sale followed in the U.S.A. and big sales globally.

RED SOVINE (country singer)
TEDDY BEAR *Gusto/Starday* [*USA*] *RCA* [*Britain*]. Written by D. Royal, B.J. Burnette, T. Hill and Red Sovine, this was released in the U.S.A. in June 1976 and in Britain in September 1975. In the U.S.A. it was No 35 for one week, staying in the charts for 14 weeks. R.I.A.A. Gold Disc award on 16 November 1976.

Woodrow Wilson, 'Red' Sovine was born on 7 July 1918 in

Charleston, West Virginia. His first engagement was with Jim Pike and the Carolina Tar Heels on the Old Farm Hour radio show on WCHS. The group moved to the WWVA Wheeling Jamboree, and in 1947 Red formed his own group, The Echo Valley Boys. His first big break came in 1949 when Hank Williams left the Louisiana Hayride radio show on KWKH to join the Grand Ole Opry. Sovine was chosen as the replacement, remaining a regular on the Hayride for five years. In 1954, he left Shreveport to join Grand Ole Opry, and frequently teamed up with Webb Pierce with whom he had hit records such as 'Little Rosa' and 'Why Baby Why'. His career included several record labels: Decca, MGM, Chart and Starday. He was best known for his story songs, of which 'Teddy Bear' was his most famous. This came at the time of the new rage in U.S.A. for CB - citizen's band radio. Thousands of drivers fitted the two-way radio sets to talk to other car drivers on home receivers. 'Teddy Bear' is the story of a truck-driving CB operator who tunes in to a little crippled boy transmitting from his daddie's receiver at home. Sung with great emotion by Red, the song is a real tear jerker, and was the hit for which he had waited a long time. He died on April 4 1980 in Nashville, Tennessee, through a heart attack and injuries suffered in an automobile accident.

STARLAND VOCAL BAND

AFTERNOON DELIGHT *Windsong/RCA* [*USA*]. Written by Bill Danoff, this was released in the U.S.A. in May 1976 and in Britain in July 1976. It went to No 1 for four weeks in the U.S.A. and stayed 29 weeks in the charts. In Britain it went to No 17 for one week and stayed ten weeks in the charts. R.I.A.A. Gold Disc award on 15 July 1976. Grammy awards: Best Arrangement for Voices (Duo, Group or Chorus), 1976; Best New Artist of the Year, Starland Vocal Band, 1976.

Starland Vocal Band was originally formed by songwriters/performers Bill and Taffy Danoff as an experiment to put some of Bill's theories on new vocal sounds into practice. They were joined by John Carroll (a well-known back-up musician in Washington D.C.) and Margot Chapman (an original member of Fat City). The resulting sound was so good that they decided to stay together as a group. They backed John Denver on U.S. concert tours. Starland's sound has exciting four-part harmonies reminiscent of the Mamas & Papas, and all members sing lead without weakening the overall sound. They recorded this soft, summery sound of 'Afternoon Delight' for John Denver's Windsong label with Milt Okun producing. Bill and Taffy will be remembered as co-writers with John Denver of his big hit 'Take Me Home Country Roads'.

THE STATLER BROTHERS (country quartet)

BEST OF THE STATLER BROTHERS (Album) *Mercury* [*USA*]. This was released in the U.S.A. in January 1976 (orig. July 1975).

The Statler Brothers are Don and Harold Reid, the two brothers of the group, Lew DeWitt and Phil Balsey. They all grew up in Staunton, Virginia. By 1955, three of the group (with Joe McDorman, an original member of the quartet later replaced by Don Reid) sang together locally as a gospel quartet. They performed under the name of the Four Stars, later as the Kingsmen, changing to the Statler Brothers because of another group having the name Kingsmen. They took their new group name from a box of tissues they spotted backstage at a performance (Statler Tissues being a regional product in Virginia State). Johnny Cash heard them in 1963 and invited them to open one of his shows, and then asked them to join his company. They toured the world with the Cash show for eight years, and later became a regular feature on Cash's ABC-TV series, so popular in the late 1960s and early 1970s. With the release of their second single, 'Flowers on the Wall' they became an established recording act. In 1965 the disc won them two Grammy awards. Many hits followed including 'I'll Go To My Grave Loving You', 'Pictures', 'Do You Remember These?', 'Class of '57', 'Monday Morning Secretary', 'Carry Me Back', 'Thank You World!'. These estab-

lished the group's tone with its unique harmonies, and original material. A third Grammy Award came for Best Performance by a Vocal Group in 1972. The Reid Brothers and DeWitt wrote most of their songs.

In 1972, The Statler Brothers began by monopolizing the Country Music Association's Award for Vocal Group of the Year, and then won it for six consecutive years, winning again in 1979 for the seventh time, an unprecedented feat. 'The Best of the Statler Brothers' was certified platinum in June 1978 by Mercury label. It was the first country album to sell the million without any activity on the pop album charts. The album was still on the country charts at the end of May 1981, a staggering 275-week run.

Contents of the album are: 'Bed of Roses'; 'Whatever Happened to Randolph Scott?'; 'Do You Remember These?'; 'Carry Me Back'; 'Flowers on the Wall'; 'The Class of '57'; 'Pictures'; 'I'll Go To My Grave Loving You'; 'Thank you World!'; 'New York City'; 'Susan When She Tried'. Sales were over two million by January 1981.

AL STEWART

YEAR OF THE CAT (Album) *GRT/Janus* [*USA*]. Written by Al Stewart and released in the U.S.A. in September 1976, this was No 5 for three weeks and stayed 34 weeks in the charts. R.I.A.A. Gold Disc award on 14 January 1977. Platinum award on 24 March 1977.

Al Stewart was born in Glasgow and played with semi-professional groups around Gloucestershire, prior to becoming a well-known soloist at London folk-clubs. He subsequently developed a somewhat monologue style of writing and a more rocking aspect in place of his usual folk music. He signed with CBS who released his first album 'Bedsitter Images' (1967, re-released with some track changes in 1970). This album featured an orchestra, never before used for a folk singer. It was acclaimed by traditional and modern audiences. 'Love Chronicles' (1969) followed – a history of his love life – then 'Zero She Flies' (1970); 'Orange' (1972) and 'Past, Present and Future' (1974). This latter album was released by the Janus label in the U.S.A., as they had then expanded their interest in English and Continental progressive rock. Stewart was a big success in Philadelphia and other cities which paved the way to his American acceptance, and with the release of his second Janus album 'Modern Times', his audiences grew. 'Modern Times' achieved mid-chart status in 1975.

'Year of the Cat' was recorded at London's Abbey Road Studios, produced by Alan Parsons and proved to be the big breakthrough for Al in the States. The album also went platinum in Holland and was a big success in other parts of the world. It includes: 'Year of the Cat'; 'On the Border'; 'Lord Grenville'; 'Sand in Your Shoes'.

ROD STEWART

A NIGHT ON THE TOWN (Album) *Riva* [*Britain*], *Warner Bros* [*USA*]. Written by Rod Stewart, this was released in Britain in June 1976 and in the U.S.A. in July 1976. It reached No 1 and stayed there for four weeks in Britain and was in the charts for 31 weeks. In the U.S.A. it went to No 2 for five weeks, staying 42 weeks in the charts. R.I.A.A. Gold Disc award on 20 October 1976. Platinum award on 23 November 1976.

Rod Stewart's success in the U.S.A. with his discs in 1971 continued over the following 10 years, and in Britain he had as many as 14 singles in the Top 10 up to 1978. 'A Night On The Town' album enhanced his reputation in the U.S.A. where it sold well over the million. It was a slow side/fast side disc, a proven format that worked well for Stewart. It includes: 'The First Cut Is The Deepest'; 'Pretty Flamingo'; 'Big Bayou'; 'Tonight's The Night'.

TONIGHT'S THE NIGHT (Gonna be alright) *Riva* [*Britain*] *Warner Bros* [*USA*]. Written by Rod Stewart, this was released in Britain in June 1976 and in the U.S.A. in September 1976. In the U.S.A. it was No 1 for eight weeks, staying in the charts for

26 weeks. In Britain it was No 4 for two weeks and stayed eight weeks in the charts.

This single release, the prime track from Stewart's successful album 'A Night on the Town', was a tremendous success in the U.S.A., having the longest stay at No 1 for the year.

BARBRA STREISAND
LOVE THEME FROM 'A STAR IS BORN' (Evergreen) *Columbia* [*USA*]. Written by Paul Williams and Barbra Streisand, this was released in the U.S.A. in December 1976 and in Britain in March 1977. It went to No 1 for two weeks in the U.S.A., staying 24 weeks in the charts. In Britain it went to No 3 for one week, staying 19 weeks in the charts. R.I.A.A. Gold Disc award on 31 March 1977. Grammy Awards: Song of the Year; Best Arrangement Accompanying Vocalists; Best Pop Vocal Performance, Female, 1976. No doubt about this being the song of the year, it scooped up many awards (*see* 'A Star Is Born' soundtrack, 1976).

THE SYLVERS (male and female sextet)
HOT LINE *Capitol* [*USA*]. Written by K. St Lewis and F. Perren and released in the U.S.A. in October 1976, this went to No 2 for two weeks, staying 24 weeks in the charts. R.I.A.A. Gold Disc award on 3 January 1977.

Second million seller for this group with a successful brand of 'bubblegum' soul.

TAVARES (male rhythm and blues quintet)
HEAVEN MUST BE MISSING AN ANGEL *Capitol* [*USA*]. Written by K. St Lewis and F. Perren, this was released in the U.S.A. in May 1976 and in Britain in July 1976. In the U.S.A. it was No 10 for one week and stayed in the charts for 24 weeks. In Britain it was No 3 for one week, staying 11 weeks in the charts. R.I.A.A. Gold Disc award on 22 September 1976.

There was never any doubt that the five Boston brothers: Ralph; Arthur 'Pooch'; Antone 'Chubby'; Feliciano 'Batch'; and Perry Lee 'Tiny' would break into the international market. The Tavares brothers started singing as youngsters and took their musical cues from older brother John who no longer performs with the group. Vocalist Johnny Bristol produced their first album 'Check It Out', a major R & B hit which sold almost a half a million copies. The group signed with Capitol in 1973. Since then, Tavares have had ten Top 15 R & B singles in a row, and of these, 'She's Gone' and 'It Only Takes a Minute' went to No 1 on the R & B charts in the U.S.A. Their second album for Capitol was 'Hard Core Poetry' followed by 'In The City' and

'Sky High'. All soared in to the best sellers on both R & B and pop charts. It was a great achievement for Capitol Records' soul campaign starting in 1975. Brian Panella, manager of Tavares, had brought the group to Capitol for whom he had previously worked for seven years. With the disco boom in the U.S.A., soul music, with its rhythmic form for dancing, enjoyed a massive upsurge in popularity, and crossed over to the pop market. Fred Perren became Tavares' new producer, and he wrote 'Heaven Must Be Missing an Angel'. He was already on the crest of a wave with his 'Boogie Fever' hit for the Sylvers. Perren's masterminded hit was also Tavares' first British hit. 'Heaven Must Be Missing an Angel' was the prime track from their album 'Sky High'. Tavares visited Britain in this year for concert dates in London and Manchester with another Capitol soul artist, Natalie Cole.

JAMES TAYLOR
GREATEST HITS (Album) *Warner Bros* [*USA*]. Written by James Taylor and released in the U.S.A. in November 1976, it went to No 16 for two weeks, staying in the charts for 18 weeks. R.I.A.A. Gold Disc award on 22 December 1976. Platinum award on 21 November 1977.

Contents of the album are: 'Carolina on My Mind'; 'Something in the Way She Moves'; 'Fire and Rain'; 'Sweet Baby James'; 'Country Road'; 'You've Got a Friend'; 'Don't Let Me Be Lonely Tonight'; 'Walking Man'; 'How Sweet It Is'; 'Mexico'; 'Shower the People'; 'Steamroller'.

JOHNNY TAYLOR
DISCO LADY *Columbia* [*USA*]. Written by Vance and Davis, this was released in the U.S.A. in February 1976 and in Britain in May 1976. It reached No 1 for three weeks in the U.S.A. and stayed 20 weeks in the charts. In Britain it was No 25 for one week and stayed seven weeks in the charts. R.I.A.A. Gold Disc award on 11 March 1976. Platinum award on 22 April 1976.

1976 was Johnny Taylor's biggest year in an already distinguished career. 'Disco Lady', his debut Columbia single, was the label's fastest selling single. At one period, it was reportedly being played once every ten minutes on the Top 40 radio stations in the States. Its tremendous success generated incredible audience response on his 1976 nationwide tour. It was the first platinum singles award from R.I.A.A. for two million sales. His first Columbia album 'Eargasm' also shipped 'gold'.

10 CC
THE THINGS WE DO FOR LOVE *Mercury* [*Britain*], *Phonogram/Mercury* [*USA*]. Written by Eric Stewart and Graham Gouldman, this was released in Britain in November 1976 and in the U.S.A. in January 1977. In the U.S.A. it went to No 3 for two weeks and stayed 23 weeks in the charts. In Britain it went to No 4 for two weeks and stayed 13 weeks in the charts. R.I.A.A. Gold Disc award on 18 April 1977.

The members of 10 CC are: Eric Stewart (guitar/vocals); Lol Creme (guitar/vocals); Graham Gouldman (bass/vocals); Kevin Godley (drums/vocals). Formed in Manchester in 1972 when four former colleagues returned to their home town. Godley, Creme and Stewart had been together in the pop group Hot Legs. Gouldman had been to the U.S.A. for a number of years to further his songwriting career, following early hits for The Yardbirds ('For Your Love') and The Hollies ('Bus Stop'). Their prowess and professionalism was unmistakable as 10 CC – a top entertainment group since the mid-1960s. They had a string of Top 10 hits in Britain from 1972 – eleven up to 1978. 'The Things We do for Love' was their first million seller in the U.S.A., and also a big success in the U.K.

ANDREA TRUE CONNECTION
MORE, MORE, MORE *Buddah* [*USA*]. Written by Gee Diamond, this was released in the U.S.A. in January 1976 and in Britain in March 1976. It was No 1 for one week in the U.S.A., staying 34 weeks in the charts. It was No 3 for one week in

Britain and stayed ten weeks in the charts. R.I.A.A. Gold Disc award on 28 September 1976.

Andrea True was born and raised in Nashville, and educated at a local boarding school designed for the performing arts. She also studied the piano and drama. As a teenager she hosted a show called 'Teen Beat' for WLAC-TV. She then moved into radio work as a regular co-host for WLAC on the Junior Achievement Show. At 15 Andrea won a college scholarship and the Paderewski Medal from the Fraternity of Student Musicians, and continued to study at Nashville's George Peabody College, gaining a B.Sc. degree in music.

After leaving college, Andrea moved to New York City and taught music theory at the Berghof Studio, and then wrote commercials. She later moved to Nashville Teleprojects and worked on the musical show 'Country Suite', devoting her spare time to modelling, designing clothes, writing magazine articles and starting a movie career. The latter was launched in 1972 with *Illusions of A Lady* for Times Square movies, an X-rated adult only film. National magazine reviews hailed her as the most versatile actress in adult films. By 1975 she was writing, directing and appearing in her own films. Her singing career started in 1974 when she appeared at the Riverboat in the Empire State Building. Her singing drew the attention of Buddah Records, and by 1976 she had her first release with 'More, More, More', written, produced and arranged by Gregg (Gee) Diamond. This first topped the blues and soul charts. With its catchy tune and sensuous rhythms, it was a big hit in the discos, and then topped the national charts, becoming an international smash. It also gained a platinum disc in Canada. An album of the same title followed which contained the hit 'Party Line', and in 1978 came 'What's Your Name, What's Your Number'. Andrea created an act that played to excited audiences throughout the world. This consisted of Andrea, a male lead vocalist, seven musicians and four dancers, making up the Connection – a visually exciting stage performance.

FRANKIE VALLI & THE FOUR SEASONS
GREATEST HITS OF FRANKIE VALLI & THE FOUR SEASONS (Double album) *K-Tel* [*Canada/Britain*]. Released in Britain in November 1976, this went to No 4 for two weeks and stayed in the charts for 20 weeks.

Earlier in 1976, Private Stock Records issued 'The Four Seasons Story', but they were never granted the rights for U.K. advertising of the Four Seasons repertoire on TV and radio, although they held the rights to the recordings. An arrangement was made with K-Tel that the material should be made into a TV-promoted package for Britain – whilst 'The Four Seasons Story' also went on the normal market. 'Greatest Hits' is culled from the same basic catalogue of prime Vee Jay and Philips material for Valli and The Four Seasons and draws upon the group's 1960s material. It contains all their major U.S. and U.K. hits, many of them written by Bob Gaudio, who with Valli and Bob Crewe took over the group's entire catalogue of masters, the only major act in the music business since the 1950s – apart from Elvis Presley – to own their own masters. The combined Canada-UK sales were over the million. Britain awarded a Platinum Disc for over £1,000,000 sales.

Complete contents are: 'Opus 17 (Don't Worry 'Bout Me)'; 'Big Girls Don't Cry'; 'Dawn'; 'Silence Is Golden'; 'Toy Soldier'; 'Will You Love Me Tomorrow?'; 'Don't Think Twice'; 'Too Many Memories'; 'I've Got You Under My Skin'; 'Sherry'; 'Swearin' To God'; 'Walk Like A Man'; 'Workin' My Way Back To You'; 'Girl, Come Running'; 'Bye-Bye Baby (Baby Goodbye)'; 'Alone'; '(You're Gonna) Hurt Yourself'; 'Save It For Me'; 'Ronnie'; 'My Eyes Adored You'; 'Big Man In Town'; 'Can't Take My Eyes Off You'; 'Ain't That a Shame'; 'And That Reminds Me'; 'Huggin' My Pillow'; 'Watch the Flowers Grow'; 'A Patch of Blue'; 'Marlena'; 'Let's Hang On'; 'Fallen Angel'; 'Tell It To The Rain'; 'Connie-O'; 'Candy Girl'; 'C'mon Marianne'; 'Beggin' '; 'The Proud One'; 'You're Ready Now'; 'The Sun Ain't Gonna Shine (Anymore)'; 'Stay'; 'Rag Doll'.

WAR
SUMMER *United Artists* [*USA*]. Written by War and released in the U.S.A. in June 1976, this went to No 7 for two weeks, staying 20 weeks in the charts. R.I.A.A. Gold Disc award on 14 September 1976.

A disc with a lazy beat about the joys of summer by this outstanding group.

GREATEST HITS (Album) *United Artists* [*USA*]. Released in the U.S.A. in August 1976, it was No 7 for one week, staying in the charts for 21 weeks. R.I.A.A. Gold Disc award on 24 August 1976. Platinum award on 6 January 1977.

A most successful album for the group including all their hits.

WILD CHERRY
PLAY THAT FUNKY MUSIC *Epic/Sweet City* [*USA*]. Written by R. Parissi, this was released in the U.S.A. in June 1976 and in Britain in September 1976. It went to No 1 for three weeks in the U.S.A., staying 33 weeks in the charts. In Britain it went to No 7 for one week and stayed 11 weeks in the charts. R.I.A.A. Gold Disc award on 23 August 1976. Platinum award on 15 October 1976.

A phenomenal hit for the Wild Cherry group from Cleveland. Sweet City Records, a local label, started developing products for their area, and made an agreement with Epic Records to distribute the material. 'Wild Cherry' was the first. On release of the single the response was positive and quick, and Epic's promotion plan gave the disc wide coverage, picking up black and white Top 40 airplay, despite the line 'Play that funky music, white boy' which opened up the chorus. It was the third single to receive the new R.I.A.A. Platinum Award for two million sale. Composer Parissi was producer of the disc.

WILD CHERRY (Album) *Epic/Sweet City* [*USA*]. This was released in the U.S.A. in July 1976. It was No 5 for two weeks, staying 25 weeks in the charts. R.I.A.A. Gold Disc award on 8 September 1976. Platinum award on 17 December 1976.

Following the success of the group's single 'Play That Funky Music', the album was also a very big success. This exceptionally strong debut disc was described as 'electrified funk' i.e. music by a white group with a very full black sound. It includes 'Play That Funky Music'; '99½'; 'Nowhere To Run'; 'What in the Funk Do You See?'; 'Hold On'; 'The Lady Wants Your Money'.

WINGS
WINGS AT THE SPEED OF SOUND (Album) *Capitol* [*USA and Britain*]. This was released in the U.S.A. and Britain in March 1976. In the U.S.A. it went to No 1 for seven weeks and in Britain to No 2 for four weeks. It stayed 35 weeks in the U.S charts and 32 weeks in the British charts. R.I.A.A. Gold Disc award on 25 March 1976. Platinum award on 3 May 1976.

The demand for this disc exceeded all Wings' past efforts. It was released prior to the group's first-ever U.S. tour and recorded at EMI, Abbey Road, London. It strengthened Paul McCartney's importance as a lyricist and a recording artist in his own right. An immediate best seller, sales went over the two million mark by January 1977. Contents of the album are: (*)'Let 'Em In' (Paul McCartney); 'The Note You Never Wrote' (Paul McCartney); 'She's My Baby' (Paul McCartney); 'Beware My Love' (Paul McCartney); 'Wino Junko' (Jimmy McCulloch & Colin Allen); (*)'Silly Love Songs' (Paul McCartney); 'Cook of the House' (Paul McCartney); 'Time to Hide' (Denny Laine); 'Must Do Something About It' (Paul McCartney); 'San Ferry Anne' (Paul McCartney); 'Warm and Beautiful' (Paul McCartney).

Personnel: Paul McCartney (piano, bass, guitar, drums, vocals); Denny Laine (guitar, vocals); Jimmy McCulloch (guitars, vocals); Linda McCartney (keyboards, vocals); Joe English (drums, vocals). Plus brass and strings. Produced by Paul McCartney. (*) denotes million seller as a single release.

SILLY LOVE SONGS *Capitol [USA] Parlophone [Britain]*. This was written by Paul McCartney and released in the U.S.A. and Britain in April 1976. It reached No 1 for five weeks in the U.S.A., staying 29 weeks in the charts. In Britain it was No 1 for one week and stayed 11 weeks in the charts. R.I.A.A. Gold Disc award on 11 June 1976.

A prime track from the album 'Wings at the Speed of Sound'; a very cleverly constructed song with catchy harmonies, horns and bass.

LET 'EM IN *Capitol [USA] Parlophone [Britain]*. Written by Paul McCartney, this was released in the U.S.A. in June 1976 and in Britain in July 1976. It went to No 1 for one week both in the U.S.A. and in Britain. It was in the U.S.A. charts for 25 weeks and in the British charts for ten weeks. R.I.A.A. Gold Disc award on 25 October 1976.

The second single release from the album 'Wings at the Speed of Sound'. An impressive follow-up to 'Silly Love Songs', with a loping beat and brisk military drum sound, and one of Wings' dazzling stage numbers on their U.S. tour in this year.

WINGS OVER AMERICA (Triple album) *Capitol [USA]*. Released in the U.S.A. in December 1976, this went to No 1 for one week, staying 24 weeks in the charts. R.I.A.A. Gold Disc award on 13 December 1976. Platinum award on 20 December 1976.

1976 was the year in which Wings toured the world, including their first performances in North America, and the first time Paul McCartney had appeared on a U.S. concert stage since the last concert of the last Beatles' tour a decade earlier. The Wings tour of the U.S.A. in May and June 1976 gave 34 performances in 21 cities to over 600,000 people, grossing over £2 million. The 'Wings Over America' three-record set was recorded live during the tour and quickly received gold and platinum certification. Wings also received more gold and platinum awards from R.I.A.A. in 1976 than any other solo artist or group (two gold singles, two gold albums and two platinum albums). Paul McCartney was named the No 1 Top Featured Male Vocalist for both singles and albums, and reaffirmed his place as one of the most important figures in popular music, establishing Wings as a true supergroup of the seventies. Contents of album are: 'Venus and Mars' (1975); 'Rock Show'; 'Jet' (Paul McCartney, 1973); 'Let Me Roll It' (Paul McCartney, 1973); 'Spirits of Ancient Egypt' (Paul McCartney, 1975); 'Medicine Jar' (J. McCulloch and Allen 1975); 'Maybe I'm Amazed' (Paul McCartney); 'Call Me Back Again' (Paul McCartney); 'Lady Madonna' (Lennon and McCartney, 1968); 'Long and Winding Road' (Lennon and McCartney, 1970); 'Live and Let Die' (Paul McCartney, 1973); 'Picasso's Last Words' (Paul McCartney, 1973); 'Richard Cory' (Simon); 'Bluebird' (Paul McCartney, 1973); 'I've Just Seen a Face' (Lennon and McCartney, 1965); 'Blackbird' (Lennon and McCartney, 1968); 'Yesterday' (Lennon and McCartney, 1965); 'You Gave Me The Answer' (Paul McCartney, 1975); 'Magneto and Titanium Man (Paul McCartney, 1975); 'Go Now' (Larry Banks and M. Bennett, 1964); 'My Love' (Paul McCartney, 1973); 'Listen To What The Man Said' (Paul McCartney, 1975); 'Let 'Em In' (McCartney, 1976); 'Time To Hide' (Denny Laine, 1976); 'Silly Love Songs' (McCartney, 1976); 'Beware My Love' (McCartney, 1976); 'Letting Go' (McCartney); 'Band On The Run' (McCartney, 1973); 'Hi Hi Hi' (McCartney); 'Soily' (McCartney).

STEVIE WONDER
SONGS IN THE KEY OF LIFE (Double album) *Motown [USA]*. Written by Stevie Wonder, this was released in the U.S.A. and Britain in October 1976. In the U.S.A. it climbed to No 1 and stayed there for 12 weeks, remaining 51 weeks in the charts. In Britain it reached No 1 for four weeks, staying 41 weeks in the charts. Grammy awards: Album of the Year, 1976; Best Producer of the Year, Stevie Wonder, 1976; Best Pop Vocal (Male), Stevie Wonder, 1976.

This album demonstrated Stevie Wonder's talent as per-

former, producer and songwriter. Much of the music has a decidedly Latin flavour, a new style for Wonder, plus electronic keyboard and synthesizer instruments. Among musicians contributing to the work are: George Benson; Herbie Hancock; Bobbie Humphrey; Mike Sembello; Jim Horn; Sneaky Pete Kleinow; Minnie Riperton and Dorothy Ashby. It shipped 1,300,000 units and over two million sales by December 1977. 'Songs in the Key of Life' is a peak of creative and performing art, a giant album in many senses of the word. Initial reaction from FM radio stations was overwhelmingly positive. It was recorded at Record Plants in Los Angeles and Sausolito, and at the Hit Factory in New York. It included: 'Village Ghetto Land'; 'Confusion'; 'Sir Duke'; 'Knock Me Off My Feet'; 'Summer Soft'; 'Pastime Paradise'; 'I Wish'; 'Ordinary Pain'; 'Black Man'; 'Isn't She Lovely'; 'Joy Inside My Tears'; 'If It's Magic'; 'As'; 'Another Star'; 'All Day Sucker'; 'Saturn'; 'Ebony Eyes'; 'Easy Goin' Evening'; 'Love's In Need Of Love Today'; 'At Last'; 'Have a Talk With God'.

GARY WRIGHT
DREAM WEAVER *Warner Bros [USA]*. Written by Gary Wright and released in the U.S.A. in January 1976, this went to No 1 for one week, staying 25 weeks in the charts. R.I.A.A. Gold Disc award on 20 April 1976.

Gary's big hit single, culled from his 1975 album of the same title.

ORIGINAL THEATRE CAST

ANNIE (Album) *Columbia [USA]*. Written by Larry Morton and Charles Strouse, this obtained the R.I.A.A. Gold Disc award on 19 June 1979 and the platinum award on 22 December 1980. Grammy Award: Best Show Cast Album, 1977.

Annie was born in a strip cartoon in the *New York Daily News* in 1924, and at one period appeared in newspapers with a combined circulation of 47 million. Sponsored by Ovaltine, she moved into radio, starred in two earlier movies, and in the musical that has played in 12 countries. Annie is a plucky orphan who symbolizes all the values held to be representative of American childhood - honesty, courage, patriotism, independence, and self-reliance. The original star of the musical was Andrea McArdle, the second 'Annie' on Broadway was Shelly Bruce, who was succeeded by Allison Smith. The album sold 300,000 by 1978, and with its long run in the U.S.A. sold the million by the end of 1980. The show was still running on Broadway in 1982. It included the showstopper song 'Tomorrow', and 'Something Was Missing', 'Without a Smile', 'I Think I'm Gonna Live', 'East Street', 'Annie' and 'Maybe'.

The film rights were bought for £5,200,000, being £2,200,000 more than had ever been paid for any film before. Nine thousand girls were auditioned in 22 cities, including London, before ten year-old Aileen Quinn was selected for Annie. The potential profits from the film, scheduled for release in 1982, were estimated to set new standards for the commercial cinema, with immediate guarantees of £25 million in fees for eventual screening on cable and network TV, plus over 800 Annie-related products, ranging from dog food and chewing gum to wigs.

ORIGINAL FILM SOUNDTRACK

ROCKY (Album) *United Artists [USA]*. With songs by Sylvester Stallone, this was released in the U.S.A. in January 1977. In the U.S.A. it went to No 4 for three weeks, staying 28 weeks in the charts. Academy Award: Best Film, 1977.

This film had rave reviews, and starred composer Sylvester Stallone in the story of a boxer. The film score was written by Bill Conti, whose theme 'Gonna Fly Now' was the big hit. The album also included 'Take You Back' and 'You Take My Heart Away'.

ORIGINAL FILM SOUNDTRACK

SATURDAY NIGHT FEVER (Double album) *RSO [USA]*. This was released in the U.S.A. in November 1977 and in Britain in December 1977. It went to No 1 in the U.S.A. for 25 weeks, and stayed in the charts for 81 weeks. In Britain it stayed in the charts for 62 weeks, reaching No 1 for 18 weeks. R.I.A.A. Gold Disc award on 22 November 1977. Platinum award on 3 January 1978. Grammy award: Album of the Year, 1978.

It was English pop music critic Nik Cohn's story 'Bible Rites of The New Saturday Night' that inspired the Robert Stigwood Organization to make 'Saturday Night Fever'. Within 12 hours of the article's publication, Stigwood phoned Cohn and a contract was delivered at his door. With the disco explosion of 1976, the release of 'Saturday Night Fever' made the discos more crammed than ever, and their popularity spread throughout the world. The film starred an exceptional disco dancer, John Travolta. He became the U.S.A.'s heartthrob through the top-rated TV series 'Welcome Back Kotter' in which he played a tough-talking teenage villain. Travolta also had a parallel success as a singer, and following his hit record of 'Let Her In', he was approached to make 'Saturday Night Fever'. The girl in the film was played by Karen Lynn Gorey. Its success was unprecedented in that apart from Travolta, famous bands and artists contributed material to the double album. The sales were staggering, a global 30 million with a retail sale figure near to £150 million, almost quadrupling the gross rentals on the movie. France sold over one million, an unprecedented feat for their market, Italy almost a million, Britain two million, and there were large sales in Holland, Canada, Australia and Spain. American sales were over 12 million. It was predominantly the Bee Gees' recording of their songs for the film that made the album such a success.

The album contains: 'Stayin' Alive'; 'How Deep Is Your Love?'; 'Night Fever'; 'You Should Be Dancing' (all these were million sellers as singles); 'More Than a Woman'; 'Jive Talkin'' (written and sung by the Bee Gees); 'If I Can't Have You' (written by the Bee Gees, sung by Yvonne Elliman); 'A Fifth of Beethoven' (written and played by Walter Murphy and based on Beethoven's 5th Symphony); 'More Than a Woman' (written by the Bee Gees, sung by Tavares); 'Calypso Breakdown' (performed by Ralph McDonald); 'Open Sesame' (Kool and The Gang); 'Boogie Shoes' (K.C. and The Sunshine Band); 'K-Jee' (M.F.S.B.); 'Disco Inferno'; 'Manhattan Skyline'; 'Night on Disco Mountain' (based on 'Night on the Bare Mountain' by Mussorgsky); 'Salsation' (The Trammps). 'Saturday Night Fever' is the biggest-selling album to date. Robert Stigwood presented the Bee Gees with a platinum Cadillac when the album had sold 10 million (by May 1978). Polygram presented RSO with Gold and Platinum Albums for U.K. sales (May 1978).

ORIGINAL FILM SOUNDTRACK

STAR WARS (Double album) *20th Century [USA]*. With music by John Williams, this was released in the U.S.A. in May 1977 and in Britain in December 1977. In the U.S.A. it went to No 2 for seven weeks, staying 51 weeks in the charts. R.I.A.A. Gold Disc award on 18 July 1977. Platinum award on 17 August 1977. Grammy award: Best Pop Instrumental Recording, John Williams conducting London Symphony Orchestra, 1977.

Star Wars was described as 'the phenomenon of 1977' and has no parallel in movie history. By the end of 1977 it had grossed 200 million dollars and was seen by 30 million people in the U.S.A., with big grosses around the world. John Williams' stirring soundtrack went high up the charts and sold over two million in the U.S.A. and another million abroad.

The film is pure science-fiction escapism. For two hours, the special effects give the audience the impression of floating about the universe lost in some time capsule, hypnotized by gorilla-like creatures and dazzled by rockets and ray guns. The story starts in a mythical galaxy where Princess Leia (Carrie Fisher) is leading a revolution against the evil regime of the Galactic Empire. She is captured by Grand Moff Tarkin (Peter Cushing) and his accomplice Darth Vader. Leia had handed over the stolen plans of the Death Star to two trusted robots, Arto Detoo (Kenny Baker) and See Threepio (Anthony Daniels). They flee to a barren desert, are picked up by scavengers and sold to farmer Owen Lars and his stalwart nephew, Luke Skywalker (Mark Hamill). A wise old hermit, Obi Wan Kenobi (Alec Guiness) comes to their aid. The forces of right triumph after some breathless and spectacular thrills, Tarkin meets a grisly end, and democracy is restored. Much of the film was made at Elstree Studios, Hertfordshire, England and directed by George Lucas. The London premier was on 27 December 1977 at the Dominion Theatre and Leicester Square Theatre, London. (See Meco - 'Star Wars Theme' for data on composer John Williams.)

ABBA

KNOWING ME, KNOWING YOU *Polar [Sweden]*, *Epic [Britain]*, *Atlantic [USA]*. Written by Bjorn Ulvaeus and Benny Andersson, this was released in Britain in February 1977 and in the U.S.A. in May 1977. It was No 1 for six weeks in Britain, staying in the charts for 13 weeks. In the U.S.A. it was No 15 for one week and stayed 18 weeks in the charts.

Another prime track from ABBA's album 'Arrival'. It sold the million, mainly in Europe.

AEROSMITH

DRAW THE LINE (Album) *Columbia [USA]*. Written by Aerosmith and released in the U.S.A. in December 1977, this was No 8 for two weeks and stayed 17 weeks in the charts. R.I.A.A. Gold Disc award on 9 December 1977. Platinum award on 13 December 1977.

Another huge success for this hard rock quintet, with an almost instant million sale. It includes: 'Draw the Line'; 'Critical Mass'; 'Get It Up'; 'Bright Light Fright'; 'Kings and Queens'; 'Milk Cow Blues'.

BACCARA (female duo)

YES SIR I CAN BOOGIE *RCA [Germany]*. Written by Rolf Soja and Nestral, this was released in Britain in July 1977, going to No 1 for one week and staying 17 weeks in the charts.

This was written by Baccara's producer Rolf Soja. The duo, Spanish girls called Maria and Mayte, were born in Madrid, Spain, and started their careers in show business as dancers on Spanish TV. They developed a nightclub act singing and dancing. It was on the island of Fuerteventura, one of the Canary Islands off the Atlantic coast of Africa, a tiny holiday retreat with a few fishing villages and some luxury hotels, that Baccara were discovered by holidaymaking Leon Dean - an executive with RCA Records in Germany. He took them back to Germany for RCA to record this, their first record, and it went straight to the top of the charts in Germany for several weeks. It subsequently became No 1 in nine countries including Britain, Holland, Austria, Switzerland, Belgium, and sold over 750,000 in Japan where it was a big disco hit. 'Yes Sir I Can Boogie' is a sexy, sultry song. It dominated the juke boxes and radio throughout Europe. It was released in the U.S.A. in December 1977 on Manhattan Records, with fair success. Global sales were well over the million.

THE BEATLES

THE BEATLES AT THE HOLLYWOOD BOWL (Album) *Capitol [USA]*. This was released in the U.S.A. and in Britain in May 1977. It was No 7 for two weeks in the U.S.A. and stayed in the charts for 12 weeks. R.I.A.A. Gold Disc award in May 1977. Platinum award on 12 August 1977.

The first live Beatles album and the first never-before-released Beatles recording to appear in seven years. The recordings are of the Beatles' 1964 and 1965 concerts at the Hollywood Bowl in California. The three-track tapes had been in Capitol's vaults for 12 years, and were transferred to modern multi-track tape, re-mixed, filtered, equalized and edited by long-time producer George Martin and remix engineer Geoff Emerick. All the original vocals and instruments were kept intact and no over-dubbing was used. The album contained 13 songs - the highlights of their repertoire at that point in their career, and as producer George Martin points out in his liner notes, 'it is a piece of history that will not occur again'.

Contents are: 'Twist and Shout'; 'Dizzie Miss Lizzie'; 'Boys' (sung by Ringo); Chuck Berry's 'Roll over Beethoven'; Little Richard's 'Long Tall Sally'; and 8 Lennon & McCartney compositions: 'She's a Woman'; 'Ticket to Ride'; 'Can't Buy Me Love'; 'Things We Said Today'; 'A Hard Day's Night'; 'Help'; 'All My Loving'; 'She Loves You.'

It was the 21st album by the Beatles as a group to be distributed by Capitol in the U.S.A., but did not register in Britain after an extensive advertising campaign.

THE BEE GEES

HOW DEEP IS YOUR LOVE? *RSO/Polydor [USA]*. Written by the Bee Gees, this was released in the U.S.A. in September 1977 and in Britain in October 1977. In the U.S.A. it went to No 2 for two weeks and stayed 30 weeks in the charts. In Britain it

was No 2 for one week and stayed 15 weeks in the charts. R.I.A.A. Gold Disc award on 16 December 1977. Grammy Award: Best Pop Vocal Performance by a Duo, Group or Chorus, 1977.

This was included in the 'Saturday Night Fever' album. As a single release it sold 1,700,000 in the U.S.A. and over 250,000 in Britain.

STAYIN' ALIVE *RSO [USA]*. Written by the Bee Gees, this was released in the U.S.A. in December 1977 and in Britain in January 1978. It went to No 1 for four weeks in the U.S.A., staying 26 weeks in the charts. In Britain it was No 4 for one week and stayed 20 weeks in the charts. R.I.A.A. Gold Disc award on 26 January 1978. Platinum award on 13 March 1978. Grammy Award: Best Vocal Arrangement on 'Stayin' Alive', 1968.

Another huge seller as a single from the 'Saturday Night Fever' album. U.S. sales went over two million, British sales over a quarter of a million.

HERE AT LAST - BEE GEES 'LIVE' (Double album) *RSO/Polydor [USA]*. With songs written by the Bee Gees, this was released in the U.S.A. in May 1977 and in Britain in June 1977. In the U.S.A. it was No 14 for one week, staying in the charts for 58 weeks. R.I.A.A. Gold Disc award on 24 June 1977. Platinum award on 22 November 1977.

The Bee Gees made a tour of the U.S.A. in 1976, and this album was recorded of a concert which took place in Los Angeles in December 1976. This album underlines the quality of their output since their first transatlantic hit, 'New York Mining Disaster 1941' of a decade ago. Contents are: 'I've Gotta Get a Message To You'; 'Love So Right'; 'Edge Of The Universe'; 'Come On Over'; 'You Can't Keep A Good Man Down'; 'Wind Of Change'; 'Nights On Broadway'; 'Jive Talkin'; 'Lonely Days'; 'New York Mining Disaster 1941'; 'Medley' ('Run To Me', 'World', 'Holiday', 'I Can't See Nobody', 'I Started A Joke', 'Massachusetts'); 'How Can You Mend A Broken Heart?'; 'To Love Somebody'; 'You Should Be Dancing'; 'Boogie Child'; 'Down the Road'; 'Words'.

WILLIAM BELL

TRYIN' TO LOVE TWO *Mercury [USA]*. Written by Paul Mitchell and William Bell and released in the U.S.A. in January 1977, this went to No 7 for two weeks and stayed 20 weeks in the charts. R.I.A.A. Gold Disc award on 26 May 1977.

William Bell's first million seller. He was originally a recording artist for Stax label around 1968 in the U.S.A.

GEORGE BENSON

IN FLIGHT (Album) *Warner Bros [USA]*. This was released in the U.S.A. in February 1977 and in Britain in May 1977. It went to No 16 for two weeks in the U.S.A., staying 21 weeks in the charts. In Britain it was No 16 for two weeks, staying 13 weeks in the charts. R.I.A.A. Gold Disc award on 15 March 1977. Platinum award on 6 October 1977.

Another fine album by jazz guitarist/vocalist Benson. This one picked up where his successful 'Breezin'' album left off, with Benson singing on four of the six tracks and filling in with his inimitable fluid guitar style. The tracks include songs by Donny Hathaway and War. Prime tracks were the evergreen 'Nature Boy', 'Gonna Love You More', and 'The World Is A Ghetto'.

DEBBY BOONE

YOU LIGHT UP MY LIFE *Warner/Curb [USA]*. Written by Joe Brooks, this was released in the U.S.A. in September 1977 and in Britain in December 1977. In the U.S.A. it climbed to No 1, staying there for 13 weeks, and remained 28 weeks in the charts. In Britain it was No 48 for one week and stayed two weeks in the charts. R.I.A.A. Gold Disc award on 19 October 1977. Platinum award on 22 November 1977. Grammy Awards:

Song of the Year, Joe Brooks, 1977; Best New Artist of the Year, Debby Boone, 1977.

There was no doubt about this being the song of the year. It was 1977's biggest selling single, the title track of the film of the same name. It was Debby Boone's first solo hit, selling over three million by the year's end and a final tally of four million by May 1978. It also had the longest stay at the top of the U.S. charts since 1943. Writer Joe Brooks also produced the disc. The song was awarded the 'Oscar' for best film song of 1977. Debby Boone, singer of this slow intense ballad, is one of the daughters of star Pat Boone, and was born in 1956. All the family were singers and had a stage act, their songs consisting throughout of themes of love and togetherness, in keeping with their Christian upbringing. They were a great attraction at Knotts Berry Farm, a Disney-land style entertainment complex on the outskirts of Los Angeles, performing as The Boone Sisters Quartet. Debby's album of the same title was also a big success.

YOU LIGHT UP MY LIFE (Album) *Warner/Curb* [*USA*]. Released in the U.S.A. in September 1977, this went to No 8 for one week and stayed 29 weeks in the charts. R.I.A.A. Gold Disc award on 25 October 1977. Platinum award on 13 December 1977.

Debby's album was an immediate winner, following her success with the single. Four producers were responsible for laying down an appealing commercial sound. The album was shipped 'gold'. It included: 'You Light Up My Life'; 'A Rock and Roll Song'; 'From Me To You'; 'Micol's Theme'.

JACQUES BREL

BREL (Album) *Logo* [*France*]. Jacques Brel was the foremost singer of France, but in 1972 he deserted his public and went to live in Polynesia on the island where the famous painter Gaugin had lived a century before. In the summer of 1977 he returned to Paris incognito, went into a studio and quickly recorded a dozen new songs, then returned just as quickly to the South Pacific. His tunes have no relation to the rock era. They are indelibly in the tradition of French café singers. He was known as 'the master of the smokey boites of off-colour Paris'. One song 'Les F...' is about a nightclub singer who has to perform before an audience of 100 nationalities, who couldn't possibly understand him. It is as close to autobiography as Brel ever came. Brel was Belgian – actually Flemish. One of his most famous songs was 'Le Moribond' written in 1961 and rewritten in part by Terry Jacks with English translation (by McKuen) to become 'Seasons in the Sun', a tremendous seller in 1974. It was reported that Brel died in 1978. This Brel album sold nearly two million. The prime tracks were: 'Les F...'; 'Orly'; 'To Get Old'.

BRIGHOUSE & RASTRICK BRASS BAND

THE FLORAL DANCE *Logo* [*Britain*]. This Cornish melody written and arranged by Katie Moss (1911) was released in Britain in October 1977, going to No 2 for five weeks and staying 13 weeks in the charts.

The Furry (or Floral) Dance is held annually on May 8 in Coinagehall Street, Helston, Cornwall, notable for its picturesque street-dancing. Katie Moss's original ballad describes the scene in her lyrics and the band playing the famous melody for the street dancers. Arranger Ivor Raymonde produced this Brass Band version for the Brighouse and Rastrick Band, one of the best in Britain. It sold nearly a million in Britain by March 1978, the million sale reported in February 1981.

PETER BROWN

DO YA WANNA GET FUNKY WITH ME? *Drive/TK* [*USA*]. Written by Peter Brown, this was released in the U.S.A. in August 1977 and in Britain in January 1978. In the U.S.A. it went to No 27 for one week, staying 14 weeks in the charts. In Britain it went to No 4 for one week, staying in the charts for four weeks.

Peter Brown from Palos Heights, Chicago, taught himself to play drums at the age of 13. At high school he joined a baton-twirling corps named the Jorgensen Rangerettes, who played rock music instead of the usual marching anthems. Peter taught himself the piano, played with the corps for five years and became their musical director. He started composing, acquiring more instruments and a four-track tape recorder, and turned his bedroom into a recording studio, making tapes and overdubbing to perfect his sound. He sent a tape to TK Records producer Cory Wade which was turned down. Peter then bought a synthesizer, piano, drum kit and a dozen percussion instruments. With these he overdubbed new tracks to the tape he'd sent to Cory. This time, Cory felt Peter was right, and the song 'Do Ya Wanna Get Funky With Me?' was transferred to 24 tracks, and with added background vocals was an immediate success. At this time, the discos were using 12-inch singles, put out in a limited edition. Listeners wanted to buy them and the trend grew into a mania with all the record companies in U.S.A. Peter's disc was the first ever 12-inch single to sell a million, and was certified 'gold' by TK Productions of Hialeah, Florida. It went to No 1 on the R & B charts, and crossed over to success on the National charts.

JACKSON BROWNE

RUNNING ON EMPTY (Album) *Asylum* [*USA*]. Written by Jackson Browne and released in the U.S.A. in December 1977, this went to No 3 for four weeks, staying 49 weeks in the charts. R.I.A.A. Gold Disc award on 28 December 1977. Platinum award on 25 August 1978.

Probably the first time a major artist released a live album of entirely new material – the tracks recorded on stage, in hotel rooms and on buses. The album has a travel-weary theme in many of the songs. The title track 'Running On Empty' is one of Browne's best to date.

JIMMY BUFFETT

CHANGES IN LATITUDES, CHANGES IN ATTITUDES (Album) *ABC* [*USA*]. Written by Jimmy Buffett and released in the U.S.A. in February 1977, this went to No 15 for one week, remaining 39 weeks in the charts. R.I.A.A. Gold Disc award on 20 June 1977. Platinum award on 14 December 1977.

Jimmy Buffett is a native of Mobile, Alabama. He earned a degree in journalism from Auburn and the University of Southern Mississippi. After graduation he made the rounds of the New Orleans clubs and later got a recording contract with Barnaby Records in Nashville. Moving to Miami, he got another contract with ABC Records. His first three albums for Dunhill ('A White Sport Coat and a Pink Crustacean' 'Livin' and Dyin' in 3/4 Time' and 'A1A') were popular successes, as was his first ABC album 'Havana Daydreamin''. He re-signed with ABC in 1976 and completed 'Changes in Latitudes, Changes in Attitudes' which included a self-contained band (the Coral Reefers) recorded at Criteria Studios in Miami. The sound cuts across country rock and pop, and Buffett's wit and sensitivity stand out, particularly on 'Margaritaville'. Other prime tracks are the title track – and Jesse Winchester's 'Biloxi'. It was the single release of 'Margaritaville' that brought his type of whimsy and sarcasm to the attention of the public throughout the country, with a resulting million-selling album.

GLEN CAMPBELL

SOUTHERN NIGHTS *Capitol* [*USA*]. Written by Allen Toussaint and released in the U.S.A. in February 1977, this went to No 1 for one week and stayed 22 weeks in the charts. In Britain it went to No 28, staying six weeks in the charts. R.I.A.A. Gold Disc award on 20 April 1977.

Yet another big hit for popular Country artist, Glen Campbell, which had fair success in Britain.

SHAUN CASSIDY

DA DOO RON RON *Warner/Curb* [*USA*]. Written by Phil Spector, Ellie Greenwich and Jeff Barry (1963), this was released in the U.S.A. in March 1977, going to No 1 for one week and staying 23 weeks in the charts. R.I.A.A. Gold Disc award on 19 July 1977.

Shaun Cassidy gained international stardom with this revival of the Crystals' 1963 hit, and two subsequent million sellers. He was born on the road-show circuit of Oscar-winning parents Shirley Jones and Jack Cassidy. His half-brother is teen idol David Cassidy. Shaun was writing songs when he was 13 and also involved in the first of a series of rock bands. In 1975 he was heard by Mike Curb who signed him to Curb Records. His first singles were released in Europe, and his debut single 'Morning Girl' was a hit in Holland. The follow-up 'That's Rock and Roll' hit the Top 10 in Germany and Australia. Shortly after completing his debut album in early 1975, Shaun got the role of Joe Hardy in the TV hit 'The Hardy Boys' which confirmed his popularity. Shaun was born in 1958.

SHAUN CASSIDY (Album) *Warner/Curb* [*USA*]. This was released in the U.S.A. in June 1977 and went to No 2 for two weeks, staying in the charts for 68 weeks. R.I.A.A. Gold Disc award on 9 August 1977. Platinum award on 20 September 1977.

An album full of songs in the same vein as his hit 'Da Doo Ron Ron'. It included: 'That's Rock and Roll'; 'Take Good Care of My Baby'; and 'Da Doo Ron Ron'.

THAT'S ROCK AND ROLL *Warner/Curb* [*USA*]. Written by Eric Carmen, this was released in the U.S.A. in July 1977, going to No 3 for two weeks and staying 22 weeks in the charts. R.I.A.A. Gold Disc award on 4 October 1977.

Shaun's big hit from the album 'Shaun Cassidy', originally composed by U.S. pianist Eric Carmen in 1975.

BORN LATE (Album) *Warner/Curb* [*USA*]. Released in the U.S.A. in November 1977, this went to No 8 for two weeks and stayed 36 weeks in the charts. R.I.A.A. Gold Disc award on 22 November 1977. Platinum award on 13 December 1977.

Fine follow-up album from Shaun. It included: 'Hey Deanie'; 'A Girl Like You'; 'Teen Dream'.

HEY DEANIE *Warner/Curb* [*USA*]. Written by Shaun Cassidy and released in the U.S.A. in November 1977, this went to No 13 for one week, staying 17 weeks in the charts. R.I.A.A. Gold Disc award on 17 January 1978.

Another big hit for Shaun, from his 'Born Late' album.

CHIC (rock sextet)

DANCE, DANCE, DANCE (Yowsah, Yowsah, Yowsah) *Atlantic* [*USA*]. Written by Bernard Edwards and Nile Rodgers, this was released in the U.S.A. and Britain in November 1977. It was No 8 for three weeks in the U.S.A. and stayed 25 weeks in the charts. In Britain it was No 6 for one week and stayed 12 weeks in the charts. R.I.A.A. Gold Disc award on 16 February 1978.

Chic personnel includes Bernard Edwards and Nile Rodgers (leaders/producers/songwriters); Tony Thompson (drums); Alfa Anderson (lead singer); Luci Martin (vocalist); and Norma. The group's music had its roots in London. Rodgers and Edwards went to Gullivers and Cue Club frequently and got the idea to change their musical direction towards disco music. This decision transformed them from penniless musicians to millionaires. At the clubs, they noted that the people there were well dressed and danced all night long. They discarded their look of long hair, jeans and T-shirts for suits, came up with a nice clean appearance and a good sound to capitalize on a completely new market in disco groups that no one was exploiting. The changeover was not an immediate success. They spent 7 months trying to get a record company in New York interested in a tape of a song. Pawning their instruments, they bought two very expensive European three-piece suits, and went round the record companies again, and soon their first single 'Dance, Dance, Dance' was released. It was a big hit.

Edwards and Rodgers first got together in 1972 in the Big Apple Band, backing group for New York City. They toured the U.S.A. and Europe for three years when New York City was disbanded, but kept active by recording demos on their own and backing artists like Carl Douglas. They coined the name Chic in June 1977, and lined up several new faces as touring and recording members. Chic went on to become a major force in the recording world with the blockbuster 'Le Freak' (*see* 1978) and further successes in 1979.

CHICAGO

CHICAGO XI (Album) *Columbia* [*USA*]. The material for this disc was written by Chicago. It was released in the U.S.A. in September 1977, going to No 7 for two weeks and staying 17 weeks in the charts. R.I.A.A. Gold Disc award on 16 September 1977. Platinum award on 11 October 1977.

Another almost instant million seller for Chicago, a continuation of their success saga. It includes: 'Mississippi Delta City Blues'; 'Baby, What a Big Surprise'; 'Vote For Me'; 'Little One'; 'Take Me Back To Chicago' (with guest artist Chaka Khan).

ERIC CLAPTON

SLOWHAND (Album) *RSO* [*USA*]. This was released in the U.S.A. and Britain in November 1977. It went to No 4 for two weeks in the U.S.A. and stayed 44 weeks in the charts. In Britain it was No 35 for one week, staying five weeks in the charts. R.I.A.A. Gold Disc award on 26 January 1978. Platinum award on 14 March 1978.

This album had a similar line-up to Clapton's more recent albums with the addition of saxophonist Mel Collins. A great success in the U.S.A. where it sold two million. Notable for Clapton's punchy guitar sound, with the eight minute track 'The Core' an outstanding item. Other tracks are: 'Cocaine'; 'Wonderful Tonight'; 'Lay Down Sally'; 'Next Time You See Her'; 'We're All The Way'; 'May You Never'; 'Mean Old 'Frisco'; 'Peaches and Diesel'.

LAY DOWN SALLY *RSO* [*USA*]. This was released in the U.S.A. and Britain in December 1977. In the U.S.A. it reached No 8 for three weeks, staying in the charts for 22 weeks. In Britain it was No 39 for one week, staying six weeks in the charts. R.I.A.A. Gold Disc award on 17 April 1978.

Another success for Clapton in the U.S.A.

NATALIE COLE

I'VE GOT LOVE ON MY MIND *Capitol* [*USA*]. This was released in the U.S.A. in January 1977, going to No 5 for two weeks and staying 24 weeks in the charts. R.I.A.A. Gold Disc award on 13 April 1977.

Natalie is the daughter of Nat 'King' Cole. She was raised with music and surrounded by her father's friends Pearl Bailey, Nancy Wilson, Ella Fitzgerald, Sarah Vaughan, Count Basie and her personal favourite Harry Belafonte, all of whom made her interested in performing at a very early age. Her experience goes back to when she was six years of age, when she sang on a Christmas record with her father. At 11, she appeared and sang on the stage of Los Angeles' Greek Theater with her father and Barbara McNair in the stage play *I'm With You*. Natalie went to the University of Massachusetts at Amherst and stayed on one summer to waitress at a local club, ending up fronting a band. Her first professional engagement came on 4 July, 1971. She began to play bigger and better clubs, and doing some TV until meeting Chuck Jackson and Marvin Yancy who became her songwriting producers. She was soon signed to Capitol Records. Natalie did not try to become an imitator of her famous father, and became a star in her own right, with her own style and identity, gathering all of her musical influences of the past and those of contemporaries such as Aretha Franklin and The Pointer Sisters. Her first album 'Inseparable' was released in 1975. Her first hit 'This Will Be' was released, followed by the single 'Inseparable'. She won two Grammy Awards: New Artist of the Year and Best Female R & B Female Performance in 1975 for 'This Will Be' from her first album. In 1976 'Sophisticated Lady' from her second album 'Natalie' won her a third Grammy – Best Female Vocal Performance R & B.

International acclaim was bestowed upon her when she received the top Grand Prix award at the fifth Tokyo Music Festival, and then came her first platinum album 'Unpredictable'. She is married to Marvin Yancy, her producer. She was voted No 1 Top New Vocalist in both pop and R & B singles categories in 1976. Natalie credits her teen influences as the Jefferson Airplane, the Beatles, Stevie Wonder and Janis Joplin. 'I've Got Love On My Mind' started a run of million sellers in this year to top her other achievements.

UNPREDICTABLE (Album) *Capitol* [*USA*]. Released in the U.S.A. in February 1977, this went to No 9 for one week and stayed in the charts for 24 weeks. R.I.A.A. Gold Disc award on 1 March 1977. Platinum award on 12 August 1977.

Natalie's third album, the one that enhanced her position among the giants of the pop world.

OUR LOVE *Capitol* [*USA*]. This was released in the U.S.A. in December 1977 and reached No 6 for one week, staying 21 weeks in the charts. R.I.A.A. Gold Disc award on 6 April 1978.

Another million seller to continue Natalie's run of successes. This one crossed over from being No 2 in the R & B charts to success in the national charts.

THANKFUL (Album) *Capitol* [*USA*]. Released in the U.S.A. in December 1977, this went to No 28 for two weeks and stayed in the charts for 28 weeks. R.I.A.A. Gold Disc award on 20 December 1977. Platinum award on 21 June 1978.

In a relatively short career, Natalie proved with this album she could do no wrong. She participated in the songwriting for this disc with her songwriters Yancy and Jackson.

THE COMMODORES

THE COMMODORES (Album) *Motown* [*USA*]. With material written by The Commodores and released in the U.S.A. in March 1977, this went to No 5 for six weeks and stayed 44 weeks in the charts.

According to reports, this album was a million seller after being only six weeks on the market. It subsequently passed the two million mark. The line-up was: Lionel Richie (lead tenor and saxophone); Walter Clyde Orange (drummer and vocalist); Thomas McClary (guitar); Ronald LaPread (bass); Milan Williams (keyboards): and William King (brass). They all hail from and were born in various parts of south U.S.A. The group met at Tuskegee Institute in Alabama in the late 1960s, where all were major students in music. They called themselves The Mystics, and also performed as The Jays with an all-girl back-up group The Joyettes, gaining national attention when on a benefit tour for the Institute. Their first professional engagement was at the famous Small's Paradise, NY, where their one-night appearance turned into a month's engagement. Motown creative vice-president Suzanne de Passe first heard them in 1970 and after signing them to the label, booked them on the first three Jackson Five tours. This considerably enhanced their popularity, and their first single 'Machine Gun' was a sizeable hit in both the U.S.A. and Europe. The Commodores toured Europe, the Philippines and Japan. They performed before an audience of over 400,000 in the Philippines, and took part in the Tokyo Music Festival (1975) where their song 'Slippery When Wet' won the top award as best song. This was followed by a single hit 'Sweet Love' from their album 'Moving On' (1976). All their albums became either gold or platinum according to Motown Records (who up to 1977 were not members of R.I.A.A.). Their other big hits apart from those mentioned were singles: 'This Is Your Life'; 'Easy'; 'Brickhouse'; and 'Too Hot To Trot'. They changed their name to The Commodores in 1969, after tossing a dictionary up in the air which landed on the 'C' page and by picking a word at random. The group have successfully combined the funk sound with sophisticated uptown mood, and emerged as one of the most dynamic and musically matured groups of the seventies. They are also extremely proficient businessmen. Lionel Richie was the most successful writer of their ballads. The group's albums released were 'Machine Gun' (1973); 'Caught In The Act' (1975); 'Moving On' (1976); 'Hot on the Tracks' (1976); 'Commodores' (1977); 'Commodores Live' (1977); 'Zoom' (1978); 'Natural High' (1978); 'Midnight Magic' (1979); 'Heroes' (1980); 'In The Pocket' (1981). In an eight-year span, The Commodores sold more than 25 million albums, and became known as the Black Beatles.

The Commodores' album shows the group's versatility with its stomping rhythm and blues with funky backbeats, excellent lead and support singing and arrangements. It included 'Squeeze the Fruit'; 'Funny Feelings'; 'Won't You Come Dance With Me?'; and 'Funky Situation'.

COMMODORES 'LIVE' (Double album) *Motown* [*USA*]. Written by The Commodores, this was released in the U.S.A. in November 1977, going to No 5 for one week and staying 26 weeks in the charts.

Second huge seller for The Commodores. This sold two million by the end of 1977. It contained new versions of favourites like 'Slippery When Wet'; 'Easy'; 'Brick House'; and 'I Feel Sanctified', also 'Zoom' and 'Too Hot To Trot'. In this year they wrote the music for two films, *Greased Lightning* and *Scott Joplin*, and a lot of material for fellow Motown artists like Jerry Butler, The Temptations and Fifth Dimension.

BILL CONTI

GONNA FLY NOW (Theme from 'Rocky') *United Artists* [*USA*]. Written by Bill Conti, Ayn Robbins and Carol Connors, this was released in the U.S.A. in April 1977, going to No 4 for four weeks and staying 20 weeks in the charts. R.I.A.A. Gold Disc award on 7 July 1977.

Bill Conti was born in Providence, Rhode Island in 1943, receiving his first musical training at the age of seven from his father, a fine pianist, sculptor and painter. When he was 12 the family moved to Florida and it wasn't long before Bill organized a rock'n'roll group, playing also in his school's marching band and symphony orchestra. At Louisiana State University he played bassoon in the symphony orchestra and was staff arranger for the college band, also playing jazz piano in local clubs. He got to L.S.U. on a scholarship for bassoon playing. He next earned a Bachelor of Music degree in composition at the Julliard School of Music in New York. In 1967 Bill went to Rome playing with his own piano trio in jazz clubs, and writing scores for 'spaghetti' Westerns. As time passed in Italy, he wrote scores for *Candidate for a Killing*, *Blume in Love* and other motion pictures. The director of the latter film convinced Bill to return to the U.S.A. He scored episodes for several series on TV, and for the big screen. The director Paul Mazursky gave him the assignment for the score of *Rocky*, the film that proved to be the best film of the year, with an Oscar award. His theme 'Gonna Fly Now' was a big hit. Bill Conti's classical training and other experiences had finally paid off.

RITA COOLIDGE

ANYTIME ... ANYWHERE (Album) *A & M* [*USA*]. This was released in the U.S.A. in March 1977 and reached No 9 for two weeks, staying in the charts for 37 weeks. R.I.A.A. Gold Disc award on 18 August 1977. Platinum award on 19 October 1977.

Rita was born in Nashville, Tennessee, daughter of a preacher. She sang in church choirs from the incredibly young age of two. After leaving Florida State University, she formed the band RC and the Moonpies, and travelled to Memphis doing radio spots and jingles. She then moved to California meeting up with Delaney and Bonnie, as back-up singer, and recorded with them on their first album 'Home'. After touring with the prominent Friends' band she carried on singing with them on the Joe Cocker/Leon Russell Mad Dogs and Englishmen tour. Rita became an important back-up on U.S. super-sessions, working

with Stephen Stills and Eric Clapton on their solo albums. Her own albums leant more towards country music. Previous Coolidge albums were 'Rita Coolidge' (1971); 'Nice Feelin' (1972); 'The Lady's Not For Sale' (1973); 'Kris and Rita' (1973); 'Fall into Spring' (1974); 'Kris & Rita Full Moon' (1975). She married star singer/writer/actor Kris Kristofferson in 1973, and appeared in the film *Pat Garrett and Billy The Kid*. All her albums were on the A & M label. The 'Anytime ... Anywhere' album moved slightly toward a more black-influenced sound with four tracks arranged by Booker T., including '(Your Love Has Lifted Me) Higher and Higher'; 'The Way You Do The Things You Do'. Also included were more typical songs by this sultry vocalist such as 'Hungry Years' and 'Southern Lady'.

HIGHER AND HIGHER (Your love has lifted me) *A & M* [*USA*]. Written by Smith, Jackson and Miner (1967), this was released in the U.S.A. in April 1977 and in Britain in October 1977. In the U.S.A. it went to No 3 for three weeks, staying 27 weeks in the charts. In Britain it was No 48 for one week, staying two weeks in the charts. R.I.A.A. Gold Disc award on 30 August 1977.

The prime track from Rita's album 'Anytime ... Anywhere'. It is a cover version of Jackie Wilson's 1976 hit with a mid-tempo rendition, plus Booker T. Jones' organ solo.

WE'RE ALL ALONE *A & M* [*USA*]. Released in the U.S.A. in September 1977, this went to No 4 for two weeks and stayed in the charts for 22 weeks. R.I.A.A. Gold Disc award on 2 February 1978.

Another big hit for Rita, making it her best year to date.

CROSBY, STILLS & NASH

CROSBY, STILLS & NASH (Album) *Atlantic* [*USA*]. Written by Crosby, Stills and Nash, this was released in the U.S.A. in June 1977 and in Britain in July 1977. In the U.S.A. it went to No 2 for two weeks and stayed 26 weeks in the charts. In Britain it was No 23 for one week, staying nine weeks in the charts. R.I.A.A. Gold Disc award on 28 June 1977. Platinum award on 18 August 1977.

Crosby, Stills and Nash (or CSN) were one of the earliest supergroups when they came into prominence in 1969. Nothing before sounded like them and although many tried to fill the gap when they disbanded in 1971, nothing still sounds like them. In December 1976, CSN regrouped and were recorded with George Perry (bass); Craig Doerge (keyboards); and Joe Vitale (drums). At their initial sessions they played each other their newest songs, and realized they were going to sing real three-part again, keeping the tracks as sparse as possible. Their intention was to retain the basic magic of their first album of 1969. The resulting album was an immediate bestseller, and sold over two million by January 1978. It included 'Shadow Captain' (Crosby and Doerge); 'See the Changes' (Stills); 'Carried Away', (Nash); 'Fair Game' (Stills); 'Anything At All' (Crosby); 'Cathedral' (Nash); 'Just a Song Before I Go' (Nash); and 'Dark Star'.

JOHN DENVER

JOHN DENVER'S GREATEST HITS (Vol 2) (Title for Britain: Best of John Denver Vol 2) (Album) *RCA* [*USA*]. This was released in the U.S.A. and Britain in February 1977. In the U.S.A. it was No 22 for one week, staying in the charts for 11 weeks. R.I.A.A. Gold Disc award on 30 March 1977. Platinum award on 5 June 1981.

Another big seller for Denver, one of the world's most successful recording artists. Denver enthusiasts kept on buying this over a period of four years till it finally reached the million mark. Contents are: 'Annie's Song'; 'Welcome To My Morning (Farewell Andromeda)'; 'Fly Away'; 'Like a Sad Song'; 'Looking For Space'; 'Thank God I'm a Country Boy'; 'My Sweet Lady'; 'Back Home Again'; 'This Old Guitar'; 'Grandma's Feather Bed'; 'Calypso'; 'I'm Sorry'.

The British release did not include 'Thank God I'm a Country Boy' and 'Back Home Again' but 'Baby You Look Good Tonight' and 'I'd Rather Be a Cowboy' instead.

I WANT TO LIVE (Album) *RCA* [*USA*]. This was released in the U.S.A. in November 1977 and in Britain in January 1978. It was No 47 for two weeks in the U.S.A., staying 11 weeks in the charts. R.I.A.A. Gold Disc award on 1 December 1977. Platinum award on 12 May 1978.

This album was produced by Milt Okun with strings and orchestral arrangements by Lee Holdridge, the team whose past work enhanced most of Denver's albums. It contained seven new Denver songs: 'I want to Live'; 'Tradewinds'; 'To the Wild Country'; 'How Can I Leave You Again'; while John interprets Tom Paxton's 'Bet on the Blues' and Eric Andersen's 'Thirsty Boots'.

NEIL DIAMOND

LOVE AT THE GREEK (Double album) *Columbia* [*USA*]. Released in the U.S.A. in February 1977, this went to No 6 for two weeks and stayed 17 weeks in the charts. R.I.A.A. Gold Disc award on 1 March 1977. Platinum award on 5 July 1977.

A double album of Neil's concert performance at the Greek Theater with all the excitement it generated. It contained 20 tracks including many of his best-known songs such as 'Sweet Caroline'; 'Song Sung Blue'; 'Beautiful Noise'; and 'If You Know What I Mean', also his latest hit 'I've Been This Way Before'.

Neil had a sell-out tour including the London Palladium (June

1977) and Woburn Abbey (July 1977) (his first-ever open-air concert), plus a British Nationwide TV Special.

I'M GLAD YOU'RE HERE WITH ME TONIGHT (Album) *Columbia* [*USA*]. Released in the U.S.A. in November 1977, it went to No 10 for four weeks, staying in the charts for 26 weeks. R.I.A.A. Gold Disc award on 17 November 1977. Platinum award on 13 December 1977.

A varied collection of material that included Brian Wilson's 'God Only Knows' and Joni Mitchell's 'Free Man in Paris'. The album was produced by Bob Gaudio. Diamond's dramatic readings reached a new level of sophistication with the ten compositions, especially the title track.

EAGLES

HOTEL CALIFORNIA *Elektra/Asylum* [*USA*]. Written by Frey, Henley and Felder, this was released in the U.S.A. in March 1977 and in Britain in April 1977. In the U.S.A. it hit No 1 for one week, staying 23 weeks in the charts. In Britain it was No 5 for one week and stayed nine weeks in the charts. R.I.A.A. Gold Disc award on 12 May 1977.

Second million seller single from the group's album 'Hotel California'.

EARTH, WIND & FIRE

ALL 'N ALL (Album) *Columbia* [*USA*]. Written by the group and released in the U.S.A. in November 1977, this reached No 5 for seven weeks and stayed 36 weeks in the charts. R.I.A.A. Gold Disc award on 17 November 1977. Platinum award on 9 December 1977.

One of this group's best albums to date. It included an outstanding ballad 'Serpentine Fire', also 'I'll Write a Song For You'; 'Jupiter'; 'Magic Mind'; and 'Be Ever Wonderful'.

ELECTRIC LIGHT ORCHESTRA

TELEPHONE LINE *Jet* [*Britain*] *United Artists* [*USA*]. Written by Jeff Lynne, this was released in Britain in May 1977 and in the U.S.A. in June 1977. In both Britain and the U.S.A. it went to No 7 for two weeks, staying nine weeks in the British charts and 21 weeks in the U.S. charts. R.I.A.A. Gold Disc award on 23 September 1977.

Taken from ELO's album 'A New World Record' (1976) and released as a single, it was a great success in the U.S.A.

OUT OF THE BLUE (Double album) *Jet/United Artists* [*USA*]. Written by Jeff Lynne, this was released in the U.S.A. in November 1977 and in Britain in October 1977. In the U.S.A. it was No 7 for two weeks, staying 29 weeks in the charts. In Britain it went to No 4 for two weeks and stayed in the charts for 106 weeks. R.I.A.A. Gold Disc and platinum awards, both on 14 November 1977.

This instant million seller for ELO had advance orders of four million units and the world-wide estimate is over five million. Of this figure, the U.S.A. reported sales of two million by the end of 1977. In Britain it easily passed the £1,000,000 sale, staying in the GB charts for just over two years. The album was ELO's eighth release.

The tremendous success of their 'New World Record' album stirred global interest in the group. Jeff Lynne, their leader/writer went to Switzerland for a few weeks with only musical instruments for company, and worked. He emerged with 15 songs - far more than he needed for one album, so it was decided to do a double album. The group joined Lynne in Switzerland for a few weeks and they went to Musicland Studios in Munich, spending about 15 weeks working 12 hours a day. When the band had completed part of the recording, their string arranger, Louis Clarke, came in to work with Lynne and Richard Tandy on the string and choir arrangements. The Munich Philharmonic Strings and the choir added their contribution. It was the end of a marathon session for the whole band. The 'Out Of The Blue' stage show used the spectacular idea of a spaceship, with sensational applause and reaction from their audiences. There was no doubt that 'Out Of The Blue' was one of the most successful albums in pop history. Outstanding tracks were: 'Turn To Stone'; 'Sweet Talkin' Woman'; 'Night in the City'; 'Mr Blue Sky'; 'Jungle'; 'Birmingham Blues'; 'Concerto for a Rainy Day' (an extended piece of conceptual work).

THE EMOTIONS (female trio)

BEST OF MY LOVE *Columbia* [*USA*]. Written by Maurice White and Albert McKay, this was released in the U.S.A. in June 1977 and in Britain in September 1977. It hit No 1 for three weeks in the U.S.A., staying 28 weeks in the charts. In Britain it went to No 4 for one week, staying ten weeks in the charts. R.I.A.A. Gold Disc award on 2 August 1977.

The outstanding track from the trio's album 'Rejoice', described as 'a powerhouse squeaky chugger'. The Emotions were a new coloured group who gained prominence with this fine disc.

REJOICE (Album) *Columbia* [*USA*]. Released in the U.S.A. in June 1977, this was No 7 for one week and stayed in the charts for 27 weeks. R.I.A.A. Gold Disc award on 12 July 1977. Platinum award on 1 September 1977.

The group's gold debut that introduced the musical talents of the three singers. It was produced by Maurice White who wrote material for them, including the big hit 'Best of My Love'. Other fine tracks were: 'A Feeling Is'; 'Blessed How'd I Know That Love Would Slip Away'; 'Don't Ask My Neighbours'; 'Love's What's Happenin''.

FLEETWOOD MAC

RUMOURS (Album) *Warner Bros* [*USA*]. Written by members of Fleetwood Mac, this was released in the U.S.A. and Britain in February 1977. In the U.S.A. it hit No 1 for 35 weeks, staying 90 weeks in the charts. In Britain it was No 2 for two weeks, staying 153 weeks in the charts. R.I.A.A. Gold Disc award on 15 February 1977. Platinum award on 9 March 1977.

This incredible album with its long run in the charts on both sides of the Atlantic sold ten million units by the end of 1977. It was Canada's first ever million-seller album, and sold half a million in Germany, also half a million in Britain. In June 1980 it was reported the album had sold a global 21 million, the second highest to date. ('Saturday Night Fever' album held the position as No 1 album seller). It is a consistently beautiful sounding album, encompassing many styles and emotions. Contents are: 'The Chain' (McVie, Nicks and Fleetwood);'You Make Loving Fun' (McVie); 'I Don't Want To Know' (Nicks); 'Oh Daddy' (McVie); 'Gold Dust Woman' (Nicks); 'Second Hand News' (Buckingham); 'Dreams' (Nicks); 'Never Going Back Again' (Buckingham); 'Don't Stop' (McVie); 'Go Your Own Way'

(McVie and Buckingham); 'Songbird' (Christine McVie).

DREAMS *Warner Bros* [*USA*]. Written by Stevie Nicks, this was released in the U.S.A. in April 1977 and in Britain in July 1977. It went to No 1 for one week in the U.S.A. and stayed 21 weeks in the charts. In Britain it was No 24 for one week, staying in the charts for nine weeks. R.I.A.A. Gold Disc award on 14 September 1977.

The biggest selling single from the group's album 'Rumours'.

THE FLOATERS (vocal/instrumental quartet)

THE FLOATERS (Album) *ABC* [*USA*]. This was released in the U.S.A. in June 1977 and in Britain in August 1977. In the U.S.A. it was No 10 for one week, staying 20 weeks in the charts. In Britain it was No 17 for two weeks and stayed eight weeks in the charts. R.I.A.A. Gold Disc award on 28 July 1977. Platinum award on 7 October 1977.

Another addition to the many black groups in the U.S.A. This male quartet's first album of their material was a quick success, and spawned a hit single with 'Float On'.

FLOAT ON *ABC* [*USA*]. Written by Arnold Ingram, James Mitchell Jnr and Marvin Willis, this was released in the U.S.A. in June 1977 and in Britain in July 1977. In the U.S.A. it went to No 4 for two weeks and stayed 19 weeks in the charts. In Britain it hit No 1 for two weeks, staying 11 weeks in the charts. R.I.A.A. Gold Disc award on 25 August 1977.

The prime track from the group's album 'The Floaters'.

DAN FOGELBERG

NETHERLANDS (Album) *CBS* [*USA*]. Written by Dan Fogelberg and released in the U.S.A. in June 1977, this went to No 16 for one week and stayed 18 weeks in the charts. R.I.A.A. Gold Disc award on 9 August 1977. Platinum award on 26 December 1979.

Dan Fogelberg was born in 1952 in Peoria, Illinois. At an early age he learned piano and experimented with acoustic slide guitar. While studying painting at the University of Illinois, he devoted much time to music, and met Irving Azoff. They left together for the west coast where Azoff secured a contract for Fogelberg. The first album 'Home Free' was recorded and produced in Nashville by Norbert Putnam. Then came the 'Souvenirs' album that made Dan a nationally known performer. 'Captured Angel' was the third album. He moved from Tennessee to Boulder, Colorado. His fourth album 'Netherlands' was co-produced with Norbert Putnam, and achieved the million sale after consistent sales over a period of two years. The album included: 'Love Gone By'; 'False Faces'; 'Sketches'; 'Loose Ends'; 'Once Upon a Time'.

FOGHAT

FOGHAT - LIVE (Album) *Warner/Bearsville* [*USA*]. Written by Foghat and released in the U.S.A. in September 1977, this went to No 10 for one week, staying in the charts for 22 weeks. R.I.A.A. Gold Disc award on 11 October 1977. Platinum award on 20 December 1977.

Recordings for this album were made in May 1977 from the group's popular stage show. It included such favourites as 'Fool for the City' and 'Slow Ride'.

FOREIGNER

FOREIGNER (Album) *Atlantic* [*USA*]. Written by Foreigner (mainly Mick Jones) and released in the U.S.A. in March 1977, this was No 4 for one week and stayed 48 weeks in the charts. R.I.A.A. Gold Disc award on 16 May 1977. Platinum award on 11 August 1977.

Foreigner comprises Mick Jones (guitar); Ian McDonald; Dennis Elliott (drums) - all British, and Americans Lou Gramm (vocalist); Ed Gagliardi (bass); Al Greenwood (keyboards). The band was formed around late 1976 after a chance meeting between Jones (formerly with Spooky Tooth) and McDonald (formerly with King Crimson) - two seasoned musicians living in New York City. Greenwood was the first musician enlisted, then Lou Gramm (formerly of Black Sheep) and Elliott and Gagliardi. Being an Anglo-American group, they chose the name Foreigner. The resulting mixture of rock forms, together with the band's wide range of influences and experience proved sensational. The 'Foreigner' album was recorded in November 1976, released in March 1977, with the label deliberately maintaining a low profile, as few even knew of the existence of the group. Within two weeks, the album started climbing the charts with enormous success. A year of preparation and a month of roadwork paid off, and in 1978 a sell-out world tour taking in Japan, Hong Kong, Australia, Greece, Germany and Britain, with a debut in the U.K. at London's Rainbow theatre, and later a fantastic success at the Reading Festival. This album sold four million, the fastest selling album in Atlantic's history.

It includes: 'Feels Like the First Time'; 'Cold As Ice'; 'At War With the World'; 'Starrider'; 'Headknocker'; 'The Damage Is Done'.

Foreigner won many polls in its first year of existence and was voted No 1 New Artist, No 1 New Pop Artist, and No 1 New Male Group by the principal musical papers.

PETER FRAMPTON

I'M IN YOU (Album) *A & M* [*USA*]. Written by Peter Frampton and guests, this was released in the U.S.A. and Britain in June 1977. In the U.S.A. it was No 2 for four weeks and stayed in the charts for 25 weeks. In Britain it was No 19 for one week and stayed nine weeks in the charts. R.I.A.A. Gold Disc award and Platinum award, both on 13 June 1977.

An instant million-seller album, seasoned with ballads ('I'm In You') and mid-tempo songs like 'Won't You Be My Friend?' (by Little Feat); 'Rocky's Hot Club' (with Stevie Wonder on harmonica); and 'Signed, Sealed, Delivered'.

CRYSTAL GAYLE

WE MUST BELIEVE IN MAGIC (Album) *United Artists* [*USA*]. This was released in the U.S.A. in September 1977 and in Britain in January 1978. It was No 34 for one week in the U.S.A., staying 16 weeks in the charts. It was No 15 for one week in Britain and stayed seven weeks in the charts. R.I.A.A. Gold Disc award on 14 November 1977. Platinum award on 15 February 1978.

Crystal Gayle is the younger sister of country singer Loretta Lynn (whose best-selling biography of her life from poverty to stardom was filmed in 1980 as *A Coalminer's Daughter*, with Sissy Spacek as Loretta winning an Oscar for Best Actress 1980). She was reared, like her sister, in Van Lear, Kentucky, and at 16 became a member of big sister's road show. Straight out of high school, Crystal signed to MCA and had a Top 20 disc on the Country Charts with 'I've Cried (The Blue Right Out Of My Eyes)', written by her sister Loretta. She was later signed to United Artists, and by 1976 was hitting the Top 10 in the country charts and with some successful albums was universally recognized for her unique music. In 1976 she won several awards: Country Music Awards Show, Outstanding Vocalist (Female) by the Academy of Country Music and, in 1977, Outstanding Female Vocalist award from the Country Music Association. In this year Crystal broke through into the big time on both sides of the Atlantic, starting with 'You Never Miss A Real Good Thing' and then 'Don't It Make My Brown Eyes Blue'. The latter song was the prime track from this album 'We Must Believe In Magic'. Once the regional music of the U.S.A. - with its roots firmly entrenched in the Southern States - country music had become big business. It won far greater appeal than at any time in its 60-year commercial existence. The success of this album certainly gave Crystal the crossover from country to national and international recognition.

DON'T IT MAKE MY BROWN EYES BLUE *United Artists* [*USA*]. Written by Leigh, this was released in the U.S.A. in July

1977 and in Britain in November 1977. In the U.S.A. it went to No 2 for two weeks and in Britain to No 7 for one week. It stayed 30 weeks in the U.S. charts and 13 weeks in the British lists. R.I.A.A. Gold Disc award on 14 November 1977. Grammy Award: Best Country Vocal Performance, Female, 1977.

Well over a million sales for this in America, and Britain sold 250,000 as well. Taken from Crystal's album 'We Must Believe In Magic' which was first released as a Country Album chart hit in July 1977 where it was No 2.

ANDY GIBB

I JUST WANT TO BE YOUR EVERYTHING *RSO* [*USA*]. Written by Barry Gibb, this was released in the U.S.A. in April 1977 and in Britain in June 1977. It hit No 1 for five weeks in the U.S.A., staying 32 weeks in the charts. In Britain it was No 26 for two weeks and stayed seven weeks in the charts. R.I.A.A. Gold Disc award on 9 August 1977.

Andy Gibb, younger brother of the Bee Gees, was born in 1958. He made music his career from the age of 13. From singing in piano bars in Spain, he then in 1977 played the bigger halls. As a British citizen he received no pay for his work in Spain because of age and citizenship problems, but by 1973 had formed a rock band, playing regularly at two major clubs on the Isle of Man in Britain. Following in his brothers' footsteps, Andy went to Australia where the Bee Gees first became successful. He reorganized the band, secured a few jobs, and in a short time achieved success. In just over a year, he was appearing in large halls throughout Australia, and his self-written first single 'Words and Music' got to No 5 in Sydney's charts. Robert Stigwood, the Bee Gees' manager, had Andy flown to Miami to record some demonstration tapes with brother Barry's aid. This resulted in Andy's first album 'Flowing Rivers'. In the summer of this year he made a successful North American tour, and the big success of 'I Just Want To Be Your Everything' helped to push his debut album up the charts. Andy's first worldwide release single gave him international acclaim.

FLOWING RIVERS (Album) *RSO* [*USA*]. With material by Andy and Barry Gibb, etc., this was released in the U.S.A. in August 1977 and in Britain in September 1977. It was No 33 for one week in the U.S.A. and stayed 32 weeks in the charts. R.I.A.A. Gold Disc award on 22 November 1977. Platinum award on 4 August 1978.

Andy's debut album, recorded in Miami, includes contributions from George Terry, Joe Walsh, and an array of musicians from Miami's Criteria Studios. The outstanding tracks are: 'Words and Music'; 'I Just Want To Be Your Everything'; 'Starlight'; '(Love Is) Thicker Than Water'.

(LOVE IS) THICKER THAN WATER *RSO* [*USA*]. Written by Andy and Barry Gibb, this was released in the U.S.A. in October 1977, going to No 1 for one week and staying in the charts for 29 weeks. R.I.A.A. Gold Disc award on 16 February 1978.

The second million-seller single from the 'Flowing Rivers' album.

HEART

LITTLE QUEEN (Album) *Portrait* [*USA*]. Written by Ann and Nancy Wilson, this was released in the U.S.A. in May 1977 and was No 3 for one week, staying 30 weeks in the charts. R.I.A.A. Gold Disc award on 2 June 1977. Platinum award on 2 August 1977.

Second million-seller album for Heart, the band again fronted by the Wilson sisters, and their debut album for the Portrait label. The album includes: 'Barracuda'; 'Love Alive'; 'Sylvan Song'; 'Dream Of The Archer'; 'Kick It Out'; 'Treat Me Well'; 'Cry To Me'; 'Go On Cry'.

HEATWAVE

BOOGIE NIGHTS *Epic* [*USA*] *GTO* [*Britain*]. Written by Rod Temperton, this was released in the U.S.A. in June 1977

and in Britain in January 1978. In the U.S.A. it went to No 2 for five weeks, staying 30 weeks in the charts. In Britain it went to No 2 for one week and stayed 14 weeks in the charts. R.I.A.A. Gold Disc award on 17 October 1977. Platinum award on 22 December 1977.

One of the only three singles to receive the platinum award in 1977 for two million sales. This was the outstanding track from the group's hit album 'Too Hot To Handle' (1976).

ALWAYS AND FOREVER *Epic* [*USA*] *GTO* [*Britain*]. This was written by Johnnie Wilder and Rod Temperton and was released in the U.S.A. in December 1977 and in Britain in November 1978. In the U.S.A. it went to No 16 for one week and stayed 22 weeks in the charts. In Britain it went to No 9 for one week, staying in the charts for nine weeks. R.I.A.A. Gold Disc award on 17 March 1978.

Second million-selling single from Heatwave's 'Too Hot To Handle' album.

HIGH INERGY

IF YOU CAN'T TURN ME OFF (in the middle of turning me on) *Gordy* [*USA*]. Written by Pam Sawyer and Marilyn McLeod, this was released in the U.S.A. in September 1977, going to No 12 for one week and staying 21 weeks in the charts.

High Inergy are a female quartet – Linda Howard, Michelle Martin and sisters Vernessa and Barbara Mitchell, all from Pasadena. They were accepted into the city's Bicentennial Performing Arts Programme early in 1976. The Mitchell sisters auditioned as singers, Linda and Michelle as dancers contributing back-up vocals. The four girls got together to develop a one-hour show which they performed some 500 times during the eight months the federally funded programme lasted. Barbara and Vernessa wrote all the songs. After this, they sent a tape to Motown which reached Gwen Gordy, who brought them to Motown in October 1976. The group's first release was this lovely ballad which was immediately popular. Their coaching at Motown and the disc brought them stardom, and 'If You Can't Turn Me Off' went 'gold'. (At this time Motown were not members of R.I.A.A. for million seller certification of their records.) The single was followed by an album 'High Inergy – Turnin' On' which also went 'gold'. None of the girls were over 19 when they started their singing/performing careers.

DAN HILL

SOMETIMES WHEN WE TOUCH *20th Century* [*USA*]. Written by Dan Hill and Barry Mann, this was released in the U.S.A. in November 1977 and in Britain in January 1978. In the U.S.A. it was No 3 for two weeks and stayed in the charts for 25 weeks. In Britain it was No 13 for one week and stayed 12 weeks in the charts. R.I.A.A. Gold Disc award on 28 February 1978.

Dan Hill was born in 1945 and raised in a suburb of Toronto, Canada. He began songwriting at 14 and played professional dates at 17 in coffee houses and clubs. After a year travelling around the U.S.A., plus a short-lived deal with Canadian RCA, he decided on doing the American club circuit. On return to Toronto he found that a number of his tunes were being recorded by other artists, and his bookings became more plentiful, with subsequent appearances at Toronto's famous Riverboat. A tour soon after gained him an award – Canada's Juno – for best new singer. Dan's first album, 'Dan Hill' featured his gentle melodies played with rolling guitar arrangements, and became a Canadian Gold Disc, distributed in the U.S.A. by 20th Century, while its single 'You Make Me Want To Be' climbed the Canadian charts. Then came 'Sometimes When We Touch', a beautiful ballad, to become his first million seller. Dan is the son of a black father and white mother, and many of his songs are a tribute to them, his mixed racial background and unique upbringing.

HOT

ANGEL IN YOUR ARMS *Big Tree* [*USA*]. Written by Herbert Ivey, Terry Woodford and Thomas Brasfield and released in the U.S.A. in March 1977, this was No 17 for one week and stayed 26 weeks in the charts. R.I.A.A. Gold Disc award on 11 July 1977.

The one and only million seller for this U.S. group.

ISLEY BROTHERS

GO FOR YOUR GUNS (Album) *T-Neck* [*USA*]. Written by the Isley Brothers, this was released in the U.S.A. in April 1977, going to No 4 for one week and staying in the charts for 31 weeks. R.I.A.A. Gold Disc award on 19 April 1977. Platinum award on 2 June 1977.

Yet another big hit for the famous brothers. It included: 'The Pride'; 'Footsteps in the Dark'; 'Climbin' up the Ladder'; 'Voyage to Atlantis'; 'Livin' in the Life'.

JEAN MICHEL JARRE

OXYGENE (Album) *Polydor* [*France*]. With compositions by Jean Michel Jarre, this was released in Britain in August 1977 and in the U.S.A. in September 1977. In Britain it went to No 4 for four weeks and stayed 17 weeks in the charts.

Jean Michel Jarre was born in 1948, son of famous composer Maurice Jarre who wrote the scores for the films *Lawrence of Arabia* and *Doctor Zhivago*. Son Jean became a genuinely innovative force in electronics, and is also a talented and inspired composer. 'Oxygene' album (parts 1-6) was recorded on an eight-track machine, as it was conceived as a piece of music to be performed on stage. The album was released in France in the early part of 1977, where it became No 1. By the year's end it had sold two and a half million units, with gold certifications in Holland, England, France, Switzerland and Belgium. In 1978 it was reported to have sold a global five million, a phenomenal figure for a debut album. Strangely, although it was one of Europe's biggest albums of 1977, it did not show much sign of life in the U.S. charts. Jarre was asked how he accounted for the international success of an album composed entirely of electronic synthesizers and keyboards. He said 'I try to integrate the synthesizers into the orchestration of music rather than use them as sound effects.' As a result, Jarre's album is an emotive piece of music that is rare for a work of its kind. An unusually melodic theme is carried over on both sides with all instruments played by Jarre himself. It brought synthesizer music to mass appeal.

WAYLON JENNINGS

OL' WAYLON (Album) *RCA* [*USA*]. Released in the U.S.A. in May 1977, this was No 20 for one week and stayed in the charts for 27 weeks. R.I.A.A. Gold Disc award on 14 June 1977. Platinum award on 7 October 1977.

This album was also No 1 for 15 weeks on the U.S. country album charts. Waylon, described as 'the best country singer in the world' by Kris Kristofferson, brings a rare distinction to country music in its contemporary form. This album reinforces that opinion. It includes: 'Luckenbach Texas'; 'Satin Sheets'; 'I Think I'm Gonna Kill Myself'; 'Lucille'; 'Sweet Caroline' (written by Neil Diamond); a medley of two early Presley hits – 'That's alright Mamma' and 'My Baby Left Me' (written by Arthur Crudup); 'Belle of the Ball.' Waylon has some help from Willie Nelson and his wife Jessi Colter on one or two tracks.

BILLY JOEL

THE STRANGER (Album) *Columbia* [*USA*]. Written by Billy Joel, this was released in the U.S.A. in September 1977 and in Britain in March 1978. In the U.S.A. it reached No 2 for one week and stayed 86 weeks in the charts. In Britain it was No 24 for one week and stayed 23 weeks in the charts. R.I.A.A. Gold Disc award on 1 December 1977. Platinum award on 18 January 1978.

Billy Joel grew up in Hicksville, Long Island, where his father Howard Joel had an extensive training as a classical pianist, but worked as an electrical engineer. Billy started piano lessons at the age of four, kept them up for about 11 years, and became interested in popular music, joining his first band, The Echoes, at 14. In 1968, the Hassles heard Billy playing organ with the Lost Souls (The Echoes new name) and he joined them. In 1971 Billy recorded his first album 'Cold Spring Harbor', and moved to Los Angeles, continuing his musical career under the name of Bill Martin for a short period. In 1973 his first album for Columbia, 'Piano Man', was released and earned a Gold Disc. His second album for Columbia, 'Street-life Serenade', in 1974, was followed by 'Turnstiles', written and recorded in 1976, with Joel as producer, Liberty DeVitto (drums); Richie Canata (keyboards); Doug Stegmeyer (bass) and Russell Javors (guitar) at Long Island's Ultra-Sonic Studios. This was quite a success, and an artistic breakthrough for Joel, laying the musical background for what was to follow on, 'The Stranger' and later '52nd Street'. Joel's keyboards were up front, stylized to suit the song. Apart from his piano expertise, Billy insists he is 'a singer-songwriter man'. His astonishing repertoire stretches in style from ragtime and boogie piano to open-hearted ballads. 'Just the Way You Are' (from this album 'The Stranger') became one of the most widely interpreted tunes of the decade. He completed a 56-date tour of the USA and Canada by early 1978, and then began an extensive tour of Europe, Australia and Japan. With his band, as already mentioned, they are a most formidable and emotive outfit, and put on a dazzling show.

The contents of the album are: 'Moving Out'; 'The Stranger'; 'Just The Way You Are'; 'Scenes From An Italian Restaurant'; 'Only The Good Die Young'; 'She's Always A Woman'; 'Vienna'; 'Get It Right The First Time'; 'Everybody Has A Dream'.

'The Stranger' is the second largest seller in Columbia's history with 5 million units sold.

JUST THE WAY YOU ARE *Columbia* [*USA*]. Written by Billy Joel, this was released in the U.S.A. in November 1977 and in Britain in January 1978. It went to No 3 for two weeks in the U.S.A. and stayed 25 weeks in the charts. In Britain it was No 16 for one week and stayed nine weeks in the charts. R.I.A.A. Gold Disc award on 6 March 1978. Grammy Awards: Record of the Year, 1978; Song of the Year, 1978.

The great hit from Billy Joel's album 'The Stranger', destined to become one of the world's standards.

ELTON JOHN

GREATEST HITS (Vol 2) (Album) *MCA* [*USA*], *DJM* [*Britain*]. This was released in the U.S.A. in September 1977 and in Britain in October 1977. In the U.S.A. it was No 16 for two weeks and stayed in the charts for 24 weeks. In Britain it went to No 8 for two weeks, staying 21 weeks in the charts. R.I.A.A. Gold Disc award on 30 September 1977. Platinum award on 9 November 1977.

This million seller contained four songs (marked (*)) never before available on any of Elton's albums. Contents are: 'The Bitch Is Back'; 'Sorry Seems To Be The Hardest Word'; 'Someone Saved My Life Tonight'; 'Island Girl'; 'Grow Some Funk Of Your Own'; 'Levon' (all by Taupin and John); (*) 'Lucy in the Sky with Diamonds' (by Lennon and McCartney); (*) 'Don't Go Breaking My Heart' (by Anna Orson and Carte Blanche); (*) 'Philadelphia Freedom' (by Taupin and John); (*) 'Pinball Wizard' (by Pete Townshend) (from rock opera *Tommy*).

BROTHERS JOHNSON

RIGHT ON TIME (Album) *A & M* [*USA*]. Written by Brothers Johnson, this was released in the U.S.A. in May 1977, going to No 14 for three weeks and staying 28 weeks in the charts. R.I.A.A. Gold Disc award on 24 May 1977. Platinum award on 2 August 1977.

The follow-up to their debut album 'Look Out For Number One' (1976) again produced by Quincy Jones, but this album has a changed sound, with smooth, almost jazz-tinged music. It included 'Runnin' For Your Lovin'; 'Free Yourself, Be Yourself'. 'Right On Time' sold two million by the end of 1978.

STRAWBERRY LETTER NO 23 *A & M* [*USA*]. Written by Shuggie Otis, this was released in the U.S.A. and Britain in July 1977. In the U.S.A. it was No 7 for one week and stayed 17 weeks in the charts. In Britain it was No 35 for one week and stayed in the charts for five weeks. R.I.A.A. Gold Disc award on 19 October 1977.

The second million-seller single for the brothers.

KANSAS
POINT OF KNOW RETURN (Album) *Columbia* [*USA*]. Written by Kansas and released in the U.S.A. in October 1977, this went to No 5 for six weeks, staying in the charts for 49 weeks. R.I.A.A. Gold Disc award on 11 October 1977. Platinum award on 20 November 1977.

With this follow-up to their 'Leftoverture' album (1976), Kansas were well on their way to becoming one of the U.S.A.'s premier rock outfits. The sophisticated solos give the sextet a unique appeal. It includes: 'Sparks Of The Tempest'; 'Hopeless Human'; 'Lightning's Hand'; 'Paradox'; 'Dust in the Wind'.

K.C. & THE SUNSHINE BAND
I'M YOUR BOOGIE MAN *TK* [*USA*]. Written by Harry Casey and Richard Finch, this was released in the U.S.A. in February 1977 and in Britain in April 1977. It hit No 1 for one week in the U.S.A. and stayed 26 weeks in the charts. In Britain it was No 41 for one week and stayed four weeks in the charts.

Continuation of the success story of KC and the Sunshine Band, and their talented producers/arrangers/songwriters Casey and Finch. This distinctive new single was taken from K.C. (or Casey) and the Sunshine Band's 'Part Three' album (1976) and is the third track from it with a reported million sale.

KISS
KISS ALIVE II (Double album) *Casablanca* [*USA*]. With material by Kiss and others, this was released in the U.S.A. in November 1977, going to No 3 for three weeks and staying 31 weeks in the charts. R.I.A.A. Gold Disc award on 28 November 1977. Platinum award on 28 November 1977.

The live songs are from recent albums by Kiss and include 'Beth', 'Hard Luck Woman', 'Calling Dr Love' and 'Love Gun'. There are three sides of live material and one of studio recorded songs (including Dave Clark Five's 'Anyway You Want It'). This second concert album was as successful as the first.

LOVE GUN (Album) *Casablanca* [*USA*]. With material by Kiss and others, this was released in the U.S.A. in June 1977, going to No 4 for two weeks and staying in the charts for 19 weeks. R.I.A.A. Gold Disc award on 30 June 1977. Platinum award on 30 June 1977 too.

An almost instant million seller for Kiss. It included 'I Stole Your Love', 'Tomorrow and Tonight', and also the Barry, Greenwich and Spector hit 'Then She Kissed Me'.

KENNY LOGGINS
CELEBRATE ME HOME (Album) *Columbia* [*USA*]. Written by Kenny Loggins and released in the U.S.A. in April 1977, this was No 52 for one week and stayed 25 weeks in the charts. R.I.A.A. Gold Disc award on 20 September 1977. Platinum award on 22 December 1980.

First solo million-seller album for Kenny Loggins, originally the other half of Loggins and Messina (*see* 1972 for biographical data).

This album took over two years to reach the million sale. It includes: 'Enter My Dream'; 'Why Do People Lie?'; 'I've Got The Melody (Deep In My Heart)'; 'Daddy's Back'; 'Lady Luck'.

LTD
(EVERYTIME I TURN AROUND) BACK IN LOVE AGAIN *A & M* [*USA*]. Written by Len Hanks and Zane Grey, this was released in the U.S.A. in September 1977, going to No 6 for two weeks and staying 22 weeks in the charts. R.I.A.A. Gold Disc award on 22 December 1977.

LTD is: Lorenzo Carnegie; Jake Riley Jr; Carle Vickers; Henry Davis; Abraham Joseph Miller; Johnny McGhee; Melvin Webb; Jeff Osborne; Billy Osborne (Jeff's older brother); and D. J. Davis. Ten components of one of the hottest stage acts in the U.S.A. Several years ago, they got together determined to create their own sound – soulful rhythms and a spiritual element that was powerful but not overbearing. They are some of the finest musicians from the Los Angeles area. After several albums that helped them sort out these various elements, their A & M album 'Something to Love' in this year was No 1 on the R & B album chart, and then high in the pop album chart. The album included 'Back In Love Again', a big hit as a single release. LTD's success is due to collaboration with super-producer Bobby Martin (of A & M) who brought out the group's outstanding musicianship, with a coast-to-coast tour culminating in a massive soul-pop show at Los Angeles Forum on 29 December 1977. Their potential was, despite their name, unlimited.

LYNYRD SKYNYRD
STREET SURVIVORS (Album) *MCA* [*USA*]. With material by Lynyrd Skynyrd, this was released in the U.S.A. in October 1977, reaching No 4 for two weeks and staying in the charts for 32 weeks. R.I.A.A. Gold Disc award on 27 October 1977. Platinum award on 10 December 1977.

This album introduced guitarist Steve Gaines, who added a new dimension to their sound and contributed a good portion of the material, plus occasional lead vocals. Principal tracks: 'You Got That Right' and 'What's Your Name?'.

PETER McCANN
DO YOU WANNA MAKE LOVE? *20th Century* [*USA*]. Written by Peter McCann and released in the U.S.A. in April 1977, this was No 7 for one week and stayed 23 weeks in the charts. R.I.A.A. Gold Disc award on 17 August 1977.

First million seller for newcomer Peter McCann.

RONNIE McDOWELL
THE KING IS GONE *GRT/Scorpion* [*USA*]. Written by Ronnie McDowell and Lee Morgan, this was released in the U.S.A. in September 1977, going to No 12 for one week and staying 12 weeks in the charts. R.I.A.A. Gold Disc award on 8 September 1977.

Ronnie McDowell, long-time ardent admirer of Elvis Presley, was on his way to a date in Bowling Green, Kentucky on 16 August when he heard on his car radio of the death of Elvis. He was so overcome that he headed home and wrote a recitation to express his feelings, but had no intentions of actually using it. He then met up with songwriter Lee Morgan who had also written a tribute song. They incorporated their joint efforts and at the urging of Scorpion Records, went into the studio to put it down. The following morning acetates were delivered to the local radio stations. WSIX-FM station had an immediate response, and WESC in Greenville, South Carolina received, on 23 August, nine or ten requests an hour. The record exploded all over the U.S.A., and GRT signed a distribution deal, with orders for 75,000 the next day. Within eight days of release, it sold a million, and two million by early January 1978.

CHUCK MANGIONE (jazz trumpet/flugelhorn)
FEELS SO GOOD (Album) *A & M* [*USA*]. Released in the U.S.A. in October 1977, this went to No 2 for three weeks and stayed in the charts for 54 weeks. R.I.A.A. Gold Disc award on 27 March 1978. Platinum award on 18 May 1978.

America became jazz conscious again in 1976-77, spearheaded by the unprecedented success of such artists as George Benson and Herbie Hancock. Mangione's album was the top album of

1978. Chuck Mangione was born on 29 November 1940, and took piano lessons at the age of eight. At ten, he was taking trumpet lessons. In high school, his brother, pianist Gap, formed the Jazz Brothers (1958). They cut three albums and Chuck did one on his own in 1962. In 1965, he moved to New York City, played with various bands, and from 1968 to 1972 headed the Eastman Jazz Ensemble; he also formed his own quartet in 1968. In 1969, he presented a concert of his orchestral works called 'Kaleidoscope', and in 1971 got a contract with a major recording company. In 1976 he received the Grammy Award (Best Instrumentalist Composition) for 'Bellavia' and a 1978 Grammy for Best Pop Instrumental Performance for 'Children of Sanchez'. Chuck is a Bachelor of Music with a degree from the Eastman School of Music, and one of the best jazz trumpet/flugelhorn players around. This album included the title song hit 'Feels So Good' with over a million performances, matching the success of the million-selling album.

BARRY MANILOW

BARRY MANILOW – LIVE (Album) *Arista* [*USA*]. This was released in the U.S.A. in May 1977 and in Britain in May 1978. In the U.S.A. it hit No 1 for one week and stayed 54 weeks in the charts. R.I.A.A. Gold Disc award on 16 June 1977. Platinum award on 16 June 1977 also.

This Manilow album sold three million by the end of November 1977, and was an instant million seller on release. It is a recording of a live performance in New York. Among the tracks were: 'Studio Musician'; 'Mandy'; 'Weekend in New England'; 'It's Just Another New Year's Eve' and 'Beautiful Music'.

LOOKS LIKE WE MADE IT *Arista* [*USA*]. Written by Will Jennings and Richard Kerr, this was released in the U.S.A. in May 1977, going to No 3 for two weeks and staying 21 weeks in the charts. R.I.A.A. Gold Disc award on 7 September 1977.

BOB MARLEY & THE WAILERS

JAMMING *Island* [*Jamaica*]. Written by Bob Marley, this was released in Britain in December 1977, reaching No 9 and staying in the charts for 12 weeks.

A great number from the 'King of Reggae', immensely popular in Jamaica. It subsequently passed the global million sale, and is considered a classic of its genre.

STEVE MARTIN

LET'S GET SMALL (Album) *Warner Bros* [*USA*]. Written by Steve Martin and released in the U.S.A. in September 1977, this went to No 15 for one week and stayed 51 weeks in the charts. R.I.A.A. Gold Disc award on 29 November 1977. Platinum award on 9 May 1978. Grammy Award: Best Comedy Recording, 1977.

Steve Martin is one of America's hottest comics. This album was recorded live at the Boarding House, and features all the pieces he had mastered over the previous two years. It includes: 'Getting Small'; 'I'm Mad At My Mother' and 'Ramblin' Man'.

MEAT LOAF

BAT OUT OF HELL (Album) *Epic/Cleveland* [*USA*]. With songs by Jim Steinman, this was released in the U.S.A. in December 1977 and in Britain in March 1978. In the U.S.A. it went to No 14 for two weeks and stayed 69 weeks in the charts. In Britain it was No 11 for one week, staying in the charts for 259 weeks (to the end of 1983 and continuing into 1984), a record for Britain.

Meat Loaf is not a group. It is a man from Texas, born to a gospel singing family from the South – Dallas, in fact. He built up a reputation working with a West Coast band, and also sang on Ted Nugent's album 'Free For All', before portraying Crazy Eddie in the 'Rocky Horror Picture Show'. It was when he met Jim Steinman in the 'National Lampoon Show' that Meat Loaf started to become known worldwide. They came to the attention of Todd Rundgren who produced 'Bat Out Of Hell', Meat Loaf's first major album from Epic Records. Steinman, a composer, arranger, and pianist from Claremont, California, couldn't have found anyone better than Meat Loaf to do the vocal work on his gothic horror album. Meat Loaf, a mountain of a man with the voice of a grizzly, the power of a Bible-thumping preacher and with roots in R & B was ideal for the iron rock'n'roll required. The result was a sensation on both sides of the Atlantic. Its success in Britain was incredible. One estimate of its sales was 9 million, to October 1981.

It includes: 'Heaven Can Wait'; 'For Cryin' Out Loud'; 'Bat Out Of Hell'; 'Paradise By The Dashboard Light' and 'Two Out Of Three Ain't Bad'.

Meat Loaf's real name is Marvin Lee Day.

MECO

'STAR WARS THEME'/CANTINA BAND *Millenium/Casablanca* [*USA*], *RCA* [*Britain*]. Written by John Williams, this was released in the U.S.A. in August 1977, going to No 1 for two weeks and staying 22 weeks in the charts. In Britain it was No 7 for one week and stayed nine weeks in the charts. R.I.A.A. Gold Disc award on 28 September 1977. Platinum award on 8 June 1978. Grammy award: Best Instrumental Composition, Main Title from *Star Wars*, to John Williams, composer, 1977.

Meco Monardo, recording artist, saw the film *Star Wars* on its opening day in New York, and liked it so much that he went back for three more viewings. He got the idea of taking various excerpts to make into a contemporary disco format. Casablanca's president agreed and an album was made. Meco's version of the theme was released six weeks after the release of the original soundtrack, and the catchy disco version shot to the top of the charts, selling over two million. Meco began as a studio musician (trombonist), then arranger and producer (from 1974). He devised the modern formula of running danceable tracks to form an extended side of music. Composer John Williams was born in New York in 1932, and studied at the University of California in Los Angeles and at the Juillard School of music in New York. He started arranging in the Air Force, continuing his studies after a stint as pianist and conductor with Vic Damone. John set his sights on Hollywood and in 1958 scored his first film *Because They're Young*. From then on, he composed scores and acted as musical director for around 40 films including *Diamond Head*, *Valley of the Dolls*, *Poseidon Adventure*, *Goodbye Mr Chips*, *Earthquake*, *Towering Inferno*, *Jaws* and *Star Wars*. The latter brought him three Grammy awards – Best Pop Instrumental Recording, Best Instrumental Composition and Best Original Score Written for a Motion Picture in 1977. He also holds three Oscar awards – Best Scoring and Adaptation for *Fiddler on the Roof* (1972): Best Original Music Score for *Jaws* (1975) and Best Original Music Score for *Star Wars* (1977). He has many other awards for musical composition, notably the American TV Academy's 'Emmy' and the British Academy of Film & TV Arts Award for best original score in 1976. His symphonic works have been performed by many major American orchestras.

'STAR WARS' & OTHER GALACTIC FUNK (Album) *Millenium* [*USA*]. Released in the U.S.A. in July 1977, this went to No 22 for four weeks and stayed 20 weeks in the charts. R.I.A.A. Gold Disc award on 28 September 1977. Platinum award on 8 June 1978.

This album contained the 'Star Wars' Theme, a huge success as a single release. Meco credits a number of musicians from other galaxies for help on the album including Thur-M76 on Bontins, Krim-A23 on Hyper-Harps, the Lumen Family on Slokins, Phor Spee on Blorcas and Poe Ta Toe on Clomato. Side 1 features various themes from *Star Wars* with disco beat and electonic effects by a Buchler synthesizer. Side 2 contains 'Other Galactic Funk'.

RANDY NEWMAN

SHORT PEOPLE *Warner Bros* [*USA*]. Written by Gary Newman, this was released in the U.S.A. in October 1977, reaching No 3 for two weeks and staying 22 weeks in the charts. R.I.A.A. Gold Disc award on 24 January 1978.

Randy Newman is an eccentric in the pop business. He began by composing glossy type pop tunes, and progressed to a style firmly entrenched in America. He writes about the American

experience, bringing in all races, problems and situations. He wryly attacks everyone from 'Yellow Man' to 'Rednecks' with an individual sense of humour. Randy began playing piano at six and studied music theory at U.C.L.A. His own piano accompaniment of his songs is often performed with full orchestration. Whilst his music has often been likened to that of Stephen Foster and the classic pop of Gershwin, Porter and Hart, it is his own distinctive style with which the public identifies. He became a cult hero with a great number of supporters, first gaining a following through hit covers of songs like Three Dog Night's 'Mama Told Me Not To Come'. Three of his uncles are well-known conductors and film score composers. 'Short People' was banned by radio stations from coast to coast, but despite this, Newman broke through to international stardom.

STEVE MILLER BAND

BOOK OF DREAMS (Album) *Capitol* [*USA*]. With material by Steve Miller, this was released in the U.S.A. in May 1977, going to No 2 for one week and staying in the charts for 47 weeks. R.I.A.A. Gold Disc award on 11 May 1977. Platinum award on 10 June 1977.

The Steve Miller Band's second million-selling album. It showcases Miller's emotive vocals and exemplary guitar style, with good, melodic rock inventively arranged and performed. Of the 12 tracks, three are sufficient to display his wide talent i.e. mellow rock, mystic electronics and simple dance tune with almost Elizabethan form:- 'Threshold', 'Electro Lux Embroglio' and 'Babes in the Wood'.

OLIVIA NEWTON-JOHN

GREATEST HITS (Album) *MCA* [*USA*]. This was released in the U.S.A. in October 1977 and in Britain in January 1978. It was No 20 for two weeks in the U.S.A. and stayed in the charts for 24 weeks. In Britain it was No 19 for one week and stayed

eight weeks in the charts. R.I.A.A. Gold Disc award on 21 October 1977. Platinum award on 15 December 1977.

A superlative album of all Olivia's successes since she became a big star in the U.S.A. Contents are: 'Sam'; 'Changes'; (*) 'Let Me Be There'; 'Come On Over'; (*) 'If You Love Me (Let Me Know)'; (*) 'I Honestly Love You'; 'Something Better To Do'; (*) 'Have You Never Been Mellow?'; (*) Please Mr. Please'; 'Don't Stop Believin'; 'Let It Shine'. (* denotes sold a million as a single.)

PAUL NICHOLAS

HEAVEN ON THE 7TH FLOOR *RSO* [*USA*]. This was released in the U.S.A. and Britain in July 1977. In the U.S.A. it was No 8 for one week and in Britain it was No 40 for one week. It stayed in the U.S. charts for 28 weeks and for three weeks in the British charts. R.I.A.A. Gold Disc award on 12 December 1977.

Taken from the Paul Nicholas debut album 'Paul Nicholas'. Paul appeared in several films and shows, notably *Stardust*, *Hair* and *Sergeant Pepper's Lonely Hearts Club Band*.

TED NUGENT

CAT SCRATCH FEVER (Album) *Epic* [*USA*]. Written by Ted Nugent, this was released in the U.S.A. in June 1977, going to No 11 for three weeks and staying 30 weeks in the charts. R.I.A.A. Gold Disc award on 11 July 1977. Platinum award on 27 September 1977.

Nugent adds new emphasis on this album to the term hard rock. A triumphant disc, powerful from start to finish. It includes: 'Live It Up'; 'Death By Misadventure'; 'Home Bound'; 'A Thousand Knives'; 'Wang Dang Sweet Poontang'; 'Out Of Control'.

ALAN O'DAY

UNDERCOVER ANGEL *Pacific* [*USA*]. This was released in the U.S.A. in April 1977 and in Britain in June 1977. In the U.S.A. it hit No 1 for four weeks and stayed 26 weeks in the charts. In Britain it was No 43 for one week and stayed three weeks in the charts. R.I.A.A. Gold Disc award on 28 June 1977.

A big success for newcomer Alan O'Day and his song in the U.S.A., but not in Britain.

PABLO CRUISE

A PLACE IN THE SUN (Album) *A & M* [*USA*]. Released in the U.S.A. in March 1977, this was No 30 for one week and stayed in the charts for 33 weeks. R.I.A.A. Gold Disc award on 25 August 1977. Platinum award on 29 April 1980.

Another new U.S. group. This album took three years to reach the million sale.

(For further data on Pablo Cruise see 1978.)

PARLIAMENT

FUNKENTELECHY vs THE PLACEBO SYNDROME *Casablanca* [*USA*]. This was released in the U.S.A. in December 1977. It went to No 20 for one week and stayed 28 weeks in the charts. R.I.A.A. Gold Disc award on 10 January 1978. Platinum award on 4 May 1978.

Another adventure of Dr Funkenstein who falls prey to the Placebo Syndrome at the hands of Sir Nose D'Voidoffunk. The entire Parliament, including Bootsy's Rubber Band, up to its usual funky antics again.

THE ALAN PARSONS PROJECT

I ROBOT (Album) *Arista* [*USA*]. This was released in the U.S.A. in July 1977 and in Britain in August 1977. In the U.S.A. it was No 16 for four weeks, staying 34 weeks in the charts, and in Britain it was No 26 for one week, staying eight weeks in the charts. R.I.A.A. Gold Disc award on 16 September 1977. Platinum award on 25 October 1978.

Alan Parsons, recording engineer extraordinaire, was born in 1949. He entered the creative world of recorded music when he served as assistant engineer on the making of the Beatles' 'Abbey Road', and began a long association with the studio and Paul McCartney. He subsequently went on to engineer two Wings albums, 'Wildlife' and 'Red Rose Speedway'. He also worked with The Hollies on five albums, and his engineering style for Pink Floyd's 'Dark Side Of The Moon' earned him a Grammy nomination. He enjoyed instantaneous success as a producer with Steve Harley and Cockney Rebel, then produced two hit Pilot singles and albums for other artists. In 1976, Eric Woolfson had the idea of a rock album based on Edgar Allan Poe's horror tales, and the collaboration with Parsons became known as The Alan Parsons Project. The album 'Tales of Mystery and Imagination' took two years to produce and first appeared in the spring of 1976, receiving worldwide accolades. Parsons and Woolfson (who devised the controlling idea, wrote the lyrics, and played keyboards) proceeded to an even grander concept in 'I Robot', a haunting science-fiction vision. This album represented a new challenge for Parsons, the 28-year-old Englishman. It stunned the world of music by creating the future with an astounding impact, and is one of the most mysterious and lush works in modern music. Parsons assembled some of the world's finest musicians including Pilot, Allan Clarke and Steve Harley, and Andrew Powell as orchestra leader. For Parsons and Woolfson, The Project was a 'dream come true'. The album is distinguished by a science-fiction theme with performances by Allan Clarke on 'Breakdown', Steve Harley on 'The Voice' and members of Pilot. The opening theme has a Tangerine Dream-like quality.

DOLLY PARTON (Country artist)

HERE YOU COME AGAIN (Album) *RCA* [*USA*]. With material by Dolly Parton and others, this was released in the U.S.A. in October 1977 and in Britain in January 1978. It was No 11 for one week in the U.S.A., staying 16 weeks in the charts. R.I.A.A. Gold Disc award on 27 December 1977. Platinum award on 28 April 1978.

Dolly Parton was born in Locust Ridge, Sevier County, Tennessee, on 19 January 1946, the fourth child of 12 born to her parents. She has been singing all her life and writing songs since she was five, and singing with two of her sisters in their grandfather's church. At the age of ten, Dolly was singing on the Cass Walker TV show out of Knoxville, and first sang on record when she was 11. After school graduation, Dolly headed for Nashville in June 1964, and worked writing for Fred Foster's Combine Music company, before being given the chance to record for Foster's label, Monument. Then chart appearances entered the picture, first with Curly Putnam's song 'Dumb Blonde' and then one of her own 'Something Fishy'. She was discovered by Porter Wagoner and joined his road and TV show in late 1967 and for the following eight years the couple were frequently named as top country music duo on record and stage appearances. She quickly established herself as a major recording artist and songwriter, and one of Nashville's top entertainers. In 1968, Dolly had signed with RCA and in 1969 became a member of The Grand Ole Opry. In 1974, she shifted her management to the West Coast, despite local outcry, but finally brought a whole new dimension to country music. Her most notable shift away from the normal was the release of her self-produced album 'New Harvest, First Gathering' recorded in Nashville and mixed in Los Angeles, mostly of her own songs. Then came the 'Here You Come Again' album, to take her music to everyone - the break-out from the Nashville confines - and the perfect crossover from country to the national charts, and her first million-seller album.

This contained some of her own songs and some by other writers. It included her own 'Me and Little Andy'; 'God's Colouring Book'; 'Two Doors Down'; 'It's All Wrong, But It's All Right'; plus the Lovin' Spoonful's 'Lovin' You'; Bobby Goldsboro's 'Cowgirl and The Dandy'; and Barry Mann and Cynthia Weill's 'Here You Come Again', the supreme title track.

Dolly's many country classics such as 'Coat Of Many Colours', 'Bargain Store', 'My Tennessee Mountain Home' and 'Jolene'

of previous years stamp her as a talented songwriter as well as a singer. Her successful British tour in 1977 was highlighted when she met Queen Elizabeth II.

HERE YOU COME AGAIN *RCA* [*USA*]. Written by Barry Mann and Cynthia Weill, this was released in the U.S.A. in October 1977, going to No 6 for one week and staying 25 weeks in the charts. R.I.A.A. Gold Disc award on 1 February 1978.

Taken from her album of the same title, this was the massive crossover hit for Dolly in the U.S.A. and her first million-selling single. The disc was also No 1 for four weeks on the country charts.

TEDDY PENDERGRASS

TEDDY PENDERGRASS (Album) *Philadelphia International* [*USA*]. Released in the U.S.A. in March 1977, this was No 23 for one week and stayed in the charts for 25 weeks. R.I.A.A. Gold Disc award on 23 May 1977. Platinum award on 21 June 1978.

Teddy Pendergrass was born on 25 March 1950 in Philadelphia and comes from a rich religious background. He was singing gospel tunes from the age of two, and ordained a minister at ten. His mother worked at Shioles, a club frequented by stars such as Frank Sinatra and Connie Francis. Teddy would accompany his mother and took advantage of it by teaching himself how to read music and play drums. After a road stint with a band headed by James Brown's brother Teddy, at the age of 16, he returned to Philadelphia and joined the local Cadillacs band. Through this, he met Harold Melvin. In 1969 The Bluenotes had lost their backup band. Fate stepped in when a casual visit to a North Philly club by Melvin led to recruitment of the Cadillacs with drummer, Theodore Pendergrass. In 1970, when in the French West Indies, the Bluenotes' lead vocalist left. Pendergrass averted a crisis, and in two weeks Teddy and Harold put the act together for a commitment in Miami. In 1971, the group signed with Gamble-Huff's Philadelphia International, and in 1972 the first single was released, 'I Miss You', followed by million sellers in 1972 and 1973. In 1975, the group's album 'Wake Up Everybody' introduced Teddy's first solo effort on the title tune. In 1976, Teddy decided to go solo and this album, his first, with contributions from many Philadelphia music makers, sparkled with vitality and up-tempo numbers. It includes: 'You Can't Hide From Yourself'; 'Somebody Told Me'; 'Be Sure'; 'Don't Love You Anymore'; 'The Whole Town's Laughing At Me'; 'The More I Get, the More I Want'.

PINK FLOYD

ANIMALS (Album) *Harvest* [*Britain*] *Columbia* [*USA*]. With material written by Pink Floyd, this was released in Britain and the U.S.A. in February 1977. In the U.S.A. it was No 6 for two weeks and in Britain it was No 2 for three weeks. It stayed 23 weeks in the U.S. charts and 31 weeks in the British lists. R.I.A.A. Gold Disc award on 12 February 1977. Platinum award on 10 March 1977.

This album was masterminded by Roger Waters of the group, and is a gritty attempt to divide humankind into three categories: The Dogs, The Pigs and The Sheep, powerful images commenting on contemporary society. Waters uses a chilling vocal delivery, the acid lyrics lashing out and displaying a complete loss of faith in human nature. David Gilmour's guitar is prominent, cutting through with neat breaks over the rhythms.

PLAYER

BABY COME BACK *Polydor/RSO* [*USA*]. Written by Peter Beckett and John Crowley, this was released in the U.S.A. in September 1977 and in Britain in January 1978. In the U.S.A. it went to No 2 for four weeks and stayed 32 weeks in the charts. In Britain it was No 32 for one week and stayed seven weeks in the charts. R.I.A.A. Gold Disc award on 12 January 1978.

Player personnel: Ronn Moss (bass/vocals); Peter Beckett

(guitar/vocals); Wayne Cook (keyboards/vocals); J. C. Cowley (keyboards/bass/guitar/vocals); John Friesen (drums). They were signed to the Dennis Lambert-Brian Potter label, Haven Records, before going to RSO. Lambert and Potter then handled production for both the 'Player' album and 'Baby Come Back'. The group's music is varied - R & B, jazz, rock, folk and classical. The group began when Beckett (from Liverpool) met Crowley at a party in the U.S.A., and they decided to write together. Moss had played in a high school band, Cook played in the Daddy Warbucks and Good Thunder bands and had toured and recorded with Jackson Browne, Helen Reddy and The Osmonds. The five members were brought together in Los Angeles by manager Paul Palmer. Player has gone a long way towards realizing the big things predicted for them, as this successful first million seller proved. In this year they made a 36-date tour of Canada and the U.S.A. by joining RSO artist Eric Clapton.

ELVIS PRESLEY

MY WAY *RCA* [*USA*]. Written by Paul Anka (lyrics) and Claude Francois and Jacques Revaux (music), the original French words were by Gilles Thibaut (1967) and the title was 'Comme d'habitude'. It was released in the U.S.A. in November 1977 and in Britain in December 1977. In the U.S.A. it was in the charts for 12 weeks, reaching No 37 for one week. In Britain it was No 14 for one week and stayed eight weeks in the charts. R.I.A.A. Gold Disc award on 13 January 1978.

This was the first Presley single to be released after his death on 16 August. The lyrics of this famous song seemed particularly apt in view of his passing. Taken from the CBS documentary film shot during the months before Presley died.

WAY DOWN *RCA* [*USA*]. Written by Layng Martine, this was released in the U.S.A. in June 1977 and in Britain in August 1977. It was No 10 for one week in the U.S.A. and stayed 23 weeks in the charts. In Britain it went to No 1 for five weeks and stayed in the charts for 13 weeks. R.I.A.A. Gold Disc award on 12 September 1977.

Taken from the 'Moody Blue' album, one of Presley's biggest U.S. hits for some time. It was the last single released before his death.

MOODY BLUE (Album) *RCA* [*USA*]. This was released in the U.S.A. in July 1977 and in Britain in August 1977. It went to No 5 for three weeks in the U.S.A., staying 34 weeks in the charts. It went to No 3 for two weeks in Britain, staying in the charts for 13 weeks. R.I.A.A. platinum award on 12 September 1977.

Recorded in Memphis, at Graceland, Presley's home, and on tour. A varied set of ballads and rockers including the oldie 'Little Darlin'; 'Pledging My Love'; 'Moody Blue'; 'Let Me Be There'; 'Way Down'; and 'Unchained Melody'. Elvis was giving a concert in Indianapolis in July, and was presented with a copy of 'Moody Blue' - the two-billionth RCA record just off the presses. Last album release before Presley died.

ELVIS IN CONCERT (Double album) *RCA* [*USA*]. This was released in the U.S.A. in October 1977 and in Britain in November 1977. In the U.S.A. it went to No 3 for four weeks and stayed 25 weeks in the charts. In Britain it was No 13 for one week, staying four weeks in the charts. R.I.A.A. platinum award on 14 October 1977.

This U.S. TV special documentary on the CBS network was screened on 3 October 1977. It was scheduled for release before Elvis' untimely death as CBS had finished the production over two months prior to that event. It glued millions of Americans to their TV. It is in no sense an Elvis memorial album - it showed that Elvis' popularity with his audiences had not waned in any way in his 22 years of superstardom.

The double album consists of one record of the soundtrack of the CBS TV Special, and the second includes live recordings of Elvis' June (1977) tour. The TV soundtrack included 'My Way'; 'Jailhouse Rock'; 'Early Morning Rain'; 'Teddy Bear'/'Don't be Cruel' medley; 'Hurt'; 'That's All Right'; 'Hound Dog'. The

tour recordings includes: 'Johnny B. Goode'; 'I Got a Woman'; 'Love Me'; 'And I Love You So'; 'It's Now or Never'; 'If You Love Me Let Me Know'; 'Early Morning Rain'. It was an instant million seller.

ELVIS SINGS THE WONDERFUL WORLD OF CHRIST-MAS (Album) *RCA* [*USA*]. Put out in the U.S.A. as a tribute at Christmastime to the late Elvis. A collection of seasonal songs made up from his earlier recordings, such as the 'Christmas Album' (see 1957) and his EP 'Elvis Sings Christmas Songs', originally released in the U.S.A. in 1971. R.I.A.A. Gold Disc award on 4 November 1977. Platinum award on 1 December 1977.

The demand for Elvis' discs immediately following his death created a sales explosion. Within a week retail sales (reported 'in the millions') had cleared the shelves of every available recording by the King of Rock 'n Roll, and the following years showed that Elvis was worth more dead than alive. A worldwide avalanche of sales had by mid-1980 surpassed the billion (1,000,000,000) mark, double the output up to August 1977. Elvis was the most successful entertainer in the history of the recording industry. He changed the shape of popular music throughout the world and catapulted the music world into the rock 'n roll era, influencing the personal tastes of teenagers. He set popular music on its present-day path. For the record it is interesting to note that Elvis starred in 33 motion pictures, 32 of his albums were certified as gold or platinum by RIAA and 62 singles qualified for a Gold Disc. It has now been estimated that practically every Presley disc had reached a million sale by the end of 1980, which with single titles not already mentioned would total 85 singles. These additional singles were mostly released between 1967 and 1975.

QUEEN

NEWS OF THE WORLD (Album) *EMI* [*Britain*] *Asylum* [*USA*]. Written by Freddy Mercury and Brian May, this was released in Britain in October 1977 and in the U.S.A. in November 1977. In Britain it was No 4 for one week and stayed 19 weeks in the charts. In the U.S.A. it went to No 2 for four weeks and stayed 32 weeks in the charts. R.I.A.A. Gold Disc award on 14 November 1977. Platinum award on 28 December 1977.

This album is a departure of sorts for Queen as they explore new sounds and song structures. It includes 'Get Down, Make Love'; 'We Will Rock You'; 'We Are The Champions'.

WE ARE THE CHAMPIONS b/w WE WILL ROCK YOU *EMI* [*Britain*] *Asylum* [*USA*]. Written by Freddy Mercury and Brian May, this was released in Britain in October 1977 and in the U.S.A. in the same month. In Britain it went to No 2 for three weeks, staying 11 weeks in the charts. In the U.S.A. it hit No 1 for three weeks and stayed 30 weeks in the charts. R.I.A.A. Gold Disc award on 25 January 1978. Platinum award on 25 April 1978.

Both sides of this disc, taken from Queen's album 'News of the World', were a great success in the U.S.A. particularly. Sales there were over two million.

RAYDIO

JACK AND JILL *Arista* [*USA*]. Written by Ray Parker Jnr, this was released in the U.S.A. in December 1977 and in Britain in March 1978. It was No 7 for four weeks in the U.S.A., staying in the charts for 26 weeks. In Britain it was No 11 for one week and stayed in the charts for 12 weeks. R.I.A.A. Gold Disc award on 26 April 1978.

Raydio personnel are: Ray Parker (guitar/songwriter); Arnell Carmichael (synthesizer); Jerry Knight (bass); Vincent Bonham (piano). Parker, leader of Raydio, was born in Detroit in 1954. He started out playing the clarinet, his father then bought him a guitar and he taught himself to play it. At 13, he formed his first trio: himself, Ollie Brown and Nathan Watts; all three achieved musical success. At 14, Parker toured with the Detroit Spinners. Then he played in a back-up band at Twenty Grand, a big Detroit Club, where acts like The Temptations, Gladys Knight and the Pips and Stevie Wonder appeared. Parker started recording, first at Motown and then on all the Invictus hits. Moving to Hollywood, he did all the Barry White sessions, and sold his compositions to artists like Barry White, Nancy Wilson and Chaka Khan. Parker's career really took off when he started recording with everybody in the industry: Labelle, Boz Scaggs, Helen Reddy, etc.

Whilst he was at Motown and Invictus, Stevie Wonder called him from New York to play guitar for him on the 1972 tour with the Rolling Stones. This gave him the urge to write songs. A friend of his played a tape to Clive Davis, who signed him to Arista Records. Parker got his group Raydio together, and cut his own first, self-produced album 'Raydio' in his own studio. This was a big success and included 'Jack and Jill' which soon sold a million when released as a single.

REO SPEEDWAGON

YOU GET WHAT YOU PLAY FOR (Double album) *Epic* [*USA*]. Written by REO Speedwagon, this was released in the

U.S.A. in March 1977, going to No 42 for one week and staying 32 weeks in the charts. R.I.A.A. Gold Disc award on 9 August 1977. Platinum award on 14 December 1978.

Personnel are: Gregg Philbin (bass guitar); Alan Gratzer (drums); Gary Ricrath (lead guitar); Neal Doughty (keyboards); Kevin Cronin (lead vocals/guitar). Philbin was later replaced by Bruce Hall. REO Speedwagon is the name of the first brand of high-speed fire truck. They started in Champaign, Illinois on the bar circuit in 1971. With a 50-dollar limousine, the band set out to conquer the Midwest, performing three gigs a day. They subsequently owned a succession of planes with such names as 'The Flying Turkey' and 'The Flying Tuna'. The group graduated to supporting the Eagles, Aerosmith, Rod Stewart, and Bad Company. They became a top act and started recording. Their albums were 'REO Speedwagon'; 'REO Two'; 'Ridin' the Storm Out'; 'Lost in a Dream'; 'This Time We Mean It'; 'REO' and then the big one 'You Get What You Play For'. This took 20 months on the market before the million sale was reached. REO Speedwagon were hailed as a cult band among enthusiasts of Midwestern high-energy rock. The album included 'Keep Pushin''; 'Summer Love'; '157 Riverside Avenue'; 'Riding The Storm Out'; 'Little Queenie'.

JOHNNY RIVERS

SWAYIN' TO THE MUSIC (Slow Dancin') *Big Tree/Atlantic* [*USA*]. Released in the U.S.A. in June 1977, this went to No 11 for one week and stayed in the charts for 25 weeks. R.I.A.A. Gold Disc award on 29 December 1977.

Johnny Rivers' first million seller for five years.

KENNY ROGERS

LUCILLE *United Artists* [*USA*]. Written by Hal Bynum and Roger Bowling, this was released in the U.S.A. in March 1977 and in Britain in April 1977. In the U.S.A. it went to No 7 for one week and stayed 23 weeks in the charts. In Britain it hit No 1 for one week, staying 14 weeks in the charts. R.I.A.A. Gold Disc award on 22 June 1977. Grammy Award: Best Country Vocal Performance, Male, 'Lucille', Kenny Rogers, 1977.

Kenny Rogers, formerly with the New Christy Minstrels and the First Edition (*see* 1969) became a solo recording artist in 1976, when his first UA single came out – 'Love Lifted Me' – to become a sizeable country hit, and giving Rogers the title of his debut UA album. 'Lucille' was a smash hit that mastered both country and pop lists, establishing Kenny as a major solo recording artist.

LINDA RONSTADT

SIMPLE DREAMS (Album) *Asylum* [*USA*]. Released in the U.S.A. in September 1977, this went to No 2 for 11 weeks and stayed 39 weeks in the charts. R.I.A.A. Gold Disc award on 19 September 1977. Platinum award on 12 October 1977. Grammy award: Best Album Package, 'Simple Dreams', 1977.

Linda's finest achievement so far. The album includes: Roy Orbison's 'Blue Bayou'; Rolling Stones' 'Tumbling Dice'; Buddy Holly's 'It's So Easy'. An almost instant million seller.

BLUE BAYOU *Elektra/Asylum* [*USA*]. Written by Roy Orbison and Joe Melson (1963), this was released in the U.S.A. in September 1977 and in Britain in January 1978. In the U.S.A. it reached No 3 for two weeks and stayed 24 weeks in the charts. In Britain it was No 35 for two weeks and stayed in the charts for four weeks. R.I.A.A. Gold Disc award on 23 January 1978.

The prime track from Linda's album 'Simple Dreams', and one of the classic songs of 1963.

ROSE ROYCE

IN FULL BLOOM (Album) *Whitfield/Warner* [*USA*]. With material by Norman Whitfield, this was released in the U.S.A. in August 1977 and in Britain in February 1978. It went to No 20 for one week in the U.S.A., staying 28 weeks in the charts. In Britain it was No 18 for two weeks, staying nine weeks in the charts. R.I.A.A. Gold Disc award on 4 October 1977. Platinum award on 6 December 1977.

Rose Royce played an important part in the success of the *Car Wash* soundtrack album, but now had an album all to themselves. Norman Whitfield wrote most of the material, as well as arranging and producing the music. Principal tracks: 'Ooh Boy' and 'Do You Dance?'.

RUFUS (featuring Chaka Khan)

ASK RUFUS (Album) *ABC* [*USA*]. Written by Rufus, this was released in the U.S.A. in January 1977 and in Britain in February 1977. In the U.S.A. it went to No 14 for one week and stayed 19 weeks in the charts. R.I.A.A. Gold Disc award on 28 January 1977. Platinum award on 13 April 1977.

Chaka Khan leads the group through lush ballads and inspired rock numbers. Another big success for her and Rufus. The group had two personnel changes – David Wolinski (keyboards) and Richard Calhoun (percussion). Contents of album are: 'At Midnight (My Love Will Lift You Up)'; 'Close The Door'; 'Slow Screw Against The Wall'; 'A Flat Fry'; 'Earth Song'; 'Everlasting Love'; 'Hollywood'; 'Magic In Your Eyes'; 'Better Days'; 'Egyptian Song'.

SAMANTHA SANG

EMOTION *Private Stock* [*USA*]. Written by the Gibb Brothers, this was released in the U.S.A. in November 1977 and in Britain in January 1978. In the U.S.A. it reached No 3 for three weeks and stayed 29 weeks in the charts. In Britain it was No 11 for one week and stayed 13 weeks in the charts. R.I.A.A. Gold Disc award on 9 February 1978. Platinum award on 21 April 1978.

Samantha Sang is from Australia. This song was written for her by the Gibb brothers (The Bee Gees) and the disc was one of the biggest-selling singles of the year. It sold over two million in the U.S.A.

SANTANA

MOONFLOWER (Double album) *Columbia* [*USA*]. This was released in the U.S.A. and Britain in October 1977. It went to No 17 for one week in the U.S.A., staying in the charts for 15 weeks. In Britain it was No 7 for one week and stayed 25 weeks in the charts. R.I.A.A. Gold Disc award on 1 December 1977.

An impressive double album of live tracks and recorded studio sides. It was reported that the global sale was a million by October 1978.

The album includes: 'She's Not There'; 'Black Magic Woman'; 'Gypsy Queen'; 'Soul Sacrifice'; 'Let The Children Play'; 'Toussaint L'Overture'.

LEO SAYER

WHEN I NEED YOU *Chrysalis* [*Britain*] *Warner Bros* [*USA*]. Written by Albert Hammond and Carole Sager, this was released in Britain in January 1977 and in the U.S.A. in February 1977. In both the U.S.A. and Britain it went to No 1 for three weeks. It stayed 24 weeks in the U.S.A. charts and 13 weeks in the British charts. R.I.A.A. Gold Disc award on 10 May 1977.

This song, with its haunting melody, was culled from Leo Sayer's 1976 album 'Endless Flight'. A big hit on both sides of the Atlantic, and the second million-seller single from the album.

BOZ SCAGGS

DOWN TWO THEN LEFT (Album) *Columbia* [*USA*]. Written by Boz Scaggs, this was released in the U.S.A. in November 1977, going to No 13 for two weeks and staying 19 weeks in the charts. R.I.A.A. Gold Disc award on 19 November 1977. Platinum award on 9 December 1977.

The follow-up to Boz's 'Silk Degrees' album of 1976. Producer Joe Wissert again provides the solid musical core over which Boz exercises his distinctive tenor voice. Outstanding tracks are 'Still Falling For You' and 'Hard Times'.

CARLY SIMON

NOBODY DOES IT BETTER *Elektra/Asylum* [*USA*]. Written by Carole Bayer Sager and Marvin Hamlisch, this was released in Britain and the U.S.A. in July 1977. In the U.S.A. it was No 2 for one week and stayed in the charts for 27 weeks. In Britain it was No 7 for three weeks, staying in the charts for 13 weeks. R.I.A.A. Gold Disc award on 9 November 1977.

Another great song for Carly, written by two of America's most famous songwriters.

PAUL SIMON

GREATEST HITS etc. (Album) *Columbia* [*USA*]. This was released in the U.S.A. in November 1977, going to No 22 for one week and staying 21 weeks in the charts. R.I.A.A. Gold Disc award on 17 November 1977. Platinum award on 1 February 1978.

All the musical highlights of Paul Simon's solo career are included on this impressive compilation. In addition to his hit singles 'Kodachrome'; 'Still Crazy After All These Years'; 'American Tune'; and '50 Ways To Leave Your Lover', two new songs are included.

STEELY DAN

AJA (Album) *ABC* [*USA*]. Released in the U.S.A. in October 1977, this went to No 4 for four weeks and stayed 58 weeks in the charts. R.I.A.A. Gold Disc award on 4 October 1977. Platinum award on 27 December 1977. Grammy award: Best Engineered Recording (Non-Classical), 1977.

Songwriters Walter Becker and Donald Fagen were partners since college, and are the chief architects of the Steely Dan albums. Gary Katz signed them to ABC Music and later convinced ABC Records to record them. The Steely Dan outfit of Fagen (keyboards/vocals); Becker (bass/vocals); Denny Dias (guitar/vocals); and Jim Hodder (drums) was formed from ex-members of Ultimate Spinach and New York session players. Their first album 'Can't Buy A Thrill' (1972) was followed by 'Countdown To Ecstasy' (1973); 'Pretzel Logic' (1974); 'Katy Lied' (1975); and 'Royal Scam' (1976). From then on, with only Denny Dias of the original band, they utilized various rhythm players and soloists - around 60 musicians in all. Their albums are considered to contain some of the most accomplished rock of the 1970s. Increasing use of jazz ensemble and solo elements, harmonic technique in arrangements plus allusions to be-bop, soul music, classic pops and 20th-century avant garde classicism, makes their work impressive. This album 'AJA', their sixth, is superb. It includes their longest songs to date – the title track and 'Deacon Blues', both running over seven minutes. The album entered the Top 10 within three weeks of release, without the benefit of a single or tour – and a top FM airplay draw since release. A long chart run of over a year, and around three million sold by the end of 1978.

ROD STEWART

FOOTLOOSE AND FANCY FREE (Album) *Warner Bros* [*USA*], *Riva* [*Britain*]. With material by Rod Stewart, etc., this was released in the U.S.A. and Britain in November 1977. In the U.S.A. it reached No 4 for four weeks and stayed 39 weeks in the charts. In Britain it went to No 3 for two weeks and stayed 25 weeks in the charts. R.I.A.A. Gold Disc award on 22 November 1977. Platinum award on 20 December 1977.

An almost immediate million seller for Rod, and a success on both sides of the Atlantic. It includes: 'Hot Legs'; 'Born Loose'; 'You're In My Heart'; 'You Keep Me Hanging On'; 'If Loving You Is Wrong'.

YOU'RE IN MY HEART (The final acclaim) *Warner Bros* [*USA*], *Riva* [*Britain*]. This was released in Britain and the U.S.A. in October 1977. It was No 4 for four weeks in the U.S.A., staying 23 weeks in the charts. In Britain it went to No 3 for one week, staying in the charts for ten weeks. R.I.A.A. Gold Disc award on 8 February 1978.

The big single success from Stewart's album 'Footloose and Fancy Free'.

BARBRA STREISAND

STREISAND SUPERMAN (Album) *Columbia* [*USA*]. This was released in the U.S.A. and Britain in June 1977. It climbed to No 2 in the U.S.A., staying there for two weeks, and remained in the charts for 22 weeks. In Britain it was No 32 for one week and stayed in the charts for seven weeks. R.I.A.A. Gold Disc award on 22 June 1977. Platinum award on 9 August 1977.

In this year, Barbra Streisand was at the peak of her popularity, and this album appealed to a wide audience. It included 'New York State Of Mind' written by Billy Joel; 'Lullaby for Myself' (Rupert Holmes); 'Love Comes From Unexpected Places' (Kim Carnes); 'My Heart Belongs To Me'; 'Don't Believe What You Read'; and 'Answer Me'.

STYX

THE GRAND ILLUSION (Album) *A & M* [*USA*]. This was released in the U.S.A. in July 1977 and in Britain in May 1978. It was No 9 for two weeks in the U.S.A., staying 51 weeks in the charts. R.I.A.A. Gold Disc award on 19 October 1977. Platinum award on 22 December 1977.

The Styx story begins in Chicago, when the twin brothers Chuck and John Panozzo learned to play bass and drums respectively (1963). They were joined by Dennis De Young (accordion), called themselves Tradewinds and in 1963 were doing local dates. John Curulewski (guitar) from Chicago's south side joined in 1968, and Jim Young (lead guitar) in 1970. They then changed their name to Styx. They made a demo at RCA's recording centre in 1971. The tapes intrigued record executive/producer Bill Traut, and he signed Styx to Wooden Nickel label, a subsidiary of RCA, in 1972. They made four albums, 'Styx 1'; 'Styx 2'; 'The Serpent is Rising'; and 'Man of Miracles' at yearly intervals, and kept alive by performing locally, as the album sales were minimal. WLS radio station kept getting requests for a Styx song 'Lady'; other stations picked it up and it became the group's first hit single. Styx later signed to A & M, replacing Curulewski with Tommy Shaw, who made his recording debut on the 'Crystal Ball' album (1976), then 'Equinox'. A 200-date tour prepared the band for the next album 'The Grand Illusion', which stayed in the charts for about a year, selling more than three million copies.

The album includes: 'The Grand Illusion'; 'Fooling Yourself'; 'Superstars'; 'Miss America'; 'Come Sail Away'.

DONNA SUMMER

I FEEL LOVE *Casablanca* [*USA*]. Written by Donna Summer and Giorgio Moroeder, this was released in the U.S.A. and Britain in July 1977. In the U.S.A. it went to No 4 for two weeks and stayed 23 weeks in the charts. In Britain it hit No 1 for four weeks and stayed in the charts for 11 weeks. R.I.A.A. Gold Disc award on 9 November 1977.

Second million-seller single for Donna, extremely popular in both the U.S.A. and Britain.

JAMES TAYLOR

'JT' (Album) *Columbia* [*USA*]. Released in the U.S.A. in July 1977, this went to No 3 for two weeks and stayed 25 weeks in the charts. R.I.A.A. Gold Disc award on 5 July 1977. Platinum award on 1 September 1977.

James Taylor's debut album for Columbia, produced by Peter Asher. Although Linda Ronstadt and Carly Simon are among those who lend vocal support, it is Taylor, with his soft-spoken and understated style, who remains in the spotlight throughout. The album includes: 'Handy Man' (Grammy winner Best Pop Vocal Performance, Male: 1977); 'Bartender's Blues'; 'Your Smiling Face'; 'Terra Nova'; 'Traffic Jam'; 'Honey, Don't Leave L.A.'

Peter Asher received a Grammy award for Best Producer of the Year: 1977 for this album.

JOE TEX

AIN'T GONNA BUMP NO MORE (With No Big Fat Woman) *Epic* [*USA*]. Written by Joe Tex, this was released in the U.S.A. in March 1977 and in Britain in April 1977. In the U.S.A. it went to No 10 for one week and stayed 22 weeks in the charts. In Britain it went to No 2 for one week and stayed in the charts for 11 weeks. R.I.A.A. Gold Disc award on 9 June 1977.

Joe Tex's first big hit for over five years.

MARSHALL TUCKER BAND

CAROLINA DREAMS (Album) *Capricorn* [*USA*]. Written by members of the band, this was released in the U.S.A. in February 1977, going to No 27 for six weeks and staying 32 weeks in the charts. R.I.A.A. Gold Disc award on 2 June 1977. Platinum award on 23 May 1978.

Marshall Tucker Band members are: Doug Gray (lead singer); Toy Caldwell (guitar/songwriter); George Eubanks (saxes/flute); George McCorkle (rhythm guitar); Tommy Caldwell (bass); Paul Riddle (drums). MTB are a group of country boys from Spartanburg, South Carolina, affectionately known as the 'people's band' in their Southern American area. Their albums 'Marshall Tucker Band' (1973); 'Where We All Belong' (1974); 'Searchin' for a Rainbow' (1975); 'A New Life' (1974); and 'Together Forever' (1977) were all certified gold by R.I.A.A. Most of the material for these was written by Tom Caldwell. MTB diversified their efforts for the 'Carolina Dreams' album with songs by members Eubanks and McCorkle as well as Caldwell, and the result was national recognition for the band that had made it all the way to the top without ever leaving home. The album included: 'Carolina Dreams'; 'Desert Skies'; 'Tell It To The Devil'; 'I Should Have Never Started Loving You'; 'Live In A Song'; 'Never Trust A Stranger'.

BONNIE TYLER

IT'S A HEARTACHE *RCA* [*Britain*]. Written by Steve Wolfe and Ronnie Scott, this was released in Britain in November 1977 and in the U.S.A. in April 1978. In Britain it went to No 4 for four weeks and stayed 12 weeks in the charts. In the U.S.A. it went to No 3 for two weeks, staying 22 weeks in the charts. R.I.A.A. Gold Disc award on 16 June 1978.

sold the million by May 1979. The group's rise to prominence nationwide came through extensive TV exposure from 1978, and with sold-out concerts and popularity overseas assured international stardom. The album includes: 'Village People'; 'African Queens'; 'Fire Island'; 'San Francisco/Hollywood'; 'Arabian Nights'. It was produced by Jacques Morali.

BOB WELCH

FRENCH KISS (Album) *Capitol* [*USA*]. This was released in the U.S.A. in September 1977, going to No 20 for one week and staying in the charts for 45 weeks. R.I.A.A. Gold Disc award on 9 December 1977. Platinum award on 1 May 1978.

Bob Welch was formerly a member of Fleetwood Mac (vocals and guitar) and later one of the trio Paris, a hard rock outfit. He is more subdued and melodic on this, his first solo album. It highlights a reworking of his 'Sentimental Lady', and was produced by Lindsey Buckingham and Christine McVie of Fleetwood Mac, who also added background vocals.

BARRY WHITE

BARRY WHITE SINGS FOR SOMEONE YOU LOVE (Album) *20th Century* [*USA*]. With songs written by Barry White, etc. this was released in the U.S.A. in September 1977, going to No 12 for four weeks and staying 23 weeks in the charts. R.I.A.A. Gold Disc award on 20 September 1977. Platinum award on 15 November 1977.

This album was another big success for talented artist/songwriter/businessman Barry White. Contents are: 'Play Your Game Baby'; 'It's Ecstasy When You Lay Down Next To Me'; 'You're So Good, You're Bad'; 'I Never Thought I'd Fall In Love With You'; 'You Turned My Whole World Around'; 'Oh What A Night For Dancing'; 'Of All The Guys In The World'.

Writers respectively: A. Johnson and S. Hudman; N. Pigford and E. Paris; A. Shroeder and J. Ragovoy; R. E. Coleman; F. Wilson and D. Pearson; V. Wilson and Barry White; D. Pearson and Barry White.

IT'S ECSTASY WHEN YOU LAY DOWN NEXT TO ME *20th Century* [*USA*]. Written by N. Pigford and E. Paris, this was released in the U.S.A. in September 1977 and in Britain in October 1977. It was No 5 for one week in the U.S.A. and stayed 20 weeks in the charts. In Britain it was No 40 for one week, staying three weeks in the charts. R.I.A.A. Gold Disc award on 18 October 1977.

The prime track from Barry's album 'Barry White Sings For Someone You Love'.

MERI WILSON

TELEPHONE MAN *GRT* [*USA*]. Written by Meri Wilson, this was released in the U.S.A. in June 1977 and in Britain in July 1977. In the U.S.A. it went to No 27 for one week and stayed 19 weeks in the charts. In Britain it reached No 6 for two weeks and stayed ten weeks in the charts. R.I.A.A. Gold Disc award on 26 October 1977.

Meri Wilson is the daughter of an Air Force officer, and was born in Japan, but raised in Marietta, Georgia. At an early age she took up music, and started playing piano and flute while attending Indiana University to major in music. An automobile accident disrupted her life, and while in hospital for many months she took up playing the guitar - both six and twelve string instruments. After hospital, she finished her education and returned to Georgia, playing supper clubs by night and writing songs by day. She accepted an offer from an exclusive supper club in Dallas, and stayed on as entertainments director there. In Dallas the jingle industry heard about her and she was soon performing background vocals on commercials. The first time she ever sang the lead on a master recording session of her own, was on the hilarious hit song she wrote entitled 'Telephone Man', a story of a young lady having a telephone installed. Her unique

Bonnie Tyler was born in the village of Skewen, near Swansea, Wales. Ronnie Scott (owner of one of London's prestigious clubs) and Steve Wolfe decided, in 1976, to find a girl singer who they felt could do justice to their songs. During a visit to Wales they heard Bonnie singing in a Swansea nightclub. Bonnie had been working in Welsh clubs for almost eight years before she met Scott and Wolfe, and had never recorded before. She made a single with them for RCA which flopped. This was followed by 'Lost in France', a Top 10 hit in the U.K., which was also a European hit. The writers continued with 'It's a Heartache', a success in Britain, but when released in the U.S.A. an immediate smash, with a million sales inside two months. America was entranced by the singer's unique talents, and in a short space of time, Bonnie became an international star of the recording world. 'It's a Heartache' went to No 1 in Australia, Canada, Denmark, France, Finland, Norway, Sweden, Spain and South Africa, and was also a major hit in Portugal, Israel, Holland, West Germany, Argentina, Belgium and Brazil. She was the first non-Brazilian artist to be presented with a Gold Disc by RCA there. The distinctive hoarseness in Bonnie's voice is the result of a delicate throat operation to correct a complaint common among singers - nodules on the vocal chords. This gave her a voice rich with vibrato, and she sings with a maturity that belies her years. Bonnie is in great demand for concert tours around the world.

VILLAGE PEOPLE

VILLAGE PEOPLE (Album) *Casablanca* [*USA*]. This was released in the U.S.A. in July 1977. R.I.A.A. Gold Disc award on 18 September 1978.

Village People are an aggregation in which each member dresses a 'role': Randy Jones (cowboy); David 'Scar' Hodo (construction man); Glen Hughes (leather man); Felipe Rose (Indian); Alexander Briley (military man); and lead singer Victor Wills (a variety of costumes including police uniforms). This album, their first, was an instant hit in its first week of release, a four-cut concept album that celebrates the gay male lifestyles in San Francisco, Hollywood and Fire Island, closing with a rousing liberation song. It got a tremendous amount of disco airplay (and commensurate sales), and achieved enormous popularity without appearing in any of the charts in U.S.A. It was reported to have performance on the record was captured on the first take, and when released was a huge success.

WINGS

MULL OF KINTYRE *Parlophone [Britain]*. Written by Paul McCartney and Denny Laine and released in Britain in November 1977, this was No 1 in Britain for 8 weeks and stayed 17 weeks in the charts.

This was the fastest-selling single of 1977 and the biggest-selling single ever for Britain. It sold 110,000 in one day, 250,000 by 3 December and 500,000 by 10 December. Sales by 24 December were 1,200,000, and finally over two million. 'Mull of Kintyre' is about Paul McCartney's hideaway on the west coast of Scotland. Denny Laine and Paul decided to get a new tune together and make it sound like a traditional Scottish tune, although adding a modern sound to it. They called in the local Campbelltown Pipe Band, and wrote the tune to their own scale, because the bagpipes can play only certain keys. All traditional tunes are catchy, and 'Mull of Kintyre' was no exception. Its simple melody and lyrics, plus bagpipe accompaniment, had instant appeal. It was Paul McCartney's first release to reach the No 1 position since the Beatles' 'Ballad of John & Yoko' in 1969, and is only the 17th single to sell more than a million in Britain.

1978

ORIGINAL FILM SOUNDTRACK (VARIOUS ARTISTS)

FM (Double album) *MCA [USA]*. This was released in the U.S.A. in April 1978 and reached No 7 for two weeks, staying in the charts for 22 weeks. In Britain it was No 37 for two weeks and stayed five weeks in the charts. R.I.A.A. Gold Disc award on 24 April 1978. Platinum award on 10 May 1978.

This double album, from the film *FM*, transfers rockers to the screen. FM is a title denoting the various VHF radio stations in the USA that broadcast rock music as a serious business. Some of the biggest names in FM radio contributed to this album with either former hit singles or new recordings - a gallery of artists of rock over the previous two years. The movie is entirely about music. The complete contents are: 'More Than a Feeling' (Boston); 'Livingston Saturday Night' (Jimmy Buffett); 'It Keeps You Runnin'' (Doobie Brothers); 'Life in the Fast Lane' (Eagles); 'There's a Place in the World For a Gambler' (Dan Fogelberg); 'Cold As Ice' (Foreigner); 'Just the Way You Are' (Billy Joel); 'Bad Man' (Randy Meisner); 'Fly Like an Eagle' (Steve Miller); 'Breakdown' (Tom Petty & The Heartbreakers); 'We Will Rock You' (Queen); 'Tumbling Dice' (Linda Ronstadt); 'Poor Poor Pitiful Me' (Linda Ronstadt); 'Lido Shuffle' (Boz Scaggs); 'Night Moves' (Bob Seger & Silver Bullet Band); 'FM' (Steely Dan); 'Do It Again' (Steely Dan); 'Your Smiling Face' (James Taylor); 'Life's Been Good' (Joe Walsh).

ORIGINAL FILM SOUNDTRACK (STARRING JOHN TRAVOLTA AND OLIVIA NEWTON-JOHN)

GREASE (Album) *RSO [USA]*. This was released in the U.S.A. in April 1978 and in Britain in June 1978. In the U.S.A. it stayed in the charts for a total of 72 weeks, climbing to No 1 and staying there for 16 weeks. In Britain it went to No 1 for 13 weeks and stayed for 46 weeks in the charts. R.I.A.A. Gold Disc award on 2 May 1978. Platinum award on 9 May 1978.

Grease was originally a Broadway stage production (1973) with score by Jim Jacobs and Warren Casey. The film version contains some of their songs, but the new numbers written for the film included four hits as million-selling singles. The story of the film is superficially a celebration of the decade which gave birth to the first teenage culture independent of adults and their values in the 1950s. With John Travolta (the new star of *Saturday Night Fever*) teamed with Olivia Newton-John, plus millions being spent on promoting the film, the result was staggering. The film was premiered in London on 14 September 1978 at the Empire, Leicester Square. The album had begun to register huge sales in the U.S.A. (it had been shipped platinum) and finally sold over 10 million there. Britain sold a million, Australia over 520,000, and the global total was 19 million. The album includes: (*)'You're the One That I Want' (John Farrar) sung by Travolta/Newton-John; (*)'Summer Nights' (Jim Jacobs and Warren Casey) sung by Travolta/Newton-John; (*)'Hopelessly Devoted To You' (John Farrar) sung by Olivia Newton-John; 'Look at Me, I'm Sandra Dee' sung by Olivia Newton-John; (*)'Grease' (Barry Gibb) sung by Frankie Valli; 'Sandy' (Louis St Louis and Scott Simon) sung by John Travolta; 'It's Raining on Prom Night' (Jim Jacobs and Warren Grey); 'Blue Suede Shoes'; 'Hound Dog', 'Tears on My Pillow' (hits of the fifties) sung by Sha Na Na.

(*) denotes million seller single release.

Produced by Robert Stigwood.

ORIGINAL FILM SOUNDTRACK

SERGEANT PEPPER'S LONELY HEARTS CLUB BAND (Double album) *RSO [USA]*. Released in the U.S.A. in July 1978, it reached No 5 there for six weeks and stayed in the charts for 21 weeks. R.I.A.A. Gold and Platinum awards on 19 July 1978.

The first album to ship triple Platinum (3,000,000) in the U.S.A. It sold over four million within two weeks in the U.S.A., and sales elsewhere probably make a global total of well over five million. The film, produced by Robert Stigwood and written by Henry Edwards, was an attempt to put a collection of marvellous old Beatles tunes, most of them from the 1967 album 'Sergeant Pepper's Lonely Hearts Club Band', into the cinema. The story is about Sergeant Pepper and his three sidemen, heroic World War 1 bandsmen who return to their town of Heartland and, after many years, bequeath their instruments to the four little boys (portrayed by Peter Frampton, Barry, Robin and Maurice Gibb, the brothers who are the Bee Gees) who would grow up to become the second Sergeant Pepper band. The boys are sent to Hollywood, where they are exploited in the rock world's money splurge whilst forces of evil are in operation back home. Frampton (as Billy Shears) has forgotten all about Strawberry Fields (Sandy Farina) his girl friend. The dark forces in Heartland are subsequently foiled, although Strawberry dies.

Despite the huge album sales the film, on which 12 million dollars had been spent, was not a huge success. Many star names made guest appearances, including Frankie Howerd, Donald Pleasance, Aerosmith, Alice Cooper, Billy Preston, Earth, Wind & Fire, Stargard, Paul Nicholas and George Burns (as the town's mayor - Mr Kite) and Steve Martin. There were 29 Beatles songs in the film (nine from the original album). The film premiere was on 21 July 1978. The album was produced and arranged by George Martin. It includes: 'Oh Darling' (Robin Gibb); 'Long and Winding Road' (Peter Frampton); 'Come Together' (Aerosmith); 'Got to Get You Into My Life' (Earth, Wind & Fire); 'Carry the Weight' 'Maxwell's Silver Hammer' (Steve Martin); 'Because' (Alice Cooper); 'Get Back' (Billy Preston); 'She Came in Through the Bathroom Window' (Peter Frampton and the Bee Gees); 'Being For the Benefit of Mr Kite' (Peter Frampton and the Bee Gees); 'Polythene Pam' (Bee Gees); 'She's Leaving Home' (Bee Gees); 'Sergeant Pepper's Lonely Hearts Club Band' (The Beatles); 'Getting Better' (Peter Frampton); 'With a Little Help From My Friends' (Peter Frampton); 'I Want You', 'Nowhere Man'; 'Day in the Life'; 'When I'm 64'; 'Lucy in the Sky With Diamonds' (all written by John Lennon and Paul McCartney); 'Here Comes the Sun' (George Harrison) sung by Sandy Farina.

ORIGINAL FILM SOUNDTRACK

THANK GOD IT'S FRIDAY (Double album) *Casablanca* [*USA*]. This was released in the U.S.A. in May 1978 and in Britain in July 1978. It was No 14 for one week in the U.S.A., staying in the charts for 21 weeks. In Britain it was No 40 for one week and stayed four weeks in the charts. R.I.A.A. Gold Disc award on 16 May 1978. Platinum award on 8 June 1978.

The film is a contemporary comedy concerning a night in a Hollywood disco. Motown-Casablanca Film Works took over the Millionaires' Club on Los Angeles' famous 'restaurant row' and turned it into the exotic Zoo Disco. In the story of this one frantic and funny night, assorted types meet, compete, share their dreams, pair off, and step into the spotlight for a chance of stardom. All the characters come together in the big dance contest. The film starred Hilary Beane; Andrea Howard; Valerie Landsburg; John Friedrich; Paul Jabara (who composed the Oscar-winning song 'Last Dance'); Mark Lonow; Jeff Goldblum; DeWayne Jessie; Robin Menken; Terri Nunn; Chuck Sacci; Ray Vitte; Marya Small; Debra Winger; and guest stars, The Commodores and Donna Summer.

The album contains: 'Thank God It's Friday' (Love and Kisses); 'After Dark' (Pattie Brooks); 'With Your Love' (Donna Summer); 'Last Dance' (Donna Summer); 'Disco Queen' (Paul Jabara); 'Find My Way' (Cameo); 'Too Hot Ta Trot' (The Commodores); 'Leatherman's Theme' (Wright Bros.' Flying Machine); 'I Wanna Dance' (Marathon); 'Take It To The Zoo' (Sunshine); 'Seville Nights' (Santa Esmeralda); 'You're the Most Precious Thing in My Life' (Love and Kisses); 'Do You Want The Real Thing?' (D.C. LaRue); 'Trapped In A Stairway' (Paul Jabara); 'Floyd's Theme' (Natural Juices); 'Lovin', Livin' And Givin'' (Diana Ross); 'Love Masterpiece' (Thelma Houston); 'Last Dance (Reprise)' (Donna Summer); 'Je T'Aime (Moi Non Plus)' (Donna Summer).

The film provided a showcase for a rich variety of talent, both old and new, with an extensive roster of talent from Motown Records and Casablanca. It was directed by Robert Klane.

ORIGINAL FILM SOUNDTRACK

THE WIZ (album) *MCA* [*USA*]. With music and lyrics by Charlie Smalls, this was released in the U.S.A. in September 1978, going to No 64 for one week and staying 12 weeks in the charts. R.I.A.A. Gold Disc award on 29 September 1978.

Originally a stage show with a completely black cast, this film version of the Wizard of Oz fable starred Diana Ross; Michael Jackson; Nipsey Russell; Ted Ross; Lena Horne; and Richard Pryor (as 'The Wiz'). Based on the play *The Wiz*, and the book by William F. Brown. The film was directed by Sidney Lumet. In Britain, the gala premiere was on 4 April 1979 at the Dominion Theatre, London. It is a funky Harlem version of Dorothy's fantastic trip with the Scarecrow, The Tin Man and the Cowardly Lion, and bears little relation to Judy Garland's film *The Wizard of Oz*. The album contains two outstanding numbers: 'Ease On Down The Road' (sung by Diana Ross and Michael Jackson); and 'You Can't Win' (sung by Michael Jackson). The million sale was reported in early 1979. Music was adapted and supervised by Quincy Jones.

ABBA

ABBA – THE ALBUM (album) *Epic* [*Britain*] *Atlantic* [*USA*]. Written by B. Ulvaeus and B. Andersson, this was released in Britain and the U.S.A. in January 1978. In Britain it climbed to No 1 and stayed there for seven weeks, remaining 40 weeks in the charts. In the U.S.A. it went to No 33 for two weeks and stayed 33 weeks in the charts. R.I.A.A. Gold Disc award on 10 March 1978. Platinum award on 8 August 1978.

This album was an instant No 1 in Britain and sold £1,000,000 worth immediately. It went on to at least 750,000 copies sold by the end of the year. With worldwide sales, the tally is estimated at around 2½ million. It contains: 'Eagle'; 'Take a Chance on Me'; 'One Man, One Woman'; 'Name Of The Game'; 'Move On'; 'Hole in Your Soul'; and 'The Girl With The Golden Hair' (three scenes from a mini-musical), a 14-minute segment taking in three tracks: 'Thank You For The Music'; 'I Wonder'; and 'I'm A Marionette'. It was produced by Benny Andersson and Bjorn Ulvaeus at Marcus Music and Metronome Studio, Sweden. 'Eagle' and 'Hole in Your Soul' are from their movie, a screen record of their Australian tour, complete with ovations. (This was titled 'ABBA – THE MOVIE' and premiered in London on 17 February, 1978).

TAKE A CHANCE ON ME *Epic* [*Britain*] *Atlantic* [*USA*]. Written by B. Ulvaeus and B. Andersson, this was released in Britain in February 1978 and in the U.S.A. in March 1978. It went to No 1 for three weeks in Britain and to No 9 for two weeks in the U.S.A. R.I.A.A. Gold Disc award on 8 August 1978.

The best track from the group's 'Abba – the album'. It sold over 500,000 in Britain, over 1,000,000 in the U.S.A., and with sales elsewhere an estimated tally of over two million.

AEROSMITH

LIVE BOOTLEG (Double album) *Columbia* [*USA*]. This was released in the U.S.A. in October 1978, reaching No 7 for three weeks and staying 16 weeks in the charts. R.I.A.A. Gold Disc

award on 31 October 1978. Platinum award on 26 December 1978.

Aerosmith first earned a reputation for its exciting stage act and this double album indicates why. The tracks were recorded at various locations from 1973 to 1978 and include a new version of 'Come Together' and 'Dream On'.

ATLANTA RHYTHM SECTION

CHAMPAGNE JAM (Album) *Polydor* [*USA*]. Released in the U.S.A. in March 1978, this went to No 11 for two weeks and stayed in the charts for 28 weeks. R.I.A.A. Gold Disc award on 11 April 1978. Platinum award on 26 September 1978.

One of the South's premier rock groups for a long time. It came into its own on a commercial level with 'So Into You'. With this album, the group has a sharper sound and some exceptional rockers. It includes: 'Champagne Jam' and 'Imaginary Lover' (a Top 10 chart single); also – 'Large Time'; 'Normal Love'; 'I'm Not Gonna Let it Bother Me Tonight'; 'The Ballad of Lois Malone'; 'Evileen'; 'The Great Escape'.

THE BEE GEES

NIGHT FEVER *Polydor/RSO* [*USA*]. Written by The Bee Gees, this was released in the U.S.A. in January 1978 and in Britain in April 1978. It was No 1 for eight weeks in the U.S.A. and stayed 22 weeks in the charts. In Britain it went to No 1 for two weeks and stayed in the charts for 20 weeks. R.I.A.A. Gold Disc award on 27 February 1978. Platinum award on 2 May 1978.

Culled from the 'Saturday Night Fever' album, this was the second single from the album to sell over two million in the U.S.A. alone. It also sold over 250,000 in Britain.

TOO MUCH HEAVEN *Polydor/RSO* [*USA*]. Written by The Bee Gees, this was released in the U.S.A. and Britain in November 1978. It went to No 1 for one week in the U.S.A. and to No 3 for one week in Britain, staying 22 weeks in the U.S.A. charts and 12 weeks in the British lists. R.I.A.A. Gold Disc award on 8 November 1978. Platinum award on 9 February 1979.

This was one of the most performed songs during 1979, and is unique among the songs that have been awarded BMI Most Performed honours through the years. The Bee Gees chose it as their gift when the Founder members of UNICEF conceived a scheme to provide a continuing source of financial help to needy children of the world. Through this organization participating composers donate the publishing, performing and recording rights of one of their songs.

GEORGE BENSON
A WEEKEND IN L.A. (Album) *Warner Bros* [*USA*]. This was released in the U.S.A. in January 1978, going to No 9 for one week and staying in the charts for 31 weeks. R.I.A.A. Gold Disc award on 28 February 1978. Platinum award on 3 May 1978.

This album consists of live recordings made at the Roxy Theatre, Los Angeles in late 1977, when Benson enlisted players like Phil Upchurch, Ralph MacDonald and Ronnie Foster to accompany him. It included classics such as 'It's All in the Game', 'On Broadway' and songs like 'The Greatest Love of All'.

BLONDIE
PARALLEL LINES (Album) *Chrysalis* [*USA*]. This was released in the U.S.A. in September 1978 and in Britain in August 1978. In the U.S.A. it went to No 9 for two weeks, staying 49 weeks in the charts. In Britain it hit No 1 for four weeks, staying in the charts for a total of 103 weeks. R.I.A.A. Gold Disc award on 9 April 1979. Platinum award on 6 June 1979.

Blondie is a group, comprising Deborah Harry (vocalist) backed by Chris Stein (guitar/songwriter); Frank Infante (guitar); Jimmy Destri (keyboards); Nigel Harrison (bass); Clem Burke (drums).

Debbie Harry was born in Miami on 3 July 1947 and raised in Hawthorne, New Jersey. When Debbie left home and moved to Manhattan, her first stab at a musical career was a brief and ill-starred effort with a group called Wind in The Willows. Then came a period in New York, with various jobs as beautician, Playboy Bunny and barmaid, whilst keeping up her artistic ability by writing and painting. She found work with a band - The Stilettoes - and Chris Stein joined shortly afterwards. The band folded in the early seventies, and Debbie and Chris founded Blondie. In 1976, Richie Gottehrer, a well-known songwriter, discovered Blondie at CBGBs, a sleazy dive on the Bowery. He brought Larry Uttal, president of a small New York label, Private Stock, to the show. Result - Blondie's first record 'X Offender' which attracted enough interest to follow it with an album 'Blondie'. Blondie hired a new manager, Peter Leeds, and the group made its West Coast debut in February 1977 at Whisky in Los Angeles. Whilst in L.A. they were engaged to join Iggy Pop and David Bowie on their U.S. tour. Gary Valentine, the band's original bass player, left in July 1977 and was replaced by Frank Infante. Blondie then left the small Private Stock label and went over to the Chrysalis label, which produced their album 'Plastic Letters'. Manager Peter Leeds paid 500,000 dollars to buy out Gottehrer and Private Stock and buy the recording rights of the group. Under Leeds' guidance, Blondie toured England in 1977 and then Europe, Australia, Thailand and Japan, establishing them as international artists. The 'Parallel Lines' album took six months inching up the U.S. charts, but after almost a year, finally sold the million. Its success in Britain was phenomenal as well, selling a million there by October 1979, and it stayed two years in the charts.

The album's producer Mike Chapman was responsible for the proficient musical sound, which was an affirmation of the talents of Debbie Harry and her group. The prime cut was 'Heart of Glass' which really started Blondie's breakthrough, and that was from England, where the single reached No 1. The album was top in Britain's final 1979 listing. Other tracks on the album are: 'I'm Gonna Love You Too'; 'Hanging on the Telephone'; 'Fade Away and Radiate'.

HEART OF GLASS *Chrysalis* [*USA*]. Written by Debbie Harry and Chris Stein, this was released in the U.S.A. in November 1978 and in Britain in January 1979. It went to No 1 for one week in the U.S.A. and for four weeks in Britain, staying 23 weeks in the U.S. charts and 12 weeks in the British lists. R.I.A.A. Gold Disc award on 6 April 1979.

The hit track from Blondie's album 'Parallel Lines'. It was first released as a 12-inch disc, and subsequently (January 1979) as a 7-inch single. Blondie's long-established appeal on the international scene was underlined with 'Heart of Glass'. It achieved No 1 status in Britain, France and Germany, with a million copies sold in Britain alone, while high chart positions were registered in Austria, Switzerland, Holland and Belgium. It took another three months before it got to the top in the U.S.A. and helped album sales for the group there. Blondie at last matched their success abroad with a similar acceptance in the U.S.A.

THE BLUES BROTHERS
BRIEFCASE FULL OF BLUES (Album) *Atlantic* [*USA*]. This was released in the U.S.A. in December 1978, reaching No 2 for three weeks and staying 28 weeks in the charts. R.I.A.A. Gold Disc award on 22 December 1978. Platinum award on 5 January 1979.

A long-awaited debut from 'Jake and Elwood' Blues, since their appearance on the U.S. *Saturday Night Live* show earlier in the year, with the assistance of Steve Cropper (guitar); 'Duck' Dunn (bass); and Tom Scott (saxophone). The Blues Brothers are John Belushi and Dan Akroyd.

BONEY M
RIVERS OF BABYLON *Atlantic/Hansa* [*Britain*]. This traditional song arranged by F. Farian and Reyam was released in Britain in April 1978. It went to No 1 for four weeks and stayed in the British charts for 39 weeks.

Boney M's version of this traditional song, based on Psalm 137, was an extraordinary success. WEA Records who control the label sold one million after just four weeks on the market. Germany sold a million and France 500,000. Total tally was well over three million. Marcia Barrett of the group remembered the words from when she was very young, Frank Farian sent six tapes round the clubs in Germany, and the German disc jockeys had no doubts.

NIGHT FLIGHT TO VENUS (Album) *Atlantic/Hansa* [*Britain/Germany*]. Produced by Frank Farian, this was released in Britain in July 1978, reaching No 1 for four weeks and staying 48 weeks in the charts.

Boney M's first million-selling album. It reached that figure in Germany by January 1979. In Britain it had over £1,000,000 sale.

MARY'S BOY CHILD *Atlantic/Hansa* [*Britain/Germany*]. Written by Jester Hairston (1956) and released in Britain in December 1978, this was No 1 for four weeks and stayed in the charts for seven weeks.

Boney M completed a run of 10 sold-out concerts in eight days in Moscow during mid-December to a total audience of 20,000, and thus spearheaded an unprecedented rock revolution in Russia. Whilst this was going on, the Hansa group's seasonal single 'Mary's Boy Child' almost immediately hit the top of Britain's charts, receiving a record 220,000 orders in one day. After only three weeks on the market it reached the million sale, and went on to sell 2,500,000 copies, matching Wings' 'Mull of Kintyre' of

Christmas 1977. Western Europe's music industry hadn't seen anything like it. Germany also sold a million in three weeks, and 17 pressing plants in four countries were trying to catch up with orders. This was undoubtedly WEA's (controllers of the Atlantic label) and Boney M's biggest-ever seller. Although the original Belafonte version in 1957 was in Calypso style, Boney M's version of Jester Hairston's original had some re-arrangement by Farian, their producer, and Jay and Lorin.

BOSTON

DON'T LOOK BACK (Album) *Epic* [*USA*]. With material by Tom Scholtz, this was released in the U.S.A. in August 1978, climbing to No 2 for nine weeks and staying 25 weeks in the charts. R.I.A.A. Gold and Platinum Disc awards on 25 August 1978.

This album took two years in the making, and the group's 'architect', Tom Scholtz, still further enhanced his prestige. It was an instant million seller (it shipped two million), and sold four million in a month, an astounding feat. It contains: 'Don't Look Back'; 'Feelin' Satisfied'; 'A Man I'll Never Be'; 'It's Easy'; 'Party'; 'Used To Bad News'.

ALICIA BRIDGES

I LOVE THE NIGHT LIFE (Disco Round) *Polydor* [*USA*]. Written by Alicia Bridges and Susan Hutcheson, this was released in the U.S.A. in July 1978, going to No 7 for three weeks and staying 30 weeks in the charts. R.I.A.A. Gold Disc award on 18 December 1978.

First big hit for newcomer Alicia Bridges and her song, a tribute to disco popularity.

JIMMY BUFFETT

SON OF A SON OF A SAILOR (Album) *ABC* [*USA*]. With material by Jimmy Buffett, this was released in the U.S.A. in April 1978, going to No 10 for one week and staying in the charts for 19 weeks. R.I.A.A. Gold Disc award on 5 April 1978. Platinum award on 10 May 1978.

Another million seller for Jimmy Buffett and his band. This album is an intriguing blend of song references to the sea, the sails and the ports, and witty yet wry observations and philosophies on life. It includes: 'Son of a Son of a Sailor'; 'Fool Button'; 'Livingstone Saturday Night'; 'Cheeseburger in Paradise'; 'Mañana'.

KATE BUSH

WUTHERING HEIGHTS *EMI* [*Britain*]. Written by Kate Bush, this was released in Britain in February 1978, climbing to No 1 and staying there for four weeks, remaining in the charts for 14 weeks.

Kate Bush was born on 30 July 1958, the daughter of a doctor in Kent, England. It was Dave Gilmour of Pink Floyd who realised her talent and put up the money for proper demos of the songs she had written over a period of three years. The orchestral arrangements for her album 'The Kick Inside' were done by noted musician Andrew Powell, who also produced it. 'Wuthering Heights', taken from the album, was her first single, and had a very English story line which everyone knew because it was a classic book. It was also her strongest song musically, and had a high pitch, which suited her extraordinarily ethereal feline voice. The disc was an immediate success. Sales of the single reached 500,000 in six weeks, and the final global tally was a million.

THE CARS

THE CARS (Album) *Elektra* [*USA*]. Written by The Cars and released in the U.S.A. in June 1978, this went to No 18 for four weeks and stayed a total of 104 weeks in the charts. R.I.A.A. Gold Disc award on 16 October 1978. Platinum award on 27 December 1978.

The Cars consist of Richard Ocasek (singer/guitar/

songwriter); Elliot Easton (guitar); Greg Hakes (multi-instrumental keyboardist); David Robinson (drums); Ben Orr (vocals/bass). The idea for the band came from Ocasek who formed the nucleus of the band with Orr in early 1977 in Boston. Each member had experience with other groups. The Cars developed a following at Boston clubs, and had their first major exposure in large halls supporting Bob Seger and J. Geils. A demo tape of 'Just What I Needed' soon became a top request on two radio stations in Boston. They signed with Elektra/Asylum and that single was a success. 'The Cars' album was recorded in England with Roy Thomas Baker producing. The band toured constantly in the U.S.A., and did a brief tour of Europe (England, France, Holland, Belgium and Germany) which led to international acceptance, through their remarkable music. The album included 'Just What I Needed'; 'Good Times Roll'; 'Bye Bye Love' and 'Best Friend's Girl'. It sold a million in six months and with two years in the charts must have exceeded 1½ million. The album is considered to be the perfect music for an endless summer drive – an uncompromising hard rock attack.

SHAUN CASSIDY

UNDER WRAPS (Album) *Warner/Curb* [*USA*]. This was released in the U.S.A. in July 1978, going to No 23 for one week and staying 13 weeks in the charts. R.I.A.A. Gold Disc award on 2 August 1978. Platinum award on 10 October 1978.

Shaun's third album with excellent songs chosen by him and producer Michael Lloyd (including four of his own). A distinct development in maturity as a song stylist, and a pop sound reminiscent of the Beach Boys.

CHIC

LE FREAK *Atlantic* [*USA*]. Written by Bernard Edwards and Nile Rodgers, this was released in the U.S.A. in October 1978 and in Britain in November 1978. It hit No 1 for seven weeks in the U.S.A. and No 7 for one week in Britain. It stayed 29 weeks in the U.S.A. charts and 15 weeks in the British lists. R.I.A.A. Gold Disc award on 12 November 1978. Platinum award on 7 December 1978.

Chic really started a new disco dance craze with this, and sales were enormous, the final tally being six million. It was Atlantic's first picture record, and the first ever 12-inch picture disco-disc, available as a promotional item only, featuring different designs on each side of the record. The four-colour paper was embedded between two layers of clear vinyl rather than in the five-layer arrangement used in conventional picture records. The single was a 7-inch disc, the 12-inch commercial and promotional black vinyl disco disc also available as well as in the picture record format. 'Le Freak' was taken from Chic's second album 'C'est Chic' released shortly after.

C'EST CHIC (Album) *Atlantic* [*USA*]. Written by Bernard Edwards and Nile Rodgers, this was released in the U.S.A. in November 1978 and in Britain in January 1979. In the U.S.A. it was No 7 for four weeks, staying in the charts for 27 weeks. In Britain it went to No 2 for one week, staying in the charts for 23 weeks. R.I.A.A. Gold Disc award on 28 November 1978. Platinum award on 27 December 1978.

A stunning album by Chic, with the type of chanting and uptempo dance music that saw the group cross into the pop market. It sold two million by the year's end and went on to 4½ million in the U.S.A. alone by April 1979. British sales were over 100,000. It contained the dance craze item 'Le Freak'; 'Savoir Faire'; 'Chic Cheer'; 'Happy Man'; 'I Want Your Love'; 'At Last I'm Free'; 'Sometimes You Win'; '(Funny) Bone'.

CHICAGO

HOT STREETS (Album) *Columbia* [*USA*]. With material written by Chicago, this was released in the U.S.A. in October 1978, going to No 10 for two weeks and staying 23 weeks in the charts. R.I.A.A. Gold Disc award on 16 October 1978. Platinum award on 27 October 1978.

Another almost instant million seller for Chicago. The group had a new member - guitarist Donnie Dacus - and a new producer, Phil Ramone. The album includes: 'Alive Again'; 'No Tell Lover'; 'Gone Long Gone'; 'Show Me the Way'; 'Little Miss Lovin''.

ERIC CLAPTON

BACKLESS (Album) *RSO* [*USA*]. With material by Eric Clapton, Bob Dylan and J.J. Cale, this was released in the U.S.A. in November 1978 and in Britain in December 1978. In the U.S.A. it went to No 11 for two weeks and stayed 21 weeks in the charts. In Britain it was No 18 for one week and stayed 11 weeks in the charts. R.I.A.A. Gold and Platinum Disc awards on 14 November 1978.

Clapton's successful follow-up to his 'Slowhand' album, with pungent rhythmic guitar to material by himself and others. The album was shipped platinum, an instant million seller. Contents are: 'Promises'; 'Watch Out For Lucy'; 'Tulsa Time'; 'Roll It'; 'Tell Me That You Love Me'; 'If I Don't Be There By Morning'; 'Early in the Morning'; 'Walk Out In The Rain'; 'Golden Ring'; 'I'll Make Love To You Anytime'.

CLOUT

SUBSTITUTE *Carrere EMI* [*Britain*]. Written by Wilson, this was released in Britain in June 1978 and in the U.S.A. in September 1978. It went to No 2 for two weeks in Britain and stayed 15 weeks in the charts. In the U.S.A. it was No 61 for one week and stayed ten weeks in the charts.

Clout are a female vocal/instrumental South African group. This disc was a great favourite all over Europe. Apart from its success in Britain (over 600,000 sales) it was in the Top 5 for four months in France (400,000 sale); No 2 in Holland (100,000); No 1 in Belgium (60,000); and No 1 for seven weeks in South Africa.

IZHAR COHEN & THE ALPHABETA SINGERS

A-BI-NI-BI (A love song in the B. language) *Polydor* [*France and Britain*]. Written by Kirsch and Ehud Manaur, this disc was No 20 in Britain with seven weeks in the charts.

This was the winner of the Eurovision Song Contest held on 22 April 1978 at the Palais des Congrès, Paris - Israel's first success in this annual event. It was sung by Izhar Cohen and the quintet Alphabeta Singers. Composer Manaur is one of Israel's most successful pop music figures who appeared regularly on radio and TV there. Over the subsequent three years the disc was widely popular with the Jewish community in Europe and was reported to have sold three million by 1981.

THE COMMODORES

NATURAL HIGH (Album) *Motown* [*USA*]. This was released in the U.S.A. in May 1978 and in Britain in June 1978. It went to No 2 for two weeks in the U.S.A. and stayed 29 weeks in the

charts. In Britain it went to No 8 for two weeks, staying 23 weeks in the charts. R.I.A.A. Gold and Platinum Disc awards on 22 August 1978.

This classy collection of smooth love songs was in the U.S. Top 10 for 19 weeks. Of the eight new tunes, the most outstanding were: 'Fire Girl'; 'Three Times a Lady' and 'I Like What You Do'. It sold over two million.

NEIL DIAMOND

YOU DON'T BRING ME FLOWERS (Album) *Columbia* [*USA*]. Written by Neil Diamond, A. and M. Bergman; etc., it was released in the U.S.A. and Britain in December 1978. It went to No 8 for two weeks in the U.S.A. and to No 15 for one week in Britain, staying 24 weeks in the U.S.A. charts and 23 weeks in the British lists. R.I.A.A. Gold and Platinum Disc awards on 7 December 1978.

Instant million seller album for Neil. This included: 'You Don't Bring Me Flowers' (duet version) and 'You've Got Your Troubles'.

DIRE STRAITS

DIRE STRAITS (Album) *Vertigo* [*Britain*], *Warner Bros* [*USA*]. With material written by Mark Knopfler, this was released in Britain in mid-1978 and in the U.S.A. in October 1978. In Britain it went to No 5 for one week and stayed 32 weeks in the charts. In the U.S.A. it went to No 3 for two weeks, staying 28 weeks in the charts. R.I.A.A. Gold Disc award on 21 February 1979. Platinum award on 27 March 1979.

Dire Straits are: Mark Knopfler (songwriter/guitar); his brother David Knopfler (vocals/guitar); John Illsley (vocals/bass guitar); Pick Withers (drums). David, Mark and John got together in a small flat in Deptford, London and practised on their guitars. John was working on a degree in sociology at the University of London, David was a social worker and Mark an English teacher at Loughton College in Essex at the time. In 1977, Mark brought along some original songs for the trio to try out. In July 1977 they recorded a tape with Withers, a session player, and came out of the studio with five songs, including 'Sultans of Swing', a ballad about a forgotten Dixieland band. They left the tape at the doorstep of Charlie Gillett, host of a radio show 'Honky Tonkin'', hoping Gillett could give them some advice. Gillett put the tape in his programme, and three record companies phoned expressing interest in the group. Listener response was unprecedented. In December 1977 they were signed to a recording contract with Phonogram Records (owners of the Vertigo label) and in January 1978 opened for Talking Heads on their European tour. A month later, 'Dire Straits' was recorded, the album finished in 12 days - costing only £12,000. It received immediate airplay in Europe, but took longer to make the U.S. charts. When it did, in 1979, it was found that acceptance there was almost unanimous. The album sold four million. Their music is good, honest, unpretentious rock, and threw into focus the increasing trend of rock stars to have brains as well as sex appeal. The album included 'Sultans of Swing' and 'In the Gallery' - the two outstanding tracks.

DOCTOR HOOK

SHARING THE NIGHT TOGETHER *Capitol* [*USA*]. Written by Ava Alderidge and Edward Struzick, this was released in the U.S.A. in September 1978, going to No 4 for two weeks and remaining in the charts for 23 weeks. R.I.A.A. Gold Disc award on 26 December 1978.

The best track from Dr Hook's album 'Pleasure and Pain', written by Ava Alderidge and Edward Struzick.

DOOBIE BROTHERS

MINUTE BY MINUTE (Album) *Warner Bros* [*USA*]. Released in the U.S.A. in December 1978, this was No 1 there for one week and stayed 47 weeks in the charts. R.I.A.A. Gold Disc

award on 27 December 1978. Platinum award on 6 March 1979.

A fine album of the group's return to its rock roots, highlighted by the vocals of Michael McDonald and Nicolette Larson on 'Sweet Feelin''. U.S. sales were over three million.

EARTH, WIND & FIRE

GOT TO GET YOU INTO MY LIFE *Arc/Columbia* [*USA*]. Written by John Lennon and Paul McCartney (1966), this was released in the U.S.A. in July 1978 and in Britain in September 1978. In the U.S.A. it was No 11 for one week and stayed 11 weeks in the charts. In Britain it was No 33 for one week, staying seven weeks in the charts. R.I.A.A. Gold Disc award on 14 September 1978.

The group's version of the Beatles oldie as sung in the film *Sergeant Pepper's Lonely Hearts Club Band*, in which they appeared as guest artists. This was issued on a 12-inch disco disc in the U.S.A.

SEPTEMBER *Arc/Columbia* [*USA*]. Written by M. White, Al McKay and Willis, this was released in the U.S.A. in November

1978 and in Britain in December 1978. It went to No 4 for two weeks in the U.S.A. and to No 3 for one week in Britain, staying 22 weeks in the U.S.A. charts and 12 weeks in the British charts. R.I.A.A. Gold Disc award on 23 January 1979.

A new song by members of the group included in their album 'The Best of Earth, Wind & Fire, Vol 1.'

THE BEST OF EARTH, WIND & FIRE, Vol 1 (Album) *Arc/Columbia* [*USA*]. This was released in the U.S.A. in November 1978 and in Britain in December 1978. In the U.S.A. it went to No 5 for two weeks, staying 25 weeks in the charts. In Britain it went to No 6 for one week and stayed in the charts for 40 weeks. R.I.A.A. Gold and Platinum Disc awards on 7 December 1978.

Instant million-selling album for one of the most successful crossover stories in popular music. Contents: 'That's The Way of the World'; 'Shining Star'; 'Reasons'; 'Singasong'; 'Getaway'; 'Can't Hide Love'; 'Fantasy'; 'September'; 'Love Music'; 'Got To Get You Into My Life'. This album sold over 100,000 in Britain.

WALTER EGAN

MAGNET AND STEEL *Columbia* [*USA*]. This was released in the U.S.A. in May 1978, going to No 13 for two weeks and lasting 19 weeks in the charts. R.I.A.A. Gold Disc award on 9 November 1978.

A million-seller for Walter Egan, and another new potential star for the ever-expanding Columbia (CBS) empire.

YVONNE ELLIMAN

IF I CAN'T HAVE YOU *Polydor/RSO* [*USA*]. Written by the Gibb brothers (The Bee Gees), this was released in the U.S.A. in January 1978 and in Britain in April 1978. It went to No 2 for two weeks in the U.S.A. and to No 4 for two weeks in Britain, staying 18 weeks in the U.S. charts and 12 weeks in the British charts. R.I.A.A. Gold Disc award on 2 May 1978.

This song was featured in one of the *Saturday Night Fever* film disco sequences, sung by Yvonne. Yvonne Elliman started her professional singing career in London. She came over from Hawaii in 1969 when she was 17, and was promised stardom. That didn't happen as expected, and she actually used to busk in Piccadilly to help pay her way. Singing at The Pheasantry, a well-known club in the Kings Road, Chelsea, she was overheard by Andrew Lloyd Webber and Tim Rice. They asked if she would be interested in singing a couple of songs on a record they were making of a new rock musical called *Jesus Christ Superstar*. She went to Webber's home and they played 'I Don't Know How To Love Him'. The recording in a studio was made in a couple of takes, but Yvonne didn't think it was very good (she had been into acid rock at that time). A percentage of the profits was offered - half of one per cent, or a flat fee of £100. She chose the latter. The album of course sold several millions. Yvonne was offered the part of Mary Magdalene in the stage production, which she did for six months, and accepted the same role in the film version. She was involved in the record, stage, film and travelling road shows of the musical. She also worked with Eric Clapton, both on record and live appearances for three years, provided the female chorus for his 'I Shot the Sheriff' hit, and made several solo albums for RSO including 'Rising Sun' and 'Love Me'. In 1976 she won the Don Kirschner Rock Award as Best Female Vocalist in the U.S.A., and was nominated by *Billboard* in 1977 as top vocalist in the Easy Listening category. Her third RSO album 'Night Flight' was released and contained her hit 'If I Can't Have You'. Yvonne now lives in Los Angeles, and is a member of the close-knit Robert Stigwood Organisation (RSO).

EXILE

KISS YOU ALL OVER *Warner/Curb* [*USA*], *RAK* [*Britain*]. Written by Nicky Chinn and Mike Chapman, this was released in the U.S.A. in July 1978 and in Britain in August 1978. It was No 1 for three weeks in the U.S.A. and stayed 24 weeks in the charts. It went to No 6 for one week in Britain and stayed in the charts for 12 weeks. R.I.A.A. Gold Disc award on 4 October 1978.

The first million seller for this new U.S. male vocal and instrumental group, with a song written by two of Britain's most successful pop composers.

FATHER ABRAHAM

SMURF SONG *Dureco [Holland]*, *Decca [Britain]*, *Philips/Phonogram [Germany]*. Written by Linlec and Pierre Kartner, this was released in Britain in May 1978, going to No 2 for six weeks and staying 17 weeks in the charts.

The Smurfs are comic strip characters created by Pierre Payo Culliford and their prototype started around 1958 as Schtroumpff. Pierre, a Belgian artist, used the pseudonym Payo. It quickly spread in strip form to France, became Schlumpfe in Germany, Puffi in Italy, Pitusos in Spain and eventually got translated to Smurf in Holland. The word in any language means 'thingummybob' or 'what's-his-name'. The Smurfs had their own song written for them by Dutch composer Pierre Kartner, a successful performer working under the stage name of Father Abraham. He recorded the song in Holland, and it became No 1 there for seven weeks, selling 500,000 copies within two weeks. An album with the song included sold 250,000. Father Abraham recorded a German version – 'Das Lied Der Schlumpfe', another chart topper and certified platinum award for a million sales. Versions of the song were recorded and released in French, Swedish, Spanish, Portuguese and Japananese. Decca acquired it for U.K. release from Decca's Dutch company Dureco. In May 1978 BP petrol bought the sole U.K. rights to Smurfs and launched a million-pound advertising campaign on TV. This was largely responsible for its success in Britain where it sold over 250,000. (BP had used Smurfs as a forecourt promotion at garages in Holland in 1971.) The little gnome-like creatures attracted millions of British children, with many different Smurf characters, dolls and a hardback book for the children's market in the U.K. being on sale. A million pounds' worth (£1,000,000) of Smurf characters and accessories were sold within three months.

FIREFALL

ELAN (Album) *Atlantic [USA]*. With songs by Rick Roberts, Larry Burnett, Jock Bartley and Mark Andes, this was released in the U.S.A. in October 1978, going to No 20 for one week and staying 15 weeks in the charts. R.I.A.A. Gold Disc award on 17 October 1978. Platinum award on 10 January 1979.

Firefall comprises: Rick Roberts (vocals/guitar); Jock Bartley (guitar); Mark Andes (bass); Larry Burnett (vocals/songwriter/guitar); Michael Clarke (drums); David Muse (keyboards/wind instruments). Roberts started playing with Bartley in Boulder, Colorado, in 1974, the other members following in due course. In October 1975 the group began rehearsals for their first LP in Miami, and the 'Firefall' album (1976) steadily climbed the national charts, with the R.I.A.A. Gold Disc award in November 1976. The second album 'Luna Sea' (1977) also hit gold. By 1978 they had acquired newfound maturity and strength, and touring was again scheduled in between recording. 'Elan' is their best album so far. They are a rock band with masterful vocals, tight playing, various elements of jazz, folk, pop, R & B, country – a characteristic blend of sound patterns and moods. The album included two outstanding tracks: 'Strange Way' and a soaring rocker 'Get You Back'.

ROBERTA FLACK & DONNY HATHAWAY

THE CLOSER I GET TO YOU *Atlantic [USA]*. Written by Reggie Lucas and James Mtume, this was released in the U.S.A. in February 1978, reaching No 3 for three weeks and staying 21 weeks in the charts. R.I.A.A. Gold Disc award on 1 May 1978.

The second million seller for this duo, fifth for Roberta Flack.

DAN FOGELBERG & TIM WEISBERG

TWIN SONS OF DIFFERENT MOTHERS (Album) *Full Moon/CBS [USA]*. Released in the U.S.A. in September 1978, this went to No 7 for two weeks and stayed in the charts for 26 weeks. R.I.A.A. Gold Disc award on 29 September 1978. Platinum award on 12 December 1978.

This album features a complementary pairing of two musicians branching out in new directions, Dan's collaboration with flautist Weisberg making it a predominantly instrumental album. Emotional and personal songs had dominated Dan's first four albums, on which Tim had played. Fogelberg was always keen to establish himself as an instrumental composer and as a guitar player, and this album gave them both a lot of room to stretch out as musicians, which they had not been able to do on previous records. The experiment was a big success. The music ranges from classical-type compositions such as 'Guitar Etude No 3' to Judy Collins' 'Since You Asked' and The Hollies' 'Tell Me To My Face'. Other tracks were 'The Power Of Gold' and 'Intimidation'.

FOREIGNER

DOUBLE VISION (Album) *Atlantic [USA]*. With material by Foreigner (mainly Mick Jones), this was released in the U.S.A. in June 1978, going to No 3 for eight weeks and staying 42 weeks in the charts. R.I.A.A. Gold Disc award on 20 June 1978. Platinum award on 22 June 1978.

Advance orders for this album were 1,300,000 – the highest advance orders of any album in the history of Atlantic Records. Foreigner's meteoric rise, which started in March 1977, with the release of their first album (four million sold) continued with 'Double Vision' which sold four million by the end of 1978. It was in the U.S. Top 10 for an incredible 30 weeks of its run, and spawned two million-selling singles. It includes: 'Double Vision'; 'Hot-Blooded'; 'Spellbinder'; 'Blue Morning, Blue Day'; 'Back Where You Belong'; 'Love Has Taken Its Toll'; 'Tramontane'; 'You're All I Am'.

DOUBLE VISION *Atlantic [USA]*. Released in the U.S.A. in July 1978, this went to No 8 for two weeks and stayed 15 weeks in the charts. R.I.A.A. Gold Disc award on 13 November 1978.

Title track from the group's album 'Double Vision', this sold a million later in the year.

HOT BLOODED *Atlantic [USA]*. Written by Lou Gramm and Mick Jones, this was released in the U.S.A. in June 1978 and in Britain in October 1978. It was No 4 for two weeks in the U.S.A. and stayed 18 weeks in the charts. In Britain it was No 42 for one week and lasted three weeks in the charts. R.I.A.A. Gold Disc award on 30 September 1978.

Second million seller from Foreigner's 'Double Vision' album.

FUNKADELIC

ONE NATION UNDER A GROOVE (Album) *Warner Bros [USA]*. With material by Funkadelic, this was released in the U.S.A. in September 1978, going to No 9 for three weeks and staying 17 weeks in the charts. R.I.A.A. Gold Disc award on 4 October 1978. Platinum award on 19 December 1978.

Funkadelic had been around a long time before getting the big breakthrough with this, their first million-selling album. They had made nine albums from 1970, but none as big as this.

ONE NATION UNDER A GROOVE *Warner Bros [USA]*. This was released in the U.S.A. in August 1978, reaching No 7 for three weeks and staying in the charts for 17 weeks. R.I.A.A. Gold Disc award on 21 November 1978.

Funkadelic's single released from their album of the same title.

CRYSTAL GAYLE

WHEN I DREAM (Album) *Liberty/United Artists [USA]*. This was No 15 for two weeks and stayed 102 weeks in the U.S. country charts. R.I.A.A. Gold Disc award on 15 September

1978. Platinum award on 11 May 1982.

Crystal's second album to achieve the million sale. Crystal's acceptance as a country artist with pop audiences can be seen as a breaking down of the barriers as the music became more widespread. This is clearly demonstrated in this album which mixes country songs like 'Wayward Wind' and 'Somebody Soon' with 'Cry Me a River' and 'Heart Mender', carrying far greater pop appeal, due to artists like Waylon Jennings; Willie Nelson; Emmylou Harris; and Olivia Newton-John. They made audiences aware of country music.

GLORIA GAYNOR

I WILL SURVIVE *Polydor* [*USA*]. Written by Dino Fekaris and Freddie Perren, this was released in the U.S.A. in December 1978 and in Britain in January 1979. It was No 1 for one week in the U.S.A. and for four weeks in Britain. It stayed 24 weeks in the U.S. charts and 15 weeks in the British charts. R.I.A.A. Gold Disc award on 12 February 1979. Platinum award on 16 April 1979.

Gloria Gaynor hails from Newark, New Jersey. In 1974, her recording of 'Never Can Say Goodbye' became a great favourite with the discos, and established her as one of disco's pioneers. In 1975, she was crowned Queen of the Discos by the National Association of Discotheque Disc Jockeys. Then came several failed singles, an accident when she fell from a disco stage, and

six months in hospital with a seriously damaged spine. In August 1978 Gloria visited Fred Perren, a former staff producer/writer at Motown, with the idea of a cover version of the world-wide hit 'Substitute'. Perren suggested Fekaris as a possible producer. Polydor had been in touch with Perren to produce Gloria Gaynor. Perren and Fekaris wrote 'I Will Survive' as the 'B' side for 'Substitute', but it was the former title, a song backed by a thick, pulsating disco beat, sung with rare passion and aggression, that proved to be the hit. The song actually refers not only to Gloria's injury but many other setbacks. She said, 'I am a survivor. I've come through a lot of problems, emotional and economic, as well as the injury.' The disc was a massive hit in the U.S.A., with over two million sales, 250,000 or more in Britain, and big sales around the world, where it was a 'must' in every disco. It stayed 13 weeks in the U.S.A. Top 10. A triumph for the writer/producers and particularly for Gloria, who got her big break into the entertainment world when she was working as a beautician, and a neighbour who owned a disco heard her singing along to King Cole and Ella Fitzgerald records. Composers Fekaris and Perren received the first Grammy Award for Best Disco Recording, 1979.

ANDY GIBB

SHADOW DANCING (Album) *RSO* [*USA*]. With songs by Barry, Robin, Maurice and Andy Gibb and Blue Weaver, this

was released in the U.S.A. in May 1978 and in Britain in August 1978. In the U.S.A. it went to No 2 for two weeks and stayed 43 weeks in the charts. It went to No 15 for one week in Britain, staying nine weeks in the charts. R.I.A.A. Gold Disc award on 30 May 1978. Platinum award on 17 June 1978.

The youngest member of the Gibb family wrote most of the songs for this album himself with occasional assistance from his three brothers and Blue Weaver. It spawned three million-selling singles: 'Shadow Dancing'; 'An Everlasting Love'; 'Our Love (Don't Throw It All Away)'.

SHADOW DANCING *RSO* [*USA*]. Written by Robin, Maurice, Barry and Andy Gibb, this was released in the U.S.A. in April 1978 and in Britain in May 1978. In the U.S.A. it climbed to No 1, staying there eight weeks, and stayed 21 weeks in the charts. In Britain it was No 42 for one week and stayed six weeks in the charts. R.I.A.A. Gold Disc award on 19 May 1978. Platinum award on 12 July 1978.

From Andy Gibb's album of the same title, this was a monster seller – over two million in the U.S.A.

AN EVERLASTING LOVE *RSO* [*USA*]. Written by Barry Gibb, this was released in the U.S.A. in July 1978 and in Britain in August 1978. In the U.S.A. it went to No 9 for one week and stayed 14 weeks in the charts. In Britain it went to No 10 for one week, staying in the charts for ten weeks. R.I.A.A. Gold Disc award on 15 August 1978.

Second big hit from Andy's album.

OUR LOVE (DON'T THROW IT ALL AWAY) *RSO* [*USA*]. Written by Barry Gibb and Blue Weaver, this was released in the U.S.A. in October 1978 and in Britain in January 1979. In the U.S.A. it was No 9 for five weeks, staying 19 weeks in the charts. It was No 32 for one week in Britain and stayed seven weeks in the charts. R.I.A.A. Gold Disc award on 3 January 1979.

Third big hit from Andy's album, making it a memorable year.

NICK GILDER

HOT CHILD IN THE CITY *Chrysalis* [*USA*]. Written by James McCulloch and Nick Gilder, this was released in the U.S.A. in June 1978, going to No 1 for four weeks and staying in the charts for 30 weeks. R.I.A.A. Gold Disc award on 29 September 1978. Platinum award on 4 January 1979.

Nick Gilder was born in London, and went to Vancouver in 1971 where he was a student at a technical college – not a singer. By sheer chance, he got mixed up with a group called Sweeney Todd who soon got a recording contract. The guitarist James McCulloch and Nick became co-writers for the group's material. The first record company who signed them folded, but they soon found another. In 1976 their number 'Roxy Roller' turned the group of strictly local stars into one of Canada's hottest properties. The song was an immediate success and held the No 1 position on the Canadian charts for three weeks. Nick and James then had offers to go solo, so they signed with Chrysalis Records, whilst the rest of Sweeney Todd were enjoying their fame through a Juno Award (the Canadian Grammy) for 'Roxy'. Subsequently, Nick got together with Mike Chapman of the Chinn-Chapman team who had been a major factor in turning Sweet and Suzi Quatro into worldwide stars. Early in 1978 Gilder, Chapman and engineer Peter Coleman went into the studio and cut three singles, one of which was 'Hot Child'. This sold over two million in the U.S.A. Gilder's stage tour quartet back-up are: James McCulloch (guitar); Eric Nelson (bass); Craig Krampf (drums); Jamie Herndon (keyboards/guitar).

DAN HARTMAN

INSTANT REPLAY *CBS/Blue Star* [*USA*]. Written by Dan Hartman, this was released in the U.S.A. and Britain in October 1978. It was No 29 for two weeks in the U.S.A. and No 8 for

three weeks in Britain, staying 17 weeks in the U.S.A. charts and 11 weeks in the British lists. R.I.A.A. Gold Disc award on 23 January 1979.

First million seller for Dan Hartman, another of CBS's new artists. This single also sold 250,000 in Britain, and is taken from his album of the same title. Hartman was bass player, singer and writer for Edgar Winter.

HEART

MAGAZINE (Album) *Mushroom* [*USA*]. With material by Ann and Nancy Wilson, this was released in the U.S.A. in April 1978, going to No 14 for two weeks and staying 20 weeks in the charts. R.I.A.A. Gold and Platinum Disc awards on 2 June 1978.

Third million seller in a row for Heart, fronted by the talented Wilson Sisters.

DOG AND BUTTERFLY (Album) *Portrait* [*USA*]. With material by Ann and Nancy Wilson, this was released in the U.S.A. in September 1978, going to No 11 for one week and staying in the charts for 27 weeks. R.I.A.A. Gold Disc award on 27 September 1978. Platinum award on 27 October 1978.

Fourth consecutive million-selling album for Heart. It is tastefully divided between rock (dog side) and lighter numbers (butterfly side), again showcasing the vocals of Ann and Nancy Wilson. Highlights: 'Mistral Wind'; 'Straight On'; 'High Time'; 'Cook With Fire'; 'Dog and Butterfly'; and 'Nada One'.

HEATWAVE

CENTRAL HEATING (Album) *Epic* [*USA*] *GTO* [*Britain*]. With material written by Rod Temperton, etc., this was released in the U.S.A. and Britain in April 1978. It went to No 12 for one week in the U.S.A., staying 20 weeks in the charts. In Britain it was No 26 for two weeks and stayed 15 weeks in the charts. R.I.A.A. Gold Disc award on 10 April 1978. Platinum award on 21 June 1978.

Heatwave's successful follow-up to their debut album of 1976. Another Barry Blue production, a collection of syncopated dance numbers with catchy arrangements. It included 'Leavin' For a Dream'; 'Party Poops'; 'Central Heating'; 'The Groove Line';

'Mind Blowing Decisions'; 'Put the Word Out'; 'Send out For Sunshine'.

THE GROOVE LINE *GTO* [*Britain*] *Epic* [*USA*]. Written by Rod Temperton, this was released in Britain in January 1978 and in the U.S.A. in April 1978. It went to No 7 for three weeks in the U.S.A. and stayed in the charts for 16 weeks. In Britain it was No 12 for one week, staying eight weeks in the charts. R.I.A.A. Gold Disc award on 17 July 1978.

A big hit in the U.S.A., simultaneously with their 'Central Heating' album in which it was included. It was first released as a single in Britain.

HOT CHOCOLATE

EVERY 1's A WINNER *Infinity* [*USA*] *RAK* [*Britain*]. Written by E. Brown, this was released in Britain in February 1978 and in the U.S.A. in November 1978. In Britain it went to No 12 for one week and stayed in the charts for 11 weeks. It went to No 7 for two weeks in the U.S.A., staying 17 weeks in the charts. R.I.A.A. Gold Disc award on 2 February 1979.

Produced by Mickie Most in Britain, and written by the group's leader Errol Brown. In 1978, Hot Chocolate signed with a brand new U.S. label, Infinity, and 'Every 1's a Winner' was

its first release. The members of Hot Chocolate are: Errol Brown (lead singer/songwriter); Patrick Olive (vocal/congas/bass guitar); Larry Ferguson; Tony Connor (drums/guitar); Harvey Hinsley (lead guitar); Tony Wilson (songwriter). (See also Hot Chocolate, 1975.)

ISLEY BROTHERS

SHOWDOWN (Album) *T-Neck* [*USA*]. Written by the Isley Brothers, this was released in the U.S.A. in April 1978 and in Britain in May 1978. In the U.S.A. it reached No 3 for three weeks and stayed in the charts for 20 weeks. R.I.A.A. Gold Disc award on 10 April 1978. Platinum award on 3 May 1978.

After 20 years of producing the best of almost every type of black music, the group's polished soulful style is better than ever on this album. It included: 'Showdown'; 'Take Me To The Next Phase' (Pts 1 & 2); 'Groove With You'; 'Love Fever'; 'Rockin' With Fire'; 'Fun and Games'; 'Ain't Giving Up No Love'; 'Coolin' Me Out'.

THE JACKSONS
DESTINY (Album) *Epic* [*USA*]. With material by The Jacksons and released in the U.S.A. in November 1978, this went to No 16 for two weeks and stayed 28 weeks in the charts. R.I.A.A. Gold Disc award on 13 March 1979. Platinum award on 8 May 1979.

This is the first album completely written and produced by The Jacksons themselves. The Jacksons by this date were The Jackson Five minus Jermaine Jackson, with other relatives who were not old enough to perform in the original group.

JEAN MICHEL JARRE
EQUINOXE (Album) *Polydor* [*France*]. With compositions by Jean Michel Jarre, this was released in France in December 1978 and in Britain in the same month. In Britain it went to No 11 for three weeks and lasted 25 weeks in the charts.

The follow-up to 'Oxygene', another impressive pastiche of electronics and synthesizers, similar to his first album in that it went to the top in many countries around the world, but like its predecessor did not succeed in the U.S.A. The two albums were reported to have sold 10 million collectively by August 1979. They made Jarre a millionaire. In July 1979, Jarre achieved his

desire of giving a mass concert in Paris. The French capital came to a halt during Bastille Day celebrations when crowds gathered in the Place de la Concorde to listen to Jarre. One million people attended. Giant light shows were projected on the surrounding buildings as Jarre crouched over his bank of synthesizers. The finale was a dazzling fireworks display. The £250,000 celebration was the idea of Parisian Mayor Jacques Chirac. (See also data on 'Oxygene' 1977.) Over 100,000 copies of 'Equinoxe' were sold in Britain, the remainder of the huge sales spread around other countries – possibly three to four million. Jarre also gave four spectacular concerts in Shanghai and Peking in October 1981, the first Western pop musician to do so in China.

JEFFERSON STARSHIP
EARTH (Album) *Grunt/RCA* [*USA*]. With material by Martin Balin, Jesse Barish, Grace Slick, group members and others, this was released in the U.S.A. in February 1978 and in Britain in March 1978. In the U.S.A. it was No 8 for three weeks, staying

in the charts for 27 weeks. R.I.A.A. Gold Disc award on 28 February 1978. Platinum award on 4 May 1978.

This album is considered to be a landmark in the group's career. It contains very high-quality material, provided by various group members and others. It includes: 'Count On Me'; 'Show Yourself'; 'All Nite Long'; 'Skateboard'; 'Fire'; 'Crazy Feelin''; 'Runaway'; 'We Can Be Together'; 'Ride the Tiger'; 'Take Your Time'; 'Love Too Good'.

WAYLON JENNINGS & WILLIE NELSON
WAYLON AND WILLIE (Album) *RCA* [*USA*]. This was released in the U.S.A. in January 1978 and in Britain in April 1978. It went to No 23 for three weeks in the U.S.A. and stayed in the charts for 22 weeks. R.I.A.A. Gold Disc award on 3 February 1978. Platinum award on 11 April 1978.

A wonderful country album including duets by two country music legends. Another massive crossover record for Waylon Jennings from the country charts to the national charts. (It stayed in the country charts for over three years.) It contains: 'Mamas, Don't Let Your Babies Grow Up To Be Cowboys' (a hit as a single, and Grammy Award for Best Group Vocal in the Country field, 1978); 'I Can Get Off On You'; 'Don't Cuss the Fiddle'; 'The Year 2003 Minus 25'; 'Lookin' For a Feelin''; 'Gold Dust Woman'; 'Wurlitzer Prize'; 'It's Not Supposed To Be That Way'; 'If You Can Touch Her At All'; 'A Couple More Years'; 'Good Hearted Woman'.

BILLY JOEL
52ND STREET (Album) *Columbia* [*USA*]. Written by Billy Joel, this was released in the U.S.A. in October 1978 and in Britain the following month. It hit No 1 for eight weeks in the U.S.A., staying in the charts for 45 weeks. In Britain it went to No 10 for one week, staying 40 weeks in the charts. R.I.A.A. Gold and Platinum Disc awards on 23 October 1978.

This album contains some of the most compelling material Billy has ever written. It was an instant million seller, and sold two million in its first month on the market. The album contained his very powerful 'My Life', an outstanding song which became a big hit as a single release.

MY LIFE *Columbia* [*USA*]. Written by Billy Joel and released in the U.S.A. and Britain in November 1978, this went to No 3 for two weeks in the U.S.A. and to No 12 for two weeks in Britain. It lasted 20 weeks in the U.S.A. charts and 13 weeks in the British charts. R.I.A.A. Gold Disc award on 16 January 1979.

The prime track from Billy's album '52nd Street', and a very popular song with other recording stars.

ELTON JOHN
A SINGLE MAN (Album) *MCA* [*USA*], *Rocket* [*Britain*]. With songs by Bernie Taupin and Elton John, this was released in the U.S.A. and Britain in October 1978. In the U.S.A. it was No 16 for one week and stayed 13 weeks in the charts. In Britain it went to No 10 for three weeks, staying 25 weeks in the charts. R.I.A.A. Gold Disc award on 24 October 1978. Platinum award on 15 November 1978.

Elton John's most musical effort in many years, with exploration in several directions, including a beautiful piano instrumental, 'Song for Guy', an exemplary vocal on 'It Ain't Gonna Be Easy' and a pop classic – 'Part-Time Love'. Remainder of songs on the album are: 'Shine On Through'; 'Return To Paradise'; 'I Don't Care'; 'Big Dipper'; 'Georgia'; 'Shooting Star'; 'Madness'; 'Reverie'. Apart from the million U.S.A. sale, it sold 250,000 in Britain.

BROTHERS JOHNSON
BLAM (Album) *A & M* [*USA*]. Written by Brothers Johnson, this was released in the U.S.A. in July 1978, going to No 12 for two weeks and staying 16 weeks in the charts. R.I.A.A. Gold

Disc award on 1 August 1978. Platinum award on 19 September 1978.

Produced by the arranger and discoverer of the Brothers – Quincy Jones. An album of ballad and steamy disco-style material played by the guitar/bass duo. It included 'It's You Girl' and 'Ain't We Funkin' Now'.

QUINCY JONES

SOUNDS—AND STUFF LIKE THAT (Album) *A & M* [*USA*]. Released in the U.S.A. in June 1978, this was No 16 for one week and remained in the charts for 18 weeks. R.I.A.A. Gold Disc award on 21 June 1978. Platinum award on 10 November 1978.

An album demonstrating the talents as producer, arranger and songwriter of Quincy Jones. It includes artists like Herbie Hancock, Chaka Khan, Ralph MacDonald, Patti Austin and Ashford and Simpson.

JOURNEY

INFINITY (Album) *Columbia* [*USA*]. With material by Journey, this was released in the U.S.A. in January 1978, reaching No 26 for two weeks and staying 32 weeks in the charts. R.I.A.A. Gold Disc award on 3 May 1978. Platinum award on 10 October 1978.

Personnel of Journey: Ross Valory (bass); Neal Schon (guitar); Aynsley Dunbar (drums); Gregg Rolie (guitar/vocals); Steve Perry (lead vocals). Journey, a San Francisco-based group, started in the early 1970s. Valory, a well-known musician of the Haight-Ashbury days of the mid-sixties was a member of the Frumious Bandersnatch band. He then became bass with the Steve Miller Band before joining Journey. Valory had also played along with Santana guitarist Gregg Rolie. Another Santana player Neal Schon joined up with them. In early 1974, Dunbar came into the group replacing Prairie Prince, while guitarist George Tickner had also been added earlier. They made Journey's first album 'Journey' in 1975. 'Look Into The Future' (1976) and 'Next' (1977) followed. But it wasn't until the release of 'Infinity' that they were established as a heavy metal band and Steve Perry was chosen as lead singer to carry them away from their progressive instrumental rock. This fourth album gave them a fresh outlook and renewed vigour.

The album includes: 'Wheel In The Sky'; 'La Do Do'; 'Anytime'; 'Lights'; 'Feeling That Way'; 'Winds of March'. Roy Thomas Baker produced the album. Dunbar left later to join Jefferson Starship and was replaced by Steve Smith (1979).

KANSAS

TWO FOR THE SHOW (Album) *Kirshner/CBS* [*USA*]. Written by Kansas and released in the U.S.A. in November 1978, this went to No 24 for two weeks and stayed 15 weeks in the charts. R.I.A.A. Gold Disc award on 16 November 1978. Platinum award on 14 March 1979.

Another success for Kansas – their sixth album.

DUST IN THE WIND *Kirshner/CBS* [*USA*]. Written by Kansas and released in the U.S.A. in January 1978, this went to No 5 for one week and stayed 20 weeks in the charts. R.I.A.A. Gold Disc award on 14 July 1978.

The prime track from Kansas' album 'Point of Know Return' (1977).

EVELYN 'CHAMPAGNE' KING

SHAME *RCA* [*USA*]. Written by Fitch and Cross, this was released in the U.S.A. in May 1978 and in Britain in the same month. In the U.S.A. it was No 9 for one week and stayed 19 weeks in the charts. In Britain it was No 39 for one week, staying 23 weeks in the charts. R.I.A.A. Gold Disc award on 11 August 1978.

Evelyn was born in New York's Bronx in 1961, and reared in Philadelphia. She began her career singing within the family before joining a local group, Volume 1, who performed at a party for 'Bubbling Brown Sugar' – in which her uncle Avon Long was a star. Evelyn was a great success there. She soon took part-time employment with Philadelphia International Records and then RCA, for whom she cut her debut album 'Smooth Talk', produced by her long-time mentor T. Life, and recorded in New York and Philadelphia. This contained 'Shame', which when released as a single was a smash disco hit.

SMOOTH TALK (Album) *RCA* [*USA*]. This was released in the U.S.A. in May 1978 and in Britain in June 1978. It was No 43 for one week in the U.S.A. and stayed in the charts for 15 weeks. R.I.A.A. Gold Disc award on 6 September 1978.

This album was reported in the U.S. musical press as having sold a million by February 1979. It included her big hit 'Shame', Teddy Pendergrass's 'Dancin' Dancin' Dancin'', and 'I Don't Know If It's Right'. It was her début album, and spawned two million-selling singles.

I DON'T KNOW IF IT'S RIGHT *RCA* [*USA*]. This was released in the U.S.A. in December 1978, going to No 19 for one week and staying 20 weeks in the charts. R.I.A.A. Gold Disc award on 22 February 1979.

Evelyn's second million-selling single from her 'Smooth Talk' album.

KISS

DOUBLE PLATINUM (Double album) *Casablanca* [*USA*]. With material by Kansas, this was released in the U.S.A. in May 1978, going to No 27 for one week and remaining in the charts for 14 weeks. R.I.A.A. Gold and Platinum Disc awards on 16 May 1978.

Double album of the group's greatest hits. It contains all the familiar songs, in remixed versions, to give a fresh appeal. Tracks include the hits 'Beth'; 'Hard Luck Woman' and 'Love Gun'. An instant million seller.

SOLO ALBUMS BY MEMBERS OF THE GROUP (Albums) *Casablanca* [*USA*]. All released in the U.S.A. September 1978. Top chart positions, U.S.A.: Peter Criss: No 53 (one week); Paul Stanley: No 49 (one week); Gene Simmons: No 31 (one week); Ace Frehley: No 41 (one week). Chart longevity, U.S.A.: Peter Criss: 17 weeks; Paul Stanley: 18 weeks; Gene Simmons: 18 weeks; Ace Frehley: 22 weeks. R.I.A.A. Gold and Platinum Discs for each album on 2 October 1978, immediately after release.

Casablanca Records created a precedent by releasing four Kiss solo albums simultaneously. Each album is as individual as the personality responsible for it, and the music hardly identifiable by the quartet known as Kiss. Each album shows the awareness of melody, and is quite different from their bizarre performances on stage. Selected producers and musician friends were enlisted. Vini Poncia and Jeff Glixman worked with Peter Criss and Paul Stanley – Sean Delaney and Eddie Kramer (veteran Kiss producers) assisting Ace Frehley and Gene Simmons. Casablanca carried out an extensive marketing campaign, the biggest ever employed in the history of recorded music. The diversity of each album produced without the participation of the other group members was immediately accepted on its own musical terms.

An instant million sale for each. **Peter Criss** album – outstanding tracks: 'I'm Gonna Love You' and 'Don't You Let Me Down'. **Paul Stanley** album – outstanding tracks: 'Tonight You Belong To Me' and 'Wouldn't You Like To Know Me'. **Gene Simmons** album - outstanding tracks: 'See You In Your Dreams' and 'Radioactive'. **Ace Frehley** album - outstanding tracks: 'New York Groove' and 'I'm In Need Of Love'.

LITTLE RIVER BAND
SLEEPER CATCHER (Album) *EMI/Harvest* [*Britain*], *Harvest/Capitol* [*USA*]. With material by Little River Band, this was released in the U.S.A. in June 1978, going to No 24 for one week and staying in the charts for 24 weeks. R.I.A.A. Gold Disc award on 29 August 1978. Platinum award on 9 May 1979.

Little River Band personnel are: Glenn Shorrock (vocals); Graham Goble (guitar/vocals); Beeb Birtles (guitar); Derek Pellicci (drums); David Briggs (guitar); George McArdle (bass). (McArdle not with the band for recording after this album.) The band was formed in 1975, taking its name from a sign for the resort town of Little River, about 30 miles from Melbourne, Australia, when *en route* to a date. Shorrock and Goble helped to found Mississippi, the musical forerunner of Little River Band. Mississippi's debut album won awards in Australia as 'Best Group Album of 1972'. Shorrock moved to England and toured with bands, then returned to Australia to join the country's first super group Axiom. Axiom travelled to England but broke up, Shorrock staying on to pursue a solo career before linking with Esperanto, an ambitious 12-piece rock band with which he performed for two years. Shorrock met up with the survivors of Mississippi in England which broke up through bad management, and eventually returned in February 1974 and re-formed Mississippi, the name being changed to Little River Band. They were managed by Glenn Wheatley, a former Australian musician, who had been to the U.S.A. for a few years with talent agencies, and who returned to Australia looking for a band capable of making it on the U.S. scene. He found Little River Band. EMI signed the new ensemble to an exclusive contract, and recorded the albums 'Little River Band' (1975), 'After Hours' (1976), and 'Diamantina Cocktail' (1977) – the latter earning the group a gold award in the U.S.A. They did two world tours before making the 'Sleeper Catcher' album, the first ever to ship platinum in the history of the Australian music industry. This contained two hits 'Reminiscing' and 'Lady' which sold over 500,000 each in the U.S.A. alone, and earned the group its first platinum album in the States. ('Sleeper Catcher' is the name given to persons who retrieve the bets of tardy gamblers in the Australian game of two-up.)

KENNY LOGGINS
NIGHTWATCH (Album) *Columbia* [*USA*]. Written by Kenny Loggins and released in the U.S.A. in July 1978, this reached No 8 for two weeks and stayed in the charts for 23 weeks. R.I.A.A. Gold Disc award on 14 September 1978. Platinum award on 13 October 1978.

With this album, Kenny emerged as a solo star. It was produced by Bob James. Tracks include: 'Whenever I Call You "Friend" '; 'Easy Driver'; 'Down in the Boondocks'; 'Down'n Dirty'; 'Angelique'.

LTD
TOGETHERNESS (Album) *A & M* [*USA*]. This was released in the U.S.A. in June 1978, going to No 21 for two weeks and staying 23 weeks in the charts. R.I.A.A. Gold Disc award on 21 June 1978. Platinum award on 19 September 1978.

Second million seller for this group – now one single and one album. One of the premier crossover R & B acts in the U.S.A.

CHERYL LYNN
GOT TO BE REAL *Columbia* [*USA*]. This was released in the U.S.A. in November 1978 and went to No 9 for two weeks,

staying in the charts for 20 weeks. R.I.A.A. Gold Disc award on 16 January 1979.

Another new artist from the Columbia talent stable, and her million-selling song.

LYNYRD SKYNYRD
LYNYRD SKYNYRD'S FIRST AND ... LAST (Album) *MCA* [*USA*]. With material by Lynyrd Skynyrd, this was released in the U.S.A. in September 1978, reaching No 21 for one week and staying in the charts for ten weeks. R.I.A.A. Gold Disc award on 8 September 1978. Platinum award on 10 November 1978.

The group's first posthumous album, a collection of tracks dating back to the formative years before their rise to national stardom. All the tracks are previously unreleased and have been mixed, overdubbed by the group members to enhance the sound quality. Contents are: 'Down South Jukin'; 'Preacher's Daughter'; 'White Dove'; 'Was I Right Or Wrong?'; 'Lend a Helpin' Hand'; 'Wine'; 'Comin' Home'; 'The Seasons'; 'Things Goin' On'.

BARRY MANILOW
CAN'T SMILE WITHOUT YOU *Arista* [*USA*]. Written by Martin, Arnold and Morrow, this was released in the U.S.A. in January 1978 and in Britain in April 1978. It was No 2 for four weeks in the U.S.A. and stayed 20 weeks in the charts. In Britain it was No 43 for one week, staying seven weeks in the charts. R.I.A.A. Gold Disc award on 6 April 1978.

One of the outstanding tracks from Barry's album 'Even Now'.

EVEN NOW (Album) *Arista* [*USA*]. Written by Manilow and others, this was released in the U.S.A. in January 1978 and in Britain in April 1978. In the U.S.A. it went to No 2 for six weeks and stayed in the charts for 36 weeks. In Britain it was No 12 for one week and in the charts for 24 weeks. R.I.A.A. Gold Disc award on 15 February 1978. Platinum award on 22 February 1978.

One of Barry Manilow's biggest successes. This album sold over three million in the U.S.A. alone, and over 100,000 in Britain. The contents offer a wide range, demonstrating Barry's prowess at creating mood music.

It includes: 'Where Do I Go From Here?'; 'Losing Touch'; 'Starting Again'; 'Can't Smile Without You'; 'I Was a Fool (To Let You Go)'; 'Copacabana'. The title for the album was apparently taken from his recording of 'Even Now' on the Flashback label. It also included 'Somewhere In The Night' (written by Kerr and Jennings).

COPACABANA (At The Copa) *Arista* [*USA*]. Written by Barry Manilow, Bruce Sussman and Jack Feldman, this was released in the U.S.A. in June 1978 and in Britain in July 1978. It went to No 6 for one week in the U.S.A., staying in the charts for 16 weeks. In Britain it was No 42 for one week, staying ten weeks in the charts. R.I.A.A. Gold Disc award on 7 September 1978. Grammy award: Best Pop (Male) Vocal, 1978.

The second million-selling single from Barry's album 'Even Now'.

GREATEST HITS (Double album) *Arista* [*USA*]. This was released in the U.S.A. in November 1978. It went to No 5 for two weeks and stayed 34 weeks in the charts. R.I.A.A. Gold and Platinum Disc awards on 27 November 1978.

By 1978 Barry Manilow had emerged as one of the top male singers. Over the previous five years he had sold over 10 million albums, and was the only artist in the world who had ever achieved three triple-platinum albums in 18 months - 'This One's For You' (1977); 'Barry Manilow Live' (1977); and 'Even Now' (1978). It was inevitable that an album of his 'Greatest Hits' would appear. This was a double album containing 19 songs, covering the period from 'Mandy' (1974) to 'Ready To

Take a Chance Again' (1978). This stayed in the U.S. Top 20 for 16 weeks, after receiving awards for instant million sale on release. Britain released a single album 'Manilow Magic' (The Best of Barry Manilow) in February 1979, and this had over £1,000,000 sale, after reaching No 3 and remaining 149 weeks in their charts to 1982. It contained 12 of the songs from 'Greatest Hits': 'Mandy'; 'New York City Rhythm'; 'Looks Like We Made It'; 'Can't Smile Without You'; 'Ready To Take a Chance Again'; 'Tryin' To Get The Feeling'; 'Could It Be Magic?'; 'Copacabana'; 'Weekend in New England'; 'It's a Miracle'; 'All The Time'; 'I Write The Songs'.

STEVE MARTIN

KING TUT *Warner Bros* [*USA*]. Written by Steve Martin, this was released in the U.S.A. in May 1978, going to No 16 for two weeks and staying 18 weeks in the charts. R.I.A.A. Gold Disc award on 23 August 1978.

First million-selling single for Steve Martin, one of America's greatest comedians.

A WILD AND CRAZY GUY (Album) *Warner Bros* [*USA*]. With material by Steve Martin and released in the U.S.A. in October 1978, this reached No 2 for two weeks, remaining 23 weeks in the charts. R.I.A.A. Gold Disc award on 1 November 1978. Platinum award on 21 November. Grammy award: Best Comedy Album, 1978.

Martin shows here that he is one of the most inventive, and funniest comedians around. He wades through irreverent routines such as 'Cat Handcuffs', a discourse on college subjects, and a live version of his famous 'King Tut'.

JOHNNY MATHIS

YOU LIGHT UP MY LIFE (Album) *Columbia* [*USA*]. This was released in the U.S.A. in March 1978 and in Britain in April 1978. In the U.S.A. it went to No 14 for two weeks and in Britain to No 3 for three weeks. It stayed 21 weeks in the U.S.A. charts and 19 weeks in the British charts. R.I.A.A. Gold Disc award on 2 May 1978. Platinum award on 6 July 1978.

Another Mathis success, his usual formula and smooth interpretations of chart hits such as 'You Light Up My Life'; 'Too Much, Too Little, Too Late' (Duet with Deniece Williams); 'Emotion'; 'How Deep Is Your Love?'; 'Till Love Touches Your Life'; 'If You Believe' (from *The Wiz*). Sales in Britain were over £300,000.

JOHNNY MATHIS & DENIECE WILLIAMS

TOO MUCH, TOO LITTLE, TOO LATE *Columbia* [*USA*]. Written by Nat Kipner and John Vallins, this was released in the U.S.A. and Britain in March 1978. In the U.S.A. it hit No 1 for one week and stayed in the charts for 19 weeks. In Britain it went to No 3 for one week, staying 14 weeks in the charts. R.I.A.A. Gold Disc award on 2 May 1978.

The prime track from Mathis' album 'You Light Up My Life'. It sold 250,000 in Britain.

MEAT LOAF

TWO OUT OF THREE AIN'T BAD *Epic/Cleveland* [*USA*]. Written by Jim Steinman, this was released in the U.S.A. in March 1978 and in Britain in July 1978. In the U.S.A. it reached No 7 for one week, staying 24 weeks in the charts. It was No 32 for one week in Britain and stayed eight weeks in the charts. R.I.A.A. Gold Disc award on 20 July 1978.

The outstanding track from Meat Loaf's big album success 'Bat Out of Hell'.

STEVE MILLER BAND

GREATEST HITS 1974-1978 (Album) *Capitol* [*USA*]. This was released in the U.S.A. in November 1978, going to No 16 for two weeks and lasting in the charts for 18 weeks. R.I.A.A.

Gold and Platinum Disc awards on 27 November 1978.

A superlative album showing Steve Miller's talent and the commercial success he has enjoyed over the past five years. Contents are: 'Swingtown'; 'Jungle Love'; 'The Joker'; 'Rock'n'Me'; 'Take The Money and Run'; 'Serenade'; 'True Fine Love'; 'The Stake'; 'Fly Like an Eagle'; 'Jet Airliner'; 'Dance, Dance, Dance'; 'Winter Time'; 'Wild Mountain Honey'; 'Threshold'.

EDDIE MONEY

EDDIE MONEY (Album) *CBS* [*USA*]. With material by Eddie Money and James Lyon, this was released in the U.S.A. in February 1978, going to No 35 for three weeks and staying 30 weeks in the charts. R.I.A.A. Gold Disc award on 6 July 1978. Platinum award on 13 November 1979.

Another new recording star for the CBS line-up, and his debut album. This album included two hits: 'Baby Hold On' and 'Two Tickets To Paradise'.

MOODY BLUES

OCTAVE (Album) *London* [*USA*] *Decca* [*Britain*]. Written by the Moody Blues, this was released in the U.S.A. in May 1978 and in Britain in June 1978. It was No 13 for three weeks in the U.S.A. and stayed 16 weeks in the charts. It went to No 6 for two weeks in Britain, staying 17 weeks in the charts. R.I.A.A. Gold Disc award on 19 June 1978. Platinum award on 26 January 1979.

Second million-selling album for the Moody Blues (their first was in 1967). Their familiar lush sound is again produced by Tony Clarke. British sales were over £300,000.

ANNE MURRAY

LET'S KEEP IT THAT WAY (Album) *Capitol* [*USA*]. This was released in the U.S.A. in January 1978 and in Britain in May 1978. In the U.S.A. it was No 27 for one week and stayed 16 weeks in the charts. R.I.A.A. Gold Disc award on 12 October 1978. Platinum award on 19 December 1978.

Since Anne Murray's big success with 'Snowbird' (1970) the Canadian singer's career became one of the most successful in contemporary music, bridging the gap between pop and country. This album, her first million seller in the U.S.A., was a hit on both the pop and country charts. Anne's success had made her an international star. She made appearances outside the North American continent, with Britain an important part in her work schedules. She visited Britain in 1972 for the International Festival of Country Music at Wembley, returning on three further occasions and taping her own TV special for the BBC in 1973. Queen Elizabeth II bestowed on Anne the highest honour possible for a Canadian citizen – Officer of the Order of Canada. During these interim years, she had many awards from Canada, and elsewhere, and many hits, including a Grammy award for 'Love Song' (1974), the Best Female Country Vocalist Performance, 1974. Up to 1980, 21 of her singles were in the U.S. charts and Capitol had released 17 Murray albums. 'Let's Keep It That Way' marked the beginning of superstardom. It contained the big hit 'You Needed Me' and 'Walk Right Back'. Anne's success lies in her love for all kinds of music. She offers something for everyone, be it jazz, gospel, pop or country. (See also 'Snowbird' 1970 data.)

YOU NEEDED ME *Capitol* [*USA*]. Written by Randy Goodman, this was released in the U.S.A. in June 1978 and in Britain in November 1978. It climbed to No 2 for three weeks in the U.S.A., staying 28 weeks in the charts. In Britain it went to No 22 for one week and stayed 13 weeks in the charts. R.I.A.A. Gold Disc award on 26 October 1978. Grammy award: Best Pop Vocal Performance, Female, 1978.

The prime track from Anne's album 'Let's Keep It That Way', and one of the best songs of the year.

DAVID NAUGHTON
MAKIN' IT *RSO* [*USA*]. Written by D. Fekaris and Fred Perren, this was released in the U.S.A. in December 1978, going to No 9 for three weeks and staying 24 weeks in the charts. In Britain it was No 44 for one week and stayed six weeks in the charts. R.I.A.A. Gold Disc award on 31 July 1979.

A new U.S. artist, with his first million seller written by the ace producers/songwriters Fekaris and Perren.

WILLIE NELSON
WILLIE AND FAMILY LIVE (Album) *Columbia* [*USA*]. This was released in the U.S.A. in November 1978, going to No 42 for one week and staying in the charts for 12 weeks. R.I.A.A. Gold Disc award on 13 February 1979. Platinum award on 6 March 1980.

A fine album of Nelson's country songs. The 'Family' includes many country artists, who appeared with him in his first starring role in the film *Honeysuckle Rose* in 1980 (see 1980).

STARDUST (Album) *Columbia* [*USA*]. Released in the U.S.A. in April 1978, this was No 52 for two weeks and stayed 12 weeks in the charts. R.I.A.A. Gold Disc award on 20 July 1978. Platinum award on 26 December 1978.

Having already paved the way for his crossover success with the 'Outlaw' album, this follow-up album contained standard songs, smoothly performed with production by Booker T. Jones. In the U.S. country charts it was a very long runner, with 137 weeks in the charts to the end of 1980, and going on into 1981. It includes: 'Stardust'; 'Georgia On My Mind'; 'Unchained Melody'; 'September Song'; 'Someone To Watch Over Me'; 'Blue Skies'; 'All of Me'.

OLIVIA NEWTON-JOHN
HOPELESSLY DEVOTED TO YOU *Polydor/RSO* [*USA*]. Written by John Farrar, this was released in the U.S.A. in July 1978 and in Britain in October 1978. It went to No 4 for two weeks in the U.S.A., staying 17 weeks in the charts. In Britain it went to No 2 for two weeks and stayed in the charts for ten weeks. R.I.A.A. Gold Disc award on 31 August 1978.

One of the hit songs from the 'Grease' album. The song was produced by its writer John Farrar, who records all Olivia's songs. The disc also sold half a million in Britain.

A LITTLE MORE LOVE *MCA* [*USA*] *EMI* [*Britain*]. Written by John Farrar, this was released in the U.S.A. and Britain in November 1978. It went to No 4 for two weeks in the U.S.A. and for one week in Britain. It stayed 21 weeks in the U.S. charts and 11 weeks in the British lists. R.I.A.A. Gold Disc award on 12 February 1979.

Another million seller, written and produced by John Farrar. This sold over 250,000 in Britain.

TOTALLY HOT (Album) *MCA* [*USA*] *EMI* [*Britain*]. This was released in the U.S.A. and Britain in November 1978. In the U.S.A. it went to No 6 for five weeks and stayed 32 weeks in the charts. In Britain it was No 30 for one week, staying 13 weeks in the charts. R.I.A.A. Gold Disc award on 15 November 1978. Platinum award on 5 December 1978.

1978 was another fabulously successful year for Olivia. All her discs were million sellers, including the soundtrack 'Grease'. 'Totally Hot' reveals the 'new' Olivia fresh from her success in the film *Grease*. Producer John Farrar put together a well-rounded album with choice material covering ballads, country, disco (the title track) and good old rock'n'roll like 'Gimme Some Lovin''. It was an instant million seller in the U.S.A., and Britain had sales of over £300,000. (See also original soundtrack 'Grease' 1978.)

TED NUGENT
DOUBLE LIVE GONZO (Double album) *Epic* [*USA*]. With material by Ted Nugent, etc., this was released in the U.S.A. in January 1978, going to No 12 for two weeks and staying in the charts for 16 weeks. R.I.A.A. Gold Disc award on 14 February 1978. Platinum award on 20 July 1978.

Mostly recorded throughout the South by the Mid-Western rock and roller Ted Nugent, an album demonstrating his live raw power. It includes his classic hit 'Cat Scratch Fever' and live standards from his days with Chicago's Amboy Dukes.

WEEKEND WARRIORS (Album) *Epic* [*USA*]. Written by Ted Nugent and released in the U.S.A. in October 1978, this went to No 12 for one week and stayed 20 weeks in the charts. R.I.A.A. Gold Disc award on 30 October 1978. Platinum award on 16 November 1978.

Ted Nugent ('The Motor City Madman') and his steady drummer, Cliff Davies, are joined by two new sidemen for their first studio recording since 'Cat Scratch Fever'. Another energetic album of blistering, hard rock. It includes: 'Venom Stomp'; 'Weekend Warriors'; 'One Woman'; 'Name Your Poison'; 'Need You Bad'.

THE O'JAYS
SO FULL OF LOVE (Album) *Philadelphia International* [*USA*]. With material written by Kenny Gamble and Leon Huff, this was released in the U.S.A. in April 1978, going to No 4 for two weeks and staying 24 weeks in the charts. R.I.A.A. Gold Disc award on 2 May 1978. Platinum award on 31 May 1978.

The O'Jays come back into the million-selling circle after three years, with a fine album of Gamble and Huff songs. This contained their million-selling single 'Use Ta Be My Gal'; 'Help (Somebody Please)'; 'Brandy'; 'Cry Together'; 'Sing My Heart Out'.

USE TA BE MY GAL *Philadelphia International* [*USA*]. Written by Kenny Gamble and Leon Huff, this was released in the U.S.A. in April 1978 and in Britain in June 1978. It went to No 3 for three weeks in the U.S.A. and stayed 19 weeks in the charts. It went to No 12 for one week in Britain, staying in the charts for 12 weeks. R.I.A.A. Gold Disc award on 16 June 1978.

The prime track from the album 'So Full Of Love'.

PABLO CRUISE
WORLDS AWAY (Album) *A & M* [*USA*]. Written by Pablo Cruise and released in the U.S.A. in June 1978, this went to No 6 for four weeks, staying 28 weeks in the charts. R.I.A.A. Gold Disc award on 21 June 1978. Platinum award on 19 September 1978.

Pablo Cruise, a quartet, consists of Dave Jenkins (guitar/bass/vocals); Cory Lerios (piano); Stephen Price (drums); and Bud Cockrell (bass/vocals). They had made three albums prior to this one since 1975. 'Worlds Away' is their second million seller. It includes 'Love Will Find A Way'; 'Worlds Away'; 'Don't Want To Live Without It'.

PARLIAMENT
FLASH LIGHT *Casablanca* [*USA*]. Written by George Clinton and released in the U.S.A. in February 1978, this was No 14

for one week, remaining 17 weeks in the charts. R.I.A.A. Gold Disc award on 20 April 1978.

Second million-selling single for Parliament.

PEACHES & HERB
SHAKE YOUR GROOVE THING *Polydor [USA]*. Written by D. Fekaris and Fred Perren, this was released in the U.S.A. in December 1978 and in Britain in January 1979. In the U.S.A. it reached No 7 for two weeks and stayed 25 weeks in the charts. In Britain it was No 26 for one week, staying ten weeks in the charts. R.I.A.A. Gold Disc award on 16 February 1979.

Peaches (Francine 'Peaches' Hurd) and Herb Fame started around the mid-sixties. Both are vocalists backed by a big band. They first recorded for CBS, then MCA and finally with Polydor for whom this number was included in their debut album, '2 Hot', in early 1979.

TEDDY PENDERGRASS
LIFE IS A SONG WORTH SINGING (Album) *Philadelphia International [USA]*. This was released in the U.S.A. in June 1978, going to No 10 for two weeks and staying 24 weeks in the charts. R.I.A.A. Gold Disc award on 16 June 1978. Platinum award on 25 August 1978.

Pendergrass's second solo album is a Philadelphia family affair with seven producers and four arrangers contributing to the distinctive vocals and sound. It sold over two million in the U.S.A. The album includes: 'Close The Door'; 'Get Up, Get Down, Get Funky, Get Loose'; 'Only You'; 'When Somebody Loves You Back'.

CLOSE THE DOOR *Philadelphia International [USA]*. Written by Kenny Gamble and Leon Huff, this was released in the U.S.A. in June 1978 and in Britain in October 1978. In the U.S.A. it was No 16 for one week, staying 15 weeks in the charts. It was No 41 for one week in Britain and stayed six weeks in the charts. R.I.A.A. Gold Disc award on 25 October 1978.

The outstanding track from Pendergrass's album 'Life is a Song Worth Singing'.

POINTER SISTERS
FIRE *Planet/Elektra/Asylum [USA] Planet [Britain]*. Written by Bruce Springsteen, this was released in the U.S.A. in November 1978 and in Britain in March 1979. In the U.S.A. it went to No 2 for two weeks, staying in the charts for 27 weeks. In Britain it was No 34 for two weeks and stayed eight weeks in the charts. R.I.A.A. Gold Disc award on 5 February 1979.

The four black sisters – Bonnie, Ruth, Anita and June Pointer – hail from East Oakland, California, and appeared on the scene in 1973. They worked in Houston, Texas, before producer David Robinson took them to California for studio work as back-up singers with Elvin Bishop's group, and recording with Taj Mahal, Dave Mason, Cold Blood and Boz Scaggs. After signing with Atlantic, they went to Jackson, Mississippi, to record soul music, but this was not their style. After one single, they returned to the West Coast and decided to follow their own direction. Their style was a mixture of forties and fifties music, gospel, jazz and show-business. They made five albums for Blue Thumb label: 'The Pointer Sisters' (1973); 'That's a Plenty' (1974); 'Steppin'' (1975); 'Best Of' (1976); 'Having a Party' (1978); and one for ABC 'Live at the Opera House' (1974); then 'Energy' (1978) for Planet label. The single 'Fire' was included in the latter (released early 1979). At last, the Pointer Sisters got their first million seller with a song written by Bruce Springsteen, who also came to the fore in this year.

SUZI QUATRO & CHRIS NORMAN
STUMBLIN' IN *RAK [Britain] RSO [USA]*. Written by Nicky Chinn and Mike Chapman, this was released in Britain in November 1978 and in the U.S.A. in January 1979. It was No 41 for one week in Britain, lasting seven weeks in the charts. In the U.S.A. it went to No 8 for two weeks and lasted 23 weeks in the

charts. R.I.A.A. Gold Disc award on 7 June 1979.

Not very many women are represented consistently on the charts during the male-dominated era of the mid-seventies, but Suzi Quatro's success with her brand of high-energy rock was an exception. 'Stumblin' In', plus her album 'If You Knew Suzi' gave her greatest success so far in the U.S.A. Suzi had made tours encompassing Europe, Australia and the Orient, and TV specials in East Germany, New Zealand and Australia. Her success on U.S. TV came through her being chosen for the part of Leather Tuscadero in the special two-part episode of *Happy Days*: 'Fonzie – Rock Entrepreneur' which led to her role as the rocker in several additional episodes. She toured the U.S. and Canada in 1979, following the success of 'Stumblin' In', another hit for writers Chinn and Chapman, the disc being produced by Mike Chapman in Britain. Suzi had thus carved a special place in rock'n'roll, on the stage and screen.

QUEEN
JAZZ (Album) *Elektra [USA] EMI [Britain]*. With material by Freddy Mercury and Brian May, this was released in Britain and the U.S.A. in November 1978. In Britain it reached No 2 for one week and stayed 26 weeks in the charts. In the U.S.A. it went to No 12 for two weeks and stayed 18 weeks in the charts. R.I.A.A. Gold and Platinum Disc awards on 28 November 1978.

An instant million seller for Queen. This album was produced by Roy Thomas Baker, with the group's characteristic vocal and guitar sound, matched with strong melodies. It sold over 100,000 in Britain.

GERRY RAFFERTY
CITY TO CITY (Album) *United Artists [Britain and USA]*. Written by Gerry Rafferty, this was released in Britain in February 1978 and in the U.S.A. in March 1978. It went to No 5 for two weeks in the U.S.A. and stayed in the charts for 29 weeks. In Britain it went to No 6 for one week, staying 26 weeks in the charts. R.I.A.A. Gold Disc award on 26 May 1978. Platinum award on 20 June 1978.

Gerry Rafferty was educated in Glasgow, and was playing with various bands at 16, the first being the Humblebums in 1968. In 1971 he recorded his first album 'Can I Have My Money Back?'; a cynical review of the music industry. He then went on to found Stealer's Wheel with Joe Egan, debuting in 1972 with 'Stuck In The Middle With You'. The band broke up and Gerry's legal problems kept him from performing for three years. He retired during that period to his farm in Scotland, and made only the most necessary trips to London. In 1978 he recorded the 'Gerry Rafferty' album for Logo, and then 'City To City' for U.A., with a 16-piece band. Apart from being a vocalist, Gerry plays guitar and keyboards. This album included the big hit 'Baker Street'. It also sold over £300,000 in Britain, but it was the U.S.A. that took Gerry to its heart, leading to worldwide recognition.

BAKER STREET *United Artists [Britain and USA]*. Written by Gerry Rafferty, this was released in Britain in January 1978 and in the U.S.A. in April 1978. It went to No 3 for two weeks in Britain and stayed 15 weeks in the charts. In the U.S.A. it went to No 2 for four weeks and stayed 20 weeks in the charts. R.I.A.A. Gold Disc award on 18 July 1978.

The hit song from Rafferty's album 'City To City'. Gerry wrote this while in London, staying with musician friends in Baker Street (where the fictional detective Sherlock Holmes lived). The disc is notable for the haunting saxophone solo played by Raphael Ravenscroft.

REO SPEEDWAGON
YOU CAN TUNE A PIANO – BUT YOU CAN'T TUNA FISH *Epic [USA]*. With material by REO Speedwagon, this was released in the U.S.A. in April 1978, going to No 44 for two weeks and staying in the charts for 20 weeks. R.I.A.A. Gold Disc award on 26 June 1978. Platinum award on 7 November 1980.

Second million-selling album for REO Speedwagon, though it took two and a half years to achieve that sale. It includes: 'Roll With The Changes'; 'Sing To Me'; 'Say You Love Me or Say Goodnight'; 'Blazin' Your Own Trail Again'; 'Time For Me To Fly'.

KENNY ROGERS

TEN YEARS OF GOLD (Album) *United Artists* [*USA*]. This was released in the U.S.A. in January 1978, going to No 52 for two weeks and staying 23 weeks in the charts. R.I.A.A. Gold Disc award on 15 February 1978. Platinum award on 20 July 1978.

This album goes right back to Kenny's first hit with the First Edition, 'Just Dropped In To See What Condition My Condition Is In'. Also includes: 'Lucille'; 'Daytime Friends'; 'Today I Started Loving You Again'; 'Ruby, Don't Take Your Love To Town'; 'Love Lifted Me'; 'Somethin's Burnin''; 'Reuben James'; 'But You Know I Love You'; 'While The Feeling's Good'. The album was 155 weeks in the U.S.A. country charts to the end of 1980 and into 1981.

THE GAMBLER (Album) *United Artists* [*USA*]. Released in the U.S.A. in November 1978, this went to No 6 for two weeks and lasted a total of 98 weeks in the charts. R.I.A.A. Gold Disc award on 30 November 1978. Platinum award on 27 February 1979. Grammy award: Best Country Song 'The Gambler' to Composer Don Schlitz, 1978.

An album with a smooth balance of story-songs and ballads, making a fabulous year for Kenny. It contained the title song, best country song of the year, and was also in the U.S. country charts for 105 weeks to the end of 1980, continuing into 1981, and selling four million by 1982.

THE ROLLING STONES

SOME GIRLS (Album) *Rolling Stones* [*Britain and USA*]. This was released in Britain and the U.S.A. in June 1978. In the U.S.A. it hit No 1 for one week and in Britain No 2 for one week. It lasted 42 weeks in the U.S. charts and 24 weeks in the British charts. R.I.A.A. Gold Disc award on 12 June 1978. Platinum award on 22 June 1978.

This album was recorded at EMI Studios, Paris, and on the Rolling Stones' Mobile, during the winter and early spring of 1978. Another blockbuster for the raunchy, gutsy sound of the group, and far and away their best rock album in many years. Apart from its U.S. success, it also sold over £300,000 worth in Britain. In the U.S.A. it was in the Top 10 for 26 weeks. Contents are: 'When The Whip Comes Down'; 'Lies'; 'Respectable'; 'Miss You'; 'Before They Make Me Run'; 'Beast Of Burden'; 'Some Girls'; 'Far Away Eyes'; 'Shattered' (all written by Keith Richard and Mick Jagger); 'Imagination' (written by Barrett Strong and Norman Whitfield). Released on the EMI label in Britain.

MISS YOU *Rolling Stones* [*Britain and USA*]. Written by Keith Richard and Mick Jagger, this was released in Britain and the U.S.A. in May 1978. It was No 3 for four weeks in the U.S.A. and for one week in Britain, staying 22 weeks in the U.S. charts and 13 weeks in the British lists. R.I.A.A. Gold Disc award on 26 July 1978.

This was included on the Stones' album 'Some Girls' which was released a little later. Also a success in Britain with over 250,000 sale.

LINDA RONSTADT

LIVING IN THE U.S.A. (Album) *Elektra/Asylum* [*USA*]. This was released in the U.S.A. in September 1978, going to No 2 for two weeks and staying 26 weeks in the charts. R.I.A.A. Gold and Platinum Disc awards on 22 September 1978.

The largest shipping in the history of Elektra/Asylum - two million. It sold three million by early 1979. Linda selected material recorded by other star artists; Elvis Presley's 'Love Me Tender'; Elvis Costello's 'Alison'; Chuck Berry's 'Back In The USA'; The Hollies' 'Just One Look'; J.D. Souther's 'White

Rhythm & Blues'; Eric Kaz' 'Blowing Away' and the great oldie 'When I Grow Too Old To Dream'. The producer was Peter Asher.

BOB SEGER & THE SILVER BULLET BAND

STRANGER IN TOWN (Album) *Capitol* [*USA*]. Released in the U.S.A. in May 1978, this went to No 4 for two weeks and stayed in the charts for 50 weeks. R.I.A.A. Gold and Platinum Disc awards on 30 May 1978.

This album was shipped platinum. Seger invited two Eagles' members - Frey and Felder - to join him as part of his backing band. An album in celebration of old-time rock'n'roll. It includes: 'Hollywood Nights'; 'Till It Shines'; 'Ain't Got No Money'; 'Old Time Rock and Roll'; 'Feel Like a Number'; 'Brave Strangers'; 'Still The Same'. Produced at five different studios in the U.S.A. - Miami, Alabama, Los Angeles, Hollywood and Detroit.

CARLY SIMON

BOYS IN THE TREES (Album) *Casablanca* [*USA*]. Written by Carly Simon, this was released in the U.S.A. in April 1978, going to No 14 for one week and staying in the charts for 24 weeks. R.I.A.A. Gold Disc award on 15 May 1978. Platinum award on 2 October 1978.

A fine album, with songs maintaining a consistently high standard. Produced by Arif Mardin.

BRUCE SPRINGSTEEN

DARKNESS ON THE EDGE OF TOWN (Album) *Columbia* [*USA*]. With material by Bruce Springsteen, this was released in the U.S.A. in May 1978 and in Britain in the following month. In the U.S.A. it went to No 8 for two weeks, staying 23 weeks in the charts. In Britain it was No 14 for one week and stayed 12 weeks in the charts. R.I.A.A. Gold Disc award on 16 June 1978. Platinum award on 27 June 1978.

Bruce Springsteen was born in New Jersey, 1950. The singer/songwriter/guitarist made his first two albums 'Greetings from Asbury Park, NJ' and 'The Wild, The Innocent and the E. Street Shuffle' in 1973 (Bruce's band is The E. Street Band). These gained him a small but devoted fan following. In 1975, with the release of his third album 'Born To Run' which rose to No 10 in the charts in two weeks, he was nationally acclaimed and was the subject of cover stories in *Time* and *Newsweek* during the same week - a first in rock history. Then came legal troubles when Bruce brought a massive lawsuit against his manager, Mike Appel, which took almost 12 months to settle, finally in Bruce's favour, giving him complete control over his career. Bruce then worked on a new album 'Darkness on the Edge of Town' that quickly became a million seller, a triumph after a long lay-off, and established him as a pre-eminent songwriter. The album is in essence a profound declaration of principle. The album contains 10 songs, essential seventies rock. Some of the outstanding emotional songs of high intensity and performance are: 'Prove It All Night'; 'Badlands'; 'Racing In The Street'; 'The Promised Land'; 'Adam Raised a Cain'.

STEELY DAN

STEELY DAN'S GREATEST HITS (Double album) *ABC* [*USA*]. With material by Donald Fagen and Walter Becker, this was released in the U.S.A. in October 1978 and in Britain in November 1978. In the U.S.A. it was No 32 for two weeks and stayed 15 weeks in the charts. In Britain it was No 41 for one week and stayed 17 weeks in the charts. R.I.A.A. Gold and Platinum Disc awards on 7 December 1978.

An attractive album of 18 songs dating from 1972 to 1978, and including one previously unreleased - 'Here at the Western World' (by Becker and Fagen). Complete contents are: 'Do It Again'; 'Reeling in the Years'; 'My Old School'; 'Bodhisattva'; 'Show Biz Kids'; 'East St Louis Toodle-oo'; 'Rikki Don't Lose That Number'; 'Pretzel Logic'; 'Any Major Dude'; 'Here At The Western World'; 'Black Friday'; 'Bad Sneakers'; 'Doctor

Wu'; 'Haitian Divorce'; 'Kid Charlemagne'; 'The Fez'; 'Peg'; 'Josie'.

AL STEWART

TIME PASSAGES (Album) *Arista* [*USA*]. This was released in the U.S.A. and Britain in September 1978, going to No 14 for one week in the U.S.A. and staying in the charts for 22 weeks. R.I.A.A. Gold Disc award on 25 October 1978. Platinum award on 16 March 1979.

Considered to be Al Stewart's finest work to date. The album takes one on a journey through time and space, touching down in Revolutionary France, the era of Sir Thomas More, on the decks of the sunken Marie Celeste, a farm in the Mid-West and other assorted vignettes. The album was produced by Alan Parsons, and recorded in Los Angeles, with fine musicians featured: Peter Wood (keyboards); Al Perkins (steel guitar); Stuart Elliot (drums); Peter White (guitar/keyboards/accordion); Phil Kenzie (saxophone); Robin Lamble (bass). The title song was released as a single.

ROD STEWART

BLONDES HAVE MORE FUN (Album) *Warner Bros* [*USA*] *Riva* [*Britain*]. Written by Rod Stewart, this was released in the U.S.A. and Britain in December 1978. It hit No 1 for three weeks in the U.S.A. and No 3 for three weeks in Britain. It stayed 33 weeks in the U.S. charts and 30 weeks in the British lists. R.I.A.A. Gold Disc award 13 December 1978. Platinum award 27 December 1978.

Another huge success for Rod Stewart. This album was in the U.S. Top 10 for 16 weeks, and it sold over 300,000 units in Britain. The prime track was 'Da Ya Think I'm Sexy?', a disco-style number.

DA YA THINK I'M SEXY? *Warner Bros* [*USA*] *Riva* [*Britain*]. Written by C. Appice and Rod Stewart, this was released in Britain in November 1978 and in the U.S.A. in December 1978. It went to No 1 for five weeks in the U.S.A. and for one week in Britain. It remained 24 weeks in the U.S. charts and 12 weeks in the British charts. R.I.A.A. Gold Disc award on 30 January 1979. Platinum award on 21 February 1979.

A tremendous seller in the U.S.A. - over two million - and half a million in Britain. Brazilian singer/composer Jorge Ben claimed that it infringed his copyright 'Taj Mahal' originally recorded in Portuguese for the South American market, and registered in the U.S. Stewart agreed to ceding all rights to UNICEF for the International Year of the Child appeal.

BARBRA STREISAND

SONGBIRD (Album) *Columbia* [*USA*]. This was released in the U.S.A. in May 1978, going to No 12 for two weeks and staying in the charts for 21 weeks. R.I.A.A. Gold Disc award on 31 May 1978. Platinum award on 25 August 1978.

Another fine album of Streisand charm. It includes: 'Tomorrow'; 'You Don't Bring Me Flowers'; 'One More Night'; 'A Man I Loved'; 'Stay Away'.

GREATEST HITS, Vol 2 (Album) *Columbia* [*USA*]. This was released in the U.S.A. in October 1978 and in Britain in February 1979. It climbed to No 1 for four weeks in both the U.S.A. and Britain, staying 23 weeks in the U.S. charts and 25 weeks in the British charts. R.I.A.A. Gold and Platinum Disc awards on 16 November 1978.

Barbra Streisand's 34th album since 1962. This was a chart topper on both sides of the Atlantic, was 13 weeks in the U.S. Top 10, and 10 weeks in the U.K. Top 10. Huge sales in the U.S.A. and over £1,000,000 worth in Britain. The album contains some of her best performances on record from 1972. The tracks are: 'Love Theme from *A Star Is Born*' ('Evergreen'); 'Love Theme from *Eyes Of Laura Mars*' ('Prisoner'); 'Songbird'; 'The Way We Were' (from the film *The Way We Were*); 'My Heart Belongs To Me'; 'Superman'; 'You Don't Bring Me Flowers' (duet with Neil Diamond); 'Sweet Inspiration/Where You Lead'; 'All In Love Is Fair'; 'Stoney End'.

BARBRA STREISAND & NEIL DIAMOND

YOU DON'T BRING ME FLOWERS *Columbia* [*USA*]. Written by Neil Diamond and A. and M. Bergman, this was released in the U.S.A. in October 1978 and in Britain in November 1978. It reached No 1 for two weeks in the U.S.A. and No 5 for one week in Britain. It remained 16 weeks in the U.S. charts and 11 weeks in the British lists. R.I.A.A. Gold Disc award on 16 November 1978.

A beautiful duet by Barbra and Neil, crafted by three of America's finest songwriters.

STYX

PIECES OF EIGHT (Album) *A & M* [*USA*]. This was released in the U.S.A. in September 1978, going to No 6 for two weeks and lasting 53 weeks in the charts. R.I.A.A. Gold and Platinum Disc awards on 10 October 1978.

Second million-selling album for Styx, one of the U.S.A.'s premier attractions. The outstanding tracks are 'I'm OK' and 'Blue Collar Man'.

DONNA SUMMER

LAST DANCE *Casablanca* [*USA*]. Written by Paul Jabara, this was released in the U.S.A. in April 1978 and in Britain in July 1978. In the U.S.A. it went to No 4 for two weeks and stayed 20 weeks in the charts. In Britain it was No 51 for one week, staying eight weeks in the charts. R.I.A.A. Gold Disc award on 19 July 1978. Grammy awards: Best Rhythm and Blues Song, 1978; Best Female R & B Vocal Performance, Donna Summer, 1978.

This was sung by Donna Summer in the film *Thank God It's Friday* and was winner of the Film Oscar for Best Song of 1978. The song is generally regarded as a disco anthem.

LIVE AND MORE (Double album) *Casablanca* [*USA*]. This was released in the U.S.A. in September 1978 and in Britain in October 1978. In the U.S.A. it reached No 2 for two weeks and stayed 37 weeks in the charts. In Britain it was No 16 for one week, staying 12 weeks in the charts. R.I.A.A. Gold Disc award on 14 September 1978. Platinum award on 19 October 1978.

Three sides of this album show Donna blossoming into an engaging stage personality, singing some of her numerous hits in addition to new standards such as 'The Way We Were'. Side four is a studio effort using 'McArthur Park' as its theme.

MacARTHUR PARK *Casablanca* [*USA*]. Written by Jim Webb (1968), this was released in the U.S.A. in September 1978 and in Britain in October 1978. It was No 1 for two weeks in the U.S.A. and stayed 22 weeks in the charts. In Britain it went to No 5 for three weeks, staying ten weeks in the charts. R.I.A.A. Gold Disc award on 26 October 1978.

Single release of the theme used by Donna for part of her album 'Live and More'.

TASTE OF HONEY

BOOGIE OOGIE OOGIE *Capitol* [*USA*]. Written by Janice Johnson and Perry Kibble, it was released in the U.S.A. and Britain in June 1978. In the U.S.A. it went to No 1 for one week, staying in the charts for 27 weeks. In Britain it went to No 3 for one week, staying 16 weeks in the charts. R.I.A.A. Gold Disc award on 8 August 1978. Platinum award on 10 October 1978. Grammy award: Best New Artist of the Year, 1978.

Taste of Honey are Larry and Fonce Mizell with their group. This disc was a very big seller. It sold over two million in the U.S.A. alone. Other group members are: Janice Johnson (lead singer/bass); Hazel Payne (lead guitar/vocalist); Perry Kibble (piano); Donald Johnson (drums).

A TASTE OF HONEY (Album) *Capitol* [*USA*]. This was released in the U.S.A. in June 1978, going to No 16 for one week and staying 24 weeks in the charts. R.I.A.A. Gold Disc award on 2 August 1978. Platinum award on 4 October 1978.

Extremely popular album with the talented Larry and Fonce

Mizell and their group. It contained the big hit 'Boogie Oogie Oogie'.

TOTO

TOTO (Album) *Columbia* [*USA*]. This was released in the U.S.A. in October 1978, going to No 9 for two weeks and staying in the charts for 33 weeks. R.I.A.A. Gold Disc award on 12 December 1978. Platinum award on 23 January 1979.

Personnel of Toto are: David Paich (keyboards); Jeff Porcaro (drums); David Hungate (bass); Bobby Kimball (vocals); Steve Porcaro (keyboards); Steve Lukather (lead guitar). Most of these played together on the Los Angeles scene for several years. Paich and Steve Porcaro had worked with Boz Scaggs and others; Hungate with Barbra Streisand and Leo Sayer; Lukather with Hall and Oates; Kimball with Alice Cooper. This line-up had been together for only a short time, but the debut album was one of the most impressive in recent years. Paich originally met Jeff Porcaro through their fathers, who worked together on a Glen Campbell TV project. The album, recorded by the sextet of top West Coast session men, is unique in that its full sound is produced by two keyboard players with the other four contributing vocals. It included 'Rock Maker'; 'I'll Supply The Love' and 'Hold The Line'.

HOLD THE LINE *Columbia* [*USA*]. Written by David Paich, this was released in the U.S.A. in October 1978 and in Britain in January 1979. In the U.S.A. it was No 5 for two weeks, staying 24 weeks in the charts. In Britain it was No 14 for one week and stayed 11 weeks in the charts. R.I.A.A. Gold Disc award on 15 February 1979.

A solid Top 10 hit on the group's first time out. The prime track from their debut album 'Toto'.

JOHN TRAVOLTA & OLIVIA NEWTON-JOHN

YOU'RE THE ONE THAT I WANT *RSO* [*USA*]. Written by John Farrar, this was released in the U.S.A. in March 1978 and in Britain in May 1978. It went to No 1 for one week in the U.S.A. and for eight weeks in Britain, staying 25 weeks in the U.S. charts and 26 weeks in the British charts. R.I.A.A. Gold Disc award on 12 April 1978. Platinum award on 18 July 1978.

Included in the film *Grease*, this song was a staggering success globally. It sold well over two million in the U.S.A. and 1,750,000 in Britain. In both countries the disc was 14 weeks in their Top 10. Sales elsewhere must have achieved a global tally of well over five million.

SUMMER NIGHTS *RSO* [*USA*]. Written by J. Jacobs and W. Casey, this was released in the U.S.A. in August 1978 and in Britain in September 1978. It went to No 4 for one week in the U.S.A., lasting 17 weeks in the charts. In Britain it hit No 1 for seven weeks, staying 18 weeks in the charts. R.I.A.A. Gold Disc award on 31 August 1978.

Second million-selling single from *Grease* by the stars of the film. This also sold a million in Britain. It was 10 weeks in Britain's Top 10 and five weeks in the U.S. Top 10.

FRANKIE VALLI

GREASE *RSO* [*USA*]. Written by Barry Gibb, this was released in the U.S.A. in May 1978 and in Britain in August 1978. It went to No 1 for two weeks in the U.S.A., staying in the charts for 21 weeks, and to No 3 for two weeks in Britain, staying in the charts for 14 weeks. R.I.A.A. Gold and Platinum Disc award on 17 October 1978.

Third big hit from the film *Grease* and Frankie Valli's first platinum single. It also sold 500,000 in Britain. Writer Barry Gibb is a member of the Bee Gees. The disc was in the U.S. Top 10 for 11 weeks, and five weeks in Britain's Top 10.

VAN HALEN

VAN HALEN (Album) *Warner Bros* [*USA*]. With material by Van Halen, this was released in the U.S.A. in March 1978, going

to No 29 for two weeks and staying 81 weeks in the charts. R.I.A.A. Gold Disc award on 24 May 1978. Platinum award on 10 October 1978.

Van Halen are the two brothers Edward Van Halen (guitar) and Alex Van Halen (drums); Mike Anthony (bass); Dave Roth (vocals). The brothers hail from Amsterdam, Holland. The band were formed in 1972, playing for parties and clubs, culminating in a contract with Warner Bros. Their music is a merger of classical training and American rock and roll. With the success of this three-million-selling debut album, they went on to complete two successful world tours. On the road they used 700,000 watts of light, 40,000 watts of sound and 50 tons of equipment. The album included their frenetic hard rock numbers 'You Really Got Me', 'Jamie's Cryin' and 'Runnin' With The Devil'.

GINO VANNELLI

BROTHER TO BROTHER (Album) *A & M* [*USA*]. Written by the Vannelli Brothers, this was released in the U.S.A. in September 1978, going to No 18 for three weeks and staying in the charts for 21 weeks. R.I.A.A. Gold Disc award on 7 November 1978. Platinum award on 18 January 1979.

Gino Vannelli was reared in Montreal, his father a big band vocalist. At 14 he joined his first rock'n'roll band, and the next group included his brother Joe. At 16, Gino's first single was a Top 10 hit in Canada, and over the next few years he travelled the club circuit between Montreal and New York. His skills as a musician, songwriter, and performer impressed Herb Alpert of A & M in 1973 when his demo tape was heard. Alpert co-produced his debut album 'Crazy Life' featuring Joe on keyboards and Gino on drums. Gino was then 20. Next came the album 'Powerful People' and Gino joined the 'Soul Train' on tour with Stevie Wonder. He was the first white artist to do so. In 1975 the album 'Storm at Sun-up' was released with the synthesized sound and Joe had evolved. The fourth album was 'Gist of the Gemini' and then 'A Pauper In Paradise' which presented some of Gino's best songs. It was performed with the help of the Royal Philharmonic Orchestra. 'Brother to Brother' followed, and with it the big breakthrough for Gino in the U.S.A. A tour with a 10-piece band in the U.S.A. then established him. This album included 'I Just Wanna Stop' and 'Love and Emotion' written by the youngest brother Ross.

VILLAGE PEOPLE

MACHO MAN (Album) *Casablanca* [*USA*]. It was released in the U.S.A. in March 1978, going to No 49 for one week and remaining 35 weeks in the charts. R.I.A.A. Gold Disc award on 4 August 1978. Platinum award on 26 December 1978.

By mid-1979, this album had sold two million. A relentless drive characterizes its sound with macho vocals and thumping drum beats.

MACHO MAN *Casablanca* [*USA*]. Released in the U.S.A. in June 1978, this was No 28 for one week and stayed 14 weeks in the charts. R.I.A.A. Gold Disc award on 30 October 1978.

Taken from the group's album of the same title, this one certainly appealed to the male pop fans.

CRUISIN' (Album) *Casablanca* [*USA*]. Released in the U.S.A. in September 1978, this went to No 4 for one week, staying 41 weeks in the charts. R.I.A.A. Gold Disc award on 13 October 1978. Platinum award on 13 December 1978.

Yet another big hit for Village People in this successful year for them. Sales of this went over the three million in the U.S.A. It contained the big success 'Y.M.C.A.' and other vignettes like 'The Woman', a scintillating Jacques Morali production again.

Y.M.C.A. *Casablanca* [*USA*]. Written by J. Morali, H. Belolo and V. Willis, this was released in the U.S.A. in October 1978 and in Britain in November 1978. It went to No 2 for two weeks in the U.S.A. and lasted 32 weeks in the charts. In Britain it hit No 1 for three weeks, lasting 15 weeks in the charts. R.I.A.A.

Gold Disc award on 18 December 1978. Platinum award on 10 February 1979.

Village People finished up the year of successes with this smash hit. It sold over two million in the U.S.A., and one million in Britain. In the U.S.A. it was in the Top 10 for 14 weeks, and eight weeks in Britain's Top 10.

JOE WALSH

BUT SERIOUSLY, FOLKS (Album) *Asylum [USA]*. This was released in the U.S.A. in May 1978 and in Britain in June 1978. In the U.S.A. it went to No 9 for one week, staying 22 weeks in the charts, and in Britain it went to No 17 for two weeks, staying 17 weeks in the charts. R.I.A.A. Gold Disc award on 31 May 1978. Platinum award on 7 August 1978.

Guitarist Joe Walsh was born in Wichita. He became well known when with James Gang. In 1972 he formed Barnstorm, and recorded the album 'Barnstorm'. Four more albums

followed, for Dunhill and Anchor labels, then 'But seriously, Folks', his first solo album for Asylum. This contains examples of his guitar virtuosity. He is a competent writer on both rockers and ballads. This album included his eight-minute epic 'Life's Been Good'; 'Tomorrow'; 'At the Station' and 'Over and Over'.

JEFF WAYNE

WAR OF THE WORLDS (Double album) *CBS [Britain]*. With lyrics by Gary Osborne and music by Jeff Wayne, this was released in Britain in June 1978, going to No 5 for three weeks and staying in the charts for over two years.

One of the most ambitious projects ever undertaken by CBS in Britain. It was the concept of Jeff Wayne to produce a dramatization-with-music of the famous H.G. Wells novel about invaders from Mars. The narration was by Richard Burton, and musicians employed were Justin Hayward, Phil Lynott and David Essex amongst others. Jeff Wayne composed, orchestrated, conducted and produced, and his father Jerry Wayne (*see* Griffin & Wayne, 1948) was executive producer. The double album had big sales in addition to the £1,000,000 plus sale in Britain. It exceeded platinum in Holland, New Zealand and Australia, and was gold in Canada, Spain, Israel and Belgium. Global sales have been estimated at over three million copies. The album includes: 'Forever Autumn' (sung by Justin Hayward); 'Thunder Child'; 'The Spirit of Man'; 'Brave New World'. It also sold briskly in the U.S.A.

BARRY WHITE

THE MAN (Album) *20th Century [USA]*. Released in the U.S.A. in October 1978, this went to No 11 for one week and stayed 19 weeks in the charts. R.I.A.A. Gold and Platinum Disc awards on 22 December 1978.

A fine Barry White album of seven tracks. The principal

numbers are: 'Your Sweetness Is My Weakness' and 'Just The Way You Are'.

THE WHO

WHO ARE YOU? (Album) *MCA [USA] Polydor [Britain]*. With material by Peter Townshend, this was released in the U.S.A. and Britain in August 1978. In the U.S.A. it climbed to No 4 for four weeks and stayed 19 weeks in the charts. In Britain it went to No 6 for one week and stayed nine weeks in the charts. R.I.A.A. Gold Disc award on 24 August 1978. Platinum award on 20 September 1978.

An album demonstrating that The Who were ever-changing and were at least a year ahead of their time again. In this, they stretch the boundaries of rock, and Townshend achieves an almost symphonic quality with his masterful use of synthesizers on 'Music Must Change'; 'Guitar and Pen'; 'New Song'; and 'Who Are You?'. British sales were over £300,000.

WINGS

LONDON TOWN (Album) *Capitol [USA] Parlophone [Britain]*. Written by Paul McCartney and Denny Laine, this was released in the U.S.A. and Britain in March 1978. It went to No 2 for five weeks in the U.S.A. and stayed in the charts for 24 weeks. In Britain it went to No 4 for three weeks, staying 17 weeks in the charts. R.I.A.A. Gold Disc award on 20 March 1978. Platinum award on 30 March 1978.

This album was shipped platinum. McCartney's first studio effort for over a year, with superb studio technique. It sold over £300,000 in Britain. Contents are: 'London Town'; 'Café on the Left Bank'; 'Children, Children'; 'Girlfriend'; 'I've Had Enough'; 'With a Little Luck'; 'Famous Groupies'; 'Deliver Your Children'; 'Name and Number'; 'Don't Let It Bring You Down'; 'Morse Moose & The Grey Goose'; 'I'm Carrying'; 'Backwards Traveller'.

WINGS' GREATEST (Album) *Parlophone [Britain] Capitol [USA]*. With songs by Paul McCartney, this was released in Britain and the U.S.A. in December 1978. It was No 5 for one week in Britain and stayed 31 weeks in the charts and in the U.S.A. it went to No 23 for one week, staying 15 weeks in the charts. R.I.A.A. Gold and Platinum Disc awards on 6 December 1978.

An album of Wings' greatest hits from 1971 to 1978, an instant million seller in the U.S.A. In Britain sales were over £1,000,000 worth.

Contents are: 'Another Day'; 'Silly Love Songs'; 'Live And Let Die'; 'Junior's Farm'; 'With a Little Luck'; 'Band On The Run'; 'Uncle Albert/Admiral Halsey'; 'Hi Hi Hi'; 'Let 'Em In'; 'My Love'; 'Jet'; 'Mull of Kintyre' (McCartney and Denny Laine).

YES

TORMATO (Album) *Atlantic [USA]*. With material by Yes, this was released in the U.S.A. and Britain in October 1978. It went to No 15 for two weeks in the U.S.A., staying in the charts for ten weeks. It went to No 8 for one week in Britain, staying 11 weeks in the charts. R.I.A.A. Gold Disc award on 10 October 1978. Platinum award on 8 November 1978.

First million seller for Yes in the 13 years since their formation. The band was started in Birmingham, Britain, in 1968, and got their breakthrough via London's Marquee Club. The original members were Jon Anderson (vocals); Chris Squire (bass); Bill Bruford (drums); Peter Banks (guitar); Tony Kaye (organ). Banks left in 1971 and Steve Howe was the replacement. Kaye left and Rick Wakeman joined. Bruford was replaced by Alan White, a session drummer, in 1972. Up to 1977, the group had made 10 albums for Atlantic. Number 11, 'Tormato', was the really big break in the U.S.A. This contained eight songs, each under eight minutes in length – intriguing music, with the outstanding track 'Don't Kill the Whale'. Sales in Britain were over £300,000 worth.

ORIGINAL FILM SOUNDTRACK

THE ROSE (Album) *Atlantic [USA]*. Released in the U.S.A. in December 1979, this went to No 9 for two weeks and stayed 41 weeks in the charts. R.I.A.A. Gold Disc award on 10 April 1980. Platinum award on 11 June 1980.

Bette Midler, singer and actress, has never sounded better than on this soundtrack from the critically acclaimed feature film. It includes old and new material. 'When a Man Loves a Woman' is an outstanding track, also 'The Rose'. The film features Bette Midler, Alan Bates and Frederic Forrest.

ORIGINAL FILM SOUNDTRACK (THE WHO)

THE KIDS ARE ALRIGHT (Album) *MCA [USA] Polydor [Britain]*. With material by Peter Townshend, this was released in the U.S.A. and Britain in June 1979. In the U.S.A. it went to No 14 for one week and stayed 17 weeks in the charts. In Britain it was No 26 for one week, staying nine weeks in the charts. R.I.A.A. Gold Disc award on 26 June 1979. Platinum award on 5 October 1979.

A superior rock documentary on The Who, re-mixed by John Entwhistle. It contains 20 of the group's most familiar tunes, including Peter Townshend's 'Long Live Rock' (from album 'Odds and Sods' 1974) which sets the theme for one of rock's legends. British sales were over 300,000.

ABBA

GREATEST HITS, Vol 2 (Album) *Polar [Sweden] Epic [Britain] Atlantic [USA]*. Written by ABBA (B. Ulvaeus and B. Andersson), this was released in Britain in November 1979 and in the U.S.A. in December 1979. In Britain it went to No 1 for four weeks, lasting 49 weeks in the charts. In the U.S.A. it was No 39 for one week and stayed 19 weeks in the charts. R.I.A.A. Gold Disc award on 23 April 1980.

This was Epic's (CBS) largest-ever U.K. shipment – two million. An instant sale of over 300,000 in Britain, with a final tally estimated at well over 500,000 in Britain and around two million globally. The album contained several titles that sold a million as single releases.

Contents are: (*) 'Knowing Me, Knowing You'; 'Take a Chance On Me'; (*) 'Dancing Queen'; (*) 'Money, Money, Money'; 'Rock Me'; 'Eagle'; 'I Wonder'; (*) 'Chiquita'; (*) 'The Name of the Game'; 'Angel Eyes'; 'Does Your Mother Know?'; 'Summer Night City'; 'Thank You For the Music'; 'Gimme, Gimme, Gimme'. (*) denotes singles million seller.

CHIQUITA *Polar [Sweden]*, *Epic [Britain]*. Written by B. Ulvaeus and B. Andersson, this was released in Britain in March 1979 and in the U.S.A. in November 1979. It went to No 2 for two weeks in Britain, staying nine weeks in the charts. In the U.S.A. it was No 47 for three weeks and stayed in the charts for nine weeks.

Biggest sales for this disc were the Spanish version for the Latin market – 2,250,000 copies.

AC/DC

HIGHWAY TO HELL (Album) *Atlantic [USA]*. Written by AC/DC, this was released in the U.S.A. in August 1979, going to No 22 for one week and staying 23 weeks in the charts. R.I.A.A. Gold Disc award on 6 December 1979. Platinum award on 18 March 1980.

AC/DC is Australia's finest export. It was formed in the early 1970s by Angus Young (guitar) and his brother Malcolm Young (guitar) aided by Phil Rudd (drums); Cliff Williams (bass); Brian Johnson (vocals); and Bonn Scott (vocals). They toured the outback extensively before going to London where they played at the Red Cow, Hammersmith, near the Hammersmith Odeon where they later triumphed. At the end of 1976, the best selections from their first two Australian albums 'High Voltage' and 'TNT' were combined for world release as 'High Voltage'. Their next success was 'Dirty Deeds Done Cheap' (1976) followed by 'Let There Be Rock' (1977), 'Power Age' and 'If You Want Blood' (both 1978). 'Highway To Hell' established them worldwide as one of the 1970s great rock groups. Bonn Scott died on 19 February 1980 in London.

HERB ALPERT & TIJUANA BRASS

RISE *A & M [USA]*. Written by A. Armar and A. Radazz, this was released in the U.S.A. in July 1979 and in Britain in October 1979. In the U.S.A. it climbed to No 1 for one week and stayed 25 weeks in the charts. In Britain it went to No 13 for one week, staying 12 weeks in the charts. R.I.A.A. Gold Disc award on 25 September 1979. Grammy award: Best Pop Instrumental Performance, 1979.

The fourth million seller single for Alpert and his unique band. An outstanding instrumental disc.

RISE (Album) *A & M [USA]*. Released in the U.S.A. in October 1979 and in Britain in November 1979, this went to No 7 in the U.S.A. and stayed there for two weeks, remaining in the charts for 27 weeks. In Britain it was No 37 for two weeks and stayed six weeks in the charts. R.I.A.A. Gold Disc and Platinum awards on 5 February 1980.

Yet another big-selling album for Alpert, who hit the world musical scene way back in 1962. A great follow-up to his single of the same title.

BAD COMPANY

DESOLATION ANGELS (Album) *Swan Song [USA]*. Written by Bad Company, this was released in the U.S.A. and Britain in March 1979. In the U.S.A. it went to No 3 for two weeks and stayed 33 weeks in the charts. In Britain it went to No 10 for one week, staying nine weeks in the charts. R.I.A.A. Gold Disc award on 20 March 1979. Platinum award on 26 April 1979.

Bad Company's fifth album and fourth million seller. It was recorded in 1978, followed by a prodigious spring/summer tour in 1979. It is the group's heaviest rock album yet, featuring their no-frills style of rock and their two great assets – the brooding, soulful vocals of Paul Rodgers and the cutting guitar style of Mike Ralphs. The album includes the hit single 'Rock'n'Roll Fantasy', plus 'Early in the Morning'; 'Gone, Gone, Gone'; and 'Evil Wind'.

Bad Company remains one of rock's most enduring self-contained bands after five years in the U.S.A.

THE BEE GEES

SPIRITS HAVING FLOWN (Album) *RSO* [*USA*]. Written by the Bee Gees, this was released in the U.S.A. and Britain in January 1979. It was No 1 for ten weeks in the U.S.A., staying 45 weeks in the charts. It went to No 1 for two weeks in Britain and stayed in the charts for 32 weeks. R.I.A.A. Gold Disc and platinum awards on 30 January 1979.

The Bee Gees' first studio album since their monumental success with 'Saturday Night Fever'. It shipped two million copies and was an instant success. Within three months, sales were four million. British sales were around 500,000, and it was in the British charts' Top 10 for 14 weeks. In the U.S.A. it had a phenomenal run at No 1 for 10 weeks. It established The Bee Gees as the leading proponents of disco/soul.

Three of the tracks were million-seller singles: 'Tragedy'; 'Too Much Heaven'; and 'Love You Inside Out'.

TRAGEDY *RSO* [*USA*]. Written by Barry, Robin and Maurice Gibb, this was released in the U.S.A. and Britain in February 1979. It went to No 1 for two weeks in both the U.S.A. and Britain, staying 19 weeks in the U.S. charts and 10 weeks in the British charts. R.I.A.A. Gold Disc award on 5 February 1979. Platinum award on 14 May 1979.

This sold over two million in the U.S.A. It was shipped 'gold'. Distinguished by its classic progressions, high harmonies, and an undercurrent of synthesizers. Culled from the album 'Spirits Having Flown'.

LOVE YOU INSIDE OUT *RSO* [*USA*]. Written by Barry, Maurice and Robin Gibb, this was released in the U.S.A. and Britain in April 1979. In the U.S.A. it went to No 4 for two weeks and stayed 15 weeks in the charts. In Britain it was No 13 for two weeks, staying in the charts for nine weeks. R.I.A.A. Gold Disc award on 10 April 1979.

Another instant million seller from the album 'Spirits Having Flown'. It featured light disco overtones and high vocal harmonies.

THE BEE GEES' 'GREATEST' (British title: BEE GEES' GREATEST HITS) (Album) *RSO* [*USA*]. With material written by The Bee Gees, this was released in the U.S.A. and Britain in November 1979. It was No 3 for four weeks in the U.S.A., remaining in the charts for 27 weeks. In Britain it was No 6 for three weeks and stayed 24 weeks in the charts. R.I.A.A. Gold Disc and platinum awards on 26 February 1980.

A great album of The Bee Gees' 1970s material. It included three tunes never released before. Instant million seller in the U.S.A. with an estimated total sale of over two million. British sales were over 300,000.

BELL & JAMES

LIVIN' IT UP ON FRIDAY NIGHT *A & M* [*USA*]. Written by Le Roy Bell and Casey James, this was released in the U.S.A. in January 1979 and in Britain in March 1979. In the U.S.A. it was No 15 for two weeks, staying 18 weeks in the charts. In Britain it was No 59 for one week, staying three weeks in the charts. R.I.A.A. Gold Disc award on 6 April 1979.

Le Roy Bell and Casey James started as writers for stars like Elton John, The Spinners and The O'Jays. They soared to success with their own debut single 'Livin It Up on Friday Night'.

PAT BENATAR

IN THE HEAT OF THE NIGHT (Album) *Chrysalis* [*USA*]. This was released in the U.S.A. in November 1979, going to No 16 for one week and staying 56 weeks in the charts. R.I.A.A. Gold Disc award on 25 March 1980. Platinum award on 8 December 1980.

Pat Andrzejewski Benatar grew up on Long Island, New York. Her mother left a promising career in opera and Pat was trained to be a classical singer from the age of nine, but other types of music interested her, and when The Beatles came along, instead of classical practice, she played their records continuously. Plans were made to enroll her in the Juilliard School of Music, but Pat decided against it. She married Dennis Benatar and moved to Virginia where he was stationed in the army. After two and a half years as a bank teller, she began singing in local bars and lounges. She returned to New York, and resumed cabaret performing, winding up at the Catch A Rising Star where she met many writers and started singing their songs. She was heard by Chrysalis Records' presidents Ellis and Wright. The next day she got an amazing review in the *New York Post*, and offers came from many record companies. She signed with Chrysalis, and her first album 'In the Heat of the Night' was produced by Mike Chapman and Peter Coleman. She was partnered by Neil Geralde, an established guitarist, originally a member of Rick Derringer's group, and her band for touring included him and Scott St Clair Sheets; Roger Capps and Myren Grumbacher. Chrysalis dubbed her 'Rock and Roll Woman of the Eighties'. This debut album sold well over the million.

BLONDIE

EAT TO THE BEAT (Album) *Chrysalis* [*USA*]. With material by the Blondie group, this was released in the U.S.A. and Britain in October 1979. It was No 17 for one week in the U.S.A. and stayed in the charts for 31 weeks. In Britain it reached No 1 for one week, lasting 31 weeks in the charts. R.I.A.A. Gold Disc award on 1 February 1980. Platinum award on 10 July 1980.

Blondie's second big-selling album, again produced by Mike Chapman. It was No 1 in Britain on the first week of release, and sold over the half million, in addition to a million or more in the U.S.A.

It contains the theme song 'Union City Blues' from the movie *Union City*, and was written by Debbie Harry and the band's bassist Nigel Harrison. Debbie Harry and the band launched themselves into the film world with Debbie playing the part of a psychotic housewife in the movie.

CHUCK BROWN & THE SOUL SEARCHERS

BUSTIN' LOOSE *MCA/Source* [*USA*]. Released in the U.S.A. in January 1979, this was No 36 for three weeks and stayed in the charts for 15 weeks. R.I.A.A. Gold Disc award on 14 March 1979.

Taken from the group's R.I.A.A. Gold Disc award album of the same title. First million seller for the Source label and the group.

CAPTAIN AND TENNILLE

DO THAT TO ME ONE MORE TIME *Casablanca* [*USA*]. This was released in the U.S.A. in October 1979 and in Britain in February 1980. In the U.S.A. it hit No 1 for one week and stayed 23 weeks in the charts. In Britain it was No 7 for one week and stayed in the charts for ten weeks. R.I.A.A. Gold Disc award on 11 February 1980.

Another big success for this duo, written by Captain (Daryl Dragon).

THE CARS

CANDY-O (Album) *Elektra/Asylum* [*USA*]. With songs by Ric Ocasek, this was released in the U.S.A. in June 1979 and in Britain in July 1979. It went to No 4 for four weeks in the U.S.A., staying 33 weeks in the charts. In Britain it was No 30 for one week, staying six weeks in the charts. R.I.A.A. Gold Disc award on 24 July 1979. Platinum award on 6 August 1979.

The Cars' second album, again produced by Roy Thomas Baker. A powerful disc of group member Ocasek's sophisticated songs.

CHEAP TRICK

CHEAP TRICK AT BUDOKAN (Album) *Epic* [*USA*]. Written by Cheap Trick, this was released in the U.S.A. and Britain in February 1979. In the U.S.A. it went to No 3 for five weeks and stayed 50 weeks in the charts. In Britain it was No 29 for one week, lasting seven weeks in the charts. R.I.A.A. Gold Disc award on 13 March 1979. Platinum award on 22 May 1979.

Cheap Trick quintet are Rick Nielsen (guitar); Tom Petersson (bass); Robin Zander (vocals); Bun E. Carlos (drums); Xeno (vocals). The group became part of CBS Records' roster of new artists and were signed to their Epic label in 1977. Their first albums were 'Cheap Trick' (1977); 'In Color' (1977); 'Heaven Tonight' (1978). 'Cheap Trick at Budokan' was recorded in 1978, and became a big success after the good response it generated as an import. The group took Japan by storm, and the album when released later in 1979 in the U.S.A. stormed up the charts and was a steady seller for almost a year. It included their big hits 'I Want You to Want Me' and 'Surrender'. Other tracks were 'Big Eyes'; 'Ain't That a Shame'; 'Need Your Love'; and 'Come on, Come on'.

I WANT YOU TO WANT ME *Epic* [*USA*]. Written by Rick Nielsen, this went to No 4 for two weeks in the U.S.A. and to No 29 for one week in Britain. It was in the U.S. charts for 24 weeks and stayed nine weeks in the British charts. R.I.A.A. Gold Disc award on 13 August 1979.

Cheap Trick's big single seller, from their album 'Cheap Trick at Budokan'.

DREAM POLICE (Album) *Epic* [*USA*]. Written by Cheap Trick, this was released in the U.S.A. in September 1979 and in Britain in October 1979. In the U.S.A. it went to No 3 for three weeks, staying 19 weeks in the charts. In Britain it was No 41 for one week, staying five weeks in the charts. R.I.A.A. Gold Disc award on 6 February 1980. Platinum award on the same date.

Second million seller for the group, a superb rock'n'roll disc with a sense of humour.

CHER

TAKE ME HOME *Casablanca* [*USA*]. Written by Michèle Aller and Bob Esty, this was released in the U.S.A. in February 1979, going to No 8 for one week and staying 19 weeks in the charts. R.I.A.A. Gold Disc award on 3 May 1979.

Cher's new disco image, and a stunning production by the co-writer Bob Esty. One of the biggest hits of the year.

CHIC

I WANT YOUR LOVE *Atlantic* [*USA*]. Written by Nile Rodgers and Bernard Edwards, this was released in the U.S.A. and Britain in February 1979. It went to No 5 for two weeks in the U.S.A. and stayed in the charts for 20 weeks. It went to No 4 for one week in Britain and stayed 11 weeks in the charts. R.I.A.A. Gold Disc award on 1 March 1979.

A great follow-up to 'Le Freak' (Atlantic's biggest single ever), this disc was a quick million seller.

GOOD TIMES *Atlantic* [*USA*]. Written by Nile Rodgers and Bernard Edwards, this was released in the U.S.A. and Britain in June 1979. In the U.S.A. it went to No 2 for three weeks and stayed 18 weeks in the charts. In Britain it went to No 5 for one week, staying 11 weeks in the charts. R.I.A.A. Gold Disc award on 26 June 1979.

Yet another almost instant million seller for Chic and its talented writers, from an upcoming album. Cosy vocals, crystal piano and production.

RISQUE (Album) *Atlantic* [*USA*]. Written by Nile Rodgers and Bernard Edwards, this was released in the U.S.A. and Britain in August 1979. It reached No 10 for three weeks in the U.S.A. and stayed 13 weeks in the charts. In Britain it was No 29 for one week and stayed 12 weeks in the charts. R.I.A.A. Platinum Disc award on 6 December 1979.

This superb album includes the hit single 'Good Times'. Chic remained as one of the most successful crossover stories of recent years, and the album is geared, once again, to that market.

CHARLIE DANIELS BAND

MILLION MILE REFLECTIONS (Album) *Epic* [*USA*]. With material by The Daniels Band and released in the U.S.A. in May 1979, this went to No 9 for two weeks and stayed in the charts for 37 weeks. R.I.A.A. Gold Disc award on 28 June 1979. Platinum award on 16 August 1979.

Daniels' second million-selling album. It shows why they are regarded as one of the premier 'southern' rock bands of the time. The album contained 'Reflections' (Daniels' tribute to the late Ronnie Van Zandt of Lynyrd Skynyrd) and the big hit 'The Devil Went Down To Georgia'. The personnel for the disc are: Charlie Daniels (guitar/violin/vocals); Tom Crain (guitar/vocals); Joel DiGregorio (vocals and keyboards); Fred Edwards (drums); Charles Hayward (bass); Jim Marshall (drums).

THE DEVIL WENT DOWN TO GEORGIA *Epic* [*USA*]. Written by the Daniels' group, this was released in the U.S.A. in June 1979 and in Britain in September 1979. In the U.S.A. it went to No 3 for two weeks, staying 23 weeks in the charts. In Britain it was No 14 for one week and stayed 10 weeks in the charts. R.I.A.A. Gold Disc award on 21 August 1979. Grammy award: Best Country Vocal Performance by Duo or Group, 1979.

The prime track from Daniels' album 'Million Mile Reflections', composed by Daniels and the five members of his band. On this, Daniels demonstrates his unparalleled singing of a story and fiddle playing.

TERI DeSARIO WITH KC

YES I'M READY *Casablanca* [*USA*]. This was released in the U.S.A. in November 1979 and was No 1 for one week, staying 22 weeks in the charts. R.I.A.A. Gold Disc award on 21 March 1980.

New female artist for the Casablanca label, teamed with KC (H.W. Casey) of KC & the Sunshine Band.

JOHN DENVER & THE MUPPETS

A CHRISTMAS TOGETHER (Album) *RCA* [*USA*]. This was released in December 1979, going to No 16 for three weeks

in the U.S.A. and staying seven weeks in the charts. R.I.A.A. Gold and Platinum Disc awards on 17 February 1980.

A superb seasonal album of John Denver with the TV Muppets. It was an inevitable million seller.

DOCTOR HOOK

WHEN YOU'RE IN LOVE WITH A BEAUTIFUL WOMAN *Capitol* [*USA*]. Written by Even Steven, this was released in the U.S.A. in April 1979 and in Britain in September 1979. It went to No 4 for two weeks in the U.S.A. and to No 1 for four weeks in Britain. It stayed 25 weeks in the U.S. charts and 16 weeks in the British charts. R.I.A.A. Gold Disc award on 22 August 1979.

This song was originally on the album 'Pleasure and Pain' (1978), which also had another million-seller single with 'Sharing the Night Together'. 'Beautiful Woman' sold half a million in Britain.

THE DOOBIE BROTHERS

WHAT A FOOL BELIEVES *Warner Bros* [*USA*]. Written by Michael McDonald and Kenny Loggins, this was released in the U.S.A. in January 1979 and in Britain in February 1979. It was No 1 for one week in the U.S.A., staying 21 weeks in the charts. In Britain it was No 31 for one week and stayed in the charts for 10 weeks. R.I.A.A. Gold Disc award on 14 April 1979. Grammy awards: Record of the Year, 1979; Song of the Year, 1979; Best Arrangement, 1979; Best Arrangement Accompanying Vocalists, 1979.

One of the U.S.A.'s premier rock groups performing with an easy-going beat, distinctive lead and high harmony. One of their biggest hits with many awards.

BOB DYLAN

SLOW TRAIN COMING (Album) *Columbia* [*USA*]. Written by Bob Dylan, this was released in the U.S.A. in August 1979 and in Britain in September 1979. It went to No 9 for two weeks in the U.S.A. and stayed in the charts for 16 weeks. In Britain it went to No 2 for two weeks, staying 13 weeks in the charts. R.I.A.A. Gold Disc award on 26 December 1979. Platinum award on 9 May 1980.

One of Dylan's all-time strongest albums, similar musically to his earliest work. There are religious undertones to the lyrics. The album includes 'Gotta Serve Somebody', a song that subsequently gave him his first individual Grammy award for Best Male Vocal Performer of 1979.

EAGLES

HEARTACHE TONIGHT *Elektra/Asylum* [*USA*]. Written by Henley, Frey, Seger and Souther, this was released in the U.S.A. in September 1979 and in Britain in October 1979. In the U.S.A. it went to No 1 for one week and stayed in the charts for 16 weeks. In Britain it was No 40 for one week and stayed in the charts for five weeks. R.I.A.A. Gold Disc award on 1 February 1980. Grammy award: Best Rock Performance by Group or Duo, 1979.

The prime track from Eagles' album 'The Long Run'. It has a big beat, slashing rhythm and whining guitars to accompany Glenn Frey's tough vocals.

THE LONG RUN (Album) *Elektra/Asylum* [*USA*]. Written by the Eagles group, this was released in the U.S.A. and Britain in September 1979. It climbed to No 1 in the U.S.A. and stayed there for 14 weeks, staying 52 weeks in the charts. In Britain it went to No 4 for two weeks and stayed in the charts for 15 weeks. R.I.A.A. Gold and Platinum Disc awards on 1 February 1980.

This album was No 2 the first week, and No 1 for over three months, being 28 weeks in the Top 10, plus a chart run of one year. The album is full of channelled energy, with seductive guitar and harmonies throughout. Sales are estimated at well over three million. The outstanding tracks are 'Heartache Tonight' and 'The Long Run'.

EARTH, WIND & FIRE

AFTER THE LOVE HAS GONE *ARC/Columbia* [*USA*]. Written by David Foster, Jay Graydon and William Champlin, this was released in the U.S.A. in June 1979 and in Britain in July 1979. It went to No 4 for two weeks in the U.S.A., remaining in the charts for 17 weeks. In Britain it went to No 4 for one week and stayed 10 weeks in the charts. R.I.A.A. Gold Disc award on 19 November 1979. Grammy Awards: Best R & B Vocal Performance, 1979; Best R & B Song of the Year, 1979.

Another lovely ballad from this group, their second million-selling single of the year.

BOOGIE WONDERLAND *ARC/Columbia* [*USA*]. Written by Jonathan Lind and Allee Willis, this was released in the U.S.A. and Britain in May 1979. In the U.S.A. it went to No 11 for two weeks and stayed 19 weeks in the charts. In Britain it went to No 4 for three weeks and stayed 13 weeks in the charts. R.I.A.A. Gold Disc award on 29 May 1979. Grammy award: Best R & B Instrumental Performance, 1979.

The outstanding track from the group's album 'I Am' and an almost instant million seller.

I AM (Album) *ARC/Columbia* [*USA*]. This was released in the U.S.A. in May 1979 and in Britain in June 1979. It was No 4 for four weeks in the U.S.A., staying in the charts for 27 weeks. In Britain it went to No 5 for five weeks and stayed 40 weeks in the charts. R.I.A.A. Gold and Platinum Disc awards on 7 June 1979.

Tremendous hit album for Earth, Wind & Fire. It included the million-seller 'Boogie Wonderland', with other strong songs being: 'Can't Get in' and 'Wait'. The album also sold half a million in Britain where it was 14 weeks in the Top 10. In the U.S.A. it was 13 weeks in their Top 10, and an instant million seller on release.

ELECTRIC LIGHT ORCHESTRA
DISCOVERY (Album) *Jet/CBS* [*USA*]. With material by Jeff Lynne, this was released in the U.S.A. and Britain in June 1979. In the U.S.A. it reached No 5 for four weeks and in Britain it was No 1 for five weeks. It was in the U.S. charts for 34 weeks and stayed 44 weeks in the British charts. R.I.A.A. Gold Disc award on 11 June 1979. Platinum award on 19 June 1979.

Another album by ELO, displaying their great sense of concept production and already established sound. It was in the U.S. Top 10 for three months and in Britain for 21 weeks. It was No 1 immediately on release in Britain with instant sales of 300,000. Estimated U.S. sales are put at over two million, and British at over half a million. Recording was made at Musicland Studios, Munich, with the strings and choir arranged by Jeff Lynne, Richard Tardy and Louis Clarke and conducted by Clarke.

Contents are: 'Shine a Little Love'; 'Confusion'; 'The Diary of Horace Wimp'; 'Last Train to London'; 'Midnight Blue'; 'On the Run'; 'Wishing'; 'Don't Bring me Down'.

DON'T BRING ME DOWN *Jet/CBS* [*USA*]. Written by Jeff Lynne, this was released in the U.S.A. and Britain in July 1979. In the U.S.A. it was No 3 for three weeks and stayed 18 weeks in the charts. In Britain it was No 3 for one week and stayed nine weeks in the charts. R.I.A.A. Gold Disc award on 20 November 1979.

A spectacular single from the group's 'Discovery' album.

E.L.O.'s GREATEST HITS (Album) *Jet/CBS* [*USA*]. This was released in the U.S.A. and in Britain in December 1979. It was No 22 for one week in the U.S.A., staying 10 weeks in the charts. In Britain it went to No 7 for one week and stayed 16 weeks in the charts. R.I.A.A. Gold Disc award on 13 March 1980. Platinum award on 15 October 1980.

This album sold a million in the U.S.A. and over 300,000 in Britain.

FLEETWOOD MAC
TUSK (Double album) *Warner Bros* [*USA*]. Written by Fleetwood Mac, this was released in the U.S.A. and Britain in October 1979. In the U.S.A. it went to No 4 for three weeks and stayed 28 weeks in the charts. In Britain it climbed to No 1 for one week and stayed 20 weeks in the charts R.I.A.A. Gold and Platinum Disc awards on 12 February 1980.

Sales of over one million in the U.S.A. and over 300,000 in Britain for this highly progressive double album for Fleetwood Mac, after a wait of over two years. It was in the U.S. Top 10 for 13 weeks and Britain's Top 10 for six weeks. The group's Lindsey Buckingham wrote nine of the songs. It includes two tracks of particular note: 'Tusk' and Stevie Nicks' sultry 'Sara'. Lindsey

Buckingham's production influence and the digital recording reaffirmed their position as one of pop music's most creative and interesting groups. Other tracks are: 'What Makes You Think You're the One?'; 'Not that Funny' (both Lindsey Buckingham); 'Sisters of the Moon' (Nicks); and 'Over and Over' (McVie). Sales by 1980 were 2,500,000.

DAN FOGELBERG
PHOENIX (Album) *Columbia* [*USA*]. Written by Dan Fogelberg, this was released in the U.S.A. in November 1979, going to No 3 for three weeks and staying 30 weeks in the charts. R.I.A.A. Gold and Platinum Disc awards on 13 March 1980.

Fogelberg is one of rock's sophisticates. His sensitive lyrics and crying guitar style are the feature of this fine album, beautifully realized by fine back-up musicians.

FOREIGNER
HEAD GAMES (Album) *Atlantic* [*USA*]. With material by Foreigner, this was released in the U.S.A. in September 1979, going to No 5 for two weeks and staying in the charts for 27 weeks. R.I.A.A. Gold and Platinum Disc awards on 7 January 1980.

Foreigner's third million-seller album. Two million sold by 1980.

ART GARFUNKEL
BRIGHT EYES *CBS* [*Britain*]. Written by Mike Batt, this was No 1 for six weeks in Britain and stayed 19 weeks in the charts.

This was originally recorded for the cartoon film *Watership Down*, a charming allegorical and poignant story about rabbits. Composer Mike Batt (born Southampton 6 February 1950) is one of Britain's top creative talents. He is self-taught on guitar and all keyboard instruments, and picked up orchestration by experience. He came into prominence when he wrote the music for *The Wombles of Wimbledon Common*, fictitious litter-collecting animals created by children's authoress Elisabeth Beresford in a book called *The Wombles* written in 1967. The Wombles were Orinoco (Mike Batt) and various people playing the other characters of Wellington; Bungo; Madame Cholet; Great Uncle Bulgaria; Tomsk and Tobermory.

Art Garfunkel's 'Bright Eyes' was a tremendous success in Britain where it sold the million.

GLORIA GAYNOR

LOVE TRACKS (Album) *Polydor* [*USA*]. This was released in the U.S.A. in January 1979 and in Britain in March 1979. In the U.S.A. it was No 9 for two weeks and stayed 19 weeks in the charts. In Britain it was No 31 for one week, staying six weeks in

the charts. R.I.A.A. Gold Disc award on 5 February 1979. Platinum award on 27 March 1979.

A fine album by the Queen of the Discos, achieving million status within two months of release.

GQ

DISCO NIGHTS (Rock Freak) *Arista* [*USA*]. Written by the GQ group with lyrics by E. Raheim LeBlanc, this was No 12 for two weeks in the U.S.A. and No 42 for one week in Britain. It stayed 31 weeks in the U.S. charts and six weeks in the British charts. R.I.A.A. Gold Disc award on 23 April 1979.

This band took shape in 1968, when Emmanuel Raheim Le Blanc and Keith 'Sabu' Crier first started jamming in the Bronx area of New York. They played neighbourhood clubs and parties, going through a series of personnel name changes: Sabu & The Survivors; Sons of Darkness; The Third Chance; and Rhythm Makers. LeBlanc (guitar/vocals) and Crier (bass) recruited Herb Lane (keyboards) and then Paul Service (drums). They took on Tony Lopez as managaer and Beau Ray Fleming as producer, after a frustrating 6-year tenure with a small label DeLite. Lopez, a subscriber to *GQ* magazine (*Gentleman's Quarterly*), changed the band's name to GQ for 'Good Quality' and got together with the editor in the hope of doing joint promotions. It was in Manhattan that they played a tape over a car stereo for Ray Fleming. He invited Larkin Arnold (Arista senior vice president) to come from Los Angeles to hear the group in a cramped basement in the South Bronx. They played 'Disco Nights' and two weeks later were in the studio. 'Disco Nights' coupled with 'Boogie Oogie Oogie' was a big hit as a single, and was followed by an album so titled. This 'overnight success' plus GQ's unique instrumentation and the styling of their songs made them one of the hottest bands in the U.S.A.

'Disco Nights (Rock Freak)' inspired the hottest new dance in years - 'The Rock'.

DISCO NIGHTS (Album) *Arista* [*USA*]. With songs by Raheim LeBlanc and the GQ group, this was released in the U.S.A. in March 1979, going to No 11 for one week and staying 18 weeks in the charts. R.I.A.A. Gold Disc award on 8 May 1979. Platinum award on 19 October 1979.

GQ's fine debut album, produced by Beau Ray Fleming and Jimmy Simpson (brother of songwriter Valerie Simpson). The album was dedicated to late R & B star, Billy Stewart. The album was a big hit with the discos, and included the popular 'Disco Nights (Rock Freak)'; 'Make My Dream a Reality'; 'Wonderful'; 'This Happy Feeling' - all originals - and 'Boogie Oogie Oogie' (written by Janice Johnson and Perry Kibble in 1978 when it was a hit for Taste of Honey group), a great favourite of GQ.

MOLLY HATCHET

MOLLY HATCHET (Album) *Epic* [*USA*]. With material by Molly Hatchet and released in the U.S.A. in April 1979, this was No 72 for one week and stayed in the charts for 11 weeks. R.I.A.A. Gold Disc award on 28 June 1979. Platinum award on 30 December 1980.

This Southern rock band from Jacksonville, Florida, was formed in 1971 by Dave Hlubeck (guitar) and Steve Holland (guitar). Other members are Duane Roland (guitar) and Brice Crunp (drums). It wasn't until 1976 that the three-line guitar group became stable. They played the tough club circuit and this debut album was soon certified gold. Produced by Tom Werman and Bee Jay Studios in Orlando, Florida, it included 'Bounty Hunter'; 'Big Apple'; 'Gator Country'; 'Dreams I'll Never See'; and 'Trust Your Old Friend'. They got recognition by British audiences when they played the Reading Festival in 1979, and came back for three encores.

FLIRTIN' WITH DISASTER (Album) *Epic* [*USA*]. Written by Molly Hatchet, this was released in the U.S.A. in September 1979, going to No 22 for four weeks and staying 29 weeks in the charts. R.I.A.A. Gold Disc award on 10 January 1980. Platinum award on 22 February 1980.

Second million-selling album for the group. It contained the hit single 'Flirtin' with Disaster'.

PATRICK HERNANDEZ

BORN TO BE ALIVE *Columbia* [*USA*]. Written by Patrick Hernandez, this was released in the U.S.A. in June 1979, going to No 19 for one week and staying in the charts for 22 weeks. R.I.A.A. Gold Disc award on 13 November 1979.

Another new artist from the Columbia (CBS) roster. This disc was a huge disco hit that broke through into the pop market. Its rhythm and breathtaking strings created an awesome experience, and was No 1 in every country in Europe, also Argentina, Australia, Brazil, Canada and Mexico. Estimated global sales were 11 million. Patrick is a Frenchman from Guadeloupe, but lived in Paris from 1966.

RUPERT HOLMES

ESCAPE (The Pina Colada Song) *MCA* [*USA*]. Written by Rupert Holmes and released in the U.S.A. in October 1979, this was No 1 for two weeks and stayed 19 weeks in the charts. R.I.A.A. Gold Disc award on 7 January 1980.

Rupert Holmes was born in England to a British mother and a U.S. serviceman father, and raised outside New York City. His father became a music teacher and started Rupert on clarinet at an early age. He wrote his first song at the age of six, continued his writing over the years and formed his first band, The Nomads, in high school. He subsequently recorded five albums; his first, 'Widescreen', got Barbra Streisand's attention, and she got him to produce and arrange her album 'Lazy Afternoon' which contained four of his songs. Rupert also wrote several songs for her film *A Star Is Born*. His material has also been recorded by Barry Manilow; B. J. Thomas; Dionne Warwick; Manhattan Transfer; and Mac Davis. He also produced albums for London-based artists The Strawbs; Sparks; John Miles; and Sailor. Rupert's songs are very specific - he writes them to say exactly what he means. His versatile style rates him as one of the most popular singer-songwriters of the early 1980s, and he was named top new vocalist for 1979-80 by *Record World*. 'Escape' was taken from his album 'Partners in Crime'.

Pina Colada is a Caribbean drink made of Bacardi rum, coconut, pineapple juice and crushed ice.

INSTANT FUNK

I GOT MY MIND MADE UP (You can get it girl) *RCA/ Salsoul* [*USA*]. Written by Kim and Scotty Miller and Raymond Earl, this was released in the U.S.A. in January 1979, going to No 26 for two weeks and staying in the charts for 14 weeks. R.I.A.A. Gold Disc award on 2 April 1979.

Instant Funk's instant success is due to a solid foundation after six years as back-up band and/or recording musicians for Bunny Sigler, as well as with artists Evelyn 'Champagne' King; Lou Rawls; The O'Jays; The Salsoul Orchestra and others. It had emerged as one of the pre-eminent bands in the funk field by 1977. Their career started as members of TNJ signing with Philadelphia International label TSOP in 1972. They disbanded in 1974. Kim Miller (guitar) and Scotty Miller (drums) stayed together, and then met Bunny Sigler, and worked with him. They added Dennis Richardson (piano) and Charles Williams (conga) naming themselves Instant Funk after the style they created for themselves. Later band additions were James Carmichael (percussion/lead vocals); Larry Davis (trumpet); Johnny Onderline (saxophones); Eric Huff (trombone); and George Bell, formerly of Village People, on guitar. Sigler, their producer, got them a contract with Salsoul Records. Their blend of funk and R & B sounds in collaboration with Sigler made a unique mark on contemporary music.

MICHAEL JACKSON

DON'T STOP TILL YOU GET ENOUGH *Epic* [*USA*]. Written by Michael Jackson and Phillinganes, this was released in the U.S.A. in August 1979 and in Britain in September 1979. It was No 1 for one week in the U.S.A., staying 20 weeks in the charts. In Britain it went to No 3 for one week and stayed 12 weeks in the charts. R.I.A.A. Gold Disc award on 29 November 1979. Grammy award: Best R & B Vocal Performer, 1979.

Taken from Michael's upcoming album. Its contrasting fal-

setto vocals and prominent bass/percussion created a hypnotic effect. The disc also sold over 500,000 in Britain. It was Michael's first Grammy award.

OFF THE WALL (Album) *Epic* [*USA*]. Written by Michael Jackson, this was released in the U.S.A. in August 1979 and in Britain in September 1979. In the U.S.A. it went to No 2 for seven weeks and stayed in the charts for 64 weeks. In Britain it went to No 5 for one week, lasting 61 weeks in the charts. R.I.A.A. Gold and Platinum Disc awards on 10 December 1979.

Michael Jackson is the strongest member of the famous Jackson family which created entirely their own sound. This debut album combines disco and traditional R & B rhythm with several outstanding ballads. It includes the big hit 'Don't Stop Till you Get Enough', and was produced by Quincy Jones. An astounding success on both sides of the Atlantic, it was 43 weeks of its chart run in the U.S.A. in the Top 10, and only deprived of the No 1 spot through the success of another 'Wall' disc – 'The Wall' by Pink Floyd. In Britain it was in the Top 20 for most of the time where it sold around 500,000. U.S. sales are estimated at well over two million.

The album also included the hits 'Rock With You'; 'She's Out of My Life'; and 'Off the Wall'.

ROCK WITH YOU *Epic* [*USA*]. Written by Rod Temperton, this was released in the U.S.A. in October 1979 and in Britain in February 1980. It climbed to No 1 for two weeks in the U.S.A. and remained 22 weeks in the charts. In Britain it went to No 7 for one week and stayed nine weeks in the charts. R.I.A.A. Gold Disc award on 14 February 1980.

This second million-selling single for Michael made it a fabulous year for him. The song was composed by Temperton, the keyboards wizard of the English group Heatwave.

THE JACKSONS

SHAKE YOUR BODY (Down To The Ground) *Epic* [*USA*]. Written by Marion, Michael, Sigmund, Steven and Tariano Jackson, this was released in the U.S.A. in January 1979 and in Britain in March 1979. In the U.S.A. it went to No 3 for two weeks and stayed 28 weeks in the charts. In Britain it went to No 4 for two weeks and stayed 12 weeks in the charts. R.I.A.A. Gold and Platinum Disc awards on 12 April 1979.

A new disco release with unusual arrangements. It has a measure of gospel in the beat, and features Michael Jackson's high, distinctive vocals. U.S. sales were well over two million. In Britain, sales were 250,000. Produced by the group.

WAYLON JENNINGS

GREATEST HITS (Album) *RCA* [*USA*]. Released in the U.S.A. in April 1979, this went to No 25 for one week and stayed in the charts for 94 weeks. R.I.A.A. Gold Disc award on 16 May 1979. Platinum award on 7 September 1979.

One of the pioneers of 'outlaw' country music, this Jennings album is virtually a documentary of the genre. It includes 11 songs such as 'Mammas Don't Let your Babies Grow Up to be Cowboys', his duet with Willie Nelson. An extremely popular album, staying in the U.S. charts for almost two years.

ELTON JOHN

MAMA CAN'T BUY YOU LOVE *MCA* [*USA*]. Written by Le Roy Bell and Casey James, this was released in the U.S.A. in June 1979, going to No 7 for two weeks and staying 18 weeks in the charts. R.I.A.A. Gold Disc award on 17 August 1979.

A great number by American writers/recording artists Bell and James. In this year Elton returned with live performances, a series of historic concerts in the Soviet Union and his first major U.S. tour in four years. In these, he dropped his flamboyant appearance and used only his percussionist Ray Cooper, basing his approach on being just a singer and his songs. He made headlines as the most important pop singer to tour the Soviet Union. Disc produced by Thom Bell. The vocals fit perfectly to Bell's sparkling lyrics, production and keyboards.

ROBERT JOHN

SAD EYES *EMI/America* [*USA*]. Written by Robert John, this was released in the U.S.A. in May 1979 and in Britain in October 1979. In the U.S.A. it reached No 1 for five weeks and stayed 31 weeks in the charts. In Britain it was No 31 for one week and stayed eight weeks in the charts. R.I.A.A. Gold Disc award on 11 September 1979.

A welcome comeback for Robert John, whose last hit was 'The Lion Sleeps Tonight' in 1971. The track is taken from his album 'Robert John'. Dramatic falsetto vocals with weeping guitar and full chorus, plus an attractive hook.

RICKIE LEE JONES

RICKIE LEE JONES (Album) *Warner Bros* [*USA*]. Written by Rickie Lee Jones, this was released in the U.S.A. in March 1979 and in Britain in June 1979. It went to No 3 for two weeks in the U.S.A. and stayed 30 weeks in the charts. It was No 18 for one week in Britain, staying 21 weeks in the charts. R.I.A.A. Gold Disc award on 22 May 1979. Platinum award on 7 August 1979. Grammy award: Best New Artist, 1979.

This debut album was a success from its first week of release in the U.S.A. Singer/songwriter Rickie's debut album was produced by Lenny Waronker and Russ Titelman. Her disc embraces a style of blues, jazz and folk with polished passionate lyrics.

THE JONES GIRLS

YOU GONNA MAKE ME LOVE SOMEBODY ELSE *Philadelphia International* [*USA*]. Released in the U.S.A. in June 1979, this was No 39 for one week and stayed in the charts for 12 weeks. R.I.A.A. Gold Disc award on 30 August 1979.

Another new group, a trio, with a disc that sold a quick million.

JOURNEY

EVOLUTION (Album) *Columbia* [*USA*]. With material written by Journey and released in the U.S.A. in March 1979, this was No 19 for one week and stayed 45 weeks in the charts. R.I.A.A. Gold Disc award on 12 April 1979. Platinum award on 19 October 1979.

Journey's second million-selling album. It included the title song 'Evolution'. The album was the group's best pop-oriented record to date.

Best track: 'Lovin', Touchin', Squeezin''.

KISS

DYNASTY (Album) *Casablanca* [*USA*]. Written by Kiss, this was released in the U.S.A. in May 1979 and in Britain in July 1979. In the U.S.A. it went to No 7 for two weeks and stayed in the charts for 33 weeks. In Britain it was No 50 for one week and stayed six weeks in the charts. R.I.A.A. Gold Disc award on 6 June 1979. Platinum award on 10 July 1979.

A new collective effort by the four writer/members of Kiss. The album is a mixture of standard pounding rhythms and some disco. It included the hit 'I Was Made For Lovin' You'.

I WAS MADE FOR LOVIN' YOU *Casablanca* [*USA*]. Written by Kiss, this was released in the U.S.A. in May 1979, going to No 5 for one week and staying 20 weeks in the charts. R.I.A.A. Gold Disc award on 16 August 1979.

The outstanding track from the group's album 'Dynasty'.

THE KNACK

MY SHARONA *Capitol* [*USA*]. Written by Doug Feiger and Berton Averre, this was released in the U.S.A. and Britain in June 1979. In the U.S.A. it was No 1 for five weeks, staying 26 weeks in the charts. In Britain it was No 6 for one week and stayed 10 weeks in the charts. R.I.A.A. Gold Disc award on 16 August 1979.

The Knack quartet: Doug Feiger (lead singer/rhythm guitar); Berton Averre (lead guitar/vocalist); Bruce Gary (drums); Prescott Niles (bass). Everyone went to see them at the local Los Angeles clubs and they were exceedingly well known even before signing with a label - Capitol Records who were very excited about the group. Their brand of new rock music, one of the best examples of power pop, quickly took them to the top of the charts. Rock fans wanted to hear good, straightforward rock and roll again, and 'My Sharona' was a natural hit everywhere. The group later (1980) made a successful European and Japanese tour.

GET THE KNACK (Album) *Capitol* [*USA*]. With material by The Knack, this was released in the U.S.A. in July 1979. It reached No 1 for four weeks and stayed in the charts for 32 weeks. R.I.A.A. Gold Disc award on 11 July 1979. Platinum award on 3 August 1979.

Following The Knack's success with 'My Sharona', this debut album raced to the top of the charts, and was also in the Top 10 for fifteen weeks. It was the fastest album to be certified gold for Capitol since the historic 'Meet the Beatles' in 1964. It was produced by Mike Chapman.

KOOL AND THE GANG

LADIES' NIGHT (Album) *De-Lite* [*USA*]. With material by Kool And The Gang, this was released in the U.S.A. in September 1979, going to No 14 for two weeks and staying 46 weeks in the charts. R.I.A.A. Gold and Platinum Disc awards on 21 January 1980.

This album was released at the time the group were celebrating their tenth anniversary. Through the seventies they remained pacesetters by being continually creative and introducing more elements of their jazz background. With the advent of disco, their music changed direction and the band regrouped. They added a lead vocalist, and the personel was: Robert Earl Bell; Ronald Nathan Bell; George M. Brown; Claydes Eugene Smith; James Warren Taylor; Dennis Roland Thomas; Earl Eugene Toon Jr, and Muhammed Meekaaeel. Then they created a sound acceptable for both a pop and black market. Eumir Deodato came in as producer resulting in the new Kool And The Gang, with an irresistibly successful combination of R & B, pop and jazz.

The album included a hit track 'Ladies' Night'. First million-selling album for the group.

LADIES' NIGHT *De-Lite* [*USA*]. Written by Kool And The Gang and released in the U.S.A. in September 1979, this went to No 5 for two weeks and stayed in the charts for 26 weeks. R.I.A.A. Gold Disc award on 10 December 1979.

Principal track from their album of the same title, their third million-selling single. The band's music found its way into films, being used in both *Saturday Night Fever* and *Rocky*.

LED ZEPPELIN

IN THROUGH THE DOOR (Album) *Swan Song* [*USA*]. Written by Led Zeppelin, this was released in the U.S.A. and Britain in August 1979. It was No 1 for seven weeks in the U.S.A. and stayed 35 weeks in the charts. In Britain it was No 1 for three weeks and stayed in the charts for 15 weeks. R.I.A.A. Gold and Platinum Disc awards on 7 January 1980.

Led Zeppelin's ninth consecutive album to go gold and platinum. It was No 1 in its first week of release in both Britain and the U.S.A., and stayed in the U.S. Top 10 for 26 weeks. The only other album to achieve No 1 immediately was Elton John's 'Captain Fantastic'. The initial demand for Led Zeppelin's album was unbelievable, 1,700,000 within days in the U.S.A. with an estimated U.S. total sale of over three million. In Britain sales were an immediate 100,000. After nearly three years away from recording, the album is neither New Wave nor disco, but simply superb rock'n'roll, the group having departed from a heavy metal sound with the addition of very good acoustic work. It made a tremendous appeal to a younger generation hearing the group for the first time. The album included a superb 10-minute track 'Carouselambra'.

Led Zeppelin suffered a sad loss when drummer John Bonham died on 25 September 1980 in Windsor, Britain.

LITTLE RIVER BAND

FIRST UNDER THE WIRE (Album) *Capitol* [*USA*]. With material written by Little River Band, this was released in the U.S.A. in July 1979, going to No 7 for two weeks and staying 28 weeks in the charts. R.I.A.A. Gold and Platinum Disc awards on 20 November 1979.

Second million-selling album for this Australian group. They signed directly with Capitol early in 1979. Advance orders were over 500,000. Up to this time the group had made three world tours, and from August made a three-month tour of North America. This is a fine album, with lush instrumentation and perfect harmony.

LYNYRD SKYNYRD

GOLD AND PLATINUM (Double album) *MCA* [*USA*]. Written by Lynyrd Skynyrd, this was released in the U.S.A. in December 1979 and in Britain in February 1980. In the U.S.A. it went to No 14 for two weeks and stayed 25 weeks in the charts. In Britain it was No 49 for one week and stayed four weeks in the charts. R.I.A.A. Gold Disc award on 25 March 1980. Platinum award on 18 April 1980.

Double album of the group's greatest hits, a tribute to their creativity, and longevity in the best traditions of the Southern boogie band genre. Complete contents are: 'Free Bird'; 'Tuesday's Gone'; 'Whiskey Rock-A-Roller'; 'Down South Jukin''; 'Comin' Home'; 'Saturday Night Special'; 'Gimme Three Steps'; 'What's Your Name?'; 'Simple Man'; 'On the Hunt'; 'Gimme Back My Bullets'; 'That Smell'; 'I Ain't The One'; 'You Got That Right'; 'I Know A Little'; 'Sweet Home Alabama'.

'M'

POP MUZIK *MCA* [*Britain*], *Sire* [*USA*]. Written by Robin Scott, this was released in Britain in April 1979 and in the U.S.A. in August 1979. In the U.S.A. it went to No 4 for three weeks, staying 26 weeks in the charts, and it remained 14 weeks in the British charts. R.I.A.A. Gold Disc award on 5 December 1979.

'M' is Robin Scott, a young Englishman who writes, produces and arranges. M denotes music, muzak and muzik as in pop music. 'Pop Muzik' is considered a classic single, and Scott (as 'M') recorded a song flawless in design, a perfect three minutes of pop plus a hook that caught on. Everybody sang it. Scott cherishes his anonymity. His compositions are neither identifiably American nor European, disco, pop, New Wave or rock. He used two female vocalists and many studio techniques to produce his sound. It became an international success.

Sales in Britain were 250,000 and it was in the Top 10 for seven weeks. In the U.S. Top 10 for nine weeks.

McFADDEN & WHITEHEAD

AIN'T NO STOPPIN' US NOW *Philadelphia International* [*USA*]. Written by Gene McFadden and John Whitehead, this was released in the U.S.A. in March 1979 and in Britain in May 1979. It was No 15 for two weeks in the U.S. and stayed 19 weeks in the charts. It reached No 5 for one week in Britain and stayed 10 weeks in the charts. R.I.A.A. Gold Disc award on 8 May 1979. Platinum award on 27 July 1979.

A new U.S. duo with a tremendous hit. This disc sold over two million. They are major writers/artists/producers. Lush female chorus – a real disco disc.

PETER MAFFAY

REVANCHE (Revenge) (Album) *Metronome* [*Germany*]. Peter Maffay was Germany's male vocalist of 1979, and was the first German artist in two decades to get a gold single and a platinum album in the same year.

BARRY MANILOW

ONE VOICE (Album) *Arista* [*USA*]. Written by Barry Manilow, this was released in the U.S.A. and Britain in October 1979. In the U.S.A. it went to No 8 for two weeks and stayed 26 weeks in the charts. In Britain it was No 18 for one week, staying in the charts for seven weeks. R.I.A.A. Gold and Platinum Disc awards on 28 January 1980.

Another huge success for Barry and his fine songs, still further enhancing his tremendous popularity everywhere.

FRANK MILLS

MUSIC BOX DANCER *Polydor* [*USA*]. Written by Frank Mills and released in the U.S.A. in January 1979, this went to No 1 for one week and stayed in the charts for 23 weeks. R.I.A.A. Gold Disc award on 28 March 1979.

Taken from this Canadian artist's album of the same title, it is a piano solo, the first of that genre to hit the million for a long time. Mills' album also sold over half a million. The single was in the U.S. Top 10 for ten weeks.

MAXINE NIGHTINGALE

LEAD ME ON *Windsong* [*USA*]. Written by Allee Willis and David Lasley, this was released in the U.S.A. in June 1979, going to No 4 for one week and staying 22 weeks in the charts. R.I.A.A. Gold Disc award on 18 September 1979.

Maxine's first single in some time is a lilting ballad, beautifully recorded and orchestrated. She signed with Windsong early in the year and her album 'Lead Me On' was released. The single is taken from it, Maxine thus reaffirming her hit status.

THE O'JAYS

IDENTIFY YOURSELF (Album) *Philadelphia International* [*USA*]. This was released in the U.S.A. in August 1979, going to No 19 for two weeks and staying in the charts for 25 weeks. R.I.A.A. Gold and Platinum Disc awards on 26 December 1979.

With one of the longest recording histories in contemporary music, this group has never released a mediocre album. This one has appeal for all buyers – pop, black and disco fans – plus the group's fabulous vocals. The album is different from their previous issues in that it shows a lot of creative development by changing their sound, using some very fine musicians and assistance from other people, notably Ndugu, Mtume and Stevie Wonder. It took them 22 years to develop the polish and expertise for the album. Their collaboration with the label's famous songwriting duo Kenny Gamble and Leon Huff since the early seventies put them in a category few other groups can equal.

THOM PACE

MAYBE (Theme of TV Series *Grizzly Adams*) *DG/Polydor* [*Germany*] *RSO* [*Britain*]. Written by Thom Pace, this was No 1 in Germany for nine weeks. It was released in Britain in May 1979, reaching No 14 for one week and staying 15 weeks in the charts.

Thom Pace wrote 'Maybe' in 10 minutes in 1972, originally for a movie *The Snow Tigers*, but it was first used in the TV series *Grizzly Adams*. NBC received thousands of letters about the theme, but no U.S. record label showed any interest. They couldn't convince a record company that a single that didn't sound like anything else on the radio would be a hit. It was only when *Grizzly* was syndicated in Europe that RSO (through its London office) showed interest. In 1979 the series hit the German airwaves, and the single literally exploded. 800,000 were sold there, and it was also a hit in Britain, Australia and Switzerland. It was produced by Don Perry of DG/Polydor, and a Gold Disc was presented in Munich in February 1980. It was Thom Pace's first award.

PEACHES & HERB

2 HOT (Album) *Polydor* [*USA*]. Released in the U.S.A. in January 1979, this went to No 2 for two weeks and stayed 34 weeks in the charts. R.I.A.A. Gold Disc award on 16 February

1979. Platinum award on 28 March 1979.

Peaches and Herb's debut album was a quick success. It stayed in the U.S. Top 10 for 16 weeks, and included their hit 'Shake Your Groove Thing'.

REUNITED *Polydor* [*USA*]. Written by Dino Fekaris and Fred Perren, this was released in the U.S.A. in March 1979 and in Britain in April 1979. It went to No 1 for four weeks in the U.S.A., staying 21 weeks in the charts. In Britain it went to No 4 for one week and stayed 12 weeks in the charts. R.I.A.A. Gold Disc award on 6 April 1979. Platinum award on 11 May 1979.

A monster hit for this duo, with over two million sales in the U.S.A. and 250,000 in Britain. Eleven weeks in the U.S. Top 10, and five weeks in the British Top 10.

TEDDY PENDERGRASS

TEDDY (Album) *Philadelphia International* [*USA*]. Released in the U.S.A. in June 1979, this was No 5 for two weeks and stayed in the charts for 24 weeks. R.I.A.A. Gold Disc award on 11 June 1979. Platinum award on 27 July 1979.

Teddy's third consecutive million-selling album which still further enhanced his sexy image. As a song stylist he is in a class by himself. The disc includes a sizzling track 'Turn Off the Lights', and tunes from some of the finest new writers. It was eight weeks in U.S. Top 10.

TOM PETTY & THE HEARTBREAKERS

DAMN THE TORPEDOES (Album) *Backstreet/MCA* [*USA*]. Written by the group, this was released in the U.S.A. in October 1979, going to No 3 for two weeks and staying 45 weeks in the charts. R.I.A.A. Gold Disc award on 25 February 1980. Platinum award on 27 February 1980.

The personnel of the band are: Tom Petty (guitar/vocals); Benimont Tench (keyboards/vocals); Mike Campbell (guitar); Ron Blair (bass); Stan Lynch (drums/keyboards). They made their disc debut in 1976 with the album 'Tom Petty & The Heartbreakers' followed by 'You're Gonna Get It' (1978) and 'Official Live Bootleg' – all from the Shelter label with whom they signed. Petty's first single hit 'Breakdown' involved them in legal trouble as a result of MCA's purchase of ABC Records which had distributed Shelter. This resulted in Petty being left with a half-million dollars' debt, but he filed under the Bankruptcy Act. The legal triangle surrounding the band was solved by the newly formed Backstreet label, part of MCA, through a new contract which led to the late 1979 release of 'You're Gonna Get It'. 'Damn the Torpedoes' was co-produced by Tom Petty and Jimmy Lovine, a much richer finish resulting for the basic five-piece ensemble, balancing Petty and Campbell's classic guitar work against Tench's keyboards. With their roots in prime 1960s rock supported by their sound, the album was their big breakthrough. The upsets of 1979 were eclipsed by one of the first true success stories of 1980. Tom Petty, born 1953, hails from Gainesville, Florida. The album was 12 weeks in the U.S. Top 10. It included the hit tracks 'Don't Do Me Like That' and 'Refugee', both single releases.

PINK FLOYD

ANOTHER BRICK IN THE WALL *Harvest* [*Britain*] Columbia [*USA*]. Written by Roger Waters, this was released in the U.S.A. in December 1979 and in Britain in January 1980. In both the U.S.A. and Britain it was No 1 for five weeks. It stayed in the U.S. charts for 26 weeks and in the British charts for 12 weeks. R.I.A.A. Gold Disc award 24 March 1980.

A rare single release by Pink Floyd, taken from their huge success 'The Wall' album. It was in the U.S. Top 10 for 15 weeks and Britain's Top 10 for seven weeks. British sales were over 500,000 in addition to the U.S.A.'s million plus.

THE WALL (Double album) *Harvest* [*Britain*] *Columbia* [*USA*]. With material by Pink Floyd, this was released in Britain and the U.S.A. in December 1979. In the U.S.A. it was No 1 for

14 weeks and stayed 48 weeks in the charts. In Britain it went to No 3 for four weeks, staying 26 weeks in the charts. R.I.A.A. Gold and Platinum Disc awards on 13 March 1980. Grammy award: Best Engineered Recording, to James Guthrie, engineer, 'The Wall', 1980.

This album's long stay at No 1 in the U.S.A. and 30 weeks in the Top 10 made it a monster seller. By 1982 it was estimated to have sold over 12 million globally, at least five million of these in the U.S.A. and a million in Britain and Germany. It was the group's first release in three years, and ranks with their classic 'Dark Side Of The Moon' in 1973. In addition to the Pink Floyd quartet of Roger Waters; Richard Wright; Nick Mason; and Dave Gilmour, six vocalists were used: Bruce Johnston; Jon Joyce; Toni Tennille; Stan Farber; Joe Chemay; and Jim Hass, also the Islington Green School singers. The album deals with alienation, and in July 1982 a film based on the album was released, directed by Alan Parker. It cost £7 million to produce. *The Wall* film with Pink Floyd's music, an extraordinary fusion of live action and animation (by Gerald Scarfe), is somewhat gruesome and disturbing. This extravagant fantasy concerns Pink, a war baby whose life had been dominated by the death of his father and the possessiveness of his mother. He becomes a rock singer, but indulges in an orgy of destruction, also attempts suicide and imagines himself as a racist at a Nuremberg-type rally. The young Pink (Kevin McKeen) shows the only decent emotion. Bob Geldof portrays the grown-up Pink.

It is estimated that Pink Floyd's records since 1966 have grossed over £200 million.

THE POINTER SISTERS

ENERGY (Album) *Planet* [*USA*]. Released in the U.S.A. in January 1979, this was No 20 for two weeks and stayed in the charts for 15 weeks. R.I.A.A. Gold Disc award on 13 February 1979.

The Pointer Sisters' first album for Planet. It included the million-selling single 'Fire' (1978). A million sale of the album was reported in 1980.

POPE JOHN PAUL II

SONGS OF POPE JOHN PAUL II IN POLAND (Lieder des Papstes) (Album) *Crystal/EMI* [*Germany*] *Infinity* [*USA*]. This was released in the U.S.A. in October 1979 under the title 'Pope John Paul II Sings at the Festival Sacrosong'.

The German release of this album was one of the fastest-selling discs of the year. It sold 60,000 in West Germany in the first three days and well over 100,000 were exported. The million sale soon followed. The U.S. release was made available to coincide with the Pope's American visit in October to Boston and five other cities. The Infinity record is the same as the European one, but they completely repackaged it in a boxed set with the original title 'Lieder des Papstes', cover information and lyrics in English. Infinity ordered one million copies from MCA Distributing and they estimated between 6 and 12 million would be sold by Christmas 1979.

Crystal Records, the first to record the Pope, did so through a series of lucky coincidences. After the Pope announced plans to return to his native Poland, a representative of the Polish Roman Catholic Church in Cracow approached the West German ambassador in Warsaw, asking if a recording company might be interested in documenting the visit. Soon after, the Ambassador was in Freiburg, Germany, for a religious conference where Gerd Paulus was producing a recording at the meeting. Paulus of EOM Verlag, a local record/publishing company, had considerable experience making remote recordings at religious ceremonies. The Ambassador went to Paulus who in turn contacted Church officials in Cracow and Rome, and Bernd Goeke at Crystal, with whom he had previously worked. As the Pope journeyed through Poland, Paulus and his five-man team stayed with him, in convents, churches and at open-air gatherings. They selected six songs sung by the Pope alone for inclusion on the album. Other cuts were devoted to music written for the Pope. A third part of the album includes songs from the Sacrasong, a religious festival started in 1967 by then-Bishop Wojtyla. One of these, 'A Moment of the Whole Life' was written by the Bishop himself. Paulus and EOM Verlag control world rights to the recordings. Artists' royalties are split between the Polish Roman Catholic Church and the Polish state. In the U.S.A., a major portion of the proceeds went to the Pontifical Mission Society, a Roman Catholic charity. Infinity is an MCA-owned company.

PRINCE
PRINCE (Album) *Warner Bros* [*USA*]. Written by Prince, this was released in the U.S.A. in November 1979, going to No 20 for one week and staying 21 weeks in the charts. R.I.A.A. Gold Disc award on 21 February 1980. Platinum award on 13 March 1980.

Prince grew up in Minneapolis, Minnesota. His father was a musician, so Prince experimented on the piano and began learning other instruments. He subsequently played 26. Songwriting came very easy to him. At 18 he signed with Warners, probably the youngest artist ever to produce his own album. He found it easier to play all the instruments on his albums, later teaching his 5-piece band the parts. His lyrics are controversial; he expresses himself and his experiences, always writing truthfully about himself. With a spectacular stage presentation plus his musical prowess, he became one of the most intriguing figures in pop music. This album was a big success, and contained the track 'I Wanna be Your Lover', a big hit as a single release. His full name is Prince Nelson.

I WANNA BE YOUR LOVER *Warner Bros* [*USA*]. Written by Prince (Prince Nelson), this was released in the U.S.A. in November 1979, going to No 13 for two weeks and staying in the charts for 21 weeks. R.I.A.A. Gold Disc award 18 March 1980.

The prime track from Prince's album 'Prince'.

QUEEN
CRAZY LITTLE THING CALLED LOVE *EMI* [*Britain*] *Elektra* [*USA*]. Written by Freddie Mercury, this was released in Britain in October 1979 and in the U.S.A. in December 1979. In Britain it went to No 2 for two weeks, staying 13 weeks in the charts. In the U.S.A. it was No 1 for two weeks and stayed 22 weeks in the charts. R.I.A.A. Gold Disc award on 12 May 1980.

A big hit on both sides of the Atlantic for composer Freddie Mercury and his outstandingly successful group Queen. It was 11 weeks in the U.S. Top 10 and six weeks in the British Top 10. Sales in Britain were over 500,000.

RACEY
SOME GIRLS *RAK* [*Britain*]. Written by Nicky Chinn and Mike Chapman, this was released in Britain in March 1979,

going to No 2 for three weeks and staying in the charts for 11 weeks.

Racey is a male quartet in Britain. They had their first success in 1978 with 'Lay Your Love On Me'. 'Some Girls', a bouncy pop-rocker, sold half a million in Britain. Estimated global sales were two million.

CLIFF RICHARD
WE DON'T TALK ANYMORE *EMI* [*Britain*]. Written by Alan Tarney, this was released in Britain in July 1979 and in the U.S.A. in October 1979. In Britain it was No 1 for four weeks, staying 14 weeks in the charts. It was No 9 for three weeks in the U.S.A., staying 18 weeks in the charts.

Cliff's first big hit in the U.S.A. was 'Devil Woman' (1976) so this new disc made a welcome return for him. Over 250,000 were sold in Britain and the global tally by November 1979 was two million. Eight weeks in the Top 10 in Britain, and five in the U.S. Top 10.

KENNY ROGERS
SHE BELIEVES IN ME *United Artists* [*USA*]. Written by Steve Gibb, this was released in the U.S.A. in April 1979 and in Britain in May 1979. It went to No 4 for one week in the U.S.A. and stayed in the charts for 22 weeks. In Britain it was No 24 for one week and stayed seven weeks in the charts. R.I.A.A. Gold Disc award on 6 August 1979.

A romantic new tune sung by Kenny in his inimitable style, and a winner with both pop and country fans.

KENNY (Album) *United Artists* [*USA*]. This was released in the U.S.A. in September 1979 and in Britain in February 1980. It went to No 3 for two weeks and stayed 52 weeks in the charts in the U.S.A. In Britain it went to No 7 for one week and stayed nine weeks in the charts. R.I.A.A. Gold and Platinum Disc awards on 16 January 1980.

A superb album and collection of new tunes suitable for everyone. It included 'You Turn the Light On', which shows off Kenny's rock roots, and some fine tracks for his country audience. It was 16 weeks in the U.S. Top 10, and a consistent seller for a year. Sales by 1980 were three million.

COWARD OF THE COUNTY *United Artists* [*USA*]. Written by Roger Bowling and Billy Edd Wheeler, this was released in the U.S.A. in November 1979 and in Britain in January 1980. It went to No 1 for one week in the U.S.A. and to No 1 for two weeks in Britain. It stayed 20 weeks in the U.S. charts and 12 weeks in the British lists. R.I.A.A. Gold Disc award on 7 March 1980.

A most unusual and clever song that reached the top of the charts on both sides of the Atlantic. It sold 500,000 in Britain and was in the Top 10 for six weeks. In the U.S.A. it was 11 weeks in the Top 10. 1979 was an outstanding year for Kenny.

SHALAMAR
SECOND TIME AROUND *Solar* [*USA*] *RCA* [*Britain*]. Written by L. Sylvers and W. Shelby, this was released in the U.S.A. and Britain in November 1979. It went to No 13 for one week in the U.S.A., staying in the charts for 20 weeks. In Britain it was No 45 for one week and stayed eight weeks in the charts. R.I.A.A. Gold Disc award on 7 February 1980.

First major success for this U.S. male vocal/instrumental group.

SHEILA & B. DEVOTION
SPACER *Carrere* [*France*]. Written by Nile Rodgers and Bernard Edwards, this was released in Britain in November 1979 and in the U.S.A. in April 1980. In Britain it reached No 18 for one week and stayed 14 weeks in the charts.

Another big hit for Chic's Rodgers and Edwards. Sheila is the French model-star who had been singing since the mid-1960s (*see* Sheila data, 1963). The disc sold over two million in Europe

before the U.S. release (where it was not a chart entry). It showcases Sheila's sensuous voice.

SISTER SLEDGE

WE ARE FAMILY (Album) *Cotillion* [*USA*] *Atlantic* [*Britain*]. Written by Nile Rodgers and Bernard Edwards, this was released in the U.S.A. in February 1979 and in Britain in August 1979. In the U.S.A. it went to No 5 for two weeks and stayed 24 weeks in the charts. In Britain it was No 36 for one week and stayed in the charts for 10 weeks. R.I.A.A. Gold Disc award on 10 April 1979. Platinum award on 23 May 1979.

Sister Sledge is definitely a family affair. The four sisters, Kathie, Debbie, Joni and Kim come from a close-knit family

with a long musical tradition. They made their debut at an early age at the Second Macedonia Church in their hometown of northeast Philadelphia. Their grandmother, a former opera singer, had the girls entertaining guests at functions when the youngest was only two years old. Encouraged by their grandmother and singer/dancer/actress mother, they excelled in both music and academic pursuits, all graduating from Temple University. They attracted the attention of Henry Allen, then senior vice president of Atlantic Records and later to be Cotillion's president. The girls were signed to their first contract in 1973 while still in high school. Their first album was 'Circle Of Love' (Atlantic, 1975) and after its release they started on a tour that won them enthusiasm from audiences in the U.S. and Europe. They won the fourth Annual Tokyo Music Festival International Contest in Japan in 1975. Each sister can take lead vocals or sing background harmonies, and they play various instruments and arrange their own choreography and stage routines.

They were subsequently introduced to Nile Rodgers and Bernard Edwards, the duo behind the success of Chic, who were on the same label. Collaboration produced this platinum album, which contained three hit singles, including the title song 'We Are Family' and 'He's the Greatest Dancer'. The talented quartet are accompanied on the album by a 12-piece band that included Rodgers and Edwards.

WE ARE FAMILY *Cotillion* [*USA*] *Atlantic* [*Britain*]. Written by Bernard Edwards and Nile Rodgers, this was released in the U.S.A. in April 1979 and in Britain in May 1979. In the U.S.A. it went to No 3 for two weeks and stayed in the charts for 19 weeks. In Britain it went to No 8 for one week, staying 10 weeks in the charts. R.I.A.A. Gold Disc award on 18 June 1979.

The prime track from the Sister Sledge album of the same title.

REX SMITH

YOU TAKE MY BREATH AWAY *Columbia* [*USA*]. This was released in the U.S.A. in May 1979, going to No 4 for three weeks and staying 23 weeks in the charts. R.I.A.A. Gold Disc award on 20 July 1979.

Rex Smith is yet another new artist from Columbia, and one of the best in 1979. His song soon sold the million.

THE SPINNERS

WORKING MY WAY BACK TO YOU *Atlantic* [*USA*]. Written by Sandy Linzer and Denny Randall, this was released in the U.S.A. in December 1979 and in Britain in February 1980. In the U.S.A. it reached No 2 for two weeks and stayed in the charts for 25 weeks. It Britain it was No 1 for two weeks and stayed 14 weeks in the charts. R.I.A.A. Gold Disc award on 10 April 1980.

The Spinners' music-making has, since they started in 1957, never lost its appeal. Their classic sound has always been in tune with the times. Originally named The Domonicos, they became The Detroit Spinners, but are now known simply as The Spinners. In 1977 St Louis-born John Edwards (a stand-in for sick members on the road since 1975) became a fully-fledged Spinner.

This disc (actually a medley of 'Working My Way Back To You' and 'Forgive Me, Girl') was a big success. The Spinners (about to enter their 25th year in 1980) were more popular than ever. 'Working My Way' was a classic for The Four Seasons in 1966, and only The Spinners could cover this with so much soulful imagination and verve. British sales were over 250,000. It was in the British Top 10 for three weeks and the U.S. for 10 weeks.

AMII STEWART

KNOCK ON WOOD *Ariola* [*USA*] *Atlantic/Hansa* [*Britain*]. Written by Eddie Floyd and Steve Cropper, this was released in the U.S.A. in January 1979 and in Britain in March 1979. In the U.S.A. it was No 1 for one week and stayed 24 weeks in the charts. In Britain it was No 6 for one week, staying 12 weeks in the charts. R.I.A.A. Gold Disc award on 22 March 1979. Platinum award on 1 August 1979.

Amii Stewart was born in 1956 in Washington, DC, and after a theatre/dance/film career that began at the age of 16, travelled to Europe with the cast of *Bubbling Brown Sugar*. She spent two years in London (1977–79) and met producer/songwriters Barry Leng and Simon May who asked her to record a demo of 'You Really Touched My Heart'. This aroused immediate interest with Trudy Meisel of Hansa Productions. They signed her to a contract and released the song backed with the same writers' 'Closest Thing To Heaven' as a single in Britain. A promotional tour followed in Germany, Italy and the U.K., after which Amii returned to London to record 'Knock on Wood', the rock classic written in 1966 by Eddie Floyd who had a big hit with it then. Her complex, thundering disco version, when released by Ariola American, found immediate success with an avalanche of attention. Ariola released two versions, and sold over two million in the U.S.A. and 250,000 in Britain. It set alight her music career and changed everything for the multi-talented artist. She resigned from her leading role in *Bubbling Brown Sugar* in London to devote all her time to promoting an album and single that struck gold in six weeks. Amii returned to the U.S.A. (from her London-based home) to become one of the most requested artists on TV and other shows. She was voted one of the top Female New Singers of 1979.

'Knock on Wood' (a German production) was 10 weeks in the U.S. Top 10 and three weeks in the British.

ROD STEWART

GREATEST HITS (Album) *Riva* [*Britain*] *Warner Bros* [*USA*]. This was released in Britain and the U.S.A. in November 1979. In Britain it climbed to No 1 and stayed there for five weeks, staying in the charts for 23 weeks. In the U.S.A. it went to No 13 for six weeks and stayed 17 weeks in the charts. R.I.A.A. Gold and Platinum Disc awards on 26 February 1980.

A new collection of Rod Stewart's hits traces the progression from the days of 'Maggie May' and 'Sailing' up to the hits of 'Da Ya Think I'm Sexy?' and 'I Was only Joking'. In the U.S.A. it sold well over the million and in Britain over 500,000. It was in the British Top 10 for 12 weeks. The global sales were well over two million.

NICK STRAKER BAND

A WALK IN THE PARK *Pinnacle* [*Britain*]. Written by N. Bailey and released in Britain in May 1979 (re-released August 1980, CBS label), this went to No 1 for five weeks in Germany

and stayed in the charts there for 37 weeks. In Britain it was No 20 for three weeks and stayed 12 weeks in the charts.

Nick Straker spent four years with school friend Dennis Bovell in Matumbi before leaving to concentrate on studio work in 1975. This disc was a huge hit in Europe with estimated sales of nine million, over one million in Germany alone. Its first release in Britain was disappointing, but after its success on the Continent, CBS licensed the track from Pinnacle with fair success in Britain. London-based Pinnacle were national distributors of many independent labels.

BARBRA STREISAND

THE MAIN EVENT/FIGHT *Columbia* [*USA*]. Written by Bruce Roberts, Bob Esty and Paul Jabara, this was released in the U.S.A. in June 1979, going to No 3 for one week and staying 20 weeks in the charts. R.I.A.A. Gold Disc award on 30 August 1979.

The theme from Barbra Streisand's film *The Main Event* exhibits her stylish vocals plus a punchy disco beat.

WET (Album) *Columbia* [*USA*]. This was released in the U.S.A. in October 1979 and in Britain in November 1979. It went to No 6 for two weeks in the U.S.A. and stayed 25 weeks in the charts. In Britain it was No 25 for one week, staying 12 weeks in the charts. R.I.A.A. Gold and Platinum Disc awards on 20 February 1980.

An intricate 'theme' album demonstrating Barbra's vocal expertise and mood changes, with sophistication and some rock. Her duet on the album with Donna Summer gave her a whole new audience, and the rest of the songs were absolutely right for her thousands of fans. British sales over 100,000.

BARBRA STREISAND & DONNA SUMMER

NO MORE TEARS (Enough is Enough) *Columbia & Casablanca* [*USA*]. Written by Bruce Roberts and Paul Jabara, this was released in the U.S.A. and Britain in October 1979. It was No 1 for three weeks in the U.S.A., staying in the charts for 19 weeks. It went to No 3 for two weeks in Britain, staying 13 weeks in the charts. R.I.A.A. Gold Disc award on 11 February 1980.

As Barbra Streisand is a Columbia artist and Donna Summer signed to Casablanca, this disc was put out by both companies, there being a 7-inch and a 12-inch disco record. They were the first ever to receive individual awards for a disc of the same title and artists. British sale was around 250,000, and it was four weeks in their Top 10 and 10 weeks in U.S. Top 10. British release was on Casablanca label.

STYX

CORNERSTONE (Album) *A & M* [*USA*]. With material by Styx, this was released in the U.S.A. in October 1979 and in Britain in January 1980. In the U.S.A. it was No 3 for nine weeks, staying 39 weeks in the charts. In Britain it was No 36 for one week and stayed in the charts for seven weeks. R.I.A.A. Gold and Platinum Disc awards on 5 February 1980.

An extremely successful album for Styx. It entered the charts at No 8 and stayed in the Top 10 in the U.S.A. for 22 weeks. It included the hit track 'Babe'.

BABE *A & M* [*USA*]. Written by Dennis De Young, this was released in the U.S.A. in October 1979 and in Britain in December 1979. It went to No 1 for two weeks in the U.S.A. and stayed 21 weeks in the charts. It went to No 6 for two weeks in Britain and stayed in the charts for 10 weeks. R.I.A.A. Gold Disc award on 28 January 1980.

The composer of this number is the leading vocalist/keyboard player of Styx. It was a swift success in the U.S.A. and stayed 13 weeks in their Top 10. The disc was also the group's first hit in Britain, and sold 250,000. The prime track from Styx album 'Cornerstone'.

THE SUGARHILL GANG

RAPPER'S DELIGHT *Sugarhill* [*USA*]. Written by Robins, Jackson, Wright and O'Brien, this was released in the U.S.A. in October 1979 and in Britain in November 1979. In the U.S.A. it was No 45 for three weeks and stayed 20 weeks in the charts. In Britain it went to No 3 for one week, staying 10 weeks in the charts.

'Rapper's Delight' bears the distinction of being the first 12-inch disc to sell over a million. A tremendous success with disco fans and particularly the DJs. Rappers are the street disc jockeys who improvise rhymes and fast talk to the extended breaks of disco records.

The disc was also a hit in Britain where it sold over 250,000. The disco customers bought it in a big way in the U.S.A. to make it a million seller there (though not certified by R.I.A.A. as the label were not members).

The composition was later credited on the 'Sugarhill Gang' album to Chic's Nile Rodgers and Bernard Edwards. It is probable that the quartet originally named as the writers were members of Sugarhill Gang, though this has not been confirmed.

This was in Britain's Top 10 for five weeks.

DONNA SUMMER

HOT STUFF *Casablanca* [*USA*]. Written by Peter Bellotte, Harold Faltermeier and Keith Forsey, this was released in the U.S.A. in April 1979 and in Britain in May 1979. It hit No 1 for five weeks in the U.S.A., staying 23 weeks in the charts. In Britain it was No 11 for two weeks, staying 10 weeks in the charts. R.I.A.A. Gold Disc award on 20 April 1979. Platinum award on 1 August 1979. Grammy award: Best Female Rock Performance, 'Hot Stuff', 1979.

A stunning hit for Donna with over two million sale. A splendid rock disco tune in her now fully developed style, and one of the three tracks from her album 'Bad Girls' to pass the million sale. As usual produced by Peter Bellotte and Giorgio Moroder. It was 14 weeks in the U.S. Top 10, and features a blazing guitar solo from Jeff 'Skunk' Baxter, formerly of Steely Dan.

BAD GIRLS (Double album) *Casablanca* [*USA*]. This was released in the U.S.A. in April 1979 and in Britain in May 1979. It went to No 1 for four weeks in the U.S.A., staying 39 weeks in the charts. In Britain it was No 23 for one week and stayed in the charts for 23 weeks. R.I.A.A. Gold and Platinum Disc awards on 3 May 1979.

This album was shipped platinum and has been described as sheer magic. The Moroder-Bellotte production is exquisite, and Donna shows that she is as adept at rock, as at ballad and disco. Her meteoric rise paralleled the extraordinary growth of disco as the dominant force in contemporary music. She is an artist of great stature internationally. The album contains 15 songs, eight of which Donna had a hand in writing, and all of which took Donna and her producers on to new stylistic sound. It included three tracks which became million-selling singles: 'Bad Girls'; 'Hot Stuff'; 'Dim All The Lights'. It closes with a poem to the recording people's new playground, Sunset Strip, entitled 'Sunset People'. Its conclusion in sound and volume is positively explosive.

The album was in the U.S. Top 10 for 20 weeks, and sales were estimated at over three million. In Britain it sold over 60,000.

Other high energy tracks are 'Our Love' and 'Lucky'.

BAD GIRLS *Casablanca* [*USA*]. Written by Joseph Esposito, Edward Hokenson, Bruce Sudano and Donna Summer, this was released in the U.S.A. in May 1979 and in Britain in June 1979. In the U.S.A. it hit No 1 for four weeks and stayed in the charts for 21 weeks. It went to No 14 for one week in Britain and stayed in the charts for eight weeks. R.I.A.A. Gold Disc award on 19 June 1979. Platinum award on 4 September 1979.

Another two-million-plus single from Donna's 'Bad Girls' album. With this, Donna became the first artist in history to have a number one single and a second hit single in the Top 5 at the same time. 'Bad Girls' was 12 weeks in the U.S. Top 10 and this threatening sultry street theme also sold 250,000 in Britain.

DIM ALL THE LIGHTS *Casablanca* [*USA*]. Written by Donna Summer, this was released in the U.S.A. in August 1979 and in Britain in October 1979. In the U.S.A. it reached No 2 for two weeks, staying 21 weeks in the charts. In Britain it was No 29 for one week and stayed nine weeks in the charts. R.I.A.A. Gold Disc award on 11 December 1979.

The third track from Donna's 'Bad Girls' album to sell the million. It is a real joyous disco-pop record. It was in the U.S. Top 10 for eight weeks.

ON THE RADIO - GREATEST HITS (Vols 1 & 2) (double album) *Casablanca* [*USA*]. This was released in the U.S.A. in October 1979 and in Britain in November 1979. In the U.S.A. it hit No 1 for one week and stayed 41 weeks in the charts. In Britain it was No 24 for one week, staying 21 weeks in the charts. R.I.A.A. Platinum Disc award on 21 February 1980.

This 'Greatest Hits' album was 18 weeks in the U.S. Top 10, and made seven million-selling discs for Donna in 1979 (two albums, three singles, one single with Barbra Streisand and one single with The Brooklyn Dreams). She had dominated the season, and was the first female artist with three individual singles and two individual albums in the same year. This album also sold around 150,000 in Britain. The U.S. sales are estimated at well over two million.

DONNA SUMMER WITH THE BROOKLYN DREAMS

HEAVEN KNOWS *Casablanca* [*USA*]. Written by Peter Bellotte, Donna Summer, Giorgio Moroder and Gregg Mathieson, this was released in the U.S.A. in January 1979 and in Britain in

February 1979. In the U.S.A. it went to No 5 for one week and stayed in the charts for 20 weeks. In Britain it was No 34 for one week and stayed eight weeks in the charts. R.I.A.A. Gold Disc award on 5 March 1979.

This disc by Donna and her friends started 1979 in a big way for her. It was in the U.S. Top 10 for seven weeks. The Brooklyn Dreams are Joe Esposito (guitar); Eddie Hokenson (percussion); Bruce Sudano (keyboards), all from Brooklyn, N.Y.

SUPERTRAMP

BREAKFAST IN AMERICA (Album) *A & M* [*USA*]. With material written by R. Davies and R. Hodgson, this was released in the U.S.A. and Britain in March 1979. It went to No 1 for nine weeks in the U.S.A., lasting 57 weeks in the charts. In Britain it went to No 3 for six weeks and stayed 52 weeks in the

charts. R.I.A.A. Gold Disc award on 9 April 1979. Platinum award on 8 May 1979. Grammy awards: Best album Package, 1979; Best Engineered Recording (Non-Classical), 1979.

Supertramp was originally formed in London in the early 1970s, with founder members Rick Davies (keyboards) and Roger Hodgson (vocals/guitar) teaming up after Davies' band The Joint failed. They were joined by Richard Palmer and Bob Millar, and made two albums for A & M 'Supertramp' (1970) and 'Indelibly Stamped' (1971) before change of personnel and their first hit album 'Crime of the Century' (1974) for A & M. The latter topped the British charts and was a long-term chart item in the U.S.A. The revised Supertramp was then songwriters Davies and Hodgson; John Helliwell (sax); Doug Thomson (bass); and Bob Benberg (from Glendale, California) on drums. They settled in an English cottage named Southcombe and devised the intricate keyboard/sax/guitar ensemble for 'Crime of the Century' and the following 'Crisis? What Crisis?' (1975).

This preceded their first extensive international tour, and introduced U.S. and Canadian audiences to the band's massive sound system. This was developed together with several British equipment firms. All profits from the first concert were invested in developing new recording and performing equipment. Between 'Crisis ...' and 'Even in The Quietest Moments' (1977) the group moved to the Los Angeles area, the inspiration for the themes of 'Breakfast In America'. This was first recorded in almost entire demo form at their Burbank facility (named Southcombe after their English origins) and then produced at the Village Recorder. This emerged with the razor-sharp sonic finish, the Supertramp signature. A & M organized an extensive promotion campaign around the album's distinctive cover - a happy heroine, Libby, holding high a glass of orange juice in emulation of the Statute of Liberty. Together with a singles hit 'The Logical Song' from the album, the campaign boosted sales tremendously and renewed activity for 'Crime', 'Crisis?' and 'Moments'. 'Breakfast In America' shipped one million in the U.S.A. and immediately raced up the charts to the top for nine weeks, plus 26 weeks in the Top 10. It shipped gold in Belgium, France, Holland, Norway, Canada and Australia. Double gold in

Spain and Portugal, and then gold in Germany. In Britain it went platinum (300,000 units) and then platinum in Holland and Canada. The U.S. sales are estimated at at least three million, and over six million outside the U.S., three million of these in Europe. Supertramp has remained an international force ever since the release of 'Crime of The Century' in 1974 and the strong international sales since then. Their global success story is therefore no surprise, nor their conquest of America.

The album was also 20 weeks in Britain's Top 10.

VAN HALEN

VAN HALEN II (Album) *Warner Bros* [*USA*]. Written by the Van Halen group, this was released in the U.S.A. and Britain in April 1979. In the U.S.A. it went to No 6 for two weeks and stayed 31 weeks in the charts. It was No 23 for one week in Britain and stayed seven weeks in the charts. R.I.A.A. Gold Disc award on 3 April 1979. Platinum award on 8 May 1979.

Second million-selling album for the Dutch group. They rock through nine originals and a cover version of 'You're No Good'. Edward Van Halen's guitar virtuosity is also to the fore. It was 10 weeks in the U.S. Top 10.

RANDY VANWARMER

JUST WHEN I NEEDED YOU MOST *Bearsville* [*USA*]. Written by Randy Vanwarmer, this was released in the U.S.A. in February 1979 and in Britain in July 1979. In the U.S.A. it went to No 5 for two weeks and in Britain to No 5 for one week. It stayed in the U.S. charts for 21 weeks and the British charts for 11 weeks. R.I.A.A. Gold Disc award on 31 July 1979.

A strong debut single for Randy and a mighty hit for the first single he ever recorded. Randy first sang this publicly in 1977 in Cornwall, England, in a room above and behind a public house called the Monmouth, to a small audience who paid 30 pence for the privilege. These are the places where modern ballads are traditionally sung. The audience knows most of the artist's repertoire by heart. Randy's songs are absolute naturals. In 1978 he left his beautiful village of East Looe, Cornwall, and went to the record company Bearsville. Never was a cheap air fare better spent. Randy (a Colorado boy from birth to 15) was happy to be back after eight years in the U.S.A. The Scottish expatriate who originally signed him to Bearsville in London – Ian Kimmet – was there. Randy's songs, mostly love songs, have an instant and universal appeal. In addition to the million or more U.S. sale, it sold 250,000 in Britain.

VILLAGE PEOPLE

IN THE NAVY *Casablanca* [*USA*] *Mercury* [*Britain*]. Written by Morali, Belolo and Willis, this was released in the U.S.A. and Britain in March 1979. It was No 2 for two weeks in the U.S.A. and stayed 19 weeks in the charts. In Britain it was No 4 for one week, staying nine weeks in the charts. R.I.A.A. Gold Disc award on 15 March 1979.

An infectious, catchy melody, extremely popular with disco fans. It was eight weeks in the U.S. Top 10. British sales were 250,000. The global tally is estimated at over two million. An instant million seller in the U.S.A.

GO WEST (Album) *Casablanca* [*USA*] *Mercury* [*Britain*]. Written by Morali, Belolo and Willis, this was released in the U.S.A. in April 1979 and in Britain in May 1979. In the U.S.A. it went to No 5 for two weeks, staying 21 weeks in the charts. In Britain it was No 15 for one week and stayed 19 weeks in the charts. R.I.A.A. Gold and Platinum Disc awards on 4 April 1979.

Another instant million seller, an album this time, the group's biggest yet. It was five weeks in the U.S. Top 10 and estimated sales were over two million. In Britain, sales were over 100,000. An infectious beat and tongue-in-cheek humour is again evident in their performance. It included 'In the Navy'; 'Go West'; 'YMCA'; 'Get Away Holiday'; 'I Wanna Shake Your Hand'; 'Manhattan Woman'.

LIVE AND SLEAZY (Double album) *Casablanca* [*USA*]. With material by Morali, Belolo, Hurtt and Whitehead, this was released in the U.S.A. in October 1979, going to No 37 for two weeks and staying 14 weeks in the charts. R.I.A.A. Gold Disc award on 25 January 1980.

This album sold over two million globally (800,000 of these in the U.S.A.). Two sides of this double album feature the band doing all their hits live. The other two sides feature the new lead singer Ray Simpson (brother of songwriter Valerie) and taking on rock'n'roll styles as well. It includes the title track 'Sleazy'. At this time the group were involved in their first film venture, *Can't Stop The Music*, described as a fictionalized documentary that traces the group's history and success (*see* Village People, original film soundtrack, 1980).

DIONNE WARWICK

DIONNE (Album) *Arista* [*USA*]. This was released in the U.S.A. in June 1979, going to No 15 for one week and staying in the charts for 25 weeks. R.I.A.A. Gold Disc award on 23 September 1979. Platinum award on 11 March 1980.

Dionne made a triumphant return after a recording hiatus of around three years, with this her first album for Arista. With a new producer, Barry Manilow, she showed once again that she is one of the finest singers. The album included the big hit 'I'll Never Love Like This Again'; 'Déjà Vu'; 'In Your Eyes'; and 'Who, What, Where, Why?' Composers such as Manilow; Rupert Holmes; Isaac Hayes; Richard Kerr; and Cissy Houston are represented on it, making a superb disc.

I'LL NEVER LOVE THIS WAY AGAIN *Arista* [*USA*]. Written by Richard Kerr and Will Jennings, this was released in the U.S.A. in June 1979, going to No 5 for one week and lasting 26 weeks in the charts. R.I.A.A. Gold Disc award on 19 October 1979. Grammy award: Best Pop Vocal Performance, Female, 1979.

Brilliant vocals on this initial Arista release plus expert production by Barry Manilow. The prime track from her 'Dionne' album, it was seven weeks in the U.S. Top 10.

THE WHISPERS

THE WHISPERS (Album) *Solar* [*USA*]. Written by The Whispers and released in the U.S.A. in December 1979, this was No 6 for two weeks and stayed 24 weeks in the charts. R.I.A.A. Gold and Platinum Disc awards on 18 March 1980.

The Whispers are Walter and Wallace Scott (identical twins); Nicholas Caldwell; Leaveil Degree; and Marcus Hutson. A Los Angeles-based vocal group, they became an 'overnight' success, after having performed together for 12 years. This was their sixth album, produced by the group with Solar president Dick Griffey. It crossed over to the pop charts after having sold 350,000 copies on the Black Music charts, and soon sold the million. The album includes the hits 'Lady'; 'And The Beat Goes On', a big disco success; and an updated version of 'My Girl' (a hit for The Temptations in 1965); also 'A Song for Donny (Hathaway)', released previously by Griffey to benefit the family of the late Donny Hathaway and to establish, with Solar distributor RCA Records, a musical scholarship in Hathaway's honour. The group then went on a 70-city tour named 'The Solar Galaxy Of Stars' produced by Griffey with Solar's other artists – Shalamar, Lakeside and Dynasty.

WINGS

GOODNIGHT TONIGHT *Columbia* [*USA*] *CBS* [*Britain*]. Written by Paul McCartney, this was released in Britain and the U.S.A. in March 1979. In the U.S.A. it was No 7 for two weeks and stayed 16 weeks in the charts. In Britain it went to No 5 for one week, staying in the charts for seven weeks. R.I.A.A. Gold Disc award on 15 May 1979.

Another quick million seller for Paul McCartney and Wings. It was Paul's first single for Columbia – a disco tune – featuring every conceivable studio technique. It was in the British and U.S. Top 10 for four weeks.

BACK TO THE EGG (Album) *Columbia [USA] Parlophone [Britain]*. Written by Paul McCartney, this was released in the U.S.A. and Britain in June 1979. It went to No 7 for two weeks in the U.S.A., staying in the charts for 20 weeks. In Britain it went to No 6 for one week, staying 15 weeks in the charts. R.I.A.A. Gold and Platinum Disc awards on 18 June 1979.

An instant million seller for Wings, and their first Columbia album. McCartney and friends (including Pete Townshend and many others on two tracks) recorded a lush, tuneful album. British sales were around 200,000, U.S. sales estimated at two million or more. It was in the Top 10 for four weeks in both countries. Contents are: 'Reception'; 'Getting Closer'; 'We're Open Tonight'; 'Spin It On'; 'Again and Again'; 'Old Siam'; 'Sir Arrow Through Me'; 'Rockestra Theme'; 'To You'; 'After the Ball'; 'Million Miles'; 'Winter Rose, Love Awake'; 'The Broadcast'; 'So Glad to See You Here'; 'Baby's Request'.

NEIL YOUNG & CRAZY HORSE

RUST NEVER SLEEPS (Album) *Reprise [USA]*. With material by Neil Young, this was released in the U.S.A. and Britain in July 1979. In the U.S.A. it reached No 13 for one week, staying 21 weeks in the charts. In Britain it was also No 13 for one week and stayed 12 weeks in the charts. R.I.A.A. Gold Disc award on 28 August 1979. Platinum award on 7 February 1980.

A collection of all new material in Neil's country-rock style. Fine lyrics and acoustic/electrics make this a great album.

Individually Crazy Horse are: Billy Talbot; Ralph Holina; and Frank Sampredo. They were originally known as the Rockets. Young has recorded with Crazy Horse since the demise of Buffalo Springfield.

Facing page, top, left to right: Leo Sayer, The Police; bottom: ABBA.

THE 1980s

ORIGINAL FILM SOUNDTRACK (VILLAGE PEOPLE)

CAN'T STOP THE MUSIC (Album) *Casablanca* [*USA*]. Music and production by Jacques Morali, released in the U.S.A. June 1980, where it was No 33 for one week and seven weeks in the charts.

After Village People had become big stars with their rousing anthems and visual impact, a film was inevitable. The album included all new music (except their famous 'Y.M.C.A.' song) and was reported by the label to have sold two million globally by March 1981.

The large cast also included Hot Gossip (group); The Ritchie Family; June Havoc. Village People sang most of the songs, including: 'New York'; 'Samantha'; 'I love you to death'; 'Celebration'; 'Milk Shake'; 'You can't stop the music'.

ORIGINAL FILM SOUNDTRACK

FAME (Album) *RSO* [*USA*]. With musical score by Michael Gore, this was released in the U.S.A. in May 1980. It reached No 11 in the U.S.A. for three weeks, staying in the charts for 24 weeks. R.I.A.A. Gold Disc award on 19 August 1980. Platinum award on 15 September 1980.

This musical film is about eight adolescents struggling through the Performing Arts High School in New York City. Michael Gore, brother of the 1960s pop star Lesley Gore, wrote nine original songs along with his sister and lyricist Dean Pitchford. The film was produced by Alan Marshall and directed by Alan Parker, both best known for the Academy Award winning film *Midnight Express*. The film opened nationally in hundreds of theatres in the U.S.A. and Canada on 20 June 1980. It contained the hit song 'Fame', winner of the Oscar 1980 for Best Film Song, and recorded by Irene Cara, written by Michael Gore and Dean Pitchford. Gore's own background included a curriculum spanning theory, composition, orchestration and conducting at Yale, studies with composer Max Deutsch in Paris, and pianist for the European premiere of Leonard Bernstein's 'Mass', followed by a tenure as a producer for CBS Records International. He was also a staff writer for Screen Gems-EMI. It was through his sister that he got his first look at music as a career when he was 11 and she had her big hit 'It's My Party'. His score for 'Fame' reflects his pop recording sessions and conservatory training, a perfect mixture for the film, blending pop, dance music and classical music dictated by the screen action.

The album contains: 'Fame'; 'Out Here On My Own'; 'Dogs in the Yard'; 'Red Light' (sung by Linda Clifford)'; 'Is It OK If I Call You Mine?'; 'Never Alone'; 'Ralph and Monty' (Dressing Room Piano); 'I Sing the Body Electric'. Irene Cara also recorded 'Out Here on My Own'.

A subsequent series on TV was a big success.

ORIGINAL FILM SOUNDTRACK (WILLIE NELSON & FAMILY)

HONEYSUCKLE ROSE (Double album) *Columbia* [*USA*]. Released in the U.S.A. in August 1980, it reached No 7 for three weeks, staying in the charts for a total of 35 weeks. R.I.A.A. Gold Disc award on 15 October 1980. Platinum award on 12 November 1980. Grammy award: Willie Nelson for 'On the Road Again', Best Country Song, 1980.

Willie Nelson's first starring role, premiered on 3 July at the Capital Plaza Theatre in Austin, Texas. The film was shot mainly in dance halls, saloons and motels from San Antonio to Corpus Christi, Texas, and draws heavily on Nelson's own past and his life on the road. Nelson wrote his first tune for the movie 'On the Road Again' on the back of a plane ticket during a plane trip from Atlanta to Austin. The film got its title from Willie's mailbox, which has 'Honeysuckle Rose Bonham' printed on its side. Willie plays Buck Bonham, and Honeysuckle Rose is the name of his home estate in Texas. Willie's 'Family' includes his co-stars Dyan Cannon; Slim Pickens; Emmylou Harris; Johnny Gimble; Hank Cochran; Amy Irving; and others. The soundtrack includes: 'On the Road Again'; 'Blue Eyes Crying In the Rain'; 'Angel Eyes'; 'Two Sides to Every Story'; 'Angel Flying Close to the Ground'; 'So You Think You're a Cowboy'; plus two songs 'I Guess I've Come to Live Here in Your Eyes' and 'If You Want Me to I Will', both written for the film but cut out of the final film print. Nelson wrote several of these. Other performers on the album were Jeannie Seely; Jody Payne; and Kenneth Threadgill. Nelson's road band appears with him on the album and in the film. The film includes at least another dozen songs by various artists such as Kris Kristofferson; Leon Russell; Rodney Crowell; Lee Clayton; Mickey Rooney Jr; John Bush Shinn; and Nelson, Cochran, Threadgill, and Gimble.

ORIGINAL FILM SOUNDTRACK (NEIL DIAMOND)

THE JAZZ SINGER (Album) *Capitol* [*USA*]. With songs by Neil Diamond and others, this was released in the U.S.A. and Britain in November 1980. It was in the U.S. charts for 37 weeks and the British for 72 weeks, reaching No 3 in the U.S.A. for six weeks and No 3 for one week in Britain. R.I.A.A. Gold and Platinum Disc awards on 14 January 1981.

The idea for this film stems from Al Jolson's film of the early talkies (1928) but with an up-to-date approach and new songs. Neil Diamond in the star role gave a dramatic performance and the film was a box office blockbuster. This album was 25 weeks in the U.S. Top 10 and 13 weeks in Britain's Top 10. It included the hits 'Love on the Rocks' (by Diamond and Becaud); 'Hello Again (Love Theme)' and 'America'.

It sold over three million in the U.S.A. and well over 500,000 in Britain.

ORIGINAL FILM SOUNDTRACK (JOHN TRAVOLTA & VARIOUS ARTISTS)

URBAN COWBOY (Double album) *Full Moon/Asylum* [*USA*]. This was released in the U.S.A. in April 1980, reaching No 1 for five weeks and staying in the charts for 46 weeks. R.I.A.A. Gold Disc award on 14 July 1980. Platinum award on 24 July 1980.

A novel idea for a film – the big city cowboy, portrayed by John Travolta, with a host of country stars, and bands. The double album includes: 'Stand By Me' (written by Lieber and Stoller) sung by Mickey Gilley and B.E. King; 'All Night Long' (written and sung by Joe Walsh); 'Love the World Away' (written by Morrison and Wilson), sung by Kenny Rogers; 'Look What You've Done to Me' (written and sung by Boz Scaggs); 'Could I Have This Dance?' (by W. Holyfield and B. House) sung by Anne Murray (Grammy award for this song to Anne Murray – Best Country Female Vocalist, 1980); 'Orange Blossom Special' and 'Hoedown'; sung by Mickey Gilley (Grammy award to Mickey Gilley & Urban Cowboy Band for Best Country Instrumental Performance, 1980).

Other artists on the album were Jimmy Buffett; Charlie Daniels Band; Eagles; Dan Fogelberg; Gilley's Urban Cowboy Band; Johnny Lee; Bonnie Raitt; Linda Ronstadt/J.D. Souther; Bob Seger & Silver Bullet Band.

The album was also in the U.S. Top 10 for 17 weeks. Sales were around two million. Johnny Lee also sang his song 'Lookin' for Love' (on the soundtrack).

An additional album 'Urban Cowboy 2' was released in December 1980 and included 'Ride Hard and Put Up Wet' by Johnny Lee; 'Jukebox Argument'; and 'Honky Tonk Wine' by Mickey Gilley; two Charlie Daniels Band tracks and a Gilley/Lee duet.

ORIGINAL SOUNDTRACK (STARRING OLIVIA NEWTON-JOHN & ELECTRIC LIGHT ORCHESTRA, GENE KELLY, MICHAEL BECK)

XANADU (musical fantasy) (Album) *MCA* [*USA*]. With music by Electric Light Orchestra composed by Jeff Lynne and John Farrar, this was released in the U.S.A. in June 1980 and in Britain in July 1980. It stayed in the U.S. charts for 38 weeks and was No 1 for one week. It reached No 2 in the British charts for one week, staying in the charts for 17 weeks. R.I.A.A. Gold and Platinum Disc awards on 19 August 1980.

Based on the fabulous Kubla Khan stories of the Far East – 'In Xanadu did Kubla Khan a stately pleasure dome decree' – this film, described as 'a musical fantasy of all time to transport you beyond your dreams' was premiered on 8 August 1980. It was produced and written by John Farrar. The title song 'Xanadu' was performed by Olivia Newton-John backed by E.L.O., and written by Jeff Lynne of the group. The complete contents are: 'Magic' (written by Jeff Lynne); 'Xanadu'; 'When You're Away'; 'Suspended in Time' all sung by Olivia Newton-John who also duets with Cliff Richard on 'Suddenly' (written by John Farrar); 'Dancin'' with The Tubes; and 'I'm Alive'; 'The Fall'; 'Don't Walk Away'; and 'All Over the World' (all written by Jeff Lynne) performed by E.L.O.

It was 10 weeks in the U.S. Top 10 and eight weeks in Britain's Top 10. British sales were over 100,000 and the U.S.A.'s over two million.

The album yielded five Top 20 singles; 'Xanadu'; 'Magic'; 'I'm Alive'; 'Suddenly'; 'All Over the World'.

ABBA

SUPER TROUPER (Album) *Polar* [*Sweden*] *Epic* [*Britain*] *Atlantic* [*USA*]. With songs by Benny Andersson and Bjorn Ulvaeus, this was released in Britain and the U.S.A. in November 1980. In Britain it hit No 1 for eight weeks, staying in the charts for 41 weeks. In the U.S.A. it reached No 26 for two weeks, staying in the charts for 27 weeks. R.I.A.A. Gold Disc award on 6 February 1981.

With remarkable consistency, ABBA again produce a big seller by their own recipe and blend of sound. This album contained 'Lay All Your Love on Me', a kind of electro-disco Christmas carol. The album was 10 weeks in Britain's Top 10 after being an instant No 1, and sold 300,000 by its second week, and well over 500,000 altogether. U.S. sales were also around half a million. Total global sales estimated at well over two million. Epic announced the million sale in December 1980.

Contents are: 'Super Trouper'; 'The Winner Takes it All'; 'Me and I'; 'On and On and On'; 'Andante, Andante'; 'Happy New Year'; 'Our Last Summer'; 'The Piper'; 'Lay All Your Love on Me'; 'The Way Old Friends Do'.

AC/DC

BACK IN BLACK (Album) *Atlantic* [*USA*]. Written by Angus Young, Michael Young and Brian Johnston, this was released in the U.S.A. and Britain in August 1980. It stayed in the U.S. charts for 52 weeks, and the British for 29 weeks, reaching No 4 for one week in the U.S.A. and No 1 for two weeks in Britain. R.I.A.A. Gold and Platinum Disc awards on 13 October 1980.

Another million seller for this heavy metal quintet. It was an instant No 1 in Britain where it sold over 100,000 and six weeks in the Top 10. In the U.S.A. it was 24 weeks in the Top 10. The two principal tracks are: 'Back in Black' and 'You Shook Me All Night Long'.

AIR SUPPLY

LOST IN LOVE (Album) *Arista* [*USA*]. With material by Graham Russell, this was released in the U.S.A. in May 1980, staying in the charts for 46 weeks, reaching No 24 for one week. R.I.A.A. Gold Disc award on 1 October 1980. Platinum on 12 January 1981.

Composer/vocalist Graham Russell, British-bred Australian citizen, was born in 1951. He moved to Australia in the late 1960s to find success as a songwriter. As this failed, he went into acting

and secured the role of Peter in a production of *Jesus Christ Superstar*. Here he met co-vocalist/guitarist Russell Hitchcock, who alternated playing Jesus and Judas in the show. The duo teamed as Air Supply and in late 1976 had a top-three single in Australia with Russell's 'Love and Other Bruises'. The subsequent album 'Air Supply' achieved gold status in Australia. Around this time, Air Supply was chosen as supporting act for Rod Stewart's Australian tour, and the duo opened for Stewart's North American tour, where in 1977 they did around 50 concerts with Stewart from L.A. Forum to Madison Square Garden, and found time to record. Their second and third singles in Australia, 'Empty Pages' and 'Do What You Want to Do' were both hits, and spawned a second gold album. Up to this time the duo were backed by studio musicians on recording and stage, but in 1978 recruited David Moyse (guitar); Ralph Cooper (drums); and Criston Barker (bass) to complete Air Supply. The first single with the new line-up was 'Bring Out the Magic', the second was 'Lost in Love' from album number three 'Life Support'.

'Lost in Love' was a continent-wide hit. It was heard by Clive Davis, President of Arista, in the U.S.A., was remixed under his supervision and became the band's big breakthrough American hit.

Criston Barker left and was replaced by David Green. Frank Esler-Smith was recruited to handle keyboards and Rex Goh added on guitar, to complete the sextet.

The 'Lost in Love' album included the group's single of the same title, which was first released in the U.S.A. in January 1980. The single and this album captivated the music world in a very short time.

ALL OUT OF LOVE *Arista* [*USA*]. Written by Graham Russell and Clive Davis, this was released in the U.S.A. in June 1980 and in Britain in September 1980. In the U.S.A. it was No 1 for two weeks and stayed 32 weeks in the charts. In Britain it was No 11 for one week and stayed ten weeks in the charts. R.I.A.A. Gold Disc award on 10 October 1980.

Arista's president, Clive Davis, worked on the lyrics with composer Graham Russell, as he did not find the lyrics as effective as 'Lost in Love'. The result was Air Supply's second hit record. It was 11 weeks in the U.S. Top 10.

ALABAMA

MY HOME'S IN ALABAMA (Album) *RCA* [*USA*]. This was released in the U.S.A. in April 1980 and stayed in the country charts for over 12 months. R.I.A.A. Gold Disc award on 14 July 1981. Platinum award on 30 June 1982.

Alabama, a quartet consisting of cousins Randy Owen (lead vocal and guitar); Jeff Cook (guitar and vocals); Teddy Gentry (bass and vocals); and Mark Herndon who settled in as drummer in 1979. The cousins were born and raised near Fort Payne, Ala., and pursued separate musical interests until 1973, when Jeff (working for Western Electric), Randy (in school), and Teddy (carpet layer) decided to form a group. They played various clubs in nearby Myrtle Beach, sometimes opening for such acts as Bobby Bare and other Nashville artists. They cut their own records and sold them from the stage, and promoted them to radio stations themselves. GRT Records released their 'I Want To Be With You' in 1977, and this caught the attention of MDJ Records of Dallas who signed the group and released 'I Wanna Come Over' in late 1979 which achieved No 34, and was swiftly followed by 'My Home's in Alabama' which got to number 16. RCA signed Alabama in April 1980, releasing 'Tennessee River' and this album 'My Home's in Alabama'. The group became one of country music's most impressive success stories of the year, with 'Tennessee River' a number two single and the album at No 15 for two weeks with a long run in the country charts. They received two CMA nominations (Group of the Year and Instrumental Group) and were virtually the most successful group on country singles and album charts still dominated by solo artists, duets and other front-singer arrangements.

One of the band members summed up the group's success when he said 'We're right in the middle of what people like as country.'

PAT BENATAR

CRIMES OF PASSION (Album) *Chrysalis* [*USA*]. Released in the U.S.A. in August 1980, this went to No 2 for five weeks and stayed in the charts for 42 weeks. R.I.A.A. Gold Disc award on 21 October 1980. Platinum award on 30 October 1980. Grammy award: Best Rock (Female) Vocal for 'Crimes of Passion', 1980.

Pat Benatar at her best with a tough, no-nonsense vocal, plus her band with its explosive rhythm kick. The album stayed in the U.S. Top 10 for 30 weeks. Her second million-selling album.

HIT ME WITH YOUR BEST SHOT *Chrysalis* [*USA*]. Written by Schwartz, this was released in the U.S.A. in September 1980, going to No 5 for two weeks and staying 30 weeks in the charts. R.I.A.A. Gold Disc award on 26 January 1981.

First million-selling single for Pat, the rock'n'roller with the sometimes aggressive, sometimes gentle voice. In the U.S. Top 10 for 13 weeks.

GEORGE BENSON

GIVE ME THE NIGHT (Album) *Quest/Warner Bros* [*USA*]. This was released in the U.S.A. and Britain in July 1980. It went to No 6 in the U.S.A. for two weeks and No 3 in Britain for one week. It stayed 34 weeks in the U.S.A. charts and 36 weeks in the British lists. R.I.A.A. Gold Disc award on 16 September 1980. Platinum Disc award on 14 October 1980. Grammy awards: Best Rhythm and Blues Vocal Performance for 'Give Me The Night' album, 1980; Best Jazz Vocal Performance, 'Moody's Mood', 1980; Best Rhythm and Blues Performance, 'Off Broadway', 1980; Best Instrumental Arrangement by Quincy Jones and Jerry Hey for 'Dinorah, Dinorah', 1980.

Benson and Quincy Jones, producer, in one of the best collaborations of 1980, as evinced by the four Grammy awards. Benson gives one of his most exacting performances on record, which abounds in variety and something for everyone. The album includes 'Give Me the Night' (written by Rod Temperton) with Benson's vocal and instrumental talents displayed on this crisp, Sly-flavoured vocal and powerful bass line hit. Other prime tracks: 'Moody's Mood'; 'Dinorah, Dinorah'; and 'Off Broadway'. The album was seven weeks in the U.S. Top 10 and eight weeks in Britain's Top 10.

In addition to U.S.A.'s over one million sale, it sold over 100,000 in Britain.

BLONDIE

CALL ME *Chrysalis* [*USA*]. Written by G. Moroder and Debbie Harry, this was released in the U.S.A. in February 1980 and in Britain in April 1980. It reached No 1 for six weeks in the U.S.A. and for one week in Britain, staying 26 weeks in the U.S. charts and nine weeks in the British charts. R.I.A.A. Gold Disc award on 7 April 1980.

Theme song from the film *American Gigolo*, a stirring electronic dance track and among the best in progressive rock-disco fusion. Giorgio Moroder wrote all the music for the film and Debbie Harry co-wrote 'Call Me'. Blondie performs this in the film, Moroder's synthesizer tracks supporting and propelling the group to make a perfect pairing. Blondie lead Deborah Harry, together with Moroder, further enhanced their reputations as stylistic pioneers. The track has a duration of 8.04 minutes. It was an almost instant hit, staying in the U.S. Top 10 for 13 weeks, and in Britain's Top 10 for four weeks. British sales of over 100,000 added to the over a million sale in the U.S.A.

THE TIDE IS HIGH *Chrysalis* [*USA*]. Written by Reid and Holt, this was released in the U.S.A. and Britain in November 1980. It was No 1 for two weeks in both the U.S.A. and Britain and stayed 27 weeks in the U.S. charts, with 12 weeks in the British charts. R.I.A.A. Gold Disc award on 26 January 1981.

A surprising and pleasing track from the group's subsequent album, 'Autoamerican'. Debbie Harry's soothing vocals plus danceable rhythm made the reggae track another big hit. It was nine weeks in the U.S. Top 10 and six weeks in Britain's Top 10 where its over 100,000 sale added to the U.S. million.

AUTOAMERICAN (Album) *Chrysalis* [*USA*]. This was released in the U.S.A. and Britain in November 1980. In the U.S.A. it was No 9 for five weeks and stayed 26 weeks in the charts. In Britain it was No 3 for one week, staying 16 weeks in the charts. R.I.A.A. Gold and Platinum Disc awards on 26 January 1981.

Produced by Blondie's new producer, Mike Chapman, at the height of the group's popularity. The quintet's album covers every style from funk to orchestral, from show tunes to dance hall music. It was eight weeks in the U.S. Top 10 and three weeks in Britain's Top 10. British sales added over 300,000 to the American million plus.

It contained: 'The Tide is High'; 'Rapture'; 'Angels on the Balcony'; 'T-Birds' (the latter two with backing by Flo and Eddie); and other numbers. In addition to 'The Tide is High', 'Rapture' also achieved a Gold Disc in 1981, when released as a single.

KURTIS BLOW

THE BREAKS (Part 1) *Mercury* [*USA*]. Written by Moore, Smith, Walker, Ford and Simmons, this was released in the U.S.A. in June 1980 and in Britain in October 1980. In the U.S.A. it was No 58 for one week and lasted 11 weeks in the charts. In Britain it was No 47 for one week, staying four weeks in the charts. R.I.A.A. Gold Disc award on 19 August 1980.

Blow (real name Kurt Walker) was a well-known personality in upper Manhattan and the Bronx. He enjoyed a reputation as one of the best of the 'rappers', the street disc jockeys who improvise rhymes and fast talk to the extended rhythm breaks of disco records. Blow's career as a recording artist began in 1979 when J.B. Moore and Robert Ford Jr decided to produce a Christmas rap record. Moore wrote lyrics and music with Denzil Miller and Larry Smith over two evenings, and Moore invested his savings in the recording of 'Christmas Rappin''. They were going to release it themselves, when Phonogram's Los Angeles office phoned for a British contract on the disc. It finally appeared on Mercury in the U.S.A. It was, however, 'The Breaks' that proved to be the big hit. It generated tremendous excitement and dance power via black radio stations and many white, black, straight and gay dance floors. DJs were always looking for discs with 30-40-second percussion breaks. Blow's disc was in immediate demand in the discos, an amusing string of rhymes that tell hard-luck stories. The inspiration for 'The Breaks' came primarily from Eddie Lawrence's 'Old Philosopher' records which were litanies of personal misfortune. The 12-inch disc sold 590,000 in two months and went on easily to pass the million sale immediately. A 7-inch version for jukeboxes sold 250,000 instantly to retailers.

It was in the U.S. Top 10 for 11 weeks, and Britain's Top 10 for four weeks. 'The Breaks' is only the second single to be certified gold: the first was the Summer/Streisand duet, 'No More Tears (Enough is Enough)', although Summerhill Gang's 'Rapper's Delight' was the first 12-inch single to sell a million, but not officially certified gold by R.I.A.A.

JACKSON BROWNE

HOLD OUT (Album) *Asylum/Elektra* [*USA*]. With material by Jackson Browne, this was released in the U.S.A. in June 1980 and in Britain in July 1980. It went to No 4 for seven weeks in the U.S.A., staying in the charts for 30 weeks. In Britain it was No 44 for one week and stayed five weeks in the charts. R.I.A.A. Platinum Disc award on 15 September 1980.

Jackson Browne's first album since 'Running on Empty' (1977). This new album includes a great rock track 'Boulevard' with a razor-edged guitar and irresistible melody line, backed by a fervent chorus to his distinctive vocal. Other prime tracks are 'Disco Apocalypse' and 'Hold On, Hold Out', an anthem to human tenacity. It was 11 weeks in the U.S. Top 10.

THE CARS

PANORAMA (Album) *Elektra* [*USA*]. With material by Ric Ocasek, this was released in the U.S.A. in August 1980, going to No 8 for three weeks and lasting 23 weeks in the charts. R.I.A.A. Gold and Platinum Disc awards on 15 October 1980.

Yet another big success to further the group's explosive career, produced by Roy Thomas Baker. There are thick guitar sounds and an array of electronic percussion to the high-power blend of Ric Ocasek's stylish songs.

THE CHIPMUNKS

CHIPMUNK PUNK (Album) *Excelsior/Pickwick International* [*USA*]. Released in the U.S.A. in June 1980, this went to No 18 for one week and stayed in the charts for 32 weeks. R.I.A.A. Gold Disc award on 14 October 1980.

In 1958, Ross Bagdasarian created The Chipmunks by means of sound recordings at varying speeds and the recordings were issued under his pseudonym of David Seville (see 1958). They were a tremendous success, and worldwide sales for the group consisting of Alvin, Simon and Theodore were over 30 million. The group that never was was revived with great effect in 1980 with this album of 'Chipmunk Punk'. The mastermind behind the project, Pickwick A & R Director, Steve Vining, was responsible for the label's budget line of oldies as well as for the Quintessence classical series. He produced rhythm tracks for 'Chipmunk Punk' in Nashville and singing on the vocal tracks overdubbed in Minneapolis, where Excelsior Records were based. It took only two months for the album's release, after arranging clearance with Ross Bagdasarian Jr (the Chipmunk creator's son). The album was actually completed in 30 days. There was amazing nationwide reaction. It sold over 300,000 by August and was reported a million seller by the end of the year.

On the album jacket, Alvin is credited with lead guitar and vocals, Simon with bass, and Theodore with drums. On it, the Chipmunks perform recent hits by the Knack ('My Sharona';

'Good Girls Don't'; 'Frustrated') Linda Ronstadt ('How Do I Make You') and Blondie ('Call Me') among others.

THE COMMODORES

HEROES (Album) *Motown* [*USA*]. With songs by Richie and Jones, this was released in the U.S.A. in June 1980, going to No 7 for two weeks and staying in the charts for 26 weeks. R.I.A.A. Gold and Platinum Disc awards on 3 February 1981.

The Commodores' tenth album, a balance of funk, rock, gospel and ballads for a broad audience. The gospel-flavoured chorus

resounds over a grand piano and the cherished lead vocal by Lionel Richie in 'Jesus is Love' and 'Mighty Spirit', and he sings with loving sincerity on the title track 'Heroes', the role fitting the dramatic mood perfectly. The other tracks are: 'Got to Be Together'; 'Celebrate'; 'Old-Fashioned Love'; 'All the Way Down'; 'Sorry to Say'; 'Wake up Children'. It was in the U.S. Top 10 for six weeks. Production by James Carmichael.

CHRISTOPHER CROSS

CHRISTOPHER CROSS (Album) *Warner Bros* [*USA*]. With material by Christopher Cross, this was released in the U.S.A. in January 1980 and in Britain in February 1981. It went to No 8 for six weeks in the U.S.A., staying 87 weeks in the charts. In Britain it went to No 14 for one week and stayed in the charts for 76 weeks (to September 1983). R.I.A.A. Gold Disc award on 6 May 1980. Platinum award on 19 August 1980. Grammy awards: Album of the Year, 1980; Christopher Cross, Best New Artist, 1980; Record of the Year, 'Sailing', 1980; Song of the Year, 'Sailing', 1980; Best Arrangement Accompanying a Vocalist to Michael Omartian for 'Sailing', 1980.

The Christopher Cross story is one of meteoric rise from obscurity to stardom, winning four personal Grammy awards (the fifth went to his producer/arranger Michael Omartian). Born in Austin, Texas, hardly anyone outside Austin knew who Cross was up to the early part of 1980. His success story has all the elements of a fairy tale. He played in several Texas 'cover' bands in the seventies, singing the current hits in bars while working on his own simple, pretty, melodic songs. During this period he met Tim Meece, who became his manager. After the initial rejections from Warner Bros (he liked the A & R staff and styles of acts and producers for the label) Meece suggested signing with Austin-based Free Flow Productions. This proved to be a smart move, because Cross's next demo caught the attention of Warners' A & R staffer Michael Ostin. Ostin liked the tape and the label suggested he go down to Austin to hear Cross perform. It was the summer of 1978, and Cross was playing at Austin's Alamo Roadhouse when Ostin and staff producer Russ Titelman decided he was a refreshing new talent who had to be signed. Several months later work began on the album with producer

Michael Omartian. This was completed in October 1979, but Warners' decided to launch it on 27 December 1979 for sale in the first week of 1980. It immediately took off at AOR and retail in Texas, then spread to southest U.S.A. Because the album was very melodic, much of the momentum during the first two months was lost, as rock music was preferred in that area. The label decided to release 'Ride Like The Wind' from the album as a single in late January which quickly entered the charts, and then consistently jumped each week until it reached No 3 on 26 April. It was a different sounding single, and its success spurred album sales, followed by another track 'Sailing' as a single release which reached No 1 in August. A third track 'Never Be the Same' also became a single chart hit. Cross's debut album soon sold the million. It was 12 weeks in the U.S. Top 10 and a long run in the charts in both the U.S.A. and Britain.

Christopher Cross toured throughout May and June as an

opening act for Fleetwood Mac and The Eagles, but his most important national, and indeed international exposure was when he sang at the Oscar presentation for 1981 the song 'Arthur's Theme' (The Best That You Can Do) which he co-wrote with Bacharach, Allen and Bayer Sager for the film *Arthur*. This won the Oscar for best film song of that year. He had achieved the impossible as a debut artist by breaking into the Top 10 album charts with little fanfare. British sales were well over 100,000. Warners' attributed the success of Christopher Cross mainly to their entire staff's good old-fashioned promotion, and that the public liked Cross' music. No extensive promotion campaigns, contests or gimmicks were used to sell the album.

CHARLIE DANIELS BAND

FULL MOON (Album) *Epic* [*USA*]. With material by Daniels' Band, this was released in the U.S.A. in July 1980, going to No 10 for three weeks and staying 29 weeks in the charts. R.I.A.A. Gold Disc award on 29 September 1980. Platinum award on 7 November 1980.

Big success for the Daniels' Band, following the release of the single track 'In America', the lyrics of which roused the fighting spirit and started radio coverage from coast to coast for the album as well.

The band paint vivid scenes and characters in this high-energy collection of country, blues, and rock-influenced tunes. A second outstanding track was 'South Sea Song'.

DEVO

WHIP IT *Warner Bros* [*USA*]. Written by Mark Mothersbaugh and Jerry Casale, this was released in the U.S.A. in August 1980 and in Britain in November 1980. In the U.S.A. it was No 17 for one week and stayed 29 weeks in the charts. In Britain it was No 51 for one week, staying six weeks in the charts. R.I.A.A. Gold Disc award on 12 December 1980.

The prime track from Devo's album 'Freedom of Choice'. Its crisp drum crashes sparked a sharp rhythm crack, and the melodic 'hook' invited repeated listening.

Devo quintet are: Mark Mothersbaugh (vocals); Bob Mothersbaugh (guitar); Jerry Casale (guitar); Bob Casale (guitar); Alan Myers (drums). The band's name is derived from their so-called 'theory of de-evolution' – a theory that manifested itself in weird ways. Their music is described by Warner Bros as 'the sound of things falling apart'. Devo actually hail from Spudsville, U.S.A. (also known as Akron, Ohio). Their first album (named after their slogan 'Are we not Men? We are Devo') featured semi-classics such as 'Jocko Homo' and a zany 'I Can't Get No Satisfaction'. It became a cult item. Spuds everywhere mimicked singer Mark's stilted vocal delivery and the whole band's stiff robot-like posturing and oddly fascist salute. Devo became one of the few acts in pop other than Elvis Presley to spawn imitators. A disc of Devo clones was actually released by a local Los Angeles label, Rhino Records. Devo's second album was 'Duty Now For The Future' (1979). With 'Freedom of Choice' their music changed to sound more mainstream, with vocals closer to actual singing than the previous drone effect. The single 'Whip It' is an example.

Devo made successful appearances for two months in Japan and Europe, and subsequently on their U.S. tour in 1980.

NEIL DIAMOND

SEPTEMBER MORN (Album) *Columbia* [*USA*]. Written by Neil Diamond, this was released in the U.S.A. and Britain in January 1980. It went to No 10 for two weeks in the U.S.A. and remained in the charts for 17 weeks. In Britain it went to No 14 for one week, staying 11 weeks in the charts. R.I.A.A. Gold Disc award on 13 March 1980. Platinum award on 9 May 1980.

A fine Diamond album showing off his unique ability as a songwriter. The title cut 'September Morn' is outstanding. British sales were over 100,000.

DOCTOR HOOK

SEXY EYES *Capitol* [*USA*]. Written by Bob Mather, Keith Steagall and Chris Waters, this was released in the U.S.A. in February 1980 and in Britain in March 1980. It reached No 3 for two weeks in the U.S.A. and was in the charts for 24 weeks. In Britain it went to No 4 for one week and stayed nine weeks in the charts. R.I.A.A. Gold Disc award on 10 July 1980.

An infectious dance beat with sparkling keyboards and flirtatious vocals made this a winner for Doctor Hook. It was seven weeks in the U.S. Top 10 and five weeks in Britain's Top 10.

THE DOOBIE BROTHERS

ONE STEP CLOSER (Album) *Warner Bros* [*USA*]. Written by Knudsen, McFree and Carter, this was released in the U.S.A. in October 1980, going to No 3 for three weeks and staying in the charts for 23 weeks. R.I.A.A. Gold and Platinum Disc awards on 18 November 1980.

The Doobies elaborate on their most imitated sound of the year with saxophone and percussion. Mike McDonald's vocals are influential and other members contribute. It was nine weeks in the U.S. Top 10.

THE DOORS

GREATEST HITS (Album) *Elektra* [*USA*]. This was released in the U.S.A. in November 1980 and went to No 41 for one week, staying 24 weeks in the charts. R.I.A.A. Gold Disc award on 30 December 1980. Platinum award on 18 September 1981.

Welcome revival of the famous Doors' hits. The album included their most famous song 'Light My Fire' and other big hits such as 'Hello, I Love You' and 'Touch Me'.

THE EAGLES

EAGLES 'LIVE' (Album) *Asylum* [*USA*]. With material by The Eagles, this was released in the U.S.A. and Britain in November 1980. It was No 9 for four weeks in the U.S.A., lasting 22 weeks in the charts. In Britain it was No 24 for one week and stayed 12 weeks in the charts. R.I.A.A. Gold and Platinum Disc awards on 7 January 1981.

This album shows The Eagles' proficiency in concert, the quality of the recording making it difficult to distinguish the package from a studio album. It included live versions of their hits ranging from 'Take it Easy' to 'The Long Run'. Another outstanding track, 'Seven Bridges Road' a new song (written by Young), is a harmony-rich number with nimble acoustic guitar backing. The album was six weeks in the U.S. Top 10. British sales were over 60,000.

Remainder of tracks on the album are: 'Hotel California'; 'Heartache Tonight'; 'I Can't Tell You Why'; 'New Kid in Town'; 'Life's Been Good'; 'Wasted Time'; 'Take it to the Limit'; 'Doolin-Dalton (Reprise No 2)'; 'Desperado'; 'Saturday Night'; 'All Night Long'; 'Life in the Fast Lane'.

SHEENA EASTON

MORNING TRAIN (9 to 5) *EMI* [*Britain*]. Written by F. Palmer, this was released in Britain in July 1980 and in the U.S.A. in February 1981. In Britain it went to No 3 for two weeks and stayed 15 weeks in the charts. In the U.S.A. it hit No 1 for three weeks, staying 19 weeks in the charts. R.I.A.A. Gold Disc award on 8 May 1981.

Scottish singer Sheena Easton (born 1959) achieved national acclaim in Britain after featuring in a TV documentary – the story of a pop star's struggle for success. Her debut single release was 'Modern Girl' - only a mild success, but when the TV show was repeated, that single and '9 to 5' both shot up Britain's charts together. The latter's success in the U.S.A. was even bigger. The title there was changed to 'Morning Train' as Dolly Parton had a hit also titled '9 to 5'. The disc was six weeks in the British Top 10 and eight weeks in the U.S. Top 10. Sheena subsequently recorded the theme song for the James Bond film *For Your Eyes Only*, and she became an international star. British sales of '9 to 5' were over 250,000 for this bright timely ballad.

ELECTRIC LIGHT ORCHESTRA

I'M ALIVE *MCA* [*USA*] *Jet* [*Britain*]. Written by Jeff Lynne, this was released in the U.S.A. and Britain in May 1980. In the U.S.A. it went to No 14 for one week, remaining 15 weeks in the charts. In Britain it was No 20 for two weeks and stayed nine weeks in the charts. R.I.A.A. Gold Disc award on 15 July 1980.

One of the outstanding tracks from the musical fantasy film *Xanadu*, this abounds with keyboard magic to a Beatlesque melody, plus heavenly falsetto choruses. A vintage ELO disc.

LARRY GRAHAM

ONE IN A MILLION YOU *Warner Bros* [*USA*]. Written by Sam Dees, this was released in the U.S.A. in June 1980, going to No 16 for two weeks and staying 21 weeks in the charts. R.I.A.A. Gold Disc award on 24 September 1980.

The title track from Graham's album, a dramatic ballad, one of the best of the year. His musical career started at the age of 16

in the San Francisco area when he joined his mother in the Dell Graham Trio, playing guitar and organ. When the organ broke down one night, he went out to rent another one, but all they had was a bass guitar. He has played bass guitar ever since. When he and his mother became a duet, he thumped and hit the strings to compensate for the lack of a drummer. He developed a style of playing that was uniquely his own. Thanks to his mother he was already an all-round musician. She gave him dancing lessons when he was five, and at eight introduced him to the piano. By the time he was a teenager, Larry played all keyboards, guitar, harmonica, saxophone, and drums and had a three-and-a-half-octave vocal range. Word of his talent reached Sylvester Stewart, then a DJ at Oakland's KSOL station. Stewart was impressed and recruited him for his band Sly and the Family Stone. The band was one of the most influential during the seventies, and one of the most imitated aspects of its sound was Graham's bass playing. After six years with Sly, Larry left to form Graham Central Station, and the group made six albums and achieved international fame for their special blend of 'progressive funk'. After six years with his group, he decided to 'go back to his roots' and sing ballads, and he went into his own studio and came up with his first solo album 'One In a Million You'. The title song made a huge impact on both pop and black charts. The band continued under its own entity with Graham producing, while he continued on a solo career. People have likened his voice to Lou Rawls, Arthur Prysock and Billy Eckstine.

DARYL HALL & JOHN OATES

VOICES (Album) *RCA* [*USA*]. This album was released in the U.S.A. in June 1980, going to No 17 for one week and staying in the charts for 53 weeks. R.I.A.A. Gold Disc award on 6 May 1981. R.I.A.A. Platinum Disc award on 22 January 1982.

1980 was the year that saw the duo return to the Top 10 with their single release of 'You've Lost That Lovin' Feeling' from the album, and expanded their acclaim globally. In January 1980 they played six shows at London's prestigious Venue, all sold out in two days, and when a seventh was added it sold out also. By the time they left England they had a hit single in 'Running from Paradise'. On return to England in September, they played a 15-city tour (which sold out), ending with two shows at the Hammersmith Odeon in London which brought 'You've Lost That Lovin' Feeling' and 'Kiss on My List' to the fore - both from the 'Voices' album. Further performances in Paris followed. They gave performances in Japan (February 1980) and the return trip (October 1980) spawned the hit single 'Hard To Be' also from the 'Voices' album. Australia brought further acclaim in 1980 on their first tour of that country. The year ended with TV, press and radio interviews in Germany and Spain.

While Hall and Oates had been conquering abroad, they also

had great success in the U.S.A. on three tours, and by 1981 achieved international stardom.

The album includes: 'How Does it Feel to be Back?'; 'Hard to Be'; 'You've Lost That Lovin' Feeling'; 'You Make my Dreams'; 'Kiss on my List', all these titles bringing phenomenal success to the duo.

THE ISLEY BROTHERS
GO ALL THE WAY (Album) *T-Neck* [*USA*]. With material by the group and released in the U.S.A. in April 1980, this climbed to No 5 for two weeks and stayed 17 weeks in the charts. R.I.A.A. Gold and Platinum Disc awards on 4 June 1980.

The Isley Brothers continue their success with this fine album of driving funk and seductive, sensuous ballads. It includes three outstanding tracks: 'Go All the Way'; 'Don't Say Goodnight (It's Time for Love) (Parts 1 & 2)'- and 'Say You Will (Part 1)'. The album was 7 weeks in the U.S. Top 10.

THE JACKSONS
TRIUMPH (Album) *Epic* [*USA*]. With songs by Michael and Randy Jackson, this was released in the U.S.A. and Britain in October 1980. It went to No 9 for two weeks in the U.S.A. and to No 13 for one week in Britain. It stayed in the U.S. charts for 26 weeks and for eight weeks in the British charts. R.I.A.A. Gold and Platinum Disc awards on 10 December 1980.

Following his huge solo success, Michael Jackson leads his brothers in an outstanding album of nine numbers. This self-produced collection features mostly uptempo original works, with Michael as principal writer. The album includes: 'Can You Feel It?'; 'Lovely One'; 'Heartbreak Hotel'; 'Everybody'; and 'Time Waits For No One'. It was five weeks in the U.S. Top 10.

WAYLON JENNINGS
THEME FROM 'THE DUKES OF HAZZARD' (Good Ol' Boys) *RCA* [*USA*]. Written by Waylon Jennings, this was released in the U.S.A. in August 1980, reaching No 7 for seven weeks and staying 27 weeks in the charts. R.I.A.A. Gold Disc award on 9 December 1980.

Jennings' first million-selling single, and the most successful single of the year for RCA's country division. Jennings applies his own unique country philosophy to the popular TV show, the result being a twangy folk culture jewel. It was seven weeks in the U.S. Top 10.

BILLY JOEL
GLASS HOUSES (Album) *Columbia* [*USA*]. With material by Billy Joel, this was released in the U.S.A. in March 1980 and in Britain in July 1980. It climbed to No 1 in the U.S.A., staying there for 11 weeks, and remained in the charts for a total of 60 weeks. In Britain it went to No 20 for one week, staying 12 weeks in the charts. R.I.A.A. Gold and Platinum Disc awards on 5 May 1980. Grammy awards: Best Rock (Male) Vocal for 'Glass Houses', 1980; Producer of the Year, Phil Ramone, for 'Glass Houses', 1980.

This was a blockbuster for Billy Joel, one of music's most successful performer/writers. Its reign at the top of the charts and staying in them for over a year, plus half that time (29 weeks) in the U.S. Top 10 generated a sale of at least two million. Sales in Britain were over 100,000. It included songs familiar and some not, but 'It's Still Rock And Roll To Me' was the prime track. Joel surveys the current rock scene with sharp vocal phrasing and a pulsating rhythm, driving home his pointed lyrical observations.

IT'S STILL ROCK AND ROLL TO ME *Columbia* [*USA*]. Written by Billy Joel, this was released in the U.S.A. in May 1980 and in Britain in July 1980. It hit No 1 for four weeks in the U.S.A., staying in the charts for 23 weeks. In Britain it went to No 14 for one week, staying 11 weeks in the charts. R.I.A.A. Gold Disc award on 23 July 1980.

The best track from Billy's album 'Glass Houses'. It was 11 weeks in the U.S. Top 10.

ELTON JOHN
LITTLE JEANNIE *MCA* [*USA*]. Written by John and Osborne, this was released in the U.S.A. and Britain in May 1980. In the U.S.A. it went to No 4 for three weeks and stayed 20 weeks in the charts. It was No 33 for one week in Britain and stayed seven weeks in the charts. R.I.A.A. Gold Disc award on 12 August 1980.

The initial release from Elton's subsequent album '21 at 33'. In the U.S. Top 10 for eight weeks.

BROTHERS JOHNSON
LIGHT UP THE NIGHT (Album) *A & M* [*USA*]. Written by the Brothers Johnson and Temperton, this was released in the U.S.A. and Britain in February 1980. It went to No 8 for two weeks in the U.S.A., staying 22 weeks in the charts. In Britain it was No 22 for one week, staying 13 weeks in the charts. R.I.A.A. Gold Disc award on 19 April 1980. Platinum award on 25 September 1980.

Superb nine-track release by the brothers, produced by Quincy Jones with strings and horns arranged by Jerry Hey. Another example of the progression of R & B music, mixing traditional rhythms with rock and disco influences. It includes the outstanding tracks 'Stomp' (an irresistible vocal chant); 'Light Up the Night'; 'All About Heaven'. It was in the U.S. Top 10 for five weeks.

JOURNEY
DEPARTURE (Album) *Columbia* [*USA*]. With material by the group, this was released in the U.S.A. in March 1980, going to No 10 for three weeks and staying 32 weeks in the charts. R.I.A.A. Gold Disc award on 5 May 1980. Platinum award on 3 July 1980.

Another Journey album full of high-energy tunes, drawn from traditional U.S. rock'n'roll rhythms, with powerful vocals by Steve Perry. It includes: 'Any Way You Want It'; 'Precious Time'; 'Good Morning, Girl'; 'Stay Awhile'. In the U.S. Top 10 for three weeks.

KOOL & THE GANG
CELEBRATE (Album) *De-Lite/Phonogram* [*USA*]. This was released in the U.S.A. in October 1980, going to No 11 for two

weeks and staying in the charts for 32 weeks. R.I.A.A. Gold Disc award on 16 December 1980. Platinum award on 25 February 1981.

Another solid package with selections evenly balanced between moderate tempo and dance numbers that appealed to both R & B and pop audiences. Again produced by Eumir Deodato. It included the huge hit 'Celebration'.

CELEBRATION *De-Lite/Phonogram* [*USA*]. Written by Ronald Bell and the group, it was released in the U.S.A. and Britain in October 1980. It was No 1 for one week in the U.S.A., lasting 32 weeks in the charts, and in Britain it was No 7 for one week, staying 13 weeks in the charts. R.I.A.A. Gold Disc award on 14 January 1981. Platinum award on 19 March 1981.

This was one of the only two singles to receive a platinum award in 1981 for a two million sale. It also sold 250,000 in Britain. The title cut from their album 'Celebrate'. A big party hook with chorus chants and insistent bass. It was in the U.S. Top 10 for 12 weeks and the British for three weeks.

JOHNNY LEE

LOOKIN' FOR LOVE *Full Moon/Asylum* [*USA*]. Written by Johnny Lee and released in the U.S.A. in July 1980, this went to No 3 for one week and lasted 21 weeks in the charts. R.I.A.A. Gold Disc award on 18 November 1980.

Johnny Lee's debut single was a hit. It was originally released on the *Urban Cowboy* soundtrack, the film in which he also appeared. Johnny was formerly a trumpet player/vocalist for Mickey Gilley. The disc was six weeks in the U.S. Top 10.

JOHN LENNON & YOKO ONO

DOUBLE FANTASY (Album) *Geffen* [*USA*]. With songs by John Lennon and Yoko Ono, this was released in the U.S.A. and Britain in November 1980. It went to No 1 for two weeks in both the U.S.A. and Britain, staying 35 weeks in the U.S. charts and 34 weeks in the British charts. R.I.A.A. Gold and Platinum Disc awards on 10 January 1981. Grammy award: Album of the Year, 1981.

This album, John Lennon's last, was released just one month before he was assassinated outside his flat in New York on 8 December 1980. The songs were written during the summer of 1980 in a Bermuda resort called Fairylands, and the subsequent album was his first for five years. After his death by being gunned down outside the Dakota Apartments by Central Park, it became a huge seller everywhere, over two million in the U.S.A. and half a million in Britain by early February 1981. Global sales by June 1981 were over eight million. It was an astounding 19 weeks in the U.S. Top 10 and 17 weeks in Britain's Top 10. The album also spawned two million-seller singles: 'Just Like Starting Over' in 1980; and 'Woman' in 1981. It is virtually a pop music dialogue on love and marriage by one of rock'n'roll's most notable couples, John's romantic visions alternating tracks with Yoko's tender observations. The complete contents are: 'Starting Over'; 'Every Man Has a Woman Who Loves Him'; 'Cleanup Time'; 'Give Me Something'; 'I'm Losing You'; 'Beautiful Boy (Darling Boy)'; 'Watching the Wheels'; 'I'm Your Angel'; 'Dear Yoko'; 'Beautiful Boys'; 'Kiss, Kiss, Kiss'; 'Woman'; 'Hard Times are Over'.

As with Presley's demise, there was a huge demand for Lennon's old material. John Lennon left £2,500,000 in Britain, but the division of his total estate is estimated at £125,000,000. His record royalties were said to grow by £100,000 a day. In the U.S.A. 37-year-old multi-millionaire David Geffen controls virtually all Lennon's latest records and merchandising. Geffen, a one-time messenger boy, became chairman of Elektra Asylum before forming his own Geffen Records label and signing Lennon in this year. Lennon was in the process of completing a new album when he was shot and his widow Yoko started remixing some of the tracks - under Geffen's guidance - for the album to be released later. This would 'add to one of the greatest private fortunes on earth', as one observer predicted.

(Just Like) STARTING OVER *Geffen* [*USA*]. Written by John Lennon, this was released in the U.S.A. and Britain in November 1980. In the U.S.A. it was No 1 for six weeks, staying 22 weeks in the charts. In Britain it was No 1 for one week and stayed 14 weeks in the charts. R.I.A.A. Gold Disc award on 24 December 1980.

This glorious pop-rocker was released prior to the 'Double Fantasy' album. It was 10 weeks in the U.S. Top 10, and six weeks in Britain's Top 10. British sales were over 500,000.

LIPPS INC.

FUNKY TOWN *Casablanca* [*USA*]. Written by Steven Greenberg, this was released in the U.S.A. in March 1980 and in Britain in May 1980. It climbed to No 1 for four weeks in the U.S.A. and to No 2 for two weeks in Britain, staying 28 weeks in the U.S. charts and 13 weeks in the British lists. R.I.A.A. Gold Disc award on 23 May 1980. Platinum award on 17 July 1980.

'Funky Town' was written, produced, arranged and played by 29-year-old studio musician Steven Greenberg, and is one of the cleverest singles to get into the charts. According to one report, the disc manages to combine a Moroder-type synthesizer track with Blue Mink vocals, Silver Convention strings and riffs from 'Boogie Nights' and 'Sunshine of Your Love'. Greenberg also recruited vocalist Cynthia Johnson and guitarist Tom Riopelle. It is a track from Lipps Inc.'s album 'Mouth to Mouth', and sold over two million in the U.S.A., plus another 250,000 in Britain. Its appeal to discos was immense, and radio stations were dumbfounded to see it zoom towards the top so quickly when they started playing it, particularly as many programmers and critics were convinced that disco was finished. 'Funky Town' was the first club disco record to cross over to pop. It was in the U.S. Top 10 for 13 weeks and the British for seven weeks.

LOVERBOY

LOVERBOY (Album) *Columbia* [*USA*]. This was released in the U.S.A. in December 1980, going to No 13 for two weeks and staying 24 weeks in the charts. R.I.A.A. Gold Disc award on 8 May 1981. R.I.A.A. platinum award on 8 February 1982.

This was the hottest debut album of 1981 by a new rock group comprising five young men - a group with no past but with a giant future. The album burst onto the rock scene with considerable impact. It contained 'Turn me Loose' which subsequently triggered off a demand for it as a single release.

THE MANHATTANS

SHINING STAR *Columbia* [*USA*]. Written by Leo Graham and Paul Richmond, this was released in the U.S.A. in April 1980 and in Britain in July 1980. In the U.S.A. it went to No 4 for two weeks, staying 26 weeks in the charts. It was No 45 for one week in Britain and stayed four weeks in the charts. R.I.A.A. Gold Disc award on 18 July 1980. Grammy award: Best Duo or Group with Vocal, 'Shining Star', 1980.

A great disc by The Manhattans, masters of the ballad. It is highlighted by sympathetic falsetto vocals and repetitive acoustic guitar line that becomes an understated hook. This moving, though not maudlin, song was eight weeks in the U.S. Top 10, and a well-deserved Grammy winner. Produced by the composer Leo Graham.

BARRY MANILOW

BARRY (Album) *Arista* [*USA*]. Material by Barry Manilow and others. This was released in the U.S.A. and Britain in November 1980, going to No 11 for five weeks in the U.S.A. and to No 8 for one week in Britain. It stayed 20 weeks in the U.S. charts and 31 weeks in the British lists. R.I.A.A. Gold and Platinum Disc awards on 4 February 1981.

Manilow continues his success on the pop scene with this fine album. It contains: 'I Made It In the Rain'; 'Lonely Together'; 'Bermuda Triangle'; '24 Hours a Day'; 'Dance Away'; 'Life Will

Go On'; 'We Still Have Time'; 'London'; and two special touches, 'Only in Chicago' (written with Maurice White) and Broadway-style humour in 'The Last Duet' (with Lily Tomlin). In Britain it was six weeks in the Top 10 and sold over 300,000.

PAUL McCARTNEY
COMING UP Columbia [USA]. Written by Paul McCartney, this was released in the U.S.A. and Britain in April 1980. It reached No 3 for six weeks in the U.S.A. and stayed 20 weeks in the charts. In Britain it went to No 2 for one week and stayed nine weeks in the charts. R.I.A.A. Gold Disc award on 21 July 1980.

Taken from Paul's subsequent album 'McCartney 2', a taste of his first one-man project in years. Electronic keyboards plus dance beat and Paul's vocals give a contemporary sound. It was 10 weeks in the U.S. Top 10 and four weeks in Britain's. British sales were over 250,000.

MICKEY MOUSE
MICKEY MOUSE DISCO (Album) Disneyland/Vista [USA]. This was released in the U.S.A. in March 1980, going to No 14 for one week and staying a total of 56 weeks in the charts. R.I.A.A. Gold Disc award on 11 April 1980. Platinum award on 30 May 1980.

An astute idea of the Disneyworld label to produce this album based on the popularity of their famous cartoon character, Mickey Mouse. It was intended for sale for the young and had a great success. It was the bestselling children's album of the year and sold two million by the year's end.

BETTE MIDLER
THE ROSE Columbia [USA]. Written by Amanda McBroom, this single was released in the U.S.A. in March 1980, reaching No 1 there for two weeks. It was in the charts for 23 weeks. R.I.A.A. Gold Disc award on 25 June 1980. Grammy award: Best Pop Vocal Performance (Female), 'The Rose', 1980.

The title theme from the hit film The Rose, this single is a remixed version from the soundtrack album. The lonely piano setting puts Bette Midler at her breathtaking best. The disc was in the U.S. Top 10 for 11 weeks.

Bette Midler, self-styled The Divine Miss M (also the title of her first album in 1973) was born 1 December 1945 in Hawaii. She went to New York in the 1960s with an ambition for acting. She secured the part of Tzeitel in Fiddler on the Roof for three years, but it was at the nightclub Continental in New York where she had her first major engagement. Johnny Carson, host of the late-night TV show, featured her on TV in his Las Vegas engagement. Her act took in a wide range of material, from Bessie Smith's 'Empty Red Blues' to Shangri-La's 'Leader of the Pack'. Barry Manilow became her musical director, conductor and pianist and produced and arranged her bestselling album 'Divine Miss M' (1973). He also went on tour with her as a support act. Bette's star role in the film The Rose (1979) enhanced her career, and she achieved national and international acclaim.

STEPHANIE MILLS
NEVER KNEW LOVE LIKE THIS BEFORE 20th Century-Fox [USA]. Written by James Mtume and Reggie Lucas, this was released in the U.S.A. in August 1980 and in Britain in October 1980. In the U.S.A. it went to No 8 for two weeks and stayed 29 weeks in the charts. In Britain it went to No 4 for one week, staying in the charts for 13 weeks. R.I.A.A. Gold Disc award on 16 January 1981. Grammy awards: Best R & B Female Vocalist, 'Never Knew Love Like This', 1980; Best Rhythm and Blues song, 'Never Knew Love Like This', to Composers Mtume and Lucas, 1980.

Stephanie hails from Mount Vernon, New York, and was born in 1958. She has always been immersed in music and was honoured while still in grammar school for her artistic and vocal ability with a prize that had been given to only one other in the school's history – Barbra Streisand. Her career started at the age of 10, when she won the Apollo Theatre's amateur night contest. The theatre management gave her her first professional booking – a week's engagement with the Isley Brothers. Soon afterwards, she was one of the children in the musical Maggie Flynn on Broadway with Shirley Jones and Jack Cassidy. Irene Cara of Fame was also one of the children. This Broadway debut resulted in the part of Dorothy in The Wiz when she was 15. She played the part for four years on Broadway, but the film part was given to Diana Ross. She spent a couple of years at Motown under Burt Bacharach and Hal David, who saw her as a successor to Dionne Warwick, writing and producing the album 'For The First Time' before the partnership was dissolved. She then teamed with Mtume and Lucas and made her first two albums for 20th Century-Fox – 'Whatcha Gonna Do With My Lovin'' and 'Sweet Sensation', both of which went 'gold'. Then came the single 'Never Knew Love Like This Before', her first million seller, with its keyboards, angelic chorus and Stephanie's lovely fairytale quality voice.

Since her success in The Wiz and subsequently as a concert and nightclub artist, Stephanie became an international celebrity, travelling over 100,000 miles each year – Paris, Rome, London. Her British debut in 1981 was marked by a steamy duet with soul singer Teddy Pendergrass. She recorded two duets with him for his album 'T.P.'

This single was also a hit in Britain where it sold over 250,000. It was in the U.S. Top 10 for three weeks and the British for four weeks.

With sell-out concert appearances and numerous TV appearances, she has fans all over the world.

RONNIE MILSAP
GREATEST HITS (Album) RCA [USA]. This was released in the U.S.A. in October 1980, going to No 36 for one week and staying 21 weeks in the charts. R.I.A.A. Gold Disc award on 12 February 1981. Platinum award on 14 July 1981.

Country artist Ronnie Milsap was born in Robbinsville, North Carolina, U.S.A., and was blind from birth. He discovered an aptitude for music at the age of five at the State School for the blind in Raleigh. He was a violin virtuoso at seven, played piano when eight and mastered the guitar at twelve. He now plays most of the keyboard, stringed, percussion and woodwind instruments. During school, Milsap studied classical music, but the strong influence of country music was so inherent that he decided to return to his roots. This did not meet the approval of his teachers, but they finally gave in and allowed him to form his own rock group with three other boys. They called themselves the Apparitions and frequently performed at high school and college assemblies in the Raleigh area. Milsap's love of music won out over a legal career, and he stayed in Atlanta where he went to junior college, picking up odd engagements. His first job was with H.H. Cale. By 1966 Ronnie had formed his own band and played the Playboy circuit and college dates, and got a contract with Scepter Records. He moved to Memphis in 1969 and his group worked there at T.J.s, a popular nightclub. Here he wrote the hits 'Denver' and 'Loving You is a Natural Thing'. Later he recorded for Chip Records and then with Warner Bros. After finally deciding to go country, he moved to Nashville where Tom Collins of Pi-Gem Music helped him to establish a career in country music. In April 1973 Ronnie signed a contract with RCA, his first release being 'I Hate You', followed by such singles as 'The Girl That Waits on Tables'; 'Pure Love'; 'Please Don't Tell Me How the Story Ends'; and 'Legend in My Time'. From 1976 all nine of Milsap's RCA singles were No 1 on the country charts. His RCA albums were 'Where My Heart Is'; 'Pure Love'; 'A Legend In My Time'; 'Night Things'; '20-20 Vision'; 'Ronnie Milsap Live'; 'It Was Almost Like a Song'; 'Only One Love In My Life'; and 'Images'.

Ronnie won the Country Music Association's award for Best Male Vocalist of 1974, again in 1976 and 1977, also Entertainer of the Year 1977 and Best Album of the Year 'Ronnie Milsap

national charts, staying there for a total of 22 weeks. R.I.A.A. Gold Disc award on 4 February 1981. R.I.A.A. Platinum Disc award on 16 April 1982.

A true success story in music of the brisk triumphs by this gospel group as they made the transition to country music contenders. The quartet, headed by lead singer Duane Allen, made their first single 'Y'all Come Back Saloon' for ABC (now MCA). This was a big hit across the board. In 1979 came hit single 'Dream On' and their third LP 'The Oak Ridge Boys Have Arrived'. They received major industry awards, broke records in concert performances and became frequent TV guest stars. Their show is a delight – visually and auditory – with driving rhythm and tight-knit harmony, generating excitement to every audience. They were named by the Country Music Association as Vocal Group of the year (1979) while the Oak Ridge Band (a four-man group) were Instrumental Group of the Year as well. They are produced by expert Ron Chancey.

The album contains: 'You're the One'; 'I'll be True to You'; 'Trying to Love Two Women'; 'Cryin' Again'; 'Dream On'; 'Leaving Louisiana in the Broad Daylight'; 'Heart of Mine'; 'Come On In'; 'Sail Away'; 'Y'all Come Back Saloon'.

ALAN PARSONS PROJECT
THE TURN OF A FRIENDLY CARD (Album) *Arista* [*USA*]. With material by Alan Parsons, this was released in the U.S.A. and Britain in November 1980. It went to No 14 for one week in the U.S.A. and stayed 29 weeks in the charts. In Britain it went to No 38 for one week, staying three weeks in the charts. R.I.A.A. Gold Disc award on 18 February 1981. Platinum award on 12 August 1981.

The effectiveness of Parsons' writing and production illustrates the album's scheme with a variety of moods, methods and lead vocalists.

DOLLY PARTON
9 TO 5 *MCA* [*USA*]. Written by Dolly Parton, this was released in the U.S.A. in December 1980, going to No 1 for five weeks and staying 26 weeks in the charts. R.I.A.A. Gold Disc award on

Live'. His fame as a pianist/singer had been spreading throughout the world. In 1978 Ronnie made his debut appearance at the Wembley Country Music Festival, London.

This 'Greatest Hits' collection is outstanding. It contains: '(I'd Be) A Legend in My Time'; '(I'm A) Stand By My Woman Man'; 'I Hate You'; 'Pure Love'; 'It was Almost Like a Song'; 'Daydreams about Night Things'; 'Let's Take The Long Way Round The World'; 'Let My Love Be Your Pillow'; 'Please Don't Tell Me How The Story Ends'; 'Back On My Mind Again'; 'What A Difference You've Made To My Life' and a new hit single 'Smoky Mountain Rain'.

These made Ronnie Milsap a star, and built a legend.

ANNE MURRAY
GREATEST HITS (Album) *Capitol* [*USA*]. This was released in the U.S.A. in September 1980 and in Britain in October 1981. In the U.S.A. it went to No 11 for two weeks and stayed 35 weeks in the charts. It went to No 14 for one week in Britain, staying in the charts for ten weeks. R.I.A.A. Gold Disc award on 10 November 1980. Platinum award on 26 November 1980. Grammy award: Best Country (Female) Vocalist, 1980, for 'Could I Have This Dance?'.

One of the greatest hit packages, an impressive track record catalogued in this album, spanning Anne's work with producers Brian Ahern and Jim Ed Norman, and containing all her hits. The album includes: 'Snowbird'; 'You Needed Me'; 'Could I Have This Dance?' (from the film *Urban Cowboy*).

Sales in Britain were over 60,000.

OLIVIA NEWTON-JOHN
MAGIC *MCA* [*USA*] *Jet* [*Britain*]. Written by John Farrar, this was released in the U.S.A. in May 1980 and in Britain in August 1980. It hit No 1 for three weeks in the U.S.A., staying in the charts for 25 weeks. In Britain it went to No 32 for one week, staying seven weeks in the charts. R.I.A.A. Gold Disc award on 15 July 1980.

One of the great tracks from the film *Xanadu* soundtrack. An infectious pop ballad with a big beat. It was in the U.S. Top 10 for 11 weeks.

THE OAK RIDGE BOYS
GREATEST HITS (Album) *MCA* [*USA*]. This was released in the U.S.A. in November 1980, going to No 5 for two weeks in the U.S. country charts and to No 37 for two weeks in the

19 February 1981. Grammy awards: Best Country Song, '9 to 5', 1981; Best Country Vocal (Female) Performance, '9 to 5', 1981.

This self-penned song won Dolly Parton all the country awards in the U.S.A. A cut from the subsequent soundtrack of the film *9 to 5*, it had instant appeal in the U.S.A. and universally. The track to Dolly's vocal is accompanied by a lively rhythm, punctuated by horns. It was in the U.S. Top 10 for 13 weeks.

The film *9 to 5* gave Dolly her first movie role. It co-starred Jane Fonda and Lily Tomlin.

TEDDY PENDERGRASS

'T.P.' (Album) *Philadelphia International* [*USA*]. With material by various writers and released in the U.S.A. in August 1980, this went to No 11 for two weeks and lasted 30 weeks in the charts. R.I.A.A. Gold Disc award on 29 September 1980. Platinum award on 12 November 1980.

The most exploratory album Teddy has made, consisting of a variety of material, and joined by other artists, Stephanie Mills and Ashford and Simpson. He brings to mind several of the R & B greats while maintaining his own distinct tone and colour. The LP includes: 'Feel the Fire' (duet with Stephanie Mills); 'Take Me in Your Arms Again' (duet with Stephanie Mills); 'Girl You Know'; 'Can't we Try?'; 'Just Called to Say'; 'Is It Still Good to You?'; 'Love T.K.O.' (written by Womack and Nobel).

THE POINTER SISTERS

HE'S SO SHY *Planet/Elektra/Asylum* [*USA*]. Written by Tom Snow and Cynthia Weill, this was released in the U.S.A. in July 1980, going to No 5 for four weeks and staying in the charts for 31 weeks. R.I.A.A. Gold Disc award on 25 November 1980.

The prime track from the Pointer Sisters' subsequent album. June Pointer is lead singer supported by an irresistible keyboard riff and snappy percussion drive. It was in the U.S. Top 10 for nine weeks.

THE POLICE

ZENYATTA MONDATTA (Album) *A & M* [*USA*]. With material by Sting and the group, this was released in the U.S.A. and Britain in October 1980. In the U.S.A. it went to No 8 for two weeks and in Britain it climbed to No 1 for four weeks. It stayed 38 weeks in the U.S. charts and 31 weeks in the British lists. R.I.A.A. Gold Disc award on 12 December 1980. Platinum award on 27 February 1981.

Police is composed of Gordon Sumner ('Sting') born in Wallsend, Northumberland, England, 2 October 1951, (vocals/ bass); Andy Summers from Blackpool, England (guitar); Stewart Copeland, son of former CIA Chief of Operations in the Middle East (drums). Sumner attended Warwick University and subsequently was a teacher in Newcastle. Summers was a precocious musician at school and became a session man before joining The Police. Copeland attended the American School in St John's Wood, London, and started playing in the school band. Copeland played with Curved Air and noticed Sting playing in Last Exit in Newcastle. He enticed Sting down to London where they rehearsed with French guitarist Henri Padovani (who later joined Wayne County's Electric Chairs). They played with Cherry Vanilla and in their own right at the Roxy Club in early 1977, supplementing their income with session work. Andy Summers saw them at the Marquee and was enlisted. They made their debut as a quartet at the Mont de Marsan festival in France, the only Continental haven for British New Wave bands. Summers' melodic guitar style, Sting's plain bass lines and Copeland's heavy beat made them the most danceable of London's new wave bands. During some concerts for Eberhard Schoener's Laser Theatre in Germany, they were asked to appear in a Wrigley's Spearmint Gum advert for American TV. They had their own label, Illegal Records, and made their first single 'Fall Out' in 1977. It sold 15,000. Copeland's brother Miles became their manager after hearing them record 'Roxanne' in 1978 for A & M Records with whom he secured them a deal. They then started

recording their first album 'Outlandos D'Amour'. Sting began filming for *Quadrophenia*. The album was recorded for less than £3,000 but eventually made a massive profit for them and their recording company.

In Britain, the playlisting system barred 'Roxanne' because it was the story of a prostitute, and 'Can't Stand Losing You' because it referred to suicide. A & M having signed them for an album deal started their big record company exploitation. Both the singles began to get heavy airplay on American college radio and the FM stations, then Britain started taking notice. Police made their first American tour, taking in Boston, Detroit, Dayton, Pittsburgh, Washington, Philadelphia and New York. They ended 1978 with a big nationwide British tour, with three singles in the British chart, and another assault on America. In January 1979, they had 20 dates at the Laser Theatre in Germany, various radio sessions, and on 13 February began recording the album 'Regatta De Blanc' again at Surrey Sound on another low budget, paid by themselves. It became 'gold' in the U.S.A.

'Roxanne' began making an impression in Britain, and the band made their debut on 'Top of the Pops'. 'Outlandos' was storming up the U.S. charts, and Police began another extensive tour. Sting did many broadcasts and *Quadrophenia* was premiered. He played the role of Ace from which for a total of 10 minutes on screen he received rave reviews. Police topped the bill at the Reading Festival, and 'Message In A Bottle' (from 'Regatta de Blanc' album) was released as a single, in September 1979, to be No 1 in Britain. 1979 ended with Police on another U.S. tour (October and November) followed by a world tour around Christmas 1979. The Police, with their Spartan approach to the business of recording, touring and breaking records, personified the spirit of the new rock'n'roll. They broke all the rules – violating those that made expensive, elaborate recording sessions and lavish tours an imperative for aspiring rock bands. To quote their manager: 'The philosophy of The Police has been three-piece, condensed, recording cheaply, keeping everything basically as simple as possible and capturing that element of what made rock music great in the first place.'

'Zenyatta Mondatta' album contains: 'Don't Stand so Close to Me'; 'When the World is Running Down'; 'Voices Inside My Head'; 'Driven to Tears'; 'You Make the Best of What's Still Around'; 'Canary in a Coalmine'; 'Bombs Away'; 'De Do Do Do, De Da Da Da'; 'Behind my Camel'; 'Man in a Suitcase'; 'Shadows in the Rain'; 'The Other Way of Stepping'.

It was six weeks in the U.S. Top 10 and 15 weeks in Britain's Top 10. The album was an instant No 1 on both sides of the Atlantic, selling over 500,000 in Britain and over three million by March 1981 in the U.S.A.

PRETENDERS

PRETENDERS (Album) *Sire/Warner* [*USA*] *Real* [*Britain*]. This was released in the U.S.A. and Britain in January 1980. It was No 11 for two weeks in the U.S.A. and stayed 31 weeks in the charts. In Britain it reached No 1 for four weeks and stayed 35 weeks in the charts. R.I.A.A. Gold Disc award on 2 June 1980. R.I.A.A. Platinum Disc award on 11 August 1982.

Akron-born rock singer Chrissie Hynde is one of the wave of new 'rock' women. This album was formulating months before release, due to airplay for Chrissie's U.K. singles with her band. The singles were cut for the newly-formed Real label, and were the payoff after five frustrating years for the singer/guitarist. Chrissie first journeyed to England in 1974, but her projects launched there, in Paris, and back in the U.S.A. all failed. She added her Mid-Western rock roots and R & B with traces of reggae and New Wave, yet by 1978 this all resulted in nothing but false starts and near misses.

Former Anchor A & R executive sponsored the turnaround, after hearing a solo demo of Hynde's 'The Phone Call', one of the songs subsequently recorded for this album. He signed her as one of the first three acts on Real label, and soon after she linked up with Pete Farndon (bassist); Martin Chambers (drums); and James Honeyman Scott (guitar/keyboards) with

Farndon as backing vocalist. The band's first single was a new version of Ray Davies' 'Stop Your Sobbing'. The next English singles 'The Wait' and 'Tattooed Love Boys' clearly showed that the band were even more powerful than their soaring debut single suggested. With their New Wave drive of uptempo songs, the quartet added shifts in time signatures, off-centre harmonic progressions and subtle electronic dissonances. By mid-1980, Pretenders made their first U.S. tour, with the album making its mark on both sides of the Atlantic. British sales were well over 100,000 and the U.S.A. passed the million two years later. It included the outstanding track 'Brass in Pocket' driven by Chrissie Hynde's chilling vocals, also 'The Phone Call'. The whole album is new English rock at its best, a great triumph for a debut album.

After a tour of the Far East in 1982, Scott died on 16 June. Further misfortune was Pete Farndon leaving the group two days before and his subsequent death, making the group's future uncertain, even with their new album 'Pretenders 2' on the market.

QUEEN

THE GAME (Album) *Elektra* [*USA*] *EMI* [*Britain*]. Written by John Deacon and Freddie Mercury, this was released in Britain and the U.S.A. in July 1980. It was No 1 for two weeks in both Britain and the U.S.A., staying 18 weeks in the British charts and 42 weeks in the U.S. charts. R.I.A.A. Gold Disc award on 15 September 1980. Platinum award on 1 October 1980.

A masterful album by Queen. It was 25 weeks in the U.S. Top 10 and a huge hit there. The album included two million-seller singles 'Crazy Little Thing Called Love' and 'Another One Bites the Dust'. Other tracks included were: 'Need Your Loving Tonight'; 'Play the Game'; 'The Game'; 'Save Me'. In Britain it was four weeks in the Top 10, and entered the charts at No 2 the first week, selling an instant 100,000. U.S. sales were well over two million, global over three million.

ANOTHER ONE BITES THE DUST *Elektra* [*USA*] *EMI* [*Britain*]. Written by John Deacon, this was released in the U.S.A and Britain in August 1980. In the U.S.A. it hit No 1 for six weeks and stayed 35 weeks in the charts. In Britain it went to No 7 for one week, staying in the charts for nine weeks. R.I.A.A. Gold Disc award on 1 October 1980. Platinum award on 25 November 1980.

This cut from Queen's album 'The Game' was a tremendous hit in the U.S.A., and one of the only three discs of the year to go platinum for a singles release and sell over two million. The disc has a powerful bass combining with the sing-along hook to make it a thoroughly contagious song. In the U.S. Top 10 for 21 weeks, Britain for three weeks.

EDDIE RABBITT

DRIVIN' MY LIFE AWAY *Elektra* [*USA*]. Written by Eddie Rabbitt, David Malloy and Even Stevens, this was released in the U.S.A. in June 1980, going to No 5 for three weeks and staying in the charts for 26 weeks. R.I.A.A. Gold Disc award on 25 March 1981.

By this year, Eddie Rabbitt had become a mainstay of the country scene. His story begins with songwriting. He achieved success in this field with 'Kentucky Rain' (Elvis Presley, 1970) and 'Pure Love' (Ronnie Milsap, 1974) and then made the transition to country recording star. After 1974 he had seven No 1 singles including 'Drinkin' My Baby Off My Mind' (1976); 'I Just Want To Love You' (1978); 'Suspicions' (1979); and 'Gone Too Far' (1980). In all, there were 13 Top 10 Rabbitt country hits.

The Rabbitt success story is actually one of teamwork. Around 1970, Rabbit and Stevens didn't mean much in Nashville. They spent three years collaborating on songs. This resulted in the unique format of the Rabbitt hits and the layered harmony sound on his recordings. It was just the two writers, a couple of guitars, and a sound-on-sound tape recorder in the early days. Third team member David Malloy was learning to be an engineer at Nashville's Sound Lab Studio nearby. Rabbitt and Stevens visited him after midnight to experiment in the studio. Malloy was impressed, added some of his own ideas, refined the sound and collaborated on the songs, ultimately becoming musically bound to the duo. Using the technology of the studio, the early demos sounded almost like finished records. The trio took them to Elektra Records. Seven albums later, Malloy became Rabbitt's regular producer and collaborator. Even Stevens was Eddie's regular songwriting partner and a source of inspiration also. None had any big Nashville industry connections. Rabbitt and Stevens are not even Southerners (Stevens is from a small town in Ohio and Rabbitt has New York/New Jersey roots). Their song 'Suspicions' was BMI's most performed country song of 1980. Randy McCormick, arranger/pianist with a group of musicians from Muscle Shoals (Alabama) was in Los Angeles for recording, and the Rabbitt team were working and taping in the studio. During a meal, McCormick experimented with chords at the piano. The trio exchanged ideas inspired by the chords. Lyrics were suggested and a song took shape. Later McCormick's explorations were transformed into one of Eddie's most successful records. The quartet's 'Suspicions' was a winner right away.

'Drivin' my Life Away' is a smooth rocker with chorus harmonies and lyrical guitar to Rabbitt's slick vocal. The song is a prime track from the 'Roadie' soundtrack. It was five weeks in the U.S. Top 10.

HORIZON (Album) *Elektra* [*USA*]. Written by Rabbitt, Malloy, Stevens and McCormick, this was released in the U.S.A. in July 1980 and went to No 20 for three weeks. It stayed in the U.S. charts for 39 weeks. R.I.A.A. Gold Disc award on 24 October 1980. Platinum award on 23 February 1981.

McCormick worked with the Rabbitt team on this album at Caribou Ranch Recording Studio in Colorado. It is an interesting blend of modern rockabilly and strong country ballads. The standout tracks are: 'Drivin' my Life Away'; 'So Deep in Your Love'; 'I Love a Rainy Night'. It was first a country chart success, then crossed over to the national charts. Two of the songs were million-seller singles.

I LOVE A RAINY NIGHT *Elektra* [*USA*]. Written by Rabbitt, Stevens and Malloy, this was released in the U.S.A. in November 1980, going to No 3 for four weeks and staying 28 weeks in the charts. R.I.A.A. Gold Disc award on 10 March 1981.

Taken from the album 'Horizon' this rockabilly-flavoured follow-up to Rabbitt's crossover hit 'Drivin' my Life Away' is straight from the fifties and gives the listener an instant urge to get up and dance. It was in the U.S. Top 10 for nine weeks.

RAY, GOODMAN & BROWN

SPECIAL LADY *Polydor* [*USA*]. Written by Willie Goodman, Harry Ray and Lee Walter, this was released in the U.S.A. in January 1980, reaching No 9 for three weeks and lasting 20 weeks in the charts. R.I.A.A. Gold Disc award on 13 May 1980.

Ray, Goodman and Brown had been favourites with the U.S. audiences for more than a decade as The Moments (see 1970) with such hits as 'Love on a Two-Way Street'; 'Sexy Mama'; 'Look at Me' and 'Girls'. 'Special Lady' is the outstanding track from their album of the same title. They were in their teens when they started singing professionally. Harry Ray performed with the Sound of Soul band while in the Army's Special Services, and then with The Establishments. Al (Willie) Goodman grew up singing spirituals in a Mississippi church and was later a featured singer with the Corvettes. Billy Brown was born in Atlanta where his father was a minister. He sang with a group known as the Broadways. They were a chart success as a trio from the beginning, and performed with major acts such as Earth, Wind and Fire; The Supremes; The Temptations; Smokey Robinson; and others. The black trio's recordings were not only successful in the U.S.A., but also in England, France, most of Europe and Japan. A French recording of their 'Look at Me' was an international hit. They also scored with 16 charted singles and with 10 albums. With the Moments they were always in the middle of the road, so the trio went out on their own to take their music to a different level.

This disc of 'Special Lady' earned them an award as 'Best New Group of 1980'. It was five weeks in the U.S. Top 10.

REO SPEEDWAGON

KEEP ON LOVING YOU *Epic* [*USA*]. Written by Cronin, Ricrath and Beamish, this was released in the U.S.A. in December 1980 and in Britain in April 1981. It went to No 1 for one week in the U.S.A. and stayed 30 weeks in the charts. In Britain it went to No 7 for two weeks and stayed 14 weeks in the charts. R.I.A.A. Gold Disc award on 16 March 1981.

A dramatic single from the group's subsequent 'Hi Infidelity' album. It has majestic keyboards, with Kevin Cronin's heart-throb vocals. It was 14 weeks in the U.S. Top 10 and three weeks in the British.

HI INFIDELITY (Album) *Epic* [*USA*]. With material by REO Speedwagon, this was released in the U.S.A. in December 1980 and in Britain in April 1981. In the U.S.A. it was No 1 for a total of 17 weeks and stayed 60 weeks in the charts. In Britain it went to No 6 for one week, staying 29 weeks in the charts. R.I.A.A. Gold and Platinum Disc awards on 2 February 1981.

This eleventh album for REO Speedwagon was a real block-buster with its long stay at the top of the U.S. charts and long spell in the charts of over a year. It included the hit 'Keep on Loving You'; 'Don't Let Him Go'; and a novel track with a gospel touch 'I Wish You Were There'. Sales were big also in Britain - over 60,000. It was in the U.S. Top 10 for 26 weeks, and Britain's for eight weeks.

KENNY ROGERS

GIDEON (Album) *United Artists* [*USA*]. Written by Kim Carnes and Dave Ellingson, this was released in the U.S.A. in April 1980. It was No 8 for six weeks there and stayed 32 weeks in the charts. R.I.A.A. Gold and Platinum Disc awards on 28 May 1980.

This advance platinum award album is all about 'Gideon'. It includes 'Don't Fall in Love with a Dreamer', a duet with Kim Carnes. From modest beginnings as a singer, Rogers emerged as a mass phenomenon. This album was eight weeks in the U.S. Top 10. A concept album, telling the story of a West Texas man who died a cowboy, looking back on his life.

LADY *Liberty* [*USA*]. Written by Lionel Richie Jnr, this was released in the U.S.A. in September 1980 and in Britain in November 1980. In the U.S.A. it was at No 1 for five weeks, staying 27 weeks in the charts. In Britain it was No 12 for one week and stayed 12 weeks in the charts. R.I.A.A. Gold Disc award on 25 November 1980.

This is a beautiful ballad, written and produced by the leader of The Commodores. It was in the U.S. Top 10 for 14 weeks and was included in his 'Greatest Hits' album.

GREATEST HITS (Album) *Liberty* [*USA*]. Released in the U.S.A. in September 1980, this was No 1 for a total of 14 weeks and stayed in the charts for 73 weeks (to end of March 1982). R.I.A.A. Gold and Platinum Disc awards on 2 December 1980.

Kenny's album traces the gold and platinum path of his highly successful career, and includes his 'best of' classics from his early days with First Edition, such as 'Reuben James' (1969) up to his 1977 breakthrough 'Lucille'. The other tracks are: 'Ruby'; 'The Gambler'; 'Coward of the County'; 'She Believes in Me'; 'You Decorated my Life'; 'Don't Fall in Love with a Dreamer'; 'Love the World Away'; 'Every Time Two Fools Collide'. 'Long Arm of the Law'; and 'Lady' were two new songs.

It was 32 weeks in the U.S. Top 10 and actually went on to a chart stay of two years. The album was produced by Lionel Richie Jr (of The Commodores) and Larry Butler.

THE ROLLING STONES

EMOTIONAL RESCUE (Album) *Rolling Stones* [*Britain*] *Atlantic* [*USA*]. With material by Mick Jagger and Keith Richard, this was released in Britain and the U.S.A. in June 1980. It went to No 1 for one week in the U.S.A. and for four weeks in Britain. It stayed 31 weeks in the U.S. charts and 18 weeks in the British charts. R.I.A.A. Platinum Disc award on 10 September 1980.

No 1 chart entry in Britain the first week of its release, and No 2 in the U.S.A. The popularity of the Rolling Stones is never-ending, their subsequent tours all being sell-outs. This album contains: 'Dance'; 'Summer Romance'; 'Send It to Me'; 'Let Me Go'; 'Indian Girl'; 'Where the Boys Go'; 'Down in the Hole'; 'Emotional Rescue'; 'She's So Cold'; 'All About You'. British sales were over 100,000.

LINDA RONSTADT

MAD LOVE (Album) *Asylum* [*USA*]. With material by Steinberg, Taylor, Gorgoni and Costello, this was released in the U.S.A. in March 1980, going to No 3 for two weeks and staying 31 weeks in the charts. R.I.A.A. Gold and Platinum Disc awards on 12 May 1980.

A change of image for Linda, showing how the New Wave rock had revitalized her incomparable talent. It included: 'How Do I Make You'; 'Rambler Gambler'; 'I Can't Let Go'; and three Elvis Costello songs as well as other New-Wavish tunes. Linda's double-tracked vocals are supreme. The album was 11 weeks in the U.S. Top 10.

DIANA ROSS

DIANA (Album) *Motown* [*USA*]. Written by Nile Rodgers and Bernard Edwards, this was released in the U.S.A. and Britain in June 1980. In the U.S.A. it went to No 4 for three weeks and stayed in the charts for 39 weeks. In Britain it went to No 13 for one week, staying 26 weeks in the charts. R.I.A.A. Gold and Platinum Disc awards on 3 February 1981.

Diana's new album pairs her with the most influential team in R & B music of the day, Chic's Rodgers and Edwards. They wrote the songs and brought along their entire entourage (notably drummer Tony Thompson, and singers Alfa Anderson and Luci Martin) weaving Ross' voice into their sound. The principal tracks are: 'Upside Down'; 'Have Fun'; 'No One Gets the Prize'; 'I'm Coming Out'; 'Tenderness'. The composers varied their style slightly by eliminating hand claps and employing reggae influences on one track, plus New-Wave-sounding echo on the background singing. The album was 13 weeks in the U.S. Top 10 and also sold over 100,000 in Britain.

UPSIDE DOWN *Motown* [*USA*]. Written by Nile Rodgers and Bernard Edwards, this was released in the U.S.A. and Britain in July 1980. In the U.S.A. this stayed in the charts for 30 weeks, going to No 1 for two weeks. In Britain it stayed six weeks in the charts, going to No 2 for two weeks. R.I.A.A. Gold Disc award on 16 December 1981.

The big hit track from her 'Diana' album. It presents Diana in a low register, singing/chanting in front of the chorus, with razor-sharp phrasing and surprising force in her voice. It was 11 weeks in the U.S. Top 10 and six weeks in Britain's. British sales were 250,000.

LEO SAYER

MORE THAN I CAN SAY *Chrysalis* [*Britain*] *Warner Bros* [*USA*]. Written by Jerry Allison and Sonny Curtis, this was released in Britain in June 1980 and in the U.S.A. in September 1980. It reached No 2 for one week in Britain, lasting 11 weeks in the charts. In the U.S.A. it went to No 3 for four weeks, staying 28 weeks in the charts. R.I.A.A. Gold Disc award on 24 December 1980.

Leo Sayer continues his success with this fine disc, on both sides of the Atlantic. It was 11 weeks in the U.S Top 10 and five weeks in Britain's. An additional 250,000 sale in Britain to add to the over one million in the U.S.A.

BOZ SCAGGS

MIDDLE MAN (Album) *Columbia* [*USA*] *CBS* [*Britain*]. With material by Boz Scaggs, this was released in the U.S.A. and Britain in April 1980. In the U.S.A. it was No 11 for three weeks and stayed 25 weeks in the charts. In Britain it was No 52 for one week and stayed four weeks in the charts. R.I.A.A. Gold Disc award on 4 June 1980. Platinum award on 6 February 1981.

Scaggs' album is as smooth as his former 'Silk Degrees' album but does not produce the latter's formula. This album has fine guitar solos from Steve Lukather and Carlos Santana. It includes a great track 'Breakdown Dead Ahead'.

BOB SEGER & SILVER BULLET BAND

AGAINST THE WIND (Album) *Capitol* [*USA*]. With material by Bob Seger, this was released in the U.S.A. and Britain in March 1980. It hit No 1 for two weeks in the U.S.A., staying in the charts for 58 weeks. In Britain it went to No 26 for one week and stayed six weeks in the charts. R.I.A.A. Gold and Platinum Disc awards on 29 April 1980. Grammy awards: Best Country Duo or Group (Vocal) for 'Against The Wind', 1980; Best Album Package to Art Director Roy Kohara, 'Against The Wind', 1980.

Seger maintains his reputation as one of rock's finest story-tellers on this fine album. He is assisted by three Eagles to make 'Fire Lake' the blockbuster number. It also includes 'Against the Wind'; 'You'll Accompn'y Me'; and 'The Horizontal Bop', all released as successful singles. The album was No 2 in its third week in the U.S.A. and of its long run in the charts of over a year, was 24 weeks in the Top 10.

CARLY SIMON

JESSE *Warner Bros* [*USA*]. Written by Carly Simon and Nain-eri, this was released in the U.S.A. in July 1980, going to No 6 for one week and remaining 25 weeks in the charts. R.I.A.A. Gold Disc award on 5 December 1980.

A fine lively record about a one-sided love affair that won't go away, and sharp slide guitar effects plus chorus, brings Carly back to the million-selling lists once more. It was 10 weeks in the U.S. Top 10.

THE S.O.S. BAND

TAKE YOUR TIME (Do it Right) (Part 1) *Tabu/CBS* [*USA*]. Written by Sigidi and Harold Clayton, this was released in the U.S.A. in April 1980 and in Britain in July 1980. In the U.S.A. it went to No 3 for two weeks and stayed 24 weeks in the charts. It was No 51 for one week in Britain and stayed four weeks in the charts. R.I.A.A. Gold Disc award on 20 June 1980. Platinum Disc award on 19 September 1980.

One of the only three two-million-seller singles of the year. Writer and producer Sigidi and arranger Fred Wesley (see Wesley & The JBs, 1973) and a seven-piece band produced a fresh, midtempo cut of space-age funk, with handclapping and a doodling percussion of brilliant melodic elements. It embraces an instrumental break, framed by synthesizer and bass on the bottom and pretty xylophone accenting, all immediately effective. This debut disc by S.O.S. was a blockbuster favourite with the discos, hence its big sale. It was seven weeks in the U.S. Top 10. The group hails from Atlanta, California. The lead vocal – 'first mate' – is Mary Davis.

BRUCE SPRINGSTEEN & THE E STREET BAND

THE RIVER (Double album) *Columbia* [*USA*]. With material by Bruce Springsteen, this was released in the U.S.A. and Britain in October 1980. It went to No 2 for three weeks in the U.S.A., staying 28 weeks in the charts. In Britain it went to No 2 for one week, staying 51 weeks in the charts. R.I.A.A. Gold and Platinum Disc awards on 12 December 1980.

The radio stations eagerly pounced on this long-awaited double album, the rock'n'roll hero's first for two years. It was his fifth album, and entered the U.S. charts immediately at No 2 and similarly in Britain. Bruce is a national phenomenon and one of the most potent forces in popular music. His stunning performance in the film *No Nukes* set the stage for the release of 'The River' album. It contained 20 new songs, displaying the awesome power of his music. At the same time, a single 'Hungry Heart' was released, a Top 10 song and somewhat of an anthem at every one of his sold-out four-hour concerts. Without prompting, the audience sings the entire first verse while the band waits for Bruce to join in the chorus.

The album was 13 weeks in the U.S. Top 10 and three weeks in Britain. British sales added another 100,000 plus to the U.S. over a million.

STEELY DAN

GAUCHO (Album) *MCA* [*USA*]. With material by the group, this was released in the U.S.A. and Britain in November 1980. In the U.S.A. it was No 9 for three weeks, staying in the charts for 26 weeks. In Britain it was No 27 for two weeks and stayed 12 weeks in the charts. R.I.A.A. Gold and Platinum Disc awards on 22 January 1981.

The richness and detail of Becker and Fagen's sound (with producer Gary Katz) is without equal. An outstanding album, it includes: 'Hey Nineteen'; and 'Third World Man' and was in the U.S. Top 10 for five weeks.

ROD STEWART

FOOLISH BEHAVIOUR (Album) *Warner Bros* [*USA*] *Riva* [*Britain*]. Written by Stewart, Chen, Savigar, Cregan and Grainger, this was released in the U.S.A. and Britain in November 1980. It went to No 14 for four weeks in the U.S.A. and to No 3 for one week in Britain, staying 20 weeks in the U.S. charts and 13 weeks in the British lists. R.I.A.A. Gold Disc award on 14 January 1981. Platinum Disc award on 4 March 1981.

Another hit album for Stewart, with his unmistakable voice on sentimental and rock numbers. The prime track 'Passion' includes menacing guitar runs, and percussion. Other outstanding tracks are: 'My Girl'; and 'Foolish Behaviour'. Sales in Britain added another 300,000 or more to the U.S. million.

BARBRA STREISAND

GUILTY (Album) *Columbia* [*USA*]. Written by the Gibb brothers, this was released in the U.S.A. and Britain in October 1980. It went to No 1 for three weeks in the U.S.A. and for two weeks in Britain. It stayed in the U.S. charts for 36 weeks and for 83 weeks in the British charts. R.I.A.A. Platinum Disc award on 19 November 1980.

Another instant success in both Britain and the U.S.A. for Barbra. It was No 1 in its second week in the U.S.A. A triumph also for the Gibb brothers (of the Bee Gees) and their fine songs. The album was produced by Barry Gibb, and with Barbra he created one of the most formidable pop alliances in recent years. It included 'Guilty' and 'Woman in Love', both scintillating tracks that sold over a million each when released as singles. The 'Guilty' album was 28 weeks in the U.S. Top 10 and 18 weeks in Britain's. British sales went well over 500,000, with over 18 months in their charts. Global sales were over four million by March 1981.

WOMAN IN LOVE *Columbia* [*USA*]. Written by Robin and Barry Gibb, this was released in the U.S.A. and Britain in September 1980. In the U.S.A. it went to No 1 for one week and stayed 25 weeks in the charts. In Britain it was No 1 for three weeks and stayed 15 weeks in the charts. R.I.A.A. Gold Disc award on 7 November 1980.

The Gibb brothers give Barbra a luscious backing on this single release from her 'Guilty' album. It was 10 weeks in the U.S. Top 10 and seven in Britain's. Another 500,000 were sold in Britain in addition to the U.S. million plus.

BARBRA STREISAND & BARRY GIBB

GUILTY *Columbia* [*USA*]. Written by Barry and Robin Gibb and released in the U.S.A. and Britain in November 1980, this went to No 6 for six weeks in the U.S.A., staying in the charts for 22 weeks. In Britain it was No 34 for one week and stayed nine weeks in the charts. R.I.A.A. Gold Disc award on 3 March 1981. Grammy award: Best Pop Vocal Performance by Duo or Group for 'Guilty', 1980.

The disc was particularly popular in the U.S.A., where it was eight weeks in the Top 10.

DONNA SUMMER

ON THE RADIO *Casablanca* [*USA*]. Written by Giorgio Moroder and Donna Summer, this was released in the U.S.A. and Britain in February 1980. In the U.S.A. it went to No 1 for one week and stayed 16 weeks in the charts. It was No 32 for one week in Britain and lasted four weeks in the charts. R.I.A.A. Gold Disc award on 11 March 1980.

Donna's first No 1 single of the year, a cut from her album of the same title (1979). The radio reaction to this disc was fantastic. It was in the U.S. Top 10 for seven weeks.

THE WANDERER *Geffen* [*USA*] *Warner Bros* [*Britain*]. Written by Giorgio Moroder and Pete Bellotte, this was released in the U.S.A. and Britain in September 1980, going to No 4 for three weeks in the U.S.A. and to No 48 for one week in Britain. It stayed 25 weeks in the U.S. charts and six weeks in the British lists. R.I.A.A. Gold Disc award on 2 December 1980.

Donna's first single on her new label, a cut from the album of the same title, produced by the creative Moroder and Bellotte. It was eight weeks in the U.S. Top 10.

VAN HALEN

WOMEN AND CHILDREN FIRST (Album) *Warner Bros* [*USA*]. With material by Van Halen, this was released in the U.S.A. in March 1980 and in Britain in the following month. In the U.S.A. it went to No 4 for two weeks, staying 26 weeks in the charts. In Britain it went to No 15 for one week and stayed seven weeks in the charts. R.I.A.A. Gold Disc award on 29 May 1980. Platinum Disc award on 2 June 1980.

Another million-selling album for Van Halen, who in a few short years became one of the industry's hottest acts. A perfect album, lean and powerful, for their massive audience. It was 10 weeks in the U.S. Top 10.

GROVER WASHINGTON JNR

WINELIGHT (Album) *Elektra* [*USA*]. Written by Ralph Mac-Donald, Grover Washington, Bill Salter and Bill Withers, this was released in the U.S.A. in November 1980 and in Britain in May 1981. It went to No 5 for two weeks in the U.S.A., staying in the charts for 37 weeks. In Britain it was No 34 for one week, staying nine weeks in the charts. R.I.A.A. Gold Disc award on 10 March 1981. Platinum Disc award on 6 May 1981.

Grover Washington Jr has for many years represented the best in pop-jazz. He was an influential force in making musicians aware of the commercial potential of this contemporary music. From 1973, he made nine albums for the Kudu label up to 1978, then one for Tamla (1978) and two for Elektra, of which this was the second (1980). Writer Salter, percussionist producer Mac-Donald and arranger Bill Eaton share production credit on this 'Winelight' album which was cut at Ralph MacDonald's studio in New York, Rosebud. Washington provided the brilliant saxophone work and MacDonald the percussion. It included 'Just the Two of Us', a winner with the jazz audience, with the words written by Bill Withers who adds the vocals.

A worthy million seller, the first, for the popular saxophonist's special blend of fusion. It was six weeks in the U.S. Top 10, and also reached No 1 on the Black Oriented Album Chart.

THE WHISPERS

AND THE BEAT GOES ON *Solar* [*USA*]. Written by Sylvers, Shockley and Shelby, this was released in the U.S.A. and Britain in January 1980. In the U.S.A. it was No 23 for one week and stayed 15 weeks in the charts. It went to No 2 for one week in Britain and stayed 12 weeks in the charts. R.I.A.A. Gold Disc award on 18 March 1980.

The prime cut from The Whispers' album of that title (1979) caught on in the discos and soon sold the million to their fans. The quintet, with their crafty harmonies, agile vocal interplay, plus big bass beat to the smooth, soft falsettos and classy percussion, are unbeatable at this type of music. The disc was very successful in Britain as well, selling over 250,000 and staying in their Top 10 for five weeks.

STEVIE WONDER

HOTTER THAN JULY (Album) *Tamla* [*USA*] *Motown* [*Britain*]. Written by Stevie Wonder, this was released in the U.S.A. and Britain in November 1980. It went to No 3 for five weeks in the U.S.A., staying in the charts for 29 weeks. In Britain it went to No 2 for one week and stayed 54 weeks in the charts. R.I.A.A. Gold and Platinum Disc awards on 3 February 1981.

Stevie Wonder's 25th original album consists of songs with lyrics focusing on politics, love, prejudice and the celebration of life. The ten selections cover a wide range, from reggae, as in 'Master Blaster' (Jammin') to the country style of 'I Ain't Gonna Stand for It'. Other outstanding tracks are: 'Happy Birthday' (a joyous tribute to Martin Luther King, with Stevie playing all the instruments himself on an uplifting riff) and 'Lately'. The album was 17 weeks in the U.S. Top 10 and 16 in Britain, where it added over 500,000 to the total tally of an estimated 3 million. It was No 2 in Britain the first week of release, and stayed in their charts for over a year. Its appeal was universal.

Appendix A: Million sellers released in 1981

The following list of discs released in 1981 are those so far reported as having sold a million copies at the time of going to press, in the order *Artist, Title, Original label.*

† Denotes million-seller album: R.I.A.A. Platinum Disc award.
* Denotes million-seller single: R.I.A.A. Gold Disc award.
** Denotes two-million-seller single: R.I.A.A. Platinum Disc award.

ABBA
The Visitors (album)
Polar (Sweden)

AC/DC
Dirty Deeds Done Dirt Cheap (album)
For Those About to Rock We Salute You
(R.I.A.A. certified 1982)
Atlantic (U.S.A.)

Air Supply
The One That You Love (album)
The One That You Love
Arista (U.S.A.)

Alabama
Feels So Right (album)
RCA (U.S.A.)

April Wine
The Nature of the Beast (Album)
(R.I.A.A. certified 1982)
Capitol (U.S.A.)

Benatar, Pat
Precious Time (album)
Chrysalis (U.S.A.)

Blondie
Rapture
Chrysalis (U.S.A.)

Carlton, Carl
She's a Bad Mama Jama
20th Century (U.S.A.)

Carnes, Kim
Bette Davis' Eyes
Mistaken Identity (album)
EMI/America (U.S.A.)

Cars, The
†Shake It Up (album)
(R.I.A.A. certified 1982)
Elektra/Asylum (U.S.A.)

Commodores, The
†In The Pocket (album)
Motown (U.S.A.)

Cross, Christopher
*'Arthur's Theme' (The Best You Can Do)
(R.I.A.A. certified 1982)
Warner (U.S.A.)

Diamond, Neil
†On the Way to the Stars (album)
(R.I.A.A. certified 1982)
Columbia (U.S.A.)

Earth, Wind & Fire
†Raise (album)
Columbia (U.S.A.)
*Let's Groove
(R.I.A.A. certified 1982)
ARC/Columbia (U.S.A.)

Fogelberg, Dan
†The Innocent Age (album)
Full Moon/Epic (U.S.A.)

Foreigner
†4 (album)
*Waiting for a Girl Like You
(R.I.A.A. certified 1982)
Atlantic (U.S.A.)

Gap Band
†Gap Band III (album)
Mercury/Phonogram (U.S.A.)

J. Geils Band
†Freeze-Frame (album)
(R.I.A.A. certified 1982)
*Freeze-Frame
(R.I.A.A. certified 1982)
*Centerfold
(R.I.A.A. certified 1982)
EMI/America (U.S.A.)

Genesis
†ABACAB (album)
(R.I.A.A. certified 1982)
Atlantic (U.S.A.)

Go Go's, The
†Beauty and the Beat (album)
(R.I.A.A. certified 1982)
IRS/A&M (U.S.A.)

Hall, Daryl, & Oates, John
*Kiss On My List
*Private Eyes
†Private Eyes (album)
*I Can't Go For That (No Can Do)
(R.I.A.A. certified 1982)
RCA (U.S.A.)

Human League, The
*Don't You Want Me?
(R.I.A.A. certified 1982)
Virgin (Britain)
A & M (U.S.A.)

Iglesias, Julio
Begin the Beguine
CBS (Britain)

James, Rick
†Street Songs (album)
Gordy (U.S.A.)

The Human League

Jarreau, Al
†Breakin' Away (album)
(R.I.A.A. certified 1982)
Warner (U.S.A.)

Jett, Joan
†I Love Rock 'n' Roll (album)
(R.I.A.A. certified 1982)
Boardwalk (U.S.A.)

Joel, Billy
†Songs in the Attic (album)
Columbia (U.S.A.)

Jones, Quincy
†The Dude (album)
(R.I.A.A. certified 1982)
A & M (U.S.A.)

Journey
†Escape (album)
†Captured (album)
Columbia (U.S.A.)

Kool & The Gang
†Something Special (album)
De-Lite/Polygram (U.S.A.)

Lennon, John
Imagine (Original in 'Imagine'
(album), 1971, released as single
1975, on Apple label and
Parlophone 1981)
*Woman
Geffen (U.S.A.)

Loggins, Ken, & Messina, Jim
†Best of Friends (album)
Columbia (U.S.A.)

Moody Blues
†Long Distance Voyager (album)
Threshold/Polygram (U.S.A.)

Nelson, Willie
†Greatest Hits (and some that will
be) (album)
(R.I.A.A. certified 1982)
†Somewhere Over the Rainbow
(album)
Columbia (U.S.A.)

Newton, Juice
†Juice (album)
(R.I.A.A. certified 1982)
*Angel of the Morning
*Queen of Hearts
Capitol (U.S.A.)

Newton-John, Olivia
†Physical (album)
**Physical
MCA (U.S.A.)

Nicks, Stevie
†Bella Donna (album)
Modern (U.S.A.)

The Police

Oak Ridge Boys, The
**Elvira
†Fancy Free (album)
RCA (U.S.A.)

Osbourne, Ozzy
†Diary of a Madman (album)
(R.I.A.A. certified 1982)
†Blizzard of Oz (album)
(R.I.A.A. certified 1982)
Jet/CBS (U.S.A.)

**Petty, Tom & The
Heartbreakers**
†Hard Promises (album)
Backstreet (U.S.A.)

Pointer Sisters, The
*Slowhand
Planet (U.S.A.)

Police
†Ghost in the Machine (album)
A & M (U.S.A.)

Quarterflash
†Quarterflash (album)
(R.I.A.A. certified 1982)
Geffen/Warner (U.S.A.)

Queen
†Greatest Hits (album)
Elektra (U.S.A.)

Robinson, Smokey
*Being With You
Tamla (U.S.A.)

Rogers, Kenny
†Christmas (album)
(R.I.A.A. certified 1982)
†Share Your Love (album)
Liberty (U.S.A.)

Rolling Stones, The
†Tattoo You (album)
Rolling Stones (U.S.A.)

Ross, Diana
†Why Do Fools Fall in Love?
(album)
(R.I.A.A. certified 1982)
RCA (U.S.A.)

Ross, Diana & Richie, Lionel
**Endless Love
Motown (U.S.A.)

**Royal Philharmonic Orchestra
(Cond. Louis Clarke)**
†Hooked on Classics (album)
(R.I.A.A. certified 1982)
RCA (U.S.A.)
K-Tel (Britain)

Rush
†Moving Pictures (album)
Mercury/Polygram (U.S.A.)

Scarbury, Joey
*Greatest American Hero Theme
Elektra (U.S.A.)

**Seger, Bob & Silver Bullet
Band**
†Nine Tonight (album)
Capitol (U.S.A.)

Smith, Frankie
*Double Dutch Bus (12-inch disc)
*Double Dutch Bus (7-inch disc)
Shot (U.S.A.)

Springfield, Rick
*Jessie's Girl
†Working Class Dog (album)
RCA (U.S.A.)

Squier, Billy
†Don't Say No (album)
Capitol (U.S.A.)

Stars On
*Stars On 45
Radio (U.S.A.)

Stewart, Rod
†Tonight I'm Yours (album)
(R.I.A.A. certified 1982)
Warner (U.S.A.)

Streisand, Barbra
†Memories (album)
(R.I.A.A. certified 1982)
Columbia (U.S.A.)

Styx
†Paradise Theater (album)
A & M (U.S.A.)

Taste of Honey
*Sukiyaki
Capitol (U.S.A.)

'38 Special
†Wild-Eyed Southern Boys (album)
(R.I.A.A. certified 1982)
Warner (U.S.A.)

Van Halen
†Fair Warning (album)
Warner (U.S.A.)

Who, The
†Face Dances (album)
Warner (U.S.A.)

Winwood, Steve
†Arc of a Diver (album)
Island (U.S.A.)

Yarbrough & Peoples
*Don't Stop the Music
Mercury/Polygram (U.S.A.)

Soundtrack, Vangelis
†*Chariots of Fire* (album)
(R.I.A.A. certified 1982)
Polydor (U.S.A. & Britain)

Various Artists
**Star Wars*
**The Empire Strikes Back*
(Both R.I.A.A certified in 1982)
Buena Vista (U.S.A.)
(These two 7-inch discs issued by
the label in their Storyteller Series.)

Styx

Appendix B: Million sellers released in

1982

Afrika Bambaattaa & Soulsonic Force
*Planet Rock
Tommy Boy (U.S.A.)

Air Supply
†Now and Forever (album)
(R.I.A.A. certified 1983)
Arista (U.S.A.)

Alabama
†Mountain Music (album)
RCA (U.S.A.)

Asia
†Asia (album)
Geffen/Warner (U.S.A.)

Vangelis

Austin, Patty, & Ingram, James
*Baby come to me
(R.I.A.A. certified 1983)
Quest (U.S.A.)

Basil, Toni
* & **Mickey
(R.I.A.A. certified 1982 (gold)
and 1983 (platinum))
Chrysalis (U.S.A.)

Benatar, Pat
†Get Nervous (album)
(R.I.A.A. certified 1983)
Chrysalis (U.S.A.)

Branigan, Laura
*Gloria
(R.I.A.A. certified 1983)
Atlantic (U.S.A.)

Buckner & Garcia
*Pac-Man Fever
Columbia (U.S.A.)

Chicago
*Hard to Say I'm Sorry
†16 (album)
Full Moon/Warner (U.S.A.)

Clash, The
†Combat Rock
(R.I.A.A. certified 1983) (album)
Epic (U.S.A.)

Cougar, John
†American Fool (album)
*Hurts So Good
*Jack and Diane
Riva/Polygram (U.S.A.)

Crosby, Stills & Nash
†Daylight Again (album)
(R.I.A.A. certified 1983)
Atlantic (U.S.A.)

**Dexy's Midnight Runners &
The Emerald Express**
Come On Eileen
Mercury/Phonogram (Britain)

Diamond, Neil
†Heartlight (album)
Columbia (U.S.A.)

Fleetwood Mac
†Mirage (album)
Columbia (U.S.A.)

Fogelberg, Dan
†Greatest Hits (album)
(R.I.A.A. certified 1983)
Epic (U.S.A.)

Fonda, Jane
†Jane Fonda Workout (album)
(R.I.A.A. certified 1983)
Columbia (U.S.A.)

Gap Band
†Gap Band IV (album)
Polygram (U.S.A.)

Gaye, Marvin
*Sexual Healing
†Midnight Love (album)
Columbia (U.S.A.)

Go Go's, The
*We Got the Beat
IRS/A & M (U.S.A.)

Hall, Daryl, & Oates, John
†H2O
RCA (U.S.A.)
*Maneater
(R.I.A.A. certified 1983)
RCA (U.S.A.)

Henley, Don
*Dirty Laundry
(R.I.A.A. certified 1983)
Asylum (U.S.A.)

Jackson, Michael
*Billie Jean
(R.I.A.A. certified 1983)
*Beat It
(R.I.A.A. certified 1983)
†Thriller (album)
(R.I.A.A. certified 1983)
(Note: One of the world's biggest-
selling albums. Global sale by June
1984 was over 30 million)
Epic (U.S.A.)

**Jackson, Michael, &
McCartney, Paul**
*The Girl is Mine
(R.I.A.A. certified 1983)
Epic (U.S.A.)

Jett, Joan
**I Love Rock 'n' Roll
Boardwalk (U.S.A.)

Joel, Billy
†The Nylon Curtain (album)
Columbia (U.S.A.)

Judas Priest
†Screaming for Vengeance (album)
(R.I.A.A. certified 1983)
Columbia (U.S.A.)

Led Zeppelin
†Coda (album)
(R.I.A.A. certified 1983)
Swan Song (U.S.A.)

Loverboy
†Get Lucky (album)
Columbia (U.S.A.)

**McCartney, Paul, & Wonder,
Stevie**
†Tug of War (album)
*Ebony and Ivory
Columbia (U.S.A.)

Men at Work
†Business as Usual (album)
*Down Under
(R.I.A.A. certified 1983)
Columbia (U.S.A.)

Miller Band, Steve
†Abracadabra (album)
*Abracadabra
Capitol (U.S.A.)

Musical Youth
Pass the Dutchie
MCA (Britain)

Nelson, Willie
†Always On My Mind (album)
Columbia (U.S.A.)

Newton-John, Olivia
†Greatest Hits Vol. 2 (album)
MCA (U.S.A.)

Dexy's Midnight Runners

Musical Youth

Parsons, Alan, Project
*Eye in the Sky (album)
(R.I.A.A. certified 1983)
Arista (U.S.A.)

Presley, Elvis
*Welcome to my World (album)
(R.I.A.A. certified 1983)
RCA (U.S.A.)

Prince
*1999 (album)
(R.I.A.A. certified 1983)
Warner Bros (U.S.A.)

Renee & Renato
Save Your Love
Hollywood (Britain)

REO Speedwagon
*Good Trouble (album)
Epic (US.A.)

Richie, Lionel
Lionel Richie (album)
Truly
Motown (U.S.A.)

**Seger, Bob and the Silver
Bullet Band**
The Distance (album)
(R.I.A.A. certified 1983)
Capitol (U.S.A.)

Simmons, Richard
Reach (album)
Elektra/Asylum (U.S.A.)

Springfield, Rick
Success Hasn't Spoiled Me Yet
(album)
RCA (U.S.A.)

Squier, Billy
†Emotions in Motion (album)
Capitol (U.S.A.)

Stray Cats
†Built For Speed (album)
EMI/America (U.S.A.)

Survivor
†Eye of the Tiger (album)
**Eye of the Tiger
Scotti Bros/CBS (U.S.A.)

Sylvia
*Nobody
RCA (U.S.A.)

Thirty-Eight Special (.38)
†Special Forces (album)
(R.I.A.A. certified 1983)
A & M (U.S.A.)

Toto
†Toto IV (album)
Columbia (U.S.A.)

Vandross, Luther
†Forever, For Always, For Love
(album)
(R.I.A.A. certified 1983)
Epic (U.S.A.)

Van Halen
†Diver Down (album)
Warner (U.S.A.)

Soundtrack
†*Annie* (album)
Columbia (U.S.A.)

Rick Springfield

Various Artists
The Kids From Fame (TV series)
(album)
BBC REP (Britain)

The following discs of excerpts
from Disney cartoons all achieved a
million sale by 1983 with R.I.A.A.
certification:
The Fox and the Hound
Peter Pan
Bambi
Cinderella
The Lady and the Tramp
Snow White
Pinocchio
Dumbo
Mary Poppins (Film)
Disney (U.S.A.)

Appendix C:
Million Sellers
released in

1983

Adams, Bryan
†Cuts Like a Knife (album)
A & M (U.S.A.)

Air Supply
†Greatest Hits (album)
*Making Love Out Of Nothing At
All
Arista (U.S.A.)

Anderson, John
*Swingin'
Warner Bros (U.S.A.)

Alabama
†The Closer You Get (album)
RCA (U.S.A.)

Asia
†Alpha (album)
Geffen (U.S.A.)

Benatar, Pat
†Live From Earth (album)
Chrysalis (U.S.A.)

Bowie, David
†Let's Dance (album)
*Let's Dance
EMI-America (U.S.A.)

Cara, Irene
*Flashdance (What a feeling)
Casablanca (U.S.A.)

Cougar (Mellencamp), John
†Uh-Uh (album)
Riva (U.S.A.)

Culture Club
†Kissing to be Clever (album)
†Colour by Numbers (album)
Karma Chameleon
Virgin (Britain)

Def Leppard
†Pyromania (album)
†High 'N' Dry (album)
Mercury (U.S.A)

Duran Duran
†Rio (album)
(Orig. released in Britain 1982)
Capitol (U.S.A.)

Eurythmics
*Sweet Dreams (are made of this)
RCA (U.S.A.)

Genesis
†Genesis (album)
Atlantic (U.S.A.)

Grant, Eddy
*Electric Avenue
Portrait/Ice (U.S.A.)

Hall, Daryl, & Oates, John
†Rock 'n' Soul Part I (album)
RCA (U.S.A.)

Joel, Billy
†An Innocent Man (album)
Columbia (U.S.A.)

The Eurythmics

Culture Club

Def Leppard

Journey
†Frontiers (album)
Columbia (U.S.A.)

Loverboy
†Keep it up (album)
Columbia (U.S.A.)

McCartney, Paul, & Jackson, Michael
*Say Say Say
Columbia (U.S.A.)

Men At Work
†Cargo (album)
Columbia (U.S.A.)

Midnight Star
†No Parking on the Dance Floor
(album)
Solar (U.S.A.)

Mtume
*Juicy Fruit
Epic (U.S.A.)

Nicks, Stevie
†The Wild Heart (album)
Modern (U.S.A.)

Pink Floyd
†The Final Cut (album)
Columbia (U.S.A.)

Police
†Synchronicity (album)
*Every Breath you Take
A & M (U.S.A.)

Presley, Elvis
(Re-issues of his former million
sellers, again selling a million since
his demise in 1977)
*I Got Stung (orig. 1958)

*Are You Lonesome Tonight? (orig. 1960)
*Don't (orig. 1958)
*Return to Sender (orig. 1962)
*It's Now or Never (orig. 1960)
*A Fool Such as I (orig. 1959)
*Wear my Ring Around Your Neck (orig. 1958)
RCA (U.S.A.)

Quiet Riot
†Metal Health (album)
*Cum on Feel the Noize
Pasha (U.S.A.)

Richie, Lionel
†Can't Slow Down (album)
*All Night Long
Motown (U.S.A)

Rogers, Kenny
†Eyes That See in the Dark (album)
RCA (U.S.A.)

Rogers, Kenny & Parton, Dolly
* & **Islands in the Stream
RCA (U.S.A.)

Ronstadt, Linda
†What's New? (album)
Asylum (U.S.A.)

Springfield, Rick
†Living in Oz (album)
RCA (U.S.A.)

Styx
†Kilroy Was Here (album)
*Mr Roboto
A & M (U.S.A.)

Taco
*Puttin' on the Ritz
RCA (U.S.A.)

Tyler, Bonnie
†Faster Than the Speed of Night (album)
*Total Eclipse of the Heart
Columbia (U.S.A.)

Young, Paul
No Parlez (album)
CBS (Britain)

ZZ Top
†Eliminator (album)
Warner Bros (U.S.A.)

Soundtracks
†Flashdance (album)
Casablanca (U.S.A.)
†Staying Alive (album)
RSO (U.S.A.)

Various Artists
Further releases of excerpts from Disney cartoons etc., all with million-sale R.I.A.A. certification in 1983:
*The Three Little Pigs
*Sleeping Beauty
*It's a Small World
*Pete's Dragon
*Winnie the Pooh & Tigger Too
*Brer Rabbit & The Tar Baby
Disney (U.S.A)
*Return of the Jedi
Polydor (U.S.A)
*ET - The Extra Terrestrial
Warner Bros (U.S.A.)

Appendix D: Previous releases with certified million sale by 1982

Alabama
†My Home's in Alabama (album)
Released 1980 on RCA (U.S.A.)

Beach Boys, The
*I Get Around
Released 1964 on Capitol (U.S.A.)

Gayle, Crystal
†When I Dream (album)
Released 1978 on Capitol (U.S.A.)

Hall, Daryl & Oates, John
†Voices (album)
Released 1980 on RCA (U.S.A.)

Loverboy
†Loverboy (album)
Released 1980 on Columbia
(U.S.A.)

Oak Ridge Boys, The
†Greatest Hits (album)
Released 1980 on MCA (U.S.A.)

Pretenders, The
†Pretenders (album)
Released 1980 on Sire/Warner
(U.S.A.)

Soundtrack, Village People
Can't Stop the Music (album)
(Million seller globally by 1981)
Released 1980 on Casablanca
(U.S.A.)

Appendix E: Previous releases with certified million sale by 1983 (R.I.A.A.)

Jones, George
†I Am What I Am (album)
(R.I.A.A. certified 1983)
Released 1980 on Epic (U.S.A.)

Rogers, Kenny
†20 Greatest Hits (album)
(R.I.A.A. certified 1983)
Released 1980 on Liberty (U.S.A.)

**The Pretenders (photo does
not show original line-up)**

Title Index 1903–1980

Titles in CAPITALS indicate albums, LPs and EPs. An asterisk* indicates that a million-units sale in the U.S.A. has been certified by the Record Industry Association of America (R.I.A.A.).

A

Aba daba honeymoon (Reynolds–Carpenter) 1951
ABBA (ABBA) LP 1975
ABBEY ROAD (Beatles) LP 1969
ABC (Jackson 5) 1970
ABC (Jackson 5) LP 1970
A-Bi-Na-Ba (Cohen/Alphabeta Singers) 1978
*Abraham, Martin and John (Dion) 1968
Abraham, Martin and John (Clay) 1971
A chi (Leali) 1967
Action (Sweet) 1975
Act naturally (Ringo Starr–Beatles) 1965
Adeste fideles (Crosby) 1942
Adieu Jolie Candy (Michael) 1970
*Admiral Halsey (Paul & Linda McCartney) 1971
AEROSMITH (Aerosmith) LP 1973
AFTERMATH (Rolling Stones) LP 1966
*Afternoon delight (Starland Vocal Band) 1976
*After the lovin' (Humperdinck) 1976
*AFTER THE LOVIN' (Humperdinck) LP 1976
*After the love has gone (Earth, Wind & Fire) 1979
*AGAINST THE WIND (Seger/Silver Bullet band) LP 1980
Again (Damone) 1949
*AGENTS OF FORTUNE (Blue Oyster Cult) LP 1976
AGE OF AQUARIUS (Fifth Dimension) LP 1969
Ahab the Arab (Ray Stevens) 1962
A-hubba-hubba-hubba, dig you later (Como) 1945
*Ain't gonna bump no more (Tex) 1977
Ain't no mountain high enough (Diana Ross) 1970
*Ain't no sunshine (Withers) 1971
*Ain't no woman (Four Tops) 1973
Ain't that a shame (Domino) 1955
Ain't that a shame (Boone) 1955
Ain't that loving you baby (Presley) 1964
Ain't understanding mellow (Butler & Eager) 1971
'Airport' Theme (Bell) 1970
*Air that I breathe, The (Hollies) 1974
*AJA (Steely Dan) LP 1977
Albatross (Fleetwood Mac) 1968
*ALBUM, THE (ABBA) LP 1978
ALBUM 1700 (Peter, Paul & Mary) LP 1967
Al di la (Pericoli) 1961
Alexander's ragtime band (Jolson–Crosby) 1947
All alone am I (Brenda Lee) 1962
All by myself (Domino) 1955
*All by myself (Eric Carmen) 1975
Allegheny moon (Patti Page) 1956
Alley cat (Bent Fabric) 1962
*Alley-oop (Hollywood Argyles) 1960
*All I ever need is you (Sonny & Cher) 1971
All I have to do is dream (Everly Bros) 1958
All in white (see 'Ganz in weiss')
All I want for Christmas (Spike Jones) 1948
All kinds of everything (Dana) 1970
All my love (Patti Page) 1950
*ALL'N ALL (Earth, Wind & Fire) LP 1977

All or nothing at all (Sinatra) 1943
*All out of love (Air Supply) 1980
All shook up (Presley) 1957
ALL STAR FESTIVAL (Various artists) LP 1963
All that I am (Presley) 1966
All the boys and girls (see 'Tous les garcons')
All the way (Sinatra) 1957
*ALL THE WORLD'S A STAGE (Rush) LP 1976
*ALL THINGS IN TIME (Rawls) LP 1976
ALL THINGS MUST PASS (Harrison) Triple LP 1970
*All you need is love (Beatles) 1967
Almost (Morgan) 1952
ALOHA FROM HAWAII VIA SATELLITE (Presley) 2 LP 1973
*Alone again, naturally (O'Sullivan) 1972
Alright now (Free) 1970
Alvin's harmonica (Seville & Chipmunks) 1959
*Always and forever (Heatwave) 1977
Amapola (Jimmy Dorsey) 1941
Amazing grace (Collins) 1970
Amazing grace (Royal Scots Dragoon Guards) 1972
Ame no midosuji (Ouyang) 1971
AMERICAN GRAFFITI – Soundtrack 1973
AMERICAN IN PARIS, AN – Soundtrack LP 1952
American patrol (Glenn Miller) 1942
*American Pie (McLean) 1971
AMERICAN PIE (McLean) LP 1971
*Americans (MacGregor) 1973
*American woman (Guess Who) 1970
AMERICA (America) LP 1972
Among my souvenirs (Francis) 1959
*Amos Moses (Reed) 1970
*And the beat goes on (Whispers) 1980
*And when I die (Blood, Sweat & Tears) 1969
*Angel in your arms (Hot) 1977
Angel of the morning (Rush) 1968
*Angie baby (Helen Reddy) 1974
*Angie (Rolling Stones) 1973
*ANIMALS (Pink Floyd) LP 1977
Anna – El negro zambon (Sylvano Mangano) 1953
Annie had a baby (Ballard) 1954
*Annie's song (Denver) 1974
*'ANNIE' (Stage show) LP 1977
Anniversary song (Jolson) 1946
*Another brick in the wall (Pink Floyd) 1979
Another day (McCartney) 1971
*Another one bites the dust (Queen) 1980
*Another somebody done somebody wrong song (Thomas) 1975
Answer me my love (Nat King Cole) 1954
*Anyone who had a heart (Cilla Black) 1964
Anyone who had a heart (Dionne Warwick) 1963
Anything that's part of you (Presley) 1962
Any time (Arnold) 1948
Any time (Fisher) 1951
*ANYTIME . . . ANYWHERE (Coolidge) LP 1977
Any way you want it (Dave Clark) 1964
Any way you want me (Presley) 1956
Aoi hitomi (Yoshikawa & Blue Comets) 1966
Apache (Shadows) 1960
'Apartment, The' – theme (Ferrante & Teicher) 1960
Applause (see 'Kassai')
Apples, peaches, pumpkin pie (Jay & Techniques) 1967

Après toi (see 'Come what may')
April love (Boone) 1957
April showers (Jolson) 1945
AQUALUNG (Jethro Tull) LP 1971
*Aquarius/Let the sunshine in (Fifth Dimension) 1969
Are you lonesome tonight? (Presley) 1960
Are you sure? (Allisons) 1961
*Arizona (Lindsay) 1969
ARRIVAL (ABBA) LP 1976
Artistry in rhythm (Kenton) 1945
ASK ME WHY (Beatles) EP 1963
*ASK RUFUS (Rufus) LP 1977
As tears go by (Rolling Stones) 1965
As years go by (Mashmakan) 1970
AT FOLSOM PRISON (Johnny Cash) LP 1968
A tisket, a-tasket (Ella Fitzgerald) 1938
AT SAN QUENTIN (Johnny Cash) LP 1969
At the hop (Danny and Juniors) 1957
At the woodchoppers ball (Woody Herman) 1939
Auctioneer, The (Van Dyke) 1956
Aufwiederseh'n, sweetheart (Vera Lynn) 1952
*AUTOAMERICAN (Blondie) LP 1980
Autumn leaves (Roger Williams) 1955
Avalon (Jolson) 1946
AVERAGE WHITE BAND (Average White Band) LP 1974

B

BBabe (Styx) 1979
Baby come back (Equals) 1968
*Baby come back (Player) 1977
Baby come close (Robinson/Miracles) 1973
*Baby don't get hooked on me (Davis) 1972
Baby face (Mooney) 1948
*Baby, I love you (Franklin) 1967
*Baby, I love you (Kim) 1969
*Baby, I'm a-want you (Bread) 1971
Baby, I'm yours (Barbara Lewis) 1965
Baby, I need your loving (Four Tops) 1964
Baby, it's cold outside (Williams/Montalban) 1949
*Baby it's you (Smith) 1969
Baby love (Supremes) 1964
Baby, now that I've found you (Foundations) 1967
Babysittin' Boogie (Bendix) 1961
Baby, you got what it takes (Washington/Benton) 1960
Bachelor boy (Cliff Richard) 1962
BACHMAN-TURNER OVERDRIVE 2 (Bachman-Turner Overdrive) LP 1974
Back Bay shuffle (Artie Shaw) 1938
*Backfield in motion (Mel and Tim) 1969
*Back home again (Denver) 1974
BACK HOME AGAIN (Denver) LP 1974
*Back in love again (Every time I turn around) (LTD) 1977
*BACK IN BLACK (AC/DC) LP 1980
Back in my arms again (Supremes) 1965
*BACKLESS (Clapton) LP 1978
*Back stabbers (O'Jays) 1972
*BACK TO THE EGG (Wings) LP 1979
*Bad, Bad Leroy Browne (Croce) 1973
BAD COMPANY (Bad Company) LP 1974
*BAD GIRLS (Summer) LP 1979
*Bad Girls (Summer) 1979
*Bad moon rising (Creedence Clearwater Revival) 1969
Bad to me (Kramer) 1963
*Baker Street (Rafferty) 1978
Ballad of Bonnie and Clyde (Fame) 1967

Ballad of Davy Crockett (Hayes) 1955
*Ballad of John & Yoko (Beatles) 1969
*Ballad of the Green Berets (Sadler) 1966
BALLADS OF THE GREEN BERETS (Sadler) LP 1966
Ballerina – Dance ballerina, dance (Monroe) 1947
Ballo del mattone, Il (Pavone) 1963
Ball of confusion (Temptations) 1970
Ballroom blitz (Sweet) 1973
Bamba, La (Valens) 1958
Bambola, La (Pravo) 1968
Banana boat song – Day-O (Belafonte) 1957
Band of gold (Cherry) 1955
*Band of gold (Payne) 1970
Band on the run (McCartney & Wings) 1974
BAND ON THE RUN (McCartney & Wings) LP 1973
Bang-a-gong (see 'Get it on')
Banjo boy (Jan & Kjeld) 1960
Barbara Ann (Beach Boys) 1965
Barefootin' (Parker) 1966
*BARRY MANILOW – LIVE (Manilow) LP 1977
*BARRY WHITE SINGS FOR SOMEONE YOU LOVE (White) LP 1977
*BARRY (Manilow) LP 1980
*BAT OUT OF HELL (Meat Loaf) LP 1977
*Battle hymn of Lieut. Calley (Nelson) 1971
*Battle of New Orleans (Horton) 1959
BAY CITY ROLLERS (Bay City Rollers) LP 1975
BAYOU COUNTRY (Creedence Clearwater Revival) LP 1969
BEACH BOYS' 20 GOLDEN GREATS (Beach Boys) LP 1977
Beat goes on, The (Sonny and Cher) 1967
*BEATLES AT THE HOLLYWOOD BOWL, THE (Beatles) LP 1977
BEATLES FOR SALE (Beatles) LP 1964
BEATLES SECOND ALBUM (Beatles) LP 1964
BEATLES STORY, THE (Beatles) Double LP 1964
BEATLES, THE (Beatles) Double LP 1968
BEATLES 1962-1966 (Beatles) 2 LP 1973
BEATLES VI (Beatles) LP 1965
BEATLES 1967-1972 2 LP 1973
BEATLES '65 (Beatles) LP 1964
BEAT OF THE BRASS (Alpert) LP 1968
*BEAUTIFUL NOISE (Diamond) LP 1976
Beautiful Sunday (Daniel Boone) 1972
*Beautiful morning, A (Rascals) 1968
Be-bop-a-lula (Vincent) 1956
Be-bop baby (Ricky Nelson) 1957
Because of you (Bennett) 1951
Because they're young (Eddy) 1960
Because you're mine (Lanza) 1952
Because (Como) 1948
Because (Dave Clark 5) 1964
Beep beep (Playmates) 1958
Beer barrel polka (Glahe) 1938
*Before the next teardrop falls (Fender) 1975
Begin the beguine (Heywood) 1944
Begin the beguine (Shaw) 1938
*Behind closed doors (Rich) 1973
BEHIND CLOSED DOORS (Rich) LP 1973
Bei mir bist du schön (Andrews Sisters) 1937
BELAFONTE AT CARNEGIE HALL (Belfonte) LP 1959
BELFONTE SINGS OF THE CARIBBEAN (Belfonte) LP 1957
Believe what you say (Ricky Nelson) 1958
*Bells, The (Originals) 1970
Be my baby (Ronettes) 1963

509

Be my guest (Domino) 1959
Be my love (Lanza) 1950
Bend it (Dee, Dozy, Beaky, Mick, Tich) 1966
*Bend me, shape me (American Breed) 1967
*Bennie and the Jets (Elton John) 1974
Ben (Michael Jackson) 1972
Besame mucho – Kiss me (Jimmy Dorsey) 1943
BEST OF CHARLEY PRIDE (Charley Pride) LP 1969
*BEST OF EARTH, WIND & FIRE (Earth, Wind & Fire) LP 1978
BEST OF HERMAN'S HERMITS (Herman's Hermits) LP 1965
*BEST OF JETHRO TULL (Jethro Tull) LP 1978
*Best of my love (Emotions) 1977
BEST OF THE ANIMALS (Animals) LP 1966
*BEST OF THE DOOBIES (Doobie Brothers) LP 1976
BEST OF THE GUESS WHO (Guess Who) LP 1971
BEST OF THE STATLER BROTHERS (Statler Brothers) LP 1976
BEST OF THE STYLISTICS (Stylistics) LP 1975
*Best thing that ever happened to me (Knight/Pips) 1974
*Betcha by golly, wow (Stylistics) 1972
*Be thankful for what you've got (De Vaughn) 1974
*Beth (Kiss) 1976
Be true to your school (Beach Boys) 1963
BETWEEN THE LINES (Ian) LP 1975
Beware, brother, beware (Jordan) 1946
Bewitched, bothered and bewildered (Snyder) 1940
Beyond the sea – La mer (Darin) 1960
*Big bad John (Dean) 1961
BIG BAMBU (Cheech and Chong) LP 1972
Big girls don't cry (Four Seasons) 1962
BIG HITS – High tide and green grass (Rolling Stones) LP 1966
Big hunk o'love, A (Presley) 1959
BILL COSBY IS A VERY FUNNY FELLOW (Cosby) LP 1964
*Billy, don't be a hero (Donaldson & Heywoods) 1974
Bimbo (Reeves) 1953
Bird dog (Everly Bros) 1958
Birds and the bees (Akens) 1965
Bits and pieces (Dave Clark 5) 1964
*BLACK AND BLUE (Rolling Stones) LP 1976
Black and white rag (Atwell) 1952
*Black and white (Three Dog Night) 1972
Black cat tango (see 'Kuro Neko No Tango')
Black is black (Los Bravos) 1966
BLACK SABBATH (Black Sabbath) LP 1970
*Black water (Doobie Bros) 1974
Blacksmith blues (Morse) 1952
Blame it on the bossa nova (Gorme) 1963
*BLAM (Brothers Johnson) LP 1978
*Blinded by the light (Mann) 1976
Blockbuster (Sweet) 1973
*BLONDES HAVE MORE FUN (Rod Stewart) LP 1978
BLOOD ON THE TRACKS (Dylan) LP 1975
BLOOD, SWEAT AND TEARS (Blood, Sweat and Tears) LP 1969
BLOOD, SWEAT AND TEARS. 3 (Blood, Sweat and Tears) LP
BLOOD, SWEAT AND TEARS. 4 (Blood, Sweat and Tears) LP 1971
BLOOMING HITS (Mauriat) LP 1967
Blossom fell, A (Nat King Cole) 1955
Blowin' in the wind (Peter, Paul and Mary) 1963

Blue Angel (Orbison) 1960
Blue bayou (Orbison) 1963
*Blue bayou (Ronstadt) 1977
Blueberry Hill (Domino) 1956
Bluebird of happiness (Mooney) 1948
Blue chateau (Yoshikawa & Blue Comets) 1967
Blue Danube (Stokowski) 1939
Blue eyes (see 'Aoi hitomi') 1951
'BLUE HAWAII' (Presley) LP 1961
Blue jean bop (Vincent) 1956
Blue monday (Domino) 1956
Blue moon (Kendricks) 1975
Blue moon (Marcels) 1961
*BLUE MOVES (Elton John) 2 LP 1976.
Blues in the night (Dinah Shore) 1941
Blue skirt waltz (Yankovic) 1948
Blue star (Stapleton) 1955
Blue suede shoes (Perkins) 1956
Blue tango (Anderson) 1951
Blue velvet (Vinton) 1963
Blue yodel (Jimmy Rodgers) 1928
Bobby's girl (Blaine) 1962
Body and soul (Hawkins) 1939
*Bohemian rhapsody (Queen) 1975
Bony Moronie (Larry Williams) 1957
Boogie chillun (Hooker) 1948
Boogie down (Kendricks) 1973
*Boogie fever (Sylvers) 1975
*Boogie nights (Heatwave) 1977
Boogie on reggae woman (Wonder) 1974
*Boogie oogie oogie (Taste of Honey) 1978
*Boogie wonderland (Earth, Wind & Fire) 1979
Boogie woogie (Tommy Dorsey) 1938
*BOOK OF DREAMS (Miller Band) LP 1977
Book of love (Monotones) 1958
Born a woman (Posey) 1966
*BORN LATE (Shaun Cassidy) LP 1977
*Born to be alive (Hernandez) 1979
*Born to be wild (Steppenwolf) 1968
Born to lose (Daffan) 1943
Bossa nova baby (Presley) 1963
Botch-a me (Clooney) 1952
Bouquet of roses (Arnold) 1948
*Boy named Sue, A (Cash) 1969
*BOYS IN THE TREES (Carly Simon) LP 1978
Bo(ll) weevil (Domino) 1956
Bo(ll) weevil (Benton) 1961
BRAIN SALAD SURGERY (Emerson, Lake & Palmer) LP 1973
Brakeman's blues (Jimmie Rodgers) 1928
*Brand new key (Melanie) 1971
*Brandy (Looking Glass) 1972
*BRASS CONSTRUCTION (Brass Construction) LP 1976
Bread and butter (Newbeats) 1964
*BREAKFAST IN AMERICA (Supertramp) LP 1979
BREAKFAST AT TIFFANY'S Soundtrack (Mancini) LP 1961
Breaking up is hard to do (Sedaka) 1962
*Breaks, The (Blow) 1980
Break up to make up (Stylistics) 1973
Breathless (Jerry Lee Lewis) 1958
Breeze and I, The (Valente) 1955
*BREEZIN' (Benson) LP 1977
BREL (Brel) LP 1977
Bridge on the River Kwai, March (Mitch Miller) 1957
*Bridge over troubled water (Franklin) 1971
*Bridge over troubled water (Simon & Garfunkel) 1970
BRIDGE OVER TROUBLED WATER (Simon & Garfunkel) LP 1970
*BRIEFCASE FULL OF BLUES (Blues Brothers) LP 1978
Bright Eyes (Garfunkel) 1979
Bring the boys home (Payne) 1971
Bristol stomp (Dovells) 1961
Broken hearted melody (Sarah Vaughan) 1959
*Brother Louie (Stories) 1973

BROTHERS AND SISTERS (Allman Bros) LP 1973
*BROTHER TO BROTHER (Vannelli) LP 1978
Brown eyed girl (Van Morrison) 1967
Brown sugar (Rolling Stones) 1971
BUDDY HOLLY STORY, THE (Buddy Holly) LP 1959
*Build me up Buttercup (Foundations) 1968
*Burning love (Presley) 1972
Bus stop (Hollies) 1966
Busted (Ray Charles) 1963
*Bustin' loose (Chick Brown) 1979
*BUT SERIOUSLY? FOLKS (Walsh) LP 1978
Butterfly (Andy Williams) 1957
Butterfly (Gracie) 1957
Butterfly (Gerard) 1971
Buttons and bows (Dinah Shore) 1948
Buttons and bows (Dinning Sisters) 1948
By the light of the silvery moon (Ray Noble) 1941
Bye bye baby (Bay City Rollers) 1975
Bye bye love (Everly Bros) 1957

C

CADEAU DE LA VIE
*Calcutta (Welk) 1961
Caldonia (Jordan) 1945
*California dreamin' (Mamas and Papas) 1965
California, here I come (Jolson) 1946
*Call me (Blondie) 1980
*Call me (Green) 1973
Call on me (Bland) 1963
CALYPSO (Belafonte) LP 1956
Calypso melody (David Rose) 1957
'CAMELOT' (stage show) LP 1961
CAMPBELL, GLEN – LIVE (Campbell) LP 1969
Canadian sunset (Winterhalter) 1956
*Candida (Dawn) 1970
Candy kisses (Morgan) 1949
Candy man (Orbison) 1961
*Candy man (Sammy Davis) 1972
*CANDY-O (Cars) LP 1979
*Can I change my mind (Tyrone Davis) 1968
*Can't buy me love (Beatles) 1964
CAN'T GET ENOUGH (White) LP 1974
*Can't get enough of your love, babe (White) 1974
Can't get used to losing you (Andy Williams) 1963
Can the can (Quatro) 1973
*Can't help falling in love (Presley) 1961
*Cantina Band (Meco) 1977
Can't keep it in (Cat Stevens) 1972
*Can't smile without you (Manilow) 1978
'CAN'T STOP THE MUSIC' (Soundtrack) LP (Village People) 1980
*Can't take my eyes off you (Valli) 1967
Can't you hear my heartbeat (Herman's Hermits) 1965
Can't you see that she's mine (Dave Clark 5) 1964
CAPTAIN AND ME (Doobie Bros) LP 1973
CAPTAIN FANTASTIC & BROWN DIRT COWBOY (Elton John) LP 1975
Cara mia (Whitfield) 1954
Caravan (Eckstine) 1949
Caravan (Marterie) 1952
CARIBOU (Elton John) LP 1974
Carnival is over, The (Seekers) 1965
CAROLE KING MUSIC (Carol King) LP 1971
*CAROLINA DREAMS (Tucker Band) LP 1977
Carrie Anne (Hollies) 1967
Carry me back to old Virginny (Gluck) 1915
*CARS, THE (Cars) LP 1978
*Car wash (Rose Royce) 1976
Casatschok (Dourakine) 1969

CASS, JOHN, MICHELLE, DENNY LP (See MAMAS AND PAPAS)
Cast your fate to the wind (Pearson Sounds orchestra) 1964
*Catch a falling star (Como) 1958
Catch us if you can (Dave Clark 5) 1965
Cathy's clown (Everly Bros) 1960
*CAT SCRATCH FEVER (Nugent) LP 1977
*Cat's in the cradle (Chapin) 1974
Cattle call (Arnold) 1955
Cave man (see 'Troglodyte')
*Cecilia (Simon & Garfunkel) 1970
*CELEBRATE ME HOME (Loggins) LP 1977
*CELEBRATE (Kool & Gang) LP 1980
*Celebration (Kool & Gang) 1980
*CENTRAL HEATING (Heatwave) LP 1978
*C'EST CHIC (Chic) LP 1978
C'est ma chanson (see 'This is my song')
Chain gang (Bobby Scott) 1956
Chain gang (Cooke) 1960
*Chain of fools (Franklin) 1967
Chains of love (Turner) 1951
*CHAMPAGNE JAM (Atlanta Rhythm Section) LP 1978
Chances are (Mathis) 1957
*CHANGES IN LATITUDES, CHANGES IN ATTITUDES (Buffett) LP 1977
*CHANGESONEBOWIE (Bowie) LP 1976
Changing partners (Patti Page) 1953
Chanson d'amour (Art and Dotty Todd) 1957
Chantilly lace (Big Bopper) 1958
Chapel in the moonlight (in the) (Kitty Kallen) 1954
Chapel of love (Dixie Cups) 1964
Chariot (Petula Clark) 1962
Chariot (see 'I will follow him')
Charlie Brown (Coasters) 1959
Charmaine (Mantovani) 1951
Chattanooga choo choo (Glen Miller) 1941
Chattanoogie shoe-shine boy (Foley) 1950
CHEAP THRILLS (Big Brother & Holding Co) LP 1968
*CHEAP TRICK AT BUDOKAN (Cheap Trick) LP 1979
CHEECH AND CHONG (Cheech & Chong) LP 1971
Cherie I love you (Boone) 1958
*Cherish (Association) 1966
Cherish (Cassidy) 1971
Cherry, Cherry (Diamond) 1966
Cherry pink and apple blossom white (Alan Dale) 1956
Cherry pink and apple blossom white (Perez Prado) 1955
*Chevy van (Johns) 1975
*Chewy, Chewy (Ohio Express) 1968
CHICAGO II (Chicago) LP 1970
CHICAGO III (Chicago) 2LP 1971
CHICAGO live at CARNEGIE HALL (Chicago) 4LP 1971
CHICAGO'S GREATEST HITS (Chicago) LP 1975
CHICAGO TRANSIT AUTHORITY (Chicago) 2LP 1969
CHICAGO V (Chicago) LP 1972
CHICAGO VI (Chicago) LP 1973
CHICAGO VII (Chicago) 2LP 1974
CHICAGO VIII (Chicago) LP 1975
*CHICAGO X (Chicago) LP 1976
*CHICAGO XI (Chicago) LP 1977
Chicago (Sinatra) 1957
*CHILDREN OF THE WORLD (Bee Gees) LP 1976
Children's marching song (Stapleton) 1959
CHIPMUNK PUNK (Chipmunks) LP 1980
Chipmunk song (Seville & Chipmunks) 1958
Chiquita (ABBA) 1979
Chirpy chirpy cheep cheep (Middle of the Road) 1971
Cho choo ch'boogie (Jordan) 1946

DREAM WEAVER (Gary Wright) LP 1975
Dreamy melody (Art Landry) 1922
Dream (Pied Pipers) 1945
*Drift away (Dobie Gray) 1973
*Drivin' my life away (Rabbitt) 1980
*Drowning in the Sea of Love (Simon) 1971
*Duelling banjos (Weissberg & Mandell) 1973
Duke of Earl (Chandler) 1962
*'Dukes of Hazzard' Theme (Jennings) 1980
Dungaree doll (Fisher) 1955
Du sollst nicht weinen (Heintje) 1968
*Dust in the wind (Kansas) 1978
Du (Maffey) 1970
*DYNASTY (Kiss) LP 1979

E

Early autumn (Stafford) 1952
Early in the morning (Vanity Fare) 1969
Earth angel (Penguins) 1954
*EARTH (Jefferson Starship) LP 1978
Easier said than done (The Essex) 1963
Easter parade (Harry James) 1942
Easter parade (Lombardo) 1947
*Easy come, easy go (Sherman) 1970
*Easy loving (Hart) 1971
EASY RIDER Soundtrack LP 1969
Easy to be hard (Three Dog Night) 1969
EAT A PEACH (Allman Brothers) LP 1972
*EAT TO THE BEAT (Blondie) LP 1979
Ebb tide (Chacksfield) 1953
Ebb tide (Grant) 1961
Ebony eyes (Everly Bros) 1961
*EDDIE MONEY (Money) LP 1978
Eh Campari (La Rosa) 1953
*Eight days a week (Beatles) 1965
1812 Festival Overture (Dorati) LP 1956
*ELAN (Firefall) LP 1978
El Bimbo (Bimbo Jet) 1974
Eleanor Rigby (Beatles) 1966
Eli's coming (Three Dog Night) 1969
El negro zumben ('Anna') (Sylvano Mangano) 1953
Eloise (Ryan) 1968
El Paso (Robbins) 1959
ELTON JOHN (Elton John) LP 1970
ELVIS' CHRISTMAS ALBUM (Presley) LP 1957
ELVIS' GOLDEN RECORDS (Presley) LP 1958
*ELVIS IN CONCERT (Presley) 2 LP 1977
*ELVIS SINGS THE WONDERFUL WORLD OF CHRISTMAS (Presley) LP 1977
ELVIS (Presley) LP 1957
Emerald no densetsu (Tempters) 1968
EMERSON, LAKE & PALMER (Emerson, Lake & Palmer) LP 1970
*EMOTIONAL RESCUE (Rolling Stones) LP 1980
*Emotion (Sang) 1977
Empty arms (Ivory Joe Hunter) 1957
*ENDLESS FLIGHT (Sayer) LP 1976
ENDLESS SUMMER (Beach Boys) 2LP 1974
End of our road (Knight/Pips) 1968
End of the world (Davis) 1962
ENERGY (Pointer Sisters) LP 1979
*Enjoy yourselves (Jacksons) 1976
*Entertainer, The (Hamlisch) 1974
E PLURIBUS FUNK (Grand Funk Railroad) LP 1971
EQUINOXE (Jarre) LP 1978
*Escape – Pina colada song (Holmes) 1979
EVENING WITH JOHN DENVER, AN (Denver) 2LP 1975
*EVEN NOW (Manilow) LP 1978
Even the bad times are good (Tremeloes) 1967
Eve of destruction (McGuire) 1965
*Evergreen – Theme from 'A Star Is Born' (Streisand) 1976

*Everlasting love, An (Andy Gibb) 1978
Every beat of my heart (Knight/Pips) 1961
*Everybody loves somebody (Dean Martin) 1964
*Everybody is a star (Sly & Family Stone) 1969
Everybody's somebody's fool (Connie Francis) 1960
*Everybody plays the fool (Main Ingredient) 1972
Every day I have the blues (B. B. King) 1955
*Everyday people (Sly & Family Stone) 1968
Everyone's gone to the moon (Jonathan King) 1965
EVERY PICTURE TELLS A STORY (Rod Stewart) LP 1971
Everything I own (Bread) 1972
Everything I have is yours (Eckstine) 1947
*Everything is beautiful (Stevens) 1970
Every time (see 'Ogni volta')
*Every 1's a winner (Hot Chocolate) 1978
*EVOLUTION (Journey) LP 1979
EXILE ON MAIN STREET (Rolling Stones) 2LP 1972
'Exodus' and other great themes (Mantovani) LP 1960
'Exodus' main theme (Ferrante & Teicher) 1960
Exordium and terminus (see 'In the year 2525')
Expressway to your heart (Soul Survivors) 1967
·*Express (B. T. Express) 1975
Eye level (Simon Park) 1973

F

Falling (Orbison) 1963
*Fallin' in love (Hamilton, Frank, Reynolds) 1975
*Fame (David Bowie) 1975
*'FAME' (Soundtrack) LP 1980
Family affair (Sly & Family Stone) 1971
FAMILY ALBUM (Partridge Family) LP 1970
FAMILY REUNION (O'Jays) LP 1975
Famous Original Hits Vol 1 (Country/Western artists) LP 1965
Fancy (Gentry) 1969
FANDANGO (Z. Z. Top) LP 1975
FANTASY (Carole King) LP 1973
Fascination (Jane Morgan) 1957
Fat man, The (Domino) 1948
*Feelings (Albert) 1975
*Feel like making love (Flack) 1974
*FEELS SO GOOD (Mangione) LP 1977
Fernando (ABBA) 1976
FESTIVAL (1812) OVERTURE (Dorati) LP 1956
FEVER ZONE (Tom Jones) LP 1968
Fever (Little Willie John) 1956
Fever (Peggy Lee) 1958
'FIDDLER ON THE ROOF' – Original Theatre cast. LP 1964
'FIDDLER ON THE ROOF' – Film Soundtrack. LP 1971
*Fifth of Beethoven, A (Murphy) 1976
*Fifty ways to leave your lover (Paul Simon) 1975
*52nd STREET (Joel) LP 1978
*Fight (Streisand) 1979
*Fight the power (Isley Bros) 1975
FILM ENCORES (Mantovani) LP 1957
Fine brown frame (Lutcher) 1948
Finger poppin' time (Hank Ballard) 1960
Fingertips Pt. 2 (Little Stevie Wonder) 1963
FIRE ON THE MOUNTAIN (Daniels Band) LP 1974
*Fire (Arthur Brown) 1968
Fire (Ohio Players) 1974

FIRE (Ohio Players) LP 1974
*Fire (Pointer Sisters) 1978
FIRST FAMILY? THE (Vaughan Meader) LP 1962
First man on the moon (Apollo 11 Astronauts) 1969
*First time ever I saw your face (Flack) 1972
Five hundred miles away from home (Bare) 1963
(See also 'J'entends siffler le train' – Richard Anthony)
Five, ten, fifteen hours (Ruth Brown) 1952
Flamingo (Bostic) 1952
*Flash light (Parliament) 1978
FLEETWOOD MAC (Fleetwood Mac) LP 1975
Flip flop and fly (Turner) 1955
*FLIRTIN' WITH DISASTER (Molly Hatchet) 1979 LP
*FLOATERS, THE (Floaters) LP 1977
*Float on (Floaters) 1977
Floral Dance (Brighouse & Rastrick Band) 1977
FLOWER DRUM SONG – Original theatre cast (LP) 1959
*FLOWING RIVERS (Andy Gibb) LP 1977
Floy joy (Supremes) 1972
Flying saucer (Buchanan & Goodman) 1956
*FLY LIKE AN EAGLE (Miller Band) LP 1976
*Fly like an eagle (Miller Band) 1976
*Fly robin, fly (Silver Convention) 1975
Fly, The (Checker) 1961
*'FM' Soundtrack 2 LP 1978
*FOGHAT – LIVE (Foghat) LP 1977
*Fooled around and fell in love (Bishop) 1976
FOOL FOR THE CITY (Foghat) 1976 LP
Fool in love, A (Ike & Tina Turner) 1960
Fool such as I, A (Presley) 1959
Football match, The (see 'Partita di pallone')
*FOOTLOOSE AND FANCY FREE (Rod Stewart) LP 1977
*For all we know (Carpenters) 1971
*FOREIGNER (Foreigner) LP 1977
Forever with you (see 'Kimi to itsumademo')
Forever (Drake) 1964
Forget him (Rydell) 1963
For me and my gal (Godfrey) 1947
For once in my life (Wonder) 1968
FOR THE GOOD TIMES (Price) LP 1970
*For the love of money (O'Jays) 1974
*Fortunate son (Creedence Clearwater Revival) 1969
Forty eight crash (Quatro) 1973
FORTY GREATEST HITS (Como) LP 1975
FORTY GREATEST HITS (Presley) LP 1974
For what it's worth (Buffalo Springfield) 1967
For your love (Yardbirds) 1965
Four in the morning (Faron Young) 1972
Four leaf clover (I'm looking over a) (Mooney) 1948
Four strong winds (Bare) 1964
Four walls (Reeves) 1957
*Fox on the run (Sweet) 1975
*FRAMPTON COMES ALIVE (Frampton) 2 LP 1976
*Frankenstein (Edgar Winter group) 1973
Frankie and Johnny (Presley) 1966
Frankie (Connie Francis) 1959
*Freddie's dead, 'Superfly' theme (Mayfield) 1972
*FREE FOR ALL (Nugent) LP 1976
Free wheelin' (Bachman-Turner Overdrive) 1974
*FREHLEY, ACE LP (see 'Kiss' 1978)
Freight train (Nancy Whisky/Chas. McDevitt) 1957

*FRENCH KISS (Welch) LP 1977
French song, The (Starr) 1964
Frenesi (Artie Shaw) 1940
Friday on my mind (Easybeats) 1966
Friendly persuasion – Thee I love (Boone) 1956
From a jack to a king (Ned Miller) 1962
From me to you (Beatles) 1963
Frosty the snow man (Autry) 1950
FULFILLINGNESS FIRST FINALE (Wonder) LP 1974
*FULL MOON (Daniels Band) LP 198·
Fun, fun, fun (Beach Boys) 1964
*FUNKENTELECHY VS PLACEBO SYNDROME (Parliament) LP 1977
Funky Broadway (Pickett) 1967
Funky Nassau (Beginning of the End) 1973
*Funky town (Lipps Inc) 1980
*Funky worm (Ohio Players) 1973
Funny (Elledge) 1961
Funny (Hinton) 1964
*Funny face (Fargo) 1972
Funny, funny (Sweet) 1971

G

*Galveston (Campbell) 1969
Galway Bay (Crosby) 1948
Gambler's guitar (Draper) 1953
*GAMBLER, THE (Kenny Rogers) LP 1978
Game of love (Fontana) 1965
*Games people play (see 'They just can't stop it')
*GAME, THE (Queen) LP 1980
Ganz in weisse (Roy Black) 1966
*Garden party (Rick Nelson) 1972
*GAUCHO (Steely Dan) LP 1980
Geh alte schau ni net so depat on (Three Meckys) 1968
GEMS FOREVER (Mantovani) LP 1958
GENIUS OF JANKOWSKI, THE (Jankowski) LP 1965
Georgia on my mind (Charles) 1960
*Georgy girl (Seekers) 1966
Get a job (Silhouettes) 1958
*Getaway (Earth, Wind & Fire) 1976
*Get back (Beatles) 1969
*Get down (O'Sullivan) 1973
Get down tonight (KC & Sunshine Band) 1975
Get it on (T. Rex) 1971
Get off my cloud (Rolling Stones) 1965
*Get on the good foot (James Brown) 1972
Get ready (Rare Earth) 1970
*GET THE KNACK (The Knack) LP 1979
*Get together (Youngbloods) 1969
*Get up and boogie (Silver Convention) 1976
GET YOUR WINGS (Aerosmith) LP 1974
'G.I. BLUES' (Presley) LP 1960
*GIDEON (Kenny Rogers) LP 1980
GIFT OF LIFE (LP) (see CADEAU DE LA VIE)
Gimme little sign (Wood) 1967
Gimme some lovin' (Spencer Davis) 1966
Girl from Ipanema (Gilberto/Getz) 1964
*Girl watcher (Okaysians) 1968
Gitarre und das meer, Die (Freddy) 1959
*Gitarzan (Stevens) 1969
*Give me just a little more time (Chairmen of the Board) 1969
*GIVE ME THE NIGHT (Benson) LP 1980
Give peace a chance (Plastic Ono Band) 1969
*Give your baby a standing ovation (Dells) 1973
Glad all over (Dave Clark 5) 1963
*GLASS HOUSES (Joel) LP 1980
GLEN CAMPBELL – LIVE (Campbell) L 1969
Glendora (Como) 1956

GLENN MILLER STORY, THE (Miller) LP 1954
Gloria (Shadows of Knight) 1966
Glow worm (Mills Bros) 1952
Glow worm (Spike Jones) 1946
*Go all the way (Raspberries) 1972
*GO ALL THE WAY (Isley Brothers) LP 1980
Go away little girl (Happenings) 1966
Go away little girl (Lawrence) 1962
Go away little girl (Donny Osmond) 1971
*GO FOR YOUR GUNS (Isley Brothers) LP 1977
*Going in circles (Friends of Distinction) 1969
GOING PLACES (Alpert) LP 1965
Going to a go go (Miracles) 1965
Going to the river (Domino) 1953
Goin' home (Domino) 1952
*GOLD AND PLATINUM (Lynyrd Skynyrd) 2 LP 1979
Goldfinger (Shirley Bassey) 1964
GOLDFINGER Soundtrack LP 1964
Gone, forgotten, all over (see 'Vergangen, vergessen')
Gone (Husky) 1957
Gonna find me a bluebird (Rainwater) 1956
*Gonna fly now (Conti) 1977
Go now (Moody Blues) 1964
Goodbye cruel world (Darren) 1961
GOODBYE YELLOW BRICK ROAD (Elton John) LP 1973
*Goodbye Yellow Brick Road (Elton John) 1973
Good golly, Miss Molly (Little Richard) 1958
Good lovin' (Young Rascals) 1966
Good luck charm (Presley) 1962
Good morning starshine (Oliver) 1969
Goodnight Irene (Jenkins and Weavers) 1950
*Goodnight tonight (Wings) 1979
Good, the bad and the ugly, The (Montenegro) 1968
Good time Charley's got the blues (O'Keefe) 1972
*Good times (Chic) 1979
Good timin' (Jimmy Jones) 1960
Good vibrations (Beach Boys) 1966
*Got to be real (Lynn) 1978
Got to be there (Michael Jackson) 1972
*Got to get you into my life (Earth, Wind & Fire) 1978
*Go WEST (Village People) LP 1979
GRAND FUNK RAILROAD – LIVE (Grand Funk Railroad) LP 1970
*GRAND ILLUSION, THE (Styx) LP 1977
*Grazing in the grass (Friends of Distinction) 1969
*Grazing in the grass (Masekela) 1968
*'GREASE' Soundtrack LP 1978
*Grease (Valli) 1978
Great balls of fire (Jerry Lee Lewis) 1957
*GREATEST OF EDDIE ARNOLD (Eddie Arnold) LP 1974
*GREATEST HITS (ABBA) LP 1975
*GREATEST HITS (ABBA) Vol 2 LP 1979
*GREATEST HITS – HISTORY (America) LP 1975
*GREATEST HITS (Bee Gees) LP 1979
*GREATEST HITS (Glen Campbell) LP 1971
*GREATEST HITS, Vol 1 LP (Cash) 1967
*GREATEST HITS (Chicago) LP 1975
*GREATEST HITS, 40 (Perry Como) LP 1975
*GREATEST HITS (John Denver) LP 1973
*GREATEST HITS (John Denver) Vol 2 LP 1977
*GREATEST HITS (The Doors) LP 1980
*GREATEST HITS (Eagles) LP 1976
*GREATEST HITS (Electric Light Orchestra) LP 1979

*GREATEST HITS (Waylon Jennings) LP 1979
*GREATEST HITS (Elton John) LP 1974
*GREATEST HITS (Elton John) Vol 2 LP 197
*GREATEST HITS (Barry Manilow) 2 LP 1978
*GREATEST HITS (Mathis) 1958
*GREATEST HITS (Steve Miller Band) LP 1978
*GREATEST HITS (Ronnie Milsap) LP 1980
*GREATEST HITS (Anne Murray) LP 1980
*GREATEST HITS (Olivia Newton-John) LP 1977
*GREATEST HITS (Oak Ridge Boys) LP 1980
*GREATEST HITS, 40 (Elvis Presley) LP 1974
*GREATEST HITS (Helen Reddy) LP 1975
*GREATEST HITS (Kenny Rogers) LP 1980
*GREATEST HITS (Linda Ronstadt) LP 1976
*GREATEST HITS (Diana Ross/Supremes) LP 1967
*GREATEST HITS (Seals & Crofts) LP 1975
*GREATEST HITS (Paul Simon) LP 1977
*GREATEST HITS (Simon & Garfunkel) LP 1972
*GREATEST HITS (Sly & Family Stone) LP 1970
*GREATEST HITS (Steely Dan) LP 1978
*GREATEST HITS (Cat Stevens) LP 1975
*GREATEST HITS (Rod Stewart) LP 1979
*GREATEST HITS (Barbra Streisand) Vol 2 LP 1978
*GREATEST HITS (Donna Summer) 2 LP 1979
*GREATEST HITS (James Taylor) LP 1976
*GREATEST HITS (Frankie Valli/Four Seasons) 2 LP 1976
*GREATEST HITS (War) LP 1976
*GREATEST HITS (Wings) LP 1978
GREATEST HITS (Tammy Wynette) LP 1969
(See also 'BEST OF . . .' Albums)
Great pretender, The (Platters) 1956
Green door (Lowe) 1956
Green eyes (Jimmy Dorsey) 1941
Green fields (Brothers Four) 1960
Green green (New Christy Minstrels) 1963
Green green grass of home (Tom Jones) 1966
*Green onions (Booker T & MG's) 1962
Green river (Creedence Clearwater Revival) 1969
GREEN RIVER (Creedence Clearwater Revival) LP 1969
Greensleeves (Mantovani) 1952
*Green tambourine (Lemon Piper) 1967
*Groove line, The (Heatwave) 1978
*Groove me (King Floyd) 1970
*Groovin' (Young Rascals) 1967
Groovy kind of love (Mindbenders) 1966
Groovy situation (Gene Chandler) 1970
G. T. O. (Ronny and Daytonas) 1964
*GUILTY (Streisand) LP 1980
*Guilty (Streisand/Gibb) 1980
Guitar and the sea, The (Freddy) 1959
Guitar boogie (Arthur Smith) 1945
Guitar man, Dance with the (Eddy) 1962
Guy is a guy, A (Doris Day) 1951
*Gypsies, Tramps and Thieves (Cher) 1971
Gypsy cried, The (Christie) 1962
Gypsy, The (Ink Spots) 1946
*Gypsy woman (Hyland) 1970

H
'Hair' Original theatre cast. LP 1968
*Hair (Cowsills) 1969
Half as much (Clooney) 1952
Half breed (Rainwater) 1959
*Half breed (Cher) 1973
Handy man (Jimmy Jones) 1960
Hang on Sloopy (McCoys) 1965
Hang on Sloopy (Ramsey Lewis) 1965
Hanky panky (James/Shondells) 1966
Happening, The (Supremes) 1967
*Happiest girl in the whole USA (Fargo) LP 1972
HAPPIEST GIRL IN THE WHOLE USA (Fargo) LP 1972
Happy Christmas, war is over (Lennon/Ono) 1972
*Happy together (Turtles) 1967
Happy whistler (Robertson) 1956
*Hard day's night, A (Beatles) 1964
'HARD DAY'S NIGHT, A' (Beatles) LP 1964
*Hard headed woman (Presley) 1958
Hard luck blues (Roy Brown) 1950
*Harper Valley P.T.A. (Jeannie Riley) 1968
HARPER VALLEY P.T.A. (Riley) LP 1968
*Harry Hippie (Womack) 1972
Harry Lime – 'Third Man' theme (Lombardo) 1950
Harry Lime – 'Third Man' theme (Anton Karas) 1950
HARVEST FOR THE WORLD (Isley Brothers) LP 1976
HARVEST (Neil Young) LP 1972
*HASTEN DOWN THE WIND (Ronstadt) LP 1976
Hats off to Larry (Shannon) 1961
Have I the right (Honeycombs) 1964
*Have you ever seen the rain (Creedence Clearwater Revival) 1971
Have you heard? (Joni James) 1953
*Have you never been mellow (Newton-John) 1975
HAVE YOU NEVER BEEN MELLOW (Newton-John) LP 1975
Have you seen her? (Chi-Lites) 1971
Have you seen my wife, Mr Jones? (see 'New York mining disaster')
Have you seen your mother, baby, standing in the shadow (Rolling Stones) 1966
Hawaiian wedding song (Andy Williams) 1959
Hawaii Five-O (Ventures) 1969
*HEAD MACHINE (Foreigner) LP 1979
HEADHUNTERS (Hancock) LP 1974
HEADQUARTERS (Monkees) LP 1967
He ain't heavy – he's my brother (Hollies) 1969
Hear my prayer (Ernest Lough) 1927
Heartaches (Ted Weems) 1933
*Heartache tonight (Eagles) 1979
Heartaches by the number (Mitchell) 1959
*Heartbeat (De Franco Family) 1973
Heartbreak Hotel (Presley) 1956
Heart of glass (Blondie) 1978
*Heart of gold (Neil Young) 1972
Hearts of stone (Fontane Sisters) 1954
Hearts of stone (Otis Williams/Charms) 1955
Heart (see 'Cuore')
HEAT IS ON, THE (Isley Bros) LP 1975
Heat wave (Martha/Vandellas) 1963
*Heaven knows (Summer/Brooklyn Dreams) 1979
HEAVENLY (Matthis) LP 1959
*Heaven must be missing an angel (Tavares) 1976
*Heaven on the 7th floor (Nicholas) 1977
Heavy makes you happy (Staple Singers) 1971
*He don't love you (Orlando/Dawn) 1975
Heidschi Bumbeidschi (Heintje) 1968
Heimatlos (Freddy) 1958

Heimweh (Freddy) 1956
HEINTJE (Heintje) LP 1968
Heisser sand (Mina) 1962
He'll have to stay (Jeanne Black) 1960
He'll have to go (Reeves) 1959
Hello Dolly (Louis Armstrong) 1964
*Hello goodbye (Beatles) 1967
*Hello, I love you (Doors) 1960
Hello Mary Lou (Ricky Nelson) 1961
Hello Muddah., hello Faddah (Sherman) 1963
Hello walls (Young) 1961
Hell raiser (Sweet) 1973
Help, get me some help (Ringo Willie Cat) 1972
*Help me make it through the night (Sammi Smith) 1971
Help me Rhonda (Beach Boys) 1965
*Help (Beatles) 1965
'HELP' (Beatles) LP 1965
Henery the eighth I am (see I'm Henery the eighth)
Here am I broken-hearted (Johny Ray) 1951
*HERE AT LAST – BEE GEES 'LIVE' (Bee Gees) 2 LP 1977
Here comes summer (Keller) 1959
Here comes Santa Claus (Autry) 1917
Here comes my baby (Tremeloes) 1967
*Here I am (Green) 1973
Here in my heart (Martino) 1952
*HERE YOU COME AGAIN (Parton) LP 1977
*Here you come again (Parton) 1977
*HEROES (Commodores) LP 1980
He's a rebel (Crystals) 1962
He's got the whole world in His hands (Mahalia Jackson) 1958
*He's got the whole world in His hands (Laurie London) 1958
He's so fine (Chiffons) 1963
*He's so shy (Pointer Sisters) 1980
Hey, baby (Channel) 1962
*Hey, Deanie (Shaun Cassidy) 1977
Hey, girl (Donny Osmond) 1971
Hey, good lookin' (Hank Williams) 1951
*Hey Jude (Beatles) 1968
HEY JUDE (Beatles) LP 1970
*Hey, Paula (Paul & Paula) 1962
*Hey there, lonely girl (Holman) 1969
Hey there (Clooney) 1954
*Hey, tonight (Creedence Clearwater Revival) 1971
High and mighty, The (Leroy Holmes) 1954
*Higher and higher – Your love has lifted me (Coolidge) 1977
High noon – Do not forsake me oh my darling (Lane) 1952
High school confidential (Jerry Lee Lewis) 1958
'HIGH SOCIETY' Soundtrack LP 1956
*HIGHWAY TO HELL (AC/DC) LP 1979
*HI INFIDELITY (REO Speedwagon) LP 1980
Hi lili, hi lo (Caron/Ferrer) 1953
*Himno a la alegria (Rios) 1969
His latest flame (Presley) 1961
HISTORY – AMERICA'S GREATEST HITS (America) LP 1975
*Hitchin' a ride (Vanity Fare) 1970
*Hit me with your best shot (Benatar) 1980
Hit the road, Jack (Charles) 1961
Hokkaido skies (Okumura) 1966
Hold me, thrill me, kiss me (Karen Chandler) 1952
Hold me, thrill me, kiss me (Carter) 1965
Hold my hand (Cornell) 1954
Hold on, I'm coming (Sam & Dave) 1966
*HOLD OUT (Browne) LP 1980
*Hold the line (Toto) 1978
Hold what you've got (Tex) 1964
Hold your head up (Argent) 1972
Holiday for strings (David Rose) 1944

*Holly Holy (Diamond) 1969
HOLLY STORY, BUDDY (Buddy Holly) LP 1959
*Hollywood swinging (Kool & The Gang) 1974
Homburg (Procol Harum) 1967
HOMECOMING (America) LP 1972
Homeless – Heimatlos (Freddy) 1958
Honey babe (Mooney) 1955
Honeydripper (Jimmy Rodgers) 1957
Honeydripper (Liggins) 1950
Honey honey (ABBA) 1974
Honey hush (Turner) 1953
HONEY IN THE HORN (Al Hirt) LP 1963
*'HONEYSUCKLE ROSE' Soundtrack 2 LP 1980
*Honey (Goldsboro) 1968
HONEY (Ohio Players) LP 1975
Honky cat (Elton John) 1972
HONKY CHÂTEAU (Elton John) LP 1972
Honky tonk blues (Hank Williams) 1952
*Honky tonk women (Rolling Stones) 1969
Honky tonk (Doggett) 1956
Hooked on a feeling (Blue Swede) 1973
*Hooked on a feeling (B. J. Thomas) 1968
*Hopelessly devoted to you (Newton-John) 1978
HORIZON (Carpenters) LP 1975
*HORIZON (Rabbitt) LP 1980
*Horse, The (Nobles & Co) 1968
*Horse with no name, A (American) 1972
HOT AUGUST NIGHT (Diamond) 2 LP 1972
*Hot blooded (Foreigner) 1978
Hot canary (Zabach) 1950
*Hot child in the city (Gilder) 1978
Hot diggity (Como) 1956
*HOTEL CALIFORNIA (Eagles) LP 1976
*Hotel California (Eagles) 1977
*Hot Line (Sylvers) 1976
Hot pants (James Brown) 1971
HOT ROCKS, 1964–1971 (Rolling Stones) 2 LP 1971
*HOT STREETS (Chicago) LP 1978
*Hot stuff (Summer) 1979
*HOTTER THAN JULY (Wonder) LP 1980
Hound dog (Presley) 1956
HOUR OF THE STARS LP (see 'STUNDE DER STARS')
House of bamboo (Andy Williams) 1959
House of the Rising Sun (Animals) 1964
*House of the Rising Sun (Frijid Pink) 1970
HOUSES OF THE HOLY (Led Zeppelin) LP 1973
House that Jack built (Franklin) 1968
*How can you mend a broken heart? (Bee Gees) 1971
*How could I let you get away (Spinners) 1972
How could you believe me – Liar Song (Astaire/Powell) 1951
*How deep is your love (Bee Gees) 1977
*How do you do (Mouth & MacNeal) 1972
How high the moon (Paul and Ford) 1951
How important can it be (Joni James) 1955
Hubba-hubba-hubba, A – Dig you later (Como) 1945
Humoresque (Lombardo) 1946
Humpty Dumpty heart (Thompson) 1948
Hurry on down (Lutcher) 1948
Hurt (see 'A chi')
Hush (Deep Purple) 1968
*Hustle, The (McCoy/Soul City Symph.) 1975

HYMNS (Tennessee Ernie Ford) LP 1956

I
H
I almost lost my mind (Boone) 1956
I almost lost my mind (Ivory Joe Hunter) 1950
I am the walrus (Beatles) 1967
*I am woman (Reddy) 1972
I AM WOMAN (Helen Reddy) LP 1972
*I AM (Earth Wind & Fire) LP 1979
I apologise (Eckstine) 1951
I beg of you (Presley) 1958
*I believe in you (Taylor) 1973
I believe (Bachelors) 1964
I believe (Mahalia Jackson) 1958
I believe (Laine) 1953
I can dream, can't I? (Andrews Sisters) 1949
I CAN HEAR IT NOW (Ed Murrow) Album of singles discs, 1948
*I can help (Swan) 1974
*I can see clearly now (Nash) 1972
I can't begin to tell you (Crosby) 1945
I can't get next to you (Temptations) 1969
*I can't get no satisfaction (Rolling Stones) 1965
I can't go on (Domino) 1955
I can't help myself (Four Tops) 1965
*I can't stop loving you (Ray Charles) 1962
I can't stop loving you (Don Gibson) 1958
Ich will einem cowboy als mann (Gitte) 1963
I could have danced all night (Syms) 1956
I cried a tear (La Vern Baker)
Ida, sweet as apple cider (Red Nicholls) 1927
*IDENTIFY YOURSELF (O'Jays) LP 1979
*I'd like to teach the world to sing (New Seekers) 1971
I'd like to teach the world to sing (Hillside Singers) 1971
*I'd love you to want me (Lobo) 1972
I do, I do, I do (ABBA) 1975
I don't care what the world may do (Bradford) 1954
I don't hurt any more (Snow) 1954
*I don't know if it's right (Evelyn King) 1978
I don't want to spoil the party (Beatles) 1965
*I'd really love to see you tonight (Dan & Coley) 1976
I dream of Naomi (Hedva & David) 1971
I'd've baked a cake – If I knew you were coming (Barton) 1950
*I feel fine (Beatles) 1964
*I feel love (Summer) 1977
I feel so bad (Presley) 1961
If every day was like Christmas (Presley) 1966
If I can dream (Presley) 1968
*If I can't have you (Elliman) 1978
If I didn't have a dime (Pitney) 1962
IF I EMBARRASS YOU, TELL YOUR FRIENDS (Barth) LP 1960
If I had a hammer (Lopez) 1963
If I knew you were coming, I'd've baked a cake (Barton) 1950
If I loved you (Como) 1945
If loving you is wrong (Ingram) 1972
IF YOU CAN BELIEVE YOUR EYES AND EARS (Mamas & Papas) LP 1966
If you can't turn me off (High Inergy) 1977
If you could read my mind (Lightfoot) 1970
*If you don't know me by now (Melvin/Blue Notes) 1972
*If you leave me now (Chicago) 1976
*If you love me let me know (Newton-John) 1974
IF YOU LOVE ME LET ME KNOW (Newton-John) LP 1974
*If you're ready (Staple Singers) 1973

If you wanna be happy (Soul) 1963
*If you want me to stay (Sly & Family Stone) 1973
If (Bread) 1971
If (Como) 1951
I get around (Beach Boys) 1964
I get so lonely (see 'Oh baby mine')
I go ape (Sedaka) 1959
*I gotcha (Tex) 1972
*I got my mind made up (Instant Funk) 1979
I got rhythm (Happenings) 1967
I got stung (Presley) 1958
I gotta go get my baby (Teresa Brewer) 1955
I gotta know (Presley) 1960
I gotta right to cry (Liggins) 1950
*I got you babe (Sonny and Cher) 1965
I got you, I feel good (James Brown) 1965
I had the craziest dream (Harry James) 1942
I hear a symphony (Supremes) 1965
I heard it through the grapevine (Knight/Pips) 1967
I heard it through the grapevine (Gaye) 1968
I hear you knocking (Gale Storm) 1955
I hear you knocking (Edmunds) 1970
*I honestly love you (Newton-John) 1974
*I just want to be your everything (Andy Gibb) 1977
Il ballo del mattone (Pavone) 1963
I left my heart in San Francisco (Bennett) 1962
I like it like that (Kenner) 1961
I like it like that (Dave Clark 5) 1965
I lived my life (Domino) 1963
*I'll be around (Detroit Spinners) 1972
*I'll be good to you (Brothers Johnson) 1976
I'll be home (Boone) 1956
I'll be home for Christmas (Crosby) 1943
I'll be there (Jackson 5) 1970
I'll come running back to you (Cooke) 1957
I'll hold you in my dreams (Arnold) 1947
*I'll never fall in love again (Tom Jones) 1969
I'll never find another you (Seekers) 1965
I'll never get out of this world alive (Hank Williams) 1952
*I'll never love this way again (Warwick) 1979
I'll sail my ship alone (Mullican) 1950
I'll take you there (Staple Singers) 1972
*I love a rainy night (Rabbitt) 1980
*I love how you love me (Vinton) 1968
*I love music (O'Jays) 1975
I loves you Porgy (Nina Simone) 1959
*I love the night life (Bridges) 1978
I love you because (Reeves) 1964
I love you, love me love (Glitter) 1973
Il silenzio (Rosso) 1965
*I'm a believer (Monkees) 1966
I'm a fool to care (Barry) 1961
IMAGINATION (Gladys Knight & The Pips) LP 1973
IMAGINE (Lennon) LP 1971
*I'm alive (Electric Light Orchestra) 1980
I'm always chasing rainbows (Como) 1946
I'm a man (Spencer Davis) 1967
I may never pass this way again (Como) 1958
I'm down (Beatles) 1965
*I'M GLAD YOU'RE HERE WITH ME TONIGHT (Diamond) LP 1977
I'm gonna get married (Lloyd Price) 1959
I'm gonna love that gal (Como) 1943

*I'm gonna love you just a little bit more (White) 1973
*I'm gonna make you love me (Supremes/Temptations) 1968
I'm gonna sit right down and write myself a letter (Billy Williams) 1957
*I'm Henery the Eighth, I am (Herman's Hermits) 1965
I'm hurtin' (Orbison) 1961
I'm in love again (Domino) 1956
I'm in the mood (Hooker) 1948
I'm into something good (Herman's Hermits) 1964
*I'M IN YOU (Frampton) LP 1977
I'm leaving it up to you (Dale and Grace) 1963
*I'm leaving it all up to you (Donny & Marie Osmond) 1974
I'm looking over a four leaf clover (Mooney) 1947
IMMORTAL CLASSICS, MANTOVANI PLAYS (Mantovani) LP 1954
IMMORTAL LADIES (Melachrino) LP 1956
I'm movin' on (Snow) 1950
I'm not old enough to love you (see 'Non ho l'età') 1964
I'm so lonesome I could cry (B. J. Thomas) 1966
I'm sorry (Brenda Lee) 1960
*I'm sorry (Denver) 1975
I'm sticking with you (Bowen) 1957
*I'm still in love with you (Green) 1972
I'M STILL IN LOVE WITH YOU (Al Green) LP 1972
*I'm stone in love with you (Stylistics) 1972
I'm telling you now (Freddie and Dreamers) 1963
I'm walking (Domino) 1957
I'm walking behind you (Fisher) 1953
I'm walking (Ricky Nelson) 1957
I'm your Boogie man (KC & Sunshine Band) 1977
I'm your puppet (Purify) 1966
I'm yours (Cornell) 1952
I'm yours (Presley) 1965
IN-A-GADDA-DA-VIDA (Iron Butterfly) LP 1968
In a shanty in old Shanty Town (Long) 1940
*Incense and peppermints (Strawberry Alarm Clock) 1967
IN CONCERT (Peter, Paul & Mary) LP 1964
In-crowd, The (Ramsey Lewis) 1965
Indescribably blue (Presley) 1967
*Indian giver (1910 Fruitgum Co) 1969
Indian love call (Slim Whitman) 1951
Indian love call (Jeanette MacDonald & Nelson Eddy) 1936
Indian love call (Artie Shaw) 1938
Indian Reservation (Fardon) 1968
*Indian Reservation (Revere & Raiders) 1971
In dreams (Orbison) 1963
I need you now (Fisher) 1954
I need your love tonight (Presley) 1959
*I never cry (Cooper) 1976
*I never loved a man (Franklin) 1967
I never see Maggie alone (Roberts) 1949
*INFINITY (Journey) LP 1978
*IN FLIGHT (Benson) LP 1977
*IN FULL BLOOM (Rose Royce) LP 1977
In ginocchio da te (Morandi) 1964
In my little corner of the world (Anita Bryant) 1960
Inner city blues (Gaye) 1971
INNERVISIONS (Stevie Wonder) LP 1973
In old Lisbon – Lisbon antigua (Riddle) 1956
*Instant Karma (Lennon) 1970
*Instant replay (Hartman) 1978

In the chapel in the moonlight (Kitty Kallen) 1954
*In the ghetto (Presley) 1969
*IN THE HEAT OF THE NIGHT (Benatar) LP 1979
In the middle of an island (Bennett) 1957
In the midnight hour (Pickett) 1965
In the mood (Glenn Miller) 1939
In the mood (Ernie Fields) 1959
In the Navy (Village People) 1979
In the rain (Dramatics) 1972
In the still of the night (Five Satins) 1956
*In the summertime (Mungo Jerry) 1970
In the sun (see 'Nel sole')
IN THE WIND (Peter, Paul & Mary) LP 1963
*In the year 2525 (Zager and Evans) 1969
*IN THROUGH THE DOOR (Led Zeppelin) LP 1979
Into each life some rain must fall (Ella Fitzgerald & Ink Spots) 1944
INTRODUCING THE BEATLES (Beatles) LP 1963
I only live twice (see 'Kaette kita yopparai')
I only want to be with you (Springfield) 1963
I.O.U. (Dean) 1976
I remember you (Ifield) 1962
*I ROBOT (Parsons Project) LP 1977
I saw Mommy kissing Santa Claus (Boyd) 1952
*I say a little prayer (Warwick) 1967
I say a little prayer (Franklin) 1968
I second that emotion (Robinson/ Miracles) 1967
*I shot the sheriff (Clapton) 1974
*Island girl (Elton John) 1975
Israelites (Dekker) 1969
I STARTED OUT AS A CHILD (Cosby) LP 1964
Is this the way to Amarillo? (Christie) 1971
I still love you (Domino) 1957
Is you is or is you ain't my baby (Jordan) 1944
It ain't gonna rain no mo' (Hall) 1923
ITALIA MIA (Mantovani) LP 1961
Itchykoo Park (Small Faces) 1967
It doesn't matter any more (Holly) 1958
*It don't come easy (Ringo Starr) 1971
I thank you (Sam and Dave) 1968
*I think I love you (Partridge Family) 1970
It isn't fair (Cornell) 1950
It mek (Dekker) 1969
It must be him (Vikki Carr) 1967
*It never rains in Southern California (Hammond) 1972
*It's a heartache (Tyler) 1977
It's all in the game (Edwards) 1958
It's all over now (Rolling Stones) 1964
It's almost tomorrow (Dream Weavers) 1955
It's a long long lonely highway (Presley) 1965
*It's ecstasy when you lay down next to me (White) 1977
It's impossible (Como) 1970
It's in the book (Standley) 1952
It's just a matter of time (Benton) 1959
It's late (Ricky Nelson) 1959
It's magic (Doris Day) 1948
It's my party (Gore) 1963
It's no sin (Howard) 1951
It's no sin (Four Acres) 1951
It's not for me to say (Mathis) 1957
It's not unusual (Tom Jones) 1965
It's now or never (Presley) 1960
It's only make believe (Twitty) 1958
It's over (Orbison) 1964
*It's still rock'n roll to me (Joel) 1980
It's too late (Carole King) 1971
It's too late (Goldsboro) 1966

It's too soon to know (Boone) 1958
Itsy bitsy teenie weenie yellow polka dot bikini (Hyland) 1960
It's you I love (Domino) 1959
*It's your thing (Isley Bros) 1969
It wasn't God who made honky tonk angels (Kitty Wells) 1952
I understand (Four Tunes) 1954
I understand (Freddie and Dreamers) 1964
I've got a Humpty Dumpty heart (Thompson) 1948
I've got a lovely bunch of coco-nuts (Freddy Martin) 1949
*I've got love on my mind (Natalie Cole) 1977
I've got my love to keep me warm (Les Brown) 1949
I've gotta get a message to you (Bee Gees) 1968
*I've got to use my imagination (Knight/Pips) 1973
I've heard that song before (Harry James) 1942
I've told every little star (Linda Scott) 1961
Ivory tower (Otis Williams and Charms) 1956
I walk the line (Cash) 1956
I wanna play house with you (Arnold) 1951
*I want to be your lover (Prince) 1979
I want to be a cowboy's sweetheart (Montana) 1936
I want to hold your hand (Beatles) 1963
*I WANT TO LIVE (Denver) LP 1977
I want to marry a cowboy (see 'Ich will einem cowboy als mann')
I WANT YOU BACK LP (see 'DIANA ROSS PRESENTS THE JACKSON 5')
I want you back (Jackson 5) 1969
I want you, I need you, I love you (Presley) 1956
*I want your love (Chic) 1979
*I want you to want me (Cheap Trick) 1979
I was Kaiser Bill's batman (Jack Smith) 1967
*I was made for lovin' you (Kiss) 1979
I was made to love her (Wonder) 1967
I was the one (Presley) 1956
I went to your wedding (Patti Page) 1952
I will follow him (Little Peggy March) 1963
*I will survive (Gaynor)
I wish I didn't love you so (Hutton) 1947
I wish it would rain (Temptations) 1968
I wonder what she's doing tonight? (Boyce/Hart) 1967
I won't forget you (Reeves) 1964
*I write the songs (Manilow) 1975
I yust go nuts at Christmas (Yorgesson) 1949

J

*Jack and Jill (Raydio) 1977
Jailhouse rock (Presley) 1957
Jalousie (Laine) 1951
Jalousie - Jealousy (Fiedler) 1938
Jambalaya (Jo Stafford) 1952
Jambalaya (Hank Williams) 1952
Jamming (Marley) 1977
Jam up jelly tight (Roe) 1969
Japanese Sandman (Whiteman) 1920
Java (Hirt) 1963
'JAZZ SAMBA' (Getz and Byrd) LP 1962
*"JAZZ SINGER, THE" (Soundtrack) LP 1980
*JAZZ (Queen) LP 1978
Jealousy (see 'Jalousie')
Jealous kind of fella (Greene) 1969
Jealous of you (Connie Francis) 1960
*Jean (Oliver) 1969
Jenny, Jenny (Little Richard) 1957

Jenny take a ride (Ryder/Detroit Wheels) 1965
J'entends siffler le train (Richard Anthony) 1962
*Jesse (Carly Simon) 1980
JESUS CHRIST SUPERSTAR (various artists) LP 1970
JESUS CHRIST SUPERSTAR – Film soundtrack LP 1973
Jesus (Faith) 1971
Je t'aime - moi non plus (Birkin/ Gainsbourg) 1969
Jezebel (Laine) 1951
Jim Dandy (LaVern Baker) 1957
Jingle bells - Yingle bells (Yorgesson) 1949
Jingle bell rock (Helms) 1958
Jingle bells (Singing Dogs) 1955
Jingle bells (Crosby) 1943
*Jingle, jangle (Archies) 1969
Jingle jangle jingle (Kay Kyser) 1942
*Jive talkin' (Bee Gees) 1975
Johnny Angel (Fabares) 1962
Johnny B. Goode (Berry) 1958
JOHNNY'S GREATEST HITS (Johnny Mathis) 1958
*Joker, The (Steve Miller band) 1973
JOLSON STORY, THE (Al Jolson) Album of singles discs 1946
JONATHAN LIVINGSTONE SEAGULL – Soundtrack (Diamond) LP 1973
Josephine (Bill Black) 1960
*Joy to the world (Three Dog Night) 1971
*J.T. (James Taylor) LP 1977
JUDY AT CARNEGIE HALL (Judy Garland) LP 1961
*Judy in disguise (John Fred & Playboys) 1967
*Julie, do ya love me? (Sherman) 1970
Jumpin' Jack Flash (Rolling Stones) 1968
Jumpin' jive (Caloway) 1939
Junge komm bald wieder (Freddy) 1962
*Jungle boogie (Kool & The Gang) 1973
*Jungle fever (Chakachas) 1971
Just a baby's prayer at twilight (Burr) 1918
Just a closer walk with Thee (Foley) 1950
Just a dream (Clanton) 1958
Just a little bit better (Herman's Hermits) 1965
Just a little lovin' will go a long way (Arnold) 1948
Just a little too much (Ricky Nelson) 1959
Just ask your heart (Avalon) 1959
*Just don't want to be lonely (Main Ingredient) 1974
*Just like starting over (Lennon) 1980
Just loving you (Anita Harris) 1967
Just my imagination (Temptations) 1971
*Just the way you are (Joel) 1977
Just walkin' in the rain (Johnny Ray) 1956
*Just when I needed you most (Vanwarmer) 1979
*Just you'n me (Chicago) 1973

K

Kaette kita yopparai (Folk Crusaders) 1967
Kalamazoo – I've got a gal in (Glenn Miller) 1942
Kansas City (Wilbert Harrison) 1959
Kassai - Applause (Chiaki) 1972
Kaw-Liga (Hank Williams) 1952
KC & SUNSHINE BAND (KC & Sunshine Band) LP 1975
Keep a-knockin' (Little Richard) 1957
Keeper of the castle (Four Tops) 1972
Keep it comin' love (KC & Sunshine Band) 1976

*Keep loving you (REO Speedwagon) 1980
Keep on dancing (Gentrys) 1965
Keep on truckin' (Kendricks) 1973
Keep searchin' (Shannon) 1964
Keep the ball rollin' (Jay & Techniques) 1967
*KENNY (Kenny Rogers) LP 1979
Kentucky rain (Presley) 1970
Kewpie doll (Como) 1958
*"KIDS ARE ALRIGHT, THE" (Soundtrack) 1979 LP
Kili-watch (The Cousins) 1961
*Killing me softly with his song (Flack) 1973
Kimi to itsumademo (Kayama) 1965
Kind of a drag (Buckinghams) 1966
KING AND I, THE - Soundtrack LP 1956
KING CREOLE (Presley) EP 1958
*King is gone, The (McDowell) 1977
*King of the road (Roger Miller) 1965
KINGSTON TRIO, THE (Kingston Trio) LP 1958
*King Tut (Martin) 1978
Kinijirareta koi (Moriyama) 1969
*Kiss Alive II (Kiss) 2-LP 1977
*Kiss an angel good morning (Pride) 1971
*Kiss and say goodbye (Manhattans) 1976
Kisses sweeter than wine (Jimmy Rodgers) 1957
Kissin' cousins (Presley) 1964
Kiss me - Besame mucho (Jimmy Dorsey) 1943
Kiss of fire (Georgia Gibbs) 1952
*Kiss you all over (Exile) 1978
*KISS (Solo Albums) for Criss (Peter), Stanley (Paul), Simmons (Gene), Frehley (Ace) 1978
KISS - ALIVE (Kiss) LP 1975
KNOCKERS UP (Rusty Warren) LP 1959
*Knock on wood (Amii Stewart) 1979
*Knock three times (Dawn) 1970
Knowing me knowing you (ABBA) 1977
Koi no kisetsu (Pinky & The Killers) 1968
Kookie, Kookie, lend me your comb (Byrnes/Stevens) 1959
*Kung Fu fighting (Carl Douglas) 1974
Kyoto Bojyo (Kyoto guy) (Nagisa) 1971
Kyoto doll (see 'Kyoto no koi')
Kyoto no koi (Nagisa) 1970

L

La Bamba (Valens) 1958
La Bambola (Pravo) 1968
Lachend vagabond, Der (Bertelmann) 1958
La coppia piu bella del mondo (Celentano) 1967
*Ladies night (Kool & the Gang) 1979
*LADIES NIGHT (Kool & the Gang) LP 1979
Lady D'Arbanville (Cat Stevens) 1970
Lady Godiva (Peter & Gordon) 1966
Lady is a tramp, The (Greco) 1961
Lady Jane (Rolling Stones) 1966
*Lady Madonna (Beatles) 1968
*Lady Marmalade (Labelle) 1974
Lady of Spain (Fisher) 1952
LADY SINGS THE BLUES (Diana Ross) Soundtrack 2LP 1972
*Lady Willpower (Union Gap) 1968
*Lady (Kenny Rogers) 1980
Lah dee dah (Billie & Lillie) 1957
La, la, la (Sherman) 1969
La la means I love you (Delfonics) 1968
La mama (Charles Aznavour) 1963
La mer—Beyond the sea (Darin) 1960
La'amour est bleu (see 'Love is blue')
Land of a thousand dances (Pickett) 1966
La Paloma (Billy Vaughn) 1958
La Paloma (Freddy) 1961

*Last dance (Summer) 1978
Last date (Cramer) 1960
Last kiss (Wilson) 1964
Last night (Mar-Keys) 1961
*Last night I didn't get to sleep at all (5th Dimension) 1972
*Last song (Bear) 1972
Last time, The (Rolling Stones) 1965
*Last train to Clarksville (Monkees) 1966
Last waltz, The (Humperdinck) 1967
La Tramontana (Antoine) 1968
Laughing song (Shepard) 1910
Laughing vagabond—Der lachende vagabond (Bertelmann) 1958
*Laughing (Guess Who) 1969
Laura (Woody Herman) 1945
L'aventura (Stone & Chardon) 1972
La vie en rose (Piaf) 1950
Lawdy, Miss Clawdy (Lloyd Price) 1952
*Lay down Sally (Clapton) 1977
Lazy day (Spanky & Our Gang) 1967
Lazy river (Mills Brothers) 1948
Leader of the gang (I'm the) (Glitter) 1973
Leader of the pack (Shangri-Las) 1964
*Lead me on (Nightingale) 1979
*Lean on me (Bill Withers) 1972
Learnin' the blues (Sinatra) 1955
*Leave me alone Ruby Red Dress (Reddy) 1973
*Leaving me (Independents) 1973
*Leaving on a jet plane (Peter, Paul & Mary) 1969
L'ecole est fini (Sheila) 1963
LED ZEPPELIN III (Led Zeppelin) LP 1970
LED ZEPPELIN (Led Zeppelin) LP 1969
LED ZEPPELIN II (Led Zeppelin) LP 1969
LED ZEPPELIN IV (Led Zeppelin) LP 1971
*Le Freak (Chic) 1978
*LEFTOVERTURE (Kansas) LP 1976
Left right out of your heart (Patti Page) 1958
Legend of the emerald (see 'Emerald-no densetsu')
Legend of Xanadu (Dee, Dozy, Beaky, Mick, Tich) 1965
Leroy (Jack Scott) 1958
Les oignons—The onions (Bechet) 1949
*Let 'em in (Wings) 1976
*Let it be (Beatles) 1970
LET IT BE (Beatles) Soundtrack LP 1970
LET IT BLEED (Rolling Stones) LP 1969
*Let me be there (Newton-John) 1973
Let me be your teddy bear (Presley) 1957
Let me go over (Brewer) 1955
Let me go over (Joan Weber) 1954
Let's dance (Montez) 1962
*Let's do it again (Staple Singers) 1975
Let's get it on (Gaye) 1973
LET'S GET IT ON (Gaye) LP 1973
*LET'S GET SMALL (Steve Martin) LP 1977
Let's go, let's go, let's go (Ballard) 1960
Let's hang on (Four Seasons) 1965
Let's have a party—Song medley (Atwell) 1953
Let's have another party—song melody (Atwell) 1954
*LET'S KEEP IT THAT WAY (Murray) LP 1978
Let's live for today (Grass Roots) 1967
Let's spend the night together (Rolling Stones) 1967
*Let's stay together (Green) 1971
Let's twist again (Checker) 1961
Let's twist again (Johnny Hallyday) 1961
Let's work together (Canned Heat) 1970

Letter from Sherry, A (Dale Ward) 1963
*Letter, The (Box Tops) 1967
Letter to an angel (Clanton) 1958
Let the good times roll (Shirley & Lee) 1956
Let there be drums (Sandy Nelson) 1961
Let the sunshine in (see 'Aquarius')
LET'S STAY TOGETHER (Al Green) LP 1972
Liar song ('See 'How could you believe me')
Liar (Three Dog Night) 1971
Liebeskummer lohnt sich nicht (Malmquist) 1964
*LIFE IS A SONG WORTH SINGING (Pendergrass) LP 1978
Light my fire (Feliciano) 1968
*Light my fire (Doors) 1967
*Lightnin' strikes (Christie) 1965
*LIGHT UP THE NIGHT (Brothers Johnson) LP 1980
Like a rolling stone (Dylan) 1965
Lili Marlene (Andersen) 1939
*Li'l Red Riding Hood (Sam the Sham & Pharaohs) 1966
Lily the Pink (Scaffold) 1968
Limbo rock (Checker) 1962
'Limelight' Theme—Terry's theme (Chacksfield) 1953
Linger awhile (Whiteman) 1923
*Lion sleeps tonight, The (Robert John) 1971
*Lion sleeps tonight, The (The Tokens) 1961
Lipstick on your collar (Connie Francis) 1959
Lisbon antigua—In old Lisbon (Riddle) 1956
Listen people (Herman's Hermits) 1966
*Listen to what the man said (Wings/McCartney) 1975
Little arrows (Leapy Lea) 1968
Little bird told me so, A (Knight) 1948
*Little bit me, little bit you (Monkees) 1967
*Little bit o'soul, A (Music Explosion) 1967
Little bitty girl (Rydell) 1959
Little bitty pretty one (Thurston Harris) 1957
Little Blue Riding Hood (Freberg) 1953
Little brown jug (Glenn Miller) 1939
Little children (Kramer) 1964
Little darling (Diamonds) 1957
Little drummer boy (Simeone) 1959
LITTLE DRUMMER BOY—LP (see 'Sing we now of Christmas', 1958)
Little girl (Cole) 1948
*Little green apples (O.C. Smith) 1968
Little green bag (George Baker Selection) 1970
*Little Jeannie (Elton John) 1980
*Little more love, A (Newton-John) 1978
Little ole man—Uptight (Cosby) 1967
*LITTLE QUEEN (Heart) LP 1977
Little sister (Presley) 1961
Little star (Elegants) 1958
Little things (Goldsboro) 1965
Little things mean a lot (Kallen) 1954
Little white cloud that cried (Ray) 1951
Little white lies (Haymes) 1948
*Little Willy (Sweet) 1972
Little woman (Sherman) 1969
Live and let die (McCartney/Wings) 1973
*LIVE AND MORE (Summer) LP 1978
LIVE AND SLEEZY (Village People) 2LP 1979
LIVE - AT CARNEGIE HALL (Chicago) LP 1971
*LIVE BOOTLEG (Aerosmith) 2LP 1978
*LIVE BULLET (Seger & Silver Bullet Band) LP 1976

*LIVE (Eagles) LP 1980
LIVE—AT LAS VEGAS (Tom Jones) LP 1969
LIVE—GLEN CAMPBELL (Glen Campbell) LP 1969
LIVE—GRAND FUNK RAILROAD (Grand Funk Railroad) LP 1970
Living doll (Cliff Richard) 1959
LIVING IN THE MATERIAL WORLD (Harrison) LP 1973
*LIVING IN THE U.S.A. (Ronstadt) LP 1978
*Livin' it up Friday night (Bell & James) 1979
Loco-motion, The (Grand Funk Railroad) 1974
Loco-motion, The (Little Eva) 1962
Lollipop (Chordettes) 1958
Lonely ballerina (Mantovani) 1954
Lonely blue boy (Twitty) 1960
Lonely boy (Anka) 1959
Lonely bull (Alpert) 1962
LONELY BULL, THE (Alpert) LP 1962
Lonely days (Bee Gees) 1970
*Lonely nights (Captain & Tennille) 1976
Lonely teardrops (Jackie Wilson) 1959
Lonely week-ends (Rich) 1960
Lonesome town (Ricky Nelson) 1958
Long and winding road, The (Beatles) 1970
Long cool woman (Hollies) 1972
Long gone lonesome blues (Hank Williams) 1950
Long gone (Sonny Thompson) 1948
LONG HARD CLIMB (Helen Reddy) LP 1973
Long long lonely highway (Presley) 1965
*LONG RUN, THE (Eagles) LP 1979
LONG TALL SALLY (Beatles) EP 1964
Long tall Sally (Little Richard) 1956
LOOK AT US (Sonny and Cher) LP 1965
*Lookin' for a love (Womack) 1974
*Lookin' for love (Johnny Lee) 1980
*Looking out my back door (Creedence Clearwater Revival) 1970
Looking through the eyes of love (Pitney) 1965
*LOOK OUT FOR NO. 1 (Brothers Johnson) LP 1976
*Looks like we made it (Manilow) 1977
*Look what you done for me (Al Green) 1972
Looky looky (Giorgio) 1969
*Lord's Prayer, The (Sister Janet Mead) 1974
LOS COCHINOS (Cheech & Chong) LP 1973
Losing you (Brenda Lee) 1963
*LOST IN LOVE (Air Supply) LP 1980
Louie Louie (Kingsmen) 1963
Love affair (see 'One of a kind')
Love and marriage (Sinatra) 1955
Love at first sight (see 'Je t'aime - moi non plus')
*LOVE AT THE GREEK (Diamond) 2LP 1977
*Love can make you happy (Mercy) 1969
Love child (Ross/Supremes) 1968
Love forever (see 'Kimi to itsumademo')
*Love grows (Edison Lighthouse) 1970
*LOVE GUN (Kiss) LP 1977
*Love hurts (Nazareth) 1975
*Love I lost, The (Melvin/Blue Notes) 1973
Love is a many splendored thing (Four Aces) 1955
*Love is blue (Mauriat) 1967
Love is here and now you're gone (Supremes) 1967
Love is love (Ryan) 1969
Love is strange (Mickey and Sylvia) 1956

*Love is thicker than water (Andy Gibb) 1977
Love Jones (Brighter Side of Darkness) 1972
Love letters in the sand (Boone) 1957
Love letters (Ketty Lester) 1962
Love letters (Presley) 1966
Loveliest night of the year (Mario Lanza) 1951
Love machine (Miracles) 1975
Love me do (Beatles) 1962
Love me tender (Presley) 1956
Love me (Domino) 1954
*Love on a two-way street (Moments) 1970
Love problems aren't worthwhile (see Liebeskummer lohnt sich nicht')
*LOVERBOY (Loverboy) LP 1980
*Love Rollercoaster (Ohio Players) 1975
Lovers and fools (Ozaki) 1972
*Lover's concerto (The Toys) 1965
Lover's question, A (McPhater) 1958
Lover (Peggy Lee) 1952
Lovesick blues (Hank Williams) 1949
Lovesick blues (Ifield) 1962
*Loves me like a rock (Paul Simon) 1973
Love somebody (Doris Day) 1947
*Love so right (Bee Gees) 1976
*Love's theme (Love Unlimited Orch.) 1973
LOVE STORY—Film Soundtrack LP 1970
'Love Story' Theme—'Where do I begin?' (Andy Williams) 1971
*Love Theme—'A Star Is Born' (Streisand) 1976
*Love Theme—'Romeo & Juliet' (Mancini) 1969
*Love to love you, baby (Donna Summer) 1975
*LOVE TRACKS (Gaynor) LP 1979
*Love train (O'Jays) 1973
*Love will keep us together (Captain & Tennille) 1975
LOVE WILL KEEP US TOGETHER (Captain & Tennille) LP 1975
*Love won't let me wait (Major Harris) 1975
*Love you inside out (Bee Gees) 1979
Love you save me, The (Jackson 5) 1970
Love (Al Green) 1975
Loving you (Presley) 1957
*Lovin' you (Ripperton) 1975
*Lowdown (Scaggs) 1976
LOW SPARK OF HIGH HEELED BOYS (Traffic) LP 1971
*Lucille (Kenny Rogers) 1977
Lucille (Little Richard) 1957
Lucky lips (Ruth Brown) 1957
Lucky lips (Cliff Richard) 1961
*Lucy in the sky with diamonds (Elton John) 1974
*LYNYRD SKYNYRD'S FIRST...AND LAST (Lynyrd Skynyrd) LP 1978

M

*MacArthur Park (Summer) 1978
MacArthur Park (Richard Harris) 1968
*Macho Man (Village People) 1978
McNamara's band (Crosby) 1946
Mack the knife (Darin) 1959
Ma belle amie (Tee-Set) 1969
MACHINE HEAD (Deep Purple) LP 1972
*MACHO MAN (Village People) LP 1978
MADE IN JAPAN (Deep Purple) LP 1972
*MAD LOVE (Ronstadt) LP 1980
MADMAN ACROSS THE WATER (Elton John) LP 1971
*MAGAZINE (Heart) LP 1978
*Maggie May (Rod Stewart) 1971
MAGICAL MYSTERY TOUR (Beatles) LP 1967
*Magic carpet ride (Steppenwolf) 1968

Magic moments (Como) 1958
*Magic (Newton-John) 1980
*Magic (Pilot) 1975
*Magnet and Steel (Egan) 1978
'Mahogany' Theme—'Do you know where you are going to?' (Diana Ross) 1975
Main Course (Bee Gees) LP 1975
*Main Event, The (Streisand) 1979
Majesty of love (Rainwater/Connie Francis) 1957
Make it easy on yourself (Walker Bros) 1965
*Make it with you (Bread) 1970
Make love to me (Jo Stafford) 1954
Make me know it (see 'It's now or never' (Presley)
Make me smile (Harley/Cockney Rebel) 1975
*Makin' it (Naughton) 1978
*Mama can't buy you love (Elton John) 1979
Mama, he treats your daughter mean (Ruth Brown) 1953
Mama, La (see La Mama)
Mama look a boo boo (Belafonte) 1957
Mama mia (ABBA) 1975
Mamas and the Papas, The (Mamas & Papas) LP 1966
Mama's pearl (Jackson 5) 1971
*Mama told me not to come (Three Dog Night) 1970
Mama (Connie Francis) 1960
Mama (Heintje) 1967
Mambo Italiano (Clooney) 1954
Mammy Blue (Los Pop Tops) 1971
Mam'selle (Art Lund) 1947
'Man and a Woman, A' LP (see 'Un homme et une femme')
Manana (Peggy Lee) 1948
*Mandy (Manilow) 1974
Man of La Mancha (Stage Show) LP 1966
Man that got away, The (Garland) 1954
*Man, the (White) LP 1978
Mantovani Plays the Immortal Classics (LP) 1954
Man who shot Liberty Valance (Pitney) 1962
Man with the golden arm (Jacobs) 1956
Many tears ago (Connie Francis) 1960
Marble breaks and iron bends (see 'Marmor, stein und eisen')
Marble, stone and iron break (see 'Marmor, stein und eisen')
Mardi Gras (Creedence Clearwater Revival) LP 1972
Maria Elena (Jimmy Dorsey) 1941
Maria Elena (Los Indios Tabajaras) 1963
Marianne (Gilkyson) 1957
Marie (Four Tunes) 1954
Marie (Tommy Dorsey) 1937
Marina (Granata) 1960
'Mary Poppins' Soundtrack LP 1964
Mary's Boy Child (Boney M) 1978
Mary's Boy Child (Belafonte) 1957
Mashed potato time (Dee Dee Sharp) 1962
Massachusetts (Bee Gees) 1967
Master of Reality (Black Sabbath) LP 1971
Mata au Himade (see 'Lovers and fools')
Matsunoki kouta (Ninomiya) 1965
Maybe baby (Crickets) 1958
Maybellene (Berry) 1955
Maybe you'll be there (Jenkins) 1947
Maybe (Chantels) 1958
Maybe (Pace) 1979
May I (Williams/Zodiacs) 1961
McCartney (Paul McCartney) LP 1970
*Me and Mrs Jones (Billy Paul) 1972
Me and you and a dog named Boo (Lobo) 1971
Mean woman blues (Orbison) 1963
Meet the Beatles (Beatles) LP 1963
Melancholy serenade (Gleason) 1953

*Mellow yellow (Donovan) 1956
Melodie d'amour (Ames Bros.) 1957
Melody of love (Billy Vaughn) 1955
Memorial Album (John F. Kennedy) 1963
Memories are made of this—Heimweh (Freddy) 1956
Memories are made of this (Dean Martin) 1955
Memories Sing Along (Mitch Miller) LP 1960
Memphis (Mack) 1963
Memphis (Rivers) 1964
Mendocino (Sir Douglas Quintet) 1968
Mendocino (Holm) 1969
Merci cherie (Jurgens) 1966
Mercy, mercy me (Gaye) 1971
Mer, La—Beyond the sea (Darin) 1960
Merry Christmas everybody (Slade) 1973
Merry Christmas (Mathis) LP 1959
Merry Christmas (Crosby) LP 1947
Mess of blues (see 'It's now or never'—Presley) 1960
Mexican Joe (Reeves) 1953
Mexico (Reeves) 1961
Mi casa, su casa (Como) 1957
Michael, row the boat ashore (Highwaymen) 1961
Mickey's monkey (Miracles) 1963
Mickey (Ted Weems) 1947
*Micky Mouse Disco (Mickey Mouse) LP 1980
*Middle Man (Scaggs) LP 1980
*Midnight confessions (Grassroots) 1968
Midnight cowboy (Ferrante & Teicher) 1969
Midnight in Moscow (Kenny Ball) 1961
*Midnight train to Georgia (Knight/Pips) 1973
Mighty Joe (Shocking Blue) 1970
Mighty Quinn (Manifred Mann) 1968
Miller Story, Glenn (Miller) LP 1954
*Million Mile Reflections (Daniels Band) LP 1979
Minnie the Moocher (Calloway) 1931
*Minute by Minute (Doobie Brothers) LP 1978
Mirage (James/Shondells) 1967
Misa Criolla (Ramirez) LP 1974
*Miss you (Rolling Stones) 1978
Mister and Mississippi (Patti Page) 1951
Mister Big Stuff (Jean Knight) 1971
Mister Blue (Fleetwoods) 1959
Mister Custer (Verne) 1960
Mister Jaws (Goodman) 1975
Mister Sandman (Chordettes) 1954
Misty Blue (Moore) 1976
Misty (Mathis) 1959
Moanin' the blues (Hank Williams) 1950
Mockin' Bird Hill (Paul/Ford) 1951
Mockin' Bird Hill (Patti Page) 1951
Mockingbird (Foxx) 1963
*Mockingbird (James Taylor/Carly Simon) 1974
Modern Sounds in Country and Western Music (Ray Charles) LP 1962
*Molly Hatchet (Molly Hatchet) LP 1979
Moments to remember (Four Lads) 1955
Mona Lisa (Nat Cole) 1950
*Monday, Monday (Mamas and Papas) 1966
Money, Honey (Drifters) 1953
Money, Money, Money (ABBA) 1976
Money (Strong) 1959
Monkees, The (Monkees) LP 1966
Monsieur (Petula Clark) 1962
Monster mash (Pickett) 1962, 1973
Mony Mony (James/Shondells) 1968
Moods (Diamond) LP 1972
*Moody Blue (Presley) LP 1977

Moody River (Boone) 1961
Moon Flower (Santana) 2LP 1977
Moonglow and 'Picnic' Theme (McGuire Sisters) 1956
Moonglow and theme from 'Picnic' (Stoloff) 1956
Moonglow and 'Picnic' Theme (Gates) 1956
Moonlight in Vermont (Margaret Whiting) 1944
Moonlight serenade (Glenn Miller) 1939
Moonlight becomes you (Harry James) 1942
Moonlight gambler (Laine) 1957
Moon River (Butler) 1961
'Moon River' and other movie themes (Andy Williams) LP 1962
More and more (Pierce) 1954
More Hot Rocks (Rolling Stones) 2LP 1972
*More, more, more (True Connection) 1976
More of the Monkees (The Monkees) LP 1967
More Sing Along with Mitch (Mitch Miller) LP 1958
*More than I can say (Sayer) 1980
More today than yesterday (Spiral Staircase) 1969
More (Como) 1956
Morgen (Robic) 1959
Moritat (Hyman) 1956
*Morning after, The (Maureen McGovern) 1973
*Morning Train—9 to 5 (Easton) 1980
Most beautiful couple in the world (see 'La coppia piu bella')
*Most beautiful girl (Pich) 1973
Most of the Animals, the (see 'Best of the Animals')
Mother of mine (Neil Reid) 1971
*Mothership Connection (Parliament) LP 1976
Mother's little helper (Rolling Stones) 1966
Mountain's high, The (Dick & Dee Dee) 1961
Move on up a little higher (Mahalia Jackson) 1947
Move two mountains, You've gotta (Johnson) 1960
Moving (Peter, Paul & Mary) LP 1963
*Mrs Brown you've got a lovely daughter (Herman's Hermits) 1965
*Mrs Robinson (Simon and Garfunkel) 1968
Mr Tambourine Man (Byrds) 1965
Mule train (Laine) 1949
Mull of Kintyre (Wings) 1977
*Music Box Dancer (Mills) 1979
'Music Man, the' (Stage show) LP 1958
Music, music, music (Brewer) 1950
Music to watch girls go by (Crewe Generation) 1966
*Muskrat love (Captain & Tennille) 1976
Mustang Sally (Pickett) 1966
*M.U.—The Best of Jethro Tull (Jethro Tull) LP 1976
My blue heaven (Austin) 1927
My Bonnie (Sheridan/Beatles) 1961
My boy friend's back (Angels) 1963
My boy Lollipop (Millie) 1964
My brand of blues (Rainwater) 1959
My bucket's got a hole in it (Hank Williams) 1949
My cherie amour (Wonder) 1969
*My ding-a-ling (Chuck Berry) 1972
*My eyes adored you (Valli) 1974
'My Fair Lady' (Stage show) LP 1956
'My Fair Lady' (Sound-track) LP 1964
My foolish heart (Eckstine) 1950
My girl (Temptations) 1965
My guy (Wells) 1964
My happiness (Jon and Sandra Steele) 1948

My happiness (Pied Pipers) 1948
My happiness (Connie Francis) 1959
My heart cries for you (Mitchell) 1950
My heart has a mind of its own (Connie Francis) 1960
My heart is an open book (Dobkins) 1959
*My Home's in Alabama (Alabama) LP 1980
My home town (Anka) 1960
My house is your house—Mi casa su casa (Como) 1957
*My life (Joel) 1978
My love is real (Rainwater) 1959
*My love (McCartney/Wings) 1973
My love (Petula Clark) 1965
My Mammy (Happenings) 1967
My Mammy (Jolson) 1946
*My melody of love (Vinton) 1974
My old man's a dustman (Donegan) 1960
My prayer (Platters) 1956
*My Sharona (The Knack) 1970
My song (Franklin) 1968
My Son the Folk Singer (Allan Sherman) LP 1962
My special angel (Helms) 1957
*My Sweet Lord (George Harrison) 1970
My true love (Jack Scott) 1958
My truly truly fair (Mitchell) 1951
My two front teeth—All I want for Christmas is, (Spike Jones) 1948
My way (Frank Sinatra) 1969
*My way (Presley) 1977
My wish came true (Presley) 1959
My world is empty without you (Supremes) 1966
My Yiddishe Momme (Sophie Tucker) 1938

N

*Nadia's Theme (DeVorzon & Butler) 1976
*Na Na Hey Hey, kiss him goodbye (Steam) 1969
Nathan Jones (Supremes) 1971
*Natural High (Commodores) LP 1978
*Natural high (Bloodstone) 1973
Nature boy (Nat King Cole) 1948
Naughty lady of Shady Lane, The (Ames Bros.) 1954
Neanderthal man (Hotlegs) 1970
Near you (Craig) 1947
Needles and pins (Searchers) 1964
Neither one of us wants to say goodbye (Knight/Pips) 1973
Nel blu dipinto di blue—Volare (Modugno) 1958
Nel blu dipinto di blue—Volare (Dean Martin) 1958
Nel blu dipinto di blue—Volare (Rydell) 1960
Nel sole (Bano) 1967
Nessuno mi puo giudicare (Caselli) 1966
*Netherlands (Fogelberg) LP 1977
Never be anyone else but you (Ricky Nelson) 1959
Never can say goodbye (Jackson 5) 1971
*Never knew love like this before (Stephanie Mills)
Never marry a railroad man (Shocking Blue) 1970
*Never my love (Association) 1967
*Never never gonna give you up (Barry White) 1973
Never on Sunday (Don Costa) 1960
New Jole Blon (Mullican) 1947
*New kid in town (Eagles) 1976
New pretty blonde—New Jole Blon (Mullican) 1947
*News of the World (Queen) LP 1977
*New World Record (Electric Light Orchestra) 2LP 1976
New York mining disaster (Bee Gees) 1967

PRESIDENTIAL YEARS, THE (John F. Kennedy) LP 1963
*PRETENDER, THE (Brown) LP 1976
*PRETENDERS (Pretenders) LP 1980
Pretend (Marterie) 1953
Primrose Lane (Wallace) 1959
*PRINCE (Prince) LP 1979
Prisoner of love (Como) 1946
Prisoner of love (Eckstine) 1945
Prisoner's song, The (Dalhart) 1924
Problems (Everly Bros.) 1958
PRONOUNCED LEH-NERD SKIN-NERD (Lynyrd Skynyrd) LP 1973
*Proud Mary (Ike & Tina Turner) 1971
*Proud Mary (Creedence Clearwater Revival) 1969
P.S. I love you (Beatles) 1962
P.S. I love you (Hilltoppers) 1953
Puff, the magic dragon (Peter, Paul & Mary) 1963
Puppet on a string (Sandy Shaw) 1967
*Puppy love (Donny Osmond) 1972
Puppy love (Anka) 1960
Puppy song (Cassidy) 1973
Purple people eater (Wooley) 1958
*Put a little love in your heart (De Shannon) 1969
*Put your hand in the hand (Ocean) 1971
Put your head on my shoulder (Anka) 1959

Q

QUADROPHENIA (The Who) 2LP 1973
Quarter to three (Bonds) 1961
Queen of the hop (Darin) 1958
Que sera, sera—Whatever will be, will be (Doris Day) 1956
Quiet village (Denny) 1959

R

Racing with the moon (Monroe) 1941
RADIO BLOOPERS ALBUM (Schafer) 1953
*Rag doll (Four Seasons) 1964
Ragging the baby to sleep (Jolson) 1912
Rag mop (Ames Bros) 1950
Rags to riches (Bennett) 1953
RAGS TO RUFUS (Rufus) LP 1974
Ragtime cowboy Joe (Seville & Chipmunks) 1959
Rain and tears (Aphrodite's Child) 1968
Rainbow (Russ Hamilton) 1957
*Raindrops keep fallin' on my head (B. J. Thomas) 1969
Raindrops (Dee Clark) 1961
*Rain, the park and other things, The (Cowsills) 1967
*Rainy days and Mondays (Carpenters) 1971
*Rainy night in Georgia (Benton) 1969
Rain (Beatles) 1966
*Ramblin' man (Allman Brothers) 1973
Ramblin' man (Hank Williams) 1951
Ramblin' rose (Nat Cole) 1962
RAMBLIN' ROSE (Nat Cole) LP 1962
Ramona (Austin) 1928
Ramona (Blue Diamonds) 1960
RAM (Paul and Linda McCartney) 1971
Rapper's delight (Sugarhill Gang) 1979
*Rapper, The (Jaggerz) 1969
Raunchy (Justis) 1957
Rawhide (Wray) 1959
Reach out, I'll be there (Four Tops) 1966
*Reason to believe (Rod Stewart) 1971
Rebel rouser (Eddy) 1958
RED HEADED STRANGER (Nelson) LP 1975
RED OCTOPUS (Jefferson Starship) LP 1975
Red River rock (Johnny and Hurricanes) 1959

Red roses for a blue lady (Kaempfert) 1965
Red rubber ball (Cyrkle) 1966
Reflections (Ross/Supremes) 1967
Reflections of my life (Marmalade) 1969
*REJOICE (Emotions) LP 1977
Release me (Humperdinck) 1967
Release me (Esther Phillips) 1962
Remember, walkin' in the sand (Shangri-Las) 1964
Remember you're mine (Boone) 1956
Rescue me (Bass) 1965
Respect yourself (Staple Singers) 1971
*Respect (Franklin) 1967
Return to me (Dean Martin) 1958
Return to sender (Presley) 1962
*Reunited (Peaches & Herb) 1979
REVANCHE (Maffay) LP 1979
REVENGE (Cosby) 1967
Revolution (Beatles) 1968
REVOLVER (Beatles) LP 1966
*Rhinestone cowboy (Glen Campbell) 1975
RHYMES AND REASONS (Carole King) LP 1972
Rhythm of the rain (Cascades) 1963
*Rich Girl (Hall & Oates) 1976
*RICKIE LEE JONES (Rickie Lee Jones) LP 1979
Ricochet (Brewer) 1953
*Ride Captain, ride (Blues Image) 1970
Riders in the sky (Monroe) 1949
Ride (Dee Dee Sharp) 1962
*Right back where we started (Nightingale) 1976
*RIGHT ON TIME (Brothers Johnson) LP 1977
Ring of fire (Cash) 1963
Ring of gold – Wir wollen niemals (Bruhl) 1960
Ringo (Greene) 1964
RINGO (Ringo Starr) LP 1973
Rip it up (Little Richard) 1956
*RISE (Alpert) LP 1979
*Rise (Alpert) 1979
*RISQUE (Chic) LP 1979
Rivers of Babylon (Boney M) 1978
*RIVER, THE (Springsteen) LP 1980
R.M. Blues (Milton) 1945
Rock-a-bye your baby with a Dixie melody (Jolson) 1946
Rock-a-bye your baby with a Dixie melody (Jerry Lewis) 1956
Rock-a-hula baby (Presley) 1961
*ROCK AND ROLL OVER (Kiss) LP 1976
Rock and roll waltz (Kay Starr) 1956
Rock and roll – Parts 1 & 2 (Glitter) 1972
Rock and roll music (Berry) 1957
Rock around the clock (Haley & Comets) 1954
Rocket man (Elton John) 1972
Rockin' around the Christmas tree (Brenda Lee) 1958
Rockin' chair (McCrae) 1975
Rockin' little angel (Ray Smith) 1960
*Rockin' pneumonia (Rivers) 1972
Rockin' pneumonia (Huey Smith) 1957
Rockin' robin (Bobby Day) 1958
Rockin' robin (Michael Jackson) 1972
Rock island line (Donegan) 1955
*Rock me gently (Kim) 1974
Rock me (Steppenwolf) 1969
*ROCK'N ROLL MUSIC (Beatles) 2 LP 1976
ROCK OF THE WESTIES (Elton John) LP 1975
*Rock on (David Essex) 1973
*Rock steady (Aretha Franklin) 1971
*ROCKS (Aerosmith) LP 1976
*Rock the boat (Hues Corporation) 1974
*Rock with you (Michael Jackson) 1979
*Rocky mountain high (Denver) 1972
ROCKY MOUNTAIN HIGH (Denver) LP 1972

ROCKY MOUNTAIN CHRISTMAS (Denver) LP 1975
*Rock your baby (McCrae) 1974
*'ROCKY' (Soundtrack) LP 1977
Roll over Beethoven (Berry) 1956
*'Romeo and Juliet' Love Theme (Mancini) 1969
'ROMEO AND JULIET' Soundtrack LP 1969
Romeo (Petula Clark) 1961
Rose and a baby Ruth, A (G. Hamilton IV) 1956
*Rose garden (Lynn Anderson) 1970
ROSE GARDEN (Lynn Anderson) LP 1971
Rose Marie (Whitman) 1954
Rose O'Day (Kate Smith) 1941
Rose, Rose I love you (Laine/Luboff Choir) 1951
*Roses are red (Vinton) 1962
*Rose, The (Midler) 1980
'ROSE, THE' (Soundtrack) LP 1979
ROSS (DIANA) AND SUPREMES GREATEST HITS (see 'GREATEST HITS')
Round and round (Como) 1957
Roving kind, The (Mitchell) 1951
Rubber ball (Vee) 1960
*Rubberband man (Detroit Spinners) 1976
*Rubberneckin' (Presley) 1969
RUBBER SOUL (Beatles) LP 1965
Ruby, don't take your love to town (K. Rogers/First Edition) 1969
*Ruby Tuesday (Rolling Stones) 1967
Rudolph, the red-nosed reindeer (Gene Autry) 1949
RUFUS, featuring Chaka Khan (Rufus) LP 1975
RUFUSIZED (Rufus) LP 1974
Rum and Coca Cola (Andrews Sisters) 1944
Rumble (Wray) 1954
*RUMOURS (Fleetwood Mac) LP 1977
Runaround Sue (Dion) 1961
Runaway (Shannon) 1961
Running bear (Preston) 1960
*RUNNING ON EMPTY (Browne) 1977
Runnin' scared (Orbison) 1961
Run to him (Vee) 1961
*RUN WITH THE PACK (Bad Company) LP 1976
*RUST NEVER SLEEPS (Young and Crazy Horse) LP 1979

S

*Sad eyes (Robert John) 1979
Sad movies (Sue Thompson) 1961
Sad sunset (see 'Yuhi ga naiteiru')
Sail along silv'ry moon (Billy Vaughn) 1957
Sailor – Seeman (Lolita) 1960
Sam's song (Bing and Gary Crosby) 1950
San Antonio Rose (Wills) 1940
San Antonio Rose (Crosby) 1940
San Francisco, wear some flowers in your hair (McKenzie) 1967
SANTANA III (Santana) LP 1971
SANTANA (Santana) LP 1969
*Sara Smile (Hall & Oates) 1976
*Satisfaction, I can't get no (Rolling Stones) 1965
*Saturday in the park (Chicago) 1972
*'SATURDAY NIGHT FEVER' (Soundtrack) 2 LP 1977
Saturday night fish fry (Jordan) 1969
*Saturday night (Bay City Rollers) 1975
Saved by the bell (Gibb) 1969
Save the last dance for me (Drifters) 1960
Save your kisses for me (Brotherhood of Man) 1976
*Say, has anybody seen my sweet Gypsy Rose? (Orlando/Dawn) 1973
Say something sweet to your sweetheart (Stafford/MacRae) 1948
Scat in the dark (Yuki) 1969

Scende la poggia – It's raining (Morandi) 1969
Schlafe mein prinzchen (Papa Bue) 1960
School days (Berry) 1957
School is over (see 'L'ecole est fini')
*Scorpio (Coffey) 1971
Sea cruise (Frankie Ford) 1959
Sealed with a kiss (Hyland) 1962
Sea of love (Phillips) 1959
Searchin' (Coasters) 1957
*Seasons in the sun (Terry Jacks) 1974
SECOND HELPING (Lynyrd Skynyrd) LP 1974
*Second time around (Shalamar) 1979
Secret agent man (Rivers) 1966
Secret love (Doris Day) 1954
Secret love (Whitman) 1954
Secretly (Jimmy Rodgers) 1958
Seeman – Sailor (Lolita) 1960
See my baby jive (Wizzard) 1973
*See saw (Franklin) 1968
See the funny little clown (Goldsboro) 1964
See you in September (Happenings) 1966
See you later alligator (Haley) 1956
SENTIMENTAL SING ALONG (Mitch Miller) LP 1960
Sentimental me (Ames Bros) 1950
Sentimental journey (Les Brown/Doris Day) 1945
*September (Earth, Wind & Fire) 1978
*SEPTEMBER MORN (Diamond) LP 1980
September in the rain (Shearing) 1949
SERENADE (Diamond) LP 1974
*'SERGEANT PEPPER'S LONELY HEARTS CLUB BAND' (Soundtrack) 2 LP 1978
SERGEANT PEPPER'S LONELY HEARTS CLUB BAND (Beatles) 1967
SESAME STREET (Original TV Cast) LP 1970
Seven little girls sitting in the back seat (Evans) 1959
*Sexy eyes (Dr Hook) 1980
Sexy ways (Ballard) 1954
*SHADOW DANCING (Andy Gibb) LP 1978
*Shadow dancing (Andy Gibb) 1978
'Shaft' Theme (Hayes) 1971
'SHAFT' – Film soundtrack 2LP (Hayes) 1971
Shake a hand (Adams) 1953
Shake rattle and roll (Haley & Comets) 1954
Shake, shake, shake your booty (KC & Sunshine Band) 1976
*Shake your body (Jacksons) 1979
*Shake your groove thing (Peaches & Herb) 1978
Sha la la makes me happy (Green) 1974
Sha la la (Mann) 1964
*Shambala (Three Dog Night) 1973
*Shame (King) 1978
*Shannon (Gross) 1976
Share the land (Guess Who) 1970
*Sharing the night together (Dr Hook) 1978
*SHAUN CASSIDY (Shaun Cassidy) LP 1977
Sh-Boom (Crew Cuts) 1954
*She believes in me (Kenny Rogers) 1979
She'd rather be with me (Turtles) 1967
*Sheila (Roe) 1962
She loves you (Beatles) 1963
Sherry (Four Seasons) 1962
*She's a lady (Tom Jones) 1971
She's a woman (Beatles) 1964
*She's not just another woman (8th Day) 1971
She's not there (Zombies) 1964
She's not you (Presley) 1962
She (Aznavour) 1974

Shifting whispering sands (Draper) 1955

Shine (Laine) 1948

*Shining star (Earth, Wind & Fire) 1975

*Shining star (Manhattans) 1980

SHIP AHOY (O'Jays) LP 1973

Ship on a stormy sea, A (Clanton) 1959

Shoo fly pie and apple pan dowdy (Kenton) 1946

Shop around (Miracles) 1961

*Shop around (Captain & Tennille) 1976

Short fat Fanny (Larry Williams) 1956

*Short People (Newman) 1957

Shot gun boogie (Tennessee Ernie Ford) 1950

Shout (Isley Brothers) 1959

Shout (Joey Doe) 1962

*SHOWDOWN (Isley Bros) 1978

*Show must go on, The (Three Dog Night) 1974

Shrimp boats (Stafford) 1951

*Sideshow (Blue Magic) 1974

Signed sealed and delivered (Copas) 1948

Signed sealed and delivered (Wonder) 1970

*Signs (5 Man Electrical Band) 1971

Silence is golden (Tremeloes) 1967

Silent night (Crosby) 1942

Silhouettes (Diamonds) 1957

Silhouettes (Herman's Hermits) 1965

Silhouettes (The Rays) 1957

*SILK DEGREES (Scaggs) LP 1976

*Silly love songs (Wings) 1976

Silver-haired Daddy, That (Gene Autry) 1939

Silver threads and golden needles (Springfields) 1963

*SIMMONS (GENE) LP (see 'Kiss' 1978)

*Simon says (1910 Fruitgum Co.) 1968

*SIMPLE DREAMS (Ronstadt) 1977

Since I met you baby (Ivory Joe Hunter) 1957

Sincerely (McGuire Sisters) 1955

*Since you've been gone (Franklin) 1968

SING ALONG WITH MITCH (Mitch Miller) LP 1958

Sing along with Mao (Mao Tze Tung) 1966

*Sing a song (Earth, Wind & Fire) 1975

Singing Dogs 1955

SINGING NUN, THE (Singing Nun) LP 1963

Singing the blues (Mitchell) 1956

Single girl (Posey) 1966

*SINGLE MAN, A (Elton John) LP 1978

SINGLES, THE 1969–1973 (LP) (Carpenters) 1974

SING WE NOW OF CHRISTMAS (Simeone) LP 1958

*Sing (Carpenters) 1973

Sinking of the Titanic (Stoneman) 1924

Sin – It's no sin (Four Aces) 1951

Sin – It's no sin (Howard) 1951

Sittin' in the balcony (Cochran) 1957

Sittin' on the dock of the bay (Redding) 1968

Six days on the road (Dudley) 1963

Sixteen candles (Crests) 1958

Sixteen reasons (Connie Stevens) 1960

Sixteen tons (Tennessee Ernie Ford) 1955

SIXTY YEARS OF MUSIC AMERICA LOVES BEST (Various Artists) on two LPs 1959

*Skinny legs and all (Tex) 1967

*Skin tight (Ohio Players) 1974

SKIN TIGHT (Ohio Players) LP 1974

Sky high (Jigsaw) 1975

*SLEEPCATCHER (Little River Band) LP 1978

Sleep walk (Santo & Johnny) 1959

Slightly out of tune (see 'Desafinado') 1962

*Slip away (Clarence Carter) 1968

Slipping around (Whiting and Wakely) 1949

*Slippin' into darkness (War) 1971

Sloop John B (Beach Boys) 1966

*SLOWHAND (Clapton) LP 1977

Slow poke (Pee Wee King) 1951

*SLOW TRAIN COMING (Dylan) LP 1979

Slow twistin' (Checker) 1962

SLY & FAMILY STONE GREATEST HITS (Sly/Family Stone) LP 1970

*Smile a little smile (Flying Machine) 1969

Smoke gets in your eyes (Platters) 1958

*Smoke on the water (Deep Purple) 1973

Smoke, smoke, smoke that cigarette (Tex Williams) 1947

Smokie (Bill Black) 1959

*Smokin' in the boys' room (Brownsville Station) 1973

*SMOOTH TALK (Evelyn King) LP 1978

Smurf song (Father Abraham) 1978

*Snoopy versus the Red Baron (Royal Guardsmen) 1966

*Snowbird (Ann Murray) 1970

*So FULL OF LOVE (O'Jays) LP 1978

Soldier boy (Shirelles) 1962

Soldier's sweetheart, The (Jimmie Rodgers) 1927

Soley Soley (Middle of the road) 1971

So long (ABBA) 1975

So many ways (Benton) 1959

*Somebody's been sleeping (100 Proof Aged in Soul) 1970

Somebody stole my gal (Weems) 1923

*Someday we'll be together (Ross/Supremes) 1969

*SOME GIRLS (Rolling Stones) LP 1978

*Some girls (Racey) 1979

Some kinda fun (Montez) 1962

Some of these days (Sophie Tucker) 1926

*Someone saved my life tonight (Elton John) 1975

SOMETHING NEW (Beatles) LP 1964

Something special (Stone) 1960

*Something (Beatles) 1969

*Somethin' stupid (Frank and Nancy Sinatra) 1967

*Sometimes when we touch (Hill) 1977

SOMEWHERE MY LOVE (Conniff) LP 1966

So much in love (Tymes) 1963

Son, come home soon – Junge komm bald wieder (Freddy) 1962

*SONGBIRD (Streisand) LP 1978

Song from 'Moulin Rouge' Where is your heart? (Mantovani) 1953

Song from 'Moulin Rouge' Where is your heart? (Faith) 1955

SONG HITS FROM THEATRELAND (Mantovani) LP 1955

Song of joy (see 'Himno a la alegria')

*SONG OF JOY (Captain & Tennille) LP 1976

*'SONG REMAINS THE SAME' (Soundtrack) 2 LP 1976

SONGS FOR SINGERS (Rusty Warren) LP 1958

SONGS HE MADE FAMOUS (Jolson) EP 1950

*SONGS IN THE KEY OF LIFE (Wonder) 2 LP 1976

SONGS OF POPE JOHN PAUL 2ND IN POLAND (Pope John Paul) LP 1979

*Song sung blue (Diamond) 1972

Sonny boy (Jolson) 1928 & 1946

*SON OF A SON OF A SAILOR (Buffett) LP 1978

Son of my father (Chicory Tip) 1972

So rare (Jimmy Dorsey) 1957

Sorry, I ran all the way home (Impalas) 1959

*Sorry seems to be the hardest word (Elton John) 1976

S.O.S. (ABBA) 1975

*Soul and inspiration (Righteous Bros) 1966

*Soulful strut (Young-Holt Unlimited) 1968

*Soul man (Sam and Dave) 1967

*SOUL SEARCHING (Average White Band) LP 1976

SOUND MAGAZINE (Partridge Family) LP 1971

'SOUND OF MUSIC', THE (Original stage cast) LP 1960

'SOUND OF MUSIC', THE (Film soundtrack) LP 1965

*Sound of Philadelphia – T.S.O.P. (M.F.S.B.) 1973

*Sound of silence, The (Simon and Garfunkel) 1965

*SOUNDS . . . AND STUFF LIKE THAT (Quincy Jones) LP 1978

South America, take it away (Crosby and Andrews Sisters) 1946

*Southern nights (Campbell) 1977

SOUTH OF THE BORDER (Alpert) LP 1965

'SOUTH PACIFIC' (Film track) LP 1958

'SOUTH PACIFIC' (Stage show) LP 1949

South Street (Orlons) 1963

*Space race (Billy Preston) 1973

Spacer (Sheila & B. Devotion) 1979

Spaniard that blighted my life, The (Jolson) 1913

Spaniard that blighted my life, The (Jolson–Crosby) 1947

Spanish eyes (Martino) 1965

Spanish flea (Alpert) 1965

*Spanish Harlem (Franklin) 1971

*Special lady (Ray, Goodman & Brown) 1980

Speedy Gonzalez (Boone) 1962

*Spiders and snakes (Jim Stafford) 1973

*Spill the wine (Eric Burdon & War) 1970

*Spinning wheel (Blood, Sweat & Tears) 1969

*SPIRIT (Denver) LP 1976

*Spirit in the sky (Greenbaum) 1970

SPIRIT OF AMERICA (Beach Boys) 2LP 1975

*SPIRITS HAVING FLOWN (Bee Gees) LP 1979

*SPITFIRE (Jefferson Starship) LP 1976

Splish splash (Darin) 1958

Spooky (Classics IV) 1967

S.R.O. (Alpert) LP 1966

Stagger Lee (Lloyd Price) 1959

Stand by your man (Wynette) 1968

Standing in the shadows of love (Four Tops) 1966

*Stand Tall (Cummings) 1976

*STANLEY (Paul) LP (see 'Kiss' 1978)

Stardust (Artie Shaw) 1940

Stardust (Billy Ward & Dominoes) 1957

*STARDUST (Nelson) LP 1978

*'Star is born, A' – Love Theme (Streisand) 1976

*'STAR IS BORN, A' (Soundtrack) LP 1976

STARS FOR US (Various Artists) LP 1973

Starting all over again (Mel & Tim) 1972

*Starting over (Lennon) 1980

Start movin' (Mineo) 1957

*'STAR WARS' AND OTHER GALACTIC FUNK (Meco) LP 1977

*'Star Wars' Theme (Meco) 1977

*'STAR WARS' (Soundtrack) 2 LP 1977

Stasera mi butto (Roberts) 1967

*Stay awhile (The Bells) 1971

*Stayin' alive (Bee Gees) 1977

Stay (Maurice Williams) 1960

Steal away (Foley) 1950

St George and the Dragonet (Freberg) 1953

*Stick-up (Honey Cone) 1971

STICKY FINGERS (Rolling Stones) LP 1971

STILL MORE SING ALONG (Mitch Miller) LP 1959

STING, THE (Film Soundtrack) LP 1974

Stoned love (Supremes) 1970

*Stoned soul picnic (Fifth Dimension) 1968

Stood up (Ricky Nelson) 1957

Stop in the name of love (Supremes) 1965

Stop, stop, stop (Hollies) 1966

*Stormy (Classic IV) 1968

STRAIGHT SHOOTER (Bad Company) LP 1975

Stranger in Midosuji (see 'Ame no Midosuji')

Stranger in paradise (Four Acres) 1954

Stranger in paradise (Tony Bennett) 1953

*STRANGER IN TOWN (Seger) LP 1978

*Stranger on the shore (Acker Bilk) 1961

Strangers in the night (Frank Sinatra) 1966

*STRANGER, THE (Joel) LP 1977

STRAUSS WALTZES (Mantovani) LP 1953

Strawberry fields forever (Beatles) 1967

*Strawberry letter No 23 (Brothers Johnson) 1977

*Streak, The (Ray Stevens) 1974

*STREET SURVIVORS (Lynyrd Skynyrd) LP 1977

*STREISAND SUPERMAN (Streisand) LP 1977

Stripper, The (David Rose) 1962

Strip polka (Kay Kyser) 1942

Stroll, The (Diamonds) 1958

Stuck in the middle with you (Stealers Wheel) 1973

Stuck on you (Presley) 1960

'STUDENT PRINCE' AND OTHER GREAT MUSICAL COMEDY SONGS (Lanza) LP 1954

*Stumblin' in (Quatro & Norman) 1978

STUNDE DER STARS (LP) 1969

Substitute (Clout) 1978

Suddenly there's a valley (Gogi Grant) 1955

Sugar baby love (Rubettes) 1974

Sugar blues (McCoy) 1936

Sugarbush (Laine/Day) 1952

Sugar lips (Hirt) 1964

*Sugar shack (Gilmer) 1963

*Sugar, sugar (Archies) 1969

Sugartime (McGuire Sisters) 1958

*Sugar town (Nancy Sinatra) 1966

Sukiyaki (Sakamoto) 1962

SUMMER BREEZE (Seals & Crofts) LP 1972

*Summer in the city (Lovin' Spoonful) 1966

*Summer nights (Travolta & Newton-John) 1978

*Summer place, A (Theme) (Percy Faith) 1960

*SUMMERTIME DREAM (Lightfoot) LP 1976

*Summer (War) 1976

Summit Ridge Drive (Artie Shaw) 1940

Sunday, Monday or always (Crosby) 1943

Sunday will never be the same (Spanky/Our Gang) 1967

*Sundown (Lightfoot) 1974

SUNDOWN (Lightfoot) LP 1974

*Sunny (Hebb) 1966

Sunrise serenade (Glenn Miller) 1939

*Sunshine on my shoulders (Denver) 1974

*Sunshine of your love (The Cream) 1967

Sunshine Superman (Donovan) 1966

TOULOUSE STREET (Doobie Bros) LP 1972
Tous les garcons et les filles (Hardy) 1962
Town without pity (Pitney) 1961
TOYS IN THE ATTIC (Aerosmith) 1975
*T.P. (Pendergrass) LP 1980
Traces (Classics IV) 1969
Tracks of my tears (Miracles) 1965
Tracy (Cuff Links) 1969
Traffic jam (Artie Shaw) 1939
*Tragedy (Bee Gees) 1979
Tragedy (Wayne) 1959
Tramontana, La (Antoine) 1968
*Trapped by a thing called love (La-Salle) 1971
*Travellin' man (Ricky Nelson) 1961
*Travellin' band (Creedence Clearwater Revival) 1970
Treasure of love (McPhatter) 1956
*Treat her like a lady (Cornelius Bros/Sister Rose) 1971
Treat me nice (Presley) 1957
Tree in the meadow, A (Margaret Whiting) 1948
TRES HOMBRES (Z. Z. Top) LP 1973
TRILOGY (Emerson, Lake, Palmer) LP 1972
*TRIUMPH (Jacksons) LP 1980
*Troglodyte (J. Castor Bunch) 1972
True love, true love (Drifters) 1960
True love ways (Peter & Gordon) 1965
True love (Grace Kelly/Bing Crosby) 1956
TRYIN' TO GET THE FEELIN' (Barry Manilow) LP 1975
*Tryin' to love two (Bell) 1977
Try me - I need you (James Brown) 1958
*T.S.O.P. (M.F.S.B.) 1973
Tubby the Tuba (Jory) 1946
Tubular bells (Mike Oldfield) 1974
TUBULAR BELLS (Mike Oldfield) LP 1973
TUMBLEWEED CONNECTION (Elton John) LP 1970
Turn around, look at me (Vogues) 1968
*Turn back the hands of time (Davis) 1970
*TURN OF A FRIENDLY CARD, THE (Parsons Project) LP 1980
Turn, turn, turn (Byrds) 1965
*TUSK (Fleetwood Mac) 2 LP 1979
Tutti frutti (Little Richard) 1957
Tuxedo Junction (Glenn Miller) 1940
T'was the night before Christmas (Fred Waring) 1942
T'WAS THE NIGHT BEFORE CHRISTMAS (Fred Waring) - Album 1946
Tweedle dee (Georgia Gibbs) 1955
Tweedle dee, Tweedle-dum (Middle of the Road) 1971
Tweedle dee (LaVern Baker) 1955
*Twelfth of never (Donny Osmond) 1973
Twelfth Street Rag (Pee Wee Hunt) 1948
Twenty four hours from Tulsa (Pitney) 1963
TWENTY GOLDEN GREATS (Campbell) LP 1976
TWENTY GOLDEN GREATS (Beach Boys) LP 1976
Twenty six miles (Four Preps) 1957
TWENTY TWO (22) EXPLOSIVE HITS - Vol. 2 (Various artists) LP 1972
Twilight time (Three Suns) 1950
Twilight time (Platters) 1958
*TWIN SONS OF DIFFERENT MOTHERS (Fogelberg & Weisberg) LP 1978
Twist and shout (Isley Bros) 1962
Twist and shout (Beatles) 1963
TWIST AND SHOUT (Beatles) EP 1963
Twistin' the night away (Sam Cooke) 1962
Twist, The (Checker) 1960
Twist, The (Ballard) 1960
Two black crows (Moran and Mack) 1926

Two different worlds (Rondo) 1956
Two faces have I (Christie) 1963
*TWO FOR THE SHOW (Kansas) LP 1978
*2 HOT (Peaches & Herb) LP 1979
Two little Italians - Zwei kleiner Italien (Connie Froboess) 1962
Two little boys (Rolf Harris) 1969
Two lovers (Wells) 1963
*Two out of three ain't bad (Meat Loaf) 1978
Tzena, Tzena, Tzena (Jenkins and Weavers) 1950

U

Ue O Mui Te Amo (see 'Sakiyaki') (Sakamoto) 1962
Una lacrima sul viso (Bobby Solo) 1964
Una Paloma Blanca (Baker Selection) 1975
Unchained melody (Baxter) 1955
Unchained melody (Hibbler) 1955
*Uncle Albert (Paul & Linda McCartney) 1971
Undecided (Ames Bros and Les Brown) 1951
*Undercover angel (O'Day) 1977
Under foreign stars - Unter fremden sternen (Freddy) 1960
Under the moon of love (Showaddywaddy) 1976
*UNDER WRAPS (Shaun Cassidy) LP 1978
UN HOMME et une FEMME Soundtrack LP 1966
Unpermitted love (see 'Kinijirtareta koi')
*UNPREDICTABLE (Natalie Cole) LP 1977
Unter fremden sternen - Under foreign stars (Freddy) 1960
*Until you come back to me (Franklin) 1973
*Up around the bend (Creedence Clearwater Revival) 1970
Up on the roof (Drifters) 1963
Up the ladder to the roof (Supremes) 1970
Up tight (Little Stevie Wonder) 1965
UP TO DATE (Partridge Family) LP 1971
Up, up and away (Fifth Dimension) 1967
*'URBAN COWBOY' (Soundtrack) LP 1980
*Use me (Bill Withers) 1972
*Use-ta be my gal (O'Jays) 1978

V

*Valleri (Monkees) 1968
Valley of the Dolls - Theme (Warwick) 1967
*VAN HALEN (Van Halen) LP 1978
*VAN HALEN 2 (Van Halen) LP 1979
Vaya con Dios (Paul & Ford) 1953
Vehicle (Ides of March) 1970
VENUS AND MARS (Wings/McCartney) LP 1975
Venus (Avalon) 1959
*Venus (Shocking Blue) 1969
Vergangen, vergessen, voruber (Freddy) 1960
Vesti la giubba - On with the motley (from 'Pagliacci') (Caruso) 1903
Vie en rose, La (Edith Piaf) 1950
Viens danser le Twist (Hallyday) 1961
VILLAGE PEOPLE (Village People) LP 1977
Viva Espana (Sylvia) 1974
Viva Las Vegas (Presley) 1964
*VOICES (Hall & Oates) LP 1980
Volare - Nel blu di pinto di blu (Dean Martin) 1958
Volare - Nel blu di pinto di blu (Modugno) 1958
Volare - Nel blu di pinto di blu (Rydell) 1960

W

Wabash blues (Isham Jones) 1921
Wabash cannon ball (Acuff) 1942

Wade in the water (Ramsey Lewis Trio) 1966
Wah-Watusi, The (Orlons) 1962
Waitin' in school (Ricky Nelson) 1957
Wake up little Susie (Everly Bros) 1957
Walk away from love (Ruffin) 1975
Walk, don't run (Ventures) 1960 & 1964
Walking back to happiness (Shapiro) 1961
Walking in rhythm (Blackbyrds) 1975
*Walkin' in the rain with the one I love (Love Unlimited) 1972
Walk in the Black Forest, A (Jankowski) 1965
Walk in the park, A (Straker Band) 1979
Walkin' the floor over you (Tubb) 1941
Walkin' to New Orleans (Domino) 1960
Walk like a man (Four Seasons) 1963
Walk on by (Warwick) 1964
Walk on by (Van Dyke) 1961
Walk right back (Everly Bros) 1961
Walk right in (Rooftop Singers) 1963
WALLS AND BRIDGES (Lennon) LP 1974
*WALL, THE (Pink Floyd) 1979 2 LP
Wanderer, The (Dion) 1961
*Wanderer, The (Summer) 1980
Wand'rin' star (Marvin) 1970
Wang Wang Blues (Busse) 1920
*Want Ads (Honey Cone) 1971
Wanted (Como) 1954
War (Edwin Starr) 1970
*WANTED - THE OUTLAWS (Jennings, Nelson, Colter & Glaser) LP 1976
War Child (Jethro Tull) LP 1974
WAR OF THE WORLDS (Wayne) 2 LP 1978
WAR - LIVE (War) LP 1974
*Wasted days and wasted nights (Fender) 1975
Watching Scotty grow (Goldsboro) 1970
Waterloo (Jackson) 1959
Waterloo (ABBA) 1974
WATERLOO (ABBA) LP 1974
Way down yonder in New Orleans (Cannon) 1959
*Way down (Presley) 1977
*Way I want to touch you, The (Captain & Tennille) 1975
*WAYLON AND WILLIE (Jennings & Nelson) LP 1978
Way of women (see 'Onna no michi')
Wayward wind, The (Gogi Grant) 1956
*Way we were, The (Streisand) 1973
WAY WE WERE, THE (Streisand) LP 1974
*We are family (Sister Sledge) 1979
*WE ARE FAMILY (Sister Sledge) LP 1979
*We are the champions (Queen) 1977
Wear my ring round your neck (Presley) 1958
Wear my ring (Vincent) 1957
*We can work it out (Beatles) 1965
*Wedding bell blues (Fifth Dimension) 1969
Wedding samba (Ros) 1949
Wedding, The (Julie Rogers) 1964
We don't talk any more (Cliff Richard) 1979
*WEEKEND IN L.A. (Benson) LP 1978
*WEEKEND WARRIORS (Nugent) LP 1978
We got love (Rydell) 1959
WEIHNACHTEN MIT HEINTJE (Heintje) LP 1968
Weisse rosen aus Athene (Mouskouri) 1961
WELCOME BACK MY FRIENDS (Emerson, Lake, Palmer) LP 1974
*Welcome back (Sebastian) 1976
WELCOME TO THE L.B.J. RANCH (Doud/Robin) LP 1965

We'll sing in the sunshine (Garnett) 1964
We love you (Rolling Stones) 1967
*WE MUST BELIEVE IN MAGIC (Gayle) LP 1977
*We're all alone (Coolidge) 1977
*We're an American band (Grand Funk Railroad) 1973
'WEST SIDE STORY' (Film soundtrack) LP 1961
'WEST SIDE STORY' (Original stage cast) LP 1957
*WET (Streisand) LP 1979
We've only just begun (Carpenters) 1970
We will make love (Russ Hamilton) 1957
We will never part—Wir wollen niemals (Bruhl) 1960
*We will rock you (Queen) 1977
*What a fool believes (Doobie Brothers) 1979
What am I living for? (Willis) 1958
What a wonderful world (Armstrong) 1967
Whatcha see is whatcha get (Dramatics) 1971
What'd I say? (Charles) 1959
What do you want to make those eyes at me for? (Emile Ford) 1959
Whatever will be, will be - Que sera sera (Doris Day) 1956
What goes on (Beatles) 1966
What in the world's come over you (Jack Scott) 1960
What kind of fool am I? (Sammy Davis) 1962
WHAT NOW, MY LOVE (Alpert) LP 1966
What's going on (Gaye) 1971
What's new pussycat? (Jones) 1965
What the world needs now is love (Clay) 1971
WHAT WERE ONCE VICES ARE NOW HABITS (Doobie Bros) LP 1974
Wheel of fortune (Kay Starr) 1952
Wheels (Billy Vaughn) 1961
Wheels (String-a-long) 1961
*When a child is born (Mathis) 1976
*When a man loves a woman (Sledge) 1966
*WHEN I DREAM (Gayle) LP 1978
*When I need you (Sayer) 1977
When my blue moon turns to gold (Walker and Sullivan) 1941
When the saints go marching in (Sheridan/Beatles) 1961
When the swallows come back to Capistrano (Boone) 1957
*When will I see you again (Three Degrees) 1974
When you're hot, you're hot (Jerry Reed) 1971
*When you're in love with a beautiful woman (Dr Hook) 1979
When you're smiling (Laine) 1948
When you were sweet 16 (Como) 1947
When? (Kalin Twins) 1958
Where did our love go (Supremes) 1964
Where do I begin? (see 'Theme from "Love Story"')
Where do you come from? (Presley) 1962
*Where is the love (Flack/Hathaway) 1972
Where is your heart? - song from 'Moulin Rouge' (Faith) 1953
Where is your heart? - song from 'Moulin Rouge' (Mantovani) 1953
Where the boys are (Connie Francis) 1961
*Which way you goin' Billy? (Poppy Family) 1969
Whiffenpoof song (Crosby and Waring) 1947
*Whip it (Devo) 1980
WHIPPED CREAM AND OTHER DELIGHTS (Alpert) LP 1965
Whispering hope (Stafford/McRae) 1949

Whispering (Whiteman) 1920
*Whispers, The (Whispers) LP 1979
White Christmas (Crosby) 1942
White Christmas (Freddy Martin) 1942
White Christmas (Sinatra) 1944
White dove (see 'Una paloma blanca')
White room (Cream) 1968
White rose of Athens – Weisse rosen aus Athene (Mouskouri) 1961
Whiter shade of pale, A (Procol Harum) 1967
White silver sands (Bill Black) 1960
White sport coat and a pink carnation (Robbins) 1957
*Who Are You? (The Who) LP 1978
Whole lotta love (Led Zeppelin) 1969
Whole lotta lovin' (Domino) 1958
Whole lotta shakin' goin' on (Jerry Lee Lewis) 1957
*Who's making love (Johnny Taylor) 1968
Who's sorry now? (Connie Francis) 1958
Who? (Olsen) 1926
Who wouldn't love you? (Kay Kyser) 1942
Why, baby, why? (Boone) 1957
Why can't we live together? (Timmy Thomas) 1972
Why can't we be friends? (War) 1975
Why do fools fall in love? (Teenagers and Lymon) 1956
Why don't they understand? (G. Hamilton IV) 1958
Why don't you believe me? (Joni James) 1952
Why don't you do right (Peggy Lee/Benny Goodman) 1942
Why Is There Air? (Cosby) LP 1965
*Why me, Lord? (Kristofferson) 1973
Why? (Avalon) 1959
*Wichita lineman (Glen Campbell) 1968
Wight is Wight (Delpec) 1970
Wig-Wam Bam (Sweet) 1972
*Wild and Crazy Guy, A (Martin) LP 1978
*Wild Cherry (Wild Cherry) LP 1976
*Wild fire (Murphy) 1975
Wild in the country (Presley) 1961
Wild one (Rydell) 1950
Wild side of life (Hank Thompson) 1952
Wildwood flower (Carter Family) 1928
*Willie and Family 'Live' (Nelson) LP 1978
*Will it go round in circles? (Billy Preston) 1973
Willy and the Poor Boys (Creedence Clearwater Revival) LP 1969
Will you be staying after Sunday? (Peppermint Rainbow) 1968
Will you love me tomorrow? (Shirelles) 1960
*Winchester Cathedral (New Vaudeville Band) 1966
Windsong (Denver) LP 1975
*Windy (Association) 1967
*Winelight (Washington Jr) LP 1980
*Wings at the Speed of Sound (Wings) LP 1976
*Wings Over America (Wings) 3 LP 1976
Winter wonderland (Lombardo and Andrews Sisters) 1946
Wipe out (Surfaris) 1963

Wir wollen riemals anseinandergeh'n (Bruhl) 1960
Wish you were here (Fisher) 1952
Wish You Were Here (Pink Floyd) LP 1975
Witch doctor (Seville) 1958
Witch, The (The Rattles) 1970
With a girl like you (Troggs) 1966
With my eyes wide open I'm dreaming (Patti Page) 1949
*Without love (Tom Jones) 1969
*Without you (Nilsson) 1971
With the Beatles (Beatles) LP 1963
Wolverton Mountain (Claude King) 1962
*Woman in love (Streisand) 1980
Woman to woman (Shirley Brown) 1974
*Woman, woman (Union Gap) 1967
*Women and Children First (Van Halen) LP 1980
Wonderful land (The Shadows) 1972
Wonderfulness (Crosby) LP 1966
Wonderful time up there, A (Boone) 1958
Wonderful, wonderful (Mathis) 1956
Wonderful world (Cooke) 1960
Wonderful world (Herman's Hermits) 1965
Wonderland by night (Kaempfert) 1960
*Wonder of you, The (Presley) 1970
Woodchoppers' Ball, At the (Herman) 1939
Wooden heart (Dowell) 1961
Wooden heart (Presley) 1960
'Woodstock' (Various artists) 3 LP Soundtrack 1970
Woody Woodpecker song (Kay Kyser) 1948
*Wooly bully (Sam the Sham and Pharaohs) 1965
Words (Bee Gees) 1968
Workin' for the man (Orbison) 1962
*Working my way back to you (Spinners) 1979
Work with me, Annie (Ballard) 1953
*World is a ghetto, The (War) 1972
World is a Ghetto, The (War) LP 1972
World is waiting for the sunrise, The (Paul & Ford) 1961
World of our own, A (Seekers) 1965
*Worlds Away (Pablo Cruise) LP 1978
World Star Festival (Various Artists) LP 1969
World without love (Peter and Gordon) 1964
World (Bee Gees) 1967
*Worst that could happen, The (Brooklyn Bridge) 1968
Would I love you (Patti Page) 1951
Wreck of the old 97, The (Dalhart) 1924
Wuthering Heights (Kate Bush) 1978

Wynette, Tammy 'Greatest Hits' LP 1969
Wyoming (Mantovani) 1951

X

*'Xanadu' (Soundtrack) LP 1980

Y

Yakety yak (Coasters) 1958
Ya-Ya (Lee Dorsey) 1961
*Year of the Cat (Al Stewart) LP 1976

Yeh, yeh (Fame and Blue Flames) 1964
Yellow polka dot bikini, Itsy bitsy teenie weenie (Hyland) 1960
Yellow river (Christie) 1970
Yellow rose of Texas, The (Mitch Miller) 1955
*Yellow submarine (Beatles) 1966
'Yellow Submarine' Soundtrack (Beatles) LP 1968
*Yes, I'm ready (De Sario & KC) 1979
Yes it is (Beatles) 1965
Yes sir, I can boogie (Baccara) 1979
Yesterday Man (Andrews) 1965
Yesterday . . . and Today (Beatles) LP 1966
*Yesterday once more (Carpenters) 1973
*Yesterday (Paul McCartney of the Beatles) 1965
Yester me, yester you, yesterday (Wonder) 1969
Yingle bells (Yorgesson) 1949
*Y.M.C.A. (Village People) 1978
Yoake – no skat – Scat in the dark (Yuki) 1969
*You ain't seen nothing yet 'Bachman-Turner Overdrive) 1974
You always hurt the one you love (Mills Bros) 1944
*You are everything (Stylistics) 1971
You are my destiny (Anka) 1958
You are the sunshine of my life (Wonder) 1973
You belong to me (Jo Stafford) 1952
You call everybody darling (J. Smith/Clark Sisters) 1947
You can't be true dear (Griffin/Wayne) 1948
You can't do that (Beatles) 1964
You can't hurry love (Supremes) 1966
You can't sit down. Part 2 (Upchurch) 1961
*You Can Tune a Piano But You Can't Tuna Fish (REO Speedwagon) LP 1978
*You don't bring me flowers (Diamond & Streisand) 1978
*You Don't Bring Me Flowers (Diamond) LP 1978
You don't have to say you love me (Presley) 1970
*You don't have to be a star (McCoo & Davis) 1976
You don't have to say you love me (Springfield) 1966
You don't know me (Charles) 1962
You don't know (Shapiro) 1961
You don't own me (Gore) 1963
*You Get What You Play For (REO Speedwagon) LP 1977
*You gonna make me love somebody else (Jones Girls) 1979
You got what it takes (Johnson) 1959
You haven't done nothin' (Wonder) 1974
You keep me hanging on (Supremes) 1966
*You Light Up My Life (Johnny Mathis) LP 1978
*You light up my life (Debby Boone) 1977
*You Light Up My Life (Debby Boone) LP 1977
You'll never know (Haymes) 1943
*You'll never find another love like mine (Rawls) 1976

You made me love you (Al Jolson) 1946
You made me love you (Harry James) 1941
*You make me feel brand new (Stylistics) 1974
*You make me feel like dancing (Sayer) 1976
*You needed me (Murray) 1978
Young at heart (Sinatra) 1953
Young blood (Coasters) 1957
*Young girl (Union Gap) 1968
Young love (Sonny James) 1957
Young love (Tab Hunter) 1957
Young ones, The (Cliff Richard) 1962
*You ought to be with me (Al Green) 1972
Your cheatin' heart (Joni James) 1953
Your cheatin' heart (Hank Williams) 1952
You're a big girl now (Stylistics) 1971
You really got me (Kinks) 1964
You're breaking my heart (Damone) 1949
*You're having my baby (Anka) 1974
*You're in my heart (Rod Stewart) 1977
*You're my soul and inspiration (Righteous Bros) 1966
You're my world (Cilla Black) 1964
*You're sixteen (Burnette) 1960
*You're sixteen (Ringo Starr) 1973
You're so fine (Falcons) 1959
*You're so vain (Carly Simon) 1972
You're the devil in disguise (Presley) 1963
You're the first, the last, my everything (White) 1974
*You're the one that I want (Travolta and Newton-John) 1978
Your good thing (Rawls) 1969
*Your Mama don't dance (Loggins & Messina) 1972
Yours (Vera Lynn) 1952
You said you loved me (Domino) 1953
You send me (Cooke) 1957
*You sexy thing (Hot Chocolate) 1975
*You should be dancing (Bee Gees) 1976
You shouldn't cry (see 'Du sollst nicht weinen')
*You take my breath away (Rex Smith) 1979
You've got a friend (James Taylor) 1971
You've got to move two mountains (Johnson) 1960
You've lost that lovin' feelin' (Righteous Bros) 1964
*You've made me so very happy (Blood, Sweat and Tears) 1969
You've really got a hold on me (Miracles) 1962
You were made for me (Freddie and Dreamers) 1963
You were on my mind (We Five) 1965
You will never miss your Mother until she is gone (Carson) 1923
You you you (Ames Bros) 1953
*Yo Yo (Osmonds) 1971
Yuhi ga naiteriru (Spiders) 1966
*Yummy Yummy (Ohio Express) 1968

Z

Zenyatta Mondatta (Police) LP 1980
Zwei kleiner Italiener – Two little Italians (Froboess) 1962

Artist Index 1903–1980: Section 1

An index to artists appearing in theatre-cast, film-soundtrack and collective-artist million-selling albums is given separately (page 530).

A

ABBA 1974, 1975, 1976, 1977, 1978, 1979, 1980
AC/DC 1979, 1980
Acuff, Roy 1942
Adamo 1969
Aerosmith 1973, 1974, 1975, 1976, 1977, 1978
Air Supply 1980
Airedales (*see* Roberts 1967)
Akens, Jewel 1965
Alabama 1980
Albert Morris 1975
Alberts, Al (*see* Four Aces 1951)
Alive'n Kickin' 1970
Allen, Rex 1953
Allisons, The 1961
Allman Brothers, 1972, 1973
Alpert, Herb 1962, 1965, 1966, 1968, 1979
Alphabeta Singers (*see* Cohen)
American Breed 1967
Americans, The (*see* Jay & Americans)
America, 1972, 1975
Ames Brothers 1950, 1951, 1953, 1954, 1957
Andersen, Lale 1939
Anderson, Leroy 1951
Anderson, Lynn 1970, 1971
Andrews Sisters 1937, 1944 (*see also* Crosby 1943, 1944, 1946 and Lombardo 1946)
Andrews, Chris 1965
Andrews, Patty 1949
Angels, The 1963
Animals, The 1964, 1966
Anka, Paul 1957, 1958, 1959, 1960, 1964, 1974
Anthony (see Little Anthony)
Anthony, Richard 1962
Antoine 1968
Aphrodite's Child 1968
Apollo II Astronauts 1969
Applebaum, Stan (see Vinton 1963, Francis 1960)
Archies, The 1969
Arden, Toni 1968
Argent 1972
Armstrong, Louis 1964, 1967
Arnold, Eddy 1947, 1948, 1951, 1955, 1974
Arthey, Johnny (*see* Rogers 1964)
Association, The 1966, 1967
Astaire, Fred 1951
Atlanta Rhythm Section 1978
Atwell, Winifred 1952, 1953, 1954
Austin, Gene 1927, 1928
Autry, Gene 1939, 1947, 1949, 1950
Avalon, Frankie 1958, 1959
Average White Band 1974, 1976
Ayres, Mitchell (*see* Como 1956)
Aznavour, Charles 1963, 1974
Azpiazu, Don 1931

B

Babbitt, Harry (*see* Kyser 1948)
Baccara 1977
Bacharach, Burt (*see* Warwick 1963, 1964; Vinton 1963 and Pitney 1962, 1963)
Bachelors, The 1964
Bachman-Turner Overdrive 1974
Bad Company, 1974, 1975, 1976, 1979
Badfinger 1970, 1971
Baez, Joan 1971, 1975
Baker (George) Selection 1970, 1975
Baker, Bonnie (*see* Tucker 1939)
Baker, LaVern 1955, 1957, 1959
Ballard, Hank 1954, 1960
Ball, Kenny 1961
Ball, Thalben (*see* Lough 1927)

Bano, Al 1967
Barber, Chris 1959
Barbour, Dave (*see* Peggy Lee 1948)
Bare, Bobby 1963, 1964
Barron, Blue 1949
Barry, Joe 1961
Barry, Len 1965
Barth, Belle 1960
Barton, Eileen 1950
Bassey, Shirley 1964
Bass, Fontella 1965
Baxter, Les 1955, 1956 (*see also* Cole 1950, 1951)
Bay City Rollers 1975
B. Devotion (*see* Sheila 1979)
Beach Boys 1963, 1964, 1965, 1966, 1974, 1975, 1976
Bear, Edward 1972
Beatles, The 1962, 1963, 1964, 1965, 1966, 1967, 1968, 1969, 1970, 1973, 1976, 1977 (*see also* Sheridan 1961)
Bechet, Sidney 1949
Bee Gees, The 1967, 1968, 1970, 1971, 1975, 1976, 1977, 1978, 1979
Beginning of the End 1973
Belafonte, Harry 1956, 1957, 1959
Bell & James 1979
Bell (Archie) & The Drells 1968
Bells, The 1971
Bell, Vincent 1970
Bell, William 1977
Belmonts, The (*see* Dion 1959)
Benatar, Pat 1979, 1980
Bendix, Ralf 1961
Beneke, Tex (*see* Miller 1941, 1952)
Bennett, Tony 1951, 1953, 1957, 1962
Benson, George 1976, 1977, 1978, 1980
Benton, Brook 1959, 1961, 1969 (*see also* Washington 1960)
Berry, Chuck 1955, 1956, 1957, 1958, 1972
Bertelmann, Fred 1958
Big Apple Band (*see* Murphy 1976)
Big Brother & Holding Co 1968
Bilk, Acker 1961
Billie & Lillie 1957
Bimbo Jet 1974
Birkin (Jane) & Gainsbourg (Serge) 1969
Bishop, Elvin 1976
Black Sabbath 1970, 1971
Black, Bill 1959, 1960
Blackbyrds 1975
Black, Cilla 1964
Black, Jeanne 1960
Black, Roy 1966, 1969
Blaine, Marcia 1962
Bland, Bobby 1963
Blondie 1978, 1979, 1980
Blood, Sweat & Tears 1969, 1970, 1971
Bloodstone 1973
Blow, Kurtis 1980
Blue Caps (*see* Vincent 1956, 1957)
Blue Comets (*see* Yoshikawa)
Blue Diamonds, The 1960
Blue Flames (*see* Fame)
Blue Image 1970
Blue Magic 1974
Blue Notes (*see* Melvin 1972, 1973)
Blue Oyster Cult 1976
Blue Swede 1973
Blues Brothers 1978
Bob Crewe Generation 1966
Bonds, Gary 1961
Bonney, Graham 1966
Boney M 1976, 1978
Booker, T. 1962
Boone, Daniel 1972
Boone, Debby 1977
Boone, Pat 1955, 1956, 1957, 1958, 1961, 1962
Borelly, Jean Claude 1974
Bostic, Earl 1952
Boston 1976, 1978
Botkin, Perry (*see* De Vorzo 1976)

Botkin, Perry (*see* Crosby 1949)
Bowen, Jimmy 1957
Bowie, David 1975, 1976
Box Tops, The 1967, 1968
Boyce (Tommy) & Hart (Bobby) 1967
Boyd, Jimmy 1952 (*see also* Laine 1953)
Bradford, Alex 1954
Brass Construction 1976
Bravos, Los 1966
Brazilians, The (*see* Lee 1948)
Brazos Valley Boys (*see* Thompson 1952)
Bread, 1970, 1971, 1972
Brel, Jacques 1977
Brewer, Teresa 1950, 1952, 1953, 1955, 1956
Bridges, Alicia 1978
Brighouse & Rastrick Band 1977
Brighter Side of Darkness, The 1972
Britt, Elton 1942
Brooklyn Bridge 1968
Brooklyn Dreams (*see* Summer 1979)
Brossart, Naomi (*see* Meader 1962)
Brotherhood of Man 1976
Brothers Four, 1960
Brothers Johnson (*see* Johnson Brothers)
Brown (*see* Ray, Goodman & Brown, 1980)
Brown, Arthur 1968
Brown, Charles 1960
Brown, Chuck 1979
Browne, Jackson 1976, 1977
Brown, James 1956, 1958, 1965, 1967, 1971, 1972, 1974
Brown, Les 1945, 1949 (*see also* Ames Bros 1952)
Brown, Peter 1977
Brown, Roy 1950
Brown, Ruth 1952, 1953, 1957
Brown, Shirley 1974
Browns, The 1959
Brownsville Station 1973
Brubeck, Dave 1961
Bruhl, Heidi 1960
Bryant, Anita 1960
B. T. Express 1974, 1975
Buchanan 1956
Buckinghams, The 1966
Bue, Papa 1960
Buffalo Springfield 1967
Buffett, Jimmy 1977, 1978
Burdon (Eric) & War 1970
Burnette, Johnny 1960
Burr, Henry 1918
Bush, Kate 1978
Busse, Henry 1920
Butler, Daws (*see* Freberg 1953)
Butler, Jerry 1969, 1971
Butterfield, Billy (*see* Whiting 1944)
Byrd, Charlie (*see* Getz 1962)
Byrds, The 1965
Byrnes, Edd 1959

C

Call of the North Orchestra (*see* Landry 1922)
Calloway, Cab 1939, 1931
Calvert, Eddie 1953
Campbell, Glen 1968, 1969, 1971, 1975, 1976, 1977
Canned Heat 1970
Cannon, Freddy 1959, 1962, 1965
Captain & Tennille 1975, 1976, 1979
Carlos, Walter 1968
Carmen, Eric 1975
Caron, Leslie 1953
Carpenter, Carleton (*see* Reynolds 1951)
Carpenters, The 1970, 1971, 1972, 1973, 1974, 1975
Carroll, Jimmy (*see* Weber 1954)
Carr, Vikki 1967
Cars, The 1978, 1979, 1980
Carter Family 1928
Carter, Clarence 1968, 1970

Carter, Mel 1965
Caruso, Enrico 1903
Cascades, The 1963
Caselli, Caterina 1966
Case, Russ (*see* Como 1945, 1946, 1948)
Cash and Carry (*see* Setter 1974)
Cash, Johnny 1956, 1963, 1967, 1968, 1969
Cassidy, David 1971, 1973
Cassidy, Shaun 1977, 1978
Cast of Idiots (*see* Dees, Rick, 1976)
Castor (Jimmy) Bunch, 1972
Cates, George 1956
Cavaliers (*see* Wilson)
Cavallaro, Carmen 1945 (*see also* Crosby 1945)
Celentano, Adriano 1967
Chacksfield, Frank 1953
Chairman of the Board 1969
Chakachas, The 1971
Champs, The 1958
Chandler, Gene 1962, 1970
Chandler, Karen 1952
Channel, Bruce 1962
Chantels, The 1958
Chapin, Harry 1974
Charden (*see* Stone 1972)
Charles (Ray) Singers (*see* Como 1965)
Charles, Ray 1959, 1960, 1961, 1962, 1963
Charms, The (*see* Williams, Otis 1955, 1956)
Cheap Trick 1979
Checker, Chubby 1960, 1961, 1962
Checkmates (*see* Ford, Emile 1959)
Cheech & Chong 1971, 1972, 1973
Cher 1971, 1973, 1974 (*see also* Sonny & Cher) 1979
Cherry, Don 1955
Chevalier, Christian (*see* Anthony 1961)
Chiaki, Naomi 1972
Chic 1977, 1978, 1979
Chicago 1969, 1970, 1971, 1972, 1973, 1974, 1975, 1976, 1977, 1978
Chicory Tip 1972
Chiffons, The 1963
Chipmunks, The (*see also* Seville 1959) 1980
Chi-Lites, The 1971, 1972
Chordettes, The 1954, 1958
Christie 1970
Christie, Lou 1962, 1963, 1965
Christie, Tony 1971
Christy, June (*see* Kenton 1945, 1946)
Cinquetti, Gigliola 1964
City Slickers (*see* Jones 1942, 1944, 1946, 1948)
Clanton, Jimmy 1958, 1959, 1962
Clapton, Eric 1974, 1977, 1978
Clark Sisters (*see* Jack Smith 1947)
Clark, Buddy (*see* Doris Day 1947)
Clark, Dave 1963, 1964, 1965
Clark, Dee, 1961
Clark, Petula 1961, 1962, 1964, 1965, 1967
Classics IV 1967, 1968, 1969
Clay, Tom 1971
Cliburn, Van (*see* Van Cliburn)
Climax 1971
Clooney, Rosemary 1951, 1952, 1954
Clout 1978
Clowns, The (*see* Smith 1957)
Coasters, The 1957, 1958, 1959
Cochran, Eddie 1957
Cocker, Joe 1970
Cockney Rebel (*see* Harley 1975)
Coffey, Dennis 1971
Cohen, Izhar & Alphabeta Singers 1978
Cole, Buddy (*see* Clooney 1954)
Cole, Cozy 1958
Cole, Nat King 1948, 1950, 1951, 1954, 1955, 1962
Cole, Natalie 1977
Coley, John Ford (*see* Dan, England 1976)

Artist Index 1903–1980: Section 2

Index to artists on theatre-cast film-soundtrack and collective-artist albums